SEVENTH EDITION

Development Through the Lifespan

Laura E. Berk
Illinois State University

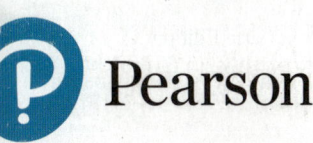

Dedication
To David, Peter, and Melissa, with love

Vice President and Senior Publisher: Roth Wilkofsky
Managing Editor: Tom Pauken
Development Editors: Judy Ashkenaz, Michelle McSweeney
Editorial Assistants: Rachel Trapp, Laura Hernandez
Manager, Content Production: Amber Mackey
Team Lead/Senior Content Producer: Elizabeth Gale Napolitano
Program Management: Barbara Freirich
Digital Studio Product Manager: Chris Fegan, Elissa Senra-Sargent
Senior Operations Specialist: Carol Melville, LSC
Photo Researcher: Sarah Evertson—ImageQuest
Rights and Permissions Manager: Ben Ferrini
Interior Designer: Carol Somberg
Cover Design: PreMedia Global
Project Coordination and Editorial Services: Ohlinger Publishing Services, Inc.
Full-Service Project Management: Aptara
Electronic Page Makeup: Jeff Miller
Copyeditor and References Editor: Loretta Palagi
Proofreader: Julie Hotchkiss
Indexer: Linda Herr Hallinger
Supplements Project Manager: Stephanie Laird, Ohlinger Publishing Services, Inc.
Printer/Binder and Cover Printer: LSC Communications, Kendallville, IN
Text Font: Times
Cover Art: Harold Gregor, "No Words for Where," 2012

Copyright © 2018 by Laura E. Berk. Copyrights © 2014, 2010, 2007, 2004, 2001, 1998 by Pearson Education, Inc.

All rights reserved. Printed in the United States of America. This publication is protected by Copyright and permission should be obtained from the publisher prior to any prohibited reproduction, storage in a retrieval system, or transmission in any form or by any means, electronic, mechanical, photocopying, recording, or likewise. To obtain permission(s) to use material from this work, please submit a written request to Pearson Education, Inc., Permissions Department, 221 River Street, Hoboken NJ 07030.

Library of Congress Cataloging-in-Publication Data
Names: Berk, Laura E., author.
Title: Development through the lifespan / Laura E. Berk, Illinois State
   University.
Description: Seventh Edition. | Boston : Pearson, 2018. | Revised edition of
   the author's Development through the lifespan, [2014]
Identifiers: LCCN 2016038686 | ISBN 9780134419695 (Student edition) | ISBN 0134419693
Subjects: LCSH: Developmental psychology–Textbooks.
Classification: LCC BF713 .B465 2018 | DDC 155–dc23 LC record available at
   https://lccn.loc.gov/2016038686

5   17

Student Edition
ISBN 10: 0-13-441969-3
ISBN 13: 978-0-13-441969-5

Instructor's Review Edition
ISBN 10: 0-13-441991-X
ISBN 13: 978-0-13-441991-6

À la Carte Edition
ISBN 10: 0-13-441972-3
ISBN 13: 978-0-13-441972-5

About the Author

Laura E. Berk is a distinguished professor of psychology at Illinois State University, where she has taught child, adolescent, and lifespan development for more than three decades. She received her bachelor's degree in psychology from the University of California, Berkeley, and her master's and doctoral degrees in child development and educational psychology from the University of Chicago. She has been a visiting scholar at Cornell University, UCLA, Stanford University, and the University of South Australia.

Berk has published widely on the effects of school environments on children's development, the development of private speech, and the role of make-believe play in development. Her empirical studies have attracted the attention of the general public, leading to contributions to *Psychology Today* and *Scientific American*. She has also been featured on National Public Radio's *Morning Edition* and in *Parents Magazine, Wondertime,* and *Reader's Digest.*

Berk has served as a research editor of *Young Children*, a consulting editor for *Early Childhood Research Quarterly*, and as an associate editor of the *Journal of Cognitive Education and Psychology.* She is a frequent contributor to edited volumes, having written the article on social development for *The Child: An Encyclopedic Companion* and the article on Vygotsky for *The Encyclopedia of Cognitive Science.* She is coauthor of the chapter on make-believe play and self-regulation in the *Sage Handbook of Play in Early Childhood* and the chapter on psychologists writing textbooks in *Career Paths in Psychology: Where Your Degree Can Take You*, published by the American Psychological Association.

Berk's books include *Private Speech: From Social Interaction to Self-Regulation; Scaffolding Children's Learning: Vygotsky and Early Childhood Education; Landscapes of Development: An Anthology of Readings;* and *A Mandate for Playful Learning in Preschool: Presenting the Evidence.* In addition to *Development Through the Lifespan,* she is author of the best-selling texts *Child Development* and *Infants, Children, and Adolescents,* published by Pearson. Her book for parents and teachers is *Awakening Children's Minds: How Parents and Teachers Can Make a Difference.*

Berk is active in work for children's causes. She serves on the governing boards of the Illinois Network of Child Care Resource and Referral Agencies and of Artolution, an organization devoted to engaging children, youths, and families in collaborative public art projects around the world as a means of promoting resilience and relief from trauma. Berk has been designated a YWCA Woman of Distinction for service in education. She is a fellow of the American Psychological Association, Division 7: Developmental Psychology.

Features at a Glance

SOCIAL ISSUES: HEALTH

Family Chaos Undermines Parents' and Children's Well-Being 26
The Pros and Cons of Reproductive Technologies 52
The Nurse–Family Partnership: Reducing Maternal Stress and Enhancing Child Development Through Social Support 90
A Cross-National Perspective on Health Care and Other Policies for Parents and Newborn Babies 102
Does Child Care in Infancy Threaten Attachment Security and Later Adjustment? 202
Family Stressors and Childhood Obesity 296
Children's Eyewitness Testimony 361
Lesbian, Gay, and Bisexual Youths: Coming Out to Oneself and Others 382
Childhood Attachment Patterns and Adult Romantic Relationships 480
Partner Abuse 488
The Silver Lining in Life's Adversities 523
Generative Adults Tell Their Life Stories 540
Grandparents Rearing Grandchildren: The Skipped-Generation Family 554
Interventions for Caregivers of Older Adults with Dementia 592
Elder Suicide 618

SOCIAL ISSUES: EDUCATION

Baby Learning from TV and Video: The Video Deficit Effect 157
Magnet Schools: Equal Access to High-Quality Education 327
Media Multitasking Disrupts Learning 400
Development of Civic Engagement 419
How Important Is Academic Engagement in College for Successful Transition to the Labor Market? 461
The Art of Acting Enhances Cognitive Functioning in Older Adults 603

BIOLOGY AND ENVIRONMENT

Resilience 10
The Tutsi Genocide and Epigenetic Transmission of Maternal Stress to Children 71
The Mysterious Tragedy of Sudden Infant Death Syndrome 106
Brain Plasticity: Insights from Research on Brain-Damaged Children and Adults 122
"Tuning In" to Familiar Speech, Faces, and Music: A Sensitive Period for Culture-Specific Learning 139
Infantile Amnesia 164
Parental Depression and Child Development 187
Development of Shyness and Sociability 192
Autism and Theory of Mind 243
Transgender Children 281
Children with Attention-Deficit Hyperactivity Disorder 309
Bullies and Their Victims 349
Sex Differences in Spatial Abilities 396
Two Routes to Adolescent Delinquency 431
Telomere Length: A Marker of the Impact of Life Circumstances on Biological Aging 439
Anti-Aging Effects of Dietary Calorie Restriction 511
What Factors Promote Psychological Well-Being in Midlife? 546
What Can We Learn About Aging from Centenarians? 572
Experience Corps: Promoting Retired Adults' Physical and Mental Health and Children's Academic Success 638
Music as Palliative Care for Dying Patients 653

CULTURAL INFLUENCES

The Baby Boomers Reshape the Life Course 12
Immigrant Youths: Adapting to a New Land 32
The African-American Extended Family 63
Cultural Variation in Infant Sleeping Arrangements 126
Social Origins of Make-Believe Play 168
The Role of Fathers' Involvement in Children's Development 205
Why Are Children from Asian Cultures Advanced in Drawing Skills? 226
Children in Village and Tribal Cultures Observe and Participate in Adult Work 237
Cultural Variations in Personal Storytelling: Implications for Early Self-Concept 259
Ethnic Differences in the Consequences of Physical Punishment 270
The Flynn Effect: Massive Generational Gains in IQ 319
Impact of Ethnic and Political Violence on Children 359
Identity Development Among Ethnic Minority Adolescents 412
Masculinity at Work: Men Who Choose Nontraditional Careers 464
Is Emerging Adulthood Really a Distinct Stage of Development? 474
Menopause as a Biocultural Event 514
The New Old Age 613
Cultural Variations in Mourning Behavior 664

APPLYING WHAT WE KNOW

Steps Prospective Parents Can Take Before Conception to Increase the Chances of a Healthy Baby 55
Do's and Don'ts for a Healthy Pregnancy 92
Soothing a Crying Baby 107
Reasons to Breastfeed 128
Features of a High-Quality Home Life: The HOME Infant–Toddler Subscales 170
Signs of Developmentally Appropriate Infant and Toddler Child Care 172
Supporting Early Language Learning 178
Encouraging Affectionate Ties Between Infants and Their Preschool Siblings 206
Helping Toddlers Develop Compliance and Self-Control 209
Signs of Developmentally Appropriate Early Childhood Programs 248
Helping Children Manage Common Fears of Early Childhood 262
Positive Parenting 271
Regulating Screen Media Use 275
Providing Developmentally Appropriate Organized Sports in Middle Childhood 302
Signs of High-Quality Education in Elementary School 325
Fostering a Mastery-Oriented Approach to Learning 341
Helping Children Adjust to Their Parents' Divorce 355
Handling Consequences of Teenagers' New Cognitive Capacities 393
Supporting High Achievement in Adolescence 399
Supporting Healthy Identity Development 413
Preventing Sexual Coercion 455
Resources That Foster Resilience in Emerging Adulthood 475
Keeping Love Alive in a Romantic Partnership 482
Strategies That Help Dual-Earner Couples Combine Work and Family Roles 501
Reducing Cancer Incidence and Deaths 517
Reducing the Risk of Heart Attack 518
Managing Stress 521
Facilitating Adult Reentry to College 533
Ways Middle-Aged Parents Can Promote Positive Ties with Their Adult Children 552
Relieving the Stress of Caring for an Aging Parent 558
Ingredients of Effective Retirement Planning 563
Increasing the Effectiveness of Educational Experiences for Older Adults 604
Fostering Adaptation to Widowhood in Late Adulthood 629
Discussing Concerns About Death with Children and Adolescents 644
Communicating with Dying People 650
Suggestions for Resolving Grief After a Loved One Dies 663

Contents

A Personal Note to Students xiv
Preface for Instructors xv

PART I
THEORY AND RESEARCH IN HUMAN DEVELOPMENT

chapter 1
History, Theory, and Research Strategies 2

A Scientific, Applied, and Interdisciplinary Field 5

Basic Issues 5
- Continuous or Discontinuous Development? 6
- One Course of Development or Many? 6
- Relative Influence of Nature and Nurture? 7

The Lifespan Perspective: A Balanced Point of View 7
- Development Is Lifelong 8
- Development Is Multidimensional and Multidirectional 8
- Development Is Plastic 9
- Development Is Influenced by Multiple, Interacting Forces 9

■ **BIOLOGY AND ENVIRONMENT** *Resilience* 10

■ **CULTURAL INFLUENCES** *The Baby Boomers Reshape the Life Course* 12

Scientific Beginnings 12
- Darwin: Forefather of Scientific Child Study 12
- The Normative Period 14
- The Mental Testing Movement 14

Mid-Twentieth-Century Theories 14
- The Psychoanalytic Perspective 14
- Behaviorism and Social Learning Theory 16
- Piaget's Cognitive-Developmental Theory 17

Recent Theoretical Perspectives 19
- Information Processing 19
- Developmental Neuroscience 20
- Ethology and Evolutionary Developmental Psychology 21
- Vygotsky's Sociocultural Theory 22
- Ecological Systems Theory 23

■ **SOCIAL ISSUES: HEALTH** *Family Chaos Undermines Parents' and Children's Well-Being* 25

Comparing and Evaluating Theories 26

Studying Development 26
- Common Research Methods 28
- General Research Designs 31

■ **CULTURAL INFLUENCES** *Immigrant Youths: Adapting to a New Land* 32

- Designs for Studying Development 35

Ethics in Lifespan Research 37

Summary 39

Important Terms and Concepts 41

PART II
FOUNDATIONS OF DEVELOPMENT

chapter 2
Genetic and Environmental Foundations 42

Genetic Foundations 44
- The Genetic Code 44
- The Sex Cells 44
- Boy or Girl? 45
- Multiple Offspring 45
- Patterns of Gene–Gene Interactions 46
- Chromosomal Abnormalities 50

Reproductive Choices 51
- Genetic Counseling 51

■ **SOCIAL ISSUES: HEALTH** *The Pros and Cons of Reproductive Technologies* 52

- Prenatal Diagnosis and Fetal Medicine 53
- Adoption 55

Environmental Contexts for Development 56
- The Family 57
- Socioeconomic Status and Family Functioning 58
- Poverty 58
- Affluence 60
- Beyond the Family: Neighborhoods and Schools 60
- The Cultural Context 62

■ **CULTURAL INFLUENCES** *The African-American Extended Family* 63

Understanding the Relationship Between Heredity and Environment 66
- The Question, "How Much?" 67
- The Question, "How?" 68

■ **BIOLOGY AND ENVIRONMENT** *The Tutsi Genocide and Epigenetic Transmission of Maternal Stress to Children* 71

Summary 72

Important Terms and Concepts 73

chapter 3
Prenatal Development, Birth, and the Newborn Baby 74

Prenatal Development 76
- Conception 76
- Germinal Period 76
- Period of the Embryo 78
- Period of the Fetus 79

Prenatal Environmental Influences 81
- Teratogens 81
- Other Maternal Factors 88

v

vi   Contents

■ **SOCIAL ISSUES: HEALTH** *The Nurse–Family Partnership: Reducing Maternal Stress and Enhancing Child Development Through Social Support* 90

    The Importance of Prenatal Health Care 91

Childbirth 92
    The Stages of Childbirth 93
    The Baby's Adaptation to Labor and Delivery 94
    The Newborn Baby's Appearance 94
    Assessing the Newborn's Physical Condition: The Apgar Scale 94

Approaches to Childbirth 95
    Natural, or Prepared, Childbirth 95
    Home Delivery 96

Medical Interventions 96
    Fetal Monitoring 96
    Labor and Delivery Medication 97
    Cesarean Delivery 97

Preterm and Low-Birth-Weight Infants 97
    Preterm versus Small-for-Date Infants 98
    Consequences for Caregiving 98
    Interventions for Preterm Infants 99

The Newborn Baby's Capacities 101
    Reflexes 101

■ **SOCIAL ISSUES: HEALTH** *A Cross-National Perspective on Health Care and Other Policies for Parents and Newborn Babies* 102

    States of Arousal 104

■ **BIOLOGY AND ENVIRONMENT** *The Mysterious Tragedy of Sudden Infant Death Syndrome* 106

    Sensory Capacities 108
    Neonatal Behavioral Assessment 110

Adjusting to the New Family Unit 111

Summary 111

Important Terms and Concepts 113

PART III
INFANCY AND TODDLERHOOD: THE FIRST TWO YEARS

chapter 4
Physical Development in Infancy and Toddlerhood 114

Body Growth 116
    Changes in Body Size and Muscle–Fat Makeup 116
    Changes in Body Proportions 117
    Individual and Group Differences 117

Brain Development 117
    Development of Neurons 117
    Measures of Brain Functioning 119
    Development of the Cerebral Cortex 120
    Sensitive Periods in Brain Development 121

■ **BIOLOGY AND ENVIRONMENT** *Brain Plasticity: Insights from Research on Brain-Damaged Children and Adults* 122

    Changing States of Arousal 125

■ **CULTURAL INFLUENCES** *Cultural Variation in Infant Sleeping Arrangements* 126

Influences on Early Physical Growth 127
    Heredity 127
    Nutrition 127
    Malnutrition 129

Learning Capacities 130
    Classical Conditioning 130
    Operant Conditioning 131
    Habituation 131
    Imitation 132

Motor Development 133
    The Sequence of Motor Development 134
    Motor Skills as Dynamic Systems 135
    Fine-Motor Development: Reaching and Grasping 136

Perceptual Development 137
    Hearing 138

■ **BIOLOGY AND ENVIRONMENT** *"Tuning In" to Familiar Speech, Faces, and Music: A Sensitive Period for Culture-Specific Learning* 139

    Vision 140
    Intermodal Perception 143
    Understanding Perceptual Development 144

Summary 146

Important Terms and Concepts 147

chapter 5
Cognitive Development in Infancy and Toddlerhood 148

Piaget's Cognitive-Developmental Theory 150
    Piaget's Ideas About Cognitive Change 150
    The Sensorimotor Stage 151
    Follow-Up Research on Infant Cognitive Development 153
    Evaluation of the Sensorimotor Stage 156

■ **SOCIAL ISSUES: EDUCATION** *Baby Learning from TV and Video: The Video Deficit Effect* 157

Information Processing 160
    A General Model of Information Processing 160
    Attention 161
    Memory 162
    Categorization 163

■ **BIOLOGY AND ENVIRONMENT** *Infantile Amnesia* 164
    Evaluation of Information-Processing Findings 166

The Social Context of Early Cognitive Development 166

Individual Differences in Early Mental Development 167
    Infant and Toddler Intelligence Tests 167

■ **CULTURAL INFLUENCES** *Social Origins of Make-Believe Play* 168

    Early Environment and Mental Development 169
    Early Intervention for At-Risk Infants and Toddlers 172

Language Development 173
    Theories of Language Development 174
    Getting Ready to Talk 175
    First Words 176
    The Two-Word Utterance Phase 177
    Individual and Cultural Differences 177
    Supporting Early Language Development 178

Summary 180

Important Terms and Concepts 181

chapter 6
Emotional and Social Development in Infancy and Toddlerhood 182

Erikson's Theory of Infant and Toddler Personality 184
    Basic Trust versus Mistrust 184
    Autonomy versus Shame and Doubt 184

Emotional Development 184
    Basic Emotions 185

■ **BIOLOGY AND ENVIRONMENT** *Parental Depression and Child Development* 187

    Understanding and Responding to the Emotions of Others 188
    Emergence of Self-Conscious Emotions 188
    Beginnings of Emotional Self-Regulation 189

Temperament and Development 190
    The Structure of Temperament 190
    Measuring Temperament 191
    Stability of Temperament 191

■ **BIOLOGY AND ENVIRONMENT** *Development of Shyness and Sociability* 192

    Genetic and Environmental Influences 193
    Temperament and Child Rearing: The Goodness-of-Fit Model 195

Development of Attachment 196
    Bowlby's Ethological Theory 196
    Measuring the Security of Attachment 197
    Stability of Attachment 198
    Cultural Variations 199
    Factors That Affect Attachment Security 199

■ **SOCIAL ISSUES: HEALTH** *Does Child Care in Infancy Threaten Attachment Security and Later Adjustment?* 202

    Multiple Attachments 203

■ **CULTURAL INFLUENCES** *The Role of Fathers' Involvement in Children's Development* 205

    Attachment and Later Development 205

Self-Development 206
    Self-Awareness 206
    Categorizing the Self 208
    Self-Control 208

Summary 210

Important Terms and Concepts 211

■ **MILESTONES** *Development in Infancy and Toddlerhood* 212

PART IV
EARLY CHILDHOOD: TWO TO SIX YEARS

chapter 7
Physical and Cognitive Development in Early Childhood 214

PHYSICAL DEVELOPMENT 216

A Changing Body and Brain 216
    Skeletal Growth 217
    Brain Development 217

Influences on Physical Growth and Health 219
    Heredity and Hormones 219
    Nutrition 219
    Infectious Disease 220
    Childhood Injuries 221

Motor Development 222
    Gross-Motor Development 223
    Fine-Motor Development 224
    Individual Differences in Motor Skills 225

■ **CULTURAL INFLUENCES** *Why Are Children from Asian Cultures Advanced in Drawing Skills?* 226

COGNITIVE DEVELOPMENT 227

Piaget's Theory: The Preoperational Stage 227
    Advances in Mental Representation 227
    Make-Believe Play 227
    Symbol–Real-World Relations 228
    Limitations of Preoperational Thought 229
    Follow-Up Research on Preoperational Thought 231
    Evaluation of the Preoperational Stage 232
    Piaget and Education 233

Vygotsky's Sociocultural Theory 234
    Private Speech 234
    Social Origins of Early Childhood Cognition 235
    Vygotsky and Early Childhood Education 235
    Evaluation of Vygotsky's Theory 236

Information Processing 236
    Executive Function 236

■ **CULTURAL INFLUENCES** *Children in Village and Tribal Cultures Observe and Participate in Adult Work* 237

    Memory 239
    The Young Child's Theory of Mind 241
    Early Childhood Literacy 242

■ **BIOLOGY AND ENVIRONMENT** *Autism and Theory of Mind* 243

    Early Childhood Mathematical Reasoning 244

Individual Differences in Mental Development 245
    Home Environment and Mental Development 245
    Preschool, Kindergarten, and Child Care 246
    Educational Media 248

viii Contents

Language Development 249
  Vocabulary 250
  Grammar 251
  Conversation 252
  Supporting Language Development in Early Childhood 252
Summary 253
Important Terms and Concepts 255

chapter 8
Emotional and Social Development in Early Childhood 256

Erikson's Theory: Initiative versus Guilt 258
Self-Understanding 258
  Foundations of Self-Concept 258
  ■ **CULTURAL INFLUENCES** Cultural Variations in Personal Storytelling: Implications for Early Self-Concept 259
  Emergence of Self-Esteem 260
Emotional Development 260
  Understanding Emotion 260
  Emotional Self-Regulation 261
  Self-Conscious Emotions 262
  Empathy and Sympathy 262
Peer Relations 263
  Advances in Peer Sociability 263
  First Friendships 265
  Peer Relations and School Readiness 266
  Parental Influences on Early Peer Relations 266
Foundations of Morality and Aggression 267
  The Psychoanalytic Perspective 267
  Social Learning Theory 268
  ■ **CULTURAL INFLUENCES** Ethnic Differences in the Consequences of Physical Punishment 270
  The Cognitive-Developmental Perspective 271
  The Other Side of Morality: Development of Aggression 272
Gender Typing 276
  Gender-Stereotyped Beliefs and Behavior 276
  Biological Influences on Gender Typing 277
  Environmental Influences on Gender Typing 277
  Gender Identity 279
  Reducing Gender Stereotyping in Young Children 280
  ■ **BIOLOGY AND ENVIRONMENT** Transgender Children 281
Child Rearing and Emotional and Social Development 282
  Styles of Child Rearing 282
  What Makes Authoritative Child Rearing Effective? 283
  Cultural Variations 284
  Child Maltreatment 285
Summary 288
Important Terms and Concepts 289

MILESTONES Development in Early Childhood 290

PART V
MIDDLE CHILDHOOD: SIX TO ELEVEN YEARS

chapter 9
Physical and Cognitive Development in Middle Childhood 292

PHYSICAL DEVELOPMENT 294
Body Growth 294
Common Health Problems 295
  Nutrition 295
  Overweight and Obesity 295
  ■ **SOCIAL ISSUES: HEALTH** Family Stressors and Childhood Obesity 296
  Vision and Hearing 298
  Illnesses 298
  Unintentional Injuries 298
Motor Development and Play 299
  Gross-Motor Development 299
  Fine-Motor Development 300
  Sex Differences 301
  Games with Rules 301
  Adult-Organized Youth Sports 301
  Shadows of Our Evolutionary Past 302
  Physical Education 303

COGNITIVE DEVELOPMENT 303
Piaget's Theory: The Concrete Operational Stage 304
  Concrete Operational Thought 304
  Limitations of Concrete Operational Thought 306
  Follow-Up Research on Concrete Operational Thought 306
  Evaluation of the Concrete Operational Stage 307
Information Processing 307
  Executive Function 307
  ■ **BIOLOGY AND ENVIRONMENT** Children with Attention-Deficit Hyperactivity Disorder 309
  Memory Strategies 310
  Knowledge and Memory 311
  Culture, Schooling, and Memory Strategies 311
  The School-Age Child's Theory of Mind 311
  Cognitive Self-Regulation 312
  Applications of Information Processing to Academic Learning 313
Individual Differences in Mental Development 314
  Defining and Measuring Intelligence 314
  Other Efforts to Define Intelligence 315
  Explaining Individual and Group Differences in IQ 317
  ■ **CULTURAL INFLUENCES** The Flynn Effect: Massive Generational Gains in IQ 319
Language Development 321
  Vocabulary and Grammar 321
  Pragmatics 322
  Learning Two Languages 323

Contents   ix

Learning in School   *324*
    Educational Philosophies   *324*
    Teacher–Student Interaction and Grouping Practices   *326*
    Teaching Children with Special Needs   *326*

■ **SOCIAL ISSUES: EDUCATION** *Magnet Schools: Equal Access to High-Quality Education*   *327*

    How Well Educated Are U.S. Children?   *329*

Summary   *331*

Important Terms and Concepts   *333*

chapter 10
Emotional and Social Development in Middle Childhood   334

Erikson's Theory: Industry versus Inferiority   *336*

Self-Understanding   *336*
    Self-Concept   *336*
    Self-Esteem   *337*
    Influences on Self-Esteem   *337*

Emotional Development   *341*
    Self-Conscious Emotions   *341*
    Emotional Understanding   *341*
    Emotional Self-Regulation   *342*

Moral Development   *342*
    Moral and Social-Conventional Understanding   *343*
    Understanding Individual Rights   *343*
    Culture and Moral Understanding   *344*
    Understanding Diversity and Inequality   *344*

Peer Relations   *345*
    Peer Groups   *346*
    Friendships   *346*
    Peer Acceptance   *347*

■ **BIOLOGY AND ENVIRONMENT** *Bullies and Their Victims*   *349*

Gender Typing   *350*
    Gender-Stereotyped Beliefs   *350*
    Gender Identity and Behavior   *350*

Family Influences   *351*
    Parent–Child Relationships   *351*
    Siblings   *352*
    Only Children   *352*
    Divorce   *353*
    Blended Families   *355*
    Maternal Employment and Dual-Earner Families   *356*

Some Common Problems of Development   *358*
    Fears and Anxieties   *358*
    Child Sexual Abuse   *358*

■ **CULTURAL INFLUENCES** *Impact of Ethnic and Political Violence on Children*   *359*

    Fostering Resilience in Middle Childhood   *360*

■ **SOCIAL ISSUES: HEALTH** *Children's Eyewitness Testimony*   *361*

Summary   *362*

Important Terms and Concepts   *363*

MILESTONES   *Development in Middle Childhood*   *364*

PART VI
ADOLESCENCE:
THE TRANSITION TO ADULTHOOD

chapter 11
Physical and Cognitive Development in Adolescence   366

PHYSICAL DEVELOPMENT   *368*

Conceptions of Adolescence   *368*
    The Biological Perspective   *368*
    The Social Perspective   *368*
    A Balanced Point of View   *368*

Puberty: The Physical Transition to Adulthood   *368*
    Hormonal Changes   *369*
    Body Growth   *369*
    Motor Development and Physical Activity   *370*
    Sexual Maturation   *371*
    Individual Differences in Pubertal Growth   *372*
    Brain Development   *373*
    Changing States of Arousal   *374*

The Psychological Impact of Pubertal Events   *374*
    Reactions to Pubertal Changes   *374*
    Pubertal Change, Emotion, and Social Behavior   *375*
    Pubertal Timing   *376*

Health Issues   *378*
    Nutritional Needs   *378*
    Eating Disorders   *378*
    Sexuality   *379*

■ **SOCIAL ISSUES: HEALTH** *Lesbian, Gay, and Bisexual Youths: Coming Out to Oneself and Others*   *382*

    Sexually Transmitted Infections   *383*
    Adolescent Pregnancy and Parenthood   *384*
    Substance Use and Abuse   *386*

COGNITIVE DEVELOPMENT   *388*

Piaget's Theory: The Formal Operational Stage   *388*
    Hypothetico-Deductive Reasoning   *388*
    Propositional Thought   *389*
    Follow-Up Research on Formal Operational Thought   *389*

An Information-Processing View of Adolescent Cognitive Development   *390*
    Scientific Reasoning: Coordinating Theory with Evidence   *391*
    How Scientific Reasoning Develops   *391*

Consequences of Adolescent Cognitive Changes   *392*
    Self-Consciousness and Self-Focusing   *392*
    Idealism and Criticism   *393*
    Decision Making   *393*

Sex Differences in Mental Abilities   *394*
    Verbal Abilities   *394*
    Mathematical Abilities   *395*

■ **BIOLOGY AND ENVIRONMENT** *Sex Differences in Spatial Abilities*   *396*

Learning in School 396
  School Transitions 396
  Academic Achievement 398
■ **SOCIAL ISSUES: EDUCATION** *Media Multitasking Disrupts Learning* 400
  Dropping Out 402
Summary 403
Important Terms and Concepts 405

chapter 12
Emotional and Social Development in Adolescence 406

Erikson's Theory: Identity versus Role Confusion 408
Self-Understanding 408
  Changes in Self-Concept 408
  Changes in Self-Esteem 408
  Paths to Identity 409
  Identity Status and Psychological Well-Being 410
  Influences on Identity Development 411
■ **CULTURAL INFLUENCES** *Identity Development Among Ethnic Minority Adolescents* 412
Moral Development 413
  Kohlberg's Theory of Moral Development 413
  Are There Sex Differences in Moral Reasoning? 415
  Coordinating Moral, Social-Conventional, and Personal Concerns 416
  Influences on Moral Reasoning 416
  Moral Reasoning and Behavior 417
  Religious Involvement and Moral Development 418
■ **SOCIAL ISSUES: EDUCATION** *Development of Civic Engagement* 419
  Further Challenges to Kohlberg's Theory 420
The Family 420
  Parent–Adolescent Relationships 420
  Family Circumstances 422
  Siblings 422
Peer Relations 422
  Friendships 422
  Cliques and Crowds 425
  Dating 426
Problems of Development 427
  Depression 427
  Suicide 428
  Delinquency 429
■ **BIOLOGY AND ENVIRONMENT** *Two Routes to Adolescent Delinquency* 431
Summary 432
Important Terms and Concepts 433

MILESTONES *Development in Adolescence* 434

PART VII
EARLY ADULTHOOD

chapter 13
Physical and Cognitive Development in Early Adulthood 436

PHYSICAL DEVELOPMENT 438
Biological Aging Is Under Way in Early Adulthood 438
  Aging at the Level of DNA and Body Cells 438
■ **BIOLOGY AND ENVIRONMENT** *Telomere Length: A Marker of the Impact of Life Circumstances on Biological Aging* 439
  Aging at the Level of Tissues and Organs 440
Physical Changes 440
  Cardiovascular and Respiratory Systems 440
  Motor Performance 442
  Immune System 443
  Reproductive Capacity 443
Health and Fitness 444
  Nutrition 445
  Exercise 447
  Substance Abuse 448
  Sexuality 450
  Psychological Stress 455

COGNITIVE DEVELOPMENT 456
Changes in the Structure of Thought 456
  Epistemic Cognition 456
  Pragmatic Thought and Cognitive-Affective Complexity 458
Expertise and Creativity 458
The College Experience 460
  Psychological Impact of Attending College 460
  Dropping Out 460
■ **SOCIAL ISSUES: EDUCATION** *How Important Is Academic Engagement in College for Successful Transition to the Labor Market?* 461
Vocational Choice 462
  Selecting a Vocation 462
  Factors Influencing Vocational Choice 462
■ **CULTURAL INFLUENCES** *Masculinity at Work: Men Who Choose Nontraditional Careers* 464
  Vocational Preparation of Non-College-Bound Young Adults 465
Summary 466
Important Terms and Concepts 467

chapter 14
Emotional and Social Development in Early Adulthood 468

A Gradual Transition: Emerging Adulthood 470
  Unprecedented Exploration 470
  Cultural Change, Cultural Variation, and Emerging Adulthood 473
  Risk and Resilience in Emerging Adulthood 473

Contents **xi**

■ **CULTURAL INFLUENCES** *Is Emerging Adulthood Really a Distinct Stage of Development?* 474

Erikson's Theory: Intimacy versus Isolation 476

Other Theories of Adult Psychosocial Development 477
- Levinson's Seasons of Life 477
- Vaillant's Adaptation to Life 477
- The Social Clock 478

Close Relationships 478
- Romantic Love 479

■ **SOCIAL ISSUES: HEALTH** *Childhood Attachment Patterns and Adult Romantic Relationships* 480
- Friendships 482

The Family Life Cycle 484
- Leaving Home 484
- Joining of Families in Marriage 485

■ **SOCIAL ISSUES: HEALTH** *Partner Abuse* 488
- Parenthood 489

The Diversity of Adult Lifestyles 492
- Singlehood 493
- Cohabitation 494
- Childlessness 495
- Divorce and Remarriage 495
- Varied Styles of Parenthood 496

Career Development 498
- Establishing a Career 498
- Women and Ethnic Minorities 499
- Combining Work and Family 500

Summary 502

Important Terms and Concepts 503

MILESTONES *Development in Early Adulthood* 504

PART VIII
MIDDLE ADULTHOOD

chapter 15
Physical and Cognitive Development in Middle Adulthood 506

PHYSICAL DEVELOPMENT 508

Physical Changes 508
- Vision 508
- Hearing 509
- Skin 509
- Muscle–Fat Makeup 510
- Skeleton 510
- Reproductive System 510

■ **BIOLOGY AND ENVIRONMENT** *Anti-Aging Effects of Dietary Calorie Restriction* 511

■ **CULTURAL INFLUENCES** *Menopause as a Biocultural Event* 514

Health and Fitness 514
- Sexuality 515
- Illness and Disability 515
- Hostility and Anger 519

Adapting to the Physical Challenges of Midlife 520
- Stress Management 520
- Exercise 521
- Hardiness 522
- Gender and Aging: A Double Standard 523

■ **SOCIAL ISSUES: HEALTH** *The Silver Lining in Life's Adversities* 523

COGNITIVE DEVELOPMENT 524

Changes in Mental Abilities 524
- Cohort Effects 524
- Crystallized and Fluid Intelligence 525
- Individual and Group Differences 526

Information Processing 527
- Speed of Processing 527
- Executive Function 528
- Memory Strategies 529
- Practical Problem Solving and Expertise 530
- Creativity 530
- Information Processing in Context 531

Vocational Life and Cognitive Development 531

Adult Learners: Becoming a Student in Midlife 532
- Characteristics of Returning Students 532
- Supporting Returning Students 532

Summary 534

Important Terms and Concepts 535

chapter 16
Emotional and Social Development in Middle Adulthood 536

Erikson's Theory: Generativity versus Stagnation 538

■ **SOCIAL ISSUES: HEALTH** *Generative Adults Tell Their Life Stories* 540

Other Theories of Psychosocial Development in Midlife 541
- Levinson's Seasons of Life 541
- Vaillant's Adaptation to Life 542
- Is There a Midlife Crisis? 542
- Stage or Life Events Approach 543

Stability and Change in Self-Concept and Personality 543
- Possible Selves 544
- Self-Acceptance, Autonomy, and Environmental Mastery 544
- Coping with Daily Stressors 545

■ **BIOLOGY AND ENVIRONMENT** *What Factors Promote Psychological Well-Being in Midlife?* 546
- Gender Identity 546
- Individual Differences in Personality Traits 548

Relationships at Midlife 549
- Marriage and Divorce 549
- Changing Parent–Child Relationships 551
- Grandparenthood 552
- Middle-Aged Children and Their Aging Parents 554

■ **SOCIAL ISSUES: HEALTH** *Grandparents Rearing Grandchildren: The Skipped-Generation Family* 554

- Siblings 557
- Friendships 558

Vocational Life 559
- Job Satisfaction 560
- Career Development 560
- Career Change at Midlife 562
- Unemployment 562
- Planning for Retirement 562

Summary 564

Important Terms and Concepts 565

MILESTONES *Development in Middle Adulthood* 566

PART IX
LATE ADULTHOOD

chapter 17
Physical and Cognitive Development in Late Adulthood 568

PHYSICAL DEVELOPMENT 570

Life Expectancy 570
- Variations in Life Expectancy 570
- Life Expectancy in Late Adulthood 571
- Maximum Lifespan 572

■ **BIOLOGY AND ENVIRONMENT** *What Can We Learn About Aging from Centenarians?* 572

Physical Changes 573
- Nervous System 573
- Sensory Systems 574
- Cardiovascular and Respiratory Systems 576
- Immune System 577
- Sleep 577
- Physical Appearance and Mobility 578
- Adapting to Physical Changes of Late Adulthood 578

Health, Fitness, and Disability 581
- Nutrition and Exercise 582
- Sexuality 583
- Physical Disabilities 585
- Mental Disabilities 587
- Health Care 591

■ **SOCIAL ISSUES: HEALTH** *Interventions for Caregivers of Older Adults with Dementia* 592

COGNITIVE DEVELOPMENT 594

Memory 595
- Explicit versus Implicit Memory 595
- Associative Memory 596
- Remote Memory 597
- Prospective Memory 598

Language Processing 598

Problem Solving 599

Wisdom 600

Factors Related to Cognitive Maintenance and Change 601

Cognitive Interventions 602

Lifelong Learning 602

■ **SOCIAL ISSUES: EDUCATION** *The Art of Acting Enhances Cognitive Functioning in Older Adults* 603

- Types of Programs 603
- Benefits of Continuing Education 605

Summary 605

Important Terms and Concepts 607

chapter 18
Emotional and Social Development in Late Adulthood 608

Erikson's Theory: Ego Integrity versus Despair 610

Other Theories of Psychosocial Development in Late Adulthood 610
- Peck's Tasks of Ego Integrity and Joan Erikson's Gerotranscendence 610
- The Positivity Effect 611
- Reminiscence 612

Stability and Change in Self-Concept and Personality 612
- Secure and Multifaceted Self-Concept 612

■ **CULTURAL INFLUENCES** *The New Old Age* 613

- Agreeableness, Acceptance of Change, and Openness to Experience 614
- Spirituality and Religiosity 614

Contextual Influences on Psychological Well-Being 615
- Control versus Dependency 616
- Physical Health 617
- Negative Life Changes 617
- Social Support 617

■ **SOCIAL ISSUES: HEALTH** *Elder Suicide* 618

A Changing Social World 619
- Social Theories of Aging 620
- Social Contexts of Aging: Communities, Neighborhoods, and Housing 622

Relationships in Late Adulthood 625
- Marriage 625
- Lesbian and Gay Couples 626

Divorce, Remarriage, and Cohabitation 627
Widowhood 628
Never-Married, Childless Older Adults 629
Siblings 630
Friendships 630
Relationships with Adult Children 631
Relationships with Adult Grandchildren 632
Elder Maltreatment 632

Retirement 634
The Decision to Retire 635
Adjustment to Retirement 636
Leisure and Volunteer Activities 636

Successful Aging 637

■ **BIOLOGY AND ENVIRONMENT** *Experience Corps: Promoting Retired Adults' Physical and Mental Health and Children's Academic Success* 638

Summary 639

Important Terms and Concepts 641

MILESTONES *Development in Late Adulthood* 642

PART X
THE END OF LIFE

chapter 19
Death, Dying, and Bereavement 644

How We Die 646
Physical Changes 646
Defining Death 646
Death with Dignity 647

Understanding of and Attitudes Toward Death 648
Childhood 648
Adolescence 650
Adulthood 650
Death Anxiety 651

Thinking and Emotions of Dying People 653
Do Stages of Dying Exist? 653
Contextual Influences on Adaptations to Dying 654

A Place to Die 657
Home 657
Hospital 657
Nursing Home 658
The Hospice Approach 658

■ **BIOLOGY AND ENVIRONMENT** *Music as Palliative Care for Dying Patients* 659

The Right to Die 660
Ending Life-Sustaining Treatment 660
Medical Aid-in-Dying 662
Voluntary Euthanasia 664

Bereavement: Coping with the Death of a Loved One 665
Grief Process 665
Personal and Situational Variations 666
Bereavement Interventions 668

■ **CULTURAL INFLUENCES** *Cultural Variations in Mourning Behavior* 669

Death Education 671

Summary 672

Important Terms and Concepts 673

Glossary G-1

References R-1

Name Index NI-1

Subject Index SI-1

A Personal Note to Students

My more than 30 years of teaching human development have brought me in contact with thousands of students like you—students with diverse college majors, future goals, interests, and needs. Some are affiliated with my own field, psychology, but many come from other related fields—education, sociology, anthropology, family studies, biology, social service, and nursing, to name just a few. Each semester, my students' aspirations have proved to be as varied as their fields of study. Many look toward careers in applied work—counseling, caregiving, nursing, social work, school psychology, and program administration. Some plan to teach, and a few want to do research. Most hope someday to become parents, whereas others are already parents who come with a desire to better understand and rear their children. And almost all arrive with a deep curiosity about how they themselves developed from tiny infants into the complex human beings they are today.

My goal in preparing this seventh edition of *Development Through the Lifespan* is to provide a textbook that meets the instructional goals of your course as well as your personal interests and needs. To achieve these objectives, I have grounded this book in a carefully selected body of classic and current theory and research. In addition, the text highlights the lifespan perspective on development and the interwoven contributions of biology and environment to the developing person. It also illustrates commonalities and differences among ethnic groups and cultures and discusses the broader social contexts in which we develop. I have provided a unique pedagogical program that will assist you in mastering information, integrating various aspects of development, critically examining controversial issues, applying what you have learned, and relating the information to your own life.

I hope that learning about human development will be as rewarding for you as I have found it over the years. I would like to know what you think about both the field of human development and this book. I welcome your comments; please feel free to send them to me at berklifespandevelopment@gmail.com.

Laura E. Berk

Preface for Instructors

My decision to write *Development Through the Lifespan* was inspired by a wealth of professional and personal experiences. First and foremost were the interests and concerns of hundreds of students of human development with whom I have worked in over three decades of college teaching. Each semester, their insights and questions have revealed how an understanding of any single period of development is enriched by an appreciation of the entire lifespan. Second, as I moved through adult development myself, I began to think more intently about factors that have shaped and reshaped my own life course—family, friends, mentors, co-workers, community, and larger society. My career well-established, my marriage having stood the test of time, and my children launched into their adult lives, I felt that a deeper grasp of these multiple, interacting influences would help me better appreciate where I had been and where I would be going in the years ahead. I was also convinced that such knowledge could contribute to my becoming a better teacher, scholar, family member, and citizen. And because teaching has been so central and gratifying to my work life, I wanted to bring to others a personally meaningful understanding of lifespan development.

The years since *Development Through the Lifespan* first appeared have been a period of unprecedented expansion and change in theory and research. This seventh edition represents these rapidly transforming aspects of the field, with a wealth of new content and teaching tools:

- *Diverse pathways of change are highlighted.* Investigators have reached broad consensus that variations in biological makeup and everyday tasks lead to wide individual differences in paths of change and resulting competencies. This edition pays more attention to variability in development and to recent theories—including ecological, sociocultural, dynamic systems, and epigenesis—that attempt to explain it. Multicultural and cross-cultural findings, including international comparisons, are enhanced throughout the text. Biology and Environment and Cultural Influences boxes also accentuate the theme of diversity in development.

- *The lifespan perspective is emphasized.* As in previous editions, the lifespan perspective—development as lifelong, multidimensional, multidirectional, plastic, and embedded in multiple contexts—continues to serve as a unifying approach to understanding human change and is woven thoroughly into the text.

- *The complex bidirectional relationship between biology and environment is given greater attention.* Accumulating evidence on development of the brain, motor skills, cognitive and language competencies, temperament and personality, emotional and social understanding, and developmental problems underscores the way biological factors emerge in, are modified by, and share power with experience. The interconnection between biology and environment is integral to the lifespan perspective and is revisited throughout the text narrative and in the Biology and Environment boxes with new and updated topics.

- *Inclusion of interdisciplinary research is expanded.* The move toward viewing thoughts, feelings, and behavior as an integrated whole, affected by a wide array of influences in biology, social context, and culture, has motivated developmental researchers to strengthen their ties with other fields of psychology and with other disciplines. Topics and findings included in this edition increasingly reflect the contributions of educational psychology, social psychology, health psychology, clinical psychology, neurobiology, pediatrics, geriatrics, sociology, anthropology, social service, and other fields.

- *Links among theory, research, and applications are strengthened.* As researchers intensify their efforts to generate findings relevant to real-life situations, I have placed greater weight on social policy issues and sound theory- and research-based applications. Further applications are provided in the Applying What We Know tables, which give students concrete ways of building bridges between their learning and the real world.

- *The role of active student learning is made more explicit.* Ask Yourself questions at the end of most major sections have been revised to promote three approaches to engaging with the subject matter—*Connect, Apply,* and *Reflect.* This feature assists students in thinking about what they have learned from multiple vantage points. The *Look and Listen* feature asks students to observe what real children, adolescents, and adults say and do; speak with them or with professionals invested in their well-being; and inquire into community programs and practices that influence lifespan development. In addition, highlighting of key terms within the text narrative reinforces student learning in context.

TEXT PHILOSOPHY

The basic approach of this book has been shaped by my own professional and personal history as a teacher, researcher, and parent. It consists of seven philosophical ingredients that I regard as essential for students to emerge from a course with a thorough understanding of lifespan development. Each theme is woven into every chapter:

1. **An understanding of the diverse array of theories in the field and the strengths and shortcomings of each.** The first chapter begins by emphasizing that only knowledge of multiple theories can do justice to the richness of human development. As I take up each age period and domain of development, I present a variety of theoretical perspectives, indicate how each highlights previously overlooked aspects of development, and discuss research that evaluates it. Consideration of contrasting theories also serves as the context for an even-handed analysis of many controversial issues.

2. **A grasp of the lifespan perspective as an integrative approach to development.** I introduce the lifespan perspective

as an organizing framework in the first chapter and refer to and illustrate its assumptions throughout the text, in an effort to help students construct an overall vision of development from conception to death.

3. **Knowledge of both the sequence of human development and the processes that underlie it.** Students are provided with discussion of the organized sequence of development along with processes of change. An understanding of process—how complex combinations of biological, psychological, and environmental factors produce development—has been the focus of most recent research. Accordingly, the text reflects this emphasis. But new information about the timetable of change has also emerged. In many ways, the very young and the old have proved to be more competent than they were believed to be in the past. In addition, many milestones of adult development, such as finishing formal education, entering a career, getting married, having children, and retiring, have become far less predictable. Current evidence on the sequence and timing of development, along with its implications for process, is presented for all periods of the lifespan.

4. **An appreciation of the impact of context and culture on human development.** A wealth of research indicates that people live in rich physical and social contexts that affect all domains of development. Throughout the book, students travel to distant parts of the world as I review a growing body of cross-cultural evidence. The text narrative also discusses many findings on socioeconomically and ethnically diverse people within the United States. Furthermore, the impact of historical time period and cohort membership receives continuous attention. In this vein, gender issues—the distinctive but continually evolving experiences, roles, and life paths of males and females—are granted substantial emphasis. Besides highlighting the effects of immediate settings, such as family, neighborhood, and school, I make a concerted effort to underscore the influence of larger social structures—societal values, laws, and government policies and programs—on lifelong well-being.

5. **An understanding of the joint contributions of biology and environment to development.** The field recognizes more powerfully than ever before the joint roles of hereditary/constitutional and environmental factors—that these contributions to development combine in complex ways and cannot be separated in a simple manner. Numerous examples of how biological dispositions can be maintained as well as transformed by social contexts are presented throughout the book.

6. **A sense of the interdependency of all domains of development—physical, cognitive, emotional, and social.** Every chapter emphasizes an integrated approach to human development. I show how physical, cognitive, emotional, and social development are interwoven. Within the text narrative, and in the Ask Yourself questions at the end of major sections, students are referred to other sections of the book to deepen their grasp of relationships among various aspects of change.

7. **An appreciation of the interrelatedness of theory, research, and applications.** Throughout this book, I emphasize that theories of human development and the research stimulated by them provide the foundation for sound, effective practices with children, adolescents, and adults. The link among theory, research, and applications is reinforced by an organizational format in which theory and research are presented first, followed by practical implications. In addition, a current focus in the field—harnessing knowledge of human development to shape social policies that support human needs throughout the lifespan—is reflected in every chapter. The text addresses the current condition of children, adolescents, and adults in the United States and elsewhere in the world and shows how theory and research have combined with public interest to spark successful interventions. Many important applied topics are considered, such as family planning, infant mortality, parental employment and child care, adolescent pregnancy and parenthood, domestic violence, exercise and adult health, religiosity and well-being, lifelong learning, grandparents rearing grandchildren, caring for aging adults with dementia, adjustment to retirement, successful aging, and palliative care for the dying.

TEXT ORGANIZATION

I have chosen a chronological organization for *Development Through the Lifespan*. The book begins with an introductory chapter that describes the scientific history of the field, influential theories, and research strategies. It is followed by two chapters on foundations of development. Chapter 2 combines an overview of genetic and environmental contexts into a single integrated discussion of these multifaceted influences on development. Chapter 3 is devoted to prenatal development, birth, and the newborn baby. With these foundations, students are ready to look closely at seven major age periods: infancy and toddlerhood (Chapters 4, 5, and 6), early childhood (Chapters 7 and 8), middle childhood (Chapters 9 and 10), adolescence (Chapters 11 and 12), early adulthood (Chapters 13 and 14), middle adulthood (Chapters 15 and 16), and late adulthood (Chapters 17 and 18). Topical chapters within each chronological division cover physical development, cognitive development, and emotional and social development. The book concludes with a chapter on death, dying, and bereavement (Chapter 19).

The chronological approach assists students in thoroughly understanding each age period. It also eases the task of integrating the various domains of development because each is discussed in close proximity. At the same time, a chronologically organized book requires that theories covering several age periods be presented piecemeal. This creates a challenge for students, who must link the various parts together. To assist with this task, I frequently remind students of important earlier achievements before discussing new developments, referring back to related sections with page references. Also, chapters or sections devoted to the same topic (for example, cognitive development) are similarly organized, making it easier for students to draw connections across age periods and construct an overall view of developmental change.

NEW COVERAGE IN THE SEVENTH EDITION

Lifespan development is a fascinating and ever-changing field of study, with constantly emerging new discoveries and refinements in existing knowledge. The seventh edition represents this burgeoning contemporary literature, with over 2,300 new citations. Cutting-edge topics throughout the text underscore the book's major themes. Here is a sampling:

CHAPTER 1: Introduction to the developmental systems approach, as illustrated by the lifespan perspective • Updated Cultural Influences box on baby boomers reshaping the life course • Updated Social Issues: Health box on the impact of family chaos on parents' and children's well-being • Revised section on developmental neuroscience, with special attention to developmental social neuroscience • Updated examples of research strategies, including naturalistic observation, case studies, and sequential design • Inclusion of children's assent as part of informed consent guidelines for protection of human subjects

CHAPTER 2: Updated discussion of gene–gene interactions, including the distinction between protein-coding genes and regulator genes, which greatly complicate genetic influences • New evidence on older paternal age and increased risk of DNA mutations contributing to psychological disorders, including autism and schizophrenia • Updated Social Issues: Health box on the pros and cons of reproductive technologies • Recent findings on neighborhood influences on physical and mental health • New section on contributions of schooling to development and life chances, with special attention to SES differences • Expanded attention to the role of ethnic minority extended families in promoting resilience in the face of prejudice and economic deprivation • Updated sections on public policies and development, including current statistics on the condition of children, adolescents, and older adults in the United States compared with other Western nations • Enhanced discussion of gene–environment interaction, with illustrative new research findings • Expanded section on epigenesis, including the role of methylation along with new examples of environmental influences on gene expression • New Biology and Environment box on epigenetic transmission of maternal stress to children

CHAPTER 3: Enhanced attention to development during the prenatal period, including brain growth, sensory capacities, and embryonic and fetal behavior • Expanded and updated consideration of a wide range of teratogens • New evidence on the long-term consequences of severe emotional stress during pregnancy • Updated Social Issues: Health box on the Nurse–Family Partnership—reducing maternal stress and enhancing child development through social support • New statistics and research on benefits and risks of medical interventions during childbirth • New findings on risks of late preterm birth—as little as 1 or 2 weeks early • Updated research on interventions for preterm and low-birth-weight infants, including kangaroo care and recordings of the mother's voice and heartbeat • Expanded and updated Social Issues: Health box on health care and other policies for parents and newborn babies, including cross-national infant mortality rates and the importance of generous parental leave • Updated findings on hormonal changes in both mothers and fathers around the time of birth, and in foster and adoptive mothers, that facilitate effective caregiving • Revised Biology and Environment box on sudden infant death syndrome, including the importance of public education about safe sleep environments and other protective measures

CHAPTER 4: Updated discussion of advances in brain development, with special attention to the prefrontal cortex • Revised Biology and Environment box on early brain plasticity, based on research on brain-damaged children and adults • New evidence on infant sleep, including contributions of bedtime routines to sleep quality • Enhanced attention to cultural influences on infant sleep, including updated Cultural Influences box addressing parent–infant cosleeping and bedsharing • New findings on long-term consequences of malnutrition in infancy and toddlerhood • Updated discussion of the controversy surrounding newborns' capacity to imitate • Updated evidence on how environmental factors, including caregiving practices and the baby's physical surroundings, contribute to motor development • New findings on implications of infants' capacity to analyze the speech stream for later language progress • Enhanced discussion of the impact of crawling and walking experience on perceptual and cognitive development • Expanded and updated section on intermodal perception, including its contributions to diverse aspects of learning

CHAPTER 5: New research on analogical problem solving in infants and toddlers • Updated evidence on toddlers' grasp of pictures and videos as symbols, including experiences that enhance symbolic understanding • New research on infants' numerical knowledge • Revised and enhanced introduction to the concept of executive function • New evidence on the similarity of infant and toddler memory processing to that of older children and adults • New research on cultural variations in scaffolding infant and toddler learning • New evidence on the importance of sustained high-quality child care from infancy through the preschool years for cognitive, language, literacy, and math progress at kindergarten entry • Updated findings on infants' participation in imitative exchanges and joint attention, revealing their developing capacity to engage in cooperative processes necessary for effective communication • Enhanced attention to SES differences in early vocabulary development as a predictor of vocabulary size at kindergarten entry, with implications for literacy skills and school success • New evidence highlighting the importance of a responsive adult for early language development, in both real-life and video contexts

CHAPTER 6: New research on cultural variations in development of emotional self-regulation • New findings on factors influencing the low to moderate stability of temperament, including parenting and young children's developing capacity for effortful control • Revised section on genetic and environmental influences on temperament, with special attention to ethnic and gender differences • New section on temperamental differences in susceptibility to the effects of good and poor parenting, highlighting evidence on the short 5-HTTLPR gene • Updated research on cultural variations in views of sensitive caregiving, with implications for attachment security • New findings on the joint contributions of infant genotype, temperament, and parenting to disorganized/disoriented attachment, with special attention to the short 5-HTTLPR and DRD4-7 repeat gene • New illustration of interventions that promote attachment security by teaching parents to interact sensitively with difficult-to-care-for babies • New evidence on contributions of fathers' involvement in caregiving to attachment security and to cognitive, emotional, and social competence • New research on the implications of infant–caregiver attachment for later development, with special emphasis on continuity of caregiving • Updated research on cultural variations in early self-development

CHAPTER 7: Updated consideration of advances in brain development in early childhood, with enhanced attention to the prefrontal cortex and executive function • Updated statistics and research on the health status of young children, including tooth decay and childhood immunizations • New evidence on parenting practices and young children's unintentional injuries • New Cultural Influences box addressing why children from Asian cultures are advanced in drawing progress and artistic creativity • Updated evidence on early childhood categorization, highlighting cultural differences • New section on development of executive function in early childhood, with evidence on the facilitating role of parental sensitivity and scaffolding • Updated discussion of development of memory in early childhood, including the distinction between episodic memory and semantic memory • New evidence on cognitive attainments and social experiences that contribute to young children's mastery of false belief • Updated Biology and Environment box on autism and theory of mind • Revised section on strengthening preschool intervention for economically disadvantaged children, including findings on Head Start REDI • Updated discussion of educational media, including effects on cognitive development and academic learning

CHAPTER 8: Recent findings on development of emotional understanding and emotional self-regulation in early childhood • New research on the influence of parents' elaborative reminiscing on self-concept and emotional understanding • New evidence addressing contributions of sociodramatic and rough-and-tumble play to young children's emotional and social development • Expanded and updated section on contributions of early childhood peer relations to school readiness and academic performance • New research on corporal punishment and children's adjustment, with special attention to children at high genetic risk for behavior problems • Updated Cultural Influences box on ethnic differences in the consequences of physical punishment • Recent research on moral understanding in early childhood, including contributions of language, theory of mind, peer and sibling experiences, and parenting • Expanded discussion of media exposure and young children's aggression • New Biology and Environment box on transgender children • New findings on early intervention to prevent child maltreatment, with special attention to Healthy Families America home visiting program

CHAPTER 9: New Social Issues: Health box on family stressors and childhood obesity • New evidence on contributions of children's physical fitness to executive function, memory, and academic achievement • Expanded attention to informal, child-organized games, including SES and cultural variations • Updated research on school-age children's spatial reasoning, focusing on cognitive maps of large-scale spaces • New section on gains in executive function in middle childhood, including related changes in the brain, implications for academic learning, and interventions that train executive function in children with learning difficulties • Updated evidence on the school-age child's theory of mind, with special attention to recursive thought • New Cultural Influences box on the Flynn effect, dramatic gains in IQ from one generation to the next • Updated findings on reducing cultural bias in testing through dynamic assessment and interventions that counter the negative impact of stereotype threat • Expanded discussion of the diverse cognitive benefits of bilingualism • Updated section on U.S. academic achievement in international perspective

CHAPTER 10: Updated discussion of cultural influences on self-esteem, including gender and ethnic variations • New evidence addressing effects of person praise and process praise on children's mastery orientation • New section on culture and moral understanding • Enhanced consideration of racial and ethnic prejudice in school-age children, including effective ways to reduce prejudice • Revised and updated Biology and Environment box on bullies and their victims, with special attention to cyberbullying • Updated discussion of school-age children's gender-stereotyped beliefs, including stereotypes about achievement • Expanded coverage of effects of maternal and dual-earner employment on child development • Revised and updated Cultural Influences box on the impact of ethnic and political violence on children • Updated evidence on child sexual abuse, including long-term consequences for physical and psychological health • Enhanced discussion of resilience in middle childhood, including research on social and emotional learning interventions

CHAPTER 11: Updated statistics on physical activity levels among U.S. adolescents • New research on adolescent brain development, with implications for adolescent risk-taking and susceptibility to peer influence • New evidence on effects of pubertal timing on adjustment • Recent research on nutritional needs and dietary choices of U.S. adolescents • Expanded discussion of adolescent sexuality, with new evidence on factors contributing to early sexual activity • New research on substance use and abuse, including the Strong African American Families (SAAF) program, aimed at reducing drug experimentation • Updated discussion of sex differences in mental abilities, including current evidence on reading, writing, and math achievement • Expanded discussion of school transitions, with new findings on achievement of students in K–8 versus middle schools • Updated Social Issues: Education box on effects of media multitasking on learning, with new evidence on consequences for executive function • Expanded discussion of high school students' part-time work and implications for academic and social adjustment

CHAPTER 12: Expanded consideration of influences on adolescents' self-esteem, including parents, peers, and larger social environment • New research on the process of identity development, along with personal and social influences • Updated evidence on adolescents' capacity to integrate moral, social-conventional, and personal concerns • Enhanced consideration of parental, peer, and school influences on moral maturity • Enhanced discussion of parent–adolescent relationships and development of autonomy, including cultural variations • New evidence on contributions of sibling relationships to adolescent adjustment • New research on gender differences in friendship quality among ethnic minority youths • Expanded and updated section on teenagers' online communication with friends, including consequences for friendship quality and social adjustment • Updated evidence on adolescent depression, addressing the combined influence of heredity, pubertal hormones, and family, peer, and life-event influences, with special attention to gender differences • New research on family, school, and neighborhood contributions to delinquency

CHAPTER 13: Updated Biology and Environment box on telomere length as a marker of the impact of life circumstances on biological aging • New statistics on overweight and obesity in adulthood, including international comparisons, variations among U.S. ethnic groups, and approaches to treatment • New research on substance abuse in early adulthood, including sex differences in progression to alcohol dependence • New findings on sexual attitudes and behavior among young adults, including Internet dating, sex differences in number of lifetime partners, sex without relationship commitment on U.S. college campuses, same-sex relationships, and implications of sexual activity for life satisfaction • Discussion of generational differences in acceptance of same-sex marriage, including high acceptance by Millennials • Updated section on risk of sexually transmitted infections (STIs) in early adulthood, with special attention to HIV/AIDS • Revised and updated evidence on sexual coercion • Updated evidence on cognitive ingredients of creativity, including reduced inhibition of information that, at first glance, appears irrelevant • New Social Issues: Education box on the importance of academic engagement in college for successful transition to the labor market • Enhanced consideration of women's progress in choosing male-dominated careers, with special attention to college women talented in math and science

CHAPTER 14: New evidence on emerging adults' identity development, including cultural variations in timing of identity achievement • Updated section on religion and spirituality among emerging adults, with implications for psychological adjustment • New findings on forms of love, with special attention to compassionate love and contributions of commitment to lasting intimate relationships • Updated research on cultural variations in experience of love, including arranged-marriage couples whose love grew over time • New evidence on lesbian and gay intimate relationships • Updated discussion of the challenges and rewards of parenthood • Recent findings on cohabitation, with special attention to factors linked to relationship persistence and dissolution • New research on gay and lesbian parents and their children's development • Updated findings on the challenges experienced by women who pursue male-dominated careers • Enhanced consideration of gender variations in career development, including factors contributing to the widespread gender pay gap and to differences in career advancement

CHAPTER 15: Updated Biology and Environment box on anti-aging effects of dietary calorie restriction • New evidence on physical and mental symptoms associated with the climacteric and menopause • Updated evidence on sexual activity of midlife cohabiting and married couples • Updated findings on gender bias in medical treatment of women for heart attacks • New research on developmental trends in Type A behavior • New findings on regular physical exercise and reduced mortality risk throughout adulthood, along with approaches to increasing midlife physical activity • New Social Issues: Health box on mental health benefits of modest lifetime exposure to adversity • New section on executive function in midlife, focusing on declines in working memory, inhibition, and flexible shifting of attention, and on middle-aged adults' compensatory strategies • Revised and updated section on practical problem solving and expertise in middle adulthood

CHAPTER 16: New evidence on the relationship of midlife generativity to psychological adjustment, including civic, political, and religious engagement • Updated research on life regrets and midlife psychological well-being • Enhanced Biology and Environment box on factors that promote psychological well-being in midlife, with new evidence on the link between physical activity and improved executive function • Discussion of the dramatic rise in death rates due to suicide and drug and alcohol abuse among U.S. middle-aged white men • Revised and updated section on gender identity, with special attention to cohort effects on the midlife rise in androgyny • New research on marriage and divorce in middle adulthood • Updated evidence on SES variations in support provided by middle-aged parents to their adult children • New findings on cultural variations in middle-aged children caring for aging parents • Recent research on midlife sibling relationships, with special attention to the persisting influence of parental favoritism • New evidence on gender and SES variations in the midlife rise in job satisfaction

CHAPTER 17: New evidence on the relationship of visual and hearing impairments to cognitive functioning • Updated consideration of assistive technology for older people with disabilities •

Enhanced discussion of the impact of negative stereotypes of aging on older adults' physical, cognitive, and emotional functioning • Updated evidence on sexuality in late adulthood • New findings on risk and protective factors for Alzheimer's disease, including the role of epigenetic processes • Updated findings on the associative memory deficit in late life • New findings on the reminiscence bump in autobiographical recall • Enhanced discussion of language processing, with special attention to aging adults' narrative competence • Attention to the adverse impact of "elderspeak," simplified, patronizing language often directed at aging adults • Updated discussion of cognitive interventions aimed at older adults, including those directed at improving executive function • Revised and updated Social Issues: Education box on how intensive training in the art of acting enhances cognitive functioning in aging adults

CHAPTER 18: New section on the positivity effect, older adults' bias toward emotionally positive information, plus expanded discussion of late-life expertise in emotional self-regulation • Updated findings on spirituality and religiosity in late adulthood, including aspects of religious involvement that enhance older adults' psychological well-being • New research on contributions of personal control to life satisfaction • New evidence on socioemotional selectivity theory, including age-related change in closeness of social partners • Updated discussion of assisted living, including variations in quality of U.S. facilities, with implications for aging adults with limited financial resources • Revised and updated section on late-life marriage, with special attention to diversity in marital satisfaction • New evidence on lesbian and gay older couples, including advantages of legally recognized marriage for physical and mental health • Updated research on late-life divorce, remarriage, and cohabitation, along with the growing number of couples described as living apart together • Enhanced and updated discussion of elder abuse, with updated statistics on U.S. incidence, new evidence on traits of perpetrators, and physical and mental health consequences for victims • New Biology and Environment box on Experience Corps, illustrating the benefits of volunteer service for older adults' physical and mental health

CHAPTER 19: Updated section on children's understanding of death including cultural variations in parents' candidness in discussing death with children • Attention to the role of forgiveness in relieving distress and inducing a sense of life completion among the terminally ill • Enhanced discussion of patients' and family members' experiences with dying at home • Updated evidence on the diverse benefits of hospice care for dying patients and family members • New findings on the success of music vigils in reducing pain and promoting psychological well-being among dying patients • Revised sections on medical aid-in-dying and voluntary euthanasia, including ethical issues and current public and physician opinion • Findings indicating that the typical response to loss of a loved one is resilience • Enhanced consideration of gender differences in grieving, with special attention to parents who have lost a child • Revised and updated section on death education

PEDAGOGICAL FEATURES

Maintaining a highly accessible writing style—one that is lucid and engaging without being simplistic—continues to be one of my major goals. I frequently converse with students, encouraging them to relate what they read to their own lives. In doing so, I aim to make the study of human development involving and pleasurable.

Chapter Introductions and Vignettes

To provide a helpful preview of chapter content, I include an outline and overview in each chapter introduction. To help students construct a clear image of development and to enliven the text narrative, each chronological age division is unified by case examples woven throughout that set of chapters. For example, the middle childhood section highlights the experiences and concerns of 10-year-old Joey; 8-year-old Lizzie; their divorced parents, Rena and Drake; and their classmates. In the chapters on late adulthood, students get to know Walt and Ruth, a vibrant retired couple, along with Walt's older brother, Dick, and his wife, Goldie, and Ruth's sister, Ida, a victim of Alzheimer's disease. Besides a set of main characters who bring unity to each age period, many additional vignettes offer vivid examples of development and diversity among children, adolescents, and adults.

End-of-Chapter Summaries

Comprehensive end-of-chapter summaries, organized according to the major divisions of each chapter and highlighting important terms, remind students of key points in the text discussion. Learning objectives are included in the summary to encourage active study.

Look and Listen

This active-learning feature presents students with opportunities to observe what real children, adolescents, and adults say and do; speak with them or with professionals invested in their well-being; and inquire into community programs and practices that influence development. "Look and Listen" experiences are tied to relevant text sections, with the goal of making the study of development more authentic and meaningful.

Ask Yourself Questions

Active engagement with the subject matter is also supported by study questions at the end of most major sections. Three types of questions prompt students to think about human development in diverse ways: **Connect** questions help students build an image of the whole person by integrating what they have learned across age periods and domains of development. **Apply** questions encourage application of knowledge to controversial issues and problems faced by children, adolescents, adults, and professionals who work with them. **Reflect** questions personalize study of human development by asking students to reflect on their own development and life experiences.

Learning Objectives

New to this edition, learning objectives appear below each main heading, guiding students' reading and study.

Three Types of Thematic Boxes

Thematic boxes accentuate the philosophical themes of this book:

Social Issues boxes discuss the impact of social conditions on children, adolescents, and adults, and emphasize the need for sensitive social policies to ensure their well-being. They are divided into two types: **Social Issues: Education** boxes focus on home, school, and community influences on learning—for example, *Magnet Schools: Equal Access to High-Quality Education, Media Multitasking Disrupts Learning,* and *How Important Is Academic Engagement in College for Successful Transition to the Labor Market?*

Social Issues: Health boxes address values and practices relevant to physical and mental health. Examples include *A Cross-National Perspective on Health Care and Other Policies for Parents and Newborn Babies, Family Stressors and Childhood Obesity,* and *The Silver Lining in Life's Adversities.*

Biology and Environment boxes highlight growing attention to the complex, bidirectional relationship between biology and environment. Examples include *The Tutsi Genocide and Epigenetic Transmission of Maternal Stressors to Children, Transgender Children,* and *Experience Corps: Promoting Retired Adults' Physical and Mental Health and Children's Academic Success.*

Cultural Influences boxes deepen the attention to culture threaded throughout the text. They highlight both cross-cultural and multicultural variations in human development—for example, *Immigrant Youths: Adapting to a New Land, The Flynn Effect: Massive Generational Gains in IQ,* and *Cultural Variations in Mourning Behavior.*

Applying What We Know Tables

In this feature, I summarize research-based applications on many issues, speaking directly to students as parents or future parents and to those pursuing different careers or areas of study, such as teaching, health care, counseling, or social work. The tables include *Supporting Early Language Learning, Regulating Screen Media Use,* and *Relieving the Stress of Caring for an Aging Parent.*

Milestones Tables

A Milestones table appears at the end of each age division of the text. These tables summarize major physical, cognitive, language, emotional, and social attainments, providing a convenient aid for reviewing the chronology of human development.

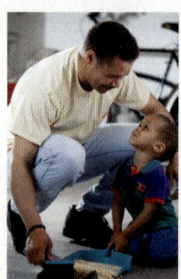

Enhanced Art and Photo Program

Colorful graphics present concepts and research findings with clarity and attractiveness, thereby aiding student understanding and retention. Each photo has been carefully selected to complement text discussion and to represent the diversity of children, adolescents, and adults around the world.

In-Text Key Terms with Definitions, End-of-Chapter Term List, and End-of-Book Glossary

In-text highlighting of key terms and definitions encourages students to review the central vocabulary of the field in greater depth by rereading related information. Key terms also appear in an end-of-chapter page-referenced term list and an end-of-book glossary.

ACKNOWLEDGMENTS

The dedicated contributions of many individuals helped make this book a reality and contributed to refinements and improvements in this seventh edition.

REVIEWERS

An impressive cast of over 150 reviewers has provided many helpful suggestions and constructive criticisms, as well as encouragement and enthusiasm for the organization and content of the text. I am grateful to each one of them.

For the Seventh Edition

Cheryl Anagnopoulos, Black Hills State University
Donna Baptiste, Northwestern University
Carolyn M. Barry, Loyola University Maryland
Gina Brelsford, Penn State–Harrisburg
Katie E. Cherry, Louisiana State University
Michelle Drouin, Indiana U. Purdue–Fort Wayne
Kathleen Dwinnells, Kent State–Trumbull
Karen Fingerman, University of Texas, Austin
Lily Halsted, Queens University of Charlotte
James Henrie, University of Wisconsin–Parkside
Janette Herbers, Villanova University
Michelle Kelley, Old Dominion University
Kristopher Kimbler, Florida Gulf Coast University
Katie Lawson, Ball State University
Joan Pendergast, Concord University
Amy Rauer, Auburn University
Celinda Reese-Melancon, Oklahoma State University
Pam Schuetze, SUNY Buffalo
Brooke Spangler, Miami University
Virginia Tompkins, Ohio State–Lima
Bridget Walsh, University of Nevada–Reno
Nona Leigh Wilson, Northwestern University

For the First Through Sixth Editions

Gerald Adams, University of Guelph
Jackie Adamson, South Dakota School of Mines and Technology
Paul C. Amrhein, University of New Mexico
Cheryl Anagnopoulos, Black Hills State University
Doreen Arcus, University of Massachusetts, Lowell
René L. Babcock, Central Michigan University
Carolyn M. Barry, Loyola University
Sherry Beaumont, University of Northern British Columbia
W. Keith Berg, University of Florida
Lori Bica, University of Wisconsin, Eau Claire
James A. Bird, Weber State University
Toni Bisconti, University of Akron
Joyce Bishop, Golden West College
Kimberly Blair, University of Pittsburgh
Tracie L. Blumentritt, University of Wisconsin–La Crosse
Ed Brady, Belleville Area College
Michele Y. Breault, Truman State University
Dilek Buchholz, Weber State University
Lanthan Camblin, University of Cincinnati
Judith W. Cameron, Ohio State University
Joan B. Cannon, University of Massachusetts, Lowell
Michael Caruso, University of Toledo
Susan L. Churchill, University of Nebraska–Lincoln
Gary Creasey, Illinois State University
Rhoda Cummings, University of Nevada–Reno
Rita M. Curl, Minot State University
Linda Curry, Texas Christian University
Carol Lynn Davis, University of Maine
Lou de la Cruz, Sheridan Institute
Manfred Diehl, Colorado State University
Byron Egeland, University of Minnesota
Mary Anne Erickson, Ithaca College
Beth Fauth, Utah State University
Karen Fingerman, University of Texas, Austin
Maria P. Fracasso, Towson University
Elizabeth E. Garner, University of North Florida
Laurie Gottlieb, McGill University
Dan Grangaard, Austin Community College
Clifford Gray, Pueblo Community College
Marlene Groomes, Miami Dade College
Laura Gruntmeir, Redlands Community College
Linda Halgunseth, Pennsylvania State University
Laura Hanish, Arizona State University
Traci Haynes, Columbus State Community College
Vernon Haynes, Youngstown State University
Bert Hayslip, University of North Texas
Melinda Heinz, Iowa State University
Bob Heller, Athabasca University
Karl Hennig, St. Francis Xavier University
Paula Hillman, University of Wisconsin–Whitewater
Deb Hollister, Valencia Community College
Hui-Chin Hsu, University of Georgia
Lera Joyce Johnson, Centenary College of Louisiana
Janet Kalinowski, Ithaca College
Kevin Keating, Broward Community College
Joseph Kishton, University of North Carolina, Wilmington
Wendy Kliewer, Virginia Commonwealth University
Marita Kloseck, University of Western Ontario
Karen Kopera-Frye, University of Nevada, Reno
Valerie Kuhlmeier, Queens University
Deanna Kuhn, Teachers College, Columbia University
Rebecca A. López, California State University–Long Beach
Dale Lund, California State University, San Bernardino
Pamela Manners, Troy State University
Debra McGinnis, Oakland University
Robert B. McLaren, California State University, Fullerton
Kate McLean, University of Toronto at Mississauga
Randy Mergler, California State University
Karla K. Miley, Black Hawk College
Carol Miller, Anne Arundel Community College
Teri Miller, Milwaukee Area Technical College
David Mitchell, Kennesaw State University
Steve Mitchell, Somerset Community College

Gary T. Montgomery, University of Texas, Pan American
Feleccia Moore-Davis, Houston Community College
Ulrich Mueller, University of Victoria
Karen Nelson, Austin College
Bob Newby, Tarleton State University
Jill Norvilitis, Buffalo State College
Patricia O'Brien, University of Illinois at Chicago
Nancy Ogden, Mount Royal College
Peter Oliver, University of Hartford
Verna C. Pangman, University of Manitoba
Robert Pasnak, George Mason University
Ellen Pastorino, Gainesville College
Julie Patrick, West Virginia University
Marion Perlmutter, University of Michigan
Warren H. Phillips, Iowa State University
Dana Plude, University of Maryland
Leslee K. Polina, Southeast Missouri State University
Dolores Pushkar, Concordia University
Leon Rappaport, Kansas State University
Celinda Reese-Melancon, Oklahoma State University
Pamela Roberts, California State University, Long Beach
Stephanie J. Rowley, University of North Carolina
Elmer Ruhnke, Manatee Community College
Randall Russac, University of North Florida
Marie Saracino, Stephen F. Austin State University
Edythe H. Schwartz, California State University–Sacramento
Bonnie Seegmiller, City University of New York, Hunter College
Richard Selby, Southeast Missouri State University
Mathew Shake, Western Kentucky University
Aurora Sherman, Oregon State University
Carey Sherman, University of Michigan
Kim Shifren, Towson University
David Shwalb, Southeastern Louisiana University
Paul S. Silverman, University of Montana
Judith Smetana, University of Rochester
Glenda Smith, North Harris College
Gregory Smith, Kent State University
Jacqui Smith, University of Michigan
Jeanne Spaulding, Houston Community College
Thomas Spencer, San Francisco State University
Bruce Stam, Chemeketa Community College
Stephanie Stein, Central Washington University
JoNell Strough, West Virginia University
Vince Sullivan, Pensacola Junior College
Bruce Thompson, University of Southern Maine
Laura Thompson, New Mexico State University
Mojisola Tiamiyu, University of Toledo
Ruth Tincoff, Harvard University
Joe Tinnin, Richland College
Catya von Károlyi, University of Wisconsin–Eau Claire
L. Monique Ward, University of Michigan
Rob Weisskirch, California State University, Fullerton
Nancy White, Youngstown State University
Ursula M. White, El Paso Community College
Carol L. Wilkinson, Whatcom Community College
Lois J. Willoughby, Miami-Dade Community College
Paul Wink, Wellesley College
Deborah R. Winters, New Mexico State University

EDITORIAL AND PRODUCTION TEAM

I cannot begin to express what a great pleasure it has been, once again, to work with Tom Pauken, Managing Editor, who oversaw the preparation of the third, fifth, and sixth editions of *Development Through the Lifespan* and who returned to edit this seventh edition along with its supplements package. Tom's unmatched dedication to my titles, keen organizational skills, responsive day-to-day communication, careful review of manuscript, insightful suggestions, interest in the subject matter, patience, and sense of humor (at just the right moments) greatly enhanced the quality of the text and made it possible for me to keep pace with Pearson's tight revision time frame. I greatly look forward to working with Tom on future projects.

My sincere thanks, as well, to Roth Wilkofsky, Senior Publisher, for crafting a caring climate at Pearson in which to prepare this revision and for bringing the publishing team together in New York for the seventh edition planning meeting. I have benefited greatly from Roth's astute problem solving and encouragement, wide-ranging knowledge and experience, and cordiality.

Donna Simons and Liz Napolitano, Senior Production Managers, coordinated the complex production tasks, transforming my manuscript into an exquisitely beautiful text. I am deeply grateful for their keen aesthetics, attention to detail, flexibility, efficiency, and thoughtfulness.

Rachel Trapp, Assistant Editor, has been nothing short of amazing. In addition to spending countless hours searching, gathering, and organizing scholarly literature, she assisted with a wide array of editorial and production tasks. Judy Ashkenaz and Michelle McSweeney, Development Editors, carefully reviewed and commented on each chapter, helping to ensure that reviewers' comments were diligently considered and that every thought would be clearly expressed and well developed. Lorretta Palagi provided outstanding copyediting and careful compilation of the references list.

The supplements package benefited from the talents and dedication of several individuals. Judy Ashkenaz wrote the new Lecture Enhancements for the Instructor's Resource Manual and revised its chapter summaries and outlines. Kimberly Michaud prepared a superb Test Bank, and Julie Hughes, Denise Wright, and Rachel Trapp carefully crafted the online assessments. Rachael Payne designed and wrote a highly attractive PowerPoint presentation. Maria Henneberry and Phil Vandiver of Contemporary Visuals in Bloomington, Illinois, prepared an inspiring set of new video segments.

A final word of gratitude goes to my family, whose love, patience, and understanding have enabled me to be wife, mother, teacher, researcher, and text author at the same time. My sons, David and Peter, grew up with my texts, passing from childhood to adolescence and then to adulthood as successive editions were written. David has a special connection with the books' subject matter as an elementary school teacher. Peter is now an experienced attorney, and his vivacious and talented wife Melissa an accomplished linguist and university professor. All three continue to enrich my understanding through reflections on events and progress in their own lives. Finally, I thank my husband, Ken, for willingly making room in our lives for the immensely demanding endeavor of authoring seven editions of *Development Through the Lifespan*.

Laura E. Berk

mydevelopmentlab

MyDevelopmentLab is a collection of online homework, tutorial, and assessment products designed to improve college and university students' learning. Authored by Laura Berk, MyDevelopmentLab for *Development Through the Lifespan*, Seventh Edition, engages students through active learning and promotes in-depth mastery of the subject matter, thereby fostering more thorough preparation for class, quizzes, and exams.

- A **Personalized Study Plan** analyzes students' study needs into three levels: Remember, Understand, and Apply.
- A **Variety of Assessments** enable continuous evaluation of students' learning.
- The **Gradebook** helps students track progress and get immediate feedback. Automatically graded assessments flow into the Gradebook, which can be viewed in MyDevelopmentLab or exported.
- The **eText** allows students to highlight relevant passages and add notes. Access the eText through a laptop, iPad®, or tablet—or download the free app to use on tablets.
- **Extensive video footage** includes NEW segments produced by author Laura Berk.
- **Multimedia simulations** include NEW topics, with simulations designed by author Laura Berk to seamlessly complement the text.
- **Careers in Human Development** explains how studying human development is essential for a wide range of career paths. This tool features more than 25 career overviews, which contain interviews with actual practitioners, educational requirements, typical day-to-day activities, and links to websites for additional information.
- **MyVirtualLife** is a pair of interactive web-based simulations. The first allows students to rear a child from birth to age 18 and monitor the effects of their parenting decisions over time. In the second, students make personal decisions and see the impact of those decisions on their simulated future selves.

For a sampling of MyDevelopmentLab's rich content, visit *www.mydevelopmentlab.com*.

REVEL™

REVEL is an immersive learning experience designed for the way today's students read, think, and learn. Built in collaboration with educators and students nationwide, REVEL is the newest, fully digital method of delivering course content.

REVEL further enlivens the text, with interactive media and assessments—integrated within the authors' narrative—that provide opportunities for students to deeply engage with course content while reading. Greater student engagement leads to more thorough understanding of concepts and improved performance throughout the course.

To learn more about REVEL, visit *www.pearsonhighered.com/REVEL*.

INSTRUCTOR RESOURCES

In addition to MyDevelopmentLab, several other author-produced instructor materials accompany *Development Through the Lifespan's* seventh edition. Altogether, these resources enhance student learning and engagement in the course content.

Instructor's Resource Manual (IRM) This thoroughly revised IRM can be used by first-time or experienced instructors to enrich classroom experiences. Two new lecture enhancements accompany each chapter, presenting cutting-edge topics, with article citations and suggestions for expanding on chapter content in class.

Test Bank The Test Bank contains over 2,000 multiple-choice and essay questions, all of which are page-referenced to the chapter content and also classified by type.

Pearson MyTest This secure online environment allows instructors to easily create exams, study guide questions, and quizzes from any computer with an Internet connection.

PowerPoint Presentation The PowerPoint presentation provides outlines and illustrations of key topics for each chapter of the text.

"Explorations in Lifespan Development" DVD and Guide This revised DVD, designed for classroom use, is over nine hours in length and contains more than 80 four- to ten-minute narrated segments, 20 of which are new to this edition, that illustrate theories, concepts, and milestones of human development. The DVD and Guide are available only to instructors who are confirmed adopters of the text.

About the Cover Art

Growing up in Depression-era Detroit, Harold Gregor displayed passion for and talent in art as a child. As early as kindergarten, he drew—so much so that he recalls being placed in the corner for wasting paper. He earned his bachelor's degree from Wayne State University, master's degree from Michigan State University, and Ph.D. from Ohio State University in painting. After a decade of teaching and experimentation with diverse artistic styles in southern California, he moved to the American heartland, joining the faculty at Illinois State University in 1970.

The Illinois farm and prairie landscape quickly became a compelling source of inspiration, and Gregor gained national prominence as one of the foremost American Photorealist painters. Starting with close-up views of corn cribs, an indigenous form of architecture that fascinated him, he soon moved to panoramas and aerial views of prairie farm scenes, introducing imaginative colors that accentuated the unique and varied beauty of the Midwestern landscape.

In 2004, while climbing a cliff trail in Italy, he fell and broke his right wrist. With his right arm in a cast, he transformed an obstacle into an opportunity: He began to paint with his left hand. Once his right arm healed, he refined his left-handed paintings, eventually arriving at brilliantly colorful, abstract stylistic innovations he calls Vibrascapes, of which the dazzling, energetic image on the cover of this text is an example.

Now a distinguished professor emeritus, Harold Gregor is the epitome of "successful aging." At age 87, he continues to paint prolifically, prepare new exhibitions, and teach. On his studio wall can be found a Chinese proverb, which reads, "What happiness to wake alive again into this same gray world of winter rain." He says the proverb reminds him that although growing older is accompanied by unforeseen challenges, he feels blessed each day to do what he enjoys most: painting and teaching.

Harold Gregor's paintings have been shown at the White House, the American Embassy in Moscow, and the Art Institute of Chicago. They have won numerous prestigious awards and can be viewed in galleries across the United States. To learn more about his life and work, visit www.hgregor.com; and watch the video segment, *Creativity in Late Life*, that accompanies this text.

Legend for Photos Accompanying Sofie's Story

Sofie's story is told in Chapters 1 and 19, from her birth to her death. The photos that appear at the beginning of Chapter 1 follow her through her lifespan and include family members of two succeeding generations.

Page 2

1. Sofie, age 18, high school graduation.
2. Sofie as a baby, with her mother.
3. Sofie, age 6, with her brother, age 8.
4. Sofie's German passport.
5. Sofie, age 60, and daughter Laura on Laura's wedding day.
6. Sofie and Phil, less than two years before Sofie died.
7. Sofie's grandsons, David and Peter, ages 5 and 2, children of Laura and Ken.
8. Laura, Ken, and sons Peter and David, ages 10 and 13, on the occasion of David's Bar Mitzvah.
9. Peter and Melissa on their wedding day.
10. David, toasting Peter and Melissa's marriage.
11. Laura and Ken, at family gathering.

Page 3
Sofie, age 30, shortly after immigrating to the United States.

Page 4
Sofie and Phil in their mid-thirties, when they became engaged.

1

chapter 1

History, Theory, and Research Strategies

This photo essay chronicles the life course and family legacy of Sofie Lentschner. It begins in the early twentieth century with Sofie's infancy and concludes in the early twenty-first century, nearly four decades after Sofie's death, with the wedding of a grandson. For a description of each photo, see the legend on page 1.

What's ahead in chapter 1

A Scientific, Applied, and Interdisciplinary Field

Basic Issues
 Continuous or Discontinuous Development? • One Course of Development or Many? • Relative Influence of Nature and Nurture?

The Lifespan Perspective: A Balanced Point of View
 Development Is Lifelong • Development Is Multidimensional and Multidirectional • Development Is Plastic • Development Is Influenced by Multiple, Interacting Forces

■ **BIOLOGY AND ENVIRONMENT** Resilience

■ **CULTURAL INFLUENCES** The Baby Boomers Reshape the Life Course

Scientific Beginnings
 Darwin: Forefather of Scientific Child Study • The Normative Period • The Mental Testing Movement

Mid-Twentieth-Century Theories
 The Psychoanalytic Perspective • Behaviorism and Social Learning Theory • Piaget's Cognitive-Developmental Theory

Recent Theoretical Perspectives
 Information Processing • Developmental Neuroscience • Ethology and Evolutionary Developmental Psychology • Vygotsky's Sociocultural Theory • Ecological Systems Theory

■ **SOCIAL ISSUES: HEALTH** Family Chaos Undermines Parents' and Children's Well-Being

Comparing and Evaluating Theories

Studying Development
 Common Research Methods • General Research Designs • Designs for Studying Development

■ **CULTURAL INFLUENCES** Immigrant Youths: Adapting to a New Land

Ethics in Lifespan Research

Sofie Lentschner was born in 1908, the second child of Jewish parents who made their home in Leipzig, Germany, a city of thriving commerce and cultural vitality. Her father was a successful businessman and community leader, her mother a socialite well-known for her charm, beauty, and hospitality. As a baby, Sofie displayed the determination and persistence that would be sustained throughout her life. She sat for long periods inspecting small objects with her eyes and hands. The single event that consistently broke her gaze was the sound of the piano in the parlor. As soon as Sofie could crawl, she steadfastly pulled herself up to finger its keys and marveled at the tinkling sounds.

By the time Sofie entered elementary school, she was an introspective child, often ill at ease at the festive parties that girls of her family's social standing were expected to attend. She immersed herself in schoolwork, especially in mastering foreign languages—a regular part of German elementary and secondary education. Twice a week, she took piano lessons from the finest teacher in Leipzig. By the time Sofie graduated from high school, she spoke English and French fluently and had become an accomplished pianist. Whereas most German girls of her time married by age 20, Sofie postponed serious courtship in favor of entering university. Her parents began to wonder whether their intense, studious daughter would ever settle into family life.

Sofie wanted marriage as well as education, but her plans were thwarted by the political turbulence of her times. When Hitler rose to power in the early 1930s, Sofie's father, fearing for the safety of his wife and children, moved the family to Belgium. Conditions for Jews in Europe quickly worsened. The Nazis plundered Sofie's family home and confiscated her father's business. By the end of the 1930s, Sofie had lost contact with all but a handful of her aunts, uncles, cousins, and childhood friends, many of whom (she later learned) were herded into cattle cars and transported to Nazi death camps. In 1939, as anti-Jewish laws and atrocities intensified, Sofie's family fled to the United States.

As Sofie turned 30, her parents, convinced that she would never marry and would need a career for financial security, agreed to support her return to school. Sofie earned two master's degrees, one in music and the other in librarianship. Then, on a blind date, she met Philip, a U.S. army officer. Philip's calm, gentle nature complemented Sofie's intensity and worldliness. Within six months they married. During the next four years, two daughters and a son were born.

When World War II ended, Philip left the army and opened a small men's clothing store. Sofie divided her time between caring for the children and helping Philip in the store. Now in her forties, she was a devoted mother, but few women her age were still rearing young children. As Philip struggled with the business, he spent longer hours at work, and Sofie often felt lonely. She rarely touched the piano, which brought back painful memories of youthful life plans shattered by war. Sofie's sense of isolation and lack of fulfillment frequently left her short-tempered. Late at night, she and Philip could be heard arguing.

As Sofie's children grew older, she returned to school again, this time earning a teaching credential. Finally, at age 50, she launched a career, teaching German and French to high school students and English to newly arrived immigrants. Besides easing her family's financial difficulties, she felt a gratifying sense of accomplishment and creativity. These years were among the most energetic and satisfying of Sofie's life. She had an unending enthusiasm for teaching—for transmitting her facility with language, her firsthand knowledge of the consequences of hatred and oppression, and her practical understanding of how to adapt to life in a new land. She watched her children, whose young lives were free of the trauma of war, adopt many of her values and commitments and begin their marital and vocational lives at the expected time.

Sofie approached age 60 with an optimistic outlook. Released from the financial burden of paying for their children's college education, she and Philip looked forward to greater leisure. Their affection and respect for each other deepened. Once again, Sofie began to play the piano. But this period of contentment was short-lived.

One morning, Sofie awoke and felt a hard lump under her arm. Several days later, her doctor diagnosed cancer. Sofie's spirited disposition and capacity to adapt to radical life changes helped her meet the illness head on. She defined it as an enemy to be fought and overcome. As a result, she lived five more years. Despite the exhaustion of chemotherapy, Sofie maintained a full schedule of teaching duties and continued to visit and run errands for her aging mother. But as she weakened physically, she no longer had the stamina to meet her classes. Bedridden for the last few weeks, she slipped quietly into death with Philip at her side. The funeral chapel overflowed with hundreds of Sofie's students.

One of Sofie's three children, Laura, is the author of this book. Married a year before Sofie died, Laura and her husband, Ken, often think of Sofie's message, spoken privately on the eve of their wedding day: "I learned from my own life and marriage that you must build a life together but also a life apart. You must grant each other the time, space, and support to forge your own identities, your own ways of expressing yourselves and giving to others. The most important ingredient of your relationship must be respect."

Laura and Ken settled in a small Midwestern city, near Illinois State University, where they served on the faculty for many years—Laura in the Department of Psychology, Ken in the Department of Mathematics. They have two sons, David and Peter, to whom Laura has related many stories about Sofie's life and who carry her legacy forward. David shares his grandmother's penchant for teaching; he is a third-grade teacher. Peter, a lawyer, shares her love of music, and his wife Melissa—much like Sofie—is both a talented linguist and a musician. When Peter asked Melissa to marry him, he placed a family heirloom on her finger—an engagement ring that had belonged to Sofie's aunt, who perished in a Nazi death camp. In the box that held the ring, Melissa found a written copy of the story of Sofie and her family.

Sofie also had a lifelong impact on many of her students. A professor of human development wrote to Laura:

> I teach a class in lifespan development. When I opened the textbook and saw the pictures of your mother, I was very surprised. I took high school German classes from her. I remember her as a very tough teacher who both held her students accountable and cared about each and every one of us. That she was an incredible teacher did not really sink in until I went to Germany during my [college] years and was able to both understand German and speak it.

Sofie's story raises a wealth of fascinating issues about human life histories:

- What determines the features that Sofie shares with others and those that make her unique—in physical characteristics, mental capacities, interests, and behaviors?
- What led Sofie to retain the same persistent, determined disposition throughout her life but to change in other essential ways?

- How do historical and cultural conditions—for Sofie, the persecution that destroyed her childhood home, caused the death of family members and friends, and led her family to flee to the United States—affect well-being throughout life?
- How does the timing of events—for example, Sofie's early exposure to multiple languages and her delayed entry into marriage, parenthood, and career—affect development?
- What factors—both genetic and environmental—led Sofie to die sooner than expected?

These are central questions addressed by **developmental science,** a field of study devoted to understanding constancy and change throughout the lifespan (Lerner et al., 2014; Overton & Molenaar, 2015). Great diversity characterizes the interests and concerns of investigators who study development. But all share a single goal: to identify those factors that influence consistencies and transformations in people from conception to death.

A Scientific, Applied, and Interdisciplinary Field

1.1 What is developmental science, and what factors stimulated expansion of the field?

The questions just listed are not just of scientific interest. Each has *applied,* or practical, importance as well. In fact, scientific curiosity is just one factor that led the study of development to become the exciting field it is today. Research about development has also been stimulated by social pressures to improve people's lives. For example, the beginning of public education in the early twentieth century led to a demand for knowledge about what and how to teach children of different ages. The interest of the medical profession in improving people's health required an understanding of physical development, nutrition, and disease. The social service profession's desire to treat emotional problems and to help people adjust to major life events, such as divorce, job loss, war, natural disasters, or the death of loved ones, required information about personality and social development. And parents have continually sought expert advice about child-rearing practices and experiences that would promote their children's well-being.

Our large storehouse of information about development is *interdisciplinary.* It has grown through the combined efforts of people from many fields of study. Because of the need for solutions to everyday problems at all ages, researchers from psychology, sociology, anthropology, biology, and neuroscience have joined forces in research with professionals from education, family studies, medicine, public health, and social service, to name just a few. Together, they have created the field as it exists today—a body of knowledge that is not only scientifically important but also relevant and useful.

Basic Issues

1.2 Identify three basic issues on which theories of human development take a stand.

Developmental science is a relatively recent endeavor. Studies of children did not begin until the late nineteenth and early twentieth centuries. Investigations into adult development, aging, and change over the life course emerged only in the 1960s and 1970s (Elder & Shanahan, 2006). But speculations about how people grow and change have existed for centuries. As they combined with research, they inspired the construction of *theories* of development. A **theory** is an orderly, integrated set of statements that describes, explains, and predicts behavior. For example, a good theory of infant–caregiver attachment would (1) *describe* the behaviors of babies of 6 to 8 months of age as they seek the affection and comfort of a familiar adult, (2) *explain* how and why infants develop this strong desire to bond with a caregiver, and (3) *predict* the consequences of this emotional bond for future relationships.

Theories are vital tools for two reasons. First, they provide organizing frameworks for our observations of people. In other words, they *guide and give meaning* to what we see. Second, theories that are verified by research provide a sound basis for practical action. Once a theory helps us *understand* development, we are in a much better position *to know how to improve* the welfare and treatment of children and adults.

As we will see, theories are influenced by the cultural values and belief systems of their times. But theories differ in one important way from mere opinion or belief: A theory's continued existence depends on *scientific verification.* Every theory must be tested using a fair set of research procedures agreed on by the scientific community, and the findings must endure, or be replicated over time.

Within the field of developmental science, many theories offer very different ideas about what people are like and how they change. The study of development provides no ultimate truth because investigators do not always agree on the meaning of what they see. Also, humans are complex beings; they change physically, mentally, emotionally, and socially. No single theory has explained all these aspects. But the existence of many theories helps advance knowledge as researchers continually try to support, contradict, and integrate these different points of view.

This chapter introduces you to major theories of human development and research strategies used to test them. In later chapters, we will discuss each theory in greater depth and also introduce other important but less grand theories. Although there are many theories, we can easily organize them by looking at the stand they take on three basic issues: (1) Is the course of development continuous or discontinuous? (2) Does one course of development characterize all people, or are there many possible courses? (3) What are the roles of genetic and environmental factors—nature and nurture—in development? Let's look closely at each of these issues.

Continuous or Discontinuous Development?

How can we best describe the differences in capacities among infants, children, adolescents, and adults? As Figure 1.1 illustrates, major theories recognize two possibilities.

One view holds that infants and preschoolers respond to the world in much the same way as adults do. The difference between the immature and mature being is simply one of *amount or complexity.* For example, when Sofie was a baby, her perception of a piano melody, memory for past events, and ability to categorize objects may have been much like our own. Perhaps her only limitation was that she could not perform these skills with as much information and precision as we can. If this is so, then changes in her thinking must be **continuous**—a process of gradually augmenting the same types of skills that were there to begin with.

According to a second view, infants and children have *unique ways of thinking, feeling, and behaving,* ones quite different from those of adults. If so, then development is **discontinuous**—a process in which new ways of understanding and responding to the world emerge at specific times. From this perspective, Sofie could not yet perceive, remember, and categorize experiences as a mature person can. Rather, she moved through a series of developmental steps, each with unique features, until she reached the highest level of functioning.

Theories that accept the discontinuous perspective regard development as taking place in **stages**—*qualitative* changes in thinking, feeling, and behaving that characterize specific periods of development. In stage theories, development is like climbing a staircase, with each step corresponding to a more mature, reorganized way of functioning. The stage concept also assumes that people undergo periods of rapid transformation as they step up from one stage to the next. In other words, change is fairly sudden rather than gradual and ongoing.

Does development actually occur in a neat, orderly sequence of stages? This ambitious assumption has faced significant challenges. Later in this chapter, we will review some influential stage theories.

One Course of Development or Many?

Stage theorists assume that people everywhere follow the same sequence of development. Yet the field of human development is becoming increasingly aware that children and adults live in distinct **contexts**—unique combinations of personal and environmental circumstances that can result in different paths of change. For example, a shy individual who fears social encounters develops in very different contexts from those of an outgoing agemate who readily seeks out other people. Children and adults in non-Western village societies have experiences in their families and communities that differ sharply from those of people in large Western cities. These different circumstances foster different intellectual capacities, social skills, and feelings about the self and others (Kagan, 2013a; Mistry & Dutta, 2015).

As you will see, contemporary theorists regard the contexts that shape development as many-layered and complex. On the personal side, they include heredity and biological makeup. On the environmental side, they include both immediate settings—home, school, and neighborhood—and circumstances more remote from people's everyday lives: community resources, societal values, and historical time period. Furthermore, new evidence is increasingly emphasizing *mutually influential relations* between individuals and their contexts: People not only are affected by but also contribute to the contexts in which they develop (Elder, Shanahan, & Jennings, 2015). Finally, researchers today are more conscious than ever before of cultural diversity in development.

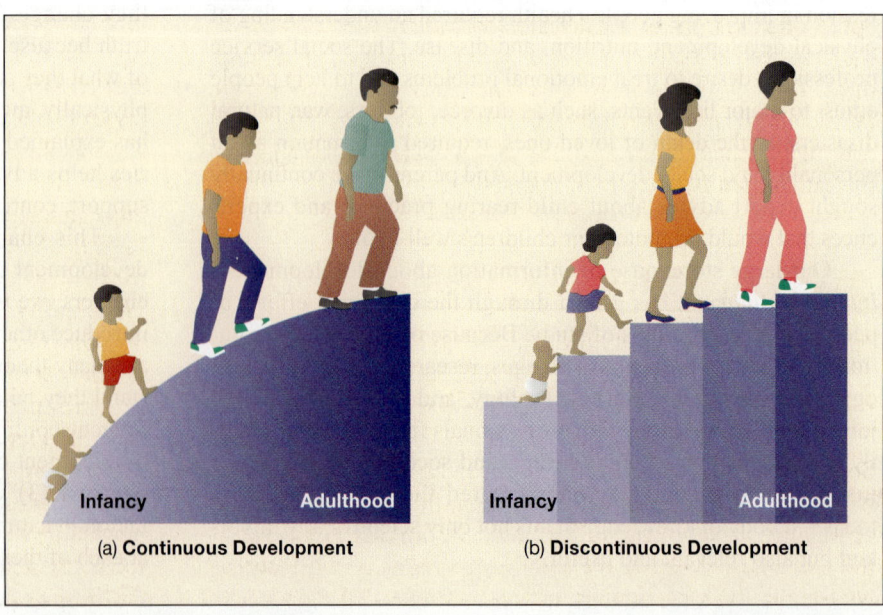

FIGURE 1.1 Is development continuous or discontinuous? (a) Some theorists believe that development is a smooth, continuous process. Individuals gradually add more of the same types of skills. (b) Other theorists think that development takes place in discontinuous stages. People change rapidly as they step up to a new level and then change very little for a while. With each new step, the person interprets and responds to the world in a reorganized, qualitatively different way. As we will see later, still other theorists believe that development is characterized by both continuous and discontinuous change.

(a) Continuous Development (b) Discontinuous Development

Relative Influence of Nature and Nurture?

In addition to describing the course of human development, each theory takes a stand on a major question about its underlying causes: Are genetic or environmental factors more important? This is the age-old **nature–nurture controversy.** By *nature,* we mean the hereditary information we receive from our parents at the moment of conception. By *nurture,* we mean the complex forces of the physical and social world that influence our biological makeup and psychological experiences before and after birth.

Although all theories grant roles to both nature and nurture, they vary in emphasis. Consider the following questions: Is the developing person's ability to think in more complex ways largely the result of a built-in timetable of growth, or is it primarily influenced by stimulation from parents and teachers? Do children acquire language rapidly because they are genetically predisposed to do so or because parents teach them from an early age? And what accounts for the vast individual differences among people—in height, weight, physical coordination, intelligence, personality, and social skills? Is nature or nurture more responsible?

A theory's position on the roles of nature and nurture affects how it explains individual differences. Theorists who emphasize *stability*—that individuals who are high or low in a characteristic (such as verbal ability, anxiety, or sociability) will remain so at later ages—typically stress the importance of *heredity*. If they regard environment as important, they usually point to *early experiences* as establishing a lifelong pattern of behavior. Powerful negative events in the first few years, they argue, cannot be fully overcome by later, more positive ones (Bowlby, 1980; Sroufe, Coffino, & Carlson, 2010). Other theorists, taking a more optimistic view, see development as having substantial **plasticity** throughout life—as open to change in response to influential experiences (Baltes, Lindenberger, & Staudinger, 2006; Overton & Molenaar, 2015).

Throughout this book, you will see that investigators disagree, often sharply, on the question of *stability versus plasticity.* Their answers often vary across *domains,* or aspects, of development. Think back to Sofie's story, and you will see that her linguistic ability and persistent approach to challenges were stable over the lifespan. In contrast, her psychological well-being and life satisfaction fluctuated considerably.

Since the 1960s, researchers have moved from focusing only on child development to investigating development over the entire life course. This woman and her companions on a river rafting trip illustrate the health, vitality, and life satisfaction of many contemporary older adults.

Many acknowledge that development has both universal features and features unique to each individual and his or her contexts. And a growing number regard heredity and environment as inseparably interwoven, each affecting the potential of the other to modify the child's traits and capacities (Lerner et al., 2014; Overton & Molenaar, 2015).

These balanced visions owe much to the expansion of research from a nearly exclusive focus on the first two decades of life to include development during adulthood. In the first half of the twentieth century, it was widely assumed that development stopped at adolescence. Infancy and childhood were viewed as periods of rapid transformation, adulthood as a plateau, and aging as a period of decline. The changing character of the North American population awakened researchers to the idea that gains in functioning are lifelong.

Because of improvements in nutrition, sanitation, and medical knowledge, *average life expectancy* (the number of years an individual born in a particular year can expect to live) gained more in the twentieth century than in the preceding 5,000 years. In 1900, U.S. life expectancy was just under age 50; in 2000, it was 76.8. Today, it is 78.8 years in the United States and even higher in most other industrialized nations, including neighboring Canada. Life expectancy continues to increase; in the United States, it is predicted to reach 84 years in 2050. Consequently, there are more older adults—a worldwide trend that is especially striking in developed countries. People age 65 and older accounted for about 4 percent of the U.S. population in 1900, 7 percent in 1950, and 14 percent in 2013 (U.S. Census Bureau, 2015d).

Older adults are not only more numerous but also healthier and more active. Challenging the earlier stereotype of the withering person, they have contributed to a profound shift in our view of human change. Increasingly, researchers are envisioning it from a *developmental systems perspective*—as a perpetually ongoing process, extending from conception to death, that is molded by a complex network of biological, psychological, and social influences (Lerner, 2015). A leading systems approach is the **lifespan perspective.** Four assumptions make up this broader

The Lifespan Perspective: A Balanced Point of View

1.3 Describe the lifespan perspective on development.

So far, we have discussed basic issues of human development in terms of extremes—solutions favoring one side or the other. But as we trace the unfolding of the field, you will see that the positions of many theorists have softened. Today, some theorists believe that both continuous and discontinuous changes occur.

view: that development is (1) lifelong, (2) multidimensional and multidirectional, (3) highly plastic, and (4) affected by multiple, interacting forces (Baltes, Lindenberger, & Staudinger, 2006; Smith & Baltes, 1999; Staudinger & Lindenberger, 2003).

Development Is Lifelong

According to the lifespan perspective, no age period is supreme in its impact on the life course. Rather, events occurring during each major period, summarized in Table 1.1, can have equally powerful effects on future change. Within each period, change occurs in three broad domains: *physical, cognitive,* and *emotional/social,* which we separate for convenience of discussion (see Figure 1.2 for a description of each). Yet these domains are not really distinct; they overlap and interact.

Every age period has its own agenda, its unique demands and opportunities that yield certain similarities in development across many individuals. Nevertheless, throughout life, the challenges people face and the adjustments they make are highly diverse in timing and pattern, as the remaining assumptions make clear.

Development Is Multidimensional and Multidirectional

Think back to Sofie's life and how she continually faced new demands and opportunities. From a lifespan perspective, the challenges and adjustments of development are *multidimensional*—affected by an intricate blend of biological, psychological, and social forces.

Lifespan development is also *multidirectional,* in at least two ways. First, development is not limited to improved performance. Rather, at every period, it is a joint expression of growth and decline. When Sofie directed her energies toward mastering languages and music as a school-age child, she gave up refining other skills to their full potential. Later, when she chose to become a teacher, she let go of other career options. Although gains are especially evident early in life, and losses during the final years, people of all ages can improve current skills and develop new ones, including skills that compensate for reduced functioning (de Frias, 2014; Stine-Morrow et al., 2014). Most older adults, for example, devise compensatory techniques for dealing with their increasing memory failures. They may rely more on external aids, such as calendars and lists, or generate new internal strategies, such as visualizing exactly where they will be and what they will be doing when they must keep an appointment or take medication.

Second, besides being multidirectional over time, change is multidirectional within each domain of development. Although some qualities of Sofie's cognitive functioning (such as memory) probably declined in her mature years, her knowledge of both English and French undoubtedly grew throughout her life. And she also developed new forms of thinking. For example, Sofie's wealth of experience and ability to cope with diverse problems led her to become expert in practical matters—a quality of reasoning called *wisdom*. Recall Sofie's wise advice to Laura and Ken on the eve of their wedding day. We will consider the development of wisdom in Chapter 17. Notice in the examples just mentioned how the lifespan perspective includes both continuous and discontinuous change.

TABLE 1.1
Major Periods of Human Development

PERIOD	APPROXIMATE AGE RANGE	BRIEF DESCRIPTION
Prenatal	Conception to birth	The one-celled organism transforms into a human baby with remarkable capacities to adjust to life in the surrounding world.
Infancy and toddlerhood	Birth–2 years	Dramatic changes in the body and brain support the emergence of a wide array of motor, perceptual, and intellectual capacities and first intimate ties to others.
Early childhood	2–6 years	During the "play years," motor skills are refined, thought and language expand at an astounding pace, a sense of morality is evident, and children establish ties with peers.
Middle childhood	6–11 years	The school years are marked by improved athletic abilities; more logical thought processes; mastery of fundamental reading, writing, math, and other academic knowledge and skills; advances in self-understanding, morality, and friendship; and the beginnings of peer-group membership.
Adolescence	11–18 years	Puberty leads to an adult-sized body and sexual maturity. Thought becomes abstract and idealistic and school achievement more serious. Adolescents begin to establish autonomy from the family and to define personal values and goals.
Early adulthood	18–40 years	Most young people leave home, complete their education, and begin full-time work. Major concerns are developing a career, forming an intimate partnership, and marrying, rearing children, or pursuing other lifestyles.
Middle adulthood	40–65 years	Many people are at the height of their careers and attain leadership positions. They must also help their children begin independent lives and their parents adapt to aging. They become more aware of their own mortality.
Late adulthood	65 years–death	People adjust to retirement, to decreased physical strength and health, and often to the death of an intimate partner. They reflect on the meaning of their lives.

FIGURE 1.2 Major domains of development. The three domains are not really distinct. Rather, they overlap and interact.

Development Is Plastic

Lifespan researchers emphasize that development is plastic at all ages. Consider Sofie's social reserve in childhood and her decision to study rather than marry as a young adult. As new opportunities arose, Sofie moved easily into marriage and childbearing in her thirties. And although parenthood and financial difficulties posed challenges, Sofie and Philip's relationship gradually became richer and more fulfilling. In Chapter 17, we will see that intellectual performance also remains flexible with advancing age. Older adults respond to special training with substantial (but not unlimited) gains in a wide variety of mental abilities (Bamidis et al., 2014; Willis & Belleville, 2016).

Evidence on plasticity reveals that aging is not an eventual "shipwreck," as has often been assumed. Instead, the metaphor of a "butterfly"—of metamorphosis and continued potential—provides a far more accurate picture of lifespan change. Still, development gradually becomes less plastic, as both capacity and opportunity for change are reduced. And plasticity varies greatly across individuals. Some children and adults experience more diverse life circumstances. Also, as the Biology and Environment box on pages 10–11 indicates, some adapt more easily than others to changing conditions.

Development Is Influenced by Multiple, Interacting Forces

According to the lifespan perspective, pathways of change are highly diverse because *development is influenced by multiple forces:* biological, historical, social, and cultural. Although these wide-ranging influences can be organized into three categories, they work together, combining in unique ways to fashion each life course.

Age-Graded Influences. Events that are strongly related to age and therefore fairly predictable in when they occur and how long they last are called **age-graded influences.** For example, most individuals walk shortly after their first birthday, acquire their native language during the preschool years, reach puberty around age 12 to 14, and (for women) experience menopause in their late forties or early fifties. These milestones are influenced by biology, but social customs—such as starting school around age 6, getting a driver's license at age 16, and entering college around age 18—can create age-graded influences as well. Age-graded influences are especially prevalent in childhood and adolescence, when biological changes are rapid and cultures impose many age-related experiences to ensure that young people acquire the skills they need to participate in their society.

History-Graded Influences. Development is also profoundly affected by forces unique to a particular historical era. Examples include epidemics, wars, and periods of economic prosperity or depression; technological advances like the introduction of television, computers, the Internet, smartphones, and tablets; and changes in cultural values, such as attitudes toward women, ethnic minorities, and older adults. These **history-graded influences** explain why people born around the same

Biology and Environment

Resilience

John and his best friend, Gary, grew up in a rundown, crime-ridden, inner-city neighborhood. By age 10, each had experienced years of family conflict followed by parental divorce. Reared from then on in mother-headed households, John and Gary rarely saw their fathers. Both dropped out of high school and were in and out of trouble with the police.

Then their paths diverged. By age 30, John had fathered two children with women he never married, had spent time in prison, was unemployed, and drank alcohol heavily. In contrast, Gary had returned to finish high school, had studied auto mechanics at a community college, and had become manager of a gas station and repair shop. Married with two children, he had saved his earnings and bought a home. He was happy, healthy, and well-adapted to life.

A wealth of evidence shows that environmental risks—poverty, negative family interactions and parental divorce, job loss, mental illness, and drug abuse—predispose children to future problems (Masten, 2013). Why did Gary "beat the odds" and bounce back from adversity?

Research on **resilience**—the ability to adapt effectively in the face of threats to development—is receiving increased attention as investigators look for ways to protect young people from the damaging effects of stressful life conditions. This interest has been inspired by several long-term studies on the relationship of life stressors in childhood to competence and adjustment in adolescence and adulthood (Werner, 2013). In each study, some individuals were shielded from negative outcomes, whereas others had lasting problems. Four broad factors seemed to offer protection from the damaging effects of stressful life events.

Personal Characteristics

A child's genetically influenced characteristics can reduce exposure to risk or lead to experiences that compensate for early stressful events. High intelligence and socially valued talents (in music or athletics, for example) increase the chances that a child will have rewarding experiences in school and in the community that offset the impact of a stressful home life. Temperament is particularly

This teenager's close, affectionate relationship with his grandfather helps foster resilience. Strong bonds with family members can shield children from the damaging effects of stressful life conditions.

powerful. Children who have easygoing, sociable dispositions and who can readily inhibit negative emotions and impulses tend to have an optimistic outlook on life and a special capacity to adapt to change—qualities that elicit positive responses from others. In contrast, emotionally reactive and irritable

---

time—called a *cohort*—tend to be alike in ways that set them apart from people born at other times.

Consider the *baby boomers,* a term used to describe people born between 1946 and 1964, the post–World War II period during which birth rates soared in most Western nations. This population increase was especially sharp in the United States: By 1960, the prewar birth rate had nearly doubled, yielding the largest gain in the nation's history. The sheer size of the baby-boom generation made it a powerful social force from the time its members became young adults; today, the baby boomers are redefining our view of middle and late adulthood (see the Cultural Influences box above).

LOOK and LISTEN

Identify a history-graded influence in your life, and speculate about its impact on people your age. Then ask someone a generation or two older than you to identify a history-graded influence in his or her life and to reflect on its impact.

Nonnormative Influences. Age-graded and history-graded influences are normative—meaning typical, or average—because each affects large numbers of people in a similar way. **Nonnormative influences** are events that are irregular: They happen to just one person or a few people and do not follow a predictable timetable. Consequently, they enhance the multidirectionality of development. Nonnormative influences that had a major impact on the direction of Sofie's life included piano lessons in childhood with an inspiring teacher; delayed marriage, parenthood, and career entry; and a battle with cancer. Because they occur irregularly, nonnormative events are difficult for researchers to capture and study. Yet, as each of us can attest from our own experiences, they can affect us in powerful ways.

Nonnormative influences have become more powerful and age-graded influences less so in contemporary adult development. Compared with Sofie's era, much greater diversity exists today in the ages at which people finish their education, enter careers, marry, have children, and retire. Indeed, Sofie's "off-time" accomplishments would have been less unusual had she been children often tax the patience of people around them (Wang & Deater-Deckard, 2013). For example, both John and Gary moved several times during their childhoods. Each time, John became anxious and angry. Gary looked forward to making new friends and exploring a new neighborhood.

A Warm Parental Relationship

A close relationship with at least one parent who provides warmth, appropriately high expectations, monitoring of the child's activities, and an organized home environment fosters resilience (Shonkoff & Garner, 2012; Taylor, 2010). But this factor (as well as the next one) is not independent of children's personal characteristics. Children who are self-controlled, socially responsive, and able to deal with change are easier to rear and more likely to enjoy positive relationships with parents and other people. At the same time, children develop more attractive dispositions as a result of parental warmth and attention (Luthar, Crossman, & Small, 2015).

Social Support Outside the Immediate Family

The most consistent asset of resilient children is a strong bond with a competent, caring adult. For children who do not have a close bond with either parent, a grandparent, aunt, uncle, or teacher who forms a special relationship with the child can promote resilience (Masten, 2013). Gary received support in adolescence from his grandfather, who listened to Gary's concerns and helped him solve problems. In addition, Gary's grandfather had a stable marriage and work life and handled stressors skillfully. Consequently, he served as a model of effective coping.

Associations with rule-abiding peers who value academic achievement are also linked to resilience (Furman & Rose, 2015). But children who have positive relationships with adults are far more likely to establish these supportive peer ties.

Community Resources and Opportunities

Community supports—supervision offered by neighborhood adults, high-quality child-care centers and public schools, convenient and affordable health care and social services, libraries, and recreation centers—foster both parents' and children's well-being. In addition, opportunities to participate in community life help older children and adolescents overcome adversity. Extracurricular activities at school, religious youth groups, scouting, and other organizations teach important social skills, such as cooperation, leadership, and contributing to others' welfare. As participants acquire these competencies, they gain in self-reliance, self-esteem, and community commitment (Leventhal, Dupéré, & Shuey, 2015). As a college student, Gary volunteered for Habitat for Humanity, joining a team building affordable housing in low-income neighborhoods. Community involvement offered Gary opportunities to form meaningful relationships, which further strengthened his resilience.

Research on resilience highlights the complex connections between heredity and environment. Armed with positive characteristics, which stem from native endowment, favorable rearing experiences, or both, children and adolescents can act to reduce stressful situations.

But when many risks pile up, they are increasingly difficult to overcome (Obradović et al., 2009). To inoculate children against the negative effects of risk, interventions must not only reduce risks but also enhance children's protective relationships at home, in school, and in the community. This means attending to both the person and the environment—strengthening the individual's capacities while also reducing hazardous experiences.

---

born two generations later. Age remains a powerful organizer of everyday experiences, and age-related expectations have certainly not disappeared. But age markers have blurred, and they vary across ethnic groups and cultures. The increasing role of nonnormative events in the life course adds to the fluid nature of lifespan development.

Notice that instead of a single line of development, the lifespan perspective emphasizes many potential pathways and outcomes—an image more like tree branches extending in diverse directions, which may undergo both continuous and stagewise transformations (see Figure 1.3). Now let's turn to scientific

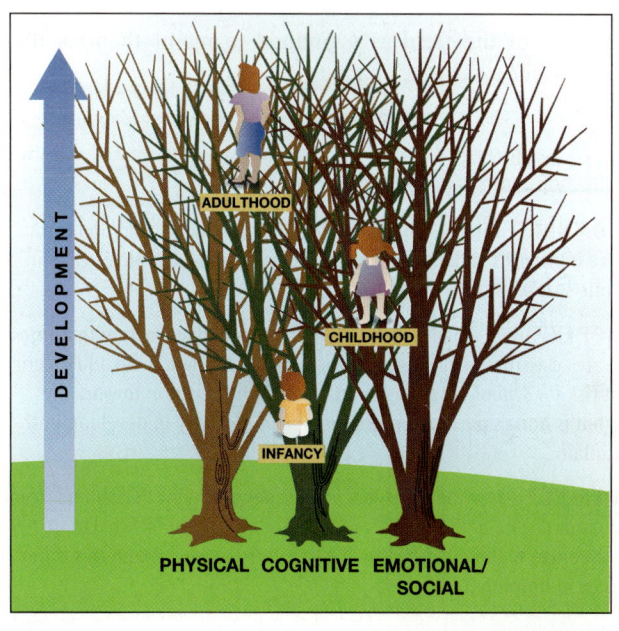

FIGURE 1.3 **The lifespan view of development.** Rather than envisioning a single line of stagewise or continuous change (see Figure 1.1 on page 6), lifespan theorists conceive of development as more like tree branches extending in diverse directions. Many pathways are possible, depending on the contexts that influence the individual's life course. Each branch in this treelike image represents a possible skill within one of the major domains of development. The crossing of the branches signifies that the domains—physical, cognitive, emotional, and social—are interrelated.

Cultural Influences

The Baby Boomers Reshape the Life Course

From 1946 to 1964, 92 percent of all American women of childbearing age gave birth, averaging almost four children each—a new baby every 8 seconds (Croker, 2007). This splurge of births, which extended for nearly two decades, yielded a unique generation often credited with changing the world. Today, the baby boomers number 74 million adults—about 23 percent of the U.S. population (Colby & Ortman, 2014). Most are middle aged, with the oldest having entered late adulthood.

Several interrelated factors sparked the post–World War II baby boom. Many people who had postponed marriage and parenthood throughout the Great Depression of the 1930s started families in the 1940s, once the economy had improved. With the end of World War II, returning GIs also began to have children. As these two cohorts focused on childbearing, they gave birth to babies who otherwise would have been spaced out over 10 to 15 years. And as economic prosperity accelerated in the 1950s, making larger families affordable, more people married at younger ages and had several children closely spaced, which led the baby boom to persist into the 1960s (Stewart & Malley, 2004). Finally, after a war, the desire to make babies generally strengthens. Besides replacing massive population loss, new births signify hope that human life will endure.

Compared with their counterparts in the previous generation, many more young baby boomers were economically privileged. They were also the recipients of deep emotional investment from their parents, who—having undergone the deprivations of depression and war—often ranked children as the most enduring benefit of their adult lives. These factors may have engendered optimism, confidence, even a sense of entitlement (Elder, Nguyen, & Caspi, 1985). At the same time, their huge numbers—evident in overflowing school classrooms—may have sparked an intense struggle for individual recognition. By the time the boomers reached early adulthood, this set of traits led critics to label them a narcissistic, indulged, "me" generation.

From the mid-1960s to the early 1970s, the "leading-edge" baby boomers (born in the late

A "trailing edge" baby-boomer nurse immunizes an infant in a village clinic high in the central mountains of Afghanistan. The country suffers from the second highest infant mortality rate in the world. Service roles are just one way this cohort contributes to society.

1940s and early 1950s) entered colleges and universities in record numbers, in part because of draft deferments offered to students during the Vietnam War. The boomers became better educated than any previous generation. This cohort—self-focused, socially aware, and in search of distinction—broke

foundations of the field as a prelude to major theories that address various aspects of change.

Ask yourself

CONNECT Distinguish age-graded, history-graded, and nonnormative influences on lifespan development. Cite an example of each in Sofie's story.

APPLY Anna, a high school counselor, devised a program that integrates classroom learning with vocational training to help adolescents at risk for school dropout stay in school and transition to work life. What is Anna's position on *stability versus plasticity* in development? Explain.

REFLECT Describe an aspect of your development that differs from a parent's or a grandparent's when he or she was your age. Using influences highlighted by the lifespan perspective, explain this difference in development.

Scientific Beginnings

1.4 Describe major early influences on the scientific study of development.

Scientific study of human development dates back to the late nineteenth and early twentieth centuries. Early observations of human change were soon followed by improved methods and theories. Each advance contributed to the firm foundation on which the field rests today.

Darwin: Forefather of Scientific Child Study

British naturalist Charles Darwin (1809–1882) observed the infinite variation among plant and animal species. He also saw that within a species, no two individuals are exactly alike. From these observations, he constructed his famous *theory of evolution*.

away from their parents' family- and marriage-centered lifestyles. Starting in the mid-sixties, marriage rates declined, age of first marriage rose, and divorce rates increased. And the baby boomers responded to the turbulence of those times—the assassination of President Kennedy in 1963, the Vietnam War, and growing racial tensions—by mobilizing around the antiwar, civil rights, and women's movements, yielding a generation of student activists.

By the time the "trailing-edge" boomers (born in the late 1950s and early 1960s) came of age, these movements had left an enduring mark. Even as they turned toward family life and career development, the boomers continued to search for personal meaning, self-expression, and social responsibility. By midlife, the generation had produced an unusually large number of socially concerned writers, teachers, filmmakers, and labor and community organizers, as well as innovative musicians and artists (Cole & Stewart, 1996). And a multitude of ordinary citizens worked to advance social causes.

As baby-boom women entered the labor market and struggled for career advancement and equal pay, their self-confidence grew, and they paved the way for the next generation: On average, younger women attained this same level of self-confidence at a much earlier age (Twenge, 2001). And as baby-boom activists pressed for gender and racial equality, they influenced national policy. The 1960s saw laws passed that banned discrimination in employment practices, in racial access to public accommodations, and in sale or rental of housing. By the 1970s, progress in civil rights served as the springboard for the gay and lesbian rights movement.

The baby boomers are healthier, better educated, and financially better off than any previous mid- or late-life cohort (New Strategist Editors, 2015). Their sense of self-empowerment and innovativeness has energized efforts to increase the personal meaningfulness of their worklives and to deepen their lifelong engagement with social causes. Yet another concern of baby-boom midlifers is an intense desire to control the physical changes of aging (Hooyman, Kawamoto, & Kiyak, 2015). Far more than their predecessors, they resist growing old, as indicated by their interest in a wide array of anti-aging products and procedures—from cosmetics to Botox to plastic surgery—that are now a multi-billion-dollar U.S. industry.

Nevertheless, it is important to note that the baby boomers—though advantaged as a generation—are diverse in health status and sense of control over their lives. Those higher in education and income are considerably better off. And because retirement savings were heavily hit by the economic recession of 2007 to 2009, and pension plans with guaranteed fixed benefits had declined over the boomers' employment years, many are working longer than they had planned.

What lies ahead as each year, millions of members of this gigantic population bulge transition to late adulthood? Most analysts focus on societal burdens, such as rising social security and health-care costs. At the same time, aging boomers have more relevant experience in caring about their world—and more years left to do so—than any previous cohort of older adults. Rather than slowing down in their sixties and seventies, many remain immersed in their careers, start new businesses, or pursue challenging volunteer and service roles (Farrell, 2014). As the boomers cast aside traditional retirement, they are redefining the last third of life as a time of continued engagement, meaning, and contributions to society.

The theory emphasized two related principles: *natural selection* and *survival of the fittest*. Darwin explained that certain species survive in particular environments because they have characteristics that fit with, or are adapted to, their surroundings. Other species die off because they are less well-suited to their environments. Individuals within a species who best meet the environment's survival requirements live long enough to reproduce and pass their more beneficial characteristics to future generations. Darwin's (1859/1936) emphasis on the adaptive value of physical characteristics and behavior found its way into important developmental theories.

During his explorations, Darwin discovered that early prenatal growth is strikingly similar in many species. Other scientists concluded from Darwin's observations that the development of the human child follows the same general plan as the evolution

Darwin's theory of evolution emphasizes the adaptive value of physical characteristics and behavior. Affection and care in families promote survival and psychological well-being throughout the lifespan. Here, a granddaughter shares a moment of intimacy with her grandmother.

of the human species. Although this belief eventually proved inaccurate, efforts to chart parallels between child growth and human evolution prompted researchers to make careful observations of all aspects of children's behavior. Out of these first attempts to document an idea about development, scientific child study was born.

The Normative Period

G. Stanley Hall (1844–1924), one of the most influential American psychologists of the early twentieth century, is generally regarded as the founder of the child study movement (Cairns & Cairns, 2006). He also foreshadowed lifespan research by writing one of the few books of his time on aging. Inspired by Darwin's work, Hall and his well-known student Arnold Gesell (1880–1961) devised theories based on evolutionary ideas. They regarded development as a *maturational process*—a genetically determined series of events that unfold automatically, much like a flower (Gesell, 1933; Hall, 1904).

Hall and Gesell are remembered less for their one-sided theories than for their intensive efforts to describe all aspects of development. They launched the **normative approach,** in which measures of behavior are taken on large numbers of individuals, and age-related averages are computed to represent typical development. Using this procedure, Hall constructed elaborate questionnaires asking children of different ages almost everything they could tell about themselves—interests, fears, imaginary playmates, dreams, friendships, everyday knowledge, and more. Similarly, through careful observations and parent interviews, Gesell collected detailed normative information on the motor achievements, social behaviors, and personality characteristics of infants and children.

Gesell was also among the first to make knowledge about child development meaningful to parents by informing them of what to expect at each age. If, as he believed, the timetable of development is the product of millions of years of evolution, then children are naturally knowledgeable about their needs. His child-rearing advice recommended sensitivity to children's cues. Along with Benjamin Spock's *Baby and Child Care,* Gesell's books became a central part of a rapidly expanding child development literature for parents.

The Mental Testing Movement

While Hall and Gesell were developing their theories and methods in the United States, French psychologist Alfred Binet (1857–1911) was also taking a normative approach to child development, but for a different reason. In the early 1900s, Binet and his colleague Theodore Simon were asked by Paris school officials to find a way to identify children with learning problems who needed to be placed in special classes. To address these practical educational concerns, Binet and Simon constructed the first successful intelligence test.

In 1916, at Stanford University, Binet's test was adapted for use with English-speaking children. Since then, the English version has been known as the *Stanford-Binet Intelligence Scale.*

Besides providing a score that could successfully predict school achievement, the Binet test sparked tremendous interest in individual differences in development. Comparisons of the scores of people who vary in gender, ethnicity, birth order, family background, and other characteristics became a major focus of research. And intelligence tests moved quickly to the forefront of the nature–nurture controversy.

Mid-Twentieth-Century Theories

1.5 What theories influenced human development research in the mid-twentieth century?

In the mid-twentieth century, the study of human development expanded into a legitimate discipline. A variety of theories emerged, each of which continues to have followers today. In these theories, the European concern with the individual's inner thoughts and feelings contrasts sharply with the North American academic focus on scientific precision and concrete, observable behavior.

The Psychoanalytic Perspective

In the 1930s and 1940s, as more people sought help from professionals to deal with emotional difficulties, a new question had to be addressed: How and why do people become the way they are? To treat psychological problems, psychiatrists and social workers turned to an emerging approach to personality development that emphasized each individual's unique life history.

According to the **psychoanalytic perspective,** people move through a series of stages in which they confront conflicts between biological drives and social expectations. How these conflicts are resolved determines the person's ability to learn, to get along with others, and to cope with anxiety. Among the many individuals who contributed to the psychoanalytic perspective, two were especially influential: Sigmund Freud, founder of the psychoanalytic movement, and Erik Erikson.

Freud's Theory. Freud (1856–1939), a Viennese physician, sought a cure for emotionally troubled adults by having them talk freely about painful events of their childhoods. Working with these recollections, he examined his patients' unconscious motivations and constructed his **psychosexual theory,** which emphasizes that how parents manage their child's sexual and aggressive drives in the first few years is crucial for healthy personality development.

In Freud's theory, three parts of the personality—id, ego, and superego—become integrated during five stages, summarized in Table 1.2. The *id,* the largest portion of the mind, is the source of basic biological needs and desires. The *ego,* the conscious, rational part of personality, emerges in early infancy to redirect the id's impulses so they are discharged in acceptable ways. Between

TABLE 1.2
Freud's Psychosexual Stages and Erikson's Psychosocial Stages Compared

APPROXIMATE AGE	FREUD'S PSYCHOSEXUAL STAGE	ERIKSON'S PSYCHOSOCIAL STAGE
Birth–1 year	*Oral:* If oral needs are not met through sucking from breast or bottle, the individual may develop such habits as thumb sucking, fingernail biting, overeating, or smoking.	*Basic trust versus mistrust:* From warm, responsive care, infants gain a sense of trust, or confidence, that the world is good. Mistrust occurs if infants are neglected or handled harshly.
1–3 years	*Anal:* Toddlers and preschoolers enjoy holding and releasing urine and feces. If parents toilet train before children are ready or make too few demands, conflicts about anal control may appear in the form of extreme orderliness or disorder.	*Autonomy versus shame and doubt:* Using new mental and motor skills, children want to decide for themselves. Parents can foster autonomy by permitting reasonable free choice and not forcing or shaming the child.
3–6 years	*Phallic:* As preschoolers take pleasure in genital stimulation, Freud's Oedipus conflict for boys and Electra conflict for girls arise: Children feel a sexual desire for the other-sex parent. To avoid punishment, they give up this desire and adopt the same-sex parent's characteristics and values. As a result, the superego is formed, and children feel guilty when they violate its standards.	*Initiative versus guilt:* Through make-believe play, children gain insight into the person they can become. Initiative—a sense of ambition and responsibility—develops when parents support their child's sense of purpose. If parents demand too much self-control, children experience excessive guilt.
6–11 years	*Latency:* Sexual instincts die down, and the superego strengthens as children acquire new social values from adults and same-sex peers.	*Industry versus inferiority:* At school, children learn to work and cooperate with others. Inferiority develops when negative experiences at home, at school, or with peers lead to feelings of incompetence.
Adolescence	*Genital:* With puberty, sexual impulses reappear. Successful development during earlier stages leads to marriage, mature sexuality, and child rearing.	*Identity versus role confusion:* By exploring values and vocational goals, young people form a personal identity. The negative outcome is confusion about future adult roles.
Early adulthood		*Intimacy versus isolation:* Young adults establish intimate relationships. Because of earlier disappointments, some individuals cannot form close bonds and remain isolated.
Middle adulthood		*Generativity versus stagnation:* Generativity means giving to the next generation through child rearing, caring for others, or productive work. The person who fails in these ways feels an absence of meaningful accomplishment.
Old age		*Integrity versus despair:* Integrity results from feeling that life was worth living as it happened. Older people who are dissatisfied with their lives fear death.

Erik Erikson

3 and 6 years of age, the *superego,* or conscience, develops as parents insist that children conform to the values of society. Now the ego faces the increasingly complex task of reconciling the demands of the id, the external world, and conscience—for example, the id impulse to grab an attractive toy from a playmate versus the superego's warning that such behavior is wrong. According to Freud, the relations established among id, ego, and superego during the preschool years determine the individual's basic personality.

Freud (1938/1973) believed that during childhood, sexual impulses shift their focus from the oral to the anal to the genital regions of the body. In each stage, parents walk a fine line between permitting too much or too little gratification of their child's basic needs. If parents strike an appropriate balance, children grow into well-adjusted adults with the capacity for mature sexual behavior and investment in family life.

Freud's theory was the first to stress the influence of the early parent–child relationship on development. But his perspective was eventually criticized. First, it overemphasized the influence of sexual feelings in development. Second, because it was based on the problems of sexually repressed, well-to-do adults in nineteenth-century Victorian society, it did not apply in other cultures. Finally, Freud had not studied children directly.

Erikson's Theory. Several of Freud's followers took what was useful from his theory and improved on his vision. The most important is Erik Erikson (1902–1994), who expanded the picture of development at each stage. In his **psychosocial theory,** Erikson emphasized that in addition to mediating between id impulses and superego demands, the ego makes a positive contribution to development, acquiring attitudes and skills that make the individual an active, contributing member of society. A basic psychosocial conflict, which is resolved along a continuum from positive to negative, determines healthy or maladaptive outcomes at each stage. As Table 1.2 shows, Erikson's first five stages parallel Freud's stages, but Erikson added three adult stages.

A child of the Kazakh people of Mongolia learns from her grandfather how to train an eagle to hunt small animals, essential for the meat-based Kazakh diet. As Erikson recognized, this parenting practice is best understood in relation to the competencies valued and needed in Kazakh culture.

Unlike Freud, Erikson pointed out that normal development must be understood in relation to each culture's life situation. For example, in the 1940s, he observed that Yurok Indians of the northwest coast of the United States deprived newborns of breastfeeding for the first 10 days, instead feeding them a thin soup. At age 6 months, infants were abruptly weaned—if necessary, by having the mother leave for a few days. From our cultural vantage point, these practices seem cruel. But Erikson explained that because the Yurok depended on salmon, which fill the river just once a year, the development of self-restraint was essential for survival. In this way, he showed that child rearing is responsive to the competencies valued and needed by an individual's society.

Contributions and Limitations of the Psychoanalytic Perspective.
A special strength of the psychoanalytic perspective is its emphasis on the individual's unique life history as worthy of study and understanding. Consistent with this view, psychoanalytic theorists accept the *clinical,* or *case study, method,* which synthesizes information from a variety of sources into a detailed picture of the personality of a single person. (We will discuss this method further at the end of this chapter.) Psychoanalytic theory has also inspired a wealth of research on many aspects of emotional and social development, including infant–caregiver attachment, aggression, sibling relationships, child-rearing practices, morality, gender roles, and adolescent identity.

Despite its extensive contributions, the psychoanalytic perspective is no longer in the mainstream of human development research. Psychoanalytic theorists may have become isolated from the rest of the field because they were so strongly committed to in-depth study of individuals that they failed to consider other methods. In addition, many psychoanalytic ideas, such as psychosexual stages and ego functioning, are too vague to be tested empirically (Crain, 2010).

Nevertheless, Erikson's broad outline of lifespan change captures key, optimal psychosocial attainments during each major period of the life course. We will return to it, along with other perspectives inspired by Erikson's theory, in later chapters.

Behaviorism and Social Learning Theory

As the psychoanalytic perspective gained in prominence, the study of development was also influenced by a very different perspective. According to **behaviorism,** directly observable events—stimuli and responses—are the appropriate focus of study. North American behaviorism began in the early twentieth century with the work of John Watson (1878–1958), who wanted to create an objective science of psychology.

Traditional Behaviorism.
Watson was inspired by Russian physiologist Ivan Pavlov's studies of animal learning. Pavlov knew that dogs release saliva as an innate reflex when they are given food. But he noticed that his dogs were salivating before they tasted any food—when they saw the trainer who usually fed them. The dogs, Pavlov reasoned, must have learned to associate a neutral stimulus (the trainer) with another stimulus (food) that produces a reflexive response (salivation). Because of this association, the neutral stimulus alone could bring about a response resembling the reflex. Eager to test this idea, Pavlov successfully taught dogs to salivate at the sound of a bell by pairing it with the presentation of food. He had discovered *classical conditioning.*

Watson wanted to find out if classical conditioning could be applied to children's behavior. In a historic experiment, he taught Albert, an 11-month-old infant, to fear a neutral stimulus—a soft white rat—by presenting it several times with a sharp, loud sound, which naturally scared the baby. Little Albert, who at first had reached out eagerly to touch the furry rat, began to cry and retreat at the sight of it (Watson & Raynor, 1920). In fact, Albert's fear was so intense that researchers eventually challenged the ethics of studies like this one. Watson concluded that environment is the supreme force in development and that adults can mold children's behavior by carefully controlling stimulus–response associations. He viewed development as continuous—a gradual increase with age in the number and strength of these associations.

Another form of behaviorism was B. F. Skinner's (1904–1990) *operant conditioning theory.* According to Skinner, the frequency of a behavior can be increased by following it with a wide variety of *reinforcers,* such as food, praise, or a friendly smile, or decreased through *punishment,* such as disapproval or withdrawal of privileges. As a result of Skinner's work, operant conditioning became a broadly applied learning principle. We will consider these basic learning capacities further in Chapter 4.

Social Learning Theory. Psychologists wondered whether behaviorism might offer a more direct and effective explanation of the development of social behavior than the less precise concepts of psychoanalytic theory. This sparked approaches that built on the principles of conditioning, providing expanded views of how children and adults acquire new responses.

Several kinds of **social learning theory** emerged. The most influential, devised by Albert Bandura (1925–), emphasizes *modeling*, also known as *imitation* or *observational learning*, as a powerful source of development. The baby who claps her hands after her mother does so, the child who angrily hits a playmate in the same way that he has been punished at home, and the teenager who wears the same clothes and hairstyle as her friends at school are all displaying observational learning. In his early work, Bandura found that diverse factors affect children's motivation to imitate: their own history of reinforcement or punishment for the behavior, the promise of future reinforcement or punishment, and even observations of the model being reinforced or punished.

Bandura's work continues to influence much research on social development. But today, his theory stresses the importance of *cognition*, or thinking. In fact, the most recent revision of Bandura's (1992, 2001) theory places such strong emphasis on how we think about ourselves and other people that he calls it a *social-cognitive* rather than a social learning approach.

In Bandura's revised view, children gradually become more selective in what they imitate. From watching others engage in self-praise and self-blame and through feedback about the worth of their own actions, children develop *personal standards* for behavior and *a sense of self-efficacy*—the belief that their own abilities and characteristics will help them succeed. These cognitions guide responses in particular situations (Bandura, 2001, 2011). For example, imagine a parent who often remarks, "I'm glad I kept working on that task, even though it was hard," and who encourages persistence by saying, "I know you can do a good job on that homework!" Soon the child starts to view herself as hardworking and high-achieving and selects people with these characteristics as models. In this way, as individuals acquire attitudes, values, and convictions about themselves, they control their own learning and behavior.

Contributions and Limitations of Behaviorism and Social Learning Theory. Behaviorism and social learning theory have been helpful in treating a wide range of adjustment problems. **Applied behavior analysis** consists of careful observations of individual behavior and related environmental events, followed by systematic changes in those events based on procedures of conditioning and modeling. The goal is to eliminate undesirable behaviors and increase desirable responses. It has been used to relieve a wide range of difficulties in children and adults, ranging from poor time management and unwanted habits to serious problems, such as language delays, persistent aggression, and extreme fears (Heron, Hewar, & Cooper, 2013).

Nevertheless, many theorists believe that behaviorism and social learning theory offer too narrow a view of important environmental influences, which extend beyond immediate reinforcement, punishment, and modeled behaviors to people's rich physical and social worlds. Behaviorism and social learning theory have also been criticized for underestimating people's contributions to their own development. Bandura, with his emphasis on cognition, is unique among theorists whose work grew out of the behaviorist tradition in granting children and adults an active role in their own learning.

Piaget's Cognitive-Developmental Theory

If one individual has influenced research on child development more than any other, it is Swiss cognitive theorist Jean Piaget (1896–1980). North American investigators had been aware of Piaget's work since 1930. But they did not grant it much attention until the 1960s, mainly because Piaget's ideas were at odds with behaviorism, which dominated North American psychology in the mid-twentieth century (Watrin & Darwich, 2012). Piaget did not believe that children's learning depends on reinforcers, such as rewards from adults. According to his **cognitive-developmental theory,** children actively construct knowledge as they manipulate and explore their world.

Piaget's Stages. Piaget's view of development was greatly influenced by his early training in biology. Central to his theory is the biological concept of *adaptation* (Piaget, 1971). Just as structures of the body are adapted to fit with the environment, so structures of the mind develop to better fit with, or represent, the external world. In infancy and early childhood, Piaget claimed, children's understanding is different from adults'. For example, he believed that young babies do not realize that an object hidden from view—a favorite toy or even the mother—continues to exist. He also concluded that preschoolers' thinking is full of

Social learning theory recognizes that children acquire many skills through modeling. By observing and imitating his father's behavior, this child learns an important skill.

TABLE 1.3
Piaget's Stages of Cognitive Development

STAGE	PERIOD OF DEVELOPMENT	DESCRIPTION
Sensorimotor	Birth–2 years	Infants "think" by acting on the world with their eyes, ears, hands, and mouth. As a result, they invent ways of solving sensorimotor problems, such as pulling a lever to hear the sound of a music box, finding hidden toys, and putting objects into and taking them out of containers.
Preoperational	2–7 years	Preschool children use symbols to represent their earlier sensorimotor discoveries. Development of language and make-believe play takes place. However, thinking lacks the logic of the two remaining stages.
Concrete operational	7–11 years	Children's reasoning becomes logical and better organized. School-age children understand that a certain amount of lemonade or play dough remains the same even after its appearance changes. They also organize objects into hierarchies of classes and subclasses. However, children think in a logical, organized fashion only when dealing with concrete information they can perceive directly.
Formal operational	11 years on	The capacity for abstract, systematic thinking enables adolescents, when faced with a problem, to start with a hypothesis, deduce testable inferences, and isolate and combine variables to see which inferences are confirmed. Adolescents can also evaluate the logic of verbal statements without referring to real-world circumstances.

Jean Piaget

faulty logic. For example, children younger than age 7 commonly say that the amount of a liquid changes when it is poured into a different-shaped container. According to Piaget, children eventually revise these incorrect ideas in their ongoing efforts to achieve an *equilibrium,* or balance, between internal structures and information they encounter in their everyday worlds.

In Piaget's theory, as the brain develops and children's experiences expand, they move through four broad stages, each characterized by qualitatively distinct ways of thinking. Table 1.3 provides a brief description of Piaget's stages. Cognitive development begins in the *sensorimotor stage* with the baby's use of the senses and movements to explore the world. These action patterns evolve into the symbolic but illogical thinking of the preschooler in the *preoperational stage.* Then cognition is transformed into the more organized, logical reasoning of the school-age child in the *concrete operational stage.* Finally, in the *formal operational stage,* thought becomes the abstract, systematic reasoning system of the adolescent and adult.

Piaget devised special methods for investigating how children think. Early in his career, he carefully observed his three infant children and presented them with everyday problems, such as an attractive object that could be grasped, mouthed, kicked, or searched for. From their responses, Piaget derived his ideas about cognitive changes during the first two years. To study childhood and adolescent thought, Piaget adapted the clinical method of psychoanalysis, conducting open-ended *clinical interviews* in which a child's initial response to a task served as the basis for Piaget's next question. We will look more closely at this technique when we discuss research methods later in this chapter.

Contributions and Limitations of Piaget's Theory.
Piaget convinced the field that children are active learners whose minds consist of rich structures of knowledge. Besides investigating children's understanding of the physical world, Piaget explored their reasoning about the social world. His stages have

In Piaget's formal operational stage, adolescents think systematically and abstractly. These high school students participating in a robotics competition solve problems by generating hypotheses about procedures that might work and conducting systematic tests to observe their real-world consequences.

sparked a wealth of research on children's conceptions of themselves, other people, and human relationships. In practical terms, Piaget's theory encouraged the development of educational philosophies and programs that emphasize discovery learning and direct contact with the environment.

Despite Piaget's overwhelming contributions, his theory has been challenged. Research indicates that Piaget underestimated the competencies of infants and preschoolers. When young children are given tasks scaled down in difficulty and relevant to their everyday experiences, their understanding appears closer to that of the older child and adult than Piaget assumed. Also, adolescents generally reach their full intellectual potential only in areas of endeavor in which they have had extensive education and experience. These findings have led many researchers to conclude that cognitive maturity depends heavily on the complexity of knowledge sampled and the individual's familiarity with the task (Miller, 2011).

Furthermore, children's performance on Piagetian problems can be improved with training—findings that call into question Piaget's assumption that discovery learning rather than adult teaching is the best way to foster development (Klahr, Matlen, & Jirout, 2013; Siegler & Svetina, 2006). Critics also point out that Piaget's stagewise account pays insufficient attention to social and cultural influences on development. Finally, lifespan theorists—challenging Piaget's conclusion that no new stages occur after adolescence—have proposed important transformations in adulthood (Heckhausen, Wrosch, & Schulz, 2010; ; Moshman, 2011; Perry, 1970/1998).

Today, the field of developmental science is divided over its loyalty to Piaget's ideas. Those who continue to find merit in Piaget's stages often accept a modified view—one in which changes in thinking take place more gradually than Piaget believed (Case, 1998; Halford & Andrews, 2011; Mascolo & Fischer, 2015). Among those who disagree with Piaget's stage sequence, some have embraced an approach that emphasizes continuous gains in children's cognition: information processing. And still others have been drawn to theories that focus on the role of children's social and cultural contexts. We take up these approaches in the next section.

Ask yourself

CONNECT Although social learning theory focuses on social development and Piaget's theory on cognitive development, each has enhanced our understanding of other domains. Mention an additional domain addressed by each theory.

APPLY A 4-year-old becomes frightened of the dark and refuses to go to sleep at night. How would a psychoanalyst and a behaviorist differ in their views of how this problem developed?

REFLECT Illustrate Bandura's ideas by describing a personal experience in which you observed and received feedback from another person that strengthened your sense of self-efficacy—belief that your abilities and characteristics will help you succeed.

Recent Theoretical Perspectives

1.6 Describe recent theoretical perspectives on human development.

New ways of understanding the developing person are constantly emerging—questioning, building on, and enhancing the discoveries of earlier theories. Today, a wealth of fresh approaches and research emphases is broadening our insights into lifespan development.

Information Processing

In the 1970s and 1980s, researchers turned to the field of cognitive psychology for ways to understand the development of thinking. The design of digital computers that use mathematically specified steps to solve problems suggested to psychologists that the human mind might also be viewed as a symbol-manipulating system through which information flows—a perspective called **information processing** (Munakata, 2006). From the time information is presented to the senses at *input* until it emerges as a behavioral response at *output,* information is actively coded, transformed, and organized.

Information-processing researchers often design flowcharts to map the precise steps individuals use to solve problems and complete tasks, much like the plans devised by programmers to get computers to perform a series of "mental operations." They seek to clarify how both task characteristics and cognitive limitations—for example, memory capacity or available knowledge—influence performance (Birney & Sternberg, 2011). To see the usefulness of this approach, let's look at an example.

In a study of problem solving, a researcher provided a pile of blocks varying in size, shape, and weight and asked school-age children to build a bridge across a "river" (painted on a floor mat) that was too wide for any single block to span (Thornton, 1999). Figure 1.4 shows one solution: Two planklike blocks span the water, each held in place by the counterweight of heavy blocks on the bridge's towers. Whereas older children easily built successful bridges, only one 5-year-old did. Careful tracking of her efforts revealed that she repeatedly tried unsuccessful strategies, such as pushing two planks together and pressing down on their ends to hold them in place. But eventually, her experimentation triggered the idea of using the blocks as counterweights. Her mistaken procedures helped her understand why the counterweight approach worked.

Many information-processing models exist. Some, like the one just considered, track mastery of one or a few tasks. Others describe the human cognitive system as a whole (Gopnik & Tenenbaum, 2007; Ristic & Enns, 2015; Westermann et al., 2006). These general models are used as guides for asking questions about broad changes in thinking: Does a child's ability to solve problems become more organized and "planful" with age? Why is information processing slower among older than younger

FIGURE 1.4 Information-processing flowchart showing the steps that a 5-year-old used to solve a bridge-building problem. Her task was to use blocks varying in size, shape, and weight, some of which were planklike, to construct a bridge across a "river" (painted on a floor mat) too wide for any single block to span. The child discovered how to counterweight and balance the bridge. The arrows reveal that, even after building a successful counterweight, she returned to earlier, unsuccessful strategies, which seemed to help her understand why the counterweight approach worked. (Based on Thornton, 1999.)

adults? Are declines in memory during old age evident on all types of tasks or only some?

Like Piaget's theory, the information-processing approach regards people as actively making sense of their own thinking (Halford & Andrews, 2011; Munakata, 2006). But unlike Piaget's theory, it does not divide development into stages. Rather, most information-processing researchers regard the thought processes studied—perception, attention, memory, categorization of information, planning, problem solving, and comprehension of written and spoken prose—as similar at all ages but present to a lesser or greater extent. Their view of development is one of continuous change.

A great strength of the information-processing approach is its commitment to rigorous research methods. Because it has provided precise accounts of how children and adults tackle many cognitive tasks, its findings have important implications for education. Currently, researchers are intensely interested in the development of an array of "executive" processes that enable children and adults to manage their thoughts, emotions, and actions. These capacities—variously labeled self-control, self-regulation, executive function, planning, delay of gratification, and more—are essential for attaining our goals in challenging situations (Carlson, Zelazo, & Faja, 2013; Chevalier, 2015; Müller & Kerns, 2015). As we will see in later chapters, executive processes are consistent predictors of academic achievement, socially competent behavior, life success, and psychological well-being.

Nevertheless, information processing has fallen short in some respects. It has been better at analyzing thinking into its components than at putting them back together into a comprehensive theory. And it has had little to say about aspects of cognition that are not linear and logical, such as imagination and creativity.

Developmental Neuroscience

Over the past three decades, as information-processing research expanded, a new area of investigation arose called **developmental cognitive neuroscience.** It brings together researchers from psychology, biology, neuroscience, and medicine to study the relationship between changes in the brain and the developing person's cognitive processing and behavior patterns.

Improved methods for analyzing brain activity while children and adults perform various tasks have greatly enhanced knowledge of relationships between brain functioning and behavior (de Haan, 2015). Armed with these brain electrical-recording and imaging techniques (which we will consider in Chapter 4), neuroscientists are tackling questions like these: How does genetic makeup combine with specific experiences at various ages to influence development and organization of the brain? What transformations in the brain make it harder for adolescents and adults than for children to acquire a second language? What neurological changes are related to declines in speed of thinking, memory, and other aspects of cognitive processing in late adulthood?

A complementary new area, **developmental social neuroscience,** is devoted to studying the relationship between changes in the brain and emotional and social development. Developmental social neuroscience emerged later than its cognitive counterpart because techniques for measuring brain activity are hard to implement in most social situations, where children and adults must move freely to interact with others (Zelazo & Paus, 2010). When researchers started to tap more convenient neurobiological measures that are sensitive to psychological state, such as heart rate, blood pressure, and hormone levels detected in saliva, an explosion of social-neuroscience investigations followed.

Active areas of investigation in developmental social neuroscience include identification of the neural systems underlying infants' capacity to imitate others, adolescents' heightened risk-taking behavior, and individual differences in impulsivity, sociability, anxiety, aggression, and depression. One particularly energetic focus is the negative impact of extreme adversity, such as early rearing in deprived orphanages or child abuse and neglect, on brain development and cognitive, emotional, and social skills (Anderson & Beauchamp, 2013; Gunnar, Doom, &

A therapist encourages a 6-year-old with autism to master the alphabet and interact socially, giving her a high five for progress. Developmental social neuroscientists are intensely interested in identifying the neurological bases of autism and using those findings to devise effective interventions.

Ethology and Evolutionary Developmental Psychology

Ethology is concerned with the adaptive, or survival, value of behavior and its evolutionary history. Its roots can be traced to the work of Darwin. Two European zoologists, Konrad Lorenz and Niko Tinbergen, laid its modern foundations. Watching diverse animal species in their natural habitats, Lorenz and Tinbergen observed behavior patterns that promote survival. The best known of these is *imprinting*, the early following behavior of certain baby birds, such as geese, that ensures that the young will stay close to the mother and be fed and protected from danger. Imprinting takes place during an early, restricted period of development (Lorenz, 1952). If the mother goose is absent during this time but an object resembling her in important features is present, young goslings may imprint on it instead.

Observations of imprinting led to a major concept in human development: the *critical period*. It is a limited time span during which the individual is biologically prepared to acquire certain adaptive behaviors but needs the support of an appropriately stimulating environment. Many researchers have investigated whether complex cognitive and social behaviors must be learned during certain time periods. For example, if children are deprived of adequate food or physical and social stimulation during their early years, will their intelligence be impaired? If language is not mastered in early childhood, is the child's capacity to acquire it reduced?

In later chapters, we will see that the term *sensitive period* applies better to human development than the strict notion of a critical period (Knudsen, 2004). A **sensitive period** is a time that is biologically optimal for certain capacities to emerge because the individual is especially responsive to environmental influences. However, its boundaries are less well-defined than those of a critical period. Development can occur later, but it is harder to induce.

Esposito, 2015). Another burgeoning interest is uncovering the neurological bases of *autism*—the disrupted brain structures and networks that lead to the impaired social skills, language delays, and repetitive motor behavior of this disorder (Stoner et al., 2014). As these efforts illustrate, researchers are forging links between cognitive and social neuroscience, identifying brain systems that affect both domains of development.

Rapid progress in clarifying the types of experiences that support or undermine brain development at diverse ages is contributing to effective interventions for enhancing cognitive and social functioning. Today, researchers are examining the impact of various training and treatment techniques on both brain functioning and behavior (Johnson & de Haan, 2015; Lustig & Lin, 2016). Although much remains to be discovered, developmental neuroscience is broadening our understanding of development and yielding major practical applications throughout the lifespan.

Nevertheless, neuroscience research has so captivated the field that it poses the risk that brain properties underlying human behavior will be granted undue importance over powerful environmental influences, such as parenting, education, and economic inequalities in families and communities. Although most neuroscientists are mindful of the complex interplay among heredity, individual experiences, and brain development, their findings have too often resulted in excessive emphasis being placed on biological processes (Kagan, 2013b).

Fortunately, an advantage of having many theories is that they encourage researchers to attend to previously neglected dimensions of people's lives. The final three perspectives we will discuss focus on *contexts* for development. The first of these views emphasizes that the environments to which humans have been exposed over their long evolutionary history influences the development of many capacities.

Ethology focuses on the adaptive, or survival, value of behavior and on similarities between human behavior and that of other species, especially our primate relatives. Observing this chimpanzee mother cuddling her infant helps us understand the human caregiver–infant relationship.

Inspired by observations of imprinting, British psychoanalyst John Bowlby (1969) applied ethological theory to the understanding of the human infant–caregiver relationship. He argued that infant smiling, babbling, grasping, and crying are built-in social signals that encourage the caregiver to approach, care for, and interact with the baby. By keeping the parent near, these behaviors help ensure that the infant will be fed, protected from danger, and provided with stimulation and affection necessary for healthy growth. The development of attachment in humans is a lengthy process involving psychological changes that lead the baby to form a deep affectionate tie with the caregiver (Thompson, 2006). Bowlby believed that this bond has lifelong consequences for human relationships. In later chapters, we will consider research that evaluates this assumption.

Observations by ethologists have shown that many aspects of social behavior, including emotional expressions, aggression, cooperation, and social play, resemble those of our primate relatives. Recently, researchers have extended this effort in a new area of research called **evolutionary developmental psychology**. It seeks to understand the adaptive value of species-wide cognitive, emotional, and social competencies as those competencies change with age (King & Bjorklund, 2010; Lickliter & Honeycutt, 2013). Evolutionary developmental psychologists ask questions like these: What role does the newborn's visual preference for facelike stimuli play in survival? Does it support older infants' capacity to distinguish familiar caregivers from unfamiliar people? Why do children play in gender-segregated groups? What do they learn from such play that might lead to adult gender-typed behaviors, such as male dominance and female investment in caregiving?

As these examples suggest, evolutionary psychologists are not just concerned with the genetic and biological roots of development. They recognize that humans' large brain and extended childhood resulted from the need to master an increasingly complex environment, so they are also interested in learning (Bjorklund, Causey, & Periss, 2009). And they realize that today's lifestyles differ so radically from those of our evolutionary ancestors that certain evolved behaviors—such as life-threatening risk taking in adolescents and male-to-male violence—are no longer adaptive (Blasi & Bjorklund, 2003).

Recently, evolutionary psychologists have begun to address the adaptiveness of human longevity—why adults live as much as one-fourth to one-third of their years after their children are grown (Croft et al., 2015). A common explanation involves the support that grandparents (especially grandmothers) offer in rearing young grandchildren, which is associated with higher birth and child-survival rates. Another emphasizes the scarcity of group resources that resulted when, in our evolutionary past, both younger and older females could reproduce, with costs for child survival.

In sum, evolutionary developmental psychology aims to understand the *person–environment system* throughout the lifespan. The next contextual perspective we will discuss, Vygotsky's sociocultural theory, serves as an excellent complement to the evolutionary viewpoint because it highlights social and cultural contexts for development.

Vygotsky's Sociocultural Theory

The field of developmental science has recently seen a dramatic increase in research demonstrating that human development and culture are closely interwoven (Mistry & Dutta, 2015). The contributions of Russian psychologist Lev Vygotsky (1896–1934) and his followers have played a major role in this trend.

Vygotsky's (1934/1987) perspective, called **sociocultural theory,** focuses on how *culture*—the values, beliefs, customs, and skills of a social group—is transmitted to the next generation. According to Vygotsky, *social interaction*—in particular, cooperative dialogues with more knowledgeable members of society—is necessary for children to acquire the ways of thinking and behaving that make up a community's culture. Vygotsky believed that as adults and more expert peers help children master culturally meaningful activities, the communication between them becomes part of children's thinking. As children internalize the features of these dialogues, they use the language within them to guide their own thought and actions and to acquire new skills (Lourenço, 2012; Winsler, Fernyhough, & Montero, 2009). The young child instructing herself while working a puzzle, preparing a table for dinner, or solving a math problem has begun to produce the same kind of guiding comments that an adult previously used to help her master culturally important tasks.

Vygotsky's theory has been especially influential in the study of cognitive development. Vygotsky agreed with Piaget that children are active, constructive beings. But whereas Piaget emphasized children's independent efforts to make sense of their world, Vygotsky viewed cognitive development as a *socially mediated process,* in which children depend on assistance from adults and more expert peers as they tackle new challenges.

Human longevity may have adaptive value. Grandparents' support in rearing young grandchildren promotes higher birth and child-survival rates.

Research stimulated by Vygotsky's theory reveals that people in every culture develop unique strengths. But Vygotsky's emphasis on culture and social experience led him to neglect the biological side of development. Although he recognized the importance of heredity and brain growth, he said little about their role in cognitive change. Furthermore, Vygotsky's focus on social transmission of knowledge meant that, compared with other theorists, he placed less emphasis on children's capacity to shape their own development. Followers of Vygotsky stress that children strive for social connection, actively participating in the conversations and social activities from which their development springs (Daniels, 2011; Rogoff, 2003). Contemporary sociocultural theorists grant the individual and society more balanced, mutually influential roles.

Ecological Systems Theory

Urie Bronfenbrenner (1917–2005) is responsible for an approach that rose to the forefront of the field because it offers the most differentiated and complete account of contextual influences on development. **Ecological systems theory** views the person as developing within a complex *system* of relationships affected by multiple levels of the surrounding environment. Because the child's biologically influenced dispositions join with environmental forces to mold development, Bronfenbrenner characterized his perspective as a *bioecological model* (Bronfenbrenner & Morris, 2006).

Bronfenbrenner envisioned the environment as a series of nested structures, including but also extending beyond the home, school, neighborhood, and workplace settings in which people spend their everyday lives (see Figure 1.5 on page 24). Each layer joins with the others to powerfully affect development.

The Microsystem.
The innermost level of the environment, the **microsystem,** consists of activities and interaction patterns in the person's immediate surroundings. Bronfenbrenner emphasized that to understand development at this level, we must keep in mind that all relationships are *bidirectional:* Adults affect children's behavior, but children's biologically and socially influenced characteristics—their physical attributes, personalities, and capacities—also affect adults' behavior. A friendly, attentive child is likely to evoke positive, patient reactions from parents, whereas an irritable or distractible child is more likely to receive impatience, restriction, and punishment. When these reciprocal interactions occur often over time, they have an enduring impact on development (Crockenberg & Leerkes, 2003).

Third parties—other individuals in the microsystem—also affect the quality of any two-person relationship. If they are supportive, interaction is enhanced. For example, when parents encourage each other in their child-rearing roles, each engages in more effective parenting. In contrast, marital conflict is associated with inconsistent discipline and hostility toward children. In response, children often react with fear and anxiety or with anger and aggression, and the well-being of both parent and child suffers (Cummings & Davies, 2010; Low & Stocker, 2012).

With her teacher's guidance, this Chinese child practices calligraphy. She acquires a culturally valued skill through interaction with an older, more experienced calligrapher.

In Vygotsky's theory, children undergo certain stagewise changes. For example, when they acquire language, they gain in ability to participate in dialogues with others, and mastery of culturally valued competencies surges forward. When children enter school, they spend much time discussing language, literacy, and other academic concepts—experiences that encourage them to reflect on their own thinking (Kozulin, 2003). As a result, they advance dramatically in reasoning and problem solving.

At the same time, Vygotsky stressed that dialogues with experts lead to continuous changes in thinking that vary greatly from culture to culture. Consistent with this view, a major finding of cross-cultural research is that cultures select tasks for their members, and social interaction surrounding those tasks leads to competencies essential for success in a particular culture. For example, in industrialized nations, teachers help people learn to read, drive a car, or use a computer. Among the Zinacanteco Indians of southern Mexico, adult experts guide young girls as they master complicated weaving techniques (Greenfield, 2004). In Brazil and other developing nations, child candy sellers with little or no schooling develop sophisticated mathematical abilities as the result of buying candy from wholesalers, pricing it in collaboration with adults and experienced peers, and bargaining with customers on city streets (Saxe, 1988).

FIGURE 1.5 Structure of the environment in ecological systems theory. The *microsystem* concerns relations between the developing person and the immediate environment; the *mesosystem*, connections among immediate settings; the *exosystem*, social settings that affect but do not contain the developing person; and the *macrosystem*, the values, laws, customs, and resources of the culture that affect activities and interactions at all inner layers. The *chronosystem* (not pictured) is not a specific context. Instead, it refers to the dynamic, ever-changing nature of the person's environment.

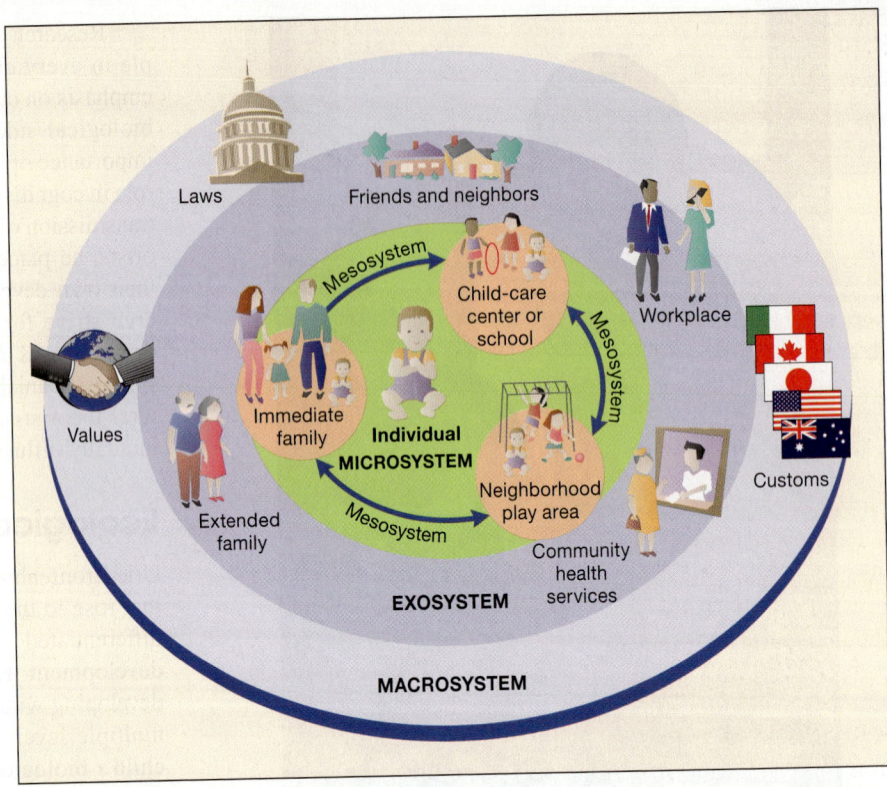

The Mesosystem.
The second level of Bronfenbrenner's model, the **mesosystem,** encompasses connections between microsystems. For example, a child's academic progress depends not just on activities that take place in classrooms but also on parent involvement in school life and on the extent to which academic learning is carried over to the home (Wang & Sheikh-Khalil, 2014). Among adults, how well a person functions as spouse and parent at home is affected by relationships in the workplace, and vice versa (Strazdins et al., 2013).

The Exosystem.
The **exosystem** consists of social settings that do not contain the developing person but nevertheless affect experiences in immediate settings. These can be formal organizations, such as the management in the individual's workplace, religious institution, or community health and welfare services. Flexible work schedules, paid maternity and paternity leave, and sick leave for parents whose children are ill are examples of ways that work settings can support child rearing and, indirectly, enhance the development of both adult and child. Exosystem supports can also be informal. Children are affected by their parents' social networks—friends and extended-family members who provide advice, companionship, and even financial assistance. Research confirms the negative impact of a breakdown in exosystem activities. Families who are affected by unemployment or who are socially isolated, with few personal or community-based ties, show increased rates of conflict and child abuse (Tomyr, Ouimet, & Ugnat, 2012). Refer to the Social Issues: Health box on the following page for an additional illustration of the power of the exosystem to affect family functioning and children's development.

The Macrosystem.
The outermost level of Bronfenbrenner's model, the **macrosystem,** consists of cultural values, laws, customs, and resources. The priority that the macrosystem gives to the needs of children and adults affects the support they receive

A mother says good-bye to her son as she drops him off at preschool. The child's experiences at preschool (microsystem) and the mother's experiences at work (exosystem) affect the parent–child relationship.

Social Issues: Health

Family Chaos Undermines Parents' and Children's Well-Being

All of us can recall days during our childhoods when family routines—regular mealtime, bedtime, homework time, and parent–child reading and playtimes—were disrupted, perhaps because of a change in a parent's job, a family illness, or a busy season of after-school sports. In some families, however, absence of daily structure is nearly constant, yielding a chaotic home life that interferes with healthy development (Fiese & Winter, 2010). An organized family life provides a supportive context for warm, involved parent–child interaction, which is essential to both parents' and children's well-being.

Family chaos is linked to economic disadvantage—especially, single mothers with limited incomes struggling to juggle the challenges of transportation, shift jobs, unstable child-care arrangements, and other daily hassles. But chaos is not limited to such families.

Surveys reveal that among U.S. families as a whole, mothers' time with children has remained fairly stable over the past four decades, while fathers' time has increased (Pew Research Center, 2015c). But the way many parents spend that time has changed. Across income levels and ethnic groups, employed mothers and fathers, but especially mothers, report more multitasking while caring for children—for example, preparing dinner while helping with homework, or reading to children while checking work-related emails (Bianchi, 2011; Offer & Schneider, 2011). Mothers who frequently multitask experience greater psychological stress.

Parental multitasking disrupts family routines—a possible reason that today's parents and children often say they have too little time together. For example, only about half of U.S. families report eating meals together regularly (Child Trends, 2013; Opinion Research Corporation, 2009). Frequency of family meals is associated with wide-ranging positive outcomes—in childhood, enhanced language development and academic achievement, fewer behavior problems, and time spent sleeping; and in adolescence, reduced sexual risk taking, alcohol and drug use, and mental health problems. Shared mealtimes also increase the likelihood of a healthy diet and protect against obesity and adolescent eating disorders (Fiese & Schwartz, 2008; Lora et al., 2014). As these findings suggest, regular mealtimes are a general indicator of an organized family life and positive parent involvement.

But family chaos can prevail even when families do engage in joint activities. Unpredictable, disorganized family routines involving harsh or lax parental discipline and hostile, disrespectful communication are associated with child and adolescent adjustment difficulties (Fiese, Foley, & Spagnola, 2006; Milkie, Nomaguchi, & Denny, 2015). As family time becomes pressured and overwhelming, its orderly structure diminishes, and parental stress escalates while warm parent–child engagement disintegrates.

Diverse circumstances can trigger a pileup of limited parental emotional resources, breeding family chaos. In addition to *microsystem* and *mesosystem* influences (parents with mental health problems, parental separation and divorce, single parents with few or no supportive relationships), the *exosystem* is powerful: When family time is at the mercy of external forces—parents commuting several hours a day to and from work, child-care arrangements often failing, parents experiencing excessive workplace pressures or job loss—family routines are threatened.

Family chaos contributes to children's behavior problems, above and beyond its negative impact on parenting effectiveness (Fiese & Winter, 2010; Martin, Razza, & Brooks-Gunn, 2012). Chaotic surroundings induce in children a sense of being hassled and feelings of powerlessness, which engender anxiety and low self-esteem.

Exosystem and macrosystem supports—including work settings with favorable family policies and high-quality child care that is affordable and reliable—can help prevent escalating demands on families that give way to chaos. In one community, a child-care center initiated a take-home dinner program. Busy parents could special-order a healthy, reasonably priced family meal, ready to go at day's end to aid in making the family dinner a routine that enhances children's development.

A chaotic home life interferes with warm, relaxed parent–child interaction and contributes to behavior problems. Exosystem influences, such as excessive workplace pressures, can trigger disorganized family routines.

at inner levels of the environment. For example, in countries that require generous workplace benefits for employed parents and set high standards for quality of child care, children are more likely to have favorable experiences in their immediate settings. And when the government provides a generous pension plan for retirees, it supports the well-being of older people.

LOOK and LISTEN

Ask a parent to explain his or her most worrisome child-rearing challenge. Describe one source of support at each level of Bronfenbrenner's bioecological model that could ease parental stress and promote child development.

A Dynamic, Ever-Changing System. According to Bronfenbrenner, the environment is not a static force that affects people in a uniform way. Instead, it is ever-changing. Whenever individuals add or let go of roles or settings in their lives, the breadth of their microsystems changes. These shifts in contexts—*ecological transitions,* as Bronfenbrenner called them—are often important turning points in development. Starting school, entering the workforce, moving in together, marrying, becoming a parent, getting divorced, and retiring are examples.

Bronfenbrenner labeled the temporal dimension of his model the **chronosystem** (the prefix *chrono* means "time"). Life changes can be imposed externally or, alternatively, can arise from within the person, since individuals select, modify, and create many of their own settings and experiences. How they do so depends on their physical, intellectual, and personality characteristics and their environmental opportunities. Therefore, in ecological systems theory, development is neither controlled by environmental circumstances nor driven solely by inner dispositions. Rather, people are both products and producers of their environments: The person and the environment form a network of interdependent effects. Our discussion of resilience on pages 10–11 illustrates this idea. You will see many more examples in later chapters.

Ask yourself

CONNECT Is ecological systems theory compatible with assumptions of the lifespan perspective—development as lifelong, multidirectional, highly plastic, and influenced by multiple, interacting forces? Explain.

APPLY Mario wants to find out precisely how children of different ages recall stories. Desiree is interested in how adult–child communication in different cultures influences children's storytelling. Which theoretical perspective has Mario probably chosen? How about Desiree? Explain.

REFLECT To illustrate the chronosystem in ecological systems theory, select an important event from your childhood, such as a move to a new neighborhood, a class with an inspiring teacher, or parental divorce. How did the event affect you? How might its impact have differed had you been five years younger? How about five years older?

Comparing and Evaluating Theories

1.7 Identify the stand taken by each major theory on the three basic issues of human development.

In the preceding sections, we reviewed major theoretical perspectives in human development research. They differ in many respects. First, they focus on different domains of development. Some, such as the psychoanalytic perspective and ethology, emphasize emotional and social development. Others, such as Piaget's cognitive-developmental theory, information processing, and Vygotsky's sociocultural theory, stress changes in thinking. The remaining approaches—behaviorism, social learning theory, evolutionary developmental psychology, ecological systems theory, and the lifespan perspective—encompass many aspects of human functioning. Second, every theory contains a point of view about development. As we conclude our review of theoretical perspectives, identify the stand that each theory takes on the basic issues discussed at the beginning of this chapter. Then check your analysis against Table 1.4.

Finally, we have seen that every theory has strengths and limitations. Perhaps you are attracted to some theories but have doubts about others. As you read more about development in later chapters, you may find it useful to keep a notebook in which you test your own theoretical likes and dislikes against the evidence. Don't be surprised if you revise your ideas many times, just as theorists have done since scientific study of development began.

Studying Development

1.8 Describe methods commonly used in research on human development.

1.9 Distinguish between correlational and experimental research designs, noting the strengths and limitations of each.

1.10 Describe designs for studying development, noting the strengths and limitations of each.

In every science, research is usually based on a *hypothesis*— a prediction drawn directly from a theory. Theories and hypotheses, however, merely initiate the many activities that result in sound evidence on human development. Conducting research according to scientifically accepted procedures involves many steps and choices. Investigators must decide which participants, and how many, to include. Then they must figure out what the participants will be asked to do and when, where, and how many times each will be seen. Finally, they must examine and draw conclusions from their data.

In the following sections, we look at research strategies commonly used to study human development. We begin with

TABLE 1.4
Stances of Major Theories on Basic Issues in Human Development

THEORY	CONTINUOUS OR DISCONTINUOUS DEVELOPMENT?	ONE COURSE OF DEVELOPMENT OR MANY?	RELATIVE INFLUENCE OF NATURE AND NURTURE?
Psychoanalytic perspective	*Discontinuous:* Psychosexual and psychosocial development takes place in stages.	*One course:* Stages are assumed to be universal.	*Both nature and nurture:* Innate impulses are channeled and controlled through child-rearing experiences. *Early experiences* set the course of later development.
Behaviorism and social learning theory	*Continuous:* Development involves an increase in learned behaviors.	*Many possible courses:* Behaviors reinforced and modeled may vary from person to person.	*Emphasis on nurture:* Development is the result of conditioning and modeling. *Both early and later experiences* are important.
Piaget's cognitive-developmental theory	*Discontinuous:* Cognitive development takes place in stages.	*One course:* Stages are assumed to be universal.	*Both nature and nurture:* Development occurs as the brain grows and children exercise their innate drive to discover reality in a generally stimulating environment. *Both early and later experiences* are important.
Information processing	*Continuous:* Children and adults change gradually in perception, attention, memory, and problem-solving skills.	*One course:* Changes studied characterize most or all children and adults.	*Both nature and nurture:* Children and adults are active, sense-making beings who modify their thinking as the brain grows and they confront new environmental demands. *Both early and later experiences* are important.
Ethology and evolutionary developmental psychology	*Both continuous and discontinuous:* Children and adults gradually develop a wider range of adaptive behaviors. Sensitive periods occur in which qualitatively distinct capacities emerge fairly suddenly.	*One course:* Adaptive behaviors and sensitive periods apply to all members of a species.	*Both nature and nurture:* Evolution and heredity influence behavior, and learning lends greater flexibility and adaptiveness to it. In sensitive periods, *early experiences* set the course of later development.
Vygotsky's sociocultural theory	*Both continuous and discontinuous:* Language acquisition and schooling lead to stagewise changes. Dialogues with more expert members of society also result in continuous changes that vary from culture to culture.	*Many possible courses:* Socially mediated changes in thought and behavior vary from culture to culture.	*Both nature and nurture:* Heredity, brain growth, and dialogues with more expert members of society jointly contribute to development. *Both early and later experiences* are important.
Ecological systems theory	*Not specified.*	*Many possible courses:* Biologically influenced dispositions join with environmental forces at multiple levels to mold development in unique ways.	*Both nature and nurture:* The individual's characteristics and the reactions of others affect each other in a bidirectional fashion. *Both early and later experiences* are important.
Lifespan perspective	*Both continuous and discontinuous:* Continuous gains and declines and discontinuous, stagewise emergence of new skills occur.	*Many possible courses:* Development is influenced by multiple, interacting biological, psychological, and social forces, many of which vary from person to person, leading to diverse pathways of change.	*Both nature and nurture:* Development is multidimensional, affected by an intricate blend of hereditary and environmental factors. Emphasizes plasticity at all ages. *Both early and later experiences* are important.

research methods—the specific activities of participants, such as taking tests, answering questionnaires, responding to interviews, or being observed. Then we turn to *research designs*—overall plans for research studies that permit the best possible test of the investigator's hypothesis. Finally, we discuss ethical issues involved in doing research with human participants.

Why learn about research strategies? There are two reasons. First, each of us must be a wise and critical consumer of knowledge. Knowing the strengths and limitations of various research strategies is important in separating dependable information from misleading results. Second, individuals who work directly with children or adults may be in a unique position to build bridges between research and practice by conducting studies, either on their own or in partnership with experienced investigators. Community agencies such as schools, mental health facilities, and parks and recreation programs sometimes collaborate with researchers in designing, implementing, and evaluating interventions aimed at enhancing development (Guerra, Graham, & Tolan, 2011). To broaden these efforts, a basic understanding of the research process is essential.

LOOK and LISTEN

Ask a teacher, counselor, social worker, or nurse to describe a question about development he or she would like researchers to address. After reading the rest of this chapter, recommend research strategies best suited to answering that question.

Common Research Methods

How does a researcher choose a basic approach to gathering information? Common methods include systematic observation, self-reports (such as questionnaires and interviews), clinical or case studies of a single individual, and ethnographies of the life circumstances of a specific group of people. Table 1.5 summarizes the strengths and limitations of each of these methods.

Systematic Observation. Observations of the behavior of children and adults can be made in different ways. One approach is to go into the field, or natural environment, and record the behavior of interest—a method called **naturalistic observation.**

A study of preschoolers' responses to their peers' distress provides a good example (Farver & Branstetter, 1994). Observing 3- and 4-year-olds in child-care centers, the researchers recorded each instance of crying and the reactions of nearby children—whether they ignored, watched, commented on the child's unhappiness, scolded or teased, or shared, helped, or expressed sympathy. Caregiver behaviors—explaining why a child was crying, mediating conflict, or offering comfort—were noted to see if adult sensitivity was related to children's caring responses. A strong relationship emerged. The great strength of naturalistic observation is that investigators can see directly the everyday behaviors they hope to explain.

Naturalistic observation also has a major limitation: Not all individuals have the same opportunity to display a particular behavior in everyday life. In the study just described, some children might have witnessed a child crying more often than others or been exposed to more cues for positive social responses from caregivers. For these reasons, they might have displayed more compassion.

Researchers commonly deal with this difficulty by making **structured observations,** in which the investigator sets up a

TABLE 1.5
Strengths and Limitations of Common Research Methods

METHOD	DESCRIPTION	STRENGTHS	LIMITATIONS
SYSTEMATIC OBSERVATION			
Naturalistic observation	Observation of behavior in natural contexts	Reflects participants' everyday lives.	Cannot control conditions under which participants are observed.
Structured observation	Observation of behavior in a laboratory, where conditions are the same for all participants	Grants each participant an equal opportunity to display the behavior of interest.	May not yield observations typical of participants' behavior in everyday life.
SELF-REPORTS			
Clinical interview	Flexible interviewing procedure in which the investigator obtains a complete account of the participant's thoughts	Comes as close as possible to the way participants think in everyday life. Great breadth and depth of information can be obtained in a short time.	May not result in accurate reporting of information. Flexible procedure makes comparing individuals' responses difficult.
Structured interview, questionnaires, and tests	Self-report instruments in which each participant is asked the same questions in the same way	Permits comparisons of participants' responses and efficient data collection. Researchers can specify answer alternatives that participants might not think of in an open-ended interview.	Does not yield the same depth of information as a clinical interview. Responses are still subject to inaccurate reporting.
CLINICAL, OR CASE STUDY, METHOD			
	A full picture of one individual's psychological functioning, obtained by combining interviews, observations, and test scores	Provides rich, descriptive insights into factors that affect development.	May be biased by researchers' theoretical preferences. Findings cannot be applied to individuals other than the participant.
ETHNOGRAPHY			
	Participant observation of a culture or distinct social group. By making extensive field notes, the researcher tries to capture the culture's unique values and social processes	Provides a more complete description than can be derived from a single observational visit, interview, or questionnaire.	May be biased by researchers' values and theoretical preferences. Findings cannot be applied to individuals and settings other than the ones studied.

CHAPTER 1 History, Theory, and Research Strategies

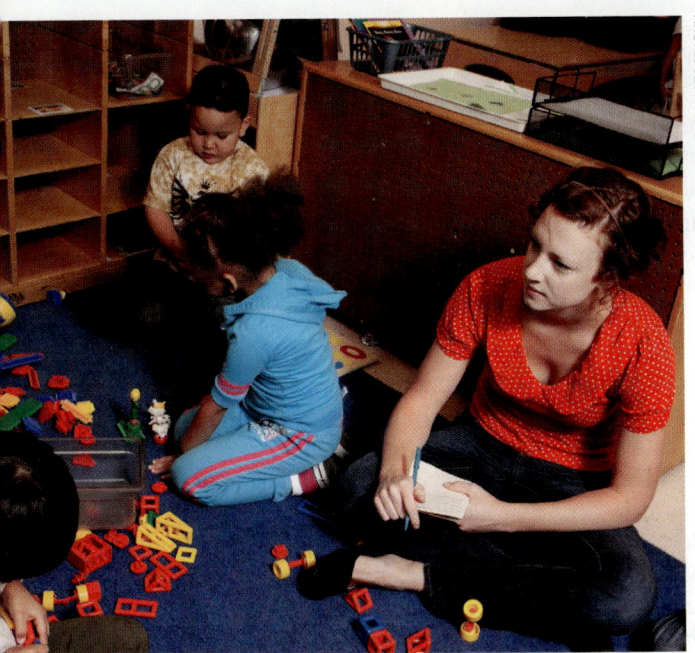

In naturalistic observation, the researcher goes into the field and records the behavior of interest. Here, a research assistant observes children at preschool. She may be focusing on their playmate choices, cooperation, helpfulness, or conflicts.

laboratory situation that evokes the behavior of interest so that every participant has equal opportunity to display the response. In one such study, 2-year-olds' emotional reactions to harm that they thought they had caused were observed by asking each of them to take care of a rag doll that had been modified so its leg would fall off when the child picked it up. To make the child feel at fault, once the leg detached, an adult "talked for" the doll, saying, "Ow!" Researchers recorded children's facial expressions of sadness and concern for the injured doll, efforts to help the doll, and body tension—responses that indicated worry, remorse, and a desire to make amends. In addition, mothers were asked to engage in brief conversations about emotions with their children (Garner, 2003). Toddlers whose mothers more often explained the causes and consequences of emotion were more likely to express concern for the injured doll.

The procedures used to collect systematic observations vary, depending on the research problem posed. Sometimes investigators choose to describe the entire stream of behavior—everything said and done over a certain time period. In one study, researchers wanted to find out whether maternal sensitivity in infancy and early childhood contributes to readiness for formal schooling at age 6 (Hirsh-Pasek & Burchinal, 2006). Between ages 6 months and 4½ years, the investigators periodically videotaped mother–child play sessions. Then they rated each session for many behaviors—maternal positive emotion, support, stimulating play, and respect for the child's autonomy. These ingredients of sensitivity did predict better language and academic progress when the children reached kindergarten.

Researchers have devised ingenious ways of observing difficult-to-capture behaviors. For example, to record instances of bullying, a group of investigators set up video cameras overlooking a classroom and a playground and had fourth to sixth graders wear small, remote microphones and pocket-sized transmitters (Craig, Pepler, & Atlas, 2000). Results revealed that bullying occurred often—at rates of 2.4 episodes per hour in the classroom and 4.5 episodes per hour on the playground. Yet only 15 to 18 percent of the time did teachers take steps to stop the harassment.

Systematic observation provides invaluable information on how children and adults actually behave, but it tells us little about the reasoning behind their responses. For this kind of information, researchers must turn to self-report techniques.

Self-Reports. Self-reports ask research participants to provide information on their perceptions, thoughts, abilities, feelings, attitudes, beliefs, and past experiences. They range from relatively unstructured interviews to highly structured interviews, questionnaires, and tests.

In a **clinical interview,** researchers use a flexible, conversational style to probe for the participant's point of view. In the following example, Piaget questioned a 5-year-old child about his understanding of dreams:

> *Where does the dream come from?*—I think you sleep so well that you dream.—*Does it come from us or from outside?*—From outside.—*When you are in bed and you dream, where is the dream?*—In my bed, under the blanket. I don't really know. If it was in my stomach, the bones would be in the way and I shouldn't see it.—*Is the dream there when you sleep?*—Yes, it is in the bed beside me. (Piaget, 1926/1930, pp. 97–98)

Although a researcher conducting clinical interviews with more than one participant would typically ask the same first question to establish a common task, individualized prompts are used to provide a fuller picture of each person's reasoning.

The clinical interview has two major strengths. First, it permits people to display their thoughts in terms that are as close as possible to the way they think in everyday life. Second, the clinical interview can provide a large amount of information in a fairly brief period (Sharp et al., 2013). For example, in an hour-long session, we can obtain a wide range of information on child rearing from a parent or on life circumstances from an older adult—much more than we could capture by observing for the same amount of time.

A major limitation of the clinical interview has to do with the accuracy with which people report their thoughts, feelings, and experiences. Some participants, wishing to please the interviewer, may make up answers that do not represent their actual thinking. When asked about past events, some may have trouble recalling exactly what happened. And because the clinical interview depends on verbal ability and expressiveness, it may underestimate the capacities of individuals who have difficulty putting their thoughts into words.

The clinical interview has also been criticized because of its flexibility. When questions are phrased differently for each participant, responses may reflect the manner of interviewing rather than real differences in the way people think about a topic.

Structured interviews (including tests and questionnaires), in which each participant is asked the same set of questions in the same way, eliminate this problem. These instruments are also much more efficient. Answers are briefer, and researchers can obtain written responses from an entire group at the same time. Furthermore, by listing answer alternatives, researchers can specify the activities and behaviors of interest—ones that participants might not think of in an open-ended clinical interview. For example, when a sample of parents was asked what they considered "the most important thing for children to prepare them for life," 62 percent checked "to think for themselves" when this choice appeared on a list. Yet only 5 percent thought of this during a clinical interview (Schwarz, 2008).

Nevertheless, structured interviews do not yield the same depth of information as a clinical interview. And they can still be affected by the problem of inaccurate reporting.

The Clinical, or Case Study, Method.
An outgrowth of psychoanalytic theory, the **clinical, or case study, method** brings together a wide range of information on one person, including interviews, observations, and test scores. The aim is to obtain as complete a picture as possible of that individual's psychological functioning and the experiences that led up to it.

The clinical method is well-suited to studying the development of certain types of individuals who are few in number but vary widely in characteristics. For example, the method has been used to find out what contributes to the accomplishments of *prodigies*—extremely gifted children who attain adult competence in a field before age 10 (Moran & Gardner, 2006).

In one investigation, researchers conducted case studies of eight child prodigies nationally recognized for talents in such areas as art, music, and mathematics (Ruthsatz & Urbach, 2012). One child began playing the violin at 28 months, had won regional competitions as a 5-year-old, and by age 7 had performed as a soloist at New York's Carnegie Hall and Lincoln Center. Another child started reading as an infant, took college-level classes beginning at age 8, and published a paper in a mathematics journal at 13. Across the eight cases, the investigators noticed interesting patterns, including above-average intelligence and exceptionally high scores on tests of memory and attention to detail. Notably, several prodigies had relatives with autism, a condition that also involves intense attention to detail. The researchers concluded that although child prodigies generally do not display the cognitive and social deficits of autism, the two groups may share an underlying genetic trait that affects the functioning of certain brain regions, heightening perception and attention.

The clinical method yields richly detailed case narratives that offer valuable insights into the many factors influencing development. Nevertheless, like all other methods, it has drawbacks. Because information often is collected unsystematically and subjectively, researchers' theoretical preferences may bias their observations and interpretations. In addition, investigators cannot assume that their conclusions apply, or generalize, to anyone other than the person studied (Stanovich, 2013). Even when patterns emerge across cases, it is wise to confirm these with other research strategies.

Methods for Studying Culture.
To study the impact of culture, researchers adjust the methods just considered or tap procedures specially devised for cross-cultural and multicultural research. Which approach investigators choose depends on their research goals.

Sometimes researchers are interested in characteristics that are believed to be universal but that vary in degree from one society to the next: Are parents warmer or more directive in some cultures than others? How strong are gender stereotypes in different nations? In each instance, several cultural groups will be compared, and all participants must be questioned or observed in the same way. Therefore, researchers draw on the observational and self-report procedures we have already considered, adapting them through translation so they can be understood in each cultural context. For example, to study cultural variation in parenting practices, the same questionnaire, asking for ratings on such items as "I often start a conversation with my parents about what happens in school" or "My parents can tell when I'm upset about something," is given to all participants (Qin & Pomerantz, 2013). Still, investigators must be mindful of cultural differences in familiarity with being observed and with responding to self-report instruments, which may bias their findings (van de Vijver, 2011).

At other times, researchers want to uncover the *cultural meanings* of children's and adults' behaviors by becoming as familiar as possible with their way of life. To achieve this goal, investigators rely on a method borrowed from the field of anthropology—**ethnography.** Like the clinical method, ethnographic research is a descriptive, qualitative technique. But instead of aiming to understand a single individual, it is directed toward understanding a culture or a distinct social group through

Using the clinical, or case study, method, this researcher interacts with a 3-year-old during a home visit. Interviews and observations will contribute to an in-depth picture of this child's psychological functioning.

CHAPTER 1 History, Theory, and Research Strategies

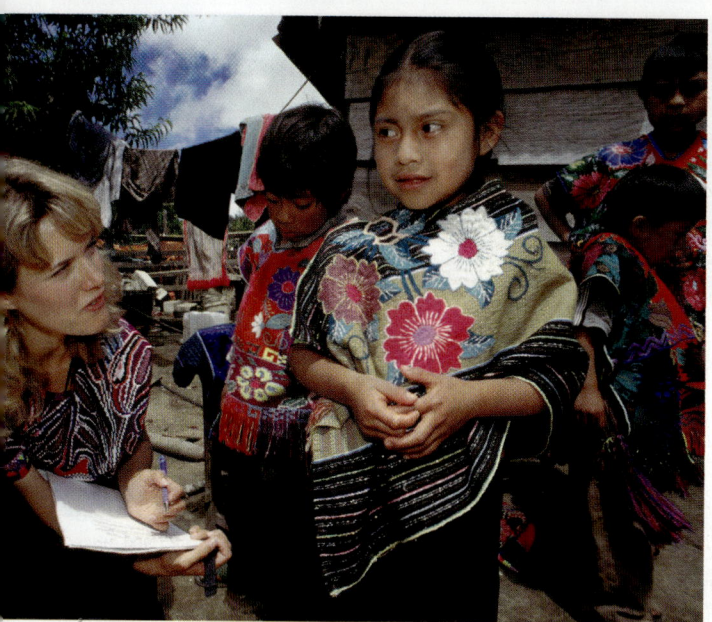

A Western researcher works with Zinacantec Mayan children in Chiapas, Mexico, using the ethnographic method to gather information about how they learn through everyday activities.

Ask yourself

CONNECT What strengths and limitations do the clinical, or case study, method and ethnography have in common?

APPLY A researcher wants to study the thoughts and feelings of parents on active duty in the military and those of their school-age and adolescent children. Which method should she use? Why?

REFLECT Reread the description of nonnormative influences on page 10, and cite an example from your own life. Which method would be best suited to studying the impact of such a nonnormative event on development?

participant observation. Typically, the researcher spends months, and sometimes years, in the cultural community, participating in its daily life. Extensive field notes are gathered, consisting of a mix of observations, self-reports from members of the culture, and careful interpretations by the investigator (Case, Todd, & Kral, 2014). Later, these notes are put together into a description of the community that tries to capture its unique values and social processes.

The ethnographic method assumes that entering into close contact with a social group will allow researchers to understand the beliefs and behaviors of its members in a way that is not possible with an observational visit, interview, or questionnaire. Some ethnographies take in many aspects of experience, as one researcher did in describing what it is like to grow up in a small American town. Others focus on one or a few settings and issues—for example, youth resilience in an economically disadvantaged Alaskan-Native community or African-Caribbean adults' reactions to a diagnosis of high blood pressure, signaling elevated risk for heart disease (Higginbottom, 2006; Peshkin, 1997; Rasmus, Allen, & Ford, 2014). Notice how such ethnographic evidence is vital for designing effective interventions. Researchers may supplement traditional self-report and observational methods with ethnography if they suspect that unique meanings underlie cultural differences, as the Cultural Influences box on page 32 reveals.

Ethnographers strive to minimize their influence on the culture they are studying by becoming part of it. Nevertheless, as with clinical research, investigators' cultural values and theoretical commitments sometimes lead them to observe selectively or misinterpret what they see. Finally, the findings of ethnographic studies cannot be assumed to generalize beyond the people and settings in which the research was conducted.

General Research Designs

In deciding on a research design, investigators choose a way of setting up a study that permits them to test their hypotheses with the greatest certainty possible. Two main types of designs are used in all research on human behavior: *correlational* and *experimental.*

Correlational Design. In a **correlational design,** researchers gather information on individuals, generally in natural life circumstances, without altering their experiences. Then they look at relationships between participants' characteristics and their behavior or development. Suppose we want to answer such questions as, Do parents' styles of interacting with their children have any bearing on children's intelligence? Does the arrival of a baby influence a couple's marital satisfaction? Does death of a spouse in late adulthood affect the surviving partner's physical health and psychological well-being? In these and many other instances, the conditions of interest are difficult or impossible to arrange and control and must be studied as they currently exist.

Retirees enjoy socializing on the riverbank in the town of Split, Croatia. How do older adults' friendships affect their well-being? A correlational design can be used to answer this question, but it does not permit researchers to determine the precise cause of their findings.

Cultural Influences

Immigrant Youths: Adapting to a New Land

Over the past several decades, increasing numbers of immigrants have come to North America, fleeing war and persecution in their homelands or seeking better life chances. Today, nearly one-fourth of U.S. children and adolescents have foreign-born parents, mostly originating from Latin America, the Caribbean, Asia, and Africa. Although some move with their parents, more than 80 percent of young people from immigrant families are U.S.-born citizens (Hernandez, Denton, & Blanchard, 2011; Hernandez et al., 2012).

How well are these youths—now the fastest-growing sector of the U.S. youth population—adapting to their new country? To find out, researchers use multiple research methods: academic testing, questionnaires assessing psychological adjustment, and in-depth ethnographies.

Academic Achievement and Adjustment

Although educators and laypeople often assume that the transition to a new country has a negative impact on psychological well-being, many children of immigrant parents adapt amazingly well. Students who are foreign-born (immigrated with their parents) or first-generation (American-born, with immigrant parents) often achieve in school as well as or better than students of native-born parents (Hao & Woo, 2012; Hernandez, Denton, & Blanchard, 2011). And compared with their agemates, adolescents from immigrant families are less likely to commit delinquent and violent acts, use drugs and alcohol, have early sex, miss school because of illness, or suffer from obesity. Furthermore, they report just as favorable, and at times higher, self-esteem as do young people with native-born parents (Saucier et al., 2002; Supple & Small, 2006).

These outcomes are strongest for Chinese, Filipino, Japanese, Korean, and East Indian youths, less dramatic for other ethnicities (Fuligni, 2004; Louie, 2001; Portes & Rumbaut, 2005). Variation in adjustment is greater among Mexican, Central American, and Southeast Asian (Hmong, Cambodian, Laotian, Thai, and Vietnamese) young people, who show elevated rates of school failure and dropout, delinquency, teenage parenthood, and drug use (García Coll & Marks, 2009; Pong & Landale, 2012). Disparities in parental economic resources, education, English-language proficiency, and support of children contribute to these trends.

Still, many first- and second-generation youths whose parents face considerable financial hardship and who speak little English are successful (Hao & Woo, 2012). Factors other than income are responsible—notably, family values and strong ethnic-community ties.

Family and Ethnic-Community Influences

Ethnographies reveal that immigrant parents view education as the surest way to improve life chances (García Coll & Marks, 2009). They typically emphasize trying hard, reminding their children that, because educational opportunities were not available in their native countries, they themselves are often limited to menial jobs.

Adolescents from these families internalize parental valuing of education more strongly than do agemates with native-born parents (Fuligni, 2004; Su & Costigan, 2008). Because minority ethnicities usually stress allegiance to family and community over individual goals, immigrant young people feel a strong sense of obligation to their parents. They view school success as an important way of repaying their parents for the hardships they have endured (Bacallao & Smokowski, 2007; van Geel & Vedder, 2011). Both family relationships and school achievement protect these youths from risky behaviors (see the Biology and Environment box on pages 10–11).

Immigrant parents of successful youths typically develop close ties to an ethnic community, which exerts additional control

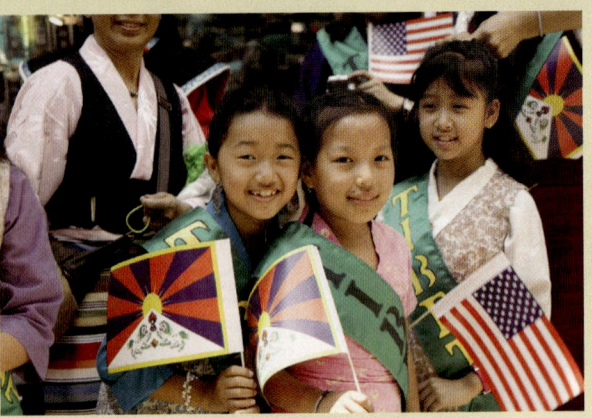

These Tibetan-American children march in an international immigrants parade in New York City. Cultural values that engender allegiance to family and community promote high achievement and protect many immigrant youths from involvement in risky behaviors.

through a high consensus on values and constant monitoring of young people's activities. The following comments capture the power of these family and community forces:

A 16-year-old girl from Central America describes the supportive adults in her neighborhood: They ask me if I need anything for school. If we go to a store and I see a notebook, they ask me if I want it. They give me advice, tell me that I should be careful of the friends I choose. They also tell me to stay in school to get prepared. They tell me I am smart. They give me encouragement. (Suárez-Orozco, Pimental, & Martin, 2009, p. 733)

A teenage boy from Mexico discusses the importance of family in his culture: A really big part of the Hispanic population [is] being close to family, and the family being a priority all the time. I hate people who say, "Why do you want to go to a party where your family's at? Don't you want to get away from them?" You know, I don't really get tired of them. I've always been really close to them. That connection to my parents, that trust that you can talk to them, that makes me Mexican. (Bacallao & Smokowski, 2007, p. 62)

The experiences of well-adjusted immigrant youths are not problem-free. Many encounter racial and ethnic prejudices and experience tensions between family values and the new culture—challenges we will take up in Chapter 12. In the long term, however, family and community cohesion, supervision, and high expectations promote favorable outcomes.

Correlational studies have one major limitation: We cannot infer cause and effect. For example, if we were to find that parental interaction is related to children's intelligence, we would not know whether parents' behavior actually *causes* intellectual differences among children. In fact, the opposite is possible. The behaviors of highly intelligent children may be so attractive that they cause parents to interact more favorably. Or a third variable that we did not even consider, such as the amount of noise and distraction in the home, may cause changes in both parental interaction and children's intelligence.

In correlational studies and in other types of research designs, investigators often examine relationships by using a **correlation coefficient**—a number that describes how two measures, or variables, are associated with each other. We will encounter the correlation coefficient in discussing research findings throughout this book, so let's look at what it is and how it is interpreted. A correlation coefficient can range in value from +1.00 to −1.00. The *magnitude, or size, of the number* shows the *strength of the relationship*. A zero correlation indicates no relationship; the closer the value is to +1.00 or −1.00, the stronger the relationship (see Figure 1.6). For instance, a correlation of −.78 is high, −.52 is moderate, and −.18 is low. Note, however, that correlations of +.52 and −.52 are equally strong. The *sign of the number* (+ or −) refers to the *direction of the relationship*. A positive sign (+) means that as one variable *increases*, the other also *increases*. A negative sign (−) indicates that as one variable *increases*, the other *decreases*.

Let's look at some examples of how a correlation coefficient works. One researcher reported a +.55 correlation between a measure of maternal language stimulation and the size of 2-year-olds' vocabularies (Hoff, 2003). This is a moderate correlation, which indicates that toddlers whose mothers spoke more to them tended to be advanced in language development. In two other studies, child-rearing practices were related to toddlers' compliance in consistent ways. First, maternal warmth and sensitivity during play correlated positively with 2-year-olds' willingness to comply with their mother's directive to clean up toys, at +.34 (Feldman & Klein, 2003). Second, the extent to which mothers spoke harshly, interrupted, and controlled their 4-year-olds' play correlated negatively with children's compliance, at −.31 for boys and −.42 for girls (Smith et al., 2004).

All these investigations found a relationship between parenting and young children's behavior. Are you tempted to conclude that the maternal behaviors influenced children's responses? Although the researchers in these studies suspected this was so, they could not be sure of cause and effect. Can you think of other possible explanations? Finding a relationship in a correlational study suggests that tracking down its cause—using a more powerful experimental strategy, if possible—would be worthwhile.

Experimental Design An **experimental design** permits inferences about cause and effect because researchers use an evenhanded procedure to assign people to two or more treatment conditions. In an experiment, the events and behaviors of interest are divided into two types: independent and dependent variables. The **independent variable** is the one the investigator expects to cause changes in another variable. The **dependent variable** is the one the investigator expects to be influenced by the independent variable. Cause-and-effect relationships can be detected because the researcher directly *controls* or *manipulates* changes in the independent variable by exposing participants to the treatment conditions. Then the researcher compares their performance on measures of the dependent variable.

In one *laboratory experiment,* researchers explored the impact of adults' angry interactions on children's adjustment (El-Sheikh, Cummings, & Reiter, 1996). They hypothesized that the way angry encounters end (independent variable) affects children's emotional reactions (dependent variable). Four- and 5-year-olds were brought one at a time to a laboratory, accompanied by their mothers. One group was exposed to an *unresolved-anger treatment,* in which two adult actors entered the room and argued but did not work out their disagreements. The other group witnessed a resolved-anger treatment, in which the adults ended their disputes by apologizing and compromising. When witnessing a follow-up adult conflict, children in the *resolved-anger treatment* showed less distress, as measured by fewer anxious facial expressions, less freezing in place, and less seeking of closeness to their mothers. The experiment revealed that anger resolution can reduce the stressful impact of adult conflict on children.

In experimental studies, investigators must take special precautions to control for participants' characteristics that could reduce the accuracy of their findings. For example, in the study just described, if a greater number of children from homes high in parental conflict ended up in the unresolved-anger treatment, we could not tell what produced the results—the independent variable or the children's family backgrounds. To protect against this problem, researchers engage in **random assignment** of participants to treatment conditions. By using an unbiased procedure, such as drawing numbers out of a hat or flipping a coin,

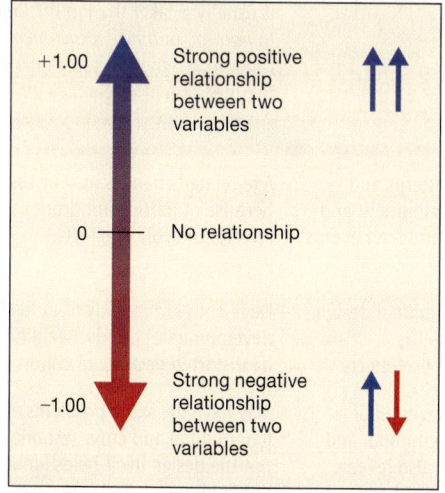

FIGURE 1.6 The meaning of correlation coefficients. The magnitude of the number indicates the *strength* of the relationship. The sign of the number (+ or −) indicates the *direction* of the relationship.

investigators increase the chances that participants' characteristics will be equally distributed across treatment groups.

Modified Experimental Designs: Field and Natural Experiments.
Most experiments are conducted in laboratories, where researchers can achieve the maximum possible control over treatment conditions. But, as we have already indicated, findings obtained in laboratories may not always apply to everyday situations. In *field experiments,* investigators capitalize on opportunities to assign participants randomly to treatment conditions in natural settings. In the experiment just described, we can conclude that the emotional climate established by adults affects children's behavior in the laboratory. But does it also do so in daily life?

Another study helps answer this question. Ethnically diverse, poverty-stricken families with a 2-year-old child were scheduled for a home visit, during which researchers assessed family functioning and child problem behaviors by asking parents to respond to questionnaires and videotaping parent–child interaction. Then the families were randomly assigned to either a brief intervention condition, called the Family Check-Up, or a no-intervention control group. The intervention consisted of three home-based sessions in which a consultant gave parents feedback about their child-rearing practices and their child's adjustment, explored parents' willingness to improve, identified community services appropriate to each family's needs, and offered follow-up sessions on parenting practices and other concerns (Brennan et al., 2013; Dishion et al., 2008). Findings showed that families assigned to the Family Check-Up (but not controls) gained in positive parenting, which predicted a reduction in child problem behaviors and higher academic achievement when the children reached school age.

Often researchers cannot randomly assign participants and manipulate conditions in the real world. Sometimes they can compromise by conducting *natural,* or *quasi-, experiments,* comparing treatments that already exist, such as different family environments, schools, workplaces, or retirement villages. These studies differ from correlational research only in that groups of participants are carefully chosen to ensure that their characteristics are as much alike as possible. In this way, investigators do their best to rule out alternative explanations for their treatment effects. But despite these efforts, natural experiments cannot achieve the precision and rigor of true experimental research.

To help you compare correlational and experimental designs, Table 1.6 summarizes their strengths and limitations. It also includes an overview of designs for studying development, to which we turn next.

TABLE 1.6
Strengths and Limitations of Research Designs

DESIGN	DESCRIPTION	STRENGTHS	LIMITATIONS
GENERAL			
Correlational	The investigator obtains information on participants without altering their experiences.	Permits study of relationships between variables.	Does not permit inferences about cause-and-effect relationships.
Experimental	Through random assignment of participants to treatment conditions, the investigator manipulates an independent variable and examines its effect on a dependent variable. Can be conducted in the laboratory or the natural environment.	Permits inferences about cause-and-effect relationships.	When conducted in the laboratory, findings may not generalize to the real world. In *field experiments,* control over the treatment is usually weaker than in the laboratory. In *natural,* or *quasi-, experiments,* lack of random assignment substantially reduces the precision of research.
DEVELOPMENTAL			
Longitudinal	The investigator studies the same group of participants repeatedly at different ages.	Permits study of common patterns and individual differences in development and relationships between early and later events and behaviors.	Age-related changes may be distorted because of participant dropout, practice effects, and cohort effects.
Cross-sectional	The investigator studies groups of participants differing in age at the same point in time.	More efficient than the longitudinal design. Not plagued by such problems as participant dropout and practice effects.	Does not permit study of individual developmental trends. Age differences may be distorted because of cohort effects.
Sequential	The investigator conducts several similar cross-sectional or longitudinal studies (called sequences). These might study participants over the same ages but in different years, or they might study participants over different ages but during the same years.	When the design includes longitudinal sequences, permits both longitudinal and cross-sectional comparisons. Also reveals cohort effects. Permits tracking of age-related changes more efficiently than the longitudinal design.	May have the same problems as longitudinal and cross-sectional strategies, but the design itself helps identify difficulties.

Designs for Studying Development

Scientists interested in human development require information about the way research participants change over time. To answer questions about development, they must extend correlational and experimental approaches to include measurements at different ages. Longitudinal and cross-sectional designs are special *developmental research strategies*. In each, age comparisons form the basis of the research plan.

The Longitudinal Design.
In a **longitudinal design,** participants are studied repeatedly, and changes are noted as they get older. The time spanned may be relatively short (a few months to several years) or very long (a decade or even a lifetime). The longitudinal approach has two major strengths. First, because it tracks the performance of each person over time, researchers can identify common patterns as well as individual differences in development. Second, longitudinal studies permit investigators to examine relationships between early and later events and behaviors. Let's illustrate these ideas.

A group of researchers wondered whether children who display extreme personality styles—either angry and explosive or shy and withdrawn—retain the same dispositions when they become adults. In addition, the researchers wanted to know what kinds of experiences promote stability or change in personality and what consequences explosiveness and shyness have for long-term adjustment. To answer these questions, the researchers delved into the archives of the Guidance Study, a well-known longitudinal investigation initiated in 1928 at the University of California, Berkeley, that continued for several decades (Caspi, Elder, & Bem, 1987, 1988).

Results revealed that the two personality styles were moderately stable. Between ages 8 and 30, a good number of individuals remained the same, whereas others changed substantially. When stability did occur, it appeared to be due to a "snowballing effect," in which children evoked responses from adults and peers that acted to maintain their dispositions. Explosive youngsters were likely to be treated with anger, whereas shy children were apt to be ignored. As a result, the two types of children came to view their social worlds differently. Explosive children regarded others as hostile; shy children regarded them as unfriendly (Caspi & Roberts, 2001). Together, these factors led explosive children to sustain or increase their unruliness and shy children to continue to withdraw.

Persistence of extreme personality styles affected many areas of adult adjustment. For men, the results of early explosiveness were most apparent in their work lives, in the form of conflicts with supervisors, frequent job changes, and unemployment. Since few women in this sample of an earlier generation worked after marriage, their family lives were most affected. Explosive girls grew up to be hotheaded wives and mothers who were especially prone to divorce. Sex differences in the long-term consequences of shyness were even greater. Men who had been withdrawn in childhood were delayed in marrying, becoming fathers, and developing stable careers. However, because a withdrawn, unassertive style was socially acceptable for females in the mid-twentieth century, women with shy personalities showed no special adjustment problems.

Problems in Conducting Longitudinal Research.
Despite their strengths, longitudinal investigations pose a number of problems. For example, participants may move away or drop out of the research for other reasons. This biases the sample so that it no longer represents the population to whom researchers would like to generalize their findings. Also, from repeated study, people may become more aware of their own thoughts, feelings, and actions and revise them in ways that have little to do with age-related change. In addition, they may become "test-wise." Their performance may improve as a result of *practice effects*—better test-taking skills and increased familiarity with the test—not because of factors commonly associated with development.

The most widely discussed threat to the accuracy of longitudinal findings is **cohort effects** (see pages 9–10): Individuals born in the same time period are influenced by a particular set of historical and cultural conditions. Results based on one cohort may not apply to people developing at other times. For example, consider the results on female shyness described in the preceding section, which were gathered in the 1950s. Today's shy adolescent girls and young women tend to be poorly adjusted—a difference that may be due to changes in gender roles in Western societies. Shy adults, whether male or female, feel more anxious and depressed, have fewer social supports, are delayed in forming romantic partnerships, and do less well in educational and

These refugees being helped ashore in Greece are among millions of Syrians who have been displaced by or have fled their country's civil war. Their lives have been dramatically altered by their wartime and migration experiences—a cohort effect deemed the largest humanitarian crisis of contemporary times.

career attainment than their agemates (Asendorpf, Denissen, & van Aken, 2008; Karevold et al., 2012; Mounts et al., 2006). Similarly, a longitudinal study of lifespan development would probably result in quite different findings if it were carried out in the second decade of the twenty-first century, around the time of World War II, or during the Great Depression of the 1930s.

Cohort effects don't just operate broadly on an entire generation. They also occur when specific experiences influence some groups of individuals but not others in the same generation. For example, children who witnessed the terrorist attacks of September 11, 2001 (either because they were near Ground Zero or because they saw injury and death on TV), or who lost a parent in the disaster, were far more likely than other children to display persistent emotional problems, including intense fear, anxiety, and depression (Mullett-Hume et al., 2008; Rosen & Cohen, 2010).

The Cross-Sectional Design.
The length of time it takes for many behaviors to change, even in limited longitudinal studies, has led researchers to turn to a more efficient strategy for studying development. In the **cross-sectional design,** groups of people differing in age are studied at the same point in time. Because participants are measured only once, researchers need not be concerned about such difficulties as participant dropout or practice effects.

A study in which students in grades 3, 6, 9, and 12 filled out a questionnaire about their sibling relationships provides a good illustration (Buhrmester & Furman, 1990). Findings revealed that sibling interaction was characterized by greater equality and less power assertion with age. Also, feelings of sibling companionship declined in adolescence. The researchers thought that several factors contributed to these age differences. As later-born children become more competent and independent, they no longer need, and are probably less willing to accept, direction from older siblings. And as adolescents move from psychological dependence on the family to greater involvement with peers, they may have less time and emotional need to invest in siblings. As we will see in Chapter 12, subsequent research has confirmed these intriguing ideas about the development of sibling relationships.

Problems in Conducting Cross-Sectional Research.
Despite its convenience, cross-sectional research does not provide evidence about development at the level at which it actually occurs: the individual. For example, in the cross-sectional study of sibling relationships just discussed, comparisons are limited to age-group averages. We cannot tell if important individual differences exist. Indeed, longitudinal findings reveal that adolescents vary considerably in the changing quality of their sibling relationships. Although many become more distant, others become more supportive and intimate, still others more rivalrous and antagonistic (Kim et al., 2006; McHale, Updegraff, & Whiteman, 2012).

Cross-sectional studies—especially those that cover a wide age span—have another problem. Like longitudinal research, they can be threatened by cohort effects. For example, comparisons of 25-year-old cohorts, 50-year-old cohorts, and 75-year-old cohorts—groups born, reared, and educated in different years—may not really represent age-related changes (MacDonald & Stawski, 2016). Instead, they may reflect unique experiences associated with the historical period in which the age groups were growing up.

Improving Developmental Designs.
Researchers have devised ways of building on the strengths and minimizing the weaknesses of longitudinal and cross-sectional approaches. Several modified developmental designs have resulted.

Sequential Designs. To overcome some of the limitations of traditional developmental designs, investigators sometimes use **sequential designs,** in which they conduct several similar cross-sectional or longitudinal studies (called *sequences*). The sequences might study participants over the same ages but in different years, or they might study participants over different ages but during the same years. Figure 1.7 illustrates the first of these options. As it also reveals, some sequential designs combine longitudinal and cross-sectional strategies, an approach that has two advantages:

- We can find out whether cohort effects are operating by comparing participants of the same age who were born in different years. In Figure 1.7, for example, we can compare the three longitudinal samples at ages 20, 30, and 40. If they do not differ, we can rule out cohort effects.
- We can make longitudinal and cross-sectional comparisons. If outcomes are similar in both, we can be especially confident about our findings.

In a study that used the design in Figure 1.7, researchers wanted to find out whether adult personality development progresses as Erikson's psychosocial theory predicts (Whitbourne et al., 1992). Questionnaires measuring Erikson's stages were given to three cohorts of 20-year-olds, each born a decade apart. The cohorts were reassessed at 10-year intervals. Consistent with Erikson's theory, longitudinal and cross-sectional gains in identity and intimacy occurred between ages 20 and 30 for all three cohorts, and sense of identity and intimacy in early adulthood predicted psychological well-being at midlife. But a powerful cohort effect emerged for consolidation of a sense of industry: At age 20, Cohort 1 scored substantially below Cohorts 2 and 3. Look at Figure 1.7 again and notice that members of Cohort 1 reached age 20 in the mid-1960s. As college students, they were part of an era of political protest that reflected disenchantment with the work ethic. Once out of college, they caught up with the other cohorts in industry, perhaps as a result of experiencing the pressures of the work world. Followed up in 2001 at age 54, Cohort 1 showed a decline in focus on identity issues and a gain in ego integrity (Sneed, Whitbourne, & Culang, 2006; Sneed et al., 2012). These trends are expected to continue through late adulthood.

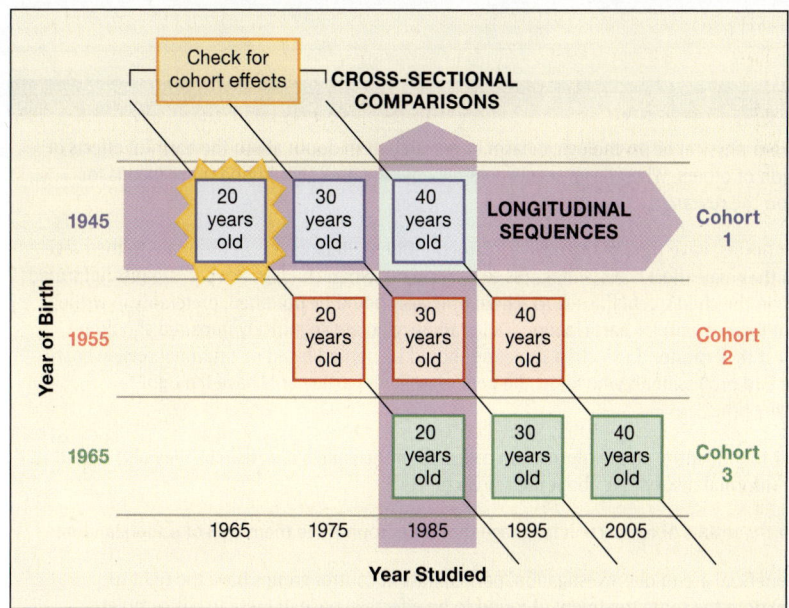

FIGURE 1.7 Example of a sequential design. Three cohorts, born in 1945 (blue), 1955 (pink), and 1965 (green), are followed longitudinally from 20 to 40 years of age. The design permits the researcher to check for cohort effects by comparing people of the same age who were born in different years. In a study that used this design, the 20-year-olds in Cohort 1 differed substantially from the 20-year-olds in Cohorts 2 and 3, indicating powerful history-graded influences. This design also permits longitudinal and cross-sectional comparisons. Similar findings lend additional confidence in the results.

By uncovering cohort effects, sequential designs help explain diversity in development. Yet to date only a small number of sequential studies have been conducted.

Combining Experimental and Developmental Designs. Perhaps you noticed that all the examples of longitudinal and cross-sectional research we have considered permit only correlational, not causal, inferences. Yet causal information is desirable, both for testing theories and for finding ways to enhance development. Sometimes researchers can explore the causal link between experiences and development by experimentally manipulating the experiences. If, as a result, development improves, then we have strong evidence for a causal association. Today, research that combines an experimental strategy with either a longitudinal or a cross-sectional approach is becoming increasingly common.

Ask yourself

CONNECT Review the study of the Family Check-Up, described on page 34. Explain how it combines an experimental with a developmental design. What are the independent and dependent variables? Is its developmental design longitudinal or cross-sectional?

APPLY A researcher compares older adults with chronic heart disease to those with no major health problems and finds that the first group scores lower on mental tests. Can the researcher conclude that heart disease causes a decline in intellectual functioning in late adulthood? Explain.

REFLECT Suppose a researcher asks you to enroll your baby in a 10-year longitudinal study. What factors would lead you to agree and to stay involved? Do your answers shed light on why longitudinal studies often have biased samples?

Ethics in Lifespan Research

1.11 What special ethical concerns arise in research on human development?

Research into human behavior creates ethical issues because, unfortunately, the quest for scientific knowledge can sometimes exploit people. For this reason, special guidelines for research have been developed by the federal government, by funding agencies, and by research-oriented associations, such as the American Psychological Association (2010) and the Society for Research in Child Development (2007). Table 1.7 on page 38 presents a summary of basic research rights drawn from these guidelines. After examining them, read about the following research situations, each of which poses a serious ethical dilemma. What precautions do you think should be taken in each instance?

- In a study of moral development, an investigator wants to assess children's ability to resist temptation by videotaping their behavior without their knowledge. She promises 7-year-olds a prize for solving difficult puzzles but tells them not to look at a classmate's correct solutions, which are deliberately placed at the back of the room. Informing children ahead of time that cheating is being studied or that their behavior is being monitored will destroy the purpose of the study.

- A researcher wants to study the impact of mild daily exercise on the physical and mental health of patients in nursing homes. He consults each resident's doctor to make sure that the exercise routine will not be harmful. But when he seeks the residents' consent, he finds that many do not comprehend the purpose of the research. And some appear to agree simply to relieve feelings of isolation and loneliness.

TABLE 1.7
Rights of Research Participants

RESEARCH RIGHT	DESCRIPTION
Protection from harm	Participants have the right to be protected from physical or psychological harm in research. If in doubt about the harmful effects of research, investigators should seek the opinion of others. When harm seems possible, investigators should find other means for obtaining the desired information or abandon the research.
Informed consent	All participants, including children and older adults, have the right to have explained to them, in language appropriate to their level of understanding, all aspects of the research that may affect their willingness to participate. When children are participants, informed consent of parents as well as others who act on the child's behalf (such as school officials) should be obtained, preferably in writing, along with the child's written or verbal assent (agreement) for participation. Older adults who are cognitively impaired should be asked to appoint a surrogate decision maker. If they cannot do so, then someone should be named by an institutional review board (IRB) after careful consultation with relatives and professionals who know the person well. All participants have the right to discontinue participation in the research at any time.
Privacy	Participants have the right to concealment of their identity on all information collected in the course of research. They also have this right with respect to written reports and any informal discussions about the research.
Knowledge of results	Participants have the right to be informed of the results of research in language that is appropriate to their level of understanding.
Beneficial treatments	If experimental treatments believed to be beneficial are under investigation, participants in control groups have the right to alternative beneficial treatments (if available) or to the same treatment (if found to be effective) once the research is complete.

Sources: American Psychological Association, 2010; Society for Research in Child Development, 2007.

As these examples indicate, when children or older adults take part in research, the ethical concerns are especially complex. Immaturity makes it difficult or impossible for children to evaluate for themselves what participation in research will mean. And because mental impairment rises with very advanced age, some older adults cannot make voluntary and informed choices (Dubois et al., 2011; Society for Research in Child Development, 2007). The life circumstances of others make them unusually vulnerable to pressure for participation.

Virtually every organization that has devised ethical principles for research has concluded that conflicts arising in research situations do not have simple right-or-wrong answers. The ultimate responsibility for the ethical integrity of research lies with the investigator. But researchers are advised—and often required—to seek advice from others. Committees for this purpose exist in colleges, universities, and other institutions. These *institutional review boards (IRBs)* follow federal guidelines for the protection of human subjects, which balance the costs of the research to participants in terms of inconvenience and possible psychological or physical harm against the study's value for advancing knowledge and improving conditions of life. If any risks to the safety and welfare of participants outweigh the worth of the research, then preference is always given to the participants' interests.

The ethical principle of *informed consent* requires special interpretation when participants cannot fully appreciate the research goals and activities. Parental consent is meant to protect the safety of children, whose ability to decide is not yet mature. But as soon as children are old enough to appreciate the purpose of the research, and certainly by age 7, their own informed *assent,* or agreement, should be obtained in addition to parental consent. Around this age, changes in children's thinking permit them to better understand basic scientific principles and the needs of others. Researchers should respect and enhance these new capacities by giving children a full explanation of research activities in language they can understand (Birbeck & Drummond, 2015). Extra care must be taken when telling children that the information they provide will be kept confidential and that they can end their participation at any time. Even adolescents may not understand, and sometimes do not believe, these promises (Bruzzese & Fisher, 2003). In certain ethnic minority communities, where deference to authority and meeting the needs of a guest (the researcher) are highly valued, children and parents may be particularly likely to consent or assent when they would rather not do so (Fisher et al., 2002).

Most older adults require no more than the usual informed-consent procedures. Yet many investigators set upper age limits in studies relevant to late adulthood, thereby excluding the oldest adults (Bayer & Tadd, 2000). Older adults should not be stereotyped as incompetent to decide about their own participation or to engage in research activities. Nevertheless, extra measures must be taken to protect those who are cognitively impaired or who reside in settings for the chronically ill. Yet participation should not be automatically withheld because it can result in personal as well as scientific benefits. In these instances, potential participants should be asked to appoint a surrogate decision maker. If they cannot do so, then someone should be named by an IRB, after careful consultation with relatives and professionals who know the person well. As an added precaution, if the older adult is incapable of consenting and the risks of the research are more than minimal, the study should not be done unless it is likely to benefit the participant directly (Dubois et al., 2011).

Older adults should not be arbitrarily excluded from research. Most require only typical informed-consent procedures, and their participation brings both personal and scientific benefits. But for some, including those who reside in settings for the chronically ill, informed consent may necessitate the assistance of a surrogate decision maker.

procedures are used with adults, *debriefing,* in which the investigator provides a full account and justification of the activities, occurs after the research session is over. But young children often lack the cognitive skills to understand the reasons for deceptive procedures and, despite explanations, even older children may leave the research situation questioning the honesty of adults. Ethical standards permit deception if investigators satisfy IRBs that such practices are necessary. Nevertheless, because deception may have serious emotional consequences for some youngsters, many experts in research ethics believe that investigators should use it with children only if the risk of harm is minimal.

Finally, all ethical guidelines advise that special precautions be taken in the use of deception and concealment, as occurs when researchers observe people from behind one-way mirrors, give them false feedback about their performance, or do not tell them the truth about the real purpose of the research. When these

Ask yourself

CONNECT Review the field experiment on the impact of the Family Check-Up on page 34. Why is it ethically important for the researchers to offer the intervention to the no-intervention control group after completion of the study? (*Hint:* Refer to Table 1.7 on page 38.)

APPLY As a researcher gathers observations of the activities of several older adults with cognitive impairments in a nursing home, one resident says, "Stop watching me!" How should the researcher respond, and why?

REFLECT What ethical safeguards do you consider vital in conducting research that requires deception of children?

Summary / chapter 1

A Scientific, Applied, and Interdisciplinary Field (p. 5)

1.1 What is developmental science, and what factors stimulated expansion of the field?

- **Developmental science** is an interdisciplinary field devoted to understanding human constancy and change throughout the lifespan. Research on human development has been stimulated by both scientific curiosity and social pressures to improve people's lives.

Basic Issues (p. 5)

1.2 Identify three basic issues on which theories of human development take a stand.

- Each **theory** of human development takes a stand on three fundamental issues: (1) Is development a **continuous** process or a series of **discontinuous stages?** (2) Does one general course of development characterize all individuals, or do many possible courses exist, depending on the **contexts** in which they live? (3) Are genetic or environmental factors more important in influencing development (the **nature–nurture controversy**), and are individual differences stable or characterized by substantial **plasticity?**

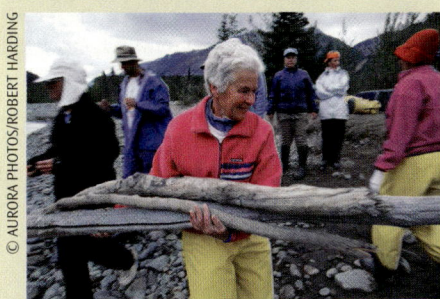

The Lifespan Perspective: A Balanced Point of View (p. 7)

1.3 Describe the lifespan perspective on development.

- The **lifespan perspective** envisions human change from a developmental systems perspective. It assumes that development is lifelong, multidimensional (affected by biological, psychological, and social forces), multidirectional (a joint expression of growth and decline), and plastic (open to change through new experiences).

- According to the lifespan perspective, the life course is influenced by multiple, interacting forces: (1) **age-graded influences,** which are predictable in timing and duration; (2) **history-graded influences,** unique to a particular historical era; and (3) **nonnormative influences,** unique to one or a few individuals.

Scientific Beginnings (p. 12)

1.4 Describe major early influences on the scientific study of development.

- Darwin's theory of evolution influenced important developmental theories and inspired scientific child study. In the early twentieth century, Hall and Gesell introduced the **normative approach,** which measured behaviors of large groups to yield descriptive facts about development.

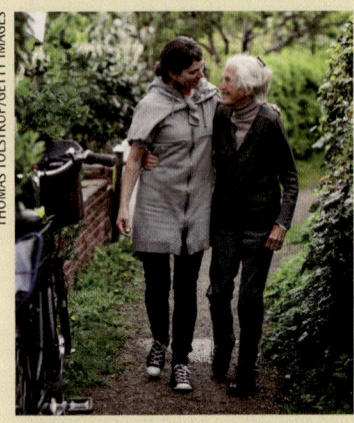

- Binet and Simon constructed the first successful intelligence test, which sparked interest in individual differences in development and led to a heated controversy over nature versus nurture.

Mid-Twentieth-Century Theories (p. 14)

1.5 What theories influenced human development research in the mid-twentieth century?

- In the 1930s and 1940s, psychiatrists and social workers turned to the **psychoanalytic perspective** for help in treating people's emotional problems. In Freud's **psychosexual theory,** the individual moves through five stages, during which three portions of the personality—id, ego, and superego—become integrated. Erikson's **psychosocial theory** expands Freud's theory, emphasizing the development of culturally relevant attitudes and skills and the lifespan nature of development.
- As the psychoanalytic perspective gained in prominence, **behaviorism** and **social learning theory** emerged, emphasizing the study of directly observable events—stimuli and responses—and the principles of conditioning and modeling. These approaches gave rise to **applied behavior analysis,** in which procedures of conditioning and modeling are used to eliminate undesirable behaviors and increase desirable responses.

- Piaget's **cognitive-developmental theory** emphasizes that children actively construct knowledge as they move through four stages, beginning with the baby's sensorimotor action patterns and ending with the abstract, systematic reasoning system of the adolescent and adult. Piaget's work has stimulated a wealth of research on children's thinking and encouraged educational programs emphasizing children's discovery learning.

Recent Theoretical Perspectives (p. 19)

1.6 Describe recent theoretical perspectives on human development.

- **Information processing** views the mind as a complex symbol-manipulating system, much like a computer. Because this approach provides precise accounts of how children and adults tackle cognitive tasks, its findings have important implications for education.
- Researchers in **developmental cognitive neuroscience** study the relationship between changes in the brain and the development of cognitive processing and behavior patterns. More recently, investigators in **developmental social neuroscience** are examining relationships between changes in the brain and emotional and social development. Findings on experiences that affect brain development at various ages are contributing to interventions for enhancing cognitive and social functioning.

- Three contemporary perspectives emphasize *contexts* for development. The first, **ethology** stresses the adaptive value of behavior and inspired the **sensitive period** concept. In **evolutionary developmental psychology,** which extends this emphasis, researchers seek to understand the adaptiveness of specieswide competencies as they change with age.

- The second perspective, Vygotsky's **sociocultural theory,** which focuses on how culture is transmitted from one generation to the next through social interaction, views cognitive development as a socially mediated process. Through cooperative dialogues with more expert members of society, children come to use language to guide their own thought and actions and acquire culturally relevant knowledge and skills.

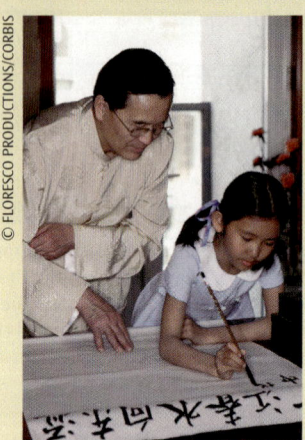

- The third perspective, **ecological systems theory,** views the individual as developing within a complex system of relationships affected by multiple, nested layers of the surrounding environment—**microsystem, mesosystem, exosystem,** and **macrosystem.** The **chronosystem** represents the dynamic, ever-changing nature of individuals and their experiences.

Comparing and Evaluating Theories (p. 26)

1.7 Identify the stand taken by each major theory on the three basic issues of human development.

- Theories vary in their focus on different domains of development, in their view of how development occurs, and in their strengths and weaknesses. (For a full summary, see Table 1.4 on page 27.)

Studying Development (p. 26)

1.8 Describe methods commonly used in research on human development.

- **Naturalistic observations,** gathered in everyday environments, permit researchers to see directly the everyday behaviors they hope to explain. **Structured observations,** which take place in laboratories, give every participant an equal opportunity to display the behaviors of interest.

CHAPTER 1 History, Theory, and Research Strategies

- Self-report methods can be flexible and open-ended like the **clinical interview,** which permits participants to express their thoughts in ways similar to their thinking in everyday life. **Structured interviews**—including tests and questionnaires—are more efficient, permitting researchers to specify activities and behaviors that participants might not think of in an open-ended interview. Investigators use the **clinical, or case study, method** to obtain an in-depth understanding of a single individual.

- Researchers have adapted observational and self-report methods to permit direct comparisons of cultures. To uncover the cultural meanings of behavior, they rely on **ethnography,** engaging in participant observation.

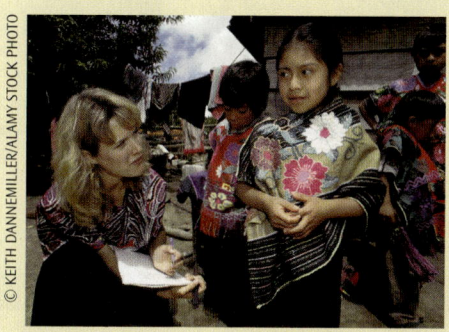

1.9 *Distinguish between correlational and experimental research designs, noting the strengths and limitations of each.*

- The **correlational design** examines relationships between variables without altering participants' experiences. The **correlation coefficient** is often used to measure the association between variables. Correlational studies do not permit inferences about cause and effect, but they can help identify relationships that are worth exploring with a more powerful experimental strategy.

- An **experimental design** permits inferences about cause and effect. Researchers manipulate an **independent variable** by exposing participants to two or more treatment conditions. Then they determine what effect this variable has on a **dependent variable. Random assignment** to treatment conditions reduces the chances that participants' characteristics will affect the accuracy of experimental findings.

- Field and natural, or quasi-, experiments compare treatments in natural environments. However, these approaches are less rigorous than laboratory experiments.

1.10 *Describe designs for studying development, noting the strengths and limitations of each.*

- In the **longitudinal design,** participants are studied repeatedly over time, revealing common patterns as well as individual differences in development and relationships between early and later events and behaviors. Longitudinal research poses several problems, including biased sampling, practice effects, and **cohort effects**—difficulty generalizing results from one cohort to people developing at other historical times.

- The **cross-sectional design,** in which groups of people differing in age are studied at the same point in time, offers a more efficient way to study development, but it is limited to comparisons of age-group averages and can be vulnerable to cohort effects.

- **Sequential designs** compare participants of the same age born in different years to determine whether cohort effects are operating. When sequential designs combine longitudinal and cross-sectional strategies, researchers can see if outcomes are similar, for added confidence in their findings.

- Combining experimental and developmental designs permits researchers to examine causal influences on development.

Ethics in Lifespan Research (p. 37)

1.11 *What special ethical concerns arise in research on human development?*

- Because the quest for scientific knowledge has the potential to exploit people, the ethical principle of informed consent requires special safeguards for children and for older adults who are cognitively impaired or who live in settings for the chronically ill.

- The use of deception in research with children is especially risky because it may undermine their basic faith in the honesty of adults.

Important Terms and Concepts

age-graded influences (p. 9)
applied behavior analysis (p. 17)
behaviorism (p. 16)
chronosystem (p. 26)
clinical interview (p. 29)
clinical, or case study, method (p. 30)
cognitive-developmental theory (p. 17)
cohort effects (p. 35)
contexts (p. 6)
continuous development (p. 6)
correlational design (p. 31)
correlation coefficient (p. 33)
cross-sectional design (p. 36)
dependent variable (p. 33)
developmental cognitive neuroscience (p. 20)
developmental science (p. 5)
developmental social neuroscience (p. 20)

discontinuous development (p. 6)
ecological systems theory (p. 23)
ethnography (p. 30)
ethology (p. 21)
evolutionary developmental psychology (p. 22)
exosystem (p. 24)
experimental design (p. 33)
history-graded influences (p. 9)
independent variable (p. 33)
information processing (p. 19)
lifespan perspective (p. 7)
longitudinal design (p. 35)
macrosystem (p. 24)
mesosystem (p. 24)
microsystem (p. 23)
naturalistic observation (p. 28)
nature–nurture controversy (p. 7)

nonnormative influences (p. 10)
normative approach (p. 14)
plasticity (p. 7)
psychoanalytic perspective (p. 14)
psychosexual theory (p. 14)
psychosocial theory (p. 15)
random assignment (p. 33)
resilience (p. 10)
sensitive period (p. 21)
sequential designs (p. 36)
social learning theory (p. 17)
sociocultural theory (p. 22)
stage (p. 6)
structured interview (p. 30)
structured observation (p. 28)
theory (p. 5)

chapter 2

Genetic and Environmental Foundations

Heredity and environment combine in intricate ways, making members of this multigenerational extended family both alike and different in physical characteristics and behavior.

What's ahead in chapter 2

Genetic Foundations
The Genetic Code • The Sex Cells • Boy or Girl? • Multiple Offspring • Patterns of Gene–Gene Interactions • Chromosomal Abnormalities

Reproductive Choices
Genetic Counseling • Prenatal Diagnosis and Fetal Medicine • Adoption

■ **SOCIAL ISSUES: HEALTH** The Pros and Cons of Reproductive Technologies

Environmental Contexts for Development
The Family • Socioeconomic Status and Family Functioning • Poverty • Affluence • Beyond the Family: Neighborhoods and Schools • The Cultural Context

■ **CULTURAL INFLUENCES** The African-American Extended Family

Understanding the Relationship Between Heredity and Environment
The Question, "How Much?" • The Question, "How?"

■ **BIOLOGY AND ENVIRONMENT** The Tutsi Genocide and Epigenetic Transmission of Maternal Stress to Children

"It's a girl!" announces the doctor, holding up the squalling newborn baby as her parents gaze with amazement at their miraculous creation.

"A girl! We've named her Sarah!" exclaims the proud father to eager relatives waiting for news of their new family member.

As we join these parents in thinking about how this wondrous being came into existence and imagining her future, we are struck by many questions. How could this baby, equipped with everything necessary for life outside the womb, have developed from the union of two tiny cells? What ensures that Sarah will, in due time, roll over, reach for objects, walk, talk, make friends, learn, imagine, and create—just like other typical children born before her? Why is she a girl and not a boy, dark-haired rather than blond, calm and cuddly instead of wiry and energetic? What difference will it make that Sarah is given a name and place in one family, community, nation, and culture rather than another?

To answer these questions, this chapter takes a close look at the foundations of development: heredity and environment. Because nature has prepared us for survival, all humans have features in common. Yet each of us is also unique. Take a moment to think about several of your friends, and jot down the most obvious physical and behavioral similarities between them and their parents. Did you find that one person shows combined features of both parents, another resembles just one parent, whereas a third is not like either parent? These directly observable characteristics are called **phenotypes.** They depend in part on the individual's **genotype**—the complex blend of genetic information that determines our species and influences all our unique characteristics. Yet phenotypes are also affected by each person's lifelong history of experiences.

We begin our discussion with a review of basic genetic principles that help explain similarities and differences among us in appearance and behavior. Then we turn to aspects of the environment that play powerful roles throughout the lifespan. As our discussion proceeds, some findings may surprise you. For example, many people believe that when children inherit unfavorable characteristics, little can be done to help them. Others are convinced that the damage done to a child by a harmful environment can easily be corrected. As we will see, neither of these assumptions is true. Rather, heredity and environment continuously collaborate, each modifying the power of the other to influence the course of development. In the final section of this chapter, we consider how nature and nurture work together. ●

Genetic Foundations

2.1 What are genes, and how are they transmitted from one generation to the next?

2.2 Describe various patterns of gene–gene interaction.

2.3 Describe major chromosomal abnormalities, and explain how they occur.

Within each of the trillions of cells in the human body (except red blood cells) is a control center, or *nucleus*, that contains rod-like structures called **chromosomes**, which store and transmit genetic information. Human chromosomes come in 23 matching pairs; an exception is the XY pair in males, which we will discuss shortly. Each member of a pair corresponds to the other in size, shape, and genetic functions. One chromosome is inherited from the mother and one from the father (see Figure 2.1).

The Genetic Code

Chromosomes are made up of a chemical substance called **deoxyribonucleic acid,** or **DNA.** As Figure 2.2 shows, DNA is a long, double-stranded molecule that looks like a twisted ladder. Each rung of the ladder consists of a specific pair of chemical substances called *bases,* joined together between the two sides. It is this sequence of base pairs that provides genetic instructions. A **gene** is a segment of DNA along the length of the chromosome. Genes can be of different lengths—perhaps 100 to several thousand ladder rungs long. An estimated 21,000 **protein-coding genes,** which directly affect our body's characteristics, lie along the human chromosomes. They send instructions for making a rich assortment of proteins to the *cytoplasm,* the area surrounding the cell nucleus. Proteins, which trigger chemical reactions throughout the body, are the biological foundation on which our characteristics are built. An additional 18,000 **regulator genes** modify the instructions given by protein-coding genes, greatly complicating their genetic impact (Pennisi, 2012).

We share some of our genetic makeup with even the simplest organisms, such as bacteria and molds, and most of it with other mammals, especially primates. About 95 percent of chimpanzee and human DNA is identical. And the genetic variation from one human to the next is even less: Individuals around the world are about 99.6 percent genetically identical (Tishkoff & Kidd, 2004). But these straightforward comparisons are misleading. Many human DNA segments that appear like those of chimpanzees have undergone duplications and rearrangements with other segments. So in actuality, the species-specific genetic material responsible for the attributes that make us human, from our upright gait to our extraordinary language and cognitive capacities, is extensive (Preuss, 2012). Furthermore, it takes a change in only a single DNA base pair to influence human traits. And such tiny changes generally combine in unique ways across multiple genes, thereby amplifying variability within the human species.

How do humans, with far fewer genes than scientists once thought (only twice as many as the worm or fly), manage to develop into such complex beings? The answer lies in the proteins our genes make, which break up and reassemble in staggering variety—about 10 to 20 million altogether. Simpler species have far fewer proteins. Furthermore, the communication system between the cell nucleus and cytoplasm, which fine-tunes gene activity, is more intricate in humans than in simpler organisms. Finally, within the cell, a wide range of environmental factors modify gene expression. Recent evidence reveals that many such effects are unique to humans and influence brain development (Hernando-Herraez et al., 2013). So even at this microscopic level, biological events of profound developmental significance are the result of *both* genetic and nongenetic forces.

The Sex Cells

New individuals are created when two special cells called **gametes,** or sex cells—the sperm and ovum—combine. A gamete contains

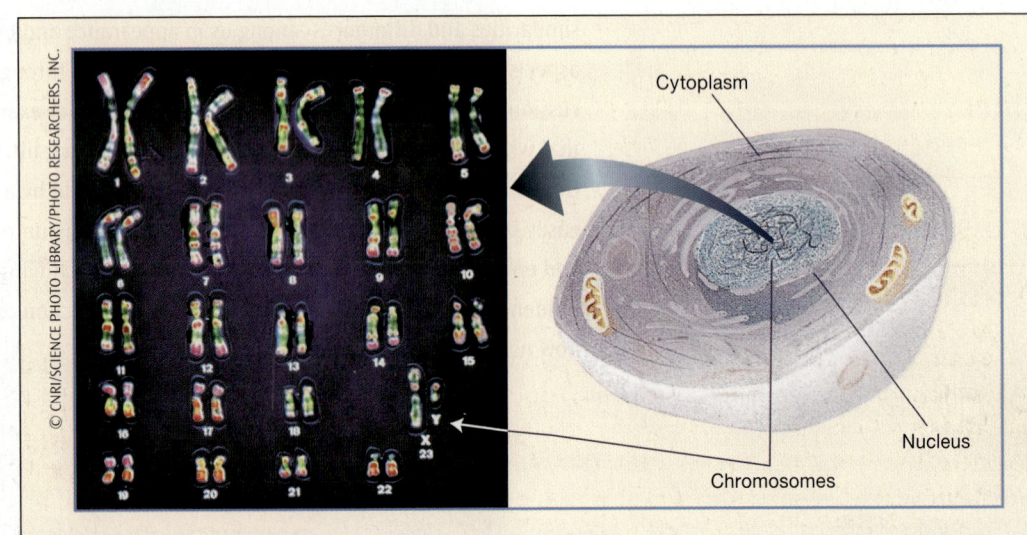

FIGURE 2.1 A karyotype, or photograph, of human chromosomes. The 46 chromosomes shown on the left were isolated from a human cell, stained, greatly magnified, and arranged in pairs according to decreasing size of the upper "arm" of each chromosome. The twenty-third pair, XY, reveals that the cell donor is a male. In a female, this pair would be XX.

CHAPTER 2 Genetic and Environmental Foundations

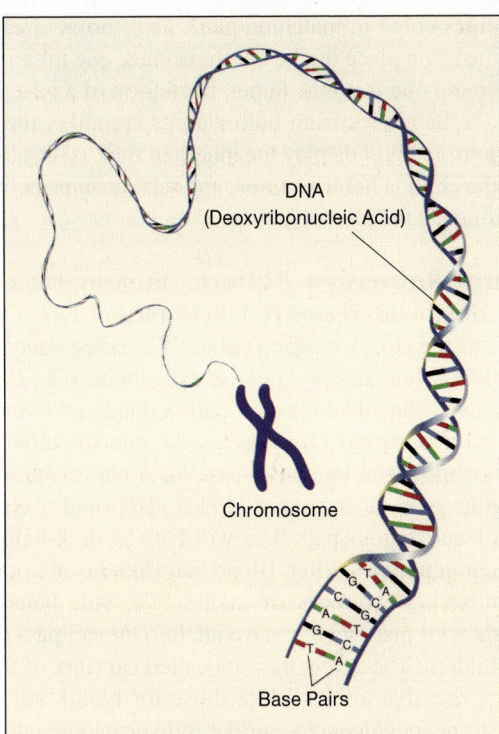

FIGURE 2.2 DNA's ladderlike structure. A gene is a segment of DNA along the length of the chromosome, varying from perhaps 100 to several thousand ladder rungs long. The pairings of bases across the rungs of the ladder are very specific: Adenine (A) always appears with thymine (T), and cytosine (C) always appears with guanine (G).

only 23 chromosomes, half as many as a regular body cell. Gametes are formed through a cell division process called **meiosis,** which halves the number of chromosomes normally present in body cells. When sperm and ovum unite at conception, the resulting cell, called a **zygote,** will again have 46 chromosomes.

In meiosis, the chromosomes pair up and exchange segments, so that genes from one are replaced by genes from another. Then chance determines which member of each pair will gather with others and end up in the same gamete. These events make the likelihood extremely low—about 1 in 700 trillion—that nontwin siblings will be genetically identical (Gould & Keeton, 1996). The genetic variability produced by meiosis is adaptive: It increases the chances that at least some members of a species will cope with ever-changing environments and will survive.

In the male, four sperm are produced when meiosis is complete. Also, the cells from which sperm arise are produced continuously throughout life. For this reason, a healthy man can father a child at any age after sexual maturity. In the female, meiosis results in just one ovum. In addition, the female is born with a bank of ova already present in her ovaries, though recent findings suggest that new ova may arise from ovarian stem cells later on (Virant-Klun, 2015). Still, there are plenty of female sex cells. About 1 to 2 million are present at birth, 40,000 remain at adolescence, and approximately 350 to 450 will mature during a woman's childbearing years (Moore, Persaud, & Torchia, 2016b).

Boy or Girl?

Return to Figure 2.1 and note that 22 of the 23 pairs of chromosomes are matching pairs, called **autosomes** (meaning *not* sex chromosomes). The twenty-third pair consists of **sex chromosomes.** In females, this pair is called XX; in males, it is called XY. The X is a relatively long chromosome, whereas the Y is short and carries little genetic material. When gametes form in males, the X and Y chromosomes separate into different sperm cells. The gametes that form in females all carry an X chromosome. Therefore, the sex of the new organism is determined by whether an X-bearing or a Y-bearing sperm fertilizes the ovum.

Multiple Offspring

Ruth and Peter, a couple I know well, tried for several years to have a child, without success. When Ruth reached age 33, her doctor prescribed a fertility drug, and twins—Jeannie and Jason—were born. Jeannie and Jason are **fraternal,** or **dizygotic, twins,** the most common type of multiple offspring, resulting from the release and fertilization of two ova. Genetically, they are no more alike than ordinary siblings. Table 2.1 summarizes genetic and environmental factors that increase the chances of giving birth to fraternal twins. Older maternal age, fertility drugs, and in vitro fertilization are major causes of the dramatic rise in fraternal twinning and other multiple births in industrialized nations over the past several decades. Currently, fraternal twins account for 1 in about every 33 births in the United States (Martin et al., 2015).

TABLE 2.1
Maternal Factors Linked to Fraternal Twinning

FACTOR	DESCRIPTION
Ethnicity	Occurs in 6 to 9 per 1,000 births among Asians and Hispanics, 9 to 12 per 1,000 births among white Europeans, and 11 to 18 or more per 1,000 births among black Africans[a]
Family history of twinning	Occurs more often among women whose mothers and sisters gave birth to fraternal twins, suggesting a hereditary influence through the female line
Age	Rises with maternal age, peaking between 35 and 39 years, and then rapidly falls
Nutrition	Occurs less often among women with poor diets; occurs more often among women who are tall and overweight or of normal weight as opposed to slight body build
Number of births	Is more likely with each additional birth
Fertility drugs and in vitro fertilization	Is more likely with fertility hormones and in vitro fertilization (see page 52), which also increase the chances of bearing higher-order multiples

[a]Worldwide rates, not including multiple births resulting from use of fertility drugs.
Sources: Kulkarni et al., 2013; Lashley, 2007; Smits & Monden, 2011.

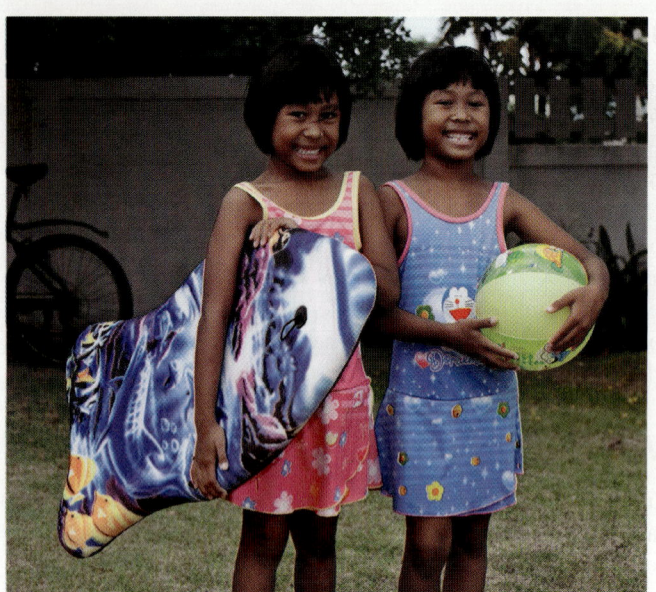

These identical, or monozygotic, twins were created when a duplicating zygote separated into two clusters of cells, which developed into two individuals with the same genetic makeup.

Twins can be created in another way. Sometimes a zygote that has started to duplicate separates into two clusters of cells that develop into two individuals. These are called **identical,** or **monozygotic, twins** because they have the same genetic makeup. The frequency of identical twins is the same around the world—about 1 in every 350 to 400 births (Kulkarni et al., 2013). Animal research has uncovered a variety of environmental influences that prompt this type of twinning, including temperature changes, variation in oxygen levels, and late fertilization of the ovum (Lashley, 2007). In a minority of cases, identical twinning runs in families, but this occurs so rarely that it is likely due to chance rather than heredity.

During their early years, children of single births often are healthier and develop more rapidly than twins. Jeannie and Jason, like most twins, were born early—three weeks before Ruth's due date. And, like other premature infants—as you will see in Chapter 3—they required special care after birth. When the twins came home from the hospital, Ruth and Peter had to divide time between them. Perhaps because neither baby received as much attention as the average single infant, Jeannie and Jason walked and talked several months later than most other children their age, though most twins catch up in development by middle childhood (Lytton & Gallagher, 2002; Nan et al., 2013). Parental energies are further strained after the birth of triplets, whose early development is slower than that of twins (Feldman, Eidelman, & Rotenberg, 2004).

Patterns of Gene–Gene Interactions

Jeannie has her parents' dark, straight hair; Jason is curly-haired and blond. The way genes from each parent interact helps explain these outcomes. Recall that except for the XY pair in males, all chromosomes come in matching pairs. Two forms of each gene occur at the same place on the chromosomes, one inherited from the mother and one from the father. Each form of a gene is called an **allele.** If the alleles from both parents are alike, the child is **homozygous** and will display the inherited trait. If the alleles differ, then the child is **heterozygous,** and relationships between the alleles influence the phenotype.

Dominant–Recessive Pattern. In many heterozygous pairings, **dominant–recessive inheritance** occurs: Only one allele affects the child's characteristics. It is called *dominant;* the second allele, which has no effect, is called *recessive*. Hair color is an example. The allele for dark hair is dominant (we can represent it with a capital *D*), whereas the one for blond hair is recessive (symbolized by a lowercase *b*). A child who inherits a homozygous pair of dominant alleles *(DD)* and a child who inherits a heterozygous pair *(Db)* will both be dark-haired, even though their genotypes differ. Blond hair (like Jason's) can result only from having two recessive alleles *(bb)*. Still, heterozygous individuals with just one recessive allele *(Db)* can pass that trait to their children. Therefore, they are called **carriers** of the trait.

Most recessive alleles—like those for blond hair, pattern baldness, or nearsightedness—are of little developmental importance. But as Table 2.2 illustrates, some cause serious disabilities and diseases. One well-known recessive disorder is *phenylketonuria,* or *PKU*, which affects the way the body breaks down proteins contained in many foods. Infants born with two recessive alleles lack an enzyme that converts one of the basic amino acids that make up proteins (phenylalanine) into a byproduct essential for body functioning (tyrosine). Without this enzyme, phenylalanine quickly builds to toxic levels that damage the central nervous system. By 1 year, infants with PKU suffer from permanent intellectual disability.

Despite its potentially damaging effects, PKU illustrates that inheriting unfavorable genes does not always lead to an untreatable condition. All U.S. states require that each newborn be given a blood test for PKU. If the disease is found, doctors place the baby on a diet low in phenylalanine. Children who receive this treatment nevertheless show mild deficits in certain cognitive skills, such as memory, planning, decision making, and problem solving, because even small amounts of phenylalanine interfere with brain functioning (DeRoche & Welsh, 2008; Fonnesbeck et al., 2013). But as long as dietary treatment begins early and continues, children with PKU usually attain an average level of intelligence and have a normal lifespan.

In dominant–recessive inheritance, if we know the genetic makeup of the parents, we can predict the percentage of children in a family who are likely to display or carry a trait. Figure 2.3 on page 48 illustrates this for PKU. For a child to inherit the condition, each parent must have a recessive allele. But because of the action of regulator genes, children vary in the degree to which phenylalanine accumulates in their tissues and in the extent to which they respond to treatment.

Only rarely are serious diseases due to dominant alleles. Think about why this is so. Children who inherit the dominant

TABLE 2.2
Examples of Dominant and Recessive Diseases

DISEASE	DESCRIPTION	MODE OF INHERITANCE	INCIDENCE	TREATMENT
AUTOSOMAL DISEASES				
Cooley's anemia	Pale appearance, retarded physical growth, and lethargic behavior begin in infancy.	Recessive	1 in 500 births to parents of Mediterranean descent	Frequent blood transfusion; death from complications usually occurs by adolescence.
Cystic fibrosis	Lungs, liver, and pancreas secrete large amounts of thick mucus, leading to breathing and digestive difficulties.	Recessive	1 in 2,000 to 2,500 European-American births; 1 in 16,000 births to North Americans of African descent	Bronchial drainage, prompt treatment of respiratory infection, dietary management. Advances in medical care allow survival with good life quality into adulthood.
Phenylketonuria (PKU)	Inability to metabolize the amino acid phenylalanine, contained in many proteins, causes severe central nervous system damage in the first year of life.	Recessive	1 in 10,000 to 20,000 births to North Americans	Placing the child on a special diet results in average intelligence and normal lifespan. Subtle deficits in memory, planning, decision making, and problem solving are often present.
Sickle cell anemia	Abnormal sickling of red blood cells causes oxygen deprivation, pain, swelling, and tissue damage. Anemia and susceptibility to infections, especially pneumonia, occur.	Recessive	1 in 500 births to North Americans of African descent	Blood transfusions, painkillers, prompt treatment of infection. No known cure; 50 percent die by age 55.
Tay-Sachs disease	Central nervous system degeneration, with onset at about 6 months, leads to poor muscle tone, blindness, deafness, and convulsions.	Recessive	1 in 3,600 births to Jews of European descent and to French Canadians	None. Death occurs by 3 to 4 years of age.
Huntington's disease	Central nervous system degeneration leads to muscular coordination difficulties, mental deterioration, and personality changes. Symptoms usually do not appear until age 35 or later.	Dominant	1 in 18,000 to 25,000 births to North Americans	None. Death occurs 10 to 20 years after symptom onset.
Marfan syndrome	Tall, slender build; thin, elongated arms and legs; and heart defects and eye abnormalities, especially of the lens. Excessive lengthening of the body results in a variety of skeletal defects.	Dominant	1 in 5,000 to 10,000 births	Correction of heart and eye defects is sometimes possible. Death from heart failure in young adulthood is common.
X-LINKED DISEASES				
Duchenne muscular dystrophy	Degenerative muscle disease. Abnormal gait, loss of ability to walk between 7 and 13 years.	Recessive	1 in 3,000 to 5,000 male births	None. Death from respiratory infection or weakening of the heart muscle usually occurs in adolescence.
Hemophilia	Blood fails to clot normally; can lead to severe internal bleeding and tissue damage.	Recessive	1 in 4,000 to 7,000 male births	Blood transfusions. Safety precautions to prevent injury.
Diabetes insipidus	Insufficient production of the hormone vasopressin results in excessive thirst and urination. Dehydration can cause central nervous system damage.	Recessive	1 in 2,500 male births	Hormone replacement.

Note: For recessive disorders listed, carrier status can be detected in prospective parents through a blood test or genetic analyses. For all disorders listed, prenatal diagnosis is available (see page 53).

Sources: Kliegman et al., 2015; Lashley, 2007; National Center for Biotechnology Information, 2015.

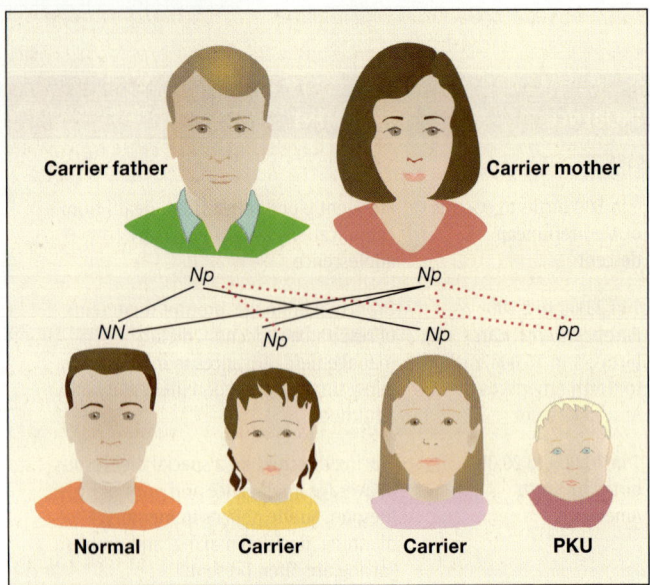

FIGURE 2.3 Dominant–recessive mode of inheritance, as illustrated by PKU. When both parents are heterozygous carriers of the recessive gene *(p)*, we can predict that 25 percent of their offspring are likely to be normal *(NN)*, 50 percent are likely to be carriers *(Np)*, and 25 percent are likely to inherit the disorder *(pp)*. Notice that the PKU-affected child, in contrast to his siblings, has light hair. The recessive gene for PKU affects more than one trait. It also leads to fair coloring.

allele always develop the disorder. They seldom live long enough to reproduce, so the harmful dominant allele is eliminated from the family's heredity in a single generation. Some dominant disorders, however, do persist. One is *Huntington's disease,* a condition in which the central nervous system degenerates. Its symptoms usually do not appear until age 35 or later, after the person has passed the dominant allele to his or her children.

Incomplete-Dominance Pattern. In some heterozygous circumstances, the dominant–recessive relationship does not hold completely. Instead, we see **incomplete dominance,** a pattern of inheritance in which both alleles are expressed in the phenotype, resulting in a combined trait, or one that is intermediate between the two.

The *sickle cell trait,* a heterozygous condition present in many black Africans, provides an example. *Sickle cell anemia* (see Table 2.2) occurs in full form when a child inherits two recessive genes. They cause the usually round red blood cells to become sickle (crescent-moon) shaped, especially under low-oxygen conditions. The sickled cells clog the blood vessels and block the flow of blood, causing intense pain, swelling, and tissue damage. Despite medical advances that today allow 85 percent of affected children to survive to adulthood, North Americans with sickle cell anemia have an average life expectancy of only 55 years (Chakravorty & Williams, 2015). Heterozygous individuals are protected from the disease under most circumstances. However, when they experience oxygen deprivation—for example, at high altitudes or after intense physical exercise—the single recessive allele asserts itself, and a temporary, mild form of the illness occurs.

The sickle cell allele is common among black Africans for a special reason. Carriers of it are more resistant to malaria than are individuals with two alleles for normal red blood cells. In Africa, where malaria is common, these carriers survived and reproduced more frequently than others, leading the gene to be maintained in the black population. But in regions of the world where the risk of malaria is low, the frequency of the gene is declining. For example, only 8 percent of African Americans are carriers, compared with 20 percent of black Africans (Centers for Disease Control and Prevention, 2015m).

X-Linked Pattern. Males and females have an equal chance of inheriting recessive disorders carried on the autosomes, such as PKU and sickle cell anemia. But when a harmful allele is carried on the X chromosome, **X-linked inheritance** applies. Males are more likely to be affected because their sex chromosomes do not match. In females, any recessive allele on one X chromosome has a good chance of being suppressed by a dominant allele on the other X. But the Y chromosome is only about one-third as long and therefore lacks many corresponding genes to override those on the X. A well-known example is *hemophilia,* a disorder in which the blood fails to clot normally. Figure 2.4 shows its greater likelihood of inheritance by male children whose mothers carry the abnormal allele.

Besides X-linked disorders, many sex differences reveal the male to be at a disadvantage. Rates of miscarriage, infant and childhood deaths, birth defects, learning disabilities, behavior disorders, and intellectual disability all are higher for boys (Boyle et al., 2011; MacDorman & Gregory, 2015). It is possible that these sex differences can be traced to the genetic code. The female, with two X chromosomes, benefits from a greater variety of genes. Nature, however, seems to have adjusted for the male's disadvantage. Worldwide, about 103 boys are born for every 100 girls, and judging from miscarriage and abortion statistics, an even greater number of males are conceived (United Nations, 2015).

In cultures with strong gender-biased attitudes that induce expectant parents to prefer a male child, the male-to-female birth sex ratio is often much larger. In China, for example, the spread of ultrasound technology (which enables prenatal sex determination) and enforcement of a one-child family policy to control population growth—both of which began in the 1980s—led to a dramatic increase in sex-selective abortion. In 2015, China announced the end of its one-child policy, substituting a two-child policy. Nevertheless, many Chinese couples continue to say they desire just one child (Basten & Jiang, 2015; Chen, Li, & Meng, 2013). Today, China's birth sex ratio is 117 boys for every 100 girls—a gender imbalance with adverse social consequences, such as rising crime rates and male competition for marriage partners.

In contrast, in many Western countries, including the United States, Canada, and European nations, the proportion of male births has declined in recent decades. Some researchers attribute this trend to a rise in stressful living conditions, which heighten spontaneous abortions, especially of male fetuses (Catalano et al., 2010). In support of this hypothesis, a California study spanning the decade of the 1990s revealed that the percentage of male fetal

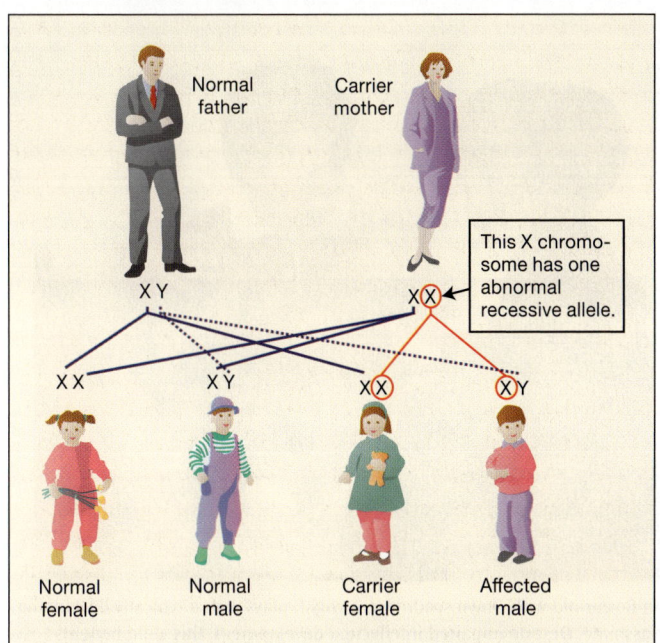

FIGURE 2.4 X-linked inheritance. In the example shown here, the allele on the father's X chromosome is normal. The mother has one normal and one abnormal recessive allele on her X chromosomes. By looking at the possible combinations of the parents' alleles, we can predict that 50 percent of these parents' male children are likely to have the disorder and 50 percent of their female children are likely to be carriers of it.

deaths increased in months in which unemployment (a major stressor) also rose above its typical level (Catalano et al., 2009).

Genomic Imprinting. More than 1,000 human characteristics follow the rules of dominant–recessive and incomplete-dominance inheritance (National Center for Biotechnology Information, 2015). For these traits, whichever parent contributes a gene to the new individual, the gene responds similarly. Geneticists, however, have identified some exceptions. In **genomic imprinting,** alleles are imprinted, or chemically marked through regulatory processes within the genome, in such a way that one pair member (either the mother's or the father's) is activated, regardless of its makeup (Hirasawa & Feil, 2010). The imprint is often temporary; it may be erased in the next generation, and it may not occur in all individuals.

The number of genes subjected to genomic imprinting is believed to be small—less than 1 percent. Nevertheless, these genes have a significant impact on brain development and physical health, as disruptions in imprinting reveal. For example, imprinting is involved in several childhood cancers and in *Prader-Willi syndrome,* a disorder with symptoms of intellectual disability and severe obesity. Imprinting also may explain why children are more likely to develop diabetes if their father, rather than their mother, suffers from it, and why people with asthma or hay fever tend to have mothers, not fathers, with the illness (Ishida & Moore, 2013).

Genomic imprinting can operate on the sex chromosomes, as *fragile X syndrome*—the most common inherited cause of intellectual disability—reveals. In this disorder, which affects about 1 in 4,000 males and 1 in 6,000 females, an abnormal repetition of a sequence of DNA bases occurs on the X chromosome, damaging a particular gene. In addition to cognitive impairments, the majority of individuals with fragile X syndrome suffer from attention deficits and high anxiety, and about 30 to 35 percent also have symptoms of autism (Wadell, Hagerman, & Hessl, 2013). The defective gene at the fragile site is expressed only when it is passed from mother to child (Hagerman et al., 2009). Because the disorder is X-linked, males are more severely affected.

Mutation. Although less than 3 percent of pregnancies result in the birth of a baby with a hereditary abnormality, these children account for about 20 percent of infant deaths and contribute substantially to lifelong impaired physical and mental functioning (Martin et al., 2015). How are harmful genes created in the first place? The answer is **mutation,** a sudden but permanent change in a segment of DNA. A mutation may affect only one or two genes, or it may involve many genes, as in the chromosomal disorders we will discuss shortly. Some mutations occur spontaneously, simply by chance. Others are caused by hazardous environmental agents.

Although nonionizing forms of radiation—electromagnetic waves and microwaves—have no demonstrated impact on DNA, ionizing (high-energy) radiation is an established cause of mutation. Women who receive repeated doses before conception are more likely to miscarry or give birth to children with hereditary defects. The incidence of genetic abnormalities, such as physical malformations and childhood cancer, is also higher in children whose fathers are exposed to radiation in their occupation. However, infrequent and mild exposure to radiation generally does not cause genetic damage (Adelstein, 2014). Rather, moderate to high doses over an extended time can impair DNA.

The examples just given illustrate *germline mutation,* which takes place in the cells that give rise to gametes. When the affected individual mates, the defective DNA is passed on to the next generation. In a second type, called *somatic mutation,* normal body cells mutate, an event that can occur at any time of life. The DNA defect appears in every cell derived from the affected body cell, eventually becoming widespread enough to cause disease (such as cancer) or disability.

It is easy to see how disorders that run in families can result from germline mutation. But somatic mutation may be involved in these disorders as well. Some people harbor a genetic susceptibility that causes certain body cells to mutate easily in the presence of triggering events (Weiss, 2005). This helps explain why some individuals develop serious illnesses (such as cancer) as a result of smoking, exposure to pollutants, or psychological stress, while others do not.

Somatic mutation shows that each of us does not have a single, permanent genotype. Rather, the genetic makeup of each cell can change over time. Somatic mutation increases with age, raising the possibility that it contributes to the age-related rise in disease and to the aging process itself (Salvioli et al., 2008).

Finally, although virtually all mutations that have been studied are harmful, some spontaneous ones (such as the sickle cell allele in malaria-ridden regions of the world) are necessary and desirable. By increasing genetic variation, they help individuals adapt to unexpected environmental challenges. Scientists, however, seldom go looking for mutations that contribute to favorable traits, such as an exceptional talent or sturdy immune system. They are far more concerned with identifying and eliminating unfavorable genes that threaten health and survival.

Polygenic Inheritance. So far, we have discussed patterns of gene–gene interaction in which people either display a particular trait or do not. These cut-and-dried individual differences are much easier to trace to their genetic origins than are characteristics that vary on a continuum among people, such as height, weight, intelligence, and personality. These traits are due to **polygenic inheritance,** in which many genes affect the characteristic in question. Polygenic inheritance is complex, and much about it is still unknown. In the final section of this chapter, we will discuss how researchers infer the influence of heredity on human attributes when they do not know the precise patterns of inheritance.

Chromosomal Abnormalities

Besides harmful recessive alleles, abnormalities of the chromosomes are a major cause of serious developmental problems. Most chromosomal defects result from mistakes during meiosis, when the ovum and sperm are formed. A chromosome pair does not separate properly or part of a chromosome breaks off. Because these errors involve far more DNA than problems due to single genes, they usually produce many physical and mental symptoms.

Down Syndrome. The most common chromosomal disorder, occurring in 1 out of every 700 live births, is *Down syndrome.* In 95 percent of cases, it results from a failure of the twenty-first pair of chromosomes to separate during meiosis, so the new individual receives three of these chromosomes rather than the normal two. For this reason, Down syndrome is sometimes called *trisomy 21.* In other, less frequent forms, an extra broken piece of a twenty-first chromosome is attached to another chromosome (called *translocation* pattern). Or an error occurs during early prenatal cell duplication, causing some but not all body cells to have the defective chromosomal makeup (called *mosaic* pattern) (U.S. Department of Health and Human Services, 2015f). Because the mosaic type involves less genetic material, symptoms may be less extreme.

The consequences of Down syndrome include intellectual disability, memory and speech problems, limited vocabulary, and slow motor development. Measures of electrical brain activity indicate that the brains of individuals with Down syndrome function in a less coordinated fashion than do the brains of typical individuals (Ahmadlou et al., 2013). The disorder is also associated with distinct physical features—a short, stocky build, a flattened face, a protruding tongue, almond-shaped eyes, and (in 50 percent of cases) an unusual crease running across the palm of the hand. In addition, infants with Down syndrome are often born with eye cataracts, hearing loss, and heart and intestinal defects (U.S. Department of Health and Human Services, 2015f).

An 8-year-old with Down syndrome, at right, plays with a typically developing classmate. Despite impaired intellectual development, this child benefits from exposure to stimulating environments and from opportunities to interact with peers.

Because of medical advances, life expectancy of individuals with Down syndrome has increased greatly: Today, it is about 60 years of age. However, about 70 percent of affected people who live past age 40 show symptoms of *Alzheimer's disease,* the most common form of dementia (Hartley et al., 2015). Genes on chromosome 21 are linked to this disorder.

Infants with Down syndrome smile less readily, show poor eye-to-eye contact, have weak muscle tone, and explore objects less persistently (Slonims & McConachie, 2006). But when parents encourage them to engage with their surroundings, children with Down syndrome develop more favorably. They also benefit from infant and preschool intervention programs, although emotional, social, and motor skills improve more than intellectual performance (Carr, 2002). Clearly, environmental factors affect how well children with Down syndrome fare.

As Figure 2.5 shows, the risk of bearing a baby with Down syndrome, as well as other chromosomal abnormalities, rises dramatically with maternal age. But exactly why older mothers are more likely to release ova with meiotic errors is not yet known (Chiang, Schultz, & Lampson, 2012). In about 5 percent of cases, the extra genetic material originates with the father. Some studies suggest a role for advanced paternal age, while others show no age effects (De Souza, Alberman, & Morris, 2009; Dzurova & Pikhart, 2005; Vranekovic et al., 2012).

Abnormalities of the Sex Chromosomes. Disorders of the autosomes other than Down syndrome usually disrupt development so severely that miscarriage occurs. When such babies are born, they rarely survive beyond early childhood. In contrast, sex chromosome disorders often are not recognized until adolescence when, in some deviations, puberty is delayed. The most common problems involve the presence of an extra chromosome (either X or Y) or the absence of one X in females.

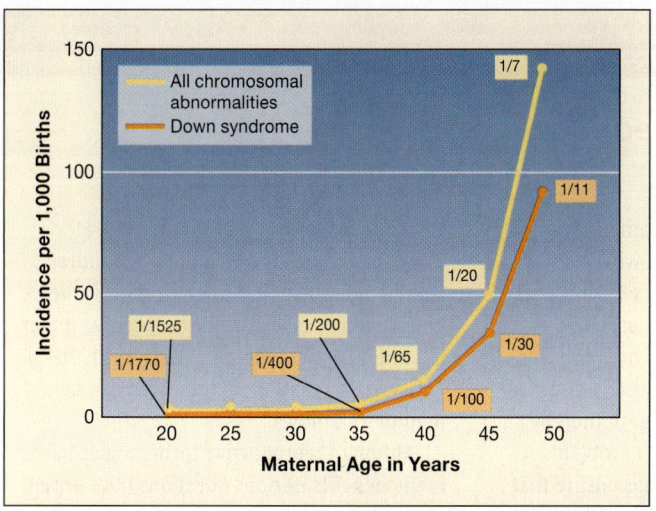

FIGURE 2.5 Risk of Down syndrome and all chromosomal abnormalities by maternal age. Risk rises sharply after age 35. (From R. L. Schonberg, 2012, "Birth Defects and Prenatal Diagnosis," from *Children with Disabilities*, 7th ed., M. L. Batshaw, N. J. Roizen, & G. R. Lotrecchiano, eds., p. 50. Baltimore: Paul H. Brookes Publishing Co, Inc.)

Research has discredited a variety of myths about individuals with sex chromosome disorders. For example, males with *XYY syndrome* are not necessarily more aggressive and antisocial than XY males (Stochholm et al., 2012). And most children with sex chromosome disorders do not suffer from intellectual disability. Rather, their cognitive challenges are usually very specific. Verbal difficulties—for example, with reading and vocabulary—are common among girls with *triple X syndrome* and boys with *Klinefelter syndrome,* both of whom inherit an extra X chromosome. In contrast, girls with *Turner syndrome,* who are missing an X, have trouble with spatial relationships—for example, drawing pictures, telling right from left, following travel directions, and noticing changes in facial expressions (Otter et al., 2013; Ross et al., 2012; Temple & Shephard, 2012). Brain-imaging evidence confirms that adding to or subtracting from the usual number of X chromosomes alters the development of certain brain structures, yielding particular intellectual deficits (Bryant et al., 2012; Hong et al., 2014).

Ask yourself

CONNECT Referring to ecological systems theory (Chapter 1, pages 23–26), explain why parents of children with genetic disorders often experience increased stress. What factors, within and beyond the family, can help these parents support their children's development?

APPLY Gilbert's genetic makeup is homozygous for dark hair. Jan's is homozygous for blond hair. What proportion of their children are likely to be dark-haired? Explain.

REFLECT Provide illustrations from our discussion, and from people you know with genetic disorders, of environmental influences on development.

Reproductive Choices

2.4 What procedures can assist prospective parents in having healthy children?

Two years after they married, Ted and Marianne gave birth to their first child. Kendra appeared to be a healthy infant, but by 4 months her growth had slowed, and she was diagnosed with Tay-Sachs disease (see Table 2.2 on page 47). When Kendra died at 2 years of age, Ted and Marianne were devastated. Although they did not want to bring another infant into the world who would endure such suffering, they badly wanted to have a child.

In the past, many couples with genetic disorders in their families chose not to bear a child at all rather than risk the birth of an abnormal baby. Today, genetic counseling and prenatal diagnosis help people make informed decisions about conceiving, carrying a pregnancy to term, or adopting a child.

Genetic Counseling

Genetic counseling is a communication process designed to help couples assess their chances of giving birth to a baby with a hereditary disorder and choose the best course of action in view of risks and family goals. Individuals likely to seek counseling are those who have had difficulties bearing children—for example, repeated miscarriages—or who know that genetic problems exist in their families. In addition, adults who delay childbearing are often candidates for genetic counseling. As maternal age rises beyond age 35, the rates of Down syndrome and other chromosomal abnormalities increase sharply (refer again to Figure 2.5). Older paternal age presents a heightened risk of DNA mutations as well. After age 40, it is associated with increased incidence of several serious psychological disorders (Zitzmann, 2013). These include *autism* (see page 21 in Chapter 1); *schizophrenia,* characterized by hallucinations, delusions, and irrational behavior; and *bipolar disorder,* marked by alternating periods of elation and depression. But because younger parents have children in far higher numbers than older parents, they still bear the majority of babies with genetic defects. Therefore, some experts argue that parental needs, not age, should determine referral for genetic counseling (Berkowitz, Roberts, & Minkoff, 2006).

If a family history of intellectual disability, psychological disorders, physical defects, or inherited diseases exists, the genetic counselor interviews the couple and prepares a *pedigree,* a picture of the family tree in which affected relatives are identified. The pedigree is used to estimate the likelihood that parents will have an affected child. For many disorders traceable to a single gene, blood tests or genetic analyses can reveal whether the parent is a carrier of the harmful allele. Carrier detection is possible for all the recessive diseases listed in Table 2.2 on page 47, as well as others, and for fragile X syndrome.

Autism, schizophrenia, and bipolar disorder have each been linked to an array of DNA-sequence deviations (called *genetic*

Social Issues: Health

The Pros and Cons of Reproductive Technologies

Some people decide not to risk pregnancy because of a history of genetic disease. Many others—in fact, one-sixth of all couples who try to conceive—discover that they are infertile. And some never-married adults and gay and lesbian couples want to bear children. Today, increasing numbers of individuals are turning to alternative methods of conception—technologies that have become the subject of heated debate.

Donor Insemination and In Vitro Fertilization

For nearly fifty years, *donor insemination*—injection of sperm from an anonymous man into a woman—has been used to overcome male reproductive difficulties. It also permits women without a male partner to become pregnant. Donor insemination is 70 percent successful, resulting in about 40,000 deliveries and 52,000 newborn babies in the United States each year (Rossi, 2014).

In vitro fertilization is another commonly used reproductive technology. Since the first "test tube" baby was born in England in 1978, 1 percent of all children in developed countries—about 65,000 babies in the United States—have been conceived through this technique annually (Sunderam et al., 2015). With in vitro fertilization, a woman is given hormones that stimulate the ripening of several ova. These are removed surgically and placed in a dish of nutrients, to which sperm are added. Once an ovum is fertilized and duplicates into several cells, it is injected into the mother's uterus.

By mixing and matching gametes, pregnancies can be brought about when either or both partners have a reproductive problem. Usually, in vitro fertilization is used to treat women whose fallopian tubes are permanently damaged. But a single sperm can now be injected directly into an ovum, thereby overcoming most male fertility problems. And a "sex sorter" method helps ensure that couples who carry X-linked diseases (which usually affect males) have a daughter. Fertilized ova and sperm can even be frozen and stored in embryo banks for use at some future time, thereby guaranteeing healthy zygotes should age or illness lead to fertility problems.

The overall success rate of assisted reproductive techniques, as measured by live births, is about 50 percent. However, success declines steadily with age, from 55 percent in women age 31 to 35 to 8 percent in women age 43 (Cetinkaya, Siano, & Benadiva, 2013; Gnoth et al., 2011).

Children conceived through these methods may be genetically unrelated to one or both of their parents. In addition, most parents who have used the procedures do not tell their children how they were conceived. Does lack of genetic ties or secrecy interfere with parent–child relationships? Perhaps because of a strong desire for parenthood, caregiving is actually somewhat warmer for young children conceived through donor insemination or in vitro fertilization. Also, these children and adolescents are as well-adjusted as their counterparts who were naturally conceived (Punamäki, 2006; Wagenaar et al., 2011). However, in one study, school-age children who had not been informed of their gamete-donor origins experienced less positive maternal interaction (Golombok et al., 2011, 2013). This suggests that open discussion can be helpful to families.

Although reproductive technologies have many benefits, serious questions have arisen about their use. In many countries, including the United States, doctors are not required to keep records of donor characteristics, though information about the child's genetic background might be critical in the case of serious disease (Murphy, 2013). Another concern is that the in vitro "sex sorter" method enables parental sex selection, thereby eroding the moral value that boys and girls are equally precious.

In vitro fertilization poses greater risks than natural conception to infant survival and healthy development. About 26 percent of in vitro procedures result in multiple births. Most are twins, but 3 percent are triplets and higher-order multiples. Consequently, among in vitro babies, the rate of low birth weight is nearly four times as high as in the general population. In response, doctors have reduced the number of fertilized ova injected into a woman's uterus, typically to no more than two (Kulkarni et al., 2013; Sunderam et al., 2015). Risk of pregnancy complications, miscarriage, and major birth defects also rises, due to the biological effects of in vitro techniques and the older age of many people seeking treatment.

---

markers) distributed across multiple chromosomes. New *genomewide testing methods,* which look for these genetic markers, enable genetic counselors to estimate risk for these conditions. But estimates are generally low because the genetic markers are found in only a minority of affected people. Also, the genetic markers are not associated with mental illness every time they appear. Their expression—as we will illustrate at the end of this chapter—seems to depend on environmental conditions. Recently, geneticists have begun to identify rare repeats and deletions of DNA bases that are more consistently related to mental illness (Gershon & Alliey-Rodriguez, 2013). These discoveries may lead to more accurate prediction of the likelihood of passing a psychological disorder from parent to child.

When all the relevant hereditary information is in, genetic counselors help people consider appropriate options. These include taking a chance and conceiving, choosing from among a variety of reproductive technologies (see the Social Issues: Health box above), or adopting a child.

Surrogate Motherhood

An even more controversial form of medically assisted conception is *surrogate motherhood*. In this procedure, in vitro fertilization may be used to impregnate a woman (called a surrogate) with a couple's fertilized ovum. Alternatively, sperm from a man whose partner is infertile may be used to inseminate the surrogate, who agrees to turn the baby over to the father. The child is then adopted by his partner. In both cases, the surrogate is paid a fee for her childbearing services.

Most surrogate arrangements proceed smoothly, and the limited evidence available suggests that families usually function well, tell their children about the surrogacy, and stay in touch with and have positive relationships with the surrogate, especially if she is genetically related to the child (Golombok et al., 2011, 2013; Jadva, Casey, & Golombok, 2012). The small number of children who have been studied are generally well-adjusted.

Nevertheless, because surrogacy usually involves the wealthy as contractors for infants and the less economically advantaged as surrogates, it may promote exploitation of financially needy women. In addition, most surrogates already have children of their own, and knowledge that their mother would give away a baby may cause these children to worry about the security of their own family circumstances.

Reproductive Frontiers

Experts are debating the ethics of other reproductive options. Doctors have used donor ova from younger women in combination with in vitro fertilization to help postmenopausal women become pregnant. Most recipients are in their forties, but some in their fifties and sixties, and a few at age 70, have given birth. These cases magnify health risks to mother and baby and bring children into the world whose parents may not live to see them reach adulthood. Based on U.S. life expectancy data, 1 in 3 mothers and 1 in 2 fathers having a baby at age 55 will die before their child enters college (U.S. Census Bureau, 2015d).

Today, customers at donor banks can select ova or sperm on the basis of physical characteristics and even IQ. And scientists are devising ways to alter the DNA of human ova, sperm, and embryos to protect against hereditary disorders—techniques that could be used to engineer other desired characteristics. Many worry that these practices are dangerous steps toward selective breeding through "designer babies"—controlling offspring traits by manipulating genetic makeup.

Although reproductive technologies permit many barren adults to become parents, laws are needed to regulate such practices. In Australia, New Zealand, and Europe, in vitro gamete donors and applicants for the procedure must undergo highly regulated screening (Murphy, 2013). Denmark, France, and Italy prohibit in vitro fertilization for women past menopause. Pressure from those working in the field of assisted reproduction may soon lead to similar policies in the United States.

The ethical problems of surrogate motherhood are so complex that 13 U.S. states and the District of Columbia sharply restrict or ban the practice (Swain, 2014). Most European nations, along with Australia and Canada, allow only "altruistic" surrogacy, in which the surrogate has no financial gain. At present, not enough is known about the consequences of being a product of these procedures. More research on how such children grow up, including later-appearing medical conditions and feelings about their origins, is important for weighing the pros and cons of these techniques.

Fertility drugs and in vitro fertilization often lead to multiple births. These quadruplets are healthy, but babies born with the aid of reproductive technologies are at high risk for low birth weight and major birth defects.

Prenatal Diagnosis and Fetal Medicine

If couples at risk for bearing a child with abnormalities decide to conceive, several **prenatal diagnostic methods**—medical procedures that permit detection of developmental problems before birth—are available (see Table 2.3 on page 54). Women of advanced maternal age are prime candidates for *amniocentesis* or *chorionic villus sampling*. Except for *maternal blood analysis*, however, prenatal diagnosis should not be used routinely because of injury risks to the developing organism.

Prenatal diagnosis has led to advances in fetal medicine. For example, by inserting a needle into the uterus, doctors can administer drugs to the fetus. Surgery has been performed to repair such problems as heart, lung, and diaphragm malformations, urinary tract obstructions, and neural defects (Sala et al., 2014). Fetuses with blood disorders have been given blood transfusions. And those with immune deficiencies have received bone

TABLE 2.3
Prenatal Diagnostic Methods

METHOD	DESCRIPTION
Amniocentesis	The most widely used technique. A hollow needle is inserted through the abdominal wall to obtain a sample of fluid in the uterus. Cells are examined for genetic defects. Can be performed by the 14th week after conception; 1 to 2 more weeks are required for test results. Small risk of miscarriage.
Chorionic villus sampling	A procedure that can be used if results are desired or needed very early in pregnancy. A thin tube is inserted into the uterus through the vagina, or a hollow needle is inserted through the abdominal wall. A small plug of tissue is removed from the end of one or more chorionic villi, the hairlike projections on the membrane surrounding the developing organism. Cells are examined for genetic defects. Can be performed at 9 weeks after conception; results are available within 24 hours. Entails a slightly greater risk of miscarriage than amniocentesis. Also associated with a small risk of limb deformities, which increases the earlier the procedure is performed.
Fetoscopy	A small tube with a light source at one end is inserted into the uterus to inspect the fetus for defects of the limbs and face. Also allows a sample of fetal blood to be obtained, permitting diagnosis of such disorders as hemophilia and sickle cell anemia, as well as neural defects (see below). Usually performed between 15 and 18 weeks after conception but can be done as early as 5 weeks. Entails some risk of miscarriage.
Ultrasound	High-frequency sound waves are beamed at the uterus; their reflection is translated into a picture on a video screen that reveals the size, shape, and placement of the fetus. By itself, permits assessment of fetal age, detection of multiple pregnancies, and identification of gross physical defects. Also used to guide amniocentesis, chorionic villus sampling, and fetoscopy. Sometimes combined with magnetic resonance imaging (see below) to detect physical abnormalities with greater accuracy. When used five or more times, may increase the chances of low birth weight.
Maternal blood analysis	By the second month of pregnancy, some of the developing organism's cells enter the maternal bloodstream. An elevated level of alpha-fetoprotein may indicate kidney disease, abnormal closure of the esophagus, or neural tube defects, such as anencephaly (absence of most of the brain) and spina bifida (bulging of the spinal cord from the spinal column). Isolated cells can be examined for genetic defects.
Ultrafast magnetic resonance imaging (MRI)	Sometimes used as a supplement to ultrasound, where brain or other abnormalities are detected and MRI can provide greater diagnostic accuracy. Uses a scanner to magnetically record detailed pictures of fetal structures. The ultrafast technique overcomes image blurring due to fetal movements. No evidence of adverse effects.
Preimplantation genetic diagnosis	After in vitro fertilization and duplication of the zygote into a cluster of about 8 to 10 cells, 1 or 2 cells are removed and examined for hereditary defects. Only if that sample is free of detectable genetic disorders is the fertilized ovum implanted in the woman's uterus.

Sources: Akolekar et al., 2015; Jokhi & Whitby, 2011; Kollmann et al., 2013; Moore, Persaud, & Torchia, 2016b; Sermon, Van Steirteghem, & Liebaers, 2004.

marrow transplants that succeeded in creating a normally functioning immune system (Deprest et al., 2010).

These techniques frequently result in complications, the most common being premature labor and miscarriage (Danzer & Johnson, 2014). Yet parents may be willing to try almost any option, even one with only a slim chance of success. Currently, the medical profession is struggling with how to help parents make informed decisions about fetal surgery.

Advances in *genetic engineering* also offer hope for correcting hereditary defects. As part of the Human Genome Project—an ambitious international research program aimed at deciphering the chemical makeup of human genetic material (genome)—researchers mapped the sequence of all human DNA base pairs. Using that information, they are "annotating" the genome—identifying all its genes and their functions, including their protein products and what these products do. A major goal is to understand the estimated 4,000 human disorders, those due to single genes and those resulting from an interplay of multiple genes and environmental factors.

A 9-year-old with cystic fibrosis undergoes a breathing test to assess lung functioning. Today, researchers are testing gene therapies aimed at regenerating the lining of the lungs to relieve symptoms of this recessive disorder.

Applying what we Know

Steps Prospective Parents Can Take Before Conception to Increase the Chances of a Healthy Baby

RECOMMENDATION	EXPLANATION
Arrange for a physical exam.	A physical exam before conception permits detection of diseases and other medical problems that might reduce fertility, be difficult to treat during pregnancy, or affect the developing organism.
Consider your genetic makeup.	Find out if anyone in your family has had a child with a genetic disease or disability. If so, seek genetic counseling before conception.
Reduce or eliminate toxins under your control.	Because the developing organism is highly sensitive to damaging environmental agents during the early weeks of pregnancy (see Chapter 3), couples trying to conceive should avoid drugs, alcohol, cigarette smoke, radiation, pollution, chemical substances in the home and workplace, and infectious diseases. Furthermore, they should stay away from ionizing radiation and household and industrial chemicals, which pose risks for mutations.
Ensure proper nutrition.	A doctor-recommended vitamin–mineral supplement, begun before conception, helps prevent many prenatal problems. It should include folic acid, which reduces the chances of neural tube defects, prematurity, and low birth weight (see Chapter 3, pages 87–88).
Consult your doctor after 12 months of unsuccessful efforts at conception.	Long periods of infertility may be due to undiagnosed spontaneous abortions, which can be caused by genetic defects in either partner. If a physical exam reveals a healthy reproductive system, seek genetic counseling.

So far, thousands of genes have been identified, including those involved in disorders of the heart, digestive, blood, eye, and nervous system and in many forms of cancer (National Institutes of Health, 2015). As a result, new treatments are being explored, such as *gene therapy*—correcting genetic abnormalities by delivering DNA carrying a functional gene to the cells. Testing of gene therapies for relieving symptoms of hemophilia and treating severe immune system dysfunction, leukemia, and several forms of cancer has been encouraging (Kaufmann et al., 2013). In another approach, called *proteomics,* scientists modify gene-specified proteins involved in biological aging and disease (Twyman, 2014).

Genetic treatments, however, seem some distance in the future for most single-gene defects and even farther off for diseases involving multiple genes that combine in complex ways with each other and the environment. Applying What We Know above summarizes steps that prospective parents can take before conception to protect the genetic health of their child.

Adoption

Adults who are infertile or likely to pass along a genetic disorder, same-sex couples, and single adults who want a family are turning to adoption in increasing numbers. Couples who have children by birth, too, sometimes choose to expand their families through adoption. Adoption agencies try to ensure a good fit by seeking parents of the same ethnic and religious background as the child and, where possible, choosing parents who are the same age as typical biological parents. Because the availability of healthy babies has declined (fewer young unwed mothers give up their babies than in the past), more people in North America and Western Europe are adopting from other countries or accepting children who are past infancy or who have known developmental problems (Palacios & Brodzinsky, 2010).

Adopted children and adolescents—whether or not they are born in their adoptive parents' country—tend to have more learning and emotional difficulties than other children, a difference that increases with the child's age at time of adoption (van den Dries et al., 2009; van IJzendoorn, Juffer, & Poelhuis, 2005;

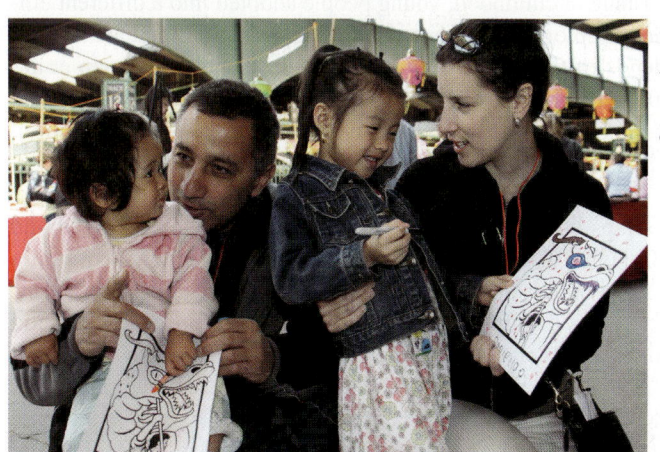

Adoption is one option for adults who are infertile or have a family history of genetic disorders. This couple, who adopted their daughters from China, can promote their children's adjustment by helping them learn about their birth heritage.

Verhulst, 2008). Various explanations exist for adoptees' more problematic childhoods. The biological mother may have been unable to care for the child because of problems believed to be partly genetic, such as alcoholism or severe depression, and may have passed this tendency to her offspring. Or perhaps she experienced stress, poor diet, or inadequate medical care during pregnancy—factors that can affect the child (as we will see in Chapter 3). Furthermore, children adopted after infancy often have a preadoptive history of conflict-ridden family relationships, lack of parental affection, neglect and abuse, or deprived institutional rearing. Finally, adoptive parents and children, who are genetically unrelated, are less alike in intelligence and personality than are biological relatives—differences that may threaten family harmony.

Despite these risks, most adopted children fare well, and those with preexisting problems who experience sensitive parenting usually make rapid progress, cognitively and socially (Arcus & Chambers, 2008; Juffer & van IJzendoorn, 2012). Overall, international adoptees develop much more favorably than birth siblings or institutionalized agemates who remain in their birth country (Christoffersen, 2012). And children with troubled family histories who are adopted at older ages generally improve in feelings of trust and affection for their adoptive parents as they come to feel loved and supported (Veríssimo & Salvaterra, 2006). As we will see in Chapter 4, however, later-adopted children—especially those with multiple early-life adversities—are more likely than their agemates to have persistent cognitive, emotional, and social problems.

By adolescence, adoptees' lives are often complicated by unresolved curiosity about their roots. As they try to integrate aspects of their birth family and their adoptive family into their emerging identity, teenagers face a challenging process of defining themselves. When parents have been warm, open, and supportive in their communication about adoption, their children typically forge a positive sense of self (Brodzinsky, 2011). And as long as their parents took steps to help them learn about their heritage in childhood, young people adopted into a different ethnic group or culture generally develop identities that are healthy blends of their birth and rearing backgrounds (Nickman et al., 2005; Thomas & Tessler, 2007). The decision to search for birth parents, however, is usually postponed until early adulthood, when marriage and childbirth may trigger it.

As we conclude our discussion of reproductive choices, perhaps you are wondering how things turned out for Ted and Marianne. Through genetic counseling, Marianne discovered a history of Tay-Sachs disease on her mother's side of the family. Ted had a distant cousin who died of the disorder. The genetic counselor explained that the chances of giving birth to another affected baby were 1 in 4. Ted and Marianne took the risk: Their son Douglas is now 12 years old. Although Douglas is a carrier of the recessive allele, he is healthy. In a few years, Ted and Marianne will tell Douglas about his genetic history and explain the importance of genetic counseling and testing before he has children of his own.

Ask yourself

CONNECT How does research on adoption reveal resilience? Which factor related to resilience (see Chapter 1, pages 10–11) is central in positive outcomes for adoptees?

APPLY Imagine that you must counsel a couple considering in vitro fertilization using donor ova to overcome infertility. What medical and ethical risks would you raise?

REFLECT Suppose you are a carrier of fragile X syndrome and want to have children. Would you choose pregnancy, adoption, or surrogacy? If you became pregnant, would you opt for prenatal diagnosis? Explain your decisions.

Environmental Contexts for Development

2.5 Describe family functioning from the perspective of ecological systems theory, along with aspects of the environment that support family well-being and development.

Just as complex as genetic inheritance is the surrounding environment—a many-layered set of influences that combine to help or hinder physical and psychological well-being. Jot down a brief description of events and people that have significantly influenced your development. Do the items on your list resemble those of my students, who mostly mention experiences that involve their families? This emphasis is not surprising, since the family is the first and longest-lasting context for development. Other influences that generally make students' top ten are friends, neighbors, school, workplace, and community and religious organizations.

Return to Bronfenbrenner's ecological systems theory, discussed in Chapter 1. It emphasizes that environments extending beyond the *microsystem*—the immediate settings just mentioned—powerfully affect development. Indeed, my students rarely mention one context, with an impact so pervasive that we seldom stop to think about it in our daily lives. This is the *macrosystem*, or broad social climate of society—its values and programs that support and protect human development. All people need help with the demands of each period of the lifespan—through affordable housing and health care, safe neighborhoods, good schools, well-equipped recreational facilities, and high-quality child care and other services that permit them to meet both work and family responsibilities. And some people, because of poverty or special tragedies, need considerably more help than others.

In the following sections, we take up these contexts for development. Because they affect every age and aspect of change, we will return to them in later chapters. For now, our discussion emphasizes that environments, as well as heredity, can enhance or create risks for development.

The Family

In power and breadth of influence, no other microsystem context equals the family. The family creates unique bonds among people. Attachments to parents and siblings are usually lifelong and serve as models for relationships in the wider world. Within the family, children learn the language, skills, and social and moral values of their culture. And people of all ages turn to family members for information, assistance, and pleasurable interaction. Warm, gratifying family ties predict physical and psychological health throughout development (Khaleque & Rohner, 2012). In contrast, isolation or alienation from the family, especially from parents, is generally associated with developmental problems.

Contemporary researchers view the family as a network of interdependent relationships (Bronfenbrenner & Morris, 2006; Russell, 2014). Recall from ecological systems theory that *bidirectional influences* exist in which the behaviors of each family member affect those of others. Indeed, the very term *system* implies that the responses of family members are related. These system influences operate both directly and indirectly.

Direct Influences. The next time you have a chance to observe family members interacting, watch carefully. You are likely to see that kind, patient communication evokes cooperative, harmonious responses, whereas harshness and impatience engender angry, resistive behavior. Each of these reactions, in turn, forges a new link in the interactive chain. In the first instance, a positive message tends to follow; in the second, a negative or avoidant one is likely.

These observations fit with a wealth of research on the family system. Studies of families of diverse ethnicities show that when parents are firm but warm, children tend to comply with their requests. And when children cooperate, their parents are likely to be warm and gentle in the future. In contrast, children whose parents discipline harshly and impatiently are likely to refuse and rebel. And because children's misbehavior is stressful, parents may increase their use of punishment, leading to more unruliness by the child (Lorber & Egeland, 2011; Shaw et al., 2012). This principle also applies to other two-person family relationships—siblings, marital partners, parent and adult child. In each case, the behavior of one family member helps sustain a form of interaction in the other that either promotes or undermines psychological well-being.

Indirect Influences. The impact of family relationships on development becomes even more complicated when we consider that interaction between any two members is affected by others present in the setting. Recall from Chapter 1 that Bronfenbrenner calls these indirect influences the effect of *third parties*.

Third parties can serve as supports for or barriers to development. For example, when a marital relationship is warm and considerate, mothers and fathers are more likely to engage in effective **coparenting,** mutually supporting each other's parenting behaviors. Such parents are warmer, praise and stimulate their children more, and nag and scold them less. Effective coparenting, in turn, fosters a positive marital relationship (Morrill et al., 2010). In contrast, parents whose marriage is tense and hostile often coparent ineptly. They interfere with each other's child-rearing efforts, are less responsive to children's needs, and are more likely to criticize, express anger, and punish (Palkovitz, Fagan, & Hull, 2013; Pruett & Donsky, 2011).

Children who are chronically exposed to angry, unresolved parental conflict have serious behavior problems resulting from disrupted emotional security (Cummings & Miller-Graff, 2015). These include both *internalizing difficulties,* such as feeling anxious and fearful and trying to repair their parents' relationship, and *externalizing difficulties,* including anger and aggression (Cummings, Goeke-Morey, & Papp, 2004; Goeke-Morey, Papp, & Cummings, 2013). These child problems can further disrupt the parents' relationship.

Yet even when third parties strain family ties, other members may help restore effective interaction. Grandparents, for example, can promote children's development both directly, by responding warmly to the child, and indirectly, by providing parents with child-rearing advice, models of child-rearing skill, and even financial assistance. Of course, as with any indirect influence, grandparents can sometimes be harmful. When relations between grandparents and parents are quarrelsome, parent–child communication may suffer.

Adapting to Change. Think back to the *chronosystem* in Bronfenbrenner's theory (see page 26 in Chapter 1). The interplay of forces within the family is dynamic and ever-changing. Important events, such as the birth of a baby, a change of jobs, or the addition to the household of an aging parent in declining health, create challenges that modify existing relationships. The way such events affect family interaction depends on the support other family members provide and on the developmental status of each participant. For example, the arrival of a new baby prompts

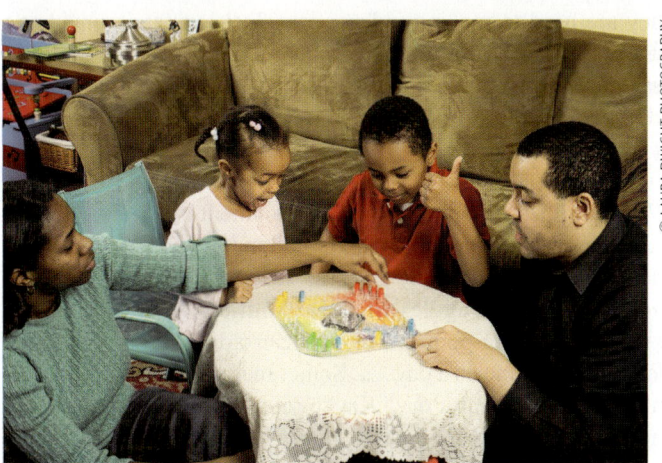

The family is a network of interdependent relationships, in which each person's behavior influences that of others. As this family plays a game, warm, considerate parental communication encourages children's cooperation, which promotes further parental warmth and caring.

very different reactions in a toddler than in a school-age child. And caring for an ill, aging parent is more stressful for a middle-aged adult still rearing children than for an adult of the same age who has no child-rearing responsibilities.

Historical time period also contributes to a dynamic family system. In recent decades, a declining birth rate, a high divorce rate, expansion of women's roles, increased acceptance of homosexuality, and postponement of parenthood have led to a smaller family size and a greater number of single parents, remarried parents, gay and lesbian parents, employed mothers, and dual-earner families. This, combined with a longer lifespan, means that more generations are alive, with fewer members in the youngest ones, leading to a "top-heavy" family structure. Young people today are more likely to have older relatives than at any time in history—a circumstance that can be enriching as well as a source of tension. In sum, as this complex intergenerational system moves through time, relationships are constantly revised as members adjust to their own and others' development as well as to external pressures.

LOOK and LISTEN

Record the number of siblings in your grandparents', parents', and own generation. Then do the same for several of your friends' families. Do you see evidence of a "top-heavy" family structure? What consequences might it have for family members of different generations?

Nevertheless, some general patterns in family functioning do exist. In the United States and other industrialized nations, one important source of these consistencies is socioeconomic status.

Socioeconomic Status and Family Functioning

People in industrialized nations are stratified on the basis of what they do at work and how much they earn for doing it—factors that determine their social position and economic well-being. Researchers assess a family's standing on this continuum through an index called **socioeconomic status (SES),** which combines three related, but not completely overlapping, variables: (1) years of education and (2) the prestige of one's job and the skill it requires, both of which measure social status; and (3) income, which measures economic status. As SES rises and falls, people face changing circumstances that profoundly affect family functioning.

SES is linked to timing of marriage and parenthood and to family size. People who work in skilled and semiskilled manual occupations (for example, construction workers, truck drivers, and custodians) tend to marry and have children earlier as well as give birth to more children than people in professional and technical occupations. The two groups also differ in child-rearing values and expectations. For example, when asked about personal qualities they desire for their children, lower-SES parents tend to emphasize external characteristics, such as obedience, politeness, neatness, and cleanliness. In contrast, higher-SES parents emphasize psychological traits, such as curiosity, happiness, self-direction, and cognitive and social maturity (Duncan & Magnuson, 2003; Hoff, Laursen, & Tardif, 2002).

These differences are reflected in family interaction. Parents higher in SES talk to, read to, and otherwise stimulate their infants and preschoolers more and grant them greater freedom to explore. With older children and adolescents, higher-SES parents use more warmth, explanations, and verbal praise; set higher academic and other developmental goals; and allow their children to make more decisions. Commands ("You do that because I told you to"), criticism, and physical punishment all occur more often in low-SES households (Bush & Peterson, 2008; Mandara et al., 2009).

Education contributes substantially to these variations in child rearing. Higher-SES parents' interest in providing verbal stimulation, nurturing inner traits, and promoting academic achievement is supported by years of schooling, during which they learned to think about abstract, subjective ideas and, thus, to invest in their children's cognitive and social development (Mistry et al., 2008). At the same time, greater economic security enables parents to devote more time, energy, and material resources to fostering their children's psychological characteristics (Duncan, Magnuson, & Votruba-Drzal, 2015).

Because of limited education and low social status, many lower-SES parents feel a sense of powerlessness in their relationships beyond the home. At work, for example, they must obey rules made by others in positions of authority. When they get home, their parent–child interaction seems to duplicate these experiences—but now they are in authority. High levels of stress sparked by economic insecurity contribute to low-SES parents' reduced provision of stimulating interaction and activities as well as greater use of coercive discipline (Belsky, Schlomer, & Ellis, 2012; Conger & Donnellan, 2007). Higher-SES parents, in contrast, typically have more control over their own lives. At work, they are used to making independent decisions and convincing others of their point of view. At home, they are more likely to teach these skills to their children.

Poverty

When families slip into poverty, development is seriously threatened. In a TV documentary on childhood poverty, a PBS filmmaker explored the daily lives of several American children, along with the struggles of their families (Frontline, 2012). Asked what being poor is like, 10-year-old Kaylie replied, "We don't get three meals a day. . . . Sometimes we have cereal but no milk and have to eat it dry." Kaylie said she felt hungry much of the time, adding, "I'm afraid if we can't pay our bills, me and my brother will starve."

Kaylie lives with her 12-year-old brother Tyler and their mother, who suffers from depression and panic attacks and cannot work. The children sometimes gather discarded tin cans from around their rural neighborhood and sell them for a small amount

Homelessness poses enormous challenges for maintaining positive family relationships and physical and mental health. This mother and her three young children prepare to move out of the motel room they share with her boyfriend and father.

of cash. When money to pay rent ran out, the family moved from its small house to an extended-stay motel. Before the move, Kaylie and Tyler tearfully gave up their pet dog to a shelter.

In the cramped motel room with family belongings piled haphazardly around her, Kaylie complained, "I have no friends, no places to play. I pass the time by." Her mother had postponed the children's school enrollment, expecting soon to move to a trailer court in a new school district. Kaylie and Tyler had few books and indoor games; no outdoor play equipment such as bicycles, bats and balls, and roller skates; and no scheduled leisure pursuits like swimming or music lessons or youth organization activities. Asked to imagine her future, Kaylie wasn't hopeful. "I see my future poor, on the streets, in a box, asking for money from everyone, stealing stuff. . . . I'd like to explore the world, but I'm never going to be able to do that."

Although poverty rates in the United States declined slightly in the 1990s, they rose over the first decade of the twenty-first century and then stabilized. Today, about 15 percent—46 million Americans—are affected. Those hit hardest are parents under age 25 with young children and older adults who live alone. Poverty is also magnified among ethnic minorities and women. For example, 21 percent of U.S. children are poor, a rate that climbs to 32 percent for Hispanic children, 36 percent for Native-American children, and 38 percent for African-American children. For single mothers with preschool children and older women on their own, the poverty rate is close to 50 percent (U.S. Census Bureau, 2015d).

Joblessness, a high divorce rate, a lower remarriage rate among women than men, widowhood, and (as we will see later) government programs with insufficient resources to meet family needs are responsible for these disheartening statistics. The poverty rate is higher among children than any other age group. And of all Western nations, the United States has the highest percentage of extremely poor children. Nearly 10 percent of U.S. children live in deep poverty (at less than half the poverty threshold, the income level judged necessary for a minimum living standard). In contrast, in most northern and central European countries, child poverty rates have remained below 10 percent for several decades, and extreme child poverty is rare (UNICEF, 2013). The earlier poverty begins, the deeper it is, and the longer it lasts, the more devastating are its effects. Children of poverty are more likely than other children to suffer from lifelong poor physical health, persistent deficits in cognitive development and academic achievement, high school dropout, mental illness, and impulsivity, aggression, and antisocial behavior (Duncan, Magnuson, & Votruba-Drzal, 2015; Morgan et al., 2009; Yoshikawa, Aber, & Beardslee, 2012).

The constant stressors that accompany poverty gradually weaken the family system. Poor families have many daily hassles: loss of welfare and unemployment payments, basic services—phone, TV, electricity, hot water—being shut off because of inability to pay bills, and limited or uncertain access to food, to name just a few. When daily crises arise, family members become depressed, irritable, and distracted; hostile interactions increase; and children's development suffers (Conger & Donnellan, 2007; Kohen et al., 2008).

Negative outcomes are especially severe in single-parent families and families who must live in poor housing and dangerous neighborhoods—conditions that make everyday existence even more difficult while reducing social supports that help people cope with economic hardship (Hart, Atkins, & Matsuba, 2008; Leventhal, Dupéré, & Shuey, 2015). On average, poverty rates are higher, neighborhood disorganization greater, and community services scarcer in rural communities—like the one where Kaylie, Tyler, and their mother live—than in urban areas (Hicken et al., 2014; Vernon-Feagans & Cox, 2013). These conditions heighten risks for disrupted family functioning and physical and psychological adjustment throughout life.

A related problem has reduced the life chances of substantial numbers of children and adults. An estimated 580,000 individuals in the United States were homeless on a given night in the most recently reported year (Henry et al., 2014). The majority are adults on their own, many of whom suffer from serious mental illness. But about one-fourth of the homeless are children and youths. Homelessness is mostly due to two factors: insufficient availability of low-cost housing and release of people with mental illness from institutions without necessary supports for adjusting to ordinary life.

Most homeless families consist of women with children under age 5. Besides health problems (which affect the majority of homeless people), many homeless children suffer from developmental delays and chronic emotional stress due to harsh, insecure daily lives (Kilmer et al., 2012). An estimated 23 percent who are old enough do not go to school, or attend irregularly. Homeless children achieve less well than other poverty-stricken children because of poor attendance, frequent moves from school to school, and physical and emotional health problems (Cutuli et al., 2010; National Coalition for the Homeless, 2012).

Although gaps in overall health and achievement between poverty-stricken children and their economically better-off peers are substantial, a considerable number of children from financially stressed families are resilient, faring well. A host of interventions aimed at helping children and youths surmount the risks of poverty exist. Some address family functioning and parenting, while others directly target children's academic, emotional, and social skills. And more programs are recognizing that because poverty-stricken children often experience multiple adversities, they benefit most from efforts that are multifaceted (Kagan, 2013a). We will discuss many such interventions later in this book.

Affluence

Despite their advanced education and great material wealth, affluent parents—those in prestigious and high-paying occupations—too often fail to engage in family interaction and parenting that promote favorable development. In several studies, researchers tracked the adjustment of youths growing up in wealthy suburbs. By seventh grade, many showed serious problems that worsened in high school (Luthar & Barkin, 2012; Racz, McMahon, & Luthar, 2011). Their school grades were poor, and they were more likely than youths in general to engage in alcohol and drug use, to commit delinquent acts, and to report high levels of anxiety and depression.

Why are so many affluent youths troubled? Compared to their better-adjusted counterparts, poorly adjusted affluent young people report less emotional closeness, less supervision, and fewer serious consequences for misbehaviors from their parents, who lead professionally and socially demanding lives. As a group, wealthy parents are nearly as physically and emotionally unavailable to their youngsters as parents coping with serious financial strain. At the same time, these parents often make excessive demands for achievement and are critical when their children perform less than perfectly (Luthar, Barkin, & Crossman, 2013). Adolescents whose parents value their accomplishments more than their character are more likely to have academic and emotional problems.

For both affluent and low-SES youths, a simple routine—eating dinner with parents—is associated with a reduction in adjustment difficulties, even after many other aspects of parenting are controlled (see Figure 2.6) (Luthar & Latendresse, 2005). Interventions that make wealthy parents aware of the high costs of a competitive lifestyle, weak involvement in children's lives, and unrealistically high expectations are badly needed.

Beyond the Family: Neighborhoods and Schools

As the concepts of *mesosystem* and *exosystem* in ecological systems theory make clear, connections between family and community are vital for psychological well-being. From our discussion of poverty, perhaps you can see why: In poverty-stricken

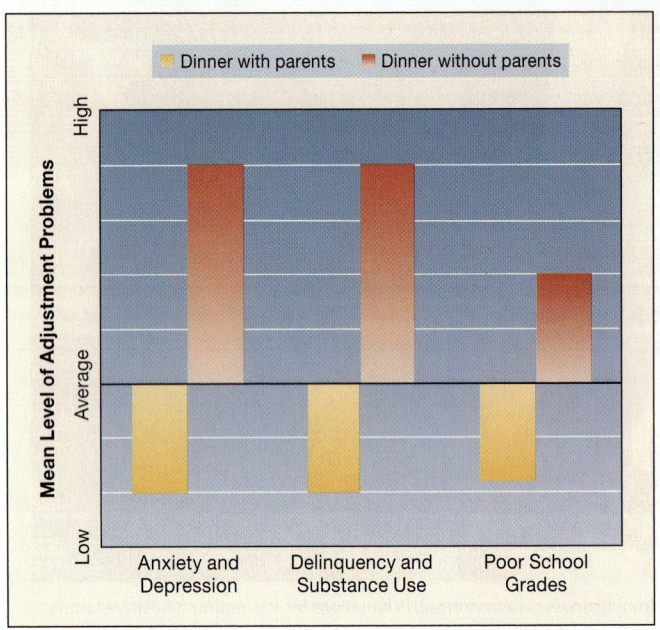

FIGURE 2.6 Relationship of regularly eating dinner with parents to affluent youths' adjustment problems. Compared with sixth graders who often ate dinner with their parents, those who rarely did so were far more likely to display anxiety and depression, delinquency and substance use, and poor school grades, even after many other aspects of parenting were controlled. In this study, frequent family mealtimes also protected low-SES youths from delinquency and substance use and from classroom learning problems. (Based on Luthar & Latendresse, 2005.)

areas, community life is usually disrupted. Families move often, parks and playgrounds are in disarray, and community centers providing organized leisure time activities do not exist. In such neighborhoods, family violence, child abuse and neglect, child and youth internalizing and externalizing difficulties, adult criminal behavior, and depression and declines in cognitive functioning in older adults are especially high (Chen, Howard, & Brooks-Gunn, 2011; Dunn, Schaefer-McDaniel, & Ramsay, 2010; Ingoldsby et al., 2012; Lang et al., 2008). In contrast, strong family ties to the surrounding social context—as indicated by frequent contact with relatives and friends and regular church, synagogue, temple, or mosque attendance—reduce stress and enhance adjustment.

Neighborhoods. Let's look closely at the functions of communities in the lives of children and adults by beginning with the neighborhood. What were your childhood experiences like in the yards, streets, parks, and other community settings surrounding your home? How did you spend your time, whom did you get to know, and how important were these moments to you?

Neighborhoods offer resources and social ties that play an important part in children's development. In an experimental study of neighborhood mobility, low-SES families were randomly assigned vouchers to move out of public housing into neighborhoods varying widely in affluence. Compared with their peers who remained in poverty-stricken areas, children and youths who moved into low-poverty neighborhoods and remained there for several years showed substantially better physical and mental health and school achievement (Goering, 2003; Leventhal & Brooks-Gunn, 2003; Leventhal & Dupéré, 2011). The ability of low-income families to integrate into the social life of their new neighborhoods was key to favorable outcomes.

Neighborhood resources have a greater impact on economically disadvantaged than on well-to-do young people. Higher-SES families depend less on their immediate surroundings for social support, education, and leisure pursuits. They can afford to transport their children to lessons and entertainment and, if necessary, to better-quality schools in distant parts of the community. In low-income neighborhoods, in-school and after-school programs that substitute for lack of other resources by providing art, music, sports, and other enrichment activities are associated with improved academic performance and a reduction in emotional and behavior problems in elementary and middle school (Durlak, Weissberg, & Pachan, 2010; Kataoka & Vandell, 2013; Vandell, Reisner, & Pierce, 2007). Neighborhood organizations, such as religious youth groups and special interest clubs, contribute to favorable development in adolescence, including increased self-confidence, school achievement, and educational aspirations (Barnes et al., 2007).

Yet in dangerous, disorganized neighborhoods, high-quality activities for children and adolescents are scarce. Even when they are available, crime and social disorder limit young people's access, and parents overwhelmed by financial and other stressors are less likely to encourage their children to participate (Dearing et al., 2009). Thus, the neediest children and youths are especially likely to miss out on these development-enhancing activities.

LOOK and LISTEN

Ask several parents to list their school-age children's regular lessons and other enrichment activities. Then inquire about home and neighborhood factors that either encourage or impede their children's participation.

The Better Beginnings, Better Futures Project of Ontario, Canada, is a government-sponsored set of pilot programs aimed at preventing the dire consequences of neighborhood poverty. The most successful of these efforts, using neighborhood elementary schools as its base, provided children ages 4 to 8 years with in-class, before- and after-school, and summer enrichment activities. Project staff also visited each child's parents regularly, informed them about community resources, and encouraged their involvement in the child's school and neighborhood life. And a community-wide component focused on improving the neighborhood as a place to live, by offering leadership training and adult education programs and organizing safety initiatives and special events and celebrations (Peters, 2005; Peters, Petrunka, & Arnold, 2003). Longitudinal follow-ups as participants reached grades 3, 6, 9, and 12 revealed wide-ranging benefits compared with children and families living in impoverished neighborhoods without this set of programs (Peters et al., 2010; Worton et al., 2014). Among these were gains in children's academic achievement and social adjustment, a reduction in adolescent delinquency, and parent-reported improved family functioning, child-rearing practices, and sense of community connection.

During late adulthood, neighborhoods become increasingly important because people spend more time at home. Despite the availability of planned housing for older adults, about 90 percent remain in regular housing, usually in the same neighborhood where they lived during their working lives (U.S. Census Bureau, 2015d). Proximity to relatives and friends is a significant factor in the decision to move or stay put late in life (Hooyman, Kawamoto, & Kiyak, 2015). In the absence of nearby family members, older adults mention neighbors and nearby friends as resources they rely on most for physical and social support.

Schools. Unlike the informal worlds of family and neighborhood, the school is a formal institution designed to transmit knowledge and skills needed to become productive members of society. Children and youths in the developed world spend much time in school—a total of about 14,000 hours, on average, by high school graduation. And today, because many children younger than age 5 attend "school-like" child-care centers or preschools, the impact of schooling begins earlier and is even more powerful than these figures suggest.

Schools are complex social systems that affect many aspects of development. Schools differ in their physical environments—student body size, number of children per class, and space available for work and play. They also vary in their educational philosophies—whether teachers regard students as passive

A 5-year-old enjoys working with volunteers at a community garden sponsored by the Boys & Girls Clubs of America. Neighborhood resources are especially important for the development of economically disadvantaged children and youths.

learners to be molded by adult instruction; as active, curious beings who determine their own learning; or as collaborative partners assisted by adult experts, who guide their mastery of new skills. Finally, the social life of schools varies—for example, in the degree to which students cooperate and compete; in the extent to which students of different abilities, SES, and ethnic backgrounds learn together; and in whether they are safe, humane settings or riddled with peer harassment and violence (Evans, 2006). We will discuss each of these aspects of schooling in later chapters.

Achieving well in elementary and secondary school is crucial for admission to and success in college. Beginning in the 1960s, obtaining a college degree became the main route to securing a highly skilled, well-paying job. In addition to elevated job status and lifetime earnings, higher education contributes to life satisfaction and longevity, and among SES variables, it probably does so uniquely. Well-educated adults tend to have larger social networks and, therefore, access to more social support. Education also enhances knowledge and decision-making skills—for example, in the realms of health behavior and family functioning. Increased education is linked to reduced likelihood of smoking, heavy drinking, unsafe driving, and overweight and obesity (Cutler & Lleras-Muney, 2010). Compared to adults with less education, college graduates less often have children out of wedlock and more often have stable marriages (Cancian & Haskins, 2013; Pew Research Center, 2010a).

As with SES and family functioning, the impact of schooling and academic achievement on development and life chances strengthens over time. Furthermore, these contextual factors are interrelated: Children living in low-income and poverty-stricken neighborhoods are more likely to attend underfunded schools and experience poorer quality education. For these reasons, educational interventions aimed at upgrading the educational experiences and school performance of economically disadvantaged children are best begun in the early years (Crosnoe & Benner, 2015). But intervening at later periods to target specific educational problems is also helpful—for example, by providing high-quality vocational education to non-college-bound youths.

Students whose parents are involved in school activities and attend parent–teacher conferences show better academic achievement. Higher-SES parents, whose backgrounds and values are similar to those of teachers, are more likely to maintain regular school contact. In contrast, low-SES and ethnic minority parents often feel uncomfortable about coming to school, and daily stressors reduce the energy they have for school involvement (Grant & Ray, 2010). Teachers and administrators must take extra steps with low-SES and ethnic minority families to build supportive family–school ties.

When these efforts lead to cultures of good parenting and teaching, they deliver an extra boost to student success. For example, students attending schools with many highly involved parents achieve especially well (Darling & Steinberg, 1997). And when excellent education becomes a team effort of teachers, administrators, and community members, its effects on learning are stronger and reach many more students (Hauser-Cram et al., 2006).

The Cultural Context

Our discussion in Chapter 1 emphasized that human development can be fully understood only when viewed in its larger cultural context. In the following sections, we expand on this theme by taking up the role of the *macrosystem* in development. First, we discuss ways that cultural values and practices affect environmental contexts for development. Then we consider how healthy development depends on laws and government programs that shield people from harm and foster their well-being.

Cultural Values and Practices. Cultures shape family interaction and community settings beyond the home—in short, all aspects of daily life. Many of us remain blind to aspects of our own cultural heritage until we see them in relation to the practices of others.

Consider the question, Who should be responsible for rearing young children? How would you answer it? Here are some typical responses from my students: "If parents decide to have a baby, then they should be ready to care for it." "Most people are not happy about others intruding into family life." These statements reflect a widely held opinion in the United States—that the care and rearing of children, and paying for that care, are the duty of parents, and only parents. This view has a long history—one in which independence, self-reliance, and the privacy of family life emerged as central American values (Dodge & Haskins, 2015; Halfon & McLearn, 2002). It is one reason, among others, that the public has been slow to endorse government-supported benefits for all families, such as high-quality child care and paid employment leave for meeting family needs. It has also contributed to the large number of U.S. families who remain poor, even though family members are gainfully employed (Gruendel & Aber, 2007; UNICEF, 2013).

Although the culture as a whole may value independence and privacy, not all citizens share the same values. Some belong to **subcultures**—groups of people with beliefs and customs that differ from those of the larger culture. Many ethnic minority groups in the United States have cooperative family structures, which help protect their members from the harmful effects of poverty. As the Cultural Influences box on the following page indicates, the African-American tradition of **extended-family households,** in which parent and child live with one or more adult relatives, is a vital feature of black family life that has promoted resilience in its members, despite a long history of prejudice and economic deprivation.

Active, involved extended families also characterize other minorities, such as Asian, Native-American, and Hispanic subcultures. Within these families, grandparents play meaningful roles in guiding younger generations; adults who face employment, marital, or child-rearing difficulties receive assistance and emotional support; and caregiving is enhanced for children and older adults (Jones & Lindahl, 2011; Mutchler, Baker, & Lee, 2007). In Hispanic extended families, for example, grandparents are even more likely to share in rearing young children than are African-American grandparents—a collaborative parenting

Cultural Influences

The African-American Extended Family

The African-American extended family can be traced to the African heritage of most black Americans. In many African societies, newly married couples do not start their own households. Instead, they live with a large extended family, which assists its members with all aspects of daily life. This tradition of maintaining a broad network of kin ties traveled to North America during the period of slavery. Since then, it has served as a protective shield against the destructive impact of poverty and racial prejudice on African-American family life. Today, more black than white adults have relatives other than their own children living in the same household. African-American parents also live closer to kin, often establish family-like relationships with friends and neighbors, see more relatives during the week, and perceive them as more important figures in their lives (Boyd-Franklin, 2006; McAdoo & Younge, 2009).

By providing emotional support and sharing essential resources, the African-American extended family helps reduce the stress of poverty and single parenthood. Extended-family members often help with child rearing, and adolescent mothers living in extended families are more likely to complete high school and get a job than mothers living on their own—factors that benefit children's well-being (Gordon, Chase-Lansdale, & Brooks-Gunn, 2004).

For single mothers rearing children and adolescents, extended-family living continues to be associated with more positive mother–child interaction. Even after establishing their own home, single mothers often invite family members or close friends to live with them. This kinship support increases the likelihood of effective parenting, which is related to gains in children's academic performance and social skills and to reduced antisocial behavior (Taylor, 2010; Washington, Gleeson, & Rulison, 2013).

Finally, the extended family plays an important role in transmitting African-American culture. Compared with nuclear-family households (which include only parents and their children), extended-family arrangements place more emphasis on cooperation and on moral and religious values. And older black adults, such as grandparents and great-grandparents,

Three generations enjoy a family picnic. Strong bonds with extended-family members have helped protect many African-American children against the destructive impact of poverty and racial prejudice.

view educating children about their African heritage as especially important (Mosely-Howard & Evans, 2000; Taylor, 2000). These influences strengthen family bonds, enhance children's development, and increase the chances that the extended-family lifestyle will carry over to the next generation.

---

arrangement that has physical and emotional health benefits for grandparents, parents, and children alike (Goodman & Silverstein, 2006). A likely reason for such far-reaching effects is that intergenerational shared parenting is consistent with the Hispanic cultural ideal of *familism,* which places an especially high priority on close, harmonious family bonds and meeting family needs.

Our discussion so far reflects two broad sets of values on which cultures and subcultures are commonly compared: *collectivism* versus *individualism* (Triandis & Gelfand, 2012). In cultures that emphasize collectivism, people stress group goals over individual goals and value *interdependent* qualities, such as social harmony, obligations and responsibility to others, and collaborative endeavors. In cultures that emphasize individualism, people are largely concerned with their own personal needs and value *independence*—personal exploration, discovery, achievement, and choice in relationships. Although it is the most common basis for comparing cultures, the collectivism–individualism distinction is controversial because both sets of values exist, in varying mixtures, in most cultures (Taras et al., 2014). Nevertheless, consistent cross-national differences in collectivism–individualism remain: The United States is more individualistic than most Western European countries, which place greater weight on collectivism. These values affect a nation's approach to protecting the well-being of its children, families, and aging citizens.

Public Policies and Lifespan Development. When widespread social problems arise, such as poverty, homelessness, hunger, and disease, nations attempt to solve them through devising **public policies**—laws and government programs designed to improve current conditions. For example, when poverty increases and families become homeless, a country might decide to build more low-cost housing, raise the minimum wage, and increase welfare benefits. When reports indicate that many children are not achieving well in school, federal and state governments might grant more tax money to school districts, strengthen teacher preparation, and make sure that help reaches children who need it most. And when older adults have difficulty making ends meet because of inflation, a nation might increase its social security benefits.

U.S. public policies safeguarding children and youths have lagged behind policies for older adults. And compared with other industrialized nations, both sets of policies have been slow to emerge in the United States.

Policies for Children, Youths, and Families. We have already seen that although many U.S. children fare well, a large number grow up in environments that threaten their development. As Table 2.4 reveals, the United States does not rank well on any key measure of children's health and well-being.

The problems of children and youths extend beyond the indicators in the table. The Affordable Care Act, signed into law in 2010, extended government-supported health insurance to all children in low-income families. But expanded coverage for low-income adults, including parents, is not mandatory for the states, leaving 13 percent of adults without an affordable coverage option. Largely because uninsured parents lack knowledge of how to enroll their children, 11 percent of children eligible for the federally supported Children's Health Insurance Program (CHIP)—more than 5 million—do not receive coverage (Kaiser Family Foundation, 2015). Furthermore, the United States has been slow to move toward national standards and funding for child care. Affordable care is in short supply, and much of it is mediocre to poor in quality (Burchinal et al., 2015; Phillips & Lowenstein, 2011). In families affected by divorce, weak enforcement of child support payments heightens poverty in mother-headed households. And 7 percent of 16- to 24-year-olds who dropped out of high school have not returned to earn a diploma (U.S. Department of Education, 2015).

Why have attempts to help children and youths been difficult to realize in the United States? A complex set of political and economic forces is involved. Cultural values of self-reliance and privacy have made government hesitant to become involved in family matters. Furthermore, good social programs are expensive, and they must compete for a fair share of a country's economic resources. Children can easily remain unrecognized in this process because they cannot vote or speak out to protect their own interests, as adult citizens do (Ripple & Zigler, 2003). They must rely on the goodwill of others to become an important government priority.

Policies for Older Adults. Until well into the twentieth century, the United States had few policies in place to protect its aging population. For example, Social Security benefits, which address the income needs of retired citizens who contributed to society through prior employment, were not awarded until the

TABLE 2.4
How Does the United States Compare to Other Nations on Indicators of Children's Health and Well-Being?

INDICATOR	U.S. RANK[a]	SOME COUNTRIES THE UNITED STATES TRAILS
Childhood poverty (among 20 industrialized nations considered)	20th	Canada, Germany, Iceland, Ireland, Norway, Sweden, United Kingdom[b]
Infant deaths in the first year of life (among 39 industrialized nations considered)	39th	Canada, Greece, Hungary, Ireland, Singapore, Spain
Teenage birth rate (among 20 industrialized nations considered)	20th	Australia, Canada, Czech Republic, Denmark, Hungary, Iceland, Poland, Slovakia
Public expenditure on education as a percentage of gross domestic product[c] (among 32 industrialized nations considered)	13th	Belgium, France, Iceland, New Zealand, Portugal, Spain, Sweden
Public expenditure on early childhood education as a percentage of gross domestic product[c] (among 34 industrialized nations considered)	21st	Austria, France, Germany, Italy, Netherlands, Sweden
Public expenditure on health as a percentage of total health expenditure, public plus private (among 34 industrialized nations considered)	34th	Australia, Austria, Canada, France, Hungary, Iceland, Switzerland, New Zealand

[a] 1 = highest, or best, rank.
[b] The U.S. childhood poverty rate of 21 percent greatly exceeds poverty in these nations, which have standards of living similar to the United States. For example, the childhood poverty rate is 13 percent in Canada, 12 percent in the United Kingdom, 11 percent in Ireland, 7 percent in Sweden, and 6 percent in Norway. Deep poverty affects just 2.5 percent of children in Canada, and a fraction of 1 percent in the other countries just listed. In contrast, 10 percent of U.S. children live in deep poverty.
[c] Gross domestic product is the value of all goods and services produced by a nation during a specified time period. It provides an overall measure of a nation's wealth.

Sources: OECD, 2013a, 2015c; Sedgh et al., 2015; UNICEF, 2013; U.S. Census Bureau, 2015d.

late 1930s. Yet most Western nations had social security systems a decade or more earlier (Karger & Stoesz, 2014). In the 1960s, U.S. federal spending on programs for older adults expanded rapidly. Medicare, a national health insurance program for older people that pays partial health-care costs, was initiated. This leaves about one-third of older adults' health expenditures to be covered by supplemental private insurance, government health insurance for low-income adults, or out-of-pocket payments (Davis, Schoen, & Bandeali, 2015).

Social Security and Medicare consume 97 percent of the U.S. federal budget for older adults. Consequently, U.S. programs have been criticized for neglecting social services. To meet this need, a national network for planning, coordinating, and delivering assistance to older adults has been established. Approximately 655 Area Agencies on Aging operate at regional and local levels, assessing community needs and offering communal and home-delivered meals, self-care education, elder abuse prevention, and a wide range of other social services. But limited funding means that the Area Agencies help far too few people in need.

As noted earlier, many older adults—especially women, ethnic minorities, and those living alone—remain in dire economic straits. Those who had interrupted employment histories, held jobs without benefits, or suffered lifelong poverty are not eligible for Social Security. Although all Americans age 65 and older are guaranteed a minimum income, the guaranteed amount is below the poverty line—the amount judged necessary for bare subsistence by the federal government. Furthermore, Social Security benefits are rarely adequate as a sole source of retirement income; they must be supplemented through other pensions and family savings. But a substantial percentage of U.S. aging citizens do not have access to these resources. Therefore, they are

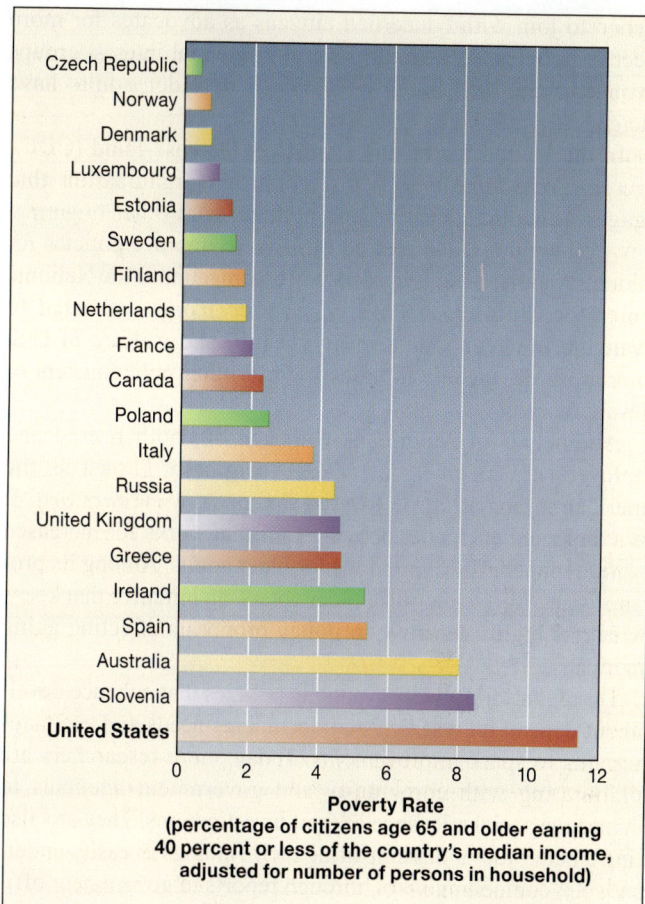

FIGURE 2.7 Percentage of older adults living in poverty in 20 industrialized nations. Among the countries listed, the United States has the highest rate of older adults living in poverty. Public expenditures on social security and other income guarantees for this group are far greater in the highly ranked nations than in the United States. (Based on Luxembourg Income Study, 2015.)

more likely than other age groups to be among the "near poor" (U.S. Department of Health and Human Services, 2015e).

Nevertheless, the U.S. aging population is financially much better off now than in the past. Today, older adults are a large, powerful, well-organized constituency, far more likely than children or low-income families to attract the support of politicians. As a result, the number of aging poor has declined from 1 in 3 people in 1960 to just under 1 in 10 today (U.S. Census Bureau, 2015d). Still, as Figure 2.7 shows, aging adults in the United States are less well off than those in many other Western nations, which provide more generous, government-funded income supplements to older adults.

Looking Toward the Future. Despite the worrisome state of many children, families, and aging citizens, efforts are being made to improve their condition. Throughout this book, we will discuss many successful programs that could be expanded. Also, growing awareness of the gap between what we know and what we do to better people's lives has led experts in developmental

Many U.S. ethnic-minority older adults are poverty-stricken. This Native American, who lives on a Navajo Reservation, depends on an itinerant doctor for routine medical care.

science to join with concerned citizens as advocates for more effective policies. As a result, several influential interest groups devoted to the well-being of children or older adults have emerged.

In the United States, the Children's Defense Fund (CDF), *www.childrensdefense.org,* is a nonprofit organization that engages in public education and partners with other organizations, communities, and elected officials to improve policies for children. Another energetic advocacy organization is the National Center for Children in Poverty, *www.nccp.org,* dedicated to advancing the economic security, health, and welfare of U.S. children in low-income families by informing policymakers of relevant research.

About half of Americans over age 50, both retired and employed, are members of AARP (originally known as the American Association of Retired Persons), *www.aarp.org.* It has a large and energetic lobbying staff that works for increased government benefits of all kinds for older adults. Among its programs is an effort to mobilize older voters, an initiative that keeps lawmakers highly sensitive to policy proposals affecting aging Americans.

Besides strong advocacy, public policies that enhance development depend on research that documents needs and evaluates programs to spark improvements. Today, more researchers are collaborating with community and government agencies to enhance the social relevance of their investigations. They are also doing a better job of disseminating their findings in easily understandable, compelling ways, through reports to government officials, websites aimed at increasing public understanding, and collaborations with the media to ensure accurate and effective reporting (Shonkoff & Bales, 2011). In these ways, researchers are helping to create the sense of immediacy about the condition of children, families, and older adults that is necessary to spur a society into action.

AARP members sign a petition, to be sent to U.S. Senators, in support of legalizing importation of cheaper prescription medications from Canada. Lobbying for policy change is one way AARP addresses the needs of older adults.

Ask yourself

CONNECT Links between family and community foster development throughout the lifespan. Provide examples and research findings that support this idea.

APPLY Check your local newspaper or one or two national news websites to see how often articles appear on the condition of children, families, and older adults. Why is it important for researchers to communicate with the public about the well-being of these sectors of the population?

REFLECT Do you agree with the widespread American sentiment that government should not become involved in family life? Explain.

Understanding the Relationship Between Heredity and Environment

2.6 Explain the various ways heredity and environment may combine to influence complex traits.

So far in this chapter, we have discussed a wide variety of genetic and environmental influences, each of which has the power to alter the course of development. Yet people who are born into the same family (and who therefore share both genes and environments) are often quite different in characteristics. We also know that some individuals are affected more than others by their homes, neighborhoods, and communities. How do scientists explain the impact of heredity and environment when they seem to work in so many different ways?

Behavioral genetics is a field devoted to uncovering the contributions of nature and nurture to this diversity in human traits and abilities. All contemporary researchers agree that both heredity and environment are involved in every aspect of development. But for polygenic traits (those due to many genes) such as intelligence and personality, scientists are a long way from knowing the precise hereditary influences involved. Although they are making progress in identifying variations in DNA sequences associated with complex traits, so far these genetic markers explain only a small amount of variation in human behavior, and a minority of cases of most psychological disorders (Plomin, 2013). For the most part, scientists are still limited to investigating the impact of genes on complex characteristics indirectly.

Some believe that it is useful and possible to answer the question of *how much each factor contributes* to differences among people. A growing consensus, however, regards that question as unanswerable. These investigators believe that heredity and environment are inseparable (Lickliter & Honeycutt, 2015; Moore, 2013). The important question, they maintain, is *how nature and nurture work together.* Let's consider each position in turn.

The Question, "How Much?"

To infer the role of heredity in complex human characteristics, researchers use special methods, the most common being the *heritability estimate*. Let's look closely at the information this procedure yields, along with its limitations.

Heritability. **Heritability estimates** measure the extent to which individual differences in complex traits in a specific population are due to genetic factors. We will take a brief look at heritability findings on intelligence and personality here, returning to them in greater detail in later chapters. Heritability estimates are obtained from **kinship studies,** which compare the characteristics of family members. The most common type of kinship study compares identical twins, who share all their genes, with fraternal twins, who, on average, share only half. If people who are genetically more alike are also more similar in intelligence and personality, then the researcher assumes that heredity plays an important role.

Kinship studies of intelligence provide some of the most controversial findings in the field of developmental science. Some experts claim a strong genetic influence, whereas others believe that heredity is barely involved. Currently, most kinship findings support a moderate role for heredity. When many twin studies are examined, correlations between the scores of identical twins are consistently higher than those of fraternal twins. In a summary of more than 10,000 twin pairs of diverse ages, the correlation for intelligence was .86 for identical twins and .60 for fraternal twins (Plomin & Spinath, 2004).

Researchers use a complex statistical procedure to compare these correlations, arriving at a heritability estimate ranging from 0 to 1.00. The typical overall value for intelligence is about .50 for twin samples in Western industrialized nations, suggesting that differences in genetic makeup explain half the variation in intelligence. However, heritability increases with age, from approximately .20 in infancy, to .40 in childhood and adolescence, to .60 in adulthood, with some late adulthood estimates as high as .80 (Plomin & Deary, 2015). As we will see later, one explanation is that, compared to children, adults exert greater personal control over their intellectual experiences—for example, how much time they spend reading or solving challenging problems. Adopted children's mental test scores are more strongly related to their biological parents' scores than to those of their adoptive parents, offering further support for the role of heredity (Petrill & Deater-Deckard, 2004).

Heritability research also reveals that genetic factors are important in personality. For frequently studied traits, such as sociability, anxiety, agreeableness, and activity level, heritability estimates obtained on child, adolescent, and young adult twins are moderate, in the .40s and .50s (Vukasović & Bratko, 2015). Unlike intelligence, however, heritability of personality does not increase over the lifespan (Loehlin et al., 2005).

Twin studies of schizophrenia, bipolar disorder, and autism generally yield high heritabilities, above .70. Heritabilities for antisocial behavior and major depression are considerably lower, in the .30s and .40s (Ronald & Hoekstra, 2014; Sullivan, Daly, & O'Donovan, 2012). Again, adoption studies are consistent with these results. Biological relatives of adoptees with schizophrenia, bipolar disorder, or autism are more likely than adoptive relatives to share the same disorder (Plomin, DeFries, & Knopik, 2013).

Limitations of Heritability. The accuracy of heritability estimates depends on the extent to which the twin pairs studied reflect genetic and environmental variation in the population. Within a population in which all people have very similar home, school, and community experiences, individual differences in intelligence and personality are assumed to be largely genetic, and heritability estimates should be close to 1.00. Conversely, the more environments vary, the more likely they are to account for individual differences, yielding lower heritability estimates. In twin studies, most twin pairs are reared together under highly similar conditions. Even when separated twins are available for study, social service agencies have often placed them in advantaged homes that are alike in many ways (Richardson & Norgate, 2006). Because the environments of most twin pairs are less diverse than those of the general population, heritability estimates are likely to exaggerate the role of heredity.

Heritability estimates can easily be misapplied. For example, high heritabilities have been used to suggest that ethnic

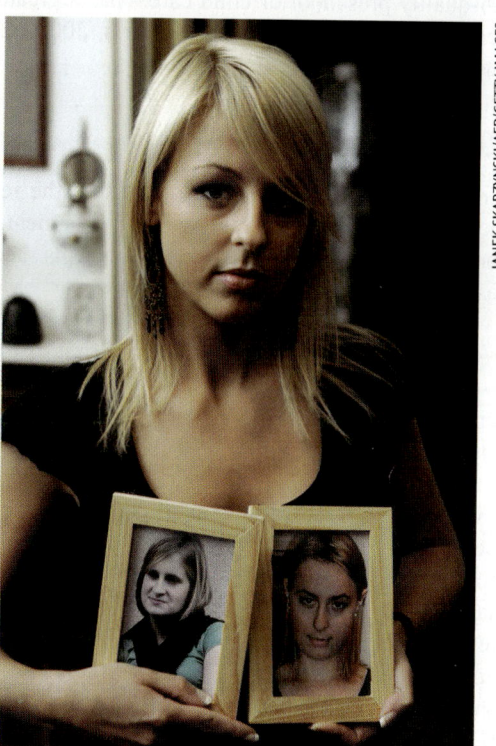

Kasia Ofmanski, of Warsaw, Poland, holds photos of Nina (right), the identical twin from whom she was mistakenly separated at birth, and Edyta (left), who was assumed to be her twin and who grew up with her. When the twins first met at age 17, Kasia exclaimed, "She's just like me." They found many similarities: Both were physically active, extroverted, and earned similar grades in school. Clearly heredity contributes to personality traits, but generalizing from twin evidence to the population is controversial.

differences in intelligence, such as the poorer performance of black children compared to white children, have a genetic basis (Jensen, 1969, 2001; Rushton, 2012; Rushton & Jensen, 2006). Yet heritabilities computed on mostly white twin samples do not explain test score differences between ethnic groups. We have already seen that large socioeconomic differences are involved. In Chapter 9, we will discuss research indicating that when black children are adopted into economically advantaged homes at an early age, their scores are well above average and substantially higher than those of children growing up in impoverished families.

Perhaps the most serious criticism of heritability estimates has to do with their limited usefulness. Though confirming that heredity contributes to a broad array of human traits, these statistics give us no precise information on how intelligence and personality develop or how children might respond to environments designed to help them develop as far as possible (Baltes, Lindenberger, & Staudinger, 2006). Indeed, the heritability of children's intelligence increases as parental education and income increase—that is, as children grow up in conditions that allow them to make the most of their genetic endowment. In impoverished environments, children are prevented from realizing their potential. Consequently, enhancing these children's experiences through interventions—such as parent education and high-quality preschool or child care—has a greater impact on development (Bronfenbrenner & Morris, 2006; Phillips & Lowenstein, 2011).

The Question, "How?"

Today, most researchers view development as the result of a dynamic interplay between heredity and environment. How do nature and nurture work together? Several concepts shed light on this question.

Gene–Environment Interaction. The first of these ideas is **gene–environment interaction,** which means that because of their genetic makeup, individuals differ in their responsiveness to qualities of the environment (Rutter, 2011). Let's explore this idea in Figure 2.8. Gene–environment interaction can apply to any characteristic; here it is illustrated for intelligence. Notice that when environments vary from extremely unstimulating to highly enriched, Ben's intelligence increases steadily, Linda's rises sharply and then falls off, and Ron's begins to increase only after the environment becomes modestly stimulating.

Gene–environment interaction highlights two important points. First, it shows that because each of us has a unique genetic makeup, we respond differently to the same environment. Notice in Figure 2.8 how a poor environment results in similarly low scores for all three individuals. But when the environment provides a moderate level of stimulation, Linda is by far the best-performing child. And in a highly enriched environment, Ben does best, followed by Ron, both of whom now outperform Linda. Second, sometimes different gene–environment combinations can make two people look the same! For example, if Linda is reared in a minimally stimulating environment, her score will

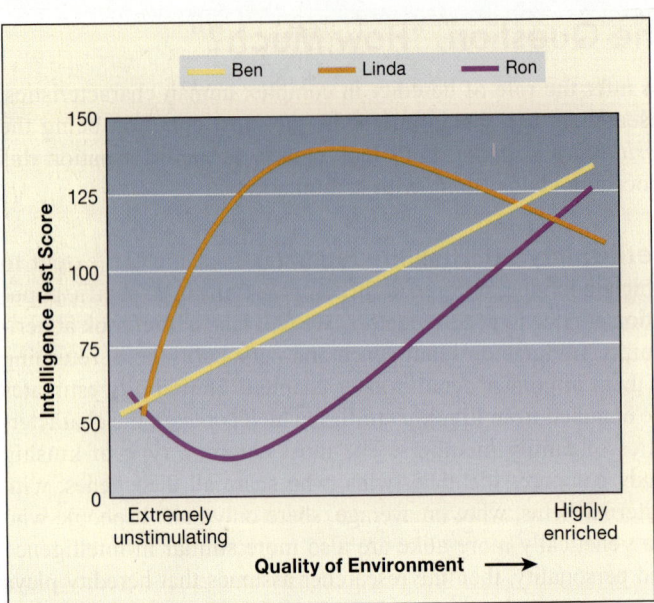

FIGURE 2.8 Gene–environment interaction, illustrated for intelligence by three children who differ in responsiveness to quality of the environment. As environments vary from extremely unstimulating to highly enriched, Ben's intelligence test score increases steadily, Linda's rises sharply and then falls off, and Ron's begins to increase only after the environment becomes modestly stimulating.

be about 100—average for people in general. Ben and Ron can also obtain this score, but to do so, they must grow up in a fairly enriched home (Gottlieb, Wahlsten, & Lickliter, 2006).

Recently, researchers have made strides in identifying gene–environment interactions in personality development. In Chapter 6 we will see that young children with certain genes that increase their risk of an emotionally reactive temperament respond especially strongly to variations in parenting quality (Bakermans-Kranenburg & van IJzendoorn, 2015). When parenting is favorable, they gain control over their emotions and adjust as well or better than other children. But when parenting is unfavorable, they become increasingly irritable, difficult, and poorly adjusted, more so than children not at genetic risk.

Gene–Environment Correlation. A major problem in trying to separate heredity and environment is that they are often correlated (Rutter, 2011; Scarr & McCartney, 1983). According to the concept of **gene–environment correlation,** our genes influence the environments to which we are exposed. The way this happens changes with age.

Passive and Evocative Correlation. At younger ages, two types of gene–environment correlation are common. The first is called *passive* correlation because the child has no control over it. Early on, parents provide environments influenced by their own heredity. For example, parents who are good athletes emphasize outdoor activities and enroll their children in swimming and gymnastics. Besides being exposed to an "athletic environment," the children may have inherited their parents' athletic ability. As a result, they are likely to become good athletes for both genetic and environmental reasons.

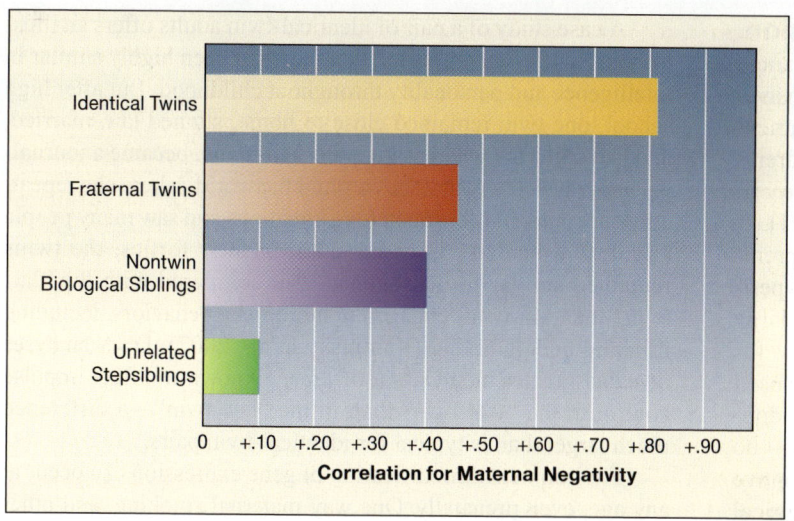

FIGURE 2.9 Similarity in mothers' interactions for pairs of siblings differing in genetic relatedness. The correlations shown are for maternal negativity. The pattern illustrates evocative gene–environment correlation. Identical twins evoke similar maternal treatment because of their identical heredity. As genetic resemblance between siblings declines, the strength of the correlation drops. Mothers vary their interactions as they respond to each child's unique genetic makeup. (Based on Reiss, 2003.)

The second type of gene–environment correlation is *evocative.* Children evoke responses that are influenced by the child's heredity, and these responses strengthen the child's original style. For example, a cooperative, attentive child probably receives more patient and sensitive interactions from parents than an inattentive, distractible child. In support of this idea, the more genetically alike siblings are, the more their parents treat them alike, in both warmth and negativity. Parents' treatment of identical twins is highly similar, whereas their treatment of fraternal twins and nontwin biological siblings is only moderately so. And little resemblance exists in parents' warm and negative interactions with unrelated stepsiblings (see Figure 2.9) (Reiss, 2003). Likewise, identical-twin pairs—who resemble each other more in sociability than fraternal twins do—tend to be more alike in the degree of friendliness they evoke from new playmates (DiLalla, Bersted, & John, 2015).

Active Correlation. At older ages, *active* gene–environment correlation becomes common. As children extend their experiences beyond the immediate family and are given the freedom to make more choices, they actively seek environments that fit with their genetic tendencies. The well-coordinated, muscular child spends more time at after-school sports, the musically talented child joins the school orchestra and practices his violin, and the intellectually curious child is a familiar patron at her local library.

This tendency to actively choose environments that complement our heredity is called **niche-picking** (Scarr & McCartney, 1983). Infants and young children cannot do much niche-picking because adults select environments for them. In contrast, older children, adolescents, and adults are increasingly in charge of their environments.

Niche-picking explains why pairs of identical twins reared apart during childhood and later reunited may find, to their surprise, that they have similar hobbies, food preferences, and vocations—a trend that is especially marked when twins' environmental opportunities are similar. Niche-picking also helps us understand why identical twins become somewhat more alike, and fraternal twins and adopted siblings less alike, in intelligence with age (Bouchard, 2004). And niche-picking sheds light on why adult identical-twin pairs, compared to fraternal twins and other adults, select more similar spouses and best friends—in height, weight, personality, political attitudes, and other characteristics (Rushton & Bons, 2005).

The influence of heredity and environment is not constant but changes over time. With age, genetic factors may become more important in influencing the environments we experience and choose for ourselves.

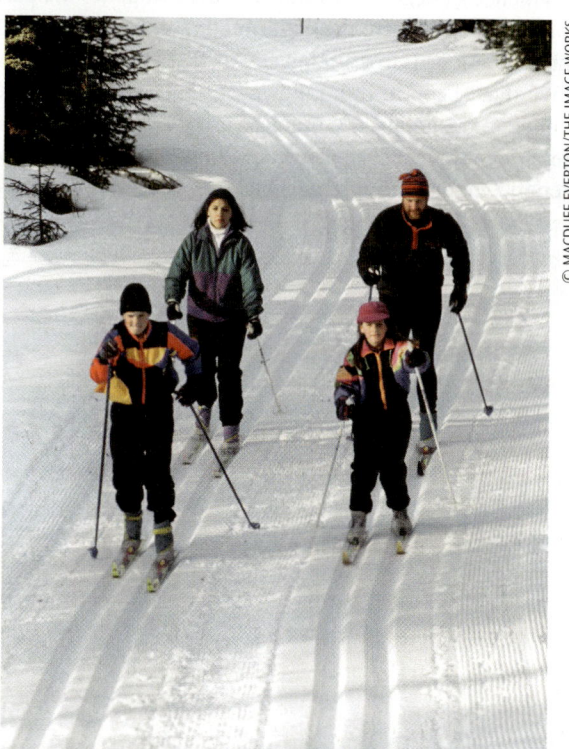

These parents share their enthusiasm for outdoor sports with their children, who may have inherited the parents' athletic ability. When heredity and environment are correlated, the influence of one cannot be separated from the influence of the other.

Environmental Influences on Gene Expression.

Notice how, in the concepts just considered, heredity is granted priority. In gene–environment interaction, it affects responsiveness to particular environments. Similarly, gene–environment correlation is viewed as driven by genetics, in that children's genetic makeup causes them to receive, evoke, or seek experiences that actualize their hereditary tendencies (Rutter, 2011).

A growing number of researchers take issue with the supremacy of heredity, arguing that it does not dictate children's experiences or development in a rigid way. For example, in a large Finnish adoption study, children with a genetic tendency for mental illness (based on having a biological mother diagnosed with schizophrenia) but who were being reared by healthy adoptive parents showed little evidence of mental disturbance—no more than a control group with healthy biological and adoptive parents. In contrast, schizophrenia and other psychological impairments piled up in adoptees whose biological and adoptive parents were both mentally ill (Tienari, Wahlberg, & Wynne, 2006; Tienari et al., 2003).

Furthermore, parents and other caring adults can *uncouple* unfavorable gene–environment correlations by providing children with positive experiences that modify the expression of heredity, yielding favorable outcomes. In a study that tracked the development of 5-year-old identical twins, pair members tended to resemble each other in level of aggression. And the more aggression they displayed, the more maternal anger and criticism they received (a gene–environment correlation). Nevertheless, some mothers treated their twins differently. When followed up at age 7, twins who had been targets of more maternal negativity engaged in even more antisocial behavior. In contrast, their better-treated, genetically identical counterparts showed a reduction in disruptive acts (Caspi et al., 2004). Good parenting protected them from a spiraling, antisocial course of development.

Accumulating evidence reveals that the relationship between heredity and environment is not a one-way street, from genes to environment to behavior. Rather, like other system influences considered in this and the previous chapter, it is *bidirectional:* Genes affect people's behavior and experiences, but their experiences and behavior also affect gene expression. This view of the relationship between heredity and environment, depicted in Figure 2.10, is called **epigenesis,** which means development resulting from ongoing, bidirectional exchanges between heredity and all levels of the environment (Cox, 2013; Gottlieb, 1998, 2007).

Biologists are beginning to clarify the precise mechanisms through which environment can alter gene expression without changing the DNA sequence—a field of research called *epigenetics.* One such mechanism is **methylation**—a biochemical process triggered by certain experiences, in which a set of chemical compounds (called a methyl group) lands on top of a gene and changes its impact, reducing or silencing its expression. Methylation levels can be measured, and they help explain why identical twins, though precisely the same in DNA sequencing, sometimes display strikingly different phenotypes with age.

A case study of a pair of identical-twin adults offers an illustration. Researchers reported that they had been highly similar in intelligence and personality throughout childhood. But after high school, one twin remained close to home, studied law, married, and had children, whereas the other left home, became a journalist, and traveled to war zones around the world, where she repeatedly encountered life-threatening situations and saw many people killed or wounded. Assessed again in their forties, the twins remained similar in intelligence. But compared with the "law twin," the "war twin" engaged in more risky behaviors, including drinking and gambling (Kaminsky et al., 2007). DNA analyses revealed greater methylation of a gene known to affect impulse control in the "war twin" than in the "law twin"—a difference much larger than is typical for identical-twin pairs.

Environmental modification of gene expression can occur at any age, even prenatally. One way maternal smoking, and other harmful prenatal environmental factors we will take up in Chapter 3, may compromise development is through altered DNA methylation (Markunas et al., 2014). And as the Biology and Environment box on the following page illustrates, severe maternal stress during pregnancy is linked to long-term impairment in children's capacity to manage stress, with gene methylation likely contributing to unfavorable outcomes. The harsh conditions associated with chronic poverty, as well, are believed to exert their impact epigenetically, leaving behind a "biological residue" that compromises the child's potential for a physically and mentally healthy life (Miller et al., 2009). Furthermore, animal evidence indicates that some methylated genes are passed to offspring at conception, thereby affecting development in subsequent generations (Grossniklaus et al., 2013).

We must keep in mind, however, that epigenetic processes also operate positively: Favorable rearing experiences alter gene expression in ways that enhance development! And some negative epigenetic modifications may be reversible through carefully

FIGURE 2.10 Epigenesis. Development takes place through ongoing, bidirectional exchanges between heredity and all levels of the environment. Genes affect behavior and experiences. Experiences and behavior also affect gene expression. (Adapted from Gottlieb, 2007.)

Biology and Environment

The Tutsi Genocide and Epigenetic Transmission of Maternal Stress to Children

In 1994, in a genocidal rampage committed by members of the Hutu majority against the Tutsi people of Rwanda, nearly 1 million perished within a three-month period. The horror was so extreme that in surveys of Rwandans during the years following the genocide, an estimated 40 to 60 percent reported symptoms of *post-traumatic stress disorder (PTSD)* (Neugebauer et al., 2009; Schaal et al., 2011). In PTSD, flashbacks, nightmares, anxiety, irritability, angry outbursts, and difficulty concentrating lead to intense distress, physical symptoms, and loss of interest in relationships and daily life.

Parental PTSD is a strong predictor of child PTSD (Brand et al., 2011; Yehuda & Bierer, 2009). In both children and adults, PTSD is associated with disruptions in the body's stress response system, reflected in abnormal blood levels of stress hormones. In appropriate concentrations, stress hormones assist our brains in managing stress effectively. In individuals with PTSD, stress hormone levels are either too high or (more often) too low, contributing to persistently disturbed stress regulation.

Mounting evidence confirms that exposure to extreme adversity increases methylation of a chromosome-5 gene called *GR*, which plays a central role in stress-hormone regulation. Might this epigenetic process contribute to parent-to-child transmission of PTSD?

To explore this question, researchers identified 50 Tutsi women who had been pregnant during the genocide (Perroud et al., 2014). Half had been directly exposed to the trauma; the other half had not been exposed due to being out of the country at the time. Eighteen years later, the mothers and their adolescent children were assessed for PTSD and depression by trained psychologists. Blood samples enabled genetic testing for methylation of the *GR* gene and assessment of stress-hormone levels (which we will discuss further in Chapter 3).

Compared with non-exposed mothers, mothers who witnessed the genocidal carnage had substantially higher PTSD and depression scores, and children of the two groups of mothers differed similarly. Also, as Figure 2.11 reveals, exposed mothers and their children displayed stronger *GR* methylation. And consistent with methylation's dampening effect on gene expression, trauma-exposed mothers and their children had much lower stress-hormone levels than their non-exposed counterparts.

These findings are consistent with other evidence, in both animals and humans, indicating that prenatal exposure to the biological consequences of severe maternal stress can induce epigenetic changes, through methylation, that impair functioning of the body's stress response system (Daskalakis & Yehuda, 2014; Mueller & Bale, 2008). In the Tutsi mothers and children, the effects of genocidal trauma were long-lasting,

This Rwandan mother gave birth shortly after the Tutsi genocide. Nine years later, she continues to suffer from PTSD caused by first-hand experience of atrocities, including repeated rape and loss of her mother, brother, and two sisters in the massacre. Her daughter's PTSD and depression might be the result of prenatal exposure to severe maternal stress, which can trigger epigenetic changes that disrupt the body's stress response system.

evident in serious psychological disorders nearly two decades later.

As the researchers noted, more remains to be discovered about exactly how maternal trauma exposure compromised the Tutsi children's capacity to manage stress. Epigenetic processes, not just prenatally but also at later ages, may have been largely responsible. Alternatively, poor-quality parenting, resulting from maternal anxiety, irritability, anger, and depression, could have been the major influence. More likely, epigenetic changes, inept parenting, and other unfavorable environmental factors combined to place the Tutsi children at high risk for PTSD and depression. In Chapter 3, we will return to the impact of prenatal stress, including evidence showing that its negative impact can be lessened or prevented through social support.

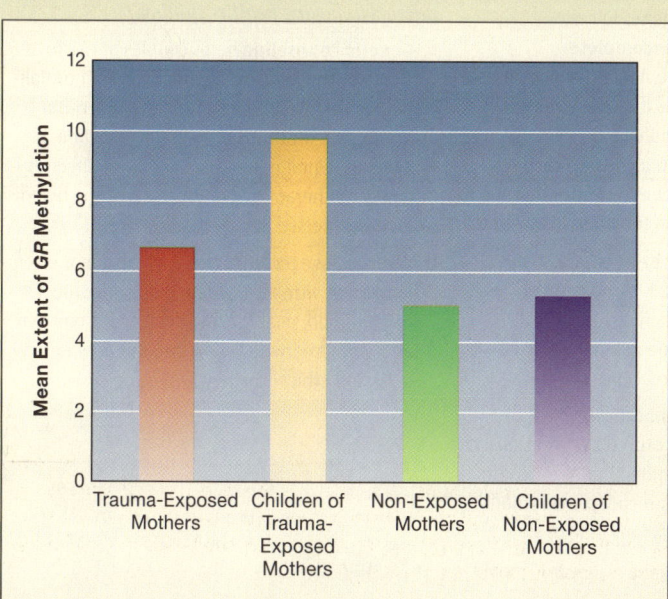

FIGURE 2.11 Methylation status of the *GR* gene in trauma-exposed and non-trauma-exposed Tutsi mothers and their children. Mothers who had been directly exposed to the Rwandan Tutsi genocide, as well as their children, showed elevated methylation of the *GR* gene, which is centrally involved in functioning of the body's stress response system. (Based on Perroud et al., 2014.)

designed interventions (van IJzendoorn, Bakermans-Kranenburg, & Ebstein, 2011). The concept of epigenesis reminds us that the genome is not static but is constantly in flux, both reflecting and affecting the individual's ever-changing environment.

Epigenetics is still an emerging field, and clarifying its mechanisms may prove to be even more complex than efforts to understand DNA sequence variations (Duncan, Pollastri, & Smoller, 2014). But from what we already know, one lesson is clear: Development is best understood as a series of complex exchanges between nature and nurture. Although people cannot be changed in any way we might desire, environments can modify genetic influences. The success of any attempt to improve development depends on the characteristics we want to change, the genetic makeup of the individual, and the type and timing of our intervention.

Ask yourself

CONNECT Explain how each of the following concepts supports the conclusion that genetic influences on human characteristics are not constant but change over time: somatic mutation (page 49), niche-picking (page 69), and epigenesis (page 70).

APPLY Bianca's parents are accomplished musicians. At age 4, Bianca began taking piano lessons. By age 10, she was accompanying the school choir. At age 14, she asked to attend a special music high school. Explain how gene–environment correlation promoted Bianca's talent.

REFLECT What aspects of your own development—for example, interests, hobbies, college major, or vocational choice—are probably due to niche-picking? Explain.

Summary / chapter 2

Genetic Foundations (p. 44)

2.1 What are genes, and how are they transmitted from one generation to the next?

- Each individual's **phenotype,** or directly observable characteristics, is a product of both **genotype** and environment. **Chromosomes,** rodlike structures within the cell nucleus, contain our hereditary endowment. Along their length are **genes,** segments of **deoxyribonucleic acid (DNA). Protein-coding genes** send instructions for making proteins to the cell's cytoplasm; **regulator genes** modify those instructions. A wide range of environmental factors also alter gene expression.

- **Gametes,** or sex cells, result from a cell division process called **meiosis,** which halves the number of chromosomes. In meiosis, genes shuffle to create new combinations, ensuring that each individual receives a unique set from each parent. Once sperm and ovum unite, the resulting **zygote** will then have the full complement of chromosomes.

- If the fertilizing sperm carries an X chromosome, the child will be a girl; if it contains a Y chromosome, a boy. **Fraternal,** or **dizygotic, twins** result when two ova are released from the mother's ovaries and each is fertilized. **Identical,** or **monozygotic, twins** develop when a zygote divides in two during the early stages of cell duplication.

2.2 Describe various patterns of gene–gene interaction.

- Traits controlled by single genes follow **dominant–recessive** and **incomplete-dominance** patterns of inheritance. **Homozygous** individuals have two identical **alleles,** or forms of a gene. **Heterozygous** individuals, with one dominant and one recessive allele, are **carriers** of the recessive trait. In **incomplete dominance,** both alleles are expressed in the phenotype.

- **X-linked inheritance** applies when recessive disorders are carried on the X chromosome and, therefore, are more likely to affect males. In **genomic imprinting,** one parent's allele is activated, regardless of its makeup.

- Harmful genes arise from **mutation,** which can occur spontaneously or be caused by hazardous environmental agents. Germline mutation occurs in the cells that give rise to gametes; somatic mutation can occur in body cells at any time of life.

- Human traits that vary on a continuum, such as intelligence and personality, result from **polygenic inheritance**—the effects of many genes.

2.3 Describe major chromosomal abnormalities, and explain how they occur.

- Most chromosomal abnormalities result from errors during meiosis. The most common, Down syndrome, leads to physical defects and intellectual disability. **Sex chromosome** disorders are milder than defects of the **autosomes** and usually cause very specific cognitive impairments.

Reproductive Choices (p. 51)

2.4 What procedures can assist prospective parents in having healthy children?

- **Genetic counseling** helps couples at risk for giving birth to children with genetic abnormalities consider reproductive options. **Prenatal diagnostic methods** allow early detection of developmental problems. Genetic engineering and gene therapy offer hope for treating hereditary disorders.

- Reproductive technologies, such as donor insemination, in vitro fertilization, and surrogate motherhood, enable individuals to become parents who otherwise would not, but they raise legal and ethical concerns.

- Many adults who cannot conceive or are likely to transmit a genetic disorder choose adoption. Although adopted children have more learning and emotional problems than children in general, most fare well in the long run. Warm, sensitive parenting predicts favorable development.

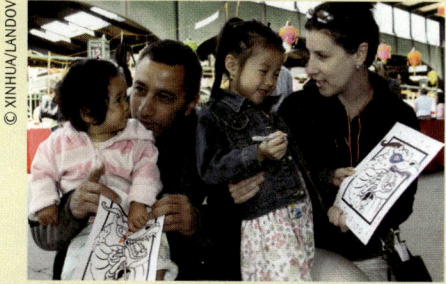

Environmental Contexts for Development (p. 56)

2.5 Describe family functioning from the perspective of ecological systems theory, along with aspects of the environment that support family well-being and development.

- The first and foremost context for development is the family, a dynamic system characterized by bidirectional influences, in which each member's behaviors affect those of others. Both direct and indirect influences operate within the family system, which must continually adjust to new events and changes in its members. Warm, gratifying family ties, which foster effective **coparenting**, help ensure children's psychological health.

- **Socioeconomic status (SES)** profoundly affects family functioning. Higher-SES families tend to be smaller, to emphasize psychological traits, and to engage in warm, verbally stimulating interaction with children. Lower-SES families often stress external characteristics and use more commands, criticism, and physical punishment.

- Children's development in affluent families may be impaired by parents' physical and emotional unavailability. Poverty and homelessness can seriously undermine development.

- Supportive ties between family and community are vital for psychological well-being. Stable, socially cohesive neighborhoods that provide constructive leisure and enrichment activities promote favorable development in both children and adults. High-quality schooling and academic achievement profoundly affect life chances, with their impact strengthening over time.

- The values and practices of cultures and **subcultures** affect all aspects of daily life. **Extended-family households,** which are common among many ethnic minority groups, help protect family members from the negative effects of poverty and other stressful life conditions.

- Consistent cross-national differences in *collectivism–individualism* powerfully affect approaches to devising **public policies** to address social problems. Largely because of its strongly individualistic values, the United States lags behind other developed nations in policies safeguarding children and families, as well as older adults.

Understanding the Relationship Between Heredity and Environment (p. 66)

2.6 Explain the various ways heredity and environment may combine to influence complex traits.

- **Behavioral genetics** examines the contributions of nature and nurture to diversity in human traits and abilities. Some researchers use **kinship studies** to compute **heritability estimates,** which attempt to quantify the influence of genetic factors on such complex traits as intelligence and personality. However, the accuracy and usefulness of this approach have been challenged.

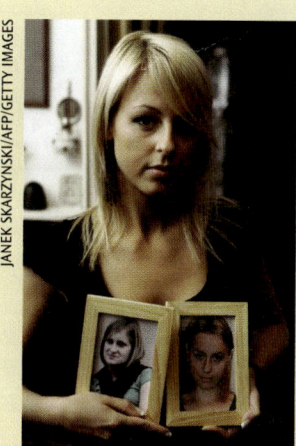

- In **gene–environment interaction,** heredity influences each individual's unique response to qualities of the environment. **Gene–environment correlation** and **niche-picking** describe how genes affect the environments to which individuals are exposed.

- **Epigenesis** reminds us that development is best understood as a series of complex exchanges between heredity and all levels of the environment. Epigenetic research is uncovering biochemical processes—such as **methylation**—through which environment can modify gene expression.

Important Terms and Concepts

allele (p. 46)
autosomes (p. 45)
behavioral genetics (p. 66)
carrier (p. 46)
chromosomes (p. 44)
coparenting (p. 57)
deoxyribonucleic acid (DNA) (p. 44)
dominant–recessive inheritance (p. 46)
epigenesis (p. 70)
extended-family household (p. 62)
fraternal, or dizygotic, twins (p. 45)
gametes (p. 44)
gene (p. 44)

gene–environment correlation (p. 68)
gene–environment interaction (p. 68)
genetic counseling (p. 51)
genomic imprinting (p. 49)
genotype (p. 43)
heritability estimate (p. 67)
heterozygous (p. 46)
homozygous (p. 46)
identical, or monozygotic, twins (p. 46)
incomplete dominance (p. 48)
kinship studies (p. 67)
meiosis (p. 45)
methylation (p. 70)

mutation (p. 49)
niche-picking (p. 69)
phenotype (p. 43)
polygenic inheritance (p. 50)
prenatal diagnostic methods (p. 53)
protein-coding genes (p. 44)
public policies (p. 64)
regulator genes (p. 44)
sex chromosomes (p. 45)
socioeconomic status (SES) (p. 58)
subculture (p. 62)
X-linked inheritance (p. 48)
zygote (p. 45)

chapter 3

Prenatal Development, Birth, and the Newborn Baby

An expectant mother observes closely as a nurse uses a portable ultrasound device to check the health of her fetus. High-quality prenatal care provided at this field clinic along the Thai–Burmese border helps protect pregnant women from serious diseases that are common in the region.

THIERRY FALISE/LIGHTROCKET VIA GETTY IMAGES

What's ahead in chapter 3

Prenatal Development
Conception • Germinal Period • Period of the Embryo • Period of the Fetus

Prenatal Environmental Influences
Teratogens • Other Maternal Factors • The Importance of Prenatal Health Care

■ **SOCIAL ISSUES: HEALTH** The Nurse–Family Partnership: Reducing Maternal Stress and Enhancing Child Development Through Social Support

Childbirth
The Stages of Childbirth • The Baby's Adaptation to Labor and Delivery • The Newborn Baby's Appearance • Assessing the Newborn's Physical Condition: The Apgar Scale

Approaches to Childbirth
Natural, or Prepared, Childbirth • Home Delivery

Medical Interventions
Fetal Monitoring • Labor and Delivery Medication • Cesarean Delivery

Preterm and Low-Birth-Weight Infants
Preterm versus Small-for-Date Infants • Consequences for Caregiving • Interventions for Preterm Infants

■ **SOCIAL ISSUES: HEALTH** A Cross-National Perspective on Health Care and Other Policies for Parents and Newborn Babies

The Newborn Baby's Capacities
Reflexes • States of Arousal • Sensory Capacities • Neonatal Behavioral Assessment

■ **BIOLOGY AND ENVIRONMENT** The Mysterious Tragedy of Sudden Infant Death Syndrome

Adjusting to the New Family Unit

One fall, Yolanda and Jay enrolled in an evening section of my child development course, when Yolanda was just two months pregnant. In their early thirties, married for several years, and with their careers well under way, they had decided to have a baby. Each week, they arrived for class full of questions: "How does the baby grow before birth?" "When is each organ formed?" "Has its heart begun to beat?" "Can it hear, feel, or sense our presence?"

Most of all, Yolanda and Jay wanted to do everything possible to make sure their baby would be born healthy. Yolanda started to wonder about her diet and whether she should keep up her daily aerobic workout. And she asked me whether an aspirin for a headache, a glass of wine at dinner, or a few cups of coffee during the workday might be harmful.

In this chapter, we answer Yolanda and Jay's questions, along with a great many more that scientists have asked about the events before birth. First, we trace prenatal development, paying special attention to supports for healthy growth as well as damaging influences that threaten the child's health and survival. Because the changes taking place during these nine months are so astounding, the prenatal environment can exert a powerful, lasting impact—for better or for worse—on physical and mental health.

Next, we turn to the events of childbirth. Today, women in industrialized nations have many choices about where and how they give birth, and hospitals go to great lengths to make the arrival of a new baby a rewarding, family-centered event.

Yolanda and Jay's son Joshua reaped the benefits of his parents' careful attention to his needs during pregnancy: He was strong, alert, and healthy at birth. Nevertheless, the birth process does not always go smoothly. We will consider the pros and cons of medical interventions, such as pain-relieving drugs and surgical deliveries, designed to ease a difficult birth and protect the health of mother and baby. Our discussion also addresses the development of infants born underweight or too early. We conclude with a close look at the remarkable capacities of newborns. ●

75

Prenatal Development

3.1 List the three periods of prenatal development, and describe the major milestones of each.

The sperm and ovum that unite to form the new individual are uniquely suited for the task of reproduction. The ovum is a tiny sphere, measuring 1/175 inch in diameter—barely visible to the naked eye as a dot the size of the period at the end of this sentence. But in its microscopic world, it is a giant—the largest cell in the human body. The ovum's size makes it a perfect target for the much smaller sperm, which measure only 1/500 inch.

Conception

About once every 28 days, in the middle of a woman's menstrual cycle, an ovum bursts from one of her *ovaries,* two walnut-sized organs located deep inside her abdomen, and is drawn into one of two *fallopian tubes*—long, thin structures that lead to the hollow, softly lined uterus (see Figure 3.1). While the ovum is traveling, the spot on the ovary from which it was released, now called the *corpus luteum,* secretes hormones that prepare the lining of the uterus to receive a fertilized ovum. If pregnancy does not occur, the corpus luteum shrinks, and the lining of the uterus is discarded two weeks later with menstruation.

The male produces sperm in vast numbers—an average of 300 million a day—in the *testes,* two glands located in the *scrotum,* sacs that lie just behind the penis. In the final process of maturation, each sperm develops a tail that permits it to swim long distances, upstream in the female reproductive tract, through the *cervix* (opening of the uterus) and into the fallopian tube, where fertilization usually takes place. The journey is difficult, and many sperm die. Only 300 to 500 reach the ovum, if one happens to be present. Once in the fallopian tube, sperm live for up to six days and can lie in wait for the ovum, which survives for only one day after its release from the ovary. However, most conceptions result from intercourse occurring during a three-day period—on the day of ovulation or during the two days preceding it (Mu & Fehring, 2014).

With conception, the story of prenatal development begins to unfold. The vast changes that take place during the 38 weeks of pregnancy are usually divided into three periods: (1) the germinal period, (2) the period of the embryo, and (3) the period of the fetus. As we look at what happens in each, you may find it useful to refer to Table 3.1, which summarizes milestones of prenatal development.

Germinal Period

The germinal period lasts about two weeks, from fertilization and formation of the zygote until the tiny mass of cells drifts down and out of the fallopian tube and attaches itself to the wall

FIGURE 3.1 Female reproductive organs, showing fertilization, early cell duplication, and implantation. (From *Before We Are Born,* 9th ed., by K. L. Moore, T. V. N. Persaud, & M G. Torchia, p. 33. Copyright © 2016 Elsevier, Inc.)

1 Zygote As the zygote moves down the fallopian tube, it duplicates, at first slowly and then more rapidly.

2 Blastocyst By the fourth day, it forms a hollow, fluid-filled ball, called a blastocyst. The inner cells, called the embryonic disk, will become the new organism. The outer cells, or trophoblast, will provide protective covering.

3 Implantation At the end of the first week, the blastocyst begins to implant in the uterine lining.

CHAPTER 3 Prenatal Development, Birth, and the Newborn Baby

TABLE 3.1
Milestones of Prenatal Development

TRIMESTER	PRENATAL PERIOD	WEEKS	LENGTH AND WEIGHT	MAJOR EVENTS
First	Germinal	1		The one-celled zygote multiplies and forms a blastocyst.
		2		The blastocyst burrows into the uterine lining. Structures that feed and protect the developing organism begin to form—*amnion, chorion, yolk sac, placenta,* and *umbilical cord.*
	Embryo	3–4	¼ inch (6 mm)	A primitive brain and spinal cord appear. Heart, muscles, ribs, backbone, and digestive tract begin to develop.
		5–8	1 inch (2.5 cm); ½ ounce (4 g)	Many external body structures (face, arms, legs, toes, fingers) and internal organs form, and production and migration of neurons in the brain begin. The sense of touch starts to develop, and the embryo can move.
	Fetus	9–12	3 inches (7.6 cm); less than 1 ounce (28 g)	Rapid increase in size begins. Nervous system, organs, and muscles become organized and connected, touch sensitivity extends to most of the body, and new behavioral capacities (kicking, thumb sucking, mouth opening, and rehearsal of breathing) appear. External genitals are well-formed, and the fetus's sex is evident.
Second		13–24	12 inches (30 cm); 1.8 pounds (820 g)	The fetus continues to enlarge rapidly. In the middle of this period, the mother can feel fetal movements. Vernix and lanugo keep the fetus's skin from chapping in the amniotic fluid. Most of the brain's neurons are in place by 24 weeks. Eyes are sensitive to light, and the fetus reacts to sound.
Third		25–38	20 inches (50 cm); 7.5 pounds (3,400 g)	The fetus has a good chance of survival if born during this time. Size increases. Lungs mature. Rapid brain development, in neural connectivity and organization, enables sensory and behavioral capacities to expand. In the middle of this period, a layer of fat is added under the skin. Antibodies are transmitted from mother to fetus to protect against disease. Most fetuses rotate into an upside-down position in preparation for birth.

Source: Moore, Persaud, & Torchia, 2016a.

Photos (from top to bottom): © Claude Cortier/Photo Researchers, Inc.; © G. Moscoso/Photo Researchers, Inc.; © John Watney/Photo Researchers, Inc.; © James Stevenson/Photo Researchers, Inc.; © Lennart Nilsson, *A Child Is Born*/TT Nyhetsbyrån.

of the uterus. The zygote's first cell duplication is long and drawn out; it is not complete until about 30 hours after conception. Gradually, new cells are added at a faster rate. By the fourth day, 60 to 70 cells exist that form a hollow, fluid-filled ball called a *blastocyst* (refer again to Figure 3.1). The cells on the inside of the blastocyst, called the *embryonic disk,* will become the new organism; the outer ring of cells, termed the *trophoblast,* will become the structures that provide protective covering and nourishment.

Implantation. Between the seventh and ninth days, **implantation** occurs: The blastocyst burrows deep into the uterine lining. Surrounded by the woman's nourishing blood, it starts to grow in earnest. At first, the trophoblast (protective outer layer) multiplies fastest. It forms a membrane, called the **amnion,** that encloses the developing organism in *amniotic fluid,* which helps keep the temperature of the prenatal world constant and provides a cushion against any jolts caused by the woman's movement. A *yolk sac* emerges that produces blood cells until the developing liver, spleen, and bone marrow are mature enough to take over this function (Moore, Persaud, & Torchia, 2016a).

The events of these first two weeks are delicate and uncertain. As many as 30 percent of zygotes do not survive this period. In some, the sperm and ovum did not join properly. In others, cell

Germinal period: seventh to ninth day. The fertilized ovum duplicates rapidly, forming a hollow ball of cells, or blastocyst, by the fourth day after fertilization. Here the blastocyst, magnified thousands of times, burrows into the uterine lining between the seventh and ninth days.

By the end of the germinal period, the developing organism has found food and shelter. These dramatic beginnings take place before most mothers know they are pregnant.

Period of the Embryo

The period of the **embryo** lasts from implantation through the eighth week of pregnancy. During these brief six weeks, the most rapid prenatal changes take place as the groundwork is laid for all body structures and internal organs.

Last Half of the First Month.
In the first week of this period, the embryonic disk forms three layers of cells: (1) the *ectoderm,* which will become the nervous system and skin; (2) the *mesoderm,* from which will develop the muscles, skeleton, circulatory system, and other internal organs; and (3) the *endoderm,* which will become the digestive system, lungs, urinary tract, and glands. These three layers give rise to all parts of the body.

At first, the nervous system develops fastest. The ectoderm folds over to form the **neural tube,** or primitive spinal cord. At 3½ weeks, the top swells to form the brain. While the nervous system is developing, the heart begins to pump blood, and muscles, backbone, ribs, and digestive tract appear. At the end of the first month, the curled embryo—only ¼ inch long—consists of millions of organized groups of cells with specific functions.

The Second Month.
In the second month, growth continues rapidly. The eyes, ears, nose, jaw, and neck form. Tiny buds become arms, legs, fingers, and toes. Internal organs are more distinct: The intestines grow, the heart develops separate chambers, and the liver and spleen take over production of blood cells so that the yolk sac is no longer needed. Changing body proportions cause the embryo's posture to become more upright.

duplication never begins. By preventing implantation in these cases, nature eliminates most prenatal abnormalities (Sadler, 2014).

The Placenta and Umbilical Cord. By the end of the second week, cells of the trophoblast form another protective membrane—the **chorion,** which surrounds the amnion. From the chorion, tiny fingerlike *villi,* or blood vessels, emerge.[1] As these villi burrow into the uterine wall, the placenta starts to develop. By bringing the embryo's and mother's blood close together, the **placenta** permits food and oxygen to reach the developing organism and waste products to be carried away. A membrane forms that allows these substances to be exchanged but prevents the mother's and embryo's blood from mixing directly.

The placenta is connected to the developing organism by the **umbilical cord,** which first appears as a primitive body stalk and, during the course of pregnancy, grows to a length of 1 to 3 feet. The umbilical cord contains one large vein that delivers blood loaded with nutrients and two arteries that remove waste products. The force of blood flowing through the cord keeps it firm, so it seldom tangles while the embryo, like a space-walking astronaut, floats freely in its fluid-filled chamber (Moore, Persaud, & Torchia, 2016a).

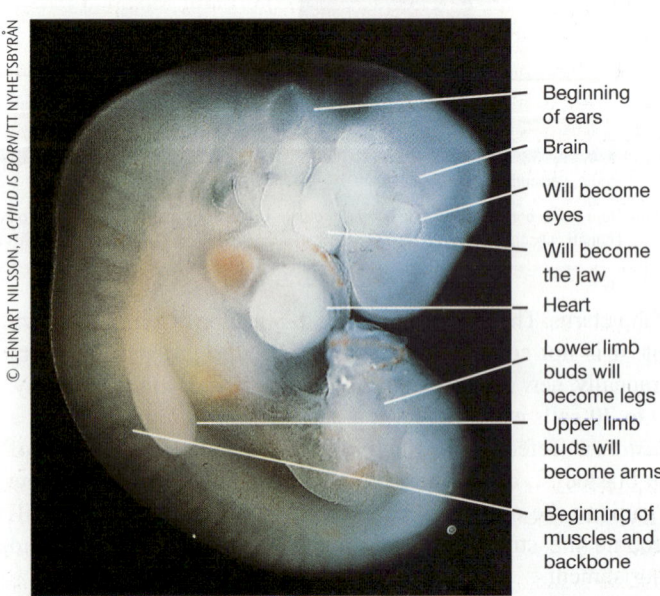

Period of the embryo: fourth week. This 4-week-old embryo is only ¼-inch long, but many body structures have begun to form.

---

[1] Recall from Table 2.3 on page 54 that *chorionic villus sampling* is the prenatal diagnostic method that can be performed earliest, at nine weeks after conception.

Period of the embryo: seventh week. The embryo's posture is more upright. Body structures—eyes, nose, arms, legs, and internal organs—are more distinct. The embryo now responds to touch and can also move, although at less than one inch long and an ounce in weight, it is still too tiny to be felt by the mother.

Period of the fetus: eleventh week. The fetus grows rapidly. At 11 weeks, the brain and muscles are better connected. The fetus can kick, bend its arms, open and close its hands and mouth, and suck its thumb. Notice the yolk sac, which shrinks as the internal organs take over its function of producing blood cells.

During the fifth week, production of *neurons* (nerve cells that store and transmit information) begins deep inside the neural tube at the astounding pace of more than 250,000 per minute (Jabès & Nelson, 2014). Once formed, neurons begin traveling along tiny threads to their permanent locations, where they will form the major parts of the brain.

By the end of this period, the embryo—about 1 inch long and ⅐ ounce in weight—can already sense its world. It responds to touch, particularly in the mouth area and on the soles of the feet. And it can move, although its tiny flutters are still too light to be felt by the mother (Moore, Persaud, & Torchia, 2016a).

Period of the Fetus

The period of the **fetus,** from the ninth week to the end of pregnancy, is the longest prenatal period. During this "growth and finishing" phase, the organism increases rapidly in size.

The Third Month.
In the third month, the organs, muscles, and nervous system start to become organized and connected. Touch sensitivity extends to most of the body (Hepper, 2015). When the brain signals, the fetus kicks, bends its arms, forms a fist, curls its toes, turns its head, opens its mouth, and even sucks its thumb, stretches, and yawns. The tiny lungs begin to expand and contract in an early rehearsal of breathing movements.

By the twelfth week, the external genitals are well-formed, and the sex of the fetus can be detected with ultrasound (Sadler, 2014). Other finishing touches appear, such as fingernails, toenails, tooth buds, and eyelids. The heartbeat can now be heard through a stethoscope.

Prenatal development is sometimes divided into **trimesters,** or three equal time periods. At the end of the third month, the *first trimester* is complete.

The Second Trimester.
By the middle of the second trimester, between 17 and 20 weeks, the new being has grown large enough that the mother can feel its movements. Already, the fetus is remarkably active—in motion nearly 30 percent of the time—which helps strengthen the joints and muscles (DiPietro et al., 2015). A white, cheeselike substance called **vernix** emerges on the skin, protecting it from chapping during the long months spent bathing in the amniotic fluid. White, downy hair called **lanugo** also appears over the entire body, helping the vernix stick to the skin.

At the end of the second trimester, many organs are well-developed. And most of the brain's billions of neurons are in place; few will be produced after this time. However, *glial cells,* which support and feed the neurons, continue to increase rapidly throughout the remaining months of pregnancy, as well as after birth. Consequently, brain weight increases tenfold from the twentieth week until birth (Roelfsema et al., 2004). At the same time, neurons begin forming *synapses,* or connections, at a rapid pace.

Brain growth means new sensory and behavioral capacities. The 20-week-old fetus can be stimulated as well as irritated by sounds. And if a doctor looks inside the uterus using fetoscopy (see Table 2.3 on page 54), fetuses try to shield their eyes from the light with their hands, indicating that sight has begun to emerge (Moore, Persaud, & Torchia, 2016a). Still, a fetus born at this time cannot survive. Its lungs are immature, and the brain cannot yet control breathing movements or body temperature.

The Third Trimester. During the final trimester, a fetus born early has a chance for survival. The point at which the baby can first survive, called the **age of viability,** occurs sometime between 22 and 26 weeks (Moore, Persaud, & Torchia, 2016a). A baby born between the seventh and eighth months, however, usually needs oxygen assistance to breathe. Although the brain's respiratory center is now mature, tiny air sacs in the lungs are not yet ready to inflate and exchange carbon dioxide for oxygen.

The brain continues to make great strides. The *cerebral cortex,* the seat of human intelligence, enlarges. As rapid gains in neural connectivity and organization continue, the fetus spends more time awake. At 20 weeks, fetal heart rate reveals no periods of alertness. But by 28 weeks, fetuses are awake about 11 percent of the time, a figure that rises to 16 percent just before birth (DiPietro et al., 1996). Between 30 and 34 weeks, fetuses show rhythmic alternations between sleep and wakefulness that gradually increase in organization (Rivkees, 2003). Around 36 weeks, synchrony between fetal heart rate and motor activity peaks: A rise in heart rate is usually followed within five seconds by a burst of motor activity (DiPietro et al., 2006, 2015). These are clear signs that coordinated neural networks are beginning to form in the brain.

By the end of pregnancy, the fetus takes on the beginnings of a personality. Fetal activity is linked to infant temperament. In one study, more active fetuses during the third trimester became 1-year-olds who could better handle frustration and 2-year-olds who were more active as well as less fearful, in that they more readily interacted with toys and with an unfamiliar adult in a laboratory (DiPietro et al., 2002). Perhaps fetal activity is an indicator of healthy neurological development, which fosters adaptability in childhood. The relationships just described, however, are modest. As we will see in Chapter 6, sensitive caregiving can modify the temperaments of children who have difficulty adapting to new experiences.

The third trimester brings greater responsiveness to external stimulation. As we will see when we discuss newborn capacities, fetuses acquire taste and odor preferences from bathing in

Period of the fetus: twenty-second week. This fetus is almost one foot long and weighs slightly more than one pound. Its movements can be felt easily by the mother and by other family members who place a hand on her abdomen. If born now, the fetus has a slim chance of survival.

Period of the fetus: thirty-sixth week. This fetus fills the uterus. To nourish it, the umbilical cord and placenta have grown large. Notice the vernix (a cheeselike substance) on the skin, which protects it from chapping. The fetus has accumulated fat to aid temperature regulation after birth. In two more weeks, it will be full-term.

and swallowing amniotic fluid (its makeup is influenced by the mother's diet). Between 23 and 30 weeks, connections form between the cerebral cortex and brain regions involved in pain sensitivity. By this time, painkillers should be used in any surgical procedures (Lee et al., 2005). Around 28 weeks, fetuses blink their eyes in reaction to nearby sounds (Saffran, Werker, & Werner, 2006). And around 30 weeks, fetuses presented with a repeated auditory stimulus against the mother's abdomen initially react with a rise in heart rate, electrical brain-wave recordings, and body movements. Then responsiveness gradually declines, indicating *habituation* (adaptation) to the sound. If a new auditory stimulus is introduced, heart rate and brain waves recover to a high level, revealing that the fetus recognizes the new sound as distinct from the original stimulus (Hepper, Dornan, & Lynch, 2012; Muenssinger et al., 2013). This indicates that fetuses can remember for at least a brief period.

Within the next six weeks, fetuses distinguish the tone and rhythm of different voices and sounds—learning that will serve as a springboard for language development. They show systematic heart-rate and brain-wave changes in response to the mother's voice versus the father's or a stranger's, to their native language (English) versus a foreign language (Mandarin Chinese), and to a simple familiar melody (descending tones) versus an unfamiliar melody (ascending tones) (Granier-Deferre et al., 2003; Kisilevsky & Hains, 2011; Kisilevsky et al., 2009; Lecanuet et al., 1993; Lee & Kisilevsky, 2013; Voegtline et al., 2013). And in one clever study, mothers read aloud Dr. Seuss's lively book *The Cat in the Hat* each day during the last six weeks of pregnancy. After birth, their infants learned to turn on recordings of the mother's voice by sucking on nipples (DeCasper & Spence, 1986). They sucked hardest to hear *The Cat in the Hat*—the sound they had come to know while still in the womb.

In the final three months, the fetus gains more than 5 pounds and grows 7 inches. In the eighth month, lanugo typically is shed. A layer of fat is added to assist with temperature regulation. The fetus also receives antibodies from the mother's blood that protect against illnesses, since the newborn's immune system will not work well until several months after birth. In the last weeks, most fetuses assume an upside-down position, partly because of the shape of the uterus and partly because the head is heavier than the feet. Growth slows, and birth is about to take place.

Ask yourself

CONNECT How is brain development related to fetal capacities and behavior? What implications do individual differences in fetal behavior have for infant temperament after birth?

APPLY Amy, two months pregnant, wonders how the embryo is being fed and what parts of the body have formed. "I don't look pregnant yet, so does that mean not much development has taken place?" she asks. How would you respond to Amy?

Prenatal Environmental Influences

3.2 Cite factors that influence the impact of teratogens, and discuss evidence on the impact of known or suspected teratogens.

3.3 Describe the impact of additional maternal factors on prenatal development.

3.4 Why is early and regular health care vital during the prenatal period?

Although the prenatal environment is far more constant than the world outside the womb, many factors can affect the embryo and fetus. Yolanda and Jay learned that parents—and society as a whole—can do a great deal to create a safe environment for development before birth.

Teratogens

The term **teratogen** refers to any environmental agent that causes damage during the prenatal period. Scientists chose this label (from the Greek word *teras*, meaning "malformation" or "monstrosity") because they first learned about harmful prenatal influences from cases in which babies had been profoundly damaged. But the harm done by teratogens is not always straightforward. It depends on the following factors:

- *Dose.* As we discuss particular teratogens, you will see that larger doses over longer time periods usually have more negative effects.
- *Heredity.* The genetic makeup of the mother and the developing organism plays an important role. Some individuals are better able than others to withstand harmful environments.
- *Other negative influences.* The presence of several negative factors at once, such as additional teratogens, poor nutrition, and lack of medical care, can worsen the impact of a harmful agent.
- *Age.* The effects of teratogens vary with the age of the organism at time of exposure. To understand this last idea, think of the *sensitive period* concept introduced in Chapter 1. A sensitive period is a limited time span in which a part of the body or a behavior is biologically prepared to develop rapidly. During that time, it is especially sensitive to its surroundings. If the environment is harmful, then damage occurs, and recovery is difficult and sometimes impossible.

Figure 3.2 on page 82 summarizes prenatal sensitive periods. In the *germinal period,* before implantation, teratogens rarely have any impact. If they do, the tiny mass of cells is usually so damaged that it dies. The *embryonic period* is the time when serious defects are most likely to occur because the foundations for all body parts are being laid down. During the *fetal period,* teratogenic damage is usually minor. However, organs such as the brain, ears, eyes, teeth, and genitals can still be strongly affected.

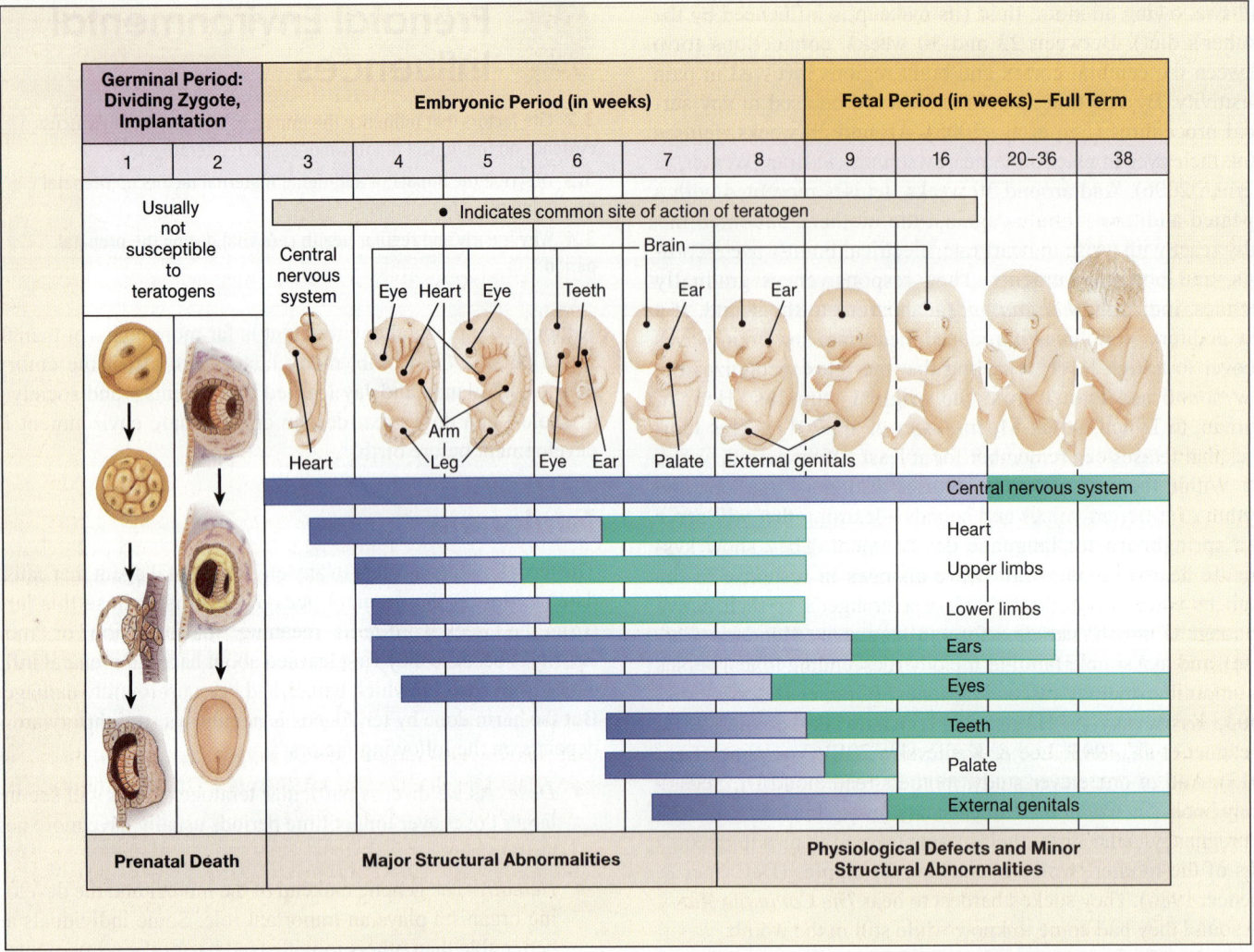

FIGURE 3.2 Sensitive periods in prenatal development. Each organ or structure has a sensitive period, during which its development may be disturbed. Blue horizontal bars indicate highly sensitive periods. Green horizontal bars indicate periods that are somewhat less sensitive to teratogens, although damage can occur. (Based on *Before We Are Born*, 9th ed., by K. L. Moore, T. V. N. Persaud, & M. G. Torchia, p. 313. Copyright © 2016 Elsevier, Inc.)

The effects of teratogens go beyond immediate physical damage. Some health effects are delayed and may not show up for decades. Furthermore, psychological consequences may occur indirectly, as a result of physical damage. For example, a defect resulting from drugs the mother took during pregnancy can affect others' reactions to the child as well as the child's ability to explore the environment. Over time, parent–child interaction, peer relations, and cognitive, emotional, and social development may suffer. Furthermore, prenatally exposed children may be less resilient in the face of environmental risks, such as single parenthood, parental emotional disturbance, or maladaptive parenting (Yumoto, Jacobson, & Jacobson, 2008). As a result, their long-term adjustment may be compromised.

Notice how an important idea about development discussed in earlier chapters is at work here: *bidirectional influences* between child and environment. Now let's look at what scientists have discovered about a variety of teratogens.

Prescription and Nonprescription Drugs. In the early 1960s, the world learned a tragic lesson about drugs and prenatal development. At that time, a sedative called *thalidomide* was widely available in Canada, Europe, and South America. When taken by mothers 4 to 6 weeks after conception, thalidomide produced gross deformities of the embryo's developing arms and legs and, less frequently, damage to the ears, heart, kidneys, and genitals. About 7,000 infants worldwide were affected (Moore, Persaud, & Torchia, 2016a). As children exposed to thalidomide grew older, many scored below average in intelligence. Perhaps the drug damaged the central nervous system directly. Or the child-rearing conditions of these severely deformed youngsters may have impaired their intellectual development.

Another medication, a synthetic hormone called *diethylstilbestrol (DES),* was widely prescribed between 1945 and 1970 to prevent miscarriages. As daughters of these mothers reached adolescence and young adulthood, they showed unusually high rates of cancer of the vagina, malformations of the uterus, and infertility. When they tried to have children, their pregnancies more often resulted in prematurity, low birth weight, and miscarriage than those of non-DES-exposed women. Young men showed an increased risk of genital abnormalities and cancer of the testes (Goodman, Schorge, & Greene, 2011; Reed & Fenton, 2013).

Currently, the most widely used potent teratogen is a vitamin A derivative called *isotretinoin,* prescribed to treat severe acne and taken by hundreds of thousands of women of childbearing age in industrialized nations. Exposure during the first trimester results in eye, ear, skull, brain, heart, and immune system abnormalities (Yook et al., 2012). U.S. regulations for prescribing isotretinoin require female users to commit to avoiding pregnancy by using two methods of birth control.

Indeed, any drug with a molecule small enough to penetrate the placental barrier can enter the embryonic or fetal bloodstream. Yet many pregnant women continue to take over-the-counter medications without consulting their doctors. Aspirin is one of the most common. Some research suggests that aspirin use is linked to brain damage leading to impaired motor control, inattention, and overactivity, though other research fails to confirm these findings (Barr et al., 1990; Kozer et al., 2003; Thompson et al., 2014; Tyler et al., 2012). Coffee, tea, cola, and cocoa contain another frequently consumed drug, caffeine. High doses increase the risk of low birth weight (Sengpiel et al., 2013). Persistent intake of antidepressant medication is associated with an elevated incidence of premature delivery, low birth weight, respiratory distress at birth, and delayed motor development, but contrary evidence exists (Grigoriadis et al., 2013; Huang et al., 2014; Robinson, 2015).

Because children's lives are involved, we must take findings like these seriously. At the same time, we cannot be sure that these frequently used drugs actually cause the problems just mentioned. Often mothers take more than one drug. If the embryo or fetus is injured, it is hard to tell which drug might be responsible or whether other factors correlated with drug taking are at fault. Until we have more information, the safest course of action is the one Yolanda took: Avoid drugs as far as possible.

Unfortunately, many women do not know that they are pregnant during the early weeks of the embryonic period, when exposure to medications (and other teratogens) can be of greatest threat. In some instances, such as antidepressant use by severely depressed mothers, the benefits of drug treatment may outweigh its risks.

Illegal Drugs. The use of highly addictive mood-altering drugs, such as cocaine and heroin, has become more widespread, especially in poverty-stricken inner-city areas, where these drugs provide a temporary escape from a daily life of hopelessness. Nearly 6 percent of U.S. pregnant women take these substances (Substance Abuse and Mental Health Services Administration, 2014).

Babies born to users of cocaine, heroin, or methadone (a less addictive drug used to wean people away from heroin) are at risk for a wide variety of problems, including prematurity, low birth weight, brain abnormalities, physical defects, breathing difficulties, and death around the time of birth (Bandstra et al., 2010; Behnke & Smith, 2013). In addition, these infants are born drug-addicted. They are often feverish and irritable and have trouble sleeping, and their cries are abnormally shrill and piercing—a common symptom among stressed newborns (Barthell & Mrozek, 2013). When mothers with many problems of their own must care for these babies, who are difficult to calm down, cuddle, and feed, behavior problems are likely to persist.

Throughout the first year, heroin- and methadone-exposed infants are less attentive to the environment than nonexposed babies, and their motor development is slow. After infancy, some children get better, while others remain jittery and inattentive (Hans & Jeremy, 2001). The kind of parenting they receive may explain why problems persist for some but not for others.

Evidence on cocaine suggests that some prenatally exposed babies develop lasting difficulties. Cocaine constricts the blood vessels, causing oxygen delivered to the developing organism to fall for 15 minutes following a high dose. It also can alter the production of neurons, formation of synaptic connections, and chemical balance in the fetus's brain. These effects may contribute to an array of cocaine-associated physical malformations, especially of the central nervous system and heart; brain hemorrhages and seizures; and growth retardation (Cain, Bornick, & Whiteman, 2013; Li et al., 2013). Several studies report perceptual, motor, attention, memory, language, and impulse-control problems that persist into adolescence (Bandstra et al., 2011; Coyle, 2013; Singer et al., 2015).

Other investigations, however, reveal no major negative effects of prenatal cocaine exposure (Ackerman, Riggins, & Black, 2010; Buckingham-Howes et al., 2013). These contradictory

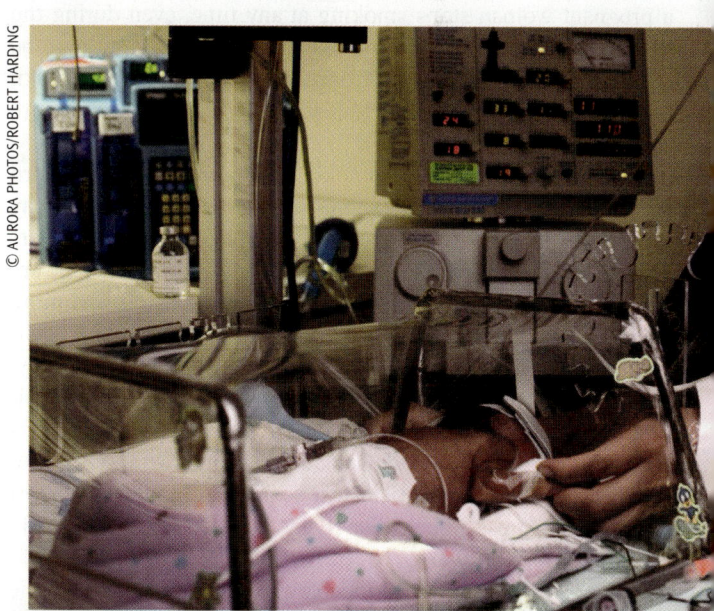

This infant, born many weeks before his due date, breathes with the aid of a respirator. Prematurity and low birth weight can result from a variety of environmental influences during pregnancy, including maternal drug and tobacco use.

findings illustrate how difficult it is to isolate the precise damage caused by illegal drugs. Cocaine users vary greatly in the amount, potency, and purity of the cocaine they ingest. Also, they often take several drugs, display other high-risk behaviors, suffer from poverty and other stresses, and engage in insensitive caregiving—factors that worsen outcomes for children (Molnar et al., 2014). But researchers have yet to determine exactly what accounts for findings of cocaine-related damage in some studies but not in others.

Another drug, marijuana, has been legalized for medical and recreational use in some U.S. states. Researchers have linked prenatal marijuana exposure to attention, memory, and academic achievement difficulties; impulsivity and overactivity; and depression as well as anger and aggression in childhood and adolescence (Behnke & Smith, 2013; Goldschmidt et al., 2004; Gray et al., 2005; Jutras-Aswad et al., 2009). As with heroin and cocaine, however, lasting consequences are not well-established. Overall, the effects of illegal drugs are far less consistent than the impact of two legal substances to which we now turn: tobacco and alcohol.

Tobacco. Although smoking has declined in Western nations, about 11 percent of U.S. women smoke during their pregnancies (Centers for Disease Control and Prevention, 2015n). The best-known effect of smoking during the prenatal period is low birth weight. But the likelihood of other serious consequences, such as miscarriage, prematurity, cleft lip and palate, blood vessel abnormalities, impaired heart rate and breathing during sleep, infant death, and asthma and cancer later in childhood, also increases (Geerts et al., 2012; Havstad et al., 2012; Howell, Coles, & Kable, 2008; Mossey et al., 2009). The more cigarettes a mother smokes, the greater the chances that her baby will be affected. If a pregnant woman stops smoking at any time, even during the third trimester, she reduces the likelihood that her infant will be born underweight and suffer from future problems (Polakowski, Akinbami, & Mendola, 2009). The earlier she stops, the more beneficial the effects.

Even when a baby of a smoking mother appears to be born in good physical condition, slight behavioral abnormalities may threaten the child's development. Newborns of smoking mothers are less attentive to sounds, display more muscle tension, are more excitable when touched and visually stimulated, and more often have colic (persistent crying). These findings suggest subtle negative effects on brain development (Espy et al., 2011; Law et al., 2003). Consistent with this view, prenatally exposed children and adolescents tend to have shorter attention spans, difficulties with impulsivity and overactivity, poorer memories, lower intelligence and achievement test scores, and higher levels of disruptive, aggressive behavior (Espy et al., 2011; Thakur et al., 2013).

Exactly how can smoking harm the fetus? Nicotine, the addictive substance in tobacco, constricts blood vessels, lessens blood flow to the uterus, and causes the placenta to grow abnormally. This reduces the transfer of nutrients, so the fetus gains weight poorly. Also, nicotine raises the concentration of carbon monoxide in the bloodstreams of both mother and fetus. Carbon monoxide displaces oxygen from red blood cells, damaging the central nervous system and slowing fetal body growth (Behnke & Smith, 2013). Other toxic chemicals in tobacco, such as cyanide and cadmium, contribute to its damaging effects.

From one-third to one-half of nonsmoking pregnant women are "passive smokers" because their husbands, relatives, or co-workers use cigarettes. Passive smoking is also related to low birth weight, infant death, childhood respiratory illnesses, and possible long-term attention, learning, and behavior problems (Best, 2009; Hawsawi, Bryant, & Goodfellow, 2015). Clearly, expectant mothers should avoid smoke-filled environments.

Alcohol. In his moving book *The Broken Cord,* Michael Dorris (1989), a Dartmouth College anthropology professor, described what it was like to rear his adopted son Adam, whose biological mother drank heavily throughout pregnancy and died of alcohol poisoning shortly after his birth. A Sioux Indian, Adam was born with **fetal alcohol spectrum disorder (FASD),** a term that encompasses a range of physical, mental, and behavioral outcomes caused by prenatal alcohol exposure. Children with FASD are given one of three diagnoses, which vary in severity:

1. **Fetal alcohol syndrome (FAS),** distinguished by (a) slow physical growth, (b) a pattern of three facial abnormalities (short eyelid openings; a thin upper lip; a smooth or flattened philtrum, or indentation running from the bottom of the nose to the center of the upper lip), and (c) brain injury, evident in a small head and impairment in at least three areas of functioning—for example, memory, language and communication, attention span and activity level (overactivity), planning and reasoning, motor coordination, or social skills. Other defects—of the eyes, ears, nose, throat, heart, genitals, urinary tract, or immune system—may also be present. Adam was diagnosed as having FAS. As is typical for this disorder, his mother drank heavily throughout pregnancy.

2. **Partial fetal alcohol syndrome (p-FAS),** characterized by (a) two of the three facial abnormalities just mentioned and (b) brain injury, again evident in at least three areas of impaired functioning. Mothers of children with p-FAS generally drank alcohol in smaller quantities, and children's defects vary with the timing and length of alcohol exposure. Furthermore, recent evidence suggests that paternal alcohol use around the time of conception can alter gene expression, thereby contributing to symptoms (Alati et al., 2013; Ouko et al., 2009).

3. **Alcohol-related neurodevelopmental disorder (ARND),** in which at least three areas of mental functioning are impaired, despite typical physical growth and absence of facial abnormalities. Again, prenatal alcohol exposure, though confirmed, is less pervasive than in FAS (Mattson, Crocker, & Nguyen, 2012).

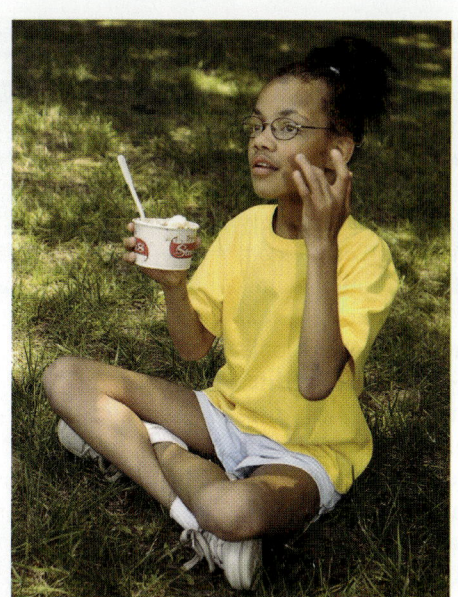

Left photo: This 5-year-old's mother drank heavily during pregnancy. The child's widely spaced eyes, thin upper lip, and flattened philtrum are typical of fetal alcohol syndrome (FAS). *Right photo:* This 12-year-old has the small head and facial abnormalities of FAS. She also shows the cognitive impairments and slow growth that accompany the disorder.

Even when provided with enriched diets, FAS babies fail to catch up in physical size during infancy or childhood. Mental impairment associated with all three FASD diagnoses is also permanent: In his teens and twenties, Adam had trouble concentrating and keeping a routine job, and he suffered from poor judgment. For example, he would buy something and not wait for change or would wander off in the middle of a task. He died at age 23, after being hit by a car.

The more alcohol a woman consumes during pregnancy, the poorer the child's motor coordination, speed of information processing, reasoning, and intelligence and achievement test scores during the preschool and school years (Burden, Jacobson, & Jacobson, 2005; Mattson, Calarco, & Lang, 2006). In adolescence and early adulthood, FASD is associated with persisting attention and motor-coordination deficits, poor school performance, trouble with the law, inappropriate social and sexual behaviors, alcohol and drug abuse, and lasting mental health problems, including depression and high emotional reactivity to stress (Bertrand & Dang, 2012; Hellemans et al., 2010; Roszel, 2015).

How does alcohol produce its devastating effects? First, it interferes with production and migration of neurons in the primitive neural tube. Brain-imaging research reveals reduced brain size, damage to many brain structures, and abnormalities in brain functioning, including electrical and chemical activity involved in transferring messages from one part of the brain to another (de la Monte & Kril, 2014; Memo et al., 2013). Second, animal research reveals widespread epigenetic changes in response to alcohol consumption, including altered methylation of many genes, that contribute to deficits in brain functioning (Kleiber et al., 2014). Third, the body uses large quantities of oxygen to metabolize alcohol. A pregnant woman's heavy drinking draws away oxygen that the developing organism needs for cell growth.

About 25 percent of U.S. mothers report drinking at some time during their pregnancies. As with heroin and cocaine, alcohol abuse is higher in poverty-stricken women. It is especially high among Native Americans, for whom the risk of a baby born with FAS is 20 to 25 times greater than for the rest of the U.S. population (Rentner, Dixon, & Lengel, 2012). Unfortunately, when affected girls later become pregnant, the poor judgment caused by the syndrome often prevents them from understanding why they themselves should avoid alcohol. Thus, the tragic cycle is likely to be repeated in the next generation.

How much alcohol is safe during pregnancy? Even mild drinking, less than one drink per day, is associated with reduced head size (a measure of brain development), slow body growth, and behavior problems (Flak et al., 2014; Martinez-Frias et al., 2004). Recall that other factors—both genetic and environmental—can make some fetuses more vulnerable to teratogens. Therefore, no amount of alcohol is safe. Couples planning a pregnancy and expectant mothers should avoid alcohol entirely.

Radiation. Defects due to ionizing radiation were tragically apparent in children born to pregnant women who survived the bombing of Hiroshima and Nagasaki during World War II. Similar abnormalities surfaced in the nine months following the 1986 Chernobyl, Ukraine, nuclear power plant accident. After each disaster, the incidence of miscarriage and babies born with brain damage, physical deformities, and slow physical growth rose dramatically (Double et al., 2011; Schull, 2003). Evacuation of residents in areas near the Japanese nuclear facility damaged by the March 2011 earthquake and tsunami was intended to prevent these devastating outcomes.

Even when a radiation-exposed baby seems normal, problems may appear later. For example, even low-level radiation, resulting from industrial leakage or medical X-rays, can increase the risk of childhood cancer (Fushiki, 2013). In middle childhood, prenatally exposed Chernobyl children had abnormal brain-wave activity, lower intelligence test scores, and rates of language and emotional disorders two to three times greater than those of nonexposed children in the surrounding area. Furthermore, the more tension parents reported, due to forced evacuation from their homes and worries about living in irradiated areas, the poorer their children's emotional functioning (Loganovskaja & Loganovsky, 1999; Loganovsky et al., 2008).

Stressful rearing conditions seemed to combine with the damaging effects of prenatal radiation to impair children's development.

Environmental Pollution. In industrialized nations, an astounding number of potentially dangerous chemicals are released into the environment, and many new pollutants are introduced each year. When 10 newborns were randomly selected from U.S. hospitals for analysis of umbilical cord blood, researchers uncovered a startling array of industrial contaminants—287 in all (Houlihan et al., 2005). They concluded that many babies are "born polluted" by chemicals that not only impair prenatal development but increase the chances of life-threatening diseases and health problems later on.

Certain pollutants cause severe prenatal damage. In the 1950s, an industrial plant released waste containing high levels of *mercury* into a bay providing seafood and water for the town of Minamata, Japan. Many children born at the time displayed physical deformities, intellectual disability, abnormal speech, difficulty in chewing and swallowing, and uncoordinated movements. High levels of prenatal mercury exposure disrupt production and migration of neurons, causing widespread brain damage (Caserta et al., 2013; Hubbs-Tait et al., 2005). Prenatal mercury exposure from maternal seafood diets predicts deficits in speed of cognitive processing, attention, and memory during the school years (Boucher et al., 2010, 2012; Lam et al., 2013). Pregnant women are wise to avoid eating long-lived predatory fish, such as swordfish, albacore tuna, and shark, which are heavily contaminated with mercury.

For many years, *polychlorinated biphenyls (PCBs)* were used to insulate electrical equipment, until research showed that, like mercury, they entered waterways and the food supply. In Taiwan, prenatal exposure to high levels of PCBs in rice oil resulted in low birth weight, discolored skin, deformities of the gums and nails, brain-wave abnormalities, and delayed cognitive development (Chen & Hsu, 1994; Chen et al., 1994). Steady, low-level PCB exposure is also harmful. Women who frequently ate PCB-contaminated fish, compared with those who ate little or no fish, had infants with lower birth weights, smaller heads, persisting attention and memory difficulties, and lower intelligence test scores in childhood (Boucher, Muckle, & Bastien, 2009; Polanska, Jurewicz, & Hanke, 2013; Stewart et al., 2008).

Another teratogen, *lead,* is present in paint flaking off the walls of old buildings and in certain materials used in industrial occupations. High levels of prenatal lead exposure are related to prematurity, low birth weight, brain damage, and a wide variety of physical defects. Even at low levels, affected infants and children show slightly poorer mental and motor development (Caserta et al., 2013; Jedrychowski et al., 2009).

Prenatal exposure to *dioxins*—toxic compounds resulting from incineration—is linked to thyroid abnormalities in infancy and to an increased incidence of breast and uterine cancers in women, perhaps through altering hormone levels (ten Tusscher & Koppe, 2004). Even tiny amounts of dioxin in the paternal bloodstream cause a dramatic change in the sex ratio of offspring: Affected men father nearly twice as many girls as boys (Ishihara et al., 2007). Dioxin seems to impair the fertility of Y-bearing sperm prior to conception.

Finally, persistent air pollution inflicts substantial prenatal harm. Exposure to traffic-related fumes and smog is associated with reduced infant head size, low birth weight, elevated infant death rates, impaired lung and immune-system functioning, and later respiratory illnesses (Proietti et al., 2013; Ritz et al., 2014).

Infectious Disease. About 5 percent of women in industrialized nations catch an infectious disease while pregnant. Although most of these illnesses, such as the common cold, seem to have no impact, a few—as Table 3.2 illustrates—can cause extensive damage.

Viruses. In the mid-1960s, a worldwide epidemic of *rubella* (three-day, or German, measles) led to the birth of more than 20,000 American babies with serious defects and to 13,000 fetal and newborn deaths. Consistent with the sensitive period concept, the greatest damage occurs when rubella strikes during the embryonic period. More than 50 percent of infants whose mothers become ill during that time show deafness; eye

This pregnant woman wears a face mask as protection against Singapore's smog, which occasionally hits life-threatening levels. Prolonged exposure to polluted air poses serious risks to prenatal development.

TABLE 3.2
Effects of Some Infectious Diseases During Pregnancy

DISEASE	MISCARRIAGE	PHYSICAL MALFORMATIONS	INTELLECTUAL DISABILITY	LOW BIRTH WEIGHT AND PREMATURITY
VIRAL				
Acquired immune deficiency syndrome (AIDS)	✔	?	✔	✔
Chickenpox	✔	✔	✔	✔
Cytomegalovirus	✔	✔	✔	✔
Herpes simplex 2 (genital herpes)	✔	✔	✔	✔
Mumps	✔	✗	✗	✗
Rubella (German measles)	✔	✔	✔	✔
BACTERIAL				
Chlamydia	✔	?	✗	✔
Syphilis	✔	✔	✔	?
Tuberculosis	✔	?	✔	✔
PARASITIC				
Malaria	✔	✗	✗	✔
Toxoplasmosis	✔	✔	✔	✔

✔ = established finding, ✗ = no present evidence, ? = possible effect that is not clearly established.
Sources: Kliegman et al., 2015; Waldorf & McAdams, 2013.

deformities, including cataracts; heart, genital, urinary, intestinal, bone, and dental defects; and intellectual disability. Infection during the fetal period is less harmful, but low birth weight, hearing loss, and bone defects may still occur. The organ damage inflicted by prenatal rubella often leads to lifelong health problems, including severe mental illness, diabetes, cardiovascular disease, and thyroid and immune-system dysfunction in adulthood (Duszak, 2009; Waldorf & McAdams, 2013). Routine vaccination in infancy and childhood has made new rubella outbreaks unlikely in industrialized nations. But over 100,000 cases of prenatal infection continue to occur each year, primarily in developing countries in Africa and Asia with weak or absent immunization programs (World Health Organization, 2015e).

The *human immunodeficiency virus (HIV)*, which can lead to *acquired immune deficiency syndrome (AIDS)*, a disease that destroys the immune system, has infected increasing numbers of women over the past three decades. In developing countries, where 95 percent of new infections occur, more than half affect women. In South Africa, for example, 30 percent of all pregnant women are HIV-positive (South Africa Department of Health, 2013). Untreated HIV-infected expectant mothers pass the deadly virus to the developing organism 10 to 20 percent of the time.

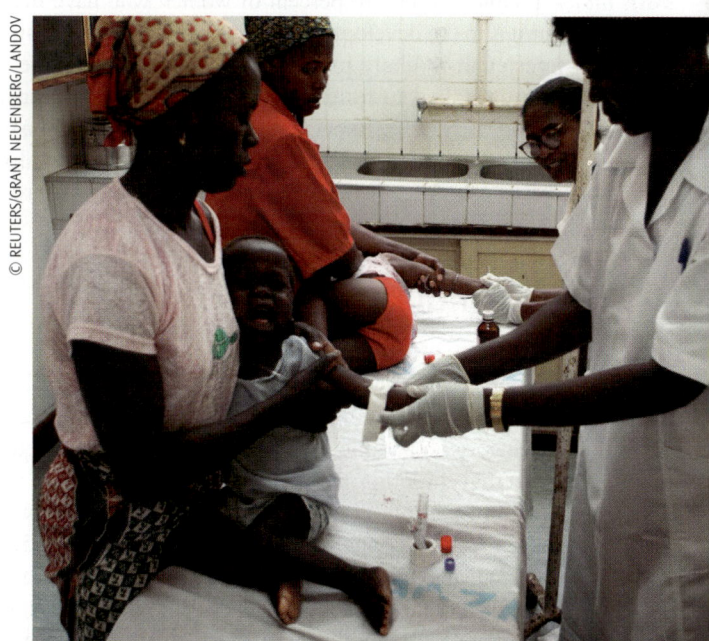

Babies are tested for the HIV virus in a clinic in Mozambique, Africa. Prenatal treatment with antiretroviral drugs reduces transmission of AIDS from mother to child to less than 1 to 2 percent.

AIDS progresses rapidly in infants. By 6 months, weight loss, diarrhea, and repeated respiratory illnesses are common. The virus also causes brain damage, as indicated by seizures, gradual loss in brain weight, and delayed cognitive and motor development. Most untreated prenatal AIDS babies die by age 3 (Siberry, 2015). Antiretroviral drug therapy reduces prenatal transmission to less than 1 to 2 percent, with no harmful consequences to the fetus. These medications have led to a dramatic decline in prenatally acquired HIV in Western nations. Recently, several babies born with HIV for whom aggressive retroviral treatment began within 2 days after birth appeared free of the disease (McNeil, 2014). Although distribution is increasing, antiretroviral drugs remain unavailable to at least one-third of HIV-infected pregnant women in developing countries (World Health Organization, 2015a).

As Table 3.2 reveals, the developing organism is especially sensitive to the family of herpes viruses, for which no vaccine or treatment exists. Among these, *cytomegalovirus* (the most frequent prenatal infection, transmitted through respiratory or sexual contact) and *herpes simplex 2* (which is sexually transmitted) are especially dangerous. In both, the virus invades the mother's genital tract, infecting babies either during pregnancy or at birth.

Bacterial and Parasitic Diseases. Table 3.2 also includes several bacterial and parasitic diseases. Among the most common is *toxoplasmosis,* caused by a parasite found in many animals. Pregnant women may become infected from handling contaminated soil while gardening, having contact with the feces of infected cats, or eating raw or undercooked meat or unwashed fruits and vegetables. About 40 percent of women who have the disease transmit it to the developing organism. If it strikes during the first trimester, it is likely to cause eye and brain damage. Later infection is linked to mild visual and cognitive impairments (Wallon et al., 2013). Expectant mothers can avoid toxoplasmosis by making sure that the meat they eat is well-cooked, having pet cats checked for the disease, and turning over the care of litter boxes and the garden to other family members.

Other Maternal Factors

Besides avoiding teratogens, expectant parents can support prenatal development in other ways. In healthy, physically fit women, regular moderate to vigorous exercise, including walking, swimming, biking, or an aerobic workout, is related to improved fetal cardiovascular functioning, higher birth weight, and a reduction in risk of certain complications, such as pregnancy-induced maternal diabetes and premature birth (Artal, 2015; Jukic et al., 2012). Most women, however, do not engage in sufficient exercise during pregnancy to promote their own and their baby's health. An expectant mother who remains fit experiences fewer physical discomforts in the final weeks.

In the following sections, we examine other maternal factors—nutrition, emotional stress, blood type, and age.

Nutrition. During the prenatal period, when children are growing more rapidly than at any other time, they depend totally on the mother for nutrients. A healthy diet that results in a weight gain of 25 to 30 pounds (10 to 13.5 kilograms) helps ensure the health of mother and baby.

Prenatal malnutrition can cause serious damage to the central nervous system. The poorer the mother's diet, the greater the loss in brain weight, especially if malnutrition occurred during the last trimester. During that time, the brain is increasing rapidly in size, and a maternal diet high in all the basic nutrients is necessary for it to reach its full potential. An inadequate diet during pregnancy can also distort the structure of the liver, kidney, pancreas, and other organs, predisposing the individual to later disease. As Figure 3.3 illustrates, large-scale studies reveal a consistent link between low birth weight and high blood pressure, cardiovascular disease, and diabetes in adulthood, even after many other prenatal and postnatal health risks were controlled (Johnson & Schoeni, 2011).

Because poor nutrition suppresses development of the immune system, prenatally malnourished babies frequently catch respiratory illnesses. In addition, they are often irritable and unresponsive to stimulation. In poverty-stricken families, these effects quickly combine with a stressful home life. With age, delays in motor, attention, and memory development, low intelligence test scores, and serious learning problems become more apparent (Monk, Georgieff, & Osterholm, 2013).

Many studies show that providing pregnant women with an adequate quantity of food has a substantial impact on the health of their newborn babies. Vitamin–mineral enrichment is also crucial. For example, taking a folic acid supplement around the

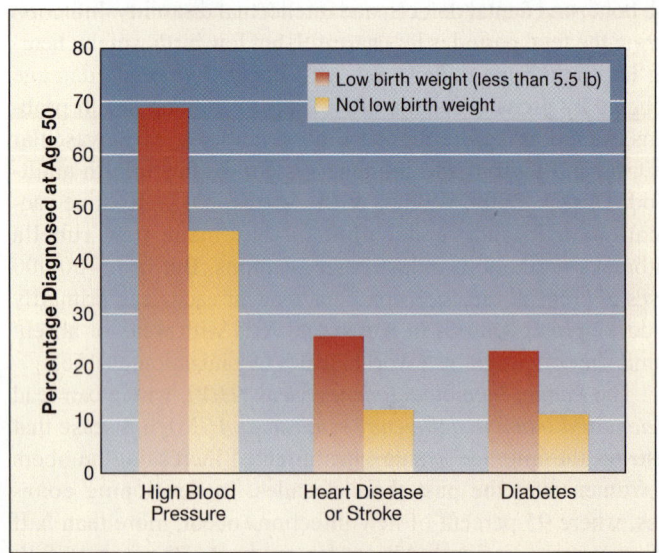

FIGURE 3.3 Relationship of low birth weight to disease risk in adulthood. In a follow-up of more than 2,000 U.S. births at age 50, low birth weight was associated with a greatly increased incidence of high blood pressure, heart disease, stroke, and diabetes after many other prenatal and postnatal health risks were controlled. (Based on Johnson & Schoeni, 2011.)

time of conception reduces by more than 70 percent abnormalities of the neural tube, such as *anencephaly* and *spina bifida* (see Table 2.3 on page 54). Folic acid supplementation early in pregnancy also lessens the risk of other physical defects, including cleft lip and palate, circulatory system and urinary tract abnormalities, and limb deformities. Furthermore, adequate folic acid intake during the last 10 weeks of pregnancy cuts in half premature delivery and low birth weight (Goh & Koren, 2008; Hovdenak & Haram, 2012).

Because of these findings, U.S. government guidelines recommend that all women of childbearing age consume 0.4 milligram of folic acid per day (Talaulikar & Arulkumaran, 2011). Because many U.S. pregnancies are unplanned, government regulations mandate that bread, flour, rice, pasta, and other grain products be fortified with folic acid.

Although prenatal malnutrition is highest in poverty-stricken regions of the world, it is not limited to developing countries. The U.S. Special Supplemental Food Program for Women, Infants, and Children (WIC), which provides food packages and nutrition education to low-income pregnant women, reaches about 90 percent of those who qualify because of their extremely low incomes (U.S. Department of Agriculture, 2015b). But many U.S. women who need nutrition intervention are not eligible for WIC.

Emotional Stress. When women experience severe emotional stress during pregnancy, their babies are at risk for a wide variety of difficulties. Intense anxiety—especially during the first two trimesters—is associated with higher rates of miscarriage, prematurity, low birth weight, infant respiratory and digestive illnesses, colic (persistent infant crying), sleep disturbances, and irritability during the child's first three years (Dunkel-Shetter & Lobel, 2012; Field, 2011; Lazinski, Shea, & Steiner, 2008). Prenatal stressors consistently found to impair later physical and psychological well-being include chronic strain due to poverty; major negative life events such as divorce or death of a family member; disasters such as earthquakes or terrorist attacks; and fears specific to pregnancy and childbirth, including persistent anxiety about the health and survival of the baby and oneself. It is important to note that mild to moderate occasional stress has no adverse impact.

How can severe maternal stress affect the developing organism? To understand this process, list changes you sensed in your own body the last time you were under substantial stress. When we experience fear and anxiety, stress hormones released into our bloodstream—such as *epinephrine* (adrenaline) and *cortisol*, known as the "flight or fight" hormones—cause us to be "poised for action." Large amounts of blood are sent to parts of the body involved in the defensive response—the brain, the heart, and the muscles in the arms, legs, and trunk. Blood flow to other organs, including the uterus, is reduced. As a result, the fetus is deprived of a full supply of oxygen and nutrients.

Maternal stress hormones also cross the placenta, causing a dramatic rise in fetal stress hormones (evident in the amniotic fluid) and, therefore, in fetal heart rate, blood pressure, blood glucose, and activity level (Kinsella & Monk, 2009; Weinstock, 2008). Excessive fetal stress may permanently alter fetal neurological functioning, thereby heightening stress reactivity in later life. Recall from Chapter 2 that epigenetic changes (gene methylation) may be partly or largely responsible. Infants and children of mothers who experienced severe prenatal anxiety display cortisol levels that are either abnormally high or abnormally low, both of which signal reduced physiological capacity to manage stress.

Maternal emotional stress during pregnancy is associated with diverse negative behavioral outcomes in children and adolescents, including anxiety, short attention span, anger, aggression, overactivity, and lower intelligence test scores, above and beyond the impact of other risks, such as maternal smoking during pregnancy, low birth weight, postnatal maternal anxiety, and low SES (Coall et al., 2015; Monk, Georgieff, & Osterholm, 2013). Furthermore, similar to prenatal malnutrition, overwhelming the fetus with maternal stress hormones heightens susceptibility to later illness, including cardiovascular disease and diabetes in adulthood (Reynolds, 2013).

But stress-related prenatal complications are greatly reduced when mothers have partners, other family members, and friends who offer social support (Bloom et al., 2013; Luecken et al., 2013). The relationship of social support to positive pregnancy outcomes and subsequent child development is particularly strong for economically disadvantaged women, who often lead highly stressful lives (see the Social Issues: Health box on page 90).

Rh Factor Incompatibility. When inherited blood types of mother and fetus differ, serious problems sometimes result. The most common cause of these difficulties is **Rh factor incompatibility.** When the mother is Rh-negative (lacks the Rh blood protein) and the father is Rh-positive (has the protein), the baby may inherit the father's Rh-positive blood type. If even a little of a fetus's Rh-positive blood crosses the placenta into the Rh-negative mother's bloodstream, she begins to form antibodies to the foreign Rh protein. If these enter the fetus's system, they destroy red blood cells, reducing the oxygen supply to organs and tissues. Intellectual disability, miscarriage, heart damage, and infant death can occur.

It takes time for the mother to produce Rh antibodies, so firstborn children are rarely affected. The danger increases with each additional pregnancy. Fortunately, Rh incompatibility can be prevented in most cases. After the birth of each Rh-positive baby, Rh-negative mothers are routinely given a vaccine to prevent the buildup of antibodies.

Maternal Age. In Chapter 2, we noted that women who delay childbearing until their thirties or forties face increased risk of infertility, miscarriage, and babies with chromosomal defects. Are other pregnancy complications more common for older mothers? Research indicates that healthy women in their thirties have about the same rates as those in their twenties. Thereafter,

Social Issues: Health

The Nurse–Family Partnership: Reducing Maternal Stress and Enhancing Child Development Through Social Support

At age 17, Denise—an unemployed high-school dropout living with her disapproving parents—gave birth to Tara. Having no one to turn to for help during pregnancy and beyond, Denise felt overwhelmed and anxious much of the time. Tara was premature and cried uncontrollably, slept erratically, and suffered from frequent minor illnesses throughout her first year. When she reached school age, she had trouble keeping up academically, and her teachers described her as distractible, unable to sit still, angry, and uncooperative.

The Nurse–Family Partnership—currently implemented in hundreds of counties across 43 U.S. states, in six tribal communities, in the U.S. Virgin Islands, and internationally in Australia, Canada, the Netherlands, and the United Kingdom—is a voluntary home visiting program for first-time, low-income expectant mothers like Denise. Its goals are to reduce pregnancy and birth complications, promote competent early caregiving, and improve family conditions, thereby protecting children from lasting adjustment difficulties.

A registered nurse visits the home weekly during the first month after enrollment, twice a month during the remainder of pregnancy and through the middle of the child's second year, and then monthly until age 2. In these sessions, the nurse provides the mother with intensive social support—a sympathetic ear; assistance in accessing health and other community services and the help of family members (especially fathers and grandmothers); and encouragement to finish high school, find work, and engage in future family planning.

To evaluate the program's effectiveness, researchers randomly assigned large samples of mothers at risk for high prenatal stress (due to teenage pregnancy, poverty, and other negative life conditions) to nurse-visiting or comparison conditions (just prenatal care, or prenatal care plus infant referral for developmental problems). Families were followed

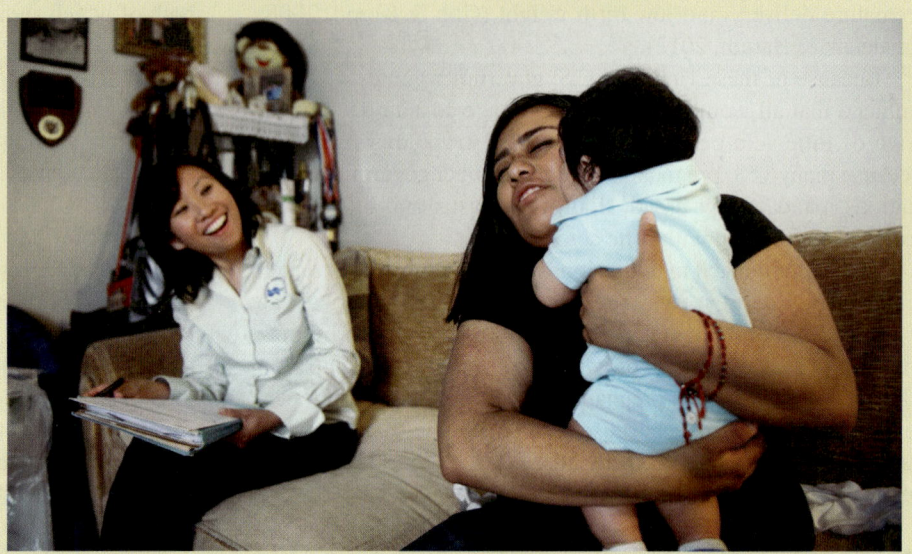

The Nurse–Family Partnership provides this first-time, low-income mother with regular home visits from a registered nurse. In follow-up research, children of home-visited mothers developed more favorably—cognitively, emotionally, and socially—than comparison children.

through their child's school-age years and, in one experiment, into adolescence (Kitzman et al., 2010; Olds et al., 2004, 2007; Rubin et al., 2011).

As kindergartners, Nurse–Family Partnership children obtained higher language and intelligence test scores. And at both ages 6 and 9, the children of home-visited mothers in the poorest mental health during pregnancy exceeded comparison children in academic achievement and displayed fewer behavior problems. Furthermore, from their baby's birth on, home-visited mothers were on a more favorable life course: They had fewer subsequent births, longer intervals between their first and second births, more frequent contact with the child's father, more stable intimate partnerships, less welfare dependence, and a greater sense of control over their lives—key factors in reducing subsequent maternal stress and in protecting children's development. Perhaps for these reasons, adolescent children of home-visited mothers continued to be advantaged in

academic achievement and reported less alcohol use and drug-taking than comparison-group agemates.

Other findings revealed that professional nurses, compared with trained paraprofessionals, were far more effective in preventing outcomes associated with prenatal stress, including high infant fearfulness to novel stimuli and delayed mental development (Olds et al., 2002). Nurses were probably more proficient in individualizing program guidelines to fit the strengths and challenges faced by each family. They also might have had unique legitimacy as experts in the eyes of stressed mothers, more easily convincing them to take steps to reduce pregnancy complications that can trigger persisting developmental problems—such as those Tara displayed.

The Nurse–Family Partnership is highly cost-effective (Miller, 2015). For $1 spent, it saves more than five times as much in public spending on pregnancy complications, preterm births, and child and youth health, learning, and behavior problems.

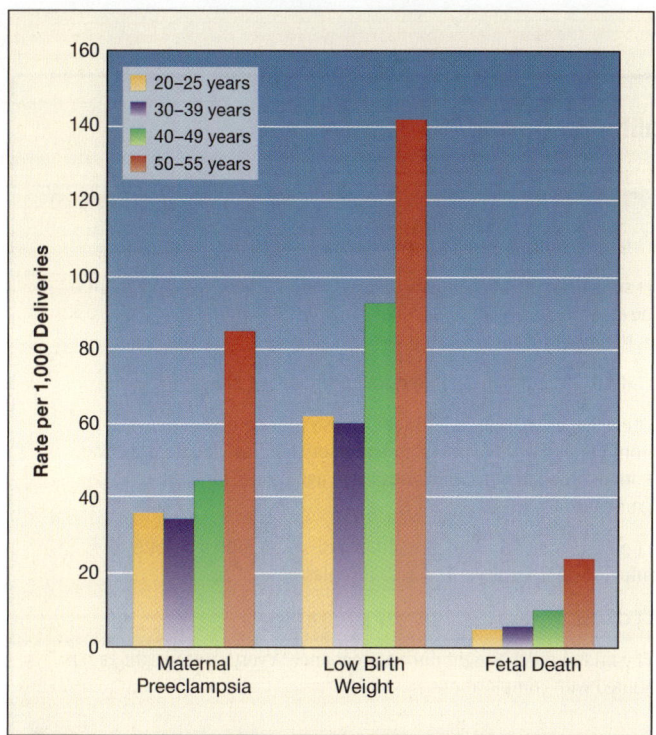

FIGURE 3.4 Relationship of maternal age to prenatal and birth complications. Complications increase after age 40, with a sharp rise between 50 and 55 years. See elsewhere on this page for a description of preeclampsia. (Based on Salihu et al., 2003.)

as Figure 3.4 reveals, complication rates increase, with a sharp rise among women age 50 to 55—an age at which, because of menopause (end of menstruation) and aging reproductive organs, few women can conceive naturally (Salihu et al., 2003; Usta & Nassar, 2008).

In the case of teenage mothers, does physical immaturity cause prenatal complications? As we will see in Chapter 11, infants born to teenagers have a higher rate of problems, but not directly because of maternal age. Most pregnant teenagers come from low-income backgrounds, where stress, poor nutrition, and health problems are common. Also, many are afraid to seek medical care. And in the United States, although the Affordable Care Act has greatly increased health insurance for pregnant adolescents, not all have full coverage.

LOOK and LISTEN

> List prenatal environmental factors that can compromise later academic performance and social adjustment. Ask several adults who hope someday to be parents to explain what they know about each factor. How great is their need for prenatal education?

The Importance of Prenatal Health Care

Yolanda's pregnancy, like most others, was free of complications. But unexpected difficulties can arise, especially if mothers have health problems. For example, the 5 percent of pregnant women who have diabetes need careful monitoring. Extra glucose in the diabetic mother's bloodstream causes the fetus to grow larger than average, making pregnancy and birth problems more common. Maternal high blood glucose also compromises prenatal brain development: It is linked to poorer memory and learning in infancy and early childhood (Riggins et al., 2009). Another complication, experienced by 5 to 10 percent of pregnant women, is *preeclampsia* (sometimes called *toxemia*), in which blood pressure increases sharply and the face, hands, and feet swell in the last half of pregnancy. If untreated, preeclampsia can cause convulsions in the mother and fetal death. Usually, hospitalization, bed rest, and drugs can lower blood pressure to a safe level (Vest & Cho, 2012). If not, the baby must be delivered at once.

Unfortunately, 6 percent of pregnant women in the United States wait until after the first trimester to seek prenatal care or receive none at all. Inadequate care is far more common among adolescent and low-income, ethnic minority mothers. Their infants are three times as likely to be born underweight and five times as likely to die as are babies of mothers who receive early medical attention (Child Trends, 2015c). Although government-sponsored health services for low-income pregnant women have expanded, some do not qualify and must pay for at least part of their care. As we will see when we take up birth complications, in nations where affordable medical care is universally available, such as Australia, Canada, Japan, and European countries, late-care pregnancies and maternal and infant health problems are greatly reduced.

Besides financial hardship, some mothers have other reasons for not seeking early prenatal care. These include *situational barriers* (difficulty finding a doctor, getting an appointment, and arranging transportation) and *personal barriers* (psychological stress, the demands of taking care of other young children, family crises, and ambivalence about the pregnancy). Many also engage in high-risk behaviors, such as smoking and drug abuse, which they do not want to reveal to health professionals (Kitsantas, Gaffney, & Cheema, 2012). These women, who receive little or no prenatal care, are among those who need it most!

Clearly, public education about the importance of early and sustained prenatal care for all pregnant women is badly needed. For women who are young, less-educated, low-income, or under stress and therefore at risk for inadequate prenatal care, assistance in making appointments, drop-in child-care centers, and free or low-cost transportation are vital.

Culturally sensitive health-care practices are also helpful. In a strategy called *group prenatal care,* after each medical checkup, trained leaders provide ethnic minority expectant mothers with a group discussion session, which is conducted in their native language and encourages them to talk about important health issues. Compared to mothers receiving traditional brief appointments with little opportunity to ask questions, participants engaged in more health-promoting behaviors and gave birth to babies with a reduced incidence of

Applying what we Know

Do's and Don'ts for a Healthy Pregnancy

DO	DON'T
Do make sure that you have been vaccinated against infectious diseases that are dangerous to the embryo and fetus, such as rubella, before you get pregnant. Most vaccinations are not safe during pregnancy.	Don't take any drugs without consulting your doctor.
Do see a doctor as soon as you suspect that you are pregnant, and continue to get regular medical checkups throughout pregnancy.	Don't smoke. If you have already smoked during part of your pregnancy, cut down or, better yet, quit. If other members of your family smoke, ask them to quit or to smoke outside.
Do eat a well-balanced diet and take vitamin–mineral supplements, as prescribed by your doctor, both prior to and during pregnancy. Gain 25 to 30 pounds gradually.	Don't drink alcohol from the time you decide to get pregnant.
Do obtain literature from your doctor, library, or bookstore about prenatal development. Ask your doctor about anything that concerns you.	Don't engage in activities that might expose your embryo or fetus to environmental hazards, such as radiation or chemical pollutants. If you work in an occupation that involves these agents, ask for a safer assignment or a leave of absence.
Do keep physically fit through moderate exercise. If possible, join a special exercise class for expectant mothers.	Don't engage in activities that might expose your embryo or fetus to harmful infectious diseases, such as toxoplasmosis.
Do avoid emotional stress. If you are a single expectant mother, find a relative or friend on whom you can rely for emotional support.	Don't choose pregnancy as a time to go on a diet.
Do get plenty of rest. An overtired mother is at risk for pregnancy complications.	Don't gain too much weight during pregnancy. A very large weight gain is associated with complications.
Do enroll in a prenatal and childbirth education class with your partner or other companion. When parents know what to expect, the nine months before birth can be one of the most joyful times of life.	

prematurity and low birth weight (Tandon et al., 2012). Refer to Applying What We Know above, which lists "do's and don'ts" for a healthy pregnancy, based on our discussion of the prenatal environment.

Expectant mothers are invited to ask questions during a group prenatal care session. Ethnic minority mothers who receive culturally sensitive prenatal care engage in more health-promoting behaviors and have healthier newborns.

Ask yourself

CONNECT Using what you learned about research strategies in Chapter 1, explain why it is difficult to determine the prenatal effects of many environmental agents, such as drugs and pollution.

APPLY Nora, pregnant for the first time, believes that a few cigarettes and a glass of wine a day won't be harmful. Provide Nora with research-based reasons for not smoking or drinking.

REFLECT If you had to choose five environmental influences to publicize in a campaign aimed at promoting healthy prenatal development, which ones would you choose, and why?

Childbirth

3.5 Describe the three stages of childbirth, the baby's adaptation to labor and delivery, and the newborn baby's appearance.

Although Yolanda and Jay completed my course three months before their baby was born, both agreed to return to share their experiences with my next class. Two-week-old Joshua came along as well. Yolanda and Jay's story revealed that the birth of a baby is one of the most dramatic and emotional events in human experience. Jay was present throughout Yolanda's labor and delivery. Yolanda explained:

> By morning, we knew I was in labor. It was Thursday, so we went in for my usual weekly appointment. The doctor said, yes, the baby was on the way, but it would be a while. He told us to go home and relax and come to the hospital in three or four hours. We checked in at 3 in the afternoon; Joshua arrived at 2 o'clock the next morning. When, finally, I was ready to deliver, it went quickly; a half hour or so and some good hard pushes, and there he was! His face was red and puffy, and his head was misshapen, but I thought, "Our son! I can't believe he's really here."

Jay was also elated by Joshua's birth. "It was awesome, indescribable. I can't stop looking and smiling at him," Jay said, holding Joshua over his shoulder and patting and kissing him gently. In the following sections, we explore the experience of childbirth, from both the parents' and the baby's point of view.

The Stages of Childbirth

It is not surprising that childbirth is often referred to as labor. It is the hardest physical work a woman may ever do. A complex series of hormonal changes between mother and fetus initiates the process, which naturally divides into three stages (see Figure 3.5):

1. *Dilation and effacement of the cervix.* This is the longest stage of labor, lasting an average of 12 to 14 hours with a first birth and 4 to 6 hours with later births. Contractions of the uterus gradually become more frequent and powerful, causing the cervix, or uterine opening, to widen and thin to nothing, forming a clear channel from the uterus into the birth canal, or vagina.
2. *Delivery of the baby.* This stage is much shorter, lasting about 50 minutes for a first birth and 20 minutes in later births. Strong contractions of the uterus continue, but the

(a) Dilation and Effacement of the Cervix
Contractions of the uterus cause dilation and effacement of the cervix.

(b) Transition
Transition is reached when the frequency and strength of the contractions are at their peak and the cervix opens completely.

(c) Pushing
With each contraction, the mother pushes, forcing the baby down the birth canal, and the head appears.

(d) Birth of the Baby
Near the end of Stage 2, the shoulders emerge, followed quickly by the rest of the baby's body.

(e) Delivery of the Placenta
With a few final pushes, the placenta is delivered.

FIGURE 3.5 The three stages of childbirth.

mother also feels a natural urge to squeeze and push with her abdominal muscles. As she does so with each contraction, she forces the baby down and out.

3. *Delivery of the placenta.* Labor comes to an end with a few final contractions and pushes. These cause the placenta to separate from the wall of the uterus and be delivered in about 5 to 10 minutes.

The Baby's Adaptation to Labor and Delivery

At first glance, labor and delivery seem like a dangerous ordeal for the baby. The strong contractions exposed Joshua's head to a great deal of pressure, and they squeezed the placenta and the umbilical cord repeatedly. Each time, Joshua's supply of oxygen was temporarily reduced.

Fortunately, healthy babies are equipped to withstand these traumas. The force of the contractions intensifies the baby's production of stress hormones. Unlike during pregnancy, when excessive stress endangers the fetus, during childbirth high levels of infant cortisol and other stress hormones are adaptive. They help the baby withstand oxygen deprivation by sending a rich supply of blood to the brain and heart (Gluckman, Sizonenko, & Bassett, 1999). In addition, stress hormones prepare the baby to breathe by causing the lungs to absorb any remaining fluid and by expanding the bronchial tubes (passages leading to the lungs). Finally, stress hormones arouse the infant into alertness. Joshua was born wide awake, ready to interact with the surrounding world.

The Newborn Baby's Appearance

Parents are often surprised at the odd-looking newborn—a far cry from the storybook image they may have had in their minds. The average newborn is 20 inches long and 7½ pounds in weight; boys tend to be slightly longer and heavier than girls. The head is

To accommodate the well-developed brain, a newborn's head is large in relation to the trunk and legs. This newborn's body readily turns pink as she takes her first few breaths.

large in comparison to the trunk and legs, which are short and bowed. This combination of a large head (with its well-developed brain) and a small body means that human infants learn quickly in the first few months of life. But, unlike most other mammals, they cannot get around on their own until much later.

Even though newborn babies may not match parents' idealized image, some features do make them attractive (Luo, Li, & Lee, 2011). Their round faces, chubby cheeks, large foreheads, and big eyes make adults feel like picking them up and cuddling them.

Assessing the Newborn's Physical Condition: The Apgar Scale

Infants who have difficulty making the transition to life outside the uterus require special help at once. To assess the newborn's physical condition quickly, doctors and nurses use the **Apgar Scale.** As Table 3.3 shows, a rating of 0, 1, or 2 on each of

TABLE 3.3
The Apgar Scale

	RATING		
SIGN[a]	**0**	**1**	**2**
Heart rate	No heartbeat	Under 100 beats per minute	100 to 140 beats per minute
Respiratory effort	No breathing for 60 seconds	Irregular, shallow breathing	Strong breathing and crying
Reflex irritability (sneezing, coughing, and grimacing)	No response	Weak reflexive response	Strong reflexive response
Muscle tone	Completely limp	Weak movements of arms and legs	Strong movements of arms and legs
Color[b]	Blue body, arms, and legs	Body pink with blue arms and legs	Body, arms, and legs completely pink

[a]To remember these signs, you may find it helpful to use a technique in which the original labels are reordered and renamed as follows: color = **A**ppearance; heart rate = **P**ulse; reflex irritability = **G**rimace; muscle tone = **A**ctivity; and respiratory effort = **R**espiration. Together, the first letters of the new labels spell **Apgar**.
[b]The skin tone of nonwhite babies makes it difficult to apply the "pink" color criterion. However, newborns of all races can be rated for pinkish glow resulting from the flow of oxygen through body tissues.

Source: Apgar, 1953.

five characteristics is made at 1 minute and again at 5 minutes after birth. A combined Apgar score of 7 or better indicates that the infant is in good physical condition. If the score is between 4 and 6, the baby needs assistance in establishing breathing and other vital signs. If the score is 3 or below, the infant is in serious danger and requires emergency medical attention (Apgar, 1953). Two Apgar ratings are given because some babies have trouble adjusting at first but do quite well after a few minutes.

Approaches to Childbirth

3.6 Describe natural childbirth and home delivery, noting benefits and concerns associated with each.

Childbirth practices, like other aspects of family life, are heavily influenced by culture. In many village and tribal societies, expectant mothers are well-acquainted with the childbirth process. For example, the Jarara of South America and the Pukapukans of the Pacific Islands treat birth as a vital part of daily life. The Jarara mother gives birth in full view of the entire community, including small children. The Pukapukan girl is so familiar with the events of labor and delivery that she frequently can be seen playing at it. Using a coconut to represent the baby, she stuffs it inside her dress, imitates the mother's pushing, and lets the nut fall at the proper moment. In most nonindustrialized cultures, women are assisted—though often not by medical personnel—during labor and delivery. Among the Mende of Sierra Leone, birth attendants, who are appointed by the village chief, visit mothers before and after birth to provide advice and practice traditional strategies during labor to quicken delivery, including massaging the abdomen and supporting the woman in a squatting position (Dorwie & Pacquiao, 2014).

In Western nations, childbirth has changed dramatically over the centuries. Before the late 1800s, birth usually took place at home and was a family-centered event. The industrial revolution brought greater crowding to cities, along with new health problems. As a result, childbirth moved from home to hospital, where the health of mothers and babies could be protected. Once doctors assumed responsibility for childbirth, women's knowledge of it declined, and relatives and friends no longer participated (Borst, 1995).

By the 1950s and 1960s, women had begun to question the medical procedures used during labor. Many felt that routine use of strong drugs and delivery instruments had robbed them of a precious experience and was often neither necessary nor safe for the baby. Gradually, a natural childbirth movement arose in Europe and spread to North America. Its purpose was to make hospital birth as comfortable and rewarding for mothers as possible. Today, most hospitals offer birth centers that are family-centered and homelike. *Freestanding birth centers,* which permit greater maternal control over labor and delivery, including choice of delivery positions, presence of family

In Sierra Leone, a new mother rests comfortably after giving birth to twins. She had her first twin at home, assisted by village birth attendants. After complications arose, the birth attendants took her to a clinic, where they collaborated with nurses in delivering her second twin. Throughout, cultural practices remained a part of this birth experience.

members and friends, and early contact between parents and baby, also exist. And a small number of North American women reject institutional birth and choose to have their babies at home.

Natural, or Prepared, Childbirth

Yolanda and Jay chose **natural, or prepared, childbirth**—a group of techniques aimed at reducing pain and medical intervention and making childbirth a rewarding experience. Most natural childbirth programs draw on methods developed by Grantly Dick-Read (1959) in England and Fernand Lamaze (1958) in France. These physicians recognized that cultural attitudes had taught women to fear the birth experience. An anxious, frightened woman in labor tenses her muscles, heightening the pain that usually accompanies strong contractions.

In a typical natural childbirth program, the expectant mother and a companion (a partner, relative, or friend) participate in three activities:

- *Classes.* Yolanda and Jay attended a series of classes in which they learned about the anatomy and physiology of labor and delivery. Knowledge about the birth process reduces a mother's fear.
- *Relaxation and breathing techniques.* During each class, Yolanda was taught relaxation and breathing exercises aimed at counteracting the pain of uterine contractions.
- *Labor coach.* Jay learned how to help Yolanda during childbirth by reminding her to relax and breathe, massaging her back, supporting her body, and offering encouragement and affection.

Social support is important to the success of natural childbirth. In Guatemalan and American hospitals that routinely isolated patients during childbirth, some mothers were randomly assigned a *doula*—a Greek word referring to a trained lay attendant—who stayed with them throughout labor and delivery, talking to them, holding their hands, and rubbing their backs to promote relaxation. These mothers had shorter labors and fewer birth complications than women not given supportive companionship. Guatemalan mothers who received doula support also interacted more positively with their newborns, talking, smiling, and gently stroking (Kennell et al., 1991; Sosa et al., 1980).

Other studies indicate that mothers who are supported during labor and delivery—either by a lay birth attendant or by a relative or friend with doula training—less often have instrument-assisted or cesarean (surgical) deliveries or need medication to control pain. Also, their babies' Apgar scores are higher, and they are more likely to be breastfeeding at a two-month follow-up (Campbell et al., 2006, 2007; Hodnett et al., 2012; McGrath & Kennell, 2008). Social support also makes Western hospital-birth customs more acceptable to women from parts of the world where assistance from family and community members is the norm (Dundek, 2006).

Home Delivery

Home birth has always been popular in certain industrialized nations, such as England, the Netherlands, and Sweden. The number of American women choosing to have their babies at home rose during the 1970s and 1980s but remains small, at less than 1 percent (Martin et al., 2015). Although some home births are attended by doctors, many more are handled by *certified nurse–midwives,* who have degrees in nursing and additional training in childbirth management.

Is it just as safe to give birth at home as in a hospital? For healthy women without pregnancy complications who are assisted by a well-trained doctor or midwife, it seems so because complications rarely occur (Cheyney et al., 2014). However, if attendants are not carefully trained and prepared to handle emergencies, the likelihood of infant disability and death is high (Grünebaum et al., 2015). When mothers are at risk for any kind of complication, the appropriate place for labor and delivery is the hospital, where life-saving treatment is available.

Medical Interventions

3.7 List common medical interventions during childbirth, circumstances that justify their use, and any dangers associated with each.

Four-year-old Melinda walks with a halting, lumbering gait and has difficulty keeping her balance. She has *cerebral palsy,* a general term for a variety of impairments in muscle coordination caused by brain damage before, during, or just after birth. One out of every 500 American children has cerebral palsy. For about 10 percent, including Melinda, the brain damage was caused by **anoxia,** or inadequate oxygen supply, during labor and delivery (Clark, Ghulmiyyah, & Hankins, 2008; McIntyre et al., 2013). Melinda was in **breech position,** turned so that the buttocks or feet would be delivered first, and the umbilical cord was wrapped around her neck. Her mother had gotten pregnant accidentally, was frightened and alone, and arrived at the hospital at the last minute. Had she come to the hospital earlier, doctors could have monitored Melinda's condition and delivered her surgically as soon as squeezing of the umbilical cord led to distress, thereby reducing the damage or preventing it entirely.

In cases like Melinda's, medical interventions are clearly justified. But in others, they can interfere with delivery and even pose new risks. In the following sections, we examine some commonly used medical procedures during childbirth.

Fetal Monitoring

Fetal monitors are electronic instruments that track the baby's heart rate during labor. An abnormal heartbeat pattern may indicate that the baby is in distress due to anoxia and needs to be delivered immediately. Continuous fetal monitoring, which is required in most U.S. hospitals, is used in over 85 percent of U.S. births (Ananth et al., 2013). The most popular type of monitor is strapped across the mother's abdomen throughout labor. A second, more accurate method involves threading a recording

After a home birth, the midwife and a lay attendant provide support to the new mother. For healthy women attended by a well-trained doctor or midwife, home birth is as safe as hospital birth.

device through the cervix and placing it directly under the baby's scalp.

Fetal monitoring is a safe medical procedure that has saved the lives of many babies in high-risk situations. But in healthy pregnancies, it does not reduce the already low rates of infant brain damage and death. Furthermore, most infants have some heartbeat irregularities during labor, so critics worry that fetal monitors identify many babies as in danger who, in fact, are not. Monitoring is linked to an increase in the number of instrument and cesarean (surgical) deliveries, practices we will discuss shortly (Alfirevic, Devane, & Gyte, 2013). In addition, some women complain that the devices are uncomfortable and interfere with the normal course of labor.

Still, fetal monitors will probably continue to be used routinely in the United States, even though they are not necessary in most cases. Doctors fear that they will be sued for malpractice if an infant dies or is born with problems and they cannot show they did everything possible to protect the baby.

Labor and Delivery Medication

Some form of medication is used in more than 80 percent of U.S. births (Declercq et al., 2014). *Analgesics,* drugs used to relieve pain, may be given in mild doses during labor to help a mother relax. *Anesthetics* are a stronger type of painkiller that blocks sensation. Currently, the most common approach to controlling pain during labor is *epidural analgesia,* in which a regional pain-relieving drug is delivered continuously through a catheter into a small space in the lower spine. Unlike older spinal block procedures, which numb the entire lower half of the body, epidural analgesia limits pain reduction to the pelvic region. Because the mother retains the capacity to feel the pressure of the contractions and to move her trunk and legs, she is able to push during the second stage of labor.

Although pain-relieving drugs help women cope with childbirth and enable doctors to perform essential medical interventions, they also can cause problems. Epidural analgesia, for example, weakens uterine contractions. As a result, labor is prolonged, and the chances of instrument delivery or cesarean (surgical) birth increase. And because drugs rapidly cross the placenta, exposed newborns are at risk for respiratory distress (Kumar et al., 2014). They also tend to have lower Apgar scores, to be sleepy and withdrawn, to suck poorly during feedings, and to be irritable when awake (Eltzschig, Lieberman, & Camann, 2003; Platt, 2014). Although no confirmed long-term consequences for development exist, the negative impact of these drugs on the newborn's adjustment supports the current trend to limit their use.

Cesarean Delivery

A **cesarean delivery** is a surgical birth; the doctor makes an incision in the mother's abdomen and lifts the baby out of the uterus. Forty years ago, cesarean delivery was rare. Since then, cesarean rates have climbed internationally, reaching 16 percent in Finland, 24 percent in New Zealand, 26 percent in Canada, 31 percent in Australia, and 33 percent in the United States (Martin et al., 2015; OECD, 2013b).

Cesareans have always been warranted by medical emergencies, such as Rh incompatibility, premature separation of the placenta from the uterus, or serious maternal infection (for example, the herpes simplex 2 virus, which can infect the baby during a vaginal delivery). Cesareans are also justified in breech births, in which the baby risks head injury or anoxia (as in Melinda's case). But the infant's exact position makes a difference: Certain breech babies fare just as well with a normal delivery as with a cesarean (Vistad et al., 2013). Sometimes the doctor can gently turn the baby into a head-down position during the early part of labor.

Until recently, many women who have had a cesarean have been offered the option of a vaginal birth in subsequent pregnancies. But growing evidence indicates that compared with repeated cesareans, a natural labor after a cesarean is associated with slightly increased rates of rupture of the uterus and infant death (Hunter, 2014). As a result, the rule "Once a cesarean, always a cesarean" has made a comeback.

Repeated cesareans, however, do not explain the worldwide rise in cesarean deliveries. Instead, medical control over childbirth is largely responsible. Because many needless cesareans are performed, pregnant women should ask questions about the procedure when choosing a doctor. Although the operation itself is safe, mother and baby require more time for recovery. Anesthetic may have crossed the placenta, making cesarean newborns sleepy and unresponsive and putting them at increased risk for breathing difficulties (Ramachandrappa & Jain, 2008).

Ask yourself

CONNECT How might natural childbirth positively affect the parent–newborn relationship? Explain how your answer illustrates bidirectional influences between parent and child, emphasized in ecological systems theory.

APPLY Sharon, a heavy smoker, has just arrived at the hospital in labor. Which medical intervention discussed in the preceding sections is her doctor justified in using? (For help in answering this question, review the prenatal effects of tobacco on page 84.)

REFLECT If you were an expectant parent, would you choose home birth? Why or why not?

Preterm and Low-Birth-Weight Infants

3.8 Describe risks associated with preterm birth and low birth weight, along with effective interventions.

Babies born three weeks or more before the end of a full 38-week pregnancy or who weigh less than 5½ pounds (2,500 grams) have for many years been referred to as "premature." A wealth of research indicates that premature babies are at risk for many

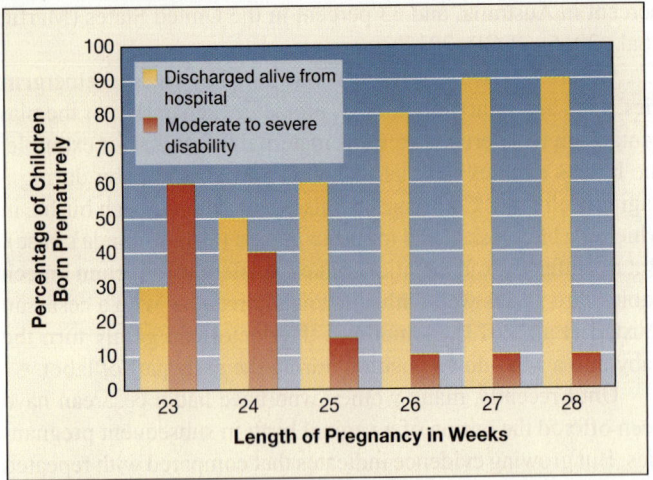

FIGURE 3.6 Rates of infant survival and child disabilities by length of pregnancy. In a follow-up of more than 2,300 babies born between 23 and 28 weeks gestation, the percentage who survived decreased and the percentage who displayed moderate to severe disabilities (assessed during the preschool years) increased with reduced length of pregnancy. Severe disabilities included cerebral palsy (unlikely to ever walk), severely delayed mental development, deafness, and blindness. Moderate disabilities included cerebral palsy (able to walk with assistance), moderately delayed mental development, and hearing impairments partially correctable with a hearing aid. (Adapted from Bolisetty et al., 2006.)

problems. Birth weight is the best available predictor of infant survival and healthy development. Many newborns who weigh less than 3½ pounds (1,500 grams) experience difficulties that are not overcome, an effect that becomes stronger as length of pregnancy and birth weight decrease (see Figure 3.6) (Bolisetty et al., 2006; Wilson-Ching et al., 2013). Brain abnormalities, delayed physical growth, frequent illness, sensory impairments, poor motor coordination, inattention, overactivity, language delays, low intelligence test scores, deficits in school learning, and emotional and behavior problems are some of the difficulties that persist through childhood and adolescence and into adulthood (Hutchinson et al., 2013; Lawn et al., 2014; Lemola, 2015).

About 11 percent of American infants are born early, and 8 percent are born underweight. The two risk factors often co-occur, and they can strike unexpectedly. But the problem is highest among poverty-stricken women (Martin et al., 2015). These mothers, as noted earlier, are more likely to be under stress, undernourished, and exposed to other harmful environmental influences. In addition, they often do not receive adequate prenatal care.

Recall from Chapter 2 that prematurity is also common in multiple births. About 55 percent of twins and more than 90 percent of triplets are born early and low birth weight (Martin et al., 2015). Because space inside the uterus is restricted, multiples gain less weight than singletons in the second half of pregnancy.

Preterm versus Small-for-Date Infants

Although preterm and low-birth-weight infants face many obstacles to healthy development, most go on to lead normal lives; about half of those born at 23 to 24 weeks gestation and weighing only a couple of pounds at birth have no disability (refer again to Figure 3.6). To better understand why some babies do better than others, researchers divide them into two groups. **Preterm infants** are born several weeks or more before their due date. Although they are small, their weight may still be appropriate, based on time spent in the uterus. **Small-for-date infants** are below their expected weight considering length of the pregnancy. Some small-for-date infants are actually full-term. Others are preterm infants who are especially underweight.

Small-for-date infants—especially those who are also preterm—usually have more serious problems. During the first year, they are more likely to die, catch infections, and show evidence of brain damage. By middle childhood, they are smaller in stature, have lower intelligence test scores, are less attentive, achieve more poorly in school, and are socially immature (Katz et al., 2013; Sullivan et al., 2008; Wilson-Ching et al., 2013). Small-for-date infants probably experienced inadequate nutrition before birth. Perhaps their mothers did not eat properly, the placenta did not function normally, or the babies themselves had defects that prevented them from growing as they should. Consequently, small-for-date infants are especially likely to suffer from neurological impairments that permanently weaken their capacity to manage stress (Osterholm, Hostinar, & Gunnar, 2012). Severe stress, in turn, heightens their susceptibility to later physical and psychological health problems.

Even among preterm newborns whose weight is appropriate for length of pregnancy, just 7 to 14 more days—from 34 to 35 or 36 weeks—greatly reduces rates of illness, costly medical procedures, and lengthy hospital stays (although they need greater medical intervention than full-term babies) (Ananth, Friedman, & Gyamfi-Bannerman, 2013). And despite being relatively low-risk for disabilities, a substantial number of 34-week preterms are below average in physical growth and mildly to moderately delayed in cognitive development in early and middle childhood (Morse et al., 2009; Stephens & Vohr, 2009). In an investigation of over 120,000 New York City births, babies born even 1 or 2 weeks early showed slightly lower reading and math scores at a third-grade follow-up than children who experienced a full-length prenatal period (Noble et al., 2012). These outcomes persisted even after controlling for other factors linked to achievement, such as birth weight and SES. Yet doctors often induce births several weeks preterm, under the misconception that these babies are developmentally "mature."

Consequences for Caregiving

Imagine a scrawny, thin-skinned infant whose body is only a little larger than the size of your hand. You try to play with the baby by stroking and talking softly, but he is sleepy and unresponsive. When you feed him, he sucks poorly. During the short, unpredictable periods he is awake, he is usually irritable.

The appearance and behavior of preterm babies can lead parents to be less sensitive in caring for them. Compared with full-term infants, preterm babies—especially those who are very ill at birth—are less often held close, touched, and talked to gently. At times, mothers of these infants resort to interfering pokes and verbal commands in an effort to obtain a higher level of response from the baby (Feldman, 2007; Forcada-Guex et al., 2006). This may explain why preterm babies as a group are at risk for child abuse.

Research reveals that distressed, emotionally reactive preterm infants are particularly susceptible to the effects of parenting quality: Among a sample of preterm 9-month-olds, the combination of infant negativity and angry or intrusive parenting yielded the highest rates of behavior problems at 2 years of age. But with warm, sensitive parenting, distressed preterm babies' rates of behavior problems were the lowest (Poehlmann et al., 2011). When they are born to isolated, poverty-stricken mothers who cannot provide good nutrition, health care, and parenting, the likelihood of unfavorable outcomes increases. In contrast, parents with stable life circumstances and social supports usually can overcome the stresses of caring for a preterm infant (Ment et al., 2003). In these cases, even sick preterm babies have a good chance of catching up in development by middle childhood.

These findings suggest that how well preterm infants develop has a great deal to do with the parent–child relationship. Consequently, interventions directed at supporting both sides of this tie are more likely to help these infants recover.

Interventions for Preterm Infants

A preterm baby is cared for in a special Plexiglas-enclosed bed called an *isolette*. Temperature is carefully controlled because these babies cannot yet regulate their own body temperature effectively. To help protect the baby from infection, air is filtered before it enters the isolette. When a preterm infant is fed through a stomach tube, breathes with the aid of a respirator, and receives medication through an intravenous needle, the isolette can be very isolating indeed! Physical needs that otherwise would lead to close contact and other human stimulation are met mechanically.

Special Infant Stimulation. In proper doses, certain kinds of stimulation can help preterm infants develop. In some intensive care nurseries, preterm babies can be seen rocking in suspended hammocks, lying on waterbeds designed to replace the gentle motion they would have received while still in the mother's uterus, or listening to soft music—experiences that promote faster weight gain, more predictable sleep patterns, and greater alertness (Arnon et al., 2006; Marshall-Baker, Lickliter, & Cooper, 1998). In one experiment, extremely preterm newborns, born between the 25th and 32nd prenatal weeks, were exposed either to recordings of their mother's voice and heartbeat for several hours each day or to routine hospital noise. At age 1 month, an ultrasound revealed that auditory areas of the brain had grown substantially larger in the maternal sounds group (see Figure 3.7) (Webb et al., 2015). Listening to womblike, familiar rhythmic maternal sounds, as

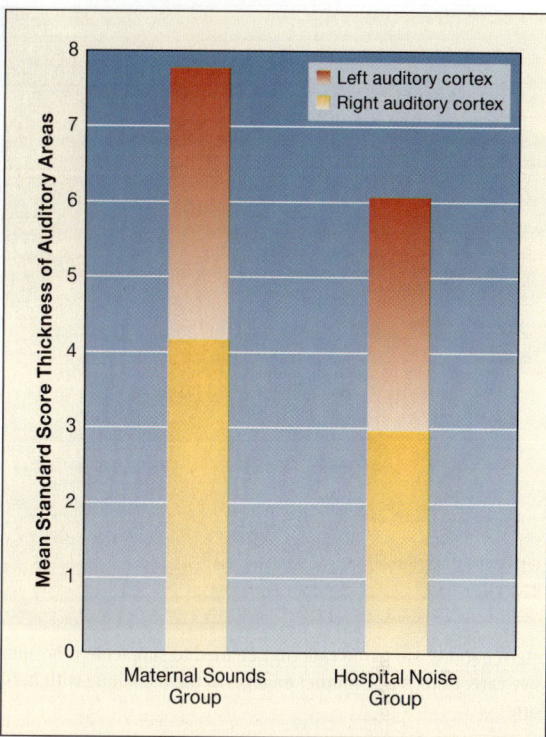

FIGURE 3.7 Listening to mother's voice and heartbeat enhances brain development in extremely preterm newborns. Infants born between the 25th and 32nd prenatal weeks were randomly assigned to hear either recordings of their mother's voice and heartbeat for several hours a day or routine, unpatterned hospital noise. After a month's exposure in the intensive care nursery, ultrasound measures showed that the left and right cerebral auditory areas were substantially thicker in the maternal sounds group than the hospital noise group. In addition to highlighting an effective intervention, the results suggest that exposure to soft, rhythmic maternal sounds during pregnancy enhances early brain development. (Based on Webb et al., 2015.)

opposed to the unpredictable din of hospital equipment, promoted brain development.

In baby animals, touching the skin releases certain brain chemicals that support physical growth—effects believed to occur in humans as well. When preterm infants were massaged several times each day in the hospital, they gained weight faster and, at the end of the first year, were advanced in mental and motor development over preterm babies not given this stimulation (Field, 2001; Field, Hernandez-Reif, & Freedman, 2004).

In developing countries where hospitalization is not always possible, skin-to-skin "kangaroo care" is the most readily available intervention for promoting the recovery of preterm babies. It involves placing the infant in a vertical position between the mother's breasts or next to the father's chest (under the parent's clothing) so the parent's body functions as a human incubator. Because of its many physical and psychological benefits, the technique is often used in Western nations as a supplement to hospital intensive care.

Kangaroo skin-to-skin contact fosters improved oxygenation of the baby's body, temperature regulation, sleep, breastfeeding, alertness, and infant survival (Conde-Agudelo, Belizan, &

In Western nations, kangaroo care may be used to supplement hospital intensive care. Here, a U.S. mother engages in the technique with her fragile newborn.

Diaz-Rossello, 2011; Kaffashi et al., 2013). In addition, the kangaroo position provides the baby with gentle stimulation of all sensory modalities: hearing (through the parent's voice), smell (through proximity to the parent's body), touch (through skin-to-skin contact), and vision (through the upright position). Mothers and fathers practicing kangaroo care feel more confident about caring for their fragile babies, interact more sensitively and affectionately, and feel more attached to them (Dodd, 2005; Feldman, 2007).

Together, these factors may explain why preterm babies given many hours of kangaroo care in their early weeks, compared to those given little or no such care, are more likely to explore novel toys and score higher in mental and motor development during the first year (Bera et al., 2014; Feldman, 2007). In an investigation that followed children born preterm until age 10, those who had experienced kangaroo care, compared with matched controls, displayed a more adaptive cortisol stress response, better organized sleep, more favorable mother–child interaction, and enhanced cognitive development (Feldman, Rosenthal, & Eidelman, 2014). Because of its diverse benefits, most U.S. hospital nurseries now offer kangaroo care to parents and preterm newborns.

Training Parents in Infant Caregiving Skills. Interventions that support parents of preterm infants generally teach them how to recognize and respond to the baby's needs. For parents with adequate economic and personal resources to care for a preterm infant, just a few sessions of coaching are linked to enhanced parent–infant interaction, reduced infant crying and improved sleep, more rapid language development in the second year, and steady gains in mental test performance that equal those of full-term children by middle childhood (Achenbach, Howell, & Aoki, 1993; Newnham, Milgrom, & Skouteris, 2009).

When preterm infants live in stressed, economically disadvantaged households, long-term, intensive intervention is necessary (Guralnick, 2012). In the Infant Health and Development Program, preterm babies born into poverty received a comprehensive intervention. It combined medical follow-up, weekly home visits in which mothers received training in infant care and everyday problem solving, and cognitively stimulating child care from 1 to 3 years of age. More than four times as many intervention children as no-intervention controls (39 versus 9 percent) were within normal range at age 3 in intelligence, psychological adjustment, and physical growth (Bradley et al., 1994). In addition, mothers in the intervention group were more affectionate and more often encouraged play and cognitive mastery in their children—reasons their 3-year-olds may have been developing so favorably (McCarton, 1998).

At ages 5 and 8, children who had attended the child-care program regularly—for more than 350 days over the three-year period—continued to show better intellectual functioning. In contrast, children who attended only sporadically gained little or even lost ground (Hill, Brooks-Gunn, & Waldfogel, 2003). These findings confirm that babies who are both preterm and economically disadvantaged require *intensive* intervention. And special strategies, such as extra adult–child interaction, may be necessary to achieve lasting changes in children with the lowest birth weights.

Nevertheless, even the best caregiving environments cannot always overcome the enormous biological risks associated with extreme preterm and low birth weight. A better course of action is prevention. The high rate of underweight babies in the United States—one of the worst in the industrialized world—could be greatly reduced by improving the health and social conditions described in the Social Issues: Health box on pages 102–103.

Ask yourself

CONNECT List factors discussed in this chapter that increase the chances that an infant will be born underweight. How many of these factors could be prevented by better health care for expectant mothers?

APPLY Cecilia and Anna each gave birth to a 3-pound baby seven weeks preterm. Cecilia is single and on welfare. Anna and her partner are happily married and earn a good income. Plan an intervention appropriate for helping each baby develop.

REFLECT Many people object to the use of extraordinary medical measures to save extremely low-birth-weight babies because of their high risk for serious developmental problems. Do you agree or disagree? Explain.

The Newborn Baby's Capacities

3.9 Describe the newborn baby's reflexes and states of arousal, noting sleep characteristics and ways to soothe a crying baby.
3.10 Describe the newborn baby's sensory capacities.
3.11 Why is neonatal behavioral assessment useful?

Newborn infants have a remarkable set of capacities that are crucial for survival and for evoking adult attention and care. In relating to their physical and social worlds, babies are active from the very start.

Reflexes

A **reflex** is an inborn, automatic response to a particular form of stimulation. Reflexes are the newborn baby's most obvious organized patterns of behavior. As Jay placed Joshua on a table in my classroom, we saw several. When Jay bumped the side of the table, Joshua reacted by flinging his arms wide and bringing them back toward his body. As Yolanda stroked Joshua's cheek, he turned his head in her direction. Look at Table 3.4 and see if you can name the newborn reflexes that Joshua displayed.

Some reflexes have survival value. The rooting reflex helps a breastfed baby find the mother's nipple. Babies display it only when hungry and touched by another person, not when they touch themselves (Rochat & Hespos, 1997). At birth, babies adjust their sucking pressure to how easily milk flows from the nipple (Craig & Lee, 1999). And if sucking were not automatic, our species would be unlikely to survive for a single generation!

Other reflexes probably aided survival during our evolutionary past. For example, the Moro, or "embracing," reflex is believed to have helped infants cling to their mothers when they were carried about all day. If the baby happened to lose support, the reflex caused the infant to embrace and, along with the palmar grasp reflex (so strong during the first week that it can support the baby's entire weight), regain its hold on the mother's body.

Several reflexes help parents and infants establish gratifying interaction. A baby who successfully finds the nipple, sucks easily during feedings, and grasps when the hand is touched encourages parents to respond lovingly and feel competent as caregivers. Reflexes can also help caregivers comfort the baby because they permit infants to control distress and amount of stimulation. For example, on outings with Joshua, Yolanda brought along a pacifier. If he became fussy, sucking helped quiet him until she could feed, change, or hold him.

TABLE 3.4
Some Newborn Reflexes

REFLEX	STIMULATION	RESPONSE	AGE OF DISAPPEARANCE	FUNCTION
Eye blink	Shine bright light at eyes or clap hand near head.	Infant quickly closes eyelids.	Permanent	Protects infant from strong stimulation
Rooting	Stroke cheek near corner of mouth.	Head turns toward source of stimulation.	3 weeks (becomes voluntary turning at this time)	Helps infant find the nipple
Sucking	Place finger in infant's mouth.	Infant sucks finger rhythmically.	Replaced by voluntary sucking after 4 months	Permits feeding
Moro	Hold infant horizontally on back and let head drop slightly, or produce a sudden loud sound against surface supporting infant.	Infant makes an "embracing" motion by arching back, extending legs, throwing arms outward, and then bringing arms in toward the body.	6 months	In human evolutionary past, may have helped infant cling to mother
Palmar grasp	Place finger in infant's hand and press against palm.	Infant spontaneously grasps finger.	3–4 months	Prepares infant for voluntary grasping
Tonic neck	Turn baby's head to one side while infant is lying awake on back.	Infant lies in a "fencing position." One arm is extended in front of eyes on side to which head is turned, other arm is flexed.	4 months	May prepare infant for voluntary reaching
Stepping	Hold infant under arms and permit bare feet to touch a flat surface.	Infant lifts one foot after another in stepping response.	2 months in infants who gain weight quickly; sustained in lighter infants	Prepares infant for voluntary walking
Babinski	Stroke sole of foot from toe toward heel.	Toes fan out and curl as foot twists in.	8–12 months	Unknown

Sources: Knobloch & Pasamanick, 1974; Prechtl & Beintema, 1965; Thelen, Fisher, & Ridley-Johnson, 1984.

Social Issues: Health

A Cross-National Perspective on Health Care and Other Policies for Parents and Newborn Babies

Infant mortality—the number of deaths in the first year of life per 1,000 live births—is an index used around the world to assess the overall health of a nation's children. Although the United States has the most up-to-date health-care technology in the world, it has made less progress in reducing infant deaths than many other countries. Over the past three decades, it has slipped in the international rankings, from seventh in the 1950s to thirty-ninth in 2015. Members of America's poor ethnic minorities are at greatest risk, with African-American infants more than twice as likely as white infants to die in the first year of life (U.S. Census Bureau, 2015c, 2015d).

Neonatal mortality, the rate of death within the first month of life, accounts for 67 percent of the infant death rate in the United States. Two factors are largely responsible for neonatal mortality. The first is serious physical defects, most of which cannot be prevented. The percentage of babies born with physical defects is about the same in all ethnic and income groups. The second leading cause of neonatal mortality is low birth weight, which is largely preventable.

Widespread poverty and inadequate health-care programs for mothers and young children are largely responsible for these trends. In addition to providing government-sponsored health-care benefits to all citizens, each country in Figure 3.8 that outranks the United States in infant survival takes extra steps to make sure that pregnant mothers and babies have access to good nutrition, high-quality medical care, and social and economic supports that promote effective parenting.

For example, all Western European nations guarantee women a certain number of prenatal visits at very low or no cost. After a baby is born, a health professional routinely visits the home to provide counseling about infant care and to arrange continuing medical services. Home assistance is especially extensive in the Netherlands (Lamkaddem

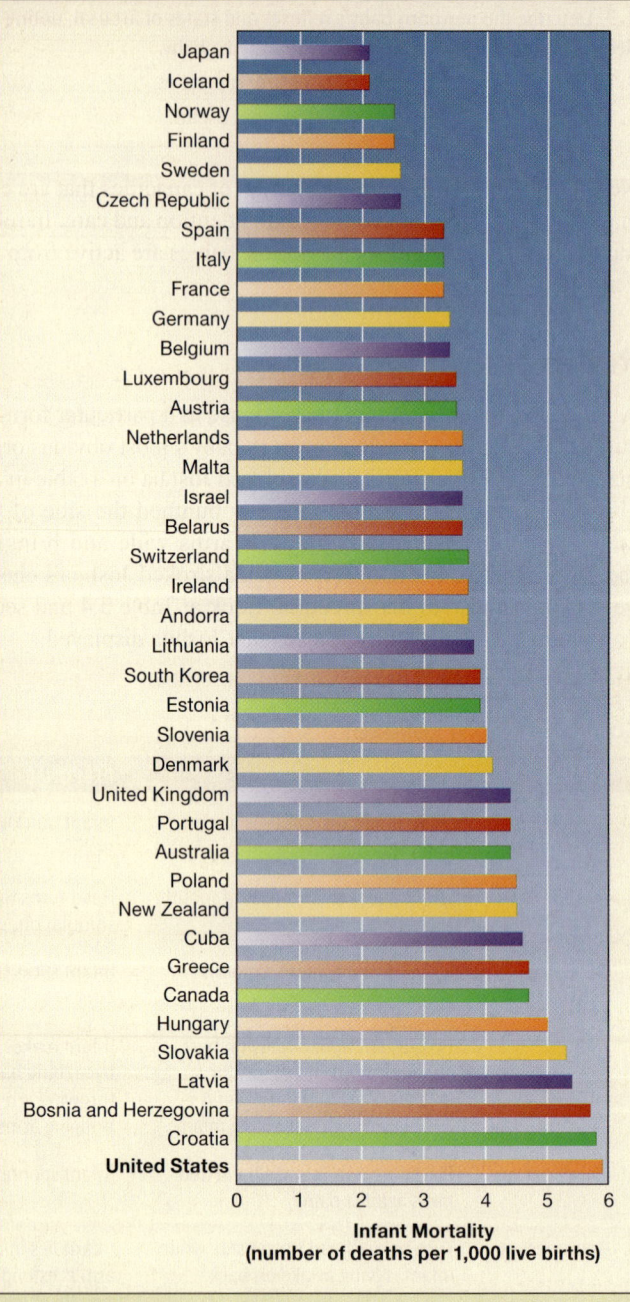

FIGURE 3.8 Infant mortality in 39 nations. Despite its advanced health-care technology, the United States ranks poorly. It is thirty-ninth in the world, with a death rate of 5.9 infants per 1,000 births. (Based on U.S. Census Bureau, 2015c.)

A few reflexes form the basis for complex motor skills that will develop later. For example, the tonic neck reflex may prepare the baby for voluntary reaching. When infants lie on their backs in this "fencing position," they naturally gaze at the hand in front of their eyes. The reflex may encourage them to combine vision with arm movements and, eventually, reach for objects.

Certain reflexes—such as the palmar grasp and stepping—drop out early, but the motor functions involved are renewed later. The stepping reflex, for example, looks like a primitive walking response. In infants who gain weight quickly in the weeks after birth, the stepping reflex drops out because thigh and calf muscles are not strong enough to lift the baby's chubby legs.

et al., 2014). For a token fee, each mother is granted a specially trained maternity helper, who assists with infant care, shopping, housekeeping, meal preparation, and the care of other children for 8 to 10 days after delivery.

Paid, job-protected employment leave is another vital societal intervention for new parents. Sweden has the most generous parental leave program in the world. Mothers can begin maternity leave 60 days prior to expected delivery, extending it to 6 weeks after birth; fathers are granted 2 weeks of birth leave. In addition, either parent can take full leave for 15 months at 80 percent of prior earnings, followed by an additional 3 months at a modest flat rate. Each parent is also entitled to another 18 months of unpaid leave. Even economically less well-off nations provide parental leave benefits. In Bulgaria, new mothers are granted 11 months paid leave, and fathers receive 3 weeks. Furthermore, many countries supplement basic paid leave. In Germany, for example, after a fully paid 3-month leave, a parent may take one more year at a flat rate and additional leave at no pay until the child reaches age 3 (Addati, Cassirer, & Gilchrist, 2014).

Yet in the United States, the federal government mandates *only 12 weeks of unpaid leave* for employees in companies with at least 50 workers. Most women, however, work in smaller businesses, and many of those who work in large enough companies cannot afford to take unpaid leave. And because of financial pressures, many new mothers who are eligible for unpaid work leave take far less than 12 weeks. Similarly, though paternal leave predicts fathers' increased involvement in infant care at the end of the first year, many fathers take little or none at all (Nepomnyaschy & Waldfogel, 2007). In 2002, California became the first state to guarantee a mother or father paid leave—up to six weeks at half salary, regardless of the size of the company. Since then, the District of Columbia, Hawaii, New Jersey, New York, Rhode Island, Washington, and the territory of Puerto Rico have passed similar legislation.

Nevertheless, 6 weeks of childbirth leave (the norm in the United States) is not enough. Leaves of 6 to 8 weeks or less are linked to increased maternal anxiety, depression, sense of role overload (conflict between work and family responsibilities), and negative interactions with the baby. A leave of 12 weeks or more predicts favorable maternal physical and mental health, supportive marital interaction, and sensitive caregiving (Chatterji & Markowitz, 2012; Feldman, Sussman, & Zigler, 2004). Single women and their babies are most hurt by the absence of a generous national paid-leave policy. These mothers, who are usually the sole source of support for their families, can least afford to take time from their jobs.

In countries with low infant mortality rates, expectant parents need not wonder how or where they will get health care and other resources to support their baby's development. The powerful impact of universal, high-quality health care, generous parental leave, and other social services on maternal and infant well-being provides strong justification for these policies. Responding to these findings, the Affordable Care Act provides generous grants to U.S. states to cover the cost of evidence-based home-visiting programs that provide comprehensive services to mothers, infants, and young children in high-risk families.

This doctor works with high-risk pregnancies, delivering babies whose poverty-stricken mothers have had little or no prenatal care. Nations with low poverty rates and government-supported, high-quality health care for pregnant mothers and babies outrank the United States in infant survival.

But if the lower part of the infant's body is dipped in water, the reflex reappears because the buoyancy of the water lightens the load on the baby's muscles (Thelen, Fisher, & Ridley-Johnson, 1984). When stepping is exercised regularly, babies make more reflexive stepping movements and are likely to walk several weeks earlier than if stepping is not practiced (Zelazo et al., 1993). However, there is no special need for infants to practice the stepping reflex because all normal babies walk in due time.

Refer to Table 3.4 again, and you will see that most newborn reflexes disappear during the first six months, due to a gradual increase in voluntary control over behavior as the cerebral cortex develops. Pediatricians test reflexes carefully because reflexes can

In the Moro reflex, loss of support or a sudden loud sound causes the baby to arch his back, extend his legs, throw his arms outward, and then return them toward the body in an "embracing" motion.

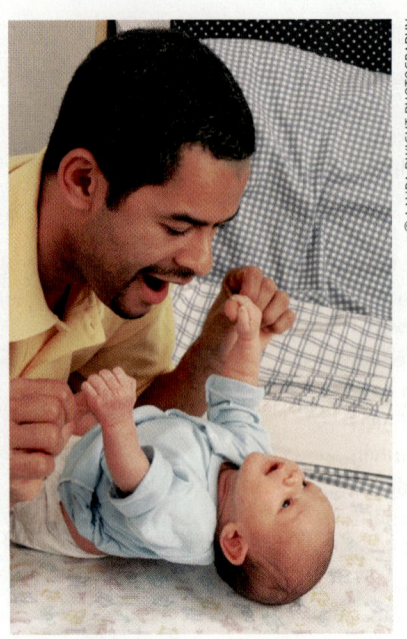
The palmar grasp reflex is so strong during the first week after birth that many infants can use it to support their entire weight.

When held upright under the arms, newborn babies show reflexive stepping movements.

reveal the health of the baby's nervous system. Weak or absent reflexes, overly rigid or exaggerated reflexes, and reflexes that persist beyond the point in development when they should normally disappear can signal brain damage (Schott & Rossor, 2003).

States of Arousal

Throughout the day and night, newborn infants move in and out of five **states of arousal,** or degrees of sleep and wakefulness, described in Table 3.5. During the first month, these states alternate frequently. The most fleeting is quiet alertness, which usually moves quickly toward fussing and crying. Much to the relief of their fatigued parents, newborns spend the greatest amount of time asleep—about 16 to 18 hours a day. Because the fetus tends to synchronize periods of rest and activity with those of the mother, newborns sleep more at night than during the day (Heraghty et al., 2008). Nevertheless, young babies' sleep–wake cycles are affected more by fullness–hunger than by darkness–light (Davis, Parker, & Montgomery, 2004).

However, striking individual differences in daily rhythms exist that affect parents' attitudes toward and interactions with the baby. A few newborns sleep for long periods, increasing the energy their well-rested parents have for sensitive, responsive care. Other babies cry a great deal, and their parents must exert great effort to soothe them. If these parents do not succeed, they may feel less competent and less positive toward their infant.

Furthermore, from birth on, arousal patterns have implications for cognitive development. Babies who spend more time alert probably receive more social stimulation and opportunities to explore and, therefore, may have a slight advantage in mental development. And as with adults, sleep enhances babies' learning and memory. In one study, eye-blink responses and brain-wave recordings revealed that sleeping newborns readily learned that a tone would be followed by a puff of air to the eye (Fifer et al., 2010). Because young infants spend so much time sleeping, the capacity to learn about external stimuli during sleep may be essential for babies' adaptation to their surroundings.

Of the states listed in Table 3.5, the two extremes—sleep and crying—have been of greatest interest to researchers. Each tells us something about normal and abnormal early development.

Sleep. Observing Joshua as he slept, Yolanda and Jay wondered why his eyelids and body twitched and his rate of breathing varied. Sleep is made up of at least two states. During irregular, or **rapid-eye-movement (REM), sleep,** brain-wave activity is remarkably similar to that of the waking state. The eyes dart beneath the lids; heart rate, blood pressure, and breathing are uneven; and slight body movements occur. In contrast, during regular, or **non-rapid-eye-movement (NREM), sleep,** the body is almost motionless, and heart rate, breathing, and brain-wave activity are slow and even.

Like children and adults, newborns alternate between REM and NREM sleep. However, they spend far more time in the REM state than they ever will again. REM sleep accounts for 50 percent of a newborn baby's sleep time. By 3 to 5 years, it has declined to an adultlike level of 20 percent (Louis et al., 1997).

Why do young infants spend so much time in REM sleep? In older children and adults, the REM state is associated with dreaming. Babies probably do not dream, at least not in the same way we do. But researchers believe that the stimulation of REM sleep is vital for growth of the central nervous system (Tarullo, Balsam, & Fifer, 2011). Young infants seem to have a special need for this stimulation because they spend little time in an alert state, when they can get input from the environment. In support of this idea, the percentage of REM sleep is especially great in the fetus and in preterm babies, who are even less able than full-term newborns to take advantage of external stimulation (Peirano, Algarin, & Uauy, 2003).

TABLE 3.5
Infant States of Arousal

STATE	DESCRIPTION	DAILY DURATION IN NEWBORN
Regular, or NREM, sleep	The infant is at full rest and shows little or no body activity. The eyelids are closed, no eye movements occur, the face is relaxed, and breathing is slow and regular.	8–9 hours
Irregular, or REM, sleep	Gentle limb movements, occasional stirring, and facial grimacing occur. Although the eyelids are closed, occasional rapid eye movements can be seen beneath them. Breathing is irregular.	8–9 hours
Drowsiness	The infant is either falling asleep or waking up. Body is less active than in irregular sleep but more active than in regular sleep. The eyes open and close; when open, they have a glazed look. Breathing is even but somewhat faster than in regular sleep.	Varies
Quiet alertness	The infant's body is relatively inactive, with eyes open and attentive. Breathing is even.	2–3 hours
Waking activity and crying	The infant shows frequent bursts of uncoordinated body activity. Breathing is very irregular. Face may be relaxed or tense and wrinkled. Crying may occur.	1–4 hours

Source: Wolff, 1966.

Because newborns' normal sleep behavior is organized and patterned, observations of sleep states can help identify central nervous system abnormalities. In infants who are brain-damaged or who have experienced birth trauma, disturbed REM–NREM sleep cycles are often present. Babies with poor sleep organization are likely to be behaviorally disorganized and, therefore, to have difficulty learning and evoking caregiver interactions that enhance their development. In follow-ups during the preschool years, they show delayed motor, cognitive, and language development (Feldman, 2006; Holditch-Davis, Belyea, & Edwards, 2005; Weisman et al., 2011). And the brain-functioning problems that underlie newborn sleep irregularities may culminate in sudden infant death syndrome, a major cause of infant mortality (see the Biology and Environment box on page 106).

Crying. Crying is the first way that babies communicate, letting parents know they need food, comfort, or stimulation. During the weeks after birth, all infants have some fussy periods when they are difficult to console. But most of the time, the nature of the cry, combined with the experiences that led up to it, helps guide parents toward its cause. The baby's cry is a complex stimulus that varies in intensity, from a whimper to a message of all-out distress (Wood, 2009). As early as the first few weeks, infants can be identified by the unique vocal "signature" of their cries, which helps parents locate their baby from a distance (Gustafson, Green, & Cleland, 1994).

Young infants usually cry because of physical needs. Hunger is the most common cause, but babies may also cry in response to temperature change when undressed, a sudden noise, or a painful stimulus. Newborns (as well as older babies up to age 6 months) often cry at the sound of another crying baby (Dondi, Simion, & Caltran, 1999; Geangu et al., 2010). Some researchers believe that this response reflects an inborn capacity to react to the suffering of others. Furthermore, crying typically increases during the early weeks, peaks at about 6 weeks, and then declines (Barr, 2001). Because this trend appears in many cultures with vastly different infant care practices, researchers believe that normal readjustments of the central nervous system underlie it.

The next time you hear an infant cry, notice your own reaction. The sound stimulates a sharp rise in blood cortisol, alertness, and feelings of discomfort in men and women, parents and nonparents alike (de Cock et al., 2015; Yong & Ruffman, 2014). This powerful response is probably innately programmed to ensure that babies receive the care and protection they need to survive.

Soothing Crying Infants. Although parents do not always interpret their baby's cry correctly, their accuracy improves with

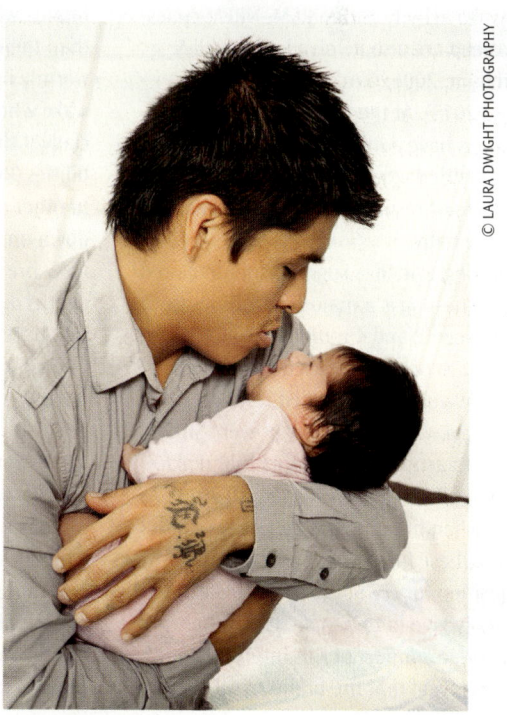

To soothe his crying infant, this father rocks her gently while talking softly.

Biology and Environment

The Mysterious Tragedy of Sudden Infant Death Syndrome

Millie awoke with a start one morning and looked at the clock. It was 7:30, and Sasha had missed both her night waking and her early morning feeding. Wondering if she was all right, Millie and her husband, Stuart, tiptoed into the room. Sasha lay still, curled up under her blanket. She had died silently during her sleep.

Sasha was a victim of **sudden infant death syndrome (SIDS),** the unexpected death, usually during the night, of an infant younger than 1 year of age that remains unexplained after thorough investigation. In industrialized nations, SIDS is the leading cause of infant mortality between 1 and 12 months, accounting for about 20 percent of these deaths in the United States (Centers for Disease Control and Prevention, 2015i).

SIDS victims usually show physical problems from the beginning. Early medical records of SIDS babies reveal higher rates of prematurity and low birth weight, poor Apgar scores, and limp muscle tone. Abnormal heart rate and respiration and disturbances in sleep–wake activity and in REM–NREM cycles while asleep are also involved (Cornwell & Feigenbaum, 2006; Garcia, Koschnitzky, & Ramirez, 2013). At the time of death, many SIDS babies have a mild respiratory infection (Blood-Siegfried, 2009). This seems to increase the chances of respiratory failure in an already vulnerable baby.

Mounting evidence suggests that impaired brain functioning is a major contributor to SIDS. Between 2 and 4 months, when SIDS is most likely to occur, reflexes decline and are replaced by voluntary, learned responses. Neurological weaknesses may prevent SIDS babies from acquiring behaviors that replace defensive reflexes (Rubens & Sarnat, 2013). As a result, when breathing difficulties occur during sleep, these infants do not wake up, shift their position, or cry out for help. Instead, they simply give in to oxygen deprivation and death. In support of this interpretation, autopsies reveal that the brains of SIDS babies contain unusually low levels of serotonin (a brain chemical that assists with arousal when survival is threatened) as well as other abnormalities in centers that control breathing and arousal (Salomonis, 2014).

Several environmental factors are linked to SIDS. Maternal cigarette smoking, both during and after pregnancy, as well as smoking by other caregivers, doubles risk of the disorder. Babies exposed to cigarette smoke arouse less easily from sleep and have more respiratory infections (Blackwell et al., 2015). Prenatal abuse of drugs that depress central nervous system functioning (alcohol, opiates, and barbiturates) increases the risk of SIDS as much as fifteenfold (Hunt & Hauck, 2006). Babies of drug-abusing mothers are especially likely to display SIDS-related brain abnormalities (Kinney, 2009).

Infant sleep practices may also be involved. Infants who sleep on their stomachs rather than their backs and who are wrapped very warmly in clothing and blankets less often wake when their breathing is disturbed, especially if they suffer from biological vulnerabilities (Richardson, Walker, & Horne, 2008). In other cases, healthy babies sleeping face down on soft bedding may die from continually breathing their own exhaled breath—deaths due to accidental suffocation and therefore incorrectly classified as SIDS.

SIDS rates are especially high among poverty-stricken minorities (U.S. Department of Health and Human Services, 2015b). In these families, parental stress, substance abuse, reduced access to health care, and lack of knowledge about safe sleep practices are widespread.

Public education efforts are vital for reducing the prevalence of SIDS. The U.S. government's Safe to Sleep campaign encourages parents to create safe sleep environments

Public education campaigns encouraging parents to put their infants on their backs to sleep have helped reduce the incidence of SIDS by more than half in many Western nations.

and engage in other protective practices, which are also endorsed by the American Academy of Pediatrics (Barsman et al., 2015). Recommendations include quitting smoking and drug taking, placing infants on their backs, using light sleep clothing, providing a firm sleep surface, and eliminating soft bedding. An estimated 20 percent of SIDS cases would be prevented if all infants had smoke-free homes. Dissemination of information to parents about putting infants down on their backs has cut the incidence of SIDS by more than half in many Western nations (Behm et al., 2012). Another protective measure is pacifier use: Sleeping babies who suck arouse more easily in response to breathing and heart-rate irregularities (Li et al., 2006).

When SIDS does occur, surviving family members require a great deal of help to overcome a sudden and unexpected death. As Millie commented six months after Sasha's death, "It's the worst crisis we've ever been through. What's helped us most are the comforting words of others who've experienced the same tragedy."

Applying what we Know

Soothing a Crying Baby

METHOD	EXPLANATION
Talk softly or play rhythmic sounds.	Continuous, monotonous, rhythmic sounds (such as a clock ticking, a fan whirring, or peaceful music) are more effective than intermittent sounds.
Offer a pacifier.	Sucking helps babies control their own level of arousal.
Massage the baby's body.	Stroking the baby's torso and limbs with continuous, gentle motions relaxes the baby's muscles.
Swaddle the baby.	Restricting movement and increasing warmth often soothe a young infant.
Lift the baby to the shoulder and rock or walk.	This combination of physical contact, upright posture, and motion is an effective soothing technique, causing young infants to become quietly alert.
Take the baby for a short car ride or a walk in a baby carriage; swing the baby in a cradle.	Gentle, rhythmic motion of any kind helps lull the baby to sleep.
Combine several of the methods just listed.	Stimulating several of the baby's senses at once is often more effective than stimulating only one.
If these methods do not work, let the baby cry for a short period.	Occasionally, a baby responds well to just being put down and will, after a few minutes, fall asleep.

Sources: Dayton et al., 2015; Evanoo, 2007; St James-Roberts, 2012.

experience. At the same time, they vary widely in responsiveness. Parents who are high in empathy (ability to take the perspective of others in distress) and who hold "child-centered" attitudes toward infant care (for example, believe that babies cannot be spoiled by being picked up) are more likely to respond quickly and sensitively (Cohen-Bendahan, van Doornen, & de Weerth, 2014; Leerkes, 2010).

Fortunately, there are many ways to soothe a crying baby when feeding and diaper changing do not work (see Applying What We Know above). The technique that Western parents usually try first, lifting the baby to the shoulder and rocking or walking, is highly effective. Another common soothing method is swaddling—wrapping the baby snugly in a blanket. The Quechua, who live in the cold, high-altitude desert regions of Peru, dress young babies in layers of clothing and blankets that cover the head and body, a practice that reduces crying and promotes sleep (Tronick, Thomas, & Daltabuit, 1994). It also allows the baby to conserve energy for early growth in the harsh Peruvian highlands.

LOOK and LISTEN

In a public setting, watch several parents soothe their crying infants. What techniques did the parents use, and how successful were they?

In many tribal and village societies and non-Western developed nations (such as Japan), babies are in physical contact with their caregivers almost continuously. Infants in these cultures

The Bedouin people of the Middle East tightly swaddle young infants, a practice that reduces crying and promotes sleep.

show shorter bouts of crying than their American counterparts (Barr, 2001). When Western parents choose to practice "proximal care" by holding their babies extensively, the amount of crying in the early months is reduced by about one-third (St James-Roberts, 2012).

Fortunately, with age, crying declines. Virtually all researchers agree that parents can lessen older babies' need to cry by encouraging more mature ways of expressing their desires, such as gestures and vocalizations.

Abnormal Crying. Like reflexes and sleep patterns, the infant's cry offers a clue to central nervous system distress. The cries of brain-damaged babies and those who have experienced prenatal and birth complications are often shrill, piercing, and shorter in duration than those of healthy infants (Green, Irwin, & Gustafson, 2000). Even newborns with a fairly common problem—*colic*, or persistent crying—tend to have high-pitched, harsh-sounding cries (Zeskind & Barr, 1997). Although the cause of colic is unknown, certain newborns, who react especially strongly to unpleasant stimuli, are susceptible. Because their crying is intense, they find it harder to calm down than other babies (St James-Roberts, 2007). Colic generally subsides between 3 and 6 months.

Most parents try to respond to a crying baby with extra care and attention, but sometimes the cry is so unpleasant and the infant so difficult to soothe that parents become frustrated, resentful, and angry. Preterm and ill babies are more likely to be abused by highly stressed parents, who sometimes mention a high-pitched, grating cry as one factor that caused them to lose control and harm the baby (Barr et al., 2014; St James-Roberts, 2012). We will discuss a host of additional influences on child abuse in Chapter 8.

Sensory Capacities

On his visit to my class, Joshua looked wide-eyed at my bright pink blouse and turned to the sound of his mother's voice. During feedings, he lets Yolanda know through his sucking rhythm that he prefers the taste of breast milk to a bottle of plain water. Clearly, Joshua has some well-developed sensory capacities. In the following sections, we explore the newborn's responsiveness to touch, taste, smell, sound, and visual stimulation.

Touch.
In our discussion of preterm infants, we saw that touch helps stimulate early physical growth. As we will see in Chapter 6, it is vital for emotional development as well. Therefore, it is not surprising that sensitivity to touch emerges early prenatally and is well-developed at birth, as the reflexes listed in Table 3.4 on page 101 reveal. Newborns even use touch to investigate their world. When small objects are placed in their palms, they can distinguish shape (prism versus cylinder) and texture (smooth versus rough), as indicated by their tendency to hold on longer to an object with an unfamiliar shape or texture than to a familiar object (Lejeune et al., 2012; Sann & Streri, 2007).

At birth, infants are highly sensitive to pain. If male newborns are circumcised, anesthetic is sometimes not used because of the risk of giving drugs to a very young infant. Babies often respond with a high-pitched, stressful cry and a dramatic rise in heart rate, blood pressure, palm sweating, pupil dilation, and muscle tension (Lehr et al., 2007; Warnock & Sandrin, 2004). Brain-imaging research suggests that because of central nervous system immaturity, preterm babies, particularly males, feel the pain of a medical injection especially intensely (Bartocci et al., 2006).

Certain local anesthetics for newborns ease the pain of these procedures. As a supplement to pain-relieving medication, offering a nipple that delivers a sugar solution is also helpful; it quickly reduces crying and discomfort in young babies, preterm and full-term alike (Roman-Rodriguez et al., 2014). Breast milk may be especially effective: Even the smell of the milk of the baby's mother reduces infant distress to a routine blood-test heel stick more effectively than the odor of another mother's milk or of formula (Badiee, Asghari, & Mohammadizadeh, 2013; Nishitani et al., 2009). And combining sweet liquid with gentle holding by the parent lessens pain even more. Research on infant mammals indicates that physical touch releases *endorphins*—painkilling chemicals in the brain (Gormally et al., 2001).

Allowing a baby to endure severe pain overwhelms the nervous system with stress hormones (Walker, 2013). The result is heightened pain sensitivity, sleep disturbances, feeding problems, and difficulty calming down when upset.

Taste and Smell.
Facial expressions reveal that newborns can distinguish several basic tastes. Like adults, they relax their facial muscles in response to sweetness, purse their lips when the taste is sour, and show an archlike mouth opening when it is bitter. Similarly, certain odor preferences are present at birth. For example, the smell of bananas or chocolate causes a pleasant facial expression, whereas the odor of rotten eggs makes the infant frown (Steiner, 1979; Steiner et al., 2001). These reactions are important for survival: The food that best supports the infant's early growth is the sweet-tasting milk of the mother's breast. Not until 4 months do babies prefer a salty taste to plain water, a change that may prepare them to accept solid foods (Mennella & Beauchamp, 1998).

During pregnancy, the amniotic fluid is rich in tastes and smells that vary with the mother's diet—early experiences that influence newborns' preferences. In a study carried out in the Alsatian region of France, where anise is frequently used to flavor foods, researchers tested newborns for their reaction to the anise odor (Schaal, Marlier, & Soussignan, 2000). The mothers of some babies had regularly consumed anise during the last two weeks of pregnancy; the other mothers had never consumed it. When presented with the anise odor on the day of birth, the babies of non-anise-consuming mothers were far more likely to turn away with a negative facial expression (see Figure 3.9). These different reactions were still apparent four days later, even though all mothers had refrained from consuming anise during this time.

FIGURE 3.9 Examples of facial expressions of newborns exposed to the odor of anise whose mothers' diets differed in anise-flavored foods during late pregnancy. (a) Babies of anise-consuming mothers spent more time turning toward the odor and sucking, licking, and chewing. (b) Babies of non-anise-consuming mothers more often turned away with a negative facial expression. (From B. Schaal, L. Marlier, & R. Soussignan, 2000, "Human Foetuses Learn Odours from Their Pregnant Mother's Diet," *Chemical Senses*, 25, p. 731. © 2000 Oxford University Press, Inc.; permission conveyed through Copyright Clearance Center, Inc.)

Young infants will readily learn to prefer a taste that at first evoked either a negative or a neutral response. Bottle-fed newborns allergic to cow's milk who are given a soy or other vegetable-based substitute (typically very sour and bitter-tasting) soon prefer it to regular formula. When first given solid foods several months later, these infants display an unusual liking for bitter-tasting cereals (Beauchamp & Mennella, 2011). This taste preference is still evident at ages 4 to 5 years, in more positive responses to foods with sour and bitter tastes than shown by agemates without early vegetable-based formula exposure.

In mammals, including humans, the sense of smell—in addition to playing an important role in feeding—helps mothers and babies identify each other. At 2 to 4 days of age, breastfed babies prefer the odors of their own mother's breast and underarm to those of an unfamiliar lactating mother (Cernoch & Porter, 1985; Marin, Rapisardi, & Tani, 2015). And both breast- and bottle-fed 3- to 4-day-olds orient more and display more mouthing to the smell of unfamiliar human milk than to formula milk, indicating that (even without postnatal exposure) the odor of human milk is more attractive to newborns (Marlier & Schaal, 2005). Newborns' dual attraction to the odors of their mother and of breast milk helps them locate an appropriate food source and, in the process, begin to distinguish their caregiver from other people.

Hearing. Newborn infants can hear a wide variety of sounds—sensitivity that improves greatly over the first few months (Johnson & Hannon, 2015). At birth, infants prefer complex sounds, such as noises and voices, to pure tones. And babies only a few days old can tell the difference between a variety of sound patterns: a series of tones arranged in ascending versus descending order; tone sequences with a rhythmic downbeat (as in music) versus those without; utterances with two versus three syllables; the stress patterns of words ("*ma*-ma" versus "ma-*ma*"); happy-sounding speech as opposed to speech with negative or neutral emotional qualities; and even two languages spoken by the same bilingual speaker, as long as those languages differ in their rhythmic features—for example, French versus Russian (Mastropieri & Turkewitz, 1999; Ramus, 2002; Sansavini, Bertoncini, & Giovanelli, 1997; Trehub, 2001; Winkler et al., 2009).

Young infants listen longer to human speech than structurally similar nonspeech sounds (Vouloumanos, 2010). And they can detect the sounds of any human language. Newborns make fine-grained distinctions among many speech sounds. For example, when given a nipple that turns on a recording of the *"ba"* sound, babies suck vigorously and then slow down as the novelty wears off. When the sound switches to *"ga,"* sucking picks up, indicating that infants detect this subtle difference. Using this method, researchers have found only a few speech sounds that newborns cannot discriminate. Their ability to perceive sounds not found in their own language is more precise than an adult's (Aldridge, Stillman, & Bower, 2001; Jusczyk & Luce, 2002). These capacities reveal that the baby is marvelously prepared for the awesome task of acquiring language.

Listen carefully to yourself the next time you talk to a young baby. You will probably speak in ways that highlight important parts of the speech stream—use a slow, high-pitched, expressive voice with a rising tone at the ends of phrases and sentences and a pause before continuing. Adults probably communicate this way with infants because they notice that babies are more attentive when they do so. Indeed, newborns prefer speech with these characteristics (Saffran, Werker, & Werner, 2006). They will also suck more on a nipple to hear a recording of their mother's voice than that of an unfamiliar woman and to hear their native language as opposed to a foreign language (Moon, Cooper, & Fifer, 1993; Spence & DeCasper, 1987). These preferences result from hearing the muffled sounds of the mother's voice before birth.

Vision. Vision is the least-developed of the newborn baby's senses. Visual structures in both the eye and the brain are not yet fully formed. For example, cells in the *retina*, the membrane lining the inside of the eye that captures light and transforms it into messages that are sent to the brain, are not as mature or densely packed as they will be in several months. The optic nerve that relays these messages, and visual centers in the brain that receive them, will not be adultlike for several years. And muscles of the *lens*, which permit us to adjust our visual focus to varying distances, are weak (Johnson & Hannon, 2015).

As a result, newborns cannot focus their eyes well, and their **visual acuity,** or fineness of discrimination, is limited. At birth, infants perceive objects at a distance of 20 feet about as clearly as adults do at 600 feet (Slater et al., 2010). In addition, unlike adults (who see nearby objects most clearly), newborn babies see unclearly across a wide range of distances (Banks, 1980; Hainline, 1998). As a result, images such as the parent's face, even from close up, look quite blurred.

Although they cannot yet see well, newborns actively explore their environment by scanning it for interesting sights and tracking moving objects. However, their eye movements are slow and inaccurate (von Hofsten & Rosander, 1998). Joshua's captivation with my pink blouse reveals that he is attracted to bright objects. But despite their preference for colored over gray stimuli, newborn babies are not yet good at discriminating colors. It will take about four months for color vision to become adultlike (Johnson & Hannon, 2015).

Neonatal Behavioral Assessment

A variety of instruments permit doctors, nurses, and researchers to assess the behavior of newborn babies. The most widely used, T. Berry Brazelton's **Neonatal Behavioral Assessment Scale (NBAS),** evaluates the newborn's reflexes, muscle tone, state changes, responsiveness to physical and social stimuli, and other reactions (Brazelton & Nugent, 2011). An instrument consisting of similar items, the *Neonatal Intensive Care Unit Network Neurobehavioral Scale (NNNS),* is specially designed for use with newborns at risk for developmental problems because of low birth weight, preterm delivery, prenatal substance exposure, or other conditions (Tronick & Lester, 2013). Scores are used to recommend appropriate interventions and to guide parents in meeting their baby's unique needs.

The NBAS has been given to many infants around the world. As a result, researchers have learned about individual and cultural differences in newborn behavior and how child-rearing practices can maintain or change a baby's reactions. For example, compared with scores of European-American infants, NBAS scores of Asian and Native-American babies reveal less irritability. Mothers in these cultures often encourage their babies' calm dispositions through holding and nursing at the first signs of discomfort (Muret-Wagstaff & Moore, 1989; Small, 1998). The Kipsigis of rural Kenya, who highly value infant motor maturity, massage babies regularly and begin exercising the stepping reflex shortly after birth. These customs contribute to Kipsigis babies' strong but flexible muscle tone at 5 days of age (Super & Harkness, 2009). In Zambia, Africa, close mother–infant contact throughout the day quickly changes the poor NBAS scores of undernourished newborns. When reassessed at 1 week of age, a once unresponsive newborn appears alert and contented (Brazelton, Koslowski, & Tronick, 1976).

Because newborn behavior and parenting combine to influence development, *changes in scores* over the first week or two of life (rather than a single score) provide the best estimate of the baby's ability to recover from the stress of birth. NBAS "recovery curves" predict intelligence and absence of emotional and behavior problems with moderate success well into the preschool

Similar to women in the Zambian culture, this mother of the El Molo people of northern Kenya carries her baby all day, providing close physical contact, a rich variety of stimulation, and ready feeding.

years (Brazelton, Nugent, & Lester, 1987; Ohgi et al., 2003a, 2003b).

In some hospitals, health professionals use the NBAS or the NNNS to help parents get to know their newborns through discussion or demonstration of the capacities these instruments assess. Parents who participate in these programs, compared with no-intervention controls, interact more confidently and effectively with their babies (Browne & Talmi, 2005; Bruschweiler-Stern, 2004). Although lasting effects on development have not been demonstrated, NBAS-based interventions are useful in helping the parent–infant relationship get off to a good start.

Ask yourself

CONNECT How do the diverse capacities of newborn babies contribute to their first social relationships? Provide as many examples as you can.

APPLY After a difficult delivery, Jackie observes her 2-day-old daughter, Kelly, being given the NBAS. Kelly scores poorly on many items. Seeing this, Jackie wonders if Kelly will develop normally. How would you respond to Jackie's concern?

REFLECT Are newborns more competent than you thought they were before you read this chapter? Which of their capacities most surprised you?

Adjusting to the New Family Unit

3.12 Describe typical changes in the family after the birth of a baby.

Because effective caregiving is crucial for infant survival and optimal development, nature helps prepare expectant mothers and fathers for their new role. Toward the end of pregnancy, mothers begin producing higher levels of the hormone *oxytocin*, which stimulates uterine contractions; causes the breasts to "let down" milk; induces a calm, relaxed mood; and promotes responsiveness to the baby (Gordon et al., 2010).

Fathers show hormonal changes around the time of birth that are compatible with those of mothers—specifically, slight increases in *prolactin* (a hormone that stimulates milk production in females) and *estrogens* (sex hormones produced in larger quantities in females) and a drop in *androgens* (sex hormones produced in larger quantities in males) (Delahunty et al., 2007; Wynne-Edwards, 2001). These changes, which are induced by fathers' contact with the mother and baby, predict positive emotional reactions and sensitivity to infants (Feldman et al., 2010; Leuner, Glasper, & Gould, 2010).

Although birth-related hormones can facilitate caregiving, their release and effects seem to depend on experiences, such as a positive couple relationship. Furthermore, as successful adoption reveals, humans can parent effectively without experiencing birth-related hormonal changes. In fact, when foster and adoptive mothers hold and interact with their nonbiological infants, they typically release oxytocin (Bick et al., 2013; Galbally et al., 2011). And the greater their oxytocin production, the more they express affection and pleasure toward the infant.

Nevertheless, the early weeks after a baby's arrival are full of profound challenges. The mother needs to recover from childbirth. If she is breastfeeding, energies must be devoted to working out this intimate relationship. The father must become a part of this new threesome while supporting the mother in her recovery. At times, he may feel ambivalent about the baby, who constantly demands and gets the mother's attention. And as we will see in Chapter 6, siblings—especially those who are young and firstborn—understandably feel displaced. They sometimes react with jealousy and anger.

While all this is going on, the tiny infant is assertive about his urgent physical needs, demanding to be fed, changed, and comforted at odd times of the day and night. The family schedule becomes irregular and uncertain, and parental sleep deprivation and consequent daytime fatigue are often major challenges (Insana & Montgomery-Downs, 2012). Yolanda spoke candidly about the changes she and Jay experienced:

> When we brought Joshua home, he seemed so small and helpless, and we worried about whether we would be able to take proper care of him. It took us 20 minutes to change the first diaper! I rarely feel rested because I'm up two to four times every night, and I spend a good part of my waking hours trying to anticipate Joshua's rhythms and needs. If Jay weren't so willing to help by holding and walking Joshua, I think I'd find it much harder.

In Chapter 14, we will see that when parents' relationship is positive and cooperative, social support is available, and families have sufficient income, the stress caused by the birth of a baby remains manageable. These family conditions consistently contribute to favorable development—in infancy and beyond.

Summary / chapter 3

Prenatal Development (p. 76)

3.1 *List the three periods of prenatal development, and describe the major milestones of each.*

- The **germinal period** lasts about two weeks, from fertilization through **implantation** of the multicelled blastocyst in the uterine lining. Structures that will support prenatal growth begin to form, including the **placenta** and the **umbilical cord**.

- During the period of the **embryo**, weeks 2 through 8, the foundations for all body structures are laid down. The **neural tube** forms and the nervous system starts to develop. Other organs follow rapidly. By the end of this period, the embryo responds to touch and can move.

- The period of the **fetus**, lasting until the end of pregnancy, involves dramatic increase in body size and completion of physical structures. High fetal activity in the middle of the second **trimester** strengthens joints and muscles. At the end of the second trimester, most of the brain's neurons are in place.

- The fetus reaches the **age of viability** at the beginning of the third trimester, between 22 and 26 weeks. The brain continues to develop rapidly, and new sensory and behavioral capacities emerge, including taste and odor preferences, pain sensitivity, and the ability to distinguish the tone and rhythm of different voices and sounds. Gradually the lungs mature, the fetus fills the uterus, and birth is near.

Prenatal Environmental Influences (p. 81)

3.2 *Cite factors that influence the impact of teratogens, and discuss evidence on the impact of known or suspected teratogens.*

- The impact of **teratogens** varies with amount and length of exposure, genetic makeup of mother and fetus, presence of other harmful agents, and age of the organism. The developing organism is especially vulnerable during the embryonic period.

- The most widely used potent teratogen is isotretinoin, a drug used to treat severe acne. The prenatal impact of other commonly used medications, such as aspirin and caffeine, is hard to separate from other correlated factors.

- Babies born to users of cocaine, heroin, or methadone are at risk for a wide variety of problems, including prematurity, low birth weight, brain abnormalities, physical defects, breathing difficulties, and infant death around the time of birth. However, negative effects of cocaine are not well-established.

- Infants whose parents use tobacco are often born underweight, may have physical defects, and are at risk for long-term attention, learning, and behavior problems. Maternal alcohol consumption can lead to **fetal alcohol spectrum disorder (FASD)**. **Fetal alcohol syndrome (FAS)**, resulting from heavy drinking throughout pregnancy, involves slow physical growth, facial abnormalities, and mental impairments. Milder forms—**partial fetal alcohol syndrome (p-FAS)** and **alcohol-related neurodevelopmental disorder (ARND)**—affect children whose mothers consumed smaller quantities of alcohol.

- Prenatal exposure to high levels of ionizing radiation, mercury, PCBs, lead, and dioxins leads to physical malformations and severe brain damage. Low-level exposure has been linked to cognitive deficits and emotional and behavioral disorders. Persistent air pollution is associated with low birth weight and impaired lung and immune-system functioning.

- Among infectious diseases, rubella causes wide-ranging abnormalities. Babies with prenatally transmitted HIV rapidly develop AIDS, leading to brain damage and early death. Antiretroviral drug therapy dramatically reduces prenatal transmission. Cytomegalovirus, herpes simplex 2, and toxoplasmosis can also be devastating to the embryo and fetus.

3.3 *Describe the impact of additional maternal factors on prenatal development.*

- Exercise during pregnancy is linked to improved fetal cardiovascular functioning and reduction in risk of pregnancy complications.

- Prenatal malnutrition can lead to low birth weight, damage to the brain and other organs, and suppression of immune system development. Vitamin–mineral supplementation, including folic acid, can prevent prenatal and birth complications.

- Severe emotional stress is linked to pregnancy complications and may permanently alter fetal neurological functioning, resulting in impaired capacity to manage stress and susceptibility to later illness. Stress-related prenatal consequences can be reduced by providing the mother with social support. **Rh factor incompatibility**—an Rh-positive fetus developing within an Rh-negative mother—can lead to oxygen deprivation, brain and heart damage, and infant death.

- Older mothers face increased risk of miscarriage, babies with chromosomal defects, and, after age 40, a rise in other pregnancy complications. Poor health and environmental risks associated with poverty explain higher rates of pregnancy complications in adolescent mothers.

3.4 *Why is early and regular health care vital during the prenatal period?*

- Unexpected difficulties, such as preeclampsia, can arise, especially when pregnant women have preexisting health problems. Prenatal health care is especially crucial for women least likely to seek it, particularly those who are young, less-educated, and low-income.

Childbirth (p. 92)

3.5 *Describe the three stages of childbirth, the baby's adaptation to labor and delivery, and the newborn baby's appearance.*

- In the first stage, contractions widen and thin the cervix. In the second stage, the mother feels an urge to push the baby through the birth canal. In the final stage, the placenta is delivered. During labor, infants produce high levels of stress hormones, which help them withstand oxygen deprivation, clear the lungs for breathing, and arouse them into alertness at birth.

- Newborn babies have large heads, small bodies, and facial features that make adults feel like cuddling them. The **Apgar Scale** assesses the baby's physical condition at birth.

Approaches to Childbirth (p. 95)

3.6 *Describe natural childbirth and home delivery, noting benefits and concerns associated with each.*

- In **natural**, or **prepared, childbirth,** the expectant mother and a companion attend classes about labor and delivery, master relaxation and breathing techniques to counteract pain, and prepare for coaching during childbirth. Social support from a doula reduces the length of labor and the incidence of birth complications and enhances newborn adjustment.

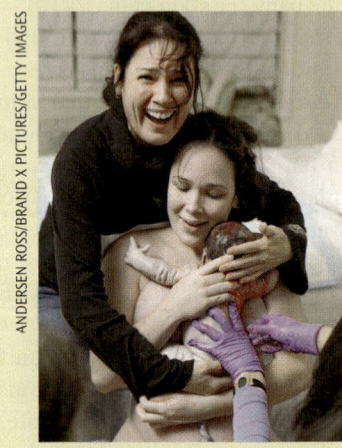

- Home birth is safe for healthy mothers who are assisted by a well-trained doctor or midwife, but mothers at risk for complications are safer giving birth in a hospital.

Medical Interventions (p. 96)

3.7 *List common medical interventions during childbirth, circumstances that justify their use, and any dangers associated with each.*

- **Fetal monitors** help save the lives of many babies at risk for **anoxia** because of pregnancy and birth complications. When used routinely, however, they may identify infants as in danger who, in fact, are not.

- Use of analgesics and anesthetics to control pain, though necessary in complicated deliveries, can prolong labor and may have negative effects on newborn adjustment.

- **Cesarean delivery** is warranted by medical emergency or serious maternal illness and for many babies who are in **breech position**. However, many unnecessary cesareans are performed.

Preterm and Low-Birth-Weight Infants (p. 97)

3.8 *Describe risks associated with preterm birth and low birth weight, along with effective interventions.*

- Low birth weight, most common in infants born to poverty-stricken women, is a major cause of neonatal and **infant mortality** and developmental problems. Compared with **preterm infants**, whose weight is appropriate for time spent in the uterus, **small-for-date infants** usually have longer-lasting difficulties.

- Some interventions provide special infant stimulation in the intensive care nursery. Others teach parents how to care for and interact with their babies. Preterm infants in stressed, low-income households need long-term, intensive intervention.

The Newborn Baby's Capacities (p. 101)

3.9 *Describe the newborn baby's reflexes and states of arousal, noting sleep characteristics and ways to soothe a crying baby.*

- **Reflexes** are the newborn baby's most obvious organized patterns of behavior. Some have survival value, others help parents and infants establish gratifying interaction, and a few provide the foundation for complex motor skills.

- Newborns experience five **states of arousal** but spend most of their time asleep. Sleep includes at least two states, **rapid-eye-movement (REM) sleep** and **non-rapid-eye-movement (NREM) sleep.** Newborns spend about 50 percent of sleep time in REM sleep, which provides them with stimulation essential for central nervous system development.

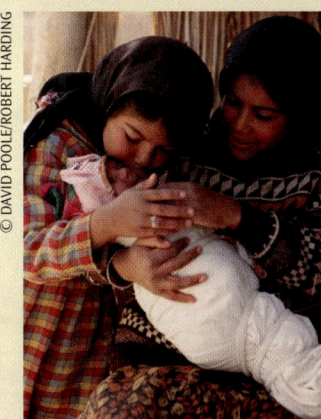

- A crying baby stimulates strong feelings of discomfort in nearby adults. Once feeding and diaper changing have been tried, a highly effective soothing technique is lifting the baby to the shoulder and rocking or walking. Extensive parent–infant physical contact substantially reduces crying in the early months.

3.10 *Describe the newborn baby's sensory capacities.*

- The senses of touch, taste, smell, and sound are well-developed at birth. Newborns use touch to investigate their world, are sensitive to pain, prefer sweet tastes and smells, and orient toward the odor of their own mother's lactating breast.

- Newborns can distinguish a variety of sound patterns and prefer complex sounds. They are especially responsive to human speech, can detect the sounds of any human language, and prefer their mother's voice.

- Vision is the least developed of the newborn's senses. At birth, focusing ability and **visual acuity** are limited. In exploring the visual field, newborn babies are attracted to bright objects but have difficulty discriminating colors.

3.11 *Why is neonatal behavioral assessment useful?*

- The most widely used instrument for assessing the newborn infant's behavior, Brazelton's **Neonatal Behavioral Assessment Scale (NBAS)**, has helped researchers understand individual and cultural differences in newborn behavior. Sometimes it is used to teach parents about their baby's capacities.

Adjusting to the New Family Unit (p. 111)

3.12 *Describe typical changes in the family after the birth of a baby.*

- The new baby's arrival is exciting but stressful, as the mother recuperates from childbirth and the family schedule becomes irregular and uncertain. When parents have a positive relationship as well as social support and adequate income, adjustment problems are usually temporary.

Important Terms and Concepts

age of viability (p. 80)
alcohol-related neurodevelopmental disorder (ARND) (p. 84)
amnion (p. 77)
anoxia (p. 96)
Apgar Scale (p. 94)
breech position (p. 96)
cesarean delivery (p. 97)
chorion (p. 78)
embryo (p. 78)
fetal alcohol spectrum disorder (FASD) (p. 84)
fetal alcohol syndrome (FAS) (p. 84)

fetal monitors (p. 96)
fetus (p. 79)
implantation (p. 77)
infant mortality (p. 102)
lanugo (p. 79)
natural, or prepared, childbirth (p. 95)
Neonatal Behavioral Assessment Scale (NBAS) (p. 110)
neural tube (p. 78)
non-rapid-eye-movement (NREM) sleep (p. 105)
partial fetal alcohol syndrome (p-FAS) (p. 84)
placenta (p. 78)

preterm infants (p. 98)
rapid-eye-movement (REM) sleep (p. 105)
reflex (p. 101)
Rh factor incompatibility (p. 89)
small-for-date infants (p. 98)
states of arousal (p. 104)
sudden infant death syndrome (SIDS) (p. 106)
teratogen (p. 81)
trimesters (p. 79)
umbilical cord (p. 78)
vernix (p. 79)
visual acuity (p. 109)

chapter 4

Physical Development in Infancy and Toddlerhood

Beginning to walk frees this 14-month-old's hands for carrying objects, grants a whole new perspective on a tantalizing physical world to explore, and enables her to interact with caregivers in new ways—for example, by showing an object or giving a hug. In the first two years, motor, perceptual, cognitive, and social development mutually influence one another.

What's ahead in chapter 4

Body Growth

Changes in Body Size and Muscle–Fat Makeup • Changes in Body Proportions • Individual and Group Differences

Brain Development

Development of Neurons • Measures of Brain Functioning • Development of the Cerebral Cortex • Sensitive Periods in Brain Development • Changing States of Arousal

■ **BIOLOGY AND ENVIRONMENT** Brain Plasticity: Insights from Research on Brain-Damaged Children and Adults

■ **CULTURAL INFLUENCES** Cultural Variation in Infant Sleeping Arrangements

Influences on Early Physical Growth

Heredity • Nutrition • Malnutrition

Learning Capacities

Classical Conditioning • Operant Conditioning • Habituation • Imitation

Motor Development

The Sequence of Motor Development • Motor Skills as Dynamic Systems • Fine-Motor Development: Reaching and Grasping

Perceptual Development

Hearing • Vision • Intermodal Perception • Understanding Perceptual Development

■ **BIOLOGY AND ENVIRONMENT** "Tuning In" to Familiar Speech, Faces, and Music: A Sensitive Period for Culture-Specific Learning

On a brilliant June morning, 16-month-old Caitlin emerged from her front door, ready for the short drive to the child-care home where she spent her weekdays while her mother, Carolyn, and her father, David, worked. Clutching a teddy bear in one hand and her mother's arm with the other, Caitlin descended the steps. "One! Two! Threeee!" Carolyn counted as she helped Caitlin down. "How much she's changed," Carolyn thought to herself, looking at the child who, not long ago, had been a newborn. With her first steps, Caitlin had passed from *infancy* to *toddlerhood*—a period spanning the second year of life. At first, Caitlin did, indeed, "toddle" with an awkward gait, tipping over frequently. But her face reflected the thrill of conquering a new skill.

As they walked toward the car, Carolyn and Caitlin spotted 3-year-old Eli and his father, Kevin, in the neighboring yard. Eli dashed toward them, waving a bright yellow envelope. Carolyn bent down to open the envelope and took out a card. It read, "Announcing the arrival of Grace Ann. Born: Cambodia. Age: 16 months." Carolyn turned to Kevin and Eli. "That's wonderful news! When can we see her?"

"Let's wait a few days," Kevin suggested. "Monica's taken Grace to the doctor this morning. She's underweight and malnourished." Kevin described Monica's first night with Grace in a hotel room in Phnom Penh. Grace lay on the bed, withdrawn and fearful. Eventually she fell asleep, gripping crackers in both hands.

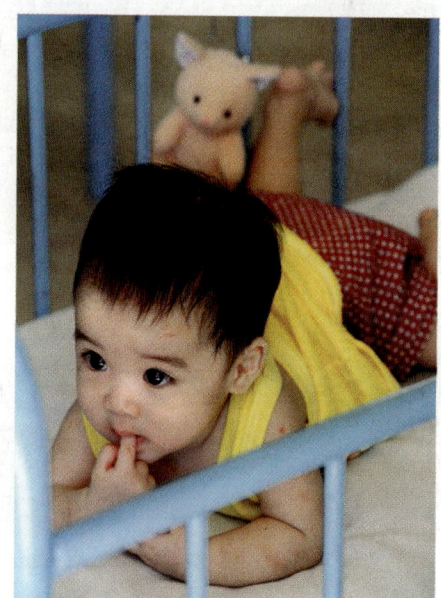

Carolyn felt Caitlin's impatient tug at her sleeve. Off they drove to child care, where Vanessa had just dropped off her 18-month-old son, Timmy. Within moments, Caitlin and Timmy were in the sandbox, shoveling sand into plastic cups and buckets with the help of their caregiver, Ginette.

A few weeks later, Grace joined Caitlin and Timmy at Ginette's child-care home. Although still tiny and unable to crawl or walk, she had grown taller and heavier, and her sad, vacant gaze had given way to an alert expression, a ready smile, and an enthusiastic desire to imitate and explore. When Caitlin headed for the sandbox, Grace stretched out her arms, asking Ginette to carry her there, too. Soon Grace was pulling herself up at every opportunity. Finally, at age 18 months, she walked!

This chapter traces physical growth during the first two years—one of the most remarkable and busiest times of development. We will see how rapid changes in the infant's body and brain support learning, motor skills, and perceptual capacities. Caitlin, Grace, and Timmy will join us along the way to illustrate individual differences and environmental influences on physical development. ●

116 CHAPTER 4 Physical Development in Infancy and Toddlerhood

Body Growth

4.1 Describe major changes in body growth over the first two years.

The next time you're walking in your neighborhood park or at the mall, note the contrast between infants' and toddlers' physical capabilities. One reason for the vast changes in what children can do over the first two years is that their bodies change enormously—faster than at any other time after birth.

Changes in Body Size and Muscle–Fat Makeup

By the end of the first year, a typical infant's height is about 32 inches—more than 50 percent greater than at birth. By 2 years, it is 75 percent greater (36 inches). Similarly, by 5 months of age, birth weight has doubled, to about 15 pounds. At 1 year it has tripled, to 22 pounds, and at 2 years it has quadrupled, to about 30 pounds.

Figure 4.1 illustrates this dramatic increase in body size. But rather than making steady gains, infants and toddlers grow in

FIGURE 4.1 Body growth during the first two years. These photos depict the dramatic changes in body size and proportions during infancy and toddlerhood in two individuals—a boy, Shanwel, and a girl, Mai. In the first year, the head is quite large in proportion to the rest of the body, and height and weight gain are especially rapid. During the second year, the lower portion of the body catches up. Notice, also, how both children added "baby fat" in the early months of life and then slimmed down, a trend that continues into middle childhood.

little spurts. In one study, children who were followed over the first 21 months of life went for periods of 7 to 63 days with no growth, then added as much as half an inch in a 24-hour period! Almost always, parents described their babies as irritable, very hungry, and sleeping more on the days before the spurt (Lampl, 1993; Lampl & Johnson, 2011).

One of the most obvious changes in infants' appearance is their transformation into round, plump babies by the middle of the first year. This early rise in "baby fat," which peaks at about 9 months, helps the small infant maintain a constant body temperature. In the second year, most toddlers slim down, a trend that continues into middle childhood (Fomon & Nelson, 2002). In contrast, muscle tissue increases very slowly during infancy and will not reach a peak until adolescence. Babies are not very muscular; their strength and physical coordination are limited.

Changes in Body Proportions

As the child's overall size increases, different parts of the body grow at different rates. Two growth patterns describe these changes. The first is the **cephalocaudal trend**—from the Latin for "head to tail." During the prenatal period, the head develops more rapidly than the lower part of the body. At birth, the head takes up one-fourth of total body length, the legs only one-third. Notice how, in Figure 4.1, the lower portion of the body catches up. By age 2, the head accounts for only one-fifth and the legs for nearly one-half of total body length.

In the second pattern, the **proximodistal trend,** growth proceeds, literally, from "near to far"—from the center of the body outward. In the prenatal period, the head, chest, and trunk grow first; then the arms and legs; and finally the hands and feet. During infancy and childhood, the arms and legs continue to grow somewhat ahead of the hands and feet.

Individual and Group Differences

In infancy, girls are slightly shorter and lighter than boys, with a higher ratio of fat to muscle. These small sex differences persist throughout early and middle childhood and are greatly magnified at adolescence. Ethnic differences in body size are apparent as well. Grace was below the *growth norms* (height and weight averages for children her age). Early malnutrition contributed, but even after substantial catch-up, Grace—as is typical for Asian children—remained below North American norms. In contrast, Timmy is slightly above average, as African-American children tend to be (Bogin, 2001).

Children of the same age differ in *rate* of physical growth; some make faster progress toward a mature body size than others. But current body size is not enough to tell us how quickly a child's physical growth is moving along. Although Timmy is larger and heavier than Caitlin and Grace, he is not physically more mature. In a moment, you will see why.

The best estimate of a child's physical maturity is *skeletal age,* a measure of bone development. It is determined by X-raying the long bones of the body to see the extent to which soft, pliable cartilage has hardened into bone—a gradual process that is completed in adolescence. When skeletal ages are examined, African-American children tend to be slightly ahead of European-American children, and girls are considerably ahead of boys. At birth, the sexes differ by about 4 to 6 weeks, a gap that widens over infancy and childhood (Tanner, Healy, & Cameron, 2001). Girls are advanced in development of other organs as well. This greater physical maturity may contribute to girls' greater resistance to harmful environmental influences. As noted in Chapter 2, girls experience fewer developmental problems than boys and have lower infant and childhood mortality rates.

Brain Development

4.2 Describe brain development during infancy and toddlerhood, current methods of measuring brain functioning, and appropriate stimulation to support the brain's potential.

4.3 How does the organization of sleep and wakefulness change over the first two years?

At birth, the brain is nearer to its adult size than any other physical structure, and it continues to develop at an astounding pace throughout infancy and toddlerhood. We can best understand brain growth by looking at it from two vantage points: (1) the microscopic level of individual brain cells and (2) the larger level of the cerebral cortex, the most complex brain structure and the one responsible for the highly developed intelligence of our species.

Development of Neurons

The human brain has 100 to 200 billion **neurons,** or nerve cells, that store and transmit information, many of which have thousands of direct connections with other neurons. Unlike other body cells, neurons are not tightly packed together. Between them are tiny gaps, or **synapses,** where fibers from different neurons come close together but do not touch (see Figure 4.2 on page 118). Neurons send messages to one another by releasing chemicals called **neurotransmitters,** which cross the synapse.

The basic story of brain growth concerns how neurons develop and form this elaborate communication system. Figure 4.3 on page 118 summarizes major milestones of brain development. In the prenatal period, neurons are produced in the embryo's primitive neural tube. From there, they migrate to form the major parts of the brain (see Chapter 3, page 79). Once neurons are in place, they differentiate, establishing their unique functions by extending their fibers to form synaptic connections with neighboring cells. During the first two years, neural fibers and synapses increase at an astounding pace (Gilmore et al., 2012; Moore, Persaud, & Torchia, 2016a). A surprising aspect of brain growth

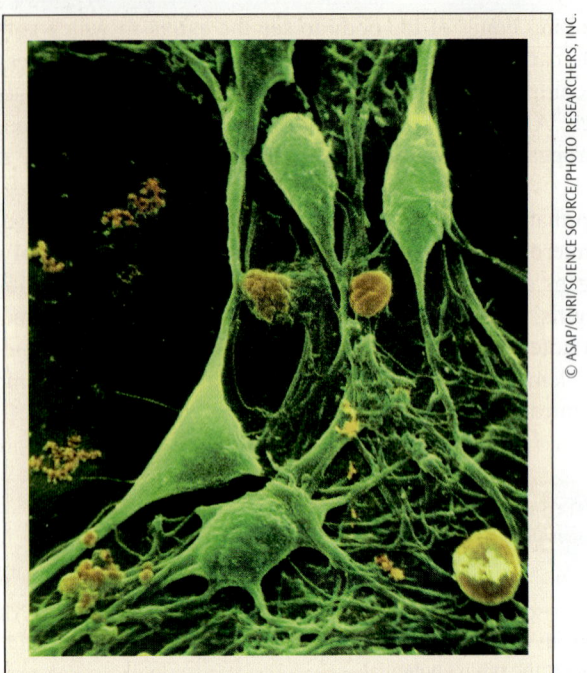

FIGURE 4.2 Neurons and their connective fibers. This photograph of several neurons, taken with the aid of a powerful microscope, shows the elaborate synaptic connections that form with neighboring cells.

As neurons form connections, *stimulation* becomes vital to their survival. Neurons that are stimulated by input from the surrounding environment continue to establish new synapses, forming increasingly elaborate systems of communication that support more complex abilities. At first, stimulation results in a massive overabundance of synapses, many of which serve identical functions, thereby ensuring that the child will acquire the motor, cognitive, and social skills that our species needs to survive. Neurons that are seldom stimulated soon lose their synapses, in a process called **synaptic pruning** that returns neurons not needed at the moment to an uncommitted state so they can support future development. In all, about 40 percent of synapses are pruned during childhood and adolescence to reach the adult level (Webb, Monk, & Nelson, 2001). For this process to advance, appropriate stimulation of the child's brain is vital during periods in which the formation of synapses is at its peak (Bryk & Fisher, 2012).

If few neurons are produced after the prenatal period, what causes the extraordinary increase in brain size during the first two years? About half the brain's volume is made up of **glial cells,** which are responsible for **myelination,** the coating of neural fibers with an insulating fatty sheath (called *myelin*) that improves the efficiency of message transfer. Glial cells multiply rapidly from the end of pregnancy through the second year of life—a process that continues at a slower pace through middle childhood and accelerates again in adolescence. Gains in neural fibers and myelination account for the overall increase in size of the brain, from nearly 30 percent of its adult weight at birth to 70 percent by age 2 (Johnson, 2011). Growth is especially dramatic during the first year, when the brain more than doubles in size.

is **programmed cell death,** which makes space for these connective structures: As synapses form, many surrounding neurons die—40 to 60 percent, depending on the brain region (Jabès & Nelson, 2014). Fortunately, during the prenatal period, the neural tube produces far more neurons than the brain will ever need.

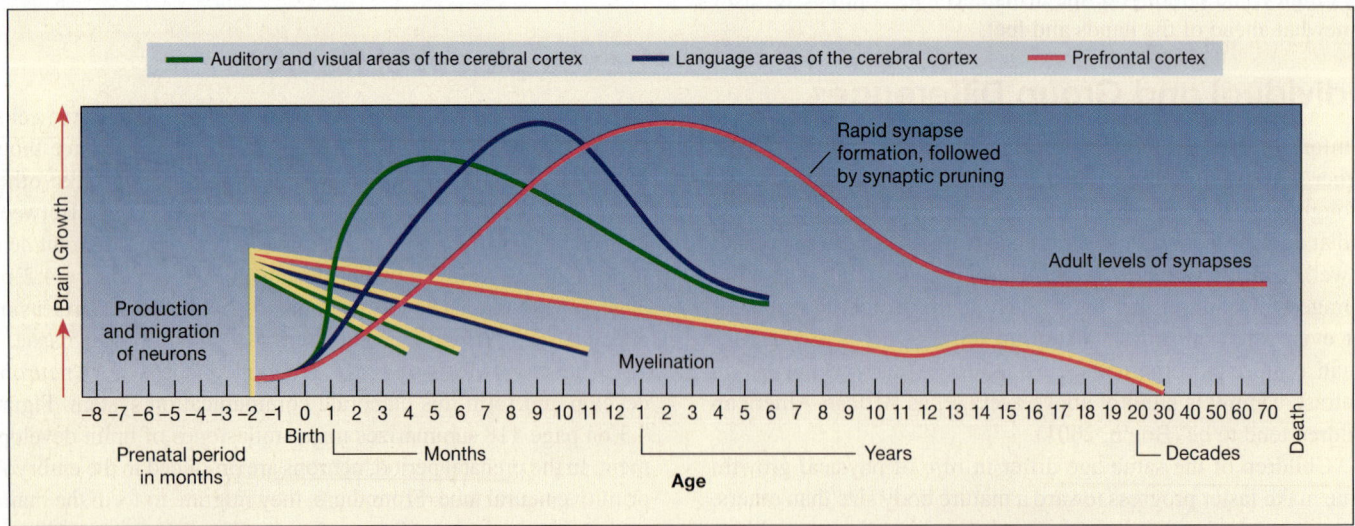

FIGURE 4.3 Major milestones of brain development. Formation of synapses is rapid during the first two years, especially in the auditory, visual, and language areas of the cerebral cortex. The prefrontal cortex, responsible for complex thought (see page 120), undergoes more extended synaptic growth. In each area, overproduction of synapses is followed by synaptic pruning. The prefrontal cortex is among the last regions to attain adult levels of synaptic connections—in mid- to late adolescence. Myelination occurs at a dramatic pace during the first two years, more slowly through childhood, followed by an acceleration at adolescence and then a reduced pace in early adulthood. The multiple yellow lines indicate that the timing of myelination varies among different brain areas. For example, neural fibers myelinate over a longer period in the language areas, and especially in the prefrontal cortex, than in the visual and auditory areas. (Based on Thompson & Nelson, 2001.)

Brain development can be compared to molding a "living sculpture." First, neurons and synapses are overproduced. Then, cell death and synaptic pruning sculpt away excess building material to form the mature brain—a process jointly influenced by genetically programmed events and the child's experiences. The resulting "sculpture" is a set of interconnected regions, each with specific functions—much like countries on a globe that communicate with one another (Johnston et al., 2001). This "geography" of the brain permits researchers to study its organization and the activity of its regions using neurobiological techniques.

Measures of Brain Functioning

Table 4.1 describes major measures of brain functioning. Among these methods, the two most frequently used detect changes in *electrical activity* in the cerebral cortex. In an *electroencephalogram (EEG),* researchers examine *brain-wave patterns* for stability and organization—signs of mature functioning of the cortex. And as the person processes a particular stimulus, *event-related potentials (ERPs)* detect the general location of brain-wave activity—a technique often used to study preverbal infants' responsiveness to various stimuli, the impact of experience on specialization of specific regions of the cortex, and atypical brain functioning in individuals with learning and emotional problems (DeBoer, Scott, & Nelson, 2007; Gunnar & de Haan, 2009).

Neuroimaging techniques, which yield detailed, three-dimensional computerized pictures of the entire brain and its active areas, provide the most precise information about which brain regions are specialized for certain capacities and about abnormalities in brain functioning. The most promising of these methods is *functional magnetic resonance imaging (fMRI).* Unlike *positron emission tomography (PET),* fMRI does not depend on X-ray photography, which requires injection of a radioactive substance. Rather, when an individual is exposed to a stimulus, fMRI detects changes in blood flow and oxygen metabolism throughout the brain magnetically, yielding a colorful, moving picture of parts of the brain used to perform a given activity (see Figure 4.4a and b on page 120).

Because PET and fMRI require that the participant lie as motionless as possible for an extended time, they are not suitable for infants and young children. A neuroimaging technique that works well in infancy and early childhood is *near-infrared spectroscopy (NIRS),* in which infrared (invisible) light is beamed at regions of the cerebral cortex to measure blood flow and oxygen metabolism while the child attends to a stimulus (refer again to Table 4.1). Because the apparatus consists only of thin, flexible optical fibers attached to the scalp using a head cap, a baby can sit on the parent's lap and move during testing—as Figure 4.4c illustrates (Hespos et al., 2010). But unlike PET and fMRI, which map activity changes throughout the brain, NIRS examines only the functioning of the cerebral cortex.

The measures just reviewed are powerful tools for uncovering relationships between the brain and psychological development. But like all research methods, they have limitations. Even

TABLE 4.1
Measuring Brain Functioning

METHOD	DESCRIPTION
Electroencephalogram (EEG)	Electrodes embedded in a head cap record electrical brain-wave activity in the brain's outer layers—the cerebral cortex. Researchers use an advanced tool called a geodesic sensor net (GSN) to hold interconnected electrodes (up to 128 for infants and 256 for children and adults) in place through a cap that adjusts to each person's head shape, yielding improved brain-wave detection.
Event-related potentials (ERPs)	Using the EEG, the frequency and amplitude of brain waves in response to particular stimuli (such as a picture, music, or speech) are recorded in the cerebral cortex. Enables identification of general regions of stimulus-induced activity.
Functional magnetic resonance imaging (fMRI)	While the person lies inside a tunnel-shaped apparatus that creates a magnetic field, a scanner magnetically detects increased blood flow and oxygen metabolism in areas of the brain as the individual processes particular stimuli. The scanner typically records images every 1 to 4 seconds; these are combined into a computerized moving picture of activity anywhere in the brain (not just its outer layers). Not appropriate for children younger than ages 5 to 6, who cannot remain still during testing.
Positron emission tomography (PET)	After injection or inhalation of a radioactive substance, the person lies on an apparatus with a scanner that emits fine streams of X-rays, which detect increased blood flow and oxygen metabolism in areas of the brain as the person processes particular stimuli. As with fMRI, the result is a computerized image of activity anywhere in the brain. Not appropriate for children younger than ages 5 to 6.
Near-infrared spectroscopy (NIRS)	Using thin, flexible optical fibers attached to the scalp through a head cap, infrared (invisible) light is beamed at the brain; its absorption by areas of the cerebral cortex varies with changes in blood flow and oxygen metabolism as the individual processes particular stimuli. The result is a computerized moving picture of active areas in the cerebral cortex. Unlike fMRI and PET, NIRS is appropriate for infants and young children, who can move within a limited range during testing.

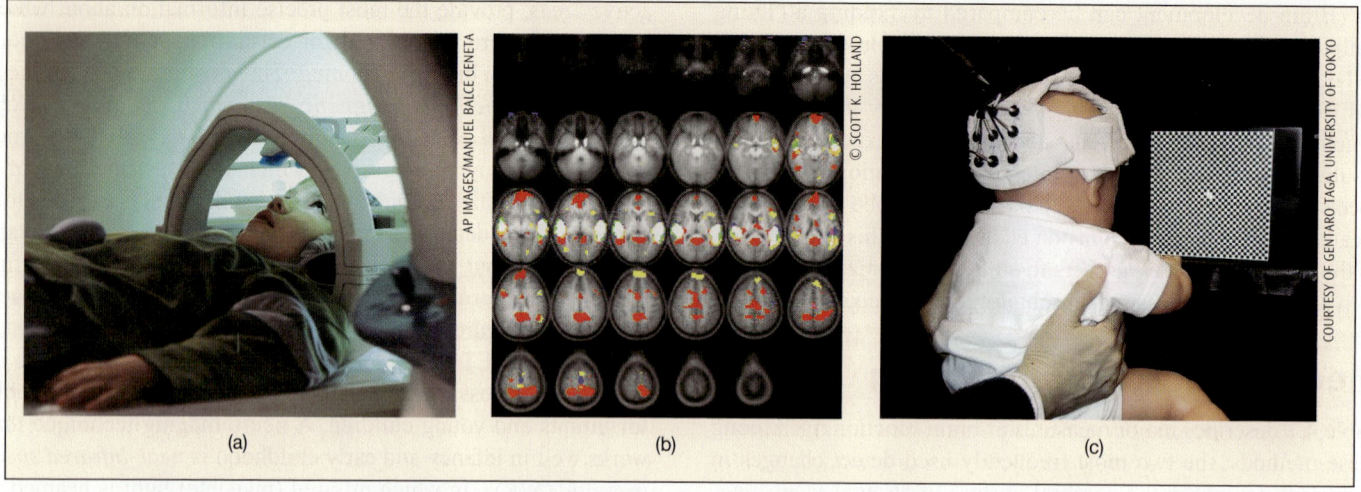

FIGURE 4.4 Functional magnetic resonance imaging (fMRI) and near-infrared spectroscopy (NIRS). (a) This 6-year-old is part of a study that uses fMRI to find out how his brain processes light and motion. (b) The fMRI image shows which areas of the child's brain are active while he views changing visual stimuli. (c) Here, NIRS is used to investigate a 2-month-old's response to a visual stimulus. During testing, the baby can move freely within a limited range. (Photo [c] from G. Taga, K. Asakawa, A. Maki, Y. Konishi, & H. Koisumi, 2003, "Brain Imaging in Awake Infants by Near-Infrared Optical Topography," *Proceedings of the National Academy of Sciences, 100,* p. 10723. Reprinted by permission.)

though a stimulus produces a consistent pattern of brain activity, investigators cannot be certain that an individual has processed it in a certain way (Kagan, 2013b). And a researcher who takes a change in brain activity as an indicator of information processing must make sure that the change was not due instead to hunger, boredom, fatigue, or body movements. Consequently, other methods must be combined with brain-wave and -imaging findings to clarify their meaning (de Haan & Gunnar, 2009). Now let's turn to the developing organization of the cerebral cortex.

Development of the Cerebral Cortex

The **cerebral cortex** surrounds the rest of the brain, resembling half of a shelled walnut. It is the largest brain structure, accounting for 85 percent of the brain's weight and containing the greatest number of neurons and synapses. Because the cerebral cortex is the last part of the brain to stop growing, it is sensitive to environmental influences for a much longer period than any other part of the brain.

Regions of the Cerebral Cortex. Figure 4.5 shows specific functions of regions of the cerebral cortex, such as receiving information from the senses, instructing the body to move, and thinking. The order in which cortical regions develop corresponds to the order in which various capacities emerge in the infant and growing child. For example, a burst of activity occurs in the auditory and visual cortexes and in areas responsible for body movement over the first year—a period of dramatic gains in auditory and visual perception and mastery of motor skills (Gilmore et al., 2012). Language areas are especially active from late infancy through the preschool years, when language development flourishes (Pujol et al., 2006).

The cortical regions with the most extended period of development are the *frontal lobes*. The **prefrontal cortex,** lying in front of areas controlling body movement, is responsible for complex thought—in particular, consciousness and various "executive" processes, including inhibition of impulses, integration of information, and memory, reasoning, planning, and problem-solving strategies. From age 2 months on, the prefrontal cortex functions more effectively. But it undergoes especially rapid myelination and formation and pruning of synapses during the preschool and school years, followed by another period of accel-

FIGURE 4.5 The left side of the human brain, showing the cerebral cortex. The cortex is divided into different lobes, each of which contains a variety of regions with specific functions. Some major regions are labeled here.

erated growth in adolescence, when it reaches an adult level of synaptic connections (Jabès & Nelson, 2014; Nelson, Thomas, & de Haan, 2006).

Lateralization and Plasticity of the Cortex.
The cerebral cortex has two *hemispheres,* or sides, that differ in their functions. Some tasks are done mostly by the left hemisphere, others by the right. For example, each hemisphere receives sensory information from the side of the body opposite to it and controls only that side.* For most of us, the left hemisphere is largely responsible for verbal abilities (such as spoken and written language) and positive emotion (such as joy). The right hemisphere handles spatial abilities (judging distances, reading maps, and recognizing geometric shapes) and negative emotion (such as distress) (Banish & Heller, 1998; Nelson & Bosquet, 2000). In left-handed people, this pattern may be reversed or, more commonly, the cerebral cortex may be less clearly specialized than in right-handers.

Why does this specialization of the two hemispheres, called **lateralization,** occur? Studies using fMRI reveal that the left hemisphere is better at processing information in a sequential, analytic (piece-by-piece) way, a good approach for dealing with communicative information—both verbal (language) and emotional (a joyful smile). In contrast, the right hemisphere is specialized for processing information in a holistic, integrative manner, ideal for making sense of spatial information and regulating negative emotion. A lateralized brain may have evolved because it enabled humans to cope more successfully with changing environmental demands (Falk, 2005). It permits a wider array of functions to be carried out effectively than if both sides processed information in exactly the same way.

Researchers study the timing of brain lateralization to learn more about **brain plasticity.** A highly *plastic* cerebral cortex, in which many areas are not yet committed to specific functions, has a high capacity for learning. And if a part of the cortex is damaged, other parts can take over tasks it would have handled. But once the hemispheres lateralize, damage to a specific region means that the abilities it controls cannot be recovered to the same extent or as easily as earlier.

At birth, the hemispheres have already begun to specialize. Most newborns show greater activation (detected with either ERP or NIRS) in the left hemisphere while listening to speech sounds or displaying a positive state of arousal. In contrast, the right hemisphere reacts more strongly to nonspeech sounds and to stimuli (such as a sour-tasting fluid) that evoke negative emotion (Fox & Davidson, 1986; Hespos et al., 2010).

Nevertheless, research on brain-damaged children and adults offers evidence for substantial plasticity in the young brain, summarized in the Biology and Environment box on page 122. Furthermore, early experience greatly influences the organization of the cerebral cortex. For example, deaf adults who, as infants and children, learned sign language (a spatial skill) depend more than hearing individuals on the right hemisphere for language processing (Neville & Bavelier, 2002). And toddlers who are advanced in language development show greater left-hemispheric specialization for language than their more slowly developing agemates (Luna et al., 2001; Mills et al., 2005). Apparently, the very process of acquiring language and other skills promotes lateralization.

In sum, the brain is more plastic during the first few years than at later ages. An overabundance of synaptic connections supports brain plasticity and, therefore, young children's ability to learn, which is fundamental to their survival (Murphy & Corbett, 2009). And although the cortex is programmed from the start for hemispheric specialization, experience greatly influences the rate and success of its advancing organization.

Sensitive Periods in Brain Development

Animal studies confirm that early, extreme sensory deprivation results in permanent brain damage and loss of functions— findings that verify the existence of sensitive periods in brain development. For example, early, varied visual experiences must occur for the brain's visual centers to develop normally. If a 1-month-old kitten is deprived of light for just 3 or 4 days, these areas of the brain degenerate. If the kitten is kept in the dark during the fourth week of life and beyond, the damage is severe and permanent (Crair, Gillespie, & Stryker, 1998). And the general quality of the early environment affects overall brain growth. When animals reared from birth in physically and socially stimulating surroundings are compared with those reared in isolation, the brains of the stimulated animals are larger and show much denser synaptic connections (Sale, Berardi, & Maffei, 2009).

Human Evidence: Victims of Deprived Early Environments.
For ethical reasons, we cannot deliberately deprive some infants of normal rearing experiences and observe the impact on their brains and competencies. Instead, we must turn to natural experiments, in which children were victims of deprived early environments that were later rectified. Such studies have revealed some parallels with the animal evidence just described.

For example, when babies are born with cataracts in both eyes (clouded lenses, preventing clear visual images), those who have corrective surgery within 4 to 6 months show rapid improvement in vision, except for subtle aspects of face perception, which require early visual input to the right hemisphere to develop (Maurer & Lewis, 2013; Maurer, Mondloch, & Lewis, 2007). The longer cataract surgery is postponed beyond infancy, the less complete the recovery in visual skills. And if surgery is delayed until adulthood, vision is severely and permanently impaired (Lewis & Maurer, 2005).

Studies of infants placed in orphanages who were later exposed to ordinary family rearing confirm the importance of a generally stimulating environment for psychological development. In one investigation, researchers followed the progress of a

---
*The eyes are an exception. Messages from the right half of each retina go to the right hemisphere; messages from the left half of each retina go to the left hemisphere. Thus, visual information from both eyes is received by both hemispheres.

Biology and Environment

Brain Plasticity: Insights from Research on Brain-Damaged Children and Adults

In the first few years of life, the brain is highly plastic. It can reorganize areas committed to specific functions in a way that the mature brain cannot. Adults who suffered injury to a part of the brain in infancy and early childhood usually show fewer cognitive impairments than adults with later-occurring injury (Huttenlocher, 2002).

Nevertheless, the young brain is not totally plastic. When it is injured, its functioning is compromised. The extent of plasticity depends on several factors, including age at time of injury, site and severity of damage, skill area, and environmental supports for recovery. Furthermore, plasticity is not restricted to childhood. Some reorganization after injury also occurs in the mature brain.

Brain Plasticity in Infancy and Early Childhood

In a large study of children with injuries to the cerebral cortex that occurred around the time of birth or in the first six months of life, language and spatial skills were assessed repeatedly into adolescence (Stiles, Reilly, & Levine, 2012; Stiles et al., 2005, 2008, 2009). All the children had experienced early brain seizures or hemorrhages. Brain-imaging techniques (fMRI and PET) revealed the precise site of damage.

Regardless of whether injury occurred in the left or right cerebral hemisphere, the children showed delays in language development that persisted until about age 3½ years. That damage to either hemisphere affected early language competence indicates that at first, language functioning is broadly distributed in the brain. But by age 5, the children caught up in vocabulary and grammatical skills. Undamaged areas—in either the left or the right hemisphere—had taken over these language functions.

Compared with language, spatial skills were more impaired. When preschool through adolescent-age youngsters were asked to copy designs, those with early right-hemispheric damage had trouble with holistic processing—accurately representing the overall shape. In contrast, children with left-hemispheric damage captured the basic shape but omitted fine-grained details. Nevertheless, the children improved in their drawing skills with age—gains that did not occur in brain-injured adults (Stiles, Reilly, & Levine, 2012; Stiles et al., 2003, 2008, 2009).

Clearly, recovery after early brain injury is greater for language than for spatial skills. Why is this so? Researchers speculate that spatial processing is the older of the two capacities in our evolutionary history and, therefore, more lateralized at birth (Stiles et al., 2008). But early brain injury has far less impact than later injury on both language and spatial skills, revealing the young brain's plasticity.

The Price of High Plasticity in the Young Brain

Despite impressive recovery of language and (to a lesser extent) spatial skills, children with early brain injuries show deficits in a wide range of complex mental abilities during the school years. For example, their reading and math progress is slow. In telling stories, they produce simpler narratives than agemates without early brain injuries. And as the demands of daily life increase, they have difficulty managing homework and other responsibilities (Anderson, Spencer-Smith, & Wood, 2011; Stiles, Reilly, & Levine, 2012).

High brain plasticity, researchers explain, comes at a price. When healthy brain regions take over the functions of damaged areas, a "crowding effect" occurs: Multiple tasks must be done by a smaller-than-usual volume of brain tissue (Stiles, 2012). Complex mental abilities of all kinds suffer because performing them well requires the collaboration of many regions in the cerebral cortex.

Brain Plasticity in Adulthood

Brain plasticity is not restricted to early childhood. Though far more limited, reorganization in the brain can occur later, even in adulthood. For example, adult stroke victims often display considerable recovery, especially in response to stimulation of language and motor

This preschooler, who experienced brain damage in infancy, has been spared massive impairments because of high plasticity of the brain. Here, a teacher encourages her to cut basic shapes to strengthen spatial skills, which remain more impaired than language after early brain injury.

skills. Brain-imaging findings reveal that structures adjacent to the permanently damaged area or in the opposite cerebral hemisphere reorganize to support the impaired ability (Kalra & Ratan, 2007; Murphy & Corbett, 2009).

In infancy and childhood, the goal of brain growth is to form neural connections that ensure mastery of essential skills. At older ages, specialized brain structures are in place, but after injury they can still reorganize to some degree. The adult brain can produce a small number of new neurons. And when an individual practices relevant tasks, the brain strengthens existing synapses and generates new ones.

Nevertheless, when brain injury is widespread, recovery for both children and adults is greatly reduced. And when damage occurs to certain regions—for example, the prefrontal cortex—recovery is also limited (Pennington, 2015). Because of its executive role in thinking and widespread connections throughout the brain, prefrontal abilities are difficult to transfer to other cortical areas. Consequently, early prefrontal lesions typically result in persisting, general intellectual deficits (Pennington, 2015). Clearly, brain plasticity is a complex process that is not equivalent throughout the brain.

large sample of children transferred between birth and 3½ years from extremely deprived Romanian orphanages to adoptive families in Great Britain (Beckett et al., 2006; O'Connor et al., 2000; Rutter et al., 1998, 2004, 2010). On arrival, most were impaired in all domains of development. Cognitive catch-up was impressive for children adopted before 6 months, who attained average mental test scores in childhood and adolescence, performing as well as a comparison group of early-adopted British-born children.

But Romanian children who had been institutionalized for more than the first six months showed serious intellectual deficits (see Figure 4.6). Although they improved in intelligence test scores during middle childhood and adolescence, they remained substantially below average. And most displayed at least three serious mental health problems, such as inattention, overactivity, unruly behavior, and autistic-like symptoms (social disinterest, stereotyped behavior) (Kreppner et al., 2007, 2010).

Neurobiological findings indicate that early, prolonged institutionalization leads to a generalized decrease in size and activity in the cerebral cortex—especially the prefrontal cortex, which governs complex cognition and impulse control. Neural fibers connecting the prefrontal cortex with other brain structures involved in control of emotion are also reduced (Hodel et al., 2014; McLaughlin et al., 2014; Nelson, 2007). And activation of the left cerebral hemisphere, governing positive emotion, is diminished relative to right cerebral activation, governing negative emotion (McLaughlin et al., 2011).

Additional evidence confirms that the chronic stress of early, deprived orphanage rearing disrupts the brain's capacity to manage stress. In another investigation, researchers followed the development of children who had spent their first eight months or more in Romanian institutions and were then adopted into Canadian homes (Gunnar & Cheatham, 2003; Gunnar et al., 2001). Compared with agemates adopted shortly after birth, these children showed extreme stress reactivity, as indicated by high concentrations of the stress hormone *cortisol* in their saliva. The longer the children spent in orphanage care, the higher their cortisol levels—even 6½ years after adoption.

In other research, orphanage children from diverse regions of the world who were later adopted by American families displayed abnormally low cortisol—a blunted physiological response that (as we saw in Chapter 3) is also a sign of impaired capacity to manage stress (Koss et al., 2014; Loman & Gunnar, 2010). Persisting abnormally high or low cortisol levels are linked to later learning, emotional, and behavior problems, including both internalizing and externalizing difficulties.

Appropriate Stimulation. Unlike the orphanage children just described, Grace, whom Monica and Kevin had adopted from Cambodia at 16 months of age, showed favorable progress. Two years earlier, they had adopted Grace's older brother, Eli. When Eli was 2 years old, Monica and Kevin sent a letter and a photo of Eli to his biological mother, describing a bright, happy child. The next day, the Cambodian mother tearfully asked an adoption agency to send her baby daughter to join Eli and his American family. Although Grace's early environment was very depleted, her biological mother's loving care—holding gently, speaking softly, playfully stimulating, and breastfeeding—likely prevented irreversible damage to her brain.

In the Bucharest Early Intervention Project, 136 institutionalized Romanian babies were randomized into conditions of

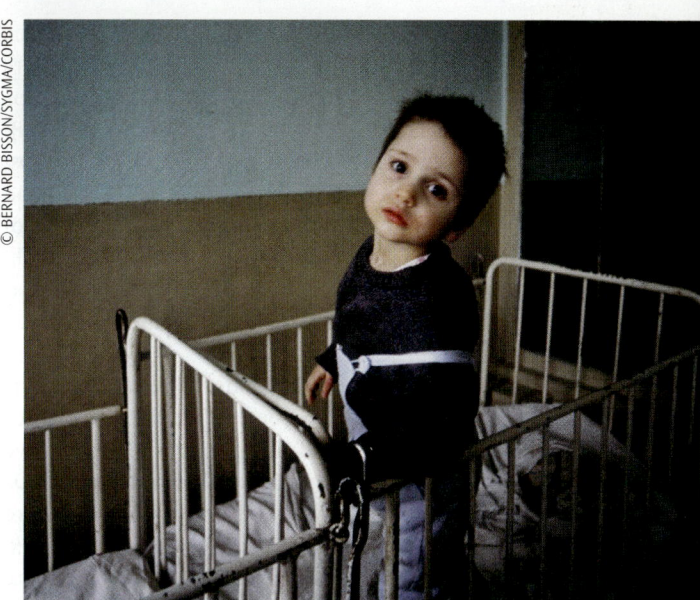

This Romanian orphan receives little adult contact or stimulation. The longer he remains in this barren environment, the greater his risk of brain damage and lasting impairments in all domains of development.

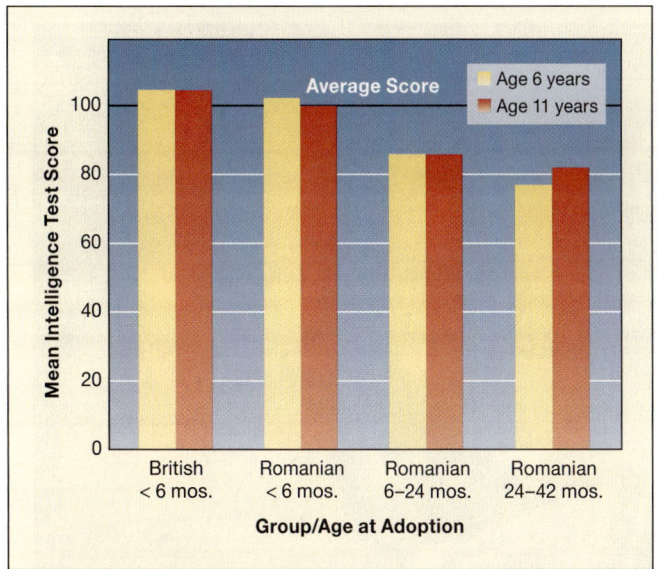

FIGURE 4.6 Relationship of age at adoption to mental test scores at ages 6 and 11 among British and Romanian adoptees. Children transferred from Romanian orphanages to British adoptive homes in the first six months of life attained average scores and fared as well as British early-adopted children, suggesting that they had fully recovered from extreme early deprivation. Romanian children adopted after 6 months of age performed well below average. And although those adopted after age 2 improved between ages 6 and 11, they continued to show serious intellectual deficits. (Adapted from Beckett et al., 2006.)

either care as usual or transfer to high-quality foster families between 6 and 31 months of age. Specially trained social workers provided foster parents with counseling and support. Follow-ups between 2½ and 12 years revealed that the foster-care group exceeded the institutional-care group in intelligence test scores, language skills, emotional responsiveness, social skills, EEG and ERP assessments of brain development, and adaptive cortisol levels (Fox, Nelson, & Zeanah, 2013; Nelson, Fox, & Zeanah, 2014; McLaughlin et al., 2015). Consistent with an early sensitive period, on all measures, earlier foster placement predicted better outcomes.

In addition to impoverished environments, ones that overwhelm children with expectations beyond their current capacities interfere with the brain's potential. In recent years, expensive early learning centers as well as "educational" tablets and DVDs have become widespread. Within these contexts, infants are trained with letter and number flash cards, and toddlers are given a full curriculum of reading, math, science, art, and more. There is no evidence that these programs yield smarter "superbabies" (Principe, 2011). To the contrary, trying to prime infants with stimulation for which they are not ready can cause them to withdraw, thereby threatening their interest in learning and creating conditions much like stimulus deprivation!

How, then, can we characterize appropriate stimulation during the early years? To answer this question, researchers distinguish between two types of brain development. The first, **experience-expectant brain growth,** refers to the young brain's rapidly developing organization, which depends on ordinary experiences—opportunities to explore the environment, interact with people, and hear language and other sounds. As a result of millions of years of evolution, the brains of all infants, toddlers, and young children *expect* to encounter these experiences and, if they do, grow normally. The second type of brain development, **experience-dependent brain growth,** occurs throughout our lives. It consists of additional growth and refinement of established brain structures as a result of specific learning experiences that vary widely across individuals and cultures (Greenough & Black, 1992). Reading and writing, playing computer games, weaving an intricate rug, and practicing the violin are examples. The brain of a violinist differs in certain ways from the brain of a poet because each has exercised different brain regions for a long time.

Experience-expectant brain development occurs early and naturally, as caregivers offer babies and preschoolers age-appropriate play materials and engage them in enjoyable daily routines—a shared meal, a game of peekaboo, a bath before bed, a picture book to talk about, or a song to sing. The resulting growth provides the foundation for later-occurring, experience-dependent development (Belsky & de Haan, 2011; Huttenlocher, 2002). No evidence exists for a sensitive period in the first few years for mastering skills that depend on extensive training, such as reading, musical performance, or gymnastics. To the contrary, rushing early learning harms the brain by overwhelming its neural circuits, thereby reducing the brain's sensitivity to the everyday experiences it needs for a healthy start in life.

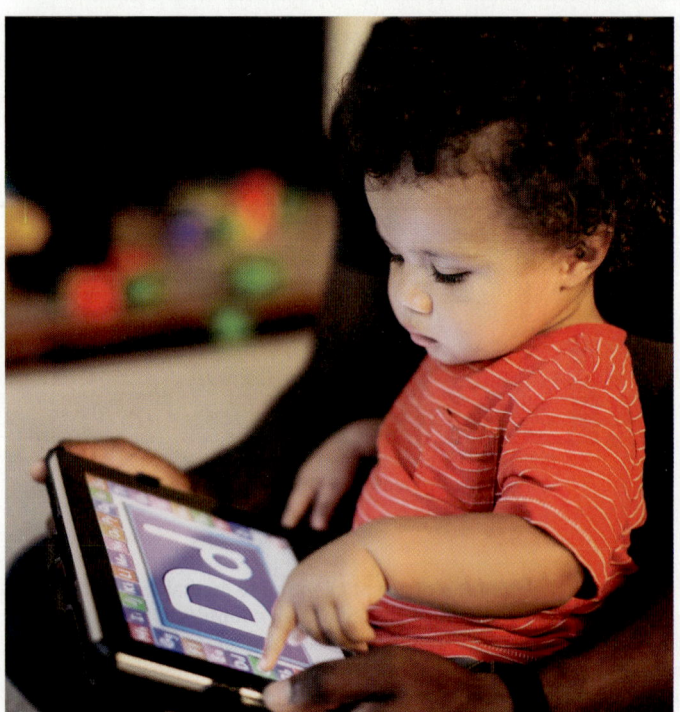

Experience-expectant brain growth depends on ordinary, stimulating experiences—like this toddler's exploration of a mossy log. It provides the foundation for experience-dependent brain growth—refinements due to culturally specific learning. But too much emphasis on training at an early age—for example, drill on mastering the ABCs—can interfere with access to everyday experiences the young brain needs to grow optimally.

Changing States of Arousal

Rapid brain growth means that the organization of sleep and wakefulness changes substantially between birth and 2 years, and fussiness and crying also decline. The newborn baby takes round-the-clock naps that total about 16 to 18 hours. Total sleep time declines slowly; the average 2-year-old still needs 12 to 13 hours. But periods of sleep and wakefulness become fewer and longer, and the sleep–wake pattern increasingly conforms to a night–day schedule. Most 6- to 9-month-olds take two daytime naps; by about 18 months, children generally need only one nap (Galland et al., 2012). Between ages 3 and 5, napping subsides.

These changing arousal patterns are due to brain development, but they are also affected by cultural beliefs and practices and by parents' needs (Super & Harkness, 2002). Dutch parents, for example, view sleep regularity as far more important than U.S. parents do. And whereas U.S. parents regard a predictable sleep schedule as emerging naturally from within the child, Dutch parents believe that a schedule must be imposed, or the baby's development might suffer (Super & Harkness, 2010; Super et al., 1996). At age 6 months, Dutch babies are put to bed earlier and sleep, on average, 2 hours more per day than their U.S. agemates.

Motivated by demanding work schedules and other needs, many Western parents try to get their babies to sleep through the night as early as 3 to 4 months by offering an evening feeding. But infants who receive more milk or solid foods during the day are not less likely to wake, though they feed less at night (Brown & Harries, 2015). Trying to induce young infants to sleep through the night is at odds with their neurological capacities: Not until the middle of the first year is the secretion of *melatonin,* a hormone within the brain that promotes drowsiness, much greater at night than during the day (Sadeh, 1997).

Furthermore, as the Cultural Influences box on page 126 reveals, isolating infants to promote sleep is rare elsewhere in the world. When babies sleep close to their parents, their average sleep period remains constant at three hours from 1 to 8 months of age. Only at the end of the first year, as REM sleep (the state that usually prompts waking) declines, do infants move in the direction of an adultlike sleep–wake schedule (Ficca et al., 1999).

Even after babies sleep through the night, they continue to wake occasionally. In studies carried out in Australia, Israel, and the United States, night wakings increased around 6 months and again between 1½ and 2 years (Armstrong, Quinn, & Dadds, 1994; Scher, Epstein, & Tirosh, 2004; Scher et al., 1995). As Chapter 6 will reveal, around the middle of the first year, infants are forming a clear-cut attachment to their familiar caregiver and begin protesting when he or she leaves. And the challenges of toddlerhood—the ability to range farther from the caregiver and increased awareness of the self as separate from others—often prompt anxiety, evident in disturbed sleep and clinginess. When parents offer comfort, these behaviors subside.

FIGURE 4.7 Relationship of bedtime routines to night-wakings in infancy/toddlerhood and the preschool years. In a large sample of mothers in 13 Western and Asian nations, the more consistently they reported using bedtime routines, the less often their infants, toddlers, and preschoolers woke during the night. Findings were similar for ease of falling asleep and amount of nighttime sleep. (From J. A. Mindell, A. M. Li, A. Sadeh, R. Kwon, & D. Y. T. Goh, 2015, "Bedtime Routines for Young Children: A Dose-Dependent Association with Sleep Outcomes," *Sleep, 38,* p. 720. Copyright © 2015 by permission of the Associated Professional Sleep Societies, LLC. Reprinted by permission.)

Finally, bedtime routines promote sleep as early as the first two years. In one study, over 10,000 mothers in 13 Western and Asian nations were asked to report on their bedtime practices and their newborn to 5-year-olds' sleep quality. Consistently engaging in bedtime routines—for example, rocking and singing in infancy, storybook reading in toddlerhood and early childhood—was associated with falling asleep more readily, waking less often, and getting more nighttime sleep throughout the entire age range (see Figure 4.7) (Mindell et al., 2015). Mothers who established regular bedtime routines in infancy and toddlerhood were more likely to maintain the practice in early childhood.

Ask yourself

CONNECT Explain how either too little or too much stimulation can impair cognitive and emotional development in the early years.

APPLY Which infant enrichment program would you choose: one that emphasizes gentle talking and touching and social games, or one that includes reading and number drills and classical music lessons? Explain.

REFLECT What is your attitude toward parent–infant cosleeping? Is it influenced by your cultural background? Explain.

Cultural Influences

Cultural Variation in Infant Sleeping Arrangements

Western child-rearing advice from experts strongly encourages nighttime separation of baby from parent. For example, the most recent edition of Benjamin Spock's *Baby and Child Care* recommends that babies sleep in their own room by 3 months of age, explaining, "By 6 months, a child who regularly sleeps in her parents' room may feel uneasy sleeping anywhere else" (Spock & Needlman, 2012, p. 62). And the American Academy of Pediatrics (2012b) has issued a controversial warning that parent–infant bedsharing increases the risk of sudden infant death syndrome (SIDS) and accidental suffocation.

Yet parent–infant cosleeping—in the same room and usually in the same bed—is the norm for approximately 90 percent of the world's population, in cultures as diverse as the Japanese, the rural Guatemalan Maya, the Inuit of northwestern Canada, and the !Kung of Botswana. Japanese and Korean children usually lie next to their mothers throughout infancy and early childhood, and many continue to sleep with a parent or other family member until adolescence (Yang & Hahn, 2002). Among the Maya, mother–infant bedsharing is interrupted only by the birth of a new baby, when the older child is moved next to the father or to another bed in the same room (Morelli et al., 1992). Bedsharing is also common in U.S. ethnic minority families (McKenna & Volpe, 2007). African-American children, for example, frequently fall asleep with their parents and remain with them for part or all of the night (Buswell & Spatz, 2007).

Cultural values strongly influence infant sleeping arrangements. In one study, researchers interviewed Guatemalan Mayan mothers and American middle-SES mothers about their sleeping practices. Mayan mothers stressed the importance of promoting an *interdependent self,* explaining that cosleeping builds a close parent–child bond, which is necessary for children to learn the ways of people around them. In contrast, American mothers emphasized an *independent self,* mentioning their desire to instill early autonomy, prevent bad habits, and protect their own privacy (Morelli et al., 1992).

Over the past two decades, cosleeping has increased in Western nations. An estimated 11 percent of U.S. infants routinely bedshare, and an additional 30 to 35 percent sometimes do (Buswell & Spatz, 2007; Colson et al., 2013). Proponents of the practice say that it helps infants sleep, makes breastfeeding more convenient, and provides valuable bonding time (McKenna & Volpe, 2007).

During the night, babies who sleep with their parents breastfeed three times longer than infants who sleep alone. Because infants arouse to nurse more often when sleeping next to their mothers, some researchers believe that cosleeping may actually help safeguard babies at risk for SIDS (see page 106 in Chapter 3). Consistent with this view, SIDS is rare in Asian cultures where bedsharing is widespread, including Cambodia, China, Japan, Korea, Thailand, and Vietnam (McKenna, 2002; McKenna & McDade, 2005).

Critics warn that bedsharing will promote emotional problems, especially excessive dependency. Yet a longitudinal study following children from the end of pregnancy through age 18 showed that young people who had bedshared in the early years were no different from others in any aspect of adjustment (Okami, Weisner, & Olmstead, 2002). A more serious concern is that infants might become trapped under the parent's body or in soft bedding and suffocate. Parents who are obese or who use alcohol, tobacco, or mood-altering drugs do pose a serious risk to bedsharing babies, as does the use of quilts and comforters or an overly soft mattress (American Academy of Pediatrics, 2012b; Carpenter et al., 2013).

But with appropriate precautions, parents and infants can cosleep safely (Ball & Volpe, 2013). In cultures where cosleeping is widespread, parents and infants usually sleep with

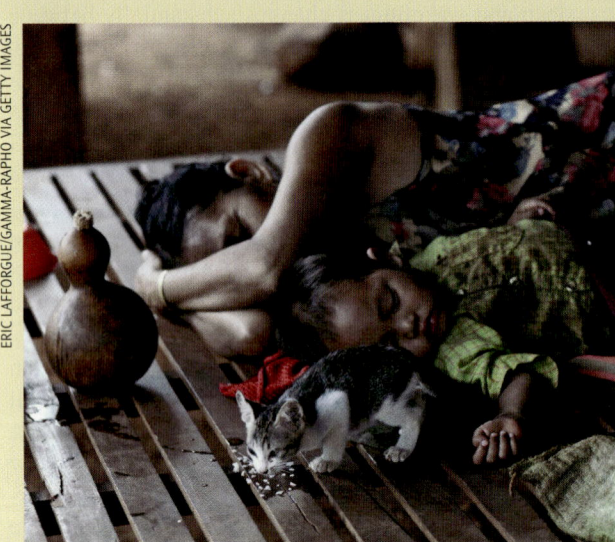

This Vietnamese mother and child sleep together—a practice common in their culture and around the globe. Hard wooden sleeping surfaces protect cosleeping children from entrapment in soft bedding.

light covering on hard surfaces, such as firm mattresses, floor mats, and wooden planks, or infants sleep in a cradle or hammock next to the parents' bed (McKenna, 2002). And when sharing the same bed, infants typically lie on their back or side facing the mother—positions that promote frequent, easy communication between parent and baby and arousal if breathing is threatened.

Finally, breastfeeding mothers usually assume a distinctive sleeping posture: They face the infant, with knees drawn up under the baby's feet and arm above the baby's head. Besides facilitating feeding, the position prevents the infant from sliding down under covers or up under pillows (Ball, 2006). Because this posture is also seen in female great apes while sharing sleeping nests with their infants, researchers believe it may have evolved to enhance infant safety.

Some researchers point out that placing too much emphasis on separate sleeping may have risky consequences—for example, inducing tired parents to avoid feeding their babies in bed in favor of using dangerously soft sofas (Bartick & Smith, 2014). Pediatricians are wise to discuss the safety of each infant's sleep environment with parents, while taking into account cultural values and motivations (Ward, 2015). Then they can work within that framework to create a safe sleep environment.

Influences on Early Physical Growth

4.4 Cite evidence that heredity and nutrition both contribute to early physical growth.

Physical growth, like other aspects of development, results from a complex interplay between genetic and environmental factors. Heredity, nutrition, and emotional well-being all affect early physical growth.

Heredity

Because identical twins are much more alike in body size than fraternal twins, we know that heredity is important in physical growth (Dubois et al., 2012). When diet and health are adequate, height and rate of physical growth are largely influenced by heredity. In fact, as long as negative environmental influences such as poor nutrition or illness are not severe, children and adolescents typically show *catch-up growth*—a return to a genetically influenced growth path once conditions improve. Still, the health of the brain, the heart, the digestive system, and many other internal organs may be permanently compromised. (Recall the consequences of inadequate prenatal nutrition for long-term health, discussed on page 88 in Chapter 3.)

Genetic makeup also affects body weight: The weights of adopted children correlate more strongly with those of their biological than of their adoptive parents (Kinnunen, Pietilainen, & Rissanen, 2006). At the same time, environment—in particular, nutrition—plays an especially important role.

Nutrition

Nutrition is especially crucial for development in the first two years because the baby's brain and body are growing so rapidly. Pound for pound, an infant's energy needs are at least twice those of an adult. Twenty-five percent of infants' total caloric intake is devoted to growth, and babies need extra calories to keep rapidly developing organs functioning properly (Meyer, 2009).

Breastfeeding versus Bottle-Feeding. Babies need both enough food and the right kind of food. In early infancy, breastfeeding is ideally suited to their needs, and bottled formulas try to imitate it. Applying What We Know on page 128 summarizes major nutritional and health advantages of breastfeeding.

Because of these benefits, breastfed babies in poverty-stricken regions are much less likely to be malnourished and 6 to 14 times more likely to survive the first year of life. The World Health Organization recommends breastfeeding until age 2 years, with solid foods added at 6 months. These practices, if widely followed, would save the lives of more than 800,000 infants annually (World Health Organization, 2015f). Even breastfeeding for just a few weeks offers some protection against respiratory and intestinal infections, which are devastating to young children in developing countries. Also, because a nursing mother is less likely to get pregnant, breastfeeding helps increase spacing between siblings, a major factor in reducing infant and childhood deaths in nations with widespread poverty. (Note, however, that breastfeeding is not a reliable method of birth control.)

Yet many mothers in the developing world do not know about these benefits. In Africa, the Middle East, and Latin America, most babies get some breastfeeding, but fewer than 40 percent are exclusively breastfed for the first six months, and one-third are fully weaned from the breast before 1 year (UNICEF, 2015). In place of breast milk, mothers give their babies commercial formula or low-grade nutrients, such as rice water or highly diluted cow or goat milk. Contamination of these foods as a result of poor sanitation is common and often leads to illness and infant death. The United Nations has encouraged all hospitals and maternity units in developing countries to promote breastfeeding as long as mothers do not have viral or bacterial infections (such as HIV or tuberculosis) that can be transmitted to the baby. Today, most developing countries have banned the practice of giving free or subsidized formula to new mothers.

Partly as a result of the natural childbirth movement, breastfeeding has become more common in industrialized nations, especially among well-educated women. Today, 79 percent of American mothers begin breastfeeding after birth, but about half stop by 6 months (Centers for Disease Control and Prevention, 2014a). Not surprisingly, mothers who return to work sooner wean their babies from the breast earlier (Smith & Forrester, 2013). But mothers who cannot be with their infants all the time can still combine breast- and bottle-feeding. The U.S. Department of Health and Human Services (2011) advises exclusive breastfeeding for the first 6 months and inclusion of breast milk in the baby's diet until at least 1 year.

Midwives in India support a mother as she learns to breastfeed her infant. Breastfeeding is especially important in developing countries, where it helps protect babies against life-threatening infections and early death.

Applying what we Know

Reasons to Breastfeed

NUTRITIONAL AND HEALTH ADVANTAGES	EXPLANATION
Provides the correct balance of fat and protein	Compared with the milk of other mammals, human milk is higher in fat and lower in protein. This balance, as well as the unique proteins and fats contained in human milk, is ideal for a rapidly myelinating nervous system.
Ensures nutritional completeness	A mother who breastfeeds need not add other foods to her infant's diet until the baby is 6 months old. The milks of all mammals are low in iron, but the iron contained in breast milk is much more easily absorbed by the baby's system. Consequently, bottle-fed infants need iron-fortified formula.
Helps ensure healthy physical growth	One-year-old breastfed babies are leaner (have a higher percentage of muscle to fat), a growth pattern that persists through the preschool years and that is associated with a reduction in later overweight and obesity.
Protects against many diseases	Breastfeeding transfers antibodies and other infection-fighting agents from mother to baby and enhances functioning of the immune system. Compared with bottle-fed infants, breastfed babies have far fewer allergic reactions and respiratory and intestinal illnesses. Breast milk also has anti-inflammatory effects, which reduce the severity of illness symptoms. Breastfeeding in the first four months (especially when exclusive) is linked to lower blood cholesterol levels in adulthood and, thereby, may help prevent cardiovascular disease.
Protects against faulty jaw development and tooth decay	Sucking the mother's nipple instead of an artificial nipple helps avoid malocclusion, a condition in which the upper and lower jaws do not meet properly. It also protects against tooth decay due to sweet liquid remaining in the mouths of infants who fall asleep while sucking on a bottle.
Ensures digestibility	Because breastfed babies have a different kind of bacteria growing in their intestines than do bottle-fed infants, they rarely suffer from constipation or other gastrointestinal problems.
Smooths the transition to solid foods	Breastfed infants accept new solid foods more easily than do bottle-fed infants, perhaps because of their greater experience with a variety of flavors, which pass from the maternal diet into the mother's milk.

Sources: American Academy of Pediatrics, 2012a; Druet et al., 2012; Ip et al., 2009; Owen et al., 2008.

Women who do not breastfeed sometimes worry that they are depriving their baby of an experience essential for healthy psychological development. Yet breastfed and bottle-fed infants in industrialized nations do not differ in quality of the mother–infant relationship or in later emotional adjustment (Jansen, de Weerth, & Riksen-Walraven, 2008; Lind et al., 2014). Some studies report a slight advantage in intelligence for children and adolescents who were breastfed, after controlling for maternal intelligence, SES, and other factors (Belfort et al., 2013; Kanazawa, 2015). Other studies, however, find no cognitive benefits (Walfisch et al., 2013).

Are Chubby Babies at Risk for Later Overweight and Obesity?

From early infancy, Timmy was an enthusiastic eater who nursed vigorously and gained weight quickly. By 5 months, he began reaching for food on his mother's plate. Vanessa wondered: Was she overfeeding Timmy and increasing his chances of becoming overweight?

Most chubby babies thin out during toddlerhood and early childhood, as weight gain slows and they become more active. Infants and toddlers can eat nutritious foods freely without risk of becoming overweight. But recent evidence does indicate a strengthening relationship between rapid weight gain in infancy and later obesity (Druet et al., 2012). The trend may be due to the rise in overweight and obesity among adults, who promote unhealthy eating habits in their young children. Interviews with 1,500 U.S. parents of 4- to 24-month-olds revealed that many routinely served older infants and toddlers french fries, pizza, candy, sugary fruit drinks, and soda. On average, infants consumed 20 percent and toddlers 30 percent more calories than they needed (Siega-Riz et al., 2010). At the same time, as many as one-fourth ate no fruits and one-third no vegetables.

How can parents prevent their infants from becoming overweight children and adults? One way is to breastfeed exclusively for the first six months, which is associated with slower weight gain over the first year, leaner body build through early childhood, and 10 to 20 percent reduced obesity risk in later life (Gunnarsdottir et al., 2010; Koletzko et al., 2013). Another strategy is to avoid giving babies foods loaded with sugar, salt, and saturated fats. Once toddlers learn to walk, climb, and run, parents can also provide plenty of opportunities for energetic play. Finally, because research shows a correlation between excessive television viewing and overweight in older children, parents should limit the time very young children spend in front of the TV.

Malnutrition

Osita is an Ethiopian 2-year-old whose mother has never had to worry about his gaining too much weight. When she weaned him at 1 year, he had little to eat besides starchy rice flour cakes. Soon his belly enlarged, his feet swelled, his hair fell out, and a rash appeared on his skin. His bright-eyed curiosity vanished, and he became irritable and listless.

In developing countries and war-torn areas where food resources are limited, malnutrition is widespread. Malnutrition contributes to one-third of worldwide infant and early childhood deaths—about 2.1 million children annually. It is also responsible for growth stunting of nearly one-third of the world's children under age 5 (World Health Organization, 2015c). The 8 percent who are severely affected suffer from two dietary diseases.

Marasmus is a wasted condition of the body caused by a diet low in all essential nutrients. It usually appears in the first year of life when a baby's mother is too malnourished to produce enough breast milk and bottle-feeding is also inadequate. Her starving baby becomes painfully thin and is in danger of dying.

Osita has **kwashiorkor**, caused by an unbalanced diet very low in protein. The disease usually strikes after weaning, between 1 and 3 years of age. It is common in regions where children get just enough calories from starchy foods but little protein. The child's body responds by breaking down its own protein reserves, which causes the swelling and other symptoms that Osita experienced.

Children who survive these extreme forms of malnutrition often suffer from lasting damage to the brain, heart, liver, pancreas, and other organs (Müller & Krawinkel, 2005; Spoelstra et al., 2012). When their diets do improve, they tend to gain excessive weight (Black et al., 2013). A malnourished body protects itself by establishing a low basal metabolism rate, which may endure after nutrition improves. Also, malnutrition may disrupt appetite control centers in the brain, causing the child to overeat when food becomes plentiful.

Learning and behavior are also seriously affected. Animal evidence reveals that a deficient diet permanently reduces brain weight and alters the production of neurotransmitters in the brain—an effect that can disrupt all aspects of development (Haller, 2005). Children who experienced marasmus or kwashiorkor show poor fine-motor coordination, have difficulty paying attention, often display conduct problems, and score low on intelligence tests into adulthood (Galler et al., 1990, 2012; Waber et al., 2014). They also display a more intense stress response to fear-arousing situations, perhaps caused by the constant, gnawing pain of hunger (Fernald & Grantham-McGregor, 1998).

Recall from our discussion of prenatal malnutrition in Chapter 3 that irritability and passivity of malnourished children compound the developmental consequences of poor diet. These behaviors may appear even when nutritional deprivation is only mild to moderate. Because government-supported supplementary food programs do not reach all families in need, an estimated 19 percent of U.S. children suffer from *food insecurity*—uncertain access to enough food for a healthy, active life. Food insecurity is especially high among single-parent families (35 percent) and low-income ethnic minority families—for example, African Americans and Hispanics (26 and 22 percent, respectively) (U.S. Department of Agriculture, 2015a). Although few of these children have marasmus or kwashiorkor, their physical growth and ability to learn are still affected.

Left photo: This baby of Niger, Africa, has marasmus, a wasted condition caused by a diet low in all essential nutrients. *Right photo:* The swollen abdomen of this toddler, also of Niger, is a symptom of kwashiorkor, which results from a diet very low in protein. If these children survive, they are likely to be growth stunted and to suffer from lasting organ damage and serious cognitive and emotional impairments.

Ask yourself

CONNECT How are bidirectional influences between parent and child involved in the impact of malnutrition on psychological development?

APPLY Eight-month-old Shaun is well below average in height and painfully thin. What serious growth disorder does he likely have, and what type of intervention, in addition to dietary enrichment, will help restore his development?

REFLECT Imagine that you are the parent of a newborn baby. Describe feeding practices you would use, and ones you would avoid, to prevent overweight and obesity.

Learning Capacities

4.5 Describe infant learning capacities, the conditions under which they occur, and the unique value of each.

Learning refers to changes in behavior as the result of experience. Babies come into the world with fundamental learning capacities that permit them to profit from experience immediately. Infants are capable of two basic forms of learning, which were introduced in Chapter 1: classical and operant conditioning. They also learn through their natural preference for novel stimulation. Finally, shortly after birth, babies learn by observing others; they can imitate the facial expressions and gestures of adults.

Classical Conditioning

Newborn reflexes, discussed in Chapter 3, make **classical conditioning** possible in the young infant. In this form of learning, a neutral stimulus is paired with a stimulus that leads to a reflexive response. Once the baby's nervous system makes the connection between the two stimuli, the neutral stimulus produces the behavior by itself. Classical conditioning helps infants recognize which events usually occur together in the everyday world, so they can anticipate what is about to happen next. As a result, the environment becomes more orderly and predictable. Let's take a closer look at the steps of classical conditioning.

As Carolyn settled down in the rocking chair to nurse Caitlin, she often stroked Caitlin's forehead. Soon Carolyn noticed that each time she did this, Caitlin made sucking movements. Caitlin had been classically conditioned. Figure 4.8 shows how it happened:

1. Before learning takes place, an **unconditioned stimulus (UCS)** must consistently produce a reflexive, or **unconditioned, response (UCR)**. In Caitlin's case, sweet breast milk (UCS) resulted in sucking (UCR).

FIGURE 4.8 The steps of classical conditioning. This example shows how a mother classically conditioned her baby to make sucking movements by stroking the baby's forehead at the beginning of feedings.

2. To produce learning, a *neutral stimulus* that does not lead to the reflex is presented just before, or at about the same time as, the UCS. Carolyn stroked Caitlin's forehead as each nursing period began. The stroking (neutral stimulus) was paired with the taste of milk (UCS).
3. If learning has occurred, the neutral stimulus by itself produces a response similar to the reflexive response. The neutral stimulus is then called a **conditioned stimulus (CS)**, and the response it elicits is called a **conditioned response (CR)**. We know that Caitlin has been classically conditioned because stroking her forehead outside the feeding situation (CS) results in sucking (CR).

If the CS is presented alone enough times, without being paired with the UCS, the CR will no longer occur, an outcome called *extinction*. In other words, if Carolyn repeatedly strokes Caitlin's forehead without feeding her, Caitlin will gradually stop sucking in response to stroking.

Young infants can be classically conditioned most easily when the association between two stimuli has survival value. In the example just described, learning which stimuli regularly accompany feeding improves the infant's ability to get food and survive (Blass, Ganchrow, & Steiner, 1984).

In contrast, some responses, such as fear, are very difficult to classically condition in young babies. Until infants have the motor skills to escape unpleasant events, they have no biological need to form these associations. After age 6 months, however, fear is easy to condition. In Chapter 6, we will discuss the development of fear and other emotional reactions.

Operant Conditioning

In classical conditioning, babies build expectations about stimulus events in the environment, but they do not influence the stimuli that occur. In **operant conditioning,** infants act, or *operate,* on the environment, and stimuli that follow their behavior change the probability that the behavior will occur again. A stimulus that increases the occurrence of a response is called a **reinforcer.** For example, sweet liquid *reinforces* the sucking response in newborns. Removing a desirable stimulus or presenting an unpleasant one to decrease the occurrence of a response is called **punishment.** A sour-tasting fluid *punishes* newborns' sucking response, causing them to purse their lips and stop sucking entirely.

Many stimuli besides food can serve as reinforcers of infant behavior. For example, newborns will suck faster on a nipple when their rate of sucking produces interesting sights and sounds, including visual designs, music, or human voices (Floccia, Christophe, & Bertoncini, 1997). As these findings suggest, operant conditioning is a powerful tool for finding out what stimuli babies can perceive and which ones they prefer.

As infants get older, operant conditioning includes a wider range of responses and stimuli. For example, researchers have hung mobiles over the cribs of 2- to 6-month-olds. When the baby's foot is attached to the mobile with a long cord, the infant can, by kicking, make the mobile turn. Under these conditions, it takes only a few minutes for infants to start kicking vigorously (Rovee-Collier, 1999; Rovee-Collier & Barr, 2001). As you will see in Chapter 5, operant conditioning with mobiles is frequently used to study infants' memory and their ability to group similar stimuli into categories. Once babies learn the kicking response, researchers see how long and under what conditions they retain it when exposed again to the original mobile or to mobiles with varying features.

Operant conditioning also plays a vital role in the formation of social relationships. As the baby gazes into the adult's eyes, the adult looks and smiles back, and then the infant looks and smiles again. As the behavior of each partner reinforces the other, both continue their pleasurable interaction. In Chapter 6, we will see that this contingent responsiveness contributes to the development of infant–caregiver attachment.

Habituation

At birth, the human brain is set up to be attracted to novelty. Infants tend to respond more strongly to a new element that has entered their environment, an inclination that ensures that they will continually add to their knowledge base. **Habituation** refers to a gradual reduction in the strength of a response due to repetitive stimulation. Time spent looking at the stimulus, heart rate, respiration rate, and brain activity may all decline, indicating a loss of interest. Once this has occurred, a new stimulus—a change in the environment—causes responsiveness to return to a high level, an increase called **recovery.** For example, when you walk through a familiar space, you notice things that are new and different—a recently hung picture on the wall or a piece of furniture that has been moved. Habituation and recovery make learning more efficient by focusing our attention on those aspects of the environment we know least about.

Researchers investigating infants' understanding of the world rely on habituation and recovery more than any other learning capacity. For example, a baby who first *habituates* to a visual pattern (a photo of a baby) and then *recovers* to a new one (a photo of a bald man) appears to remember the first stimulus and perceive the second one as new and different from it. This method of studying infant perception and cognition, illustrated in Figure 4.9 on page 132, can be used with newborns, including preterm infants (Kavšek & Bornstein, 2010). It has even been used to study the fetus's sensitivity to external stimuli in the third trimester of pregnancy—for example, by measuring changes in fetal heart rate or brain waves when various repeated sounds are presented, followed by a different sound (see page 81 in Chapter 3).

Recovery to a new stimulus, or *novelty preference,* assesses infants' *recent memory.* Think about what happens when you return to a place you have not seen for a long time. Instead of attending to novelty, you are likely to focus on aspects that are familiar: "I recognize that—I've been here before!" Like adults, infants shift from a novelty preference to a *familiarity preference*

FIGURE 4.9 Using habituation to study infant perception and cognition. In the habituation phase, infants view a photo of a baby until their looking declines. In the test phase, infants are again shown the baby photo, but this time it appears alongside a photo of a bald-headed man. (a) When the test phase occurs soon after the habituation phase (within minutes, hours, or days, depending on the age of the infants), participants who remember the baby face and distinguish it from the man's face show a *novelty preference;* they recover to (spend more time looking at) the new stimulus. (b) When the test phase is delayed for weeks or months, infants who continue to remember the baby face shift to a *familiarity preference;* they recover to the familiar baby face rather than to the novel man's face.

as more time intervenes between habituation and test phases in research. That is, babies recover to the familiar stimulus rather than to a novel stimulus (see Figure 4.9) (Colombo, Brez, & Curtindale, 2013; Flom & Bahrick, 2010; Richmond, Colombo, & Hayne, 2007). By focusing on that shift, researchers can also use habituation to assess *remote memory,* or memory for stimuli to which infants were exposed weeks or months earlier.

As Chapter 5 will reveal, habituation research has greatly enriched our understanding of how long babies remember a wide range of stimuli. And by varying stimulus features, researchers can use habituation and recovery to study babies' ability to categorize stimuli as well.

Imitation

Babies come into the world with a primitive ability to learn through **imitation**—by copying the behavior of another person. For example, Figure 4.10 shows a human newborn imitating two adult facial expressions (Meltzoff & Moore, 1977). The newborn's capacity to imitate extends to certain gestures, such as head and index-finger movements, and has been demonstrated in many ethnic groups and cultures (Meltzoff & Kuhl, 1994; Nagy et al., 2005). As the figure reveals, even newborn primates, including chimpanzees (our closest evolutionary relatives), imitate some behaviors (Ferrari et al., 2006; Myowa-Yamakoshi et al., 2004).

Nevertheless, some studies have failed to reproduce the human findings (see, for example, Anisfeld, 2005). And because newborn mouth and tongue movements occur with increased frequency to almost any arousing change in stimulation (such as lively music or flashing lights), some researchers argue that certain newborn "imitative" responses are actually mouthing—a common early exploratory response to interesting stimuli (Jones, 2009). Furthermore, imitation is harder to induce in babies 2 to 3 months old than just after birth. Therefore, skeptics believe that the newborn imitative capacity is little more than an automatic response that declines with age, much like a reflex (Heyes, 2005).

Others claim that newborns imitate a variety of facial expressions and head movements with effort and determination, even after short delays—when the adult is no longer demonstrating the behavior (Meltzoff & Williamson, 2013; Paukner, Ferrari, & Suomi, 2011). Furthermore, these investigators argue that imitation—unlike reflexes—does not decline. Human babies several months old often do not imitate an adult's behavior right away because they first try to play familiar social games—mutual gazing, cooing, smiling, and waving their arms. But when an adult models a gesture repeatedly, older human infants soon get down to business and imitate (Meltzoff & Moore, 1994). Similarly, imitation declines in baby chimps around 9 weeks of age, when mother–baby mutual gazing and other face-to-face exchanges increase.

According to Andrew Meltzoff, newborns imitate much as older children and adults do—by actively trying to match body movements they *see* with ones they *feel* themselves make. With successive tries, they imitate a modeled gesture with greater accuracy (Meltzoff & Williamson, 2013). Later we will encounter evidence that young babies are remarkably adept at coordinating information across sensory systems.

Scientists have identified specialized cells in motor areas of the cerebral cortex in primates—called **mirror neurons**—that may underlie early imitative capacities. Mirror neurons fire identically when a primate hears or sees an action and when it carries out that action on its own (Ferrari & Coudé, 2011). Brain-imaging research reveals functioning neural-mirroring systems in human infants by the middle of the first year that enable them to observe another's behavior (such as tapping a rattle or ringing a bell) while simulating the behavior in their own brain (Shimada & Hiraki, 2006). These systems are believed to be the biological basis of a variety of interrelated, complex social abilities in addition to imitation, including empathic sharing of emotions and understanding others' intentions.

Still, Meltzoff's view of newborn imitation as a flexible, voluntary capacity remains controversial. Some critics contend ment (Ferrari et al., 2013; Heyes, 2010). And as we will see in Chapter 5, the capacity to imitate expands greatly over the first two years.

However limited it is at birth, imitation is a powerful means of learning. Using imitation, infants explore their social world, learning from other people. As they notice similarities between their own actions and those of others, they experience other people as "like me" and learn about themselves (Meltzoff & Williamson, 2013). By tapping into infants' ability to imitate, adults can get infants to exhibit desirable behaviors. Finally, caregivers take great pleasure in a baby who participates in imitative exchanges—a capacity that strengthens the parent–infant bond.

Ask yourself

CONNECT Which learning capacities contribute to an infant's first social relationships? Explain, providing examples.

APPLY Nine-month-old Byron has a toy with large, colored push buttons on it. Each time he pushes a button, he hears a nursery tune. Which learning capacity is the manufacturer of this toy taking advantage of? What can Byron's play with the toy reveal about his perception of sound patterns?

Motor Development

4.6 Describe dynamic systems theory of motor development, along with factors that influence motor progress in the first two years.

Carolyn, Monica, and Vanessa each kept a baby book, filled with proud notations about when their children first held up their heads, reached for objects, sat by themselves, and walked alone. Parents are understandably excited about these new motor skills, which allow babies to master their bodies and the environment in new ways. For example, sitting upright gives infants a new perspective on the world. Reaching permits babies to find out about objects by acting on them. And when infants can move on their own, their opportunities for exploration multiply.

Babies' motor achievements have a powerful effect on their social relationships. When Caitlin crawled at 7½ months, Carolyn and David began to restrict her movements by saying no and expressing mild impatience. When she walked three days after her first birthday, the first "testing of wills" occurred (Biringen et al., 1995). Despite her mother's warnings, she sometimes pulled items from shelves that were off limits. "I said, 'Don't do that!'" Carolyn would say firmly, taking Caitlin's hand and redirecting her attention.

At the same time, newly walking babies more actively attend to and initiate social interaction (Clearfield, 2011; Karasik et al., 2011). Caitlin frequently toddled over to her parents to express a greeting, give a hug, or show them objects of interest. Carolyn

FIGURE 4.10 Imitation by human and chimpanzee newborns. The human infants in the middle row imitating (left) tongue protrusion and (right) mouth opening are 2 to 3 weeks old. The chimpanzee imitating both facial expressions is 2 weeks old. (From A. N. Meltzoff & M. K. Moore, 1977, "Imitation of Facial and Manual Gestures by Human Neonates," *Science, 198,* p. 75. Copyright © 1977 by AAAS. Reprinted with permission of the American Association for the Advancement of Science conveyed through Copyright Clearance Center, Inc., and Dr. Andrew Meltzoff. And from M. Myowa-Yamakoshi et al., 2004, "Imitation in Neonatal Chimpanzees [Pan Troglodytes]." *Developmental Science, 7,* p. 440. Copyright © 2004 by John Wiley & Sons. Reprinted with permission of John Wiley & Sons conveyed through Copyright Clearance Center, Inc.)

that babies learn to imitate gradually through rich social experiences (Ray & Heyes, 2011). And even researchers who believe that newborns can imitate agree that many opportunities to see oneself act, to watch others' responses, and to engage in imitative games with caregivers are required for infants to become proficient imitators (Marshall & Meltzoff, 2011). Consistent with this view, human neural-mirroring systems, though possibly functional at birth, undergo an extended period of develop-

and David, in turn, increased their verbal responsiveness, expressions of affection, and playful activities. And when Caitlin encountered risky situations, such as a sloping walkway or a dangerous object, Carolyn and David intervened, combining emotional warnings with rich verbal and gestural information that helped Caitlin notice critical features of her surroundings, regulate her motor actions, and acquire language (Karasik et al., 2008). Caitlin's delight as she worked on new motor skills triggered pleasurable reactions in others, which encouraged her efforts further. Motor, social, cognitive, and language competencies developed together and supported one another.

The Sequence of Motor Development

Gross-motor development refers to control over actions that help infants get around in the environment, such as crawling, standing, and walking. *Fine-motor development* has to do with smaller movements, such as reaching and grasping. Table 4.2 shows the average age at which U.S. infants and toddlers achieve a variety of gross- and fine-motor skills. It also presents the age range during which most babies accomplish each skill, indicating large individual differences in *rate* of motor progress. Also, a baby who is a late reacher will not necessarily be a late crawler or walker. We would be concerned about a child's development only if many motor skills were seriously delayed.

Historically, researchers assumed that motor skills were separate, innate abilities that emerged in a fixed sequence governed by a built-in maturational timetable. This view has long been discredited. Rather, motor skills are interrelated. Each is a product of earlier motor attainments and a contributor to new ones. And children acquire motor skills in highly individual ways. For example, before her adoption, Grace spent most of her days lying in a hammock. Because she was rarely placed on her tummy and on firm surfaces that enabled her to move on her own, she did not try to crawl. As a result, she pulled to a stand and walked before she crawled! Babies display such skills as rolling, sitting, crawling, and walking in diverse orders rather than in the sequence implied by motor norms (Adolph & Robinson, 2013).

TABLE 4.2
Gross- and Fine-Motor Development in the First Two Years

MOTOR SKILL	AVERAGE AGE ACHIEVED	AGE RANGE IN WHICH 90 PERCENT OF INFANTS ACHIEVE THE SKILL
When held upright, holds head erect and steady	6 weeks	3 weeks–4 months
When prone, lifts self by arms	2 months	3 weeks–4 months
Rolls from side to back	2 months	3 weeks–5 months
Grasps cube	3 months, 3 weeks	2–7 months
Rolls from back to side	4½ months	2–7 months
Sits alone	7 months	5–9 months
Crawls	7 months	5–11 months
Pulls to stand	8 months	5–12 months
Plays pat-a-cake	9 months, 3 weeks	7–15 months
Stands alone	11 months	9–16 months
Walks alone	11 months, 3 weeks	9–17 months
Builds tower of two cubes	11 months, 3 weeks	10–19 months
Scribbles vigorously	14 months	10–21 months
Walks up stairs with help	16 months	12–23 months
Jumps in place	23 months, 2 weeks	17–30 months
Walks on tiptoe	25 months	16–30 months

Note: These milestones represent overall age trends. Individual differences exist in the precise age at which each milestone is attained.
Sources: Bayley, 1969, 1993, 2005.

Motor Skills as Dynamic Systems

According to **dynamic systems theory of motor development**, mastery of motor skills involves acquiring increasingly complex *systems of action*. When motor skills work as a system, separate abilities blend together, each cooperating with others to produce more effective ways of exploring and controlling the environment. For example, control of the head and upper chest combine into sitting with support. Kicking, rocking on all fours, and reaching combine to become crawling. Then crawling, standing, and stepping are united into walking (Adolph & Robinson, 2015; Thelen & Smith, 1998).

Each new skill is a joint product of four factors: (1) central nervous system development, (2) the body's movement capacities, (3) the goals the child has in mind, and (4) environmental supports for the skill. Change in any element makes the system less stable, and the child starts to explore and select new, more effective motor patterns.

The broader physical environment also profoundly influences motor skills. Infants with stairs in their home learn to crawl up stairs at an earlier age and also more readily master a back-descent strategy—the safest but also the most challenging position because the baby must turn around at the top, give up visual guidance of her goal, and crawl backward (Berger, Theuring, & Adolph, 2007). And if children were reared on the moon, with its reduced gravity, they would prefer jumping to walking or running!

LOOK and LISTEN

Observe a newly crawling or walking baby. Note the goals that motivate the baby to move, along with the baby's effort and motor experimentation. Describe parenting behaviors and features of the environment that promote mastery of the skill.

When a skill is first acquired, infants must refine it. For example, in trying to crawl, Caitlin often collapsed on her tummy and moved backward. Soon she figured out how to propel herself forward by alternately pulling with her arms and pushing with her feet, "belly-crawling" in various ways for several weeks. As babies attempt a new skill, related, previously mastered skills often become less secure. As the novice walker experiments with balancing the body vertically over two small moving feet, balance during sitting may become temporarily less stable (Chen et al., 2007).

Motor mastery involves intense practice. In learning to walk, toddlers practice six or more hours a day, traveling the length of 29 football fields! They fall, on average, 17 times per hour but rarely cry, returning to motion within a few seconds (Adolph et al., 2012). Gradually their small, unsteady steps change to a longer stride, their feet move closer together, their toes point to the front, and their legs become symmetrically coordinated. As movements are repeated thousands of times, they promote new synaptic connections in the brain that govern motor patterns.

Dynamic systems theory shows us why motor development cannot be genetically determined. Because it is motivated by exploration and the desire to master new tasks and varies with context, heredity can map it out only at a general level. Rather than being *hardwired* into the nervous system, motor behaviors are *softly assembled* from multiple components, allowing for different paths to the same motor skill (Adolph & Robinson, 2015; Spencer, Perone, & Buss, 2011).

Dynamic Motor Systems in Action.

To find out how infants acquire motor capacities, some studies have tracked babies from their first attempts at a skill until it became smooth and effortless. In one investigation, researchers held sounding toys alternately in front of infants' hands and feet, from the time they showed interest until they engaged in well-coordinated reaching and grasping (Galloway & Thelen, 2004). As Figure 4.11 illustrates, the infants violated the normative sequence of arm and hand control preceding leg and foot control, shown in Table 4.2. They first reached for the toys with their feet—as early as 8 weeks of age, at least a month before reaching with their hands!

Why did babies reach "feet first"? Because the hip joint constrains the legs to move less freely than the shoulder constrains the arms, infants could more easily control their leg movements. Consequently, foot reaching required far less practice than hand reaching. As these findings confirm, rather than following a strict sequence, the order in which motor skills develop depends on the anatomy of the body part being used, the surrounding environment, and the baby's efforts.

Furthermore, in building a more effective dynamic system, babies often use advances in one motor skill to support advances

FIGURE 4.11 Reaching "feet first." When sounding toys were held in front of babies' hands and feet, they reached with their feet as early as 8 weeks of age, a month or more before they reached with their hands. This 2½-month-old skillfully explores an object with her foot.

in others. For example, beginning to walk frees the hands for carrying, and new walkers like to fetch distant objects and transport them (Karasik, Tamis-LeMonda, & Adolph, 2011). Observations of new walkers reveal that, surprisingly, they fall less often when carrying objects than when their hands are empty (Karasik et al., 2012). Toddlers integrate their object carrying into their emerging "walking system," using it to improve their balance.

Cultural Variations in Motor Development. Cross-cultural research further illustrates how early movement opportunities and a stimulating environment contribute to motor development. More than half a century ago, Wayne Dennis (1960) observed infants in Iranian orphanages who were deprived of the tantalizing surroundings that induce infants to acquire motor skills. These babies spent their days lying on their backs in cribs, without toys to play with. As a result, most did not move on their own until after 2 years of age. When they finally did move, the constant experience of lying on their backs led them to scoot in a sitting position rather than crawl on their hands and knees. Because babies who scoot come up against furniture with their feet, not their hands, they are far less likely to pull themselves to a standing position in preparation for walking. Indeed, by 3 to 4 years of age, only 15 percent of the Iranian orphans were walking alone.

Cultural variations in infant-rearing practices affect motor development. To ensure safety and ease toileting while parents work in the fields, mothers in rural northeastern China place infants on their backs in bags of sand (similar to kitty litter) for most of the day, continuing this practice into the second year. Compared with diapered infants in the same region, sandbag-reared babies are greatly delayed in sitting and walking (Mei, 1994). Among the Zinacanteco Indians of southern Mexico and the Gusii of Kenya, adults view babies who walk before they know enough to keep away from cooking fires and weaving looms as dangerous to themselves and disruptive to others (Greenfield, 1992). Zinacanteco and Gusii parents actively discourage infants' gross-motor progress.

In contrast, among the Kipsigis of Kenya and the West Indians of Jamaica, babies hold their heads up, sit alone, and walk considerably earlier than North American infants. In both societies, parents emphasize early motor maturity, practicing formal exercises to stimulate particular skills (Adolph, Karasik, & Tamis-LeMonda, 2010). In the first few months, babies are seated in holes dug in the ground, with rolled blankets to keep them upright. Walking is promoted by frequently standing babies in adults' laps, bouncing them on their feet, and exercising the stepping reflex (Hopkins & Westra, 1988; Super, 1981). As parents in these cultures support babies in upright postures and rarely put them down on the floor, their infants usually skip crawling—a motor skill regarded as crucial in Western nations!

Finally, because it decreases exposure to "tummy time," the current Western practice of having babies sleep on their backs to protect them from SIDS (see page 106 in Chapter 3) delays gross-motor milestones of rolling, sitting, and crawling (Scrutton, 2005). Regularly exposing infants to the tummy-lying position during waking hours prevents these delays.

Fine-Motor Development: Reaching and Grasping

Of all motor skills, reaching may play the greatest role in infant cognitive development. By grasping things, turning them over, and seeing what happens when they are released, infants learn a great deal about the sights, sounds, and feel of objects. Because certain gross-motor attainments vastly change infants' view of their surroundings, they promote manual coordination. When babies sit, and even more so when they stand and walk, they see the panorama of an entire room (Kretch, Franchak, & Adolph, 2014). In these positions, they focus mainly on the sights and sounds of nearby objects and want to explore them.

Reaching and grasping, like many other motor skills, start out as gross, diffuse activity and move toward mastery of fine movements. Figure 4.12 illustrates some milestones of reaching over the first nine months. Newborns make poorly coordinated swipes, called *prereaching,* toward an object in front of them, but because of poor arm and hand control they rarely contact the object. Like newborn reflexes, prereaching drops out around 7 weeks of age (von Hofsten, 2004). Yet these early behaviors suggest that babies are biologically prepared to coordinate hand with eye in the act of exploring.

At about 3 to 4 months, as infants develop the necessary eye, head, and shoulder control, reaching reappears as purposeful, forward arm movements in the presence of a nearby toy and gradually improves in accuracy (Bhat, Heathcock, & Galloway, 2005). By 5 to 6 months, infants reach for an object in a room that has been darkened during the reach by switching off the lights—a skill that improves over the next few months (Clifton

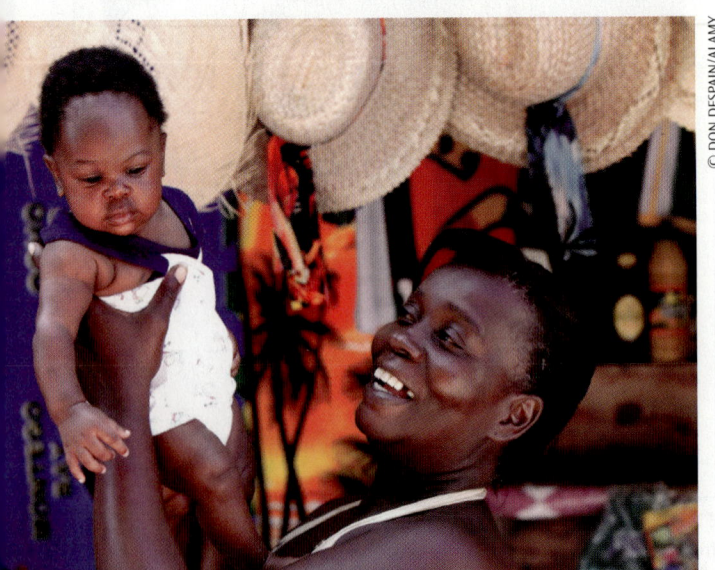

This West Indian mother of Jamaica "walks" her baby up her body in a deliberate effort to promote early mastery of walking.

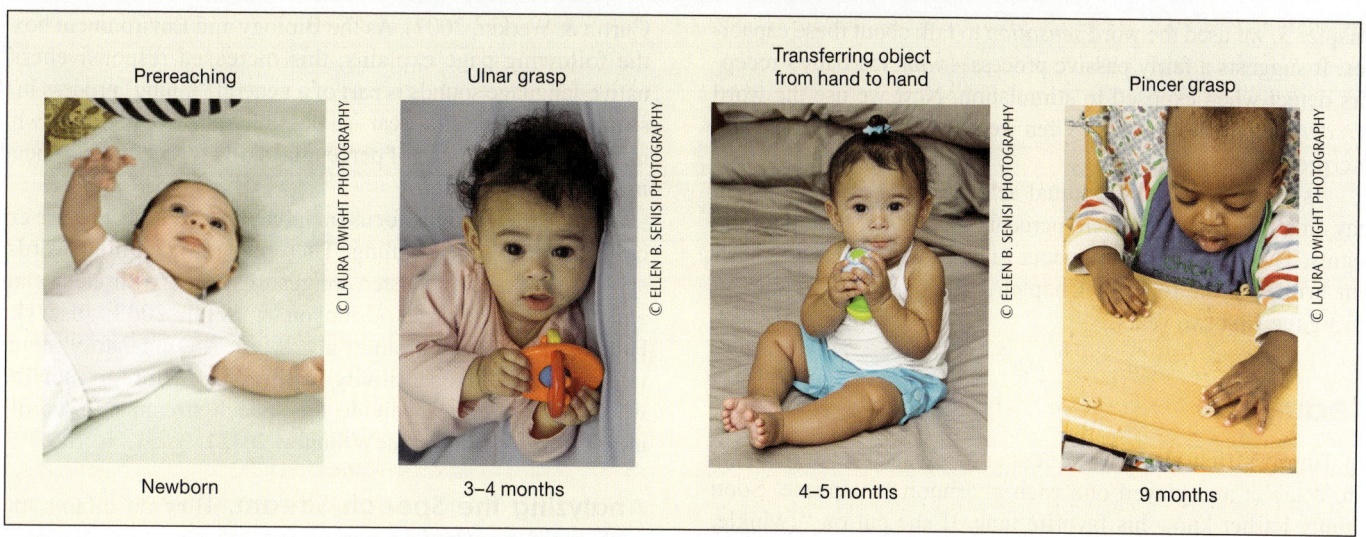

FIGURE 4.12 Some milestones of reaching and grasping. The average age at which each skill is attained is given. (Ages from Bayley, 1969; Rochat, 1989.)

et al., 1994; McCarty & Ashmead, 1999). Early on, vision is freed from the basic act of reaching so it can focus on more complex adjustments. By 7 months, the arms become more independent; infants reach for an object by extending one arm rather than both (Fagard & Pezé, 1997). During the next few months, infants become more efficient at reaching for moving objects—ones that spin, change direction, and move sideways, closer, or farther away (Fagard, Spelke, & von Hofsten, 2009; Wentworth, Benson, & Haith, 2000).

Once infants can reach, they modify their grasp. The newborn's grasp reflex is replaced by the *ulnar grasp,* a clumsy motion in which the fingers close against the palm. Still, even 4- to 5-month-olds modify their grasp to suit an object's size, shape, and texture (rigid versus soft)—a capacity that improves over the second half-year as infants adjust the hand more precisely and do so in advance of contacting the object (Rocha et al., 2013; Witherington, 2005). Around 4 to 5 months, when infants begin to sit up, both hands become coordinated in exploring objects. Babies of this age can hold an object in one hand while the other scans it with the fingertips, and they frequently transfer objects from hand to hand (Rochat & Goubet, 1995). By the end of the first year, babies use the thumb and index finger opposably in a well-coordinated *pincer grasp*. Then the ability to manipulate objects greatly expands. The 1-year-old can pick up raisins and blades of grass, turn knobs, and open and close small boxes.

Between 8 and 11 months, reaching and grasping are well-practiced, so attention is released from the motor skill to events that occur before and after attaining the object. For example, 10-month-olds modify their reach to anticipate their next action. They adjust their arm and hand to catch a ball, and they reach for a ball faster when they intend to throw it than when they intend to push it down a narrow tube (Claxton, Keen, & McCarty, 2003; Kayed & Van der Meer, 2009). Around this time, too, infants begin to solve simple problems that involve reaching, such as searching for and finding a hidden toy.

Finally, the capacity to reach for and manipulate an object increases infants' attention to the way an adult reaches for and plays with that same object (Hauf, Aschersleben, & Prinz, 2007). As babies watch what others do, they broaden their understanding of others' behaviors and of the range of actions that can be performed on various objects.

Ask yourself

CONNECT Provide several examples of how motor development influences infants' and toddlers' social experiences. How do social experiences, in turn, influence motor development?

APPLY List everyday experiences that support mastery of reaching, grasping, sitting, and crawling. Why should caregivers place young infants in a variety of waking-time body positions?

REFLECT Do you favor early, systematic training of infants in motor skills such as crawling, walking, and stair climbing? Why or why not?

Perceptual Development

4.7 What changes in hearing, depth and pattern perception, and intermodal perception take place during infancy?

4.8 Explain differentiation theory of perceptual development.

In Chapter 3, you learned that the senses of touch, taste, smell, and hearing—but not vision—are remarkably well-developed at birth. Now let's turn to a related question: How does perception change over the first year? Our discussion will address hearing and vision, the focus of almost all research. Recall that in

Chapter 3, we used the word *sensation* to talk about these capacities. It suggests a fairly passive process—what the baby's receptors detect when exposed to stimulation. Now we use the word *perception*, which is active: When we perceive, we organize and interpret what we see.

As we review the perceptual achievements of infancy, you may find it hard to tell where perception leaves off and thinking begins. The research we are about to discuss provides an excellent bridge to the topic of Chapter 5—cognitive development during the first two years.

Hearing

On Timmy's first birthday, Vanessa downloaded nursery songs into a tablet and played one each afternoon at naptime. Soon Timmy let her know his favorite tune. If she put on "Twinkle, Twinkle," he stood up in his crib and whimpered until she replaced it with "Jack and Jill." Timmy's behavior illustrates the greatest change in hearing over the first year of life: Babies start to organize sounds into complex patterns.

Between 4 and 7 months, infants display a sense of musical phrasing: They prefer Mozart minuets with pauses between phrases to those with awkward breaks (Krumhansl & Jusczyk, 1990). Around 6 to 7 months, they can distinguish musical tunes on the basis of variations in rhythmic patterns, including beat structure (duple or triple) and accent structure (emphasis on the first note of every beat unit or at other positions) (Hannon & Johnson, 2004). They are also sensitive to features conveying the purpose of familiar types of songs, preferring to listen to high-pitched playsongs (aimed at entertaining) and low-pitched lullabies (used to soothe) (Tsang & Conrad, 2010). By the end of the first year, infants recognize the same melody when it is played in different keys (Trehub, 2001). As we will see next, 6- to 12-month-olds make comparable discriminations in human speech: They readily detect sound regularities, which facilitates later language learning.

Speech Perception. Recall from Chapter 3 that newborns can distinguish nearly all sounds in human languages and that they prefer listening to human speech over nonspeech sounds and to their native tongue rather than a rhythmically distinct foreign language. Brain-imaging evidence reveals that in young infants, discrimination of speech sounds activates both auditory and motor areas in the cerebral cortex (Kuhl et al., 2014). Researchers speculate that while perceiving speech sounds, babies also generate internal motor plans that prepare them for producing those sounds.

As infants listen to people talk, they learn to focus on meaningful sound variations. ERP brain-wave recordings reveal that around 5 months, infants become sensitive to syllable stress patterns in their own language (Weber et al., 2004). Between 6 and 8 months, they start to "screen out" sounds not used in their native tongue and, in the case of bilingual infants, in both native languages (Albareda-Castellot, Pons, & Sebastián-Gallés, 2010;

Curtin & Werker, 2007). As the Biology and Environment box on the following page explains, this increased responsiveness to native-language sounds is part of a general "tuning" process in the second half of the first year—a possible sensitive period in which infants acquire a range of perceptual skills for picking up socially important information.

Soon after, infants focus on larger speech units that are critical to figuring out meaning. They recognize familiar words in spoken passages and listen longer to speech with clear clause and phrase boundaries (Johnson & Seidl, 2008; Jusczyk & Hohne, 1997; Soderstrom et al., 2003). Around 7 to 9 months, infants extend this sensitivity to speech structure to individual words: They begin to divide the speech stream into wordlike units (Jusczyk, 2002; MacWhinney, 2015).

Analyzing the Speech Stream. How do infants make such rapid progress in perceiving the structure of speech? Research shows that they have an impressive **statistical learning capacity.** By analyzing the speech stream for patterns—repeatedly occurring sequences of sounds—they acquire a stock of speech structures for which they will later learn meanings, long before they start to talk around age 12 months.

For example, when presented with controlled sequences of nonsense syllables, babies as young as 5 months listen for

A 6-month-old is a remarkable analyzer of the speech stream. While listening to her mother talk, she detects sound patterns, discriminating words and word sequences for which she will later learn meanings.

Biology and Environment

"Tuning In" to Familiar Speech, Faces, and Music: A Sensitive Period for Culture-Specific Learning

To share experiences with members of their family and community, babies must become skilled at making perceptual discriminations that are meaningful in their culture. As we have seen, at first babies are sensitive to virtually all speech sounds, but around 6 months, they narrow their focus, limiting the distinctions they make to the language they hear and will soon learn.

The ability to perceive faces shows a similar **perceptual narrowing effect**—perceptual sensitivity that becomes increasingly attuned with age to information most often encountered. After habituating to one member of each pair of faces in Figure 4.13, 6-month-olds were shown the familiar face and the novel face side by side. For both pairs, they recovered to (looked longer at) the novel face, indicating that they could discriminate individual faces of both humans and monkeys equally well (Pascalis, de Haan, & Nelson, 2002). But at 9 months, infants no longer showed a novelty preference when viewing the monkey pair. Like adults, they could distinguish only the human faces. Similar findings emerge with sheep faces: Four- to 6-months-olds easily distinguish them, but 9- to 11-month olds no longer do (Simpson et al., 2011).

This perceptual narrowing effect appears again in musical rhythm perception. Western adults are accustomed to the even-beat pattern of Western music—repetition of the same rhythmic structure in every measure of a tune—and easily notice rhythmic changes that disrupt this familiar beat. But present them with music that does not follow this typical Western rhythmic form—Baltic folk tunes, for example—and they fail to pick up on rhythmic-pattern deviations. In contrast, 6-month-olds can detect such disruptions in both Western and non-Western melodies. By 12 months, however, after added exposure to Western music, babies are no longer aware of deviations in foreign musical rhythms, although their sensitivity to Western rhythmic structure remains unchanged (Hannon & Trehub, 2005b).

Several weeks of regular interaction with a foreign-language speaker and of daily opportunities to listen to non-Western music fully restore 12-month-olds' sensitivity to wide-ranging speech sounds and music rhythms (Hannon & Trehub, 2005a; Kuhl, Tsao, & Liu, 2003). Similarly, 6-month-olds given three months of training in discriminating individual monkey faces, in which each image is labeled with a distinct name ("Carlos," "Iona") instead of the generic label "monkey," retain their ability to discriminate monkey faces at 9 months (Scott & Monesson, 2009). Adults given similar extensive experiences, by contrast, show little improvement in perceptual sensitivity.

Taken together, these findings suggest a heightened capacity—or sensitive period—in the second half of the first year, when babies are biologically prepared to "zero in" on socially meaningful perceptual distinctions. Notice how, between 6 and 12 months,

FIGURE 4.13 Discrimination of human and monkey faces. Which of these pairs is easiest for you to tell apart? After habituating to one of the photos in each pair, infants were shown the familiar and the novel face side by side. For both pairs, 6-month-olds recovered to (looked longer at) the novel face, indicating that they could discriminate human and monkey faces equally well. By 12 months, babies lost their ability to distinguish the monkey faces. Like adults, they showed a novelty preference only to human stimuli. (From O. Pascalis et al., 2002, "Is Face Processing Species-Specific During the First Year of Life?" *Science, 296*, p. 1322. Copyright © 2002 by AAAS. Republished with permission of American Association for the Advancement of Science conveyed through Copyright Clearance Center, Inc.)

learning is especially rapid across several domains (speech, faces, and music) and is easily modified by experience. This suggests a broad neurological change—perhaps a special time of experience-expectant brain growth (see page 124) in which babies analyze stimulation of all kinds in ways that prepare them to participate in their cultural community.

---

statistical regularities: They locate words by distinguishing syllables that often occur together (indicating they belong to the same word) from syllables that seldom occur together (indicating a word boundary) (Johnson & Tyler, 2010). Consider the English word sequence *pretty#baby*. After listening to the speech stream for just one minute (about 60 words), babies can distinguish a word-internal syllable pair *(pretty)* from a word-external syllable pair *(ty#ba)*. They prefer to listen to new speech that preserves the word-internal pattern (Saffran, Aslin, & Newport, 1996 ; Saffran & Thiessen, 2003).

Once infants begin locating words, they focus on the words and, around 7 to 8 months, identify regular syllable-stress patterns—for example, in English, that the onset of a strong syllable (*hap*-py, *rab*-bit) often signals a new word (Thiessen & Saffran, 2007). By 10 months, babies can detect words that start with weak syllables, such as "sur*prise*," by listening for sound regularities before and after the words (Kooijman, Hagoort, & Cutler, 2009).

Clearly, babies have a powerful ability to extract patterns from complex, continuous speech. Their remarkable statistical learning capacity also extends to visual stimuli and is present in the first weeks of life (Aslin & Newport, 2012). Statistical learning seems to be a general capacity that infants use to analyze complex stimulation.

Finally, the more rapidly 10-month-olds detect words within the speech stream (as indicated by ERP recordings), the larger their vocabulary at age 2 years (Junge et al., 2012). Parents' speech to babies, which often contains single-word utterances followed by the same words embedded in the speech stream ("Doggie!" "See the big doggie?"), aids word discrimination (Lew-Williams, Pelucchi, & Saffran, 2011). As we will see in Chapter 5, adults' style of communicating with infants greatly facilitates analysis of the structure of speech.

Vision

For exploring the environment, humans depend on vision more than any other sense. Although at first a baby's visual world is fragmented, it undergoes extraordinary changes during the first 7 to 8 months of life.

Visual development is supported by rapid maturation of the eye and visual centers in the cerebral cortex. Recall from Chapter 3 that the newborn baby focuses and perceives color poorly. Around 2 months, infants can focus on objects about as well as adults can, and their color vision is adultlike by 4 months (Johnson & Hannon, 2015). *Visual acuity* (fineness of discrimination) increases steadily, reaching 20/80 by 6 months and an adult level of about 20/20 by 4 years (Slater et al., 2010). Scanning the environment and tracking moving objects also improve over the first half-year as infants better control their eye movements and build an organized perceptual world (Johnson, Slemmer, & Amso, 2004; von Hofsten & Rosander, 1998).

As babies explore their visual field, they figure out the characteristics of objects and how they are arranged in space. To understand how they do so, let's examine the development of two aspects of vision: depth and pattern perception.

Depth Perception.
Depth perception is the ability to judge the distance of objects from one another and from ourselves. It is important for understanding the layout of the environment and for guiding motor activity.

Figure 4.14 shows the *visual cliff,* designed by Eleanor Gibson and Richard Walk (1960) and used in the earliest studies of depth perception. It consists of a Plexiglas-covered table with

FIGURE 4.14 The visual cliff. Plexiglas covers the deep and shallow sides. By refusing to cross the deep side and showing a preference for the shallow side, this infant demonstrates the ability to perceive depth.

a platform at the center, a "shallow" side with a checkerboard pattern just under the glass, and a "deep" side with a checkerboard several feet below the glass. The researchers found that crawling babies readily crossed the shallow side, but most avoided the deep side. They concluded that around the time infants crawl, most distinguish deep from shallow surfaces and steer clear of drop-offs.

The visual cliff shows that crawling and avoidance of drop-offs are linked, but not how they are related or when depth perception first appears. Subsequent research has looked at babies' ability to detect specific depth cues, using methods that do not require that they crawl.

Motion is the first depth cue to which infants are sensitive. Babies 3 to 4 weeks old blink their eyes defensively when an object moves toward their face as if it is going to hit (Nánez & Yonas, 1994). *Binocular depth cues* arise because our two eyes have slightly different views of the visual field. The brain blends these two images, resulting in perception of depth. Research in which two overlapping images are projected before the baby, who wears special goggles to ensure that each eye receives only one image, reveals that sensitivity to binocular cues emerges between 2 and 3 months and improves rapidly over the first year (Brown & Miracle, 2003). Finally, beginning at 3 to 4 months and strengthening between 5 and 7 months, babies display sensitivity to *pictorial depth cues*—the ones artists often use to make a painting look three-dimensional. Examples include receding lines that create the illusion of perspective, changes in texture (nearby textures are more detailed than faraway ones), overlapping objects (an object partially hidden by another object is perceived to be more distant), and shadows cast on surfaces (indicating a separation in space between the object and the surface) (Kavšek, Yonas, & Granrud, 2012).

Why does perception of depth cues emerge in the order just described? Researchers speculate that motor development is involved. For example, control of the head during the early weeks of life may help babies notice motion and binocular cues. Around 5 to 6 months, the ability to turn, poke, and feel the surface of objects promotes perception of pictorial cues (Bushnell & Boudreau, 1993; Soska, Adolph, & Johnson, 2010). And as we will see next, one aspect of motor progress—independent movement—plays a vital role in refinement of depth perception.

Independent Movement and Depth Perception. At 6 months, Timmy started crawling. "He's fearless!" exclaimed Vanessa. "If I put him down in the middle of my bed, he crawls right over the edge. The same thing happens by the stairs." Will Timmy become wary of the side of the bed and the staircase as he becomes a more experienced crawler? Research suggests that he will. Infants with more crawling experience (regardless of when they started to crawl) are far more likely to refuse to cross the deep side of the visual cliff (Campos et al., 2000).

From extensive everyday experience, babies gradually figure out how to use depth cues to detect the danger of falling. But because the loss of body control that leads to falling differs greatly for each body position, babies must undergo this learning separately for each posture (Adolph & Kretch, 2012). In one study, 9-month-olds who were experienced sitters but novice crawlers were placed on the edge of a shallow drop-off that could be widened (Adolph, 2008). While in the familiar sitting position, infants avoided leaning out for an attractive toy at distances likely to result in falling. But in the unfamiliar crawling posture, they headed over the edge, even when the distance was extremely wide! And newly walking babies will step repeatedly over a risky drop-off (Kretch & Adolph, 2013). They will also careen down slopes and over uneven surfaces without making necessary postural adjustments (Adolph et al., 2008; Joh & Adolph, 2006). Thus, they fall frequently. As infants and toddlers discover how to avoid falling in different postures and situations, their understanding of depth expands.

Independent movement promotes other aspects of three-dimensional understanding. For example, seasoned crawlers are better than their inexperienced agemates at remembering object locations and finding hidden objects (Campos et al., 2000). They

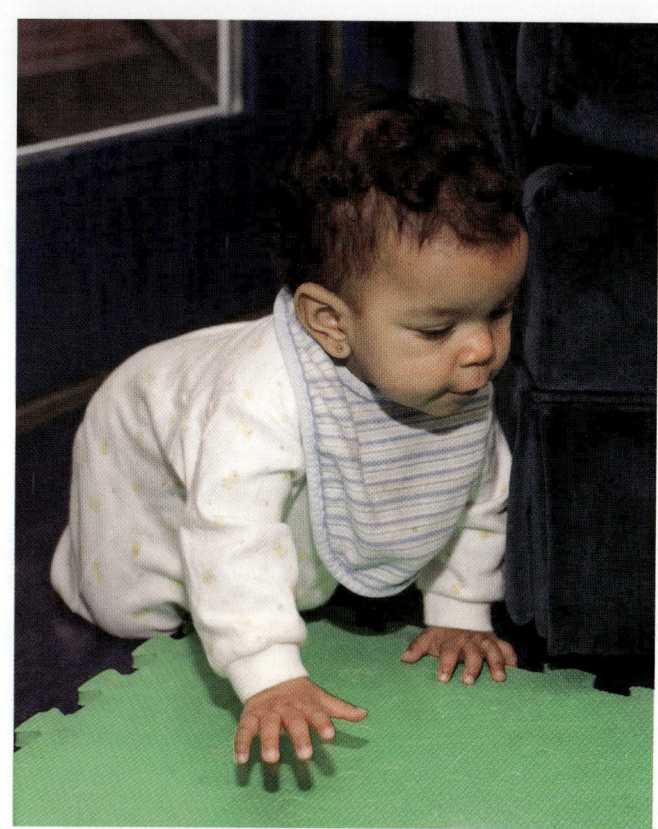

As this 8-month-old becomes adept at crawling, his experience fosters three-dimensional understanding—for example, remembering object locations and how objects appear from different viewpoints.

are also better at recognizing the identity of a previously viewed moving object when shown that object from a new angle (Schwarzer, Freitag, & Schum, 2013).

Why does crawling make such a difference? Compare your own experience of the environment when you are driven from one place to another with what you experience when you walk or drive yourself. When you move on your own, you are much more aware of landmarks and routes of travel, and you take more careful note of what things look like from different points of view. The same is true for infants. In fact, crawling promotes a new level of brain organization, as indicated by more organized EEG brain-wave activity in the cerebral cortex (Bell & Fox, 1996). Perhaps crawling strengthens certain neural connections, especially those involved in vision and understanding of space.

Pattern Perception. Even newborns prefer to look at patterned rather than plain stimuli (Fantz, 1961). As they get older, infants prefer more complex patterns. For example, 3-week-olds look longest at black-and-white checkerboards with a few large squares, whereas 8- and 14-week-olds prefer those with many squares (Brennan, Ames, & Moore, 1966).

A general principle, called **contrast sensitivity,** explains early pattern preferences (Banks & Ginsburg, 1985). *Contrast* refers to the difference in the amount of light between adjacent

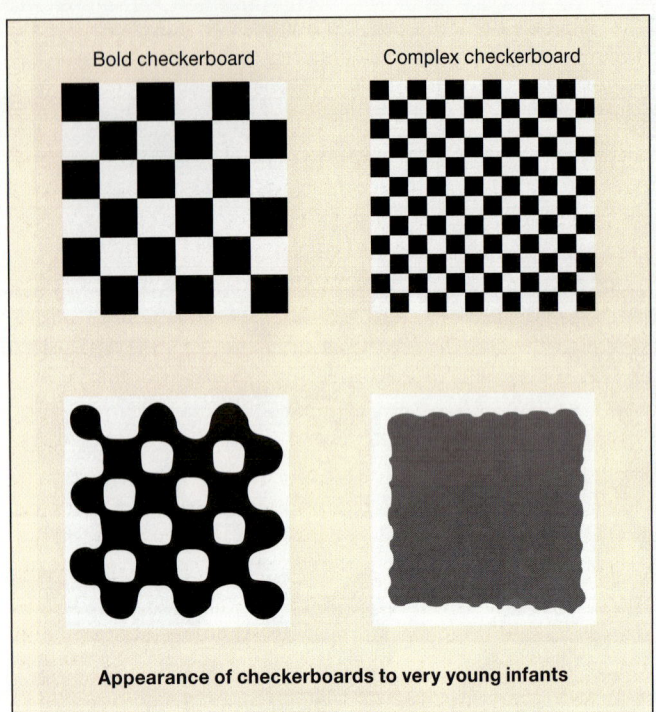

FIGURE 4.15 The way two checkerboards differing in complexity look to infants in the first few weeks of life. Because of their poor vision, very young infants cannot resolve the fine detail in the *complex checkerboard*. It appears blurred, like a gray field. The large, *bold checkerboard* appears to have more contrast, so babies prefer to look at it. (Adapted from M. S. Banks & P. Salapatek, 1983, "Infant Visual Perception," in M. M. Haith & J. J. Campos [Eds.], *Handbook of Child Psychology: Vol. 2. Infancy and Developmental Psychobiology* [4th ed.]. New York: John Wiley & Sons, p. 504. Copyright © 1983 by John Wiley & Sons, Inc. Reproduced with permission of John Wiley & Sons, Inc.)

FIGURE 4.16 Subjective boundaries in visual patterns. (a) Do you perceive a square in the middle of the figure? By 4 months of age, infants do, too. (b) What does the image, missing two-thirds of its outline, look like to you? By 12 months, infants detect a motorcycle. After habituating to the incomplete motorcycle image, they were shown an intact motorcycle figure paired with a novel form. Twelve-month-olds recovered to (looked longer at) the novel figure, indicating that they recognized the motorcycle pattern on the basis of very little visual information. (Adapted from Ghim, 1990; Rose, Jankowski, & Senior, 1997.)

regions in a pattern. If babies are *sensitive to* (can detect) the contrast in two or more patterns, they prefer the one with more contrast. To understand this idea, look at the checkerboards in the top row of Figure 4.15. To us, the one with many small squares has more contrasting elements. Now look at the bottom row, which shows how these checkerboards appear to infants in the first few weeks of life. Because of their poor vision, very young babies cannot resolve the small features in more complex patterns, so they prefer to look at the large, bold checkerboard. Around 2 months, when detection of fine-grained detail has improved, infants become sensitive to the contrast in complex patterns and spend more time looking at them (Gwiazda & Birch, 2001).

In the early weeks of life, infants respond to the separate parts of a pattern. They stare at single high-contrast features, generally on the edges, and have difficulty shifting their gaze away toward other interesting stimuli (Hunnius & Geuze, 2004a, 2004b). At 2 to 3 months, when scanning ability and contrast sensitivity improve, infants thoroughly explore a pattern's features, pausing briefly to look at each part (Bronson, 1994).

Once babies can take in all aspects of a pattern, they integrate the parts into a unified whole. Around 4 months, babies are so good at detecting pattern organization that they perceive subjective boundaries that are not really present. For example, they perceive a square in the center of Figure 4.16a, just as you do (Ghim, 1990). Older infants carry this sensitivity to subjective form further, applying it to complex, moving stimuli. For example, 9-month-olds look much longer at an organized series of blinking lights that resembles a human being walking than at an upside-down or scrambled version (Bertenthal, 1993). At 12 months, infants detect familiar objects represented by incomplete drawings, even when as much as two-thirds of the drawing is missing (see Figure 4.16b) (Rose, Jankowski, & Senior, 1997). As these findings reveal, infants' increasing knowledge of objects and actions supports pattern perception.

Face Perception. Infants' tendency to search for structure in a patterned stimulus also applies to face perception. Newborns prefer to look at photos and simplified drawings of faces with features arranged naturally (upright) rather than unnaturally (upside-down or sideways) (see Figure 4.17a) (Cassia, Turati, & Simion, 2004; Mondloch et al., 1999). They also track a facelike pattern moving across their visual field farther than they track other stimuli (Johnson, 1999). And although they rely more on outer features (hairline and chin) than inner features to distinguish real faces, newborns prefer photos of faces with eyes open and a direct gaze (Farroni et al., 2002; Turati et al., 2006). Yet another amazing capacity is their tendency to look longer at both human and animal faces judged by adults as attractive—a preference that may be the origin of the widespread social bias favoring physically attractive people (Quinn et al., 2008; Slater et al., 2010).

Some researchers claim that these behaviors reflect a built-in capacity to orient toward members of one's own species, just as many newborn animals do (Johnson, 2001; Slater et al., 2011). Others assert that newborns prefer any stimulus in which the most salient elements are arranged horizontally in the upper part of a pattern—like the "eyes" in Figure 4.17b (Cassia, Turati, & Simion, 2004). Possibly, however, a bias favoring the facial pattern promotes such preferences. Still other researchers argue that newborns are exposed to faces more often than to other stimuli—early experiences that could quickly "wire" the brain to detect faces and prefer attractive ones (Bukacha, Gauthier, & Tarr, 2006).

Although newborns respond to facelike structures, they cannot discriminate a stationary, complex facial pattern from other, equally complex patterns (see Figure 4.17c). But from repeated exposures to their mother's face, they quickly learn to prefer her face to that of an unfamiliar woman, although they mostly attend to its broad outlines. Around 2 months, when they can combine pattern elements into an organized whole, babies prefer a complex drawing of the human face to other equally complex stimulus arrangements (Dannemiller & Stephens, 1988). And they clearly prefer their mother's detailed facial features to those of another woman (Bartrip, Morton, & de Schonen, 2001).

Around 3 months, infants make fine distinctions among the features of different faces—for example, between photographs of two strangers, even when the faces are moderately similar (Farroni et al., 2007). At 5 months—and strengthening over the second half-year—infants perceive emotional expressions as meaningful wholes. They treat positive faces (happy and surprised) as different from negative ones (sad and fearful) (Bornstein & Arterberry, 2003). And by 7 months, they discriminate among a wider range of facial expressions, including happiness, surprise, sadness, fearfulness, and anger (Witherington et al., 2010).

Experience influences face processing, leading babies to form group biases at a tender age. As early as 3 months, infants prefer and more easily discriminate among female faces than among male faces (Ramsey-Rennels & Langlois, 2006). The greater time infants spend with female adults explains this effect, since babies with a male primary caregiver prefer male faces. Furthermore, 3- to 6-month-olds exposed mostly to members of their own race prefer to look at the faces of members of that race, and between 6 and 9 months their ability to discriminate other-race faces weakens (Kelly et al., 2007, 2009). This own-race bias is absent in babies who have frequent contact with members of other races, and it can be reversed through exposure to racial diversity (Anzures et al., 2013; Heron-Delaney et al., 2011). Notice how early experience promotes *perceptual narrowing* with respect to gender and racial information in faces, as occurs for species information, discussed in the Biology and Environment box on page 139.

Development of areas specialized for face processing in the right cerebral hemisphere plus extensive face-to-face interaction with caregivers contribute to infants' refinement of face perception. Face identification continues to improve throughout childhood (Stiles et al., 2015). Not until ages 10 to 11 are children as adept as adults at rapidly and accurately discriminating highly similar faces encountered in everyday life.

Up to this point, we have considered the infant's sensory systems one by one. Now let's examine their coordination.

Intermodal Perception

Our world provides rich, continuous *intermodal stimulation*—simultaneous input from more than one *modality*, or sensory system. In **intermodal perception**, we make sense of these running streams of light, sound, tactile, odor, and taste information, perceiving them as integrated wholes. We know, for example, that an object's shape is the same whether we see it or touch it, that lip movements are closely coordinated with the sound of a voice, and that dropping a rigid object on a hard surface will cause a sharp, banging sound.

Recall that newborns turn in the general direction of a sound and reach for objects in a primitive way. These behaviors suggest that infants expect sight, sound, and touch to go together. Research reveals that babies perceive input from different sensory systems in a unified way by detecting *amodal sensory properties*—information that overlaps two or more sensory systems, such as rate, rhythm, duration, intensity, temporal synchrony (for vision and hearing), and texture and shape (for vision and touch). Consider the sight and sound of a bouncing ball or

FIGURE 4.17 Early face perception. Newborns prefer to look at the photo of a face (a) and the simple pattern resembling a face (b) over the upside-down versions. (c) When the complex drawing of a face on the left and the equally complex, scrambled version on the right are moved across newborns' visual field, they follow the face longer. But if the two stimuli are stationary, infants show no preference for the face until around 2 months of age. (From Cassia, Turati, & Simion, 2004; Johnson, 1999; Mondloch et al., 1999.)

This toddler exploring a tambourine readily detects amodal relations in the synchronous sounds and visual appearance of its metal jingles.

the face and voice of a speaking person. In each event, visual and auditory information occur simultaneously and with the same rate, rhythm, duration, and intensity.

Even newborns are impressive perceivers of amodal properties. After touching an object (such as a cylinder) placed in their palms, they recognize it visually, distinguishing it from a different-shaped object (Sann & Streri, 2007). And they require just one exposure to learn the association between the sight and sound of a toy, such as a rhythmically jangling rattle (Morrongiello, Fenwick, & Chance, 1998).

Within the first half-year, infants master a remarkable range of intermodal relationships. Three- to 5-month-olds can match faces with voices on the basis of lip–voice synchrony, emotional expression, and even age and gender of the speaker. Around 6 months, infants can perceive and remember the unique face–voice pairings of unfamiliar adults (Flom, 2013).

How does intermodal perception develop so quickly? Young infants seem biologically primed to focus on amodal information. Their detection of amodal relations—for example, the common tempo and rhythm in sights and sounds—precedes and provides the basis for detecting more specific intermodal matches, such as the relation between a particular person's face and the sound of her voice or between an object and its verbal label (Bahrick, 2010).

Intermodal sensitivity is crucial for perceptual development. In the first few months, when much stimulation is unfamiliar and confusing, it enables babies to notice meaningful correlations between sensory inputs and rapidly make sense of their surroundings.

In addition to easing perception of the physical world, intermodal perception facilitates social and language processing. For example, as 3- to 4-month-olds gaze at an adult's face, they initially require both vocal and visual input to distinguish positive from negative emotional expressions (Flom & Bahrick, 2007). Only later do infants discriminate positive from negative emotion

in each sensory modality—first in voices (around 5 months), then (from 7 months on) in faces (Bahrick, Hernandez-Reif, & Flom, 2005). Furthermore, in speaking to infants, parents often provide temporal synchrony between words, object motions, and touch—for example, saying "doll" while moving a doll and having it touch the infant. This greatly increases the chances that babies will remember the association between the word and the object (Gogate & Bahrick, 2001).

LOOK and LISTEN

While watching a parent and infant playing, list instances of parental intermodal stimulation and communication. What is the baby likely learning about people, objects, or language from each intermodal experience?

In sum, intermodal perception fosters all aspects of psychological development. When caregivers provide many concurrent sights, sounds, and touches, babies process more information and learn faster (Bahrick, 2010). Intermodal perception is yet another fundamental capacity that assists infants in their active efforts to build an orderly, predictable world.

Understanding Perceptual Development

Now that we have reviewed the development of infant perceptual capacities, how can we put together this diverse array of amazing achievements? Widely accepted answers come from the work of Eleanor and James Gibson. According to the Gibsons' **differentiation theory,** infants actively search for *invariant features* of the environment—those that remain stable—in a constantly changing perceptual world. In pattern perception, for example, young babies search for features that stand out and orient toward faces. Soon they explore internal features, noticing *stable relationships* among them. As a result, they detect patterns, such as complex designs and individual faces. Similarly, infants analyze the speech stream for regularities, detecting words, word-order sequences, and—within words—syllable-stress patterns. The development of intermodal perception also reflects this principle (Bahrick & Lickliter, 2012). Babies seek out invariant relationships—first, amodal properties, such as common rate and rhythm in a voice and face, and later more detailed associations, such as unique voice–face matches.

The Gibsons described their theory as *differentiation* (where *differentiate* means "analyze" or "break down") because over time, the baby detects finer and finer invariant features among stimuli. In addition to pattern perception and intermodal perception, differentiation applies to depth perception. Recall how sensitivity to motion precedes detection of fine-grained pictorial features. So one way of understanding perceptual development is to think of it as a built-in tendency to seek order and consistency—a capacity that becomes increasingly fine-tuned with age (Gibson, 1970; Gibson, 1979).

Babies' changing motor skills tranform the way they perceive surfaces. *Left photo:* A 12-month-old who has just begun to walk proceeds feet-first down a steep incline, unaware of the high risk of falling. *Right photo:* An 18-month-old with extensive experience walking knows that it's best to sit and scoot down the incline.

Infants constantly look for ways in which the environment *affords possibilities for action* (Gibson, 2003). By exploring their surroundings, they figure out which objects can be grasped, squeezed, bounced, or stroked and which surfaces are safe to cross or present the possibility of falling. And from handling objects, babies become more aware of a variety of observable object properties (Perone et al., 2008). As a result, they differentiate the world in new ways and act more competently.

To illustrate, recall how infants' changing capabilities for independent movement affect their perception. When babies crawl, and again when they walk, they gradually realize that a sloping surface *affords the possibility of falling*. With added weeks of practicing each skill, they hesitate to crawl or walk down a risky incline. Experience in trying to keep their balance on various surfaces makes crawlers and walkers more aware of the consequences of their movements. Crawlers come to detect when surface slant places so much body weight on their arms that they will fall forward, and walkers come to sense when an incline shifts body weight so their legs and feet can no longer hold them upright.

Infants do not transfer their learning about slopes or drop-offs from crawling to walking because the affordances for each posture are different (Adolph, Kretch, & LoBue, 2014). Learning is gradual and effortful because newly crawling and walking babies cross many types of surfaces in their homes each day. As they experiment with balance and postural adjustments to accommodate each, they perceive surfaces in new ways that guide their movements. As a result, they act more competently.

As we conclude our discussion of infant perception, it is only fair to note that some researchers believe that babies do more than make sense of experience by searching for invariant features and action possibilities: They also *impose meaning* on what they perceive, constructing categories of objects and events in the surrounding environment (Johnson & Hannon, 2015). We have seen the glimmerings of this *cognitive* point of view in this chapter. For example, older babies *interpret* a familiar face as a source of pleasure and affection and a pattern of blinking lights as a human being walking. This cognitive perspective also has merit in understanding the achievements of infancy. In fact, many researchers combine these two positions, regarding infant development as proceeding from a perceptual to a cognitive emphasis over the first year of life.

Ask yourself

CONNECT Using examples, explain why intermodal perception is vital for infants' developing understanding of their physical and social worlds.

APPLY After several weeks of crawling, Ben learned to avoid going headfirst over a drop-off. Now he has started to walk. Can his parents trust him not to step over a risky drop-off? Explain, using the concept of affordances.

REFLECT Consider a new motor skill that you acquired. How do you think it changed your perceptual and cognitive capacities?

Summary / chapter 4

Body Growth (p. 116)

4.1 Describe major changes in body growth over the first two years.

- Height and weight gains are greater during the first two years than at any other time after birth. Body fat increases quickly during the first nine months, whereas muscle development is slow and gradual. Body proportions change as growth follows the **cephalocaudal** and **proximodistal trends**.

Brain Development (p. 117)

4.2 Describe brain development during infancy and toddlerhood, current methods of measuring brain functioning, and appropriate stimulation to support the brain's potential.

- Early in development, the brain grows faster than any other organ of the body. Once **neurons** are in place, they rapidly extend fibers to form **synapses**. Neurons release chemicals called **neurotransmitters**, which cross synapses to communicate with other neurons. **Programmed cell death** makes space for neural fibers and synapses. Seldom stimulated neurons lose their synapses in a process called **synaptic pruning**. **Glial cells**, responsible for **myelination**, multiply rapidly through the second year, contributing to large gains in brain weight.

- Measures of brain functioning include those that detect changes in electrical activity in the cerebral cortex (EEG, ERPs), neuroimaging techniques (PET, fMRI), and NIRS, an imaging technique suitable for infants and young children.

- The **cerebral cortex** is the largest, most complex brain structure and the last to stop growing. Its frontal lobes contain the **prefrontal cortex**, which is responsible for complex thought. Gradually, the hemispheres of the cerebral cortex specialize, a process called **lateralization**. But in the first few years of life, there is high **brain plasticity**: Many areas are not yet committed to specific functions, and the capacity for learning is high.

- Both heredity and early experience contribute to brain organization. Stimulation of the brain is essential during sensitive periods, when the brain is developing most rapidly. Prolonged early deprivation can disrupt development of the cerebral cortex, especially the prefrontal cortex, and interfere with the brain's capacity to manage stress, with long-term physical and psychological consequences.

- Appropriate early stimulation promotes **experience-expectant brain growth**, which depends on ordinary experiences. No evidence exists for a sensitive period in the first few years for **experience-dependent brain growth**, which relies on specific learning experiences. In fact, environments that overwhelm children with inappropriately advanced expectations can undermine the brain's potential.

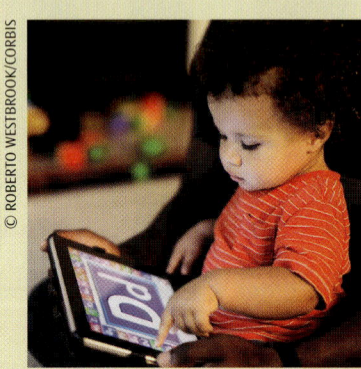

4.3 How does the organization of sleep and wakefulness change over the first two years?

- Infants' changing arousal patterns are primarily affected by brain growth, but the social environment also plays a role. Periods of sleep and wakefulness become fewer but longer, increasingly conforming to a night–day schedule.

- Most parents in Western nations try to get their babies to sleep through the night much earlier than parents throughout most of the world, who are more likely to sleep with their babies. Regular bedtime routines promote sleep in infants and toddlers.

Influences on Early Physical Growth (p. 127)

4.4 Cite evidence that heredity and nutrition both contribute to early physical growth.

- Twin and adoption studies reveal that heredity contributes to body size and rate of physical growth.

- Breast milk is ideally suited to infants' growth needs. Breastfeeding protects against disease and prevents malnutrition and infant death in poverty-stricken areas of the world.

- Most infants and toddlers can eat nutritious foods freely without risk of becoming overweight. However, the relationship between rapid weight gain in infancy and later obesity is strengthening because of the rise in unhealthy parental feeding practices.

- **Marasmus** and **kwashiorkor,** two dietary diseases caused by malnutrition, affect many children in developing countries. If prolonged, they can permanently stunt body growth and brain development.

Learning Capacities (p. 130)

4.5 Describe infant learning capacities, the conditions under which they occur, and the unique value of each.

- **Classical conditioning** is based on the infant's ability to associate events that usually occur together in the everyday world. Infants can be classically conditioned most easily when the pairing of an **unconditioned stimulus (UCS)** and a **conditioned stimulus (CS)** has survival value.

- In **operant conditioning,** infants act on the environment, and their behavior is followed by either **reinforcers,** which increase the occurrence of a preceding behavior, or **punishment,** which either removes a desirable stimulus or presents an unpleasant one to decrease the occurrence of a response. In young infants, interesting sights and sounds and pleasurable caregiver interaction serve as effective reinforcers.

- **Habituation** and **recovery** reveal that at birth, babies are attracted to novelty. Novelty preference (recovery to a novel stimulus) assesses recent memory, whereas familiarity preference (recovery to the familiar stimulus) assesses remote memory.

- Newborns have a primitive ability to imitate adults' facial expressions and gestures. **Imitation** is a powerful means of learning, which contributes to the parent–infant bond. Scientists have identified specialized cells called **mirror neurons** that may underlie infants' capacity to imitate.

Motor Development (p. 133)

4.6 Describe dynamic systems theory of motor development, along with factors that influence motor progress in the first two years.

- According to **dynamic systems theory of motor development,** children acquire new motor skills by combining existing skills into increasingly complex systems of action. Each new skill is a joint product of central nervous system development, the body's movement possibilities, the child's goals, and environmental supports for the skill.

- Movement opportunities and a stimulating environment profoundly affect motor development, as shown by observations of infants learning to crawl and walk in varying contexts. Cultural values and child-rearing customs also contribute to the emergence and refinement of motor skills.

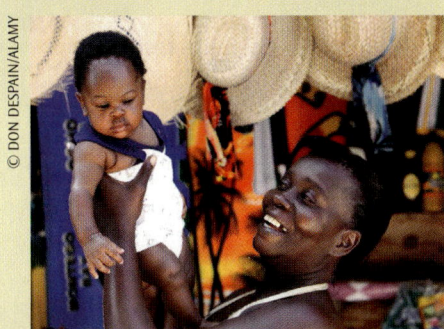

- During the first year, infants perfect reaching and grasping. Reaching gradually becomes more accurate and flexible, and the clumsy ulnar grasp is transformed into a refined pincer grasp.

Perceptual Development (p. 137)

4.7 What changes in hearing, depth and pattern perception, and intermodal perception take place during infancy?

- Infants organize sounds into increasingly complex patterns and, as part of the **perceptual narrowing effect,** begin to "screen out" sounds not used in their native language by the middle of the first year. An impressive **statistical learning capacity** enables babies to detect regular sound patterns, for which they will later learn meanings.

- Rapid maturation of the eye and visual centers in the brain supports the development of focusing, color discrimination, and visual acuity during the first half-year. The ability to scan the environment and track moving objects also improves.

- Research on depth perception reveals that responsiveness to motion cues develops first, followed by sensitivity to binocular and then to pictorial cues. Experience in independent movement enhances depth perception and other aspects of three-dimensional understanding, but babies must learn to avoid drop-offs for each body position.

- **Contrast sensitivity** explains infants' early pattern preferences. At first, babies stare at single, high-contrast features. Over time, they discriminate increasingly complex, meaningful patterns.

- Newborns prefer to look at and track simple, facelike stimuli, but researchers disagree on whether they have a built-in tendency to orient toward human faces. Around 2 months, they prefer their mother's facial features; at 3 months, they distinguish the features of different faces; and by 7 months, they discriminate various facial expressions, including happiness, sadness, and surprise.

- From the start, infants are capable of **intermodal perception**—combining information across sensory modalities. Detection of amodal relations (such as common tempo or rhythm) provides the basis for detecting other intermodal matches.

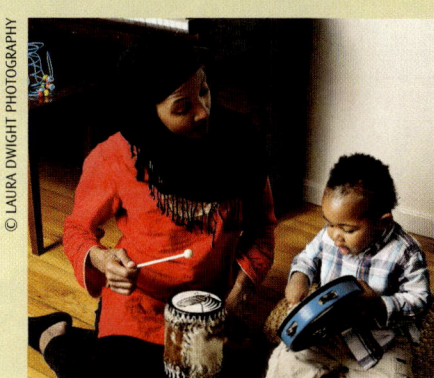

4.8 Explain differentiation theory of perceptual development.

- According to **differentiation theory,** perceptual development is a matter of detecting invariant features in a constantly changing perceptual world. Acting on the world plays a major role in perceptual differentiation. From a cognitive perspective, infants also impose meaning on what they perceive. Many researchers combine these two ideas.

Important Terms and Concepts

brain plasticity (p. 121)
cephalocaudal trend (p. 117)
cerebral cortex (p. 120)
classical conditioning (p. 130)
conditioned response (CR) (p. 131)
conditioned stimulus (CS) (p. 131)
contrast sensitivity (p. 141)
differentiation theory (p. 144)
dynamic systems theory of motor development (p. 135)
experience-dependent brain growth (p. 124)
experience-expectant brain growth (p. 124)

glial cells (p. 118)
habituation (p. 131)
imitation (p. 132)
intermodal perception (p. 143)
kwashiorkor (p. 129)
lateralization (p. 121)
marasmus (p. 129)
mirror neurons (p. 133)
myelination (p. 118)
neurons (p. 117)
neurotransmitters (p. 117)
operant conditioning (p. 131)

perceptual narrowing effect (p. 139)
prefrontal cortex (p. 120)
programmed cell death (p. 118)
proximodistal trend (p. 117)
punishment (p. 131)
recovery (p. 131)
reinforcer (p. 131)
statistical learning capacity (p. 138)
synapses (p. 117)
synaptic pruning (p. 118)
unconditioned response (UCR) (p. 130)
unconditioned stimulus (UCS) (p. 130)

chapter 5

Cognitive Development in Infancy and Toddlerhood

A father encourages his child's curiosity and delight in discovery. With the sensitive support of caring adults, infants' and toddlers' cognition and language develop rapidly.

What's ahead in chapter 5

Piaget's Cognitive-Developmental Theory

Piaget's Ideas About Cognitive Change • The Sensorimotor Stage • Follow-Up Research on Infant Cognitive Development • Evaluation of the Sensorimotor Stage

■ **SOCIAL ISSUES: EDUCATION** Baby Learning from TV and Video: The Video Deficit Effect

Information Processing

A General Model of Information Processing • Attention • Memory • Categorization • Evaluation of Information-Processing Findings

■ **BIOLOGY AND ENVIRONMENT** Infantile Amnesia

The Social Context of Early Cognitive Development

■ **CULTURAL INFLUENCES** Social Origins of Make-Believe Play

Individual Differences in Early Mental Development

Infant and Toddler Intelligence Tests • Early Environment and Mental Development • Early Intervention for At-Risk Infants and Toddlers

Language Development

Theories of Language Development • Getting Ready to Talk • First Words • The Two-Word Utterance Phase • Individual and Cultural Differences • Supporting Early Language Development

When Caitlin, Grace, and Timmy gathered at Ginette's child-care home, the playroom was alive with activity. The three spirited explorers, each nearly 18 months old, were bent on discovery. Grace dropped shapes through holes in a plastic box that Ginette held and adjusted so the harder ones would fall smoothly into place. Once a few shapes were inside, Grace grabbed the box and shook it, squealing with delight as the lid fell open and the shapes scattered around her. The clatter attracted Timmy, who picked up a shape, carried it to the railing at the top of the basement steps, and dropped it overboard, then followed with a teddy bear, a ball, his shoe, and a spoon. Meanwhile, Caitlin pulled open a drawer, unloaded a set of wooden bowls, stacked them in a pile, knocked it over, and then banged two bowls together.

As the toddlers experimented, I could see the beginnings of spoken language—a whole new way of influencing the world. "All gone baw!" Caitlin exclaimed as Timmy tossed the bright red ball down the basement steps. "Bye-bye," Grace chimed in, waving as the ball disappeared from sight. Later that day, Grace revealed the beginnings of make-believe. "Night-night," she said, putting her head down and closing her eyes, ever so pleased that she could decide for herself when and where to go to bed.

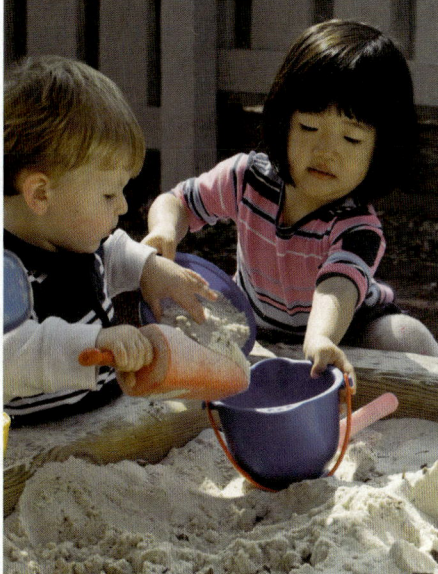

Over the first two years, the small, reflexive newborn baby becomes a self-assertive, purposeful being who solves simple problems and starts to master the most amazing human ability: language. Parents wonder, how does all this happen so quickly? This question has also captivated researchers, yielding a wealth of findings along with vigorous debate over how to explain the astonishing pace of infant and toddler cognitive development.

In this chapter, we take up three perspectives: Piaget's *cognitive-developmental theory, information processing,* and Vygotsky's *sociocultural theory*. We also consider the usefulness of tests that measure infants' and toddlers' intellectual progress. Finally, we look at the beginnings of language. We will see how toddlers' first words build on early cognitive achievements and how, very soon, new words and expressions greatly increase the speed and flexibility of their thinking. Throughout development, cognition and language mutually support each other. ●

Piaget's Cognitive-Developmental Theory

5.1 According to Piaget, how do schemes change over the course of development?

5.2 Describe major cognitive attainments of the sensorimotor stage.

5.3 What does follow-up research say about infant cognitive development and the accuracy of Piaget's sensorimotor stage?

Swiss theorist Jean Piaget inspired a vision of children as busy, motivated explorers whose thinking develops as they act directly on the environment. Influenced by his background in biology, Piaget believed that the child's mind forms and modifies psychological structures so they achieve a better fit with external reality. Recall from Chapter 1 that in Piaget's theory, children move through four stages between infancy and adolescence. During these stages, all aspects of cognition develop in an integrated fashion, changing in a similar way at about the same time.

Piaget's **sensorimotor stage** spans the first two years of life. Piaget believed that infants and toddlers "think" with their eyes, ears, hands, and other sensorimotor equipment. They cannot yet carry out many activities inside their heads. But by the end of toddlerhood, children can solve everyday practical problems and represent their experiences in speech, gesture, and play. To appreciate Piaget's view of how these vast changes take place, let's consider some important concepts.

Piaget's Ideas About Cognitive Change

According to Piaget, specific psychological structures—organized ways of making sense of experience called **schemes**—change with age. At first, schemes are sensorimotor action patterns. For example, at 6 months, Timmy dropped objects in a fairly rigid way, simply letting go of a rattle or teething ring and watching with interest. By 18 months, his "dropping scheme" had become deliberate and creative. In tossing objects down the basement stairs, he threw some in the air, bounced others off walls, released some gently and others forcefully. Soon, instead of just acting on objects, he will show evidence of thinking before he acts. For Piaget, this change marks the transition from sensorimotor to preoperational thought.

In Piaget's theory, two processes, *adaptation* and *organization*, account for changes in schemes.

Adaptation. The next time you have a chance, notice how infants and toddlers tirelessly repeat actions that lead to interesting effects. **Adaptation** involves building schemes through direct interaction with the environment. It consists of two complementary activities, *assimilation* and *accommodation*. During **assimilation,** we use our current schemes to interpret the external world. For example, when Timmy dropped objects, he was assimilating them to his sensorimotor "dropping scheme." In **accommodation,** we create new schemes or adjust old ones after

In Piaget's theory, first schemes are sensorimotor action patterns. As this 12-month-old experiments with his dropping scheme, his behavior becomes more deliberate and varied.

noticing that our current ways of thinking do not capture the environment completely. When Timmy dropped objects in different ways, he modified his dropping scheme to take account of the varied properties of objects.

According to Piaget, the balance between assimilation and accommodation varies over time. When children are not changing much, they assimilate more than they accommodate—a steady, comfortable state that Piaget called cognitive *equilibrium.* During times of rapid cognitive change, children are in a state of *disequilibrium,* or cognitive discomfort. Realizing that new information does not match their current schemes, they shift from assimilation to accommodation. After modifying their schemes, they move back toward assimilation, exercising their newly changed structures until they are ready to be modified again.

Each time this back-and-forth movement between equilibrium and disequilibrium occurs, more effective schemes are produced. Because the times of greatest accommodation are the earliest ones, the sensorimotor stage is Piaget's most complex period of development.

Organization. Schemes also change through **organization,** a process that occurs internally, apart from direct contact with the environment. Once children form new schemes, they rearrange them, linking them with other schemes to create a strongly interconnected cognitive system. For example, eventually Timmy will relate "dropping" to "throwing" and to his developing

TABLE 5.1
Summary of Piaget's Sensorimotor Stage

SENSORIMOTOR SUBSTAGE	TYPICAL ADAPTIVE BEHAVIORS
1. Reflexive schemes (birth–1 month)	Newborn reflexes (see Chapter 3, page 101)
2. Primary circular reactions (1–4 months)	Simple motor habits centered around the infant's own body; limited anticipation of events
3. Secondary circular reactions (4–8 months)	Actions aimed at repeating interesting effects in the surrounding world; imitation of familiar behaviors
4. Coordination of secondary circular reactions (8–12 months)	Intentional, or goal-directed, behavior; ability to find a hidden object in the first location in which it is hidden (object permanence); improved anticipation of events; imitation of behaviors slightly different from those the infant usually performs
5. Tertiary circular reactions (12–18 months)	Exploration of the properties of objects by acting on them in novel ways; imitation of novel behaviors; ability to search in several locations for a hidden object (accurate A–B search)
6. Mental representation (18 months–2 years)	Internal depictions of objects and events, as indicated by sudden solutions to problems; ability to find an object that has been moved while out of sight (invisible displacement); deferred imitation; and make-believe play

understanding of "nearness" and "farness." According to Piaget, schemes truly reach equilibrium when they become part of a broad network of structures that can be jointly applied to the surrounding world (Piaget, 1936/1952).

In the following sections, we will first describe infant development as Piaget saw it, noting research that supports his observations. Then we will consider evidence demonstrating that in some ways, babies' cognitive competence is more advanced than Piaget believed.

The Sensorimotor Stage

The difference between the newborn baby and the 2-year-old child is so vast that Piaget divided the sensorimotor stage into six substages, summarized in Table 5.1. Piaget based this sequence on a very small sample: his own three children. He observed his son and two daughters carefully and also presented them with everyday problems (such as hidden objects) that helped reveal their understanding of the world.

According to Piaget, at birth infants know so little that they cannot explore purposefully. The **circular reaction** provides a special means of adapting their first schemes. It involves stumbling onto a new experience caused by the baby's own motor activity. The reaction is "circular" because, as the infant tries to repeat the event again and again, a sensorimotor response that first occurred by chance strengthens into a new scheme. Consider Caitlin, who at age 2 months accidentally made a smacking sound after a feeding. Finding this new sound intriguing, she tried to repeat it until, after a few days, she became quite expert at smacking her lips.

The circular reaction initially centers on the infant's own body but later turns outward, toward manipulation of objects. In the second year, it becomes experimental and creative, aimed at producing novel outcomes. Infants' difficulty inhibiting new and interesting behaviors may underlie the circular reaction. This immaturity in inhibition seems to be adaptive, helping to ensure that new skills will not be interrupted before they strengthen (Carey & Markman, 1999). Piaget considered revisions in the circular reaction so important that, as Table 5.1 shows, he named the sensorimotor substages after them.

Repeating Chance Behaviors. Piaget saw newborn reflexes as the building blocks of sensorimotor intelligence. In Substage 1, babies suck, grasp, and look in much the same way, no matter what experiences they encounter.

Around 1 month, as babies enter Substage 2, they start to gain voluntary control over their actions through the *primary circular reaction,* by repeating chance behaviors largely motivated by basic needs. This leads to some simple motor habits, such as sucking their fist or thumb. Babies in this substage also begin to vary their behavior in response to environmental demands. For

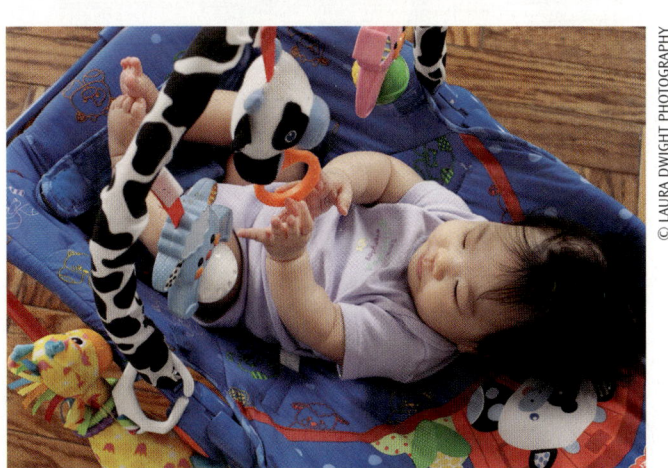

When this 3-month-old accidentally hits a toy hung in front of her, she repeatedly attempts to recapture this interesting effect. In the process, she forms a new "hitting scheme."

example, they open their mouths differently for a nipple than for a spoon. And they start to anticipate events. When hungry, 3-month-old Timmy would stop crying as soon as Vanessa entered the room—a signal that feeding time was near.

During Substage 3, from 4 to 8 months, infants sit up and reach for and manipulate objects. These motor attainments strengthen the *secondary circular reaction,* through which babies try to repeat interesting events in the surrounding environment that are caused by their own actions. For example, 4-month-old Caitlin accidentally knocked a toy hung in front of her, producing a fascinating swinging motion. Over the next three days, Caitlin tried to repeat this effect, gradually forming a new "hitting" scheme. Improved control over their own behavior permits infants to imitate others' behavior more effectively. However, Piaget noted, they usually cannot adapt flexibly and quickly enough to imitate novel behaviors. Although they enjoy watching an adult demonstrate a game of pat-a-cake, they are not yet able to participate.

Intentional Behavior. In Substage 4, 8- to 12-month-olds combine schemes into new, more complex action sequences. As a result, actions that lead to new schemes no longer have a random, hit-or-miss quality—*accidentally* bringing the thumb to the mouth or *happening* to hit the toy. Instead, 8- to 12-month-olds can engage in **intentional, or goal-directed, behavior,** coordinating schemes deliberately to solve simple problems. Consider Piaget's famous object-hiding task, in which he shows the baby an attractive toy and then hides it behind his hand or under a cover. Infants of this substage can find the object by coordinating two schemes—"pushing" aside the obstacle and "grasping" the toy. Piaget regarded these *means–end action sequences* as the foundation for all problem solving.

Retrieving hidden objects reveals that infants have begun to master **object permanence,** the understanding that objects continue to exist when out of sight. But this awareness is not yet complete. Babies still make the *A-not-B search error:* If they reach several times for an object at a first hiding place (A), then see it moved to a second (B), they still search for it in the first hiding place (A). Consequently, Piaget concluded that they do not have a clear image of the object as persisting when hidden from view.

Infants in Substage 4, who can better anticipate events, sometimes use their capacity for intentional behavior to try to change those events. At 10 months, Timmy crawled after Vanessa when she put on her coat, whimpering to keep her from leaving. Also, babies can now imitate behaviors slightly different from those they usually perform. After watching someone else, they try to stir with a spoon, push a toy car, or drop raisins into a cup (Piaget, 1945/1951).

In Substage 5, from 12 to 18 months, the *tertiary circular reaction,* in which toddlers repeat behaviors with variation, emerges. Recall how Timmy dropped objects over the basement steps, trying first this action, then that, then another. This deliberately exploratory approach makes 12- to 18-month-olds better problem solvers. For example, Grace figured out how to fit a shape through a hole in a container by turning and twisting it until it fell through and how to use a stick to get toys that were out of reach. According to Piaget, this capacity to experiment leads to a more advanced understanding of object permanence. Toddlers look for a hidden toy in several locations, displaying an accurate A–B search. Their more flexible action patterns also permit them to imitate many more behaviors—stacking blocks, scribbling on paper, and making funny faces.

Mental Representation. Substage 6 brings the ability to create **mental representations**—internal depictions of information that the mind can manipulate. Our most powerful mental representations are of two kinds: (1) *images,* or mental pictures of objects, people, and spaces; and (2) *concepts,* or categories in which similar objects or events are grouped together. We use a mental image to retrace our steps when we've misplaced something or to imitate someone's behavior long after observing it. By thinking in concepts and labeling them (for example, "ball" for all rounded, movable objects used in play), we become more efficient thinkers, organizing our diverse experiences into meaningful, manageable, and memorable units.

Piaget noted that 18- to 24-month-olds arrive at solutions suddenly rather than through trial-and-error behavior. In doing so, they seem to experiment with actions inside their heads—evidence that they can mentally represent their experiences. For example, at 19 months, Grace—after bumping her new push toy

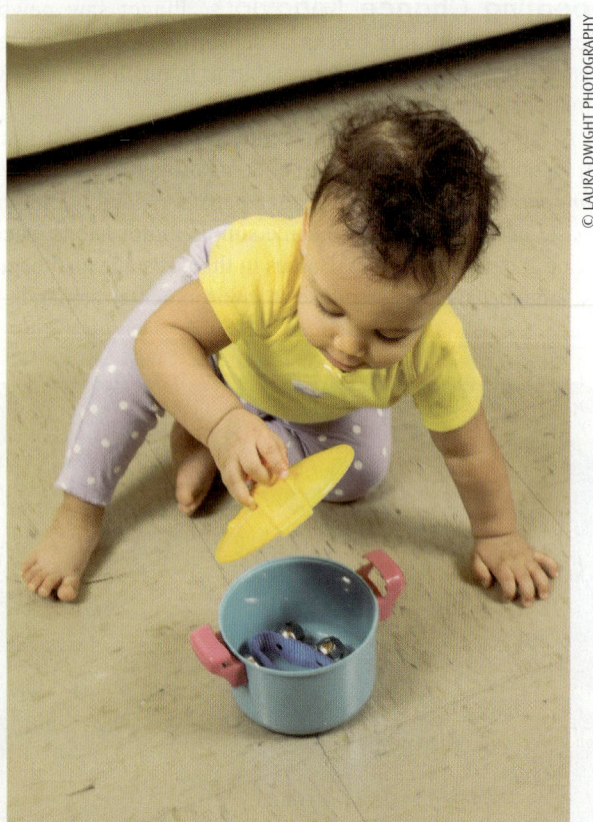

To find the toy hidden inside the pot, a 10-month-old engages in intentional, goal-directed behavior—the basis for all problem solving.

CHAPTER 5 Cognitive Development in Infancy and Toddlerhood 153

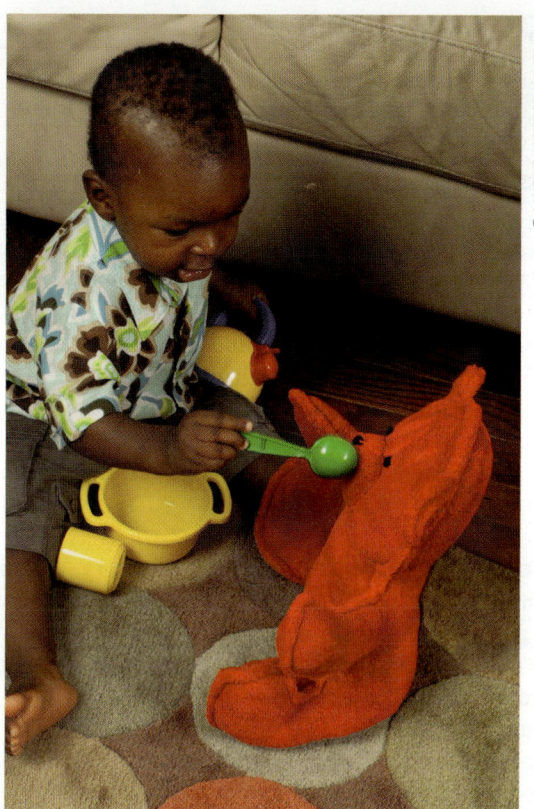

The capacity for mental representation enables this 20-month-old to engage in first acts of make-believe.

against a wall—paused for a moment as if to "think," and then immediately turned the toy in a new direction.

Representation also enables older toddlers to solve advanced object permanence problems involving *invisible displacement*—finding a toy moved while out of sight, such as into a small box while under a cover. It permits **deferred imitation**—the ability to remember and copy the behavior of models who are not present. And it makes possible **make-believe play,** in which children act out everyday and imaginary activities. As the sensorimotor stage draws to a close, mental symbols have become major instruments of thinking.

Follow-Up Research on Infant Cognitive Development

Many studies suggest that infants display a wide array of understandings earlier than Piaget believed. Recall the operant conditioning research reviewed in Chapter 4, in which newborns sucked vigorously on a nipple to gain access to interesting sights and sounds. This behavior, which closely resembles Piaget's secondary circular reaction, shows that infants explore and control the external world long before 4 to 8 months. In fact, they do so as soon as they are born.

To discover what infants know about hidden objects and other aspects of physical reality, researchers often use the **violation-of-expectation method.** They may *habituate* babies to a physical event (expose them to the event until their looking declines) to familiarize them with a situation in which their knowledge will be tested. Or they may simply show babies an *expected event* (one that is consistent with reality) and an *unexpected event* (a variation of the first event that violates reality). Heightened attention to the unexpected event suggests that the infant is "surprised" by a deviation from physical reality and, therefore, is aware of that aspect of the physical world.

The violation-of-expectation method is controversial. Some researchers believe that it indicates limited, implicit (nonconscious) awareness of physical events—not the full-blown, conscious understanding that was Piaget's focus in requiring infants to act on their surroundings, as in searching for hidden objects (Campos et al., 2008). Others maintain that the method reveals only babies' perceptual preference for novelty, not their knowledge of the physical world (Bremner, 2010; Bremner, Slater, & Johnson, 2015). Let's examine this debate in light of recent evidence.

Object Permanence. In a series of studies using the violation-of-expectation method, Renée Baillargeon and her collaborators claimed to have found evidence for object permanence in the first few months of life. Figure 5.1 describes and illustrates one of these studies, in which infants exposed to both an expected

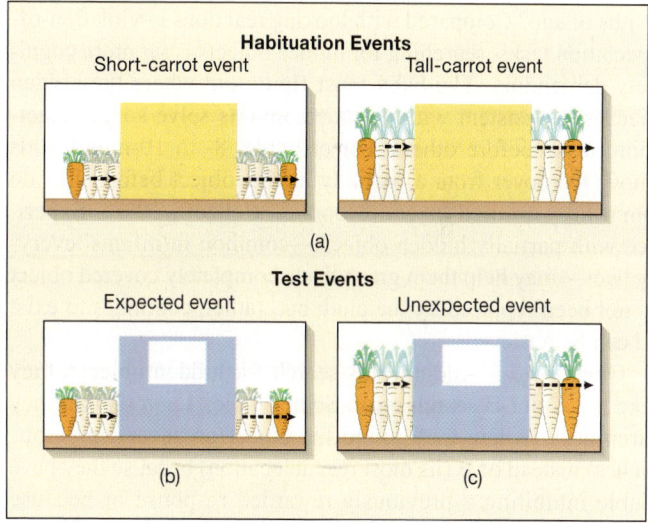

FIGURE 5.1 Testing young infants for understanding of object permanence using the violation-of-expectation method. (a) First, infants were habituated to two events: a short carrot and a tall carrot moving behind a yellow screen, on alternate trials. Next, the researchers presented two test events. The color of the screen was changed to help infants notice its window. (b) In the *expected event,* the carrot shorter than the window's lower edge moved behind the blue screen and reappeared on the other side. (c) In the *unexpected event,* the carrot taller than the window's lower edge moved behind the screen and did not appear in the window, but then emerged intact on the other side. Infants as young as 2½ to 3½ months looked longer at the *unexpected event,* suggesting that they had some understanding of object permanence. (Adapted from R. Baillargeon & J. DeVos, 1991, "Object Permanence in Young Infants: Further Evidence," *Child Development, 62,* p. 1230. © 1991, John Wiley and Sons. Reproduced with permission of John Wiley & Sons Ltd. conveyed through Copyright Clearance Center, Inc.)

and an unexpected object-hiding event looked longer at the unexpected event (Aguiar & Baillargeon, 2002; Baillargeon & DeVos, 1991).

Additional violation-of-expectation studies yielded similar results, suggesting that infants look longer at a wide variety of unexpected events involving hidden objects (Newcombe, Sluzenski, & Huttenlocher, 2005; Wang, Baillargeon, & Paterson, 2005). Still, as previously noted, critics question what these looking preferences tell us about babies' actual understandings.

But another type of looking behavior suggests that young infants are aware that objects persist when out of view. Four- and 5-month-olds will track a ball's path of movement as it disappears and reappears from behind a barrier, even gazing ahead to where they expect it to emerge. As further support for such awareness, 5- to 9-month-olds more often engaged in such predictive tracking when a ball viewed on a computer screen gradually rolled behind a barrier than when it disappeared instantaneously or imploded (rapidly decreased in size) at the barrier's edge (Bertenthal, Gredebäck, & Boyer, 2013; Bertenthal, Longo, & Kenny, 2007). With age, babies are more likely to fixate on the predicted place of the ball's reappearance and wait for it—evidence of an increasingly secure grasp of object permanence.

If young infants do have some notion of object permanence, how do we explain Piaget's finding that even babies capable of reaching do not try to search for hidden objects before 8 months of age? Compared with looking reactions in violation-of-expectation tasks, searching for hidden objects is far more cognitively demanding: The baby must figure out where the hidden object is. Consistent with this idea, infants solve some object-hiding tasks before others. For example, 8- to 10-month-olds remove the cover from a partially hidden object before they do from a fully covered object (Moore & Meltzoff, 2008). Experience with partially hidden objects—common in infants' everyday lives—may help them grasp that a completely covered object has not been replaced by the cloth but, rather, continues to exist and can be retrieved.

Once 8- to 12-month-olds search for hidden objects, they make the A-not-B search error. Some studies suggests that they search at A (where they found the object on several previous reaches) instead of B (its most recent location) because they have trouble inhibiting a previously rewarded response or because they do not attend closely when the hiding place moves from A to B (Diamond, Cruttenden, & Neiderman, 1994; Ruffman & Langman, 2002). A more comprehensive explanation is that a complex, dynamic system of factors—having built a habit of reaching toward A, continuing to look at A, having the hiding place at B appear similar to the one at A, and maintaining a constant body posture—increases the chances that the baby will make the A-not-B search error. Disrupting any one of these factors increases 10-month-olds' accurate searching at B (Thelen et al., 2001). In addition, older infants are still perfecting reaching and grasping (see Chapter 3) (Berger, 2010). If these motor skills are challenging, babies have little attention left to focus on inhibiting their habitual reach toward A.

LOOK and LISTEN

> Using an attractive toy and cloth, try several object-hiding tasks with 8- to 14-month-olds. Is their searching behavior consistent with research findings?

In sum, mastery of object permanence is a gradual achievement. Babies' understanding becomes increasingly complex with age: They must distinguish the object from the barrier concealing it, keep track of the object's whereabouts, and use this knowledge to obtain the object (Moore & Meltzoff, 2008). Success at object search tasks coincides with rapid development of the frontal lobes of the cerebral cortex (Bell, 1998). Also crucial are a wide variety of experiences perceiving, acting on, and remembering objects.

Mental Representation. In Piaget's theory, before about 18 months of age, infants are unable to mentally represent experience. Yet 8- to 10-month-olds' ability to recall the location of hidden objects after delays of more than a minute, and 14-month-olds' recall after delays of a day or more, indicate that babies construct mental representations of objects and their whereabouts (McDonough, 1999; Moore & Meltzoff, 2004). And in studies of deferred imitation and problem solving, representational thought is evident even earlier.

Deferred and Inferred Imitation. Piaget studied imitation by noting when his three children demonstrated it in their everyday behavior. Under these conditions, a great deal must be known about the infant's daily life to be sure that deferred imitation—which requires infants to represent a model's past behavior—has occurred.

Laboratory research suggests that deferred imitation is present at 6 weeks of age! Infants who watched an unfamiliar adult's facial expression imitated it when exposed to the same adult the next day (Meltzoff & Moore, 1994). As motor capacities improve, infants copy actions with objects. In one study, an adult showed 6- and 9-month-olds a novel series of actions with a puppet: taking its glove off, shaking the glove to ring a bell inside, and replacing the glove. When tested a day later, infants who had seen the novel actions were far more likely to imitate them (see Figure 5.2). And when researchers paired a second, motionless puppet with the first puppet 1 to 6 days before the demonstration, 6- to 9-month-olds generalized the novel actions to this new, very different-looking puppet (Barr, Marrott, & Rovee-Collier, 2003; Giles & Rovee-Collier, 2011).

Between 12 and 18 months, toddlers use deferred imitation skillfully to enrich their range of sensorimotor schemes. They retain modeled behaviors for at least several months, copy the actions of peers as well as adults, and imitate across a change in context—for example, enact at home a behavior seen at child care (Meltzoff & Williamson, 2010; Patel, Gaylord, & Fagen, 2013). The ability to recall modeled behaviors in the order they occurred—evident as early as 6 months—also strengthens over

FIGURE 5.2 Testing infants for deferred imitation. After researchers performed a novel series of actions with a puppet, this 6-month-old imitated the actions a day later: (a) removing the glove; (b) shaking the glove to ring a bell inside. With age, gains in recall are evident in deferred imitation of others' behaviors over longer delays.

the second year (Bauer, 2006; Rovee-Collier & Cuevas, 2009). And when toddlers imitate in correct sequence, they remember more behaviors (Knopf, Kraus, & Kressley-Mba, 2006).

Older infants and toddlers even imitate rationally, by *inferring* others' intentions! They are more likely to imitate purposeful rather than accidental or arbitrary behaviors on objects (Hamlin, Hallinan, & Woodward, 2008; Thoermer et al., 2013). And they adapt their imitative acts to a model's goals. If 12-month-olds see an adult perform an unusual action for fun (make a toy dog enter a miniature house by jumping through the chimney, even though its door is wide open), they copy the behavior. But if the adult engages in the odd behavior because she *must* (makes the dog go through the chimney after first trying the door and finding it locked), 12-month-olds typically imitate the more efficient action (putting the dog through the door) (Schwier et al., 2006).

Between 14 and 18 months, toddlers become increasingly adept at imitating actions an adult *tries* to produce, even if these are not fully realized (Bellagamba, Camaioni, & Colonnesi, 2006; Olineck & Poulin-Dubois, 2009). On one occasion, Ginette attempted to pour some raisins into a bag but missed, spilling them onto the counter. A moment later, Grace began dropping the raisins into the bag, indicating that she had inferred Ginette's goal.

Problem Solving. As Piaget indicated, around 7 to 8 months, infants develop intentional means–end action sequences that they use to solve simple problems, such as pulling on a cloth to obtain a toy resting on its far end (Willatts, 1999). Out of these explorations of object-to-object relations, the capacity for tool use in problem solving—flexibly manipulating an object as a means to a goal—emerges (Keen, 2011).

For example, 12-month-olds who were repeatedly presented with a spoon oriented so its handle pointed toward their preferred hand (usually the right) adapted their preferred-hand grip when the spoon's handle was presented in the opposite orientation (to the left). As a result, they succeeded in transporting food to their mouths most of the time (McCarty & Keen, 2005). With age, babies increasingly adjusted their grip to fit the spoon's orientation in advance, planning ahead for what they wanted to do with the tool.

By 10 to 12 months, infants can *solve problems by analogy*—apply a solution strategy from one problem to other relevant problems. In one study, babies of this age were given three similar problems, each requiring them to overcome a barrier, grasp a string, and pull it to get an attractive toy. The problems differed in many aspects of their superficial features—texture and color of the string, barrier, and floor mat and type of toy (horse, doll, or car). For the first problem, the parent demonstrated the solution and encouraged the infant to imitate (Chen, Sanchez, & Campbell, 1997). Babies obtained the toy more readily with each additional problem.

These findings suggest that at the end of the first year, infants form flexible mental representations of how to use tools to get objects. They have some ability to move beyond trial-and-error experimentation, represent a solution mentally, and use it in new contexts.

Symbolic Understanding. One of the most momentous early attainments is the realization that words can be used to cue mental images of things not physically present—a symbolic capacity called **displaced reference** that emerges around the first birthday. It greatly enhances toddlers' capacity to learn about the world through communicating with others. Observations of 12- to 13-month-olds reveal that they respond to the label of an absent toy by looking at and gesturing toward the spot where it usually rests (Saylor, 2004). As memory and vocabulary improve, skill at displaced reference expands.

But at first, toddlers have difficulty using language to acquire new information about an absent object—an ability that is essential to learn from symbols. In one study, an adult taught 19- and 22-month-olds a name for a stuffed animal—"Lucy" for a frog. Then, with the frog out of sight, each toddler was told that some water had spilled, so "Lucy's all wet!" Finally, the adult showed the toddler three stuffed animals—a wet frog, a dry frog, and a pig—and said, "Get Lucy!" (Ganea et al., 2007). Although all the children remembered that Lucy was a frog, only the 22-month-olds identified the wet frog as Lucy. This capacity to use language as a flexible symbolic tool—to modify and enrich existing mental representations—improves from the end of the second into the third year.

A beginning awareness of the symbolic function of pictures also emerges in the first year, strengthening in the second. Even newborns perceive a relation between a picture and its referent, as indicated by their preference for looking at a photo of their mother's face (see page 143 in Chapter 4). By 9 months and perhaps before, the majority of infants recognize that real objects can be grasped while pictures of objects cannot. Most touch, rub, or pat a color photo of an object but rarely try to grasp it (Ziemer, Plumert, & Pick, 2012). These behaviors suggest that 9-month-olds do not mistake a picture for the real thing, though they may not yet comprehend it as a symbol. Manual exploration of pictures declines after 9 months, becoming rare around 18 months (DeLoache & Ganea, 2009).

Around this time, toddlers clearly treat pictures symbolically, as long as pictures strongly resemble real objects. After hearing a novel label ("blicket") applied to a color photo of an unfamiliar object, most 15- to 24-month-olds—when presented with both the real object and its picture and asked to indicate the "blicket"—gave a symbolic response (Ganea et al., 2009). They selected either the real object or both the object and its picture, not the picture alone.

By the middle of the second year, toddlers often use pictures as vehicles for communicating with others and acquiring new knowledge. They point to, name, and talk about pictures, and they can apply something learned from a book with realistic-looking pictures to real objects, and vice versa (Ganea, Ma, & DeLoache, 2011; Simcock, Garrity, & Barr, 2011).

Picture-rich environments in which caregivers often direct babies' attention to the link between pictures and real objects promote pictorial understanding. In a study carried out in a village community in Tanzania, Africa, where children receive no exposure to pictures before school entry, an adult taught 1½-year-olds a new name for an unfamiliar object during picture-book interaction (Walker, Walker, & Ganea, 2012). When later asked to pick the named object from a set of real objects, not until 3 years of age did the Tanzanian children perform as well as U.S. 15-month-olds.

Even after coming to appreciate the symbolic nature of pictures, young children have difficulty grasping the meaning of some pictures (such as line drawings), as we will see in Chapter 8. How do infants and toddlers interpret another ever-present, pictorial medium—video? See the Social Issues: Education box on the following page to find out.

Evaluation of the Sensorimotor Stage

Table 5.2 on page 158 summarizes the remarkable cognitive attainments we have just considered. Compare this table with Piaget's description of the sensorimotor substages in Table 5.1 on page 151. You will see that infants anticipate events, actively search for hidden objects, master the A–B object search, flexibly vary their sensorimotor schemes, engage in make-believe play, and treat pictures and video images symbolically within Piaget's time frame. Yet other capacities—including secondary circular reactions, understanding of object properties, first signs of object permanence, deferred imitation, problem solving by analogy,

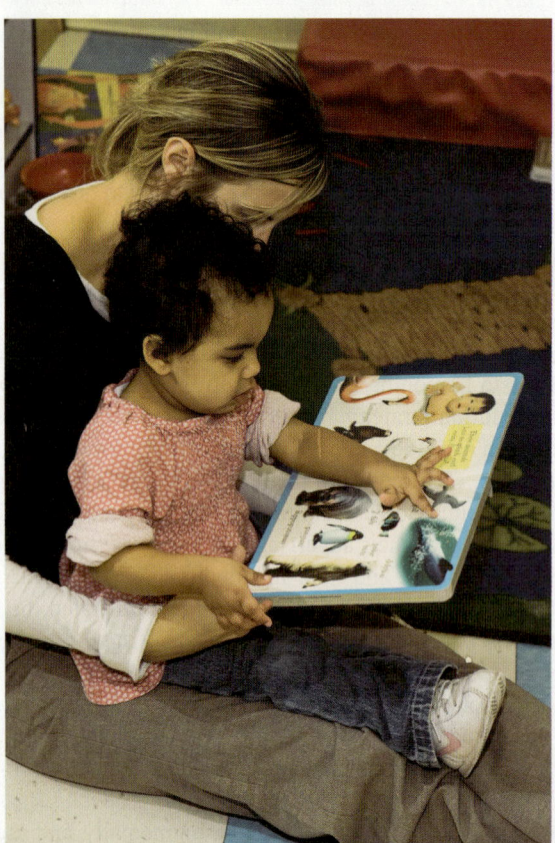

A 17-month-old points to a picture in a book, revealing her beginning awareness of the symbolic function of pictures. But pictures must be highly realistic for toddlers to treat them symbolically.

Social Issues: Education

Baby Learning from TV and Video: The Video Deficit Effect

Children first become TV and video viewers in early infancy, as they are exposed to programs watched by parents and older siblings or to shows aimed at viewers not yet out of diapers, such as the Baby Einstein products. U.S. parents report that 50 percent of 2-month-olds watch TV, a figure that rises to 90 percent by 2 years of age. Average viewing time increases from 55 minutes per day at 6 months to just under 1½ hours per day at age 2 (Anand et al., 2014; Cespedes et al., 2014). Although parents assume that babies learn from TV and videos, research indicates that babies cannot take full advantage of them.

Initially, infants respond to videos of people as if viewing people directly—smiling, moving their arms and legs, and (by 6 months) imitating actions of a televised adult (Barr, Muentener, & Garcia, 2007). But when shown videos of attractive toys, 9-month-olds touch and grab at the screen, suggesting that they confuse the images with the real thing. By the middle of the second year, manual exploration declines in favor of pointing at the images (Pierroutsakos & Troseth, 2003). Nevertheless, toddlers have difficulty applying what they see on video to real situations.

In a series of studies, some 2-year-olds watched through a window while a live adult hid an object in an adjoining room, while others watched the same event on a video screen. Children in the direct viewing condition retrieved the toy easily; those in the video condition had difficulty (Troseth, 2003; Troseth & DeLoache, 1998). This **video deficit effect**—poorer performance after viewing a video than a live demonstration—has also been found for 2-year-olds' deferred imitation, word learning, and means–end problem solving (Bellagamba et al., 2012; Hayne, Herbert, & Simcock, 2003; Krcmar, Grela, & Linn, 2007).

One explanation is that 2-year-olds typically do not view a video character as offering socially relevant information. After an adult on video announced where she had hidden a toy, few 2-year-olds searched (Schmidt, Crawley-Davis, & Anderson, 2007). In contrast, when the adult uttered the same words while standing in front of the child, 2-year-olds promptly retrieved the object.

Toddlers seem to discount information on video as relevant to their everyday experiences because people do not look at and converse with them directly or establish a shared focus on objects, as their caregivers do. In one study, researchers gave some 2-year-olds an interactive video experience (using a two-way, closed-circuit video system). An adult on video interacted with the child for five minutes—calling the child by name, talking about the child's siblings and pets, waiting for the child to respond, and playing interactive games (Troseth, Saylor, & Archer, 2006). Compared with 2-year-olds who viewed the same adult in a noninteractive video, those in the interactive condition were far more successful in

A 2-year-old looks puzzled by a video image. Perhaps she has difficulty grasping its meaning because onscreen characters do not converse with her directly, as adults in real life do.

using a verbal cue from a person on video to retrieve a toy.

Around age 2½, the video deficit effect declines. Before this age, the American Academy of Pediatrics (2001) recommends against mass media exposure. In support of this advice, amount of TV viewing is negatively related to toddlers' language progress (Zimmerman, Christakis, & Meltzoff, 2007). And 1- to 3-year-old heavy viewers tend to have attention, memory, and reading difficulties in the early school years (Christakis et al., 2004; Zimmerman & Christakis, 2005).

When toddlers do watch TV and video, it is likely to work best as a teaching tool when it is rich in social cues (Lauricella, Gola, & Calvert, 2011). These include use of familiar characters and close-ups in which the character looks directly at the camera, addresses questions to viewers, and pauses to invite a response.

---

and displaced reference of words—emerge earlier than Piaget expected. These findings show that the cognitive attainments of infancy and toddlerhood do not develop together in the neat, stepwise fashion that Piaget assumed.

Recent research raises questions about Piaget's view of how infant development takes place. Consistent with Piaget's ideas, sensorimotor action helps infants construct some forms of knowledge. For example, as we saw in Chapter 4, crawling enhances depth perception and ability to find hidden objects, and manipulating objects fosters awareness of object properties. Yet we have also seen that infants comprehend a great deal before they are capable of the motor behaviors that Piaget assumed led to those understandings. How can we account for babies' amazing cognitive accomplishments?

TABLE 5.2
Some Cognitive Attainments of Infancy and Toddlerhood

AGE	COGNITIVE ATTAINMENTS
Birth–1 month	Secondary circular reactions using limited motor skills, such as sucking a nipple to gain access to interesting sights and sounds
1–4 months	Awareness of object permanence, object solidity, and gravity, as suggested by violation-of-expectation findings; deferred imitation of an adult's facial expression over a short delay (1 day)
4–8 months	Improved knowledge of object properties and basic numerical knowledge, as suggested by violation-of-expectation findings; deferred imitation of an adult's novel actions on objects over a short delay (1 to 3 days)
8–12 months	Ability to search for a hidden object; ability to solve simple problems by analogy to a previous problem
12–18 months	Ability to search for a hidden object when it is moved from one location to another (accurate A–B search); deferred imitation of an adult's novel actions on objects after long delays (at least several months) and across a change in situation (from child care to home); rational imitation, inferring the model's intentions; displaced reference of words
18 months–2 years	Ability to find an object moved while out of sight (invisible displacement); deferred imitation of actions an adult tries to produce, even if these are not fully realized; deferred imitation of everyday behaviors in make-believe play; beginning awareness of pictures and video as symbols of reality

Alternative Explanations. Unlike Piaget, who thought young babies constructed all mental representations out of sensorimotor activity, most researchers now believe that infants have some built-in cognitive equipment for making sense of experience. But intense disagreement exists over the extent of this initial understanding. As we have seen, much evidence on young infants' cognition rests on the violation-of-expectation method. Researchers who lack confidence in this method argue that babies' cognitive starting point is limited (Bremner, Slater, & Johnson, 2015; Cohen, 2010; Kagan, 2013c). For example, some believe that newborns begin life with a set of biases for attending to certain information and with general-purpose learning procedures—such as powerful techniques for analyzing complex perceptual information (Bahrick, 2010; MacWhinney, 2015; Rakison, 2010). Together, these capacities enable infants to construct a wide variety of schemes.

Others, convinced by violation-of-expectation findings, believe that infants start out with impressive understandings. According to this **core knowledge perspective,** babies are born with a set of innate knowledge systems, or *core domains of thought.* Each of these prewired understandings permits a ready grasp of new, related information and therefore supports early, rapid development (Carey, 2009; Leslie, 2004; Spelke & Kinzler, 2007, 2013). Core knowledge theorists argue that infants could not make sense of the complex stimulation around them without having been genetically "set up" in the course of evolution to comprehend its crucial aspects.

Researchers have conducted many studies of infants' *physical knowledge,* including object permanence, object solidity (that one object cannot move through another), and gravity (that an object will fall without support). Violation-of-expectation findings suggest that in the first few months, infants have some awareness of all these basic object properties and quickly build on this knowledge (Baillargeon et al., 2009, 2011). Core knowledge theorists also assume that an inherited foundation of *linguistic knowledge* enables swift language acquisition in early childhood—a possibility we will consider later in this chapter. Furthermore, these theorists argue, infants' early orientation toward people initiates rapid development of *psychological knowledge*—in particular, understanding of mental states, such as intentions, emotions, desires, and beliefs, which we will address further in Chapter 6.

Research even suggests that infants have basic *numerical knowledge.* In the best-known study, 5-month-olds saw a screen raised to hide a single toy animal and then watched a hand place a second toy behind the screen. Finally, the screen was removed to reveal either one or two toys. If infants kept track of the two objects (requiring them to add one object to another), then they should look longer at the unexpected, one-toy display—which is what they did (see Figure 5.3) (Wynn, 1992). These findings and others suggest that babies can discriminate quantities up to three and use that knowledge to perform simple arithmetic—both addition and subtraction (in which two objects are covered and one object is removed) (Kobayashi, Hiraki, & Hasegawa, 2005; Walden et al., 2007; Wynn, Bloom, & Chiang, 2002).

Additional evidence suggests that 6-month-olds can distinguish among large sets of items, as long as the difference between those sets is very great—at least a factor of two. For example, they can tell the difference between 8 and 16 dots but not between 8 and 12 (Lipton & Spelke, 2003; Xu, Spelke, & Goddard, 2005). Consequently, some researchers believe that infants can represent approximate large-number values in addition to the small-number discriminations evident in Figure 5.3.

As with other violation-of-expectation results, this evidence is controversial. Skeptics question whether other aspects of object displays, rather than numerical sensitivity, are responsible for the findings (Clearfield & Westfahl, 2006; Langer, Gillette, & Arriaga, 2003). Furthermore, indisputable evidence for

FIGURE 5.3 Testing infants for basic number concepts. (a) First, infants saw a screen raised in front of a toy animal. Then an identical toy was added behind the screen. Next, the researchers presented two outcomes. (b) In the *expected outcome*, the screen dropped to reveal two toy animals. (c) In the *unexpected outcome*, the screen dropped to reveal one toy animal. Five-month-olds shown the unexpected outcome looked longer than did 5-month-olds shown the expected outcome. The researchers concluded that infants can discriminate the quantities "one" and "two" and use that knowledge to perform simple addition: $1 + 1 = 2$. A variation of this procedure suggested that 5-month-olds could also do simple subtraction: $2 - 1 = 1$. (From K. Wynn, 1992, "Addition and Subtraction by Human Infants." *Nature, 358*, p. 749. © 1992 by Nature Publishing Group. Adapted with permission of Nature Publishing Group in the format "Republish in a book" via Copyright Clearance Center.)

built-in core knowledge requires that it be demonstrated at birth or close to it—in the absence of relevant opportunities to learn. Yet evidence on newborns' ability to process small and large numerical values is inconsistent (Coubart et al., 2014; Izard et al., 2009). And critics point out that claims for infants' number knowledge are surprising, in view of other research indicating that before 14 to 16 months, toddlers have difficulty making less-than and greater-than comparisons between small sets. Not until the preschool years do children add and subtract small sets correctly.

The core knowledge perspective, while emphasizing native endowment, acknowledges that experience is essential for children to extend this initial knowledge. But so far, it has said little about which experiences are most important in each core domain and how those experiences advance children's thinking. Despite challenges, core knowledge investigators have sharpened the field's focus on clarifying the starting point for human cognition and on carefully tracking the changes that build on it.

Piaget's Legacy. Follow-up research on Piaget's sensorimotor stage yields broad agreement on two issues. First, many cognitive changes of infancy are gradual and continuous rather than abrupt and stagelike, as Piaget thought (Bjorklund, 2012). Second, rather than developing together, various aspects of infant cognition change unevenly because of the challenges posed by different types of tasks and infants' varying experiences with them. These ideas serve as the basis for another major approach to cognitive development—*information processing*.

Before we turn to this alternative point of view, let's recognize Piaget's enormous contributions. Piaget's work inspired a wealth of research on infant cognition, including studies that challenged his theory. Today, researchers are far from consensus on how to modify or replace his account of infant cognitive development, and some believe that his general approach continues to make sense and fits considerable evidence (Cohen, 2010). Piaget's observations also have been of great practical value. Teachers and caregivers continue to look to the sensorimotor stage for guidelines on how to create developmentally appropriate environments for infants and toddlers.

Ask yourself

CONNECT Which of the capacities listed in Table 5.2 indicate that mental representation emerges earlier than Piaget believed?

APPLY Several times, after her father hid a teething biscuit under a red cup, 12-month-old Mimi retrieved it easily. Then Mimi's father hid the biscuit under a nearby yellow cup. Why did Mimi persist in searching for it under the red cup?

REFLECT What advice would you give the typical U.S. parent about permitting an infant or toddler to watch as much as 1 to 1½ hours of TV or video per day? Explain.

Information Processing

5.4 Describe the information-processing view of cognitive development and the general structure of the information-processing system.

5.5 What changes in attention, memory, and categorization take place over the first two years?

5.6 Describe the strengths and limitations of the information-processing approach to early cognitive development.

Information-processing researchers agree with Piaget that children are active, inquiring beings. But instead of providing a single, unified theory of cognitive development, they focus on many aspects of thinking, from attention, memory, and categorization skills to complex problem solving.

Recall from Chapter 1 that the information-processing approach frequently relies on computer-like flowcharts to describe the human cognitive system. Information-processing theorists are not satisfied with general concepts, such as assimilation and accommodation, to describe how children think. Instead, they want to know exactly what individuals of different ages do when faced with a task or problem (Birney & Sternberg, 2011). The computer model of human thinking is attractive because it is explicit and precise.

A General Model of Information Processing

Most information-processing researchers assume that we hold information in three parts of the mental system for processing: the *sensory register,* the *short-term memory store,* and the *long-term memory store* (see Figure 5.4). As information flows through each, we can use *mental strategies* to operate on and transform it, increasing the chances that we will retain information, use it efficiently, and think flexibly, adapting it to changing circumstances. To understand this more clearly, let's look at each aspect of the mental system.

First, information enters the **sensory register,** where sights and sounds are represented directly and stored briefly. Look around you, and then close your eyes. An image of what you saw persists momentarily, but then it decays, or disappears, unless you use mental strategies to preserve it. For example, by *attending to* some information more carefully than to other information, you increase the chances that it will transfer to the next step of the information-processing system.

In the second part of the mind, the **short-term memory store,** we retain attended-to information briefly so we can actively "work on" it to reach our goals. One way of looking at the short-term store is in terms of its *basic capacity,* often

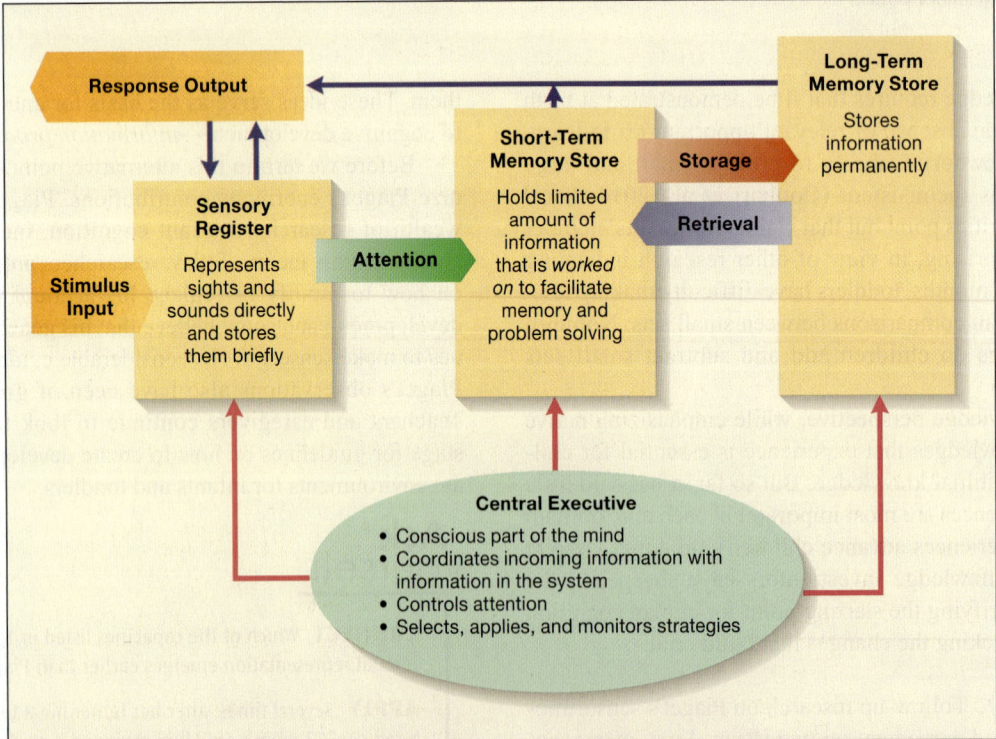

FIGURE 5.4 Model of the human information-processing system. Information flows through three parts of the mental system: the *sensory register,* the *short-term memory store,* and the *long-term memory store.* In each, mental strategies can be used to manipulate information, increasing the efficiency and flexibility of thinking and the chances that information will be retained. The *central executive* is the conscious, reflective part of the mental system. It coordinates incoming information with information already in the system, decides what to attend to, and oversees the use of strategies.

referred to as *short-term memory:* how many pieces of information can be held at once for a few seconds. But most researchers endorse a contemporary view of the short-term store, which offers a more meaningful indicator of its capacity, called **working memory**—the number of items that can be briefly held in mind while also engaging in some effort to monitor or manipulate those items. Working memory can be thought of as a "mental workspace" that we use to accomplish many activities in daily life. From childhood on, researchers assess changes in its capacity by presenting individuals with lists of items (such as numerical digits or short sentences), asking them to work on the items (for example, repeat the digits backward or remember the final word of each sentence in correct order), and seeing how well they do.

The sensory register can take in a wide panorama of information. Short-term and working memory are far more restricted, though their capacity increases steadily from early childhood to early adulthood—on a verbatim digit-span task tapping short-term memory, from about two to seven items; and on working-memory tasks, from about two to five items (Cowan & Alloway, 2009). Still, individual differences are evident at all ages. By engaging in a variety of basic cognitive procedures, such as focusing attention on relevant items and repeating (rehearsing) them rapidly, we increase the chances that information will be retained and accessible to ongoing thinking.

To manage the cognitive system's activities, the **central executive** directs the flow of information, implementing the basic procedures just mentioned and also engaging in more sophisticated activities that enable complex, flexible thinking. For example, the central executive coordinates incoming information with information already in the system, and it selects, applies, and monitors strategies that facilitate memory storage, comprehension, reasoning, and problem solving (Pressley & Hilden, 2006). The central executive is the conscious, reflective part of our mental system.

The more effectively the central executive joins with working memory to process information, the better learned cognitive activities will be and the more *automatically* we can apply them. Consider the richness of your thinking while you automatically drive a car. **Automatic processes** are so well-learned that they require no space in working memory and, therefore, permit us to focus on other information while performing them. Furthermore, the more effectively we process information in working memory, the more likely it will transfer to the third, and largest, storage area—**long-term memory,** our permanent knowledge base, which is unlimited. In fact, we store so much in long-term memory that *retrieval*—getting information back from the system—can be problematic. To aid retrieval, we apply strategies, just as we do in working memory. Information in long-term memory is *categorized* by its contents, much like a digital library reference system that enables us to retrieve items by following the same network of associations used to store them in the first place.

Information-processing researchers believe that several aspects of the cognitive system improve during childhood and adolescence: (1) the *basic capacity* of its stores, especially working memory; (2) the *speed* with which information is worked on; and (3) the *functioning of the central executive.* Together, these changes make possible more complex forms of thinking with age (Halford & Andrews, 2010).

Gains in working-memory capacity are due in part to brain development, but greater processing speed also contributes. Fast, fluent thinking frees working-memory resources to support storage and manipulation of additional information. Furthermore, researchers have become increasingly interested in studying the development of **executive function**—the diverse cognitive operations and strategies that enable us to achieve our goals in cognitively challenging situations. These include controlling attention by inhibiting impulses and irrelevant information and by flexibly directing thought and behavior to suit the demands of a task; coordinating information in working memory; and planning—capacities governed by the prefrontal cortex and its elaborate connections to other brain regions (Chevalier, 2015; Müller & Kerns, 2015). The reason for investigators' great interest is that measures of executive function in childhood predict important cognitive and social outcomes—including task persistence, self-control, academic achievement, and interpersonal acceptance—in adolescence and adulthood (Carlson, Zelazo, & Faja, 2013).

As we will see, gains in aspects of executive function are under way in the first two years. Dramatic strides will follow in childhood and adolescence.

Attention

Recall from Chapter 4 that around 2 to 3 months of age, infants shift from focusing on single, high-contrast features to exploring objects and patterns more thoroughly—visual search behavior that improves over the first year (Frank, Amso, & Johnson, 2014). Besides attending to more aspects of the environment, infants gradually become more efficient at managing their attention, taking in information more quickly. Habituation research reveals that preterm and newborn babies require a long time—about 3 to 4 minutes—to habituate and recover to novel visual stimuli. But by 4 or 5 months, they need as little as 5 to 10 seconds to take in a complex visual stimulus and recognize it as different from a previous one (Colombo, Kapa, & Curtindale, 2011).

One reason that very young babies' habituation times are so much longer is that they have difficulty disengaging attention from a stimulus (Colombo, 2002). When Carolyn held up a colorful rattle, 2-month-old Caitlin stared intently until, unable to break her gaze, she burst into tears. The ability to shift attention from one stimulus to another improves by 4 months—a change believed to be due to development of structures in the cerebral cortex controlling eye movements (Posner & Rothbart, 2007).

Over the first year, infants mostly attend to novel and eye-catching events. In the second year, as toddlers become increasingly capable of intentional behavior (refer back to Piaget's Substage 4), attraction to novelty declines (but does not disappear) and *sustained attention* increases, especially when children

By encouraging her toddler's goal-directed play, this mother promotes sustained attention.

play with toys. A toddler who engages even in simple goal-directed behavior, such as stacking blocks or putting them in a container, must sustain attention to reach the goal (Ruff & Capozzoli, 2003). As plans and activities gradually become more complex, the duration of attention increases.

Memory

Methods devised to assess infants' short-term memory, which require keeping in mind an increasingly longer sequence of very briefly presented visual stimuli, reveal that retention increases from one item at age 6 months to two to four items at 12 months (Oakes, Ross-Sheehy, & Luck, 2007). Operant conditioning and habituation techniques, which grant babies more time to process information, provide windows into early long-term memory. Both methods show that retention of visual events improves greatly with age.

Using operant conditioning, researchers study infant memory by teaching 2- to 6-month-olds to move a mobile by kicking a foot tied to it with a long cord. Two-month-olds remember how to activate the mobile for 1 to 2 days after training, and 3-month-olds for one week. By 6 months, memory increases to two weeks (Rovee-Collier, 1999; Rovee-Collier & Bhatt, 1993). Around the middle of the first year, babies can manipulate switches or buttons to control stimulation. When 6- to 18-month-olds pressed a lever to make a toy train move around a track, duration of memory continued to increase with age; 13 weeks after training, 18-month-olds still remembered how to press the lever (see Figure 5.5) (Hartshorn et al., 1998).

Even after 2- to 6-month-olds forget an operant response, they need only a brief prompt—an adult who shakes the mobile—to reinstate the memory (Hildreth & Rovee-Collier, 2002). And when 6-month-olds are given a chance to reactivate the response themselves for just a couple of minutes, their memory not only returns but extends dramatically, to about 17 weeks (Rovee-Collier & Cuevas, 2009). Perhaps permitting the baby to generate the previously learned behavior strengthens memory because it reexposes the child to more aspects of the original learning situation.

Habituation studies show that infants learn and retain a wide variety of information just by watching objects and events, without being physically active. Sometimes, their retention is much longer than in operant conditioning studies. Babies are especially captivated by the movements of objects and people. For example, 3- to 5-month-olds' retention of the unusual movements of objects (such as a metal nut swinging on the end of a string) persists for at least three months (Bahrick, Hernandez-Reif, & Pickens, 1997). By contrast, their memory for the faces of unfamiliar people and the features of objects is short-lived—only about 24 hours.

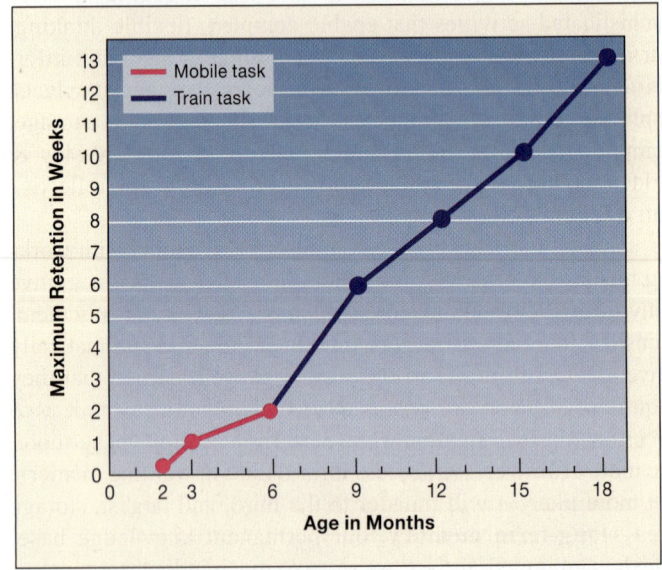

FIGURE 5.5 **Increase in retention in two operant conditioning tasks from 2 to 18 months.** Two- to 6-month-olds were trained to make a kicking response that turned a mobile. Six- to 18-month-olds were trained to press a lever that made a toy train move around a track. Six-month-olds learned both responses and retained them for an identical length of time, indicating that the tasks are comparable. Consequently, researchers could plot a single line tracking gains in retention from 2 to 18 months of age. The line shows that memory improves dramatically. (From C. Rovee-Collier & R. Barr, 2001, "Infant Learning and Memory," in G. Bremner & A. Fogel [Eds.], *Blackwell Handbook of Infant Development,* Oxford, UK: Blackwell, p. 150. © 2001, 2004 by Blackwell Publishing Ltd.)

By 10 months, infants remember both novel actions and the features of objects involved in those actions equally well (Baumgartner & Oakes, 2011). This improved sensitivity to object appearance is fostered by infants' increasing ability to manipulate objects, which helps them learn about objects' observable properties.

So far, we have discussed only **recognition**—noticing when a stimulus is identical or similar to one previously experienced. It is the simplest form of memory: All babies have to do is indicate (by kicking, pressing a lever, or looking) whether a new stimulus is identical or similar to a previous one. **Recall** is more challenging because it involves remembering something not present. But by the middle of the first year, infants are capable of recall, as indicated by their ability to find hidden objects and engage in deferred imitation.

Recall, too, improves steadily with age. For example, 1-year-olds can retain short sequences of adult-modeled behaviors for up to 3 months, and 1½-year-olds can do so for as long as 12 months. The ability to recall modeled behaviors in the order in which they occurred—evident as early as 6 months—strengthens over the second year (Bauer, Larkina, & Deocampo, 2011; Rovee-Collier & Cuevas, 2009). And when toddlers imitate in correct sequence, processing relations between actions, they remember more.

Long-term recall depends on connections among multiple regions of the cerebral cortex, especially with the prefrontal cortex. Formation of these neural circuits is under way in infancy and toddlerhood and will accelerate in early childhood (Jabès & Nelson, 2014). The evidence as a whole indicates that infants' memory processing is remarkably similar to that of older children and adults: Babies have distinct short-term and long-term memories and display both recognition and recall. And they acquire information quickly and retain it over time, doing so more effectively with age (Howe, 2015). Yet a puzzling finding is that older children and adults no longer recall their earliest experiences! See the Biology and Environment box on pages 164–165 for a discussion of *infantile amnesia*.

Categorization

Even young infants can *categorize,* grouping similar objects and events into a single representation. Categorization reduces the enormous amount of new information infants encounter every day, helping them learn and remember (Rakison, 2010).

Creative variations of operant conditioning research with mobiles have been used to investigate infant categorization. One such study, of 3-month-olds, is described and illustrated in Figure 5.6. Similar investigations reveal that in the first few months, babies categorize stimuli on the basis of shape, size, and other physical properties (Wasserman & Rovee-Collier, 2001). By 6 months of age, they can categorize on the basis of two correlated features—for example, the shape and color of an alphabet letter (Bhatt et al., 2004). This ability to categorize using clusters of features prepares babies for acquiring many complex everyday categories.

Habituation has also been used to study infant categorization. Researchers show babies a series of pictures or toys belonging to one category and then see whether they recover to (look longer at) a picture that is not a member of the category or, in the case of toys, spend more time manipulating the out-of-category item. Findings reveal that by the second half of the first year, infants group familiar objects into an impressive array of categories—food items, furniture, birds, land animals, air animals, sea animals, plants, vehicles, kitchen utensils, and spatial location ("above" and "below," "on" and "in") (Bornstein, Arterberry, & Mash, 2010; Casasola & Park, 2013; Sloutsky, 2015). Besides organizing the physical world, infants of this age categorize their emotional and social worlds. They sort people and their voices by gender and age, begin to distinguish emotional expressions, separate people's natural actions (walking) from other motions, and expect people (but not inanimate objects) to move spontaneously (Spelke, Phillips, & Woodward, 1995; see also Chapter 4, pages 141–143).

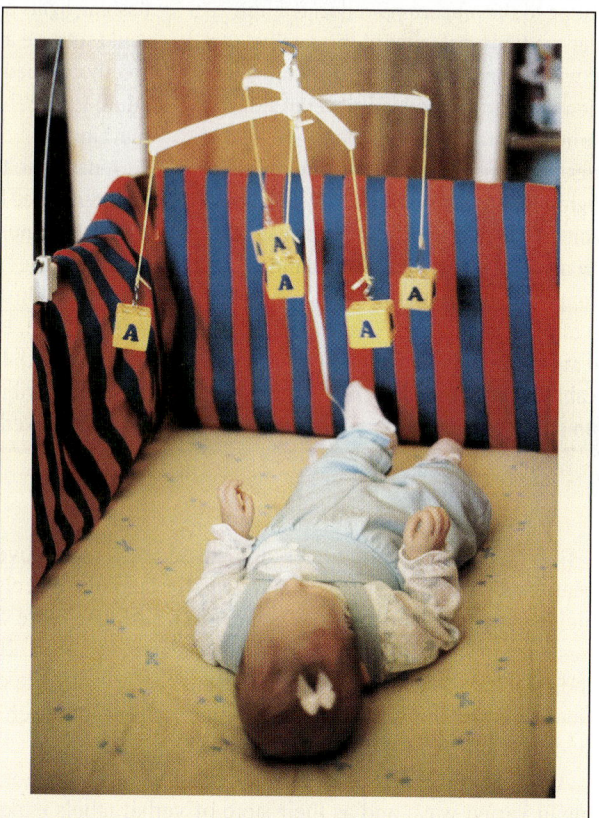

FIGURE 5.6 Investigating infant categorization using operant conditioning. Three-month-olds were taught to kick to move a mobile that was made of small blocks, all with the letter *A* on them. After a delay, kicking returned to a high level only if the babies were shown a mobile whose elements were labeled with the same form (the letter *A*). If the form was changed (from *A*s to *2*s), infants no longer kicked vigorously. While making the mobile move, the babies had grouped together its features. They associated the kicking response with the category *A* and, at later testing, distinguished it from the category *2*. (Bhatt, Rovee-Collier, & Weiner, 1994; Hayne, Rovee-Collier, & Perris, 1987.)

Biology and Environment

Infantile Amnesia

If infants and toddlers recall many aspects of their everyday lives, how do we explain **infantile amnesia**—that most of us can retrieve few, if any, events that happened to us before age 2 to 3? The reason cannot be merely the passage of time because we can recall many personally meaningful one-time events from both the recent and the distant past: the day a sibling was born or a move to a new house—recollections known as **autobiographical memory**.

Several explanations of infantile amnesia exist. One theory credits brain development, pointing to the *hippocampus* (located just under the temporal lobes of the cerebral cortex), which plays a vital role in the formation of new memories. Though its overall structure is formed prenatally, the hippocampus continues to add new neurons well after birth. Integrating those neurons into existing neural circuits is believed to disrupt already stored early memories (Josselyn & Frankland, 2012). In support of this view, the decline in production of hippocampal neurons—in monkeys and rats as well as in humans—coincides with the ability to form stable, long-term memories of unique experiences.

Another conjecture is that older children and adults often use verbal means for storing information, whereas infants' and toddlers' memory processing is largely nonverbal—an incompatibility that may prevent long-term retention of early experiences. To test this idea, researchers sent two adults to the homes of 2- to 4-year-olds with an unusual toy that the children were likely to remember: the Magic Shrinking Machine, shown in Figure 5.7. One adult showed the child how, after inserting an object in an opening on top of the machine and turning a crank that activated flashing lights and musical sounds, the child could retrieve a smaller, identical object (discreetly dropped down a chute by the second adult) from behind a door on the front of the machine.

A day later, the researchers tested the children to see how well they recalled the event. Their nonverbal memory—based on acting out the "shrinking" event and recognizing the "shrunken" objects in photos—was excellent. But even when they had the vocabulary, children younger than age 3 had trouble describing features of the "shrinking" experience. Verbal recall increased sharply between ages 3 and 4, when infantile amnesia typically subsides (Simcock & Hayne, 2003, p. 813). In a follow-up study, which assessed verbal recall 6 years later, only 19 percent—including two children who were younger than age 3—remembered the "shrinking" event (Jack, Simcock, & Hayne, 2012). Those who recalled were more likely to have participated in conversations with a parent about the experience, which could have helped them gain verbal access to the memory.

These findings help reconcile infants' and toddlers' remarkable memory skills with infantile amnesia. During the first few years, children rely heavily on nonverbal memory techniques, such as visual images and motor actions. As language develops, their ability to use it to refer to preverbal memories requires considerable support from adults. As children encode autobiographical events in verbal form, they use language-based cues to retrieve them, increasing the accessibility of these memories at later ages (Peterson, Warren, & Short, 2011).

Other evidence indicates that the advent of a clear self-image contributes to the end

---

Babies' earliest categories are based on similar overall appearance or prominent object part: legs for animals, wheels for vehicles. But as infants approach their first birthday, more categories appear to be based on subtle sets of features (Cohen, 2003; Mandler, 2004; Quinn, 2008). Older infants can even make categorical distinctions when the perceptual contrast between two categories is minimal (birds versus airplanes).

As they gain experience in comparing to-be-categorized items in varied ways and as their store of verbal labels expands, toddlers start to categorize flexibly: When 14-month-olds are given four balls and four blocks, some made of soft rubber and some of rigid plastic, their sequence of object touching reveals that after classifying by shape, they can switch to classifying by material (soft versus hard) if an adult calls their attention to the new basis for grouping (Ellis & Oakes, 2006).

In addition to touching and sorting, toddlers' categorization skills are evident in their play behaviors. After watching an adult give a toy dog a drink from a cup, most 14-month-olds shown a rabbit and a motorcycle offered the drink only to the rabbit (Mandler & McDonough, 1998). They clearly understood that certain actions are appropriate for some categories of items (animals) but not for others (vehicles).

By the end of the second year, toddlers' grasp of the animate–inanimate distinction expands. Nonlinear motions are typical of animates (a person or a dog jumping), linear motions of inanimates (a car or a table pushed along a surface). At 18 months, toddlers more often imitate a nonlinear motion with a toy that has animate-like parts (legs), even if it represents an inanimate (a bed). At 22 months, displaying a fuller understanding, they imitate a nonlinear motion only with toys in the animate category (a cat but not a bed) (Rakison, 2005). They seem to realize that whereas animates are self-propelled and therefore have varied paths of movement, inanimates move only when acted on, in highly restricted ways.

Researchers disagree on how toddlers gradually shift from categorizing on the basis of prominent perceptual features

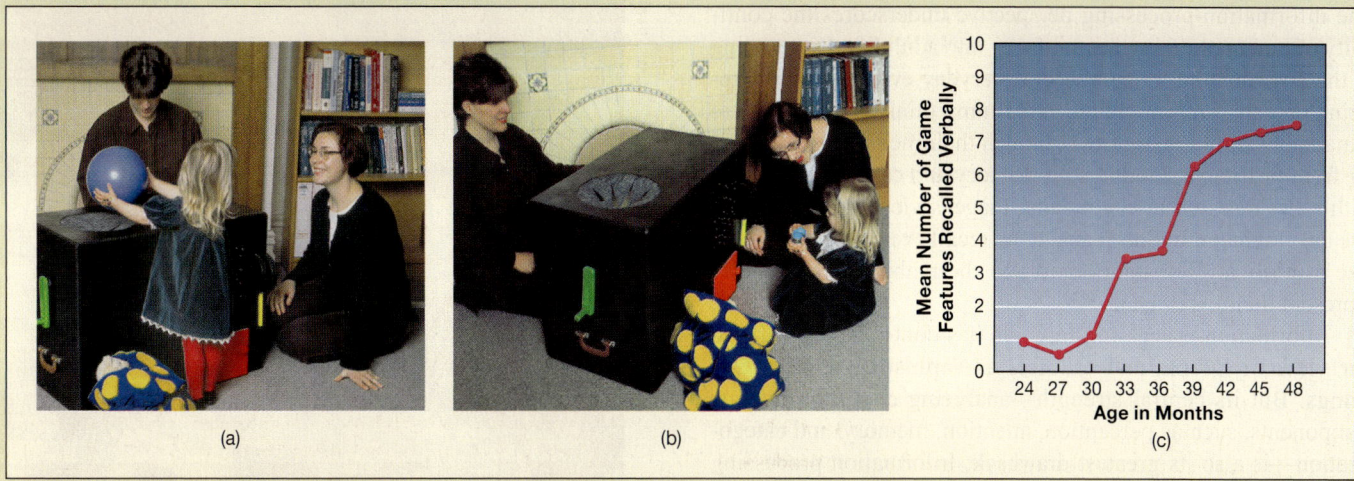

FIGURE 5.7 The Magic Shrinking Machine, used to test young children's verbal and nonverbal memory of an unusual event. After being shown how the machine worked, the child participated in selecting objects from a polka-dot bag, dropping them into the top of the machine (a), and turning a crank, which produced a "shrunken" object (b). When tested the next day, 2- to 4-year-olds' nonverbal memory for the event was excellent. But below 36 months, verbal recall was poor, based on the number of features recalled about the game during an open-ended interview (c). Recall improved between 36 and 48 months. (From G. Simcock & H. Hayne, 2003, "Age-Related Changes in Verbal and Nonverbal Memory During Early Childhood," *Developmental Psychology, 39*, pp. 807, 809. Copyright © 2003 by the American Psychological Association. *Photos:* Ross Coombes/Courtesy of Harlene Hayne.)

of infantile amnesia. For example, among children and adolescents, average age of earliest memory is around age 2 to 2½ (Howe, 2014; Tustin & Hayne, 2010). Though these recollections are sparse in information recalled, their timing coincides with the age at which toddlers display firmer self-awareness, reflected in pointing to themselves in photos and referring to themselves by name.

Very likely, both neurobiological change and social experience contribute to the decline of infantile amnesia. Brain development and adult–child interaction may jointly foster self-awareness, language, and improved memory, which enable children to talk with adults about significant past experiences (Howe, 2015). As a result, preschoolers begin to construct a long-lasting autobiographical narrative of their lives and enter into the history of their family and community.

(objects with flapping wings and feathers belong to one category; objects with rigid wings and a smooth surface to another) to categorizing on a conceptual basis, grouping objects by their common function or behavior (birds versus airplanes, dogs versus cats) (Madole, Oakes, & Rakison, 2011; Mandler, 2004; Träuble & Pauen, 2011). But all acknowledge that exploration of objects and expanding knowledge of the world contribute. In addition, adult labeling of a set of objects with a consistently applied word—"Look at the car!" "Do you see the car?"—calls babies' attention to commonalities among objects, fostering categorization as early as 3 to 4 months of age (Ferry, Hespos, & Waxman, 2010). Toddlers' vocabulary growth, in turn, promotes categorization by highlighting new categorical distinctions (Cohen & Brunt, 2009).

By age 2, toddlers can use conceptual similarity to guide behavior in increasingly novel situations, which greatly enhances the flexibility of their analogical problem solving. In one study, 24-month-olds watched as an adult constructed a toy animal resembling a monkey using wooden, Velcro, and plastic pieces and then labeled it a "thornby." A day later, the toddlers were given a different set of wooden, Velcro, and plastic materials that, when put together, resembled a rabbit (Hayne & Gross, 2015). Those asked to make a "thornby" out of "these other things" readily formed a category and applied the adult's actions with the first animal to constructing the second, novel animal. A control group not presented with verbal cues performed poorly.

Variations among languages lead to cultural differences in development of categories. Korean toddlers, who learn a language in which object names are often omitted from sentences, develop object-sorting skills later than their English-speaking counterparts (Gopnik & Choi, 1990). At the same time, Korean contains a common word, *kkita,* with no English equivalent, referring to a tight fit between objects in contact (a ring on a finger, a cap on a pen), so Korean toddlers are advanced in forming the spatial category "tight fit" (Choi et al., 1999).

Evaluation of Information-Processing Findings

The information-processing perspective underscores the continuity of human thinking from infancy into adult life. In attending to the environment, remembering everyday events, and categorizing objects, Caitlin, Grace, and Timmy think in ways that are remarkably similar to our own, though their mental processing is far from proficient. Findings on memory and categorization join with other research in challenging Piaget's view of early cognitive development. Infants' capacity to recall events and to categorize stimuli attests, once again, to their ability to mentally represent their experiences.

Information-processing research has contributed greatly to our view of infants and toddlers as sophisticated cognitive beings. But its central strength—analyzing cognition into its components, such as perception, attention, memory, and categorization—is also its greatest drawback: Information processing has had difficulty putting these components back together into a broad, comprehensive theory.

One approach to overcoming this weakness has been to combine Piaget's theory with the information-processing approach, an effort we will explore in Chapter 9. A more recent trend has been the application of a *dynamic systems view* (see Chapter 4, pages 135–136) to early cognition. In this approach, researchers analyze each cognitive attainment to see how it results from a complex system of prior accomplishments and the child's current goals (Spencer, Perone, & Buss, 2011; Thelen & Smith, 2006). Once these ideas are fully tested, they may move the field closer to a more powerful view of how the minds of infants and children develop.

The Social Context of Early Cognitive Development

5.7 How does Vygotsky's concept of the zone of proximal development expand our understanding of early cognitive development?

Recall the description at the beginning of this chapter of Grace dropping shapes into a container. Notice that she learns about the toy with Ginette's help. With adult support, Grace will gradually become better at matching shapes to openings and dropping them into the container. Then she will be able to perform this and similar activities on her own.

Vygotsky's sociocultural theory emphasizes that children live in rich social and cultural contexts that affect the way their cognitive world is structured (Bodrova & Leong, 2007; Rogoff, 2003). Vygotsky believed that complex mental activities have their origins in social interaction. Through joint activities with more mature members of their society, children master activities and think in ways that have meaning in their culture.

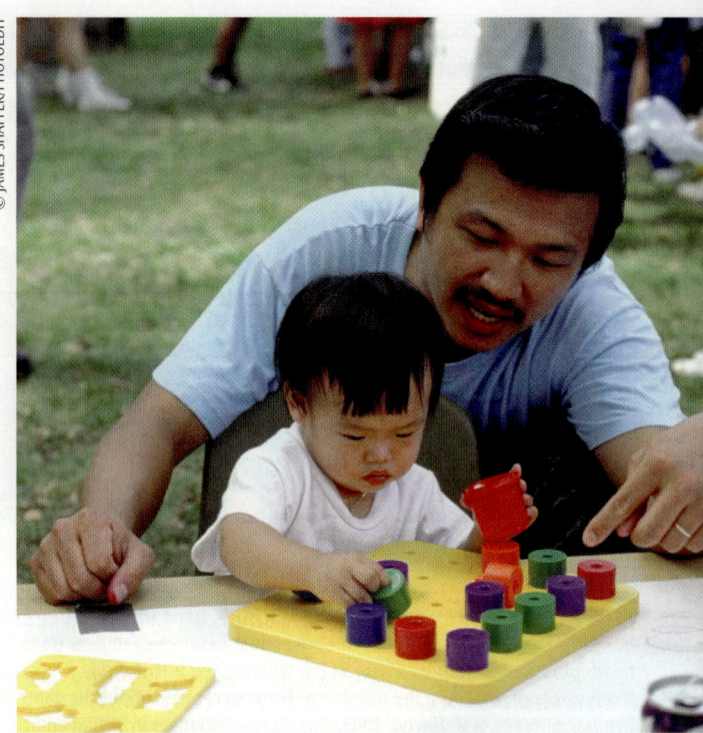

By bringing the task within his son's zone of proximal development and adjusting his communication to suit the child's needs, this father transfers mental strategies to the child, promoting his cognitive development.

A special Vygotskian concept explains how this happens. The **zone of proximal** (or potential) **development** refers to a range of tasks that the child cannot yet handle alone but can do with the help of more skilled partners. To understand this idea, think about how a sensitive adult (such as Ginette) introduces a child to a new activity. The adult picks a task that the child can master but that is challenging enough that the child cannot do it by herself. As the adult guides and supports, the child joins in the interaction and picks up mental strategies. As her competence increases, the adult steps back, permitting the child to take more responsibility for the task. This form of teaching—known as *scaffolding*—promotes learning at all ages, and we will consider it further in Chapter 7.

Vygotsky's ideas have been applied mostly to preschool and school-age children, who are more skilled in language and social communication. Recently, however, his theory has been extended to infancy and toddlerhood. Recall that babies are equipped with capabilities that ensure that caregivers will interact with them (Csibra & Gergely, 2011). Then adults adjust the task and their communication to the child's current level of performance in ways that promote learning.

Consider an adult helping a baby figure out how a jack-in-the-box works. In the early months, the adult demonstrates and, as the clown pops out, tries to capture the infant's attention by saying something like "See what happened!" By the end of the first year, when cognitive and motor skills have improved, the adult guides the baby's hand in turning the crank. During the second year, the adult helps from a distance using gestures and verbal prompts, such as pointing to the crank, making a turning motion, and verbally prompting, "Turn it!" This fine-tuned support is related to advanced play, language, and problem solving in toddlerhood and early childhood (Bornstein et al., 1992; Charman et al., 2001; Tamis-LeMonda & Bornstein, 1989).

As early as the first year, cultural variations in social experiences affect mental strategies. In the jack-in-the-box example, adults and children focus on a single activity. This strategy, common in Western middle-SES homes, is well-suited to lessons in which children master skills apart from the everyday situations in which they will later use those skills. In contrast, infants and young children in Guatemalan Mayan, Native American, and other indigenous communities often attend to several events at once. For example, one 12-month-old skillfully put objects in a jar while watching a passing truck and blowing into a toy whistle (Chavajay & Rogoff, 1999; Correa-Chávez, Roberts, & Perez, 2011).

Processing several competing events simultaneously may be vital in cultures where children largely learn through keen observation of others' ongoing activities. In a comparison of 18-month-olds from German middle-SES homes and Nso farming villages in Cameroon, the Nso toddlers copied far fewer adult-demonstrated actions on toys than did the German toddlers (Borchert et al., 2013). Nso caregivers rarely create such child-focused teaching situations. Rather they expect children to imitate adult behaviors without prompting. Nso children are motivated to do so because they want to be included in the major activities of their community.

Earlier we saw how infants and toddlers create new schemes by acting on the physical world (Piaget) and how certain skills become better developed as children represent their experiences more efficiently and meaningfully (information processing). Vygotsky adds a third dimension to our understanding by emphasizing that many aspects of cognitive development are socially mediated. The Cultural Influences box on page 168 presents additional evidence for this idea, and we will see even more in the next section.

Ask yourself

CONNECT List techniques that parents can use to promote development of categorization in infancy and toddlerhood, and explain why each is effective.

APPLY When Timmy was 18 months old, his mother stood behind him, helping him throw a large ball into a box. As his skill improved, she stepped back, letting him try on his own. Using Vygotsky's ideas, explain how Timmy's mother is supporting his cognitive development.

REFLECT Describe your earliest autobiographical memory. How old were you when the event occurred? Do your recollections fit with research on infantile amnesia?

Individual Differences in Early Mental Development

5.8 Describe the mental testing approach and the extent to which infant tests predict later performance.

5.9 Discuss environmental influences on early mental development, including home, child care, and early intervention for at-risk infants and toddlers.

Because of Grace's deprived early environment, Kevin and Monica had a child psychologist give her one of many tests available for assessing mental development in infants and toddlers. Worried about Timmy's progress, Vanessa also arranged for him to be tested. At age 22 months, he had only a handful of words in his vocabulary, played in a less mature way than Caitlin and Grace, and seemed restless and overactive.

The cognitive theories we have just discussed try to explain the *process* of development—how children's thinking changes. Mental tests, in contrast, focus on *individual differences*: They measure variations in developmental progress, arriving at scores that *predict* future performance, such as later intelligence, school achievement, and adult vocational success. This concern with prediction arose about a century ago, when French psychologist Alfred Binet designed the first successful intelligence test, which predicted school achievement (see Chapter 1). It inspired the design of many new tests, including ones that measure intelligence at very early ages.

Infant and Toddler Intelligence Tests

Accurately measuring infants' intelligence is a challenge because babies cannot answer questions or follow directions. All we can do is present them with stimuli, coax them to respond, and observe their behavior. As a result, most infant tests emphasize perceptual and motor responses. But increasingly, tests are being developed that also tap early language, cognition, and social behavior, especially with older infants and toddlers.

One commonly used test, the *Bayley Scales of Infant and Toddler Development,* is suitable for children between 1 month and 3½ years. The most recent edition, the Bayley-III, has three main subtests: (1) the Cognitive Scale, which includes such items as attention to familiar and unfamiliar objects, looking for a fallen object, and pretend play; (2) the Language Scale, which assesses understanding and expression of language—for example, recognition of objects and people, following simple directions, and naming objects and pictures; and (3) the Motor Scale, which includes gross and fine motor skills, such as grasping, sitting, stacking blocks, and climbing stairs (Bayley, 2005).

Two additional Bayley-III scales depend on parental report: (4) the Social-Emotional Scale, which asks caregivers about such behaviors as ease of calming, social responsiveness, and imitation

Cultural Influences

Social Origins of Make-Believe Play

One of the activities my husband, Ken, used to do with our two young sons was to bake pineapple upside-down cake, a favorite treat. One day when a cake was in the making, 21-month-old Peter stood on a chair at the kitchen sink, busily pouring water from one cup to another.

"He's in the way, Dad!" complained 4-year-old David.

"Maybe if we let him help, he'll give us room," Ken suggested. As David stirred the batter, Ken poured some into a small bowl for Peter, moved his chair to the side of the sink, and handed him a spoon.

"Here's how you do it, Petey," instructed David, with a superior air. Peter watched as David stirred, then tried to copy. When it was time to pour the batter, Ken helped Peter hold and tip the small bowl.

"Time to bake it," said Ken.

"Bake it, bake it," repeated Peter, watching Ken slip the pan into the oven.

Several hours later, we observed one of Peter's earliest instances of make-believe play. He got his pail from the sandbox and, after filling it with a handful of sand, carried it into the kitchen. "Bake it, bake it," Peter called to Ken. Together, father and son placed the pretend cake in the oven.

Piaget and his followers concluded that toddlers discover make-believe independently, once they are capable of representational schemes. Vygotsky challenged this view, pointing out that society provides children with opportunities to represent culturally meaningful activities in play. Make-believe, like other complex mental activities, is first learned under the guidance of experts (Meyers & Berk, 2014). In the example just described, Peter extended his capacity to represent daily events when Ken drew him into the baking task and helped him act it out in play.

In Western middle-SES families, make-believe is culturally cultivated and scaffolded by adults, who value it as a developmentally beneficial activity (Gaskins, 2014). During make-believe, mothers, especially, offer toddlers a rich array of cues that they are pretending—looking and smiling at the child more, making more exaggerated movements, and using

In cultures where sibling caregiving is common, make-believe play is more frequent and complex with older siblings than with mothers. These Afghan children play "wedding," dressing the youngest as a bride.

more "we" talk (acknowledging that pretending is a joint endeavor) than they do during the same real-life event (Lillard, 2007). These cues encourage toddlers to join in and probably facilitate their ability to distinguish pretend from real acts, which strengthens over the second and third years (Ma & Lillard, 2006).

Also, when adults participate, toddlers' make-believe is more elaborate (Keren et al., 2005). They are more likely to combine pretend acts into complex sequences, as Peter did when he put sand in the bucket (making the batter), carried it into the kitchen, and, with Ken's help, put it in the oven (baking the cake). The more parents pretend with their toddlers, the more time their children devote to make-believe (Cote & Bornstein, 2009).

In some cultures, such as those of Indonesia and Mexico, where play is viewed as solely a child's activity and sibling caregiving is common, make-believe is more frequent and complex with older siblings than with mothers. As early as age 3 to 4, children provide rich, challenging stimulation to their younger brothers and sisters, take these teaching responsibilities seriously, and, with age, become better at adjusting their playful interactions to the younger child's needs (Zukow-Goldring, 2002). In a study of Zinacanteco Indian children of southern Mexico, by age 8, sibling teachers were highly skilled at showing 2-year-olds how to play at everyday tasks, such as washing and cooking (Maynard, 2002). They often guided toddlers verbally and physically through the task and provided feedback.

In Western middle-SES families, older siblings less often teach deliberately but still serve as influential models of playful behavior. In New Zealand families of European descent, when both a parent and an older sibling were available, toddlers more often imitated the actions of the sibling, especially when siblings engaged in make-believe (Barr & Hayne, 2003).

As we will see in Chapter 7, make-believe play is a major means through which children extend their cognitive and social skills and learn about important activities in their culture (Nielsen, 2012). Vygotsky's theory, and the findings that support it, tells us that providing a stimulating physical environment is not enough to promote early cognitive development. In addition, toddlers must be invited and encouraged by more skilled members of their culture to participate in the social world around them. Parents and teachers can enhance early make-believe by playing often with toddlers, guiding and elaborating their make-believe themes.

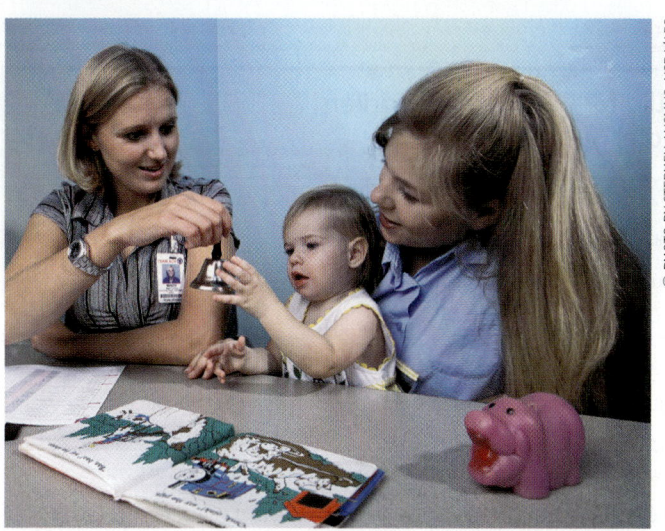

A trained examiner administers a test based on the Bayley Scales of Infant Development to a 1-year-old sitting in her mother's lap. Compared with earlier editions, the Bayley-III Cognitive and Language Scales better predict preschool mental test performance.

in play; and (5) the Adaptive Behavior Scale, which asks about adaptation to the demands of daily life, including communication, self-control, following rules, and getting along with others.

Computing Intelligence Test Scores. Intelligence tests for infants, children, and adults are scored in much the same way—by computing an **intelligence quotient (IQ)**, which indicates the extent to which the raw score (number of items passed) deviates from the typical performance of same-age individuals. To make this comparison possible, test designers engage in **standardization**—giving the test to a large, representative sample and using the results as the *standard* for interpreting scores. The standardization sample for the Bayley-III included 1,700 infants, toddlers, and young preschoolers, reflecting the U.S. population in SES and ethnic diversity.

Within the standardization sample, performances at each age level form a **normal distribution,** in which most scores cluster around the mean, or average, with progressively fewer falling toward the extremes (see Figure 5.8). This *bell-shaped distribution* results whenever researchers measure individual differences in large samples. When intelligence tests are standardized, the mean IQ is set at 100. An individual's IQ is higher or lower than 100 by an amount that reflects how much his or her test performance deviates from the standardization-sample mean.

The IQ offers a way of finding out whether an individual is ahead, behind, or on time (average) in mental development compared with others of the same age. For example, if Timmy's score is 100, then he did better than 50 percent of his agemates. A child with an IQ of 85 did better than only 16 percent, whereas a child with an IQ of 130 outperformed 98 percent. The IQs of 96 percent of individuals fall between 70 and 130; only a few achieve higher or lower scores.

Predicting Later Performance from Infant Tests. Despite careful construction, most infant tests—including previous editions of the Bayley—predict later intelligence poorly. Infants and toddlers easily become distracted, fatigued, or bored during testing, so their scores often do not reflect their true abilities. And infant perceptual and motor items differ from the tasks given to older children, which increasingly emphasize verbal, conceptual, and problem-solving skills. In contrast, the Bayley-III Cognitive and Language Scales, which better dovetail with childhood tests, are good predictors of preschool mental test performance (Albers & Grieve, 2007). But because most infant test scores do not tap the same dimensions of intelligence assessed in older children, they usually are conservatively labeled **developmental quotients (DQs)** rather than IQs.

Infant tests are somewhat better at making long-term predictions for extremely low-scoring babies. Today, they are largely used for *screening*—helping to identify for further observation and intervention babies who are likely to have developmental problems.

As an alternative to infant tests, some researchers have turned to information-processing measures, such as habituation, to assess early mental progress. Their findings show that speed of habituation and recovery to novel visual stimuli is among the best available infant predictors of IQ from early childhood through early adulthood (Fagan, Holland, & Wheeler, 2007; Kavšek, 2004). Habituation and recovery seem to be an especially effective early index of intelligence because they assess memory as well as quickness and flexibility of thinking, which underlie intelligent behavior at all ages (Colombo et al., 2004). The consistency of these findings has prompted designers of the Bayley-III to include items that tap such cognitive skills as habituation, object permanence, and categorization.

Early Environment and Mental Development

In Chapter 2, we indicated that intelligence is a complex blend of hereditary and environmental influences. Many studies have examined the relationship of environmental factors to infant and toddler mental test scores. As we consider this evidence, you will encounter findings that highlight the role of heredity as well.

FIGURE 5.8 Normal distribution of intelligence test scores. To determine what percentage of same-age individuals in the population a person with a certain IQ outperformed, add the figures to the left of that IQ score. For example, an 8-year-old child with an IQ of 115 scored better than 84 percent of the population of 8-year-olds.

Applying what we Know

Features of a High-Quality Home Life for Infants and Toddlers: The HOME Infant–Toddler Subscales

HOME SUBSCALE	SAMPLE ITEM
Organization of the physical environment	Child's play environment appears safe and free of hazards.
Provision of appropriate play materials	Parent provides toys or interesting activities for child during observer's visit.
Emotional and verbal responsiveness of the parent	Parent caresses or kisses child at least once during observer's visit.
	Parent spontaneously speaks to child twice or more (excluding scolding) during observer's visit.
Parental acceptance of the child	Parent does not interfere with child's actions or restrict child's movements more than three times during observer's visit.
Parental involvement with the child	Parent tends to keep child within visual range and to look at child often during observer's visit.
Opportunities for variety in daily stimulation	Child eats at least one meal per day with mother and/or father, according to parental report.
	Child frequently has a chance to get out of house (for example, accompanies parent on trips to grocery store).

Sources: Bradley, 1994; Bradley et al., 2001. A brief, exclusively observational HOME instrument taps the first three subscales only (Rijlaarsdam et al., 2012).

Home Environment. The **Home Observation for Measurement of the Environment (HOME)** is a checklist for gathering information about the quality of children's home lives through observation and parental interview (Caldwell & Bradley, 1994). Applying What We Know above lists factors measured by the HOME Infant–Toddler Subscales—the most widely used home environment measure during the first three years (Rijlaarsdam et al., 2012).

Each HOME subscale is positively related to toddlers' mental test performance. And although low SES is consistently linked to lower HOME scores, an organized, stimulating physical setting and parental affection, involvement, and encouragement of new skills consistently predict better language and IQ scores in toddlerhood and early childhood across SES and ethnic groups (Bornstein, 2015; Fuligni, Han, & Brooks-Gunn, 2004; Linver, Martin, & Brooks-Gunn, 2004; Tong et al., 2007). The extent to which parents talk to infants and toddlers is particularly important. It contributes strongly to early language progress, which, in turn, predicts intelligence and academic achievement in elementary school (Hart & Risley, 1995; Hoff, 2013).

Yet we must interpret these correlational findings cautiously. Parents who are more intelligent may provide better experiences while also giving birth to brighter children, who evoke more stimulation from their parents. Research supports this hypothesis, which refers to *gene–environment correlation* (see Chapter 2, pages 68–69) (Saudino & Plomin, 1997). But parent–child shared heredity does not account for the entire association between home environment and mental test scores. Family living conditions—both HOME scores and affluence of the surrounding neighborhood—continue to predict children's IQ beyond the contribution of parental IQ and education (Chase-Lansdale et al., 1997; Klebanov et al., 1998).

How can the research summarized so far help us understand Vanessa's concern about Timmy's development? Ben, the psychologist who tested Timmy, found that he scored only slightly below average. Ben talked with Vanessa about her child-rearing practices and watched her play with Timmy. A single parent who

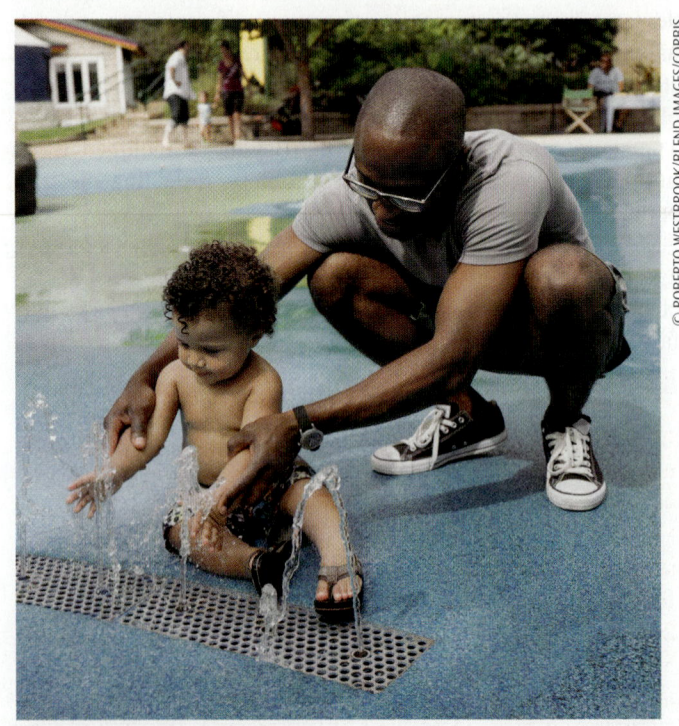

A father plays actively and affectionately with his baby. Parental warmth, attention, and verbal communication predict better language and IQ scores in toddlerhood and early childhood.

worked long hours, Vanessa had little energy for Timmy at the end of the day. Ben also noticed that Vanessa, anxious about Timmy's progress, was intrusive: She interfered with his active behavior and bombarded him with directions: "That's enough ball play. Stack these blocks."

Ben explained that young children who experience intrusive parenting are likely to be distractible and withdrawn and do poorly on mental tests—negative outcomes that persist unless parenting improves (Clincy & Mills-Koonce, 2013; Rubin, Coplan, & Bowker, 2009). Ben coached Vanessa in how to interact sensitively with Timmy while assuring her that Timmy's current performance need not forecast his future development. Warm, responsive parenting that builds on toddlers' current capacities is a much better indicator than an early mental test score of how children will do later.

Infant and Toddler Child Care.
Today, more than 60 percent of U.S. mothers with a child under age 2 are employed (U.S. Census Bureau, 2015d). Child care for infants and toddlers has become common, and its quality—though not as influential as parenting—affects mental development.

Research consistently shows that infants and young children exposed to poor-quality child care—whether they come from middle- or low-SES homes—score lower on measures of cognitive, language, academic, and social skills during the preschool, elementary, and secondary school years (Belsky et al., 2007b; Burchinal et al., 2015; Dearing, McCartney, & Taylor, 2009; NICHD Early Child Care Research Network, 2000b, 2001, 2003b, 2006; Vandell et al., 2010). In contrast, good child care can reduce the negative impact of a stressed, poverty-stricken home life, and it sustains the benefits of growing up in an economically advantaged family (Burchinal, Kainz, & Cai, 2011; McCartney et al., 2007). As Figure 5.9 illustrates, the Early Childhood Longitudinal Study, which included a large sample of U.S. children diverse in SES and ethnicity followed from birth through the preschool years, confirmed the importance of continuous high-quality child care from infancy through the preschool years (Li et al., 2013).

In contrast to most European countries and to Australia and New Zealand, where child care is nationally regulated and funded to ensure its quality, reports on U.S. child care raise serious concerns. Standards are set by the individual states and vary widely. In studies of quality, only 20 to 25 percent of U.S. child-care centers and family child-care homes provided infants and toddlers with sufficiently positive, stimulating experiences to promote healthy psychological development. Most settings offered substandard care, with infants and toddlers faring better when cared for by a relative (NICHD Early Childhood Research Network, 2000a, 2004). Furthermore, the cost of child care in the United States is high: On average, full-time center-based care for one infant consumes from 7 to 19 percent of the median income for couples and over 40 percent for single mothers (Child Care

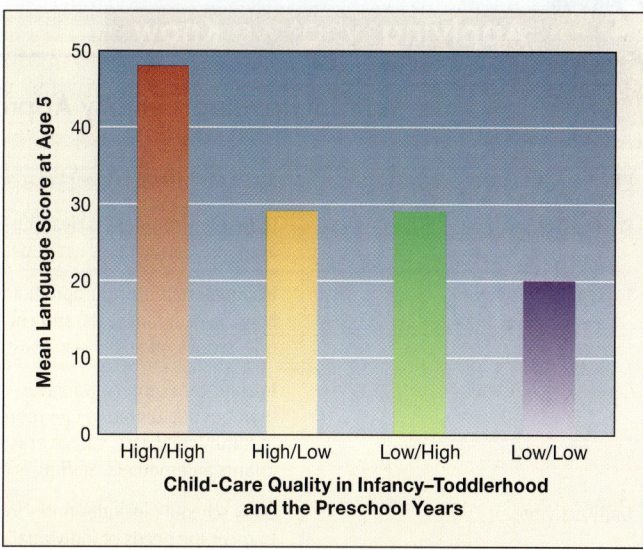

FIGURE 5.9 Relationship of child-care quality in infancy–toddlerhood and the preschool years to language development at age 5. When a nationally representative sample of more than 1,300 children was followed over the first five years, language scores were highest for those experiencing high-quality child care in both infancy–toddlerhood and the preschool years, intermediate for those experiencing high-quality care in just one of these periods, and lowest for those experiencing poor-quality care in both periods. Cognitive, literacy, and math scores also showed this pattern. (Based on Li et al, 2013)

Aware, 2015). The cost of a family child-care home is only slightly lower.

Unfortunately, many U.S. children from low-income families experience inadequate child care (NICHD Early Child Care Research Network, 2005; Torquati et al., 2011). But U.S. settings providing the very worst care tend to serve middle-income families. These parents are especially likely to place their children in for-profit centers, where quality tends to be lowest. Economically disadvantaged children more often attend publicly subsidized, nonprofit centers, which are better equipped with learning materials and have smaller group sizes and more favorable teacher–child ratios (Johnson, Ryan, & Brooks-Gunn, 2012). Still, child-care quality for low-income children is often substandard.

See Applying What We Know on page 172 for signs of high-quality care for infants and toddlers, based on standards for **developmentally appropriate practice.** These standards, devised by the U.S. National Association for the Education of Young Children, specify program characteristics that serve young children's developmental and individual needs, based on both current research and consensus among experts. Caitlin, Grace, and Timmy are fortunate to be in family child care that meets these standards.

Child care in the United States is affected by a macrosystem of individualistic values and weak government regulation and funding. Furthermore, many parents think that their children's

Applying what we Know

Signs of Developmentally Appropriate Infant and Toddler Child Care

PROGRAM CHARACTERISTICS	SIGNS OF QUALITY
Physical setting	Indoor environment is clean, in good repair, well-lighted, and well-ventilated. Fenced outdoor play space is available. Setting does not appear overcrowded when children are present.
Toys and equipment	Play materials are appropriate for infants and toddlers and are stored on low shelves within easy reach. Cribs, highchairs, infant seats, and child-sized tables and chairs are available. Outdoor equipment includes small riding toys, swings, slide, and sandbox.
Caregiver–child ratio	In child-care centers, caregiver–child ratio is no greater than 1 to 3 for infants and 1 to 6 for toddlers. Group size (number of children in one room) is no greater than 6 infants with 2 caregivers and 12 toddlers with 2 caregivers. In family child care, caregiver is responsible for no more than 6 children; within this group, no more than 2 are infants and toddlers. Staffing is consistent, so infants and toddlers can form relationships with particular caregivers.
Daily activities	Daily schedule includes times for active play, quiet play, naps, snacks, and meals. It is flexible rather than rigid, to meet the needs of individual children. Atmosphere is warm and supportive, and children are never left unsupervised.
Interactions among adults and children	Caregivers respond promptly to infants' and toddlers' distress; hold them and talk, sing, and read to them; and interact with them in a manner that respects the individual child's interests and tolerance for stimulation.
Caregiver qualifications	Caregiver has some training in child development, first aid, and safety.
Relationships with parents	Parents are welcome anytime. Caregivers talk frequently with parents about children's behavior and development.
Licensing and accreditation	Child-care setting, whether a center or a home, is licensed by the state. In the United States, voluntary accreditation by the National Association for the Education of Young Children (www.naeyc.org/accreditation), or the National Association for Family Child Care (www.nafcc.org) is evidence of an especially high-quality program.

Sources: Copple & Bredekamp, 2009.

child-care experiences are better than they really are (Torquati et al., 2011). Unable to identify good care, or without the financial means to purchase it, they do not demand it. In recent years, the U.S. federal government and some states have allocated additional funds to subsidize child-care costs, especially for low-income families (Matthews, 2014). Though far from meeting the need, this increase in resources has had a positive impact on child-care quality and accessibility.

LOOK and LISTEN

Ask several employed parents of infants or toddlers to describe what they sought in a child-care setting, along with challenges they faced in finding child care. How knowledgeable are the parents about the ingredients of high-quality care?

Early Intervention for At-Risk Infants and Toddlers

Children living in persistent poverty are likely to show gradual declines in intelligence test scores and to achieve poorly when they reach school age (Schoon et al., 2012). These problems are largely due to stressful home environments that undermine children's ability to learn and increase the likelihood that they will remain poor as adults. A variety of intervention programs have been developed to break this tragic cycle of poverty. Although most begin during the preschool years (we will discuss these in Chapter 7), some start during infancy and continue through early childhood.

In center-based interventions, children attend an organized child-care or preschool program where they receive educational, nutritional, and health services, and their parents receive child-rearing and other social service supports. In home-based interventions, a skilled adult visits the home and works with parents, teaching them how to stimulate a young child's development. In most programs of either type, participating children score higher than untreated controls on mental tests by age 2. The earlier intervention begins, the longer it lasts, and the greater its scope and intensity, the better participants' cognitive and academic performance throughout childhood and adolescence (Ramey, Ramey, & Lanzi, 2006; Sweet & Appelbaum, 2004).

The Carolina Abecedarian Project illustrates these favorable outcomes. In the 1970s, more than 100 infants from poverty-stricken families, ranging in age from 3 weeks to 3 months, were randomly assigned to either a treatment group or a control group. Treatment infants were enrolled in full-time, year-round child care through the preschool years. There they received stimulation aimed at promoting motor, cognitive, language, and social skills and, after age 3, literacy and math concepts. Special emphasis was placed on rich, responsive adult–child verbal communication. All children received nutrition and health services; the primary difference between treatment and controls was the intensive child-care experience.

By 12 months of age, treatment children scored higher in IQ, an advantage they sustained until last tested—at age 21. In addition, throughout their school years, treatment youths achieved higher scores in reading and math. These gains translated into reduced enrollment in special education, more years of schooling completed, higher rates of college enrollment and graduation, more consistent employment, and lower rates of adolescent parenthood (Campbell et al., 2001, 2002, 2012).

Recognition of the power of intervening as early as possible led the U.S. Congress to provide limited funding for services directed at infants and toddlers who already have serious developmental problems or who are at risk for problems because of poverty. Early Head Start, begun in 1995, currently has 1,000 sites serving about 110,000 low-income children and their families (Walker, 2014). A recent evaluation, conducted when children reached age 3, showed that Early Head Start led to warmer, more stimulating parenting, a reduction in harsh discipline, gains in cognitive and language development, and lessening of child aggression (Love, Chazan-Cohen, & Raikes, 2007; Love et al., 2005; Raikes et al., 2010). The strongest effects occurred at sites mixing center- and home-visiting services.

By age 5, however, the benefits of Early Head Start had declined or disappeared, and a follow-up in fifth grade showed no persisting gains (U.S. Department of Health and Human Services, 2006; Vogel et al., 2010). One speculation is that more intentional educational experiences extending through the preschool years—as in the Abecedarian project—would increase the lasting impact of Early Head Start (Barnett, 2011). Although Early Head Start is in need of refinement, it is a promising beginning at providing U.S. infants and toddlers living in poverty with publicly supported intervention.

Ask yourself

CONNECT Using what you learned about brain development in Chapter 4, explain why it is best to initiate intervention for poverty-stricken children in the first two years rather than later.

APPLY Fifteen-month-old Manuel's developmental quotient (DQ) is 115. His mother wants to know exactly what this means and what she should do to support his mental development. How would you respond?

REFLECT Suppose you were seeking a child-care setting for your baby. What would you want it to be like, and why?

Language Development

5.10 Describe theories of language development, and indicate the emphasis each places on innate abilities and environmental influences.

5.11 Describe major language milestones in the first two years, individual differences, and ways adults can support early language development.

Improvements in perception and cognition during infancy pave the way for an extraordinary human achievement—language. In Chapter 4, we saw that by the second half of the first year, infants make dramatic progress in distinguishing the basic sounds of their language and in segmenting the flow of speech into word and phrase units. They also start to comprehend some word meanings and, around 12 months of age, say their first understandable word. Sometime between 1½ and 2 years, toddlers combine two words (MacWhinney, 2015). By age 6, children understand the meaning of about 14,000 words, speak in elaborate sentences, and are skilled conversationalists.

To appreciate this awesome task, think about the many abilities involved in your own flexible use of language. When you speak, you must select words that match the underlying concepts you want to convey. To be understood, you must pronounce words correctly. Then you must combine them into phrases and sentences using a complex set of grammatical rules. Finally, you must follow the rules of everyday conversation—taking turns, making comments relevant to what your partner just said, and using an appropriate tone of voice. How do infants and toddlers make such remarkable progress in launching these skills?

This Early Head Start program provides rich, educational experiences for toddlers plus parent education and family supports. The most favorable outcomes of Early Head Start result from mixing center- and home-visiting services.

Theories of Language Development

In the 1950s, researchers did not take seriously the idea that very young children might be able to figure out important properties of language. Children's regular and rapid attainment of language milestones suggested a process largely governed by maturation, inspiring the nativist perspective on language development. In recent years, new evidence has spawned the interactionist perspective, which emphasizes the joint roles of children's inner capacities and communicative experiences.

The Nativist Perspective. According to linguist Noam Chomsky's (1957) *nativist* theory, language is a unique human accomplishment, etched into the structure of the brain. Focusing on grammar, Chomsky reasoned that the rules of sentence organization are too complex to be directly taught to or discovered by even a cognitively sophisticated young child. Rather, he proposed that all children have a **language acquisition device (LAD),** an innate system that contains a *universal grammar,* or set of rules common to all languages. It enables children, no matter which language they hear, to understand and speak in a rule-oriented fashion as soon as they pick up enough words.

Are children innately primed to acquire language? Recall from Chapter 4 that newborn babies are remarkably sensitive to speech sounds. And children everywhere reach major language milestones in a similar sequence (Parish-Morris, Golinkoff, & Hirsh-Pasek, 2013). Also, the ability to master a grammatically complex language system seems unique to humans, as efforts to teach language to nonhuman primates—using either specially devised artificial symbol systems or sign language—have met with limited success. Even after extensive training, chimpanzees (who are closest to humans in terms of evolution) master only a basic vocabulary and short word combinations, and they produce these far less consistently than human preschoolers (Tomasello, Call, & Hare, 2003).

Furthermore, evidence that childhood is a *sensitive period* for language acquisition is consistent with Chomsky's idea of a biologically based language program. Researchers have examined the language competence of deaf adults who acquired their first language—American Sign Language (ASL), a gestural system just as complex as any spoken language—at different ages. The later learners, whose parents chose to educate them through the oral method, which relies on speech and lip-reading, did not acquire spoken language because of their profound deafness. Consistent with the sensitive-period notion, those who learned ASL in adolescence or adulthood never became as proficient as those who learned in childhood (Mayberry, 2010; Newport, 1991; Singleton & Newport, 2004).

Although it is now widely accepted that humans have a unique capacity to acquire language, Chomsky's theory has been contested on several grounds. First, researchers have had great difficulty specifying Chomsky's universal grammar. Chomsky's critics doubt that one set of rules can account for the extraordinary variation in grammatical forms among the world's 5,000 to 8,000 languages. Second, children do not acquire language as quickly as nativist theory suggests. They refine and generalize many grammatical forms gradually, engaging in much piecemeal learning and making errors along the way (Evans & Levinson, 2009; MacWhinney, 2015). As we will see in Chapter 9, complete mastery of some grammatical forms, such as the passive voice, is not achieved until well into middle childhood. This suggests that more experimentation and learning are involved than Chomsky assumed.

Finally, recall from Chapter 4 that for most people, language is housed largely in the left hemisphere of the cerebral cortex, consistent with Chomsky's notion of a brain prepared to process language. But our discussion also revealed that language areas in the cortex *develop* as children acquire language. Although the left hemisphere is biased for language processing, if it is injured in the early years, other regions take over (see page 122 in Chapter 4). Thus, left-hemispheric localization, though typical, is not necessary for effective language processing.

The Interactionist Perspective. Recent ideas about language development emphasize *interactions* between inner capacities and environmental influences. One type of interactionist theory applies the information-processing perspective to language development. A second type emphasizes social interaction.

Some information-processing theorists assume that children make sense of their complex language environments by applying powerful cognitive capacities of a general kind (MacWhinney, 2015; Munakata, 2006; Saffran, 2009). These theorists note that brain regions housing language also govern similar perceptual

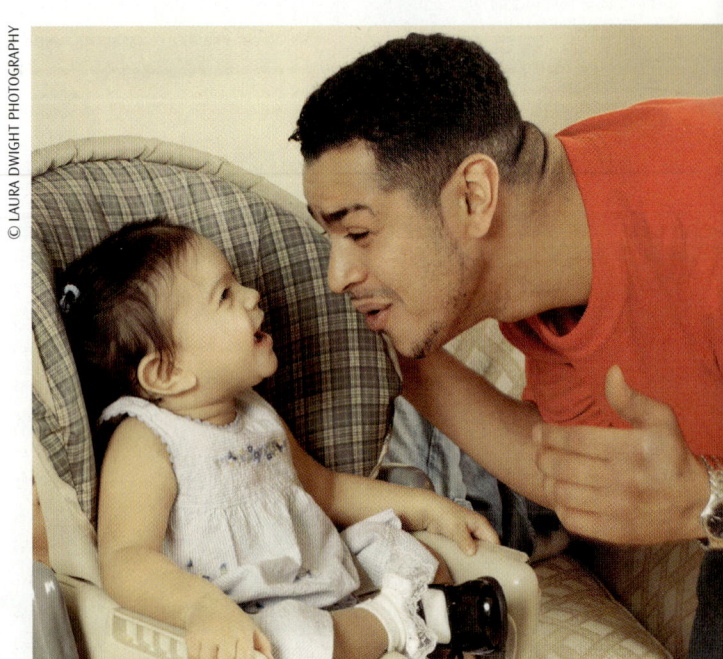

Infants communicate from the very beginning of life. How will this child become a fluent speaker of her native language within just a few years? Theorists disagree sharply.

TABLE 5.3
Milestones of Language Development During the First Two Years

APPROXIMATE AGE	MILESTONE
2 months	Infants coo, making pleasant vowel sounds.
4 months on	Infants observe with interest as the caregiver plays turn-taking games, such as pat-a-cake and peekaboo.
6 months on	Infants babble, adding consonants to their cooing sounds and repeating syllables. By 7 months, babbling starts to include many sounds of spoken languages.
	Infants begin to comprehend a few commonly heard words.
8–12 months	Infants become more accurate at establishing joint attention with the caregiver, who often verbally labels what the baby is looking at.
	Infants actively participate in turn-taking games, trading roles with the caregiver.
	Infants use preverbal gestures, such as showing and pointing, to influence others' goals and behavior and to convey information.
12 months	Babbling includes sound and intonation patterns of the child's language community.
	Speed and accuracy of word comprehension increase rapidly.
	Toddlers say their first recognizable word.
18–24 months	Spoken vocabulary expands from about 50 to 200 to 250 words.
	Toddlers combine two words.

and cognitive abilities, such as the capacity to analyze musical and visual patterns (Saygin, Leech, & Dick, 2010).

Other theorists blend this information-processing view with Chomsky's nativist perspective. They agree that infants are amazing statistical analyzers of speech and other information. But, they argue, these capacities probably are not sufficient to account for mastery of higher-level aspects of language, such as intricate grammatical structures (Aslin & Newport, 2012). They also point out that grammatical competence may depend more on specific brain structures than the other components of language. When 2- to 2½-year-olds and adults listened to short sentences—some grammatically correct, others with phrase-structure violations—both groups showed similarly distinct ERP brain-wave patterns for each sentence type in the left frontal and temporal lobes of the cerebral cortex (Oberecker & Friederici, 2006). This suggests that 2-year-olds process sentence structures using the same neural system as adults do. Furthermore, in studies of older children and adults with left-hemispheric brain damage, grammar is more impaired than other language functions (Curtiss & Schaeffer, 2005).

Still other interactionists emphasize that children's social skills and language experiences are centrally involved in language development. In this *social-interactionist* view, an active child strives to communicate, which cues her caregivers to provide appropriate language experiences. These experiences, in turn, help the child relate the content and structure of language to its social meanings (Bohannon & Bonvillian, 2013; Chapman, 2006).

Among social interactionists, disagreement continues over whether or not children are equipped with specialized language structures in the brain (Hsu, Chater, & Vitányi, 2013; Lidz, 2007; Tomasello, 2006). Nevertheless, as we chart the course of language development, we will encounter much support for their central premise—that children's social competencies and language experiences greatly affect their language progress. In reality, native endowment, cognitive-processing strategies, and social experience probably operate in different balances with respect to each aspect of language. Table 5.3 provides an overview of early language milestones that we will examine in the next few sections.

Getting Ready to Talk

Before babies say their first word, they make impressive progress toward understanding and speaking their native tongue. They listen attentively to human speech, and they make speechlike sounds. As adults, we can hardly help but respond.

Cooing and Babbling. Around 2 months, babies begin to make vowel-like noises, called **cooing** because of their pleasant "oo" quality. Gradually, consonants are added, and around 6 months, **babbling** appears, in which infants repeat consonant–vowel combinations. With age, they increasingly babble in long strings, such as "babababab" or "nanananana," in an effort to gain control over producing particular sounds.

Babies everywhere (even those who are deaf) start babbling at about the same age and produce a similar range of early sounds. But for babbling to develop further, infants must be able to hear human speech. In babies with hearing impairments, these speechlike sounds are greatly delayed and limited in diversity of sounds (Bass-Ringdahl, 2010). And a deaf infant not exposed to sign language will stop babbling entirely (Oller, 2000).

Babies initially produce a limited number of sounds and then expand to a much broader range. Around 7 months, babbling starts to include many sounds of spoken languages. As caregivers respond to infant babbles, older infants become better at matching the sounds they hear in adult speech (Goldstein & Schwade, 2008). By 8 to 10 months, babbling reflects the sound and intonation patterns of the child's language community, some of which are transferred to their first words (Boysson-Bardies & Vihman, 1991).

Deaf infants exposed to sign language from birth babble with their hands much as hearing infants do through speech (Petitto & Marentette, 1991). Furthermore, hearing babies of deaf, signing parents produce babblelike hand motions with the rhythmic patterns of natural sign languages (Petitto et al., 2001, 2004). This sensitivity to language rhythm—evident in both spoken and signed babbling—supports both discovery and production of meaningful language units.

Becoming a Communicator. At birth, infants are prepared for some aspects of conversational behavior. For example, newborns initiate interaction through eye contact and terminate it by looking away. By 3 to 4 months, infants start to gaze in the same general direction adults are looking—a skill that becomes more accurate at 10 to 11 months, as babies realize that others' focus offers information about their communicative intentions (to talk about an object) or other goals (to obtain an object) (Brooks & Meltzoff, 2005; Senju, Csibra, & Johnson, 2008). This **joint attention,** in which the child attends to the same object or event as the caregiver, who often labels it, contributes greatly to early language development. Infants and toddlers who frequently experience it sustain attention longer, comprehend more language, produce meaningful gestures and words earlier, and show faster vocabulary development (Brooks & Meltzoff, 2008; Carpenter, Nagell, & Tomasello, 1998; Flom & Pick, 2003; Silvén, 2001).

Around 3 months, interactions between caregivers and babies begin to include *give-and-take.* Infants and mothers mutually imitate the pitch, loudness, and duration of each other's sounds. Mothers take the lead, imitating about twice as often as 3-month-olds, who limit their imitations to a handful of sounds they find easier to produce (Gratier & Devouche, 2011). Between 4 and 6 months, imitation extends to social games, as in pat-a-cake and peekaboo. At first, the parent starts the game and the baby is an amused observer. Gradually, infants join in, and by the end of the first year, they participate actively, trading roles with the caregiver. Through these imitative exchanges, babies practice the turn-taking pattern of human conversation, a vital context for acquiring language and communication skills.

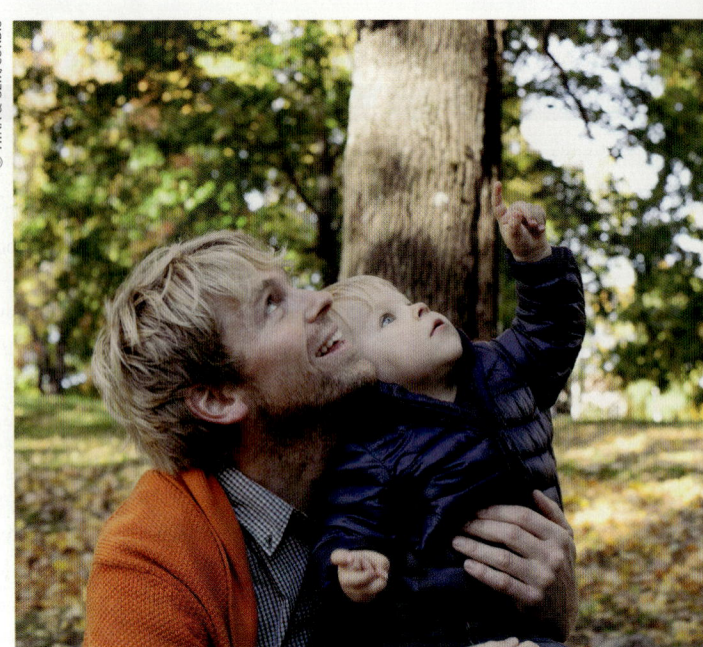

This baby uses a preverbal gesture to direct his father's attention. The father's verbal response ("I see that squirrel!") promotes the baby's transition to spoken language.

At the end of the first year, babies use *preverbal gestures* to direct adults' attention, influence their behavior, and convey helpful information (Tomasello, Carpenter, & Liszkowski, 2007). For example, Caitlin held up a toy to show it, pointed to the cupboard when she wanted a cookie, and pointed at her mother's car keys lying on the floor. Carolyn responded to these gestures and also labeled them ("That's your bear!" "You want a cookie!" "Oh, there are my keys!"). In this way, toddlers learn that using language leads to desired results.

The more time caregivers and infants spend in joint play with objects, the earlier and more often babies use preverbal gestures (Salomo & Liszkowski, 2013). Soon toddlers integrate words with gestures, using the gesture to expand their verbal message, as in pointing to a toy while saying "give" (Capirci et al., 2005). Gradually, gestures recede, and words become dominant. But the earlier toddlers form word–gesture combinations, the faster their vocabulary growth, the sooner they produce two-word utterances at the end of the second year, and the more complex their sentences at age 3½ (Huttenlocher et al., 2010; Rowe & Goldin-Meadow, 2009).

First Words

In the middle of the first year, infants begin to understand word meanings. By 5 months, they respond to their own name, preferring to listen to it than to another word matched in stress pattern (Mandel, Jusczyk, & Pisoni, 1995). And when 6-month-olds listened to the word "Mommy" or "Daddy" while viewing side-by-side videos of their parents, they looked longer at the video of the named parent (Tincoff & Jusczyk, 1999).

First recognizable spoken words, around 1 year, build on the sensorimotor foundations Piaget described and on categories children have formed. In a study tracking the first 10 words used by several hundred U.S. and Chinese (both Mandarin- and Cantonese-speaking) babies, important people ("Mama," "Dada"), common objects ("ball," "bread"), and sound effects ("woof-woof," "vroom") were mentioned most often. Action words ("hit," "grab," "hug") and social routines ("hi," "bye"), though also appearing in all three groups, were more often produced by Chinese than U.S. babies, and the Chinese babies also named more important people—differences we will consider shortly (Tardif et al., 2008). In their first 50 words, toddlers rarely name things that just *sit there*, like "table" or "vase."

When young children first learn words, they sometimes apply them too narrowly, an error called **underextension.** At 16 months, Caitlin used "bear" only to refer to the worn and tattered bear she carried nearly constantly. As vocabulary expands, a more common error is **overextension**—applying a word to a wider collection of objects and events than is appropriate. For example, Grace used "car" for buses, trains, trucks, and fire engines. Toddlers' overextensions reflect their sensitivity to categories (MacWhinney, 2005). They apply a new word to a group of similar experiences: "car" to wheeled objects, "open" to opening a door, peeling fruit, and untying shoelaces. This suggests that children often overextend deliberately because they have difficulty recalling or have not acquired a suitable word. And when a word is hard to pronounce, toddlers are likely to substitute a related one they can say (Bloom, 2000). As vocabulary expands and pronunciation improves, overextensions gradually decline.

Overextensions illustrate another important feature of language development: the distinction between language *production* (the words and word combinations children use) and language *comprehension* (the language they understand). At all ages, comprehension develops ahead of production. A 2-year-old who refers to trucks, trains, and bikes as "car" may look at or point to these objects correctly when given their names (Naigles & Gelman, 1995). Still, the two capacities are related. The speed and accuracy of toddlers' comprehension of spoken language increase dramatically over the second year. And toddlers who are faster and more accurate in comprehension tend to show more rapid growth in words understood and produced over the following year (Fernald & Marchman, 2012). Quick comprehension frees space in working memory for picking up new words and for the more demanding task of using them to communicate.

The Two-Word Utterance Phase

Young toddlers add to their spoken vocabularies at a rate of one to three words per week. Because gains in word production between 18 and 24 months are so impressive (one or two words per day), many researchers concluded that toddlers undergo a *spurt in vocabulary*—a transition from a slower to a faster learning phase. In actuality, most children show a steady increase in rate of word learning that continues through the preschool years (Ganger & Brent, 2004).

How do toddlers build their vocabularies so quickly? In the second year, they improve in ability to categorize experience, recall words, and understand others' social cues to meaning, such as eye gaze, pointing, and handling objects (Golinkoff & Hirsh-Pasek, 2006; Liszkowski, Carpenter, & Tomasello, 2007). In Chapter 7, we will consider young children's diverse strategies for word learning.

Once toddlers produce 200 to 250 words, they start to combine two words: "Mommy shoe," "go car," "more cookie." These two-word utterances are called **telegraphic speech** because, like a telegram, they focus on high-content words, omitting smaller, less important ones ("can," "the," "to").

Two-word speech consists largely of simple formulas ("more + X," "eat + X"), with different words inserted in the "X" position. Toddlers rarely make gross grammatical errors, such as saying "chair my" instead of "my chair." But their word-order regularities are usually copies of adult word pairings, as when the parent says, "How about *more sandwich*?" or "Let's see if you can *eat the berries*." This suggests that at first, young children rely on "concrete pieces of language" they often hear, gradually generalizing from those pieces to word-order and other grammatical rules (Bannard, Lieven, & Tomasello, 2009; MacWhinney, 2015). As we will see in Chapter 7, children master grammar steadily over the preschool years.

Individual and Cultural Differences

Although children typically produce their first word around their first birthday, the range is large, from 8 to 18 months—variation due to a complex blend of genetic and environmental influences. Earlier we saw that Timmy's spoken language was delayed, in part because of Vanessa's tense, directive communication with him. But Timmy is also a boy, and girls are slightly ahead of boys in early vocabulary growth (Van Hulle, Goldsmith, & Lemery, 2004). The most common explanation is girls' faster rate of physical maturation, which is believed to promote earlier development of the left cerebral hemisphere.

Temperament matters, too. For example, shy toddlers often wait until they understand a great deal before trying to speak. Once they do speak, their vocabularies increase rapidly, although they remain slightly behind their agemates (Spere et al., 2004).

Caregiver–child conversation—especially, the richness of adults' vocabularies—also plays a strong role (Huttenlocher et al., 2010). Commonly used words for objects appear early in toddlers' speech, and the more often their caregivers use a particular noun, the sooner young children produce it (Goodman, Dale, & Li, 2008). Mothers talk more to toddler-age girls than to boys, and parents converse less often with shy than with sociable children (Leaper, Anderson, & Sanders, 1998; Patterson & Fisher, 2002).

Applying what we Know

Supporting Early Language Learning

STRATEGY	CONSEQUENCE
Respond to coos and babbles with speech sounds and words.	Encourages experimentation with sounds that can later be blended into first words. Provides experience with the turn-taking pattern of human conversation.
Establish joint attention and comment on what child sees.	Predicts earlier onset of language and faster vocabulary development.
Play social games, such as pat-a-cake and peekaboo.	Provides experience with the turn-taking pattern of human conversation.
Engage toddlers in joint make-believe play.	Promotes all aspects of conversational dialogue.
Engage toddlers in frequent conversations.	Predicts faster early language development and academic success during the school years.
Read to toddlers often, engaging them in dialogues about picture books.	Provides exposure to many aspects of language, including vocabulary, grammar, communication skills, and information about written symbols and story structures.

Compared to their higher-SES agemates, children from low-SES homes usually have smaller vocabularies. By 18 to 24 months, they are slower at word comprehension and have acquired 30 percent fewer words (Fernald, Marchman, & Weisleder, 2013). Limited parent–child conversation and book reading are major factors. On average, a middle-SES child is read to for 1,000 hours between 1 and 5 years, a low-SES child for only 25 hours (Neuman, 2003).

Not surprisingly, rate of early vocabulary growth is a strong predictor of low-SES children's vocabulary size at kindergarten entry, which forecasts their later literacy skills and academic success (Rowe, Raudenbush, & Goldin-Meadow, 2012). Higher-SES toddlers who lag behind their agemates in word learning have more opportunities to catch up in early childhood. Young children have distinct styles of early language learning. Caitlin and Grace, like most toddlers, used a **referential style**; their vocabularies consisted mainly of words that refer to objects. A smaller number of toddlers use an **expressive style**; compared to referential children, they produce many more social formulas and pronouns ("thank you," "done," "I want it"). These styles reflect early ideas about the functions of language. Caitlin and Grace, for example, thought words were for naming things. In contrast, expressive-style children believe words are for talking about people's feelings and needs (Bates et al., 1994). The vocabularies of referential-style toddlers grow faster because all languages contain many more object labels than social phrases.

What accounts for a toddler's language style? Rapidly developing referential-style children often have an especially active interest in exploring objects. They also eagerly imitate their parents' frequent naming of objects (Masur & Rodemaker, 1999). Expressive-style children tend to be highly sociable, and their parents more often use verbal routines ("How are you?" "It's no trouble") that support social relationships (Goldfield, 1987).

The two language styles are also linked to culture. Object words (nouns) are particularly common in the vocabularies of English-speaking toddlers, but Chinese, Japanese, and Korean toddlers have more words for actions (verbs) and social routines. Mothers' speech in each culture reflects this difference (Chan, Brandone, & Tardif, 2009; Chan et al., 2011; Choi & Gopnik, 1995; Fernald & Morikawa, 1993). American mothers frequently label objects when interacting with their babies. Asian mothers, perhaps because of a cultural emphasis on the importance of group membership, emphasize actions and social routines. Also, in Mandarin, sentences often begin with verbs, making action words especially salient to Mandarin-speaking toddlers.

At what point should parents be concerned if their child talks very little or not at all? If a toddler's language development is greatly delayed when compared with the norms in Table 5.3 (page 175), then parents should consult the child's doctor or a speech and language therapist. Late babbling may be a sign of slow language development that can be prevented with early intervention (Rowe, Raudenbush, & Goldin-Meadow, 2012). Some toddlers who do not follow simple directions or who, after age 2, have difficulty putting their thoughts into words may suffer from a hearing impairment or a language disorder that requires immediate treatment.

Supporting Early Language Development

Consistent with the interactionist view, a rich social environment builds on young children's natural readiness to acquire language. For a summary of how caregivers can consciously support early language development, see Applying What We Know above. Caregivers also do so unconsciously—through a special style of speech.

Adults in many cultures speak to babies in **infant-directed speech (IDS),** a form of communication made up of short sentences with high-pitched, exaggerated expression, clear pronunciation, distinct pauses between speech segments, clear gestures to support verbal meaning, and repetition of new words in a variety of contexts ("See the *ball,*" "The *ball* bounced!") (Fernald et al., 1989; O'Neill et al., 2005). Deaf parents use a similar style of communication when signing to their deaf babies (Masataka, 1996). From birth on, infants prefer IDS over other adult talk, and by 5 months they are more emotionally responsive to it (Aslin, Jusczyk, & Pisoni, 1998).

IDS builds on several communicative strategies we have already considered: joint attention, turn-taking, and caregivers' sensitivity to toddlers' preverbal gestures. In this example, Carolyn uses IDS with 18-month-old Caitlin:

Caitlin:	"Go car."
Carolyn:	"Yes, time to go in the car. Where's your jacket?"
Caitlin:	*[Looks around, walks to the closet.]* "Dacket!" *[Points to her jacket.]*
Carolyn:	"There's that jacket! *[Helps Caitlin into the jacket.]* On it goes! Let's zip up. *[Zips up the jacket.]* Now, say bye-bye to Grace and Timmy."
Caitlin:	"Bye-bye, G-ace. Bye-bye, Te-te.
Carolyn:	"Where's your bear?"
Caitlin:	*[Looks around.]*
Carolyn:	*[Pointing.]* "See? By the sofa." *[Caitlin gets the bear.]*

Parents constantly fine-tune the length and content of their utterances in IDS to fit children's needs—adjustments that enable infants and toddlers to join in and that foster both language comprehension and production (Ma et al., 2011; Rowe, 2008). As we saw earlier, parent–toddler conversation strongly predicts language development and reading success during the school years.

Research also reveals that live interaction with a responsive adult is far better suited to spurring early language development than media sources. After a month's regular exposure to a commercial video for babies that labeled common household objects, 12- to 18-month-olds did not add any more words to their vocabulary than non-viewing controls. Rather, toddlers in a comparison group whose parents spent time teaching them the words in everyday activities learned best (DeLoache et al., 2010). Consistent with these findings, a video format that allows an adult to interact responsively with a 2-year-old—as in a Skype session—is an effective context for acquiring new verbs (Roseberry, Hirsh-Pasek, & Golinkoff, 2014).

But toddler viewers are unable to learn language from TV or video unless programs are specially adapted for them. For example, 2½-year-olds fail to acquire new object labels from an on-screen conversation between two adults, unless the actors show clear evidence of reciprocal interaction, such as the speaker

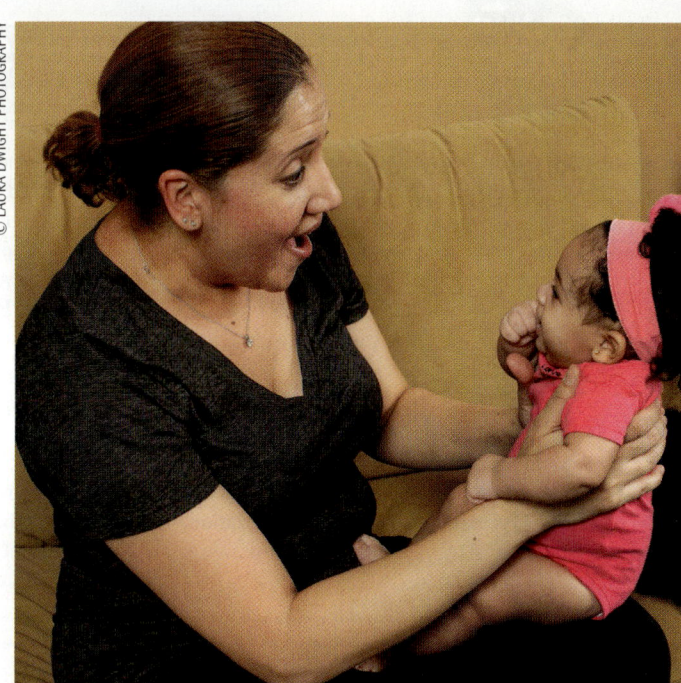

A mother speaks to her baby in short, clearly pronounced sentences with high-pitched, exaggerated intonation. This form of communication, called infant-directed speech, eases early language learning.

handing the object to her partner, who accepts it and imitates the speaker's action (O'Doherty et al., 2011). Return to page 157 to review the *video deficit effect,* noting how these findings illustrate it.

Do social experiences that promote language development remind you of those that strengthen cognitive development in general? IDS and parent–child conversation create a *zone of proximal development* in which children's language expands. In contrast, adult behaviors that are unresponsive to children's needs or impatient with their efforts to talk result in immature language skills (Baumwell, Tamis-LeMonda, & Bornstein, 1997; Cabrera, Shannon, & Tamis-LeMonda, 2007). In the next chapter, we will see that adult sensitivity supports infants' and toddlers' emotional and social development as well.

Ask yourself

CONNECT Cognition and language are interrelated. List examples of how cognition fosters language development. Next, list examples of how language fosters cognitive development.

APPLY Fran frequently corrects her 17-month-old son Jeremy's attempts to talk and—fearing that he won't use words—refuses to respond to his gestures. How might Fran be contributing to Jeremy's slow language progress?

REFLECT Find an opportunity to speak to an infant or toddler. Did you use IDS? What features of your speech are likely to promote early language development, and why?

Summary / chapter 5

Piaget's Cognitive-Developmental Theory (p. 150)

5.1 *According to Piaget, how do schemes change over the course of development?*

- By acting on the environment, children move through four stages in which psychological structures, or **schemes,** achieve a better fit with external reality.

- Schemes change in two ways: through **adaptation,** which is made up of two complementary activities—**assimilation** and **accommodation**; and through **organization,** the internal rearrangement of schemes into a strongly interconnected cognitive system.

5.2 *Describe major cognitive attainments of the sensorimotor stage.*

- In the **sensorimotor stage,** the **circular reaction** provides a means of adapting first schemes, and the newborn's reflexes gradually transform into the flexible action patterns of the older infant. Eight- to 12-month-olds develop **intentional,** or **goal-directed, behavior** and begin to understand **object permanence.**

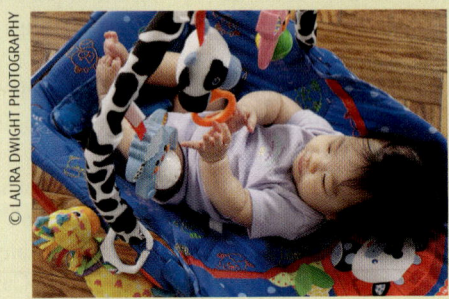

- Between 18 and 24 months, **mental representation** is evident in sudden solutions to sensorimotor problems, mastery of object permanence problems involving invisible displacement, **deferred imitation,** and **make-believe play.**

5.3 *What does follow-up research say about infant cognitive development and the accuracy of Piaget's sensorimotor stage?*

- Follow-up research suggests that infants display certain understandings earlier than Piaget believed. Some awareness of object permanence, as revealed by the **violation-of-expectation method** and object-tracking research, may be evident in the first few months. Furthermore, young infants display deferred imitation, and by 10 to 12 months, they can solve problems by analogy—attainments that require mental representation.

- Around their first birthday, babies attain **displaced reference,** the realization that words may stand for things not physically present. By the second year, toddlers treat realistic-looking pictures symbolically. Around 2½ years, the **video deficit effect** declines; children grasp the symbolic meaning of video.

- Researchers believe that newborns have more built-in equipment for making sense of their world than Piaget assumed, although they disagree on how much initial understanding infants have. According to the **core knowledge perspective,** infants are born with core domains of thought, including physical, psychological, linguistic, and numerical knowledge, that support early, rapid cognitive development.

- Broad agreement exists that many cognitive changes of infancy are continuous rather than stagelike and that aspects of cognition develop unevenly rather than in an integrated fashion.

Information Processing (p. 160)

5.4 *Describe the information-processing view of cognitive development and the general structure of the information-processing system.*

- Most information-processing researchers assume that we hold information in three parts of the mental system for processing: the **sensory register,** the **short-term memory store,** and **long-term memory.** The **central executive** joins with **working memory**—our "mental workspace"—to process information effectively. **Automatic processes** permit us to focus on other information while performing them.

- Gains in **executive function**—impulse control, flexible thinking, coordinating information in working memory, and planning—in childhood predict important cognitive and social outcomes in adolescence and adulthood.

5.5 *What changes in attention, memory, and categorization take place over the first two years?*

- With age, infants attend to more aspects of the environment and take information in more quickly. In the second year, attention to novelty declines and sustained attention improves.

- Young infants are capable of **recognition** memory. By the middle of the first year, they also engage in **recall.** Both recognition and recall improve steadily with age.

- Infants group stimuli into an expanding array of categories. In the second year, toddlers begin to categorize flexibly, switching their basis of object sorting, and their grasp of the animate–inanimate distinction expands. Gradually, they shift from a perceptual to a conceptual basis of categorizing.

5.6 *Describe the strengths and limitations of the information-processing approach to early cognitive development.*

- Information-processing findings challenge Piaget's view of infants as purely sensorimotor beings who cannot mentally represent experiences. But information processing has not yet provided a broad, comprehensive theory of children's thinking.

The Social Context of Early Cognitive Development (p. 166)

5.7 *How does Vygotsky's concept of the zone of proximal development expand our understanding of early cognitive development?*

- Vygotsky believed that infants master tasks within the **zone of proximal development**—ones just ahead of their current capacities—through the support and guidance of more skilled partners. As early as the first year, cultural variations in social experiences affect mental strategies.

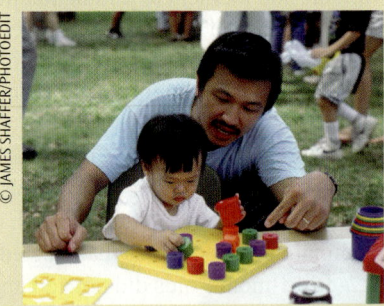

Individual Differences in Early Mental Development (p. 167)

5.8 *Describe the mental testing approach and the extent to which infant tests predict later performance.*

- The mental testing approach measures variation in developmental progress in an effort to predict future performance. Scores are arrived at by computing an **intelligence quotient (IQ),** which compares an individual's test performance with that of a **standardization** sample of same-age individuals, whose scores form a **normal distribution.**

- Infant tests consisting largely of perceptual and motor responses predict later intelligence poorly. As a result, scores on infant tests are called **developmental quotients (DQs),** rather than IQs. Speed of habituation and recovery to visual stimuli is a better predictor of future performance.

5.9 *Discuss environmental influences on early mental development, including home, child care, and early intervention for at-risk infants and toddlers.*

- Research with the **Home Observation for Measurement of the Environment (HOME)** shows that an organized, stimulating home environment and parental affection, involvement, and encouragement repeatedly predict higher mental test scores. The extent to which parents talk to infants and toddlers is especially influential.

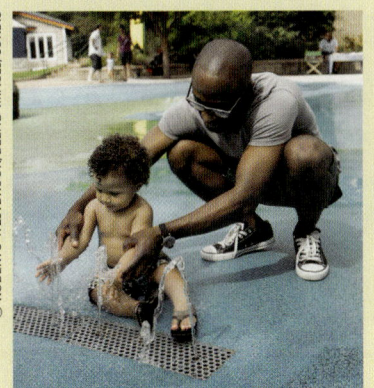

- Quality of infant and toddler child care influences later cognitive, language, academic, and social skills. Standards for **developmentally appropriate practice** specify program characteristics that meet young children's developmental needs.

- Intensive intervention beginning in infancy and extending through early childhood can prevent the gradual declines in intelligence and the poor academic performance evident in many poverty-stricken children.

Language Development (p. 173)

5.10 *Describe theories of language development, and indicate the emphasis each places on innate abilities and environmental influences.*

- Chomsky's nativist theory regards children as naturally endowed with a **language acquisition device (LAD).** Consistent with this perspective, mastery of a complex language system is unique to humans, and childhood is a sensitive period for language acquisition.

- Recent theories suggest that language development results from interactions between inner capacities and environmental influences. Some interactionists apply the information-processing perspective to language development. Others emphasize the importance of children's social skills and language experiences.

5.11 *Describe major language milestones in the first two years, individual differences, and ways adults can support early language development.*

- Infants begin **cooing** at 2 months and **babbling** at about 6 months. Around 10 months, their skill at establishing **joint attention** improves, and soon they use preverbal gestures. Adults can encourage language progress by responding to infants' coos and babbles, playing turn-taking games, establishing joint attention and labeling what babies see, and labeling their preverbal gestures.

- Around 12 months, toddlers say their first word. Young children often make errors of **underextension** and **overextension.** Once vocabulary reaches 200 to 250 words, two-word utterances called **telegraphic speech** appear. At all ages, language comprehension is ahead of production.

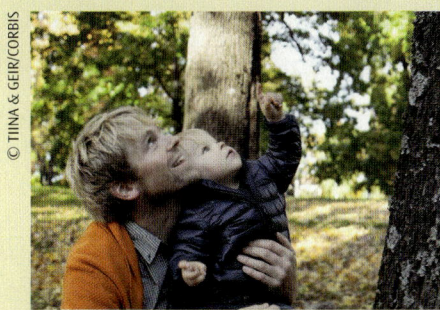

- Girls show faster language progress than boys, and reserved toddlers may wait before trying to speak. Most toddlers use a **referential style** of language learning; their early words consist largely of names for objects. Some use an **expressive style,** in which social formulas and pronouns are common and vocabulary grows more slowly.

- Adults in many cultures speak to young children in **infant-directed speech (IDS),** a simplified form of communication that is well-suited to their learning needs. Parent–toddler conversation is a good predictor of early language development and reading success during the school years. Live interaction with an adult is better suited to spurring language progress than are media sources.

Important Terms and Concepts

accommodation (p. 150)
adaptation (p. 150)
assimilation (p. 150)
autobiographical memory (p. 164)
automatic processes (p. 161)
babbling (p. 175)
central executive (p. 161)
circular reaction (p. 151)
cooing (p. 175)
core knowledge perspective (p. 158)
deferred imitation (p. 153)
developmentally appropriate practice (p. 171)
developmental quotient (DQ) (p. 169)
displaced reference (p. 156)
executive function (p. 161)

expressive style of language learning (p. 178)
Home Observation for Measurement of the Environment (HOME) (p. 170)
infant-directed speech (IDS) (p. 179)
infantile amnesia (p. 164)
intelligence quotient (IQ) (p. 169)
intentional, or goal-directed, behavior (p. 152)
joint attention (p. 176)
language acquisition device (LAD) (p. 174)
long-term memory (p. 161)
make-believe play (p. 153)
mental representation (p. 152)
normal distribution (p. 169)
object permanence (p. 152)
organization (p. 150)

overextension (p. 177)
recall (p. 163)
recognition (p. 163)
referential style of language learning (p. 178)
scheme (p. 150)
sensorimotor stage (p. 150)
sensory register (p. 160)
short-term memory store (p. 160)
standardization (p. 169)
telegraphic speech (p. 177)
underextension (p. 177)
video deficit effect (p. 157)
violation-of-expectation method (p. 153)
working memory (p. 161)
zone of proximal development (p. 166)

chapter 6

Emotional and Social Development in Infancy and Toddlerhood

This mother has forged a close, affectionate bond with her son. Her warmth and sensitivity engender a sense of security in the baby—a vital foundation for all aspects of early development.

What's ahead in chapter 6

Erikson's Theory of Infant and Toddler Personality
  Basic Trust versus Mistrust • Autonomy versus Shame and Doubt

Emotional Development
  Basic Emotions • Understanding and Responding to the Emotions of Others • Emergence of Self-Conscious Emotions • Beginnings of Emotional Self-Regulation

■ **BIOLOGY AND ENVIRONMENT** Parental Depression and Child Development

Temperament and Development
  The Structure of Temperament • Measuring Temperament • Stability of Temperament • Genetic and Environmental Influences • Temperament and Child Rearing: The Goodness-of-Fit Model

■ **BIOLOGY AND ENVIRONMENT** Development of Shyness and Sociability

Development of Attachment
  Bowlby's Ethological Theory • Measuring the Security of Attachment • Stability of Attachment • Cultural Variations • Factors That Affect Attachment Security • Multiple Attachments • Attachment and Later Development

■ **SOCIAL ISSUES: HEALTH** Does Child Care in Infancy Threaten Attachment Security and Later Adjustment?

■ **CULTURAL INFLUENCES** The Role of Fathers' Involvement in Children's Development

Self-Development
  Self-Awareness • Categorizing the Self • Self-Control

As Caitlin reached 8 months of age, her parents noticed that she had become more fearful. One evening, when Carolyn and David left her with a babysitter, she wailed as they headed for the door—an experience she had accepted easily a few weeks earlier. Caitlin and Timmy's caregiver Ginette also observed an increasing wariness of strangers. When she turned to go to another room, both babies dropped their play to crawl after her. At the mail carrier's knock at the door, they clung to Ginette's legs, reaching out to be picked up.

At the same time, each baby seemed more willful. Removing an object from the hand produced little response at 5 months. But at 8 months, when Timmy's mother, Vanessa, took away a table knife he had managed to reach, Timmy burst into angry screams and could not be consoled or distracted.

All Monica and Kevin knew about Grace's first year was that she had been deeply loved by her destitute, homeless mother. Separation from her, followed by a long journey to an unfamiliar home, had left Grace in shock. At first she was extremely sad, turning away when Monica or Kevin picked her up. But as Grace's new parents held her close, spoke gently, and satisfied her craving for food, Grace returned their affection. Two weeks after her arrival, her despondency gave way to a sunny, easygoing disposition. She burst into a wide grin, reached out at the sight of Monica and Kevin, and laughed at her brother Eli's funny faces. As her second birthday approached, she pointed to herself, exclaiming "Gwace!" and laid claim to treasured possessions. "Gwace's chicken!" she would announce at mealtimes, sucking the marrow from the drumstick, a practice she had brought with her from Cambodia.

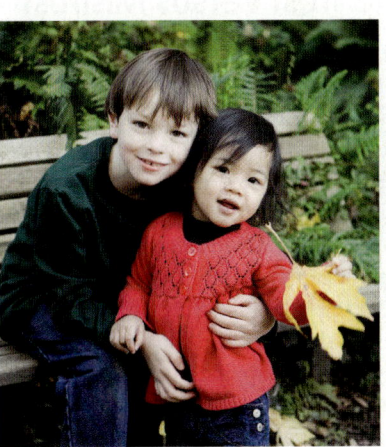

Taken together, the children's reactions reflect two related aspects of personality development during the first two years: close ties to others and a sense of self. We begin with Erikson's psychosocial theory, which provides an overview of personality development during infancy and toddlerhood. Then, as we chart the course of emotional development, we will discover why fear and anger became more apparent in Caitlin's and Timmy's range of emotions by the end of the first year. Our attention then turns to individual differences in temperament. We will examine genetic and environmental contributions to these differences and their consequences for future development.

Next, we take up attachment to the caregiver, the child's first affectionate tie. We will see how the feelings of security that grow out of this important bond support the child's exploration, self-awareness, and expanding social relationships.

Finally, we focus on early self-development. By the end of toddlerhood, Grace recognized herself in mirrors and photographs, labeled herself as a girl, and showed the beginnings of self-control. "Don't touch!" she instructed herself one day as she resisted the desire to pull a lamp cord out of its socket. Cognitive advances combine with social experiences to produce these changes during the second year. ●

Erikson's Theory of Infant and Toddler Personality

6.1 What personality changes take place during Erikson's stages of basic trust versus mistrust and autonomy versus shame and doubt?

Our discussion of major theories in Chapter 1 revealed that the psychoanalytic perspective is no longer in the mainstream of human development research. But one of its lasting contributions is its ability to capture the essence of personality during each period of development. The most influential psychoanalytic approach is Erik Erikson's *psychosocial theory*, summarized on page 15. Let's look closely at his first two stages.

Basic Trust versus Mistrust

Erikson accepted Freud's emphasis on the importance of the parent–infant relationship during feeding, but he expanded and enriched Freud's view. A healthy outcome during infancy, Erikson believed, does not depend on the *amount* of food or oral stimulation offered but rather on the *quality* of caregiving: relieving discomfort promptly and sensitively, holding the infant gently, waiting patiently until the baby has had enough milk, and weaning when the infant shows less interest in breast or bottle.

Erikson recognized that no parent can be perfectly in tune with the baby's needs. Many factors affect parental responsiveness—personal happiness, family conditions (for example, additional young children, social supports, financial well-being), and culturally valued child-rearing practices. But when the *balance of care* is sympathetic and loving, the psychological conflict of the first year—**basic trust versus mistrust**—is resolved on the positive side. The trusting infant expects the world to be good and gratifying, so he feels confident about venturing out to explore it. The mistrustful baby cannot count on the kindness and compassion of others, so she protects herself by withdrawing from people and things around her.

Autonomy versus Shame and Doubt

With the transition to toddlerhood, Freud viewed parents' manner of toilet training as decisive for psychological health. In Erikson' view, toilet training is only one of many influential experiences. The familiar refrains of newly walking, talking toddlers—"No!" "Do it myself!"—reveal that they have entered a period of budding selfhood. They want to decide for themselves, not just in toileting but also in other situations. The conflict of toddlerhood, **autonomy versus shame and doubt,** is resolved favorably when parents provide young children with suitable guidance and reasonable choices. A self-confident, secure 2-year-old has parents who do not criticize or attack him when he fails at new skills—using the toilet, eating with a spoon, or putting away toys. And they meet his assertions of independence with tolerance and understanding—for example, by giving him an extra five minutes to finish his play before leaving for the grocery store. In contrast, when parents are over- or undercontrolling, the outcome is a child who feels forced and shamed and who doubts his ability to control impulses and act competently on his own.

On a visit to a science museum, a 2-year-old insists on exploring a flight simulator. As the mother supports her toddler's desire to "do it myself," she fosters a healthy sense of autonomy.

In sum, basic trust and autonomy grow out of warm, sensitive parenting and reasonable expectations for impulse control starting in the second year. If children emerge from the first few years without sufficient trust in caregivers and without a healthy sense of individuality, the seeds are sown for adjustment problems. Adults who have difficulty establishing intimate ties, who are overly dependent on a loved one, or who continually doubt their own ability to meet new challenges may not have fully mastered the tasks of trust and autonomy during infancy and toddlerhood.

Emotional Development

6.2 Describe the development of basic emotions over the first year, noting the adaptive function of each.

6.3 Summarize changes during the first two years in understanding others' emotions, expression of self-conscious emotions, and emotional self-regulation.

Observe several infants and toddlers, noting the emotions each displays, the cues you rely on to interpret the baby's emotional state, and how caregivers respond. Researchers have conducted many such observations to find out how babies convey their emotions and interpret those of others. They have discovered that emotions play powerful roles in organizing the attainments that Erikson regarded as so important: social relationships, exploration of the environment, and discovery of the self (Saarni et al., 2006).

Think back to the *dynamic systems perspective* introduced in Chapters 1 and 4. As you read about early emotional development in the sections that follow, notice how emotions are an integral part of young children's dynamic systems of action. Emotions energize development. At the same time, they are an aspect of the system that develops, becoming more varied and complex as children reorganize their behavior to attain new goals (Campos, Frankel, & Camras, 2004; Camras, 2011).

Because infants cannot describe their feelings, determining exactly which emotions they are experiencing is a challenge. Cross-cultural evidence reveals that people around the world associate photographs of different facial expressions with emotions in the same way (Ekman & Friesen, 1972; Ekman & Matsumoto, 2011). These findings inspired researchers to analyze infants' facial patterns to determine the range of emotions they display at different ages.

But to express a particular emotion, infants, children, and adults actually use diverse responses—not just facial expressions but also vocalizations and body movements—which vary with their developing capacities, goals, and contexts. Therefore, to infer babies' emotions as accurately as possible, researchers must attend to multiple interacting expressive cues—vocal, facial, and gestural—and see how they vary across situations believed to elicit different emotions (Camras & Shuster, 2013).

Basic Emotions

Basic emotions—happiness, interest, surprise, fear, anger, sadness, and disgust—are universal in humans and other primates and have a long evolutionary history of promoting survival. Do infants come into the world with the ability to express basic emotions?

Although signs of some emotions are present, babies' earliest emotional life consists of little more than two global arousal states: attraction to pleasant stimulation and withdrawal from unpleasant stimulation (Camras et al., 2003). Only gradually do emotions become clear, well-organized signals. The dynamic systems perspective helps us understand how this happens: Children coordinate separate skills into more effective, emotionally expressive systems as the central nervous system develops and the child's goals and experiences change (Camras & Shutter, 2010).

Sensitive, contingent caregiver communication, in which parents selectively mirror aspects of the baby's diffuse emotional behavior, helps infants construct emotional expressions that more closely resemble those of adults (Gergely & Watson, 1999). With age, face, voice, and posture start to form organized patterns that vary meaningfully with environmental events. For example, Caitlin typically responded to her parents' playful interaction with a joyful face, pleasant babbling, and a relaxed posture, as if to say, "This is fun!" In contrast, an unresponsive parent often evokes a sad face, fussy sounds, and a drooping body (sending the message, "I'm despondent") or an angry face, crying, and "pick-me-up" gestures (as if to say, "Change this unpleasant event!") (Weinberg & Tronick, 1994). Gradually, emotional expressions become well-organized and specific—and therefore provide more precise information about the baby's internal state.

Four basic emotions—happiness, anger, sadness, and fear—have received the most research attention. Let's see how they develop.

Happiness. Happiness—expressed first in blissful smiles and later through exuberant laughter—contributes to many aspects of development. When infants achieve new skills, they smile and laugh, displaying delight in motor and cognitive mastery. The baby's smile encourages caregivers to smile responsively and to be affectionate and stimulating, and then the baby smiles even more (Bigelow & Power, 2014). Happiness binds parent and baby into a warm, supportive relationship that fosters the infant's motor, cognitive, and social competencies.

During the early weeks, newborn babies smile when full, during REM sleep, and in response to gentle touches and sounds, such as stroking of the skin, rocking, and a parent's soft, high-pitched voice. By the end of the first month, infants smile at dynamic, eye-catching sights, such as a bright object jumping suddenly across their field of vision. Between 6 and 10 weeks, the parent's communication evokes a broad grin called the **social smile** (Lavelli & Fogel, 2005). These changes parallel the development of infant perceptual capacities—in particular, sensitivity to visual patterns, including the human face (see Chapter 4). Social smiling becomes better-organized and stable as babies learn to use it to evoke and sustain pleasurable face-to-face interaction with their caregivers.

Laughter, which typically appears around 3 to 4 months, reflects faster processing of information than smiling. But as with smiling, the first laughs occur in response to very active stimuli, such as the parent saying playfully, "I'm gonna get you!" and kissing the baby's tummy. As infants understand more about their world, they laugh at events with subtler elements of surprise, such as a silent game of peekaboo. Soon they pick up on parents' facial and vocal cues to humor (Mireault et al., 2015). From 5 to 7 months, in the presence of those cues, they increasingly find absurd events—such as an adult wearing a ball as a clown's nose—funny.

During the second half-year, babies smile and laugh more when interacting with familiar people, a preference that strengthens the parent–child bond. And like adults, 10- to 12-month-olds have several smiles, which vary with context—a broad, "cheek-raised" smile in response to a parent's greeting; a reserved, muted smile for a friendly stranger; and a "mouth-open" smile during stimulating play (Messinger & Fogel, 2007). By the end of the first year, the smile has become a deliberate social signal.

Anger and Sadness. Newborn babies respond with generalized distress to a variety of unpleasant experiences, including hunger, painful medical procedures, changes in body temperature, and too much or too little stimulation. From 4 to 6 months into the second year, angry expressions increase in frequency and intensity (Braungart-Rieker, Hill-Soderlund, & Karrass,

2010). Older infants also react with anger in a wider range of situations—when an interesting object or event is removed, an expected pleasant event does not occur, their arms are restrained, the caregiver leaves for a brief time, or they are put down for a nap (Camras et al., 1992; Stenberg & Campos, 1990; Sullivan & Lewis, 2003).

Why do angry reactions increase with age? As infants become capable of intentional behavior (see Chapter 5), they want to control their own actions and the effects they produce (Mascolo & Fischer, 2007). Furthermore, older infants are better at identifying who caused them pain or removed a toy. Their anger is particularly intense when a caregiver from whom they have come to expect warm behavior causes discomfort. And increased parental limit setting once babies crawl and walk contributes to babies' angry responses (Roben et al., 2012). The rise in anger is also adaptive. Independent movement enables an angry infant to defend herself or overcome an obstacle to obtain a desired object. Finally, anger motivates caregivers to relieve the baby's distress and, in the case of separation, may discourage them from leaving again soon.

Although expressions of sadness also occur in response to pain, removal of an object, and brief separations, they are less frequent than anger (Alessandri, Sullivan, & Lewis, 1990). But when caregiver–infant communication is seriously disrupted, infant sadness is common—a condition that impairs all aspects of development (see the Biology and Environment box on the following page).

Fear. Like anger, fear rises from the second half of the first year into the second year (Braungart-Rieker, Hill-Soderlund, & Karrass, 2010; Brooker et al., 2013). Older infants hesitate before playing with a new toy, and newly crawling infants soon back away from heights (see Chapter 4). But the most frequent expression of fear is to unfamiliar adults, a response called **stranger anxiety.** Many infants and toddlers are quite wary of strangers, although the reaction does not always occur. It depends on several factors: temperament (some babies are generally more fearful), past experiences with strangers, and the current situation. When an unfamiliar adult picks up the infant in a new setting, stranger anxiety is likely. But if the adult sits still while the baby moves around and a parent is nearby, infants often show positive and curious behavior (Horner, 1980). The stranger's style of interaction—expressing warmth, holding out an attractive toy, playing a familiar game, and approaching slowly rather than abruptly—reduces the baby's fear.

LOOK and LISTEN

While observing an 8- to 18-month-old with his or her parent, gently approach the baby, offering a toy. Does the baby respond with stranger anxiety? To better understand the baby's behavior, ask the parent to describe his or her temperament and past experiences with strangers.

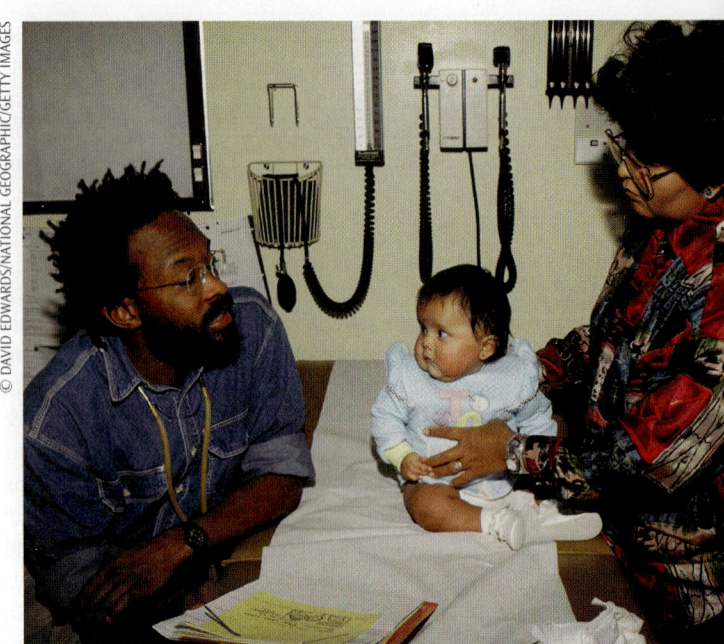

Stranger anxiety appears in many infants after 6 months of age. This baby, though safe in her mother's arms, observes her doctor with cautious curiosity.

Cross-cultural research reveals that infant-rearing practices can modify stranger anxiety. Among the Efe hunters and gatherers of the Republic of Congo, where the maternal death rate is high, infant survival is safeguarded by a collective caregiving system in which, starting at birth, Efe babies are passed from one adult to another. Consequently, Efe infants show little stranger anxiety (Tronick, Morelli, & Ivey, 1992). In contrast, among infants in Israeli kibbutzim (cooperative agricultural settlements), who live in isolated communities vulnerable to terrorist attacks, wariness of strangers is widespread. By the end of the first year, when infants look to others for cues about how to respond emotionally, kibbutz babies display greater stranger anxiety than their city-reared counterparts (Saarni et al., 2006).

The rise in fear after age 6 months keeps newly mobile babies' enthusiasm for exploration in check. Once wariness develops, infants use the familiar caregiver as a **secure base,** or point from which to explore, venturing into the environment and then returning for emotional support. As part of this adaptive system, encounters with strangers lead to two conflicting tendencies: approach (indicated by interest and friendliness) and avoidance (indicated by fear). The infant's behavior is a balance between the two.

As cognitive development enables toddlers to discriminate more effectively between threatening and nonthreatening people and situations, stranger anxiety and other fears of the first two years decline. Fear also wanes as toddlers acquire more strategies for coping with it, as we will see when we discuss emotional self-regulation.

Biology and Environment

Parental Depression and Child Development

About 8 to 10 percent of women experience chronic depression—mild to severe feelings of sadness, distress, and withdrawal that continue for months or years. Often, the beginnings of this emotional state cannot be pinpointed. In other instances, depression emerges or strengthens after childbirth but fails to subside as the new mother adjusts to hormonal changes in her body and gains confidence in caring for her baby. This is called *postpartum depression*.

Although it is less recognized and studied, fathers, too, experience chronic depression. About 3 to 5 percent of fathers report symptoms after the birth of a child (Thombs, Roseman, & Arthurs, 2010). Parental depression can interfere with effective parenting and seriously impair children's development. Genetic makeup increases the risk of depressive illness, but social and cultural factors are also involved.

Maternal Depression

During Julia's pregnancy, her husband, Kyle, showed so little interest in the baby that Julia worried that having a child might be a mistake. Then, shortly after Lucy was born, Julia's mood plunged. She felt anxious and weepy, overwhelmed by Lucy's needs, and angry at loss of control over her own schedule. When Julia approached Kyle about her own fatigue and his unwillingness to help with the baby, he snapped that she was overreacting. Julia's childless friends stopped by just once to see Lucy but did not call again.

Julia's depressed mood quickly affected her baby. In the weeks after birth, infants of depressed mothers sleep poorly, are less attentive to their surroundings, and have elevated levels of the stress hormone cortisol (Fernandes et al., 2015; Goodman et al., 2011; Natsuaki et al., 2014). The more extreme the depression and the greater the number of stressors in a mother's life (such as marital discord, little or no social support, and poverty), the more the parent–child relationship suffers. Julia rarely smiled at, comforted, or talked to Lucy, who responded to her mother's sad, vacant gaze by turning away, crying, and often looking sad or angry herself (Field, 2011; Vaever et al., 2015). By age 6 months, Lucy showed symptoms common in babies of depressed mothers—delays in motor and cognitive development, poor emotion regulation, an irritable mood, and attachment difficulties—outcomes that, without intervention, usually persist (Ibanez et al., 2015; Lefkovics, Baji, & Rigó, 2014; Vedova, 2014).

Depressed mothers view their babies negatively, which contributes to their inept caregiving (Lee & Hans, 2015). As their children get older, these mothers' lack of warmth and involvement is often accompanied by inconsistent discipline—sometimes lax, at other times too forceful (Thomas et al., 2015). As we will see in later chapters, children who experience these maladaptive parenting practices often have serious adjustment problems. Some withdraw into a depressive mood themselves; others become impulsive and aggressive. In one study, children born to mothers who were depressed during pregnancy were four times as likely as children of nondepressed mothers to have engaged in violent antisocial behavior by age 16, after other stressors in the mother's life that could contribute to youth antisocial conduct had been controlled (Hay et al., 2010).

Paternal Depression

In a study of a large representative sample of British parents and babies, researchers assessed depressive symptoms of fathers shortly after birth and again the following year. Then they tracked the children's development into the preschool years (Ramchandani et al., 2008). Persistent paternal depression was, like maternal depression, a strong predictor of child behavior problems—especially overactivity, defiance, and aggression in boys.

Paternal depression is linked to frequent marital and father–child conflict as children grow older (Gutierrez-Galve et al., 2015; Kane & Garber, 2004). Over time, children subjected to parental negativity develop a pessimistic world view—one in which they lack self-confidence and perceive their parents and other people as threatening. Children who constantly feel in danger are especially likely

This father appears disengaged from his son. Disruptions in the parent–child relationship caused by paternal depression often lead to serious child behavior problems.

to become overly aroused in stressful situations, easily losing control in the face of cognitive and social challenges (Sturge-Apple et al., 2008). Although children of depressed parents may inherit a tendency toward emotional and behavior problems, quality of parenting is a major factor in their adjustment.

Interventions

Early treatment is vital to prevent parental depression from interfering with the parent–child relationship. Julia's doctor referred her to a therapist, who helped Julia and Kyle with their marital problems. At times, antidepressant medication is prescribed.

In addition to alleviating parental depression, therapy that encourages depressed parents to revise negative views of their babies and to engage in emotionally positive, responsive caregiving is vital for reducing attachment and other developmental problems (Goodman et al., 2015). When a depressed parent does not respond easily to treatment, a warm relationship with the other parent or another caregiver can safeguard children's development.

Understanding and Responding to the Emotions of Others

Infants' emotional expressions are closely tied to their ability to interpret the emotional cues of others. We have seen that in the first few months, babies match the feeling tone of the caregiver in face-to-face communication. Around 3 months, they become sensitive to the structure and timing of face-to-face interactions (see Chapter 5, page 176). When they gaze, smile, or vocalize, they now expect their social partner to respond in kind, and they reply with positive vocal and emotional reactions (Bigelow & Power, 2014; Markova & Legerstee, 2006). Within these exchanges, infants become increasingly aware of the range of emotional expressions (Montague & Walker-Andrews, 2001). Recall from Chapter 4 (page 133) that according to some researchers, out of this early imitative communication, they start to view others as "like me"—an awareness believed to lay the foundation for understanding others' thoughts and feelings (Meltzoff, 2013).

By 4 to 5 months, infants distinguish positive from negative emotion in voices, and soon after, in facial expressions, gradually discriminating a wider range of emotions (see Chapter 4). Responding to emotional expressions as organized wholes indicates that these signals are becoming meaningful to babies. As skill at establishing joint attention improves, infants realize that an emotional expression not only has meaning but is also a meaningful reaction to a specific object or event (Thompson, 2015).

Once these understandings are in place, beginning at 8 to 10 months, infants engage in **social referencing**—actively seeking emotional information from a trusted person in an uncertain situation (Mumme et al., 2007). Many studies show that the caregiver's emotional expression (happy, angry, or fearful) influences whether a 1-year-old will be wary of strangers, play with an unfamiliar toy, or cross the deep side of the visual cliff (see page 140) (de Rosnay et al., 2006; Stenberg, 2003; Striano & Rochat, 2000). The adult's voice—either alone or combined with a facial expression—is more effective than a facial expression alone (Kim, Walden, & Knieps, 2010; Vaish & Striano, 2004). The voice conveys both emotional and verbal information, and the baby need not turn toward the adult but, instead, can focus on evaluating the novel event.

As toddlers start to appreciate that others' emotional reactions may differ from their own, social referencing allows them to compare their own and others' assessments of events. In one study, an adult showed 14- and 18-month-olds broccoli and crackers and acted delighted with one food but disgusted with the other. When asked to share the food, 18-month-olds offered the adult whichever food she appeared to like, regardless of their own preferences (Repacholi & Gopnik, 1997).

In sum, in social referencing, toddlers use others' emotional messages to evaluate the safety and security of their surroundings, to guide their own actions, and to gather information about others' intentions and preferences. These experiences, along with cognitive and language development, probably help toddlers refine the meanings of emotions—for example, happiness versus surprise, anger versus fear—during the second year (Gendler, Witherington, & Edwards, 2008).

Emergence of Self-Conscious Emotions

Besides basic emotions, humans are capable of a second, higher-order set of feelings, including guilt, shame, embarrassment, envy, and pride. These are called **self-conscious emotions** because each involves injury to or enhancement of our sense of self. We feel guilt when we have harmed someone and want to correct the wrongdoing. Envy arises when we desire something that another possesses, so we try to restore our sense of self-worth by securing that possession. When we are ashamed or embarrassed, we have negative feelings about our behavior, and we want to retreat so others will no longer notice our failings. In contrast, pride reflects delight in the self's achievements, and we are inclined to tell others what we have accomplished and to take on further challenges (Lewis, 2014).

Self-conscious emotions appear in the middle of the second year, as 18- to 24-month-olds become firmly aware of the self as a separate, unique individual. Toddlers show shame and embarrassment by lowering their eyes, hanging their head, and hiding their face with their hands. They show guiltlike reactions, too. After noticing Grace's unhappiness, 22-month-old Caitlin returned a toy she had grabbed and patted her upset playmate. Pride and envy also emerge around age 2 (Barrett, 2005; Garner, 2003; Lewis, 2014).

This 2-year-old's older sister praises his success at tower building. To experience self-conscious emotions, such as pride, young children need self-awareness as well as instruction in when to feel proud of an accomplishment.

Besides self-awareness, self-conscious emotions require an additional ingredient: adult instruction in *when* to feel proud, ashamed, or guilty. Parents begin this tutoring early when they say, "Look how far you can throw that ball!" or "You should feel ashamed for grabbing that toy!" Self-conscious emotions play important roles in children's achievement-related and moral behaviors. The situations in which adults encourage these feelings vary from culture to culture. In Western nations, most children are taught to feel pride in personal achievement—throwing a ball the farthest, winning a game, and (later on) getting good grades. In cultures such as China and Japan, which promote an interdependent self, calling attention to individual success evokes embarrassment and self-effacement. And violating cultural standards by failing to show concern for others—a parent, a teacher, or an employer—sparks intense shame (Lewis, 2014).

Beginnings of Emotional Self-Regulation

Besides expressing a wider range of emotions, infants and toddlers begin to manage their emotional experiences. **Emotional self-regulation** refers to the strategies we use to adjust our emotional state to a comfortable level of intensity so we can accomplish our goals (Eisenberg, 2006; Thompson & Goodvin, 2007). When you remind yourself that an anxiety-provoking event will be over soon, suppress your anger at a friend's behavior, or decide not to see a scary horror film, you are engaging in emotional self-regulation.

Emotional self-regulation requires voluntary, effortful management of emotions. It improves rapidly during the first few years, as the result of a *dynamic system* of influences that include development of the prefrontal cortex and its networks of connections to brain areas involved in emotional reactivity and control; and support from caregivers, who help children manage intense emotion and, as cognitive and language skills improve, teach them strategies for doing so on their own (Rothbart, Posner, & Kieras, 2006; Thompson, 2015). Individual differences in control of emotion are evident in infancy and, by early childhood, play such a vital role in adjustment that—as we will see later—they are viewed as a major dimension of temperament, called *effortful control*.

In the early months, infants have only a limited capacity to regulate their emotional states. When their feelings get too intense, they are easily overwhelmed. They depend on soothing interventions of caregivers—being lifted to the shoulder, rocked, gently stroked, and talked to softly—for distraction and reorienting of attention.

More effective functioning of the prefrontal cortex increases the baby's tolerance for stimulation. Between 2 and 4 months, caregivers build on this capacity by initiating face-to-face play and attention to objects. In these interactions, parents arouse pleasure in the baby while adjusting the pace of their behavior so the infant does not become overwhelmed and distressed (Kopp & Neufeld, 2003). As a result, the baby's tolerance for stimulation increases further.

From 3 months on, the ability to shift attention helps infants control emotion. Babies who more readily turn away from unpleasant events or engage in self-soothing are less prone to distress (Ekas, Lickenbrock, & Braungart-Rieker, 2013). And crawling and walking, which permit babies to approach or retreat from various situations, foster more effective self-regulation.

Infants whose parents "read" and respond contingently and sympathetically to their emotional cues tend to be less fussy and fearful, to express more pleasurable emotion, to be more interested in exploration, and to be easier to soothe (Braungart-Rieker, Hill-Soderlund, & Karrass, 2010; Crockenberg & Leerkes, 2004). In contrast, parents who respond impatiently or angrily or who wait to intervene until the infant has become extremely agitated reinforce the baby's rapid rise to intense distress. When caregivers fail to regulate stressful experiences for infants who cannot yet regulate such experiences for themselves, brain structures that buffer stress may fail to develop properly, resulting in an anxious, reactive child who has a reduced capacity for managing emotional problems (Blair & Raver, 2012; Frankel et al., 2015).

Caregivers also provide lessons in socially approved ways of expressing feelings. Beginning in the first few months, parents encourage infants to suppress negative emotion by imitating their expressions of interest, happiness, and surprise more often than their expressions of anger and sadness. Boys get more of this training than girls, in part because boys have a harder time regulating negative emotion (Else-Quest et al., 2006; Malatesta et al., 1986). As a result, the well-known sex difference—females as emotionally expressive and males as emotionally controlled—is promoted at a tender age.

Cultures that highly value social harmony place particular emphasis on socially appropriate emotional behavior while discouraging expression of individual feelings. Compared with Western parents, Japanese and Chinese parents, and parents in many non-Western village cultures, discourage the expression of strong emotion in babies. Nso mothers of rural Cameroon, for example, spend less time imitating infant social smiling than do German mothers, and Nso mothers are especially quick to anticipate and quiet infant distress through soothing and breastfeeding. Chinese, Japanese, and Nso babies, in turn, smile, laugh, and cry less than their Western agemates (Friedlmeier, Corapci, & Cole, 2011; Gartstein et al., 2010; Kärtner, Holodynski, & Wörmann, 2013).

Toward the end of the second year, a vocabulary for talking about feelings—"happy," "love," "surprised," "scary," "yucky," "mad"—develops rapidly, but toddlers are not yet good at using language to manage their emotions. Temper tantrums tend to occur because toddlers cannot control the intense anger that often arises when an adult rejects their demands, particularly when they are fatigued or hungry (Mascolo & Fischer, 2007). Toddlers whose parents are emotionally sympathetic but set limits (by not giving in to tantrums), who distract the child by offering acceptable alternatives, and who later suggest better ways to handle adult refusals display more effective anger-regulation strategies and social skills during the preschool years (LeCuyer & Houck, 2006).

Patient, sensitive parents also encourage toddlers to describe their internal states. Then, when 2-year-olds feel distressed, they can guide caregivers in helping them (Cole, Armstrong, & Pemberton, 2010). For example, while listening to a story about monsters, Grace whimpered, "Mommy, scary." Monica put the book down and gave Grace a comforting hug.

Ask yourself

CONNECT Why do children of depressed parents have difficulty regulating emotion (see page 187)? What implications do their weak self-regulatory skills have for their response to cognitive and social challenges?

APPLY At age 14 months, Reggie built a block tower and gleefully knocked it down. At age 2, he called to his mother and pointed proudly to his tall block tower. What explains this change in Reggie's emotional behavior?

REFLECT Describe several recent instances illustrating how you typically manage negative emotion. How might your early experiences, gender, and cultural background have influenced your style of emotional self-regulation?

Temperament and Development

6.4 What is temperament, and how is it measured?

6.5 Discuss the roles of heredity and environment in the stability of temperament, including the goodness-of-fit model.

From early infancy, Caitlin's sociability was unmistakable. She smiled and laughed while interacting with adults and, in her second year, readily approached other children. Meanwhile, Monica marveled at Grace's calm, relaxed disposition. At 19 months, she sat contentedly in a highchair through a two-hour family celebration at a restaurant. In contrast, Timmy was active and distractible. Vanessa found herself chasing him as he dropped one toy, moved on to the next, and climbed on chairs and tables.

When we describe one person as cheerful and "upbeat," another as active and energetic, and still others as calm, cautious, or prone to angry outbursts, we are referring to **temperament**—early-appearing, stable individual differences in reactivity and self-regulation. *Reactivity* refers to quickness and intensity of emotional arousal, attention, and motor activity. *Self-regulation,* as we have seen, refers to strategies that modify that reactivity (Rothbart, 2011; Rothbart & Bates, 2006). The psychological traits that make up temperament are believed to form the cornerstone of the adult personality.

In 1956, Alexander Thomas and Stella Chess initiated the New York Longitudinal Study, a groundbreaking investigation of the development of temperament that followed 141 children from early infancy well into adulthood. Results showed that temperament can increase a child's chances of experiencing psychological problems or, alternatively, protect a child from the negative effects of a highly stressful home life. At the same time, Thomas and Chess (1977) discovered that parenting practices can modify children's temperaments considerably.

These findings stimulated a growing body of research on temperament, including its stability, biological roots, and interaction with child-rearing experiences. Let's begin to explore these issues by looking at the structure, or makeup, of temperament and how it is measured.

The Structure of Temperament

Thomas and Chess's model of temperament inspired all others that followed. When detailed descriptions of infants' and children's behavior obtained from parent interviews were rated on nine dimensions of temperament, certain characteristics clustered together, yielding three types of children:

- The **easy child** (40 percent of the sample) quickly establishes regular routines in infancy, is generally cheerful, and adapts easily to new experiences.
- The **difficult child** (10 percent of the sample) is irregular in daily routines, is slow to accept new experiences, and tends to react negatively and intensely.
- The **slow-to-warm-up child** (15 percent of the sample) is inactive, shows mild, low-key reactions to environmental stimuli, is negative in mood, and adjusts slowly to new experiences.

Note that 35 percent of the children did not fit any of these categories. Instead, they showed unique blends of temperamental characteristics.

The difficult pattern has sparked the most interest because it places children at high risk for adjustment problems—both anxious withdrawal and aggressive behavior in early and middle childhood (Bates, Wachs, & Emde, 1994; Ramos et al., 2005). Nevertheless, the difficult label has been criticized because judgments of child difficulty vary widely across caregivers and cultures. Compared with difficult children, slow-to-warm-up children present fewer problems in the early years. However, they tend to show excessive fearfulness and slow, constricted behavior in the late preschool and school years, when they are expected to respond actively and quickly in classrooms and peer groups (Chess & Thomas, 1984; Schmitz et al., 1999).

Today, the most influential model of temperament is Mary Rothbart's, described in Table 6.1. It combines related traits proposed by Thomas and Chess and other researchers, yielding a concise list of just six dimensions. For example, distractibility and persistence are considered opposite ends of the same dimension, which is labeled "attention span/persistence." A unique feature of Rothbart's model is inclusion of both "fearful distress" and "irritable distress," which distinguish between reactivity triggered by fear and reactivity due to frustration. And the model deletes overly broad dimensions such as regularity of body

CHAPTER 6 Emotional and Social Development in Infancy and Toddlerhood

TABLE 6.1
Rothbart's Model of Temperament

DIMENSION	DESCRIPTION
REACTIVITY	
Activity level	Level of gross-motor activity
Attention span/persistence	Duration of orienting or interest
Fearful distress	Wariness and distress in response to intense or novel stimuli, including time to adjust to new situations
Irritable distress	Extent of fussing, crying, and distress when desires are frustrated
Positive affect	Frequency of expression of happiness and pleasure
SELF-REGULATION	
Effortful control	Capacity to voluntarily suppress a dominant, reactive response in order to plan and execute a more adaptive response
	In the first two years, called *orienting/regulation*, which refers to the capacity to engage in self-soothing, shift attention from unpleasant events, and sustain interest for an extended time

functions and intensity of reaction (Rothbart, 2011; Rothbart, Ahadi, & Evans, 2000). A child who is regular in sleeping is not necessarily regular in eating or bowel habits. And a child who smiles and laughs intensely is not necessarily intense in fear, irritability, or motor activity.

Rothbart's dimensions represent the three underlying components included in the definition of temperament: (1) *emotion* ("fearful distress," "irritable distress," "positive affect"), (2) *attention* ("attention span/persistence"), and (3) *action* ("activity level"). Individuals differ not just in their reactivity on each dimension but also in the self-regulatory dimension of temperament, **effortful control**—the capacity to voluntarily suppress a dominant response in order to plan and execute a more adaptive response (Rothbart, 2003; Rothbart & Bates, 2006). Variations in effortful control are evident in how effectively a child can focus and shift attention, inhibit impulses, and manage negative emotion.

The capacity for effortful control in early childhood predicts favorable development and adjustment in cultures as diverse as China and the United States, with some studies showing long-term effects into adolescence and adulthood (Chen & Schmidt, 2015). Positive outcomes include persistence, task mastery, academic achievement, cooperation, moral maturity (such as concern about wrongdoing and willingness to apologize), and social behaviors of cooperation, sharing, and helpfulness (Eisenberg, 2010; Kochanska & Aksan, 2006; Posner & Rothbart, 2007;

Valiente, Lemery-Chalfant, & Swanson, 2010). Effortful control is also associated with children's resistance to stress (David & Murphy, 2007). Children high in effortful control are better able to shift attention away from disturbing events and their own anxiety to more positive features of their social environments.

Turn back to page 161 in Chapter 5 to review the concept of executive function, and note its resemblance to effortful control. These converging concepts, which are associated with similar positive outcomes, reveal that the same mental activities lead to effective regulation in both the cognitive and emotional/social domains.

Measuring Temperament

Temperament is often assessed through interviews or questionnaires given to parents. Behavior ratings by pediatricians, teachers, and others familiar with the child and laboratory observations by researchers have also been used. Parental reports are convenient and take advantage of parents' depth of knowledge about their child across many situations (Chen & Schmidt, 2015). Although information from parents has been criticized as being biased, parental reports are moderately related to researchers' observations of children's behavior (Majdandžić & van den Boom, 2007; Mangelsdorf, Schoppe, & Buur, 2000). And parent perceptions are useful for understanding how parents view and respond to their child.

Observations by researchers in the home or laboratory avoid the subjectivity of parental reports but can lead to other inaccuracies. In homes, observers find it hard to capture rare but important events, such as infants' response to frustration. And in the unfamiliar lab setting, fearful children who calmly avoid certain experiences at home may become too upset to complete the session (Rothbart, 2011). Still, researchers can better control children's experiences in the lab. And they can conveniently combine observations of behavior with neurobiological measures to gain insight into the biological bases of temperament.

Most neurobiological research has focused on children who fall at opposite extremes of the positive-affect and fearful-distress dimensions of temperament: **inhibited, or shy, children,** who react negatively to and withdraw from novel stimuli, and **uninhibited, or sociable, children,** who display positive emotion to and approach novel stimuli. As the Biology and Environment box on page 192 reveals, biologically based reactivity—evident in heart rate, hormone levels, and measures of brain activity—differentiates children with inhibited and uninhibited temperaments.

Stability of Temperament

Young children who score low or high on attention span, irritability, sociability, shyness, or effortful control tend to respond similarly when assessed again several months to a few years later and, occasionally, even into the adult years (Casalin et al., 2012; Caspi et al., 2003; Kochanska & Knaack, 2003; Majdandžić &

Biology and Environment

Development of Shyness and Sociability

Two 4-month-old babies, Larry and Mitch, visited the laboratory of Jerome Kagan, who observed their reactions to a variety of unfamiliar experiences. When exposed to new sights and sounds, such as a moving mobile decorated with colorful toys, Larry tensed his muscles, moved his arms and legs with agitation, and began to cry. In contrast, Mitch remained relaxed and quiet, smiling and cooing.

As toddlers, Larry and Mitch returned to the laboratory, where they experienced several procedures designed to induce uncertainty. Electrodes were placed on their bodies and blood pressure cuffs on their arms to measure heart rate; toy robots, animals, and puppets moved before their eyes; and unfamiliar people behaved in unexpected ways or wore novel costumes. While Larry whimpered and quickly withdrew, Mitch watched with interest, laughed, and approached the toys and strangers.

On a third visit, at age 4½, Larry barely talked or smiled during an interview with an unfamiliar adult. In contrast, Mitch asked questions and communicated his pleasure at each new activity. In a playroom with two unfamiliar peers, Larry pulled back and watched, while Mitch made friends quickly.

In longitudinal research on several hundred European-American infants followed into adolescence, Kagan found that about 20 percent of 4-month-olds were, like Larry, easily upset by novelty; another 40 percent, like Mitch, were comfortable, even delighted, with new experiences. About 20 to 25 percent of these extreme groups retained their temperamental styles as they grew older (Kagan, 2003, 2013d; Kagan et al., 2007). But most children's dispositions became less extreme over time. Genetic makeup and child-rearing experiences jointly influenced stability and change in temperament.

Neurobiological Correlates of Shyness and Sociability

Individual differences in arousal of the *amygdala,* an inner brain structure devoted to processing novelty and emotional information, contribute to these contrasting temperaments. In shy, inhibited children, novel stimuli easily excite the amygdala and its connections to the prefrontal cortex and the sympathetic nervous system, which prepares the body to act in the face of threat. In sociable, uninhibited children, the same level of stimulation evokes minimal neural excitation (Schwartz et al., 2012). And additional neurobiological responses known to be mediated by the amygdala distinguish these two emotional styles:

- *Heart rate.* From the first few weeks of life, the heart rates of shy children are consistently higher than those of sociable children, and they speed up further in response to unfamiliar events (Schmidt et al., 2007; Snidman et al., 1995).
- *Cortisol.* Saliva concentrations of the stress hormone cortisol tend to be higher, and to rise more in response to a stressful event, in shy than in sociable children (Schmidt et al., 1999; Zimmermann & Stansbury, 2004).
- *Pupil dilation, blood pressure, and skin surface temperature.* Compared with sociable children, shy children show greater pupil dilation, rise in blood pressure, and cooling of the fingertips when faced with novelty (Kagan et al., 2007).

Furthermore, shy infants and preschoolers show greater EEG activity in the right than in the left frontal lobe of the cerebral cortex, which is associated with negative emotional reactivity; sociable children show the opposite pattern (Fox et al., 2008). Neural activity in the amygdala, which is transmitted to the frontal lobes, probably contributes to these differences.

Child-Rearing Practices

According to Kagan, most extremely shy or sociable children inherit a physiology that biases them toward a particular temperamental style (Kagan, 2013d). Yet heritability research indicates that genes contribute only modestly to shyness and sociability.

Child-rearing practices affect the chances that an emotionally reactive baby will become

A strong physiological response to uncertain situations prompts this toddler to cling to her father. With patient but insistent encouragement, her parents can help her overcome the urge to retreat.

a fearful child. Warm, supportive parenting reduces shy infants' and preschoolers' intense physiological reactivity to novelty, whereas cold, intrusive parenting heightens anxiety (Coplan & Arbeau, 2008; Davis & Buss, 2012). And if parents overprotect infants and young children who dislike novelty, they make it harder for the child to overcome an urge to retreat. Parents who make appropriate demands for their child to approach new experiences help shy youngsters develop strategies for regulating fear (Rubin & Burgess, 2002).

When inhibition persists, it leads to excessive cautiousness, low self-esteem, and loneliness. In adolescence, persistent shyness increases the risk of severe anxiety, depression, and other internalizing problems, including unrealistic worries about harm, illness, and criticism for mistakes as well as social phobia—intense fear of being humiliated in social situations (Kagan, 2013d; Karevold et al., 2012). For inhibited children to acquire effective social skills, parenting must be tailored to their temperaments—a theme we will encounter again in this and later chapters.

van den Boom, 2007; van den Akker et al., 2010). However, the overall stability of temperament is low in infancy and toddlerhood and only moderate from the preschool years on (Putnam, Sanson, & Rothbart, 2000).

Why isn't temperament more stable? A major reason is that temperament itself develops with age. To illustrate, let's look at irritability and activity level. Recall from Chapter 3 that the early months are a period of fussing and crying for most babies. As infants better regulate their attention and emotions, many who initially seemed irritable become calm and content. With respect to activity level, the meaning of the behavior changes. At first, an active, wriggling infant tends to be highly aroused and uncomfortable, whereas an inactive baby is often alert and attentive. Once infants move on their own, the reverse is so! An active crawler is usually alert and interested in exploration, whereas an inactive baby may be fearful and withdrawn.

These discrepancies help us understand why long-term prediction from early temperament is best achieved after age 3, when children's styles of responding are better established (Roberts & DelVecchio, 2000). In line with this idea, between age 2½ and 3, children improve substantially and also perform more consistently across a wide range of tasks requiring effortful control, such as waiting for a reward, lowering their voice to a whisper, succeeding at games like "Simon Says," and selectively attending to one stimulus while ignoring competing stimuli (Kochanska, Murray, & Harlan, 2000; Li-Grining, 2007). Researchers believe that around this time, areas in the prefrontal cortex involved in suppressing impulses develop rapidly (Rothbart, 2011).

Nevertheless, the ease with which children manage their reactivity in early childhood depends on the type and strength of the reactive emotion involved. Compared to angry, irritable toddlers, fearful toddlers generally show greater improvement in effortful control by the preschool years (Bridgett et al., 2009; Kochanska & Knaack, 2003). Child rearing is also important in modifying reactivity. Young children with either fearful or irritable temperaments who experience patient, supportive parenting gain most in capacity to manage their emotions (Kim & Kochanska, 2012; Warren & Simmens, 2005). But if exposed to insensitive or unresponsive parenting, these emotionally negative children are especially likely to score low in effortful control, placing them at high risk for adjustment problems.

In sum, many factors affect the extent to which a child's temperament remains stable, including development of the biological systems on which temperament is based, the child's capacity for effortful control, and the success of her efforts, which depend on the quality and intensity of her emotional reactivity. When we consider the evidence as a whole, the low to moderate stability of temperament makes sense. It also confirms that child rearing can modify biologically based temperamental traits considerably and that children with certain traits, such as negative emotionality, are especially susceptible to the influence of parenting—a finding we will return to shortly. With these ideas in mind, let's turn to genetic and environmental contributions to temperament and personality.

Genetic and Environmental Influences

The word *temperament* implies a genetic foundation for individual differences in personality. Identical twins are more similar than fraternal twins across a wide range of temperamental and personality traits (Caspi & Shiner, 2006; Krueger & Johnson, 2008; Roisman & Fraley, 2006). In Chapter 2, we noted that heritability estimates derived from twin studies suggest a moderate role for genetic factors in temperament and personality: About half of individual differences have been attributed to differences in genetic makeup.

Although genetic influences on temperament are clear, environment is also powerful. Recall from Chapter 4 that children exposed to severe malnutrition in infancy remain more distractible and fearful than their agemates, even after dietary improvement. And infants reared in deprived orphanages are easily overwhelmed by stressful events. Their poor regulation of emotion results in inattention and weak impulse control, including frequent expressions of anger (see page 123).

Furthermore, heredity and environment often jointly contribute to temperament, since a child's approach to the world can be intensified or lessened by experience. To illustrate, let's begin by looking at ethnic and gender differences.

Ethnic and Gender Differences.
Compared with European-American infants, Chinese and Japanese babies tend to be less active, irritable, vocal, more easily soothed when upset, and better at quieting themselves (Kagan, 2013d; Lewis, Ramsay, & Kawakami, 1993). East Asian babies are also more attentive and less distractible, and as 2-year-olds, they are more compliant and cooperative with adults and higher in effortful control—for example, able to wait longer to play with an attractive toy (Chen et al., 2003; Gartstein et al., 2006). At the same time, Chinese and Japanese babies are more fearful, remaining closer to their mothers in an unfamiliar playroom and displaying more anxiety when interacting with a stranger (Chen, Wang, & DeSouza, 2006).

These variations may have genetic roots, but they are supported by cultural beliefs and practices, yielding *gene–environment correlations* (see pages 68–69 in Chapter 2). Japanese mothers usually say that babies come into the world as independent beings who must learn to rely on their parents through close physical contact. European-American mothers, in contrast, typically believe that they must wean the baby away from dependency toward autonomy. Consistent with these beliefs, Asian mothers interact gently, soothingly, and gesturally with their babies, whereas European-American mothers use a more active, stimulating, verbal approach (Kagan, 2010). Also, recall from our discussion of emotional self-regulation that Chinese and Japanese adults discourage babies from expressing strong emotion, which contributes further to their infants' tranquility.

Similarly, gender differences in temperament are evident as early as infancy, suggesting a genetic foundation. Boys tend to be more active and daring, less fearful, more irritable when frustrated, more likely to express high-intensity pleasure in play, and more impulsive than girls—factors that contribute to boys' higher injury rates throughout childhood and adolescence. And girls' large advantage in effortful control undoubtedly contributes to their greater compliance and cooperativeness, better school performance, and lower incidence of behavior problems (Else-Quest, 2012; Olino et al., 2013). At the same time, parents more often encourage their young sons to be physically active and their daughters to seek help and physical closeness—through activities they encourage and through more positive reactions when their child exhibits temperamental traits consistent with gender stereotypes (Bryan & Dix, 2009; Hines, 2015). Perhaps for this reason, gender differences in some temperamental traits widen by adolescence.

Differential Susceptibility to Rearing Experiences.
Earlier we mentioned findings indicating that emotionally reactive toddlers function worse than other children when exposed to inept parenting, yet benefit most from good parenting. Researchers have become increasingly interested in temperamental differences in children's susceptibility (or responsiveness) to environmental influences (Pluess & Belsky, 2011). Using molecular genetic analyses, they are clarifying how these *gene–environment interactions* operate.

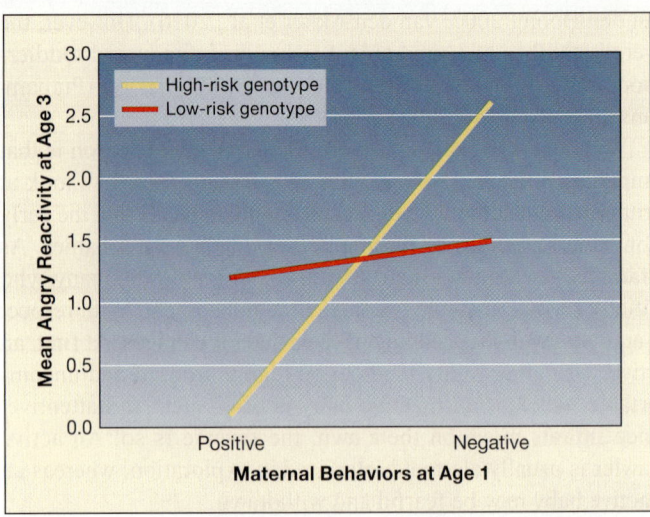

FIGURE 6.1 **Angry reactivity at age 3 in response to positive and negative maternal behaviors for children with and without the short 5-HTTLPR genotype.** Children with a high-risk genotype (with the genetic marker) were highly susceptible to parenting quality—both good and bad. They displayed little anger when exposed to maternal affection and encouragement but high anger to maternal insensitivity and hostility. Children with a low-risk genotype (without the genetic marker) responded little to quality of maternal behavior. (Adapted from P. T. Davies and D. Cicchetti, 2014, "How and Why Does the 5-HTTLPR Gene Moderate Associations Between Maternal Unresponsiveness and Children's Disruptive Problems?" *Child Development, 85*, p. 494. Adapted by permission of John Wiley & Sons.)

How will this mother respond to her daughter's anger and distress? With patience and support, emotionally reactive toddlers develop especially favorably. But when exposed to hostile, rejecting parenting, they fare worse than other children, quickly becoming aggressive and defiant.

Consistently, young children with a chromosome 7 gene containing a certain repetition of base pairs called short 5-HTTLPR—which interferes with functioning of the inhibitory neurotransmitter serotonin and, thus, greatly increases the risk of self-regulation difficulties—display high susceptibility to effects of parenting quality. Those exposed to maladaptive parenting readily develop externalizing problems. But when parenting is kind and supportive, children with the genetic marker fare exceedingly well in adjustment (Kochanska et al., 2011; van IJzendoorn, Belsky, & Bakermans-Kranenburg, 2012). Among children without the 5-HTTLPR genotype, parenting—whether positive or negative—has minimal impact on externalizing symptoms.

Findings from a two-year follow-up of 1-year-olds from poverty-stricken families provide an impressive illustration (see Figure 6.1) (Davies & Cicchetti, 2014). Toddlers with the high-risk 5-HTTLPR genotype subjected to inept parenting became increasingly reactive emotionally to their mother's hostile, rejecting behavior, responding with distress, anger, and uncontrolled screaming. Their negative emotionality, in turn, predicted a sharp rise in aggression and defiance by age 3. In contrast, high-risk toddlers of affectionate, encouraging mothers displayed effective emotion regulation and far less anger and aggression than children with a low-risk genotype! Low-risk children barely reacted to variation in parenting quality.

As these outcomes reveal, young children with the short 5-HTTLPR genetic marker show unusually high early *plasticity* (see page 9 in Chapter 1 to review). Their emotion regulation is particularly susceptible to the effects of both good and poor parenting. Because children with this "susceptibility attribute" fare better than other children when parenting is supportive, they are likely to benefit most from interventions aimed at reducing parental stress and promoting responsive child rearing.

Siblings' Unique Experiences. In families with several children, an additional influence on temperament is at work: When parents are asked to describe each of their children's personalities, they often look for differences between siblings: "She's a lot more active," "He's more sociable," "She's far more persistent." As a result, parents often regard siblings as more distinct than other observers do.

In a large study of 1- to 3-year-old twin pairs, parents rated identical twins as less alike in temperament than researchers' ratings indicated. And whereas researchers rated fraternal twins as moderately similar, parents viewed them as somewhat opposite in temperament (Saudino, 2003). This tendency to emphasize each child's unique qualities affects parenting practices. Each child, in turn, evokes responses from caregivers that are consistent with parental beliefs and the child's developing temperament.

Besides different experiences within the family, siblings have distinct experiences with teachers, peers, and others in their community that affect personality development. And as we will see in Chapter 9, in middle childhood and adolescence, siblings often seek ways to differ from one another. For all these reasons, both identical and fraternal twins tend to become increasingly dissimilar in personality with age (Loehlin & Martin, 2001). In sum, temperament and personality can be understood only in terms of complex interdependencies between genetic and environmental factors.

Temperament and Child Rearing: The Goodness-of-Fit Model

Thomas and Chess (1977) proposed a **goodness-of-fit model** to explain how temperament and environment can together produce favorable outcomes. Goodness of fit involves creating child-rearing environments that recognize each child's temperament while simultaneously encouraging more adaptive functioning. If a child's disposition interferes with learning or getting along with others, adults must gently but consistently counteract the child's maladaptive style.

Difficult children (who withdraw from new experiences and react negatively and intensely) frequently experience parenting that fits poorly with their dispositions. As infants, they are less likely to receive sensitive caregiving. By the second year, their parents tend to resort to angry, punitive discipline, which undermines the development of effortful control. As the child reacts with defiance and disobedience, parents become increasingly stressed. As a result, they continue their coercive tactics and also discipline inconsistently, at times rewarding the child's noncompliance by giving in to it (Lee et al., 2012; Paulussen-Hoogeboom et al., 2007; Pesonen et al., 2008). These practices sustain and even increase the child's irritable, conflict-ridden style.

In contrast, when parents are positive and sensitive, which helps infants and toddlers—especially those who are emotionally reactive—regulate emotion, difficultness declines by age 2 or 3 (Raikes et al., 2007). In toddlerhood and childhood, parental sensitivity, support, clear expectations, and limits foster effortful control, also reducing the likelihood that difficultness will persist and lead to emotional and social difficulties (Cipriano & Stifter, 2010; Raikes et al., 2007).

Cultural values also affect the fit between parenting and child temperament, as research in China illustrates. In the past, high valuing of social harmony, which discourages self-assertion, led Chinese adults to evaluate shy children positively. But rapid expansion of a market economy, which requires assertiveness and sociability for success, may be responsible for a change in Chinese parents' and teachers' attitudes toward childhood shyness (Chen, Wang, & DeSouza, 2006; Yu, 2002). Whereas shyness was positively correlated with teacher-rated competence, peer acceptance, leadership, and academic achievement in 1990, these relationships weakened in 1998 and reversed in 2002, when they mirrored findings of Western research (Chen et al., 2005). But positive valuing of shyness persists in rural areas of China, where shy children continue to enjoy high social status and are well-adjusted (Chen, Wang, & Cao, 2011). Cultural context makes a difference in whether shy children fare well or poorly.

An effective match between rearing conditions and child temperament is best accomplished early, before unfavorable temperament–environment relationships produce maladjustment. The goodness-of-fit model reminds us that children have unique dispositions that adults must accept. Parents can neither take full credit for their children's virtues nor be blamed for all their faults. But parents can turn an environment that exaggerates a child's problems into one that builds on the child's strengths. As we will see next, goodness of fit is also at the heart of infant–caregiver attachment. This first intimate relationship grows out of interaction between parent and baby, to which the emotional styles of both partners contribute.

Ask yourself

CONNECT Explain how findings on ethnic and gender differences in temperament illustrate gene–environment correlation, discussed on pages 68–69 in Chapter 2.

APPLY Mandy and Jeff are parents of 2-year-old inhibited Sam and 3-year-old difficult Maria. Explain the importance of effortful control to Mandy and Jeff, and suggest ways they can strengthen it in each of their children.

REFLECT How would you describe your temperament as a young child? Do you think your temperament has remained stable, or has it changed? What factors might be involved?

Development of Attachment

6.6 Describe the development of attachment during the first two years.

6.7 How do researchers measure attachment security, what factors affect it, and what are its implications for later development?

6.8 Describe infants' capacity for multiple attachments.

Attachment is the strong affectionate tie we have with special people in our lives that leads us to feel pleasure when we interact with them and to be comforted by their nearness in times of stress. By the second half-year, infants have become attached to familiar people who have responded to their needs. Consider how babies of this age single out their parents for special attention: When the parent enters the room, the baby breaks into a broad, friendly smile. When she picks him up, he pats her face, explores her hair, and snuggles against her. When he feels anxious or afraid, he crawls into her lap and clings closely.

Freud first suggested that the infant's emotional tie to the mother is the foundation for all later relationships. Contemporary research indicates that—although the parent–infant bond is vitally important—later development is influenced not just by early attachment experiences but also by the continuing quality of the parent–child relationship.

Baby monkeys reared with "surrogate mothers" preferred to cling to a soft terry-cloth "mother" over a wire-mesh "mother" holding a bottle—evidence that parent–infant attachment is based on more than satisfaction of hunger.

Attachment has also been the subject of intense theoretical debate. Recall that the *psychoanalytic perspective* regards feeding as the central context in which caregivers and babies build this close emotional bond. *Behaviorism,* too, emphasizes the importance of feeding, but for different reasons. According to a well-known behaviorist explanation, infants learn to prefer the mother's soft caresses, warm smiles, and tender words because these events are paired with tension relief as she satisfies the baby's hunger.

Although feeding is an important context for building a close relationship, attachment does not depend on hunger satisfaction. In the 1950s, a famous experiment showed that rhesus monkeys reared with terry-cloth and wire-mesh "surrogate mothers" clung to the soft terry-cloth substitute, even though the wire-mesh "mother" held the bottle and infants had to climb onto it to be fed (Harlow & Zimmerman, 1959). Human infants, too, become attached to family members who seldom feed them, including fathers, siblings, and grandparents. And toddlers in Western cultures who sleep alone and experience frequent daytime separations from their parents sometimes develop strong emotional ties to cuddly objects, such as blankets and teddy bears, that play no role in infant feeding!

Bowlby's Ethological Theory

Today, **ethological theory of attachment,** which recognizes the infant's emotional tie to the caregiver as an evolved response that promotes survival, is the most widely accepted view. John Bowlby (1969), who first applied this perspective to the infant–caregiver bond, retained the psychoanalytic idea that quality of attachment to the caregiver has profound implications for the child's feelings of security and capacity to form trusting relationships.

At the same time, Bowlby was inspired by Konrad Lorenz's studies of imprinting (see Chapter 1). Bowlby believed that the human infant, like the young of other animal species, is endowed with a set of built-in behaviors that help keep the parent nearby to protect the infant from danger and to provide support for exploring and mastering the environment. Contact with the parent also ensures that the baby will be fed, but Bowlby pointed out that feeding is not the basis for attachment. Rather, attachment can best be understood in an evolutionary context in which survival of the species—through ensuring both safety and competence—is of utmost importance.

According to Bowlby, the infant's relationship with the parent begins as a set of innate signals that call the adult to the baby's side. Over time, a true affectionate bond forms, supported by new cognitive and emotional capacities as well as by a history of warm, sensitive care. Attachment develops in four phases:

1. *Preattachment phase (birth to 6 weeks).* Built-in signals—grasping, smiling, crying, and gazing into the adult's eyes—help bring newborn babies into close contact with other humans, who comfort them. Newborns prefer their own mother's smell, voice, and face (see Chapters 3 and 4). But

they are not yet attached to her, since they do not mind being left with an unfamiliar adult.

2. *"Attachment-in-the-making" phase (6 weeks to 6–8 months).* During this phase, infants respond differently to a familiar caregiver than to a stranger. For example, at 4 months, Timmy smiled, laughed, and babbled more freely when interacting with his mother and quieted more quickly when she picked him up. As infants learn that their own actions affect the behavior of those around them, they begin to develop a *sense of trust*—the expectation that the caregiver will respond when signaled—but they still do not protest when separated from her.

3. *"Clear-cut" attachment phase (6–8 months to 18 months– 2 years).* Now attachment to the familiar caregiver is evident. Babies display **separation anxiety,** becoming upset when their trusted caregiver leaves. Like stranger anxiety (see page 186), separation anxiety does not always occur; it depends on infant temperament and the current situation. But in many cultures, separation anxiety increases between 6 and 15 months. Besides protesting the parent's departure, older infants and toddlers try hard to maintain her presence. They approach, follow, and climb on her in preference to others. And they use the familiar caregiver as a secure base from which to explore.

4. *Formation of a reciprocal relationship (18 months to 2 years and on).* By the end of the second year, rapid growth in representation and language enables toddlers to understand some of the factors that influence the parent's coming and going and to predict her return. As a result, separation protest declines. Now children negotiate with the caregiver, using requests and persuasion to alter her goals. For example, at age 2, Caitlin asked Carolyn and David to read her a story before leaving her with a babysitter. The extra time with her parents, along with a better understanding of where they were going ("to have dinner with Uncle Sean") and when they would be back ("right after you go to sleep"), helped Caitlin withstand her parents' absence.

According to Bowlby (1980), out of their experiences during these four phases, children construct an enduring affectionate tie to the caregiver that they can use as a secure base in the parents' absence. This image serves as an **internal working model,** or set of expectations about the availability of attachment figures and their likelihood of providing support during times of stress. The internal working model becomes a vital part of personality, serving as a guide for all future close relationships (Bretherton & Munholland, 2008).

Consistent with these ideas, as early as the second year, toddlers seem to form attachment-related expectations about parental comfort and support. In one study, securely attached 12- to 16-month-olds looked longer at a video of an unresponsive caregiver (inconsistent with their expectations) than a video of a responsive caregiver. Insecurely attached agemates, in contrast, either looked longer at the responsive caregiver or did not distinguish between the two (Johnson, Dweck, & Chen, 2007; Johnson

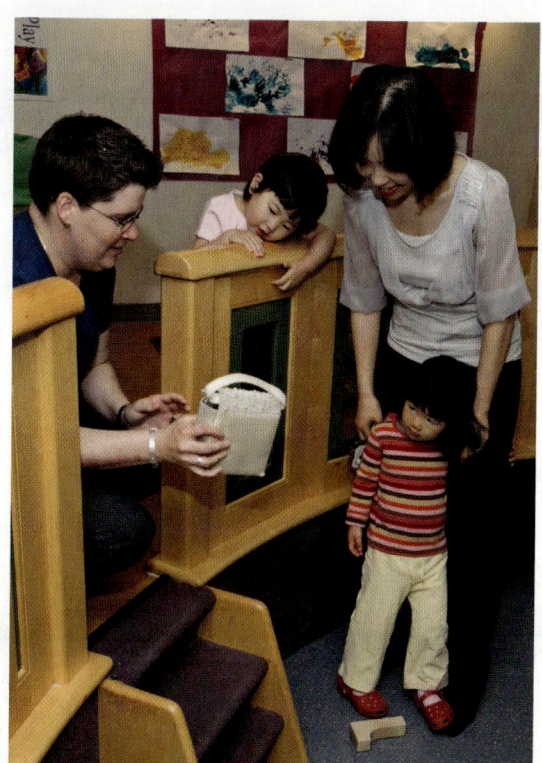

With her teacher's enticement to play and an explanation that her mother will be back soon, this 2-year-old is likely to separate without tears. Her language and representational skills enable her to predict her mother's return, so separation anxiety declines.

et al., 2010). The researchers concluded that the toddlers' visual responses reflected "surprise" at caregiver behavior at odds with their own internal working model. With age, children continually revise and expand their internal working model as their cognitive, emotional, and social capacities increase and as they interact with parents and form other close bonds with adults, siblings, and friends.

Measuring the Security of Attachment

Although all family-reared babies become attached to a familiar caregiver by the second year, the quality of this relationship varies. Some infants appear relaxed and secure in the presence of the caregiver; they know they can count on her for protection and support. Others seem anxious and uncertain.

A widely used laboratory procedure for assessing the quality of attachment between 1 and 2 years of age is the **Strange Situation.** In designing it, Mary Ainsworth and her colleagues reasoned that securely attached infants and toddlers should use the parent as a secure base from which to explore in an unfamiliar playroom. In addition, when the parent leaves, an unfamiliar adult should be less comforting than the parent. The Strange Situation takes the baby through eight short episodes in which brief separations from and reunions with the parent occur (see Table 6.2 on page 198).

TABLE 6.2
Episodes in the Strange Situation

EPISODE	EVENTS	ATTACHMENT BEHAVIOR OBSERVED
1	Researcher introduces parent and baby to playroom and then leaves.	
2	Parent is seated while baby plays with toys.	Parent as a secure base
3	Stranger enters, is seated, and talks to parent.	Reaction to unfamiliar adult
4	Parent leaves room. Stranger responds to baby and offers comfort if baby is upset.	Separation anxiety
5	Parent returns, greets baby, and offers comfort if necessary. Stranger leaves room.	Reaction to reunion
6	Parent leaves room.	Separation anxiety
7	Stranger enters room and offers comfort.	Ability to be soothed by stranger
8	Parent returns, greets baby, offers comfort if necessary, and tries to reinterest baby in toys.	Reaction to reunion

Note: Episode 1 lasts about 30 seconds; each of the remaining episodes lasts about 3 minutes. Separation episodes are cut short if the baby becomes very upset. Reunion episodes are extended if the baby needs more time to calm down and return to play.
Source: Ainsworth et al., 1978.

Observing infants' responses to these episodes, researchers identified a secure attachment pattern and three patterns of insecurity; a few babies cannot be classified (Ainsworth et al., 1978; Main & Solomon, 1990; Thompson, 2013). Although separation anxiety varies among the groups, the baby's reunion responses define attachment quality. From the description at the beginning of this chapter, which pattern do you think Grace displayed after adjusting to her adoptive family?

- **Secure attachment.** These infants use the parent as a secure base. When separated, they may or may not cry, but if they do, it is because the parent is absent and they prefer her to the stranger. When the parent returns, they convey clear pleasure—some expressing joy from a distance, others asking to be held until settling down to return to play—and crying is reduced immediately. About 60 percent of North American infants in middle-SES families show this pattern. (In low-SES families, a smaller proportion of babies show the secure pattern, with higher proportions falling into the insecure patterns.)

- **Insecure–avoidant attachment.** These infants seem unresponsive to the parent when she is present. When she leaves, they usually are not distressed, and they react to the stranger in much the same way as to the parent. During reunion, they avoid or are slow to greet the parent, and when picked up, they often fail to cling. About 15 percent of North American infants in middle-SES families show this pattern.

- **Insecure–resistant attachment.** Before separation, these infants seek closeness to the parent and often fail to explore. When the parent leaves, they are usually distressed, and on her return they combine clinginess with angry, resistive behavior (struggling when held, hitting and pushing). Many continue to cry after being picked up and cannot be comforted easily. About 10 percent of North American infants in middle-SES families show this pattern.

- **Disorganized/disoriented attachment.** This pattern reflects the greatest insecurity. At reunion, these infants show confused, contradictory behaviors—for example, looking away while the parent is holding them or approaching the parent with flat, depressed emotion. Most display a dazed facial expression, and a few cry out unexpectedly after having calmed down or display odd, frozen postures. About 15 percent of North American infants in middle-SES families show this pattern.

An alternative method, the **Attachment Q-Sort,** suitable for children between 1 and 5 years, depends on home observation (Waters et al., 1995). Either the parent or a highly trained observer sorts 90 behaviors—such as "Child greets mother with a big smile when she enters the room," "If mother moves very far, child follows along," and "Child uses mother's facial expressions as a good source of information when something looks risky or threatening"—into nine categories ranging from "highly descriptive" to "not at all descriptive" of the child. Then a score, ranging from high to low in security, is computed.

Because the Q-Sort taps a wider array of attachment-related behaviors than the Strange Situation, it may better reflect the parent–infant relationship in everyday life. However, the Q-Sort method is time-consuming, requiring a nonparent informant to spend several hours observing the child before sorting the descriptors, and it does not differentiate between types of insecurity. The Q-Sort responses of expert observers correspond well with babies' secure-base behavior in the Strange Situation, but parents' Q-Sorts do not (van IJzendoorn et al., 2004). Parents of insecure children, especially, may have difficulty accurately reporting their child's attachment behaviors.

Stability of Attachment

Research on the stability of attachment patterns between 1 and 2 years of age yields a wide range of findings (Thompson, 2006, 2013). A close look at which babies stay the same and which ones change yields a more consistent picture. Quality of attachment is usually secure and stable for middle-SES babies experiencing favorable life conditions. And infants who move from insecurity to security typically have well-adjusted mothers with positive family and friendship ties. Perhaps many became parents before they were psychologically ready but, with social support, grew into the role.

In contrast, in low-SES families with many daily stresses and little social support, attachment generally moves away from security or changes from one insecure pattern to another (Fish, 2004; Levendosky et al., 2011). And in long-term follow-ups extending from infancy to late adolescence and early adulthood, shifts from security to insecurity were associated with single parenthood, child maltreatment, maternal depression, and poor family functioning and parenting quality (Booth-LaForce et al., 2014; Weinfield, Sroufe, & Egeland, 2000; Weinfield, Whaley, & Egeland, 2004).

These findings indicate that securely attached babies more often maintain their attachment status than insecure babies. The exception is disorganized/disoriented attachment, an insecure pattern that either shows greater stability than the other patterns or consistently predicts insecurity of another type in adolescence and early adulthood (Groh et al., 2014; Hesse & Main, 2000; Weinfield, Whaley, & Egeland, 2004). Furthermore, adults with histories of attachment disorganization are at increased risk of having children who display disorganized/disoriented attachment (Raby et al., 2015). As you will soon see, many disorganized/disoriented infants and children experience extremely negative caregiving, which may disrupt emotional self-regulation so severely that confused, ambivalent feelings often persist, impairing child rearing of the next generation.

Cultural Variations

Cross-cultural evidence indicates that attachment patterns may have to be interpreted differently in certain cultures. For example, as Figure 6.2 reveals, German infants show considerably more avoidant attachment than American babies do. But German parents value independence and encourage their infants to be non-clingy (Grossmann et al., 1985). In contrast, a study of infants of the Dogon people of Mali, Africa, revealed that none showed avoidant attachment to their mothers (True, Pisani, & Oumar, 2001). Even when grandmothers are primary caregivers (as they are with firstborn sons), Dogon mothers remain available to their babies, holding them close and nursing them promptly in response to hunger and distress.

Japanese infants, as well, rarely show avoidant attachment (refer again to Figure 6.2). Rather, many are resistantly attached, but this reaction may not represent true insecurity. Japanese mothers rarely leave their babies in others' care, so the Strange Situation probably induces greater stress in them than in babies who frequently experience maternal separations (Takahashi, 1990). Also, Japanese parents view the attention seeking that is part of resistant attachment as a normal indicator of infants' efforts to satisfy dependency and security needs (Rothbaum, Morelli, & Rusk, 2011). Despite these and other cultural variations, the secure pattern is still the most common attachment quality in all societies studied (van IJzendoorn & Sagi-Schwartz, 2008).

Factors That Affect Attachment Security

What factors might influence attachment security? Researchers have looked closely at four important influences: (1) early availability of a consistent caregiver, (2) quality of caregiving, (3) the baby's characteristics, and (4) family context, including parents' internal working models.

Early Availability of a Consistent Caregiver.
What happens when a baby does not have the opportunity to establish a close tie to a caregiver? To find out, researchers followed the development of infants in an institution with a good caregiver–child ratio and a rich selection of books and toys. However, staff turnover was so rapid that the average child had 50 caregivers by age 4½. Many of these children became "late adoptees" who were placed in homes after age 4. Most developed deep ties with their adoptive parents, indicating that a first attachment can develop as late as 4 to 6 years of age (Hodges & Tizard, 1989; Tizard & Rees, 1975). But these children were more likely to display attachment difficulties, including an excessive desire for adult attention, "overfriendliness" to unfamiliar adults and peers, failure to check back with the parent in anxiety-arousing situations, and few friendships.

Children who spent their first year or more in deprived Eastern European orphanages—though also able to bond with their adoptive parents—show greatly elevated rates of attachment insecurity (Lionetti, Pastore, & Barone, 2015; Smyke et al., 2010; van den Dries et al., 2009). And they, too, are at high risk for emotional and social difficulties. Whereas many are indiscriminately friendly, others are sad, anxious, and withdrawn (Bakermans-Kranenburg et al., 2011; O'Connor et al., 2003). These symptoms typically persist and are associated with

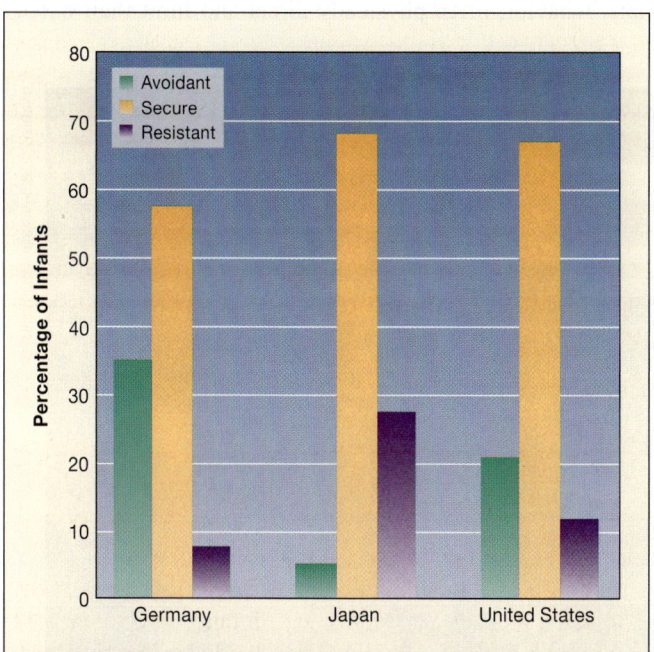

FIGURE 6.2 A cross-cultural comparison of infants' reactions in the Strange Situation. A high percentage of German babies seem avoidantly attached, whereas a substantial number of Japanese infants appear resistantly attached. Note that these responses may not reflect true insecurity. Instead, they are probably due to cultural differences in child-rearing practices. (Based on van IJzendoorn & Kroonenberg, 1988; van IJzendoorn & Sagi-Schwartz, 2008.)

wide-ranging mental health problems in middle childhood and adolescence, including cognitive impairments, inattention and overactivity, depression, and either social avoidance or aggressive behavior (Kreppner et al., 2010; Rutter et al., 2007, 2010).

Furthermore, as early as 7 months, institutionalized children show reduced ERP brain waves in response to facial expressions of emotion and have trouble discriminating such expressions—outcomes that suggest disrupted formation of neural structures involved in "reading" emotions (Parker et al., 2005). Consistent with these findings, in adopted children with longer institutional stays, the volume of the *amygdala* (see page 192) is atypically large (Tottenham et al., 2011). The larger the amygdala, the worse adopted children perform on tasks assessing understanding of emotion and the poorer their emotional self-regulation. Overall, the evidence indicates that fully normal emotional development depends on establishing a close tie with a caregiver early in life.

Quality of Caregiving.
Dozens of studies report that **sensitive caregiving**—responding promptly, consistently, and appropriately to infants and holding them tenderly and carefully—is moderately related to attachment security in diverse cultures and SES groups (Belsky & Fearon, 2008; van IJzendoorn et al., 2004). Mothers of securely attached babies also frequently refer to their infants' mental states and motives: "You really *like* that swing." "Do you *remember* Grandma?" This *maternal mind-mindedness*—tendency to treat the baby as a person with inner thoughts and feelings—seems to promote sensitive caregiving (Meins, 2013; Meins et al., 2012). In contrast, insecurely attached infants tend to have mothers who engage in less physical contact, handle them awkwardly or "routinely," and are sometimes resentful and rejecting, particularly in response to infant distress (Ainsworth et al., 1978; McElwain & Booth-LaForce, 2006; Pederson & Moran, 1996).

Also, in studies of Western babies, a special form of communication called **interactional synchrony** separates the experiences of secure from insecure babies. It is best described as a sensitively tuned "emotional dance," in which the caregiver responds to infant signals in a well-timed, rhythmic, appropriate fashion. In addition, both partners match emotional states, especially the positive ones (Bigelow et al., 2010; Isabella & Belsky, 1991). Earlier we saw that sensitive face-to-face play, in which interactional synchrony occurs, increases babies' responsiveness to others' emotional messages and also helps infants regulate emotion.

Cultures, however, vary greatly in their view of sensitivity toward infants. In Western societies that highly value independence, sensitive caregiving follows the baby's lead by being contingently responsive to infant signals, "reading" the baby's mental states, and supporting exploration. In non-Western village communities and Asian cultures, caregiving that keeps the baby physically close, dampens emotional expressiveness, and teaches social appropriateness is deemed sensitive because it advances the child's connectedness to others and promotes social harmony (Morelli, 2015; Otto & Keller, 2014). Among the Gusii people of Kenya, for example, mothers are quick to quiet their infants and satisfy their physical needs, but they rarely interact playfully with them. Yet most Gusii infants are securely attached (LeVine et al., 1994). This suggests that security depends on attentive caregiving, not necessarily on contingent interaction. Puerto Rican mothers, who highly value obedience and socially appropriate behavior, often physically direct and limit their babies'

Left: A father and baby engage in interactional synchrony, matching expressions of positive emotion in face-to-face play—a form of parental sensitivity that predicts attachment security in Western cultures. *Right:* In non-Western village communities and Asian cultures, parental sensitivity directed at physical closeness, calmness, and promptly meeting physical needs is linked to attachment security.

actions—a caregiving style linked to attachment security in Puerto Rican culture (Carlson & Harwood, 2003). Yet in Western cultures, such physical control and restriction of exploration predict insecurity (Whipple, Bernier, & Mageau, 2011).

Compared with securely attached infants, avoidant babies tend to receive overstimulating, intrusive care. Their mothers might, for example, talk energetically to them while they are looking away or falling asleep. By avoiding the mother, these infants appear to be escaping from overwhelming interaction. Resistant infants often experience inconsistent care. Their mothers are unresponsive to infant signals, yet when the baby begins to explore, they interfere, shifting the infant's attention back to themselves. As a result, the baby is overly dependent as well as angry at the mother's lack of involvement (Cassidy & Berlin, 1994).

Highly inadequate caregiving is a powerful predictor of disruptions in attachment. Child abuse and neglect (topics we will consider in Chapter 8) are associated with all three forms of attachment insecurity. Among maltreated infants, disorganized/disoriented attachment is especially common (Cyr et al., 2010). Persistently depressed mothers, mothers with very low marital satisfaction, and parents suffering from a traumatic event, such as serious illness or loss of a loved one, also tend to promote the uncertain behaviors of this pattern (Campbell et al., 2004; Madigan et al., 2006). And some mothers of disorganized/disoriented infants engage in frightening, contradictory, and unpleasant behaviors, such as looking scared, teasing the baby, holding the baby stiffly at a distance, roughly pulling the baby by the arm, or seeking reassurance from the upset child (Hesse & Main, 2006; Solomon & George, 2011).

Infant Characteristics. Because attachment is the result of a *relationship* between two partners, infant characteristics should affect how easily it is established. In Chapter 3 we saw that prematurity, birth complications, and newborn illness make caregiving more taxing. In families under stress, these difficulties are linked to attachment insecurity (Candelaria, Teti, & Black, 2011). But at-risk newborns whose parents have adequate time and patience to care for them fare quite well in attachment security (Brisch et al., 2005).

With respect to temperament, babies who are emotionally reactive are more likely to develop later insecure attachments (van IJzendoorn et al., 2004; Vaughn, Bost, & van IJzendoorn, 2008). And disorganized newborn behavior, evident in NBAS scores (see Chapter 3), increases the risk of disorganized/disoriented attachment (Spangler, Fremmer-Bomik, & Grossmann, 1996).

Again, however, evidence highlighting gene–environment interactions suggests that parental mental health and caregiving are involved. Babies with the short 5-HTTLPR genetic marker, which is associated with emotional reactivity, are more likely than infants with a low-risk genotype to exhibit disorganized/disoriented attachment, but only when caregiving is insensitive (Spangler et al., 2009). In other research, mothers' experience of trauma was associated with attachment disorganization, but only in infants with a chromosome-11 gene having a certain repetition of DNA base pairs, called DRD4 7-repeat, which is linked to impulsive, overactive behavior (van IJzendoorn & Bakermans-Kranenburg, 2006). These babies, who face self-regulation challenges, were more susceptible to the negative impact of maternal adjustment problems.

If children's temperaments alone determined attachment security, we would expect attachment, like temperament, to be at least moderately heritable. Yet the heritability of attachment is virtually nil (Roisman & Fraley, 2008). Rather, babies with certain genotypes are at increased risk for attachment insecurity when they also experience insensitive parenting. In fact, about two-thirds of siblings establish similar attachment patterns with their parent, although siblings often differ in temperament (Cole, 2006). This suggests that most parents try to adjust their caregiving to each child's individual needs.

Interventions that teach parents to interact sensitively with difficult-to-care-for babies enhance both sensitive caregiving and attachment security (van IJzendoorn & Bakermans-Kranenburg, 2015). One program that focused on both maternal sensitivity and effective discipline was particularly successful in reducing irritable distress and disruptive behavior in toddlers with the DRD4 7-repeat (Bakermans-Kranenburg & van IJzendoorn, 2008a, 2008b). These findings suggest that the DRD4 7-repeat—like the short 5-HTTLPR genetic marker—makes children more susceptible to the effects of both negative and positive parenting.

Family Circumstances. Shortly after Timmy's birth, his parents divorced and his father moved to a distant city. Anxious and distracted, Vanessa placed 2-month-old Timmy in Ginette's child-care home and began working 50-hour weeks to make ends meet. On days Vanessa stayed late at the office, a babysitter picked Timmy up, gave him dinner, and put him to bed. Once or twice a week, Vanessa retrieved Timmy from child care. As he neared his first birthday, Vanessa noticed that unlike the other children, who reached out, crawled, or ran to their parents, Timmy ignored her.

Timmy's behavior reflects a repeated finding: Job loss, a failing marriage, financial difficulties, or parental psychological problems (such as anxiety or depression) can undermine attachment indirectly by interfering with parental sensitivity. These stressors can also affect babies' sense of security directly, by altering the emotional climate of the family (for example, exposing them to angry adult interactions) or by disrupting familiar daily routines (Thompson, 2013). (See the Social Issues: Health box on pages 202–203 to find out how child care affects attachment and child adjustment.) By reducing parental stress and improving parent–child communication, social support fosters attachment security (Moss et al., 2005). Ginette's sensitivity toward Timmy was helpful, as was the parenting advice Vanessa received from Ben, a psychologist. As Timmy turned 2, his relationship with his mother seemed warmer.

Social Issues: Health

Does Child Care in Infancy Threaten Attachment Security and Later Adjustment?

Are infants who experience daily separations from their employed parents and early placement in child care at risk for attachment insecurity and development problems? Some researchers think so, but others disagree (Belsky, 2005; O'Brien et al., 2014).

The best current evidence comes from the National Institute of Child Health and Development (NICHD) Study of Early Child Care, the largest longitudinal investigation of the effects of child care to date, which included more than 1,300 infants and their families. It confirmed that use of nonparental care by itself does not affect attachment quality (NICHD Early Child Care Research Network, 2001). Rather, the relationship between child care and emotional well-being depends on both family and child-care experiences.

Family Circumstances

We have seen that family conditions affect children's attachment security and later adjustment. The NICHD Study showed that parenting quality, based on a combination of maternal sensitivity and HOME scores (see page 170 in Chapter 5), exerted a more powerful impact on children's adjustment than did exposure to child care (NICHD Early Childhood Research Network, 1998; Watamura et al., 2011).

For employed parents, balancing work and caregiving can be stressful. Mothers who are fatigued and anxious because they feel overloaded by work and family pressures may respond less sensitively to their babies, thereby risking the infant's security. As paternal involvement in caregiving has risen (see page 204), many more U.S. fathers in dual-earner families also report role overload (Galinsky, Aumann, & Bond, 2009).

Quality and Extent of Child Care

Nevertheless, poor-quality child care may contribute to a higher rate of insecure attachment. In the NICHD Study, when babies were exposed to combined home and child-care risk factors—insensitive caregiving at home along with insensitive caregiving in child care, long hours in child care, or more than one child-care arrangement—the rate of attachment insecurity increased. Overall, mother–child interaction was more favorable when children attended higher-quality child care and also spent fewer hours in child care (NICHD Early Child Care Research Network, 1997, 1999).

Furthermore, when these children reached age 3, a history of higher-quality child care predicted better social skills (NICHD Early Child Care Research Network, 2002b). However, at age 4½ to 5, children averaging more than 30 child-care hours per week displayed externalizing problems, especially defiance, disobedience, and aggression. For those who had been in child-care centers as opposed to family child-care homes, this outcome persisted through elementary school (Belsky et al., 2007b; NICHD Early Child Care Research Network, 2003a, 2006).

But these findings do not necessarily mean that child care causes behavior problems. Rather, heavy exposure to substandard care, which is widespread in the United States, may promote these difficulties, especially when combined with family risk factors. A closer look at the NICHD participants during the preschool years revealed that those in both poor-quality home and child-care environments fared worst in problem behaviors, whereas those in both high-quality home and child-care environments fared best. In between were preschoolers in high-quality child care but poor-quality homes (Watamura et al., 2011). These children benefited from the *protective influence* of high-quality child care.

Evidence from other industrialized nations confirms that full-time child care need not

---

Parents' Internal Working Models. Parents bring to the family context their own history of attachment experiences, from which they construct internal working models that they apply to the bonds they establish with their children. Monica, who recalled her mother as tense and preoccupied, expressed regret that they had not had a closer relationship. Is her image of parenthood likely to affect Grace's attachment security?

To assess parents' internal working models, researchers ask them to evaluate childhood memories of attachment experiences (Main & Goldwyn, 1998). Parents who discuss their childhoods with objectivity and balance, regardless of whether their experiences were positive or negative, tend to behave sensitively and have securely attached children. In contrast, parents who dismiss the importance of early relationships or describe them in angry, confused ways usually have insecurely attached children and are less warm, sensitive, and encouraging of learning and mastery (Behrens, Hesse, & Main, 2007; McFarland-Piazza et al., 2012; Shafer et al., 2015).

But we must not assume any direct transfer of parents' childhood experiences to quality of attachment with their own children. Internal working models are *reconstructed memories* affected by many factors, including relationship experiences over the life course, personality, and current life satisfaction. Longitudinal research reveals that negative life events can weaken the link between an individual's own attachment security in infancy and a secure internal working model in adulthood. And insecurely attached babies who become adults with insecure internal working models often have lives that, based on self-reports in adulthood, are filled with family crises (Waters et al., 2000; Weinfield, Sroufe, & Egeland, 2000).

In sum, our early rearing experiences do not destine us to become either sensitive or insensitive parents (Bretherton & Munholland, 2008). Rather, the way we *view* our childhoods—our ability to come to terms with negative events, to integrate new information into our working models, and to look back on our own parents in an understanding, forgiving way—is far more harm children's development. For example, amount of time spent in child care in Australia and Norway, which offer high-quality, government-subsidized center-based care, is unrelated to children's behavior problems (Love et al., 2003; Zachrisson et al., 2013).

Still, some children may be particularly stressed by long child-care hours. In one study, children who were rated as highly fearful by their caregivers and who attended child-care centers for full days showed a sharp increase in cortisol levels across the child-care day—a pattern that did not occur on days they spent at home (Watamura et al., 2003). Inhibited children may find the constant company of large numbers of peers particularly stressful. A secure attachment to a professional caregiver, however, is protective (Badanes, Dmitrieva, & Watamura, 2012). It is associated with falling cortisol levels across the child-care day.

Conclusions

Taken together, research suggests that some infants may be at risk for attachment insecurity and adjustment problems due to inadequate child care, long hours in such care, and parental role overload. But it is inappropriate to use these findings to justify a reduction in child-care services. When family incomes are limited or mothers who want to work are forced to stay at home, children's emotional security is not promoted.

Instead, it makes sense to increase the availability of high-quality child care and to provide parents with paid employment leave (see page 103 in Chapter 3) and opportunities for part-time work. In the NICHD Study, part-time (as opposed to full-time) employment during the baby's first year was associated with greater maternal sensitivity and a higher-quality home environment, which yielded more favorable development in early childhood (Brooks-Gunn, Han, & Waldfogel, 2010).

Finally, the professional caregiver's relationship with the baby is vital. When caregiver–child ratios are generous, group sizes are small, and caregivers are educated about child development and child rearing, caregivers' interactions are more positive, their attachments to babies are more secure, and children develop more favorably—cognitively, emotionally, and socially (Biringen et al., 2012; NICHD Early Child Care Research Network, 2000b, 2002a, 2006). Child care with these characteristics can become part of an ecological system that relieves parental and child stress, thereby promoting healthy attachment and development.

High-quality child care, with generous caregiver-child ratios, small group sizes, and knowledgeable caregivers, can be part of a system that promotes all aspects of development, including attachment security.

---

influential in how we rear our children than the actual history of care we received.

Multiple Attachments

Babies develop attachments to a variety of familiar people—not just mothers but also fathers, grandparents, siblings, and professional caregivers. Although Bowlby (1969) believed that infants are predisposed to direct their attachment behaviors to a single special person, especially when they are distressed, his theory allows for these multiple attachments.

Fathers. When anxious or unhappy, most babies prefer to be comforted by their mother. But this preference typically declines over the second year. And when babies are not distressed, they approach, vocalize to, and smile equally often at both parents, who respond similarly to these overtures (Bornstein, 2015; Parke, 2002).

Fathers' sensitive caregiving predicts attachment security, though somewhat less strongly than mothers' (Brown, Mangelsdorf, & Neff, 2012; Lucassen et al., 2011). As infancy progresses, mothers and fathers in many cultures, including Australia, Canada, Germany, India, Israel, Italy, Japan, and the United States, tend to interact differently with their babies. Mothers devote more time to physical care and expressing affection, fathers to playful interaction (Freeman & Newland, 2010; Pleck, 2012).

Also, mothers and fathers tend to play differently. Mothers more often provide toys, talk to infants, and gently play conventional games like pat-a-cake and peekaboo. In contrast, fathers—especially with their infant sons—tend to engage in highly stimulating physical play with bursts of excitement that increase as play progresses (Feldman, 2003). As long as fathers are also sensitive, this stimulating, startling play style helps babies regulate emotion in intensely arousing situations and may prepare them to venture confidently into active, unpredictable contexts, including novel physical environments and play with peers (Cabrera et al., 2007; Hazen et al., 2010). In a German study, fathers' sensitive, challenging play with preschoolers predicted favorable emotional and social adjustment from kindergarten to early adulthood (Grossmann et al., 2008).

Play is a vital context in which fathers build secure attachments (Newland, Coyl, & Freeman, 2008). It may be especially influential in cultures where long work hours prevent most fathers from sharing in infant caregiving, such as Japan (Shwalb et al., 2004). In many Western nations, however, a strict division of parental roles—mother as caregiver, father as playmate—has changed over the past several decades in response to women's workforce participation and to cultural valuing of gender equality.

> **LOOK and LISTEN**
>
> Observe parents at play with infants at home or a family gathering, describing both similarities and differences in mothers' and fathers' behaviors. Are your observations consistent with research findings?

National surveys of thousands of U.S. married couples with children reveal that fathers' family roles have changed substantially over time. As Figure 6.3 reveals, though their involvement continues to fall far short of mothers', today's fathers spend nearly three times as much time caring for children as fathers did in 1965—largely due to the dramatic rise in maternal employment (Pew Research Center, 2015e). Paternal availability to children is fairly similar across U.S. SES and ethnic groups, with one exception: Hispanic fathers spend more time engaged with their infants and young children, probably because of the particularly high value that Hispanic cultures place on family involvement (Cabrera, Aldoney, & Tamis-LeMonda, 2014; Hofferth, 2003).

A warm marital bond and supportive coparenting promote both parents' sensitivity and involvement and children's attachment security, but they are especially important for fathers (Brown et al., 2010; Laurent, Kim, & Capaldi, 2008). See the Cultural Influences box on the following page for cross-cultural evidence documenting this conclusion—and also highlighting the powerful role of paternal involvement in children's development.

Siblings. Despite declines in family size, nearly 80 percent of U.S. children grow up with at least one sibling (U.S. Census Bureau, 2015d). The arrival of a new baby is a difficult experience for most preschoolers, who often become demanding, clingy, and less affectionate with their parents for a time. Attachment security also typically declines, especially for children over age 2 (old enough to feel threatened and displaced) and for those with mothers under stress (Teti et al., 1996; Volling, 2012).

Yet resentment is only one feature of a rich emotional relationship that soon develops between siblings. Older children also show affection and concern—kissing and patting the baby and calling out, "Mom, he needs you," when the infant cries. By the end of the first year, babies usually spend much time with older siblings and are comforted by the presence of a preschool-age brother or sister during short parental absences. Throughout childhood, children continue to treat older siblings as attachment figures, turning to them for comfort in stressful situations when parents are unavailable (Seibert & Kerns, 2009).

Nevertheless, individual differences in sibling relationships emerge soon after the new baby's arrival. Certain temperamental traits—high emotional reactivity or activity level—increase the chances of sibling conflict (Brody, Stoneman, & McCoy, 1994; Dunn, 1994). And maternal warmth toward both children is related to positive sibling interaction and to preschoolers' support of a distressed younger sibling (Volling, 2001; Volling &

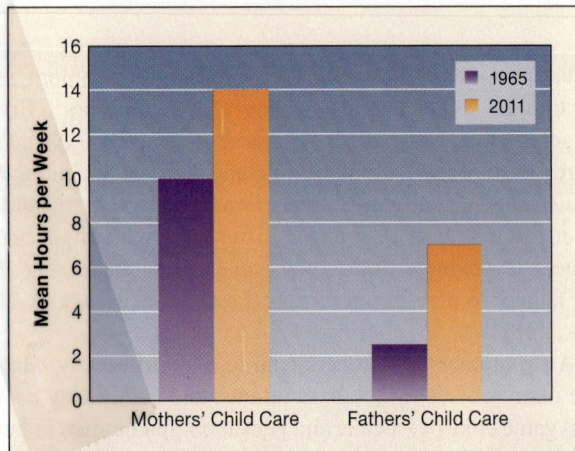

FIGURE 6.3 Average hours per week U.S. mothers and fathers reported devoting to caring for children in 1965 and 2011. In national surveys of thousands of married couples, mothers' time spent caring for children between birth and age 18 years increased moderately from 1965 to 2011. Though falling far short of mothers', fathers' time devoted to children rose nearly threefold. (Based on Pew Research Center, 2015e.)

The arrival of a baby brother or sister is a difficult experience for most preschoolers. Maternal warmth toward both children assures the older sibling of continuing parental love, models affectionate caring, and is related to positive sibling interaction.

Cultural Influences

The Role of Fathers' Involvement in Children's Development

In studies of many societies and ethnic groups around the world, researchers coded fathers' expressions of love and nurturance—evident in such behaviors as cuddling, hugging, comforting, playing, verbally expressing love, and praising the child's behavior. Fathers' sustained affectionate involvement predicted later cognitive, emotional, and social competence as strongly as did mothers'—and occasionally more strongly (Rohner & Veneziano, 2001; Veneziano, 2003). In Western cultures, paternal warmth and secure attachment are associated with higher academic achievement, better social skills, and a reduction in child and adolescent behavior problems (Bornstein, 2015; Lamb & Lewis, 2013; Michiels et al., 2010).

What factors promote fathers' involvement? Cross-cultural research reveals a consistent association between the amount of time fathers spend near infants and toddlers and their expressions of caring and affection (Rohner & Veneziano, 2001). Consider the Aka hunters and gatherers of Central Africa, where fathers spend more time in physical proximity to their babies than in any other known society. Aka fathers are within arm's reach of infants more than half the day, and they pick up, cuddle, and play with their babies at least five times as often as fathers in other hunting-and-gathering societies. Why are Aka fathers so involved? The bond between Aka husband and wife is unusually cooperative and intimate. Throughout the day, couples share hunting, food preparation, and social and leisure activities (Hewlett, 1992). The more time Aka parents are together, the greater the father's loving interaction with his baby.

In Western cultures as well, happily married fathers whose partners coparent cooperatively with them spend more time with and interact more effectively with infants. In contrast, marital dissatisfaction is associated with insensitive paternal care (Brown et al., 2010; Sevigny & Loutzenhiser, 2010). Clearly, fathers' relationships with their partners and their babies are closely linked. Evidence for the power of fathers' involvement, reported in virtually every culture and ethnic group studied, is reason to encourage and support their nurturing care of young children.

In both Western and non-Western nations, fathers' sustained, affectionate involvement predicts long-term favorable cognitive, emotional, and social development.

Belsky, 1992). In contrast, maternal harshness and lack of involvement are linked to antagonistic sibling relationships (Howe, Aquan-Assee, & Bukowski, 2001).

Finally, a good marriage is correlated with older preschool siblings' capacity to cope adaptively with jealousy and conflict (Volling, McElwain, & Miller, 2002). Perhaps good communication between parents serves as a model of effective problem solving. It may also foster a generally happy family environment, giving children less reason to feel jealous.

Refer to Applying What We Know on page 206 for ways to promote positive relationships between babies and their preschool siblings. Siblings offer a rich social context in which young children learn and practice a wide range of skills, including affectionate caring, conflict resolution, and control of hostile and envious feelings.

Attachment and Later Development

According to psychoanalytic and ethological theories, the inner feelings of affection and security that result from a healthy attachment relationship support all aspects of psychological development. Consistent with this view, an extended longitudinal study found that preschoolers who had been securely attached as babies were rated by their teachers as higher in self-esteem, empathy, and social skills than were their insecurely attached counterparts, who displayed more behavior problems. When studied again at age 11, children who had been secure infants continued to be more socially competent. And as these well-functioning school-age children became adolescents and young adults, they continued to benefit from more supportive social networks, formed more stable and gratifying romantic relationships, and attained higher levels of education (Elicker, Englund, & Sroufe, 1992; Sroufe, 2002; Sroufe et al., 2005).

For some researchers, these findings indicate that secure attachment in infancy causes improved cognitive, emotional, and social competence in later years. Yet contrary evidence exists. In other longitudinal studies, secure infants generally fared better than insecure infants, but not always (Fearon et al., 2010; McCartney et al., 2004; Schneider, Atkinson, & Tardif, 2001; Stams, Juffer, & van IJzendoorn, 2002).

Applying what we Know

Encouraging Affectionate Ties Between Infants and Their Preschool Siblings

SUGGESTION	DESCRIPTION
Spend extra time with the older child.	Parents can minimize the older child's feelings of being deprived of affection and attention by setting aside time to spend with her. Fathers can be especially helpful, planning outings with the preschooler and taking over care of the baby so the mother can be with the older child.
Handle sibling misbehavior with patience.	When parents respond patiently to the older sibling's misbehavior and demands for attention, these reactions are usually temporary. Parents can give the preschooler opportunities to feel proud of being more grown-up than the baby—for example, by encouraging the older child to assist with feeding, bathing, dressing, and offering toys, and showing appreciation for these efforts.
Discuss the baby's wants and needs.	By helping the older sibling understand the baby's point of view, parents can promote friendly, considerate behavior. They can say, for example, "He's so little that he just can't wait to be fed," or "He's trying to reach his rattle, and he can't."
Express positive emotion toward your partner and engage in effective coparenting.	When parents mutually support each other's parenting behavior, their good communication helps the older sibling cope adaptively with jealousy and conflict.

What accounts for this inconsistency? Mounting evidence indicates that *continuity of caregiving* determines whether attachment security is linked to later development (Lamb et al., 1985; Thompson, 2013). Children whose parents respond sensitively not just in infancy but also in later years generally develop favorably. In contrast, children whose parents behave insensitively or who, over a long period, are exposed to a negative family climate tend to establish lasting patterns of attachment insecurity and are at greater risk for developmental difficulties.

A close look at the relationship between parenting and children's adjustment supports this interpretation. Disorganized/disoriented attachment, a pattern associated with serious parental psychological problems and highly maladaptive caregiving, is strongly linked to internalizing and externalizing difficulties in childhood (Moss et al., 2006; Steele & Steele, 2014). And when researchers tracked a large sample of children from age 1 to 3 years, those with histories of secure attachment followed by sensitive parenting scored highest in cognitive, emotional, and social outcomes. Those with histories of insecure attachment followed by insensitive parenting scored lowest, while those with mixed histories of attachment and maternal sensitivity scored in between (Belsky & Fearon, 2002).

Although a secure attachment in infancy does not guarantee continued good parenting, it does launch the parent–child relationship on a positive path. An early warm, positive parent–child tie, sustained over time, promotes many aspects of children's development: a more confident and complex self-concept, more advanced emotional understanding, greater effortful control, more effective social skills, a stronger sense of moral responsibility, and higher motivation to achieve in school (Drake, Belsky, & Fearon, 2014; Groh et al., 2014; Viddal et al., 2015). But the effects of early attachment security are *conditional*—dependent on the quality of the baby's future relationships. Finally, as we will see again in future chapters, attachment is just one of the complex influences on children's psychological development.

Ask yourself

CONNECT Review research on emotional self-regulation on page 189. How do the caregiving experiences of securely attached infants promote emotional self-regulation?

APPLY What attachment pattern did Timmy display when Vanessa arrived home from work, and what factors probably contributed to it?

REFLECT How would you characterize your internal working model? What factors, in addition to your relationship with your parents, might have influenced it?

Self-Development

6.9 Describe the development of self-awareness in infancy and toddlerhood, along with the emotional and social capacities it supports.

Infancy is a rich formative period for the development of both physical and social understanding. In Chapter 5, you learned that infants develop an appreciation of the permanence of objects. And in this chapter, we have seen that over the first year, infants recognize and respond appropriately to others' emotions and distinguish familiar from unfamiliar people. That both objects and people achieve an independent, stable existence for infants implies that knowledge of the self as a separate, permanent entity is also emerging.

Self-Awareness

After Caitlin's bath, Carolyn often held her in front of a mirror. As early as the first few months, Caitlin smiled and returned friendly behaviors to her image. At what age did she realize that the baby smiling back was herself?

Beginnings of Self-Awareness. At birth, infants sense that they are physically distinct from their surroundings. For example, newborns display a stronger rooting reflex in response to external stimulation (an adult's finger touching their cheek) than to self-stimulation (their own hand contacting their cheek) (Rochat & Hespos, 1997). Newborns' remarkable capacity for *intermodal perception* (see page 143 in Chapter 4) supports the beginnings of self-awareness (Rochat, 2013). As they feel their own touch, feel and watch their limbs move, and feel and hear themselves cry, babies experience intermodal matches that differentiate their own body from surrounding bodies and objects.

Over the first few months, infants distinguish their own visual image from other stimuli, but their self-awareness is limited—expressed only in perception and action. When shown two side-by-side video images of their kicking legs, one from their own perspective (camera behind the baby) and one from an observer's perspective (camera in front of the baby), 3-month-olds looked longer at the observer's view (Rochat, 1998). By 4 months, infants look and smile more at video images of others than at video images of themselves, indicating that they treat another person (as opposed to the self) as a social partner (Rochat & Striano, 2002).

This discrimination of one's own limb and facial movements from those of others in real-time video reflects an *implicit* awareness that the self is distinct from the surrounding world. Implicit self-awareness is also evident in young infants' social expectations—for example, in protest or withdrawal when face-to-face interaction with a responsive adult is disrupted (see page 185). These early signs of self-experience serve as the foundation for development of *explicit* self-awareness—understanding that the self is a unique object in a world of objects.

Explicit Self-Awareness. During the second year, toddlers become consciously aware of the self's physical features. In several studies, 9- to 28-month-olds were placed in front of a mirror. Then, under the pretext of wiping the baby's face, each mother rubbed red dye on her child's nose or forehead. Younger babies typically touched the mirror as if the red mark had nothing to do with them. But the majority of those older than 18 to 20 months touched or rubbed their noses or foreheads, indicating awareness of their unique appearance (Bard et al., 2006; Lewis & Brooks-Gunn, 1979).

Around age 2, **self-recognition**—identification of the self as a physically unique being—is well under way. Children point to themselves in photos and refer to themselves by name or with a personal pronoun ("I" or "me") (Lewis & Ramsay, 2004). Soon children identify themselves in images with less detail and fidelity than mirrors. Around age 2½, most reach for a sticker surreptitiously placed on top of their heads when shown themselves in a live video, and around age 3 most recognize their own shadow (Cameron & Gallup, 1988; Suddendorf, Simcock, & Nielsen, 2007).

Nevertheless, toddlers make **scale errors,** attempting to do things that their body size makes impossible. For example, they will try to put on dolls' clothes, sit in a doll-sized chair, or walk through a doorway too narrow for them to pass through

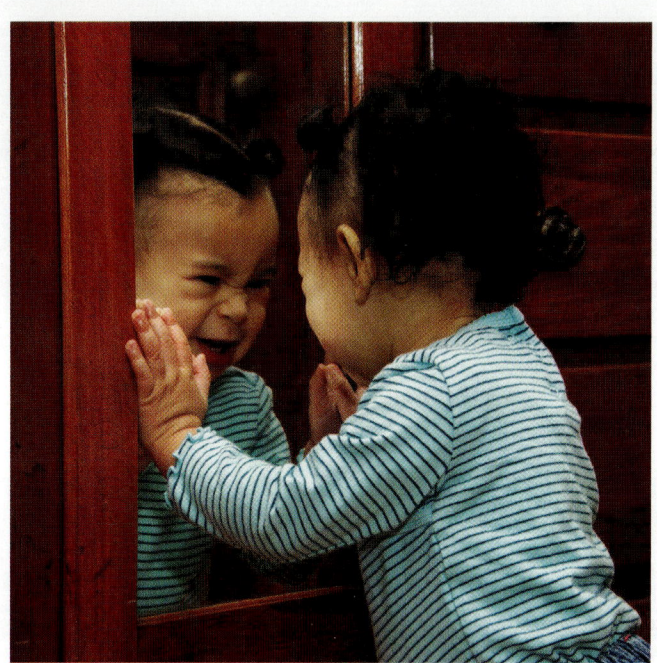

This 20-month-old makes silly faces in a mirror, a playful response to her reflection that indicates she is aware of herself as a separate being and recognizes her unique physical features.

(Brownell, Zerwas, & Ramani, 2007; DeLoache et al., 2013). Possibly, toddlers lack an accurate understanding of their own body dimensions. Alternatively, they may simply be exploring the consequences of squeezing into restricted spaces, as they are far less likely to try when the risk of harming themselves is high—for example, if the too-narrow doorway is next to a ledge where they could fall (Franchak & Adolph, 2012). Scale errors decline between ages 2 and 3½.

What experiences contribute to gains in self-awareness? During the first year, as infants act on the environment, they probably notice effects that help them sort out self, other people, and objects (Nadel, Prepin, & Okanda, 2005; Rochat, 2013). For example, batting a mobile and seeing it swing in a pattern different from the infant's own actions informs the baby about the relation between self and physical world. Smiling and vocalizing at a caregiver who smiles and vocalizes back helps clarify the relation between self and social world. The contrast between these experiences helps young infants sense that they are separate from external reality. Furthermore, 18-month-olds who often establish joint attention with caregivers are advanced in explicit self-awareness, attaining mirror self-recognition at an earlier-than-expected age (Nichols, Fox, & Mundy, 2005). Joint attention offers toddlers many opportunities to compare their own and others' reactions to objects and events, which may enhance their awareness of their own physical uniqueness.

Cultural variations exist in early self-development. In one investigation, urban middle-SES German and East Indian toddlers attained mirror self-recognition earlier than toddlers of non-Western farming communities, such as the Nso people of rural Cameroon and rural families of East India (see Figure 6.4 on page 208) (Kärtner et al., 2012). Urban German and, to a

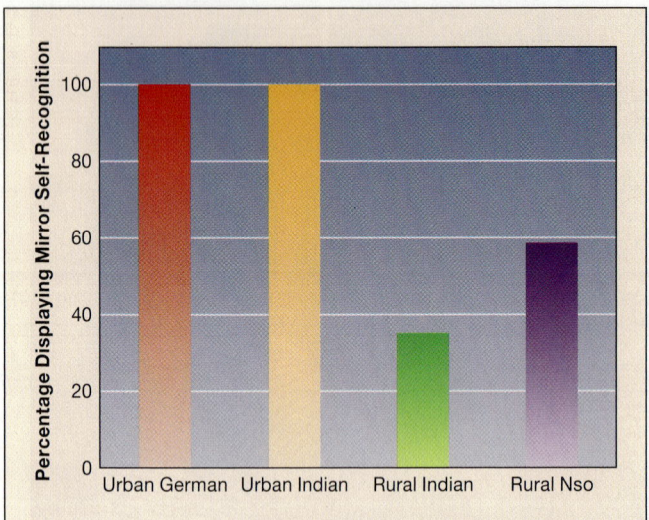

FIGURE 6.4 **Mirror self-recognition at 19 months in four cultures.** Urban middle-SES German and East Indian toddlers, whose mothers emphasized autonomous child-rearing goals, attained mirror self-recognition earlier than Nso toddlers of rural Cameroon and toddlers of rural East India, whose mothers emphasized relational child-rearing goals. (Based on Kärtner et al., 2012.)

lesser extent, urban East Indian mothers placed considerable emphasis on *autonomous child-rearing goals,* including promoting personal talents and interests and expressing one's own preferences, which strongly predicted earlier mirror self-recognition. In contrast, Nso and East Indian rural mothers valued *relational child-rearing goals*—doing what parents say and sharing with others. In related research, Nso toddlers, though delayed in mirror self-recognition, displayed an earlier capacity to comply with adult requests than did middle-SES urban Greek toddlers, whose mothers encouraged child autonomy (Keller et al., 2004).

Self-Awareness and Early Emotional and Social Development. Self-awareness quickly becomes a central part of children's emotional and social lives. Recall that self-conscious emotions depend on a strengthening sense of self. Self-awareness also leads to first efforts to understand another's perspective. Older toddlers who have experienced sensitive caregiving draw on their advancing capacity to distinguish what happens to oneself from what happens to others to express first signs of **empathy**—the ability to understand another's emotional state and *feel with* that person, or respond emotionally in a similar way. For example, they communicate concern when others are distressed and may offer what they themselves find comforting—a hug, a reassuring comment, or a favorite doll or blanket (Hoffman, 2000; Moreno, Klute, & Robinson, 2008).

Finally, the perspective taking that accompanies toddlers' firmer sense of self enables them to cooperate in resolving disputes over objects and playing games (Caplan et al., 1991). It also leads to clearer awareness of how to upset others. One 18-month-old heard her mother talking to another adult about an older sibling: "Anny is really frightened of spiders" (Dunn, 1989, p. 107). The innocent-looking toddler ran to the bedroom, returned with a toy spider, and pushed it in front of Anny's face!

Categorizing the Self

By the end of the second year, language becomes a powerful tool in self-development. Between 18 and 30 months, children develop a **categorical self** as they classify themselves and others on the basis of age ("baby," "boy," or "man"), sex ("boy" or "girl"), physical characteristics ("big," "strong"), and even goodness versus badness ("I a good girl." "Tommy mean!") and competencies ("Did it!" "I can't") (Stipek, Gralinski, & Kopp, 1990).

Toddlers use their limited understanding of these social categories to organize their own behavior. As early as 17 months, they select and play in a more involved way with toys that are stereotyped for their own gender—dolls and tea sets for girls, trucks and cars for boys. Their ability to label their own gender predicts a sharp rise in these play preferences over the next few months (Zosuls et al., 2009). Then parents encourage gender-typed behavior by responding more positively when toddlers display it (Hines, 2015). As we will see in Chapter 8, gender typing increases dramatically during early childhood.

Self-Control

Self-awareness also contributes to effortful control, the extent to which children can inhibit impulses, manage negative emotion, and behave in socially acceptable ways. To behave in a self-controlled fashion, children must think of themselves as separate, autonomous beings who can direct their own actions. And they must have the representational and memory capacities to

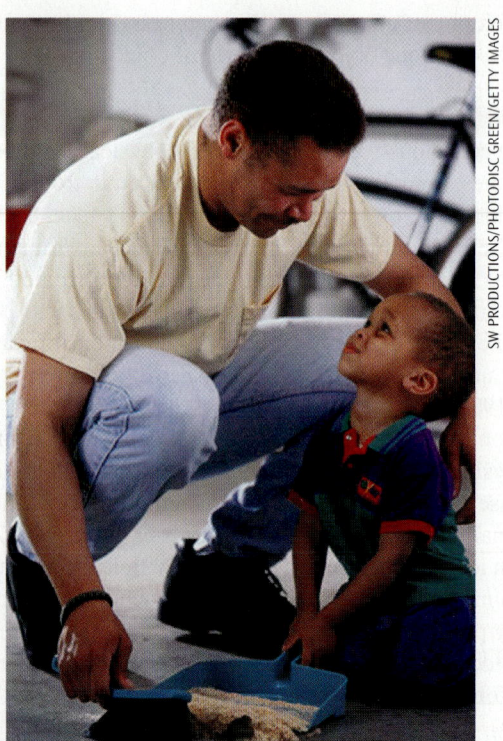

This father encourages compliance and the beginnings of self-control. The toddler joins in the task with an eager, willing spirit, which suggests he is adopting the adult's directive as his own.

Applying what we Know

Helping Toddlers Develop Compliance and Self-Control

SUGGESTION	RATIONALE
Respond to the toddler with sensitivity and encouragement.	Toddlers whose parents are sensitive and supportive sometimes actively resist, but they are also more compliant and self-controlled.
Provide advance notice when the toddler must stop an enjoyable activity.	Toddlers find it more difficult to stop a pleasant activity that is already under way than to wait before engaging in a desired action.
Offer many prompts and reminders.	Toddlers' ability to remember and comply with rules is limited; they need continuous adult oversight and patient assistance.
Respond to self-controlled behavior with verbal and physical approval.	Praise and hugs reinforce appropriate behavior, increasing the likelihood that it will occur again.
Encourage selective and sustained attention (see Chapter 5, pages 161–162).	Development of attention is related to self-control. Children who can shift attention from a captivating stimulus and focus on a less attractive alternative are better at controlling their impulses.
Support language development (see Chapter 5, pages 178–179).	In the second year, children begin to use language to remind themselves of adult expectations and to delay gratification.
Gradually increase rules in a manner consistent with the toddler's developing capacities.	As cognition and language improve, toddlers can follow more rules related to safety, respect for people and property, family routines, manners, and simple chores.

recall a caregiver's directive ("Caitlin, don't touch that light socket!") and apply it to their own behavior.

As these capacities emerge between 12 and 18 months, toddlers first become capable of **compliance.** They show clear awareness of caregivers' wishes and expectations and can obey simple requests and commands. And as every parent knows, they can also decide to do just the opposite! But for most, assertiveness and opposition occur alongside compliance with an eager, willing spirit, which suggests that the child is beginning to adopt the adult's directives as his own (Dix et al., 2007; Kochanska, Murray, & Harlan, 2000). Compliance quickly leads to toddlers' first consciencelike verbalizations—for example, correcting the self by saying "No, can't" before reaching for a cookie or jumping on the sofa.

Researchers often study the early emergence of self-control by giving children tasks that, like the situations just mentioned, require **delay of gratification**—waiting for an appropriate time and place to engage in a tempting act. Between ages 1½ and 4, children show an increasing capacity to wait before eating a treat, opening a present, or playing with a toy (Cole, LeDonne, & Tan, 2013; Vaughn, Kopp, & Krakow, 1984). Children who are advanced in development of attention, language, and suppressing negative emotion tend to be better at delaying gratification—findings that help explain why girls are typically more self-controlled than boys (Else-Quest, 2012).

Like effortful control in general, young children's capacity to delay gratification is influenced by quality of caregiving. Toddlers and preschoolers who experience parental warmth and encouragement are more likely to be cooperative and to resist temptation. Such parenting—which models patient, nonimpulsive behavior—is particularly important for emotionally reactive children (Kochanska, Aksan, & Carlson, 2005; Kochanska & Kim, 2014). Turn back to page 195, and note how these findings provide yet another example of the importance of goodness of fit between temperament and child rearing.

As self-control improves, parents gradually expand the rules they expect toddlers to follow, from safety and respect for property and people to family routines, manners, and simple chores (Gralinski & Kopp, 1993). Still, toddlers' control over their own actions depends on constant parental oversight and reminders. Several prompts ("Remember, we're going to go in just a minute") and gentle insistence were usually necessary to get Caitlin to stop playing so that she and her parents could go on an errand. Applying What We Know above summarizes ways to help toddlers develop compliance and self-control.

As the second year of life drew to a close, Carolyn, Monica, and Vanessa were delighted at their children's readiness to learn the rules of social life. As we will see in Chapter 8, advances in cognition and language, along with parental warmth and reasonable demands for maturity, lead preschoolers to make tremendous strides in this area.

Ask yourself

CONNECT What type of early parenting fosters the development of emotional self-regulation, secure attachment, and self-control? Why, in each instance, is it effective?

APPLY Len, a caregiver of 1- and 2-year-olds, wonders whether toddlers recognize themselves. List signs of self-recognition in the second year that Len can observe.

REFLECT In view of research on toddlers' compliance, active resistance, and budding capacity to delay gratification, do you think that the expression "the terrible twos"—commonly used to characterize toddler behavior—is an apt description? Explain.

Summary / chapter 6

Erikson's Theory of Infant and Toddler Personality (p. 184)

6.1 What personality changes take place during Erikson's stages of basic trust versus mistrust and autonomy versus shame and doubt?

- Warm, responsive caregiving leads infants to resolve Erikson's psychological conflict of **basic trust versus mistrust** on the positive side.

- During toddlerhood, **autonomy versus shame and doubt** is resolved favorably when parents provide appropriate guidance and reasonable choices. Adjustment problems may emerge if in the first few years children do not establish adequate trust and autonomy.

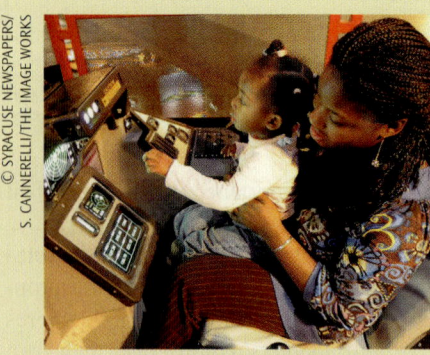

Emotional Development (p. 184)

6.2 Describe the development of basic emotions over the first year, noting the adaptive function of each.

- During the first half-year, **basic emotions** gradually become clear, well-organized signals. The **social smile** appears between 6 and 10 weeks, laughter around 3 to 4 months. Happiness strengthens the parent–child bond and both reflects and supports motor, cognitive, and social competencies.

- Anger and fear, especially in the form of **stranger anxiety,** increase in the second half-year as infants' cognitive and motor skills improve. Newly mobile babies use the familiar caregiver as a **secure base** from which to explore.

6.3 Summarize changes during the first two years in understanding others' emotions, expression of self-conscious emotions, and emotional self-regulation.

- The ability to understand others' emotional expressions improves over the first year. At 8 to 10 months, infants engage in **social referencing.** By the middle of the second year, toddlers realize that others' emotional reactions may differ from their own, and they use social referencing to gather information about others' intentions and preferences.

- During toddlerhood, self-awareness and adult instruction provide the foundation for **self-conscious emotions:** guilt, shame, embarrassment, envy, and pride. **Emotional self-regulation** emerges as the prefrontal cortex functions more effectively, as caregivers build on infants' increasing tolerance for stimulation, and as infants' ability to shift attention improves. When caregivers are emotionally sympathetic but set limits, toddlers develop more effective anger-regulation strategies in the preschool years.

Temperament and Development (p. 190)

6.4 What is temperament, and how is it measured?

- Children differ greatly in **temperament**—early-appearing, stable individual differences in reactivity and self-regulation. The pioneering New York Longitudinal Study identified three patterns: the **easy child,** the **difficult child,** and the **slow-to-warm-up child.** Today, the most influential model of temperament includes dimensions representing emotion, attention, and action, along with **effortful control,** the ability to regulate one's reactivity.

- Temperament is assessed through parental reports, behavior ratings by others familiar with the child, and laboratory observations. Most neurobiological research has focused on distinguishing **inhibited, or shy, children** from **uninhibited, or sociable, children.**

6.5 Discuss the roles of heredity and environment in the stability of temperament, including the goodness-of-fit model.

- Temperament has low to moderate stability: It develops with age and can be modified by experience. Long-term prediction from early temperament is best achieved after age 3, when children improve substantially in effortful control.

- Ethnic and gender differences in temperament may have genetic foundations but are promoted by cultural beliefs and practices.

- Temperament affects differential susceptibility to rearing experiences. Children with the short 5-HTTLPR genotype, which heightens risk of self-regulation difficulties, function worse than other children when exposed to inept parenting and benefit most from good parenting. Parents tend to emphasize temperamental differences between siblings.

- According to the **goodness-of-fit model,** child-rearing conditions that recognize the child's temperament while encouraging more adaptive functioning promote favorable adjustment.

Development of Attachment (p. 196)

6.6 Describe the development of attachment during the first two years.

- **Ethological theory,** the most widely accepted perspective on **attachment,** recognizes the infant's emotional tie to the caregiver as an evolved response that promotes survival. In early infancy, built-in signals help bring infants into close contact with other humans. Soon they communicate more freely and quiet more quickly to a familiar caregiver than a stranger.

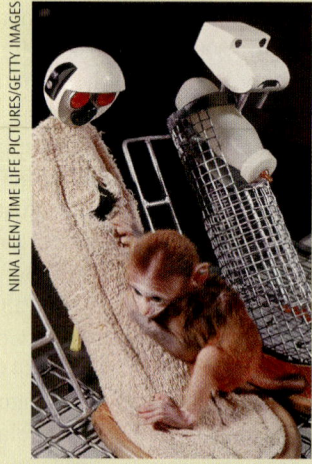

- Around 6 to 8 months, **separation anxiety** and use of the caregiver as a secure base indicate the existence of a true attachment bond. As representation and language develop, separation protest declines. From early caregiving experiences, children construct an **internal working model** that guides future close relationships.

6.7 *How do researchers measure attachment security, what factors affect it, and what are its implications for later development?*

- Using the **Strange Situation,** a laboratory technique for assessing the quality of attachment between 1 and 2 years of age, researchers have identified four attachment patterns: **secure, insecure–avoidant, insecure–resistant,** and **disorganized/disoriented attachment.** The **Attachment Q-Sort,** based on home observations of children between ages 1 and 5, yields a score ranging from low to high in security.

- Securely attached babies in middle-SES families with favorable life conditions more often maintain their attachment pattern than insecure babies. The disorganized/disoriented pattern shows greater stability than the other patterns. Cultural conditions must be considered in interpreting attachment patterns.

- Attachment security is influenced by early availability of a consistent caregiver, quality of caregiving, the fit between the baby's temperament and parenting practices, and family circumstances. **Sensitive caregiving** is moderately related to secure attachment.

- In Western cultures, **interactional synchrony** characterizes the experiences of securely attached babies. In non-Western village communities and Asian cultures, sensitive caregiving keeps the baby close and dampens emotional expressiveness.

- Continuity of caregiving is the crucial factor determining whether attachment security is linked to later development. If caregiving improves, children can recover from an insecure attachment history.

6.8 *Describe infants' capacity for multiple attachments.*

- Infants develop strong affectionate ties to fathers, who tend to engage in more exciting, physical play with babies than mothers do.

- Early in the first year, infants begin to build rich emotional relationships with siblings that combine rivalry and resentment with affection and sympathetic concern. Individual differences in quality of sibling relationships are influenced by temperament, parenting, and marital quality.

Self-Development (p. 206)

6.9 *Describe the development of self-awareness in infancy and toddlerhood, along with the emotional and social capacities it supports.*

- At birth, infants sense that they are physically distinct from their surroundings, an implicit self-awareness that expands during the first few months. In the middle of the second year, explicit awareness of the self's physical features emerges. Around age 2, **self-recognition** is clearly evident as toddlers identify themselves in photos and by name. However, **scale errors,** attempting to do things that their body size makes impossible, are common at this age.

- Self-awareness leads to toddlers' first efforts to appreciate another's perspective, including early signs of **empathy.** As language strengthens, children develop a **categorical self,** classifying themselves and others on the basis of social categories.

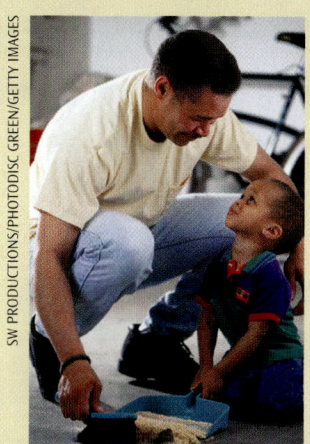

- Self-awareness also contributes to self-control. **Compliance** emerges between 12 and 18 months, followed by **delay of gratification,** which strengthens between 1½ and 4 years. Children who experience parental warmth and gentle encouragement are likely to be advanced in self-control.

Important Terms and Concepts

attachment (p. 196)
Attachment Q-Sort (p. 198)
autonomy versus shame and doubt (p. 184)
basic emotions (p. 185)
basic trust versus mistrust (p. 184)
categorical self (p. 208)
compliance (p. 209)
delay of gratification (p. 209)
difficult child (p. 190)
disorganized/disoriented attachment (p. 198)
easy child (p. 190)
effortful control (p. 191)

emotional self-regulation (p. 189)
empathy (p. 208)
ethological theory of attachment (p. 196)
goodness-of-fit model (p. 195)
inhibited, or shy, child (p. 191)
insecure–avoidant attachment (p. 198)
insecure–resistant attachment (p. 198)
interactional synchrony (p. 200)
internal working model (p. 197)
scale errors (p. 207)
secure attachment (p. 198)
secure base (p. 186)

self-conscious emotions (p. 188)
self-recognition (p. 207)
sensitive caregiving (p. 207)
separation anxiety (p. 197)
slow-to-warm-up child (p. 190)
social referencing (p. 188)
social smile (p. 185)
stranger anxiety (p. 186)
Strange Situation (p. 197)
temperament (p. 190)
uninhibited, or sociable, child (p. 191)

milestones

Development in Infancy and Toddlerhood

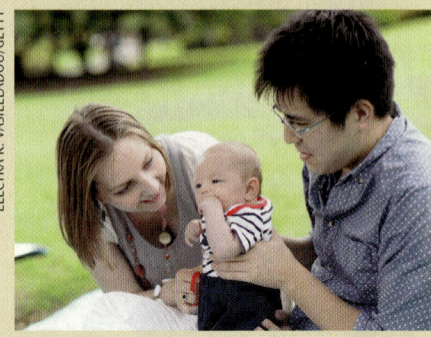

BIRTH–6 MONTHS

Physical

- Height and weight increase rapidly. (116)
- Newborn reflexes decline. (101–103)
- Distinguishes basic tastes and odors; prefers sweet-tasting foods. (108)
- Responses can be classically and operantly conditioned. (130–131)
- Habituates to unchanging stimuli; recovers to novel stimuli. (131–132)
- Sleep is increasingly organized into a night–day schedule. (125)
- Holds head up, rolls over, and grasps objects. (134, 136)
- Perceives auditory and visual stimuli as organized patterns. (138, 140, 141–142)
- Shows sensitivity to motion, then binocular, and finally pictorial depth cues. (140–141)
- Recognizes and prefers human facial pattern; recognizes features of mother's face. (143)
- Masters a wide range of intermodal (visual, auditory, and tactile) relationships. (144)

Cognitive

- Engages in immediate and deferred imitation of adults' facial expressions. (132–133, 154)
- Repeats chance behaviors that lead to pleasurable and interesting results. (151–152)
- Has some awareness of many physical properties (including object permanence) and basic numerical knowledge. (153–154, 158–159)
- Visual search behavior and recognition memory for visual events improve. (161, 162)
- Attention becomes more efficient and flexible. (161)
- Forms categories for familiar objects based on similar physical properties. (163–164)

Language

- Coos and, by end of this period, babbles. (175)
- Begins to establish joint attention with caregiver, who labels objects and events. (176)
- By end of this period, comprehends some word meanings. (176)

Emotional/Social

- Social smile and laughter emerge. (185)
- Matches feeling tone of caregiver in face-to-face communication; later, expects matched responses. (188)

- Distinguishes positive from negative emotion in voices and facial expressions. (188)
- Emotional expressions become well-organized and meaningfully related to environmental events. (185)
- Regulates emotion by shifting attention and self-soothing. (189)
- Smiles, laughs, and babbles more to caregiver than to a stranger. (197)
- Awareness of self as physically distinct from surroundings increases. (207)

7–12 MONTHS

Physical

- Approaches adultlike sleep–wake schedule. (125)
- Sits alone, crawls, and walks. (134)

- Reaching and grasping improve in flexibility and accuracy; shows refined pincer grasp. (137)
- Discriminates among a wider range of facial expressions, including happiness, surprise, sadness, fearfulness, and anger. (143)

Cognitive

- Engages in intentional, or goal-directed, behavior. (152)
- Finds object hidden in an initial location. (152)
- Recall memory improves, as indicated by gains in deferred imitation of adults' actions with objects. (154–155, 163)
- Tool use in problem solving emerges; solves simple problems by analogy to a previous problem. (155)
- Categorizes objects on the basis of subtle sets of features, even when the perceptual contrast between categories is minimal. (164)

Note: Numbers in parentheses indicate the page or pages on which each milestone is discussed.

Language

- Babbling expands to include many sounds of spoken languages and patterns of the child's language community. (176)
- Joint attention with caregiver becomes more accurate. (176)
- Takes turns in games, such as pat-a-cake and peekaboo. (176)
- Uses preverbal gestures (showing, pointing) to influence others' behavior and convey information. (176)
- Around end of this period, understands displaced reference of words and says first words. (155–156, 177)

Emotional/Social

- Smiling and laughter increase in frequency and expressiveness. (185)
- Anger and fear increase in frequency and intensity. (185)
- Stranger anxiety and separation anxiety appear. (186, 197)
- Uses caregiver as a secure base for exploration. (186)
- Shows "clear-cut" attachment to familiar caregivers. (197)
- Increasingly detects the meaning of others' emotional expressions and engages in social referencing. (188)
- Regulates emotion by approaching and retreating from stimulation. (189)

13–18 MONTHS

Physical

- Height and weight gain are rapid, but not as great as in first year. (117)
- Walking is better coordinated. (135–136)
- Manipulates small objects with improved coordination. (137)

Cognitive

- Explores the properties of objects by acting on them in novel ways. (152)
- Searches in several locations for a hidden object. (152)
- Engages in deferred imitation of adults' actions with objects over longer delays and across a change in context—for example, from child care to home. (154–155)
- Sustained attention increases. (161–162)
- Recall memory improves further. (163)
- Sorts objects into categories. (164)
- Realizes that pictures can symbolize real objects. (156)

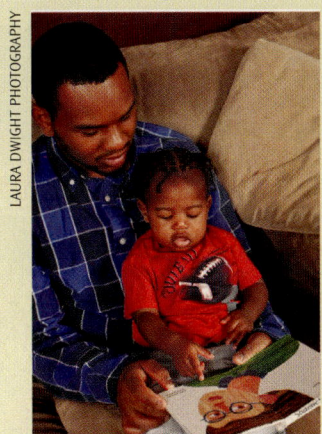

Language

- Steadily adds to vocabulary. (175, 177)
- By end of this period, produces 50 words. (175)

Emotional/Social

- Realizes that others' emotional reactions may differ from one's own. (188)

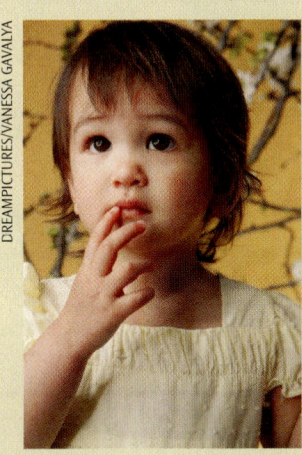

- Complies with simple directives. (209)

19–24 MONTHS

Physical

- Walks up stairs with help, jumps, and walks on tiptoe. (134)
- Manipulates small objects with good coordination. (137)

Cognitive

- Solves simple problems suddenly, through representation. (152)
- Finds a hidden object that has been moved while out of sight. (152)
- Engages in make-believe play, using simple actions experienced in everyday life. (153, 168)

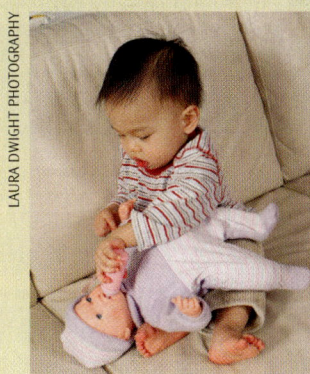

- Engages in deferred imitation of actions an adult tries to produce, even if not fully realized. (155)
- Categorizes objects conceptually, on the basis of common function or behavior. (164–165)
- Begins to use language as a flexible symbolic tool to modify existing mental representations. (156)

Language

- Produces 200 to 250 words. (175)
- Combines two words. (177)

Emotional/Social

- Self-conscious emotions (shame, embarrassment, guilt, envy, and pride) emerge. (188–189)
- Acquires a vocabulary for talking about feelings. (189)
- Begins to use language to assist with emotional self-regulation. (189–190)
- Begins to tolerate caregiver's absences more easily; separation anxiety declines. (197)
- Recognizes image of self and, by end of this period, uses own name or personal pronoun to refer to self. (207)
- Shows signs of empathy. (208)

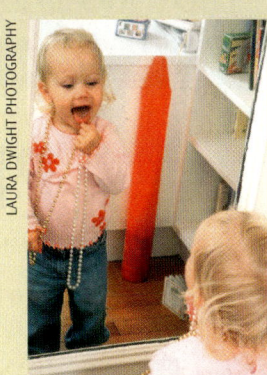

- Categorizes self and others on the basis of age, sex, physical characteristics, and goodness and badness. (208)
- Shows gender-stereotyped toy preferences. (208)
- Self-control, as indicated by delay of gratification, emerges. (209)

Note: Numbers in parentheses indicate the page or pages on which each milestone is discussed.

chapter 7

Physical and Cognitive Development in Early Childhood

On an outing with 3- and 4-year-olds to a city pond, a teacher points out features of goldfish and responds to children's observations and questions. Language and knowledge of the world expand rapidly in early childhood, supported by rich conversations with adults and peers.

What's ahead in chapter 7

PHYSICAL DEVELOPMENT

A Changing Body and Brain
Skeletal Growth • Brain Development

Influences on Physical Growth and Health
Heredity and Hormones • Nutrition • Infectious Disease • Childhood Injuries

Motor Development
Gross-Motor Development • Fine-Motor Development • Individual Differences in Motor Skills

■ **CULTURAL INFLUENCES** Why Are Children from Asian Cultures Advanced in Drawing Skills?

COGNITIVE DEVELOPMENT

Piaget's Theory: The Preoperational Stage
Advances in Mental Representation • Make-Believe Play • Symbol–Real-World Relations • Limitations of Preoperational Thought • Follow-Up Research on Preoperational Thought • Evaluation of the Preoperational Stage • Piaget and Education

Vygotsky's Sociocultural Theory
Private Speech • Social Origins of Early Childhood Cognition • Vygotsky and Early Childhood Education • Evaluation of Vygotsky's Theory

■ **CULTURAL INFLUENCES** Children in Village and Tribal Cultures Observe and Participate in Adult Work

Information Processing
Executive Function • Memory • The Young Child's Theory of Mind • Early Childhood Literacy • Early Childhood Mathematical Reasoning

■ **BIOLOGY AND ENVIRONMENT** Autism and Theory of Mind

Individual Differences in Mental Development
Home Environment and Mental Development • Preschool, Kindergarten, and Child Care • Educational Media

Language Development
Vocabulary • Grammar • Conversation • Supporting Language Learning in Early Childhood

For more than a decade, my fourth-floor office window overlooked the preschool and kindergarten play yard of our university laboratory school. On mild fall and spring mornings, classroom doors swung open, and sand table, easels, and large blocks spilled out into a small courtyard. Alongside the building was a grassy area with jungle gyms, swings, a playhouse, and a flower garden planted by the children; beyond it, a circular path lined with tricycles and wagons. Each day, the setting was alive with activity.

The years from 2 to 6 are often called "the play years," since play blossoms during this time, becoming increasingly complex, flexible, and symbolic. Our discussion opens with the physical attainments of this period—body and brain growth and improvements in motor coordination. We pay special attention to genetic and environmental factors that support these changes and to their intimate connection with other domains of development.

Then we explore early childhood cognition, beginning with Piaget's preoperational stage. Recent research, along with Vygotsky's sociocultural theory and information processing, extends our understanding of preschoolers' cognitive competencies. Next, we address factors that contribute to individual differences in mental development—the home environment, the quality of preschool and child care, and the many hours young children devote to television, computers, and other electronic media. We conclude with the dramatic expansion of language in early childhood. ●

215

PHYSICAL DEVELOPMENT

A Changing Body and Brain

7.1 Describe body growth and brain development during early childhood.

In early childhood, the rapid increase in body size of the first two years tapers off. On average, children add 2 to 3 inches in height and about 5 pounds in weight each year. Boys continue to be slightly larger than girls. As "baby fat" drops off further, children gradually become thinner, although girls retain somewhat more body fat than boys, who are slightly more muscular. As Figure 7.1 shows, by age 5 the top-heavy, bowlegged, potbellied toddler has become a more streamlined, flat-tummied, longer-legged child with body proportions similar to those of adults. Consequently, posture and balance improve—changes that support gains in motor coordination.

Individual differences in body size are even more apparent during early childhood than in infancy and toddlerhood. Speeding around the bike path in the play yard, 5-year-old Darryl—at 48 inches tall and 55 pounds—towered over his kindergarten

FIGURE 7.1 Body growth during early childhood. During the preschool years, children grow more slowly than in infancy and toddlerhood. Wilson's and Mariel's bodies became more streamlined, flat-tummied, and longer-legged. Boys continue to be slightly taller, heavier, and more muscular than girls. But generally, the two sexes are similar in body proportions and physical capacities.

classmates. (The average North American 5-year-old boy is 43 inches tall and weighs 42 pounds.) Priti, an Asian-Indian child, was unusually small because of genetic factors linked to her cultural ancestry. Hal, a European-American child from a poverty-stricken home, was well below average for reasons we will discuss shortly.

Skeletal Growth

The skeletal changes of infancy continue throughout early childhood. Between ages 2 and 6, approximately 45 new *epiphyses,* or growth centers in which cartilage hardens into bone, emerge in various parts of the skeleton. X-rays of these growth centers enable doctors to estimate children's *skeletal age,* or progress toward physical maturity (see page 117 in Chapter 4)—information helpful in diagnosing growth disorders.

By the end of the preschool years, children start to lose their primary, or "baby," teeth. The age at which they do so is heavily influenced by heredity. For example, girls, who are ahead of boys in physical development, lose their primary teeth earlier. Environmental influences also matter: Prolonged malnutrition delays the appearance of permanent teeth, whereas overweight and obesity accelerate it (Costacurta et al., 2012; Heinrich-Weltzien et al., 2013).

Diseased baby teeth can affect the health of permanent teeth, so preventing decay in primary teeth is essential—by brushing consistently, avoiding sugary foods, drinking fluoridated water, and getting topical fluoride treatments and sealants (plastic coatings that protect tooth surfaces). Another factor is exposure to tobacco smoke, which suppresses children's immune system, including the ability to fight bacteria responsible for tooth decay. Young children in homes with regular smokers are at increased risk for decayed teeth (Hanioka et al., 2011).

An estimated 23 percent of U.S. preschoolers have tooth decay, a figure that rises to 50 percent in middle childhood and 60 percent by age 18. Causes include poor diet and inadequate health care—factors that are more likely to affect low-SES children. One-third of U.S. children living in poverty have untreated dental caries (Centers for Disease Control and Prevention, 2015e).

Brain Development

Between ages 2 and 6, the brain increases from 70 percent of its adult weight to 90 percent. At the same time, preschoolers improve in a wide variety of skills—physical coordination, perception, attention, memory, language, logical thinking, and imagination.

By age 4 to 5, many parts of the cerebral cortex have overproduced synapses. In some regions, such as the prefrontal cortex, the number of synapses is nearly double the adult value. Together, synaptic growth and myelination of neural fibers result in a high energy need. In fact, fMRI evidence reveals that energy metabolism in the cerebral cortex peaks around this age (Nelson, Thomas, & de Haan, 2006). *Synaptic pruning* follows: Neurons

Genetic influences and parental acceptance may have contributed to this 5-year-old's left-handedness. Left-handed individuals show certain cognitive advantages, perhaps because their brains are less strongly lateralized than those of right-handers.

that are seldom stimulated lose their connective fibers, and the number of synapses gradually declines. By age 8 to 10, energy consumption of most cortical regions diminishes to near-adult levels (Lebel & Beaulieu, 2011). And cognitive capacities increasingly localize in distinct neural systems that become interconnected, resulting in networks of coordinated neural functioning that support children's advancing abilities (Bathelt et al., 2013; Markant & Thomas, 2013).

EEG, NIRS, and fMRI measures of neural activity reveal especially rapid growth from early to middle childhood in prefrontal-cortical areas devoted to various aspects of executive function: inhibition, working memory, flexibility of thinking, and planning—capacities that advance markedly over the preschool years (Müller & Kerns, 2015). Furthermore, for most children, the left cerebral hemisphere is especially active between 3 and 6 years and then levels off. In contrast, activity in the right hemisphere increases steadily throughout early and middle childhood (Thatcher, Walker, & Giudice, 1987).

These findings fit nicely with what we know about several aspects of cognitive development. Language skills (typically housed in the left hemisphere) expand at an astonishing pace in early childhood, and they support children's improved executive function. In contrast, spatial skills (usually located in the right hemisphere), such as giving directions, drawing pictures, and recognizing geometric shapes, develop gradually over childhood and adolescence.

Differences in rate of development between the two hemispheres suggest that they are continuing to *lateralize* (specialize in cognitive functions). Let's take a closer look at brain lateralization in early childhood by focusing on handedness.

Handedness. Research on handedness, along with other evidence covered in Chapter 4, supports the joint contribution of nature and nurture to brain lateralization. By age 6 months, infants typically display a smoother, more efficient movement when reaching with their right than their left arm—an early tendency that may contribute to the right-handed bias of most children by the end of the first year (Nelson, Campbell, & Michel, 2013; Rönnqvist & Domellöf, 2006). Gradually, handedness extends to additional skills.

Handedness reflects the greater capacity of one side of the brain—the individual's **dominant cerebral hemisphere**—to carry out skilled motor action. Other important abilities are generally located on the dominant side as well. For right-handed people—in Western nations, 90 percent of the population—language is housed in the left hemisphere with hand control. For the left-handed 10 percent, language is occasionally located in the right hemisphere or, more often, shared between the hemispheres (Szaflarski et al., 2012). This indicates that the brains of left-handers tend to be less strongly lateralized than those of right-handers.

Heritability of left-handedness is weak to modest: Left-handed parents have only a mildly elevated chance of having left-handed children (Somers et al., 2015; Suzuki & Ando, 2014). This suggests a genetic *bias* favoring right-handedness that experiences can overcome, swaying children toward a left-hand preference.

Handedness involves practice. It is strongest for complex skills requiring extensive training, such as eating with utensils, writing, and engaging in athletic activities. And wide cultural differences exist. For example, in tribal and village cultures, rates of left-handedness are relatively high. But in a study of one such society in New Guinea, individuals who had attended school in childhood were far more likely to be extremely right-handed—findings that highlight the role of experience (Geuze et al., 2012).

Although left-handedness is elevated among people with intellectual disabilities and mental illness, atypical brain lateralization is probably not responsible for these individuals' problems. Rather, early damage to the left hemisphere may have caused their disabilities while also leading to a shift in handedness. In support of this idea, left-handedness is associated with prenatal and birth difficulties that can result in brain damage, including maternal stress, prolonged labor, prematurity, Rh incompatibility, and breech delivery (Domellöf, Johansson, & Rönnqvist, 2011; Kurganskaya, 2011).

Most left-handers, however, have no developmental problems. In fact, left- and mixed-handed young people are slightly advantaged in speed and flexibility of thinking, and they are more likely than their right-handed agemates to develop outstanding verbal and mathematical talents (Beratis et al., 2013; Noroozian et al., 2012). More even distribution of cognitive functions across both brain hemispheres may be responsible.

Other Advances in Brain Development.
Besides the cerebral cortex, several other areas of the brain make strides during early childhood (see Figure 7.2). All of these changes involve establishing links between parts of the brain, increasing the coordinated functioning of the central nervous system.

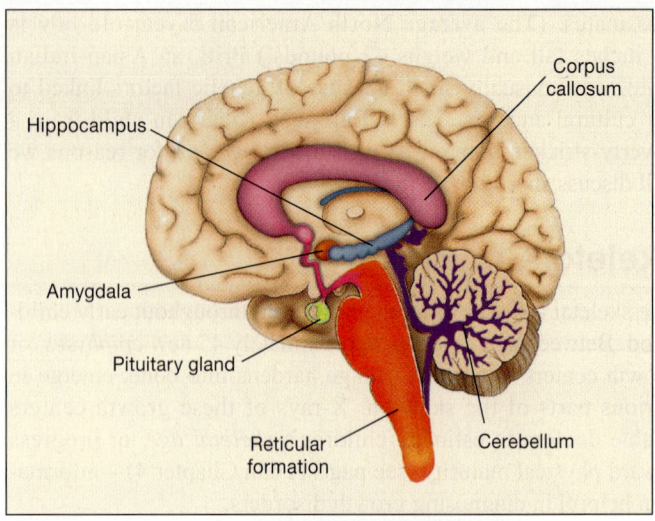

FIGURE 7.2 Cross-section of the human brain, showing the location of the cerebellum, the reticular formation, the amygdala, the hippocampus, and the corpus callosum. These structures undergo considerable development during early childhood. Also shown is the pituitary gland, which secretes hormones that control body growth (see page 219).

At the rear and base of the brain is the **cerebellum,** a structure that aids in balance and control of body movement. Fibers linking the cerebellum to the cerebral cortex grow and myelinate from birth through the preschool years, contributing to dramatic gains in motor coordination: By the end of the preschool years, children can play hopscotch, throw and catch a ball with well-coordinated movements, and print letters of the alphabet. Connections between the cerebellum and cerebral cortex also support thinking (Diamond, 2000). Children with damage to the cerebellum usually display both motor and cognitive deficits, including problems with memory, planning, and language (Hoang et al., 2014; Noterdaeme et al., 2002).

The **reticular formation,** a structure in the brain stem that maintains alertness and consciousness, generates synapses and myelinates from infancy into the twenties (Sampaio & Truwit, 2001). Neurons in the reticular formation send out fibers to other brain regions. Many go to the prefrontal cortex, contributing to improvements in sustained, controlled attention.

An inner brain structure called the **amygdala** plays a central role in processing of novelty and emotional information. The amygdala is sensitive to facial emotional expressions, especially fear (Adolphs, 2010). It also enhances memory for emotionally salient events, thereby ensuring that information vital for survival—stimuli that signify danger or safety—will be retrieved on future occasions. Throughout childhood and adolescence, connections between the amygdala and the prefrontal cortex, which governs regulation of emotion, form and myelinate (Tottenham, Hare, & Casey, 2009).

Also located in the inner-brain, adjacent to the amygdala, is the **hippocampus,** which plays a vital role in memory and in images of space that help us find our way, undergoes rapid

CHAPTER 7 Physical and Cognitive Development in Early Childhood 219

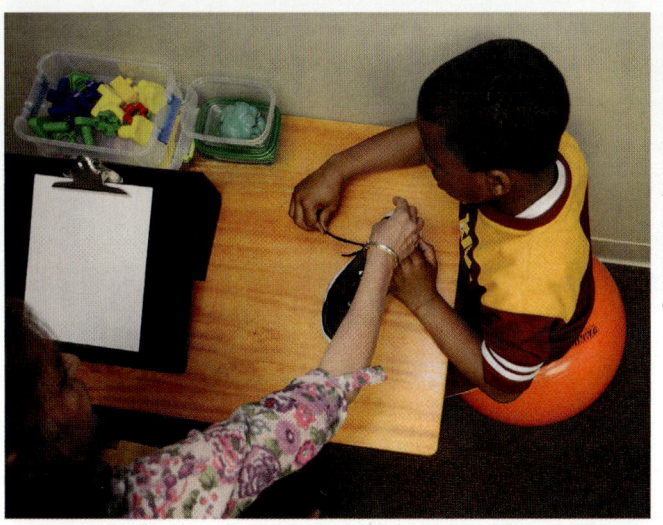

This child has been diagnosed with a rare condition in which part of the corpus callosum is absent. He has difficulty with tasks that have multiple steps and that require coordinated movements on both sides of the body. Here, a therapist helps him learn to tie shoes.

synapse formation and myelination in the second half of the first year, when recall memory and independent movement emerge. Over the preschool and elementary school years, the hippocampus and surrounding areas of the cerebral cortex continue to develop swiftly, establishing connections with one another and with the prefrontal cortex and lateralizing toward greater right-sided activation (Hopf et al., 2013; Nelson, Thomas, & de Haan, 2006). These changes support the dramatic gains in memory and spatial understanding of early and middle childhood.

The **corpus callosum** is a large bundle of fibers connecting the two cerebral hemispheres. Production of synapses and myelination of the corpus callosum peak between 3 and 6 years, continuing at a slower pace through adolescence (Thompson et al., 2000). The corpus callosum supports smooth coordination of movements on both sides of the body and integration of many aspects of thinking, including perception, attention, memory, language, and problem solving. The more complex the task, the more essential is communication between the hemispheres.

 ## Influences on Physical Growth and Health

7.2 Describe the effects of heredity, nutrition, and infectious disease on physical growth and health in early childhood.

7.3 What factors increase the risk of unintentional injuries, and how can childhood injuries be prevented?

As we consider factors affecting growth and health in early childhood, you will encounter some familiar themes. Heredity remains important, but good nutrition, relative freedom from disease, and physical safety are also essential.

Heredity and Hormones

The impact of heredity on physical growth is evident throughout childhood. Children's physical size and rate of growth are related to those of their parents (Bogin, 2001). Genes influence growth by controlling the body's production of hormones. Figure 7.2 on page 218 shows the **pituitary gland,** located at the base of the brain, which plays a crucial role by releasing two hormones that induce growth.

The first, **growth hormone (GH),** is necessary for development of almost all body tissues. Without medical intervention, children who lack GH reach an average mature height of only 4 to 4½ feet. When treated early with injections of GH, such children show catch-up growth and then grow at a normal rate, becoming much taller than they would have without treatment (Bright, Mendoza, & Rosenfeld, 2009).

A second pituitary hormone, **thyroid-stimulating hormone (TSH),** prompts the thyroid gland in the neck to release *thyroxine,* which is necessary for brain development and for GH to have its full impact on body size. Infants born with inadequate thyroxine must receive it at once, or they will be intellectually disabled. Once the most rapid period of brain development is complete, children with too little thyroxine grow at a below-average rate, but the central nervous system is no longer affected (Donaldson & Jones, 2013). With prompt treatment, such children catch up in body growth and eventually reach normal size (Høybe et al., 2015).

Nutrition

With the transition to early childhood, many children become unpredictable, picky eaters. One father I know wistfully recalled how his son, as a toddler, eagerly sampled Chinese food: "Now, at age 3, the only thing he'll try is the ice cream!"

Preschoolers' appetites decline because their growth has slowed. And their wariness of new foods is adaptive. If they stick to familiar foods, they are less likely to swallow dangerous substances when adults are not around to protect them. With the transition to middle childhood, picky eating usually subsides (Birch & Fisher, 1995; Cardona Cano et al., 2015).

Though they eat less, preschoolers require a high-quality diet, including the same nutrients adults need, but in smaller quantities. Fats, oils, salt, and sugar should be kept to a minimum because of their link to high blood pressure and heart disease in adulthood. And foods high in sugar should be eaten sparingly to prevent tooth decay and overweight and obesity—a topic we will take up in Chapter 9.

Children tend to imitate the food choices of people they admire, both adults and peers. For example, in Mexico, where children often see family members enjoying peppery foods, preschoolers enthusiastically eat chili peppers, whereas most U.S. children reject them (Birch, Zimmerman, & Hind, 1980). Repeated, unpressured exposure to new foods also promotes acceptance (Lam, 2015). For example, serving broccoli or tofu increases children's liking for these healthy foods. In contrast,

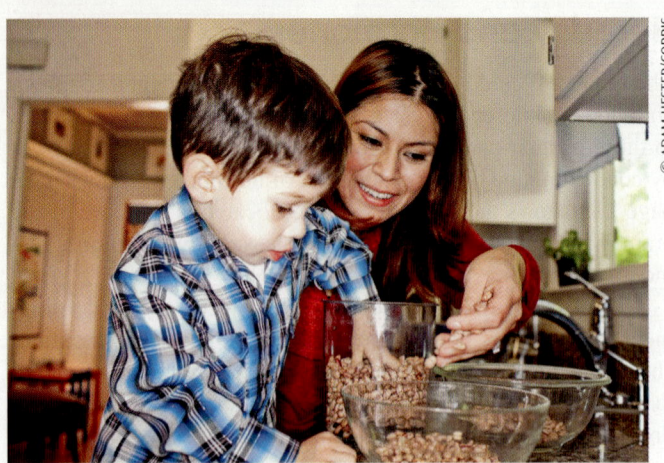

This Mexican 3-year-old helps his mother prepare refried beans for dinner. Children tend to imitate the food preferences of those they admire—both adults and peers.

offering sweet fruit drinks or soft drinks promotes "milk avoidance" (Black et al., 2002).

Although children's healthy eating depends on a wholesome food environment, offering bribes—"Finish your vegetables, and you can have an extra cookie"—leads children to like the healthy food less and the treat more (Birch, Fisher, & Davison, 2003). In general, coercing children to eat results in withdrawal from food, whereas food restriction leads to excessive eating. In a study of nearly 5,000 Dutch 4-year-olds, the more mothers reported pressuring their child to eat, the greater the likelihood of an underweight child. And the more mothers reported restricting their child's eating, the greater the chances of an overweight or obese child (see Figure 7.3) (Jansen et al., 2012).

LOOK and LISTEN

Arrange to join a family with at least one preschooler for a meal, and closely observe parental mealtime practices. Are they likely to promote healthy eating habits? Explain.

Finally, as indicated in earlier chapters, many children in the United States and in developing countries lack access to sufficient high-quality food to support healthy growth. Five-year-old Hal rode a bus from a poor neighborhood to our laboratory preschool. His mother's welfare check barely covered her rent, let alone food. Hal's diet was deficient in protein and in essential vitamins and minerals—iron (to prevent anemia), calcium (to support development of bones and teeth), zinc (to support immune system functioning, neural communication, and cell duplication), vitamin A (to help maintain eyes, skin, and a variety of internal organs), and vitamin C (to facilitate iron absorption and wound healing). These are the most common dietary deficiencies of the preschool years (Yousafzai, Yakoob, & Bhutta, 2013).

Hal was small for his age, pale, inattentive, and disruptive at preschool. By the school years, low-SES U.S. children are, on average, ½ to 1 inch shorter than their economically advantaged counterparts (Cecil et al., 2005). And throughout childhood and

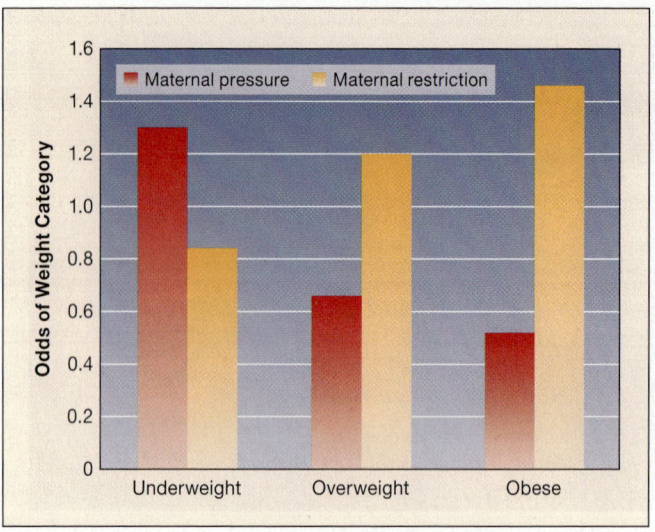

FIGURE 7.3 Relationship of maternal feeding practices to underweight, overweight, and obesity among preschoolers. In a Dutch study of nearly 5,000 4-year-olds, mothers who pressured their child to eat were more likely to have an underweight child. Mothers who restricted their child's eating increased their chances of having an overweight or obese child. These relationships held even after controlling for many factors that could have influenced maternal feeding practices and preschoolers' weight gain, including parents' SES, ethnicity, height and weight, and children's enjoyment of eating. (Based on Jansen et al., 2012.)

adolescence, a nutritionally deficient diet is associated with attention and memory difficulties, poorer intelligence and achievement test scores, and behavior problems—especially hyperactivity and aggression—even after family factors that might account for these relationships are controlled (Liu et al., 2004; Lukowski et al., 2010).

Infectious Disease

One day, I noticed that Hal had been absent from the play yard for several weeks, so I asked Leslie, his preschool teacher, what was wrong. "Hal's been hospitalized with the measles," she explained. "He's had difficulty recovering—lost weight when there wasn't much to lose in the first place." In well-nourished children, ordinary childhood illnesses have no effect on physical growth. But when children are undernourished, disease interacts with malnutrition in a vicious spiral, with potentially severe consequences.

Infectious Disease and Malnutrition. Hal's reaction to the measles is commonplace in developing countries, where a large proportion of the population lives in poverty and many children do not receive routine immunizations. Illnesses such as measles and chickenpox, which typically do not appear until after age 3 in industrialized nations, occur much earlier. Poor diet depresses the body's immune system, making children far more susceptible to disease. Of the 5.9 million annual deaths of children under age 5 worldwide, 98 percent are in developing countries and about half are due to infectious diseases (World Health Organization, 2015d).

Disease, in turn, is a major contributor to malnutrition, hindering both physical growth and cognitive development. Illness reduces appetite and limits the body's ability to absorb foods, especially in children with intestinal infections. In developing countries, widespread diarrhea, resulting from unsafe water and contaminated foods, leads to growth stunting and an estimated 1 million childhood deaths each year (Unger et al., 2014). Studies carried out in the slums and shantytowns of Brazil and Peru reveal that the more persistent diarrhea is in early childhood, the shorter children are in height and the lower their intelligence test scores during the school years (Checkley et al., 2003; Lorntz et al., 2006).

Most developmental impairments and deaths due to diarrhea can be prevented with nearly cost-free *oral rehydration therapy (ORT)*, in which sick children are given a glucose, salt, and water solution that quickly replaces fluids the body loses. Since 1990, public health workers have taught nearly half the families in the developing world how to administer ORT. Also, low-cost supplements of zinc (essential for immune system functioning) substantially reduce the incidence of severe and prolonged diarrhea, especially when combined with ORT (Galvao et al., 2013).

Immunization. In industrialized nations, childhood diseases have declined dramatically during the past half-century, largely as a result of widespread immunization of infants and young children. Hal got the measles because he did not receive a full program of immunizations.

In the United States, routine childhood immunizations have prevented an estimated 322 million illnesses and 700,000 deaths over the past two decades (Whitney et al., 2014). Yet about 17 percent of U.S. preschoolers lack essential immunizations. The rate rises to 22 percent for poverty-stricken children, many of whom do not receive full protection until age 5 or 6, when it is required for school entry (Centers for Disease Control and Prevention, 2015j). In contrast, fewer than 10 percent of preschoolers lack immunizations in Australia, Denmark, and Norway, and fewer than 5 percent in Canada, the Netherlands, Sweden, and the United Kingdom (World Health Organization, 2015b).

Why does the United States lag behind these countries? Although the U.S. Affordable Care Act of 2010 greatly improved health insurance coverage for American children, many low-income children remain without coverage and, therefore, may not receive timely vaccinations. Beginning in 1994, all U.S. children whose parents were unable to pay were guaranteed free immunizations, a program that has led to gains in immunization rates.

But inability to afford vaccines is not the only cause of inadequate immunization. Parents with little education and with stressful daily lives often fail to schedule vaccination appointments, and those without a primary-care physician do not want to endure long waits in crowded U.S. public health clinics (Falagas & Zarkadoulia, 2008). Some parents have been influenced by media reports—now widely discredited—suggesting a link between a mercury-based preservative used for decades in vaccines and a rise in the number of children diagnosed with autism. In fact, large-scale studies show no association with autism and no consistent effects on cognitive performance (Hensley & Briars, 2010; Richler et al., 2006; Thompson et al., 2007). Still, as a precautionary measure, mercury-free versions of childhood vaccines are now available. Other parents have religious or philosophical objections—for example, the belief that children should develop immunities naturally.

In areas where many parents have refused to immunize their children, outbreaks of whooping cough and rubella have occurred, with life-threatening consequences. Public education programs directed at increasing parental knowledge about the importance and safety of timely immunizations are badly needed. The Netherlands achieves its high child immunization rate by giving parents of every newborn baby a written schedule of when and where the child should be immunized (Lernout et al., 2013). If a parent does not bring the child at the specified time, a public health nurse goes to the home to ensure that the child remains in step with the schedule.

Childhood Injuries

Unintentional injuries are the leading cause of childhood mortality in industrialized nations. Although U.S. childhood injury fatalities have declined steadily over the past 35 years due to policies aimed at improving child safety, the United States ranks poorly among Western nations in these largely preventable events. About 35 percent of U.S. childhood deaths and 50 percent of adolescent deaths result from injuries, causing over 8,000 children to die annually (Child Trends, 2014c). And among the hundreds of thousands of injured children and youths who survive, many suffer pain, brain damage, and permanent physical disabilities.

Auto and traffic accidents, suffocation, drowning, and poisoning are the most common injuries resulting in childhood deaths (Safe Kids Worldwide, 2015). Motor vehicle collisions are by far the most frequent overall source of injury. They rank as the second leading U.S. cause of mortality from birth to age 5 (after suffocation among infants and drowning among toddlers and preschoolers) and as the leading cause among school-age children and adolescents.

Factors Related to Childhood Injuries. The common view of childhood injuries as "accidental" suggests they are due to chance and cannot be prevented. In fact, these injuries occur within a complex *ecological system* of individual, family, community, and societal influences—and we can do something about them.

Because of their higher activity level and greater impulsivity and risk taking, boys are nearly twice as likely as girls to be injured, and their injuries are more severe (Child Trends, 2014c). Children with certain temperamental and personality characteristics—inattentiveness, overactivity, irritability, defiance, and aggression—are also at greater risk (Ordonana, Caspi, & Moffitt, 2008; Schwebel & Gaines, 2007). As we saw in Chapter 6, these children present child-rearing challenges. They are likely to protest when placed in auto seat restraints, to refuse to take a companion's hand when crossing the street, and to disobey even after repeated instruction and discipline.

Childhood injury rates are highest in areas with extensive poverty, lack of high-quality child care, and weak parental vigilance, as illustrated by these children's makeshift playground.

Poverty, single parenthood, and low parental education are also strongly associated with injury (Dudani, Macpherson, & Tamim, 2010; Schwebel & Brezausek, 2007). Parents who must cope with many daily stresses often have little time or energy to monitor the safety of their children. And their homes and neighborhoods are likely to be noisy, crowded, and rundown, posing further risks.

Broad societal conditions also affect childhood injury. In developing countries, the rate of childhood death from injury is far greater than in developed nations (Kahn et al., 2015). Rapid population growth, overcrowding in cities, and heavy road traffic combined with weak safety measures are major causes. Safety devices, such as car safety seats and bicycle helmets, are neither readily available nor affordable.

Childhood injury rates are high in the United States because of extensive poverty, shortages of high-quality child care (to supervise children in their parents' absence), and a high rate of births to teenagers, who are not ready for parenthood (Child Trends, 2014a; Höllwarth, 2013). But U.S. children from advantaged families are also at considerably greater risk for injury than children in Western Europe. This indicates that besides reducing poverty and teenage pregnancy and upgrading the status of child care, additional steps are needed to ensure children's safety.

Preventing Childhood Injuries. Childhood injuries have many causes, so a variety of approaches are needed to reduce them. Laws prevent many injuries by requiring car safety seats, child-resistant caps on medicine bottles, flameproof clothing, and fencing around backyard swimming pools. Communities can help by modifying their physical environments. Playgrounds, a common site of injury, can be covered with protective surfaces. Free, easily installed window guards can be given to families in high-rise apartment buildings to prevent falls. And media campaigns can inform parents and children about safety issues.

But even though they know better, many parents and children behave in ways that compromise safety. About 27 percent of U.S. parents fail to place their children in car safety seats, and nearly 75 percent of infant seats and 40 percent of child booster seats are improperly used (Macy et al., 2015; Safe Kids Worldwide, 2011). American parents, especially, seem willing to ignore familiar safety practices, perhaps because of the high value they place on individual rights and personal freedom.

Furthermore, many parents overestimate young children's knowledge of safety rules, engaging in too little monitoring of their access to hazards. And when parents teach safety rules to preschoolers, they frequently fail to explain the basis for the rules—despite evidence that explanations enhance children's retention, understanding, and compliance (Morrongiello, Ondejko, & Littlejohn, 2004; Morrongiello et al., 2014). Even with well-learned rules, preschoolers need supervision to ensure that they comply (Morrongiello, Midgett, & Shields, 2001).

Interventions aimed at parents that highlight risk factors and that model and reinforce safety practices are effective in reducing home hazards and childhood injuries (Kendrick et al., 2008). Attention must also be paid to family conditions that can prevent childhood injury: relieving crowding in the home, providing social supports to ease parental stress, and teaching parents to use effective discipline—a topic we will take up in Chapter 8.

Ask yourself

CONNECT Using research on handedness, malnutrition, or unintentional injuries, show how physical growth and health in early childhood result from a complex interplay between heredity and environment.

APPLY One day, Leslie prepared a new snack to serve at preschool: celery stuffed with ricotta cheese. The first time she served it, few children touched it. How can Leslie encourage her students to accept the snack? What tactics should she avoid?

REFLECT Ask a parent or other family member whether, as a preschooler, you were a picky eater, suffered from many infectious diseases, or sustained any serious injuries. What factors might have been responsible?

Motor Development

7.4 Cite major milestones of gross- and fine-motor development, along with factors that affect motor progress, in early childhood.

Observe several 2- to 6-year-olds at play in a neighborhood park, preschool, or child-care center. You will see that an explosion of new motor skills occurs in early childhood, each of which builds on the simpler movement patterns of toddlerhood.

During the preschool years, children continue to integrate previously acquired skills into more complex, *dynamic systems*. Then they revise each new skill as their bodies grow larger and stronger, their central nervous systems develop, their environments present new challenges, and they set new goals.

Gross-Motor Development

As children's bodies become more streamlined and less top-heavy, their center of gravity shifts downward, toward the trunk. As a result, balance improves greatly, paving the way for new motor skills involving large muscles of the body. By age 2, children's gaits become smooth and rhythmic—secure enough that soon they leave the ground, at first by running and later by jumping, hopping, galloping, and skipping.

As children become steadier on their feet, their arms and torsos are freed to experiment with new skills—throwing and catching balls, steering tricycles, and swinging on horizontal bars and rings. Then upper- and lower-body skills combine into more refined actions. Five- and 6-year-olds simultaneously steer and pedal a tricycle and flexibly move their whole body when throwing, catching, hopping, and jumping. By the end of the preschool years, all skills are performed with greater speed and endurance. Table 7.1 provides a closer look at gross-motor development in early childhood.

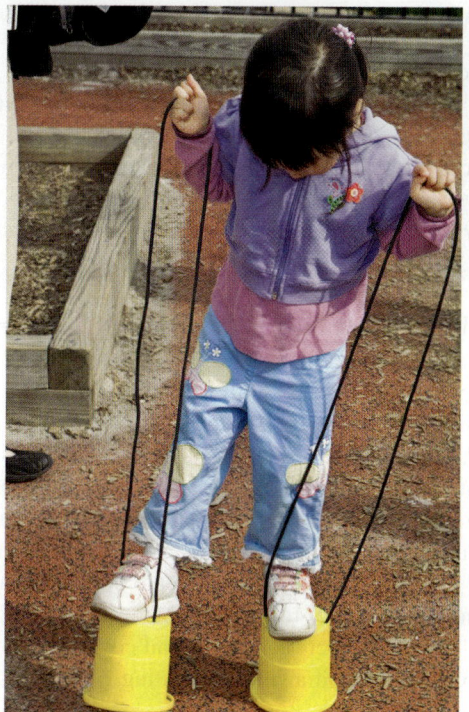

As balance improves, preschoolers can combine upper- and lower-body skills into more refined actions, such as walking on stilts.

TABLE 7.1
Changes in Gross- and Fine-Motor Skills During Early Childhood

AGE	GROSS-MOTOR SKILLS	FINE-MOTOR SKILLS
2–3 years	Walks more rhythmically; hurried walk changes to run Jumps, hops, throws, and catches with rigid upper body Pushes riding toy with feet; little steering	Puts on and removes simple items of clothing Zips and unzips large zippers Uses spoon effectively
3–4 years	Walks up stairs, alternating feet, and down stairs, leading with one foot Jumps and hops, flexing upper body Throws and catches with slight involvement of upper body; still catches by trapping ball against chest Pedals and steers tricycle	Fastens and unfastens large buttons Serves self food without assistance Uses scissors Copies vertical line and circle Draws first picture of person, using tadpole image
4–5 years	Walks down stairs, alternating feet Runs more smoothly Gallops and skips with one foot Throws ball with increased body rotation and transfer of weight from one foot to the other; catches ball with hands Rides tricycle rapidly, steers smoothly	Uses fork effectively Cuts with scissors following line Copies triangle, cross, and some letters
5–6 years	Increases running speed to 12 feet per second Gallops more smoothly; engages in true skipping Displays mature throwing and catching pattern Rides bicycle with training wheels	Uses knife to cut soft food Ties shoes Draws person with six parts Copies some numbers and simple words

Sources: Cratty, 1986; Haywood & Getchell, 2014.

Fine-Motor Development

Fine-motor skills, too, take a giant leap forward in the preschool years. As control of the hands and fingers improves, young children put puzzles together, build with small blocks, cut and paste, and string beads. To parents, fine-motor progress is most apparent in two areas: (1) children's care of their own bodies, and (2) the drawings and paintings that fill the walls at home, child care, and preschool.

Self-Help Skills. As Table 7.1 shows, young children gradually become self-sufficient at dressing and feeding. But parents must be patient about these abilities: When tired and in a hurry, young children often revert to eating with their fingers. And the 3-year-old who dresses himself may end up with his shirt on inside out, his pants on backward, and his left snow boot on his right foot! The most complex self-help skill of early childhood is shoe tying, mastered around age 6. Success requires a longer attention span, memory for an intricate series of hand movements, and the dexterity to perform them. Shoe tying illustrates the close connection between motor and cognitive development, as do two other skills: drawing and writing.

Drawing. When given crayon and paper, even toddlers scribble in imitation of others. Gradually, marks on the page take on meaning. A variety of cognitive factors combine with fine-motor control in the development of children's artful representations (Golomb, 2004). These include the realization that pictures can serve as symbols, and improved planning and spatial understanding.

Typically, drawing progresses through the following sequence:

1. *Scribbles.* At first, children's gestures rather than the resulting scribbles contain the intended representation. For example, one 18-month-old made her crayon hop and, as it produced a series of dots, explained, "Rabbit goes hop-hop" (Winner, 1986).

2. *First representational forms.* Around age 3, children's scribbles start to become pictures. Often children make a gesture with the crayon, notice that they have drawn a recognizable shape, and then label it (Winner, 1986). Few 3-year-olds spontaneously draw so others can tell what their picture represents. But when adults draw with children and point out the resemblances between drawings and objects, preschoolers' pictures become more comprehensible and detailed (Braswell & Callanan, 2003).

   A major milestone in drawing occurs when children use lines to represent the boundaries of objects, enabling 3- and 4-year-olds to draw their first picture of a person. Fine-motor and cognitive limitations lead the preschooler to reduce the figure to the simplest form that still looks human: the universal "tadpole" image, a circular shape with lines attached, shown on the left in Figure 7.4. Four-year-olds add features, such as eyes, nose, mouth, hair, fingers, and feet.

3. *More realistic drawings.* Five- and 6-year-olds create more complex drawings, like the one on the right in Figure 7.4, containing more conventional human and animal figures, with the head and body differentiated. Older preschoolers' drawings contain perceptual distortions because they have just begun to represent depth. This free depiction of reality makes their artwork look fanciful and inventive.

LOOK and LISTEN

Visit a preschool, child-care center, or children's museum where artwork by 3- to 5-year-olds is plentiful. Note developmental progress in drawings of human and animal figures and in the complexity of children's drawings.

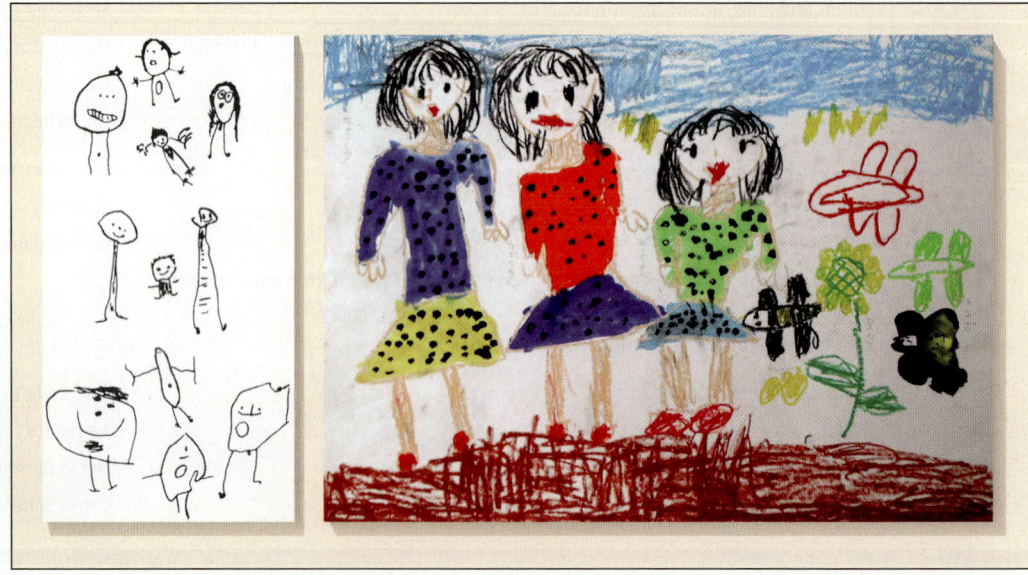

FIGURE 7.4 Examples of young children's drawings. The universal tadpolelike shape that children use to draw their first picture of a person is shown on the left. The tadpole soon becomes an anchor for details that sprout from the basic shape. By the end of the preschool years, children produce more complex, differentiated pictures like the one on the right, by a 5-year-old child. (*Left:* From H. Gardner, 1980, *Artful Scribbles: The Significance of Children's Drawing*, New York: Basic Books, p. 64. Copyright © 1980 by Howard Gardner. Reprinted by permission of Basic Books, a member of the Perseus Books Group, conveyed through Copyright Clearance Center. *Right:* © Children's Museum of the Arts New York, Permanent Collection.)

Cultural Variations in Development of Drawing.
In cultures that have rich artistic traditions and that highly value artistic competence, children create elaborate drawings that reflect cultural conventions. Adults encourage young children by guiding them in mastering basic drawing skills, modeling ways to draw, and discussing their pictures. Peers, as well, talk about one another's drawings and copy from one another's work (Boyatzis, 2000; Braswell, 2006). All of these practices enhance drawing progress. And as the Cultural Influences box on page 226 reveals, they help explain why, from an early age, children in Asian cultures are advanced over Western children in drawing skills.

In cultures with little interest in art, even older children and adolescents produce simple forms. In the Jimi Valley, a remote region of Papua New Guinea with no indigenous pictorial art, many children do not go to school and therefore have little opportunity to develop drawing skills. When a Western researcher asked nonschooled Jimi 10- to 15-year-olds to draw a human figure for the first time, most produced nonrepresentational scribbles and shapes or simple "stick" images resembling preschoolers' tadpolelike shapes (Martlew & Connolly, 1996). These forms seem to be a universal beginning in drawing. Once children realize that lines must evoke human features, they find solutions to figure drawing that follow the general sequence described earlier.

Early Printing.
When preschoolers first try to write, they scribble, making no distinction between writing and drawing. Around age 4, writing shows some distinctive features of print, such as separate forms arranged in a line on the page. But children often include picturelike devices—for example, a circular shape to write "sun" (Ehri & Roberts, 2006). Only gradually, between ages 4 and 6, as they learn to name alphabet letters and link them with language sounds, do children realize that writing stands for language.

Preschoolers' first attempts to print often involve their name, generally using a single letter. "How do you make a *D*?" my older son, David, asked at age 3½. When I printed a large uppercase *D*, he tried to copy. "*D* for David," he proclaimed, quite satisfied with his backward, imperfect creation. By age 5, David printed his name clearly enough for others to read it, but, like many children, he continued to reverse some letters well into second grade. Until children start to read, they do not find it useful to distinguish between mirror-image forms, such as *b* and *d* or *p* and *q* (Bornstein & Arterberry, 1999).

Individual Differences in Motor Skills
Wide individual differences exist in the ages at which children reach motor milestones. A tall, muscular child tends to move more quickly and to acquire certain skills earlier than a short, stocky youngster. And as in other domains, parents and teachers probably provide more encouragement to children with biologically based motor-skill advantages.

Sex differences in motor skills are evident in early childhood. Boys are ahead of girls in skills that emphasize force and power. By age 5, they can broad-jump slightly farther, run slightly faster, and throw a ball about 5 feet farther. Girls have an edge in fine-motor skills and in certain gross-motor skills that require a combination of good balance and foot movement, such as hopping and skipping (Fischman, Moore, & Steele, 1992; Haywood & Getchell, 2014). Boys' greater muscle mass and, in the case of throwing, slightly longer forearms contribute to their skill advantages. And girls' greater overall physical maturity may be partly responsible for their better balance and precision of movement.

From an early age, boys and girls are usually encouraged into different physical activities. For example, fathers are more likely to play catch with their sons than with their daughters. Sex differences in motor skills increase with age, but they remain small throughout childhood (Greendorfer, Lewko, & Rosengren, 1996). This suggests that social pressures for boys, more than girls, to be active and physically skilled exaggerate small, genetically based sex differences.

Children master the gross-motor skills of early childhood through everyday play. Aside from throwing (where direct instruction is helpful), preschoolers exposed to gymnastics, tumbling, and other formal lessons do not make faster progress. When children have access to play spaces and equipment appropriate for running, climbing, jumping, and throwing and are encouraged to use them, they respond eagerly to these challenges. Similarly, fine-motor skills can be supported through daily routines, such as dressing and pouring juice, and through richly equipped early childhood environments that include puzzles, construction sets, drawing, painting, sculpting, cutting, and pasting. And as the Cultural Influences box on page 226 shows, adults who guide and support children in acquiring drawing skills foster artistic development.

Finally, the social climate created by adults can enhance or dampen preschoolers' motor development. When parents and teachers criticize a child's performance, push specific motor skills, or promote a competitive attitude, they risk undermining children's self-confidence and, in turn, their motor progress (Berk, 2006). Adult involvement in young children's motor activities should focus on fun rather than on winning or perfecting the "correct" technique.

Ask yourself

CONNECT How are experiences that best support preschoolers' gross-motor development consistent with experience-expectant brain growth of the early years? (Return to page 124 in Chapter 4 to review.)

APPLY Mabel and Chad want to do everything they can to support their 3-year-old daughter's motor development. What advice would you give them?

REFLECT Do you think that American children should be provided with systematic instruction in drawing skills beginning in early childhood, similar to the direct teaching Chinese children receive?

Cultural Influences

Why Are Children from Asian Cultures Advanced in Drawing Skills?

Observations of young children's drawings in Asian cultures, such as China, Japan, Korea, the Philippines, Taiwan, and Vietnam, reveal skills that are remarkably advanced over those of their Western agemates. What explains such early artistic ability?

To answer this question, researchers examined cultural influences on children's drawings, comparing China to the United States. Artistic models offered by the culture, teaching strategies, valuing of the visual arts, and expectations for children's artistic development have a notable impact on the art that children produce.

In China's 4,000-year-old artistic tradition, adults showed children how to draw, encouraging them to master the precise steps required to depict people, butterflies, fish, birds, and other images. When taught to paint, Chinese children follow prescribed brush strokes, at first copying their teacher's model. To learn to write, they must concentrate hard on the unique details of each Chinese character—a requirement that likely enhances their drawing ability. Chinese parents and teachers believe that children can be creative only after they have acquired a foundation of artistic knowledge and technique (Golomb, 2004). To that end, China has devised a national art curriculum with standards and teaching materials extending from age 3 through secondary school.

The United States, as well, has a rich artistic tradition, but its styles and conventions are enormously diverse compared with those of Asian cultures. Children everywhere try to imitate the art around them as a way to acquire their culture's "visual language." But American children face a daunting imitative task, much like a child growing up in a context where each person speaks a different language (Cohn, 2014). Furthermore, U.S. art education emphasizes independence—finding one's own style. American teachers typically assume that copying others' drawings stifles creativity, so they discourage children from doing so (Copple & Bredekamp, 2009). Rather than promoting correct ways to draw, U.S. teachers emphasize imagination and self-expression.

The complex drawings of these kindergartners in Shanghai, China, benefit from adult expectations that young children learn to draw well, careful teaching of artistic knowledge and technique, and the rich artistic tradition of Chinese culture.

Does the Chinese method of teaching drawing skills beginning in early childhood interfere with children's creativity? To find out, researchers followed a group of Chinese-American children of immigrant parents and a group of European-American children, all from middle-SES two-parent families, from ages 5 to 9. At two-year intervals, the children's human-figure drawings were rated for maturity and originality—inclusion of novel elements (Huntsinger et al., 2011). On each occasion, the Chinese-American children's drawings were more advanced and also more creative.

Interviews revealed that European-American parents more often provided their children with a rich variety of art materials, whereas Chinese-American parents more often enrolled their children in art lessons, rating the development of artistic competence as more important. The Chinese-American children also spent more time as preschoolers and kindergartners in focused practice of fine-motor skills, including drawing. And the more time they spent practicing, especially when their parents taught and modeled drawing at home, the more mature their drawing skills.

At the same time, Chinese-American children's artistic creativity flourished under this systematic approach to promoting artistic maturity. Once they succeeded at drawing basic forms, they spontaneously added unusual details of their own.

In sum, even though young Chinese children are taught how to draw, their artistic products are original. Although Western children may come up with rich ideas about what to draw, until they acquire the necessary skills, they cannot implement those ideas. Cross-cultural research suggests that children benefit from adult guidance in learning to draw, just as they do in learning to talk.

COGNITIVE DEVELOPMENT

One rainy morning, as I observed in our laboratory preschool, Leslie, the children's teacher, joined me at the back of the room. "Preschoolers' minds are such a blend of logic, fantasy, and faulty reasoning," Leslie reflected. "Every day, I'm startled by the maturity and originality of what they say and do. Yet at other times, their thinking seems limited and inflexible."

Leslie's comments sum up the puzzling contradictions of early childhood cognition. Hearing a loud thunderclap outside, 3-year-old Sammy exclaimed, "A magic man turned on the thunder!" Even after Leslie explained that thunder is caused by lightning, not by a person turning it on, Sammy persisted: "Then a magic lady did it."

In other respects, Sammy's thinking was surprisingly advanced. At snack time, he accurately counted, "One, two, three, four!" and then got four boxes of raisins, one for each child at his table. But when his snack group included more than four children, Sammy's counting broke down. And after Priti dumped out her raisins, scattering them on the table, Sammy asked, "How come you got lots, and I only got this little bit?" He didn't realize that he had just as many raisins; his were simply all bunched up in a tiny red box. While Priti washed her hands after snack time, Sammy stuffed her remaining raisins back in the box and placed it in her cubby. When Priti returned and looked for her raisins, Sammy insisted, "You know where they are!" He failed to consider that Priti, who hadn't seen him move the raisins, would expect them to be where she had left them.

To understand Sammy's reasoning, we turn first to Piaget's and Vygotsky's theories along with evidence highlighting the strengths and limitations of each. Then we take up additional research on young children's cognition inspired by the information-processing perspective, address factors that contribute to individual differences in mental development, and conclude with the dramatic expansion of language in early childhood.

Piaget's Theory: The Preoperational Stage

7.5 Describe advances in mental representation, and limitations of thinking, during the preoperational stage.

7.6 What does follow-up research imply about the accuracy of Piaget's preoperational stage?

7.7 What educational principles can be derived from Piaget's theory?

As children move from the sensorimotor to the **preoperational stage**, which spans the years 2 to 7, the most obvious change is an extraordinary increase in representational, or symbolic, activity. Infants and toddlers' mental representations are impressive, but in early childhood, these capacities blossom.

Advances in Mental Representation

Piaget acknowledged that language is our most flexible means of mental representation. By detaching thought from action, it permits far more efficient thinking than was possible earlier. When we think in words, we overcome the limits of our momentary experiences. We can deal with past, present, and future at once and combine concepts in unique ways, as when we imagine a hungry caterpillar eating bananas or monsters flying through the forest at night.

But Piaget did not regard language as the primary ingredient in childhood cognitive change. Instead, he believed that sensorimotor activity leads to internal images of experience, which children then label with words (Piaget, 1936/1952). In support of Piaget's view, recall from Chapter 5 that children's first words have a strong sensorimotor basis. And toddlers acquire an impressive range of categories long before they use words to label them (see page 165). But as we will see, Piaget underestimated the power of language to spur children's cognition.

Make-Believe Play

Make-believe play is another excellent example of the development of representation in early childhood. Piaget believed that through pretending, young children practice and strengthen newly acquired representational schemes. Drawing on his ideas, several investigators have traced changes in make-believe play during the preschool years.

Development of Make-Believe. One day, Sammy's 20-month-old brother, Dwayne, visited the classroom. Dwayne wandered around, picked up a toy telephone receiver, said, "Hi, Mommy," and then dropped it. Next, he found a cup, pretended to drink, and toddled off again. Meanwhile, Sammy joined Vance and Priti in the block area for a space shuttle launch.

Make-believe play increases in sophistication during the preschool years. Children pretend with less realistic toys and increasingly coordinate make-believe roles, such as school bus driver and passengers.

"That can be our control tower," Sammy suggested, pointing to a corner by a bookshelf. "Countdown!" he announced, speaking into his "walkie-talkie"—a small wooden block. "Five, six, two, four, one, blastoff!" Priti made a doll push a pretend button, and the rocket was off!

Comparing Dwayne's pretend play with Sammy's, we see three important changes that reflect the preschool child's growing symbolic mastery:

- *Play detaches from the real-life conditions associated with it.* In early pretending, toddlers use only realistic objects—a toy telephone to talk into or a cup to drink from. Their earliest pretend acts usually imitate adults' actions and are not yet flexible. Children younger than age 2, for example, will pretend to drink from a cup but refuse to pretend a cup is a hat (Rakoczy, Tomasello, & Striano, 2005). They have trouble using an object (cup) that already has an obvious use as a symbol of another object (hat).

  After age 2, children pretend with less realistic toys (a block for a telephone receiver). Gradually, they can imagine objects and events without any support from the real world, as Sammy's imaginary control tower illustrates (Striano, Tomasello, & Rochat, 2001). And by age 3, they flexibly understand that an object (a yellow stick) may take on one fictional identity (a toothbrush) in one fictional game and another fictional identity (a carrot) in a different pretend game (Wyman, Rakoczy, & Tomasello, 2009).

- *Play becomes less self-centered.* At first, make-believe is directed toward the self—for example, Dwayne pretends to feed only himself. Soon, children direct pretend actions toward other objects, as when a child feeds a doll. Early in the third year, they become detached participants, making a doll feed itself or pushing a button to launch a rocket (McCune, 1993). Increasingly, preschoolers realize that agents and recipients of pretend actions can be independent of themselves.

- *Play includes more complex combinations of schemes.* Dwayne can pretend to drink from a cup, but he does not yet combine pouring and drinking. Later, children combine schemes with those of peers in **sociodramatic play,** the make-believe with others that is under way by the end of the second year and increases rapidly in complexity during early childhood (Kavanaugh, 2006). Already, Sammy and his classmates can create and coordinate several roles in an elaborate plot. By the end of early childhood, children have a sophisticated understanding of role relationships and story lines.

LOOK and LISTEN

Observe the make-believe play of several preschoolers at a family gathering, a preschool or child-care center, or in another community setting. Describe pretend acts that illustrate important developmental changes.

In sociodramatic play, children display awareness that make-believe is a representational activity—an understanding that strengthens over early childhood (Rakoczy, Tomasello, & Striano, 2004; Sobel, 2006). Listen closely to a group of preschoolers as they assign roles and negotiate make-believe plans: "You *pretend to be* the astronaut, I'll *act like* I'm operating the control tower!" In communicating about pretend, children think about their own and others' fanciful representations—evidence that they have begun to reason about people's mental activities, a topic we will return to later in this chapter.

Benefits of Make-Believe. Today, many researchers regard Piaget's view of make-believe as mere practice of representational schemes as too limited. In their view, play not only reflects but also contributes to children's cognitive and social skills.

Research reveals that preschoolers who devote more time to sociodramatic play are rated by observers as more socially competent a year later (Lindsey & Colwell, 2013). And make-believe predicts a wide variety of cognitive capacities, including executive function, memory, logical reasoning, language and literacy (including story comprehension and storytelling skills), imagination, creativity, and the ability to reflect on one's own thinking, regulate emotions, and take another's perspective (Berk & Meyers, 2013; Buchsbaum et al., 2012; Carlson & White, 2013; Mottweiler & Taylor, 2014; Nicolopoulou & Ilgaz, 2013; Roskos & Christie, 2013).

Critics, however, point out that the evidence just summarized is largely correlational, with too many studies failing to control all factors that might alternatively explain their findings (Lillard et al., 2013). In response, play investigators note that decades of research are consistent with a positive role for make-believe play in development and that new, carefully conducted research strengthens that conclusion (Berk, 2015; Carlson, White, & Davis-Unger, 2015). Furthermore, make-believe is difficult to study experimentally, by training children to engage in it. Besides alterations of reality, true make-believe *play* involves other qualities, including intrinsic motivation (doing it for fun, not to please an adult), positive emotion, and child control (Bergen, 2013).

Finally, much make-believe takes place when adults are not around to observe it! For example, an estimated 25 to 45 percent of preschoolers and young school-age children spend much time creating imaginary companions—special fantasized friends endowed with humanlike qualities. Yet more than one-fourth of parents are unaware of their child's invisible friend (Taylor et al., 2004). Children with imaginary companions display more complex and imaginative make-believe play; more often describe others in terms of their internal states, including desires, thoughts, and emotions; and are more sociable with peers (Bouldin, 2006; Davis, Meins, & Fernyhough, 2014; Gleason, 2013).

Symbol–Real-World Relations

To make believe and draw—and to understand other forms of representation, such as photographs, models, and maps—

preschoolers must realize that each symbol corresponds to something specific in everyday life. In Chapter 5, we saw that by the middle of the second year, children grasp the symbolic function of realistic-looking pictures, and around age 2½, of TV and video. When do children comprehend other challenging symbols—for example, three-dimensional models of real-world spaces?

In one study, 2½- and 3-year-olds watched an adult hide a small toy (Little Snoopy) in a scale model of a room and then were asked to retrieve it. Next, they had to find a larger toy (Big Snoopy) hidden in the room that the model represented. Not until age 3 could most children use the model as a guide to finding Big Snoopy in the real room (DeLoache, 1987). The 2½-year-olds did not realize that the model could be both *a toy room* and *a symbol of another room*. They had trouble with **dual representation**—viewing a symbolic object as both an object in its own right and a symbol. In support of this interpretation, when researchers made the model room less prominent as an object, by placing it behind a window and preventing children from touching it, more 2½-year-olds succeeded at the search task (DeLoache, 2002). Recall, also, that in make-believe play, 1½- to 2-year-olds cannot use an object that has an obvious use (cup) to stand for another object (hat).

How do children grasp the dual representation of symbolic objects? When adults point out similarities between models and real-world spaces, 2½-year-olds perform better on the find-Snoopy task (Peralta de Mendoza & Salsa, 2003). Also, insight into one type of symbol–real-world relation helps preschoolers master others. For example, children regard realistic-looking pictures as symbols early because a picture's primary purpose is to stand for something; it is not an interesting object in its own right (Simcock & DeLoache, 2006). And 3-year-olds who can use a model of a room to locate Big Snoopy readily transfer their understanding to a simple map (Marzolf & DeLoache, 1994).

In sum, experiences with diverse symbols—picture books, photographs, drawings, make-believe, and maps—help preschoolers appreciate that one object can stand for another. With age, children come to understand a wide range of symbols that have little physical similarity to what they represent. As a result, doors open to vast realms of knowledge.

Limitations of Preoperational Thought

Aside from gains in representation, Piaget described preschoolers in terms of what they *cannot* understand. As the term *pre*operational suggests, he compared them to older, more competent children who have reached the concrete operational stage. According to Piaget, young children are not capable of *operations*—mental representations of actions that obey logical rules. Rather, their thinking is rigid, limited to one aspect of a situation at a time, and strongly influenced by the way things appear at the moment.

Egocentrism.
For Piaget, the most fundamental deficiency of preoperational thinking is **egocentrism**—failure to distinguish others' symbolic viewpoints from one's own. He believed that

FIGURE 7.5 Piaget's three-mountains problem. Each mountain is distinguished by its color and by its summit. One has a red cross, another a small house, and the third a snow-capped peak. Children at the preoperational stage respond egocentrically. They cannot select a picture that shows the mountains from the doll's perspective. Instead, they simply choose the photo that reflects their own vantage point.

when children first mentally represent the world, they tend to focus on their own viewpoint and simply assume that others perceive, think, and feel the same way they do.

Piaget's most convincing demonstration of egocentrism involves his *three-mountains problem,* described in Figure 7.5. He also regarded egocentrism as responsible for preoperational children's *animistic thinking*—the belief that inanimate objects have lifelike qualities, such as thoughts, wishes, feelings, and intentions (Piaget, 1926/1930). Recall Sammy's insistence that someone must have turned on the thunder. According to Piaget, because young children egocentrically assign human purposes to physical events, magical thinking is common during the preschool years.

Piaget argued that preschoolers' egocentric bias prevents them from *accommodating,* or reflecting on and revising their faulty reasoning in response to their physical and social worlds. To understand this shortcoming, let's consider some additional tasks that Piaget gave to children.

Inability to Conserve.
Piaget's famous conservation tasks reveal a variety of deficiencies of preoperational thinking. **Conservation** refers to the idea that certain physical characteristics of objects remain the same, even when their outward appearance changes. At snack time, Priti and Sammy had identical boxes of raisins, but when Priti spread her raisins out on the table, Sammy was convinced that she had more.

In another conservation task involving liquid, the child is shown two identical tall glasses of water and asked if they contain equal amounts. Once the child agrees, the water in one glass is poured into a short, wide container, changing its appearance

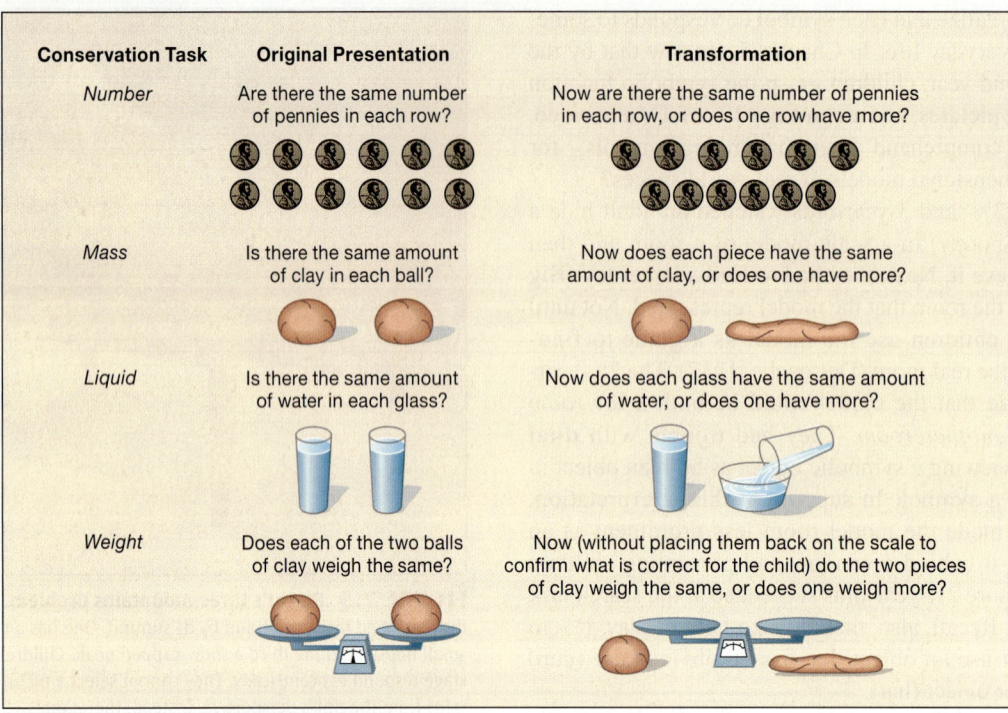

FIGURE 7.6 Some Piagetian conservation tasks. Children at the preoperational stage cannot yet conserve. These tasks are mastered gradually over the concrete operational stage. Children in Western nations typically acquire conservation of number, mass, and liquid sometime between 6 and 7 years and conservation of weight between 8 and 10 years.

but not its amount. Then the child is asked whether the amount of water has changed. Preoperational children think the quantity has changed. They explain, "There is less now because the water is way down here" (that is, its level is so low) or, "There is more now because it is all spread out." Figure 7.6 illustrates other conservation tasks that you can try with children.

The inability to conserve highlights several related aspects of preoperational children's thinking. First, their understanding is *centered,* or characterized by **centration.** They focus on one aspect of a situation, neglecting other important features. In conservation of liquid, the child *centers* on the height of the water, failing to realize that changes in width compensate for changes in height. Second, children are easily distracted by the *perceptual appearance* of objects. Third, children treat the initial and final states of the water as unrelated events, ignoring the *dynamic transformation* (pouring of water) between them.

The most important illogical feature of preoperational thought is its **irreversibility**—an inability to mentally go through a series of steps in a problem and then reverse direction, returning to the starting point. *Reversibility* is part of every logical operation. After Priti spills her raisins, Sammy cannot reverse by thinking, "I know that Priti doesn't have more raisins than I do. If we put them back in that little box, her raisins and my raisins would look just the same."

Lack of Hierarchical Classification. Preoperational children have difficulty with **hierarchical classification**—the organization of objects into classes and subclasses on the basis of similarities and differences. Piaget's famous *class inclusion problem,* illustrated in Figure 7.7, demonstrates this limitation. Preoperational children center on the overriding feature, red. They do not think reversibly by moving from the whole class (flowers) to the parts (red and blue) and back again.

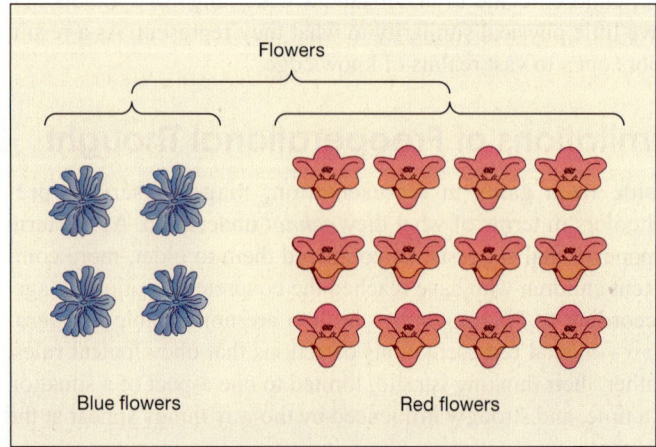

FIGURE 7.7 A Piagetian class inclusion problem. Children are shown 16 flowers, 4 of which are blue and 12 of which are red. Asked, "Are there more red flowers or flowers?" the preoperational child responds, "More red flowers," failing to realize that both red and blue flowers are included in the category "flowers."

Follow-Up Research on Preoperational Thought

Over the past three decades, researchers have challenged Piaget's view of preschoolers as cognitively deficient. Because many Piagetian problems contain unfamiliar elements or too many pieces of information for young children to handle at once, preschoolers' responses do not reflect their true abilities. Piaget also missed many naturally occurring instances of effective reasoning by preschoolers.

Egocentric, Animistic, and Magical Thinking. Do young children really believe that a person standing elsewhere in a room sees exactly what they see? When researchers use simplified tasks with familiar objects, 3-year-olds show clear awareness of others' vantage points, such as recognizing how something appears to another person who is looking at it through a color filter (Moll & Meltzoff, 2011).

Nonegocentric responses also appear in young children's conversations. For example, 4-year-olds use shorter, simpler expressions when talking to 2-year-olds than to agemates or adults (Gelman & Shatz, 1978). And in describing objects, preschoolers do not use such words as "big" and "little" in a rigid, egocentric fashion. Instead, they *adjust* their descriptions to allow for context. By age 3, they judge a 2-inch shoe as little when seen by itself (because it is much smaller than most shoes) but as big for a tiny 5-inch-tall doll (Ebeling & Gelman, 1994).

In Chapter 5, we saw that toddlers have already begun to infer others' intentions (see page 155). And in his later writings, Piaget (1945/1951) did describe preschoolers' egocentrism as a *tendency* rather than an inability. As we revisit the topic of perspective taking, we will see that it develops gradually throughout childhood and adolescence.

Piaget also overestimated preschoolers' animistic beliefs. Even infants have begun to distinguish animate from inanimate, as indicated by their developing categorical distinctions between living and nonliving things (see page 164). By age 2½, children give psychological explanations ("he likes to" or "she wants to") for people and occasionally for other animals, but rarely for objects (Hickling & Wellman, 2001). In addition, preschoolers rarely attribute biological properties (like eating and growing) to robots, indicating that they are well aware that even a self-moving object with lifelike features is not alive. But unlike adults, they often say that robots have perceptual and psychological capacities—for example, seeing, thinking, and remembering (Jipson & Gelman, 2007; Subrahmanyam, Gelman, & Lafosse, 2002). These responses result from incomplete knowledge about certain objects, and they decline with age.

Similarly, preschoolers think that magic accounts for events they otherwise cannot explain, as in Sammy's magical explanation of thunder in the opening to this chapter. But their notions of magic are flexible and appropriate. For example, 3- and 4-year-olds are more likely to say that a magical process—wishing—caused an event (an object to appear in a box) when a person made the wish before the event occurred, the event is consistent with the wish (the wished-for object rather than another object appeared in the box), and no alternative causes were apparent (Woolley, Browne, & Boerger, 2006). These features of causality are the same ones preschoolers rely on in ordinary situations.

Between ages 4 and 8, as children gain familiarity with physical events and principles, their magical beliefs decline. They figure out who is behind Santa Claus and the Tooth Fairy, realize that magicians' feats are due to trickery, and say that characters and events in fantastical stories aren't real (Woolley & Cornelius, 2013; Woolley & Cox, 2007). Still, because children entertain the possibility that something they imagine might materialize, they may react with anxiety to scary stories, TV shows, and nightmares.

Preschoolers distinguish between animate and inanimate and realize, for example, that a robot with lifelike features cannot eat or grow. But because of incomplete knowledge, they often claim that robots have perceptual and psychological capacities, such as seeing, thinking, and remembering.

Logical Thought. Many studies show that when preschoolers are given tasks that are simplified and relevant to their everyday lives, they do not display the illogical characteristics that Piaget saw in the preoperational stage. For example, when a conservation-of-number task is scaled down to include only three items instead of six or seven, 3-year-olds perform well (Gelman, 1972). And when asked carefully worded questions about what happens to a substance (such as sugar) after it is dissolved in water, most 3- to 5-year-olds know that the substance is conserved—that it continues to exist, can be tasted, and makes the liquid heavier, even though it is invisible in the water (Au, Sidle, & Rollins, 1993; Rosen & Rozin, 1993).

LOOK and LISTEN

Try the conservation of number and mass tasks in Figure 7.6 with a 3- or 4-year-old. Next, simplify conservation of number by reducing the number of pennies, and relate conservation of mass to the child's experience by pretending the clay is baking dough and transforming it into cupcakes. Did the child perform more competently?

Preschoolers' ability to reason about transformations is evident on other problems. They can engage in impressive *reasoning by analogy* about physical changes. Presented with the picture-matching problem "Play dough is to cut-up play dough as apple is to . . . ?," even 3-year-olds choose the correct answer (a cut-up apple) from a set of alternatives, several of which (a bitten apple, a cut-up loaf of bread) share physical features with the right choice (Goswami, 1996). These findings indicate that in familiar contexts, preschoolers can overcome appearances and think logically about cause and effect.

Finally, even without detailed biological or mechanical knowledge, preschoolers understand that the insides of animals are responsible for certain cause–effect sequences (such as willing oneself to move) that are impossible for nonliving things, such as machines (Gelman, 2003). They seem to use illogical reasoning only when grappling with unfamiliar topics, too much information, or contradictory facts that they cannot reconcile.

Categorization. Despite their difficulty with Piagetian class inclusion tasks, preschoolers organize their everyday knowledge into nested categories at an early age. By the beginning of early childhood, children's categories include objects that go together because of their common function, behavior, or natural kind (animate versus inanimate), despite varying widely in perceptual features.

Indeed, 2- to 5-year-olds readily draw appropriate inferences about nonobservable characteristics shared by category members (Gopnik & Nazzi, 2003). For example, after being told that a bird has warm blood and that a stegosaurus (dinosaur) has cold blood, preschoolers infer that a pterodactyl (labeled a dinosaur) has cold blood, even though it closely resembles a bird.

Nevertheless, when most instances of a category have a certain perceptual property (such as long ears), preschoolers readily categorize on the basis of perceptual features. This indicates that they flexibly use different types of information to classify, depending on the situation (Rakison & Lawson, 2013). And past experiences influence the information they decide to use. Native-American 5-year-olds growing up on the Menominee Reservation in northern Wisconsin often use relations in the natural world to categorize animals—for example, grouping together wolves and eagles because of their shared forest habitat (Ross et al., 2003). European-American children, in contrast, mostly rely on the animals' common features.

During the second and third years, and perhaps earlier, children's categories differentiate. They form many *basic-level categories*—ones that are at an intermediate level of generality, such as "chairs," "tables," and "beds." By the third year, children easily move back and forth between basic-level categories and *general categories,* such as "furniture." And they break down basic-level categories into *subcategories,* such as "rocking chairs" and "desk chairs."

Preschoolers' rapidly expanding vocabularies and general knowledge support their impressive skill at categorizing, and they benefit greatly from conversations with adults, who frequently label and explain categories to them. When adults use the word *bird* for hummingbirds, turkeys, and swans, they signal to children that something other than physical similarity binds these instances together (Gelman & Kalish, 2006). Children also ask many questions about their world, the majority of which are information-seeking: "What's that? What does it do?" (Chouinard, 2007). Usually, parents give informative answers that advance conceptual understanding. Picture-book reading is an especially rich context for category learning. In conversing about books, parents provide information that guides children's inferences about the structure of categories: "Penguins live at the South Pole, swim, catch fish, and have thick layers of fat and feathers that help them stay warm."

In sum, although preschoolers' category systems are less complex than those of older children and adults, they already have the capacity to classify hierarchically and on the basis of nonobvious properties. And they use logical, causal reasoning to identify the interrelated features that form the basis of a category and to classify new members.

Evaluation of the Preoperational Stage

Table 7.2 provides an overview of the cognitive attainments of early childhood. Compare them with Piaget's description of the preoperational child on pages 229–230. The evidence as a whole indicates that Piaget was partly wrong and partly right about young children's cognitive capacities. When given simplified tasks based on familiar experiences, preschoolers show the

These 4-year-olds understand that a category ("dinosaurs") can be based on underlying characteristics ("cold-blooded"), not just on perceptual features such as upright posture and scaly skin.

TABLE 7.2
Some Cognitive Attainments of Early Childhood

APPROXIMATE AGE	COGNITIVE ATTAINMENTS
2–4 years	Shows a dramatic increase in representational activity, as reflected in the development of language, make-believe play, understanding of dual representation, and categorization
	Takes the perspective of others in simplified, familiar situations and in everyday, face-to-face communication
	Distinguishes animate beings from inanimate objects; prefers natural over supernatural explanations for events
	Grasps conservation, notices transformations, reverses thinking, and understands many cause-and-effect relationships in simplified, familiar situations
	Categorizes objects on the basis of common function, behavior, and natural kind as well as perceptual features, depending on context; uses inner causal features to categorize objects varying widely in external appearance
	Sorts familiar objects into hierarchically organized categories
4–7 years 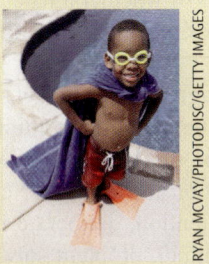	Becomes increasingly aware that make-believe and other thought processes are representational activities
	Replaces beliefs in magical creatures and events with plausible explanations
	Passes Piaget's conservation of number, mass, and liquid problems

beginnings of logical thinking, which suggest that they attain logical operations gradually.

Evidence that preschoolers can be trained to perform well on Piagetian problems also supports the idea that operational thought is not absent at one point in time and present at another (Ping & Goldin-Meadow, 2008). Over time, children rely on increasingly effective mental (as opposed to perceptual) approaches to solving problems. For example, children who cannot use counting to compare two sets of items do not conserve number (Rouselle, Palmers, & Noël, 2004). Once preschoolers can count, they apply this skill to conservation-of-number tasks involving just a few items. As counting improves, they extend the strategy to problems with more items. By age 6, they understand that number remains the same after a transformation as long as nothing is added or taken away (Halford & Andrews, 2011). Consequently, they no longer need to count to verify their answer.

The gradual development of logical operations poses yet another challenge to Piaget's assumption of abrupt change toward logical reasoning around age 6 or 7. Does a preoperational stage really exist? Some no longer think so. Recall from Chapter 5 that according to the information-processing perspective, children work out their understanding of each type of task separately, and their thought processes are basically the same at all ages—just present to a greater or lesser extent.

Other experts think the stage concept is still valid, with modifications. For example, some *neo-Piagetian theorists* combine Piaget's stage approach with the information-processing emphasis on task-specific change (Case, 1998; Halford & Andrews, 2011). They believe that Piaget's strict stage definition must be transformed into a less tightly knit concept, one in which a related set of competencies develops over an extended period, depending on brain development and specific experiences. These investigators point to evidence that as long as the complexity of tasks and children's exposure to them are carefully controlled, children approach those tasks in similar, stage-consistent ways (Andrews & Halford, 2002; Case & Okamoto, 1996). For example, in drawing pictures, preschoolers depict objects separately, ignoring their spatial arrangement. In understanding stories, they grasp a single story line but have trouble with a main plot plus one or more subplots.

This flexible stage notion recognizes the unique qualities of early childhood thinking. At the same time, it provides a better account of why, as Leslie put it, "Preschoolers' minds are such a blend of logic, fantasy, and faulty reasoning."

Piaget and Education

Three educational principles derived from Piaget's theory continue to influence teacher training and classroom practices, especially during early childhood:

- *Discovery learning.* In a Piagetian classroom, children are encouraged to discover for themselves through spontaneous interaction with the environment. Instead of presenting ready-made knowledge verbally, teachers provide a rich variety of activities designed to promote exploration, including art, puzzles, table games, dress-up clothing, building blocks, books, measuring tools, natural science tasks, and musical instruments.

- *Sensitivity to children's readiness to learn.* In a Piagetian classroom, teachers introduce activities that build on children's current thinking, challenging their incorrect ways of viewing the world. But they do not try to speed up development by imposing new skills before children indicate interest or readiness.
- *Acceptance of individual differences.* Piaget's theory assumes that all children go through the same sequence of development, but at different rates. Therefore, teachers must plan activities for individual children and small groups, not just for the whole class. In addition, teachers evaluate educational progress in relation to each child's previous development, rather than on the basis of attaining normative standards.

Like his stages, educational applications of Piaget's theory have met with criticism, especially his insistence that young children learn primarily through acting on the environment (Brainerd, 2003). In the next section, we will see that they also rely on language-based routes to knowledge.

Ask yourself

CONNECT Select two of the following features of preoperational thought: egocentrism, a focus on perceptual appearances, difficulty reasoning about transformations, and lack of hierarchical classification. Present evidence indicating that preschoolers are more capable thinkers than Piaget assumed.

APPLY Three-year-old Will understands that his tricycle isn't alive and can't feel or move on its own. But at the beach, while watching the sun dip below the horizon, Will exclaimed, "The sun is tired. It's going to sleep!" What explains this apparent contradiction in Will's reasoning?

REFLECT Did you have an imaginary companion as a young child? If so, what was your companion like, and why did you create it?

Vygotsky's Sociocultural Theory

7.8 Describe Vygotsky's perspective on the social origins and significance of children's private speech.

7.9 Describe applications of Vygotsky's theory to education, and evaluate his major ideas.

Piaget's de-emphasis on language as a source of cognitive development brought on yet another challenge, this time from Vygotsky's sociocultural theory, which stresses the social context of cognitive development. During early childhood, rapid expansion of language broadens preschoolers' participation in social dialogues with more knowledgeable individuals, who encourage them to master culturally important tasks. Soon children start to communicate with themselves in much the same way they converse with others. This greatly enhances their thinking and ability to control their own behavior. Let's see how this happens.

Private Speech

Watch preschoolers as they play and explore the environment, and you will see that they frequently talk out loud to themselves. For example, as Sammy worked a puzzle, he said, "Where's the red piece? Now, a blue one. No, it doesn't fit. Try it here."

Piaget (1923/1926) called these utterances *egocentric speech,* reflecting his belief that young children have difficulty taking the perspectives of others. Their talk, he said, is often "talk for self" in which they express thoughts in whatever form they happen to occur, regardless of whether a listener can understand. As egocentrism declines, so does this poorly adapted speech.

Vygotsky (1934/1987) disagreed with Piaget's conclusions. He maintained that language helps children think about their mental activities and behavior and select courses of action, thereby serving as the foundation for all higher cognitive processes, including controlled attention, deliberate memorization and recall, categorization, planning, problem solving, and self-reflection. In Vygotsky's view, children speak to themselves for self-guidance. As they get older and find tasks easier, their self-directed speech is internalized as silent, *inner speech*—the internal verbal dialogues we carry on while thinking and acting in everyday situations.

Because almost all studies support Vygotsky's perspective, children's self-directed speech is now called **private speech** instead of egocentric speech. Research shows that children use

A 4-year-old talks to herself as she draws. Research supports Vygotsky's theory that children use private speech to guide their thinking and behavior.

more of it when tasks are appropriately challenging (neither too easy nor too hard), after they make errors, or when they are confused about how to proceed. With age, as Vygotsky predicted, private speech goes underground, changing into whispers and silent lip movements. Furthermore, children who freely use private speech during a challenging activity are more attentive and involved and show better task performance than their less talkative agemates (Benigno et al., 2011; Lidstone, Meins, & Fernyhough, 2010; Winsler, 2009).

Social Origins of Early Childhood Cognition

Where does private speech come from? Recall from Chapter 5 that Vygotsky believed that children's learning takes place within the *zone of proximal development*—a range of tasks too difficult for the child to do alone but possible with the help of others. Consider the joint activity of Sammy and his mother as she helps him put together a difficult puzzle:

> *Sammy:* I can't get this one in. *[Tries to insert a piece in the wrong place.]*
>
> *Mother:* Which piece might go down here? *[Points to the bottom of the puzzle.]*
>
> *Sammy:* His shoes. *[Looks for a piece resembling the clown's shoes but tries the wrong one.]*
>
> *Mother:* Well, what piece looks like this shape? *[Points again to the bottom of the puzzle.]*
>
> *Sammy:* The brown one. *[Tries it, and it fits; then attempts another piece and looks at his mother.]*
>
> *Mother:* Try turning it just a little. *[Gestures to show him.]*
>
> *Sammy:* There! *[Puts in several more pieces while his mother watches.]*

Sammy's mother keeps the puzzle within his zone of proximal development, at a manageable level of difficulty. To do so, she engages in **scaffolding**—adjusting the support offered during a teaching session to fit the child's current level of performance. When the child has little notion of how to proceed, the adult uses direct instruction, breaking the task into manageable units, suggesting strategies, and offering rationales for using them. As the child's competence increases, effective scaffolders gradually and sensitively withdraw support, turning over responsibility to the child. Then children take the language of these dialogues, make it part of their private speech, and use this speech to organize their independent efforts.

Although preschoolers freely use private speech when alone or with others, they use more in the presence of others (McGonigle-Chalmers, Slater, & Smith, 2014). This suggests that some private speech retains a social purpose, perhaps as an indirect appeal for renewed scaffolding should the child need additional help. In several studies, children whose parents were effective scaffolders engaged in higher rates of private speech, were more likely to succeed when attempting challenging tasks on their own, and were advanced in overall cognitive development (Berk & Spuhl, 1995; Conner & Cross, 2003; Mulvaney et al., 2006).

Nevertheless, effective scaffolding can take different forms in different cultures. In an investigation of Hmong families who had emigrated from Southeast Asia to the United States, once again, parental cognitive support was associated with children's advanced reasoning skills. But unlike European-American parents, who emphasize independence by encouraging their children to think of ways to approach a task, Hmong parents—who highly value interdependence and child obedience—frequently tell their children what to do (for example, "Put this piece here, then this piece on top of it") (Stright, Herr, & Neitzel, 2009). Among European-American children, such directive scaffolding is associated with kindergartners' lack of self-control and behavior problems (Neitzel & Stright, 2003). Among the Hmong children, it predicted capacity to follow rules, be organized, and finish assignments.

Vygotsky and Early Childhood Education

Both Piagetian and Vygotskian classrooms emphasize active participation and acceptance of individual differences. But a Vygotskian classroom goes beyond independent discovery to promote *assisted discovery*. Teachers guide children's learning, tailoring their interventions to each child's zone of proximal development. Assisted discovery is aided by *peer collaboration*, as children of varying abilities work in groups, teaching and helping one another.

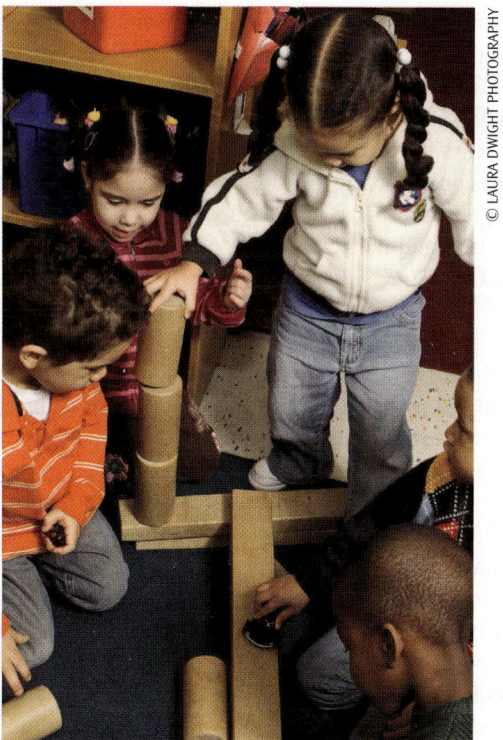

In this Vygotsky-inspired classroom, preschoolers benefit from peer collaboration as they jointly create an elaborate block structure.

Vygotsky (1933/1978) saw make-believe play as the ideal social context for fostering cognitive development in early childhood. As children create imaginary situations, they learn to follow internal ideas and social rules rather than impulses. For example, a child pretending to go to sleep follows the rules of bedtime behavior. A child imagining himself as a father and a doll as a child conforms to the rules of parental behavior (Meyers & Berk, 2014). According to Vygotsky, make-believe play is a unique, broadly influential zone of proximal development in which children try out a wide variety of challenging activities and acquire many new competencies.

Turn back to page 228 to review evidence on the contributions of make-believe play to cognitive and social development. Pretending is also rich in private speech—a finding that supports its role in helping children bring action under the control of thought (Krafft & Berk, 1998). Preschoolers who spend more time engaged in sociodramatic play are better at inhibiting impulses, regulating emotion, and taking personal responsibility for following classroom rules (Elias & Berk, 2002; Kelly & Hammond, 2011; Lemche et al., 2003). These findings support the role of make-believe in children's increasing self-control.

Evaluation of Vygotsky's Theory

In granting social experience a fundamental role in cognitive development, Vygotsky's theory underscores the power of teaching and helps us understand the wide cultural variation in children's cognitive skills. Nevertheless, his theory has not gone unchallenged. In some cultures, verbal dialogues are not the only—or even the most important—means through which children learn. When Western parents scaffold their young children's mastery of challenging tasks, their verbal communication resembles the teaching that occurs in school, where their children will spend years preparing for adult life. In cultures that place less emphasis on schooling and literacy, parents often expect children to take greater responsibility for acquiring new skills through keen observation and participation in community activities (Rogoff, Correa-Chavez, & Silva, 2011). See the Cultural Influences box on the following page for research illustrating this difference.

To account for children's diverse ways of learning through involvement with others, Barbara Rogoff (2003) suggests the term **guided participation,** a broader concept than scaffolding. It refers to shared endeavors between more expert and less expert participants, without specifying the precise features of communication. Consequently, it allows for variations across situations and cultures.

Finally, Vygotsky's theory says little about how basic motor, perceptual, attention, memory, and problem-solving skills, discussed in Chapters 4 and 5, contribute to socially transmitted higher cognitive processes. For example, his theory does not address how these elementary capacities spark changes in children's social experiences, from which more advanced cognition springs (Daniels, 2011; Miller, 2009). Piaget paid far more attention than Vygotsky to the development of basic cognitive processes. It is intriguing to speculate about the broader theory that might exist today had Piaget and Vygotsky—the two twentieth-century giants of cognitive development—had a chance to meet and weave together their extraordinary accomplishments.

Ask yourself

CONNECT Explain how Piaget's and Vygotsky's theories complement each other. How would classroom practices inspired by these theories be similar? How would they differ?

APPLY Tanisha sees her 5-year-old son, Toby, talking aloud to himself as he plays. She wonders whether she should discourage this behavior. Use Vygotsky's theory to explain to Tanisha why Toby talks to himself.

REFLECT When do you use private speech? Does it serve a self-guiding function for you, as it does for children? Explain.

Information Processing

7.10 How do executive function and memory change during early childhood?

7.11 Describe the young child's theory of mind.

7.12 Summarize children's literacy and mathematical knowledge during early childhood.

Return to the model of information processing discussed on page 160 in Chapter 5. Recall that information processing focuses on cognitive operations and mental strategies that children use to transform stimuli flowing into their mental systems. As we have already seen, early childhood is a period of dramatic strides in mental representation. And the various components of *executive function* that help us succeed in cognitively challenging situations—inhibiting impulses and distracting stimuli, flexibly shifting attention depending on task demands, coordinating information in working memory, and planning—show impressive gains (Carlson, Zelazo, & Faja, 2013). Preschoolers also become more aware of their own mental life and begin to acquire academically relevant knowledge important for school success.

Executive Function

As parents and teachers know, preschoolers—compared with school-age children—spend shorter times involved in tasks and are more easily distracted. Control of attention improves substantially during early childhood, as studies of inhibition and flexible shifting reveal. As we will see, expansion of working memory supports these attainments. The components of executive function are closely interrelated in early childhood, and they contribute vitally to academic social skills from early childhood on (Shaul & Schwartz, 2014).

Cultural Influences

Children in Village and Tribal Cultures Observe and Participate in Adult Work

In Western societies, the role of equipping children with the skills they need to become competent workers is assigned to school. In early childhood, middle-SES parents' interactions with children emphasize child-focused activities designed to prepare them to succeed academically—especially adult–child conversations and play that enhance language, literacy, and other school-related knowledge. In village and tribal cultures, children receive little or no schooling, spend their days in contact with or participating in adult work, and start to assume mature responsibilities in early childhood (Gaskins, 2014). Consequently, parents have little need to rely on conversation and play to teach children.

A study comparing 2- and 3-year-olds' daily lives in four cultures—two U.S. middle-SES suburbs, the Efe hunters and gatherers of the Republic of Congo, and a Mayan agricultural town in Guatemala—documented these differences (Morelli, Rogoff, & Angelillo, 2003). In the U.S. communities, young children had little access to adult work and spent much time conversing and playing with adults. The Efe and Mayan children spent their days close to—and frequently observing—adult work, which often took place in or near the Efe campsite or the Mayan family home.

An ethnography of a remote Mayan village in Yucatán, Mexico, shows that when young children are legitimate onlookers and participants in a daily life structured around adult work, their competencies differ from those of Western preschoolers (Gaskins, 1999; Gaskins, Haight, & Lancy, 2007). Yucatec Mayan adults are subsistence farmers. Men tend cornfields, aided by sons age 8 and older. Women prepare meals, wash clothes, and care for the livestock and garden, assisted by daughters and by sons too young to work in the fields. Children join in these activities from the second year on. When not participating, they are expected to be self-sufficient.

Young children make many nonwork decisions for themselves—how much to sleep and eat, what to wear, and even when to start school. As a result, Yucatec Mayan preschoolers are highly competent at self-care. In contrast, their make-believe play is limited; when it occurs, they usually imitate adult work. Otherwise, they watch others—for hours each day.

Yucatec Mayan parents rarely converse or play with preschoolers or scaffold their learning. Rather, when children imitate adult tasks, parents conclude that they are ready for more responsibility. Then they assign chores, selecting tasks the child can do with little help so that adult work is not disturbed. If a child cannot do a task, the adult takes over and the child observes, reengaging when able to contribute.

In a South-African village, a young child intently watches his mother grind grain. Children in village and tribal cultures observe and participate in the work of their community from an early age.

Expected to be autonomous and helpful, Yucatec Mayan children seldom display attention-getting behaviors or ask others for something interesting to do. From an early age, they can sit quietly for long periods—through a lengthy religious service or a three-hour truck ride. And when an adult interrupts their activity and directs them to do a chore, they respond eagerly to the type of command that Western children frequently avoid or resent. By age 5, Yucatec Mayan children spontaneously take responsibility for tasks beyond those assigned.

Inhibition. With age, preschoolers gain steadily in ability to inhibit impulses and keep their mind on a competing goal. Consider a task in which the child must tap once when the adult taps twice and tap twice when the adult taps once or must say "night" to a picture of the sun and "day" to a picture of the moon with stars. As Figure 7.8 on page 238 shows, 3- and 4-year-olds make many errors. But by age 6 to 7, children find such tasks easy (Diamond, 2004; Montgomery & Koeltzow, 2010). They can resist the "pull" of their attention toward a dominant stimulus— a skill that, as early as age 3 to 5, predicts social maturity as well as reading and math achievement from kindergarten through high school (Blair & Razza, 2007; Duncan et al., 2007; Rhoades, Greenberg, & Domitrovich, 2009).

Flexible Shifting. Children's ability to flexibly shift their focus of attention, depending on what's important at the moment, is often studied through categorization and sorting behaviors. As we saw in Chapter 5, even toddlers have a beginning ability to

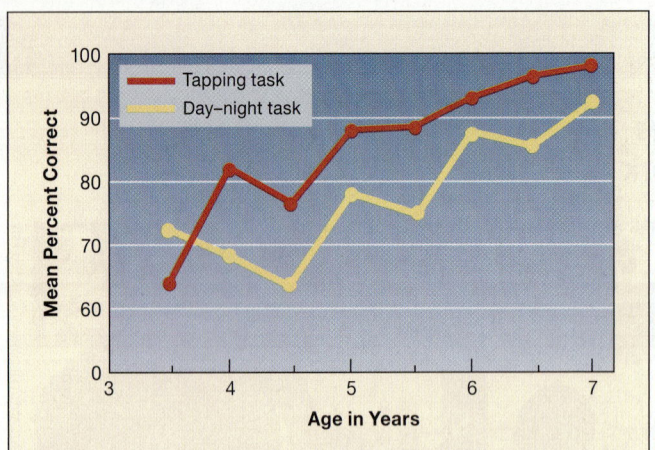

FIGURE 7.8 Gains between ages 3 and 7 in performance on tasks requiring children to inhibit an impulse and focus on a competing goal. In the tapping task, children had to tap once when the adult tapped twice and tap twice when the adult tapped once. In the day–night task, children had to say "night" to a picture of the sun and "day" to a picture of the moon with stars. (From A. Diamond, 2004, "Normal Development of Prefrontal Cortex from Birth to Young Adulthood: Cognitive Functions, Anatomy, and Biochemistry," as appeared in D. T. Stuss & R. T. Knight [Eds.], *Principles of Frontal Lobe Function*, New York: Oxford University Press, p. 474. Reprinted by permission of Adele Diamond.)

shift their basis of sorting a small set of objects after an adult calls their attention to a second way of grouping (see page 164).

In preschoolers and school-age children, flexible shifting is often studied through rule-use tasks (Zelazo et al., 2013). In this procedure, children are asked to switch the rules they use to sort picture cards in the face of conflicting cues. For example, children might first be asked to sort pictures of boats and flowers using color rules, by placing all the blue boats and flowers in a box marked with a blue boat and all the red boats and flowers in a box marked with a red flower. Then the child is asked to switch to shape rules, placing all the boats (irrespective of color) into the box marked with the blue boat and all the flowers into the box marked with the red flower. Three-year-olds persist in sorting by color; not until age 4 do children succeed in switching rules (Zelazo, 2006). And when researchers increase the complexity of the rules—for example, requiring children to shift from color to shape rules only on a subset of picture cards with an added black border—most 6-year-olds have difficulty (Henning, Spinath, & Aschersleben, 2011).

As these findings confirm, flexible shifting improves greatly during the preschool years, with gains continuing in middle childhood. Note that inhibition contributes to preschoolers' flexible shifting (Kirkham, Cruess, & Diamond, 2003; Zelazo et al., 2013). To switch rules, children must inhibit attending to the previously relevant dimension while focusing on the dimension they had just ignored.

Working Memory. Gains in working memory, enabling preschoolers to hold in mind and manipulate more information at once (see page 161 in Chapter 5), contribute to control of attention. Greater working-memory capacity eases effort in keeping several rules in mind, ignoring ones not currently important, and flexibly shifting focus to new rules, thereby improving performance.

With age, the ability to hold and combine information in working memory becomes increasingly important in problem solving. In one study, both inhibition and working-memory scores predicted 2½- to 6-year-olds' solutions to a problem-solving task requiring multistep planning. But working memory was a stronger predictor for the 4- to 6-year-olds than for the younger children (Senn, Espy, & Kaufmann, 2004). Older preschoolers were able to deploy their larger working memories to solve more challenging problems involving planning.

Planning. As the findings just described suggest, early childhood is a time of marked gains in *planning*—thinking out a sequence of acts ahead of time and performing them accordingly to reach a goal. Because successful planning requires that basic executive processes be integrated with other cognitive operations, it is regarded as a complex executive function activity (Müller & Kerns, 2015). As long as tasks are not too difficult, older preschoolers can follow a plan.

Consider a task, devised to resemble real-world planning, in which 3- to 5-year-olds were shown a doll named Molly, a camera, and a miniature zoo with a path, along which were three animal cages. The first and third cages had storage lockers next to them; the middle cage, with no locker, housed a kangaroo (see Figure 7.9). The children were told that Molly could follow the path only once and that she wanted to take a picture of the kangaroo. Then they were asked, "What locker could you leave the camera in so Molly can get it and take a photo of the kangaroo?" (McColgan & McCormack, 2008). Not until age 5 were children able to plan effectively, selecting the locker at the first cage.

On this and other planning tasks, young preschoolers have difficulty (McCormack & Atance, 2011). By the end of early childhood, children make strides in postponing action in favor of mapping out a sequence of future moves, evaluating the consequences of each, and adjusting their plan to fit task requirements.

Parenting and Development of Executive Function. Parental sensitivity and scaffolding foster preschoolers' executive function skills, as many investigations reveal (Carlson, Zelazo, & Faja, 2013). In one study, parental scaffolding of 2- and 3-year-olds while jointly solving a challenging puzzle predicted higher scores on diverse executive function tasks at age 4 (Hammond et al., 2012). Among the 2-year-olds, effective scaffolding led to gains in language, which in turn promoted executive function, perhaps by augmenting children's ability to verbally regulate their behavior through private speech.

With respect to planning, children learn much from cultural tools that support it—directions for playing games, patterns for construction, recipes for cooking—especially when they collaborate with expert planners. When mothers were observed constructing a toy with their 4- to 7-year-olds, they often pointed out the usefulness of plans and how to implement specific steps: "Do

FIGURE 7.9 **Miniature zoo used to assess children's planning.** After having been told that Molly wanted to take a picture of the kangaroo but could follow the path only once, preschoolers were asked which locker the camera should be left in so Molly could get it and take the photo. Not until age 5 did children plan, more often selecting the first locker. (Based on McColgan & McCormack, 2008.)

you want to look at the picture and see what goes where? What piece do you need first?" After working with their mothers, younger children more often referred to the plan while building on their own (Gauvain, de la Ossa, & Hurtado-Ortiz, 2001). When parents encourage planning in everyday activities, from loading the dishwasher to packing for a vacation, they help children plan more effectively.

Poverty exerts a negative impact on executive function, in part through maladaptive parenting practices and chronic stress. In a socioeconomically and ethnically diverse sample, poverty-stricken mothers more often interacted harshly and intrusively with their 7- to 24-month-olds—parenting behaviors associated with children's elevated cortisol levels and with poor executive function scores during a follow-up at age 3 (Blair et al., 2011). As the authors noted, poverty and negative parenting undermined early stress regulation, promoting "reactive and inflexible rather than reflective and flexible forms of behavior and cognition" (p. 1980).

Memory

Unlike infants and toddlers, preschoolers have the language skills to describe what they remember, and they can follow directions on memory tasks. As a result, memory becomes easier to study in early childhood. The memory changes of the first two years are largely *implicit*, taking place without conscious awareness. This enables researchers to focus on *explicit*, or conscious, memory which undergoes the greatest change throughout development.

Recognition and Recall. Show a young child a set of 10 pictures or toys. Then mix them up with some unfamiliar items, and ask the child to point to the ones in the original set. You will find that preschoolers' *recognition* memory—ability to tell whether a stimulus is the same as or similar to one they have seen before—is remarkably good. In fact, 4- and 5-year-olds perform nearly perfectly.

Now keep the items out of view, and ask the child to name the ones she saw. This more demanding task requires *recall*—generating a mental image of an absent stimulus. Young children's recall is much poorer than their recognition. At age 2, they can recall no more than one or two items and at age 4 only about three or four (Perlmutter, 1984).

A grandfather engages in scaffolding by breaking a challenging construction task into manageable units and suggesting strategies to his 3-year-old grandchild—support that consistently promotes diverse executive function skills.

Improvement in recall in early childhood is strongly associated with language development, which greatly enhances long-lasting representations of past experiences (Melby-Lervag & Hulme, 2010). But even preschoolers with good language skills recall poorly because they are not skilled at using **memory strategies**—deliberate mental activities that improve our chances of remembering. Preschoolers do not yet *rehearse*, or repeat items over and over, to remember. Nor do they *organize*, intentionally grouping items that are alike (all the animals together, all the vehicles together) so they can easily retrieve those items by thinking of their similar characteristics—even after they are trained to do so (Bauer, 2013).

Why do young children seldom use memory strategies? One reason is that strategies tax their limited working memories. Preschoolers have difficulty holding on to pieces of information and applying a strategy at the same time.

Memory for Everyday Experiences.
Think about the difference between your recall of listlike information and your memory for everyday experiences—what researchers call **episodic memory**. In remembering everyday experiences, you recall information in context—linked to a particular time, place, or person. In remembering lists, you recall isolated pieces—information removed from the context in which it was first learned that has become part of your general knowledge base. Researchers call this type of memory **semantic memory**.

Between 3 and 6 years, children improve sharply in memory for relations among stimuli. For example, in a set of photos, they remember not just the animals they saw but their contexts, such as a bear emerging from a tunnel or a zebra tied to a tree (Lloyd, Doydum, & Newcombe, 2009). The capacity to bind together stimuli supports an increasingly rich episodic memory in early childhood.

Memory for Routine Events. Like adults, preschoolers remember familiar, repeated events—what you do when you go to preschool or have dinner—in terms of **scripts**, general descriptions of what occurs and when it occurs in a particular situation. Young children's scripts begin as a structure of main acts. For example, when asked to tell what happens at a restaurant, a 3-year-old might say, "You go in, get the food, eat, and then pay." Although children's first scripts contain only a few acts, they are almost always recalled in correct sequence (Bauer, 2006, 2013). With age, scripts become more elaborate, as in this 5-year-old's account of going to a restaurant: "You go in. You can sit in a booth or at a table. Then you tell the waitress what you want. You eat. If you want dessert, you can have some. Then you pay and go home" (Hudson, Fivush, & Kuebli, 1992).

Scripts help children (and adults) organize and interpret routine experiences. Once formed, scripts can be used to predict what will happen in the future. Children rely on scripts in make-believe play and when listening to and telling stories. Scripts also support children's earliest efforts at planning by helping them represent sequences of actions that lead to desired goals (Hudson & Mayhew, 2009).

Memory for One-Time Events. In Chapter 5, we considered a second type of episodic memory—*autobiographical memory*, or representations of personally meaningful, one-time events. As preschoolers' cognitive and conversational skills improve, their descriptions of special events become better organized in time, more detailed, enriched with a personal perspective, and related to the larger context of their lives. A young preschooler simply reports, "I went camping." Older preschoolers include specifics: where and when the event happened and who was present. And with age, preschoolers increasingly include subjective information that explains the event's personal significance (Bauer, 2013; Pathman et al., 2013). For example, they might say, "I *loved* sleeping all night in the tent."

Adults use two styles to elicit children's autobiographical narratives. In the *elaborative style,* they follow the child's lead, ask varied questions, add information to the child's statements, and volunteer their own recollections and evaluations of events, assisting the child in weaving together a story. For example, after a trip to the zoo, the parent might say, "What was the first thing we did? Why weren't the parrots in their cages? I thought the lion was scary. What did you think?" In contrast, adults who use the *repetitive style* provide little information and keep repeating the same questions: "Do you remember the zoo? What did we do at the zoo?" Elaborative-style parents *scaffold* the autobiographical memories of their young children, who produce more organized and detailed personal stories when followed up later in childhood and in adolescence (Reese, 2002).

As children talk with adults about the past, they not only improve their autobiographical memory but also create a shared history that strengthens close relationships and self-understanding. Parents and preschoolers with secure attachment bonds engage in more elaborate reminiscing (Bost et al., 2006). And 5- and 6-year-olds of elaborative-style parents describe themselves in clearer, more consistent ways (Bird & Reese, 2006).

As this toddler talks with his mother about past experiences, she responds in an elaborative style, asking varied questions and contributing her own recollections. Through such conversations, she enriches his autobiographical memory.

Girls tend to produce more organized and detailed personal narratives than boys. Compared with Asian children, Western children produce narratives with more talk about their own thoughts and emotions. These differences fit with variations in parent–child conversations. Parents reminisce in greater detail and talk more about the emotional significance of events with daughters (Fivush & Zaman, 2014). And cultural valuing of an interdependent self leads many Asian parents to discourage children from talking about themselves (Fivush & Wang, 2005).

Consistent with these early experiences, women report an earlier age of first memory and more vivid early memories than men. And Western adults' autobiographical memories include earlier, more detailed events that focus more on their own roles than do the memories of Asians, who tend to highlight the roles of others (Wang, 2008).

The Young Child's Theory of Mind

As representation of the world, memory, and problem solving improve, children start to reflect on their own thought processes. They begin to construct a *theory of mind,* or coherent set of ideas about mental activities. This understanding is also called **metacognition,** or "thinking about thought" (the prefix *meta-* means "beyond" or "higher"). As adults, we have a complex appreciation of our inner mental worlds, which we use to interpret our own and others' behavior and to improve our performance on various tasks. How early are children aware of their mental lives, and how complete and accurate is their knowledge?

Awareness of Mental Life. At the end of the first year, babies view people as intentional beings who can share and influence one another's mental states, a milestone that opens the door to new forms of communication—joint attention, social referencing, preverbal gestures, and spoken language. These early milestones serve as the foundation for later mental understandings.

As they approach age 2, children display a clearer grasp of others' emotions and desires, evident in their realization that people often differ from one another and from themselves in likes, dislikes, wants, needs, and wishes. As 2-year-olds' vocabularies expand, their first verbs include such words as *want, think, remember,* and *pretend* (Wellman, 2011).

By age 3, children realize that thinking takes place inside their heads and that a person can think about something without seeing, touching, or talking about it (Flavell, Green, & Flavell, 1995). But 2- to 3-year-olds' verbal responses indicate that they assume people always behave in ways consistent with their *desires.* Not until age 4 do most realize that less obvious, more interpretive mental states, such as *beliefs,* also affect behavior.

Dramatic evidence for this advance comes from games that test whether preschoolers realize that *false beliefs*—ones that do not represent reality accurately—can guide people's actions. For example, show a child two small closed boxes—a familiar Band-Aid box and a plain, unmarked box (see Figure 7.10). Then say,

FIGURE 7.10 Example of a false-belief task. (a) An adult shows a child the contents of a Band-Aid box and of an unmarked box. The Band-Aids are in the unmarked container. (b) The adult introduces the child to a hand puppet named Pam and asks the child to predict where Pam would look for the Band-Aids and to explain Pam's behavior. The task reveals whether children understand that without having seen that the Band-Aids are in the unmarked container, Pam will hold a false belief.

"Pick the box you think has the Band-Aids in it." Children usually pick the marked container. Next, open the boxes and show the child that, contrary to her own belief, the marked one is empty and the unmarked one contains the Band-Aids. Finally, introduce the child to a hand puppet and explain, "Here's Pam. She has a cut, see? Where do you think she'll look for Band-Aids? Why would she look in there? Before you looked inside, did you think that the plain box contained Band-Aids? Why?" (Bartsch & Wellman, 1995). Only a handful of 3-year-olds can explain Pam's—and their own—false beliefs, but many 4-year-olds can.

Some researchers claim that the procedures just described, which require verbal responses, underestimate younger children's ability to attribute false beliefs to others. For example, in a study relying on active behavior (helping), most 18-month-olds—after observing an adult reach for a box previously used for blocks that now contained a spoon—based their choice of how to help on her false belief about the contents of the box: They gave her a block rather than a spoon (Buttelmann et al., 2014). This suggests that toddlers *implicitly* understand that people's actions can be guided by false beliefs, though more evidence is needed to confirm this conclusion (Astington & Hughes, 2013). Researchers cannot yet explain the striking contrast between toddlers' success on nonverbal tasks and 3-year-olds' consistent failure on verbal assessments.

Among children of diverse cultural and SES backgrounds, *explicit* false-belief understanding strengthens after age 3½, becoming more secure between ages 4 and 6 (Wellman, 2012). During that time, it becomes a powerful tool for reflecting on the thoughts and emotions of oneself and others and a good predictor of social skills (Hughes, Ensor, & Marks, 2010). It is also associated with early reading ability, probably because it helps children comprehend story narratives (Astington & Pelletier, 2005). Following a story line often requires children to link plot actions with characters' motives and beliefs.

Factors Contributing to Preschoolers' Theory of Mind. How do children develop a theory of mind at such a young age? Language, executive function, make-believe play, and social experiences all contribute.

Many studies indicate that language ability strongly predicts preschoolers' false-belief understanding (Milligan, Astington, & Dack, 2007). Children who spontaneously use, or who are trained to use, mental-state words in conversation are especially likely to pass false-belief tasks (Hale & Tager-Flusberg, 2003; San Juan & Astington, 2012). Among the Quechua people of the Peruvian highlands, whose language lacks mental-state terms, children have difficulty with false-belief tasks for years after children in industrialized nations have mastered them (Vinden, 1996).

Several aspects of preschoolers' executive function—inhibition, flexible shifting of attention, and planning—predict mastery of false belief because they enhance children's ability to reflect on experiences and mental states (Benson et al., 2013; Drayton, Turley-Ames, & Guajardo, 2011; Müller et al., 2012). Inhibition is strongly related to false-belief understanding, perhaps because false-belief tasks require suppression of an irrelevant response—the tendency to assume that others' knowledge and beliefs are the same as one's own (Carlson, Moses, & Claxton, 2004).

Social experiences also made a difference. In longitudinal research, the maternal "mind-mindedness" experienced by securely attached babies (frequent commentary on their mental states) is positively associated with later performance on false-belief and other theory-of-mind tasks (Laranjo et al., 2010; Meins et al., 2003; Ruffman et al., 2006). Securely attached children also experience more elaborative parent–child narratives, including discussions of mental states (Ontai & Thompson, 2008). These conversations expose preschoolers to concepts and language that help them think about their own and others' mental lives.

Also, preschoolers with siblings who are children (but not infants)—especially those with older siblings or two or more siblings—tend to be more aware of false belief because they are exposed to more family talk about varying thoughts, beliefs, and emotions (Hughes et al., 2010; McAlister & Peterson, 2006, 2007). Similarly, preschool friends who often engage in mental-state talk—as children do during make-believe play—are advanced in false-belief understanding (de Rosnay & Hughes, 2006). These exchanges offer children extra opportunities to talk about inner states, receive feedback, and become increasingly aware of their own and others' mental activities.

Core knowledge theorists (see Chapter 5, page 158) believe that to profit from the social experiences just described, children must be biologically prepared to develop a theory of mind. Children with *autism,* for whom mastery of false belief is either greatly delayed or absent, are deficient in the brain mechanism that enables humans to detect mental states. See the Biology and Environment box on the following page to find out more about the biological basis of reasoning about the mind.

Limitations of the Young Child's Understanding of Mental Life. Though surprisingly advanced, preschoolers' awareness of mental activities is far from complete. For example, 3- and 4-year-olds are unaware that people continue to think while they wait, look at pictures, listen to stories, or read books—that is, when there are no obvious cues that they are thinking (Eisbach, 2004; Flavell, Green, & Flavell, 1995, 2000). Furthermore, children younger than age 6 pay little attention to the *process* of thinking. When asked about subtle distinctions between mental states, such as *know* and *forget,* they express confusion (Lyon & Flavell, 1994). And they often insist that all events must be directly observed to be known. They do not understand that *mental inferences* can be a source of knowledge (Miller, Hardin, & Montgomery, 2003).

These findings suggest that preschoolers view the mind as a passive container of information. As they move into middle childhood, they will increasingly see it as an active, constructive agent—a change we will consider further in Chapter 9.

Early Childhood Literacy

One week, Leslie's students created a make-believe grocery store. They brought empty food boxes from home, placed them on shelves in the classroom, labeled items with prices, and wrote checks at the cash register. A sign at the entrance announced the daily specials: "APLS BNS 5¢" ("apples bananas 5¢").

As such play reveals, preschoolers understand a great deal about written language long before they learn to read or write in conventional ways. This is not surprising: Children in industrialized nations live in a world filled with written symbols. Each day, they observe and participate in activities involving storybooks, calendars, lists, and signs. Children's active efforts to construct literacy knowledge through informal experiences are called **emergent literacy.**

Young preschoolers search for units of written language as they "read" memorized versions of stories and recognize familiar signs ("PIZZA"). But they do not yet understand the symbolic

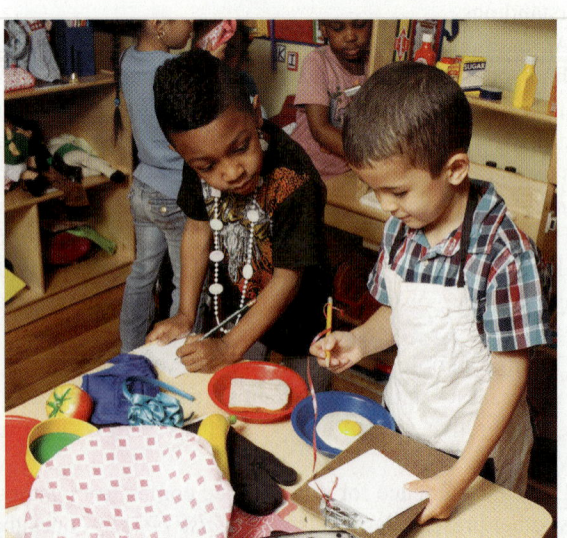

Preschoolers acquire literacy knowledge by participating in everyday activities involving written symbols. These young chefs "write down" orders they need to fill.

Biology and Environment

Autism and Theory of Mind

Michael stood at the water table in Leslie's classroom, repeatedly filling a plastic cup and dumping out its contents—dip–splash, dip–splash—until Leslie came over and redirected his actions. Without looking at Leslie's face, Michael moved to a new repetitive pursuit: pouring water from one cup into another and back again. As other children entered the play space and conversed, Michael hardly noticed. He rarely spoke, and when he did, he usually used words to get things he wanted, not to exchange ideas.

Michael has *autism* (a term meaning "absorbed in the self"). Autism varies in severity along a continuum, called *autism spectrum disorder*. Michael's difficulties are substantial. Like other similarly affected children, by age 3 he displayed deficits in two core areas of functioning. First, he had only limited ability to engage in social interaction—evident in his difficulty with nonverbal communication, such as eye gaze, facial expressions, gestures, imitation, and give-and-take, and in his delayed and stereotyped language. Second, his interests were narrow and overly intense. For example, one day he sat for more than an hour spinning a toy Ferris wheel. And Michael showed another typical feature of autism: He engaged in much less make-believe play than other children (American Psychiatric Association, 2013; Tager-Flusberg, 2014).

Researchers agree that autism stems from abnormal brain functioning, usually due to genetic or prenatal environmental causes. Beginning in the first year, children with the disorder have larger-than-average brains, with the greatest excess in brain-region volume in the prefrontal cortex (Courchesne et al., 2011). This brain overgrowth is believed to result from lack of synaptic pruning, which accompanies typical development of cognitive, language, and communication skills. Furthermore, preschoolers with autism show a deficient left-hemispheric response to speech sounds (Eyler, Pierce, & Courchesne, 2012). Failure of the left hemisphere of the cerebral cortex to lateralize for language may underlie these children's language deficits.

The amygdala, devoted to emotion processing (see page 192 in Chapter 6), also grows abnormally large in childhood, followed by a greater than average reduction in size in adolescence and adulthood. This deviant growth pattern is believed to contribute to deficits in emotion processing involved in the disorder (Alley, Gillberg, & Wilson, 2014). fMRI studies reveal that autism is associated with weaker connections between the amygdala and the temporal lobes, which are important for interpreting facial expressions (Monk et al., 2010).

Mounting evidence reveals that children with autism are impaired in theory of mind. As early as the first two years, they show deficits in emotional and social capacities believed to contribute to an understanding of mental life, including interest in observing people's actions, joint attention, and social referencing (Chawarska, Macari, & Shic, 2013; Warreyn, Roeyers, & De Groote, 2005). Long after they reach the intellectual level of an average 4-year-old, they have great difficulty with false belief. Most find it hard to attribute mental states to themselves or others (Steele, Joseph, & Tager-Flusberg, 2003). They rarely use mental-state words such as *believe, think, know, feel,* and *pretend*.

Do these findings indicate that autism is due to impairment in an innate, core brain function that leaves the child unable to detect others' mental states and therefore deficient in human sociability? Some researchers think so (Baron-Cohen, 2011; Baron-Cohen & Belmonte, 2005). But others point out that individuals with general intellectual disability but not autism also do poorly on tasks

This child, who has autism, is barely aware of his teacher and classmates. Researchers disagree on whether the deficient emotional and social capacities of autism result from a basic impairment in ability to detect others' mental states, a deficit in executive function, or a style of information processing that focuses on parts rather than coherent wholes.

assessing mental understanding (Yirmiya et al., 1998). This suggests that cognitive deficits are largely responsible.

One hypothesis with growing research support is that children with autism are impaired in executive function (Kimhi et al., 2014; Pugliese et al., 2016). This leaves them deficient in skills involved in flexible, goal-oriented thinking, including shifting attention to relevant aspects of a situation, inhibiting irrelevant responses, applying strategies, and generating plans (Robinson et al., 2009).

Another possibility is that children with autism display a peculiar style of information processing, preferring to process the parts of stimuli over coherent wholes (Booth & Happé, 2016). Deficits in thinking flexibly and in holistic processing of stimuli would each interfere with understanding the social world because social interaction requires quick integration of information from various sources and evaluation of alternative possibilities.

It is not clear which of these hypotheses is correct. Perhaps several biologically based deficits underlie the tragic social isolation of children like Michael.

function of the elements of print (Bialystok & Martin, 2003). Many preschoolers think that a single letter stands for a whole word or that each letter in a person's signature represents a separate name. Children revise these ideas as their cognitive capacities improve, as they encounter writing in many contexts, and as adults help them with written communication. Gradually, they notice more features of written language and depict writing that varies in function, as in one child's horizontal line of letters to represent "a story" and vertical line to represent a "grocery list."

Eventually, children figure out that letters are parts of words and are linked to sounds in systematic ways, as 5- to 7-year-olds' invented spellings illustrate. At first, children rely on sounds in the names of letters: "ADE LAFWTS KRMD NTU A LAVATR" ("eighty elephants crammed into a[n] elevator"). Over time, they grasp sound–letter correspondences and learn that some letters have more than one common sound and that context affects their use (McGee & Richgels, 2012).

Literacy development builds on a broad foundation of spoken language and knowledge about the world (Dickinson, Golinkoff, & Hirsh-Pasek, 2010). **Phonological awareness**—the ability to reflect on and manipulate the sound structure of spoken language, as indicated by sensitivity to changes in sounds within words, to rhyming, and to incorrect pronunciation—is a strong predictor of emergent literacy knowledge and later reading and spelling achievement (Dickinson et al., 2003; Paris & Paris, 2006). When combined with sound–letter knowledge, it enables children to isolate speech segments and link them with their written symbols. Vocabulary and grammatical knowledge are also influential. And narrative competence, assessed by having preschoolers retell stories, fosters diverse language skills essential for literacy progress, including phonological awareness (Hipfner-Boucher et al., 2014). Coherent storytelling requires attention to large language structures, such as character, setting, problem, and resolution. This seems to support the smaller-scale analysis involved in awareness of sound structures.

The more informal literacy experiences young children have, the better their language and literacy development (Dickinson & McCabe, 2001; Speece et al., 2004). Pointing out letter–sound correspondences and playing language–sound games enhance children's awareness of the sound structures of language and how they are represented in print (Ehri & Roberts, 2006). *Interactive reading,* in which adults discuss storybook content with preschoolers, and adult-supported writing activities that focus on narrative, such as preparing a letter or a story, also have wide-ranging benefits (Hood, Conlon, & Andrews, 2008; Senechal & LeFevre, 2002; Storch & Whitehurst, 2001). Each is linked to improved reading achievement in middle childhood.

Preschoolers from low-SES families have far fewer home and preschool language and literacy learning opportunities—a gap that translates into large differences in reading readiness at kindergarten entry (see Figure 7.11) and into widening disparities in reading achievement during the school years (Cabell et al., 2013; Hoff, 2013). But high-quality intervention can reduce the SES gap in early literacy development substantially. Providing low-SES parents with children's books, along with guidance in how to stimulate emergent literacy, greatly enhances literacy

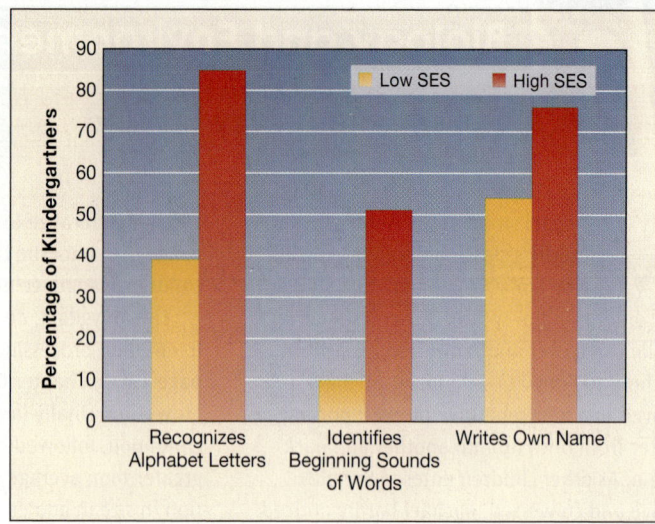

FIGURE 7.11 Some reading readiness skills at kindergarten entry by SES. The SES gap in emergent literacy development is large. (Adapted from Lee & Burkam, 2002.)

activities in the home (Huebner & Payne, 2010). And when teachers are shown how to engage in effective instruction of diverse literacy skills, low-SES preschoolers gain in emergent literacy components included in their classroom experiences (Hilbert & Eis, 2014; Lonigan et al., 2013).

Early Childhood Mathematical Reasoning

Mathematical reasoning, like literacy, builds on informally acquired knowledge. Between 14 and 16 months, toddlers display a beginning grasp of **ordinality,** or order relationships between quantities—for example, that 3 is more than 2, and 2 is more than 1. In the early preschool years, children attach verbal labels (*lots, little, big, small*) to amounts and sizes. Sometime in the third year, they begin to count. By the time children turn 3, most can count a row of about five objects, although they do not yet know exactly what the words mean. For example, when asked for *one,* they give one item, but when asked for *two, three, four,* or *five,* they usually give a larger, but incorrect, amount. Nevertheless, 2½- to 3½-year-olds realize that a number word refers to a unique quantity (Sarnecka & Gelman, 2004). They know that when a number label changes (for example, from *five* to *six*), the number of items should also change.

By age 3½ to 4, most children have mastered the meaning of numbers up to 10, count correctly, and grasp the vital principle of **cardinality**—that the last number in a counting sequence indicates the quantity of items in a set (Sarnecka & Wright, 2013). Mastery of cardinality increases the efficiency of children's counting.

Around age 4, children use counting to solve simple arithmetic problems. At first, their strategies are tied to the order of numbers as presented; to add 2 + 4, they count on from 2 (Bryant & Nunes, 2002). But soon they experiment with other strategies and eventually arrive at the most efficient, accurate approach—

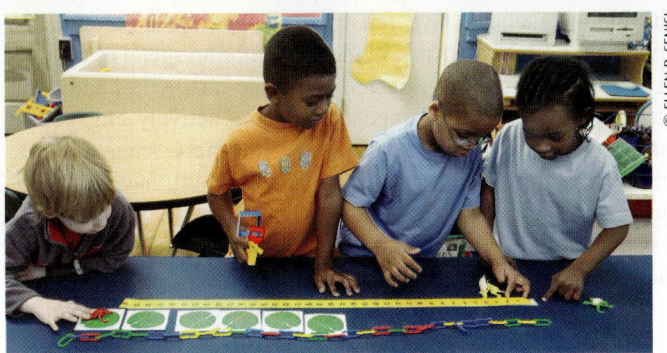

Preschoolers "hop" a toy frog along a number line, measuring the length of each jump. Through informal exploration of number concepts, they construct basic understandings essential for learning math skills later on.

in this example, beginning with the higher digit. Around this time, children realize that subtraction cancels out addition. Knowing, for example, that 4 + 3 = 7, they can infer without counting that 7 − 3 = 4 (Rasmussen, Ho, & Bisanz, 2003). Grasping basic arithmetic rules facilitates rapid computation, and with enough practice, children recall answers automatically.

When adults provide many occasions for counting, comparing quantities, and talking about number concepts, children acquire these understandings sooner (Ginsburg, Lee, & Boyd, 2008). Math proficiency at kindergarten entry predicts math achievement years later, in elementary and secondary school (Duncan et al., 2007; Romano et al., 2010).

As with emergent literacy, children from low-SES families begin kindergarten with considerably less math knowledge than their economically advantaged agemates—a gap due to differences in home learning environments (DeFlorio & Beliakoff, 2015). In an early childhood math curriculum called *Building Blocks,* materials that promote math concepts and skills through three types of media—computers, manipulatives, and print—enable teachers to weave math into many preschool daily activities, from building blocks to art and stories (Clements et al., 2011). Compared with agemates randomly assigned to other preschool programs, low-SES preschoolers experiencing Building Blocks showed substantially greater year-end gains in math concepts and skills, including counting, sequencing, and arithmetic computation.

Ask yourself

CONNECT Cite evidence on the development of preschoolers' memory, theory of mind, executive function, and literacy and mathematical understanding that is consistent with Vygotsky's sociocultural theory.

APPLY Lena wonders why her 4-year-old son Gregor's teacher provides extensive playtime in learning centers during each preschool day. Explain to Lena how adult-supported play can promote literacy and math skills essential for academic success.

REFLECT Describe informal experiences important for literacy and math development that you experienced while growing up.

 # Individual Differences in Mental Development

7.13 Describe early childhood intelligence tests and the impact of home, preschool and kindergarten programs, child care, and educational media on mental development.

Five-year-old Hal sat in a testing room while Sarah gave him an intelligence test. Some of Sarah's questions were *verbal*. For example, she showed Hal a picture of a shovel and said, "Tell me what this is"—an item measuring vocabulary. She tested his working memory by asking him to repeat sentences and lists of numbers back to her. She probed his quantitative knowledge and problem solving by seeing if he could count and solve simple addition and subtraction problems. To assess Hal's spatial reasoning, Sarah used *nonverbal* tasks: Hal copied designs with special blocks, figured out the pattern in a series of shapes, and indicated what a piece of paper folded and cut would look like when unfolded (Roid, 2003; Wechsler, 2012).

Sarah knew that Hal came from an economically disadvantaged family. When low-SES and certain ethnic minority preschoolers are bombarded with questions by an unfamiliar adult, they sometimes react with anxiety. Also, such children may not define the testing situation in achievement terms (Ford, Kozey, & Negreiros, 2012). Instead, they may look for attention and approval from the adult and may settle for lower performance than their abilities allow. Sarah spent time playing with Hal before she began testing and encouraged him while testing was in progress (Bracken & Nagle, 2006). Under these conditions, low-SES preschoolers improve in performance.

The questions Sarah asked Hal tap knowledge and skills that not all children have equal opportunity to learn. In Chapter 9, we will take up the hotly debated issue of *cultural bias* in mental testing. For now, keep in mind that intelligence tests do not sample all human abilities, and cultural and situational factors affect performance. Nevertheless, test scores remain important: By age 6 to 7, they are good predictors of later IQ and academic achievement, which are related to vocational success in industrialized societies. Let's see how the environments in which preschoolers spend their days—home, preschool, and child care—affect mental test performance.

Home Environment and Mental Development

A special version of the *Home Observation for Measurement of the Environment (HOME),* covered in Chapter 5, assesses aspects of 3- to 6-year-olds' home lives that foster intellectual growth. Research with the HOME early childhood subscales reveals that preschoolers who develop well intellectually have homes rich in educational toys and books. Their parents are warm and affectionate, stimulate language and academic knowledge, and arrange interesting outings. They also make reasonable demands for socially mature behavior—for example, that the child perform simple chores and behave courteously toward others. And these parents resolve conflicts with reason instead of physical force and punishment (Bradley & Caldwell, 1982; Espy, Molfese, & DiLalla, 2001; Roberts, Burchinal, & Durham, 1999).

When low-SES parents manage, despite life challenges, to obtain high HOME scores, their preschoolers do substantially better on tests of intelligence and measures of language and emergent literacy skills (Berger, Paxson, & Waldfogel, 2009; Mistry et al., 2008). In a study of African-American 3- and 4-year-olds from low-income families, HOME cognitive stimulation and emotional support subscales predicted reading achievement four years later (Zaslow et al., 2006). These findings highlight the vital contribution of home environmental quality to children's overall intellectual development.

Preschool, Kindergarten, and Child Care

Children between ages 2 and 6 spend even more time away from their homes and parents than infants and toddlers do. Largely because of the rise in maternal employment, over the past several decades the number of young children enrolled in preschool or child care has steadily increased to more than 65 percent in the United States (U.S. Census Bureau, 2015d).

A *preschool* is a program with planned educational experiences aimed at enhancing the development of 2- to 5-year-olds. In contrast, *child care* refers to a variety of arrangements for supervising children, from care in the caregiver's or the child's home to a center-based program. The line between preschool and child care is fuzzy. Parents often select a preschool as a child-care option. And in response to the needs of employed parents, many U.S. preschools, as well as most public school kindergartens, have increased their hours from half to full days (Child Trends, 2015b).

With age, preschoolers tend to shift from home-based to center-based programs. In the United States, children of higher-income parents and children of very-low-income parents are especially likely to be in preschools or child-care centers (Child Trends, 2015b). Many low-income working parents rely on care by relatives because they are not eligible for public preschool or government-subsidized child-care centers. A few states offer government-funded prekindergarten programs located within public schools to all 4-year-olds. The goal of these universal pre-kindergartens is to ensure that as many children as possible, from all SES levels, enter kindergarten prepared to succeed.

Types of Preschool and Kindergarten. Preschool and kindergarten programs range along a continuum from child-centered to teacher-directed. In **child-centered programs,** teachers provide activities from which children select, and much learning takes place through play. In contrast, in **academic programs,** teachers structure children's learning, teaching letters, numbers, colors, shapes, and other academic skills through formal lessons, often using repetition and drill.

Despite evidence that formal academic training undermines young children's motivation and emotional well-being, early childhood teachers have felt increased pressure to take this approach. Preschoolers and kindergartners who spend much time in large-group, teacher-directed academic instruction and completing worksheets—as opposed to being actively engaged in learning centers by warm, responsive teachers—display more stress behaviors (such as wiggling and rocking), have less confidence in their abilities, prefer less challenging tasks, and are less advanced in motor, academic, language, and social skills at the end of the school year (Stipek, 2011; Stipek et al., 1995). Follow-ups reveal lasting effects through elementary school in poorer study habits and achievement (Burts et al., 1992; Hart et al., 1998, 2003). These outcomes are strongest for low-SES children.

Although government spending for universal prekindergarten is controversial in the United States, in Western Europe such programs are widespread and child-centered in their daily activities. Enrolled preschoolers of all SES backgrounds show gains in cognitive and social development still evident in elementary and secondary school (Rindermann & Ceci, 2008; Waldfogel & Zhai, 2008). Findings on some U.S. universal prekindergarten programs that meet rigorous state standards of quality—especially, provision of rich teacher–child interactions and stimulating learning activities—reveal up to a one-year advantage in kindergarten and first-grade language, literacy, and math scores relative to those of children not enrolled (Gormley & Phillips, 2009; Weiland & Yoshikawa, 2013). Children from low-SES families benefit most.

As for the dramatic rise in full-day kindergartens, the longer school day is associated with better academic achievement through elementary school. But benefits for social development are mixed (Brownell et al., 2015; Cooper et al., 2010). Some evidence suggests that kindergartners in full-day as opposed to half-day classrooms have more behavior problems.

Early Intervention for At-Risk Preschoolers. In the 1960s, as part of the "War on Poverty" in the United States, many intervention programs for low-SES preschoolers were initiated in an effort to address learning problems prior to school entry. The most extensive of these federal programs, **Project Head Start,** began in 1965. A typical Head Start center provides children with a year or two of preschool, along with nutritional and health services. Parent involvement is central to the Head Start philosophy. Parents serve on policy councils, contribute to program planning, work directly with children in classrooms, attend special programs on parenting and child development, and receive services directed at their own emotional, social, and vocational needs. Currently, Head Start serves about 904,000 children and their families across the nation (Office of Head Start, 2014).

More than two decades of research have established the long-term benefits of preschool intervention. The most extensive study combined data from seven programs implemented by universities or research foundations. Results showed that poverty-stricken children who attended programs scored higher in IQ and achievement than controls during the first 2 to 3 years of elementary school. After that, differences declined (Lazar & Darlington,

1982). But on real-life measures of school adjustment, children and adolescents who had received intervention remained ahead. They were less likely to be placed in special education or retained in grade, and a greater number graduated from high school.

A separate report on one program—the High/Scope Perry Preschool Project—revealed benefits lasting well into adulthood. Two years' exposure to cognitively enriching preschool was associated with increased employment and reduced pregnancy and delinquency rates in adolescence. At age 27, those who had attended preschool were more likely than their no-preschool counterparts to have earned both high school and college degrees, have higher incomes, be married, and own their own home—and less likely to have been involved with the criminal justice system. In the most recent follow-up, at age 40, the intervention group sustained its advantage on all measures of life success, including education, income, family life, and law-abiding behavior (Schweinhart, 2010; Schweinhart et al., 2005).

Do effects on school adjustment of these excellent interventions generalize to Head Start and other community-based preschool interventions? Gains are similar, though not as strong. Head Start preschoolers, who are more economically disadvantaged than children in other programs, have more severe learning and behavior problems. And quality of Head Start—though better than in most preschool programs serving low-SES children—often does not equal that of model university-based programs (Barnett, 2011; Resnick, 2010). But community-based interventions of high quality are associated with diverse life-success outcomes, including higher rates of high school graduation and college enrollment and lower rates of adolescent drug use and delinquency (Yoshikawa et al., 2013).

A consistent finding is that gains in IQ and achievement test scores from attending Head Start and other interventions quickly dissolve. In the Head Start Impact Study, a nationally representative sample of 5,000 Head Start–eligible 3- and 4-year-olds was randomly assigned to one year of Head Start or to a control group that could attend other types of preschool programs (Puma et al., 2012; U.S. Department of Health and Human Services, 2010). By year's end, Head Start 3-year-olds exceeded controls in vocabulary, emergent literacy, and math skills; 4-year-olds in vocabulary, emergent literacy, and color identification. But except for language skills, academic test-score advantages were no longer evident by the end of first grade. And Head Start graduates did not differ from controls on any achievement measures at the end of third grade.

What explains these disappointing results? Head Start children typically enter inferior public schools in poverty-stricken neighborhoods, which undermine the benefits of preschool education (Ramey, Ramey, & Lanzi, 2006). And recall from Chapter 5 that when intensive intervention begins in infancy, IQ gains are more likely to endure into adulthood (see page 173).

A few supplementary programs have responded to the need to intensify preschool intervention to augment its impact. One of the most widely implemented is *Head Start REDI* (Research-Based Developmentally Informed), an enrichment curriculum designed for integration into existing Head Start classrooms.

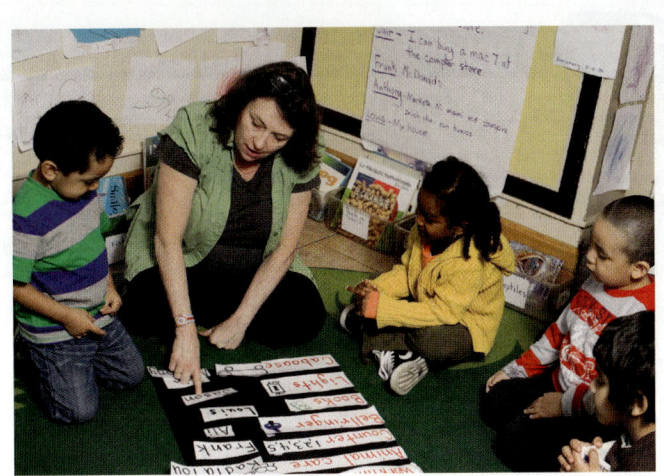

This teacher integrates Head Start REDI into her preschool classroom. By delivering extra educational enrichment, Head Start REDI yields greater gains in language, literacy, and social skills than typical Head Start classrooms.

Before school begins, Head Start teachers—60 percent of whom do not have teaching certificates—take workshops in which they learn strategies for enhancing language, literacy, and social skills. Throughout the school year, they receive one-to-one mentoring from master teachers, aimed at ensuring effective delivery of REDI.

Relative to typical Head Start classrooms, Head Start plus REDI yields higher year-end language, literacy, and social development scores—advantages still evident at the end of kindergarten (Bierman et al., 2008, 2014). REDI's impact on teaching quality is likely responsible. Teachers trained in REDI converse with preschoolers in more cognitively complex ways and more often use management strategies that prevent disruptive behavior (Domitrovich et al., 2009).

Head Start is highly cost-effective when compared to the price of providing special education, treating criminal behavior, and supporting unemployed adults. Because of limited funding, however, only 46 percent of 3- and 4-year-olds living in poverty attend preschool, with Head Start serving just half of these children (Child Trends, 2014b).

Child Care. We have seen that high-quality early intervention can enhance the development of economically disadvantaged children. As noted in Chapter 5, however, much U.S. child care lacks quality. Preschoolers exposed to substandard care, especially for long hours in crowded child-care centers, score lower in cognitive and social skills and display more behavior problems (Burchinal et al., 2015; NICHD Early Child Care Research Network, 2003b, 2006). Externalizing difficulties are especially likely to endure into the school years after extensive exposure to mediocre care (Belsky et al., 2007b; Vandell et al., 2010).

In contrast, good child care enhances cognitive, language, and social development, especially for low-SES children—effects that persist into elementary school and, for academic achievement, adolescence (Burchinal et al., 2015; Dearing, McCartney, & Taylor, 2009; Vandell et al., 2010). Center-based

Applying what we Know

Signs of Developmentally Appropriate Early Childhood Programs

PROGRAM CHARACTERISTICS	SIGNS OF QUALITY
Physical setting	Indoor environment is clean, in good repair, and well-ventilated. Classroom space is divided into richly equipped activity areas, including make-believe play, blocks, science, math, games and puzzles, books, art, and music. Fenced outdoor play space is equipped with swings, climbing equipment, tricycles, and sandbox.
Group size	In preschools and child-care centers, group size is no greater than 18 to 20 children with two teachers.
Teacher–child ratio	In preschools and child-care centers, teacher is responsible for no more than 8 to 10 children. In family child-care homes, caregiver is responsible for no more than 6 children.
Daily activities	Children select many of their own activities and learn through experiences relevant to their own lives, mainly in small groups or individually. Teachers facilitate children's involvement, accept individual differences, and adjust expectations to children's developing capacities.
Interactions between adults and children	Teachers move among groups and individuals, asking questions, offering suggestions, and adding more complex ideas. Teachers use positive guidance techniques, such as modeling and encouraging expected behavior and redirecting children to more acceptable activities.
Teacher qualifications	Teachers have college-level specialized preparation in early childhood development, early childhood education, or a related field.
Relationships with parents	Parents are encouraged to observe and participate. Teachers talk frequently with parents about children's behavior and development.
Licensing and accreditation	Preschool and child-care programs are licensed by the state. Voluntary accreditation by the National Association for the Education of Young Children (www.naeyc.org/academy) or the National Association for Family Child Care (www.nafcc.org) is evidence of an especially high-quality program.

Source: Copple & Bredekamp, 2009.

care is more strongly associated with cognitive gains than are other child-care arrangements (Abner et al., 2013). Good-quality child-care centers are more likely than family child-care homes to provide a systematic educational program.

Applying What We Know above summarizes characteristics of high-quality early childhood programs, based on standards for developmentally appropriate practice devised by the U.S. National Association for the Education of Young Children. These standards offer a set of worthy goals as the United States strives to upgrade child-care and educational services for young children.

Educational Media

Besides home and preschool, young children spend much time in another learning environment: screen media, including both television and computers. In the industrialized world, nearly all homes have at least one television set, and most have two or more. And more than 90 percent of U.S. children live in homes with one or more computers, 80 percent of which have an Internet connection, usually a high-speed link (Rideout, Foehr, & Roberts, 2010; U.S. Census Bureau, 2015d).

Educational Television. Sammy's favorite TV program, *Sesame Street,* uses lively visual and sound effects to stress basic literacy and number concepts and puppet and human characters to teach general knowledge, emotional and social understanding, and social skills. Today, *Sesame Street* is broadcast in more than 140 countries, making it the most widely viewed children's program in the world (Sesame Workshop, 2015).

Time devoted to watching children's educational programs, including *Sesame Street,* is associated with gains in early literacy and math skills and academic progress in elementary school (Ennemoser & Schneider, 2007; Mares & Pan, 2013). One study reported a link between preschool viewing of *Sesame Street* (and similar educational programs) and getting higher grades, reading more books, and placing more value on achievement in high school (Anderson et al., 2001).

Sesame Street modified its previous, rapid-paced format in favor of more leisurely episodes with a clear story line. Programs with slow-paced action and easy-to-follow narratives, such as *Arthur* and *The Magic School Bus,* are associated with improved executive function, greater recall of program content, gains in vocabulary and reading skills, and more elaborate make-believe play than programs presenting quick, disconnected bits of information (Lillard & Peterson, 2011; Linebarger & Piotrowski, 2010). Narratively structured educational TV eases processing demands, facilitating attention and freeing up space in working memory for applying program content to real-life situations.

Despite the spread of computers, television remains the dominant form of youth media. The average U.S. 2- to 6-year-old watches TV programs and videos from 1½ to 2⅔ hours a day. In middle childhood, viewing time increases to an average of 3½ hours a day and then declines slightly in adolescence (Common Sense Media, 2013; Rideout, Foehr, & Roberts, 2010).

Low-SES children are more frequent TV viewers, perhaps because few alternative forms of entertainment are available in their neighborhoods or affordable for their parents. On the positive side, preschoolers in low-SES families watch as much educational television as their economically advantaged agemates (Common Sense Media, 2013). But parents with limited education are more likely to engage in practices that heighten TV viewing of all kinds, including leaving the TV on all day and eating family meals in front of it (Rideout, Foehr, & Roberts, 2010).

About 35 percent of U.S. preschoolers and 45 percent of school-age children have a TV set in their bedroom. These children are exposed to even more background TV than their agemates and spend from 40 to 90 minutes more per day watching programs, usually with no parental restrictions on what they view (Common Sense Media, 2013; Rideout & Hamel, 2006).

Does extensive TV viewing take children away from worthwhile activities? Persistent background TV distracts infants and preschoolers from their play, diminishing time spent in focused attention and involvement with a set of toys (Courage & Howe, 2010). The more preschool and school-age children watch primetime shows and cartoons, the less time they spend reading and interacting with others and the poorer their academic skills (Ennemoser & Schneider, 2007; Huston et al., 1999; Wright et al., 2001). Whereas educational programs can be beneficial, watching entertainment TV—especially heavy viewing—detracts from children's school success and social experiences.

Learning with Computers. The majority of 2- to 4-year-olds have used a computer at one time or another, and more than one-third do so regularly—from once a week to every day. But although almost all young children from higher-income families have access to a computer at home, only about half of those from low-income families do (Common Sense Media, 2013; Fletcher et al., 2014).

Because computers can have rich educational benefits, most early childhood classrooms include computer-learning centers. Computer literacy and math programs, including online storybooks, expand children's general knowledge and encourage diverse language, literacy, and arithmetic skills (Karemaker, Pitchford, & O'Malley, 2010; Li, Atkins, & Stanton, 2006). Kindergartners who use computers to draw or write produce more elaborate pictures and text and make fewer writing errors.

Simplified computer languages that children can use to make designs or build structures introduce them to programming skills. As long as adults support children's efforts, these activities promote problem solving and metacognition because children must plan and reflect on their thinking to get their programs to work. Furthermore, while programming, children are especially likely to help one another and to persist in the face of challenge (Resnick & Silverman, 2005; Tran & Subrahmanyam, 2013).

As with television, children spend much time using computers and other screen media for entertainment—especially

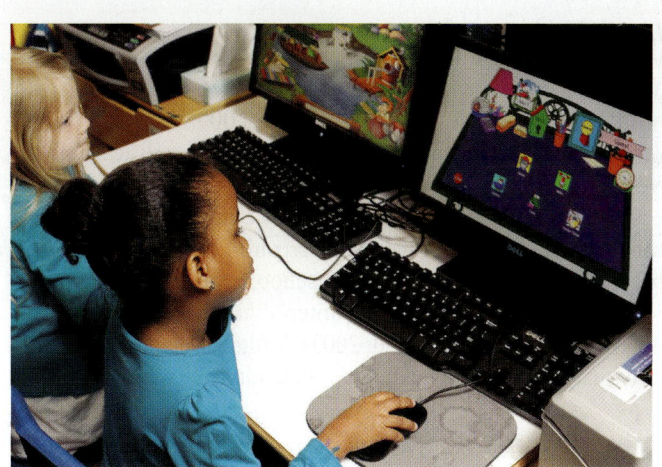

In a preschool computer-learning center, children jointly play a game aimed at strengthening math concepts and problem solving. They are likely to gain in both math and collaborative skills.

game playing, which more than triples from early to middle childhood, when it consumes, on average, 1¼ hours per day. Boys are two to three times more likely than girls to be daily players (Common Sense Media, 2013; Rideout, Foehr, & Roberts, 2010). Both TV and game media are rife with gender stereotypes and violence. We will consider the impact of screen media on emotional and social development in the next chapter.

Ask yourself

CONNECT Compare outcomes resulting from preschool intervention programs with those from interventions beginning in infancy (see pages 172–173 in Chapter 5). Which are more likely to lead to lasting cognitive gains? Explain.

APPLY Your senator has heard that IQ gains resulting from Head Start do not last, so he plans to vote against additional funding. Write a letter explaining why he should support Head Start.

REFLECT How much and what kinds of TV viewing and computer use did you engage in as a child? How do you think your home media environment influenced your development?

Language Development

7.14 Trace the development of vocabulary, grammar, and conversational skills in early childhood.

7.15 Cite factors that support language learning in early childhood.

Language is intimately related to virtually all cognitive changes discussed in this chapter. Between ages 2 and 6, children make momentous advances in language. Their remarkable achievements, as well as their mistakes along the way, reveal their active, rule-oriented approach to mastering their native tongue.

Vocabulary

At age 2, Sammy had a spoken vocabulary of about 250 words. By age 6, he will have acquired around 10,000 words (Byrnes & Wasik, 2009). To accomplish this feat, Sammy will learn about five new words each day. How do children build their vocabularies so quickly? Research shows that they can connect new words with their underlying concepts after only a brief encounter, a process called **fast-mapping**. Preschoolers can even fast-map two or more new words encountered in the same situation (Wilkinson, Ross, & Diamond, 2003). Still, fast-mapping does not imply that children immediately acquire adultlike word meanings.

Types of Words.
Children in many Western and non-Western language communities fast-map labels for objects especially rapidly because these refer to concepts that are easy to perceive (McDonough et al., 2011; Parish-Morris et al., 2010). Soon children add verbs (*go, run, broke*), which require more complex understandings of relationships between objects and actions (Scott & Fisher, 2012). Children learning Chinese, Japanese, and Korean—languages in which nouns are often omitted from adult sentences, while verbs are stressed—acquire verbs much sooner (early in the second year) and more readily than their English-speaking agemates (Chan et al., 2011; Ma et al., 2009).

As young children acquire verbs, they also add modifiers (*red, round, sad*). Among those that are related in meaning, first they make general distinctions (*big–small*), then more specific ones (*tall–short, high–low, wide–narrow*) (Stevenson & Pollitt, 1987).

Strategies for Word Learning.
Preschoolers figure out the meanings of new words by contrasting them with words they already know. How do they discover which concept each word picks out? One speculation is that early in vocabulary growth, children adopt a *mutual exclusivity bias*—the assumption that words refer to entirely separate (nonoverlapping) categories (Markman, 1992). Consistent with this idea, when 2-year-olds hear the labels for two distinct novel objects (for example, *clip* and *horn*), they assign each word correctly, to the whole object and not just a part of it (Waxman & Senghas, 1992).

Indeed, children's first several hundred nouns refer mostly to objects well-organized by shape. The process of learning nouns based on the perceptual property of shape heightens young children's attention to the distinctive shapes of other objects (Smith et al., 2002; Yoshida & Smith, 2003). This *shape bias* helps preschoolers master additional names of objects, and vocabulary accelerates.

Once the name of a whole object is familiar, on hearing a new name for the object, 2- and 3-year-olds set aside the mutual exclusivity assumption. For example, if the object (*bottle*) has a distinctively shaped part (*spout*), children readily apply the new label to it (Hansen & Markman, 2009). Still, mutual exclusivity and object shape cannot account for preschoolers' remarkably flexible responses when objects have more than one name. In these instances, children often call on other components of language.

According to one proposal, preschoolers discover many word meanings by observing how words are used in the structure of sentences (Gleitman et al., 2005; Naigles & Swenson, 2007). Consider an adult who says, "This is a *citron* one," while showing the child a yellow car. Two- and 3-year-olds conclude that a new word used as an adjective for a familiar object (car) refers to a property of that object (Imai & Haryu, 2004). As children hear the word in various sentence structures ("That lemon is bright *citron*"), they refine its meaning and generalize it to other categories.

Young children also take advantage of rich social information that adults frequently provide, while drawing on their own expanding ability to infer others' intentions, desires, and perspectives. In one study, an adult performed an action on an object and then used a new label while looking back and forth between the child and the object, as if inviting the child to play. Two-year-olds concluded that the label referred to the action, not the object (Tomasello & Akhtar, 1995). By age 3, children can even use a speaker's recently expressed desire ("I really want to play with the *riff*") to figure out the label belonging to one of two novel objects (Saylor & Troseth, 2006).

Adults also inform children directly about which of two or more words to use—by saying, for example, "You can call it a sea creature, but it's better to say *dolphin*." Preschoolers' vocabularies grow more quickly when they have parents who provide such clarifying information (Callanan & Sabbagh, 2004).

Furthermore, to fill in for words they have not yet learned, children as young as age 3 coin new words using ones they already know—"plant-man" for a gardener, "crayoner" for a child using crayons. Preschoolers also extend language meanings through metaphors based on concrete sensory comparisons: "Clouds are pillows," "Leaves are dancers." Once vocabulary and general knowledge expand, children also appreciate nonsensory comparisons: "Friends are like magnets," "Time flies by" (Keil, 1986; Özçaliskan, 2005). Metaphors permit young children to communicate in amazingly vivid and memorable ways.

Explaining Vocabulary Development.
Children acquire vocabulary so efficiently and accurately that some theorists believe that they are innately biased to induce word meanings using certain principles, such as mutual exclusivity (Lidz, Gleitman, & Gleitman, 2004). But critics point out that a small set of built-in, fixed principles cannot account for the varied, flexible manner in which children master vocabulary (MacWhinney, 2015; Parish-Morris, Golinkoff, & Hirsh-Pasek, 2013). And many word-learning strategies cannot be innate because children acquiring different languages use different approaches to mastering the same meanings.

An alternative view is that vocabulary growth is governed by the same cognitive strategies that children apply to nonlinguistic information. According to one account, children draw on a *coalition* of cues—perceptual, social, and linguistic—which shift in importance with age (Golinkoff & Hirsh-Pasek, 2006, 2008). Infants rely solely on perceptual features. Toddlers and young preschoolers, while still sensitive to perceptual features (such as object shape and physical action), increasingly attend to social

Young children rely on any useful information available to add to their vocabularies. As this child observes her father creating a sculpture, she attends to a variety of perceptual, social, and linguistic cues to grasp the meanings of unfamiliar words, such as *plaster, statue, base, form, sculpt, mold,* and *studio.*

cues—the speaker's direction of gaze, gestures, and expressions of intention and desire (Hollich, Hirsh-Pasek, & Golinkoff, 2000; Pruden et al., 2006). And as language develops further, linguistic cues—sentence structure and intonation (stress, pitch, and loudness)—play larger roles.

Preschoolers are most successful at figuring out new word meanings when several kinds of information are available (Parish-Morris, Golinkoff, & Hirsh-Pasek, 2013). Researchers have just begun to study the multiple cues that children use for different kinds of words and how their combined strategies change with development.

Grammar

Between ages 2 and 3, English-speaking children use simple sentences that follow a subject–verb–object word order. Children learning other languages adopt the word orders of the adult speech to which they are exposed.

Basic Rules. Toddlers' greater looking times at scenes that match sentences they hear reveal that they comprehend the meaning of basic grammatical structures that they cannot yet produce, such as "Big Bird is tickling Cookie Monster" or "What did the ball hit?" (Seidl, Hollich, & Jusczyk, 2003). First use of grammatical rules, however, is piecemeal—limited to just a few verbs. As children listen for familiar verbs in adults' speech, they expand their own utterances containing those verbs, relying on adult speech as their model (Gathercole, Sebastián, & Soto, 1999). Sammy, for example, added the preposition *with* to the verb *open* ("You open with scissors") but not to the word *hit* ("He hit me stick").

To test preschoolers' ability to generate novel sentences that conform to basic English grammar, researchers had them use a new verb in the subject–verb–object form after hearing it in a different construction, such as passive: "Ernie is getting *gorped* by the dog." When children were asked what the dog was doing, the percentage who could respond "He's *gorping* Ernie" rose steadily with age. But not until age 3½ to 4 could the majority of children apply the fundamental subject–verb–object structure broadly, to newly acquired verbs (Chan et al., 2010; Tomasello, 2006).

Once children form three-word sentences, they make small additions and changes to words that enable them to express meanings flexibly and efficiently. For example, they add *–ing* for ongoing actions (*playing*), add *-s* for plural (*cats*), use prepositions (*in* and *on*), and form various tenses of the verb *to be* (*is, are, were, has been, will*). English-speaking children master these grammatical markers in a regular sequence, starting with those that involve the simplest meanings and structures (Brown, 1973).

When preschoolers acquire these markers, they sometimes overextend the rules to words that are exceptions—a type of error called **overregularization.** "My toy car *breaked*" and "We each got two *foots*" are expressions that appear between ages 2 and 3 (Maratsos, 2000; Marcus, 1995).

Complex Structures. Gradually, preschoolers master more complex grammatical structures, although they do make mistakes. In first creating questions, 2- to 3-year-olds use many formulas: "Where's *X*?" "Can I *X*?" (Dabrowska, 2000; Tomasello, 2003). Question asking remains variable for the next couple of years. An analysis of one child's questions revealed that he inverted the subject and verb when asking certain questions ("What she will do?" "Why he can go?") but not others. The correct expressions were the ones he heard most often in his mother's speech (Rowland & Pine, 2000). And sometimes children produce errors in subject–verb agreement ("Where does the dogs play?") and subject case ("Where can me sit?") (Rowland, 2007).

Similarly, children have trouble with some passive sentences. When told, "The car is pushed by the truck," young preschoolers often make a toy car push a truck. By age 4½, they understand such expressions, whether they contain familiar or novel verbs (Dittmar et al., 2014). But full mastery of the passive form is not complete until the end of middle childhood.

Nevertheless, preschoolers' grasp of grammar is remarkable. By age 4 to 5, they form embedded sentences ("I think *he will come*"), tag questions ("Dad's going to be home soon, *isn't he?*"), and indirect objects ("He showed *his friend* the present") (Zukowski, 2013). As the preschool years draw to a close, children use most of the grammatical constructions of their language competently.

Explaining Grammatical Development. Evidence that grammatical development is an extended process has raised questions about Chomsky's nativist theory (to review, see page 174 in Chapter 5). Some experts believe that grammar is a product of general cognitive development—children's tendency to search the environment for consistencies and patterns of all sorts. These *information-processing theorists* believe that children notice which words appear in the same positions in sentences and are combined in the same way with other words (Howell & Becker, 2013; MacWhinney, 2015; Tomasello, 2011). Over time, they group words into grammatical categories and use them appropriately in sentences.

Other theorists, while also focusing on how children process language, agree with the essence of Chomsky's theory—that the grammatical categories into which children group word meanings are innate, present at the outset (Pinker, 1999; Tien, 2013). Critics, however, point out that toddlers' two-word utterances do not reflect a flexible grasp of grammar and that preschoolers make many errors in their gradual mastery of grammar. In sum, controversy persists over whether a universal, built-in language acquisition device exists or whether children draw on general cognitive-processing procedures, devising unique strategies adapted to the specific language that they hear.

Conversation

Besides acquiring vocabulary and grammar, children must learn to engage in effective and appropriate communication. This practical, social side of language is called **pragmatics,** and preschoolers make considerable headway in mastering it.

As early as age 2, children are skilled conversationalists. In face-to-face interaction, they take turns and respond appropriately to their partners' remarks. With age, the number of turns over which children can sustain interaction, ability to maintain a topic over time, and responsiveness to queries requesting clarification increase (Comeau, Genesee, & Mendelson, 2010; Snow et al., 1996). By age 3, children can infer a speaker's intention when the speaker expresses it indirectly. For example, most know that an adult who, in response to an offer of cereal, says, "We have no milk," is declining the cereal (Schulze, Grassmann, & Tomasello, 2013). These surprisingly advanced abilities probably grow out of early interactive experiences.

By age 4, children adjust their speech to fit the age, sex, and social status of their listeners. For example, in acting out roles with hand puppets, they use more commands when playing socially dominant and male roles (teacher, doctor, father) but speak more politely and use more indirect requests when playing less dominant and female roles (student, patient, mother) (Anderson, 2000).

Preschoolers' conversations appear less mature in highly demanding situations in which they cannot see their listeners' reactions or rely on typical conversational aids, such as gestures or objects to talk about. When asked in a phone conversation what he received for his birthday, one 3-year-old held up a new toy and said, "This!" But 3- to 6-year-olds give more specific directions about how to solve a puzzle over the phone than in person, indicating that they realize that more verbal description is necessary on the phone (Cameron & Lee, 1997). Between ages 4 and 8, both conversing and giving directions over the phone improve greatly.

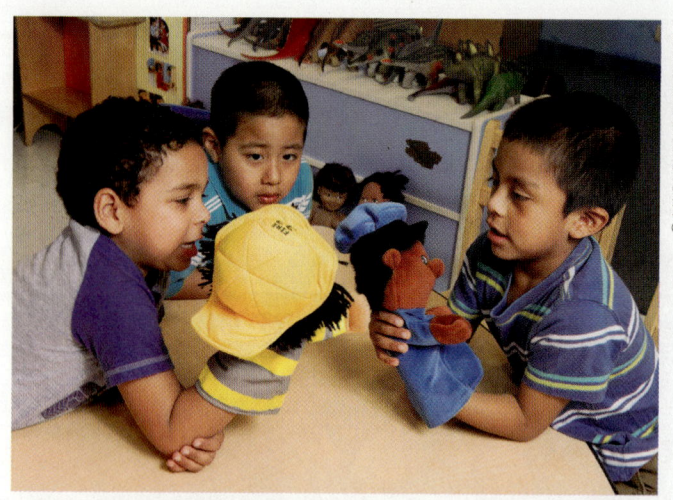

These preschoolers likely use more assertive language when speaking for a male puppet than they would if speaking for a female puppet. In doing so, they reveal their early grasp of stereotypic features of social roles in their culture.

Supporting Language Learning in Early Childhood

As in toddlerhood, conversational give-and-take with adults, either at home or in preschool, is consistently related to language progress (Hart & Risley, 1995; Huttenlocher et al., 2010). In addition, sensitive, caring adults use specific techniques that promote early language skills. When children use words incorrectly or communicate unclearly, they give helpful, explicit feedback: "I can't tell which ball you want. Do you mean the large red one?" But they do not overcorrect, especially when children make grammatical mistakes. Criticism discourages children from freely using language in ways that lead to new skills.

Instead, adults generally provide indirect feedback about grammar by using two strategies, often in combination: **recasts**—restructuring inaccurate speech into correct form, and **expansions**—elaborating on children's speech, increasing its complexity (Bohannon & Stanowicz, 1988; Chouinard & Clark, 2003). For example, if a child says, "I gotted new red shoes," the parent might respond, "Yes, you got a pair of new red shoes." In one study, after such corrective input, 2- to 4-year-olds often shifted to correct forms—improvements still evident several months later (Saxton, Backley, & Gallaway, 2005). However, the impact of such feedback has been challenged. The techniques are not used in all cultures and, in a few investigations, had no impact on children's grammar (Strapp & Federico, 2000; Valian, 1999). Rather than eliminating errors, perhaps expansions and recasts model grammatical alternatives and encourage children to experiment with them.

Do the findings just described remind you once again of Vygotsky's theory? In language, as in other aspects of cognitive development, parents and teachers gently prompt children to take the next step forward. Children strive to master language because they want to connect with other people. Adults, in turn, respond to children's desire to become competent speakers by listening attentively, elaborating on what children say, modeling correct usage, and stimulating children to talk further. In the next chapter, we will see that this combination of warmth and encouragement of mature behavior is at the heart of early childhood emotional and social development as well.

Ask yourself

CONNECT Explain how children's strategies for word learning support the interactionist perspective on language development, described on pages 174–175 in Chapter 5.

APPLY Sammy's mother explained to him that the family would take a vacation in Miami. The next morning, Sammy announced, "I gotted my bags packed. When are we going to Your-ami?" What explains Sammy's errors?

Summary / chapter 7

PHYSICAL DEVELOPMENT

A Changing Body and Brain (p. 216)

7.1 Describe body growth and brain development during early childhood.

- Gains in body size taper off in early childhood as children become longer and leaner. New epiphyses emerge in the skeleton, and by the end of the preschool years, children start to lose their primary teeth.

- Neural fibers in the brain continue to form synapses and to myelinate, followed by synaptic pruning and increasing localization of cognitive capacities in regions of the cerebral cortex. Prefrontal-cortical areas devoted to various aspects of executive function develop rapidly. The left cerebral hemisphere is especially active, supporting preschoolers' expanding language skills and improved executive function.

- Hand preference, reflecting an individual's **dominant cerebral hemisphere,** strengthens during early childhood. Research on handedness supports the joint contribution of nature and nurture to brain lateralization.

- Fibers linking the **cerebellum** to the cerebral cortex grow and myelinate, enhancing motor coordination and thinking. The **reticular formation,** responsible for alertness and consciousness; the **hippocampus,** which plays a vital role in memory and spatial understanding; the **amygdala,** which plays a central role in processing novelty and emotional information; and the **corpus callosum,** connecting the two cerebral hemispheres, also form synapses and myelinate.

Influences on Physical Growth and Health (p. 219)

7.2 Describe the effects of heredity, nutrition, and infectious disease on physical growth and health in early childhood.

- Heredity controls production and release of two hormones by the **pituitary gland: growth hormone (GH),** which is necessary for development of almost all body tissues, and **thyroid-stimulating hormone (TSH),** which affects brain development and body size.

- As growth rate slows, preschoolers' appetites decline, and they often become wary of new foods. Repeated, unpressured exposure to new foods promotes healthy, varied eating.

- Dietary deficiencies, especially in protein, vitamins, and minerals, are associated with stunted physical growth, attention and memory difficulties, and academic and behavior problems. Disease also contributes to malnutrition, especially when intestinal infections cause persistent diarrhea.

- Immunization rates are lower in the United States than in other industrialized nations because many low-income children lack access to health care. Parental stress and misconceptions about vaccine safety also contribute.

7.3 What factors increase the risk of unintentional injuries, and how can childhood injuries be prevented?

- Unintentional injuries are the leading cause of childhood mortality in industrialized nations. Victims are more likely to be boys; to be temperamentally inattentive, overactive, irritable, defiant, and aggressive; and to be growing up in poverty-stricken homes and neighborhoods.

- Effective injury prevention includes passing laws that promote child safety; creating safer home, travel, and play environments; improving public education; changing parent and child behaviors; and providing social supports to ease parental stress.

Motor Development (p. 222)

7.4 Cite major milestones of gross- and fine-motor development, along with factors that affect motor progress, in early childhood.

- As the child's center of gravity shifts toward the trunk, balance improves, paving the way for new gross-motor achievements. Preschoolers run, jump, hop, gallop and eventually skip, throw, and catch, and generally become better coordinated.

- Improved control of the hands and fingers leads to dramatic gains in fine-motor skills. Preschoolers gradually become self-sufficient at dressing and feeding.

- By age 3, children's scribbles become pictures. With age, drawings increase in complexity and realism, influenced by gains in children's cognitive and fine-motor capacities and by their culture's artistic traditions. Cognitive advances and exposure to written materials contribute to progress in accurately printing alphabet letters.

- Body build and opportunity for physical play affect motor development. Sex differences favoring boys in force and power and girls in balance and fine movements are partly genetic, but environmental pressures exaggerate them. Children master the motor skills of early childhood through informal play experiences.

COGNITIVE DEVELOPMENT

Piaget's Theory: The Preoperational Stage (p. 227)

7.5 *Describe advances in mental representation, and limitations of thinking, during the preoperational stage.*

- Rapid advances in mental representation mark the beginning of Piaget's **preoperational stage**. Make-believe, which supports many aspects of development, becomes increasingly complex, evolving into **sociodramatic play** with peers. **Dual representation** improves rapidly over the third year as children realize that models, drawings, and simple maps correspond to circumstances in the real world.

- Preoperational children's cognitive limitations include **egocentrism, centration,** a focus on one aspect of a situation and on perceptual appearances, and **irreversibility.** As a result, they fail **conservation** and **hierarchical classification** tasks.

7.6 *What does follow-up research imply about the accuracy of Piaget's preoperational stage?*

- When young children are given simplified tasks relevant to their everyday lives, their performance appears more mature than Piaget assumed. Preschoolers recognize others' perspectives, distinguish animate from inanimate objects, have flexible and appropriate notions of magic, reason by analogy about physical transformations, understand cause-and-effect relationships, and organize knowledge into hierarchical categories.

- Evidence that operational thinking develops gradually over the preschool years challenges Piaget's stage concept. Some theorists propose a more flexible view of stages.

7.7 *What educational principles can be derived from Piaget's theory?*

- A Piagetian classroom promotes discovery learning, sensitivity to children's readiness to learn, and acceptance of individual differences.

Vygotsky's Sociocultural Theory (p. 234)

7.8 *Describe Vygotsky's perspective on the social origins and significance of children's private speech.*

- Unlike Piaget, Vygotsky regarded language as the foundation for all higher cognitive processes. According to Vygotsky, **private speech,** or language used for self-guidance, emerges out of social communication as adults and more skilled peers help children master appropriately challenging tasks. Private speech is eventually internalized as silent, inner speech.

- **Scaffolding**—adjusting teaching support to fit children's current needs and suggesting strategies—promotes gains in children's thinking.

7.9 *Describe applications of Vygotsky's theory to education, and evaluate his major ideas.*

- A Vygotskian classroom emphasizes assisted discovery—verbal guidance from teachers and peer collaboration. Make-believe play is a vital zone of proximal development in early childhood.

- **Guided participation,** a broader concept than scaffolding, recognizes situational and cultural variations in shared endeavors between more expert and less expert participants.

Information Processing (p. 236)

7.10 *How do executive function and memory change during early childhood?*

- Executive function improves markedly over the preschool years. Children gain in inhibition, ability to flexibly shift their focus of attention, and working-memory capacity—executive function components that are closely interconnected and that contribute vitally to academic and social skills. Older preschoolers also gain in planning, a complex executive function activity.

- Parental scaffolding supports preschoolers' executive function skills. Poverty exerts a negative impact, in part through maladaptive parenting and chronic stress.

- Young children's recognition memory is remarkably accurate, but their recall of listlike information is poor because they use **memory strategies** less effectively than older children.

- **Episodic memory**—memory for everyday experiences—improves greatly in early childhood. Like adults, preschoolers remember recurring events as **scripts,** which become increasingly elaborate with age.

- As cognitive and conversational skills improve, children's autobiographical memories become more organized and detailed, especially when adults use an elaborative style in talking about the past.

7.11 *Describe the young child's theory of mind.*

- Preschoolers begin to construct a theory of mind, evidence of their capacity for **metacognition.** Between ages 4 and 6, explicit false-belief understanding becomes more secure, enhancing children's capacity to reflect on their own and others' thoughts and emotions. Language, executive function, and social experiences contribute.

- Preschoolers regard the mind as a passive container of information rather than as an active, constructive agent.

7.12 *Summarize children's literacy and mathematical knowledge during early childhood.*

- Preschoolers' **emergent literacy** reveals that they revise their ideas about the meaning of print as their cognitive capacities improve, as they encounter writing in many contexts, and as adults help them with written communication. **Phonological awareness** is a strong predictor of emergent literacy knowledge and later spelling and reading achievement. Informal literacy experiences, including adult–child interactive storybook reading, foster literacy development.

CHAPTER 7 Physical and Cognitive Development in Early Childhood

- Toddlers display a beginning grasp of **ordinality**. By age 3½ to 4, preschoolers understand **cardinality** and use counting to solve arithmetic problems, eventually arriving at the most efficient, accurate approach. Adults promote children's mathematical knowledge by providing many occasions for counting, comparing quantities, and talking about number concepts.

Individual Differences in Mental Development (p. 245)

7.13 *Describe early childhood intelligence tests and the impact of home, preschool and kindergarten programs, child care, and educational media on mental development.*

- Intelligence tests for young children sample a range of verbal and nonverbal skills. By age 6 to 7, scores are good predictors of later IQ and academic achievement. Children growing up in warm, stimulating homes with parents who make reasonable demands for mature behavior develop well intellectually.

- Preschool and kindergarten programs include both **child-centered programs,** in which much learning occurs through play, and **academic programs,** in which teachers structure children's learning, often using repetition and drill. Emphasizing formal academic training undermines young children's motivation and negatively influences later achievement.

- **Project Head Start** is the most extensive U.S. federally funded preschool program for low-income children. High-quality preschool intervention results in immediate IQ and achievement gains and long-term improvements in school adjustment.

- Enriching Head Start classrooms with Head Start REDI yields higher year-end language, literacy, and social skills. Good child care enhances cognitive, language, and social development, especially for low-SES children.

- Children gain in diverse cognitive skills from educational television and computer software. TV programs with slow-paced action and easy-to-follow story lines foster executive function, vocabulary and reading skills, and elaborate make-believe play. Computer programs that introduce children to programming skills promote problem solving and metacognition. But heavy exposure to prime-time TV and cartoons is associated with poorer academic skills.

Language Development (p. 249)

7.14 *Trace the development of vocabulary, grammar, and conversational skills in early childhood.*

- Supported by **fast-mapping,** preschoolers' vocabularies increase dramatically. Initially, they rely heavily on the perceptual cue of object shape to expand their vocabulary. With age, they increasingly draw on social and linguistic cues.

- Between ages 2 and 3, children adopt the basic word order of their language. As preschoolers gradually master grammatical rules, they sometimes overextend them in a type of error called **overregularization.** By the end of early childhood, children have acquired complex grammatical forms.

- **Pragmatics** is the practical, social side of language. Two-year-olds are already skilled conversationalists in face-to-face interaction. By age 4, children adapt their speech to their listener's age, sex, and social status.

7.15 *Cite factors that support language learning in early childhood.*

- Conversational give-and-take with adults fosters language progress. Adults provide explicit feedback on the clarity of children's language and indirect feedback about grammar through **recasts** and **expansions.**

Important Terms and Concepts

academic programs (p. 246)
amygdala (p. 218)
cardinality (p. 244)
centration (p. 230)
cerebellum (p. 218)
child-centered programs (p. 246)
conservation (p. 229)
corpus callosum (p. 219)
dominant cerebral hemisphere (p. 218)
dual representation (p. 229)
egocentrism (p. 229)
emergent literacy (p. 242)
episodic memory (p. 240)

expansions (p. 252)
fast-mapping (p. 250)
growth hormone (GH) (p. 219)
guided participation (p. 236)
hierarchical classification (p. 230)
hippocampus (p. 218)
irreversibility (p. 230)
memory strategies (p. 240)
metacognition (p. 241)
ordinality (p. 244)
overregularization (p. 251)
phonological awareness (p. 244)
pituitary gland (p. 219)

pragmatics (p. 252)
preoperational stage (p. 227)
private speech (p. 234)
Project Head Start (p. 246)
recasts (p. 252)
reticular formation (p. 218)
scaffolding (p. 235)
scripts (p. 240)
semantic memory (p. 240)
sociodramatic play (p. 228)
thyroid-stimulating hormone (TSH) (p. 219)

chapter 8

Emotional and Social Development in Early Childhood

During the preschool years, children make great strides in understanding the thoughts and feelings of others, and they build on these skills as they form first friendships—special relationships marked by attachment and common interests.

What's ahead in chapter 8

Erikson's Theory: Initiative versus Guilt

Self-Understanding
Foundations of Self-Concept • Emergence of Self-Esteem

■ **CULTURAL INFLUENCES** Cultural Variations in Personal Storytelling: Implications for Early Self-Concept

Emotional Development
Understanding Emotion • Emotional Self-Regulation • Self-Conscious Emotions • Empathy and Sympathy

Peer Relations
Advances in Peer Sociability • First Friendships • Peer Relations and School Readiness • Parental Influences on Early Peer Relations

Foundations of Morality and Aggression
The Psychoanalytic Perspective • Social Learning Theory • The Cognitive-Developmental Perspective • The Other Side of Morality: Development of Aggression

■ **CULTURAL INFLUENCES** Ethnic Differences in the Consequences of Physical Punishment

Gender Typing
Gender-Stereotyped Beliefs and Behaviors • Biological Influences on Gender Typing • Environmental Influences on Gender Typing • Gender Identity • Reducing Gender Stereotyping in Young Children

■ **BIOLOGY AND ENVIRONMENT** Transgender Children

Child Rearing and Emotional and Social Development
Styles of Child Rearing • What Makes Authoritative Child Rearing Effective? • Cultural Variations • Child Maltreatment

As the children in Leslie's classroom moved through the preschool years, their personalities took on clearer definition. By age 3, they voiced firm likes and dislikes as well as new ideas about themselves. "Stop bothering me," Sammy said to Mark, who had reached for Sammy's beanbag as Sammy aimed it toward the mouth of a large clown face. "See, I'm great at this game," Sammy announced with confidence, an attitude that kept him trying, even though he missed most of the throws.

The children's conversations also revealed early notions about morality. Often they combined statements about right and wrong with forceful attempts to defend their own desires. "You're 'posed to share," stated Mark, grabbing the beanbag out of Sammy's hand.

"I was here first! Gimme it back," demanded Sammy, pushing Mark. The two boys struggled until Leslie intervened, provided an extra set of beanbags, and showed them how they could both play.

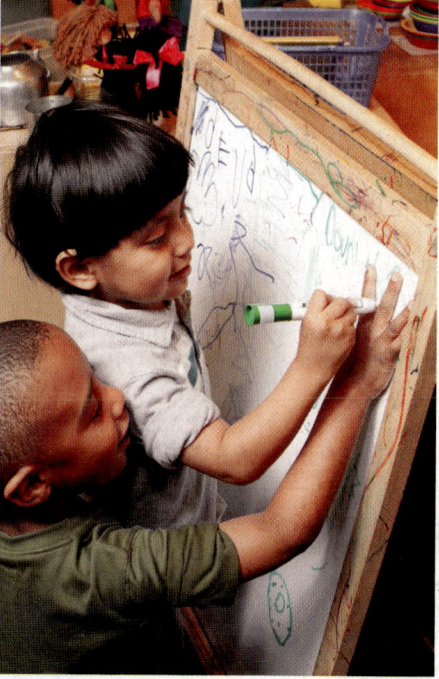

As the interaction between Sammy and Mark reveals, preschoolers quickly become complex social beings. Young children argue, grab, and push, but cooperative exchanges are far more frequent. Between ages 2 and 6, first friendships form, in which children converse, act out complementary roles, and learn that their own desires for companionship and toys are best met when they consider others' needs and interests.

The children's developing understanding of their social world was especially apparent in their growing attention to the dividing line between male and female. While Priti and Karen cared for a sick baby doll in the housekeeping area, Sammy, Vance, and Mark transformed the block corner into a busy intersection. "Green light, go!" shouted police officer Sammy as Vance and Mark pushed large wooden cars and trucks across the floor. Already, the children preferred peers of their own gender, and their play themes mirrored their culture's gender stereotypes.

This chapter is devoted to the many facets of early childhood emotional and social development. We begin with Erik Erikson's theory, which provides an overview of personality change in the preschool years. Then we consider children's concepts of themselves, their insights into their social and moral worlds, their gender typing, and their increasing ability to manage their emotional and social behaviors. Finally, we ask, What is effective child rearing? And we discuss the complex conditions that support good parenting or lead it to break down, including the serious and widespread problems of child abuse and neglect. ●

Erikson's Theory: Initiative versus Guilt

8.1 What personality changes take place during Erikson's stage of initiative versus guilt?

Erikson (1950) described early childhood as a period of "vigorous unfolding." Once children have a sense of autonomy, they become less contrary than they were as toddlers. Their energies are freed for tackling the psychological conflict of the preschool years: **initiative versus guilt.** As the word *initiative* suggests, young children have a new sense of purposefulness. They are eager to tackle new tasks, join in activities with peers, and discover what they can do with the help of adults. They also make strides in conscience development.

Erikson regarded play as a means through which young children learn about themselves and their social world. Play permits preschoolers to try new skills with little risk of criticism and failure. It also creates a small social organization of children who must cooperate to achieve common goals. Around the world, children act out family scenes and highly visible occupations—police officer, doctor, and nurse in Western societies, rabbit hunter and potter among the Hopi Indians, hut builder and spear maker among the Baka of West Africa (Gaskins, 2013).

Recall that Erikson's theory builds on Freud's psychosexual stages (see Chapter 1, page 15). In Freud's Oedipus and Electra conflicts, to avoid punishment and maintain parents' affection, children form a *superego,* or conscience, by *identifying* with the same-sex parent. As a result, they adopt the moral and gender-role standards of their society. For Erikson, the negative outcome of early childhood is an overly strict superego that causes children to feel too much guilt because they have been threatened, criticized, and punished excessively by adults. When this happens, preschoolers' exuberant play and bold efforts to master new tasks break down.

Although Freud's ideas are no longer accepted as satisfactory explanations of conscience development, Erikson's image of initiative captures the diverse changes in young children's emotional and social lives. Early childhood is, indeed, a time when children develop a confident self-image, more effective control over their emotions, new social skills, the foundations of morality, and a clear sense of themselves as boy or girl.

Self-Understanding

8.2 Describe the development of self-concept and self-esteem in early childhood.

The development of language enables young children to talk about their own subjective experience of being. In Chapter 7, we noted that young children acquire a vocabulary for talking about their inner mental lives and refine their understanding of mental states. As self-awareness strengthens, preschoolers focus more intently on qualities that make the self unique. They begin to develop a **self-concept,** the set of attributes, abilities, attitudes, and values that an individual believes defines who he or she is.

Foundations of Self-Concept

Ask a 3- to 5-year-old to tell you about himself, and you are likely to hear something like this: "I'm Tommy. I'm 4 years old. I can wash my hair all by myself. I have a new Lego set, and I made this big, big tower." Preschoolers' self-concepts consist largely of observable characteristics, such as their name, physical appearance, possessions, and everyday behaviors (Harter, 2012).

By age 3½, children also describe themselves in terms of typical emotions and attitudes ("I'm happy when I play with my friends"; "I don't like scary TV programs"; "I usually do what Mommy says"), suggesting a beginning understanding of their unique psychological characteristics (Eder & Mangelsdorf, 1997). And by age 5, children's degree of agreement with such statements coincides with maternal reports of their personality traits, indicating that older preschoolers have a sense of their own

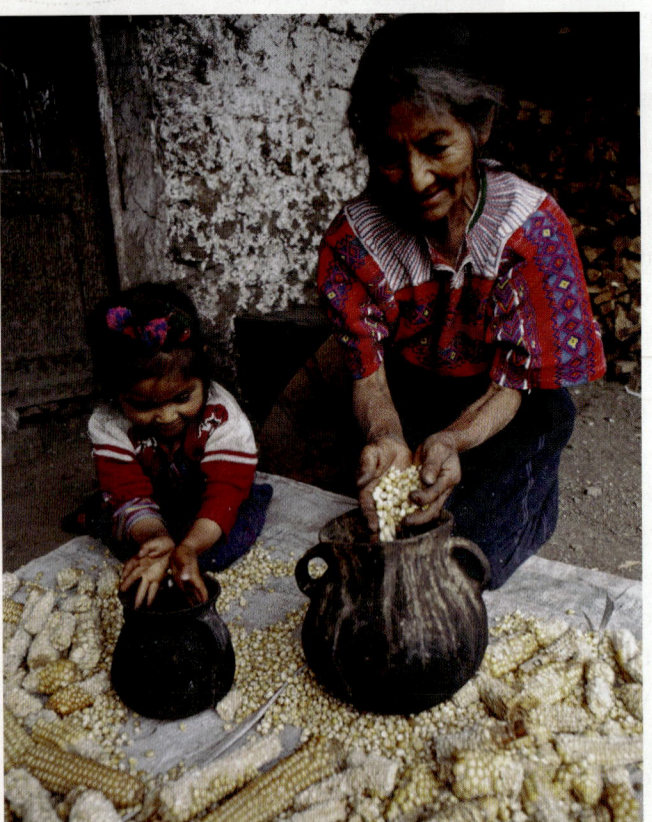

A Guatemalan 3-year-old pretends to shell corn. By acting out family scenes and highly visible occupations, young children around the world develop a sense of initiative, gaining insight into what they can do and become in their culture.

Cultural Influences

Cultural Variations in Personal Storytelling: Implications for Early Self-Concept

Preschoolers of many cultural backgrounds participate in personal storytelling with their parents. Striking cultural differences exist in parents' selection and interpretation of events in these narratives, affecting the way children view themselves.

In one study, researchers spent hundreds of hours over a two-year period studying the storytelling practices of six middle-SES Irish-American families in Chicago and six middle-SES Chinese families in Taiwan. From extensive videotapes of adults' conversations with the children from ages 2½ to 4, the investigators identified personal stories and coded them for content, quality of their endings, and evaluation of the child (Miller, Fung, & Mintz, 1996; Miller et al., 1997, 2012b).

Parents in both cultures discussed pleasurable holidays and family excursions in similar ways and with similar frequency. But five times more often than the Irish-American parents, the Chinese parents told long stories about their preschooler's previous misdeeds—using impolite language, writing on the wall, or playing in an overly rowdy way. These narratives, often sparked by a current misdeed, were conveyed with warmth and caring, stressed the impact of misbehavior on others ("You made Mama lose face"), and often ended with direct teaching of proper behavior ("Saying dirty words is not good"). By contrast, in the few instances in which Irish-American stories referred to transgressions, parents downplayed their seriousness, attributing them to the child's spunk and assertiveness.

Early narratives about the child launch preschoolers' self-concepts on culturally distinct paths (Miller, 2014). Influenced by Confucian traditions of strict discipline and social obligations, Chinese parents integrated these values into their stories, affirming the importance of not disgracing the family and explicitly conveying expectations for improvement in the story's conclusion. Although Irish-American parents disciplined their children, they rarely dwelt on misdeeds in storytelling. Rather, they cast the child's shortcomings in a positive light, perhaps to promote self-esteem.

Whereas most Americans believe that favorable self-esteem is crucial for healthy development, Chinese adults generally see it as unimportant or even negative—as impeding the child's willingness to listen and be corrected (Miller et al., 2002). Consistent with this view, the Chinese parents did little to cultivate their child's individuality. Instead, they used storytelling to guide the child toward responsible behavior. Hence, the Chinese child's self-image emphasizes obligations to others, whereas the American child's is more autonomous.

A Chinese mother speaks gently to her child about proper behavior. Chinese parents often tell preschoolers stories that point out the negative impact on others of the child's misdeeds. The Chinese child's self-concept, in turn, emphasizes social obligations.

---

timidity, agreeableness, and positive or negative affect (Brown et al., 2008). But most preschoolers do not yet say, "I'm helpful" or "I'm shy." Direct references to personality traits must wait for greater cognitive maturity.

A warm, sensitive parent–child relationship fosters a more positive, coherent early self-concept. Recall from Chapter 7 that securely attached preschoolers participate in more elaborative parent–child conversations about personally experienced events, which help them understand themselves (see page 242). Elaborative reminiscing that focuses on children's internal states—thoughts, feelings, and subjective experiences—plays an especially important role in early self-concept development. For example, when parents reminisce with preschoolers about times they successfully resolved upsetting feelings, 4- and 5-year-olds describe their emotional tendencies more favorably ("I'm not scared—not me!") (Goodvin & Romdall, 2013). By emphasizing the personal meaning of past events, conversations about internal states facilitate self-knowledge.

As early as age 2, parents use narratives of past events to impart rules, standards for behavior, and evaluative information about the child: "You added the milk when we made the mashed potatoes. That's a very important job!" (Nelson, 2003). As the Cultural Influences box above reveals, these self-evaluative narratives are a major means through which caregivers imbue the young child's self-concept with cultural values.

As they talk about personally significant events and as their cognitive skills advance, preschoolers gradually come to view themselves as persisting over time—a change evident in their improved ability to anticipate their own future states and needs. When asked to select from three items (a raincoat, money, a blanket) the one they need to bring with them to a future event (walking next to a waterfall), children's performance—along with future-state justifications ("I'm gonna get wet")—increased sharply between ages 3 and 4 (Atance & Meltzoff, 2005). And by age 5, children better understand that their future preferences are likely to differ from their current ones. Most realize that when they grow up, they will prefer reading newspapers to reading picture books and drinking coffee to drinking grape juice (Bélanger et al., 2014). By the end of the preschool years, children can set aside their current state of mind and take a future perspective.

Emergence of Self-Esteem

Another aspect of self-concept emerges in early childhood: **self-esteem,** the judgments we make about our own worth and the feelings associated with those judgments. These evaluations are among the most important aspects of self-development because they affect our emotional experiences, future behavior, and long-term psychological adjustment.

By age 4, preschoolers have several self-judgments—for example, about learning things in school, making friends, getting along with parents, and treating others kindly (Marsh, Ellis, & Craven, 2002). But they lack the cognitive maturity to combine these evaluations into a global sense of self-esteem. Also, because they have difficulty distinguishing between their desired and their actual competence, they usually rate their own ability as extremely high and underestimate task difficulty, as Sammy did when he asserted, despite his many misses, that he was great at beanbag throwing (Harter, 2012).

High self-esteem contributes greatly to preschoolers' initiative during a period in which they must master many new skills. By age 3, children whose parents patiently encourage while offering information about how to succeed are enthusiastic and highly motivated. In contrast, children whose parents criticize their worth and performance give up easily when faced with challenges and express shame and despondency after failing (Kelley, Brownell, & Campbell, 2000). Adults can avoid promoting these self-defeating reactions by adjusting their expectations to children's capacities, scaffolding children's attempts at difficult tasks (see Chapter 7, page 235), and pointing out effort and improvement in children's behavior.

Emotional Development

8.3 Identify changes in understanding and expressing emotion during early childhood, citing factors that influence those changes.

Gains in representation, language, and self-concept support emotional development in early childhood. Between ages 2 and 6, children make strides in emotional abilities that, collectively, researchers refer to as *emotional competence* (Denham et al., 2011). First, preschoolers gain in emotional understanding, becoming better able to talk about feelings and to respond appropriately to others' emotional signals. Second, they become better at emotional self-regulation—in particular, at coping with intense negative emotion. Finally, preschoolers more often experience *self-conscious emotions* and *empathy,* which contribute to their developing sense of morality.

Parenting strongly influences preschoolers' emotional competence. Emotional competence, in turn, is vital for successful peer relationships and overall mental health.

Understanding Emotion

Early in the preschool years, children refer to causes, consequences, and behavioral signs of emotion (Thompson, Winer, & Goodvin, 2011). Over time, their understanding becomes more accurate and complex.

By age 4 to 5, children correctly judge the causes of many basic emotions ("He's happy because he's swinging very high"; "He's sad because he misses his mother"). Preschoolers' explanations tend to emphasize external factors over internal states, a balance that changes with age (Rieffe, Terwogt, & Cowan, 2005). In Chapter 7, we saw that after age 4, children appreciate that both desires and beliefs motivate behavior. Once these understandings are secure, children's grasp of how internal factors can trigger emotion expands.

Preschoolers are good at inferring how others are feeling based on their behavior. For example, they can tell that a child who jumps up and down and claps his hands is probably happy and that a child who is tearful and withdrawn is sad (Widen & Russell, 2011). And they are beginning to realize that thinking

This preschooler confidently prepares to slide down the pole of a playground jungle gym. Her high self-esteem contributes greatly to her initiative in mastering new skills.

and feeling are interconnected—that focusing on negative thoughts ("I broke my arm, so now I have to wear this itchy cast that makes it hard to play") is likely to make a person feel worse, but thinking positively ("Now I have a cool cast my friends can write their names on!") can help a person feel better (Bamford & Lagattuta, 2012). Furthermore, preschoolers come up with effective ways to relieve others' negative emotions, such as hugging to reduce sadness (Fabes et al., 1988). Overall, preschoolers have an impressive ability to interpret, predict, and change others' feelings.

At the same time, preschoolers have difficulty interpreting situations that offer conflicting cues about how a person is feeling. When asked what might be happening in a picture of a happy-faced child with a broken bicycle, 4- and 5-year-olds tended to rely only on the emotional expression: "He's happy because he likes to ride his bike." Older children more often reconciled the two cues: "He's happy because his father promised to help fix his broken bike" (Gnepp, 1983; Hoffner & Badzinski, 1989). This capacity requires improved executive function—retaining in working memory two conflicting sources of information while drawing on one's knowledge base to integrate them.

The more parents label and explain emotions and express warmth when conversing with preschoolers, the more "emotion words" children use and the better developed their emotion understanding (Fivush & Haden, 2005; Laible & Song, 2006). Discussions of negative experiences or disagreements are particularly helpful because they evoke more elaborative dialogues that include validation of children's feelings (Laible, 2011). In one study, mothers who explained emotions and negotiated and compromised during conflicts with their 2½-year-olds had children who, at age 3, were advanced in emotional understanding and used similar strategies to resolve disagreements (Laible & Thompson, 2002). Such dialogues seem to help children reflect on the causes and consequences of emotion while modeling mature communication skills.

Knowledge about emotion helps children in their efforts to get along with others. As early as 3 to 5 years of age, it is related to friendly, considerate behavior, constructive responses to disputes with agemates, and perspective-taking ability (Garner & Estep, 2001; Hughes & Ensor, 2010; O'Brien et al., 2011). And as children learn about emotion from interacting with adults, they engage in more emotion talk with agemates and siblings. Preschoolers who refer to feelings when interacting with playmates are better liked by their peers (Fabes et al., 2001). Children seem to recognize that acknowledging others' emotions and explaining their own enhance the quality of relationships.

Emotional Self-Regulation

Language, along with preschoolers' growing understanding of the causes and consequences of emotion, contributes to gains in *emotional self-regulation* (Thompson, 2015). By age 3 to 4, children verbalize a variety of strategies for alleviating negative emotion that they tailor to specific situations (Davis et al., 2010; Dennis & Kelemen, 2009). For example, they know they can restrict sensory input (cover their eyes or ears to block out a scary sight or sound), talk to themselves ("Mommy said she'll be back soon"), change their goals (decide that they don't want to play anyway after being excluded from a game), or repair the situation ("stop fighting and share" to resolve a conflict with a peer). The effectiveness of preschoolers' recommended strategies improves with age.

As children use these strategies, emotional outbursts decline. Gains in executive function—in particular, inhibition, flexible shifting of attention, and manipulating information in working memory—contribute greatly to managing emotion in early childhood. Three-year-olds who can distract themselves when upset and focus on how to handle their feelings tend to become cooperative school-age children with few problem behaviors (Gilliom et al., 2002).

By watching parents manage emotion, children learn strategies for regulating their own. Parents who are in tune with their own emotional experiences tend to be supportive with their preschoolers, offering suggestions and explanations of emotion-regulation strategies that strengthen children's capacity to handle stress (Meyer et al., 2014; Morris et al., 2011). In contrast, when parents rarely express positive emotion, dismiss children's feelings as unimportant, and fail to control their own anger, children's emotion management and psychological adjustment suffer (Hill et al., 2006; Thompson & Meyer, 2007).

Adult–child conversations that prepare children for difficult experiences by discussing what to expect and ways to handle anxiety also foster emotional self-regulation (Thompson & Goodman, 2010). Nevertheless, preschoolers' vivid imaginations and incomplete grasp of the distinction between fantasy and reality make fears common in early childhood. See Applying What We Know on page 262 for ways to help young children manage fears.

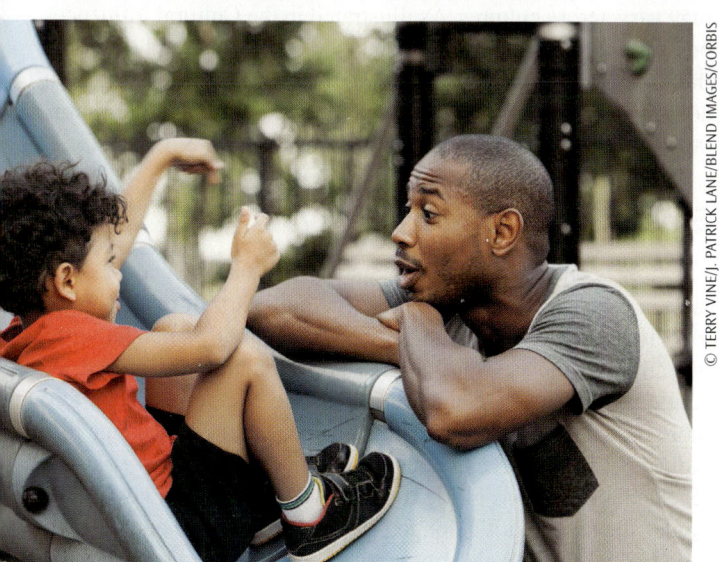

Warm, elaborative conversations in which parents label and explain emotions enhance preschoolers' emotional understanding.

Applying what we Know

Helping Children Manage Common Fears of Early Childhood

FEAR	SUGGESTION
Monsters, ghosts, and darkness	Reduce exposure to frightening stories and TV programs until the child is better able to understand that fantastical beings are not real. "Search" the child's room for monsters, showing him that none are there. Use a night-light, sit by the child's bed until he falls asleep, and tuck in a favorite toy for protection.
Preschool or child care	If the child resists going to preschool but seems content once there, the fear is probably separation. Provide a sense of warmth and caring while gently encouraging independence. If the child fears being at preschool, find out why—the teacher, the children, or a crowded, noisy environment. Provide support by accompanying the child and gradually lessening the amount of time you stay.
Animals	Do not force the child to approach a dog, cat, or other animal that arouses fear. Let the child move at her own pace. Demonstrate how to hold and pet the animal, showing that when treated gently, the animal is friendly. If the child is larger than the animal, emphasize this: "You're so big. That kitty is probably afraid of *you!*"
Intense fears	If a child's fear is intense, persists for a long time, interferes with daily activities, and cannot be reduced in any of the ways just suggested, it has reached the level of a *phobia*. Sometimes phobias are linked to family problems and require counseling. Other phobias diminish without treatment as the child's emotional self-regulation improves.

Self-Conscious Emotions

One morning in Leslie's classroom, a group of children crowded around for a bread-baking activity. Leslie asked them to wait patiently while she got a baking pan. But Sammy reached over to feel the dough, and the bowl tumbled off the table. When Leslie returned, Sammy looked at her, then covered his eyes with his hands and said, "I did something bad." He felt ashamed and guilty.

As their self-concepts develop, preschoolers become increasingly sensitive to praise and blame or to the possibility of such feedback. They more often experience *self-conscious emotions*—feelings that involve injury to or enhancement of their sense of self (see Chapter 6). By age 3, self-conscious emotions are clearly linked to self-evaluation (Lagattuta & Thompson, 2007; Lewis, 1995). But because preschoolers are still developing standards of excellence and conduct, they depend on the messages of parents, teachers, and others who matter to them to know *when* to feel proud, ashamed, or guilty, often viewing adult expectations as obligatory rules ("Dad said you're 'posed to take turns") (Thompson, Meyer, & McGinley, 2006).

When parents repeatedly comment on the worth of the child and her performance ("That's a bad job! I thought you were a good girl!"), children experience self-conscious emotions intensely—more shame after failure, more pride after success. In contrast, when parents focus on how to improve performance ("You did it this way; now try doing it that way"), they induce moderate, more adaptive levels of shame and pride and greater persistence on difficult tasks (Kelley, Brownell, & Campbell, 2000; Lewis, 1998).

Among Western children, intense shame is associated with feelings of personal inadequacy ("I'm stupid"; "I'm a terrible person") and with maladjustment—withdrawal and depression as well as intense anger and aggression toward those who participated in the shame-evoking situation (Muris & Meesters, 2014). In contrast, guilt—when it occurs in appropriate circumstances and is neither excessive nor accompanied by shame—is related to good adjustment. Guilt helps children resist harmful impulses, and it motivates a misbehaving child to repair the damage and behave more considerately (Mascolo & Fischer, 2007; Tangney, Stuewig, & Mashek, 2007). But overwhelming guilt—involving such high emotional distress that the child cannot make amends—is linked to depressive symptoms as early as age 3 (Luby et al., 2009).

Finally, the consequences of shame for children's adjustment may vary across cultures. As illustrated in the Cultural Influences box on page 259, people in Asian societies, who tend to define themselves in relation to their social group, view shame as an adaptive reminder of an interdependent self and of the importance of others' judgments (Friedlmeier, Corapci, & Cole, 2011).

Empathy and Sympathy

Empathy is another emotional capacity that becomes more common in early childhood. It serves as a motivator of **prosocial, or altruistic, behavior**—actions that benefit another person without any expected reward for the self (Eisenberg, Spinrad, & Knafo-Noam, 2015). Compared with toddlers, preschoolers rely more on words to communicate empathic feelings, a change that indicates a more reflective level of empathy. When a 4-year-old received a Christmas gift that she hadn't included on her list for Santa, she assumed it belonged to another little girl and pleaded with her parents, "We've got to give it back—Santa's made a big mistake. I think the girl's crying 'cause she didn't get her present!"

Yet for some children, empathizing—*feeling with* an upset adult or peer and responding emotionally in a similar way—does not yield acts of kindness and helpfulness but, instead, escalates into personal distress. In trying to reduce these negative feelings, the child focuses on his own anxiety rather than on the person in need. As a result, empathy does not lead to **sympathy**—feelings of concern or sorrow for another's plight.

Temperament plays a role in whether empathy prompts sympathetic, prosocial behavior or a personally distressed, self-focused response. Children who are sociable, assertive, and good at regulating emotion are more likely to help, share, and comfort others in distress. But poor emotion regulators less often display sympathetic concern and prosocial behavior (Eisenberg, Spinrad, & Knafo-Noam, 2015; Valiente et al., 2004). When faced with someone in need, they react with behavioral and physiological distress—frowning, lip biting, thumb sucking, comfort seeking, a rise in heart rate, and a sharp increase in EEG brain-wave activity in the right cerebral hemisphere, which houses negative emotion—indications that they are overwhelmed by their feelings (Liew et al., 2010; Pickens, Field, & Nawrocki, 2001).

Preschoolers' empathic concern strengthens in the context of a secure parent–child attachment relationship (Murphy & Laible, 2013). When parents are warm and sensitive and respond to their preschoolers' feelings with empathy and sympathy, children react with concern to others' distress—a response that persists into adolescence and early adulthood (Michalik et al., 2007; Newton et al., 2014; Taylor et al., 2013). Besides modeling empathy and sympathy, parents can teach children the importance of kindness and can intervene when they display inappropriate emotion—strategies that predict high levels of sympathetic responding (Eisenberg, 2003).

In contrast, angry, punitive parenting can disrupt the development of empathy and sympathy at an early age (Knafo & Plomin, 2006). Physically abused preschoolers, who experience negative parenting to an extreme, rarely express concern at a peer's unhappiness but, rather, are likely to withdraw or react with verbal and physical attacks (Anthonysamy & Zimmer-Gembeck, 2007). Their behavior resembles their parents' insensitive responding to others' suffering.

Peer Relations

8.4 Describe peer sociability and friendship in early childhood, along with cultural and parental influences on early peer relations.

As children become increasingly self-aware and better at communicating and understanding others' thoughts and feelings, their skill at interacting with peers improves rapidly. Peers provide young children with learning experiences they can get in no other way. Because peers interact on an equal footing, children must keep a conversation going, cooperate, and set goals in play. With peers, children form friendships—special relationships marked by attachment and common interests. Let's look at how peer interaction changes over the preschool years.

Advances in Peer Sociability

Mildred Parten (1932), one of the first to study peer sociability among 2- to 5-year-olds, noticed a dramatic rise with age in joint, interactive play. She concluded that social development proceeds in a three-step sequence. It begins with **nonsocial activity**—unoccupied, onlooker behavior and solitary play. Then it shifts to **parallel play,** in which a child plays near other children with similar materials but does not try to influence their behavior. At the highest level are two forms of true social interaction. In **associative play,** children engage in separate activities but exchange toys and comment on one another's behavior. Finally, in **cooperative play,** a more advanced type of interaction, children orient toward a common goal, such as acting out a make-believe theme.

Follow-Up Research on Peer Sociability.
Longitudinal evidence indicates that these play forms emerge in the order suggested by Parten but that later-appearing ones do not replace earlier ones in a developmental sequence (Rubin, Bukowski, & Parker, 2006). Rather, all types coexist in early childhood.

During classroom free-play periods, preschoolers often transition from onlooker to parallel to cooperative play and back again (Robinson et al., 2003). They seem to use parallel play as a way station—a respite from the demands of complex social interaction and a crossroad to new activities. And although nonsocial activity declines with age, it is still the most frequent form among 3- to 4-year-olds and accounts for one-third of kindergartners' free-play time. Also, both solitary and parallel play remain fairly stable from 3 to 6 years, accounting for as much of the child's play as cooperative interaction (Rubin, Fein, & Vandenberg, 1983).

As children's language skills and capacity to take the perspective of others improve, empathy also increases, motivating prosocial, or altruistic, behavior.

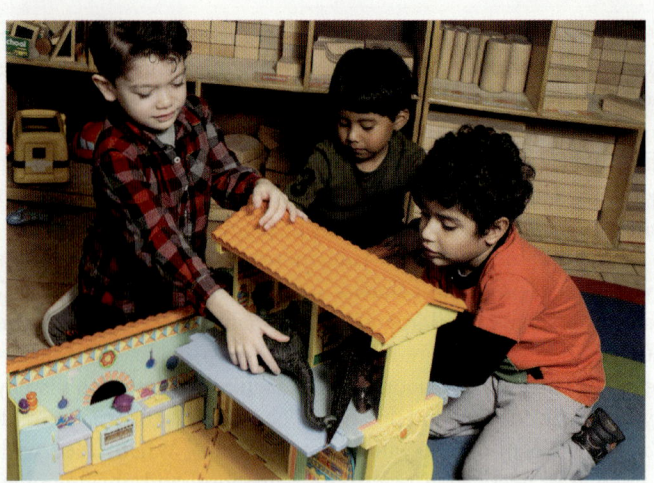

Four-year-olds (left) engage in parallel play. Cooperative play (right) develops later than parallel play, but preschool children continue to move back and forth between the two types of sociability, using parallel play as a respite from the complex demands of cooperation.

We now understand that the *type*, not the amount, of solitary and parallel play changes during early childhood. In studies in Taiwan and the United States, researchers rated the *cognitive maturity* of nonsocial, parallel, and cooperative play, using the categories shown in Table 8.1. Within each of Parten's play types, older children displayed more cognitively mature behavior than younger children (Pan, 1994; Rubin, Watson, & Jambor, 1978).

Often parents wonder whether a preschooler who spends much time playing alone is developing normally. But only *certain types* of nonsocial activity—aimless wandering, hovering near peers, and functional play involving repetitive motor action—are cause for concern. Children who behave reticently, by watching peers without playing, are usually temperamentally inhibited—high in social fearfulness (Coplan & Ooi, 2014). And preschoolers who engage in solitary, repetitive behavior (banging blocks, making a doll jump up and down) tend to be immature, impulsive children who find it difficult to regulate anger and aggression (Coplan et al., 2001). In the classroom, both reticent and impulsive children tend to experience peer ostracism (Coplan & Arbeau, 2008).

But other preschoolers with low rates of peer interaction are not socially anxious or impulsive. They simply like to play alone, and their solitary activities are positive and constructive. Children who prefer solitary play with art materials, puzzles, and building toys are typically well-adjusted youngsters who, when they do play with peers, show socially skilled behavior (Coplan & Armer, 2007). Still, a few preschoolers who engage in such age-appropriate solitary play—more often boys—are rebuffed by peers (Coplan et al., 2001, 2004). Perhaps because quiet play is inconsistent with the "masculine" gender role, boys who engage in it are at risk for negative reactions from both parents and peers and, eventually, for adjustment problems.

As noted in Chapter 7, *sociodramatic play*—an advanced form of cooperative play—becomes especially common over the preschool years. In joint make-believe, preschoolers act out and respond to one another's pretend feelings. They also explore and gain control of fear-arousing experiences when they play doctor or pretend to search for monsters in a magical forest. As a result, sociodramatic play helps them understand others' feelings and regulate their own (Meyers & Berk, 2014). Furthermore, preschoolers spend much time negotiating roles and rules in socio-

TABLE 8.1
Developmental Sequence of Cognitive Play Categories

PLAY CATEGORY	DESCRIPTION	EXAMPLES
Functional play	Simple, repetitive motor movements with or without objects, especially common during the first two years	Running around a room, rolling a car back and forth, kneading clay with no intent to make something
Constructive play	Creating or constructing something, especially common between 3 and 6 years	Making a house out of toy blocks, drawing a picture, putting together a puzzle
Make-believe play	Acting out everyday and imaginary roles, especially common between 2 and 6 years	Playing house, school, or police officer; acting out storybook or television characters

Source: Rubin, Fein, & Vandenberg, 1983.

dramatic play. To create and manage complex plots, they must resolve disputes through compromise.

When researchers observed free-play periods in preschools, they found that girls participated more in sociodramatic play, whereas boys participated more in friendly, vigorous interactions called *rough-and-tumble play*. Each type of play was associated with expressions of positive emotion and predicted children's emotional understanding and self-regulation one year later (Lindsey & Colwell, 2013). Both sociodramatic play and rough-and-tumble play require children to exercise self-control and to respond to peers' verbal and nonverbal emotional cues. We will return to the topic of rough-and-tumble play in Chapter 11.

Cultural Variations. Peer sociability takes different forms, depending on the relative importance cultures place on group harmony as opposed to individual autonomy (Chen, 2012). For example, children in India generally play in large groups. Much of their behavior is imitative, occurs in unison, and involves close physical contact—a play style requiring high levels of cooperation. In a game called Bhatto Bhatto, children act out a script about a trip to the market, touching one another's elbows and hands as they pretend to cut and share a tasty vegetable (Roopnarine et al., 1994).

As another example, young Chinese children—unlike their North American agemates, who tend to reject reticent peers—are typically accepting of quiet, reserved behavior by their playmates (Chen et al., 2006; French et al., 2011). In Chapter 6, we saw that until recently, cultural values that discourage self-assertion led to positive evaluations of shyness in China (see page 195). Apparently, this benevolent attitude is still evident in the play behaviors of young Chinese children.

Agta village children in the Philippines play a tug-of-war game. Large-group, highly cooperative play occurs more often in societies that value group harmony over individual autonomy.

Cultural beliefs about the importance of play also affect early peer associations. Caregivers who view play as mere entertainment are less likely to provide props or to encourage pretend than those who value its cognitive and social benefits (Gaskins, 2014). Recall the description of children's daily lives in a Mayan village culture on page 237 in Chapter 7. When Mayan children do pretend, their play themes are *interpretive* of daily life—involving a limited number of scripts that reflect everyday roles and experiences. Children in industrialized, urban contexts more often engage in *inventive* play, generating make-believe scenarios unconstrained by actual experience (Gaskins, 2013). Perhaps Western-style sociodramatic play, with its elaborate materials and wide-ranging imaginative themes, is particularly important for social development in societies where the worlds of adults and children are distinct. It may be less crucial in village cultures where children participate in adult activities from an early age.

First Friendships

As preschoolers interact, first friendships form that serve as important contexts for emotional and social development. To adults, friendship is a mutual relationship involving companionship, sharing, understanding of thoughts and feelings, and caring for and comforting each other in times of need. In addition, mature friendships endure over time and survive occasional conflicts.

Preschoolers understand something about the uniqueness of friendship. They say that a friend is someone "who likes you," with whom you spend a lot of time playing, and with whom you share toys. But friendship does not yet have a long-term, enduring quality based on mutual trust (Damon, 1988a; Hartup, 2006). "Mark's my best friend," Sammy declared on days when the boys got along well. But when a dispute arose, he reversed himself: "Mark, you're not my friend!" Nevertheless, preschool friendships can be remarkably stable across early childhood, as long as peers remain in the same social group. In one study, nearly one-third mentioned the same best friends—the children they like to play with most—a year later (Dunn, 2004a; Eivers et al., 2012).

Already, interactions between preschoolers who mutually name each other as friends are especially positive, reflecting greater support and intimacy than do other peer relationships (Furman & Rose, 2015; Hartup, 2006). Preschoolers give far more reinforcement—greetings, praise, and compliance—to their friends, and they also receive more from them. Friends are also more cooperative and emotionally expressive—talking, laughing, and looking at each other more often than nonfriends do.

As early as the preschool years, children with a mutual friendship are better adjusted and more socially competent (Shin et al., 2014). Furthermore, children entering kindergarten who have friends in their class or who readily make new friends adjust to school more favorably (Ladd, Birch, & Buhs, 1999; Proulx & Poulin, 2013). Perhaps the company of friends serves as a secure base from which to develop new relationships, enhancing children's feelings of comfort in the new classroom.

Peer Relations and School Readiness

The ease with which kindergartners make new friends and are accepted by classmates predicts cooperative participation in classroom activities and self-directed completion of learning tasks (Ladd, Buhs, & Seid, 2000). Socially competent preschoolers are more motivated and persistent, exceeding their less socially skilled peers in academic performance in kindergarten and the early school grades (Walker & Henderson, 2012; Ziv, 2013). Because social maturity in early childhood contributes to academic performance, readiness for kindergarten must be assessed in terms of not only academic skills but also social skills.

Young children's positive peer interactions occur most often in unstructured situations such as free play, making it important for preschools and kindergartens to provide space, time, materials, and adult scaffolding to support child-directed activities (Booren, Downer, & Vitiello, 2012). Warm, responsive teacher–child interaction is also vital, especially for shy children and for impulsive, emotionally negative, and aggressive children, who are at high risk for social difficulties (Brendgen et al., 2011; Vitaro et al., 2012). In studies involving several thousand 4-year-olds in public preschools in six states, teacher sensitivity and emotional support were strong predictors of children's social competence, both during preschool and in a follow-up after kindergarten entry (Curby et al., 2009; Mashburn et al., 2008). Along with excellent teacher preparation, other indicators of program quality—small group sizes, generous teacher–child ratios, and developmentally appropriate daily activities (see page 248 in Chapter 7)—create classroom conditions that make positive teacher and peer relationships more likely.

Parental Influences on Early Peer Relations

Children first acquire skills for interacting with peers within the family. Parents influence children's peer sociability both *directly*, through attempts to influence children's peer relations, and *indirectly*, through their child-rearing practices and play.

Direct Parental Influences.
Preschoolers whose parents frequently arrange informal peer play activities tend to have larger peer networks and to be more socially skilled (Ladd, LeSieur, & Profilet, 1993). In providing play opportunities, parents show children how to initiate peer contacts. And parents' skillful suggestions for managing conflict, discouraging teasing, and entering a play group are associated with preschoolers' social competence and peer acceptance (Mize & Pettit, 2010; Parke et al., 2004).

Indirect Parental Influences.
Many parenting behaviors not directly aimed at promoting peer sociability nevertheless influence it. For example, secure attachments to parents are linked to more responsive, harmonious peer interaction, larger peer networks, and warmer, more supportive friendships during the

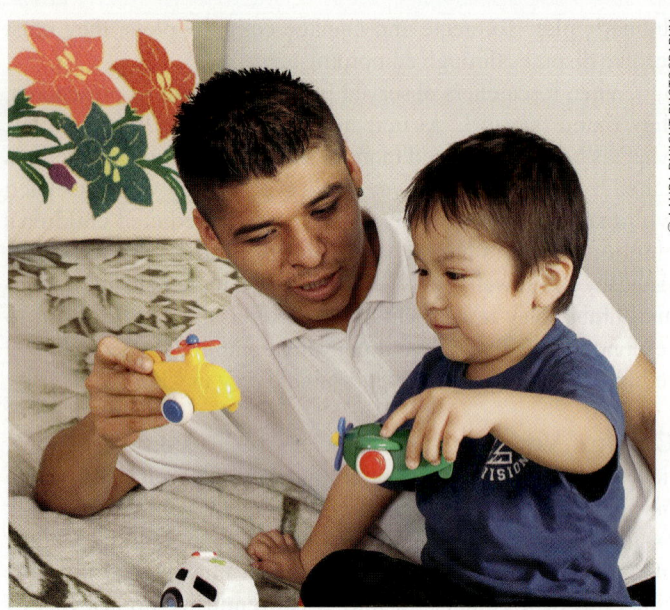

Parents' play with children, especially same-sex children, contributes to social competence. By playing with his father as he would with a peer, this child acquires social skills that facilitate peer interaction.

preschool and school years (Laible, 2007; Lucas-Thompson & Clarke-Stewart, 2007; Wood, Emmerson, & Cowan, 2004). The sensitive, emotionally expressive communication that contributes to attachment security is likely responsible.

Warm, collaborative parent–child play seems particularly effective for promoting peer interaction skills. During play, parents interact with their child on a "level playing field," much as peers do. And perhaps because parents play more with children of their own sex, mothers' play is more strongly linked to daughters' competence, fathers' play to sons' competence (Lindsey & Mize, 2000; Pettit et al., 1998).

As we have seen, some preschoolers already have great difficulty with peer relations. In Leslie's classroom, Robbie was one of them. Wherever he happened to be, comments like "Robbie ruined our block tower" and "Robbie hit me for no reason" could be heard. As we take up moral development and aggression in the next section, you will learn more about how parenting contributed to Robbie's peer problems.

Ask yourself

CONNECT How does emotional self-regulation affect the development of empathy and sympathy? Why are these emotional capacities vital for positive peer relations?

APPLY Three-year-old Ben lives in the country, with no other preschoolers nearby. His parents wonder whether it is worth driving Ben into town once a week to participate in a peer play group. What advice would you give Ben's parents, and why?

REFLECT What did your parents do, directly and indirectly, that might have influenced your earliest peer relationships?

Foundations of Morality and Aggression

8.5 What are the central features of psychoanalytic, social learning, and cognitive-developmental approaches to moral development?

8.6 Describe the development of aggression in early childhood, including family and media influences and effective approaches to reducing aggressive behavior.

Young children's behavior provides many examples of their budding moral sense. We have seen that toddlers show empathic concern for others in distress and will try to help. They also expect others to act fairly, by dividing resources equally among peers (Geraci & Surian, 2011). As children reach age 2, they often use language to evaluate their own and others' actions: "I naughty. I wrote on the wall" or (after being hit by another child) "Connie not nice." And we have seen that children of this age share toys, help others, and cooperate in games—early indicators of considerate, responsible, prosocial attitudes.

Adults everywhere take note of this developing capacity to distinguish right from wrong. Some cultures have special terms for it. The Utku Indians of Hudson Bay say the child develops *ihuma* (reason). The Fijians believe that *vakayalo* (sense) appears. In response, parents hold children more responsible for their actions (Dunn, 2005). By the end of early childhood, children can state many moral rules: "Don't take someone's things without asking!" "Tell the truth!" In addition, they argue over matters of justice: "You sat there last time, so it's my turn." "It's not fair. He got more!"

All theories of moral development recognize that conscience begins to take shape in early childhood. And most agree that at first, the child's morality is *externally controlled* by adults. Gradually, it becomes regulated by *inner standards*. Truly moral individuals do not do the right thing just to conform to others' expectations. Rather, they have developed compassionate concerns and principles of good conduct, which they follow in many situations.

Each major theory of development emphasizes a different aspect of morality. Psychoanalytic theory stresses the *emotional side* of conscience development—in particular, identification and guilt as motivators of good conduct. Social learning theory focuses on how *moral behavior* is learned through reinforcement and modeling. Finally, the cognitive-developmental perspective emphasizes *thinking*—children's ability to reason about justice and fairness.

The Psychoanalytic Perspective

Recall that according to Freud, young children form a *superego*, or conscience, by *identifying* with the same-sex parent, whose moral standards they adopt. Children obey the superego to avoid *guilt*, a painful emotion that arises each time they are tempted to misbehave. Moral development, Freud believed, is largely complete by 5 to 6 years of age.

Today, most researchers disagree with Freud's view of conscience development. In his theory (see page 14), fear of punishment and loss of parental love motivate conscience formation and moral behavior. Yet children whose parents frequently use threats, commands, or physical force tend to violate standards often and feel little guilt (Kochanska et al., 2005, 2008). And if a parent withdraws love after misbehavior—for example, refuses to speak to or states a dislike for the child—children often respond with high levels of self-blame, thinking "I'm no good" or "Nobody loves me." Eventually, to protect themselves from overwhelming guilt, these children may deny the emotion and, as a result, also develop a weak conscience (Kochanska, 1991; Zahn-Waxler et al., 1990).

Inductive Discipline. In contrast, conscience formation is promoted by a type of discipline called **induction,** in which an adult helps make the child aware of feelings by pointing out the effects of the child's misbehavior on others. For example, a parent might say, "She's crying because you won't give back her doll" (Hoffman, 2000). When generally warm parents provide explanations that match the child's capacity to understand, while firmly insisting that the child listen and comply, induction is effective as early as age 2. Preschoolers whose parents use it are more likely to refrain from wrongdoing, confess and repair damage after misdeeds, and display prosocial behavior (Choe, Olson, & Sameroff, 2013; Volling, Mahoney, & Rauer, 2009).

The success of induction may lie in its power to motivate children's active commitment to moral standards. Induction gives children information about how to behave that they can use in future situations. By emphasizing the impact of the child's actions on others, it encourages empathy and sympathetic concern. And giving children reasons for changing their behavior encourages them to adopt moral standards because those standards make sense.

In contrast, discipline that relies too heavily on threats of punishment or withdrawal of love makes children so anxious and

A teacher uses inductive discipline to explain to a child the impact of her transgression on others, pointing out classmates' feelings. Induction encourages empathy, sympathetic concern, and commitment to moral standards.

frightened that they cannot think clearly enough to figure out what they should do. As a result, these practices do not get children to internalize moral rules and—as noted earlier—also interfere with empathy and prosocial responding (Eisenberg, Spinrad, & Knafo-Noam, 2015).

The Child's Contribution.
Although good discipline is crucial, children's characteristics also affect the success of parenting techniques. Twin studies suggest a modest genetic contribution to empathy (Knafo et al., 2009). More empathic children require less power assertion and are more responsive to induction.

Temperament is also influential. Mild, patient tactics—requests, suggestions, and explanations—are sufficient to prompt guilt reactions in anxious, fearful preschoolers (Kochanska et al., 2002). But with fearless, impulsive children, gentle discipline has little impact. Power assertion also works poorly. It undermines children's effortful control, or capacity to regulate their emotional reactivity, which is linked to good conduct, empathy, sympathy, and prosocial behavior (Kochanska & Aksan, 2006). Parents of impulsive children can foster conscience development by ensuring a warm, harmonious relationship and combining firm correction of misbehavior with induction (Kochanska & Kim, 2014). When children are so low in anxiety that parental disapproval causes them little discomfort, a close parent–child bond motivates them to listen to parents as a means of preserving an affectionate, supportive relationship.

The Role of Guilt.
Although little support exists for Freudian ideas about conscience development, Freud was correct that guilt motivates moral action. Inducing *empathy-based guilt*—expressions of personal responsibility and regret, such as "I'm sorry I hurt him"—by explaining that the child is harming someone and has disappointed the parent is particularly effective (Eisenberg, Eggum, & Edwards, 2010). Empathy-based guilt reactions are associated with stopping harmful actions, repairing damage caused by misdeeds, and engaging in future prosocial behavior.

But contrary to what Freud believed, guilt is not the only force that compels us to act morally. Nor is moral development complete by the end of early childhood. Rather, it is a gradual process that extends into adulthood.

Social Learning Theory

According to social learning theory, morality does not have a unique course of development. Rather, moral behavior is acquired through modeling, just like any other set of responses.

Importance of Modeling.
Many studies show that having helpful or generous models increases young children's prosocial responses. Nevertheless, certain characteristics of models affect children's willingness to imitate:

- *Warmth and responsiveness.* Preschoolers are more likely to copy the prosocial actions of warm, responsive (as opposed to cold, distant) adults (Yarrow, Scott, & Waxler, 1973). Warmth seems to make children more attentive and receptive to the model and is itself an example of a prosocial response.

- *Competence and power.* Children admire and therefore tend to imitate competent, powerful models—especially older peers and adults (Bandura, 1977).

- *Consistency between assertions and behavior.* When models say one thing and do another—for example, announce that "it's important to help others" but rarely engage in helpful acts—children generally choose the most lenient standard of behavior (Mischel & Liebert, 1966).

Models are most influential in the early years. In one study, toddlers' eager, willing imitation of their mothers' behavior predicted moral conduct (not cheating in a game) and guilt following transgressions at age 3 (Forman, Aksan, & Kochanska, 2004). At the end of early childhood, children who have had consistent exposure to caring adults tend to behave prosocially whether or not a model is present (Mussen & Eisenberg-Berg, 1977). They have internalized prosocial rules from repeated observations and encouragement by others.

At the same time, reinforcing young children with attention or praise appears unnecessary to induce them to help others. Most 2-year-olds will readily help an unfamiliar adult obtain an out-of-reach object, regardless of whether their parent encourages them, remains silent, or is absent from the room (Warneken & Tomasello, 2013). And giving children material rewards for helping undermines their prosocial responding (Warneken & Tomasello, 2009). Children who are materially rewarded come to expect something in return for helping and, therefore, rarely help spontaneously, out of kindness to others.

Effects of Punishment.
Many parents realize that yelling at, slapping, and spanking children for misbehavior are ineffective disciplinary tactics. A sharp reprimand or physical force to restrain or move a child is justified when immediate obedience is necessary—for example, when a 3-year-old is about to run into the street. In fact, parents are most likely to use forceful methods under these conditions. But to foster long-term goals, such as acting kindly toward others, they tend to rely on warmth and reasoning (Kuczynski, 1984; Lansford et al., 2012). And in response to serious transgressions, such as lying and stealing, they often combine power assertion with reasoning (Grusec, 2006).

Frequent punishment promotes immediate compliance but not lasting changes in behavior. For example, Robbie's parents often punished by hitting, shouting, and criticizing. But as soon as they stopped punishing and turned away, Robbie—like most children subjected to corporal punishment—misbehaved again (Holden, Williamson, & Holland, 2014). The more harsh threats, angry physical control, and physical punishment children experience, the more likely they are to develop serious, lasting problems. These include weak internalization of moral rules; depression, aggression, antisocial behavior, and poor academic performance in childhood and adolescence; and depression, alcohol abuse, criminality, physical health problems, and family violence in adulthood (Afifi et al., 2013; Bender et al., 2007; Kochanska, Aksan, & Nichols, 2003).

Repeated harsh punishment has wide-ranging undesirable side effects:

- Parents often spank in response to children's aggression. Yet the punishment itself models aggression!
- Harshly treated children develop a chronic sense of being personally threatened, which prompts a focus on their own distress rather than a sympathetic orientation to others' needs.
- Children who are frequently punished learn to avoid the punitive parent, who, as a result, has little opportunity to teach desirable behaviors.
- By stopping children's misbehavior temporarily, harsh punishment gives adults immediate relief. For this reason, a punitive adult is likely to punish with greater frequency over time, a course of action that can spiral into serious abuse.
- Children, adolescents, and adults whose parents used *corporal punishment*—physical force that inflicts pain but not injury—are more accepting of such discipline (Deater-Deckard et al., 2003; Vitrup & Holden, 2010). In this way, use of physical punishment may transfer to the next generation.

Although corporal punishment spans the SES spectrum, its frequency and harshness are elevated among less-educated, economically disadvantaged parents (Giles-Sims, Straus, & Sugarman, 1995; Lansford et al., 2009). And consistently, parents with conflict-ridden marriages and with mental health problems (who are emotionally reactive, depressed, or aggressive) are more likely to be punitive and also to have hard-to-manage children, whose disobedience evokes more parental harshness (Berlin et al., 2009; Taylor et al., 2010). But even after controlling for child, parenting, and family characteristics that might otherwise account for the relationship, longitudinal findings reveal a link between physical punishment and later child and adolescent aggression (Lansford et al., 2011; Lee et al., 2013; MacKenzie et al., 2013).

Physical punishment affects children with certain temperaments more than others. In a longitudinal study extending from 15 months to 3 years, early corporal punishment predicted externalizing behavior in preschoolers of diverse temperaments, but negative outcomes were considerably greater for temperamentally difficult children (Mulvaney & Mebert, 2007). Similar findings emerged in a twin study in which physical punishment was most detrimental for children at high genetic risk for behavior problems (Boutwell et al., 2011). Return to page 70 in Chapter 2 to review findings indicating that good parenting can shield children at risk for aggression and antisocial activity from developing those behaviors.

In view of these findings, the widespread use of corporal punishment by American parents is cause for concern. Surveys of nationally representative samples of U.S. families reveal that

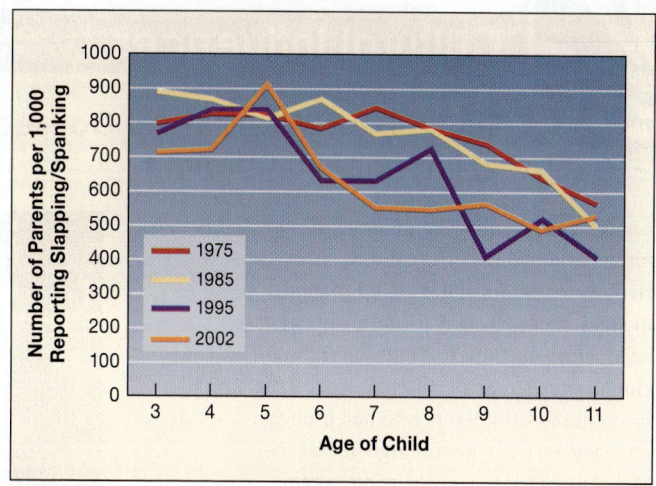

FIGURE 8.1 **Prevalence of corporal punishment in early and middle childhood by year of survey.** Five large surveys of U.S. parents show little change in use of corporal punishment over nearly three decades. Estimates are based on the number of parents per 1,000 reporting one or more instances of spanking or slapping their child during the past year. Rates are not shown for infants and toddlers, though other evidence indicates that 50 to 80 percent experience physical punishment. (From A. J. Zolotor, A. D. Theodore, D. K. Runyan, J. J. Chang, & A. L. Laskey, 2011, "Corporal Punishment and Physical Abuse: Population-Based Trends for Three- to 11-Year-Old Children in the United States," *Child Abuse Review, 20,* p. 61. Reprinted by permission of John Wiley & Sons, Ltd.)

although corporal punishment typically increases from infancy to age 5 and then declines, it is high at all ages (see Figure 8.1) (Gershoff et al., 2012; Straus & Stewart, 1999; Zolotor et al., 2011). Furthermore, more than one-third of physically punishing parents report having used a hard object, such as a brush or a belt.

A prevailing American belief is that corporal punishment, if implemented by caring parents, is harmless, perhaps even beneficial. But as the Cultural Influences box on page 270 reveals, this assumption is valid only under conditions of limited use in certain social contexts.

Alternatives to Harsh Punishment. Alternatives to criticism, slaps, and spankings can reduce the side effects of punishment. A technique called **time out** involves removing children from the immediate setting—for example, by sending them to their rooms—until they are ready to act appropriately. When a child is out of control, a few minutes in time out can be enough to change behavior while also giving angry parents time to cool off (Morawska & Sanders, 2011). Another approach is *withdrawal of privileges,* such as watching a favorite TV program. Like time out, removing privileges allows parents to avoid using harsh techniques that can easily intensify into violence.

When parents do decide to use mild punishment, they can increase its effectiveness in three ways:

- *Consistency.* Permitting children to act inappropriately on some occasions but scolding them on others confuses them, and the unacceptable act persists (Acker & O'Leary, 1996).

Cultural Influences

Ethnic Differences in the Consequences of Physical Punishment

In an African-American community, six older adults, who had volunteered to serve as mentors for parents facing child-rearing challenges, met to discuss parenting issues at a social service agency. Their attitudes toward discipline were strikingly different from those of the white social workers who had brought them together. Each mentor argued that successful child rearing required appropriate physical tactics. At the same time, they voiced strong disapproval of screaming or cursing at children, calling such out-of-control parental behavior "abusive." Ruth, the oldest and most respected member of the group, characterized good parenting as a complex combination of warmth, teaching, talking nicely, and disciplining physically. She related how an older neighbor advised her to handle her own children when she was a young parent:

> She said to me says, don't scream … you talk to them real nice and sweet and when they do something ugly … she say you get a nice little switch and you won't have any trouble with them and from that day that's the way I raised 'em. (Mosby et al., 1999, pp. 511–512)

In several studies, corporal punishment predicted externalizing problems similarly among white, black, Hispanic, and Asian children (Gershoff et al., 2012; MacKenzie et al., 2013). But other studies point to ethnic variations. In one longitudinal investigation, researchers followed several hundred families, collecting information from mothers on disciplinary strategies and from teachers on children's problem behaviors from kindergarten through fourth grade (Lansford et al., 2012). Regardless of ethnicity, reasoning was the most common approach to discipline, spanking the least common. But predictors and outcomes of spanking varied, depending on family ethnicity.

Among white families, externalizing behavior in kindergarten predicted parental physical punishment in first through third grades, which in turn led to more externalizing behavior by fourth grade. In contrast, among African-American families, kindergarten externalizing behavior was unrelated to later physical punishment, and physical punishment did not augment externalizing behavior (Lansford et al., 2012). The investigators concluded that white parents more often use physical discipline in reaction to challenging behaviors, causing those behaviors to escalate. African-American parents, in contrast, seem to use physical punishment to prevent child difficulties, thereby reducing its negative consequences.

Consistent with this interpretation, African-American and European-American parents report meting out physical punishment differently. In black families, such discipline is typically culturally approved, mild, delivered in a context of parental warmth, accompanied by verbal teaching, and aimed at helping children become responsible adults. White parents, in contrast, usually consider physical punishment to be wrong, so when they resort to it, they are often highly agitated and rejecting of the child (Dodge, McLoyd, & Lansford, 2006; LeCuyer et al., 2011). As a result, most black children may view spanking as a practice carried out with their best interests in mind, whereas white children may regard it as an act of aggression.

In African-American families, physical discipline is often culturally approved, generally mild, and delivered in a context of parental warmth. As a result, children may view it as an effort to encourage maturity, not as an act of aggression.

In support of this view, when several thousand ethnically diverse children were followed from the preschool through the early school years, spanking was associated with a rise in behavior problems if parents were cold and rejecting, but not if they were warm and supportive (McLoyd & Smith, 2002). In another study, spanking predicted depressive symptoms only among a small number of African-American children whose mothers disapproved of the practice and, as a result, tended to use it when they were highly angry and frustrated (McLoyd et al., 2007).

These findings are not an endorsement of physical punishment. Other forms of discipline, including time out, withdrawal of privileges, and the positive parenting strategies listed on page 271, are far more effective. In adolescence, ethnic differences in physical punishment fade: It is broadly associated with depression and misconduct among teenagers (Wang & Kenny, 2014). But it is noteworthy that the meaning and impact of physical discipline to children can vary sharply with its intensity level, context of warmth and support, and cultural approval.

Applying what we Know

Positive Parenting

STRATEGY	EXPLANATION
Use transgressions as opportunities to teach.	When a child engages in harmful or unsafe behavior, intervene firmly, and then use induction, which motivates children to make amends and behave prosocially.
Reduce opportunities for misbehavior.	On a long car trip, bring back-seat activities that relieve children's restlessness. At the supermarket, converse with children and let them help with shopping. Children then learn to occupy themselves constructively when options are limited.
Provide reasons for rules.	When children appreciate that rules are rational, not arbitrary, they are more likely to strive to follow the rules.
Arrange for children to participate in family routines and duties.	By joining with adults in preparing a meal, clearing the table, or raking leaves, children develop a sense of responsible participation in family and community life and acquire many practical skills.
When children are obstinate, try compromising and problem solving.	When a child refuses to obey, express understanding of the child's feelings ("I know it's not fun to clean up"), suggest a compromise ("You put those away, I'll take care of these"), and help the child think of ways to avoid the problem in the future. Responding firmly but kindly and respectfully increases the likelihood of willing cooperation.
Encourage mature behavior.	Express confidence in children's capacity to learn and appreciation for effort and cooperation: "You gave that your best!" "Thanks for cleaning up on your own!" Adult encouragement fosters pride and satisfaction in succeeding, thereby inspiring children to improve further.

Sources: Berk, 2001; Grusec, 2006.

- *A warm parent–child relationship.* Children of involved, caring parents find the interruption in parental affection that accompanies punishment especially unpleasant. They want to regain parental warmth and approval as quickly as possible.
- *Explanations.* Providing reasons for mild punishment helps children relate the misdeed to expectations for future behavior (Larzelere et al., 1996). This approach leads to a far greater reduction in misbehavior than using punishment alone.

Positive Relationships, Positive Parenting. The most effective forms of discipline encourage good conduct—by building a mutually respectful bond with the child, letting the child know ahead of time how to act, and praising mature behavior. When sensitivity, cooperation, and shared positive emotion are evident in joint activities between parents and preschoolers, children show firmer conscience development—expressing empathy after transgressions, playing fairly in games, and considering others' welfare (Kochanska et al., 2008; Thompson, 2014). Parent–child closeness leads children to heed parental demands because the child feels a sense of commitment to the relationship.

See Applying What We Know above for ways to parent positively. After experiencing a training program in these strategies, parents felt more confident about their ability to handle child-rearing challenges and were less approving of physical punishment (Durrant et al., 2014). When parents focus on promoting children's long-term social and life skills—cooperation, problem solving, and consideration for others—they greatly reduce the need for punishment.

The Cognitive-Developmental Perspective

The psychoanalytic and behaviorist approaches to morality focus on how children acquire ready-made standards of good conduct from adults. In contrast, the cognitive-developmental perspective regards children as *active thinkers* about social rules. As early as the preschool years, children make moral judgments, deciding what is right or wrong on the basis of concepts they construct about justice and fairness (Gibbs, 2010; Helwig & Turiel, 2011).

Young children have some well-developed ideas about morality. As long as researchers emphasize people's intentions, 3-year-olds say that a person with bad intentions—someone who deliberately frightens, embarrasses, or otherwise hurts another—is more deserving of punishment than a well-intentioned person. They also protest when they see one person harming another (Helwig, Zelazo, & Wilson, 2001; Vaish, Missana, & Tomasello, 2011). Around age 4, children know that a person who expresses an insincere intention—saying, "I'll come over and help you rake leaves," while not intending to do so—is lying (Maas, 2008). And 4-year-olds approve of telling the truth and disapprove of lying, even when a lie remains undetected (Bussey, 1992).

This preschooler understands that his choice of a toy is a matter of personal choice, distinct from moral imperatives and social conventions.

several studies, understanding of false belief was associated with 4- and 5-year-olds' moral justifications that focused on the harmed individual's emotions and well-being (Dunn, Cutting, & Demetriou, 2000; Lane et al., 2010). But advances in theory of mind, though influencing preschoolers' explanations, are not sufficient to account for gains in moral understanding.

In addition, morally relevant social experiences are vital, contributing to gains in both theory of mind and moral understanding and to their integration (Killen & Smetana, 2015). Disputes with siblings and peers over rights, possessions, and property allow preschoolers to express emotions and perspectives, negotiate, compromise, and work out their first ideas about justice and fairness. Children also learn from warm, sensitive parental communication and from observing how adults respond to children's rule violations (Turiel & Killen, 2010). Children who are advanced in moral thinking tend to have parents who adapt their discussions about fighting, honesty, and ownership to what their children can understand, tell stories with moral implications, point out injustices, encourage prosocial behavior, and gently stimulate the child to think further, without being hostile or critical (Dunn, 2014; Janssens & Deković, 1997).

Preschoolers who verbally and physically assault others, often with little or no provocation, are already delayed in moral reasoning (Helwig & Turiel, 2004). Without special help, such children show long-term disruptions in moral development, deficits in self-control, and ultimately an antisocial lifestyle.

Furthermore, preschoolers distinguish **moral imperatives,** which protect people's rights and welfare, from two other types of rules and expectations: **social conventions,** customs determined solely by consensus, such as table manners and politeness rituals (saying "please" and "thank you"); and **matters of personal choice,** such as choice of friends, hairstyle, and leisure activities, which do not violate rights and are up to the individual (Killen, Margie, & Sinno, 2006; Nucci & Gingo, 2011; Smetana, 2006). Interviews with 3- and 4-year-olds reveal that they consider moral violations (stealing an apple) as more wrong than violations of social conventions (eating ice cream with your fingers). And preschoolers' concern with personal choice, conveyed through statements like "I'm gonna wear *this* shirt," serves as the springboard for moral concepts of individual rights, which will expand greatly in middle childhood and adolescence.

Young children's moral reasoning tends to be *rigid*, emphasizing salient features and consequences while neglecting other important information. For example, they have difficulty distinguishing between accidental and intentional transgressions (Killen et al., 2011). And they are more likely than older children to claim that stealing and lying are always wrong, even when a person has a morally sound reason for engaging in these acts (Lourenço, 2003). Furthermore, their explanations for why hitting others is wrong are simplistic and centered on physical harm: "When you get hit, it hurts, and you start to cry" (Nucci, 2008).

Still, preschoolers' ability to distinguish moral imperatives from social conventions is impressive. Researchers speculate that children's commitment to the wrongness of moral transgressions builds on their early concern for others' welfare. With language and cognitive development—especially, in theory of mind and in understanding of emotion—older preschoolers start to reason morally by referring to others' perspectives and feelings. In

The Other Side of Morality: Development of Aggression

Beginning in late infancy, all children display aggression from time to time, and as opportunities to interact with siblings and peers increase, aggressive outbursts occur more often (Naerde et al., 2014). By the second year, aggressive acts with two distinct purposes emerge. Initially, the most common is **proactive** (or *instrumental*) **aggression,** in which children act to fulfill a need or desire—to obtain an object, privilege, space, or social reward, such as adult or peer attention—and unemotionally attack a person to achieve their goal. The other type, **reactive** (or *hostile*) **aggression,** is an angry, defensive response to provocation or a blocked goal and is meant to hurt another person (Eisner & Malti, 2015; Vitaro & Brendgen, 2012).

Proactive and reactive aggression come in three forms, which are the focus of most research:

- **Physical aggression** harms others through physical injury—pushing, hitting, kicking, or punching others, or destroying another's property.

- **Verbal aggression** harms others through threats of physical aggression, name-calling, or hostile teasing.

- **Relational aggression** damages another's peer relationships through social exclusion, malicious gossip, or friendship manipulation.

Although verbal aggression is always direct, physical and relational aggression can be either *direct* or *indirect*. For example, hitting injures a person directly, whereas destroying property inflicts physical harm indirectly. Similarly, saying, "Do what I say, or I won't be your friend," conveys relational aggression directly, while spreading rumors, refusing to talk to a peer, or manipulating friendships by saying behind someone's back, "Don't play with her; she's a nerd," do so indirectly.

Physical aggression rises sharply between ages 1 and 3 and then diminishes as verbal aggression replaces it (Alink et al., 2006; Vitaro & Brendgen, 2012). And proactive aggression declines as preschoolers' improved capacity to delay gratification enables them to resist grabbing others' possessions. But reactive aggression in verbal and relational forms tends to rise over early and middle childhood (Côté et al., 2007; Tremblay, 2000). Older children are better able to recognize malicious intentions and, as a result, more often retaliate in hostile ways.

By age 17 months, boys are more physically aggressive than girls—a difference found throughout childhood in many cultures (Baillargeon et al., 2007; Card et al., 2008). The sex difference is due in part to biology—in particular, to male sex hormones (androgens) and temperamental traits (activity level, irritability, impulsivity) on which boys exceed girls. Gender-role conformity is also important. For example, parents respond far more negatively to physical fighting in girls (Arnold, McWilliams, & Harvey-Arnold, 1998).

Although girls have a reputation for being both verbally and relationally more aggressive than boys, the sex difference is small (Crick, Ostrov, & Werner, 2006; Crick et al., 2006). Beginning in the preschool years, girls concentrate most of their aggressive acts in the relational category. Boys inflict harm in more variable ways. Physically and verbally aggressive boys also tend to be relationally aggressive (Card et al., 2008). Therefore, boys display overall rates of aggression that are much higher than girls'.

At the same time, girls more often use indirect relational tactics that—in disrupting intimate bonds especially important to girls—can be particularly mean. Whereas physical attacks are usually brief, acts of indirect relational aggression may extend for hours, weeks, or even months (Nelson, Robinson, & Hart, 2005; Underwood, 2003). In one instance, a 6-year-old girl formed a "pretty-girls club" and—for nearly an entire school year—convinced its members to exclude several classmates by saying they were "dirty and smelly."

An occasional aggressive exchange between preschoolers is normal. But children who are emotionally negative, impulsive, and disobedient and who score low in cognitive abilities—especially, language and executive function skills necessary for self-regulation—are at risk for early, high rates of physical or relational aggression (or both) that can persist. Persistent aggression, in turn, predicts later internalizing and externalizing difficulties and social skills deficits, including loneliness, anxiety, depression, peer relationship problems, and antisocial activity in middle childhood and adolescence (Côté et al., 2007; Eisner & Malti, 2015; Ostrov et al., 2013).

The Family as Training Ground for Aggressive Behavior. "I can't control him, he's impossible," Robbie's mother, Nadine, complained to Leslie one day. When Leslie asked if Robbie might be troubled by something happening at home, she discovered that his parents fought constantly and resorted to harsh, inconsistent discipline. Parental power assertion, critical remarks, physical punishment, and inconsistency are linked to aggression from early childhood through adolescence in many cultures, with most of these practices predicting both physical and relational forms (Côté et al., 2007; Gershoff et al., 2010; Kuppens et al., 2013; Nelson et al., 2013; Olson et al., 2011).

In families like Robbie's, anger and punitiveness quickly create a conflict-ridden family atmosphere and an "out-of-control" child. The pattern begins with forceful discipline, which occurs more often with stressful life experiences (such as economic hardship or an unhappy marriage), parental mental health problems, or a temperamentally difficult child (Eisner & Malti, 2015). Typically, the parent threatens, criticizes, and punishes, and the child angrily resists until the parent "gives in," so the behaviors repeat and escalate.

As these cycles generate anxiety and irritability among other family members, they join in the hostile interactions. Compared with siblings in typical families, preschool siblings who have critical, punitive parents are more aggressive toward each other. Destructive sibling conflict, in turn, spreads to peer relationships, contributing to poor impulse control and antisocial behavior by the early school years (Miller et al., 2012a).

These preschoolers display proactive aggression, pushing and grabbing as they argue over a game. As children learn to compromise and share, and as their capacity to delay gratification improves, proactive aggression declines.

Boys are more likely than girls to be targets of harsh, inconsistent discipline because they are more active and impulsive and therefore harder to control. When children who are extreme in these characteristics are exposed to emotionally negative, inept parenting, their capacity for emotional self-regulation, empathic responding, and guilt after transgressions is seriously disrupted (Eisenberg, Eggum, & Edwards, 2010). Consequently, they lash out when disappointed, frustrated, or faced with a sad or fearful victim.

Children subjected to these family processes acquire a distorted view of the social world, often seeing hostile intent where it does not exist and, as a result, making many unprovoked attacks (Lochman & Dodge, 1998; Orbio de Castro et al., 2002). And some, who conclude that aggression "works" to access rewards and control others, callously use it to advance their own goals and are unconcerned about causing suffering in others—an aggressive style associated with later more severe conduct problems, violent behavior, and delinquency (Marsee & Frick, 2010).

Highly aggressive children tend to be rejected by peers, to fail in school, and (by adolescence) to seek out deviant peers. Together, these factors contribute to the long-term stability of aggression. We will consider this life-course path of antisocial activity in Chapter 12.

Media Violence and Aggression. In the United States, an estimated 60 percent of TV programs contain violent scenes, often portraying repeated aggressive acts that go unpunished. TV victims of violence are rarely shown experiencing serious harm, and few programs condemn violence or depict other ways of solving problems (Calvert, 2015; Center for Communication and Social Policy, 1998). Verbally and relationally aggressive acts are particularly frequent in reality TV shows (Coyne, Robinson, & Nelson, 2010). And violent content is 10 percent above average in children's programming, with cartoons being the most violent.

LOOK and LISTEN

Watch a half-hour of cartoons and a prime-time movie on TV, and tally the number of violent acts, including those that go unpunished. How often did violence occur in each type of program? What do young viewers learn about the consequences of violence?

Reviewers of thousands of studies have concluded that TV violence increases the likelihood of hostile thoughts and emotions and of verbally, physically, and relationally aggressive behavior (Bushman & Huesmann, 2012; Comstock, 2008). A growing number of studies show that playing violent video and computer games has similar effects (Anderson et al., 2010; Hofferth, 2010). Although young people of all ages are susceptible, preschool and young school-age children are especially likely to imitate TV violence because they believe that much TV fiction is real and accept what they see uncritically.

Watching TV violence increases the likelihood of hostile thoughts and emotions and aggressive behavior. Playing violent video and computer games has similar effects.

Violent programming not only creates short-term difficulties in parent and peer relations but also has lasting negative consequences. In several longitudinal studies, time spent watching TV in childhood and adolescence predicted aggressive behavior in adulthood, after other factors linked to TV viewing (such as prior child and parent aggression, IQ, parent education, family income, and neighborhood crime) were controlled (see Figure 8.2) (Graber et al., 2006; Huesmann et al., 2003; Johnson et al., 2002). Aggressive children and adolescents have a greater

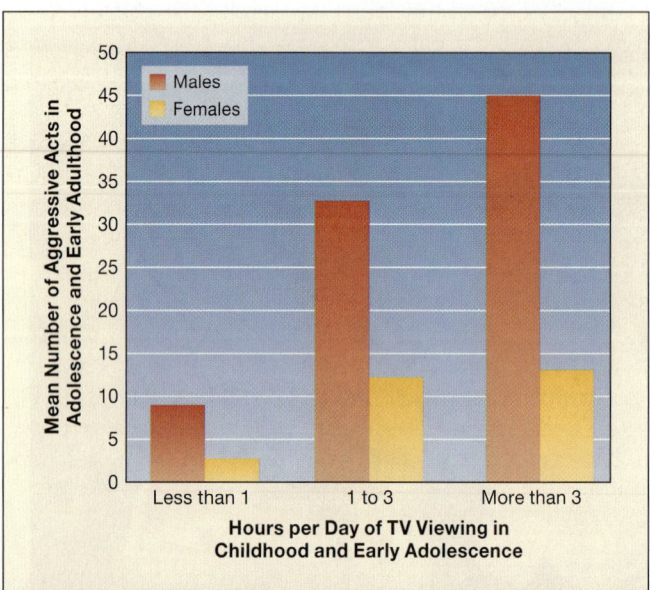

FIGURE 8.2 Relationship of television viewing in childhood and early adolescence to aggressive acts in adolescence and early adulthood. Interviews with more than 700 parents and youths revealed that the more TV watched in childhood and early adolescence, the greater the annual number of aggressive acts committed by the young person, as reported in follow-up interviews at ages 16 and 22. (Adapted from Johnson et al., 2002.)

Applying what we Know

Regulating Screen Media Use

STRATEGY	DESCRIPTION
Limit TV viewing and computer and tablet use.	Parents should provide clear rules limiting children's TV viewing and computer and tablet use, based on age guidelines and exposure to program and game content, and should stick to the rules. The TV or computer should not be used as a babysitter. Placing a TV or a computer in a child's bedroom substantially increases use and makes the child's activity hard to monitor.
Avoid using screen media as a reward.	When media access is used as a reward or withheld as a punishment, children become increasingly attracted to it.
When possible, watch TV and view online content with children, helping them understand what they see.	By raising questions about realism in media depictions, expressing disapproval of on-screen behavior, and encouraging discussion, adults help children understand and critically evaluate TV and online content.
Link TV and online content to everyday learning experiences.	Parents can extend TV and online learning in ways that encourage children to engage actively with their surroundings. For example, a program on animals might spark a trip to the zoo, a visit to the library for a book about animals, or new ways of observing and caring for the family pet.
Model good media practices.	Parents' media behavior influences children's behavior. Parents should avoid excessive media use, limit their own exposure to harmful content, and limit mobile device use during family interactions.

appetite for violent media fare. And boys devote more time to violent media than girls, in part because of male-oriented themes of conquest and adventure. But even in nonaggressive children, violent TV sparks hostile thoughts and behavior; its impact is simply less intense.

Surveys of U.S. parents indicate that 20 to 30 percent of preschoolers and about half of school-age children experience no limits on TV, computer, or tablet use (Rideout & Hamel, 2006; Roberts, Foehr, & Rideout, 2005; Varnhagen, 2007). And parents often model excessive, inappropriate use of screen media. In observations of adults with children in fast-food restaurants, almost one-third of the adults spent the entire meal absorbed with mobile devices rather than engaged with children in their care (Radesky et al., 2014).

To help parents improve their preschoolers' "media diet," one group of researchers devised a year-long intervention in which they guided parents in replacing violent programs with age-appropriate educational and prosocial programs. Compared to a control group, children in intervention families displayed lower rates of externalizing behavior and improved social competence (Christakis et al., 2013). Applying What We Know above lists strategies parents can use to regulate children's screen media use.

Helping Children and Parents Control Aggression.

Treatment for aggressive children is best begun early, before their behavior becomes well-practiced and difficult to change. Breaking the cycle of hostilities between family members and promoting effective ways of relating to others are crucial.

Leslie suggested that Robbie's parents enroll in a training program aimed at improving the parenting of children with conduct problems. In one approach, called *Incredible Years*, parents complete 18 weekly group sessions facilitated by two professionals, who teach positive parenting techniques for promoting children's academic, emotional, and social skills and for managing disruptive behaviors (Webster-Stratton & Reid, 2010). A special focus is positive parenting, including guidance and encouragement for prosocial behaviors.

Evaluations in which families with aggressive children were randomly assigned to either Incredible Years or control groups reveal that the program is highly effective at improving parenting and reducing child behavior problems. And the effects endure. In one long-term follow-up, 75 percent of young children with serious conduct problems whose parents participated in Incredible Years were well-adjusted as teenagers (Webster-Stratton, Rinaldi, & Reid, 2011).

At preschool, Leslie began teaching Robbie more successful ways of relating to peers, had him practice these skills, and praised him for using them. As opportunities arose, she encouraged Robbie to talk about playmates' feelings and to express his own. As he increasingly took the perspective of others, empathized, and felt sympathetic concern, his lashing out at peers declined (Izard et al., 2008). Robbie also participated in a social problem-solving intervention. Throughout the school year, he met weekly with Leslie and a small group of classmates to act out common conflicts using puppets, discuss alternatives for settling disputes, and practice successful strategies. Preschoolers who receive such training show gains in emotional and social competence still present after entering kindergarten (Bierman & Powers, 2009; Moore et al., 2015).

Finally, relieving stressors that stem from economic disadvantage and neighborhood disorganization and providing families with social supports help prevent childhood aggression (Bugental, Corpuz, & Schwartz, 2012). When parents better cope with stressors in their own lives, interventions aimed at reducing children's aggression are more effective.

Ask yourself

CONNECT What must parents do to foster conscience development in fearless, impulsive children? How does this illustrate the concept of goodness of fit (see page 195 in Chapter 6)?

APPLY Alice and Wayne want their two children to become morally mature, caring individuals. List some parenting practices they should use and some they should avoid.

REFLECT Which types of punishment for a misbehaving preschooler do you endorse, and which types do you reject? Why?

Gender Typing

8.7 Discuss biological and environmental influences on preschoolers' gender-stereotyped beliefs and behavior.

8.8 Describe and evaluate major theories that explain the emergence of gender identity.

Gender typing refers to any association of objects, activities, roles, or traits with one sex or the other in ways that conform to cultural stereotypes (Blakemore, Berenbaum, & Liben, 2009). In Leslie's classroom, girls spent more time in the housekeeping, art, and reading corners, while boys gathered more often in spaces devoted to blocks, woodworking, and active play. Already, the children had acquired many gender-linked beliefs and preferences and tended to play with peers of their own sex.

The same theories that provide accounts of morality have been used to explain children's gender typing: *social learning theory*, with its emphasis on modeling and reinforcement, and *cognitive-developmental theory*, with its focus on children as active thinkers about their social world. As we will see, neither is adequate by itself. *Gender schema theory*, a third perspective that combines elements of both, has gained favor. In the following sections, we consider the early development of gender typing.

Gender-Stereotyped Beliefs and Behavior

Even before children can label their own sex consistently, they have begun to acquire common associations with gender—men as rough and sharp, women as soft and round. In one study, 18-month-olds linked such items as fir trees and hammers with males, although they had not yet learned comparable feminine associations (Eichstedt et al., 2002). Recall from Chapter 6 that around age 2, children use such words as *boy, girl, lady,* and *man* appropriately. As soon as gender categories are established, young children's gender-typed learning accelerates.

Preschoolers associate toys, clothing, tools, household items, games, occupations, colors (pink and blue), and behaviors (physical and relational aggression) with one sex or the other (Banse et al., 2010; Giles & Heyman, 2005; Poulin-Dubois et al., 2002). And their actions reflect their beliefs, not only in play preferences but also in personality traits. As we have seen, boys tend to be more active, impulsive, assertive, and physically aggressive. Girls tend to be more fearful, dependent, emotionally sensitive, compliant, advanced in effortful control, and skilled at inflicting indirect relational aggression (Else-Quest, 2012).

During early childhood, gender-stereotyped beliefs strengthen—so much so that many children apply them as blanket rules rather than as flexible guidelines (Halim et al., 2013; Trautner et al., 2005). When children were asked whether gender stereotypes could be violated, half or more of 3- and 4-year-olds answered "no" to clothing, hairstyle, and play with certain toys (Barbie dolls and G.I. Joes) (Blakemore, 2003). Furthermore, most 3- to 6-year-olds are firm about not wanting to be friends with a child who violates a gender stereotype (a boy who wears nail polish, a girl who plays with trucks) or to attend a school where such violations are allowed (Ruble et al., 2007).

The rigidity of preschoolers' gender stereotypes helps us understand some commonly observed everyday behaviors. When Leslie showed her class a picture of a Scottish bagpiper wearing a kilt, the children insisted, "Men don't wear skirts!" During free play, they often exclaimed that girls can't be police officers and boys don't take care of babies. These one-sided judgments are a joint product of gender stereotyping in the environment and young children's cognitive limitations. Most

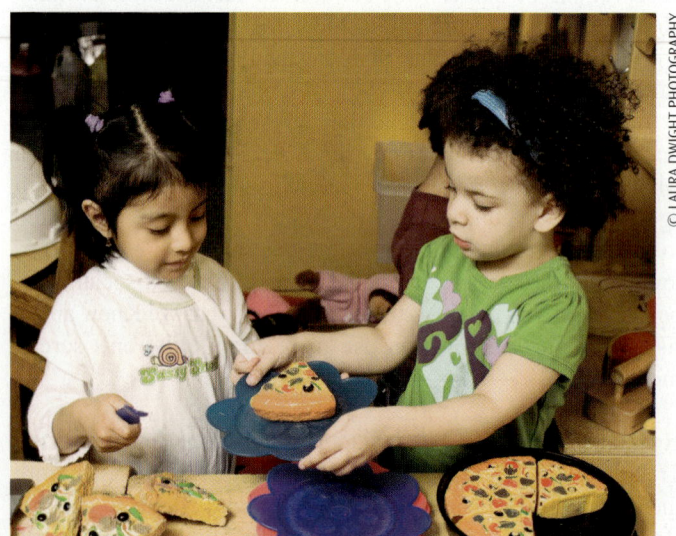

Early in the preschool years, gender typing is well under way. Girls tend to play with girls and are drawn to toys and activities that emphasize nurturance and cooperation.

preschoolers do not yet realize that characteristics *associated with* being male or female—activities, toys, occupations, hairstyle, and clothing—do not *determine* a person's sex.

Biological Influences on Gender Typing

The sex differences in personality traits and behavior described earlier appear in many cultures around the world (Munroe & Romney, 2006; Whiting & Edwards, 1988). Certain ones—male activity level and physical aggression, female emotional sensitivity, and preference for same-sex playmates—are widespread among mammalian species (de Waal, 2001). According to an evolutionary perspective, the adult life of our male ancestors was largely oriented toward competing for mates, that of our female ancestors toward rearing children. Therefore, males became genetically primed for dominance and females for intimacy, responsiveness, and cooperativeness (Konner, 2010; Maccoby, 2002). Evolutionary theorists claim that family and cultural forces can influence the intensity of biologically based sex differences. But experience cannot eradicate those aspects of gender typing that served adaptive functions in human history.

Experiments with animals reveal that prenatally administered androgens increase active play and aggression and suppress maternal caregiving in both male and female mammals (Arnold, 2009). Research with humans reveals similar patterns. Girls exposed prenatally to high levels of androgens, due to normal variation in hormone levels or to a genetic defect, show more "masculine" behavior—a preference for trucks and blocks over dolls, for active over quiet play, and for boys as playmates—even when parents encourage them to engage in gender-typical play (Berenbaum & Beltz, 2011; Hines, 2011a). And boys with reduced prenatal androgen exposure, either because production by the testes is reduced or because body cells are androgen insensitive, tend to engage in "feminine" behaviors, including toy choices, play behaviors, and preference for girl playmates (Jürgensen et al., 2007; Lamminmaki et al., 2012).

Some researchers argue that biologically based sex differences, which affect children's play styles, cause children to seek out same-sex playmates whose interests and behaviors are compatible with their own (Maccoby, 1998; Mehta & Strough, 2009). Preschool girls like to play in pairs with other girls because they share a preference for quieter activities involving cooperative roles. Boys prefer larger-group play with other boys, due to a shared desire to run, climb, play-fight, compete, and build up and knock down.

Research confirms that preschoolers are drawn to peers who engage in similar levels of gender-typed activities. But they also like to spend time with same-sex peers regardless of type of activity—perhaps because they expect a playmate who is like themselves in so basic a way to be more enjoyable (Martin et al., 2013). At age 4, children spend three times as much time with same-sex as with other-sex playmates. By age 6, this ratio has climbed to 11 to 1 (Martin & Fabes, 2001).

Environmental Influences on Gender Typing

A wealth of evidence reveals that environmental forces—at home, at school, with peers, and in the community—build on genetic influences to promote vigorous gender typing in early childhood.

Parents. Beginning at birth, parents have different expectations of sons than of daughters. Many parents prefer that their children play with "gender-appropriate" toys (Blakemore & Hill, 2008). And they tend to describe achievement, competition, and control of emotion as important for sons and warmth, polite behavior, and closely supervised activities as important for daughters (Brody, 1999; Turner & Gervai, 1995).

Actual parenting practices reflect these beliefs. Parents give their sons toys that stress action and competition (cars, tools, footballs) and their daughters toys that emphasize nurturance, cooperation, and physical attractiveness (dolls, tea sets, jewelry) (Leaper, 1994; Leaper & Friedman, 2007). Fathers of preschoolers report more physical activities (chasing, playing ball) with sons and more literacy activities (reading, storytelling) with daughters (Leavell et al., 2011). Furthermore, parents tend to react more positively when a son plays with cars and trucks, demands attention, runs and climbs, or tries to take toys from others. When interacting with daughters, parents more often direct play activities, provide help, encourage participation in household tasks, make supportive statements (approval, praise, and agreement), and refer to emotions (Clearfield & Nelson, 2006; Fagot & Hagan, 1991; Leaper, 2000).

Furthermore, parents provide children with indirect cues about gender stereotypes through the language they use. In a study of picture book reading with toddlers and preschoolers, mothers frequently expressed *generic utterances,* which referred

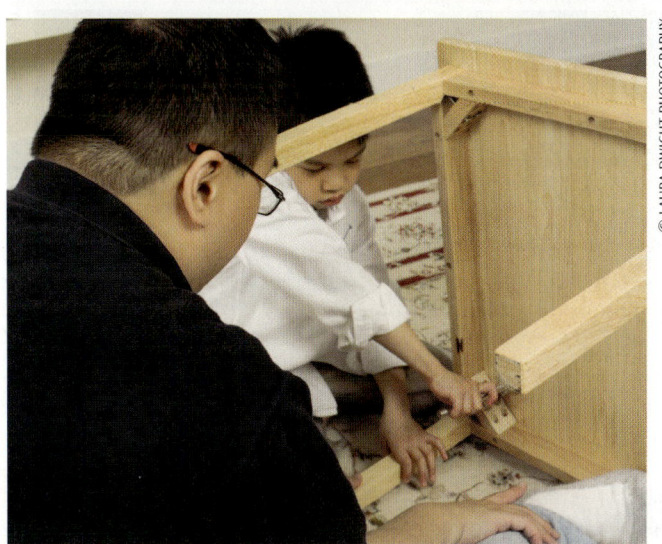

This father teaches his son carpentry skills. Of the two sexes, boys are more gender-typed. Fathers, especially, promote "masculine" behavior in their sons by insisting that they conform to gender roles.

to nearly all same-sex individuals as alike, ignoring exceptions ("Boys can be sailors." "Most girls don't like trucks.") (Gelman, Taylor, & Nguyen, 2004). Children picked up these expressions from their mother's speech, and older preschoolers often made stereotyped generic statements, which their mothers affirmed (Child: "Only boys can drive trucks." Mother: "O.K.").

Of the two sexes, boys are more gender-typed. Fathers, especially, are more insistent that boys conform to gender roles. They place more pressure to achieve on sons than on daughters and are less tolerant of "cross-gender" behavior in sons—more concerned when a boy acts like a "sissy" than when a girl acts like a "tomboy" (Blakemore & Hill, 2008; Wood, Desmarais, & Gugula, 2002).

Parents who hold nonstereotyped values and behave accordingly have children who are less gender-typed (Tenenbaum & Leaper, 2002). Children of gay or lesbian parents tend to be less gender-typed than agemates of heterosexual parents, perhaps because of their parents' more gender-equitable expectations and behaviors (Fulcher, Sutfin, & Patterson, 2008; Goldberg, Kashy, & Smith, 2012).

Teachers. Teachers often act in ways that extend gender-role learning. Several times, Leslie caught herself emphasizing gender distinctions when she called out, "Will the girls line up on one side and the boys on the other?" or pleaded, "Boys, I wish you'd quiet down like the girls!" These practices increase preschoolers' gender-stereotyped beliefs while reducing their liking for and willingness to play with other-sex peers (Hilliard & Liben, 2010).

Like parents, preschool teachers encourage girls to participate in adult-structured activities. Girls frequently cluster around the teacher, following directions, while boys are attracted to play areas where adults are minimally involved (Campbell, Shirley, & Candy, 2004). As a result, boys and girls engage in different social behaviors. Compliance and bids for help occur more often in adult-structured contexts; assertiveness, leadership, and creative use of materials in unstructured pursuits.

As early as kindergarten, teachers give more overall attention (both positive and negative) to boys than to girls—a difference evident in diverse countries, including China, England, and the United States. They praise boys more for their academic knowledge but also use more disapproval and controlling discipline with them (Chen & Rao, 2011; Davies, 2008; Swinson & Harrop, 2009). Teachers seem to expect boys to misbehave more often—a belief based partly on boys' actual behavior and partly on gender stereotypes.

Peers. The more preschoolers play with same-sex partners, the more their behavior becomes gender-typed—in toy choices, activity level, aggression, and adult involvement (Martin et al., 2013). By age 3, same-sex peers positively reinforce one another for gender-typed play by praising, imitating, or joining in. In contrast, when preschoolers engage in "cross-gender" activities—for example, when boys play with dolls or girls with cars and trucks—peers criticize them. Boys are especially intolerant of cross-gender play in other boys (Thorne, 1993). A boy who frequently crosses gender lines is likely to be ignored by other boys, even when he does engage in "masculine" activities.

Children also develop different styles of social influence in gender-segregated peer groups. To get their way in large-group play, boys often rely on commands, threats, and physical force. Girls' preference for playing in pairs leads to greater concern with a partner's needs, evident in girls' use of polite requests, persuasion, and acceptance. Girls soon find that gentle tactics succeed with other girls but not with boys, who ignore their courteous overtures (Leaper, 1994; Leaper, Tenenbaum, & Shaffer, 1999). Boys' unresponsiveness gives girls another reason to stop interacting with them.

Over time, children come to believe in the "correctness" of gender-segregated play and to perceive themselves as more similar to same-sex than other-sex peers, which further strengthens gender segregation and gender-stereotyped activities (Martin et al., 2011). As boys and girls separate, *in-group favoritism*—more positive evaluations of members of one's own gender—becomes another factor that sustains the separate social worlds of boys and girls, resulting in "two distinct subcultures" of knowledge, beliefs, interests, and behaviors (Maccoby, 2002).

Although gender segregation is pervasive, cultural variations exist in the extent of gender-typed communication within such groups. African-American and Hispanic girls from low-SES families tend to be more assertive and independent when interacting with one another and with boys than are European-American girls (Goodwin, 1998). Similarly, in a comparison of Chinese and U.S. preschoolers' play, Chinese girls used more direct commands and criticism when interacting with same- and other-sex peers (Kyratzis & Guo, 2001). In cultures where interdependence is highly valued, perhaps children do not feel a need to work as hard at maintaining same-sex peer relations through traditional interaction.

In this preschool classroom, girls cluster around the teacher for instruction while boys play independently. As a result, children practice gender-typed behaviors—compliance and bids for attention by girls, assertiveness and leadership by boys.

The Broader Social Environment. Finally, children's everyday environments present many examples of gender-typed behavior—in occupations, leisure activities, media portrayals, and achievements of men and women. Media stereotypes, which are especially prevalent in cartoons and video games, contribute to young children's biased beliefs about roles and behaviors suitable for males and females (Calvert, 2015; Leaper, 2013). As we will see next, children soon come to view not just their social surroundings but also themselves through a "gender-biased lens"—a perspective that can seriously restrict their interests and learning opportunities.

Gender Identity

As adults, each of us has a **gender identity**—an image of oneself as relatively masculine or feminine in characteristics. By middle childhood, researchers can measure gender identity by asking children to rate themselves on personality traits. A child or adult with a "masculine" identity scores high on traditionally masculine items (such as *ambitious, competitive,* and *self-sufficient*) and low on traditionally feminine items (such as *affectionate, cheerful,* and *soft-spoken*). Someone with a "feminine" identity does the reverse. And a substantial minority (especially females) have a gender identity called **androgyny**, scoring high on both masculine and feminine personality characteristics.

Gender identity is a good predictor of psychological adjustment. "Masculine" and androgynous children and adults have higher self-esteem than "feminine" individuals (DiDonato & Berenbaum, 2011; Harter, 2012). Also, androgynous individuals are more adaptable—able to show masculine independence or feminine sensitivity, depending on the situation (Huyck, 1996; Taylor & Hall, 1982). The existence of an androgynous identity demonstrates that children can acquire a mixture of positive qualities traditionally associated with each gender—an orientation that may best help them realize their potential.

Emergence of Gender Identity. How do children develop a gender identity? According to *social learning theory,* behavior comes before self-perceptions. Preschoolers first acquire gender-typed responses through modeling and reinforcement and only later organize these behaviors into gender-linked ideas about themselves. In contrast, *cognitive-developmental theory* maintains that self-perceptions come before behavior. Over the preschool years, children acquire **gender constancy**—a full understanding of the biologically based permanence of their gender, including the realization that sex remains the same even if clothing, hairstyle, and play activities change. Then children use this knowledge to guide their gender-related behavior.

Children younger than age 6 who watch an adult dress a doll in "other-gender" clothing typically insist that the doll's sex has also changed (Chauhan, Shastri, & Mohite, 2005; Fagot, 1985). Full attainment of gender constancy is strongly related to ability to pass Piagetian conservation tasks (DiLisi & Gallagher, 1991). Indeed, gender constancy tasks can be considered a type of conservation problem, in that children must conserve a person's sex despite a superficial change in his or her appearance.

Is cognitive-developmental theory correct that gender constancy is responsible for children's gender-typed behavior? Evidence for this assumption is weak. Some evidence suggests that attaining gender constancy actually contributes to more flexible gender-role attitudes, perhaps because children then realize that engaging in gender-atypical behavior cannot cause their sex to change (Ruble et al., 2007). But overall, the impact of gender constancy on gender typing is not great. As research in the following section reveals, gender-role adoption is more powerfully affected by children's beliefs about how close the connection must be between their own gender and their behavior.

Gender Schema Theory. **Gender schema theory** is an information-processing approach that combines social learning and cognitive-developmental features. It explains how environmental pressures and children's cognitions work together to shape gender-role development (Martin & Halverson, 1987; Martin, Ruble, & Szkrybalo, 2002). At an early age, children pick up gender-stereotyped preferences and behaviors from others. At the same time, they organize their experiences into *gender schemas,* or masculine and feminine categories, that they use to interpret their world. As soon as preschoolers can label their own gender, they select gender schemas consistent with it ("Only boys can be doctors" or "Cooking is a girl's job") and apply those categories to themselves. Their self-perceptions then become gender-typed and serve as additional schemas that children use to process information and guide their own behavior.

We have seen that individual differences exist in the extent to which children endorse gender-typed views. Figure 8.3 on page 280 shows different cognitive pathways for children who often apply gender schemas to their experiences and those who rarely do (Liben & Bigler, 2002). Consider Billy, who encounters a doll. If Billy is a *gender-schematic child,* his *gender-salience filter* immediately makes gender highly relevant. Drawing on his prior learning, he asks himself, "Should boys play with dolls?" If he answers "yes" and the toy interests him, he will explore it and learn more about it. If he answers "no," he will avoid the "gender-inappropriate" toy. But if Billy is a *gender-aschematic child*—one who seldom views the world in gender-linked terms—he simply asks himself, "Do I like this toy?" and responds on the basis of his interests.

Gender-schematic thinking is so powerful that when children see others behaving in "gender-inconsistent" ways, they often distort their memory to make it "gender-consistent." For example, when shown a picture of a male nurse, they may remember him as a doctor (Martin & Ruble, 2004). And because gender-schematic preschoolers typically conclude, "What I like, children of my own sex will also like," they often use their own preferences to add to their gender biases (Liben & Bigler, 2002). For example, a girl who dislikes oysters may declare, "Only boys like oysters!" even though she has never actually been given information promoting such a stereotype. At least partly for this reason, young children's gender schemas contain both culturally

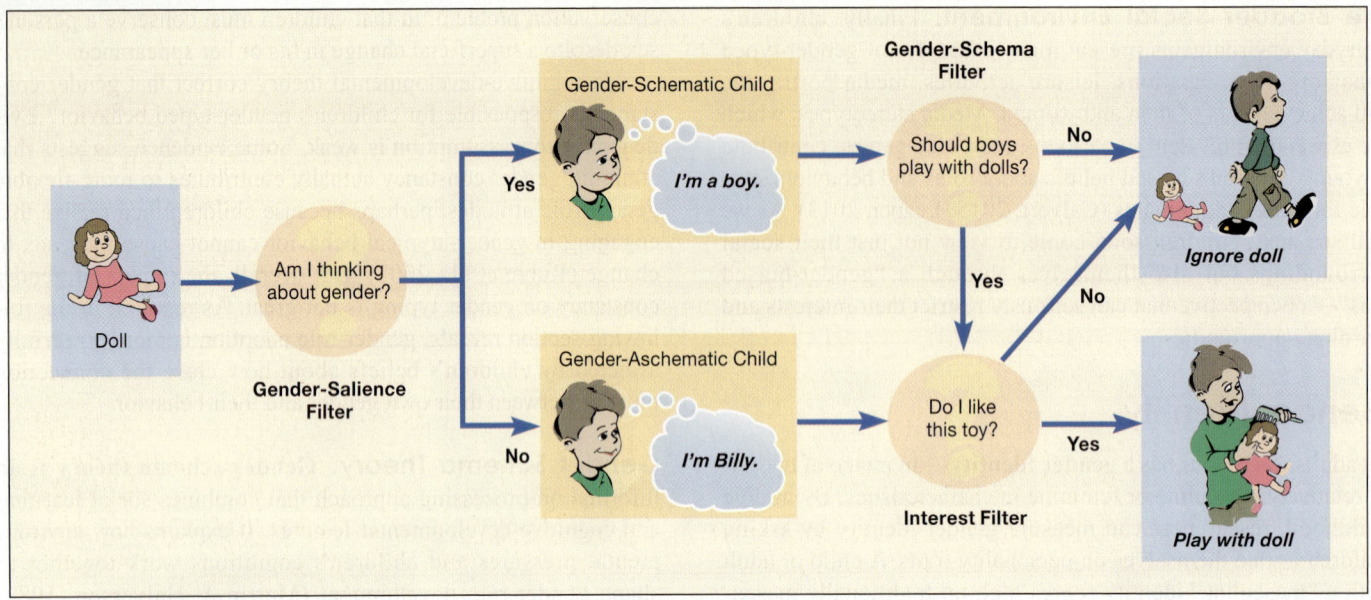

FIGURE 8.3 Cognitive pathways for gender-schematic and gender-aschematic children. In *gender-schematic children,* the gender-salience filter immediately makes gender highly relevant: Billy sees a doll and thinks, "I'm a boy. Should boys play with dolls?" Drawing on his experiences, he answers "yes" or "no." If he answers "yes" and the doll interests him, he plays with the doll. If he answers "no," he avoids the "gender-inappropriate" toy. *Gender-aschematic children* rarely view the world in gender-linked terms: Billy simply asks, "Do I like this toy?" and responds on the basis of his interests. (Reprinted by permission of Rebecca Bigler.)

standard and nonstandard ideas (Tenenbaum et al., 2010). Not until well into the school years do children's gender schemas fully resemble those of adults.

Gender identity involves self-perceptions that build on a core sense of one's own gender. A few children, however, express great discomfort with the gender they were assigned at birth and want to live as the other gender, expressing this desire as early as the preschool years. For research on transgender children, refer to the Biology and Environment box on the following page.

Reducing Gender Stereotyping in Young Children

How can we help young children avoid rigid gender schemas that restrict their behavior and learning opportunities? No easy recipe exists. Biology clearly affects children's gender typing, channeling boys, on average, toward active, competitive play and girls toward quieter, more intimate interaction. At the same time, differential treatment of boys and girls begins as soon as they are born, amplifying biologically based tendencies and promoting a great many aspects of gender typing that are unrelated to human nature (Hines, 2015).

Because young children's cognitive limitations lead them to assume that cultural practices determine gender, parents and teachers are wise to try to delay preschoolers' exposure to gender-stereotyped messages. Adults can begin by limiting traditional gender roles in their own behavior and can provide children with nontraditional alternatives. For example, parents can take turns making dinner, bathing children, and driving the family car, and they can give their sons and daughters both trucks and dolls and both pink and blue clothing. Teachers can ensure that all children spend time in mixed-gender play activities and unstructured pursuits, as children's behavior tends to be less gender-typed in these contexts (Goble et al., 2012). Finally, adults can avoid using language that conveys gender stereotypes and can shield children from media presentations that do so.

Once children notice the vast array of gender stereotypes in their society, adults can point out exceptions. For example, they can arrange for children to see men and women pursuing nontraditional careers and can explain that interests and skills, not sex, should determine a person's occupation. Research shows that such reasoning reduces children's gender-biased views. By middle childhood, children who hold flexible beliefs about what boys and girls can do are more likely to notice instances of gender discrimination (Brown & Bigler, 2004). And as we will see next, a rational approach to child rearing promotes healthy, adaptable functioning in many other areas as well.

Ask yourself

CONNECT In addition to gender-stereotyped beliefs, what other aspects of preschoolers' social understanding tend to be rigid and one-sided?

APPLY List findings indicating that language and communication—between parents and children, between teachers and children, and between peers—powerfully affect children's gender typing. What recommendations would you make to counteract these influences?

REFLECT Would you describe your own gender identity as "masculine," "feminine," or "androgynous"? What biological and social factors might have influenced your gender identity?

Biology and Environment

Transgender Children

Jacob, who began life as a girl named Mia, firmly insisted at age 2, "I am a boy!" in opposition to his parents' suggestion that he was merely "pretending." At preschool, he became increasingly angry at being identified as a girl. When his teacher asked him to write his name, he would print M-I-A but then vigorously cross it out. Gradually, his parents sensed the strength of his expressed identity. With guidance from a therapist, they began following his lead, providing boys' clothes, a short haircut, superhero action figures, and toy cars. At age 4, after his parents presented him with several options, one of which was living as a boy, he affirmed that he wanted to change his name to Jacob and go to a different school, where he could start a new public life as a boy (Lemay, 2015). "I want to be a boy always," Jacob declared. His problematic behavior at home and school quickly subsided.

The number of transgender children, adolescents, and adults in Western nations, though few, has risen recently—perhaps because more stories like Jacob's are appearing in the media and because seeking treatment has become more acceptable. Individuals dissatisfied with their natal (birth) sex who strongly identify as the other sex experience substantial distress—a condition called *gender dysphoria*. Estimates based on large samples of Dutch and North American children suggest that about 1.5 percent of natal boys and 2 percent of natal girls suffer from gender dysphoria (Ristori & Steensma, 2016; Van Beijsterveldt, Hudziak, & Boomsma, 2006). Some researchers speculate that the sex difference has to do with greater cultural acceptance of gender nonconformity in girls, leading girls who experience gender dysphoria to express it more readily.

People who change gender in adulthood often trace the emergence of their gender dysphoria to early childhood. Although contributing factors are not well understood, the prenatal hormone environment seems to play a role. For example, genetic females known to have been exposed to high levels of prenatal androgens are more likely than other women to be transgender (Dessens, Slijper, & Drop, 2005). But many females prenatally exposed to high androgen levels, and many males exposed to low levels, do not express discomfort with their natal sex.

Although some studies claim that most cases of childhood gender dysphoria subside in adolescence and adulthood, their samples failed to distinguish between gender-dysphoric children and children who merely display gender-nonconforming behavior. Children who are severely troubled over the mismatch between their natal sex and core gender identity, who insist that they are the other gender, and who also engage in high levels of "other-gender" behavior generally experience persisting dysphoria (Ristori & Steensma, 2016; Steensma et al., 2011). These persisters are likely to transition mostly or entirely—as Jacob did—to their desired gender role.

Transgender children are not pretending, confused, or delayed in gender understanding. When questioned about their peer preferences, gender-typed object choices, and gender identity, their responses are identical to those of nontransgender agemates who share their expressed gender (Olson, Key, & Eaton, 2015).

During early adolescence, gender dysphoria typically deepens as persisters encounter changes in their bodies and first feelings of sexual attraction (Leibowitz & de Vries, 2016). Some desire, and may be deemed eligible for, psychological and medical sex-change treatment, involving suppression of pubertal sex hormones, cross-sex hormone treatment after age 16, and surgery after age 18. Others go through a period of questioning, including hesitancy over invasive treatments, and take additional time to assess their feelings about transitioning physically (Steensma & Cohen-Kettenis, 2015). A number of these young people find their gender dysphoria so overwhelming that they eventually decide on treatment in their twenties and thirties.

Jacob, who began life as a girl, changed his name and transitioned to living as a boy in early childhood. Transgender children whose parents support their desire to express their identified gender are more content and better-adjusted.

Controversy exists over therapies for gender-dysphoric children. One approach is directed at lessening their cross-gender identity and behavior and increasing their comfort with their natal sex. These therapies, however, have yielded poor results (Adelson, 2012; Byne et al., 2012). Gender-dysphoric children react with heightened distress to efforts to suppress or deny their identified gender.

Increasing numbers of health professionals are convinced that therapies must be aimed at permitting children to follow their gender-identity inclinations and helping parents protect their children from the negative reactions of others. These efforts are motivated by the tragic circumstances of many contemporary transgender adults, who experienced family rejection and social ostracism from childhood on and who face high rates of unemployment, poverty, homelessness, depression, and suicide (Byne et al., 2012; Di Ceglie, 2014; Haas, Rodgers, & Herman, 2014). Current evidence suggests that embracing transgender children's expressed identity leads to contented, better-adjusted children and adolescents. Follow-up research is needed to assess long-term outcomes in the coming generation of transgender adults.

Child Rearing and Emotional and Social Development

8.9 Describe the impact of child-rearing styles on development, and explain why authoritative parenting is effective.

8.10 Discuss the multiple origins of child maltreatment, its consequences for development, and prevention strategies.

In this and previous chapters, we have seen how parents can foster children's competence—by building a parent–child relationship based on affection and cooperation, by modeling mature behavior, by using reasoning and inductive discipline, and by guiding and encouraging mastery of new skills. Now let's put these practices together into an overall view of effective parenting.

Styles of Child Rearing

Child-rearing styles are combinations of parenting behaviors that occur over a wide range of situations, creating an enduring child-rearing climate. In a landmark series of studies, Diana Baumrind (1971) gathered information on child rearing by watching parents interact with their preschoolers. Her findings, and those of others who have extended her work, reveal three features that consistently differentiate an effective style from less effective ones: (1) acceptance and involvement, (2) control, and (3) autonomy granting (Gray & Steinberg, 1999; Hart, Newell, & Olsen, 2003). Table 8.2 shows how child-rearing styles differ in these features.

Authoritative Child Rearing. The **authoritative child-rearing style**—the most successful approach—involves high acceptance and involvement, adaptive control techniques, and appropriate autonomy granting. Authoritative parents are warm, attentive, and sensitive to their child's needs. They establish an enjoyable, emotionally fulfilling parent–child relationship that draws the child into close connection. At the same time, authoritative parents exercise firm, reasonable control. They insist on mature behavior, give reasons for their expectations, and use disciplinary encounters as "teaching moments" to promote the child's self-regulation. Finally, authoritative parents engage in gradual, appropriate autonomy granting, allowing the child to make decisions in areas where he is ready to do so (Baumrind, 2013; Kuczynski & Lollis, 2002; Russell, Mize, & Bissaker, 2004).

Throughout childhood and adolescence, authoritative parenting is linked to many aspects of competence—an upbeat mood, self-control, task persistence, cooperativeness, high self-esteem, social and moral maturity, and favorable school performance (Amato & Fowler, 2002; Aunola, Stattin, & Nurmi, 2000; Gonzalez & Wolters, 2006; Jaffe, Gullone, & Hughes, 2010; Mackey, Arnold, & Pratt, 2001; Milevsky et al., 2007).

TABLE 8.2
Features of Child-Rearing Styles

CHILD-REARING STYLE	ACCEPTANCE AND INVOLVEMENT	CONTROL	AUTONOMY GRANTING
Authoritative	Is warm, responsive, attentive, and sensitive to the child's needs	Engages in adaptive behavioral control: Makes reasonable demands for mature behavior and consistently enforces and explains them	Permits the child to make decisions in accord with readiness Encourages the child to express thoughts, feelings, and desires When parent and child disagree, engages in joint decision making when possible
Authoritarian	Is cold and rejecting and frequently degrades the child	Engages in coercive behavioral control: Makes excessive demands for mature behavior, uses force and punishment Often uses psychological control, withdrawing love and intruding on the child's individuality and attachment to parents	Makes decisions for the child Rarely listens to the child's point of view
Permissive	Is warm but overindulgent or inattentive	Is lax in behavioral control: Makes few or no demands for mature behavior	Permits the child to make many decisions before the child is ready
Uninvolved	Is emotionally detached and withdrawn	Is lax in behavioral control: Makes few or no demands for mature behavior	Is indifferent to the child's decision making and point of view

Authoritarian Child Rearing. The **authoritarian child-rearing style** is low in acceptance and involvement, high in coercive control, and low in autonomy granting. Authoritarian parents appear cold and rejecting. To exert control, they yell, command, criticize, and threaten. "Do it because I said so!" is their attitude. They make decisions for their child and expect the child to accept their word unquestioningly. If the child resists, authoritarian parents resort to force and punishment.

Children of authoritarian parents are more likely to be anxious, unhappy, and low in self-esteem and self-reliance. When frustrated, they tend to react with hostility and, like their parents, use force to get their way. Boys, especially, show high rates of anger and defiance. Although girls also engage in acting-out behavior, they are more likely to be dependent, lacking interest in exploration, and overwhelmed by challenging tasks (Hart, Newell, & Olsen, 2003; Kakihara et al., 2010; Thompson, Hollis, & Richards, 2003). Children and adolescents exposed to the authoritarian style typically do poorly in school. However, because of their parents' concern with control, they tend to achieve better and to commit fewer antisocial acts than peers with undemanding parents—that is, those whose parents use one of the two styles we will consider next (Steinberg, Blatt-Eisengart, & Cauffman, 2006).

In addition to unwarranted direct control, authoritarian parents engage in a more subtle type called **psychological control,** in which they attempt to take advantage of children's psychological needs by intruding on and manipulating their verbal expressions, individuality, and attachments to parents. These parents frequently interrupt or put down the child's ideas, decisions, and choice of friends. When they are dissatisfied, they withdraw love, making their affection contingent on the child's compliance. Children subjected to psychological control exhibit adjustment problems involving both anxious, withdrawn behavior and defiance and aggression—especially the relational form, which (like parental psychological control) damages relationships through manipulation and exclusion (Barber, Stolz, & Olsen, 2005; Barber & Xia, 2013; Kuppens et al., 2013).

Permissive Child Rearing. The **permissive child-rearing style** is warm and accepting but uninvolved. Permissive parents are either overindulgent or inattentive and, thus, engage in little control. Instead of gradually granting autonomy, they allow children to make many of their own decisions at an age when they are not yet capable of doing so. Their children can eat meals and go to bed whenever they wish and can watch as much television as they want. They do not have to learn good manners or do any household chores. Although some permissive parents truly believe in this approach, many others simply lack confidence in their ability to influence their child's behavior (Oyserman et al., 2005).

Children of permissive parents tend to be impulsive, disobedient, and rebellious. They are also overly demanding and dependent on adults, and they show less persistence on tasks, poorer school achievement, and more antisocial behavior. The link between permissive parenting and dependent, nonachieving, rebellious behavior is especially strong for boys (Barber & Olsen, 1997; Steinberg, Blatt-Eisengart, & Cauffman, 2006).

Uninvolved Child Rearing. The **uninvolved child-rearing style** combines low acceptance and involvement with little control and general indifference to issues of autonomy. Often these parents are emotionally detached and depressed and so overwhelmed by life stress that they have little time and energy for children. At its extreme, uninvolved parenting is a form of child maltreatment called *neglect.* Especially when it begins early, it disrupts virtually all aspects of development (see Chapter 6, page 187). Even with less extreme parental disengagement, children and adolescents display many problems—poor emotional self-regulation, school achievement difficulties, depression, and antisocial behavior (Aunola, Stattin, & Nurmi, 2000; Schroeder et al., 2010).

What Makes Authoritative Child Rearing Effective?

Like all correlational findings, the association between authoritative parenting and children's competence is open to interpretation. Perhaps parents of well-adjusted children are authoritative because their youngsters have especially cooperative dispositions. But although temperamentally fearless, impulsive children and emotionally negative children are more likely to evoke coercive, inconsistent discipline, extra warmth and firm control succeed in modifying these children's maladaptive styles (Cipriano & Stifter, 2010; Larzelere, Cox, & Mandara, 2013). With inhibited, fearful children, parents must suppress their tendency to overprotect their child. Instead, inhibited children benefit from extra encouragement to be assertive and express their autonomy (Nelson et al., 2006; Rubin & Burgess, 2002).

Longitudinal research indicates that among children of diverse temperaments, authoritative child rearing predicts maturity and adjustment into adolescence. The warmth and caring that authoritative parents accord their children are linked to favorable child functioning in many cultures and seem universally necessary (Khaleque & Rohner, 2002). And a variant of authoritativeness in which parents exert strong control over the child's behavior—becoming directive but not coercive—yields just as favorable long-term outcomes as a more democratic approach (Baumrind, Larzelere, & Owens, 2010). Indeed, some children, because of their dispositions, require "heavier doses" of certain authoritative features.

In sum, authoritative child rearing seems to create a positive emotional context for parental influence in the following ways:

- Warm, involved parents who are secure in the standards they hold for their children model caring concern as well as confident, self-controlled behavior.

- Children are far more likely to comply with and internalize control that appears fair and reasonable, not arbitrary.
- By adjusting demands and autonomy granting to children's capacities, authoritative parents convey to children that they are competent and can do things successfully for themselves. In this way, parents foster favorable self-esteem and cognitive and social maturity.
- Supportive aspects of the authoritative style, including parental acceptance, involvement, and rational control, are a powerful source of *resilience,* protecting children from the negative effects of family stress and poverty (Luthar, Crossman, & Small, 2015).

LOOK and LISTEN

Ask several parents to explain their style of child rearing, inquiring about acceptance and involvement, control, and autonomy granting. Look, especially, for variations in amount and type of control over children's behavior along with parents' rationales.

Cultural Variations

Although authoritative parenting is broadly advantageous, ethnic minority parents often have distinct child-rearing beliefs and practices that reflect cultural values. Let's look at some examples.

Compared with Western parents, Chinese parents describe their parenting as more controlling. They are more directive in teaching and scheduling their children's time, as a way of fostering self-control and high achievement. Chinese parents may appear less warm than Western parents because they withhold praise, which they believe results in self-satisfied, poorly motivated children (Cheah & Li, 2010; Ng, Pomerantz, & Deng, 2014). Chinese parents report expressing affection and concern and using induction and other reasoning-oriented discipline as much as American parents do, but they more often shame a misbehaving child, withdraw love, and use physical punishment (Cheah et al., 2009; Shwalb et al., 2004). When these practices become excessive, resulting in an authoritarian style high in psychological or coercive control, Chinese children display the same negative outcomes as Western children: poor academic achievement, anxiety, depression, impaired self-regulation, and aggressive behavior (Chan, 2010; Lee et al., 2012; Pong, Johnston, & Chen, 2010; Sorkhabi & Mandara, 2013).

In Hispanic families, Asian Pacific Island families, and Caribbean families of African or East Indian origin, firm insistence on respect for parental authority is paired with high parental warmth—a combination suited to promoting cognitive and social competence and family loyalty (Roopnarine & Evans, 2007; Tamis-LeMonda & McFadden, 2010). Hispanic fathers

In Caribbean families of African origins, respect for parental authority is paired with high parental warmth—a combination that promotes competence and family loyalty.

typically spend much time with their children and are warm and sensitive (Cabrera & Bradley, 2012).

Although wide variation exists, low-SES African-American parents tend to expect immediate obedience. They believe that strict parenting fosters self-control and vigilance in risky surroundings. African-American parents who use controlling strategies tend to have cognitively and socially competent children who view parental control as a sign of love and concern. And among African-American youths, controlling parenting protects against delinquency and disruptive behaviors at school (Mason et al., 2004; Roche, Ensminger, & Cherlin, 2007). Recall, also, that a history of mild physical punishment is not associated with behavior problems among African-American children (refer to the Cultural Influences box on page 270). Most African-American parents who use strict, "no-nonsense" discipline use physical punishment sparingly and combine it with warmth and reasoning.

These cultural variations remind us that child-rearing styles must be viewed in their larger contexts. As we have seen, many factors contribute to good parenting: personal characteristics of both child and parent, SES, access to extended family and community supports, cultural values and practices, and public policies.

As we turn to the topic of child maltreatment, our discussion will underscore, once again, that effective child rearing is sustained not just by the desire of mothers and fathers to be good parents. Almost all want to be. Unfortunately, when vital supports for parenting break down, children—as well as parents—can suffer terribly.

Child Maltreatment

Child maltreatment is as old as human history, but only in recent decades has the problem been widely acknowledged and studied. Perhaps public concern has increased because child maltreatment is especially common in large industrialized nations. In the most recently reported year, about 680,000 U.S. children (9 out of every 1,000) were identified as victims (U.S. Department of Health and Human Services, 2015c). Because most cases go unreported, the true figures are much higher.

Child maltreatment takes the following forms:

- *Physical abuse:* Assaults, such as kicking, biting, shaking, punching, or stabbing, that inflict physical injury
- *Sexual abuse:* Fondling, intercourse, exhibitionism, commercial exploitation through prostitution or production of pornography, and other forms of sexual exploitation
- *Neglect:* Failure to meet a child's basic needs for food, clothing, medical attention, education, or supervision
- *Emotional abuse:* Acts that could cause serious emotional harm, including social isolation, repeated unreasonable demands, ridicule, humiliation, intimidation, or terrorizing

Neglect accounts for about 80 percent of reported cases, physical abuse for 18 percent, emotional abuse for 9 percent, and sexual abuse for 9 percent (U.S. Department of Health and Human Services, 2015c). But these figures are only approximate, as many children experience more than one form.

Parents commit more than 80 percent of abusive incidents. Other relatives account for about 5 percent, and the remainder are perpetrated by parents' unmarried partners, child-care providers, and other adults. Infants, toddlers, and preschoolers are at greatest risk for neglect, physical abuse, and emotional abuse. Sexual abuse is perpetrated more often against school-age and early adolescent children. But each type occurs at every age (Trocmé & Wolfe, 2002; U.S. Department of Health and Human Services, 2015c). Because many sexual abuse victims are identified in middle childhood, we will pay special attention to this form of maltreatment in Chapter 10.

Origins of Child Maltreatment. Early findings suggested that child maltreatment was rooted in adult psychological disturbance (Kempe et al., 1962). But although child maltreatment is more common among disturbed parents, it soon became clear that a single "abusive personality type" does not exist. Parents who were abused as children do not necessarily become abusers (Jaffee et al., 2013). And sometimes even "normal" parents harm their children.

For help in understanding child maltreatment, researchers turned to *ecological systems theory* (see Chapters 1 and 2). They discovered that many interacting variables—at the family, community, and cultural levels—contribute. The more risks present, the greater the likelihood of abuse or neglect (see Table 8.3).

The Family. Within the family, children whose characteristics make them more challenging to rear are more likely to become targets of abuse. These include premature or very sick babies and children who are temperamentally difficult, are inattentive and overactive, or have other developmental problems. Child factors, however, only slightly increase the risk of abuse (Jaudes & Mackey-Bilaver, 2008; Sidebotham et al., 2003). Whether such children are maltreated largely depends on parents' characteristics.

TABLE 8.3
Factors Related to Child Maltreatment

FACTOR	DESCRIPTION
Parent characteristics	Psychological disturbance; alcohol and drug abuse; history of abuse as a child; belief in harsh physical discipline; desire to satisfy unmet emotional needs through the child; unreasonable expectations for child behavior; young age (most under 30); low educational level; lack of parenting skills
Child characteristics	Premature or very sick baby; difficult temperament; inattentiveness and overactivity; other developmental problems
Family characteristics	Low income or poverty; homelessness; marital instability; social isolation; partner abuse; frequent moves; large families with closely spaced children; overcrowded living conditions; presence of nonbiological caregivers; disorganized household; lack of steady employment; other signs of high life stress
Community	Characterized by violence and social isolation; few parks, child-care centers, preschool programs, recreation centers, or religious institutions to serve as family supports
Culture	Approval of physical force and violence as ways to solve problems

Sources: Centers for Disease Control and Prevention, 2015c; Wekerle & Wolfe, 2003; Whipple, 2006.

High parental stress, low income and education, and extreme household disorganization are often associated with child maltreatment. Abusive parents are more likely to live in rundown neighborhoods that offer few sources of social support.

Maltreating parents are less skillful than other parents in handling discipline confrontations. They also suffer from biased thinking about their child. For example, they often attribute their baby's crying or their child's misdeeds to a stubborn or bad disposition, evaluate children's transgressions as worse than they are, and feel powerless in parenting—perspectives that lead them to move quickly toward physical force (Bugental & Happaney, 2004; Crouch et al., 2008).

Most parents have enough self-control not to respond with abuse to their child's misbehavior or developmental problems. Other factors combine with these conditions to prompt an extreme response. Abusive parents react to stressful situations with high emotional arousal. And low income, low education (less than a high school diploma), unemployment, alcohol and drug use, marital conflict, overcrowded living conditions, frequent moves, and extreme household disorganization are common in abusive and neglectful homes (Dakil et al., 2012; Wulczyn, 2009). These conditions increase the chances that parents will be too overwhelmed to meet basic child-rearing responsibilities or will vent their frustrations by lashing out at their children.

The Community. The majority of abusive and neglectful parents are isolated from both formal and informal social supports. Because of their life histories, many have learned to mistrust and avoid others and are poorly skilled at establishing and maintaining positive relationships. Also, maltreating parents are more likely to live in unstable, rundown neighborhoods that provide few links between family and community, such as parks, recreation centers, and religious institutions (Guterman et al., 2009; Tomyr, Ouimet, & Ugnat, 2012). They lack "lifelines" to others and have no one to turn to for help during stressful times.

The Larger Culture. Cultural values, laws, and customs profoundly affect the chances that child maltreatment will occur when parents feel overburdened. Societies that view violence as an appropriate way to solve problems set the stage for child abuse.

Although the United States has laws to protect children from maltreatment, widespread support exists for use of physical force with children (refer back to page 269). Twenty-three European countries have outlawed corporal punishment, a measure that dampens both physical discipline and abuse (duRivage et al., 2015; Zolotor & Puzia, 2010). Furthermore, all industrialized nations except the United States prohibit corporal punishment in schools. The U.S. Supreme Court has twice upheld the right of school officials to use corporal punishment. Fortunately, 31 U.S. states and the District of Columbia have passed laws that ban it.

Consequences of Child Maltreatment.

The family circumstances of maltreated children impair the development of emotional self-regulation, empathy and sympathy, self-concept, social skills, and academic motivation. Over time, these youngsters show serious adjustment problems—cognitive deficits including impaired executive function, school failure, deficits in processing emotional and social signals, peer difficulties, severe depression, aggressive behavior, substance abuse, and violent crime (Cicchetti & Toth, 2015; Nikulina & Widom, 2013; Stronach et al., 2011).

How do these damaging consequences occur? Recall our earlier discussion of hostile cycles of parent–child interaction. For abused children, these are especially severe. Also, a family characteristic strongly associated with child abuse is partner abuse (Graham-Bermann & Howell, 2011). Clearly, the home lives of abused children overflow with adult conduct that leads to profound distress and to use of aggression to solve problems.

Furthermore, the sense of abandonment conveyed by neglectful parenting and the humiliating, terrorizing behaviors of abusive adults result in low self-esteem, high anxiety, self-blame, and efforts to escape from extreme psychological pain—at times severe enough to lead to post-traumatic stress disorder (PTSD) and attempted suicide in adolescence. At school, maltreated children present serious discipline problems (Nikulina, Widom, & Czaja, 2011; Wolfe, 2005). Their noncompliance, poor motivation, and cognitive immaturity interfere with academic achievement, further undermining their chances for life success.

Finally, chronic abuse is associated with central nervous system damage, including abnormal EEG brain-wave activity; fMRI-detected reduced size and impaired functioning of the cerebral cortex, corpus callosum, cerebellum, and hippocampus; and atypical production of the stress hormone cortisol—initially too high but, after months of abuse, often too low. Over time, the massive trauma of persistent abuse seems to blunt children's normal physiological response to stress (Cicchetti & Toth, 2015; Jaffee & Christian, 2014). These effects increase the chances that cognitive and emotional problems will endure.

Preventing Child Maltreatment. Because child maltreatment is embedded in families, communities, and society as a whole, efforts to prevent it must be directed at each of these levels. Many approaches have been suggested, from teaching high-risk parents effective child-rearing strategies to developing broad social programs aimed at improving economic conditions and community services.

We have seen that providing social supports to families is effective in easing parental stress. This approach sharply reduces child maltreatment as well. Parents Anonymous, a U.S. organization with affiliate programs around the world, helps child-abusing parents learn constructive parenting practices, largely through social supports. Its local chapters offer self-help group meetings, daily phone calls, and regular home visits to relieve social isolation and teach child-rearing skills.

Early intervention aimed at strengthening both child and parent competencies can prevent child maltreatment. Healthy Families America, a program that began in Hawaii and has spread to 430 sites across the United States and Canada, identifies families at risk for maltreatment during pregnancy or at birth. Each receives three years of home visitation, in which a trained worker helps parents manage crises, encourages effective child rearing, and puts parents in touch with community services (Healthy Families America, 2011). In evaluations of sites verified to provide high-quality program delivery, parents randomly assigned to Healthy Families home visitation, compared with no-intervention controls, more often engaged their child in developmentally supportive activities and used effective discipline strategies; less often displayed harsh, coercive tactics; and reported less parenting stress—factors that reduce the risk of child maltreatment (Green et al., 2014; LeCroy & Krysik, 2011). Another home-visiting program that prevents child abuse and neglect is the Nurse–Family Partnership, discussed on page 90 in Chapter 3 (Olds et al., 2009).

Even with intensive treatment, some adults persist in their abusive acts. An estimated 1,600 U.S. children, most of them infants and preschoolers, die from maltreatment annually (U.S. Department of Health and Human Services, 2015c). When parents are unlikely to change their behavior, the drastic step of separating parent from child and legally terminating parental rights is the only justifiable course of action.

Child maltreatment is a sad note on which to end our discussion of a period of childhood that is so full of excitement, awakening, and discovery. But there is reason to be optimistic. Great strides have been made over the past several decades in understanding and preventing child maltreatment.

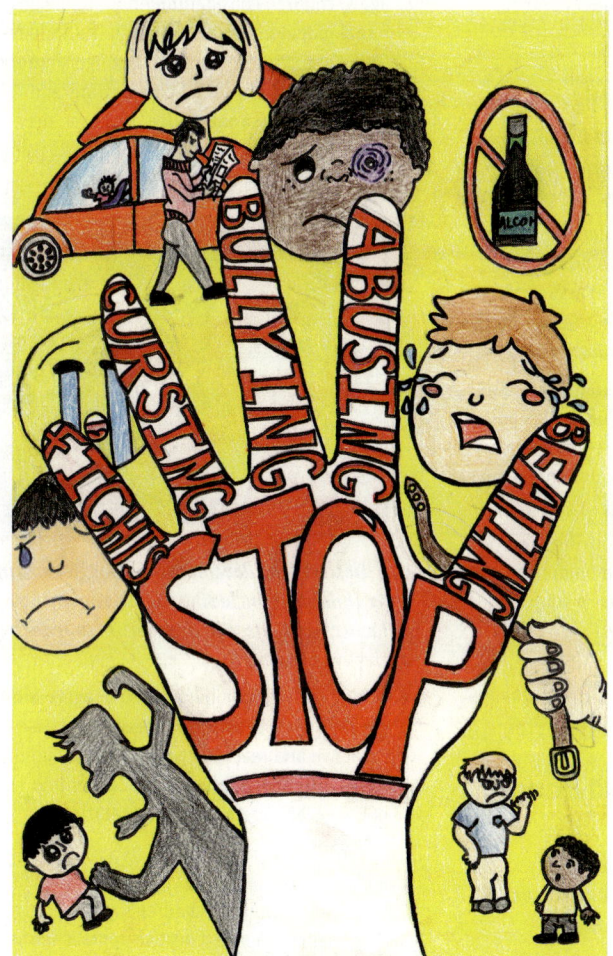

Each year, fourth to sixth graders across Los Angeles County enter a poster contest to celebrate Child Abuse Prevention Month. This recent winner urges parents not to commit acts of physical and emotional abuse.(Jonathan Chin, 0th Grade, Yaya Fine Art Studio, Temple City, CA. Courtesy ICAN Associates, Los Angeles County Inter-Agency Council on Child Abuse and Neglect, *ican4kids.org*.)

Ask yourself

CONNECT Which child-rearing style is most likely to be associated with inductive discipline, and why?

APPLY Chandra heard a news report about 10 severely neglected children, living in squalor in an inner-city tenement. She wondered, "Why would parents so mistreat their children?" How would you answer Chandra?

REFLECT How would you classify your parents' child-rearing styles? What factors might have influenced their approach to parenting?

Summary / chapter 8

Erikson's Theory: Initiative versus Guilt (p. 258)

8.1 What personality changes take place during Erikson's stage of initiative versus guilt?

- Preschoolers develop a new sense of purposefulness as they grapple with Erikson's psychological conflict of **initiative versus guilt.** A healthy sense of initiative depends on exploring the social world through play, cooperating with peers to achieve common goals, and forming a conscience through identification with the same-sex parent.

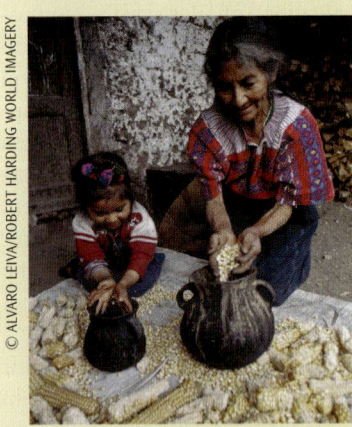

Self-Understanding (p. 258)

8.2 Describe the development of self-concept and self-esteem in early childhood.

- As preschoolers think more intently about themselves, they construct a **self-concept** consisting largely of observable characteristics and typical emotions and attitudes. A warm, sensitive parent–child relationship fosters a more positive, coherent early self-concept.

- Preschoolers' high **self-esteem** consists of several self-judgments and contributes to a mastery-oriented approach to the environment.

Emotional Development (p. 260)

8.3 Identify changes in understanding and expressing emotion during early childhood, citing factors that influence those changes.

- Preschoolers' impressive understanding of the causes, consequences, and behavioral signs of basic emotions is supported by cognitive and language development, secure attachment, and conversations about feelings.

- By age 3 to 4, children are aware of various strategies for emotional self-regulation. Temperament, parental modeling, and parental communication about coping strategies influence preschoolers' capacity to handle stress and negative emotion.

- As their self-concepts develop, preschoolers more often experience self-conscious emotions. They depend on feedback from parents and other adults to know when to feel these emotions.

- Empathy also becomes more common in early childhood. The extent to which empathy leads to **sympathy** and results in **prosocial,** or **altruistic, behavior** depends on temperament and parenting.

Peer Relations (p. 263)

8.4 Describe peer sociability and friendship in early childhood, along with cultural and parental influences on early peer relations.

- During early childhood, peer interaction increases as children move from **nonsocial activity** to **parallel play,** then to **associative** and **cooperative play.** Nevertheless, both solitary and parallel play remain common.

- Sociodramatic play seems especially important in societies where child and adult worlds are distinct. In collectivist cultures, play generally occurs in large groups and is highly cooperative.

- Interactions between preschool friends are unusually positive, but friendship does not yet have an enduring quality based on mutual trust. Early childhood social competence contributes to later academic performance.

- Parents affect peer sociability both directly, by influencing their child's peer relations, and indirectly, through their child-rearing practices.

Foundations of Morality and Aggression (p. 267)

8.5 What are the central features of psychoanalytic, social learning, and cognitive-developmental approaches to moral development?

- The psychoanalytic perspective stresses the emotional side of conscience development, especially identification and guilt as motivators of moral action. But contrary to Freud's view that morality develops out of fear of punishment and loss of parental love, conscience formation is promoted by **induction,** in which adults point out the effects of the child's misbehavior on others.

- Social learning theory focuses on how moral behavior is learned through modeling by warm, powerful, and consistent adults. Giving children material rewards undermines prosocial behavior.

- Alternatives to harsh punishment such as **time out** and withdrawal of privileges can help parents avoid undesirable side effects of punishment. Parents can increase the effectiveness of mild punishment by being consistent, maintaining a warm parent–child relationship, and offering explanations.

- The cognitive-developmental perspective views children as active thinkers about social rules. By age 4, children consider intentions in making moral judgments and distinguish truthfulness from lying. Preschoolers also distinguish **moral imperatives** from **social conventions** and **matters of personal choice.** However, they tend to reason rigidly about morality, focusing on outcomes and on physical harm.

8.6 Describe the development of aggression in early childhood, including family and media influences and effective approaches to reducing aggressive behavior.

- During early childhood, **proactive aggression** declines while **reactive aggression** increases. Proactive and reactive aggression come in three forms: **physical aggression** (more common in boys), **verbal aggression,** and **relational aggression.**

- Ineffective discipline and a conflict-ridden family atmosphere promote children's aggression, as does media violence. Effective approaches to reducing aggressive behavior include training parents in effective child-rearing practices, teaching children conflict-resolution skills, helping parents cope with stressors in their own lives, and shielding children from violent media.

Gender Typing (p. 276)

8.7 *Discuss biological and environmental influences on preschoolers' gender-stereotyped beliefs and behavior.*

- **Gender typing** is well under way in early childhood. Preschoolers acquire a wide range of gender-stereotyped beliefs, often applying them rigidly.

- Prenatal hormones contribute to boys' higher activity level and rougher play and to children's preference for same-sex playmates. But parents, teachers, peers, and the broader social environment also encourage many gender-typed responses.

8.8 *Describe and evaluate major theories that explain the emergence of gender identity.*

- Although most people have a traditional **gender identity**, some are **androgynous**, combining both masculine and feminine characteristics. Masculine and androgynous identities are linked to better psychological adjustment.

- According to social learning theory, preschoolers first acquire gender-typed responses through modeling and reinforcement and then organize these behaviors into gender-linked ideas about themselves. Cognitive-developmental theory suggests that children must master **gender constancy** before developing gender-typed behavior, but evidence for this assumption is weak.

- **Gender schema theory** combines features of social learning and cognitive-developmental perspectives. As children acquire gender-typed preferences and behaviors, they form masculine and feminine categories, or gender schemas, that they apply to themselves and their world.

- A few children express great discomfort with the gender they were assigned at birth and, as early as the preschool years, express a desire to live as the other gender.

Child Rearing and Emotional and Social Development (p. 282)

8.9 *Describe the impact of child-rearing styles on development, and explain why authoritative parenting is effective.*

- Three features distinguish **child-rearing styles**: degree of (1) acceptance and involvement, (2) control, and (3) autonomy granting. Compared with the **authoritarian, permissive,** and **uninvolved** styles, the **authoritative style** promotes cognitive, emotional, and social competence. Warmth, reasonable rather than coercive control, and gradual autonomy granting account for the effectiveness of this style. **Psychological control,** which is associated with authoritarian parenting, contributes to adjustment problems.

- Although some ethnic groups effectively combine parental warmth with high levels of control, harsh and excessive control impairs academic and social competence.

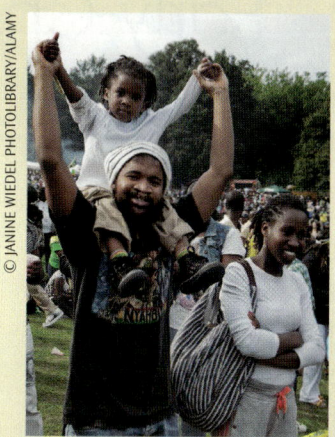

8.10 *Discuss the multiple origins of child maltreatment, its consequences for development, and prevention strategies.*

- Maltreating parents use ineffective discipline, hold a negatively biased view of their child, and feel powerless in parenting. Unmanageable parental stress and social isolation greatly increase the likelihood of abuse and neglect. Societal approval of corporal punishment promotes child abuse.

- Maltreated children are impaired in emotional self-regulation, empathy and sympathy, self-concept, social skills, and academic motivation. The trauma of repeated abuse is associated with central nervous system damage and serious, lasting adjustment problems. Successful prevention requires efforts at the family, community, and societal levels.

Important Terms and Concepts

androgyny (p. 279)
associative play (p. 263)
authoritarian child-rearing style (p. 283)
authoritative child-rearing style (p. 282)
child-rearing styles (p. 282)
cooperative play (p. 263)
gender constancy (p. 279)
gender identity (p. 279)
gender schema theory (p. 279)
gender typing (p. 276)

induction (p. 267)
initiative versus guilt (p. 258)
matters of personal choice (p. 272)
moral imperatives (p. 272)
nonsocial activity (p. 263)
parallel play (p. 263)
permissive child-rearing style (p. 283)
physical aggression (p. 272)
proactive aggression (p. 272)
prosocial, or altruistic, behavior (p. 262)

psychological control (p. 283)
reactive aggression (p. 272)
relational aggression (p. 272)
self-concept (p. 258)
self-esteem (p. 260)
social conventions (p. 272)
sympathy (p. 263)
time out (p. 269)
uninvolved child-rearing style (p. 283)
verbal aggression (p. 272)

milestones
Development in Early Childhood

3–4 YEARS

Physical
- Running, jumping, hopping, throwing, and catching become better coordinated. (223)
- Pedals and steers tricycle. (223)

- Galloping and one-foot skipping appear. (223)
- Fastens and unfastens large buttons. (223)
- Uses scissors. (223)
- Uses fork effectively. (223)
- Draws first picture of a person, using tadpole image. (224)

Cognitive
- Understands the symbolic function of drawings and of models of real-world spaces. (224, 228–229)
- Grasps conservation, reasons about transformations, reverses thinking, and understands cause–effect sequences in simplified, familiar situations. (231–233)
- Sorts familiar objects into hierarchically organized categories. (232)
- Uses private speech to guide behavior during challenging tasks. (234–235)
- Gains in executive function, including inhibition, flexible shifting of attention, and working memory capacity. (236–238)
- Uses scripts to recall routine events. (240)
- Understands that both beliefs and desires determine behavior. (241)
- Knows the meaning of numbers up to 10, counts correctly, and grasps cardinality. (244)

2 YEARS

Physical
- Throughout early childhood, height and weight increase more slowly than in toddlerhood. (216)
- Balance improves; walks more rhythmically; hurried walk changes to run. (223)
- Jumps, hops, throws, and catches with rigid upper body. (223)
- Puts on and removes simple items of clothing. (223)
- Uses spoon effectively. (223)
- First drawings are gestural scribbles. (224)

Cognitive
- Make-believe becomes less dependent on realistic objects, less self-centered, and more complex; sociodramatic play increases. (228)
- Understands the symbolic function of photos and realistic-looking pictures. (229)
- Takes the perspective of others in simplified, familiar situations and in face-to-face communication. (231, 252)
- Recognition memory is well-developed. (239)
- Shows awareness of the distinction between inner mental and outer physical events. (241)
- Attaches verbal labels to amounts and sizes; begins to count. (244)

Language
- Vocabulary increases rapidly. (250)
- Uses a coalition of cues—perceptual and, increasingly, social and linguistic—to figure out word meanings. (250–251)
- Speaks in simple sentences that follow basic word order of native language, gradually adding grammatical markers. (251)
- Displays effective conversational skills. (252)

Emotional/Social
- Understands causes, consequences, and behavioral signs of basic emotions. (260)

- Begins to develop self-concept and self-esteem. (258–260)
- Shows early signs of developing moral sense—verbal evaluations of own and others' actions and distress at harmful behaviors. (267)
- May display proactive (instrumental) aggression. (272–273)
- Gender-stereotyped beliefs and behavior increase. (276)

Note: Numbers in parentheses indicate the page or pages on which each milestone is discussed.

Language

- Aware of some meaningful features of written language. (244)

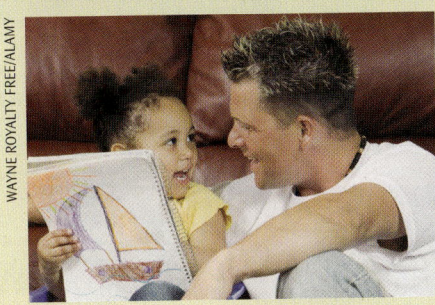

- Coins new words based on known words; extends language meanings through metaphor. (250)
- Masters increasingly complex grammatical structures, occasionally overextending grammatical rules to exceptions. (251–252)
- Adjusts speech to fit the age, sex, and social status of listeners. (252)

Emotional/Social

- Describes self in terms of observable characteristics and typical emotions and attitudes. (258–259)
- Has several self-esteems, such as learning things in school, making friends, getting along with parents, and treating others kindly. (260)
- Emotional self-regulation improves. (261)
- Experiences self-conscious emotions more often. (262)
- Relies more on language to express empathy. (262)
- Proactive aggression declines, while reactive aggression (verbal and relational) increases. (272–273)
- Engages in associative and cooperative play with peers, in addition to parallel play. (263)

- Forms first friendships, based on pleasurable play and sharing of toys. (265)
- Distinguishes truthfulness from lying. (271)
- Distinguishes moral imperatives from social conventions and matters of personal choice. (272)
- Preference for same-sex playmates strengthens. (277)

5–6 YEARS

Physical

- Starts to lose primary teeth. (217)
- Increases running speed, gallops more smoothly, and engages in true skipping. (223)
- Displays mature, flexible throwing and catching patterns. (223)
- Uses knife to cut soft foods. (223)
- Ties shoes. (223, 224)
- Draws more complex pictures. (224)

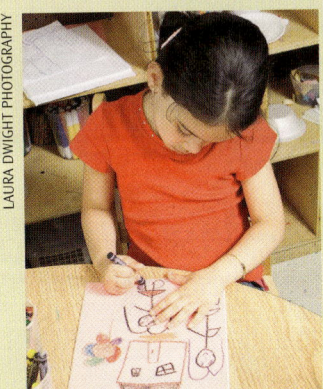

- Copies some numbers and simple words; prints name. (223, 225)

Cognitive

- Magical beliefs decline. (231)
- Improves in ability to distinguish appearance from reality. (228)
- Gains further in executive function, including planning. (237–238)

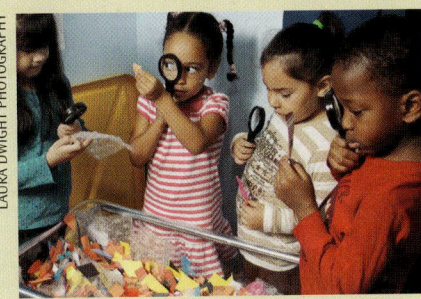

- Improves in recognition, recall, scripted memory, and autobiographical memory. (239–240)
- Understanding of false belief strengthens. (241)

Language

- Understands that letters and sounds are linked in systematic ways. (244)
- Uses invented spellings. (244)
- By age 6, has acquired a vocabulary of about 10,000 words. (250)
- Uses most grammatical constructions competently. (251)

Emotional/Social

- Improves in emotional understanding, including the ability to interpret, predict, and influence others' emotional reactions. (260–261)

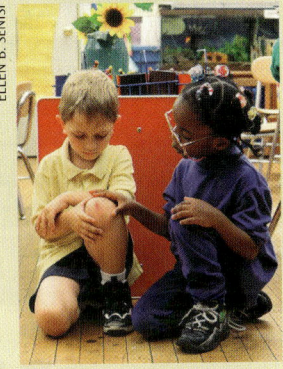

- Has acquired many morally relevant rules and behaviors. (268)
- Gender-stereotyped beliefs and behavior and preference for same-sex playmates continue to strengthen. (277)
- Understands gender constancy. (279)

Note: Numbers in parentheses indicate the page or pages on which each milestone is discussed.

chapter 9

Physical and Cognitive Development in Middle Childhood

During a first grade math activity, students work together to take measurements and record data. An improved capacity to remember, reason, and reflect on one's thinking makes middle childhood a time of dramatic advances in academic learning and problem solving.

What's ahead in chapter 9

PHYSICAL DEVELOPMENT

Body Growth

Common Health Problems
Nutrition • Overweight and Obesity • Vision and Hearing • Illnesses • Unintentional Injuries

■ **SOCIAL ISSUES: HEALTH** Family Stressors and Childhood Obesity

Motor Development and Play
Gross-Motor Development • Fine-Motor Development • Sex Differences • Games with Rules • Adult-Organized Youth Sports • Shadows of Our Evolutionary Past • Physical Education

COGNITIVE DEVELOPMENT

Piaget's Theory: The Concrete Operational Stage
Concrete Operational Thought • Limitations of Concrete Operational Thought • Follow-Up Research on Concrete Operational Thought

Information Processing
Executive Function • Memory Strategies • Knowledge and Memory • Culture, Schooling, and Memory Strategies • The School-Age Child's Theory of Mind • Cognitive Self-Regulation • Applications of Information Processing to Academic Learning

■ **BIOLOGY AND ENVIRONMENT** Children with Attention-Deficit Hyperactivity Disorder

Individual Differences in Mental Development
Defining and Measuring Intelligence • Other Efforts to Define Intelligence • Explaining Individual and Group Differences in IQ

■ **CULTURAL INFLUENCES:** The Flynn Effect: Massive Generational Gains in IQ

Language Development
Vocabulary and Grammar • Pragmatics • Learning Two Languages

Learning in School
Educational Philosophies • Teacher–Student Interaction and Grouping Practices • Teaching Children with Special Needs • How Well-Educated Are U.S. Children?

■ **SOCIAL ISSUES: EDUCATION** Magnet Schools: Equal Access to High-Quality Education

"I'm on my way, Mom!" hollered 10-year-old Joey as he stuffed the last bite of toast into his mouth, slung his book bag over his shoulder, dashed out the door, jumped on his bike, and headed down the street for school. Joey's 8-year-old sister Lizzie followed, pedaling furiously until she caught up with Joey. Rena, the children's mother and one of my colleagues at the university, watched from the front porch as her son and daughter disappeared in the distance.

"They're branching out," Rena commented to me over lunch that day as she described the children's expanding activities and relationships. Homework, household chores, soccer teams, music lessons, scouting, friends at school and in the neighborhood, and Joey's new paper route were all part of the children's routine. "It seems the basics are all there. I don't have to monitor Joey and Lizzie so constantly anymore. Being a parent is still challenging, but it's more a matter of refinements—helping them become independent, competent, and productive individuals."

Joey and Lizzie have entered middle childhood—the years from 6 to 11. Around the world, children of this age are assigned new responsibilities. For children in industrialized nations, middle childhood is often called the "school years" because its onset is marked by the start of formal schooling. In village and tribal cultures, the school may be a field or a jungle. But universally, mature members of society guide children of this age period toward real-world tasks that increasingly resemble those they will perform as adults.

This chapter focuses on physical and cognitive development in middle childhood. By age 6, the brain has reached 90 percent of its adult weight, and the body continues to grow slowly. In this way, nature gives school-age children the mental powers to master challenging tasks as well as added time—before reaching physical maturity—to acquire fundamental knowledge and skills for life in a complex social world.

We begin by reviewing typical growth trends, gains in motor skills, and special health concerns. Then we return to Piaget's theory and the information-processing approach for an overview of cognitive changes. Next, we examine genetic and environmental contributions to IQ scores, which often influence important educational decisions. Our discussion continues with the further blossoming of language. Finally, we consider the role of schools in children's learning and development. ●

PHYSICAL DEVELOPMENT

Body Growth

9.1 Describe major trends in body growth during middle childhood.

Physical growth during the school years continues at the slow, regular pace of early childhood. At age 6, the average North American child weighs about 45 pounds and is 3½ feet tall. Over the next few years, children will add about 2 to 3 inches in height and 5 pounds in weight each year (see Figure 9.1). Between ages 6 and 8, girls are slightly shorter and lighter than boys. By age 9, this trend reverses as girls approach the dramatic adolescent growth spurt, which occurs two years earlier in girls than in boys.

Because the lower portion of the body is growing fastest, Joey and Lizzie appeared longer-legged than they had in early childhood. They grew out of their jeans more quickly than their jackets and frequently needed larger shoes. As in early childhood, girls have slightly more body fat and boys more muscle. After age 8, girls begin accumulating fat at a faster rate, and they will add even more during adolescence (Hauspie & Roelants, 2012).

During middle childhood, the bones of the body lengthen and broaden. However, ligaments are not yet firmly attached to bones. This, combined with increasing muscle strength, gives children the unusual flexibility needed to perform cartwheels and handstands. As their bodies become stronger, many children experience a greater desire for physical exercise. Nighttime "growing pains"—stiffness and aches in the legs—are common as muscles adapt to an enlarging skeleton (Uziel et al., 2012).

Between ages 6 and 12, all 20 primary teeth are lost and replaced by permanent ones, with girls losing their teeth slightly earlier than boys. For a while, the permanent teeth seem much too large. Gradually, growth of facial bones causes the child's face to lengthen and mouth to widen, accommodating the newly erupting teeth.

FIGURE 9.1 Body growth during middle childhood. Mai and Henry continue to display the slow, regular pattern of growth they showed in early childhood. Around age 9, girls begin to grow at a faster rate than boys as the adolescent growth spurt draws near.

Common Health Problems

9.2 Describe the causes and consequences of serious nutritional problems in middle childhood, giving special attention to obesity.

9.3 What vision and hearing problems are common in middle childhood?

9.4 What factors contribute to illness during the school years, and how can these health problems be reduced?

9.5 Describe changes in the occurrence of unintentional injuries in middle childhood, and cite effective interventions.

Children from economically advantaged homes, like Joey and Lizzie, are at their healthiest in middle childhood, full of energy and play. Growth in lung size permits more air to be exchanged with each breath, so children are better able to exercise vigorously without tiring. The cumulative effects of good nutrition, combined with rapid development of the body's immune system, offer greater protection against disease.

Not surprisingly, poverty continues to be a powerful predictor of ill health during middle childhood. Because economically disadvantaged U.S. families often lack health insurance (see Chapter 7), many children do not have regular access to a doctor. A substantial number also lack such basic necessities as a comfortable home and regular meals.

Nutrition

Children need a well-balanced, plentiful diet to provide energy for successful learning in school and increased physical activity. With their increasing focus on friendships and new activities, many children spend little time at the table, and the number who eat dinner with their families drops sharply between ages 9 and 14. Family dinnertimes have waned in general, yet eating an evening meal with parents leads to a diet higher in fruits, vegetables, grains, and milk products and lower in soft drinks and fast foods (Burgess-Champoux et al., 2009; Hammons & Fiese, 2011).

School-age children report that they "feel better" and "focus better" after eating healthy foods and that they feel sluggish, "like a blob," after eating junk foods. In a longitudinal study of nearly 14,000 U.S. children, a parent-reported diet high in sugar, fat, and processed food in early childhood predicted slightly lower IQ at age 8, after many factors that might otherwise account for this association were controlled (Northstone et al., 2012). Even mild nutritional deficits can affect cognitive functioning. Among school-age children from middle- to high-SES families, insufficient dietary iron and folate are related to poorer concentration and mental test performance (Arija et al., 2006; Low et al., 2013).

As we saw in earlier chapters, many poverty-stricken children in developing countries and in the United States suffer from serious and prolonged malnutrition. Unfortunately, malnutrition that persists from infancy or early childhood into the school years usually results in permanent physical and mental damage (Grantham-McGregor, Walker, & Chang, 2000; Liu et al., 2003). Government-sponsored supplementary food programs from the early years through adolescence can prevent these effects.

Overweight and Obesity

Mona, a very heavy child in Lizzie's class, often watched from the sidelines during recess. When she did join in games, she was slow and clumsy, the target of unkind comments: "Move it, Tubs!" Most afternoons, she walked home from school alone while her schoolmates gathered in groups, talking, laughing, and chasing. At home, Mona sought comfort in high-calorie snacks.

Mona suffers from **obesity,** a greater-than-20-percent increase over healthy weight, based on *body mass index (BMI)*—a ratio of weight to height associated with body fat. A BMI above the 85th percentile for a child's age and sex is considered *overweight,* a BMI above the 95th percentile *obese*. During the past several decades, a rise in overweight and obesity has occurred in many Western nations, with large increases in Canada, Germany, Greece, Ireland, Israel, New Zealand, the United Kingdom, and the United States. Since the 1970s, U.S. childhood obesity has tripled. Today, 32 percent of U.S. children and adolescents are overweight, more than half of them extremely so: 17 percent are obese (Ogden et al., 2014; World Health Organization, 2015g).

Obesity rates have also risen in developing countries, as urbanization shifts the population toward sedentary lifestyles and diets high in meats and energy-dense refined foods (World Health Organization, 2015g). In China, for example, where obesity was nearly nonexistent a generation ago, today 20 percent of children are overweight and 8 percent obese, with two to three times as many boys as girls affected (Sun et al., 2014). In addition to lifestyle changes, a prevailing belief in Chinese culture that excess body fat signifies prosperity and health—carried over from a half-century ago, when famine caused millions of deaths—has contributed to this alarming upsurge. High valuing of sons may induce Chinese parents to offer boys especially generous portions of energy-dense foods.

Overweight rises with age, from 23 percent among U.S. preschoolers to 35 percent among school-age children and adolescents to an astronomical 69 percent among adults (Ogden et al., 2014). Overweight preschoolers are five times more likely than their normal-weight peers to be overweight at age 12, and few persistently overweight adolescents attain a normal weight in adulthood (Nader et al., 2006; Patton et al., 2011).

Causes of Obesity. Not all children are equally at risk for excessive weight gain. Identical twins are more likely than fraternal twins to resemble each other in BMI, and adopted children tend to resemble their biological parents (Min, Chiu, & Wang, 2013). Although heredity clearly contributes to children's risk, the importance of environment is apparent in the consistent relationship of low SES to overweight and obesity in industrialized nations, especially among ethnic minorities—in the United States, African-American, Hispanic, and Native-American

Social Issues: Health

Family Stressors and Childhood Obesity

In response to chronic stress, many adults and children increase their food consumption—especially foods high in sugar and fat—and gain excessive weight. How can a stressful daily life prompt overeating?

One route is through elevated stress hormones, including cortisol, which signal the body to increase energy expenditure and the brain, in turn, to boost caloric intake (Zellner et al., 2006). In a second pathway, chronic stress triggers insulin resistance—a prediabetic condition that frequently induces a raging appetite (Dallman et al., 2003).

Furthermore, the effort required to manage persistent stress can easily strain self-regulatory capacity, leaving the individual unable to limit excessive eating. Deficits in inhibition and a related capacity, delay of gratification (ability to wait for a reward), are associated with childhood obesity (Liang et al., 2014). And in several studies, the greater the number of home-life stressors in school-age children's lives, the poorer their regulation of negative emotion and behavior (Evans, 2003; Evans et al., 2005). Impaired self-regulation, then, might be a major intervening factor in the link between childhood chronic stress and obesity. To find out, researchers followed several hundred children from economically disadvantaged families, assessing family stressors and self-regulatory ability at age 9 and change in BMI four years later, at age 13 (Evans et al., 2012). Number of stressors experienced—including poverty, single-parent household, residential crowding, noise, household clutter, lack of books and play materials, child separation from the family, and exposure to violence—strongly predicted impaired self-regulation, as indicated by children's delay of gratification. Poor self-regulation, in turn, largely accounted for the relationship between family stressors and gain in BMI over time.

In obesity prevention programs, children given self-regulation training—instructions to "stop and think" in eating situations—show

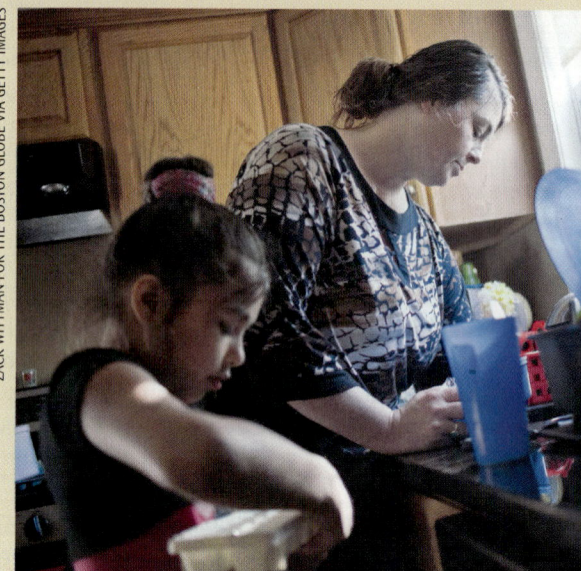

This 9-year-old, living in shelter housing with her mother, is at high risk for obesity. Home-life stressors, including poverty, single parenthood, noise, crowding, and clutter, contribute to overeating by impairing children's self-regulation.

beneficial outcomes in terms of improved eating behaviors and weight control (Johnson, 2000). But such training is likely to be fully effective only when stressors in children's family lives are manageable, not overwhelming.

---

children and adults (Ogden et al., 2014). Factors responsible include lack of knowledge about healthy diet; a tendency to buy high-fat, low-cost foods; and family stress, which can prompt overeating. Recall, also, that children who were undernourished in their early years are at risk for later excessive weight gain (see page 129 in Chapter 4).

Parental feeding practices also contribute to childhood obesity. Overweight children are more likely to eat sugary and fatty foods, perhaps because these foods are plentiful in the diets offered by their parents, who also tend to be overweight (Kit, Ogden, & Flegal, 2014). Frequent eating out—which increases parents' and children's consumption of high-calorie fast foods—is linked to overweight. And eating out likely plays a major role in the relationship between mothers' employment hours and elevated BMI among school-age children (Morrissey, Dunifon, & Kalil, 2011). Demanding work schedules reduce the time parents have for healthy meal preparation.

Furthermore, some parents anxiously overfeed, interpreting almost all their child's discomforts as a desire for food—a practice common among immigrant parents and grandparents who, as children themselves, may have survived periods of food deprivation. Still other parents are overly controlling, restricting when, what, and how much their child eats and worrying about weight gain (Couch et al., 2014; Jansen et al., 2012). In each case, parents undermine children's ability to regulate their own food intake.

Because of these experiences, obese children soon develop maladaptive eating habits. They are more responsive than normal-weight individuals to external stimuli associated with food—taste, sight, smell, time of day, and food-related words—and less responsive to internal hunger cues (Temple et al., 2007). Furthermore, a stressful family life contributes to children's diminished self-regulatory capacity, amplifying uncontrolled eating (see the Social Issues: Health box above).

Another factor implicated in weight gain is insufficient sleep (Hakim, Kheirandish-Gozal, & Gozal, 2015). Reduced sleep may increase time available for eating while leaving children too fatigued for physical activity. It also disrupts the brain's regulation of hunger and metabolism.

The rise in childhood obesity is due in part to the many hours U.S. children devote to screen media. In a study that tracked children's TV viewing from ages 4 to 11, the more TV children watched, the more body fat they added: By age 11, children who devoted more than 3 hours per day to TV accumulated 40 percent more fat than those devoting less than 1¾ hours (Proctor et al., 2003). TV and Internet ads encourage children to eat unhealthy snacks: The more ads they watch, the greater their consumption of high-calorie snack foods. Children permitted to have a TV in their bedroom—a practice linked to especially high TV viewing—are at even further risk for overweight (Borghese et al., 2015; Soos et al., 2014). And heavy viewing likely subtracts from time spent in physical exercise.

Consequences of Obesity. Obese children are at risk for lifelong health problems. Symptoms that begin to appear in the early school years—high blood pressure, high cholesterol levels, respiratory abnormalities, insulin resistance, and inflammatory reactions—are powerful predictors of heart disease, circulatory difficulties, type 2 diabetes, gallbladder disease, sleep and digestive disorders, many forms of cancer, and premature death. Furthermore, obesity has caused a dramatic rise in cases of diabetes in children, sometimes leading to early, severe complications, including stroke, kidney failure, and circulatory problems that heighten the risk of eventual blindness and leg amputation (Biro & Wien, 2010; Yanovski, 2015).

Unfortunately, physical attractiveness is a powerful predictor of social acceptance. In Western societies, both children and adults stereotype obese youngsters as lazy, sloppy, ugly, stupid, self-doubting, and deceitful (Penny & Haddock, 2007; Tiggemann & Anesbury, 2000). In school, obese children and adolescents are often socially isolated. They report more emotional, social, and school difficulties, including peer teasing, rejection, and consequent low self-esteem (van Grieken et al., 2013; Zeller & Modi, 2006). They also tend to achieve less well than their healthy-weight agemates (Datar & Sturm, 2006).

Persistent obesity from childhood into adolescence predicts serious psychological disorders, including severe anxiety and depression, defiance and aggression, and suicidal thoughts and behavior (Lopresti & Drummond, 2013; Puhl & Latner, 2007). As we will see in Chapter 13, these consequences combine with continuing discrimination to further impair physical health and to reduce life chances in close relationships and employment.

Treating Obesity. In Mona's case, the school nurse suggested that Mona and her obese mother enter a weight-loss program together. But Mona's mother, unhappily married for many years, had her own reasons for overeating and rejected this idea. In one study, nearly 70 percent of parents judged their overweight or obese children to have a normal weight (Jones et al., 2011). Consistent with these findings, most obese children do not get any treatment.

The most effective interventions are family-based and focus on changing weight-related behaviors (Seburg et al., 2015). In one program, both parent and child revised eating patterns, exercised daily, and reinforced each other with praise and points for progress, which they exchanged for special activities and times together. The more weight parents lost, the more their children lost. Follow-ups after 5 and 10 years showed that children maintained their weight loss more effectively than adults—a finding that underscores the importance of early intervention (Epstein, Roemmich, & Raynor, 2001; Wrotniak et al., 2004). Monitoring dietary intake and physical activity is important. Small wireless sensors that sync with mobile devices, enabling individualized goal-setting and tracking of progress through game-like features, are effective (Calvert, 2015; Seburg et al., 2015). But these interventions work best when parents' and children's weight problems are not severe.

Children consume one-third of their daily caloric intake at school. Therefore, schools can help reduce obesity by serving healthier meals and ensuring regular physical activity (Lakshman, Elks, & Ong, 2012). Because obesity is expected to rise further without broad prevention strategies, many U.S. states and cities have passed obesity-reduction legislation. Among measures taken are weight-related school screenings for all children, improved school nutrition standards that include food and beverages sold outside of meals, additional school recess time and physical education, and obesity awareness and weight-reduction programs as part of school curricula. A review of these

A mother and son reinforce each other's efforts to lose weight and get in shape. The most effective interventions for childhood obesity focus on changing the whole family's behaviors, emphasizing fitness and healthy eating.

school-based efforts reported impressive benefits (Waters et al., 2011). Obesity prevention in schools was more successful in reducing 6- to 12-year-olds' BMIs than programs delivered in other community settings, perhaps because schools are better able to provide long-term, comprehensive intervention.

> **LOOK and LISTEN**
>
> Contact your state and city governments to find out about their childhood obesity-prevention legislation. Can policies be improved?

Vision and Hearing

The most common vision problem in middle childhood is *myopia,* or nearsightedness. By the end of the school years, it affects nearly 25 percent of children—a rate that rises to 60 percent by early adulthood (Rahi, Cumberland, & Peckham, 2011).

Heritability estimates based on comparisons of twins and other family members reveal a moderate genetic influence (Guggenheim et al., 2015). And worldwide, myopia occurs far more frequently in Asian than in white populations (Morgan, Ohno-Matsui, & Saw, 2012). Early biological trauma also can induce myopia. School-age children with low birth weights show an especially high rate, believed to result from immaturity of visual structures, slower eye growth, and a greater incidence of eye disease (Molloy et al., 2013).

When parents warn their children not to read in dim light or sit too close to the TV or computer screen, their concern ("You'll ruin your eyes!") is well-founded. In diverse cultures, the more time children spend reading, writing, using the computer, and doing other close work, the more likely they are to be myopic. In school-age children who spend more time playing outdoors, the incidence of myopia is reduced (Russo et al., 2014). Myopia is one of the few health conditions to increase with SES. Fortunately, it can be overcome easily with corrective lenses.

During middle childhood, the Eustachian tube (canal that runs from the inner ear to the throat) becomes longer, narrower, and more slanted, preventing fluid and bacteria from traveling so easily from the mouth to the ear. As a result, middle-ear infections, common in infancy and early childhood, become less frequent. Still, about 3 to 4 percent of the school-age population, and as many as 20 percent of low-SES children, develop persistent hearing loss as a result of repeated untreated infections (Aarhus et al., 2015; Ryding et al., 2002). With regular screening for both vision and hearing, defects can be corrected before they lead to serious learning difficulties.

Illnesses

Children experience a somewhat higher rate of illness during the first two years of elementary school than later because of exposure to sick children and an immune system that is still developing. About 20 to 25 percent of U.S. children have chronic diseases and conditions (including physical disabilities) (Compas et al., 2012). By far the most common—accounting for about one-third of childhood chronic illness and the most frequent cause of school absence and childhood hospitalization—is *asthma,* in which the bronchial tubes (passages that connect the throat and lungs) are highly sensitive (Basinger, 2013). In response to a variety of stimuli, such as cold weather, infection, exercise, allergies, and emotional stress, they fill with mucus and contract, leading to coughing, wheezing, and serious breathing difficulties.

The prevalence of asthma in the United States has increased steadily over the past several decades, with nearly 8 percent of children affected. Although heredity contributes to asthma, researchers believe that environmental factors are necessary to spark the illness. Boys, African-American children, and children who were born underweight, whose parents smoke, and who live in poverty are at greatest risk (Centers for Disease Control and Prevention, 2015a). The higher rate and greater severity of asthma among African-American and poverty-stricken children may be the result of pollution in inner-city areas (which triggers allergic reactions), stressful home lives, and lack of access to good health care. Childhood obesity is also related to asthma (Hampton, 2014). High levels of blood-circulating inflammatory substances associated with body fat and the pressure of excess weight on the chest wall may be responsible.

About 2 percent of U.S. children have more severe chronic illnesses, such as sickle cell anemia, cystic fibrosis, diabetes, arthritis, cancer, and AIDS. Painful medical treatments, physical discomfort, and changes in appearance often disrupt the sick child's daily life, making it difficult to concentrate in school and separating the child from peers. As the illness worsens, family and child stress increases (Marin et al., 2009; Rodriguez, Dunn, & Compas, 2012). For these reasons, chronically ill children are at risk for academic, emotional, and social difficulties.

A strong link exists between good family functioning and child well-being for chronically ill children, just as it does for physically healthy children (Compas et al., 2012). Interventions that foster positive family relationships help parent and child cope with the disease and improve adjustment. These include health education, counseling, parent and peer support groups, and disease-specific summer camps, which teach children self-help skills and give parents time off from the demands of caring for an ill youngster.

Unintentional Injuries

As we conclude our discussion of threats to school-age children's health, let's return to the topic of unintentional injuries (discussed in detail in Chapter 7). As Figure 9.2 shows, injury fatalities increase from middle childhood into adolescence, with rates for boys rising considerably above those for girls.

Motor vehicle accidents, involving children as passengers or pedestrians, continue to be the leading cause of injury, followed

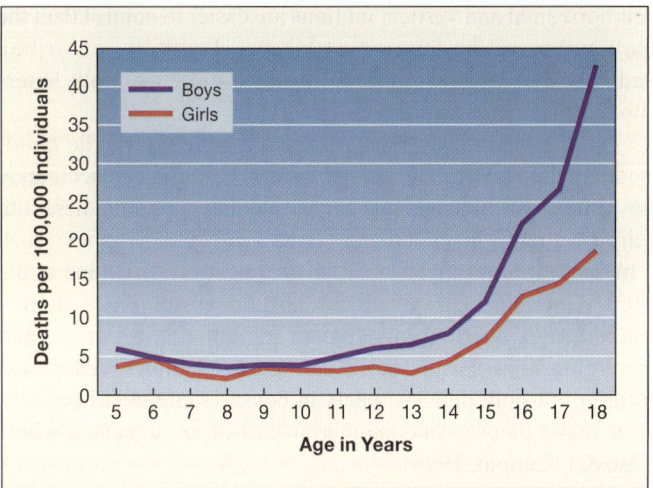

FIGURE 9.2 **U.S. rates of injury mortality from middle childhood to adolescence.** Injury fatalities increase with age, and the gap between boys and girls expands. Motor vehicle (passenger and pedestrian) accidents are the leading cause, with bicycle injuries next in line. (Based on Centers for Disease Control and Prevention, 2015p.)

by bicycle accidents (Bailar-Heath & Valley-Gray, 2010). Pedestrian injuries most often result from midblock dart-outs, bicycle accidents from disobeying traffic signals and rules. When many stimuli impinge on young school-age children at once, they often fail to think before they act. They need frequent reminders, supervision, and prohibitions against venturing into busy traffic on their own.

Effective school- and community-based prevention programs use extensive modeling and rehearsal of safety practices, give children feedback about their performance along with praise and tangible rewards for acquiring safety skills, and provide occasional booster sessions. Targeting specific injury risks (such as traffic safety) rather than many risks at once yields longer-lasting results (Nauta et al., 2014). As part of these programs, parents, who often overestimate their child's safety knowledge and physical abilities, must be educated about children's age-related safety capacities.

One vital safety measure is legally requiring that children wear protective helmets while bicycling, in-line skating, skateboarding, or using scooters. This precaution leads to a 9 percent reduction in head injuries, a leading cause of permanent disability and death in school-age children (Karkhaneh et al., 2013). Combining helmet use with other community-based prevention strategies is especially effective.

Highly active, impulsive, risk-taking children, many of whom are boys, remain particularly susceptible to injury in middle childhood. Parents tend to be lax in intervening in the dangerous behaviors of such children, especially under conditions of marital conflict or other forms of stress (Schwebel et al., 2011, 2012). The greatest challenge for injury-control programs is reaching these youngsters and reducing their exposure to hazardous situations.

 Motor Development and Play

9.6 Cite major changes in motor development and play during middle childhood.

Visit a park on a pleasant weekend afternoon, and watch several preschool and school-age children at play. You will see that gains in body size and muscle strength support improved motor coordination in middle childhood. And greater cognitive and social maturity enables older children to use their new motor skills in more complex ways. A major change in children's play takes place at this time.

Gross-Motor Development

During the school years, running, jumping, hopping, and ball skills become more refined. Third to sixth graders burst into sprints as they race across the playground, jump quickly over rotating ropes, engage in intricate hopscotch patterns, kick and dribble soccer balls, bat at balls pitched by their classmates, and balance adeptly as they walk heel-to-toe across narrow ledges. These diverse skills reflect gains in four basic motor capacities:

- *Flexibility.* Compared with preschoolers, school-age children are physically more pliable and elastic, a difference evident as they swing bats, kick balls, jump over hurdles, and execute tumbling routines.

Improved physical flexibility, balance, agility, and force, along with more efficient information processing, promote gains in school-age children's gross-motor skills.

- *Balance.* Improved balance supports many athletic skills, including running, hopping, skipping, throwing, kicking, and the rapid changes of direction required in many team sports.
- *Agility.* Quicker and more accurate movements are evident in the fancy footwork of dance and cheerleading and in the forward, backward, and sideways motions used to dodge opponents in tag and soccer.
- *Force.* Older youngsters can throw and kick a ball harder and propel themselves farther off the ground when running and jumping than they could at earlier ages (Haywood & Getchell, 2014).

Along with body growth, more efficient information processing plays a vital role in improved motor performance. During middle childhood, the capacity to react only to relevant information increases. And steady gains in reaction time occur, including anticipatory responding to visual stimuli, such as a thrown ball or a turning jump rope. Ten-year-olds react twice as quickly as 5-year-olds (Debrabant et al., 2012; Kail, 2003). Because 5- to 7-year-olds are seldom successful at batting a thrown ball, T-ball is more appropriate for them than baseball. Similarly, handball, four-square, and kickball should precede instruction in tennis, basketball, and football.

Children's gross-motor activity not only benefits from but contributes to cognitive development. Physical fitness predicts improved executive function, memory, and academic achievement in middle childhood (Chaddock et al., 2011). Exercise-induced changes in the brain seem to be responsible: Brain-imaging research reveals that structures supporting attentional control and memory are larger, and myelination of neural fibers within them greater, in better-fit than in poorly-fit children (Chaddock et al., 2010a, 2010b; Chaddock-Heyman et al., 2014). Furthermore, children who are physically fit—and those assigned to a yearlong, one-hour-per-day school fitness program—activate these brain structures more effectively while performing executive function tasks (Chaddock et al., 2012; Chaddock-Heyman et al., 2013). Mounting evidence supports the role of vigorous exercise in optimal brain and cognitive functioning in childhood—a relationship that persists throughout the lifespan.

Fine-Motor Development

Fine-motor development also improves over the school years. On rainy afternoons, Joey and Lizzie experimented with yo-yos, built model airplanes, and wove potholders on small looms. Like many children, they took up musical instruments, which demand considerable fine-motor control.

Gains in fine-motor skill are especially evident in children's writing and drawing. By age 6, most children can print the alphabet, their first and last names, and the numbers from 1 to 10 with reasonable clarity. Their writing is large, however, because they make strokes using the entire arm rather than just the wrist and fingers. Children usually master uppercase letters first because their horizontal and vertical motions are easier to control than the small curves of the lowercase alphabet. Legibility of writing gradually increases as children produce more accurate letters with uniform height and spacing.

Children's drawings show dramatic gains in middle childhood. By the end of the preschool years, children can accurately copy many two-dimensional shapes, and they integrate these into their drawings. Some depth cues have also begun to appear, such as making distant objects smaller than near ones (Braine et al., 1993). Around 9 to 10 years, the third dimension is clearly evident through overlapping objects, diagonal placement, and converging lines. Furthermore, as Figure 9.3 shows, school-age children not only depict objects in considerable detail but also better relate them to one another as part of an organized whole (Case & Okamoto, 1996).

FIGURE 9.3 Increase in organization, detail, and depth cues in school-age children's drawings. Compare both drawings to the one by a 5-year-old in Figure 7.4 on page 224. In the drawing by an 8-year-old on the top, notice how all parts are depicted in relation to one another and with greater detail. Integration of depth cues increases dramatically over the school years, as shown in the drawing on the bottom, by an 11-year-old. Here, depth is indicated by overlapping objects, diagonal placement, and converging lines, as well as by making distant objects smaller than near ones.

Sex Differences

Sex differences in motor skills extend into middle childhood and, in some instances, become more pronounced. Girls have an edge in fine-motor skills of handwriting and drawing and in gross-motor capacities that depend on balance and agility, such as hopping and skipping (Haywood & Getchell, 2014). But boys outperform girls on all other gross-motor skills, especially throwing and kicking.

School-age boys' genetic advantage in muscle mass is not large enough to account for their gross-motor superiority. Rather, the social environment plays a larger role. Parents hold higher expectations for boys' athletic performance, and children readily absorb these messages. From first through twelfth grades, girls are less positive than boys about the value of sports and their own sports ability—differences explained in part by parental beliefs (Anderson, Hughes, & Fuemmeler, 2009; Fredricks & Eccles, 2002). The more strongly girls believe that females are incompetent at sports (such as hockey or soccer), the lower they judge their own ability and the poorer they actually perform (Belcher et al., 2003; Chalabaev, Sarrazin, & Fontayne, 2009).

Educating parents about the minimal differences between school-age boys' and girls' physical capacities and sensitizing them to unfair biases against promotion of girls' athletic ability may help increase girls' self-confidence and participation in athletics. Greater emphasis on skill training for girls, along with increased attention to their athletic achievements, is also likely to help. As a positive sign, compared with a generation ago, many more girls now participate in individual and team sports, though their involvement continues to lag behind boys' (Kanters et al., 2013; Sabo & Veliz, 2011). Middle childhood is a crucial time to encourage girls' sports participation because during this period, children start to discover what they are good at and make some definite skill commitments.

Games with Rules

The physical activities of school-age children reflect an important advance in quality of play: Games with rules become common. Children around the world engage in an enormous variety of informally organized games, including variants on popular sports such as soccer, baseball, and basketball. In addition to the best-known childhood games, such as tag, jacks, and hopscotch, children have invented hundreds of other games, including red rover, statues, leapfrog, kick the can, and prisoner's base.

Gains in perspective taking—in particular, the ability to understand the roles of several players in a game—permit this transition to rule-oriented games. These play experiences, in turn, contribute greatly to emotional and social development. Child-invented games usually rely on simple physical skills and a sizable element of luck. As a result, they rarely become contests of individual ability. Instead, they permit children to try out different styles of cooperating, competing, winning, and losing with little personal risk. Also, in their efforts to organize a game, children discover why rules are necessary and which ones work well.

Compared with past generations, school-age children today spend less time engaged in informal outdoor play—a change that reflects parental concern about neighborhood safety as well as competition for children's time from TV and other screen media. Another factor is the rise in adult-organized sports, such as Little League baseball and soccer and hockey leagues, which fill many hours that children from economically advantaged families used to devote to spontaneous play.

In village societies and developing countries and in many low-SES communities in industrialized nations, children's informal sports and games remain common. In an ethnographic study in two communities—a refugee camp in Angola, Africa, and a Chicago public housing complex—the overwhelming majority of 6- to 12-year-olds engaged in child-organized games at least once a week, and half or more did so nearly every day. Play in each context reflected cultural values (Guest, 2013). In the Angolan community, games emphasized imitation of social roles, such as soccer moves of admired professional players. Games in Chicago, in contrast, were competitive and individualistic. In ballgames, for example, children often made sure peers noticed when they batted or fielded balls particularly well.

Adult-Organized Youth Sports

Nearly half of U.S. children—60 percent of boys and 47 percent of girls—participate in organized sports outside of school hours at some time between ages 5 and 18 (SFIA, 2015). Children in low-SES communities, however, are profoundly underserved, with girls and ethnic minorities having especially limited opportunities. In a comparison of two neighborhoods in Oakland,

A group of boys gather in their schoolyard for a pick-up basketball game. Unlike their economically advantaged agemates, children in low-SES communities often play child-organized games, which serve as rich contexts for social learning.

Applying what we Know

Providing Developmentally Appropriate Organized Sports in Middle Childhood

SUGGESTION	DESCRIPTION
Build on children's interests.	Permit children to select from among appropriate activities the ones that suit them best. Do not push children into sports they do not enjoy.
Teach age-appropriate skills.	For children younger than age 9, emphasize basic skills, such as kicking, throwing, and batting, and simplified games that grant all participants adequate playing time.
Emphasize enjoyment.	Permit children to progress at their own pace and to play for the fun of it, whether or not they become expert athletes.
Limit the frequency and length of practices.	Adjust practice time to children's attention spans and need for unstructured time with peers, with family, and for homework. Two practices a week, each no longer than 30 minutes for younger school-age children and 60 minutes for older school-age children, are sufficient.
Focus on personal and team improvement.	Emphasize effort, skill gains, and teamwork rather than winning. Avoid criticism for errors and defeat, which promotes anxiety and avoidance of athletics.
Discourage unhealthy competition.	Avoid all-star games and championship ceremonies that recognize individuals. Instead, acknowledge all participants.
Permit children to contribute to rules and strategies.	Involve children in decisions aimed at ensuring fair play and teamwork. To strengthen desirable responses, reinforce compliance rather than punishing noncompliance.

California, 67 percent of teenage girls in a well-to-do area were members of athletic teams (Team Up for Youth, 2014). Just a few miles away, in a poverty-stricken, largely minority part of the city, a mere 11 percent were involved in organized sports.

For most children, joining community athletic teams is associated with increased self-esteem and social skills (Daniels & Leaper, 2006). Children who view themselves as good at sports are more likely to continue playing on teams in adolescence, which predicts greater participation in sports and other physical fitness activities in early adulthood (Kjønniksen, Anderssen, & Wold, 2009).

In some cases, though, the arguments of critics—that youth sports overemphasize competition and substitute adult control for children's natural experimentation with rules and strategies—are valid. Coaches and parents who criticize rather than encourage can prompt intense anxiety in some children, setting the stage for emotional difficulties and early athletic dropout, not elite performance (Wall & Côté, 2007). See Applying What We Know above for ways to ensure that athletic leagues provide children with positive learning experiences.

LOOK and LISTEN

Observe a youth athletic-league game, such as soccer, baseball, or hockey. Do coaches and parents encourage children's effort and skill gains, or are they overly focused on winning? Cite examples of adult and child behaviors.

Shadows of Our Evolutionary Past

While watching children in your neighborhood park, notice how they sometimes wrestle, roll, hit, and run after one another, alternating roles while smiling and laughing. This friendly chasing and play-fighting is called **rough-and-tumble play.** It emerges in the preschool years and peaks in middle childhood (Pellegrini, 2006). Children in many cultures engage in it with peers whom they like especially well.

Children's rough-and-tumble play resembles the social behavior of many other young mammals. It seems to originate in parents' physical play with babies, especially fathers' with sons (see pages 203–204 in Chapter 6). And it is more common among boys, probably because prenatal exposure to androgens predisposes boys toward active play (see Chapter 8).

In our evolutionary past, rough-and-tumble play may have been important for developing fighting skill. It also helps children form a **dominance hierarchy**—a stable ordering of group members that predicts who will win when conflict arises. Observations of arguments, threats, and physical attacks between children reveal a consistent lineup of winners and losers that becomes increasingly stable in middle childhood, especially among boys. Once school-age children establish a dominance hierarchy, hostility is rare. Children seem to use play-fighting as a safe context to assess the strength of a peer before challenging that peer's dominance (Fry, 2014; Roseth et al., 2007). Rough-and-tumble play offers lessons in how to handle combative interactions with restraint.

In our evolutionary past, rough-and-tumble play—which can be distinguished from aggression by its friendly quality—may have been important for developing fighting skill and establishing dominance hierarchies.

As children reach puberty, individual differences in strength become apparent, and rough-and-tumble play declines. When it does occur, its meaning changes: Adolescent boys' rough-and-tumble is linked to aggression (Pellegrini, 2003). Unlike children, teenage rough-and-tumble players "cheat," hurting their opponent. In explanation, boys often say that they are retaliating, apparently to reestablish dominance. Thus, a play behavior that limits aggression in childhood becomes a context for hostility in adolescence.

Physical Education

Physical activity supports many aspects of children's development—physical health, self-esteem, and cognitive and social skills. Yet to devote more time to academic instruction, 80 percent of U.S. school districts no longer require a daily recess in the elementary school grades (Centers for Disease Control and Prevention, 2014b). Although most U.S. states require some physical education, only six do so in every grade, and only one mandates at least 30 minutes per school day in elementary school and 45 minutes in middle and high school. Not surprisingly, physical inactivity among school-age children is pervasive: Fewer than 30 percent of 6- to 17-year-olds engage in at least moderate-intensity activity for 60 minutes per day, including some vigorous activity (involving breathing hard and sweating) on three of those days—the U.S. government recommendations for good health (Centers for Disease Control and Prevention, 2014f). With the transition to adolescence, physical activity declines, more for girls than for boys.

Many experts believe that schools should not only offer more frequent physical education classes but also reduce the emphasis placed on competitive sports, which are unlikely to reach the least physically fit youngsters. Instead, programs should emphasize informal games and individual exercise—pursuits most likely to endure. Physically active children tend to become active adults who reap many benefits (Kjønniksen, Torsheim, & Wold, 2008). These include greater physical strength, resistance to many illnesses (from colds and flu to cancer, diabetes, and heart disease), enhanced psychological well-being, and a longer life.

Ask yourself

CONNECT Select one of the following health problems of middle childhood: obesity, myopia, asthma, or unintentional injuries. Explain how both genetic and environmental factors contribute to it.

APPLY Nine-year-old Allison thinks she isn't good at sports, and she doesn't like physical education class. Suggest strategies her teacher can use to improve her pleasure and involvement in physical activity.

REFLECT Did you participate in adult-organized sports as a child? If so, what kind of climate for learning did coaches and parents create?

COGNITIVE DEVELOPMENT

"Finally!" 6-year-old Lizzie exclaimed the day Rena enrolled her in elementary school. "Now I get to go to real school, just like Joey!" Lizzie confidently walked into a combined kindergarten–first-grade class in her neighborhood school, ready for a more disciplined approach to learning. In a single morning, she and her classmates met in reading groups, wrote in journals, worked on addition and subtraction, and sorted leaves gathered for a science project. As Lizzie and Joey moved through the elementary school grades, they tackled increasingly complex projects and became more accomplished at reading, writing, math skills, and general knowledge of the world.

To understand the cognitive attainments of middle childhood, we turn to research inspired by Piaget's theory and the information-processing perspective. Then we look at expanding definitions of intelligence that help us appreciate individual differences. Our discussion continues with language, which blossoms further in these years. Finally, we consider the role of schools in children's development.

Piaget's Theory: The Concrete Operational Stage

9.7 What are the major characteristics of concrete operational thought?

9.8 Discuss follow-up research on concrete operational thought.

When Lizzie visited my child development class at age 4, Piaget's conservation problems confused her (see Chapter 7, page 229). For example, when water was poured from a tall, narrow container into a short, wide one, she insisted that the amount of water had changed. But when Lizzie returned at age 8, she found this task easy. "Of course it's the same!" she exclaimed. "The water's shorter, but it's also wider. Pour it back," she instructed the college student who was interviewing her. "You'll see, it's the same amount!"

Concrete Operational Thought

Lizzie has entered Piaget's **concrete operational stage,** which extends from about 7 to 11 years. Compared with early childhood, thought is more logical, flexible, and organized.

Conservation. The ability to pass *conservation tasks* provides clear evidence of *operations*—mental actions that obey logical rules. Notice how Lizzie is capable of *decentration,* focusing on several aspects of a problem and relating them, rather than centering on just one. She also demonstrates **reversibility,** the capacity to think through a series of steps and then mentally reverse direction, returning to the starting point. Recall from Chapter 7 that reversibility is part of every logical operation. It is solidly achieved in middle childhood.

Classification. Between ages 7 and 10, children pass Piaget's *class inclusion problem* (see page 230). This indicates that they are more aware of classification hierarchies and can focus on relations between a general category and two specific categories at the same time—on three relations at once. They are better able to inhibit their habitual strategy of perceptually comparing the two specific categories (blue flowers and yellow flowers) in favor of relating each specific category to its less-obvious general category (Borst et al., 2013). School-age children's enhanced classification skills are evident in their enthusiasm for collecting treasured objects. At age 10, Joey spent hours sorting and resorting his baseball cards, grouping them first by league and team, then by playing position and batting average. He could separate the players into a variety of classes and subclasses and easily rearrange them.

Seriation. The ability to order items along a quantitative dimension, such as length or weight, is called **seriation.** To test for it, Piaget asked children to arrange sticks of different lengths from shortest to longest. Older preschoolers can put the sticks

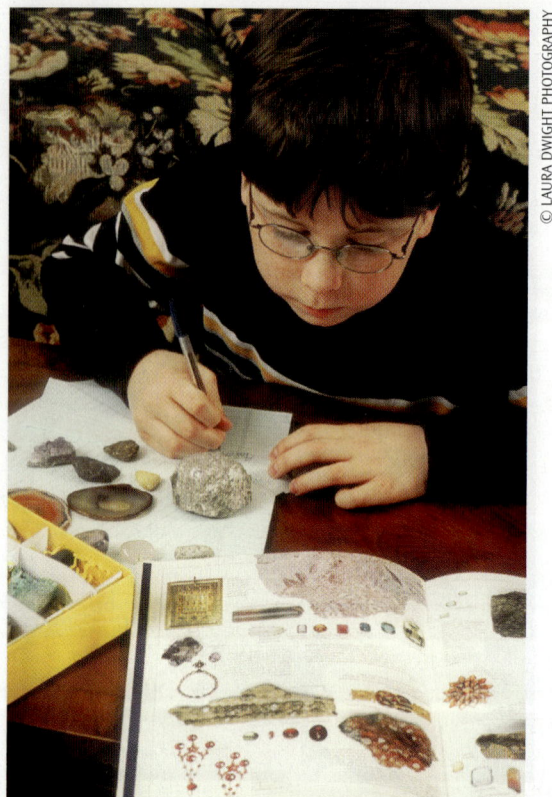

An improved ability to categorize underlies children's interest in collecting objects during middle childhood. This 10-year-old sorts and organizes his extensive rock and mineral collection.

in a row, but they do so haphazardly, making many errors. In contrast, 6- to 7-year-olds create the series efficiently, moving in an orderly sequence from the smallest stick, to the next largest, and so on.

The concrete operational child can also seriate mentally, an ability called **transitive inference.** In a well-known transitive inference problem, Piaget showed children pairings of sticks of different colors. From observing that Stick *A* is longer than Stick *B* and Stick *B* is longer than Stick *C,* children must infer that *A* is longer than *C.* Like Piaget's class inclusion task, transitive inference requires children to integrate three relations at once—in this instance, *A–B, B–C,* and *A–C.* As long as they receive help in remembering the premises (*A–B* and *B–C*), 7- to 8-year-olds can grasp transitive inference (Wright, 2006). And when the task is made relevant to children's everyday experiences—for example, based on winners of races between pairs of cartoon characters—6-year-olds perform well (Wright, Robertson, & Hadfield, 2011).

Spatial Reasoning. Piaget found that school-age children's understanding of space is more accurate than that of preschoolers. To illustrate, let's consider children's **cognitive maps**—their mental representations of spaces such as a classroom, school, or neighborhood. Drawing or reading a map of a large-scale space (school or neighborhood) requires considerable perspective-taking skill. Because the entire space cannot be seen at once, children must infer its overall layout by relating its separate parts.

Preschoolers and young school-age children include *landmarks* on the maps they draw of a single room, but their arrangement is not always accurate. They do better when asked to place stickers showing the location of furniture and people on a map of the room. But if the map is rotated to a position other than the room's orientation, they have difficulty (Liben & Downs, 1993). In identifying landmarks on a rotated map, 7-year-olds are aided by the opportunity to walk through the room (Lehnung et al., 2003). Actively exploring it permits them to experience landmarks from different vantage points, which fosters a more flexible mental representation.

With respect to large-scale outdoor environments, not until age 9 can many children accurately place stickers on a map to indicate landmarks. Children who spontaneously use strategies that help them align the map with their current location in the space—rotating the map or tracing their route on it—show better performance (Liben et al., 2013). Around this age, the maps children draw of large-scale spaces become better organized, showing landmarks along an *organized route of travel*. At the same time, children are able to give clear, well-organized instructions for getting from one place to another.

At the end of middle childhood, most children can form an accurate *overall view of a large-scale space*. And they readily draw and read maps, even when the orientation of the map and the space it represents do not match (Liben, 2009). Ten- to 12-year-olds also grasp the notion of *scale*—the proportional relation between a space and its representation on a map (Liben, 2006). And they appreciate that in interpreting map symbols, a mapmaker's assigned meaning supersedes physical resemblance—for example, that green dots (not red dots) may indicate where fire trucks are located (Myers & Liben, 2008).

LOOK and LISTEN

Ask a 6- to 8-year-old and a 9- to 12-year-old to draw a neighborhood map showing important landmarks, such as the school, a friend's house, or a shopping area. In what ways do the children's maps differ?

Cultural frameworks influence children's map making. In many non-Western communities, people rarely use maps for way-finding but rely on information from neighbors, street vendors, and shopkeepers. Also, compared to their Western age-mates, non-Western children less often ride in cars and more often walk, which results in intimate neighborhood knowledge. When a researcher had 12-year-olds in small cities in India and in the United States draw maps of their neighborhoods, the Indian children represented a rich array of landmarks and aspects of social life, such as people and vehicles, in a small area surrounding their home. The U.S. children, in contrast, drew a more formal, extended space, highlighting main streets and key directions (north–south, east–west) but including few landmarks (see Figure 9.4) (Parameswaran, 2003). Although the U.S. children's

FIGURE 9.4 **Maps drawn by older school-age children from India and the United States.** (a) The Indian child depicted many landmarks and features of social life in a small area near her home. (b) The U.S. child drew a more extended space and highlighted main streets and key directions but included few landmarks and people. (From G. Parameswaran, 2003, "Experimenter Instructions as a Mediator in the Effects of Culture on Mapping One's Neighborhood," *Journal of Environmental Psychology*, 23, pp. 415–416. Copyright © 2003, reprinted with permission from Elsevier, Ltd., conveyed through Copyright Clearance Center, Inc.)

maps scored higher in cognitive maturity, this difference reflected cultural interpretations of the task. When asked to create a map to "help people find their way," the Indian children drew spaces as far-reaching and organized as the U.S. children's.

Limitations of Concrete Operational Thought

As the name of this stage suggests, concrete operational thinking suffers from one important limitation: Children think in an organized, logical fashion only when dealing with concrete information they can perceive directly. Their mental operations work poorly with abstract ideas—ones not apparent in the real world. Consider children's solutions to transitive inference problems. When shown pairs of sticks of unequal length, Lizzie easily engaged in transitive inference. But she had difficulty with a hypothetical version of this task: "Susan is taller than Sally, and Sally is taller than Mary. Who is the tallest?" Not until age 11 or 12 can children typically solve this problem.

That logical thought is at first tied to immediate situations helps account for a special feature of concrete operational reasoning: Children master concrete operational tasks step by step. For example, they usually grasp conservation of number first, followed by length, liquid, and mass, and then weight. This *continuum of acquisition* (or gradual mastery) of logical concepts is another indication of the limitations of concrete operational thinking (Fischer & Bidell, 1991). Rather than coming up with general logical principles that they apply to all relevant situations, school-age children seem to work out the logic of each problem separately.

Follow-Up Research on Concrete Operational Thought

According to Piaget, brain development combined with experience in a rich and varied external world should lead children everywhere to reach the concrete operational stage at about the same time. Yet much evidence indicates that specific cultural and school practices have much to do with mastery of Piagetian tasks (Rogoff, 2003). And information-processing research helps explain the gradual mastery of logical concepts in middle childhood.

The Impact of Culture and Schooling. In village societies, conservation is often delayed. Among the Hausa of Nigeria, who live in small agricultural settlements and rarely send their children to school, even basic conservation tasks—number, length, and liquid—are not understood until age 11 or later (Fahrmeier, 1978). This suggests that participating in relevant everyday activities helps children master conservation and other Piagetian problems. Joey and Lizzie, for example, think of fairness in terms of equal distribution—a value emphasized in their culture. They frequently divide materials, such as Halloween

A Zinacanteco Indian girl of southern Mexico learns the centuries-old practice of backstrap weaving. Although Zinacanteco children might do poorly on Piaget's tasks, they are adept at the complex mental transformations involved in converting warp strung on a loom into woven cloth.

treats or lemonade, equally among their friends. Because they often see the same quantity arranged in different ways, they grasp conservation early.

The experience of going to school promotes mastery of Piagetian tasks. When children of the same age are tested, those who have been in school longer do better on transitive inference problems (Artman & Cahan, 1993). Opportunities to seriate objects, to learn about order relations, and to remember the parts of complex problems are probably responsible. Yet certain informal nonschool experiences can also foster operational thought. Around age 7 to 8, Zinacanteco Indian girls of southern Mexico, who learn to weave elaborately designed fabrics as an alternative to schooling, engage in mental transformations to figure out how a warp strung on a loom will turn out as woven cloth—reasoning expected at the concrete operational stage (Maynard & Greenfield, 2003). North American children of the same age, who do much better than Zinacanteco children on Piagetian tasks, have great difficulty with these weaving problems.

On the basis of such findings, some investigators have concluded that the forms of logic required by Piagetian tasks are heavily influenced by training, context, and cultural conditions. Does this view remind you of Vygotsky's sociocultural theory, discussed in earlier chapters?

An Information-Processing View of Concrete Operational Thought. The gradual mastery of logical concepts in middle childhood raises a familiar question about Piaget's theory: Is an abrupt stagewise transition to logical thought the best way to describe cognitive development in middle childhood?

Some *neo-Piagetian theorists* argue that the development of operational thinking can best be understood in terms of expansion of information-processing capacity rather than a sudden shift to a new stage. For example, Robbie Case (1996, 1998) proposed that change within each Piagetian stage and movement between stages are largely due to gains in the efficiency with which children use their limited working memories. According to Case, with brain development and practice, cognitive schemes are applied more rapidly, gradually demanding less attention and becoming automatic. This frees up space in working memory so children can focus on combining old schemes and generating new ones. For instance, as children's understanding that the height of a liquid changes after it is poured into a differently shaped container becomes routine, they notice that the width of the water changes as well. Soon they coordinate these observations, and they grasp conservation of liquid. Then, as this logical idea becomes well-practiced, children transfer it to more demanding situations, such as weight.

Once the schemes of a Piagetian stage are sufficiently automatic, enough working memory is available to integrate them into an improved, broadly applicable representation. As a result, children transition from concrete operations to the complex, systematic reasoning of formal operational thought, which enables them to think effectively in a wider range of situations. We will discuss the formal operational stage in Chapter 11.

Case's theory, along with similar neo-Piagetian perspectives, helps explain why children's understandings appear in specific situations at different times rather than being mastered all at once (Andrews & Halford, 2011; Barrouillet & Gaillard, 2011a). First, different forms of the same logical insight, such as the various conservation tasks, vary in their processing demands, with those acquired later requiring more space in working memory. Second, as we have seen, children's experiences with different types of tasks vary widely, affecting their performance. Compared with Piaget's theory, neo-Piagetian approaches better account for unevenness in cognitive development.

Evaluation of the Concrete Operational Stage.
Piaget was correct that school-age children approach many problems in more organized, rational ways than preschoolers. But disagreement continues over whether this difference occurs because of *continuous* improvement in logical skills or *discontinuous* restructuring of children's thinking (as Piaget's stage idea assumes). Many researchers think that both types of change may be involved (Andrews & Halford, 2011; Barrouillet & Gaillard, 2011b; Case, 1998; Mascolo & Fischer, 2015).

During the school years, children apply logical schemes to many more tasks. In the process, their thought seems to change qualitatively—toward a more comprehensive grasp of the underlying principles of logical thought. Piaget himself recognized this possibility in evidence for gradual mastery of conservation and other tasks. So perhaps some blend of Piagetian and information-processing ideas holds the greatest promise for explaining cognitive development in middle childhood.

Ask yourself

CONNECT Explain how advances in perspective taking and understanding of symbols contribute to school-age children's improved ability to draw and use maps.

APPLY Nine-year-old Adrienne spends many hours helping her father build furniture in his woodworking shop. How might this experience facilitate Adrienne's advanced performance on Piagetian seriation problems?

REFLECT Which aspects of Piaget's description of the concrete operational child do you accept? Which do you doubt? Explain, citing research evidence.

Information Processing

9.9 Describe gains in executive function and memory in middle childhood, along with factors that influence children's progress.

9.10 Describe the school-age child's theory of mind and capacity to engage in self-regulation.

9.11 Discuss current perspectives on teaching reading and mathematics to elementary school children.

In contrast to Piaget's focus on overall cognitive change, the information-processing perspective examines separate aspects of thinking. As noted in our discussion of Case's theory, working-memory capacity continues to increase in middle childhood. And school-age children make strides in other facets of executive function, including control of attention and planning. Dramatic gains also occur in strategic memory and self-regulation. Each advance contributes vitally to academic learning.

Executive Function

The school years are a time of continued development of the prefrontal cortex, which increases its connections with more distant parts of the brain. Myelination of neural fibers rises steadily, especially in the prefrontal cortex and in the corpus callosum, which connects the two cerebral hemispheres (Giedd et al., 2009; Smit et al., 2012). As interconnectivity between the prefrontal cortex and other brain areas strengthens, the prefrontal cortex becomes a more effective "executive," overseeing the integrated functioning of neural networks.

Consequently, executive function undergoes marked improvement (Xu et al., 2013). Children handle increasingly difficult tasks that require the integration of working memory, inhibition, and flexible shifting of attention, which, in turn, support gains in planning, strategic thinking, and self-monitoring and self-correction of behavior.

Heritability evidence suggests considerable genetic contribution to executive function (Polderman et al., 2009; Young

School-age children undergo marked gains in executive function. They can perform increasingly complex tasks—such as this science project on how flood plains are formed—that require the integration of working memory, inhibition, and flexible shifting of attention.

et al., 2009). And molecular genetic analyses are identifying specific genes related to severely deficient executive function components, such as inhibition and flexible thinking, which (as we will soon see) contribute to learning and behavior disorders, including attention-deficit hyperactivity disorder (ADHD) (refer to the Biology and Environment box on the following page).

But in both typically and atypically developing children, heredity combines with environmental contexts to influence executive function. In Chapter 3, we reviewed evidence indicating that prenatal teratogens can impair executive processes, including impulse control, attention, and planning. And as noted in Chapter 7, poverty, through chronic stress and poor parenting, undermines executive function. As we turn now to the development of executive function components in middle childhood, our discussion will confirm once more that supportive home and school experiences are essential for optimal development.

Inhibition and Flexible Shifting. During middle childhood, children become better at deliberately attending to relevant aspects of a task and inhibiting irrelevant responses. One way researchers study this increasing selectivity of attention is by introducing irrelevant stimuli into a task and seeing how well children attend to its central elements. Performance improves sharply between ages 6 and 10, with gains continuing throughout adolescence (Gomez-Perez & Ostrosky-Solis, 2006; Tabibi & Pfeffer, 2007; Vakil et al., 2009).

Older children are also better at flexibly shifting their attention in response to task requirements. When given rule-use tasks that require frequent switching of the rules used to sort picture cards containing conflicting cues (return to page 238 in Chapter 7 for an example), schoolchildren gain steadily with age in the complexity of rules they can keep in mind and in the speed and accuracy with which they shift between rules. Recall that flexible shifting benefits from gains in inhibition (enabling children to ignore rules not momentarily relevant) and expansion of working memory (helping children keep multiple rules in mind).

In sum, selectivity and flexibility of attention become better controlled and more efficient over middle childhood (Carlson, Zelazo, & Faja, 2013). Children adapt their attention more quickly in the face of increasingly complex distractors—skills that contribute to more organized, strategic approaches to challenging tasks.

Working Memory. As Case's theory emphasizes, working memory profits from increased efficiency of thinking. Time needed to process information on a wide variety of cognitive tasks declines rapidly between ages 6 and 12 in diverse cultures, likely due to myelination and enhanced connectivity among regions of the cerebral cortex (Kail & Ferrer, 2007; Kail et al., 2013). A faster thinker can hold on to and operate on more information at once. Still, individual differences in working-memory capacity exist, and they are of particular concern because they predict intelligence test scores and academic achievement in many subjects (DeMarie & Lopez, 2014).

Children with persistent learning difficulties in reading and math are often deficient in working memory (Alloway et al., 2009). Observations of elementary school children with limited working memories revealed that they often failed at school assignments that made heavy memory demands (Gathercole, Lamont, & Alloway, 2006). They could not follow complex instructions, lost their place in tasks with multiple steps, and frequently gave up before finishing their work. The children struggled because they could not hold in mind sufficient information to complete assignments.

Compared to their economically advantaged agemates, children from poverty-stricken families are more likely to score low on working-memory tasks. In one study, years of childhood spent in poverty predicted reduced working memory in early adulthood (Evans & Schamberg, 2009). Childhood neurobiological measures of stress—elevated blood pressure and stress hormone levels, including cortisol—largely explained this poverty–working-memory association. Chronic stress, as we saw in Chapter 4, can impair brain structure and function, especially in the prefrontal cortex and its connections with the hippocampus, which govern working-memory capacity.

About 15 percent of children have very low working-memory scores, and the majority struggle in school (Holmes, Gathercole, & Dunning, 2010). Scaffolding in which parents and teachers modify tasks to reduce memory load is essential so these children can learn. Effective approaches include communicating in short sentences with familiar vocabulary, repeating task instructions, breaking complex tasks into manageable parts, and encouraging children to use external memory aids—for example, lists of useful spellings while writing or number lines while doing math (Gathercole & Alloway, 2008).

Training Executive Function. An increasing number of studies confirm that children's executive function skills can be improved through training, with benefits for both academic

Biology and Environment

Children with Attention-Deficit Hyperactivity Disorder

While the other fifth graders worked quietly at their desks, Calvin squirmed, dropped his pencil, looked out the window, and fiddled with his shoelaces. "Hey Joey," he yelled across the room, "wanna play ball after school?" But the other children weren't eager to play with Calvin, who was physically awkward and failed to follow the rules of the game. He had trouble taking turns at bat and, in the outfield, looked elsewhere when the ball came his way. Calvin's desk was a chaotic mess. He often lost pencils, books, and other school materials, and he had difficulty remembering assignments and due dates.

Symptoms of ADHD

Calvin is one of about 5 percent of U.S. school-age children with **attention-deficit hyperactivity disorder (ADHD),** which involves inattention, impulsivity, and excessive motor activity resulting in academic and social problems (American Psychiatric Association, 2013; Goldstein, 2011). Boys are diagnosed two to three times as often as girls. However, many girls with ADHD seem to be overlooked, either because their symptoms are less flagrant or because of a gender bias: A difficult, disruptive boy is more likely to be referred for treatment (Faraone, Biederman, & Mick, 2006).

Children with ADHD cannot stay focused on a task that requires mental effort for more than a few minutes. They often act impulsively, ignoring social rules and lashing out with hostility when frustrated. Many, though not all, are *hyperactive,* exhausting parents and teachers and irritating other children with their excessive motor activity. For a child to be diagnosed with ADHD, these symptoms must have appeared before age 12 as a persistent problem.

Because of their difficulty concentrating, children with ADHD score lower in IQ than other children, though the difference is mostly accounted for by a small subgroup with substantially below-average scores (Biederman et al., 2012). Researchers agree that deficient executive function underlies ADHD symptoms. Children with ADHD are impaired in ability to inhibit distracting behaviors and irrelevant information and score low in working-memory capacity (Antshel, Hier, & Barkley, 2015). Consequently, they have difficulty with sustained attention, planning, memory, reasoning, and problem solving in academic and social situations and often fail to manage frustration and intense emotion.

This child frequently engages in disruptive behaviors at school. Children with ADHD have great difficulty staying on task and often act impulsively, ignoring social rules.

Origins of ADHD

ADHD runs in families and is highly heritable: Identical twins share it more often than fraternal twins (Freitag et al., 2010). Children with ADHD show abnormal brain functioning, including reduced electrical and blood-flow activity and structural abnormalities in the prefrontal cortex and in other areas involved in attention, inhibition of behavior, and other aspects of motor control (Mackie et al., 2007). Also, the brains of children with ADHD grow more slowly and are about 3 percent smaller in overall volume, with a thinner cerebral cortex, than the brains of unaffected agemates (Narr et al., 2009; Shaw et al., 2007). Several genes that disrupt functioning of the neurotransmitters serotonin (involved in inhibition and self-control) and dopamine (required for effective cognitive processing) have been implicated in the disorder (Akutagava-Martins et al., 2013).

At the same time, ADHD is associated with environmental factors. Prenatal teratogens—such as tobacco, alcohol, illegal drugs, and environmental pollutants—are linked to inattention and hyperactivity. Furthermore, children with ADHD are more likely to have parents with psychological disorders and to come from homes where family stress is high (Law et al., 2014). These circumstances often intensify the child's preexisting difficulties.

Treating ADHD

Calvin's doctor eventually prescribed stimulant medication, the most common treatment for ADHD. These drugs seem to increase activity in the prefrontal cortex, thereby reducing impulsivity and hyperactivity and improving attention for most children who take them (Connor, 2015).

By itself, drug treatment is insufficient for helping children compensate for inattention and impulsivity in everyday situations. So far, the most effective treatments combine medication with interventions that provide training in executive function skills and that model and reinforce appropriate academic and social behavior (Smith & Shapiro, 2015; Tamm, Nakonezny, & Hughes, 2014).

Family intervention is also vital. Inattentive, hyperactive children strain the patience of parents, who are likely to react punitively and inconsistently—a child-rearing style that strengthens defiant, aggressive behavior. In fact, in 50 to 75 percent of cases, these two sets of behavior problems occur together (Goldstein, 2011).

ADHD is usually a lifelong disorder. Adults with ADHD continue to need help in structuring their environments, regulating negative emotion, selecting appropriate careers, and understanding their condition as a biological deficit rather than a character flaw.

These fourth graders take a break from school work to meditate, a practice that requires focused attention and reflection. Mindfulness training such as meditation leads to gains in executive function, school grades, prosocial behavior, and positive peer relations.

achievement and social competence (Müller & Kerns, 2015). Both direct and indirect training approaches are effective.

To enhance control of attention and working memory, researchers often embed direct training in interactive computer games. In one investigation, 10-year-olds with learning difficulties who played a game providing working-memory training four times a week for eight weeks showed substantially greater improvement in working-memory capacity, IQ, and spelling and math achievement over agemates who played less often or did not play at all (Alloway, Bibile, & Lau, 2013). Working memory, IQ, and spelling gains were still evident eight months after the training ended.

Executive function can also be enhanced indirectly, by increasing children's participation in activities—such as exercise—known to promote it (see page 300). Another indirect method attracting growing interest is *mindfulness training,* which—similar to meditation- and yoga-based exercises for adults—encourages children to focus attention on their current thoughts, feelings, and sensations, without judging them. For example, children might be asked to attend to their own breathing or to manipulate an object held behind their backs while noticing how it feels (Zelazo & Lyons, 2012). If their attention wanders, they are told to bring it back to the current moment. Mindfulness training leads to gains in executive function, school grades, prosocial behavior, and positive peer relations in school-age children (Schonert-Reichl & Lawlor, 2010; Schonert-Reichl et al., 2015) The sustained attention and reflection that mindfulness requires seem to help children avoid snap judgments, distracting thoughts and emotions, and impulsive behavior.

Planning. Planning on multistep tasks improves over the school years. On tasks with multiple parts, older children make decisions about what to do first and what to do next in a more orderly fashion. By the end of middle childhood, children engage in *advance planning*—evaluating an entire sequence of steps to see if it will get them to their goal (Tecwyn, Thorpe, & Chappell, 2014). Nine- and 10-year-olds can project ahead, predicting how early steps in their plan will affect success at later steps and adjust their overall plan accordingly.

As Chapter 7 revealed, children learn much about planning from collaborating with more expert planners. With age, they take more responsibility in these joint endeavors, such as suggesting planning strategies and organizing task materials. The demands of school tasks—and parents' and teachers' explanations of how to plan—contribute to gains in school-age children's planning.

But adult-controlled activities may rob children of opportunities to plan. In one study, researchers videotaped small groups of first and second graders devising plays they would perform for their class (Baker-Sennett, Matusov, & Rogoff, 2008). Some groups were child-led, whereas others were led by adult volunteers. Child-led groups engaged in extensive planning, brainstorming themes and working out the details of their plays. But when adults planned the play in advance, the children spent most of their time in nonplanning pursuits, such as rehearsing lines. The adults missed a rich opportunity to scaffold planning by turning over responsibility for it to the children and guiding and supporting, as needed.

Memory Strategies

As attention improves, so do *memory strategies,* deliberate mental activities we use to store and retain information. When Lizzie had a list of things to learn, such as the state capitals of the United States, she immediately used **rehearsal**—repeating the information to herself. Soon after, a second strategy becomes common: **organization**—grouping related items together (for example, all state capitals in the same part of the country), an approach that greatly improves recall (Schneider, 2002).

Perfecting memory strategies requires time and effort. Eight-year-old Lizzie rehearsed in a piecemeal fashion. After being given the word *cat* in a list of items, she said, "Cat, cat, cat." But 10-year-old Joey combined previous words with each new item, saying, "Desk, man, yard, cat, cat." This active, cumulative approach, in which neighboring words create contexts for each other that trigger recall, yields much better memory (Lehman & Hasselhorn, 2012). And whereas Lizzie often organized by everyday association (hat–head, carrot–rabbit), Joey grouped items *taxonomically,* based on common properties (clothing, food, animals), thus using fewer categories—an efficient procedure yielding dramatic memory gains (Bjorklund et al., 1994). Furthermore, Joey often combined several strategies—for example, organizing items, stating the category names, and finally rehearsing (Schwenck, Bjorklund, & Schneider, 2007). The more strategies children apply simultaneously, the better they remember.

By the end of middle childhood, children start to use **elaboration**—creating a relationship, or shared meaning, between two or more pieces of information that do not belong to the same category. For example, to learn the words *fish* and *pipe*, you might generate the verbal statement or mental image, "The fish is smoking a pipe" (Schneider & Pressley, 1997). This highly effective memory technique, which requires considerable effort and space in working memory, becomes increasingly common in adolescence.

Because organization and elaboration combine items into *meaningful chunks*, they permit children to hold onto much more information and, as a result, further expand working memory. In addition, when children link a new item to information they already know, they can *retrieve* it easily by thinking of other items associated with it. As we will see, this also contributes to improved memory during the school years.

Knowledge and Memory

During middle childhood, children's general knowledge base, or *semantic memory,* grows larger and becomes organized into increasingly elaborate, hierarchically structured networks. This rapid growth of knowledge helps children use strategies and remember (Schneider, 2002). Knowing more about a topic makes new information more meaningful, so it is easier to store and retrieve.

To investigate this idea, researchers classified fourth graders as either experts or novices in knowledge of soccer and then gave both groups lists of soccer and nonsoccer items to learn. Experts remembered far more items on the soccer list (but not on the nonsoccer list) than novices. And during recall, the experts' listing of items was better organized, as indicated by clustering of items into categories (Schneider & Bjorklund, 1992). This superior organization at retrieval suggests that highly knowledgeable children organize information in their area of expertise with little or no effort. Consequently, experts can devote more working-memory resources to using recalled information for reasoning and problem solving.

But knowledge is not the only important factor in children's strategic memory processing. Children who are expert in an area are usually highly motivated. As a result, they not only acquire knowledge more quickly but also *actively use what they know* to add more. In contrast, academically unsuccessful children fail to ask how previously stored information can clarify new material. This, in turn, interferes with the development of a broad knowledge base (Schneider & Bjorklund, 1998). So extensive knowledge and use of memory strategies support each other.

Culture, Schooling, and Memory Strategies

A repeated finding is that people in village cultures who have little formal schooling do not use or benefit from instruction in memory strategies because they see no practical reason to use these techniques (Rogoff, 2003). Tasks requiring children to recall isolated pieces of information, which are common in classrooms, strongly motivate use of memory strategies.

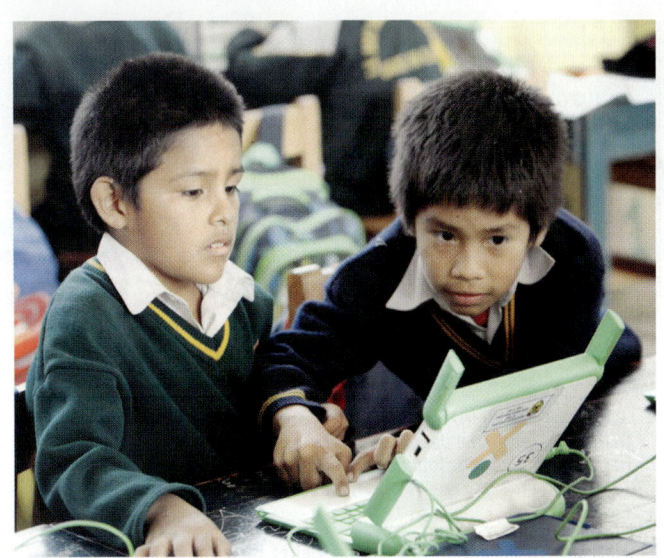

Children in a shanty town on the outskirts of Lima use laptops provided by the Peruvian government. Societal modernization—access to contemporary resources for communication and literacy—is broadly associated with improved cognitive performance.

Societal modernization—indicated by the presence of books, writing tablets, electricity, radio, TV, and other economically advantageous resources in homes—is broadly associated with performance on cognitive tasks commonly given to children in industrialized nations. In an investigation in which researchers rated towns in Belize, Kenya, Nepal, and American Samoa for degree of modernization, Belize and American Samoa exceeded Kenya and Nepal (Gauvain & Munroe, 2009). Modernization predicted both extent of schooling and 5- to 9-year-olds' cognitive scores on a memory test plus an array of other measures.

In sum, the development of memory strategies is not just a product of a more competent information-processing system. It also depends on task demands, schooling, and cultural circumstances.

The School-Age Child's Theory of Mind

During middle childhood, children's *theory of mind,* or set of ideas about mental activities, becomes more elaborate and refined. Recall from Chapter 7 that this awareness of thought is often called *metacognition.* Children's improved ability to reflect on their own mental life is another reason that their thinking advances.

Unlike preschoolers, who view the mind as a passive container of information, older children regard it as an active, constructive agent that selects and transforms information (Astington & Hughes, 2013). Consequently, they have a much better understanding of cognitive processes and the impact of psychological factors on performance. For example, with age, elementary school children become increasingly aware of effective memory strategies and why they work (Alexander et al., 2003). And

FIGURE 9.5 A second-order false-belief task. After relating the story in the sequence of pictures, the researcher asks a second-order false-belief question: "Where does Lisa think Jason will look for the letter? Why?" Around age 7, children answer correctly—that Lisa thinks Jason will look under his pillow because Lisa doesn't know that Jason saw her put the letter in the desk. (Adapted from Astington, Pelletier, & Homer, 2002.)

gradually they grasp relationships between mental activities—for example, that remembering is crucial for understanding and that understanding strengthens memory (Schwanenflugel, Henderson, & Fabricius, 1998).

Furthermore, school-age children's understanding of sources of knowledge expands. They realize that people can extend their knowledge not just by directly observing events and talking to others but also by making *mental inferences* (Miller, Hardin, & Montgomery, 2003). This grasp of inference enables knowledge of *false belief* to expand. In several studies, researchers told children complex stories involving one character's belief about a second character's belief. Then the children answered questions about what the first character thought the second character would do (see Figure 9.5). By age 6 to 7, children were aware that people form beliefs about other people's beliefs and that these second-order beliefs can be wrong!

Appreciation of *second-order false belief* enables children to pinpoint the reasons that another person arrived at a certain belief (Miller, 2009; Naito & Seki, 2009). Notice how it requires the ability to view a situation from at least two perspectives—that is, to reason simultaneously about what two or more people are thinking, a form of perspective taking called **recursive thought.** We think recursively when we make such statements as "*Lisa believes that Jason believes* the letter is under his pillow, but that's *not what Jason really believes; he knows* the letter is in the desk."

The capacity for recursive thought greatly assists children in appreciating that people can harbor quite different interpretations of the same reality. For example, around ages 7 to 8, children realize that two people are likely to interpret the same event quite differently, regardless of the beliefs and biases they bring to the situation (Lalonde & Chandler, 2002). Indeed, school-age children's newfound awareness of varying viewpoints is so powerful that, at first, they overextend it (Lagattuta, Sayfan, & Blattman, 2010). They often overlook the fact that people with different past experiences sometimes agree!

As with other cognitive attainments, schooling contributes to a more reflective, process-oriented view of mental activities. In school, teachers often call attention to the workings of the mind by asking children to remember mental steps, share points of view with peers, and evaluate their own and others' reasoning.

Cognitive Self-Regulation

Although metacognition expands, school-age children frequently have difficulty putting what they know about thinking into action. They are not yet good at **cognitive self-regulation,** the process of continuously monitoring progress toward a goal, checking outcomes, and redirecting unsuccessful efforts. For example, Lizzie is aware that she should group items when memorizing and reread a complicated paragraph to make sure she understands it. But she does not always engage in these activities.

To study cognitive self-regulation, researchers sometimes look at the impact of children's awareness of memory strategies on how well they remember. By second grade, the more children know about memory strategies, the more they recall—a relationship that strengthens over middle childhood (DeMarie et al., 2004). And when children apply a strategy consistently, their knowledge of it strengthens, resulting in a bidirectional relationship between metacognition and strategy use that enhances self-regulation (Schlagmüller & Schneider, 2002).

Cognitive self-regulation develops gradually because monitoring and controlling task outcomes is highly demanding, requiring constant evaluation of effort and progress. Throughout elementary and secondary school, self-regulation predicts academic success (Zimmerman & Labuhn, 2012). Students who do well in school know when they encounter obstacles to learning and take steps to address them—for example, by organizing the learning environment, reviewing confusing material, or seeking support from more expert adults or peers (Schunk & Zimmerman, 2013). This active, purposeful approach contrasts sharply with the passive orientation of students who achieve poorly.

Parents and teachers can foster self-regulation. In one study, researchers observed parents instructing their children on a problem-solving task during the summer before third grade. Parents who patiently pointed out important features of the task and suggested strategies had children who, in the classroom, more often discussed ways to approach problems and monitored their own performance (Stright et al., 2002). Explaining the effectiveness of strategies is particularly helpful because it provides a rationale for future action.

Children who acquire effective self-regulatory skills develop a sense of *academic self-efficacy*—confidence in their own ability, which supports future self-regulation (Zimmerman & Moylan, 2009). Unfortunately, some children receive messages from parents and teachers that seriously undermine their academic self-esteem and self-regulatory skills. We will consider these *learned-helpless* students, along with ways to help them, in Chapter 10.

Applications of Information Processing to Academic Learning

Fundamental discoveries about the development of information processing have been applied to children's learning of reading and mathematics. Researchers are identifying the cognitive ingredients of skilled performance, tracing their development, and distinguishing good from poor learners by pinpointing differences in cognitive skills. They hope, as a result, to design teaching methods that will improve children's learning.

Reading. Reading makes use of many skills at once, taxing all aspects of our information-processing system. Joey and Lizzie must perceive single letters and letter combinations, translate them into speech sounds, recognize the visual appearance of many common words, hold chunks of text in working memory while interpreting their meaning, and combine the meanings of various parts of a text passage into an understandable whole. Because reading is so demanding, most or all of these skills must be done automatically. If one or more are poorly developed, they will compete for space in our limited working memories, and reading performance will decline.

As children make the transition from emergent literacy to conventional reading, *phonological awareness* (see page 244 in Chapter 7) continues to facilitate their progress. Other information-processing skills also contribute. Gains in processing speed foster children's rapid conversion of visual symbols into sounds (Moll et al., 2014). Visual scanning and discrimination play important roles and improve with reading experience (Rayner, Pollatsek, & Starr, 2003). Performing all these skills efficiently releases working memory for higher-level activities involved in comprehending the text's meaning.

Until recently, researchers were involved in an intense debate over how to teach beginning reading. Those who took a **whole-language approach** argued that from the beginning, children should be exposed to text in its complete form—stories, poems, letters, posters, and lists. According to this view, as long as reading is kept whole and meaningful, children will be motivated to discover the specific skills they need. Other experts advocated a **phonics approach,** believing that children should first be coached on *phonics*—the basic rules for translating written symbols into sounds. Only after mastering these skills should they get complex reading material.

Many studies confirm that children learn best with a mixture of both approaches. In kindergarten, first, and second grades, teaching that includes phonics boosts reading scores, especially for children who lag behind in reading progress (Block, 2012; Brady, 2011). Learning letter–sound relationships enables children to *decode,* or decipher, words they have never seen before. Yet too much emphasis on basic skills may cause children to lose sight of the goal of reading: understanding. Children who read aloud fluently without registering meaning know little about effective metacognitive reading strategies—for example, that they must read more carefully if they will be tested than if they are reading for pleasure, that relating ideas in the text to personal experiences and general knowledge will deepen understanding, and that explaining a passage in their own words is a good way to assess comprehension. Teaching aimed at increasing awareness and use of reading strategies enhances reading performance from third grade on (Lonigan, 2015; McKeown & Beck, 2009).

Mathematics. Mathematics teaching in elementary school builds on and greatly enriches children's informal knowledge of number concepts and counting. Written notation systems and formal computational procedures enhance children's ability to represent numbers and compute. Over the early elementary school years, children acquire basic math facts through a combination of frequent practice, experimentation with diverse computational procedures (through which they discover faster, more accurate techniques), reasoning about number concepts, and teaching that conveys effective strategies. Eventually children retrieve answers automatically and apply this knowledge to more complex problems.

Arguments about how to teach mathematics resemble those in reading, pitting drill in computing against "number sense," or understanding. Again, a blend of both approaches is most beneficial (Fuson, 2009). In learning basic math, poorly performing students use cumbersome, error-prone techniques or try to retrieve answers from memory too soon. They have not sufficiently experimented with strategies to see which are most effective and to reorganize their observations in logical, efficient ways—for example, noticing that multiplication problems involving the number 2 (2 × 8) are equivalent to addition doubles (8 + 8). On tasks assessing their grasp of math concepts, their performance is weak (Clements & Sarama, 2012). This suggests

This fourth grader uses paper cut in different sizes to clarify the concept of fractions. The most effective math teaching combines frequent practice with instruction emphasizing conceptual understanding.

that encouraging students to apply strategies and making sure they understand why certain strategies work well are essential for solid mastery of basic math.

A similar picture emerges for more complex skills, such as carrying in addition, borrowing in subtraction, and operating with decimals and fractions. Children taught by rote persistently make mistakes, following a "math rule" that they recall incorrectly because they do not understand it (Carpenter et al., 1999).

In one study, the more teachers emphasized conceptual knowledge, by having children actively construct meanings in word problems before practicing computation and memorizing math facts, the more children gained in math achievement from second to third grade (Staub & Stern, 2002). Children taught in this way draw on their solid knowledge of relationships between operations—for example, that the inverse of division is multiplication—to generate efficient, flexible procedures. And because they have been encouraged to estimate answers, if they go down the wrong track in computation, they are usually self-correcting. They also select math operations that are appropriate for problem contexts. They can solve a word problem ("Jesse spent $3.45 for bananas, $2.62 for bread, and $3.55 for peanut butter. Can he pay for it all with a $10 bill?") quickly through estimation instead of exact calculation (De Corte & Verschaffel, 2006).

In Asian countries, students receive a variety of supports for acquiring mathematical knowledge and often excel at math computation and reasoning. Use of the metric system helps Asian children grasp place value. The consistent structure of number words in Asian languages (*ten-two* for 12, *ten-three* for 13) also makes this idea clear (Miura & Okamoto, 2003). And because Asian number words are shorter and more quickly pronounced, more digits can be held in working memory at once, increasing speed of thinking. Furthermore, Chinese parents provide their preschoolers with extensive practice in counting and computation—experiences that contribute to the superiority of Chinese over U.S. children's math knowledge even before school entry (Siegler & Mu, 2008; Zhou et al., 2006). Finally, as we will see later in this chapter, compared with lessons in the United States, those in Asian classrooms devote more time to exploring math concepts and strategies and less to drill and repetition.

Ask yourself

CONNECT Explain why gains in executive function are vital for mastery of reading and math in middle childhood.

APPLY Lizzie knows that if you have difficulty learning part of a task, you should devote extra attention to that part. But she plays each of her piano pieces from beginning to end instead of practicing the hard parts. What explains Lizzie's failure to engage in cognitive self-regulation?

REFLECT In your elementary school math education, how much emphasis was placed on computational drill and how much on understanding concepts? How do you think that balance affected your interest and performance in math?

Individual Differences in Mental Development

9.12 Describe major approaches to defining and measuring intelligence.

9.13 Describe evidence indicating that both heredity and environment contribute to intelligence.

Around age 6, IQ becomes more stable than it was at earlier ages, and it correlates moderately with academic achievement, typically around .50 to .60. And children with higher IQs are more likely to attain higher levels of education and enter more prestigious occupations in adulthood (Deary et al., 2007). Because IQ predicts school performance and educational attainment, it often enters into educational decisions. Do intelligence tests accurately assess school-age children's ability to profit from academic instruction? Let's look closely at this controversial issue.

Defining and Measuring Intelligence

Virtually all intelligence tests provide an overall score (the IQ), which represents *general intelligence,* or reasoning ability, along with an array of separate scores measuring specific mental abilities. But intelligence is a collection of many capacities, not all of which are included on currently available tests (Carroll, 2005; Sternberg, 2008). Test designers use a complicated statistical technique called *factor analysis* to identify the various abilities that intelligence tests measure. It identifies which sets of test items cluster together, meaning that test-takers who do well on one item in a cluster tend to do well on the others. Distinct clusters are called *factors,* each of which represents an ability. See Figure 9.6 for items typically included in intelligence tests for children.

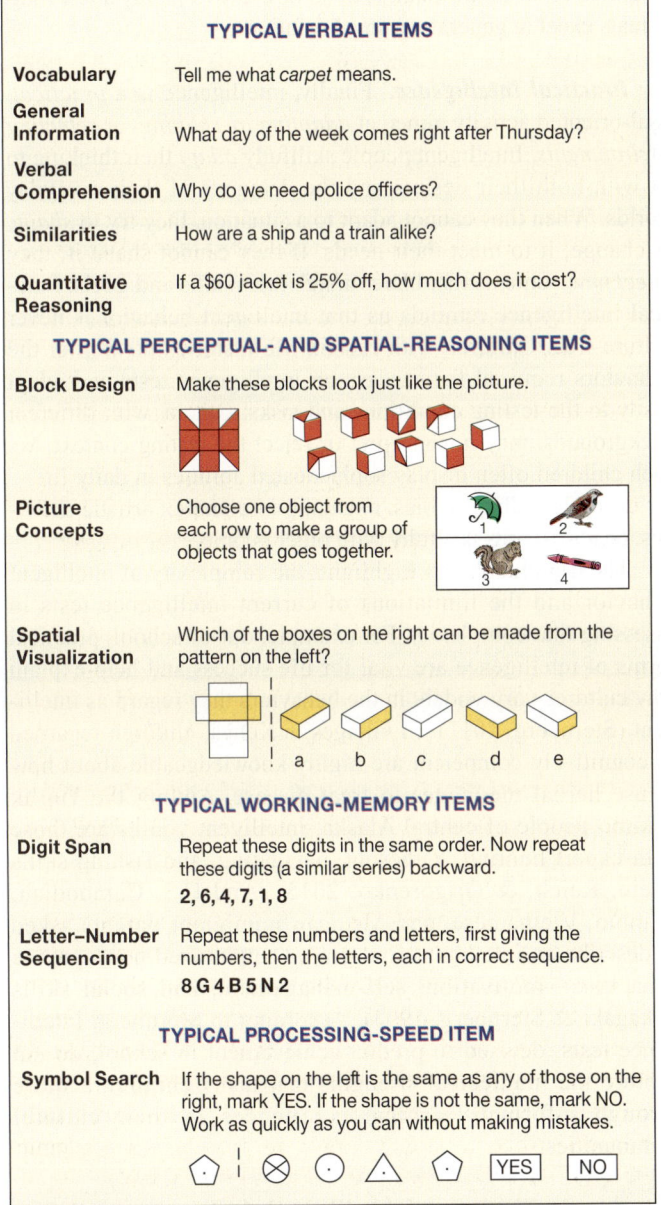

FIGURE 9.6 Test items like those on commonly used intelligence tests for children. The verbal items emphasize culturally loaded, fact-oriented information. The perceptual- and spatial-reasoning, working-memory, and processing-speed items emphasize aspects of information processing and are assumed to assess more biologically based skills.

Although *group-administered* intelligence tests are available that permit large numbers of students to be tested at once, intelligence is most often assessed with *individually administered* tests, which are best suited for identifying highly intelligent children and diagnosing children with learning problems. During an individually administered test, a well-trained examiner not only considers the child's answers but also observes the child's behavior, noting such reactions as attention to and interest in the tasks and wariness of the adult. These observations provide insight into whether the test results accurately reflect the child's abilities. Two individual tests—the Stanford-Binet and the Wechsler—are used especially often.

The contemporary descendant of Alfred Binet's first successful intelligence test is the *Stanford-Binet Intelligence Scales,* Fifth Edition, for individuals from age 2 to adulthood. In addition to general intelligence, it assesses five intellectual factors: general knowledge, quantitative reasoning, visual–spatial processing, working memory, and basic information processing (such as speed of analyzing information). Each factor includes both a verbal mode and a nonverbal mode of testing, yielding 10 subtests in all (Roid, 2003; Roid & Pomplun, 2012). The nonverbal subtests, which do not require spoken language, are particularly useful when assessing individuals with limited English, hearing impairments, or communication disorders. The knowledge and quantitative reasoning factors emphasize culturally loaded, fact-oriented information, such as vocabulary and arithmetic problems. In contrast, the visual–spatial processing, working-memory, and basic information-processing factors are assumed to be less culturally biased (see the spatial visualization item in Figure 9.6).

The *Wechsler Intelligence Scale for Children (WISC-V)* is the fifth edition of a widely used test for 6- through 16-year-olds. It measures general intelligence and an array of intellectual factors, five of which are recommended for a comprehensive evaluation of a child's intellectual ability: verbal comprehension, visual–spatial reasoning, fluid reasoning (tapping ability to apply rules in reasoning and to detect conceptual relationships among objects), working memory, and processing speed (Weiss et al., 2015). The WISC-V was designed to downplay culture-dependent information, which is emphasized on only one factor (verbal comprehension). The goal is to provide a test that is as "culture-fair" as possible.

Other Efforts to Define Intelligence

As we have seen, mental tests now tap important aspects of information processing. In line with this trend, some researchers have combined the mental-testing approach to defining intelligence with the information-processing approach. They believe that once we identify the processing skills that separate individuals who test well from those who test poorly, we will know more about how to intervene to improve performance.

Processing speed, assessed in terms of reaction time on diverse cognitive tasks, is moderately related to IQ (Coyle, 2013; Li et al., 2004). Individuals whose nervous systems function more efficiently, permitting them to take in more information and manipulate it quickly, have an edge in intellectual skills. And not surprisingly, executive function strongly predicts general intelligence (Brydges et al., 2012; Schweizer, Moosebrugger, & Goldhammer, 2006). We have seen that the components of executive function are vital for success on a great many cognitive tasks.

Individual differences in intelligence, however, are not entirely due to causes within the child. Throughout this book, we have seen how cultural and situational factors affect children's thinking. Robert Sternberg has devised a comprehensive theory that regards intelligence as a product of both inner and outer forces.

Sternberg's Triarchic Theory. As Figure 9.7 shows, Sternberg's (2005, 2008, 2013) **triarchic theory of successful intelligence** identifies three broad, interacting intelligences: (1) *analytical intelligence,* or information-processing skills; (2) *creative intelligence,* the capacity to solve novel problems; and (3) *practical intelligence,* application of intellectual skills in everyday situations. Intelligent behavior involves balancing all three intelligences to achieve success in life according to one's personal goals and the requirements of one's cultural community.

Analytical Intelligence. Analytical intelligence consists of the information-processing skills that underlie all intelligent acts: executive function, strategic thinking, knowledge acquisition, and cognitive self-regulation. But on intelligence tests, processing skills are used in only a few of their potential ways, resulting in far too narrow a view of intelligent behavior.

Creative Intelligence. In any context, success depends not only on processing familiar information but also on generating useful solutions to new problems. People who are *creative* think more skillfully than others when faced with novelty. Given a new task, they apply their information-processing skills in exceptionally effective ways, rapidly making these skills automatic so that working memory is freed for more complex aspects of the situation. Consequently, they quickly move to high-level performance. Although all of us are capable of some creativity, only a few individuals excel at generating novel solutions.

Practical Intelligence. Finally, intelligence is a *practical,* goal-oriented activity aimed at *adapting to, shaping,* or *selecting environments.* Intelligent people skillfully *adapt* their thinking to fit with both their desires and the demands of their everyday worlds. When they cannot adapt to a situation, they try to *shape,* or change, it to meet their needs. If they cannot shape it, they *select* new contexts that better match their skills and goals. Practical intelligence reminds us that intelligent behavior is never culture-free. Children with certain life histories do well at the behaviors required for success on intelligence tests and adapt easily to the testing conditions and tasks. Others, with different backgrounds, may misinterpret or reject the testing context. Yet such children often display sophisticated abilities in daily life—for example, telling stories, engaging in complex artistic activities, or interacting skillfully with other people.

The triarchic theory highlights the complexity of intelligent behavior and the limitations of current intelligence tests in assessing that complexity. For example, out-of-school, practical forms of intelligence are vital for life success and help explain why cultures vary widely in the behaviors they regard as intelligent (Sternberg, 2011). In villages in Kenya, children regarded as cognitively competent are highly knowledgeable about how to use herbal medicines to treat disease. Among the Yup'ik Eskimo people of central Alaska, intelligent youths are those with expert hunting, gathering, navigating, and fishing skills (Hein, Reich, & Grigorenko, 2015). And U.S. Cambodian, Filipino, Vietnamese, and Mexican immigrant parents asked to describe an intelligent first grader emphasized noncognitive capacities—motivation, self-management, and social skills (Okagaki & Sternberg, 1993). According to Sternberg, intelligence tests, devised to predict achievement in school, do not capture the intellectual strengths that many children acquire through informal learning experiences in their cultural communities.

Gardner's Theory of Multiple Intelligences. In yet another view of how information-processing skills underlie intelligent behavior, Howard Gardner's (1983, 1993, 2011) **theory of multiple intelligences** defines intelligence in terms of distinct sets of processing operations that permit individuals to engage in

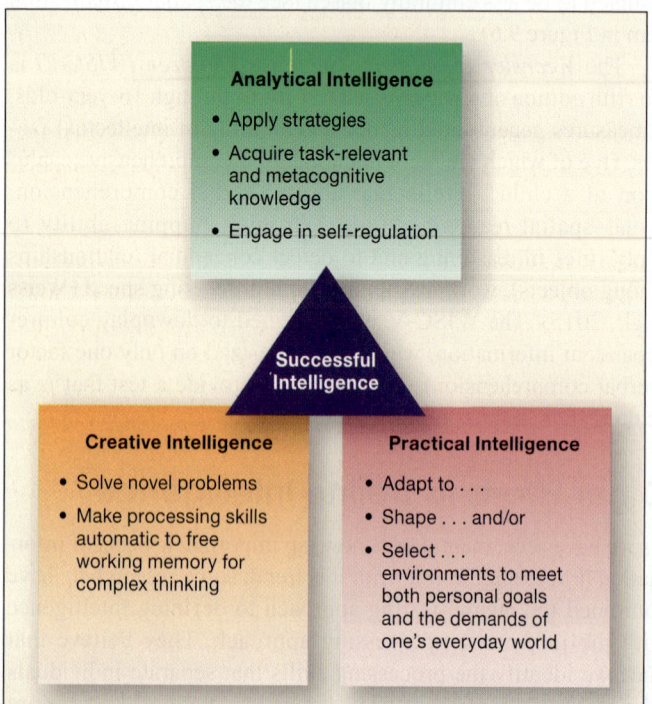

FIGURE 9.7 Sternberg's triarchic theory of successful intelligence. People who behave intelligently balance three interrelated intelligences—analytical, creative, and practical—to achieve success in life, defined by their personal goals and the requirements of their cultural communities.

TABLE 9.1
Gardner's Multiple Intelligences

INTELLIGENCE	PROCESSING OPERATIONS	END-STATE PERFORMANCE POSSIBILITIES
Linguistic	Sensitivity to the sounds, rhythms, and meaning of words and the functions of language	Poet, journalist
Logico-mathematical	Sensitivity to, and capacity to detect, logical or numerical patterns; ability to handle long chains of logical reasoning	Mathematician
Musical	Ability to produce and appreciate pitch, rhythm (or melody), and aesthetic quality of the forms of musical expressiveness	Instrumentalist, composer
Spatial	Ability to perceive the visual–spatial world accurately, to perform transformations on those perceptions, and to re-create aspects of visual experience in the absence of relevant stimuli	Sculptor, navigator
Bodily-kinesthetic	Ability to use the body skillfully for expressive as well as goal-directed purposes; ability to handle objects skillfully	Dancer, athlete
Naturalist	Ability to recognize and classify all varieties of animals, minerals, and plants	Biologist
Interpersonal	Ability to detect and respond appropriately to the moods, temperaments, motivations, and intentions of others	Therapist, salesperson
Intrapersonal	Ability to discriminate complex inner feelings and to use them to guide one's own behavior; knowledge of one's own strengths, weaknesses, desires, and intelligences	Person with detailed, accurate self-knowledge

Sources: Gardner, 1983, 1993, 2011.

a wide range of culturally valued activities. Dismissing the idea of general intelligence, Gardner proposes at least eight independent intelligences (see Table 9.1).

Gardner believes that each intelligence has a unique neurological basis, a distinct course of development, and different expert, or "end-state," performances. At the same time, he emphasizes that a lengthy process of education is required to transform any raw potential into a mature social role (Gardner, 2011). Cultural values and learning opportunities affect the extent to which a child's intellectual strengths are realized and the ways they are expressed.

Gardner's list of abilities has yet to be firmly grounded in research. Neurological evidence for the independence of his abilities is weak. Some exceptionally gifted individuals have abilities that are broad rather than limited to a particular domain (Piirto, 2007). And research with mental tests suggests that several of Gardner's intelligences (linguistic, logico-mathematical, and spatial) have at least some features in common. Nevertheless, Gardner calls attention to several intelligences not tapped by IQ scores.

For example, Gardner's interpersonal and intrapersonal intelligences include a set of skills for accurately perceiving, reasoning about, and regulating emotion that has become known as *emotional intelligence.* Among school-age children and adolescents, measures of emotional intelligence are positively associated with self-esteem, empathy, prosocial behavior, cooperation, leadership skills, and academic performance and negatively associated with internalizing and externalizing problems (Brackett, Rivers, & Salovey, 2011; Ferrando et al., 2011). These findings have increased teachers' awareness that providing classroom lessons that coach students in emotional abilities can improve their adjustment.

Explaining Individual and Group Differences in IQ

When we compare individuals in terms of academic achievement, years of education, and occupational status, it quickly becomes clear that certain sectors of the population are advantaged over others. In trying to explain these differences,

According to Gardner, people are capable of at least eight distinct intelligences. Through a project aimed at improving sea turtle nesting habitats, these children expand and enrich their naturalist intelligence.

researchers have compared the IQ scores of ethnic and SES groups. American black children and adolescents score, on average, 10 to 12 IQ points below American white children. Although the difference has been shrinking over the past several decades, a substantial gap remains (Nisbett, 2009; Nisbett et al., 2012). Hispanic children fall midway between black and white children, and Asian Americans score slightly higher than their white counterparts—about 3 points (Ceci, Rosenblum, & Kumpf, 1998).

The gap between middle- and low-SES children—about 9 points—accounts for some of the ethnic differences in IQ, but not all (Brooks-Gunn et al., 2003). Of course, IQ varies greatly *within* each ethnic and SES group, and minority top performers are typically indistinguishable from top performers in the white majority. Still, these group differences are large enough and of serious enough consequence that they cannot be ignored.

Beginning in the 1970s, the IQ nature–nurture controversy escalated after psychologist Arthur Jensen (1969) claimed that heredity is largely responsible for individual, ethnic, and SES variations in intelligence—a position others asserted as well (Herrnstein & Murray, 1994; Jensen, 2001; Rushton & Jensen, 2006, 2010). These contentions prompted an outpouring of research studies and responses, including ethical challenges reflecting deep concern that the conclusions would fuel social prejudices. Let's look closely at some important evidence.

Nature versus Nurture. In Chapter 2, we introduced the *heritability estimate*. The most powerful evidence on the heritability of IQ involves twin comparisons. The IQ scores of identical twins (who share all their genes) are more similar than those of fraternal twins (who are genetically no more alike than ordinary siblings). On the basis of this and other kinship evidence, researchers estimate that about half the differences in IQ among children can be traced to their genetic makeup.

Recall, however, that heritabilities risk overestimating genetic influences and underestimating environmental influences. Although these measures offer convincing evidence that genes contribute to IQ, disagreement persists over how large a role heredity plays. As we saw in Chapter 2, the heritability of children's intelligence rises with parental education and income—conditions that enable children to realize their genetic potential. And heritability estimates do not reveal the complex processes through which genes and experiences influence intelligence as children develop.

Adoption studies offer a wider range of information. When young children are adopted into caring, stimulating homes, their IQs rise substantially compared with the IQs of nonadopted children who remain in economically deprived families (Hunt, 2011). But adopted children benefit to varying degrees. In one investigation, children of two extreme groups of biological mothers—those with IQs below 95 and those with IQs above 120—were adopted at birth by parents who were well above average in income and education. During the school years, the children of the low-IQ biological mothers scored above average in IQ. But they did not do as well as children of high-IQ biological mothers placed in similar adoptive families (Loehlin, Horn, & Willerman, 1997). Adoption research confirms that heredity and environment jointly contribute to IQ.

Adoption studies also shed light on the black–white IQ gap. In two investigations, African-American children adopted into economically well-off white homes during the first year of life scored high on intelligence tests, attaining mean IQs of 110 and 117 by middle childhood (Moore, 1986; Scarr & Weinberg, 1983). The IQ gains of black children "reared in the culture of the tests and schools" are consistent with a wealth of evidence that poverty severely depresses the intelligence of ethnic minority children (Nisbett et al., 2012).

Dramatic gains in IQ from one generation to the next offer additional support for the conclusion that, given new experiences and opportunities, members of oppressed groups can move far beyond their current test performance. See the Cultural Influences box on the following page to learn about the Flynn effect.

Cultural Influences. A controversial question raised about ethnic differences in IQ has to do with whether they result from *test bias*. If a test samples knowledge and skills that not all groups of children have had equal opportunity to learn, or if the testing situation impairs the performance of some groups but not others, then the resulting score is a biased, or unfair, measure.

Some experts claim that because IQ predicts academic achievement equally well for majority and minority children, intelligence tests are fair to both groups. The tests, they say, represent success in the common culture (Edwards & Oakland, 2006; Jensen, 2002). Others believe that lack of exposure to certain communication styles and knowledge, along with negative stereotypes about the test-taker's ethnic group, can undermine children's performance (McKown, 2013; Sternberg, 2005).

Language and Communication Styles. Ethnic minority families often foster unique language skills that do not match the expectations of most classrooms and testing situations.

The majority of African-American children enter school speaking African-American English. Their home discourse differs from standard English, on which school learning is based.

Cultural Influences

The Flynn Effect: Massive Generational Gains in IQ

After gathering IQ scores from diverse nations that had either military mental testing or frequent testing of other large, representative samples, James Flynn (1999, 2007) reported a finding so consistent and intriguing that it became known as the **Flynn effect:** IQs have increased steadily from one generation to the next. Evidence for the Flynn effect now exists for 30 nations (Nisbett et al., 2012). This dramatic *secular trend* in intelligence test performance holds for industrialized and developing nations, both genders, and individuals varying in ethnicity and SES (Ang, Rodgers, & Wänström, 2010; Rodgers & Wänstrom, 2007). Gains are greatest on tests of spatial reasoning—tasks often assumed to be "culture-fair" and, therefore, mostly genetically based.

The amount of increase depends on extent of societal modernization (see page 311 to review). Among European and North American nations that modernized by the early twentieth century, IQ gains have been about 3 points per decade (Flynn, 2007). IQ has continued to increment at that pace in England and the United States, but gains have slowed in certain nations with especially favorable economic and social conditions, such as Norway and Sweden (Schneider, 2006; Sundet, Barlaug, & Torjussen, 2004).

Among nations that modernized later, around the mid-twentieth century (such as Argentina), IQ gains tend to be larger, as much as 5 to 6 points per decade (Flynn & Rossi-Casé, 2011). And nations that began to modernize in the late twentieth century (Caribbean countries, Kenya, Sudan) show even greater increments, especially in spatial reasoning (Daley et al., 2003; Khaleefa, Sulman, & Lynn, 2009). The degree of societal modernity possible today is far greater than it was a century ago.

Diverse aspects of modernization probably underlie the better reasoning ability of each successive generation. These include improved education, health, and technology (TV, computers, the Internet); more cognitively demanding jobs and leisure activities (reading, chess, video games); a generally more stimulating world; and greater test-taking motivation.

As developing nations continue to advance in IQ, they are projected to catch up with the industrialized world by the end of the twenty-first century (Nisbett et al., 2012). Large, envi-

Dramatic generational gains in IQ may result, in part, from greater participation by each successive generation in cognitively stimulating leisure activities.

ronmentally induced gains in IQ over time present a major challenge to the assumption that black–white and other ethnic variations in IQ are genetic.

African-American English is a complex, rule-governed dialect used by most African Americans in the United States (Craig & Washington, 2006). Nevertheless, it is often inaccurately viewed as a deficient form of standard American English rather than as different from it.

The majority of African-American children entering school speak African-American English, though they vary in the extent to which they use it. Greater users tend to come from low-SES families, who quickly learn that the language they bring from home is devalued in school. Teachers frequently try to "correct" or eliminate their use of African-American English forms, replacing these with standard English (Washington & Thomas-Tate, 2009). Because their home discourse is distinctly different from the linguistic knowledge required to learn to read, children who speak mostly African-American English in school generally progress slowly in reading and achieve poorly (Charity, Scarborough, & Griffin, 2004).

Many African-American children learn to flexibly shift between African-American English and standard English by third grade. But those who continue to speak mostly their African-American dialect through the later grades—the majority of whom live in poverty and therefore have few opportunities outside of school for exposure to standard English—fall further behind in reading and in overall achievement (Washington & Thomas-Tate, 2009). These children have a special need for school programs that facilitate mastery of standard English while respecting and accommodating their home language in the classroom.

Research also reveals that many ethnic minority parents without extensive education prefer a *collaborative style of communication* when completing tasks with children. They work together in a coordinated, fluid way, each focused on the same aspect of the problem. This pattern of adult–child engagement has been observed in Native-American, Canadian Inuit, Hispanic, and Guatemalan Mayan cultures (Chavajay & Rogoff, 2002; Crago, Annahatak, & Ningiuruvik, 1993; Paradise & Rogoff, 2009). With increasing education, parents establish a *hierarchical style of communication,* like that of classrooms and tests. The parent directs each child to carry out an aspect of the task, and children work independently (Greenfield, Suzuki, & Rothstein-Fish, 2006). This sharp discontinuity between home and school communication practices likely contributes to low-SES minority children's lower IQs and school performance.

Knowledge. Many researchers argue that IQ scores are affected by specific information acquired as part of majority-culture upbringing. Knowledge affects ability to reason effectively. In one study, researchers assessed black and white community college students' familiarity with vocabulary taken from items on an intelligence test. When verbal comprehension, similarities, and analogies items depended on words that the white students knew better, the whites scored higher than the blacks. When the same types of items involved words that the two groups knew equally well, the two groups did not differ (Fagan & Holland, 2007). Prior knowledge, not reasoning ability, fully explained ethnic differences in performance.

Even nonverbal test items, such as spatial reasoning, depend on learning opportunities. For example, among children, adolescents, and adults alike, playing video games that require fast responding and mental rotation of visual images increases success on spatial test items (Uttal et al., 2013). Low-income minority children may lack opportunities to use games and objects that promote certain intellectual skills.

Furthermore, the sheer amount of time children spend in school predicts IQ. In comparisons of children of the same age who are in different grades, those who have been in school longer score higher in verbal intelligence—a difference that increases as the children advance further in school (Bedard & Dhuey, 2006). Taken together, these findings indicate that children's exposure to the knowledge and ways of thinking valued in classrooms has a sizable impact on their intelligence test performance.

Stereotypes. Imagine trying to succeed at an activity when the prevailing attitude is that members of your group are incompetent. **Stereotype threat**—the fear of being judged on the basis of a negative stereotype—can trigger anxiety that interferes with performance. Mounting evidence confirms that stereotype threat undermines test taking in children and adults (McKown & Strambler, 2009). For example, researchers gave African-American, Hispanic-American, and European-American 6- to 10-year-olds verbal tasks. Some children were told that the tasks were "not a test." Others were told they were "a test of how good children are at school problems"—a statement designed to induce stereotype threat in the ethnic minority children. Among children who were aware of ethnic stereotypes (such as "black people aren't smart"), African Americans and Hispanics performed far worse in the "test" condition than in the "not a test" condition (McKown & Weinstein, 2003). European-American children, in contrast, performed similarly in both conditions.

From third grade on, children become increasingly conscious of ethnic stereotypes, and those from stigmatized groups are especially mindful of them. By early adolescence, many low-SES minority students start to devalue doing well in school, saying it is not important to them (Killen, Rutland, & Ruck, 2011). Self-protective disengagement, sparked by stereotype threat, may be responsible. This weakening of motivation can have serious, long-term consequences. Research shows that self-discipline—effort and delay of gratification—predicts school performance, as measured by report card grades, better than IQ does (Duckworth, Quinn, & Tsukayama, 2012).

Reducing Cultural Bias in Testing. Although not all experts agree, many acknowledge that IQ scores can underestimate the intelligence of children from ethnic minority groups. A special concern exists about incorrectly labeling minority children as slow learners and assigning them to remedial classes, which are far less stimulating than regular school experiences. To avoid this danger, test scores need to be combined with assessments of children's adaptive behavior—their ability to cope with the demands of their everyday environments. The child who does poorly on an intelligence test yet plays a complex game on the playground or figures out how to rewire a broken TV is unlikely to be intellectually deficient.

In addition, flexible testing procedures enhance minority children's performance. In an approach called **dynamic**

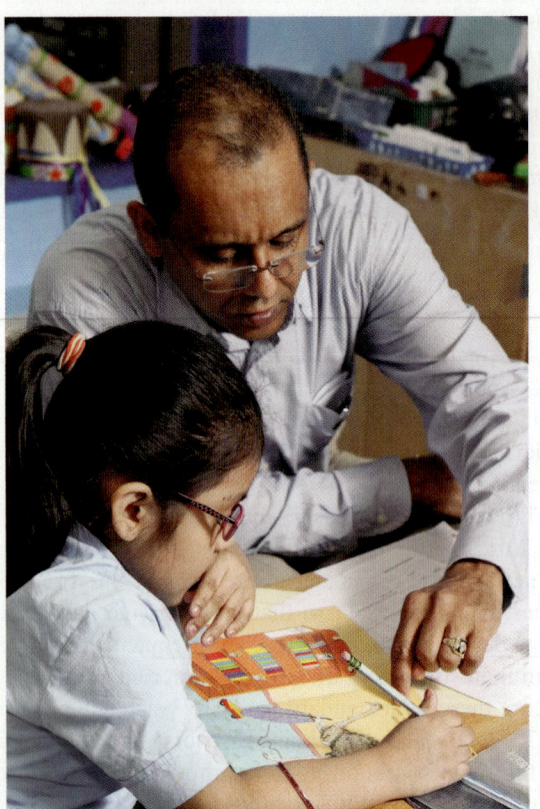

This teacher uses dynamic assessment, tailoring instruction to students' individual needs—an approach that reveals what each child can learn with social support.

assessment, an innovation consistent with Vygotsky's zone of proximal development, the adult introduces purposeful teaching into the testing situation to find out what the child can attain with social support (Robinson-Zañartu & Carlson, 2013).

Research shows that children's receptivity to teaching and capacity to transfer what they have learned to novel problems contribute substantially to gains in test performance (Haywood & Lidz, 2007). In one study, first graders diverse in SES and ethnicity participated in dynamic assessment in which they were asked to solve a series of unfamiliar math equations that increased in difficulty, such as __ + 1 = 4 (easier) and 3 + 6 = 5 + __ (difficult). When a child could not solve an equation, an adult provided increasingly explicit teaching until the child either succeeded or still had trouble, in which case the session ended. Beyond static IQ-like measures of children's verbal, math, and reasoning abilities, performance during dynamic assessment strongly predicted end-of-year scores on a test of math story problems, which children usually find highly challenging (Seethaler et al., 2012). Dynamic assessment seemed to evoke skills and understandings that children readily applied to a very different and demanding type of math.

Cultural bias in testing can also be reduced by countering the negative impact of stereotype threat. In one approach, researchers encouraged African-American students to affirm their self-worth by writing a short essay about their most important values—for example, a close friendship or a self-defining skill. This self-affirmation intervention was just as successful in boosting end-of-term grades of poorly performing middle school students as it was for students doing moderately well in school (see Figure 9.8).

In view of its many problems, should intelligence testing in schools be suspended? Most experts reject this solution. Without testing, important educational decisions would be based only on subjective impressions, perhaps increasing discriminatory placement of minority children. Intelligence tests are useful when interpreted carefully by psychologists and educators who are sensitive to cultural influences on test performance. And despite their limitations, IQ scores continue to be fairly accurate measures of school learning potential for the majority of Western children.

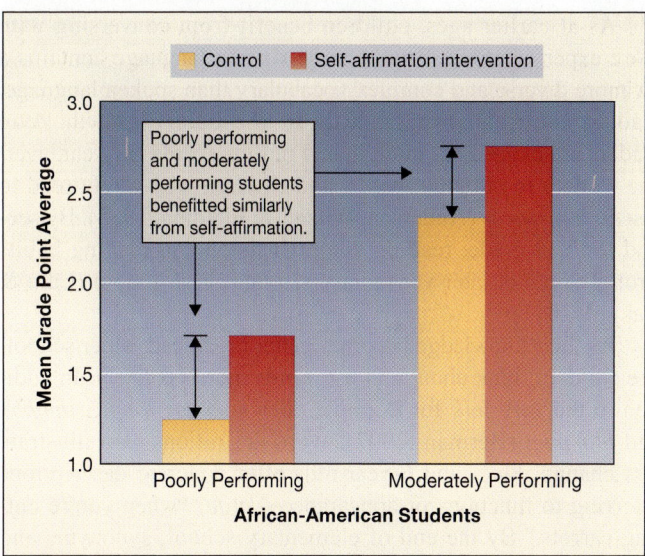

FIGURE 9.8 Impact of a self-affirmation intervention on African-American middle-school students' end-of-term grade-point average. In the fall, several hundred students were randomly assigned to either a self-affirmation intervention, in which they wrote brief essays about the personal meaning of their most important values, or a control condition, in which they wrote essays about why their least important values might be meaningful to someone else. African-American students experiencing the self-affirmation condition earned substantially higher end-of-term course grades than did controls; poorly performing and moderately performing students benefitted similarly. White students' grades were unaffected, indicating that the treatment succeeded by lessening the negative impact of stereotype threat on the African Americans. (Based on Cohen, Garcia, & Master, 2006.)

Language Development

9.14 Describe changes in school-age children's vocabulary, grammar, and pragmatics, and cite the advantages of bilingualism for development.

Vocabulary, grammar, and pragmatics continue to develop in middle childhood, though less obviously than at earlier ages. In addition, children's attitude toward language undergoes a fundamental shift: They develop language awareness.

Vocabulary and Grammar

During the elementary school years, vocabulary increases fourfold, eventually reaching comprehension of 40,000 words. On average, children learn about 20 new words each day, a rate of growth greater than in early childhood. In addition to the word-learning strategies discussed in Chapter 7, school-age children add to their vocabularies by analyzing the structure of complex words. From *happy* and *decide,* they quickly derive the meanings of *happiness* and *decision* (Larsen & Nippold, 2007). They also figure out many more word meanings from context (Nagy & Scott, 2000).

Ask yourself

CONNECT Explain how dynamic assessment is consistent with Vygotsky's zone of proximal development and with scaffolding. (See Chapter 7, page 235.)

APPLY Josefina, a Hispanic fourth grader, does well on homework assignments. But when her teacher announces, "It's time for a test to see how much you've learned," Josefina usually does poorly. How might stereotype threat explain this inconsistency?

REFLECT Do you think that intelligence tests are culturally biased? What observations and evidence influenced your conclusions?

As at earlier ages, children benefit from conversing with more expert speakers. But because written language contains a far more diverse and complex vocabulary than spoken language, reading contributes enormously to vocabulary growth. Avid readers are exposed to more than 4 million words per year, average readers to 600,000 words, and children who rarely read to just 50,000 words (Anderson, Wilson, & Fielding, 1988). By second to third grade, reading comprehension and reading habits strongly predict later vocabulary size into high school (Cain & Oakhill, 2011).

As their knowledge becomes better organized, older school-age children think about and use words more precisely: In addition to the verb *fall*, for example, they also use *topple, tumble,* and *plummet* (Berman, 2007). Word definitions also illustrate this change. Five- and 6-year-olds offer concrete descriptions referring to functions or appearance—*knife:* "when you're cutting carrots." By the end of elementary school, synonyms and explanations of categorical relationships appear—for example, *knife:* "something you could cut with. A saw is like a knife. It could also be a weapon" (Uccelli & Pan, 2013). This advance reflects older children's ability to deal with word meanings on an entirely verbal plane. They can add new words to their vocabulary simply by being given a definition.

School-age children's more reflective and analytical approach to language permits them to appreciate the multiple meanings of words—to recognize, for example, that many words, such as *cool* or *neat,* have psychological as well as physical meanings: "Cool shirt!" or "That movie was really neat!" This grasp of double meanings permits 8- to 10-year-olds to comprehend subtle metaphors, such as "sharp as a tack" and "spilling the beans" (Nippold, Taylor, & Baker, 1996; Wellman & Hickling, 1994). It also leads to a change in children's humor. Riddles and puns that alternate between different meanings of a key word are common: "Hey, did you take a bath?" "Why, is one missing?"

> **LOOK and LISTEN**
>
> Record examples of 8- to 10-year-olds' humor, or examine storybooks for humor aimed at second through fourth graders. Does it require a grasp of the multiple meanings of words?

Mastery of complex grammatical constructions also improves. For example, English-speaking children use the passive voice more frequently, and they more often extend it from an abbreviated form ("It broke") into full statements ("The glass was broken by Mary") (Tomasello, 2006). Another grammatical achievement of middle childhood is advanced understanding of infinitive phrases—the difference between "John is eager to please" and "John is easy to please" (Berman, 2007; Chomsky, 1969). Like gains in vocabulary, appreciation of these subtle grammatical distinctions is supported by an improved ability to analyze and reflect on language.

Pragmatics

A more advanced theory of mind—in particular, the capacity for recursive thought—enables children to understand and use increasingly subtle, indirect expressions of meaning with age. Around age 8, children begin to grasp irony and sarcasm (Glenright & Pexman, 2010). After Rena prepared a dish for dinner that Joey didn't like, he quipped sarcastically, "Oh boy, my favorite!" Notice how this remark requires the speaker to consider at least two perspectives simultaneously—in Joey's case, his mother's desire to serve a particular dish despite his objection, expressed through a critical comment with a double meaning.

Furthermore, as a result of improved memory, ability to take the perspective of listeners, and conversations with adults about past experiences, children's narratives increase in organization, detail, and expressiveness. A typical 4- or 5-year-old's narrative states what happened: "We went to the lake. We fished and waited. Paul caught a huge catfish." Six- and 7-year-olds add orienting information (time, place, participants) and connectives ("next," "then," "so," "finally") that lend coherence to the story. Gradually, narratives lengthen into a *classic form* in which events not only build to a high point but resolve: "After Paul reeled in the catfish, Dad cleaned and cooked it. Then we ate it all up!" And evaluative comments rise dramatically, becoming common by age 8 to 9: "The catfish tasted great. Paul was so proud!" (Melzi & Schick, 2013; Ukrainetz et al., 2005).

Because children pick up the narrative styles of significant adults in their lives, their narratives vary widely across cultures. For example, instead of the *topic-focused style* of most European-American children, who describe an experience from beginning to end, African-American children often use a

In families who regularly eat meals together, children are advanced in language and literacy development. Mealtimes offer many opportunities to relate complex, extended personal stories.

topic-associating style in which they blend several similar experiences. One 9-year-old related having a tooth pulled, then described seeing her sister's tooth pulled, next told how she had removed one of her own baby teeth, and concluded, "I'm a pullin-teeth expert . . . call me, and I'll be over" (McCabe, 1997, p. 164). Like adults in their families and communities, African-American children are more attuned to keeping their listeners interested than to relating a linear sequence of events. They often embellish their narratives by including fictional elements and many references to characters' motives and intentions (Gorman et al., 2011). As a result, African-American children's narratives are usually longer and more complex than those of white children.

The ability to generate clear oral narratives enhances reading comprehension and prepares children for producing longer, more explicit written narratives. In families who regularly eat meals together, children are advanced in language and literacy development, perhaps because mealtimes offer many opportunities to relate personal stories (Snow & Beals, 2006).

Learning Two Languages

Joey and Lizzie speak only one language—English, their native tongue. Yet throughout the world, many children grow up *bilingual*, and some acquire more than two languages. An estimated 22 percent of U.S. children—11.2 million in all—speak a language other than English at home (U.S. Census Bureau, 2015d).

Bilingual Development. Children can become bilingual in two ways: (1) by acquiring both languages at the same time in early childhood or (2) by learning a second language after acquiring the first. Children of bilingual parents who teach them both languages in infancy and early childhood separate the language systems early on and attain early language milestones according to a typical timetable (Hoff et al., 2012). When preschool and school-age children from immigrant families acquire a second language after they already speak the language of their cultural heritage, the time required to master the second language to the level of native-speaking agemates varies greatly, from 1 to 5 or more years (MacWhinney, 2015; Páez & Hunter, 2015). Influential factors include child motivation, knowledge of the first language (which supports mastery of the second), and quality of communication and of literacy experiences in both languages at home and at school.

As with first-language development, a *sensitive period* for second-language development exists. Mastery must begin sometime in childhood for most second-language learners to attain full proficiency (Hakuta, Bialystok, & Wiley, 2003). But a precise age cutoff for a decline in second-language learning has not been established. Rather, a continuous age-related decrease from childhood to adulthood occurs.

Children who become fluent in two languages develop denser synaptic connections in areas of the left hemisphere devoted to language. And compared to monolinguals, bilinguals show greater activity in these areas and in the prefrontal cortex during linguistic tasks, likely due to the high executive-processing demands of controlling two languages (Costa & Sebastián-Gallés, 2014). Because both languages are always active, bilingual speakers must continuously decide which one to use in particular social situations, resisting attention to the other.

This increase in executive processing has diverse cognitive benefits as bilinguals acquire more efficient executive function skills and apply them to other tasks (Bialystok, 2011). Bilingual children and adults outperform others on tests of inhibition, sustained and selective attention, flexible shifting, analytical reasoning, concept formation, and false-belief understanding (Bialystok, Craik, & Luk, 2012; Carlson & Meltzoff, 2008). They are also advanced in certain aspects of language awareness, such as detection of errors in grammar, meaning, and conventions of conversation (responding politely, relevantly, and informatively). And children transfer their phonological awareness skills in one language to the other, especially if the two languages share phonological features and letter–sound correspondences, as Spanish and English do (Bialystok, 2013; Siegal, Iozzi, & Surian, 2009). These capacities, as noted earlier, enhance reading achievement.

Bilingual Education. The advantages of bilingualism provide strong justification for bilingual education programs in schools. In Canada, about 7 percent of elementary school students are enrolled in *language immersion programs,* in which English-speaking children are taught entirely in French for several years. This strategy succeeds in developing children who are proficient in both languages and who, by grade 6, achieve as well in reading, writing, and math as their counterparts in the regular English program (Genesee & Jared, 2008; Lyster & Genesee, 2012).

In the United States, fierce disagreement exists over how best to educate dual language learning children. Some believe that time spent communicating in the child's native tongue detracts from English-language achievement. Other educators, committed to developing minority children's native language while fostering mastery of English, note that providing instruction in the native tongue lets minority children know that their heritage is respected. It also prevents inadequate proficiency in both languages. Minority children who gradually lose the first language as a result of being taught the second end up limited in both languages (McCabe et al., 2013). This circumstance leads to severe academic difficulties and is believed to contribute to the high rates of school failure and dropout among low-SES Hispanic young people, who make up over 70 percent of the U.S. language-minority population.

At present, public opinion and educational practice favor English-only instruction. Many U.S. states have passed laws declaring English to be their official language, creating conditions in which schools have no obligation to teach minority students in languages other than English. Where bilingual education exists, usually its goal is to transition students to English-only

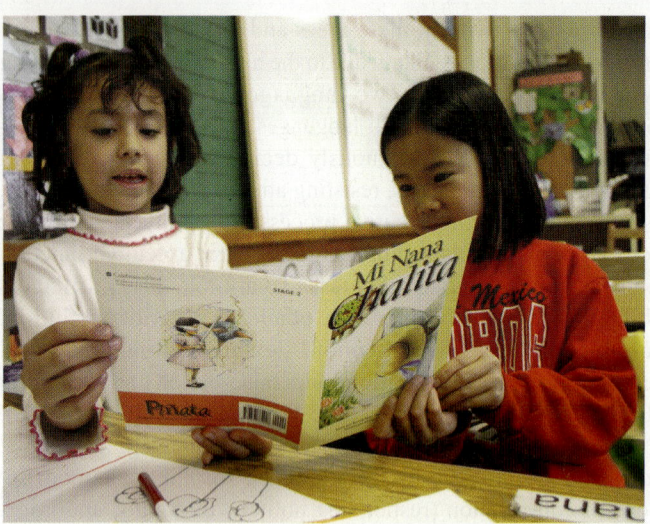

The child on the left, a native Spanish speaker, benefits from an English–Spanish bilingual classroom, which sustains her native language while she masters English. And her native-English-speaking classmate has the opportunity to begin learning Spanish!

instruction as soon as possible (Wright, 2013). Yet in classrooms where both languages are integrated into the curriculum, minority children are more involved in learning and acquire the second language more easily—gains that result in better academic achievement (Guglielmi, 2008). In contrast, when teachers speak only in a language that children can barely understand, minority children display frustration, boredom, and escalating academic difficulties (Paradis, Genesee, & Crago, 2011). This downward spiral in achievement is greatest in high-poverty schools, where resources to support the needs of language-minority children are scarce.

Supporters of U.S. English-only education often point to the success of Canadian language immersion programs, in which classroom lessons are conducted in the second language. But Canadian parents enroll their children in immersion classrooms voluntarily, and students in those programs are native speakers of the dominant language of their region. Furthermore, teaching in the child's native language is merely delayed, not ruled out. For U.S. non-English-speaking minority children, whose native languages are not valued by the larger society, a different strategy is necessary—one that promotes children's native-language and -literacy skills while they learn English.

Ask yourself

CONNECT How can bilingual education promote ethnic minority children's cognitive and academic development?

APPLY After soccer practice, 10-year-old Shana remarked, "I'm wiped out!" Megan, her 5-year-old sister, responded, "What did'ya wipe out?" Explain Shana's and Megan's different understandings.

REFLECT Considering research on bilingualism, what changes would you make in your second-language learning, and why?

 Learning in School

9.15 Describe the influence of educational philosophies on children's motivation and academic achievement.

9.16 Discuss the role of teacher–student interaction and grouping practices in academic achievement.

9.17 Under what conditions is placement of children with learning difficulties in regular classrooms successful?

9.18 Describe the characteristics of gifted children and current efforts to meet their educational needs.

9.19 How well-educated are U.S. children compared with children in other industrialized nations?

Evidence cited throughout this chapter indicates that schools are vital forces in children's cognitive development. How do schools exert such a powerful influence? Research looking at schools as complex social systems, varying in educational philosophies, teacher–student relationships, and larger cultural context, provides important insights. As you read about these topics, refer to Applying What We Know on the following page, which summarizes characteristics of high-quality education in elementary school.

Educational Philosophies

Teachers' educational philosophies play a major role in children's learning. Two philosophical approaches have received most research attention. They differ in what children are taught, the way they are believed to learn, and how their progress is evaluated.

Traditional versus Constructivist Classrooms. In a **traditional classroom,** the teacher is the sole authority for knowledge, rules, and decision making. Students are relatively passive—listening, responding when called on, and completing teacher-assigned tasks. Their progress is evaluated by how well they keep pace with a uniform set of standards for their grade.

A **constructivist classroom,** in contrast, encourages students to *construct* their own knowledge. Although constructivist approaches vary, many are grounded in Piaget's theory, which views children as active agents who reflect on and coordinate their own thoughts rather than absorbing those of others. A glance inside a constructivist classroom reveals richly equipped learning centers, small groups and individuals solving self-chosen problems, and a teacher who guides and supports in response to children's needs. Students are evaluated by considering their progress in relation to their own prior development.

In the United States, the pendulum has swung back and forth between these two views. In the 1960s and early 1970s, constructivist classrooms gained in popularity. Then, as concern arose over the academic progress of children and youths, classrooms returned to traditional instruction—a style that has become increasingly pronounced as a result of the 2001 No Child Left Behind Act, followed by its 2015 replacement, the Every Child

Applying what we Know

Signs of High-Quality Education in Elementary School

CLASSROOM CHARACTERISTICS	SIGNS OF QUALITY
Physical setting	Space is divided into richly equipped activity centers—for reading, writing, playing math or language games, exploring science, working on construction projects, using computers, and engaging in other academic pursuits. Spaces are used flexibly for individual and small-group activities and whole-class gatherings.
Curriculum	The curriculum helps children both achieve academic standards and make sense of their learning. Subjects are integrated so that children apply knowledge in one area to others. The curriculum is implemented through activities responsive to children's interests, ideas, and everyday lives, including their cultural backgrounds.
Daily activities	Teachers provide challenging activities that include opportunities for small-group and independent work. Groupings vary in size and makeup of children, depending on the activity and on children's learning needs. Teachers encourage cooperative learning and guide children in attaining it.
Interactions between teachers and children	Teachers foster each child's progress and use intellectually engaging strategies, including posing problems, asking thought-provoking questions, discussing ideas, and adding complexity to tasks. They also demonstrate, explain, coach, and assist in other ways, depending on each child's learning needs.
Evaluations of progress	Teachers regularly evaluate children's progress through written observations and work samples, which they use to enhance and individualize teaching. They help children reflect on their work and decide how to improve it. They also seek information and perspectives from parents on how well children are learning and include parents' views in evaluations.
Relationship with parents	Teachers forge partnerships with parents. They hold periodic conferences and encourage parents to visit the classroom anytime, to observe and volunteer.

Source: Copple & Bredekamp, 2009.

Succeeds Act. These policies, by placing heavy pressure on teachers and school administrators to improve achievement test scores, have narrowed the curricular focus in many schools to preparing students to take such tests (Kew et al., 2012).

Although older elementary school children in traditional classrooms have a slight edge in achievement test scores, constructivist settings are associated with many other benefits—gains in critical thinking, greater social and moral maturity, and more positive attitudes toward school (DeVries, 2001; Rathunde & Csikszentmihalyi, 2005; Walberg, 1986). And as noted in Chapter 7, when teacher-directed instruction is emphasized in preschool and kindergarten, it actually undermines motivation and achievement, especially in low-SES children.

Recent Philosophical Directions. Recent approaches to education, grounded in Vygotsky's sociocultural theory, capitalize on the rich social context of the classroom to spur children's learning. In these **social-constructivist classrooms,** children participate in a wide range of challenging activities with teachers and peers, with whom they jointly construct understandings. As children acquire knowledge and strategies through working together, they become competent, contributing members of their classroom community and advance in cognitive and social development (Bodrova & Leong, 2007; Lourenço, 2012). Vygotsky's emphasis on the social origins of complex mental activities has inspired the following educational themes:

- *Teachers and children as partners in learning.* A classroom rich in both teacher–child and child–child collaboration transfers culturally valued ways of thinking to children.

- *Experiences with many types of symbolic communication in meaningful activities.* As children master reading, writing, and mathematics, they become aware of their culture's communication systems, reflect on their own thinking, and bring it under voluntary control. Can you identify research presented earlier in this chapter that supports this theme?

- *Teaching adapted to each child's zone of proximal development.* Assistance that both responds to current understandings and encourages children to take the next step helps ensure that each child makes the best progress possible.

According to Vygotsky, besides teachers, more expert peers can spur children's learning, as long as they adjust the help they provide to fit the less mature child's zone of proximal development. Consistent with this idea, mounting evidence confirms that peer collaboration promotes development only under certain conditions. A crucial factor is **cooperative learning,** in which small groups of classmates work toward common goals—by considering one another's ideas, appropriately challenging one another, providing sufficient explanations to correct misunderstandings, and resolving differences of opinion on the basis of reasons and evidence. When teachers explain, model, and have children role-play how to work together effectively, cooperative

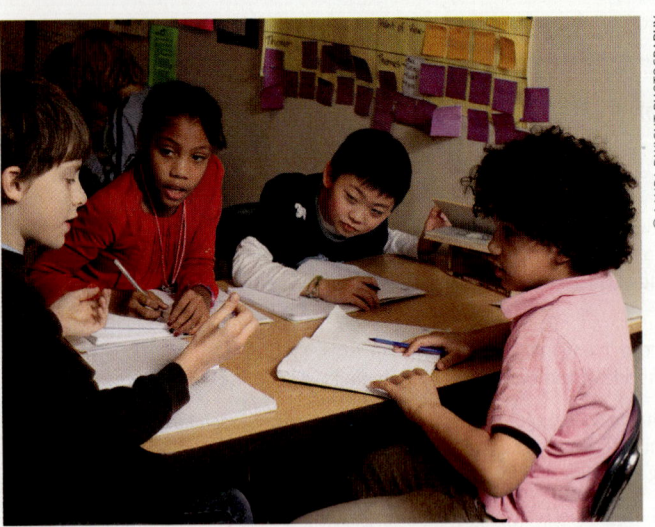

Fourth graders work together to complete an assignment. Cooperative learning enhances children's complex reasoning skills as well as their enjoyment of learning and academic achievement.

learning among heterogeneous peers results in more complex reasoning, greater enjoyment of learning, and achievement gains across a wide range of subjects (Jadallah et al., 2011; Webb et al., 2008).

Teacher–Student Interaction and Grouping Practices

Elementary school students describe good teachers as caring, helpful, and stimulating—behaviors associated with gains in motivation, achievement, and positive peer relations (Hughes & Kwok, 2006, 2007; Hughes, Zhang, & Hill, 2006; O'Connor & McCartney, 2007). But too many U.S. teachers—especially those in schools with many students from low-income families—emphasize repetitive drill over higher-level thinking, such as grappling with ideas and applying knowledge to new situations (Valli, Croninger, & Buese, 2012). This focus on low-level skills becomes increasingly pronounced over the school year as state-mandated achievement testing draws nearer.

Of course, teachers do not interact in the same way with all children. Well-behaved, high-achieving students typically get more encouragement and praise, whereas unruly students have more conflicts with teachers and receive more criticism from them (Henricsson & Rydell, 2004). Warm, low-conflict teacher–student relationships have an especially strong impact on the academic self-esteem, achievement, and social behavior of low-SES minority students and other children at risk for learning difficulties (Hughes, 2011; Hughes et al., 2012; Spilt et al., 2012). But overall, higher-SES students—who tend to be higher-achieving and to have fewer learning and behavior problems—have more sensitive and supportive relationships with teachers (Jerome, Hamre, & Pianta, 2008).

Unfortunately, once teachers' attitudes toward students are established, they can become more extreme than is warranted by students' behavior. Of special concern are **educational self-fulfilling prophecies:** Children may adopt teachers' positive or negative views and start to live up to them. This effect is especially strong when teachers emphasize competition and publicly compare children, regularly favoring the best students (Weinstein, 2002).

Teacher expectations have a greater impact on low-achieving than high-achieving students (McKown, Gregory, & Weinstein, 2010). When a teacher is critical, high achievers can fall back on their history of success. Low-achieving students' sensitivity to self-fulfilling prophecies can be beneficial when teachers believe in them. But biased teacher judgments are usually slanted in a negative direction. In one study, African-American and Hispanic elementary school students taught by high-bias teachers (who expected them to do poorly) showed substantially lower end-of-year achievement than their counterparts taught by low-bias teachers (McKown & Weinstein, 2008). Recall our discussion of *stereotype threat*. A child in the position of confirming a negative stereotype may respond with especially intense anxiety and reduced motivation, amplifying a negative self-fulfilling prophecy.

In many schools, students are assigned to *homogeneous* groups or classes in which children of similar ability levels are taught together. Homogeneous grouping can be a potent source of self-fulfilling prophecies. Low-group students—who as early as first grade are more likely to be low-SES, minority, and male—get more drill on basic facts and skills, engage in less discussion, and progress at a slower pace. Gradually, they decline in self-esteem and motivation and fall further behind in achievement (Lleras & Rangel, 2009; Worthy, Hungerford-Kresser, & Hampton, 2009).

Unfortunately, widespread SES and ethnic segregation in U.S. schools consigns large numbers of low-SES, minority students to a form of schoolwide homogeneous grouping. Refer to the Social Issues: Education box on the following page to find out how magnet schools foster heterogeneous learning contexts, thereby reducing achievement differences between SES and ethnic groups.

Teaching Children with Special Needs

We have seen that effective teachers flexibly adjust their teaching strategies to accommodate students with a wide range of characteristics. These adjustments are especially challenging at the very low and high ends of the ability distribution. How do schools serve children with special learning needs?

Children with Learning Difficulties.
U.S. legislation mandates that schools place children who require special supports for learning in the "least restrictive" (as close to normal as possible) environments that meet their educational needs. In **inclusive classrooms,** students with learning difficulties learn alongside typical students in the regular educational setting for all or part of the school day—a practice designed to prepare them for participation in society and to combat prejudices against individuals

Social Issues: Education

Magnet Schools: Equal Access to High-Quality Education

Each school-day morning, Emma leaves her affluent suburban neighborhood, riding a school bus 20 miles to a magnet school in an impoverished, mostly Hispanic inner-city neighborhood. In her fifth-grade class, she settles into a science project with her friend, Maricela, who lives in the local neighborhood. For the first hour of the day, the children use a thermometer, ice water, and a stopwatch to determine which of several materials is the best insulator, recording and graphing their data. Throughout the school, which specializes in innovative math and science teaching, students diverse in SES and ethnicity learn side-by-side.

Despite the 1954 U.S. Supreme Court *Brown v. Board of Education* decision ordering schools to desegregate, school integration receded over the 1990s as federal courts canceled their integration orders and returned this authority to states and cities. Since 2000, the racial divide in American education has improved only modestly (Stroub & Richards, 2013). When minority students attend ethnically mixed schools, they typically do so with other minorities.

U.S. schools in inner-city, low-income neighborhoods are vastly disadvantaged in funding and therefore in educational opportunities, largely because public education is primarily supported by local property taxes. Consequently, in inner-city segregated neighborhoods, dilapidated school buildings; inexperienced teachers; outdated, poor-quality educational resources; and school cultures that fail to encourage strong teaching are widespread (Condron, 2013). The negative impact on student achievement is severe.

Magnet schools offer a solution. In addition to the usual curriculum, they emphasize a specific area of interest—such as performing arts, math and science, or technology. Families outside the school neighborhood are attracted to magnet schools (hence the name) by their rich academic offerings. Often magnets are located in low-income, minority areas, where they serve the neighborhood student population. Other students, who apply and are admitted by lottery, are bussed in—many from well-to-do city and suburban neighborhoods. In another model, all students—including those in the surrounding neighborhood—must apply. In either case, magnet schools are voluntarily desegregated.

Do magnet schools enhance minority student achievement? A Connecticut study comparing students enrolled in magnet schools with those whose lottery numbers were not drawn and who therefore attended other city schools confirmed that the magnet students showed greater gains in reading and math achievement over a two-year period (Bifulco, Cobb, & Bell, 2009). These outcomes were strongest for low-SES, ethnic minority students.

By high school, the higher-achieving peer environments of ethnically diverse schools encourage more students to pursue higher education (Franklin, 2012). In sum, magnet schools are a promising approach to overcoming the negative forces of SES and ethnic isolation in American schools.

A magnet-school teacher receives hugs from her first-grade students at a party celebrating news that she is a finalist for Texas Elementary Teacher of the Year. Magnet schools typically attract students diverse in ethnicity and SES because of their rich academic offerings and innovative teaching.

---

with disabilities. Largely as the result of parental pressures, an increasing number of students experience *full inclusion*—full-time placement in regular classrooms.

Students with *mild intellectual disability* are sometimes integrated into inclusive classrooms. Typically, their IQs fall between 55 and 70, and they also show problems in adaptive behavior, or skills of everyday living (American Psychiatric Association, 2013). But the largest number designated for inclusion—5 to 10 percent of school-age children—have **learning disabilities**, great difficulty with one or more aspects of learning, usually reading. As a result, their achievement is considerably behind what would be expected on the basis of their IQ. Often these deficits express themselves in other ways—for example, as deficiencies in processing speed, attention, and working memory, which depress both intelligence and achievement test scores (Cornoldi et al., 2014). The problems of students with learning disabilities cannot be traced to any obvious physical or emotional difficulty or to environmental disadvantage. Instead, deficits in brain functioning are involved (Waber, 2010). In many instances, the cause is unknown.

Although some students benefit academically from inclusion, many do not. Achievement gains depend on both the severity of the disability and the support services available (Downing, 2010). Furthermore, children with disabilities are often rejected by regular-classroom peers. Students with intellectual disability are overwhelmed by the social skills of their classmates; they cannot interact adeptly in a conversation or game. And the processing deficits of some students with learning disabilities lead

In this inclusive first-grade classroom, a teacher encourages special-needs students' active participation. They are likely to do well if they receive support from a special education teacher and if their regular classroom teacher minimizes comparisons and promotes positive peer relations.

to problems in social awareness and responsiveness (Nowicki, Brown, & Stepien, 2014).

Does this mean that students with special needs cannot be served in regular classrooms? Not necessarily. Often these children do best when they receive instruction in a resource room for part of the day and in the regular classroom for the remainder (McLeskey & Waldron, 2011). In the resource room, a special education teacher works with students on an individual and small-group basis. Then, depending on their progress, children join typically developing classmates for different subjects and amounts of time.

Special steps must to be taken to promote peer relations in inclusive classrooms. Peer tutoring experiences in which teachers guide typical students in supporting the academic progress of classmates with learning difficulties lead to friendly interaction, improved peer acceptance, and achievement gains (Mastropieri et al., 2013). And when teachers prepare their class for the arrival of a student with special needs, inclusion may foster emotional sensitivity and prosocial behavior among regular classmates.

Gifted Children. Some children are **gifted,** displaying exceptional intellectual strengths. An IQ score above 130 is the standard definition of giftedness based on intelligence test performance (Pfeiffer & Yermish, 2014). High-IQ children have an exceptional capacity to solve challenging academic problems. Yet recognition that intelligence tests do not sample the entire range of human mental skills has led to an expanded conception of giftedness.

Creativity and Talent. **Creativity** is the ability to produce work that is *original* yet *appropriate*—something others have not thought of that is useful in some way (Kaufman & Sternberg, 2007). A child with high potential for creativity can be designated as gifted. Tests of creative capacity tap **divergent thinking**—the generation of multiple and unusual possibilities when faced with a task or problem. Divergent thinking contrasts sharply with **convergent thinking,** which involves arriving at a single correct answer and is emphasized on intelligence tests (Guilford, 1985).

Because highly creative children (like high-IQ children) are often better at some tasks than others, a variety of tests of divergent thinking are available (Runco, 1992; Torrance, 1988). A verbal measure might ask children to name uses for common objects (such as a newspaper). A figural measure might ask them to create drawings based on a circular motif (see Figure 9.9). A "real-world problem" measure requires students to suggest solutions to everyday problems. Responses can be scored for the number of ideas generated and their originality.

Yet critics point out that these measures are poor predictors of creative accomplishment in everyday life because they tap only one of the complex cognitive contributions to creativity (Plucker & Makel, 2010). Also involved are defining new and important problems, evaluating divergent ideas, choosing the most promising, and calling on relevant knowledge to understand and solve problems (Lubart, Georgsdottir, & Besançon, 2009).

Consider these ingredients, and you will see why people usually demonstrate creativity in only one or a few related areas. Partly for this reason, definitions of giftedness have been extended to include **talent**—outstanding performance in a specific field. Case studies reveal that excellence in such endeavors as creative writing, mathematics, science, music, visual arts, athletics, and leadership has roots in specialized interests and skills that first appear in childhood (Moran & Gardner, 2006). Highly

FIGURE 9.9 Responses of an 8-year-old who scored high on a figural measure of divergent thinking. This child was asked to make as many pictures as she could from the circles on the page. The titles she gave her drawings, from left to right, are as follows: "Dracula," "one-eyed monster," "pumpkin," "Hula-Hoop," "poster," "wheelchair," "earth," "stop-light," "planet," "movie camera," "sad face," "picture," "beach ball," "the letter O," "car," "glasses." Tests of divergent thinking tap only one of the complex cognitive contributions to creativity. (Reprinted by permission of Laura E. Berk.)

talented children are biologically prepared to master their domain of interest, and they display a passion for doing so.

But talent must be nurtured. Studies of the backgrounds of talented children and highly accomplished adults often reveal warm, sensitive parents who provide a stimulating home life, are devoted to developing their child's abilities, and provide models of hard work. These parents are reasonably demanding but not overly ambitious (Winner, 2003). They arrange for caring teachers while the child is young and for more rigorous master teachers as the child's talent develops.

Although most are well-adjusted, many gifted children and adolescents experience social isolation, partly because their highly driven, independent styles leave them out of step with peers and partly because they enjoy solitude, which is necessary to develop their talents (Pfeiffer & Yermish, 2014). Still, gifted children desire gratifying peer relationships, and some—more often girls than boys—try to become better-liked by hiding their abilities (Reis, 2004).

Finally, whereas many talented youths become experts in their fields, few become highly creative. Rapidly mastering an existing field requires different skills than innovating in that field (Moran & Gardner, 2006). The world, however, needs both experts and creators.

Educating the Gifted. Debate about the effectiveness of school programs for the gifted typically focuses on factors irrelevant to giftedness—whether to provide enrichment in regular classrooms, pull children out for special instruction (the most common practice), or advance brighter students to a higher grade. Overall, gifted children fare well within each of these models, as long as special activities promote problem solving, critical thinking, and creativity (Guignard & Lubart, 2006).

Gardner's theory of multiple intelligences has inspired several model programs that provide enrichment to all students in diverse disciplines. Meaningful activities, each tapping a specific intelligence or set of intelligences, serve as contexts for assessing strengths and weaknesses and, on that basis, teaching new knowledge and original thinking (Gardner, 2000; Hoerr, 2004). For example, linguistic intelligence might be fostered through storytelling or playwriting; spatial intelligence through drawing, sculpting, or taking apart and reassembling objects; and kinesthetic intelligence through dance or pantomime.

Evidence is still needed on how well these programs nurture children's talents and creativity. But they have already succeeded in one way—by highlighting the strengths of some students who previously had been considered unexceptional or even at risk for school failure (Ford, 2012). Consequently, they may be especially useful in identifying talented low-SES, ethnic minority children, who are underrepresented in school programs for the gifted.

How Well-Educated Are U.S. Children?

Our discussion of schooling has largely focused on how teachers can support the education of children. Yet many factors—both within and outside schools—affect children's learning. Societal

	Country	Average Math Achievement Score
High-Performing Nations	China (Shanghai)	613
	Singapore	573
	China (Hong Kong)	561
	Taiwan	560
	Korea	554
	China (Macao)	538
	Japan	536
	Switzerland	531
	Netherlands	523
	Estonia	521
	Finland	519
	Canada	518
	Poland	518
	Belgium	515
	Germany	514
Intermediate-Performing Nations	Austria	506
	Australia	504
	Ireland	501
	Slovenia	501
	Denmark	500
	New Zealand	500
	Czech Republic	499
	France	495
International Average = 494	United Kingdom	494
	Iceland	493
	Luxembourg	490
	Norway	489
	Portugal	487
	Italy	485
	Spain	484
	Russian Federation	482
	United States	**481**
	Sweden	478
	Hungary	477
Low-Performing Nations	Israel	466
	Greece	453
	Turkey	448
	Romania	445

FIGURE 9.10 Average mathematics scores of 15-year-olds by country. The Programme for International Student Assessment measured achievement in many nations around the world. In recent comparisons of countries' performance, the United States performed below the international average in math; in reading and science, its performance was about average. (Adapted from Programme for International Student Assessment, 2012.)

values, school resources, quality of teaching, and parental encouragement all play important roles. These multiple influences are especially apparent when schooling is examined in cross-cultural perspective.

In international studies of reading, mathematics, and science achievement, young people in China, Korea, and Japan are consistently top performers. Among Western nations, Canada, Finland, the Netherlands, and Switzerland are also in the top tier. But U.S. students typically perform at or below the international averages (see Figure 9.10) (Programme for International Student Assessment, 2012).

Why do U.S. students fall behind in academic accomplishment? According to international comparisons, instruction in the United States is less challenging, more focused on absorbing facts, and less focused on high-level reasoning and critical thinking than in other countries. A growing number of experts believe that U.S. educational policies directed at getting students to meet targeted goals on achievement tests by holding schools and teachers accountable for student performance have contributed to these trends (Darling-Hammond, 2010; Kew et al., 2012).

Furthermore, countries with large socioeconomic inequalities (such as the United States) rank lower in achievement, in part because low-SES children tend to live in less favorable family and neighborhood contexts (Condron, 2013). But the United States is also far less equitable than top-achieving countries in the quality of education it provides its low-SES and ethnic minority students. U.S. teachers, for example, vary much more in training, salaries, and teaching conditions.

Finland is a case in point. Its nationally mandated curricula, teaching practices, and assessments are aimed at cultivating initiative, problem solving, and creativity—vital abilities needed for success in the twenty-first century. Finnish teachers are highly trained: They must complete several years of graduate-level education at government expense (Ripley, 2013). And Finnish education is grounded in equal opportunity for all—a policy that has nearly eliminated SES variations in achievement, despite an influx of immigrant students from low-income families into Finnish schools over the two past decades.

In-depth research on learning environments in Asian nations, such as Japan, Korea, and Taiwan, also highlights social forces that foster strong student learning. Among these is cultural valuing of effort. Whereas American parents and teachers tend to regard native ability as the key to academic success, Japanese, Korean, and Taiwanese parents and teachers believe that all children can succeed academically as long as they try hard. Asian children, influenced by interdependent values, typically view striving to achieve as a moral obligation—part of their responsibility to family and community (Hau & Ho, 2010).

As in Finland, all students in Japan, Korea, and Taiwan receive the same nationally mandated, high-quality instruction, delivered by teachers who are well-prepared, highly respected in their society, and far better paid than U.S. teachers (Kang & Hong, 2008; U.S. Department of Education, 2015).

The Finnish and Asian examples underscore the need for American families, schools, and the larger society to work together to upgrade education. Recommended strategies, verified by research, include:

- supporting parents in attaining economic security, creating stimulating home learning environments, monitoring their children's academic progress, and communicating often with teachers

- investing in high-quality preschool education, so every child arrives at school ready to learn

- strengthening teacher education

- providing intellectually challenging, relevant instruction with real-world applications

- vigorously pursuing school improvements that reduce the large inequities in quality of education between SES and ethnic groups.

A Finnish teacher passes out materials to her second-grade students. Finland's teachers are highly trained, and their education system—designed to cultivate initiative, problem solving, and creativity in all students—has nearly eliminated SES variations in achievement.

Ask yourself

CONNECT Review research on child-rearing styles on pages 282–283 in Chapter 8. What style do gifted children who realize their potential typically experience? Explain.

APPLY Sandy wonders why her daughter Mira's teacher often has students work on assignments in small, cooperative groups. Explain the benefits of this approach to Sandy.

REFLECT What grouping practices were used in your elementary education—homogeneous, heterogeneous, or a combination? What impact do you think those practices had on your motivation and achievement?

Summary

PHYSICAL DEVELOPMENT

Body Growth (p. 294)

9.1 *Describe major trends in body growth during middle childhood.*

- During middle childhood, physical growth continues at a slow, regular pace. Bones lengthen and broaden, and permanent teeth replace the primary teeth. By age 9, girls overtake boys in physical size.

Common Health Problems (p. 295)

9.2 *Describe the causes and consequences of serious nutritional problems in middle childhood, giving special attention to obesity.*

- Many poverty-stricken children suffer from serious and prolonged malnutrition, which can permanently impair physical and mental development.

- Overweight and **obesity** have increased dramatically in both industrialized and developing nations, with large gains in the United States. Although heredity contributes to obesity, parental feeding practices, maladaptive eating habits, reduced sleep, lack of exercise, and unhealthy diets are powerful influences. Obesity leads to serious physical health and adjustment problems.

- The most effective approaches to treating childhood obesity are family-based interventions aimed at changing parents' and children's eating patterns and lifestyles. Schools can help by serving healthier meals and ensuring regular physical activity.

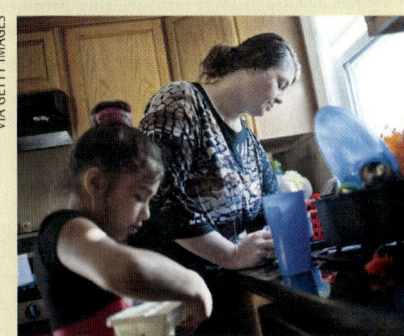

9.3 *What vision and hearing problems are common in middle childhood?*

- The most common vision problem, myopia, is influenced by heredity, early biological trauma, and time spent doing close work. It is one of the few health conditions that increases with SES.

- Although ear infections decline during the school years, many low-SES children experience some hearing loss because of repeated untreated middle-ear infections.

9.4 *What factors contribute to illness during the school years, and how can these health problems be reduced?*

- Children experience more illnesses during the first two years of elementary school than later because of exposure to sick children and an immature immune system.

- The most common cause of school absence and childhood hospitalization is asthma. It occurs more often among African-American and poverty-stricken children, as well as obese children.

- Children with severe chronic illnesses are at risk for academic, emotional, and social difficulties, but positive family relationships improve adjustment.

9.5 *Describe changes in the occurrence of unintentional injuries in middle childhood, and cite effective interventions.*

- Unintentional injuries increase from middle childhood into adolescence, especially for boys. Auto and bicycle accidents account for most of the rise.

- Effective school-based injury-prevention programs use modeling, rehearsal, and rewards for acquiring safety skills.

Motor Development and Play (p. 299)

9.6 *Cite major changes in motor development and play during middle childhood.*

- Gains in flexibility, balance, agility, and force, along with more efficient information processing, contribute to school-age children's improved gross-motor performance.

- Fine-motor development also improves. Handwriting becomes more legible, and children's drawings increase in organization, detail, and representation of depth.

- Although girls outperform boys in fine-motor skills, boys outperform girls in all gross-motor skills except those requiring balance and agility. Parents' higher expectations for boys' athletic performance play a large role.

- Games with rules become common during the school years, contributing to emotional and social development. Children, especially boys, also engage in **rough-and-tumble play**—friendly play-fighting that helps establish a **dominance hierarchy** among group members.

- Most U.S. school-age children are not active enough for good health, in part because of cutbacks in recess and physical education.

COGNITIVE DEVELOPMENT

Piaget's Theory: The Concrete Operational Stage (p. 304)

9.7 *What are the major characteristics of concrete operational thought?*

- In the **concrete operational stage**, children's thought becomes more logical, flexible, and organized. Mastery of conservation demonstrates decentration and **reversibility** in thinking.

- School-age children are also better at hierarchical classification and **seriation**, including **transitive inference**. Their spatial reasoning improves, evident in their ability to create **cognitive maps** representing familiar large-scale spaces.

- Concrete operational thought is limited in that children do not come up with general logical principles. They master concrete operational tasks step by step.

9.8 *Discuss follow-up research on concrete operational thought.*

- Specific cultural practices, especially those associated with schooling, promote children's mastery of Piagetian tasks.

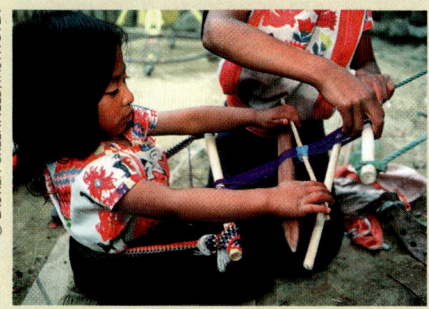

- Some researchers attribute the gradual development of operational thought to expansion of information-processing capacity. Case's neo-Piagetian theory proposes that with brain development and practice, cognitive schemes become more automatic, freeing up space in working memory for combining old schemes and generating new ones that are integrated into improved, broadly applicable representations.

CHAPTER 9 Physical and Cognitive Development in Middle Childhood

Information Processing (p. 307)

9.9 *Describe gains in executive function and memory in middle childhood, along with factors that influence children's progress.*

- As the prefrontal cortex continues to develop, children make great strides in executive function, enabling them to handle increasingly complex tasks that require integration of working memory, inhibition, and flexible shifting of attention. Planning on multistep tasks also improves.

- Heredity and environmental factors, including home and school experiences, combine to influence children's executive-function skills. Deficits in executive function underlie symptoms of **attention-deficit hyperactivity disorder (ADHD).**

- Memory strategies also improve. **Rehearsal** appears first, followed by **organization** and then **elaboration.** With age, children combine memory strategies.

- Development of children's general knowledge base, or semantic memory, facilitates strategic memory processing, as does their motivation to use what they know. Societal modernization is broadly associated with cognitive performance, including on memory tasks.

9.10 *Describe the school-age child's theory of mind and capacity to engage in self-regulation.*

- School-age children regard the mind as an active, constructive agent, yielding a better understanding of cognitive processes, including effective memory strategies, mental inference, and second-order false belief, which requires **recursive thought. Cognitive self-regulation** develops gradually, improving with adult instruction in strategy use.

9.11 *Discuss current perspectives on teaching reading and mathematics to elementary school children.*

- Skilled reading draws on all aspects of the information-processing system. A combination of **whole language** and **phonics** is most effective for teaching beginning reading. Teaching that blends practice in basic skills with conceptual understanding also is best in mathematics.

Individual Differences in Mental Development (p. 314)

9.12 *Describe major approaches to defining and measuring intelligence.*

- In middle childhood, IQ becomes more stable and correlates moderately with academic achievement. Most intelligence tests yield an overall score as well as scores for separate intellectual factors. Processing speed and executive function predict IQ.

- Sternberg's **triarchic theory of successful intelligence** identifies three broad, interacting intelligences: analytical intelligence (information-processing skills), creative intelligence (capacity to solve novel problems), and practical intelligence (application of intellectual skills in everyday situations).

- Gardner's **theory of multiple intelligences** identifies at least eight distinct mental abilities. It has stimulated efforts to define, measure, and foster emotional intelligence.

9.13 *Describe evidence indicating that both heredity and environment contribute to intelligence.*

- Heritability estimates and adoption research indicate that intelligence is a product of both heredity and environment. Adoption studies suggest that environmental factors underlie the black–white IQ gap. The **Flynn effect,** steady generational changes in IQ in many nations, is closely associated with extent of societal modernization.

- IQ scores are affected by culturally influenced language communication styles, knowledge, and amount of time spent in school. **Stereotype threat** triggers anxiety that interferes with test performance. **Dynamic assessment** helps many minority children perform more competently on mental tests.

Language Development (p. 322)

9.14 *Describe changes in school-age children's vocabulary, grammar, and pragmatics, and cite the advantages of bilingualism for development.*

- Language awareness contributes to language progress. School-age children have a more precise and flexible understanding of word meanings and use more complex grammatical constructions and conversational strategies. Narratives increase in organization, detail, and expressiveness.

- Mastery of a second language must begin in childhood for full proficiency to occur. Bilingualism has positive consequences for executive function, various other cognitive skills, and aspects of language awareness.

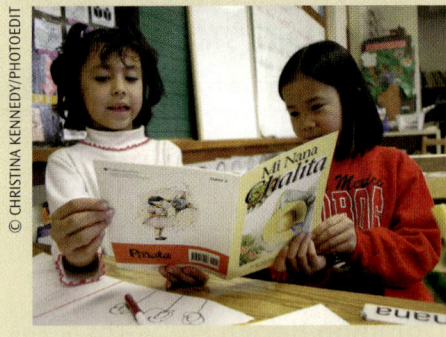

Learning in School (p. 324)

9.15 *Describe the influence of educational philosophies on children's motivation and academic achievement.*

- Older students in **traditional classrooms** have a slight edge in achievement test scores over those in **constructivist classrooms,** who gain in critical thinking, social and moral maturity, and positive attitudes toward school.

- Students in **social-constructivist classrooms** benefit from working collaboratively in meaningful activities and from teaching adapted to each child's zone of proximal development. Children benefit from teacher support for **cooperative learning** with peers, which promotes complex reasoning and achievement gains.

9.16 *Discuss the role of teacher–student interaction and grouping practices in academic achievement.*

- Caring, helpful, and stimulating teaching fosters children's motivation, achievement, and peer relations. **Educational self-fulfilling prophecies** have a greater impact on low than high achievers and are especially likely to occur in classrooms that emphasize competition and public evaluation. Homogeneous grouping can induce self-fulfilling prophecies in low-group students, who decline in self-esteem and achievement.

9.17 Under what conditions is placement of children with learning difficulties in regular classrooms successful?

- The success of **inclusive classrooms** for students with mild intellectual disability and **learning disabilities** depends on meeting individual learning needs and promoting positive peer relations.

9.18 Describe the characteristics of gifted children and current efforts to meet their educational needs.

- **Giftedness** includes high IQ, **creativity,** and **talent.** Tests of creativity that tap **divergent thinking** rather than **convergent thinking** focus on only one of the ingredients of creativity. Highly talented children generally have parents and teachers who nurture their exceptional abilities.

9.19 How well-educated are U.S. children compared with children in other industrialized nations?

- In international studies, U.S. students typically perform at or below international averages. Compared with education in top-achieving nations, education in the United States is less focused on high-level reasoning and critical thinking, and less equitable across SES groups.

Important Terms and Concepts

attention-deficit hyperactivity disorder (ADHD) (p. 309)
cognitive maps (p. 304)
cognitive self-regulation (p. 312)
concrete operational stage (p. 304)
constructivist classroom (p. 324)
convergent thinking (p. 328)
cooperative learning (p. 325)
creativity (p. 328)
divergent thinking (p. 328)
dominance hierarchy (p. 302)
dynamic assessment (pp. 320–321)

educational self-fulfilling prophecies (p. 326)
elaboration (p. 310)
Flynn effect (p. 319)
gifted (p. 328)
inclusive classrooms (p. 326)
learning disabilities (p. 327)
obesity (p. 295)
organization (p. 310)
phonics approach (p. 313)
recursive thought (p. 312)
rehearsal (p. 310)
reversibility (p. 304)

rough-and-tumble play (p. 302)
seriation (p. 304)
social-constructivist classroom (p. 324)
stereotype threat (p. 320)
talent (p. 328)
theory of multiple intelligences (p. 316)
traditional classroom (p. 324)
transitive inference (p. 304)
triarchic theory of successful intelligence (p. 316)
whole-language approach (p. 313)

chapter 10

Emotional and Social Development in Middle Childhood

Having fled their war-torn homeland of Syria, school-age friends nestle together in a barren refugee camp in Jordan. In middle childhood, trust—mutual kindness and assistance—becomes a defining feature of friendship. For children experiencing the dislocation and losses of war, friends can serve as a source of resilience.

What's ahead in chapter 10

Erikson's Theory: Industry versus Inferiority

Self-Understanding
Self-Concept • Self-Esteem • Influences on Self-Esteem

Emotional Development
Self-Conscious Emotions • Emotional Understanding • Emotional Self-Regulation

Moral Development
Moral and Social-Conventional Understanding • Understanding Individual Rights • Culture and Moral Understanding • Understanding Diversity and Inequality

Peer Relations
Peer Groups • Friendships • Peer Acceptance

■ **BIOLOGY AND ENVIRONMENT** Bullies and Their Victims

Gender Typing
Gender-Stereotyped Beliefs • Gender Identity and Behavior

Family Influences
Parent–Child Relationships • Siblings • Only Children • Divorce • Blended Families • Maternal Employment and Dual-Earner Families

Some Common Problems of Development
Fears and Anxieties • Child Sexual Abuse • Fostering Resilience in Middle Childhood

■ **CULTURAL INFLUENCES** Impact of Ethnic and Political Violence on Children

■ **SOCIAL ISSUES: HEALTH** Children's Eyewitness Testimony

One afternoon as school dismissed, Joey urgently tapped his best friend Terry on the shoulder. "Gotta talk to you," Joey pleaded. "Everything was going great until I got that word—*porcupine*," Joey went on, referring to the fifth-grade spelling bee that day. "Just my luck! *P-o-r-k*, that's how I spelled it! I can't believe it. I *know* I'm one of the best spellers in our class, better than that stuck-up Belinda Brown. I knocked myself out studying those spelling lists. Then *she* got all the easy words. If I *had* to lose, why couldn't it be to a nice person?"

Joey's conversation reflects new emotional and social capacities. By entering the spelling bee, he shows *industriousness,* the energetic pursuit of meaningful achievement in his culture—a major change of middle childhood. Joey's social understanding has also expanded: He can size up strengths, weaknesses, and personality characteristics. Furthermore, friendship means something different to Joey than it did earlier: He counts on his best friend, Terry, for understanding and emotional support.

For an overview of the personality changes of middle childhood, we return to Erikson's theory. Then we look at children's views of themselves and of others, their moral understanding, and their peer relationships. Each increases in complexity as children reason more effectively and spend more time in school and with agemates.

Despite changing parent–child relationships, the family remains powerfully influential in middle childhood. Today, family structures are more diverse than ever before. Through Joey and his younger sister Lizzie's experiences with parental divorce, we will see that family functioning is far more important than family structure in ensuring children's well-being. Finally, we look at some common emotional problems of middle childhood. ●

Erikson's Theory: Industry versus Inferiority

10.1 What personality changes take place during Erikson's stage of industry versus inferiority?

According to Erikson (1950), children whose previous experiences have been positive enter middle childhood prepared to focus their energies on realistic accomplishment. Erikson believed that the combination of adult expectations and children's drive toward mastery sets the stage for the psychological conflict of middle childhood, **industry versus inferiority**, which is resolved positively when experiences lead children to develop a sense of competence at useful skills and tasks. In cultures everywhere, adults respond to children's improved physical and cognitive capacities by making new demands, and children are ready to benefit from those challenges.

In most of the world, the transition to middle childhood is marked by the beginning of formal schooling, where children discover their own and others' unique capacities, learn the value of division of labor, and develop a sense of moral commitment and responsibility. The danger at this stage is *inferiority,* reflected in the pessimism of children who lack confidence in their ability to do things well. This sense of inadequacy can develop when family life has not prepared children for school life or when teachers and peers destroy children's self-confidence with negative responses.

Erikson's sense of industry combines several developments of middle childhood: a positive but realistic self-concept, pride in accomplishment, moral responsibility, and cooperative participation with agemates. How do these aspects of self and social relationships change over the school years?

The industriousness of middle childhood involves responding to new expectations for realistic accomplishment. In the informal, encouraging atmosphere of this classroom in India, children come to view themselves as responsible, capable, and cooperative.

Self-Understanding

10.2 Describe school-age children's self-concept and self-esteem, and discuss factors that affect their achievement-related attributions.

In middle childhood, children begin to describe themselves in terms of psychological traits, compare their own characteristics with those of their peers, and speculate about the causes of their strengths and weaknesses. These transformations in self-understanding have a major impact on self-esteem.

Self-Concept

During the school years, children refine their self-concept, organizing their observations of behaviors and internal states into general dispositions. A major change takes place between ages 8 and 11, as the following self-description by a fourth grader illustrates:

> I'm pretty popular, at least with the girls who I spend time with, but not with the super-popular girls who think they are cooler than everyone else. With my friends, I know what it takes to be liked, so I'm nice to people and helpful and can keep secrets. . . . Sometimes, if I get in a bad mood I'll say something that can be a little mean and then I'm ashamed of myself. At school, I'm feeling pretty smart in certain subjects like language arts and social studies, someday I will probably get a job that depends on having good English skills. . . . But I'm feeling pretty dumb in math and science, especially when I see how well a lot of the other kids are doing. I now understand that I can be both smart and dumb, you aren't just one or the other. (Harter, 2012, p. 59).

Instead of specific behaviors, this child emphasizes competencies: "smart in certain subjects like language arts and social studies" and "having good English skills." She also describes her personality, mentioning both positive and negative traits: "helpful" and "can keep secrets" but sometimes "a little mean." Older school-age children are far less likely than younger children to describe themselves in extreme, all-or-none ways (Harter, 2012a).

These evaluative self-descriptions result from school-age children's frequent **social comparisons**—judgments of their appearance, abilities, and behavior in relation to those of others. Notice, in the introduction to this chapter, Joey's observation that he is "one of the best spellers" in his class. Similarly, our fourth grader's self-description mentions feeling "smart" at some subjects but not at others, especially when she sees "how well a lot of the other kids are doing." Whereas 4- to 6-year-olds can compare their own performance to that of a single peer, older children can compare multiple individuals, including themselves (Harter, 2012).

What factors account for these revisions in self-concept? Cognitive development affects the changing *structure* of the self. School-age children can better coordinate several aspects of a situation in reasoning about their physical world. Similarly, in the social realm, they combine typical experiences and behaviors into stable psychological dispositions, blend positive and negative characteristics, and compare their own characteristics with those of many peers.

The changing *content* of self-concept is a product of both cognitive capacities and feedback from others. Sociologist George Herbert Mead (1934) proposed that a well-organized psychological self emerges when children adopt a view of the self that resembles others' attitudes toward the child. Mead's ideas indicate that *perspective-taking skills*—in particular, an improved ability to infer what other people are thinking and to distinguish those viewpoints from one's own—are crucial for developing a self-concept based on personality traits. In Chapter 9, we saw that middle childhood brings the capacity for recursive thought, which enables school-age children to "read" others' messages more accurately and internalize their expectations. As they do so, they form an *ideal self* that they use to evaluate their real self. A large discrepancy between the two, as we will soon see, can undermine self-esteem.

Parental support for self-development continues to be vitally important. School-age children with a history of elaborative parent–child conversations about past experiences construct rich, positive narratives about the self and therefore have more complex, favorable, and coherent self-concepts (Baddeley & Singer, 2015). Children also look to more people beyond the family for information about themselves as they enter a wider range of settings in school and community. And self-descriptions now include frequent reference to social groups: "I'm a Boy Scout, a paper boy, and a Prairie City soccer player," said Joey. As children move into adolescence, although parents and other adults remain influential, self-concept is increasingly vested in feedback from close friends (Oosterwegel & Oppenheimer, 1993).

But recall that the content of self-concept varies from culture to culture. In earlier chapters, we noted that Asian parents stress harmonious interdependence, whereas Western parents emphasize independence and self-assertion. When asked to recall personally significant past experiences (their last birthday, a time their parent scolded them), U.S. school-age children gave longer accounts including more personal preferences, interests, skills, and opinions. Chinese children, in contrast, more often referred to social interactions and to others. Similarly, in their self-descriptions, U.S. children listed more personal attributes ("I'm smart," "I like hockey"), Chinese children more attributes involving group membership and relationships ("I'm in second grade," "My friends are crazy about me") (Wang, 2006; Wang, Shao, & Li, 2010).

Self-Esteem

Recall that most preschoolers have extremely high self-esteem. But as children enter school and receive much more feedback about how well they perform compared with their peers, self-esteem differentiates and also adjusts to a more realistic level.

To study school-age children's self-esteem, researchers ask them to indicate the extent to which statements such as "I'm good at reading" or "I'm usually the one chosen for games" are true of themselves. By age 6 to 7, children in diverse Western cultures have formed at least four broad self-evaluations: academic competence, social competence, physical/athletic competence, and physical appearance. Within these are more refined categories that become increasingly distinct with age (Marsh, 1990; Marsh & Ayotte, 2003; Van den Bergh & De Rycke, 2003). Furthermore, the capacity to view the self in terms of stable dispositions permits school-age children to combine their separate self-evaluations into a general psychological image of themselves—an overall sense of self-esteem (Harter, 2012). As a result, self-esteem takes on the hierarchical structure shown in Figure 10.1 on page 338.

Children attach greater importance to certain self-evaluations than to others. Although individual differences exist, during childhood and adolescence, perceived physical appearance correlates more strongly with overall self-worth than does any other self-esteem factor (O'Dea, 2012; Shapka & Keating, 2005). Emphasis on appearance—in the media, by parents and peers, and in society—has major implications for young people's overall satisfaction with themselves.

Self-esteem generally remains high during elementary school but becomes more realistic and nuanced as children evaluate themselves in various areas (Marsh, Craven, & Debus, 1998; Wigfield et al., 1997). These changes occur as children receive more competence-related feedback, as their performances are increasingly judged in relation to those of others, and as they become cognitively capable of social comparison (Harter, 2012a).

Influences on Self-Esteem

From middle childhood on, individual differences in self-esteem become increasingly stable (Trzesniewski, Donnellan, & Robins, 2003). And positive relationships among self-esteem, valuing of various activities, and success at those activities emerge and strengthen. Academic self-esteem predicts how important, useful, and enjoyable children judge school subjects to be, willingness to try hard, achievement, and eventual career choice (Denissen, Zarrett, & Eccles, 2007; Valentine, DuBois, & Cooper, 2004; Whitesell et al., 2009). Children with high social self-esteem are consistently better-liked by classmates (Jacobs et al., 2002). And as Chapter 9 revealed, sense of athletic competence is positively associated with investment in and performance at sports.

A profile of low self-esteem in all areas is linked to anxiety, depression, and increasing antisocial behavior (Kim & Cicchetti, 2006; Robins et al., 2001; Sowislo & Orth, 2013). What social influences might lead self-esteem to be high for some children and low for others?

Culture, Gender, and Ethnicity.
Cultural forces profoundly affect self-esteem. An especially strong emphasis on social comparison in school may explain why Chinese and Japanese children, despite their higher academic achievement, score lower than U.S. children in self-esteem—a difference that widens with age (Harter, 2012; Twenge & Crocker, 2002). At the same time, because their cultures value social harmony, Asian children tend to be reserved in positive self-judgments but generous in praise of others (Falbo et al., 1997).

FIGURE 10.1 Hierarchical structure of self-esteem in the mid-elementary school years. From their experiences in different settings, children form at least four separate self-esteems: academic competence, social competence, physical/athletic competence, and physical appearance. These differentiate into additional self-evaluations and combine to form a general sense of self-esteem.

Gender-stereotyped expectations also affect self-esteem. In one study, the more 5- to 8-year-old girls talked with friends about the way people look, watched TV shows focusing on physical appearance, and perceived their friends as valuing thinness, the greater their dissatisfaction with their physical self and the lower their overall self-esteem a year later (Dohnt & Tiggemann, 2006). In another investigation, being overweight was more strongly linked to negative body image for third-grade girls than for boys (Shriver et al., 2013). By the end of middle childhood, girls feel less confident than boys about their physical appearance and athletic abilities. With respect to academic self-esteem, boys, again, are somewhat advantaged: Whereas girls score higher in language arts self-esteem, boys have higher math and science self-esteem—even when children of equal skill levels are compared (Jacobs et al., 2002; Kurtz-Costes et al., 2008). At the same time, girls exceed boys in self-esteem dimensions of close friendship and social acceptance.

Compared with their European-American agemates, African-American children tend to have slightly higher self-esteem, possibly because of warm extended families and a stronger sense of ethnic pride (Gray-Little & Hafdahl, 2000). Consistent with this interpretation, African-American 7- to 10-year-olds randomly assigned to a 10-session, small-group program celebrating black family life and culture gained in self-esteem relative to agemates assigned to a no-intervention control (Okeke-Adeyanju et al., 2014). Finally, children and adolescents who attend schools or live in neighborhoods where their SES and ethnic groups are well-represented feel a stronger sense of belonging and have fewer self-esteem problems (Gray-Little & Carels, 1997).

Child-Rearing Practices.
School-age children with a strong sense of attachment security and whose parents use an *authoritative* child-rearing style (see Chapter 8) feel especially good about themselves (Kerns, Brumariu, & Seibert, 2011;

Children learn African drumming skills at a community center during Kwanzaa, a holiday honoring their African heritage. A stronger sense of ethnic pride may contribute to slightly higher self-esteem among African-American children compared with their European-American agemates.

Yeung et al., 2016). Warm, positive parenting lets children know that they are accepted as competent and worthwhile. And firm but appropriate expectations, backed up with explanations, help them evaluate their own behavior against reasonable standards.

Controlling parents—those who too often help or make decisions for their child, often because their own sense of self-worth hinges on their child's performance—communicate a sense of inadequacy to children. Having parents who are repeatedly disapproving and insulting is also linked to low self-esteem (Kernis, 2002; Wuyts et al., 2015). Children subjected to such parenting need constant reassurance, and many rely heavily on peers to affirm their self-worth—a risk factor for adjustment difficulties, including aggression and antisocial behavior (Donnellan et al., 2005). In contrast, indulgent parenting is associated with unrealistically high self-esteem. These children are vulnerable to temporary, sharp drops in self-esteem when their overblown self-images are challenged (Thomaes et al., 2013). They tend to lash out at peers who express disapproval and to display adjustment problems, including meanness and aggression (Hughes, Cavell, & Grossman, 1997; Thomaes et al., 2008).

American cultural values have increasingly emphasized a focus on the self that may lead parents to indulge children and boost their self-esteem too much. The self-esteem of U.S. youths has risen sharply in recent decades—a period in which much popular parenting literature, educational policies, and social programs have advised promoting children's self-esteem (Gentile, Twenge, & Campbell, 2010). Research, however, confirms that children do not benefit from compliments ("You're terrific") that have no basis in real accomplishment (Wentzel & Brophy, 2014). Rather, the best way to foster a positive, secure self-image is to encourage children to strive for worthwhile goals. Over time, a bidirectional relationship emerges: Achievement fosters self-esteem, which contributes to further effort and gains in performance (Marsh et al., 2005).

What can adults do to promote, and to avoid undermining, this mutually supportive relationship between motivation and self-esteem? Some answers come from research on the precise content of adults' messages to children in achievement situations.

Achievement-Related Attributions. *Attributions* are our common, everyday explanations for the causes of behavior. Notice how Joey, in talking about the spelling bee at the beginning of this chapter, attributes his disappointing performance to *luck* (Belinda got all the easy words) and his usual success to *ability* (he *knows* he's a better speller than Belinda). Joey also appreciates that *effort* matters: "I knocked myself out studying those spelling lists."

The combination of improved reasoning skills and frequent evaluative feedback permits 10- to 12-year-olds to separate all these variables in explaining performance. Those who are high in academic self-esteem and motivation make **mastery-oriented attributions,** crediting their successes to ability—a characteristic they can improve through trying hard and can count on when faced with new challenges. And they attribute failure to factors that can be changed or controlled, such as insufficient effort or a difficult task (Dweck & Molden, 2013). Whether these children succeed or fail, they take an industrious, persistent approach to learning.

In contrast, children who develop **learned helplessness** attribute their failures, not their successes, to ability. When they succeed, they conclude that external factors, such as luck, are responsible. Unlike their mastery-oriented counterparts, they believe that ability is fixed and cannot be improved by trying hard (Dweck & Molden, 2013). When a task is difficult, these children experience an anxious loss of control—in Erikson's terms, a pervasive sense of inferiority. They give up without really trying.

Children's attributions affect their goals. Mastery-oriented children seek information on how best to increase their ability through effort. Hence, their performance improves over time (Dweck & Molden, 2013). In contrast, learned-helpless children focus on obtaining positive and avoiding negative evaluations of their fragile sense of ability. Gradually, their ability ceases to predict how well they do. In one study, the more fourth to sixth graders held self-critical attributions, the lower they rated their competence, the less they knew about effective study strategies, the more they avoided challenge, and the poorer their academic performance (Pomerantz & Saxon, 2001). Because learned-helpless children fail to connect effort with success, they do not develop the metacognitive and self-regulatory skills necessary for high achievement (see Chapter 9). Lack of effective learning strategies, reduced persistence, and a sense of loss of control sustain one another in a vicious cycle.

Influences on Achievement-Related Attributions. What accounts for the different attributions of mastery-oriented and learned-helpless children? Adult communication plays a key role (Pomerantz & Dong, 2006.) Children with a learned-helpless style often have parents who believe that their child is not very capable and must work harder than others to succeed. When the child fails, the parent might say, "You can't do that, can you? It's OK if you quit" (Hokoda & Fincham, 1995). Similarly, students with unsupportive teachers often regard their performance as externally controlled (by their teachers or by luck), withdraw from learning activities, decline in achievement, and come to doubt their ability (Skinner, Zimmer-Gembeck, & Connell, 1998).

When a child succeeds, adults can offer **person praise,** which emphasizes the child's traits ("You're so smart!"), or **process praise,** which emphasizes behavior and effort ("You figured it out!"). Children—especially those with low self-esteem—feel more shame following failure if they previously received person praise, less shame if they previously received process praise or no praise at all (Brummelman et al., 2014). Consistent with a learned-helpless orientation, person praise teaches children that abilities are fixed, which leads them to question their competence and retreat from challenges (Pomerantz & Kempner, 2013). In contrast, process praise—consistent with a mastery orientation—implies that competence develops through effort (Pomerantz, Grolnick, & Price, 2013).

For some children, performance is especially likely to be undermined by adult feedback. Despite their higher achievement, girls more often than boys attribute poor performance to lack of ability. When girls do not do well, they tend to receive messages from teachers and parents that their ability is at fault, and negative stereotypes (for example, that girls are weak at math) undermine their interest and effort (Gunderson et al., 2012; Tomasetto, Alparone, & Cadinu, 2011). And as Chapter 9 revealed, low-SES ethnic minority students often receive less favorable feedback from teachers, especially when assigned to homogeneous groups of poorly achieving students—conditions that result in a drop in academic self-esteem and achievement.

LOOK and LISTEN

> Observe a school-age child working on a challenging homework assignment under the guidance of a parent or other adult. What features of the adult's communication likely foster mastery-oriented attributions? How about learned helplessness? Explain.

Finally, cultural values influence children's views about success and failure. Asian parents and teachers are more likely than their American counterparts to view effort as key to success. Asian children, in turn, feel a stronger sense of obligation toward parents, internalizing their messages (Mok, Kennedy, & Moore, 2011; Qu & Pomerantz, 2015). Asians also attend more to failure than to success because failure indicates where corrective action is needed. Americans, in contrast, focus more on success because it enhances self-esteem. Observations of U.S. and Chinese mothers' responses to their fourth and fifth graders' puzzle solutions revealed that the U.S. mothers offered more

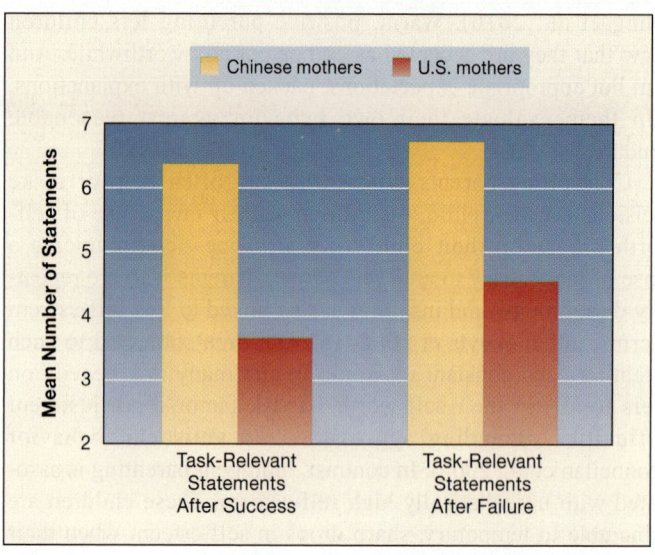

FIGURE 10.2 Chinese and U.S. mothers' task-relevant statements in response to their fourth-grade child's success or failure on puzzle tasks. Observations revealed that regardless of whether their child had just succeeded or failed, Chinese mothers were more likely than U.S. mothers to make task-relevant statements aimed at ensuring that the child exerted high effort. (Based on Ng, Pomerantz, & Lam, 2007.)

praise after success, whereas the Chinese mothers more often pointed out the child's inadequate performance. And Chinese mothers made more task-relevant statements aimed at ensuring that children exerted sufficient effort ("You concentrated on it"; "You only got 6 out of 12") (see Figure 10.2) (Ng, Pomerantz, & Lam, 2007). When children continued with the task after mothers left the room, the Chinese children showed greater gains in performance.

Fostering a Mastery-Oriented Approach. An intervention called *attribution retraining* encourages learned-helpless children to believe that they can overcome failure by exerting more effort and using more effective strategies. Children are given tasks difficult enough that they will experience some failure, followed by repeated feedback that helps them revise their attributions: "You can do it if you try harder." After they succeed, children are given process praise—"Your strategies worked"; "You really tried hard on that one"—so that they attribute their success to both effort and effective strategies, not chance. Another approach is to encourage low-effort students to focus on mastering a task for its own sake, not on grades, and on individual improvement, not on comparisons with classmates (Wentzel & Brophy, 2014). Instruction in effective strategies and self-regulation is also vital, to compensate for development lost in this area and to ensure that renewed effort pays off (Berkeley, Mastropieri, & Scruggs, 2011).

Attribution retraining is best begun early, before children's views of themselves become hard to change. An even better approach is to prevent learned helplessness, using the strategies summarized in Applying What We Know on the following page.

When adults offer process praise emphasizing behavior and effort, children learn that persistence builds competence. Teacher remarks, such as "You found a good way to solve that problem!" will foster a mastery-oriented approach in this student.

Applying what we Know

Fostering a Mastery-Oriented Approach to Learning

STRATEGY	DESCRIPTION
Provision of tasks	Select tasks that are meaningful, responsive to a diversity of student interests, and appropriately matched to current competence so that the child is challenged but not overwhelmed.
Parent and teacher encouragement	Communicate warmth, confidence in the child's abilities, the value of achievement, and the importance of effort in success. Resist praising children's personal qualities, focusing instead on their competent behavior, sustained effort, and successful strategies. Model high effort in overcoming failure. *For teachers:* Communicate often with parents, suggesting ways to foster children's effort and progress. *For parents:* Monitor schoolwork; provide scaffolded assistance that promotes knowledge of effective strategies and self-regulation.
Performance evaluations	Make evaluations private; avoid publicizing success or failure through wall posters, stars, privileges for "smart" children, or prizes for "best" performance. Emphasize individual progress and self-improvement. Provide accurate, constructive feedback to children about their performance.
School environment	Provide for cooperative learning and peer tutoring, in which children assist one another; avoid ability grouping, which makes evaluations of children's progress public. Accommodate individual and cultural differences in learning styles. Create an atmosphere that sends a clear message that all students can learn.

Sources: Wentzel & Brophy, 2014; Wigfield et al., 2006.

Ask yourself

CONNECT What cognitive changes, described in Chapter 9, support the transition to a self-concept emphasizing competencies, personality traits, and social comparisons?

APPLY Should parents try to promote children's self-esteem by telling them they're "smart" or "wonderful"? Are children harmed if they do not feel good about everything they do? Explain.

REFLECT Recall your own attributions for academic successes and failures when you were in elementary school. What are those attributions like now? What messages from others may have contributed to your attributions?

Emotional Development

10.3 Cite changes in self-conscious emotions, emotional understanding, and emotional self-regulation in middle childhood.

Greater self-awareness and social sensitivity support advances in emotional competence in middle childhood. Gains take place in experience of self-conscious emotions, emotional understanding, and emotional self-regulation.

Self-Conscious Emotions

As school-age children integrate social expectations into their self-concepts, self-conscious emotions of pride and guilt become clearly governed by personal responsibility. Children experience pride in a new accomplishment and guilt over a transgression, even when no adult is present (Harter, 2012). Also, children no longer report guilt for any mishap, as they did earlier, but only for intentional wrongdoing, such as ignoring responsibilities, cheating, or lying (Ferguson, Stegge, & Damhuis, 1991). These changes reflect the older child's more mature sense of morality, a topic addressed later in this chapter.

Pride motivates children to take on further challenges, whereas guilt prompts them to make amends and to strive for self-improvement. But in Chapter 8 we noted that excessive guilt is linked to depressive symptoms. And harsh, insensitive reprimands from adults ("Everyone else can do it! Why can't you?") can lead to intense shame, which is particularly destructive, yielding both internalizing and externalizing problems (see page 262).

Emotional Understanding

School-age children's understanding of mental activity means that, unlike preschoolers, they are likely to explain emotion by referring to internal states, such as happy or sad thoughts, rather than to external events (Flavell, Flavell, & Green, 2001). Also, between ages 6 and 12, children become more aware of circumstances

Third graders help prepare meal packages to be sent to Africa to feed children in need. Gains in emotional understanding and perspective taking enable children to respond with empathy to people's general life condition.

likely to spark mixed emotions, each of which may be positive or negative and may differ in intensity (Pons et al., 2003; Zadjel et al., 2013). For example, recalling the birthday present he received from his grandmother, Joey reflected, "I was very happy that I got something but a little sad that I didn't get just what I wanted."

Appreciating mixed emotions helps children realize that people's expressions may not reflect their true feelings (Misailidi, 2006). It also fosters awareness of self-conscious emotions. For example, between ages 6 and 7, children improve sharply in ability to distinguish pride from happiness and surprise (Tracy, Robins, & Lagattuta, 2005). And 8- and 9-year-olds understand that pride combines two sources of happiness—joy in accomplishment and joy that a significant person recognized that accomplishment (Harter, 1999). Furthermore, children of this age can reconcile contradictory facial and situational cues in figuring out another's feelings (see page 261 in Chapter 8).

As with self-understanding, gains in emotional understanding are supported by cognitive development and social experiences, especially adults' sensitivity to children's feelings and willingness to discuss emotions. Together, these factors lead to a rise in empathy as well. As children move closer to adolescence, advances in recursive perspective taking permit an empathic response not just to people's immediate distress but also to their general life condition (Hoffman, 2000). As Joey and Lizzie imagined how people who are chronically ill or hungry feel and evoked those emotions in themselves, they gave part of their allowance to charity and joined in fundraising projects through school, community center, and scouting.

Emotional Self-Regulation

In Chapter 8, we saw that emotional understanding, along with parents' modeling and teaching of emotion-regulation strategies, contributes to young children's ability to manage emotions. These factors continue to play important roles during middle childhood, a period of rapid gains in emotional self-regulation (Zalewski et al., 2011).

By age 10, most children shift adaptively between two general strategies for managing emotion. In **problem-centered coping,** they appraise the situation as changeable, identify the difficulty, and decide what to do about it. If problem solving does not work, they engage in **emotion-centered coping,** which is internal, private, and aimed at controlling distress when little can be done about an outcome (Kliewer, Fearnow, & Miller, 1996; Lazarus & Lazarus, 1994). For example, when faced with an anxiety-provoking test or an angry friend, older school-age children view problem solving and seeking social support as the best strategies. But when outcomes are beyond their control—after receiving a bad grade—they opt for distraction or try to redefine the situation: "Things could be worse. There'll be another test." School-age children's improved ability to appraise situations and reflect on thoughts and feelings means that, compared with preschoolers, they more often use these internal strategies to manage emotion (Brenner & Salovey, 1997).

Furthermore, through interacting with parents, teachers, and peers, school-age children become more knowledgeable about socially approved ways to display negative emotion. They increasingly prefer verbal expression ("Please stop pushing and wait your turn") to crying, sulking, or aggression (Waters & Thompson, 2014). Young school-age children justify these more mature displays of emotion by mentioning avoidance of punishment or adult approval, but by third grade, they begin to emphasize concern for others' feelings. Children with this awareness are rated as especially helpful, cooperative, and socially responsive by teachers and as better-liked by peers (Garner, 1996; McDowell & Parke, 2000).

When emotional self-regulation has developed well, school-age children acquire a sense of *emotional self-efficacy*—a feeling of being in control of their emotional experience (Thompson & Goodman, 2010). This fosters a favorable self-image and an optimistic outlook, which further help children face emotional challenges. As at younger ages, school-age children whose parents respond sensitively and helpfully when the child is distressed are emotionally well-regulated—generally upbeat in mood and also empathic and prosocial. In contrast, poorly regulated children often experience hostile, dismissive parental reactions to distress (Morris et al., 2007; Vinik, Almas, & Grusec, 2011). These children are overwhelmed by negative emotion, a response that interferes with empathy and prosocial behavior.

Moral Development

10.4 Describe changes in moral understanding during middle childhood, including children's understanding of diversity and inequality.

Recall from Chapter 8 that preschoolers pick up many morally relevant behaviors through modeling and reinforcement. By middle childhood, they have had time to internalize rules for good conduct: "It's good to help others in trouble" or "It's wrong to take something that doesn't belong to you." This change leads children to become considerably more independent and trustworthy.

In Chapter 8, we also saw that children do not just copy their morality from others. As the cognitive-developmental approach emphasizes, they actively think about right and wrong. An expanding social world, the capacity to consider more information when reasoning, and gains in recursive perspective taking lead moral understanding to advance greatly in middle childhood.

Moral and Social-Conventional Understanding

During middle childhood, children construct a flexible appreciation of moral rules. They take into account an increasing number of variables—not just the action and its immediate impact, but also the actor's intentions and the context of his behavior (Killen & Smetana, 2015). For example, between ages 7 and 11, children say it is acceptable to hit another child in certain situations—in self-defense, to protect someone else from serious bodily injury, or to prevent the other child from hurting herself (Jambon & Smetana, 2014). Older children focus less on the actor's transgression (hitting) and more on the aim of his behavior (trying to prevent harm).

Similarly, by age 7 to 8, children no longer say that truth telling is always good and lying is always bad but consider prosocial and antisocial intentions and the context of the behavior. They evaluate certain types of truthfulness very negatively—for example, blunt statements, particularly in public contexts where they are especially likely to have negative social consequences (telling a classmate that you don't like her drawing) (Ma et al., 2011).

Although both Chinese and Canadian schoolchildren consider lying about antisocial acts "very naughty," Chinese children more often rate lying favorably when the intention is modesty, as when a student who has thoughtfully picked up litter from the playground says, "I didn't do it" (Cameron et al., 2012; Lee et al., 2001). Similarly, Chinese children are more likely to favor lying to support the group at the expense of the individual (saying you're sick so, as a poor singer, you won't harm your class's chances of winning a singing competition). In contrast, Canadian children more often favor lying to support the individual at the expense of the group (claiming that a friend who is a poor speller is actually a good speller because the friend wants to participate in a spelling competition) (Fu et al., 2007; Lau et al., 2012).

These judgments reflect school-age children's enhanced understanding of varied reasons for deception (Mills, 2013). They realize that people may convey inaccurate information because they are biased, trying to be persuasive, concerned about how others may react, or protecting others' welfare. Notice how such perspective taking is *recursive*: Children must consider simultaneously the viewpoints of two or more people—the person who lies and the recipients of the lie.

Appreciation of second-order false belief, which depends on recursive thought (see page 312 in Chapter 9), is related to gains in moral judgment in middle childhood. In one study, researchers gave children a morally relevant second-order false-belief task: A child, while helping her teacher clean up, accidently throws out a bag containing a treasured cupcake belonging to a classmate who is out of the room (Fu et al., 2014). School-age children who reasoned accurately about the helper's belief about the bag's contents (trash) and the cupcake owner's belief about the cupcake's location (in a bag in the classroom) assigned less blame to the helper. Using their recursive capacity, these children inferred that *the cupcake owner would understand that the helper thought the bag had trash in it.*

As children construct more advanced ideas about justice, they clarify and link moral imperatives and social conventions. School-age children distinguish social conventions with a clear *purpose* (not running in school hallways to prevent injuries) from ones with no obvious justification (crossing a "forbidden" line on the playground) (Buchanan-Barrow & Barrett, 1998). They regard violations of purposeful social conventions as closer to moral transgressions.

Understanding Individual Rights

When children challenge adult authority, they typically do so within the personal domain (Nucci, 2005). As their grasp of moral imperatives and social conventions strengthens, so does their conviction that certain choices, such as hairstyle, friends, and leisure activities, are up to the individual.

Notions of personal choice, in turn, enhance children's moral understanding. As early as age 6, children view freedom of speech and religion as individual rights, even if laws exist that deny those rights (Helwig, 2006). And they regard laws that discriminate against individuals—for example, denying certain people access to medical care or education—as wrong and worthy of violating (Helwig & Jasiobedzka, 2001). In justifying their responses, children appeal to personal privileges and, by the end of middle childhood, to the importance of individual rights for maintaining a fair society.

At the same time, older school-age children place limits on individual choice. Fourth graders faced with conflicting moral

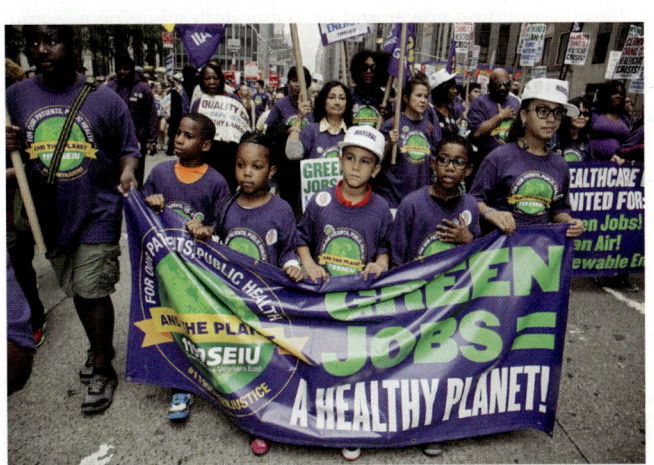

New York City schoolchildren participate in the People's Climate March, which advocates for global action to prevent climate change. By age 6, children's more sophisticated grasp of personal choice enhances moral understanding, including freedom of speech.

and personal concerns—such as whether or not to befriend a classmate of a different race or gender—typically decide in favor of kindness and fairness (Killen et al., 2002). Indeed, high-quality friendships may play an important role in facilitating children's moral sensibilities (McDonald et al., 2014). The cooperativeness, responsiveness, and empathic understanding between good friends promotes concern for others' rights and welfare, while also highlighting the circumstances in which some transgressions ought to be forgiven.

Culture and Moral Understanding

Children and adolescents in diverse cultures use similar criteria to reason about moral, social-conventional, and personal concerns (Nucci, 2005, 2008). For example, Chinese young people, whose culture places a high value on respect for adult authority, nevertheless say that adults have no right to interfere in children's personal matters, such as how they spend free time (Hasebe, Nucci, & Nucci, 2004). A Colombian child illustrated this passionate defense of personal control when asked if a teacher had the right to tell a student where to sit during circle time. In the absence of a moral reason from the teacher, the child declared, "She should be able to sit wherever she wants" (Ardila-Rey & Killen, 2001, p. 249).

Furthermore, when a directive is fair and caring, such as telling children to share candy or to return lost money to its owner, school-age children view it as right, regardless of who states it—even a child with no authority. And even in Korean culture, which promotes children's deference to adults, 7- to 11-year-olds evaluate negatively a teacher's or principal's order to engage in immoral acts, such as stealing or refusing to share (Kim, 1998). In sum, children everywhere seem to realize that higher principles, independent of rule and authority, must prevail when people's personal rights and welfare are at stake.

Understanding Diversity and Inequality

By the early school years, children absorb prevailing societal attitudes, associating power and privilege with white people and poverty and inferior status with people of color. They do not necessarily acquire these views directly from parents or friends, whose attitudes often differ from their own (Aboud & Doyle, 1996; Pahlke, Bigler, & Suizzo, 2012). Rather, children seem to pick up mainstream beliefs from implicit messages in the media and elsewhere in their environments. Powerful sources include social contexts that present a world sorted into groups, such as racial and ethnic segregation in schools and communities.

In-Group and Out-Group Biases: Development of Prejudice.
Studies in diverse Western nations confirm that by age 5 to 6, white children generally evaluate their own racial group favorably and other racial groups less favorably or negatively. *In-group favoritism* emerges first; children simply prefer their own group, generalizing from self to similar others (Buttelmann & Böhm, 2014; Dunham, Baron, & Carey, 2011; Nesdale et al., 2004).

The ease with which a trivial group label supplied by an adult can induce in-group favoritism is striking. In one study, European-American 5-year-olds were told that they were members of a group based on T-shirt color. Although no information was provided about group status and the children never met any group members, they still displayed vigorous in-group favoritism (Dunham, Baron, & Carey, 2011). When shown photos of unfamiliar agemates wearing either an in-group or an out-group shirt, the children claimed to like members of their own group better, gave them more resources, and engaged in positively biased recall of group members' behavior.

Out-group prejudice requires a more challenging social comparison between in-group and out-group. But it does not take long for white children to acquire negative attitudes toward ethnic minority out-groups when such attitudes are encouraged by circumstances in their environments. When white Canadian 4- to 7-year-olds living in a white community and attending nearly all-white schools sorted positive and negative adjectives into boxes labeled as belonging to a white child and a black child, out-group prejudice emerged at age 5 (Corenblum, 2003). Unfortunately, many minority children show a reverse pattern: *out-group favoritism,* in which they assign positive characteristics to the privileged white majority and negative characteristics to their own group (Averhart & Bigler, 1997; Newheiser et al., 2014).

But recall that with age, children pay more attention to inner traits. The capacity to classify the social world in multiple ways enables school-age children to understand that people can be both "the same" and "different"—those who look different need not think, feel, or act differently. Consequently, voicing of negative attitudes toward minorities declines after age 7 or 8 (Aboud, 2008; Raabe & Beelmann, 2011). Around this time, both majority and minority children express *in-group favoritism,* and white children's *prejudice against out-group members* often weakens (Nesdale et al., 2005; Ruble et al., 2004).

Yet even in children aware of the injustice of discrimination, prejudice often operates unintentionally and without awareness—as it does in many adults (Dunham, Baron, & Banaji, 2006). Consider a study in which U.S. children and adults were shown pictures of computer-generated racially ambiguous faces displaying happy and angry expressions and asked to classify them by race. White participants more often categorized happy faces as white and angry faces as African American or Asian. These implicit biases were evident across all ages tested—as early as 3 or 4. In contrast, African-American participants did not show any racial biases in their responses (Dunham, Chen, & Banaji, 2013). The absence of any in-group favoritism (classifying happy faces as black) suggests an early-emerging, implicit sensitivity to prevailing racial attitudes among African Americans.

These findings raise the question of whether the decline in white children's explicit racial bias during middle childhood is a true decrease or whether it reflects their growing awareness of widely held standards that deem prejudice to be inappropriate—or both. Around age 10, white children start to avoid talking about race in order to appear unbiased, just as many adults do (Apfelbaum et al., 2008). At least to some degree, then, older school-age children's desire to present themselves in a socially

Palestinian and Israeli children and adolescents take a break from mural painting to sing and dance together. Intergroup contact, in which racially and ethnically different children have equal status, work toward common goals, and become personally acquainted, is an effective way to reduce prejudice.

acceptable light may contribute to reduced explicit out-group prejudice, while implicit racial bias persists.

Nevertheless, the extent to which children hold racial and ethnic biases varies, depending on the following personal and situational factors:

- *A fixed view of personality traits.* Children who believe that people's personality traits are fixed rather than changeable often judge others as either "good" or "bad." Ignoring motives and circumstances, they readily form prejudices based on limited information. For example, they might infer that "a new child at school who tells a lie to get other kids to like her" is simply "a bad kid" (Levy & Dweck, 1999).

- *Overly high self-esteem.* Children (and adults) with very high self-esteem are more likely to hold racial and ethnic prejudices (Baumeister et al., 2003; Bigler, 2013). These individuals seem to belittle disadvantaged people or groups to justify their own extremely favorable, yet insecure, self-evaluations. Children who say their own ethnicity makes them feel especially "good"—and thus perhaps socially superior—are more likely to display in-group favoritism and out-group prejudice (Pfeifer et al., 2007).

- *A social world in which people are sorted into groups.* The more adults highlight group distinctions and the less interracial contact children experience, the more likely white children will express in-group favoritism and out-group prejudice (Aboud & Brown, 2013).

Reducing Prejudice. Research confirms that an effective way to reduce prejudice is through intergroup contact, in which racially and ethnically different children have equal status, work toward common goals, and become personally acquainted, and in which parents and teachers expect them to engage in such interaction (Tropp & Page-Gould, 2015). Children assigned to cooperative learning groups with peers of diverse backgrounds show low levels of prejudice in their expressions of likability and in their behavior. For example, they form more cross-race friendships (Pettigrew & Tropp, 2006). Sharing thoughts and feelings with close, cross-race friends, in turn, reduces even subtle, unintentional prejudices (Turner, Hewstone, & Voci, 2007). But positive effects seem not to generalize to out-group members who are not part of these learning teams.

Long-term contact and collaboration among neighborhood, school, and community groups may be the best way to reduce prejudice (Rutland, Killen, & Abrams, 2010). School environments that expose children to broad ethnic diversity, teach them to understand and value those differences, directly address the damage caused by prejudice, emphasize moral values of justice and fairness, and encourage perspective taking and empathy both prevent children from forming negative biases and lessen already acquired biases (Beelmann & Heinemann, 2014). Unfortunately, as noted in Chapter 9, segregation is widespread in U.S. schools, which seldom offer exposure to the diversity necessary for countering negative racial and ethnic biases. Return to page 327 to review efforts of magnet schools to reduce this racial divide.

Finally, inducing children to view others' traits as changeable, by discussing with them the many possible influences on those traits, is helpful. The more children believe that people can change their personalities, the more they report liking and perceiving themselves as similar to members of disadvantaged outgroups. Furthermore, children who believe that human attributes are changeable spend more time volunteering to help people in need (Karafantis & Levy, 2004). Volunteering may, in turn, promote a view of others as changeable by helping children take the perspective of the underprivileged and appreciate the social conditions that lead to disadvantage.

Ask yourself

CONNECT Cite examples of how older children's capacity to take more information into account enhances their emotional and moral understanding.

APPLY Ten-year-old Marla says her classmate Bernadette will never get good grades because she's lazy. Jane believes that Bernadette tries but can't concentrate because her parents are divorcing. Why is Marla more likely than Jane to develop prejudices?

REFLECT Did you attend an integrated elementary school? Why is school integration vital for reducing racial and ethnic prejudice?

Peer Relations

10.5 How do peer sociability and friendship change in middle childhood?

10.6 Describe major categories of peer acceptance and ways to help rejected children.

In middle childhood, the society of peers becomes an increasingly important context for development. The capacity for recursive perspective taking permits more sophisticated understanding of self and others, which, in turn, contributes to peer interaction. Compared with preschoolers, school-age children resolve conflicts more effectively, using persuasion and compromise (Mayeux & Cillessen, 2003). Sharing, helping, and other prosocial acts also increase. In line with these changes, aggression declines. But the drop is greatest for physical attacks (Côté et al., 2007). As we will see, verbal and relational aggression continue as children organize into peer groups.

Peer Groups

By the end of middle childhood, children display a strong desire for group belonging. They form **peer groups,** collectives that generate unique values and standards for behavior and a social structure of leaders and followers. Peer groups organize on the basis of proximity (being in the same classroom) and similarity in sex, ethnicity, academic achievement, popularity, and aggression (Rubin et al., 2013).

The practices of these informal groups lead to a "peer culture" that typically involves a specialized vocabulary, dress code, and place to "hang out." As children develop these exclusive associations, the codes of dress and behavior that grow out of them become more broadly influential. Peers who deviate—by "kissing up" to teachers, wearing the wrong clothes, or tattling on classmates—are often rebuffed, becoming targets of critical glances and comments. These customs bind peers together, creating a sense of group identity. Within the group, children acquire many social skills—cooperation, leadership, followership, and loyalty to collective goals.

Most school-age children believe a group is wrong to exclude a peer on the basis of unconventional appearance or behavior— a view that strengthens with age (Killen, Crystal, & Watanabe, 2002). Nevertheless, children do exclude, often using relationally aggressive tactics. Peer groups—at the instigation of their leaders, who can be skillfully aggressive—frequently oust no longer "respected" children. Some of these castouts, whose own previous behavior toward outsiders reduces their chances of being included elsewhere, turn to other low-status peers with poor social skills (Farmer et al., 2010). Socially anxious children, when ousted, often become increasingly peer-avoidant and thus more isolated (Buhs, Ladd, & Herald-Brown, 2010). In either case, opportunities to acquire socially competent behavior diminish.

School-age children's desire for group membership can also be satisfied through formal group ties such as scouting, 4-H, and religious youth groups. Adult involvement holds in check the negative behaviors associated with children's informal peer groups. And through working on joint projects and helping in their communities, children gain in social and moral maturity (Vandell & Shumow, 1999).

Friendships

Whereas peer groups provide children with insight into larger social structures, friendships contribute to the development of trust and sensitivity. During the school years, friendship becomes more complex and psychologically based. Consider the following 8-year-old's ideas:

Why is Shelly your best friend? Because she helps me when I'm sad, and she shares. . . . *What makes Shelly so special?* I've known her longer, I sit next to her and got to know her better. . . . *How come you like Shelly better than anyone else?* She's done the most for me. She never disagrees, she never eats in front of me, she never walks away when I'm crying, and she helps me with my homework. . . . *How do you get someone to like you?* . . . If you're nice to [your friends], they'll be nice to you. (Damon, 1988b, pp. 80–81)

As these responses show, friendship has become a mutually agreed-on relationship in which children like each other's personal qualities and respond to one another's needs and desires. And once a friendship forms, *trust* becomes its defining feature. School-age children state that a good friendship is based on acts of kindness, signifying that each person can be counted on to support the other (Hartup & Abecassis, 2004). Consequently, older children regard violations of trust, such as not helping when others need help, breaking promises, and gossiping behind the other's back, as serious breaches of friendship.

Because of these features, school-age children's friendships are more selective. Whereas preschoolers say they have lots of friends, by age 8 or 9, children name only a handful of good friends. Girls, who demand greater closeness than boys, are more exclusive in their friendships. In addition, children tend to select friends similar to themselves in age, sex, race, ethnicity, and SES. Friends also resemble one another in personality (sociability, inattention/hyperactivity, aggression, depression), peer popularity, academic achievement, and prosocial behavior (Rubin et al., 2013). But friendship opportunities encouraged by children's environments also affect their choices. Children whose parents have cross-race friends form more cross-race friendships

Peer groups first form in middle childhood. These boys have probably established a peer-group structure of leaders and followers as they gather for a soccer game. Their relaxed body language and similar dress suggest a strong sense of group belonging.

CHAPTER 10 Emotional and Social Development in Middle Childhood

School-age children tend to select friends who are similar to themselves in personality and academic achievement. And friendships are fairly stable: These boys are likely to remain friends for at least a full school year.

(Pahlke, Bigler, & Suizzo, 2012). And as noted earlier, in integrated classrooms with mixed-race collaborative learning groups, students develop more cross-race friendships.

> **LOOK and LISTEN**
>
> Ask an 8- to 11-year-old to tell you what he or she looks for in a best friend. Is *trust* centrally important? Does the child mention personality traits, just as school-age children do in describing themselves?

Over middle childhood, high-quality friendships remain fairly stable. About 50 to 70 percent endure over a school year, and some last for several years. Gains in friendship support—including compromise, sharing of thoughts and feelings, and prosocial behavior—contribute to this stability (Berndt, 2004; Furman & Rose, 2015). But context is also influential: Friendships spanning several situations—such as school, religious institution, and children of parents' friends—are more likely to endure (Troutman & Fletcher, 2010).

Through friendships, children learn the importance of emotional commitment. They come to realize that close relationships can survive disagreements if friends are secure in their liking for each other and resolve disputes in ways that meet both partners' needs. Yet the impact of friendships on children's development depends on the nature of those friends. Children who bring kindness and compassion to their friendships strengthen each other's prosocial tendencies.

But when aggressive children make friends, the relationship is often riddled with hostile exchanges and is at risk for breakup, especially when just one member of the pair is aggressive. And within these close ties, children's aggressive tendencies worsen (Ellis & Zarbatany, 2007; Salmivalli, 2010). Aggressive girls' friendships are high in exchange of private feelings but also full of jealousy, conflict, and betrayal. Aggressive boys' friendships involve frequent expressions of anger, coercive statements, physical attacks, and enticements to rule-breaking behavior (Rubin et al., 2013; Werner & Crick, 2004). As we will see next, aggressive children often acquire negative reputations in the wider world of peers.

Peer Acceptance

Peer acceptance refers to likability—the extent to which a child is viewed by a group of agemates, such as classmates, as a worthy social partner. Unlike friendship, likability is not a mutual relationship but a one-sided perspective, involving the group's view of an individual. Nevertheless, better-accepted children tend to be socially competent and, as a result, have more friends and more positive relationships with them (Mayeux, Houser, & Dyches, 2011).

To assess peer acceptance, researchers usually use self-reports that measure *social preferences*—for example, asking children to identify classmates whom they "like most" or "like least" (Cillessen, 2009). These self-reports yield five general categories of peer acceptance:

- **Popular children,** who get many positive votes (are well-liked)
- **Rejected children,** who get many negative votes (are disliked)
- **Controversial children,** who receive many votes, both positive and negative (are both liked and disliked)
- **Neglected children,** who are seldom mentioned, either positively or negatively
- *Average children,* who receive average numbers of positive and negative votes and account for about one-third of children in a typical elementary school classroom

Another approach assesses *perceived popularity*—children's judgments of whom most of their classmates admire. Only moderate correspondence exists between the classmates children perceive as popular (believe are admired by many others) and those classified as popular based on peer preferences (receive many "like most" ratings) (Mayeux, Houser, & Dyches, 2011).

Peer acceptance is a powerful predictor of psychological adjustment. Rejected children, especially, are anxious, unhappy, disruptive, and low in self-esteem. Both teachers and parents rate them as having a wide range of emotional and social problems. Peer rejection in middle childhood is also strongly associated with poor school performance, absenteeism, dropping out, substance use, depression, antisocial behavior, and delinquency in adolescence and with criminality in adulthood (Ladd, 2005; Rubin et al., 2013).

However, earlier influences—children's characteristics combined with parenting practices—may largely explain the link between peer acceptance and adjustment. School-age children with peer-relationship problems are more likely to have weak emotional self-regulation skills and to have experienced family stress due to low income and insensitive parenting, including coercive discipline (Blair et al., 2014; Trentacosta & Shaw, 2009). Nevertheless, as we will see, rejected children evoke reactions from peers that contribute to their unfavorable development.

Determinants of Peer Acceptance. Why is one child liked while another is rejected? A wealth of research reveals that social behavior plays a powerful role.

Popular Children. **Popular-prosocial children** are both well-liked (socially preferred) and admired (high in perceived popularity). They combine academic and social competence, performing well in school and communicating with peers in friendly and cooperative ways (Cillessen & Bellmore, 2004; Mayeux, Houser, & Dyches, 2011).

But other popular children are admired for their socially adept yet belligerent behavior. **Popular-antisocial children** include "tough" boys—athletically skilled but poor students who cause trouble and defy adult authority—and relationally aggressive boys and girls who enhance their own status by ignoring, excluding, and spreading rumors about other children (Rose, Swenson, & Waller, 2004; Vaillancourt & Hymel, 2006). Despite their aggressiveness, peers often view these youths as "cool," perhaps because of their athletic abilities and sophisticated but devious social skills. Although peer admiration gives these children some protection against lasting adjustment difficulties, their antisocial acts require intervention (Rodkin et al., 2006). With age, peers like these high-status, aggressive youths less and less, eventually condemning their nasty tactics and rejecting them.

Rejected Children. Rejected children display a wide range of negative social behaviors. The largest subtype, **rejected-aggressive children,** show high rates of conflict, physical and relational aggression, and hyperactive, inattentive, and impulsive behavior. They are usually deficient in perspective taking, misinterpreting the innocent behaviors of peers as hostile and blaming others for their social difficulties (Dodge, Coie, & Lynam, 2006; Rubin et al., 2013). Compared with popular-antisocial children, they are more extremely antagonistic.

In contrast, **rejected-withdrawn children** are passive and socially awkward. Overwhelmed by social anxiety, they hold negative expectations about interactions with peers and worry about being scorned and attacked (Rubin et al., 2013; Troop-Gordon & Asher, 2005).

Rejected children are excluded by peers as early as kindergarten. Soon their classroom participation declines, their feelings of loneliness rise, their academic achievement falters, and they want to avoid school (Buhs, Ladd, & Herald-Brown, 2010; Gooren et al., 2011). Most have few friends, and some have none—a circumstance that predicts severe adjustment difficulties (Ladd et al., 2011; Pedersen et al., 2007).

Both types of rejected children are at risk for peer harassment. But as the Biology and Environment box on the following page reveals, rejected-aggressive children also act as bullies, and rejected-withdrawn children are especially likely to be victimized.

LOOK and LISTEN

Contact a nearby elementary school or a school district to find out what practices are in place to prevent bullying. Inquire about a written antibullying policy, and request a copy.

Controversial and Neglected Children. Consistent with the mixed peer opinion they engender, controversial children display a blend of positive and negative social behaviors. They are hostile and disruptive, but they also engage in positive, prosocial acts. Even though some peers dislike them, they have qualities that protect them from social exclusion. They have many friends and are happy with their peer relationships (de Bruyn & Cillessen, 2006). But like their popular-antisocial and rejected-aggressive counterparts, they often bully others and engage in calculated relational aggression to sustain their dominance (Putallaz et al., 2007).

Perhaps the most surprising finding on peer acceptance is that neglected children, once thought to be in need of treatment, are usually well-adjusted. Although they engage in low rates of interaction, most are just as socially skilled as average children and do not report feeling unhappy about their social life. When they want to, they can break away from their usual pattern of playing alone, cooperating well with peers and forming positive, stable friendships (Ladd & Burgess, 1999; Ladd et al., 2011). Neglected, socially competent children remind us that an outgoing, gregarious personality style is not the only path to emotional well-being.

Helping Rejected Children.

A variety of interventions exist to improve the peer relations and psychological adjustment of rejected children. Most involve coaching, modeling, and reinforcing positive social skills, such as how to initiate interaction with a peer, cooperate in play, and respond to another child with friendly emotion and approval. Several of these programs have produced lasting gains in social competence and peer acceptance (Asher & Rose, 1997; DeRosier, 2007). Combining social-skills training with other treatments increases its effectiveness. Rejected children are often poor students, whose low academic self-esteem magnifies their negative interactions with teachers and classmates. Intensive academic tutoring improves both school achievement and social acceptance (O'Neill et al., 1997).

Still another approach focuses on training in perspective taking and in solving social problems. But many rejected-aggressive children are unaware of their poor social skills and do not take responsibility for their social failures (Mrug, Hoza, & Gerdes, 2001). Rejected-withdrawn children, in contrast, are likely to develop a *learned-helpless* approach to peer difficulties—concluding, after repeated rebuffs, that they will never be liked (Wichmann, Coplan, & Daniels, 2004). Both types of children need help attributing their peer difficulties to internal, changeable causes.

As rejected children gain in social skills, teachers must encourage peers to alter their negative opinions. Accepted children often selectively recall their negative acts while overlooking their positive ones (Mikami, Lerner, & Lun, 2010). Consequently, even in the face of contrary evidence, rejected children's negative reputations tend to persist. Teachers' praise and expressions of liking can modify peer judgments (De Laet et al., 2014).

Finally, because rejected children's socially incompetent behaviors often originate in a poor fit between the child's temperament and parenting practices, interventions focusing on the child alone may not be sufficient. Without improving the quality of parent–child interaction, rejected children may soon return to their old behavior patterns.

Biology and Environment

Bullies and Their Victims

Follow the activities of aggressive children over a school day, and you will see that they reserve their hostilities for certain peers. A particularly destructive form of interaction is **peer victimization,** in which certain children become targets of verbal and physical attacks or other forms of abuse. What sustains these repeated assault–retreat cycles between pairs of children? About 20 percent of children are bullies, while 25 percent are repeatedly victimized. Most bullies who engage in face-to-face physical and verbal attacks are boys, but a considerable number of girls bombard vulnerable classmates with verbal and relational hostility (Cook et al., 2010).

As bullies move into adolescence, an increasing number attack through electronic means. About 20 to 40 percent of youths have experienced "cyberbullying" through text messages, e-mail, social media sites, or other electronic tools (Kowalski & Limber, 2013). Compared with face-to-face bullying, gender differences in cyberbullying are less pronounced; the indirectness of online aggression may lead girls to prefer it (Menesini & Spiel, 2012). Girls more often cyberbully with words, whereas boys typically distribute embarrassing photos or videos.

Perpetrators and victims of "traditional" bullying are frequently involved in cyberbullying. But electronic bullying is not always an extension of traditional bullying (Smith et al., 2008). And victims are far less likely to report cyberbullying to parents or adults at school. In many instances, the cyberbully's identity is unknown to the victim and audience.

Many bullies are disliked, or become so, because of their cruelty. But a substantial number are socially powerful youngsters who are broadly admired by peers. These high-status bullies often target already-peer-rejected children, whom classmates are unlikely to defend (Veenstra et al., 2010). Not only do peers rarely intervene to help victims, but about 20 to 30 percent of onlookers encourage bullies, even joining in (Salmivalli & Voeten, 2004).

Bullying occurs more often in schools where teachers are viewed as unfair and uncaring and where many students judge bullying behavior to be "OK" (Guerra, Williams, & Sadek, 2011). Indeed, bullies and the peers who assist them typically display social information-processing deficits, including overly high self-esteem, pride in their acts, and indifference to harm done to their victims (Hymel et al., 2010).

Chronic victims tend to be passive when active behavior is expected. Biologically based traits—an inhibited temperament and a frail physical appearance—contribute. But victims also have histories of resistant attachment, overly controlling child rearing, and maternal overprotection—parenting that prompts anxiety, low self-esteem, and dependency, resulting in a fearful demeanor that marks these children as vulnerable (Snyder et al., 2003).

Consequences of victimization include loneliness, low peer acceptance, poor school performance, disruptive behavior, and school avoidance (Kochel, Ladd, & Rudolph, 2012; Paul & Cillessen, 2003). Like persistent child abuse, victimization is linked to impaired production of cortisol, suggesting a disrupted physiological response to stress (Vaillancourt, Hymel, & McDougall, 2013).

As instances of traditional bullying and cyberbullying accumulate, victims report substantial interference with daily functioning. Both traditional bullying and cyberbullying are related to rising anxiety, depression, and suicidal thoughts (Menesini, Calussi, & Nocentini, 2012; van den Eijnden et al., 2014). Repeated cyberattacks directed at causing widespread damage to the victim's reputation—for example, circulating malicious videos on cell phones or social networking sites—magnify these effects.

Aggression and victimization are not polar opposites. One-third to one-half of victims are also aggressive, meting out physical, relational, or cyberhostilities. Bullies usually respond by abusing them again—a cycle that sustains their victim status. Among rejected children, these bully/victims are the most despised. They often have histories of

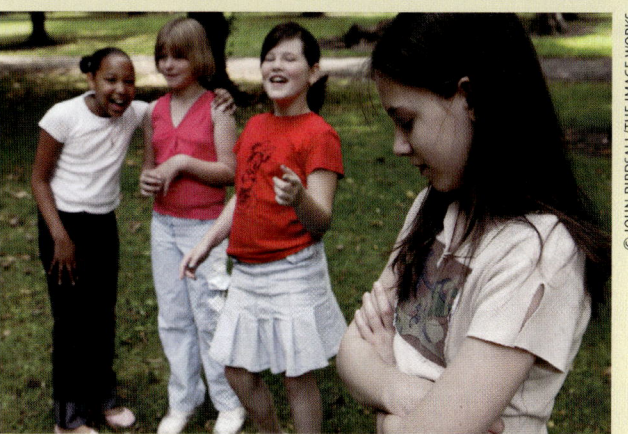

Bullies and the peers who assist them typically display overly high self-esteem, pride in their acts, and indifference to the harm done to their victims. And chronic victims are often easy targets—physically weak, passive, and inhibited.

extremely maladaptive parenting, including child abuse. This combination of highly negative home and peer experiences places them at severe risk for maladjustment (Kowalski, Limber, & Agatston, 2008).

Interventions that change victimized children's negative opinions of themselves and that teach them to respond in nonreinforcing ways to their attackers are helpful. Another way to assist victimized children is to help them form and maintain a gratifying friendship (Fox & Boulton, 2006). When children have a close friend to whom they can turn for help, bullying episodes usually end quickly.

Although modifying victimized children's behavior can help, the best way to reduce bullying is to promote prosocial attitudes and behaviors in youth environments (including school, sports programs, recreation centers, and neighborhoods). Effective approaches include developing school and community codes against both traditional bullying and cyberbullying; teaching child bystanders to intervene; strengthening parental oversight of children's use of cell phones, computers, and the Internet; and increasing adult supervision of high-bullying areas in schools, such as hallways, lunchroom, and schoolyard (Kärnä et al., 2011; Kiriakidis & Kavoura, 2010).

The U.S. Department of Health and Human Services manages an antibullying website, *www.stopbullying.gov*, that raises awareness of the harmfulness of bullying and provides information on prevention.

Gender Typing

10.7 What changes in gender-stereotyped beliefs and gender identity occur during middle childhood?

Children's understanding of gender roles broadens in middle childhood, and their gender identities (views of themselves as relatively masculine or feminine) change as well. We will see how gender stereotypes influence children's attitudes, behaviors, peer relations, and self-perceptions.

Gender-Stereotyped Beliefs

Research in many countries reveals that stereotyping of personality traits increases steadily in middle childhood, becoming adultlike around age 11 (Best, 2001; Heyman & Legare, 2004). For example, children regard "tough," "aggressive," "rational," and "dominant" as masculine and "gentle," "sympathetic," and "dependent" as feminine.

Children derive these distinctions from observing sex differences in behavior as well as from adult treatment. When helping a child with a task, for example, parents (especially fathers) behave in a more mastery-oriented fashion with sons, setting higher standards, explaining concepts, and pointing out important features of tasks—particularly during gender-typed pursuits, such as science activities (Tenenbaum & Leaper, 2003; Tenenbaum et al., 2005).

Furthermore, elementary school teachers tend to stereotype girls who display "feminine" behavior as diligent and compliant and boys who display "masculine" behavior as lazy and troublesome (Heyder & Kessels, 2015). These perceptions may contribute to boys' reduced academic engagement and lower school grades relative to girls'. At the same time, when teachers are presented with a boy and a girl who are equally successful at math, they tend to see the girl as having to work harder (Robinson-Cimpian et al., 2014). As we saw in our discussion of achievement-related attributions, this downrating of girls' ability negatively affects their performance.

Also in line with adult stereotypes, school-age children often regard reading, spelling, art, and music as subjects girls are good at and mathematics, athletics, and mechanical skills as subjects boys are good at (Cvencek, Meltzoff, & Greenwald, 2011; Eccles, Jacobs, & Harold, 1990). These attitudes influence children's preferences for and sense of competence at various subjects.

An encouraging sign is that children's gender-stereotyped beliefs about achievement may be changing. In several investigations carried out in Canada, France, and the United States, a majority of elementary and secondary students disagreed with the idea that math is a "masculine" subject (Kurtz-Costes et al., 2014; Martinot, Bagès, & Désert, 2012; Plante, Théoret, & Favreau, 2009; Rowley et al., 2007). The overwhelming majority of these young people, however, continued to view language arts traditionally—as largely "feminine." And they still perceived girls as doing better in language arts than in math.

Although school-age children are aware of many stereotypes, they also develop a more open-minded view of what males and females *can do.* As with racial stereotypes (see page 344), the ability to classify flexibly contributes to this change. School-age children realize that a person's sex is not a certain predictor of his or her personality traits, activities, and behavior (Halim & Ruble, 2010; Trautner et al., 2005). Similarly, by the end of middle childhood, most children regard gender typing as socially rather than biologically influenced (Taylor, Rhodes, & Gelman, 2009).

Nevertheless, acknowledging that people *can* cross gender lines does not mean that children always *approve* of doing so. In one longitudinal study, between ages 7 and 13, children generally became more open-minded about girls being offered the same opportunities as boys (Crouter et al., 2007). But this change was less pronounced for boys than girls, and for children whose parents held more traditional gender attitudes. Furthermore, many school-age children take a harsh view of certain violations—boys playing with dolls and wearing girls' clothing, girls acting noisily and roughly (Blakemore, 2003). They are especially intolerant when boys engage in these "cross-gender" acts.

Gender Identity and Behavior

Children who were more strongly gender-typed relative to their agemates in early childhood usually remain so in middle childhood (Golombok et al., 2008). Nevertheless, overall changes do occur, with boys' and girls' gender identities following different paths.

From third to sixth grade, boys tend to strengthen their identification with "masculine" personality traits, whereas girls' identification with "feminine" traits declines. While still leaning toward the "feminine" side, girls are more *androgynous* than boys—more likely to describe themselves as having some

An 8-year-old launches the rocket she made in her school's Young Astronaut Club. Whereas school-age boys usually stick to "masculine" pursuits, girls experiment with a wider range of options.

"other-gender" characteristics (Serbin, Powlishta, & Gulko, 1993). And whereas boys usually stick to "masculine" pursuits, many girls experiment with a wider range of options—from cooking and sewing to sports and science projects—and more often consider traditionally male future work roles, such as firefighter or astronomer (Liben & Bigler, 2002).

These changes are due to a mixture of cognitive and social forces. School-age children of both sexes are aware that society attaches greater prestige to "masculine" characteristics. For example, they rate "masculine" occupations as having higher status than "feminine" occupations and an unfamiliar job as higher in status when portrayed with a male worker than a female worker (Liben, Bigler, & Krogh, 2001; Weisgram, Bigler, & Liben, 2010). Messages from adults and peers are also influential. In Chapter 8, we saw that parents (especially fathers) are more disapproving when sons, as opposed to daughters, cross gender lines. Similarly, a tomboyish girl can interact with boys without losing the approval of her female peers, but a boy who hangs out with girls is likely to be ridiculed and rejected.

As school-age children make social comparisons and characterize themselves in terms of stable dispositions, their gender identity expands to include the following self-evaluations, which greatly affect their adjustment:

- *Gender typicality*—the degree to which the child feels similar to others of the same gender. Although children need not be highly gender-typed to view themselves as gender-typical, their psychological well-being depends, to some degree, on feeling that they "fit in" with their same-sex peers.
- *Gender contentedness*—the degree to which the child feels comfortable with his or her gender assignment, which also promotes happiness.
- *Felt pressure to conform to gender roles*—the degree to which the child feels parents and peers disapprove of his or her gender-related traits. Because such pressure reduces the likelihood that children will explore options related to their interests and talents, children who feel strong gender-typed pressure are often distressed.

In a longitudinal study of third through seventh graders, gender-typical and gender-contented children gained in self-esteem over the following year, whereas gender-atypical and gender-discontented children declined in self-worth. Furthermore, *gender-atypical* children, especially those who report *intense pressure to conform to gender roles,* experience serious adjustment difficulties—withdrawal, sadness, disappointment, and anxiety (Corby, Hodges, & Perry, 2007; Yunger, Carver, & Perry, 2004). Clearly, school-age children who experience rejection because of their gender-atypical traits suffer profoundly.

Because felt pressure to conform to gender roles predicts maladjustment among gender-atypical children, more experts are advocating interventions that help parents and peers become more accepting of children's gender-atypical interests and behaviors (Bigler, 2007; Conway, 2007; Hill et al., 2010). Return to page 281 in Chapter 8 to review related evidence on gender-dysphoric children, who feel profoundly discontented with their natal (birth) sex and who strongly identify as the other sex, along with evidence on the best therapeutic approach to help them.

Ask yourself

CONNECT Describe similarities in development of self-concept, attitudes toward racial and ethnic minorities, and gender-stereotyped beliefs in middle childhood.

APPLY What changes in parent–child and teacher–child relationships are likely to help rejected children?

REFLECT As a school-age child, did you have classmates you would classify as popular-antisocial? What were they like, and why do you think peers admired them?

Family Influences

10.8 How do parent–child communication and sibling relationships change in middle childhood?

10.9 What factors influence children's adjustment to divorce and blended family arrangements?

10.10 How do maternal employment and life in dual-earner families affect school-age children?

As children move into school, peer, and community contexts, the parent–child relationship changes. At the same time, children's well-being continues to depend on the quality of family interaction. In the following sections, we will see that contemporary diversity in family life—divorce, remarriage, maternal employment, and dual-earner families—can have positive as well as negative effects on children. In later chapters, we take up other family structures, including gay and lesbian families, never-married single-parent families, and the increasing numbers of grandparents rearing grandchildren.

Parent–Child Relationships

In middle childhood, the amount of time children spend with parents declines dramatically. Children's growing independence means that parents must deal with new issues. "I've struggled with how many chores to assign, how much allowance to give, whether their friends are good influences, and what to do about problems at school," Rena remarked. "And then there's the challenge of keeping track of them when they're out—or even when they're home and I'm not there to see what's going on."

Despite these new concerns, child rearing becomes easier for parents who established an authoritative style during the early years. Reasoning is more effective with school-age children because of their greater capacity for logical thinking and their increased respect for parents' expert knowledge. And children of parents who engage in joint decision making where possible are more likely to listen to parents' perspectives in situations where compliance is vital (Russell, Mize, & Bissaker, 2004).

As children demonstrate that they can manage daily activities and responsibilities, effective parents gradually shift control from adult to child. They do not let go entirely but, rather, engage in **coregulation,** a form of supervision in which they exercise general oversight while letting children take charge of moment-by-moment decision making. Coregulation grows out of a warm, cooperative relationship between parent and child based on give-and-take. Parents must guide and monitor from a distance and effectively communicate expectations when they are with their children. And children must inform parents of their whereabouts, activities, and problems so parents can intervene when necessary (Collins, Madsen, & Susman-Stillman, 2002). Coregulation supports and protects children while preparing them for adolescence, when they will make many important decisions themselves.

As at younger ages, mothers tend to spend more time than fathers with school-age children and know more about children's everyday activities, although many fathers are highly involved (Pew Research Center, 2015e). Both parents, however, tend to devote more time to children of their own sex (Lam, McHale, & Crouter, 2012). And parents are more vigilant about monitoring the activities of same-sex children while their children are away from home.

Although school-age children often press for greater independence, they know how much they need their parents' support. A positive parent–child relationship is linked to improved emotional self-regulation in children, reducing the negative impact of stressful events (Brumariu, Kerns, & Seibert, 2012; Hazel et al., 2014). School-age children often turn to parents for affection, advice, affirmation of self-worth, and assistance with everyday problems.

Siblings

In addition to parents and friends, siblings continue to be important sources of support. Yet sibling rivalry tends to increase in middle childhood. As children participate in a wider range of activities, parents often compare siblings' traits and accomplishments. The child who gets less parental affection, more disapproval, or fewer material resources is likely to be resentful and show poorer adjustment (Dunn, 2004b; McHale, Updegraff, & Whiteman, 2012).

For same-sex siblings who are close in age, parental comparisons are more frequent, resulting in more quarreling and antagonism. This effect is particularly strong when parents are under stress as a result of financial worries, marital conflict, single parenthood, or child negativity (Jenkins, Rasbash, & O'Connor, 2003). Parents whose energies are drained become less careful about being fair. Perhaps because fathers, overall, spend less time with children than mothers, children react especially intensely when fathers prefer one child (Kolak & Volling, 2011).

To reduce rivalry, siblings often strive to be different from one another (McHale, Updegraff, & Whiteman, 2012). For example, two brothers I know deliberately selected different athletic pursuits and musical instruments. If the older one did

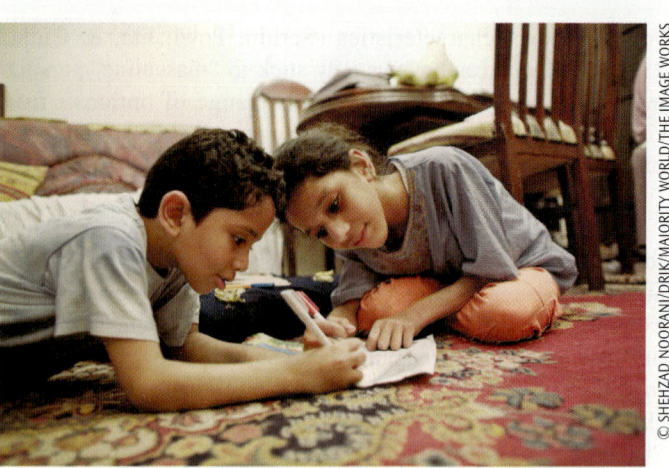

An older sister helps her 6-year-old brother with homework. Although sibling rivalry tends to increase in middle childhood, siblings also provide each other with emotional support and help with difficult tasks.

especially well at an activity, the younger one did not want to try it. Parents can limit these effects by making an effort not to compare children, but some feedback about their competencies is inevitable. As siblings strive to win recognition for their own uniqueness, they shape important aspects of each other's development.

Although conflict rises, school-age siblings continue to rely on each other for companionship, assistance, and emotional support. But for siblings to reap these benefits, parental encouragement of warm, considerate sibling ties is vital. The more positive their relationship, the more siblings resolve disagreements constructively, provide help with family, academic, and peer challenges, and contribute to resilience in the face of major stressors, such as parental divorce (Conger, Stocker, & McGuire, 2009; Soli, McHale, & Feinberg, 2009).

When siblings get along well, the older sibling's academic and social competence tends to "rub off on" the younger sibling, fostering more favorable achievement and peer relations. And both older and younger siblings benefit in empathy and prosocial behavior (Brody & Murry, 2001; Lam, Solmeyer, & McHale, 2012; Padilla-Walker, Harper, & Jensen, 2010). But destructive sibling conflict in middle childhood is associated with negative outcomes, including conflict-ridden peer relationships, anxiety, depressed mood, and later substance use and delinquency, even after other family relationship factors are controlled (Kim et al., 2007; Ostrov, Crick, & Stauffacher, 2006).

Only Children

Although sibling relationships bring many benefits, they are not essential for healthy development. Contrary to popular belief, only children are not spoiled, and in some respects, they are advantaged. U.S. children growing up in one-child and multi-child families do not differ in self-rated personality traits (Mottus, Indus, & Allik, 2008). And compared to children with siblings, only children are higher in self-esteem and achievement motivation, do better in school, and attain higher levels of education. One reason may be that only children have somewhat closer relationships with parents, who may exert more pressure for mastery and accomplishment and can invest more time in their child's educational experiences (Falbo, 2012). However, only children tend to be less well-accepted in the peer group, perhaps because they have not had opportunities to learn effective conflict-resolution strategies through sibling interactions (Kitzmann, Cohen, & Lockwood, 2002).

Favorable development also characterizes only children in China, where a one-child family policy was enforced in urban areas for more than three decades, until it was abolished in 2015. Compared with agemates who have siblings, Chinese only children are slightly advantaged in cognitive development and academic achievement. They also feel more emotionally secure, perhaps because government disapproval led to tension in families with more than one child (Falbo, 2012; Yang et al., 1995). Chinese mothers usually ensure that their children have regular contact with first cousins (who are considered siblings). Perhaps as a result, Chinese only children do not differ from agemates with siblings in social skills and peer acceptance (Hart, Newell, & Olsen, 2003).

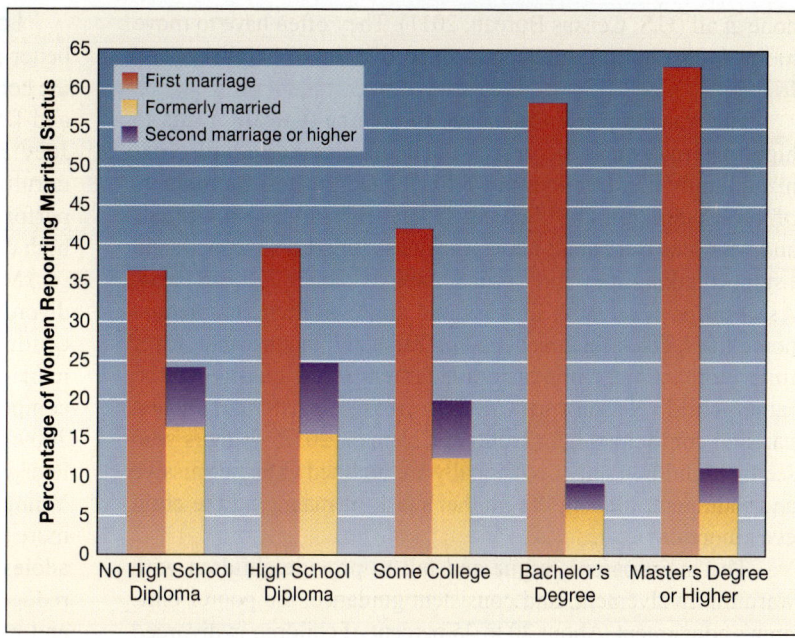

FIGURE 10.3 Divorce rates among U.S. women by level of education. A survey of over 10,000 U.S. women between ages 15 and 44 revealed that increased education is linked to marital stability, limited education to divorce, remarriage, and subsequent divorce. (Based on Lundberg & Pollak, 2015.)

Divorce

Children's interactions with parents and siblings are affected by other aspects of family life. When Joey was 8 and Lizzie 5, their father, Drake, moved out. During the preceding months, Joey began pushing, hitting, taunting, and calling Lizzie names. Although she tried to retaliate, she was no match for Joey's larger size. The arguments usually ended with Lizzie running in tears to her mother. Joey and Lizzie's fighting coincided with their parents' growing marital unhappiness.

Between 1960 and 1985, divorce rates in Western nations rose dramatically before stabilizing in most countries. The United States has experienced a decline in divorce over the past twenty years, largely due to a rise in age at first marriage and a drop in marriage rates. However, this decrease largely applies to well-educated, financially secure families. As Figure 10.3 shows, individuals with less education experience substantially greater marital instability (Lundberg & Pollak, 2015). Because educational and economic disadvantage increases family fragility, divorce rates are higher among African Americans, Hispanic Americans, and Native Americans than among European Americans (Raley, Sweeny, & Wondra, 2015).

Among developed nations, the United States has one of the highest divorce rates. Of the estimated 42 to 45 percent of American marriages that end in divorce, half involve children. More than one-fourth of U.S. children live in divorced, single-parent households. Although most reside with their mothers, the percentage in father-headed households has increased steadily, to about 14 percent (U.S. Census Bureau, 2015d).

Children of divorce spend an average of five years in a single-parent home—almost a third of childhood. For many, divorce leads to new family relationships. About 10 percent of U.S. children live with one parent (usually their mother) and a married or cohabiting stepparent (Kreider & Ellis, 2011). Many of these children eventually experience a third major change—the end of their parent's second marriage or cohabiting partnership.

These figures reveal that divorce is not a single event in the lives of parents and children. Instead, it is a transition that leads to a variety of new living arrangements, accompanied by changes in housing, income, and family roles and responsibilities. Although divorce is stressful for children and increases the risk of adjustment problems, most adjust favorably (Greene et al., 2012; Lamb, 2012). How well children fare depends on many factors: the custodial parent's psychological health and financial resources, the child's characteristics, and social supports within the family and surrounding community.

Immediate Consequences. "Things were worst after Drake and I decided to separate," Rena reflected. "We fought over division of our belongings and custody of the children, and the kids suffered. Sobbing, Lizzie told me she was 'sorry she made Daddy go away.' Joey kicked and threw things at home and didn't do his work at school. In the midst of everything, I could hardly deal with their problems. We had to sell the house, and I needed a better-paying job."

Family conflict often rises in newly divorced households as parents try to settle disputes over children and possessions. Once one parent moves out, additional events threaten supportive interactions between parents and children. Mother-headed households typically experience a sharp drop in income. In the United States, nearly 30 percent of divorced mothers with young children live in poverty, and many more are low-income, getting less than the full amount of child support from the absent father or none at all (U.S. Census Bureau, 2011). They often have to move to lower-cost housing, reducing supportive ties to neighbors and friends.

The transition from marriage to divorce typically leads to high maternal stress, depression, and anxiety and to a disorganized family life. Declines in well-being are greatest for mothers of young children (Williams & Dunne-Bryant, 2006). "Meals and bedtimes were at all hours, the house didn't get cleaned, and I stopped taking Joey and Lizzie on weekend outings," said Rena. As children react with distress and anger to their less secure home lives, discipline may become harsh and inconsistent. Over time, contact with noncustodial fathers—and quality of the father–child relationship—often decreases, particularly when parental conflict is high (Troilo & Coleman, 2012). Fathers who see their children only occasionally are inclined to be permissive and indulgent, making the mother's task of managing the child even more difficult.

The more parents argue and fail to provide children with warmth, involvement, and consistent guidance, the poorer children's adjustment. About 20 to 25 percent of children in divorced families display severe problems, compared with about 10 percent in nondivorced families (Golombok & Tasker, 2015; Lansford, 2009). At the same time, reactions vary with children's age, temperament, and sex.

Children's Age. Preschool and young school-age children often blame themselves for a marital breakup and fear that both parents may abandon them. And although older children have the cognitive maturity to understand that they are not responsible for their parents' divorce, many react strongly, declining in school performance, becoming unruly, and escaping into undesirable peer activities, especially when family conflict is high and parental supervision is low (Kleinsorge & Covitz, 2012; Lansford et al., 2006). Some older children—especially the oldest child in the family—display more mature behavior, willingly taking on extra household tasks, care of younger siblings, and emotional support of a depressed, anxious mother. But if these demands are too great, these children may eventually become resentful, withdraw from the family, and engage in angry, acting-out behavior (Hetherington & Kelly, 2002).

Children's Temperament and Sex. Exposure to stressful life events and inadequate parenting magnifies the problems of temperamentally difficult children (see Chapter 6). In contrast, easy children are less often targets of parental anger and also cope more effectively with adversity.

These findings help explain sex differences in response to divorce. Girls sometimes respond as Lizzie did, with internalizing reactions such as crying, self-criticism, and withdrawal. More often, children of both sexes show demanding, attention-getting behavior. But in mother-custody families, boys are at slightly greater risk for serious adjustment problems (Amato, 2010). Recall from Chapter 8 that boys are more active and noncompliant—behaviors that increase with exposure to parental conflict and inconsistent discipline. Coercive maternal behavior and defiance by sons are common in divorcing households.

Long-Term Consequences. Rena eventually found better-paying work and gained control over the daily operation of the household. And after several meetings with a counselor, Rena and Drake realized the harmful impact of their quarreling on Joey and Lizzie. Drake visited regularly and handled Joey's unruliness with firmness and consistency. Soon Joey's school performance improved, his behavior problems subsided, and both children seemed calmer and happier.

Most children show improved adjustment by two years after divorce. Yet overall, children and adolescents of divorced parents continue to score slightly lower than children of continuously married parents in academic achievement, self-esteem, social competence, and emotional and behavior problems (Lansford, 2009; Weaver & Schofield, 2015). And divorce is linked to problems with adolescent sexuality and development of intimate ties. Young people who experienced parental divorce—especially more than once—display higher rates of early sexual activity and adolescent parenthood. Some show other lasting difficulties—reduced educational attainment, troubled romantic relationships and marriages, divorce in adulthood, and unsatisfying parent–child relationships (Amato, 2010).

The overriding factor in positive adjustment following divorce is effective parenting—shielding the child from family conflict and using authoritative child rearing (Lamb, 2012). Parent-training programs can help custodial parents support their children's development. One eleven-session parent-training intervention for mothers of school-age children yielded improved parent–child relationships and child coping skills, with effects persisting for six years (Velez et al., 2011).

Where the custodial parent is the mother, regular contact with fathers is also important. But only about one-third of children experience at least weekly visits (Amato & Dorius, 2010). The more paternal contact and the warmer the father–child relationship, the less children react with defiance and aggression (Dunn et al., 2004). For girls, a good father–child relationship protects against early sexual activity and unhappy romantic involvements. For boys, it seems to affect overall psychological

Regular contact with both parents and effective coparenting—supporting each other in their child-rearing roles—greatly improve adjustment in children of divorce.

Applying what we Know

Helping Children Adjust to Their Parents' Divorce

SUGGESTION	EXPLANATION
Shield children from conflict.	Witnessing intense parental conflict is very damaging to children. If one parent insists on expressing hostility, children fare better if the other parent does not respond in kind.
Provide children with as much continuity, familiarity, and predictability as possible.	Children adjust better during the period surrounding divorce when their lives have some stability—for example, the same school, bedroom, babysitter, playmates, and daily schedule.
Explain the divorce, and tell children what to expect.	Children may develop fears of abandonment if they are not prepared for their parents' separation. They should be told that their parents will not be living together anymore, which parent will be moving out, and when they will be able to see that parent. If possible, parents should explain the divorce together, providing a reason that each child can understand and assuring children that they are not to blame.
Emphasize the permanence of the divorce.	Fantasies of parents getting back together can prevent children from accepting the reality of their current life. Children should be told that the divorce is final and that they cannot change this fact.
Respond sympathetically to children's feelings.	Children need supportive, understanding responses to their feelings of sadness, fear, and anger. For children to adjust well, their painful emotions must be acknowledged, not denied or avoided.
Engage in authoritative parenting.	Authoritative parenting—providing affection and acceptance, reasonable demands for mature behavior, and consistent, rational discipline—greatly reduces children's risk of maladjustment following divorce.
Promote a continuing relationship with both parents.	When parents disentangle their lingering hostility toward the former spouse from the child's need for a continuing relationship with the other parent, children adjust well.

well-being. In fact, some studies report that outcomes for sons are better when the father is the custodial parent (Clarke-Stewart & Hayward, 1996; McLanahan, 1999). Fathers' greater economic security and image of authority seem to help them engage in effective parenting with sons. And boys in father-custody families may benefit from greater involvement of both parents because noncustodial mothers participate more in their children's lives than do noncustodial fathers.

Although divorce is painful for children, remaining in an intact but high-conflict family is much worse than making the transition to a low-conflict, single-parent household (Lamb, 2012; Strohschein, 2005). Divorcing parents who manage to engage in *effective coparenting* (see page 57 in Chapter 2), supporting each other in their child-rearing roles, greatly improve their children's chances of growing up competent, stable, and happy (Lamb, 2012). Caring extended-family members, teachers, siblings, and friends also reduce the likelihood that divorce will result in long-term difficulties (Hetherington, 2003).

Divorce Mediation, Joint Custody, and Child Support.

Awareness that divorce is highly stressful for children and families has led to community-based services aimed at helping them through this difficult time. One such service is *divorce mediation*, a series of meetings between divorcing adults and a trained professional aimed at reducing family conflict, including legal battles over property division and child custody. Mediation increases out-of-court settlements, cooperation and involvement of both parents in child rearing, and parents' and children's feelings of well-being (Douglas, 2006; Emery, Sbarra, & Grover, 2005).

Joint custody, which grants parents equal say in important decisions about the child's upbringing, is becoming increasingly common. Children usually reside with one parent and see the other on a fixed schedule, similar to the typical sole-custody situation. In other cases, parents share physical custody, and children move between homes. Joint-custody parents report little conflict—fortunately so, since the success of the arrangement depends on effective coparenting (Bauserman, 2012). And their children, regardless of living arrangements, tend to be better-adjusted than children in sole-maternal-custody homes (Bauserman, 2002).

Finally, many single-parent families depend on child support from the noncustodial parent to relieve financial strain. All U.S. states have procedures for withholding wages from parents who fail to make these payments. Although child support is usually not enough to lift a single-parent family out of poverty, it can ease its burdens substantially. Noncustodial fathers who have generous visitation schedules and who often see their children are more likely to pay child support regularly (Amato & Sobolewski, 2004). And increases in paternal contact and in child support over time predict better coparenting relationships (Hofferth, Forry, & Peters, 2010). Applying What We Know above summarizes ways to help children adjust to their parents' divorce.

Blended Families

"If you get married to Wendell, and Daddy gets married to Carol," Lizzie wondered aloud to Rena, "then I'll have two sisters and one more brother. And let's see, how many grandmothers and grandfathers? A lot!" exclaimed Lizzie.

About 60 percent of divorced parents remarry within a few years. Others *cohabit,* or share a sexual relationship and a residence with a partner outside of marriage. Parent, stepparent, and children form a new family structure called the **blended, or reconstituted, family.** For some children, this expanded family network is positive, bringing greater adult attention. But children in blended families usually have more adjustment problems than children in stable, first-marriage families (Pryor, 2014). Switching to stepparents' new rules and expectations can be stressful, and children often view steprelatives as intruders. How well they adapt is, again, related to the quality of family functioning. This depends on which parent forms a new relationship, the child's age and sex, and the complexity of blended-family relationships. As we will see, older children and girls seem to have the hardest time.

Mother–Stepfather Families.
Because mothers generally retain custody of children, the most common form of blended family is a mother–stepfather arrangement. Boys tend to adjust quickly, welcoming a stepfather who is warm, who refrains from exerting his authority too quickly, and who offers relief from coercive cycles of mother–son interaction. Mothers' friction with sons also declines as a result of greater economic security, another adult to share household tasks, and an end to loneliness (Visher, Visher, & Pasley, 2003). Stepfathers who marry rather than cohabit are more involved in parenting, perhaps because men who choose to marry a mother with children are more interested in and skilled at child rearing (Hofferth & Anderson, 2003). Girls, however, often have difficulty with their custodial mother's remarriage. Stepfathers disrupt the close ties many girls have established with their mothers, and girls often react with sulky, resistant behavior (Pryor, 2014).

But age affects these findings. Older school-age children and adolescents of both sexes display more irresponsible, acting-out behavior than their peers not in stepfamilies (Hetherington & Stanley-Hagan, 2000; Robertson, 2008). If parents are warmer and more involved with their biological children than with their stepchildren, older children are more likely to notice and challenge unfair treatment. And adolescents often view the new stepparent as a threat to their freedom, especially if they experienced little parental monitoring in the single-parent family. But when teenagers have affectionate, cooperative relationships with their mothers, many develop good relations with their stepfathers—a circumstance linked to more favorable adolescent well-being (King, 2009; Yuan & Hamilton, 2006).

Father–Stepmother Families.
Remarriage of noncustodial fathers often leads to reduced contact with their biological children, especially when fathers remarry quickly, before they have established postdivorce parent–child routines (Dunn, 2002; Juby et al., 2007). When fathers have custody, children typically react negatively to remarriage. One reason is that children living with fathers often start out with more problems. Perhaps the biological mother could no longer handle the difficult child (usually a boy), so the father and his new partner are faced with the child's behavior problems. In other instances, the father has custody because of a very close relationship with the child, and his remarriage disrupts this bond (Buchanan, Maccoby, & Dornbusch, 1996).

Girls, especially, have a hard time getting along with their stepmothers, either because the remarriage threatens the girl's bond with her father or because she becomes entangled in loyalty conflicts between the two mother figures. But the longer girls live in father–stepmother households, the more positive their interaction with stepmothers becomes (King, 2007). With time and patience, children of both genders benefit from the support of a second mother figure.

Support for Blended Families.
Parenting education and couples counseling can help parents and children adapt to the complexities of blended families. Effective approaches encourage stepparents to move into their new roles gradually by first building a warm relationship with the child, which makes more active parenting possible (Pasley & Garneau, 2012). Counselors can offer couples guidance in effective coparenting to limit loyalty conflicts and provide consistency in child rearing. And tempering parents' unrealistic expectations for children's rapid adjustment—by pointing out that building a unified blended family often takes years—makes it easier for families to endure the transition and succeed.

Unfortunately, the divorce rate for second marriages is higher than for first marriages. Parents with antisocial tendencies and poor child-rearing skills are particularly likely to have several divorces and remarriages. The more marital transitions children experience, the greater their adjustment difficulties (Amato, 2010). These families usually require prolonged, intensive therapy.

Maternal Employment and Dual-Earner Families

Today, U.S. single and married mothers are in the labor market in nearly equal proportions, and more than three-fourths of those with school-age children are employed (U.S. Census Bureau, 2015d). In previous chapters, we saw that the impact of maternal employment on early development depends on the quality of child care and the parent–child relationship. The same is true in middle childhood.

Maternal Employment and Child Development.
When employed mothers remain committed to parenting, children develop favorably, displaying higher self-esteem and less gender-stereotyped beliefs. Girls, especially, perceive women's roles as involving more freedom of choice and satisfaction and are more career-oriented (Hoffman, 2000). Furthermore, stable maternal employment begun in early childhood is linked to higher achievement and fewer behavior problems in elementary school, especially for children of low-income mothers (Lombardi & Coley, 2013; Lucas-Thompson, Goldberg, & Prause, 2010). Parenting practices and improved financial well-being likely contribute to these benefits. Employed mothers who

feel economically more secure are more likely to engage in warm, involved parenting.

In dual-earner households, maternal employment often leads fathers to take on greater child-rearing responsibilities. Paternal involvement is associated in childhood and adolescence with higher achievement, more mature social behavior, and a flexible view of gender roles; and in adulthood with generally better mental health (Bornstein, 2015; Lamb & Lewis, 2013).

But when employment places heavy demands on parents' schedules or is stressful for other reasons, children are at risk for ineffective parenting (Strazdins et al., 2013). Working many hours, working a nonstandard schedule (such as night or weekend shifts), or experiencing a negative workplace atmosphere is associated with lower-quality parenting, fewer joint parent–child activities, poorer cognitive development, and increased behavior problems throughout childhood and adolescence (Li et al., 2014; Strazdins et al., 2006).

In contrast, part-time employment and flexible work schedules are associated with good child adjustment (Buehler & O'Brian, 2011; Youn, Leon, & Lee, 2012). By preventing role overload, these arrangements help parents meet children's needs.

Support for Employed Parents and Their Families.
In dual-earner families, the father's willingness to share responsibilities is crucial. If he helps little or not at all, the mother carries a double load, at home and at work, leading to fatigue, distress, and little time and energy for children. Fortunately, compared to several decades ago, today's U.S. fathers are far more involved in child care (see page 204 in Chapter 6). But their increased participation has resulted in a growing number of fathers who also report role overload (Galinsky, Aumann, & Bond, 2009).

Employed parents need assistance from work settings and communities in their child-rearing roles. Part-time employment, flexible schedules, job sharing, on-site child care, and paid leave when children are ill help parents juggle the demands of work and child rearing (Butts, Casper, & Yang, 2013). Equal pay and employment opportunities for women are also important. Because these policies enhance financial status and morale, they improve the way mothers feel and behave when they arrive home at the end of the working day.

Child Care for School-Age Children.
High-quality child care is vital for parents' peace of mind and children's well-being, even in middle childhood. An estimated 4.5 million 5- to 14-year-olds in the United States are **self-care children,** who regularly look after themselves for some period of time after school (Laughlin, 2013). Self-care increases with age and also with SES, perhaps because of the greater safety of higher-income neighborhoods. But when lower-SES parents lack alternatives to self-care, their children spend more hours on their own (Casper & Smith, 2002).

The implications of self-care for development depend on children's maturity and the way they spend their time. Among younger school-age children, those who spend more hours alone have more adjustment difficulties (Vandell & Posner, 1999). As

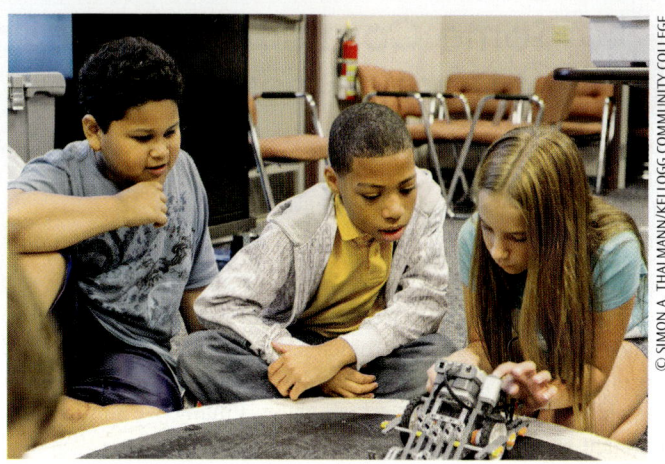

High-quality after-school programs with enrichment activities yield academic and social benefits, especially for low-SES children.

children become old enough to look after themselves, those whose parents engage in authoritative child rearing, monitor their activities through telephone calls, and assign regular after-school chores appear responsible and well-adjusted (Coley, Morris, & Hernandez, 2004; Vandell et al., 2006). In contrast, children left to their own devices are more likely to bend to peer pressures and engage in antisocial behavior.

Throughout middle childhood, attending after-school programs with well-trained and supportive staffs, generous adult–child ratios, and skill-building activities is linked to good school performance and emotional and social adjustment (Durlak, Weissberg, & Pachan, 2010; Kantaoka & Vandell, 2013). Low-SES children who participate in "after-care" programs offering academic assistance and enrichment activities (scouting, music and art lessons, clubs) show special benefits. They exceed their self-care counterparts in classroom work habits, academic achievement, and prosocial behavior and display fewer behavior problems (Lauer et al., 2006; Vandell et al., 2006).

Yet good after-care is in especially short supply in low-income neighborhoods (Greenberg, 2013). A special need exists for well-planned programs in these areas—ones that provide safe environments, warm relationships with adults, and enjoyable, goal-oriented activities.

Ask yourself

CONNECT How does each level in Bronfenbrenner's ecological systems theory—microsystem, mesosystem, exosystem, and macrosystem—contribute to effects of parents' employment on children's development?

APPLY Steve and Marissa are in the midst of an acrimonious divorce. Their 9-year-old son Dennis has become hostile and defiant. How can Steve and Marissa help Dennis adjust?

REFLECT What after-school child-care arrangements did you experience in elementary school? How do you think they influenced your development?

Some Common Problems of Development

10.11 Cite common fears and anxieties in middle childhood.

10.12 Discuss factors related to child sexual abuse, its consequences for children's development, and its prevention and treatment.

10.13 Cite factors that foster resilience in middle childhood.

We have considered a variety of stressful experiences that place children at risk for future problems. Next, we address two more areas of concern: school-age children's fears and anxieties and the consequences of child sexual abuse. Finally, we sum up factors that help children cope effectively with stress.

Fears and Anxieties

Although fears of the dark, thunder and lightning, and supernatural beings persist into middle childhood, older children's anxieties are also directed toward new concerns. As children begin to understand the realities of the wider world, the possibility of personal harm (being robbed, stabbed, or shot) and media events (war and disasters) often trouble them. Other common worries include academic failure, physical injuries, separation from parents, parents' health, the possibility of dying, and peer rejection (Muris & Field, 2011; Weems & Costa, 2005).

As long as fears are not too intense, most children handle them constructively, using the more sophisticated emotional self-regulation strategies that develop in middle childhood. Consequently, overall number of fears declines with age, especially for girls, who express more fears than boys throughout childhood and adolescence (Gullone, 2000; Muris & Field, 2011). But about 5 percent of school-age children develop an intense, unmanageable fear called a **phobia.** Children with inhibited temperaments are at high risk, displaying phobias five to six times as often as other children (Ollendick, King, & Muris, 2002).

Some children with phobias and other anxieties develop *school refusal*—severe apprehension about attending school, often accompanied by physical complaints such as dizziness, nausea, stomachaches, and vomiting (Wimmer, 2013). About one-third of children with school refusal are 5- to 7-year-olds for whom the real fear is maternal separation (Elliott, 1999). Family therapy helps these children, whose difficulty can often be traced to parental overprotection.

Most cases of school refusal appear around age 11 to 13, in children who usually find a particular aspect of school frightening—an overcritical teacher, a school bully, or too much parental pressure to achieve. A change in school environment or parenting practices may be needed. Firm insistence that the child return to school, along with training in how to manage anxiety and cope with difficult situations, is also helpful (Kearney, Spear, & Mihalas, 2014).

Severe childhood anxieties may arise from harsh living conditions. In inner-city ghettos and in war-torn areas of the world, large numbers of children live in the midst of constant danger, chaos, and deprivation. As the Cultural Influences box on the following page reveals, they are at risk for long-term emotional distress and behavior problems. Finally, as we saw in our discussion of child abuse in Chapter 8, too often violence and other destructive acts become part of adult–child relationships. During middle childhood, child sexual abuse increases.

Child Sexual Abuse

Until recently, child sexual abuse was considered rare, and adults often dismissed children's claims of abuse. In the 1970s, efforts by professionals and media attention led to recognition of child sexual abuse as a serious and widespread problem. About 61,000 cases in the United States were confirmed in the most recently reported year (U.S. Department of Health and Human Services, 2015c).

Characteristics of Abusers and Victims. Sexual abuse is committed against children of both sexes, but more often against girls. Most cases are reported in middle childhood, but for some victims, abuse begins early in life and continues for many years (Collin-Vézina, Daigneault, & Hébert, 2013).

In the vast majority of cases, the abuser is male, often a parent or someone the parent knows well—a father, stepfather, live-in boyfriend, uncle, or older brother (Olafson, 2011). If the abuser is a nonrelative, the person is usually someone the child has come to know and trust, such as a teacher, caregiver, clergy member, or family friend (Sullivan et al., 2011). The Internet and mobile phones have become avenues through which some perpetrators commit sexual abuse—for example, by exposing children and adolescents to pornography and online sexual advances as a way of "grooming" them for sexual acts offline (Kloess, Beech, & Harkins, 2014).

Abusers make the child comply in a variety of distasteful ways, including deception, bribery, verbal intimidation, and physical force. You may wonder how any adult—especially a parent or close relative—could violate a child sexually. Many offenders deny their own responsibility, blaming the abuse on the willing participation of a seductive youngster. Yet children are not capable of making a deliberate, informed decision to enter into a sexual relationship! Even older children and adolescents are not free to say yes or no. Rather, the responsibility lies with abusers, who tend to have characteristics that predispose them toward sexual exploitation of children. They have great difficulty controlling their impulses and may suffer from psychological disorders, including alcohol and drug abuse. Often they pick out children who are unlikely to defend themselves or to be believed—those who are physically weak, emotionally deprived, socially isolated, or affected by disabilities (Collin-Vézina, Daigneault, & Hébert, 2013).

Reported cases of child sexual abuse are linked to poverty, marital instability, and resulting weakening of family ties. Children who live in homes with a constantly changing cast of characters—repeated marriages, separations, and new partners—are especially vulnerable (Murray, Nguyen, & Cohen, 2014). But children in economically advantaged, stable homes are also victims, although their abuse is more likely to escape detection.

Cultural Influences

Impact of Ethnic and Political Violence on Children

Around the world, many children live with armed conflict, terrorism, and other acts of violence stemming from ethnic and political tensions. Some children participate in fighting, either because they are forced or because they want to please adults. Others are kidnapped, assaulted, and tortured. Child bystanders often come under direct fire and may be killed or physically maimed. And many watch in horror as family members, friends, and neighbors flee, are wounded, or die. An estimated 25 million children live in conflict-ridden, poor countries. In the past decade, wars have left 6 million physically disabled, 20 million homeless, and more than 1 million separated from their parents (Masten et al., 2015; UNICEF, 2011).

When war and social crises are temporary, most children can be comforted and do not show long-term emotional difficulties. But chronic danger requires children to make substantial adjustments that can seriously impair their psychological functioning.

The greater children's exposure to life-threatening experiences, the more likely they are to display post-traumatic stress symptoms—extreme fear and anxiety, terrifying intrusive memories, depression, irritability, anger, aggression, and a pessimistic view of the future (Dimitry, 2012; Eisenberg & Silver, 2011). These outcomes appear to be culturally universal, emerging among children in every war zone studied—from Bosnia, Rwanda, and the Sudan to the West Bank, Gaza, Iraq, Afghanistan, and Syria.

Parental affection and reassurance are the best protection against lasting problems. When parents offer security, discuss traumatic experiences sympathetically, and serve as role models of calm emotional strength, most children can withstand even extreme war-related violence (Gewirtz, Forgatch, & Wieling, 2008). Children separated from their parents, who are at greatest risk for maladjustment, must rely on help from their communities. Orphans in Eritrea who were placed in residential settings where they could form a close emotional tie with an adult showed less emotional stress five years later than orphans placed in impersonal settings (Wolff & Fesseha, 1999). Education and recreation programs are powerful safeguards, too, providing children with consistency in their lives along with teacher and peer supports.

With the September 11, 2001, terrorist attacks on the World Trade Center, some U.S. children experienced extreme wartime violence firsthand. Most children, however, learned about the attacks indirectly—from the media or from caregivers or peers. Both direct and indirect exposure triggered child and adolescent distress, but extended exposure—having a family member affected or repeatedly witnessing the attacks on TV—resulted in more severe symptoms (Agronick et al., 2007; Rosen & Cohen, 2010). During the following months, distress reactions declined, though more slowly for children with pre-existing adjustment problems.

Unlike many war-traumatized children in the developing world, students in New York's

A refugee camp volunteer teaches Syrian students in a makeshift school. Educational and recreational programs provide children with consistency in severely stressful environments, helping to protect them from lasting adjustment problems.

Public School 31, who watched from their classroom windows as the towers collapsed, received immediate intervention—a "trauma curriculum" in which they expressed their emotions through writing, drawing, and discussion and participated in experiences aimed at helping them manage stress and restore trust and tolerance. Evaluations of similar school-based interventions in war-torn regions reveal that they are highly effective in lessening children's and adolescents' post-traumatic stress symptoms (Peltonen & Punamäki, 2010; Qouta et al., 2012).

When wartime drains families and communities of resources, international organizations must step in and help children. The Children and War Foundation, www.childrenandwar.org, offers programs and manuals that train local personnel in how to promote children's adaptive coping. Efforts to preserve children's physical, psychological, and educational well-being may be the best way to stop transmission of violence to the next generation.

Consequences. The adjustment problems of child sexual abuse victims—including anxiety, depression, low self-esteem, mistrust of adults, and anger and hostility—are often severe and can persist for years after the abusive episodes. Younger children frequently react with sleep difficulties, loss of appetite, and generalized fearfulness. Adolescents may run away and show suicidal reactions, eating disorders (including weight gain and obesity), substance abuse, and delinquency. At all ages, persistent abuse accompanied by force, violence, and a close relationship to the perpetrator (incest) has a more severe impact. And sexual abuse, like physical abuse, is associated with central nervous system damage (Gaskill & Perry, 2012).

Sexually abused children frequently display precocious sexual knowledge and behavior. In adolescence, abused young people often become promiscuous, and as adults, they show increased arrest rates for sex crimes (mostly against children)

and prostitution. Furthermore, women who were sexually abused are likely to choose partners who abuse them and their children. As mothers, they often engage in irresponsible and coercive parenting, including child abuse and neglect (Collin-Vézina, Daigneault, & Hébert, 2013; Trickett, Noll, & Putnam, 2011). In these ways, the harmful impact of sexual abuse is transmitted to the next generation.

Prevention and Treatment. Because sexual abuse typically appears in the midst of other serious family problems, specialized trauma-focused therapy with both children and parents is usually needed (Saunders, 2012). The best way to reduce the suffering of victims is to prevent sexual abuse from continuing. Today, courts are prosecuting abusers more vigorously and taking children's testimony more seriously (see the Social Issues: Health box on the following page).

Educational programs that teach children to recognize inappropriate sexual advances and identify sources of help reduce the risk of abuse (Finkelhor, 2009). Yet because of controversies over educating children about sexual abuse, few schools offer these interventions. New Zealand is the only country with a national, school-based prevention program targeting sexual abuse. In Keeping Ourselves Safe, children and adolescents learn that abusers are rarely strangers. Parent involvement ensures that home and school collaborate in teaching children self-protection skills. Evaluations reveal that virtually all New Zealand parents and children support the program and that it has helped many children avoid or report abuse (Sanders, 2006).

Fostering Resilience in Middle Childhood

Throughout middle childhood—and other periods of development—children encounter challenging and sometimes threatening situations that require them to cope with psychological stress. In this and the previous chapter, we have considered such topics as chronic illness, learning disabilities, achievement expectations, divorce, harsh living conditions and wartime trauma, and sexual abuse. Each taxes children's coping resources, creating serious risks for development.

Nevertheless, only a modest relationship exists between stressful life experiences and psychological disturbance in childhood (Masten, 2014). In our earlier discussions of poverty, troubled family lives, and birth complications, we noted that some children manage to surmount their negative impact. The same is true for school difficulties, family transitions, the experience of war, and child maltreatment. Recall from Chapter 1 that four broad factors protect against maladjustment: (1) the child's personal characteristics, including an easygoing temperament and a mastery-oriented approach to new situations; (2) a warm parental relationship; (3) an adult outside the immediate family who offers a support system; and (4) community resources, such as good schools, social services, and youth organizations and recreation centers.

Often just one or a few of these ingredients account for why one child is resilient and another is not. Usually, however, personal and environmental factors are interconnected: Each resource favoring resilience strengthens others. For example, safe, stable neighborhoods with family-friendly community services reduce parents' daily hassles and stress, thereby promoting good parenting (Chen, Howard, & Brooks-Gunn, 2011). In contrast, unfavorable home, school, and neighborhood experiences increase the chances that children will act in ways that expose them to further hardship. And when negative conditions pile up, such as marital discord, poverty, crowded living conditions, school and neighborhood violence, and abuse and neglect, the rate of maladjustment multiplies (Masten & Cicchetti, 2010).

Several highly effective school-based social and emotional learning programs promote children's resilience by increasing academic motivation, social competence, and supportive relationships (Durlak et al., 2011). Among these is the 4Rs (Reading, Writing, Respect, and Resolution) Program, which provides elementary school students with weekly lessons in emotional and social understanding and skills. Topics include managing anger, responding with empathy, being assertive, resolving social conflicts, and standing up against prejudice and bullying. High-quality children's literature, selected for relevance to program themes, complements each lesson. Discussion, writing, and role-playing of the stories deepen students' understanding.

An evaluation of 4Rs in New York City public schools revealed that teachers implementing the intervention used more supportive instructional techniques, including making concepts relevant to students' everyday lives and providing feedback that acknowledges effort. And relative to controls, children who participated in 4Rs became less depressed, less aggressive, more attentive, and more socially competent (Aber et al., 2011). In unsafe neighborhoods, 4Rs transforms schools into places of safety and mutual respect, where learning can occur.

Programs like 4Rs recognize that *resilience* is not a preexisting attribute but rather a capacity that develops, enabling children to use internal and external resources to cope with adversity (Luthar, Crossman, & Small, 2015). Throughout our discussion, we have seen how families, schools, communities, and society as a whole can enhance or undermine school-age children's developing sense of competence. As the next two chapters will reveal, young people whose childhood experiences helped them learn to control impulses, overcome obstacles, strive for self-direction, and respond considerately and sympathetically to others meet the challenges of the next period—adolescence—quite well.

Ask yourself

CONNECT Explain how factors that promote resilience contribute to favorable adjustment following divorce.

APPLY Claire told her 6-year-old daughter never to talk to or take candy from strangers. Why is Claire's warning unlikely to protect her daughter from sexual abuse?

REFLECT Describe a challenging time during your childhood. What aspects of the experience increased stress? What resources helped you cope with adversity?

Social Issues: Health

Children's Eyewitness Testimony

Increasingly, children are being called on to testify in court cases involving child abuse and neglect, child custody, and similar matters. The experience can be traumatic, requiring children to report on highly stressful events and sometimes to speak against a parent or other relative to whom they feel loyal. In some family disputes, they may fear punishment for telling the truth. In addition, child witnesses are faced with an unfamiliar situation—at the very least an interview in the judge's chambers and at most an open courtroom with judge, jury, spectators, and the possibility of unsympathetic cross-examination. Not surprisingly, these conditions can compromise the accuracy of children's recall.

Age Differences

As a result of societal reactions to rising rates of child abuse and the difficulty of prosecuting perpetrators, age requirements for child testimony have been relaxed in the United States (Klemfuss & Ceci, 2012). Children as young as age 3 frequently serve as witnesses.

Compared with preschoolers, school-age children are better at giving accurate, detailed narrative accounts of past experiences and correctly inferring others' motives and intentions. Older children are also more resistant to misleading questions that attorneys may ask when probing for more information or, in cross-examination, trying to influence the child's response (Hobbs & Goodman, 2014).

Nevertheless, when properly questioned, even 3-year-olds can recall recent events accurately (Peterson & Rideout, 1998). And in the face of biased interviewing, adolescents and adults often form elaborate, false memories of events (Ceci et al., 2007).

Suggestibility

Court testimony often involves repeated questioning—a procedure that, by itself, negatively affects children's response consistency and accuracy (Krähenbühl, Blades, & Eiser, 2009). When adults lead child witnesses by suggesting incorrect "facts," interrupt their denials, reinforce them for giving desired answers, ask complex and confusing questions, or use a confrontational style, they further increase the likelihood of incorrect reporting (Zajac, O'Neill, & Hayne, 2012).

By the time children appear in court, weeks, months, or even years have passed since the target events. When a long delay is combined with biased interviewing and with stereotyping of the accused ("He's in jail because he's been bad"), children can easily be misled into giving false information (Quas et al., 2007). The more distinctive, emotional, and personally relevant an event is, the more likely children are to recall it accurately over time, even after exposure to misleading suggestions (Goodman et al., 2014).

In many sexual abuse cases, anatomically correct dolls or body diagrams are used to prompt children's recall. Although these methods may help older children provide more detail, they increase the suggestibility of preschoolers, who may then report physical and sexual contact that never happened (Poole & Bruck, 2012).

Interventions

Adults must prepare child witnesses so they understand the courtroom process and know what to expect. In some places, "court schools" take children through the setting and give them an opportunity to role-play court activities. Practice interviews—in which children learn to provide the most accurate, detailed information possible and to admit

School-age eyewitnesses are better able than preschoolers to give accurate, detailed descriptions and correctly infer others' motives and intentions. This juvenile court judge can promote accurate recall by using a warm, supportive tone and avoiding leading questions.

not knowing rather than agreeing or guessing—are helpful (Zajac, O'Neill, & Hayne, 2012).

At the same time, legal professionals must use interviewing procedures that increase children's accurate reporting. Unbiased, open-ended questions that prompt children to disclose details—"Tell me what happened" or "You said there was a man; tell me about the man"—reduce suggestibility (Goodman et al., 2014; Steele, 2012). Also, a warm, supportive interview tone fosters accurate recall, perhaps by easing children's anxiety so they feel freer to disagree with an interviewer's false suggestions (Ceci, Bruck, & Battin, 2000).

If children are likely to experience emotional trauma or later punishment (as in a family dispute), courtroom procedures are sometimes adapted to protect them. For example, children can testify over closed-circuit TV so they do not have to face an abuser. When it is not wise for a child to participate directly, impartial expert witnesses can provide testimony that reports on the child's psychological condition and includes important elements of the child's story.

Summary / chapter 10

Erikson's Theory: Industry versus Inferiority (p. 336)

10.1 *What personality changes take place during Erikson's stage of industry versus inferiority?*

- Children who successfully resolve Erikson's psychological conflict of **industry versus inferiority** develop a positive but realistic self-concept, pride in their accomplishments, a sense of moral responsibility, and cooperative participation with agemates.

Self-Understanding (p. 336)

10.2 *Describe school-age children's self-concept and self-esteem, and discuss factors that affect their achievement-related attributions.*

- As school-age children gain in perspective-taking skills, their self-concepts increasingly include competencies, personality traits (both positive and negative), and **social comparisons.** Although parental support remains vital, children increasingly look to more people beyond the family for information about themselves.

- Self-esteem differentiates further and becomes hierarchically organized and more realistic. Cultural forces, gender-stereotyped expectations, and child-rearing practices contribute to variations in self-esteem. Authoritative parenting is linked to favorable self-esteem.

- Children who hold **mastery-oriented attributions** believe ability can be improved by trying hard and attribute failure to controllable factors, such as insufficient effort. In contrast, children who receive negative feedback about their ability are likely to develop **learned helplessness,** attributing success to external factors, such as luck, and failure to low ability.

- **Process praise,** which emphasizes behavior and effort, encourages mastery-oriented attributions, whereas **person praise,** which focuses on fixed abilities, is linked to learned helplessness. Cultural valuing of effort also promotes a mastery-oriented approach.

Emotional Development (p. 341)

10.3 *Cite changes in self-conscious emotions, emotional understanding, and emotional self-regulation in middle childhood.*

- Self-conscious emotions of pride and guilt become clearly governed by personal responsibility. Intense shame is particularly destructive, yielding both internalizing and externalizing problems.

- School-age children develop an appreciation of mixed emotions, which enables them to reconcile contradictory cues in interpreting another's feelings. Empathy increases and includes sensitivity to both people's immediate distress and their general life condition.

- By age 10, most children shift adaptively between **problem-centered** and **emotion-centered coping** to regulate emotion. Children who acquire a sense of emotional self-efficacy are upbeat, empathic, and prosocial.

Moral Development (p. 342)

10.4 *Describe changes in moral understanding during middle childhood, including children's understanding of diversity and inequality.*

- By middle childhood, children have internalized rules for good conduct. They construct a flexible appreciation of moral rules based on intentions and context and develop a better understanding of personal choice and individual rights.

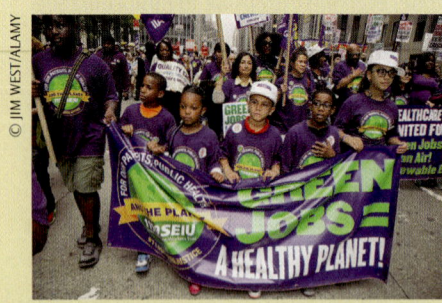

- School-age children absorb prevailing societal attitudes about race and ethnicity. With age, they pay more attention to inner traits, although implicit racial bias may persist. Children most likely to hold biases are those who believe that personality traits are fixed, who have inflated self-esteem, and who live in a social world that highlights group differences. Long-term intergroup contact is most effective at reducing prejudice.

Peer Relations (p. 345)

10.5 *How do peer sociability and friendship change in middle childhood?*

- Peer interaction becomes more prosocial, and physical aggression declines. By the end of middle childhood, children organize into **peer groups.**

- Friendships develop into mutual relationships based on trust. Children tend to select friends similar to themselves in multiple ways.

10.6 *Describe major categories of peer acceptance and ways to help rejected children.*

- On measures of **peer acceptance, popular children** are well-liked by many agemates; **rejected children** are strongly disliked; **controversial children** are both liked and disliked; **neglected children** arouse little reaction, positive or negative; and *average children* receive average numbers of positive and negative votes.

- **Popular-prosocial children** combine academic and social competence, while **popular-antisocial children** are aggressive but admired. **Rejected-aggressive children** are especially high in conflict and hostility; in contrast, **rejected-withdrawn children** are passive, socially awkward, and frequent targets of **peer victimization.**

- Coaching in social skills, academic tutoring, and training in perspective taking and social problem solving can help rejected children gain in social competence and peer acceptance. Intervening to improve the quality of parent–child interaction is often necessary.

CHAPTER 10 Emotional and Social Development in Middle Childhood

Gender Typing (p. 350)

10.7 What changes in gender-stereotyped beliefs and gender identity occur during middle childhood?

- School-age children extend their awareness of gender stereotypes to personality traits and academic subjects. But they also broaden their view of what males and females can do.

- Boys strengthen their identification with masculine traits, whereas girls more often experiment with "other-gender" activities. Gender identity includes self-evaluations of gender typicality, contentedness, and felt pressure to conform to gender roles—each of which affects adjustment.

Family Influences (p. 351)

10.8 How do parent–child communication and sibling relationships change in middle childhood?

- Despite declines in time spent with parents, **coregulation** allows parents to exercise general oversight over children, who increasingly make their own decisions.

- Sibling rivalry tends to increase with participation in a wider range of activities and more frequent parental comparisons. Only children do not differ from children with siblings in self-rated personality traits and are higher in self-esteem, school performance, and educational attainment.

10.9 What factors influence children's adjustment to divorce and blended family arrangements?

- Marital breakup is often quite stressful for children. Individual differences are affected by parental psychological health, financial well-being, child characteristics (age, temperament, and sex), and social supports. Children with difficult temperaments are at greater risk for adjustment problems. Divorce is linked to early sexual activity, adolescent parenthood, and long-term relationship difficulties.

- The overriding factor in positive adjustment following divorce is effective parenting. Positive father–child relationships are protective, as are supports from extended-family members, teachers, siblings, and friends. Divorce mediation can foster parental conflict resolution in the period surrounding divorce. The success of joint custody depends on effective coparenting.

- In **blended,** or **reconstituted, families,** girls, older children, and children in father–stepmother families tend to have more adjustment problems. Stepparents who move into their roles gradually help children adjust.

10.10 How do maternal employment and life in dual-earner families affect school-age children?

- When employed mothers remain committed to parenting, children display higher self-esteem, less gender-stereotyped beliefs, better achievement, and fewer behavior problems. In dual-earner families, the father's willingness to share responsibilities is a crucial factor. Workplace supports help parents in their child-rearing roles.

- Authoritative child rearing, parental monitoring, and regular after-school chores lead **self-care children** to be responsible and well-adjusted. Good "after-care" programs also aid school performance and emotional and social adjustment, especially for low-SES children.

Some Common Problems of Development (p. 358)

10.11 Cite common fears and anxieties in middle childhood.

- School-age children's fears include physical harm, media events, academic failure, parents' health, the possibility of dying, and peer rejection. Children with inhibited temperaments are at higher risk of developing **phobias.** Harsh living conditions can also cause severe anxiety.

10.12 Discuss factors related to child sexual abuse, its consequences for children's development, and its prevention and treatment.

- Child sexual abuse is typically committed by male family members, more often against girls than boys. Abusers have characteristics that predispose them toward sexual exploitation of children. Reported cases are strongly associated with poverty and marital instability. Abused children often have severe adjustment problems.

- Treatment for abused children typically requires long-term therapy with both children and parents. Educational programs that teach children to recognize inappropriate sexual advances and identify sources of help reduce the risk of sexual abuse.

10.13 Cite factors that foster resilience in middle childhood.

- Only a modest relationship exists between stressful life experiences and psychological disturbance in childhood. Children's personal characteristics, a warm family life, authoritative parenting, and school, community, and societal resources predict resilience.

Important Terms and Concepts

- blended, or reconstituted, families (p. 356)
- controversial children (p. 347)
- coregulation (p. 352)
- emotion-centered coping (p. 342)
- industry versus inferiority (p. 336)
- learned helplessness (p. 339)
- mastery-oriented attributions (p. 339)
- neglected children (p. 347)
- peer acceptance (p. 347)
- peer group (p. 346)
- peer victimization (p. 349)
- person praise (p. 339)
- phobia (p. 358)
- popular-antisocial children (p. 348)
- popular children (p. 347)
- popular-prosocial children (p. 348)
- problem-centered coping (p. 342)
- process praise (p. 330)
- rejected-aggressive children (p. 348)
- rejected children (p. 347)
- rejected-withdrawn children (p. 348)
- self-care children (p. 357)
- social comparisons (p. 336)

milestones
Development in Middle Childhood

6–8 YEARS

Physical

- Slow gains in height and weight continue. (294)
- Permanent teeth gradually replace primary teeth. (294)
- Legibility of writing increases. (300)
- Drawings become more organized and detailed and include some depth cues. (300)
- Games with rules and rough-and-tumble play become common. (301, 302)

Cognitive

- Thought becomes more logical, as shown by the ability to pass Piagetian conservation, class inclusion, and seriation problems. (304)

- Improves dramatically in speed of information processing. (308)
- Gains further in executive function, with marked improvements in inhibition, flexible shifting of attention, working memory capacity, and planning on multistep tasks. (308, 310)
- Uses memory strategies of rehearsal and then organization. (310)
- Views the mind as an active, constructive agent, capable of transforming information. (311)
- Awareness of memory strategies and of the impact of psychological factors, such as mental inferences, on performance improve. (311–312)
- Understands second-order false belief; capable of recursive thought. (312)
- Uses informal knowledge of number concepts and counting to master increasingly complex mathematical skills. (313)

Language

- Vocabulary increases rapidly throughout middle childhood, eventually reaching comprehension of 40,000 words. (321)
- Word definitions are concrete, referring to functions and appearance. (322)
- Transitions from emergent literacy to conventional reading. (313)

- Language awareness develops. (321)
- Understands and uses increasingly subtle, indirect expressions of meaning, such as irony and sarcasm. (322)
- Narratives increase in organization, detail, and expressiveness. (322)

Emotional/Social

- Self-concept begins to include personality traits, competencies, and social comparisons. (336)
- Self-esteem differentiates, becomes hierarchically organized, and adjusts to a more realistic level. (337)
- Self-conscious emotions of pride and guilt are governed by personal responsibility. (341)
- Recognizes that individuals can experience more than one emotion at a time and that their expressions may not reflect their true feelings. (341–342)

- Reconciles contradictory facial and situational cues in understanding another's feelings. (342)
- Empathy increases. (342)
- Becomes more independent and trustworthy. (342–343)
- Constructs a flexible appreciation of moral rules, taking prosocial and antisocial intentions into account. (343)
- Physical aggression declines; verbal and relational aggression continue. (345–346)
- Resolves conflicts more effectively. (345–346)

9–11 YEARS

Physical

- Adolescent growth spurt begins two years earlier in girls than in boys. (294)
- Executes gross-motor skills of running, jumping, throwing, catching, kicking, batting, and dribbling more quickly and with better coordination. (299–300)

Note: Numbers in parentheses indicate the page or pages on which each milestone is discussed.

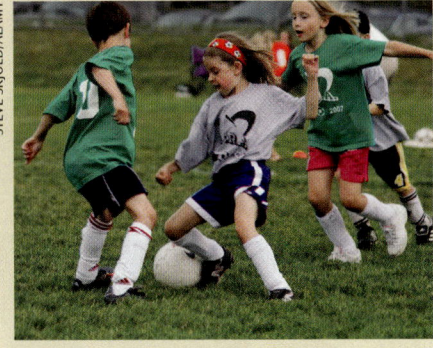

- Ability to represent depth in drawings expands. (300)
- Dominance hierarchies become more stable, especially among boys. (302)

Cognitive

- Continues to master concrete operational tasks in a step-by-step fashion. (306)
- Spatial reasoning improves; readily draws and reads maps of large-scale spaces, grasps the notion of scale, and understands map symbols. (304–305)

- Continues to improve in speed of information processing. (308)
- Continues to gain in executive function. (308, 309)
- Uses memory strategies of rehearsal and organization more effectively. (310)
- Applies several memory strategies simultaneously; begins to use elaboration. (310–311)

- General knowledge base (semantic memory) grows larger and becomes better organized. (311)
- Theory of mind becomes more elaborate and refined. (311–312)
- Cognitive self-regulation improves. (312–313)

Language

- Thinks about and uses words more precisely; word definitions emphasize synonyms and categorical relations. (322)
- Grasps multiple meanings of words, as reflected in comprehension of metaphors and humor. (322)
- Continues to master complex grammatical constructions. (322)

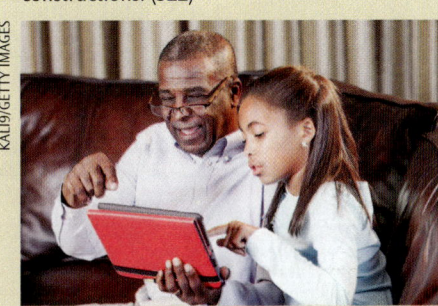

- Narratives lengthen, become more coherent, and include more evaluative comments. (322)

Emotional/Social

- Self-esteem remains high but continues to become more realistic and nuanced. (337)
- Distinguishes ability, effort, and external factors (such as luck) in attributions for success and failure. (339)
- Empathic responding extends to general life conditions. (342)
- Shifts adaptively between problem-centered and emotion-centered strategies in regulating emotion. (342)
- Becomes more knowledgeable about socially approved ways to display negative emotion. (342)

- Clarifies and links moral rules and social conventions. (343)
- Convictions about matters of personal choice strengthen, and understanding of individual rights expands. (343–344)
- Explicit outgroup prejudice declines. (344–345)
- Friendships become more selective and are based on mutual trust. (346)
- Peer groups emerge. (346)

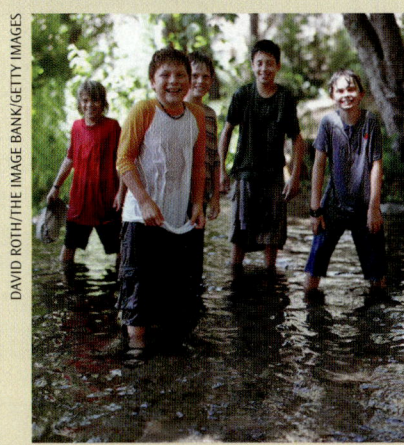

- Becomes aware of more gender stereotypes, including personality traits and achievement, but has a flexible appreciation of what males and females can do. (350)
- Gender identity expands to include self-evaluations of typicality, contentedness, and felt pressure to conform. (351)
- Sibling rivalry tends to increase. (352)

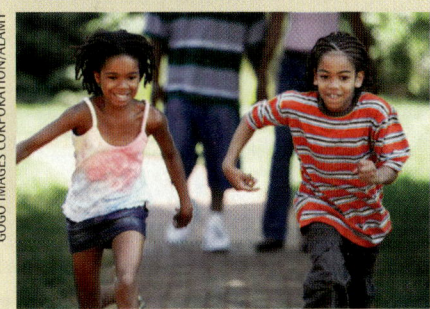

Note: Numbers in parentheses indicate the page or pages on which each milestone is discussed.

chapter 11

Physical and Cognitive Development in Adolescence

The dramatic physical and cognitive changes of adolescence make it both an exhilarating and apprehensive period of development. Although their bodies are full-grown and sexually mature, these teenagers have many skills to acquire and hurdles to surmount before they are ready for full assumption of adult roles.

What's ahead in chapter 11

PHYSICAL DEVELOPMENT

Conceptions of Adolescence
The Biological Perspective • The Social Perspective • A Balanced Point of View

Puberty: The Physical Transition to Adulthood
Hormonal Changes • Body Growth • Motor Development and Physical Activity • Sexual Maturation • Individual Differences in Pubertal Growth • Brain Development • Changing States of Arousal

The Psychological Impact of Pubertal Events
Reactions to Pubertal Changes • Pubertal Change, Emotion, and Social Behavior • Pubertal Timing

Health Issues
Nutritional Needs • Eating Disorders • Sexuality • Sexually Transmitted Infections • Adolescent Pregnancy and Parenthood • Substance Use and Abuse

■ **SOCIAL ISSUES: HEALTH** Lesbian, Gay, and Bisexual Youths: Coming Out to Oneself and Others

COGNITIVE DEVELOPMENT

Piaget's Theory: The Formal Operational Stage
Hypothetico-Deductive Reasoning • Propositional Thought • Follow-Up Research on Formal Operational Thought

An Information-Processing View of Adolescent Cognitive Development
Scientific Reasoning: Coordinating Theory with Evidence • How Scientific Reasoning Develops

Consequences of Adolescent Cognitive Changes
Self-Consciousness and Self-Focusing • Idealism and Criticism • Decision Making

Sex Differences in Mental Abilities
Verbal Abilities • Mathematical Abilities

■ **BIOLOGY AND ENVIRONMENT**
Sex Differences in Spatial Abilities

Learning in School
School Transitions • Academic Achievement • Dropping Out

■ **SOCIAL ISSUES: EDUCATION** Media Multitasking Disrupts Learning

On Sabrina's eleventh birthday, her friend Joyce gave her a surprise party, but Sabrina seemed somber during the celebration. Although Sabrina and Joyce had been close friends since third grade, their relationship was faltering. Sabrina was a head taller and some 20 pounds heavier than most girls in her sixth-grade class. Her breasts were well-developed, her hips and thighs had broadened, and she had begun to menstruate. In contrast, Joyce still had the short, lean, flat-chested body of a school-age child.

Ducking into the bathroom while the other girls put candles on the cake, Sabrina frowned at her image in the mirror. "I'm so big and heavy," she whispered. At church youth group on Sunday evenings, Sabrina broke away from Joyce and joined the eighth-grade girls. Around them, she didn't feel so large and awkward.

Once a month, parents gathered at Sabrina's and Joyce's school to discuss child-rearing concerns. Sabrina's parents, Franca and Antonio, attended whenever they could. "How you know they are becoming teenagers is this," volunteered Antonio. "The bedroom door is closed, and they want to be alone. Also, they contradict and disagree. I tell Sabrina, 'You have to go to Aunt Gina's on Saturday for dinner with the family.' The next thing I know, she's arguing with me."

Sabrina has entered **adolescence,** the transition between childhood and adulthood. In industrialized societies, the skills young people must master are so complex and the choices confronting them so diverse that adolescence is greatly extended. But around the world, the basic tasks of this period are much the same. Sabrina must accept her full-grown body, acquire adult ways of thinking, attain greater independence from her family, develop more mature ways of relating to peers of both sexes, and begin to construct an identity—a secure sense of who she is in terms of sexual, vocational, moral, ethnic, religious, and other life values and goals.

The beginning of adolescence is marked by **puberty,** a flood of biological events leading to an adult-sized body and sexual maturity. As Sabrina's reactions suggest, entry into adolescence can be an especially trying time for some young people. In this chapter, we trace the events of puberty and take up a variety of health concerns—physical exercise, nutrition, sexual activity, substance use and abuse, and other challenges that many teenagers encounter on the path to maturity.

Adolescence also brings with it vastly expanded powers of reasoning. Teenagers can grasp complex scientific and mathematical principles, grapple with social and political issues, and delve deeply into the meaning of a poem or story. The second part of this chapter traces these extraordinary changes from both Piaget's and the information-processing perspective. Next, we examine sex differences in mental abilities. Finally, we turn to the main setting in which adolescent thought takes shape: the school. ●

PHYSICAL DEVELOPMENT

Conceptions of Adolescence

11.1 How have conceptions of adolescence changed over the past century?

Why is Sabrina self-conscious, argumentative, and in retreat from family activities? Historically, theorists explained the impact of puberty on psychological development by resorting to extremes—either a biological or a social explanation. Today, researchers realize that biological and social forces jointly determine adolescent psychological change.

The Biological Perspective

Ask several parents of young children what they expect their sons and daughters to be like as teenagers, and you will probably get answers like these: "Rebellious and irresponsible," "Full of rages and tempers." This widespread storm-and-stress view dates back to major early-twentieth-century theorists. The most influential, G. Stanley Hall (1904), who based his ideas on Darwin's theory of evolution, described adolescence as a period so turbulent that it resembled the era in which humans evolved from savages into civilized beings. Similarly, in Freud's psychosexual theory, sexual impulses reawaken in the *genital stage*, triggering psychological conflict and volatile behavior. As adolescents find intimate partners, inner forces gradually achieve a new, mature harmony, and the stage concludes with marriage, birth, and child rearing. In this way, young people fulfill their biological destiny: sexual reproduction and survival of the species.

The Social Perspective

Contemporary research suggests that the storm-and-stress notion of adolescence is exaggerated. Certain problems, such as eating disorders, depression, suicide, and lawbreaking, do occur more often than earlier. But the overall rate of serious psychological disturbance rises only slightly from childhood to adolescence, reaching 15 to 20 percent (Merikangas et al., 2010). Though much greater than the adulthood rate (about 6 percent), emotional turbulence is not a routine feature of the teenage years.

The first researcher to point out the wide variability in adolescent adjustment was anthropologist Margaret Mead (1928). She returned from the Pacific islands of Samoa with a startling conclusion: Because of the culture's relaxed social relationships and openness toward sexuality, adolescence "is perhaps the pleasantest time the Samoan girl (or boy) will ever know" (p. 308). In Mead's alternative view, the social environment is entirely responsible for the range of teenage experiences, from erratic and agitated to calm and stress-free. Later researchers found that Samoan adolescence was not as untroubled as Mead had assumed (Freeman, 1983). Still, she showed that to understand adolescent development, researchers must pay greater attention to social and cultural influences.

A Balanced Point of View

Today we know that biological, psychological, and social forces combine to influence adolescent development (Hollenstein & Lougheed, 2013). Biological changes are universal—found in all primates and all cultures. These internal stresses and the social expectations accompanying them—that the young person give up childish ways, develop new interpersonal relationships, and take on greater responsibility—are likely to prompt moments of uncertainty, self-doubt, and disappointment in all teenagers. Adolescents' prior and current experiences affect their success in surmounting these challenges.

At the same time, the length of adolescence and its demands and pressures vary substantially among cultures. Most tribal and village societies have only a brief intervening phase between childhood and full assumption of adult roles (Lancy, 2008). In industrialized nations, young people face prolonged dependence on parents and postponement of sexual gratification while they prepare for a productive work life. As a result, adolescence is greatly extended—so much so that researchers commonly divide it into three phases:

1. *Early adolescence* (11 to 14 years): This is a period of rapid pubertal change.
2. *Middle adolescence* (14 to 16 years): Pubertal changes are now nearly complete.
3. *Late adolescence* (16 to 18 years): The young person achieves full adult appearance and anticipates assumption of adult roles.

The more the social environment supports young people in achieving adult responsibilities, the better they adjust. For all the biological tensions and uncertainties about the future that teenagers feel, most negotiate this period successfully. With this in mind, let's look closely at puberty, the dawning of adolescent development.

Puberty: The Physical Transition to Adulthood

11.2 Describe body growth, motor performance, and sexual maturation during puberty.
11.3 What factors influence the timing of puberty?
11.4 What changes in the brain take place during adolescence?

The changes of puberty are dramatic. Within a few years, the school-age child's body transforms into that of a full-grown adult. Genetically influenced hormonal processes regulate pubertal growth. Girls, who have been advanced in physical maturity since the prenatal period, reach puberty, on average, two years earlier than boys.

Hormonal Changes

The complex hormonal changes that underlie puberty occur gradually and are under way in middle childhood. Secretions of *growth hormone (GH)* and *thyroxine* (see Chapter 7, page 219) increase, eventually leading to tremendous gains in body size and to attainment of skeletal maturity.

Sexual maturation is controlled by the sex hormones. Although we think of *estrogens* as female hormones and *androgens* as male hormones, both types are present in each sex but in different amounts. Sex hormones begin to rise long before physical changes are visible, typically between ages 6 and 8, when the adrenal glands on top of each kidney start to release increasing levels of *adrenal androgens*. By age 10, levels of adrenal androgens have increased tenfold, and some children experience their first feelings of sexual attraction (Best & Fortenberry, 2013).

Adrenal androgens influence girls' height spurt, and they stimulate growth of underarm and pubic hair. (Adrenal androgens have little visible impact on boys, whose physical characteristics are mainly influenced by androgen secretions from the testes.) Estrogens released by girls' maturing ovaries contribute to the height spurt by stimulating GH secretion, and they cause the breasts, uterus, and vagina to mature, the body to take on feminine proportions, and fat to accumulate. In addition, estrogens play a crucial role in regulating the menstrual cycle.

Boys' maturing testes release large quantities of the androgen *testosterone,* which leads to muscle growth, body and facial hair, and other male sex characteristics. Androgens (especially testosterone) exert a GH-enhancing effect, contributing greatly to gains in body size. The testes secrete small amounts of estrogen as well, which add to the growth spurt and lead many boys to experience temporary breast enlargement. In both sexes, estrogens in combination with androgens stimulate gains in bone density, which continue into early adulthood (Ambler, 2013; Cooper, Sayer, & Dennison, 2006).

As you can see, pubertal changes are of two broad types: (1) overall body growth and (2) maturation of sexual characteristics. We have seen that the hormones responsible for sexual maturity also affect body growth, making puberty the time of greatest sexual differentiation since prenatal life.

Body Growth

The first outward sign of puberty is the rapid gain in height and weight known as the **growth spurt**. On average, it is under way for North American and Western European girls shortly after age 10, for boys around age 12½. Because estrogens trigger and then restrain GH secretion more readily than androgens, the typical girl is taller and heavier during early adolescence. By age 13½, however, she is surpassed by the typical boy, whose

Sex differences in pubertal growth are obvious among these 11-year-olds. Compared with the boys, the girls are taller and more mature-looking.

adolescent growth spurt has now started, whereas hers is almost finished (Ambler, 2013). Growth in body size is complete for most girls by age 16 and for boys by age 17½, when the epiphyses at the ends of the long bones close completely (see Chapter 7, page 217). Altogether, adolescents add 10 to 11 inches in height and 50 to 75 pounds—nearly 50 percent of adult body weight. Figure 11.1 on page 370 illustrates pubertal changes in general body growth.

Body Proportions. During puberty, the cephalocaudal growth trend of infancy and childhood reverses. The hands, legs, and feet accelerate first, followed by the torso, which accounts for most of the adolescent height gain. This pattern helps explain why early adolescents often appear awkward and out of proportion—long-legged, with giant feet and hands.

Large sex differences in body proportions also appear, caused by the action of sex hormones on the skeleton. Boys' shoulders broaden relative to the hips, whereas girls' hips broaden relative to the shoulders and waist. Of course, boys also end up larger than girls, and their legs are longer in relation to the rest of the body—mainly because boys have two extra years of preadolescent growth, when the legs are growing the fastest.

Muscle–Fat Makeup and Other Internal Changes. Around age 8, girls start to add fat on their arms, legs, and trunk, a trend that accelerates between ages 11 and 16. In contrast, arm and leg fat decreases in adolescent boys. Although both sexes gain in muscle, this increase is much greater in boys, who develop larger skeletal muscles, hearts, and lung capacity (Rogol, Roemmich, & Clark, 2002). Also, the number of red blood cells—and therefore the ability to carry oxygen from the lungs to the muscles—increases in boys but not in girls. Altogether, boys gain far more muscle strength than girls, a difference that contributes to boys' superior athletic performance during the teenage years (Greydanus, Omar, & Pratt, 2010).

FIGURE 11.1 Body growth during adolescence. Because the pubertal growth spurt takes place earlier for girls than for boys, Mariel reached her adult body size earlier than Steven. Rapid pubertal growth is accompanied by large sex differences in body proportions.

Motor Development and Physical Activity

Puberty brings steady improvements in gross motor performance, but the pattern of change differs for boys and girls. Girls' gains are slow and gradual, leveling off by age 14. In contrast, boys show a dramatic spurt in strength, speed, and endurance that continues through the teenage years. By midadolescence, few girls perform as well as the average boy in running speed, broad jump, or throwing distance. And practically no boys score as low as the average girl (Greydanus, Omar, & Pratt, 2010; Haywood & Getchell, 2014).

Among boys, athletic competence is strongly related to peer admiration and self-esteem. Some adolescents become so obsessed with physical prowess that they turn to performance-enhancing drugs. In recent large-scale studies, more than 9 percent of U.S. high school seniors, mostly boys, reported using creatine, an over-the-counter substance that enhances short-term muscle power but is associated with serious side effects, including muscle tissue disease, brain seizures, and heart irregularities. About 2 percent of seniors, again mostly boys, have taken anabolic steroids or a related substance, androstenedione—powerful prescription medications that boost muscle mass and strength (Johnston et al., 2015). Teenagers usually obtain steroids illegally, ignoring side effects, which range from acne, excess body hair, and high blood pressure to mood swings, aggressive behavior, and damage to the liver, circulatory system, and reproductive organs (Denham, 2012). Coaches and health professionals should inform teenagers of the dangers of these performance-enhancing substances.

In 1972, the U.S. federal government required schools receiving public funds to provide equal opportunities for males and females in all educational programs, including athletics. Since then, high school girls' sports participation has increased, although it still falls far short of boys'. According to a recent survey of all 50 U.S. state high school athletic associations, 42 percent of sports participants are girls, 58 percent boys (National Federation of State High School Associations, 2016). In Chapter 9, we saw that girls get less encouragement and recognition for athletic achievement, a pattern that starts early and persists into the teenage years (see page 301).

Furthermore, when researchers followed a large, representative sample of U.S. youths from ages 9 to 17, daily free-time physical activity declined with age, more so for girls than boys.

High school students run in their school's cross country invitational. Endurance sports that do not require an organized team or special facilities are especially likely to be sustained into adulthood.

And at every age, only a minority of participants engaged in regular exercise outside of school hours (see Figure 11.2) (Wall et al., 2011). In high school, just 55 percent of U.S. boys and 48 percent of girls receive any physical education, with just 30 percent of all students experiencing a daily physical education class (Kann et al., 2016).

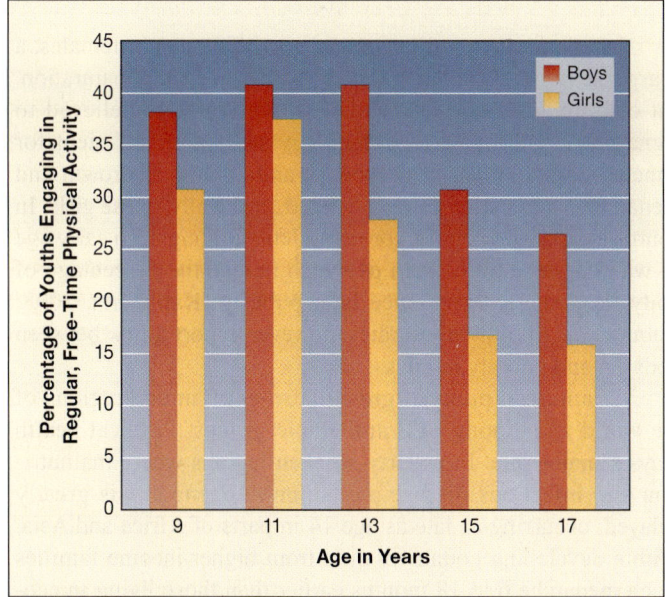

FIGURE 11.2 Decline in free-time physical activity from ages 9 to 17 among U.S. boys and girls. In a longitudinal-sequential investigation of a U.S. nationally representative sample of over 1,600 youths followed from ages 9 to 17, the percentage engaging in at least seven sessions of free-time daily exercise (sports, free-time daily exercise, playing actively with friends) in the previous week declined from 38 to 27 percent among boys and 31 to 16 percent among girls. Throughout adolescence, boys exceeded girls in regular daily exercise. (Based on Wall et al., 2011.)

Besides improving motor performance, sports and exercise influence cognitive and social development. Interschool and intramural athletics provide important lessons in teamwork, problem solving, assertiveness, and competition. And regular, sustained physical activity—which required physical education can ensure—is associated with lasting physical and mental health benefits (Brand et al., 2010).

Adolescents vary in their enjoyment of sports and exercise, leading to differences in continued involvement. In one study, participating in team or individual sports at age 14 at least once a week for girls and twice a week for boys predicted high physical activity rates at age 31. Endurance sports, such as running and cycling—activities that do not require an organized team or special facilities—were especially likely to continue into adulthood (Tammelin et al., 2003). And adolescent exertion during exercise, defined as sweating and breathing heavily, is one of the best predictors of adult physical exercise, perhaps because it fosters high *physical self-efficacy*—belief in one's ability to sustain an exercise program (Motl et al., 2002; Telama et al., 2005).

Sexual Maturation

Accompanying rapid body growth are changes in physical features related to sexual functioning. Some, called **primary sexual characteristics,** involve the reproductive organs (ovaries, uterus, and vagina in females; penis, scrotum, and testes in males). Others, called **secondary sexual characteristics,** are visible on the outside of the body and serve as additional signs of sexual maturity (for example, breast development in females and the appearance of underarm and pubic hair in both sexes). As Table 11.1 on page 372 shows, these characteristics develop in a fairly standard sequence, although the ages at which each begins and is completed vary greatly. Typically, pubertal development takes about 4 years, but some adolescents complete it in 2 years, whereas others take 5 to 6 years.

Sexual Maturation in Girls. Female puberty usually begins with the budding of the breasts and the growth spurt. **Menarche,** or first menstruation, typically occurs around age 12½ for North American girls, 13 for Western Europeans. But the age range is wide, from 10½ to 15½ years. Following menarche, breast and pubic hair growth are completed, and underarm hair appears.

Notice in Table 11.1 that nature delays sexual maturity until the girl's body is large enough for childbearing; menarche takes place after the peak of the height spurt. As an extra measure of security, for 12 to 18 months following menarche, the menstrual cycle often occurs without the release of an ovum from the ovaries (Fuqua & Rogol, 2013). But this temporary period of sterility does not occur in all girls, and it does not provide reliable protection against pregnancy.

Sexual Maturation in Boys. The first sign of puberty in boys is the enlargement of the testes (glands that manufacture sperm), accompanied by changes in the texture and color of the scrotum. Pubic hair emerges soon after, about the same time the penis begins to enlarge (Fuqua & Rogol, 2013).

TABLE 11.1
Pubertal Development in North American Girls and Boys

GIRLS	AVERAGE AGE ATTAINED	AGE RANGE	BOYS	AVERAGE AGE ATTAINED	AGE RANGE
Breasts begin to "bud"	10	8–13	Testes begin to enlarge	11.5	9.5–13.5
Height spurt begins	10	8–13	Pubic hair appears	12	10–15
Pubic hair appears	10.5	8–14	Penis begins to enlarge	12	10.5–14.5
Peak strength spurt	11.6	9.5–14	Height spurt begins	12.5	10.5–16
Peak height spurt	11.7	10–13.5	Spermarche (first ejaculation) occurs	13.5	12–16
Menarche (first menstruation) occurs	12.5	10.5–15.5	Peak height spurt	14	12.5–15.5
Peak weight spurt	12.7	10–14	Peak weight spurt	14	12.5–15.5
Adult stature reached	13	10–16	Facial hair begins to grow	14	12.5–15.5
Pubic hair growth completed	14.5	14–15	Voice begins to deepen	14	12.5–15.5
Breast growth completed	15	10–17	Penis and testes growth completed	14.5	12.5–16
			Peak strength spurt	15.3	13–17
			Adult stature reached	15.5	13.5–17.5
			Pubic hair growth completed	15.5	14–17

Sources: Boswell, 2014; Herman-Giddens, 2006; Rogol, Roemmich, & Clark, 2002; Rubin et al., 2009.
Photos: (left) © Laura Dwight Photography; (right) Bill Aron/PhotoEdit

As Table 11.1 reveals, the growth spurt occurs much later in the sequence of pubertal events for boys than for girls. When it reaches its peak around age 14, enlargement of the testes and penis is nearly complete, and underarm hair appears. So do facial and body hair, which increase gradually for several years. Another landmark of male physical maturity is the deepening of the voice as the larynx enlarges and the vocal cords lengthen. (Girls' voices also deepen slightly.) Voice change usually takes place at the peak of the male growth spurt and often is not complete until puberty is over (Archibald, Graber, & Brooks-Gunn, 2006).

While the penis is growing, the prostate gland and seminal vesicles (which together produce semen, the fluid containing sperm) enlarge. Then, around age 13½, **spermarche,** or first ejaculation, occurs (Rogol, Roemmich, & Clark, 2002). For a while, the semen contains few living sperm. So, like girls, boys have an initial period of reduced fertility.

Individual Differences in Pubertal Growth

Heredity contributes substantially to the timing of pubertal changes. Identical twins are more similar than fraternal twins in attainment of most pubertal milestones (Eaves et al., 2004; Jahanfar, Lye, & Krishnarajah, 2013).

Nutrition and exercise also make a difference. In females, a sharp rise in body weight and fat may hasten sexual maturation. Fat cells release a protein called *leptin,* which is believed to signal the brain that the girl's energy stores are sufficient for puberty—a likely reason that breast and pubic hair growth and menarche occur earlier for heavier and, especially, obese girls. In contrast, girls who begin rigorous athletic training at an early age or who eat very little (both of which reduce the percentage of body fat) usually experience later puberty (Kaplowitz, 2008; Rubin et al., 2009). Few studies, however, report a link between body fat and puberty in boys.

Variations in pubertal growth also exist among regions of the world and among SES and ethnic groups. Physical health plays a major role. In poverty-stricken regions where malnutrition and infectious disease are common, menarche is greatly delayed, occurring as late as age 14 in parts of Africa and Asia. Within developing countries, girls from higher-income families reach menarche 6 to 18 months earlier than those living in economically disadvantaged homes (Parent et al., 2003; Zhu et al., 2016).

But in industrialized nations where food is abundant, the joint roles of heredity and environment in pubertal growth are apparent. For example, breast and pubic hair growth begin, on average, around age 9 in African-American girls—a year earlier than in European-American girls. And African-American girls reach menarche about six months earlier, around age 12 (Ramnitz & Lodish, 2013). Although widespread overweight and obesity in the black population contribute, a genetically influenced faster rate of physical maturation is also involved. Black girls usually reach menarche before white girls of the same age and body weight (Reagan et al., 2012).

Early family experiences may also affect pubertal timing. One theory suggests that humans have evolved to be sensitive to the emotional quality of their childhood environments. When children's safety and security are at risk, it is adaptive for them to reproduce early. Research indicates that girls and (less consistently) boys with a history of family conflict, harsh parenting, parental separation, or single mothers tend to reach puberty early. In contrast, those with warm, stable family ties reach puberty relatively late (Belsky et al., 2007a; Boynton-Jarrett et al., 2013; Ellis & Essex, 2007; Ellis et al., 2011; Webster et al., 2014). For girls, two longitudinal studies confirm this chain of influence from adverse childhood family environments to earlier pubertal timing to increased adolescent sexual risk taking (Belsky et al., 2010; James et al., 2012).

In the research we have considered, threats to emotional health accelerate puberty, whereas threats to physical health delay it. A **secular trend,** or generational change, in pubertal timing lends added support to the role of physical well-being in pubertal development. In industrialized nations, age of menarche declined steadily—by about 3 to 4 months per decade—from 1900 to 1970, a period in which nutrition, health care, sanitation, and control of infectious disease improved greatly. Boys, too, have reached puberty earlier in recent decades (Herman-Giddens et al., 2012). And as developing nations make socioeconomic progress, they also show secular gains.

In most industrialized nations, the trend toward earlier menarche has stopped or undergone a slight reversal (Sørensen et al., 2012). But in the United States and a few European countries, soaring rates of overweight and obesity are responsible for a modest, continuing trend toward earlier menarche (Gonzalez-Feliciano, Maisonet, & Marcus, 2013; Henk et al., 2013). A worrisome consequence is that girls who reach sexual maturity at age 10 or 11 will feel pressure to act much older than they are. As we will see shortly, early-maturing girls are at risk for unfavorable peer involvements, including sexual activity.

Brain Development

The physical transformations of adolescence include major changes in the brain. Brain-imaging research reveals continued pruning of unused synapses in the cerebral cortex, especially the prefrontal cortex. Growth and myelination of stimulated neural fibers accelerate, further strengthening connections among various brain regions. In particular, linkages between the prefrontal cortex and other areas in the cerebral cortex and the inner brain (including the amygdala and hippocampus) expand and attain rapid communication (Blakemore, 2012; Chavarria et al., 2014; Goddings & Giedd, 2014). Consequently, adolescents gain in diverse cognitive skills, including executive function, reasoning, problem solving, and decision making.

But these advances in cognitive control occur gradually over the teenage years. fMRI evidence reveals that adolescents recruit the prefrontal cortex's network of connections with other brain areas less effectively than adults do. Because the *prefrontal cognitive-control network* still requires fine-tuning, teenagers' performance on tasks requiring inhibition, planning, and delay of gratification (rejecting a smaller immediate reward in favor of a larger, later reward) is not yet fully mature (Luna, Padmanabhan, & Geier, 2014; Smith, Xiao, & Bechara, 2012; Steinberg et al., 2009).

Adding to these executive function and self-regulation difficulties are changes in the brain's *emotional/social network.* As humans and other mammals become sexually mature, neurons become more responsive to excitatory neurotransmitters. As a result, adolescents react more strongly to stressful events and experience pleasurable stimuli more intensely. Changes in the emotional/social network also increase adolescents' sensitivity to social stimuli, making them highly reactive to peer influence and evaluation (Somerville, 2013).

Because the cognitive-control network is not yet functioning optimally, most teenagers find it especially difficult to manage these powerful feelings and impulses (Albert, Chein, & Steinberg, 2013; Casey, Jones, & Somerville, 2011). This imbalance contributes to teenagers' unchecked drive for novel experiences, including drug taking, reckless driving, unprotected sex, and delinquent activity. In a longitudinal study of a large, representative sample of U.S. youths, researchers tracked changes in self-reported impulsivity and sensation seeking between ages 12 and 24 (Harden & Tucker-Drob, 2011). As Figure 11.3 shows, impulsivity declined steadily with age—evidence of gradual improvement

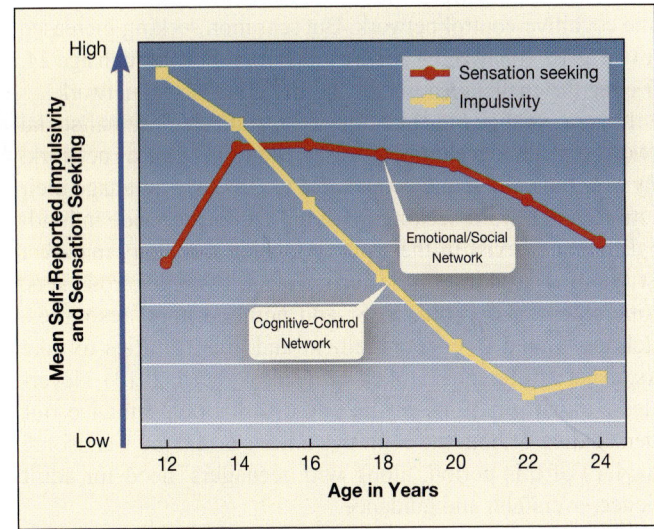

FIGURE 11.3 Development of impulsivity and sensation seeking from 12 to 24 years. In this longitudinal study of a large, representative sample of 7,600 U.S. youths, impulsivity declined steadily, while sensation seeking increased in early adolescence and then diminished more gradually. Findings confirm the challenge that the emotional/social network poses to the cognitive-control network. (From K. P. Harden and E. M. Tucker-Drob, 2011, "Individual Differences in the Development of Sensation Seeking and Impulsivity During Adolescence: Further Evidence of a Dual Systems Model," *Developmental Psychology, 47,* p. 742. Copyright © 2011 by the American Psychological Association. Adapted with permission of the American Psychological Association.)

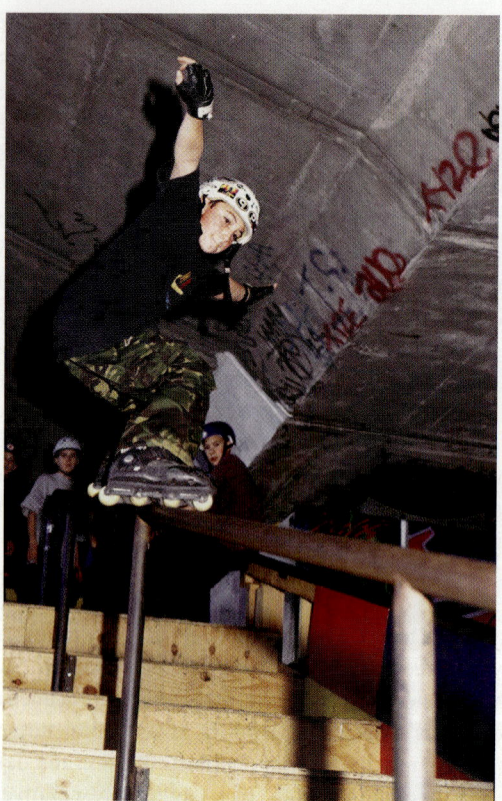

Changes in the brain's emotional/social network outpace development of the prefrontal cognitive-control network, contributing to teenagers' drive for novel experiences, receptiveness to peer influence, and risk-taking behavior.

of the cognitive-control network. But sensation seeking increased from 12 to 16, followed by a more gradual decline through age 24, reflecting the challenge posed by the emotional/social network.

In sum, changes in the adolescent brain's emotional/social network outpace development of the cognitive-control network. Only over time are young people able to effectively manage their emotions and reward-seeking behavior. Of course, wide individual differences exist in the extent to which teenagers manifest this rise in risk taking in the form of careless, dangerous acts. Temperament, parenting, SES, and neighborhood resources, which are linked to encouragement and opportunities to take risks, make a difference (Hollenstein & Lougheed, 2013). Nevertheless, transformations in the adolescent brain enhance our understanding of both the cognitive advances and the worrisome behaviors of this period, along with teenagers' need for adult patience, oversight, and guidance.

Changing States of Arousal

At puberty, revisions occur in the way the brain regulates the timing of sleep, perhaps because of increased neural sensitivity to evening light. As a result, adolescents go to bed much later than they did as children. Yet they need almost as much sleep as they did in middle childhood—about nine hours. When the school day begins early, their sleep needs are not satisfied.

This sleep "phase delay" strengthens with pubertal growth. But today's teenagers—with more evening social activities, part-time jobs, and bedrooms equipped with screen media—get much less sleep than teenagers of previous generations. Sleep-deprived adolescents display declines in executive function and both cognitive and emotional self-regulation. As a result, they are more likely to achieve less well in school; suffer from anxiety, irritability, and depressed mood; and engage in high-risk behaviors that result in motor vehicle collisions and arrests for delinquency (Bryant & Gómez, 2015; Carskadon, 2011; Meldrum, Barnes, & Hay, 2015). Sleep rebound on weekends sustains the pattern by leading to difficulty falling asleep on subsequent evenings. Later school start times ease but do not eliminate sleep loss (Wahlstrom et al., 2014). Educating teenagers about the importance of sleep is vital.

The Psychological Impact of Pubertal Events

11.5 Explain adolescents' reactions to the physical changes of puberty.
11.6 Describe the impact of pubertal timing on adolescent adjustment, noting sex differences.

Think back to your late elementary and middle school days. As you reached puberty, how did your feelings about yourself and your relationships with others change? Research reveals that pubertal events affect adolescents' self-image, mood, and interaction with parents and peers. Some outcomes are a response to dramatic physical change, whenever it occurs. Others have to do with pubertal timing.

Reactions to Pubertal Changes

Two generations ago, menarche was often traumatic. Today, girls commonly react with "surprise," undoubtedly due to the sudden onset of the event. Otherwise, they typically report a mixture of positive and negative emotions (Chang, Hayter, & Wu, 2010; DeRose & Brooks-Gunn, 2006). Yet wide individual differences exist that depend on prior knowledge and support from family members, which in turn are influenced by cultural attitudes toward puberty and sexuality.

For girls who have no advance information, menarche can be shocking and disturbing. And cultural or religious views of menstruation as unclean, embarrassing, or a source of weakness requiring restriction of activities also promote distressed reactions (Marván & Alcalá-Herrera, 2014). Unlike 50 to 60 years ago, today few girls in developed countries are uninformed, a shift that is probably due to parents' greater willingness to discuss sexual matters and to the spread of health education classes (Omar, McElderry, & Zakharia, 2003). Almost all girls get some information from their mothers. And some evidence suggests that compared with European-American families, African-American families may better prepare girls for menarche, treat it as an important milestone, and express less conflict over girls reaching sexual maturity—factors that lead African-American girls to react more favorably (Martin, 1996).

Like girls' reactions to menarche, boys' responses to spermarche reflect mixed feelings. Virtually all boys know about ejaculation ahead of time, but many say that no one spoke to them before or during puberty about physical changes (Omar, McElderry, & Zakharia, 2003). Usually they get their information from reading material or websites. Even boys who had advance information often say that their first ejaculation occurred earlier than they expected and that they were unprepared for it. Whereas almost all girls eventually tell a friend that they are menstruating, far fewer boys tell anyone about spermarche (DeRose & Brooks-Gunn, 2006; Downs & Fuller, 1991). Overall, boys get much less social support than girls for the changes of puberty. They might benefit, especially, from opportunities to ask questions and discuss feelings with a sympathetic parent or health professional.

Many tribal and village societies celebrate the onset of puberty with an *initiation ceremony*, a ritualized announcement to the community that marks an important change in privilege and responsibility. Consequently, young people know that reaching puberty is a significant milestone in their culture. In contrast, Western societies grant little formal recognition to movement from childhood to adolescence or from adolescence to adulthood. Ceremonies such as the Jewish bar or bat mitzvah and the *quinceañera* in Hispanic communities (celebrating a 15-year-old girl's sexual maturity and marriage availability) resemble initiation ceremonies, but only within the ethnic or religious subculture. They do not mark a significant change in social status in the larger society.

Instead, Western adolescents are granted partial adult status at many different ages—for example, an age for starting employment, for driving, for leaving high school, for voting, and for drinking. And in some contexts (at home and at school), they may still be regarded as children. The absence of a widely accepted marker of physical and social maturity makes the process of becoming an adult more confusing.

Pubertal Change, Emotion, and Social Behavior

A common belief is that puberty has something to do with adolescent moodiness and the desire for greater physical and psychological separation from parents. Let's see what research says about these relationships.

Adolescent Moodiness.
Higher pubertal hormone levels are linked to greater moodiness, but only modestly so (Graber, Brooks-Gunn, & Warren, 2006). What other factors might contribute? In several studies, the moods of children, adolescents, and adults were monitored by having them carry electronic pagers, beeping them at random intervals, and asking them to write down what they were doing, whom they were with, and how they felt.

As expected, adolescents reported less favorable moods than school-age children and adults (Larson & Lampman-Petraitis, 1989; Larson et al., 2002). But negative moods were linked to a greater number of negative life events, such as difficulties with parents, disciplinary actions at school, and breaking up with a boyfriend or girlfriend. Negative events increased steadily from childhood to adolescence, and teenagers also reacted to them with greater emotion than children (Larson & Ham, 1993). (Recall that stress reactivity is heightened by changes in the brain's emotional/social network during puberty.)

Compared with the moods of older adolescents and adults, those of younger adolescents (ages 12 to 16) were less stable, often shifting between cheerful and sad. These mood swings were strongly related to situational changes. High points of adolescents' days were times spent with peers and in self-chosen leisure activities. Low points tended to occur in adult-structured settings—class, job, and religious services. Furthermore, emotional highs coincided with Friday and Saturday evenings, especially in high school. Going out with friends and romantic partners increases so dramatically during adolescence that it becomes a "cultural script" for what is *supposed* to happen (Larson & Richards, 1998). Consequently, teenagers who spend weekend evenings at home often feel profoundly lonely. Fortunately, frequent reports of negative mood level off in late adolescence (Natsuaki, Biehl, & Ge, 2009).

In Hispanic communities, the quinceañera, celebrated at age 15, is a rite of passage honoring a girl's journey from childhood to maturity. However, the ceremony does not mark a meaningful change in social status in the larger society.

Parent–Child Relationships. Sabrina's father noticed that as his children entered adolescence, they kept their bedroom doors closed, resisted spending time with the family, and became more argumentative. Sabrina and her mother squabbled over Sabrina's messy room ("It's *my* room, Mom. You don't have to live in it!"). And Sabrina protested the family's regular weekend visit to Aunt Gina's ("Why do I have to go *every* week?"). Research shows that puberty is related to a rise in intensity of parent–child conflict, and to fluctuations between positive and negative parent–child interaction, that persists into middle adolescence (Gure, Ucanok, & Sayil, 2006; Marceau, Ram, & Susman, 2015; McGue et al., 2005).

Why should young teenagers' more adultlike appearance trigger these disputes? The association may have adaptive value. Among nonhuman primates, the young typically leave the family group around the time of puberty. The same is true in many village and tribal cultures (Lancy, 2008; Schlegel & Barry, 1991). Departure of young people discourages sexual relations between close blood relatives. But adolescents in industrialized nations, who are still economically dependent on parents, cannot leave the family. Consequently, a substitute seems to have emerged: psychological distancing.

As children become physically mature, they demand to be treated in adultlike ways. And as we will see, adolescents' new powers of reasoning may also contribute to a rise in family tensions. Parent–adolescent disagreements focus largely on everyday matters such as driving, dating partners, and curfews (Adams & Laursen, 2001). But beneath these disputes lie serious concerns: parental efforts to protect teenagers from substance use, auto accidents, and early sexual activity. The larger the gap between parents' and adolescents' views of teenagers' readiness for new responsibilities, the more they quarrel (Deković, Noom, & Meeus, 1997).

Puberty brings an increase in parent–child conflict—psychological distancing that may, in part, be a modern substitute for physical departure from the family. Parents and adolescents often argue over the young person's readiness for new responsibilities.

Parent–daughter conflict tends to be more intense than conflict with sons, perhaps because parents place more restrictions on girls (Allison & Schultz, 2004). But most disputes are mild, and by late adolescence, only a small minority of families experience continuing friction. In a longitudinal investigation of parent–child conflict-resolution strategies spanning early to late adolescence, after an initial increase, adolescents displayed fewer angry behaviors, and parents' angry responses also declined. At the same time, teenagers and parents increasingly used positive problem solving, such as compromise and reasoning (Van Doorn, Branje, & Meeus, 2011). And throughout adolescence, positive problem solving greatly exceeded angry confrontations.

LOOK and LISTEN

Interview several parents and/or 12- to 14-year-olds about recent changes in parent–child relationships. Has intensity of conflict increased? Over what issues?

Pubertal Timing

"All our children were early maturers," said Franca during the parents' discussion group. "The three boys were tall by age 12 or 13, but it was easier for them. They felt big and important. Sabrina was skinny as a little girl, but now she says she is too fat and needs to diet. She thinks about boys and doesn't concentrate on her schoolwork."

Findings of several studies match the experiences of Sabrina and her brothers. Both adults and peers viewed early-maturing boys as relaxed, independent, self-confident, and physically attractive. Popular with agemates, they tended to hold leadership positions in school and to be athletic stars. Late-maturing boys often experienced transient emotional difficulties, until they caught up physically with their peers (Brooks-Gunn, 1988; Huddleston & Ge, 2003). But early-maturing boys, though viewed as well-adjusted, reported more psychological stress, depressed mood, and problem behaviors (sexual activity, smoking, drinking, aggression, delinquency) than both their on-time and later-maturing agemates (Natsuaki, Biehl, & Ge, 2009; Negriff, Susman, & Trickett, 2011; Susman & Dorn, 2009).

In contrast, early-maturing girls were unpopular, withdrawn, lacking in self-confidence, anxious, and prone to depression, and they held few leadership positions (Blumenthal et al., 2011; Galvao et al., 2014; Ge, Conger, & Elder, 1996; Graber, Brooks-Gunn, & Warren, 2006; Jones & Mussen, 1958). And like early-maturing boys, they were more involved in deviant behavior (smoking, drinking, sexual activity, delinquency) (Arim et al., 2011; Mrug et al., 2014; Negriff, Susman, & Trickett, 2011). In contrast, their later-maturing counterparts were regarded as physically attractive, lively, sociable, and leaders at school.

Two factors largely account for these trends: (1) how closely the adolescent's body matches cultural ideals of physical attractiveness, and (2) how well young people fit in physically with their peers.

The Role of Physical Attractiveness. Flip through your favorite popular magazine. You will see evidence of our society's view of an attractive female as thin and long-legged and of a good-looking male as tall, broad-shouldered, and muscular. The female image is a girlish shape that favors the late developer. The male image fits the early-maturing boy.

Consistent with these preferences, early-maturing European-American girls tend to report a less positive **body image**—conception of and attitude toward their physical appearance—than their on-time and late-maturing agemates. Compared with African-American and Hispanic girls, European-American girls are more likely to have internalized the cultural ideal of a thin female body (Rosen, 2003; Williams & Currie, 2000). Although boys are less consistent, early, rapid maturers are more likely to be satisfied with their physical characteristics (Alsaker, 1995; Sinkkonen, Anttila, & Siimes, 1998).

Body image is a strong predictor of young people's self-esteem (Harter, 2012). But the negative effects of pubertal timing on body image and—as we will see next—emotional adjustment are greatly amplified when accompanied by other stressors (Stice, 2003).

The Importance of Fitting in with Peers. Because early-maturing adolescents of both sexes feel physically "out of place" when with their agemates, they often seek out older companions, who may encourage them into activities they are not yet ready to handle. And pubertal hormonal influences on the brain's emotional/social network are stronger for early maturers, further magnifying their receptiveness to sexual activity, drug and alcohol use, and delinquent acts (Ge et al., 2002; Steinberg, 2008). Perhaps as a result, early maturers of both sexes more often report feeling emotionally stressed and decline in academic performance (Mendle, Turkheimer, & Emery, 2007; Natsuaki, Biehl, & Ge, 2009).

At the same time, the young person's context greatly increases the likelihood that early pubertal timing will lead to negative outcomes. Early maturers in economically disadvantaged neighborhoods are especially vulnerable to establishing ties with deviant peers—associations that heighten defiant, hostile behavior (Obeidallah et al., 2004). And because families in such neighborhoods tend to be exposed to chronic, severe stressors and to have few social supports, these early maturers are also more likely to experience harsh, inconsistent parenting, which, in turn, predicts deviant peer associations as well as antisocial behavior and depressive symptoms (Benoit, Lacourse, & Claes, 2013; Ge et al., 2002, 2011).

Long-Term Consequences. Do the effects of pubertal timing last? Follow-up research reveals that early-maturing girls, especially, are at risk for lasting difficulties. In one study, depression and frequently changing sexual partners persisted into early adulthood among early-maturing girls, with depression evident mainly in those who had displayed the severest adolescent conduct problems (Copeland et al., 2010). In another study, which followed young people from age 14 to 24,

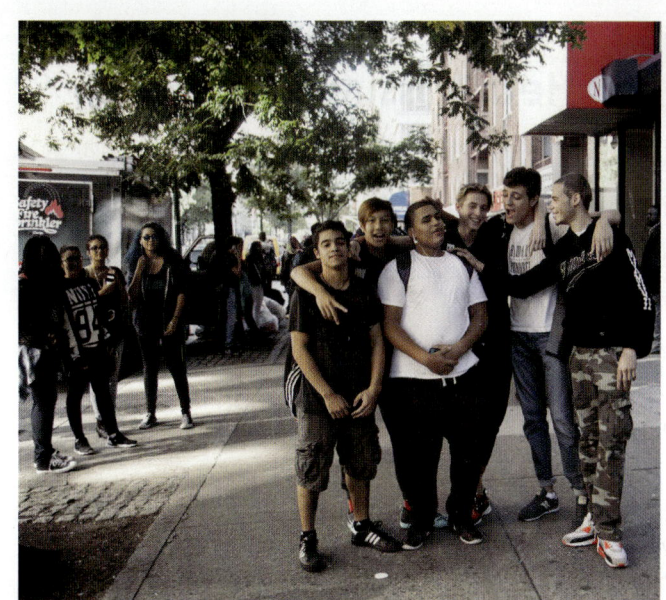

Early maturers often seek out the companionship of older adolescents, who increase their risk for early sexual activity, drug use, and delinquency. In economically disadvantaged neighborhoods, early maturers are especially vulnerable to establishing ties with deviant peers.

early-maturing boys showed good adjustment. But early-maturing girls reported poorer-quality relationships with family and friends, smaller social networks, and lower life satisfaction in early adulthood than did their on-time counterparts (Graber et al., 2004).

Recall that childhood family conflict and harsh parenting are linked to earlier pubertal timing, more so for girls than for boys (see page 373). Perhaps many early-maturing girls enter adolescence with emotional and social difficulties. As the stresses of puberty interfere with school performance and lead to unfavorable peer pressures, poor adjustment may extend and deepen.

Clearly, interventions that target at-risk early-maturing youths are needed. These include educating parents and teachers and providing adolescents with counseling and social supports so they will be better prepared to handle the emotional and social challenges of this transition.

Ask yourself

CONNECT How might adolescent moodiness contribute to psychological distancing between parents and adolescents? (*Hint:* Think about bidirectional influences in parent–child relationships.)

APPLY As a school-age child, Chloe enjoyed leisure activities with her parents. Now, as a 14-year-old, she spends hours in her room and resists going on weekend family excursions. Explain Chloe's behavior.

REFLECT Recall your own reactions to the physical changes of puberty. Are they consistent with research findings? Explain.

Health Issues

11.7 Describe nutritional needs during adolescence, and cite factors related to eating disorders.

11.8 Discuss social and cultural influences on adolescent sexual attitudes and behavior.

11.9 Cite factors involved in development of sexual orientation.

11.10 Discuss factors related to sexually transmitted infections and teenage pregnancy and parenthood, noting prevention and intervention strategies.

11.11 What personal and social factors are related to adolescent substance use and abuse?

The arrival of puberty brings new health issues related to the young person's efforts to meet physical and psychological needs. As adolescents attain greater autonomy, their personal decision making becomes important, in health as well as other areas. Yet none of the health concerns we are about to discuss can be traced to a single cause. Rather, biological, psychological, family, peer, and cultural factors jointly contribute.

Nutritional Needs

When their sons reached puberty, Franca and Antonio reported a "vacuum cleaner effect" in the kitchen as the boys routinely emptied the refrigerator. Rapid body growth leads to a dramatic increase in nutritional requirements, at a time when the diets of many young people are the poorest. Of all age groups, adolescents are the most likely to skip breakfast (a practice linked to overweight and obesity), eat on the run, and consume empty calories (Piernas & Popkin, 2011; Ritchie et al., 2007).

Fast-food restaurants, where teenagers often gather, have begun to offer some healthy menu options, and many schools now offer more nutritious choices (French & Story, 2013). But adolescents need guidance in selecting these alternatives. Sweets, soft drinks, pizza, and French fries still figure prominently in the diets of many young people, especially those from low-SES families (Poti, Slining, & Popkin, 2014; Slining, Mathias, & Popkin, 2013).

One of the most common nutritional problems of adolescence is iron deficiency. Iron requirements increase to a maximum during the growth spurt and remain high among girls because of iron loss during menstruation. A tired, irritable teenager may be suffering from anemia rather than unhappiness and should have a medical checkup. Many adolescents—especially girls—do not get enough calcium and are also deficient in riboflavin (vitamin B_2) and magnesium, both of which support metabolism (Rozen, 2012).

Frequency of family meals is strongly associated with greater intake of fruits, vegetables, grains, and calcium-rich foods and reduced soft drink and fast-food consumption (Burgess-Champoux et al., 2009; Fiese & Schwartz, 2008). But compared to families with younger children, those with adolescents eat fewer meals together. In addition to their other benefits (see page 60 in Chapter 2 and page 295 in Chapter 9), family meals can greatly improve teenagers' diets.

Eating Disorders

Concerned about her daughter's desire to lose weight, Franca explained to Sabrina that she was really quite average in build for an adolescent girl and reminded her that her Italian ancestors had considered a plump female body more beautiful than a thin one. Girls who reach puberty early, who are very dissatisfied with their body image, and who grow up in homes where concern with weight and thinness is high are at risk for eating problems. Body dissatisfaction and severe dieting are strong predictors of an eating disorder in adolescence (Rohde, Stice, & Marti, 2014). Disturbed eating is highest in Western nations, but with the spread of Western media and cultural values, Africa, Asia, and the Middle East are increasingly affected (Pike, Hoek, & Dunne, 2014). The three most serious eating disorders are anorexia nervosa, bulimia nervosa, and binge-eating disorder.

Anorexia Nervosa.
Anorexia nervosa is a tragic eating disorder in which young people starve themselves because of a compulsive fear of getting fat. About 1 percent of North American and Western European teenage girls are affected. During the past half-century, cases have increased sharply, fueled by cultural admiration of female thinness. In the United States, Asian-American, European-American, and Hispanic girls are at greater risk than African-American girls, whose greater satisfaction with their body image may offer some protection (American Psychiatric Association, 2013; Martin et al., 2015; Ozer & Irwin, 2009). Boys account for 10 to 15 percent of anorexia cases; up to half of these are gay or bisexual young people, who may be uncomfortable with a strong, bulky appearance or influenced by the cultural ideal of a lean but muscular male body (Darcy, 2012; Raevuori et al., 2009).

Individuals with anorexia have an extremely distorted body image. Even after becoming severely underweight, they see themselves as too heavy. Most go on self-imposed diets so strict that they struggle to avoid eating in response to hunger. To enhance weight loss, they exercise strenuously.

In their attempt to reach "perfect" slimness, individuals with anorexia lose 25 to 50 percent of their body weight. A normal menstrual cycle requires about 15 percent body fat, so many girls with anorexia experience delayed menarche or disrupted menstrual cycles. Malnutrition causes pale skin, brittle discolored nails, fine dark hairs all over the body, and extreme sensitivity to cold. If it continues, the heart muscle can shrink, the kidneys can fail, and irreversible brain damage and loss of bone mass can occur. About 5 percent of individuals with anorexia eventually die of the disorder, due to physical complications or suicide (American Psychiatric Association, 2013).

Forces within the person, the family, and the larger culture give rise to anorexia nervosa. Identical twins share the disorder more often than fraternal twins, indicating a genetic influence. Abnormalities in neurotransmitters in the brain, linked to anxiety and impulse control, may make some individuals more

(a) (b)

Aiva, a 16-year-old anorexia nervosa patient, is shown at left on the day she entered treatment—weighing just 77 pounds—and, at right, after a 10-week treatment program. Less than 50 percent of young people with anorexia recover fully.

susceptible (Phillipou, Rossell, & Castle, 2014; Pinheiro, Root, & Bulik, 2011). Many young people with anorexia have unrealistically high standards for their own behavior and performance, are emotionally inhibited, and avoid intimate ties outside the family. Consequently, they are often excellent students who are responsible and well-behaved. But as we have also seen, the societal image of "thin is beautiful" contributes to the poor body image of many girls—especially early-maturing girls, who are at greatest risk (Hoste & Le Grange, 2013).

In addition, parent–adolescent interactions reveal problems related to adolescent autonomy. Often the mothers of these girls have high expectations for physical appearance, achievement, and social acceptance and are overprotective and controlling. Fathers tend to be either controlling or uninvolved. These parental attributes may contribute to affected girls' persistent anxiety and fierce pursuit of perfection in achievement, respectable behavior, and thinness (Deas et al., 2011; Kaye, 2008). Nevertheless, it remains unclear whether maladaptive parent–child relationships precede the disorder, emerge as a response to it, or both.

Because individuals with anorexia usually deny or minimize the seriousness of their disorder, treatment is difficult. Hospitalization is often necessary to prevent life-threatening malnutrition. The most successful treatment is family therapy and medication to reduce anxiety and neurotransmitter imbalances (Hoste & Le Grange, 2013). Still, less than 50 percent of young people with anorexia recover fully. For many, eating problems continue in less extreme form. About 10 percent show signs of a less severe, but nevertheless debilitating, disorder: bulimia nervosa.

Bulimia Nervosa. In **bulimia nervosa,** young people (again, mainly girls, but gay and bisexual boys are also vulnerable) engage in binge eating, followed by compensatory efforts to avoid weight gain, such as deliberate vomiting, purging with laxatives, excessive exercise, or fasting (American Psychiatric Association, 2013). Bulimia typically appears in late adolescence and is more common than anorexia nervosa, affecting about 2 to 4 percent of teenage girls, only 5 percent of whom previously suffered from anorexia. Bulimia is not consistently linked to ethnicity.

Twin studies show that bulimia, like anorexia, is influenced by heredity (Thornton, Mazzeo, & Bulik, 2011). Overweight and early menarche increase the risk. Some adolescents with bulimia, like those with anorexia, are perfectionists. But most are impulsive, sensation-seeking young people who are especially prone to act irrationally when distressed and who engage in petty shoplifting, alcohol abuse, and other risky behaviors (Pearson, Wonderlich, & Smith, 2015). And although girls with bulimia, like those with anorexia, are pathologically anxious about gaining weight, they may have experienced their parents as disengaged and emotionally unavailable rather than as controlling (Fassino et al., 2010).

In contrast to young people with anorexia, those with bulimia usually feel depressed and guilty about their abnormal eating habits, and many report suicidal thoughts (Bodell, Joiner, & Keel, 2013). Because affected individuals desperately want help, bulimia is usually easier to treat than anorexia, through support groups, nutrition education, training in changing eating habits, and anti-anxiety, antidepressant, and appetite-control medication (Hay & Bacaltchuk, 2004).

Binge-Eating Disorder. Between 2 and 3 percent of adolescent girls and close to 1 percent of boys experience episodes of **binge-eating disorder**—binging at least once a week for three months or longer, without compensatory purging, exercise, or fasting (American Psychiatric Association, 2013; Smink et al., 2014). Binge-eating disorder, like bulimia, is unrelated to ethnicity. It typically leads to overweight and obesity, but binge eaters do not engage in the prolonged, restrictive dieting characteristic of anorexia and bulimia.

As with other eating disorders, binge-eating disorder is associated with social adjustment difficulties, and many binge eaters—similar to individuals with bulimia—experience severe emotional distress and suicidal thoughts (Stice, Marti, & Rohde, 2013). Effective treatments resemble those used for bulimia.

Sexuality

Sabrina's 16-year-old brother Louis and his girlfriend Cassie hadn't planned to have intercourse—it "just happened." After dating Louis for two months, Cassie began to wonder, "Will he think I'm normal if I don't have sex with him? If he wants to and I say no, will I lose him?" Both young people knew their parents wouldn't approve. In fact, when Franca and Antonio noticed how attached Louis was to Cassie, they talked to him about the importance of waiting and the dangers of pregnancy. But that Friday evening, Louis and Cassie's feelings for each other seemed overwhelming. "If I don't make a move," Louis thought, "will she think I'm a wimp?"

Cultural attitudes will profoundly affect the way these teenagers, who are just beginning to explore their sexual attraction to each other, learn to manage sexuality in social relationships.

With the arrival of puberty, hormonal changes—in particular, the production of androgens in young people of both sexes—lead to an increase in sex drive (Best & Fortenberry, 2013). In response, adolescents become very concerned about managing sexuality in social relationships. Improved cognitive capacities involving perspective taking and self-reflection affect their efforts to do so. Yet like the eating behaviors we have just discussed, adolescent sexuality is heavily influenced by the young person's social context.

The Impact of Culture.
When did you first learn about sex, and how? Was sex discussed openly in your family, or was it treated with secrecy? Exposure to sex, education about it, and efforts to limit the sexual curiosity of children and adolescents vary widely around the world.

Despite the prevailing image of sexually free adolescents, sexual attitudes in North America are relatively restrictive. Typically, parents provide little or no information about sex, discourage sex play, and rarely talk about sex in children's presence. When young people become interested in sex, only about half report getting information from parents about intercourse, pregnancy prevention, and sexually transmitted infections. Many parents avoid meaningful discussions about sex out of fear of embarrassment or concern that the adolescent will not take them seriously (Wilson et al., 2010). Yet warm, open give-and-take is associated with teenagers' adoption of parents' views, discussions about sexual health with dating partners, and reduced sexual risk taking (Commendador, 2010; Widman et al., 2014).

Adolescents who do not get information about sex from their parents are likely to learn from friends, siblings, books, magazines, movies, TV, and the Internet (Sprecher, Harris, & Meyers, 2008). Among TV shows that adolescents prefer, more than 80 percent contain sexual content. Most depict partners as spontaneous and passionate, taking no steps to avoid pregnancy or sexually transmitted infections, and experiencing no negative consequences. Teenagers' exposure to sexualized media predicts increased sexual activity, pregnancy, and sexual harassment behaviors (offensive name-calling or touching, pressuring a peer for a date), even after many other relevant factors are controlled (Brown & L'Engle, 2009; Roberts, Henriksen, & Foehr, 2009; Wright, Malamuth, & Donnerstein, 2012).

Not surprisingly, adolescents who are prone to engage in early sex choose to consume more sexualized media (Steinberg & Monahan, 2011; Vandenbosch & Eggermont, 2013). Still, the Internet is a hazardous "sex educator." In a survey of a large sample of U.S. 10- to 17-year-old Web users, 42 percent said they had viewed online pornographic websites (images of naked people or people having sex) while surfing the Internet in the past 12 months. Of these, 66 percent indicated they had encountered the images accidentally and did not want to view them (Wolak, Mitchell, & Finkelhor, 2007). Youths who felt depressed, had been bullied by peers, or were involved in delinquent activities had more encounters with Internet pornography, which may have intensified their adjustment problems.

Consider the contradictory messages young people receive. On one hand, adults express disapproval of sex at a young age and outside of marriage. On the other hand, the social environment extols sexual excitement, experimentation, and promiscuity. American teenagers are left bewildered, poorly informed about sexual facts, and with little sound advice on how to conduct their sex lives responsibly.

Adolescent Sexual Attitudes and Behavior.
Although differences among subcultural groups exist, sexual attitudes of U.S. adolescents and adults have become more liberal over the past half century. Compared with previous generations, more people approve of sexual intercourse before marriage (Elias, Fullerton, & Simpson, 2013; Rifkin, 2014). During the past 15 years, adolescents have swung slightly back toward more conservative sexual beliefs, largely in response to the risk of sexually transmitted infections, especially AIDS, and to teenage sexual abstinence programs sponsored by schools and religious organizations (Akers et al., 2011; Ali & Scelfo, 2002).

Trends in adolescents' sexual behavior are consistent with their attitudes. Rates of nonmarital sex among U.S. young people rose for several decades but have recently declined (Martinez & Abma, 2015). Nevertheless, as Figure 11.4 illustrates, a substantial percentage of U.S. young people are sexually active by ages 15 to 16.

The quality of adolescent sexual experiences varies, depending on circumstances. About 70 percent of sexually active teenagers report that they first had sex with a steady dating partner, and most have only one or two partners during high school. But 12 percent of high school students report having sexual relations

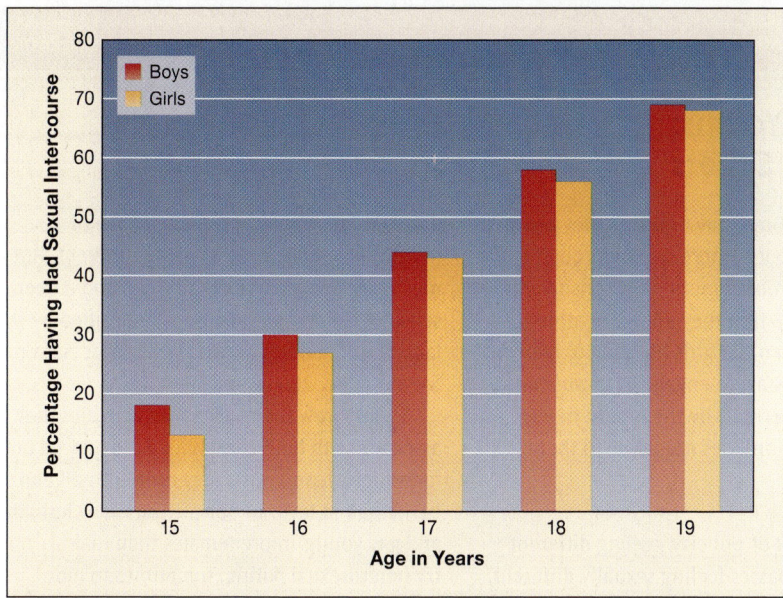

FIGURE 11.4 **U.S. adolescents who report ever having had sexual intercourse.** Most U.S. adolescents become sexually active during the high school years. Boys tend to have their first intercourse earlier than girls, but in general, boys and girls' rates of sexual intercourse are similar. (Based on Martinez & Abma, 2015.)

with four or more partners (Kann et al., 2016; Wildsmith et al., 2012). Mutually consensual sexual activity in the context of a stable, caring romantic relationship can be a positive and satisfying experience for older adolescents. But when teenagers engage in casual sex, or have sex when they have been drinking or using drugs, they often report negative feelings, including guilt and depression (Harden, 2014).

Characteristics of Adolescents Who Engage in Early Sexual Activity. A variety of adverse personal, family, peer, and educational characteristics are linked to early and frequent teenage sexual activity. These include childhood impulsivity, weak sense of personal control over life events, early pubertal timing, parental divorce, single-parent and stepfamily homes, large family size, little or no religious involvement, weak parental monitoring, disrupted parent–child communication, sexually active friends and older siblings, poor school performance, lower educational aspirations, and tendency to engage in norm-violating acts, including alcohol and drug use and delinquency (Conduct Problems Prevention Research Group, 2014; Diamond, Bonner, & Dickenson, 2015; Zimmer-Gembeck & Helfand, 2008).

Because many of these factors are associated with growing up in a low-income family, it is not surprising that early sexual activity is more common among young people from economically disadvantaged homes. Living in a neighborhood high in physical deterioration, crime, and violence also increases the likelihood that teenagers will be sexually active (Best & Fortenberry, 2013). In such neighborhoods, social ties are weak, adults exert little oversight and control over adolescents' activities, negative peer influences are widespread, and teenagers are unlikely to consider the impact of early parenthood on their current and future lives. In fact, the high rate of early sexual activity among African-American teenagers—8 percent report having had sexual intercourse before age 13, compared with 4 percent of all U.S. young people—may be largely explained by widespread poverty in the black population (Kann et al., 2016; Kaplan et al., 2013).

Contraceptive Use. Although adolescent contraceptive use has increased in recent years (see Figure 11.5), about 14 percent of sexually active teenagers in the United States are at risk for unintended pregnancy because they do not use contraception consistently (Kann et al., 2016). Why do so many fail to take precautions? Typically, teenagers respond, "I was waiting until I had a steady boyfriend" or "I wasn't planning to have sex."

As our discussion of cognitive development will reveal, although adolescents can consider many possibilities when faced with a problem, they often fail to apply this reasoning to everyday situations. We have seen that in the midst of everyday peer pressures and heightened emotion, self-regulation is difficult for teenagers, who often overlook the potential consequences of risky behaviors. They are least likely to use condoms in relatively new relationships in which they feel high trust or love and are having sex often (Ewing & Bryan, 2015).

Adolescents who report good relationships with parents and who talk openly with them about sex and contraception are more likely to use birth control (Widman et al., 2014). But few believe their parents would be understanding and supportive. School sex

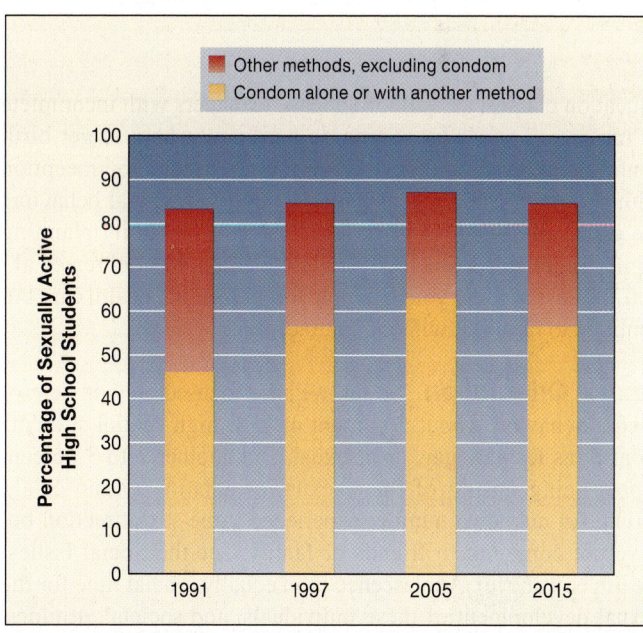

FIGURE 11.5 **Contraceptive use at last intercourse among sexually active U.S. high school students, 1991 to 2015.** Adolescents' use of contraceptives—especially condoms—increased throughout the 1990s and early 2000s. More recently, overall rates of contraceptive use stabilized. At the same time, adolescents increasingly chose methods other than the condom that are effective, most commonly hormonal options—the pill, patch, or vaginal ring. (Based on Kann et al., 2016.)

Social Issues: Health

Lesbian, Gay, and Bisexual Youths: Coming Out to Oneself and Others

Cultures vary widely in their acceptance of sexual minorities. In the United States, societal attitudes toward lesbian, gay, and bisexual people have become more accepting, but prejudice remains widespread (Pew Research Center, 2013d). This makes forming a sexual identity more challenging for sexual minority youths than for their heterosexual counterparts.

Wide variation in sexual identity formation exists, depending on personal, family, and community factors. Yet interviews with gay and lesbian adolescents and adults reveal that many (though not all) move through a three-phase sequence in coming out to themselves and others.

Feeling Different

Many gay men and lesbians say that they felt different from other children when they were young. Typically, this first sense of their biologically determined sexual orientation appears between ages 6 and 12, in play interests more like those of the other gender (Rahman & Wilson, 2003). Boys may find that they are less interested in sports, more drawn to quieter activities, and more emotionally sensitive than other boys; girls that they are more athletic and active than other girls. By age 10, many of these children start to engage in *sexual questioning*—wondering why the typical heterosexual orientation does not apply to them.

Confusion

With the arrival of puberty, feeling different clearly encompasses feeling sexually different. Although wide variation exists, on average, boys begin to think they are gay at around age 10 and know for sure at around age 15 (Pew Research Center, 2013d). Awareness tends to emerge a few years later for girls, around 13 and 18, respectively, perhaps because social pressures toward heterosexuality are particularly intense for adolescent girls.

Realizing that same-sex attraction has personal relevance generally sparks additional confusion. A few adolescents resolve their discomfort by crystallizing a lesbian, gay, or bisexual identity quickly, with a flash of insight into their sense of being different. But most experience an inner struggle and a deep sense of isolation—outcomes intensified by lack of role models and social support (Safren & Pantalone, 2006).

Some throw themselves into activities they associate with heterosexuality. Boys may go out for athletic teams; girls may drop softball and basketball in favor of dance. And many lesbian and gay youths (more females than males) try heterosexual dating, sometimes to hide their sexual orientation and at other times to develop intimacy skills that they later apply to same-sex relationships (D'Augelli, 2006). Those who are extremely troubled and guilt-ridden may escape into alcohol, drugs, and suicidal thinking. As Chapter 16 will reveal, suicide attempts are unusually high among lesbian, gay, and bisexual young people.

Self-Acceptance

By the end of adolescence, the majority of lesbian, gay, and bisexual teenagers accept

---

education classes, as well, often leave teenagers with incomplete or incorrect knowledge. Some do not know where to get birth control counseling and devices or how to discuss contraception with a partner. And those engaged in high-risk sexual behaviors are especially likely to worry that a doctor or family planning clinic might not keep their visits confidential (Lehrer et al., 2007). Most of these young people forgo essential health care but continue to have sex without contraception.

Sexual Orientation. So far, we have focused only on heterosexual behavior. About 5 percent of U.S. high school students identify as lesbian, gay, or bisexual, and another 2 to 3 percent report being unsure of their sexual orientation (Kann et al., 2011). An unknown number experience same-sex attraction but have not come out to friends or family (see the Social Issues: Health box above). Adolescence is an equally crucial time for the sexual development of these individuals, and societal attitudes, again, loom large in how well they fare.

Heredity makes an important contribution to sexual orientation: Identical twins of both sexes are more likely than fraternal twins to share a homosexual orientation; so are biological (as opposed to adoptive) relatives (Kendler et al., 2000; Långström et al., 2010). Furthermore, male homosexuality tends to be more common on the maternal than on the paternal side of families, suggesting that it may be X-linked (see Chapter 2). Indeed, one gene-mapping study found that among 40 pairs of gay brothers, 33 (82 percent) had an identical segment of DNA on the X chromosome (Hamer et al., 1993). One or several genes in that region might predispose males to develop same-sex attraction.

How might heredity influence sexual orientation? According to some researchers, certain genes affect the level or impact of prenatal sex hormones, which modify brain structures in ways that induce homosexual feelings and behavior (Bailey et al., 1995; LeVay, 1993). Keep in mind, however, that environmental factors can also alter prenatal hormones. Girls exposed prenatally to very high levels of androgens or estrogens—either because of a genetic defect or from drugs given to the mother to prevent miscarriage—are more likely to develop lesbian or bisexual orientations (Hines, 2011b). Furthermore, gay men tend to be later in birth order and to have a higher-than-average number of older brothers (Bogaert & Skorska, 2011; VanderLaan et al., 2014). Perhaps mothers with several male children sometimes produce antibodies to androgens, reducing the prenatal impact of male sex hormones on the brains of later-born boys.

Stereotypes and misconceptions about homosexuality and bisexuality persist. For example, contrary to common belief, their sexual identity. But they face another crossroad: whether to tell others. Stigma against their sexual orientation leads some to decide that disclosure is impossible. When they do come out, sexual minority youths often face peer hostility, including verbal abuse and physical attacks. These experiences trigger intense emotional distress, depression, school truancy, and drug use in victims (Dragowski et al., 2011; Rosario & Schrimshaw, 2013).

Nevertheless, many young people eventually acknowledge their sexual orientation publicly, usually by telling trusted friends first. Once teenagers establish a same-sex sexual or romantic relationship, many come out to parents. Few parents respond with severe rejection; most are either positive or slightly negative and disbelieving. Still, lesbian, gay, and bisexual young people report lower levels of family support than their heterosexual agemates (McCormack, Anderson, & Adams, 2014; Needham & Austin, 2010). Yet parental understanding is a key predictor of favorable adjustment—including reduced *internalized homophobia,* or societal prejudice turned against the self (Bregman et al., 2013).

When people react positively, coming out strengthens the young person's sexual identity as valid, meaningful, and fulfilling. Contact with lesbian, gay, and bisexual peers is important for reaching this phase, and changes in society permit many adolescents in urban areas to attain it earlier than their counterparts did a decade or two ago. Gay and lesbian communities exist in large cities, along with specialized interest groups, social clubs, religious groups, newspapers, and periodicals. But teenagers in small towns and rural areas may have difficulty meeting other sexual minority youths and finding a supportive environment. These adolescents have a special need for caring adults and peers who can help them find self- and social acceptance.

Lesbian, gay, and bisexual teenagers who succeed in coming out to themselves and others integrate their sexual orientation into a broader sense of identity, a process we will address in Chapter 12. As a result, energy is freed for other aspects of psychological growth. In sum, coming out can foster many facets of adolescent development, including self-esteem, psychological well-being, and relationships with family and friends.

Lesbian, gay, bisexual, and transgender high school students and their allies participate in an annual Youth Pride Festival and March. When peers react with acceptance, coming out strengthens the young person's sexual identity as valid, meaningful, and fulfilling.

most sexual minority adolescents and adults are not "gender-deviant" in dress or behavior. And attraction to members of the same sex is not limited to lesbian, gay, and bisexual teenagers. In recent surveys, between 17 and 78 percent of teenagers who reported sexual experiences with same-sex partners identified as heterosexual (Kann et al., 2011). And a study of lesbian, bisexual, and "unlabeled" young women confirmed that bisexuality is not, as often assumed, a transient state (Diamond, 2008). Over a 10-year period, most reported stable proportions of same-sex versus other-sex attractions over time.

The evidence to date indicates that genetic and prenatal biological influences contribute substantially to homosexuality. The origins of bisexuality are not yet known.

Sexually Transmitted Infections

Sexually active adolescents, regardless of sexual orientation, are at risk for sexually transmitted infections (STIs). Young people from 15 to 24 have the highest rates of STIs of all age groups (Centers for Disease Control and Prevention, 2015l). In recent years, U.S. rates have risen: 1 out of 5 sexually active teenagers contracts an STI each year—a rate three or more times that of Canada and Western Europe (Greydanus et al., 2012; Public Health Agency of Canada, 2015). Teenagers at greatest risk are the same ones most likely to engage in irresponsible sexual behavior: economically disadvantaged young people who feel a sense of hopelessness. Left untreated, STIs can lead to sterility and life-threatening complications.

By far the most serious STI is HIV/AIDS. In contrast to other Western nations, where the incidence of HIV infection among people under age 30 is low, one-fourth of U.S. HIV cases are young people between ages 13 and 24. Because AIDS symptoms typically do not emerge until 8 to 10 years after HIV infection, many young adults diagnosed with HIV or AIDS contracted the virus during adolescence. Males who have sex with HIV-positive same-sex partners account for most of these cases. But one-fourth are due to heterosexual spread of the disease, mostly through male-to-female transmission (Centers for Disease Control and Prevention, 2015h). It is at least twice as easy for a male to infect a female with any STI, including HIV, as for a female to infect a male.

As a result of school courses and media campaigns, most adolescents are aware of basic facts about HIV and AIDS. But they have limited understanding of other STIs, underestimate their own susceptibility, and are poorly informed about how to protect themselves (Kann et al., 2014). Furthermore, high school students report engaging in oral sex much more often than intercourse, and with more partners. But few consistently use STI protection during oral sex, which is a significant mode of transmission for several STIs (Vasilenko et al., 2014). Concerted efforts are needed to educate young people about the full range of STIs and risky sexual behaviors.

Adolescent Pregnancy and Parenthood

Cassie didn't get pregnant after having sex with Louis, but some of her classmates were less fortunate. About 625,000 U.S. teenage girls (almost 11,000 of them younger than age 15)—an estimated 13 percent of those who had sexual intercourse—became pregnant in the most recently reported year (U.S. Department of Health and Human Services, 2016a). Despite a decline of more than 50 percent since 1990, the U.S. adolescent pregnancy rate remains higher than that of most other industrialized countries (Sedgh et al., 2015).

Because about one-fourth of U.S. adolescent pregnancies end in abortion, the number of teenage births is considerably lower than it was 50 years ago (Guttmacher Institute, 2015). Still, the United States greatly exceeds most other developed nations in adolescent birth rate (see Figure 11.6). And teenage parenthood remains a problem today because contemporary adolescents rarely marry before childbirth. In 1960, only 15 percent of teenage births were to unmarried females, compared with 89 percent today (Child Trends, 2015a). Increased social acceptance of single motherhood, along with the belief of many teenage girls that a baby might fill a void in their lives, means that very few girls give up their infants for adoption.

Correlates and Consequences of Adolescent Parenthood.
Becoming a parent is especially challenging for adolescents, who have not yet established a clear sense of direction for their own lives. Life conditions and personal attributes jointly contribute to adolescent childbearing and also interfere with teenagers' capacity to parent effectively.

Teenage parents are far more likely to come from poverty-stricken homes than agemates who postpone parenthood. Their backgrounds often include low parental warmth and involvement, domestic violence, child abuse and neglect, repeated parental divorce and remarriage, adult models of unmarried parenthood, and residence in neighborhoods where other adolescents also display these risks. Girls at risk for early pregnancy also do poorly in school, use drugs and alcohol, have a childhood history of aggressive and antisocial behavior, associate with deviant peers, and experience high rates of depression (Hillis et al., 2004; Luster & Haddow, 2005; Noll & Shenck, 2013). A high percentage of births are to economically disadvantaged ethnic minority teenagers. Many turn to early parenthood as a pathway to adulthood when educational and career avenues are unavailable.

The lives of expectant teenagers, already troubled in many ways, tend to worsen in several respects after the baby is born. Adolescent mothers are less likely than their peers to finish high school, get married, or secure employment. About 35 percent become pregnant again within two years; of these, about half go on to deliver a second child (Child Trends, 2015a; Ruedinger & Cox, 2012). Teenage mothers who do marry are more likely to divorce and, consequently, spend more of their child-rearing years as single parents. Because of low educational attainment, marital instability, and poverty, many teenage mothers are on welfare or work in unsatisfying, low-paid jobs.

Many adolescent fathers, too, are unemployed or work at unskilled jobs, usually earning too little to provide their children with basic necessities (Futris, Nielsen, & Olmstead, 2010). About half have been incarcerated (Elfenbein & Felice, 2003). And for both mothers and fathers, reduced educational and occupational attainment often persists well into adulthood (Taylor, 2009).

Because many pregnant teenage girls have inadequate diets, smoke, use alcohol and other drugs, and do not receive early prenatal care, their babies often experience pregnancy and birth complications—especially low birth weight (Khashan, Baker, & Kenny, 2010). And compared with adult mothers, adolescent mothers know less about child development, have unrealistically high expectations of their infants, perceive their babies as more difficult, interact less effectively with them, and more often engage in harsh or abusive parenting (Lee, 2013; Ruedinger & Cox, 2012). Their children typically score low on intelligence tests, achieve poorly in school, and engage in disruptive social behavior.

Furthermore, because adolescent parenthood is linked to a set of unfavorable family conditions and personal characteristics that negatively affect development over an extended time, it often transfers to the next generation (Meade, Kershaw, & Ickovics, 2008; Wildsmith et al., 2012). One particularly influential factor

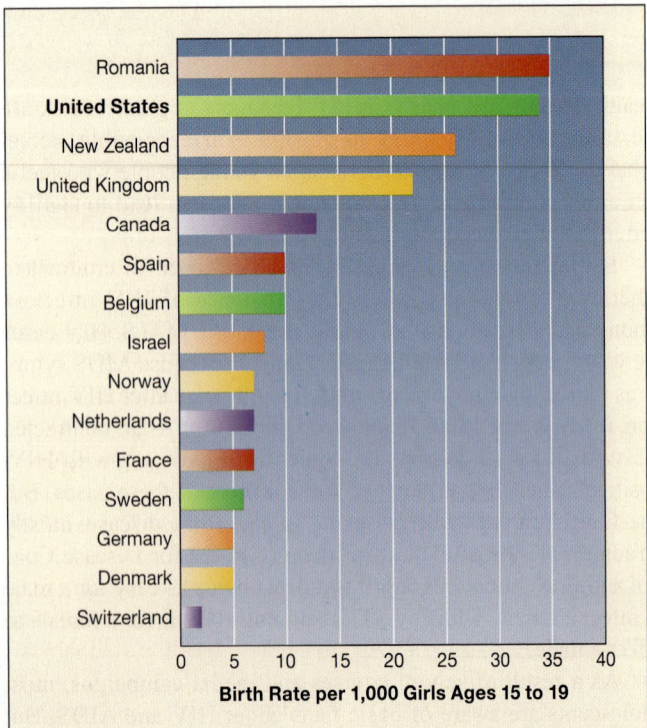

FIGURE 11.6 Birth rates among 15- to 19-year-olds in 15 industrialized nations. The U.S. adolescent birth rate greatly exceeds that of most other industrialized nations. (Based on Sedgh et al., 2015.)

is father absence. Consistent with findings reported earlier for sexual activity and pregnancy, far greater intergenerational continuity, especially for daughters, occurs when teenage mothers remain unmarried.

Even when children born to teenage mothers do not become early childbearers, their development is often compromised. Many drop out of school, struggle financially, and experience long-term physical and mental health difficulties. The circumstances that lead to adolescent parenthood are likely responsible for many of the negative consequences associated with it (Morinis, Carson, & Quigley, 2013; Ruedinger & Cox, 2012). Young people from severely disadvantaged backgrounds tend to experience poor social, educational, and economic outcomes; to struggle with the challenges of child rearing; and to have children with cognitive, emotional, and behavior problems, whether they give birth as teenagers or delay parenthood until their twenties.

Still, outcomes vary widely. If a teenage parent finishes high school, secures gainful employment, avoids additional births, and finds a stable partner, long-term disruptions in her own and her child's development will be less severe.

Prevention Strategies. Preventing teenage pregnancy means addressing the many factors underlying early sexual activity and lack of contraceptive use. Too often, sex education courses are given late (after sexual activity has begun), last only a few sessions, and are limited to a catalog of facts about anatomy and reproduction. Sex education that goes beyond this minimum does not encourage early sex, as some opponents claim (Chin et al., 2012). It does improve awareness of sexual facts—knowledge that is necessary for responsible sexual behavior.

Knowledge, however, is not enough: Sex education must also help teenagers build a bridge between what they know and what they do. Effective sex education programs include several key elements:

- They teach techniques for handling sexual situations—including refusal skills for avoiding risky sexual behaviors and communication skills for improving contraceptive use—through role-playing and other activities in which young people practice those behaviors.
- They deliver clear, accurate messages that are appropriate in view of participating adolescents' culture and sexual experiences.
- They last long enough to have an impact.
- They provide specific information about contraceptives and ready access to them.

Many studies show that sex education with these components can delay the initiation of sexual activity, increase contraceptive use, and reduce pregnancy rates (Chin et al., 2012; Kirby, 2002, 2008).

LOOK and LISTEN

Contact a nearby public school district for information about its sex education curriculum. Considering research findings, do you think it is likely to be effective in delaying initiation of sexual activity and reducing adolescent pregnancy rates?

Proposals to increase access to contraceptives are the most controversial aspect of U.S. adolescent pregnancy prevention efforts. Many adults argue that placing birth control pills or condoms in the hands of teenagers is equivalent to approving of early sex. Yet sex education programs promoting abstinence without also advocating contraceptive use have little or no impact on delaying teenage sexual activity or preventing pregnancy (Rosenbaum, 2009; Trenholm et al., 2008). In Canada and Western Europe, where community- and school-based clinics offer adolescents contraceptives and where universal health insurance helps pay for them, teenage sexual activity is no higher than in the United States—but pregnancy, childbirth, and abortion rates are much lower (Schalet, 2007).

Efforts to prevent adolescent pregnancy and parenthood must go beyond improving sex education and access to contraception to build academic and social competence (Cornell, 2013). In a program called Teen Outreach, adolescents participated in a year-long community service class in which they spent at least 20 hours per week in volunteer work tailored to their interests, returning to school for discussions that focused on enhancing their sense of connection to the community, ability to cope with everyday challenges, social skills, and self-respect. Compared to controls in regular classes, adolescents randomly assigned to Teen Outreach displayed substantially lower end-of-year rates of pregnancy, school failure, and school suspension (Allen et al., 1997; Allen & Philliber, 2001). The program appeared most beneficial for youths at greatest risk for school failure and conduct problems, based on their history of school suspensions.

Finally, teenagers who look forward to a promising future are far less likely to engage in early and irresponsible sex. By expanding educational, vocational, and employment opportunities, society can give young people good reasons to postpone childbearing.

Intervening with Adolescent Parents. The most difficult and costly way to deal with adolescent parenthood is to wait until it happens. Young parents need health care, encouragement to stay in school, job training, instruction in parenting and life-management skills, and high-quality, affordable child care. Schools that provide these services reduce the incidence of low-birth-weight babies, increase educational success, and prevent additional childbearing (Cornell, 2013; Key et al., 2008).

Adolescent mothers also benefit from relationships with family members and other adults who are sensitive to their developmental needs. Those with more social support report reduced levels of depression during the year after giving birth (Brown et al., 2012). In one study, African-American teenage mothers who had a long-term "mentor" relationship—an aunt, neighbor, or teacher who provided emotional support and guidance—were far more likely than those without a mentor to stay in school and graduate (Klaw, Rhodes, & Fitzgerald, 2003). Home visiting programs are also effective. Return to page 90 in Chapter 3 to review the Nurse–Family Partnership, which helps launch teenage mothers and their babies on a favorable life course.

Programs focusing on fathers attempt to increase their financial and emotional commitment to the baby. Although half of

Early parenthood imposes lasting hardships on adolescent parents and their newborn babies. But the involvement of a caring father and a stable partnership between the parents can improve outcomes for young families.

young fathers visit their children during the first few years, contact usually diminishes over time (Ng & Kaye, 2012). As with teenage mothers, support from family members helps fathers stay involved. Mothers who receive financial and child-care assistance and emotional support from their child's father are less distressed and more likely to sustain a relationship with him (Easterbrooks et al., 2016; Gee & Rhodes, 2003). And children with lasting ties to their teenage fathers show better long-term adjustment (Martin, Brazil, & Brooks-Gunn, 2012).

Substance Use and Abuse

At age 14, Louis waited until he was alone at home, took some cigarettes from his uncle's pack, and smoked them. At an unchaperoned party, he and Cassie drank several cans of beer and lit up marijuana joints. Louis got little physical charge out of these experiences. A good student, who was well-liked by peers and got along well with his parents, he did not need drugs as an escape valve. But he knew of other teenagers who started with alcohol and cigarettes, moved on to harder substances, and eventually were hooked.

Teenage alcohol and drug use is pervasive in industrialized nations. According to the most recent nationally representative survey of U.S. high school students, 20 percent of tenth graders have tried smoking, 47 percent drinking, and 37 percent at least one illegal drug (usually marijuana). At the end of high school, 6 percent smoke cigarettes regularly, 17 percent have engaged in heavy drinking during the past month, and 21 percent have used marijuana. About 21 percent have tried at least one highly addictive and toxic substance, such as amphetamines, cocaine, phencyclidine (PCP), Ecstasy (MDMA), inhalants, heroin, sedatives (including barbiturates), or OxyContin (a narcotic painkiller) (Johnston et al., 2015).

These figures represent a substantial decline since the mid-1990s, probably resulting from greater parent, school, and media focus on the hazards of drug taking. An exception is use of marijuana, which began to rise in the mid-2000s but has recently leveled off. Many states have passed medical use laws and a few have legalized recreational use, making it easier for young people to obtain marijuana (Johnston et al., 2015).

In part, drug taking reflects the sensation seeking of the teenage years. But adolescents also live in drug-dependent cultural contexts. They see adults relying on caffeine to stay alert, alcohol and cigarettes to cope with daily hassles, and other remedies to relieve stress, depression, and physical discomfort. They also encounter high rates of cigarette, alcohol, and drug use in TV programs, movies, and advertisements (Strasburger, 2012). And compared to a decade or two ago, today doctors more often prescribe—and parents frequently seek—medication to treat children's problems (Olfman & Robbins, 2012). In adolescence, these young people may readily "self-medicate" when stressed.

Most teenagers who try alcohol, tobacco, or marijuana are not headed for a life of addiction. These *occasional experimenters* are usually psychologically healthy, sociable, curious young people. Nevertheless, adolescent experimentation with any drug should not be taken lightly. Because most drugs impair perception and thought processes, a single heavy dose can lead to permanent injury or death. And a worrisome minority of teenagers move from substance *use* to *abuse*—taking drugs regularly, requiring increasing amounts to achieve the same effect, moving on to harder substances, and using enough to interfere with their ability to meet daily responsibilities.

Correlates and Consequences of Adolescent Substance Abuse.
Unlike experimenters, drug abusers are seriously troubled young people. Their impulsive, disruptive, hostile style is often evident in early childhood, and they are inclined to express their unhappiness through antisocial acts. Compared with other young people, their drug taking starts earlier and may have genetic roots (Patrick & Schulenberg, 2014). In a longitudinal study of ethnically diverse early adolescents, a large imbalance between the brain's cognitive-control network and its emotional/social network—indicated by weak executive function against elevated sensation seeking of this period—predicted a rapid rise in alcohol, tobacco, and marijuana use by midadolescence (see Figure 11.7) (Khurana et al., 2015). These teenagers, at high risk of becoming abusers, contrasted sharply with minimal experimenters and nonusers, who displayed similar sensation seeking but much stronger cognitive control.

But environmental factors also contribute. These include low SES, family mental health problems, parental and older sibling drug abuse, lack of parental warmth and involvement, physical and sexual abuse, and poor school performance. Especially among teenagers with family difficulties, encouragement from friends who use and provide drugs increases substance abuse (Ohannessian & Hesselbrock, 2008; Patrick & Schulenberg, 2014).

Introducing drugs while the adolescent brain is still a work-in-progress can have profound, lasting consequences, impairing

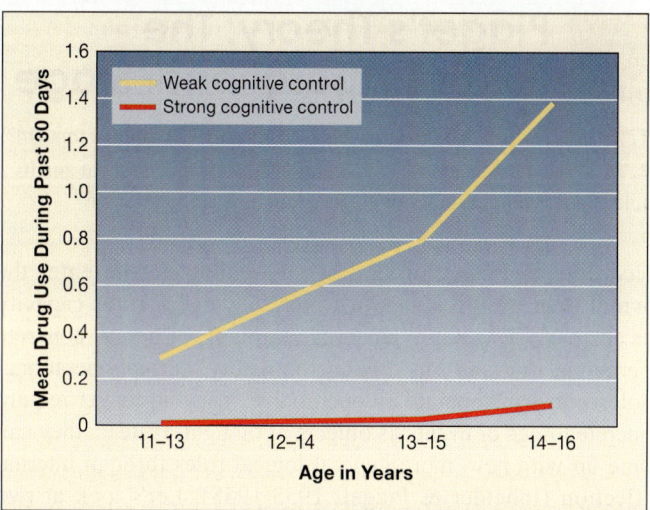

FIGURE 11.7 Weak cognitive control predicts a rapid rise in drug use from early to middle adolescence. When several hundred ethnically diverse adolescents were followed from early to middle adolescence, a large imbalance between the brain's cognitive-control network and emotional/social network (weak executive function against high sensation seeking) predicted a dramatic rise in drug taking, signifying high risk for abuse. Elevated sensation seeking against strong cognitive control predicted minimal use or nonuse over time (Based on Khurana et al., 2015.)

The Strong African American Families (SAAF) program strengthens parent–adolescent relationships through discussions like this one, which pave the way toward more effective parenting, including communicating and enforcing clear expectations and resolving disputes through cooperative problem solving.

neurons and their connective networks. At the same time, teenagers who use substances to deal with daily stresses fail to learn responsible decision-making skills and alternative coping techniques. They show serious adjustment problems, including chronic anxiety, depression, and antisocial behavior, that are both cause and consequence of heavy drug taking (Kassel et al., 2005; Luciana et al., 2013). And they often enter into marriage, childbearing, and the work world prematurely and fail at these challenges—painful outcomes that further promote addictive behavior.

Prevention and Treatment. School and community programs that reduce drug experimentation typically combine several components:

- They promote effective parenting, including monitoring of teenagers' activities.
- They teach skills for resisting peer pressure.
- They reduce the social acceptability of drug taking by emphasizing health and safety risks (Stephens et al., 2009).

One intervention, the Strong African American Families (SAAF) program, teaches parents to monitor their adolescents' behavior, communicate and enforce clear expectations, and use cooperative problem solving to resolve disputes. Evaluations revealed that SAAF reduced substance use among African-American youths, and it was most effective for adolescents with the DRD4 7-repeat or the short 5-HTTLPR gene (see pages 194 and 201 in Chapter 6), which placed them at risk for self-regulation difficulties (Brody et al., 2009, 2014). Does this remind you of evidence discussed in previous chapters indicating that good parenting can protect the development of genetically vulnerable children?

Programs that teach at-risk teenagers effective strategies for handling life stressors and that build competence through community service reduce alcohol and drug use, just as they reduce teenage pregnancy. Providing appealing substitute activities is also helpful. Physical activity works especially well as a substitute for cigarette smoking. In a program aimed at helping teenagers stop smoking, participants were most likely to cut back or quit when the intervention also helped them exercise more (Horn et al., 2013).

When an adolescent becomes a drug abuser, family and individual therapy are generally needed to treat maladaptive parent–child relationships, impulsivity, low self-esteem, anxiety, and depression. Academic and vocational training to improve life success also helps. But even comprehensive programs have alarmingly high relapse rates—from 35 to 85 percent (Brown & Ramo, 2005; Sussman, Skara, & Ames, 2008).

Adolescents who are motivated at the start of treatment have better outcomes (Joe et al., 2014). One recommendation is to initiate treatment gradually, through support-group sessions that focus on reducing drug taking. Modest improvements may boost the young person's sense of self-efficacy for behavior change and, as a result, increase motivation to make longer-lasting changes through intensive treatment.

Ask yourself

CONNECT What adverse personal attributes and life conditions do teenagers who engage in early and frequent sexual activity have in common with those who abuse drugs?

APPLY After 17-year-old Veronica gave birth to Ben, her parents told her they didn't have room for the baby. Veronica dropped out of school and moved in with her boyfriend, who soon left. Why are Veronica and Ben likely to experience long-term hardships?

REFLECT Describe your experiences with peer pressure to experiment with alcohol and drugs. What factors influenced your response?

COGNITIVE DEVELOPMENT

One mid-December evening, a knock at the front door announced the arrival of Franca and Antonio's oldest son, Jules, home for vacation after the fall semester of his sophomore year at college. The family gathered around the kitchen table. "How did it all go, Jules?" asked Antonio as he served slices of apple pie.

"Well, physics and philosophy were awesome," Jules responded with enthusiasm. "The last few weeks, our physics prof introduced us to Einstein's theory of relativity. Boggles my mind, it's so incredibly counterintuitive."

"Counter-what?" asked 11-year-old Sabrina.

"Counterintuitive. Unlike what you'd normally expect," explained Jules. "Imagine you're on a train, going unbelievably fast, like 160,000 miles a second. The faster you go, approaching the speed of light, the slower time passes and the denser and heavier things get relative to on the ground. The theory revolutionized the way we think about time, space, matter—the entire universe."

Sabrina wrinkled her forehead, baffled by Jules's otherworldly reasoning. "Time slows down when I'm bored, like right now, not on a train when I'm going somewhere exciting. No speeding train ever made me heavier, but this apple pie will if I eat any more of it," Sabrina announced, leaving the table.

Sixteen-year-old Louis reacted differently. "Totally cool, Jules. So what'd you do in philosophy?"

"It was a course in philosophy of technology. We studied the ethics of futuristic methods in human reproduction. For example, we argued the pros and cons of a world in which all embryos develop in artificial wombs."

"What do you mean?" asked Louis. "You order your kid at the lab?"

"That's right. I wrote my term paper on it. I had to evaluate it in terms of principles of justice and freedom. I can see some advantages but also lots of dangers...."

As this conversation illustrates, adolescence brings with it vastly expanded powers of reasoning. At age 11, Sabrina finds it difficult to move beyond her firsthand experiences to a world of possibilities. During the coming years, her thinking will acquire the complex qualities that characterize the cognition of her older brothers. Jules and Louis consider multiple variables simultaneously and think about situations that are not easily detected in the real world or that do not exist at all. As a result, they can grasp advanced scientific and mathematical principles and grapple with social and political issues. Compared with school-age children's thinking, adolescent thought is more enlightened, imaginative, and rational.

Systematic research on adolescent cognitive development began with testing of Piaget's ideas (Keating, 2012; Kuhn, 2009). Information-processing research has greatly enhanced our understanding.

Piaget's Theory: The Formal Operational Stage

11.12 What are the major characteristics of formal operational thought?

11.13 Discuss follow-up research on formal operational thought and its implications for the accuracy of Piaget's formal operational stage.

According to Piaget, around age 11 young people enter the **formal operational stage,** in which they develop the capacity for abstract, systematic, scientific thinking. Whereas concrete operational children can "operate on reality," formal operational adolescents can "operate on operations." They no longer require concrete things or events as objects of thought. Instead, they can come up with new, more general logical rules through internal reflection (Inhelder & Piaget, 1955/1958). Let's look at two major features of the formal operational stage.

Hypothetico-Deductive Reasoning

Piaget believed that at adolescence, young people first become capable of **hypothetico-deductive reasoning.** When faced with a problem, they start with a *hypothesis,* or prediction about variables that might affect an outcome, from which they *deduce* logical, testable inferences. Then they systematically isolate and combine variables to see which of these inferences are confirmed in the real world. Notice how this form of problem solving begins with possibility and proceeds to reality. In contrast, concrete operational children start with reality—with the most obvious predictions about a situation. If these are not confirmed, they usually cannot think of alternatives and fail to solve the problem.

Adolescents' performance on Piaget's famous *pendulum problem* illustrates this approach. Suppose we present several school-age children and adolescents with strings of different lengths, objects of different weights to attach to the strings, and a bar from which to hang the strings (see Figure 11.8). Then we ask each of them to figure out what influences the speed with which a pendulum swings through its arc.

Formal operational adolescents hypothesize that four variables might be influential: (1) the length of the string, (2) the weight of the object hung on it, (3) how high the object is raised before it is released, and (4) how forcefully the object is pushed. By varying one factor at a time while holding the other three constant, they test each variable separately and, if necessary, also in combination. Eventually they discover that only string length makes a difference.

In contrast, concrete operational children cannot separate the effects of each variable. They may test for the effect of string length without holding weight constant—comparing, for example, a short, light pendulum with a long, heavy one. Also, they typically fail to notice variables that are not immediately suggested by the concrete materials of the task—for example, how high the object is raised or how forcefully it is released.

FIGURE 11.8 Piaget's pendulum problem. Adolescents who engage in hypothetico-deductive reasoning think of variables that might possibly affect the speed with which a pendulum swings through its arc. Then they isolate and test each variable, as well as testing the variables in combination. Eventually they deduce that the weight of the object, the height from which it is released, and how forcefully it is pushed have no effect on the speed with which the pendulum swings through its arc. Only string length makes a difference.

Propositional Thought

A second important characteristic of Piaget's formal operational stage is **propositional thought**—adolescents' ability to evaluate the logic of propositions (verbal statements) without referring to real-world circumstances. In contrast, children can evaluate the logic of statements only by considering them against concrete evidence in the real world.

In a study of propositional reasoning, a researcher showed children and adolescents a pile of poker chips and asked whether statements about the chips were true, false, or uncertain (Osherson & Markman, 1975). In one condition, the researcher hid a chip in her hand and presented the following propositions:

"*Either* the chip in my hand is green or it is not green."
"The chip in my hand is green *and* it is not green."

In another condition, the experimenter made the same statements while holding either a red or a green chip in full view.

School-age children focused on the concrete properties of the poker chips. When the chip was hidden, they replied that they were uncertain about both statements. When it was visible, they judged both statements to be true if the chip was green and false if it was red. In contrast, most adolescents analyzed the logic of the statements. They understood that the "either-or" statement is always true and the "and" statement is always false, regardless of the chip's color.

Although Piaget did not view language as playing a central role in children's cognitive development (see Chapter 7), he acknowledged its importance in adolescence. Formal operations require language-based and other symbolic systems that do not stand for real things, such as those in higher mathematics. Secondary school students use such systems in algebra and geometry. Formal operational thought also involves verbal reasoning about abstract concepts. Jules was thinking in this way when he pondered relationships among time, space, and matter in physics and wondered about justice and freedom in philosophy.

Follow-Up Research on Formal Operational Thought

Research on formal operational thought poses questions similar to those we discussed with respect to Piaget's earlier stages: Does formal operational thinking appear earlier than Piaget expected? Do all individuals reach formal operations during their teenage years?

Are Children Capable of Hypothetico-Deductive and Propositional Thinking?
School-age children show the glimmerings of hypothetico-deductive reasoning, although they are less competent at it than adolescents. In simplified situations involving no more than two possible causal variables, 6-year-olds understand that hypotheses must be confirmed by appropriate evidence (Ruffman et al., 1993). But without direct instruction, school-age children cannot sort out evidence that bears on three or more variables at once (Lorch et al., 2010; Matlen & Klahr, 2013). And as we will see when we take up information-processing research, children have difficulty explaining why a pattern of observations supports a hypothesis, even when they recognize the connection between the two.

With respect to propositional thought, when a simple set of premises defies real-world knowledge ("All cats bark. Rex is a cat. Does Rex bark?") but is presented with the support of props in make-believe play, 4- to 6-year-olds can reason logically. To justify their answer, they are likely to say, "We can pretend cats bark!" (Dias & Harris, 1988, 1990). But in an entirely verbal mode, children have great difficulty reasoning from premises that contradict reality or their own beliefs.

Consider this set of statements: "If dogs are bigger than elephants and elephants are bigger than mice, then dogs are bigger than mice." Children younger than 10 judge this reasoning to be false because some of the relations specified do not occur in real life (Moshman & Franks, 1986; Pillow, 2002). They automatically think of well-learned knowledge ("Elephants are larger than dogs") that casts doubt on the truthfulness of the premises. Children find it more difficult than adolescents to inhibit activation of such knowledge (Klaczynski, Schuneman, & Daniel, 2004; Simoneau & Markovits, 2003). Partly for this reason, they fail to grasp the *logical necessity* of propositional reasoning—that the accuracy of conclusions drawn from premises rests on the rules of logic, not on real-world confirmation.

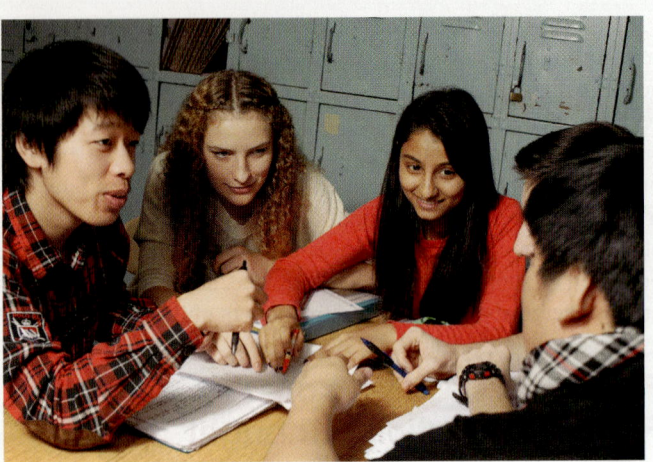

Adolescents gradually improve in propositional thought. As these students discuss problems in a social studies class, they show that they can analyze the logic of propositions, independent of their content.

In an Israeli study of seventh to ninth graders, after controlling for participants' age, researchers found that years of schooling fully accounted for early adolescent gains in propositional thought (Artman, Cahan, & Avni-Babad, 2006). School tasks, the investigators speculated, provide crucial experiences in setting aside the "if ... then" logic of everyday conversations that is often used to convey intentions, promises, and threats ("If you don't do your chores, then you won't get your allowance") but that conflicts with the logic of academic reasoning. In school, then, adolescents encounter rich opportunities to realize their neurological potential to think more effectively.

An Information-Processing View of Adolescent Cognitive Development

11.14 How do information-processing researchers account for cognitive changes in adolescence?

As with hypothetico-deductive reasoning, in early adolescence, young people become better at analyzing the *logic* of propositions, regardless of their *content*. And they handle problems requiring increasingly complex mental operations. In justifying their reasoning, they more often explain the logical rules on which it is based (Müller, Overton, & Reese, 2001; Venet & Markovits, 2001). But these capacities do not appear suddenly at puberty. Rather, gains are gradual from childhood on—findings that call into question the emergence of a new stage of cognitive development at adolescence (Kuhn, 2009; Moshman, 2005).

Do All Individuals Reach the Formal Operational Stage?
Try giving one or two of the formal operational tasks just described to your friends. How well do they do? Even well-educated adults often have difficulty (Kuhn, 2009; Markovits & Vachon, 1990).

Why are so many adults not fully formal operational? One reason is that people are most likely to think abstractly and systematically on tasks in which they have had extensive guidance and practice in using such reasoning (Kuhn, 2013). This conclusion is supported by evidence that taking college courses leads to improvements in formal reasoning related to course content. Math and science prompt gains in propositional thought, social science in methodological and statistical reasoning (Lehman & Nisbett, 1990). Like concrete reasoning in children, formal operations do not emerge in all contexts at once but are specific to situation and task (Keating, 2004, 2012).

Individuals in tribal and village societies rarely do well on tasks typically used to assess formal operational reasoning (Cole, 1990). Piaget acknowledged that without the opportunity to solve hypothetical problems, people in some societies might not display formal operations. Still, researchers ask, Does formal operational thought largely result from children's and adolescents' independent efforts to make sense of their world, as Piaget claimed? Or is it a culturally transmitted way of thinking that is specific to literate societies and taught in school?

Information-processing theorists refer to a variety of specific mechanisms, including components of executive function, as underlying cognitive gains in adolescence. As noted in previous chapters, each mechanism promotes advances in others (Keating, 2012; Kuhn, 2009, 2013; Kuhn & Franklin, 2006). Now let's draw them together:

- *Working memory* increases, enabling more information to be held in mind at once and combined into increasingly complex, efficient representations, "opening possibilities for growth" in the capacities listed below and also improving as a result of gains in those capacities (Demetriou et al., 2002, p. 97).
- *Inhibition*—both of irrelevant stimuli and of well-learned responses in situations where they are inappropriate—improves, supporting gains in attention and reasoning.
- *Attention* becomes more *selective* (focused on relevant information) and *flexible*—better-adapted to the changing demands of tasks.
- *Planning* on complex tasks with multiple steps improves, becoming better-organized and efficient.
- *Strategies* become more effective, enhancing storage, representation, and retrieval of information.
- *Knowledge* increases, easing strategy use.
- *Metacognition* (awareness of thought) expands, leading to new insights into effective strategies for acquiring information and solving problems.
- *Cognitive self-regulation* improves, yielding better moment-by-moment monitoring, evaluation, and redirection of thinking.

As we look at influential findings from an information-processing perspective, we will see some of these changes in action. And we will discover that researchers regard one of them—*metacognition*—as central to adolescent cognitive development.

Scientific Reasoning: Coordinating Theory with Evidence

During a free moment in physical education class, Sabrina wondered why more of her tennis serves and returns passed the net and dropped in her opponent's court when she used a particular brand of balls. "Is it something about their color or size?" she asked herself. "Hmm … or maybe it's their surface texture—that might affect their bounce."

The heart of scientific reasoning is coordinating theories with evidence. Researchers have conducted extensive research into the development of scientific reasoning, using problems that, like Piaget's tasks, involve several variables that, alone or in combination, might affect an outcome (Lehrer & Schauble, 2015). How does evaluation of theories in light of evidence change with age?

In one series of studies, third, sixth, and ninth graders and adults were first presented with evidence—sometimes consistent and sometimes conflicting with theories—and then questioned about the accuracy of each theory (Kuhn, 2002). For example, participants were given a problem much like Sabrina's: to theorize about which of several features of sports balls—size (large or small), color (light or dark), texture (rough or smooth), or presence or absence of ridges on the surface—influences the quality of a player's serve. Next, they were told about the theory of Mr. (or Ms.) S, who believes the ball's size is important, and the theory of Mr. (or Ms.) C, who thinks color matters. Finally, the interviewer presented evidence by placing balls with certain characteristics in two baskets, labeled "good serve" and "bad serve" (see Figure 11.9).

The youngest participants often discounted obviously causal variables, ignored evidence conflicting with their own initial judgment, and distorted evidence in ways consistent with their preferred theory. These findings, and others like them, suggest that on complex, multivariable tasks, children—instead of viewing evidence as separate from and bearing on a theory—often blend the two into a single representation of "the way things are." Children are especially likely to overlook evidence that does not match their prior beliefs when a causal variable is implausible (like color affecting the performance of a sports ball) and when task demands (number of variables to be evaluated) are high (Yang & Tsai, 2010). The ability to distinguish theory from evidence and use logical rules to examine their relationship improves steadily from childhood into adolescence, continuing into adulthood (Kuhn & Dean, 2004; Zimmerman & Croker, 2013).

How Scientific Reasoning Develops

What factors support skill at coordinating theory with evidence? Greater working-memory capacity, permitting a theory and the effects of several variables to be compared at once, is vital. Adolescents also benefit from exposure to increasingly complex problems and to instruction that highlights critical features of scientific reasoning—for example, why a scientist's expectations in a particular situation are inconsistent with everyday beliefs and experiences (Chinn & Malhotra, 2002). This explains why scientific reasoning is strongly influenced by years of schooling, whether individuals grapple with traditional scientific tasks (like

FIGURE 11.9 Which features of these sports balls—size, color, surface texture, or presence or absence of ridges—influence the quality of a player's serve? This set of evidence suggests that color might be important, since light-colored balls are largely in the good-serve basket and dark-colored balls in the bad-serve basket. But the same is true for texture! The good-serve basket has mostly smooth balls; the bad-serve basket, rough balls. Since all light-colored balls are smooth and all dark-colored balls are rough, we cannot tell whether color or texture makes a difference. But we can conclude that size and presence or absence of ridges are not important, since these features are equally represented in the good-serve and bad-serve baskets. (Adapted from Kuhn, Amsel, & O'Loughlin, 1988.)

the sports-ball problem) or engage in informal reasoning—for example, justifying a theory about what causes children to fail in school (Amsel & Brock, 1996).

Sophisticated *metacognitive understanding* is vital for scientific reasoning (Kuhn, 2011, 2013). When adolescents regularly pit theory against evidence over many weeks, they experiment with various strategies, reflect on and revise them, and become aware of the nature of logic. Then they apply their appreciation of logic to an increasingly wide variety of situations. The ability to think about theories, deliberately isolate and control variables, and inhibit an initial choice long enough to actively seek disconfirming evidence and weigh alternative possibilities is rarely present before adolescence (Kuhn, 2000; Kuhn et al., 2008; Moshman, 1998).

Though far more competent than children, adolescents and adults vary widely in scientific reasoning skills (Kuhn, 2011). Many continue to show a self-serving bias, applying logic more effectively to ideas they doubt than to ideas they favor. Reasoning scientifically requires the metacognitive capacity to evaluate one's objectivity—to be fair-minded rather than self-serving (Moshman, 2011). As we will see in Chapter 12, this flexible, open-minded approach is not just a cognitive attainment but a personality trait—one that assists teenagers greatly in forming an identity and developing morally.

Adolescents develop scientific reasoning skills in a similar step-by-step fashion on different types of tasks. In a series of studies, 10- to 20-year-olds were given sets of problems graded in difficulty. One set contained causal-experimental tasks like the sports-ball problem in Figure 11.9, another contained quantitative-relational tasks like the pendulum problem in Figure 11.8, and still another consisted of propositional tasks like the poker chip problem on page 389 (Demetriou et al., 1993, 1996, 2002). In each type of task, adolescents mastered component skills in sequential order by expanding their metacognitive awareness. For example, on causal-experimental tasks, they first became aware of the many variables that—separately and in combination—could influence an outcome. This enabled them to formulate and test hypotheses. Over time, adolescents combined separate skills into a smoothly functioning system, constructing a general model that they could apply to many instances of a given type of problem.

LOOK and LISTEN

> Describe one or more memorable experiences from your high school classes that helped you advance in scientific reasoning—pit theory against evidence and become receptive to disconfirming evidence, even for theories you favored.

Piaget underscored the role of metacognition in formal operational thought when he spoke of "operating on operations" (see page 388). But information-processing findings confirm that scientific reasoning does not result from an abrupt, stagewise change. Instead, it develops gradually out of many specific experiences that require children and adolescents to match theories against evidence and reflect on and evaluate their thinking.

Consequences of Adolescent Cognitive Changes

11.15 Describe typical reactions of adolescents that result from their advancing cognition.

The development of increasingly complex, effective thinking leads to dramatic revisions in the way adolescents see themselves, others, and the world in general. But just as adolescents are occasionally awkward in using their transformed bodies, so they initially falter in their abstract thinking. Teenagers' self-concern, idealism, criticism, and faulty decision making, though perplexing to adults, are usually beneficial in the long run. Applying What We Know on the following page suggests ways to handle the everyday consequences of teenagers' newfound cognitive capacities.

Self-Consciousness and Self-Focusing

Adolescents' ability to reflect on their own thoughts, combined with physical and psychological changes, leads them to think more about themselves. Piaget believed that a new form of egocentrism arises, in which adolescents again have difficulty distinguishing their own and others' perspectives (Inhelder & Piaget, 1955/1958). Piaget's followers suggest that two distorted images of the relation between self and other appear.

The first is called the **imaginary audience,** adolescents' belief that they are the focus of everyone else's attention and concern (Elkind & Bowen, 1979). As a result, they become extremely self-conscious. The imaginary audience helps explain why adolescents spend long hours inspecting every detail of their appearance and why they are so sensitive to public criticism. To teenagers, who believe that everyone is monitoring their performance, a critical remark from a parent or teacher can be mortifying.

A second cognitive distortion is the **personal fable.** Certain that others are observing and thinking about them, teenagers develop an inflated opinion of their own importance—a feeling that they are special and unique. Many adolescents view themselves as reaching great heights of omnipotence and also sinking to unusual depths of despair—experiences that others cannot possibly understand (Elkind, 1994). One teenager wrote in her diary, "My parents' lives are so ordinary, so stuck in a rut. Mine will be different. I'll realize my hopes and ambitions." Another, upset when a boyfriend failed to return her affections, rebuffed her mother's comforting words: "Mom, you don't know what it's like to be in love!"

Although imaginary-audience and personal-fable ideation is common in adolescence, these distorted visions of the self do not result from egocentrism, as Piaget suggested. Rather, they are partly an outgrowth of advances in perspective taking, which cause young teenagers to be more concerned with what others think (Vartanian & Powlishta, 1996). Recall, also, that changes in the brain's emotional/social network spark increased sensitivity to social feedback.

In fact, certain aspects of the imaginary audience may serve positive, protective functions. When asked why they worry about the views of others, adolescents responded that others' evaluations have important *real* consequences—for self-esteem, peer

This teenager appears self-confident and delighted that all eyes are on him. When the personal fable engenders a view of oneself as highly capable and influential, it may help young people cope with the challenges of adolescence.

Applying what we Know

Handling Consequences of Teenagers' New Cognitive Capacities

THOUGHT EXPRESSED AS …	SUGGESTION
Sensitivity to public criticism	Avoid finding fault with the adolescent in front of others. If the matter is important, wait until you can speak to the teenager alone.
Exaggerated sense of personal uniqueness	Acknowledge the adolescent's unique characteristics. At opportune times, encourage a more balanced perspective by pointing out that you had similar feelings as a teenager.
Idealism and criticism	Respond patiently to the adolescent's grand expectations and critical remarks. Point out positive features of targets, helping the teenager see that all societies and people are blends of virtues and imperfections.
Difficulty making everyday decisions	Refrain from deciding for the adolescent. Model effective decision making, and offer diplomatic suggestions about the pros and cons of alternatives, the likelihood of various outcomes, and learning from poor choices.

acceptance, and social support (Bell & Bromnick, 2003). The idea that others care about their appearance and behavior also has emotional value, helping teenagers hold onto important relationships as they struggle to establish an independent sense of self (Galanki & Christopoulos, 2011).

With respect to the personal fable, in a study of sixth through tenth graders, sense of omnipotence predicted self-esteem and overall positive adjustment. Viewing the self as highly capable and influential helps young people cope with challenges of adolescence. In contrast, sense of personal uniqueness was modestly associated with depression and suicidal thinking (Aalsma, Lapsley, & Flannery, 2006). Focusing on the distinctiveness of one's own experiences may interfere with forming close, rewarding relationships, which provide social support in stressful times. And when combined with a sensation-seeking personality, the personal fable seems to contribute to adolescent risk taking by reducing teenagers' sense of vulnerability (Alberts, Elkind, & Ginsberg, 2007). Young people with high personal-fable and sensation-seeking scores tend to take more sexual risks, more often use drugs, and commit more delinquent acts than their age-mates (Greene et al., 2000).

Idealism and Criticism

Adolescents' capacity to think about possibilities opens up the world of the ideal. Teenagers can imagine alternative family, religious, political, and moral systems, and they want to explore them. They often construct grand visions of a world with no injustice, discrimination, or tasteless behavior. The disparity between teenagers' idealism and adults' greater realism creates tension between parent and child. Envisioning a perfect family against which their parents and siblings fall short, adolescents become fault-finding critics.

Overall, however, teenage idealism and criticism are advantageous. Once adolescents come to see other people as having both strengths and weaknesses, they have a much greater capacity to work constructively for social change and to form positive, lasting relationships (Elkind, 1994). Parents can help teenagers forge a better balance between the ideal and the real by tolerating their criticism while reminding them that all people are blends of virtues and imperfections.

Decision Making

Think back, once again, to evidence indicating that puberty triggers changes in the brain's emotional/social network that outpace development of the prefrontal cognitive-control network. Consequently, teenagers often perform less well than adults in decision making, where they must inhibit emotion and impulses in favor of thinking rationally.

Good decision making involves (1) recognizing the range of possible response options, (2) identifying pros and cons of each alternative, (3) assessing the likelihood of various outcomes, (4) evaluating one's choice in terms of whether one's goals were met and, if not, (5) learning from the mistake and making a better future decision. When researchers modified a card game to trigger strong emotion by introducing immediate feedback about gains and losses after each choice, teenagers behaved more irrationally, taking far greater risks than adults in their twenties (Figner et al., 2009). Additional evidence confirms that in decision-making contexts, adolescents—especially early adolescents—are far more enticed than adults are by the possibility of immediate reward (see page 373)—more willing to take risks and less likely to avoid potential losses (Christakou et al., 2013; Defoe et al., 2015).

Nevertheless, teenagers are less effective than adults at decision making even under "cool," unemotional conditions (Huizenga, Crone, & Jansen, 2007). They less often carefully evaluate alternatives, instead falling back on well-learned intuitive judgments (Jacobs & Klaczynski, 2002). Consider a hypothetical problem requiring a choice, on the basis of two arguments, between taking a traditional lecture class and taking a computer-based class. One argument contains large-sample information: course evaluations from 150 students, 85 percent of whom liked the computer class. The other argument contains small-sample personal reports: complaints of two honor-roll students who both hated the computer class and enjoyed the traditional class (Klaczynski, 2001). Most adolescents, even those who knew that selecting the large-sample argument was "more intelligent,"

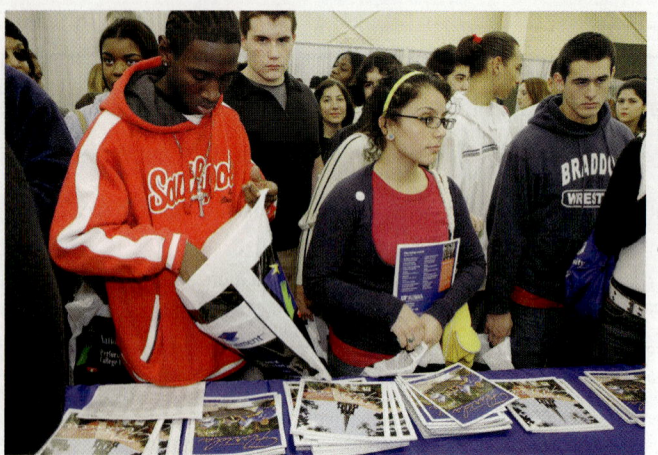

These high school students attending a college fair will face many choices over the next few years. But in making decisions, teenagers are less likely than adults to carefully weigh the pros and cons of each alternative.

based their choice on the small-sample argument, which resembled the informal opinions they depend on in everyday life.

Earlier we noted that processing skills governed by the prefrontal cognitive-control network, such as decision making, develop gradually. Like other aspects of cognitive development, decision making is affected by experience. As "first-timers" in many situations, adolescents do not have sufficient knowledge to consider pros and cons and predict likely outcomes. And after engaging in risky behavior without negative consequences, teenagers rate its benefits higher and its risks lower than peers who have not tried it (Halpern-Felsher et al., 2004). These faulty judgments increase the chances of continued risk taking.

Over time, young people learn from their successes and failures and gather information from others about factors that affect decision making (Reyna & Farley, 2006). School and community interventions that teach effective decision-making skills can help adolescents apply their capacity for metacognition by reflecting on and monitoring the decision process (Bruine de Bruin, 2012). But because taking risks without experiencing harmful outcomes can heighten adolescents' sense of invulnerability, they need supervision and protection from high-risk experiences until their decision making improves.

Ask yourself

CONNECT How does evidence on adolescent decision making help us understand teenagers' risk taking in sexual activity and drug use?

APPLY Clarissa, age 14, is convinced that no one appreciates how hurt she feels at not being invited to the homecoming dance. Meanwhile, 15-year-old Justine, alone in her room, pantomimes being sworn in as student body president with her awestruck parents looking on. Which aspect of the personal fable is each adolescent displaying? Which one is more likely to be well-adjusted, and which poorly adjusted? Explain.

REFLECT Cite examples of your own idealistic thinking or poor decision making as a teenager. How has your thinking changed?

 # Sex Differences in Mental Abilities

11.16 What factors contribute to sex differences in mental abilities at adolescence?

Sex differences in mental abilities have sparked almost as much controversy as the ethnic and SES differences in IQ considered in Chapter 9. In most areas of cognitive functioning, including general intelligence, girls and boys are similar (Hyde, 2014). Still, they vary in certain specific mental abilities, most notably reading, writing, mathematical, and spatial skills.

Verbal Abilities

Throughout the school years, girls attain higher scores in reading and writing achievement and account for a lower percentage of children referred for remedial reading instruction. Girls continue to score slightly higher on tests of verbal ability in middle childhood and adolescence in every country in which assessments have been conducted (Reilly, 2012; Wai et al., 2010). And when verbal tests are heavily weighted with writing, girls' advantage is large (Halpern et al., 2007).

A special concern is that girls' advantage in reading and writing achievement increases in adolescence, with boys doing especially poorly in writing—trends evident in the United States and other industrialized nations (Stoet & Geary, 2013; U.S. Department of Education, 2012a, 2016). These differences in literacy skills are believed to be major contributors to a widening gender gap in college enrollments. Whereas 40 years ago, males accounted for 60 percent of U.S. undergraduate students, today they are in the minority, at 44 percent (U.S. Department of Education, 2015).

Recall from Chapter 5 that girls have a biological advantage in earlier development of the left hemisphere of the cerebral cortex, where language is usually localized. And fMRI research indicates that in tackling language tasks (such as deciding whether two spoken or written words rhyme), 9- to 15-year-old girls show concentrated activity in language-specific brain areas. Boys, in contrast, display more widespread activation—in addition to language areas, considerable activity in auditory and visual areas, depending on how words are presented (Burman, Bitan, & Booth, 2008). This suggests that girls are more efficient language processors than boys, who rely heavily on sensory brain regions and process spoken and written words differently.

But girls also receive more verbal stimulation from early childhood through adolescence (Peterson & Roberts, 2003). Furthermore, children view language arts as a "feminine" subject. And as a result of the high-stakes testing movement, students today spend more time at their desks being taught in a regimented way—an approach particularly at odds with boys' higher activity level, assertiveness, and incidence of learning problems. Clearly, reversing boys' weakening literacy skills is a high priority, requiring a concerted effort by families, schools, and communities.

Mathematical Abilities

Studies of mathematical abilities in the early school grades are inconsistent. Some find no disparities, others slight differences depending on the math skill assessed (Lachance & Mazzocco, 2006). Girls tend to be advantaged in counting, arithmetic computation, and mastery of basic concepts, perhaps because of their better verbal skills and more methodical approach to problem solving (Wei et al., 2012). But by late childhood to early adolescence, when math concepts become more abstract and spatial, boys outperform girls. The difference is especially evident on tests requiring complex reasoning (Lindberg et al., 2010; Reilly, Neumann, & Andrews, 2016). In science achievement, too, boys' advantage increases as problems become more difficult.

The male advantage is evident in most countries where boys and girls have equal access to secondary education. But the gap is typically small, varies considerably across nations, and has diminished over the past 30 years (Else-Quest, Hyde, & Linn, 2010; Halpern, 2012; Reilly, 2012). Among the most capable, however, the gender gap is larger. On average, twice as many twelfth-grade boys as girls attain very high math achievement scores—a difference that extends to science achievement as well (Reilly, Neumann, & Andrews, 2016; Wai et al., 2010).

Some researchers believe that heredity contributes to the gender gap in math, especially the tendency for more boys to be extremely talented. Accumulating evidence indicates that boys' advantage originates in two skill areas: (1) their more rapid numerical memory, which permits them to devote more working-memory resources to complex mental operations; and (2) their superior spatial reasoning, which enhances their mathematical problem solving (Halpern et al., 2007). Longitudinal evidence on nationally representative samples of U.S. high school students tracked for a decade or more reveals that high spatial ability in adolescence predicts subsequent advanced educational attainment in math-intensive fields and entry into science, technology, engineering, and math (STEM) careers, beyond the contributions of verbal and math ability (Wai, Lubinski, & Benbow, 2009). See the Biology and Environment box on pages 396–397 for further consideration of this issue.

Social pressures are also influential. Long before sex differences in math achievement appear, many children view math as a "masculine" subject. Also, parents typically think boys are better at it—an attitude that encourages girls to blame their errors on lack of ability and to consider math less useful for their future lives. These beliefs, in turn, reduce girls' confidence and interest in math and their willingness to consider STEM careers (Ceci & Williams, 2010; Kenney-Benson et al., 2006; Parker et al., 2012). Furthermore, *stereotype threat*—fear of being judged on the basis of a negative stereotype (see page 320 in Chapter 9)—causes girls to do worse than their abilities allow on difficult math problems (Picho, Rodriguez, & Finnie, 2013). As a result of these influences, even girls who are highly talented are less likely to develop effective math reasoning skills.

A positive sign is that today, American boys and girls reach advanced levels of high school math and science study in equal proportions—a crucial factor in reducing sex differences in knowledge and skill (U.S. Department of Education, 2015). But boys spend more time than girls with screen media, and boys tend to use them differently—more often playing video games, creating Web pages, writing computer programs, analyzing data, and using graphics programs (Lenhart et al., 2010; Looker & Thiessen, 2003; Rideout, Foehr, & Roberts, 2010). As a result, boys acquire more specialized computer knowledge.

Clearly, extra steps must be taken to promote girls' interest in and confidence at math and science. As Figure 11.11 shows, in cultures that value gender equality, sex differences in math achievement are much smaller and, in two nations, reversed! Swedish and Icelandic high school girls exceed boys in math scores (Guiso et al., 2008; OECD, 2012). Similarly, math and science achievement gaps are smaller in countries with higher proportions of women in research-related professions, and in countries where few individuals view science as "masculine" (Else-Quest, Hyde, & Linn, 2010; Nosek et al., 2009; Reilly, 2012).

Finally, a math curriculum beginning in kindergarten that teaches children how to apply effective spatial strategies—

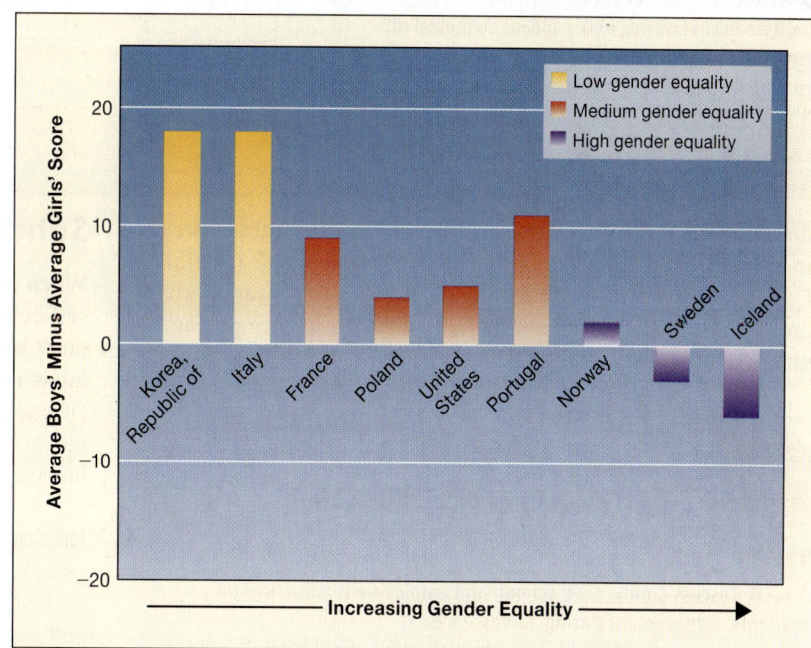

FIGURE 11.11 Math achievement gender gaps in nine industrialized nations, arranged in order of increasing gender equality. Math achievement scores are based on 15-year-olds' performance on an identical test in each country. Country gender equality is a composite measure that includes cultural attitudes toward women, women's participation in the labor force and in politics and government, and women's educational attainment and economic opportunities. As country gender equality increases, boys' advantage in math achievement tends to decline; in Sweden and Iceland, girls' math scores exceed boys'. (Adapted from Guiso et al., 2008; OECD, 2012.)

Biology and Environment

Sex Differences in Spatial Abilities

Spatial skills are a key focus of researchers' efforts to explain sex differences in complex mathematical reasoning. The gender gap favoring males is large for *mental rotation tasks*, in which individuals must rotate a three-dimensional figure rapidly and accurately inside their heads (see Figure 11.10). Males also do considerably better on *spatial perception tasks*, in which people must determine spatial relationships by considering the orientation of the surrounding environment. Sex differences on *spatial visualization tasks*, involving analysis of complex visual forms, are weak or nonexistent. Because many strategies can be used to solve these tasks, both sexes may come up with effective procedures (Maeda & Yoon, 2013; Miller & Halpern, 2014).

Sex differences in spatial abilities emerge as early as the first few months of life, in male

FIGURE 11.10 Types of spatial tasks. Large sex differences favoring males appear on mental rotation, and males do considerably better than females on spatial perception. In contrast, sex differences on spatial visualization are weak or nonexistent.

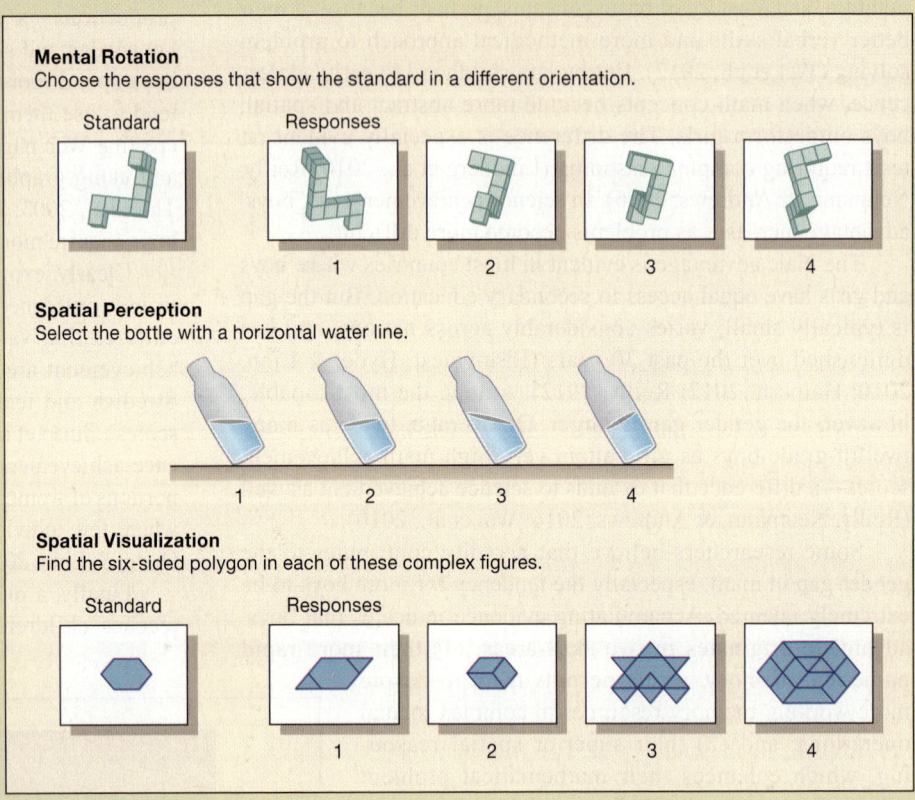

drawing diagrams, mentally manipulating visual images, searching for numerical patterns, and graphing—is vital (Nuttall, Casey, & Pezaris, 2005). Because girls are biased toward verbal processing, they may not attain their math and science potential unless they are specifically taught how to think spatially.

Learning in School

11.17 Discuss the impact of school transitions on adolescent adjustment.
11.18 Discuss family, peer, school, and employment influences on academic achievement during adolescence.
11.19 What factors increase the risk of high school dropout?

In complex societies, adolescence coincides with entry into secondary school. Most young people move into either a middle or a junior high school and then into a high school. With each change, academic achievement increasingly determines higher education options and job opportunities. In the following sections, we take up various aspects of secondary school life.

School Transitions

When Sabrina started middle school, she left a small, intimate, self-contained sixth-grade classroom for a much larger school. "I don't know most of the kids in my classes, and my teachers don't know me," Sabrina complained to her mother at the end of the first week. "Besides, there's too much homework. I get assignments in all my classes at once. I can't do all this!" she shouted, bursting into tears.

Impact of School Transitions. As Sabrina's reactions suggest, school transitions can create adjustment problems. With each school change—from elementary to middle or junior high and then to high school—adolescents' grades decline (Benner, 2011; Ryan, Shim, & Makara, 2013). The drop is partly due to tighter academic standards, but school transitions are also associated with reductions in achievement test scores and attendance, which cannot be explained by tougher grading (Benner & Wang, 2014; Schwerdt & West, 2013). The transition to secondary school often means less personal attention, more whole-class instruction, and less chance to participate in classroom decision making.

infants' superior ability to recognize a familiar object from a new perspective—a capacity requiring mental rotation (Moore & Johnson, 2011; Quinn & Liben, 2014). The male spatial advantage is present throughout childhood, adolescence, and adulthood in many cultures (Levine et al., 1999; Silverman, Choi, & Peters, 2007). One hypothesis is that heredity, perhaps through prenatal exposure to androgen hormones, underlies this finding. However, a large number of studies testing this idea have produced inconsistent findings (Hines, 2015). Although heredity likely plays a role, its path of influence remains unclear.

Growing evidence confirms that experience contributes to males' superior spatial performance. Children who engage in manipulative activities, such as block play, model building, and carpentry, do better on spatial tasks (Baenninger & Newcombe, 1995). Playing action video games enhances many cognitive processes important for spatial skills, including visual discrimination, speed of thinking, attention shifting, tracking of multiple objects, mental rotation, and wayfinding—gains that persist and generalize to diverse situations (Spence & Feng, 2010). Boys spend far more time than girls at these pursuits.

These teenagers take part in a science research competition for high school seniors. With supportive experiences, girls can excel in math and science.

Furthermore, adults seem to encourage spatial reasoning in boys more than girls, even during activities that are not gender typed. For example, when researchers observed preschoolers in their homes, boys and girls were equally likely to play with puzzles. But parents were more engaged and referred more often to spatial concepts with sons, who more often tackled difficult puzzles (Levine et al., 2012). Complex puzzle play predicted children's performance on a test of spatial abilities several months later.

Spatial skills respond readily to training, with improvements often larger than the sex differences themselves. But because boys and girls usually show similar training effects, sex differences typically persist (Uttal et al., 2013). In one study of first graders, however, training in mental rotation strategies over several months—a more intensive approach than previously tried—led girls to reach the same performance level as boys (Tzuriel & Egozi, 2010). This suggests that the right kind of early intervention can override genetically based sex differences in spatial skills.

It is not surprising, then, that students often rate their middle and high school experiences less favorably than their elementary school experiences. They also report that their teachers care less about them, are less friendly, grade less fairly, and stress competition more. Consequently, many young people feel less academically competent, and their motivation and liking for school decline (Barber & Olsen, 2004; De Wit et al., 2011; Otis, Grouzet, & Pelletier, 2005).

Adolescents facing added strains—family disruption, poverty, low parent involvement, high parental conflict, low social support, or learned helplessness on academic tasks—at either transition are at greatest risk for self-esteem and academic difficulties (de Bruyn, 2005; De Wit et al., 2011; Seidman et al., 2003). Furthermore, the high school transition is especially challenging for African-American and Hispanic students who move to a new school with substantially fewer same-ethnicity peers (Benner & Graham, 2009). Under these conditions, minority adolescents report decreased feelings of belonging and school liking, and they show steeper declines in grades.

Distressed youths whose school performance either remains low or drops sharply after school transition often show a persisting pattern of poor self-esteem, motivation, and achievement. In another study, researchers compared "multiple-problem" youths (those having both academic and mental health problems), youths having difficulties in just one area (either academic or mental health), and well-adjusted youths (those doing well in both areas) across the transition to high school (Roeser, Eccles, & Freedman-Doan, 1999). Although all groups declined in grade point average, well-adjusted students continued to get high marks and multiple-problem youths low marks, with the others falling in between. In addition, the multiple-problem youths showed a far greater rise in truancy and out-of-school problem behaviors.

Adolescents with academic and emotional difficulties often turn to similarly alienated peers for the support they lack in other spheres of life (Rubin et al., 2013). For these vulnerable youths, the transition to high school may initiate a downward spiral in academic performance and school involvement that leads to failure and dropping out.

Helping Adolescents Adjust to School Transitions.
As these findings reveal, school transitions often lead to environmental changes that fit poorly with adolescents' developmental needs (Eccles & Roeser, 2009). They disrupt close relationships with teachers at a time when adolescents need adult support.

On the first day of school, a teacher's caring attention helps this sixth grader deal with the stress of moving from a small, self-contained elementary school classroom to a large middle school.

They emphasize competition during a period of heightened self-focusing. They reduce decision making and choice as the desire for autonomy is increasing. And they interfere with peer networks as young people become more concerned with peer acceptance.

LOOK and LISTEN

Ask several secondary school students to describe their experiences after school transition. What supports for easing the stress of transition did their teachers and school provide?

Support from parents, teachers, and peers can ease these strains (Waters, Lester, & Cross, 2014). Parental involvement, monitoring, gradual autonomy granting, and emphasis on mastery rather than merely good grades are associated with better adjustment (Gutman, 2006). Adolescents with close friends are more likely to sustain these friendships across the transition, which increases social integration and academic motivation in the new school (Aikens, Bierman, & Parker, 2005).

Some school districts reduce the number of school transitions by combining elementary and middle school into K–8 buildings. Compared with agemates who transition to middle school, K–8 sixth and seventh graders score higher in achievement (Kleffer, 2013; Schwerdt & West, 2013). Furthermore, teachers and administrators in K–8 buildings report more positive social contexts—less chaos, fewer conduct problems, and better overall working conditions (Kim et al., 2014). These factors predict students' favorable school attitudes, academically and socially.

Other less extensive changes are also effective. Forming smaller units within larger schools promotes closer relationships with both teachers and peers along with greater extracurricular involvement (Seidman, Aber, & French, 2004). And a "critical mass" of same-ethnicity peers—according to one suggestion, at least 15 percent of the student body—helps teenagers feel socially accepted and reduces fear of out-group hostility (National Research Council, 2007). In the first year after a school transition, homerooms can be provided in which teachers offer academic and personal counseling. Assigning students to classes with several familiar peers or a constant group of new peers strengthens emotional security and social support. In schools that take these steps, students are less likely to decline in academic performance or display other adjustment problems (Felner et al., 2002).

Academic Achievement

Adolescent achievement is the result of a long history of cumulative effects. Early on, positive educational environments, both family and school, lead to personal traits that support achievement—intelligence, confidence in one's own abilities, the desire to succeed, and high educational aspirations. Nevertheless, improving an unfavorable environment can foster resilience among poorly performing young people. See Applying What We Know on the following page for a summary of environmental factors that enhance achievement during the teenage years.

Child-Rearing Styles.
Authoritative parenting is linked to higher grades and achievement test scores in school among adolescents varying widely in SES, just as it predicts mastery-oriented behavior in childhood (Collins & Steinberg, 2006; Pinquart, 2016). In contrast, authoritarian, permissive, and uninvolved styles are associated with poorer achievement and declines in academic performance over time.

The link between authoritative parenting and adolescents' academic competence has been confirmed in countries with diverse value systems, including Argentina, Australia, China, the Netherlands, Pakistan, and the United Kingdom (Chan & Koo, 2011; de Bruyn, Deković, & Meijnen, 2003; Steinberg, 2001). In Chapter 8, we noted that authoritative parents adjust their expectations to children's capacity to take responsibility for their own behavior. Warmth, open discussion, firmness, and monitoring of adolescents' whereabouts and activities make young people feel cared about and valued, encourage reflective thinking and self-regulation, and increase awareness of the importance of doing well in school. These factors, in turn, are related to mastery-oriented attributions, effort, achievement, and high educational aspirations (Gauvain, Perez, & Beebe, 2013; Gregory & Weinstein, 2004).

Parent–School Partnerships.
In response to teenagers' desire for greater autonomy, parents' volunteering at school and contact with teachers tend to decline over adolescence. Nevertheless, high-achieving students typically have parents who remain invested in their teenager's education (Hill & Taylor, 2004). They keep tabs on academic progress, regularly attend parent–teacher conferences, make sure the young person is enrolled in challenging, well-taught classes, and emphasize the importance of doing well in school and engaging in academic planning.

Applying what we Know

Supporting High Achievement in Adolescence

FACTOR	DESCRIPTION
Child-rearing practices	Authoritative parenting
	Joint parent–adolescent decision making
	Parent involvement in the adolescent's education
Peer influences	Peer valuing of and support for high achievement
School characteristics	Warm, supportive teachers who develop personal relationships with parents and show them how to support their teenager's learning
	Learning activities that encourage high-level thinking
	Active student participation in learning activities and classroom decision making
Employment schedule	Job commitment limited to less than 15 hours per week
	High-quality vocational education for non-college-bound adolescents

In a large sample of U.S. tenth graders, students whose parents encouraged educational pursuits and high achievement more often completed homework on time, less often skipped class, and expressed greater interest and enjoyment in school learning (Wang & Sheikh-Khalil, 2014). When followed up nearly two years later, they gained in grade point average relative to agemates with less involved parents, beyond the influence of SES and previous academic performance. Academically involved parents send a message to their youth about the value of education, model constructive solutions to academic problems, and promote wise educational decisions.

Compared to parents in neighborhoods with ample resources, parents in depleted, high-risk neighborhoods tend to report higher levels of academic involvement with their teenagers at home. They seem to work harder at conveying to their children the value of education, even though daily stressors reduce their energy for such involvement (Bhargava & Witherspoon, 2015; Bunting et al., 2013). Yet stronger home–school links can relieve some of this stress. Schools can build parent–school partnerships by strengthening relationships between teachers and parents, organizing communities of parents who mutually support one another, and including parents in school governance so they remain aware of and invested in school goals.

Peer Influences. Peers play an important role in adolescent achievement, in a way that relates to both family and school. Teenagers whose parents value achievement generally choose friends who share those values (Kiuru et al., 2009; Rubin et al., 2013). For example, when Sabrina began to make new friends in middle school, she often studied with her girlfriends. Each girl wanted to do well and reinforced this desire in the others.

Peer support for high achievement also depends on the overall climate of the peer culture, which, for ethnic minority youths, is powerfully affected by the surrounding social order. In one study, integration into the school peer network predicted higher grades among European-American and Hispanic students but not among Asians and African Americans (Faircloth & Hamm, 2005). Asian cultural values stress respect for family and teacher expectations over close peer ties. African-American minority adolescents may observe that their ethnic group is worse off than the white majority in educational attainment, jobs, income, and housing. And discriminatory treatment by teachers and peers, often resulting from stereotypes that they are "not intelligent," triggers anger, anxiety, self-doubt, declines in motivation and achievement, association with peers who are not interested in school, and increases in problem behaviors (Wong, Eccles, & Sameroff, 2003).

Schools that build close networks of support between teachers and peers can prevent these negative outcomes. One high school

While waiting for her husband to get off work, this mother helps her daughter with homework in front of a convenience store as her son plays nearby. Parents in depleted, high-risk neighborhoods work harder at conveying to their children the value of education, even though daily stressors reduce their energy for such involvement.

Social Issues: Education

Media Multitasking Disrupts Learning

"Mom, I'm going to study for my biology test now," called 16-year-old Ashley while shutting her bedroom door. Sitting down at her desk, she accessed a popular social media site on her laptop, donned headphones and began listening to a favorite song on her tablet, and placed her cell phone next to her elbow so she could hear it chime if any text messages arrived. Only then did she open her textbook and begin to read.

In a survey of a nationally representative sample of U.S. 8- to 18-year-olds, more than two-thirds reported engaging in two or more media activities at once, some or most of the time (Rideout, Foehr, & Roberts, 2010). When observed studying in their homes for just 15 minutes, adolescents diverted, on average, every 5 to 6 minutes to texting, social media sites, phone calling, or watching TV (Rosen, Carrier, & Cheever, 2013). The presence of a television in the young person's bedroom is a strong predictor of this behavior, as is access to a mobile device—especially a smartphone. Nearly three-fourths of U.S. teenagers have smartphones, and one-fourth report being online "almost constantly" (Foehr, 2006; Pew Research Center, 2015g).

Research confirms that media multitasking greatly reduces learning. In one experiment, participants were given two tasks: learning to predict the weather in two different cities using colored shapes as cues and keeping a mental tally of how many high-pitched beeps they heard through headphones. Half the sample performed the tasks simultaneously, the other half separately (Foerde, Knowlton, & Poldrack, 2006). Both groups learned to predict the weather in the two-city situation, but the multitaskers were unable to apply their learning to new weather problems.

fMRI evidence revealed that the participants working only on the weather task activated the hippocampus, which plays a vital role in *explicit memory*—conscious, strategic recall, which enables new information to be used flexibly and adaptively in contexts outside the original learning situation (see page 239 in Chapter 7). In contrast, the multitaskers activated subcortical areas involved in *implicit memory*—a shallower, automatic form of learning that takes place unconsciously.

Adolescents who often media multitask report problems with each aspect of executive function in everyday life—working memory ("I forget what I'm doing in the middle of things"), inhibition ("It's hard for me to wait my turn"), and flexibly shifting attention ("I have trouble changing from one activity to another") (Baumgartner et al., 2014). Consequently, beyond superficial preparation for her biology test, Ashley is likely to have difficulty concentrating and strategically

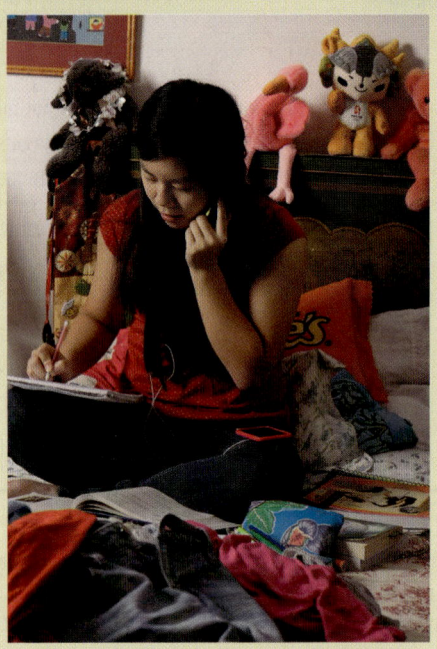

Media multitasking while doing homework fragments attention, yielding superficial learning. Frequent multitaskers are likely to have trouble filtering out irrelevant stimuli even when they are not multitasking.

processing new information after turning off her electronic devices.

Experienced teachers often complain that compared to students of a generation ago, today's teenagers are more easily distracted and learn less thoroughly. One teacher reflected, "It's the way they've grown up—working short times on many different things at one time" (Clay, 2009, p. 40).

---

with a largely low-income ethnic minority student body (65 percent African American) reorganized into "career academies"—learning communities within the school, each offering a different career-related curriculum (for example, one focusing on health, medicine, and life sciences, another on computer technology). The vocationally relevant academic program combined with more caring teacher–student relationships helped create a school climate in which peers valued school engagement, collaborated on projects, and were motivated to do well academically (Conchas, 2006). High school graduation and college enrollment rates rose from a small minority to over 90 percent.

Finally, teenagers' use of text messaging, e-mail, and social media sites to remain continuously in touch with peers—even during class and while working on homework—is an aspect of contemporary peer-group life that poses risks to achievement. See the Social Issues: Education box above to find out about the impact of "media multitasking" on learning.

School Characteristics. Adolescents need school environments that are responsive to their expanding powers of reasoning and their emotional and social needs. Without appropriate learning experiences, their cognitive potential is unlikely to be realized.

Classroom Learning Experiences. As noted earlier, in large, departmentalized secondary schools, many adolescents report that their classes lack warmth and supportiveness, which dampens their motivation. Of course, an important benefit of separate classes in each subject is that adolescents can be taught by experts, who are more likely to encourage high-level thinking, teach effective learning strategies, and emphasize content relevant to students' experiences—factors that contribute to interest, effort, and achievement (Crosnoe & Benner, 2015; Eccles, 2004). But many classrooms do not consistently provide stimulating, challenging teaching.

Wide variability in quality of instruction has contributed to increasing numbers of seniors who graduate from high school deficient in basic academic skills. Although the achievement gap separating African-American, Hispanic, and Native-American students from white students has declined since the 1970s, mastery of reading, writing, mathematics, and science by low-SES ethnic minority students remains disappointing (U.S. Department of Education, 2012a, 2012b, 2016). Too often these young people attend underfunded schools with rundown buildings, outdated equipment, and textbook shortages. In some, crime and discipline problems receive more attention than teaching and learning. By middle school, many low-SES minority students have been placed in low academic tracks, compounding their learning difficulties.

Tracking. Ability grouping, as we saw in Chapter 9, is detrimental during the elementary school years. At least into middle school, mixed-ability classes are desirable. They support the motivation and achievement of students varying widely in academic progress (Gillies, 2003; Gillies & Ashman, 1996).

By high school, some grouping is unavoidable because certain aspects of education must dovetail with the young person's future educational and vocational plans. In the United States, high school students are counseled into college preparatory, vocational, or general education tracks. Unfortunately, low-SES minority students are assigned in large numbers to noncollege tracks, perpetuating educational inequalities of earlier years.

Once assigned to a low academic track, students are "locked out" of advanced courses in later grades because they have not taken prerequisite courses, which restricts them to a lower-quality curriculum (Kelly & Price, 2011). Even in secondary schools with no formal tracking program, low-SES minority students tend to be assigned to lower course levels in most or all academic subjects, resulting in *de facto* (unofficial) *tracking* (Kalogrides & Loeb, 2013).

Breaking out of a low academic track is difficult, even when students try to do so. Interviews with African-American students revealed that many thought their previous performance did not reflect their ability. Yet teachers and counselors, overburdened with other responsibilities, had little time to reconsider individual cases (Ogbu, 2003). And compared to students in higher tracks, those in low tracks decline in academic self-esteem and exert substantially less effort—differences due in part to less stimulating classroom experiences and reduced teacher expectations (Chiu et al., 2008; Worthy, Hungerford-Kresser, & Hampton, 2009).

High school students are separated into academic and vocational tracks in virtually all industrialized nations. In China, Japan, and most Western European countries, students' placement is determined by a national exam, which usually establishes the young person's future possibilities. In the United States, students who are not assigned to a college preparatory track or who do poorly in high school can still attend college. Ultimately, however, many young people do not benefit from the more open U.S. system. By adolescence, SES differences in quality of education and academic achievement are greater in the United States than in most other industrialized countries. And the United States has a higher percentage of young people who see themselves as educational failures and drop out of high school (OECD, 2013c).

Part-Time Work. The number of U.S. high school students employed during the school year rises with age, from 40 percent of tenth graders to nearly 50 percent of twelfth graders—rates that exceed youth employment in other developed nations (Bachman, Johnston, & O'Malley, 2014). Most are middle-SES youths in pursuit of spending money rather than vocational exploration and training. Low-SES teenagers who need to contribute to family income or to support themselves find it harder to get jobs (Staff, Mont'Alvao, & Mortimer, 2015). But when African-American and Hispanic teenagers from economically disadvantaged homes are employed, they generally put in more work hours.

Adolescents typically hold jobs that involve low-level, repetitive tasks and provide little contact with adult supervisors. A heavy commitment to such jobs is harmful. The more hours students work, the poorer their school attendance, the lower their grades, the less likely they are to participate in extracurricular activities, and the more likely they are to drop out (Marsh & Kleitman, 2005). Students who spend many hours at such jobs also report more drug and alcohol use and delinquent acts (Monahan, Lee, & Steinberg, 2011; Samuolis et al., 2013). In contrast, steady, moderate hours of employment predict higher grades and greater likelihood of attending and completing college, especially among students who began high school with weak academic records (Staff & Mortimer, 2007). For these youths, perhaps paid work promotes effective time management, sense of responsibility, and self-confidence.

Work–study programs or other jobs that combine academic and vocational learning opportunities are also linked to favorable outcomes—positive school and work attitudes, improved academic performance, and reduced delinquency (Hamilton & Hamilton, 2000; Staff & Uggen, 2003). Yet high-quality vocational preparation for non-college-bound U.S. adolescents is scarce; just 6 percent of twelfth graders report participating in work–study programs (Bachman, Johnston, & O'Malley, 2014). Unlike some European nations, the United States has no widespread training system to prepare youths for skilled business and industrial occupations and manual trades. Although U.S. federal and state governments support some job-training programs, most are too brief to make a difference and serve too few young people in need of assistance.

Dropping Out

Across the aisle from Louis in math class sat Norman, who daydreamed, crumpled his notes into his pocket after class, and rarely did his homework. On test days, he twirled a good luck charm but left most questions blank. Louis and Norman had been classmates since fourth grade, but they had little to do with each other. To Louis, who was quick at schoolwork, Norman seemed to live in another world. Once or twice a week, Norman cut class; one spring day, he stopped coming altogether.

Norman is one of about 7 percent of U.S. 16- to 24-year-olds who dropped out of high school and remain without a diploma or a GED (U.S. Department of Education, 2015). The overall dropout rate has declined since the mid-2000s, largely due to substantial gains in Hispanic teenagers' graduation rates. Nevertheless, as Figure 11.12 shows, dropout rates remain elevated among low-SES ethnic minority youths, especially Native-American and Hispanic teenagers. Also, boys drop out at considerably higher rates than girls.

The decision to leave school has dire consequences. Youths without upper secondary education have much lower literacy scores than high school graduates, and they lack the skills valued by employers in today's knowledge-based economy. Consequently, dropouts have much lower employment rates than high school graduates. Even when employed, dropouts are far more likely to remain in menial, low-paid jobs and to be out of work from time to time.

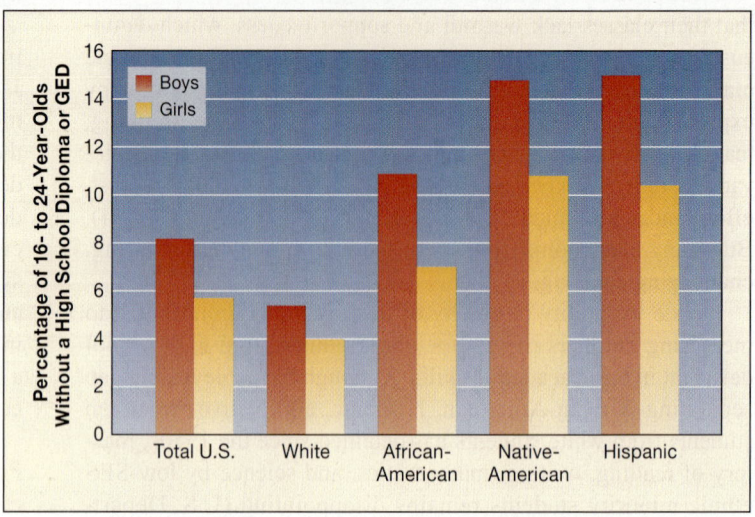

FIGURE 11.12 U.S. high school dropout rates by ethnicity and gender. Because many African-American, Hispanic, and Native-American young people come from economically disadvantaged families and attend underfunded, poor-quality schools, their dropout rates are above the national average. Rates for Native-American and Hispanic youths are especially high. Across all ethnicities, boys' dropout rates exceed girls'. (Stark & Noel, 2015.)

Factors Related to Dropping Out. Many dropouts show a persistent pattern of disruptive behavior combined with poor academic performance (Hawkins, Jaccard, & Needle, 2013). But others, like Norman, have few behavior problems; they simply experience academic difficulties and quietly disengage from school (Balfanz, Herzog, & MacIver, 2007). The pathway to dropping out starts early. Risk factors in first grade predict dropout nearly as well as risk factors in secondary school (Entwisle, Alexander, & Olson, 2005).

Norman—like other dropouts—had a long history of marginal-to-failing school grades and low academic self-esteem (Wexler & Pyle, 2013). As Norman got older, he attended class less regularly, paid little attention when he was there, and rarely did his homework. He didn't join school clubs or participate in sports. As a result, few teachers or students got to know him well. By the day he left, Norman felt alienated from all aspects of school life.

As with other dropouts, Norman's family background contributed to his problems. Compared with other students, even those with the same grade profile, dropouts are more likely to have parents who are uninvolved in their teenager's education and engage in little monitoring of their youngster's daily activities. Many are single parents, never finished high school themselves, and are unemployed (Pagani et al., 2008; Song, Benin, & Glick, 2012).

Students who drop out often have school experiences that undermine their chances for success: grade retention, which marks them as academic failures; classes with unsupportive teachers and few opportunities for active participation; and frequent peer victimization (Brown & Rodriguez, 2009; Peguero, 2011). In such schools, rule breaking is common and often results in suspension, which—by excluding students from classes—contributes further to academic failure (Christie, Jolivette, & Nelson, 2007). Students in general education and vocational tracks, where teaching tends to be the least stimulating, are three times as likely to drop out as those in a college preparatory track (U.S. Department of Education, 2015). Boys' higher rates of learning and behavior problems from early childhood on contribute to their greater school leaving relative to girls.

Prevention Strategies. Among the diverse strategies available for helping teenagers at risk of dropping out, several common themes are related to success:

- *Supplementary academic instruction and counseling that offer personalized attention.* Most potential dropouts need intensive remedial instruction in small classes that permit warm, caring teacher–student relationships to form (Wilson & Tanner-Smith, 2013). In one successful approach, at-risk students are matched with retired adults, who serve as tutors, mentors, and role models in addressing academic and vocational needs (Prevatt, 2003).

- *High-quality vocational education.* For many marginal students, the real-life nature of vocational education is more comfortable and effective than purely academic work (Levin, 2012). To work well, vocational education must carefully integrate academic and job-related instruction so students see the relevance of classroom experiences to their future goals.

- *Efforts to address the many factors in students' lives related to leaving school early.* Programs that strengthen parent involvement, offer flexible work–study arrangements, and provide on-site child care for teenage parents can make staying in school easier for at-risk adolescents.

- *Participation in extracurricular activities.* Another way of helping marginal students is to draw them into the community life of the school. The most powerful influence on extracurricular involvement is small school size (Crosnoe, Johnson, & Elder, 2004; Feldman & Matjasko, 2007). As high school student body declines—dropping from 2,000 students to 500 to 700 students—at-risk youths are more likely to be needed to help staff activities. As a result, they feel more attached to their school. In large schools, creation of smaller "schools within schools" has the same effect.

  Moderate (but not excessive) participation in arts, community service, or vocational development activities promotes diverse aspects of adjustment (Fredricks, 2012; Fredricks & Eccles, 2006). Among these are improved academic performance, reduced antisocial behavior, more favorable self-esteem and initiative, and increased peer acceptance.

As we conclude our discussion of academic achievement, let's place the school dropout problem in historical perspective. Over the second half of the twentieth century, the percentage of U.S. young people completing high school by age 24 increased steadily, from less than 50 percent to more than 90 percent. Although many dropouts get caught in a vicious cycle in which their lack of self-confidence and skills prevents them from seeking further education and training, of the 25 percent of high school freshmen who do not graduate on time, more than two-thirds return to finish their secondary education by their mid-twenties (U.S. Department of Education, 2015). And some extend their schooling further as they come to realize how essential education is for a rewarding job and a satisfying adult life.

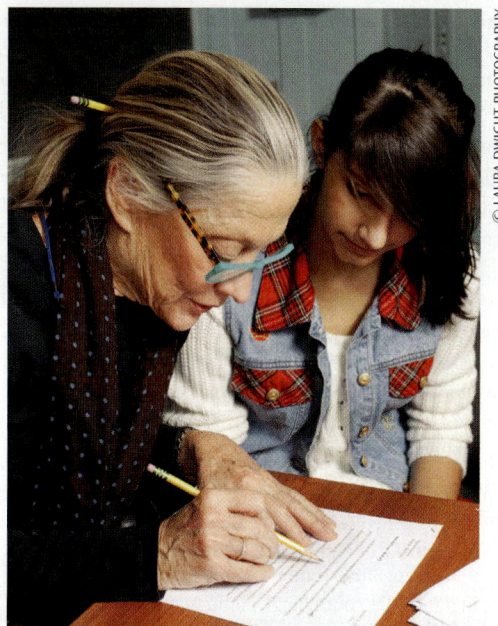

A teenager receives additional academic support from a caring retired teacher—a successful strategy for preventing struggling students from dropping out of school.

Ask yourself

CONNECT How are educational practices that prevent school dropout similar to those that improve learning for adolescents in general?

APPLY Tanisha is finishing sixth grade. She can either continue in her current school through eighth grade or switch to a much larger seventh- to ninth-grade middle school. Which choice would you suggest, and why?

REFLECT Describe your own experiences in making the transition to middle school and then to high school. What did you find stressful? What helped you adjust?

Summary / chapter 11

PHYSICAL DEVELOPMENT

Conceptions of Adolescence (p. 368)

11.1 How have conceptions of adolescence changed over the past century?

- **Adolescence** is the transition between childhood and adulthood. Early theorists viewed adolescence as either a biologically determined period of storm and stress or entirely influenced by the social environment. Contemporary researchers view adolescence as a joint product of biological, psychological, and social forces.

- In industrialized societies, adolescence is greatly extended.

Puberty: The Physical Transition to Adulthood (p. 368)

11.2 Describe body growth, motor performance, and sexual maturation during puberty.

- Hormonal changes in middle childhood initiate **puberty**, on average, two years earlier for girls than for boys. As the body enlarges during the **growth spurt**, girls' hips and boys' shoulders broaden. Girls add more fat, boys more muscle.

- Puberty brings slow, gradual improvements in gross-motor performance for girls, dramatic gains for boys.

- At puberty, changes in **primary** and **secondary sexual characteristics** accompany rapid body growth. **Menarche** occurs late in the girl's sequence of pubertal events, after the growth spurt peaks. In boys, the peak in growth occurs later, preceded by enlargement of the sex organs and **spermarche**.

11.3 What factors influence the timing of puberty?

- Heredity, nutrition, exercise, and overall physical health influence the timing of puberty. The emotional quality of family experiences may play a role.

- A **secular trend** toward earlier puberty has occurred in industrialized nations as physical well-being increased. In some countries, rising obesity rates have extended this trend.

11.4 What changes in the brain take place during adolescence?

- Synaptic pruning in the cerebral cortex continues, and growth and myelination of stimulated neural fibers accelerates, strengthening connections within the brain, particularly those involving the prefrontal cortex. Consequently, adolescents gain in diverse cognitive skills, but gains are gradual, and self-regulation is not yet fully mature.

- Neurons become more responsive to excitatory neurotransmitters, heightening emotional reactivity and reward seeking. Changes in the brain's emotional/social network outpace development of the prefrontal cognitive-control network, resulting in difficulties controlling emotions and impulses.

- Revisions occur in brain regulation of sleep timing, leading to a sleep "phase delay." Sleep deprivation contributes to poorer achievement, anxiety, irritability, depressed mood, and high-risk behaviors.

The Psychological Impact of Pubertal Events (p. 374)

11.5 Explain adolescents' reactions to the physical changes of puberty.

- Girls typically react to menarche with mixed emotions, although those who receive advance information and support from family members respond more positively. Boys, who receive little social support for pubertal changes, react to spermarche with mixed feelings.

- Besides higher hormone levels, negative life events and adult-structured situations are associated with adolescents' negative moods. Psychological distancing between parent and child at puberty may be a modern substitute for physical departure from the family.

11.6 Describe the impact of pubertal timing on adolescent adjustment, noting sex differences.

- Early-maturing boys and late-maturing girls have a more positive **body image** and usually adjust well. In contrast, early-maturing girls and late-maturing boys tend to experience emotional and social difficulties, which—for girls—persist into early adulthood.

Health Issues (p. 378)

11.7 Describe nutritional needs during adolescence, and cite factors related to eating disorders.

- Nutritional requirements increase with rapid body growth, and vitamin and mineral deficiencies may result from poor eating habits. Frequency of family meals is associated with healthy eating.

- Early puberty, certain personality traits, maladaptive family interactions, and societal emphasis on thinness heighten risk of eating disorders such as **anorexia nervosa**, **bulimia nervosa**, and **binge-eating disorder.** Heredity also plays a role.

11.8 Discuss social and cultural influences on adolescent sexual attitudes and behavior.

- North American attitudes toward adolescent sex are relatively restrictive. Parents and the mass media deliver contradictory messages.

- Early, frequent sexual activity is linked to factors associated with economic disadvantage. Adolescent cognitive processes and weak social supports for responsible sexual behavior underlie the failure of many sexually active teenagers to practice contraception consistently.

11.9 Cite factors involved in development of sexual orientation.

- Biological factors, including heredity and prenatal hormone levels, play an important role in sexual orientation. Lesbian, gay, and bisexual teenagers face special challenges in establishing a positive sexual identity.

11.10 Discuss factors related to sexually transmitted infections and teenage pregnancy and parenthood, noting prevention and intervention strategies.

- Early sexual activity, combined with inconsistent contraceptive use, results in high rates of sexually transmitted infections (STIs) among U.S. adolescents.

- Life conditions linked to poverty and personal attributes jointly contribute to adolescent childbearing. Teenage parenthood is associated with school dropout, reduced chances of marriage, greater likelihood of divorce, and long-term economic disadvantage.

- Effective sex education, access to contraceptives, and programs that build academic and social competence help prevent early pregnancy. Adolescent mothers need school programs that provide job training, instruction in life-management skills, and child care. When teenage fathers stay involved, children develop more favorably.

11.11 What personal and social factors are related to adolescent substance use and abuse?

- Teenage alcohol and drug use is pervasive in industrialized nations. Drug taking reflects adolescent sensation seeking and drug-dependent cultural contexts. The minority who move to substance abuse tend to start using drugs early and to have serious personal, family, school, and peer problems.

- Effective prevention programs work with parents early to reduce family adversity, strengthen parenting skills, and build teenagers' competence.

COGNITIVE DEVELOPMENT

Piaget's Theory: The Formal Operational Stage (p. 388)

11.12 What are the major characteristics of formal operational thought?

- In Piaget's **formal operational stage,** adolescents become capable of **hypothetico-deductive reasoning.** To solve problems, they form a hypothesis; deduce logical, testable inferences; and systematically isolate and combine variables to see which inferences are confirmed.

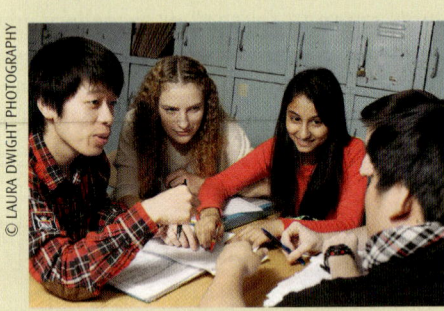

- Adolescents also develop **propositional thought**—the ability to evaluate the logic of verbal statements without referring to real-world circumstances.

11.13 Discuss follow-up research on formal operational thought and its implications for the accuracy of Piaget's formal operational stage.

- Individuals are most likely to think abstractly and systematically in situations in which they have had extensive guidance and practice. Learning activities in school provide adolescents with rich opportunities to acquire formal operations. Gains occur gradually rather than as a sudden stage shift.

An Information-Processing View of Adolescent Cognitive Development (p. 390)

11.14 How do information-processing researchers account for cognitive changes in adolescence?

- Information-processing researchers believe that a variety of specific mechanisms underlie cognitive gains in adolescence: increased working memory, improved inhibition, more selective and flexible attention, improved planning, more effective strategies, increased knowledge, expanded metacognition, and improved cognitive self-regulation.

- Scientific reasoning—the ability to coordinate theory with evidence–improves as adolescents solve increasingly complex problems and acquire more sophisticated metacognitive understanding.

Consequences of Adolescent Cognitive Changes (p. 392)

11.15 Describe typical reactions of adolescents that result from their advancing cognition.

- As adolescents reflect on their own thoughts, two distorted images of the relation between self and other appear—the **imaginary audience** and the **personal fable**. Both result from heightened social sensitivity and gains in perspective taking.

- Adolescents' capacity to think about possibilities prompts idealistic visions at odds with reality, and teenagers often become fault-finding critics.

- Adolescents are less effective at decision making than adults. They take greater risks in emotionally charged situations, less often weigh alternatives, and more often fall back on intuitive judgments.

Sex Differences in Mental Abilities (p. 394)

11.16 What factors contribute to sex differences in mental abilities at adolescence?

- Girls' advantage in reading and writing achievement increases, probably due to more efficient language processing and greater verbal stimulation. Gender stereotyping of language arts as "feminine" and regimented teaching may weaken boys' literacy skills.

- By early adolescence, when concepts become more abstract and spatial, boys surpass girls in mathematical performance. Overall, the gender difference is small, but it is larger among the most capable. Boys' superior spatial reasoning enhances their mathematical problem solving. Americans' gender stereotyping of math as "masculine" contributes to boys' greater self-confidence and interest in pursuing STEM careers.

Learning in School (p. 396)

11.17 Discuss the impact of school transitions on adolescent adjustment.

- School transitions bring larger, more impersonal school environments, in which grades and feelings of competence decline. Teenagers coping with added stressors are at greatest risk for self-esteem and academic problems.

11.18 Discuss family, peer, school, and employment influences on academic achievement during adolescence.

- Authoritative parenting and parents' school involvement promote high achievement. Teenagers whose parents value achievement generally choose friends who share those values. Schools can help by promoting a peer culture that values school engagement.

- Warm, supportive classroom environments that encourage student interaction and high-level thinking enable adolescents to reach their academic potential.

- By high school, separate educational tracks that dovetail with students' future plans are necessary. However, U.S. high school tracking usually extends the educational inequalities of earlier years.

- Steady, moderate hours of part-time employment predict higher grades and greater likelihood of attending and completing college. But a heavy commitment to low-level jobs with little adult supervision can impair school attendance, academic performance, and extracurricular participation.

11.19 What factors increase the risk of high school dropout?

- Factors related to dropping out include lack of parental support for achievement, a history of poor school performance, classes with unsupportive teachers, and frequent peer victimization.

Important Terms and Concepts

adolescence (p. 367)
anorexia nervosa (p. 378)
binge-eating disorder (p. 379)
body image (p. 377)
bulimia nervosa (p. 379)
formal operational stage (p. 388)
growth spurt (p. 369)
hypothetico-deductive reasoning (p. 388)
imaginary audience (p. 392)
menarche (p. 371)
personal fable (p. 392)
primary sexual characteristics (p. 371)
propositional thought (p. 389)
puberty (p. 367)
secondary sexual characteristics (p. 371)
secular trend (p. 373)
spermarche (p. 372)

chapter 12

Emotional and Social Development in Adolescence

As adolescents spend less time with family members, peer groups become more tightly knit into cliques. Mixed-sex cliques prepare teenagers for dating by providing models of how to interact and opportunities to do so without having to be intimate.

What's ahead in chapter 12

Erikson's Theory: Identity versus Role Confusion

Self-Understanding
Changes in Self-Concept • Changes in Self-Esteem • Paths to Identity • Identity Status and Psychological Well-Being • Influences on Identity Development

■ **CULTURAL INFLUENCES** Identity Development Among Ethnic Minority Adolescents

Moral Development
Kohlberg's Theory of Moral Development • Are There Sex Differences in Moral Reasoning? • Coordinating Moral, Social-Conventional, and Personal Concerns • Influences on Moral Reasoning • Moral Reasoning and Behavior • Religious Involvement and Moral Development • Further Challenges to Kohlberg's Theory

■ **SOCIAL ISSUES: EDUCATION** Development of Civic Engagement

The Family
Parent–Adolescent Relationships • Family Circumstances • Siblings

Peer Relations
Friendships • Cliques and Crowds • Dating

Problems of Development
Depression • Suicide • Delinquency

■ **BIOLOGY AND ENVIRONMENT** Two Routes to Adolescent Delinquency

Louis sat on the grassy hillside overlooking the high school, waiting for his best friend, Darryl, to arrive. The two boys often had lunch together. Watching as hundreds of students poured onto the school grounds, Louis reflected on what he had learned in government class that day: "Suppose I *had* been born in the People's Republic of China. I'd be sitting here, speaking a different language, being called by a different name, and thinking about the world in different ways. Wow," Louis pondered. "I am who I am through some quirk of fate."

Louis awoke from his thoughts with a start to see Darryl standing in front of him. "Hey, dreamer! I've been shouting and waving from the bottom of the hill for five minutes. How come you're so spaced out lately, Louis?"

"Oh, just wondering about stuff—what I want, what I believe in. My older brother Jules—I envy him. He seems to know more about where he's going. I'm up in the air about it. You ever feel that way?"

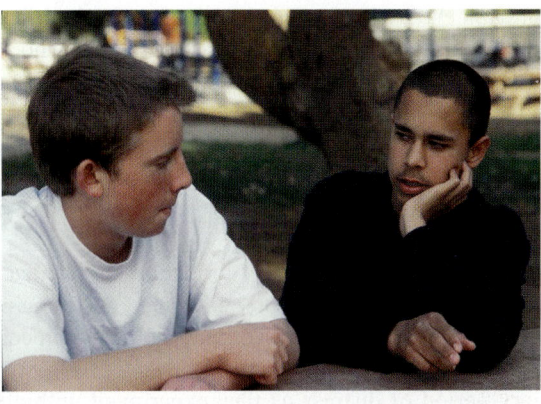

"Yeah, a lot," Darryl admitted, looking at Louis seriously. "I wonder, what am I really like? Who will I become?"

Louis and Darryl's introspective remarks are signs of a major reorganization of the self at adolescence: the development of identity. Both young people are attempting to formulate who they are—their personal values and the directions they will pursue in life. The restructuring of the self that begins in adolescence is profound. Rapid physical changes prompt teenagers to reconsider what they are like as people. And the capacity to think hypothetically enables them to project themselves into the distant future. They start to realize the significance of their choice of values, beliefs, and goals for their later lives.

We begin this chapter with Erikson's account of identity development and the research it has stimulated on teenagers' thoughts and feelings about themselves. The quest for identity extends to many aspects of development. We will see how a sense of cultural belonging and moral understanding are refined during adolescence. And as parent–child relationships are revised and young people become increasingly independent of the family, friendships and peer networks become crucial contexts for bridging the gap between childhood and adulthood. Our chapter concludes with a discussion of several serious adjustment problems of adolescence: depression, suicide, and delinquency. ●

Erikson's Theory: Identity versus Role Confusion

How does social media use impact an adolescent's sense of identity?

12.1 According to Erikson, what is the major personality attainment of adolescence?

Erikson (1950, 1968) was the first to recognize **identity** as the major personality attainment of adolescence and as a crucial step toward becoming a productive, content adult. Constructing an identity involves defining who you are, what you value, and the directions you choose to pursue in life. One expert described it as an explicit theory of oneself as a rational agent—one who acts on the basis of reason, takes responsibility for those actions, and can explain them (Moshman, 2011). This search for what is true and real about the self drives many choices—vocation, interpersonal relationships, community involvement, ethnic-group membership, and expression of one's sexual orientation, as well as moral, political, and religious ideals.

Although the seeds of identity formation are planted early, not until late adolescence and early adulthood do young people become absorbed in this task. According to Erikson, in complex societies, young people often experience an *identity crisis*—a temporary period of distress as they experiment with alternatives before settling on values and goals. They go through a process of inner soul-searching, sifting through characteristics that defined the self in childhood and combining them with emerging traits, capacities, and commitments. Then they mold these into a solid inner core that provides a mature identity—a sense of self-continuity as they move through various roles in daily life. Once formed, identity continues to be refined in adulthood as people reevaluate earlier commitments and choices.

Erikson called the psychological conflict of adolescence **identity versus role confusion.** He believed that successful psychosocial outcomes of infancy and childhood pave the way toward a positive resolution. If young people's earlier conflicts were resolved negatively or if society limits their choices to ones that do not match their abilities and desires, they are likely to appear shallow, directionless, and unprepared for the challenges of adulthood.

Current theorists agree with Erikson that questioning of values, plans, and priorities is necessary for a mature identity, but they no longer describe this process as a "crisis." In fact, Erikson himself did not believe that the adolescent's inner struggle need be severe to form a clear, unified identity (Kroger, 2012). For most young people, identity development is not traumatic and disturbing but, rather, a process of *exploration* followed by *commitment*. As young people try out life possibilities, they gather important information about themselves and their environment and move toward making enduring decisions (Moshman, 2011). In the following sections, we will see that adolescents go about the task of defining the self in ways that closely match Erikson's description.

Self-Understanding

12.2 Describe changes in self-concept and self-esteem during adolescence.

12.3 Describe the four identity statuses, along with factors that promote identity development.

During adolescence, the young person's vision of the self becomes more complex, well-organized, and consistent. Compared with children, adolescents engage in evaluations of an increasing variety of aspects of the self. Over time, they construct a balanced, integrated representation of their strengths and limitations (Harter, 2012). Changes in self-concept and self-esteem set the stage for developing a unified personal identity.

Changes in Self-Concept

Recall that by the end of middle childhood, children describe themselves in terms of personality traits. In early adolescence, they unify separate traits ("smart" and "curious") into more abstract descriptors ("intelligent"). But these generalizations are not interconnected and are often contradictory. For example, 12- to 14-year-olds might mention opposing traits—"intelligent" and "clueless," "extrovert" and "introvert." These disparities result from the expansion of adolescents' social world, which creates pressure to display different selves in different relationships. As adolescents' awareness of these inconsistencies grows, they frequently agonize over "which is the real me" (Harter, 2012).

By late adolescence, cognitive changes enable teenagers to combine their traits into an organized system. Their use of qualifiers ("I have a *fairly* quick temper," "I'm not *thoroughly* honest") reveals an increasing awareness that psychological qualities can vary from one situation to the next. Older adolescents also add integrating principles that make sense of formerly troublesome contradictions. "I'm very adaptable," said one young person. "When I'm around my friends, who think what I say is important, I'm talkative; but around my family I'm quiet because they're never interested enough to really listen to me" (Damon, 1990, p. 88).

Compared with school-age children, teenagers place more emphasis on social virtues, such as being friendly, considerate, kind, and cooperative—traits that reflect adolescents' increasing concern with being viewed positively by others. Among older adolescents, personal and moral values also appear as key themes. As young people revise their views of themselves to include enduring beliefs and plans, they move toward the unity of self that is central to identity development.

Changes in Self-Esteem

Self-esteem, the evaluative side of self-concept, continues to differentiate in adolescence. Teenagers add several new dimensions of self-evaluation—close friendship, romantic appeal, and job competence—to those of middle childhood (see Chapter 10, pages 337–338) (Harter, 2012).

Level of general self-esteem also changes. Though some adolescents experience temporary or persisting declines after school transitions (see Chapter 11, page 397), self-esteem rises from mid- to late adolescence for most young people, who report feeling especially good about their peer relationships, physical appearance, and athletic capabilities (Birkeland et al., 2012; Cole et al., 2001; Impett et al., 2008). Teenagers often assert that they have become more mature, capable, personable, and attractive. In longitudinal research on a nationally representative sample of U.S. youths, an increasing sense of mastery—feeling competent and in control of one's life—strongly predicted this rise in self-esteem (Erol & Orth, 2011). With greater independence and opportunities to emphasize pursuits in which they experience success, older adolescents are better able to discount the importance of doing well in areas in which they feel inadequate.

Teenagers with mostly favorable self-esteem profiles tend to be well-adjusted, whereas low self-esteem in all areas is linked to adjustment difficulties. But certain self-esteem factors are more strongly related to well-being. Adolescents with poor academic self-esteem tend to be anxious and unfocused, and those with negative peer relationships are likely to be anxious and depressed (Marsh, Parada, & Ayotte, 2004; Rudolph, Caldwell, & Conley, 2005).

What factors influence self-esteem? In Chapter 11, we saw that adolescents who are off time in pubertal development, who are heavy drug users, and who fail in school feel poorly about themselves. And as in middle childhood, adolescent girls score lower than boys in overall sense of self-worth, though the difference remains slight (Bachman et al., 2011; Shapka & Keating, 2005). Recall that girls feel less positively about their physical appearance and athletic skills and less competent at math and science (see Chapter 10). At the same time girls continue to outscore boys on self-esteem dimensions of language arts, close friendship, and social acceptance.

But the contexts in which young people find themselves can modify these group differences. Authoritative parenting continues to predict stable, favorable self-esteem, as does encouragement from teachers (Lindsey et al., 2008; McKinney, Donnelly, & Renk, 2008; Wilkinson, 2004). In contrast, teenagers whose parents are critical and insulting have highly unstable and generally low self-esteem (Kernis, 2002). Peer acceptance can have a protective effect on general self-esteem for teenagers experiencing low parental warmth and approval (Birkeland, Breivik, & Wold, 2014). But adolescents exposed to highly negative parental feedback tend to rely excessively on peers to affirm their self-worth—a risk factor for adjustment difficulties (DuBois et al., 1999, 2002).

The larger social environment also influences self-esteem. Sustaining a middle-childhood trend, European-American adolescents' self-esteem is less positive than that of African-African teenagers, who may benefit from greater extended family support and ethnic pride (Gray-Little & Hafdahl, 2000). And Asians score lower in self-esteem relative to European Americans as adolescence progresses—a decline reflecting cultural valuing of modesty and disapproval of boastfulness rather than sense of personal competence (Bachman et al., 2011). Finally, teenagers who attend schools or live in neighborhoods where their ethnic group is well-represented have fewer self-esteem problems (Gray-Little and Carels, 1997).

Paths to Identity

Adolescents' well-organized self-descriptions and differentiated sense of self-esteem provide the cognitive foundation for forming an identity. Using a clinical interviewing procedure devised by James Marcia (1980) or briefer questionnaire measures, researchers commonly evaluate progress in identity development on two key criteria derived from Erikson's theory: *exploration* and *commitment*. Their various combinations yield four *identity statuses*, summarized in Table 12.1: **identity achievement,** commitment to values and goals following a period of exploration; **identity moratorium,** exploration without having reached commitment; **identity foreclosure,** commitment in the absence of exploration; and **identity diffusion,** characterized by lack of both exploration and commitment.

Identity development follows many paths. Some young people remain in one status, whereas others experience multiple status transitions. And the pattern often varies across *identity domains,* such as sexual orientation, vocation, and religious and political values. When assessed periodically between the mid-teens and mid-twenties, many young people change from "lower"

From mid- to late adolescence, self-esteem typically rises, fostered by pride in new competencies and growing self-confidence. This teenager beams as she displays the blue ribbon she won at an agricultural fair.

TABLE 12.1
The Four Identity Statuses

IDENTITY STATUS	DESCRIPTION	EXAMPLE
Identity achievement	Having explored alternatives, identity-achieved individuals are committed to clearly formulated self-chosen values and goals. They feel a sense of psychological well-being, of sameness through time, and of knowing where they are going.	When asked about her willingness to give up pursuing her chosen occupation if something better came along, Lauren responded, "Well, I might, but I doubt it. I've thought long and hard about law as a career. I'm pretty certain it's for me."
Identity moratorium	*Moratorium* means "delay or holding pattern." These individuals have not yet made definite commitments. They are in the process of exploring—gathering information and trying out activities, with the desire to find values and goals to guide their lives.	When asked whether he had ever had doubts about his religious beliefs, Ramón said, "Yes, I guess I'm going through that right now. I just don't see how there can be a God and yet so much evil in the world."
Identity foreclosure	Identity-foreclosed individuals have committed themselves to values and goals without exploring alternatives. They accept a ready-made identity chosen for them by authority figures—usually parents but sometimes teachers, religious leaders, or romantic partners.	When asked if she had ever reconsidered her political beliefs, Emily answered, "No, not really, our family is pretty much in agreement on these things."
Identity diffusion	Identity-diffused individuals lack clear direction. They are not committed to values and goals, nor are they actively trying to reach them. They may never have explored alternatives or may have found the task too threatening and overwhelming.	When asked about his attitude toward nontraditional gender roles, Justin responded, "Oh, I don't know. It doesn't make much difference to me. I can take it or leave it."

statuses (foreclosure or diffusion) to higher ones (moratorium or achievement), but nearly as many remain stable, and some move in the reverse direction (Kroger, 2012; Kroger, Martinussen, & Marcia, 2010; Meeus et al., 2010).

The process of identity formation typically involves exploring a range of alternatives, making provisional commitments, engaging in in-depth evaluation of one's choices, and—if those choices fit poorly with one's capacities and potentials—refocusing on possible alternative commitments (Crocetti & Meeus, 2015; Luyckx et al., 2011). Consequently, young people often cycle between in-depth exploration and reconsideration—which can involve intense uncertainty and, thus, temporary diffusion—before eventually arriving at enduring commitments.

Because attending college offers expanded opportunities to explore values, career options, and lifestyles, college students usually make more identity progress than they did in high school (Klimstra et al., 2010; Montgomery & Côté, 2003). After college, many young people continue to sample a broad range of life experiences before making clear commitments. Those who go to work immediately after high school graduation generally settle on a self-definition earlier. But if non-college-bound youths encounter obstacles to realizing their occupational goals because of lack of training or vocational choices, they are at risk for identity foreclosure or diffusion (Eccles et al., 2003).

With respect to gender, some girls show more sophisticated reasoning than boys in identity domains related to intimacy, such as sexuality and family versus career priorities. Otherwise, consistent with Erikson's psychosocial stages (see page 15 in Chapter 1), adolescents of both sexes typically make progress on identity concerns before experiencing genuine intimacy in romantic relationships (Arseth et al., 2009; Beyers & Seiffge-Krenke, 2010).

Identity Status and Psychological Well-Being

A wealth of research verifies that both identity achievement and moratorium are psychologically healthy routes to a mature self-definition. Long-term foreclosure and diffusion, in contrast, are maladaptive.

Although young people in moratorium are at times anxious and depressed about finding commitments, they resemble identity-achieved individuals in using an active, *information-gathering cognitive style* to make personal decisions and solve problems: They seek out relevant information, evaluate it carefully, and critically reflect on their views (Berzonsky, 2011). Individuals who are identity-achieved or exploring tend to have higher self-esteem, are more open to alternative ideas and values, feel more in control of their lives, are more likely to view school and work as feasible avenues for realizing their aspirations, and are more advanced in moral reasoning and more concerned with social justice (Berzonsky et al., 2011; Crocetti et al., 2013). But an exception to these favorable outcomes exists: If exploration becomes ruminative—excessively concerned with making the right choice so the young person makes no choice at all—it is associated with distress and poor adjustment (Beyers & Luyckx, 2016).

Because foreclosure involves commitment, it offers a sense of security in the face of important life choices (Meeus et al., 2012). Although typically low in anxiety and highly satisfied with life, foreclosed individuals display a *dogmatic, inflexible cognitive style,* internalizing the values and beliefs of parents and others without deliberate evaluation and resisting information that threatens their position (Berzonsky, 2011; Berzonsky et al., 2011). Most fear rejection by people on whom they depend for affection and self-esteem. A few foreclosed teenagers who are alienated from their families and society may join cults or other extremist groups, uncritically adopting a way of life different from their past.

Long-term diffused individuals are the least mature in identity development. They typically use a *diffuse-avoidant cognitive style* in which they avoid dealing with personal decisions and problems and, instead, allow current situational pressures to dictate their reactions (Berzonsky, 2011; Crocetti et al., 2013). Taking an "I don't care" attitude, they entrust themselves to luck or fate and tend to go along with the crowd. As a result, they often experience time management and academic difficulties, are low in self-esteem and prone to depression, and, of all young people, are the most likely to commit antisocial acts and to use and abuse drugs (Meeus et al., 2012). Often at the heart of their apathy is a sense of hopelessness about the future.

Influences on Identity Development

Adolescent identity formation begins a lifelong, dynamic process in which a change in either the individual or the context opens up the possibility of reformulating identity. A wide variety of factors influence identity development.

Identity status, as we have just seen, is both cause and consequence of personality characteristics. Adolescents who assume that absolute truth is always attainable tend to be foreclosed, while those who doubt that they will ever feel certain about anything are more often identity-diffused. Young people who are curious, open-minded, and persistent in the face of obstacles, and who appreciate that they can use rational criteria to choose among alternatives, are likely to be in a state of moratorium or identity achievement (Berzonsky et al., 2011; Schwartz et al., 2013).

Identity development is enhanced when families serve as a "secure base" from which adolescents can confidently move out into the wider world. Young people who feel attached to their parents but also free to voice their own opinions tend to have committed to values and goals and are on their way to identity achievement (Crocetti et al., 2014; Luyckx, Goossens, & Soenens, 2006). Foreclosed teenagers often have close bonds with parents but lack opportunities for healthy separation. And diffused young people report the lowest levels of parental support and of warm, open communication (Arseth et al., 2009).

Interaction with diverse peers through school and community activities encourages adolescents to explore values and role possibilities (Barber et al., 2005). And close friends, like parents, can act as a secure base, providing emotional support, assistance, and models of identity development. In one study, 15-year-olds with warm, trusting peer ties were more involved in exploring relationship issues (Meeus, Oosterwegel, & Vollebergh, 2002). They thought seriously about what they valued in close friends and in a life partner.

Identity development also depends on schools and communities that offer rich and varied opportunities for exploration. Supportive experiences include classrooms that promote high-level thinking, teachers and counselors who encourage low-SES and ethnic minority students to go to college, elective classes and extracurricular and community activities that enable teenagers to pursue their interests and talents, and vocational training that immerses adolescents in the real world of adult work (Hardy et al., 2011; McIntosh, Metz, & Youniss, 2005; Sharp et al., 2007).

Culture strongly influences an aspect of mature identity not captured by the identity-status approach: constructing a sense of self-continuity despite significant personal changes. In one study, researchers asked Native Canadian and cultural-majority 12- to 20-year-olds to describe themselves in the past and in the present and then to justify why they regarded themselves as the same continuous person (Lalonde & Chandler, 2005). Most cultural-majority adolescents used an individualistic approach: They described an *enduring personal essence,* a core self that remained the same despite change. In contrast, Native Canadian youths took an interdependent approach that emphasized a *constantly transforming self,* resulting from new roles and relationships. They typically constructed a *coherent narrative* in which they linked together various time slices of their life with a thread that explained how they had changed in meaningful ways.

Finally, societal forces also are responsible for the special challenges faced by lesbian, gay, and bisexual youths (see Chapter 11) and by ethnic minority adolescents in forming a secure identity (see the Cultural Influences box on page 412). Applying What We Know on page 413 summarizes ways that adults can support adolescents in their quest for identity.

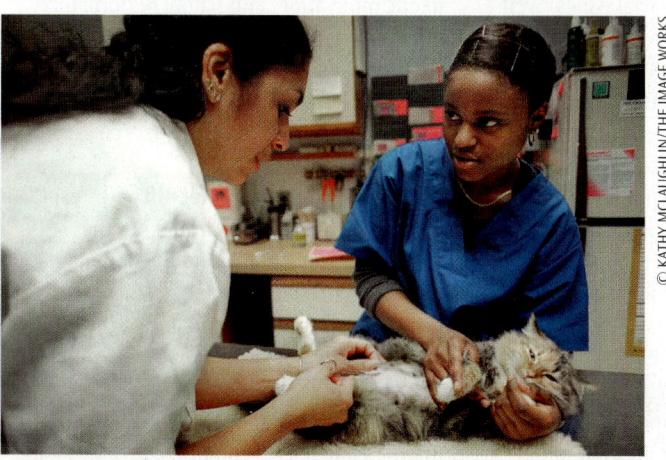

An internship in a veterinary office enables this teenager to explore a real-world career related to her love of animals, thereby fostering identity development.

Ask yourself

CONNECT Explain the close link between adolescent identity development and cognitive processes.

APPLY Return to the conversation between Louis and Darryl in the opening of this chapter. Which identity status best characterizes each of the two boys, and why?

REFLECT Does your identity progress vary across the domains of sexuality, close relationships, vocation, religious beliefs, and political values? Describe factors that may have influenced your identity development in an important domain.

Cultural Influences

Identity Development Among Ethnic Minority Adolescents

For teenagers who are members of minority groups, **ethnic identity**—a sense of ethnic-group membership and the attitudes, beliefs, and feelings associated with that membership—is central to the quest for identity. As minority youths develop cognitively and become more sensitive to feedback from the social environment, they become painfully aware of how their ethnicity and race compromise their life chances. This discovery complicates their efforts to develop a sense of cultural belonging and a set of personally meaningful goals.

In many immigrant families from cultures that value interdependent qualities, adolescents' commitment to obeying their parents and fulfilling family obligations lessens the longer the family has been in the immigrant-receiving country. This circumstance induces **acculturative stress**—psychological distress resulting from conflict between the minority and the host culture (Phinney, Ong, & Madden, 2000). When immigrant parents tightly restrict their teenagers through fear that assimilation into the larger society will undermine their cultural traditions, their youngsters often rebel, rejecting aspects of their ethnic background.

At the same time, discrimination can interfere with the formation of a positive ethnic identity. In one study, Mexican-American youths who had experienced more discrimination were less likely to explore their ethnicity (Romero & Roberts, 2003). Those with low ethnic pride showed a sharp drop in self-esteem in the face of discrimination.

With age, many minority young people strengthen their ethnic identity. But because the process of forging an ethnic identity can be painful and confusing, others show no change, and still others regress (Huang & Stormshak, 2011). Young people with parents of different ethnicities face extra challenges. In a large survey of high school students, part-black biracial teenagers reported as much discrimination as their monoracial black counterparts, yet they felt less positively about their ethnicity. And compared with monoracial minorities, many biracial adolescents—including black–white, black–Asian, white–Asian, black–Hispanic, and white–Hispanic—regarded their ethnicity as less central to their identities (Herman, 2004). Perhaps these adolescents encountered fewer opportunities in their homes and communities to forge a strong sense of belonging to either culture.

Adolescents whose family members encourage them to disprove ethnic stereotypes of low achievement or antisocial behavior typically surmount the threat that discrimination poses to a favorable ethnic identity. These young people manage experiences of unfair treatment effectively, by seeking social support and engaging in direct problem solving (Scott, 2003). Also, minority adolescents whose families have taught them the history, traditions, values, and language of their ethnic group are more likely to explore and progress toward ethnic identity achievement (Douglass & Umaña-Taylor, 2015; Else-Quest & Morse, 2015).

Interacting with same-ethnicity peers is also vital. Ethnic identity progress tends to be similar among same-ethnicity friends, and it can be predicted by the frequency with which they talk about ethnic and racial issues (Syed & Juan, 2012). In a study of Asian-American adolescents, contact with other Asians strengthened positive feelings about their own ethnic group in a mostly white or a racially mixed school but not in a mostly Asian school (Yip, Douglass, & Shelton, 2013). Ethnic identity concerns become especially salient in racially diverse settings.

How can society help minority adolescents resolve identity conflicts constructively? Here are some relevant approaches:

- Promote effective parenting, in which children and adolescents benefit from family ethnic pride yet are encouraged to explore the meaning of ethnicity in their own lives.

Adolescents of the Iroquois Tuscarora tribe perform a traditional dance at the New York State Fair. Minority youths whose cultural heritage is respected in their communities are more likely to develop a strong, secure ethnic identity.

- Ensure that schools respect minority youths' native languages and right to high-quality education.
- Foster contact with peers of the same ethnicity, along with respect between ethnic groups.

A strong, secure ethnic identity is associated with higher self-esteem, optimism, academic motivation, and school performance, and with more positive peer relations and prosocial behavior (Ghavami et al., 2011; Rivas-Drake et al., 2014). For teenagers faced with adversity, ethnic identity is a powerful source of resilience.

Forming a **bicultural identity**—by exploring and adopting values from both the adolescent's subculture and the dominant culture—offers added benefits. Biculturally identified adolescents tend to be achieved in other identity domains, to have a more secure ethnic identity, and to have especially positive relations with members of other ethnic groups (Basilio et al., 2014; Phinney, 2007). In sum, achievement of ethnic identity enhances many aspects of emotional and social development.

Applying what we Know

Supporting Healthy Identity Development

STRATEGY	EXPLANATION
Engage in warm, open communication.	Provides both emotional support and freedom to explore values and goals.
Initiate discussions that promote high-level thinking at home and at school.	Encourages rational and deliberate selection among beliefs and values.
Provide opportunities to participate in extracurricular activities and vocational training programs.	Permits young people to explore the real world of adult work.
Provide opportunities to talk with adults and peers who have worked through similar identity questions.	Offers models of identity achievement and advice on how to resolve identity concerns.
Refrain from gender stereotyping and exerting pressure to conform to gender roles, instead emphasizing exploration of options based on values, interests, and talents.	Frees young people to form a gender identity based on inner traits rather than societal expectations, thereby fostering gender contentedness and psychological well-being (see page 351 in Chapter 10).
Create safe, affirming school and community environments for sexual minority youths.	Promotes integration of sexual orientation into a broader sense of personal identity (see page 382 in Chapter 11).
Provide opportunities to explore ethnic heritage and learn about other cultures in an atmosphere of respect.	Fosters identity achievement in all areas as well as valuing of ethnic diversity, which supports the identity explorations of others.

Moral Development

12.4 Describe Kohlberg's theory of moral development, and evaluate its accuracy.

12.5 Describe influences on moral reasoning and its relation to moral behavior.

Eleven-year-old Sabrina sat at the kitchen table reading the Sunday newspaper, her eyes wide with interest. "Look at this!" she said to 16-year-old Louis, who was munching cereal. Sabrina held up a page of large photos showing a 70-year-old woman standing in her home. The floor and furniture were piled with stacks of newspapers, cardboard boxes, tin cans, glass containers, food, and clothing. The accompanying article described crumbling plaster on the walls, frozen pipes, and nonfunctioning sinks, toilet, and furnace. The headline read: "Loretta Perry: My Life Is None of Their Business."

"Look what they're trying to do to this poor lady," exclaimed Sabrina. "They're throwing her out of her house and tearing it down! Those city inspectors must not care about anyone. Here it says, 'Mrs. Perry has devoted much of her life to doing favors for people.' Why doesn't someone help *her?*"

"Sabrina, you're missing the point," Louis responded. "She's violating 30 building code standards. The law says you're supposed to keep your house clean and in good repair."

"But Louis, she's old, and she needs help. She says her life will be over if they destroy her home."

"The building inspectors aren't being mean, Sabrina. She's refusing to obey the law. And she's not just a threat to herself—she's a danger to her neighbors, too. Suppose her house caught on fire. You can't live around other people and say your life is nobody's business."

"You don't just knock someone's home down," Sabrina replied with exasperation. "Why aren't her friends and neighbors over there fixing up that house? You're just like those building inspectors, Louis. You've got no feelings!"

As Louis and Sabrina's discussion illustrates, cognitive development and expanding social experiences permit adolescents to better understand larger social structures—societal institutions and law-making systems—that govern moral responsibilities. As their grasp of social arrangements expands, adolescents construct new ideas about what should be done when the needs and desires of people conflict. As a result, they move toward increasingly just, fair, and balanced solutions to moral problems.

Kohlberg's Theory of Moral Development

Early work by Piaget on the moral judgment of the child inspired Lawrence Kohlberg's more comprehensive cognitive-developmental theory of moral understanding. Kohlberg used a clinical interviewing procedure in which he presented European-American 10- to 16-year-old boys with hypothetical *moral dilemmas*—stories involving a conflict between two moral values—and asked them what the main actor should do and why. Then he followed the participants longitudinally, reinterviewing them at 3- to 4-year intervals over the next 20 years. The best known of Kohlberg's dilemmas, the "Heinz dilemma," pits the value of obeying the law (not stealing) against the value of human life (saving a dying person):

In Europe a woman was near death from cancer. There was one drug the doctors thought might save her. A druggist in the same town had discovered it, but he was charging ten times what the drug cost him to make. The sick woman's husband, Heinz, went to everyone he knew to borrow the money, but he could only get together half of what it cost. The druggist refused to sell the drug for less or let Heinz pay later. So Heinz became desperate and broke into the man's store to steal the drug for his wife. Should Heinz have done that? Why or why not? (paraphrased from Colby et al., 1983, p. 77)

Kohlberg emphasized that it is *the way an individual reasons about the dilemma,* not *the content of the response* (whether or not to steal), that determines moral maturity. Individuals who believe Heinz should take the drug and those who think he should not can be found at each of Kohlberg's first four stages. Only at the two highest stages do moral reasoning and content come together in a coherent ethical system (Kohlberg, Levine, & Hewer, 1983). Given a choice between obeying the law and preserving individual rights, the most advanced moral thinkers support individual rights (in the Heinz dilemma, stealing the drug to save a life). Does this remind you of adolescents' efforts to formulate a sound, well-organized set of personal values in constructing an identity? According to some theorists, the development of identity and moral understanding are part of the same process (Bergman, 2004; Blasi, 1994).

Kohlberg's Stages of Moral Understanding.

Kohlberg organized moral development into three levels, each with two stages, yielding six stages in all. He believed that moral understanding is promoted by the same factors Piaget thought were important for cognitive development: (1) actively grappling with moral issues and noticing weaknesses in one's current reasoning, and (2) gains in perspective taking, which permit individuals to resolve moral conflicts in more effective ways.

The Preconventional Level. At the **preconventional level,** morality is externally controlled. Children accept the rules of authority figures and judge actions by their consequences. Behaviors that result in punishment are viewed as bad, those that lead to rewards as good.

- *Stage 1: The punishment and obedience orientation.* Children find it difficult to consider two points of view in a moral dilemma. As a result, they overlook people's intentions and focus on fear of authority and avoidance of punishment as reasons for behaving morally. To the Heinz dilemma, an individual who opposes stealing the drug might say, "If you steal, you'll either be sent to jail or have to live in fear of the police finding you."
- *Stage 2: The instrumental purpose orientation.* Children become aware that people can have different perspectives in a moral dilemma, but at first this understanding is concrete. They view right action as flowing from self-interest and understand reciprocity as equal exchange of favors: "You do this for me and I'll do that for you." They might argue that Heinz should steal the drug because "then he'll still have his wife to keep him company."

The Conventional Level. At the **conventional level,** individuals regard conformity to social rules as important, but not for reasons of self-interest. Rather, they believe that actively maintaining the current social system ensures positive relationships and societal order.

- *Stage 3: The "good boy–good girl" orientation, or the morality of interpersonal cooperation.* The desire to obey rules because they promote social harmony first appears in the context of close personal ties. Stage 3 individuals want to maintain the affection and approval of friends and relatives by being a "good person"—trustworthy, helpful, and nice. The capacity to view a relationship from the vantage point of an impartial, outside observer, which requires recursive thought (see page 312 in Chapter 9), supports this new approach to morality. Individuals now understand *ideal reciprocity:* They express the same concern for the welfare of another as they do for themselves—a standard of fairness summed up by the Golden Rule: "Do unto others as you would have them do unto you." An individual favoring Heinz stealing might explain, "Your family will think you're a decent, caring husband if you do."
- *Stage 4: The social-order-maintaining orientation.* At this stage, the individual takes into account a larger perspective—that of societal laws. Moral choices no longer depend on close ties to others. Instead, rules must be enforced in the same evenhanded fashion for everyone, and each member of society has a personal duty to uphold them. The Stage 4

If this teenager helps a preschooler climb an amusement park rope ladder because she expects a favor from someone in return, she is at Kohlberg's preconventional level. If she is guided by ideal reciprocity—"Do unto others as you would have them do unto you"—she has advanced to the conventional level.

individual believes that laws should never be disobeyed because they are vital for ensuring societal order and cooperation between people. Arguing against Heinz stealing, a person might say, "Heinz has a duty like everyone else to obey the law. If he's allowed to break the law because of a tough situation, others will think they can, too. We'll have chaos, not a law-abiding society."

The Postconventional or Principled Level. Individuals at the **postconventional level** move beyond unquestioning support for their own society's rules and laws. They define morality in terms of abstract principles and values that apply to all situations and societies.

- *Stage 5: The social contract orientation.* At Stage 5, individuals can imagine alternatives to their own social order, and they emphasize fair procedures for interpreting and changing the law. When laws are consistent with individual rights and the interests of the majority, each person follows them because of a *social contract orientation*—free and willing participation in the system because it brings about more good for people than if it did not exist. A person favoring Heinz stealing might explain, "Although there is a law against stealing, it wasn't meant to violate a person's right to life. If Heinz is prosecuted, the law needs to be reinterpreted to take into account people's natural right to keep on living."

- *Stage 6: The universal ethical principle orientation.* At this highest stage, right action is defined by self-chosen ethical principles of conscience that are valid for all people, regardless of law and social agreement. Stage 6 individuals typically mention such abstract principles as respect for the worth and dignity of each person, as in this response defending Heinz stealing the drug: "It doesn't make sense to put respect for property above respect for life. People could live together without private property at all. Respect for human life is absolute and accordingly people have a mutual duty to save one another from dying" (paraphrased from Rest, 1979, p. 37).

Research on Kohlberg's Stage Sequence. Kohlberg's original research and other longitudinal studies confirm that with few exceptions, individuals move through his first four stages in the predicted order (Boom, Wouters, & Keller, 2007; Dawson, 2002; Walker & Taylor, 1991). Moral development is slow and gradual: Reasoning at Stages 1 and 2 decreases in early adolescence, while Stage 3 increases through midadolescence and then declines. Stage 4 reasoning rises over the teenage years until, among college-educated young adults, it is the typical response.

Few people move beyond Stage 4. In fact, postconventional morality is so rare that no clear evidence exists that Kohlberg's Stage 6 actually follows Stage 5. This poses a key challenge to Kohlberg's theory: If people must reach Stages 5 and 6 to be considered truly morally mature, few individuals anywhere would measure up! According to one reexamination of Kohlberg's stages, moral maturity can be found in a revised understanding of Stages 3 and 4 (Gibbs, 2014). These stages are not "conventional"—based on social conformity—as Kohlberg assumed. Rather, they require profound moral constructions—an understanding of ideal reciprocity as the basis for relationships (Stage 3) and for widely accepted moral standards, set forth in rules and laws (Stage 4). In this view, "postconventional" morality is a highly reflective endeavor limited to a handful of people who have attained advanced education, usually in philosophy.

Think of an actual moral dilemma you faced recently. Real-life conflicts often elicit moral thinking below a person's actual capacity because they involve practical considerations. Although adolescents and adults mention reasoning as their most frequent strategy for resolving these dilemmas, they also refer to other strategies—talking through issues with others, relying on intuition, and calling on religious and spiritual ideas. And they report feeling drained, confused, and torn by temptation—an emotional side of moral judgment not tapped by hypothetical situations (Walker, 2004). Hypothetical dilemmas evoke the upper limits of moral thought because they allow reflection without the interference of personal risk.

The influence of situational factors on moral judgments indicates that like Piaget's cognitive stages, Kohlberg's moral stages are loosely organized and overlapping. Rather than developing in a neat, stepwise fashion, people draw on a range of moral responses that vary with context. With age, this range shifts upward as less mature moral reasoning is gradually replaced by more advanced moral thought.

Are There Sex Differences in Moral Reasoning?

As we have seen, real-life moral dilemmas often highlight the role of emotion in moral judgment. In the discussion at the beginning of this section, notice how Sabrina's moral argument focuses on caring and commitment to others. Carol Gilligan (1982) is the best-known of those who have argued that Kohlberg's theory does not adequately represent the morality of girls and women. Gilligan believes that feminine morality emphasizes an "ethic of care" that Kohlberg's system devalues. Sabrina's reasoning falls at Stage 3 because it is based on mutual trust and affection, whereas Louis's is at Stage 4 because he emphasizes following the law. According to Gilligan, a concern for others is a *different* but no less valid basis for moral judgment than a focus on impersonal rights.

Many studies have tested Gilligan's claim that Kohlberg's approach underestimates the moral maturity of females, and most do not support it (Walker, 2006). On hypothetical dilemmas as well as everyday moral problems, adolescent and adult females display reasoning at the same stage as their male agemates, and often at a higher stage. Themes of justice and caring appear in the responses of both sexes and when females do raise interpersonal concerns, they are not downgraded in Kohlberg's system (Walker, 1995). These findings suggest that although Kohlberg emphasized justice rather than caring as the highest moral ideal, his theory taps both sets of values.

Nevertheless, some evidence indicates that although the morality of males and females taps both orientations, females do tend to emphasize care, whereas males either stress justice or focus equally on justice and care (You, Maeda, & Bebeau, 2011). This difference in emphasis, which appears more often in real-life than in hypothetical dilemmas, may reflect women's greater involvement in daily activities involving care and concern for others.

Indeed, context profoundly affects use of a care orientation. In one study, researchers presented 18- to 38-year-old university students with one of three versions of a moral dilemma, in which the main character varied in familiarity: (1) a close friend in class, (2) a person "known only vaguely" from class, or (3) a classmate whose relationship was unspecified (Ryan, David, & Reynolds, 2004). When asked whether they would permit the character, who was in danger of failing the course, to borrow a copy of their recently completed assignment despite risk of cheating, both males and females gave more care responses when considering a close friend than a socially distant classmate. Gender differences emerged only in the unspecified condition, where females—who tend to forge closer relationships and, thus, may have assumed greater familiarity—expressed more caring.

Coordinating Moral, Social-Conventional, and Personal Concerns

Adolescents' moral advances are also evident in their reasoning about situations that raise competing moral, social-conventional, and personal issues. In diverse Western and non-Western cultures, concern with matters of personal choice strengthens during the teenage years—a reflection of adolescents' quest for identity and increasing independence (Rote & Smetana, 2015). As young people firmly insist that parents not encroach on the personal arena (dress, hairstyle, diary records, friendships), disputes over these issues increase. Teenagers whose parents frequently intrude into their personal affairs report greater psychological stress. In contrast, adolescents typically say that parents have a right to tell them what to do in moral and social-conventional situations (Helwig, Ruck, & Peterson-Badali, 2014). And when these issues spark disagreements, teenagers seldom challenge parental authority.

As they enlarge the range of issues they regard as personal, adolescents think more intently about conflicts between personal choice and community obligation—for example, whether, and under what conditions, it is permissible to restrict speech, religion, marriage, group membership, and other individual rights. When asked if it is OK to exclude a child from a peer group on the basis of race or gender, fourth graders usually say exclusion is always unfair. But by tenth grade, young people, though increasingly mindful of fairness, indicate that under certain conditions—in intimate relationships (friendship) and private contexts (at home or in a small club), and on the basis of gender more often than race—exclusion is OK (Killen et al., 2002, 2007; Rutland, Killen, & Abrams, 2010). In explaining, they mention the right to personal choice as well as concerns about effective group functioning.

As adolescents integrate personal rights with ideal reciprocity, they demand that the protections they want for themselves extend to others. For example, older high school students are more likely than their younger counterparts to believe that gay and lesbian youths have the right to be free of discrimination in school, and they justify with moral reasoning: "We should treat others as we wish to be treated ourselves" (Horn & Heinze,

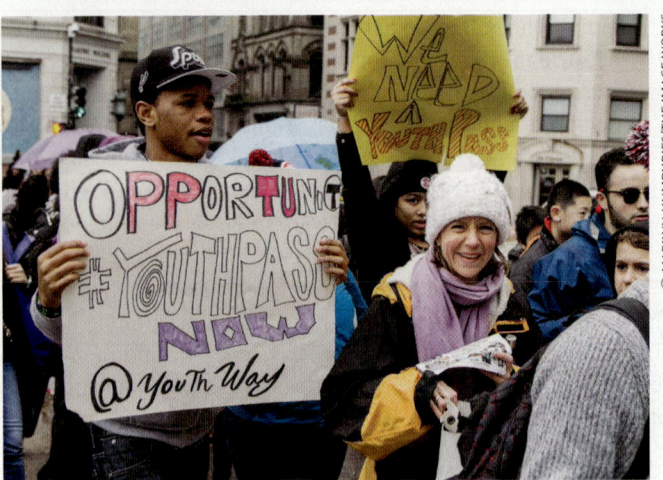

Boston teenagers protest against rising public transportation fares and in favor of a discounted youth pass. Adolescent moral development involves demanding that the protections one wants for oneself extend to others.

2011). And with age, teenagers increasingly defend the government's right to limit individual freedom to engage in risky health behaviors, such as smoking and drinking, in the interest of the larger public good (Flanagan, Stout, & Gallay, 2008).

Similarly, adolescents are increasingly mindful of the overlap between moral imperatives and social conventions. Eventually they realize that violating strongly held conventions—showing up at a wedding in a T-shirt, talking out of turn at a student council meeting—can harm others, either by inducing distress or by undermining fair treatment. As their grasp of fairness deepens, young people understand that many social conventions have moral implications: They are vital for maintaining a just and peaceful society (Nucci, 2001). Notice how this understanding is central to Kohlberg's Stage 4, which is typically attained as adolescence draws to a close.

Influences on Moral Reasoning

Many factors affect maturity of moral reasoning, including child-rearing practices, peer interaction, schooling, and culture. Growing evidence suggests that, as Kohlberg believed, these experiences work by presenting young people with cognitive challenges, which stimulate them to think about moral problems in more complex ways.

Parenting Practices. Adolescents who gain most in moral understanding have parents who engage in moral discussions, encourage prosocial behavior, insist that others be treated respectfully and fairly, and create a supportive atmosphere by listening sensitively, asking clarifying questions, and presenting higher-level reasoning (Carlo, 2014; Pratt, Skoe, & Arnold, 2004). In one study, 11-year-olds were asked what they thought an adult would say to justify a moral rule, such as not lying, stealing, or breaking a promise. Those with warm, demanding, communicative parents were far more likely than their agemates to point to the importance of ideal reciprocity: "You wouldn't like it if I did it to you" (Leman, 2005).

Peer Interaction. Interaction among peers who present differing viewpoints promotes moral understanding. When young people negotiate and compromise, they realize that social life can be based on cooperation between equals. Adolescents who report more close friendships and who more often participate in conversations with their friends are advanced in moral reasoning (Schonert-Reichl, 1999). The mutuality and intimacy of friendship, which foster decisions based on consensual agreement, may be particularly important for enhancing adolescents' understanding of fairness and justice.

Furthermore, recall from Chapter 10 that intergroup contact—cross-race friendships and interactions in schools and communities—reduces racial and ethnic prejudice. It also affects young people morally, strengthening their conviction that race-based, sexual orientation-based, and other forms of peer exclusion are wrong (Horn & Sinno, 2014; Ruck et al., 2011).

Peer discussions and role-playing of moral problems have provided the basis for interventions aimed at improving high school and college students' moral understanding. For these discussions to be effective, young people must be highly engaged—confronting, critiquing, and attempting to clarify one another's viewpoints, as Sabrina and Louis did when they argued over Mrs. Perry's plight (Berkowitz & Gibbs, 1983; Comunian & Gielen, 2006). And because gains in maturity of moral reasoning occur gradually, many peer interaction sessions over weeks or months typically are needed to produce moral change.

Schooling. Secondary schools with nondiscrimination and antibullying policies and student organizations that support the rights of minorities (such as gay–straight alliances) enhance adolescents' moral reasoning about discrimination. In one study, students attending a high school with these practices in place were more likely than those in a school without such practices to view exclusion and harassment of gay and lesbian peers as unjust (Horn & Szalacha, 2009). Teachers who create classroom climates of fairness and respect are similarly influential. Tenth graders who reported fair teacher treatment were more likely than those who had experienced unjust treatment (an undeserved detention or low grade) to view excluding a peer on the basis of race as a moral transgression (Crystal, Killen, & Ruck, 2010). When schools convey explicit messages about the harm inflicted by prejudice and harassment, they induce students to think about those behaviors in ethical terms.

Furthermore, moral reasoning typically progresses to Kohlberg's higher stages the longer a person remains in school (Gibbs et al., 2007). College environments are especially influential because they introduce young people to social issues that extend beyond personal relationships to entire political and cultural groups. In line with this idea, college students who report more perspective-taking opportunities—classes that emphasize open discussion of opinions and friendships with others of different cultural backgrounds—and who indicate that they have become more aware of social diversity tend to be advanced in moral reasoning (Comunian & Gielen, 2006; Mason & Gibbs, 1993a, 1993b).

Culture. Individuals in industrialized nations move through Kohlberg's stages more quickly and progress to higher stages

In Japan, a country that highly values interdependence, responses to moral dilemmas tend to emphasize caring as a communal responsibility. These high school students express their student body's collective empathy during a memorial visit to a school devastated by the 2011 tsunami.

than do individuals in village societies, who rarely move beyond Stage 3. One explanation for these cultural differences is that in village societies, moral cooperation is based on direct relations between people and does not allow for the development of advanced moral understanding (Stages 4 to 6), which depends on appreciating the role of larger social structures, such as laws and government institutions (Gibbs et al., 2007).

A second possible reason for cultural variation is that in both village societies and industrialized cultures that highly value interdependence, responses to moral dilemmas are more other-directed than in North America and Western Europe (Miller & Bland, 2014). In one study, both male and female Japanese adolescents, who almost always integrated care- and justice-based reasoning, placed greater weight on caring, which they regarded as a communal responsibility (Shimizu, 2001). Similarly, in research conducted in India, even highly educated people (expected to have attained Kohlberg's Stages 4 and 5) viewed solutions to moral dilemmas as the responsibility of the entire society, not of a single person (Miller & Bersoff, 1995).

These findings raise the question of whether Kohlberg's highest level represents a culturally specific way of thinking—one limited to Western societies that emphasize individualism and an appeal to an inner, private conscience. At the same time, a review of over 100 studies confirmed an age-related trend consistent with Kohlberg's Stages 1 to 4 across diverse societies (Gibbs et al., 2007). A common morality of justice is clearly evident in the dilemma responses of people from vastly different cultures.

Moral Reasoning and Behavior

A central assumption of the cognitive-developmental perspective is that moral understanding should affect moral action. According to Kohlberg, mature moral thinkers realize that behaving in line with their beliefs is vital for creating and maintaining a just social world (Gibbs, 2014). Consistent with this idea, higher-stage adolescents more often act prosocially by helping, sharing, and defending victims of injustice and by volunteering in their communities (Carlo et al., 2011; Comunian & Gielen, 2000, 2006). Also, they less often engage in cheating, aggression, and other antisocial behaviors (Raaijmakers, Engels, & van Hoof, 2005; Stams et al., 2006).

Yet the connection between more mature moral reasoning and action is only modest. As we have seen, moral behavior is influenced by many factors besides cognition, including the emotions of empathy, sympathy, and guilt; individual differences in temperament; and cultural experiences and intuitive beliefs that affect moral decision making. Compared with children, adolescents increasingly say they would feel negatively after committing a moral transgression and positively after acting morally (Krettenauer et al., 2014). Moral decisions and anticipated emotions become better coordinated over time, contributing to gains in teenagers' motivation to act morally.

Moral identity—the degree to which morality is central to self-concept—also affects moral behavior (Hardy & Carlo, 2011). In a study of low-SES African-American and Hispanic teenagers, those who emphasized moral traits and goals in their self-descriptions displayed exceptional levels of community service (Hart & Fegley, 1995). And when 10- to 18-year-olds rated moral traits on the basis of whether each reflected the kind of person they wanted to be, those with a stronger *moral ideal self* were viewed by their parents as more ethical and altruistic in behavior (Hardy et al., 2012).

Researchers are identifying factors that strengthen moral identity in hopes of capitalizing on them to promote moral commitment. Certain parenting practices—inductive discipline (see page 267 in Chapter 8) and clearly conveyed moral expectations—augment adolescents' moral identity (Patrick & Gibbs, 2011). Also, opportunities to enact moral behaviors through community service enhance adolescents' self-understanding, thereby contributing to a stronger moral identity and, in turn, to moral motivation (Matsuba, Murzyn, & Hart, 2014). As the Social Issues: Education box on the following page reveals, civic engagement can help young people see the connection between their personal interests and the public interest—an insight that may foster all aspects of morality.

Religious Involvement and Moral Development

Recall that in resolving real-life moral dilemmas, many people express religious and spiritual ideas. Though the percentage of religiously unaffiliated U.S. adults rose over the past decade, about 70 percent of Americans continue to rate religion as very important in their lives. Comparable figures are 50 percent in Canada and Germany, 40 percent in Great Britain, and 30 percent in Sweden, making the United States the most religious Western nation (Pew Research Center, 2012, 2015a; Pickel, 2013). People who regularly attend religious services include many parents with children. But as adolescents search for a personally meaningful identity, formal religious involvement declines—for U.S. youths, from 55 percent at ages 13 to 15 to 36 percent at age 18 (Pew Research Center, 2010c, 2015a).

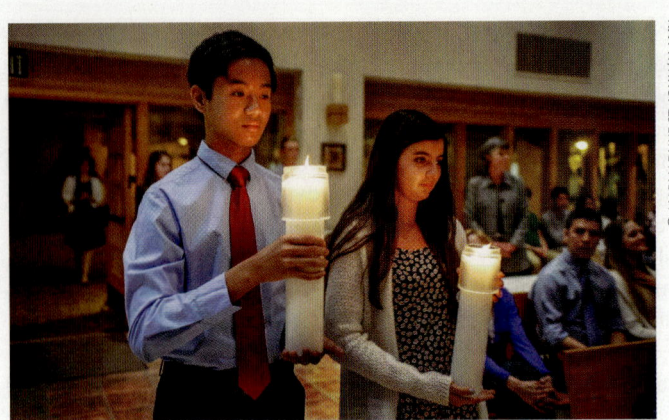

Singing in a church choir gives these youths a sense of connection to their faith and to adults and peers who hold similar values. Adolescents who participate in a religious community are more likely to engage in community service activities and to display responsible academic and social behavior.

Nevertheless, teenagers who remain part of a religious community are advantaged in moral values and behavior. Compared with nonaffiliated youths, they are more involved in community service activities aimed at helping the less fortunate (Kerestes, Youniss, & Metz, 2004). And religious involvement promotes responsible academic and social behavior and discourages misconduct (Dowling et al., 2004). It is associated with lower levels of drug and alcohol use, early sexual activity, and antisocial behavior (Good & Willoughby, 2014; Salas-Wright, Vaughn, & Maynard, 2014).

A variety of factors contribute to these favorable outcomes. In a study of inner-city high school students, religiously involved young people were more likely to report trusting relationships with parents, other adults, and friends who hold similar worldviews. The more activities they shared with this network, the higher they scored in empathy and prosocial behavior (King & Furrow, 2004). Furthermore, religious education and youth activities directly teach concern for others and provide opportunities for moral discussions and civic engagement. And adolescents who feel connected to a higher being may develop certain inner strengths, including sense of self-efficacy, prosocial values, and a strong moral identity, that help them translate their thinking into action (Hardy & Carlo, 2005; Sherrod & Spiewak, 2008).

At the same time, religious or political messages that convey stereotypes and prejudices about minorities work against youths' moral maturity. In focus groups addressing the impact of religion in their lives, Muslim adolescents from U.S. immigrant families, while recognizing the support their religious communities provided, frequently mentioned negative experiences of profiling and other forms of discrimination at the hands of non-Muslims (Abo-Zena & Barry, 2013).

Finally, religious cults that target alienated youths as potential members, rigidly indoctrinating them into the group's beliefs, estranging them from former social ties, and suppressing individuality, interfere with virtually all developmental tasks of adolescence, including moral progress (Scarlett & Warren, 2010). Although religious communities may be uniquely suited to foster teenagers' moral and prosocial commitments, not all have these effects.

CHAPTER 12 Emotional and Social Development in Adolescence 419

Social Issues: Education

Development of Civic Engagement

On Thanksgiving Day, Jules, Martin, Louis, and Sabrina joined their parents to serve a holiday dinner to poverty-stricken people. Throughout the year, Sabrina volunteered on Saturday mornings at a nursing home. During a congressional election campaign, all four adolescents raised questions about issues at special youth meetings with candidates. At school, Louis and his girlfriend, Cassie, formed an organization devoted to promoting ethnic and racial tolerance.

These young people show a strong sense of *civic engagement*—a complex combination of cognition, emotion, and behavior. Civic engagement involves knowledge of social and political issues, commitment to making a difference in the community, and skills for achieving civic goals, such as how to resolve differing views fairly (Zaff et al., 2010).

When young people engage in community service that exposes them to people in need or to public issues, they are especially likely to express a commitment to future service. And youth volunteers—who tend to be advanced in moral reasoning—gain further in moral maturity as a result of participating (Gibbs et al., 2007; Hart, Atkins, & Donnelly, 2006). Family, school, and community experiences contribute to adolescents' civic engagement.

Family Influences

Adolescents whose parents stress compassion for the less fortunate and engage in community service tend to hold socially responsible values. When asked what causes unemployment or poverty, these teenagers more often mention situational and societal factors (lack of education, government policies, or the state of the economy) than individual factors (low intelligence or personal problems). Youths who endorse situational and societal causes, in turn, have more altruistic life goals, such as working to eradicate poverty or to preserve the earth for future generations (Flanagan & Tucker, 1999).

Parents' open communication, discussion of social problems, and own civic engagement carry over to their adolescent children's civic commitment and behavior (van Goethem et al., 2014). These young people not only volunteer but do so especially often.

School and Community Influences

A democratic climate at school, in which teachers promote respectful discussion of controversial issues, fosters knowledge and critical analysis of social and political concerns and participation in organizations with a civic purpose (Lenzi et al., 2012; Torney-Purta, Barber, & Wilkenfeld, 2007). Furthermore, high school students who view their community as one in which adults care about youths and work to make the community better report higher levels of civic participation (Kahne & Sporte, 2008). Participation in extracurricular activities at school whose primary objectives are to induce social change outside the organization itself is also associated with civic commitment that persists into adulthood (Obradović & Masten, 2007).

Two aspects of these involvements seem to account for their lasting impact. First, they introduce adolescents to the vision and skills required for mature civic engagement. Within student government, political and vocational clubs, service organizations, and student newspaper and yearbook staffs, young people see how their actions affect the wider school and community. They realize that collectively they can achieve results greater than any one person can accomplish alone. And they learn to work together, balancing strong convictions with compromise (Kirshner, 2009). Second, while engaged in these activities, young people explore political and moral ideals. Often they redefine their identities to include a

A high school student plays music for a hospice patient as part of a service project he started. Youths who volunteer in their communities gain in moral maturity and are especially likely to engage in future service.

responsibility to combat others' misfortunes, which further strengthens civic engagement (Crocetti, Jahromi, & Meeus, 2012).

The majority of U.S. public schools provide students with community service opportunities. Many schools have *service-learning programs*, which integrate service activities into the academic curriculum. High school students who are required to serve their communities express as strong a desire to remain engaged as do students who volunteer. And when they reach early adulthood, they are equally likely to vote and participate in community organizations (Hart et al., 2007).

Still, most U.S. schools offering service learning do not have policies encouraging or mandating enrollment in such programs. Furthermore, low-SES, inner-city youths attend schools and live in neighborhoods with fewer civic-training opportunities. And students without plans to go to college may be less motivated to enroll in service-learning programs. As a result, these youths score substantially lower than higher-SES and college-oriented youths in civic knowledge and participation (Lenzi et al., 2012; Syvertsen et al., 2011). A broad societal commitment to fostering civic character must pay special attention to supportive school and community experiences for these young people.

Further Challenges to Kohlberg's Theory

Although much evidence is consistent with the cognitive-developmental approach to morality, Kohlberg's theory has faced major challenges. The most radical opposition comes from researchers who—referring to wide variability in moral reasoning across situations—claim that Kohlberg's stage sequence inadequately accounts for morality in everyday life. These investigators favor abandoning Kohlberg's stages for a *pragmatic approach to morality* (Krebs, 2011). They assert that each person makes moral judgments at varying levels of maturity, depending on the individual's current context and motivations: Conflict over a business deal is likely to evoke Stage 2 (instrumental purpose) reasoning, a friendship or romantic dispute Stage 3 (ideal reciprocity) reasoning, and a breach of contract Stage 4 (social-order-maintaining) reasoning.

According to the pragmatic view, everyday moral judgments—rather than being efforts to arrive at just solutions—are practical tools that people use to achieve their goals. To benefit personally, they often must advocate cooperation with others. But people often act first and then invoke moral judgments to rationalize their actions, regardless of whether their behavior is self-centered or prosocial (Haidt, 2013). And sometimes people use moral judgments for immoral purposes—for example, to excuse their transgressions.

Is the pragmatic approach correct that people strive to resolve moral conflicts fairly only when they themselves have nothing to lose? Supporters of the cognitive-developmental perspective point out that people frequently rise above self-interest to defend others' rights. Also, adolescents and adults are well aware of the greater adequacy of higher-stage moral reasoning, which some people act on despite highly corrupt environments. And individuals who engage in sudden altruistic action may have previously considered relevant moral issues so thoroughly that their moral judgment activates automatically, triggering an immediate response (Gibbs, 2014; Gibbs et al., 2009). In these instances, people who appear to be engaging in after-the-fact moral justification are actually behaving with great forethought.

In sum, the cognitive-developmental approach to morality has done much to clarify our profound moral potential. And despite opposition, Kohlberg's central assumption—that with age, humans everywhere construct a deeper understanding of fairness and justice that guides moral action—remains powerfully influential.

Ask yourself

CONNECT What advance in perspective taking contributes to an understanding of ideal reciprocity, and why is that understanding vital for mature moral reasoning?

APPLY Tam grew up in a small village culture, Lydia in a Western industrial city. At age 15, Tam reasons at Kohlberg's Stage 3, Lydia at Stage 4. What factors might account for the difference?

REFLECT Do you favor a cognitive-developmental or a pragmatic approach to morality, or both? Explain, drawing on research evidence and personal experiences.

The Family

12.6 Discuss changes in parent–child and sibling relationships during adolescence.

Franca and Antonio remember their son Louis's freshman year of high school as a difficult time. Because of a demanding project at work, Franca was away from home many evenings and weekends. In her absence, Antonio took over, but when business declined and he had to cut costs at his hardware store, he, too, had less time for the family. That year, Louis and two friends used their computer know-how to gain entry to their classmates' systems to pirate video game software. Louis's grades fell, and he often left the house without saying where he was going. Franca and Antonio began to feel uncomfortable about the long hours Louis spent at his computer and their lack of contact with him. One day, when Franca and Antonio noticed the video game icons covering Louis's computer desktop, they knew they had cause for concern.

Development at adolescence involves striving for **autonomy**—a sense of oneself as a separate, self-governing individual. Adolescent autonomy has two vital aspects: (1) an *emotional component*—relying more on oneself and less on parents for support and guidance, and (2) a *behavioral component*—making decisions independently by carefully weighing one's own judgment and the suggestions of others to arrive at a personally satisfying, well-reasoned course of action (Collins & Laursen, 2004). Nevertheless, relationships with parents remain vital for helping adolescents become autonomous, responsible individuals.

Parent–Adolescent Relationships

A variety of changes within the adolescent support autonomy. In Chapter 11, we saw that puberty triggers psychological distancing from parents. In addition, as young people look more mature, parents give them more freedom to think and decide for themselves, more opportunities to regulate their own activities, and more responsibility (McElhaney et al., 2009). Cognitive development also contributes: Gradually, adolescents make decisions more effectively, and an improved ability to reason about social relationships leads teenagers to *deidealize* their parents, viewing them as "just people." Consequently, they no longer bend as easily to parental authority. Yet as Franca and Antonio's episode with Louis reveals, teenagers still need guidance and protection from dangerous situations.

Effective Parenting. Think back to the type of parenting that fosters academic achievement (Chapter 11), identity formation, and moral maturity. You will find a common theme: Effective parenting of adolescents strikes a balance between *connection* and *separation*. Autonomy is fostered by warm, supportive parent–adolescent ties that make appropriate demands for maturity while permitting young people to explore ideas and social roles—across diverse ethnic and SES groups, nationalities, and family structures (including single-parent, two-parent, and stepparent). Autonomy, in turn, predicts high self-reliance, self-regulation, academic achievement, positive work orientation, favorable self-esteem, and ease of separation in the transition to college (Bean, Barber, & Crane, 2007; Eisenberg et al., 2005; Supple et al., 2009; Vazsonyi, Hibbert, & Snider, 2003; Wang, Pomerantz, & Chen, 2007).

Conversely, parents who are coercive or psychologically controlling interfere with the development of autonomy. These tactics are linked to low self-esteem, depression, drug and alcohol use, and antisocial behavior—outcomes that often persist into early adulthood (Allen et al., 2012; Barber, Stolz, & Olsen, 2005; Lansford et al., 2014).

In Chapter 2, we described the family as a *system* that must adapt to changes in its members. The rapid physical and psychological changes of adolescence trigger conflicting expectations in parent–child relationships. Earlier we noted that interest in making choices about personal matters strengthens in adolescence. Yet parents and teenagers—especially young teenagers—differ sharply on the appropriate age for granting certain privileges, such as control over clothing, school courses, going out with friends, and dating (Smetana, 2002). Consistent parental monitoring of the young person's daily activities, through a cooperative relationship in which the adolescent willingly discloses information, is linked to a variety of favorable outcomes—prevention of delinquency, reduction in sexual activity, improved school performance, and positive psychological well-being (Crouter & Head, 2002; Lippold et al., 2014).

LOOK and LISTEN

Ask an early adolescent and his or her parent for their views on when the young person is mature enough to begin dating, create a Facebook page, and be given other privileges. Do adolescent and parent perspectives differ?

Effective parenting, which balances connection and separation, promotes autonomy in adolescence. Teenagers benefit from freedom to explore ideas and make their own decisions, but they still need guidance and protection from dangerous situations.

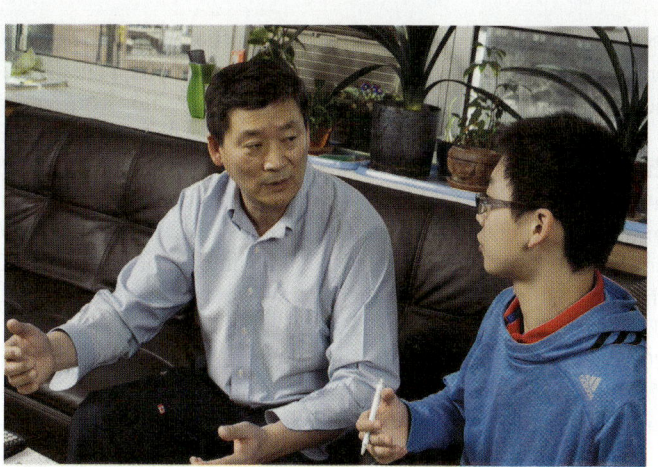

Chinese adolescents tend to readily accept their parents' decisions because they value parents' opinions, not because they feel pressured to comply.

Culture. In cultures that place a high priority on interdependence, autonomy remains a central adolescent motive, but teenagers conceive of it differently than in Western nations. Rather than equating it with independent decision making, they view autonomy as *self-endorsed* decision making—engaging in actions that are consistent with authentic personal values. In an investigation of adolescents from both urban and rural regions of China, self-endorsed motives for both independent and "dependent" decision making (following parents' advice) were related to high self-esteem and a positive outlook (Chen et al., 2013). Chinese adolescents often accept their parents' decisions because they value parents' opinions, not because they feel pressured to comply.

Immigrant parents from cultures that emphasize obedience to authority have greater difficulty adapting to their teenagers' push for independent decision making, often reacting strongly to adolescent disagreement. And as adolescents acquire the Western host culture's language and are increasingly exposed to its individualistic values, immigrant parents may become even more critical, prompting teenagers to rely less on the family network for social support and to disclose less about personal feelings, peer relationships, and potentially risky activities (Yau, Tasopoulos-Chan, & Smetana, 2009). The resulting *acculturative stress* is associated with a decline in self-esteem and a rise in anxiety, depressive symptoms, and deviant behavior, including alcohol use and delinquency (Park, 2009; Suarez-Morales & Lopez, 2009; Warner et al., 2006).

But most adolescents from immigrant families attain sufficient psychological separation from their parents to enable healthy psychological development (Fuligni & Tsai, 2015). At the same time, they sustain the strong sense of family obligation instilled by their home culture, flexibly balancing those commitments with the pursuit of autonomy valued in their new society.

A Reorganized Relationship. Throughout adolescence, the quality of the parent–child relationship is the single most consistent predictor of mental health (Collins & Steinberg, 2006). The mild to moderate conflict that typically arises facilitates adolescent identity and autonomy by helping family members learn to express and tolerate disagreement. Conflicts also inform parents of teenagers' changing needs and expectations, signaling a need for adjustments in the parent–child relationship.

By mid- to late adolescence, harmonious interaction is on the rise. The reduced time that Western teenagers spend engaged in activities with their parents—an estimated one-third less than in middle childhood for U.S. adolescents—has little to do with conflict. Rather, it results from the large amount of unstructured time available to Western teenagers—on average, nearly half their waking hours (Larson, 2001; Milkie, Nomaguchi, & Denny, 2015). Young people tend to fill these free hours with activities that take them away from home—part-time jobs, leisure and volunteer pursuits, and time with friends.

Type of shared parent–adolescent activities is more important than quantity of time together. In an investigation of middle-SES white families, engaging in leisure pursuits and eating meals together (especially with both parents) enhanced teenagers' well-being (Offer, 2013). These contexts probably afford parents and adolescents greater opportunity to discuss important concerns in a relaxed atmosphere and to emphasize shared values.

Finally, the drop in family time over the teenage years is not universal. In one study, urban low- and middle-SES African-American youths showed no decline in hours spent with family—a pattern typical in cultures stressing interdependence and family closeness (Larson et al., 2001). Furthermore, teenagers living in risky neighborhoods tend to have more trusting relationships with parents and adjust more favorably when parents maintain tighter control and pressure them not to engage in worrisome behaviors (McElhaney & Allen, 2001). In harsh surroundings, adolescents seem to interpret more measured granting of autonomy as a sign of parental caring.

Family Circumstances

As Franca and Antonio's experience with Louis reminds us, adult life stress can interfere with warm, involved parenting and, in turn, with children's adjustment during any period of development. But parents who are financially secure, not overloaded with job pressures, and content with their marriages usually find it easier to grant teenagers appropriate autonomy and experience less conflict with them (Cowan & Cowan, 2002). When Franca and Antonio's work stress eased and they recognized Louis's need for more involvement and guidance, his problems subsided.

Among the minority of families with seriously troubled parent–adolescent relationships, most difficulties began in childhood (Collins & Laursen, 2004). Think back to family conditions considered in earlier chapters that pose challenges for adolescents—for example, economic hardship, divorce, single parenthood, blended families, and child maltreatment. Teenagers who develop well despite family stressors continue to benefit from factors that fostered resilience in earlier years: an appealing, easy-going disposition; a parent who combines warmth with high expectations; and (especially if parental supports are lacking) bonds with prosocial adults outside the family who care deeply about the adolescent's well-being (Luthar, Crossman, & Small, 2015).

Siblings

Like parent–child relationships, sibling interactions adapt to development at adolescence. As younger siblings become more self-sufficient, they accept less direction from their older brothers and sisters. Also, as teenagers become more involved in friendships and romantic relationships, they invest less time and energy in siblings, who are part of the family from which they are trying to establish autonomy. As a result, sibling relationships often become less intense, in both positive and negative feelings (Kim et al., 2006; Whiteman, Solmeyer, & McHale, 2015).

Nevertheless, attachment between siblings remains strong for most young people. Overall, siblings who established a positive bond in early childhood continue to display greater affection and caring, which contribute to more favorable adolescent adjustment, including increased academic engagement, empathy, and prosocial behavior (Lam, Solmeyer, & McHale, 2012; McHale, Updegraff, & Whiteman, 2012). In contrast, sibling negativity—frequent conflict, coercive exchanges, and aggression—is associated with internalizing symptoms (anxiety and depression) and externalizing difficulties (conduct problems, bullying, and drug use) (Criss & Shaw, 2005; Solmeyer, McHale, & Crouter, 2014).

Finally, culture influences the quality of adolescent sibling ties. For example, the Hispanic cultural ideal of *familism,* which highly values close family bonds, fosters harmonious sibling relationships. In one study, Mexican-American adolescents who expressed a strong Mexican cultural orientation resolved sibling conflicts more cooperatively than did those more oriented toward U.S. individualistic values (Killoren, Thayer, & Updegraff, 2008).

Peer Relations

12.7 Describe adolescent friendships, peer groups, and dating relationships and their consequences for development.

As adolescents spend less time with family members, peers become increasingly important. In industrialized nations, young people spend most of each weekday with agemates in school as well as much out-of-class time together. In the following sections, we will see that at their best, peers serve as critical bridges between the family and adult social roles. But as with parent and sibling relationships, peer associations vary in quality and in their consequences for teenagers' well-being and adjustment.

Friendships

Number of best friends declines from about four to six in early adolescence to one or two in adulthood (Gomez et al., 2011). At the same time, the nature of the relationship changes.

Characteristics of Adolescent Friendships.
When asked about the meaning of friendship, teenagers stress three characteristics. The most important is *intimacy,* or psychological closeness, which is supported by *mutual understanding* of each other's

values, beliefs, and feelings. In addition, more than younger children, teenagers want their friends to be *loyal*—to stick up for them and not leave them for somebody else (Collins & Madsen, 2006).

Teenagers' strong desire for friendship closeness likely explains why they say friends are their most important sources of social support (Brown & Larson, 2009). As frankness and faithfulness increase, *self-disclosure* (sharing of private thoughts and feelings) between friends rises over the adolescent years. As a result, teenage friends get to know each other better as personalities. In addition to the many characteristics that school-age friends share (see page 346 in Chapter 10), adolescent friends tend to be alike in identity status, educational aspirations, political beliefs, depressive symptoms, and willingness to try drugs and engage in lawbreaking acts. Over time, they become increasingly similar in these ways, and the more similar they are, the greater the chances that their friendships will be long-lasting (Bagwell & Schmidt, 2011; Hartl, Laursen, & Cillessen, 2015). Occasionally, however, teenagers choose friends with differing attitudes and values, which permits them to explore new perspectives within the security of a compatible relationship.

During adolescence, cooperation and mutual affirmation between friends increase and negative interaction declines—changes that reflect greater skill at preserving the relationship and sensitivity to a friend's needs and desires (De Goede, Branje, & Meeus, 2009). Adolescents also are less possessive of their friends than they were in childhood (Parker et al., 2005). Desiring a certain degree of autonomy for themselves, they recognize that friends need this, too.

Gender Differences in Friendship Quality.
Ask several adolescents to describe their close friendships. You are likely to find that emotional closeness is more common between girls than boys (Hall, 2011). Girls frequently get together to "just talk," and their interactions contain more self-disclosure and mutually supportive statements. In contrast, boys more often gather for an activity—usually sports and competitive games. Boys' discussions usually focus on successes in sports and school and involve more competition and conflict (Brendgen et al., 2001; Rubin, Bukowski, & Parker, 2006).

Because of gender-role expectations, girls' friendships typically focus on communal concerns, boys' on achievement and status. Boys do form close friendship ties, but the quality of their friendships is more variable. When ethnically diverse boys from low-income families were asked to describe their friendships, African Americans, Asian Americans, and Hispanics mentioned closeness, mutual support, and self-disclosure more often than their white counterparts. But as ethnic minority boys transitioned from mid- to late adolescence, many reported a decline in friendship closeness (Way, 2013). Their remarks revealed that masculine stereotypes—to be tough and unemotional—interfered with these bonds. But perhaps because of cultural valuing of emotional expressiveness between male friends, Hispanic boys were more likely than others to resist conforming to gender stereotypes (Way et al., 2014). Such resistance, by permitting boys to benefit from the supportiveness of intimate friends, is consistently related to better adjustment.

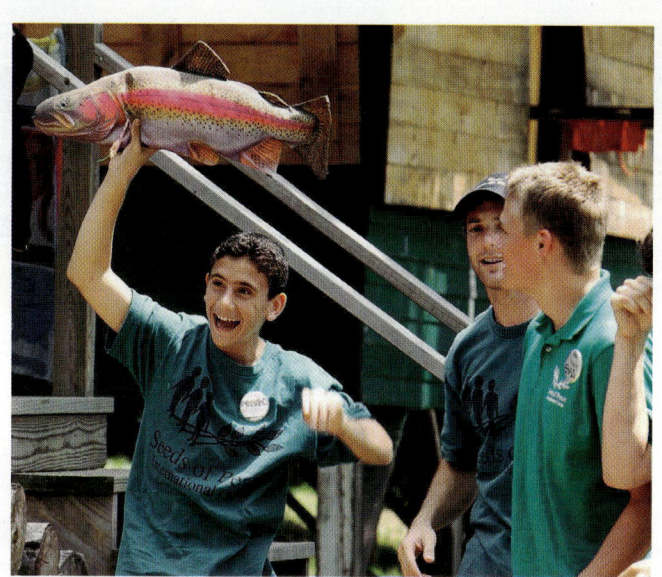

Whereas girls tend to emphasize emotional closeness in their friendships, boys more often gather for an activity, such as sports or competitive games. This camper holds up a reward for catching the largest fish, presented to him by his friends.

Friendship closeness, however, can have costs. When friends focus on deeper thoughts and feelings, they tend to *coruminate*, or repeatedly mull over problems and negative emotions, with girls doing so more than boys. Corumination, while contributing to high friendship quality, also triggers anxiety and depression—symptoms more common in girls (Hankin, Stone, & Wright, 2010; Rose et al., 2014). And when conflict arises between intimate friends, more potential exists for one party to harm the other through relational aggression—for example, by divulging sensitive personal information to outsiders. Partly for these reasons, girls' closest same-sex friendships tend to be of shorter duration than boys' (Benenson & Christakos, 2003).

Friendships, Cell Phones, and the Internet.
Teenagers frequently use cell phones and the Internet to communicate with friends. About 73 percent of U.S. 13- to 17-year-olds own or have access to a smartphone, an additional 15 percent to a basic phone; 58 percent own or have access to a tablet. Although smartphone and tablet ownership is higher among teenagers from economically advantaged families, use of these mobile devices is widespread. They serve as adolescents' primary route to the Internet: 94 percent say they go online daily or more often (Lenhart & Page, 2015).

Texting has become the preferred means of electronic interaction between teenage friends: Most adolescents engage in it, sending and receiving, on average, 30 texts per day. Cell calling ranks second, followed by instant messaging and social media sites: Facebook is favored, but the majority of teenagers also use other platforms. Though used less frequently, e-mailing, video chatting, and online gaming are additional ways teenagers spend time online with friends (see Figure 12.1). Girls text and call their friends more often than boys, and they more often use social media sites to share information (Lenhart et al., 2015). Boys are more avid gamers with friends and other peers.

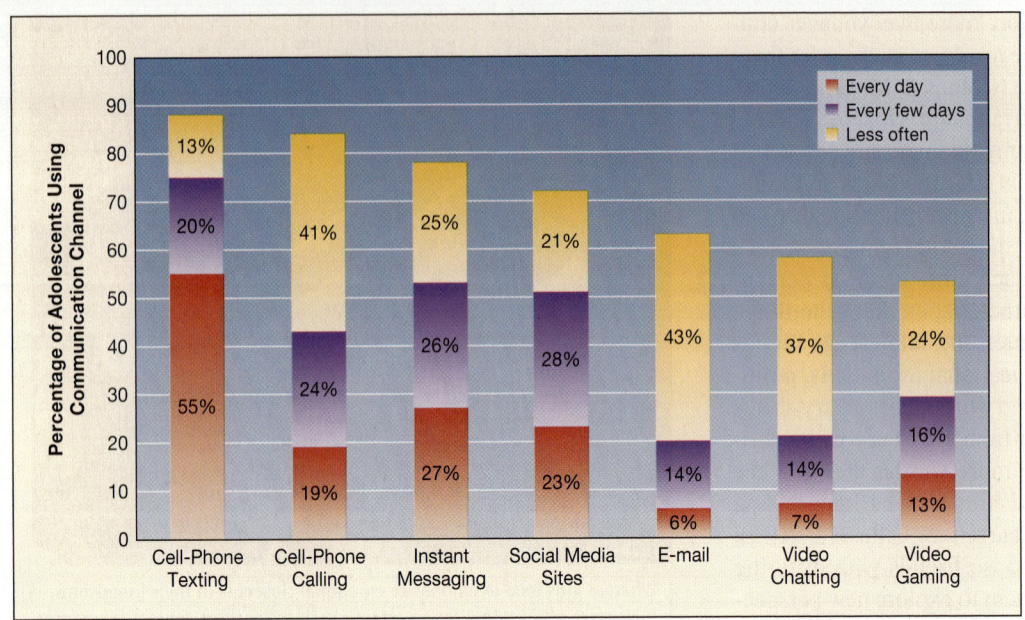

FIGURE 12.1 Percentage of U.S. 13- to 17-year-olds using various communication channels to spend time with friends. A sample of more than 1,000 adolescents responded to a survey about their communication strategies with friends. Cell-phone texting was the preferred means of electronic communication, with over half reporting that they used it daily. (Based on Lenhart & Page, 2015.)

Online interaction can contribute to friendship closeness. For example, in several studies, as amount of online messaging between preexisting friends increased, so did young people's perceptions of intimacy in the relationship and sense of well-being (Reich, Subrahmanyam, & Espinoza, 2012; Valkenburg & Peter, 2009). The effect is probably due to friends' online disclosure of personal information, such as worries, secrets, and romantic feelings. But sharing an online activity can also enhance friendship. Most teenage gamers say that playing online games with preexisting friends makes them feel more connected to those friends (Lenhart et al., 2015). While playing, they often voice-chat or video-chat to converse and collaborate.

Social media sites such as Facebook and Twitter are a major avenue through which teenagers meet new friends: Over one-third of U.S. adolescents report developing friendships this way, often connecting through friends they already know (Lenhart et al., 2015). Girls are especially likely to form new friendships through social media sites; boys more often do so during online gaming.

The quality of adolescents' face-to-face relationships tends to be reproduced in social media communication. In a study of U.S. middle school students diverse in ethnicity and SES, those with positive face-to-face peer relationships had larger networks of social media friends who frequently posted supportive comments (Mikami et al., 2010). Teenagers who reported engaging in delinquent acts tended to post hostile comments to their "About Me" section. And those with depressive symptoms more often uploaded photos of themselves engaging in inappropriate behaviors.

While online communication can augment friendships, clearly it poses risks, which teenage social media users readily verbalize. In a focus group addressing communication technology, one high school student reflected, "You don't know how to interact with people anymore because you're always texting." Others said that social media sites too often become contexts for sexually uninhibited posts and for expressed jealousies between friends over dating partners (Rueda, Lindsay, & Williams, 2015). And some mentioned that dialogues through texts and social media sites, which are abbreviated and devoid of nonverbal cues to their sincerity, contribute to misunderstandings and conflicts.

Although 60 percent of U.S. adolescent Facebook users keep their profiles private and 70 percent are friends with their parents, most are relatively unconcerned that information they share might be accessed by third parties without their knowledge. Over half post their e-mail address and one-fifth their cell-phone number. And one-fifth have shared their social media passwords with friends. About 17 percent report contact from strangers that made them feel scared or uncomfortable (Lenhart et al., 2015; Madden et al., 2013).

Finally, adolescent time devoted to social media is rising. For example, nearly one-fourth of U.S. teenagers report using the Internet almost constantly, with 30 percent sending more than 100 texts per day and half of these exceeding 200. On average, adolescent users are on social media sites for nearly 40 minutes per day. Very high social media use is linked to unsatisfying face-to-face social experiences, boredom, and depression (Madden et al., 2013; Pea et al., 2012; Smahel, Brown, & Blinka, 2012). In a longitudinal study, compulsive Internet users (who find it difficult to stop using the Internet and feel frustrated when they don't have access) experienced a rise in mental health problems from grades 8 to 11, irrespective of their preexisting mental health status. Compared to boys, girls were more addicted to social media and reported more impaired mental health (Ciarrochi et al., 2016). These findings suggest that excessive Internet use, especially social media, amplifies adjustment difficulties.

In sum, the Internet's value for enabling convenient and satisfying interaction among teenage friends must be weighed against its potential for facilitating harmful emotional and social consequences. Parents are wise to point out the risks of Internet communication, including harassment, exploitation, and excessive use, and to insist that teenagers follow Internet safety rules (see www.safeteens.com).

Friendship and Adjustment. As long as adolescent friendships are high in trust, intimate sharing, and support and not characterized by relational aggression or attraction to antisocial behavior, they contribute to many aspects of psychological health and competence into early adulthood (Bagwell & Schmidt, 2011; Furman & Rose, 2015), for several reasons:

- *Close friendships provide opportunities to explore the self and develop a deep understanding of another.* Through open, honest communication, friends become sensitive to each other's strengths and weaknesses, needs and desires—a process that supports the development of self-concept, perspective taking, and identity.
- *Close friendships provide a foundation for future intimate relationships.* Conversations with teenage friends about sexuality and romance, along with the intimacy of friendship itself, may help adolescents establish and work out problems in romantic partnerships (Connolly & Goldberg, 1999).
- *Close friendships help young people deal with the stresses of adolescence.* By enhancing sensitivity to and concern for another, supportive friendships promote empathy, sympathy, and prosocial behavior. As a result, friendships contribute to involvement in constructive youth activities, avoidance of antisocial acts, and psychological well-being (Barry & Wentzel, 2006; Lansford et al., 2003).
- *Close friendships can improve attitudes toward and involvement in school.* Close friendships promote good school adjustment, academically and socially (Wentzel, Barry, & Caldwell, 2004). Teenagers who enjoy interacting with friends at school may begin to view all aspects of school life more positively.

LOOK and LISTEN

> Interview several adolescents about qualities they value most in their best friends. Ask how friendships have helped them cope with stress and resulted in other personal benefits.

Cliques and Crowds

In early adolescence, *peer groups* (see Chapter 10) become increasingly common and tightly knit. They are organized into **cliques**—groups of about five to seven members who are friends and, therefore, usually resemble one another in family background, attitudes, values, and interests (Brown & Dietz, 2009). At first, cliques are limited to same-sex members. Among girls but not boys, being in a clique predicts academic and social competence. Clique membership is more important to girls, who use it as a context for expressing emotional closeness (Henrich et al., 2000). By midadolescence, mixed-sex cliques are common.

Among Western adolescents attending high schools with complex social structures, often several cliques with similar values form a larger, more loosely organized group called a **crowd**. Unlike the more intimate clique, membership in a crowd is based on reputation and stereotype, granting the adolescent an identity within the larger social structure of the school. Prominent crowds in typical North American and European high schools include "brains" (nonathletes who enjoy academics), "jocks" (who are very involved in sports), "populars" (class leaders with high peer

These high school drama club members form a crowd, establishing relationships on the basis of shared interests. Crowd membership grants them an identity within the larger social structure of the school.

acceptance), "partyers" (who value socializing but care little about schoolwork), "nonconformists" (who like unconventional clothing and music), "burnouts" (who frequently use alcohol and drugs, engage in sexual risk taking, and otherwise get into trouble), and "normals" (average to good students who get along with most other peers) (Stone & Brown, 1999; Sussman et al., 2007).

What influences the sorting of teenagers into cliques and crowds? Crowd affiliations are linked to strengths in adolescents' self-concepts, which reflect their abilities and interests (Prinstein & La Greca, 2002). Ethnicity also plays a role. Minority teenagers who associate with an ethnically defined crowd, as opposed to a crowd reflecting their abilities and interests, sometimes are motivated by discrimination in their school or neighborhood. Alternatively, they may be expressing a strong ethnic identity (Brown et al., 2008). Family factors are important, too. Negative relationships with parents that suppress adolescents' expression of autonomy predict difficulties in establishing favorable relationships and autonomy with peers (Allen & Loeb, 2015). As a result, teenagers are more likely to join peer groups that reject conventional values and promote risk-taking and rebellious behavior.

Once adolescents join a clique or crowd, it can modify their beliefs and behavior. In a Dutch longitudinal study, membership in nonconventional crowds (such as nonconformists and burnouts) predicted a rise in internalizing and externalizing problems (Doornwaard et al., 2012). Perhaps nonconventional youths respond with anxiety and depressive symptoms to feeling disliked by members of higher-status crowds. And within their own crowds, they experience frequent peer modeling and encouragement for antisocial activity.

Although conventional-crowd membership (brains, jocks, and populars) tends to be associated with better adjustment, the positive impact of having academically and socially skilled peers is greatest for teenagers whose own parents use an authoritative style. And the negative impact of having antisocial, drug-using friends is strongest for teenagers whose parents use less effective child-rearing styles (Mounts & Steinberg, 1995). In sum, family experiences affect the extent to which adolescents become like their peers over time.

Among heterosexual teenagers, as interest in dating increases, boys' and girls' cliques come together. Mixed-sex cliques provide boys and girls with models of how to interact and a chance to do so without having to be intimate (Connolly et al., 2004). By late adolescence, when boys and girls feel comfortable enough about approaching each other directly, the mixed-sex clique disappears.

Crowds also decline in importance. As adolescents settle on personal values and goals, they no longer feel a need to broadcast, through dress, language, and preferred activities, who they are. From tenth to twelfth grade, many young people switch crowds, mostly in conventional directions (Doornwaard et al., 2012; Strouse, 1999). Brains, popular, and normal crowds grow and deviant crowds lose members as teenagers focus more on their future.

Dating

The hormonal changes of puberty increase sexual interest, but cultural expectations determine when and how dating begins. Asian youths start dating later and have fewer dating partners than young people in Western societies, which tolerate and even encourage romantic involvements from middle school on (see Figure 12.2). At age 12 to 14, these relationships are usually casual, lasting only briefly. By age 16, they have become steady relationships, continuing, on average, for one to two years, though breakups remain common for about one-third (Carver, Joyner, & Udry, 2003; Manning et al., 2014). Early adolescents tend to mention recreation and achieving peer status as reasons for dating. By late adolescence, as young people are ready for greater psychological intimacy, they look for dating partners who offer personal compatibility, companionship, affection, and social support (Collins & van Dulmen, 2006b; Meier & Allen, 2009).

The achievement of intimacy between dating partners typically lags behind that between friends. And positive relationships with parents and friends contribute to warm romantic ties, whereas conflict-ridden parent–adolescent and peer relationships forecast hostile dating interactions (Furman & Collins, 2009; Linder & Collins, 2005).

Recall from Chapter 6 that according to ethological theory, early attachment bonds lead to an *internal working model,* or set of expectations about attachment figures, that guides later close relationships. Consistent with these ideas, secure attachment to parents in infancy and childhood—together with recollections of that security in adolescence—predicts higher-quality teenage friendships and romantic ties (Collins & van Dulmen, 2006a; Collins, Welsh, & Furman, 2009).

Parents' marital interactions make a difference, too, likely through modeling important relationship skills. In longitudinal research, parents' approach to marital conflict resolution predicted teenagers' conflict resolution with friends 1 year later and with romantic partners up to 7 years later (Miga, Gdula, & Allen, 2012). Impressively, parents' marital conflict-resolution strategies also forecast qualities of young people's interactions with their own marital partners 17 years later (Whitton et al., 2008).

Perhaps because early adolescent romantic involvements are shallow and stereotyped, early dating is related to drug use, delinquency, and poor academic achievement (Miller et al., 2009). These factors, along with a history of uninvolved parenting and aggression in family and peer relationships, increase the likelihood of dating violence. About 10 to 20 percent of adolescents are physically or sexually abused by dating partners; boys and girls are equally likely to report being victims, and violence by one partner is often returned by the other (Narayan, Englund, & Egeland, 2013; Narayan et al., 2014). Mental health consequences are severe, including increased anxiety, depression, and suicide attempts in victims of both genders, plus antisocial behavior in boys and unhealthy weight control (vomiting and use of laxatives) in girls (Exner-Cortens, Eckenrode, & Rothman, 2012). Young teenagers are better off sticking with group activities, such as parties and dances, before becoming involved with a steady boyfriend or girlfriend.

Lesbian and gay youths face special challenges in initiating and maintaining visible romances. Recall from Chapter 11 that because of prejudice, sexual minority adolescents sometimes retreat into heterosexual dating. Although more are identifying their sexual orientation to others than in the past, many have difficulty finding a partner because their peers with same-sex romantic interests have not yet come out (Glover, Galliher, & Lamere, 2009). Similar to heterosexual youths, security of attachment to parents and friends predicts gratifying romantic ties among lesbian, gay, and bisexual adolescents (Starks, Newcomb, & Mustanski, 2015). And again, prediction from teenagers' attachments to parents is persistent, still evident in

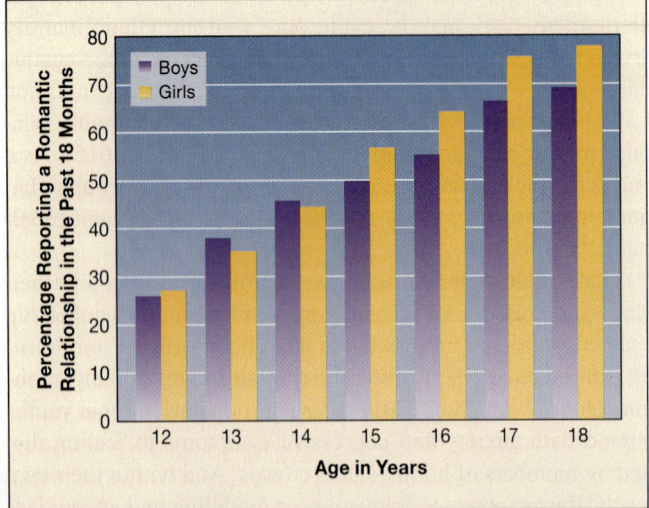

FIGURE 12.2 Increase in romantic relationships during adolescence. More than 16,000 U.S. youths responded to an interview in which they indicated whether they had been involved in a romantic relationship during the past 18 months. At age 12, about one-fourth of young people reported romantic involvement, a figure that rose to about three-fourths at age 18. (Based on Carver, Joyner, & Udry, 2003; Connolly & McIsaac, 2011.)

This young Native American couple has been dating for about a week. In addition to enhancing the quality of other peer relationships, close romantic ties promote sensitivity, empathy, self-esteem, social support, and identity progress.

sexual minority couples' romantic relationship satisfaction in early adulthood.

After high school graduation, many adolescent romances dissolve, and those that survive usually become less satisfying (Connolly & McIsaac, 2011). Because young people are still forming their identities, high school couples often find that they have little in common later. Nevertheless, among older teenagers, close romantic ties promote sensitivity, empathy, self-esteem, social support, and identity progress. In addition, teenagers' increasing capacity for caring and compromise with dating partners enhances the quality of other peer relationships (Collins, Welsh, & Furman, 2009). Thus, as long as dating leads to warm, supportive romantic bonds, it fosters adjustment and provides beneficial lessons in relating to people generally.

Ask yourself

CONNECT Discuss the many links between adolescents' parental and peer relationships.

APPLY Thirteen-year-old Mattie's parents are warm, firm in their expectations, and consistent in monitoring her activities. At school, Mattie met some girls who want her to tell her parents she's going to a friend's house and then, instead, join them at the beach for a party. Is Mattie likely to comply? Explain.

REFLECT What factors likely influenced your crowd membership in high school? How did crowd membership influence your values and behavior?

 # Problems of Development

12.8 Describe factors related to adolescent depression and suicide.
12.9 Discuss factors related to delinquency.

Most young people move through adolescence with little disturbance. But as we have seen, some encounter major disruptions in development, such as early parenthood, substance abuse, and school failure. In each instance, biological and psychological changes, families, schools, peers, communities, and culture combine to yield particular outcomes. Serious difficulties rarely occur in isolation but are usually interrelated—as is apparent in three additional problems of the teenage years: depression, suicide, and delinquency.

Depression

Depression—feeling sad, frustrated, and hopeless about life, accompanied by loss of pleasure in most activities and disturbances in sleep, appetite, concentration, and energy—is the most common psychological problem of adolescence. Among U.S. teenagers, 20 to 50 percent experience mild to moderate feelings of depression, bouncing back after a short time. More worrisome are the 15 to 20 percent who have had one or more major depressive episodes, a rate comparable to that of adults. About 5 percent are chronically depressed—gloomy and self-critical for many months and sometimes years (American Psychiatric Association, 2013; Tharpar et al., 2012).

Serious depression affects only 1 to 2 percent of children, who are far less likely than their adolescent counterparts to remain depressed when reassessed at older ages, including into adulthood (Carballo et al., 2011). In industrialized nations, depression increases sharply from ages 12 to 16. Teenage girls are twice as likely as boys to report persistent depressed mood—a difference sustained throughout the lifespan (Hyde, Mezulis, & Abramson, 2008).

If allowed to continue, depression seriously impairs social, academic, and vocational functioning. Unfortunately, the stereotypical view of adolescence as a period of storm and stress leads many adults to minimize the seriousness of adolescent depression, misinterpreting the despondency and irritability that accompany it as just a passing phase. As a result, the overwhelming majority of depressed teenagers do not receive treatment.

Factors Related to Adolescent Depression. The precise combination of biological and environmental factors leading to depression varies from one individual to the next. Twin studies indicate that depression is moderately heritable. Furthermore, the onset of depression in girls is more closely associated with the hormonal changes of puberty than with age (Angold et al., 1999). This suggests that the impact of estrogens on the adolescent brain is involved.

But pubertal hormone changes alone rarely trigger depression. Rather, genetic and hormonal risk factors seem to sensitize

Depression in adolescence is often misinterpreted as just a passing phase. As a result, the overwhelming majority of depressed teenagers do not receive treatment.

the brain to react more strongly to stressful experiences (Natsuaki, Samuels, & Leve, 2014). In support of this view, mounting evidence indicates that the short 5-HTTLPR gene, which increases the likelihood of self-regulation difficulties (see page 194 in Chapter 6), is linked to adolescent depression, but only in the presence of negative life stressors (Karg et al., 2011; Li, Berk, & Lee, 2013). This gene–environment interaction operates more consistently in adolescent girls than in boys.

Although depression runs in families, recall from earlier chapters that depressed or otherwise stressed parents often engage in maladaptive parenting. As a result, their child's attachment, emotional self-regulation, and self-esteem may be impaired, with serious consequences for cognitive and social skills (Yap, Allen, & Ladouceur, 2008). Depressed youths usually display a learned-helpless attributional style (see Chapter 10) (Graber, 2004). In a vulnerable young person, numerous negative life events may spark depression—for example, failing at something important, parental divorce, the end of a close friendship or romantic partnership, victimization through bullying, or other abusive experiences.

Gender Differences. Why are girls more prone to depression than boys? Besides greater stress reactivity, girls' gender-typed coping styles—passivity, dependency, and tendency to ruminate on anxieties and problems—seem to be involved. In line with this explanation, adolescents who identify strongly with "feminine" traits ruminate more and tend to be more depressed, regardless of their sex (Lopez, Driscoll, & Kistner, 2009; Papadakis et al., 2006). In contrast, girls with either an androgynous or a "masculine" gender identity show low rates of depressive symptoms (Priess, Lindberg, & Hyde, 2009).

Having friends with depressive symptoms is linked to a rise in teenagers' own depressive symptoms, perhaps because corumination is high in such relationships (Conway et al., 2011). Girls who repeatedly feel overwhelmed by life challenges become even more physiologically reactive to stress and cope increasingly poorly (Hyde, Mezulis, & Abramson, 2008; Natsuaki, Samuels, & Leve, 2014). In this way, stressful experiences and stress reactivity feed on each other, sustaining depression.

Profound depression in adolescence predicts depression in adulthood and serious impairments in work, family life, and social life. And depression can lead to suicidal thoughts, which all too often are translated into action.

Suicide

The U.S. suicide rate increases from childhood into middle adulthood, but it jumps sharply at adolescence. Currently, suicide is the third-leading cause of death among American youths, after motor vehicle collisions and homicides. Perhaps because U.S. teenagers experience more stress and fewer supports than in the past, the adolescent suicide rate tripled between the mid-1960s and mid-1990s. This was followed by a period of little change and, from the mid-2000s on, a slight increase (Centers for Disease Control and Prevention, 2015k, 2016d). At the same time, rates of adolescent suicide vary widely among industrialized nations—low in Greece, Italy, and Spain; intermediate in Australia, Canada, Japan, and the United States; and high in Finland, Ireland, New Zealand, Norway, and Russia (Patton et al., 2012; Värnik et al., 2012). These international differences remain unexplained.

Factors Related to Adolescent Suicide. Despite girls' higher rates of depression, the number of boys who kill themselves exceeds the number of girls by a ratio of over 4 to 1. Boys have more risk factors for suicide, including substance abuse and aggression. Also, girls make more unsuccessful suicide attempts and use methods from which they are more likely to be revived, such as a sleeping pill overdose. In contrast, boys more often choose techniques that lead to instant death, such as firearms or hanging (Esposito-Smythers et al., 2014). Gender-role expectations may contribute; less tolerance exists for feelings of helplessness and failed efforts in males than in females.

Perhaps because of greater support from extended families, African Americans, Asian Americans, and Hispanics have slightly lower suicide rates than European Americans. Recently, however, suicide has risen among African-American adolescent boys; the current rate approaches that of European-American boys. And Native-American youths commit suicide at rates two to six times national averages (Centers for Disease Control and Prevention, 2015k). High rates of profound family poverty, school failure, alcohol and drug abuse, and depression probably underlie these trends.

Lesbian, gay, bisexual, and transgender youths also are at high risk, attempting suicide three times as often as other adolescents. Those who have tried to kill themselves report more family conflict, problems in romantic relationships, and peer victimization (Liu & Mustanski, 2012).

Suicide tends to occur in two types of young people. The first group includes adolescents who are highly intelligent but solitary, withdrawn, and unable to meet their own standards or those of important people in their lives. Members of a second, larger group show antisocial tendencies and express their unhappiness through bullying, fighting, stealing, increased risk taking, and drug abuse (Spirito et al., 2012). Besides being hostile and destructive toward others, they turn their anger and disappointment inward.

Suicidal adolescents often have a family history of emotional and antisocial disorders and suicide, and they typically suffer from chronic depression, anxiety, and unresolved anger. In addition, they are likely to have experienced multiple stressful life events, including economic disadvantage, parental divorce, frequent parent–child conflict, and abuse and neglect. Stressors typically increase during the period preceding a suicide attempt or completion (Kaminski et al., 2010). Triggering events include parental blaming of the teenager for family problems, the breakup of an important peer relationship, or the humiliation of having been caught engaging in antisocial acts.

Public policies resulting in cultural disintegration have amplified suicide rates among Native-American youths. From the late 1800s to the 1970s, Native-American families were forced to enroll their children in government-run residential boarding schools designed to erase tribal affiliations. In these repressive institutions, children were not allowed to "be Indian" in any way—culturally, linguistically, artistically, or spiritually (Goldston et al., 2008). The experience left many young people academically unprepared and emotionally scarred, contributing to family and community disorganization in current and succeeding generations (Barnes, Josefowitz, & Cole, 2006; Howell & Yuille, 2004). Consequently, alcohol abuse, youth crime, and suicide rates escalated.

Why does suicide increase in adolescence? In addition to the rise in depressed mood, teenagers' improved ability to plan ahead is a major factor. Although some act impulsively, many young people take purposeful steps toward killing themselves. Other cognitive changes also contribute. Belief in the personal fable (see Chapter 11) leads many depressed young people to conclude that no one could possibly understand their intense pain. As a result, despair, hopelessness, and isolation deepen.

Prevention and Treatment. To prevent suicides, parents and teachers must be trained to pick up on the signals that a troubled teenager sends (see Table 12.2). Schools and community settings, such as recreational and religious organizations, can help by strengthening adolescents' connections with their cultural heritage and providing knowledgeable, approachable, and sympathetic adults, peer support groups, and information about telephone hot lines (Miller, 2011; Spirito et al., 2012). Once a teenager takes steps toward suicide, staying with the young person, listening, and expressing compassion and concern until professional help can be obtained are essential.

Treatments for depressed and suicidal adolescents range from antidepressant medication to individual, family, and group therapy. Until the adolescent improves, removing weapons, knives, razors, scissors, and drugs from the home is vital. On a broader scale, gun-control legislation that limits adolescents' access to the most frequent and deadly suicide method in the

TABLE 12.2
Warning Signs of Suicide

Efforts to put personal affairs in order—smoothing over troubled relationships, giving away treasured possessions
Verbal cues—saying goodbye to family members and friends, making direct or indirect references to suicide ("I won't have to worry about these problems much longer"; "I wish I were dead")
Feelings of sadness, despondency, "not caring" anymore
Extreme fatigue, lack of energy, boredom
No desire to socialize; withdrawal from friends and family
Easily frustrated
Volatile mood swings—spells of crying or laughing, angry outbursts
Inability to concentrate, distractibility
Decline in grades, absence from school, discipline problems
Neglect of personal appearance
Sleep change—loss of sleep or excessive sleepiness
Obtaining a weapon or other means of self-harm, such as prescription medications

United States would greatly reduce both the number of suicides and the high teenage homicide rate (Lewiecki & Miller, 2013).

After a suicide, family and peer survivors need support to help them cope with grief, anger, and guilt over not having been able to help the victim. Teenage suicides often occur in clusters, with one death increasing the likelihood of others among depressed peers who knew the young person or heard about the suicide through the media (Feigelman & Gorman, 2008). In view of this trend, an especially watchful eye must be kept on vulnerable adolescents after a suicide happens. Restraint by journalists in publicizing teenage suicides also aids prevention.

Delinquency

Juvenile delinquents are children or adolescents who engage in illegal acts. Since the mid-1990s, youth crime has declined sharply in the United States. Currently, 12- to 17-year-olds account for about 9 percent of police arrests, one-third less than two decades ago (U.S. Department of Justice, 2015). Yet when asked directly and confidentially about lawbreaking, almost all teenagers admit to having committed some sort of offense—usually a minor crime, such as petty stealing or disorderly conduct (Flannery et al., 2003).

Police arrests and self-reports show that delinquency rises over adolescence and then declines from the early twenties on—a trend found in many Western countries (Eisner & Malti, 2015). Recall that antisocial behavior increases among teenagers as a result of heightened reward seeking and desire for peer approval. Over time, peers become less influential; decision

Delinquency rises over adolescence and then declines. Teenagers commit more crimes in poverty-stricken neighborhoods where they have easy access to drugs, firearms, and deviant peers.

making, emotional self-regulation, and moral reasoning improve; and young people enter social contexts (such as higher education, work, marriage, and career) that are less conducive to lawbreaking.

For most adolescents, a brush with the law does not forecast long-term antisocial behavior. But repeated arrests are cause for concern. Teenagers are responsible for 11 percent of violent offenses in the United States (U.S. Department of Justice, 2015). A small percentage become recurrent offenders, who commit most of these crimes, and some enter a life of crime. As the Biology and Environment box on the following page reveals, childhood-onset conduct problems are far more likely to persist than conduct problems that first appear in adolescence.

Factors Related to Delinquency. In adolescence, the gender gap in physical aggression widens. Although girls account for about one in five adolescent arrests for violence, their offenses are largely limited to simple assault (such as pushing and spitting). Serious violent crime is mostly the domain of boys (U.S. Department of Justice, 2015). SES and ethnicity are strong predictors of arrests but only mildly related to teenagers' self-reports of antisocial acts. The difference is due to the tendency to arrest, charge, and punish low-SES ethnic minority youths more often than their higher-SES white and Asian counterparts (Farrington, 2009; Hunt, 2015).

Difficult temperament, low intelligence, poor school performance, peer rejection in childhood, and association with antisocial peers are linked to chronic delinquency (Laird et al., 2005). How do these factors fit together? One of the most consistent findings is that delinquent youths, regardless of ethnicity

and SES, experience parenting that is low in warmth, high in conflict, and characterized by harsh, inconsistent discipline and weak control and monitoring (Deutsch et al., 2012; Harris-McKoy & Cui, 2013). Because marital transitions often contribute to family discord and disrupted parenting, boys who experience parental separation and divorce are especially prone to delinquency (Farrington, 2009). And youth crime peaks on weekdays between 2:00 and 8:00 P.M., when many teenagers are unsupervised (U.S. Department of Justice, 2015).

Our discussion on pages 273–274 in Chapter 8 explained how ineffective parenting can promote and sustain children's aggression, with boys—who are more active and impulsive—more often targets of parental anger, physical punishment, and inconsistency. When these child temperamental traits combine with emotionally negative, inept parenting, aggression rises sharply during childhood, leads to violent offenses in adolescence, and persists into adulthood (again, see the Biology and Environment box).

Teenagers commit more crimes in poverty-stricken neighborhoods with poor-quality schools, limited recreational and employment opportunities, and high adult criminality (Leventhal, Dupéré, & Brooks-Gunn, 2009). In such neighborhoods, adolescents have easy access to deviant peers, drugs, and firearms and are likely to be recruited into antisocial gangs, whose members commit the vast majority of violent delinquent acts. Schools in these locales typically fail to meet students' developmental needs (Chung, Mulvey, & Steinberg, 2011). Large classes, weak instruction, rigid rules, and reduced academic expectations and opportunities are associated with higher rates of lawbreaking, even after other influences are controlled.

Prevention and Treatment. Because delinquency has roots in childhood and results from events in several contexts, prevention must start early and take place at multiple levels (Frey et al., 2009). Positive family relationships, authoritative parenting, high-quality teaching in schools, and communities with healthy economic and social conditions go a long way toward reducing adolescent antisocial acts.

Lacking resources for effective prevention, many U.S. schools have implemented *zero tolerance policies,* which severely punish all disruptive and threatening behavior, major and minor, usually with suspension or expulsion. Yet often these policies are implemented inconsistently: Low-SES minority students are two to three times as likely to be punished, especially for minor misbehaviors. No evidence exists that zero tolerance achieves its objective of reducing youth aggression and other forms of misconduct (Reppucci, Meyer, & Kostelnik, 2011; Teske, 2011). To the contrary, some studies find that by excluding students from school, zero tolerance heightens high school dropout and antisocial behavior.

Treating serious offenders requires an intensive, often lengthy approach, also directed at the multiple determinants of delinquency. The most effective interventions include training parents in communication, monitoring, and discipline strategies and providing youths with experiences that improve cognitive and social skills, moral reasoning, anger management, and

Biology and Environment

Two Routes to Adolescent Delinquency

Persistent adolescent delinquency follows two paths of development, one involving a small number of youths with an onset of conduct problems in childhood, the second a larger number with an onset in adolescence. The early-onset type is far more likely to lead to a life-course pattern of aggression and criminality (Moffitt, 2007). The late-onset type usually does not persist beyond the transition to early adulthood.

Both childhood-onset and adolescent-onset youths engage in serious offenses; associate with deviant peers; participate in substance abuse, unsafe sex, and dangerous driving; and spend time in correctional facilities. Why does antisocial activity more often continue and escalate into violence in the first group?

Most research has focused on boys, but several investigations report that girls who were physically aggressive in childhood are also at risk for later problems—occasionally violent delinquency but more often other norm-violating behaviors and psychological disorders (Broidy et al., 2003; Chamberlain, 2003). Early relational aggression is linked to adolescent conduct problems as well.

Early-Onset Type

Early-onset youngsters usually inherit traits that predispose them to aggressiveness (Eisner & Malti, 2015). For example, violence-prone children (mostly boys) are emotionally negative, restless, willful, and physically aggressive as early as age 2. They also show subtle deficits in cognitive functioning that seem to contribute to disruptions in language, executive function, emotional self-regulation, and morally relevant emotions of empathy and guilt (Malti & Krettenauer, 2013; Moffitt, 2007; Reef et al., 2011). Some have attention-deficit hyperactivity disorder (ADHD), which compounds their learning and self-control problems.

Yet most early-onset boys decline in aggression over time. Among those who follow the life-course path, harsh parenting transforms their undercontrolled style into defiance and persistent aggression (Beyers et al., 2003). As they fail academically and are rejected by peers, they befriend other deviant youths, who facilitate one another's violent behavior while relieving loneliness (see Figure 12.3) (Dodge et al., 2008; Hughes, 2010). Limited cognitive and social skills result in high rates of school dropout and unemployment, contributing further to antisocial involvements.

Children high in relational aggression also tend to be hyperactive, subjected to harsh parenting, and frequently in conflict with peers and adults (Spieker et al., 2012; Willoughby, Kupersmidt, & Bryant, 2001). As these behaviors trigger peer rejection, relationally aggressive girls befriend other girls high in relational hostility, and their aggression rises (Werner & Crick, 2004). Adolescents high in relational aggression are often angry and defiant of adult rules. Among teenagers who combine physical and relational hostility, these oppositional reactions intensify, increasing the likelihood of serious antisocial activity (Harachi et al., 2006; McEachern & Snyder, 2012).

Late-Onset Type

Other youths first display antisocial behavior around the time of puberty, gradually increasing their involvement. Their conduct problems arise from the peer context of early adolescence. For some, quality of parenting may decline for a time, perhaps due to family stresses or the challenges of disciplining an unruly teenager (Moffitt, 2007). When age brings gratifying adult privileges, these youths draw on prosocial skills mastered before adolescence and abandon their antisocial ways.

A few late-onset youths do continue to engage in antisocial acts. The seriousness of their adolescent offenses seems to trap them in situations that close off opportunities for responsible behavior. Being employed or in school and forming positive, close relationships predict an end to criminal offending by age 20 to 25 (Farrington, Ttofi, & Coid, 2009). In contrast, the longer antisocial young people spend in prison, the more likely they are to sustain a life of crime.

These findings suggest a need for a fresh look at policies aimed at stopping youth crime. Keeping youth offenders locked up for many years disrupts their educational and vocational lives and access to positive, caring relationships with adults during a crucial period of development (Bernstein, 2014). In this way, juvenile incarceration condemns them to a bleak future.

FIGURE 12.3 **Path to chronic delinquency for adolescents with childhood-onset antisocial behavior.** Difficult temperament and cognitive deficits characterize many of these youths in early childhood; some have attention-deficit hyperactivity disorder. Inept parenting transforms biologically based self-control difficulties into hostility and defiance.

other aspects of emotional self-regulation (DiBiase et al., 2011; Heilbrun, Lee, & Cottle, 2005). Yet even these multidimensional treatments can fall short if young people remain embedded in hostile home lives, poor-quality schools, antisocial peer groups, and violent neighborhoods.

In a program called *multisystemic therapy,* counselors combined family intervention with integrating violent youths into positive school, work, and leisure activities and disengaging them from deviant peers. Compared with conventional services or individual therapy, random assignment to the intervention led to improved parent–adolescent relationships and school performance, a dramatic drop in number of arrests that persisted for two decades after treatment, and—when participants did commit crimes—a reduction in their severity (see Figure 12.4). Multisystemic therapy also helped limit family instability once youth offenders reached adulthood, as measured by involvement in civil suits over divorce, paternity, or child support (Henggeler et al., 2009; Sawyer & Borduin, 2011). Efforts to create nonaggressive environments—at the family, community, and cultural levels—are needed to help delinquent youths and to foster healthy development of all young people.

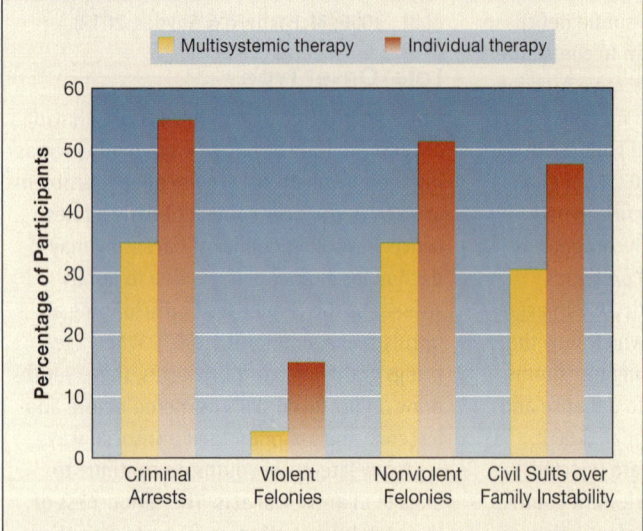

FIGURE 12.4 Impact of multisystemic therapy on arrests and family-related civil suits 22 years after treatment. A follow-up of violent youths two decades after treatment revealed that, compared to participants receiving individual therapy, those assigned to multisystemic therapy had fewer criminal arrests overall, and the crimes they did commit were far less violent. Multisystemic therapy recipients also displayed reduced family instability. (Based on Sawyer & Borduin, 2011.)

Ask yourself

CONNECT Why are adolescent girls at greater risk for depression and adolescent boys at greater risk for suicide?

APPLY Zeke had been well-behaved in elementary school, but at age 13 he started spending time with the "wrong crowd." At 16, he was arrested for property damage. Is Zeke likely to become a long-term offender? Why or why not?

REFLECT During adolescence, did you or your friends engage in any lawbreaking acts? If so, at what age? Were you motivated by a desire for excitement and/or peer approval?

Summary / chapter 12

Erikson's Theory: Identity versus Role Confusion (p. 408)

12.1 According to Erikson, what is the major personality attainment of adolescence?

- Erikson viewed **identity** as the major personality attainment of adolescence. Young people who successfully resolve the psychological conflict of **identity versus role confusion** construct a unified self-definition based on self-chosen values and goals.

Self-Understanding (p. 408)

12.2 Describe changes in self-concept and self-esteem during adolescence.

- Cognitive changes enable adolescents to develop more organized, consistent self-descriptions, with social, personal, and moral values as key themes.

- Self-esteem further differentiates and, for most adolescents, rises. Pubertal timing, academic performance, peer acceptance, parenting style, and the larger social environment all influence self-esteem.

12.3 Describe the four identity statuses, along with factors that promote identity development.

- **Identity achievement** (exploration followed by commitment to values, beliefs, and goals) and **identity moratorium** (exploration without having reached commitment) are psychologically healthy identity statuses. Long-term **identity foreclosure** (commitment without exploration) and **identity diffusion** (lack of both exploration and commitment) are related to adjustment difficulties.

- An information-gathering cognitive style, healthy parental attachment, interaction with diverse peers, close friendships, and schools and communities offering rich and varied opportunities promote healthy identity development. Supportive families and communities can foster a strong, secure **ethnic identity** among minority adolescents, who often must overcome **acculturative stress.** A **bicultural identity** offers additional emotional and social benefits.

Moral Development (p. 413)

12.4 Describe Kohlberg's theory of moral development, and evaluate its accuracy.

- At Kohlberg's **preconventional level,** morality is externally controlled and actions are judged by their consequences; at the **conventional level,** conformity to laws and rules is regarded as necessary for positive human relationships and societal order; and at the **postconventional level,** morality is defined by abstract, universal principles.

- A reexamination of Kohlberg's stages suggests that moral maturity can be found at Stages 3 and 4; few people attain the post-conventional level. Because situational factors influence moral judgments, Kohlberg's stages are best viewed as loosely organized and overlapping.
- Contrary to Gilligan's claim, Kohlberg's theory does not underestimate the moral maturity of females but instead taps both justice and caring orientations.
- Compared with children, teenagers display more subtle reasoning about conflicts between personal choice and community obligation and are increasingly aware of the moral implications of following social conventions.

12.5 *Describe influences on moral reasoning and its relationship to moral behavior.*

- Factors contributing to moral maturity include warm, rational parenting, peer discussions of moral issues, and school environments with nondiscrimination policies. In village societies, where moral cooperation is based on direct relations between people, moral reasoning rarely moves beyond Kohlberg's Stage 3. In both village cultures and industrialized societies that value interdependence, moral dilemma responses are more other-directed than in Western societies.

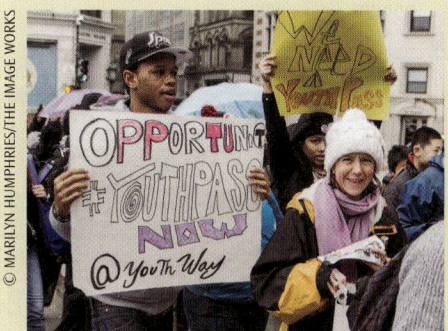

- Maturity of moral reasoning is only modestly related to moral behavior. Moral behavior is also influenced by empathy and guilt, temperament, cultural experiences, and **moral identity.** Although formal religious involvement declines in adolescence, most religiously affiliated teenagers are advantaged in moral values and behavior.

- Researchers favoring a pragmatic approach to morality assert that moral maturity varies depending on context and motivations.

The Family (p. 420)

12.6 *Discuss changes in parent–child and sibling relationships during adolescence.*

- In their quest for **autonomy,** adolescents rely more on themselves and less on parents for decision making. As teenagers deidealize their parents, they often question parental authority. Warm, supportive parenting that balances connection and separation, makes appropriate demands for maturity, and provides consistent monitoring predicts favorable outcomes.
- Sibling influence declines as adolescents separate from the family and turn toward peers. Still, attachment to siblings remains strong for most young people.

Peer Relations (p. 422)

12.7 *Describe adolescent friendships, peer groups, and dating relationships and their consequences for development.*

- Adolescent friendships are based on intimacy, mutual understanding, and loyalty and contain more self-disclosure. Girls place greater emphasis on emotional closeness, boys on shared activities and accomplishments.
- Though online interaction can augment friendship, it also poses risks. Very high social media use is linked to unsatisfying face-to-face social experiences, and excessive Internet use amplifies adjustment difficulties.
- Adolescent friendships—when not characterized by relational aggression or attraction to antisocial behavior—promote self-concept, perspective taking, identity, and the capacity for intimate relationships. They also help young people deal with stress and can foster improved attitudes toward and involvement in school.
- Adolescent peer groups are organized into **cliques,** particularly important to girls, and **crowds,** which grant teenagers an identity within the larger social structure of the school. With interest in dating, mixed-sex cliques increase in importance. Both cliques and crowds diminish as teenagers settle on personal values and goals.

- Intimacy in dating relationships lags behind that between friends. Positive relationships with parents and friends contribute to secure romantic ties.

Problems of Development (p. 427)

12.8 *Describe factors related to adolescent depression and suicide.*

- Depression is the most common psychological problem of adolescence, with girls at greater risk in industrialized nations. Combinations of biological and environmental factors are implicated, including heredity, maladaptive parenting, a learned-helpless attributional style, and negative life events.
- The suicide rate increases sharply at adolescence. Although teenage girls make more unsuccessful suicide attempts, boys account for more deaths. Teenagers at risk for suicide may be withdrawn but more often are antisocial. Family turmoil is common in the backgrounds of suicidal adolescents.

12.9 *Discuss factors related to delinquency.*

- Delinquency rises over adolescence and then declines. But only a few teenagers are serious repeat offenders—usually boys with a childhood history of conduct problems.
- A family environment low in warmth, high in conflict, and characterized by inconsistent discipline and low monitoring is consistently related to delinquency, as are poverty-stricken neighborhoods with high crime rates and ineffective schools.

Important Terms and Concepts

acculturative stress (p. 412)
autonomy (p. 420)
bicultural identity (p. 412)
clique (p. 425)
conventional level (p. 414)
crowd (p. 425)

ethnic identity (p. 412)
identity (p. 408)
identity achievement (p. 409)
identity diffusion (p. 409)
identity foreclosure (p. 409)
identity moratorium (p. 409)

identity versus role confusion (p. 408)
moral identity (p. 418)
postconventional level (p. 415)
preconventional level (p. 414)

milestones
Development in Adolescence

EARLY ADOLESCENCE: 11–14

Physical

- If a girl, reaches peak of growth spurt. (369)
- If a girl, adds more body fat than muscle. (369)
- If a girl, starts to menstruate. (371–372)
- If a boy, begins growth spurt. (369)
- If a boy, starts to ejaculate seminal fluid. (372)
- If a sexual minority, awareness of sexual orientation emerges. (382)
- If a girl, motor performance increases gradually, leveling off by age 14. (370)
- Reacts more strongly to stressful events; shows heightened sensation-seeking and risk-taking behavior. (373–374)
- Sleep "phase delay" strengthens. (374)

Cognitive

- Gains in hypothetico-deductive reasoning and propositional thought. (389–390)
- Gains in scientific reasoning—coordinating theory with evidence—on complex, multivariable tasks. (391)

- Becomes more self-conscious and self-focused. (392–393)
- Becomes more idealistic and critical. (393)
- Improves in executive function, metacognition, and cognitive self-regulation. (373–374, 390–392)

Emotional/Social

- Self-concept includes abstract descriptors unifying separate personality traits, but these are not interconnected and are often contradictory. (408)
- Moodiness and parent–child conflict tend to increase. (375–376, 420–421)
- In striving for autonomy, spends less time with parents and siblings and more time with peers. (422)

- Friendships decline in number and are based on intimacy, mutual understanding, and loyalty. (422–423)
- Peer groups become organized into same-sex cliques. (425)
- In high schools with complex social structures, cliques with similar values form crowds. (425)

MIDDLE ADOLESCENCE: 14–16

Physical

- If a girl, completes growth spurt. (369)
- If a boy, reaches peak of growth spurt. (369)
- If a boy, voice deepens. (372)
- If a boy, adds muscle while body fat declines. (369)
- If a boy, motor performance improves dramatically. (370)
- May be sexually active. (380–381)
- If a sexual minority boy, is likely certain of sexual orientation. (382)

Cognitive

- Continues to improve in hypothetico-deductive reasoning and propositional thought. (389–390)

- Continues to improve in executive function, metacognition, and cognitive self-regulation (373–374, 390–392).
- Continues to improve in scientific reasoning, following a similar sequence of mastery on different types of tasks. (391–392)
- Becomes less self-conscious and self-focused. (386–387)
- Improves in decision making. (393–394)

Note: Numbers in parentheses indicate the page or pages on which each milestone is discussed.

Emotional/Social

- Combines features of the self into an organized self-concept. (408)
- Self-esteem differentiates further and tends to rise. (408–409)
- In many cases, begins to move from lower to higher identity statuses. (409–410)
- Increasingly emphasizes ideal reciprocity and societal laws as the basis for resolving moral dilemmas. (414–415)

- Engages in more subtle reasoning about conflicts between moral, social-conventional, and personal-choice issues. (416)
- Mixed-sex cliques become common. (425–426)
- Has probably started dating. (426)

LATE ADOLESCENCE: 16–18

Physical

- If a boy, completes growth spurt. (369)
- If a boy, gains in motor performance continue. (370)

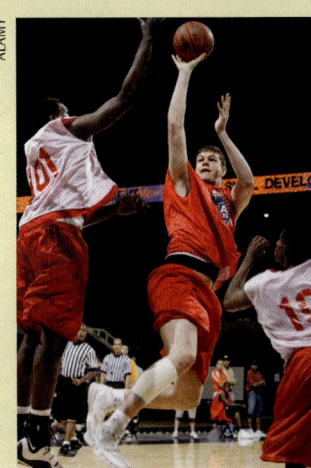

- If a sexual minority girl, is likely certain of sexual orientation. (382)

Cognitive

- Continues to improve in executive function, metacognition, cognitive self-regulation, and scientific reasoning. (373–374, 390–392)
- Improves in decision making. (393–394)

Emotional/Social

- Self-concept emphasizes personal and moral values. (408)
- Continues to construct an identity, typically moving to higher identity statuses. (409–410)
- Continues to advance in maturity of moral reasoning; motivation to act morally increases. (414–415, 418)
- Cliques and crowds decline in importance. (426)
- Seeks psychological intimacy in romantic ties, which last longer. (426–427)

Note: Numbers in parentheses indicate the page or pages on which each milestone is discussed.

chapter 13

Physical and Cognitive Development in Early Adulthood

Early adulthood brings momentous changes—among them, choosing a vocation, starting full-time work, and attaining economic independence. This Dutch computer game designer and animator works in a field that combines an interest in gaming with artistic abilities.

What's ahead in chapter 13

PHYSICAL DEVELOPMENT

Biological Aging Is Under Way in Early Adulthood
Aging at the Level of DNA and Body Cells • Aging at the Level of Tissues and Organs

■ **BIOLOGY AND ENVIRONMENT** Telomere Length: A Marker of the Impact of Life Circumstances on Biological Aging

Physical Changes
Cardiovascular and Respiratory Systems • Motor Performance • Immune System • Reproductive Capacity

Health and Fitness
Nutrition • Exercise • Substance Abuse • Sexuality • Psychological Stress

COGNITIVE DEVELOPMENT

Changes in the Structure of Thought
Epistemic Cognition • Pragmatic Thought and Cognitive-Affective Complexity

Expertise and Creativity

The College Experience
Psychological Impact of Attending College • Dropping Out

■ **SOCIAL ISSUES: EDUCATION** How Important Is Academic Engagement in College for Successful Transition to the Labor Market?

Vocational Choice
Selecting a Vocation • Factors Influencing Vocational Choice • Vocational Preparation of Non-College-Bound Young Adults

■ **CULTURAL INFLUENCES** Masculinity at Work: Men Who Choose Nontraditional Careers

---

The back seat and trunk piled high with belongings, 23-year-old Sharese hugged her mother and brother goodbye, jumped in the car, and headed toward the interstate with a sense of newfound freedom mixed with apprehension. Three months earlier, the family had watched proudly as Sharese received her bachelor's degree in chemistry from a small university 40 miles from her home. Her college years had been a time of gradual release from economic and psychological dependency on her family. She returned home periodically on weekends and lived there during the summer months. Her mother supplemented Sharese's loans with a monthly allowance. But this day marked a turning point. She was moving to her own apartment in a city 800 miles away, with plans to work on a master's degree. With a teaching assistantship and a student loan, Sharese felt more "on her own" than at any previous time in her life.

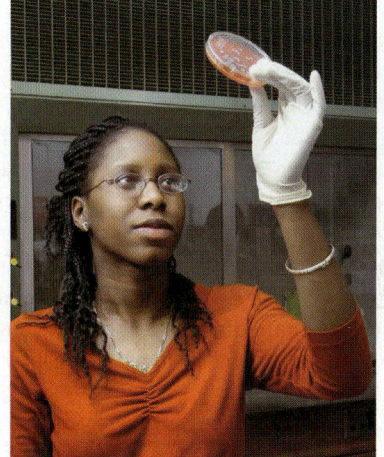

During her college years, Sharese made lifestyle changes and settled on a vocational direction. Overweight throughout high school, she lost 20 pounds in her sophomore year, revised her diet, and began an exercise regimen by joining the university's Ultimate Frisbee team, eventually becoming its captain. A summer spent as a counselor at a camp for chronically ill children helped convince Sharese to apply her background in science to a career in public health.

Still, two weeks before she was to leave, Sharese confided in her mother that she had doubts about her decision. "Sharese," her mother advised, "we never know if our life choices are going to suit us just right, and most times they aren't perfect. It's what we make of them—how we view and mold them—that turns them into successes." So Sharese embarked on her journey and found herself face-to-face with a multitude of exciting challenges and opportunities.

In this chapter, we take up the physical and cognitive sides of early adulthood, which extends from ages 18 to 40. As noted in Chapter 1, the adult years are difficult to divide into discrete periods because the timing of important milestones varies greatly among individuals—much more so than in childhood and adolescence. But for most people, early adulthood involves a common set of tasks: leaving home, completing education, beginning full-time work, attaining economic independence, establishing a long-term sexually and emotionally intimate relationship, and starting a family. These are energetic decades filled with momentous decisions that, more than any other time of life, offer the potential for living to the fullest. ●

PHYSICAL DEVELOPMENT

Throughout childhood and adolescence, the body grows larger and stronger, coordination improves, and sensory systems gather information more effectively. Once body structures reach maximum capacity and efficiency, **biological aging,** or **senescence,** begins—genetically influenced declines in the functioning of organs and systems that are universal in all members of our species. Like physical growth, however, biological aging varies widely across parts of the body, and individual differences are great—variation that the *lifespan perspective* helps us understand. A host of contextual factors—including each person's genetic makeup, lifestyle, living environment, and historical period—can accelerate or slow age-related declines (Arking, 2006). As a result, the physical changes of the adult years are, indeed, *multidimensional* and *multidirectional* (see page 8 in Chapter 1).

In the following sections, we examine the process of biological aging. Then we turn to physical and motor changes already under way in early adulthood. As you will see, biological aging can be modified substantially through behavioral and environmental interventions. During the twentieth century, improved nutrition, medical treatment, sanitation, and safety added 25 to 30 years to *average life expectancy* in industrialized nations, a trend that is continuing (see Chapter 1, page 7). We will take up life expectancy in greater depth in Chapter 17.

Biological Aging Is Under Way in Early Adulthood

13.1 Describe current theories of biological aging, both at the level of DNA and body cells and at the level of tissues and organs.

At an intercollegiate tournament, Sharese dashed across the playing field, leaping high to catch Frisbees sailing her way. In her early twenties, she is at her peak in strength, endurance, sensory acuteness, and immune system responsiveness. Yet over the next two decades, she will age and, as she moves into middle and late adulthood, will show more noticeable declines. Biological aging is the combined result of many causes, some operating at the level of DNA, others at the level of cells, and still others at the level of tissues, organs, and the whole organism. Despite hundreds of theories and the efforts of many researchers, our understanding of the mechanisms of biological aging is incomplete.

Aging at the Level of DNA and Body Cells

Current explanations of biological aging at the level of DNA and body cells are of two types: (1) those that emphasize the *programmed effects of specific genes* and (2) those that emphasize the *cumulative effects of random events* that damage genetic and cellular material. Support for both views exists, and a combination may eventually prove to be correct.

This whitewater kayaker, in his early twenties, is at his peak in strength, endurance, and sensory acuteness.

Genetically programmed aging receives some support from kinship studies indicating that longevity is a family trait. People whose parents had long lives tend to live longer themselves. And greater similarity exists in the lifespans of identical than fraternal twins. But the heritability of longevity is low to moderate, ranging from .15 to .50 for age at death and from .15 to .55 for various measures of current biological age, such as hand-grip muscle strength, respiratory capacity, blood pressure, bone density, and overall physical health (Dutta et al., 2011; Finkel et al., 2014). Rather than inheriting longevity directly, people probably inherit risk and protective factors, which influence their chances of dying earlier or later.

One "genetic programming" theory proposes the existence of "aging genes" that control biological changes, such as menopause, efficiency of gross motor skills, and deterioration of body cells. The strongest evidence for this view comes from research showing that human cells allowed to divide in the laboratory have a lifespan of 50 divisions, plus or minus 10 (Hayflick, 1998). With each duplication, a special type of DNA called **telomeres**—located at the ends of chromosomes, serving as a

A young adult takes a selfie with her 85-year-old grandmother. Longevity tends to run in families, though people probably inherit risk and protective factors rather than length of life directly.

Biology and Environment

Telomere Length: A Marker of the Impact of Life Circumstances on Biological Aging

In the not-too-distant future, your annual physical exam may include an assessment of the length of your *telomeres*—DNA at the ends of chromosomes—which safeguard the stability of your cells. Telomeres shorten with each cell duplication; when they drop below a critical length, the cell can no longer divide and becomes senescent (see Figure 13.1). Although telomeres shorten with age, the rate at which they do so varies greatly. An enzyme called *telomerase* prevents shortening and can even reverse the trend, lengthening telomeres and protecting the aging cell.

Over the past decade, research examining the influence of life circumstances on telomere length has exploded. A well-established finding is that chronic illnesses, such as cardiovascular disease and cancer, hasten telomere shortening in white blood cells, which play a vital role in the immune response (see page 443) (Corbett & Alda, 2015). Telomere shortening, in turn, predicts more rapid disease progression and earlier death.

Accelerated telomere shortening has been linked to a variety of unhealthy behaviors, including cigarette smoking, excessive alcohol use, and the physical inactivity and overeating that lead to obesity and to insulin resistance, which often precedes type 2 diabetes (Epel et al., 2006; Ludlow, Ludlow, & Roth, 2013). Unfavorable health conditions may alter telomere length as early as the prenatal period, with possible long-term negative consequences for biological aging. In research on rats, poor maternal nutrition during pregnancy resulted in low birth weight and development of shorter telomeres in kidney and heart tissue (Tarry-Adkins et al., 2008). In related human investigations, children and adolescents who had been low-birth-weight had shorter telomeres in their white blood cells than did their normal-birth-weight agemates (Raqib et al., 2007; Strohmaier et al., 2015).

Persistent emotional stress—in childhood, abuse, bullying, or exposure to family violence; in adulthood, parenting a child with a chronic illness, caring for an older adult with dementia, or experiences of racial discrimination or violence—is linked to telomere shortness in white blood cells and swabbed cheek cells (Chae et al., 2014; Drury et al., 2014; Price et al., 2013; Shalev et al., 2013). In other research, maternal severe emotional stress during pregnancy predicted shortened telomere length in children's white blood cells at birth and in follow-ups in early adulthood, even after other possible contributing factors (such as low birth weight and childhood and adult stress levels) were controlled (Entringer et al., 2011, 2012).

Fortunately, when adults make positive lifestyle changes, telomeres respond accordingly. Healthy eating behaviors; physical activity that increases fitness; reduced alcohol intake and cigarette smoking; and a decline in emotional stress are all associated with gains in telomerase activity and longer telomeres (Lin, Epel, & Blackburn, 2012; Shalev et al., 2013).

Currently, researchers are working on identifying sensitive periods of telomere change—times when telomeres are most susceptible to modification. Early intervention—for example, enhanced prenatal care and treatments aimed at reducing childhood obesity and exposure to stressors—may be particularly powerful. But telomeres are changeable through intervention well into late adulthood (Epel et al., 2009; Price et al., 2013). As our understanding of predictors and consequences of telomere length expands, it may become an important index of health and aging throughout life.

FIGURE 13.1 Telomeres at the ends of chromosomes. (a) Telomeres in a newly created cell. (b) With each cell duplication, telomeres shorten; when too short, they expose DNA to damage, and the cell dies.

"cap" to protect the ends from destruction—shortens. Eventually, so little remains that the cells no longer duplicate at all. Telomere shortening acts as a brake against somatic mutations (such as those involved in cancer), which become more likely as cells duplicate. But an increase in the number of senescent cells (ones with short telomeres) also contributes to age-related disease, loss of function, and earlier mortality (Epel et al., 2009; Tchkonia et al., 2013). As the Biology and Environment box above reveals, researchers have begun to identify health behaviors and psychological states that accelerate telomere shortening—powerful biological evidence that certain life circumstances compromise longevity.

According to an alternative, "random events" theory, DNA in body cells is gradually damaged through spontaneous or externally caused mutations. As these accumulate, cell repair and replacement become less efficient, and abnormal cancerous cells are often produced. Animal studies confirm an increase in DNA breaks and deletions and damage to other cellular material with age. Similar evidence is accruing for humans (Freitas & Magalhães, 2011).

One hypothesized cause of age-related DNA and cellular abnormalities is the release of **free radicals**—naturally occurring, highly reactive chemicals that form in the presence of oxygen. When oxygen molecules break down within the cell, the reaction strips away an electron, creating a free radical. As it seeks a replacement from its surroundings, it destroys nearby cellular material, including DNA, proteins, and fats essential for cell functioning, thereby increasing the individual's vulnerability to wide-ranging disorders of aging, including cardiovascular disease, neurological impairments, cancer, cataracts, and arthritis (Stohs, 2011). Genes for longevity, some researchers have speculated, might work by defending against free radicals.

But mounting evidence indicates that free radicals are not a major contributor to DNA mutations, cellular damage, and reduced longevity. To the contrary, in some species, elevated free-radical activity—as long as it does not reach toxic levels—is associated with longer life, likely because it serves as a "stress signal" that activates DNA repair systems within cells (Shokolenko, Wilson, & Alexeyev, 2014). These findings may explain why antioxidant dietary supplements, such as vitamin A, beta-carotene, and vitamin E, have consistently failed to reduce the incidence of disease or extend length of life (Bjelakovic, Nikolova, & Gluud, 2013).

Furthermore, scientists have identified certain species with reduced genetic defenses against free-radical activity but with exceptional longevity (Liu, Long, & Liu, 2014). The naked mole rat, the longest-living rodent, has a lifespan of up to 31 years, despite displaying greater age-related DNA damage in some of its organs than seen in the ordinary mouse, which lives no more than 4 years.

In sum, although free-radical damage increases with age, no clear evidence indicates that it triggers biological aging. Rather, it may at times contribute to longevity.

Aging at the Level of Tissues and Organs

What consequences might age-related DNA and cellular deterioration have for the overall structure and functioning of organs and tissues? There are many possibilities. Among those with clear support is the **cross-linkage theory of aging**. Over time, protein fibers that make up the body's connective tissue form bonds, or links, with one another. When these normally separate fibers cross-link, tissue becomes less elastic, leading to many negative outcomes, including loss of flexibility in the skin and other organs, clouding of the lens of the eye, clogging of arteries, and damage to the kidneys (Diggs, 2008; Kragstrup, Kjaer, & Mackey, 2011). Like other aspects of aging, cross-linking can be reduced by external factors, including regular exercise and a healthy diet.

Gradual failure of the endocrine system, which produces and regulates hormones, is yet another route to aging. An obvious example is decreased estrogen production in women, which culminates in menopause. Because hormones affect many body functions, disruptions in the endocrine system can have widespread effects on health and survival. For example, a gradual drop in growth hormone (GH) is associated with loss of muscle and bone mass, addition of body fat, thinning of the skin, and decline in cardiovascular functioning. In adults with abnormally low levels of GH, hormone therapy can slow these symptoms, but it has serious side effects, including increased risk of fluid retention in tissues, muscle pain, and cancer (Ceda et al., 2010; Sattler, 2013). So far, diet and physical activity are safer ways to limit these aspects of biological aging.

Finally, declines in immune system functioning contribute to many conditions of aging, including increased susceptibility to infectious disease and cancer, changes in blood vessel walls associated with cardiovascular disease, and chronic inflammation of body tissues, which leads to tissue damage and plays a role in many diseases. Decreased vigor of the immune response seems to be genetically programmed, but other aging processes we have considered (such as weakening of the endocrine system) can intensify it (Alonso-Fernández & De la Fuente, 2011; Franceschi & Campisi, 2014). Indeed, combinations of theories—the ones just reviewed as well as others—are needed to explain the complexities of biological aging. With this in mind, let's turn to physical signs and other characteristics of aging.

Physical Changes

13.2 Describe the physical changes of aging, paying special attention to the cardiovascular and respiratory systems, motor performance, the immune system, and reproductive capacity.

During the twenties and thirties, changes in physical appearance and declines in body functioning are so gradual that most are hardly noticeable. Later, they will accelerate. The physical changes of aging are summarized in Table 13.1. We will examine several here and take up others in later chapters. Before we begin, let's note that these trends are derived largely from cross-sectional studies. Because younger cohorts have experienced better health care and nutrition, cross-sectional evidence can exaggerate impairments associated with aging. Fortunately, longitudinal evidence is expanding, helping to correct this picture.

Cardiovascular and Respiratory Systems

During her first month in graduate school, Sharese pored over research articles on cardiovascular functioning. In her African-American extended family, her father, an uncle, and three aunts had died of heart attacks in their forties and fifties. These

TABLE 13.1
Physical Changes of Aging

ORGAN OR SYSTEM	TIMING OF CHANGE	DESCRIPTION
Sensory		
Vision	From age 30	As the lens stiffens and thickens, ability to focus on close objects declines. Yellowing of the lens, weakening of muscles controlling the pupil, and clouding of the vitreous (gelatin-like substance that fills the eye) reduce light reaching the retina, impairing color discrimination and night vision. Visual acuity, or fineness of discrimination, decreases, with a sharp drop between ages 70 and 80.
Hearing	From age 30	Sensitivity to sound declines, especially at high frequencies but gradually extending to all frequencies. Change is more than twice as rapid for men as for women.
Taste	From age 60	Sensitivity to the four basic tastes—sweet, salty, sour, and bitter—is reduced as number and distribution of taste buds on the tongue decline.
Smell	From age 60	Loss of smell receptors reduces ability to detect and identify odors.
Touch	Gradual	Loss of touch receptors reduces sensitivity on the hands, particularly the fingertips.
Cardiovascular	Gradual	As the heart muscle becomes more rigid, maximum heart rate decreases, reducing the heart's ability to meet the body's oxygen requirements when stressed by exercise. As artery walls stiffen and accumulate plaque, blood flow to body cells is reduced.
Respiratory	Gradual	Under physical exertion, respiratory capacity decreases and breathing rate increases. Stiffening of connective tissue in the lungs and chest muscles makes it more difficult for the lungs to expand to full volume.
Immune	Gradual	Shrinking of the thymus limits maturation of T cells and disease-fighting capacity of B cells, impairing the immune response.
Muscular	Gradual	As nerves stimulating them die, fast-twitch muscle fibers (responsible for speed and explosive strength) decline in number and size to a greater extent than slow-twitch fibers (which support endurance). Tendons and ligaments (which transmit muscle action) stiffen, reducing speed and flexibility of movement.
Skeletal	Begins in the late thirties, accelerates in the fifties, slows in the seventies	Cartilage in the joints thins and cracks, leading bone ends beneath it to erode. New cells continue to be deposited on the outer layer of the bones, and mineral content of bone declines. The resulting broader but more porous bones weaken the skeleton and make it more vulnerable to fracture. Change is more rapid in women than in men.
Reproductive	In women, accelerates after age 35; in men, begins after age 40	Fertility problems (including difficulty conceiving and carrying a pregnancy to term) and risk of having a baby with a chromosomal disorder increase.
Nervous	From age 50	Brain weight declines as neurons lose water content and die, mostly in the cerebral cortex, and as ventricles (spaces) within the brain enlarge. Development of new synapses and limited generation of new neurons can, in part, compensate for these declines.
Skin	Gradual	Epidermis (outer layer) is held less tightly to the dermis (middle layer); fibers in the dermis and hypodermis (inner layer) thin; fat cells in the hypodermis decline. As a result, the skin becomes looser, less elastic, and wrinkled. Change is more rapid in women than in men.
Hair	From age 35	Grays and thins.
Height	From age 50	Loss of bone strength leads to collapse of disks in the spinal column, leading to a height loss of as much as 2 inches by the seventies and eighties.
Weight	Increases to age 50; declines from age 60	Weight change reflects a rise in fat and a decline in muscle and bone mineral. Since muscle and bone are heavier than fat, the resulting pattern is weight gain followed by loss. Body fat accumulates on the torso and decreases on the extremities.

Sources: Arking, 2006; Feng, Huang, & Wang, 2013; Lemaitre et al., 2012.

tragedies prompted Sharese to enter the field of public health in hopes of finding ways to relieve health problems among black Americans. The prevalence of *hypertension,* or high blood pressure, is 13 percent higher in the U.S. black than in the U.S. white population; the African-American rate of death from heart disease (the number one cardiovascular cause) is 40 percent higher (Mozaffarian et al., 2015).

Sharese was surprised to learn that fewer age-related changes occur in the heart than we might expect, given that heart disease is a leading cause of death throughout adulthood, responsible for as many as 10 percent of U.S. male and 5 percent of U.S. female deaths between ages 20 and 34—figures that more than double in the following decade and, thereafter, continue to rise steadily with age (Mozaffarian et al., 2015). In healthy individuals, the heart's ability to meet the body's oxygen requirements under typical conditions (as measured by heart rate in relation to volume of blood pumped) does not change during adulthood. Only during stressful exercise does heart performance decline with age—a change due to a decrease in maximum heart rate and greater rigidity of the heart muscle (Arking, 2006). Consequently, the heart has difficulty delivering enough oxygen to the body during high activity and bouncing back from strain.

One of the most serious diseases of the cardiovascular system is *atherosclerosis*, in which heavy deposits of plaque containing cholesterol and fats collect on the walls of the main arteries. If present, it usually begins early in life, progresses during middle adulthood, and culminates in serious illness. Atherosclerosis is multiply determined, making it hard to separate the contributions of biological aging from individual genetic and environmental influences. The complexity of causes is illustrated by research indicating that before puberty, a high-fat diet produces only fatty streaks on the artery walls (Oliveira, Patin, & Escrivao, 2010). In sexually mature adults, however, it leads to serious plaque deposits, suggesting that sex hormones may heighten the insults of a high-fat diet.

Cardiovascular disease has decreased considerably since the mid-twentieth century, with a larger drop during the past two decades due to a decline in cigarette smoking, improved diet and exercise among at-risk individuals, and better medical detection and treatment of high blood pressure and cholesterol (Mozaffarian et al., 2015). And as a longitudinal follow-up of an ethnically diverse sample of U.S. black and white 18- to 30-year-olds revealed, those at low risk—defined by not smoking, normal body weight, healthy diet, and regular physical activity—were far less likely to be diagnosed with symptoms of heart disease over the succeeding two decades (Liu et al., 2012). Later, when we consider health and fitness, we will see why heart attacks were so common in Sharese's family—and why they occur at especially high rates in the African-American population.

Like the heart, the lungs show few age-related changes in functioning at rest, but during physical exertion, respiratory volume decreases and breathing rate increases with age. Maximum vital capacity (amount of air that can be forced in and out of the lungs) declines by 10 percent per decade after age 25. Connective tissue in the lungs, chest muscles, and ribs stiffens with age, making it more difficult for the lungs to expand to full volume (Lowery et al., 2013; Wilkie et al., 2012). Fortunately, under normal conditions, we use less than half our vital capacity. Nevertheless, aging of the lungs contributes to older adults' difficulty in meeting the body's oxygen needs while exercising.

Motor Performance

Declines in heart and lung functioning under conditions of exertion, combined with gradual muscle loss, lead to changes in motor performance. In most people, the impact of biological aging on motor skills is difficult to separate from decreases in motivation and practice. Therefore, researchers study competitive athletes, who try to attain their very best performance in real life (Tanaka & Seals, 2008). As long as athletes continue intensive training, their attainments at each age approach the limits of what is biologically possible.

Many athletic skills peak between ages 20 and 35, then gradually decline. In several investigations, the mean ages for best performance of Olympic and professional athletes in a variety of sports were charted over time. Absolute performance in most events improved over the past century. Athletes continually set new world records, suggesting improved training methods. But ages of best performance remained relatively constant. Athletic tasks that require speed of limb movement, explosive strength, and gross-motor coordination—sprinting, jumping, and tennis—typically peak in the early twenties. Those that depend on endurance, arm–hand steadiness, and aiming—long-distance running, baseball, and golf—usually peak in the late twenties and early thirties (Morton, 2014; Schulz & Curnow, 1988). Because these skills require either stamina or precise motor control, they take longer to perfect.

Research on outstanding athletes tells us that the upper biological limit of motor capacity is reached in the first part of early adulthood. How quickly do athletic skills weaken in later years? Longitudinal research on master runners reveals that as long as practice continues, speed drops only slightly from the mid-thirties into the sixties, when performance falls off at an accelerating pace (see Figure 13.2) (Tanaka & Seals, 2003, 2008; Trappe, 2007). In the case of long-distance triathlon performance, which combines

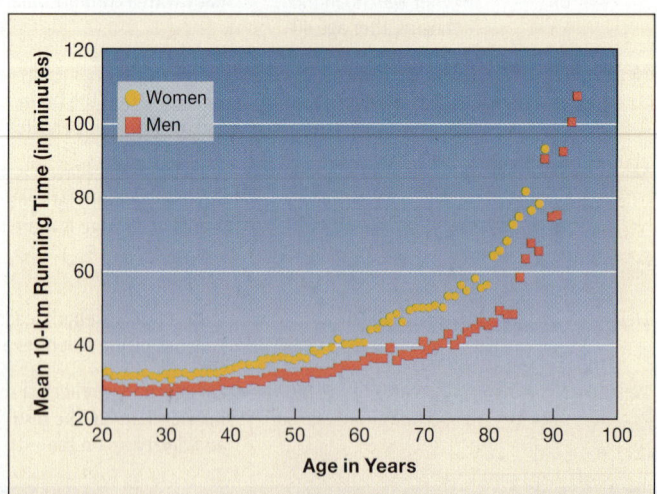

FIGURE 13.2 Ten-kilometer running times with advancing age, based on longitudinal performances of hundreds of master athletes. Runners maintain their speed into the mid-thirties, followed by modest increases in running times into the sixties, with a progressively steeper increase thereafter. (From H. Tanaka & D. R. Seals, 2003, "Dynamic Exercise Performance in Masters Athletes: Insight into the Effects of Primary Human Aging on Physiological Functional Capacity," *Journal of Applied Physiology, 5,* p. 2153. © The American Physiological Society (APS). All rights reserved. Adapted with permission.)

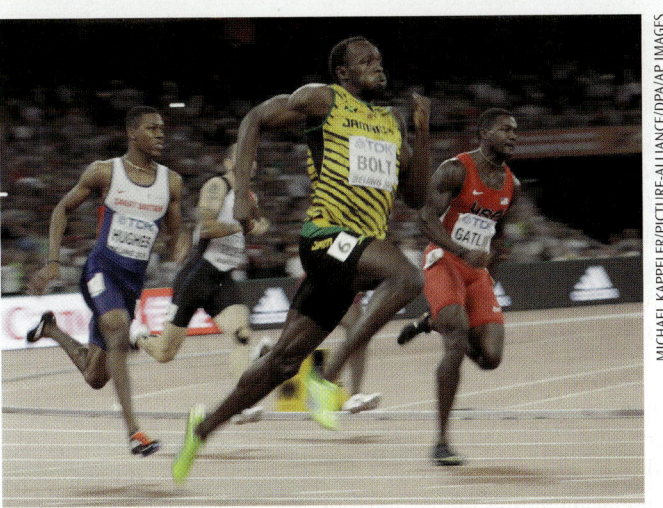

These professional athletes, ranging in age from 21 to 30 years, compete for the title of 2015 world champion in the men's 200-meter finals. Sprinting, which requires speed of limb movement and explosive strength, typically peaks in the early twenties.

running, swimming, and cycling, the decline in speed is even more gradual: The accelerating performance drop-off is delayed until the seventies, due to its non-weight-bearing swimming and cycling components (Lepers, Knechtle, & Stapley, 2013).

Indeed, sustained training leads to adaptations in body structures that minimize motor declines. For example, vital capacity is one-third greater in both younger and older active sports participants than in healthy, inactive agemates (Zaccagni, Onisto, & Gualdi-Russo, 2009). Training also slows muscle loss, increases speed and force of muscle contraction, and leads fast-twitch muscle fibers to be converted into slow-twitch fibers, which support excellent long-distance running performance and other endurance skills (Faulkner et al., 2007). In a study of hundreds of thousands of amateur marathon competitors, 25 percent of the 65- to 69-year-old runners were faster than 50 percent of the 20- to 54-year-old runners (Leyk et al., 2010). And in exceptional instances, outstanding older athletes show startling performance gains with age. For example, in the Ironman Triathlon World Championship, the top male finisher in the 70- to 74-year-old age group in 2010 improved his 2012 performance by nearly an hour (Lepers, Knechtle, & Stapley, 2013). Modest gains have even been observed among 80-year-old competitors.

In sum, although athletic skills are at their best in early adulthood, biological aging accounts for only a small part of age-related declines until advanced old age. Lower levels of performance by healthy people into their sixties and seventies largely reflect reduced capacities resulting from adaptation to a less physically demanding lifestyle.

Immune System

The immune response is the combined work of specialized cells that neutralize or destroy antigens (foreign substances) in the body. Two types of white blood cells play vital roles. *T cells,* which originate in the bone marrow and mature in the thymus (a small gland located in the upper part of the chest), attack antigens directly. *B cells,* manufactured in the bone marrow, secrete antibodies into the bloodstream that multiply, capture antigens, and permit the blood system to destroy them. Because receptors on their surfaces recognize only a single antigen, T and B cells come in great variety. They join with additional cells to produce immunity.

The capacity of the immune system to offer protection against disease increases through adolescence and declines after age 20. The trend is partly due to changes in the thymus, which is largest during the teenage years, then shrinks until it is barely detectable by age 50. As a result, production of thymic hormones is reduced, and the thymus is less able to promote full maturity and differentiation of T cells (Denkinger et al., 2015). Because B cells release far more antibodies when T cells are present, the immune response is compromised further.

Withering of the thymus is not the only reason that the body gradually becomes less effective in warding off illness. The immune system interacts with the nervous and endocrine systems. For example, psychological stress can weaken the immune response. During final exams, Sharese was less resistant to colds. And in the month after her father died, she had great difficulty recovering from the flu. Conflict-ridden relationships, caring for an ill aging parent, sleep deprivation, and chronic depression can also reduce immunity. And physical stress—from pollution, allergens, poor nutrition, and rundown housing—undermines immune functioning throughout adulthood (Cruces et al., 2014; Fenn, Corona, & Godbout, 2014). When physical and psychological stressors combine, the risk of illness is magnified.

Reproductive Capacity

Sharese was born when her mother was in her early twenties. At the same age a generation later, Sharese was embarking on several years of graduate school, prioritizing education and career. Many people believe that pregnancy during the twenties is ideal, not only because of lower risk of miscarriage and chromosomal disorders (see Chapter 2) but also because younger parents have more energy to keep up with active children. Nevertheless, as Figure 13.3 on the following page reveals, first births to women in their thirties have increased greatly over the past three decades. Many people are delaying childbearing until their education is complete, their vocational lives are well-established, and they know they can support a child.

Nevertheless, reproductive capacity does decline with age. Between ages 15 and 29, 11 percent of U.S. married childless women report fertility problems, a figure that rises to 14 percent among 30- to 34-year-olds, 39 percent among 35- to 39-year-olds, and 47 percent among 40- to 44-year-olds. Recall, also, that after 35, the success of reproductive technologies drops sharply with age (see page 52 in Chapter 2) (Chandra, Copen, & Stephen, 2013). Because the uterus shows no consistent changes from the late thirties through the forties, the decline in female fertility is

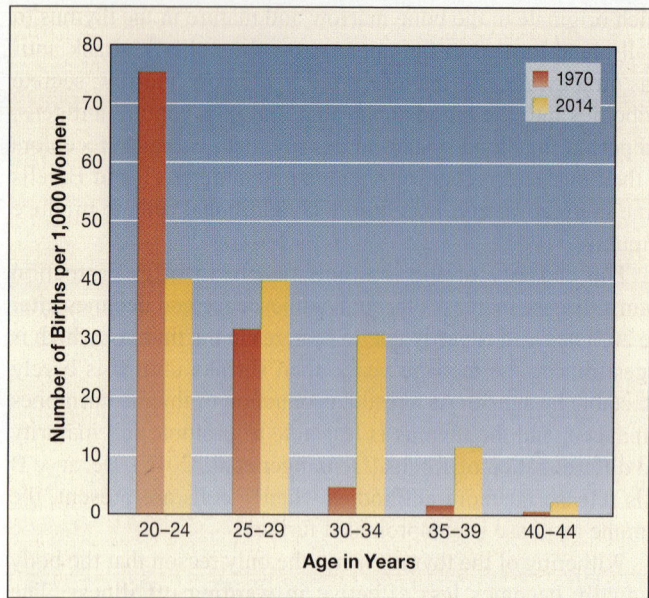

FIGURE 13.3 First births to American women of different ages in 1970 and 2014. The birthrate decreased for women 20 to 24 years of age, whereas it increased for women 25 years of age and older. For women in their thirties, the birthrate increased sixfold, and for those in their early forties, it doubled. Similar trends have occurred in other industrialized nations. (Based on Hamilton et al., 2015.)

largely due to reduced number and quality of ova. In many mammals, including humans, a certain level of reserve ova in the ovaries is necessary for conception (American College of Obstetricians and Gynecologists, 2014; Balasch, 2010). Some women have normal menstrual cycles but do not conceive because their reserve of ova is too low.

In males, semen volume and sperm motility decrease gradually after age 35, contributing to reduced fertility. In addition, the percentage of abnormal sperm rises, which elevates miscarriage rates and diminishes the success of reproductive technologies, irrespective of maternal age (Belloc et al., 2014). Although there is no best time in adulthood to begin parenthood, individuals who postpone childbearing until their late thirties or their forties risk having fewer children than they desired or none at all.

Ask yourself

CONNECT How do heredity and environment jointly contribute to age-related changes in cardiovascular, respiratory, and immune system functioning?

APPLY Penny is a long-distance runner for her college track team. What factors will affect Penny's running performance 30 years from now?

REFLECT Before reading this chapter, had you thought of early adulthood as a period of aging? Why is it important for young adults to be aware of influences on biological aging?

Health and Fitness

13.3 Describe the influence of SES, nutrition, and exercise on health, and discuss obesity in adulthood.

13.4 What are the most commonly abused substances, and what health risks do they pose?

13.5 Describe sexual attitudes and behavior of young adults, and discuss sexually transmitted infections and sexual coercion.

13.6 How does psychological stress affect health?

Figure 13.4 displays leading causes of death in early adulthood in the United States. Death rates for all causes exceed those of many other industrialized nations (OECD, 2015d). A combination of factors, including higher rates of poverty and extreme obesity, more lenient gun-control policies, and historical lack of universal health insurance in the United States, is likely responsible. In later chapters, we will see that homicide rates decline with age, while disease and physical disability rates rise. Biological aging clearly contributes to this trend. But, as we have noted, wide individual and group differences in physical changes are linked to environmental risks and health-related behaviors.

SES variations in health over the lifespan reflect these influences. With the transition from childhood to adulthood, health inequalities associated with SES increase; income, education, and occupational status show strong, continuous relationships with almost every disease and health indicator (Agigoroaei, 2016). Furthermore, SES largely accounts for the sizable health

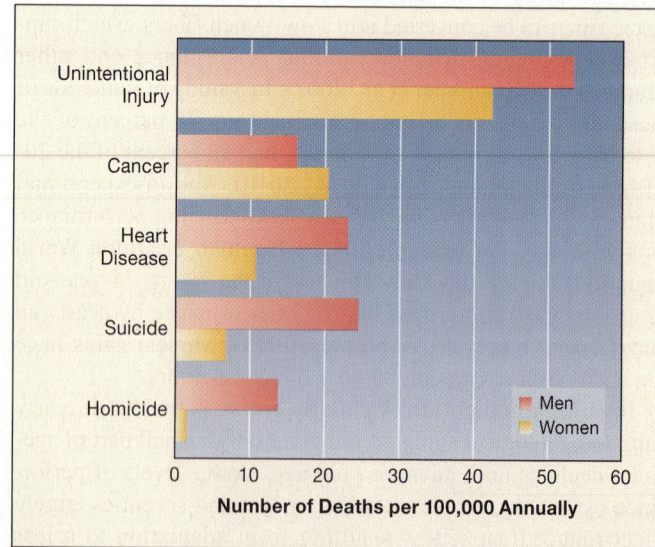

FIGURE 13.4 Leading causes of death between 25 and 44 years of age in the United States. Nearly half of unintentional injuries are motor vehicle accidents. As later chapters will reveal, unintentional injuries remain a leading cause of death at older ages, rising sharply in late adulthood. Rates of cancer and cardiovascular disease rise steadily during middle and late adulthood. Except for cancer, men are more vulnerable than women to each leading cause. From what you learned in earlier chapters, can you explain these sex differences? (Based on Heron, 2015.)

CHAPTER 13 Physical and Cognitive Development in Early Adulthood 445

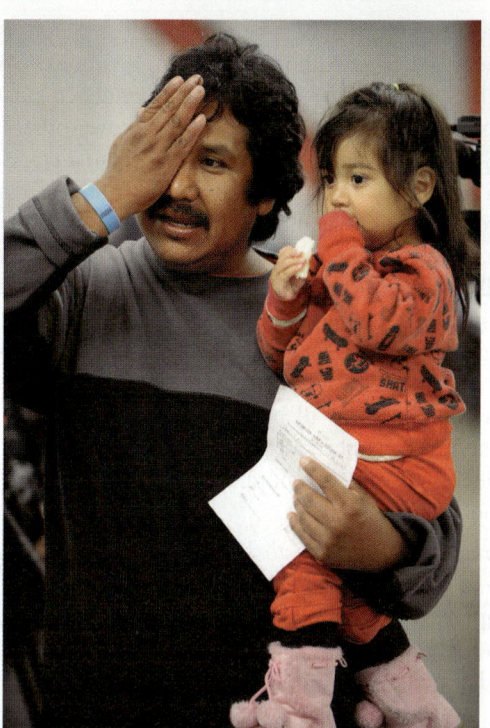

SES variations in health in the United States—larger than in other industrialized nations—are due to diverse health-related circumstances and habits plus insufficient access to high-quality, affordable health care. This Los Angeles free clinic helps address these problems by offering preventive services, including eye exams, to over 1,200 patients per day.

advantage of white over ethnic minority adults in the United States (Phuong, Frank, & Finch, 2012). Consequently, improving socioeconomic conditions is essential for closing ethnic gaps in health.

Health-related circumstances and habits—stressful life events, crowding, pollution, diet, exercise, overweight and obesity, substance abuse, jobs with numerous health risks, and availability of supportive social relationships—underlie SES health disparities (Smith & Infurna, 2011). Furthermore, poor health in childhood, which is linked to low SES, affects health in adulthood. The overall influence of childhood factors lessens if SES improves. But in most instances, child and adult SES remain fairly consistent, exerting a cumulative impact that amplifies SES differences in health with age (Matthews & Gallo, 2011; Wickrama et al., 2015).

Why are SES variations in health and mortality larger in the United States than in other industrialized nations? Besides lack of universal health insurance, low-income and poverty-stricken U.S. families are financially less well-off than families classified in these ways in other countries (Avendano & Kawachi, 2014). In addition, SES groups in the United States experience greater inequalities in environmental factors that affect health, such as housing, pollution, education, and community services.

These findings reveal, once again, that the living conditions that nations and communities provide combine with those that people create for themselves to affect physical aging. Because the incidence of health problems is much lower during the twenties and thirties than later on, early adulthood is an excellent time to prevent later problems. In the following sections, we take up a variety of major health concerns—nutrition, exercise, substance abuse, sexuality, and psychological stress.

Nutrition

Bombarded with advertising claims and an extraordinary variety of food choices, adults find it increasingly difficult to make wise dietary decisions. An abundance of food, combined with a heavily scheduled life, means that most Americans eat because they feel like it or because it is time to do so rather than to maintain the body's functions (Donatelle, 2015). As a result, many eat the wrong types and amounts of food. Overweight and obesity and diets high in sugar, fat, and processed foods are widespread nutritional problems with long-term consequences for adult health.

Overweight and Obesity.
In Chapter 9, we noted that obesity (a greater than 20 percent increase over average body weight, based on age, sex, and physical build) has increased dramatically in many Western nations, and it is on the rise in the developing world as well. Among adults, a body mass index (BMI) of 25 to 29 constitutes overweight, a BMI of 30 or greater (amounting to 30 or more excess pounds) constitutes obesity. The U.S. adult obesity rate has continued to climb, recently reaching 38 percent. Obesity is especially prevalent among certain ethnic minorities, including Native Americans (41 percent), Hispanics (43 percent), and African Americans (48 percent) (Ogden et al., 2014). More African-American and Hispanic women than men are affected.

Overweight—a less extreme but nevertheless unhealthy condition—affects an additional 34 percent of Americans. Combine the rates of overweight and obesity and the total, 72 percent, makes Americans the heaviest people in the world (OECD, 2015c; Ogden et al., 2014). Notice that the U.S. obesity rate exceeds its rate of overweight—a blatant indicator of the epidemic scale of the problem.

Recall from Chapter 9 that overweight children and adolescents are very likely to become overweight adults. But a substantial number of people show large weight gains in adulthood, most often between ages 25 and 50. And young adults who were already overweight or obese typically get heavier, leading obesity rates to rise steadily between ages 20 and 60 (Ogden et al., 2014). Among immigrants, rates of overweight and obesity increase with length of time in the United States (Singh & Linn, 2013). First-generation adults (U.S. born with immigrant parents) have much higher odds of becoming obese than their foreign-born counterparts.

Causes and Consequences.
As noted in Chapter 9, heredity makes some people more vulnerable to obesity than others. But environmental pressures underlie the rising rates of obesity in

industrialized nations: With the decline in need for physical labor in the home and workplace, our lives have become more sedentary. Meanwhile, the average number of calories and amount of sugar and fat consumed by Americans rose over most of the twentieth and early twenty-first century, with a sharp increase after 1970 (Cohen, 2014). Since then, low-cost, calorie-dense convenience foods and portion-supersizing have become widespread; eating out has escalated with women's increased participation in the labor force; and physical activity has declined as adults spend more time in sedentary transportation, jobs, and leisure activities—driving to and from work; sitting throughout the day, often behind a computer; and watching, on average, four hours of TV per day.

Adding some weight between ages 25 and 50 is a normal part of aging because **basal metabolic rate (BMR),** the amount of energy the body uses at complete rest, gradually declines as the number of active muscle cells (which create the greatest energy demand) drops off. But excess weight is strongly associated with serious health problems—including type 2 diabetes, heart disease, and many forms of cancer—and with early death (see page 297 in Chapter 9).

Furthermore, overweight adults suffer enormous social discrimination. Compared with their normal-weight agemates, they are less likely to find mates, be rented apartments, receive financial aid for college, or be offered jobs. And they report frequent mistreatment by family members, peers, co-workers, and health professionals (Ickes, 2011; Puhl, Heuer, & Brownell, 2010). Since the mid-1990s, discrimination experienced by overweight Americans has increased, with serious physical and mental health consequences. Weight stigma triggers anxiety, depression, and low self-esteem, which increase the likelihood that unhealthy eating behaviors will worsen. The more discrimination overweight people report, the greater their chances for becoming obese or—if already obese—remaining so (Sutin & Terracciano, 2013). The widespread but incorrect belief, perpetuated by the media, that obesity is a personal choice promotes negative stereotyping of obese persons.

Treatment. Because obesity climbs in early and middle adulthood, treatment for adults should begin as soon as possible—preferably in the early twenties. Even moderate weight loss reduces health problems substantially (Poobalan et al., 2010). But successful intervention is difficult. Most individuals who start a weight-loss program return to their original weight, and sometimes to a heavier weight, within two years (Wadden et al., 2012). The high rate of failure is partly due to limited evidence on just how obesity disrupts the complex neural, hormonal, and metabolic factors that maintain a normal body-weight set point. Until more information is available, researchers are examining the features of treatments and participants linked to greater success. The following elements promote lasting behavior change:

- *A lifestyle change to a nutritious diet lower in calories, plus regular exercise.* To lose weight and maintain the loss, Sharese sharply reduced calories in her diet and exercised regularly. The precise balance of dietary protein, carbohydrates, and fats that best helps adults lose weight is a matter of heated debate. Although scores of diet books offer different recommendations, no clear-cut evidence exists for the long-term superiority of one approach over others (Wadden et al., 2012). Calorie reduction rather than dietary composition predicts weight loss, though restricting sugar and fat yields substantial health benefits.

  A permanent lifestyle alteration that restricts calorie intake while increasing physical activity is essential for countering a genetic tendency toward overweight. The weight regain experienced by most dieters is sharply reduced when high levels of regular, sustained physical activity (such as an hour per day of brisk walking) become part of their lifestyle (Kushner, 2012). But most people mistakenly believe that only temporary lifestyle changes are needed (MacLean et al., 2011).

- *Training participants to keep an accurate record of food intake and body weight.* About 30 to 35 percent of obese people are convinced they eat less than they do. And although they have continued to gain weight, American adults generally report weight losses—suggesting that they are in denial about the seriousness of their weight condition (Wetmore & Mokdad, 2012). Furthermore, about 30 percent have problems with binge eating—a behavior associated with weight-loss failure (Pacanowski et al., 2014).

  As Sharese recognized how often she ate when not actually hungry and regularly recorded her weight, she was better able to limit food intake. Following a diet that prescribes

A young adult has her weight checked by a nutrition counselor near the end of a 90-day weight-loss program. Keeping an accurate record of food intake and body weight is an important element in losing weight and keeping it off.

portion-controlled servings to help control intake is associated with considerably greater weight loss (Kushner, 2012).

- *Social support.* Group or individual counseling and encouragement from friends and relatives help sustain weight-loss efforts by fostering self-esteem and self-efficacy (Poobalan et al., 2010). Once Sharese decided to act, with the support of her family and a weight-loss counselor, she felt better about herself even before the first pounds were shed.

- *Teaching problem-solving skills.* Most overweight adults do not realize that because their body has adapted to overweight, difficult periods requiring high self-control and patience are inevitable in successful weight loss (MacLean et al., 2011). Acquiring cognitive and behavioral strategies for coping with tempting situations and periods of slowed progress is associated with long-term change (Poelman et al., 2014). Weight-loss maintainers are more likely than individuals who relapse to be conscious of their behavior, to use social support, and to confront problems directly.

- *Extended intervention.* Longer treatments (from 25 to 40 weeks) that include the components listed here grant people time to develop new habits.

Although many Americans on weight-reduction diets are overweight, an estimated 25 to 65 percent of normal-weight adults view themselves as too heavy and are trying to lose weight (Nissen & Holm, 2015). Recall from Chapter 11 that the high value placed on thinness creates unrealistic expectations about desirable body weight and contributes to anorexia, bulimia, and binge eating disorder, which remain common in early adulthood (see pages 378–379). Throughout adulthood, both underweight and obesity are associated with increased mortality (Cao et al., 2014). A sensible body weight—neither too low nor too high—predicts physical and psychological health and longer life.

Dietary Fat. During college, Sharese altered the diet of her childhood and adolescent years, sharply limiting red meat, eggs, butter, and fried foods. The federal government's Dietary Guidelines for Americans recommend that no more than 10 percent of total caloric intake be made up of saturated fat, which generally comes from meat and dairy products and is solid at room temperature (U.S. Department of Agriculture, 2016). No dietary limits are placed on healthy, unsaturated fats, found in most types of vegetable oil.

Research indicates that saturated fat, especially from meat, plays a role in the age-related rise in cardiovascular disease, breast cancer, and colon cancer (Ferguson, 2010; Sieri et al., 2014). In contrast, consuming unsaturated fat, especially in the form of linoleic acid—which is plentiful in corn, soybean, and safflower oils and in nuts and seeds—is linked to reduced cardiovascular disease mortality (Guasch-Ferré et al., 2015; Wu et al., 2014).

When we consume excessive saturated fat, some is converted to cholesterol, which accumulates as plaque on the arterial walls in atherosclerosis. Earlier in this chapter, we noted that atherosclerosis is determined by multiple biological and environmental factors. But saturated fat consumption (along with other

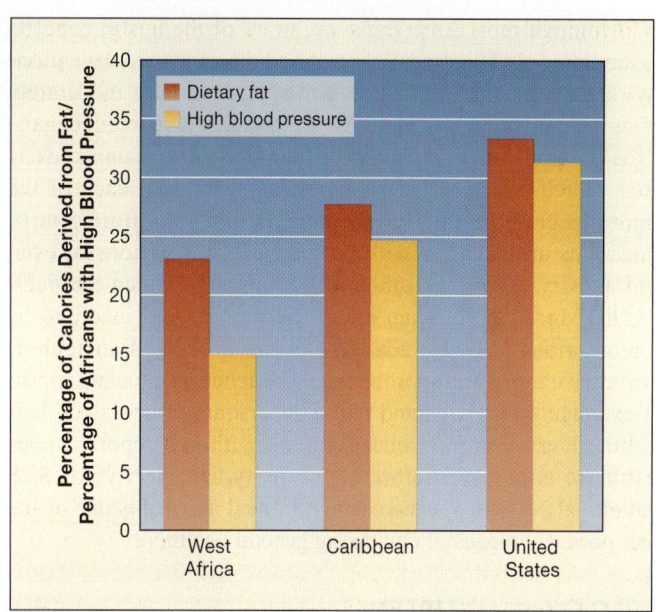

FIGURE 13.5 **Dietary fat and prevalence of high blood pressure among Africans in West Africa, the Caribbean, and the United States.** The three regions represent the historic path of the slave trade and, therefore, have genetically similar populations. As dietary fat increases, high blood pressure and heart disease rise. Both are particularly high among African Americans. (Based on Luke et al., 2001.)

societal conditions) is an important contributor to the high rate of heart disease in the U.S. black population. As Figure 13.5 shows, when researchers compared Africans in West Africa, the Caribbean, and the United States (the historic path of the slave trade), dietary fat increased, and so did high blood pressure and heart disease (Luke et al., 2001). In a survey of a large sample of inner-city African Americans experiencing financial and other stressors, those who consumed foods lower in fat said that neighborhood availability and affordability influenced their dietary choices (Eyler et al., 2004).

A vital goal of public health strategies aimed at improving nutrition and reducing the risk of chronic diseases is inducing people to replace saturated fat with unsaturated fat and with complex carbohydrates (whole grains, fruits, and vegetables), which are beneficial to cardiovascular health and protective against colon cancer (Kaczmarczyk, Miller, & Freund, 2012). Furthermore, regular exercise can reduce the harmful influence of saturated fat because it creates chemical byproducts that help eliminate cholesterol from the body.

Exercise

Three times a week over the noon hour, Sharese delighted in running, making her way to a wooded trail that cut through a picturesque area of the city. Regular exercise kept her fit and slim, and she noticed that she caught fewer respiratory illnesses than in previous years, when she had been sedentary and overweight. As Sharese explained to a friend, "Exercise gives me a positive outlook and calms me down. Afterward, I feel a burst of energy that gets me through the day."

Although most Americans are aware of the health benefits of exercise, only 50 percent of young adults engage in the nationally recommended 150 minutes per week of at least moderately intense leisure-time physical activity. And just 24 percent engage in the recommended two sessions per week of resistance exercises, which place a moderately stressful load on each of the major muscle groups. In early adulthood, about 40 percent of Americans are inactive, with no regular brief sessions of even light activity (U.S. Department of Health and Human Services, 2015d). More women than men are inactive. And inactivity is greater among low-SES adults, who live in less safe neighborhoods, have more health problems, experience less social support for exercising regularly, and feel less personal control over their health. Overweight and obesity along with self-reported poor health are strong predictors of inactivity, irrespective of SES (Valle et al., 2015). Yet increasing physical activity is one of the most powerful means of enhancing general health.

LOOK and LISTEN

Contact your local parks and recreation department to find out what community supports and services exist to increase adult physical activity. Are any special efforts made to reach low-SES adults?

Besides reducing body fat and building muscle, exercise fosters resistance to disease. Frequent bouts of moderate-intensity exercise enhance the immune response, lowering the risk of colds or flu and promoting faster recovery from these illnesses (Donatelle, 2015). Furthermore, physical activity is linked to reduced incidence of several types of cancer, with the strongest findings for breast and colon cancer (Fedewa et al., 2015). Physically active people are also less likely to develop diabetes and cardiovascular disease (Mehanna, Hamik, & Josephson, 2016). If they do, these illnesses typically occur later and are less severe than among their inactive agemates.

How does exercise help prevent these serious illnesses? First, it reduces the incidence of obesity—a risk factor for heart disease, diabetes, and cancer. In addition, people who exercise probably adopt other healthful behaviors, thereby lowering the risk of diseases associated with high-fat diets, alcohol consumption, and smoking. In animal studies, exercise directly inhibits growth of cancerous tumors—beyond the impact of diet, body fat, and the immune response (de Lima et al., 2008). Exercise also promotes cardiovascular functioning by strengthening the heart muscle, decreasing blood pressure, and producing a form of "good cholesterol" (high-density lipoproteins, or HDLs) that helps remove "bad cholesterol" (low-density lipoproteins, or LDLs) from the artery walls (Donatelle, 2015).

Yet another way that exercise guards against illness is through its mental health benefits. Physical activity reduces anxiety and depression and improves mood, alertness, and energy. Furthermore, EEG and fMRI evidence indicates that exercise enhances neural activity in the cerebral cortex, and it improves overall cognitive functioning (Etnier & Labban, 2012; Kim et al.,

Regular exercise of at least moderate intensity predicts a healthier, longer life. These young adults doing box jumps as part of a fitness program reap both physical and mental health benefits.

2012). The impact of exercise on a "positive outlook," as Sharese expressed it, is most obvious just after a workout and can last for several hours (Acevedo, 2012). The stress-reducing properties of exercise undoubtedly strengthen immunity to disease. And as physical activity enhances cognitive functioning and psychological well-being, it promotes on-the-job productivity, self-esteem, ability to cope with stress, and life satisfaction.

When we consider the evidence as a whole, it is not surprising that physical activity is associated with substantially lower death rates from all causes. The contribution of exercise to longevity cannot be accounted for by preexisting illness in inactive people. In a Danish longitudinal study of a nationally representative sample of 7,000 healthy 20- to 79-year-olds followed over several decades, mortality was lower among those who increased their leisure-time physical activity from low to either moderate or high than among those who remained consistently inactive (Schnohr, Scharling, & Jensen, 2003).

Substance Abuse

Alcohol and drug use peaks among U.S. 19- to 25-year-olds and then declines steadily with age. Eager to try a wide range of experiences before settling down to the responsibilities of adulthood, young people of this age are more likely than younger or older individuals to smoke cigarettes, chew tobacco, use marijuana, and take stimulants to enhance cognitive or physical performance (U.S. Department of Health and Human Services, 2015a). Binge drinking, driving under the influence, and experimentation with prescription drugs (such as OxyContin, a highly addictive painkiller) and "party drugs" (such as LSD and MDMA, or Ecstasy, and new substances produced to mimic their effects) also increase, at times with tragic consequences. Risks include brain damage, lasting impairments in cognitive and emotional functioning, and liver, kidney, and heart failure resulting in death (Karila et al., 2015; National Institute on Drug Abuse, 2016a).

Furthermore, when alcohol and drug taking become chronic, they intensify the psychological problems that underlie addiction. As many as 16 percent of 19- to 25-year-olds are substance abusers, with similar rates of men and women seeking treatment (U.S. Department of Health and Human Services, 2014, 2015). Return to Chapter 11, pages 386–387, to review factors that lead to alcohol and drug abuse in adolescence. The same personal and situational conditions are predictive in the adult years. Tobacco, marijuana, and alcohol are the most commonly abused substances.

Tobacco and Marijuana. Dissemination of information on the harmful effects of cigarette smoking has helped reduce its prevalence among U.S. adults from 40 percent 50 years ago to 17 percent today (Centers for Disease Control and Prevention, 2015d). Still, smoking has declined very slowly, and most of the drop is among college graduates, with far less change among those who did not finish high school. Furthermore, more men than women smoke, but the gender gap is much smaller today than in the past, reflecting a sharp increase in smoking among young women who did not finish high school.

Although college students' cigarette smoking has decreased over the past 15 years, their use of other forms of tobacco (e-cigarettes and cigars) and, especially, of marijuana has risen (Johnston et al., 2014). Young people seem to have absorbed messages about the health risks of cigarettes, though they minimize the dangers of alternative tobacco sources. And because of legalization of recreational marijuana use in some U.S. states, many young people view marijuana as safe. Yet 30 percent of users experience problematic withdrawal symptoms that result in dependency (National Institute on Drug Abuse, 2016b). And moderate to high marijuana use predicts becoming a chronic cigarette smoker in early adulthood (Brook, Lee, & Brook, 2015).

Compared to marijuana, tobacco use is much more addictive. Of young people who smoke cigarettes, the overwhelming majority started before age 21 (U.S. Department of Health and Human Services, 2015a). And the earlier they began smoking, the greater their daily cigarette use and likelihood of continuing, an important reason that preventive efforts with adolescents and young adults are vital.

The ingredients of cigarette smoke—nicotine, tar, carbon monoxide, and other chemicals—leave their damaging mark throughout the body. As smokers inhale, oxygen delivery to tissues is reduced, and heart rate and blood pressure rise. Over time, exposure to toxins and insufficient oxygen result in damage to the retina of the eye; constriction of blood vessels leading to painful vascular disease; skin abnormalities, including premature aging, poor wound healing, and hair loss; decline in bone mass; decrease in reserve ova, uterine abnormalities, and earlier menopause in women; and reduced sperm count and higher rate of sexual impotence in men (Carter et al., 2015; Dechanet et al., 2011). Other deadly outcomes include increased risk of heart attack, stroke, acute leukemia, melanoma, and cancer of the mouth, throat, larynx, esophagus, lungs, stomach, pancreas, kidneys, and bladder.

Cigarette smoking is the single most important preventable cause of death in industrialized nations. One out of every three young people who become regular smokers will die from a smoking-related disease, and the vast majority will suffer from at least one serious illness (Adhikari et al., 2009). The chances of premature death rise with earlier age of smoking initiation and number of cigarettes consumed. At the same time, the benefits of quitting in early adulthood include return of most disease risks to near-nonsmoker levels within 1 to 10 years. In a study of 1.2 million British women, those who had been regular smokers but stopped before they reached age 30 avoided 97 percent of the elevated risk of premature death from cigarettes. And those who quit before age 40 avoided 90 percent of the added risk (Pirie et al., 2013). Continuing to smoke throughout adulthood reduced life expectancy by 11 years.

Nearly 70 percent of U.S. smokers report having tried to quit during the past year, though just half who saw their doctors in the past year received advice to do so (Centers for Disease Control and Prevention, 2015o; Danesh, Paskett, & Ferketich, 2014). Although millions have stopped without help, those who use cessation aids (for example, nicotine gum, nasal spray, or patches, designed to reduce dependency gradually) or enter treatment programs often fail: As many as 90 percent start smoking again within six months (Jackson et al., 2015). Unfortunately, too few treatments last long enough, effectively combine counseling with medications that reduce nicotine withdrawal symptoms, and teach skills for avoiding relapse.

Alcohol. National surveys reveal that about 9 percent of men and 5 percent of women in the United States are heavy drinkers, defined as weekly consumption of 15 drinks or more for men and 8 drinks or more for women (U.S. Department of Health and Human Services, 2015a). About one-third of heavy drinkers are *alcoholics*—people who cannot limit their alcohol use.

Alcohol consumption peaks in the late teens and early twenties and then declines steadily with age. Excessive use is particularly high among 18- to 22-year-old college students: 14 percent report heavy drinking and 39 percent binge drinking during the past month, compared with 9 and 33 percent for other people of the same age (National Institute on Alcohol Abuse and Alcoholism, 2015). Alcoholism usually begins during this age range and worsens over the following decade.

Rates of heavy drinking are similar for male and female college students, though women tend to "mature out" of harmful levels of use later than men (Hoeppner et al., 2013). Women also progress more quickly than men to alcohol dependence, in part because their bodies metabolize alcohol more slowly and, therefore, they experience alcohol-related problems at lower drinking levels. Also, whereas men more often drink to enhance positive emotions in social situations, women more often do so in response to stress and negative mood (Brady & Lawson, 2012). As we will see, consuming alcohol to dull awareness of life's problems is more strongly linked to sustained and increased use.

Twin and adoption studies support a moderate genetic contribution to alcoholism. Genes affecting alcohol metabolism and those promoting impulsivity and sensation seeking (temperamental traits linked to alcohol and other addictions) are involved (Iyer-Eimerbrink & Nurnberger, 2014). But half of alcoholics have no family history of problem drinking.

Alcoholism crosses SES and ethnic lines but is higher in some groups than others. In cultures where alcohol is a traditional part of religious or ceremonial activities, people are less likely to abuse it. Where access to alcohol is carefully controlled and viewed as a sign of adulthood, dependency is more likely—factors that may, in part, explain why college students drink more heavily than young people not enrolled in college (Slutske et al., 2004). Poverty, hopelessness, and a history of physical or sexual abuse in childhood are among factors that sharply increase the risk of excessive drinking (Donatelle, 2015; U.S. Department of Health and Human Services, 2015a).

Alcohol acts as a depressant, impairing the brain's ability to control thought and action. In a problem drinker, it relieves anxiety at first but then induces it as the effects wear off, so the person drinks again, often at higher levels. Chronic alcohol use does widespread physical damage. Its best-known complication is liver disease, but it is also linked to cardiovascular disease, inflammation of the pancreas, irritation of the intestinal tract, bone marrow problems, disorders of the blood and joints, and some forms of cancer. Over time, alcohol causes brain damage, leading to confusion, apathy, inability to learn, and impaired memory (O'Connor, 2012). The costs to society are enormous. About one-third of fatal motor vehicle crashes in the United States involve drivers who have been drinking (U.S. Department of Transportation, 2014). Nearly half of convicted felons are alcoholics, and about half of police activities in large cities involve alcohol-related offenses (McKim & Hancock, 2013). Alcohol frequently plays a part in sexual coercion, including date rape, and in domestic violence.

The most successful treatments combine personal and family counseling, group support, and aversion therapy (use of medication that produces a physically unpleasant reaction to alcohol, such as nausea and vomiting). Alcoholics Anonymous, a community support approach, helps many people exert greater control over their lives through the encouragement of others with similar problems. Nevertheless, breaking an addiction that has dominated a person's life is difficult; about 50 percent of alcoholics relapse within a few months (Kirshenbaum, Olsen, & Bickel, 2009).

Sexuality

At the end of the teenage years, nearly 70 percent of U.S. young people have had sexual intercourse; by age 25, nearly all have done so, and the link between sexual activity and economic disadvantage apparent in adolescence (see page 381 in Chapter 11) has diminished (Copen, Chandra, & Febo-Vazquez, 2016). Compared with earlier generations, contemporary adults display a wider range of sexual choices and lifestyles, including non-marital experiences, cohabitation, marriage, and orientation toward a heterosexual or same-sex partner. In this chapter, we explore the attitudes, behaviors, and health concerns that arise as sexual activity becomes a regular event in young people's lives. In Chapter 14, we focus on the emotional side of close relationships.

Heterosexual Attitudes and Behavior.
One Friday evening, Sharese accompanied her roommate Heather to a young singles bar, where two young men soon joined them. Faithful to her boyfriend, Ernie, whom she had met in college and who worked in another city, Sharese remained aloof for the next hour. In contrast, Heather was talkative and gave one of the men, Rich, her phone number. The next weekend, Heather went out with Rich. On the second date, they had intercourse, but the romance lasted only a few weeks. Aware of Heather's more adventurous sex life, Sharese wondered whether her own was normal. Only after several months of dating exclusively had she and Ernie slept together.

Since the 1950s, public displays of sexuality in movies and the media have steadily increased, fostering the impression that Americans are more sexually active than ever before. What are contemporary adults' sexual attitudes and behaviors really like? Answers were difficult to find until interviews addressing U.S. adults' sex lives first began to be conducted in the late 1980s with large, nationally representative samples. Today, the U.S. federal government regularly gathers such information from samples as large as 10,000 to 30,000 participants (Copen, Chandra, & Febo-Vazquez, 2016; Smith et al., 1972–2014). Additional, smaller-scale survey research has also enhanced our knowledge.

Recall from Chapter 11 that the sex lives of most teenagers do not dovetail with exciting media images. Similarly, although their sexual practices are diverse, adults are far less sexually active than we have come to believe. Monogamous, emotionally committed couples like Sharese and Ernie are more typical (and more satisfied) than couples like Heather and Rich.

Sexual partners, whether dating, cohabiting, or married, tend to be similar in age (within five years), education, ethnicity,

College students gather for an impromptu spring party. Alcohol consumption peaks in the late teens and early twenties. Among heavy drinkers, women progress more quickly than men to alcohol dependence.

Although online dating sites have become increasingly popular, direct social interaction is vital for assessing one's compatibility with a potential partner.

and (to a lesser extent) religion. In addition, people who establish lasting relationships often meet in conventional ways—through friends or family members, or at school or social events where people similar to themselves congregate (Sprecher et al., 2015). The powerful influence of social networks on sexual choice is adaptive. Sustaining an intimate relationship is easier when adults share interests and values and people they know approve of the match.

Over the past decade, the Internet has become an increasingly popular way to initiate relationships. Among a sample of 2,200 Americans, 11 percent said they had used online dating sites or mobile dating apps. One-fourth of these had met their spouse or a long-term partner in this way, making the Internet the second most common route to meeting a partner, just behind meeting through friends. Furthermore, nearly 30 percent of participants knew someone who had formed an enduring relationship through Internet dating (Pew Research Center, 2013b). Knowing someone who has successfully met a partner online strongly predicts single adults' willingness to engage in Internet dating (Sprecher, 2011). Young people between 25 and 34 are the most avid users of dating sites and apps; 20 percent report having used them.

Nevertheless, online dating services sometimes undermine, rather than enhance, the chances of forming a successful relationship. Relying on Internet profiles and online communication omits aspects of direct social interaction that are vital for assessing one's compatibility with a potential partner. Especially when online communication persists for a long time (six weeks or more), people form idealized impressions that often lead to disappointment at face-to-face meetings (Finkel et al., 2012). Furthermore, having a large pool of potential partners from which to choose can promote a persistent "shopping mentality," which reduces online daters' willingness to make a commitment (Heino, Ellison, & Gibbs, 2010). Finally, the techniques that matching sites claim to use to pair partners—sophisticated analyses of information daters provide—have not demonstrated any greater success than conventional off-line means of introducing people.

Consistent with popular belief, lifetime number of sexual partners (from age 18 on) reported by American adults has risen steadily over the past several decades, from an average of 7 in the late 1980s to 11 in the early 2010s, with men exceeding women by threefold—currently, 18 to 6. As Figure 13.6 shows, acceptance of premarital sex increased, with a sharp rise after the mid-2000s (Twenge, Sherman, & Wells, 2015). Nevertheless, when adults of any age are asked how many partners they have had in the past year, the usual reply—including from 18- to 25-year-olds—is one (Copen, Chandra, & Febo-Vazquez, 2016; Lefkowitz & Gillen, 2006).

What explains the trend toward more relationships in the context of sexual commitment? In the past, dating several partners was followed by marriage. Today, dating more often gives way to cohabitation, which typically leads either to marriage or to breakup. In addition, people are marrying later, and the divorce rate remains high. Together, these factors create more opportunities for new partners.

The college years are marked by an increase in uncommitted sexual encounters, including "hookups" (emotionally uninvolved, casual sex) and "friends with benefits" (casual sex as an add-on to an existing friendship). Estimates indicate that two-thirds or more of contemporary U.S. college students have experienced at least 1 hookup, and as many as one-fourth 10 or more (Halpern & Kaestle, 2014). Although some young people report positive reactions, these encounters often have negative emotional consequences (more so for women), including lower self-esteem, regret, and depressed mood (Lewis et al., 2012). The

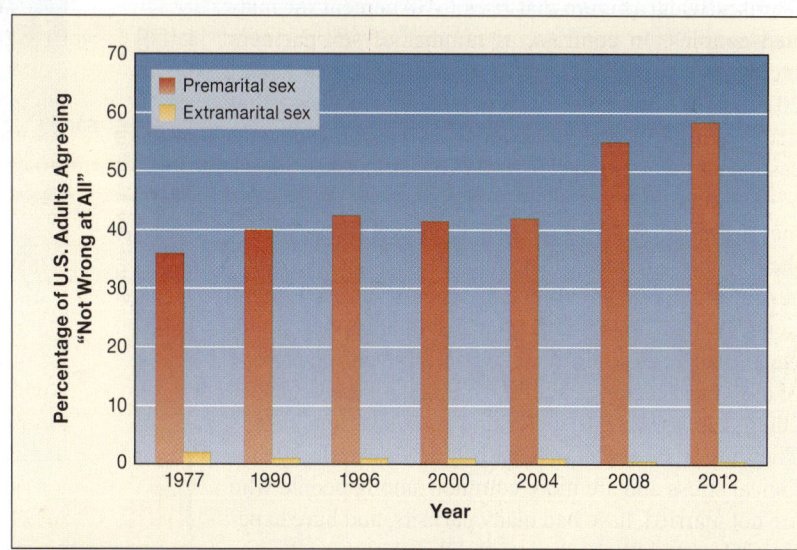

FIGURE 13.6 Percentage of U.S. adults agreeing that premarital sex and extramarital sex are "not wrong at all." In surveys of nationally representative samples of many thousands of Americans age 18 and older over the past four decades, acceptance of premarital sex increased, rising sharply after the mid-2000s. In contrast, approval of extramarital sex remained consistently low, even showing a recent decline. (Based on Smith et al., 1972–2014.)

prevalence of casual sex on college campuses suggests that young people often use it to gratify sexual needs during a time in which they are not yet ready to invest in an intimate bond.

Still, the majority of U.S. 18- to 29-year-olds say they eventually want to settle down with a mutually exclusive lifetime sexual partner (Halpern & Kaestle, 2015). In line with this goal, most people spend the majority of their lives with one partner. And as Figure 13.6 reveals, approval of extramarital sex remains low among U.S. adults of all ages, even showing a slight recent decline.

How frequently do Americans have sex? Not nearly as often as the media would suggest. One-third of 18- to 59-year-olds have intercourse as often as twice a week, another third have it a few times a month, and the remaining third have it a few times a year or not at all. Three factors affect frequency of sexual activity: age, whether people are cohabiting or married, and how long the couple has been together. Single people have more partners, but this does not translate into more sex! Sexual activity increases through the twenties and (for men) the thirties as people either cohabit or marry. Then it declines, even though hormone levels have not changed much (Herbenick et al., 2010; Langer, 2004). The demands of daily life—working, commuting, taking care of home and children—are probably responsible. Despite the common assumption that sexual practices vary greatly across social groups, the patterns just described are unaffected by education, SES, or ethnicity.

Furthermore, sexual frequency predicts life satisfaction only in the context of a satisfying relationship. But beyond once a week, more frequent sex does not add to happiness (Muise, Schimmack, & Impett, 2015). Among adults in committed relationships, who range considerably in quantity of sexual activity, more than 80 percent report feeling "extremely physically and emotionally satisfied" with their sex lives, a figure that rises to 88 percent for married couples. In contrast, as number of sex partners increases, sexual satisfaction declines sharply (Paik, 2010). These findings challenge two stereotypes—that marriage is sexually dull and that people who engage in casual dating have the "hottest" sex.

A minority of U.S. adults—women more often than men—report persistent sexual problems. For women, the two most frequent difficulties are lack of interest in sex and inability to achieve orgasm. Most often mentioned by men are climaxing too early and anxiety about performance. Sexual difficulties are linked to an array of biological factors, including chronic illnesses such as atherosclerosis and diabetes and use of various drugs. They are also associated with low SES and psychological stress and are more common among people who are not married, have had many partners, and have experienced sexual abuse during childhood or sexual coercion in adulthood (Wincze & Weisberg, 2015). As these findings suggest, a history of unfavorable relationships and sexual experiences increases the risk of sexual dysfunction.

But overall, a completely untroubled physical experience is not essential for sexual happiness. Satisfying sex involves more than technique; it is attained in the context of love and fidelity. In sum, happiness with partnered sex is linked to an emotionally fulfilling relationship, good mental health, and overall contentment with life.

Sexual Minority Attitudes and Behavior.
The majority of Americans support civil liberties and equal employment opportunities for lesbians, gay men, and bisexuals. And attitudes toward sex and romantic relationships between adults of the same sex have gradually become more accepting: Overall, more than half of U.S. adults favor allowing same-sex couples to marry legally—society's official recognition of a sexual relationship (Pew Research Center, 2015f). As Figure 13.7 shows, members of the Millennial generation, born after 1980, are the most accepting of same-sex marriage, though acceptance has risen dramatically among all generations.

Sexual minorities' political activism and greater openness about their sexual orientation have contributed to gains in acceptance. Exposure and interpersonal contact reduce negative attitudes; those who know many lesbian and gay people are highly accepting. Other than Millennials, who show no gender difference in acceptance, heterosexual men judge sexual minorities (especially gay men) more negatively than do heterosexual women, likely because of men's greater concern with gender-role conformity (Clarke, Marks, & Lykins, 2015; Pew Research Center, 2010). Acceptance is greatest among highly educated people who are low in religiosity.

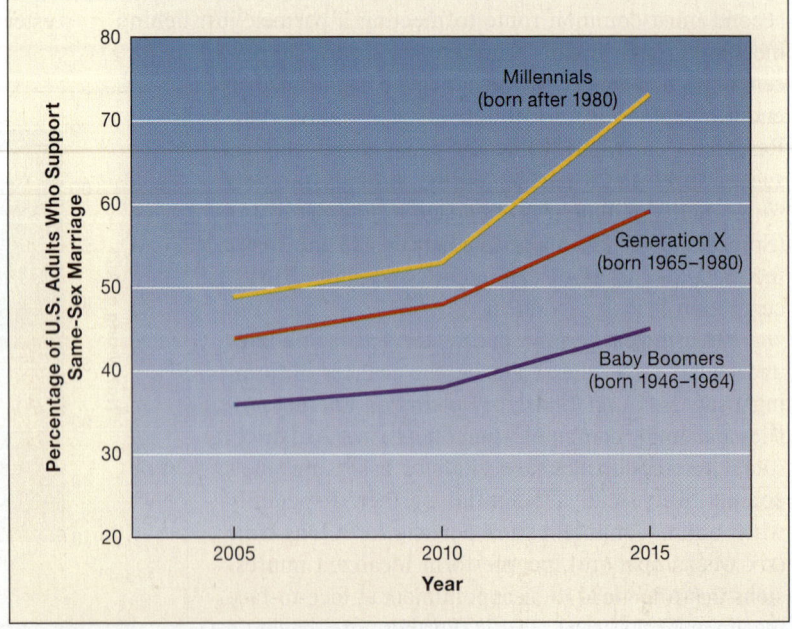

FIGURE 13.7 Percentage of U.S. adults who support same-sex marriage, by generation. In surveys of nationally representative samples of several thousand Americans age 18 and older, support for allowing same-sex couples to marry legally increased from 2005 to 2015 among all generations. Younger cohorts are the most accepting; nearly three-fourths of Millennials approve of legalized same-sex marriage. (Based on Pew Research Center, 2010b, 2015f.)

Gay and lesbian romantic partners, like heterosexual partners, tend to be similar in education and background. With greater openness and political activism, attitudes toward same-sex relationships have become more accepting.

An estimated 3.8 percent of U.S. men and women—more than 8 million adults—identify as lesbian, gay, bisexual, or transgender, with women substantially more likely than men to report a bisexual orientation (Gallup, 2015a). But many sexual minority adults do not reveal their sexual orientation in survey research. This unwillingness to answer questions, engendered by a climate of discrimination, has limited researchers' access to information about the sex lives of gay men and lesbians.

The little evidence available indicates that relationships between same-sex partners follow the same patterns as other-sex relationships: People tend to seek out partners similar in education and background to themselves; partners in committed relationships have sex more often and are more satisfied; and the overall frequency of sex is generally moderate, though higher for gay than lesbian couples in early adulthood (Joyner, Manning, & Prince, 2015; Laumann et al., 1994). And in a survey of over 20,000 ethnically diverse men whose most recent sexual event involved a male partner, those who reported feeling love or affection rated sex as more pleasurable. Furthermore, expressions of love or affection for a partner, especially one's regular partner, were common among gay men of all ethnicities—African American, Asian, European American, and Hispanic (Calabrese et al., 2015). These findings challenge negative stereotypes of gay relationships, especially those of black men, as focused on sexual gratification without warmth and tenderness.

Sexual minorities tend to live in or near large cities, where many others share their sexual orientation, or in college towns, where attitudes are more accepting (Hubbard, Gorman-Murray, & Nash, 2015). Living in small communities where prejudice is intense and no social network exists through which to find compatible same-sex partners is isolating, lonely, and predictive of mental health problems (Swank, Frost, & Fahs, 2012). People who identify themselves as gay, lesbian, or bisexual also tend to be well-educated (McGarrity, 2014). This probably reflects greater social and sexual liberalism among the more highly educated and therefore greater willingness to disclose a minority sexual orientation.

Sexually Transmitted Infections.
In the United States, one in every four individuals is likely to contract a sexually transmitted infection (STI) at some point in life. Although the incidence is highest between ages 15 and 24 (see page 383 in Chapter 11), STIs continue to be prevalent throughout the twenties, when people accumulate most of their sexual partners yet often do not take appropriate measures to prevent disease transmission (Centers for Disease Control and Prevention, 2015b). Although both men and women are seriously affected, women are at greater risk for long-term health consequences. They are less likely to experience symptoms of the most common infections, which—left untreated—cause infertility and pregnancy complications.

HIV/AIDS remains a serious risk, with gay men bearing the greatest burden for this disease. Many have responded by changing their sexual practices—limiting number of sexual partners, choosing partners more carefully, and using condoms consistently and correctly. Heterosexuals at elevated risk due to a history of many partners have done the same, resulting in declines in HIV diagnoses in some subgroups. Still, the annual number of U.S. new HIV infections—about 50,000—has remained stable since the late 1990s (Centers for Disease Control and Prevention, 2015g). And the incidence of HIV-positive adults is higher in the United States than in any other industrialized nation (OECD, 2015d).

HIV largely spreads through men having sex with men and through heterosexual contact in poverty-stricken minority groups, among whom high rates of intravenous drug abuse coexist with poor health, inadequate education, high life stress, and hopelessness. People overwhelmed by these problems are least likely to take preventive measures. Among low-income African Americans and Hispanics, HIV diagnoses have risen by over 20 percent in the past decade (Centers for Disease Control and Prevention, 2016a).

Yet HIV/AIDS can be contained and reduced—through sex education extending from childhood into adulthood and through access to health services, condoms, and clean needles and syringes for high-risk individuals. In view of susceptibility among women, who account for one-fourth of cases in North America and Western Europe and more than half in developing countries, a special need exists for female-controlled preventive measures (Wiringa, Gondwe, & Haggerty, 2015). Drug-based vaginal gels and rings that kill or inactivate the virus have shown promising results and are undergoing further testing.

Sexual Coercion.
To celebrate the end of final exams, Kelsey, a sophomore at a large university, went to a party at a friend's off-campus apartment, consumed alcohol, and lapsed into a stupor, fading in and out of consciousness. When she awoke, she found herself in a bedroom with another partyer—a male student—on top of her. Though she shouted "no" and tried to push him off, he used force. Then several more men

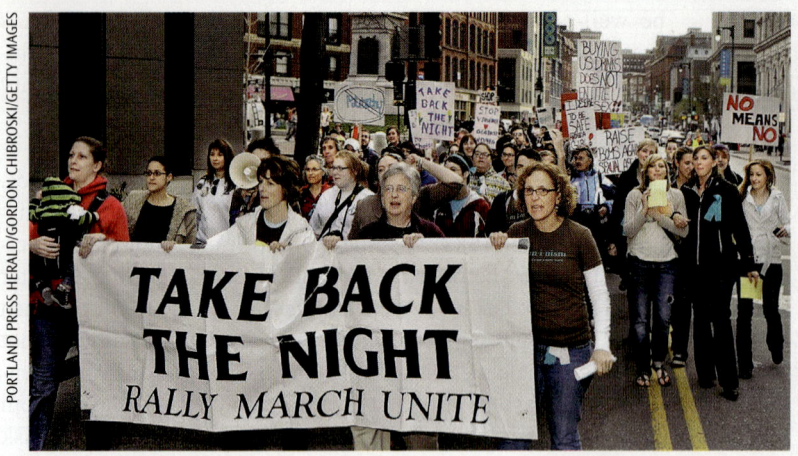

Cultural forces, including gender stereotyping and societal acceptance of violence, contribute to the high incidence of sexual coercion. Organizations like Take Back the Night aim to make communities safer by increasing awareness about sexual violence.

joined in (Krakauer, 2015). Hours later, Kelsey reported the attack, but the police suggested that because she was partially conscious, the sex might have been consensual.

An estimated 19 percent of U.S. women, sometime in their lives, have endured *rape,* legally defined as vaginal, anal, or oral penetration with a body part or object by force, by threat of harm, or when the victim is incapable of giving consent (because of alcohol consumption, mental illness, or intellectual disability). About 45 percent of women have experienced other forms of sexual coercion. The majority of victims (nearly 8 out of 10) were first victimized before age 25. The incidence is especially high on college campuses (Centers for Disease Control and Prevention, 2014d; Fedina, Holmes, & Backes, 2016). Like Kelsey, women are vulnerable to acquaintances and strangers, although in most instances their abusers are men they know well. Sexual coercion crosses SES and ethnic lines; people of all walks of life are offenders and victims.

Personal characteristics of perpetrators are far more dependable predictors of sexual coercion than those of victims. Men who commit these acts tend to be manipulative of others, lack empathy and remorse, pursue casual sexual relationships rather than emotional intimacy, approve of violence against women, and accept rape myths (such as "Women really want to be raped"). Perpetrators also interpret women's social behaviors inaccurately, viewing friendliness as seductiveness, assertiveness as hostility, and resistance as desire (Abbey & Jacques-Tiura, 2011). Furthermore, sexual abuse in childhood, promiscuity in adolescence, and alcohol abuse in adulthood are associated with sexual coercion. Approximately half of all sexual assaults take place while people are intoxicated (Black, 2011).

LOOK and LISTEN

Obtain from your campus student services or police department the number of sexual assaults reported during the most recent year. What percentage involved alcohol? What prevention and intervention services does your college offer?

Cultural forces also contribute. When men are taught from an early age to be dominant, competitive, and aggressive and women to be submissive and cooperative, the themes of rape are reinforced. Societal acceptance of violence also sets the stage for rape, which typically occurs in relationships in which other forms of aggression are commonplace. Exposure to sexually aggressive pornography and other media images, which portray women desiring and enjoying the assault, also promote sexual coercion by dulling sensitivity to its harmful consequences.

About 2 percent of U.S. men have been victims of rape, and 23 percent victims of other forms of sexual coercion. As with women, men under age 25 are at highest risk (Centers for Disease Control and Prevention, 2014d). Although rape victims report mostly male perpetrators, women are largely responsible for other forms of sexual coercion against men. Victimized men often say that women who committed these acts used threats of physical force or actual force, encouraged them to get drunk, or threatened to end the relationship unless they complied (French, Tilghman, & Malebranche, 2015). Social attitudes toward male victims are especially unsympathetic and blaming. Not surprisingly, few report these crimes.

Consequences. Women's and men's psychological reactions to rape resemble those of survivors of extreme trauma. Responses include shock, confusion, and symptoms of post-traumatic stress disorder (PTSD)—flashbacks, nightmares, irritability, psychological numbing, and difficulty concentrating—along with chronic fatigue, depression, substance abuse, social anxiety, difficulties with sexuality and intimacy, and suicidal thoughts (Gavey & Senn, 2014; Judson, Johnson, & Perez, 2013). Victims of ongoing sexual coercion may fall into a pattern of extreme passivity and fear of taking any action.

One-third to one-half of female rape victims are physically injured. From 4 to 30 percent contract STIs, and pregnancy results in about 5 percent of cases. Furthermore, victims of rape (and other sexual crimes) report more symptoms of illness across almost all body systems. And they are more likely to engage in negative health behaviors, including smoking and alcohol use (Black, 2011; Schewe, 2007).

Prevention and Treatment. Many female rape victims do not get help because fear over provoking another attack keeps them from confiding even in trusted family members and friends. A variety of community services, including safe houses, crisis hotlines, support groups, and legal assistance, exist to help women take refuge from abusive partners, but most are underfunded and cannot reach out to everyone in need. Practically no services are available for victimized men, who are often too embarrassed to come forward.

The trauma induced by rape is severe enough that therapy is vital—both individual treatment to reduce anxiety and depression and group sessions where contact with other survivors helps

Applying what we Know

Preventing Sexual Coercion

SUGGESTION	DESCRIPTION
Reduce gender stereotyping and gender inequalities.	The roots of men's sexual coercion of women lie in the historically subordinate status of women, which keeps women economically dependent on men and therefore poorly equipped to avoid partner violence. At the same time, increased public awareness that women commit sexually aggressive acts is needed.
Mandate treatment for both male and female perpetrators.	Ingredients of effective intervention include combating rape myths that victims "wanted it" and are to blame; inducing personal responsibility for coercive behavior; teaching social awareness, social skills, and anger management; and developing a support system to prevent future attacks.
Expand interventions for children and adolescents who have witnessed violence between their parents.	Although most child witnesses to parental violence do not become involved in abusive relationships as adults, they are at increased risk.
Teach both men and women to take precautions that lower the risk of sexual assault.	Risk of sexual assault can be reduced by communicating sexual limits clearly to a date; developing supportive ties to neighbors; increasing the safety of the immediate environment (for example, installing deadbolt locks, checking the back seat of the car before entering); avoiding deserted areas; not walking alone after dark; and leaving parties where alcohol use is high.
Broaden definitions of rape to be gender-neutral.	In a few U.S. states, where the definition of rape is limited to vaginal or anal penetration with a body part, a woman legally cannot rape a man. A universally applied definition that encompasses women as both victims and perpetrators is needed.

counter isolation and self-blame (Street, Bell, & Ready, 2011). Other critical features that foster recovery include

- *Routine screening for victimization* during health-care visits to ensure referral to community services and protection from future harm
- *Validation of the experience,* by acknowledging that many others have been similarly physically and sexually assaulted; that such assaults lead to a wide range of persisting symptoms, are illegal and inappropriate, and should not be tolerated; and that the trauma can be overcome
- *Safety planning,* even when the abuser is no longer present, to prevent recontact and reassault. This includes information about how to obtain police protection, legal intervention, a safe shelter, and other aid should a rape survivor be at risk again.

Finally, many steps can be taken at the level of the individual, the community, and society to prevent sexual coercion. Some are listed in Applying What We Know above.

Psychological Stress

A final health concern, threaded throughout previous sections, has such a broad impact that it merits a comment of its own. Psychological stress, measured in terms of adverse social conditions, traumatic experiences, negative life events, or daily hassles, is related to a wide variety of unfavorable health outcomes—both unhealthy behaviors and clear physical consequences. Recall from earlier chapters that intense, persistent stress, from the prenatal period on, disrupts the brain's inherent ability to manage stress, with long-term consequences. For individuals with childhood histories of stress, continuing stressful experiences combine with an impaired capacity to cope with stress, heightening the risk of adult health impairments.

As SES decreases, exposure to diverse stressors rises—an association that plays an important role in the strong connection between low SES and poor health (see pages 444–445). Chronic stress is linked to overweight and obesity, diabetes, hypertension, and atherosclerosis. And in susceptible individuals, acute stress can trigger cardiac events, including heartbeat rhythm abnormalities and heart attacks (Bekkouche et al., 2011; Kelly & Ismail, 2015). These relationships contribute to the high incidence of heart disease in low-income groups, especially African Americans. Compared with higher-SES individuals, low-SES adults show a stronger cardiovascular response to stress, perhaps because they more often perceive stressors as unsolvable (Carroll et al., 2007). Earlier we mentioned that stress interferes with immune system functioning, a link that may underlie its relationship to several forms of cancer. And by reducing digestive activity as blood flows to the brain, heart, and extremities, stress can cause gastrointestinal difficulties, including constipation, diarrhea, colitis, and ulcers (Donatelle, 2015).

The many challenging tasks of early adulthood make it a particularly stressful time of life. Young adults more often report depressive symptoms than middle-aged people, many of whom have attained vocational success and financial security and are enjoying more free time as parenting responsibilities decline (Nolen-Hoeksema & Aldao, 2011). Also, as we will see in Chapters 15 and 16, because of their longer life experience, middle-aged and older adults are better than young adults at coping with stress.

In previous chapters, we repeatedly noted the stress-buffering effect of social support, which continues throughout life. Helping young adults establish and maintain satisfying, caring social ties is as important a health intervention as any we have mentioned.

Ask yourself

CONNECT Describe history-graded influences that have contributed to the obesity epidemic. (To review this aspect of the lifespan perspective, refer to pages 9–10 in Chapter 1.)

APPLY Tom had been going to a health club three days a week after work, but job pressures convinced him that he no longer had time for regular exercise. Explain to Tom why he should keep up his exercise regimen, and suggest ways to fit it into his busy life.

REFLECT Have you used online dating sites or dating apps? Do you know others who have used them? In your view, what are the strengths and limitations of Internet dating as a way to find a compatible romantic partner?

COGNITIVE DEVELOPMENT

The cognitive changes of early adulthood are supported by further development of the cerebral cortex, especially the prefrontal cortex and its connections with other brain regions. Pruning of synapses along with growth and myelination of stimulated neural fibers continue, though at a slower pace than in adolescence. These changes result in continued fine-tuning of the *prefrontal cognitive-control network,* which achieves a better balance with the brain's *emotional/social network* as sensation seeking gradually diminishes (see pages 373–374 in Chapter 11). Consequently, planning, reasoning, and decision making improve, supported by major life events of this period—including attaining higher education, entering a career, and grappling with the demands of marriage and child rearing (Taber-Thomas & Perez-Edgar, 2016). Furthermore, fMRI evidence reveals that as young adults become increasingly proficient in a chosen field of endeavor, regions of the cerebral cortex specialized for those activities undergo further *experience-dependent brain growth* (see page 124 in Chapter 4). Besides more efficient functioning, structural changes occur as greater knowledge and refinement of skills result in more cortical tissue devoted to the task and, at times, reorganization of brain areas governing the activity (Lenroot & Giedd, 2006).

How does cognition change in early adulthood? Lifespan theorists have examined this question from three familiar vantage points. First, they have proposed transformations in the structure of thought—new, qualitatively distinct ways of thinking that extend the cognitive-developmental changes of adolescence. Second, adulthood is a time of acquiring advanced knowledge in a particular area, an accomplishment that has important implications for information processing and creativity. Finally, researchers are interested in the extent to which the diverse mental abilities assessed by intelligence tests remain stable or change during the adult years—a topic addressed in Chapter 15.

Changes in the Structure of Thought

13.7 Explain how thinking changes in early adulthood.

Sharese described her first year in graduate school as a "cognitive turning point." As part of her internship in a public health clinic, she observed firsthand the many factors that affect human health-related behaviors. For a time, the realization that everyday dilemmas did not have clear-cut solutions made her intensely uncomfortable. "Working in this messy reality is so different from the problem solving I did in my undergraduate classes," she told her mother over the phone one day.

Piaget (1967) recognized that important advances in thinking follow the attainment of formal operations. He observed that adolescents prefer an idealistic, internally consistent perspective on the world to one that is vague, contradictory, and adapted to particular circumstances (see Chapter 11, page 393). Sharese's reflections fit the observations of researchers who have studied **postformal thought**—cognitive development beyond Piaget's formal operational stage. To clarify how thinking is restructured in adulthood, let's look at some influential theories, along with supportive research. Together, they show how personal effort and social experiences combine to spark increasingly rational, flexible, and practical ways of thinking that accept uncertainties and vary across situations.

Epistemic Cognition

The work of William Perry (1981, 1970/1998) provided the starting point for an expanding research literature on the development of *epistemic cognition*. *Epistemic* means "of or about knowledge," and **epistemic cognition** refers to our reflections on how we arrived at facts, beliefs, and ideas. When mature, rational thinkers reach conclusions that differ from those of others, they consider the justifiability of their conclusions. When they cannot justify their approach, they revise it, seeking a more balanced, adequate route to acquiring knowledge.

Development of Epistemic Cognition.
Perry wondered why young adults respond in dramatically different ways to the diversity of ideas they encounter in college. To find out, he interviewed Harvard University undergraduates at the end of each of their four years, asking "what stood out" during the previous year. Responses indicated that students' reflections on knowing changed as they experienced the complexities of university life and moved closer to adult roles—findings confirmed in many subsequent studies (King & Kitchener, 2002; Magolda, Abes, & Torres, 2009; Magolda et al., 2012).

Younger students regarded knowledge as made up of separate units (beliefs and propositions), whose truth could be determined by comparing them to objective standards—standards that exist apart from the thinking person and his or her situation. As a result, they engaged in **dualistic thinking,** dividing information, values, and authority into right and wrong, good and bad, we and they. As one first-year college student put it, "When I went to my first lecture, what the man said was just like God's word. I believe everything he said because he is a professor ... and this is a respected position" (Perry, 1981, p. 81). When asked, "If two people disagree on the interpretation of a poem, how would you decide which one is right?" a sophomore replied, "You'd have to ask the poet. It's his poem" (Clinchy, 2002, p. 67). Dualistic thinkers approach learning by accepting what they are given.

Older students, in contrast, had moved toward **relativistic thinking,** viewing all knowledge as embedded in a framework of thought. Aware of a diversity of opinions on many topics, they gave up the possibility of absolute truth in favor of multiple truths, each relative to its context. As a result, their thinking became more flexible and tolerant. As one college senior put it, "Just seeing how [famous philosophers] fell short of an all-encompassing answer, [you realize] that ideas are really individualized. And you begin to have respect for how great their thought could be, without its being absolute" (Perry, 1970/1998, p. 90). Relativistic thinking leads to the realization that one's own beliefs are often subjective because several frameworks may satisfy the criterion of internal logical consistency (Sinnott, 2003). Thus, the relativistic thinker is acutely aware that each person, in arriving at a position, creates her own "truth."

Eventually, the most mature individuals progress to **commitment within relativistic thinking.** Instead of choosing between opposing views, they try to formulate a more personally satisfying perspective that synthesizes contradictions. When considering which of two theories studied in a college course is better or which of several movies most deserves an Oscar, the individual moves beyond the stance that everything is a matter of opinion and generates rational criteria against which options can be evaluated (Moshman, 2013). At the same time, mature thinkers willingly revise their internal belief system when presented with relevant evidence.

By the end of the college years, some students reach this extension of relativism. Adults who attain it generally display a more sophisticated approach to learning, in which they actively seek differing perspectives to deepen their knowledge and understanding and to clarify the basis for their own perspective. Notice how commitment within relativistic thinking involves the information-gathering cognitive style (see page 410 in Chapter 12) and pursuit of personally meaningful beliefs, values, and goals essential to healthy identity development. Mature epistemic cognition also contributes greatly to effective decision making and problem solving.

Importance of Peer Interaction and Reflection.

Advances in epistemic cognition depend on further gains in metacognition, which are likely to occur in situations that challenge young people's perspectives and induce them to consider the rationality of their thought processes (Barzilai & Zohar, 2015). In a study of the college learning experiences of seniors scoring low and high in epistemic cognition, high-scoring students frequently reported activities that encouraged them to struggle with realistic but ambiguous problems in a support-

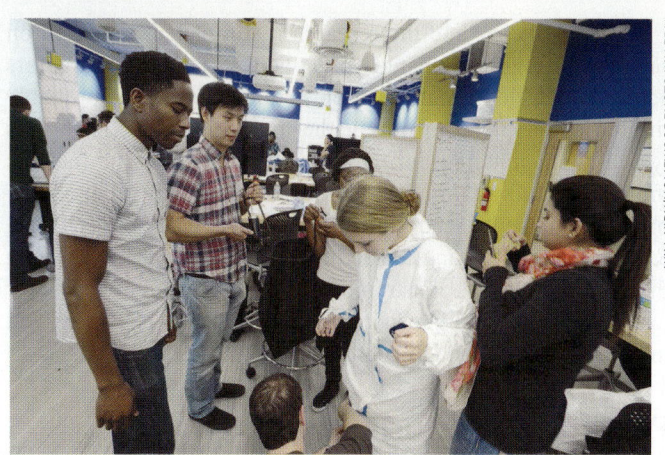

A team of university students participates in a global competition to design a more protective, lightweight, and comfortable suit for Ebola workers. Collaboratively tackling challenging, real-world problems leads to gains in epistemic cognition.

ive environment, in which faculty were committed to helping them understand how knowledge is constructed and why it must be subject to revision. For example, an engineering major, in describing an airplane-design project that required advanced epistemic cognition, mentioned his discovery that "you can design 30 different airplanes and each one's going to have its benefits and there's going to be problems with each one" (Marra & Palmer, 2004, p. 116). Low-scoring students rarely mentioned such experiences.

In tackling challenging, ill-structured problems, interaction among individuals who are roughly equal in knowledge and authority is beneficial because it prevents acceptance of another's reasoning simply because of greater power or expertise. When college students were asked to devise the most effective solution to a difficult logical problem, only 3 out of 32 students (9 percent) in a "work-alone" condition succeeded. But in an "interactive" condition, 15 out of 20 small groups (75 percent) arrived at the best answer following extensive discussion (Moshman & Geil, 1998). Whereas few students working alone reflected on their solution strategies, most groups engaged in a process of "collective rationality" in which members challenged one another to justify their reasoning and collaborated in working out the most effective strategy.

Of course, reflection on one's own thinking can also occur individually. But peer interaction fosters the necessary type of individual reflection: arguing with oneself over competing ideas and strategies and coordinating opposing perspectives into a new, more effective structure. As at earlier ages, peer collaboration remains a highly effective basis for education in early adulthood.

LOOK and LISTEN

Describe learning experiences in one of your college courses that advanced your epistemic cognition. How did your thinking change?

Perry's theory and the research it stimulated are based on samples of highly educated young adults. These investigators acknowledge that progress in epistemic cognition is probably limited to people confronting the multiplicity of viewpoints typically encountered during a college education and that the most advanced attainment—commitment within relativism—often requires advanced graduate study (Greene, Torney-Purta, & Azevedo, 2010; King & Kitchener, 2002). But the underlying theme—thought less constrained by the need to find one answer to a question and more responsive to its context—is also evident in another theory of adult cognition.

Pragmatic Thought and Cognitive-Affective Complexity

Gisella Labouvie-Vief's (1980, 1985) portrait of adult cognition echoes features of Perry's theory. Adolescents, she points out, operate within a world of possibility. Adulthood involves movement from hypothetical to **pragmatic thought,** a structural advance in which logic becomes a tool for solving real-world problems.

The need to specialize motivates this change. As adults select one path out of many alternatives, they become more aware of the constraints of everyday life. And in the course of balancing various roles, they accept contradictions as part of existence and develop ways of thinking that thrive on imperfection and compromise. Sharese's friend Christy, a married graduate student and parent of her first child at age 26, illustrates:

> I've always been a feminist, and I wanted to remain true to my beliefs in family and career. But this is Gary's first year of teaching high school, and he's saddled with four preparations and coaching the school's basketball team. At least for now, I've had to settle for "give-and-take feminism"—going to school part-time and shouldering most of the child-care responsibilities while he gets used to his new job. Otherwise, we'd never make it financially.

Labouvie-Vief (2003, 2005, 2015) also points out that young adults' enhanced reflective capacities alter the dynamics of their emotional lives: They become more adept at integrating cognition with emotion and, in doing so, again make sense of discrepancies. Examining the self-descriptions of 10- to 80-year-olds diverse in SES, Labouvie-Vief found that from adolescence through middle adulthood, people gained in **cognitive-affective complexity**—awareness of conflicting positive and negative feelings and coordination of them into a complex, organized structure that recognizes the uniqueness of individual experiences (see Figure 13.8) (Labouvie-Vief, 2008; Labouvie-Vief et al., 2007). For example, one 34-year-old combined roles, traits, and diverse emotions into this coherent self-description: "With the recent birth of our first child, I find myself more fulfilled than ever, yet struggling in some ways. My elation is tempered by my gnawing concern over meeting all my responsibilities in a satisfying way while remaining an individualized person with needs and desires."

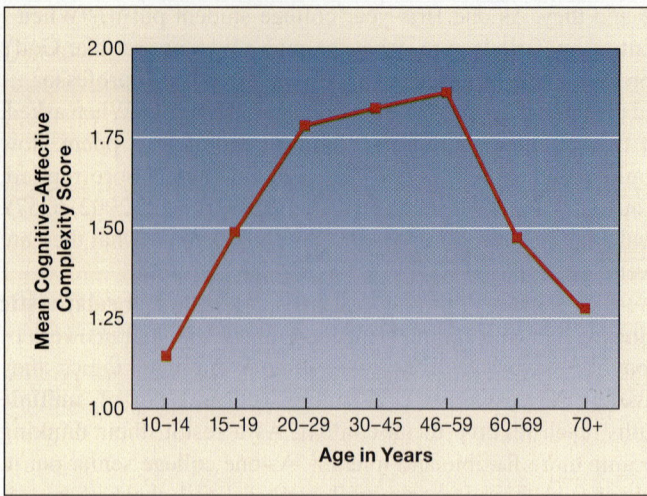

FIGURE 13.8 Changes in cognitive-affective complexity from adolescence to late adulthood. Performance, based on responses of several hundred 10- to 80-year-olds' descriptions of their roles, traits, and emotions, increased steadily from adolescence through early adulthood, peaked in middle age, and fell off in late adulthood when (as we will see in later chapters) basic information-processing skills decline. (From G. Labouvie-Vief, 2003, "Dynamic Integration: Affect, Cognition, and the Self in Adulthood," *Current Directions in Psychological Science, 12,* p. 203, copyright © 2003, Sage Publications. Reprinted by permission of SAGE Publications.)

Cognitive-affective complexity promotes greater awareness of one's own and others' perspectives and motivations. As Labouvie-Vief notes, it is a vital aspect of adult *emotional intelligence* (see page 317 in Chapter 9) and is valuable in solving many pragmatic problems. Individuals high in cognitive–affective complexity view events and people in a tolerant, open-minded fashion. And because cognitive–affective complexity involves accepting and making sense of both positive and negative feelings, it helps people regulate intense emotion and, therefore, think rationally about real-world dilemmas, even those that are laden with negative information (Labouvie-Vief, Grühn, & Studer, 2010).

Awareness of multiple truths, integration of logic with reality, and cognitive–affective complexity sum up qualitative transformations in thinking under way in early adulthood. As we will see next, adults' increasingly specialized and context-bound thought, although it closes off certain options, opens new doors to higher levels of competence.

 ## Expertise and Creativity

13.8 What roles do expertise and creativity play in adult thought?

In Chapter 9, we noted that children's expanding knowledge improves their ability to remember new information related to what they already know. For young adults, **expertise**—acquisition of extensive knowledge in a field or endeavor—is supported by the specialization that begins with selecting a college major or an occupation, since it takes many years to master any complex domain. Experts' curiosity, even passion, for their field fuels this sustained learning. As expertise is attained, it has a profound impact on information processing.

Compared with novices, experts remember and reason more quickly and effectively. The expert knows more domain-specific concepts and represents them in richer ways—at a deeper and more abstract level and as having more features that can be linked to other concepts. As a result, unlike novices, whose understanding is superficial, experts approach problems with underlying principles in mind. For example, a highly trained physicist notices when several problems deal with conservation of energy and can therefore be solved similarly. In contrast, a beginning physics student focuses only on surface features—whether the problem contains a disk, a pulley, or a coiled spring (Chi, 2006; Mayer, 2013). Experts can use what they know to arrive at many solutions automatically—through quick and easy remembering. And when a problem is challenging, they tend to plan ahead, systematically analyzing and categorizing elements and selecting the best from many possibilities, while the novice proceeds more by trial and error.

In addition to effective problem solving, expertise is necessary for creativity (Weissberg, 2006). The creative products of adulthood differ from those of childhood in that they are not just original but also directed at a social or aesthetic need. Mature creativity requires a unique cognitive capacity—the ability to formulate new, culturally meaningful problems and to ask significant questions that have not been posed before (Rostan, 1994). Movement from *problem solving* to *problem finding* is a core feature of postformal thought evident in highly creative artists and scientists.

Case studies support the 10-year rule in development of master-level creativity—a decade between initial exposure to a field and sufficient expertise to produce a creative work. Furthermore, a century of research reveals that creative productivity typically rises in early adulthood, peaks in the late thirties or early forties, and gradually declines, though creative individuals near the end of their careers are usually more productive than those just starting their careers (Simonton, 2012). But exceptions exist. Those who get an early start in creativity tend to peak and drop off sooner, whereas "late bloomers" reach their full stride at older ages. This suggests that creativity is more a function of "career age" than of chronological age.

The course of creativity also varies across disciplines and individuals (Simonton, 2012; Simonton & Damian, 2013). For example, poets, visual artists, and musicians typically show an early rise in creativity, perhaps because they do not need extensive formal education before they begin to produce. Academic scholars and scientists, who must earn higher academic degrees and spend years doing research to make worthwhile contributions, tend to display their achievements later and over a longer time. And whereas some creators are highly productive, others make only a single lifetime contribution.

Though creativity is rooted in expertise, not all experts are creative. Creativity also requires other qualities. A vital ingredient is the capacity to "think intuitively" with a reduced filter—to avoid dismissing information that, at first glance, appears irrelevant. Although this lessened inhibition is a liability in other forms of cognition, it contributes to creators' capacity to think "outside the box"—to come up with numerous, unusual associations that they can capitalize on during the creative process (Carson, Peterson, & Higgins, 2003; Dane et al., 2011).

In personality, creative individuals are tolerant of ambiguity, open to new experiences, persistent and driven to succeed, capable of deep task involvement, and willing to try again after failure (Zhang & Sternberg, 2011). Finally, creativity demands time and energy. For women especially, it may be postponed or disrupted by child rearing, divorce, or an unsupportive partner.

In sum, creativity is multiply determined. When personal and situational factors jointly promote it, creativity can continue for many decades, well into old age.

Visual artists as well as poets and musicians typically show an early rise in creativity, though they may need a decade or more to produce master-level creative works.

Ask yourself

CONNECT Why is expertise necessary for creativity? What additional ingredients are essential for creative thought?

APPLY For her lifespan development course, Marcia wrote a paper discussing the differing implications of Piaget's and Vygotsky's theories for education. Next, she reasoned that combining the two perspectives is more effective than relying on either position by itself. Explain how Marcia's reasoning illustrates advanced epistemic cognition.

REFLECT Describe a classroom experience or assignment in one of your college courses that promoted relativistic thinking.

The College Experience

13.9 Describe the impact of a college education on young people's lives, and discuss the problem of dropping out.

Looking back at the trajectory of their lives, many people view the college years as formative—more influential than any other period of adulthood. This is not surprising. College serves as a "developmental testing ground," a time for devoting full attention to exploring alternative values, roles, and behaviors. To facilitate this exploration, college exposes students to a form of "culture shock"—encounters with new ideas and beliefs, new freedoms and opportunities, and new academic and social demands.

Nearly 70 percent of U.S. recent high school graduates enrolled in an institution of higher education. Among college students, 60 percent followed this traditional route of starting college shortly after finishing high school, earning their undergraduate degree by age 24. The remaining 40 percent, who range widely in age, delayed college entry because of financial constraints, family responsibilities, or other life circumstances (U.S. Department of Education, 2015). Most research on the transforming impact of attending college focuses on traditional students between ages 18 and 24. We will consider nontraditional students in Chapter 15.

Psychological Impact of Attending College

Thousands of studies reveal broad psychological changes from the freshman to the senior year of college (Montgomery & Côté, 2003; Pascarella & Terenzini, 1991, 2005). As research on epistemic cognition revealed, students become better at reasoning about problems that have no clear solution, identifying the strengths and weaknesses of opposing sides of complex issues, and reflecting on the quality of their thinking. Their attitudes and values also broaden. They show increased interest in literature, the performing arts, and philosophical and historical issues and greater tolerance for racial and ethnic diversity. Also, as noted in Chapter 12, college leaves its mark on moral reasoning by fostering concern with individual rights and human welfare, sometimes expressed in political activism. Finally, exposure to multiple worldviews encourages young people to look more closely at themselves. During the college years, students develop greater self-understanding, enhanced self-esteem, and a firmer sense of identity.

How do these interrelated changes come about? The impact of college is jointly influenced by the richness of campus academic and out-of-class offerings and students' engagement in those experiences. The more students study and interact with both faculty and diverse peers in academic and extracurricular settings, the more they benefit cognitively—in grasping the complex causes of events, thinking critically, and generating effective problem solutions (Bowman, 2011a). Also, interacting with racially and ethnically mixed peers—both in courses exploring

Community college students join in a Peace Week activity, keeping pace with the beat of a drum circle. The more students interact with diverse peers in academic and extracurricular settings, the more they benefit cognitively from attending college.

diversity issues and in out-of-class settings—predicts gains in civic engagement. And students who connect their community service experiences with their classroom learning show large cognitive gains (Bowman, 2011b; Parker & Pascarella, 2013). These findings underscore the importance of programs that integrate commuting students into extracurricular campus life.

To what extent are U.S. college students sufficiently engaged in educationally meaningful experiences to transition successfully to the labor market? For research that bears on this question, refer to the Social Issues: Education box on the following page.

Dropping Out

In the 1970s, the United States ranked first in the world in percentage of young adults with college degrees; today it is twelfth, with just 44 percent of 25- to 34-year-olds having graduated. It lags far behind such countries as Canada, Japan, and South Korea, the global leader—where the rate is 66 percent (OECD, 2014). Major contributing factors are the high U.S. child poverty rate; poor-quality schools in low-income neighborhoods; and high rates of high school dropout among economically disadvantaged, ethnic minority teenagers (see page 402 in Chapter 11). College leaving is also influential: Six years after enrolling at a four-year institution, 42 percent of U.S. students have not earned their degrees. Most dropouts leave within the first year and many within the first six weeks. Dropout rates are higher in colleges with less selective admission requirements (U.S. Department of Education, 2015). And ethnic minority students from low-SES families are, once again, at increased risk of dropping out.

Both personal and institutional factors contribute to college leaving. Most entering freshmen have high hopes for college life but find the transition difficult. Those who have trouble adapting—because of lack of motivation, poor study skills, financial pressures, or emotional dependence on parents—quickly develop negative attitudes toward the college environment. Often these exit-prone students do not meet with their

Social Issues: Education

How Important Is Academic Engagement in College for Successful Transition to the Labor Market?

Do critical thinking, complex reasoning, and written communication—skills designated by educators and employers as crucial for success in the twenty-first century economy—really matter in college graduates' efforts to secure a satisfying, well-paid job? To find out, researchers gave 1,600 students at 25 U.S. four-year colleges and universities a test of general collegiate learning in the fall of their first year and, again, around the time they graduated (Arum & Roksa, 2014). The students also responded to surveys and in-depth interviews about the meaningfulness of their college experiences. Two years after graduation, they reported on employment outcomes.

Participants' post-college paths varied widely. Some transitioned successfully to challenging work roles that launched them on a career track. But more than half were underemployed (in jobs not requiring a college education) or unemployed. Across institutions varying widely in admission requirements, senior-year collegiate learning scores predicted success at securing jobs requiring bachelor's level skills, along with student reports that their work was both cognitively challenging and personally fulfilling.

Successful graduates were keenly aware of this link between collegiate learning and post-college success. Ashley, who landed a well-paid job as a program coordinator at a senior center, commented that her college in-class and out-of-class experiences taught her how "to work in groups, ... to think critically and be able to solve problems [and] to understand different perspectives" (Arum & Roksa, 2014, p. 77). In contrast, students with low collegiate learning scores found it hard to articulate the benefits of their college experiences. After an unsuccessful search for work related to his business degree, Nathan accepted a low-wage job as a delivery driver for a retail chain. Although he graduated with a high grade point average, he mentioned going to lots of parties, could think of little that stood out about his courses, and did not participate in any educationally relevant extracurricular activities.

Like Nathan, most participants gained little in collegiate learning during their four years of college. Since the 1970s, the time U.S. college students spend studying has declined by half, while the time they devote to socializing and other forms of entertainment has risen dramatically (Brint & Cantwell, 2010). As institutions redefined students as consumers, academic demands receded and grade inflation increased.

Surveys of employers indicate that less than one-fourth of U.S. college graduates enter the labor market with excellent collegiate skills (Fischer, 2013). Clear evidence that critical thinking, complex reasoning, and written communication have substantial labor market payoffs underscores the need for colleges to promote students' involvement in academics and career-relevant extracurricular experiences, and to upgrade the rigor of their courses.

A Baylor University forensic science professor (center) and her students work to identify the remains of unidentified migrants who died trying to enter the United States without legal documents. Students who find their coursework both cognitively challenging and personally fulfilling are more likely to experience success in their post-college careers.

---

advisers or professors (Stewart, Lim, & Kim, 2015). At the same time, colleges that do little to help high-risk students, through developmental courses and other support services, have a higher percentage of dropouts.

Beginning to prepare young people in early adolescence with the necessary visions and skills can do much to improve college success. In a study that tracked nearly 700 young people from sixth grade until two years after high school graduation, a set of factors—grade point average, academic self-concept, persistence in the face of challenge, and parental SES and valuing of a college education—predicted college enrollment at age 20 (Eccles, Vida, & Barber, 2004). Although parental SES is difficult to modify, improving parents' attitudes and behaviors and students' academic motivation and educational aspirations is within reach, through a wide array of strategies considered in Chapters 11 and 12.

Once young people enroll in college, reaching out to them, especially during the early weeks and throughout the first year, is crucial. Programs that forge bonds between teachers and students and that generously fund student services—providing academic support, counseling to address academic and personal challenges, part-time work opportunities, and meaningful extracurricular roles—increase retention. Membership in campus-based social and religious organizations is especially helpful in strengthening minority students' sense of belonging (Chen, 2012; Kuh, Cruce, & Shoup, 2008). Students who feel that their college community is concerned about them as individuals are far more likely to graduate.

Vocational Choice

13.10 Trace the development of vocational choice, and cite factors that influence it.

13.11 What problems do U.S. non-college-bound young people face in preparing for a vocation?

Young adults, college-bound or not, face a major life decision: the choice of a suitable work role. Being a productive worker calls for many of the same qualities as being an active citizen and a nurturant family member—good judgment, responsibility, dedication, and cooperation. What influences young people's decisions about careers? What is the transition from school to work like, and what factors make it easy or difficult?

Selecting a Vocation

In societies with an abundance of career possibilities, occupational choice is a gradual process that begins long before adolescence and often extends into the mid-twenties. Major theorists view the young person as moving through several periods of vocational development (Gottfredson, 2005; Super, 1994):

1. The **fantasy period:** In early and middle childhood, children gain insight into career options by fantasizing about them (Howard & Walsh, 2010). Their preferences, guided largely by familiarity, glamour, and excitement, bear little relation to the decisions they will eventually make.
2. The **tentative period:** Between ages 11 and 16, adolescents think about careers in more complex ways, at first in terms of their *interests,* and soon—as they become more aware of personal and educational requirements for different vocations—in terms of their *abilities* and *values.* "I like science and the process of discovery," Sharese thought as she neared high school graduation. "But I'm also good with people, and I'd like to do something to help others. So maybe teaching or medicine would suit my needs."
3. The **realistic period:** By the late teens and early twenties, with the economic and practical realities of adulthood just around the corner, young people start to narrow their options. A first step is often further *exploration*—gathering more information about possibilities that blend with their personal characteristics. In the final phase, *crystallization,* they focus on a general vocational category and experiment for a time before settling on a single occupation (Stringer, Kerpelman, & Skorikov, 2011). As a college sophomore, Sharese pursued her interest in science, but she had not yet selected a major. Once she decided on chemistry, she considered whether to pursue teaching, medicine, or public health.

Factors Influencing Vocational Choice

Most, but not all, young people follow this pattern of vocational development. A few know from an early age just what they want to be and follow a direct path to a career goal. Some decide and later change their minds, and still others remain undecided for an extended period. College students are granted added time to explore various options. In contrast, the life conditions of many low-SES youths restrict their range of choices.

Making an occupational choice is not simply a rational process in which young people weigh abilities, interests, and values against career options. Like other developmental milestones, it is the result of a dynamic interaction between person and environment (Sharf, 2013). A great many influences feed into the decision, including personality, family, teachers, and gender stereotypes, among others.

Personality. People are attracted to occupations that complement their personalities. John Holland (1985, 1997) identified six personality types that affect vocational choice:

- The *investigative person,* who enjoys working with ideas, is likely to select a scientific occupation (for example, anthropologist, physicist, or engineer).
- The *social person,* who likes interacting with people, gravitates toward human services (counseling, social work, or teaching).
- The *realistic person,* who prefers real-world problems and working with objects, tends to choose a mechanical occupation (construction, plumbing, or surveying).
- The *artistic person,* who is emotional and high in need for individual expression, looks toward an artistic field (writing, music, or the visual arts).
- The *conventional person,* who likes well-structured tasks and values material possessions and social status, has traits well-suited to certain business fields (accounting, banking, or quality control).
- The *enterprising person,* who is adventurous, persuasive, and a strong leader, is drawn to sales and supervisory positions or to politics.

Young architects work on their award-winning model that shows how Los Angeles might look in the year 2106. Vocational choice is moderately influenced by personality, with external factors such as parenting, education, job opportunities, and life circumstances all playing important roles.

Research confirms a relationship between personality and vocational choice in diverse cultures, but it is only moderate (Spokane & Cruza-Guet, 2005; Tang, 2009). Many people are blends of several personality types and can do well at more than one kind of occupation.

Furthermore, career decisions are made in the context of family influences, financial resources, educational and job opportunities, and current life circumstances. For example, Sharese's friend Christy scored high on Holland's investigative dimension. But after she married, had her first child, and faced increasing financial pressures, she postponed her dream of becoming a college professor and chose a human services career that required fewer years of education and offered reasonable likelihood of employment after graduation. Thus, personality takes us only partway in understanding vocational choice.

Family Influences. Young people's vocational aspirations correlate strongly with their parents' jobs. Individuals who grew up in higher-SES homes are more likely to select high-status, white-collar occupations, such as doctor, lawyer, scientist, or engineer. In contrast, those with lower-SES backgrounds tend to choose less prestigious, blue-collar careers—for example, plumber, construction worker, food service employee, or office worker. Parent–child vocational similarity is partly a function of similarity in personality, intellectual abilities, and—especially—educational attainment (Ellis & Bonin, 2003; Schoon & Parsons, 2002). Number of years of schooling completed is a powerful predictor of occupational status.

Other factors also promote family resemblance in occupational choice. Higher-SES parents are more likely to give their children important information about the worlds of education and work and to have connections with people who can help the young person obtain a high-status position (Kalil, Levine, & Ziol-Guest, 2005; Levine & Sutherland, 2013). In a study of African-American mothers' influence on their daughters' academic and career goals, college-educated mothers engaged in a wider range of strategies to promote their daughters' progress, including gathering information on colleges and areas of study and identifying knowledgeable professionals who could help (Kerpelman, Shoffner, & Ross-Griffin, 2002).

Parenting practices also shape work-related preferences. Recall from Chapter 2 that higher-SES parents tend to promote curiosity and self-direction, which are required in many high-status careers. Still, all parents can foster higher aspirations. Parental guidance, pressure to do well in school, college-going expectations, and encouragement toward high-status occupations predict confidence in career choice and educational and career attainment beyond SES (Bryant, Zvonkovic, & Reynolds, 2006; Gregory & Huang, 2013; Stringer & Kerpelman, 2010).

Teachers. Young adults preparing for or engaged in careers that require extensive education often report that teachers influenced their educational aspirations and career choice. High school students who say that most of their teachers are caring and accessible, interested in their future, and demand that they work hard feel more confident about choosing a personally suitable career and succeeding at it (Metheny, McWhirter, & O'Neil, 2008). And in longitudinal research, teacher expectations for educational attainment predicted students' enrollment in college two years after high school graduation more strongly than did parents' expectations (Gregory & Huang, 2013; Sciarra & Ambrosina, 2011). Teacher expectations mattered most for low-SES students.

These findings provide yet another reason to promote positive teacher–student relations, especially for high school students from low-SES families. Teachers who offer encouragement and communicate with students about their potential can serve as an important source of resilience for these young people.

Gender Stereotypes. Over the past four decades, young women have expressed increasing interest in nontraditional occupations (Gati & Perez, 2014; Gottfredson, 2005). Changes in gender-role attitudes, along with a dramatic rise in numbers of employed mothers who serve as career-oriented models for their daughters, are common explanations for women's attraction to nontraditional careers.

But women's progress in entering and excelling at male-dominated professions has been slow. As Table 13.2 shows, although the percentage of women architects, engineers, lawyers, doctors, and business executives has risen in the United States over the past three decades, it still falls far short of equal representation. Women remain concentrated in less-well-paid, traditionally feminine professions such as social work, education,

TABLE 13.2

Percentage of Women in Various Professions in the United States, 1983 and 2015

PROFESSION	1983	2015
Architect or engineer	5.8	15.1
Lawyer	15.8	34.5
Physician	15.8	37.9
Business executive	32.4	39.2[a]
Author, artist, entertainer	42.7	47.6
Social worker	64.3	83.8
Elementary or middle school teacher	93.5	80.7
Secondary school teacher	62.2	59.2
College or university professor	36.3	46.5
Librarian	84.4	83.0
Registered nurse	95.8	89.4
Psychologist	57.1	70.3

Source: U.S. Department of Labor, 2016a.

[a]This percentage includes executives and managers at all levels. As of 2016, women made up only 4 percent of chief executive officers at Fortune 500 companies, although that figure represents twice as many as 10 years ago.

Cultural Influences

Masculinity at Work: Men Who Choose Nontraditional Careers

Ross had always planned to major in engineering, but in his sophomore year of college, he startled his family and friends by deciding to pursue a nursing degree instead. "I've never looked back," Ross said. "I love the work." He noted some benefits of being a male in a female work world, including rapid advancement and the high regard of women colleagues. "But as soon as they learn what I do," Ross remarked with disappointment, "guys on the outside question my abilities and masculinity."

What factors influence the slowly increasing number of men who, like Ross, enter careers dominated by women? Compared to their traditional-career counterparts, these men tend to be more liberal in their social attitudes, less gender-typed, less focused on the social status of their work, and more interested in working with people (Dodson & Borders, 2006; Jome, Surething, & Taylor, 2005). Perhaps their gender-stereotype flexibility allows them to choose occupations they find satisfying, even if those jobs are not typically regarded as appropriate for men. However, they do take into account the probable financial returns of their choice (Hardie, 2015). They orient more toward nontraditional careers with higher average incomes.

Interviews with male nurses, flight attendants, primary school teachers, and librarians confirm Ross's observations: In line with stereotypes of men's greater desire for promotion and leadership, co-workers tend to assume they are more knowledgeable than they actually are. These men often report being offered choice job placements and opportunities to move quickly into supervisory positions, although many did not seek such advancement (Simpson, 2004; Williams, 2013). As one teacher commented, "I just want to be a good classroom teacher. What's wrong with that?"

But when asked to reflect on how others reacted to their choice, many men express anxiety about being stigmatized—mostly by other men. To reduce these feelings, they frequently describe their job in ways that minimize its feminine image. For example, several librarians emphasized technical requirements by referring to their title as "information scientist" or "researcher." Nurses sometimes distance themselves from a feminine work identity by specializing in "adrenaline-charged" areas such as accident or emergency (Simpson, 2005). Despite these tensions, as with Ross, a high level of private comfort with their career choice seems to prevail over uneasiness about the feminine public image of their work.

Still, men face certain barriers that resemble those of women preparing for nontraditional careers. For example, male students in college nursing programs often mention lack of male mentors and a "cooler" educational climate, which they attribute to implicit gender discrimination and unsupportive behaviors of women nurse educators (Meadus & Twomey, 2011). And many encounter the view

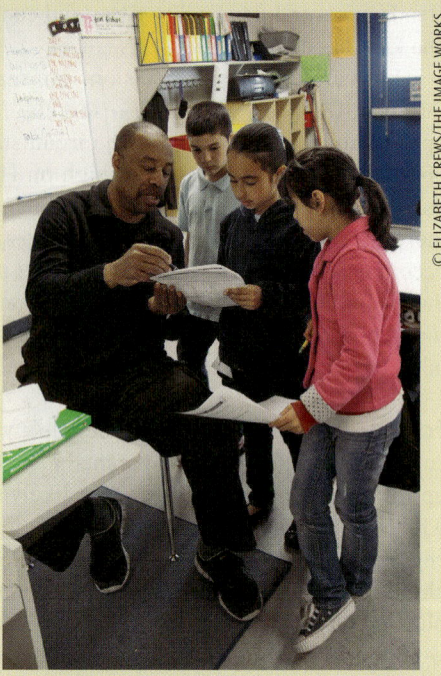

This elementary school teacher is among the increasing number of men entering careers dominated by women. Compared with his traditional-career counterparts, he is likely to be less gender-typed and more interested in working with people.

that they are less able than women to perform stereotypically "feminine" aspects of their jobs, such as those requiring sensitivity and caring—experiences that can increase work-related stress (Sobiraj et al., 2015). These findings reveal that to facilitate entry into nontraditional careers, men, too, would benefit from supportive relationships with same-gender role models and an end to gender-biased beliefs and behaviors.

---

librarianship, and nursing (U.S. Department of Labor, 2016a). In virtually all fields, women's achievements lag behind those of men, who write more books, make more discoveries, hold more positions of leadership, and produce more works of art.

Ability cannot account for these dramatic sex differences. Recall from Chapter 11 that girls are advantaged in reading and writing achievement, and the gender gap favoring boys in math is small and has been shrinking. Rather, gender-stereotyped messages play a key role. Although girls earn higher grades than boys, they reach secondary school less confident of their abilities, more likely to underestimate their achievement, and less likely to express interest in STEM careers (see page 395).

In college, the career aspirations of many women decline further as they question their capacity and opportunities to succeed in male-dominated fields and worry about combining a highly demanding career with family responsibilities (Chhin, Bleeker, & Jacobs, 2008; Sadler et al., 2012). Many college women talented in math and science settle on nonscience majors or non-STEM fields. An investigation of science-oriented young people in 50 nations revealed uniform findings: In every country, female students preferred careers in biology, agriculture, medicine, or another health profession, whereas male students favored computing, engineering, or math. And almost without exception, males expressed greater confidence in their science ability—

a gender difference that was considerably larger in industrialized than developing nations (Sikora & Pokropek, 2012). In economically advanced countries, the researchers speculated, gender-typed beliefs about science ability had far greater opportunity to become deeply ingrained and widespread.

These findings reveal a pressing need for programs that sensitize educators to the special problems women face in developing and maintaining high vocational aspirations and selecting nontraditional careers. Young women's aspirations rise in response to career guidance that encourages them to set goals that match their abilities and faculty who take steps to enhance their experiences in math and science courses. Contact with women scientists and engineers adds to female students' interest in and expectancies for success in STEM fields (Holdren & Lander, 2012). And such mentoring may help them see how altruistic values—which are particularly important to females—can be fulfilled within STEM occupations.

Compared to women, men have changed little in their interest in nontraditional occupations. See the Cultural Issues box on the previous page for research on the motivations and experiences of men who do choose female-dominated careers.

Vocational Preparation of Non-College-Bound Young Adults

Sharese's younger brother Leon graduated from high school in a vocational track. Like approximately one-third of U.S. young people with a high school diploma, he had no current plans to go to college. While in school, Leon held a part-time job selling candy at the local shopping mall. He hoped to work in data processing after graduation, but six months later he was still a part-time sales clerk at the candy store. Although Leon had filled out many job applications, he got no interviews or offers.

Leon's inability to find a job other than the one he held as a student is typical for U.S. non-college-bound high school graduates. Although they are more likely to find employment than youths who drop out, they have fewer work opportunities than high school graduates of several decades ago. Nearly 20 percent of U.S. recent high school graduates who do not continue their education are unemployed (U.S. Department of Labor, 2015a). When they do find work, most hold low-paid, unskilled jobs. In addition, they have few alternatives for vocational counseling and job placement as they transition from school to work.

American employers regard recent high school graduates as unprepared for skilled business and industrial occupations and manual trades. And there is some truth to this impression. As noted in Chapter 11, unlike European nations, the United States has no widespread training system for non-college-bound youths. As a result, most graduate without work-related skills.

In Germany, young people who do not go to a Gymnasium (college-preparatory high school) have access to one of the most successful work–study apprenticeship systems in the world for entering business and industry. About 60 percent of German youths participate. After completing full-time schooling at age 15 or 16, they spend the remaining two years of compulsory education in the Berufsschule, combining part-time vocational courses with an apprenticeship that is jointly planned by educators and employers. Students train in work settings for more than 300 blue- and white-collar occupations. Apprentices who complete the program and pass a qualifying examination are certified as skilled workers and earn union-set wages. Businesses provide financial support because they know that the program guarantees a competent, dedicated work force. Many apprentices are hired into well-paid jobs by the firms that train them (Audretsch & Lehmann, 2016). Because of the apprenticeship system, Germany has the lowest unemployment rate among 18- to 25-year-olds in Europe—less than 8 percent.

The success of the German system—and of similar systems in Austria, Denmark, Switzerland, and several East European countries—suggests that a national apprenticeship program would improve the transition from high school to work for U.S. young people. The many benefits of bringing together the worlds of schooling and work include helping non-college-bound young people establish productive lives right after graduation, motivating at-risk youths to stay in school, and contributing to the nation's economic growth. Nevertheless, implementing an apprenticeship system poses major challenges: overcoming the reluctance of employers to assume part of the responsibility for vocational training, ensuring cooperation between schools and businesses, and preventing low-SES youths from being concentrated in the lowest-skilled apprenticeship placements or from being unable to find any placement, an obstacle that Germany itself has not yet fully overcome (Lang, 2010). Currently, small-scale school-to-work projects in the United States are attempting to solve these problems and build bridges between learning and working.

Although vocational development is a lifelong process, adolescence and early adulthood are crucial periods for defining occupational goals and launching a career. Young people who are well-prepared for an economically and personally satisfying work life are much more likely to become productive citizens, devoted family members, and contented adults. The support of families, schools, businesses, communities, and society as a whole can contribute greatly to a positive outcome. In Chapter 14, we will take up the challenges of establishing a career and integrating it with other life tasks.

Ask yourself

CONNECT What have you learned in previous chapters about development of gender stereotypes that helps explain women's slow progress in entering and excelling at male-dominated professions? (*Hint:* See Chapter 10, page 338, and Chapter 11, page 395.)

APPLY Diane, a first-year college student, knows that she wants to "work with people" but doesn't yet have a specific career in mind. Her father is a chemistry professor, her mother a social worker. What can Diane's parents do to broaden her awareness of the world of work and help her focus on an occupational goal?

REFLECT Describe personal and environmental influences on your progress in choosing a vocation.

Summary / chapter 13

PHYSICAL DEVELOPMENT

Biological Aging Is Under Way in Early Adulthood (p. 438)

13.1 *Describe current theories of biological aging, both at the level of DNA and body cells and at the level of tissues and organs.*

- Once body structures reach maximum capacity and efficiency in the teens and twenties, **biological aging,** or **senescence,** begins.

- The programmed effects of specific genes may control certain age-related biological changes. For example, **telomere** shortening results in senescent cells, which contribute to disease and loss of function.

- DNA may also be damaged as random mutations accumulate, leading to less efficient cell repair and replacement and to abnormal cancerous cells. Release of **free radicals**, once thought to be a major contributor to age-related DNA and cellular damage, may instead activate DNA repair systems within cells, thereby lengthening life.

- The **cross-linkage theory of aging** suggests that over time, protein fibers form links and become less elastic, producing negative changes in many organs. Declines in the endocrine and immune systems may also contribute to aging.

Physical Changes (p. 440)

13.2 *Describe the physical changes of aging, paying special attention to the cardiovascular and respiratory systems, motor performance, the immune system, and reproductive capacity.*

- Gradual physical changes take place in early adulthood and later accelerate. Declines in heart and lung performance are evident during exercise. Heart disease is a leading cause of death in adults, although it has decreased since the mid-twentieth century due to lifestyle changes and medical advances.

- Athletic skills requiring speed, strength, and gross-motor coordination peak in the early twenties; those requiring endurance, arm–hand steadiness, and aiming peak in the late twenties and early thirties. Inactivity rather than biological aging is largely responsible for age-related declines in motor performance.

- The immune response declines after age 20 because of shrinkage of the thymus gland and increased difficulty coping with physical and psychological stress.

- Women's reproductive capacity declines with age due to reduced quality and quantity of ova. In men, semen volume and sperm motility decrease gradually after age 35, and the percentage of abnormal sperm rises.

Health and Fitness (p. 444)

13.3 *Describe the influence of SES, nutrition, and exercise on health, and discuss obesity in adulthood.*

- Health inequalities associated with SES increase in adulthood. Health-related circumstances and habits underlie these disparities.

- Sedentary lifestyles and diets high in sugar and fat have contributed to the U.S. overweight and obesity epidemic. Excess weight is associated with serious health problems, social discrimination, and early death.

- Some weight gain in adulthood reflects a decrease in **basal metabolic rate (BMR),** but many young adults add excess weight. Effective treatment includes a nutritious diet low in calories plus regular exercise, recording of food intake and body weight, social support, and teaching problem-solving skills.

- Regular exercise reduces body fat, builds muscle, fosters resistance to disease, and enhances cognitive functioning and psychological well-being.

13.4 *What are the most commonly abused substances, and what health risks do they pose?*

- Tobacco, marijuana, and alcohol are the most commonly abused substances. Cigarette smokers, most of whom began before age 21, are at increased risk for many health problems, including decline in bone mass, heart attack, stroke, and numerous cancers.

- About one-third of heavy drinkers suffer from alcoholism, to which both heredity and environment contribute. Alcohol is implicated in liver and cardiovascular disease, certain cancers and other physical disorders, motor vehicle fatalities, crime, and sexual coercion.

13.5 *Describe sexual attitudes and behavior of young adults, and discuss sexually transmitted infections and sexual coercion.*

- Most adults are less sexually active than media images suggest, but they display a wider range of sexual choices and lifestyles and have had more sexual partners than earlier generations. The Internet has become a popular way to initiate relationships.

- Adults in committed relationships report high satisfaction with their sex lives. Only a minority report persistent sexual problems—difficulties linked to biological factors and to low SES and psychological stress.

- Attitudes toward same-sex couples have become more accepting. Same-sex partners, like heterosexual partners, tend to be similar in education and background and more satisfied in committed relationships.

- Sexually transmitted infections (STIs) continue to be prevalent throughout the twenties; women are at great risk for lasting health consequences. AIDS, the most deadly STI, is spreading most rapidly through men having sex with men and through heterosexual contact in poverty-stricken minority groups.

- Most rape victims are women under age 25 who have been harmed by men they know well. Personal characteristics of perpetrators and cultural acceptance of strong gender typing and of violence contribute to sexual coercion. Although less often reported and recognized by authorities, men are also victims. Regardless of gender, rape survivors experience extreme trauma.

13.6 How does psychological stress affect health?

- Chronic psychological stress induces physical responses that contribute to cardiovascular disease, several types of cancer, and gastrointestinal problems. The challenges of early adulthood increase stress; young people can reduce stress by forming supportive social ties.

COGNITIVE DEVELOPMENT

Changes in the Structure of Thought (p. 456)

13.7 Explain how thinking changes in early adulthood.

- Development of the cerebral cortex in early adulthood results in continued fine-tuning of the prefrontal cognitive-control network, which achieves a better balance with the brain's emotional/social network, contributing to improvements in planning, reasoning, and decision making.

- Cognitive development beyond Piaget's formal operations is known as **postformal thought**. In early adulthood, personal effort and social experiences combine to spark increasingly rational, flexible, and practical ways of thinking.

- In Perry's theory of **epistemic cognition**, college students move from **dualistic thinking**, dividing information into right and wrong, to **relativistic thinking**, awareness of multiple truths. The most mature individuals progress to **commitment within relativistic thinking**, which synthesizes contradictions.

- Advances in epistemic cognition depend on gains in metacognition. Peer collaboration on challenging, ill-structured problems is especially beneficial.

- In Labouvie-Vief's theory, the need to specialize motivates adults to move from hypothetical to **pragmatic thought,** which uses logic as a tool for solving real-world problems and accepts contradiction, imperfection, and compromise. Adults' enhanced reflective capacities permit gains in **cognitive-affective complexity**—coordination of positive and negative feelings into a complex, organized structure.

Expertise and Creativity (p. 458)

13.8 What roles do expertise and creativity play in adult thought?

- Specialization in college and in an occupation leads to **expertise,** which is necessary for both problem solving and creativity. Although creativity tends to rise in early adulthood and to peak in the late thirties or early forties, its development varies across disciplines and individuals. Diverse personal and situational factors jointly promote creativity.

The College Experience (p. 460)

13.9 Describe the impact of a college education on young people's lives, and discuss the problem of dropping out.

- College students' explorations, both academic and nonacademic, yield gains in knowledge and reasoning ability, broadening of attitudes and values, enhanced self-understanding and self-esteem, and a firmer sense of identity.

- Personal and institutional factors contribute to college dropout, which is more common in less selective colleges and among ethnic minority students from low-SES families. High-risk students benefit from interventions that show concern for them as individuals.

Vocational Choice (p. 462)

13.10 Trace the development of vocational choice, and cite factors that influence it.

- Vocational choice moves through a **fantasy period,** in which children explore career options by fantasizing about them; a **tentative period,** in which teenagers evaluate careers in terms of their interests, abilities, and values; and a **realistic period,** in which young people settle on a vocational category and then a specific occupation.

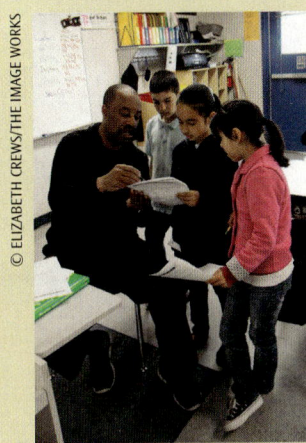

- Vocational choice is influenced by personality; parents' provision of educational opportunities, vocational information, and encouragement; and close relationships with teachers who hold high educational expectations.

- Women's progress in male-dominated professions has been slow, and their achievements lag behind those of men in virtually all fields. Gender-stereotyped messages play a key role.

13.11 What problems do U.S. non-college-bound young people face in preparing for a vocation?

- Most U.S. non-college-bound high school graduates are limited to low-paid, unskilled jobs, and many are unemployed. Work–study apprenticeships, like those widely available in Europe, would improve the transition from school to work for these young people.

Important Terms and Concepts

basal metabolic rate (BMR) (p. 446)
biological aging, or senescence (p. 438)
cognitive-affective complexity (p. 458)
commitment within relativistic thinking (p. 457)
cross-linkage theory of aging (p. 440)
dualistic thinking (p. 456)
epistemic cognition (p. 456)
expertise (p. 458)
fantasy period (p. 462)
free radicals (p. 440)
postformal thought (p. 456)
pragmatic thought (p. 458)
realistic period (p. 462)
relativistic thinking (p. 157)
telomeres (p. 438)
tentative period (p. 462)

chapter 14

Emotional and Social Development in Early Adulthood

This 19-year-old volunteer for a Nicaraguan nonprofit organization teaches children in a small village to write. For many young people in industrialized nations, the transition to early adulthood is a time of prolonged exploration of attitudes, values, and life possibilities.

What's ahead in chapter 14

A Gradual Transition: Emerging Adulthood

Unprecedented Exploration • Cultural Change, Cultural Variation, and Emerging Adulthood • Risk and Resilience in Emerging Adulthood

■ **CULTURAL INFLUENCES** Is Emerging Adulthood Really a Distinct Stage of Development?

Erikson's Theory: Intimacy versus Isolation

Other Theories of Adult Psychosocial Development

Levinson's Seasons of Life • Vaillant's Adaptation to Life • The Social Clock

Close Relationships

Romantic Love • Friendships

■ **SOCIAL ISSUES: HEALTH** Childhood Attachment Patterns and Adult Romantic Relationships

The Family Life Cycle

Leaving Home • Joining of Families in Marriage • Parenthood

■ **SOCIAL ISSUES: HEALTH** Partner Abuse

The Diversity of Adult Lifestyles

Singlehood • Cohabitation • Childlessness • Divorce and Remarriage • Varied Styles of Parenthood

Career Development

Establishing a Career • Women and Ethnic Minorities • Combining Work and Family

After completing her master's degree at age 26, Sharese returned to her hometown, where she and Ernie would soon be married. During their yearlong engagement, Sharese had wavered about whether to follow through. At times, she looked with envy at Heather, still unattached and free to choose from an array of options before her. After graduating from college, Heather accepted a Peace Corps assignment in a remote region of Ghana, forged a romance with another Peace Corps volunteer that she ended at the conclusion of her tour of duty, and then traveled for eight months before returning to the United States to contemplate next steps.

Sharese also pondered the life circumstances of her friend Christy and Christy's husband, Gary—married and first-time parents by their mid-twenties. Despite his good teaching performance, Gary's relationship with his high school principal deteriorated, and he quit his job at the end of his first year. A tight job market impeded Gary's efforts to find another teaching position, and financial pressures and parenthood put Christy's education and career plans on hold. Sharese wondered whether it was really possible to combine family and career.

As her wedding approached, Sharese's ambivalence intensified, and she admitted to Ernie that she didn't feel ready to marry. Ernie's admiration for Sharese had strengthened over their courtship, and he reassured her of his love. His career as an accountant had been under way for two years, and at age 28, he looked forward to marriage and starting a family. Uncertain and conflicted, Sharese felt swept toward the altar as relatives and friends began to arrive—and even as she walked down the aisle on the appointed day.

In this chapter, we take up the emotional and social sides of early adulthood. Notice that Sharese, Ernie, and Heather moved toward adult roles slowly, at times vacillating along the way. Not until their mid- to late twenties did they make lasting career and romantic choices and attain full economic independence—broadly accepted markers of adulthood that young people of previous generations reached considerably earlier. Each received financial and other forms of support from parents and other family members, which enabled them to postpone taking on adult roles. We consider whether prolonged exploration of life options has become so widespread that it merits a new developmental period—*emerging adulthood*—to describe and understand it.

Recall from Chapter 12 that identity development continues to be a central focus from the late teens into the mid-twenties (see page 410). As they achieve a secure identity, young adults seek close, affectionate ties. Yet the decade of the twenties is accompanied by a rise in feelings of personal control over events in their lives—in fact, a stronger sense of control than they may ever experience again (Ross & Mirowsky, 2012). Perhaps for this reason, like Sharese, they often fear losing their freedom. Once this struggle is resolved, early adulthood leads to new family units and parenthood, accomplished in the context of diverse lifestyles. At the same time, young adults must master the tasks of their chosen career.

Our discussion will reveal that identity, love, and work are intertwined. In negotiating these arenas, young adults do more choosing, planning, and changing course than any other age group. When their decisions are in tune with themselves and their social and cultural worlds, they acquire many new competencies, and life is full and rewarding.

A Gradual Transition: Emerging Adulthood

14.1 Discuss emotional and social development during emerging adulthood, along with cultural influences and individual variations.

Think about your own development. Do you consider yourself to have reached adulthood? When a sample of 1,000 U.S. 18- to 29-year-olds diverse in SES and ethnicity was asked this question, the majority of those between 18 and 21 gave an ambiguous answer: "yes and no"—a proportion that declined with age as an increasing number replied with certainty, "yes" (see Figure 14.1) (Arnett & Schwab, 2013). Similar findings are evident in a wide range of industrialized nations (Arnett, 2007a; Buhl & Lanz, 2007; Nelson, 2009; Sirsch et al., 2009). The life pursuits and subjective judgments of many contemporary young people indicate that the transition to adult roles has become so delayed and prolonged that it has spawned a new transitional period extending from the late teens to the mid- to late twenties, called **emerging adulthood.**

Unprecedented Exploration

Psychologist Jeffrey Arnett (2011) is the leader of a movement that regards emerging adulthood as a distinct period of life—a new stage between adolescence and adulthood defined by five features: *feeling in between* (neither adolescent nor adult), *identity exploration* (especially in love, work, and worldview), *self-focused* (not self-centered but lacking obligations to others), *instability* (frequent changes in living arrangements, relationships, education, and work), and *possibilities* (able to choose among multiple life directions). As Arnett explains, emerging adults have left adolescence but are still a considerable distance from taking on adult responsibilities. Rather, young people who have the economic resources to do so explore alternatives in education, work, and personal values and behavior more intensely than they did as teenagers.

Not yet immersed in adult roles, many emerging adults can engage in activities of the widest possible scope. Because so little is normative, or socially expected, routes to adult responsibilities are highly diverse in timing and order across individuals (Côté, 2006). For example, more college students than in past generations pursue their education in a drawn-out, nonlinear way—changing majors as they explore career options, taking courses while working part-time, or interrupting school to work, travel, or participate in national or international service programs. About one-third of U.S. college graduates enter graduate school, taking even longer to settle into their desired career track (U.S. Department of Education, 2015).

As a result of these experiences, young people's interests, attitudes, and values broaden (see page 460 in Chapter 13). Exposure to multiple viewpoints also encourages young people to look more closely at themselves. Consequently, they develop a more complex self-concept that includes awareness of their own changing traits and values over time, and self-esteem rises (Labouvie-Vief, 2006; Orth, Robins, & Widaman, 2012). Together, these developments contribute to advances in identity.

Identity Development. During the college years, young people refine their approach to constructing an identity. Besides exploring in *breadth* (weighing multiple possibilities and making commitments), they increasingly explore in *depth*—evaluating existing commitments (Crocetti & Meeus, 2015; Luyckx et al., 2006; Schwartz et al., 2013). For example, if you have not yet selected your major, you may be taking classes in a broad array of disciplines. Once you commit to a major, you are likely to embark on an in-depth evaluation of your choice—reflecting on your interest, motivation, and performance and on your career

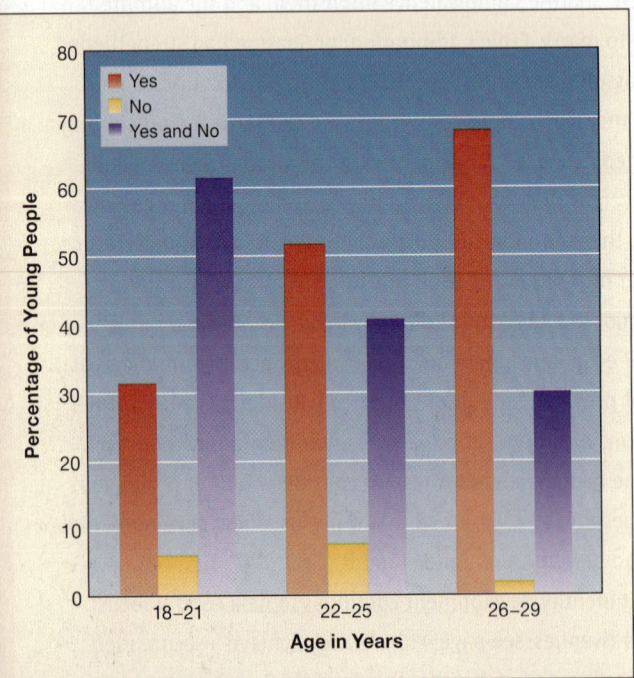

FIGURE 14.1 American young people's responses to the question, "Do you feel you have reached adulthood?" Between ages 18 and 21, the majority answered "yes and no." Even in their late twenties, 30 percent judged that they had not completed the transition to adulthood. (From J. J. Arnett & J. Schwab, 2013, *Clark University Poll of Emerging Adults, 2012: Thriving, Struggling, and Hopeful*, p. 7, Worcester, MA: Clark University. Adapted by permission of Jeffrey Jensen Arnett.)

prospects as you take additional classes in that field. Depending on the outcome of your evaluation, either your commitment to your major strengthens and you integrate it into your sense of self, or you return to a reconsideration of options as you search for alternative commitments.

Investigations conducted with over 6,000 university students from a diverse array of cultures in Europe, the Middle East, and Asia revealed that most cycled between in-depth evaluation of commitments and—if these fit poorly with their talents and potentials or were otherwise dissatisfying—reconsideration of commitments (Crocetti et al., 2015). Consider your own identity progress. Does it fit this *dual-cycle model,* in which identity formation is a process of feedback loops between in-depth exploration and reconsideration until you feel certain of your choices? Notice how the model helps explain the shifts between identity statuses displayed by many young people, described in Chapter 12. College students who move from in-depth exploration to certainty of commitment provide more coherent descriptions of themselves and are higher in self-esteem, psychological well-being, and academic, emotional, and social adjustment. Those who spend much time exploring in breadth or depth without making enduring commitments, or who are identity diffused (engage in no exploration), tend to be poorly adjusted—anxious, depressed, and higher in alcohol and drug use, casual and unprotected sex, and other health-compromising behaviors (Kunnen et al., 2008; Schwartz et al., 2011).

Many aspects of the life course that were once socially structured—marriage, parenthood, religious beliefs, and career paths—are increasingly left to individuals to decide on their own. As a result, emerging adults are required to "individualize" their identities—a process that requires a sense of self-efficacy, planfulness and purpose, determination to overcome obstacles, and responsibility for outcomes. Among young people of diverse ethnicities and SES levels, this set of qualities, termed *personal agency,* is positively related to an information-gathering cognitive style and identity exploration followed by certainty of commitments (Luyckx & Robitschek, 2014).

Nevertheless, making enduring commitments can take longer in some cultures. In Italy, for example, young people typically live at home until about age 30, even when they earn enough to live independently; most leave home only when they marry. Italians in their twenties often put identity commitments "on hold"—engaging in an extended moratorium encouraged by parents, who grant them much freedom, approval, and economic support to experiment with identity alternatives (Crocetti, Rabaglietti, & Sica, 2012). As a result, Italian emerging adults who display prolonged, in-depth exploration tend to be better adjusted than their counterparts in other cultures.

Worldview. Most emerging adults say that constructing a worldview, or a set of beliefs and values to live by, is essential for attaining adult status—even more important than finishing their education and settling into a career and marriage (Arnett, 2007b). Do today's young people forge self-centered worldviews, as the descriptor "generation me" suggests?

This issue has generated heated controversy. Analyses of large, nationally representative samples of U.S. young people, collected repeatedly over several decades, suggest that compared to past generations, Millennials report greater narcissism (egotistical self-admiration) and materialism—valuing of money and leisure and reduced empathy for the less fortunate (Gentile, Twenge, & Campbell, 2010; Twenge, 2013).

But other researchers claim that generational changes in egotism and other traits are so small as not to be meaningful (Paulsen et al., 2016). And gradual, age-related gains in self-esteem extending from adolescence through emerging adulthood and into midlife are similar across generations, with average self-esteem of today's young people no higher than that of past cohorts (Orth, Robins, & Widaman, 2012; Orth, Trzesniewski, & Robins, 2010). Over these years, adults derive a greater sense of competence from making identity commitments, entering and succeeding at their careers, having families, and becoming involved in their communities.

Furthermore, the importance to college students of attaining material wealth has not risen over the past three decades (Arnett, Trzesniewski, & Donnellan, 2013). In one investigation, the overwhelming majority of a national sample of U.S. 18- to 29-year-olds indicated that enjoyment of their work would be more important than making a lot of money, and that it was important to have a career that "does some good in the world" (Arnett & Schwab, 2013). Emerging adults do rate highly certain individualistic goals, such as career success and finding purpose in life, but these are balanced by high valuing of relationship goals, including a good marriage and strong friendships (Trzesniewski & Donnellan, 2010).

> **LOOK and LISTEN**
>
> Ask 10 to 15 of your college classmates to answer the following question: What would you do if you had a million dollars? How often do respondents mention prosocial as opposed to self-centered acts?

Civic and Political Commitments. Evidence also supports the view that many emerging adults are committed to improving their communities, nation, and world. In a survey of 165,000 first-year students enrolled in more than 200 U.S. colleges and universities, a record number expected to participate in community service, with nearly 35 percent saying that there is "a very good chance" they will do so—double the number a generation ago (Eagan et al., 2013). Among those who expect to volunteer, the overwhelming majority actually do so within their first year (DeAngeleo, Hurtado, & Pryor, 2010). Overall, emerging adults are about as likely as contemporary older adults to work with others on local projects in their communities and raise funds for charitable causes (Flanagan & Levine, 2010).

Furthermore, compared to young people in previous generations, today's emerging adults have a stronger *pluralistic orientation*—disposition for living in a diverse society that promotes

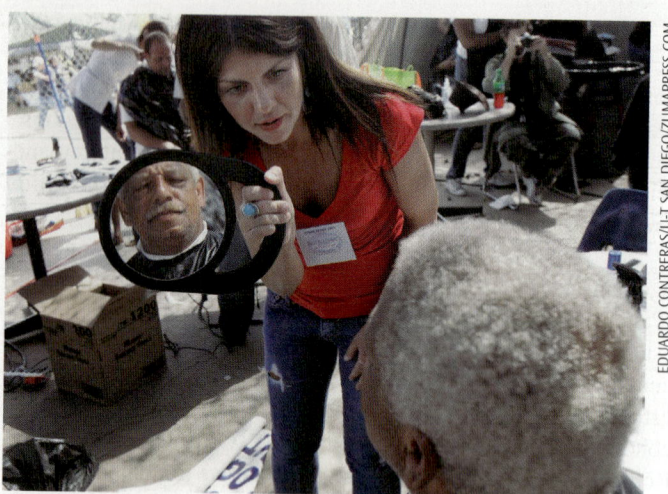

During a community event that provides services for homeless veterans, a cosmetology student shows an older adult the haircut she just gave him. Many emerging adults participate in community service and are committed to improving their world.

individual respect and equality of opportunity, regardless of race, ethnicity, gender, and sexual orientation. They are also more concerned about addressing global problems (Arnett, 2013). Overall, the intentions and behaviors of emerging adults reflect considerable caring and concern for others and civic engagement, from which they reap wide-ranging benefits—enhanced self-esteem, sense of purpose and meaning, social skills, and social networks and declines in stress, anxiety, depression, and antisocial behavior (Núñez & Flanagan, 2016).

Finally, contemporary U.S. 18- to 29-year-olds have been labeled "apathetic no shows" when it comes to voting. After declining over the 1990s, their turnout rose in the 2000s, reaching 51 percent in 2008, then dropped to 45 percent in 2012, but rose again in 2016. Throughout, participation remained below the 66 percent rate of 30-and-older citizens (Circle, 2013; Pew Research Center, 2016b). Emerging adults' longer road to adulthood likely contributes to their comparatively low voting rate. Adult commitments and responsibilities—marriage, career progress, and financial stability—increase people's stake in the political process, strengthening voter participation (Flanagan & Levine, 2010). Compared with older people, fewer young people vote in nearly all established democracies. Of those who do, most have at least some college education. Less educated adults of all ages feel least connected politically.

Religion and Spirituality. Extending a trend under way in adolescence, attendance at religious services declines further in the late teens and twenties as young people question beliefs acquired in their families and search for personally meaningful alternatives. More than one-third of U.S. 18- to 29-year-olds are unaffiliated with a particular faith, considerably more than in their parents' generation at the same age (see Figure 14.2) (Pew Research Center, 2014a, 2015a). Many are children of baby boomer parents, who encouraged them to think for themselves.

Increasing numbers of Millennials express concern that religious (and other) institutions have become too judgmental, political, and focused on money and power.

Yet about half of U.S. young people remain stable in their religious commitment (or lack thereof) from adolescence into emerging adulthood (Pew Research Center, 2015a; Smith & Snell, 2009). And in certain ways, U.S. emerging adults are quite traditional in their religious beliefs and practices. Religion is more important in their lives than it is for young people in other developed countries. Similar to previous generations, most—including many who are unaffiliated—say they believe in God and describe themselves as religious, spiritual, or both. Furthermore, more than one-third of those who are affiliated with a religion say they are "strong" members of their faith (Pew Research Center, 2010c, 2014a). Women and ethnic minorities tend to be more religious (Barry & Abo-Zena, 2014). Of the small number of young people who increase in religiosity during the late teens and early twenties, many are women, African American, or Hispanic.

Whether or not they are involved in organized religion, many young people begin to construct their own individualized faith and, if attending college, discuss religious and spiritual beliefs and experiences more often with friends than with parents or other adults. These peer dialogues promote spiritual development (Barry & Abo-Zena, 2016; Barry & Christofferson, 2014). Often emerging adults weave together beliefs and practices from diverse sources—Eastern and Western religious traditions, science, and popular culture, including music and other media images.

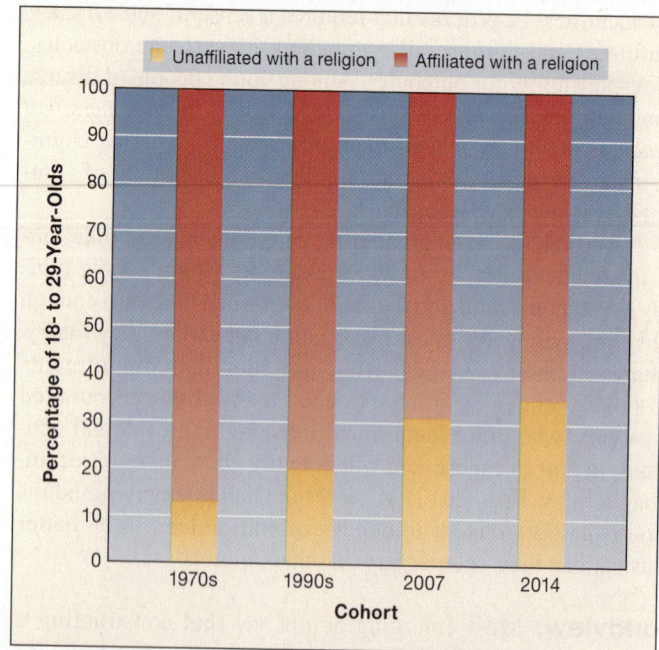

FIGURE 14.2 U.S. 18- to 29-year-olds' religiosity across generations. The percentage of unaffiliated young people rose substantially from the 1970s to 2014. Still, the majority express a religious affiliation. (Based on Pew Research Center, 2015a.)

Emerging adults who say their parents used an authoritative child-rearing style are more likely to hold religious or spiritual beliefs and engage in religious practices similar to their parents' (Nelson, 2014). The warmth, explanations, and autonomy granting of authoritative parenting seem to provide young people with a fuller understanding of their parents' religious ideology, along with greater freedom to evaluate it against alternatives. Consequently, they are more likely to integrate their parents' perspectives into their own worldview.

> **LOOK and LISTEN**
>
> Interview several of your classmates about how their religious or spiritual beliefs and practices have changed in emerging adulthood, along with factors they see as having influenced those changes.

As with adolescents, U.S. emerging adults who are religious or spiritual tend to be better adjusted. They are higher in self-esteem and psychological well-being; less often engage in substance use, antisocial acts, or hookup and friends-with-benefits relationships; and are more often involved in community service (Barry & Christofferson, 2014; Salas-Wright, Vaughn, & Maynard, 2015). But outcomes vary: Those experiencing profound religious and spiritual struggles are at risk for physical and mental health difficulties (Magyar-Russell, Deal, & Brown, 2014). And among sexual minority young people, religiosity is less protective against poor adjustment. A possible reason is that their religious communities often do not support (and sometimes condemn) their sexual orientation (Ream & Rodriguez, 2014). They benefit from religious affiliations where sexual minority status is valued as contributing to congregational diversity.

Cultural Change, Cultural Variation, and Emerging Adulthood

Rapid cultural change explains the recent appearance of emerging adulthood. First, entry-level positions in many fields require more education than in the past, prompting young adults to seek higher education in record numbers and thus delaying financial independence and career commitment. Second, wealthy nations with longer-lived populations have no pressing need for young people's labor, freeing those who are financially able for rich, extended exploration.

Indeed, emerging adulthood is limited to cultures that postpone entry into adult roles until the twenties. In developing nations, only a privileged minority—usually those from wealthier families who are admitted to universities—experience it, often for a shorter time span than their Western counterparts (Arnett, 2011). Furthermore, the overwhelming majority of young people in regions of Africa, Asia, and South America with traditional economies—that have few economic resources and are largely rural and farm-based—have no emerging adulthood. With limited education, they typically enter lifelong work, marriage, and parenthood early.

In industrialized countries, many young people experience these transitional years. Typically, their families are sufficiently well-off to provide them with financial support, without which few could advance their education, explore career possibilities, or travel the country and world to—as one emerging adult put it—"experience as much as possible." And although most emerging adults are pursuing higher education or have earned an advanced degree, some non-college-bound young people also benefit from this extended transition to adult roles (Tanner, Arnett, & Leis, 2009). But they may do so by trying out different types of work rather than college majors or travel.

Nevertheless, for low-SES youths in Western nations who are burdened by early parenthood, do not finish high school, are otherwise academically unprepared for college, or do not have access to vocational training, emerging adulthood is limited or nonexistent (see Chapters 11 and 13). Instead of excitement, exploration, and personal expansion, these individuals often alternate between unemployment and dead-end, low-paying jobs (Arnett & Tanner, 2011).

Because of its strong association with SES and higher education, some researchers reject the notion of emerging adulthood as a distinct life stage (see the Cultural Influences box on page 474). Others disagree, predicting that emerging adulthood will become increasingly common as *globalization*—the exchange of ideas, information, trade, and immigration among nations—accelerates. As globalization proceeds, gains in higher education and the formation of a common "global identity" among young people may lead to the spread of emerging adulthood (Marshall & Butler, 2016). But an emerging adulthood abundant in opportunity depends to a great extent on socioeconomic conditions.

Risk and Resilience in Emerging Adulthood

Most young people with access to the opportunities of emerging adulthood experience it as a time of flourishing, in which they solidify beliefs and values, succeed educationally, participate in prosocial activities, and launch a career. But a sizable number flounder: Their lack of direction is evident in persisting low self-esteem; high anxiety and depression; poor academic performance; and high levels of risky behaviors (Nelson & Padilla-Walker, 2013; Smith et al., 2011). What factors might differentiate emerging adults who flourish from those who flounder?

Longitudinal research indicates that the personal attributes and social supports listed in Applying What We Know on page 475 foster successful passage through these years, as indicated by completing a college degree or vocational certification, finding and keeping a well-paying job, forging warm, stable relationships with friends and intimate partners, volunteering in one's community, and feeling generally satisfied with life (Tanner, 2016). Notice how the resources in the table overlap with ones

Cultural Influences

Is Emerging Adulthood Really a Distinct Stage of Development?

Although broad consensus exists that cultural change has prolonged the transition to adult roles for many young people, disagreement exists over whether these years of "emergence" should be designated a new life stage (Côté, 2014; Kloep & Hendry, 2011). Critics of the concept of emerging adulthood offer the following arguments.

First, burgeoning higher education enrollment, delayed career entry, and later marriage and parenthood are cultural trends that began as early as the 1970s in industrialized nations, only gradually becoming more conspicuous. At no time has adulthood in complex societies been attained at a distinct moment. Rather, young people in the past reached adult status earlier in some domains and later in others, just as they do today. They also may reverse direction—for example, move back to the parental home to get their bearings after finishing college or abandon a career in favor of renewed study (Côté & Bynner, 2008; du Bois-Reymond, 2016). In accord with the lifespan perspective, development is multidimensional and multidirectional for 18- to 29-year-olds as it is for adults of all ages. Transitions occur during all periods of adult life, with societal conditions heavily influencing their timing, length, and complexity.

Second, the term *emerging adulthood* fails to describe the experiences of most of the world's youths (Nelson & Luster, 2016). In developing countries, the majority of young people—particularly women—are limited in education and marry and have children early. According to one estimate, about 1 billion individuals—nearly 70 percent of young people—follow this traditional route to adulthood (World Health Organization, 2015h). We have also seen that many low-SES youths in industrialized nations lack the academic preparation and financial resources to experience an emerging adulthood.

Third, research on emerging adulthood largely emphasizes its personal and societal benefits. But the extended exploration that defines this period might be largely a coping mechanism on the part of young people who cannot find rewarding jobs, even after college graduation. When college graduates find satisfying work enabling financial independence, most choose not to postpone these responsibilities (Arum & Roksa, 2014). Furthermore, an extended emerging adulthood is risky for those who have not developed the personal agency to make good choices and acquire adult skills (Smith et al., 2011). These young people may remain uncommitted for too long—an outcome that impedes the focused learning required for a successful work life.

Finally, the financial upheaval of the late 2000s left large numbers of bachelor's degree holders with restricted options. In 2015, over 7 percent of recent college graduates were unemployed, and 15 percent were underemployed—in low-paid jobs not requiring a college degree (Davis, Kimball, & Gould, 2015). Thus, they remain without work experiences necessary for advancing their skills. Rather than a "natural," self-chosen period of unparalleled opportunities, these graduates' delayed entry into adult roles resulted from a national economic crisis. One young person, who might have been high in personal agency in a stable economy, remarked, "It has been tough finding a job that keeps me wanting to stick with something" (Kotkin, 2012).

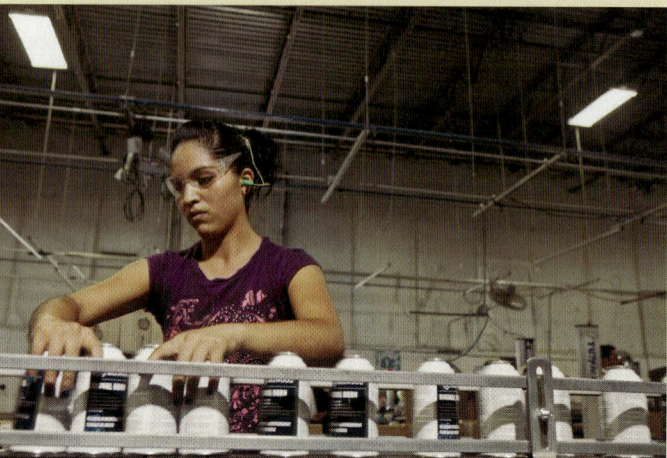

This 22-year-old performs unskilled work for low wages. Many low-SES young people lack the academic preparation and financial resources to experience an emerging adulthood.

Proponents of emerging adulthood as a distinct stage respond that, though not universal, it applies to most young people in industrialized societies and is spreading in developing nations that play major roles in our global economy (Tanner & Arnett, 2011). But skeptics counter that emerging adulthood is unlikely to become prominent in developing countries with high concentrations of poverty or, in industrialized nations, among low-income youths or those not involved in higher education (du Bois-Reymond, 2016; Kloep & Hendry, 2011). And for college graduates, societal conditions can readily restrict the prospects and rewards of this period.

Critics also emphasize that in developed nations, age-graded influences have declined in favor of nonnormative influences throughout contemporary adulthood (see page 10 in Chapter 1 to review). In their view, rather than being unique, emerging adults are part of a general trend toward blurring of age-related expectations, yielding multiple transitions and increased diversity in development throughout the adult years.

Applying what we Know

Resources That Foster Resilience in Emerging Adulthood

TYPE OF RESOURCE	DESCRIPTION
Cognitive attributes	Effective planning and decision making
	Information-gathering cognitive style and mature epistemic cognition
	Good school performance
	Knowledge of vocational options and necessary skills
Emotional and social attributes	Positive self-esteem
	Good emotional self-regulation and flexible coping strategies
	Good conflict-resolution skills
	Confidence in one's ability to reach one's goals
	Sense of personal responsibility for outcomes
	Persistence and effective use of time
	Healthy identity development—movement toward exploration in depth and certainty of commitment
	Strong moral character
	Sense of meaning and purpose in life, engendered by religion, spirituality, or other sources
	Desire to contribute meaningfully to one's community
Social and financial supports	Warm, autonomy-supportive relationship with parents
	Positive relationships with peers, teachers, and mentors
	Financial assistance from parents or others
	Sense of connection to social institutions, such as school, religious institution, workplace, and community center

discussed in previous chapters that promote development through *resilience,* the capacity to overcome challenge and adversity. Young people with more of these resources—and with resources in all three categories—probably make an especially smooth transition to adulthood. But some emerging adults with only a few resources also fare well.

As in childhood and adolescence, certain resources strengthen others. Relationships with parents have an especially wide-ranging influence. A secure, affectionate parent–emerging adult bond that extends the balance of connection and separation established in adolescence promotes many aspects of adaptive functioning: favorable self-esteem, identity progress, successful transition to college life, higher academic achievement, and more rewarding friendships and romantic ties. Autonomy-supportive parenting in particular—an empathic approach in which parents recognize the weighty decisions the young person faces and encourage personally valued choices—is linked to emerging adults' psychological well-being (Kins et al., 2009). As one reviewer of research summed up, "What seems advantageous for emerging adults' achievement of independence is feeling connected, secure, understood, and loved in their families, and having the willingness to call on parental resources" (Aquilino, 2006, p. 201).

In contrast, parental overprotection, expressed through excessive contact and psychological control—including taking over when the young person encounters challenges—is linked to the indicators of poor adjustment we have just considered, including low self-esteem, inability to make commitments in identity formation, and increased anxiety, depression, and alcohol use (Luyckx et al., 2007; Nelson et al., 2011; Patock-Peckam & Morgan-Lopez, 2009). In another form of parenting—called *helicopter parenting* in popular culture—warm, well-intentioned parents "hover" over the emerging adult out of excessive concern for his or her well-being. They might, for example, take the young person to college but refuse to leave and contact professors to discuss the young person's grades. Perhaps because helicopter parenting is motivated by strong parental affection and involvement, it is not associated with the negative outcomes just noted. But it is related to reduced school engagement (going to class, completing assignments) (Padilla-Walker & Nelson, 2012). And it likely interferes with emerging adults' ability to acquire the skills they need to act on their own.

Finally, exposure to multiple negative life events—family conflict, abusive intimate relationships, repeated romantic break-ups, academic or employment difficulties, and financial strain—undermines development, even in emerging adults whose

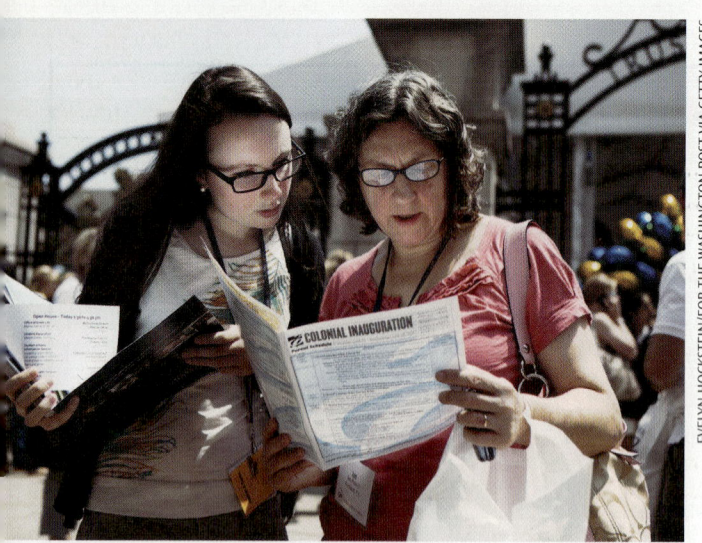

An incoming first-year college student joins her mother in checking their respective orientation-week schedules before fall classes begin. Warm, autonomy-supportive parenting—encouraging the young person to make personally valued choices—promotes adaptive functioning in emerging adulthood.

childhood and adolescence prepared them well for this transition (Tanner, 2016). In sum, supportive family, school, and community environments are crucial, just as they were at earlier ages. The majority of young people with these resources are optimistic about their future (Arnett & Schwab, 2013). Now let's turn to theories of psychosocial development in early adulthood.

Ask yourself

CONNECT How are resources that foster resilience in emerging adulthood similar to those that promote resilience in childhood and adolescence? (See pages 10–11 in Chapter 1, page 360 in Chapter 10, and page 422 in Chapter 12.)

APPLY List supports that your college environment offers emerging adults in its health and counseling services, academic advising, residential living, and extracurricular activities. How does each help young people transition to adult roles?

REFLECT Should emerging adulthood be considered a distinct developmental stage? Why or why not?

Erikson's Theory: Intimacy versus Isolation

14.2 According to Erikson, what personality changes take place during early adulthood?

Erikson's vision has influenced all contemporary theories of adult personality development. His psychological conflict of early adulthood is **intimacy versus isolation,** evident in the young person's thoughts and feelings about making a long-term commitment to an intimate partner and in close, mutually gratifying friendships.

As Sharese discovered, building an emotionally fulfilling romantic bond is challenging. Most young adults are still grappling with identity issues. Yet intimacy requires that they give up some of their independent self and redefine their identity to include both partners' values and interests. Those in their late teens through mid-twenties frequently say they don't feel ready for a lasting romantic tie, mentioning concerns about career and financial security and emotional readiness, including limits on their freedom (Arnett, 2015; Willoughby & Carroll, 2016). During their first year of marriage, Sharese separated from Ernie twice as she tried to reconcile her desire for self-determination with her desire for intimacy. Maturity involves balancing these forces. Without intimacy, young adults face the negative outcome of Erikson's early adulthood stage: loneliness and self-absorption. Ernie's patience and stability helped Sharese realize that committed love requires generosity and compromise but not total surrender of the self.

Research confirms that—as Erikson emphasized—a secure identity fosters attainment of intimacy. Among large samples of college students, identity achievement was positively correlated with fidelity (loyalty in relationships) and love, for both men and women. In contrast, identity moratorium—exploration without commitment—was negatively associated with fidelity and love (Markstrom et al., 1997; Markstrom & Kalmanir, 2001). Other studies show that advanced identity development strongly predicts involvement in a deep, committed love partnership or readiness to establish such a partnership (Beyers & Seiffge-Krenke, 2010; Montgomery, 2005).

In friendships and work ties, too, young people who have achieved intimacy are cooperative, agreeable, communicative, and accepting of differences in background and values (Barry, Madsen, & DeGrace, 2016). In contrast, those with a sense of isolation hesitate to form close ties because they fear loss of their own identity, tend to compete rather than cooperate, are not accepting of differences, and are easily threatened when others get too close.

Erikson believed that successful resolution of intimacy versus isolation prepares the individual for the middle adulthood stage, which focuses on *generativity*—caring for the next generation and helping to improve society. But as noted previously, few adults follow a fixed series of tasks tied neatly to age. Some aspects of generativity—childbearing and child rearing, as well as contributions to society through work and community service—are under way in the twenties and thirties. Still, in line with Erikson's ideas, high friendship or romantic intimacy in early adulthood does predict a stronger generative orientation (Mackinnon, De Pasquale, & Pratt, 2015).

In sum, identity, intimacy, and generativity are concerns of early adulthood, with shifts in emphasis that differ among individuals. Recognizing that Erikson's theory provides only a broad sketch of adult personality development, other theorists elaborated on his stage approach, adding detail.

Other Theories of Adult Psychosocial Development

14.3 Describe and evaluate Levinson's and Vaillant's psychosocial theories of adult personality development.

14.4 What is the social clock, and how does it affect development in adulthood?

In the 1970s, growing interest in adult development led to several widely read books on the topic. Daniel Levinson's *The Seasons of a Man's Life* (1978) and *The Seasons of a Woman's Life* (1996), and George Vaillant's *Adaptation to Life* (1977), *Aging Well* (2002), and *Triumphs of Experience* (2012) present psychosocial theories in the tradition of Erikson.

Levinson's Seasons of Life

On the basis of in-depth biographical interviews with 35- to 45-year-old men—and, later, similar interviews with women in the same age range—Levinson (1978, 1996) depicted adult development as a sequence of qualitatively distinct eras (or "seasons") coinciding with Erikson's stages and separated by *transitions*. The *life structure*, a key concept in Levinson's theory, is the underlying design of a person's life, consisting of relationships with individuals, groups, and institutions. Of its many components, usually only a few, relating to family, close friendships, and occupation, are central.

Levinson found that during the transition to early adulthood, most young people constructed a *dream*—an image of themselves in the adult world that guides their decision making. For men, the dream usually emphasized achievement in a career, whereas most career-oriented women had "split dreams" in which both marriage and career were prominent—findings confirmed in subsequent investigations (Heppner, 2013). Young adults also formed a relationship with a *mentor* who facilitated realization of their dream—often a senior colleague at work but occasionally a more experienced friend, neighbor, or relative. According to Levinson, men oriented toward high-status careers spent their twenties acquiring professional skills, values, and credentials. In contrast, for many women, career development extended into middle age.

Around age 30, a second transition occurred: Young people who had been preoccupied with career and were single usually focused on finding a life partner, while women who had emphasized marriage and family often developed more individualistic goals. For example, Christy, who had dreamed of becoming a professor, finally earned her doctoral degree in her mid-thirties and secured a college teaching position.

To create an early adulthood culminating life structure, men usually "settled down" by focusing on certain relationships and aspirations, in an effort to establish a niche in society consistent with their values, whether those were wealth, prestige, artistic or scientific achievement, or forms of family or community participation. In his late thirties, Ernie became a partner in his firm, coached his son's soccer team, and was elected treasurer of his church. He paid less attention to travel and playing the guitar than previously.

Many women, however, remained unsettled in their thirties, often because they added an occupational or relationship commitment. When her two children were born, Sharese felt torn between her research position in the state health department and her family. She took three months off after the arrival of each baby. When she returned to work, she did not pursue attractive administrative openings that required travel and time away from home. And shortly after Christy began teaching, she and Gary divorced. Becoming a single parent while starting her professional life introduced new strains.

Vaillant's Adaptation to Life

Vaillant (1977) followed the development of nearly 250 men born in the 1920s, selected for study while they were students at a competitive liberal arts college. Participants were interviewed extensively while in college and answered lengthy questionnaires during each succeeding decade. Then Vaillant (2002, 2012) conducted periodic interviews with them about work, family, and physical and mental health at ages 47, 60, 70, and 85.

Looking at how the men altered themselves and their social world to adapt to life, Vaillant—like Levinson—built on Erikson's stages. After focusing on intimacy concerns in their twenties, the men turned to career consolidation in their thirties. During their forties, they became more generative. In their fifties and sixties, they extended that generativity; they became "keepers of meaning," expressing a deep need to preserve and pass on

A furniture designer teaches a new technique to a younger coworker. For young people starting out in a career, an experienced colleague can be an especially effective mentor, serving as a role model and guide in overcoming challenges.

cultural traditions and lessons learned from life experience. Finally, in late adulthood, the men became more spiritual and reflective about the meaning of life. In a subsequent lifelong study of a sample of well-educated women, Vaillant (2002) identified a similar series of changes.

Nevertheless, the developmental patterns Vaillant and Levinson described are based largely on interviews with people born in the first few decades of the twentieth century, many of whom were educationally and economically advantaged. As our discussion of emerging adulthood illustrates, development is far more variable today—so much so that researchers increasingly doubt that adult psychosocial changes can be organized into distinct stages. Rather, people may assemble the themes and dilemmas identified by these theorists into individualized arrangements, in a *dynamic system* of interacting biological, psychological, and social forces.

The Social Clock

As we have seen, cultural changes from one generation to the next can affect the life course. Yet all societies have some kind of **social clock**—age-graded expectations for major life events, such as beginning a first job, getting married, birth of the first child, buying a home, and retiring (Neugarten, 1979). Among economically better-off young people, finishing one's education, marrying, and having children occur much later in the lifespan than they did a generation or two ago. Furthermore, large departures from social-clock life events have become increasingly common.

These conditions can create intergenerational tensions if parents expect their young-adult children to attain adult milestones on an outdated schedule. Young adults may also feel distressed because their own timing of major milestones is not widely shared by their contemporaries or supported by current public policies, thereby weakening availability of both informal and formal social supports (Settersten, 2007). And while rendering greater flexibility and freedom to young people's lives, an ill-defined social clock likely causes them to feel inadequately grounded—unsure of what others expect and of what to expect of themselves.

LOOK and LISTEN

Describe your social clock, listing major life events along with the age you expect to attain each. Then ask a parent and/or grandparent to recall his or her own early adulthood social clock. Analyze generational differences.

In sum, following a social clock of some kind seems to foster confidence and social stability because it guarantees that young people will develop skills, engage in productive work, and gain in understanding of self and others. In contrast, "crafting a life of one's own," whether self-chosen or the result of circumstances, is risky—more prone to breakdown (Settersten, 2007, p. 244). With this in mind, let's take a closer look at how men and women traverse major tasks of young adulthood.

Ask yourself

CONNECT Return to pages 409–410 in Chapter 12 and review the contributions of exploration and commitment to a mature identity. Using the two criteria, explain why identity achievement is positively related to attainment of intimacy (fidelity and love), whereas identity moratorium is negatively predictive.

APPLY In view of contemporary changes in the social clock, explain Sharese's conflicted feelings about marrying Ernie.

REFLECT Describe your early adulthood dream. Then ask a friend or classmate of the other gender to describe his or her dream, and compare the two. Discuss the extent to which they are consistent with Levinson's findings.

Close Relationships

14.5 Describe factors affecting mate selection, the components of romantic love, and the changing forms of love as relationships develop, noting cultural variations.

14.6 Describe young adults' friendships and sibling relationships and their influence on psychological well-being.

To establish an intimate tie, people must find a partner and build an emotional bond that they sustain over time. Although young adults are especially concerned with romantic love, the need for intimacy can also be satisfied through other relationships involving mutual commitment—with friends, siblings, and co-workers.

Because the social clock has become increasingly flexible, this 30-year-old attorney, committed to her demanding career, may not feel pressure to conform to a strict timetable for major life events such as marriage and parenthood.

Romantic Love

At a party during her third year of college, Sharese fell into conversation with Ernie, a senior and one of the top students in her government class. Sharese had already noticed Ernie in class, and as they talked, she discovered that he was as warm and interesting as he had seemed from a distance. Ernie found Sharese to be lively, intelligent, and attractive. By the end of the evening, the two realized that they had similar opinions on important social issues and liked the same leisure activities. They began dating steadily. Six years later, they married.

Finding a life partner is a major milestone of early adult development, with profound consequences for self-concept and psychological well-being. As Sharese and Ernie's relationship reveals, it is also a complex process that unfolds over time and is affected by a variety of events.

Selecting a Mate. Recall from Chapter 13 that intimate partners generally meet in places where they are likely to find people of their own age, level of education, ethnicity, and religion, or they connect through online dating services. People usually select partners who resemble themselves in other ways—attitudes, personality, educational plans, intelligence, mental health, physical attractiveness, and even height (Butterworth & Rodgers, 2006; Gorchoff, 2016; Lin & Lundquist, 2013; Watson et al., 2004). Romantic partners sometimes have complementary personality traits—one self-assured and dominant, the other hesitant and submissive. Because this difference permits each to sustain their preferred style of behavior, it contributes to compatibility (Sadler, Ethier, & Woody, 2011). But partners differing in other ways generally are not complementary! For example, a warm, agreeable person and an emotionally cool person usually react with discomfort to each other. Overall, little support exists for the idea that "opposites attract" (Furnham, 2009). Rather, partners who are similar in personality and other attributes tend to be more satisfied with their relationship and more likely to stay together.

Nevertheless, in choosing a long-term partner, men and women differ in the importance they place on certain characteristics. In research carried out in diverse industrialized and developing countries, women assign greater weight to financial status, intelligence, ambition, and moral character, whereas men place more emphasis on physical attractiveness and domestic skills. In addition, women prefer a same-age or slightly older partner, men a younger partner (Buss et al., 2001; Conroy-Beam et al., 2015).

According to an evolutionary perspective, because their capacity to reproduce is limited, women seek a mate with traits, such as earning power and emotional commitment, that help ensure children's survival and well-being. In contrast, men look for a mate with traits that signal youth, health, sexual pleasure, and ability to give birth to and care for offspring. As further evidence for this difference, men often want a relationship to move quickly toward physical intimacy (Buss, 2012). Women, in contrast, prefer to take time to achieve psychological intimacy.

In an alternative view, gender roles, jointly influenced by evolutionary and cultural pressures, affect criteria for mate selection. Beginning in childhood, men learn to be assertive and independent—behaviors needed for success in the work world. Women acquire nurturant behaviors, which facilitate caregiving. Then each sex learns to value traits in the other that fit with this traditional division of labor (Eagly & Wood, 2012, 2013). In support of this perspective, in cultures and in younger generations experiencing greater gender equity, men and women are more alike in their mate preferences. For example, compared with men in China and Japan, American men place more emphasis on their mate's financial prospects, less on her domestic skills. Also, when either male or female young adults are asked to imagine themselves as a future homemaker, their preferences for a good provider and an older partner strengthen (Eagly, Eastwick, & Johannesen-Schmidt, 2009).

But neither men nor women put good looks, earning power, and mate's age relative to their own at the top of their wish list. Rather, they place a higher value on attributes that contribute to relationship satisfaction: mutual attraction, caring, dependability, emotional maturity, and a pleasing disposition (Toro-Morn & Sprecher, 2003). Nevertheless, men continue to emphasize physical attractiveness more than women do, and women earning capacity more than men do. Furthermore, these gender differences—along with gender similarity in desire for a caring partner—also characterize gay men and lesbians (Impett & Peplau, 2006; Lawson et al., 2014). In sum, both biological and social forces contribute to mate selection.

As the Social Issues: Health box on page 480 reveals, young people's choice of an intimate partner and the quality of their relationship also are affected by memories of their early parent–child bond. Finally, for romance to lead to a lasting partnership, it must happen at the right time. Two people may be right for each other, but if one or both do not feel ready to marry, the relationship is likely to dissolve.

The Components of Love. How do we know that we are in love? Robert Sternberg's (2006) **triangular theory of love** identifies three components—passion, intimacy, and commitment—that shift in emphasis as romantic relationships develop. *Passion*, the desire for sexual activity and romance, is the physical- and psychological-arousal component. *Intimacy* is the emotional component, consisting of warm, tender communication and caring, self-disclosure, plus a desire for the partner to reciprocate. *Commitment*, the cognitive component, leads partners to decide that they are in love and to maintain that love.

At the beginning of a relationship, **passionate love**—intense sexual attraction—is strong. Gradually, passion declines in favor of intimacy and commitment, which form the basis for two additional forms of love. The first is **companionate love**—warm, trusting affection and valuing of the other (Sprecher & Regan, 1998). The second, and perhaps the most fundamental type of love in any deeply satisfying close relationship, is **compassionate love**—concern for the other's well-being, expressed through caring efforts to alleviate the other's distress and promote the other's growth and flourishing (Berscheid, 2010; Sprecher & Fehr, 2005).

Romantic partners' self-reports reveal that expressions of these types of love are moderately to highly correlated, with each

Social Issues: Health

Childhood Attachment Patterns and Adult Romantic Relationships

In Bowlby's ethological theory of attachment, the early attachment bond leads to an *internal working model*, or set of expectations about attachment figures, that serves as a guide for close relationships throughout life. Adults' evaluations of their early attachment experiences are related to their parenting behaviors—specifically, to the quality of attachments they build with their children (see page 202 in Chapter 6). Additional evidence indicates that recollections of childhood attachment patterns predict romantic relationships in adulthood.

In studies carried out in Australia, Israel, and the United States, researchers asked people about their early parental bonds (attachment history), their attitudes toward intimate relationships (internal working model), and their actual experiences with romantic partners. In a few instances, investigators also observed couples' behaviors. Consistent with Bowlby's theory, adults' memories and interpretations of childhood attachment patterns were good indicators of internal working models and relationship experiences. (To review patterns of attachment, see page 198.)

Secure Attachment

Adults who described their attachment history as secure (warm, loving, and supportive parents) had internal working models that reflected this security. They viewed themselves as likable and easy to get to know, were comfortable with intimacy, and rarely worried about abandonment. They characterized their most important love relationship in terms of trust, happiness, and friendship (Cassidy, 2001). Their behaviors toward their partner were empathic and supportive and their conflict resolution strategies constructive. They were also at ease in turning to their partner for comfort and assistance and reported mutually initiated, enjoyable sexual activity (Collins & Feeney, 2010; Pietromonaco & Beck, 2015).

Avoidant Attachment

Adults who reported an avoidant attachment history (demanding, disrespectful, and critical parents) displayed internal working models that stressed independence, mistrust of love partners, and anxiety about people getting too close. They were convinced that others disliked them and that romantic love is hard to find and rarely lasts. Jealousy, emotional distance, lack of support in response to their partner's distress, and little enjoyment of physical contact pervaded their most important love relationship (Pietromonaco & Beck, 2015). Avoidant adults often deny attachment needs through casual sexual encounters (Genzler & Kerns, 2004; Sprecher, 2013). They endorse many unrealistic beliefs about relationships—for example, that partners cannot change, that men's and women's needs differ, and that "mind reading" is expected (Stackert & Bursik, 2003).

Resistant Attachment

Adults recalling a resistant attachment history (parents who responded unpredictably and unfairly) presented internal working models in which they sought to merge completely with another person (Cassidy, 2001). At the same time, they worried that their desire for intense intimacy would overwhelm others, who really did not love them and would not want to stay with them. Their most important love relationship was riddled with jealousy, emotional highs and lows, and desperation about whether the partner would return their affection (Collins & Feeney, 2010). Resistant adults, though offering support, do so in ways that fit poorly with their partner's needs. They are also quick to express fear and anger, and they disclose information about themselves at inappropriate times (Pietromonaco & Beck, 2015).

Are adults' descriptions of their childhood attachment experiences accurate, or are they distorted or even completely invented? In several longitudinal studies, quality of parent–child interactions, observed or assessed through family interviews 5 to 23 years earlier, were good predictors of internal working models and romantic-relationship quality in early adulthood (Donnellan, Larsen-Rife, & Conger, 2005; Roisman et al., 2001; Zayas et al., 2011). These findings suggest that adult recollections bear some resemblance to actual parent–child experiences. However, attributes of the current partner also influence internal working models and intimate ties. When generally insecure individuals manage to form a secure representation of their partner, they report stronger feelings of affection and concern and reduced relationship conflict and anxiety (Simpson & Overall, 2014; Sprecher & Fehr, 2011).

In sum, negative parent–child experiences can be carried forward into adult close relationships. At the same time, internal working models are continuously "updated." When adults with a history of unhappy love lives have a chance to form a satisfying intimate tie, they may revise their internal working model. As the new partner approaches the relationship with a secure state of mind and sensitive, supportive behavior, the insecure partner may reappraise her expectations and respond in kind. This reciprocity creates a feedback loop through which a revised, more favorable internal working model, along with mutually gratifying interaction, persists over time.

Did the internal working model constructed by this baby, held tenderly by his father, influence the relationship he later forged with his wife? Research indicates that early attachment pattern is one of several factors associated with the quality of later intimate ties.

Romantic relationships become more intimate, committed, satisfying, and long-lasting as they move from passionate love into the trusting affection of companionate love and the caring bond of compassionate love.

helping to sustain the relationship (Fehr & Sprecher, 2013). Early passionate love is a powerful predictor of whether partners keep dating. Without the quiet intimacy, predictability, and shared attitudes and values of companionate love, most romances eventually break up (Hendrick & Hendrick, 2002). And the combination of intimacy and commitment inherent in compassionate love is strongly linked to partners' relational happiness and plans to remain together over the long term (Fehr, Harasymchuk, & Sprecher, 2014).

An ongoing relationship requires effort by both partners. Research on newlyweds' feelings and behavior over the first few years of marriage reveals that despite couples' optimistic forecasts that their marital satisfaction would remain stable or improve, partners gradually felt less "in love" and less pleased with married life (Huston et al., 2001; Lavner, Karney, & Bradbury, 2013). A variety of factors contributed, including a sharp drop in time spent talking to each other and expressing affection. Joint leisure pursuits gave way to more household tasks and chores and, therefore, fewer enjoyable times together. Also, when discussing areas of conflict, partners declined in accurate reading of each other's thoughts and feelings (Kilpatrick, Bissonnette, & Rusbult, 2002). Perhaps after an increasing number of such interactions, they tried less hard to grasp the other's point of view and resorted to well-established habits, such as giving in or withdrawing.

But couples whose relationships endure generally report that they love each other more than they did earlier (Sprecher, 1999). In the transformation from a passionate to a companionate and compassionate bond, *commitment* may be the component of love that determines whether a relationship survives. Communicating that commitment in ways that strengthen *intimacy*—through warmth, attentiveness, understanding, acceptance, and respect—strongly predicts relationship maintenance and satisfaction (Lavner & Bradbury, 2012; Neff & Karney, 2008). For example,

Sharese's doubts about getting married subsided largely because of Ernie's expressions of commitment. He assured her that he understood her needs and would support her career aspirations and individuality in other ways. Sharese returned Ernie's sentiments, and the strength of their bond deepened.

An important feature of expressing commitment is constructive conflict resolution—directly expressing wishes and needs, listening patiently, asking for clarification, compromising, accepting responsibility, forgiving one's partner, using humor, and otherwise avoiding the escalation of negative interaction sparked by criticism, contempt, defensiveness, and stonewalling (Dennison, Koerner, & Segrin, 2014; Gottman, Driver, & Tabares, 2015). In a longitudinal study, newlyweds' negativity during problem solving predicted marital dissatisfaction and divorce over the following decade (Sullivan et al., 2010). Those who displayed little concern and caring often resorted to anger and contempt when dealing with problems.

Although the capacity for constructive conflict resolution is a vital ingredient of enduring marriages, a tender, affectionate bond seems to energize that capacity, motivating couples to resolve conflicts in ways that preserve a gratifying sense of intimacy. Compared with women, men are less skilled at communicating in ways that foster intimacy, offering less comfort and helpful support in their close relationships. Men also tend to be less effective at negotiating conflict, frequently avoiding discussion (Burleson & Kunkel, 2006; Wood, 2009).

Sexual minority and heterosexual couples are similar in expressions of commitment, intimacy, and conflict and in the contributions of each to relationship satisfaction (Kurdek, 2004). But for lesbian and gay couples, widespread social stigma complicates the process of forging a gratifying, committed bond. Those who worry most about being stigmatized or harbor negative attitudes toward their own sexual orientation report lower-quality and less enduring love relationships (Mohr & Daly, 2008; Mohr & Fassinger, 2006). Applying What We Know on page 482 lists ways that all couples can help keep the embers of love aglow in a romantic partnership.

Culture and the Experience of Love. Passionate love, with its intense feelings of ecstasy and longing, is recognized in virtually all contemporary cultures, though its importance varies. Passion, which forms the basis for romantic love, along with respect for the other's unique qualities, became the dominant basis for marriage in twentieth-century Western nations as the value of individualism strengthened (Hatfield, Rapson, & Martel, 2007). Trying to satisfy dependency needs through a close relationship is regarded as immature.

This Western view contrasts sharply with the perspectives of Eastern cultures. In Japan, for example, lifelong dependency is accepted and viewed positively. The Japanese word *amae*, or love, means "to depend on another's benevolence." The traditional Chinese interdependent view defines the self through role relationships—son or daughter, brother or sister, husband or wife. Feelings of affection are distributed across a broad social network, reducing the emotional intensity of any one relationship.

Applying what we Know

Keeping Love Alive in a Romantic Partnership

SUGGESTION	DESCRIPTION
Make time for your relationship.	To foster relationship satisfaction and a sense of being "in love," plan regular times to be together.
Tell your partner of your love.	Express warmth and affection, including the powerful words "I love you," at appropriate times. These messages increase perceptions of commitment, strengthen intimacy, and encourage your partner to respond in kind.
Be available to your partner in times of need.	Provide emotional support, giving of yourself when your partner is distressed and supporting your partner in attaining personal goals.
Communicate constructively and positively about relationship problems.	When you or your partner is dissatisfied, suggest ways of overcoming difficulties, and ask your partner to collaborate in choosing and implementing a course of action. Avoid the four enemies of relationship satisfaction: criticism, contempt, defensiveness, and stonewalling.
Show an interest in important aspects of your partner's life.	Ask about your partner's work, friends, family, and leisure pursuits and express appreciation for his or her special abilities and achievements. In doing so, you grant your partner a sense of being valued.
Confide in your partner.	Share innermost feelings, keeping intimacy alive.
Forgive minor offenses and try to understand major offenses.	Whenever possible, overcome feelings of anger through forgiveness. In this way, you acknowledge unjust behavior but avoid becoming preoccupied with it.

In choosing a lifelong partner, Chinese and Japanese young people are expected to consider obligations to others, especially parents. Compared with their Western counterparts, college students of Asian heritage place less emphasis on physical attraction and deep emotion and more weight on companionship and practical matters—similarity of background, career promise, and likelihood of being a good parent (Hatfield, Rapson, & Martel, 2007).

Still, even in Eastern countries such as China, India, and Japan where arranged marriages are still fairly common, parents and prospective brides and grooms consult one another before moving forward. If parents try to force their children into a marriage with little chance of love, most of the time children resist, emphasizing the importance of love (Hatfield, Mo, & Rapson, 2015). Nevertheless, arranged marriages offer certain advantages in the cultures in which they occur, including greater family and community approval and support.

Furthermore, many arranged marriages succeed, with marital satisfaction as high as, and occasionally higher than, in self-chosen marriages (Madathil & Benshoff, 2008; Schwartz, 2007). In interviews with arranged-marriage couples from diverse countries who reported that their love gradually grew over time, the contributing factor most often mentioned was commitment (Epstein, Pandit, & Thakar, 2013). Participants explained that commitment helped bring about other qualities that strengthened their love, including good communication, accommodation (caring and concern), and pleasurable physical intimacy. A substantial number stated that building love in their marriages was an intentional act. Although not a defense of arranged marriages, the findings suggest conditions under which love between self-chosen newlyweds might be induced to grow, rather than decline as it typically does.

Friendships

Like romantic partners and childhood friends, adult friends are usually similar in age, sex, and SES—factors that contribute to common interests, experiences, and needs and therefore to the pleasure derived from the relationship. As in earlier years, friends in adulthood enhance self-esteem and psychological well-being through affirmation, acceptance, autonomy support (permitting disagreement and choice), and support in times of stress (Barry, Madsen, & DeGrace, 2016). Friends also make life more interesting by expanding social opportunities and access to knowledge and points of view.

Trust, intimacy, and loyalty, along with shared interests and values and enjoyment of each other's company, continue to be

An Indian brahmin (priest) marries a young couple. Although arranged marriages are still common in some Eastern countries, many couples emphasize the importance of love, which often grows over time.

important in adult friendships, as they were in adolescence (Blieszner & Roberto, 2012). Sharing thoughts and feelings is sometimes greater in friendship than in marriage, although commitment is less strong as friends come and go over the life course. Even so, some adult friendships continue for many years, at times throughout life. Seeing each other often contributes to friendship continuity. Partly because female friends get together more often than male friends, adult friendship ties tend to be longer-lasting among women (Sherman, de Vries, & Lansford, 2000).

Because of a dramatic rise in social media use, today's friendships are no longer as constrained by physical proximity. Among 18- to 29-year-olds, 90 percent use social media sites (Pew Research Center, 2016d). Consequently, networks of "friends" have expanded. These include friends who meet through online groups and may never meet in person but who share interests and offer emotional support (Lefkowitz, Vukman, & Loken, 2012). As yet, little is known about the role of these online ties in adults' lives.

Do social media sites lead young adults to form a large number of acquaintances at the expense of intimate friendships? Research reveals that people with 500 or more Facebook friends actually interact individually—by "liking" posts, leaving comments on walls, or engaging in chats—with far fewer. Among these large-network Facebook users, men engaged in one-on-one communication with an average of just 10 friends, women with just 16 (Henig & Henig, 2012). Facebook use was associated with an increase in passive tracking of casual relationships but no change in the number of core friendships.

LOOK and LISTEN

Ask your friends on social media to indicate the size of their online network along with the number of friends they interacted with individually during the past month. Do large-network users have only a limited number of core friendships?

Same-Sex Friendships.
Throughout life, women have more intimate same-sex friendships than men. Extending a pattern evident in childhood and adolescence, female friends often say they prefer to "just talk," whereas male friends say they like to "do something" such as play sports (see Chapter 12, page 423). Barriers to intimacy between male friends include competitiveness, which may make men unwilling to disclose weaknesses. Because of greater intimacy and give-and-take, women generally evaluate their same-sex friendships more positively than men do. But they also have higher expectations of friends (Blieszner & Roberto, 2012). Thus, they are more disapproving if friends do not meet their expectations.

Of course, individual differences exist in friendship quality. The longer-lasting men's friendships are, the closer they become and the more they include disclosure of personal information (Sherman, de Vries, & Lansford, 2000). Furthermore, involvement in family roles affects reliance on friends. For single adults, friends are the preferred companions and confidants. The more intimate young adults' same-sex friendships are in terms of

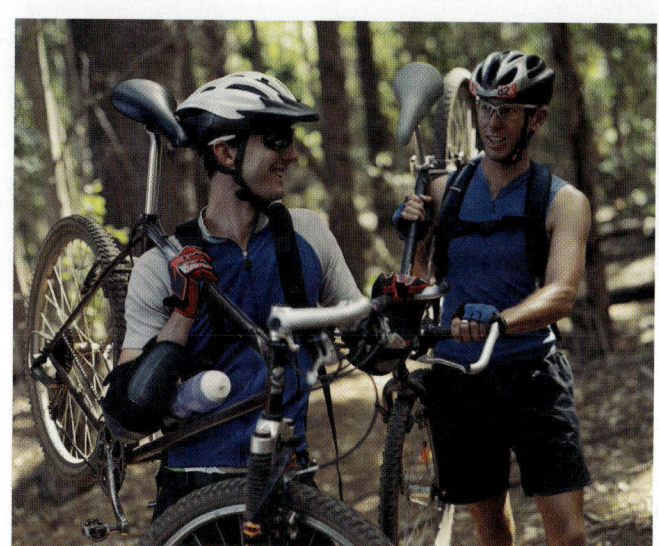

Male friends usually like to "do something" together, whereas female friends prefer to "just talk." But the longer-lasting men's friendships are, the more intimate they become, increasingly including disclosure of personal information.

warmth, social support, and self-disclosure, the more satisfying and longer-lasting the relationship and the greater its contribution to psychological well-being (Perlman, Stevens, & Carcedo, 2015). Gay and lesbian romantic relationships often develop out of close same-sex friendships, with lesbians, especially, forging compatible friendships before becoming involved romantically (Diamond, 2006).

As they develop romantic ties and marry, young adults—especially men—direct more of their disclosures toward their partners. Still, friendships continue to be vital contexts for personal sharing throughout adulthood. A best friendship can augment well-being when a marriage is not fully satisfying (but not when the marriage is low in quality) (Birditt & Antonucci, 2007).

Other-Sex Friendships.
From the college years through career exploration and settling into work roles, other-sex friendships increase. After marriage, they decline for men but continue to rise for women, who more often form them in the workplace. Highly educated, employed women have the largest number of other-sex friends. Through these relationships, young adults often gain in companionship and self-esteem and learn about masculine and feminine styles of intimacy (Bleske & Buss, 2000). Because men confide especially easily in their female friends, such friendships offer them a unique opportunity to broaden their expressive capacity. And women sometimes say male friends offer objective points of view on problems and situations—perspectives not available from female friends (Monsour, 2002).

Many people try to keep other-sex friendships platonic to safeguard their integrity. But sometimes the relationship changes into a romantic bond. When a solid other-sex friendship does evolve into a romance, it may be more stable and enduring than a romantic relationship formed without a foundation in friendship. And emerging adults, especially, are flexible about people they include in their friendship networks (Barry, Madsen, & DeGrace, 2016). After a breakup, they may even keep a former romantic partner on as a friend.

Siblings as Friends. Whereas intimacy is essential to friendship, commitment—willingness to maintain a relationship and care about the other—is the defining characteristic of family ties. As young people marry and invest less time in developing a romantic partnership, siblings—especially sisters whose earlier bond was positive—become more frequent companions than in adolescence (Birditt & Antonucci, 2007). Often, friend and sibling roles merge. For example, Sharese described Heather's practical assistance—helping with moving and running errands during an illness—in kinship terms: "She's like a sister to me. I can always turn to her." And adult sibling ties resemble friendships, in which the main concerns are staying in contact, offering social support, and enjoying being together.

A childhood history of intense parental favoritism and sibling rivalry can disrupt sibling bonds in adulthood (Panish & Stricker, 2002). But when family experiences have been positive, relationships between adult siblings can be especially close and are important sources of psychological well-being (Sherman, Lansford, & Volling, 2006). A shared background promotes similarity in values and perspectives and the possibility of deep mutual understanding.

In families with five to ten siblings, common in industrialized nations in the past and still widespread in some cultures, close sibling bonds may replace friendships (Fuller-Iglesias, 2010). One 35-year-old with five siblings, who all—with their partners and children—resided in the same small city, remarked, "With a family like this, who needs friends?"

Ask yourself

CONNECT How might recollections and evaluations of childhood attachment history, discussed on page 480, affect intimate partners' readiness to develop companionate and compassionate love?

APPLY Compared to two years earlier, when they had just met, Mindy and Graham reported an increase in relationship satisfaction. What changes in love and features of communication might have deepened their bond?

REFLECT Do you have a nonromantic, close other-sex friendship? If so, how has it enhanced your emotional and social development?

The Family Life Cycle

14.7 Trace phases of the family life cycle that are prominent in early adulthood, and cite factors that influence these phases today.

For most young people, the life course takes shape within the **family life cycle**—a series of phases characterizing the development of most families around the world. In early adulthood, people typically live on their own, marry, and bear and rear children. In middle age, as their children leave home, their parenting responsibilities diminish. Late adulthood brings retirement, growing old, and (more often for women) death of one's spouse (McGoldrick & Shibusawa, 2012). Stress tends to be greatest during transitions between phases, as family members redefine and reorganize their relationships.

But as our earlier discussion made clear, we must be careful not to view the family life cycle as a fixed progression. Wide variations exist in the sequence and timing of its phases—high rates of out-of-wedlock births, delayed marriage and parenthood, divorce, and remarriage, among others. And some people, voluntarily or involuntarily, do not experience all family life-cycle phases. Still, the family life-cycle model is useful. It offers an organized way of thinking about how the family system changes over time and the impact of each phase on the family unit and the individuals within it.

Leaving Home

During her first semester of college, Sharese noticed a change in how she related to her mother. She found it more enjoyable to discuss daily experiences and life goals, sought advice and listened with greater openness, and expressed affection more freely.

Departure from the parental home is a major step toward assuming adult responsibilities. The average age of leaving has risen since the 1960s; today, it resembles the departure age at the beginning of the twentieth century. But reasons for coresidence have changed: Early twentieth-century young adults resided with parents so they could contribute to the family economy. Twenty-first-century young people living at home are typically financially dependent on their parents. This trend toward later home-leaving is evident in most industrialized nations, though substantial variation in timing exists. Because government support is available, young adults in the Scandinavian countries move out relatively early (Furstenberg, 2010). In contrast, cultural traditions in Mediterranean countries promote lengthy coresidence, extending into the thirties.

Departures for education tend to occur at earlier ages, those for full-time work and marriage later. Because the majority of U.S. young adults enroll in higher education, many leave home around age 18. Those from divorced, single-parent homes tend to be early leavers, perhaps because of family stress (Seiffge-Krenke, 2013). Compared with the previous generation, fewer North American and Western European young people leave home to marry; more do so just to be "independent"—to express their adult status.

Slightly over half of U.S. 18- to 25-year-olds return to their parents' home for brief periods after first leaving (U.S. Census Bureau, 2015a). Usually, role transitions, such as the end of college or military service, bring young people back. But tight job markets, high housing costs, mental health problems, failures in work or love, or desire by young people launching their work lives to conserve economic resources can also prompt a temporary return home (Sandberg-Thoma, Snyder, & Jang, 2015). Also, young people who left because of family conflict often return—largely because they were not ready for independent living.

A family dinner in this Italian home includes two grown sons. Mediterranean cultural traditions promote later home-leaving, with many young adults staying into their thirties.

Residential independence rises steadily with age; by the early thirties, 90 percent of U.S. young adults live on their own (U.S. Census Bureau, 2015a). Still, the percentage of U.S. young adults residing with parents is higher today than at any time in the past 60 years. Major contributing factors include reduced employment opportunities in the aftermath of the economic recession of 2007 to 2009 and postponement of committed romantic relationships and marriage (Pew Research Center, 2016a). As young people encounter unexpected twists and turns on the road to independence, the parental home offers a safety net and base of operations for launching adult life.

The extent to which young people live on their own before marriage varies with SES and ethnicity. Those who have a bachelor's degree and are employed are more likely to establish their own residence. Among African-American, Hispanic, and Native-American groups, poverty and a cultural tradition of extended-family living lead to markedly lower rates of leaving home, even among young people in college or working (Fingerman et al., 2015; Pew Research Center, 2016a). Unmarried Asian young adults also tend to live with their parents. But the longer Asian families have lived in the United States, where they are exposed to individualistic values, the more likely young people are to move out before marriage (Lou, Lalonde, & Giguère, 2012).

Parents of young adults living at home are usually highly committed to helping their children move into adult roles. Many provide wide-ranging assistance—not just financial support, but material resources, advice, companionship, and emotional support as well. A survey of a large sample of U.S. parents diverse in SES and ethnicity and their adult children revealed that parents gave more to those with greater needs (because of problems or younger age) and to those they perceived as more successful in education and career progress. Furthermore, most parents and young-adult children judged the amount of parental support to be appropriate, though a sizable minority viewed intense support (provided several times a week) as excessive (Fingerman et al., 2009, 2012c). Nevertheless, children receiving intense support adjusted especially well, expressing firmer goals and greater life satisfaction—perhaps because the intense support matched their needs and they used it to advance their independence.

Still, in homes where parents and young adults live together, conflict over personal and moral values related to the young person's future tends to rise (Rodríguez & López, 2011). But when young adults feel securely attached to parents and well-prepared for independence, departure from the home is linked to more satisfying parent–child interaction and successful transition to adult roles, even among ethnic minorities that strongly emphasize family loyalty and obligations (Smetana, Metzger, & Campione-Barr, 2004; Whiteman, McHale, & Crouter, 2010). And regardless of living arrangements, young people doing well often have close, enjoyable relationships with their parents, who offer help because they see it as key to their child's future success (Fingerman et al., 2012b).

In contrast, resistantly attached young adults generally have difficulty with healthy separation. They often remain in the parental home for an extended time, and after leaving, they report greater parental contact than their agemates do (Seiffge-Krenke, 2006). Although avoidantly attached young people appear to adjust well to leaving home, they sometimes describe themselves as more self-sufficient than they actually are (Bernier, Larose, & Whipple, 2005; Seiffge-Krenke, 2013). They tend to be less well-adjusted than their securely attached counterparts.

Finally, leaving home very early can contribute to long-term disadvantage because it is associated with lack of parental financial and emotional support, job seeking rather than education, and earlier childbearing. Not surprisingly, U.S. non-college-bound youths who move out in their late teens tend to have less successful educational, marriage, and work lives. U.S. poverty-stricken young people are more likely than their nonpoor counterparts to leave home by age 18 (Berzin & De Marco, 2010). But if still at home beyond that age, they are less likely to move out well into their thirties—a trend that may reflect the steep challenges they face in attaining self-sufficiency and exiting poverty.

Joining of Families in Marriage

The average age of first marriage in the United States has risen from about 20 for women and 23 for men in 1960 to 27 for women and 29 for men today. Consequently, just 16 percent of contemporary U.S. 18- to 29-year-olds are married, compared to 60 percent a half-century ago (Gallup, 2015b; U.S. Census Bureau, 2016b). Postponement of marriage is even more marked in Western Europe—to the early thirties.

The number of first and second marriages has declined over the last few decades as more people stay single, cohabit, or do not remarry after divorce. In 1960, 85 percent of Americans had been married at least once; today, the figure is 70 percent. At present, 49 percent of U.S. adults, slightly less than half, live together as married couples (U.S. Census Bureau, 2015a). Nevertheless, marriage remains a central life goal for young people (Pew Research Center, 2013a). Irrespective of SES and ethnicity, most U.S. unmarried young adults say they want to marry and have children.

Same-sex marriages are recognized nationwide in 20 nations: Argentina, Belgium, Brazil, Canada, Colombia, Denmark, France, Iceland, Ireland, Luxembourg, the Netherlands, New Zealand, Norway, Portugal, South Africa, Spain, Sweden, Uruguay, the United Kingdom (except for Northern Ireland), and the United States. Because legalization is recent, research on same-sex couples in the context of marriage is scant. But so far, evidence suggests that the same factors contribute to happiness in same-sex as in other-sex marriages. And both sexual majority and minority couples perceive marriage as important for the same reasons: because it confers public legitimacy to the relationship, demonstrates commitment, and offers financial and legal benefits (Haas & Whitton, 2015).

Marriage is more than the joining of two individuals. It also requires that two systems—the spouses' families—adapt and overlap to create a new subsystem. Consequently, marriage presents complex challenges. This is especially so today because husband–wife roles are only gradually moving toward true partnership—educationally, occupationally, and in emotional connectedness. Among same-sex couples, acceptance of the relationship by parents, inclusion of the partner in family events, and living in a supportive community where they can be open about their bond benefit relationship satisfaction and durability (Rith & Diamond, 2013).

Marital Roles. Their honeymoon over, Sharese and Ernie turned to a multitude of issues they had previously decided individually or their families of origin had prescribed—from everyday matters (when and how to eat, sleep, talk, work, relax, have sex, and spend money) to family traditions and rituals (which to retain, which to work out for themselves). And as they related to their social world as a couple, they modified relationships with parents, siblings, extended family, friends, and co-workers.

Contemporary alterations in the context of marriage, including changing gender roles and living farther from family members, mean that couples must work harder than in the past to define their relationships. Although partners are usually similar in religious and ethnic background, "mixed" marriages are increasingly common today. Among new marriages in the United States, 12 percent are between partners of a different race, double the rate in 1980 (Pew Research Center, 2015d). Because of increased opportunities for interracial contact in colleges, workplaces, and neighborhoods and more positive attitudes toward intermarriage, highly educated young adults are more likely than their less educated counterparts to marry partners of another race or ethnicity (Qian & Lichter, 2011). Nevertheless, couples whose backgrounds differ face extra challenges in transitioning to married life.

Because many couples live together beforehand, marriage has become less of a turning point in the family life cycle. Still, defining marital roles can be difficult. Age of marriage is the most consistent predictor of marital stability. Young people who marry in their teens to mid-twenties are more likely to divorce than those who marry later (Lehrer & Chen, 2011; Røsand et al., 2014). Most of those who marry early have not developed a secure identity or sufficient independence to form a mature marital bond. Furthermore, early marriage is associated with low education and income—factors strongly linked to marital breakup (see page 353 in Chapter 10).

Despite progress in the area of women's rights, **traditional marriages**, involving a clear division of roles—husband as head of household responsible for family economic well-being, wife as caregiver and homemaker—still exist in Western nations. In recent decades, however, these marriages have changed, with many women who focused on motherhood while their children were young returning to the work force later. In **egalitarian marriages**, partners relate as equals, sharing power and authority. Both try to balance the time and energy they devote to their occupations, their children, and their relationship. Most well-educated, career-oriented women expect this form of marriage.

In Western nations, men in dual-earner marriages participate much more in child care than in the past, although on average they put in just 60 percent of weekly hours that mothers do (see pages 202–203 in Chapter 6). Similarly, recent surveys indicate women in the United States and European nations spend, on average, nearly twice as much time as men on housework (Pew Research Center, 2015e; Sayer, 2010).

But wide variations exist. In an investigation of over 7,500 European men and women who were married, cohabiting, or in civil unions, researchers gathered information on housework hours and gender-role attitudes. More egalitarian attitudes were strongly associated with women doing less housework (Treas & Tai, 2016). As Figure 14.3 shows, women's weekly housework hours ranged from a low of 11 to 13 in Norway, Finland, Sweden,

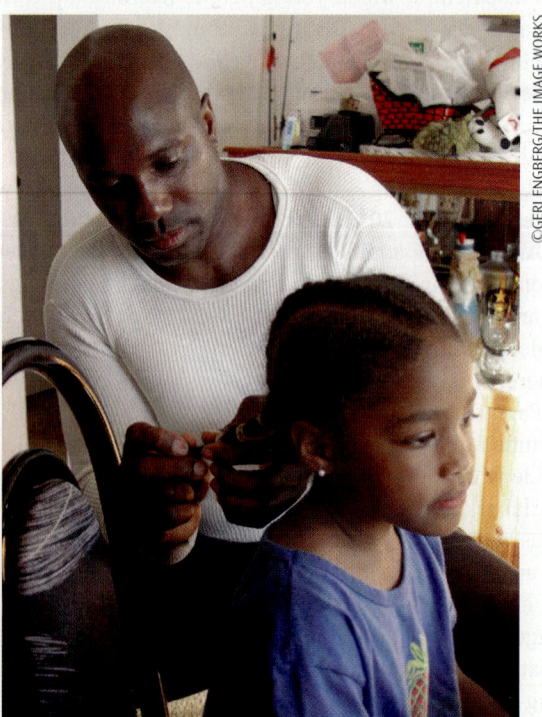

A father braids his daughter's hair. In Western nations, men in dual-earner marriages participate much more in child care than in the past, although they still contribute far less than women do.

CHAPTER 14 Emotional and Social Development in Early Adulthood 487

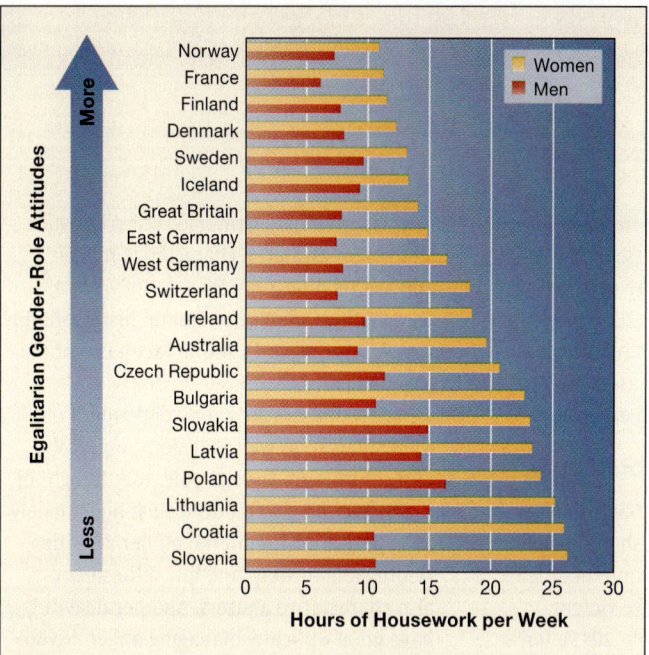

FIGURE 14.3 Women's and men's housework hours in European nations varying in gender-role attitudes. When over 7,500 men and women in European countries reported on housework hours and gender-role attitudes, women's weekly time devoted to housework was greatly reduced in countries with more egalitarian attitudes. Across all countries, women devoted substantially more time to housework than did men. (From J. Treas & T. Tai, 2016, "Gender Inequality in Housework Across 20 European Nations: Lessons from Gender Stratification Theories," *Sex Roles, 74,* p. 502. Adapted with permission.).

Research in North America and Europe confirms that women's housework hours decline modestly as their employment hours and income increase (Cooke, 2010; Treas & Tai, 2016; Van der Lippe, 2010). Employed women's reduced time doing housework is likely made possible by either purchase of time-saving services (cleaning help, prepackaged meals) or greater tolerance for unkempt homes, or both. Perhaps women continue to do the lion's share of housework because their paid work is viewed as secondary to their husband's, regardless of how much they earn. And men's greater investment in household tasks in certain Eastern European countries (Latvia, Poland, Slovakia) may largely stem from lower family incomes and poorer quality housing than elsewhere. These factors require men to invest more in household labor, especially when their partners are employed.

In the United States, African-American and European-American men devote more time to housework than Asian and Hispanic men (Wight, Bianchi, & Hunt, 2012). Although gender-role attitudes may explain these variations, men are substantially less involved than women across all ethnic groups.

Finally, although a common assumption is that among same-sex couples, one partner assumes a traditionally "male" and the other a "female" role, this is rarely so. Rather egalitarian relationships, with equal sharing of authority and household tasks, are more common in same-sex than in other-sex relationships (Patterson, 2013). In sum, in heterosexual marriages, true equality is still rare, and couples who strive for it usually attain a form of marriage in between traditional and egalitarian.

Marital Satisfaction. Despite its rocky beginnings, Sharese and Ernie's marriage grew to be especially happy. In contrast, Christy and Gary became increasingly discontented. What distinguishes satisfying marriages from less successful partnerships? Differences between these two couples mirror the findings of a large body of research on personal and contextual factors, summarized in Table 14.1.

and Iceland (Nordic nations that highly value gender equality) to a high of 24 to 26 in Poland, Lithuania, Croatia, and Slovenia (Eastern European countries more traditional in gender-role attitudes). Men's housework hours, however, did not rise in gender-egalitarian countries to compensate for women's reduced hours, and across all nations most home labor fell to women.

TABLE 14.1
Factors Related to Marital Satisfaction

FACTOR	HAPPY MARRIAGE	UNHAPPY MARRIAGE
Backgrounds	Partners similar in SES, education, religion, and age	Partners very different in SES, education, religion, and age
Age at marriage	After mid-20s	Before mid-20s
Timing of first pregnancy	After first year of marriage	Before or within first year of marriage
Relationship to extended family	Warm and positive	Negative; wish to maintain distance
Marital patterns in extended family	Stable	Unstable; frequent separations and divorces
Financial and employment status	Secure	Insecure
Family responsibilities	Shared; perception of fairness	Largely the woman's responsibility; perception of unfairness
Personality characteristics and behavior	Emotionally positive; common interests; good conflict-resolution skills	Emotionally negative and impulsive; lack of common interests; poor conflict-resolution skills

Note: The more factors present, the greater the likelihood of marital happiness or unhappiness.
Sources: Diamond, Fagundes, & Butterworth, 2010; Gere et al., 2011.

Social Issues: Health

Partner Abuse

Violence in families is a widespread health and human rights issue, occurring in all cultures and SES groups. Often one form of domestic violence is linked to others. Consider Karen, whose husband, Mike, not only assaulted her physically and sexually but also abused her psychologically—isolating, humiliating, and demeaning her. Violent adults also break their partner's favorite possessions, punch holes in walls, or throw objects. "It was a control thing," Karen explained. "He complained that I wouldn't always do what he wanted. I didn't leave because I was sure he would come after me and get more violent."

Partner abuse in which husbands are perpetrators and wives are physically injured is most likely to be reported to authorities. But in studies spanning many countries in which people are asked directly, rates of assault experienced by men and women are similar. Women victims are more often physically injured, but sex differences in severity of abuse are small (Dutton, 2012; Esquivel-Santoveña, Lambert, & Hamel, 2013). Partner abuse also occurs at similar rates in same-sex and other-sex relationships (Stiles-Shields & Carroll, 2015).

Although self-defense is a frequently reported cause of domestic assault by women, American men and women are equally likely to "strike first" (Dutton et al., 2015). "Getting my partner's attention," "gaining control," and "expressing anger" are reasons that partners typically give for abusing each other.

Factors Related to Partner Abuse

In abusive relationships, dominance–submission sometimes proceeds from husband to wife, sometimes from wife to husband. In at least half of cases, both partners are violent (Bartholomew, Cobb, & Dutton, 2015). Roy's and Pat's relationship helps us understand how partner abuse escalates. Shortly after their wedding, Pat complained about the demands of Roy's work and insisted that he come home early to spend time with her. When he resisted, she hurled epithets, threw objects, and slapped him. One evening, Roy became so angry at Pat's hostilities that he smashed a dish against the wall, threw his wedding ring at her, and left the house. The next morning, Pat apologized and promised not to attack again. But her outbursts became more frequent and desperate.

These violence–remorse cycles, in which aggression escalates, characterize many abusive relationships. Why do they occur? Personality and developmental history, family circumstances, and cultural factors combine to make partner abuse more likely.

Many abusers are overly dependent on their spouses, as well as jealous, possessive, and controlling. For example, the thought of Karen ever leaving induced such high anxiety in Mike that he monitored all her activities. Depression, anxiety, and low self-esteem also characterize abusers. And because they have great difficulty managing anger, trivial events—such as an unwashed shirt or a late meal—can trigger abusive episodes. When asked to explain their offenses, they attribute greater blame to their partner than to themselves (Henning, Jones, & Holdford, 2005).

A substantial proportion of spouse abusers grew up in homes where parents engaged in hostile interactions, used coercive discipline, and were abusive toward their children (Ehrensaft, 2009). Perhaps this explains why violent delinquency in adolescence also predicts partner abuse (Charles et al., 2011). Adults with childhood exposure to domestic

---

Christy and Gary had children early and struggled financially. Gary's negative, critical personality led him to get along poorly with Christy's parents and to feel threatened when he and Christy disagreed. Christy tried to offer Gary encouragement and support, but her own needs for nurturance and individuality were not being met. Gary was uncomfortable with Christy's career aspirations. As she came closer to attaining them, the couple grew further apart. In contrast, Sharese and Ernie married later, after their educations were complete. They postponed having children until their careers were under way and they had built a sense of togetherness that allowed each to thrive as an individual. Patience, caring, common values and interests, humor, affection, sharing of personal experiences through conversation, cooperating in household responsibilities, and good conflict-resolution skills contributed to their compatibility.

Overall, men report feeling slightly happier with their marriages than women do, but the difference is largely limited to couples in marital therapy (Jackson et al., 2014). When a marriage is distressed, women are more likely to express dissatisfaction and seek professional help. Women feel particularly dissatisfied with marriage when their husbands disagree with them about the extent to which household tasks should be shared and when conflict between the demands of family and work feels overwhelming. Role overload, however, is also linked to men's marital dissatisfaction (Minnotte, Minnotte, & Bonstrom, 2015; Ogolsky, Dennison, & Monk, 2014). Research in both Western and non-Western industrialized nations reveals that equal power in the relationship and sharing of family responsibilities usually enhance both partners' satisfaction, largely by strengthening marital harmony (Amato & Booth, 1995; Xu & Lai, 2004).

Of course, from time to time, individuals are bound to say or do something upsetting to their partner. When this happens, the partner's attributions, or explanations for the behavior, make a difference. For example, a wife who interprets her husband's critical remark about her weight as unintentional ("He just isn't aware I'm sensitive about that") is far more likely to express both current and long-term marital satisfaction than a wife who views such comments as malicious ("He's trying to hurt my feelings") (Barelds & Dijkstra, 2011; Fincham & Bradbury, 2004).

violence are not doomed to repeat it. But their parents provided them with negative expectations and behaviors that they often transfer to their close relationships. Stressful life events, such as job loss or financial difficulties, increase the likelihood of partner abuse. Because of widespread poverty, rates of abuse are elevated among African Americans and Native Americans (Black et al., 2011). Alcohol abuse is another related factor.

At a societal level, cultural norms that endorse male dominance and female submissiveness promote partner abuse (Esquivel-Santoveña, Lambert, & Hamel, 2013). In developing countries with widespread poverty that also sanction gender inequality, partner violence against women is especially high, affecting nearly half or more of the female population.

Victims are chronically anxious and depressed and experience frequent panic attacks (Warshaw, Brashler, & Gil, 2009). Why don't they simply leave these destructive relationships? A variety of situational factors discourage them from doing so. A victimized wife may depend on her husband's earning power or fear even worse harm to herself or her children. Extreme assaults, including homicide, tend to occur after partner separation (Duxbury, 2014). And victims of both sexes, but especially men, are deterred by the embarrassment of going to the police. Also, victims may falsely believe that their partner will change.

Intervention and Treatment

Community services available to battered women include crisis telephone lines that provide anonymous counseling and social support and shelters that offer safety and treatment (see page 454). Because many women return to their abusive partners several times before making their final move, community agencies usually offer therapy to perpetrators. Most rely on several months to a year of group sessions that confront rigid gender stereotyping; teach communication, problem solving, and anger control; and use social support to motivate behavior change (Hamel, 2014).

Although existing treatments are better than none, most are not effective at dealing with relationship difficulties or alcohol abuse. Consequently, many treated perpetrators repeat their violent behavior with the same or a new partner (Hamberger et al., 2009). At present, few interventions acknowledge that men also are victims. Yet ignoring their needs perpetuates domestic violence. When victims do not want to separate from a violent partner, a whole-family treatment approach that focuses on changing partner interaction and reducing high life stress is crucial.

Although partner abuse in which husbands physically harm their wives is most likely to be reported, wives assault their husbands at similar rates. Abusers' emotional problems include great difficulty managing anger.

In fact, partners who hold overly positive (but still realistic) biases concerning each other's attributes are happier with their relationships (Claxton et al., 2011). As they turn to each other for feedback about themselves, these "positive illusions" enhance self-esteem and psychological well-being. And over time, positive illusions favorably influence behavior, as partners modify their actions to bring them closer to their partner's generous perceptions.

In contrast, people who feel devalued by their partner tend to react with anxiety and insecurity—more so when they are low in self-esteem, which heightens fear of rejection. To protect themselves, they often mete out criticism and contempt in kind, setting in motion hostile, defensive exchanges that create the very rejection they fear (Murray, 2008). Alternatively, individuals may disengage emotionally, suppressing negative feelings so as not to poison the relationship (Driver et al., 2012). In the process, shared positive emotion also declines, and intimacy erodes.

At their worst, marital relationships can become contexts for intense opposition, dominance–submission, and emotional and physical violence. As the Social Issues: Health box above explains, although women are more often targets of severe partner abuse, both men and women play both roles: perpetrator and victim.

High school and college courses in family life education can promote better mate selection and teach communication skills that contribute to gratifying romantic partnerships and marriages. And counseling aimed at helping couples listen to each other with understanding and empathy, focus on positive traits and memories, and use effective conflict-resolution strategies can cultivate the self-esteem, affection, and respect needed for the relationship to be resilient and enduring (Gottman, 2011).

Parenthood

In the past, having children was, for many adults, a biological given or a compelling social expectation. Today, in Western industrialized nations, it is a matter of true individual choice. Effective birth control techniques enable adults to avoid having children in most instances. And changing cultural values allow people to remain childless with far less fear of social criticism and rejection than a generation or two ago. Nevertheless, the 6 percent of American 18- to 40-year-olds who currently say they do not want children is just slightly higher than the 5 percent who said so a quarter century ago (Gallup, 2013).

Among U.S. adults age 40 and older, 85 percent of women and 76 percent of men are parents (U.S. Census Bureau, 2015b). At the same time, increasing numbers of young adults in industrialized nations are delaying parenthood or not having children. Consistent with this trend and with the decision of most mothers to divide their energies between family and work, family size has declined to an all-time low. In 1950, the average number of children per woman was 3.1; currently, it is 1.9 in the United States and Sweden, 1.8 in the United Kingdom, 1.6 in Canada, and 1.4 in Germany, Italy, and Japan (World Bank, 2016). Nevertheless, the vast majority of married people continue to embrace parenthood as one of life's most meaningful experiences. Why do they do so, and how do the challenges of child rearing affect the adult life course?

The Decision to Have Children. The choice of parenthood is affected by a complex array of factors, including financial circumstances, personal and religious values, career goals, health conditions, and availability of supportive government and workplace family policies. Women with traditional gender identities usually decide to have children. Those in high-status, demanding careers less often choose parenthood and, when they do, more often delay it than women with less consuming jobs. Parenthood typically reduces work hours and slows career progress among career-oriented women but has no impact on men (Abele, 2014; Abele & Spurk, 2011). Professional women often consider these consequences in decision making about parenthood.

Besides these influences, a vital personal factor called childbearing motivations—each person's disposition to respond positively or negatively to the idea of parenthood—affects the decision to have children. In Western nations, these motivations have changed over time, increasingly emphasizing individual fulfillment and de-emphasizing obligation to society (Frejka et al., 2008).

When Americans and Europeans are asked about their desire to have children, they mention a variety of advantages and disadvantages. Although some ethnic and regional differences exist, in all groups highly rated reasons for having children include personal rewards—for example, the warm, affectionate relationship and opportunities for care and teaching that children provide. Also frequently mentioned are social returns, such as affirmation of one's adult status and children as a source of caregiving in later life (Guedes et al., 2013). Less important, but still mentioned, is a sense of future continuity—having someone carry on after one's own death. And occasionally, couples look to parenthood as a gratifying opportunity to share in a challenging but important life task and to deepen their relationship.

Most adults also realize that having children means years of extra burdens and responsibilities. Among disadvantages, they most often cite concerns about role overload, doubts about their own readiness for parenthood, and worries about bringing up children in a troubled world. The financial strains of child rearing follow close behind. According to a conservative estimate, today's new parents in the United States will spend about $300,000 to rear a child from birth to age 18, and many will incur substantial additional expense for higher education and financial dependency during emerging adulthood (U.S. Department of Agriculture, 2014).

Greater freedom to choose whether and when to have children makes contemporary family planning more challenging as well as intentional than it was in the past. Still, about 35 percent of U.S. births are the result of unintended pregnancies, with most born to low-income, less-educated mothers (Guttmacher Institute, 2013). Opportunities to explore childbearing motivations in high school, college, and community-based health education classes and through family-planning counseling might encourage more adults to make informed and personally meaningful decisions—a trend that would increase the chances that they would have children when ready and find parenting an enriching experience.

Transition to Parenthood. The early weeks after a baby enters the family are full of profound changes: constant caregiving, added financial responsibilities, and less time for the couple's relationship. In response, gender roles of husband and wife usually become more traditional—even for couples like Sharese and Ernie who are strongly committed to gender equality (Katz-Wise, Priess, & Hyde, 2010; Yavorsky, Dush, & Schoppe-Sullivan, 2015).

First and Second Births. For most new parents, the arrival of a baby—though often followed by mild declines in relationship and overall life satisfaction—does not cause significant marital strain (Doss et al., 2009; Lawrence et al., 2008; Luhmann et al., 2012). Marriages that are gratifying and supportive tend to remain so. But troubled marriages usually become even more distressed after childbirth (Houts et al., 2008; Kluwer & Johnson, 2007). And when expectant mothers anticipate lack of partner support in parenting, their prediction generally becomes reality, yielding an especially difficult post-birth adjustment (Driver et al., 2012; McHale & Rotman, 2007).

In dual-earner marriages, the larger the difference in men's and women's caregiving responsibilities, the greater the decline in marital satisfaction after childbirth, especially for women—with negative consequences for parent–infant interaction. In contrast, sharing caregiving predicts greater parental happiness and sensitivity to the baby (McHale et al., 2004; Moller, Hwang, & Wickberg, 2008). An exception exists, however, for employed lower-SES women who endorse traditional gender roles. When their husbands take on considerable child-care responsibilities, these mothers tend to report more distress, perhaps because of disappointment at being unable to fulfill their desire to do most of the caregiving (Goldberg & Perry-Jenkins, 2003).

Postponing childbearing until the late twenties or thirties, as more couples do today, eases the transition to parenthood. Waiting permits couples to pursue occupational goals, gain life experience, and strengthen their relationship. Under these circumstances, men are more enthusiastic about becoming fathers

Couples are increasingly postponing childbearing until their late twenties or thirties. This later transition to parenthood gives them time to pursue occupational goals, gain life experience, and strengthen their relationship.

and therefore more willing to participate. And women whose careers are well under way and whose marriages are happy are more likely to encourage their husbands to share housework and child care, which fosters fathers' involvement (Lee & Doherty, 2007; Schoppe-Sullivan et al., 2008).

A second birth typically requires that fathers take an even more active role in parenting—by caring for the firstborn while the mother is recuperating and by sharing in the high demands of tending to both a baby and a young child. Consequently, well-functioning families with a newborn second child typically pull back from the traditional division of responsibilities that occurred after the first birth. Fathers' willingness to place greater emphasis on the parenting role is strongly linked to mothers' adjustment after the arrival of a second baby (Stewart, 1990). And the support and encouragement of family, friends, and spouse are crucial for fathers' well-being.

Interventions. Couples' groups led by counselors are effective in easing the transition to parenthood (Gottman, Gottman, & Shapiro, 2010). Therapists report that many couples know little about caring for infants, perhaps because they grew up in small families where they had few sibling caregiving responsibilities. They are also unaware of the potential impact of a new baby on their relationship.

In one program, first-time expectant couples gathered once a week for 4 to 6 months to discuss their dreams for the family and changes in relationships sparked by the baby's arrival. Eighteen months after the program ended, participating fathers described themselves as more involved with their child than did fathers in a no-intervention condition. Perhaps because of fathers' caregiving assistance, participating mothers maintained their prebirth satisfaction with family and work roles. Three years after the birth, the marriages of participating couples were intact and just as happy as they had been before parenthood. In contrast, 15 percent of couples receiving no intervention had divorced (Cowan & Cowan, 1997; Schulz, Cowan, & Cowan, 2006).

High-risk parents struggling with poverty or the birth of a child with disabilities need more intensive interventions aimed at enhancing social support and parenting skills. Many low-income single mothers benefit from programs that focus on sustaining the father's involvement (Jones, Charles, & Benson, 2013).

Generous, paid employment leave—widely available in industrialized nations but not in the United States—is crucial for parents of newborns. But as we saw in Chapter 3, financial pressures mean that many new mothers who are eligible for unpaid work leave take far less than they are guaranteed, while new fathers take little or none. When favorable workplace policies exist and parents take advantage of them, couples are more likely to support each other and experience family life as gratifying (Feldman, Sussman, & Zigler, 2004). As a result, the stress caused by the birth of a baby stays at manageable levels.

Families with Young Children.
A year after the birth of their first child, a friend asked Sharese and Ernie how they liked parenthood: "Is it a joy, a dilemma, a stressful experience—how would you describe it?"

Chuckling, Sharese and Ernie responded in unison, "All of the above!"

In today's complex world, men and women are less certain about how to rear children than in previous generations. Clarifying child-rearing values and implementing them in warm, involved, and appropriately demanding ways are crucial for the welfare of the next generation and society. Yet cultures do not always place a high priority on parenting, as indicated by lack of societal supports for children and families (see Chapter 2, page 64). Furthermore, changing family forms mean that the lives of today's parents differ substantially from those of past generations.

In previous chapters, we discussed a wide variety of influences on child-rearing styles, including personal characteristics of children and parents, SES, and ethnicity. The couple's relationship is also vital. Parents who engage in effective *coparenting*, collaborating in parenting roles, are more likely to feel competent as parents, use effective child-rearing practices, and have children who are developing well. And they also gain in marital satisfaction (see page 57).

For employed parents, major struggles include finding good child care and, when their child is ill or otherwise in need of emergency care, taking time off from work or making other urgent arrangements. The younger the child, the greater parents' sense of risk and difficulty—especially low-income parents, who must work longer hours to pay bills; who often, in the United States, have no workplace benefits (health insurance or paid sick leave); who typically cannot afford the cost of child care; and who experience more immediate concerns about their children's safety (Nomaguchi & Brown, 2011). When competent, convenient child care is not available, the woman usually faces added pressures. She must either curtail or give up her work or endure unhappy children, missed workdays, and constant searches for new arrangements.

Despite its challenges, rearing young children is a powerful source of adult development. Parents report that it expands their emotional capacities, makes life more meaningful, and enhances psychological well-being (Nelson et al., 2013; Nomaguchi & Milkie, 2003). Ernie remarked that through sharing in child rearing, he felt "rounded out" as a person. Other involved parents say that parenthood helped them tune in to others' feelings and needs, required that they become more tolerant, self-confident, and responsible, and broadened their extended family, friendship, and community ties. In a survey of a large, nationally representative sample of U.S. fathers, paternal history of engagement with children predicted greater community service and assistance of extended family members in middle adulthood (Eggebeen, Dew, & Knoester, 2010).

Families with Adolescents.
Adolescence brings sharp changes in parental roles. In Chapters 11 and 12, we noted that parents must establish a revised relationship with their adolescent children—blending guidance with freedom and gradually loosening control. As adolescents gain in autonomy and explore values and goals in their search for identity, parents often complain that their teenager is too focused on peers and no longer cares about being with the family. Heightened parent–child bickering over everyday issues takes a toll, especially on mothers, who do most of the negotiating with teenagers.

Overall, children seem to navigate the challenges of adolescence more easily than parents, many of whom report a dip in marital and life satisfaction (Cui & Donnellan, 2009). More people seek family therapy during this phase of the family life cycle than during any other.

Parenting Education.
In the past, family life changed little from one generation to the next, and adults learned what they needed to know about parenting through modeling and direct experience. Today's world confronts adults with a host of factors that impinge on their ability to succeed as parents.

Contemporary parents eagerly seek information on child rearing. In addition to popular parenting books, magazines, and websites, new mothers access knowledge about parenting through social media. They also reach out to family members and networks of other women for assistance. Fathers, by contrast, less often have social networks through which they can learn about child rearing. Consequently, they frequently turn to their partner to figure out how to relate to their child, especially if they have a close, confiding marriage (McHale, Kuersten-Hogan, & Rao, 2004; Radey & Randolph, 2009). Recall from Chapter 6 that marital harmony fosters both parents' positive engagement with babies but is especially important for fathers.

Parent education courses exist to help parents clarify child-rearing values, improve family communication, understand how children develop, and apply more effective parenting strategies. A variety of programs yield positive outcomes, including enhanced knowledge of effective parenting practices, improved parent–child interaction, heightened awareness by parents of

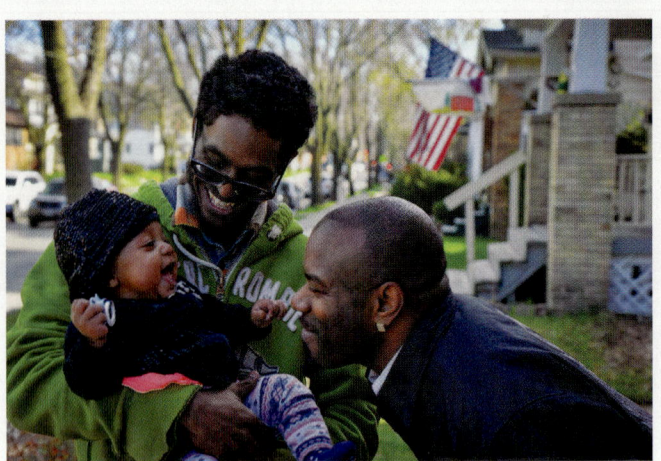

Fathers are less likely than mothers to have social networks they can access to learn about child rearing. This young father and his son interact with an older neighbor, who models effective parenting.

their role as educators of their children, and gains in psychological well-being (Bennett et al., 2013; Smith, Perou, & Lesesne, 2002). Another benefit is social support—opportunities to discuss concerns with experts and other dedicated parents, who share the view that no job is more important to the future of society than child rearing.

Ask yourself

CONNECT What aspects of adolescent development make rearing teenagers stressful for parents, leading to a dip in marital and life satisfaction? (See Chapter 11, page 376, and Chapter 12, pages 420–422.)

APPLY After her wedding, Sharese was convinced she had made a mistake. Cite factors that sustained her marriage and led it to become highly satisfying.

REFLECT Do you live with your parents or on your own? Describe factors that contributed to your current living arrangements. How would you characterize the quality of your relationship with your parents? Do your responses match the findings of research?

The Diversity of Adult Lifestyles

14.8 Discuss the diversity of adult lifestyles, focusing on singlehood, cohabitation, and childlessness.

14.9 Cite factors that contribute to high rates of divorce and remarriage.

14.10 Discuss challenges associated with varied styles of parenthood, including stepparents, never-married parents, and gay and lesbian parents.

The current array of adult lifestyles dates back to the 1960s, when young people began to question the conventional wisdom of previous generations and to ask, "How can I find happiness? What kinds of commitments should I make to live a full and rewarding life?" As the public became more accepting of diverse lifestyles, choices such as staying single, cohabiting, remaining childless, and divorcing seemed more available.

Today, nontraditional family options have penetrated the American mainstream. Many adults experience not just one but several. As we will see, some adults make a deliberate decision to adopt a lifestyle, whereas others drift into it. The lifestyle may be culturally imposed, as is the case for cohabiting same-sex couples who live in countries or regions where they cannot marry legally. Or people may choose a certain lifestyle because they feel pushed away from another, such as a marriage gone sour. In sum, the adoption of a lifestyle can be within or beyond the person's control.

Singlehood

On finishing her education, Heather joined the Peace Corps and spent four years in Ghana. Though open to a long-term relationship, she had only fleeting romances. After she returned to the United States, she went from one temporary job to another until, at age 30, she finally secured steady employment in a large international travel company as a tour director. A few years later, she advanced into a management position. At age 35, over lunch with Sharese, she reflected on her life: "I was open to marriage, but after I got my career going, it would have interfered. Now I'm so used to independence that I question whether I could adjust to living with another person. I like being able to pick up and go where I want, when I want, without having to ask anyone or think about caring for anyone. But there's a trade-off: I sleep alone, eat most of my meals alone, and spend a lot of my leisure time alone."

Singlehood—not living with an intimate partner—has increased in recent years, especially among young adults. For example, the rate of never-married Americans age 25 and older has more than doubled since 1960, to 23 percent of men and 17 percent of women. Today, more people marry later or not at all, and divorce has added to the numbers of single adults—slightly more than half when adults of all ages are considered. In view of these trends, it is likely that most Americans will spend a substantial part of their adult lives single, and a growing minority—about 8 to 10 percent—will stay that way (Pew Research Center, 2014b).

Because they marry later, more young-adult men than women are single. But women are far more likely than men to remain single for many years or their entire life. With age, fewer men are available with characteristics that most women seek in a mate—the same age or older, equally or better educated, and professionally successful. In contrast, men can choose partners from a large pool of younger unmarried women. Because of the tendency for women to "marry up" and men to "marry down," men with a high school diploma or less and highly educated women in prestigious careers are overrepresented among singles after age 30.

Ethnic differences also exist. For example, more than one-third of African Americans age 25 and older have never married, a figure more than double that of European Americans (Pew Research Center, 2014b). As we will see later, high unemployment among black men interferes with marriage. Many African Americans eventually marry in their late thirties and forties, a period in which black and white marriage rates move closer together.

Singlehood can have a variety of meanings. At one extreme are people who choose it deliberately; at the other are those who see themselves as single because of circumstances beyond their control. Most, like Heather, are in the middle—adults who want to marry but made choices that took them in a different direction or say they have not found the right person. In interviews with never-married women, some said they focused on occupational goals instead of marriage (Baumbusch, 2004; Pew Research Center, 2014b). Others reported that they found singlehood preferable to their disappointing intimate relationships.

The most commonly mentioned advantages of singlehood are freedom and mobility. But singles also recognize drawbacks—loneliness, the dating grind, limited sexual and social life, reduced sense of security, and feelings of exclusion from the world of married couples. Single men have more physical and mental health problems than single women, who more easily come to terms with their lifestyle, in part because of the greater social support available to women through intimate same-sex friendships. But overall, people over age 35 who have always been single are content with their lives (DePaulo & Morris, 2005; Pinquart, 2003). Though not quite as happy as married people, they report feeling considerably happier than people recently widowed or divorced.

Nevertheless, many single people go through a stressful period in their early thirties, when most of their friends have married and they become increasingly mindful of their own departure from society's marital social clock. Widespread veneration of marriage, along with negative stereotyping of singles as socially immature and self-centered, contributes (Morris et al., 2008). The mid-thirties is another trying time, as the biological deadline for pregnancy approaches. Interviews with 28- to 34-year-old single women revealed that they were acutely aware of pressures from family members, the shrinking pool of eligible

Compared with single men, single women more easily come to terms with their lifestyle, in part because of the greater social support available to women through intimate same-sex friendships.

men, the risks of later childbearing, and a sense of being different (Sharp & Ganong, 2011). A few decide to become parents through artificial insemination or a love affair. And an increasing number are adopting, often from overseas countries.

Cohabitation

Cohabitation refers to the lifestyle of unmarried couples who have a sexually intimate relationship and who share a residence. Until the 1960s, cohabitation in Western nations was largely limited to low-SES adults. Since then, it has increased in all groups, with an especially dramatic rise among well-educated, economically advantaged young people. Today's young adults are much more likely than those of a generation ago to form their first conjugal union through cohabitation. Among U.S. young people, cohabitation is now the preferred mode of entry into an intimate partnership, chosen by over 70 percent of couples age 30 and younger (Copen, Daniels, & Mosher, 2013). Cohabitation rates are even higher among adults with failed marriages; about one-third of these households include children.

For some couples, cohabitation serves as *preparation for marriage*—a time to test the relationship and get used to living together. For many others, it is an *alternative to marriage*, offering the rewards of sexual intimacy and companionship along with the possibility of easy departure if satisfaction declines. It is not surprising, then, that cohabiters vary greatly in the extent to which they share money and possessions and take responsibility for each other's children.

Although Americans have become increasingly favorable toward cohabitation, with more than 60 percent expressing approval, their attitudes are not as positive as those of Western Europeans. In the Netherlands, Norway, and Sweden, cohabitation is thoroughly integrated into society. Cohabiters have many of the same legal rights and responsibilities as married couples and express nearly the same level of commitment to each other (Daugherty & Copen, 2016; Perelli-Harris & Gassen, 2012). Whereas about 60 percent of American cohabiting unions break up within three years, only 6 to 16 percent dissolve in Western Europe (Guzzo, 2014; Kiernan, 2002). When they decide to marry, Dutch, Norwegian, and Swedish cohabiters more often do so to legalize their relationships, especially for the sake of children. American cohabiters typically marry to affirm their love and commitment—sentiments that Western Europeans attach to cohabitation.

As cohabitation has risen in acceptability in the United States, cohabiting relationships have become more prone to dissolution. Two decades ago, U.S. cohabiters who were engaged were more likely than their non-engaged counterparts to stay together and transition to lasting marriages. But today, the majority of both types of cohabiting relationships dissolve at a similarly high rate (60 percent) and less often lead to marriage (Guzzo, 2014). Furthermore, engagement at the start of cohabitation is declining while cohabitation is on the rise—trends suggesting that contemporary cohabitation is less often serving as preparation for marriage (Vespa, 2014). More U.S. young adult

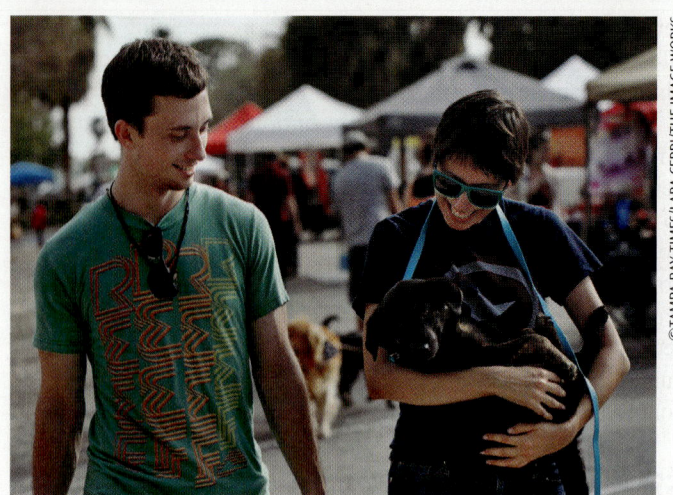

Cohabitation is common throughout Western industrialized nations. As this cohabiting couple brings home a newly adopted dog, the longevity of their relationship will depend on how committed they are to each other.

cohabiters are entering these unions without expectations or plans to marry, perhaps motivated instead by a desire to increase the cost-effectiveness and convenience of life with their current romantic partner.

Furthermore, couples who do transition from cohabitation to marriage are at slightly greater risk of divorce than couples who marry directly, without cohabiting. But the difference is largely explained by the earlier age at which premarital cohabiters, compared with direct marriers, began living together (Kuperberg, 2014). Premarital cohabitation before age 25, like early marriage, is associated with reduced readiness to select a compatible partner and forge a committed romantic bond. Also, young premarital cohabiters are more likely than direct marriers to be non-college-educated, to come from single-parent families, to differ in age and background from their partner, and to have previously cohabited with a partner other than their spouse. Among couples in general, all these factors are linked to risk of divorce.

Lesbian and gay cohabiters are exceptions to the high risk for breakup just described. The legal right to marry, granted to same-sex couples throughout the United States in 2015, is so recent that many already viewed their cohabiting relationships as symbols of long-term commitment (Haas & Whitton, 2015). When marriage became broadly available, nearly 100,000 same-sex couples transitioned from cohabitation to marriage within the following four months, yielding an 8 percent marriage-rate gain (Gallup, 2015c). If this trend continues, perhaps marriage will supplant cohabitation as the more common relationship status among committed same-sex couples, as it is among committed heterosexual couples.

In sum, cohabitation combines the rewards of a close relationship with the opportunity to avoid legal marital obligations. But cohabiting couples can encounter difficulties precisely because they do not have these obligations. Disputes over property, money, rental contracts, and responsibility for children are the rule rather than the exception when unmarried couples split up.

Childlessness

At work, Sharese got to know Beatrice and Daniel. Married for seven years and in their mid-thirties, they did not have children and were not planning any. To Sharese, their relationship seemed especially caring and affectionate. "At first, we were open to becoming parents," Beatrice explained, "but eventually we decided to focus on our marriage."

Childlessness among U.S. women in their mid-forties increased from 10 percent in 1975 to 20 percent in 2006, and then declined to 15 percent in 2014 (Pew Research Center, 2015b). Some people are *involuntarily childless* because they did not find a partner with whom to share parenthood or their efforts at fertility treatments did not succeed. Beatrice and Daniel are in another category—men and women who are *voluntarily childless*.

But voluntary childlessness is not always a permanent condition. A few people decide early that they do not want to be parents and stick to their plans. But most, like Beatrice and Daniel, make their decision after they are married and have developed a lifestyle they do not want to give up. Later, some change their minds. The voluntarily childless are usually highly educated, have prestigious occupations, are very committed to their work, and are less traditional in gender-role attitudes (Gold, 2012). At the same time, the recent decline in childlessness is largely due to more educated, career-focused women, who are more numerous than in the past, eventually opting for parenthood.

Negative stereotypes of nonparenthood—as a sign of self-indulgence and irresponsibility—have weakened in Western nations as people have become more accepting of diverse lifestyles (Dykstra & Hagestad, 2007). In line with this trend, voluntarily childless adults are just as content with their lives as parents who have warm relationships with their children. But adults who cannot overcome infertility are likely to be dissatisfied—some profoundly disappointed, others more ambivalent, depending on compensations in other areas of their lives (Letherby, 2002; Luk & Loke, 2015). Childlessness seems to interfere with adjustment and life satisfaction only when it is beyond a person's control.

Divorce and Remarriage

Divorce rates have declined over the past two decades, partly because of rising age at marriage, which is linked to greater financial stability and marital satisfaction. In addition, the increase in cohabitation has curtailed divorce: Many relationships that once would have been marriages now break up before marriage. Still, from 42 to 45 percent of U.S. marriages dissolve (U.S. Census Bureau, 2015b). Because most divorces occur within seven years of marriage, many involve young children. Divorces are also common during the transition to midlife, when people have adolescent children—a period (as noted earlier) of reduced marital satisfaction.

Nearly 60 percent of divorced adults remarry. But marital failure is even greater during the first few years of second marriages—10 percent above that for first marriages. Afterward, the divorce rates for first and second marriages are similar (Lewis & Kreider, 2015).

Factors Related to Divorce. Why do so many marriages fail? As Christy and Gary's divorce illustrates, the most obvious reason is a disrupted relationship. Christy and Gary did not argue more than Sharese and Ernie. But their problem-solving style was ineffective, and it weakened their attachment to each other. When Christy raised concerns, Gary reacted with contempt, defensiveness, and refusal to communicate. This demand–withdraw pattern is found in many partners who split up, with women more often insisting on change and men more often retreating. Another typical style involves little conflict (Gottman & Gottman, 2015). Rather, partners increasingly disengage emotionally from each other, leading separate lives because they have different expectations of family life and few shared interests, activities, or friends.

What problems underlie these maladaptive communication patterns? In a nine-year longitudinal study, researchers asked a nationally representative sample of 2,000 U.S. married people about relationship problems and followed up 3, 6, and 9 years later to find out who had separated or divorced (Amato & Rogers, 1997). Compared to men, women reported more problems, largely involving their emotions, such as anger and hurt feelings. Men seemed to have difficulty sensing their wife's distress, which contributed to her view of the marriage as unhappy. Regardless of which spouse reported the problem or was judged responsible for it, the strongest predictors of divorce during the following decade were infidelity, spending money foolishly, drinking or using drugs, expressing jealousy, engaging in irritating habits, and moodiness.

Background factors that increase the chances of divorce are younger age at marriage, being previously divorced, and having parents who had divorced—all of which are linked to marital difficulties. For example, couples who married at younger ages are more likely to report infidelity and jealousy. And research conducted in diverse industrialized nations consistently confirms that parental divorce elevates risk of divorce in the next generation, in part because it promotes child adjustment problems and reduces commitment to the norm of lifelong marriage (Diekmann & Schmidheiny, 2013). As a result, when adult children marry, they are more likely to engage in inconsiderate behaviors and to have conflict-ridden relationships and less likely to try to work through these difficulties or (if they do try) to have the skills to do so. Marriage to a caring spouse from a stable family background reduces these negative outcomes.

Poorly educated, economically disadvantaged couples who suffer multiple life stresses are especially likely to split up (Lewis & Kreider, 2015). But Christy's case represents another trend—elevated marital breakup among career-oriented, economically independent women whose education and income exceed their husband's—an outcome explained by differing gender-role beliefs between the spouses. However, the tendency for these couples to divorce at higher rates is subsiding (Schwartz & Han,

An ineffective problem-solving style can lead to divorce. Partners who split up often follow a pattern in which one partner raises concerns, and the other reacts with contempt, defensiveness, and refusal to communicate.

2014). The likely reason is a cultural shift toward more egalitarian partnerships in contemporary marriages.

In addition to the factors just described, American individualism—which includes the belief that each person has the right to pursue self-expression and personal happiness—contributes to the unusually high U.S. divorce rate (see page 353 in Chapter 10) (Amato, 2014). When people are dissatisfied with their intimate relationship, the cultural value of individualism encourages moving on.

Consequences of Divorce. Divorce involves the loss of a way of life and therefore a part of the self sustained by that way of life. As a result, it provides opportunities for both positive and negative change. Immediately after separation, both men and women experience disrupted social networks, a decline in social support, and increased anxiety and depression (Braver & Lamb, 2013). For most, these reactions subside within two years. Nonworking women who organized their identities around their husbands have an especially hard time. And some noncustodial fathers feel disoriented and rootless as a result of decreased contact with their children (Coleman, Ganong, & Leon, 2006). Others distract themselves with a frenzy of social activity.

Finding a new partner contributes most to the psychological well-being of divorced adults (Gustavson et al., 2014). But it is more crucial for men, who adjust less well than women to living on their own. Despite loneliness and a drop in income (see Chapter 10), women—especially those who were in very low-quality marriages—tend to bounce back more easily from divorce (Bourassa, Sbarra, & Whisman, 2015). Christy, for example, developed new friendships and a gratifying sense of self-reliance. However, a few women—especially those who are anxious and fearful, who remain strongly attached to their ex-spouses, or who lack education and job skills—experience a drop in self-esteem and persistent depression (Coleman, Ganong, & Leon, 2006). Job training, continued education, career advancement, and social support from family and friends play vital roles in the economic and psychological well-being of many divorced women.

Remarriage. On average, people remarry within four years of divorce, men somewhat faster than women. As noted earlier, remarriages are especially vulnerable to breakup, for several reasons. First, practical matters—financial security, help in rearing children, relief from loneliness, and social acceptance—figure more heavily into choice of a second-marriage partner than a first. As a result, remarried couples are more likely than first-marriage couples to differ in age, education level, ethnicity, religion, and other background factors. These conditions do not provide a sound footing for a lasting partnership. Second, some people transfer the negative patterns of interaction learned in their first marriage to the second. Third, people with a failed marriage behind them are even more likely to view divorce as an acceptable solution when marital difficulties resurface. Finally, remarried couples experience more stress from stepfamily situations (Coleman, Ganong, & Russell, 2013). As we will see, stepparent–stepchild ties are powerful predictors of marital happiness.

Blended families generally take 3 to 5 years to develop the connectedness and comfort of intact biological families. Family life education, couples counseling, and group therapy can help divorced and remarried adults adapt to the complexities of their new circumstances (Pryor, 2014).

Varied Styles of Parenthood

Diverse family forms result in varied styles of parenthood. Each type of family—blended, never-married, gay or lesbian, among others—presents unique challenges to parenting competence and adult psychological well-being.

Stepparents. Whether stepchildren live in the household or visit only occasionally, stepparents are in a difficult position. Stepparents enter the family as outsiders and, too often, move into their new parental role too quickly. Lacking a warm attachment bond to build on, their discipline is usually ineffective. Stepparents frequently criticize the biological parent for being too lenient, while the biological parent may view the stepparent as too harsh (Ganong & Coleman, 2004). Compared with first-marriage parents, remarried parents typically report higher levels of tension and disagreement, most centering on child-rearing issues. When both adults have children from prior marriages, rather than only one, more opportunities for conflict exist and relationship quality tends to be poorer.

Stepmothers, particularly the 10 percent who live in the same residence as stepchildren, are especially likely to experience conflict. Those who have not previously been married and had children may have an idealized image of family life, which is quickly shattered. Expected to be in charge of family relationships, stepmothers quickly find that stepparent–stepchild ties do not develop instantly. After divorce, biological mothers are frequently jealous and uncooperative. Even when their husbands do not have custody, stepmothers feel stressed. As stepchildren go in and out of the nonresident home, stepmothers find life easier without uncooperative children and then may feel guilty about their "unmaternal" feelings (Church, 2004; Pryor, 2014). A stepmother may eventually succeed in building a close parent–child bond, but her efforts are likely to meet with resistance in the short run.

Stepfathers with children of their own tend to establish positive bonds with stepchildren, especially stepsons, more readily, perhaps because they are experienced in building warm parent–child ties and feel less pressure than stepmothers to plunge into parenting (Ganong et al., 1999; van Eeden-Moorefield & Pasley, 2013). But stepfathers without biological children (like their stepmother counterparts) can have unrealistic expectations. Or their wives may push them into the father role, sparking negativity from children. After making several overtures that are ignored or rebuffed, these stepfathers frequently withdraw from parenting (Hetherington & Clingempeel, 1992).

In interviews in which young-adult stepchildren provided retrospective accounts of their stepparent relationships, the quality of these ties varied widely, from warm and loving, to ambivalent, to coexisting, to critical and rejecting. A caring relationship between remarried or cohabiting couples, sensitive relationship-building behaviors by the stepparent, cooperation from the biological parent, and supportive extended family members all affected the development of stepparent–stepchild ties. Over time, many couples built a coparenting partnership that improved interactions with stepchildren (Ganong, Coleman, & Jamison, 2011). But establishing stepparent–stepchild bonds is challenging, contributing to a higher divorce rate for remarried couples with stepchildren than for those without them.

Never-Married Single Parents.
Over the past several decades, births to unmarried mothers in industrialized nations have increased dramatically. Today, about 40 percent of U.S. births are to single mothers, more than double the percentage in 1980. Whereas teenage parenthood has declined steadily since 1990 (see page 384 in Chapter 11), births to single adult women have increased, with a particularly sharp rise during the first decade of the twenty-first century (Hamilton et al., 2015).

A growing number of nonmarital births are planned and occur to cohabiting couples. But these relationships—common among young adults with low education—are often unstable (Cherlin, 2010; Gibson-Davis & Rackin, 2014). In addition, more than 12 percent of U.S. children live with a single parent who has never married and does not have a partner. Of these parents, about 90 percent are mothers, 10 percent fathers (Curtin, Ventura, & Martinez, 2014).

Single motherhood is especially prevalent among African-American young women, who are considerably more likely than white women to give birth outside of marriage and less likely to live with the baby's father. As a result, more than half of births to black mothers in their twenties are to women without a partner, compared with about 14 percent of births to white women (Child Trends, 2015a; Hamilton et al., 2015). Job loss, persisting unemployment, and consequent inability of many black men to support a family have contributed to the number of African-American never-married, single-mother families.

Never-married African-American mothers tap the extended family, especially their own mothers and sometimes male relatives, for help in rearing their children (Anderson, 2012). Compared with their white counterparts, low-SES African-American women tend to marry later—within a decade after birth of the first child—but not necessarily to the child's biological father (Dixon, 2009; Wu, Bumpass, & Musick, 2001).

Still, for low-SES women, never-married parenthood generally increases financial hardship; about half live in poverty (Mather, 2010). Nearly 50 percent of white mothers and 60 percent of black mothers have a second child while unmarried. And they are far less likely than divorced mothers to receive paternal child support payments, although child support enforcement both reduces financial stress and increases father involvement (Huang, 2006).

Many children in single-mother homes display adjustment problems associated with economic disadvantage (Lamb, 2012). Furthermore, children of never-married mothers who lack a father's consistent warmth and involvement show less favorable cognitive development and engage in more antisocial behavior than children in low-SES, first-marriage families—problems that make life more difficult for mothers (Waldfogel, Craigie, & Brooks-Gunn, 2010). But marriage to the child's biological father benefits children only when the father is a reliable source of economic and emotional support. For example, adolescents who feel close to their nonresident father fare better in school performance and emotional and social adjustment than do those in two-parent homes where a close father tie is lacking (Booth, Scott, & King, 2010).

Unfortunately, most unwed fathers—who usually have no more than a modest education and are doing poorly financially—gradually spend less and less time with their children (Lerman, 2010). Strengthening parenting skills, social support, education, and employment opportunities for low-SES parents would greatly enhance the well-being of unmarried mothers and their children.

Lesbian and Gay Parents.
According to recent estimates, about 20 to 35 percent of lesbian couples and 5 to 15 percent of gay couples are parents, most through previous heterosexual marriages, some through adoption, and a growing number through reproductive technologies (Brewster, Tillman, & Jokinen-Gordon, 2014; Gates, 2013). In the past, because of laws assuming that gay men and lesbians could not be adequate parents, those who divorced a heterosexual partner lost custody of their children. Today, the majority of U.S. states hold that sexual orientation is irrelevant to custody or adoption—a change likely spurred by the increasing acceptance of same-sex marriage. Custody and adoption by same-sex couples are also legal in many other industrialized nations.

Most research on families headed by same-sex couples is limited to volunteer samples. Findings indicate that lesbian and gay parents are as committed to and effective at child rearing as heterosexual parents and sometimes more so (Bos, 2013). Also, whether born to or adopted by their parents or conceived through donor insemination, children in lesbian and gay families do not

Lesbian and gay parents are as committed to and effective at child rearing as heterosexual parents. Overall, families headed by same-sex couples can be distinguished from other families mainly by issues related to living in discriminatory contexts.

differ from the children of heterosexual parents in mental health, peer relations, gender-role behavior, or quality of life (Bos & Sandfort, 2010; Farr, Forssell, & Patterson, 2010; Goldberg, 2010; van Gelderen et al., 2012).

To surmount the potential bias associated with volunteer samples, some researchers take advantage of large, nationally representative data banks to study lesbian and gay families. Findings confirm that children with same-sex and other-sex parents develop similarly, and that children's adjustment is linked to factors other than parental sexual orientation (Moore & Stambolis-Ruhstorfer, 2013). For example, close parent–child relationships predict better peer relations and a reduction in adolescent delinquency, whereas family transitions (such as parental divorce or remarriage) predict academic difficulties, regardless of family form (Potter, 2012; Russell & Muraco, 2013).

The large majority of children of lesbian and gay parents identify as heterosexual (Patterson, 2013). But some evidence suggests that more adolescents from lesbian and gay families experiment for a time with partners of both sexes, perhaps as a result of being reared in families and communities especially tolerant of nonconformity and difference (Bos, van Balen, & van den Boom, 2004; Gartrell, Bos, & Goldberg, 2011).

When extended-family members withhold acceptance, lesbian and gay parents often build "families of choice" through friends, who assume the roles of relatives. Usually, however, parents of sexual minorities cannot endure a permanent rift (Fisher, Easterly, & Lazear, 2008). With time, extended family relationships become more positive and supportive.

A major concern of lesbian and gay parents is that their children will be stigmatized by their parents' sexual orientation. Peer teasing and disapproval are problems for some children of same-sex parents, but close parent–child relationships, supportive school environments, and connections with other lesbian and gay families protect children from the negative effects of these experiences (Bos, 2013). Overall, lesbian and gay families can be distinguished from other families mainly by issues related to living in discriminatory contexts.

Ask yourself

CONNECT Return to Chapter 10, pages 353–356, and review the impact of divorce and remarriage on children and adolescents. How do those findings resemble outcomes for adults? What might account for the similarities?

APPLY After dating for three months, Wanda and Scott decided to live together. What questions would you ask Wanda and Scott to predict the likelihood that their cohabiting relationship will be gratifying and eventually transition to a lasting marriage?

REFLECT Do your own experiences or those of your friends match research findings on cohabitation, singlehood, never-married parents, or gay and lesbian parents? Select one instance and discuss.

Career Development

14.11 Discuss patterns of career development, and cite difficulties faced by women, ethnic minorities, and dual-earner couples.

Besides family life, vocational life is a vital domain of social development in early adulthood. After choosing an occupation, young people must learn how to perform its tasks well, get along with co-workers, respond to authority, and protect their own interests. When work experiences go well, adults develop new competencies, feel a sense of personal accomplishment, make new friends, and become financially independent and secure. And as we have seen, especially for women but also for men who support their partner's career development, aspirations and accomplishments in the workplace and the family are interwoven.

Establishing a Career

Our discussion earlier in this chapter highlighted diverse paths and timetables for career development. Consider, once again, the wide variations among Sharese, Ernie, Christy, and Gary. Notice that Sharese and Christy, like many women, had *discontinuous* career paths—ones that were interrupted or deferred by child rearing and other family needs (Heppner & Jung, 2013; Huang & Sverke, 2007). Furthermore, not all people embark on the vocation of their dreams. For example, the economic recession of 2007 to 2009 greatly increased the number of young people in jobs that did not match their educational preparation.

Even when adults in their twenties with bachelor's or graduate degrees enter their chosen field, initial experiences can be discouraging. At the health department, Sharese discovered that paperwork consumed much of her day. Because each project had a deadline, the pressure of productivity weighed heavily on her. Adjusting to unanticipated disappointments in salary, supervisors, and co-workers is difficult. As new employees become aware of the gap between their expectations and reality, resignations are common. Furthermore, in careers with opportunities for promotion, high aspirations must often be revised downward because the structure of most work settings resembles a pyramid, with fewer management and supervisory jobs. For these reasons—in addition to layoffs due to financial exigencies—workers in their twenties typically change jobs several times; three or four changes are not unusual.

Recall from our discussion of Levinson's theory that career progress often depends on the quality of a mentoring relationship. Access to an effective mentor—a person with greater experience and knowledge who is invested in the junior person's career success and who fosters a bond of trust—is jointly affected by the availability of willing people and the individual's capacity to select an appropriate individual. Most of the time, professors and senior colleagues at work fill this role. Occasionally, knowledgeable friends or relatives provide mentoring. Mentors sometimes act as teachers who enhance the person's career-related skills. At other times they serve as guides who acquaint the person with the values and customs of the work setting. When young adults have varied mentors, each providing unique forms of assistance, they benefit more in terms of career-related learning (Hall & Las Heras, 2011). Furthermore, mentoring early in a worker's career increases the likelihood of mentoring later on (Bozionelos et al., 2011). The professional and personal benefits of mentoring induce employees to provide it to others and to seek it again for themselves.

Women and Ethnic Minorities

Women and ethnic minorities have penetrated nearly all professions, but their talents often are not developed to the fullest. Women, especially those who are members of economically disadvantaged minorities, remain concentrated in occupations that offer little opportunity for advancement, and they are underrepresented in executive and managerial roles (see Chapter 13, page 463). And although the overall difference between men's and women's earnings is smaller today than 30 years ago, it remains considerable in the majority of industrialized countries (OECD, 2015b). Currently in the United States, the average woman working full-time earns just 83 percent as much as the average man. When only workers with a bachelor's degree or higher are considered, the difference diminishes but is still substantial—88 percent (U.S. Department of Labor, 2015b).

What factors contribute to the widespread, persistent gender pay gap? In college, women more often major in education and social service fields, men in higher-paying scientific and technical fields—choices influenced by gender-stereotyped messages (see pages 464–465 in Chapter 13). And unlike the continuous career lives of most well-educated men, many women enter and exit the labor market several times, or reduce their work hours from full-time to part-time as they give birth to and rear children. Time away from a career greatly hinders advancement—a major reason that women in prestigious, male-dominated careers tend to delay or avoid childbearing.

Yet an increasing number of accomplished professional women are leaving their jobs to devote themselves full-time to child rearing—a trend that has generated mistaken, gender-stereotyped interpretations of their "choice." Interviews with such women reveal that the decision to leave their careers is almost always agonizing. The most common reason given is a high-pressured, inflexible work environment that offers no leeway for work–family balance (Lovejoy & Stone, 2012; Rubin & Wooten, 2007). When these women eventually return to the labor force, they often reorient, entering female-dominated occupations in the social services sector that are lower paid.

In addition, low self-efficacy with respect to male-dominated fields limits women's career progress. Women who pursue nontraditional careers usually have "masculine" traits—high achievement orientation, self-reliance, and belief that their efforts will result in success. But even those with high self-efficacy are less certain than their male counterparts that they can overcome barriers to career success. In traditionally masculine fields, newly hired women whose training is equivalent to that of newly hired men are nevertheless paid less (Lips, 2013). Also, these women may have difficulty finding supportive mentors. In one study, science professors at a broad sample of U.S. universities were sent an undergraduate student's application for a lab manager position. For half, the application bore a male name; for the other half, a female name (Moss-Racusin et al., 2012). Professors of both genders viewed the female student as less competent, less deserving of mentoring, and meriting a lower salary, though her accomplishments were identical to those of the male.

Gender-stereotyped images of women as followers rather than leaders slow advancement into top-level management positions. Mentoring by a senior-male executive predicts progress into management roles and pay gains more strongly for women in male-dominated industries than for men (Ramaswami et al., 2010). When a powerful male leader *sponsors* the advancement of a talented woman, designating her as having the qualities to succeed, senior-level decision makers are far more likely to take notice. Nevertheless, once in those positions, women are evaluated more harshly than men (Tharenou, 2013). This is especially

Women in male-dominated fields, such as this scientist, usually have "masculine" traits, including high achievement orientation and self-reliance. Nevertheless, many encounter workplace barriers to career success.

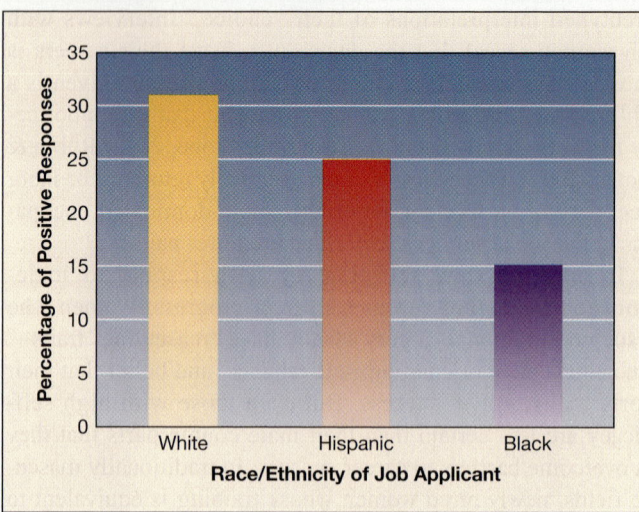

FIGURE 14.4 Relationship of job applicant race/ethnicity to employer callbacks and job offers. The white applicant received slightly more positive responses from employers than did the Hispanic applicant, both of whom greatly exceeded the black applicant, though all three submitted the same résumé and had been matched on verbal and interpersonal skills and physical attractiveness. (From D. Pager, B. Western, & B. Bonikowski, "Discrimination in a Low-Wage Labor Market: A Field Experiment," *American Sociological Review, 74,* p. 785, copyright © 2009, American Sociological Association. Adapted by permission of SAGE Publications.)

so when women display stereotypically masculine behaviors, such as an assertive leadership style.

Despite laws guaranteeing equality of opportunity, racial and ethnic bias in career opportunities remains strong. In one study, researchers recruited two three-member teams consisting of a white, a black, and a Hispanic male job applicant, each 22 to 26 years old and matched on verbal and interpersonal skills and physical attractiveness. The applicants were assigned identical fictitious résumés (with the exception that the résumé of the white member of the second team disclosed a criminal record) and sent out to apply for 170 entry-level jobs in New York City (Pager, Western, & Bonikowski, 2009). As Figure 14.4 shows, the white applicant received callbacks or job offers from employers slightly more often than the Hispanic applicant, with the black applicant trailing far behind. When the experiment was repeated with the second team, the white felon remained slightly preferred over both minority applicants, despite their clean records.

In another similar investigation, which varied applicant qualifications within résumés, white men and women with high-quality résumés received substantially more employer callbacks than those with low-quality résumés. In contrast, having a high-quality résumé made little difference for African Americans. As the researchers noted, "Discrimination appears to bite twice, making it harder for African Americans to find a job and to improve their employability" (Bertrand & Mullainathan, 2004, p. 3). Consistent with this conclusion, African Americans spend more time searching for work, search more broadly across types of jobs to increase their chances of getting an offer, experience less stable employment, and acquire less work experience than European Americans with equivalent qualifications (Pager & Pedulla, 2015; Pager & Shepherd, 2008).

Ethnic minority women often must surmount combined gender and racial discrimination to realize their career potential (O'Brien, Franco, & Dunn, 2014). Those who succeed frequently display an unusually high sense of self-efficacy, attacking problems head-on despite repeated obstacles to achievement. In interviews with African-American women who had become leaders in diverse fields, all reported intense persistence, fueled by supportive relationships with other women, including teachers and peers. Many described their mothers as inspiring role models who had set high standards and offered valuable advice and encouragement (Richie et al., 1997). Others mentioned support from their African-American communities and were strongly motivated to give back (Nickels & Kowalski-Braun, 2012). After having experienced positive mentoring, successful African-American women take on especially heavy mentoring obligations.

Combining Work and Family

The majority of women with children are in the work force (see page 356 in Chapter 10), most in dual-earner marriages or cohabiting relationships. More women than men report moderate to high levels of stress in trying to meet both work and family responsibilities (Mitchell, Eby, & Lorys, 2015; Zhao, Settles, & Sheng, 2011).

When Sharese returned to her job after her children were born, she immediately felt a sense of role overload. In addition to a challenging career, she also (like most employed women) shouldered more household and child-care tasks. And both Sharese and Ernie felt torn between the desire to excel at their jobs and the desire to spend more time with each other, their children, and their friends and relatives. Persistent stress caused by role overload is linked to poorer marital relations, less effective parenting, child behavior problems, poorer job performance,

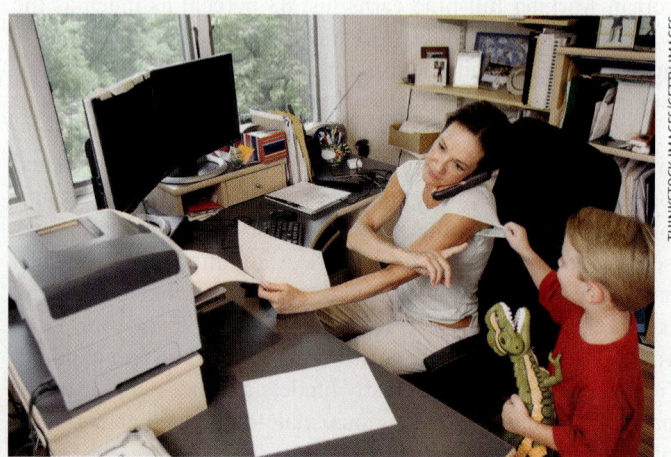

Time-flexible policies enabling employees to work from home help parents adjust work roles to meet family needs. As a result, employees feel less stressed and are more productive at work.

Applying what we Know

Strategies That Help Dual-Earner Couples Combine Work and Family Roles

STRATEGY	DESCRIPTION
Devise a plan for sharing household tasks.	As soon as possible in the relationship, discuss relative commitment to work and family and division of household responsibilities. Decide who does a particular chore on the basis of who has the needed skill and time, not on the basis of gender. Schedule regular times to rediscuss your plan.
Begin sharing child care right after the baby's arrival.	For fathers, strive to spend equal time with the baby early. For mothers, refrain from imposing your standards on your partner. Instead, share the role of "child-rearing expert" by discussing parenting values and concerns often. Attend a parent education course together.
Talk over conflicts about decision making and responsibilities.	Face conflict through communication. Clarify your feelings and needs and express them to your partner. Listen and try to understand your partner's point of view. Then be willing to negotiate and compromise.
Establish a balance between work and family.	Critically evaluate the time you devote to work in view of your family values and priorities. If it is too much, cut back.
Make sure your relationship receives regular loving care.	See Applying What We Know on page 482.
Press for workplace and public policies that support dual-earner-family roles.	Difficulties faced by dual-earner couples are partly due to lack of workplace and societal supports. Encourage your employer to provide benefits that help combine work and family, such as flexible work hours, parental leave with pay, and on-site high-quality, affordable child care. Communicate with lawmakers and other citizens about improving public policies for children and families.

and physical health problems (Saginak & Saginak, 2005; ten Brummelhuis et al., 2013).

Role overload is magnified for women in low-status work roles with rigid schedules and little autonomy (Repetti & Wang, 2014). Couples in prestigious careers have more control over both work and family domains. For example, Sharese and Ernie devised ways to spend more time with their children. They picked them up at child care early one day a week, compensating by doing certain work tasks on evenings and weekends. But in a Canadian study of more than 3,000 individuals in dual-earner families who were employed full-time, most coped with role overload by scaling back at home (leaving things undone) or restructuring family roles (taking over responsibilities for each other, as needed), with women doing more of this than men (Higgins, Duxbury, & Lyons, 2010). Overall, couples expected family life to accommodate to work demands. They seldom adjusted work roles to meet family needs. Although some had little flexibility at work, others simply prioritized work over family life.

Workplace supports can greatly reduce role overload, yielding substantial payoffs for employers. Among large, nationally representative samples of U.S. working adults, the more time-flexible policies available in their work settings (for example, time off to care for a sick child, choice in start and stop times, and opportunities to work from home), the less work–family conflict participants reported and the better their work performance (Banerjee & Perrucci, 2012; Halpern, 2005). Employees with several time-flexible options missed fewer days of work, less often arrived at work late or left early, felt more committed to their employer, and worked harder. They also reported fewer stress-related health symptoms.

LOOK and LISTEN

Talk with one or more dual-earner couples about workplace supports for good parenting. Which policies are available? Which additional ones would they find especially helpful?

Effectively balancing work and family brings many benefits—a better standard of living, improved work productivity, enhanced psychological well-being, greater self-fulfillment, and happier marriages. Ernie took great pride in Sharese's dedication to both family life and career. And the skills, maturity, and self-esteem each derived from coping successfully with challenges at home strengthened their capacity to surmount difficulties at work, enhancing both career and life satisfaction (Erdogan et al., 2012; Graves, Ohlott, & Ruderman, 2007). Applying What We Know above lists strategies that help dual-earner couples attain mastery and pleasure in both spheres of life.

Ask yourself

CONNECT Generate a list of capacities and skills derived from high commitment to family roles (both partner and parent) that can enhance work performance and satisfaction.

APPLY Write an essay aimed at convincing a company executive that family-friendly policies are "win–win" situations for both workers and employers.

REFLECT Ask someone who has succeeded in a career of interest to you to describe mentoring relationships that aided his or her progress.

Summary / chapter 14

A Gradual Transition: Emerging Adulthood (p. 470)

14.1 Discuss emotional and social development during emerging adulthood, along with cultural influences and individual variations.

- In **emerging adulthood**, many young people do not view themselves as fully adult. Rather, those with economic resources engage in extended exploration of alternatives in education, work, and personal values. Identity development continues into the college years, with young people exploring in depth and revisiting commitments that fit poorly with their talents and potentials.

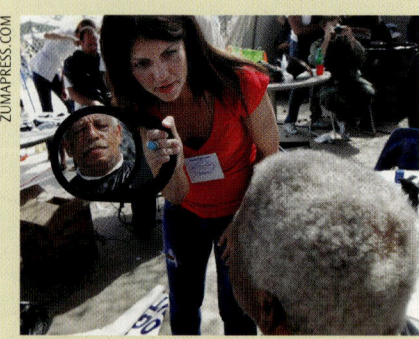

- Many emerging adults express a strong commitment to improving their communities, nation, and world, and large numbers participate in community service. Nevertheless, compared with older people, they vote in fewer numbers.

- During the late teens and twenties, religious attendance declines, continuing the trend that was under way in adolescence, though women and ethnic minority young people express greater religiosity. Regardless of religious participation, many emerging adults begin to construct an individualized faith. Those who are religious or spiritual tend to be better adjusted.

- Increased education required for entry-level jobs, gains in economic prosperity, and reduced need for young people's labor in industrialized nations have prompted the appearance of emerging adulthood. But because of its strong association with SES and higher education, some researchers do not view emerging adulthood as a distinct stage of development.

- A sizable number of emerging adults flounder, suffering from lack of direction and engaging in high levels of risky behaviors. But most young people with access to the opportunities of emerging adulthood experience it as a time of flourishing. A wide array of personal attributes and social supports, especially a warm, autonomy-supportive relationship with parents, foster resilience.

Erikson's Theory: Intimacy versus Isolation (p. 476)

14.2 According to Erikson, what personality changes take place during early adulthood?

- In Erikson's theory, young adults must resolve the conflict of **intimacy versus isolation** as they form a close relationship with a partner. The negative outcome is loneliness and self-absorption.

- Young people also focus on aspects of generativity, including parenting and contributions to society through work and community service.

Other Theories of Adult Psychosocial Development (p. 477)

14.3 Describe and evaluate Levinson's and Vaillant's psychosocial theories of adult personality development.

- Expanding Erikson's stage approach, Levinson described a series of eras in which people revise their life structure. Young adults usually construct a dream, typically involving career for men and both marriage and career for women, and form a relationship with a mentor. In their thirties, men tend to settle down, whereas many women remain unsettled.

- Also in the tradition of Erikson, Vaillant portrayed the twenties as devoted to intimacy, the thirties to career consolidation, the forties to strengthening generativity, the fifties and sixties to extending generativity in passing on cultural values, and late adulthood to reflecting on life's meaning.

- Young adults' development is far more variable today than Levinson's and Vaillant's theories depict.

14.4 What is the social clock, and how does it affect development in adulthood?

- Following a **social clock**—age-graded expectations for major life events—grants confidence to young adults. Deviating from it can bring psychological distress. As age-graded expectations have become increasingly flexible, departures from social-clock life events are common and can create intergenerational tensions.

Close Relationships (p. 478)

14.5 Describe factors affecting mate selection, the components of romantic love, and the changing forms of love as relationships develop, noting cultural variations.

- Romantic partners tend to resemble each other in age, education level, ethnicity, religion, and various personal and physical attributes.

- According to an evolutionary perspective, women seek a mate with traits that help ensure children's survival, while men look for characteristics signaling sexual pleasure and ability to bear offspring. From an alternative perspective, gender roles, jointly influenced by evolutionary and cultural pressures, influence criteria for mate selection.

- According to Sternberg's **triangular theory of love,** the balance among passion, intimacy, and commitment in romantic ties changes over time. As **passionate love** gives way to **companionate love** and **compassionate love,** relationships become more intimate, committed, satisfying, and long-lasting.

- Rather than romantic love, Eastern cultures emphasize dependency and family obligation in lifelong partnerships. Many arranged marriages succeed, with couples reporting that commitment helped strengthen their love.

14.6 Describe young adults' friendships and sibling relationships and their influence on psychological well-being.

- Adult friendships, like earlier friendships, are based on trust, intimacy, and loyalty. Women's same-sex friendships tend to be more intimate than men's. After marriage, other-sex friendships decline with age for men but increase for women, who often form them in the workplace. When family experiences have been positive, adult sibling relationships often resemble friendships.

The Family Life Cycle (p. 484)

14.7 Trace phases of the family life cycle that are prominent in early adulthood, and cite factors that influence these phases today.

- Wide variations exist in the sequence and timing of the **family life cycle.** Delayed home-leaving has occurred in most industrialized nations. Departures generally occur earlier for education than for full-time work or marriage; role transitions and financial circumstances often prompt a move back. Parents of young adults living at home are usually highly committed to helping their children move into adult roles.

- The average age of first marriage in the United States and Western Europe has risen. Same-sex marriages are recognized nationwide in 20 countries, including the United States.

- Both sexual majority and minority couples perceive marriage as important because it confers public legitimacy to the relationship, demonstrates commitment, and offers financial and legal benefits.

- Both **traditional marriages** and **egalitarian marriages** are affected by women's participation in the work force. Women in Western nations spend nearly twice as much time as men on housework, although men participate much more in child care than in the past. Women experiencing role overload feel particularly dissatisfied with their marriages, though equal sharing of family responsibilities enhances both partners' satisfaction.

- The transition to parenthood brings increased responsibilities, often prompting a shift to more traditional roles. After the birth of a second child, this may reverse. Gratifying marriages tend to remain so after childbirth, but troubled marriages usually become more distressed. Shared caregiving predicts greater parental happiness and positive parent–infant interaction.

- Couples with young children who engage in effective coparenting are more likely to use effective child-rearing practices, have children who are developing well, and gain in marital satisfaction.

- Parents of adolescents must establish revised relationships with their increasingly autonomous teenagers. Marital satisfaction often declines in this phase.

The Diversity of Adult Lifestyles (p. 492)

14.8 Discuss the diversity of adult lifestyles, focusing on singlehood, cohabitation, and childlessness.

- Postponement of marriage has contributed to a rise in singlehood. Despite an array of drawbacks, singles typically appreciate their freedom and mobility.

- **Cohabitation** has increased, becoming the preferred mode of entry into a committed intimate partnership for young people. Compared with their Western European counterparts, Americans who cohabit before marriage tend to be less committed to their partner, and their subsequent marriages are more likely to fail. U.S. lesbian and gay cohabiting couples, however, are exceptions: Many are highly committed, with large numbers marrying after legalization of same-sex marriage in the United States.

- Voluntarily childless adults tend to be highly educated, career-oriented, and content with their lives. But involuntary childlessness interferes with adjustment and life satisfaction.

14.9 Cite factors that contribute to high rates of divorce and remarriage.

- Maladaptive communication patterns, younger ages at marriage, a family history of divorce, low education, economic disadvantage, and American individualism all contribute to divorce.

- Remarriages are especially vulnerable to breakup. Reasons include emphasis on practical concerns in the decision to remarry, the persistence of negative patterns of communication, the acceptance of divorce as a solution to marital difficulties, and problems adjusting to a stepfamily.

14.10 Discuss challenges associated with varied styles of parenthood, including stepparents, never-married parents, and gay and lesbian parents.

- Establishing stepparent–stepchild ties is difficult, especially for stepmothers and for stepfathers without children of their own. A caring relationship between remarried or cohabiting couples that includes effective coparenting, cooperation from the biological parent, and extended-family support promotes positive stepparent–stepchild ties.

- Never-married single parenthood is especially high among African-American young women. Unemployment among black men contributes to this trend. Even with help from extended family members, these mothers find it difficult to overcome poverty.

- Lesbian and gay parents are as effective at child rearing as heterosexual parents, and their children are as well-adjusted as those reared by heterosexual parents.

Career Development (p. 498)

14.11 Discuss patterns of career development, and cite difficulties faced by women, ethnic minorities, and dual-earner couples.

- Men's career paths are usually continuous, whereas women's are often interrupted by family needs. Once young adults settle into an occupation, their progress is affected by opportunities for promotion, the broader economic environment, and access to effective mentors.

- Women and ethnic minorities have penetrated most professions, but their career advancement has been hampered by time away from the labor market, low self-efficacy with respect to male-dominated fields, lack of mentoring, and gender stereotypes. Racial and ethnic bias remains strong. Ethnic minority women who succeed display an unusually high sense of self-efficacy.

- Employed parents often experience role overload, which can be greatly reduced by workplace supports such as time-flexible policies. Effectively balancing work and family enhances standard of living, psychological well-being, marital happiness, and work performance.

Important Terms and Concepts

cohabitation (p. 494)
companionate love (p. 479)
compassionate love (p. 479)
egalitarian marriage (p. 486)
emerging adulthood (p. 470)
family life cycle (p. 484)
intimacy versus isolation (p. 476)
passionate love (p. 479)
social clock (p. 478)
traditional marriage (p. 486)
triangular theory of love (p. 479)

milestones
Development in Early Adulthood

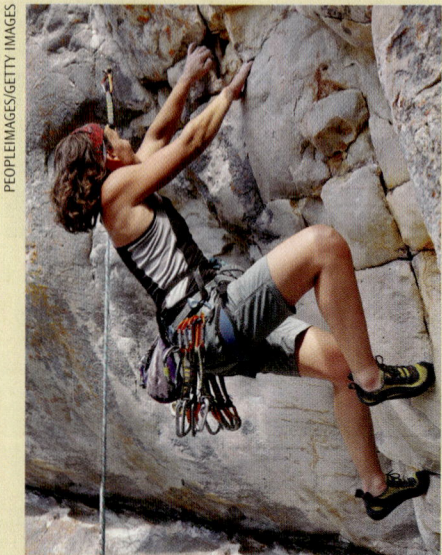

18–30 YEARS

Physical

- Athletic skills that require speed of limb movement, explosive strength, and gross motor coordination peak early in this time period, then decline. (442)
- Athletic skills that depend on endurance, arm–hand steadiness, and aiming peak at the end of this time period, then decline. (442)
- Declines in touch sensitivity, cardiovascular and respiratory capacity, immune system functioning, and skin elasticity begin and continue throughout adulthood. (441)
- As basal metabolic rate declines, gradual weight gain begins in the middle of this decade and continues through middle adulthood. (446)
- Sexual activity increases. (452)

Cognitive

- If college educated, dualistic thinking declines in favor of relativistic thinking; may progress to commitment within relativistic thinking. (456–457)
- Moves from hypothetical to pragmatic thought. (458)

- Narrows vocational options and settles on a specific career. (462)
- Gains in cognitive–affective complexity. (458)
- Develops expertise in a field of endeavor, which enhances problem solving. (458–459)
- May increase in creativity. (459)

Emotional/Social

- If life circumstances permit, may engage in the extended exploration that characterizes emerging adulthood. (470–471)
- Forms a more complex self-concept that includes awareness of own changing traits and values. (470)
- If a high school graduate, is likely to enroll in higher education. (460)
- Is likely to achieve a personally meaningful identity. (470–471)
- Leaves the parental home permanently. (484–485)
- Strives to make a long-term commitment to an intimate partner. (476, 479)

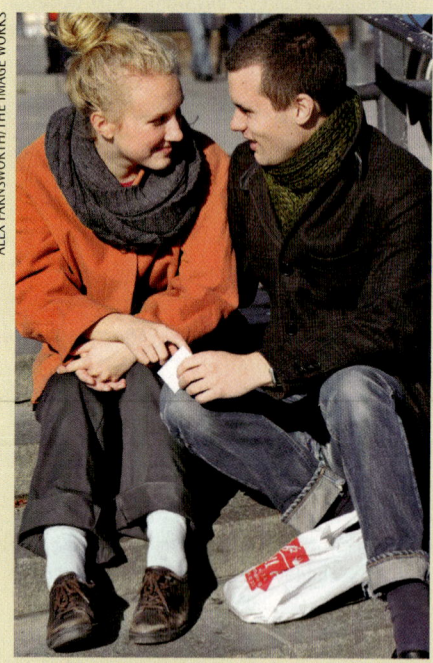

Note: Numbers in parentheses indicate the page or pages on which each milestone is discussed.

- Usually constructs a dream—an image of the self in the adult world that guides decision making. (477)
- Typically forms a relationship with a mentor. (477, 499)
- If in a high-status career, acquires professional skills, values, and credentials. (477)
- Develops mutually gratifying adult friendships and work ties. (482–483)
- May cohabit, marry, and become parents. (485–486, 489–491)
- Sibling relationships become more companionate. (484)

30–40 YEARS

Physical

- Declines in vision, hearing, and the skeletal system begin and continue throughout adulthood. (441)
- In women, reproductive capacity declines, and fertility problems increase sharply after the middle of this decade. (443–444)
- In men, semen volume and sperm motility decrease gradually in the second half of this decade; percentage of abnormal sperm rises. (444)
- Hair begins to gray and thin in the middle of this decade. (441)
- Sexual activity declines, probably as a result of the demands of daily life. (452)

Cognitive

- Continues to develop expertise in a field of endeavor. (458–459)

- Creative accomplishment often peaks in the second half of this decade, although this varies across disciplines. (459)

Emotional/Social

- May cohabit, marry, and become parents. (485–486, 489–491)

- Increasingly establishes a niche in society through family, occupational, and community commitments. (477)

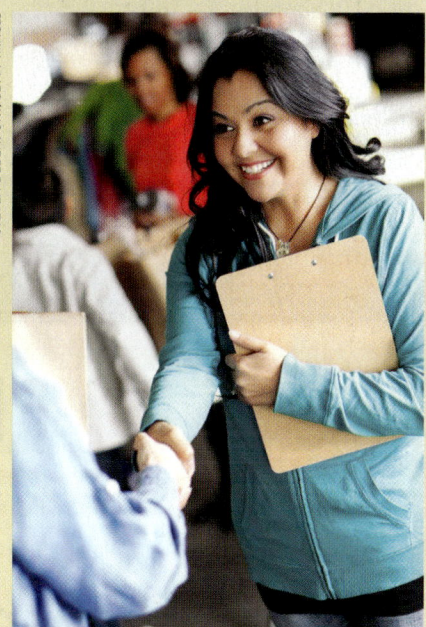

Note: Numbers in parentheses indicate the page or pages on which each milestone is discussed.

chapter 15

Physical and Cognitive Development in Middle Adulthood

A choreographer for the Dutch National Ballet works with a dancer during rehearsal. Though his body may have begun to show physical signs of aging, this middle-aged adult with decades of training is at the peak of expertise in his field.

What's ahead in chapter 15

PHYSICAL DEVELOPMENT

Physical Changes
Vision • Hearing • Skin • Muscle–Fat Makeup • Skeleton • Reproductive System

- **BIOLOGY AND ENVIRONMENT** Anti-Aging Effects of Dietary Calorie Restriction
- **CULTURAL INFLUENCES** Menopause as a Biocultural Event

Health and Fitness
Sexuality • Illness and Disability • Hostility and Anger

Adapting to the Physical Challenges of Midlife
Stress Management • Exercise • Hardiness • Gender and Aging: A Double Standard

- **SOCIAL ISSUES: HEALTH** The Silver Lining in Life's Adversities

COGNITIVE DEVELOPMENT

Changes in Mental Abilities
Cohort Effects • Crystallized and Fluid Intelligence • Individual and Group Differences

Information Processing
Speed of Processing • Executive Function • Memory Strategies • Practical Problem Solving and Expertise • Creativity • Information Processing in Context

Vocational Life and Cognitive Development

Adult Learners: Becoming a Student in Midlife
Characteristics of Returning Students • Supporting Returning Students

On a snowy December evening, Devin and Trisha sat down to read the holiday cards piled high on the kitchen counter. Devin's 55th birthday had just passed; Trisha would turn 48 in a few weeks. During the past year, they had celebrated their 24th wedding anniversary. These milestones, along with the annual updates they received from friends, brought the changes of midlife into bold relief.

Instead of new births or a first promotion at work, holiday cards and letters sounded new themes. Jewel's recap of the past year reflected growing awareness of a finite life-span, prompting her to reevaluate the meaningfulness of her personal life and career. She wrote:

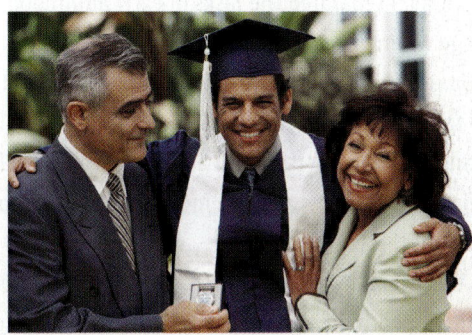

My mood has been lighter ever since I celebrated my forty-ninth birthday. My mother passed away when she was 48, so it all feels like a gift now. I'm thinking of leaving the corporate world and starting my own business. Still dating off and on, but I haven't found anyone special.

George and Anya reported on their son's graduation from law school and their daughter Michelle's first year of university:

Anya is filling the gap created by the children's departure by returning to college for a nursing degree. After enrolling this fall, she was surprised to find herself in the same psychology class as Michelle. At first, Anya worried about handling the academic work, but after a semester of success, she's feeling more confident.

Tim's message conveyed continuing robust health, acceptance of physical changes, and a new challenge: caring for aging parents:

I used to be a good basketball player in college, but recently I noticed that my 20-year-old nephew, Brent, can dribble and shoot circles around me. It must be my age! But I ran our city marathon in September and came in seventh in the over-50 division. Brent ran, too, but he opted out a few miles short of the finish line to get some pizza while I pressed on. That must be my age, too!

The saddest news is that my dad had a bad stroke. His mind is clear, but his body is partially paralyzed. It's really upsetting because he was getting to enjoy the computer I gave him, and it was so upbeat to talk with him about it in the months before the stroke.

Middle adulthood, which begins around age 40 and ends at about 65, is marked by narrowing life options and a shrinking future as children leave home and career paths become more determined. In other ways, middle age is hard to define because wide variations in attitudes and behaviors exist. Some individuals seem physically and mentally young at age 65—active and optimistic, with fulfilling work and leisure pursuits. Others feel old at age 40—as if their lives had peaked and were on a downhill course.

Another reason middle adulthood eludes definition is that it is a contemporary period of life. Before the twentieth century, only a brief interval separated the tasks of early adulthood from those of old age. Women were often widows by their mid-fifties, before their youngest child left home. And harsh living conditions led people to accept a ravaged body as a natural part of life. As life expectancy—and, with it, health and vigor—increased over the previous century, adults became more aware of their own aging and mortality.

In this chapter, we trace physical and cognitive development in midlife. In both domains, we will encounter not just progressive declines but also sustained performance and compensating gains. As in earlier chapters, we will see that change occurs in manifold ways. Besides heredity and biological aging, our personal approach to passing years combines with family, community, and cultural contexts to affect the way we age.

PHYSICAL DEVELOPMENT

Physical development in middle adulthood is a continuation of the gradual changes under way in early adulthood. Even vigorous adults notice an older body when looking in the mirror or at family photos. Hair grays and thins, new lines appear on the face, and a fuller, less youthful body shape is evident. During midlife, many individuals begin to experience life-threatening health episodes—if not in themselves, then in their partners and friends. And a shift in subjective time orientation, from "time since birth" to "time left to live" occurs, increasing consciousness of aging (Demiray & Bluck, 2014; Neugarten, 1996).

These factors lead to a revised physical self-image, with somewhat less emphasis on hoped-for gains and more on feared declines (Bybee & Wells, 2003; Frazier, Barreto, & Newman, 2012). Prominent concerns of 40- to 65-year-olds include getting a fatal disease, being too ill to maintain independence, and losing mental capacities. Unfortunately, many middle-aged adults fail to embrace realistic alternatives—becoming more physically fit and developing into healthy, energetic older adults. Although certain aspects of aging cannot be controlled, people can do much to promote physical vigor and good health in midlife.

Physical Changes

15.1 Describe the physical changes of middle adulthood, paying special attention to vision, hearing, the skin, muscle–fat makeup, and the skeleton.

15.2 Describe reproductive changes in both sexes, along with associated physical and emotional symptoms, during middle adulthood.

As she dressed for work one morning, Trisha remarked jokingly to Devin, "I think I'll leave the dust on the mirror so I can't see the wrinkles and gray hairs." Catching sight of her image, she continued in a more serious tone. "And look at this fat—it just doesn't want to go! I need to fit some regular exercise into my life." In response, Devin glanced soberly at his own enlarged midriff.

At breakfast, Devin took his glasses on and off and squinted while reading the paper. "Trish—what's the eye doctor's phone number? I've got to get these bifocals adjusted again." As they conversed between the kitchen and the adjoining den, Devin sometimes asked Trisha to repeat herself. And he kept turning up the radio and TV volume. "Does it need to be that loud?" Trisha would ask. Devin's hearing seemed less keen than before.

In the following sections, we look closely at the major physical changes of midlife. As we do so, you may find it helpful to refer back to Table 13.1 on page 441, which provides a summary.

Vision

During the forties, difficulty reading small print is common, due to thickening of the lens combined with weakening of the muscle that enables the eye to *accommodate* (adjust its focus) to nearby objects. As new fibers appear on the surface of the lens, they compress older fibers toward the center, creating a thicker, denser, less pliable structure. By age 50, the accommodative ability of the lens is one-sixth of what it was at age 20. Around age 60, the lens loses its capacity to adjust to objects at varying distances entirely, a condition called **presbyopia** (literally, "old eyes"). As the lens loses elasticity, the eye rapidly becomes more farsighted between ages 40 and 60 (Charman, 2008). Corrective lenses—or, for nearsighted people, bifocals—ease reading problems.

A second set of changes limits ability to see in dim light, which declines at twice the rate of daylight vision. Throughout adulthood, the size of the pupil shrinks and the lens yellows. In addition, starting at age 40, the *vitreous* (transparent gelatin-like substance that fills the eye) develops opaque areas, reducing the amount of light reaching the retina. Changes in the lens and vitreous also cause light to scatter within the eye, increasing sensitivity to glare. Devin had always enjoyed driving at night, but now he sometimes had trouble making out signs and moving objects (Owsley, 2011; Sörensen, White, & Ramchandran, 2016). And his vision was more disrupted by bright light sources, such as headlights of oncoming cars. Yellowing of the lens and increasing density of the vitreous also limit color discrimination, especially at the green–blue–violet end of the spectrum (Paramei, 2012). Occasionally, Devin had to ask whether his sport coat, tie, and socks matched.

Besides structural changes in the eye, neural changes in the visual system occur. Gradual loss of rods and cones (light- and color-receptor cells) in the retina and of neurons in the optic nerve (the pathway between the retina and the cerebral cortex) contributes to visual declines. By midlife, half the *rods* (which enable vision in dim light) are lost (Grossniklaus et al., 2013; Owsley, 2011). And because rods secrete substances necessary for survival of *cones* (which enable daylight and color vision), gradual loss of cones follows. In addition, decreased blood supply to the retina, due to degeneration of retinal blood vessels, causes it to thin and become less sensitive.

Middle-aged adults are at increased risk of **glaucoma**, a disease in which poor fluid drainage leads to a buildup of pressure within the eye, damaging the optic nerve. Glaucoma affects nearly 2 percent of people over age 40, more often women than men. It typically progresses without noticeable symptoms and is a leading cause of blindness. Heredity contributes to glaucoma, which runs in families: Siblings of people with the disease have a tenfold increased risk, and it occurs three to four times as often in African Americans and Hispanics as in European Americans (Guedes, Tsai, & Loewen, 2011). Starting in midlife, eye exams should include a glaucoma test. Drugs that promote release of fluid and surgery to open blocked drainage channels prevent vision loss.

Hearing

An estimated 14 percent of Americans between ages 45 and 64 suffer from hearing loss, often resulting from adult-onset hearing impairments (Center for Hearing and Communication, 2016). Although some conditions run in families and may be hereditary, most are age-related, a condition called **presbycusis** ("old hearing").

As we age, inner-ear structures that transform mechanical sound waves into neural impulses deteriorate through natural cell death or reduced blood supply caused by atherosclerosis. Processing of neural messages in the auditory cortex also weakens. The first sign of hearing loss, around age 50, is a noticeable decline in sensitivity to high-frequency sounds, which gradually extends to all frequencies. The ability to distinguish sounds occurring in close succession also recedes. Gradually, human speech becomes more difficult to make out, especially rapid speech and speech against a background of voices (Ozmerai et al., 2016; Wettstein & Wahl, 2016). Still, throughout middle adulthood, most people hear reasonably well across a wide frequency range. And African tribal peoples display little age-related hearing loss (Jarvis & van Heerden, 1967; Rosen, Bergman, & Plester, 1962). These findings suggest factors other than biological aging are involved.

Men's hearing tends to decline earlier and more rapidly than women's, a difference associated with cigarette smoking, intense

A worker uses a grinder to smooth a metal surface in a steel manufacturing facility. Men's hearing declines more rapidly than women's, a difference associated with several factors, including intense noise in some male-dominated occupations.

noise and chemical pollutants in some male-dominated occupations, and (at older ages) high blood pressure and cerebrovascular disease, or strokes that damage brain tissue (Van Eyken, Van Camp, & Van Laer, 2007; Wettstein & Wahl, 2016). Government regulations requiring industries to implement such safeguards as noise monitoring, provision of earplugs, pollution control, and regular hearing tests have greatly reduced hearing damage (U.S. Department of Labor, 2016b). But some employers do not comply fully.

Most mid- and late-life adults with hearing difficulties benefit from hearing aids, though only a minority wear them. Many regard a hearing aid as embarrassing, are unwilling to take time to adjust to using it, judge that it is not effective enough, or find it too costly (Li-Korotky, 2012). When perception of the human voice is affected, speaking to the person patiently, clearly, and with good eye contact, in an environment with reduced background noise, aids understanding.

Skin

Our skin consists of three layers: (1) the *epidermis,* or outer protective layer, where new skin cells are constantly produced; (2) the *dermis,* or middle supportive layer, consisting of connective tissue that stretches and bounces back, giving the skin elasticity; and (3) the *hypodermis,* an inner fatty layer that adds to the soft lines and shape of the skin. As we age, the epidermis becomes less firmly attached to the dermis, fibers in the dermis thin and lose their elasticity, cells in both the epidermis and dermis decline in water content, and fat in the hypodermis diminishes, leading the skin to wrinkle, loosen, and feel dry.

In the thirties, lines develop on the forehead as a result of smiling, furrowing the brow, and other facial expressions. In the forties, these become more pronounced, and "crow's-feet" appear around the eyes. Gradually, the skin loses elasticity and begins to sag, especially on the face, arms, and legs (Khavkin & Ellis, 2011). After age 50, "age spots," collections of pigment under the skin, increase. Blood vessels in the skin become more visible as the fatty layer thins.

Because sun exposure hastens wrinkling, loosening, and spotting, individuals who have spent much time outdoors without proper skin protection look older than their contemporaries. And partly because the dermis of women is not as thick as that of men and estrogen loss accelerates thinning and decline in elasticity, women's skin ages more quickly (Thornton, 2013).

Muscle–Fat Makeup

As Trisha and Devin make clear, weight gain—"middle-age spread"—is a concern for both men and women. A common pattern of change is an increase in body fat and a loss of lean body mass (muscle and bone). The rise in fat largely affects the torso and occurs as fatty deposits within the body cavity; as noted earlier, fat beneath the skin on the limbs declines. On average, size of the abdomen increases 7 to 14 percent. Although a large portion is due to weight gain, age-related changes in muscle–fat makeup also contribute (Stevens, Katz, & Huxley, 2010). In addition, sex differences in fat distribution appear. Men accumulate more on the back and upper abdomen, women around the waist and upper arms (Sowers et al., 2007). Muscle mass declines very gradually in the forties and fifties, largely due to atrophy of fast-twitch fibers, responsible for speed and explosive strength.

Yet, as indicated in Chapter 13, large weight gain and loss of muscle power are not inevitable. With age, people must gradually reduce caloric intake to adjust for the age-related decline in basal metabolic rate (see page 446). In nonhuman animals, dietary restraint dramatically increases longevity while sustaining health and vitality. Currently, researchers are identifying the biological mechanisms involved and studying their relevance to humans (see the Biology and Environment box on the following page).

Women, who tend to be less active than men, experience a more rapid age-related decline in muscle mass and function (Charlier et al., 2015). But weight-bearing exercise that includes resistance training (placing a moderately stressful load on the muscles) can offset both excess weight and muscle loss. Consider Devin's 57-year-old friend Tim, who for years has ridden his bike to and from work on weekdays, jogged on weekends, and engaged in a twice-a-week weight-lifting regimen—averaging an hour of vigorous activity each day. Like many endurance athletes, he maintained the same weight and muscular physique throughout early and middle adulthood.

Skeleton

As new cells accumulate on their outer layers, the bones broaden with age, but their mineral content declines, so they become more porous. This leads to a gradual loss in bone density that begins around age 40 and accelerates in the fifties, especially among women (Clarke & Khosla, 2010). Women's reserve of bone minerals is lower than men's to begin with. And following menopause, the favorable impact of estrogen on bone mineral absorption is lost. Among men, testosterone is similarly protective, and as they age, testosterone and bone density decline (Gold, 2016). Reduction in bone density during middle and late adulthood is substantial—about 8 to 12 percent in men and 20 to 30 percent in women.

Loss of bone strength causes the disks in the spinal column to collapse. Consequently, height may drop by as much as 1 inch by age 60, a change that will hasten thereafter. In addition, the weakened bones cannot support as much load: They fracture more easily and heal more slowly. A healthy lifestyle—including weight-bearing exercise, adequate calcium and vitamin D intake, and avoidance of smoking and heavy alcohol consumption—can slow bone loss in postmenopausal women by as much as 30 to 50 percent (Rizzoli, Abraham, & Brandi, 2014).

When bone loss is very great, it leads to a debilitating disorder called *osteoporosis*. We will take up this condition shortly when we consider illness and disability.

Reproductive System

The midlife transition in which fertility declines is called the **climacteric**. In women, it brings an end to reproductive capacity; in men, by contrast, fertility diminishes but is retained.

Reproductive Changes in Women.
The changes involved in women's climacteric occur gradually over a 10-year period, during which the production of estrogen drops. As a result, the number of days in a woman's monthly cycle shortens from about 28 in her twenties and thirties to perhaps 23 by her late forties, and her cycles become more irregular. In some, ova are not released; when they are, more are defective (see Chapter 2, page 50). The climacteric concludes with **menopause, the end of menstruation and reproductive capacity.** This occurs, on average, in the early fifties among North American, European, and East Asian women, although the age range extends from the late thirties to the late fifties (Rossi, 2004a; Siegel, 2012). Women who smoke or who have not borne children tend to reach menopause earlier.

African-American women, who generally view menopause as normal, inevitable, and even welcome, experience less irritability and moodiness during this transition than European-American women.

Biology and Environment

Anti-Aging Effects of Dietary Calorie Restriction

Scientists have long known that dietary calorie restriction in nonprimate animals slows aging while maintaining good health and body functions. Rats and mice fed 30 to 50 percent fewer calories than they would freely eat beginning in early life show various physiological health benefits, lower incidence of chronic diseases, and up to 50 percent increase in length of life (Fontana & Hu, 2014). Mild to moderate calorie restriction begun after rodents reach physical maturity also slows aging and extends longevity, though to a lesser extent. Other studies reveal similar dietary-restriction effects in mice, fleas, spiders, worms, fish, and yeast.

Nonhuman Primate Research

Would primates, especially humans, also benefit from a restricted diet? Researchers have been tracking health indicators in rhesus monkeys after placing some on regimens of 30 percent reduced calories starting at a young age and sustained into adulthood. More than two decades of longitudinal findings revealed that, compared with freely eating controls, dietary-restricted monkeys were smaller but not overly thin. They accumulated body fat differently—less on the torso, a type of fat distribution that reduces middle-aged humans' risk of heart disease.

Calorie-restricted monkeys also had a lower body temperature and basal metabolic rate—changes that suggest they shifted physiological processes away from growth to maintenance and repair functions. Consequently, like calorie-restricted rodents, they seemed better able to withstand severe physical stress, such as surgery and infectious disease (Rizza, Veronese, & Fontana, 2014).

Among physiological processes mediating these benefits, three seem most powerful. First, calorie restriction inhibited production of free radicals, which at high levels cause cellular deterioration (see page 440 in Chapter 13) (Carter et al., 2007). Second, calorie restriction protected against chronic inflammation of body tissues, which results in tissue damage and is involved in many diseases of aging (Chung et al., 2013). Third, calorie restriction reduced blood glucose and improved insulin sensitivity, thereby lessening the risk of diabetes and cardiovascular disease (Fontana, 2008). Lower blood pressure and cholesterol and a high ratio of "good" to "bad" cholesterol in calorie-restricted primates strengthened these effects.

Tracking of the monkeys' ages at death revealed inconsistent findings on whether calorie-restriction extended length of life. But limiting food intake dramatically reduced the incidence of age-related diseases, including arthritis, cancer, cardiovascular disease, and diabetes, as well as decline in brain volume, sensory functioning, and muscle mass (Colman et al., 2009; Mattison et al., 2012). In sum, the calorie-restricted monkeys clearly benefited from more years of healthy life.

Human Research

Prior to World War II, residents of the island of Okinawa consumed an average of 20 percent fewer calories (while maintaining a healthy diet) than mainland Japanese citizens. Their restricted diet was associated with a 60 to 70 percent reduction in incidence of deaths due to cancer and cardiovascular disease. Recent generations of Okinawans no longer show these health and longevity advantages (Gavrilova & Gavrilov, 2012). The reason, some researchers speculate, is the introduction of Westernized food, including fast food, to Okinawa.

Similarly, normal-weight and overweight people who engaged in self-imposed calorie restriction for 1 to 12 years display health benefits. These include reduced blood glucose, cholesterol, blood pressure, and plaque accumulation on the walls of the arteries, and a stronger immune-system response than individuals eating a typical Western diet (Fontana, Klein, & Holloszy, 2010). And experimental evidence involving random assignment to calorie-restricted and nonrestricted conditions reveals that restricted participants again display improved cardiovascular and other health indicators, suggesting reduced risk of age-related disease (Redman & Ravussin, 2011; Rizza, Veronese, & Fontana, 2014).

Though life-extending effects remain uncertain in primates (including humans), the diverse health benefits of limiting calorie intake are now well-established. They seem to result from a physiological response to food scarcity that evolved to enhance the body's capacity to survive adversity. Nevertheless, few people would be willing to maintain a substantially reduced diet for most of their lifespan. As a result, scientists have begun to explore *calorie-restriction mimetics*—natural and synthetic drug compounds that might yield the same health effects as calorie restriction, without dieting (Ingram & Roth, 2015). These investigations are still in their early stages.

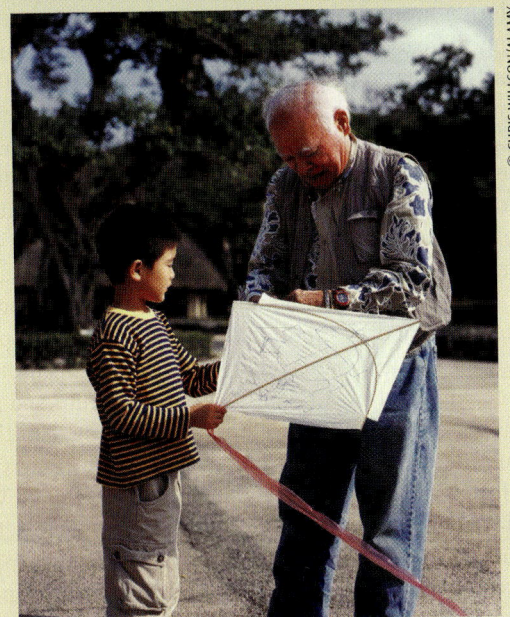

An Okinawan grandfather and grandson enjoy an afternoon of kite flying. Before World War II, residents of Okinawa consumed a restricted diet that was associated with health benefits and longer life. Recent generations no longer show these advantages, possibly due to the introduction of Westernized food to Okinawa.

Following menopause, estrogen declines further, causing the reproductive organs to shrink in size, the genitals to be less easily stimulated, and the vagina to lubricate more slowly during arousal. As a result, complaints about sexual functioning increase, with about 35 to 40 percent of women reporting difficulties, especially among those with health problems or whose partners have sexual performance problems (Thornton, Chervenak, & Neal-Perry, 2015). The drop in estrogen also means that it no longer helps protect against aging of the skin, loss of bone mass, and accumulation of plaque on the walls of the arteries by boosting "good cholesterol" (high-density lipoprotein).

The period leading up to and following menopause is often accompanied by emotional and physical symptoms, including mood fluctuations and *hot flashes*—sensations of warmth accompanied by a rise in body temperature and redness in the face, neck, and chest, followed by sweating. Hot flashes—which may occur during the day and also, as *night sweats*, during sleep—affect more than 50 percent of women in Western industrialized nations (Takahashi & Johnson, 2015). Typically, they are not severe: Only about 1 in 12 women experiences them every day. On average, hot flashes persist for four years, but in some women, they continue for a decade. Although women approaching menopause tend to report increased irritability and less satisfying sleep, research using EEG and other neurobiological measures finds no links between menopause and changes in quantity or quality of sleep (Baker et al., 2015; Lamberg, 2007). Frequent hot flashes, however, are associated with repeated night wakings and poor sleep.

Furthermore, longitudinal evidence reveals that depressive episodes rise during the climacteric, though women who have a history of depression, who are experiencing highly stressful life events, or who harbor negative attitudes toward menopause and aging are at greatest risk (Bromberger et al., 2011; Freeman et al., 2006; Vivian-Taylor & Hickey, 2014). The hormonal changes of the climacteric seem to elevate depressive symptoms, especially in vulnerable women. With the final menstrual period, as hormone levels stabilize, the incidence of depression diminishes (Freeman et al., 2014; Gibson et al., 2012). But as Figure 15.1 reveals, women with a previous history of depression are far more likely than those with no history to continue feeling depressed after menopause. Their difficulties merit serious evaluation and treatment.

Compared with North American, European, African, and Middle Eastern women, Asian women report fewer menopausal complaints, including hot flashes (Obermeyer, 2000; Richard-Davis & Wellons, 2013). Asian diets, which are high in soy-based foods—a rich source of plant estrogen—may be involved.

Hormone Therapy.
To reduce the physical discomforts of menopause, doctors may prescribe **hormone therapy**, or low daily doses of estrogen. Hormone therapy comes in two types: (1) estrogen alone, or *estrogen replacement therapy (ERT)*, for women who have had hysterectomies (surgical removal of the uterus); and (2) estrogen plus progesterone, or *hormone replacement therapy (HRT)*, for other women. Combining estrogen with progesterone lessens the risk of cancer of the endometrium (lining of the uterus), which has long been known as a serious side effect of hormone therapy.

Hormone therapy is highly successful at counteracting hot flashes and vaginal dryness. It also offers some protection against bone deterioration. Nevertheless, more than 20 experiments, in which nearly 43,000 women had been randomly assigned to take hormone therapy (ERT or HRT) or a sugar pill for at least one year and were followed for an average of seven years, revealed an array of negative consequences. Hormone therapy was associated with an increase in heart attack, stroke, blood clots, breast cancer, gallbladder disease, and deaths from lung cancer. ERT, when compared with HRT, intensified the risk of blood clots, stroke, and gallbladder disease. And women age 65 and older taking HRT showed an elevated risk of Alzheimer's disease and other dementias (Marjoribanks et al., 2012).

On the basis of available evidence, women and their doctors should make decisions about hormone therapy carefully. For those who opt to use it, taking the lowest dose possible for the shortest time possible in the early menopausal years minimizes risk (Mirkin et al., 2014). Women with family histories of cardiovascular disease or breast cancer are advised against hormone therapy. Fortunately, the number of alternative treatments is increasing. New estrogen-based drugs with fewer side effects reduce hot flashes and vaginal dryness and protect the bones (Mintziori, 2015). A relatively safe migraine-headache medica-

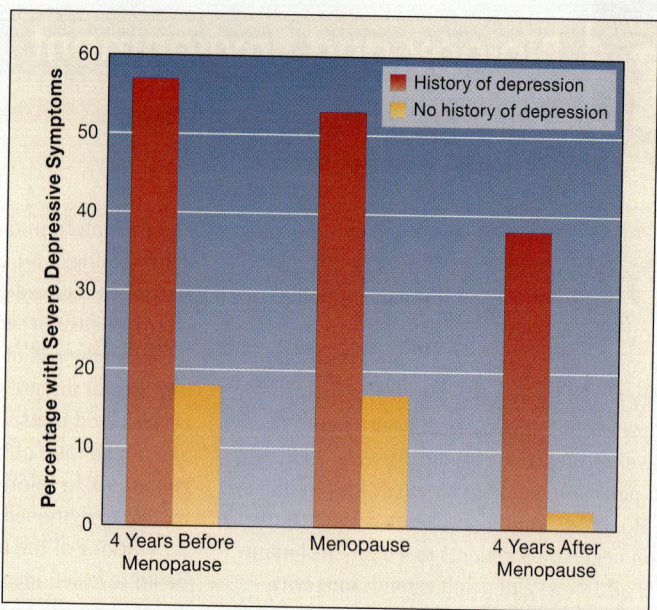

FIGURE 15.1 Percentage of women with severe depressive symptoms in the years leading up to and following menopause. A longitudinal investigation of 200 randomly selected women residing in Philadelphia revealed an elevated incidence of severe depression during the years preceding menopause (climacteric) that diminished after menopause. Women with a previous history of depression were at far greater risk: Following menopause, most who had been severely depressed during the climacteric continued to feel depressed. In contrast, depressive symptoms nearly evaporated in women with no history of depression. (Based on Freeman et al., 2014.)

tion, gabapentin, substantially lessens hot flashes, perhaps by acting on the brain's temperature regulation center. At high doses, which still appear safe, gabapentin is nearly as effective as hormone therapy. Several antidepressant drugs are helpful as well (Roberts & Hickey, 2016).

Women's Attitudes Toward Menopause.
Wide variations exist in the meanings women assign to menopause, depending on how they interpret the event in relation to their past and future lives. Jewel, who had wanted marriage and family but not attained these goals, viewed menopause as traumatic. Her sense of physical competence was still bound up with the ability to have children. Physical symptoms, or the expectation of those symptoms, can also trigger negative attitudes, such as stereotyped views of menopausal women as "irritable," "depressed," "old," or having "lost femininity" (Elavsky & McAuley, 2007; Marván, Castillo-López, & Arroyo, 2013; Sievert & Espinosa-Hernandez, 2003).

Many women, however, find menopause to be little or no trouble, regard it as a new beginning, and report improved quality of life (Mishra & Kuh, 2006). When more than 2,000 U.S. women were asked what their feelings were about no longer menstruating, nearly 50 percent of those experiencing changes in their menstrual cycles, and 60 percent of those whose periods had ceased, said they felt relieved (Rossi, 2004a). Most do not want more children and are thankful to be freed from worry about birth control. And highly educated women usually have more positive attitudes toward menopause than those with less education (Pitkin, 2010).

Compared with previous generations, the baby-boom generation seems more accepting of menopause (Avis & Crawford, 2006). Their strong desire to cast aside previous gender-stereotyped views (such as menopause as a sign of decay and disease), their more active approach to seeking health information, and their greater willingness to openly discuss sexual topics may contribute to their generally positive adaptation.

Other research suggests that African-American women hold favorable views. In several studies, they reported less irritability and moodiness than European Americans. They rarely spoke of menopause in terms of physical aging but, instead, regarded it as normal, inevitable, and even welcome (Melby, Lock, & Kaufert, 2005; Sampselle et al., 2002). Several African Americans expressed exasperation at society's readiness to label as "crazy" middle-aged women's authentic reactions to work- or family-based stressors that often coincide with menopause. And in an investigation of more than 13,000 U.S. women, ages 40 to 55 and diverse in ethnicity, other factors—SES, physical health, lifestyle factors (smoking, diet, exercise, weight gain), and especially psychological stress—overshadowed menopausal status and three common symptoms (hot flashes, night sweats, and vaginal dryness) in impact on self-rated quality of life (Avis et al., 2004).

The wide variation in physical symptoms and attitudes indicates that menopause is not just a hormonal event; it is also affected by cultural beliefs and practices. The Cultural Influences box on page 514 provides a cross-cultural look at women's experience of menopause.

Reproductive Changes in Men.
Although men also experience a climacteric, no male counterpart to menopause exists. Both quantity and motility of sperm decrease from the twenties on, and quantity of semen diminishes after age 40, negatively affecting fertility in middle age (Gunes et al., 2016). Still, sperm production continues throughout life, and men in their nineties have fathered children. Testosterone production also declines with age, though less so in healthy men who continue to engage in sexual activity, which stimulates cells that release testosterone.

Reduced testosterone plays a major role in diminishing blood flow to and changes in connective tissue in the penis. As a result, more stimulation is required for an erection, and it may be harder to maintain. The inability to attain an erection when desired can occur at any age, but it becomes more common in midlife: By age 60, 20 to 40 percent of men report difficulties, with frequency and severity rising with age (Shamloul & Ghanem, 2013).

An episode or two of impotence is not serious, but repeated bouts can lead some men to fear that their sex life is over and undermine their self-image. Viagra, Cialis, and other drugs that increase blood flow to the penis offer temporary relief from erectile dysfunction. Publicity surrounding these drugs has prompted more open discussion of erectile dysfunction and encouraged more men to seek treatment. But those taking the medications are often not adequately screened for the host of factors besides declining testosterone that contribute to impotence, including disorders of the nervous, cardiovascular, and endocrine systems; anxiety and depression; pelvic injury; and loss of interest in one's sexual partner (Mola, 2015). Although drugs for impotence are generally safe, a few users have experienced serious vision or hearing loss (Lambda & Anderson-Nelson, 2014; Shamloul & Ghanem, 2013). In men with high blood pressure or atherosclerosis, the medications heighten the risk of constricting blood vessels in the retina and optic and auditory nerves, causing permanent damage.

Ask yourself

CONNECT Compare ethnic variations in attitudes toward menopause with ethnic variations in reactions to menarche and early pubertal timing (pages 374–375 and page 377 in Chapter 11). Did you find similarities? Explain.

APPLY Between ages 40 and 50, Nancy gained 20 pounds. She also began to have trouble opening tightly closed jars, and her calf muscles ached after climbing a flight of stairs. "Exchanging muscle for fat must be an inevitable part of aging," Nancy thought. Is she correct? Why or why not?

REFLECT What factors would you consider, or advise others to consider, before using hormone therapy to reduce menopausal symptoms?

Cultural Influences

Menopause as a Biocultural Event

Biology and culture join forces to influence women's response to menopause, making it a *biocultural event*. In Western industrialized nations, menopause is "medicalized"—regarded as a syndrome of physical and emotional symptoms requiring treatment.

Yet change the circumstances in which menopause is evaluated, and attitudes change as well. In one study, nearly 600 men and women between ages 19 and 85 described their view of menopause in one of three contexts—as a medical problem, as a life transition, or as a symbol of aging (Gannon & Ekstrom, 1993). The medical context evoked many more negative statements than the other contexts.

Research in non-Western cultures reveals that middle-aged women's social status also affects the experience of menopause. In societies where older women are respected and mother-in-law and grandmother roles bring new privileges and responsibilities, complaints about menopausal symptoms are rare (Fuh et al., 2005). Perhaps in part for this reason, women in Asian nations report fewer discomforts. And their symptoms usually differ from those of Western women.

Though they rarely complain of hot flashes, the most frequent symptoms of Asian women are back, shoulder, and joint pain—a possible biological variation from other ethnic groups (Haines et al., 2005; Huang, 2010). In midlife, women in Asian cultures attain peak respect and responsibility. Typically their days are filled with monitoring the household economy, attending to grandchildren, caring for dependent parents-in-law, and employment. Asian women seem to interpret menopausal distress in light of these socially valued commitments. In Japan, neither women nor their doctors consider menopause to be a significant marker of female middle age. Rather, midlife is viewed as an extended period of "socially recognized, productive maturity" (Menon, 2001, p. 58).

A comparison of rural Mayan women of the Yucatán with rural Greek women on the island of Evia reveals additional biocultural influences on the menopausal experience (Beyene, 1992; Beyene & Martin, 2001; Mahady et al., 2008). In both societies, aging is associated with increased status, and menopause brings release from child rearing and more time for leisure activities. Otherwise, the Mayan and Greek women differ greatly.

Yucatán Mayan women marry as teenagers. By 35 to 40, they have given birth to many children but rarely menstruated because of repeated pregnancies and breastfeeding. They also experience menopause up to 10 years earlier than their counterparts in developed nations, perhaps because of additional physical stressors, such as poor nutrition and heavy physical work. Eager for childbearing to end, they look forward to menopause, describing it with such phrases as "being happy" and "free like a young girl again." None report hot flashes or any other symptoms.

Like North Americans, rural Greek women use birth control to limit family size, and most report hot flashes and sweating at menopause. But they regard these as temporary discomforts that will stop on their own, not as medical symptoms requiring treatment. When asked what they do about hot flashes, the Greek women reply, "Pay no attention," "Go outside for fresh air," and "Throw off the covers at night."

Does frequency of childbearing affect menopausal symptoms, as this contrast between Mayan and Greek women suggests? More research is needed to be sure. At the same time, the difference between North American and Greek women in attitudes toward and management of hot flashes is striking. This—along with other cross-cultural findings—highlights the combined impact of biology and culture on menopausal experiences.

For these rural Mayan women of the Yucatán, menopause brings freedom. After decades of childbearing, Mayan women look forward to menopause, describing it as "being happy" and "free like a young girl again."

Health and Fitness

15.3 Discuss sexuality in middle adulthood and its association with relationship satisfaction.

15.4 Discuss cancer, cardiovascular disease, and osteoporosis, noting risk factors and interventions.

15.5 Discuss the association of hostility and anger with heart disease and other health problems.

In midlife, about 85 percent of Americans rate their health as either "excellent" or "good"—still a large majority, but lower than the 95 percent figure in early adulthood (Zajacova & Woo, 2016). Whereas younger people usually attribute health complaints to temporary infections, middle-aged adults more often point to chronic diseases. As we will see, among those who rate their health unfavorably, men are more likely to suffer from fatal illnesses, women from nonfatal, limiting health problems.

In addition to typical negative indicators—major diseases and disabling conditions—our discussion takes up sexuality as a positive indicator of health. Before we begin, it is important to note that our understanding of health in middle and late adulthood is limited by insufficient research on women and ethnic minorities. Most studies of illness risk factors, prevention, and treatment have been carried out on men. Fortunately, this situation is changing. For example, the Women's Health Initiative (WHI)—a commitment by the U.S. federal government, extending from 1993 to 2005, to study the impact of various lifestyle and medical prevention strategies on the health of nearly 162,000 postmenopausal women of all ethnic groups and SES levels—has led to important findings, including health risks associated with hormone therapy, discussed earlier. Two five-year extensions, involving annual health updates from 115,000 WHI participants in 2005–2010, and 94,000 participants in 2010–2015, continue to yield vital information.

Sexuality

The overwhelming majority of research on sexuality in midlife focuses on heterosexual married couples and, to a lesser extent, cohabiting couples. Little is known about the sexual activity of the growing numbers of middle-aged adults who are single and dating. Research on middle-aged dating, cohabiting, and married same-sex couples is also sparse.

Frequency of sexual activity among heterosexual couples tends to decline in midlife, but for most, the drop is modest. Surveys of large, nationally representative samples of U.S. adults reveal that even in the latter years of middle adulthood (ages 55 to 64), the overwhelming majority of married and cohabiting adults are sexually active (about 90 percent of men and 80 percent of women) (Thomas, Hess, & Thurston, 2015; Waite et al., 2009). And as Figure 15.2 reveals, most sexually active midlifers report having sex regularly—more than once a month or once a week.

Longitudinal research reveals that stability of sexual activity is far more typical than dramatic change. Couples who have sex often in early adulthood continue to do so in midlife (Dennerstein & Lehert, 2004). And the best predictor of sexual frequency is relationship satisfaction, an association that is probably bidirectional (Karraker & DeLamater, 2013; Thomas, Hess, & Thurston, 2015). Sex is more likely in the context of a happy intimate bond, and couples who have sex often probably view their relationship more positively.

Nevertheless, *intensity* of sexual response diminishes in midlife due to physical changes of the climacteric. Both men and women take longer to feel aroused and to reach orgasm. If partners perceive each other as less attractive, this may contribute to a drop in sexual desire. Yet in the context of a positive outlook, sexual activity can become more satisfying. Devin and Trisha, for example, viewed each other's aging bodies with acceptance and affection—as a sign of their enduring and deepening relationship. And with greater freedom from the demands of work and family, their sex life became more spontaneous. The majority of married people over age 50 say that sex is an important component of a healthy couple relationship (Das, Waite, & Laumann, 2012). And most find ways to overcome difficulties with sexual functioning. One happily married 52-year-old woman commented, "We know what we are doing, we've had plenty of practice (laughs), and I would never have believed

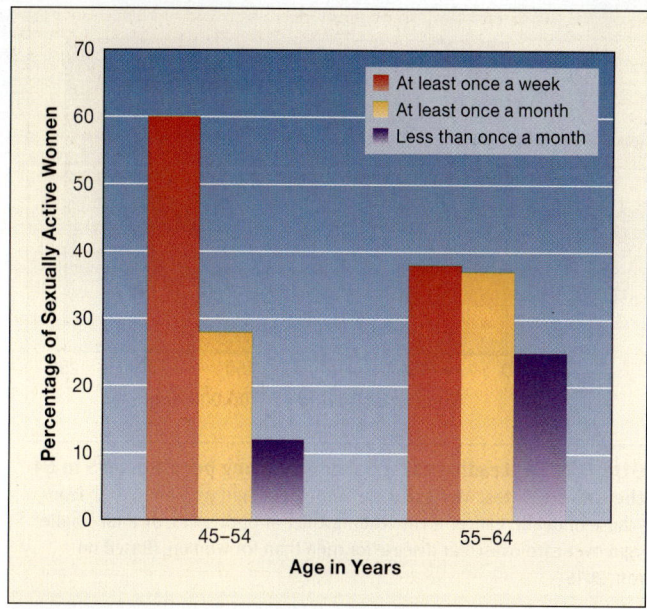

FIGURE 15.2 Frequency of sexual activity among sexually active middle-aged women. In a survey of a nationally representative sample of over 1,000 U.S. women, those who were sexually active declined in frequency with which they engaged in sex over middle adulthood. Still, among 55- to 64-year-olds, more than one-third reported having sex at least once a week, and a similar percentage at least once a month. (Based on Thomas, Hess, & Thurston, 2015.)

that it gets better as you get older, but it does" (Gott & Hinchliff, 2003, p. 1625).

When surveys include married, cohabiting, and single people, a striking gender difference in age-related sexual activity appears. The proportion of U.S. men with no sexual partners in the previous year increases only slightly from the thirties to the late fifties, from 8 to 12 percent. In contrast, the rise for women is dramatic, from 9 to about 35 to 40 percent, a gender gap that becomes even larger in late adulthood (Lindau et al., 2007; Thomas, Hess, & Thurston, 2015; Waite et al., 2009). A higher male mortality rate and the value women place on affection and continuity in sexual relations make partners less available to them. Taken as a whole, the evidence reveals that sexual activity in midlife, as in earlier periods, is the combined result of biological, psychological, and social forces.

Illness and Disability

As Figure 15.3 on page 516 shows, cancer and cardiovascular disease are the leading causes of U.S. deaths in middle age. Unintentional injuries, though still a major health threat, occur at a lower rate than in early adulthood, largely because motor vehicle collisions decline. Despite a rise in vision problems, middle-aged adults' many years of driving experience and greater cautiousness may reduce these deaths. In contrast, falls resulting in bone fractures and death more than double from early to middle adulthood (Centers for Disease Control and Prevention, 2014e).

As in earlier decades, economic disadvantage is a strong predictor of poor health and premature death, with SES differences widening in midlife (Agigoroaei, 2016). And largely because of

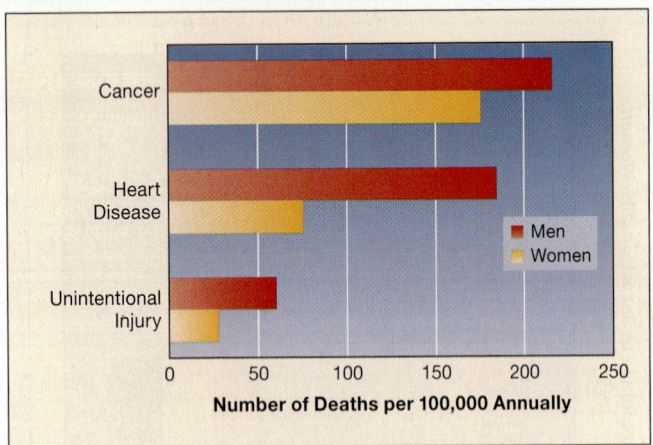

FIGURE 15.3 Leading causes of death among people age 45 to 64 in the United States. Men are more vulnerable than women to each leading cause of death. Cancer is the leading killer of both sexes, by a far smaller margin over cardiovascular disease for men than for women. (Based on Heron, 2015.)

more severe poverty and lack of universal health insurance, the United States continues to exceed most other industrialized nations in death rates from major causes (OECD, 2015d). Furthermore, men are more vulnerable than women to most health problems. Among middle-aged men, cancer deaths exceed cardiovascular disease deaths by a small margin; among women, cancer is by far the leading cause of death (refer again to Figure 15.3). Finally, as we take a closer look at illness and disability in the following sections, we will encounter yet another familiar theme: the close connection between psychological and physical well-being. Personality traits that magnify stress—especially hostility and anger—are serious threats to health in midlife.

Cancer. From early to middle adulthood, the death rate due to cancer multiplies tenfold, accounting for about 30 percent of all midlife deaths in the United States (Heron, 2015). Although the incidence of many types of cancer is currently leveling off or declining, cancer mortality was on the rise for many decades, largely because of a dramatic increase in lung cancer due to cigarette smoking. Lung cancer is the most common cause of cancer deaths in both genders, worldwide. Over the past 25 years, its incidence dropped in men; 60 percent fewer smoke today than in the 1950s. In contrast, lung cancer has only recently begun to decrease in women after a long period of increase, due to large numbers of women taking up smoking in the decades after World War II (American Cancer Society, 2015c).

Cancer occurs when a cell's genetic program is disrupted, leading to uncontrolled growth and spread of abnormal cells that crowd out normal tissues and organs. Why does this happen? Mutations of three main kinds contribute to cancer. Some result in *oncogenes* (cancer genes) that directly undergo abnormal cell duplication. Others interfere with the activity of *tumor suppressor genes* so they fail to keep oncogenes from multiplying. And a third type of mutation disrupts the activity of *stability genes*, which normally keep genetic alterations to a minimum by repairing subtle DNA mistakes that occur either during normal cell duplication or as a result of environmental agents (Ewald & Ewald, 2012). When stability genes do not function, mutations in many other genes occur at a higher rate.

Each of these cancer-linked mutations can be either *germline* (due to an inherited predisposition) or *somatic* (occurring in a single cell, which then multiplies) (see page 49 in Chapter 2 to review). Recall from Chapter 13 that according to one theory, error in DNA duplication increases with age, with cell repair becoming less efficient. Environmental toxins may initiate or intensify this process.

Figure 15.4 shows the incidence of the most common types of cancer. For cancers that affect both sexes, men are generally more vulnerable than women. The difference may be due to genetic makeup, exposure to cancer-causing agents as a result of lifestyle or occupation, and men's greater tendency to delay going to the doctor. Although the relationship of SES to cancer varies with site (for example, lung and stomach cancers are linked to lower SES, breast and prostate cancers to higher SES),

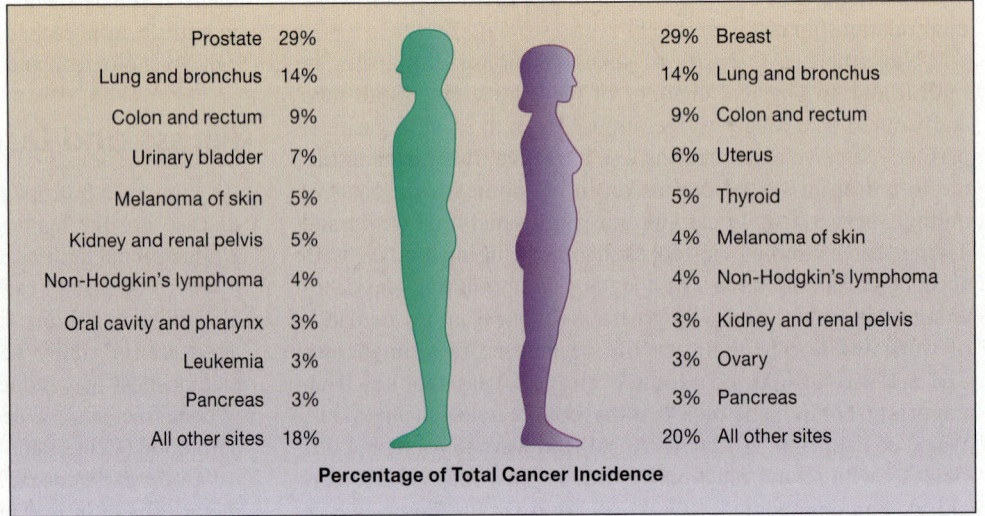

FIGURE 15.4 Incidence of 10 leading cancer types among men and women in the United States, 2012. (From R. Siegel, K. D. Miller, & A. Jemal, 2016, "Cancer Statistics, 2016," *CA: A Cancer Journal for Clinicians,* 66, p. 11. Copyright © 2016 American Cancer Society, Inc. Reproduced with permission of Wiley, Inc.)

Applying what we Know

Reducing Cancer Incidence and Deaths

INTERVENTION	DESCRIPTION
Know the seven warning signs of cancer.	The signs are change in bowel or bladder habits, sore that does not heal, unusual bleeding or discharge, thickening or lump in a breast or elsewhere in your body, indigestion or swallowing difficulty, obvious change in a wart or mole, nagging cough or hoarseness. If you have any of these signs, consult your doctor immediately.
Schedule regular medical checkups and cancer-screening tests.	Women should have a mammogram and Pap test every 1 to 2 years. Beginning at age 50, men should have an annual prostate screening test. Both men and women should be screened periodically for colon cancer, as recommended by their doctor.
Avoid tobacco.	Cigarette smoking causes 90 percent of lung cancer deaths and 30 percent of all cancer deaths. Smokeless (chewing) tobacco increases risk of cancers of the mouth, larynx, throat, and esophagus.
Limit alcohol consumption.	Consuming more than one drink per day for women or two drinks per day for men increases risk of cancers of the breast, kidney, liver, head, and neck.
Avoid excessive sun exposure.	Sun exposure causes many cases of skin cancer. When in the sun for an extended time, wear sunglasses, use sunscreen that protects against both UVA and UVB rays, and cover exposed skin.
Avoid unnecessary X-ray exposure.	Excessive exposure to X-rays increases risk of many cancers. Most medical X-rays are adjusted to deliver the lowest possible dose but should not be used unnecessarily.
Avoid exposure to industrial chemicals and other pollutants.	Exposure to nickel, chromate, asbestos, vinyl chloride, radon, and other pollutants increases risk of various cancers.
Weigh the benefits versus risks of hormone therapy.	Because estrogen replacement increases risk of uterine and breast cancers, carefully consider hormone therapy with your doctor.
Maintain a healthy diet.	Eating vegetables, fruits, and whole grains, while avoiding excess dietary fat and salt-cured, smoked, and nitrite-cured foods, reduces risk of colon and rectal cancers.
Avoid excessive weight gain.	Overweight and obesity increase risk of many cancers, including of the breast, colon, esophagus, kidney, pancreas, and uterus.
Adopt a physically active lifestyle.	Physical activity offers protection against cancers at all body sites except the skin, with the strongest evidence for cancers of the breast, rectum, and colon.

Source: American Cancer Society, 2015a.

cancer death rates increase sharply as SES decreases and are especially high among African Americans (Fernandes-Taylor & Bloom, 2015). Poorer medical care and reduced ability to fight the disease due to factors associated with poverty, including high life stress, inadequate diet, and co-occurrence of other illnesses, are responsible. Consequently, although African Americans have a lower incidence of breast cancer than European Americans, the African-American breast cancer death rate is higher.

Overall, a complex interaction of heredity, biological aging, and environment contributes to cancer. For example, many patients with familial breast cancer who respond poorly to treatment have defective forms of particular tumor-suppressor genes (either BRCA1 or BRCA2). Women with these mutations are especially likely to develop early-onset breast cancer, before age 40 (Haley, 2016). But their risk remains elevated throughout middle and late adulthood, when breast cancer rises among women in general. Genetic screening is available, permitting prevention efforts to begin early. Nevertheless, breast cancer susceptibility genes account for only 5 to 10 percent of all cases; most women with breast cancer do not have a family history (American Cancer Society, 2015b). Other genes and lifestyle factors—including alcohol consumption, overweight, physical inactivity, never having had children, use of oral contraceptives, and hormone therapy to treat menopausal symptoms—heighten the risk.

People often fear cancer because they believe it is incurable. Yet 60 percent of affected individuals are cured—free of the disease for five years or longer. Survival rates, however, vary widely with type of cancer (Siegel, Miller, & Jemal, 2016). For example, they are relatively high for breast and prostate cancers, intermediate for uterine and colon cancers, and low for lung and pancreatic cancers.

Breast cancer is the leading malignancy for women, prostate cancer for men. Lung cancer ranks second for both genders; it causes more deaths (largely preventable through avoiding tobacco) than any other cancer type. It is followed closely by colon and rectal cancer. Scheduling annual medical checkups that screen for these and other forms of cancer and taking the additional steps listed in Applying What We Know above can reduce cancer illness and death rates considerably. An increasing

Applying what we Know

Reducing the Risk of Heart Attack

INTERVENTION	RISK REDUCTION
Quit smoking.	Five years after quitting, nonsmokers show a greatly reduced risk compared to current smokers. Chemicals in tobacco damage the heart and blood vessels and greatly increase the risk of atherosclerosis.
Reduce blood cholesterol level.	Reductions in cholesterol average 10 percent with transition to a healthy diet.
Treat high blood pressure.	A combination of healthy diet and drug therapy can lower blood pressure substantially. When allowed to persist, high blood pressure places added force against the artery walls, damaging them.
Maintain ideal weight.	Greatly reduced risk for people who maintain ideal body weight compared to those who are obese.
Exercise regularly.	Greatly reduced risk for people who maintain an active rather than a sedentary lifestyle. In addition to contributing to healthy weight, lowers cholesterol and blood pressure and helps prevent type 2 diabetes, which is strongly linked to heart disease.
Drink an occasional glass of wine or beer.[a]	Modestly reduced risk for people who consume small-to-moderate amounts of alcohol. Believed to promote high-density lipoproteins (a form of "good cholesterol" that lowers "bad cholesterol") and to prevent clot formation.
If medically recommended, take low-dose aspirin.	Modestly reduced risk for people with a previous heart attack or stroke, by lowering the likelihood of blood clots (should be doctor advised; long-term use can have serious side effects).
Reduce hostility and other forms of psychological stress.	People under stress are more likely to engage in high-risk behaviors, such as overeating and smoking, and to display high-risk symptoms, such as high blood pressure.

[a]Recall from Chapter 13 that heavy alcohol use increases the risk of cardiovascular disease as well as many other diseases.
Source: Mozaffarian et al., 2016.

number of cancer-promoting mutations are being identified, and promising new therapies targeting these genes are being tested.

Surviving cancer is a triumph, but it also brings emotional challenges. During cancer treatment, relationships focus on the illness. Afterward, they must refocus on health and full participation in daily life. Unfortunately, stigmas associated with cancer exist (Daher, 2012). Friends, family, and co-workers may need reminders that cancer is not contagious and that with patience and support from supervisors and co-workers, cancer survivors regain their on-the-job productivity.

Cardiovascular Disease. Despite a decline over the last few decades (see Chapter 13), each year about 25 percent of middle-aged Americans who die succumb to cardiovascular disease (Heron, 2015). We associate cardiovascular disease with heart attacks, but Devin, like many middle-aged and older adults, learned of the condition during an annual checkup. His doctor detected high blood pressure, high blood cholesterol, and *atherosclerosis*—a buildup of plaque in his coronary arteries, which encircle the heart and provide its muscles with oxygen and nutrients. These indicators of cardiovascular disease are known as "silent killers" because they often have no symptoms.

When symptoms *are* evident, they take different forms. The most extreme is a *heart attack*—blockage of normal blood supply to an area of the heart, usually brought on by a blood clot in one or more plaque-filled coronary arteries. Intense pain results as muscle in the affected region dies. A heart attack is a medical emergency; over 50 percent of victims die before reaching the hospital, another 15 percent during treatment, and an additional 15 percent over the next few years (Mozaffarian et al., 2016). Among other, less extreme symptoms of cardiovascular disease are *arrhythmia,* or irregular heartbeat. When it persists, it can prevent the heart from pumping enough blood and result in faintness. It can also allow clots to form within the heart's chambers, which may break loose and travel to the brain. In some individuals, indigestion-like pain or crushing chest pain, called *angina pectoris,* reveals an oxygen-deprived heart.

Today, cardiovascular disease can be treated in many ways—including coronary bypass surgery, medication, and pacemakers to regulate heart rhythm. To relieve arterial blockage, Devin had *angioplasty,* a procedure in which a surgeon threaded a needle-thin catheter into his arteries and inflated a balloon at its tip, which flattened fatty deposits to allow blood to flow more freely. Unless Devin took other measures to reduce his risk, his doctor warned, the arteries would clog again within a year. As Applying What We Know above indicates, adults can do much to prevent heart disease or slow its progress.

Some risks, such as heredity, advanced age, and being male, cannot be changed. But cardiovascular disease is so disabling and deadly that people must be alert for it where they least expect it—for example, in women. Because men account for over 70 percent of cases in middle adulthood, doctors often view a heart attack as a "male problem" and frequently overlook women's unique symptoms. Rather than chest pain, many women experience extreme fatigue, dizziness, palpitations, pain in the upper back or arm, as well as intense anxiety—symptoms often mistaken for a panic attack. Women themselves are less likely to recognize symptoms and, therefore, often delay in seeking help.

In follow-ups of victims of heart attacks, women—especially African-American women, who are at increased risk—were less likely to be offered drugs to treat blood clots and costly, invasive therapies, such as angioplasty and bypass surgery (Mehta et al., 2016). As a result, treatment outcomes—including rehospitalization and death—tend to be worse for women, particularly black women.

Osteoporosis. When age-related bone loss is severe, a condition called **osteoporosis** develops. The disorder, affecting 10 percent of U.S. adults age 50 and older—amounting to 10 million people, most of whom are women—greatly magnifies the risk of bone fractures. An additional 44 percent are at risk for osteoporosis because they have bone density levels low enough to be of concern. From middle to late adulthood, osteoporosis increases fivefold in women, from 7 to 35 percent, and triples in men, from 3 to 11 percent (Wright et al., 2014). Because the bones gradually become more porous over many years, osteoporosis may not be evident until fractures—typically in the spine, hips, and wrist—occur or are discovered through X-rays.

A major factor related to osteoporosis is the drop in estrogen associated with menopause. In middle and late adulthood, women lose about 50 percent of their bone mass, about half of it in the first 10 years following menopause—a decline that, by the late sixties, is two to five times greater than in men (Drake, Clark, & Lewiecki, 2015). The earlier a woman reaches menopause, the greater her chances of developing osteoporosis related to estrogen loss. In men, the age-related decrease in testosterone—though much more gradual than estrogen loss in women—contributes to bone loss because the body converts some to estrogen.

Heredity plays an important role. A family history of osteoporosis increases risk, with identical twins more likely than fraternal twins to share the disorder (Ralston & Uitterlinden, 2010). People with thin, small-framed bodies are more likely to be affected because they typically attain a lower peak bone mass in adolescence. In contrast, higher bone density makes African Americans less susceptible than other U.S. ethnic groups (Wright et al., 2014). An unhealthy lifestyle also contributes: A diet deficient in calcium and vitamin D (essential for calcium absorption), excess intake of sodium and caffeine, and physical inactivity reduce bone mass. Cigarette smoking and alcohol consumption are also harmful because they interfere with replacement of bone cells (Drake, Clark, & Lewiecki, 2015).

When major bone fractures (such as the hip) occur, many people suffer permanent loss in function and quality of life, and they are at high risk for additional fractures. Furthermore, a serious fracture triples the chances of dying within a year (Cauley, 2013). Osteoporosis usually develops earlier in women than in men, so it has become known as a "women's disease." Men are far less likely to be screened and treated for it, even after a hip fracture. Compared with women, men with hip fractures tend to be older and to lack a history of interventions aimed at preserving bone density. Probably for these reasons, the one-year mortality rate after hip fracture is greater for men than for women.

To treat osteoporosis, doctors recommend a diet enriched with calcium and vitamin D, weight-bearing exercise (walking rather than swimming), resistance training, and bone-strengthening medications (Drake, Clark, & Lewiecki, 2015). A better way to reduce lifelong risk is through early prevention: maximizing peak bone density by increasing calcium and vitamin D intake and engaging in regular exercise in childhood, adolescence, and early adulthood.

A physical therapist guides this middle-aged patient through a resistance training regimen, one recommended intervention for osteoporosis. Because women are at much greater risk for the disease, men are less likely to be screened and treated.

Hostility and Anger

Whenever Trisha's sister Dottie called, she seemed like a powder keg ready to erupt. Dottie was critical of her boss at work, impatient with anything that interfered with her progress at getting tasks done, intensely competitive about succeeding, and explosive when she was dissatisfied. Once, when Dottie was displeased with the way Trisha, a lawyer, had handled some family legal affairs after their father died, she angrily hurled a stream of insulting remarks: "Any lawyer knows that, Trisha. How could you be so stupid! I should have called a *real* lawyer."

At age 53, Dottie had high blood pressure, difficulty sleeping, and back pain. In the past five years, she had been hospitalized five times—twice for treatment of digestive problems, twice for an irregular heartbeat, and once for a benign tumor on her thyroid gland. Trisha wondered whether Dottie's personal style was partly responsible for her health problems.

That hostility and anger might have negative effects on health is a centuries-old idea. Several decades ago, researchers first tested this notion by identifying 35- to 59-year-old men who displayed the **Type A behavior pattern**—extreme competitiveness, ambition, impatience, hostility, angry outbursts, and sense of eagerness, hurriedness, and time pressure. They found that within the next eight years, Type As were more than twice as likely as Type Bs (people with a more relaxed disposition) to develop heart disease (Rosenman et al., 1975).

Later studies, however, often failed to confirm these outcomes. Type A is actually a mix of behaviors, only one or two of which affect health. Current evidence pinpoints hostility as a "toxic" ingredient of Type A, since isolating it from global Type A consistently predicts heart disease and other health problems, even after factors that might otherwise account for these outcomes—such as smoking, alcohol consumption, overweight, and life stressors—are controlled (Eaker et al., 2004; Matthews et al., 2004; Smith et al., 2004; Smith & Mackenzie, 2006). The risks of high blood pressure, atherosclerosis, and stroke are several times greater in adults scoring high on hostility measures than in those scoring low (Räikkönen et al., 2004; Yan et al., 2003).

Expressed hostility in particular—frequent angry outbursts; rude, disagreeable behavior; critical and condescending nonverbal cues during social interaction, including glares; and expressions of contempt and disgust—predicts greater cardiovascular arousal, coronary artery plaque buildup, and heart disease (Haukkala et al., 2010; Smith & Cundiff, 2011; Smith et al., 2012). A related feature of the Type A pattern that also predicts heart disease is a socially dominant interactive style, evident in rapid, loud insistent speech and impatiently cutting off and talking over others (Smith, 2006). As people engage in these behaviors, heart rate, blood pressure, and stress hormones escalate.

Type A individuals become increasingly recognizable during the busiest years of career achievement. In a Finnish study tracking a nationally representative sample of several thousand participants, Type A behavior intensified from adolescence into the mid-thirties, followed by only a slight decline into the mid-forties (Hinsta et al., 2014). As the Type A pattern becomes clearly evident, age-related risk of heart disease rises.

Can Dottie preserve her health by bottling up her hostility instead of expressing it? Repeatedly suppressing overt anger or ruminating about past anger-provoking events is also associated with high blood pressure and heart disease (Eaker et al., 2007; Hogan & Linden, 2004). A better alternative, as we will see, is to develop effective ways of handling stress and conflict.

Stress Management

Turn back to Chapter 13, page 455, and review the negative consequences of psychological stress on the cardiovascular, immune, and gastrointestinal systems. As adults encounter problems at home and at work, daily hassles can add up to a serious stress load. Stress management is important at any age, but in middle adulthood it can limit the age-related rise in illness and, when disease strikes, reduce its severity.

Applying What We Know on the following page summarizes effective ways to reduce stress. Even when stressors cannot be eliminated, people can change how they handle some and view others. At work, Trisha focused on problems she could control—not on her boss's irritability but on ways to delegate routine tasks to her staff so she could concentrate on challenges that required her knowledge and skills. When Dottie phoned, Trisha learned to distinguish normal emotional reactions from unreasonable self-blame. Instead of interpreting Dottie's anger as a sign of her own incompetence, she reminded herself of Dottie's difficult temperament and hard life. And greater life experience helped her accept change as inevitable, so that she was better-equipped to deal with the jolt of sudden events, such as Devin's hospitalization for treatment of heart disease.

Notice how Trisha called on two general strategies for coping with stress, discussed in Chapter 10: (1) *problem-centered coping,* in which she appraised the situation as changeable, identified the difficulty, and decided what to do about it; and (2) *emotion-centered coping,* which is internal, private, and aimed at controlling distress when little can be done about a situation. Research reveals that adults who effectively reduce stress move flexibly between problem-centered and emotion-centered techniques, depending on the situation (Zakowski et al., 2001). Their approach is deliberate, thoughtful, and respectful of both themselves and others.

Notice, also, that problem-focused and emotion-focused coping, though they have different immediate goals, facilitate each other. Effective problem-focused coping reduces emotional

Adapting to the Physical Challenges of Midlife

15.6 Discuss the benefits of stress management, exercise, and hardiness in dealing effectively with the physical challenges of midlife.

15.7 Explain the double standard of aging.

Middle adulthood is often a productive time of life, when people attain their greatest accomplishments and satisfactions. Nevertheless, it takes considerable stamina to cope with the full array of changes this period can bring. Devin responded to his expanding waistline and cardiovascular symptoms by leaving his desk twice a week to attend a low-impact aerobics class and by reducing work-related stress through daily 10-minute meditation sessions. Aware of her sister Dottie's difficulties, Trisha resolved to handle her own angry and impatient feelings more adaptively. And her generally optimistic outlook enabled her to cope successfully with the physical changes of midlife, the pressures of her legal career, and Devin's cardiovascular disease.

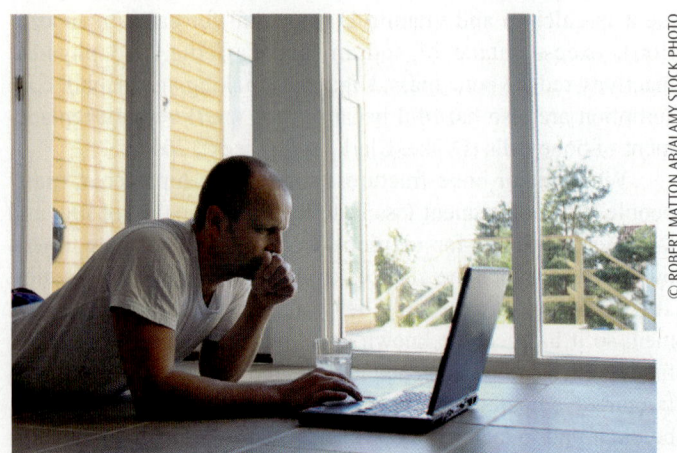

Stress management in middle adulthood helps limit the age-related rise in illness. This midlifer reduces stress by periodically leaving his high-pressure office environment to work in a sunny, relaxing space.

Applying what we Know

Managing Stress

STRATEGY	DESCRIPTION
Reevaluate the situation.	Learn to differentiate appropriate reactions from those based on irrational beliefs.
Focus on events you can control.	Don't worry about things you cannot change or that may never happen; focus on strategies for handling events under your control.
View life as fluid.	Expect change and accept it as inevitable; then many unanticipated changes will have less emotional impact.
Consider alternatives.	Don't rush into action; think before you act.
Set reasonable goals for yourself.	Aim high, but be realistic about your capacities, motivation, and the situation.
Exercise regularly.	A physically fit person can better handle stress, both physically and emotionally.
Master relaxation techniques.	Relaxation helps refocus energies and reduce the physical discomfort of stress. Classes and self-help books teach these techniques.
Use constructive approaches to anger reduction.	Delay responding ("Let me check into that and get back to you"); use mentally distracting behaviors (counting to 10 backwards) and self-instruction (a covert "Stop!") to control anger arousal; then engage in calm, self-controlled problem solving ("I should call him rather than confront him personally").
Seek social support.	Friends, family members, co-workers, and organized support groups can offer information, assistance, and suggestions for coping with stressful situations.

distress, while effective emotion-focused coping helps people face problems more calmly and, thus, generate better solutions. Ineffective coping, in contrast, is largely emotion-focused and self-blaming, impulsive, or escapist.

Constructive approaches to anger reduction are a vital health intervention (refer again to Applying What We Know). Teaching people to be assertive rather than hostile and to negotiate rather than explode interrupts the intense physiological response that intervenes between psychological stress and illness. Sometimes it is best to delay responding by simply leaving a provocative situation, taking time to think through how to handle it.

As noted in Chapter 13, people tend to cope with stress more effectively as they move from early to middle adulthood. They may become more realistic about their ability to change situations and more skilled at anticipating stressful events and at preparing to manage them (Aldwin, Yancura, & Boeninger, 2010). Furthermore, when middle-aged adults surmount a highly stressful experience, they often report lasting personal benefits as they look back with amazement at what they were able to accomplish under extremely trying conditions. A serious illness and brush with death commonly bring changes in values and perspectives, such as clearer life priorities, a greater sense of personal strength, and closer ties to others. Interpreting trauma as growth-promoting is related to more effective coping with current stressors and with increased physical and mental health years later (Aldwin & Yancura, 2011; Proulx & Aldwin, 2016). In this way, managing intense stress can serve as a context for positive development.

But for people who do have difficulty handling midlife's challenges, communities provide fewer social supports than for younger or older adults. For example, Jewel had little knowledge of what to expect during the climacteric. "It would have helped to have a support group so I could have learned about menopause and dealt with it more easily," she told Trisha. Community programs addressing typical midlife concerns, such as those of adult learners returning to college and caregivers of aging parents, can reduce stress during this period.

LOOK and LISTEN

Interview a middle-aged adult who has overcome a highly stressful experience, such as a serious illness, about how he or she coped. Inquire about any resulting changes in outlook on life. Do the adult's responses fit with research findings?

Exercise

Regular exercise, as noted in Chapter 13, has a range of physical and psychological benefits—among them, equipping adults to handle stress more effectively and reducing the risk of many diseases. Heading for his first aerobics class, Devin wondered, Can starting to exercise at age 50 counteract years of physical inactivity? To shed light on this question, researchers combined six longitudinal studies in which 660,000 European and U.S. adults, ranging in age from 21 to 98 years, were asked about how much time they typically devote to various leisure-time physical activities each week. The greater participants' weekly energy expenditure through physically active pursuits, the lower their chances of dying during the following 14 years (Arem et al., 2015). And compared with no activity, any amount of exercise had longevity benefits, even after many factors—such as SES, health status, alcohol and tobacco use, and BMI—that might account for the findings were controlled.

Yet more than half of U.S. middle-aged adults are sedentary. Furthermore, many who begin an exercise program discontinue it within the first six months. Even among those who stay active, fewer than 18 percent engage in the nationally recommended levels of leisure-time physical activity and resistance exercises (see page 448 in Chapter 13) (U.S. Department of Health and Human Services, 2015d).

A person beginning to exercise in midlife must overcome initial barriers and ongoing obstacles—lack of time and energy, inconvenience, work conflicts, and health factors (such as overweight). *Self-efficacy*—belief in one's ability to succeed—is just as vital in adopting, maintaining, and exerting oneself in an exercise regimen as it is in career progress (see Chapter 14). An important outcome of starting an exercise program is that sedentary adults gain in self-efficacy, which further promotes physical activity (McAuley & Elavsky, 2008; Parschau et al., 2014). Enhanced physical fitness, in turn, prompts middle-aged adults to feel better about their physical selves. Over time, their physical self-esteem—sense of body conditioning and attractiveness—rises (Elavsky & McAuley, 2007; Gothe et al., 2011).

A variety of group and individualized approaches are successful in increasing middle-aged adults' physical activity. Among these are workplace-based programs offering rewards for reaching exercise goals and web or mobile-phone-based interventions with tools for goal setting, self-monitoring, and feedback on progress (Duncan et al., 2014; Morgan et al., 2011). One innovative program focused on middle-aged adults who had been active in sports as youths but had disengaged from physical activity. Relative to controls, those who viewed a short video on the diverse benefits of adult team sports (such as health, skill gains, and likeminded friendships) attached greater value to becoming a sports participant in their hoped-for self-images (Lithopoulos, Rathwell, & Young, 2015). As Chapter 18 will reveal, future-oriented self-descriptions are good predictors of midlife behavior change.

Accessible, attractive, and safe exercise environments—parks, walking and biking trails, and community recreation centers—and frequent opportunities to observe others using them also promote physical activity. Besides health problems and daily stressors, low-SES adults often mention inconvenient access to facilities, expense, unsafe neighborhoods, and unclean streets as barriers to exercise—important reasons that activity level declines sharply with SES (Taylor et al., 2007; Wilbur et al., 2003). Interventions aimed at increasing physical activity among low-SES adults must address these issues in addition to lifestyle and motivational factors.

Hardiness

What type of individual is likely to cope adaptively with stress brought on by the inevitable changes of life? Researchers interested in this question have identified a set of three personal qualities—control, commitment, and challenge—that, together, they call **hardiness** (Maddi, 2007, 2011, 2016). Together, the three hardiness attributes motivate people to try their best to turn life's stressors into opportunities for resilience.

Trisha fit the pattern of a hardy individual. First, she regarded most experiences as *controllable*. "You can't stop all bad things from happening," she advised Jewel after hearing about her menopausal symptoms, "but you can try to do something about them." Second, Trisha displayed a *committed*, involved approach to daily activities, finding meaning in almost all of them, even during stressful times. Finally, she viewed stressful changes as *challenges*—as occasions for learning and self-improvement.

Hardiness influences the extent to which people appraise stressful situations as manageable, interesting, even enjoyable. These optimistic appraisals, in turn, predict health-promoting behaviors, tendency to seek social support, reduced physiological arousal to stress, and fewer physical and emotional symptoms (Maddi, 2006; Maruta et al., 2002; Räikkönen et al., 1999; Smith, Young, & Lee, 2004). Furthermore, high-hardy individuals are likely to use active, problem-centered coping strategies in situations they can control. In contrast, low-hardy people more often use emotion-centered and avoidant coping strategies—for example, saying, "I wish I could change how I feel" or eating and drinking to distract themselves from the stressful event (Maddi, 2007; Soderstrom et al., 2000).

In this and previous chapters, we have seen that many factors act as stress-resistant resources—among them heredity, diet, exercise, social support, and coping strategies. Research on hardiness emphasizes an additional ingredient: a generally optimis-

In cities across the United States, barriers to physical activity are being overcome through the creation of attractive, safe parks and trails. But low-SES adults need greater access to convenient, pleasant exercise environments.

Social Issues: Health

The Silver Lining in Life's Adversities

Many adults, in recounting a difficult time in their lives, say that ultimately it made them stronger—an outcome confirmed by research. As long as serious adversity is not frequent and overwhelming, it can lead to remarkable personal benefits.

In a study carried out in France, researchers followed a nationally representative sample of 2,000 adults, ranging in age from 18 to 101, for four years (Seery, Holman & Silver, 2010). To assess *lifetime exposure to adversity*, participants were given a list of 37 negative life events and asked to indicate which ones they had experienced, how often, and the age at which each had occurred. The list focused on serious stressors—for example, violent assault, death of a loved one, severe financial difficulties, divorce, and major disasters such as fire, flood, or earthquake.

A year later, the researchers returned for a measure of *recent exposure to adversity*, asking participants to indicate how many negative life events they had experienced in the previous six months. Finally, once each year, participants' mental health and well-being were assessed.

Findings revealed that adults with a history of modest lifetime adversity exposure, compared to no adversity or high adversity, reported more favorable adjustment—less overall psychological distress, less functional impairment (compromised work and social activities due to poor physical and mental health), fewer post-traumatic stress symptoms, and greater life satisfaction (see Figure 15.5). Furthermore, people with modest lifetime adversity were less negatively affected by exposure to recent adversity. These outcomes remained after controlling for diverse factors that might influence experiences of adversity, including age, gender, ethnicity, marital status, SES, and physical health.

Experiencing modest levels of lifetime adversity seems to foster a sense of mastery, generating in people the hardiness, or toughness, needed to overcome future stressors (Mineka & Zinbarg, 2006). Adults with no history of adversity are deprived of vital opportunities for learning to manage life stressors, so they respond less optimally when faced with them. And high levels of lifetime adversity overtax people's coping skills, engulfing them with feelings of hopelessness and loss of control and interfering substantially with mental health and well-being.

In sum, having to grapple with occasional adverse life events is a vital source of resilience. It fortifies people with the personal attributes they need to surmount life stressors they are almost certain to encounter in the future.

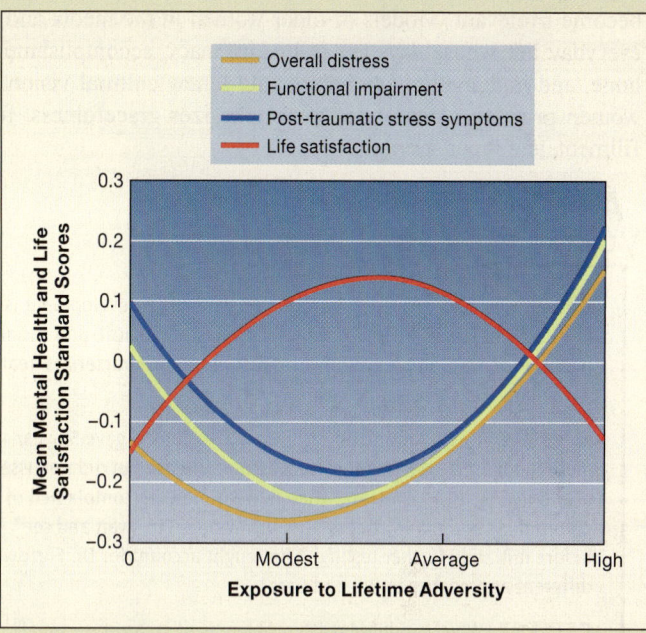

FIGURE 15.5 Relationship of lifetime adversity to mental health and life satisfaction. Among a large, nationally representative sample of French adults, modest lifetime adversity, compared to no or high adversity, predicted reduced overall distress, functional impairment, and post-traumatic stress symptoms and greater life satisfaction. (From M. D. Seery, E. A. Holman, & R. C. Silver, 2010, "Whatever Does Not Kill Us: Cumulative Lifetime Adversity, Vulnerability, and Resilience," *Journal of Personality and Social Psychology, 99*, p. 1030. Copyright © 2010 by the American Psychological Association. Adapted by permission.)

---

tic, determined, zestful approach to life. See the Social Issues: Health box above for research suggesting that experiencing a modest level of adversity can actually be life-enriching, perhaps because it promotes hardiness.

Gender and Aging: A Double Standard

Negative stereotypes of aging, which lead many middle-aged adults to fear physical changes, are more likely to be applied to women than to men, yielding a double standard (Antonucci, Blieszner, & Denmark, 2010). Though many women in midlife say they have "hit their stride"—feel assertive, confident, versatile, and capable of resolving life's problems—people often rate them as less attractive and as having more negative personality characteristics than middle-aged men (Denmark & Klara, 2007; Kite et al., 2005; Lemish & Muhlbauer, 2012).

The ideal of a sexually attractive woman—smooth skin, good muscle tone, lustrous hair—is the heart of the double standard of aging. The end of a woman's capacity to bear children contributes to negative judgments of physical appearance, especially by men (Marcus-Newhall, Thompson, & Thomas, 2001). Societal forces exaggerate this view. For example, middle-aged adults in media ads are usually male executives, fathers, and grandfathers—handsome images of competence and security. And the much larger array of cosmetic products and medical treatments offered to women to hide signs of aging may induce many to feel ashamed of their age and appearance (Chrisler, Barney, & Palatino, 2016).

At one time in our evolutionary history, this double standard may have been adaptive. Today, as many couples limit childbearing and devote more time to career and leisure pursuits, it has become irrelevant. Models of older women in the media and in everyday life whose days are full of intimacy, accomplishment, hope, and imagination can help create a new cultural vision of women growing older—one that emphasizes gracefulness, fulfillment, and inner strength.

Ask yourself

CONNECT According to the lifespan perspective, development is multidimensional—affected by biological, psychological, and social forces. Provide examples of how this assumption characterizes health at midlife.

APPLY During a routine physical exam, Dr. Furrow gave 55-year-old Bill a battery of tests for cardiovascular disease but did not assess his bone density. In contrast, when 60-year-old Cara complained of palpitations and panic attacks, Dr. Furrow opted to "wait and see" before initiating further testing. What might account for Dr. Furrow's different approaches to Bill and Cara?

REFLECT Which midlife health problem is of greatest personal concern to you? What steps can you take now to help prevent it?

COGNITIVE DEVELOPMENT

In middle adulthood, the cognitive demands of everyday life extend to new and sometimes more challenging situations. Consider a typical day in the lives of Devin and Trisha. Recently appointed dean of faculty at a small college, Devin was at his desk by 7:00 a.m. In between strategic-planning meetings, he reviewed files of applicants for new positions, worked on the coming year's budget, and spoke at an alumni luncheon. Meanwhile, Trisha prepared for a civil trial, participated in jury selection, and then joined other top lawyers at her firm for a conference about management issues. That evening, Trisha and Devin advised their 20-year-old son, Mark, who had dropped by to discuss his uncertainty over changing his college major. By 7:30 p.m., Trisha was off to an evening meeting of the local school board. And Devin left for a biweekly gathering of an amateur quartet in which he played the cello.

Middle adulthood is a time of expanding responsibilities—on the job, in the community, and at home. To juggle diverse roles effectively, Devin and Trisha called on a wide array of intellectual abilities, including accumulated knowledge, verbal fluency, memory, rapid analysis of information, reasoning, problem solving, and expertise in their areas of specialization. What changes in thinking take place in middle adulthood? How does vocational life—a major arena in which cognition is expressed—influence intellectual skills? And what can be done to support the rising tide of adults who are returning to higher education in hopes of enhancing their knowledge and quality of life?

Changes in Mental Abilities

15.8 Describe cohort effects on intelligence revealed by Schaie's Seattle Longitudinal Study.

15.9 Describe changes in crystallized and fluid intelligence in middle adulthood, and discuss individual and group differences in intellectual development.

At age 50, when he occasionally couldn't recall a name or had to pause in the middle of a lecture or speech to think about what to say next, Devin wondered, Are these signs of an aging mind? Twenty years earlier, he had taken little notice of the same events. His questioning stems from widely held stereotypes of older adults as forgetful and confused. Most cognitive aging research has focused on deficits while neglecting cognitive stability and gains.

As we examine changes in thinking in middle adulthood, we will revisit the theme of diversity in development. Different aspects of cognitive functioning show different patterns of change. Although declines occur in some areas, most people display cognitive competence, especially in familiar contexts, and some attain outstanding accomplishment. As we will see, certain apparent decrements in cognitive aging result from weaknesses in the research itself! Overall, the evidence supports an optimistic view of adult cognitive potential.

The research we are about to consider illustrates core assumptions of the lifespan perspective: development as *multidimensional*, or the combined result of biological, psychological, and social forces; development as *multidirectional*, or the joint expression of growth and decline, with the precise mix varying across abilities and individuals; and development as *plastic*, or open to change, depending on how a person's biological and environmental history combines with current life conditions.

Cohort Effects

Research using intelligence tests sheds light on the widely held belief that intelligence inevitably declines in middle and late adulthood as the brain deteriorates. Many early cross-sectional studies showed this pattern—a peak in performance at age 35 followed by a steep drop into old age. But widespread testing of college students and soldiers in the 1920s provided a convenient opportunity to conduct longitudinal research, retesting participants in middle adulthood. These findings revealed an age-related increase! To explain this contradiction, K. Warner Schaie (1998, 2005, 2016) used a sequential design, combining longitudinal and cross-sectional approaches (see page 36 in Chapter 1) in the Seattle Longitudinal Study.

In 1956, people ranging in age from 22 to 70 were tested cross-sectionally. Then, at regular intervals, longitudinal follow-ups were conducted and new samples added, yielding a total of 6,000 participants, five cross-sectional comparisons, and longitudinal data spanning more than 60 years. Findings on five

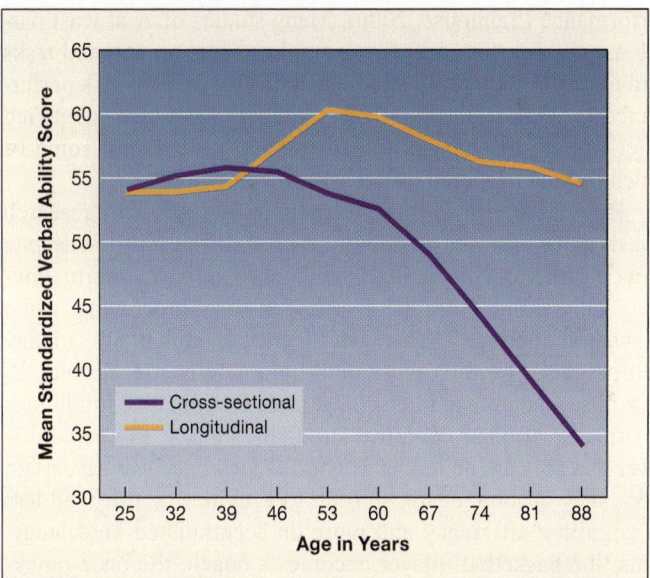

FIGURE 15.6 Cross-sectional and longitudinal trends in verbal ability, illustrating cohort effects. The steep cross-sectional decline is largely due to better health and education in younger generations. When adults are followed longitudinally, their verbal scores rise during early and middle adulthood and gradually decline during later years. However, this longitudinal trend does not hold for all abilities. (From K. W. Schaie, 1988, "Variability in Cognitive Functioning in the Elderly," in M. A. Bender, R. C. Leonard, & A. D. Woodhead [Eds.], *Phenotypic Variation in Populations*, p. 201. Adapted with kind permission from Springer Science+Business Media B. V. and K. W. Schaie.)

mental abilities showed the typical cross-sectional drop after the mid-thirties. But longitudinal trends for those abilities revealed modest gains in midlife, sustained into the fifties and the early sixties, after which performance decreased gradually.

Figure 15.6 illustrates Schaie's cross-sectional and longitudinal outcomes for just one intellectual factor: verbal ability. How can we explain the seeming contradiction in findings? *Cohort effects* are largely responsible for this difference. In cross-sectional research, each new generation experienced better health and education and more cognitively stimulating everyday experiences than the one before it (Schaie, 2013). Also, the tests given may tap abilities less often used by older individuals, whose lives no longer require that they learn information for its own sake but, instead, skillfully solve real-world problems.

Crystallized and Fluid Intelligence

A close look at diverse mental abilities shows that only certain ones follow the longitudinal pattern identified in Figure 15.6. To appreciate this variation, let's consider two broad mental abilities, each of which includes an array of specific intellectual factors.

The first of these broad abilities, **crystallized intelligence**, refers to skills that depend on accumulated knowledge and experience, good judgment, and mastery of social conventions—abilities acquired because they are valued by the individual's culture. Devin made use of crystallized intelligence when he expressed himself articulately at the alumni luncheon and suggested effective ways to save money in budget planning. On intelligence tests, vocabulary, general information, verbal comprehension, and logical reasoning items measure crystallized intelligence.

In contrast, **fluid intelligence** depends more heavily on basic information-processing skills—ability to detect relationships among visual stimuli, speed of analyzing information, and capacity of working memory. Though fluid intelligence often combines with crystallized intelligence to support effective reasoning and problem solving, it is believed to be influenced less by culture than by conditions in the brain and by learning unique to the individual (Horn & Noll, 1997). Intelligence test items reflecting fluid abilities include spatial visualization, digit span, letter–number sequencing, and symbol search. (Refer to page 315 in Chapter 9 for examples.)

Many cross-sectional studies show that crystallized intelligence increases steadily through middle adulthood, whereas fluid intelligence begins to decline in the twenties. These trends have been found repeatedly in investigations in which younger and older participants had similar education and general health status, largely correcting for cohort effects (Hartshorne & Germine, 2015; Miller et al., 2009; Park et al., 2002). In one such investigation, including nearly 2,500 mentally and physically healthy 16- to 85-year-olds, verbal (crystallized) IQ peaked between ages 45 and 54 and did not decline until the eighties! Nonverbal (fluid) IQ, in contrast, dropped steadily over the entire age range (Kaufman, 2001).

The midlife rise in crystallized abilities makes sense because adults are constantly adding to their knowledge and skills at work, at home, and in leisure activities. In addition, many crystallized skills are practiced almost daily. But does longitudinal evidence confirm the progressive falloff in fluid intelligence? And if so, how can we explain it?

Don Clarke, who flew attack helicopters in the U.S. army, fulfilled a long-held dream when he became an emergency medical service helicopter pilot. Flying search-and-rescue missions requires Clarke, in his early sixties, to make use of complex mental abilities that are at their peak in midlife.

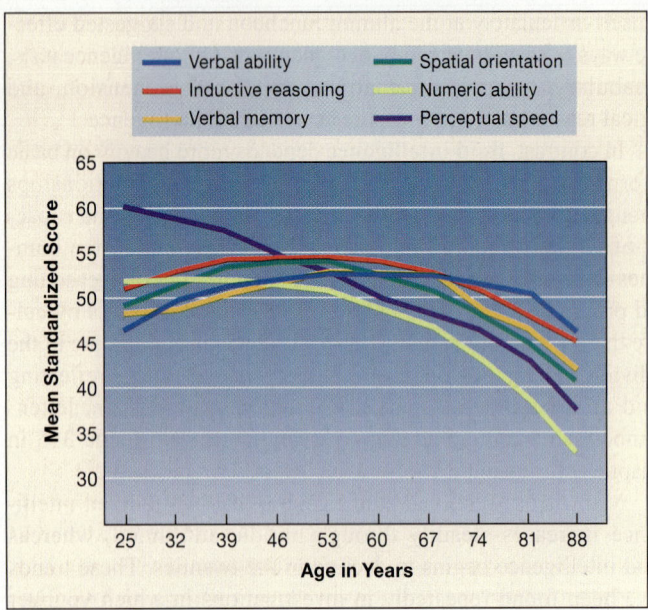

FIGURE 15.7 Longitudinal trends in six mental abilities, from the Seattle Longitudinal Study. In five abilities, modest gains occurred into the fifties and early sixties, followed by gradual declines. The sixth ability—perceptual speed—decreased steadily from the twenties to the late eighties. And late in life, fluid factors (spatial orientation, numeric ability, and perceptual speed) showed greater decrements than crystallized factors (verbal ability, inductive reasoning, and verbal memory). (From K. W. Schaie, 1994, "The Course of Adult Intellectual Development," *American Psychologist, 49,* p. 308. Copyright © 1994 by the American Psychological Association. Reprinted with permission of American Psychological Association.)

Schaie's Seattle Longitudinal Study. Figure 15.7 shows Schaie's longitudinal findings in detail. The five factors that gained in early and middle adulthood—verbal ability, inductive reasoning, verbal memory, spatial orientation, and numeric ability—include both crystallized and fluid skills. Their paths of change confirm that midlife is a time when some of the most complex mental abilities are at their peak (Schaie, 2013). According to these findings, middle-aged adults are intellectually "in their prime," not—as stereotypes would have it—"over the hill."

Figure 15.7 also shows a sixth ability, *perceptual speed*—a fluid skill in which participants must, for example, identify within a time limit which of five shapes is identical to a model or whether pairs of multidigit numbers are the same or different. Perceptual speed decreased from the twenties to the late eighties—a pattern that fits with a wealth of research indicating that cognitive processing slows as people get older (Schaie, 1998, 2005, 2013). Also notice in Figure 15.7 how, late in life, fluid factors (spatial orientation, numeric ability, and perceptual speed) show greater decrements than crystallized factors (verbal ability, inductive reasoning, and verbal memory). These trends have been confirmed in short-term longitudinal follow-ups of individuals varying widely in age (McArdle et al., 2002).

Explaining Changes in Mental Abilities. Some theorists believe that a general slowing of central nervous system functioning underlies nearly all age-related declines in cognitive performance (Salthouse, 2006). Many studies offer at least partial support for this idea. For example, scores on speeded tasks tend to mirror the overall age-related decline in fluid-task performance (Finkel et al., 2009). Researchers have also identified other important changes in information processing, some of which may be triggered by declines in speed.

Before we turn to this evidence, let's clarify why research reveals gains followed by stability in crystallized abilities, despite a much earlier decline in fluid intelligence, or basic information-processing skills. First, the decrease in basic processing, while substantial after age 45, may not be great enough to affect many well-practiced performances until quite late in life. Second, as we will see, adults can often compensate for cognitive limitations by drawing on their cognitive strengths. Finally, as people discover that they are no longer as good as they once were at certain tasks, they accommodate, shifting to activities that depend less on cognitive efficiency and more on accumulated knowledge. Thus, the basketball player becomes a coach, the once quick-witted salesperson a manager.

Individual and Group Differences

The age trends just described mask large individual differences. Some adults, because of illness or unfavorable environments, decline intellectually much earlier than others. And others sustain high functioning, even in fluid abilities, at advanced ages.

Adults who use their intellectual skills seem to maintain them longer. In the Seattle Longitudinal Study, declines were delayed for people with above-average education; complex, self-directed occupations; and stimulating leisure pursuits that included reading, traveling, attending cultural events, and participating in clubs and professional organizations. People with flexible personalities, lasting marriages (especially to a cognitively high-functioning partner), and absence of cardiovascular and other chronic diseases were also likely to maintain mental abilities well into late adulthood (Schaie, 2011, 2013, 2016). And being economically well-off was linked to favorable cognitive development, undoubtedly because SES is associated with many of the factors just mentioned.

Several gender differences also emerged, consistent with those found in childhood and adolescence. In early and middle adulthood, women outperformed men on verbal tasks and perceptual speed, whereas men excelled at spatial skills (Maitland et al., 2000). Overall, however, changes in mental abilities over the adult years were remarkably similar for the two sexes, defying the stereotype that older women are less competent than older men.

Furthermore, when the baby-boom generation, mostly middle-aged, was compared with the previous generation at the same age, cohort effects were evident. On verbal memory, inductive reasoning, and spatial orientation, baby boomers performed substantially better, reflecting generational advances in education, technology, environmental stimulation, and health care (Schaie, 2013, 2016). These gains are expected to continue: Today's children, adolescents, and adults of all ages attain higher mental test scores than same-age individuals born a decade or two earlier—differences that are largest for fluid-ability tasks (see page 319 in Chapter 9 to review evidence on the Flynn effect).

Finally, adults who maintained higher levels of perceptual speed tended to be advantaged in other cognitive capacities. As we turn to information processing in midlife, we will pay special attention to the impact of processing speed on other aspects of cognitive functioning.

Information Processing

15.10 How does information processing change in midlife?

15.11 Discuss the development of practical problem solving, expertise, and creativity in middle adulthood.

Many studies confirm that as processing speed slows, basic components of executive function decline. Yet midlife is also a time of great expansion in cognitive competence as adults apply their vast knowledge and life experience to problem solving in the everyday world.

Speed of Processing

Devin watched with fascination as his 20-year-old son, Mark, played a computer game, responding to multiple on-screen cues in rapid-fire fashion. When Devin tried it, though he practiced over several days, his performance remained well behind Mark's. Similarly, on a family holiday in Australia, Mark adjusted quickly to driving on the left side of the road, but after a week, Trisha and Devin still felt confused at intersections, where rapid responses were needed.

These real-life experiences fit with laboratory findings. On both simple reaction-time tasks (pushing a button in response to a light) and complex ones (pushing a left-hand button to a blue light, a right-hand button to a yellow light), response time increases steadily from the early twenties into the nineties. The more complex the reaction time task, the more disadvantaged older adults are. Although the decline in speed is gradual and quite small—less than 1 second in most studies—it is nevertheless of practical significance (Dykiert et al., 2012; Nissan, Liewald, & Deary, 2013).

What causes this age-related slowing of cognitive processing? Researchers agree that changes in the brain are responsible but disagree on the precise explanation. According to one view, aging is accompanied by withering of the myelin coating on neural fibers within the cerebral cortex, leading to deteriorating neural connections, especially in the prefrontal cortex and the corpus callosum. Mounting evidence indicates that in healthy older adults, extent of myelin breakdown—appearing as small, high-intensity bright spots within fMRIs—predicts decrements in reaction time and other cognitive abilities (Lu et al., 2013; Papp et al., 2014; Salami et al., 2012).

Another approach to age-related cognitive slowing suggests that older adults experience greater loss of information as it moves through the cognitive system. As a result, the whole system must slow down to inspect and interpret the information. Imagine making a photocopy, then using it to make another copy. Each subsequent copy is less clear. Similarly, with each step of thinking, information degrades. The older the adult, the more exaggerated this effect (Myerson et al., 1990). Complex tasks, which have more processing steps, are more affected by information loss. Possibly, multiple neural changes that vary across individuals underlie such information loss and associated declines in processing speed (Hartley, 2006; Salthouse, 2011).

Processing speed predicts adults' performance on many tests of complex abilities. The slower their reaction time, the lower people's scores on tests of memory, reasoning, and problem solving, with relationships greater for fluid- than crystallized-ability items (Nissan, Liewald, & Deary, 2013; Salthouse & Madden, 2008). Indeed, as adults get older, correlations between processing speed and other cognitive performances strengthen (see Figure 15.8) (Li et al., 2004). This suggests that processing speed contributes broadly to declines in cognitive functioning, which become more widespread and pronounced with aging.

Yet as Figure 15.8 shows, processing speed correlates only moderately with older adults' performances, including fluid-ability tasks. And it is not the only major predictor of age-related cognitive changes. Other factors—declines in vision and

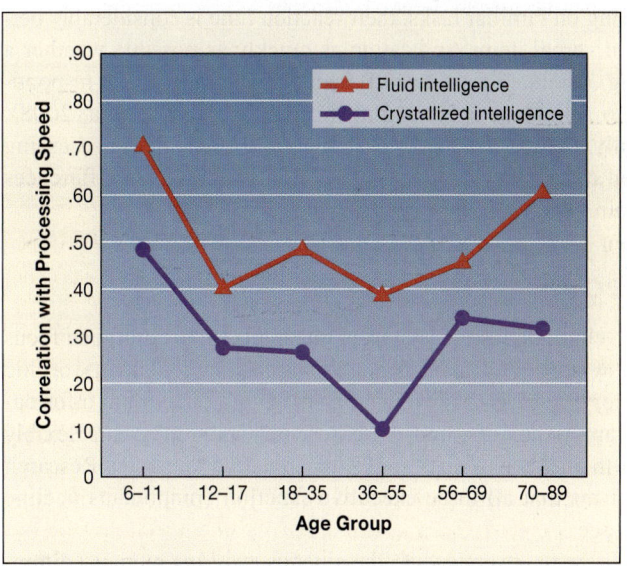

FIGURE 15.8 Age-related changes in correlations of processing speed with measures of fluid and crystallized intelligence. Correlations are higher at younger and at older ages. During childhood, gains in processing speed support development of other abilities and are related to mental test performance (see Chapter 9, page 315). As people age, declines in processing speed limit many abilities, but more so for fluid than crystallized skills. Note, however, that even at the oldest ages, correlations between processing speed and other abilities are moderate. (From S.-C. Li et al., 2004, "Transformations in the Couplings Among Intellectual Abilities and Constituent Cognitive Processes Across the Life Span," *Psychological Science, 15,* p. 160. Copyright © 2004, Sage Publications. Reprinted by Permission of SAGE Publications.)

hearing and in executive function, especially working-memory capacity—also predict diverse age-related cognitive performances (Reuter-Lorenz, Festini, & Jantz, 2016; Verhaeghen, 2016). Nevertheless, processing speed, as we will see in the following sections, contributes to decrements in working memory. Still, disagreement persists over whether age-related cognitive changes have one common cause, best represented by processing speed, or multiple independent causes.

Furthermore, processing speed is a weak predictor of the skill with which older adults perform complex, familiar tasks in everyday life, which they continue to do with considerable proficiency. Devin, for example, played a Mozart quartet on his cello with great speed and dexterity, keeping up with three other players 10 years his junior. How did he manage? Compared with the others, he more often looked ahead in the score (Krampe & Charness, 2007). Using this compensatory approach, he could prepare a response in advance, thereby minimizing the importance of speed. In one study, researchers asked 19- to 72-year-olds to perform a variety of typing tasks and also tested their reaction time. Although reaction time slowed with age, typing speed did not change (Salthouse, 1984). Like Devin, older typists look further ahead in the material to be typed, anticipating their next keystrokes. Knowledge and experience can also compensate for impairments in processing speed. Devin's many years of playing the cello undoubtedly supported his ability to play swiftly and fluidly.

Because older adults find ways to compensate for cognitive slowing on familiar tasks, their reaction time is considerably better on verbal items (indicating as quickly as possible whether a string of letters forms a word) than on nonverbal items (responding to a light or other signal) (Verhaeghen & Cerella, 2008). Finally, as we will see in Chapter 17, older adults' processing speed can be improved through training, though age differences remain.

Executive Function

As in childhood, studies of executive function in adulthood focus on how much information individuals can manipulate in working memory; the extent to which they can inhibit irrelevant information and behaviors; and the ease with which they can flexibly shift their focus of attention as the situation demands. Research confirms that all three executive function components decline with age.

From the twenties into the nineties, working memory diminishes steadily. Whether given verbal or spatial working-memory tasks, middle-aged and older adults perform less well than young adults. However, verbal working memory (for example, repeating a list of numerical digits backward) suffers much less than spatial working memory (remembering the locations of Xs, shown one at a time, in a computer-screen grid): Spatial performance declines at double the rate of verbal performance (Hale et al., 2011; Verhaeghen, 2014, 2016). As with reaction time on verbal items, verbal working memory may be better preserved because of task familiarity. Older adults have previously formed and often used verbal representations of the to-be-manipulated information (Kalpouzos & Nyberg, 2012). The necessary spatial representations, in contrast, are far less familiar.

Declines in working memory are strongly related to the slowdown in information processing described earlier (Verhaeghen, 2014). Reduced processing speed limits the amount of information a person can focus on at once. But other components of executive function also contribute to working-memory limitations.

As adults get older, inhibition—resistance to irrelevant information and impulses—is harder (Gazzaley et al., 2005; Hasher, Lustig, & Zacks, 2007). On *continuous performance tasks,* in which participants are shown a series of stimuli on a computer screen and asked to press the space bar only after a particular sequence occurs (for example, the letter *K* immediately followed by the letter *A*), performance declines steadily from the thirties on, with older adults making more errors of commission (pressing the space bar in response to incorrect letter sequences). And when extraneous noise is introduced, errors of omission (not pressing the space bar after a *K–A* sequence) also rise with age (Mani, Bedwell, & Miller, 2005). In everyday life, inhibitory difficulties cause older adults to appear distractible—inappropriately diverted from the task at hand by a thought or a feature of the environment.

Age-related deficits in inhibition lead working memory to be cluttered with irrelevant items, thereby reducing its capacity. And with age, adults not only have greater difficulty ignoring irrelevant stimuli but find it harder to remove no longer needed items from working memory (Verhaeghen, 2012; Verhaeghen & Cerella, 2002). In other words, they become less effective at *updating* their working memories as task conditions change and certain information becomes irrelevant.

Finally, flexibly shifting one's focus of attention becomes more challenging with age and is especially evident in situations where people must divide their attention between two activities. When Trisha tried to check her e-mail inbox while talking on the phone, the speed and accuracy with which she performed

In midlife, people require more effort to stay focused on relevant information and to flexibly shift their attention between activities. Years of experience in performing several activities at once enables this high school math teacher to compensate for age-related declines in executive function.

each activity declined considerably. Consistent with Trisha's experience, laboratory research reveals that sustaining two tasks simultaneously, when at least one of the tasks is complex, becomes more challenging with age. Older adults have difficulty even when they have recently engaged in extensive practice of one of the tasks and it is therefore expected to be automatic (Maquestiaux, 2016). Though not as large, an age-related decrement also occurs in switching back and forth between mental operations within a single task, such as judging one of a pair of numbers as "odd or even" on some trials, "more or less" on others (Verhaeghen & Cerella, 2008; Wasylyshyn, Verhaeghen, & Sliwinski, 2011). These declines in flexible shifting are likely affected by less effective inhibition, requiring older adults to exert more effort to stay focused on currently relevant aspects of tasks and to update that focus, as necessary.

But again, adults can compensate for these changes. People highly experienced in attending to critical information and performing several tasks at once, such as air traffic controllers and pilots, show smaller declines in inhibition and task-switching with age (Tsang & Shaner, 1998). Similarly, older adults handle two tasks proficiently when they have extensively practiced both of those activities over their lifetimes (Kramer & Madden, 2008).

Finally, practice can improve the ability to inhibit irrelevant information, divide attention between two tasks, and switch back and forth between mental operations. When older adults receive training in these skills, they improve as much as younger adults do, although training does not close the gap between age groups (Bherer et al., 2006; Erickson et al., 2007; Kramer, Hahn, & Gopher, 1998).

Memory Strategies

Memory is crucial for all aspects of information processing—an important reason that we place great value on a good memory in middle and late adulthood. But older adults' ability to recall studied information is impaired relative to younger adults', a change affected by a decline in use of memory strategies. Older individuals rehearse less than younger individuals—a difference believed to be affected by a slower rate of thinking, in that older people cannot repeat new information to themselves as quickly as younger people. A reduction in working-memory capacity is another influence, leading to difficulties in retaining to-be-remembered items and processing them at the same time (Basak & Verhaeghen, 2011).

Memory strategies of organization and elaboration, which require people to link incoming information with already stored information, are also applied less often and less effectively with age (Hertzog et al., 2010; Troyer et al., 2006). An additional reason older adults are less likely to use these techniques is that they find it harder to retrieve information from long-term memory that would help them recall. For example, given a list of words containing *parrot* and *blue jay*, they don't immediately access the category "bird," even though they know it well (Hultsch et al., 1998). Why does this happen? Greater difficulty keeping one's attention on relevant information seems to be involved (Hasher, Lustig, & Zacks, 2007). As irrelevant stimuli take up space in working memory, less is available for the memory task at hand.

But keep in mind that the memory tasks given by researchers require strategies that many adults seldom use and may not be motivated to use, since most are not in school (see Chapter 9, page 311). When a word list has a strong category-based structure, older adults organize as well as younger adults do (Naveh-Benjamin et al., 2005). And when given training in strategic memorizing, middle-aged and older people use strategies willingly, and they show improved performance over long periods, though age differences remain (Naveh-Benjamin, Brav, & Levy, 2007).

Furthermore, tasks can be designed to help older people compensate for age-related declines in working memory—for example, by slowing the pace at which information is presented or cuing the link between new and previously stored information ("To learn these words, try thinking of the category 'bird'"). In one study, adults ranging in age from 19 to 68 were shown a video and immediately tested on its content (a pressured, classroomlike condition). Then they were given a packet of information on the same topic as the video to study at their leisure and told to return three days later to be tested (a self-paced condition) (Beier & Ackerman, 2005). Performance declined with age only in the pressured condition, not in the self-paced condition. And although topic-relevant knowledge predicted better recall in both conditions, it did so more strongly in the self-paced condition, which granted participants ample time to retrieve and apply what they already knew.

LOOK and LISTEN

Ask several adults in their fifties or early sixties to list their top three everyday memory challenges and to explain what they do to enhance recall. How knowledgeable are these midlifers about effective memory strategies?

As these findings illustrate, assessing older adults in highly structured, constrained conditions substantially underestimates what they can remember when given opportunities to pace and direct their own learning. When we consider the variety of memory skills we call on in daily life, the decrements just described are limited in scope. *Semantic memory* (general knowledge base), *procedural memory* (such as how to drive a car or solve a math problem), and memory related to one's occupation either remain unchanged or increase into midlife.

Furthermore, middle-aged people who have trouble recalling something often draw on decades of accumulated *metacognitive knowledge* about how to maximize memory—reviewing major points before an important presentation, organizing notes and files so information can be found quickly, and focusing on the most useful information to retain at the expense of less useful information. Research confirms that aging has little impact on metacognitive knowledge and the ability to apply such knowledge to improve learning (Blake & Castel, 2016; Horhota et al., 2012).

In sum, age-related changes in memory vary widely across tasks and individuals as people use their cognitive capacities to meet the requirements of their everyday worlds. Does this remind you of Sternberg's *theory of successful intelligence,* described in Chapter 9—in particular, his notion of *practical intelligence* (see page 316)? Intelligent people adapt their information-processing skills to fit with their personal desires and the demands of their environments. Therefore, to understand memory development (and other aspects of cognition) in adulthood, we must view it in context. As we turn to problem solving, expertise, and creativity, we will encounter this theme again.

Practical Problem Solving and Expertise

One morning, Devin and Trish noticed a front-page article about their local circuit court chief justice. Elected to the bench when she turned 50, Beth had spearheaded a succession of groundbreaking programs during the previous decade. To prevent clogging of the courts with small claims, she brought judicial leaders together to create a small claims mediation program. To lessen prison overcrowding and promote recovery, she formed a criminal justice council and guided it in establishing a drug court program for nonviolent substance abusers. In lieu of a sentence, they reported to a treatment center, submitted to frequent drug testing, and met regularly with their probation officer. In these and other ways, Beth made the court system more efficient and effective, saving millions in tax dollars.

Beth's story is impressive, but many middle-aged adults display continued cognitive growth in the realm of **practical problem solving,** which requires people to size up real-world situations and analyze how best to achieve goals that have a high degree of uncertainty. Gains in *expertise*—an extensive, highly organized, and integrated knowledge base that can be used to support a high level of performance—help us understand why practical problem solving takes this leap forward.

The development of expertise is under way in early adulthood and reaches its height in midlife, leading to highly efficient and effective approaches to solving problems that are organized around abstract principles and intuitive judgments. Saturated with experience, the expert intuitively feels when an approach to a problem will work and when it will not. This rapid, implicit application of knowledge is typically the result of high ability in the domain of expertise plus years of learning, experience, and effortful practice (Krampe & Charness, 2007; Wai, 2014). It cannot be assessed by laboratory tasks or mental tests that do not call on this knowledge.

Expertise is not just the province of the highly educated and of those who rise to the top of administrative ladders. In a study of food service workers, researchers identified the diverse ingredients of expert performance in terms of physical skills (strength and dexterity); technical knowledge (of menu items, ordering, and food presentation); organizational skills (setting priorities, anticipating customer needs); and social skills (confident presentation and a pleasant, polished manner). Next, 20- to 60-year-olds with fewer than two to more than ten years of experience were evaluated on these qualities. Although physical strength and dexterity declined with age, job knowledge and organizational and social skills increased (Perlmutter, Kaplan, & Nyquist, 1990). Compared to younger adults with similar years of experience, middle-aged employees performed more competently, serving customers in especially adept, attentive ways.

Midlife advantages are also evident in solutions to everyday problems (Mienaltowski, 2011; Thornton, Paterson, & Yeung, 2013). Drawing on their greater life experience, middle-aged adults are especially adept at examining everyday dilemmas from different perspectives and solving them through logical analysis. Perhaps for these reasons, midlifers are more rational everyday decision makers—less likely than younger adults, and often older adults as well, to select attractive-looking options that, on further reflection, are not the best. Consider, for example, financial decision making: In evaluating options for home and auto loans and credit cards, middle-aged adults make better choices than both their younger and older counterparts, borrowing at lower interest rates and paying lower fees—even after other relevant factors, such as credit rating and income, are controlled (Agarwal et al., 2007).

Creativity

As noted in Chapter 13, creative accomplishment tends to peak in the late thirties or early forties and then decline, but with considerable variation across individuals and disciplines. Some people produce highly creative works in later decades: In her early sixties, Martha Graham choreographed *Clytemnestra,* recognized as one of the great full-length modern-dance dramas. Igor Stravinsky composed his last major musical work at age 84. Charles Darwin finished *On the Origin of Species* at age 50 and

Middle-aged adults may experience a decrease in creative output, but their creativity often becomes more deliberately thoughtful. This glassblower produces handcrafted works of art involving multiple steps, great patience, and technical precision.

continued to write groundbreaking books and papers in his sixties and seventies. Harold Gregor, who painted the dazzling image on the cover of this book, continues to invent new styles and to be a highly productive artist at age 87. And as with problem solving, the *quality* of creativity may change with advancing age—in at least three ways.

First, youthful creativity in literature and the arts is often spontaneous and intensely emotional, while creative works produced after age 40 often appear more deliberately thoughtful. Perhaps for this reason, poets produce their most frequently cited works at younger ages than do authors of fiction and nonfiction (Kozbelt, 2016; Lubart & Sternberg, 1998). Poetry depends more on language play and "hot" expression of feelings, whereas story- and book-length works require extensive planning and molding.

Second, with age, many creators shift from generating unusual products to combining extensive knowledge and experience into unique ways of thinking (Sasser-Coen, 1993). Creative works by older adults more often sum up or integrate ideas. Mature academics typically devote less energy to new discoveries in favor of writing memoirs, histories of their field, and other reflective works. And in older creators' novels, scholarly writings, and commentaries about their paintings and musical compositions, learning from life experience and living with old age are common themes (Lindauer, Orwoll, & Kelley, 1997; Sternberg & Lubart, 2001).

Finally, creativity in middle adulthood frequently reflects a transition from a largely egocentric concern with self-expression to more altruistic goals (Tahir & Gruber, 2003). As the middle-aged person overcomes the youthful illusion that life is eternal, the desire to give to humanity and enrich the lives of others increases.

Taken together, these changes may contribute to an overall decline in creative output in later decades. In reality, however, creativity takes new forms.

Information Processing in Context

Cognitive gains in middle adulthood are especially likely in areas involving experience-based buildup and transformation of knowledge and skills. As the evidence just reviewed confirms, processing speed varies with the situation. When given challenging real-world problems related to their expertise, middle-aged adults are likely to win out in both efficiency and excellence of thinking. Furthermore, on tasks and test items relevant to their real-life endeavors, intelligent, cognitively active midlifers respond as competently and nearly as quickly as their younger counterparts do!

By middle age, people's past and current experiences vary enormously—more so than in previous decades—and thinking is characterized by an increase in specialization as people branch out in various directions. Yet to reach their cognitive potential, adults must have opportunities for continued growth. Let's see how vocational and educational environments can support cognition in midlife.

Ask yourself

CONNECT In which aspects of cognition do middle-aged adults typically decline, and in which do they gain? How do those changes reflect assumptions of the lifespan perspective?

APPLY Asked about hiring middle-aged sales personnel, a department store manager replied, "They're my best employees!" Why does this manager find older employees desirable, despite age-related declines in processing speed and executive function?

Vocational Life and Cognitive Development

15.12 Describe the relationship between vocational life and cognitive development.

Vocational settings are vital contexts for maintaining previously acquired skills and learning new ones. Yet work environments vary in the degree to which they are cognitively stimulating and promote autonomy. And inaccurate, negative stereotypes of age-related problem-solving and decision-making skills can result in older employees being assigned less challenging work.

Recall from Chapter 13 that personality characteristics, including preference for certain cognitive activities, influence occupational choice. Once a person is immersed in a job, it influences cognition. In a study of a large sample of U.S. men in diverse occupations, researchers asked about the complexity and self-direction of their jobs. During the interview, they also assessed cognitive flexibility, based on logical reasoning, awareness of both sides of an issue, and independence of judgment. Two decades later, the job and cognitive variables were remeasured, permitting a look at their effects on each other (Schooler, Mulatu, & Oates, 2004). Findings revealed that complex work augmented later cognitive flexibility more than cognitive flexibility influenced preference for complex work.

Similar findings emerged in large-scale studies carried out in Japan and Poland—cultures quite different from the United States (Kohn, 2006; Kohn et al., 1990). In each nation, having a stimulating, nonroutine job helped explain the relationship between SES and flexible, abstract thinking. Furthermore, people in their fifties and early sixties benefit cognitively from challenging work just as much as those in their twenties and thirties (Avolio & Sosik, 1999; Miller, Slomczynski, & Kohn, 1985).

Mentally stimulating work requires middle-aged and older adults to grapple with novel situations. Continuously confronting complex, novel tasks predicts gains in cognitive flexibility and reduces the age-related decline in fluid abilities, with these effects extending for a decade or more after retirement (Bowen, Noack, & Staudinger, 2011; Fisher et al., 2014). And in an investigation of World War II veterans, those scoring lower in IQ in early adulthood derived greater long-term benefits from an intellectually demanding work life (Potter, Helms, & Plassman,

2008). Compared to their higher-IQ agemates, they showed a stronger positive association between stimulating work and cognitive performance after retiring.

Once again, we are reminded of the plasticity of development. Cognitive flexibility is responsive to work experiences well into middle adulthood and perhaps beyond. Designing jobs to promote intellectual stimulation and challenge may be a powerful means of fostering higher cognitive functioning later in the lifespan.

Adult Learners: Becoming a Student in Midlife

15.13 Discuss the challenges that adults face in returning to college, ways to support returning students, and benefits of earning a degree in midlife.

Adults are returning to undergraduate and graduate study in record numbers. During the past three decades, students age 25 and older in U.S. colleges and universities increased from 27 to 40 percent of total enrollment, with an especially sharp rise in those over age 35 (U.S. Department of Education, 2015). Life transitions often trigger a return to formal education, as with Devin and Trisha's friend Anya, who entered a nursing program after her last child left home. Early marriage (which often disrupts women's educational pathways), divorce, widowhood, a job layoff, a return from military service, a family move, a youngest child reaching school age, older children entering college, and rapid changes in the job market are other events that commonly precede reentry (Hostetler, Sweet, & Moen, 2007; Lorentzen, 2014).

Characteristics of Returning Students

Nearly 60 percent of adult learners are women (U.S. Department of Education, 2015). As Anya's concerns about being able to handle class work suggest (see page 507), many reentry women report feeling self-conscious, inadequate, and hesitant to talk in class. Their anxiety stems partly from not having practiced academic learning for many years and partly from negative aging and gender stereotypes—erroneous beliefs that traditional-age students are smarter or that men are more logical and therefore more academically capable (Compton, Cox, & Laanan, 2006). And for minority students, ethnic stereotypes about ability to learn and prejudicial treatment are also factors.

Role demands outside of school—from children, spouses, other family members, friends, and employers—pull many returning women in conflicting directions. Those reporting high stress typically are single parents with limited financial resources, or married women with high career aspirations, young children, and nonsupportive partners (Deutsch & Schmertz, 2011). When couples fail to rework divisions of household and child-care responsibilities to accommodate the woman's return to school, marital satisfaction declines (Sweet & Moen, 2007). As a classmate remarked to Anya, "I tried keeping the book open and reading, cooking, and talking to the kids. It didn't work. So I had to say to Bill, 'Can't you put in a load of laundry once in a while, get home earlier on just some nights?' He forgets—I went through his going to graduate school!"

Because of multiple demands on their time, mature-age women, especially those with children still at home, tend to take fewer credits, experience more interruptions in their academic programs, and progress at a slower pace than mature-age men. Role overload is the most common reason for not completing their degrees (Bergman, Rose, & Shuck, 2015). But many express high motivation to work through those difficulties, referring to the excitement of learning, to the fulfillment academic success brings, and to their hope that a college education will improve both their work and family lives (Kinser & Deitchman, 2007).

> **LOOK and LISTEN**
>
> Interview a nontraditional student on your campus about the personal challenges and rewards of working toward a degree at a later age.

Supporting Returning Students

As these findings suggest, social supports for returning students can make the difference between continuing in school and dropping out. Adult students need family members and friends who encourage their efforts and enable them to find time for uninterrupted study. Anya's classmate explained, "My doubts subsided when one day, Bill volunteered, 'You take your books and do what you need to do. I can cook dinner and do the laundry.'" Institutional services for returning students are

This 50-year-old, a full-time undergraduate at Mount Holyoke College, is one of many nontraditional students in U.S. colleges and universities. Appropriate academic advising and encouragement from family members, friends, and faculty help middle-aged learners succeed.

Applying what we Know

Facilitating Adult Reentry to College

SOURCES OF SUPPORT	DESCRIPTION
Partner and children	Value and encourage educational efforts.
	Help with household tasks to permit time for uninterrupted study.
Extended family and friends	Value and encourage educational efforts.
Educational institution	Provide orientation programs and written information that inform adult students about services and social supports.
	Provide counseling and intervention addressing academic weaknesses, self-doubts about success, and matching courses to career goals.
	Facilitate peer networks through regular meetings, phone, and online contacts.
	Promote personal relationships with faculty.
	Encourage active engagement and discussion in classes and integration of course content with real-life experiences.
	Offer evening, Saturday, and off-campus classes and online courses.
	Provide financial aid for returning students, including those enrolled part-time.
	Initiate campaigns to recruit returning students, including those from low-income families and ethnic minority groups.
	Help students with young children find child-care arrangements and provide on-campus child care.
Workplace	Value and encourage educational efforts.
	Offer flexible work schedules to make possible coordination of job, educational, and family responsibilities.

also essential. Personal relationships with faculty, peer networks with other nontraditional students, evening and Saturday classes, online courses, and financial aid for returning students, including those enrolled part-time, increase the chances of academic success.

Although nontraditional students rarely require assistance in settling on career goals, they report a strong desire for help in choosing the most appropriate courses and for small, discussion-based classes that meet their learning and relationship needs. Academic advising and professional internship opportunities are vital, strongly affecting persistence (Bergman, Rose, & Shuck, 2015). Students from low-SES backgrounds often need special assistance, such as academic tutoring, sessions in confidence building and assertiveness, and—in the case of ethnic minorities—help adjusting to styles of learning that are at odds with their cultural background.

Applying What We Know above suggests ways to facilitate adult reentry to college. When support systems are in place, most returning students reap great personal benefits and do well academically. Succeeding at coordinating education, family, and work demands leads to gains in self-efficacy and admiration from family members, friends, and co-workers (Chao & Good, 2004). Nontraditional students especially value forming new relationships, sharing opinions and experiences, and relating subject matter to their own lives. Their greater ability to integrate knowledge results in an enhanced appreciation of classroom experiences and assignments (Knowles, Swanson, & Holton, 2011). And their presence in college classes provides valuable intergenerational contact. As younger students observe the capacities and talents of older classmates, unfavorable stereotypes of aging decline.

After finishing her degree, Anya secured a position as a parish nurse with creative opportunities to counsel members of a large congregation about health concerns. Education granted her new life options, financial rewards, and higher self-esteem as she reevaluated her own competencies. Sometimes (though not in Anya's case) these revised values and increased self-reliance can spark other changes, such as a divorce or a new intimate partnership. In middle adulthood as in earlier years, education transforms development, often profoundly reshaping the life course.

Ask yourself

CONNECT Most high-level government and corporate positions are held by middle-aged and older adults rather than by young adults. What cognitive capacities enable mature adults to perform these jobs well?

APPLY Marcella completed one year of college in her twenties. Now, at age 42, she has returned to earn a degree. Plan a set of experiences for Marcella's first semester that will increase her chances of success.

REFLECT What range of services does your institution offer to support nontraditional-age students? What additional supports would you recommend?

Summary / chapter 15

PHYSICAL DEVELOPMENT

Physical Changes (p. 508)

15.1 Describe the physical changes of middle adulthood, paying special attention to vision, hearing, the skin, muscle–fat makeup, and the skeleton.

- The gradual physical changes begun in early adulthood continue in midlife, contributing to a revised physical self-image, with less emphasis on hoped-for gains and more on feared declines.

- Vision is affected by **presbyopia** (loss of the accommodative ability of the lens), reduced vision in dim light, increased sensitivity to glare, and diminished color discrimination. Risk of **glaucoma** increases.

- Age-related hearing loss, or **presbycusis,** begins with a decline in detection of high frequencies and then spreads to other tones. The ability to distinguish sounds occurring in close succession also recedes, and eventually, human speech becomes harder to decipher.

- The skin wrinkles, loosens, and dries. Age spots develop, especially in women and in people exposed to the sun.

- Muscle mass declines and fat deposits increase, with notable sex differences in fat distribution. A low-fat diet and regular exercise, including resistance training, can offset both excess weight and muscle loss.

- Bone density declines, especially in women after menopause. Height loss and bone fractures can result.

15.2 Describe reproductive changes in both sexes, along with associated physical and emotional symptoms, during middle adulthood.

- The **climacteric** in women, which occurs gradually as estrogen production drops and concludes with **menopause,** is often accompanied by physical and emotional symptoms, including hot flashes and depressive episodes. These reactions, however, vary widely with ethnicity and culture, SES, psychological stress, attitudes toward menopause, and other factors.

- **Hormone therapy** can reduce the discomforts of menopause, but its use increases the risk of cardiovascular disease, certain cancers, and cognitive declines.

- Although sperm production continues throughout life, quantity of semen diminishes, and more stimulation is required for an erection. Drugs are available to combat impotence, a condition that can undermine self-image.

Health and Fitness (p. 514)

15.3 Discuss sexuality in middle adulthood and its association with relationship satisfaction.

- Frequency of sexual activity among heterosexual couples declines only modestly in middle adulthood. Intensity of sexual response also diminishes, yet most married people over age 50 say that sex is an important part of a healthy couple relationship.

15.4 Discuss cancer, cardiovascular disease, and osteoporosis, noting risk factors and interventions.

- The death rate from cancer multiplies tenfold from early to middle adulthood. Heredity, biological aging, and environment all contribute to cancer. Today, 60 percent of affected individuals are cured. Regular screenings and various preventive steps can reduce the incidence of cancer and cancer deaths.

- Cardiovascular disease is a major cause of death in middle adulthood, especially among men. Symptoms include high blood pressure, high blood cholesterol, atherosclerosis, heart attack, arrhythmia, and angina pectoris. Quitting smoking, reducing blood cholesterol, exercising, and reducing stress can decrease risk and aid in treatment. Women experiencing a heart attack are often overlooked, misdiagnosed, or insufficiently treated.

- **Osteoporosis** affects 10 percent of people age 50 and older, primarily women. Adequate calcium and vitamin D, weight-bearing exercise, resistance training, and bone-strengthening medications can help prevent and treat osteoporosis.

15.5 Discuss the association of hostility and anger with heart disease and other health problems.

- Expressed hostility and a socially dominant interactive style, components of the **Type A behavior pattern,** predict heart disease and other health problems. Anger suppression is also related to health problems; a better alternative is to develop effective ways of handling stress and conflict.

Adapting to the Physical Challenges of Midlife (p. 520)

15.6 Discuss the benefits of stress management, exercise, and hardiness in dealing effectively with the physical challenges of midlife.

- Effective stress management includes both problem-centered and emotion-centered coping, constructive approaches to anger reduction, and social support. In middle adulthood, people tend to cope with stress more effectively, often reporting lasting personal benefits.

- Regular exercise offers physical and psychological advantages, making it worthwhile for sedentary middle-aged people to begin exercising. Developing a sense of self-efficacy and having access to convenient, safe, and attractive exercise environments promote physical activity.

- **Hardiness** includes three personal qualities—control, commitment, and challenge—that motivate people to turn life's stressors into opportunities for resilience. A modest level of lifetime adversity seems to promote hardiness.

15.7 *Explain the double standard of aging.*

- Middle-aged women are more likely than their male counterparts to be viewed unfavorably, especially by men.

COGNITIVE DEVELOPMENT

Changes in Mental Abilities (p. 524)

15.8 *Describe cohort effects on intelligence revealed by Schaie's Seattle Longitudinal Study.*

- Early cross-sectional research showed a peak in intelligence test performance at age 35 followed by a steep decline, whereas longitudinal evidence revealed modest gains in midlife. Using a sequential design, Schaie found that the cross-sectional, steep drop-off largely resulted from cohort effects, as each new generation experienced better health and education and more cognitively stimulating experiences.

15.9 *Describe changes in crystallized and fluid intelligence in middle adulthood, and discuss individual and group differences in intellectual development.*

- **Crystallized intelligence,** which depends on accumulated knowledge and experience, gains steadily through middle adulthood. In contrast, **fluid intelligence,** which depends more on basic information-processing skills, begins to decline in the twenties.
- In the Seattle Longitudinal Study, perceptual speed undergoes a steady, continuous decline. But other fluid skills, in addition to crystallized abilities, increase through middle adulthood, confirming that midlife is a time of peak performance on a variety of complex abilities.
- Midlifers' intellectual development is multidimensional, multidirectional, and plastic. Illness and unfavorable environments are linked to intellectual declines; stimulating occupations and leisure pursuits, flexible personalities, lasting marriages, good health, and economic advantage predict favorable cognitive development.

- In early and middle adulthood, women outperform men on verbal tasks and perceptual speed, whereas men excel at spatial skills. Gains in certain intellectual skills by baby boomers relative to the previous generation reflect advances in education, technology, environmental stimulation, and health care.

Information Processing (p. 527)

15.10 *How does information processing change in midlife?*

- Speed of cognitive processing slows with age. According to one view, deteriorating neuronal connections, due to myelin breakdown, reduce reaction time. Another approach suggests that older adults experience greater loss of information as it moves through the cognitive system, resulting in slower processing.
- As processing speed slows, people perform less well on memory, reasoning, and problem-solving tasks, especially fluid-ability items. But other factors also predict age-related cognitive performances.
- Executive function declines with age: working memory diminishes, and inhibition and flexible shifting of attention become more challenging.

- Compared with younger individuals, older adults less often use memory strategies, resulting in decreased recall of studied information. But training, improved design of tasks, and metacognitive knowledge enable older adults to compensate for age-related decrements.

15.11 *Discuss the development of practical problem solving, expertise, and creativity in middle adulthood.*

- Middle-aged adults display continued growth in **practical problem solving,** largely due to gains in expertise. Creativity becomes more deliberately thoughtful and often shifts from generating unusual products to integrating ideas, and from concern with self-expression to more altruistic goals.

Vocational Life and Cognitive Development (p. 531)

15.12 *Describe the relationship between vocational life and cognitive development.*

- Well into middle adulthood, stimulating, complex work augments flexible, abstract thinking. It also reduces the age-related decline in fluid abilities.

Adult Learners: Becoming a Student in Midlife (p. 532)

15.13 *Discuss the challenges that adults face in returning to college, ways to support returning students, and benefits of earning a degree in midlife.*

- Adults returning to college and graduate school are more often women. Returning students must cope with a lack of recent practice at academic work; negative stereotypes of aging, gender, and ethnicity; and demands of multiple roles.
- Social support from family and friends and institutional services can help returning students succeed. Further education results in enhanced competencies, new relationships, intergenerational contact, and reshaped life paths.

Important Terms and Concepts

climacteric (p. 510)
crystallized intelligence (p. 525)
fluid intelligence (p. 525)
glaucoma (p. 509)

hardiness (p. 522)
hormone therapy (p. 512)
menopause (p. 510)
osteoporosis (p. 519)

practical problem solving (p. 530)
presbycusis (p. 509)
presbyopia (p. 508)
Type A behavior pattern (p. 519)

chapter 16

Emotional and Social Development in Middle Adulthood

Midlife is a time of increased generativity—giving to and guiding younger generations. At a nonprofit bike store in an economically disadvantaged neighborhood, a volunteer derives a deep sense of satisfaction from providing youths with free bikes, and teaching them how to care for them.

What's ahead in chapter 16

Erikson's Theory: Generativity versus Stagnation

- ■ **SOCIAL ISSUES: HEALTH** Generative Adults Tell Their Life Stories

Other Theories of Psychosocial Development in Midlife

Levinson's Seasons of Life • Vaillant's Adaptation to Life • Is There a Midlife Crisis? • Stage or Life Events Approach

Stability and Change in Self-Concept and Personality

Possible Selves • Self-Acceptance, Autonomy, and Environmental Mastery • Coping with Daily Stressors • Gender Identity • Individual Differences in Personality Traits

- ■ **BIOLOGY AND ENVIRONMENT** What Factors Promote Psychological Well-Being in Midlife?

Relationships at Midlife

Marriage and Divorce • Changing Parent–Child Relationships • Grandparenthood • Middle-Aged Children and Their Aging Parents • Siblings • Friendships

- ■ **SOCIAL ISSUES: HEALTH** Grandparents Rearing Grandchildren: The Skipped-Generation Family

Vocational Life

Job Satisfaction • Career Development • Career Change at Midlife • Unemployment • Planning for Retirement

One weekend when Devin, Trisha, and their 24-year-old son, Mark, were vacationing together, the two middle-aged parents knocked on Mark's hotel room door. "Your dad and I are off to see a crafts exhibit," Trisha explained. "Feel free to stay behind," she offered, recalling Mark's dislike for such events as an adolescent. "We'll be back around noon for lunch."

"That exhibit sounds great!" Mark replied. "I'll meet you in the lobby."

"Sometimes I forget he's an adult!" exclaimed Trisha as she and Devin returned to their room to grab their coats. "It's been great to have Mark with us—like spending time with a good friend."

In their forties and fifties, Trisha and Devin built on earlier strengths and intensified their commitment to leave a legacy for others. When Mark faced a difficult job market after graduating from college, he returned home to live with Trisha and Devin and remained there for several years. With their support, he took graduate courses while working part-time, found steady employment in his late twenties, fell in love, and married in his mid-thirties. With each milestone, Trisha and Devin felt a sense of pride at having escorted a member of the next generation into responsible adult roles. Family activities, which had declined during Mark's adolescent and college years, increased as Trisha and Devin related to their son as an enjoyable adult companion. Challenging careers and more time for community involvement, leisure pursuits, and each other contributed to a richly diverse and gratifying time of life.

The midlife years were not as smooth for two of Trisha and Devin's friends. Approaching age 50 and fearing that she might grow old alone, Jewel frantically pursued her quest for an intimate partner. She attended singles events, used online dating services, and traveled in hopes of meeting a like-minded companion. Jewel also had compensating satisfactions—friendships that had grown more meaningful, a warm relationship with a nephew and niece, and a successful consulting business.

Tim, Devin's best friend from graduate school, had been divorced for over five years. Recently, he had met Elena and had come to love her deeply. But Elena was in the midst of major life changes. In addition to her own divorce, she was dealing with a troubled daughter and a career change. Whereas Tim had reached the peak of his career and was ready to enjoy life, Elena wanted to recapture much of what she had missed in earlier decades, including opportunities to realize her talents. "I don't know where I fit into Elena's plans," Tim wondered aloud on the phone with Trisha.

With the arrival of middle adulthood, half or more of the lifespan is over. Increasing awareness of limited time ahead prompts adults to reevaluate the meaning of their lives, refine and strengthen their identities, and reach out to future generations. Most middle-aged people make modest adjustments in their outlook, goals, and daily lives.

But some experience profound inner turbulence and initiate major changes, often in an effort to make up for lost time. Together with advancing years, family and work transitions contribute greatly to emotional and social development.

More midlifers are addressing these tasks than ever before, now that the majority of baby boomers are in their fifties and sixties (see page 12 in Chapter 1 to review how baby boomers have reshaped the life course). And the current midlife generation is healthier, better educated, and—despite the late-2000s economic recession—more financially secure than any previous midlife cohort (Mitchell, 2016). As our discussion will reveal, they have brought increased self-confidence, social consciousness, and vitality—along with great developmental diversity—to this period of the lifespan.

A monumental survey called *Midlife Development in the United States (MIDUS),* conducted in the mid-1990s, has contributed enormously to our understanding of midlife emotional and social development. Conceived by a team of researchers spanning diverse fields, including psychology, sociology, anthropology, and medicine, the aim of MIDUS was to generate new knowledge on the challenges faced by middle-aged adults. Its nationally representative sample included over 7,000 U.S. 25- to 75-year-olds, enabling those in the middle years to be compared with younger and older individuals. Through telephone interviews and self-administered questionnaires, participants responded to over 1,100 items addressing wide-ranging psychological, health, and background factors, yielding unprecedented breadth of information in a single study. The research endeavor also included "satellite" studies, in which subsamples of respondents were questioned in greater depth on key topics. And it was extended longitudinally, with 75 percent of the sample recontacted in the early to mid-2000s. In the early 2010s, researchers expanded the MIDUS sample to include over 3,500 additional U.S. participants (Delaney, 2014). Around the same time, they launched a Japanese offshoot, called Midlife in Japan (MIDJA), consisting of over 1,000 participants.

MIDUS has greatly enriched our knowledge of the *multidimensional* and *multidirectional* nature of midlife change, and it promises to be a rich source of information about middle adulthood and beyond for many years to come. Hence, our discussion repeatedly draws on MIDUS, at times delving into its findings, at other times citing them alongside those of other investigations. Let's turn now to Erikson's theory and related research, to which MIDUS has contributed. ●

Erikson's Theory: Generativity versus Stagnation

16.1 According to Erikson, how does personality change in middle age?

Erikson's psychological conflict of midlife is called **generativity versus stagnation.** Generativity involves reaching out to others in ways that give to and guide the next generation. Recall from Chapter 14 that generativity is under way in early adulthood through work, community service, and childbearing and child rearing. Generativity expands greatly in midlife, when adults focus more intently on extending commitments beyond oneself (identity) and one's life partner (intimacy) to a larger group—family, community, or society. The generative adult combines the need for self-expression with the need for communion, integrating personal goals with the welfare of the larger social world (McAdams, 2014). The resulting strength is the capacity to care for others in a broader way than previously.

Erikson (1950) selected the term *generativity* to encompass everything generated that can outlive the self and ensure society's continuity and improvement: children, ideas, products, works of art. Although parenting is a major means of realizing generativity,

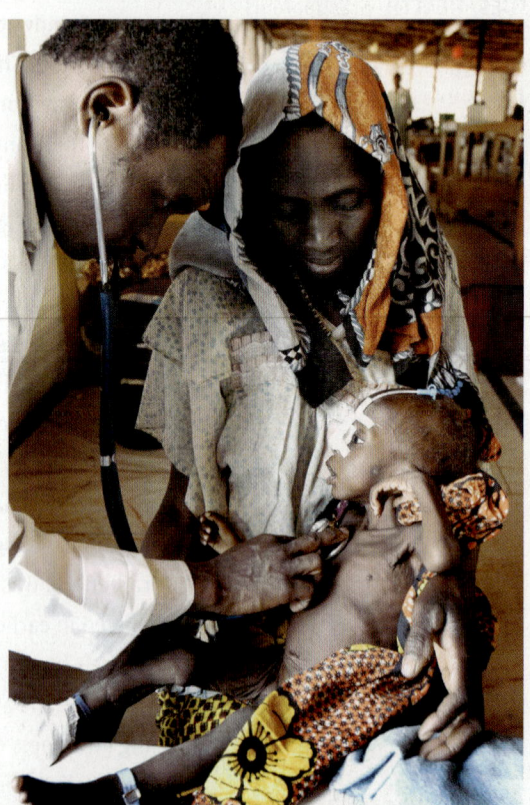

Through his work with severely malnourished children in Niger, this nurse, affiliated with the Nobel Prize–winning organization Doctors Without Borders, integrates personal goals with a broader concern for society.

it is not the only means: Adults can be generative in other family relationships (as Jewel was with her nephew and niece), as mentors in the workplace, in volunteer endeavors, and through many forms of productivity and creativity.

Notice, from what we have said so far, that generativity brings together personal desires and cultural demands. On the personal side, middle-aged adults feel a need to be needed—to attain symbolic immortality by making a contribution that will survive their death (Kotre, 1999; McAdams, Hart, & Maruna, 1998). This desire may stem from a deep-seated evolutionary urge to protect and advance the next generation. On the cultural side, society imposes a social clock for generativity in midlife, requiring adults to take responsibility for the next generation through their roles as parents, teachers, mentors, leaders, and coordinators (McAdams & Logan, 2004). And according to Erikson, a culture's "belief in the species"—the conviction that life is good and worthwhile, even in the face of human destructiveness and deprivation—is a major motivator of generative action. Without this optimistic worldview, people would have no hope of improving humanity.

The negative outcome of this stage is stagnation: Once people attain certain life goals, such as marriage, children, and career success, they may become self-centered and self-indulgent. Adults with a sense of stagnation express their self-absorption in many ways—through lack of interest in young people (including their own children), through a focus on what they can get from others rather than what they can give, and through taking little interest in being productive at work, developing their talents, or bettering the world in other ways.

Some researchers study generativity by asking people to rate themselves on generative characteristics, such as feelings of duty to help others in need or obligation to be an involved citizen. Others ask open-ended questions about life goals, major high points, and most satisfying activities, rating people's responses for generative references. And still others look for generative themes in people's narrative descriptions of themselves (Keyes & Ryff, 1998a, 1998b; McAdams, 2011, 2014; Newton & Stewart, 2010; Rossi, 2001, 2004b). Whichever method is used, generativity tends to increase in midlife among people diverse in SES and ethnicity. And as the Social Issues: Health box on page 540 illustrates, generativity is a major unifying theme in middle-aged adults' life stories.

Just as Erikson's theory suggests, highly generative people appear especially well-adjusted—low in anxiety and depression; high in autonomy, self-acceptance, and life satisfaction; more open to different viewpoints; and more likely to have successful marriages and close friends (An & Cooney, 2006; Grossbaum & Bates, 2002; Versey & Newton, 2013; Westermeyer, 2004). They also demonstrate workplace leadership qualities aimed at enhancing the success of younger colleagues, and they care greatly about the welfare of others in general (Peterson, 2002; Zacher et al., 2011). For example, generativity is associated with more effective child rearing—higher valuing of trust, open communication, transmission of generative values to children, and an authoritative style (Peterson, 2006; Peterson & Duncan, 2007;

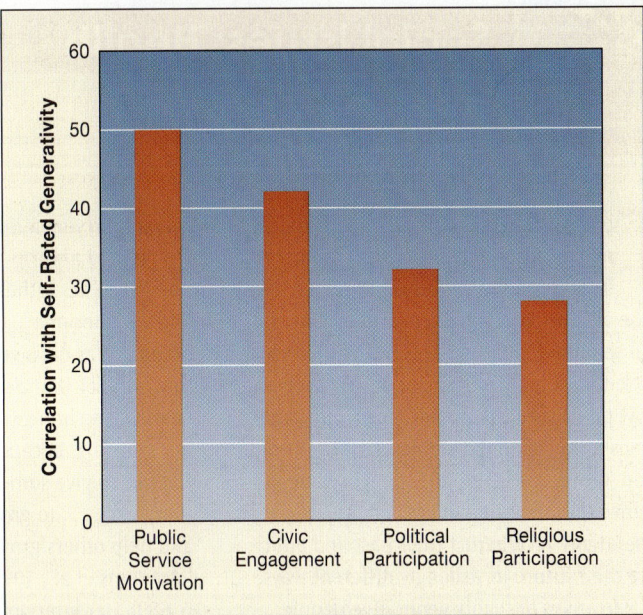

FIGURE 16.1 Relationship of middle-aged adults' generativity to civic, political, and religious engagement. Among a sample of European-American and African-American 55- to 59-year-olds, self-rated generativity was positively correlated with diverse measures of involvement in community and society—especially, public service motivation (attraction to public policy making, commitment to public interest causes) and civic engagement (participating in community organizations, raising money for charity), but also political participation (voting, expressing political opinions to others) and participation in a religious community. (Based on Jones & McAdams, 2013.)

Pratt et al., 2008). And as Figure 16.1 illustrates, midlife generativity is positively correlated with broad engagement in community and society (Jones & McAdams, 2013).

Although these findings characterize adults of all backgrounds, individual differences in contexts for generativity exist. Having children seems to foster generative development in both men and women. In some studies, including the MIDUS survey, fathers scored higher in generativity than childless men (Marks, Bumpass, & Jun, 2004; McAdams & de St. Aubin, 1992). Similarly, in an investigation of well-educated women from ages 43 to 63, those with family commitments (with or without a career) expressed greater generative concerns than childless women who were solely focused on their careers (Newton & Stewart, 2010). Perhaps parenting spurs especially tender, caring attitudes toward succeeding generations.

For low-SES men with troubled pasts as sons, students, workers, and intimate partners, fatherhood can provide a context for highly generative, positive life change (Roy & Lucas, 2006). At times, these fathers express this generativity as a refusal to pass on their own history of suffering. As one former gang member, who earned an associate's degree and struggled to keep his teenage sons off the streets, explained, "I came through the depths of hell to try to be a father. I let my sons know, 'You're never without a daddy, don't you let anybody tell you that.' I tell them that if me and your mother separate, I make sure that wherever I go, I build something for you to come to" (p. 153).

Social Issues: Health

Generative Adults Tell Their Life Stories

To clarify how highly generative adults make sense of their lives, researchers interviewed two groups of midlifers: those who often behave generatively and those who seldom do. Participants were asked to relate their life stories, including a high point, a low point, a turning point, and important scenes from childhood, adolescence, and adulthood (McAdams, 2011, 2013b). Story lines and themes revealed that adults high and low in generativity reconstruct their past and anticipate their future in strikingly different ways.

Narratives of highly generative people usually contained an orderly sequence of events that the researchers called a commitment story, in which adults give to others as a means of giving back to family, community, and society. The generative storyteller typically describes an early special advantage (such as a supportive family or a talent), along with early awareness of the suffering of others. This clash between blessing and suffering motivates the person to view the self as "called," or morally committed, to being good to others. In commitment stories, the theme of redemption is prominent. Highly generative adults frequently describe scenes in which extremely negative life events, involving frustration, failure, loss, or death, are redeemed, or made better, by good outcomes—personal renewal, improvement, and enlightenment.

Consider a story related by Diana, a 49-year-old fourth-grade teacher. Born in a small town to a minister and his wife, Diana was a favorite among the parishioners, who showered her with attention and love. When she was 8, however, her life hit its lowest point: As she looked on in horror, her younger brother ran into the street and was hit by a car; he died later that day. Afterward, Diana, sensing her father's anguish, tried—unsuccessfully—to be the "son" he had lost. But the scene ends on an upbeat note, with Diana marrying a man who forged a warm bond with her father and who became accepted "as his own son." One of Diana's life goals was to improve her teaching, because "I'd like to give something back . . . to grow and help others grow" (McAdams et al., 1997, p. 689). Her interview overflowed with expressions of generative commitment.

Whereas highly generative adults tell stories in which bad scenes turn good, less generative adults relate stories with themes of contamination, in which good scenes turn bad. For example, a good first year of college turns sour when a professor grades unfairly. A young woman loses weight and looks good but can't overcome her low self-esteem.

Why are life-story redemption events linked to generativity? First, some adults may view their generative activities as a way to redeem negative aspects of their lives. In a study of the life stories of ex-convicts who turned away from crime, many spoke of a strong desire to do good works as penance for their transgressions (Maruna, LeBel, & Lanier, 2004). Second, generativity seems to entail the conviction that the imperfections of today can be transformed into a better tomorrow. Through guiding and giving to the next generation, mature adults increase the chances that the mistakes of the past will not happen again. Finally, interpreting one's own life in terms of redemption may help sustain the perseverance needed to overcome the difficult challenges that generative activities—from rearing children to advancing societies—usually present.

Former heroin addict Harry Olsen spent eight years in and out of prison for drug convictions and other crimes. When he was released at age 39, he was overwhelmed by the prospect of reentering society but determined to transform himself. In search of direction and purpose, Olsen founded a nonprofit organization dedicated to helping other ex-convicts transition to life outside prison.

Life stories offer insight into how people imbue their lives with meaning and purpose. Although adults high and low in generativity do not differ in the number of positive and negative events included in their narratives, they interpret those events differently. Commitment stories, filled with redemption, involve a way of thinking about the self that fosters a caring, compassionate approach to others (McAdams & Logan, 2004). Such stories help people realize that although their own personal story will someday end, other stories will follow, due in part to their own generative efforts.

The more redemptive events adults include in their life stories, the higher their self-esteem, life satisfaction, and certainty that the challenges of life are meaningful, manageable, and rewarding (Lilgendahl & McAdams, 2011; McAdams & Guo, 2015). Researchers still have much to learn about factors that lead people to view good as emerging from adversity.

Finally, compared with European Americans, African Americans more often engage in certain types of generativity. They express a stronger desire to leave a legacy to their broader community (rather than just their immediate family) and, consistent with that goal, offer more social support to community members (Hart et al., 2001; Newton & Jones, 2016). A life history of greater support from church and extended family may strengthen these generative values and actions. Among European Americans, religiosity and spirituality are also positively associated with generative activity (Son & Wilson, 2011; Wink & Dillon, 2008). Highly generative middle-aged adults often indicate that as children and adolescents, they internalized moral values rooted in a religious tradition and sustained their commitment to those values, which provided lifelong encouragement for generative action (McAdams, 2013a). Especially in individualistic societies, belonging to a religious community or believing in a higher being may help preserve generative commitments.

Other Theories of Psychosocial Development in Midlife

16.2 Describe Levinson's and Vaillant's views of psychosocial development in middle adulthood, and discuss similarities and differences between men and women.

16.3 Does the term *midlife crisis* reflect the typical experience of middle adulthood, and is midlife accurately characterized as a stage?

Erikson's broad sketch of psychosocial change in midlife has been extended by Levinson and Vaillant. Let's revisit their theories, which were introduced in Chapter 14.

Levinson's Seasons of Life

Return to page 447 to review Levinson's eras (seasons of life). His interviews revealed that with the transition to middle age, adults become more aware that from now on, more time will lie behind than ahead, so they view the remaining years as increasingly precious. This leads some to make drastic revisions in their life structure: divorcing, remarrying, changing careers, or displaying enhanced creativity. Others make smaller changes in the context of marital and occupational stability.

Whether these years bring a gust of wind or a storm, most people turn inward for a time, focusing on personally meaningful living. According to Levinson, to reassess and rebuild their life structure, middle-aged adults must confront four developmental tasks. Each requires the individual to reconcile two opposing tendencies within the self, attaining greater internal harmony.

- *Young–old:* The middle-aged person must seek new ways of being both young and old. This means giving up certain youthful qualities, transforming others, and finding positive meaning in being older. Perhaps because of the double standard of aging (see pages 523–524 in Chapter 15), most middle-aged women express concern about appearing less attractive as they grow older (Rossi, 2004a). But middle-aged men—particularly non-college-educated men, who often hold blue-collar jobs requiring physical strength and stamina—are also highly sensitive to physical aging (Miner-Rubino, Winter, & Stewart, 2004).

   Compared with previous midlife cohorts, U.S. baby boomers are especially interested in controlling physical changes—a desire that has helped energize a huge industry of anti-aging cosmetic products and medical treatments (Jones, Whitbourne, & Skultety, 2006). And sustaining a youthful *subjective age* (feeling younger than one's actual age) is positively related to self-esteem and psychological well-being, with stronger associations among American than Western-European middle-aged and older adults (Keyes & Westerhof, 2012; Westerhof & Barrett, 2005; Westerhof, Whitbourne, & Freeman, 2012). In the more individualistic U.S. context, a youthful self-image seems more important for viewing oneself as self-reliant and capable of planning for an active, fulfilling late adulthood.

- *Destruction–creation:* With greater awareness of mortality, the middle-aged person focuses on ways he or she has acted destructively. Past hurtful acts toward parents, intimate partners, children, friends, and co-workers are countered by an intensified desire to be generative, through charitable giving, community volunteering, mentoring young people, or fashioning creative products.

- *Masculinity–femininity:* The middle-aged person must better balance masculine and feminine parts of the self. For men, this means greater acceptance of "feminine" traits of nurturance and caring, which enhance close relationships and compassionate exercise of authority in the workplace. For women, it generally means greater openness to "masculine" characteristics of autonomy and assertiveness. Recall from Chapter 8 that people who combine masculine and feminine traits have an androgynous gender identity. Later we will see that androgyny is associated with favorable personality traits and adjustment.

- *Engagement–separateness:* The middle-aged person must forge a better balance between engagement with the external world and separateness. For many men, and for women with successful careers, this may mean reducing concern with achievement in favor of attending more fully to oneself. But some women who have been devoted to child rearing or an unfulfilling job may feel compelled to move in the other direction, pursuing a long-desired ambition (Etaugh, 2013). At age 48, Elena left her position as a reporter for a small-town newspaper, earned an advanced degree in creative writing, accepted a college teaching position, and began writing a novel. Tim, in contrast, recognized his intense desire for a gratifying romantic partnership. By scaling back his own career, he realized he could grant Elena the time and space she needed to rebuild her work life—and that doing so might deepen their attachment to each other.

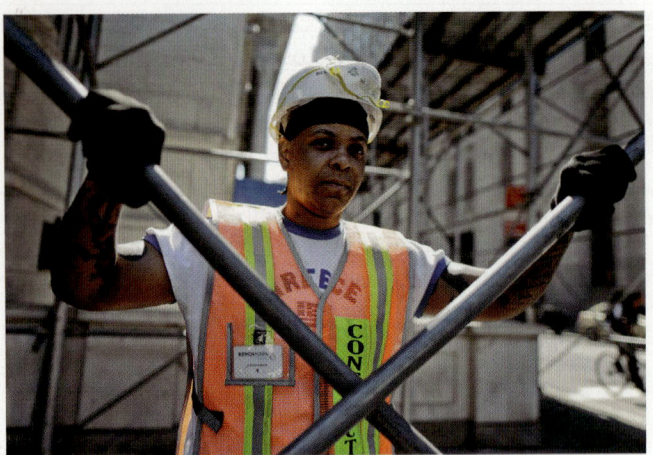

Individuals in blue-collar jobs with few possibilities for advancement may seek alternative ways to make their work more meaningful. This construction worker became a union shop steward, representing the interests of her coworkers in dealings with management.

People who flexibly modify their identities in response to age-related changes yet maintain a sense of self-continuity are more aware of their own thoughts and feelings and are higher in self-esteem and life satisfaction (Sneed et al., 2012). But adjusting one's life structure to incorporate the effects of aging requires supportive social contexts. When poverty, unemployment, and lack of a respected place in society dominate the life course, energies are directed toward survival rather than realistically addressing age-related changes. And even adults whose jobs are secure and who live in economically advantaged neighborhoods may find that employment conditions restrict possibilities for growth by placing too much emphasis on productivity and profit and too little on the meaning of work. In her early forties, Trisha left a large law firm, where she felt constant pressure to bring in high-fee clients and received little acknowledgment of her efforts, for a small practice.

Opportunities for advancement ease the transition to middle adulthood. Yet these are less available to women than to men. Individuals of both sexes in blue-collar jobs also have few possibilities for promotion. Consequently, they make whatever vocational adjustments they can—becoming active union members, shop stewards, or mentors of younger workers (Christensen & Larsen, 2008). Many men find compensating rewards in moving to the senior generation of their families.

Vaillant's Adaptation to Life

Whereas Levinson interviewed 35- to 45-year-olds, Vaillant (1977, 2002)—in his longitudinal research on well-educated men and women—followed participants past the half-century mark. Recall from Chapter 14 how adults in their late fifties and sixties extend their generativity, becoming "keepers of meaning," or guardians of their culture (see page 477). Vaillant reported that the most-successful and best-adjusted entered a calmer, quieter time of life. "Passing the torch"—concern that the positive aspects of their culture survive—became a major preoccupation.

In societies around the world, older people are guardians of traditions, laws, and cultural values. This stabilizing force holds in check too-rapid change sparked by the questioning and challenging of adolescents and young adults. As people approach the end of middle age, they focus on longer-term, less-personal goals, such as the state of human relations in their society. And they become more philosophical, accepting the fact that not all problems can be solved in their lifetime.

Is There a Midlife Crisis?

Levinson (1978, 1996) reported that most men and women in his samples experienced substantial inner turmoil during the transition to middle adulthood. Yet Vaillant (1977, 2002) saw few examples of crisis but, rather, slow and steady change. These contrasting findings raise the question of how much personal upheaval actually accompanies entry to midlife. Are self-doubt and stress especially great during the forties, and do they prompt major restructuring of the personality, as the term **midlife crisis** implies?

Trisha and Devin moved easily into this period, whereas Jewel, Tim, and Elena engaged in considerable questioning of their situations and sought alternative life paths. Clearly, wide individual differences exist in response to midlife. Yet Americans often assume that a midlife crisis will occur between ages 40 and 50, perhaps because of culturally induced apprehension of aging. But little evidence supports this view of middle age as a turbulent time.

When MIDUS participants were asked to describe "turning points" (major changes in the way they felt about an important aspect of their lives) that had occurred during the past five years, most were positive, involving fulfilling a dream or learning something good about oneself (Wethington, Kessler, & Pixley, 2004). Overall, turning points rarely resembled midlife crises. Even negative turning points generally led to personal growth—for example, a layoff that sparked a positive career change or a shift in energy from career to personal life.

Asked directly if they had ever experienced something they would consider a midlife crisis, only one-fourth of the MIDUS respondents said yes. And they defined such events more loosely than researchers do. Some reported a crisis well before age 40, others well after age 50. And most attributed it not to age but rather to challenging life events (Wethington, 2000). For example, Elena had considered both a divorce and a new career long before she initiated these changes. In her thirties, she separated from her husband; later she reconciled with him and told him that she desired to return to school, which he firmly opposed. She put her own life on hold because of her daughter's academic and emotional difficulties and her husband's resistance.

Another way of exploring midlife questioning is to ask adults about life regrets—attractive opportunities for life-changing activities they did not pursue or lifestyle changes they did not make. Among a nationally representative sample of Americans, life regrets centered mainly on romantic and family relationships, followed by education, career, finances, parenting, and health (see Figure 16.2) (Morrison & Roese, 2011). Experiencing

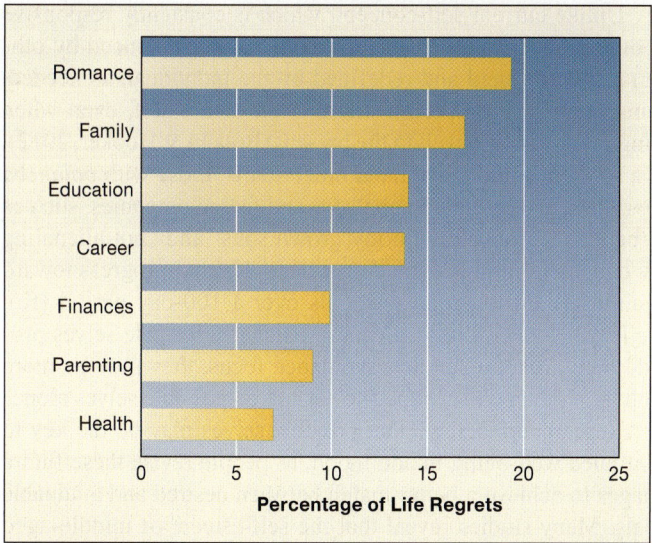

FIGURE 16.2 Life regrets most often mentioned by a nationally representative sample of Americans. Researchers telephoned 370 U.S. adults diverse in SES and ethnicity and asked each to describe one life salient regret. (Based on Morrison & Roese, 2011.)

regrets is consistently associated with less favorable psychological well-being (Schiebe & Epstude, 2016). But regrets can also serve a positive function if people mull over what went wrong in the past and, based on new insights, take whatever corrective action is possible.

By late midlife, with less time ahead to make life changes, people's interpretation of regrets plays a major role in their well-being. Mature, contented adults acknowledge a past characterized by some lost opportunities, have thought deeply about them, and feel stronger because of them. At the same time, they are able to disengage from them, investing in currently attainable, personally rewarding goals (King & Hicks, 2007). Among a sample of several hundred 60- to 65-year-olds diverse in SES, about half expressed at least one regret. Compared to those who had not resolved their disappointments, those who had come to terms with them (accepted and identified some eventual benefits) or had "put the best face on things" (identified benefits but still had some lingering regret) reported better physical health and greater life satisfaction (Torges, Stewart, & Miner-Rubino, 2005).

In sum, life evaluation is common during middle age. Most people make changes that are best described as turning points rather than drastic alterations of their lives. By midlife, an increasing number find that aspects of their life paths can no longer be modified, but they often come to see the "silver lining" in their circumstances (King & Hicks, 2007; Morrison & Roese, 2011). The few midlifers who are in crisis typically have had early adulthoods in which gender roles, family pressures, or low income and poverty severely limited their ability to realize personal goals, at home or in the wider world.

Stage or Life Events Approach

That crisis and major restructuring in midlife are rare raises, once again, a question we considered in Chapter 14: Can adult psychosocial changes be organized into stages, as Erikson's, Levinson's, and Vaillant's theories indicate? A growing number of researchers believe the mid-adult transition is not stagelike (Freund & Ritter, 2009; McAdams, 2014; Srivastava et al., 2003). Some regard it as simply an adaptation to normative life events, such as children growing up, reaching the crest of a career, and impending retirement.

Yet recall from earlier chapters that life events are no longer as age-graded as they were in the past. Their timing is so variable that they cannot be the sole cause of midlife change. Today, most experts view adaptation during midlife as the combined result of growing older and social experiences (Lachman, 2004; Sneed, Whitbourne, & Culang, 2006). Return to our discussion of the rise in generativity in middle adulthood on pages 538–539, and notice how both factors are involved.

Finally, in describing their lives, the large majority of middle-aged people report troubling times that prompt new understandings and goals. As we look closely at emotional and social development in middle adulthood, we will see that this period, like others, is characterized by both continuity and change. With this in mind, let's turn to the diverse inner concerns and outer experiences that contribute to psychological well-being and decision making in midlife.

Ask yourself

CONNECT Describe evidence on life regrets illustrating that adaptation to midlife is the combined result of growing older and social experiences.

APPLY After years of experiencing little personal growth at work, 42-year-old Mel looked for a new job and received an attractive offer in another city. Although he felt torn between leaving close friends and pursuing a long-awaited career opportunity, after several weeks of soul searching, he took the new job. Was Mel's dilemma a midlife crisis? Why or why not?

REFLECT Think of a middle-aged adult whom you admire. Describe the various ways that individual expresses generativity.

Stability and Change in Self-Concept and Personality

16.4 Describe changes in self-concept, personality, and gender identity in middle adulthood.

16.5 Discuss stability and change in the "big five" personality traits in adulthood.

Midlife changes in self-concept and personality reflect growing awareness of a finite lifespan, longer life experience, and generative concerns. Yet certain aspects of personality remain stable, revealing the persistence of individual differences established during earlier periods.

Possible Selves

On a business trip, Jewel found a spare afternoon to visit Trisha. Sitting in a coffee shop, the two women reminisced about the past and thought aloud about the future. "It's been tough living on my own and building the business," Jewel said. "What I hope for is to become better at my work, to be more community-oriented, and to stay healthy and available to my friends. Of course, I would rather not grow old alone, but if I don't find that special person, I suppose I can take comfort in the fact that I'll never have to face divorce or widowhood."

Jewel is discussing **possible selves,** future-oriented representations of what one hopes to become and what one is afraid of becoming. Possible selves are the temporal dimension of self-concept—what the individual is striving for and attempting to avoid. To lifespan researchers, these hopes and fears are just as vital in explaining behavior as people's views of their current characteristics. Indeed, possible selves may be an especially strong motivator of action in midlife, as adults attach increased meaning to time (Frazier & Hooker, 2006). As we age, we may rely less on social comparisons in judging our self-worth and more on temporal comparisons—how well we are doing in relation to what we had planned.

Throughout adulthood, the personality traits people assign to their current selves show considerable stability. A 30-year-old who says he is cooperative, competent, outgoing, or successful is likely to report a similar picture at a later age. But reports of possible selves change greatly. Adults in their early twenties mention many possible selves, and their visions are lofty and idealistic—being "perfectly happy," "rich and famous," "healthy throughout life," and not being "down and out" or "a person who does nothing important." With age, possible selves become fewer in number, more modest and concrete, and less far-off in realization. Most middle-aged people no longer desire to be the best or the most successful in life. Instead, they are largely concerned with performance of roles and responsibilities already begun—"being competent at work," "being a good husband and father," "putting my children through college," "staying healthy," and not being "a burden to my family" or "without enough money to meet my daily needs" (Bybee & Wells, 2003; Chessell et al., 2014; Cross & Markus, 1991).

What explains these shifts in possible selves? Because the future no longer holds limitless opportunities, adults preserve mental health by adjusting their hopes and fears. To stay motivated, they must maintain a sense of unachieved possibility, yet they must still manage to feel good about themselves and their lives despite disappointments (Lachman & Bertrand, 2002). For example, Jewel no longer desired to be an executive in a large company, as she had in her twenties. Instead, she wanted to grow in her current occupation. And although she feared loneliness in old age, she reminded herself that marriage can lead to equally negative outcomes, such as divorce and widowhood—possibilities that made not having attained an important interpersonal goal easier to bear.

Unlike current self-concept, which is constantly responsive to others' feedback, possible selves (though influenced by others) can be defined and redefined by the individual, as needed. Consequently, they permit affirmation of the self, even when things are not going well in the present (Bolkan & Hooker, 2012). In a study of middle-aged and older adults, those with *balanced possible selves*—related hoped-for and feared outcomes, such as "a better relationship with my grown sons" and "not alienating my daughters-in-law"—made greater self-rated progress toward attaining their self-relevant goals over a 100-day period (Ko, Mejía, & Hooker, 2014). Because balanced possible selves provide both an approach and avoidance focus, they may be more motivating than either hoped-for or feared possible selves alone.

Researchers believe that possible selves may be the key to continued well-being in adulthood, as people revise these future images to achieve a better match between desired and attainable goals. Many studies reveal that the self-esteem of middle-aged and older individuals equals or surpasses that of younger people (Robins & Trzesniewski, 2005). A major reason may be the protective effect of possible selves.

Self-Acceptance, Autonomy, and Environmental Mastery

An evolving mix of competencies and experiences leads to changes in certain aspects of personality during middle adulthood. In Chapter 15, we noted that midlife brings gains in expertise and practical problem solving. Middle-aged adults also offer more complex, integrated descriptions of themselves than do younger and older individuals (Labouvie-Vief, 2003, 2015). Furthermore, midlife is typically a period in which the number of social roles peaks—spouse, parent, worker, and engaged community member. And status at work and in the community typically rises, as adults take advantage of opportunities for leadership and other complex responsibilities.

These changes in cognition and breadth of roles undoubtedly contribute to other gains in personal functioning. In research on adults ranging in age from the late teens into the seventies, and in cultures as distinct as the United States and Japan, three qualities increased from early to middle adulthood:

- *Self-acceptance:* More than young adults, middle-aged people acknowledged and accepted both their good and bad qualities and felt positively about themselves and life.
- *Autonomy:* Middle-aged adults saw themselves as less concerned about others' expectations and evaluations and more concerned with following self-chosen standards.
- *Environmental mastery:* Middle-aged people saw themselves as capable of managing a complex array of tasks easily and effectively (Karasawa et al., 2011; Ryff & Keyes, 1995).

As these findings indicate, midlife is generally a time of increased comfort with the self, independence, assertiveness, and commitment to personal values (Helson, Jones, & Kwan, 2002; Keyes,

Shmotkin, & Ryff, 2002; Stone et al., 2010). Many midlifers seem to conclude that through effort and self-discipline, they have come close to fulfilling their potential—a likely reason for the rise in overall life satisfaction from early to middle adulthood in longitudinal research (Galambos et al., 2015). Increased contentment with oneself and one's life accomplishments might explain why middle age is sometimes referred to as "the prime of life."

At the same time, factors contributing to psychological well-being differ substantially among cohorts, as self-reports gathered from 25- to 65-year-old MIDUS survey respondents reveal (Carr, 2004). Among women who were born during the baby-boom years or later, and who thus benefited from the women's movement, balancing career with family predicted greater self-acceptance and environmental mastery. But also consider that women born before or during World War II who sacrificed career to focus on child rearing—expected of young mothers in the 1950s and 1960s—were similarly advantaged in self-acceptance. Likewise, men who were in step with prevailing social expectations scored higher in well-being. Baby-boom and younger men who modified their work schedules to make room for family responsibilities—who fit their cohort's image of the "good father"—were more self-accepting. But older men who made this accommodation scored much lower in self-acceptance than those who focused on work and conformed to the "good provider" ideal of their times. (See the Biology and Environment box on pages 546–547 for additional influences on midlife psychological well-being.)

Notions of well-being, however, vary among cultures. In comparisons of Japanese and Korean adults with same-age U.S. MIDUS participants, the Japanese and Koreans reported lower levels of psychological well-being, largely because they were less willing than the Americans to endorse individualistic traits, such as self-acceptance and autonomy, as characteristic of themselves (Karasawa et al., 2011; Keyes & Ryff, 1998b). Consistent with their interdependent orientation, Japanese and Koreans' highest well-being scores were on positive relations with others. The Korean participants clarified that they viewed personal fulfillment as achieved through family, especially the success of children. Americans also regarded family relations as relevant to well-being but placed greater emphasis on their own traits and accomplishments than on their children's.

Coping with Daily Stressors

In Chapter 15, we discussed the importance of stress management in preventing illness. It is also vital for psychological well-being. In a MIDUS satellite study in which more than 1,000 participants were interviewed on eight consecutive evenings, researchers found an early- to mid-adulthood plateau in frequency of daily stressors, followed by a decline as work and family responsibilities ease and leisure time increases (see Figure 16.3) (Almeida & Horn, 2004). Women reported more frequent role overload (conflict among roles of employee, spouse, parent, and caregiver of an aging parent) and family-network and child-

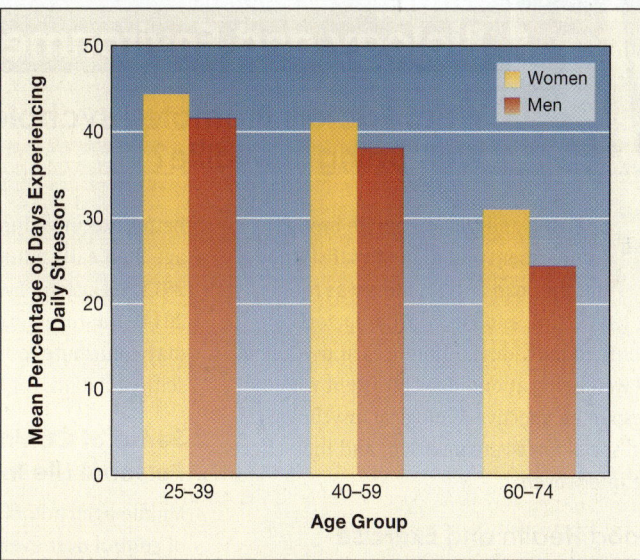

FIGURE 16.3 Age-related changes in daily stressors among men and women. In a MIDUS satellite study, researchers interviewed more than 1,000 adults on eight consecutive evenings. Findings revealed an early- to mid-adulthood plateau, followed by a decline as work and family responsibilities ease and leisure time increases. (From D. M. Almeida & M. C. Horn, 2004, "Is Daily Life More Stressful During Middle Adulthood?" in O. G. Brim, C. D. Ruff, and R. C. Kessler [Eds.], *How Healthy Are We? A National Study of Well-Being at Midlife*. Chicago: The University of Chicago Press, p. 438. Adapted by permission of The University of Chicago Press.)

related stressors, men more work-related stressors, but both genders experienced all varieties. Compared with older people, young and midlife adults also perceived their stressors as more disruptive and unpleasant, perhaps because they often experienced several at once, and many involved financial risks and children.

But recall, also, from Chapter 15 that midlife brings an increase in effective coping strategies. Middle-aged individuals are more likely to identify the positive side of difficult situations, postpone action to permit evaluation of alternatives, anticipate and plan ways to handle future discomforts, and use humor to express ideas and feelings without offending others (Diehl, Coyle, & Labouvie-Vief, 1996; Proulx & Aldwin, 2016). Notice how these efforts flexibly draw on both problem-centered and emotion-centered strategies.

Why might effective coping increase in middle adulthood? Other personality changes seem to support it. Complex, integrated, coherent self-descriptions—which increase in midlife, indicating an improved ability to blend strengths and weaknesses into an organized picture—predict a stronger sense of personal control over outcomes and good coping strategies (Hay & Diehl, 2010; Labouvie-Vief, 2015). Midlife gains in emotional stability and confidence in handling life's problems may also contribute (Roberts et al., 2007; Roberts & Mroczek, 2008). These attributes predict work and relationship effectiveness—outcomes that reflect the sophisticated, flexible coping of middle age.

Some midlifers, however, experience stressors so intense that their capacity to cope disintegrates. Over the past 15 years,

Biology and Environment

What Factors Promote Psychological Well-Being in Midlife?

For Trisha and Devin, midlife brought contentment and high life satisfaction. But the road to happiness was rockier for Jewel, Tim, and Elena. What factors contribute to individual differences in psychological well-being at midlife? Consistent with the lifespan perspective, biological, psychological, and social forces are involved, and their effects are interwoven.

Good Health and Exercise

Good health affects energy and zest for life at any age. But during middle and late adulthood, taking steps to improve health and prevent disability becomes a better predictor of psychological well-being. Many studies confirm that engaging in regular exercise—walking, dancing, jogging, or swimming—is more strongly associated with self-rated health and a positive outlook in older than in younger adults (Bherer, 2012). Middle-aged people who maintain an exercise regimen are likely to perceive themselves as particularly active for their age and, therefore, to feel a special sense of accomplishment (Netz et al., 2005). In addition, physical activity enhances self-efficacy and effective stress management (see page 521 in Chapter 15). And sustained, moderate intensity physical activity is linked to better executive function, more so in middle age than early adulthood (Maxwell & Lynn, 2015; Weinstein, Lydick, & Biswabharati, 2014). Improved executive function, in turn, may contribute to midlifers' self-efficacy and self-regulation.

Sense of Control and Personal Life Investment

Middle-aged adults who report a high sense of control over events in various aspects of their lives—health, family, and work—also report more favorable psychological well-being. Sense of control contributes further to self-efficacy (Lang, 2016). It also predicts use of more effective coping strategies, including seeking social support, and thereby helps sustain a positive outlook in the face of health, family, and work difficulties (Lachman, Neupert, & Agrigoroaei, 2011).

Personal life investment—firm commitment to goals and involvement in pursuit of those goals—also adds to mental health and life satisfaction (Staudinger & Bowen, 2010). According to Mihaly Csikszentmihalyi, a vital wellspring of happiness is *flow*—the psychological state of being so engrossed in a demanding, meaningful activity that one loses all sense of time and self-awareness. People describe

Complex endeavors that offer potential for growth engender flow—a pleasurable psychological state of deep engrossment. The perseverance and skill essential for flow are well-developed at midlife.

flow as the height of enjoyment, even as an ecstatic state. The more people experience flow, the more they judge their lives to be gratifying (Nakamura & Csikszentmihalyi, 2009). Although flow is common in people engaged in creative endeavors, many others report it—

suicides among U.S. middle-aged adults rose by 25 percent. Currently, the suicide rate for middle-aged people nearly matches that of people 85 and older (whose rate is the highest). White men between 45 and 64 showed the sharpest rise, while also displaying elevated death rates from drug and alcohol abuse. Most were poorly educated, economically disadvantaged, and suffered from physical and mental health problems (American Society for Suicide Prevention, 2016; Centers for Disease Control and Prevention, 2016d). Although causes are not yet clear, experts speculate that these trends may reflect strengthening associations among poverty, declining health, and hopelessness in middle adulthood that are unique to the United States. Steady declines in midlife mortality occurred in Australia, Canada, and Western Europe during the same time period.

Gender Identity

In her forties and early fifties, Trisha appeared more assertive at work. She spoke out more freely at meetings and took a leadership role when a team of lawyers worked on an especially complex case. She was also more dominant in family relationships, expressing her opinions to her husband and son more readily than she had 10 or 15 years earlier. In contrast, Devin's sense of empathy and caring became more apparent, and he was less assertive and more accommodating to Trisha's wishes than before.

Many studies report an increase in "masculine" traits in women and "feminine" traits in men across middle age. Women became more confident, self-sufficient, and forceful, men more emotionally sensitive, caring, considerate, and dependent. These students who love studying, employees who like their jobs, adults involved in challenging leisure pursuits, and parents and grandparents engaged in pleasurable learning activities with children. Flow depends on perseverance and skill at complex endeavors that offer potential for growth (Rich, 2013). These qualities are well-developed in middle adulthood.

Positive Social Relationships

Developing gratifying social ties is closely linked to midlife psychological well-being. High-quality relationships with relatives and friends improve mental health by promoting positive emotions and protecting against stress (Fiori, Antonucci, & Cortina, 2006; Fuller-Iglesias, Webster, & Antonucci, 2015). Enjoyable social ties can even strengthen the impact of an exercise regimen on well-being. Among an ethnically diverse sample of women using a private gym or an African Caribbean community center, exercising with likeminded companions contributed to happiness and life satisfaction (Wray, 2007). The social side of going to the gym appeared especially important to minority women, who were less concerned with physical-appearance benefits than their European-American agemates.

A Good Marriage

Although support from relatives and friends is important, a good marriage boosts psychological well-being even more. The role of marriage in mental health increases with age, becoming a powerful predictor by late midlife (Marks & Greenfield, 2009; Rauer & Albers, 2016). U.S. middle-aged adults in cohabiting relationships do not necessarily benefit similarly. But in Western Europe, where cohabitation signifies high relationship commitment, cohabitors and married people report equally positive well-being (Hansen, Moum, & Shapiro, 2007).

Longitudinal research suggests that a good marriage actually brings about well-being. For example, in a British study of a nationally representative sample of middle-aged and older couples, marital adjustment more strongly predicted life satisfaction at a two-year follow-up than life satisfaction predicted later marital adjustment (Be, Whisman, & Uebelacker, 2013). And when interviews with over 13,000 U.S. adults were repeated five years later, people who remained married reported greater happiness than those who remained single (Marks & Lambert, 1998). Those who separated or divorced became less happy, reporting considerable depression.

Although not everyone is better off married, the link between marriage and well-being is similar in many nations, suggesting that marriage changes people's behavior in ways that make them better off (Diener et al., 2000). Married partners monitor each other's health and offer care in times of illness. They also earn and save more money than single people, and income is linked to higher well-being (Sacks, Stevenson, & Wolfers, 2012). Furthermore, sexual satisfaction predicts mental health, and married couples have more satisfying sex lives than singles (see Chapter 13).

Mastery of Multiple Roles

Success in handling multiple roles—spouse, parent, worker, community volunteer—is linked to psychological well-being. In the MIDUS survey, as role involvement increased, both men and women reported greater environmental mastery, more rewarding social relationships, heightened sense of purpose in life, and more positive emotion. Furthermore, adults who occupied multiple roles and who also reported high control (suggesting effective role management) scored especially high in well-being—an outcome that was stronger for less-educated adults (Ahrens & Ryff, 2006). Control over roles may be vital for individuals with lower educational attainment, whose role combinations may be particularly stressful and who have fewer economic resources.

Finally, among nonfamily roles, community volunteering in the latter part of midlife contributes uniquely to psychological well-being (Choi & Kim, 2011; Ryff et al., 2012). It may do so by strengthening self-efficacy, generativity, and altruism.

---

tendencies emerged in cross-sectional and longitudinal research, in people varying in SES, and in diverse cultures—not just Western industrialized nations but also village societies such as the Maya of Guatemala, the Navajo of the United States, and the Druze of the Middle East (Fry, 1985; Gutmann, 1977; James et al., 1995; Jones, Peskin, & Livson, 2011). Consistent with Levinson's theory, gender identity in midlife seemed to become more androgynous—a mixture of "masculine" and "feminine" characteristics.

But in more recently gathered self-reports, men's and women's endorsement of "masculine" and "feminine" traits showed little change throughout adulthood (Lemaster, Delaney, & Strough, 2015; Strough et al., 2007). Cohort effects may explain the contradictory findings: More recent participants were mostly adolescents or young adults during the women's movement of the 1970s and 1980s, or were born after it. Influenced by this time of major social change, adults of diverse ages—and especially women—may have been more likely than previous cohorts to endorse an androgynous mix of "masculine" and "feminine" traits.

The demands of middle age may help explain why, in a wealth of earlier research, it is associated with increased androgyny. For example, some evidence reveals a link between children's departure from the home and men's greater openness to the "feminine" side of their personalities (Huyck, 1998). Perhaps men's need to enrich a marital relationship after children depart, along with reduced chances for career advancement, prompt an awakening of emotionally sensitive traits. In other research, women who attained high status in their careers gained most in dominance, assertiveness, and outspokenness by their early

Individual Differences in Personality Traits

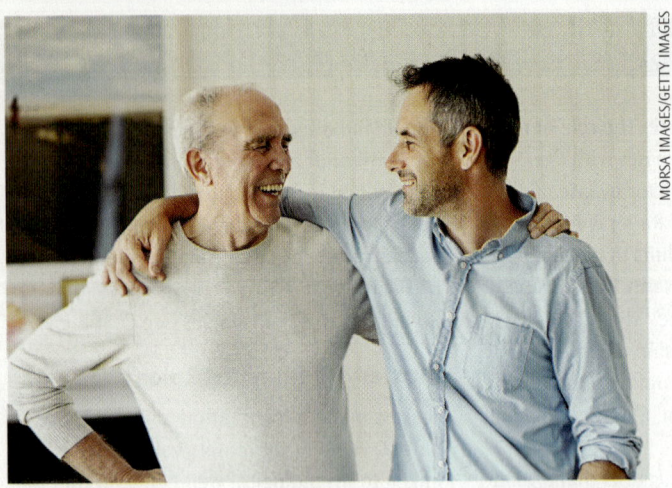

This middle-aged son comfortably expresses affection for his father. In midlife, men tend to show an increase in "feminine" traits, becoming more emotionally sensitive, caring, considerate, and dependent.

Although Trisha and Jewel both became more self-assured and assertive in midlife, in other respects they differed. Trisha had always been more organized and hard-working, Jewel more gregarious and fun-loving. Once, the two women traveled together. At the end of each day, Trisha was disappointed if she had not kept to a schedule and visited every tourist attraction. Jewel liked to "play it by ear"—wandering through streets and stopping to talk with shopkeepers and residents.

In previous sections, we considered personality changes common to many middle-aged adults, but stable individual differences also exist. Through factor analysis of self-report ratings, the hundreds of personality traits on which people differ have been reduced to five basic factors, often referred to as the **"big five" personality traits:** neuroticism, extroversion, openness to experience, agreeableness, and conscientiousness. Table 16.1 provides a description of each. Notice that Trisha is high in conscientiousness, whereas Jewel is high in extroversion.

Longitudinal and cross-sectional studies of U.S. men and women reveal that agreeableness and conscientiousness increase from adolescence through middle age, whereas neuroticism declines, and extroversion and openness to experience do not change or decrease slightly—changes that reflect "settling down" and greater maturity. Similar trends have been identified in more than 50 countries varying widely in cultural traditions, including Canada, Germany, Italy, Japan, Russia, and South Korea (McCrae & Costa, 2006; Roberts, Walton, & Viechtbauer, 2006; Schmitt et al., 2007; Soto et al., 2011; Srivastava et al., 2003).

The consistency of these cross-cultural findings has led some researchers to conclude that adult personality change is genetically influenced. They also note that individual differences in the "big five" traits are large and highly stable: A person who scores high or low at one age is likely to do the same at another, over intervals ranging from 3 to 30 years (McCrae & Costa, 2006).

fifties (Wink & Helson, 1993). Also, midlife women are more likely than men to face economic and social disadvantages. A greater number remain divorced, are widowed, or encounter discrimination in the workplace. Self-reliance and assertiveness are vital for coping with these circumstances.

In sum, a complex combination of social roles and life conditions underlies the midlife rise in androgyny, which seems to have spread to other age periods in response to cultural changes favoring gender equality. In Chapter 8, we noted that androgyny predicts high self-esteem. In adulthood, it is also associated with cognitive flexibility, creativity, advanced moral reasoning, and psychosocial maturity (Prager & Bailey, 1985; Runco, Cramond, & Pagnani, 2010; Waterman & Whitbourne, 1982). People who integrate the masculine and feminine sides of their personalities tend to be psychologically healthier, perhaps because they are able to adapt more easily to life's challenges.

TABLE 16.1
The "Big Five" Personality Traits

TRAIT	DESCRIPTION
Neuroticism	Individuals who are high on this trait are worrying, temperamental, self-pitying, self-conscious, emotional, and vulnerable. Individuals who are low are calm, even-tempered, self-content, comfortable, unemotional, and hardy.
Extroversion	Individuals who are high on this trait are affectionate, talkative, active, fun-loving, and passionate. Individuals who are low are reserved, quiet, passive, sober, and emotionally unreactive.
Openness to experience	Individuals who are high on this trait are imaginative, creative, original, curious, and liberal. Individuals who are low are down-to-earth, uncreative, conventional, uncurious, and conservative.
Agreeableness	Individuals who are high on this trait are soft-hearted, trusting, generous, acquiescent, lenient, and good-natured. Individuals who are low are ruthless, suspicious, stingy, antagonistic, critical, and irritable.
Conscientiousness	Individuals who are high on this trait are conscientious, hard-working, well-organized, punctual, ambitious, and persevering. Individuals who are low are negligent, lazy, disorganized, late, aimless, and nonpersistent.

Source: McCrae & Costa, 2006; Soto, Kronauer, & Liang, 2016.

How can there be high stability in personality traits, yet significant changes in aspects of personality discussed earlier? Look closely at the "big five" traits in Table 16.1, and you will see that they differ from the attributes considered in previous sections: They do not take into account motivations, preferred tasks, and coping styles, nor do they consider how certain aspects of personality, such as masculinity and femininity, are integrated. Theorists concerned with change due to experience focus on how personal needs and life events induce new strategies and goals; their interest is in "the human being as a complex adaptive system" (Block, 2011, p. 19). In contrast, those who emphasize stability due to heredity measure personality traits on which individuals can easily be compared and that are present at any time of life.

To resolve this apparent contradiction, we can think of adults as changing in overall organization and integration of personality as they adapt to changing life circumstances but doing so on a foundation of basic, enduring dispositions. But even the "big five" traits are responsive to life experiences: For example, people in stable jobs and romantic relationships, compared to those without these commitments, show greater gains in conscientiousness and agreeableness and declines in neuroticism over time (Hudson & Fraley, 2016; Lodi-Smith & Roberts, 2007). These findings confirm that personality remains an "open system," responsive to the pressures of life experiences.

Ask yourself

CONNECT List cognitive gains that typically occur during middle adulthood. (See Chapter 15, pages 524–526 and 530–531.) How might they support midlife personality changes?

APPLY Jeff, age 46, suggested to his wife, Julia, that they set aside time once a year to discuss their relationship—both positive aspects and ways to improve. Julia was surprised because Jeff had never before expressed interest in working on their marriage. What midlife developments probably fostered this new concern?

REFLECT List your hoped-for and feared possible selves. Then ask family members in early and middle adulthood to do the same. Are their reports consistent with age-related research findings? Explain.

Relationships at Midlife

16.6 Describe the middle adulthood phase of the family life cycle, including marriage, divorce, parent–child relationships, and grandparenthood.

16.7 Describe midlife sibling relationships and friendships.

The emotional and social changes of midlife take place within a complex web of family relationships and friendships and an intensified personal focus on generative concerns. Although some middle-aged people live alone, the vast majority—about 90 percent in the United States—live in families, about 65 percent with a spouse, 15 percent with a cohabiting partner, and 10 percent as unmarried or formerly married adults residing with children and/or other relatives (U.S. Census Bureau, 2016a). Partly because they have ties to older and younger generations in their families and partly because their friendships are well-established, midlifers have a larger number of close relationships than adults of other age periods do (Antonucci, Akiyama, & Takahashi, 2004).

The middle adulthood phase of the family life cycle is often referred to as "launching children and moving on." In the past, it was called the "empty nest," but this phrase implies a negative transition, especially for women who have devoted themselves entirely to their children and for whom the end of active parenting can trigger feelings of emptiness and regret. But for most people, middle adulthood is a liberating time, offering a sense of completion and opportunities to strengthen social ties and rekindle interests.

As our discussion in Chapter 14 revealed, increasing numbers of young adults are living at home due to role transitions and financial challenges, yielding launch–return–relaunch patterns for many middle-aged parents. Still, a declining birthrate and longer life expectancy mean that many contemporary parents do launch children a decade or more before retirement and then turn to other rewarding activities. As adult children depart and marry, middle-aged parents must adapt to new roles of parent-in-law and grandparent. At the same time, they must establish a different type of relationship with their aging parents, who may become ill or infirm and die.

Middle adulthood is marked by the greatest number of exits and entries of family members. Let's see how ties within and beyond the family change during this time of life.

Marriage and Divorce

Although not all couples are financially comfortable, middle-aged households are well-off economically compared with other age groups. Americans between 45 and 54 have the highest average annual income, and contemporary middle-aged adults—more of whom have earned college and postgraduate degrees and live in dual-earner families—are financially better off than previous midlife generations (U.S. Census Bureau, 2016a). Partly because of increased education and financial security, the contemporary social view of marriage in midlife is one of expansion and new horizons.

These forces strengthen the need to review and adjust the marital relationship. For Devin and Trisha, this shift was gradual. By middle age, their marriage had permitted satisfaction of family and individual needs, endured many changes, and culminated in deeper feelings of love. Elena's marriage, in contrast, became more conflict-ridden as her teenage daughter's problems introduced added strains and as departure of children made marital difficulties more obvious. Tim's failed marriage revealed yet another pattern. With passing years, the number of problems declined, but so did the love expressed (Gottman & Gottman, 2015; Rokach, Cohen, & Dreman, 2004). As less happened in the

For many middle-aged couples, having forged a relationship that permits satisfaction of both family and individual needs results in deeper feelings of love.

relationship, good or bad, the couple had little to keep them together.

As the Biology and Environment box on pages 546–547 revealed, marital satisfaction is a powerful predictor of midlife psychological well-being. Marital happiness is more strongly associated with life satisfaction than happiness in other domains, including vocation, children, friendships, and health (Fleeson, 2004; Heller, Watson, & Ilies, 2004). Consequently, middle-aged men who have focused mostly on career often realize the limited nature of their pursuits. At the same time, women may insist on a more gratifying relationship. And having grown children who are engaged in adult roles reminds middle-aged parents that they are in the latter part of their lives, prompting many to decide that the time for improving their marriages is now.

As with early adulthood, evidence on same-sex middle-aged couples is scarce. But some research suggests that compared to other couples, lesbian partners use more effective communication styles (Zdaniuk & Smith, 2016). In interviews with over 200 heterosexual and same-sex couples in their forties, fifties, and sixties, the lesbian couples described more openness and honesty in sharing thoughts and feelings with their partner (Mackey, Diemer, & O'Brien, 2000). Across heterosexual, lesbian, and gay participants, physical affection, low conflict, and sense of fairness predicted a deeper sense of psychological intimacy.

Divorce has increasingly become a route to resolving an unsatisfactory marriage in midlife. Although the overall U.S. divorce rate has declined over the past two decades, the divorce rate of U.S. adults age 50 and older has doubled over this period (Brown & Lin, 2013). A longer life expectancy, widespread social acceptance of marital breakup, and greater financial security (making it easier to leave an unhappy marriage) have contributed to this surge in later-life divorces.

Divorce at any age takes a heavy psychological toll, but midlifers seem to adjust more easily than younger people. A survey of more than 13,000 Americans revealed that following divorce, middle-aged men and women reported less decline in psychological well-being than their younger counterparts (Marks & Lambert, 1998). Midlife gains in practical problem solving and effective coping strategies may reduce the stressful impact of divorce.

Still, individual differences in adjustment exist, with middle-aged adults who end a highly distressed marriage fairing best (Amato, 2010). Many ultimately report gains in happiness—an outcome stronger among women than men (Bourassa, Sbarra, & Whisman, 2015). In Chapter 14, we saw that women's happiness suffers more than men's in a poor-quality marriage with unequal sharing of authority and responsibilities. When these and other relationship difficulties cannot be solved, divorce eventually brings emotional relief.

What do recently divorced middle-aged people say about why their marriages ended? Women frequently mention communication problems, inequality in the relationship, adultery, gradual distancing, substance abuse, physical and verbal abuse, or their own desire for autonomy. Men also bring up poor communication, and they sometimes admit that their "workaholic" lifestyle or emotional inattentiveness played a major role in the marital failure. Women are more likely than men to initiate divorce, and those who do fare somewhat better in psychological well-being (Sakraida, 2005; Schneller & Arditti, 2004). Men who initiate a split often already have another romantic involvement to turn to.

Because the divorce rate is greater among remarried couples than those in first marriages, about half of midlife divorces involve people who have had one or more previous unsuccessful marriages. Although many middle-aged divorcing adults are in comfortable economic circumstances, for a considerable number of women, marital breakup—especially when it is repeated—severely reduces standard of living (see pages 353–354 in Chapter 10). Consequently, in midlife and earlier, divorce contributes to the **feminization of poverty**—a trend in which women who support themselves or their families have become the majority of the adult population living in poverty, regardless of age and ethnic group. The gender gap in poverty has declined in Western nations, due to women's increased labor market participation, a reduction in the gender pay gap (see page 499 in Chapter 14), and public policies supporting women and families. But because of weaker U.S. public policies (see Chapter 2), the gender gap in poverty remains higher in the United States than in other Western countries (Kim & Choi, 2013).

Longitudinal evidence reveals that middle-aged women who weather divorce successfully tend to become more tolerant, comfortable with uncertainty, nonconforming, and self-reliant in personality—factors believed to be fostered by divorce-forced independence. And both men and women reevaluate what they consider important in a healthy relationship, placing greater weight on equal friendship and less on passionate love than they had the first time. As in earlier periods, divorce represents both a time of trauma and a time of growth (Baum, Rahav, & Sharon, 2005; Lloyd, Sailor, & Carney, 2014; Schneller & Arditti, 2004). Less is known about long-term adjustment following divorce among middle-aged men, perhaps because most enter new relationships and remarry within a short time.

Changing Parent–Child Relationships

Parents' positive relationships with their grown children are the result of a gradual process of "letting go," starting in childhood, gaining momentum in adolescence, and culminating in children's independent living. As noted earlier, most parents "launch" adult children sometime in midlife. But because more people are delaying having children to their thirties and even forties (see page 444 in Chapter 13), the age at which midlifers experience their children's departure varies widely. Most parents adjust well; only a minority have difficulty. Investment in nonparental relationships and roles, children's characteristics, parents' marital and economic circumstances, and cultural forces affect the extent to which this transition is expansive and rewarding or sad and distressing.

After their son Mark secured a career-entry job and moved out of the family home permanently, Devin and Trisha felt a twinge of nostalgia combined with a sense of pride in their grown son's maturity and success. Beyond this, they returned to rewarding careers and community participation and delighted in having more time for each other. Parents who have developed gratifying alternative activities typically welcome their children's adult status (Mitchell & Lovegreen, 2009). A strong work orientation, especially, predicts gains in life satisfaction after children depart from the home.

Wide cultural variations exist in the social clock for children's departure. Recall from Chapter 13 that many young people from low-SES homes and with cultural traditions of extended-family living do not leave home early. In the Southern European countries of Greece, Italy, and Spain, parents often actively delay their children's leaving. In Italy, for example, parents believe that moving out without a "justified" reason, usually marriage, signifies that something is wrong in the family. At the same time, Italian adults grant their grown children extensive freedom (Crocetti, Rabaglietti, & Sica, 2012). Parent–adult-child relationships are usually positive, making living with parents attractive.

With the end of parent–child coresidence comes a substantial decline in parental authority. Devin and Trisha no longer knew of Mark's daily comings and goings or expected him to inform them. Nevertheless, like most young adults, Mark visited regularly and telephoned, texted, and e-mailed often to report on events in his life, seek advice, and keep abreast of his parents' lives. Although the parental role changes, its continuation is important to middle-aged adults. Departure of children is a relatively minor event as long as parent–child contact and pleasurable interaction are sustained (Fingerman et al., 2016; Mitchell & Lovegreen, 2009). When communication seldom occurs or is negative, parents' psychological well-being declines.

Whether or not they reside with parents, young-adult children who are "off-time" in development—who deviate from parental expectations about how the path to adult responsibilities should unfold—can prompt parental strain (Settersten, 2003). Consider Elena, whose daughter was doing poorly in her college courses and in danger of not graduating. The need for extensive parental guidance, at a time when she expected her daughter to be more responsible and independent, caused anxiety and unhappiness for Elena, who was ready to reduce time devoted to active parenting.

In one study, researchers asked a large sample of 40- to 60-year-old parents to report on their grown children's problems and successes along with their own psychological well-being. Consistent with the familiar saying, "parents are only as happy as their least happy child," having even one problematic child dampened parents' well-being, but having a successful child did not have a compensating positive effect. The more grown children with problems, the poorer parents' well-being (Fingerman et al., 2012a). In contrast, it took multiple successful grown children to sway parents' well-being in a favorable direction. As with marriages, negative, conflict-ridden experiences with grown children are particularly salient, profoundly affecting midlife parents' psychological states.

Throughout middle adulthood, parents continue to give more assistance to children than they receive, especially while children are unmarried or when they face difficulties, such as marital breakup or unemployment (Ploeg et al., 2004; Zarit & Eggebeen, 2002). Support in Western countries typically flows "downstream": Although ethnic variations exist, most middle-aged parents provide more financial, practical, emotional, and social support to their offspring than to their aging parents, unless a parent has an urgent need (declining health or other crises) (Fingerman & Birditt, 2011; Fingerman et al., 2011a). In explaining their generous support of adult children, parents usually mention the importance of the relationship. And providing adult children with assistance enhances midlife psychological well-being (Marks & Greenfield, 2009). Clearly, middle-aged adults remain invested in their adult children's development and continue to reap deep personal rewards from the parental role.

However, the amount and type of support middle-aged adults provide vary with SES. Parents with more education and income give more financial assistance (Fingerman et al., 2012b). But low-SES parents give more overall support, usually consisting of coresidence plus various types of intangible assistance—advice, help with child care, emotional encouragement, and companionship. Nevertheless, because of widespread single parenthood plus larger families, low-SES parents must divide their supportive resources among more offspring. Consequently, on average, low-SES parents are able to give less tangible and intangible support to each child than their higher-SES counterparts (Fingerman et al., 2015). Finding themselves devoting much time to giving support that is thinly spread and, therefore, less effective in

Applying what we Know

Ways Middle-Aged Parents Can Promote Positive Ties with Their Adult Children

SUGGESTION	DESCRIPTION
Emphasize positive communication.	Let adult children and their intimate partners know of your respect, support, and interest. This not only communicates affection but also permits conflict to be handled in a constructive context.
Avoid unnecessary comments that are a holdover from childhood.	Adult children, like younger children, appreciate an age-appropriate relationship. Comments that have to do with safety, eating, and self-care ("Be careful on the freeway," "Don't eat those foods," "Make sure you wear a sweater—it's cold out today") annoy adult children and can stifle communication.
Accept the possibility that some cultural values and practices and aspects of lifestyle will be modified in the next generation.	In constructing a personal identity, most adult children have gone through a process of evaluating the meaning of cultural values and practices for their own lives. Traditions and lifestyles cannot be imposed on adult children.
When an adult child encounters difficulties, resist the urge to "fix" things.	Accept the fact that no meaningful change can take place without the willing cooperation of the adult child. Stepping in and taking over communicates a lack of confidence and respect. Find out whether the adult child wants your help, advice, and decision-making skills.
Be clear about your own needs and preferences.	When it is difficult to arrange for a visit, babysit, or provide other assistance, say so and negotiate a reasonable compromise rather than letting resentment build.

helping children launch their lives is likely draining and disappointing to many low-SES parents.

After children marry, parents must adjust to an enlarged family network that includes in-laws. Difficulties occur when parents do not approve of their child's partner or when the young couple adopts a way of life inconsistent with parents' values. Parents who take steps to forge a positive tie with a future daughter- or son-in-law generally experience a closer relationship after the couple marries (Fingerman et al., 2012d). And when warm, supportive relationships endure, intimacy between parents and children increases over the adult years, with great benefits for parents' life satisfaction (Ryff, Singer, & Seltzer, 2002). Members of the middle generation, especially mothers, usually take on the role of **kinkeeper,** gathering the family for celebrations and making sure everyone stays in touch.

Parents of adult children expect a mature relationship, marked by tranquility and contentment. Yet many factors—on both the child's and the parent's sides and also having to do with family circumstances—affect whether that goal is achieved. Applying What We Know above suggests ways middle-aged parents can increase the chances that bonds with adult children will be loving and rewarding and serve as contexts for personal growth.

Grandparenthood

Two years after Mark married, Devin and Trisha were thrilled to learn that a granddaughter was on the way. Compared with a generation ago, the arrival of grandparenthood occurs a decade or more later, due to postponement of marriage and childbearing. Currently, the average age of becoming a grandparent for U.S. women is 49; for U.S. men, 52. In Canada and many Western European nations, grandparenthood is further delayed, to the mid- to late fifties, likely because of factors linked to reduced childbearing, including lower rates of poverty, unintended births, and religiosity (Leopold & Skopek, 2015; Margolis, 2016). Yet a longer life expectancy means that many adults will spend one-third or more of their lifespan in the grandparent role.

Meanings of Grandparenthood. Middle-aged adults typically rate grandparenthood as highly important, following closely behind the roles of parent and spouse but ahead of worker, son or daughter, and sibling (Reitzes & Mutran, 2002). Why did Trisha and Devin, like many others their age, greet the announcement of a grandchild with such enthusiasm? Most people experience grandparenthood as a significant milestone, mentioning one or more of the following gratifications:

- *Valued older adult*—being perceived as a wise, helpful person
- *Immortality through descendants*—leaving behind not just one but two generations after death
- *Reinvolvement with personal past*—being able to pass family history and values to a new generation
- *Indulgence*—having fun with children without major child-rearing responsibilities (Hebblethwaite & Norris, 2011)

Grandparent–Grandchild Relationships. Grandparents' styles of relating to grandchildren vary as widely as the meanings they derive from their new role. The grandparent's and grandchild's age and sex make a difference. When their granddaughter was young, Trisha and Devin enjoyed an affectionate, playful relationship with her. As she got older, she looked to them for information and advice in addition to warmth and caring. By the time their granddaughter reached adolescence, Trisha and Devin had become role models, family historians, and conveyers of social, vocational, and religious values.

Living nearby is the strongest predictor of frequent, face-to-face interaction with young grandchildren and a major contributor to feelings of closeness with older grandchildren. Despite high family mobility in Western industrialized nations, most grandparents live near enough to at least one grandchild to enable regular visits. But because time and resources are limited, number of "grandchild sets" (households with grandchildren) reduces grandparent visits (Bangerter & Waldron, 2014; Uhlenberg & Hammill, 1998). A strong desire to affect the development of grandchildren can motivate grandparents' involvement. As grandchildren get older, distance becomes less influential and relationship quality more so: The extent to which adolescent or young-adult grandchildren believe their grandparent values contact is a good predictor of a close bond (Brussoni & Boon, 1998).

Maternal grandmothers report more frequent visits with grandchildren than do paternal grandmothers, who are slightly advantaged over both maternal and paternal grandfathers (Uhlenberg & Hammill, 1998). Typically, relationships are closer between grandparents and grandchildren of the same sex and, especially, between maternal grandmothers and granddaughters—a pattern found in many countries (Brown & Rodin, 2004). Grandmothers also report higher satisfaction with the grandparent role than grandfathers, perhaps because grandmothers are more likely to participate in recreational, religious, and family activities with grandchildren (Reitzes & Mutran, 2004; Silverstein & Marenco, 2001). The grandparent role may be a vital means through which women satisfy their kinkeeping function.

SES and ethnicity also influence grandparent–grandchild ties. In higher-income families, where the grandparent role is not central to family maintenance and survival, it is fairly unstructured and takes many forms. In low-income families, by contrast, grandparents often perform essential activities. For example, many single parents live with their families of origin and depend on grandparents' assistance, including help with caregiving, to reduce the impact of poverty (Masten, 2013). As children experience family stressors, bonds with grandparents can take on increasing importance, serving as a vital source of resilience.

In cultures that stress interdependence among generations of family members, grandparents are absorbed into an extended-family household and often become actively involved in child rearing. When a Chinese, Korean, or Mexican-American maternal grandmother is a homemaker, she is the preferred caregiver while parents of young children are at work (Low & Goh, 2015; Williams & Torrez, 1998). Similarly, involvement in child care is high among Native-American grandparents. In the absence of a biological grandparent, an unrelated aging adult may be integrated into the family to serve as a mentor and disciplinarian for children (Werner, 1991). (See Chapter 2, page 63, for a description of the grandmother's role in the African-American extended family.)

Increasingly, grandparents have stepped in as primary caregivers in the face of serious family problems. As the Social Issues: Health box on page 554 reveals, a rising number of American children live apart from their parents in grandparent-headed households. Despite their willingness to help and their competence at child rearing, grandparents who take full responsibility for young children experience considerable emotional and financial strain. They need more assistance from community and government agencies than is currently available.

Because parents usually serve as gatekeepers of grandparents' contact with grandchildren, relationships between grandparents and their daughter-in-law or son-in-law strongly affect the closeness of grandparent–grandchild ties. A positive bond with a daughter-in-law seems particularly important in the relationship between grandparents and their son's children (Fingerman, 2004; Sims & Rofail, 2013). And after a marital breakup, grandparents who are related to the custodial parent (typically the mother) have more frequent contact with grandchildren.

When family relationships are positive, grandparenthood provides an important means of fulfilling personal and societal needs in midlife and beyond. Typically, grandparents are a frequent source of pleasure, support, and knowledge for children, adolescents, and young adults. They also provide the young with firsthand experience in how older people think and function. In return, grandchildren become deeply attached to grandparents and keep them abreast of social change. Clearly, grandparenthood is a vital context for sharing between generations.

Many grandparents derive great joy from an affectionate, playful relationship with young grandchildren. As this grandchild gets older, he may look to his grandfather for advice, as a role model, and for family history.

Social Issues: Health

Grandparents Rearing Grandchildren: The Skipped-Generation Family

Nearly 2.7 million U.S. grandparents live with grandchildren but apart from the children's parents in **skipped-generation families** (Ellis & Simmons, 2014). The number of grandparents with primary responsibility for rearing grandchildren has increased over the past two decades, with an especially sharp rise during the economic recession of 2007 to 2009. The arrangement occurs in all ethnic groups, but more often in African-American, Hispanic, and Native-American families than in European-American families. Although grandparent caregivers are more likely to be women than men, many grandfathers participate (Fuller-Thomson & Minkler, 2005, 2007). Grandparents generally step in when parents' troubled lives—severe financial hardship, substance abuse, child abuse and neglect, family violence, or physical or mental illness—threaten children's safety and security (Smith, 2016). Often these families take in two or more children.

As a result, grandparents usually assume the parenting role under highly stressful life circumstances. Unfavorable child-rearing experiences have left their mark on the children, who show high rates of learning difficulties, depression, and antisocial behavior. Absent parents' adjustment difficulties strain family relationships. Parents may interfere by violating the grandparents' behavioral limits, taking grandchildren away without permission, or making promises to children that they do not keep. These children also introduce financial burdens into households that often are already low-income (Hayslip, Blumenthal, & Garner, 2014; Henderson & Bailey, 2015). All these factors heighten grandparents' emotional distress.

Grandparents struggle with daily dilemmas—wanting to be grandparents, not parents; wanting the parent to be present in the child's life but fearing for the child's well-being if the parent returns and does not provide good care (Templeton, 2011). And grandparent caregivers, at a time when they anticipated having more time for spouses, friends, and leisure, instead have less. Many report feeling emotionally drained, depressed, and worried about what will happen to the children if their own health fails (Henderson & Bailey, 2015). Some families are extremely burdened. Native-American caregiving grandparents are especially likely to be unemployed, to have a disability, to be caring for several grandchildren, and to be living in extreme poverty (Fuller-Thomson & Minkler, 2005).

Despite great hardship, these grandparents seem to realize their widespread image as "silent saviors," often forging close emotional bonds with their grandchildren and using effective child-rearing practices (Gibson, 2005). Compared with children in divorced, single-parent families, blended families, or foster families, children reared by grandparents fare better in adjustment (Rubin et al., 2008; Solomon & Marx, 1995).

Skipped-generation families have a tremendous need for social and financial support and intervention services for troubled children. Custodial grandparents with relatives and friends they can count on benefit in physical and mental health (Hayslip, Blumenthal, & Garner, 2015). Others say that support

Although custodial grandparents usually assume the parenting role under highly stressful circumstances, most find compensating rewards in rearing grandchildren.

groups—for themselves and for their grandchildren—are especially helpful, yet only a minority make use of such interventions (Smith, Rodriguez, & Palmieri, 2010). This suggests that grandparents need special help in finding out about and accessing support services.

Although their everyday lives are often stressful, caregiving grandparents—even those rearing children with serious problems—report as much fulfillment in the grandparent role as typical grandparents do (Hayslip & Kaminski, 2005). The warmer the grandparent–grandchild bond, the greater grandparents' long-term life satisfaction (Goodman, 2012). Many grandparents mention joy from sharing children's lives and feelings of pride at children's progress, which help compensate for difficult circumstances. And some grandparents view the rearing of grandchildren as a "second chance"—an opportunity to make up for earlier, unfavorable parenting experiences and "do it right" (Dolbin-MacNab, 2006).

Middle-Aged Children and Their Aging Parents

The number of middle-aged Americans with at least one living parent has risen dramatically—from 10 percent in 1900 to more than 60 percent today (Wiemers & Bianchi, 2015). A longer life expectancy means that adult children and their parents are increasingly likely to grow old together. What are middle-aged children's relationships with their aging parents like? And how does life change for adult children when an aging parent's health declines?

Frequency and Quality of Contact.
A widespread myth is that adults of past generations were more devoted than today's

adults to their aging parents. Although adult children spend less time in physical proximity to their parents, the reason is not neglect or isolation. Because of a desire to be independent, made possible by gains in health and financial security, fewer aging adults live with younger generations now than in the past. Nevertheless, nearly two-thirds of older adults in the United States live close to at least one of their children, and frequency of contact is high through both visits and telephone calls (U.S. Department of Health and Human Services, 2016b). Proximity increases with age: Aging adults who move usually do so in the direction of kin, and younger people tend to move in the direction of their aging parents.

Middle age is a time when adults reassess relationships with their parents, just as they rethink other close ties. Many adult children become more appreciative of their parents' strengths and generosity and mention positive changes in the quality of the relationship, even after parents show physical declines. A warm, enjoyable relationship contributes to both parent and adult-child well-being (Fingerman et al., 2007, 2008; Pudrovska, 2009). Trisha, for example, felt closer to her parents and often asked them to tell her more about their earlier lives.

Middle-aged daughters forge closer, more supportive relationships with aging parents, especially mothers, than do middle-aged sons (Suitor, Gilligan, & Pillemer, 2015). But this gender difference may be declining. Sons report closer ties and greater assistance to aging parents in recent than in previous studies. Changing gender roles are likely responsible. Because the majority of contemporary middle-aged women are employed, they face many competing demands on their time and energy. Consequently, men are becoming more involved in family responsibilities, including with aging parents (Fingerman & Birditt, 2011; Pew Research Center, 2013c). Despite this shift, women's investment continues to exceed men's.

In cultures that emphasize interdependence, parents often live with their married children. For example, traditionally, Chinese, Japanese, and Korean aging parents moved in with a son and his wife, who tended to her in-laws' needs; today, many parents live with a daughter and her family, too. This tradition of coresidence, however, is declining in some parts of Asia and in the United States, as more Asian and Asian-American aging adults choose to live on their own. And in a growing number of these families, both the husband's and wife's aging parents receive support, though a bias toward providing greater practical and financial help to the son's parents remains (Davey & Takagi, 2013; Kim et al., 2015; Zhang, Gu, & Luo, 2014). In African-American and Hispanic families as well, coresidence is common. Regardless of whether coresidence and daily contact are typical, relationship quality usually reflects patterns established earlier: Positive parent–child ties generally remain so, as do conflict-ridden interactions.

Help exchanged between adult children and their aging parents is responsive to past and current family circumstances. The more positive the history of the parent–child tie, the more help given and received. Also, aging parents give more help to unmarried adult children and to those with disabilities. Similarly, adult children give more practical help and emotional support to aging

In midlife, many adults develop warmer, more supportive relationships with their aging parents. At a birthday party for her mother, this daughter expresses love and appreciation for her mother's strengths and generosity.

parents who are widowed or in poor health (Suitor et al., 2016). At the same time, middle-aged adults do what they can to maximize the overall quantity of help offered, as needed: While continuing to provide generous assistance to their children because of the priority placed on the parent–child tie (see page 551), midlifers augment the aid they give to their parents as parental health problems increase (Stephens et al., 2009).

Even when parent–child relationships have been emotionally distant, many adult children offer more support as parents age, out of a sense of altruism and family duty. And parent–child bonds often become closer as parents get older (Fingerman et al., 2011a; Ward, Spitz, & Deane, 2009).

In sum, as long as multiple roles are manageable and the experiences within each are generally positive, midlife intergenerational assistance as family members (aging parents) have increased needs is best characterized as *resource expansion* rather than as merely conflicting demands that inevitably drain energy and detract from psychological well-being (Pew Research Center, 2013c; Stephens et al., 2009). Recall from the Biology and Environment box on pages 546–547 that midlifers derive great personal benefits from successfully managing multiple roles. Their enhanced self-esteem, mastery, and sense of meaning and purpose expand their motivation and energy to handle added family-role demands, from which they reap additional personal rewards.

Caring for Aging Parents. About one-fourth of U.S. adult children provide unpaid care to an ill or disabled aging adult (Stepler, 2015). The burden of caring for aging parents can be great. In Chapter 2, we noted that as birthrates have declined, the family structure has become increasingly "top-heavy," with more generations alive but fewer younger members. Consequently, more than one older family member is likely to need assistance, with fewer younger adults available to provide it.

The term **sandwich generation** is widely used to refer to the idea that middle-aged adults must care for multiple generations above and below them at the same time. Although only a minority of contemporary middle-aged adults who care for aging parents have children younger than age 18 at home, many are providing assistance to young-adult children and to grandchildren—obligations that, when combined with work and community responsibilities, can lead middle-aged caregivers to feel "sandwiched," or squeezed, between the pressures of older and younger generations. As more baby boomers move into late adulthood and as their adult children continue to delay childbearing, the number of midlifers who are working, rearing children, and caring for aging parents will increase.

Middle-aged adults living far from aging parents who are in poor health often substitute financial help for direct care, if they have the means. But when parents live nearby and have no spouse to meet their needs, adult children usually engage in direct care. Regardless of family income level, African-American, Asian-American, and Hispanic adults give aging parents more direct care and financial help than European-American adults do. And compared with their white counterparts, African Americans and Hispanics express a stronger sense of obligation, and find it more personally rewarding, to support their aging parents (Fingerman et al., 2011b; Roth et al., 2015; Shuey & Hardy, 2003). African Americans often draw on close, family-like relationships with friends and neighbors for caregiving assistance.

In all ethnic groups, responsibility for providing care to aging parents falls more on daughters than on sons. Why are women usually the principal caregivers? Families turn to the person who seems most available—living nearby and with fewer commitments that might interfere with the ability to assist. These unstated rules, in addition to parents' preference for same-sex caregivers (aging mothers live longer), lead more women to fill the role (see Figure 16.4). Daughters also feel more obligated than sons to care for aging parents (MetLife, 2011a; Pillemer & Suitor, 2013; Suitor et al., 2015). And although couples strive to be fair to both sides of the family, they tend to provide more direct care for the wife's parents. This bias, however, is weaker in ethnic minority families and not evident in Asian nations with cultural traditions specifying that daughters-in-law provide care to their husband's parents (Chu, Xie, & Yu, 2011; Shuey & Hardy, 2003).

As Figure 16.4 shows, nearly one-fourth of American working women are caregivers; others quit their jobs to provide care. And the time they devote to caring for a chronically ill or disabled aging parent is substantial, averaging 20 hours per week (AARP, 2015; MetLife, 2011a). Nevertheless, men—although doing less than women—do contribute. In one investigation, employed men spent an average of 7½ hours per week caring for parents or parents-in-law (Neal & Hammer, 2007). Tim, for example, looked in on his father, a recent stroke victim, every evening, reading to him, running errands, making household repairs, and taking care of finances. His sister, however, provided more hands-on care—cooking, feeding, bathing, managing medication, and doing laundry. The care sons and daughters provide tends to be divided along gender-role lines. About 10 percent of the time—generally when no other family member can do so—sons become primary caregivers, heavily involved in basic-care tasks (Pinquart & Sörensen, 2006).

As adults move from early to later middle age, the sex difference in parental caregiving declines. Perhaps as men reduce their vocational commitments and feel less need to conform to a "masculine" gender role, they grow more able and willing to provide basic care (Marks, 1996; MetLife, 2011a). At the same time, parental caregiving may contribute to men's greater openness to the "feminine" side of their personalities. A man who cared for his mother, severely impaired by dementia, commented on how the experience altered his outlook: "When this caregiving journey started, I felt scared and unprepared. Now I feel privileged and empowered. I feel fortunate to be able to hold my mom and kiss her . . . she continues to teach me, every day" (Colbert, 2014).

Most adult children help willingly, and many benefit personally (Brown & Brown, 2014). At the same time, caring for a chronically ill or disabled parent is highly stressful. Over time, the parent usually gets worse, and the caregiving task escalates. As Tim explained to Devin and Trisha, "One of the hardest aspects is the emotional strain of seeing my father's physical and mental decline up close."

Caregivers who share a household with ill parents—about 23 percent of U.S. adult children—experience the most stress. When a parent and child who have lived separately for years must move in together, conflicts generally arise over routines and lifestyles. But the greatest source of stress is problem behavior, especially for caregivers of parents who have deteriorated mentally (Bastawrous et al., 2015). Tim's sister reported that their father would wake during the night, ask repetitive questions, follow her around the house, and become agitated and combative.

Parental caregiving often has emotional, physical, and financial consequences. It leads to role overload, high job

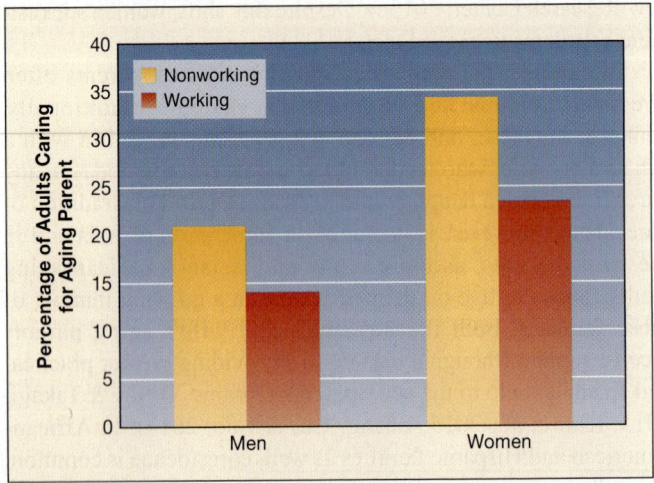

FIGURE 16.4 Baby boomers, by work status and gender, who provide basic personal care to an aging parent in poor health. A survey of a nationally representative sample of 1,100 U.S. men and women over age 50 with at least one parent living revealed that more nonworking than working adults engaged in basic personal care (assistance with such activities as dressing, feeding, and bathing). Regardless of work status, many more women than men were caregivers. (Adapted from *The MetLife Study of Caregiving Costs to Working Caregivers: Double Jeopardy for Baby Boomers Caring for Their Parents,* June 2011, Figure 3. Reprinted by permission of the MetLife Mature Market Institute, New York, NY.)

As midlife progresses, more men become involved in caring for an aging parent with a chronic illness or disability. Although the experience is stressful, most help willingly and benefit personally, perhaps becoming more open to the "feminine" side of their personalities.

LOOK and LISTEN

Ask a middle-aged adult caring for an aging parent in declining health to describe both the stressful and rewarding aspects of caregiving. What strategies does he or she use to reduce stress? To what extent does the caregiver share caregiving burdens with family members and enlist the support of community organizations?

absenteeism, exhaustion, inability to concentrate, feelings of hostility, anxiety about aging, and high rates of depression, with women more profoundly affected than men (Pinquart & Sörensen, 2006; Wang & Shi, 2016). Caregivers who must reduce their employment hours or leave the labor force to provide care (mostly women) face not just lost wages but also diminished retirement benefits. Despite having more time to care for an ill parent, women who quit work fare especially poorly in adjustment, probably because of social isolation and financial strain (Bookman & Kimbrel, 2011). Positive experiences at work can actually reduce the stress of parental care as caregivers bring a favorable self-evaluation and a positive mood home with them.

In cultures and subcultures where adult children feel an especially strong sense of obligation to care for aging parents, the emotional toll is also high (Knight & Sayegh, 2010). In research on Korean, Korean-American, and European-American caregivers of parents with mental disabilities, the Koreans and Korean Americans reported higher levels of family obligation and care burden—and also higher levels of anxiety and depression—than the European Americans (Lee & Farran, 2004; Youn et al., 1999). And among African-American caregivers, women who strongly endorsed cultural reasons for providing care ("It's what my people have always done") fared less well in mental health two years later than women who moderately endorsed cultural reasons (Dilworth-Anderson, Goodwin, & Williams, 2004).

Social support is highly effective in reducing caregiver stress. Tim's encouragement, assistance, and willingness to listen helped his sister cope with in-home care of their father so that she could find satisfactions in it. When caregiving becomes a team effort with multiple family members trading off, caregivers cope more effectively. Under these conditions, despite being demanding and stressful, it can enhance psychological well-being (Roberto & Jarrott, 2008; Roth et al., 2015). Adult children feel gratified at having helped and gain in self-understanding, problem solving, sense of competence, and appreciation of life's meaning.

In Denmark, Sweden, and Japan, a government-sponsored home helper system eases the burden of parental care by making specially trained nonfamily caregivers available, based on older adults' needs (Saito, Auestad, & Waerness, 2010). In the United States, in-home care by a nonfamily caregiver is too costly for most families; less than one-third of nonpaid family caregivers report receiving supplementary paid help from others (AARP, 2015). And unless they must, few people want to place their parents in formal care, such as nursing homes, which also are expensive. Applying What We Know on page 558 summarizes ways to relieve the stress of caring for an aging parent—at the individual, family, community, and societal levels. We will address additional care options, along with interventions for caregivers, in Chapter 17.

Siblings

As Tim's relationship with his sister reveals, siblings are ideally suited to provide social support. Nevertheless, a survey of a large sample of ethnically diverse Americans revealed that sibling contact and support decline from early to middle adulthood, rebounding only after age 70 for siblings living near each other (White, 2001). Decreased midlife contact is probably due to the demands of middle-aged adults' diverse roles. However, most adult siblings report getting together or talking on the phone at least monthly (Antonucci, Akiyama, & Merline, 2002).

Despite reduced contact, many siblings feel closer in midlife, often in response to major life events (Stewart et al., 2001). Launching and marriage of children seem to prompt siblings to think more about each other. As Tim commented, "It helped our relationship when my sister's children were out of the house and married. I'm sure she cared about me. I think she just didn't have time!" And when parents die, adult children often realize that they have become the oldest generation and must look to each other to sustain family ties.

Not all sibling bonds improve, of course. Recollections of parental favoritism in childhood, and fathers' current favoritism, are associated with negativity in adult sibling relationships (Gilligan et al., 2013; Suitor et al., 2009). The influence of mothers' current favoritism is complex. In one study, middle-aged children expressed greater closeness to siblings whom they perceived their mother favored, and reduced closeness to siblings their mother disfavored (Gilligan, Suitor, & Nam, 2015). Perhaps adult children were drawn toward or away from certain siblings by the same traits that had affected their mothers. Or they might have attempted to improve their own status with their mothers

Applying what we Know

Relieving the Stress of Caring for an Aging Parent

STRATEGY	DESCRIPTION
Use effective coping strategies.	Use problem-centered coping to manage the parent's behavior and caregiving tasks. Delegate responsibilities to other family members, seek assistance from friends and neighbors, and recognize the parent's limits while calling on capacities the parent does have. Use emotion-centered coping to reinterpret the situation in a positive way, such as emphasizing the opportunity it offers for personal growth and for giving to parents in the last years of their lives. Avoid denial of anger, depression, and anxiety in response to the caregiving burden, which heightens stress.
Seek social support.	Confide in family members and friends about the stress of caregiving, seeking their encouragement and help. So far as possible, avoid quitting work to care for an ill parent; doing so is associated with social isolation and loss of financial resources.
Make use of community resources.	Contact community organizations to seek information and assistance, in the form of caregiver support groups, in-home respite help, home-delivered meals, transportation, and adult day care.
Press for workplace and public policies that relieve the emotional and financial burdens of caring for an aging parent.	Encourage your employer to provide benefits, such as flexible work hours and employment leave, for caregiving. Communicate with lawmakers and other citizens about the need for public policies to help pay for caregiving. Emphasize the need for improved health insurance plans that reduce the financial strain of caring for an aging parent on middle- and low-income families.

by bonding with favored siblings and avoiding disfavored ones. Large inequities in parental caregiving can also unleash sibling tensions (Silverstein & Giarrusso, 2010; Suitor et al., 2013). And when aging parents need care, sibling conflict worsens if perceptions of parental favoritism are present.

As in early adulthood, sister–sister relationships tend to be closer than sister–brother and brother–brother ties, a difference apparent in many industrialized nations (Cicirelli, 1995; Fowler, 2009). But a comparison of middle-aged men of the baby-boom generation with those of the preceding cohort revealed warmer, more expressive ties between baby-boom brothers (Bedford & Avioli, 2006). A contributing factor may be baby boomers' more flexible gender-role attitudes.

In industrialized nations, sibling relationships are voluntary. In village societies, they are generally involuntary and basic to family functioning. For example, among Asian Pacific Islanders, family social life is organized around strong brother–sister attachments. A brother–sister pair is often treated as a unit in exchange marriages with another family. After marriage, brothers are expected to protect sisters, and sisters serve as spiritual mentors to brothers. Families not only include biological siblings but bestow on other relatives, such as cousins, the status of brother or sister, creating an unusually large network of lifelong sibling support (Cicirelli, 1995). Cultural norms reduce sibling conflict, thereby ensuring family cooperation.

Friendships

As family responsibilities declined in middle age, Devin found he had more time to spend with friends. On Friday afternoons, he met several male friends at a coffee house, and they chatted for a couple of hours. But most of Devin's friendships were couple-based—relationships he shared with Trisha. Compared with Devin, Trisha more often got together with friends on her own.

Middle-aged friendships reflect the same trends discussed in Chapter 14. At all ages, men's friendships are less intimate than women's. Men tend to talk about sports, politics, and business, whereas women focus on feelings and life's challenges. Women report a greater number of close friends and say they both receive from and provide their friends with more emotional support (Fiori & Denckla, 2015).

These middle-aged sisters express their mutual affection at a reunion. Even when they have only limited contact, siblings, especially sisters, often feel closer in midlife.

Because of their demanding everyday lives, many midlifers welcome the ease of keeping in touch with friends through social media. Though falling short of young adults' use, connecting regularly with friends through Facebook and other social media sites has risen rapidly among U.S. middle-aged adults (see Figure 16.5) (Perrin, 2015). As in early adulthood, women tend to be more active users. And users have more offline close relationships, sometimes using Facebook to revive "dormant" friendships.

Still, for both sexes, number of friends declines from middle to late adulthood, probably because people become less willing to invest in nonfamily ties unless they are very rewarding. As selectivity of friendship increases, older adults try harder to get along with friends (Antonucci & Akiyama, 1995). Having chosen a friend, middle-aged people attach great value to the relationship and take extra steps to protect it.

LOOK and LISTEN

Ask a middle-aged couple you know well to describe the number and quality of their friendships today compared with their friendships in early adulthood. Does their report match research findings? Explain.

By midlife, family relationships and friendships support different aspects of psychological well-being. Family ties protect against serious threats and losses, offering security within a long-term timeframe. In contrast, friendships serve as current sources of pleasure and satisfaction, with women benefiting somewhat more than men (Levitt & Cici-Gokaltun, 2011). As middle-aged couples renew their sense of companionship, they may combine the best of family and friendship.

Ask yourself

CONNECT Cite evidence that early family relationships affect middle-aged adults' bonds with adult children, aging parents, and siblings.

APPLY Raylene and her brother Walter live in the same city as their aging mother, Elsie. When Elsie could no longer live independently, Raylene took primary responsibility for her care. What factors probably contributed to Raylene's involvement in caregiving and Walter's lesser role?

REFLECT Ask one of your parents for his or her view of how the parent–child relationship changed as you transitioned to new adult roles, such as college student, career-entry worker, married partner, or parent. Do you agree?

Vocational Life

16.8 Discuss job satisfaction and career development in middle adulthood, with special attention to gender differences and experiences of ethnic minorities.

16.9 Discuss career change and unemployment in middle adulthood.

16.10 Discuss the importance of planning for retirement.

Work continues to be a salient aspect of identity and self-esteem in middle adulthood. More so than in earlier or later years, people attempt to increase the personal meaning and self-direction of their vocational lives. At the same time, certain aspects of job performance improve. Middle-aged employees have lower rates of absenteeism, turnover, and accidents. They are also more effective workplace citizens—more often helping colleagues and trying to improve group performance and less often complaining about trivial issues. And because of their greater knowledge and experience, their work productivity typically equals or exceeds that of younger workers (Ng & Feldman, 2008). Consequently, an older employee ought to be as valuable as a younger employee, and possibly more so.

The large tide of baby boomers currently moving through midlife and (as we will see in Chapter 18) the desire of most to work longer than the previous generation means that the number of older workers will rise dramatically over the next few decades (Leonesio et al., 2012). Yet a favorable transition from adult worker to older worker is hindered by negative stereotypes of aging—incorrect assumptions of limited learning capacity, slower decision making, and resistance to change and supervision (Posthuma & Campion, 2009). Furthermore, gender discrimination continues to restrict the career attainments of many women. Let's take a close look at middle-aged work life.

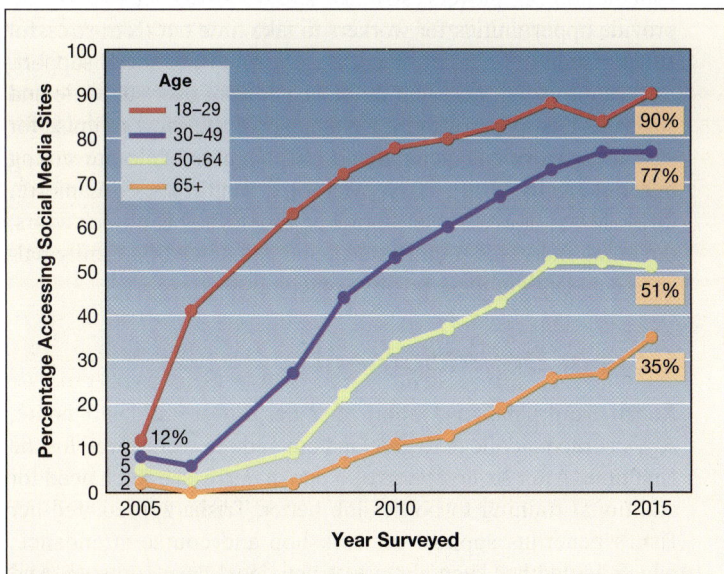

FIGURE 16.5 Gains in use of social media sites by age group from 2005 to 2015. Repeated surveys of large representative samples of U.S. adults revealed that use of social media sites increased substantially for all age groups. Though not as avid users as young adults, most middle-aged adults use social media sites, primarily Facebook. (From A. Perrin, 2015, "Social Media Usage: 2005–2015." Pew Research Center's Internet & American Life Project, Washington, D.C., October 8, 2015, www.pewinternet.org. Adapted by permission.)

Job Satisfaction

Job satisfaction has both psychological and economic significance. If people are dissatisfied at work, the consequences include absenteeism, turnover, grievances, and strikes, all of which are costly to employers.

Research shows that job satisfaction increases in midlife in diverse nations and at all occupational levels, from executives to hourly workers (see Figure 16.6). When different aspects of jobs are considered, intrinsic satisfaction—happiness with the work itself—shows a strong age-related gain (Barnes-Farrell & Matthews, 2007). Extrinsic satisfaction—contentment with supervision, pay, and promotions—changes very little.

But the age-related increase in job satisfaction is weaker for women than for men. More women take leaves from work, drop to part-time, or use flexible schedule arrangements to meet family obligations, deviating from the U.S. "ideal-worker" expectation of complete commitment to their job, through long work hours. In response, employers may penalize them—circumstances that lead them to feel unfairly treated (Kmec, O'Connor, & Schieman, 2014). Women's reduced chances for advancement may also lessen contentment with work life. The midlife rise in job satisfaction is also weaker for blue-collar than for white-collar workers, perhaps because blue-collar workers have less control over their own work schedules and activities (Avolio & Sosik, 1999).

What explains the overall rise in job satisfaction during middle adulthood? An improved capacity to cope effectively with difficult situations and a broader time perspective probably contribute. "When I first started teaching, I complained about a lot of things," remarked Devin. "From my current vantage point, I can tell a big problem from a trivial one." Moving out of unrewarding work roles, as Trisha did when she moved from a large to a small law firm, where she felt appreciated, can also boost morale. Key characteristics that predict job well-being include involvement in decision making, reasonable workloads, and good physical working conditions. Older people may have greater access to jobs that are attractive in these ways. Furthermore, having fewer alternative positions into which they can move, older workers generally reduce their career aspirations (Warr, 2001, 2007). As the perceived gap between actual and possible achievements narrows, job involvement—importance of one's work to self-esteem—increases.

Although emotional engagement with work is usually seen as psychologically healthy, it can also result in **burnout**—a condition in which long-term job stress leads to mental exhaustion, a sense of loss of personal control, and feelings of reduced accomplishment. Burnout occurs more often in the helping professions, including health care, human services, and teaching, which place high emotional demands on employees. Although people in interpersonally demanding jobs are as psychologically healthy as other people, sometimes a worker's dedication exceeds his or her coping skills, especially in an unsupportive work environment (Schmidt, Neubach, & Heuer, 2007). Burnout is associated with excessive work assignments for available time and lack of encouragement and feedback from supervisors.

Burnout is a serious occupational hazard, linked to impaired attention and memory, severe depression, on-the-job injuries, physical illnesses, poor job performance, absenteeism, and turnover (Ahola & Hakanen, 2014; Sandström et al., 2005). To prevent burnout, employers can make sure workloads are reasonable, provide opportunities for workers to take time out from stressful situations, limit hours of stressful work, and offer social support. Interventions that augment employee control over schedule and supervisor support for family and personal life show promise for sustaining work engagement and effectiveness while preventing burnout (Kelly et al., 2014; Margolis, Matthews, & Lapierre, 2014; Moen et al., 2011). Improved employee health behaviors, including increased nightly sleep, and gains in work–family balance help explain these positive outcomes.

Career Development

Recall from Chapter 15 that after her oldest child left home, Anya earned a college degree and entered the work force for the first time. After several years as a parish nurse, she felt a need for additional training to do her job better. Trisha appreciated her firm's generous support of workshop and course attendance, which helped her keep abreast of new legal developments. And as college dean, Devin took a summer seminar on management effectiveness. As these experiences reveal, career development is vital throughout work life.

Job Training.
Anya's 35-year-old supervisor, Roy, was surprised when she asked for time off to upgrade her skills. "You're

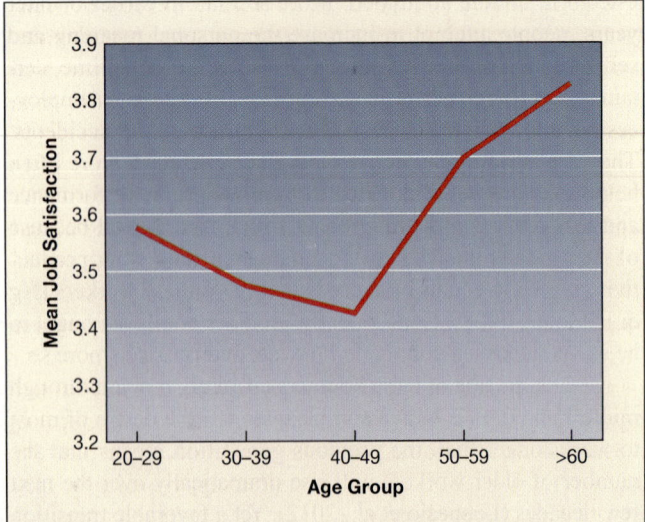

FIGURE 16.6 Age-related gain in job satisfaction from early to middle adulthood. In this study of more than 2,000 university employees at all levels, from secretary to university president, job satisfaction dropped slightly in early adulthood as people encountered some discouraging experiences (see Chapter 14). In middle age, job satisfaction showed a steady rise. (From W. A. Hochwarter et al., 2001, "A Note on the Nonlinearity of the Age–Job-Satisfaction Relationship," *Journal of Applied Social Psychology,* 31, p. 1232. Copyright © 2001, John Wiley and Sons. Reproduced with permission of Wiley Inc.)

in your fifties," he replied. "What're you going to do with so much new information at this point in your life?"

Roy's insensitive, narrow-minded response, though usually unspoken, is all too common among managers—even some who are older themselves! Research suggests that training and on-the-job career counseling are less available to older workers. And when career development activities are offered, older employees may be less likely to volunteer for them (Barnes-Farrell & Matthews, 2007; Cappelli & Novelli, 2010). What influences willingness to engage in job training and updating?

Personal characteristics are important: With age, growth needs give way somewhat to security needs. Consequently, learning and challenge may have less intrinsic value to many older workers. Perhaps for this reason, older employees depend more on co-worker and supervisor encouragement for vocational development (Claes & Heymans, 2008). Yet as we have seen, they are less likely to have supportive supervisors. Furthermore, negative stereotypes of aging reduce older workers' self-efficacy, or confidence, that they can get better at their jobs (Maurer, Wrenn, & Weiss, 2003). Self-efficacy is a powerful predictor of employees' efforts to renew and expand career-relevant skills.

Workplace characteristics matter, too. An employee given work that requires new learning must pursue that learning to complete the assignment. Unfortunately, older workers sometimes receive more routine tasks than younger workers. Therefore, some of their reduced motivation to engage in career-relevant learning may be due to the type of assignments they receive. In companies with a more favorable *age climate* (view of older workers), mature employees participate frequently in further education, and they also report greater self-efficacy, work commitment, and job satisfaction (Bowen, Noack, & Staudinger, 2011; MacDonald & Levy, 2016).

Gender and Ethnicity: The Glass Ceiling. In her thirties, Jewel became a company president by starting her own business. Having concluded that, as a woman, she had little chance of rising to a top executive position in a large corporation, she didn't even try. Although women and ethnic minorities have gradually gained in access to managerial careers, they remain a long distance from gender and ethnic equality.

From career entry on, inequalities in promotion between men and women and between whites and blacks become more pronounced over time—findings still evident after education, work skills, and work productivity have been controlled (Barreto, Ryan, & Schmitt, 2009; Huffman, 2012). Women who are promoted usually get stuck in mid-level positions. When the most prestigious high-level management jobs are considered, white men are overwhelmingly advantaged: They account for 72 percent of chief executive officers at large corporations and 96 percent at Fortune 500 companies (U.S. Department of Labor, 2016a).

Women and ethnic minorities face a **glass ceiling,** or invisible barrier to advancement up the corporate ladder. Why is this so? Management is an art and skill that must be taught. Yet women and ethnic minorities have less access to mentors, role

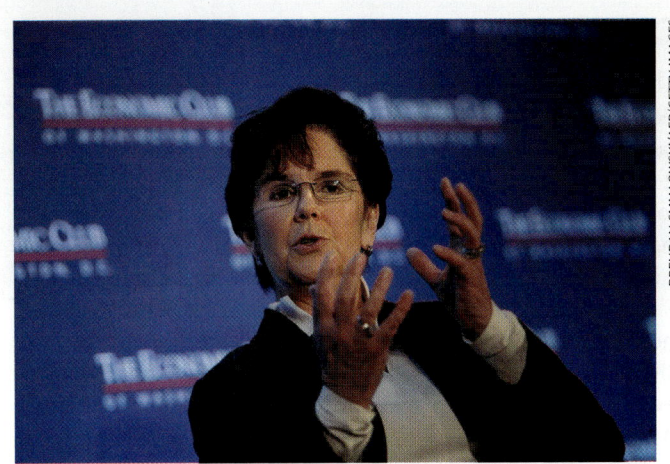

Phebe Novakovic became CEO of General Dynamics at age 55. She is among a handful of women who have attained the top leadership position in a major corporation.

models, and informal networks that serve as training routes (Baumgartner & Schneider, 2010). And stereotyped doubts about women's career commitment and ability to become strong managers (especially women with children) also contribute, leading supervisors to underrate their competence and not to recommend them for formal management training programs (Hoobler, Lemmon, & Wayne, 2011). Furthermore, challenging, high-risk, high-visibility assignments that require leadership and open the door to advancement, such as startup ventures, international experience, and troubleshooting, are less often granted to both women and minorities.

Finally, women who demonstrate qualities linked to leadership and advancement—assertiveness, confidence, forcefulness, and ambition—encounter prejudice because they deviate from traditional gender roles, even though they more often combine these traits with a democratic, collaborative style of leading than do men (Carli, 2015; Cheung & Halpern, 2010). To overcome this bias, women in line for top positions must demonstrate greater competence than their male counterparts. In an investigation of several hundred senior managers at a multinational financial services corporation, promoted female managers had earned higher performance ratings than promoted male managers (Lyness & Heilman, 2006). In contrast, no gender difference existed in performance of managers not selected for promotion.

Like Jewel, many women have dealt with the glass ceiling by going around it, leaving the corporate environment and going into business for themselves. Over the past two decades, startup businesses in the United States owned and operated by women grew at 1½ times the national average. And today, one-third of women-owned firms have ethnic minority owners. The large majority of women entrepreneurs are successful, meeting or exceeding their earnings goals (American Express Open, 2014). But when women and ethnic minorities leave the corporate world to further their careers, companies not only lose valuable talent but also fail to address the leadership needs of an increasingly diverse work force.

Career Change at Midlife

Although most people remain in the same vocation through middle age, career change does occur, as with Elena's shift from journalism to teaching and creative writing. Recall that circumstances at home and at work motivated Elena's decision to pursue a new vocation. Like other career changers, she wanted a more satisfying life—a goal she attained by ending an unhappy marriage and initiating a long-awaited vocational move at the same time.

As noted earlier, midlife career changes are seldom radical; they typically involve leaving one line of work for a related one. Elena sought a more stimulating, involving job, a direction pursued by more middle-aged professional women than men (Mainiero & Sullivan, 2005). But other people move in the reverse direction—to careers that are more relaxing, free of painful decisions, and less demanding (Juntunen, Wegner, & Matthews, 2002). The decision to change is often difficult. The individual must weigh years invested in one set of skills, current income, and job security against present frustrations and hoped-for gains.

An extreme career shift, by contrast, usually signals a personal crisis (Young & Rodgers, 1997). In a study of professionals who abandoned their well-paid, prestigious positions for routine, poorly paid, semiskilled work, nonwork problems contributed to radical change. An eminent 55-year-old TV producer became a school bus driver, a New York banker a waiter in a ski resort (Sarason, 1977). Each was responding to feelings of personal meaninglessness—escaping from family conflict, difficult relationships with colleagues, and work that had become unsatisfying to a less burdensome life.

Among blue-collar workers—such as those employed in construction, manufacturing, mining, maintenance, or food-service work—midlife career shifts are seldom freely chosen. In one investigation, researchers followed a large sample of blue-collar men in their fifties over a seven-year period; all were employed by Alcoa, the world's largest producer of aluminum. One-third had highly physically taxing jobs. Of the small minority who transitioned to less physically demanding work, an injury usually preceded the change (Modrek & Cullen, 2012). Transitioners appeared to change jobs to stay in the work force, rather than being forced to retire early because of their disability, at less than full pension benefits.

Yet opportunities to shift to less physically demanding work are usually limited. A strong predictor of middle-aged workers' eligibility for such jobs is education—at least a high school diploma (Blau & Goldstein, 2007). Less educated workers with a physical disability face greatly reduced chances of remaining in the labor force.

Unemployment

As companies downsize, eliminating jobs, the majority of people affected are middle-aged and older. Although unemployment is difficult at any time, middle-aged adults show a sharper decline in physical and mental health than their younger counterparts. Those who perceive a company's layoff process as unfair and inconsiderate—for example, giving them little time to prepare—often experience the event as highly traumatic. Older job-seekers receive fewer job offers and remain jobless longer (McKee-Ryan et al., 2009; Wanberg et al., 2016). In addition, people over age 40 who must reestablish occupational security find themselves "off-time" in terms of the social clock. Consequently, job loss can disrupt major tasks of midlife, including generativity and reappraisal of life goals and accomplishments. Finally, having been more involved in and committed to an occupation, the older unemployed worker has also lost something of greater value.

People who lose their jobs in midlife, whether executives or blue-collar workers, seldom duplicate the status and pay of their previous positions. As they search, they encounter age discrimination and find that they are overqualified for many openings—experiences that weaken their motivation to continue searching. Those also facing financial difficulties are at risk for deepening depression and physical health declines over time (Gallo et al., 2006; Kanfer, Beier, & Ackerman, 2013). Counseling that focuses on financial planning, reducing feelings of humiliation due to the stigma of unemployment, and training in effective job search strategies, including social networking and use of social media, can help people implement effective problem-centered coping strategies in their search for alternative work roles.

Planning for Retirement

One evening, Devin and Trisha met Anya and her husband, George, for dinner. Halfway through the meal, Devin inquired, "George, tell us what you and Anya are going to do about retirement. Are you planning to close down your business or work part-time? Do you think you'll stay here or move out of town?"

Three generations ago, the two couples would not have had this conversation. Because of government-sponsored retirement benefits (begun in the United States in 1935), retirement is no longer a privilege reserved for the wealthy. The federal

In his mid-forties, after many years as a professor of ancient Greek philosophy, Abe Schoener transformed his passion for winemaking into a new career as a vintner. This radical shift prompted the breakup of his marriage but ultimately led to a more satisfying life.

Applying what we Know

Ingredients of Effective Retirement Planning

ISSUE	DESCRIPTION
Finances	Ideally, financial planning for retirement should start with the first paycheck; at a minimum, it should begin 10 to 15 years before retirement.
Fitness	Starting a fitness program in middle age is important because good health is crucial for well-being in retirement.
Role adjustment	Retirement is more challenging for people who strongly identify with their work role. Preparing for a radical role adjustment reduces stress.
Where to live	The pros and cons of moving should be considered carefully because where one lives affects access to health care, friends, family, recreation, entertainment, and part-time employment.
Leisure and volunteer activities	A retiree typically gains an additional 50 hours per week of free time. Careful planning of what to do with that time has a major impact on psychological well-being.
Health insurance	Finding out about government-sponsored health insurance options helps protect quality of life after retirement.
Legal affairs	The preretirement period is an excellent time to finalize a will and begin estate planning.

government pays Social Security to the majority of retired adults, and others are covered by employer-based private pension plans.

As the trend just noted suggests, the average age of retirement declined over the twentieth century, but over the past two decades, it has risen from age 57 to 62 in the United States. A similar rise has occurred in other Western nations, where average retirement age hovers between 60 and 63. Many U.S. baby boomers say they expect to delay retirement (Gallup, 2014; Kojola & Moen, 2016). But even with the negative impact of the economic recession of 2007 to 2009, most will need to work just a few extra years to be financially ready to retire (Munnell et al., 2012). For the healthy, active, long-lived baby-boom generation, up to one-fourth of their lives may lie ahead after they leave their jobs.

Retirement is a lengthy, complex process that begins as soon as the middle-aged person first thinks about it. Planning is important because retirement leads to a loss of two important work-related rewards—income and status—and to a change in many other aspects of life. Like other life transitions, retirement can be stressful. Clarifying goals for the future and acquiring financial-planning knowledge consistently predict better retirement savings, adjustment, and satisfaction (Hershey et al., 2007; Mauratore & Earl, 2015). Yet half or more of U.S. adults over age 50 have not engaged in any concrete retirement planning (Brucker & Leppel, 2013).

Applying What We Know above lists the variety of issues addressed in a typical retirement preparation program. Financial planning is especially vital in the United States where (unlike Western European nations) the federal government does not offer a pension system that guarantees an adequate standard of living (see page 65 in Chapter 2). Hence, U.S. retirees' income typically drops by 50 percent. But even midlifers who attend financial education programs often fail to look closely at their financial well-being and to make wise decisions (Keller & Lusardi, 2012). Many could benefit from an expert's financial analysis and counsel.

LOOK and LISTEN

Contact the human resources division of a company or institution in your community, and inquire about the retirement planning services it offers. How comprehensive are those services, and what percentage of its recent retirees made use of them?

Retirement leads to ways of spending time that are largely guided by one's interests rather than one's obligations. Individuals who have not thought carefully about how to fill this time may find their sense of purpose in life seriously threatened. Planning for an active life has an even greater impact on happiness after retirement than financial planning (Mauratore & Earl, 2015). Participation in activities promotes many factors essential for psychological well-being, including a structured time schedule, social contact, and self-esteem. Carefully considering whether or not to relocate at retirement is related to an active life, since it affects access to health care, friends, family, recreation, entertainment, and part-time work.

Devin retired at age 62, George at age 66. Though several years younger, Trisha and Anya—like many married women—coordinated their retirements with those of their husbands. In contrast, Jewel—in good health but without an intimate partner to share her life—kept her consulting business going until age 75. Tim took early retirement and moved to be near Elena, where he devoted himself to public service—tutoring second graders in a public school, transporting inner-city children to museums, and coaching after-school and weekend youth sports. For Tim, retirement offered new opportunities to give generously to his community.

Unfortunately, less well-educated people with lower lifetime earnings are least likely to attend retirement preparation programs—yet they stand to benefit the most. And compared with men, women do less planning for retirement, instead relying on their husband's preparations. This gender gap seems to be narrowing, however, as women increasingly contribute to family income (Adams & Rau, 2011; Wöhrman, Deller, & Wang, 2013). Employers must take extra steps to encourage lower-paid workers and women to participate in planning activities. In addition, enhancing retirement adjustment among the economically disadvantaged depends on access to better vocational training, jobs, and health care at early ages. Clearly, a lifetime of opportunities and experiences affects the transition to retirement. In Chapter 18, we will consider the decision to retire and retirement adjustment in greater detail.

Ask yourself

CONNECT Supervisors sometimes assign more routine tasks to older workers, believing that they can no longer handle complex assignments. Cite evidence from this and the previous chapter indicating that this assumption is incorrect.

APPLY An executive wonders how his large corporation can foster advancement of women and ethnic minorities to upper management positions. What strategies would you recommend?

Summary / chapter 16

Erikson's Theory: Generativity versus Stagnation (p. 538)

16.1 *According to Erikson, how does personality change in middle age?*

- Generativity expands as middle-aged adults face Erikson's psychological conflict of **generativity versus stagnation.** Personal desires and cultural demands jointly shape adults' generative activities.

- Highly generative people, who demonstrate workplace leadership, deep concern for others' welfare, and engagement in community and society, appear especially well-adjusted. Stagnation occurs when people become self-centered and self-indulgent in midlife.

Other Theories of Psychosocial Development in Midlife (p. 541)

16.2 *Describe Levinson's and Vaillant's views of psychosocial development in middle adulthood, and discuss similarities and differences between men and women.*

- According to Levinson, middle-aged adults confront four developmental tasks requiring them to reconcile opposing tendencies: young–old, destruction–creation, masculinity–femininity, and engagement–separateness.

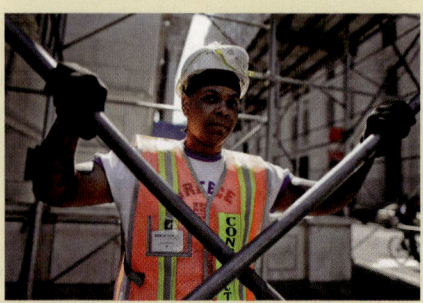

- Middle-aged men show greater acceptance of "feminine" traits of nurturance and caring, while women are more open to "masculine" characteristics of autonomy and assertiveness. Men and successful career-oriented women may reduce their concern with achievement, but some women who have devoted themselves to child rearing or an unfulfilling job may pursue a long-desired ambition.

- Vaillant found that adults in their late fifties and sixties become guardians of their culture, "passing the torch" to later generations.

16.3 *Does the term* midlife crisis *reflect the typical experience of middle adulthood, and is midlife accurately characterized as a stage?*

- Most midlifers make changes best described as "turning points." Only a minority experience a **midlife crisis**—intense self-doubt and stress leading to drastic life alterations.

- Life regrets are associated with less favorable psychological well-being, but they can also prompt corrective action.

- Because major restructuring in midlife is rare, most experts do not view midlife as stagelike.

Stability and Change in Self-Concept and Personality (p. 543)

16.4 *Describe changes in self-concept, personality, and gender identity in middle adulthood.*

- Middle-aged individuals maintain self-esteem and stay motivated by revising their **possible selves,** which become fewer in number as well as more modest and concrete. Balanced possible selves, consisting of related hoped-for and feared outcomes, seem to enhance motivation to attain self-relevant goals.

- Midlife typically brings enhanced psychological well-being through greater self-acceptance, autonomy, and environmental mastery.

- Daily stressors plateau in early to mid-adulthood, and then decline as work and family responsibilities ease. Midlife gains in emotional stability and confidence in handling life's problems lead to increased effectiveness in coping with stressors. But some midlifers are overwhelmed by intense stress, as indicated by the rise in U.S. suicides during middle age.

- In earlier research, both men and women became more androgynous in middle adulthood, likely due to a combination of social roles and life conditions. This rise in androgyny seems to have spread to other age periods in response to cultural changes favoring gender equality.

16.5 *Discuss stability and change in the "big five" personality traits in adulthood.*

- Among the **"big five" personality traits,** agreeableness and conscientiousness increase into middle age, while neuroticism declines, and extroversion and openness to experience do not change or decrease slightly. Although adults change in overall organization and integration of personality, they do so on a foundation of basic, enduring dispositions.

CHAPTER 16 Emotional and Social Development in Middle Adulthood

Relationships at Midlife (p. 549)

16.6 *Describe the middle adulthood phase of the family life cycle, including marriage, divorce, parent–child relationships, and grandparenthood.*

- "Launching children and moving on" is the midlife phase of the family life cycle. Adults must adapt as their children launch–return–relaunch, marry, and produce grandchildren, and as their own parents age and die.

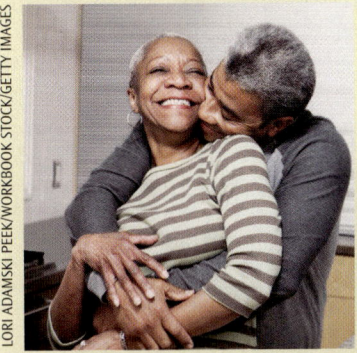

- Marital satisfaction is a powerful predictor of midlife psychological well-being. Compared to younger people, middle-aged adults seem to adjust more easily to divorce. Marital breakup often severely reduces women's standard of living, contributing to the **feminization of poverty**.

- Most middle-aged parents adjust well to launching adult children, especially if positive parent–child relationships are sustained, but adult children who are "off-time" in development can prompt parental strain. Low-SES parents are able to give less tangible and intangible support to their adult children, and they must divide it among more offspring. As children marry, middle-aged parents, especially mothers, often become **kinkeepers**.

- Grandparents' relationships with grandchildren depend on proximity, number of grandchild sets, sex of grandparent and grandchild, and in-law relationships. In low-income families and in some ethnic groups, grandparents provide essential child-rearing assistance. When serious family problems exist, grandparents may become primary caregivers in **skipped-generation families**.

- Middle-aged adults reassess their relationships with aging parents, often becoming more appreciative. Mother–daughter relationships tend to be closer than other parent–child ties. The more positive the history of the parent–child tie and the greater the need for assistance, the more help exchanged.

- Middle-aged adults, often caught between caring for aging parents, assisting young-adult children and grandchildren, and meeting work and community responsibilities, are called the **sandwich generation**. The burden of caring for ill or frail parents falls most heavily on adult daughters, though the sex difference declines in later middle age.

- Parental caregiving has emotional and health consequences, especially in cultures and subcultures where adult children feel a particularly strong obligation to provide care. Social support is highly effective in reducing caregiver stress and helping adult children derive benefits from caregiving.

16.7 *Describe midlife sibling relationships and friendships.*

- Sibling contact and support decline from early to middle adulthood, but many middle-aged siblings feel closer, often in response to major life events. Past and current parental favoritism influences the quality of sibling bonds.

- In midlife, friendships become fewer, more selective, and more deeply valued. Men continue to be less expressive with their friends than women, who have more close friendships.

Vocational Life (p. 559)

16.8 *Discuss job satisfaction and career development in middle adulthood, with special attention to gender differences and experiences of ethnic minorities.*

- Vocational readjustments are common as middle-aged people seek to increase the personal meaning and self-direction of their work lives. Certain aspects of job performance improve. Job satisfaction increases at all occupational levels, more so for men than for women.

- **Burnout** is a serious occupational hazard, especially for those in helping professions. It can be prevented by ensuring reasonable workloads, limiting hours of stressful work, and providing workers with social support.

- Both personal and workplace characteristics influence older workers' engagement in career development. In companies with a more favorable age climate, mature employees report greater self-efficacy, work commitment, and job satisfaction.

- Women and ethnic minorities face a **glass ceiling** because of limited access to management training and prejudice against women who demonstrate leadership qualities. Many women, including ethnic minorities, further their careers by leaving the corporate world, often to start their own businesses.

16.9 *Discuss career change and unemployment in middle adulthood.*

- Midlife career change typically involves leaving one line of work for a related one. Radical career change often signals a personal crisis. Among blue-collar workers, midlife career shifts are seldom freely chosen.

- Unemployment is especially difficult for middle-aged adults, who constitute the majority of laid-off workers. Counseling can help them find alternative jobs, but these rarely match their previous status and pay.

16.10 *Discuss the importance of planning for retirement.*

- Retirement brings major life changes, including loss of income and status and increased free time. Besides financial planning, preparing for an active retirement is vital, with a strong impact on happiness. Low-paid workers and women need extra encouragement to engage in retirement planning.

Important Terms and Concepts

"big five" personality traits (p. 548)
burnout (p. 560)
feminization of poverty (p. 550)
generativity versus stagnation (p. 538)

glass ceiling (p. 561)
kinkeeper (p. 552)
midlife crisis (p. 542)
possible selves (p. 544)

sandwich generation (p. 555)
skipped-generation family (p. 554)

milestones

Development in Middle Adulthood

40–50 YEARS

Physical

- Accommodative ability of the lens of the eye, ability to see in dim light, and color discrimination decline; sensitivity to glare increases. (508–509)
- Hearing loss at high frequencies occurs, and ability to distinguish sounds in close succession recedes. (509)
- Hair grays and thins. (508)
- Lines on the face become more pronounced; skin loses elasticity and begins to sag. (509–510)
- Weight gain continues, accompanied by a rise in fatty deposits in the torso, while fat beneath the skin declines. (510)
- Loss of lean body mass (muscle and bone) occurs. (510)

- In women, production of estrogen drops, leading to shortening and irregularity of the menstrual cycle. (510)
- In men, quantity of semen and sperm declines. (513)
- Intensity of sexual response declines, but frequency of sexual activity drops only modestly. (515)
- Rates of cancer and cardiovascular disease increase. (516–519)

Cognitive

- Consciousness of aging increases. (508, 541)
- Crystallized intelligence increases; fluid intelligence declines. (525)

- Speed of processing declines, but adults can compensate through experience and practice. (527–528)
- Executive function—working memory capacity, inhibition, and flexible shifting of attention—declines, but adults can compensate through experience and practice. (528–529)
- Recall of studied information declines, in part because of reduced use of memory strategies. (529)
- Retrieving information from long-term memory becomes more difficult. (529)
- Semantic memory (general knowledge base), procedural memory ("how-to" knowledge), memory related to one's occupation, and metacognitive knowledge remain unchanged or may increase. (529)

- Practical problem solving and expertise increase. (530)

- Creativity may become more deliberately thoughtful, emphasize integrating ideas, and shift from self-expression to more altruistic goals. (530–531)

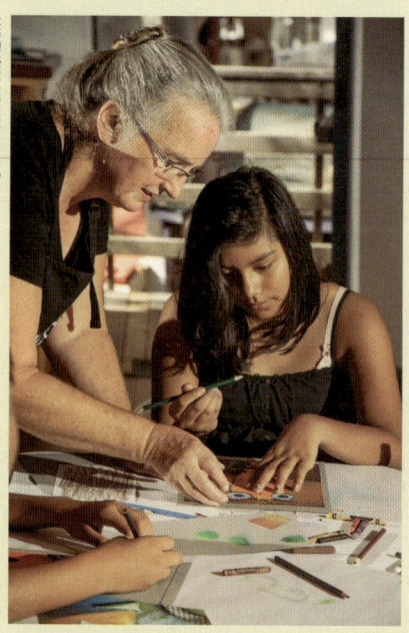

Note: Numbers in parentheses indicate the page or pages on which each milestone is discussed.

Emotional/Social

- Generativity increases. (538–539)

- Focus shifts toward personally meaningful living. (541)
- Possible selves become fewer in number, more modest and concrete, and less far-off in realization. (544)
- Self-acceptance, autonomy, and environmental mastery increase. (544–545)
- Strategies for coping with stressors become more effective. (545)
- May become more androgynous in gender identity, with "masculine" traits increasing in women, "feminine" traits in men. (541, 546–548)
- Agreeableness and conscientiousness increase, while neuroticism declines. (548)
- May launch children. (551)
- May become a kinkeeper, especially if a mother. (552)
- May become a parent-in-law and a grandparent. (552–553)
- Becomes more appreciative of parents' strengths and generosity; quality of relationships with parents increases. (554–555)
- May care for a parent with a disability or chronic illness. (555–557)
- Siblings may feel closer. (557–558)

- Number of friends generally declines. (559)
- Intrinsic job satisfaction—happiness with one's work—typically increases. (560)

50–65 YEARS

Physical

- Lens of the eye loses its capacity to adjust to objects at varying distances entirely. (508)
- Hearing loss gradually extends to all frequencies but remains greatest for high frequencies. (509)
- Skin continues to wrinkle and sag, "age spots" increase, and blood vessels in the skin become more visible. (510)
- In women, menopause occurs; as estrogen declines further, genitals are less easily stimulated, and the vagina lubricates more slowly during arousal. (510–512)
- In men, inability to attain an erection when desired becomes more common. (513)
- Loss of bone mass continues; rates of osteoporosis rise. (510, 519)

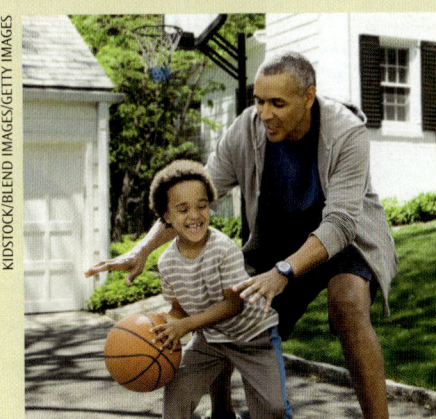

- Collapse of disks in the spinal column causes height to drop by as much as 1 inch. (510)
- Rates of cancer and cardiovascular disease continue to increase. (515–519)

Cognitive

- Cognitive changes previously listed continue.

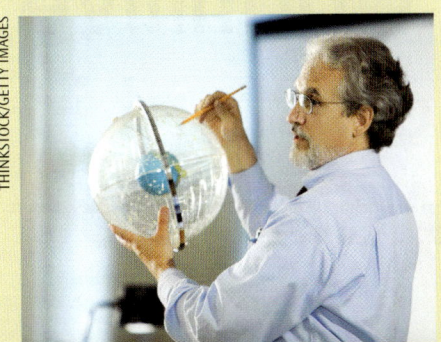

Emotional/Social

- Emotional and social changes previously listed continue.

- Emotional support and practical assistance of aging parents increase. (555)

- May retire. (562–564)

Note: Numbers in parentheses indicate the page or pages on which each milestone is discussed.

chapter 17

Physical and Cognitive Development in Late Adulthood

Cultures around the world connect age with wisdom. In most societies, leadership positions are typically held by older adults, whose life experience enhances their ability to solve human problems. Here, Liberian president and Nobel Peace laureate Ellen Johnson Sirleaf meets with the family of a teenage civilian who was fatally shot while protesting an Ebola quarantine.

What's ahead in chapter 17

PHYSICAL DEVELOPMENT

Life Expectancy
Variations in Life Expectancy • Life Expectancy in Late Adulthood • Maximum Lifespan

■ **BIOLOGY AND ENVIRONMENT** What Can We Learn About Aging from Centenarians?

Physical Changes
Nervous System • Sensory Systems • Cardiovascular and Respiratory Systems • Immune System • Sleep • Physical Appearance and Mobility • Adapting to Physical Changes of Late Adulthood

Health, Fitness, and Disability
Nutrition and Exercise • Sexuality • Physical Disabilities • Mental Disabilities • Health Care

■ **SOCIAL ISSUES: HEALTH** Interventions for Caregivers of Older Adults with Dementia

COGNITIVE DEVELOPMENT

Memory
Explicit versus Implicit Memory • Associative Memory • Remote Memory • Prospective Memory

Language Processing

Problem Solving

Wisdom

Factors Related to Cognitive Maintenance and Change

Cognitive Interventions

■ **SOCIAL ISSUES: EDUCATION** The Art of Acting Enhances Cognitive Functioning in Older Adults

Lifelong Learning
Types of Programs • Benefits of Continuing Education

At age 67, Walt gave up his photography business and looked forward to more spare time with 64-year-old Ruth, who retired from her position as a social worker at the same time. For Walt and Ruth, this culminating period of life was filled with volunteer work, golfing three times a week, and joint vacations with Walt's older brother Dick and his wife, Goldie. Walt also took up activities he had always loved but had little time to pursue—writing poems and short stories, attending theater performances, enrolling in a class on world politics, and cultivating a garden that became the envy of the neighborhood. Ruth read voraciously and served on the board of directors of an adoption agency.

Over the next 20 years, Walt and Ruth amazed nearly everyone who met them with their energy and vitality. Their warmth and concern for others led extended family and friends to seek them out. On weekends, their home was alive with visitors.

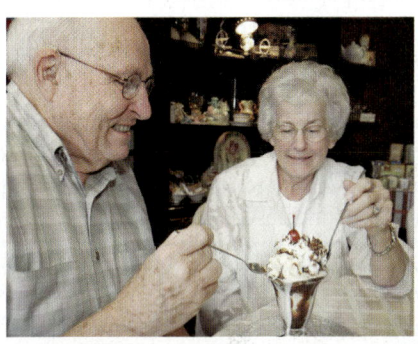

Then, in their early eighties, the couple's lives changed profoundly. Walt had surgery to treat a cancerous prostate gland and within three months was hospitalized again after a heart attack. He lingered for six weeks and then died. Ruth's grieving was interrupted by the need to care for her sister Ida. Alert and spry at age 78, Ida declined mentally in her seventy-ninth year, despite otherwise excellent physical health. Meanwhile, Ruth's arthritis worsened, and her vision and hearing weakened.

As Ruth turned 85, certain activities had become difficult—but not impossible. "It just takes a little adjustment!" Ruth exclaimed in her usual upbeat manner. Reading was harder, so she downloaded audiobooks to her smartphone. Her gait was slower and her eyesight less reliable, making her hesitant to go out alone. At dinner in a noisy restaurant with her daughter and family, Ruth felt overwhelmed and participated little in the fast-moving conversation. But in one-to-one interactions in a calm environment, she showed the same intelligence, wit, and astute insights that she had displayed all her life.

Late adulthood stretches from age 65 to the end of the lifespan. Unfortunately, popular images fail to capture the quality of these final decades. Instead, many myths prevail—that older people have entered a period of deterioration and dependency, that they are no longer able to learn, and that their families isolate them in nursing homes.

As we trace physical and cognitive development in late adulthood, we will see that the balance of gains and declines shifts as death approaches. But in industrialized nations, the typical 65-year-old can anticipate nearly two healthy, rewarding decades before this shift affects everyday life. And as Ruth illustrates, even after older adults become frail, many find ways to surmount physical and cognitive challenges.

Late adulthood is best viewed as an extension of earlier periods, not a break with them. As long as social and cultural contexts give older adults support, respect, and purpose in life, these years are a time of continued potential. ●

PHYSICAL DEVELOPMENT

Do you know older adults who "seem young" or "seem old" for their age? In using these descriptors, we acknowledge that chronological age is an imperfect indicator of **functional age,** or actual competence and performance. Because people age biologically at different rates, some 80-year-olds appear younger than many 65-year-olds. Also, recall from Chapter 13 that within each person, change differs across parts of the body. For example, Ruth became infirm physically but remained active mentally, whereas Ida, though physically fit for her age, found it hard to converse with others, keep appointments, or complete familiar tasks.

So much variation exists between and within individuals that researchers have not yet identified any single biological measure that predicts the overall rate at which a person will age. But we do have estimates of how much longer older adults can expect to live, and our knowledge of factors affecting longevity in late adulthood has increased rapidly.

People age biologically at different rates, making them look and feel younger or older than their agemates. Although these World War II veterans are the same age, the one on the left appears older than the one on the right.

Life Expectancy

17.1 Distinguish between chronological age and functional age, and discuss changes in life expectancy since the beginning of the twentieth century.

Dramatic gains in **average life expectancy**—the number of years that an individual born in a particular year can expect to live, starting at any age—provide powerful support for the multiplicity of factors considered in previous chapters that slow biological aging, including improved nutrition, medical treatment, sanitation, and safety. Recall from Chapter 1 that in 1900, life expectancy was just under 50 years; in the United States today, it is 78.8—76 for U.S. men and 81 for women. A major factor in this extraordinary gain is a steady decline in infant mortality (see Chapter 3), but death rates among adults have decreased as well. For example, heart disease, the leading cause of overall adult death in the United States, has dropped by nearly 70 percent in the past four decades, due to declines in risk factors (such as high blood pressure and cigarette smoking) and, mostly, advances in medical treatment (Wilmot et al., 2016).

Variations in Life Expectancy

Consistent group differences in life expectancy underscore the joint contributions of heredity and environment to biological aging. In countries around the globe, women outlive men, by an average of five years (Rochelle et al., 2015). This life expectancy advantage characterizes females of most species. The protective value of females' extra X chromosome (see Chapter 2), along with their reduced risk taking and physical aggression (Chapters 6 and 8), are believed to be responsible. Yet since the 1990s, the gender gap in life expectancy has narrowed in industrialized nations (Deeg, 2016). Because men are at higher risk for disease and early death, they reap somewhat larger generational gains from positive lifestyle changes and new medical discoveries.

Life expectancy varies substantially with SES. As education and income increase, so does length of life (Chetty et al., 2016; Whitfield, Thorpe, & Szanton, 2011). In the United States, the gap in life expectancy at birth between the wealthiest and the poorest individuals is 14½ years for men and 10 years for women. SES also accounts for the 2- to 3-year advantage in life expectancy for European-American over African-American adults age 65 and older (Centers for Disease Control and Prevention, 2016b). As noted in Chapter 13, stressful life events, wide-ranging unhealthy behaviors, jobs with health risks, and weak social supports are associated with low SES.

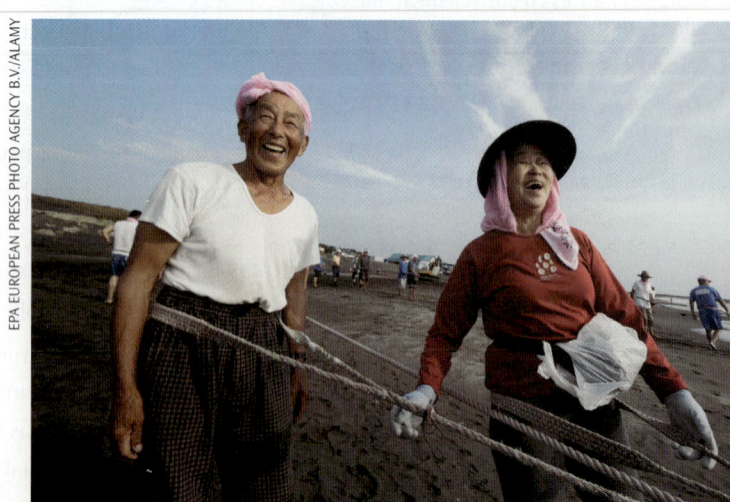

In a Japanese seaside city, a spry aging couple practice their local tradition of net fishing. Japan's low rates of obesity and heart disease and favorable health-care policies contribute to its worldwide leading status in healthy life expectancy.

Length of life—and, even more important, *quality of life* in old age—can be predicted by a country's health care, housing, and social services, along with lifestyle factors. When researchers estimate **average healthy life expectancy**, the number of years a person born in a particular year can expect to live in full health, without disease or injury, Japan ranks first, with the United States falling below the overwhelming majority of industrialized nations (see Figure 17.1). Japan's leading status in this overall measure of population health has been attributed to its low rates of obesity and heart disease (linked to its low-fat diet) along with its favorable health-care policies. Because the United States falls short in these respects, Americans spend somewhat more time disabled and die earlier than older adults in most other developed countries.

In developing nations with widespread poverty, malnutrition, disease, and armed conflict, average life expectancy hovers around 55 years. And healthy life expectancy is reduced by three to four decades compared with the industrialized world—for example, for males, 69 years in Japan, 67 years in Sweden, 65 years in the United States, but only 48 in Afghanistan, 47 in Sierra Leone, and 28 in Haiti, where overall health recently declined because of the 2010 catastrophic earthquake (Salomon et al., 2012).

Life Expectancy in Late Adulthood

Although poverty-stricken groups lag behind the economically advantaged, the proportion of older adults has risen dramatically in the industrialized world. From 1900 to 2014, people age 65 and older increased from 4 percent to 15 percent of the U.S. population. Because of aging baby boomers, older adults are projected to rise to 20 percent by 2030. Among older Americans, the fastest-growing segment is the 85-and-older group, which has increased by 30 percent during the past decade and currently makes up nearly 2 percent of the U.S. population. By 2050, they are expected to swell to more than double their current number (U.S. Department of Health and Human Services, 2015e).

Americans reaching age 65 in the early twenty-first century can look forward to, on average, to 19 more years of life. As at earlier ages, life expectancy is greater for older women than for men. Today, the 65- to 69-year age group includes 114 women for every 100 men; for people age 85 and older, this number climbs to 195 (U.S. Census Bureau, 2016c). Similar discrepancies exist throughout the world, with the exception of a few developing countries where death rates of women during childbirth are high or women experience severe discrimination and deprivation.

Although women outnumber men by a greater margin at older ages, women's advantage in life expectancy shrinks with age—in the United States, from 3 years at age 65 to 1 year at age 85. Over age 100, the gender difference disappears (Arias, 2015). Similarly, differences in rates of chronic illness and in life expectancy between European Americans and African Americans lessen with age. After age 80, a *life expectancy crossover* occurs—surviving African Americans live longer than members of the white majority (Masters, 2012; Roth et al., 2016; Sautter et al., 2012). Researchers speculate that among men and economically disadvantaged African Americans, only the biologically sturdiest survive into very old age.

Throughout this book, we have seen that genetic and environmental factors jointly affect aging. With respect to heredity, identical twins typically die within 3 years of each other, whereas fraternal twins of the same sex differ by more than 6 years. Also, longevity runs in families. When both parents survive to age 70 or older, the chances that their children will live to 90 or 100 are double that of the general population (Cevenini et al., 2008; Hayflick, 1994; Mitchell et al., 2001). At the same time, evidence from twin studies suggests that once people pass 75 to 80 years, the contribution of heredity to length of life decreases in favor of

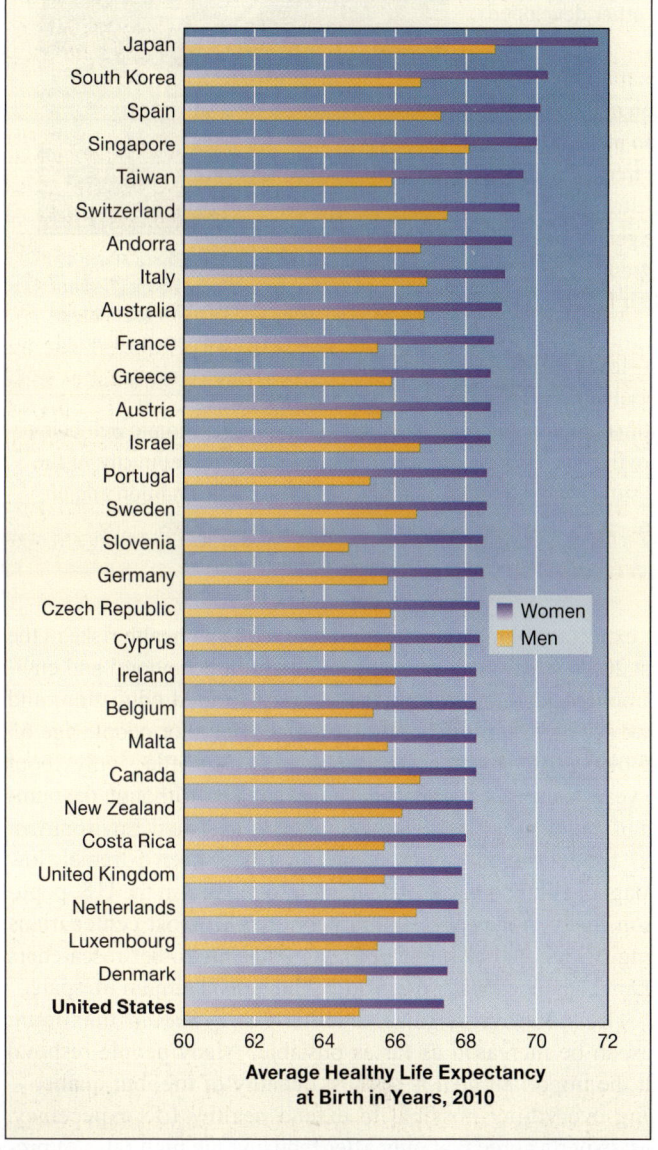

FIGURE 17.1 Average healthy life expectancy at birth in 30 nations, ranked on measures for women. Japan ranks first, the United States a disappointing thirtieth. In each nation, women's healthy life expectancy is about 2 to 3 years longer than men's. (From Salomon et al., 2012.)

Biology and Environment

What Can We Learn About Aging from Centenarians?

Jeanne Louise Calment, listed in *Guinness World Records* as the longest-lived person whose age could be documented, was born in Arles, France, in 1875 and died there in 1997, at age 122. Heredity undoubtedly contributed to her longevity: Her father lived to age 94, her mother to 86. Her family was middle-SES, and in her twenties, she married a prosperous merchant (Robine & Allard, 1999). As a young woman, she was healthy and energetic; she bicycled, swam, roller-skated, played tennis, and ran up the steps of the cathedral to attend daily Mass.

Jeanne attributed her longevity to a diet rich in olive oil and an occasional glass of port wine. Others credit her agreeable disposition and resistance to stress. "If you can't do anything about it," she once said, "don't worry about it." Jeanne took up fencing at age 85 and rode a bicycle until 100. Shortly thereafter, she moved into assisted living (see pages 593–594), where she blossomed, becoming a celebrity because of both her age and her charming personality. Alert and quick-witted until her final year, she recommended laughter as the best recipe for long life. Asked once about the effects of aging, she quipped, "I've only one wrinkle, and I am sitting on it."

The past 25 years have seen a nearly five-fold increase in the world's centenarian population, with women outnumbering men by 5 to 1. Currently, U.S. centenarians, though still rare (a fraction of 1 percent of the population), number about 72,000 (Stepler, 2016). The proportion of centenarians in the United States is smaller than in most other developed nations.

In a study of 96 U.S. centenarians, one-fourth reached age 100 with no major chronic disease, nearly as many had no physical disabilities, and 55 percent were free of cognitive impairments (Alishaire, Beltrán-Sánchez, & Crimmins, 2015). They were generally healthier than a comparison group of very old adults who died before their hundredth birthday.

These robust centenarians—leading active, autonomous lives—are of special interest because they represent the ultimate potential of the human species. What are they like? Results of several longitudinal studies reveal that they are diverse in years of education (none to postgraduate), economic well-being (very poor to very rich), and ethnicity. At the same time, their physical condition and life stories reveal common threads.

Jeanne Louise Calment, shown here at age 121, took up fencing at age 85, rode a bicycle until age 100, and maintained a quick wit until her final year. The longest-lived person on record, she died at age 122.

---

environmental factors—a healthy diet; normal body weight; regular exercise; little or no tobacco, alcohol, and drug use; an optimistic outlook; low psychological stress; and social support (Yates et al., 2008; Zaretsky, 2003). As the Biology and Environment box above reveals, the study of centenarians—people who cross the 100-year mark—offers special insights into how biological, psychological, and social influences work together to promote a long, satisfying life.

Maximum Lifespan

Finally, perhaps you are wondering: For humans, what is the **maximum lifespan**, or species-specific biological limit to length of life (in years), corresponding to the age at which the oldest known individual died? As the Biology and Environment box indicates, the oldest verified age is 122 years.

Does this figure actually reflect the upper bound of human longevity, or can it be extended? Some scientists believe that 122 years is close to the maximum, and 85 to 90 years is as much as most humans can expect. They point out that gains in average life expectancy are largely the result of reducing health risks in the first 20 or 30 years—especially, the harmful behavioral and environmental conditions linked to poverty, limited education, and weak access to health care (Olshansky, 2011). For people age 65 and older, life expectancy has increased very little—only about 1½ years—over the past decade and a half. And although the number of centenarians is rising (see the Biology and Environment box), the odds of becoming a centenarian have been extremely low throughout human history and remain so today—in the U.S. population, just 5 for every 10,000 people, with most centenarians dying by age 103 (Arias, 2015). Nevertheless, other researchers remain convinced that we can add to human maximum lifespan.

This controversy raises another issue: *Should* maximum lifespan be increased as far as possible? Many people respond that the important goal is not just quantity of life, but quality—doing everything possible to extend healthy life expectancy. Most experts agree that only after reducing the high rates of preventable illness and disability among low-SES individuals and wiping out age-related diseases should we invest in lengthening the maximum lifespan.

Health

Centenarians usually have grandparents, parents, and siblings who reached very old age, indicating a genetically based survival advantage. Likewise, their children, who are typically in their seventies and eighties, display fewer physical and cognitive impairments compared with older adults of similar age (Cosentino et al., 2013; Perls et al., 2002). Some centenarians share with siblings a segment of identical DNA on the fourth chromosome, suggesting that a certain gene, or several genes, may increase the likelihood of exceptionally long life (Perls & Terry, 2003).

Robust centenarians have a low incidence of genes associated with immune-deficiency disorders, cancer, and Alzheimer's disease. Consistent with these findings, they usually have efficiently functioning immune systems, and after-death examinations reveal few brain abnormalities (Silver & Perls, 2000). Other robust centenarians function well despite underlying chronic disease—typically atherosclerosis, other cardiovascular problems, and brain pathology (Berzlanovich et al., 2005; Evert et al., 2003). Compared with the general population, about four times as many centenarian women gave birth to healthy children after age 40 (Perls et al., 2000). Late childbearing may indicate that the body, including the reproductive system, is aging slowly.

As a group, robust centenarians are of average or slender build and practice moderation in eating. Many have most or all of their own teeth—another sign of unusual physical health. The large majority report having never smoked, engaging in no more than moderate wine consumption, and sustaining a lifelong pattern of physical activity past age 100 (Hagberg & Samuelson, 2008; Kropf & Pugh, 1995).

Personality

In personality, these very senior citizens appear highly optimistic (Jopp & Rott, 2006). In a study in which robust centenarians retook personality tests after 18 months, they reported more fatigue and depression, perhaps in response to increased frailty at the very end of their lives. But they also scored higher in tough-mindedness, independence, emotional security, and openness to experience—traits that may be vital for surviving beyond 100 (Martin, Long, & Poon, 2002). An important contributor to their favorable mental health and longevity is social support, especially close family bonds and a long and happy marriage (Margrett et al., 2011). An unusually large percentage of centenarian men—about one-fourth—are still married.

Activities

Robust centenarians have a history of community involvement—working for just causes that are central to their growth and happiness. Their past and current activities often include stimulating work, leisure pursuits, and learning, which may help sustain their good cognition and life satisfaction (Antonini et al., 2008; Weiss-Numeroff, 2013). Writing letters, poems, plays, and memoirs; making speeches; teaching music lessons and Sunday school; nursing the sick; chopping wood; selling merchandise, bonds, and insurance; painting; practicing medicine; and preaching sermons are among robust centenarians' varied involvements. In several cases, illiterate centenarians learned to read and write.

In sum, robust centenarians illustrate typical development at its best. These independent, mentally alert, happy 100-year-olds reveal how a healthy lifestyle, personal resourcefulness, and close ties to family and community can build on biological strengths, thereby pushing the limits of an active, fulfilling life.

Physical Changes

17.2 Describe physical declines of late adulthood, and changes in the nervous and sensory systems.

17.3 Describe cardiovascular, respiratory, and immune system changes and sleep difficulties in late adulthood.

17.4 Describe changes in physical appearance and mobility in late adulthood, along with effective adaptations to these changes.

The programmed effects of specific genes and the random cellular events believed to underlie biological aging (see Chapter 13) make physical declines more apparent in late adulthood. The majority of people age 65 and older are capable of living active, independent lives, but with age, growing numbers need assistance. After age 75, about 9 percent of Americans have difficulty carrying out **activities of daily living (ADLs)**—basic self-care tasks required to live on one's own, such as bathing, dressing, getting in and out of bed or a chair, or eating. And about 17 percent cannot carry out **instrumental activities of daily living (IADLs)**—tasks necessary to conduct the business of daily life and also requiring some cognitive competence, such as telephoning, shopping, food preparation, housekeeping, and paying bills. The proportion of older adults with these limitations rises sharply with age (U.S. Department of Health and Human Services, 2015d). Nevertheless, most body structures can last into our eighties and beyond, if we take good care of them. For an overview of the physical changes we are about to discuss, return to Table 13.1 on page 441.

Nervous System

On a routine office visit, 80-year-old Ruth's doctor asked her how she was getting along. "I think I might be losing my mind," Ruth replied anxiously. "Yesterday, I forgot the name of the family who just moved in next door. And the day before, I had trouble finding the right words to explain to a delivery service how to get to my house."

"Ruth, everyone forgets those sorts of things from time to time," Dr. Wiley reassured her. "When we were young and had a memory lapse, we reprimanded ourselves for being scatter-brained and thought no more about it. Now, when we do the same thing, we attribute it to having 'a senior moment,' and we worry."

Ruth also wondered why extremes of hot and cold weather felt more uncomfortable than in earlier years. And she needed more time to coordinate a series of movements and had become less sure of her balance.

Aging of the central nervous system affects a wide range of complex activities. Although brain weight declines throughout adulthood, brain-imaging research and after-death autopsies reveal that the loss becomes greater starting in the fifties and amounts to as much as 5 to 10 percent by age 80, due to withering of the myelin coating on neural fibers, loss of synaptic connections, death of neurons, and enlargement of ventricles (spaces) within the brain (Fiocco, Peck, & Mallya, 2016; Rodrigue & Kennedy, 2011).

Neuron loss occurs throughout the cerebral cortex but at different rates among different regions and often inconsistently within parts of those regions. In longitudinal studies, the frontal lobes, especially the prefrontal cortex (responsible for executive function and strategic thinking), and the corpus callosum (which connects the two cortical hemispheres), tended to show greater shrinkage than the parietal, temporal, and occipital lobes (see page 120 in Chapter 4 for a visual image of these regions) (Fabiani, 2012; Lockhart & DeCarli, 2014). The cerebellum (which controls balance and coordination and supports cognitive processes) and the hippocampus (involved in memory and spatial understanding) also lose neurons (Fiocco, Peck, & Mallya, 2016). And EEG measures reveal gradual slowing and reduced intensity of brain waves—signs of diminished efficiency of the central nervous system (Kramer, Fabiani, & Colcombe, 2006).

But brain-imaging research reveals wide individual differences in the extent of these losses, which are moderately associated with declines in cognitive functioning (Ritchie et al., 2015). And the brain can overcome some decline. In several studies, growth of neural fibers in the brains of older adults unaffected by illness took place at the same rate as in middle-aged people. Aging neurons established new synapses after other neurons had degenerated (Flood & Coleman, 1988). Furthermore, the aging cerebral cortex can, to a limited degree, generate new neurons (Snyder & Cameron, 2012). And fMRI evidence reveals that compared with younger adults, older people who do well on memory and other cognitive tasks show more widely distributed activity across areas of the cerebral cortex, particularly in the prefrontal cortex and in regions mirroring typically active sites but located in the opposite hemisphere (Fabiani, 2012; Reuter-Lorenz & Cappell, 2008). This suggests that one way older adults compensate for neuron loss is to call on additional brain regions to support cognitive processing.

The autonomic nervous system, involved in many life-support functions, also performs less well, placing older adults at risk during heat waves and cold spells. For example, Ruth's reduced tolerance for hot weather was due to decreased sweating. And her body found it harder to raise its core temperature during cold exposure. However, among physically fit older people who are free of disease, these declines are mild (Blatteis, 2012). The autonomic nervous system also releases higher levels of stress hormones into the bloodstream than it did earlier, perhaps to arouse body tissues that have become less responsive to these hormones over the years (Whitbourne, 2002). As we will see, this change may contribute to decreased immunity and to sleep problems.

Sensory Systems

Changes in sensory functioning become increasingly noticeable in late life. Older adults see and hear less well, and their taste, smell, and touch sensitivity also decline. As Figure 17.2 shows, in late life, hearing impairments are more common than visual impairments. Extending trends in middle adulthood, more women than men report being visually impaired, more men than women hearing impaired.

Vision. In Chapter 15 (see pages 508–509), we noted that structural changes in the eye make it harder to focus on nearby objects, see in dim light, and perceive color. In late adulthood, vision diminishes further. The cornea (clear covering of the eye) becomes more translucent and scatters light, which blurs images and increases sensitivity to glare. The lens continues to yellow, leading to further impairment in color discrimination. The number of individuals with **cataracts**—cloudy areas in the lens, resulting in foggy vision and (without surgery) eventual blindness—increases tenfold from middle to late adulthood, affecting 25

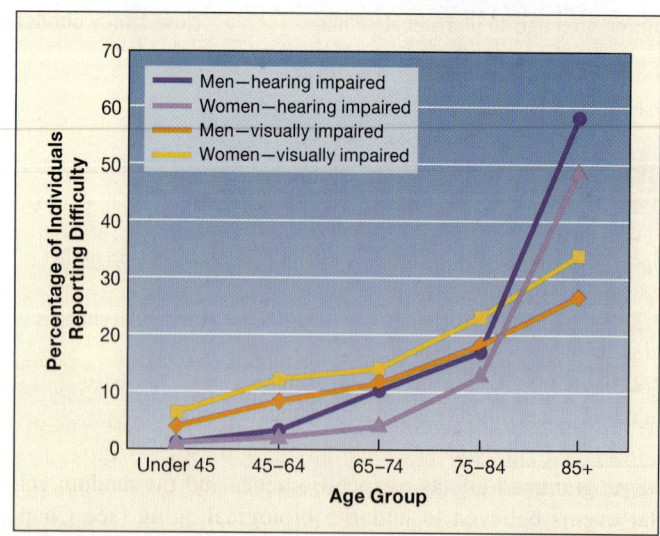

FIGURE 17.2 Rates of visual and hearing impairments among U.S. men and women by age. Among a large, nationally representative sample, those reporting that they had trouble seeing, even when wearing glasses or contact lenses, were judged visually impaired; those reporting "a lot of trouble" hearing were judged hearing impaired. Women report more visual impairments; men report more hearing impairments, a gap that widens considerably in late adulthood. In late life, hearing impairments become more common than visual impairments. (Based on U.S. Census Bureau, 2014.)

percent of people in their seventies and 50 percent of those in their eighties (Owsley, 2011; Sörensen, White, & Ramchandran, 2016). Besides biological aging, heredity, sun exposure, cigarette smoking, alcohol consumption, and certain diseases (such as hypertension and diabetes) increase the risk of cataracts (Thompson & Lakhani, 2015). Fortunately, removal of the lens and replacement with an artificial lens implant is highly successful in restoring vision.

Impaired eyesight in late adulthood largely results from a reduction in light reaching the retina (caused by yellowing of the lens, shrinking of the pupil, and clouding of the vitreous) and from cell loss in the retina and optic nerve (refer again to Chapter 15). Dark adaptation—moving from a brightly lit to a dim environment, such as a movie theater—becomes harder. A decline in binocular vision (the brain's ability to combine images received from both eyes) makes depth perception less reliable. And visual acuity (fineness of discrimination) worsens, dropping sharply after age 70 (Owsley, 2011).

When light-sensitive cells in the macula, or central region of the retina, break down, older adults may develop **macular degeneration,** in which central vision blurs and gradually is lost. Macular degeneration is the leading cause of blindness among older adults. About 10 percent of 65- to 74-year-olds, and 30 percent of 75- to 85-year-olds, have symptoms. If diagnosed early, macular degeneration can sometimes be treated with laser therapy. As with cataracts, heredity (including several identified genes) increases risk, especially when combined with cigarette smoking or obesity (Schwartz et al., 2016; Wysong, Lee, & Sloan, 2009). Atherosclerosis also contributes by constricting blood flow to the retina. Protective factors include regular, brisk physical activity and a diet emphasizing fish high in omega-3 fatty acids, which promote cardiovascular health, and fruits and vegetables high in vitamins A, C, E, and carotenoids (yellow and red plant pigments), which help shield cells in the macula from toxic levels of free radicals (Broadhead et al., 2015).

Visual difficulties have a profound impact on older people's self-confidence and everyday behavior. As she approached age 80, Ruth gave up driving, and she worried about Walt, who found it hard to shift focus between the road and the dashboard or to make out pedestrians at dusk and at night. On foot, problems with depth perception and dark adaptation increase older adults' chances of stumbling.

When vision loss is extensive, it can affect leisure pursuits and be very isolating. Because of her poor vision, Ruth could no longer enjoy museums, movies, playing bridge, or working crossword puzzles, and she depended on others for help with housekeeping and shopping. But even among people age 85 and older, only 30 percent experience visual impairment severe enough to interfere with daily living (U.S. Census Bureau, 2014). For many, however, reduced vision goes undetected. Treatment is vital for sustaining quality of life.

Hearing. "Mom, I'd like you to meet Joe's cousin Leona," said Ruth's daughter Sybil at a Thanksgiving gathering. But in the clamor of boisterous children, television sounds, and nearby conversations, 85-year-old Ruth didn't catch Leona's name or her relationship to Sybil's husband, Joe.

"Tell me your name again?" Ruth asked, adding, "Let's go into the other room, where it's quieter, so we can speak a bit."

Reduced blood supply and natural cell death in the inner ear and auditory cortex, discussed in Chapter 15, along with stiffening of membranes (such as the eardrum), cause hearing to decline in late adulthood. Decrements are greatest at high frequencies, although detection of soft sounds diminishes throughout the frequency range (see page 509). In addition, responsiveness to startling noises lessens, and discriminating complex tone patterns becomes harder (Wettstein & Wahl, 2016).

Although hearing loss has less impact on self-care than vision loss, it affects safety and enjoyment of life. In the din of city traffic, 80-year-old Ruth didn't always correctly interpret warnings, whether spoken ("Watch it, don't step out yet") or nonspoken (the beep of a horn). And when she turned up the radio or television volume, she sometimes missed the ring of the telephone or a knock at the door.

As hearing declines, older people report lower self-efficacy, more loneliness and depressive symptoms, and a smaller social network than their normally hearing peers (Kramer et al., 2002; Mikkola et al., 2015). Of all hearing difficulties, the age-related decline in speech perception has the greatest impact on life satisfaction. After age 70, ability to detect the content and emotionally expressive features of conversation declines, especially in noisy settings (Gosselin & Gagne, 2011).

Although Ruth used problem-centered coping to increase her chances of hearing conversation, she wasn't always successful. At the family's Thanksgiving reunion, fewer relatives took time to talk with Ruth, and she felt some pangs of loneliness. And sometimes people were inconsiderate. On a dinner outing, when Ruth asked Joe to repeat himself, he turned to Sybil and said loudly, "Be honest, Syb, Ruth's going deaf, isn't she?" Because aging adults with hearing loss frequently misunderstand verbal

Declines in hearing, especially the ability to perceive human speech, greatly reduce older adults' enjoyment of life. Availability of assistive listening devices can help ensure that this couple gets the most out of a movie-going experience.

communication, others may conclude they are mentally impaired. Those with hearing loss, as well as those who are visually impaired, do obtain lower scores on tests of executive function and memory (Li & Bruce, 2016). The effort they must devote to perceiving information likely detracts from other cognitive processes needed to perform the tasks.

Yet an investigation that followed several thousand older people for up to 15 years revealed that the presence of hearing or visual impairments did not predict cognitive declines, once other factors linked to cognitive functioning (such as age, educational attainment, and chronic illnesses) were controlled (Hong et al., 2016). Assuming that older adults who hear or see poorly are mentally deficient is a mistaken, negative stereotype of aging.

Most older people do not suffer from hearing loss great enough to disrupt their daily lives until after age 85. For those who do, compensating with a hearing aid and using an assistive listening device at lectures, movies, and theater performances are helpful. Furthermore, recall from Chapter 4 (pages 143–144) that beginning at birth, our perception is *intermodal* (combines information from more than one sensory system). By attending to facial expressions, gestures, and lip movements, older adults can use vision to help interpret the spoken word. Finally, when family members and others speak in quiet environments, older people are far more likely to convey an image of alertness and competence than of reduced sensitivity to the surrounding world.

Taste and Smell. Walt's brother Dick was a heavy smoker. In his sixties, he poured salt and pepper over his food and asked for "extra hot" in Mexican and Indian restaurants.

Dick's reduced sensitivity to the four basic tastes—sweet, salty, sour, and bitter—is evident in more than half of adults after age 60 and up to 80 percent after age 80, largely due to a decline in number and distribution of taste buds on the tongue. Older adults also have greater difficulty recognizing familiar foods by taste alone (Correia et al., 2016; Methven et al., 2012). Cigarette smoking, dentures, medications, and environmental pollutants can affect taste perception. When taste is harder to detect, food is less enjoyable, increasing the likelihood of dietary deficiencies. Flavor additives can help make food more attractive.

Besides enhancing food enjoyment, smell has a self-protective function. An aging person who has difficulty detecting rancid food, gas fumes, or smoke may be in a life-threatening situation. A decrease in the number of smell receptors, along with loss of neurons in brain regions involved in processing odors, contributes to declines in odor sensitivity after age 60, with one-fourth of people over age 70 affected (Attems, Walker, & Jellinger, 2015; Correia et al., 2016). Researchers believe that odor perception not only wanes but becomes distorted, a change that may promote complaints that "food no longer smells and tastes right." But older adults experiencing greater difficulty with verbal recall, including retrieval of odor labels, have greater difficulty with odor recognition tasks (Larsson, Öberg, & Bäckman, 2005). So cognitive changes may make the decline in odor perception appear greater than it actually is.

Touch. Object recognition through touch occurs many times each day, as adults identify common objects after manually exploring them—keys or credit card in a pocket, corkscrew at the back of a drawer—within 2 to 3 seconds. Touch discrimination is especially crucial for certain adults, such as the severely visually impaired reading Braille and people making fine judgments about texture—for example, in art and handicraft activities.

In later life, capacity to discriminate detailed surface properties and identify unfamiliar objects by touch declines. Waning of touch perception on the hands, especially the fingertips—believed to be due to loss of touch receptors in certain regions of the skin and slowing of blood circulation to the extremities—contributes (Stevens & Cruz, 1996). In addition, decrements in fluid abilities, especially spatial orientation, are influential (see page 526 in Chapter 15) (Kalisch et al., 2012). Fluid skills are strongly correlated with older adults' tactile performance.

Compared to their sighted counterparts, blind readers of Braille retain high touch sensitivity well into old age (Legge et al., 2008). Years of experience in picking up detailed tactile information seem to protect their tactile discrimination skills.

Although touch sensitivity typically diminishes in late adulthood, responsiveness to the emotionally pleasant quality of soft, gentle stroking is an exception: Older adults rate it as more pleasurable than younger people (Sehlstedt et al., 2016). Perhaps fewer touches from others in late life enhance enjoyment of sensitive touching when it happens.

Cardiovascular and Respiratory Systems

Aging of the cardiovascular and respiratory systems proceeds gradually and usually unnoticed in early and middle adulthood. In late adulthood, changes become more apparent. In their sixties, Ruth and Walt noticed that they felt more physically stressed after running to catch a bus or to cross a street before the light changed.

As the years pass, the heart muscle becomes more rigid, and some of its cells die while others enlarge, leading the walls of the left ventricle (the largest heart chamber, from which blood is pumped to the body) to thicken. In addition, artery walls stiffen and accumulate some plaque (cholesterol and fats) due to normal aging (much more in those with atherosclerosis). Finally, the heart muscle becomes less responsive to signals from pacemaker cells within the heart, which initiate each contraction (Larsen, 2009).

As a combined result of these changes, the heart pumps with less force, maximum heart rate decreases, and blood flow throughout the circulatory system slows. This means that sufficient oxygen may not be delivered to body tissues during high physical activity. (Recall from Chapter 13 that a healthy heart supports typical levels of exertion well into old age.)

Changes in the respiratory system compound the effects of reduced oxygenation. Because lung tissue gradually loses its elasticity, vital capacity (amount of air that can be forced in and out of the lungs) is reduced by half between ages 25 and 80. As a result, the lungs fill and empty less efficiently, causing the blood

These mountain hikers need frequent rests to catch their breath and regain their energy. With aging of the cardiovascular and respiratory systems, sufficient oxygen may not be delivered to body tissues during physical exertion.

to absorb less oxygen and give off less carbon dioxide. This explains why older people increase their breathing rate more and feel more out of breath while exercising.

Cardiovascular and respiratory deficiencies are more extreme in lifelong smokers and in people who have failed to reduce dietary fat or have had many years of exposure to environmental pollutants. As we have seen in previous chapters, exercise is a powerful means of slowing cardiovascular aging (Galetta et al., 2012). Exercise also facilitates respiratory functioning, as we will see later when we discuss health and fitness.

Immune System

As the immune system ages, T cells, which attack antigens (foreign substances) directly, become less numerous and effective (see Chapter 13, page 443). In addition, the immune system is more likely to malfunction by turning against normal body tissues in an **autoimmune response.** A less competent immune system reduces the effectiveness of available vaccines and increases the risk of a variety of illnesses—in addition to infectious diseases (such as the flu), cardiovascular disease, certain forms of cancer, and various autoimmune disorders, such as rheumatoid arthritis and diabetes (Herndler-Brandstetter, 2014). But an age-related decline in immune functioning is not the cause of most late-life illnesses. It merely permits disease to progress, whereas a stronger immune reaction would stamp out the disease agent.

Although older adults vary greatly in immunity, most experience some loss, ranging from partial to profound (Ponnappan & Ponnappan, 2011). The strength of the aging person's immune system seems to be a sign of overall physical vigor. Certain immune indicators, such as high T cell activity, predict better physical functioning and survival over the next two years in very old people (Moro-García et al., 2012; Wikby et al., 1998).

Recall from Chapter 13 that stress hormones undermine immunity. With age, the autonomic nervous system releases higher levels of these into the bloodstream. As the immune response declines with age, stress-induced susceptibility to infection rises dramatically (Archer et al., 2011). A healthy diet and exercise help protect the immune response in old age, whereas obesity aggravates the age-related decline.

Sleep

When Walt went to bed at night, he usually lay awake for a half-hour to an hour before falling asleep, remaining in a drowsy state longer than when he was younger. During the night, he spent less time in the deepest phase of NREM sleep (see Chapter 3, page 104) and awoke several times—again sometimes lying awake for a half-hour or more before drifting back to sleep.

Older adults require about as much total sleep as younger adults: around seven hours per night. Yet as people age, they have more difficulty falling asleep, staying asleep, and sleeping deeply. Insomnia affects about half of older adults. The timing of sleep tends to change as well, toward earlier bedtime and earlier morning wakening (McCrae et al., 2015). Changes in brain structures controlling sleep and higher levels of stress hormones in the bloodstream, which have an alerting effect on the central nervous system, are believed to be responsible.

Until age 70 or 80, men experience more sleep disturbances than women, for several reasons. First, enlargement of the prostate gland, which occurs in almost all aging men, constricts the urethra (the tube draining the bladder) and leads to a need to urinate more often, including during the night. Second, men—especially those who are overweight and use alcohol heavily—are more prone to **sleep apnea,** a condition in which breathing ceases for 10 seconds or longer, resulting in many brief awakenings. An estimated 45 percent of older adults are affected (Okuro & Morimoto, 2014).

Poor sleep can feed on itself. Walt's nighttime wakefulness led to daytime fatigue and short naps, which made it harder to fall asleep the following evening. And because Walt expected to have trouble sleeping, he worried about it, which also interfered with sleep. Insomnia in older adults is of special concern because it increases the risk of falls and cognitive impairments (Crowley, 2011). Those who are poor sleepers more often report slower reaction times and attention and memory difficulties.

Fortunately, there are ways to foster restful sleep, such as establishing a consistent bedtime and waking time, exercising regularly, and using the bedroom only for sleep (not for eating, reading, or watching TV). Older adults receive more prescription sedatives for sleep complaints than do people under age 60. Used briefly, these drugs can help relieve temporary insomnia. But long-term medication can make matters worse by inducing drug dependence, daytime sleepiness, and rebound insomnia after the drug is discontinued (Wennberg et al., 2013). Finally, discomfort due to an enlarged prostate, including frequent urination at night, can be corrected with laser surgical procedures that relieve symptoms without complications (Zhang et al., 2012).

Aging brings changes in appearance, evident in these portraits of Jimmy Carter, former U.S. president, at ages 52, 63, and 91. The skin creases and sags, "age spots" increase, the nose and ears broaden, and hair on the head thins.

Physical Appearance and Mobility

In earlier chapters, we saw that changes leading to an aged appearance are under way as early as the twenties and thirties. Because these occur gradually, older adults may not notice that they look older until the changes have become obvious. Each year during their summer travels, Walt and Ruth observed that Dick and Goldie's skin appeared more wrinkled. Their hair turned from gray to white as all pigment was lost; their bodies grew rounder and their arms and legs thinner. When they returned home, Walt and Ruth were more aware that they themselves had aged.

Creasing and sagging of the skin, described in Chapter 15, extends into old age. In addition, oil glands that lubricate the skin become less active, leading to dryness and roughness. "Age spots" increase; in some individuals, the arms, backs of the hands, and face may be dotted with these pigmented marks. Blood vessels can be seen beneath the more transparent skin, which has largely lost its layer of fatty support (Robert, Labat-Robert, & Robert, 2009). This further limits ability to adapt to hot and cold temperatures.

The face is especially likely to show these effects, as it is frequently exposed to the sun, which accelerates aging. Other factors that contribute to facial wrinkling and age spots include long-term alcohol use, cigarette smoking, and psychological stress. Additional facial changes occur: The nose and ears broaden as new cells are deposited on the outer layer of the skeleton. And especially in older adults with a history of poor dental care, teeth may be yellowed, cracked, and chipped, and gums may have receded (Whitbourne, 2002). As hair follicles under the skin's surface die, hair on the head thins in both sexes, and the scalp may be visible.

Body build changes as well. Height continues to decline, especially in women, as loss of bone mineral content leads to further collapse of the spinal column. Weight generally drops after age 60 because of additional loss of lean body mass (bone density and muscle), which is heavier than the fat deposits accumulating on the torso.

Several factors affect mobility. The first is muscle strength, which generally declines at a faster rate in late adulthood than in middle age. On average, by 60 to 70 years of age, 10 to 20 percent of muscle power has been lost, a figure that climbs to 30 to 50 percent after age 70 to 80 (Reid & Fielding, 2012). Second, bone strength deteriorates because of reduced bone mass, and tiny cracks in response to stress weaken the bones further. Third, strength and flexibility of the joints and the ligaments and tendons (which connect muscle to bone) diminish. In her eighties, Ruth's reduced ability to support her body, flex her limbs, and rotate her hips made walking at a steady, moderate pace, climbing stairs, and rising from a chair difficult.

In Chapter 13, we noted that endurance athletes who continue training throughout adulthood retain their muscular physiques and much of their strength into their sixties and seventies. These especially active people, like other aging individuals, lose fast-twitch muscle fibers. But they compensate by strengthening remaining slow-twitch fibers so they work more efficiently, yielding muscle function comparable to active people four decades younger (Sandri et al., 2014). Among nonathletes as well, a history of regular leisure time physical activity translates into greater mobility in late life (McGregor, Cameron-Smith, & Poppitt, 2014). At the same time, a carefully planned exercise program for older adults can enhance joint flexibility and range of movement.

Adapting to Physical Changes of Late Adulthood

Great diversity exists in older adults' adaptation to the physical changes of aging. People who are more anxious about growing older monitor their physical state more closely and are more concerned about their appearance (Montepare, 2006). Dick and

Goldie took advantage of an enormous industry designed to stave off outward signs of old age, including cosmetics, wigs, and plastic surgery, plus various "anti-aging" dietary supplements, herbal products, and hormonal medications offered by "longevity" clinics—none with any demonstrated benefits and some of them harmful (Olshansky, Hayflick, & Perls, 2004). In contrast, Ruth and Walt were relatively unconcerned about their thinning white hair and wrinkled skin. Their identities were less bound up with their appearance than with their ability to remain actively engaged in their surroundings.

Most older people sustain a favorable *subjective age*—say they feel younger than they look and than they actually are (Kleinspehn-Ammerlahn, Kotter-Grühn, & Smith, 2008; Westerhof, 2008). In several investigations, 75-year-olds reported feeling about 15 years younger! At follow-ups from a few years to two decades later, youthful self-evaluation predicted more favorable psychological well-being, better physical health and health behaviors, and slightly longer survival (Keyes & Westerhof, 2012; Westerhof et al., 2014).

Clearly, older adults vary in the aspects of physical aging that matter most to them. *Wanting* to be younger (as opposed to *feeling* younger) than one's actual age is associated with less positive well-being (Keyes & Westerhof, 2012). Compared with Dick and Goldie, Ruth and Walt approached aging with a more positive outlook and greater peace of mind, resolving to intervene in those aspects of physical aging that could be changed and to accept those that could not.

Research shows that the most obvious outward signs of aging—graying hair, facial wrinkles, and baldness—bear no relationship to cognitive functioning or to longevity (Schnohr et al., 1998). In contrast, neurological, cardiovascular, respiratory, metabolic, immune-system, and skeletal and muscular health are strongly associated with cognitive performance and both quality and length of later life (Bergman, Blomberg, & Almkvist, 2007; Garcia-Pinillos et al., 2016; Herghelegiu & Prada, 2014; Qui, 2014). Furthermore, people can do more to prevent declines in the functioning of these internal body systems than they can do to prevent gray hair and baldness!

Effective Coping Strategies. Think back to our discussion of problem-centered and emotion-centered coping in Chapter 15. It applies here as well. As Walt and Ruth prevented and compensated for age-related changes through diet, exercise, environmental adjustments, and an active, stimulating lifestyle, they felt a sense of personal control over their fates. This prompted additional active coping and improved physical functioning.

Older people who report a high sense of personal control usually deal with physical changes through problem-centered coping strategies. One 75-year-old who lost sight in one eye consulted an occupational therapist for advice and, to compensate for reduced depth perception and visual field, trained himself to use more side-to-side head movements. In contrast, older adults who consider age-related declines inevitable and uncontrollable tend to be passive when faced with them, to report more physical and mental health difficulties, and to experience steeper late-life declines in health (Gerstorf et al., 2014; Lachman, Neupert, & Agrigoroaei, 2011; Ward, 2013).

Sense of control varies across cultures: U.S. individualistic values emphasize the power of one's own actions and choices. Consequently, Americans score higher in personal control than adults in Asian nations and in Mexico (Angel, Angel, & Hill, 2009; Yamaguchi et al., 2005). Furthermore, we have seen that the United States is less generous than other industrialized nations in government-supported health care and social security benefits (see pages 64–65 in Chapter 2). In one study, sense of personal control was a stronger predictor of older adults' health status in the United States than it was in England, where government policies do more to support good health throughout the lifespan (Clarke & Smith, 2011).

When physical disabilities become severe, sense of control has diminishing returns, no longer having as much impact on health status. Aging adults with substantial physical impairments cope more effectively when they acknowledge reduced control and accept the need for caregiver or equipment assistance (Clarke & Smith, 2011; Slagsvold & Sørensen, 2013). But doing so may be more difficult for many older Americans, who are accustomed to a "culture of personal control," than for older people elsewhere in the world.

Assistive Technology. A rapidly expanding **assistive technology,** or array of devices that permit people with disabilities to improve their functioning, is available to help older people cope with physical declines. Computers and smart devices are the greatest sources of these innovative products (Czaja, 2016). Smartphones that respond to voice commands to make and answer calls help those with visual or motor difficulties. For older people who take multiple medications, a tiny computer chip called a "smart cap" can be placed on medicine bottles that beeps periodically as a reminder to take the drug and tracks how many and at what time pills have been taken. Smart watches and smart clothing can monitor diverse health indicators, improving prevention, early detection, and treatment. These devices can also recognize emergency situations, including falls, and summon help automatically. Robots are available that assist older adults with diverse tasks, such as retrieving objects, reading documents, and doing routine housework.

Architects have also designed homes that can adapt to changing physical needs—equipping them with movable walls that expand and contract, plumbing that enables a full bathroom to be added on the main floor, and "smart-home" technologies that promote safety and mobility, such as sensors in floors that activate room lights when an older person gets up at night, temperature sensors that detect whether the stove is left on, and alarm systems that detect falls. Another remarkable device is a bathroom scale that helps monitor health status. It sends a signal to a control box, which reads the person's weight aloud. After comparing weight with previous readings, the box asks relevant questions—"Are you more tired than usual?" "Are you having trouble sleeping?"—that can be answered by pressing a "yes" or "no" button. The box also works with equipment that measures blood pressure, activity level, and other health indicators. Data collected are sent electronically to whomever the older adult gives access.

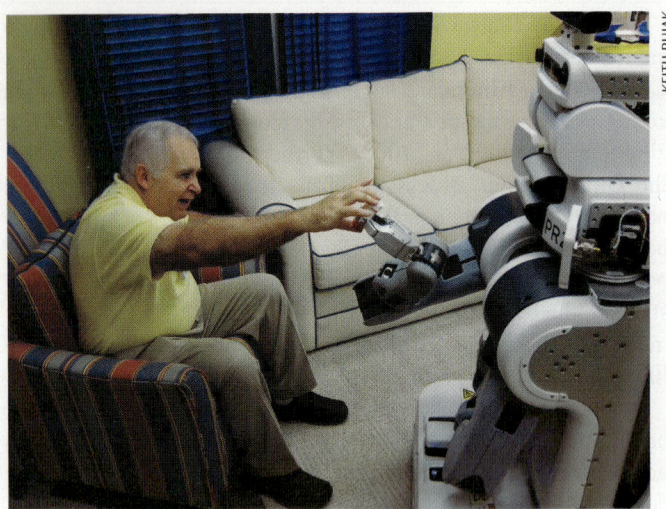

A robot hands medication to an adult with a physical disability, helping him sustain his independence and continue living in his own home.

Use of assistive devices slows physical declines and reduces the need for personal caregiving (Agree, 2014; Wilson et al., 2009). Do older people with disabilities regard some technologies as invasions of privacy? The majority weigh privacy concerns against potential benefits—saying, for example, "If this device would keep me independent longer, I wouldn't mind" (Brown, Rowles, & McIlwain, 2016). Sustaining an effective *person–environment fit,* or match between older people's current capabilities and the demands of their living environments, enhances psychological well-being (Lin & Wu, 2014).

At present, U.S. government-sponsored health-care coverage is largely limited to essential medical equipment; smart-home technologies are beyond the financial means of most older people. Sweden's health-care system, in contrast, covers many assistive devices that promote function and safety, and its building code requires that new homes include a full bathroom on the main floor (Swedish Institute, 2016). In this way, Sweden strives to maximize person–environment fit for its older adults, helping them remain as independent as possible.

Overcoming Stereotypes of Aging.
Negative stereotypes that view older adults as weak, boring, and debilitated and "deterioration as inevitable" are widespread in Western nations. Overcoming this pessimistic picture is vital for helping people adapt favorably to late-life physical changes. Many older adults report experiences of prejudice and discrimination (Perdue, 2016). These include being ignored, talked down to, or assumed to be unable to hear or understand, and exposure to disparaging jokes about older people.

Like gender stereotypes, aging stereotypes often operate automatically, without awareness; people "see" older adults in stereotypical ways, even when they appear otherwise (Kite et al., 2005). As older people encounter negative messages about aging, they experience *stereotype threat,* which results in diminished performance on tasks related to the stereotype (see page 320 in Chapter 9). In a growing number of studies, aging adults were exposed to words associated with either negative aging stereotypes ("decrepit," "confused") or positive aging stereotypes ("sage," "enlightened"). Those in negative-stereotype conditions displayed a more intense physiological response to stress, greater help-seeking and feelings of loneliness, and worse self-efficacy, physical performance, recall memory, and appraisals of their own health and memory capacity (Bouazzaoui et al., 2015; Coudin & Alexopoulos, 2010; Levy & Leifheit-Limson, 2009; Mazerolle et al., 2015). Stereotype threat triggers anxiety about one's own abilities, depleting cognitive resources needed to perform well on tasks at hand.

The stressful, disorganizing impact of negative aging stereotypes can be long-lasting. In a longitudinal study lasting several decades, older people who endorsed many negative stereotypes displayed a 30 percent greater decline in memory performance than those who endorsed few stereotypes (Levy et al., 2012). The memory decrement was especially steep for individuals who viewed themselves as old—that is, for whom negative stereotypes were personally relevant.

Positive stereotypes, in contrast, reduce stress and foster physical and mental competence (Bolkan & Hooker, 2012). In another longitudinal investigation, people with positive self-perceptions of aging—who, for example, agreed with such statements as "As I get older, things are better than I thought they'd be"—lived, on average, 7½ years longer than those with negative self-perceptions. This survival advantage remained after gender, SES, loneliness, and physical health status were controlled (Levy et al., 2002). Adults with less education are especially susceptible to the detrimental effects of aging stereotypes, perhaps because they tend to accept those messages uncritically (Andreoletti & Lachman, 2004).

Older adults rarely appear in television programs, but when they do, they typically play minor roles and are portrayed as weak, unhealthy, or dependent. TV commercials aim to sell older people products and, therefore, usually depict them in stereotypically positive roles, most commonly as an "adventurous golden ager" (fun-loving, sociable, and active), "perfect grandparent" (family-oriented, kind, and generous), or "productive golden ager" (intelligent, capable, and successful) (Kotter-Grühn, 2015). Still, the products promoted in such ads are mostly medications and medical services and "anti-aging" cosmetics and treatments—images that reinforce negative views of older adults as preoccupied with physical declines and dissatisfied with their appearance.

In cultures where older adults are treated with deference and respect, aging can be a source of pride. In the native language of the Inuit people of Canada, the closest word to "elder" is *isumataq,* or "one who knows things"—a high status that begins when a couple becomes head of the extended family unit. When Inuit older adults were asked for their thoughts on aging well, they mentioned attitudes—a positive approach to life, interest in transmitting cultural knowledge to young people, and community involvement—nearly twice as often as physical health (Collings, 2001).

Japan honors its older citizens with an annual celebration, Respect for the Aged Day. Also, a ritual called *kanreki* recognizes

CHAPTER 17 Physical and Cognitive Development in Late Adulthood

An older adult of the Inuit people of Canada lights a traditional oil lamp, a symbol of warmth and light in the arctic climate, as her granddaughter observes. Inuit culture confers high status on the aged, who serve as important sources of cultural knowledge for younger generations.

the older person's new freedoms and competencies and senior place in the family and society. Japanese extended families in the United States often plan the kanreki as a surprise sixtieth birthday party, incorporating elements of both the traditional ritual (such as dress) and the Western birthday (a special cake). A positive attitude toward aging prompts a welcoming approach to late adulthood, including some of its physical transitions.

Despite inevitable declines, physical aging can be viewed with either optimism or pessimism. As Walt commented, "You can think of your glass as half full or half empty." Cultural valuing of older adults greatly increases the likelihood that they will adopt the "half full" alternative.

Ask yourself

CONNECT Review research on stereotype threat on page 320 in Chapter 9. How do stereotypes of aging similarly affect older adults' behavior?

APPLY "The best way to adjust to this is to learn to like it," thought 65-year-old Herman, inspecting his thinning hair in the mirror. "I remember reading that bald older men are viewed as leaders." What type of coping is Herman using, and why is it effective?

REFLECT While watching TV during the coming week, keep a log of portrayals of older adults in commercials. How many images were positive? How many negative? Compare your observations with research findings.

Health, Fitness, and Disability

17.5 Discuss health and fitness in late life, paying special attention to nutrition, exercise, and sexuality.

17.6 Discuss physical disabilities associated with late adulthood.

17.7 Discuss mental disabilities associated with late adulthood.

17.8 Discuss health-care issues that affect older adults.

At Walt and Ruth's fiftieth wedding anniversary, 77-year-old Walt thanked a roomful of well-wishers for joining in the celebration. Then, with emotion, he announced, "I'm so grateful Ruth and I are still healthy enough to give to our family, friends, and community."

As Walt's remarks affirm, health is central to psychological well-being in late life. When researchers ask older adults about possible selves (see Chapter 16, page 544), number of hoped-for physical selves declines with age and number of feared physical selves increases. Nevertheless, because older people compare themselves to same-age peers, the majority rate their health favorably. And aging adults' self-rated health does not decline as much as would be expected on the basis of objective health assessments (French, Sargent-Cox, & Luszcz, 2012; U.S. Department of Health and Human Services, 2015d). As for protecting their health, older adults' sense of self-efficacy is as high as that of young adults and higher than that of middle-aged people (Frazier, 2002).

Self-efficacy and optimism about one's health promote continued health-enhancing behaviors and reduced incidence of chronic illness (Kubzansky & Boehm, 2016). Furthermore, disability need not inevitably lead to further disability and dependency. In longitudinal research, 10 to 50 percent of older adults with disabilities showed substantial improvement 2 to 6 years later (Johnston et al., 2004; Ostir et al., 1999).

SES continues to predict physical functioning. African-American and Hispanic older people (one-fifth of whom live in poverty) remain at greater risk for various health problems, including cardiovascular disease, diabetes, and certain cancers. Native-American aging adults are even worse off (Cubanski, Casillas, & Damico, 2015; Mehta, Sudharsanan, & Elo, 2014). The majority are poor, and chronic health conditions—including diabetes, kidney disease, liver disease, tuberculosis, and hearing and vision impairments—are so widespread that in the United States, the federal government grants Native Americans special health benefits. These begin as early as age 45, reflecting a much harder and shorter lifespan.

Unfortunately, low-SES and ethnic minority older adults are more likely than their higher-SES and white counterparts to delay or forgo medical treatment, particularly taking prescription medications and undergoing complex surgical procedures (Weech-Maldonado, Pradhan, & Powell, 2014). One reason is cost: On average, U.S. Medicare beneficiaries devote 18 percent of their income to out-of-pocket health-care expenses—a figure that escalates among those with the fewest resources

(Noel-Miller, 2015). Another reason is perceived discriminatory treatment by health-care providers, which undermines ethnic minority patients' trust (Guerrero, Mendes de Leon, & Evans, 2015). Furthermore, low-SES and minority older people often do not comply with doctors' directions because they feel less in control of their health and less optimistic that treatment will work. Their low self-efficacy further impairs their physical condition.

The sex differences noted in Chapter 15 extend into late adulthood: Men are more prone to fatal diseases, women to non-life-threatening disabling conditions—especially, mobility limitations due to osteoporosis and arthritis. By very old age (80 to 85 and beyond), women are more impaired than men because only the sturdiest men have survived (Deeg, 2016). In addition, with fewer physical limitations, older men are better able to remain independent and to engage in exercise, leisure and volunteer pursuits, and social activities, all of which promote better health.

Widespread health-related optimism among older people suggests that substantial inroads into preventing disability can be made even in the last few decades of life. Ideally, as life expectancy extends, we want the average period of diminished vigor before death—especially, the number of months or years of ill-health and suffering—to decrease. This public health goal is called the **compression of morbidity**. Several large-scale studies indicate that over the past several decades, compression of morbidity has occurred in industrialized nations (Fries, Bruce, & Chakravarty, 2011; Taylor & Lynch, 2011). Medical advances and improved socioeconomic conditions are largely responsible.

In addition, the impact of good health habits on postponement of disability is large. In one investigation, researchers followed a large sample of university alumni from their late sixties over the next two decades. In those who were low risk (no risk factors of smoking, obesity, or lack of exercise), disability was delayed by nearly 5 years compared with those who were moderate risk (had one of these risk factors). Compared to high-risk participants (with two or three risk factors), postponement of disability in the low-risk group exceeded 8 years (see Figure 17.3) (Chakravarty et al., 2012). Although good health habits lengthened life by about 3½ years, their impact on functional ability was greater.

Consequently, researchers believe that the most promising route to further compression of morbidity in developed countries is to reduce negative lifestyle factors. Progress in this respect, however, has been disappointing. Certain unhealthy conditions, such as a high-fat diet, overweight and obesity, and a sedentary lifestyle, have been increasing. Without modifying these factors, future gains in compression of morbidity will be hard to achieve. Rather, we may see a trend in the reverse direction: an *expansion of morbidity*, in which people live longer with debilitating illnesses because of improved medical treatments (Utz & Tabler,

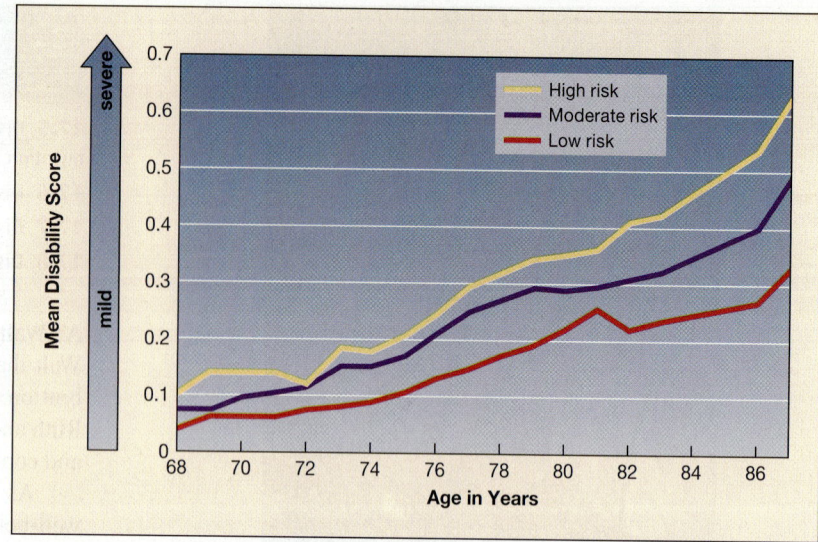

FIGURE 17.3 Development of disability in older adults with low, moderate, and high risk factors. More than 2,300 university alumni were followed from age 68 over the next two decades. The low-risk group had no risk factors (smoking, obesity, or lack of exercise). The moderate-risk group had one risk factor, and the high-risk group had two or three risk factors. Emergence of disability (at the 0.1 level) in the low-risk group was delayed by nearly 5 years compared to the moderate-risk group, and by more than 8 years compared to the high-risk group. Compression of morbidity occurred among the low-risk participants relative to their higher-risk counterparts, even though all participants were socioeconomically advantaged. (Adapted from E. F. Chakravarty et al., 2012, "Lifestyle Risk Factors Predict Disability and Death in Healthy Aging Adults," *American Journal of Medicine, 125,* p. 193. Copyright © 2012, Elsevier. Reprinted with permission from Elsevier, Inc.)

2016). As we look closely at health, fitness, and disability in late adulthood, we will add to our discussion of health promotion, taking up additional routes to this vital objective.

Comprehensive strategies are needed in the developing world, where 70 percent of older people will reside by 2025. In these nations, poverty is rampant, chronic diseases occur earlier, even routine health interventions are unavailable or too costly for many, and most public health programs do not focus on late adulthood (Rinaldo & Ferraro, 2012). As a result, disability rates among older adults are especially high, and as yet, no progress has been made in compression of morbidity.

Nutrition and Exercise

The physical changes of late life lead to an increased need for certain nutrients—calcium and vitamin D to protect the bones; zinc and vitamins B_6, C, and E to protect the immune system; and vitamins A, C, and E to protect against excess free radicals. Yet declines in physical activity, in the senses of taste and smell, and in ease of chewing (because of deteriorating teeth) can reduce the quantity and quality of food eaten. Furthermore, the aging digestive system has greater difficulty absorbing certain nutrients, such as protein, calcium, and vitamin D. And older adults who live alone may have problems shopping or cooking and may feel less like eating by themselves. Together, these physical and environmental conditions increase the risk of dietary deficiencies.

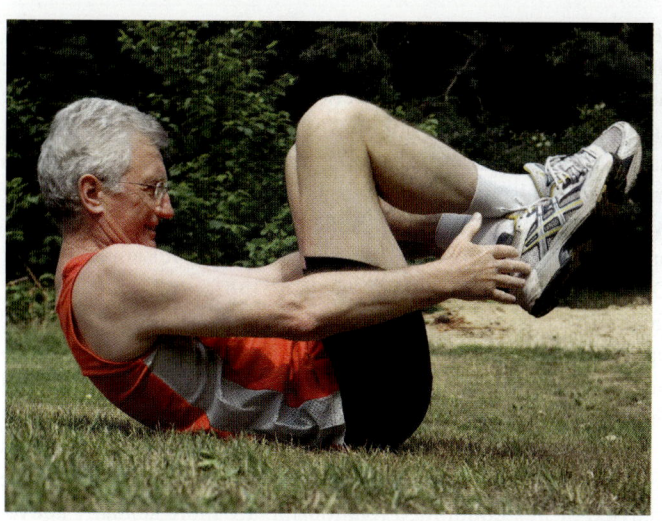

A 70-year-old does abdominal exercises after going for a run. Previously sedentary older adults who engage in regular, moderate-to-vigorous exercise gain in muscle size and strength as well as executive function and memory.

utive function and memory (Erickson, Leckie, & Weinstein, 2014). These findings offer clear biological evidence for the role of late-life physical activity in preserving central nervous system health.

Older people who come to value the intrinsic benefits of physical activity—feeling stronger, healthier, and more energetic—are likely to engage in it. Yet about 60 percent of U.S. 65- to 74-year-olds and 75 percent of those over age 75 do not exercise regularly (U.S. Department of Health and Human Services, 2015d). Often, those with chronic disease symptoms believe that exercise actually will do harm. In planning exercise programs for aging adults, it is important to instill a sense of control—by stressing the health-enhancing rewards of physical activity and by changing negative beliefs that interfere with sustained effort (Lachman, Neupert, & Agrigoroaei, 2011). Active older people can serve as positive role models and sources of encouragement for others.

Except for calcium and vitamin D, a daily vitamin–mineral supplement is recommended only for older adults suffering from malnutrition. Vitamin–mineral supplements do not reduce the incidence of cardiovascular disease or cancer (Neuhouser et al., 2009). Furthermore, supplemental nutrients and herbs identified as "cognitive enhancers"—including B and E vitamins, folic acid, and ginkgo biloba—do not improve cognitive functioning and neither prevent nor slow the progression of Alzheimer's disease (DeKosky et al., 2008; McDaniel, Maier, & Einstein, 2002). Rather, a diet high in nutrients is most effective in fostering physical and cognitive health in late adulthood. And regularly eating fish high in omega-3 fatty acids (which aid cardiovascular health) offers some protection against mental disabilities (Cederholm, Salem, & Palmblad, 2013; Morris et al., 2016).

In addition to a healthy diet, exercise continues to be a powerful health intervention. Sedentary healthy older adults up to age 80 who begin endurance training (walking, cycling, aerobic dance) show gains in vital capacity that compare favorably with those of much younger individuals. And weight-bearing exercise begun in late adulthood—even as late as age 90—promotes muscle size and strength (deJong & Franklin, 2004; Pyka et al., 1994). This translates into improved walking speed, balance, posture, and ability to carry out everyday activities, such as opening a stubborn jar lid, carrying an armload of groceries, or lifting a 30-pound grandchild.

Exercise also increases blood circulation to the brain, which helps preserve brain structures and behavioral capacities. Brain scans show that physically fit older people experience less tissue loss—in both neurons and glial cells—in the cerebral cortex (Erickson et al., 2010; Miller et al., 2012). And compared with physically inactive agemates, previously sedentary older adults who initiated a program of regular, moderate to vigorous exercise displayed gains in size of diverse cortical areas, including the prefrontal cortex and hippocampus, with benefits for exec-

Sexuality

When Walt turned 60, he asked his 90-year-old Uncle Louie at what age sexual desire and activity cease. Walt's question stemmed from a widely held myth that sex drive disappears in late adulthood. Louie corrected this impression. "My sexual interest has never gone away," he explained to Walt. "I can't do it as often, and it's a quieter experience than it was in my youth. But Rachella and I have led a happy intimate life, and it's still that way."

As in other surveys of large, nationally representative samples of U.S. older people, the National Social Life, Health, and Aging Project revealed an age-related decline in frequency of sexual activity—especially among women, who are less likely

Most married older adults report continued, regular sexual enjoyment. In addition to intercourse, feeling sensual, enjoying close companionship, and being loved and wanted are all part of sexuality at the most advanced ages.

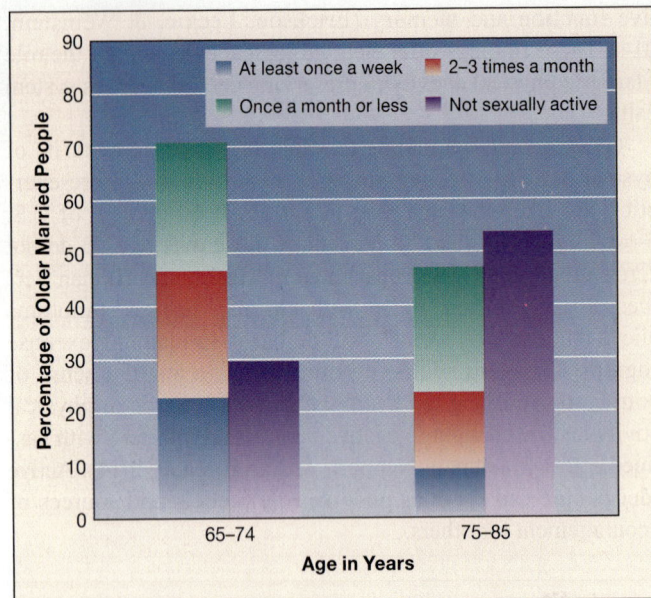

FIGURE 17.4 Age-related changes in sexual activity among U.S. married older adults. In the National Social Life, Health, and Aging Project, which included 1,500 married U.S. older people, most reported engaging in sexual activity at least two to three times per month. Sexual activity declined with age. Still, nearly half of 75- to 85-year-olds were sexually active. (Based on Karraker & DeLamater, 2013.)

than men to be in a marital or other intimate relationship. At the same time, the majority of respondents attributed at least some importance to sex, and those who had been sexually active in the previous year mostly rated sex as "very" or "extremely" important. Consistent with these attitudes, most married older adults reported continued, regular sexual enjoyment. Nearly half of the oldest survey participants, age 75 to 85, were sexually active, with more than 20 percent indicating that they engaged in some type of sexual activity (usually intercourse) at least two to three times per month (see Figure 17.4) (Karraker & DeLamater, 2013). Note that these trends are probably influenced by cohort effects: A new generation of older people, accustomed to viewing sexuality positively, will probably be more sexually active.

The same generalizations we discussed for midlife apply to late life: Good sex in the past predicts good sex in the future, and continued sexual activity is linked to relationship satisfaction. Furthermore, using intercourse as the only measure of sexual activity promotes a narrow view of pleasurable sex. Even at the most advanced ages, there is more to sexuality than the sex act itself—feeling sensual, enjoying close companionship, and being loved and wanted. Both older men and older women report that the male partner is usually the one who ceases to interact sexually (DeLamater, 2012; Karraker & DeLamater, 2013). In a culture that emphasizes an erection as necessary for being sexual, a man may withdraw from all erotic activity when he finds that erections are harder to achieve and more time must elapse between them.

Disabilities that disrupt blood flow to the penis—most often, disorders of the autonomic nervous system, cardiovascular disease, and diabetes—are largely responsible for dampening sexuality in older men. But as noted in Chapter 15, availability of drug treatments, such as Viagra, has increased men's willingness to discuss erectile dysfunction with their doctors. Cigarette smoking, excessive alcohol intake, mental health problems such as persistent anxiety and depression, and a variety of prescription medications also lead to diminished sexual performance. Among women, poor physical and mental health and absence of a partner are major factors that reduce sexual activity (DeLamater, 2012; DeLamater & Koepsel, 2014). Because the sex ratio increasingly favors females, aging heterosexual women have fewer and fewer opportunities for sexual encounters. Older adults who lack partners for an extended time tend to drift into a state of sexual disinterest.

The little evidence available on lesbian and gay older adults resembles findings on heterosexual individuals: Those who are married or in a committed relationship are more sexually active. And as sexual minority couples grow old, their focus shifts from sexual acts that lead to climax to those that convey deep affection, such as kissing, embracing, caressing, and sleeping together (Slevin & Mowery, 2012).

In Western industrialized nations, sexual expression in old age frequently meets with disapproval. Educational programs that inform older people about typical age-related changes in sexual functioning and that promote a view of sex as extending throughout adulthood are vital for encouraging positive sexual attitudes. In nursing homes, education for caregivers can help ensure residents' rights to privacy and other living conditions that permit sexual activity (DeLamater & Koepsel, 2014). A special need exists to increase staff acceptance of sexual contact between lesbian and gay couples.

Physical Disabilities

Compare the death rates shown in Figure 17.5 with those in Figure 15.3 on page 516. You will see that illness and disability

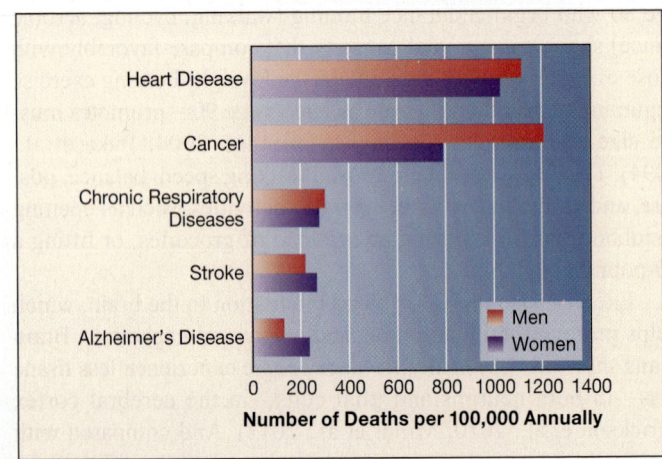

FIGURE 17.5 Leading causes of death among people age 65 and older in the United States. In late adulthood, heart disease and cancer are leading causes of death. Stroke, chronic respiratory diseases, and Alzheimer's disease also claim the lives of many older adults. Women exceed men in deaths due to stroke and Alzheimer's disease. (Based on Heron, 2015.)

climb as the end of the lifespan approaches. Heart disease and cancer remain the leading causes of death, increasing dramatically from mid- to late life. As before, death rates from heart disease and cancer are higher for men than for women (Heron, 2015).

Respiratory diseases, which rise sharply with age, are the third most common cause of death among older adults. Among such diseases is *emphysema,* caused by extreme loss of elasticity in lung tissue, which results in serious breathing difficulty. Although a few cases of emphysema are inherited, most result from long-term cigarette smoking. *Stroke* and *Alzheimer's disease* follow; both are unique in being more prevalent among women, largely because women live longer. Stroke occurs when a blood clot blocks a blood vessel or a blood vessel hemorrhages in the brain, causing damage to brain tissue. It is a major cause of late-life disability and, after age 75, death. Alzheimer's disease, the leading cause of dementia, also rises sharply with age; we will consider it in-depth shortly.

Other diseases are less frequent killers, but they limit older adults' ability to live fully and independently. We have already noted the increase after age 65 in macular degeneration, which severely impairs vision and leads to blindness (see page 575). Osteoporosis, discussed in Chapter 15, continues to rise in late adulthood; recall that it affects the majority of men and women after age 70. Yet another bone disorder—*arthritis*—adds to the physical limitations of many older people. And *type 2 diabetes* and *unintentional injuries* also multiply in late adulthood. In the following sections, we take up these last three conditions.

Finally, an important point must be kept in mind as we discuss physical and mental disabilities of late adulthood: That these conditions are strongly *related to age* does not mean that they are *entirely caused by aging.* To clarify this distinction, experts distinguish between **primary aging** (another term for *biological aging*), or genetically influenced declines that affect all members of our species and take place even in the context of overall good health, and **secondary aging,** declines due to hereditary defects and negative environmental influences, such as poor diet, lack of exercise, disease, substance abuse, environmental pollution, and psychological stress.

Throughout this book, we have seen that it is difficult to distinguish primary from secondary aging. Undoubtedly you have, at one time or another, encountered *frail older adults*— people with extreme infirmity who display wasted muscle mass and strength, weight loss, severe mobility problems, and perhaps cognitive impairment. **Frailty** involves weakened functioning of diverse organs and body systems, yielding symptoms that profoundly interfere with everyday competence—unintentional weight loss, self-reported exhaustion, muscle weakness, slow walking speed, and low physical activity. Frailty leaves older people highly vulnerable in the face of infection, extremely hot or cold weather, or injury (Moorehouse & Mallery, 2016). Although primary aging contributes to frailty, researchers agree that secondary aging plays a larger role, through genetic disorders, unhealthy lifestyle (including obesity and sedentary behavior), and chronic disease (Fried et al., 2009; Song et al.,

The frail older adult on the left has limited mobility that interferes with her everyday competence. Although biological aging contributes to frailty, secondary aging plays a larger role.

2015). The serious conditions we are about to discuss are major sources of frailty in late adulthood.

Arthritis. Beginning in her late fifties, Ruth felt a slight morning stiffness in her neck, back, hips, and knees. In her sixties, she developed bony lumps on the end joints of her fingers. As the years passed, she experienced joint pain, swelling, and some loss of flexibility—changes that affected her ability to move quickly and easily.

Arthritis, a condition of inflamed, painful, stiff, and sometimes swollen joints and muscles, becomes more common in late adulthood. It occurs in several forms. Ruth has **osteoarthritis,** the most common type, which involves deteriorating cartilage on the ends of bones of frequently used joints. Otherwise known as "wear-and-tear arthritis" or "degenerative joint disease," it is one of the few age-related disabilities in which years of use make a difference. Although a genetic proneness exists, the disease usually does not appear until the forties or fifties. In frequently used joints, cartilage on the ends of the bones, which reduces friction during movement, gradually deteriorates. Or obesity places abnormal pressure on the joints and damages cartilage. Almost all older adults show some osteoarthritis on X-rays, although wide individual differences in severity exist (Baker & Mingo, 2016). It is the most common cause of mobility problems and of surgical hip and knee replacements in older adults.

Unlike osteoarthritis, which is limited to certain joints, **rheumatoid arthritis** involves the whole body. An autoimmune response leads to inflammation of connective tissue, particularly the membranes that line the joints, resulting in overall aching, inflammation, and stiffness. Tissue in the cartilage tends to grow, damaging surrounding ligaments, muscles, and bones. The result is deformed joints and often serious loss of mobility. Sometimes other organs, such as the heart and lungs, are affected (Goronzy, Shao, & Weyand, 2010). Worldwide, about ½ to 1 percent of older adults have rheumatoid arthritis.

Overall, 45 percent of U.S. men over age 65 have been diagnosed with arthritis, about 20 percent of whom experience disability due to the disease. Among women age 65 and older, the disease incidence is higher, at 55 percent, and so is the rate of disability among diagnosed individuals, at 25 percent (Hootman et al., 2016). Although rheumatoid arthritis can strike at any age, it increases after age 60. Twin studies support a strong hereditary contribution. Presence of certain genes heightens disease risk, possibly by triggering a late-life defect in the immune system (Frisell, Saevarsdottir, & Askling, 2016; Yarwood et al., 2015). However, identical twins differ widely in disease severity, indicating that environment makes a difference. So far, cigarette smoking is the only confirmed lifestyle influence, greatly increasing risk in people without a family history of the disease (Di Giuseppe et al., 2014). Early treatment with powerful anti-inflammatory medications helps slow progression of rheumatoid arthritis.

Managing arthritis requires a balance of rest when the disease flares, pain relief, and physical activity. Regular aerobic exercise and strength training lessen pain and improve physical functioning (Semanik, Chang, & Dunlop, 2012). In obese people, weight loss is essential. Although osteoarthritis responds to these interventions more easily than rheumatoid arthritis, the course of each varies greatly. With proper analgesic medication, joint protection, lifestyle changes, and surgery to replace badly damaged hip or knee joints, many people with either form of the illness lead long, productive lives.

Diabetes. After a meal, the body breaks down the food, releasing glucose (the primary energy source for cell activity) into the bloodstream. Insulin, produced by the pancreas, keeps the blood concentration of glucose within set limits by stimulating muscle and fat cells to absorb it. When this balance system fails, either because not enough insulin is produced or because body cells become insensitive to it, *type 2 diabetes* (otherwise known as *diabetes mellitus*) results. Over time, abnormally high blood glucose damages the blood vessels, increasing the risk of heart attack, stroke, circulatory problems in the legs (which impair balance and gait), and injury to the eyes, kidneys, and nerves.

Impaired glucose tolerance also accelerates degeneration of neurons and synapses (Petrofsky, Berk, & Al-Nakhli, 2012). In several longitudinal studies, diabetes was associated with more rapid cognitive declines in older people and an elevated risk of dementia, especially Alzheimer's disease—an association we will soon revisit when we take up Alzheimer's (Baglietto-Vargas et al., 2016; Cheng et al., 2012). Cognitive deficits may even be under way in the prediabetic state, prior to a diabetic diagnosis.

From middle to late adulthood, the incidence of type 2 diabetes nearly doubles; it affects one-fourth of Americans age 65 and older (Centers for Disease Control and Prevention, 2014c). Diabetes runs in families, suggesting that heredity is involved. But inactivity and abdominal fat deposits greatly increase the risk. Higher rates of type 2 diabetes are found among African-American, Mexican-American, and Native-American aging adults for both genetic and environmental reasons, including high-fat diets and obesity associated with poverty. More than one-third have the disease.

Treating type 2 diabetes requires lifestyle changes, including a carefully controlled diet and regular exercise, which promote weight loss and glucose reabsorption. In many people with recent disease onset (less than one year), sustaining these behaviors partially or completely reverses the course of the illness (Ades, 2015).

Unintentional Injuries. At age 65 and older, the death rate from unintentional injuries is at an all-time high—more than twice as great as in adolescence and early adulthood. Motor vehicle collisions and falls are largely responsible.

Motor Vehicle Accidents. Motor vehicle collisions account for just 15 percent of U.S. injury mortality in late life, compared with 50 percent in middle adulthood. But a look at individual drivers tells a different story. Older adults have higher rates of traffic violations, accidents, and fatalities per mile driven than any other age group, with the exception of drivers under age 25. The high rate of injury persists, even though many older people, especially women, limit their driving after noticing that their ability to drive safely is slipping (Heron, 2015). Deaths due to injuries—motor vehicle and otherwise—continue to be much higher for men than for women.

Recall that visual declines led Walt to have difficulty seeing the dashboard and identifying pedestrians at night. The greater older adults' visual processing difficulties, the higher their rate of moving violations and crashes (Friedman et al., 2013). Compared with young drivers, older people are less likely to drive quickly and recklessly but more likely to fail to heed signs, yield the right of way, and turn appropriately. They often try to compensate for their difficulties by being more cautious. Slowed reaction time and indecisiveness pose hazards, too. In Chapter 15, we noted that executive function declines with age: Tasks requiring spatial working memory, inhibition of irrelevant

Visual processing difficulties, slowed reaction time, and declines in executive function contribute to high rates of traffic violations, accidents, and fatalities per mile driven in late adulthood. Still, aging adults usually try to drive as long as possible.

information and impulses, and flexible shifting of attention between activities become increasingly challenging (see page 528). Because these skills are essential for safe driving, aging adults are at high risk for collisions at busy intersections and in other complex traffic situations.

Nevertheless, older people usually try to drive as long as possible. Giving up driving results in loss of personal control over daily life and decline in productive roles, such as paid work and volunteering (Curl et al., 2014). Specially trained driver rehabilitation consultants—affiliated with hospitals, drivers licensing agencies, or U.S. Area Agencies on Aging (see page 65 in Chapter 2)—can help assess older adults' capacity to continue driving, provide driver retraining, or counsel them to retire from driving and use other transportation options.

Aging adults also make up nearly 20 percent of all U.S. pedestrian deaths (Centers for Disease Control and Prevention, 2016f). Confusing intersections, especially signals that do not allow older people enough time to cross the street, are often involved.

Falls. One day, Ruth fell down the basement steps and lay there with a broken ankle until Walt arrived home an hour later. Ruth's tumble represents the leading type of accident in late life. About one-third of adults over age 65 and half of those over age 80 have experienced a fall within the past year (Centers for Disease Control and Prevention, 2016c). Declines in vision, hearing, mobility, muscle strength, and cognitive functioning; depressed mood; use of medications that affect mental processing; and development of certain chronic illnesses, such as arthritis—all of which make it harder to avoid hazards and keep one's balance—increase the risk of falling (Rubenstein, Stevens, & Scott, 2008). The more of these factors that are present, the greater the risk of falling.

Because of weakened bones and difficulty breaking a fall, serious injury results about 20 percent of the time. The most common is hip fracture. It increases fifteenfold from age 65 to 85 and frequently leads to reduced mobility, increased weakness, and serious health complications. One in five older hip fracture patients dies within a year of the injury (Centers for Disease Control and Prevention, 2015f). Of those who survive, half never regain the ability to walk without assistance.

Falling can also impair health indirectly, by promoting fear of falling. Nearly half of older adults who have fallen admit that they purposefully avoid activities because they are afraid of falling again. In this way, a fall can limit mobility and social contact, undermining both physical and psychological well-being (Painter et al., 2012). Although an active lifestyle may expose older people to more situations that can cause a fall, the health benefits of activity far outweigh the risk of serious injury due to falling.

Preventing Unintentional Injuries. Many steps can be taken to reduce unintentional injury in late adulthood. Designing motor vehicles and street signs to accommodate older adults' visual needs is a goal for the future. Meanwhile, training that enhances visual and cognitive skills essential for safe driving and that helps older adults avoid high-risk situations (such as busy intersections and rush hour) can save lives.

Similarly, efforts to prevent falls must address risks within the person and the environment—through corrective eyewear, strength and balance training, and improved safety in homes and communities. Consult the National Resource Center for Safe Aging, *www.safeaging.org*, for a wealth of information on safety in late adulthood.

Mental Disabilities

Normal age-related cell death in the brain, described earlier, does not lead to loss of ability to engage in everyday activities. But when cell death and structural and chemical abnormalities are profound, serious deterioration of mental and motor functions occurs.

Dementia refers to a set of disorders occurring almost entirely in old age in which many aspects of thought and behavior are so impaired that everyday activities are disrupted. Dementia strikes 13 percent of adults over age 65. Approximately 2 to 3 percent of people age 65 to 69 are affected; the rate doubles every 5 to 6 years until it reaches about 22 percent among those age 85 to 89 and over half after age 90—trends that apply to the United States and other Western nations (Prince et al., 2013). Beyond age 80, a larger proportion of women than men have dementia, perhaps reflecting the biological sturdiness of the oldest men. Although dementia rates are similar across most ethnic groups, older African Americans have about twice the incidence, and Hispanics about one and one-half times the incidence, as whites (Alzheimer's Association, 2016a). Associated risk factors, not race, are responsible, as we will see shortly.

About a dozen types of dementia have been identified. Some are reversible with proper treatment, but most are irreversible and incurable. A few forms, such as Parkinson's disease,[1] involve deterioration in subcortical brain regions (primitive structures below the cortex) that often extends to the cerebral cortex and, in many instances, results in brain abnormalities resembling Alzheimer's disease. Research suggests that Parkinson's and Alzheimer's are related (Goedert, 2015). But in the majority of dementia cases, subcortical brain regions are intact, and progressive damage occurs only to the cerebral cortex. The two most common forms of *cortical dementia* are Alzheimer's disease and vascular dementia.

Alzheimer's Disease.
When Ruth took 79-year-old Ida to the ballet, an occasion the two sisters eagerly anticipated each year, she noticed a change in Ida's behavior. Ida, who had forgotten the engagement, reacted angrily when Ruth arrived unannounced at her door. Driving to the theater, which was in a familiar part of town, Ida got lost—all the while insisting that she knew the way perfectly. As the lights dimmed and the music began, Ida talked loudly and dug noisily in her purse.

---

[1] In Parkinson's disease, neurons in the part of the brain that controls muscle movements deteriorate. Symptoms include tremors, shuffling gait, loss of facial expression, rigidity of limbs, difficulty maintaining balance, and stooped posture. Over time, the disease often results in dementia.

"Shhhhhh," responded a dozen voices from surrounding seats.

"It's just the music!" Ida snapped at full volume. "You can talk all you want until the dancing starts." Ruth was astonished and embarrassed at the behavior of her once socially sensitive sister.

Six months later, Ida was diagnosed with **Alzheimer's disease,** the most common form of dementia, in which structural and chemical brain deterioration is associated with gradual loss of many aspects of thought and behavior. Alzheimer's accounts for an estimated 70 percent of all dementia cases. Approximately 11 percent of Americans over age 65—about 5.2 million people—have the disorder. Of those over age 85, about one-third are affected. In 2030, when all baby boomers will have reached late adulthood, the number of Americans with Alzheimer's is expected to rise to 7.7 million—an increase of more than 50 percent. About 5 to 15 percent of all deaths among older adults involve Alzheimer's, making it a significant cause of late-life mortality (Alzheimer's Association, 2016a).

Symptoms and Course of the Disease. The earliest symptoms are often progressively worsening memory problems—forgetting names, dates, appointments, familiar routes of travel, or the need to turn off the kitchen stove. At first, recent memory is most impaired (Bilgel et al., 2014). But as serious disorientation sets in, recall of distant events and such basic facts as time, date, and place evaporates. Faulty judgment puts the person in danger. For example, Ida insisted on driving after she was no longer competent to do so. Personality changes occur—loss of spontaneity and sparkle, anxiety in response to uncertainties created by mental problems, aggressive outbursts, reduced initiative, and social withdrawal. Depression often appears in the early phase of Alzheimer's and other forms of dementia and seems to be part of the disease process (Serra et al., 2010). However, depression may worsen as the older adult reacts to disturbing mental changes.

As the disease progresses, skilled and purposeful movements disintegrate. When Ruth took Ida into her home, she had to help her dress, bathe, eat, brush her teeth, and (eventually) walk and use the bathroom. Ida's sleep was disrupted by delusions and imaginary fears. She often awoke in the night and banged on the wall, insisting that it was dinnertime, or cried out that someone was choking her. Over time, Ida lost the ability to comprehend and produce speech. And when her brain ceased to process information, she could no longer recognize objects and familiar people. In the final months, Ida became increasingly immobile, vulnerable to infections, lapsed into a coma, and died.

The course of Alzheimer's varies greatly, from a year to as long as 20 years, with those diagnosed in their sixties and early seventies typically surviving longer than those diagnosed at later ages (Brodaty, Seeher, & Gibson, 2012). The average life expectancy for a 70-year-old man with the disease is about 4½ years, for a 70-year-old woman about 8 years.

Brain Deterioration. A diagnosis of Alzheimer's disease is made through exclusion, after ruling out other causes of dementia by a physical examination and psychological testing—an approach that is more than 90 percent accurate. To confirm Alzheimer's, doctors inspect the brain after death for a set of abnormalities that either cause or result from the disease (Hyman et al., 2012). In about 90 percent of cases, however, MRI and PET images of brain volume and activity predict whether individuals will receive an after-death confirmation of Alzheimer's (Vitali et al., 2008). Assessments of the chemical makeup of the blood or cerebrospinal fluid are also strongly predictive (Mattsson et al., 2015; Olsson et al., 2016). These procedures offer hope of very early diagnosis, opening the door to more successful interventions.

Two major structural changes in the cerebral cortex, especially in memory and reasoning areas, are associated with Alzheimer's. Inside neurons, **neurofibrillary tangles** appear—bundles of twisted threads that are the product of collapsed neural structures and that contain abnormal forms of a protein called tau. Outside neurons, **amyloid plaques,** dense deposits of a deteriorated protein called *amyloid,* surrounded by clumps of dead neurons and glial cells, develop. Although some neurofibrillary tangles and amyloid plaques are present in the brains of normal middle-aged and older people and increase with age, they are far more abundant in Alzheimer's victims. A major thrust of current research is understanding exactly how abnormal amyloid and tau damage neurons, so treatments can be developed to slow or block these processes.

Researchers once thought that amyloid plaques contributed to the neuronal damage of Alzheimer's. But recent findings suggest that they reflect the brain's effort to get harmful amyloid away from neurons. Instead, a major culprit seems to be abnormal breakdown of amyloid remaining *within* neurons (National Institute on Aging, 2016). In both Alzheimer's disease and Parkinson's disease, disruptions occur in a key neuronal process responsible for chopping up and disposing of abnormal proteins (Sagare et al., 2013). These damaged proteins (including amyloid) build to toxic levels. Abnormal amyloid causes the

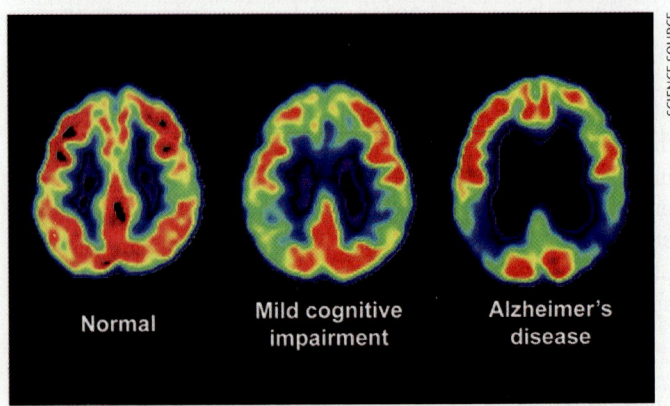

These PET images contrast a normal brain (left) with those showing structural and chemical deterioration. With widespread synaptic damage and neuronal death, overall brain volume decreases and the ventricles expand. Mild cognitive impairment (center) commonly precedes a more dramatic decline in brain volume (right), which is highly predictive of an after-death confirmation of Alzheimer's disease.

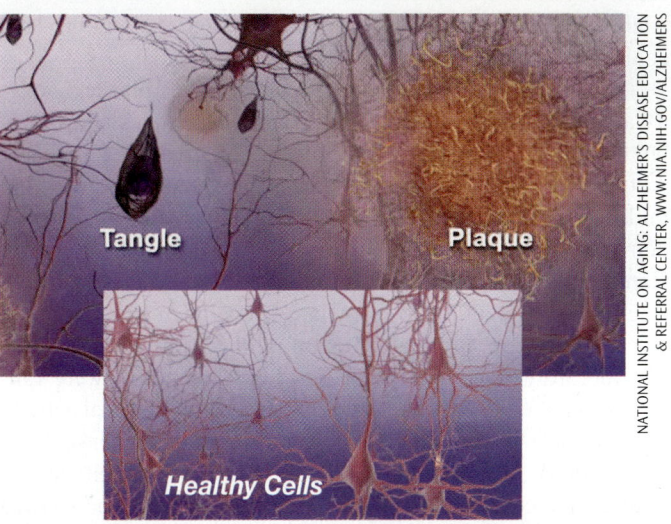

An image of tissue in the Alzheimer's brain reveals amyloid plaques between neurons, and dead and dying neurons containing neurofibrillary tangles. Compare these cell changes with healthy brain cells.

generation of signals within neurons and their transfer across synapses to malfunction (Kopeikina et al., 2011). Eventually, damaged amyloid induces heightened, abnormal electrical activity throughout the brain, contributing to broad neural network malfunctioning.

Abnormal tau in neurofibrillary tangles adds to neuronal breakdown. Tangles disrupt the transport of nutrients and signals from the neuron to its connective fibers, thereby joining with amyloid to block synaptic communication. Furthermore, abnormal tau triggers disintegration of nearby normal tau (de Calignon et al., 2012; Liu et al., 2012). Gradually, tau pathology moves across synapses, spreading from neuron to neuron and, over time, from one brain region to the next—thereby amplifying damage.

As synapses deteriorate, levels of neurotransmitters decline, neurons die in massive numbers, and brain volume shrinks. Destruction of neurons that release the neurotransmitter acetylcholine, involved in transporting messages between distant brain regions, further disrupts neuronal networks. A drop in serotonin, a neurotransmitter that regulates arousal and mood, may contribute to sleep disturbances, aggressive outbursts, and depression (Rothman & Mattson, 2012). These problems may intensify cognitive and motor symptoms.

Risk Factors. Alzheimer's disease comes in two types: *familial,* which runs in families, and *sporadic,* which has no obvious family history. Familial Alzheimer's, responsible for 1 percent or fewer cases, generally has an early onset—between ages 30 and 60—and progresses more rapidly than the later-appearing sporadic type, which typically appears after age 65. Researchers have identified genes on chromosomes 1, 14, and 21, involved in generation of harmful amyloid, that are related to familial Alzheimer's. In each case, the abnormal gene is dominant; if it is present in only one of the pair of genes inherited from parents, the person will develop early-onset Alzheimer's (National Institute on Aging, 2016). Recall that chromosome 21 is involved in Down syndrome. Individuals with this chromosomal disorder who live past age 40 almost always have the brain abnormalities and symptoms of Alzheimer's.

Heredity plays a different role in sporadic Alzheimer's, through somatic mutation. About half of people with this form of the disease have an abnormal gene on chromosome 19, which results in excess levels of APOE ε4, a blood protein that carries cholesterol throughout the body. Researchers believe that a high blood concentration of APOE ε4 affects the expression of a gene involved in regulating insulin. Deficient insulin and resulting glucose buildup in the bloodstream (conditions that, when extreme, lead to diabetes) are linked to brain damage, especially in areas regulating memory, and to high buildup of harmful amyloid in brain tissue (Liu et al., 2013; National Institute on Aging, 2016). In line with these findings, individuals with diabetes have a greatly increased risk of developing Alzheimer's.

At present, the abnormal APOE ε4 gene is the most widely known risk factor for sporadic Alzheimer's: Those who inherit one APOE ε4 allele have a threefold greater risk; those who inherit two alleles have an eight- to twelvefold greater risk (Loy et al., 2014). But genetic testing has revealed many other genes that seem to make an equal or greater contribution. For example, in older adults with Alzheimer's, genes involved in clearing abnormal proteins from neurons often are altered, enabling excessive amyloid and tau buildup. And some genes impair nutrient and signal transfer from neurons to connective fibers, without affecting amyloid (National Institute on Aging, 2016).

Nevertheless, many sporadic Alzheimer's victims show no known genetic marker, and some individuals with the APOE ε4 gene do not develop the disease. Evidence is increasing for the role of a variety of largely modifiable risk factors, including excess dietary fat, physical inactivity, overweight and obesity, smoking, chronic depression, cardiovascular disease, stroke, and (as just noted) diabetes (Baumgart et al., 2015; Institute of Medicine, 2015). Moderate to severe head injuries, possibly by accelerating deterioration of amyloid and tau, also increase Alzheimer's risk, especially among people with the APOE ε4 gene (Mckee & Daneshvar, 2015). Although a single injury is sufficient for long-term, debilitating consequences, individuals subjected to repeated instances, such as boxers, football players, and combat veterans, are especially likely to be affected.

Still, some older adults with an abundance of amyloid plaques in their brains never develop Alzheimer's. The disease is believed to result from different combinations of genetic and environmental factors, each leading to a somewhat different course of the disease. The high incidence of Alzheimer's and other forms of dementia among African Americans illustrates the complexity of potential causes.

Compared with African Americans, Yoruba village dwellers of Nigeria show a much lower Alzheimer's incidence and a much weaker association between the APOE ε4 gene and the disease (Hendrie et al., 2014). Some investigators speculate that intermarriage with European Americans heightened genetic risk among African Americans and that environmental factors translated that risk into reality. Whereas the Yoruba of Nigeria eat a low-fat diet, the African-American diet is high in fat. Eating fatty foods may increase the chances that the APOE ε4 gene will lead to Alzheimer's. And even for Yoruba and African Americans without the APOE ε4, a high-fat diet is risky (Hall et al., 2006). The more fat consumed and the higher the blood level of "bad" cholesterol (low-density lipoproteins), the greater the incidence of Alzheimer's.

New findings indicate that a substantial number of sporadic Alzheimer's cases are due to epigenetic processes, in which environmental influences modify gene expression (see page 70 in Chapter 2). In one study, researchers examined over 700 donated brains of older adults who had died. In many brains with Alzheimer's abnormalities, elevated methylation levels, which reduce or silence a gene's impact, were linked to genetic markers of the disease and predicted extent of amyloid plaque buildup (De Jager et al., 2014). The next step is to identify factors that trigger gene methylation associated with the disease.

Protective Factors. Researchers are testing both drug and nondrug approaches to preventing or slowing the progress of Alzheimer's. Among promising drug therapies are compounds that interfere with amyloid and tau breakdown and that suppress brain inflammation resulting from these toxic proteins, which worsens neuronal damage (Bachstetter, Watterson, & Van Eldik, 2014; Lou et al., 2014). Insulin therapy, delivered via a nasal spray to the brain, helps regulate neuronal use of glucose (Ribarič, 2016). Research indicates that it has memory benefits and slows cognitive decline, at least in the short term, among older adults with *mild cognitive impairment*—diminished mental abilities that are noticeable to the affected person, friends, and family members but that do not affect capacity to carry out everyday activities, which commonly precede Alzheimer's.

A "Mediterranean diet" emphasizing fish, unsaturated fat (olive oil), vegetables, and moderate consumption of red wine is linked to a 30 to 50 percent reduced incidence of Alzheimer's disease, to slower disease progression in diagnosed individuals, and also to a reduction in vascular dementia (which we will turn to next) (Lourida et al., 2013; Morris et al., 2015). These foods contain antioxidants and other substances that help promote the health of the cardiovascular and central nervous systems.

Education and an active lifestyle are beneficial as well. The rate of Alzheimer's is reduced by more than half in older adults with higher education, though this protective effect is not as great for those with the APOE ε4 gene (Beydoun et al., 2014). Some researchers speculate that complex cognitive activities of better-educated people lead to reorganization of brain areas devoted to cognitive processes and to richer synaptic connections, which act as a **cognitive reserve,** giving the aging brain greater tolerance for injury before it crosses the threshold into mental disability. In support of this view, compared to their less-educated counterparts, the highly educated display a faster rate of decline following an Alzheimer's or other dementia diagnosis, suggesting that they show symptoms only after very advanced brain deterioration (Karbach & Küper, 2016). Late-life cognitively stimulating social and leisure activities also protect against Alzheimer's and dementia in general (Bennett et al., 2006; Hall et al., 2009; Sattler et al., 2012).

Finally, persistence, intensity, and variety of physical activity are associated with decreased risk of Alzheimer's and vascular dementia, with larger benefits for older people with the APOE ε4 gene. In longitudinal research, exercising regularly in midlife predicted reduced late-life dementia, after many other dementia-linked lifestyle factors were controlled (Blondell, Hammersley-Mather, & Veerman, 2014; Smith et al., 2013). Beginning regular exercise in late life is also protective. In one investigation, older adults with mild cognitive impairment and therefore judged to be at risk for Alzheimer's were randomly assigned to either a 24-week home-based physical activity program or to a usual home-care control group (Lautenschlager et al., 2008). At a six-month follow-up, those experiencing the intervention continued to engage in regular exercise and showed slight cognitive improvement, whereas controls had declined in cognitive functioning.

Helping Alzheimer's Victims and Their Caregivers. As Ida's Alzheimer's worsened, the doctor prescribed a mild sedative and an antidepressant to help control her behavior. Drugs that increase levels of the neurotransmitters acetylcholine and serotonin show promise in limiting challenging dementia symptoms—especially agitation and disruptiveness, which are particularly stressful for caregivers (National Institute on Aging, 2016). Providing stimulation through engaging activities, exercise, and sensory experiences (touch, music, and videos) also helps reduce inappropriate behaviors (Camp, Cohen-Mansfield, & Capezuti, 2002).

But with no cure available, family interventions ensure the best adjustment possible for the Alzheimer's victim, spouse, and other relatives. Dementia caregivers devote substantially more time to caregiving and experience more stress than do people caring for older adults with physical disabilities (Alzheimer's Association, 2016a). They need assistance and encouragement from extended-family members, friends, and community agencies. The Social Issues: Health box on pages 592–593 describes a variety of helpful interventions for family caregivers. In addition to these strategies, avoiding dramatic changes in living conditions, such as moving to a new location, rearranging furniture, or modifying daily routines, helps people with Alzheimer's disease feel as secure as possible in a cognitive world that is gradually disintegrating.

LOOK and LISTEN

Investigate formal respite services, providing temporary relief to caregivers of older adults with dementia, in your community. Visit a respite program, and talk to several family caregivers about its impact on the patient's and their own adjustment.

Vascular Dementia. In **vascular dementia,** a series of strokes leaves areas of dead brain cells, producing step-by-step degeneration of mental ability, with each step occurring abruptly after a stroke. Approximately 15 percent of all dementia cases in Western nations are vascular. The disorder affects 1.5 percent of Americans over age 65 (Sullivan & Elias, 2016). At the same time, many victims of Alzheimer's disease also show vascular damage, and in some instances, the two types of dementia are difficult to distinguish.

Vascular dementia is the combined result of genetic and environmental influences. The effects of heredity are indirect, through high blood pressure, cardiovascular disease, and diabetes, each of which increases the risk of stroke. And environmental factors—including cigarette smoking, heavy alcohol use, high salt intake, very low dietary protein, obesity, inactivity, and psychological stress—also heighten stroke risk (Sahathevan, Brodtmann, & Donnan, 2011).

Because of their greater susceptibility to cardiovascular disease, more men than women have vascular dementia. The disease also varies among countries. For example, the occurrence of vascular dementia is particularly high in Japan. Although a low-fat diet reduces Japanese adults' risk of cardiovascular disease, high intake of alcohol and salt and a diet very low in animal protein increase the risk of stroke. As Japanese consumption of alcohol and salt declined and intake of meat rose in recent decades, rates of vascular dementia and stroke-caused deaths dropped (Ikejima et al., 2014; Sekita et al., 2010). However, they remain higher than in other developed nations.

Although Japan presents a unique, contradictory picture (there, cardiovascular disease is low, and stroke is high), in most cases vascular dementia is caused by atherosclerosis. Prevention is the only effective way to stop the disease. The incidence of vascular dementia has dropped in the last two decades, largely as a result of the decline in heart disease and more effective stroke prevention methods (U.S. Department of Health and Human Services, 2015d). Signs that a stroke might be coming are weakness, tingling, or numbness in an arm, a leg, or the face; sudden vision loss or double vision; speech difficulty; and severe dizziness and imbalance. Doctors may prescribe drugs to reduce the tendency of the blood to clot. Once strokes occur, paralysis and loss of speech, vision, coordination, memory, and other mental abilities are common.

Misdiagnosed and Reversible Dementia. Careful diagnosis of dementia is crucial because other disorders can be mistaken for it. And some forms of dementia can be treated and a few reversed.

Depression is the disorder most often misdiagnosed as dementia. Between 1 and 5 percent of people over age 65 are severely depressed—a rate lower than for young and middle-aged adults. As we will see in Chapter 18, however, depression rises with age, is often related to physical illness and pain, and can lead to cognitive deterioration. As at younger ages, the support of family members and friends, antidepressant medication, and individual, family, and group therapy can help relieve depression. However, U.S. older adults often do not receive the mental health services they need—partly because Medicare offers reduced coverage for treating mental health problems and partly

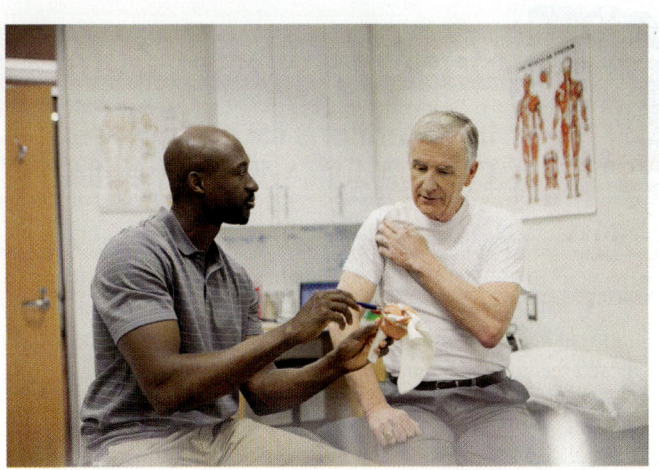

Depression—often related to physical illness and pain—may be misdiagnosed as dementia. With his therapist's support, this older adult has a good chance of avoiding depression during his slow recovery from a shoulder injury.

because doctors rarely refer older people for mental health services (Hinrichsen, 2016; Robinson, 2010). These circumstances increase the chances that depression will deepen and be confused with dementia.

The older we get, the more likely we are to be taking drugs that may have side effects resembling dementia. For example, some medications for coughs, diarrhea, and nausea inhibit the neurotransmitter acetylcholine, leading to Alzheimer's-like symptoms. In addition, some diseases can cause temporary memory loss and mental symptoms, especially among older people, who often become confused and withdrawn when ill (Grande et al., 2016; Tveito et al., 2016). Treating the underlying illness relieves the problem. Finally, environmental changes and social isolation can trigger mental declines (Hawton et al., 2011). When supportive ties are restored, cognitive functioning usually bounces back.

Health Care

Health-care professionals and lawmakers in industrialized nations worry about the economic consequences of rapid increase in the older population. Rising government-supported health-care costs and demand for certain health-care services, particularly long-term care, are of greatest concern.

Cost of Health Care for Older Adults. Adults age 65 and older make up just 14 percent of the U.S. population but account for about one-third of government health-care spending. According to current estimates, the cost of government-sponsored health insurance, or Medicare, for older people will nearly double by 2030 as more baby boomers enter late adulthood and average life expectancy extends further (Centers for Medicare and Medicaid Services, 2016).

Medicare expenses rise steeply with age. People age 75 and older receive, on average, 70 percent more benefits than those who are younger. Most of this increase reflects the need for long-term care—in hospitals and nursing homes—resulting from an

Social Issues: Health

Interventions for Caregivers of Older Adults with Dementia

Margaret, wife and caregiver of a 71-year-old Alzheimer's patient, sent a desperate plea to an advice columnist at her local newspaper: "My husband can't feed or bathe himself, or speak to anyone or ask for assistance. I must constantly anticipate his needs and try to meet them. Please help me. I'm at the end of my rope."

The effects of Alzheimer's disease are devastating not just to victims but also to family members who provide care with little or no outside assistance. Caregiving under these conditions has been called the "36-hour day" because of its constant demands. Although the majority of family caregivers are middle-aged, an estimated one-third are older adults caring for a spouse or an aging parent. Many are in poor health themselves, yet the number of hours dedicated to caregiving increases with caregiver age and is especially high among ethnic minority older adults, whose cultures emphasize care as a family obligation (Alzheimer's Association, 2016a).

Family members who exceed their caregiving capacities suffer greatly in physical and mental health and are at risk for early mortality (Sörensen & Pinquart, 2005). Severity of cognitive impairments and behavior problems in care recipients are strong predictors of weakening caregiver health (AARP, 2015). And the close relationship between the caregiver and the suffering individual—involving shared memories, experiences, and emotions—seems to heighten caregiver risk for physical and psychological problems (Monin & Schulz, 2009).

Most communities offer interventions designed to support family caregivers, but they need to be expanded and made more cost-effective. Those that work best address multiple needs: knowledge, coping strategies, caregiving skills, and respite.

Knowledge

Virtually all interventions try to enhance knowledge about the disease, caregiving challenges, and available community resources. Knowledge is usually delivered through classes, but websites with wide-ranging information on caregiving, and online communication technologies through which caregivers can obtain and share information, also exist (Czaja, 2016). Gains in knowledge, however, must be combined with other approaches to improve caregivers' well-being.

Coping Strategies

Many interventions teach caregivers everyday problem-solving strategies for managing the dependent person's behavior, along with techniques for dealing with their own negative thoughts and feelings, such as resentment about having to provide constant care. Modes of delivery include support groups, individual therapy, and classes providing coaching in effective coping strategies (Roche, MacCann, & Croot, 2016; Selwood et al., 2007). All yield improvements in caregivers' adjustment and in patients' disturbing behaviors, both immediately and in follow-ups more than a year later.

This daughter cares for her father, who has Alzheimer's disease. Although the task has compensating rewards, it is physically demanding and emotionally draining. A great need exists for interventions that support caregivers.

---

age-related rise in disabling chronic diseases and acute illnesses. Because Medicare funds only about half of their medical needs, older Americans spend several times as much on health care as their counterparts do in other industrialized nations (OECD, 2015a). And Medicare provides far less support for long-term care than U.S. older people with severe disabilities need.

Long-Term Care. When Ida moved into Ruth's home, Ruth promised never to place Ida in an institution. But as Ida's condition worsened and Ruth faced health problems of her own, she couldn't keep her word. Reluctantly, Ruth placed Ida in a nursing home.

Advancing age is strongly associated with use of long-term care services, especially nursing homes. Almost half of U.S. nursing home residents are age 85 and older. Dementia—especially Alzheimer's disease—most often leads to nursing home placement; frailty is another strong predictor (Harris-Kojetin et al., 2016; Kojima, 2016). Greater use of nursing homes is also prompted by loss of informal caregiving support through widowhood—which mostly affects women—and aging of adult children and other relatives.

Overall, only 3 percent of Americans age 65 and older are institutionalized, less than half the rates in other Western nations, such as Australia, Belgium, the Netherlands, Switzerland, Sweden, and New Zealand, which provide more generous public financing of institutional care (OECD, 2016). Unless nursing home placement follows hospitalization for an acute illness, U.S. older adults must pay for it until their resources are exhausted. At that point, Medicaid (health insurance for the poor) takes

Caregiving Skills

Caregivers benefit from lessons in how to communicate with older adults who can no longer express thoughts and emotions clearly and handle everyday tasks—for example, sustaining good eye contact to convey interest and caring; speaking slowly, with short, simple words; using gestures to reinforce meaning; waiting patiently for a response; refraining from interrupting, correcting, criticizing, or talking about the older adult as if he or she isn't there; and introducing pleasant activities, such as music and slow-paced children's TV programs, that relieve agitation (Alzheimer's Association, 2016b). Interventions that teach communication skills through active practice reduce patients' troublesome behavior and, as a result, lessen caregivers' distress and boost their sense of self-efficacy (Eggenberger, Heimerl, & Bennett, 2013; Irvine, Ary, & Bourgeois, 2003).

Respite

Caregivers usually say that *respite*—time away from providing care—is the assistance they most desire. But they may be reluctant to accept friends' and relatives' informal offers to help because of guilt, or to use formal services (such as adult day care or temporary placement in a care facility) because of cost or worries about the older adult's adjustment. Yet respite at least twice a week for several hours improves physical and mental health for most caregivers by enabling them to maintain friendships, engage in enjoyable activities, and sustain a balanced life (Lund et al., 2010b).

For respite to be most effective, caregivers must start using services before they become overwhelmed. Once a rewarding, enjoyable life has been lost, it is difficult to restore. Furthermore, frequent, regular respite is far more helpful than infrequent, irregular use. And planning how best to use respite time is crucial. Caregivers who end up spending respite hours doing housework, shopping, or working usually remain dissatisfied (Lund et al., 2009). Those who engage in activities they had wanted and planned to do gain in psychological well-being.

In addition to time away from the caregiving situation, caregivers benefit from short periods of relief from the unrelenting demands of in-home care. One group of researchers devised a unique tool called Video Respite—a series of videotapes suited to the interests of Alzheimer's patients that provide caregivers with a half-hour to an hour break. On each tape, an actor conducts a slow-paced, simple conversation about familiar experiences, people, and objects, pausing occasionally for the impaired person to respond (Caserta & Lund, 2002). Evaluations show that the videos capture the attention of people with Alzheimer's and reduce problem behaviors, such as wandering, agitation, and aggression.

Intervention Programs

Multifaceted intervention programs that begin early in the caregiving process, that continue for many weeks or months, and that are tailored to caregivers' individual needs greatly reduce stress while helping them find satisfactions in caring for a declining loved one. Such interventions usually delay institutional placement of dementia patients as well.

In the Resources for Enhancing Alzheimer's Caregiver Health (REACH) initiative, an array of "active" intervention programs, each including some or all of the ingredients just described, were evaluated against "passive" interventions providing only information and referral to community agencies. Among more than 1,200 participating caregivers, those receiving six months of active intervention declined more in self-reported burden. And one program providing family therapy in the home—through a telephone system facilitating frequent communication among therapist, caregiver, family members, and other support systems—substantially reduced caregiver depressive symptoms (Gitlin et al., 2003; Schultz et al., 2003). Caregivers with greater care responsibility—women versus men, lower-SES versus higher-SES, spouses versus nonspouses—benefited most from active intervention. In additional evaluations, REACH active intervention programs enhanced physical and mental health among caregivers of diverse ethnicities—African American, European American, and Hispanic (Basu, Hochhalter, & Stevens, 2015; Belle et al., 2006; Elliott, Burgio, & DeCoster, 2010).

---

over. Consequently, the largest users of nursing homes in the United States are people with either very low or high incomes. Middle-income aging adults and their families are more likely to try to protect their savings from being drained by high nursing home costs.

Nursing home use also varies across ethnic groups. For example, European Americans are more likely to be institutionalized than African Americans and Hispanics, who often have large, close-knit extended families with a strong sense of caregiving responsibility. Similarly, Asian and Native-American older adults use nursing homes less often than European Americans (Centers for Medicare and Medicaid Services, 2013; Thomeer, Mudrazija, & Angel, 2014). Overall, families provide at least 60 to 80 percent of all long-term care in Australia, Canada, New Zealand, the United States, and Western Europe. As we have seen, families of diverse ethnic and SES backgrounds willingly step in to care for older people in times of need.

To reduce institutionalized care of older adults and its associated high cost, experts advocate alternatives, such as publicly funded in-home help for family caregivers (see Chapter 16, page 557). Another option that has increased dramatically over the past two decades is **assisted living**—homelike housing arrangements for older adults who require more help than can be provided at home but less than is usually provided in nursing homes. Assisted living is a cost-effective alternative to nursing homes that prevents unnecessary institutionalization. It also can enhance residents' autonomy, social life, community involvement, and life satisfaction—benefits that we will take up in Chapter 18.

In a nursing home in the Netherlands, a patient enjoys moving landscapes displayed on a screen in an area resembling a train compartment. Institutional care is far less common in the United States than in other Western nations, where public financing is more generous.

In Denmark, the combination of a government-sponsored home-helper system and expansion of assisted-living housing resulted in a substantial reduction in the need for nursing home beds (Hastrup, 2007; Rostgaard, 2012). Strengthening caregiving and health-care services in U.S. assisted-living facilities would result in similarly favorable outcomes, while also enhancing older adults' happiness. The overwhelming majority of residents want to stay in assisted living rather than move to a nursing home.

When nursing home placement is necessary, steps can be taken to improve its quality. For example, the Netherlands has established separate facilities designed to meet the different needs of patients with mental and physical disabilities. And every older person, no matter how disabled, benefits from opportunities to maintain existing strengths and acquire new skills that can compensate for declines. Institutionalized individuals—like aging adults everywhere—desire a sense of personal control, gratifying social relationships, and meaningful and enjoyable daily activities (Alkema, Wilber, & Enguidanos, 2007). As Chapter 18 will reveal, designing nursing homes to meet these needs promotes both physical and psychological well-being.

Ask yourself

CONNECT Explain how each level of ecological systems theory (Chapter 1, pages 23–26) contributes to caregiver well-being and quality of home care for older adults with dementia.

APPLY Marissa complained to a counselor that at age 68, her husband, Wendell, no longer initiated sex or cuddled her. Why might Wendell have ceased to interact sexually? What interventions—both medical and educational—could be helpful to Marissa and Wendell?

REFLECT What care and living arrangements have been made for older adults needing assistance in your family? How did culture, personal values, financial means, health, and other factors influence those decisions?

COGNITIVE DEVELOPMENT

17.9 Describe overall changes in cognitive functioning in late adulthood.

Ruth's complaints to her doctor about difficulties with memory and verbal expression reflect common concerns about cognitive functioning in late adulthood. Decline in speed of processing, under way throughout the adult years, is believed to affect many aspects of cognition in old age. In Chapter 15, we noted that reduced efficiency of thinking contributes to (but may not fully explain) decrements in executive function, especially working-memory capacity and working-memory updating. Declines in inhibition of irrelevant information and impulses, in flexibly shifting between tasks and mental operations, in use of memory strategies, and in retrieval from long-term memory continue in the final decades of life, affecting many aspects of cognitive aging.

Return to Figure 15.7 on page 526, and note that the more a mental ability depends on fluid intelligence (biologically based information-processing skills), the earlier it starts to decline. In contrast, mental abilities that rely on crystallized intelligence (culturally based knowledge) are sustained longer. But maintenance of crystallized intelligence depends on continued opportunities to use and enhance cognitive skills. When these are available, crystallized abilities—vocabulary, general information, and expertise in specific endeavors—can offset losses in fluid intelligence.

Look again at Figure 15.7. In advanced old age, decrements in fluid intelligence limit what people can accomplish even with

These musicians continue to perform in late adulthood, as they have for most of their adult lives, through selective optimization with compensation. They carefully select pieces within range of their current skill, shorten the length of playing sessions to optimize their limited energy, and compensate for reduced playing speed by including just a few well-practiced, rapid passages.

cultural supports, including a rich background of experience, knowledge of how to remember and solve problems, and a stimulating daily life. Consequently, crystallized intelligence shows a modest decline.

Generally, loss outweighs improvement and maintenance as people approach the end of life, but plasticity is still possible: Some individuals display high maintenance and minimal loss at very old ages (Baltes & Smith, 2003; Schaie, 2013). Research reveals greater individual variation in cognitive functioning in late adulthood than at any other time of life (Riediger, Li, & Lindenberger, 2006). Besides fuller expression of genetic and lifestyle influences, increased freedom to pursue self-chosen courses of action—some that enhance and others that undermine cognitive skills—may be responsible.

How can older adults make the most of their cognitive resources? According to one view, those who sustain high levels of functioning engage in **selective optimization with compensation:** Narrowing their goals, they select personally valued activities to optimize (or maximize) returns from their diminishing energy. They also find new ways to compensate for losses (Baltes, Lindenberger, & Staudinger, 2006; Napolitano & Freund, 2016). For example, when famed pianist Arthur Rubinstein was asked at age 80 how he managed to sustain such extraordinary playing, he replied that he was *selective*; he played fewer pieces, carefully choosing those within range of his current skill and stamina. This enabled him to *optimize* his energy; he could practice each piece more. He also devised *compensatory* techniques for a decline in playing speed. For example, before a fast passage, he played extra slowly, so the fast section appeared to his audience to move more quickly.

In late adulthood, personal goals—while still including gains—increasingly focus on maintaining abilities and preventing losses. In one study, researchers asked people to rate their most important physical and cognitive goals for emphasis on growth ("With this goal, I want to improve something or achieve something new") and maintenance/prevention of losses ("With this goal, I want to maintain something or prevent a loss") (Ebner, Freund, & Baltes, 2006). As Figure 17.6 shows, compared with young adults, older adults accentuated maintenance and loss prevention.

As we review major changes in memory, language processing, and problem solving, we will consider ways that older adults optimize and compensate in the face of declines. We will also see that certain abilities that depend on extensive life experience, not processing efficiency, are sustained or increase in old age. Last, we take up programs that recognize older people as lifelong learners empowered by new knowledge, just as they were at earlier periods of development.

LOOK and LISTEN

Interview an older adult about memory and other cognitive challenges, asking for examples. For each instance, invite the older person to describe his or her efforts to optimize cognitive resources and compensate for losses.

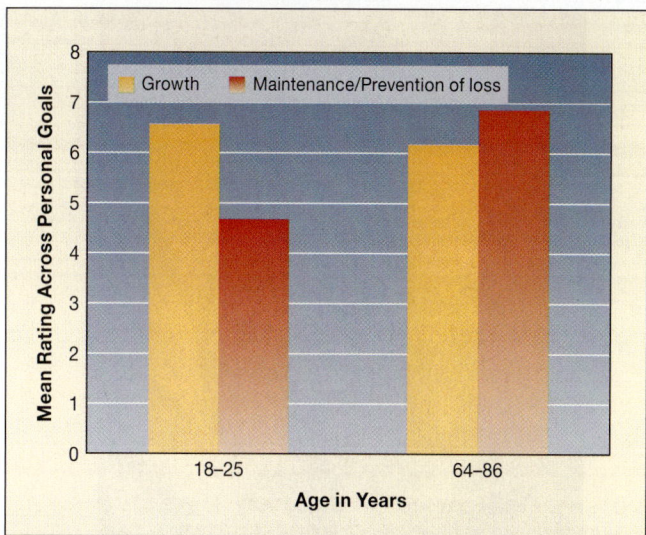

FIGURE 17.6 Personal goal orientation toward growth and maintenance/prevention of loss in young and older adults. Participants were asked to list two physical and two cognitive goals and then to rate each for emphasis on growth and on maintenance or prevention of loss, using an 8-point scale. Older adults—while continuing to pursue growth—placed much greater emphasis on maintenance and loss prevention than did young adults. (From N. C. Ebner, A. M. Freund, & P. B. Baltes, 2006, "Developmental Changes in Personal Goal Orientation from Young to Late Adulthood: From Striving for Gains to Maintenance and Prevention of Losses," *Psychology and Aging, 21,* p. 671. Adapted by permission of American Psychological Association.)

Memory

17.10 How does memory change in late life?

As older adults take in information more slowly, retain less in working memory, and find it harder to engage in inhibition, apply strategies, and retrieve relevant knowledge from long-term memory, the chances of memory failure increase (Naveh-Benjamin, 2012; Verhaeghen, 2012). Difficulties with *episodic memory*— retrieval of everyday experiences—rise substantially. In comparison, *semantic memory*—general knowledge removed from the context in which it was first learned—is better preserved.

Explicit versus Implicit Memory

"Ruth, you know that movie we saw—the one with the little 5-year-old boy who did such a wonderful acting job. I'd like to suggest it to Dick and Goldie. But what was it called?" asked Walt.

"I can't think of it, Walt. We've seen a few movies lately. Which theater was it at? Who'd we go with? Tell me more about the little boy—maybe it'll come to me."

Although everyone occasionally has memory failures like this, diverse aspects of episodic recall become more challenging in late life. When Ruth and Walt watched the movie, their slower cognitive processing meant that they retained fewer details. And

A grandmother and her granddaughter attend a festival in Sri Lanka. Declines in processing speed and working-memory capacity lead older adults to take in less about a stimulus and its context. As a result, this grandmother may find details of the event difficult to recall.

because their working memories could hold less at once, they attended poorly to *context*—where they saw the movie and who went with them (Zacks & Hasher, 2006). When we try to remember, context serves as an important retrieval cue.

Because older adults take in less about a stimulus and its context, their recall is reduced in relation to that of younger people. For example, they sometimes cannot distinguish an imagined event from one they actually experienced (Rybash & Hrubi-Bopp, 2000). They find it harder to recall the source of information, particularly when potential sources are similar—which member of their bridge club made a certain statement, to whom and on which occasion they previously told a certain joke or story, and—in laboratory research—within which of two 10-word lists they had just studied particular words had appeared (Wahlheim & Huff, 2015). Temporal memory—recall of the order in which events occurred or how recently they happened—suffers as well (Hartman & Warren, 2005; Rotblatt et al., 2015).

Older adults' limited working memories increase the likelihood of another type of episodic memory difficulty: They may, for example, travel from the den to the kitchen intending to get something but then not recall what they intended to get. When the context in which they formed the memory intention (the den) differs from the retrieval context (the kitchen), they often experience memory lapses (Verhaeghen, 2012). Once they return to the first context (the den), it serves as a strong cue for their memory intention because that is where they first encoded it, and they say, "Oh, now I remember why I went to the kitchen!"

A few days later, when Ruth saw a TV ad for the movie whose title she had forgotten, she recognized its name immediately. Recognition—a fairly automatic type of memory that demands little mental effort—suffers less than recall in late adulthood because a multitude of environmental supports for remembering are present. Age-related declines in memory are greatest on **explicit memory** tasks, which require controlled, strategic processing (Hoyer & Verhaeghen, 2006).

Consider another automatic form of memory: **implicit memory,** or memory without conscious awareness. In a typical implicit memory task, you would be shown a list of words, then asked to fill in a word fragment (such as t– –k). You would probably complete the sequence with a word you had just seen (*task*) rather than another word (*took* or *teak*). Without trying to do so, you would engage in recall.

Age differences in implicit memory are much smaller than in explicit memory. Memory that depends on familiarity rather than on consciously controlled use of strategies is better preserved in old age (Koen & Yonelinas, 2013; Ward, Berry, & Shanks, 2013). This helps explain why semantic memory—recall of vocabulary and general information, which are mostly well-learned and highly familiar—declines far less, and does so at later ages, than recall of everyday experiences (Small et al., 2012). The episodic memory problems aging adults report—for names of people, places where they put important objects, directions for getting from one place to another, and (as we will see) appointments and medication schedules—all place high demands on their more limited working memories and on other executive processes.

Associative Memory

The memory difficulties just described are part of a general, age-related decline in binding information into complex memories (Smyth & Naveh-Benjamin, 2016). Researchers call this an **associative memory deficit,** or difficulty creating and retrieving links between pieces of information—for example, two items or an item and its context, such as Ruth's attempt to remember the name of the movie with the child actor or where she had seen the movie.

To find out whether older adults have greater difficulty with associative memory than younger adults, researchers show them pairs of unrelated words or pictures of objects (such as *table–overcoat* or *sandwich–radio*) and ask that they study the pairs for an upcoming memory test. During the test, one group of participants is given *single items,* some that had appeared in the study phase and some that had not, and asked to indicate the ones they had studied. The other group is given *item pairs,* some intact from the study phase (*table–overcoat*) and some rearranged (*overcoat–radio*), and asked to indicate which pairs they had studied. As Figure 17.7 illustrates, older adults do almost as well as younger adults on single-item memory tests (Guez & Lev, 2016; Old & Naveh-Benjamin, 2008; Ratcliff & McKoon, 2015).

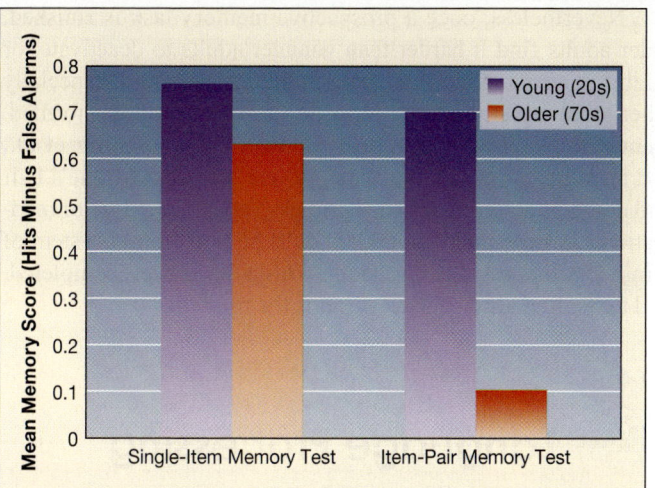

FIGURE 17.7 Young and older adults' performance on single-item and item-pair memory tests, supporting an associative memory deficit in late adulthood. After studying pairs of items (in this case, pictures of objects), some participants were asked to identify single items they had seen. Others were asked to identify the item pairs they had seen. Older adults performed almost as well as young adults on the single-item memory test. But they did far worse on the item-pair memory test. (Based on Guez & Lev, 2016.)

tigate remote recall, researchers probe *autobiographical memory*, or recall of personally meaningful events, such as what you did on your first date or how you celebrated your college graduation. Sometimes participants varying in age are given a series of words (such as *book, machine, sorry, surprised*) and asked to report a personal memory cued by each. Or they may simply be asked to describe important life events, noting the age at which each occurred.

Older adults recall both remote and recent events more often than intermediate events, with recent events mentioned most frequently in word-cue studies. The important-memories method evokes a larger number of remote events because it induces people to search their memories thoroughly for significant experiences (see Figure 17.8). Among remote events recalled, most happened between ages 10 and 30—a period of heightened autobiographical memory called the **reminiscence bump** (Janssen, Rubin, & St. Jacques, 2011; Koppel & Berntsen, 2014; Koppel & Rubin, 2016).

The reminiscence bump is evident in the autobiographical recall of older adults from diverse cultures—Bangladesh, China, Japan, Turkey, and the United States (Conway et al., 2005; Demiray, Gülgöz, & Bluck, 2009). Why are adolescent and early adulthood experiences retrieved more readily than those of middle adulthood? Youthful events occur during a period of rapid life change filled with novel experiences that stand out from the humdrum of daily life. Adolescence and early adulthood are also times of identity development, when many personally significant experiences occur. Furthermore, the reminiscence bump characterizes emotionally positive, but not negative, memories. Culturally shared, important life events—school proms, graduations, marriage, birth of children—are usually positive and cluster earlier in life (Dickson, Pillemer, & Bruehl, 2011). In contrast,

But they perform far worse on item-pair tests—findings that support an associative memory deficit.

The memory tasks just described rely on recognition. Older adults perform well when they are required only to recognize single pieces of information. But when researchers complicate recognition tasks by making them depend on associations between unrelated items, older people have difficulty with widely varying associations, including face–name, face–face, word–voice, and person–action pairings (Naveh-Benjamin, 2012). In addition to reduced use of memory strategies, sensory declines make associative memory more challenging. Older adults who see or hear less well must devote extra effort to perceiving information (Naveh-Benjamin & Kilb, 2014). This subtracts from working-memory resources available for processing associations between items.

Easing task demands by providing older adults with helpful memory cues improves their associative memory. For example, to associate names with faces, older people profit from mention of relevant facts about those individuals. And when older adults are directed to use the memory strategy of *elaboration* (relating word pairs by generating a verbal statement or mental image of their relationship), the young–old difference in memory is greatly reduced (Bastin et al., 2013; Naveh-Benjamin, Brav, & Levy, 2007). Clearly, associative deficits are substantially affected by lack of strategy use that helps bind information into integrated wholes.

Remote Memory

Although older people often say that their **remote memory**, or very long-term episodic recall, is clearer than their memory for recent events, research does not support this conclusion. To inves-

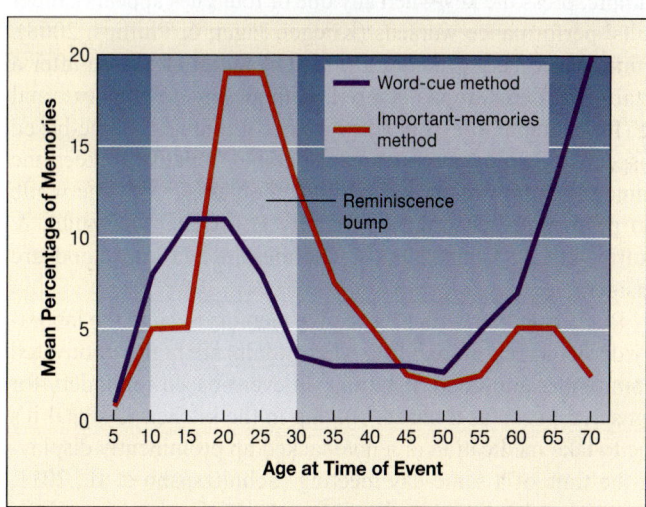

FIGURE 17.8 Distribution of autobiographical memories by reported age at time of the event, using word-cue and important-memories methods. The distributions reflect overall findings of many studies. Most early events recalled occurred between ages 10 and 30, known as the reminiscence bump. The word-cue method evokes a larger number of recent events, the important-memories method a larger number of remote events. (Based on Koppel & Berntsen, 2014.)

negative events—a serious illness, a car accident—are generally unanticipated and are not overrepresented during any life period.

Finally, the richness of older adults' remote autobiographical memories—mentions of people, objects, places, times, feelings, and other details—modestly exceeds that of younger people (Gardner, Mainetti, & Ascoli, 2015). Important early life events are usually recalled many times throughout life, on one's own and in elaborative conversations with others, which strengthen them.

Prospective Memory

So far, we have considered various aspects of *retrospective memory* (remembrance of things past). **Prospective memory** refers to remembering to engage in planned actions in the future. The amount of mental effort required determines whether older adults have trouble with prospective memory. Because Ruth and Walt knew they were prone to forget appointments, they often asked about them repeatedly. "What time is our dinner engagement, Sybil?" Walt queried several times over the preceding two days. Remembering the dinner date was challenging because Walt typically ate dinner with his daughter on Thursday evenings at 6 p.m., but this time, dinner was set for Tuesday at 7:15 p.m. His questioning was not a sign of dementia. He simply wanted to be sure to keep an important date.

In the laboratory, older adults do better on *event-based* than on *time-based* prospective memory tasks. In an event-based task, an event (such as a certain word appearing on a computer screen) serves as a cue for remembering to do something (pressing a key) while the participant engages in an ongoing activity (reading paragraphs). As long as the event-based task is not complex, older adults do as well as younger adults. But when researchers introduce extra attentional and working-memory demands (for example, press the key when any one of four cues appears), older adults' performance worsens (Kliegel, Jäger, & Phillips, 2008). In time-based tasks, the adult must engage in an action after a certain time interval has elapsed, without any obvious external cue (for example, pressing a key every 10 minutes). Time-based prospective memory requires considerable initiative to keep the planned action in mind and monitor the passage of time while also performing an ongoing activity (Einstein, McDaniel, & Scullin, 2012). Consequently, declines in late adulthood are considerable.

But difficulties with prospective memory seen in the laboratory do not appear in real life, where adults are highly motivated to remember and good at setting up event-based reminders for themselves, such as a buzzer ringing in the kitchen to signal it's time to take medication or a note tacked up prominently displaying the time of a same-day meeting (Schnitzspahn et al., 2011, 2016). In trying to remember a future activity, younger adults rely more on strategies like rehearsal, older adults on external memory aids (Dixon, de Frias, & Bäckman, 2001). In this way, they compensate for their reduced-capacity working memories and the challenge of dividing attention between what they are doing now and what they must do in the future.

Nevertheless, once a prospective memory task is finished, older adults find it harder than younger adults to deactivate, or inhibit, their intention to engage in the future action, especially when cues are still present after the task has been performed. Hence, they sometimes repeat the task again (Scullin et al., 2011). Whereas forgetting whether one has washed one's hair and doing so a second time is harmless, repeating a dose of medication can be dangerous. Older adults benefit from a system of reminders that regularly scheduled tasks have been completed, and they often arrange such systems themselves.

Language Processing

17.11 Describe changes in language processing in late adulthood.

Language and memory skills are closely related. In language comprehension (understanding the meaning of spoken or written prose), we recollect what we have heard or read without conscious awareness. Like implicit memory, language comprehension changes little in late life, as long as conversational partners do not speak too quickly and older adults are given enough time to process written text accurately, which enables them to compensate for reduced working-memory capacity. Older readers make a variety of adjustments to ensure comprehension, such as devoting more processing time to new concepts than younger readers do, pausing more often to integrate information, and making good use of story organization to help them recall both main ideas and details. Those who have invested more time in reading and other literacy activities over their lifetimes display faster and more accurate reading comprehension (Payne et al., 2012; Stine-Morrow & Payne, 2016). They benefit from years of greater practice at this highly skilled activity.

Two aspects of language production show age-related losses. The first is retrieving words from long-term memory. When conversing with others, Ruth and Walt sometimes had trouble finding the right words to convey their thoughts—even well-known words they had used many times in the past. Consequently, their speech contained more pronouns and other unclear references than it did at younger ages. They also spoke more slowly and paused more often, partly because they needed time to search their memories for certain words (Kemper, 2015). And compared to younger people, they more often reported a *tip-of-the-tongue state*—certainty that they knew a word accompanied by an inability to produce it.

Second, planning what to say and how to say it in everyday conversation is harder in late adulthood. As a result, Walt and Ruth displayed slightly more hesitations, false starts, word repetitions, and sentence fragments as they aged. Their statements were also less grammatically complex and less well-organized than before (Kemper, 2016).

What explains these changes? Whereas the meanings older people want to convey have many "mental connections" with references to the story's contemporary significance (Kemper et al., 1990). As a result, listeners tend to prefer older adults' stories to those of young people.

Nevertheless, when conversational partners detect an older person's slowed speech and shorter, at times fragmented sentences, negative stereotypes of aging often lead them to engage in *elderspeak*—a form of communication resembling infant-directed speech, consisting of a limited vocabulary, simplified expressions, and high-pitched, exaggerated expression. Lacking coherence and connectives between sentences, this distorted way of speaking actually impairs aging adults' comprehension and conversational engagement. Furthermore, older people readily detect the patronizing undertone of elderspeak (Williams et al., 2008). Even those who are cognitively impaired and in nursing homes react by withdrawing or expressing anger.

In Alberta, Canada, a First Nations older adult speaks out against environmental destruction caused by the oil industry. To compensate for language-production problems, older people speak more slowly and use simplified grammatical structures. However, they tend to be better storytellers than younger people.

Problem Solving

17.12 How does problem solving change in late life?

Problem solving is another cognitive skill that illustrates how aging brings not only declines but also adaptive changes. Problem solving in the laboratory, where tasks have goals set by the researcher, declines in late adulthood (Finucane et al., 2005). Older adults' memory limitations make it hard to keep all relevant facts in mind when dealing with a complex hypothetical problem. For similar reasons, financial decision making—evaluating loan and investment options—tends to be less effective than it was in midlife (see page 530 in Chapter 15).

Yet the everyday problems older adults encounter differ from hypothetical problems devised by researchers—and also from everyday problems experienced at earlier ages. After retirement, older adults do not have to deal with workplace problems. Their children are typically grown and living on their own, and their marriages have endured long enough to have fewer difficulties. With age, major concerns involve dealing with extended-family relationships (for example, expectations of adult children that they babysit grandchildren) and managing IADLs, such as preparing nutritious meals, paying bills, and attending to health concerns.

How do older people solve problems of daily living? Their strategies extend the adaptive problem solving of midlife. As long as they perceive problems as under their control and as important, they are active and effective in solving them (Berg & Strough, 2011). Older adults generate a smaller number of strategies compared to young and middle-aged adults, perhaps because they include only strategies they have previously found helpful, based on their long life experience (Strough et al., 2008). At the same time, older adults are particularly good at adapting strategies to fit problem conditions—home, relatives, and friends (Skinner, Berg, & Uchino, 2014). And because they are especially concerned with maintaining positive relationships, as we

other meanings, the sound of a word has only one mental connection to the word's underlying concept. Consequently, as associative memory declines with age, memory difficulties in everyday conversation are especially apparent in word retrieval (Burke & Shafto, 2004). Also, diminished working-memory capacity is involved. Because less information can be held at once, older adults have difficulty coordinating the multiple tasks required to produce complex, coherent speech.

As with memory, older adults develop compensatory techniques for their language production problems. For example, they speak more slowly so they can devote more effort to retrieving words and organizing their thoughts. Sacrificing efficiency for greater clarity, they use more sentences, but shorter ones, to convey their message (Griffin & Spieler, 2006). As older people monitor their word-retrieval failures and try hard to overcome them, they more often resolve tip-of-the-tongue states than younger people do (Schwartz & Frazier, 2005).

Most aspects of language production, including its content, grammatical correctness, and pragmatics (social appropriateness), are unaffected by aging. And aging adults are advantaged in narrative competence. In telling a story, they draw on their extensive life experience, constructing elaborate, hierarchically organized episodes with rich information about a main character's goals, actions, and motivations and with summarizing will see in Chapter 18, they usually do what they can to avoid interpersonal conflicts.

The health arena illustrates the adaptiveness of everyday problem solving in late life. Older adults make faster decisions about whether they are ill, seek medical care sooner, and select treatments more quickly. In contrast, young and middle-aged adults are more likely to adopt a "wait and see" approach in favor of gathering more facts, even when a health problem is serious (Meyer, Russo, & Talbot, 1995). This swift response of older people is interesting in view of their slower cognitive processing. Research reveals that they have accumulated more health-related knowledge, which enables them to move ahead with greater certainty (Meyer, Talbot, & Ranalli, 2007). Acting decisively when faced with health risks is sensible in old age.

Finally, older adults report that they often consult others—generally spouses and adult children, but also friends, neighbors, and members of their religious congregation—for advice about everyday problems (Strough et al., 2003). And compared with younger married couples, older couples more often collaborate in problem solving, and researchers judge their jointly generated strategies as highly effective—even on demanding tasks that require complex memory and reasoning (Peter-Wight & Martin, 2011; Rauers et al., 2011). In jointly solving problems, older people seem to compensate for moments of cognitive difficulty, yielding enhanced performance.

tions," she exclaimed. "I'm thinking of calling Ken and telling him about Steve."

"This is not a good time, Marci," Ruth advised. "You'll break Ken's heart before you've had a chance to size up your feelings for Steve. And you said Ken's taking some important exams in two weeks. If you tell him now and he's distraught, it could affect the rest of his life."

Wisdom—whether applied to personal problems or to community, national, and international concerns—requires the "pinnacle of insight into the human condition" (Baltes & Staudinger, 2000; Birren, 2009). Not surprisingly, cultures around the world assume that age and wisdom go together. In village and tribal societies, the most important social positions, such as chieftain and shaman (religious leader), are reserved for the old. Similarly, in industrialized nations, older adults are chief executive officers of large corporations, high-level religious leaders, members of legislatures, and supreme court justices. What explains this widespread trend? According to an evolutionary view, the genetic program of our species grants health, fitness, and strength to the young. Culture tames this youthful advantage in physical power with the insights of the old (Csikszentmihalyi & Nakamura, 2005). As wise older adults identify useful knowledge and reflections to transmit to younger people, they ensure balance and interdependence between generations.

In the most extensive research to date on development of wisdom, adults ranging in age from 20 to 89 responded to

Wisdom

17.13 What capacities make up wisdom, and how is it affected by age and life experience?

We have seen that a wealth of life experience enhances the storytelling and problem solving of older adults. It also underlies another capacity believed to reach its height in old age: **wisdom**. When researchers ask people to describe wisdom, most mention breadth and depth of practical knowledge, ability to reflect on and apply that knowledge in ways that make life more bearable and worthwhile; emotional maturity, including the ability to listen patiently and empathetically and give sound advice; and the altruistic form of creativity discussed in Chapter 15 that involves contributing to humanity and enriching others' lives. One group of researchers summed up the multiple cognitive and personality traits that make up wisdom as "expertise in the conduct and meaning of life" (Baltes & Smith, 2008; Baltes & Staudinger, 2000, p. 124; Kunzmann, 2016).

During her college years, Ruth and Walt's granddaughter Marci telephoned with a pressing personal dilemma. Ruth's advice reflected the features of wisdom just mentioned. After her boyfriend Ken moved to another city to attend medical school, Marci, unsure whether her love for Ken would endure, had begun dating another student. "I can't stand being pulled in two direc-

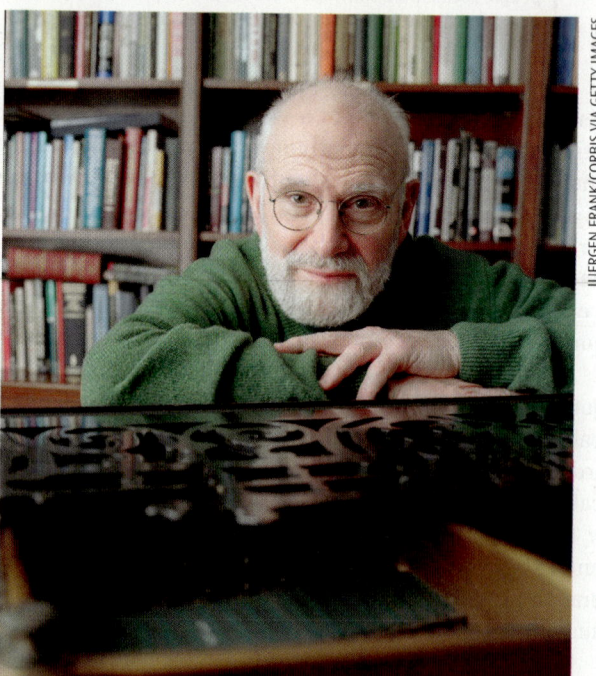

British-born neurologist Oliver Sacks died in 2015 at age 82. Through his work with patients suffering from neurological disorders, Sacks exemplified the cognitive, reflective, and emotional qualities that make up wisdom. "In examining disease," Sacks wrote, "we gain wisdom about anatomy and physiology and biology. In examining the person with disease, we gain wisdom about life."

uncertain real-life situations—for example, what to consider and do if a good friend is about to commit suicide or if, after reflecting on your life, you discover that you have not achieved your goals (Staudinger, 2008; Staudinger, Dörner, & Mickler, 2005). Responses were rated for five ingredients of wisdom:

- Knowledge about fundamental concerns of life, including human nature, social relations, and emotions
- Effective strategies for applying that knowledge to making life decisions, handling conflict, and giving advice
- A view of people that considers the multiple demands of their life contexts
- A concern with ultimate human values, such as the common good, as well as respect for individual differences in values
- Awareness and management of the uncertainties of life—that many problems have no perfect solution

Results revealed that age is no guarantee of wisdom. A small number of adults of diverse ages ranked among the wise. But type of life experience made a difference. People in human-service careers who had extensive training and practice in grappling with human problems tended to attain high wisdom scores. Other high-scorers held leadership positions (Staudinger, 1996; Staudinger & Glück, 2011). And when age and relevant life experiences were considered together, more older than younger people scored in the top 20 percent.

In addition to age and life experience, having faced and overcome adversity appears to be an important contributor to late-life wisdom (Ardelt & Ferrari, 2015). In one study, low- and moderate-income older adults nominated by aging-services providers as wise reported deriving valuable life lessons from coping with hardships, including patience, perseverance, forgiveness, and willingness to accept advice and support from others (Choi & Landeros, 2011). One participant, who in her thirties had lost her husband to cancer, became a single parent of four children, and worked for low wages as a nurse's aid while earning a college degree in nursing, said, "It was hard. . . . I had a lot of help from my classmates. . . . When I became a nurse, I already understood what pain was, and this made me better able to relate to my patients. You have got to have empathy and be able to listen when people suffer from pain and guilt" (p. 606).

Compared to their agemates, older adults with the cognitive, reflective, and emotional (compassionate) qualities that make up wisdom are better educated, forge more positive relations with others, and score higher on the personality dimension of openness to experience (Kramer, 2003). Wisdom is also linked to personal growth (continued desire to expand as a person), sense of autonomy and purpose in life (enabling resistance to social pressures to think and act in certain ways), generativity, and favorable adjustment to aging (Ardelt & Ferrari, 2015; Wink & Staudinger, 2016). Wise older people seem to flourish, even when faced with physical and cognitive challenges. This suggests that finding ways to promote wisdom would be a powerful means of both contributing to human welfare and fostering a gratifying old age.

Factors Related to Cognitive Maintenance and Change

17.14 Cite factors related to cognitive maintenance and change in late adulthood.

Heritability research suggests a modest genetic contribution to individual differences in cognitive change in late adulthood (Deary et al., 2012). At the same time, as in middle adulthood, a mentally active life is vital for preserving cognitive resources. Above-average education; frequent contact with family members and friends; stimulating work, leisure pursuits, and community participation; and a flexible personality predict higher mental test scores and reduced cognitive decline into advanced old age (Schaie, 2013; Wang et al., 2013). Today's aging adults in industrialized nations are better educated than any previous generation. As more baby boomers enter late adulthood, this trend is expected to continue, forecasting improved preservation of cognitive functions.

As noted earlier, health status powerfully predicts older adults' cognitive functioning. In longitudinal research, cigarette smokers declined cognitively at a faster rate than their nonsmoking counterparts, as did overweight and obese people, even after initial health status, SES, and mental test performance were controlled (Dahl et al., 2010; Smith et al., 2013). And a wide variety of chronic conditions, including cardiovascular disease, diabetes, osteoporosis, and arthritis, are strongly associated with cognitive declines (O'Connor & Kraft, 2013). But we must be cautious in interpreting this link between physical and cognitive deterioration. The relationship may be exaggerated by the fact that brighter adults are more likely to engage in health-protective behaviors, which postpone the onset of serious disease.

As people grow older, their cognitive scores show larger fluctuations from one occasion to the next. This rising instability of performance—especially in speed of response—accelerates in the seventies and is associated with cognitive declines, along with neurobiological signs of shrinkage in the prefrontal cortex and deficient brain functioning (Bielak et al., 2010; Lövdén et al., 2012; MacDonald, Li, & Bäckman, 2009). It seems to signal end-of-life brain degeneration.

In the year before Walt died, those close to him noticed that he had become less active and more withdrawn, even in the company of friends. **Terminal decline** refers to acceleration in deterioration of cognitive functioning prior to death. Some investigations indicate that it is limited to a few aspects of intelligence, others that it occurs generally, across many abilities. Findings also differ greatly in its estimated length—from 1 to 3 to as long as 14 years, with an average of 4 to 5 years (Lövdén et al., 2005; MacDonald, Hultsch, & Dixon, 2011; Rabbitt, Lunn, & Wong, 2008). In several studies, a sharp drop in psychological well-being, including diminished sense of personal control and social participation and increased negative affect, predicted mortality

(Gerstorf & Ram, 2013; Schilling, Wahl, & Wiegering, 2013). The downturn is especially steep in people age 85 and older and is only weakly related to mental deterioration or chronic illnesses.

Perhaps different kinds of terminal decline exist—one type arising from disease processes, another reflecting general biological breakdown due to normal aging. What we do know is that an accelerating falloff in cognitive performance or in emotional investment in life is a sign of loss of vitality and impending death.

Cognitive Interventions

17.15 Discuss outcomes of interventions aimed at helping older adults sustain cognitive skills.

For most of late adulthood, cognitive declines are gradual. Although aging of the brain contributes to them, recall from our earlier discussion that the brain can compensate by growing new neural fibers and recruiting additional regions to support cognitive functions. Furthermore, some cognitive decrements may be due to disuse of particular skills rather than biological aging. If plasticity of development is possible, then interventions that train older people in cognitive strategies should at least partially reverse the age-related declines we have discussed.

Older adults' relatively well-preserved *metacognition* is a powerful asset in training efforts. Most, for example, are aware of memory declines, report troublesome anxiety when faced with demanding memory situations, and know they must take extra steps to ensure recall of important information (Blake & Castel, 2016). Their impressive metacognitive understanding is also evident in the wide-ranging techniques they devise to compensate for everyday cognitive challenges.

The Adult Development and Enrichment Project (ADEPT) is the most extensive cognitive intervention program conducted to date (Schaie, 2005). By using participants in the Seattle Longitudinal Study (see Chapter 15, pages 524–525), researchers were able to do what no other investigation has done: assess the effects of cognitive training on long-term development.

Intervention began with adults over age 64, some of whom had maintained their scores on tests of two mental abilities (inductive reasoning and spatial orientation) over the previous 14 years and others who had shown declines. After just five one-hour training sessions in one of two types of mental test items, two-thirds of participants improved their performance on the trained skill. Gains for decliners were dramatic: Forty percent returned to the level at which they had been functioning 14 years earlier! A follow-up after 7 years revealed that although scores dropped somewhat, participants remained advantaged in their trained skill over agemates trained in the other ability. Finally, "booster" training at this time led to further gains, although these were smaller than the earlier gains.

In another large-scale intervention study called ACTIVE (Advanced Cognitive Training for Independent and Vital Elderly), more than 2,800 65- to 84-year-olds were randomly assigned to a 10-session training program focusing on one of three abilities—speed of processing, memory strategies, or reasoning—or to a no-intervention control group. Again, trained older adults showed an immediate advantage in the trained skill over controls that was still evident—though smaller in magnitude—at a 5-year follow-up and, for speed and reasoning, at a 10-year follow-up. Furthermore, 5 and 10 years after intervention, cognitive training was associated with reduced declines in ability to perform IADLs—outcomes strongest for the speed-of-processing group and, secondarily, the reasoning group (Rebok et al., 2014; Wolinsky et al., 2006). Speed gains also predicted other aspects of everyday functioning, including more favorable self-rated health, reduced depressive symptoms, fewer at-fault motor vehicle collisions, and longer time to giving up driving (Tennstedt & Unverzagt, 2013). The investigators speculated that speed-of-processing training induces a broad pattern of brain activation, affecting many regions.

Clearly, many cognitive skills can be enhanced in old age. Small-scale studies targeting executive function that provide intensive training over multiple weeks show promising improvements, especially on working-memory tasks. In some research, gains lasted for several months following intervention and transferred to other cognitive skills, such as sustained attention and episodic memory (Brehmer, Westerberg, & Bäckman, 2012; Grönholm-Nyman, 2015). A vital goal is to shift intervention from the laboratory to the community, weaving it into aging adults' recurring experiences. Community programs in the participatory arts—including dance, music, and theater training—yield gains on a broad range of cognitive measures (Noice, Noice, & Kramer, 2014). Refer to the Social Issues: Education box on the following page for a "dramatic" illustration.

Extending the focus of training to include beliefs that promote sustained effort may be helpful. Targeting self-efficacy in training programs by emphasizing late-life cognitive potential boosts both self-efficacy and cognitive gains in older people (West, Bagwell, & Dark-Freudeman, 2008). Furthermore, working in groups may offer unique opportunities for strengthening self-efficacy ("If they can do it, so can I") along with social support for persisting (Hastings & West, 2009). As we will see in the next section, another promising approach is to provide older adults with well-designed, highly stimulating educational experiences in which cognitive training in socially rich contexts is an integral part.

Lifelong Learning

17.16 Discuss types of continuing education and benefits of such programs in late life.

The competencies aging adults need to live in our complex, changing world are the same ones younger people need: communicating effectively through spoken and written systems; locating

Social Issues: Education

The Art of Acting Enhances Cognitive Functioning in Older Adults

Actors face a daunting task: They must memorize massive quantities of dialogue and then reproduce it accurately and spontaneously, as if they genuinely mean what they say. No wonder the most common question asked of actors is, "How did you learn all those lines?"

Interviews with professional actors reveal that most don't memorize lines as many people assume—by rote, or rehearsing the lines many times. Instead, they focus on the meaning of the words. First, they analyze the script for the character's intentions, breaking it down into what they call "beats"—small, goal-directed chunks of dialogue. Then they represent the role as a sequence of goals, one leading to the next. When actors recall this chain of goals, lines become easier to remember (Noice & Noice, 2006; Noice, Noice, & Kramer, 2014). For example, one actor divided a half-page of dialogue into three beats: "to put [the other character] at ease," "to start a conversation with him," "to flatter/draw him out."

To create a beat sequence, actors engage in extensive elaboration of dialogue segments. For example, to the line, "Perhaps he's in love with me but doesn't know it," an actor might create a visual image of an uncertain lover, relate the material to a past love affair of her own, and match her own mood to the feeling tone of the statement. Deep elaborative processing of the dialogue segment, along with analysis of its beat goal, yields verbatim recall without rote memorization.

Actors' script learning is so successful that on stage, they are free to "live in the moment," focusing on communicating authentic meaning through action, emotion, and utterance while speaking verbatim lines. This intermodal integration of spoken word with facial expression, tone of voice, and body language contributes further to script retention.

Can aging adults benefit from exercises that teach the essence of acting—thorough mastery of a script, enabling complete immersion in performance? In a series of studies, several hundred adults, diverse in SES and ranging in age from their sixties to nineties, were randomly assigned to either theater-arts training, singing lessons, or no-intervention control groups. The theater-arts training consisted of twice-weekly group sessions over a month's time in which participants engaged in cognitively demanding acting exercises: They analyzed the goals of brief scenes so they could become fully engrossed in acting out their meaning, and were explicitly instructed not to memorize the script by rote repetition (Noice & Noice, 2006, 2013; Noice, Noice, & Staines, 2004). Compared with singing-lesson and wait-list controls, theater-training participants showed greater gains on tests of working-memory capacity, word and prose recall, verbal fluency, problem solving, and IADLs. In a follow-up, cognitive improvements were still evident four months after the intervention ended.

The theater training required highly effortful intermodal processing, which may explain its cognitive benefits. fMRI research indicates that deeply processing verbal meanings strongly activates certain areas in the frontal lobes of the cerebral cortex in aging adults, yielding levels of neural activity close to those of younger people (Park, 2002). These findings lend neurobiological support to the power of acting, with its challenging intermodal processing of meaning, to enhance human memory.

These community-theater actors master their lines by focusing on the meaning of a character's words in goal-directed chunks. Teaching these script-learning techniques to aging adults results in diverse cognitive benefits that persist for at least several months after intervention ends.

---

information, sorting through it, and selecting what is needed; using math strategies, such as estimation; planning and organizing activities, including making good use of time and resources; mastering new technologies; and understanding past and current events and the relevance of each to their own lives. Older people also need to acquire new, problem-centered coping strategies—ways to sustain health and operate their households efficiently and safely—and updated vocational skills, for those who continue to work.

Participation by people age 65 and older in continuing education has increased substantially over the past few decades. Successful programs include a wide variety of offerings responsive to the diversity of older people and teaching methods suited to their developmental needs.

Types of Programs

One summer, Walt and Ruth attended a Road Scholar program at a nearby university. After moving into a dormitory room, they joined 30 others for two weeks of morning classes on Shakespeare, afternoon visits to points of interest, and evening performances of plays at a nearby Shakespeare festival.

Applying what we Know

Increasing the Effectiveness of Educational Experiences for Older Adults

TECHNIQUE	DESCRIPTION
Provide a positive learning environment.	Many older adults have internalized negative stereotypes of their own abilities and come to the learning environment with low self-efficacy. A supportive group atmosphere helps convince them that they can learn.
Allow ample time to learn new information.	Rate of learning varies widely among older adults. Presenting information over multiple sessions or allowing for self-paced instruction aids mastery.
Present information in a well-organized fashion.	Older adults do not organize information as effectively as younger adults. Material that is outlined, presented, and then summarized enhances memory and understanding. Digressions make a presentation harder to comprehend.
Relate information to older adults' knowledge and experiences.	Relating new material to what older adults have already learned, by drawing on their extensive knowledge and experiences and giving many vivid examples, enhances recall.
Adapt the learning environment to fit changes in sensory systems.	Adequate lighting, availability of large-print reading materials, appropriate sound amplification, reduced background noise, and clear, well-organized visual aids to supplement verbal teaching ease information processing.

In its most recently reported year, Road Scholar campus-based programs, and their recent extension to travel experiences around the world, attracted more than 100,000 American and Canadian older adults. Some programs make use of community resources through classes on local ecology or folk life. Others focus on innovative topics and experiences—writing one's own life story, discussing contemporary films with screenwriters, whitewater rafting, Chinese painting and calligraphy, or acquiring French language skills. Travel programs are enriched by in-depth lectures and expert-led field trips.

Similar educational programs have sprung up in the United States and elsewhere. The Bernard Osher Foundation collaborates with more than 120 U.S. universities to establish Osher Lifelong Learning Institutes on campuses. Each offers older adults a wide array of stimulating learning experiences, from auditing regular courses, to forming learning communities that address common interests, to helping to solve community problems. Originating in France, the University of the Third Age[2] provides Western European, British, and Australian older people with university- and community-sponsored courses, workshops on special topics, and excursions, with older adults often doing the teaching.

LOOK and LISTEN

Find out if your college or university hosts a lifelong learning program, and attend an on-campus session. What did you observe about older adults' capacity for complex learning?

Participants in the programs just mentioned tend to be active, well-educated, and financially well-off. Much less is available for older people with little education and limited income. Community senior centers with inexpensive offerings related to everyday living attract more low-SES people than programs such as Road Scholar or Universities of the Third Age (Formosa, 2014). Regardless of course content and which older adults attend, using the techniques summarized in Applying What We Know above increases the effectiveness of educational experiences.

Active, adventurous older adults explore the sights, sounds, streets, and monuments of Dublin's authors, poets, and playwrights as part of a Road Scholar travel program to Ireland.

---

[2]The term *Third Age*, as we will see in Chapter 18, refers to the period after the "Second Age" of midlife, when older people are freed from responsibilities of earning a living and rearing children to focus on personal fulfillment.

Benefits of Continuing Education

Older participants in continuing education report a rich array of benefits—understanding new ideas in many disciplines, learning new skills that enrich their lives, making new friends, and developing a broader perspective on the world (Preece & Findsen, 2007). Furthermore, participants come to see themselves differently. Many abandon their own ingrained negative stereotypes of aging when they realize that adults in late life—including themselves—can still engage in complex learning.

Older adults' willingness to acquire new knowledge and skills is apparent in the recent, rapid rise in their use of computers and the Internet. They are now the fastest growing age group to embrace online technology as they discover its many practical benefits, including assistance with shopping, banking, health-care management, and communication. Currently, about 60 percent of adults age 65 and older access the Internet, with the majority of these going online on a daily basis. As noted on page 559 in Chapter 16, 35 percent of aging adults are users of social media sites, primarily Facebook (Charness & Boot, 2016; Perrin, 2015). Still, older people have joined the computer and Internet community to a lesser extent than younger people. Those who are less well-educated and have lower incomes, and those over age 75, are especially reluctant, with many perceiving the technology as too complicated—an attitude that continuing education can overcome (Smith, 2014). With patient training, support, and modified equipment and software to suit their physical and cognitive needs, older adults readily enter the online world, often becoming nearly as devoted and skilled as younger users.

The educational needs of aging adults are likely to be given greater attention in coming decades, as their numbers grow and they assert their right to lifelong learning. Once this happens, false stereotypes—"they are too old to learn" or "education is for the young"—are likely to weaken and, perhaps, disappear.

Ask yourself

CONNECT Describe cognitive functions that are maintained or that improve in late adulthood. What aspects of aging contribute to them?

APPLY Estelle complained that she had recently forgotten two of her regular biweekly hair appointments and sometimes had trouble finding the right words to convey her thoughts. What cognitive changes account for Estelle's difficulties? What can she do to compensate?

REFLECT Interview an older adult in your family, asking about ways the individual engages in selective optimization with compensation to make the most of declining cognitive resources. Describe several examples.

Summary / chapter 17

PHYSICAL DEVELOPMENT

Life Expectancy (p. 570)

17.1 Distinguish between chronological age and functional age, and discuss changes in life expectancy since the beginning of the twentieth century.

- People age biologically at different rates, making chronological age an imperfect indicator of **functional age.** Dramatic gains in **average life expectancy** confirm that biological aging can be modified by environmental factors, including improved nutrition, medical treatment, sanitation, and safety.

- Length of life and, especially, **average healthy life expectancy** can be predicted by a country's health care, housing, and social services, along with lifestyle factors. In developing nations, both are shortened by poverty, malnutrition, disease, and armed conflict.

- With advancing age, the gender gap in average life expectancy declines, as do differences between European Americans and African Americans.

- Longevity runs in families, but environmental factors become increasingly important after age 75 to 80. Scientists disagree on whether **maximum lifespan** can be extended beyond 122 years—the oldest verified age.

Physical Changes (p. 573)

17.2 Describe physical declines of late adulthood, and changes in the nervous and sensory systems.

- With age, growing numbers of older adults experience physical declines, evident in difficulties carrying out **activities of daily living (ADLs),** or basic self-care tasks, and **instrumental activities of daily living (IADLs),** which are necessary to conduct the business of daily life.

- Neuron loss occurs throughout the cerebral cortex, with greater shrinkage in the frontal lobes, especially the prefrontal cortex, and the corpus callosum. The cerebellum and the hippocampus also lose neurons. The brain compensates by forming new synapses and, to a limited degree, generating new neurons. The autonomic nervous system functions less well and releases more stress hormones.

- Older adults tend to suffer from impaired vision and may experience **cataracts** and **macular degeneration.** Hearing impairments are more common than visual impairments, with decline in speech perception having the greatest impact on life satisfaction.

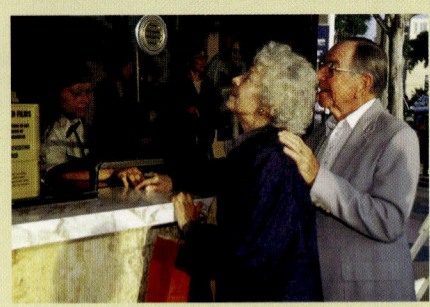

- Taste and odor sensitivity wane, making food less appealing. Touch sensitivity also deteriorates, particularly on the fingertips.

17.3 *Describe cardiovascular, respiratory, and immune system changes and sleep difficulties in late adulthood.*

- Reduced capacity of the cardiovascular and respiratory systems becomes more apparent in late adulthood, especially in lifelong smokers and in people who have not reduced dietary fat or who have had extensive exposure to environmental pollutants. Exercise can slow cardiovascular aging and facilitate respiratory functioning.

- The immune system functions less effectively in late life, permitting diseases to progress and making **autoimmune responses** and stress-induced infection more likely.

- Older adults find it harder to fall asleep, stay asleep, and sleep deeply. Until age 70 or 80, men have more trouble sleeping than women because of prostate enlargement (initiating frequent urination) and **sleep apnea.**

17.4 *Describe changes in physical appearance and mobility in late adulthood, along with effective adaptations to these changes.*

- Outward signs of aging—white hair, wrinkled and sagging skin, age spots, and decreased height and weight—become more noticeable. Mobility diminishes as muscle and bone strength and joint flexibility decline.

- Wanting to be younger (as opposed to feeling younger) than one's actual age is associated with less positive well-being. High sense of personal control, which is linked to problem-centered coping strategies, yields improved physical functioning.

- **Assistive technology** helps older people cope with physical declines, sustaining an effective person–environment fit that enhances psychological well-being.

- Negative stereotypes of aging have a stressful, disorganizing impact on older adults' functioning, whereas positive stereotypes reduce stress and foster physical and mental competence.

Health, Fitness, and Disability
(p. 581)

17.5 *Discuss health and fitness in late life, paying special attention to nutrition, exercise, and sexuality.*

- Most older adults rate their health favorably and have a high sense of self-efficacy about protecting it. Low-SES ethnic minority older people remain at greater risk for certain health problems, are less trusting of health-care providers, and are less likely to believe they can control their health.

- In late life, men continue to be more prone to fatal diseases and women to disabling conditions. In industrialized nations, **compression of morbidity** has occurred, largely as a result of medical advances and improved socioeconomic conditions; further gains will depend on reducing negative lifestyle factors. In the developing world, comprehensive strategies are needed.

- Risk of dietary deficiencies increases in late life, but except for calcium and vitamin D, a daily vitamin–mineral supplement is recommended only for those suffering from malnutrition. Exercise, even when begun in late adulthood, is a powerful health intervention.

- Though sexual activity declines, especially among women, most married older adults report continued, regular sexual enjoyment.

17.6 *Discuss physical disabilities associated with late adulthood.*

- Illness and disability increase toward the end of life. Heart disease and cancer are the leading causes of death, followed by respiratory diseases. **Primary aging** contributes to **frailty** in the elderly, but **secondary aging** (declines due to hereditary defects and negative environmental influences) plays a larger role.

- **Osteoarthritis** and **rheumatoid arthritis** are widespread among older adults, especially women. Type 2 diabetes also increases.

- The death rate from unintentional injuries reaches an all-time high from age 65 on, largely due to motor vehicle collisions and falls. Visual declines and slowed reaction time often contribute.

17.7 *Discuss mental disabilities associated with late adulthood.*

- **Alzheimer's disease,** the most common form of **dementia,** often starts with severe memory problems. It brings personality changes, depression, disintegration of purposeful movements, loss of ability to comprehend and produce speech, and death. Underlying these changes are abundant **neurofibrillary tangles** and **amyloid plaques** and lowered neurotransmitter levels in the brain.

- Familial Alzheimer's, related to genes involved in generation of harmful amyloid, generally has an early onset and progresses rapidly. About half of sporadic Alzheimer's victims have an abnormal gene that results in insulin deficiency linked to brain damage.

- Diverse environmental factors, including a high-fat diet, physical inactivity, overweight and obesity, smoking, chronic depression, cardiovascular disease, stroke, diabetes, and head injuries increase the risk of Alzheimer's. A "Mediterranean diet," education, and an active lifestyle are associated with lower incidence. Better-educated people may develop a **cognitive reserve** that increases the aging brain's tolerance to injury.

- Heredity contributes to **vascular dementia** indirectly, through high blood pressure, cardiovascular disease, and diabetes. Because of their greater susceptibility to cardiovascular disease, more men than women are affected.

- Treatable problems, such as depression, side effects of medication, and reactions to social isolation, can be mistaken for dementia.

17.8 *Discuss health-care issues that affect older adults.*

- Only a small percentage of older Americans are institutionalized, less than half the rates in other Western nations with more generous public financing of institutional care. Though ethnic differences exist, family members provide most long-term care in Western nations. Publicly funded in-home help and **assisted living** can reduce the high costs of institutional placement and increase older adults' life satisfaction.

COGNITIVE DEVELOPMENT

17.9 *Describe overall changes in cognitive functioning in late adulthood.* (p. 594)

- Individual differences in cognitive functioning are greater in late adulthood than at any other time of life. Older adults can make the most of their cognitive resources through **selective optimization with compensation.** Personal goals increasingly emphasize maintaining abilities and preventing loss.

Memory (p. 595)

17.10 *How does memory change in late life?*

- Memory failure increases with age, especially on **explicit memory** tasks, which require controlled, strategic processing. Recall of context, source, and temporal order of episodic events declines. Automatic forms of memory, such as recognition and **implicit memory,** suffer less. In general, an **associative memory deficit** characterizes older adults' memory difficulties.

- Contrary to what older people often report, **remote memory** is not clearer than recent memory. Remote memory is best for events that occurred between ages 10 and 30, a period of heightened autobiographical recall called the **reminiscence bump.**

- In the laboratory, older adults do better on event-based than on time-based **prospective memory** tasks. In everyday life, they compensate for declines in prospective memory by using external memory aids.

Language Processing (p. 598)

17.11 *Describe changes in language processing in late adulthood.*

- Language comprehension changes little in late life. Age-related losses occur in two aspects of language production: retrieving words from long-term memory and planning what to say and how to say it in everyday conversation. Older people compensate by speaking more slowly and using shorter sentences. Aging adults are advantaged in narrative competence.

Problem Solving (p. 599)

17.12 *How does problem solving change in late life?*

- Hypothetical problem solving declines in late adulthood. In everyday problem solving, older adults are effective as long as they perceive problems as under their control and as important. Older people make faster decisions about health than younger people and often consult others about everyday problems.

Wisdom (p. 600)

17.13 *What capacities make up wisdom, and how is it affected by age and life experience?*

- **Wisdom** involves extensive practical knowledge, ability to reflect on and apply that knowledge in ways that make life more bearable and worthwhile, emotional maturity, and altruistic creativity. When age and relevant life experience are combined, more older than younger people rank among the wise. Having faced and overcome adversity appears to contribute to late-life wisdom.

Factors Related to Cognitive Maintenance and Change (p. 601)

17.14 *Cite factors related to cognitive maintenance and change in late adulthood.*

- Healthy, mentally active people are likely to maintain their cognitive abilities into advanced old age. A wide array of chronic health conditions are associated with cognitive declines.

- With age, older adults' cognitive scores become increasingly unstable. As death approaches, **terminal decline** often occurs.

Cognitive Interventions (p. 602)

17.15 *Discuss outcomes of interventions aimed at helping older adults sustain cognitive skills.*

- Training in cognitive skills can offer large, persisting benefits for older people who have experienced cognitive declines. Targeting self-efficacy enhances cognitive gains.

Lifelong Learning (p. 602)

17.16 *Discuss types of continuing education and benefits of such programs in late life.*

- Increasing numbers of older people continue their education through university courses, community offerings, and other programs. Participants acquire new knowledge and skills, new friends, a broader perspective on the world, and an image of themselves as more competent. Unfortunately, fewer continuing-education opportunities are available to low-SES older adults.

Important Terms and Concepts

activities of daily living (ADLs) (p. 573)
Alzheimer's disease (p. 588)
amyloid plaques (p. 588)
assisted living (p. 593)
assistive technology (p. 579)
associative memory deficit (p. 596)
autoimmune response (p. 577)
average healthy life expectancy (p. 571)
average life expectancy (p. 570)
cataracts (p. 574)
cognitive reserve (p. 590)

compression of morbidity (p. 582)
dementia (p. 587)
explicit memory (p. 596)
frailty (p. 585)
functional age (p. 570)
implicit memory (p. 596)
instrumental activities of daily living (IADLs) (p. 573)
macular degeneration (p. 575)
maximum lifespan (p. 572)
neurofibrillary tangles (p. 588)
osteoarthritis (p. 585)

primary aging (p. 585)
prospective memory (p. 598)
reminiscence bump (p. 597)
remote memory (p. 597)
rheumatoid arthritis (p. 585)
secondary aging (p. 585)
selective optimization with compensation (p. 595)
sleep apnea (p. 577)
terminal decline (p. 601)
vascular dementia (p. 590)
wisdom (p. 600)

chapter 18

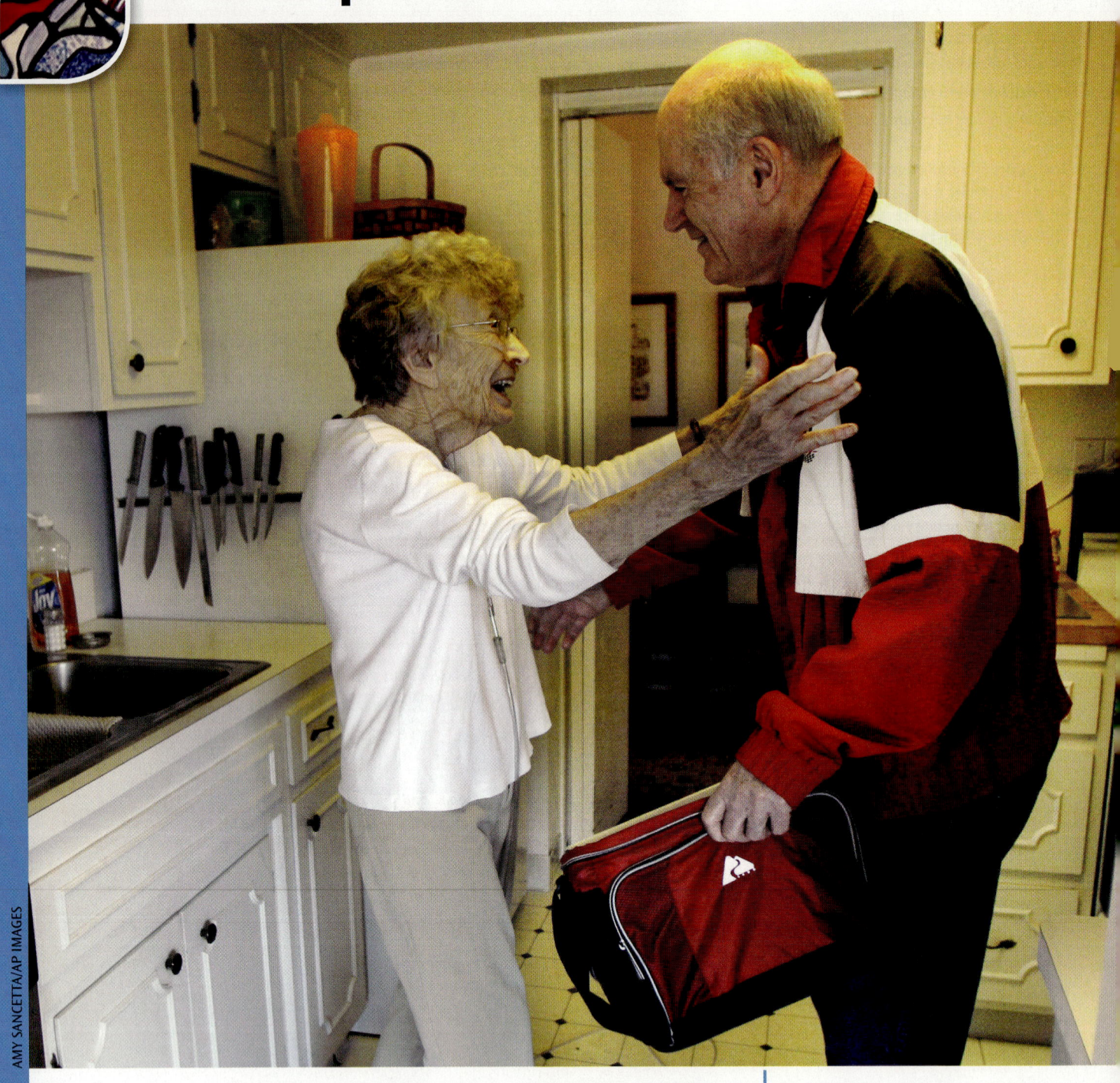

Emotional and Social Development in Late Adulthood

A familiar volunteer for Meals on Wheels delivers prepared, nutritious meals, along with a friendly visit, to this 86-year-old, helping her remain in her own home. Social support that fits with older adults' needs and desires promotes physical health and psychological well-being.

What's ahead in chapter 18

Erikson's Theory: Ego Integrity versus Despair

Other Theories of Psychosocial Development in Late Adulthood

Peck's Tasks of Ego Integrity and Joan Erikson's Gerotranscendence • The Positivity Effect • Reminiscence

■ **CULTURAL INFLUENCES** The New Old Age

Stability and Change in Self-Concept and Personality

Secure and Multifaceted Self-Concept • Agreeableness, Acceptance of Change, and Openness to Experience • Spirituality and Religiosity

Contextual Influences on Psychological Well-Being

Control versus Dependency • Physical Health • Negative Life Changes • Social Support

■ **SOCIAL ISSUES: HEALTH** Elder Suicide

A Changing Social World

Social Theories of Aging • Social Contexts of Aging: Communities, Neighborhoods, and Housing

Relationships in Late Adulthood

Marriage • Lesbian and Gay Couples • Divorce, Remarriage, and Cohabitation • Widowhood • Never-Married, Childless Older Adults • Siblings • Friendships • Relationships with Adult Children • Relationships with Adult Grandchildren • Elder Maltreatment

Retirement

The Decision to Retire • Adjustment to Retirement • Leisure and Volunteer Activities

■ **BIOLOGY AND ENVIRONMENT** Experience Corps: Promoting Retired Adults' Physical and Mental Health and Children's Academic Success

Successful Aging

With Ruth at his side, Walt spoke to the guests at their sixtieth-anniversary party. "Even when things were hard," he reflected, "the time of life I liked best always seemed to be the current one. When I was a kid, I adored playing baseball. In my twenties, I loved learning the photography business. And of course," Walt continued, glancing affectionately at Ruth, "our wedding was the most memorable day of all."

He went on: "We never had much money for luxuries, but we found ways to have fun anyway—singing in the church choir and acting in community theater. And then Sybil was born. It meant so much to me to be a father—and now a grandfather and a great-grandfather. Looking back at my parents and grandparents and forward at Sybil, Marci, and Marci's son Jamel, I feel a sense of unity with past and future generations." With a smile, Walt added, "We keep up with Marci and Jamel through Facebook and Twitter!"

Walt and Ruth greeted old age with calm acceptance, grateful for the gift of long life and loved ones. Yet not all older adults find such peace of mind. Walt's brother Dick was contentious, complaining about petty issues and major disappointments alike: "Goldie, why'd you serve cheesecake? No one eats cheesecake on birthdays!" "Know why we've got financial worries? Uncle Louie wouldn't lend me the money to keep the bakery going, so I *had* to retire."

A mix of gains and losses characterizes these twilight years, extending the multi-directionality of development begun early in life. On one hand, old age is usually a time of pleasure and tranquility, when children are grown, life's work is nearly done, and responsibilities are lightened. On the other hand, it brings concerns about declining physical functions, unwelcome loneliness, and the growing specter of imminent death.

In this chapter, we consider how older adults reconcile these opposing forces. Although some are weary and discontented, most traverse this period with poise and calm composure. They attach deeper significance to life and reap great benefits from family and friendship bonds, leisure activities, and community involvement. We will see how personal attributes and life history combine with home, neighborhood, community, and societal conditions to mold emotional and social development in late life. ●

Erikson's Theory: Ego Integrity versus Despair

18.1 According to Erikson, how does personality change in late adulthood?

The final psychological conflict of Erikson's (1950) theory, **ego integrity versus despair,** involves coming to terms with one's life. Adults who arrive at a sense of integrity feel whole, complete, and satisfied with their achievements. They have adapted to the mix of triumphs and disappointments that are an inevitable part of love relationships, child rearing, work, friendships, and community participation. They realize that the paths they followed, abandoned, and never selected were necessary for fashioning a meaningful life course.

The capacity to view one's life in the larger context of all humanity—as the chance combination of one person and one segment in history—contributes to the serenity and contentment that accompany integrity. "These last few decades have been the happiest," Walt murmured, clasping Ruth's hand—only weeks before the heart attack that would end his life. At peace with himself, his wife, and his children, Walt had accepted his life course as something that had to be the way it was.

In a study that followed a sample of women diverse in SES throughout adulthood, midlife generativity predicted ego integrity in late adulthood. Ego integrity, in turn, was associated with more favorable psychological well-being—a more upbeat mood, greater self-acceptance, higher marital satisfaction, closer relationships with adult children, greater community involvement, and increased ease in accepting help from others when it is needed (James & Zarrett, 2007). As Erikson's theory indicates, psychosocial maturity in late life brings increased contentment, affectionate, enjoyable bonds with others, and continued service to society.

Scanning the newspaper, Walt pondered, "I keep reading these percentages: One out of five people will get heart disease, one out of three will get cancer. But the truth is, one out of one will die. We are all mortal and must accept this fate." The year before, Walt had given his granddaughter, Marci, his collection of prized photos, which had absorbed him for over half a century. With the realization that the integrity of one's own life is part of an extended chain of human existence, Erikson suggested, death loses its sting (Vaillant, 2002, 2012). In support of this view, older adults who report having attained intrinsic (personally gratifying) life goals typically express acceptance of their own death (Van Hiel & Vansteenkiste, 2009). Those who emphasize attainment of extrinsic goals (such as money or prestige) more often fear life's end.

The negative outcome of this stage, despair, occurs when aging adults feel they have made many wrong decisions, yet time is too short to find an alternate route to integrity. Without another chance, the despairing person finds it hard to accept that death is near and is overwhelmed with bitterness, defeat, and hopelessness. According to Erikson, these attitudes are often expressed as anger and contempt for others, which disguise contempt for oneself. Dick's argumentative, fault-finding behavior, tendency to blame others for his personal failures, and regretful view of his own life reflect this deep sense of despair.

Erik Erikson and his wife Joan exemplified the ideal of Erikson's final stage. They aged gracefully, felt satisfied with their achievements, and were often seen together, contented and deeply in love.

Other Theories of Psychosocial Development in Late Adulthood

18.2 Discuss Robert Peck's and Joan Erikson's views of psychosocial development in late adulthood, along with implications of the positivity effect and reminiscence for older adults' lives.

As with Erikson's stages of early and middle adulthood, other theorists have clarified and refined his vision of late adulthood, specifying the tasks, thought processes, and behaviors that contribute to aging adults' sense of ego integrity and psychological well-being.

Peck's Tasks of Ego Integrity and Joan Erikson's Gerotranscendence

According to Robert Peck (1968), attaining ego integrity involves three distinct tasks:

- *Ego differentiation:* For those who invested heavily in their careers, finding other ways to affirm self-worth—through family, friendship, and community life

- *Body transcendence:* Surmounting physical limitations by emphasizing the compensating rewards of cognitive, emotional, and social powers
- *Ego transcendence:* As contemporaries die, facing the reality of death constructively through efforts to make life more secure, meaningful, and gratifying for younger generations

In Peck's theory, ego integrity requires older adults to move beyond their life's work, their bodies, and their separate identities by investing in a future that extends beyond their own lifespan. Research suggests that as people grow older, both *body transcendence* (focusing on psychological strengths) and *ego transcendence* (orienting toward a better life for those who will follow) increase. In a study of women, those in their eighties and nineties stated with greater certainty than those in their sixties that they "accept the changes brought about by aging," "have moved beyond fear of death," "have a clearer sense of the meaning of life," and "have found new, positive spiritual gifts to explore" (Brown & Lowis, 2003).

Erikson's widow Joan Erikson suggested that these attainments actually represent development beyond ego integrity (which requires satisfaction with one's past life) to an additional psychosocial stage that she calls **gerotranscendence**—a cosmic and transcendent perspective directed beyond the self to affinity with past and future generations and oneness with the universe. Drawing on her own experience of aging, her observations of her husband's final years, and the work of others, Joan Erikson speculated that success in attaining gerotranscendence is apparent in heightened inner calm and contentment and additional time spent in quiet reflection (Erikson, 1998; Tornstam, 2000, 2011).

But more research is needed to confirm the existence of a distinct, transcendent late-life stage. Beyond getting older, major negative life events, such as declines in health or financial difficulties, are associated with reports of cosmic, gerotranscendent reflections. This suggests that inner contemplation is one means older adults use to adapt to stressful, unchangeable circumstances (Read et al., 2014). Furthermore, besides focusing intently on life's meaning, many of the very old continue to be invested in the real world—strengthening bonds with intimate partners and friends, keeping up with current events, and engaging in leisure, volunteer, and career pursuits. One participant in Vaillant's (2012) longitudinal investigation of college men (see page 477 in Chapter 14), reinterviewed in his mid-eighties, reported recently marrying his long-time partner and regularly giving paid public lectures in his field. In response to Vaillant's telephone call, he remarked that Vaillant was fortunate to have reached him on his day off!

The Positivity Effect

In Chapter 13, we discussed research on development of adults' reasoning about emotion (see page 458). Recall that cognitive-affective complexity (awareness and coordination of positive and negative feelings into an organized self-description) increases from adolescence through middle adulthood and then declines as basic information-processing skills diminish in late adulthood.

In Lijiang, China, an aging adult joins her daughter in watching a street performer. Older people selectively attend to emotionally positive over negative information, which contributes to their remarkable resilience.

But older people display a compensating emotional strength, called the **positivity effect:** Compared with younger people, they selectively attend to and better recall emotionally positive over negative information (Hilimire et al., 2014; Mather & Carstensen, 2005). This bias toward the emotionally positive, also evident in more rapid ERP brain waves in response to emotionally positive than negative stimuli, contributes to older adults' remarkable resilience. Despite physical declines, increased health problems, a restricted future, and death of loved ones, most older adults maintain a sense of optimism, gaining in enjoyment, happiness, and general psychological well-being with age (Carstensen et al., 2011; Murray & Isaacowitz, 2016).

What explains this late-life rise in positivity? According to one view, aging adults' wealth of life experiences has enabled them to become expert in emotional self-regulation (Blanchard-Fields, 2007). For example, in describing interpersonal conflicts, older adults, compared with younger people, more often report using constructive strategies, such as expressing affection or disengaging to let the situation blow over, that prevent lasting negative affect (Birditt & Fingerman, 2005; Charles et al., 2009; Luong, Charles, & Fingerman, 2011). And when they cannot avoid negative experiences, older people are especially effective at emotion-centered coping (controlling distress internally). In one study, patients ranging in age from the late twenties to the late eighties, who were recently diagnosed with colon cancer, completed measures of emotion regulation. Those age 60 and older, compared to their younger counterparts, appraised the situation as less threatening and as more of a positive challenge (Hart & Charles, 2013). These more adaptive interpretations predicted more rapid reduction in distress over the following 18 months.

In addition to greater competence at regulating emotion, awareness of less time left to live motivates older adults to accentuate positive affect (Schiebe & Carstensen, 2010). A shortened time perspective induces people to focus on gratifying, meaningful experiences in the present—a finding we will return to later in this chapter.

Of course, circumstances do occur in which older people cannot take advantage of their strengths in regulating emotion. Cognitive declines or chronic stressors can overwhelm their capacity to manage negative experiences (Charles & Carstensen, 2014; Charles & Luong, 2013). And as noted in Chapter 17, when intense, persistent stress arises, it is more taxing for older adults: Age-related changes in cardiovascular and endocrine system functioning lead blood pressure and cortisol levels to remain elevated for longer periods, with negative consequences for both physical and mental health that heighten stress further.

Nevertheless, the positivity effect is a significant late-life psychosocial attainment. Much research confirms that high levels of emotional stability and well-being are the norm rather than the exception among older people, at least into their seventies or early eighties.

Reminiscence

We often think of older adults as engaged in **reminiscence**—telling stories about people and events from their past and reporting associated thoughts and feelings. Indeed, the widespread image of a reminiscing older person ranks among negative stereotypes of aging. In this common view, older people live in the past to escape the realities of a shortened future and the nearness of death. Yet research reveals no age differences in total quantity of reminiscing! Rather, younger and older adults often use reminiscence for different purposes (Westerhof, Bohlmeijer, & Webster, 2010). And certain types of reminiscence are positive and adaptive.

In his comments on major events in his life at the beginning of this chapter, Walt was engaging in a form of reminiscence called *life review*—calling up past experiences with the goal of achieving greater self-understanding. According to Robert Butler (1968), most older adults engage in life review as part of attaining ego integrity—a notion that has led many therapists to encourage life-review reminiscence. Older adults who participate in counselor-led life-review interventions, aimed at integrating positive and negative memories from all life periods, report increased self-esteem, greater sense of purpose in life, and reduced depression (Latorre et al., 2015; O'Rourke, Cappeliez, & Claxton, 2011). Life-review interventions can also help bereaved adults find a place for lost loved ones in their emotional lives, reinvest energy in other relationships, and move on with life (Worden, 2009).

Although life review occurs more often among older than younger adults, many older people who are high in self-acceptance and life satisfaction spend little time evaluating their past (Wink, 2007). In several studies in which older adults were asked what they considered to be the best time of life, 10 to 30 percent identified one of the decades of late adulthood. Early and middle adulthood received especially high marks, whereas childhood and adolescence ranked as less satisfying (Field, 1997; Mehlson, Platz, & Fromholt, 2003). These findings challenge the widespread belief that aging adults inevitably focus on the past and wish to be young again. To the contrary, contemporary older people in industrialized nations are largely present- and future-oriented: They seek avenues for personal growth and fulfillment (see the Cultural Influences box on the next page).

Clearly, life review is not essential for adapting well to late adulthood. Indeed, reminiscence that is *self-focused*, engaged in to reduce boredom and revive bitter events, is linked to adjustment problems. Compared with younger people, older adults less often engage in this ruminative form of reminiscence, and those who do are often anxious and depressed from dwelling on painful past experiences (O'Rourke, Cappeliez, & Claxton, 2011). Life-review therapy, aimed at helping them focus on positive memories, improves psychological well-being (Lamers et al., 2015; Pinquart & Forstmeier, 2012).

In contrast, extroverted people favor *other-focused* reminiscence directed at social goals, such as solidifying family and friendship ties and reliving relationships with lost loved ones. And at times, older adults—especially those who score high in openness to experience—engage in *knowledge-based* reminiscence, drawing on their past for effective problem-solving strategies and for teaching younger people. These socially engaged, mentally stimulating forms of reminiscence help make life rich and rewarding (Cappeliez, Rivard, & Guindon, 2007). Perhaps because of their strong storytelling traditions, African-American and Chinese immigrant older adults are more likely than their European-American counterparts to use reminiscence to teach others about the past (Shellman, Ennis, & Bailey-Addison, 2011; Webster, 2002).

For young and old alike, reminiscence often occurs during times of life transition. Older adults who have recently retired, been widowed, or moved to a new residence may turn temporarily to the past to sustain a sense of personal continuity (Westerhof & Bohlmeijer, 2014). As long as they do not get stuck in mulling over unresolved difficulties, reminiscence probably helps them recapture a sense of meaning.

Stability and Change in Self-Concept and Personality

18.3 Cite stable and changing aspects of self-concept and personality, and discuss spirituality and religiosity in late adulthood.

Longitudinal research reveals continuing stability of the "big five" personality traits from mid- to late life (see Chapter 16, page 548). Yet the ingredients of ego integrity—wholeness, contentment, and image of the self as part of a larger world order—are reflected in several significant late-life changes in both self-concept and personality.

Secure and Multifaceted Self-Concept

Older adults have accumulated a lifetime of self-knowledge, leading to more secure, multifaceted conceptions of themselves than at earlier ages (Diehl et al., 2011). Ruth, for example, knew

Cultural Influences

The New Old Age

After retiring, pediatrician Jack McConnell tried a relaxing lifestyle near a lake and golf course, but it worked poorly for the energetic 64-year-old. As his desire for a more fulfilling retirement grew, he noticed that outside his comfortable, gated neighborhood were many people serving community needs as gardeners, laborers, fast-food workers, and the like, yet who lived in or near poverty. The contrast galvanized Jack to found Volunteers in Medicine, a free clinic for working-poor adults and their families who lack health insurance (Croker, 2007). Five years later, at age 69, Jack was overseeing a highly cost-effective operation involving 200 retired doctors, nurses, and lay volunteers, who treat 6,000 patients a year.

Jack exemplifies a revised approach to late adulthood, one infused with new cultural meanings: Increasingly, older adults are using their freedom from work and parenting responsibilities to pursue personally enriching interests and goals. In doing so, they are giving back to their communities in significant ways, serving as role models for younger generations, and strengthening their sense of ego integrity with images of themselves as living ethical, worthy lives.

Added years of longevity and health plus financial stability have granted this active, opportunistic time of life to so many contemporary older adults that some experts believe a new phase of late adulthood has evolved called the **Third Age**—a term originating over a decade ago in France that spread through Western Europe and recently has stretched to North America. According to this view, the First Age is childhood, the Second Age is the adult period of earning a living and rearing children, and the Third Age—extending from ages 65 to 79, and sometimes longer—is a time of personal fulfillment (Gilleard & Higgs, 2011). The Fourth Age brings physical decline and need for care.

The baby boomers—healthier and financially better off than any preceding aging generation—are moving into the latter decades of their lives with expectations of continued aspirations and accomplishment. This has helped define the Third Age as a time of self-realization and high life satisfaction.

But even people a decade or two ahead of the oldest baby boomers are experiencing the Third Age as a phase of new goal setting and purpose rather than as an extended vacation in anticipation of decline (Winter et al., 2007). As we will see later in this chapter, retirement is no longer a one-way, age-graded event. Instead, many older adults are building hybrid lives—leaving career jobs to work at different jobs that utilize their skills and that they experience as more meaningful than the work they left. Consider Lucille Shulklapper, who as a child dreamed of becoming a writer but, after marrying, became a teacher while rearing three children. Retiring in her late fifties, Lucille published six books of poetry and fiction and, at age 80, her first children's book. "I am living beyond my dreams," she reflected (Ellin, 2015, p. B5).

Although policy makers often express concern about the huge, impending baby-boomer burden on Social Security and Medicare, this large pool of vigorous, publicly minded future aging adults has the potential to make enormous economic and social contributions. Today's Third Agers donate billions to the global economy in volunteer work, continue to participate in the work force in large numbers, make creative contributions, and give generously to their families through monetary support and other forms of help—far more than they receive (see page 631).

But as midlife roles shrink and terminate, too few alternatives are available for the many older people eager to make a difference (Bass, 2011). Societies need to provide abundant volunteer, national service, and other public interest opportunities, thereby harnessing their rich older adult resources to solve pressing problems. The U.S. Senior Corps, which offers expanded service incentives and options to adults age 55 and older—tutoring children, teaching English to immigrants, assisting victims of disasters, and engaging with their communities in many other ways—is a major step in that direction.

Finally, although the majority of U.S. adults in their sixties and seventies have more energy and choice than ever before, others—more often women and ethnic minorities—suffer from financial hardship and distress and have little chance for new beginnings (Cubanski, Casillas, & Damico, 2015). When social security, health care, and housing policies ensure a comfortable Third Age to all older adults, benefits accrue to the entire nation.

Lucille Shulklapper grew up dreaming of becoming a writer, a goal she finally attained at age 60, after retiring from her teaching career. Over the next two decades, she published six poetry and fiction books and, at age 80, her first children's book.

---

with certainty that she was independent, well-organized, empathetic, and good at budgeting money, counseling others, giving dinner parties, and figuring out who could be trusted and who couldn't. Furthermore, when young and older adults were asked for several life-defining memories, 65- to 85-year-olds were more likely to mention events with a common theme—such as the importance of relationships or personal independence—and to explain how the events were interrelated (McLean, 2008). Their autobiographical selves emphasized coherence and consistency, despite physical, cognitive, and occupational changes. As

Ruth remarked humorously, "I know who I am. I've had plenty of time to figure it out!"

The firmness and multifaceted nature of Ruth's self-concept enabled her to compensate for lack of skill in domains she had never tried, had not mastered, or could no longer perform as well as before. Consequently, it allowed for self-acceptance—a key feature of integrity. In a study of old (70 to 84 years) and very old (85 to 103 years) Germans asked to respond to the question "Who am I?," participants mentioned a broad spectrum of life domains, including hobbies, interests, social participation, family, health, and personality traits. Adults in both age groups expressed more positive than negative self-evaluations (Freund & Smith, 1999). Positive, multifaceted self-definitions predicted psychological well-being.

As the future shortens, most older adults, into their eighties and nineties, continue to mention—and actively pursue—hoped-for selves in the areas of physical health, cognitive functioning, personal characteristics, relationships, social responsibility, and leisure (Frazier, 2002; Markus & Herzog, 1991). With respect to feared selves, physical health is even more prominent than it was in midlife.

At the same time, possible selves reorganize well into old age. When the German 70- to 103-year-olds just mentioned were followed longitudinally for four years, the majority deleted some possible selves and replaced them with new ones (Smith & Freund, 2002). Although future expectations become more modest and concrete with age ("taking a daily thirty-minute walk" rather than "getting in better shape"), older adults usually take steps to attain their goals. Engaging in hope-related activities, in turn, is associated with gains in life satisfaction and with longer life (Brown, 2016b; Hoppmann et al., 2007). Clearly, late adulthood is not a time of withdrawal from future planning!

Agreeableness, Acceptance of Change, and Openness to Experience

During late adulthood, shifts occur in personality characteristics that, once again, defy aging stereotypes. Old age is not a time in which the personality inevitably becomes rigid and morale declines. Rather, a flexible, optimistic approach to life, which fosters resilience in the face of adversity, is common.

Longitudinal research reveals that older adults gain modestly in *agreeableness* into their seventies, becoming more generous, acquiescent, and good-natured. However, declines in agreeableness tend to occur after age 80 as more people face physical and cognitive challenges (Allemand, Zimprich, & Martin, 2008; Mõtus, Johnson, & Deary, 2012; Weiss et al., 2005; Wortman, Lucas, & Donellan, 2012). Agreeableness seems to characterize healthy aging adults who accentuate the positive, despite life's imperfections.

At the same time, older adults show age-related dips in *extroversion*, perhaps reflecting a narrowing of social contacts as people become more selective about relationships—a trend we will take up in a later section. Older people also tend to decline in *openness to experience*, likely due to awareness of cognitive changes (Allemand, Zimprich, & Martin, 2008; Donnellan & Lucas, 2008). But engaging in cognitively challenging activities can promote openness to experience! In one study, 60- to 94-year-olds participated in a 16-week cognitive training program in reasoning, which included experience in solving challenging but enjoyable puzzles. During the program, the trained group showed steady gains in both reasoning and openness to experience not displayed by untrained controls. Sustained intellectual engagement seemed to induce older adults to view themselves as more open (Jackson et al., 2012). Openness, in turn, predicts pursuit of intellectual stimulation, thereby contributing to enhanced cognitive functioning.

Another late-life development is greater *acceptance of change*—an attribute older adults frequently mention as important to psychological well-being (Rossen, Knafl, & Flood, 2008). When asked about dissatisfactions in their lives, many say they are not unhappy about anything! Acceptance of change is also evident in most older people's effective coping with the loss of loved ones. The capacity to accept life's twists and turns, many of which are beyond one's control, is vital for adaptive functioning in late adulthood.

Most aging adults are resilient, bouncing back in the face of adversity—especially if they did so earlier in their lives. And their generally positive outlook contributes to their resilience by protecting them from stress and enabling them to conserve physical and mental resources needed for effective coping (Ong, Mroczek, & Riffin, 2011). The minority who are high in neuroticism—emotionally negative, short-tempered, and dissatisfied—tend to cope poorly with stressful events and are at risk for health problems and earlier death (Mroczek, Spiro, & Turiano, 2009).

Spirituality and Religiosity

How do older adults manage to accept declines and losses yet still feel whole, complete, and calmly composed in the face of a shrinking future? One possibility, consistent with Erikson's and Peck's emphasis on a transcendent perspective in late adulthood, is the development of a more mature sense of spirituality—an inspirational sense of life's meaning. But for many people, religion provides beliefs, symbols, and rituals that guide this quest for meaning.

Older adults attach great value to religious beliefs and behaviors. In a recent survey of a large, nationally representative sample of Americans, 65 percent of those age 65 and older said that religion is very important in their lives, and nearly half reported attending religious services at least once a week—the highest of any age group (Pew Research Center, 2016c). Similar cross-sectional trends exist in countries as diverse as Belize, Germany, India, Russia, and Togo (Deaton, 2009). Although health and transportation difficulties reduce organized religious participation in advanced old age, older people generally become more religious or spiritual as they age.

The late-life increase in religiosity, however, is usually modest, and it is not universal. Longitudinal research reveals that many people show stability in religiosity throughout adulthood, while others follow diverse paths of change—gaining or declining to varying degrees (Ai, Wink, & Ardelt, 2010; Kashdan & Nezleck, 2012; Krause & Hayward, 2016; Wang et al., 2014). For example, in a British investigation following adults for two decades, one-fourth of older adults said they had become less religious, with some citing disappointment at the support they had received from their religious institution during stressful times (such as bereavement) as the reason (Coleman, Ivani-Chalian, & Robinson, 2004).

Despite these variations, spirituality and faith may advance to a higher level in late adulthood—away from prescribed beliefs toward a more reflective approach that emphasizes links to others and is at ease with mystery and uncertainty. According to James Fowler's theory of faith development, mature adults develop new faith capacities, including awareness of their own belief system as just one of many possible worldviews, contemplation of the deeper significance of religious symbols and rituals, openness to other religious perspectives as sources of inspiration, and (especially in late life) an enlarged vision of a common good that serves the needs of all humanity (Fowler & Dell, 2006). For example, as a complement to his Catholicism, Walt became intensely interested in Buddhism, especially its focus on attaining perfect peace and happiness by mastering thoughts and feelings, never harming others, and resisting attachment to worldly objects.

Involvement in both organized and informal religious activities is especially high among low-SES ethnic minority older people, including African-American, Hispanic, and Native-American groups. In African-American communities, churches not only provide contexts for deriving meaning from life but also are centers for education, health, social welfare, and political activities aimed at improving life conditions. Aging African Americans look to religion as a powerful resource for social support beyond the family and for the inner strength to withstand daily stresses and physical impairments (Armstrong & Crowther, 2002). Compared with their European-American agemates, more African-American older adults report feeling closer to God and engaging in prayer as a means of overcoming life's problems (Krause & Hayward, 2016).

As at earlier ages, in late adulthood women are more likely than men to say that religion is very important to them, to participate in religious activities, and to engage in a personal quest for connectedness with a higher power (Pew Research Center, 2016c; Wang et al., 2014). Women's higher rates of poverty, widowhood, and participation in caregiving, including caring for chronically ill family members, expose them to higher levels of stress and anxiety. As with ethnic minorities, they turn to religion for social support and for a larger vision of community that places life's challenges in perspective.

Religious involvement is associated with diverse benefits, including better physical and psychological well-being, more time devoted to exercising and leisure activities, increased sense of closeness to family and friends, greater generativity (care for others), and deeper sense of meaning (or purpose) in

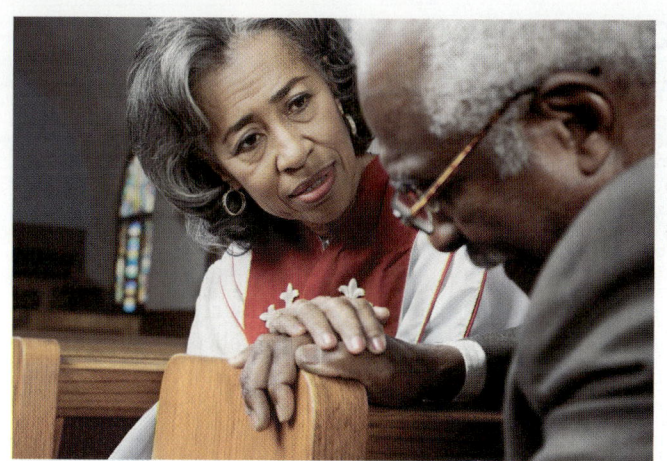

This aging parishioner seeks counsel from his church minister. For many people in late adulthood, religiosity strengthens their capacity to cope with life's hardships, reducing distress and enhancing quality of life.

life (Boswell, Kahana, & Dilworth-Anderson, 2006; Krause, 2012; Krause et al., 2013; Wink, 2006, 2007). In longitudinal research, both organized and informal religious participation predicted longer survival, after family background, health, social, and psychological factors known to affect mortality were controlled (Helm et al., 2000; Sullivan, 2010).

But aspects of religion that make a difference in aging adults' lives are not always clear. In some research, religious *activity*—not religious belief or membership in a congregation—was associated with declines in distress following negative life events, such as loss of a spouse or a life-threatening illness (Kidwai et al., 2014; Lund, Caserta, & Dimond, 1993). Increased social engagement and social support brought about by religious participation were believed to be responsible. Other evidence, however, indicates that among religious older people, belief in God's powers strengthens during late adulthood and contributes substantially to reduced distress and higher self-esteem, optimism, and life satisfaction, especially among low-SES, ethnic minorities (Hayward & Krause, 2013b; Schieman, Bierman, & Ellison, 2010, 2013). Their personal relationship with God seems to help them cope with life's hardships.

Contextual Influences on Psychological Well-Being

18.4 Discuss the influence of control versus dependency, physical health, negative life changes, and social support on older adults' psychological well-being.

As we have seen in this and the previous chapter, most adults adapt well to old age, yet some feel dependent, incompetent, and worthless. Personal and situational factors combine to affect aging adults' psychological well-being. Identifying these contextual influences is vital for designing interventions that foster positive adjustment.

Control versus Dependency

As Ruth's eyesight, hearing, and mobility declined in her eighties, Sybil visited daily to help with self-care and household tasks. During the hours mother and daughter were together, Sybil interacted most often with Ruth when she asked for help with activities of daily living. When Ruth handled tasks on her own, Sybil usually withdrew.

Observations of people interacting with older adults in both private homes and institutions reveal two highly predictable, complementary behavior patterns. In the first, called the **dependency–support script,** dependent behaviors are attended to immediately. In the second, the **independence–ignore script,** independent behaviors are mostly ignored. Notice how these sequences reinforce dependent behavior at the expense of independent behavior, regardless of the older person's competencies (Baltes, 1995, 1996). Even a self-reliant individual like Ruth did not always resist Sybil's unnecessary help because it brought about social contact.

Among older people who experience no difficulty with daily activities, opportunities to interact with others are related to high satisfaction with everyday life. In contrast, among aging adults who have trouble performing daily activities, social contact is frequently associated with a less positive everyday existence (Lang & Baltes, 1997). This suggests that social interaction while assisting older people with physical care, household chores, and errands is often not meaningful and rewarding but, rather, demeaning and unpleasant. Older adults' negative reactions to caregiving can result in persisting depression (Newsom & Schulz, 1998). But whether assistance from others undermines well-being depends on many factors, including the social and cultural context in which helping occurs, the quality of help offered, and the caregiver–older adult relationship.

Why do family members and other caregivers often respond in ways that promote excessive dependency in old age? Stereotypes of older people as passive and incompetent appear to be responsible. After reading passages that activated these stereotypes (by portraying aging adults as inept), older people responded with more frequent help-seeking behavior (Coudin & Alexopoulos, 2010).

In Western societies, which highly value independence, many older adults fear relinquishing control and becoming dependent on others. This is especially so for those with a high need for self-determination (Curtiss, Hayslip, & Dolan, 2007). As physical and cognitive limitations rise, granting older adults the freedom to choose those activities in which they desire help preserves their autonomy (Lachman, Neupert, & Agrigoroaei, 2011). In this way, they can conserve their strength by investing it in self-chosen, highly valued activities, using a set of strategies considered in Chapter 17: *selective optimization with compensation.*

Much research confirms that feelings of personal control diminish in late life (Kandler et al., 2015; Lachman, Neupert, & Agrigoroaei, 2011). But retaining as much control as they can helps older adults protect their well-being for as long as possible. In a longitudinal study of a nationally representative sample of 1,600 German adults, those who expressed a high sense of control (being able to determine most of what happens to them) reported greater life satisfaction during the three years prior to their death (Gerstorf et al., 2014). Yet typically, well-being drops sharply during the final few years.

Think about the varied ways aging adults optimize their functioning while compensating for declines. Notice how they adaptively modify their personal goals: They invest in goals that enable them to remain active and self-determining, adjust those goals to suit their changing capacities, and disengage from goals that overextend their capacities, turning toward other, attainable goals (Heckhausen, Wrosch, & Schultz, 2010). In doing so, older people strive to remain active agents in the direction of their own lives. When family and caregiving environments support their efforts, most aging adults are resilient, sustaining a sense of optimism, self-efficacy, purpose, and investment in overcoming obstacles until very late in life.

Assistance aimed at enabling older adults to use their capacities fully in pursuit of their goals creates an effective **person–environment fit**—a good match between their abilities and the demands of their living environments, which promotes adaptive behavior and psychological well-being (Fry & Debats, 2010). When people cannot maximize use of their capacities (have become excessively dependent), they react with boredom and passivity. When they encounter environmental demands that are too great (receive too little assistance), they experience overwhelming stress.

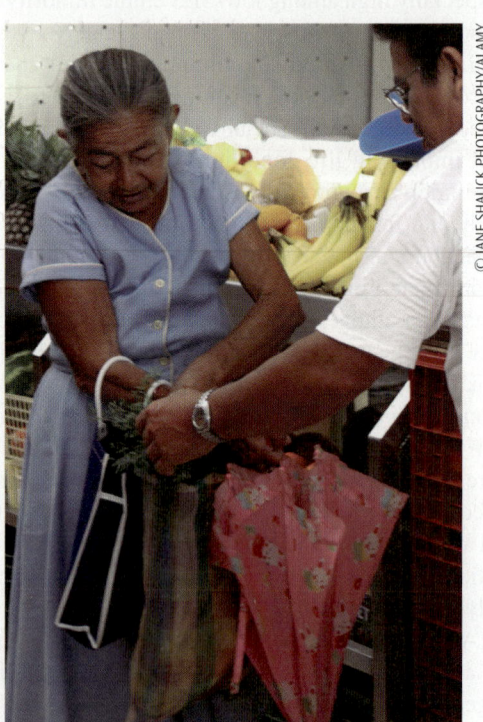

By letting her son help with grocery shopping, will this Mexican 80-year-old become too dependent? Not necessarily. When older adults assume personal control over areas of dependency, they can conserve their strength for highly valued activities.

Physical Health

As noted in Chapter 16, physical health is a powerful predictor of psychological well-being. Physical declines and chronic disease are among the strongest risk factors for late-life depression (Whitbourne & Meeks, 2011). Although fewer older than young and middle-aged adults are depressed (see Chapter 17), profound feelings of hopelessness rise with age as physical disability leads to diminished personal control and increased social isolation. But more than actual physical limitations, *perceived negative physical health* predicts depressive symptoms (Verhaak et al., 2014; Weinberger & Whitbourne, 2010). This helps explain the stronger physical impairment–depression relationship among higher-SES aging adults (Schieman & Plickert, 2007). Because of their lifetime of better physical health, they may experience physical limitations as more unexpected and challenging.

The relationship between physical and mental health problems can become a vicious cycle, each intensifying the other. In survey research conducted in 15 countries, adults of all ages reported that mental health problems actually interfered more than physical disabilities with activities of daily living, including home management and social life (Ormel et al., 2008). At times, despondency and "giving up" trigger rapid physical decline in a sick aging adult. This downward spiral can be hastened by a move to a nursing home, yielding reduced control over daily life and greater distance from family and friends. In the months after admission, many residents judge their quality of life to have worsened substantially, become severely anxious and depressed, and deteriorate rapidly. The stress of illness together with institutionalization is associated with escalating physical and mental health problems and with mortality (Miu & Chan, 2011; Scocco, Rapattoni, & Fantoni, 2006).

Depression in old age is often lethal. People age 85 and older have the highest suicide rate of all age groups (see the Social Issues: Health box on pages 618–619). What factors enable people like Ruth to surmount the physical impairment–depression relationship, remaining content? Personal characteristics discussed in this and earlier chapters—optimism, sense of self-efficacy, and effective coping—are vitally important (Morrison, 2008). But for frail aging adults to display these attributes, families and caregivers must avoid the dependency–support script and, instead, encourage their autonomy.

Unfortunately, older adults generally do not get the mental health care they need—even in nursing homes, where depression and other mental health problems are widespread (Hoeft et al., 2016; Karel, Gatz, & Smyer, 2012). More than half of U.S. nursing home residents receive no regular mental health intervention.

Negative Life Changes

Ruth lost Walt to a heart attack, cared for her sister Ida as her Alzheimer's symptoms worsened, and faced health problems of her own—all within a span of a few years. Older people are at risk for a variety of negative life changes—death of loved ones, illness and physical disabilities, declining income, and greater dependency. Negative life changes are difficult for everyone but may actually evoke less stress and depression in older than in younger adults (Charles, 2011). Many older people have learned to cope with hard times, to appraise negative changes as common and expected in late life, and to accept loss as part of human existence.

Still, when negative changes pile up, they test the coping skills of older adults. In very old age, such changes are greater for women than for men. Women over age 75 are far less likely to be married, more often have lower incomes, and suffer from more illnesses—especially ones that restrict mobility. Furthermore, older women (as at younger ages) more often say that others depend on them for caregiving and emotional support. Consequently, their social relations, even in very old age, are more often a source of stress (Antonucci, Ajrouch, & Birditt, 2008). And because of their own declining health, older women may not be able to meet others' needs for care—circumstances associated with chronic, high distress (Charles, 2010). Not surprisingly, women of advanced age tend to report lower psychological well-being than do men (Henning-Smith, 2016).

Social Support

In late adulthood, social support continues to reduce stress, thereby promoting physical health and psychological well-being. Availability of social support increases the odds of living longer (Fry & Debats, 2006, 2010). And it helps explain the relationship of religious participation to survival, discussed earlier. Usually, older adults receive informal assistance with tasks of daily living from family members—first from their spouse or, if none exists, from children and then from siblings. If these individuals are not available, other relatives and friends may step in.

Nevertheless, many older people place such high value on independence that they do not want extensive help from others close to them unless they can reciprocate. In one investigation, providing intangible assistance (such as errands, transportation, or child care) to friends and relatives and emotional support to one's spouse better predicted reduced mortality than receiving social support (Brown et al., 2003). When assistance is excessive or cannot be returned, it often interferes with self-efficacy and amplifies psychological stress (Warner et al., 2011). Perhaps for this reason, adult children express a deeper sense of obligation toward their aging parents than their parents expect from them (see Chapter 16, page 555). Formal support—a paid home helper or agency-provided services—as a complement to informal assistance not only helps relieve caregiving burden but also spares aging adults from feeling overly dependent in their close relationships.

Ethnic minority older adults, however, do not readily accept formal assistance. But they are more willing to do so when home helpers are connected to a familiar neighborhood organization, especially their religious community. Although African-American older people say they rely more on their families than on the

Social Issues: Health

Elder Suicide

When Abe's wife died, he withdrew from life, mostly spending his days alone. As grandchildren were born, Abe visited his daughters' families from time to time, carrying his despondent behavior with him. "Look at my new pajamas, Grandpa!" Abe's grandson Tony exclaimed on one occasion. Abe didn't respond.

When in his eighties, Abe developed painful digestive difficulties. His depression deepened, but he refused to see a doctor. "Don't need to," he said abruptly when one of his daughters begged him to get medical attention. Answering her invitation to Tony's tenth birthday party, Abe wrote, "Maybe—if I'm still around next month." Two weeks later, Abe died from an intestinal blockage. His body was found in the living room chair where he habitually spent his days. Although it may seem surprising, Abe's self-destructive acts are a form of suicide.

Factors Related to Elder Suicide

In most countries around the world, suicide increases over the lifespan, with older adults at greatest risk, though regional variations exist. As noted in Chapter 16, the United States is distinguished by a sharp rise in suicide in middle adulthood (see page 546). Thereafter, the suicide rate levels off or drops slightly, increasing once again from age 75 on to a level that, at age 85 and older, slightly exceeds the midlife incidence (American Foundation for Suicide Prevention, 2016).

U.S. suicides among the very old have risen by 15 percent over the past few years—a trend (as in middle adulthood) largely accounted for by white men. Furthermore, the sex difference in suicide widens in old age: Nearly 10 times as many U.S. aging men as women take their own lives (Centers for Disease Control and Prevention, 2016d). Compared with the white majority, most ethnic minority older adults have low suicide rates.

What explains these differences? Despite the lifelong pattern of higher rates of depression among females, older women's closer ties to family and friends, willingness to seek social support, and greater religiosity prevent many from taking their own lives. High levels of social support through extended families and religious institutions may prevent suicide among ethnic minorities (Conwell, Van Orden, & Caine, 2011). And within certain groups, such as Alaskan Natives, deep respect for and reliance on older adults to teach cultural traditions strengthen self-esteem and social integration. This reduces suicide, making it almost nonexistent after age 80 (Herne, Bartholomew, & Weahkee, 2014; Kettl, 1998).

Failed suicides are rare in old age. The ratio of attempts to completions for adolescents and young adults is as high as 200 to 1; for aging adults, it is 4 to 1 or lower (Conwell & O'Reilly, 2013). When older people decide to die, they are especially determined to succeed.

Underreporting of suicides probably occurs at all ages, but it is more common in old age. Many older adults, like Abe, engage in indirect self-destructive acts rarely classified as suicide—deciding not to go to a doctor when ill or refusing to eat or take prescribed medications. Among institutionalized older adults, these efforts to hasten death are widespread (Reiss & Tishler, 2008b). Consequently, suicide in late life is a larger problem than statistics indicate.

Two types of events prompt suicide in late life. Losses—retirement from a highly valued occupation, widowhood, or social isolation—place older adults who have difficulty coping with change at risk for persistent depression. Most suicides, however, stem from chronic and terminal illnesses that severely reduce physical functioning or cause intense pain

---

church for assistance, those with support and meaningful roles in both contexts fare best in mental health (Chatters et al., 2015). Compared to their white counterparts, African-American aging adults who attend church regularly are more involved in both giving and receiving diverse forms of social support—a difference largely explained by stronger social networks and shared values and goals among black congregants (Hayward & Krause, 2013a). But support from religious congregants has psychological benefits for older adults of all backgrounds, perhaps because the warm atmosphere of religious organizations fosters a sense of social acceptance.

Overall, for social support to foster well-being, older adults must take personal control of it. Help that is not wanted or needed or that exaggerates weaknesses results in poor person–environment fit, undermines mental health, and—if existing skills fall into disuse—accelerates physical disability. In contrast, help that increases autonomy—that frees up energy for endeavors that are personally satisfying and that lead to growth—enhances quality of life. These findings clarify why *perceived social support* (older adults' sense of being able to count on family or friends in times of need) is associated with a positive outlook in older adults with disabilities, whereas sheer *amount* of help family and friends provide has little impact (Uchino, 2009).

Finally, besides various types of assistance, older adults benefit from social support that offers affection, affirmation of their self-worth, and sense of belonging. Extroverted older people are more likely to take advantage of opportunities to engage with others, thereby reducing loneliness and depression and fostering self-esteem and life satisfaction (Mroczek & Spiro, 2005). But as we will see in the next section, gratifying social ties in old age have little to do with quantity of contact. Instead, high-quality relationships, involving expressions of kindness, encouragement, respect, and emotional closeness, have the greatest impact on mental health in late life.

(Conwell et al., 2010). As comfort and quality of life diminish, feelings of hopelessness and helplessness deepen.

Mild cognitive declines, especially in executive function, make some individuals susceptible to impulsivity and poor problem solving, heightening suicidal risk when losses or illnesses arise (Dombrovski et al., 2008). Dementia is also linked to suicide, especially shortly after diagnosis (Haw, Harwood, & Hawton, 2009).

The chances of suicide are further elevated when a sick older person is socially isolated—living alone or in a nursing home with high staff turnover, minimal caregiver support, and little opportunity for personal control over daily life. Suicide rates are lower in European countries where older people more often live with their families (Yur'yev et al., 2010). At the same time, when ill aging adults perceive themselves to be a burden to their families, the risk of suicide rises (Yip et al., 2010).

Prevention and Treatment

Warning signs of suicide in late adulthood, like those at earlier ages, include statements about dying, despondency, and sleep and appetite changes. But family members, friends, caregivers, and health professionals must also watch for indirect self-destructive acts that are unique to old age, such as refusing food or medical treatment.

When suicidal aging adults are depressed, the most effective treatment combines antidepressant medication with therapy, including help in coping with role transitions, such as retirement, widowhood, and dependency brought about by illness. Distorted ways of thinking ("I'm old—nothing can be done about my problems," "I'm burdening my children") must be countered and revised. Meeting with the family to find ways to reduce loneliness and desperation is also helpful.

Communities are beginning to recognize the importance of preventive steps, such as community-wide screenings for risk factors, programs that help aging adults cope with life transitions, telephone hot lines with trained volunteers who provide emotional support, and agencies that arrange for regular home visitors or "buddy system" phone calls (Draper, 2014). But so far, most of these efforts benefit women more than men because women are more likely to tell health professionals about high-risk symptoms, such as despondency, and to use social resources.

Finally, suicide in late life raises a controversial ethical issue: Do people with incurable illnesses have the right to take their own lives? We will take up this topic in Chapter 19.

U.S. suicide rates among the very old have recently increased, especially among white men. Most late-life suicides arise from illnesses that severely interfere with comfort and quality of life. Social isolation further increases suicide risk.

Ask yourself

CONNECT Why is it important to understand aging adults' *perceptions* of their circumstances—physical changes (see page 579 in Chapter 17), health, negative life changes, and social support? How do the perceptions of most older people promote psychological well-being?

APPLY At age 85, Miriam took a long time to get dressed. Joan, her home helper, said, "From now on, don't get dressed until I get there. Then I can help, and it won't take so long." What impact is Joan's approach likely to have on Miriam's personality? What alternative approach would you recommend?

REFLECT Among older people you know, do any fit the description of a Third Ager? Explain.

A Changing Social World

18.5 Describe the limitations of disengagement theory and activity theory, and explain the more recent perspectives of continuity theory and socioemotional selectivity theory.

18.6 How do communities, neighborhoods, and housing arrangements affect older adults' social lives and adjustment?

Walt and Ruth's outgoing personalities led many family members and friends to seek them out, and they often reciprocated. In contrast, Dick's stubborn nature meant that he and Goldie, for many years, had had a far more restricted network of social ties.

As noted earlier, extroverts (like Walt and Ruth) continue to interact with a wider range of people than do introverts and people (like Dick) with poor social skills. Nevertheless, both cross-sectional and longitudinal research confirms that size of social networks and, therefore, amount of social interaction decline for virtually everyone (Antonucci, Akiyama, & Takahashi, 2004; Charles & Carstensen, 2009). This finding presents a curious paradox: If social interaction and social support are essential for mental health, how is it possible for older adults to interact less yet be generally satisfied with life and less depressed than younger adults?

Social Theories of Aging

Social theories of aging offer explanations for changes in aging adults' social activity. Two older perspectives interpret declines in social interaction in opposite ways.

According to *disengagement theory*, older people decrease their activity levels and interact less frequently, becoming more preoccupied with their inner lives in anticipation of death (Cumming & Henry, 1961). Yet clearly, most older adults don't disengage! Many sustain aspects of their work, with some moving into new positions of prestige and power (see Chapter 17). And others develop new, rewarding roles in their communities.

Attempting to overcome the flaws of disengagement theory, *activity theory* proposes that social barriers to engagement, not the desires of older adults, cause declining rates of interaction. Older people who lose certain roles and relationships (for example, through retirement or widowhood) try to find others in an effort to stay active—conditions that promote life satisfaction (Maddox, 1963). However, when health status is controlled, older people who have larger social networks and engage in more activities are not necessarily happier (Charles & Carstensen, 2009). Recall that quality, not quantity, of relationships predicts psychological well-being in old age.

More recent approaches—continuity theory and socioemotional selectivity theory—view older adults' social engagement as influenced by both late-life psychological changes and social contexts. Consequently, they account for a wider range of findings.

Continuity Theory. According to **continuity theory**, most aging adults strive to maintain a personal system—an identity and a set of personality dispositions, interests, roles, and skills—that promotes life satisfaction by ensuring consistency between their past and anticipated future. This striving for continuity does not mean that older people's lives are static. To the contrary, aging produces inevitable change, but older adults try to minimize stress and disruptiveness by integrating those changes into a coherent, consistent life path, drawing on well-practiced strategies acquired over a lifetime. As much as possible, they choose to use familiar skills and engage in familiar activities with familiar people—preferences that provide a secure sense of routine and direction in life.

Research confirms a high degree of continuity in older adults' everyday pursuits and relationships. For most, friends and family members with whom they interact remain much the same, as do work, volunteer, leisure, and social activities. Even after a change (such as retirement), people usually make choices that

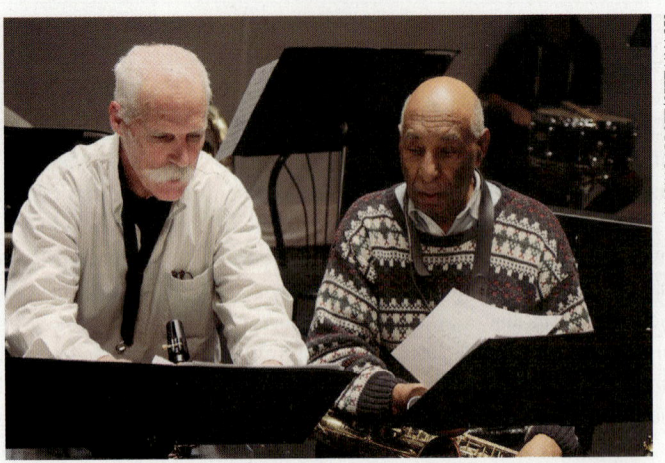

These career musicians perform after retirement as members of a community band—continuity that affirms their identity, sustains rewarding relationships and interests, and promotes self-esteem and life satisfaction.

extend the previous direction of their lives, engaging in new activities but often within familiar domains. For example, a retired manager of a children's bookstore collaborated with friends to build a children's library and donate it to an overseas orphanage. A musician who, because of arthritis, could no longer play the violin arranged regular get-togethers with musically inclined friends to listen to and talk about music. Robert Atchley (1989), originator of continuity theory, noted, "Everyday life for most older people is like long-running improvisational theater in which … changes are mostly in the form of new episodes [rather] than entirely new plays" (p. 185).

Aging adults' reliance on continuity has many benefits. Participating in familiar activities with familiar people provides repeated practice that helps preserve physical and cognitive functioning, fosters self-esteem and mastery, and affirms identity (Finchum & Weber, 2000; Vacha-Haase, Hill, & Bermingham, 2012). Investing in long-standing, close relationships provides comfort, pleasure, and a network of social support. Finally, striving for continuity is essential for attaining Erikson's sense of ego integrity, which depends on preserving a sense of personal history (Atchley, 1999).

As we explore social contexts and relationships of aging, we will encounter many examples of how older adults use continuity to experience aging positively, as a "gentle slope." We will also address ways that communities can help them do so. As our discussion will reveal, people experiencing the greatest disruption to desired continuity in activities and lifestyle preferences have the most difficulty adapting to growing older.

Socioemotional Selectivity Theory. How do people's social networks sustain continuity while also narrowing as they age? According to **socioemotional selectivity theory,** social interaction in late life extends lifelong selection processes. In middle adulthood, marital relationships deepen, siblings feel closer, and number of friendships declines. As people age, contacts with family and friends are sustained until the eighties, when they diminish gradually in favor of a few very close relationships. In contrast, as Figure 18.1 shows, relationships with

CHAPTER 18 Emotional and Social Development in Late Adulthood

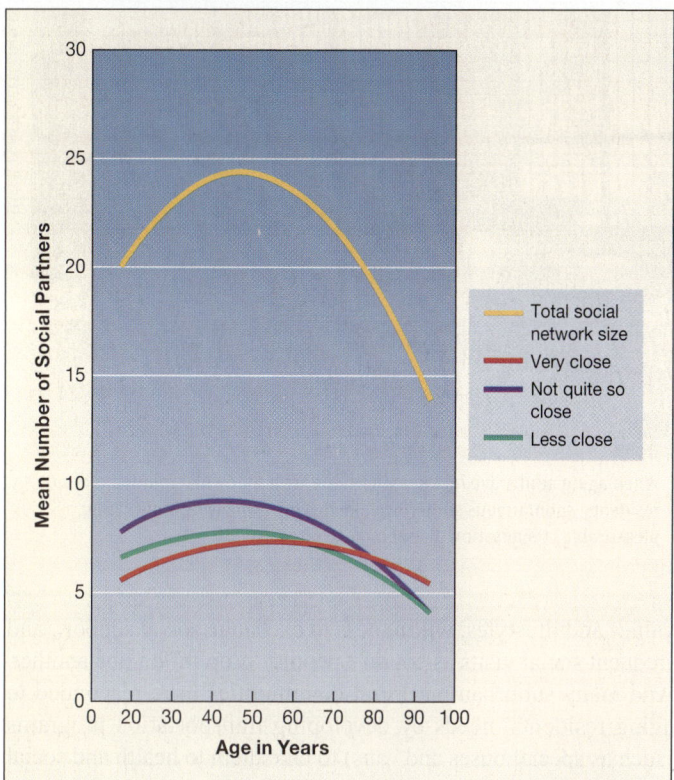

FIGURE 18.1 Age-related changes in number of social partners varying in closeness. Nearly 200 adults ranging in age from early to late adulthood were followed for a decade, during which they were periodically asked to list people in their social networks whom they felt "very close to," "not quite so close to," and "less close to." Total social network size decreased sharply from middle to late adulthood. The drop was largely accounted for by "not quite so close" and "less close" social partners. "Very close" partners declined minimally. (From T. English & L. L. Carstensen, 2014, "Selective Narrowing of Social Networks Across Adulthood Is Associated with Improved Emotional Experience in Daily Life," *International Journal of Behavioral Development, 38*, p. 199. Adapted by permission of Sage Publications.)

people to whom one feels less close decline steeply from middle through late adulthood (Carstensen, 2006; English & Carstensen, 2014; Wrzus et al., 2013).

What explains these changes? Socioemotional selectivity theory states that aging leads to changes in the functions of social interaction. Consider the reasons you interact with members of your social network. At times, you approach them to get information. At other times, you seek affirmation of your worth as a person. You also choose social partners to regulate emotion, approaching those who evoke positive feelings and avoiding those who make you feel sad, angry, or uncomfortable. For older adults, who have gathered a lifetime of information, the information-gathering function becomes less significant. Also, they realize it is risky to approach people they do not know for self-affirmation: Negative stereotypes of aging increase the odds of receiving a condescending, hostile, or indifferent response.

Instead, older adults emphasize the emotion-regulating function of interaction. In one study, younger and older adults were asked to categorize their social partners. Younger people more often sorted them on the basis of information seeking and future contact, whereas older people emphasized anticipated feel-

ings (Frederickson & Carstensen, 1990). They appeared highly motivated to approach pleasant relationships and avoid unpleasant ones. Notice how, by interacting mostly with close relatives and friends, older people engage in a form of anticipatory emotion regulation: They increase the chances that their emotional equilibrium will be preserved.

Within close bonds, aging adults actively apply their emotional expertise to promote harmony. Recall from our discussion of the positivity effect that older adults are more likely than younger people to resolve interpersonal conflicts constructively (see page 611). They also reinterpret conflict in less stressful ways—often by identifying something positive in the situation (Labouvie-Vief, 2003). Consequently, despite their smaller social networks, they are happier than younger people with their number of friends and report fewer problematic relationships and less distress when they encounter interpersonal tensions (Blanchard-Fields & Coats, 2008; Fingerman & Birditt, 2003).

Extensive research confirms that people's perception of time is strongly linked to their social goals. If you faced a shortened future, with whom would you choose to spend time? When remaining time is limited, adults *of all ages* place more emphasis on the emotional quality of their social experiences. They shift from focusing on long-term goals to emphasizing emotionally fulfilling relationships in the here and now (Charles & Carstensen, 2010). Similarly, aging adults—aware that time is "running out"—don't waste it on unlikely future payoffs but, instead, turn to close friends and family members. Furthermore, we generally take special steps to facilitate positive interaction with people dear to us whose time is limited—for example, treating older friends and relatives more kindly than younger ones, easily excusing or forgiving their social transgressions (Luong,

These sisters—ages 93 and 89—greet each other with enthusiasm. The one on the right traveled from Poland to New York City for this reunion. To preserve emotional equilibrium and reduce stress, older adults increasingly emphasize familiar, emotionally rewarding relationships.

Charles, & Fingerman, 2011). In this way, social partners contribute to older adults' gratifying relationship experiences.

Aging adults' emphasis on *relationship quality* helps explain a cultural exception to the restriction of social relationships just described. In collectivist societies, where people value an interdependent self and attach great importance to remaining embedded in their social group, older people may be motivated to sustain high-quality ties with all partners! In line with this prediction, in a Hong Kong study, aging adults scoring high in interdependence both expanded their number of emotionally close social partners and preserved the same number of peripheral social partners into advanced old age (Yeung, Fung, & Lang, 2008). In contrast, Hong Kong older people scoring low in interdependence resembled their Western counterparts: They gradually limited their social ties to a few close relationships.

In sum, socioemotional selectivity theory views older adults' preference for high-quality, emotionally fulfilling relationships as largely due to their contracting future and the preciousness of time. But the meaning of relationship quality and, therefore, the number and variety of people to whom older people turn for pleasurable interaction and self-affirmation vary with culture.

Social Contexts of Aging: Communities, Neighborhoods, and Housing

The physical and social contexts in which aging adults live affect their social experiences and, consequently, their development and adjustment. Communities, neighborhoods, and housing arrangements vary in the extent to which they enable older residents to satisfy their social needs.

Communities and Neighborhoods.
About half of U.S. ethnic minority older adults live in cities, compared with just one-third of European Americans. The majority of older people reside in suburbs, where they moved earlier in their lives and usually remain after retirement. Suburban older adults have higher incomes and report better health than their inner-city counterparts do. But inner-city older people are better off in terms of public transportation. As declines in physical functioning compromise out-of-home mobility, convenient bus, tram, and rail lines become increasingly important to life satisfaction and psychological well-being (Eibich et al., 2016; Mollenkopf, Hieber, & Wahl, 2011). Furthermore, city-dwelling aging adults fare better in terms of health, income, and proximity of cultural activities and social services than do the one-fifth of U.S. older people who live in small towns and rural areas (U.S. Department of Health and Human Services, 2015e). In addition, small-town and rural aging adults are less likely to live near their children, who often leave these communities in early adulthood.

Yet small-town and rural older people compensate for distance from children and social services by establishing closer relationships with nearby extended family and by interacting more with neighbors and friends (Hooyman, Kawamoto, & Kiyak, 2015; Shaw, 2005). Smaller communities have features that foster gratifying relationships—stability of residents, shared

When aging adults live in a neighborhood with many like-minded older residents, spontaneous gatherings like this one, involving stimulating, pleasurable conversation, happen more often.

values and lifestyles, willingness to exchange social support, and frequent social visits as country people "drop in" on one another. And many suburban and rural communities have responded to aging residents' needs by developing transportation programs (such as special buses and vans) to take them to health and social services, senior centers, and shopping centers.

Both urban and rural older people report greater life satisfaction when many aging adults reside in their neighborhood and are available as like-minded companions. Presence of family is less crucial when neighbors and nearby friends provide social support (Gabriel & Bowling, 2004). This does not mean that neighbors replace family relationships. But older adults are content as long as their children and other relatives who live far away arrange occasional visits and otherwise stay in touch through phone calls and social media (Hooyman, Kawamoto, & Kiyak, 2015).

Compared with those in urban areas, aging adults in quiet neighborhoods in small and midsized communities tend to be more satisfied with life. In addition to a friendlier, more supportive atmosphere, smaller communities have lower crime rates (Eibich et al., 2016; Krause, 2004). As we will see next, fear of crime has profound, negative consequences for older people's sense of security and comfort.

Victimization and Fear of Crime.
Walt and Ruth's single-family home stood in an urban neighborhood, five blocks from the business district where Walt's photography shop had been prior to his retirement. As the neighborhood aged, some homes fell into disrepair, and the population became more transient. Although they had never been victimized, crime was on Walt and Ruth's minds and affected their behavior: They avoided neighborhood streets after sundown.

Media attention has led to a widely held belief that crime against older adults is common. In reality, they are less often targets of crime, especially violent crime, than other age groups. In urban areas, however, purse snatching and pickpocketing are more often committed against aging adults (especially women) than younger people (U.S. Department of Justice, 2015). A single incident can strike intense anxiety into the hearts of older people because of its potential for physical injury and its financial consequences for those with low incomes.

Among frail aging adults living alone and in inner-city areas, fear of crime, which is sometimes greater than worries about income, health, and housing, restricts activities and undermines morale (Beaulieu, Leclerc, & Dube, 2003). In one study, older adults who had experienced a violent crime were more likely than those with physical and cognitive impairments to enter a nursing home (Lachs et al., 2006). Neighborhood Watch and other programs that encourage residents to look out for one another increase communication among neighbors, strengthen sense of neighborhood cohesion, and reduce fear (Oh & Kim, 2009).

Housing Arrangements. Older people's housing preferences reflect a strong desire for **aging in place**—remaining in a familiar setting where they have control over their everyday life. Overwhelmingly, aging adults in Western nations want to stay in the neighborhoods where they spent their adult lives; in fact, 90 percent remain in or near their old home. In the United States, only about 4 percent relocate to other communities (U.S. Department of Health and Human Services, 2015e). These moves are usually motivated by a desire to live closer to children or, among the more economically advantaged and healthy, a desire for a more temperate climate and a place to pursue leisure interests.

Most relocations occur within the same town or city and are prompted by declining health, widowhood, or disability (Bekhet, 2016). As we look at housing arrangements for older adults, we will see that the more a setting deviates from home life, the harder it is for older people to adjust.

Ordinary Homes. For the majority of aging adults, who are not physically impaired, staying in their own homes affords the greatest possible personal control—freedom to arrange space and schedule daily events as one chooses. More older people in Western countries live on their own today than ever before—a trend due to improved health and economic well-being (U.S. Department of Health and Human Services, 2015e). But when health and mobility problems appear, independent living poses risks to an effective person–environment fit. Most homes are designed for younger people. They are seldom modified to suit the physical capacities of their older residents.

When Ruth reached her mid-eighties, Sybil begged her to move into her home. Like many adult children of Southern, Central, and Eastern European descent (Greek, Italian, Polish, and others), Sybil felt an especially strong obligation to care for her frail mother. Older adults of these cultural backgrounds, as well as African Americans, Asians, Hispanics, and Native Americans, more often live in extended families (see page 555 in Chapter 16).

Yet increasing numbers of ethnic minority older people want to live on their own, although poverty often prevents them from doing so. For example, two decades ago, most Asian-American aging adults were living with their children, whereas today 65 percent live independently—a trend also evident in certain Asian nations, such as Japan (Federal Interagency Forum on Aging Related Statistics, 2012; Takagi & Silverstein, 2011). With sufficient income to keep her home, Ruth refused to move in with Sybil. Continuity theory helps us understand why many older adults react this way, even after health problems accumulate. As the site of memorable life events, the home strengthens continuity with the past, preserving a sense of identity in the face of physical declines and social losses. And it permits older adults to adapt to their surroundings in familiar, comfortable ways. Older people also value their independence, privacy, and network of nearby friends and neighbors.

Over the past half century, the number of unmarried, divorced, and widowed aging adults living alone has increased dramatically. Nearly 30 percent of U.S. older adults live by themselves, a figure that rises to nearly 50 percent for those age 85 and older (U.S. Department of Health and Human Services, 2015e). This trend, though evident in all segments of the aging population, is less pronounced among men, who are far more likely than women to be living with a spouse into advanced old age.

Over 35 percent of U.S. older adults who live alone are poverty-stricken—a rate far greater than among older couples. More than 70 percent are widowed women. Because of lower earnings in earlier years, some entered old age this way. Others became poor for the first time, often because they outlived a spouse who suffered a lengthy, costly illness. With age, their financial status worsens as their assets shrink and their own health-care costs rise (National Institute on Retirement Security, 2016). Under these conditions, isolation, loneliness, and depression can pile up. Poverty among lone aging women is deeper in the United States than in other Western nations because of less generous government-sponsored income and health benefits. Consequently, the feminization of poverty deepens in old age.

Residential Communities. About 12 percent of U.S. adults age 65 and older live in residential communities, a proportion that rises with age as functional limitations increase. Among people age 85 and older, 27 percent live in these communities, which come in great variety (Freedman & Spillman, 2014). Housing developments for aging adults, either single-dwelling or apartment complexes, differ from ordinary homes only in that they have been modified to suit older adults' capacities (featuring, for example, single-level living space and grab bars in bathrooms). Some are federally subsidized units for low-income residents, but most are privately developed retirement villages with adjoining recreational facilities.

For older adults who need more help with everyday tasks, *assisted-living* arrangements are available (see Chapter 17, page 593). **Independent living communities**—an increasingly popular option—provide a variety of hotel-like support services, including meals in a common dining room, housekeeping, laundry services, transportation assistance, and recreational activities. **Life-care communities** offer a continuum of housing alternatives: independent living, residences providing personal and health-related services to accommodate older adults with physical and mental disabilities, and full nursing home care. For a large initial payment and additional monthly fees, life care

Residents of a life-care community gather for a meal in the common dining room. By providing a range of housing alternatives plus personal and health-related services and care, life-care communities meet older adults' changing needs within the same facility as they age.

guarantees that individuals' changing needs will be met within the same facility as they age.

Unlike Ruth and Walt, who remained in their own home, Dick and Goldie decided in their late sixties to move to a nearby life-care community. For Dick, the move was a positive turn of events that permitted him to relate to peers on the basis of their current life together, setting aside past failures in the outside world. Dick found gratifying leisure pursuits—leading an exercise class, organizing a charity drive with Goldie, and using his skills as a baker to make cakes for birthday and anniversary celebrations.

By sustaining an effective person–environment fit as older adults' capacities change, life-care communities have positive effects on physical and mental health. A specially designed physical space plus personal and health-related assistance on an as-needed basis help older people cope with mobility and self-care limitations, enabling greater social participation and a more active lifestyle (Croucher, Hicks, & Jackson, 2006; Jenkins, Pienta, & Horgas, 2002). And in societies where old age leads to reduced status, age-segregated living is gratifying to most who choose it. It may open up useful roles and leadership opportunities. The more older adults perceive the environment as socially supportive, the more they collaborate with one another in coping with stressors of aging and in providing assistance to other residents (Lawrence & Schigelone, 2002). Residential communities appear to be well-suited to promoting mutually supportive relationships.

Nevertheless, no U.S. federal regulations govern assisted-living facilities, which vary widely in quality. Low-income ethnic minority aging adults are less likely to use assisted living. When older people with limited financial resources do transition to assisted living, they usually lack control over when and where they move and enter lower-quality settings—conditions associated with high stress. Nearly 42 percent of residents in assisted-living facilities report having experienced an unmet need during the past month, mostly related to self-care but also to getting around inside and getting outside (Ball et al., 2009; Freedman & Spillman, 2014). And in some states, assisted-living facilities are prohibited from providing any nursing care and medical monitoring, requiring residents to leave when their health declines (National Center for Assisted Living, 2013).

Yet physical designs and support services that enable aging in place are vital for older adults' well-being. These include homelike surroundings, division of large environments into smaller units to facilitate meaningful activities, social roles and relationships, and the latest assistive technologies to permit adaptation to changing health needs (Oswald & Wahl, 2013).

Shared values and goals among residents with similar backgrounds also enhance life satisfaction. Older adults who feel socially integrated into the setting are more likely to consider it their home. But those who lack like-minded companions are unlikely to characterize it as home and are at high risk for loneliness and depression (Adams, Sanders, & Auth, 2004; Cutchin, 2013).

Nursing Homes. About 3 percent of Americans age 65 and older live in nursing homes, nearly half of whom are 85 and older (Bern-Klug & Manthai, 2016). They experience the most extreme restriction of autonomy and social integration. Although potential companions are abundant, interaction is low. To regulate emotion in social interaction (so important to aging adults), personal control over social experiences is vital. Yet nursing home residents have little opportunity to choose their social partners, and timing of contact is generally determined by staff rather than by residents' preferences. Social withdrawal is an adaptive response to these often overcrowded, hospital-like settings, which typically provide few ways for residents to use their competencies. Although interaction with people in the outside world predicts nursing home residents' life satisfaction, interaction within the institution does not (Baltes, Wahl, & Reichert, 1992). Not surprisingly, nursing home residents with physical but not mental impairments are far more depressed, anxious, and lonely than their community-dwelling counterparts (Guildner et al., 2001).

Designing more homelike nursing homes could help increase residents' sense of security and control. U.S. nursing homes, usually operated for profit, are often packed with residents and institutional in their operation. In contrast, European facilities are liberally supported by public funds and resemble high-quality assisted living.

In a radically changed U.S. nursing home concept called THE GREEN HOUSE® model, a large, outdated nursing home in Mississippi was replaced by 10 small, self-contained houses (Rabig et al., 2006). Each is limited to 10 or fewer residents, who live in private bedroom–bathroom suites that surround a family-style communal space. Besides providing personal care, a stable staff of nursing assistants fosters aging adults' control and independence. Residents determine their own daily schedules and are invited to join in both recreational and household activities, including planning and preparing meals, cleaning, gardening, and caring for pets. A professional support team—including

CHAPTER 18 Emotional and Social Development in Late Adulthood 625

THE GREEN HOUSE® model blurs distinctions among nursing home, assisted living, and "independent" living. In this homelike setting, residents determine their own daily schedules and help with household tasks. Green House living environments now exist in more than 30 U.S. states.

licensed nurses, therapists, social workers, physicians, and pharmacists—visits regularly to serve residents' health needs. In comparisons of Green House residents with traditional nursing home residents, Green House older adults reported substantially better quality of life, and they also showed less decline over time in ability to carry out activities of daily living (Kane et al., 2007).

The Green House model—and other models like it—is blurring distinctions among nursing home, assisted living, and "independent" living. By making the home a central, organizing principle, the Green House approach includes all the aging-in-place and effective person–environment fit features that ensure late-life well-being: physical and emotional comfort, enjoyable daily pursuits enabling residents to maximize use of their capacities, and meaningful social relationships.

Ask yourself

CONNECT According to socioemotional selectivity theory, when time is limited, adults focus on the emotional quality of their social relationships. How do older people apply their emotional expertise (discussed on page 621) to attain this goal?

APPLY Sam lives alone in the same home he has occupied for over 30 years. His adult children cannot understand why he won't move across town to a modern apartment. Using continuity theory, explain why Sam prefers to stay where he is.

REFLECT Imagine yourself as a resident in an assisted-living facility. List all the features you would want your living context to have, explaining how each helps ensure effective person–environment fit and favorable psychological well-being.

 ## Relationships in Late Adulthood

18.7 Describe changes in relationships in late adulthood, including marriage, lesbian and gay partnerships, divorce, remarriage, and widowhood, and discuss never-married, childless older adults.

18.8 How do sibling relationships and friendships change in late life?

18.9 Describe older adults' relationships with adult children and adult grandchildren.

18.10 Discuss elder maltreatment, including risk factors, consequences, and prevention strategies.

The **social convoy** is an influential model of changes in our social networks as we move through life. Picture yourself in the midst of a cluster of ships traveling together, granting one another safety and support. Ships in the inner circle represent people closest to you, such as a spouse, best friend, parent, or child. Those less close, but still important, travel on the outside. With age, ships exchange places in the convoy, and some drift off while others join the procession (Antonucci, Birditt, & Ajrouch, 2011; Antonucci, Birditt, & Akiyama, 2009). As long as the convoy continues to exist, you adapt positively.

In the following sections, we examine the ways older adults with diverse lifestyles sustain social networks of family members and friends. As ties are lost, older adults draw others closer, and most cultivate new network members, though not at the rate they did at younger ages (Cornwell & Laumann, 2015). Although size of the convoy decreases as agemates die, aging adults are rarely left without people in their inner circle who contribute to their well-being—a testament to their resilience in maintaining effective social networks (Fiori, Smith, & Antonucci, 2007). But for some, tragically, the social convoy breaks down. We will also explore the circumstances in which older people experience abuse and neglect at the hands of those close to them.

Marriage

It has long been believed, on the basis of cross-sectional research, that marital satisfaction rises from middle to late adulthood. Longitudinal evidence, however, reveals that this seeming upturn in marital happiness is due to a cohort effect (Proulx, 2016; VanLaningham, Johnson, & Amato, 2001). Walt's comment to Ruth that "the last few decades have been the happiest" may have resulted in part from the time period in which they married—the 1950s. By the 1980s, an array of societal changes presented substantial challenges to marital contentment: a rise in U.S. families experiencing financial hardship, increased role overload as more married women moved into the work force, greater disagreement over gender-role expectations related to marital roles, and more individualistic attitudes toward marriage (see Chapters 14 and 16).

As in early and middle adulthood, paths of late-life marital satisfaction are diverse (Proulx, 2016). In one study, 700 people who remained continuously married were first interviewed in 1980 and then reinterviewed periodically over the next two decades, enabling researchers to track satisfaction in marriages that had endured for as long as 40 to 50 years. As Figure 18.2 reveals, participants fell into five patterns: two high and stable, one lower and stable, one declining followed by a rise in late life, and one declining steadily from early into late adulthood (Anderson, Van Ryzin, & Doherty, 2010). Reported marital problems and time spent in shared activities tended to parallel these paths. In addition, the steadily declining pattern had the highest percentage of individuals with financial difficulties.

Notice in Figure 18.2 that two-thirds of the participants maintained stable, happy marriages throughout adulthood. Also, lower marital quality reversed in late adulthood only for individuals who early on had experienced a rewarding marriage. Perhaps the memory of former happier times created a goal for older couples to strive for once stressful responsibilities, such as rearing children and balancing the demands of career and family, had diminished.

How do the majority of aging adults maintain highly satisfying marriages? Greater emphasis on regulating emotion in relationships may lead to more positive interactions between spouses. Aging couples, compared to younger couples, resolve their differences in more constructive ways (Hatch & Bulcroft, 2004). Even in poor-quality marriages, older adults attempt to prevent disagreements from escalating into expressions of anger and resentment (Hatch & Bulcroft, 2004). For example, when Dick complained about Goldie's cooking, Goldie tried to appease him: "All right, Dick, next birthday I won't make cheesecake." And when Goldie brought up Dick's bickering and criticism, Dick usually said, "I know, dear," and retreated to another room. As in other relationships, older people try to protect themselves from stress by molding marital ties to make them as pleasant as possible.

Aging married couples do admit to times their partner gets on their nerves or makes too many demands—more so than they say their adult children or best friends do (Birditt, Jackey, & Antonucci, 2009). But these expressions are usually mild, and they likely result from frequent contact, yielding greater opportunity for minor annoyances.

Finally, compared to their single agemates, married older people generally have larger social networks of both family members and friends, with whom they interact more frequently. As long as aging adults report mostly high-quality ties, this relationship profile provides for social engagement and support from a variety of sources and is linked to higher psychological well-being (Birditt & Antonucci, 2007). These benefits, combined with a long history of caring concern from an intimate partner, may explain the strengthening association of marriage with good health in late adulthood (Holt-Lunstad, Smith, & Layton, 2010; Yorgason & Stott, 2016). Late-life marriage is linked to lower rates of chronic illness and disability and increased longevity.

When marital dissatisfaction exists, however, even having close, high-quality friendships cannot reduce its profoundly negative impact on well-being. A poor marriage often takes a greater toll on women than on men (Birditt & Antonucci, 2007; Boerner et al., 2014). Recall from Chapter 14 that women more often try to work on a troubling relationship, yet in late life, expending energy in this way is especially taxing, both physically and mentally. Men, in contrast, are more likely to protect themselves by withdrawing and avoiding discussion.

Lesbian and Gay Couples

Older lesbians and gay men in long-term partnerships have sustained their relationships through a historical period of hostility and discrimination, finally gaining the right to marry in the United States in 2015. Nevertheless, most report happy, highly fulfilling relationships, pointing to their partner as their most important source of social support. Like their heterosexual counterparts, sexual minority older couples rate their physical and mental health more favorably than do their single lesbian and gay agemates (Williams & Fredriksen-Goldsen, 2014).

A lifetime of effective coping with an oppressive social environment may have strengthened lesbian and gay couples' skills at managing late-life physical and cognitive changes, thereby contributing to relationship satisfaction (Gabbay & Wahler, 2002). And changing social conditions, including the ease with which younger generations are embracing their sexual minority identities and "coming out," may have encouraged more older adults to do the same. Compared with same-sex couples not in a legally recognized relationship, those who are married are advantaged in physical and psychological well-being (Wight, LeBlanc, & Lee Badget, 2013). Their more favorable mental health is equivalent to that of older couples in long-term heterosexual marriages.

Because of strain in family relationships when they told others about their sexual orientation, lesbian and gay older adults

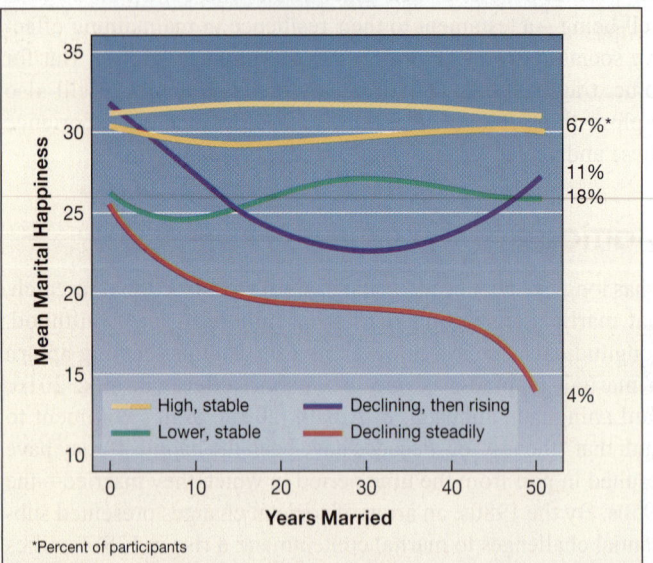

FIGURE 18.2 Paths of marital happiness. In a study of 700 continuously married people followed over two decades, participants displayed five patterns. Two thirds maintained high and stable marital satisfaction, whereas less than one-fifth displayed lower and stable satisfaction. A small minority showed a low, steadily declining pattern. Marital quality improved in late adulthood only for those who had experienced a happy marriage early on. (From J. R. Anderson, M. J. Van Ryzin, & W. J. Doherty, 2010, "Developmental Trajectories of Marital Happiness in Continuously Married Individuals: A Group-Based Modeling Approach," *Developmental Psychology, 5*, p. 591. Copyright ©2010 by the American Psychological Association. Adapted by permission.)

CHAPTER 18 Emotional and Social Development in Late Adulthood

The majority of aging adults in marriages and long-term partnerships, including same-sex couples, maintain highly satisfying relationships, which are associated with good health and increased longevity.

less often assumed during the course of their lives that family members would provide support in old age. Consequently, many have forged strong friendships to replace or supplement family ties (Richard & Brown, 2006). Sexual minority couples with gratifying friendship networks report high life satisfaction and reduced fear of aging (Slusher, Mayer, & Dunkle, 1996).

Nevertheless, because of continuing prejudice, aging lesbians and gay men face unique challenges. Health-care systems are often unresponsive to their unique needs. And those caring for a partner in poor health may be less likely to seek help from community agencies offering formal support services because of real or perceived discrimination (Zdaniuk & Smith, 2016). These circumstances can make late-life declines and losses especially stressful.

Divorce, Remarriage, and Cohabitation

When Walt's uncle Louie was 65, he divorced his wife Sandra after 32 years of marriage. Although she knew the marriage was far from perfect, Sandra had lived with Louie long enough that the divorce came as a shock. A year later, Louie married Rachella, a divorcée who shared his enthusiasm for sports and dance.

Couples who divorce in late adulthood constitute less than 5 percent of all U.S. divorces in any given year. But divorce among people age 65 and older has quadrupled over the past three decades, currently affecting 13 percent of women and 11 percent of men (Mather, Jacobsen, & Pollard, 2015). New generations of older adults—especially the baby boomers—have become more accepting of late-life marital breakup as a means of attaining self-fulfillment and as the divorce risk increased for second and subsequent marriages.

Although one-fifth of older adults' dissolving marriages are of less than 10 years duration, about half are lengthy—30 years or more (Brown & Lin, 2012). Compared with younger adults, longtime married older people

have given their adult lives to the relationship. Following divorce, they find it harder to separate their identity from that of their former spouse and, therefore, may experience a greater sense of personal failure. Relationships with family and friends shift at a time when close bonds are crucial for psychological well-being.

As in middle adulthood, aging women are more likely than men to initiate divorce. This is despite the fact that the financial consequences for women generally are severe—greater than for widowhood because many accumulated assets are lost in property settlements (Sharma, 2015). Still, older people of both genders seldom express regret over leaving an unhappy marriage (Bair, 2007). Usually, they experience a sense of relief.

An estimated 14 percent of U.S. older adults, more men than women, are in a dating relationship, though dating declines with age (Brown & Shinohara, 2013). Aging baby boomers—accustomed to using the Internet for many purposes—are turning to online dating services and personal ads to search for new partners, though they use dating sites far less often than younger people do (Pew Research Center, 2013b). Older adults' personal ads indicate that they are more selective with respect to the age, race, religion, and income of a potential dating partner (McIntosh et al., 2011). And as Figure 18.3 shows, they more often refer to their own health issues and loneliness and less often to romance, sex, desire for a soulmate, and adventure than middle-aged people do (Alterovitz & Mendelsohn, 2013). In their search for the right person, they seem to take a candid, no-nonsense approach!

Remarriage rates are low in late adulthood, though widowed older adults remarry at a higher rate than divorcees (Brown, Bulanda, & Lee, 2012). Men more often succeed in finding a partner than women, as their opportunities to do so are far greater. Nevertheless, increasing age makes remarriage less

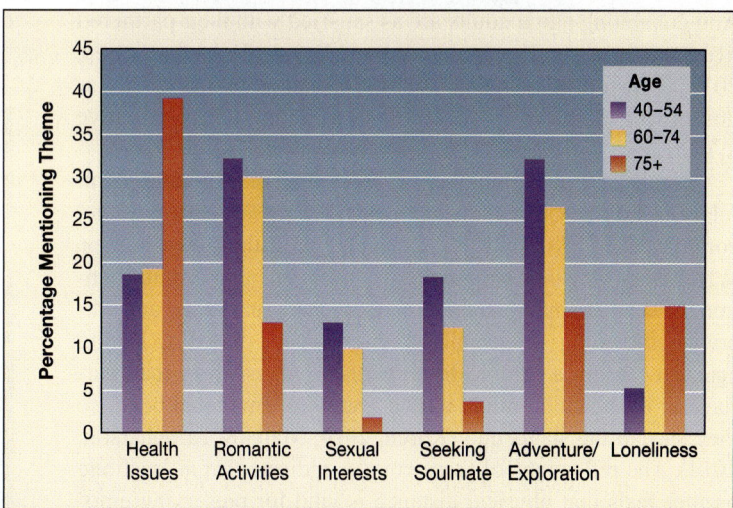

FIGURE 18.3 Themes in online personal ads of middle-aged and older adults seeking dating partners. An analysis of themes in 450 ads revealed that older adults more often mention health issues and loneliness, whereas middle-aged adults place greater emphasis on romance, sex, finding a soulmate, and adventure. Older adults appear to be practical and direct in their search for a partner. (From S. S. R. Alterovitz and G. A. Mendelsohn, 2013, "Relationship Goals of Middle-Aged, Young–Old, and Old–Old Internet Daters: An Analysis of Online Personal Ads," *Journal of Aging Studies, 27*, p. 163. Copyright © 2013, Elsevier. Reprinted by permission of Elsevier, Inc.)

likely for both men and women, who frequently say they don't want to marry again (Mahay & Lewin, 2007). Common reasons include poorer health, a shortened future (making it hard to justify radical life change), concerns about adult children's acceptance of the new partner, desire to protect assets they have accumulated over their lifetime, and (especially for women) apprehension over the caregiving burden marriage might bring (Wu & Schimmele, 2007). Divorced men who remain single, however, no longer benefit from their former wives' kinkeeping role, are more likely to experience reduced contact and support from adult children, and more often move away from friends and neighbors (Daatland, 2007). For these reasons, they are at greater risk for adjustment difficulties.

Compared with younger people who remarry, older adults who do so enter more stable relationships, as their divorce rate is much lower. In Louie and Rachella's case, the second marriage lasted for 28 years! Perhaps late-life remarriages are more successful because they involve more maturity, patience, and a better balance of romantic with practical concerns. Good health and financial stability also contribute: Healthy, economically advantaged older people are more likely to repartner than those in declining health or experiencing financial strains (Brown, Bulanda, & Lee, 2012; Vespa, 2012). Remarried older couples are generally very satisfied with their new relationships, although men tend to be more content than women (Connidis, 2010). With fewer potential mates, perhaps women who remarry in late life settle for less desirable partners.

Rather than remarrying, older people who enter a new relationship are increasingly choosing cohabitation, a trend expected to continue as more baby boomers—the first generation to cohabit at high rates in early adulthood—reach late life. Like remarriage, cohabitation results in more stable relationships and higher relationship quality than it did at younger ages. And cohabiting aging adults are as satisfied with their partnered lives as are their married counterparts (Brown, Bulanda, & Lee, 2012; Brown & Kawamura, 2010). This suggests that cohabitation in late adulthood typically serves as a long-term alternative to marriage.

Finally, a growing number of repartnered older couples form relationships described as *living apart together*—an intimate, committed tie involving living separately, in their own homes. When asked why they choose this arrangement, aging adults mention the desire to maintain their independence, financially and otherwise, including—especially among women—avoiding having again to care for a chronically ill partner. Others worry that marriage or cohabitation might alter a gratifying emotional bond, so they sustain the status quo (Koren, 2014; Malta & Farquharson, 2014). The reflections of these couples indicate that at least one partner feels that physical distance is vital for preserving emotional closeness.

Widowhood

Walt died shortly after Ruth turned 80. Ruth, like the majority of widowed aging adults, described the loss of her spouse as the most stressful event of her life. Being widowed means losing "the role and identity of being a spouse" (being married and doing things as a couple), which is "potentially one of the most pervasive, intense, intimate, and personal roles" in life (Lund & Caserta, 2004, p. 29). Ruth felt lonely, anxious, and depressed for several months after the funeral.

Because women live longer than men and are less likely to remarry, 34 percent of U.S. women age 65 and older are widowed, compared with just 12 percent of men. At the same time, widowhood rates have declined over the past several decades as divorce among aging adults rose (Mather, Jacobsen, & Pollard, 2015). Ethnic minorities with high rates of poverty and chronic disease are more likely to be widowed.

Earlier we mentioned that most widows and widowers live alone rather than in extended families, a trend that is stronger for whites than for ethnic minorities. Though less well-off financially than married aging adults, most want to retain control over their time and living space and to avoid disagreements with their adult children. Widowed older people who relocate usually move closer to family but not into the same residence.

The greatest problem for recently widowed older people is profound loneliness (Connidis, 2010). But adaptation varies widely. Aging adults have fewer lasting problems than younger individuals who are widowed, probably because death in later life is viewed as less unfair (Bennett & Soulsby, 2012). And most widowed older people—especially those with outgoing personalities and high self-esteem—are resilient in the face of loneliness (Moore & Stratton, 2002; van Baarsen, 2002). To sustain continuity with their past, they try to preserve social relationships that were important before the spouse's death. Social support is vital for favorable adjustment: Greater ease of contact with family and friends, and satisfaction with the support they provide, are associated with a reduction in symptoms of grief and depression and higher sense of self-efficacy in handling tasks of daily living (de Vries et al., 2014).

Men are less prepared than women for the challenges of widowhood, in part because most relied on their wives for household tasks. This widower has learned to cook—a skill likely to help him connect socially and adapt favorably to his dramatically changed life circumstances.

Applying what we Know

Fostering Adaptation to Widowhood in Late Adulthood

SUGGESTION	DESCRIPTION
Self Mastery of new skills of daily living	Especially for men, learning how to perform household tasks such as shopping and cooking, to sustain existing family and friendship ties, and to build new relationships is vital for positive adaptation.
Family and Friends Social support and interaction	Social support and interaction must extend beyond the grieving period to ongoing assistance and caring relationships. Family members and friends can help most by making support available while encouraging the widowed older adult to use effective coping strategies.
Community Senior centers	Senior centers offer communal meals and other social activities, enabling widowed and other older adults to connect with people in similar circumstances and to gain access to other community resources.
Support groups	Support groups can be found in senior centers, religious institutions, and other agencies. Besides new relationships, they offer an accepting atmosphere for coming to terms with loss, effective role models, and assistance with developing skills for daily living.
Religious activities	Involvement in a religious institution can help relieve the loneliness associated with loss of a spouse and offer social support, new relationships, and meaningful roles.
Volunteer activities	One of the best ways for widowed older adults to find meaningful roles is through volunteer activities. Some are sponsored by formal service organizations, such as the Red Cross or the U.S. Senior Corps. Other volunteer programs exist in hospitals, senior centers, schools, and charitable organizations.

Widowed individuals must reorganize their lives, reconstructing an identity that is separate from the deceased spouse. Wives who depended on their husbands for home maintenance and financial decision making typically find this harder than those who were not dependent (Carr et al., 2000). But overall, men show more physical and mental health problems and greater risk of mortality than women, especially when the death was unexpected (Shor et al., 2012; Sullivan & Fenelon, 2014). First, because most men relied on their wives for social connectedness, household tasks, promotion of healthy behaviors, and coping with stressors, they are less prepared than women for the challenges of widowhood. A wife's sudden death heightens this unpreparedness. Second, gender-role expectations lead men to feel less free to express their emotions or to ask for help with meals, housework, and social relationships (Bennett, 2007). Finally, men tend to be less involved in religious activities—a vital source of social support and inner strength.

African-American widowers, however, show no elevated risk of mortality over their married agemates, and they report less depression than European-American widowers (Elwert & Christakis, 2006). Perhaps greater support from extended family and religious community is responsible.

Gender differences in the experience of widowhood contribute to men's higher remarriage rate. Women's kinkeeper role (see Chapter 16, page 552) and ability to form close friendships may lead them to feel less need to remarry. In addition, because many women share the widowed state, they probably offer one another helpful advice and sympathy. In contrast, men often lack skills for maintaining family relationships, forming emotionally satisfying ties outside marriage, and handling the chores of their deceased wives.

Still, most widowed older adults fare well within a few years, resembling their married counterparts in psychological well-being. Older widows and widowers who participated in several months of weekly classes providing information and support in acquiring daily living skills felt better prepared to manage the challenges of widowed life (Caserta, Lund, & Obray, 2004). Those who emerge from this traumatic event with a sense of purpose in life and with confidence in their ability to meet everyday challenges often experience stress-related personal growth (Caserta et al., 2009). Many report a newfound sense of inner strength, greater appreciation of close relationships, and reevaluation of life priorities. Applying What We Know above suggests a variety of ways to foster adaptation to widowhood in late adulthood.

Never-Married, Childless Older Adults

About 5 percent of older Americans have remained unmarried and childless throughout their lives (Mather, Jacobsen, & Pollard, 2015). Almost all are conscious of being different from the norm, but most have developed alternative meaningful relationships. Ruth's sister Ida, for example, formed a strong bond with a neighbor's son. In his childhood, she provided emotional support and financial assistance, which helped him overcome a stressful home life. He included Ida in family events and visited her regularly until she died. Other nonmarried aging adults speak of the centrality of extended family and of younger people in their social networks—often nieces and nephews—and of

As part of a community service project, an older adult collaborates with her nephew in planting flowers at a local park. Never-married, childless older people, especially women, typically lead socially satisfying lives.

influencing them in enduring ways (Wenger, 2009). In addition, same-sex friendships are key in never-married older women's lives (McDill, Hall, & Turell, 2006). These tend to be unusually close and often involve joint travel, periods of coresidence, and associations with each other's extended families.

Never-married, childless men, who are fewer in number than never-married, childless women, are at increased risk for loneliness and depression. And without pressure from a partner to maintain a healthy lifestyle, these men engage in more unhealthy behaviors. Hence, their physical and mental health tends to be less favorable than their married counterparts' (Kendig et al., 2007). But overall, never-married older people report a level of social connectedness and psychological well-being equivalent to that of married aging adults (Hank & Wagner, 2013). These findings hold across various cohorts and Western nations.

Because friendships are not the same as blood ties when it comes to caregiving, being unmarried and childless in very old age reduces the likelihood of informal personal care (Chang, Wilber, & Silverstein, 2010; Wenger, 2009). And with close ties weighted toward friends, nonmarried childless individuals lose more network members with increasing age (Dykstra, 2006). Still, most say that some informal support is available.

Siblings

The majority of Americans age 65 and older have at least one living sibling. Typically, aging siblings live within 100 miles of each other, communicate regularly, and visit at least several times a year. Both men and women describe closer bonds with sisters than with brothers. Perhaps because of women's greater emotional expressiveness and nurturance, the closer the tie to a sister, the higher older people's psychological well-being (Van Volkom, 2006).

Aging siblings in industrialized nations are more likely to socialize than to provide each other with direct assistance because most older adults turn first to their spouse and children. Nevertheless, siblings seem to be an important "insurance policy" in late adulthood. After age 70, exchanges of support rise between siblings with a warm relationship (Bedford & Avioli, 2016). Widowed and never-married older people have more contacts with siblings, perhaps because of fewer competing family relationships, and they also are more likely to receive sibling support when their health declines (Connidis, 2010). For example, when Ida's Alzheimer's symptoms worsened, Ruth came to her aid. Although Ida had many friends, Ruth was her only living relative.

Friendships

As family responsibilities and vocational pressures lessen, friendships take on increasing importance. Having friends is an especially strong predictor of positive emotion and life satisfaction in late adulthood. Older adults report more favorable experiences with friends than with family members, in part because of the pleasurable leisure activities shared with friends (Huxhold, Miche, & Schüz, 2014; Rawlins, 2004). Unique qualities of friendship interaction—openness, spontaneity, mutual caring, and common interests—are also influential.

Functions of Late-Life Friendships.
The diverse functions of friendship in late adulthood clarify its profound significance:

- *Intimacy and companionship are basic to meaningful late-life friendships.* As Ida and her best friend, Rosie, took walks, went shopping, or visited each other, they disclosed their deepest sources of happiness and worry, engaged in enjoyable conversation, laughed, and had fun. Older adults' descriptions of their close friendships reveal that mutual interests, feelings of belongingness, and opportunities to confide in each other sustain these bonds over time (Field, 1999).

- *Late-life friends help shield each other from negative judgments stemming from stereotypes of aging.* "Where's your cane, Rosie?" Ida asked when the two women were about to leave for a restaurant. "Come on, don't be self-conscious!" Ida reminded Rosie that in the Greek village where her mother grew up, there was no separation between generations, so young people got used to wrinkled skin and weak knees. In fact, older women—as midwives, matchmakers, and experts in herbal medicine, for example—were regarded as the wise ones (Deveson, 1994).

- *Friendships link aging adults to the larger community.* For those unable to go out as often, interactions with friends can keep them abreast of events in the wider world. "Rosie," Ida reported, "did you know there's going to be a new branch of the public library in the train station, and the city council is voting on the living-wage act tonight?" Friends can also open up new experiences, such as travel or participation in community activities.

- *Friendships help protect older adults from the psychological consequences of loss.* Older people in declining health who remain in contact with friends through phone calls and visits show improved psychological well-being (Fiori, Smith, & Antonucci, 2007). Similarly, when close relatives die, friends offer compensating social supports.

Characteristics of Late-Life Friendships. Although friendship formation continues throughout life, aging adults prefer familiar, established relationships over new ones. Ties to old and dear friends who live far away are maintained, with growing numbers of older people staying in touch with the aid of e-mail and social media sites, such as Facebook (see page 605 in Chapter 17). With age, the friends they interact with most and feel closest to live in the same community. Similarly, Facebook social networks narrow, containing a greater percentage of individuals considered to be actual friends—people with whom aging adults have a stronger offline connection (Chang et al., 2015). These changes are consistent with socioemotional selectivity theory.

As in earlier years, older people tend to choose friends whose age, sex, ethnicity, and values resemble their own. Compared with younger people, fewer report other-sex friendships. But some have them—usually long-standing ones dating back several decades. Aging adults continue to benefit uniquely from these ties, obtaining an insider's view of the thoughts, feelings, and behavior of members of the other sex (Monsour, 2002). As agemates die, the very old report more intergenerational friends—both same- and other-sex (Johnson & Troll, 1994). In her eighties, Ruth spent time with Margaret, a 55-year-old widow she met while serving on the board of an adoption agency. Two or three times a month, Margaret came to Ruth's home for tea and lively conversation.

Gender differences in friendship extend into late adulthood. Women are more likely to have intimate friends; men depend on their wives and, to a lesser extent, their sisters for warm, open communication (Waite & Das, 2013). Also, older women have more **secondary friends**—people who are not intimates but with whom they spend time occasionally, such as a group that meets for lunch, bridge, or museum tours (Blieszner & Roberto, 2012). Through these associates, older adults meet new people, remain socially involved, and gain in psychological well-being.

On a village street in Cyprus, these older adults meet often to play backgammon. Spending time with friends they know well who live in the same community is especially gratifying.

In late-life friendships, affection and emotional support are both given and received to maintain balance in the relationship. Although friends call on each other for help with tasks of daily living, they generally do so only in emergencies or for occasional, limited assistance. Aging adults with physical limitations whose social networks consist mainly of friends and who therefore must frequently rely on them for help tend to report low psychological well-being (Fiori, Smith, & Antonucci, 2007). Feelings of excessive dependency and of being unable to reciprocate are probably responsible.

Relationships with Adult Children

About 80 percent of older adults in Western nations are parents of living children, most of whom are middle-aged. In Chapter 16, we noted that exchanges of help vary with the closeness of the parent–child bond and the needs of the parent and adult child. Recall, also, that over time, parent-to-child help declines, whereas child-to-parent assistance increases.

Aging adults and their adult children are often in touch, even when they live at a distance. But as with other ties, quality rather than quantity of interaction affects older parents' life satisfaction. In diverse ethnic groups and cultures, warm bonds with adult children reduce the negative impact of physical impairments and other losses (such as death of a spouse) on psychological well-being. And adult children who live nearby and therefore have more face-to-face contact can add substantially to the life satisfaction of aging adults, especially those living alone (Ajrouch, 2007; Milkie, Bierman, & Schieman, 2008; van der Pers, Mulder, & Steverink, 2015). Alternatively, conflict or unhappiness with adult children contributes to poor physical and mental health.

Although aging parents and adult children in Western nations provide each other with various forms of help, level of assistance is typically modest. Older adults in their sixties and seventies—especially those who own their own home and who are married or widowed as opposed to divorced—are more likely to be providers than recipients of help, suggesting SES variations in the balance of support (Grundy, 2005). This balance shifts as older adults age, but well into late adulthood, individuals in Western nations give more than they receive, especially in financial support but also in practical assistance—a circumstance that contradicts stereotypes of older adults as "burdens" on younger generations.

Interviews with parents age 75 and older in five Western nations revealed that in all countries, aid received from adult children most often took the form of emotional support. Fewer than one-third said their children assisted with household chores and errands. Aging parents who provided more help of various kinds than they received scored highest in life satisfaction, those receiving more help than they gave scored lowest, while those in a balanced exchange fell in between (Lowenstein, Katz, & Gur-Yaish, 2007). To avoid dependency, older people usually do not seek children's practical assistance in the absence of a pressing need, and they express annoyance when children are overprotective or help unnecessarily (Spitze & Gallant, 2004). Moderate support, with many opportunities to reciprocate, is beneficial, fostering self-esteem and sense of family connection.

Gender differences in older parent–adult child interaction are evident. Both mothers and fathers feel ambivalent toward adult offspring with problematic lives—who are financially needy, emotionally troubled, or experiencing marital problems. But mothers are more likely to have adult children who feel similarly ambivalent toward them (Fingerman et al., 2006). Perhaps mothers more often express their mixed feelings.

Cultural expectations can also engender ambivalence. For example, because their high valuing of interdependence among generations meets with challenges in the new society, Cambodian aging immigrants to the United States frequently report ambivalent feelings toward their adult children (Lewis, 2008). And in rural China, where the expectation that sons provide care for their aging parents remains strong, parents harbor more ambivalence toward their rural-residing sons than daughters. Rural sons' greater contact with and support of parents offer myriad opportunities for not living up to expectations! When sons of rural parents move to urban areas, parental ambivalence declines (Guo, Chi, & Silverstein, 2013). Urban residence is associated with more prestigious and secure jobs, perhaps fulfilling rural parents' higher expectations for sons' success and, thus, overcoming shortcomings in providing care.

Feelings of ambivalence undermine the psychological well-being of both adult children and their aging parents (Fingerman et al., 2008). But aging parents' ambivalence toward children is typically mild. Consistent with socioemotional selectivity theory, older parents do their best to accentuate positive emotion.

As social networks shrink in size, relationships with adult children become more important sources of family involvement. People 85 years and older with children have substantially more contacts with relatives than do those without children (Hooyman, Kawamoto, & Kiyak, 2015). Why is this so? Consider Ruth, whose daughter Sybil linked her to grandchildren, great-grandchildren, and relatives by marriage. When childless adults reach their eighties, siblings, other same-age relatives, and close friends may have become frail or died and hence may no longer be available as companions.

Relationships with Adult Grandchildren

Older people with adult grandchildren and great-grandchildren benefit from a wider potential network of support. Ruth and Walt saw their granddaughter, Marci, and their great-grandson, Jamel, at family gatherings. In between, they occasionally Skyped and regularly used Facebook to keep up with Marci and Jamel's activities. Staying in touch with grandchildren and other family members is the primary reason aging adults say they use social media sites (Zickuhr & Madden, 2012).

In developed nations, slightly more than half of adults over age 65 have a grandchild who is at least 18 years old. In the few studies available on grandparent–adult grandchild relationships, the overwhelming majority of grandchildren say their grandparents positively influenced their values and behavior, and most also expressed an obligation to assist grandparents in need (Even-Zohar, 2011; Fruhauf, Jarrott, & Allen, 2006). Grandparents expect affection (but not practical help) from grandchildren, and

A bride and groom take time to express their affection for the bride's grandmother on their wedding day. Grandparents view adult grandchildren as a vital link between themselves and the future.

they usually receive it. They regard the adult grandchild tie as very gratifying—a vital link between themselves and the future.

Still, grandparent–adult grandchild relationships vary greatly. Degree of grandparent involvement during childhood strongly predicts current relationship quality. Often, the tie with one grandchild is "special," characterized by more frequent contact, affection, and enjoyable times together—factors that enhance older adults' psychological well-being (Mahne & Huxhold, 2015). Relationships with grandmothers tend to be closer, with maternal grandmother–granddaughter bonds the closest, as was so when grandchildren were younger (Sheehan & Petrovic, 2008). However, as grandparents and grandchildren move through life, contact declines. Many grandchildren establish distant homes and become immersed in work, family, and friendship roles that compete for their time.

LOOK and LISTEN

Interview one or two older people with adult grandchildren about the quality and personal meaning of those relationships.

But despite less contact, grandparents' affection for their adult grandchildren strengthens with age, usually exceeding grandchildren's expressed closeness toward their grandparents (which is still strong) (Harwood, 2001). This difference in emotional investment reflects each generation's needs and goals—adult grandchildren in establishing independent lives, grandparents in preserving family relationships and continuity of values across generations. Grandchildren become increasingly important sources of emotional meaning in the last decade or two of life.

Elder Maltreatment

Although the majority of older adults enjoy positive relationships with family members, friends, and professional caregivers, some suffer maltreatment at the hands of these individuals. Through media attention, elder maltreatment has become a serious public concern.

Reports from many industrialized nations reveal widely varying rates of maltreatment, from 3 to 28 percent in general population studies. At least 10 percent of U.S. older adults say they were targets during the past year, amounting to over 4 million victims. Elder maltreatment occurs at similar rates across U.S. ethnic groups (Hernandez-Tejada et al., 2013; Roberto, 2016b). All figures are substantial underestimates because most abusive acts take place in private, and victims are often unable or unwilling to complain.

Elder maltreatment usually takes the following forms:

- *Physical abuse.* Intentional infliction of pain, discomfort, or injury, through hitting, cutting, burning, physical force, restraint, or other physically aggressive acts
- *Physical neglect.* Intentional or unintentional failure to fulfill caregiving obligations, resulting in lack of food, medication, or health services or in the older person being left alone or isolated
- *Emotional abuse.* Verbal assaults (such as name calling), humiliation (being treated as a child), and intimidation (threats of isolation or placement in a nursing home)
- *Sexual abuse.* Unwanted sexual contact of any kind
- *Financial abuse.* Illegal or improper exploitation of the aging person's property or financial resources, through theft or use without consent

Emotional abuse, financial abuse, and neglect are the most frequently reported types. Often several forms occur in combination (Kaplan & Pillemer, 2015). The perpetrator is usually a person the older adult trusts and depends on for care and assistance.

Most abusers are family members—spouses (more often men), children of both sexes, and other relatives. Others are friends, neighbors, and people whom aging adults rely on for help and services, such as in-home caregivers and investment counselors (Roberto, 2016a). Abuse in nursing homes is a major concern: From 6 to 40 percent of caregivers admit to having committed at least one act in the previous year (Schiamberg et al., 2011).

Frail aging adults are at high risk for elder maltreatment. Regular home visitors like this nurse can relieve social isolation and help older people take steps to avoid further harm.

Over the past several decades, another form of neglect—referred to in the media as "granny dumping"—has risen: abandonment of older adults with severe disabilities by family caregivers, usually at hospital emergency rooms (Phelan, 2013). Overwhelmed, their caregivers seem to have concluded that they have no other option but to take this drastic step. (See page 557 in Chapter 16 and pages 592–593 in Chapter 17 for related research.)

Risk Factors. Characteristics of the victim, the abuser, their relationship, and its social context are related to the incidence and severity of elder maltreatment. The more risk factors present, the greater the likelihood that abuse and neglect will occur.

Dependency of Victims. Very old, frail, and mentally and physically impaired older adults are more vulnerable to maltreatment, with as many as 25 percent affected (Dong et al., 2011; Selwood & Cooper, 2009). This does not mean that declines in functioning cause abuse. Rather, when other conditions are ripe for maltreatment, older people with severe disabilities are least able to protect themselves. Those with physical or cognitive impairments may also have personality traits that make them vulnerable—a tendency to lash out when angry or frustrated, a passive or avoidant approach to handling problems, and a low sense of self-efficacy (Salari, 2011). The more negative a caregiver–recipient relationship, the greater the risk of elder abuse of all kinds, particularly when that relationship has a long unfavorable history.

Dependency of Perpetrators. Within late-life parent–child relationships especially, abusers are often dependent, financially or emotionally, on their victims. This dependency, experienced as powerlessness, can lead to aggressive, exploitative behavior. Often the perpetrator–victim relationship is one of mutual dependency (Jackson & Hafemeister, 2012). The adult-child abuser needs the aging parent for money, housing, or emotional support, and the aging parent needs the abuser for assistance with everyday tasks or to relieve loneliness.

Psychological Disturbance and Other Traits of Perpetrators. Salient factors underlying the dependency of abusive adult children are mental illness and alcohol or other drug addictions (Jogerst et al., 2012). Often these perpetrators are socially isolated, have difficulties at work, or are unemployed, with resulting financial worries. These factors increase the likelihood that they will lash out when caregiving is highly demanding or the behavior of an older adult with dementia is irritating or hard to manage.

Abusers who are paid caregivers or professionals rendering other services are usually amiable but manipulative, on the lookout for opportunities to take advantage of older adults, especially those with cognitive declines (Lichtenberg, 2016). Perpetrators may overcharge, scam, or have access to financial accounts or valuables. When opportunities arise, they steal from the victim.

History of Family Violence. Elder abuse by family members is often part of a long history of family violence. Adults who were abused as children are at increased risk of abusing older adults

(Reay & Browne, 2008). In Chapter 8, we showed how aggressive cycles between family members can easily become self-sustaining, leading to the development of individuals who cope with anger through hostility toward others. In many instances, elder abuse is an extension of years of partner abuse (Walsh et al., 2007).

Institutional Conditions. Elder maltreatment is more likely to occur in nursing homes that are rundown and overcrowded and that have staff shortages, minimal staff supervision, high staff turnover, and few visitors (Schiamberg et al., 2011). Highly stressful work conditions combined with minimal oversight of caregiving quality set the stage for abuse and neglect.

Consequences of Elder Maltreatment.
All forms of elder maltreatment have profound, lasting consequences on victims' health and adjustment. Persisting anxiety, depression, post-traumatic stress symptoms, and heightened physical and cognitive impairments are common outcomes (Roberto, 2016a). Consequently, victims are at risk for premature institutionalization and shortened survival.

Financial exploitation deprives older Americans of an estimated three billion dollars annually (MetLife, 2011b). It may engender family disputes, reduced health-care options, and declining mental health.

Preventing Elder Maltreatment.
Preventing elder maltreatment by family members is especially challenging. Victims may fear retribution, wish to protect abusers who are spouses or adult children, or feel embarrassed that they cannot control the situation. And they may be intimidated into silence or not know where to turn for help (Roberto et al., 2015). Once abuse is discovered, intervention involves immediate protection and provision of unmet needs for the older adult and of mental health services and social support for the spouse or caregiver.

Prevention programs offer caregivers counseling, education, and respite services, such as day care and in-home help for aging adults. Trained volunteer "buddies" who make visits to the home can relieve social isolation and assist older people with problem solving to avoid further harm. Support groups help them identify abusive acts, practice appropriate responses, and form new relationships. And agencies that provide informal financial services to older people who are unable to manage on their own, such as writing and cashing checks and holding valuables in a safe, reduce financial abuse.

When elder abuse is extreme, legal action offers the best protection, yet it is rare. Many victims are reluctant to initiate court procedures or, because of mental impairments, cannot do so. In these instances, social service professionals must induce caregivers to rethink their role and assist in finding alternatives. In nursing homes, improving staff selection, training, and working conditions can greatly reduce abuse and neglect.

LOOK and LISTEN

Contact your state's department on aging. Find out about its policies and programs aimed at preventing elder abuse.

Combating elder maltreatment also requires efforts at the level of the larger society, including public education to encourage reporting of suspected cases and improved understanding of the needs of older people. As part of this effort, aging adults benefit from information on where to go for help (National Center on Elder Abuse, 2016). Finally, countering negative stereotypes of aging reduces maltreatment because recognizing older adults' dignity, individuality, and autonomy is incompatible with acts of physical and psychological harm.

Ask yourself

CONNECT Why is adjustment to late-life divorce usually more difficult for women and adjustment to widowhood more difficult for men?

APPLY At age 51, Mae lost her job, couldn't afford to pay rent, and moved in with her 78-year-old widowed mother, Beryl. Although Beryl welcomed Mae's companionship, Mae grew depressed, drank heavily, and stopped looking for work. When Beryl complained about Mae's behavior, Mae insulted and slapped her. Explain why this mother–daughter relationship led to elder abuse.

REFLECT If you have living grandparents, describe your relationship with one or more of them. How have you and your grandparent contributed to each other's development?

Retirement

18.11 Discuss the decision to retire, adjustment to retirement, and involvement in leisure and volunteer activities.

In Chapter 16, we noted that increased life expectancy led the period of retirement to lengthen over the twentieth century. In recent decades, however, age of retirement has risen in the United States and Western nations. The economic recession of 2007 to 2009 extended this trend, modestly raising the retirement age of the baby boomers (see page 563). Irrespective of financial need, however, the majority of baby boomers say they want to work longer, with one-third indicating that devoting some time to work is important for a happy retirement (Mather, Jacobsen, & Pollard, 2015). The distinction between work and retirement has blurred: Nearly 40 percent of U.S. adults age 65 to 69, and nearly 20 percent of those in their seventies, are still working in some capacity—rates anticipated to increase markedly over the next decade.

As these figures suggest, the contemporary retirement process is highly variable: It may include a planning period, the decision itself, diverse acts of retiring, and continuous adjustment and readjustment of activities for the rest of the life course. The majority of U.S. older adults with career jobs retire gradually by cutting down their hours and responsibilities. Many take *bridge jobs* (new part-time jobs or full-time jobs of shorter duration) that serve as transitions between full-time career and retirement (Rudolph & Toomey, 2016). About 15 percent leave their jobs but later return to paid work and even start new careers, desiring to introduce interest and challenge into their lives, to supplement limited financial resources, or both (Sterns & McQuown, 2015). Today, retirement is not a single event but rather a dynamic process with multiple transitions serving different purposes.

In the following sections, we examine factors that affect the decision to retire, happiness during the retirement years, and leisure and volunteer pursuits. We will see that the process of retirement and retired life reflect an increasingly diverse retired population.

The Decision to Retire

Walt and Ruth's retirement was preceded by extensive planning (see Chapter 16, pages 562–563), including a projected date for leaving the work force and financial preparation guaranteeing comfortable income-replacement benefits. In contrast, Walt's brother Dick was forced to retire as the operating costs of his bakery rose while his clientele declined. He looked for temporary employment in sales while his wife, Goldie, kept her part-time job as a bookkeeper to help cover living expenses.

Affordability of retirement is usually the first consideration in the decision to retire. Yet despite financial concerns, many preretirees decide to let go of a steady work life in favor of alternative, personally meaningful work, leisure, or volunteer activities. "I had been working since I was 10 years old," said one retired auto worker. "I wanted a rest." Exceptions to this positive outlook are people like Dick—forced into retirement or earning very low wages—who reluctantly take bridge jobs in another field to make ends meet. Bridge employment seems to have a favorable impact on psychological well-being only when people engage in work related to their former career (Wang & Shultz, 2010). Preservation of vocational interests, roles, and expertise is key to older adults taking a phased approach to retirement.

Figure 18.4 summarizes personal and workplace factors in addition to income that influence the decision to retire. People in good health, for whom vocational life is central to self-esteem, and whose work environments are pleasant and interesting are likely to keep on working. For these reasons, individuals in high-earning professional occupations usually retire later than those in blue-collar or clerical positions. And when they do retire, they more often shift to stimulating bridge jobs, with some retiring and returning to the work force multiple times (Feldman & Beehr, 2011; Wang, Olson, & Shultz, 2013). Self-employed older adults also work longer, probably because they can flexibly adapt their job's demands to fit their changing capacities and needs (Feldman & Vogel, 2009). In contrast, people in declining health, who are engaged in routine, boring work, who have pleasurable leisure or family pursuits, or who otherwise perceive a decline in the fit of their work with their skills and interests often opt for retirement.

Societal factors also affect retirement decisions. When many younger, less costly workers are available to replace older workers, industries are likely to offer added incentives for people to retire, such as increments to pension plans and earlier benefits—a trend that has, until recently, contributed to many early retirements in Western nations. But when concern increases about the burden on younger generations of an expanding population of retirees, eligibility for retirement benefits may be postponed to a later age. In the United States, for example, the current retirement age of 66 for full Social Security benefits will rise to 67 for individuals born in 1960 or later.

Retirement decisions vary with gender and ethnicity. On average, women retire earlier than men, largely because family events—a spouse's retirement or the need to care for an ill partner or parent—play larger roles in their decisions. However, single women and ethnic minorities, who are overrepresented among older adults in or near poverty, often lack financial resources to retire (Griffin, Loh, & Hesketh, 2013). Many continue working into old age.

In most Western nations, generous social security benefits make retirement feasible for the economically disadvantaged and sustain the standard of living of most workers after they retire. The United States is an exception: Many U.S. retirees, especially those who held low-income jobs without benefits, experience

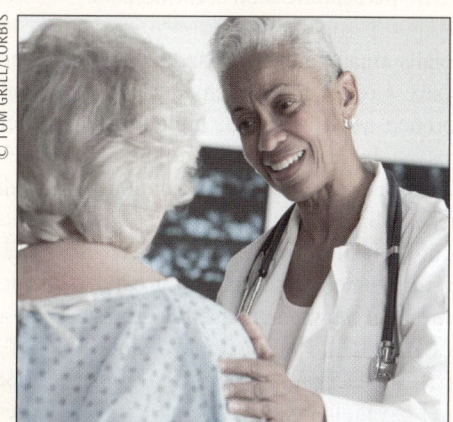

Retire
- Adequate retirement benefits
- Compelling leisure interests or family pursuits
- Low work commitment
- Declining health
- Spouse retiring
- Routine, boring job

Continue Working
- Limited or no retirement benefits
- Few leisure interests or family pursuits
- High work commitment
- Good health
- Spouse working
- Flexible job demands and work schedule
- Pleasant, stimulating work environment

A recent retiree enjoys an adult-education class in bookbinding.

This doctor, in her sixties, continues to enjoy her fulfilling career.

FIGURE 18.4 Personal and workplace factors that influence the decision to retire.

falling living standards. Denmark, France, Germany, Finland, and Sweden have gradual retirement programs in which older employees reduce their work hours, receive a partial pension to make up income loss, and continue to accrue pension benefits. Besides strengthening financial security, this approach introduces a transitional phase that fosters retirement planning and well-being (Peiró, Tordera, & Potocnik, 2012). And some countries' retirement policies are sensitive to women's more interrupted work lives. In Canada, France, and Germany, for example, time devoted to child rearing is given some credit when figuring retirement benefits.

In sum, individual preferences shape retirement decisions. At the same time, older adults' opportunities and limitations greatly affect their choices.

Adjustment to Retirement

Because retirement involves giving up roles that are a vital part of identity and self-esteem, it is often assumed to be a stressful process that contributes to declines in physical and mental health. Consider Dick, who reacted to the closing of his bakery with anxiety and depression. His adjustment difficulties resemble those of younger people experiencing job loss (see Chapter 16, page 562). But recall that Dick had a cranky, disagreeable personality. In this respect, his psychological well-being after retirement was similar to what it had been before!

We must be careful not to assume a cause-and-effect relationship each time retirement is paired with unfavorable reactions. For example, a wealth of evidence confirms that physical health problems lead older adults to retire, rather than the reverse (Shultz & Wang, 2007). And for most people, mental health and perceived quality of life are fairly stable from the pre- to postretirement years, with little change prompted by retirement itself. The widely held belief that retirement inevitably leads to adjustment problems is contradicted by countless research findings indicating that most people adapt well. Contemporary older people view retirement as a time of opportunity and personal growth and describe themselves as active and socially involved—major determinants of retirement satisfaction (Salami, 2010; Wang & Shultz, 2010). Still, about 10 to 30 percent mention some adjustment difficulties.

Workplace factors—especially financial worries and having to give up one's job—predict stress following retirement. Pressures at work also make a difference. Moving out of a high-stress job is associated with gains in psychological well-being following retirement, whereas leaving a pleasant, low-stress job or a highly satisfying job before one is ready is linked to greater difficulties during the retirement transition, typically followed by recovery (Wang, 2007). And especially for women, who take on greater caregiving responsibilities, retirement may not relieve the stress of family burdens (Coursolle et al., 2010). Rather, it may reduce work-based avenues of personal satisfaction, thereby triggering depressive symptoms and poorer psychological well-being.

Among psychological factors, a sense of personal control over life events, including deciding to retire for internally motivated reasons (to do other things), is strongly linked to retirement satisfaction (Kubicek et al., 2011; van Solinge, 2013). At the same time, those who find it hard to give up the predictable schedule and social contacts of the work setting or who have few nonwork social ties experience discomfort. Overall, however, well-educated people with complex jobs adjust more favorably (Kim & Moen, 2002). Perhaps the satisfactions derived from challenging, meaningful work readily transfer to nonwork pursuits.

As with other major life events, social support reduces stress associated with retirement. Although social network size typically shrinks as relationships with co-workers decline, quality of relationships remains fairly stable for most people. And many add to their social networks through leisure and volunteer pursuits (Kloep & Hendry, 2007). In Dick's case, entering a life-care community eased a difficult postretirement period, leading to new friends and rewarding leisure activities, some of which he shared with Goldie.

Finally, marital happiness generally fosters a favorable retirement transition. When a couple's relationship is positive, it can buffer the uncertainty of retirement. And retirement can enhance marital satisfaction by granting happily married couples more time for companionship (van Solinge & Henkens, 2008; Wang, 2007). Marital dissatisfaction, in contrast, interferes with retirement adjustment, in part because it heightens exposure to an unhappy relationship.

In line with continuity theory, people try to sustain gratifying lifestyle patterns, self-esteem, and values following retirement and, in favorable economic and social contexts, usually succeed. Return to Chapter 16, page 563, for ways adults can plan ahead to increase the chances of a positive transition to retirement.

Leisure and Volunteer Activities

With retirement, most older adults have more time for leisure and volunteer activities than ever before. After a "honeymoon period" of trying out new options, many discover that interests and skills do not develop suddenly. Instead, meaningful leisure and community service pursuits are usually formed earlier and sustained or expanded during retirement (Pinquart & Schindler, 2009). For example, Walt's fondness for writing, theater, and gardening dated back to his youth. And Ruth's strong focus on her social work career led her to become an avid community volunteer.

Involvement in leisure activities and, especially, volunteer service is related to better physical and mental health and reduced mortality (Cutler, Hendricks, & O'Neill, 2011). But simply participating does not explain this relationship. Instead, older adults select these pursuits because they permit self-expression, new achievements, the rewards of helping others, pleasurable social interaction, and a structured daily life. And those high in sense of self-efficacy are more engaged (Diehl & Berg, 2007). These factors account for gains in well-being.

As mobility limitations increase, the frequency and variety of leisure pursuits tend to decline, with activities increasingly becoming less strenuous (Dorfman, 2016). Older adults in residential communities participate more than those in ordinary homes because activities are conveniently available. But regardless of living arrangements, aging adults choose activities not for convenience but rather on the basis of whether they are personally gratifying.

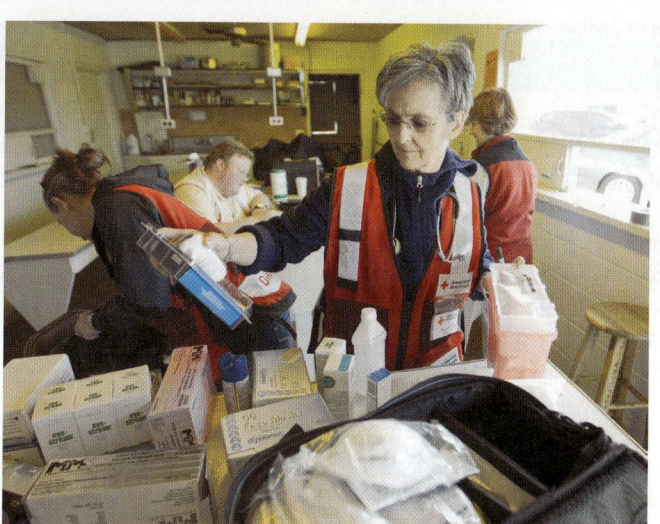

Time devoted to volunteering is higher in late adulthood than at any other time of life. This Red Cross disaster-relief volunteer traveled to Texas to provide medical assistance to victims of a fertilizer plant explosion.

Older people contribute enormously to society through volunteer work, a trend that is strengthening. About one-third of those in their sixties and seventies in industrialized nations report volunteering. Of those who do, over half give 200 or more hours per year (HSBC & Oxford Institute of Ageing, 2007; U.S. Bureau of Labor Statistics, 2016). Younger, better-educated, and financially secure older adults with social interests are more likely to volunteer, women more often than men. Although most extend an earlier pattern of civic engagement, nonvolunteers are especially receptive to volunteer activities in the first few years after retiring as they look for ways to compensate for work-role losses (Mutchler, Burr, & Caro, 2003). The retirement transition is a prime time to recruit older people into these personally rewarding, socially useful pursuits.

LOOK and LISTEN

Interview an older adult participating in a significant community service role about the personal meaning of the experience at this time of life.

Volunteering grants older adults a continuing sense of making valuable contributions to society, and most sustain high commitment through their seventies. In a survey of a large, nationally representative U.S. sample, time spent volunteering rose steadily over adulthood, not declining until the eighties (Hendricks & Cutler, 2004). Even then, it remained higher than at any other period of life! In accord with socioemotional selectivity theory, older people eventually narrow their volunteering to fewer roles, concentrating on one or two that mean the most to them (Windsor, Anstey, & Rodgers, 2008). They seem to recognize that excessive volunteering reduces its emotional rewards and, therefore, its benefits. See the Biology and Environment box on page 638 to find out about an innovative service program has impressive effects on older adults' physical, cognitive, and social functioning while also enhancing children's academic success.

Finally, when Walt and Ruth got together with Dick and Goldie, the two couples often discussed politics. Older adults report greater awareness of and interest in public affairs and typically vote at a higher rate than any other age group. Even in late old age, political knowledge shows no sign of decline. After retiring, they have more time to keep abreast of current events. They also have a major stake in debates over policies central to their welfare. But older adults' political concerns are far broader than those that serve their own age group, and their voting behavior is not driven merely by self-interest (Campbell & Binstock, 2011). Rather, their political involvement may stem from a deep desire for a safer, more secure world for future generations.

Successful Aging

18.12 Discuss the meaning of successful aging.

Walt, Ruth, Dick, Goldie, and Ida, and the research findings they illustrate, reveal great diversity in development during the final decades of life. Walt and Ruth fit contemporary experts' view of **successful aging**, in which gains are maximized and losses minimized, enabling realization of individual potential. Both were actively engaged with their families and communities, coped well with negative life changes, enjoyed a happy intimate partnership and other close relationships, and led daily lives filled with gratifying activities. Ida, too, aged successfully until the onset of Alzheimer's symptoms overwhelmed her ability to manage life's challenges. As a single adult, she built a rich social network that sustained her into old age. In contrast, Dick and Goldie reacted with despondency to physical aging and other losses (such as Dick's forced retirement). And Dick's angry outbursts restricted their social contacts, although the couple's move to a life-care community eventually led to an improved social life.

People age well when their growth, vitality, and strivings limit and, at times, overcome physical, cognitive, and social declines. Researchers want to know more about factors that contribute to successful aging so they can help more people experience it. Yet theorists disagree on the precise ingredients of a satisfying old age. Some focus on easily measurable outcomes, such as excellent cardiovascular functioning, absence of disability, superior cognitive performance, and creative achievements. But this view has been heavily criticized (Brown, 2016a). Not everyone can become an outstanding athlete, an innovative scientist, or a talented artist. And many older adults do not want to keep on accomplishing and producing—the main markers of success in Western nations. Each of us is limited by our genetic potential as it combines with a lifetime of environments we encounter and select for ourselves. Furthermore, outcomes valued in one culture may not be valued in others.

Perspectives on successful aging have turned away from specific achievements toward processes people use to reach personally valued goals (Freund & Baltes, 1998; Kahana et al., 2005; Lang, Rohr, & Williger, 2011). Instead of identifying one set of

Biology and Environment

Experience Corps: Promoting Retired Adults' Physical and Mental Health and Children's Academic Success

Experience Corps is an innovative, community-based intergenerational intervention aimed at slowing biological aging and enhancing the well-being of retired adults while also strengthening the academic success of kindergarten through third-grade children (Rebok et al., 2014). To attain maximum impact, the program is intensive and stimulating, for retirees and children alike.

Volunteers join teams of 7 to 10 for a rigorous 30-hour training program, where they acquire skills in tutoring and behavior management of children. Teams are then placed in low-income inner-city schools, where each volunteer devotes at least 15 hours per week throughout the school year to helping students identified by their teachers as in need of academic support. Teams meet at least every two weeks for problem solving and refresher training, to enhance impact on children while also fostering a sense of community among volunteers.

Currently, Experience Corps has nearly 3,000 volunteers working in 22 U.S. cities. How effective is it in attaining its intergenerational goals?

To find out, several hundred adults age 60 and older were randomly assigned to the program in the Baltimore, New York, and Port Arthur, Texas, public schools or to a wait-list control group. Outcomes were impressive: Schools where children received Experience Corps tutoring and mentoring showed higher end-of-year reading achievement and a reduction in disruptive classroom behavior, relative to other schools with similar student bodies (Gattis et al., 2010; Lee et al., 2012).

Simultaneously, older adults benefitted in wide-ranging ways, in Baltimore and in an expanded evaluation carried out in 17 U.S. cities. After 4 to 8 months of service, volunteers reported gains in physical activity and strength, whereas controls reported declines (Fried et al., 2004). And after two years of service, program participants indicated fewer physical limitations and depressive symptoms relative to controls (Hong & Morrill-Howell, 2010). From serving on teams and connecting with school personnel, volunteers also reported enhanced social support.

Furthermore, in studies addressing neurobiological outcomes, Experience Corps volunteers, but not controls, showed changes in fMRI brain activity over a school year that coincided with gains in executive function. And two years of program participation was associated with mild gains in size of the cerebral cortex and hippocampus (centrally involved in memory), whereas controls declined (Carlson et al.,

Experience Corps provides intensive training to older adult volunteers, who join teams that provide academic support to low-income inner-city schoolchildren. Intergenerational benefits are impressive: Children improve academically and behaviorally, and volunteers gain in physical, cognitive, and social well-being.

2009, 2015). Sustained, physically active and cognitively challenging volunteering appeared to increase the plasticity of brain regions supporting vital late-life cognitive skills.

Experience Corps demonstrates the powerful impact of a "high-dose" volunteer program on aging adults' physical, cognitive, and social well-being, while also improving children's academic functioning in ways that forecast life success. Recently, Experience Corps joined forces with AARP, the largest organization for older Americans, with plans to extend the program to many more older adults and children in need.

---

standards as "successful," this view focuses on how people minimize losses while maximizing gains. From this vantage point, *optimal aging* might be a better descriptor than the commonly used term *successful aging*. Optimal aging reflects the reality that aging well involves not only achievement of desirable outcomes but also effective coping with life's challenges and losses.

In research on diverse samples of adults followed over the lifespan, George Vaillant looked at how various life-course factors contributed to late-life physical and psychological well-being (Vaillant & Mukamal, 2001). Findings revealed that factors people can control to some degree (such as health habits, coping strategies, marital stability, and years of education) far outweighed uncontrollable factors (parental SES, family warmth in childhood, early physical health, and longevity of family members) in predicting a satisfying, active old age.

Consider one participant, who in childhood had experienced low SES, parental discord, a depressed mother, and seven siblings crowded into a tenement apartment. Despite these early perils, he became happily married and, through the GI bill, earned an accounting degree. At 70, he was aging well:

Anthony Pirelli may have been *ill* considering his heart attack and open-heart surgery, but he did not feel *sick*. He was as physically active as ever, and he continued to play tennis. Asked what he missed about his work, he exulted, "I'm so busy doing other things that I don't have time to miss work. . . . Life is not boring for me." He did not smoke or abuse alcohol; he loved his wife; he used mature [coping strategies]; he obtained 14 years of education; he watched his waistline; and he exercised regularly. (Adapted from Vaillant, 2002, pp. 12, 305.)

Vaillant concluded, "The past often predicts but never determines our old age" (p. 12). Successful aging is an expression of remarkable resilience during this final period of the lifespan.

In this and the previous chapter, we have considered many ways that older adults realize their goals. Look back and review the most important ones:

- Optimism and sense of self-efficacy in improving health and physical functioning (page 581)
- Selective optimization with compensation to make the most of limited physical energies and cognitive resources (pages 595 and 616)
- Strengthening of self-concept, which promotes self-acceptance and pursuit of hoped-for possible selves (pages 612–614)
- Enhanced emotional self-regulation and emotional positivity, which support meaningful, rewarding social ties (pages 611–612)
- Acceptance of change, which contributes to effective coping and life satisfaction (page 614)
- A mature sense of spirituality and faith, permitting anticipation of death with calm composure (pages 614–615)
- Personal control over domains of dependency and independence, enabling investment in self-chosen, highly valued activities (pages 616, 618)
- High-quality relationships, which offer pleasurable companionship and social support (page 622)
- Personally meaningful leisure and volunteer pursuits, which contribute to physical, cognitive, and social well-being (pages 636–637)

Aging well is facilitated by societal contexts that promote effective person–environment fit, enabling older people to manage life changes. Older adults need well-funded social security plans, good health care, safe housing, and diverse social services. (See, for example, the description of the U.S. Area Agencies on Aging in Chapter 2, page 65.) Yet because of inadequate funding and difficulties reaching rural communities, many older adults' needs remain unmet. Isolated aging adults with little education may not know how to gain access to available assistance. Furthermore, the U.S. Medicare system of sharing health-care costs with older adults strains the financial resources of many. And housing that adjusts to changes in older people's capacities, permitting them to age in place without disruptive and disorienting moves, is available only to the economically well-off.

Besides improving policies that meet older adults' basic needs, new future-oriented approaches must prepare for increased aging of the population. More emphasis on lifelong learning for workers of all ages would help people maintain and expand their skills as they grow older. Also, reforms that prepare for expected growth in the number of frail aging adults are vital, including affordable help for family caregivers, adapted housing, and sensitive nursing home care.

All these changes involve recognizing, supporting, and enhancing the contributions that seniors make to society—both the older adults of today and those of tomorrow. A nation that takes care of its aging citizens and grants them a multitude of opportunities for personal growth maximizes the chances that each of us, when our time comes to be old, will age optimally.

Ask yourself

CONNECT Leisure and volunteer interests and skills usually form early and persist over the lifespan. Referring back to earlier parts of this book, cite examples of childhood, adolescent, and early adulthood experiences that are likely to foster meaningful pursuits after retirement.

APPLY Provide research-based advice to a couple considering retirement about steps they might take to promote favorable retirement adjustment.

REFLECT Think of someone you know who is aging successfully. What personal qualities led you to select that person?

Summary / chapter 18

Erikson's Theory: Ego Integrity versus Despair (p. 610)

18.1 According to Erikson, how does personality change in late adulthood?

- Erikson's final psychological conflict, **ego integrity versus despair,** involves coming to terms with one's life. Adults who arrive at a sense of integrity feel whole and satisfied with their achievements. Despair occurs when older people feel time is too short to find an alternate route to integrity.

Other Theories of Psychosocial Development in Late Adulthood (p. 610)

18.2 Discuss Robert Peck's and Joan Erikson's views of psychosocial development in late adulthood, along with implications of the positivity effect and reminiscence for older adults' lives.

- According to Robert Peck, attaining ego integrity involves three distinct tasks: ego differentiation, body transcendence, and ego transcendence.

- Joan Erikson believes these attainments represent an additional psychosocial stage, **gerotranscendence,** evident in inner calm and quiet reflection. More evidence, however, is needed to confirm this late-life stage.

- Most older people display a **positivity effect**— a bias toward emotionally positive information— likely because they have become expert in emotional self-regulation.

- **Reminiscence** about one's past can be positive and adaptive for older people. But many well-adjusted older adults spend little time seeking greater self-understanding through life review. Rather, as the term **Third Age** conveys, they are largely present- and future-oriented, seeking opportunities for personal fulfillment.

Stability and Change in Self-Concept and Personality (p. 612)

18.3 *Cite stable and changing aspects of self-concept and personality, and discuss spirituality and religiosity in late adulthood.*

- The "big five" personality traits remain stable from mid- to late life. Older adults' accumulation of a lifetime of self-knowledge leads to more secure, multifaceted self-concepts. Those who continue to actively pursue hoped-for possible selves gain in life satisfaction. A flexible, optimistic approach to life fosters resilience, and engaging in cognitively challenging activities promotes openness to experience.

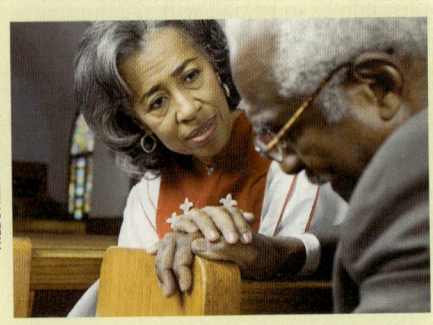

- While older people generally become more religious or spiritual as they age, this increase is usually modest and is not universal. For many, religiosity is stable throughout adulthood. Faith and spirituality may become more reflective, accepting uncertainty and emphasizing links to others. Religious involvement is especially high among low-SES ethnic minority older people and women and is linked to better physical and psychological well-being and longer survival.

Contextual Influences on Psychological Well-Being (p. 615)

18.4 *Discuss the influence of control versus dependency, physical health, negative life changes, and social support on older adults' psychological well-being.*

- In patterns of behavior called the **dependency–support script** and the **independence–ignore script,** older adults' dependency behaviors are attended to immediately while their independent behaviors are ignored. But permitting older adults to select areas in which they desire help enables them to use their capacities fully in pursuit of their goals and creates an effective **person–environment fit,** which fosters psychological well-being.

- Physical health is a powerful predictor of late-life psychological well-being. The relationship between physical and mental health problems can become a vicious cycle, each intensifying the other. People age 85 and older have the highest suicide rate of all age groups.

- Although aging adults are at risk for a variety of negative life changes, these events evoke less stress and depression in older than in younger people. But when negative changes pile up, they test older adults' coping resources.

- Social support promotes physical health and psychological well-being, but excessive assistance or help that cannot be returned often interferes with self-efficacy and amplifies psychological stress. Consequently, perceived social support, rather than sheer amount of help, is associated with a positive outlook.

A Changing Social World (p. 619)

18.5 *Describe the limitations of disengagement theory and activity theory, and explain the more recent perspectives of continuity theory and socioemotional selectivity theory.*

- Disengagement theory holds that mutual withdrawal between older people and society occurs in anticipation of death. Most older adults, however, do not disengage. Activity theory states that social barriers to engagement cause declining rates of interaction. Yet older people with more social contact are not necessarily happier.

- **Continuity theory** proposes that most aging adults strive to maintain consistency between their past and anticipated future. By using familiar skills and engaging in familiar activities with familiar people, older people integrate late-life changes into a coherent, consistent life path.

- **Socioemotional selectivity theory** states that social networks become more selective with age. Older adults, who face a shortened future, emphasize the emotion-regulating function of interaction, preferring high-quality, emotionally fulfilling relationships.

18.6 *How do communities, neighborhoods, and housing arrangements affect older adults' social lives and adjustment?*

- Suburban older adults have higher incomes and report better health than their inner-city counterparts, but the latter benefit from access to public transportation. Small-town and rural aging adults, who are less likely to live near their children, compensate by interacting more with nearby relatives, neighbors, and friends. Living in neighborhoods with like-minded older people promotes life satisfaction.

- Most older people prefer **aging in place,** but for those with health and mobility problems, independent living poses risks, and many older adults who live alone are poverty-stricken.

- Residential settings for older adults who need assisted living include **independent living communities,** which provide a variety of hotel-like support services, and **life-care communities,** which offer a range of housing alternatives guaranteeing that residents' changing needs will be met as they age.

- The small number of U.S. older adults living in nursing homes experience extreme restriction of autonomy and low social interaction. Homelike nursing homes that achieve an effective person–environment fit foster late-life well-being.

Relationships in Late Adulthood (p. 625)

18.7 *Describe changes in relationships in late adulthood, including marriage, lesbian and gay partnerships, divorce, remarriage, and widowhood, and discuss never-married, childless older adults.*

- The **social convoy** is an influential model of changes in individuals' social networks as they move through life. As ties are lost, aging adults seek ways to maintain gratifying relationships and cultivate new ones, though not as many as they did at younger ages.

- Paths of late-life marital satisfaction are diverse and depend on such factors as shared activities and financial difficulties. Married older people usually have larger social networks linked to psychological well-being and good health.

- Most lesbian and gay older couples also report happy, highly fulfilling relationships. Compared with couples not in a legally recognized relationship, those who are married are advantaged in physical and psychological well-being.

- Divorce in late life brings greater stress than for younger people. Although older adults' remarriage rates are low, those who do remarry enter into more stable relationships. Increasingly, older couples in a new relationship choose cohabitation or "living apart together" as long-term alternatives to marriage.
- Adaptation to widowhood varies widely. Aging adults fare better than younger individuals, and women better than men. Efforts to maintain social ties, an outgoing personality, high self-esteem, and a sense of self-efficacy in handling tasks of daily living promote resilience.
- Most older adults who have remained unmarried and childless throughout their lives develop alternative meaningful relationships. Never-married childless women are better-adjusted than men, but both find social support.

18.8 How do sibling relationships and friendships change in late life?

- In late adulthood, aging siblings typically live nearby, communicate regularly, and visit at least several times a year. Especially for widowed and never-married older people, siblings provide an important "insurance policy."

- Late-life friendships serve diverse functions: intimacy and companionship, a shield against negative judgments, a link to the larger community, and protection from the psychological consequences of loss. Older adults prefer established same-sex friendships, and women, more than men, have both intimate friends and **secondary friends**, with whom they spend time occasionally.

18.9 Describe older adults' relationships with adult children and adult grandchildren.

- Older adults are often in touch with their adult children, who more often provide emotional support than direct assistance. Aging parents who provide more help than they receive score highest in life satisfaction. Though typically mild, ambivalent feelings toward adult children undermine psychological well-being.
- Older people with adult grandchildren benefit from a wider potential network of support. Grandparents typically expect affection, but not practical help, from grandchildren. Although grandparent–grandchild contact declines over time, grandparents' emotional investment often strengthens.

18.10 Discuss elder maltreatment, including risk factors, consequences, and prevention strategies.

- Some older adults suffer maltreatment at the hands of family members, friends, or professional caregivers. Risk factors include a dependent perpetrator–victim relationship, perpetrator psychological disturbance, a history of family violence, and inadequate institutional conditions. All forms of elder maltreatment have profound, lasting consequences on victims' physical and mental health.
- Elder-abuse prevention programs provide counseling, education, and respite services for caregivers. Trained volunteers and support groups can help victims avoid future harm. Societal efforts that encourage reporting of suspected cases and increase understanding of older people's needs are also vital.

Retirement (p. 634)

18.11 Discuss the decision to retire, adjustment to retirement, and involvement in leisure and volunteer activities.

- The decision to retire depends on diverse factors, including affordability, health status, nature of the work environment, opportunities to pursue meaningful activities, gender, ethnicity, and societal retirement policies.

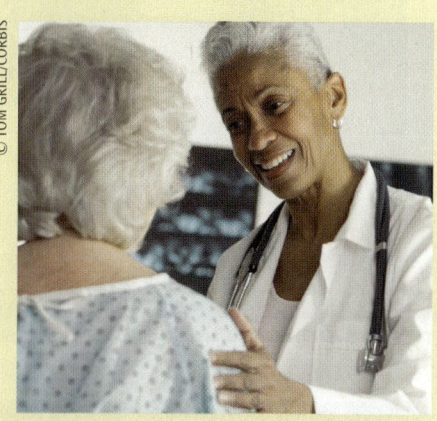

- Factors affecting adjustment to retirement include satisfactions previously derived from work, caregiving responsibilities, a sense of personal control over life events, social support, and marital happiness.
- Meaningful leisure and volunteer pursuits are typically sustained or expanded during retirement. Involvement is related to better physical and mental health and to reduced mortality.

Successful Aging (p. 637)

18.12 Discuss the meaning of successful aging.

- Older adults who experience **successful aging** minimize losses and maximize gains, enabling realization of individual potential. Societal contexts that permit older adults to manage life changes—including well-funded social security plans, good health care, safe housing, diverse social services, and opportunities for lifelong learning—foster aging well.

Important Terms and Concepts

aging in place (p. 623)
continuity theory (p. 620)
dependency–support script (p. 616)
ego integrity versus despair (p. 610)
gerotranscendence (p. 611)
independence–ignore script (p. 616)

independent living communities (p. 623)
life-care communities (p. 623)
person–environment fit (p. 616)
positivity effect (p. 611)
reminiscence (p. 612)
secondary friends (p. 631)

social convoy (p. 625)
socioemotional selectivity theory (p. 620)
successful aging (p. 637)
Third Age (p. 613)

milestones
Development in Late Adulthood

65–80 YEARS

Physical

- Performance of autonomic nervous system declines, impairing tolerance for extremes of heat and cold. (574)
- Declines in vision continue, with increased sensitivity to glare and impaired color discrimination, dark adaptation, depth perception, and visual acuity. (574–575)
- Declines in hearing continue throughout the frequency range. (575)
- Sensitivity to taste and odor may decline. (576)
- Touch sensitivity declines on the hands, especially the fingertips. (576)
- Declines in cardiovascular and respiratory functioning lead to greater physical stress during exercise. (576–577)

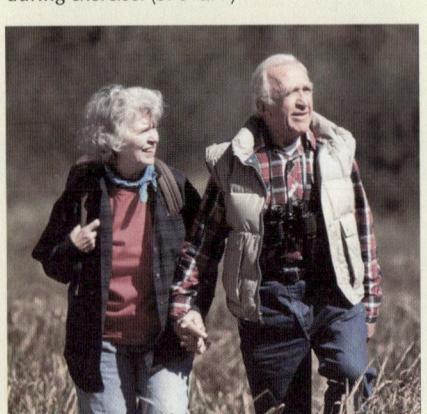

- Declines in immune system functioning increase risk for a variety of illnesses, including infectious diseases, cardiovascular disease, certain forms of cancer, and several autoimmune disorders. (577)
- Timing of sleep shifts to earlier bedtime and earlier morning wakening; sleep difficulties increase. (577)
- Graying and thinning of the hair continue; the skin wrinkles and sags further and becomes more transparent as it loses its fatty layer of support; "age spots" increase. (578)
- Height and weight decline because of loss of lean body mass. (578)

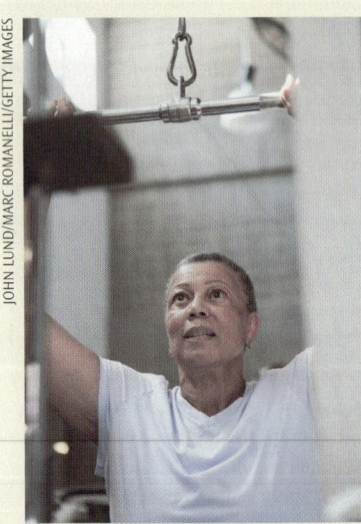

- Continued loss of bone mass leads to rising rates of osteoporosis. (578, 585)
- Frequency of sexual activity and intensity of sexual response decline, although most married older adults report regular sexual enjoyment. (583–584)

Cognitive

- Processing speed and other aspects of fluid intelligence decline; crystallized intelligence (including semantic memory, or general knowledge base) is largely sustained. (594)

- Executive function, including working memory capacity, inhibition, and flexible shifting of attention, continues to decline. (594)
- Failures in retrieving information from long-term memory increase; problems are greatest for episodic memory (memory for everyday experiences), associative memory, and explicit memory (tasks requiring memory strategies). (595–596)
- Memory for significant, remote autobiographical experiences is largely sustained. (597)
- Time-based prospective memory declines; to compensate, increasingly uses external aids as reminders. (598)

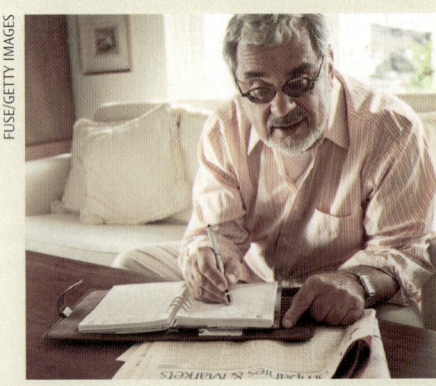

- Retrieving words from long-term memory and planning what to say and how to say it in everyday conversation become more difficult; language comprehension and narrative competence are largely sustained. (598, 599)

Note: Numbers in parentheses indicate the page or pages on which each milestone is discussed.

- Hypothetical problem solving declines, but everyday problem solving remains adaptive. (599)
- May hold an important position of leadership in society, such as chief executive officer, religious leader, or court justice. (600)

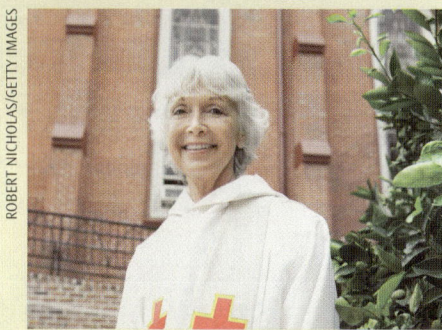

- May develop wisdom. (600–601)
- Can improve a wide range of cognitive skills through training. (602)

Emotional/Social

- Comes to terms with life, developing ego integrity. (610–611)
- Cognitive-affective complexity declines as basic information-processing skills diminish. (611)
- Displays positivity effect, selectively attending to and better recalling emotionally positive over negative information. (611)
- May engage in life-review reminiscence, but continues to seek avenues for personal growth and fulfillment. (612)

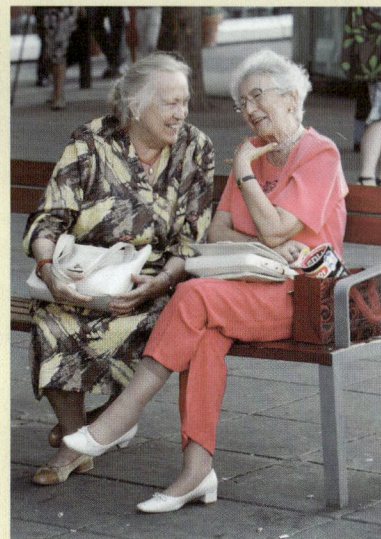

- Self-concept strengthens, becoming more secure and multifaceted. (612)
- Agreeableness and acceptance of change increase, while extroversion and openness to experience tend to decline. (614)

- Spirituality and faith may advance to a higher level, away from prescribed beliefs toward a more reflective approach. (614–615)

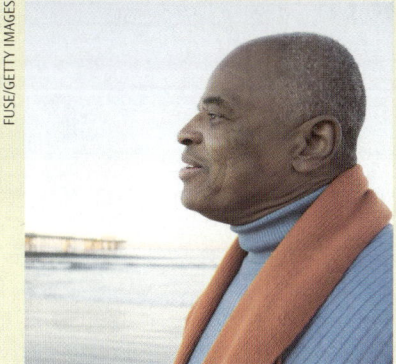

- Size of social network declines, emphasizing emotionally positive, close relationships. (620–621)
- May be widowed. (628)
- Visits and support from siblings living nearby may increase. (630)
- With additional time to devote to them, friendships take on increasing importance. (630)
- May retire. (634–635)
- Likely to increase involvement in leisure and volunteer activities. (636)
- More likely to be knowledgeable about politics and to vote. (637)

80 YEARS AND OLDER

Physical

- Physical changes previously listed continue.

- Mobility diminishes as muscle and bone strength and joint flexibility decline. (578)

Cognitive

- Cognitive changes previously listed continue.
- Fluid intelligence declines further; crystallized intelligence drops as well, though only modestly. (594–595)

Emotional/Social

- Emotional and social changes previously listed continue. (614)
- May develop gerotranscendence, a cosmic perspective directed beyond the self. (611)

- Relationships with adult children become more important. (632)
- Frequency and variety of leisure and volunteer activities may decline. (636)

Note: Numbers in parentheses indicate the page or pages on which each milestone is discussed.

chapter 19

Death, Dying, and Bereavement

In this Hindu funeral procession in Manipur, India, women wear white and light pink to mark the sadness of the occasion. All cultures have customs and rituals for commemorating the end of life and helping the bereaved cope with profound loss.

What's ahead in chapter 19

How We Die
Physical Changes • Defining Death • Death with Dignity

Understanding of and Attitudes Toward Death
Childhood • Adolescence • Adulthood • Death Anxiety

Thinking and Emotions of Dying People
Do Stages of Dying Exist? • Contextual Influences on Adaptations to Dying

A Place to Die
Home • Hospital • Nursing Home • The Hospice Approach

■ **BIOLOGY AND ENVIRONMENT** Music as Palliative Care for Dying Patients

The Right to Die
Ending Life-Sustaining Treatment • Medical Aid-in-Dying • Voluntary Euthanasia

Bereavement: Coping with the Death of a Loved One
Grief Process • Personal and Situational Variations • Bereavement Interventions

■ **CULTURAL INFLUENCES** Cultural Variations in Mourning Behavior

Death Education

As every life is unique, so each death is unique. The final forces of the human spirit separate themselves from the body in manifold ways.

My mother Sofie's death was the culmination of a five-year battle against cancer. In her last months, the disease invaded organs throughout her body, attacking the lungs in its final fury. She withered slowly, with the mixed blessing of time to prepare against certain knowledge that death was just around the corner. My father, Philip, lived another 18 years. At age 80, he was outwardly healthy, active, and about to depart on a long-awaited vacation when a heart attack snuffed out his life suddenly, without time for last words or deathbed reconciliations.

As I set to work on this chapter, my 65-year-old neighbor Nicholas gambled for a higher quality of life. To be eligible for a kidney transplant, he elected bypass surgery to strengthen his heart. Doctors warned that his body might not withstand the operation. But Nicholas knew that without taking a chance,

he would live only a few years, in debilitated condition. Shortly after the surgery, infection set in, traveling throughout his system and so weakening him that only extreme measures—a respirator to sustain breathing and powerful drugs to elevate his fading blood pressure—could keep him alive.

"Come on, Dad, you can do it," encouraged Nicholas's daughter Sasha, standing by his bedside and stroking his hand. But Nicholas could not. After two months in intensive care, he experienced brain seizures and slipped into a coma. Three doctors met with his wife, Giselle, to tell her there was no hope. She asked them to disconnect the respirator, and within half an hour Nicholas drifted away.

Death is essential for the survival of our species. We die so that our own children and the children of others may live. When it comes to this fate, nature treats humankind, with all its unique capabilities, just as it treats every other living creature. As hard as it is to accept the reality that we too will die, our greatest solace lies in knowing that death is part of ongoing life.

In this chapter, we address the culmination of lifespan development. Medical advances during the twentieth and early twenty-first centuries have provided so many means to keep death at bay that many people regard it as a forbidden topic. But pressing social and economic dilemmas that are an outgrowth of the dramatic increase in life expectancy are forcing us to attend to life's end—its quality, its timing, and ways to help people adjust to their own and others' final leave taking. The interdisciplinary field of **thanatology,** devoted to the study of death and dying, has expanded tremendously over the past three decades.

Our discussion addresses the physical changes of dying; understanding of and attitudes toward death in childhood, adolescence, and adulthood; the thoughts and feelings of people as they stand face to face with death; where people die; hopelessly ill patients' right to die; coping with the death of a loved one; and death education. The experiences of Sofie, Philip, Nicholas, their families, and others illustrate how each person's life history joins with social and cultural contexts to shape death and dying, lending great diversity to this universal experience. ●

How We Die

19.1 Describe the physical changes of dying, along with their implications for defining death and the meaning of death with dignity.

In industrialized countries, opportunities to witness the physical aspects of death are less available today than in previous generations. Most people in the developed world die in hospitals, where doctors and nurses, not loved ones, typically attend their last moments. Nevertheless, many want to know how we die, either to anticipate their own end or grasp what is happening to a dying loved one. As we look briefly at physical dying, we must keep in mind that the dying person is more than a physical being requiring care of and attention to bodily functions. The dying are also mind and spirit—for whom the end of life is still life. They benefit profoundly in their last days and hours from social support responsive to their needs for emotional and spiritual closure.

Physical Changes

My father's fatal heart attack came suddenly during the night. When I heard the news, I longed for reassurance that his death had been swift and without suffering.

When asked how they would like to die, most people say they want "death with dignity"—either a quick, agony-free end during sleep or a clear-minded final few moments in which they can say farewell and review their lives. In reality, death is the culmination of a straightforward biological process. For about 20 percent of people, it is gentle—especially when narcotic drugs ease pain and mask the destructive events taking place (Nuland, 1993). But most of the time it is not.

Recall that unintentional injuries are the leading cause of death in childhood and adolescence, cardiovascular disease and cancer in adulthood. Of the one-quarter of deaths in industrialized nations that are sudden, 65 to 85 percent are due to heart attacks (Mozaffarian et al., 2015; Sanchis-Gomar et al., 2016). My yearning for a painless death for my father was probably not fulfilled. Undoubtedly he felt the sharp, crushing sensation of a heart deprived of oxygen. As his heart twitched uncontrollably (called *fibrillation*) or stopped entirely, blood circulation slowed and ceased, and he was thrust into unconsciousness. A brain starved of oxygen for more than 2 to 4 minutes is irreversibly damaged—an outcome indicated by the pupils of the eyes becoming unresponsive to light and widening into large, black circles. Other oxygen-deprived organs stop functioning as well.

Death is long and drawn out for three-fourths of people—many more than in times past, as a result of life-saving medical technology. They succumb in different ways. Of those with heart disease, most have congestive heart failure, the cause of Nicholas's death (Murray & McLoughlin, 2012). His scarred heart could no longer contract with the force needed to deliver enough oxygen to his tissues. As it tried harder, its muscle weakened further. Without sufficient blood pressure, fluid backed up in Nicholas's lungs. This hampered his breathing and created ideal conditions for inhaled bacteria to multiply, enter the bloodstream, and run rampant in his system, leading many organs to fail.

Cancer also chooses diverse paths to inflict its damage. When it metastasizes, bits of tumor travel through the bloodstream and implant and grow in vital organs, disrupting their functioning. Medication made my mother's final days as comfortable as possible, granting a relatively easy death. But the preceding weeks involved physical suffering, including impaired breathing and digestion and turning and twisting to find a comfortable position in bed.

In the days or hours before death, activity declines; the person moves and communicates less and shows little interest in food, water, and surroundings. At the same time, body temperature, blood pressure, and circulation to the limbs fall, so the hands and feet feel cool and skin color changes to a duller, grayish hue (Hospice Foundation of America, 2011). When the transition from life to death is imminent, the person often moves through three phases:

1. **The agonal phase.** The Greek word *agon* means "struggle." Here agonal refers to a rattled breathing sound, due to fluid buildup in the throat, and to gasps and muscle spasms during the first moments in which the regular heartbeat disintegrates (Manole & Hickey, 2006).
2. **Clinical death.** A short interval follows in which heartbeat, circulation, breathing, and brain functioning stop, but resuscitation is still possible.
3. **Mortality.** The individual passes into permanent death. Within a few hours, the newly lifeless being appears shrunken, not at all like the person he or she was when alive.

Defining Death

Consider what we have said so far, and note the dilemma of identifying just when death occurs. Death is not an event that happens at a single point in time but, rather, a process in which organs stop functioning in a sequence that varies from person to person. Because the dividing line between life and death is fuzzy, societies need a definition of death to help doctors decide when life-saving measures should be terminated, to signal survivors that they must begin to grieve their loss and reorganize their lives, and to establish when donated organs can be removed.

In a Chinese cemetery, family members pray and bring offerings to their deceased ancestors as a sign of respect. Buddhist, Confucian, and Shinto beliefs, which emphasize ancestor worship and time for the spirit to leave the corpse, may partly explain why brain death is not legally recognized in China.

Several decades ago, loss of heartbeat and respiration signified death. But these criteria are no longer adequate because resuscitation techniques frequently permit vital signs to be restored. Today, **brain death,** irreversible cessation of all activity in the brain and the brain stem (which controls reflexes), is used in most industrialized nations.

But not all countries accept this standard. In China and Japan, for example, doctors rely on traditional criteria—absence of heartbeat and respiration. This approach has hindered the development of national organ transplant programs because few organs can be salvaged from bodies without artificially maintaining vital signs. Buddhist, Confucian, and Shinto beliefs about death, which stress ancestor worship and time for the spirit to leave the corpse, may be partly responsible for this discomfort with brain death and organ donation (Yang & Miller, 2015). Today, Japanese law uses the brain death standard only when the dying person is a potential organ donor (Kumaido, Sugiyama, & Tsutsumi, 2015). Otherwise, people are considered to be alive until the heart stops beating. Brain death is still not legally recognized in China.

The brain death standard, however, does not always solve the problem of when to halt treatment. Consider Nicholas, who, though not brain dead, had entered a **persistent vegetative state,** in which the cerebral cortex no longer registered electrical activity but the brain stem remained active. Doctors were certain they could not restore consciousness or body movement. Because thousands of people in the United States and other nations are in a persistent vegetative state, with health-care costs totaling many millions of dollars annually, some experts believe that absence of activity in the cerebral cortex should be sufficient to declare a person dead. But others point to a few cases in which patients who had been vegetative for months regained cortical responsiveness and consciousness, though usually with very limited functioning (Laureys & Boly, 2007). In still other instances of illness, a fully conscious but suffering person refuses life-saving measures—an issue we will consider later when we take up the right to die.

Death with Dignity

We have seen that nature rarely delivers the idealized, easy end most people want, nor can medical science guarantee it. Therefore, the greatest dignity in death is in the integrity of the life that precedes it—an integrity we can foster by the way we communicate with and care for the dying person.

First, we can assure the majority of dying people, who succumb gradually, that we will support them through their physical and psychological distress. We can treat them with respect by taking interest in those aspects of their lives that they most value and by addressing their greatest concerns (Keegan & Drick, 2011). And we can do everything possible to ensure the utmost compassionate care through their last months, weeks, and even final hours—restful physical surroundings, soothing emotional and social support, closeness of loved ones, and pastoral care that helps relieve worries about the worth of one's life, important relationships, and mortality.

Second, we can be candid about death's certainty. Unless people are aware that they are dying and understand (as far as possible) the likely circumstances of their death, they cannot plan for end-of-life care and decision making and share the sentiments that bring closure to relationships they hold most dear. Because Sofie knew how and when her death would probably take place, she chose a time when she and Philip could express what their lives had meant to each other. Among those precious bedside exchanges was Sofie's last wish that Philip remarry after her death so he would not live out his final years alone. Openness about impending death granted Sofie a final generative act,

Dying patient Dick Warner's wife, Nancy, wears a nurse's hat she crafted from paper to symbolize her dual roles as medical and emotional caregiver. The evening of this photo, Nancy heard Dick's breaths shortening. She kissed him and whispered, "It's time to let go." Dick died as he wished, with his loving wife at his bedside.

helped her let go of the person closest to her, and offered comfort as she faced death.

Finally, doctors and nurses can help dying people learn enough about their condition to make reasoned choices about whether to fight on or say no to further treatment. An understanding of how the normal body works simplifies comprehension of how disease affects it—education that can begin as early as the childhood years.

In sum, when the conditions of illness do not permit an easy death, we can still ensure the most dignified exit possible by offering the dying person care, affection, companionship, and esteem; the truth about diagnosis; and the maximum personal control over this final phase of life (American Hospice Foundation, 2013). These are essential ingredients of a "good death," and we will revisit them throughout this chapter.

Understanding of and Attitudes Toward Death

19.2 Discuss age-related changes in conceptions of and attitudes toward death, and cite factors that influence death anxiety.

A century ago, when most deaths occurred at home, people of all ages, including children, helped with care of the dying family member and were present at the moment of death. They saw their loved one buried on family property or in the local cemetery, where the grave could be visited regularly. Because infant and childhood mortality rates were high, all people were likely to know someone their own age, or even younger, who had died. And it was common for children to experience the death of a parent.

Compared with earlier generations, today more young people reach adulthood without having experienced the death of someone they know well (Morgan, Laungani, & Palmer, 2009). When a death does occur, professionals in hospitals and funeral homes take care of most tasks that involve confronting it directly.

This distance from death undoubtedly contributes to a sense of uneasiness about it. Despite frequent images of death in television shows, movies, and news reports of accidents, murders, wars, and natural disasters, Americans live in a death-avoidant culture. Adults are often reluctant to talk about death with children and adolescents. And substitute expressions, such as "passing away," "going out," or "departing," permit us to evade candid acknowledgment of death. In the following sections, we examine the development of conceptions of and attitudes toward death, along with ways to foster increased understanding and acceptance.

Childhood

Four-year-old Miriam arrived at preschool the day after her dog Pepper died. Instead of joining the other children, she stayed close to her teacher, Leslie, who noticed Miriam's discomfort. "What's wrong?" Leslie asked.

"Daddy said Pepper was so sick the vet had to put him to sleep." For a moment, Miriam looked hopeful. "When I get home, Pepper might wake up."

Leslie answered directly, "No, Pepper won't get up again. He's not asleep. He's dead, and that means he can't sleep, eat, run, or play anymore."

Miriam wandered off but later returned to Leslie and, sobbing, confessed, "I chased Pepper too hard."

Leslie put her arm around Miriam. "Pepper didn't die because you chased him," she explained. "He was very old and sick."

Over the next few days, Miriam asked many questions: "When I go to sleep, will I die?" "Can a tummy ache make you die?" "Does Pepper feel better now?" "Will Mommy and Daddy die?"

Development of the Death Concept. An accurate, biological understanding of death is based on five subconcepts:

1. *Nonfunctionality.* All living functions, including thought, feeling, movement, and bodily processes, cease at death.
2. *Finality.* Once a living thing dies, it cannot be brought back to life.
3. *Universality.* All living things eventually die.
4. *Applicability.* Death applies only to living things.
5. *Causation.* Death is caused by a breakdown of bodily functioning, which can be brought about by a wide variety of internal and external causes.

To master these subconcepts, children must acquire some basic notions of biology—that animals and plants contain body parts (brain, heart, stomach; leaf, stem, roots) essential for maintaining life. They must also break down their global category of *not alive* into *dead, inanimate, unreal,* and *nonexistent.* Until children grasp these ideas, they tend to interpret death in terms of familiar experiences—as a change in behavior (Slaughter, Jaakkola, & Carey, 1999; Slaughter & Lyons, 2003). As a result, they are vulnerable to inaccurate beliefs—for example, that they caused a relative's or pet's death or that death is like sleep.

Children actively seek to make sense of death, and from age 3½ on, they make dramatic progress in acquiring its subconcepts, with most attaining a sophisticated understanding by age 6. Young children's acquisition of biological knowledge about death is associated with reduced anxiety about death (Slaughter & Griffiths, 2007). These findings support discussing death truthfully with children, as Leslie did with Miriam.

Nonfunctionality (especially of bodily processes) and *finality* are generally understood early, even among children with little exposure to the death of relatives or pets, perhaps because preschoolers see evidence for these subconcepts in everyday situations—for example, in the dead butterflies and beetles they pick up and inspect while playing outside. Appreciation of *universality* soon follows. At first, many preschoolers think that

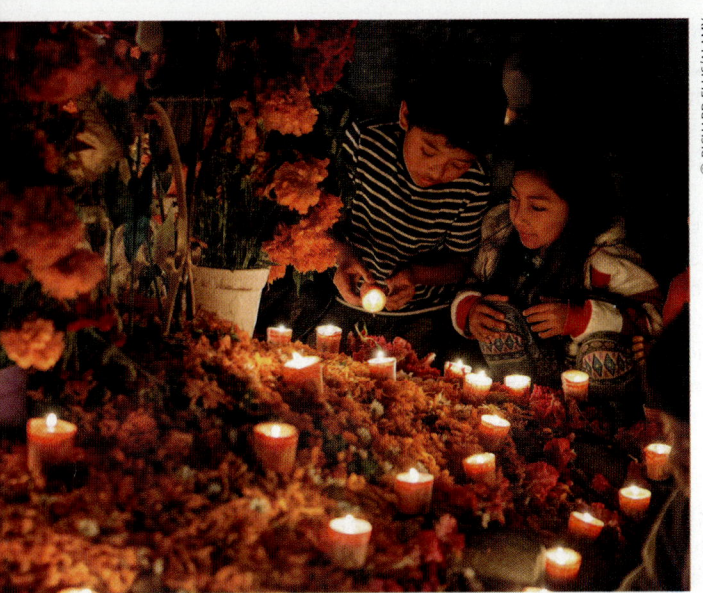

Children light candles in remembrance of a deceased family member during the annual *Dia de los Muertos* ("Day of the Dead") celebration. Because their parents value forthright discussions, Mexican-American children freely ask questions about the biology of death and death-related cultural traditions.

certain people will not die—themselves, people like themselves (other children), and people with whom they have close emotional ties. *Applicability* and *causation* are more challenging (Kenyon, 2001; Panagiotaki et al., 2015; Rosengren, Gutiérrez, & Schein, 2014). As preschoolers refine the distinction between animate and inanimate, they realize that dolls, robots, and other lifelike inanimate objects cannot die. And by age 6, their grasp of internal (illness, old age) and external (accidents) causes of death is substantial (Lazar & Torney-Purta, 1991).

Regardless of religious background, nearly 65 percent of U.S. adults believe in some kind of persistence of a spirit or soul after death (Harris Poll, 2013). When researchers asked American preschoolers whether some aspect remains after living beings die, most gave biological answers, mentioning the body, body parts, or bones. But some spoke of a spirit that "goes to heaven" (Nguyen & Rosengren, 2004; Rosengren, Gutiérrez, & Schein, 2014). These afterlife beliefs strengthen over early and middle childhood, with the majority of 10- to 12-year-olds expressing belief in the survival of a soul that enables the dead to perceive, think, and feel (Bering & Bjorklund, 2004; Harris & Giménez, 2005). Because many adults also believe in the persistence of mental activity and consciousness after death, they probably encourage these ideas in children (Harris, 2011). It is not surprising, then, that most older children conclude that even after biological functions cease at death, thoughts and feelings continue in some form.

Cultural and Individual Variations.
Although children typically attain an adultlike, biological understanding of death by the end of early childhood, individual differences exist. Cultural and religious ideas influence children's rate of mastery and how they acquire information.

Interviews with European-American parents of preschoolers revealed that parent's talk about death is often indirect and avoidant. For example, when one child asked where his dead pet mouse had gone, his mother responded, "Someplace happy" (Miller et al., 2014). The majority of parents also said they shielded their children from movies and TV programs depicting death. They defended their protective stance by arguing that young children lack the cognitive and emotional capacities to understand and cope with death—opinions at odds with research evidence. The children nevertheless picked up information through conversations with siblings and peers and overheard fragments of radio and TV broadcasts. Their parents were unable to shield them completely.

In contrast, responses of Mexican-American immigrant parents emphasized the importance of informative, forthright discussions about death from an early age and access to media depictions (except where content is violent). Death, they explained, is natural and inevitable, and opportunities to recall deceased loved ones and be reminded of an emotional and spiritual connection to them are comforting. In keeping with Mexican cultural traditions, most parents reported participating in the annual *Dia de los Muertos* ("Day of the Dead") celebration, during which many symbols of death are displayed. One tradition involves welcoming the spirits of departed relatives by making an altar, which contains photos, food offerings, decorations, and images of skulls and skeletons (Gutiérrez, Rosengren, & Miller, 2014). Compared to their European-American counterparts, the Mexican-American parents reported that their preschoolers asked many more questions about death, mostly pertaining to biological subconcepts and cultural traditions.

Other research highlights ways that religious teachings affect children's understanding. In a comparison of four ethnic groups in Israel, Druze and Muslim children's ideas about death differed from those of Christian and Jewish children (Florian & Kravetz, 1985). The Druze emphasis on reincarnation, and the greater religiosity of both Druze and Muslim groups, likely led more of their children to deny that death is final and that the body ceases to function.

Terminally ill children under age 6 usually have a well-developed biological understanding of death (Linebarger, Sahler, & Egan, 2009; Nielson, 2012). If parents and health professionals have not been forthright, the children discover they are deathly ill in other ways—through nonverbal communication, eavesdropping, talking with other child patients, and perceiving physiological changes in their bodies. Children growing up on Israeli kibbutzim (agricultural settlements) who have witnessed terrorist attacks, family members' departure on army tours, and parental anxiety about safety express a mature grasp of death by age 5 (Mahon, Goldberg, & Washington, 1999).

Enhancing Children's Understanding.
We have seen that children with a good grasp of the facts of death express less anxiety about it. Direct explanations, like Leslie's, that fit the child's capacity to understand work best. Sometimes children ask difficult questions, such as "Will I die?" "Will you die?" Parents

can be truthful as well as comforting by taking advantage of the child's sense of time: "Someday I will die, but I hope not for many, many years. First I want to enjoy you as a grownup and be a grandparent."

Another way to foster an accurate appreciation of death is to teach young children about human biology. Three- to 5-year-olds given lessons in the role of the heart, brain, lungs, stomach, and other organs in sustaining life have more advanced death concepts than children not given such lessons (Slaughter & Lyons, 2003).

Adult–child discussions should also be culturally sensitive. Rather than presenting scientific evidence as negating religious beliefs, parents and teachers can help children blend the two sources of knowledge. As noted earlier, preschool and school-age children often combine their biological appreciation of death with religious and spiritual views, which offer solace in times of bereavement (Talwar, 2011). As we will see later, open, honest discussions not only contribute to a realistic understanding of death but also facilitate grieving after a child has experienced a loss.

Adolescence

Teenagers can easily explain death subconcepts of nonfunctionality and finality, but they are attracted to alternatives. For example, adolescents often describe death as an enduring abstract state—"darkness," "eternal light," "transition," or "nothingness" (Brent et al., 1996). They also formulate personal theories about life after death. Besides images of heaven and hell influenced by their religious background, they speculate about reincarnation, transmigration of souls, and spiritual survival on earth or at another level (Noppe & Noppe, 1997; Yang & Chen, 2002).

Although mortality in adolescence is low compared with that in infancy and adulthood, teenage deaths are typically sudden and human-induced; unintentional injuries, homicide, and suicide are leading causes. Adolescents are clearly aware that death happens to everyone and can occur at any time. But as their high-risk activities suggest, they do not take death personally.

What explains teenagers' difficulty integrating logic with reality in the domain of death? First, adolescence is a period of rapid growth and onset of reproductive capacity—attainments that are the opposite of death! Second, recall that in adolescent brain development, the prefrontal cognitive control network is not yet able to manage the stress reactivity and sensation-seeking impulses emanating from the brain's emotional/social network—an imbalance that contributes to teenagers' tendency to take unnecessary chances with their lives. When they drive recklessly or play "chicken" with a speeding train and survive, they may experience the illusion of control over death, which prompts them to take additional death-defying risks. Finally, the adolescent personal fable—teenagers' conviction that they are special and unique—may also convince them that they are beyond reach of death.

By encouraging adolescents to discuss concerns about death, adults can help them build a bridge between death as a logical possibility and their everyday actions. Taking up adolescents' thoughts and feelings can be part of everyday conversation, sparked by a news report or the death of an acquaintance. Parents can capitalize on these moments to express their own views, listen closely, accept teenagers' feelings, and correct misconceptions. Such mutual sharing deepens bonds of love and provides the basis for further exploration when the need arises. Applying What We Know on the following page suggests ways to discuss concerns about death with children and adolescents.

Adulthood

In early adulthood, many people brush aside thoughts of death (Corr & Corr, 2013). This avoidance may be prompted by death anxiety, which we will consider in the next section. Alternatively, it may be due to relative lack of interest in death-related issues, given that young adults typically do not know very many people who have died and (like adolescents) think of their own death as a long way off.

In Chapters 15 and 16, we described midlife as a time of stock taking in which people begin to view the lifespan in terms of time left to live and focus on tasks to be completed. Middle-aged people no longer have a vague conception of their own death. They know that in the not-too-distant future, it will be their turn to grow old and die.

In late adulthood, adults think and talk more about death because it is much closer. Increasing evidence of mortality comes from physical changes, higher rates of illness and disability, and loss of relatives and friends (see Chapter 17). Compared with middle-aged people, older adults spend more time pondering the process and circumstances of dying than the state of death (Kastenbaum, 2012). Nearness to death seems to lead to a practical concern with how and when it might happen.

These British youths carry the coffin of a 16-year-old who was stabbed to death during a gang attack. Although teenagers grasp death's finality and nonfunctionality, they may speculate about alternative possibilities for life after death.

Applying what we Know

Discussing Concerns About Death with Children and Adolescents

SUGGESTION	DESCRIPTION
Take the lead.	Be alert to the child's or adolescent's nonverbal behaviors, bringing up the subject sympathetically, especially after a death-related situation has occurred.
Listen perceptively.	Give full attention to the child or adolescent and the feelings underlying his or her words. When adults pretend to listen while thinking about other things, young people quickly pick up this sign of indifference and withdraw their confidence.
Acknowledge feelings.	Accept the child's or adolescent's emotions as real and important; avoid being judgmental. For example, paraphrase sentiments you detect, such as "I see you're very puzzled about that. Let's talk more about it."
Provide factual information in a candid, culturally sensitive fashion.	For children who do not yet have a realistic understanding of death, provide simple, direct, and accurate explanations. Avoid misleading statements, such as "went for a rest" or "sleeping." Do not contradict the young person's religious beliefs. Rather, assist him or her in blending biological with religious knowledge.
Engage in joint problem solving.	When questions do not have easy answers, such as "Where does your soul go when you die?," convey your belief in the young person's worth by indicating that you do not want to impose a point of view but rather to help him or her come to personally satisfying conclusions. To questions you cannot answer, say, "I don't know." Such honesty shows a willingness to generate and evaluate solutions jointly.

Finally, although we have traced overall age-related changes, large individual differences exist. Some adults focus on life and death issues early on; others are less reflective, moving into old age without giving these matters much attention.

Death Anxiety

As you read the following statements, do you find yourself agreeing, disagreeing, or reacting neutrally?

> "Never feeling anything again after I die upsets me."
>
> "I hate the idea that I will be helpless after I die."
>
> "The total isolation of death is frightening to me."
>
> "The feeling that I will be missing out on so much after I die disturbs me." (Thorson & Powell, 1994, pp. 38–39)

Items like these appear on questionnaires used to measure **death anxiety**—fear and apprehension of death. Even people who clearly accept the reality of death may fear it.

What predicts whether thoughts of our own demise trigger intense distress, relative calm, or something in between? To answer this question, researchers measure both general death anxiety and specific factors—fear of no longer existing, loss of control, a painful death, decay of the body, separation from loved ones, and the unknown (Neimeyer, 1994). Findings reveal large individual and cultural variations in aspects of death that arouse fear. For example, in a study of devout Islamic Saudi Arabians, certain factors that appear repeatedly in the responses of Westerners, such as fear of the body decaying and of the unknown, were entirely absent (Long, 1985).

Among Westerners, spirituality—a sense of life's meaning—seems more important than religious commitment in limiting death anxiety (Ardelt, 2003; Routledge & Juhl, 2010). And in two studies, Christian older adults whose religious beliefs and behavior were contradictory—who believed in a rewarding afterlife but rarely prayed or attended services, or who regularly prayed and attended services but doubted the existence of an afterlife—reported higher death anxiety (Wink, 2006; Wink & Scott, 2005). Together, these findings indicate that both firmness of beliefs and consistency between beliefs and practices, rather than religiousness itself, reduce fear of death. Death anxiety is especially low among adults with deep faith in some form of higher force or being—faith that may or may not be influenced by religion (Cicirelli, 2002; Neimeyer et al., 2011).

People with a well-developed, positive personal philosophy of death are also less fearful. In one study, researchers distinguished between two philosophies: a *participatory perspective*, in which death and dying are viewed as natural and life-promoting, as fulfillment of life goals, and as a time to share one's experiences with others; and an *overcoming perspective*, in which death is seen as imposed on people, as defeat or failure, and as robbing them of opportunities to achieve their goals (Petty et al., 2015). Among adults ranging in age from 18 to 83, "participators" were less fearful of death than "overcomers."

From what you have learned about adult psychosocial development, how do you think death anxiety might change with age? If you predicted it would decline, reaching its lowest level in late adulthood, you are correct (see Figure 19.1 on page 652) (Russac et al., 2007; Tomer, Eliason, & Smith, 2000). This age-related drop has been found in many cultures and ethnic groups.

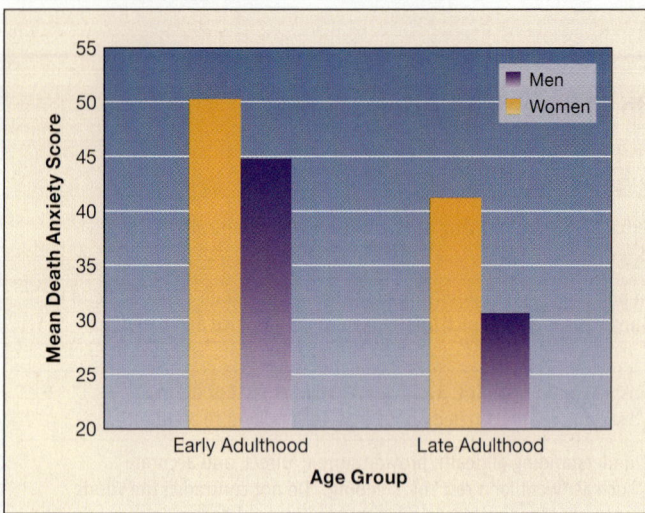

FIGURE 19.1 Relationship of age and gender to death anxiety. In this study comparing young and older adults, death anxiety declined with age. Women expressed greater fear of death than men. Many other studies show similar findings. (Based on Tomer, Eliason, & Smith, 2000.)

Experiencing some anxiety about death is normal and adaptive. But like other fears, very intense death anxiety can undermine effective adjustment. Although physical health in adulthood is not related to death anxiety, mental health clearly is. In cultures as different as China and the United States, people who are depressed or generally anxious tend to have more severe death concerns (Neimeyer & Van Brunt, 1995; Wu, Tang, & Kwok, 2002). In contrast, people who are good at inhibition (keeping their minds from straying to irrelevant thoughts) and at emotional self-regulation report less death anxiety (Bodner et al., 2015; Gailliot, Schmeichel, & Baumeister, 2006). They are better able to manage their concerns about death.

Death anxiety is largely limited to adolescence and adulthood. Children rarely display it unless they live in high-crime neighborhoods or war-torn areas where they are in constant danger (see the Cultural Influences box on the impact of ethnic and political violence on children on page 359 in Chapter 10). Terminally ill children are also at risk for high death anxiety. Compared with other same-age patients, children with cancer express more destructive thoughts and negative feelings about death (Malone, 1982). For those whose parents make the mistake of not telling them they are going to die, loneliness and death anxiety can be extreme (O'Halloran & Altmaier, 1996).

Recall from Chapter 18 that older adults are especially effective at regulating negative emotion. As a result, most cope with anxieties, including fear of death, effectively. Furthermore, attainment of ego integrity reduces death anxiety. Older people have had more time to develop *symbolic immortality*—the belief that one will continue to live on through one's children or through one's work or personal influence (see Chapter 16, page 539).

As long as it is not overly intense, death anxiety can motivate people to strive to live up to internalized cultural values—for example, to be kind to others and to work hard to reach one's goals. These efforts increase adults' sense of self-esteem, self-efficacy, and purpose in life—powerful antidotes against the terrifying thought that, in the overall scheme of things, they "are no more important or enduring than any individual potato, pineapple, or porcupine" (Fry, 2003; Pyszczynski et al., 2004, p. 436). In a study of Israeli adults, symbolic immortality predicted reduced fear of death, especially among those with secure attachments (Florian & Mikulincer, 1998). Gratifying, close interpersonal ties seem to help people feel worthwhile and forge a sense of symbolic immortality. And people who view death as an opportunity to pass a legacy to future generations are less likely to fear it (Cicirelli, 2001; Mikulincer, Florian, & Hirschberger, 2003).

Regardless of age, in both Eastern and Western cultures, women appear more anxious about death than men do (refer again to Figure 19.1) (Madnawat & Kachhawa, 2007; Tomer, Eliason, & Smith, 2000). Women may be more likely to admit and men more likely to avoid troubled feelings about mortality—an explanation consistent with females' greater emotional expressiveness throughout the lifespan. Furthermore, in one study, women showed a temporary rise in death anxiety in their early fifties not seen in men (Russac et al., 2007). Perhaps menopause, in marking the end of reproductive capacity, provides women with a stark reminder of their mortality.

Death anxiety declines in old age, and this 81-year-old from the Netherlands seems to have very little! She had this coffin made to serve as a bookshelf because, she said, "It's a waste to use a coffin just for burial." The pillow on the top will support her head after she dies.

Ask yourself

CONNECT How do advances in cognition contribute to adolescents' understanding of death? (Refer to Chapter 11, pages 388–389 and 392–393.)

APPLY When 4-year-old Chloe's aunt died, Chloe asked, "Where's Aunt Susie?" Her mother explained, "Aunt Susie is taking a long, peaceful sleep." For the next two weeks, Chloe refused to go to bed, and, when finally coaxed into her room, lay awake for hours. What is the likely reason for Chloe's behavior? What might be a better way of answering her question?

REFLECT Ask members of earlier generations in your family about their childhood experiences with death. Compare these to your own experiences. What differences did you find, and how would you explain them?

Thinking and Emotions of Dying People

19.3 Describe and evaluate Kübler-Ross's theory of typical responses to dying, and cite factors that influence dying patients' responses.

In the year before her death, Sofie did everything possible to surmount her illness. In between treatments to control the cancer, she tested her strength. She continued to teach high school, traveled to visit her children, cultivated a garden, and took weekend excursions with Philip. Hope pervaded Sofie's approach to her deadly condition, and she spoke often about the disease—so much so that her friends wondered how she could confront it so directly.

As Sofie deteriorated physically, she moved in and out of various mental and emotional states. She was frustrated, and at times angry and depressed, about her inability to keep on fighting. I recall her lamenting anxiously on a day when she was in pain, "I'm sick, so very sick! I'm trying so hard, but I can't keep on." Once she asked when my husband and I, who were newly married, would have children. "If only I could live long enough to hold them in my arms!" she cried. In the last week, she appeared tired but free of struggle. Occasionally, she spoke of her love for us and commented on the beauty of the hills outside her window. But mostly, she looked and listened, rather than actively participating in conversation. One afternoon, she fell permanently unconscious.

Do Stages of Dying Exist?

As dying people move closer to death, do they go through a series of changes that are the same for everyone, or are their thoughts and feelings unique?

Kübler-Ross's Theory. Although her theory has been heavily criticized, Elisabeth Kübler-Ross (1969) is credited with awakening society's sensitivity to the psychological needs of dying patients. From interviews with over 200 terminally ill people, she devised a theory of five typical responses—initially proposed as stages—to the prospect of death and the ordeal of dying: (1) *denial*—refusing to accept the diagnosis and avoiding discussions with doctors and family members, as a means of escaping from the prospect of death; (2) *anger*—resentment and fury that time is short, that goals may be left unattained, and at the unfairness of death; (3) *bargaining*—striking bargains with doctors, nurses, family members, friends, or God for extra time; (4) *depression*—with realization of the inevitability of death, despondency about the impending loss of one's life; and (5) *acceptance*—the weakened patient reaches a state of peace, usually in the last few days, and disengages from all but a few family members, friends, and caregivers.

Although Kübler-Ross cautioned that her five stages should not be viewed as a fixed sequence and that not all people display each response, her choice of the term *stages* has made it easy for her theory to be interpreted simplistically, as steps a "normal" dying person follows. Decades of research have yielded no evidence for a universal, linear sequence of stages experienced by dying people (Corr, 2015b). Yet some health professionals, unaware of diversity in dying experiences, have insensitively tried to push patients through Kübler-Ross's stages. And caregivers, through callousness or ignorance, can too easily dismiss a dying patient's legitimate complaints about treatment as "just what you would expect in Stage 2" (Corr & Corr, 2013; Kastenbaum, 2012).

Rather than stages, the five reactions Kübler-Ross observed are best viewed as coping strategies that anyone may call on in the face of threat. Furthermore, dying people respond in many additional ways—for example, through efforts to conquer the disease, as Sofie displayed; through an overwhelming need to control what happens to their bodies during the dying process; through acts of generosity and caring; through shifting their focus to living in a fulfilling way—"seizing the day" because so little time is left; and through sadness, relief, isolation, hope, and other emotional reactions (Silverman, 2004; Wright, 2003).

Consider Tony, a 15-year-old leukemia patient, who said to his mother, "I don't want to die yet. Gerry [youngest brother] is only 3 and not old enough to understand. If I could live just one more year, I could explain it to him myself and he will understand" (Komp, 1996, pp. 69–70). Tony's adaptation stresses compassion and altruism; bargaining fails to capture it. Following a diagnosis of terminal lung cancer, my friend Paul devoted as much time as possible to drafting a new book. One way he coped with dying was to immerse himself in work he found intensely satisfying, nearly completing the project several weeks before he died. As these examples suggest, the most serious drawback to Kübler-Ross's theory is that it looks at dying patients' thoughts and feelings outside the contexts that give them meaning.

Kübler-Ross's legacy lies in convincing professionals and the general public that the dying are living people who usually have "unfinished needs" they want to address. As we will see next, people's adaptations to impending death can be understood only in relation to the multidimensional influences that have contributed to their life course and that also shape this final phase.

Contextual Influences on Adaptations to Dying

From the moment of her diagnosis, Sofie spent no time denying the deadliness of her disease. Instead, she met it head on, just as she had dealt with other challenges of life. Her impassioned plea to hold her grandchildren in her arms was not a bargain with fate but rather an expression of profound defeat that on the threshold of late adulthood, she would not live to enjoy its rewards. At the end, her quiet, withdrawn demeanor was probably resignation, not acceptance. All her life, she had been a person with a fighting spirit, unwilling to give in to challenge.

According to recent theorists, a single strategy, such as acceptance, is not best for every dying patient. Rather, an **appropriate death** is one that makes sense in terms of the individual's pattern of living and values and, at the same time, preserves or restores significant relationships and is as free of suffering as possible (Worden, 2000). When asked about a "good death," most patients are clear about what, ideally, they would like to happen. They mention the following goals:

- Maintaining a sense of identity, or inner continuity with one's past
- Clarifying the meaning of one's life and death
- Maintaining and enhancing close relationships
- Achieving a sense of control over the time that remains
- Confronting and preparing for death (Goldsteen et al., 2006; Kleespies, 2004; Proulx & Jacelon, 2004; Reinke et al., 2013)

Dr. Paul Kalanithi, shown here with his wife, Lucy, and daughter, Cady, was diagnosed with incurable lung cancer at age 36. He continued to practice neurosurgery as long as possible, became a father, and authored the memoir *When Breath Becomes Air*, in which he urged others to make the most of their life and time. He died less than two years later, having approached his death in a way that suited his pattern of living and deepest values.

Research reveals that biological, psychological, and social and cultural forces affect people's coping with dying and, therefore, the extent to which they attain these goals. Let's look at some important influences on how people fare.

Nature of the Disease. The course of the illness and its symptoms affect the dying person's reactions. For example, the extended nature of Sofie's illness and her doctor's initial optimism about achieving a remission undoubtedly contributed to her attempts to try to conquer the disease. During the final month, when cancer had spread to Sofie's lungs and she could not catch her breath, she was agitated and fearful until oxygen and medication relieved her uncertainty about being able to breathe. In contrast, Nicholas's weakened heart and failing kidneys so depleted his strength that he responded only with passivity.

Because of the toll of the disease, about 25 percent of cancer patients show symptoms of severe depression—reactions distinct from the sadness, grief, and worry that typically accompany the dying process (Walker et al., 2014). Profound depression amplifies pain, impairs the immune response, interferes with the patient's capacity for pleasure, meaning, and connection, and is associated with poorer survival (Satin, Linden, & Phillips, 2009; Williams & Dale, 2006). It therefore requires immediate treatment. Among the most successful approaches are meaning-focused life review (see page 612 in Chapter 18), medical control of pain, and advance care planning with the patient that ensures that his or her end-of-life wishes are known and respected (Rosenstein, 2011).

Personality and Coping Style. Understanding the way individuals view stressful life events and have coped with them in the past helps us appreciate the way they manage the dying process. In a study in which terminally ill patients discussed their images of dying, responses varied greatly. For example,

- Beth regarded *dying as imprisonment:* "I felt like the clock started ticking … like the future has suddenly been taken.… In a way, I feel like I'm already dead."
- To Faith, dying was *a mandate to live ever more fully:* "I have a saying: … 'You're not ready to live until you're ready to die.' … It never meant much to me until I … looked death in the eye, and now I'm living.… This life is a lot better than the one before."
- Dawn viewed dying as *part of life's journey:* "I learned all about my disease.… I would read, read, read.… I wanted to know as much as I can about it, and I don't think hiding … behind the door … could help me at all. And, I realized for the first time in my life—*really, really, really realized* that I could handle anything."
- Patty approached dying as *an experience to be transformed* so as to make it more bearable: "I am an avid, rabid fan of *Star Trek*, a trekkie like there never has been.… I watch it to the point that I've memorized it.… [In my mind, I play the various characters so] I'm not [always] thinking about cancer or dying.… I think that's how I get through it." (Wright, 2003, pp. 442–444, 447)

Each patient's view of dying helps explain his or her responses to worsening illness. Poorly adjusted individuals—those with conflict-ridden relationships and many disappointments in life—are usually more distressed (Kastenbaum, 2012).

Family Members' and Health Professionals' Behavior.
Earlier we noted that a candid approach, in which everyone close to and caring for the dying person acknowledges the terminal illness, is best. Yet this also introduces the burden of participating in the work of dying with the patient—bringing relationships to closure, reflecting on life, and dealing with fears and regrets.

People who find it hard to engage in these tasks may pretend that the disease is not as bad as it is. In patients inclined toward denial, a "game" can be set in motion in which participants are aware that the patient is dying but act as though it were not so. Though this game softens psychological pain for the moment, it makes dying much more difficult. Besides impeding communication, it frequently leads to futile medical interventions, in which the patient has little understanding of what is happening and is subjected to great physical and emotional suffering. One attending physician provided this account of a cancer patient's death:

> The problem was that she had a young husband and parents who were pretty much in complete denial. We were trying to be aggressive up to the end. To the point that we actually hung a new form of chemotherapy about four hours before she died, even though everybody knew except her immediate family that she was going to die within the next four to eight hours. (Jackson et al., 2005, p. 653)

At other times, the patient suspects what he or she has not been told. In one instance, a terminally ill child flew into a rage because his doctor and a nurse spoke to him in ways that denied the fact that he would not grow up. Trying to get the child to cooperate with a medical procedure, the doctor said,

> "I thought you would understand, Sandy. You told me once you wanted to be a doctor."
>
> He screamed back, "I'm not going to be anything!" and threw an empty syringe at her.
>
> The nurse standing nearby asked, "What are you going to be?"
>
> "A ghost," said Sandy, and turned away from them. (Bluebond-Langner, 1977, p. 59)

The behavior of health professionals impeded Sandy's efforts to form a realistic time perspective and intensified his anger at the injustice of his premature death.

When doctors want to inform patients of their prognosis, they may encounter resistance from family members, especially in certain cultures. Withholding information is common in Southern and Eastern Europe, Central and South America, much of Asia, and the Middle East. In China, Korea, and Japan, terminally ill patients are often not told the truth, out of concern that telling might disrupt family relationships and harm patients' well-being (Mo et al., 2011; Seki et al., 2009). Although attitudes

A doctor listens sympathetically to the concerns of a terminally ill patient. Through sensitive, open communication, health professionals help dying people prepare for death by bringing relationships to closure, reflecting on life, and dealing with fears and regrets.

are changing among U.S. immigrant groups, a substantial minority of Korean Americans and Mexican Americans continue to believe that informing patients is wrong and that health-care decisions should instead be made by family members (Ko et al., 2014; Mead et al., 2013). In these instances, providing information is complex. When a family insists that a patient not be told, the doctor can first offer information to the patient and then, if the patient refuses, ask who should receive information and make health-care decisions. The patient's preference can be honored and reassessed at regular intervals.

Care of the terminally ill is demanding and stressful. Nurses who respond effectively to the psychological needs of dying patients and their families benefit from inservice training aimed at strengthening interpersonal skills, day-to-day mutual support among staff, and development of a personal philosophy of death (Efstathiou & Clifford, 2011; Hebert, Moore, & Rooney, 2011; Morris, 2011). Extensive experience working with dying patients in a sensitive, supportive environment is associated with low death anxiety, perhaps because such caregivers observe their patients' distress decline and, thus, gradually learn that their own previous fears are less founded (Bluck et al., 2008; Peters et al., 2013).

Social support from family members also affects adaptation to dying. Dying patients who feel they have much unfinished business to attend to are more anxious about impending death. Family contact reduces their sense of urgency to prolong life, likely by permitting them to work through at least some incomplete tasks (Mutran et al., 1997; Zimmerman, 2012). Granting and seeking forgiveness for past hurts is a powerful means of relieving distress and inducing life closure among the terminally ill. Unresolved forgiveness issues, in contrast, are linked to greater anger and anxiety and reduced sense of life completion (Baker, 2005; Prince-Paul, Zyzanski, & Exline, 2013). When counselors help family members express end-of-life forgiveness, terminally ill patients gain in psychological well-being.

Applying what we Know

Communicating with Dying People

SUGGESTION	DESCRIPTION
Be truthful about the diagnosis and course of the disease.	Be honest about what the future is likely to hold, thereby permitting the dying person to bring closure to his or her life by expressing sentiments and wishes and participating in decisions about treatment.
Listen perceptively and acknowledge feelings.	Be truly present, focusing full attention on what the dying person has to say and accepting the patient's feelings. Patients who sense another's presence and concern are more likely to relax physically and emotionally and express themselves.
Maintain realistic hope.	Assist the dying person in maintaining hope by encouraging him or her to focus on a realistic goal that might yet be achieved—for example, resolution of a troubled relationship or special moments with a loved one. Knowing the dying person's hope, family members and health professionals can often help fulfill it.
Assist in the final transition.	Assure the dying person that he or she is not alone, offering a sympathetic touch, a caring thought, or just a calm presence. Some patients who struggle may benefit from being given permission to die—the message that giving up and letting go are all right.

Source: Lugton, 2002.

Effective communication with the dying person is honest, fostering a trusting relationship, yet also oriented toward maintaining hope. Many dying patients move through a hope trajectory—at first, hope for a cure; later, hope for prolonging life; and finally, hope for a peaceful death with as few burdens as possible (Fanslow, 1981). Once patients near death stop expressing hope, those close to them must accept this. Family members who find letting go very difficult may benefit from expert guidance. Applying What We Know above offers suggestions for communicating with the dying.

Spirituality, Religion, and Culture. Earlier we noted that a sense of spirituality reduces fear of death. Research indicates that this is as true for the dying as for people in general. Terminally ill patients who score higher in spiritual well-being (belief in life's meaning) express a greater sense of inner peace (feeling relaxed, positive, forgiving of themselves and others, and accepting of their life situation) and less end-of-life despair (desire for a hastened death and suicidal thoughts) (McClain, Rosenfeld, & Breitbart, 2003; McClain-Jacobson et al., 2004; Selman et al., 2013). As one experienced nurse commented,

> At the end, those [patients] with a faith—it doesn't really matter in what, but a faith in something—find it easier. Not always, but as a rule. I've seen people with faith panic and I've seen those without faith accept it [death]. But, as a rule, it's much easier for those with faith. (Samarel, 1991, pp. 64–65)

Vastly different cultural beliefs, guided by religious ideas, also shape people's dying experiences:

- Buddhism, widely practiced in China, India, and Southeast Asia, emphasizes that all physical and mental states are transient, which fosters acceptance of death. By chanting sutras (teachings of Buddha) to the dying to calm the mind and emphasizing that death leads to rebirth (moving through a variety of lives on a journey toward enlightenment), Buddhists believe that it is possible for the dying person to attain Nirvana, a transcendent state in which there is no suffering, desire, or sense of self (Goin, 2015; Kubotera, 2004).

- In many Native-American groups, death is met with stoic self-control, an approach taught at an early age through stories that emphasize a circular, rather than linear, relationship between life and death and the importance of making way for others (Sharp et al., 2015).

- For African Americans, a dying loved one signals a crisis that unites family members in caregiving (Jenkins et al., 2005). The terminally ill person remains an active and vital force within the family until he or she can no longer carry out this role—an attitude of respect that eases the dying process.

- Among the Maori of New Zealand, relatives and friends gather around the dying person to give spiritual strength and comfort. Older adults, clergy, and other experts in tribal customs conduct a *karakia* ceremony, in which they recite prayers asking for peace, mercy, and guidance from the creator. After the ceremony, the patient is encouraged to discuss important matters with closest loved ones—giving away of personal belongings, directions for interment, and completion of other unfinished tasks (Ngata, 2004; Oetzel et al., 2015).

In sum, dying prompts a multitude of thoughts, emotions, and coping strategies. Which ones are emphasized depends on a wide array of contextual influences. A vital assumption of the lifespan perspective—that development is multidimensional and multidirectional—is just as relevant to this final phase as to each earlier period.

A Place to Die

19.4 Evaluate the extent to which homes, hospitals, nursing homes, and the hospice approach meet the needs of dying people and their families.

Whereas in the past most deaths occurred at home, in the United States today about 40 percent take place in hospitals and another 20 percent in long-term care facilities, usually nursing homes. Nearly 30 percent of people age 65 and older experience a hospital intensive care unit (ICU) in the last month of life, most of whom die there (Centers for Disease Control and Prevention, 2016e; Teno et al., 2013). In the large, impersonal hospital environment, meeting the human needs of dying patients and their families is usually secondary, not because professionals lack concern, but because their work focuses on saving lives. A dying patient represents a failure.

In the 1960s, a death awareness movement arose as a reaction to hospitals' death-avoiding practices—attachment of complicated machinery to patients with no chance of survival and avoidance of communication with dying patients. This movement soon led to medical care better suited to the needs of dying people and also to hospice programs, which have spread to many countries in the industrialized world. Let's visit each of these settings for dying.

Home

Had Sofie and Nicholas been asked where they wanted to die, undoubtedly each would have responded, "At home"—the preference of 80 percent of Americans (NHPCO, 2013). The reason is clear: The home can offer an atmosphere of intimacy and loving care in which the terminally ill person is unlikely to feel abandoned or humiliated by physical decline or dependence on others.

Although U.S. home deaths have increased over the past two decades, dying at home remains a distant reality for many: Only about one-fourth of Americans experience it, more often those who are financially better off (Centers for Disease Control and Prevention, 2016e). And it is important not to romanticize dying at home. Because of dramatic improvements in medicine, dying people tend to be sicker or much older than in the past. Consequently, their bodies may be extremely frail, making ordinary activities—eating, sleeping, taking a pill, toileting, and bathing—major ordeals for informal caregivers (Milligan et al., 2016). Health problems of aging spouses, work and other responsibilities of family members, and the physical, psychological, and financial strain of providing home care can make it difficult to honor a terminally ill person's wish to die at home.

For many family members, the chance to be with the dying person until the very end is a rewarding tradeoff for the high demands of caregiving. But to make dying at home feasible, adequate support for the caregiver is essential (Karlsson & Berggren, 2011). A specially trained home health aide is usually necessary—a service (as we will see shortly) that hospice programs have made more accessible. Furthermore, even with professional help, most homes are poorly equipped to handle the medical and comfort-care needs of the dying. Hospital-based equipment and technical support often must be transported to the home.

Overall, the evidence is inconsistent on whether home deaths are associated with less pain and increased satisfaction for patients and reduced distress for family members than deaths occurring in hospitals (Higginson et al., 2013; Shepperd et al., 2016). Contributing to these mixed outcomes, a considerable number of aging adults, rather than dying in their own home, die in a family member's home—often an adult child's. Modifications to the physical structure and addition of equipment to accommodate the dying person's needs, along with the intensity of caregiving tasks, can disrupt caregivers' own sense of home, with negative consequences for psychological well-being (Milligan et al., 2016). And dying older adults' concerns about burdening their adult children, along with regret at having lost the identity, security, privacy, and personal control they had in their own home, can contribute to anxiety and dissatisfaction as well.

Hospital

Hospital dying takes many forms. Each is affected by the physical state of the dying person, the hospital unit in which it takes place, and the goal and quality of care.

Sudden deaths, due to injury or critical illness, typically occur in emergency rooms. Doctors and nurses must evaluate the problem and take action quickly. Little time is available for contact with family members. When staff break the news of death in a sympathetic manner and provide explanations, family members are grateful. Otherwise, feelings of anger, frustration, and confusion can add to their grief (Walsh & McGoldrick, 2004). Crisis intervention services are needed to help survivors cope with sudden death.

Dying in intensive care is a depersonalizing experience unique to technologically sophisticated societies. In such settings, medical responses supersede privacy and communicating with patient and family.

Nicholas died in an ICU focused on preventing death in patients whose condition can worsen quickly. Privacy and communication with the family were secondary to monitoring his condition. To avoid disruption of nurses' activities, Giselle and Sasha could be at Nicholas's side only at scheduled times. Dying in intensive care—an experience unique to technologically sophisticated societies—is especially depersonalizing for patients like Nicholas, who linger between life and death while hooked to machines, sometimes for weeks or months.

Cancer patients, who account for most cases of prolonged dying, typically die in general or specialized cancer-care hospital units. When hospitalized for a long time, they reach out for help with physical and emotional needs, too often with mixed success. In these hospital settings, as in ICUs, a conflict of values is apparent (Hillman, 2011). The tasks associated with dying must be performed efficiently so all patients can be served and health professionals are not drained emotionally by repeated attachments and separations.

Although hospital comprehensive treatment programs aimed at easing physical, emotional, and spiritual suffering at the end of life have increased steadily over the past decade, one-third of U.S. hospitals still do not have them (Dumanovsky et al., 2016). And because most U.S. and Canadian medical schools do not offer even a single pain-focused course (usually an elective), few doctors and nurses are specially trained in managing pain in chronically ill and dying people (Horowitz, Gramling, & Quill, 2014). At present, many people die in painful, frightening, and depersonalizing hospital conditions, without their wishes being met.

Nursing Home

Though deaths in U.S. nursing homes—mostly very old patients—are common, care emphasizes rehabilitation rather than high-quality terminal care. Too often, residents' end-of-life preferences are not gathered and recorded in medical records. The few studies that have addressed what it is like to die in nursing homes concur that many patients suffer from inattention to their emotional and spiritual needs, high levels of untreated pain, and aggressive end-of-life medical intervention (Miller, Lima, & Thompson, 2015).

The hospice approach—which we consider next—aims to reduce profound caregiving failures in hospitals and nursing homes. When combined with hospice, nursing home care of the dying improves greatly in pain management, prevention of hospitalizations, emotional and spiritual support, and family satisfaction (Zheng et al., 2012, 2015). But referrals of dying nursing-home residents to hospice, though increasing, are often not made—or made too late to be useful.

The Hospice Approach

In medieval times, a *hospice* was a place where travelers could find rest and shelter. In the nineteenth and twentieth centuries, the word referred to homes for dying patients. Today, **hospice** is not a place but a comprehensive program of support services for terminally ill people and their families. It aims to provide a caring community sensitive to the dying person's needs so patients and family members can prepare for death in ways that are satisfying to them. Quality of life is central to the hospice approach, which includes these main features:

- The patient and family as a unit of care
- Emphasis on meeting the patient's physical, emotional, social, and spiritual needs, including controlling pain, retaining dignity and self-worth, and feeling cared for and loved
- Care provided by an interdisciplinary team: a doctor, a nurse or home health aide, a chaplain, a counselor or social worker, and a trained volunteer
- The patient kept at home or in an inpatient setting with a homelike atmosphere where coordination of care is possible
- Focus on protecting the quality of remaining life with **palliative,** or **comfort, care** that relieves pain and other symptoms (nausea, breathing difficulties, insomnia, and depression) rather than prolonging life
- In addition to regularly scheduled care visits, on-call services available 24 hours a day, 7 days a week
- Follow-up bereavement services offered to families in the year after a death

Because hospice care is a philosophy, not a facility, it can be applied in diverse ways. In Great Britain, care in a special hospice inpatient unit, sometimes associated with a hospital, is typical. In the United States, both home and hospice inpatient units are emphasized: About 36 percent of hospice patients die at home, 32 percent in a hospice inpatient unit, 14 percent in a nursing home, 9 percent in another type of residential setting, and 9 percent in a typical hospital room (NHPCO, 2013).

A son and his dying mother share recollections as he shows her a photograph of her long-ago graduation. By creating opportunities for unpressured closeness and connection, hospice care enhances dying patients' quality of life rather than extending life.

Biology and Environment

Music as Palliative Care for Dying Patients

When Peter visits 82-year-old Stuart to play the harp, Stuart reports being transported to an idyllic place with water, children, and trees—far from the lung tumors that will soon take his life. "When Peter plays for me, … I am no longer frightened," Stuart says.

Peter is a specialist in *music thanatology,* an emerging specialty in music therapy that focuses on providing palliative care to the dying through music. He uses his harp, and sometimes his voice, to induce calm and give solace to the dying, their families, and their caregivers. Peter applies music systematically—matching it to each patient's breathing patterns and other responses, delivering different sounds to uplift or comfort, depending on his assessment of the patient's moment-by-moment needs.

Research consistently shows that music vigils have diverse benefits. In one investigation, older adults suffering from advanced cancer who had been admitted to a hospital palliative care unit for end-of-life pain and other symptom management were assigned to one of two groups: standard care plus music therapy or standard care alone. Each music therapy participant experienced four music sessions over the course of 8 to 10 days. Relative to controls, the music group gained in patient-reported relaxation and psychological well-being and declined in emotional and physical symptoms, including anxiety, depression, insomnia, nausea, and shortness of breath (Domingo et al., 2015).

Other evidence indicates that music therapy can reduce pain in dying patients, with one experiment demonstrating the effectiveness of just a single session (Gutgsell et al., 2013; Horne-Thompson & Grocke, 2008). Why

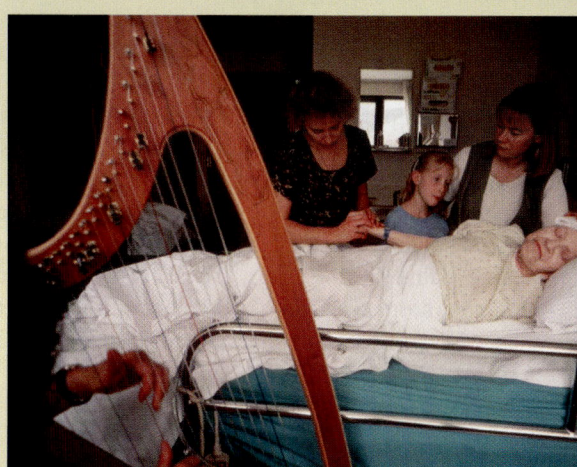

Music thanatology focuses on providing palliative care for the dying through music. This practitioner uses her harp, and sometimes her voice, to induce calm and provide solace.

is music helpful in easing end-of-life physical and emotional distress? In patients close to death, hearing typically functions longer than other senses. Consequently, responsiveness to music may persist through the individual's final days and hours (Berry & Griffie, 2016). For this reason, music vigils may be an especially effective end-of-life therapy.

But hospice programs everywhere have expanded to include a continuum of care, from home to inpatient options, including hospitals and nursing homes. Central to the hospice approach is that the dying person and his or her family be offered choices that guarantee an appropriate death. Contact with others facing terminal illness is a supportive byproduct of many hospice arrangements. And to find out about a comforting, palliative care intervention for patients near death, consult the Biology and Environment box above.

LOOK and LISTEN

> Contact a nearby hospice program, and find out about the varied ways it delivers comprehensive services to meet the needs of dying patients and their families.

Currently, the United States has over 6,000 hospice programs serving approximately 1.2 million terminally ill patients annually. About 37 percent of hospice patients have cancer. The top non-cancer diagnoses are dementia (15 percent), heart disease (15 percent), and lung disease (9 percent) (NHPCO, 2013). Because hospice care is a cost-effective alternative to expensive life-saving treatments, U.S. government health-care benefits (Medicare and Medicaid) cover it, as do most private insurance plans. In addition, community and foundation contributions allow many hospices to provide free services to uninsured patients who cannot pay (Hospice Foundation of America, 2016). Consequently hospice is affordable for most dying patients and their families. Hospices also serve dying children—a tragedy so devastating that social support and bereavement intervention are vital.

Besides reducing patient physical suffering, hospice contributes to improved family functioning. The majority of patients and families report high satisfaction with quality of care. Compared to other dying patients, those who receive hospice care experience better pain management, enhanced sense of social support, higher quality of life, longer survival, greater correspondence between their preferred and actual place of death, and reduced medical expenditures (Candy et al., 2011; Churchman et al., 2014; Connor et al., 2007). Six months to two years after their loved one's death, family members experiencing hospice score higher than their nonhospice counterparts in psychological well-being (Ragow-O'Brien, Hayslip, & Guarnaccia, 2000; Wright et al., 2008).

As a long-range goal, hospice organizations are striving for broader acceptance of their patient- and family-centered approach. Culturally sensitive approaches are needed to reach more ethnic minority patients, who are far less likely than white patients to participate in hospice (NHPCO, 2013). Canada has a Web-based hospice outreach service, the Canadian Virtual Hospice (www.virtualhospice.ca), to support patients, families, and care providers—whether or not they are part of a hospice program—with information, resources, and connections to others with similar concerns.

In developing countries, where millions of children and adults die of cancer and other devastating illnesses each year, community-based teams working under a health professional's supervision are making progress in delivering hospice and palliative care services. But they face many obstacles, including lack of funding, pain-relieving drugs, and professional and public education about hospice (WPCA, 2014). As a result, they are "islands of excellence," accessible to far too few patients and families.

Ask yourself

CONNECT Reread the description of Sofie's mental and emotional reactions to dying on pages 653 and 654. Then review the story of Sofie's life on pages 3–4 in Chapter 1. How were Sofie's responses consistent with her personality and lifelong style of coping with adversity?

APPLY When 5-year-old Timmy's kidney failure was diagnosed as terminal, his parents couldn't accept the tragic news. Their hospital visits became shorter, and they evaded his anxious questions. Eventually, Timmy blamed himself. He died with little physical pain, but alone, and his parents suffered prolonged guilt. How could hospice care have helped Timmy and his family?

REFLECT If you were terminally ill, where would you want to die? Explain.

The Right to Die

19.5 Discuss end-of-life medical practices, along with ethical controversies surrounding them.

In 1976, the parents of Karen Ann Quinlan, a young woman who had fallen into an irreversible coma after taking drugs at a party, sued to have her respirator turned off. The New Jersey Supreme Court, invoking Karen's right to privacy and her parents' power as guardians, complied with this request. Although Karen was expected to die quickly, she breathed independently, continued to be fed intravenously, and lived another 10 years in a persistent vegetative state.

In 1990, 26-year-old Terri Schiavo's heart stopped briefly, temporarily cutting off oxygen to her brain. Like Karen, Terri lay in a persistent vegetative state. Her husband and guardian, Michael, claimed that she had earlier told him she would not want to be kept alive artificially, but Terri's parents disagreed. In 1998, the Florida Circuit Court granted Michael's petition to have Terri's feeding tube removed. In 2001, after her parents had exhausted their appeals, the tube was taken out. But on the basis of contradictory medical testimony, Terri's parents convinced a circuit court judge to order the feeding tube reinserted, and the legal wrangling continued. In 2002, Michael won a second judgment to remove the tube.

By that time, publicity over the case and its central question—who should make end-of-life decisions when the patient's wishes are unclear—had made Terri a political issue. In 2003, the Florida legislature passed a law allowing the governor to stay the circuit court's order to keep Terri alive, but on appeal, the law was declared unconstitutional. In 2005, the U.S. Congress entered the fray, passing a bill that transferred Terri's fate to the U.S. District Court. When the judge refused to intervene, the feeding tube was removed for a third time. In 2005—15 years after losing consciousness—Terri Schiavo died. The autopsy confirmed the original persistent vegetative state diagnosis: Her brain was half normal size.

Before the 1950s, the right to die was of little concern because medical science could do little to extend the lives of terminally ill patients. Today, medical advances mean that the same procedures that preserve life can prolong inevitable death, diminishing both quality of life and personal dignity.

The Quinlan and Schiavo cases—and others like them—brought right-to-die issues to the forefront of public attention. Today, all U.S. states have laws that honor patients' wishes concerning withdrawal of life-sustaining treatment in cases of terminal illness and, sometimes, in cases of a persistent vegetative state, thereby permitting the patient to die naturally. But no uniform right-to-die policy covering other situations exists, and heated debate persists over how to handle the diverse circumstances in which patients and family members make requests. The various practices that are the focus of right-to-die ethical debates are summarized in Table 19.1. Let's discuss each in turn.

TABLE 19.1
Ethically Debated End-of-Life Medical Practices

PRACTICE	DESCRIPTION
Ending life-sustaining treatment	With the terminally ill patient's permission, or the permission of the patient's substitute decision maker, a doctor withholds or withdraws life-sustaining treatment, thereby permitting the patient to die naturally. For example, the doctor does not perform surgery, insert a feeding tube, or administer medication that could prolong life, or the doctor turns off the respirator of a patient who cannot breathe independently.
Medical aid-in-dying	At an incurably ill patient's request, a doctor provides a prescription for a lethal dose of medication that the patient self-administers to end his or her life.
Voluntary euthanasia	At a suffering patient's request, a doctor ends the patient's life in a painless way. For example, the doctor administers a lethal dose of medication.
Involuntary euthanasia	A doctor ends a suffering patient's life by some medical means, such as a lethal dose of medication, without the patient's consent.

Ending Life-Sustaining Treatment

Do you think Terri Schiavo should have been allowed to die sooner? Was it right for Nicholas's doctors to turn off his respirator at Giselle's request? When an Alzheimer's victim has lost all awareness and bodily functions, should life support be withheld?

Surveys reveal that more than 70 percent of U.S. adults and 95 percent of physicians support the right of patients or family members to end treatment when there is no hope of recovery (Curlin et al., 2008; Pew Research Center, 2006). In 1986, the American Medical Association endorsed withdrawing all forms of treatment from the terminally ill when death is imminent and from those in a permanent vegetative state. Consequently, ending treatment in situations like those just described is now widely practiced as part of ordinary medical procedure, in which doctors exercise professional judgment.

Still, a minority of Americans oppose the practice. Religious denomination has surprisingly little effect on people's opinions. For example, most Catholics hold favorable views, despite slow official church acceptance because of fears that ending treatment might be a first step toward government-approved mercy killing. However, ethnicity makes a difference: Many more African Americans than European Americans say they desire all medical means possible, regardless of the patient's condition, and African Americans more often receive life-sustaining intervention, such as feeding tubes (Haley, 2013; Wicher & Meeker, 2012). Their reluctance to forgo treatment reflects strong religious belief in the power of God to promote healing, mistrust of the health-care system, and limited knowledge of how to express end-of-life treatment preferences.

Because of controversial court cases like Terri Schiavo's, many doctors and health-care institutions are unwilling to withhold or withdraw treatment without legal protection. In the absence of consensus on the practice, people can best ensure that their wishes will be followed by preparing an **advance medical directive**—a written statement of desired medical treatment should they become incurably ill. U.S. states recognize two types of advance directives: a *living will* and a *durable power of attorney for health care*. Sometimes these are combined into one document.

In a **living will,** people specify the treatments they do or do not want in case of a terminal illness, coma, or other near-death situation (see Figure 19.2). For example, a person might state that without reasonable expectation of recovery, he or she should not be kept alive through medical intervention of any kind. In addition, a living will sometimes specifies that pain-relieving medication be given, even though it might shorten life. In Sofie's case, her doctor administered a powerful narcotic to relieve labored breathing and quiet her fear of suffocation. The narcotic induced unconsciousness and suppressed respiration, causing death to occur hours or days earlier than if the medication had not been prescribed. Such palliative care is accepted as appropriate and ethical medical practice.

Although living wills help ensure personal control, they do not guarantee it. Recognition of living wills is usually limited to patients who are terminally ill or are otherwise expected to die shortly. Only a few U.S. states cover people in a persistent vegetative state or aging adults who linger with many chronic problems, including Alzheimer's disease, because these conditions are not classified as terminal. Even when terminally ill patients have living wills, doctors often do not follow them for a variety of reasons (Saitta & Hodge, 2013). These include fear of lawsuits, their own moral beliefs, failure to inquire about patients' directives, and inaccessibility of those directives—for example, located in the family safe or family members unaware of them.

LIVING WILL

THIS DECLARATION is made this _____ day of _____, 20 ___.

I, _____, being of sound mind, willfully and voluntarily make known my desires that my moment of death shall not be artificially postponed. If at any time I should have an incurable and irreversible injury, disease, or illness judged to be a terminal condition by my attending physician who has personally examined me and has determined that my death is imminent except for death delaying procedures, I direct that such procedures which would only prolong the dying process be withheld or withdrawn, and that I be permitted to die naturally with only the administration of medication, sustenance, or the performance of any medical procedure deemed necessary by my attending physician to provide me with comfort care.

In the absence of my ability to give directions regarding the use of such death delaying procedures, it is my intention that this declaration shall be honored by my family and physician as the final expression of my legal right to refuse medical or surgical treatment and accept the consequences from such refusal.

Signed: _____

City, County and State of Residence: _____

_____

_____

The declarant is personally known to me and I believe him or her to be of sound mind. I saw the declarant sign the declaration in my presence (or the declarant acknowledged in my presence that he or she had signed the declaration) and I signed the declaration as a witness in the presence of the declarant. At the date of this instrument, I am not entitled to any portion of the estate of the declarant according to the laws of intestate succession or, to the best of my knowledge and belief, under any will of declarant or other instrument taking effect at declarant's death, or directly financially responsible for declarant's medical care.

Witness: _____

Witness: _____

FIGURE 19.2 Example of a living will. This document is legal in the State of Illinois. Each person completing a living will should use a form specific to the U.S. state or Canadian province in which he or she resides because laws vary widely. (Courtesy of Office of the Attorney General, State of Illinois.)

Because living wills cannot anticipate all future medical conditions and can easily be ignored, a second form of advance directive has become common. A **durable power of attorney for health care** authorizes appointment of another person (usually, though not always, a family member) to make health-care decisions on one's behalf. It generally requires only a short signed and witnessed statement like this:

> I hereby appoint [name] as my attorney-in-fact (my "agent") to act for me and in my name (in any way I could act in person) to make any and all decisions for me concerning my personal care, medical treatment, hospitalization, and health care and to require, withhold, or withdraw any type of medical treatment or procedure, even though my death may ensue. (Courtesy of Office of the Attorney General, State of Illinois)

The durable power of attorney for health care is more flexible than the living will because it permits a trusted spokesperson to confer with the doctor as medical circumstances arise. Because authority to speak for the patient is not limited to terminal illnesses, more latitude exists for dealing with unexpected situations. And for couples who are not legally married, the durable power of attorney can ensure the partner's role in decision making and in advocating for the patient's health-care needs.

Whether or not a person supports ending treatment when natural death is imminent, it is important to have a living will, durable power of attorney, or both, because most deaths occur in hospitals or long-term care facilities. Yet only 45 percent of Americans over age 40 have executed such documents, perhaps because of widespread uneasiness about bringing up the topic of death, especially with relatives. The percentage with advance directives increases with age; nearly 55 percent of adults over age 65 have them (Government Accountability Office, 2015). To encourage people to make decisions about potential treatment while they are able, U.S. federal law now requires that all medical facilities receiving federal funds provide information at admission about state laws and institutional policies on patients' rights and advance directives.

As happened with Karen Quinlan and Terri Schiavo, health professionals—when uncertain about a patient's intent and fearing liability—will probably decide to continue treatment regardless of cost and a person's prior oral statements. Perhaps for this reason, some U.S. states permit appointment of a health-care proxy, or substitute decision maker, if a patient failed to provide an advance medical directive while competent. Proxies are an important means of covering children and adolescents, who cannot legally execute advance medical directives.

Medical Aid-in-Dying

Shortly after her wedding in 2012, Brittany Maynard began experiencing headaches that increased in severity. In early 2014, at age 29, she was diagnosed with an aggressive, incurable form of brain cancer. At first, doctors estimated that Brittany had several years left to live—an exceedingly short time to any 29-year-old. But additional tests revealed that the cancer was spreading rapidly, causing her medical team to revise its forecast to just six months.

No available treatment could save Brittany's life, and treatments doctors recommended to extend it, she concluded, would have destroyed her quality of life. So Brittany decided to live as long as she could and then, with the aid of prescription sleeping medication, end her own life legally and gently before suffering became unbearable—a choice she discussed with her husband, Dan, who respected it.

In **medical aid-in-dying,** at an incurably ill patient's request, a doctor provides a prescription for a lethal dose of drugs, which the patient self-administers to end his or her life. Brittany and Dan lived in California, where at the time the practice was illegal, so they uprooted to Oregon, where doctors could, by law, prescribe drugs to assist terminally ill patients in ending their own lives gently. She spent her remaining days doing what she loved most—in the outdoors, including visiting several national parks, with people closest to her. She also advocated for terminally ill patients' right to choose when to die, explaining that having that choice gave her the sense of peace that enabled her to live fully.

As Brittany's brain seizures intensified and she experienced sleeplessness, nausea, and medication-resistant pain, she worried about waiting too long—that the growing tumor would cause sensory, cognitive, verbal, and motor losses and rob her of her autonomy. On November 1, 2014, she took the medication and died peacefully within 30 minutes, surrounded by her family and dearest friends.

In the United States, medical aid-in-dying is legal in five states: Oregon, Washington, Montana, Vermont, and—as of 2016—California. Oregon, the first state to pass legislation, in 1998, limits the practice to patients who are incurably ill; they need not be in unbearable pain. Patients must have two doctors agree that they have six months or less to live, and must wait

A terminally ill patient discusses a durable power of attorney with his son and daughter. This advance directive authorizes a trusted spokesperson to make health-care decisions and helps ensure that one's desires will be granted.

CHAPTER 19 Death, Dying, and Bereavement

At a right-to-die rally in Sacramento, California, Dan Diaz holds a picture of his late wife, Brittany Maynard, while hugging a terminally ill cancer patient who spoke at the event. Dan's advocacy was instrumental in the passage of California's End of Life Option Act, which legalized medical aid-in-dying and went into effect in 2016.

15 days following an oral request and 48 hours following a written request before being given the drugs. In Washington, Vermont, and California, legal requirements resemble Oregon's (Emanuel et al., 2016). Montana has no specified requirements because legalization resulted from a court ruling, not legislation.

Six other nations—Belgium, the Netherlands, Luxembourg, Switzerland, Colombia, and Canada—have passed medical aid-in-dying legislation. Although patients in these countries need not be terminally ill, they must be experiencing "unbearable" physical or mental suffering without prospect for improvement.

Over the past decade, about 55 percent of Americans have expressed approval of medical aid-in-dying for patients with a terminal illness, a rate that rose to 68 percent following widespread publicity of Brittany Maynard's story (Dugan, 2015). In a review of U.S., Canadian, and Western European surveys, level of support among terminally ill patients was about the same as for the general public, with one-third of patients saying they would consider it for themselves (Hendry et al., 2012). People who support the practice, as well as patients who request it, tend to be higher in SES, white, and less religious.

Oregon has the most extended, detailed records on patients who ended their own lives by taking a legal, physician-prescribed dose of drugs. Their numbers have risen over time, though they account for less than one-half of 1 percent of all deaths. Most (68 percent) were age 65 or older, and the overwhelming majority (90 percent) were enrolled in hospice and died at home. Their most common diagnosis (78 percent) was cancer. As Figure 19.3 shows, patients' most frequently expressed reasons for request-

ing medical aid-in-dying were loss of autonomy, decreasing ability to participate in activities that make life enjoyable, loss of dignity, and loss of control of bodily functions (Oregon Public Health Division, 2016). Inadequate pain control was of far less concern; most knew they had access to palliative care through hospice.

In medical aid-in-dying, the final act is solely the patient's, reducing the possibility of coercion. Still, intense disagreement surrounds the practice. Until recently, it was widely referred to as *physician-assisted suicide*. But proponents of legalization point out that terminally ill patients who gain access to medical aid-in-dying under current U.S. state laws are not suicidal; they do not want to die, nor are they motivated by emotional distress or mental illness. Each state statute specifies that medical aid-in-dying does not constitute suicide and that the patient's incurable disease must be entered as the cause of death on the death certificate.

Opponents of legalization claim that in an atmosphere of high family-caregiving burdens and pressure to contain health-care expenditures (see Chapter 17), legalizing medical aid-in-dying poses risks. For example, patients might seek it out of escalating health-care costs or fear of becoming a burden to their families. Trained as healers, U.S. doctors are less favorable than the general public, but their openness to medical aid-in-dying has grown. In a recent survey of more than 17,000 physicians representing 28 medical specialties, 54 percent indicated that they would support an incurably and terminally ill patient's decision to end his or her life and would want the same option to be available for themselves (Kane, 2014).

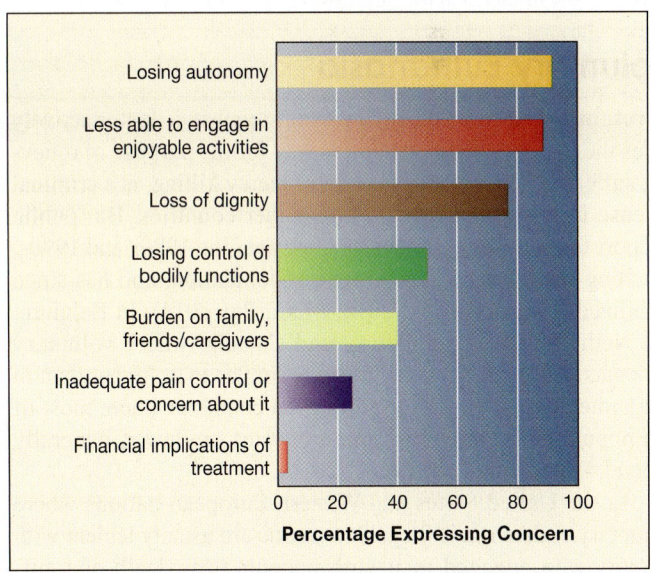

FIGURE 19.3 Reasons given by Oregon patients requesting medical aid-in-dying. Responses gathered between 1998 and 2014 from over 850 patients who ended their own lives under the Oregon Death with Dignity Act revealed that the majority were concerned about loss of autonomy, reduced capacity to engage in activities making life enjoyable, and loss of dignity. (Based on Oregon Public Health Division, 2016.)

The American Academy of Hospice and Palliative Medicine (2016), though taking a position of neutrality on legalization, has expressed concern about aid-in-dying becoming part of routine medical practice. It advises great caution on the part of doctors practicing in regions where medical aid-in-dying is legal, including making sure before engaging in it that the following conditions are met:

- The patient has access to the best possible palliative care and will continue to receive such care throughout the dying process.
- The patient has full decision-making capacity, requests medical aid-in-dying voluntarily, and has a limited life expectancy; health-care financial pressures and coercive influences from family members or others play no role.
- All reasonable alternatives have been considered and implemented, if acceptable to the patient.
- The practice is consistent with the doctor's fundamental values, and he or she is willing to participate. (If not, the doctor should recommend transfer of care, while taking into account professional obligations of nonabandonment.)

Still, evidence confirms that palliative care does not relieve pain in all cases, as it failed to do for Brittany. Nor does palliative care address dying patients' concerns about loss of autonomy and dignity, including the desire of some to avoid an extended period of palliative sedation once suffering intensifies (Kon, 2011). Finally, because the life-ending act is solely the patient's, many supporters of medical aid-in-dying believe that legalizing it is preferable to legalizing voluntary euthanasia, the practice we take up next.

Voluntary Euthanasia

In **voluntary euthanasia,** at a patient's request, a doctor actively takes the patient's life in a painless way for the purpose of relieving suffering. The practice, a form of mercy killing, is a criminal offense in all U.S. states and most other countries. But public support for voluntary euthanasia grew over the 1980s and 1990s, reaching two-thirds of the American population, and has since stabilized (Emanuel et al., 2016; McCarthy, 2014). In Belgium, the Netherlands, Luxembourg, and Canada, where voluntary euthanasia is legal, public approval is similar to or higher than in the United States. In Eastern European countries where most of the population is religious, approval rates are lower, generally around 45 percent (Cohen et al., 2014).

In the United States and Western European nations where voluntary euthanasia is illegal, the courts are usually lenient with doctors who engaged in it with patients near death and suffering profoundly, generally granting suspended sentences or probation. Nevertheless, attempts to legalize the practice have prompted heated controversy. Supporters believe it represents the most compassionate option for terminally ill people enduring great suffering. Opponents stress the moral difference between "letting die" and "killing" and argue that permitting doctors to take patients' lives may impair people's trust in health professionals. Finally, a fear exists that legalizing the practice—even when strictly monitored to ensure it does not arise out of depression, loneliness, coercion, or a desire to relieve the burden of caregiving on others—could result in broadening of euthanasia. Initially limited to the terminally ill, it might be applied involuntarily to the frail and disabled—outcomes that most people find unacceptable and immoral.

Will legalizing voluntary euthanasia lead us down a "slippery slope" to the killing of vulnerable people who either did not ask to die or were not mentally fit to make the decision? In Canada and Western Europe, safeguards are in place to prevent such deaths. In the Netherlands, for example, legal practice of euthanasia requires that physical or mental suffering be severe, with no prospect of relief; the patient's decision be well-informed and stable over time; all other options for care have been exhausted or refused; and a second doctor be consulted. These restrictions appear to have sharply reduced instances of *involuntary euthanasia* (without patient consent). Prior to legalization, Dutch physicians reported administering lethal drugs without patient approval in nearly 1 percent of deaths, a rate that declined fourfold after legalization. A substantial decrease also occurred in Belgium, where before legalization the doctor-reported incidence of involuntary euthanasia was as high as 3 percent (Chambaere et al., 2015; Onwuteaka-Philipsen et al., 2012).

Still, intense disagreement persists over voluntary euthanasia. A survey of Dutch doctors revealed that 86 percent dread the emotional burden of performing it (Van der Heide & Onwuteaka-Philipsen, 2012, as cited by Emanuel et al., 2016). Patients with dementia and mental illness, terminally ill minors, and older adults who say they are "tired of life" are of special concern. Even where voluntary euthanasia is legal in restricted circumstances, challenges in monitoring and regulating it remain. Helping suffering patients who yearn for death poses profound ethical and legal dilemmas.

Ask yourself

APPLY Thinking ahead to the day she dies, Noreen imagines a peaceful scene in which she says goodbye to loved ones. What social and medical practices are likely to increase Noreen's chances of dying in the manner she desires?

APPLY Ramón is certain that, if he ever became terminally ill, he would want doctors to halt life-saving treatment. To best ensure that his wish will be granted, what should Ramón do?

REFLECT If you were terminally ill, would you consider medical aid-in-dying or voluntary euthanasia? If so, under what conditions? Explain.

Bereavement: Coping with the Death of a Loved One

19.6 Describe the process of grieving, factors that contribute to individual variations, and bereavement interventions.

Loss is an inevitable part of existence throughout the lifespan. Even when change is for the better, we must let go of some aspects of experience so we can embrace others. In this way, our development prepares us for profound loss.

Bereavement is the experience of losing a loved one by death. The root of this word means "to be robbed," suggesting unjust and injurious theft of something valuable. Consistent with this image, we respond to loss with **grief**—intense physical and psychological distress. When we say someone is grief-stricken, we imply that his or her total way of being is affected.

Because grief can be overwhelming, cultures have devised ways of helping their members move beyond it to deal with the life changes demanded by death of a loved one. **Mourning** is the culturally specified expression of the bereaved person's thoughts and feelings. Customs—such as gathering with family and friends, dressing in black, attending the funeral, and observing a prescribed mourning period with special rituals—vary greatly among societies and ethnic groups. But all have in common the goal of helping people work through their grief and learn to live in a world that does not include the deceased.

Clearly, grief and mourning are closely linked—in everyday language, we often use the two words interchangeably. Let's look closely at how people respond to the death of a loved one.

Grief Process

Theorists formerly believed that bereaved individuals, both children and adults, moved through three phases of grieving—avoidance, confrontation, and restoration—each characterized by a different set of responses (Bowlby, 1980; Rando, 1995). In reality, however, people vary greatly in emotional reactions, behavior, and timing. An estimated 60 to 70 percent experience mild distress that resolves within a few months. Another 15 to 25 percent experience moderate distress, depression, and difficulties in everyday functioning and recover gradually, usually within a year. Only about 5 to 15 percent experience severe, prolonged distress, depression, and lack of acceptance of the death that persists for years, impairing physical and mental health—termed **complicated grief** (Bonanno, 2004; Bonanno, Westphal, & Mancini, 2011; Newson et al., 2011). As these findings reveal, the typical response to loss of a loved one is resilience.

Grievers generally move back and forth between emotional reactions, with many ups and downs. Rather than phases, the grief process is best conceived as a set of *tasks*—actions the person must take to recover and return to a fulfilling life: (1) to accept the reality of the loss, (2) to work through the pain of grief, (3) to adjust to a world without the loved one, and (4) to develop an inner bond with the deceased and move on with life (Worden, 2009). According to this view, people can take active steps to overcome grief—a powerful remedy for the distress that the bereaved often experience.

Avoidance and Confrontation. On hearing the news, many survivors react with shock followed by disbelief—a numbed feeling that serves as "emotional anesthesia" while the person begins the first task of grieving: becoming aware of and confronting the loss. Avoidance is generally short-lived, lasting from hours to weeks. Those who get stuck in it—for example, by ruminating about their own loss-related problems as a way to distract themselves from the reality of the death—are at risk for intense, long-lasting grief reactions that interfere with recovery (Eisma et al., 2013).

As grievers confront the reality of the death, they may experience a cascade of emotional reactions, including anxiety, sadness, protest, anger, helplessness, frustration, abandonment, and yearning for their loved one. Typical responses include obsessively reviewing the circumstances of death, asking how it might have been prevented, and searching for meaning in it (Neimeyer, 2001). In addition, grief-stricken people may be absentminded, unable to concentrate, and preoccupied with thoughts of the deceased, and may experience loss of sleep and appetite. Self-destructive behaviors, such as taking drugs or driving too fast, may occur. Most of these responses are symptoms of depression—a common component of grieving.

Although confrontation is difficult, it enables mourners to grapple with the second task: working through the pain of grief. Each surge of anguish that results from an unmet wish to be reunited with the deceased brings them closer to accepting that the loved one is gone and that a cherished relationship must be transformed from a physical presence to an inner representation. As a result, they make progress on the third task: adjusting to a world in which the deceased is missing.

Restoration. Adapting to loss is more than an internal, emotional task. The bereaved must also deal with stressors that are secondary outcomes of the death—overcoming loneliness by reaching out to others; mastering skills (such as finances or cooking) that the deceased had performed; reorganizing daily life without the loved one; and revising one's identity from "spouse" to "widow" or from "parent" to "parent of a deceased child."

According to a perspective called the **dual-process model of coping with loss,** effective coping requires people to oscillate between dealing with the emotional consequences of loss and attending to life changes, which—when handled successfully—have restorative, or healing, effects (Hansson & Stroebe, 2007; Stroebe & Schut, 1999, 2010). Moving back and forth offers temporary distraction and relief from painful grieving. Much research indicates that confronting grief without relief has severe negative consequences for physical and mental health (Corr & Corr, 2007). Consistent with the dual-process model, in a study that assessed widowed older adults at 6, 18, and 48 months after the death of their spouses, both loss-oriented and restoration-oriented activities occurred throughout bereavement. As predicted, restoration-oriented activities—such as visiting friends, attending religious services, and volunteering—reduced distress (Richardson, 2007). Using the dual-process model, one approach to intervention for grieving individuals addresses both emotional and life-change issues, alternating between them.

As grief subsides, emotional energies increasingly shift toward the fourth task—forging a symbolic bond with the deceased and moving on with life by meeting everyday responsibilities, investing in new activities and goals, strengthening old ties, and building new relationships. On certain days, such as family celebrations or the anniversary of death, grief reactions may resurface and require attention, but they do not interfere with a healthy, positive approach to life.

In fact, throughout the grief process, resilient individuals report experiencing both positive and negative emotions, with happiness and humor aiding in coping with grief (Ong, Bergeman, & Bisconti, 2004). In an investigation of several hundred people age 50 and older whose spouse or partner had died within the previous six months, 90 percent agreed that positive emotion in daily life is important, and more than 75 percent said they had experienced humor, laughter, or happiness during the past week. The greater participants' valuing and experience of positive emotion, the better their bereavement adjustment (Lund et al., 2008–2009). Expressions of happiness can be viewed as a restoration-oriented activity, offering distraction from grieving and strengthening bonds with others.

Personal and Situational Variations

Like dying, grieving is affected by many factors, including personality, coping style, and religious and cultural background. Gender differences are also evident. Compared with women, men typically express distress and depression less directly and seek social support less readily (Doka & Martin, 2010).

Furthermore, the quality of the person's relationship with the deceased is important. An end to a loving, fulfilling bond often leads to anguished confrontation with loss, but this soon resolves. The dissolution of a conflict-ridden, ambivalent tie, in contrast, is more likely to leave a long-term residue of anger, guilt, and regret (Abakoumkin, Stroebe, & Stroebe, 2010; Bonanno et al., 2002; Mikulincer & Shaver, 2008). And end-of-life care makes a difference: Widowed older adults whose spouses experienced a painful death report more anxiety, intrusive thoughts, and yearning for the loved one six months later (Carr, 2003).

Circumstances surrounding the death—whether it is sudden and unanticipated or follows a prolonged illness—also shape mourners' responses. The nature of the lost relationship and the timing of the death within the life course make a difference as well.

Sudden, Unanticipated Deaths versus Prolonged, Expected Deaths. In instances of sudden, unexpected deaths—usually the result of murder, suicide, war, accident, or natural disaster—avoidance may be especially pronounced and confrontation highly traumatic because shock and disbelief are extreme. In a survey of a large representative sample of 18- to 45-year-olds in Detroit, the trauma most often reported as prompting an intense, debilitating stress reaction was the sudden, unanticipated death of a loved one (Breslau et al., 1998). In contrast, during prolonged dying, the bereaved person has had time to engage in **anticipatory grieving**—acknowledging that the loss is inevitable and preparing emotionally for it. Survivors may feel less overwhelmed immediately following the death (Johansson & Grimby, 2013). Still, they may be vulnerable to persistent anxiety due to long-term stressors, such as highly demanding caregiving and having watched a loved one suffer from a debilitating illness.

Adjusting to a sudden death is easier when the survivor understands the reasons for it. This barrier to confronting loss is tragically apparent in cases of sudden infant death syndrome (SIDS), in which doctors cannot tell parents exactly why their baby died (see Chapter 3, page 106). That death seems "senseless" also complicates grieving after suicides, terrorist attacks, school and drive-by shootings, natural disasters, and motor vehicle fatalities. In Western societies, people tend to believe that momentous events should be comprehensible and nonrandom (Lukas & Seiden, 2007). A death that is sudden and unexpected can threaten basic assumptions about a just, benevolent, and controllable world.

Suicide, particularly that of a young person, is especially hard to bear. Compared with survivors of other sudden deaths, people grieving a suicidal loss are more likely to conclude that they contributed to or could have prevented it—self-blame that can trigger profound guilt and shame. These reactions are likely to be especially intense and persistent when the griever's culture or religion condemns suicide as immoral (Dunne & Dunne-Maxim, 2004). Individuals who have survived a suicide typically score higher than those who have experienced other types of losses in feelings of guilt and shame, sense of rejection by the deceased, and desire to conceal the cause of death (Dyregrov et al., 2014; Sveen & Walby, 2008). Typically, recovery from grief after a suicide is prolonged.

Parents Grieving the Loss of a Child. The death of a child, whether unexpected or foreseen, is the most difficult loss an adult can face. Children are extensions of parents' feelings about themselves—a vital part of their identity and focus of their hopes and dreams, including their sense of immortality (Price & Jones, 2015). Also, because children depend on, admire, and appreciate their parents in a deeply gratifying way, they are an unmatched source of love. Finally, the death of a child is unnatural: Children are not supposed to die before their parents.

Parents who have lost a child often report considerable distress and resurgence of grief for years. The guilt and sense of unfairness triggered by outliving their child frequently become

A father weeps while holding the body of his son, killed during the Syrian armed conflict. The death of a child, whether unexpected or foreseen, is the most difficult loss an adult can face.

tremendous burdens. Compared to fathers, mothers report more intense distress, especially when they lack opportunities to share thoughts and feelings with their spouse (Lang, Gottlieb, & Amsel, 1996; Moriarty, Carroll, & Cotroneo, 1996). (Recall that men generally grieve less openly than women.) These emotional consequences negatively affect parents' lives and likely contribute to the higher divorce rate among bereaved parents than other parents (Lyngstad, 2013; Wheeler, 2001). Risk of marital breakup tends to strengthen over time and is greatest for couples whose relationship was problematic before the child's death.

If parents can reorganize the family system and reestablish a sense of life's meaning through valuing the lost child's impact on their lives, and investing in other children and activities, then the result can be firmer family commitments and personal growth. The process, which can be lengthy, is associated with improved physical and mental health and gains in marital satisfaction (Murphy, 2008; Price et al., 2011). Five years after her son's death, one parent reflected on her progress:

> I was afraid to let go [of my pain, which was] a way of loving him.... Finally I had to admit that his life meant more than pain, it also meant joy and happiness and fun—and living.... When we release pain we make room for happiness in our lives. My memories of S. became lighter and more spontaneous. Instead of hurtful, my memories brought comfort, even a chuckle.... realized S. was still teaching me things. (Klass, 2004, p. 87)

Children and Adolescents Grieving the Loss of a Parent or Sibling.
The loss of an attachment figure has long-term consequences for children. When a parent dies, children's basic sense of security and being cared for is threatened. And the death of a sibling not only deprives children of a close emotional tie but also informs them, often for the first time, of their own vulnerability.

Children grieving a family loss describe frequent crying, trouble concentrating in school, sleep difficulties, headaches, and other physical symptoms several months to years after a death. And clinical studies suggest that persistent depression, anxiety, angry outbursts, social withdrawal, loneliness, and worries about dying themselves are common (Luecken, 2008; Marshall & Davies, 2011). At the same time, many children say they have actively maintained mental contact with their dead parent or sibling, dreaming about and speaking to them regularly (Martinson, Davies, & McClowry, 1987; Silverman & Nickman, 1996). These images, reported by bereaved adults as well, seem to facilitate coping with loss.

Cognitive development contributes to the ability to grieve. For example, children who have not yet acquired a biological understanding of death may believe the dead parent left voluntarily, perhaps in anger, and that the other parent may also disappear. For these reasons, young children need careful, repeated explanations assuring them that the parent did not want to die and was not angry at them (Christ, Siegel, & Christ, 2002). Keeping the truth from children about an impending death can lead to profound regret. One 8-year-old who learned only a half-hour in advance that his sick brother was dying reflected, "If only I'd known, I could have said goodbye."

Regardless of children's level of understanding, honesty, affection, and reassurance help them tolerate painful feelings of loss. Grief-stricken school-age children are usually more willing than adolescents to confide in parents. To appear "normal," teenagers tend to keep their grieving from both adults and peers (Barrera et al., 2013). Consequently, they are more likely than children to become depressed or to escape from grief through acting-out behavior.

Overall, effective parenting—warm, empathetic support combined with rational discipline—fosters adaptive coping and positive long-term adjustment in both children and adolescents (Luecken, 2008). Peer support is also helpful, though girls experience it more often than boys, due to greater closeness and self-disclosure in girls' friendships (LaFreniere & Cain, 2015).

Adults Grieving the Loss of an Intimate Partner.
Recall from Chapter 18 that after the death of a spouse, adaptation to widowhood varies greatly, with age, gender, social support, and personality making a difference. After a period of grieving, most widowed older adults in Western nations fare well, while younger individuals display more negative outcomes (see page 628 to review). Older widows and widowers have many more contemporaries in similar circumstances. And most have already attained important life goals or adjusted to the fact that some goals will not be attained.

In contrast, loss of a spouse or partner in early or middle adulthood is a nonnormative event that profoundly disrupts life plans. Interviews with a large, nationally representative sample of U.S. adults who had been widowed from less than 1 to 64 years previously (typically in middle adulthood) revealed that thoughts about and conversations with the lost spouse occurred often in the first few years, then declined gradually (Carnelley et al., 2006). But they did not reach their lowest level for several decades, when the typical respondent still thought about the deceased partner once every week or two and conversed with him or her about once a month.

In addition to dealing with feelings of loss, young and middle-aged widows and widowers often must assume a greater role in comforting others, especially children. They also face the stresses of single parenthood and rapid shrinking of the social network established during their life as a couple.

In countries where same-sex marriage is not legal, the death of a lesbian or gay partner presents unique challenges. When relatives limit or bar the partner from participating in funeral services, the survivor experiences **disenfranchised grief**—a sense of loss without the opportunity to mourn publicly and benefit from others' support—which can profoundly disrupt the grief process (Doka, 2008; Jenkins et al., 2014). Fortunately, gay and lesbian communities provide helpful alternative support in the form of memorial services and other rituals.

Bereavement Overload.
When a person experiences several deaths at once or in close succession, bereavement overload can occur. Multiple losses deplete the coping resources of even well-adjusted people, leaving them emotionally overwhelmed, severely depressed, and vulnerable to post-traumatic stress symptoms and complicated grief.

Because old age often brings the death of spouse, siblings, and friends in close succession, aging adults are at risk for bereavement overload (Kastenbaum, 2012). But recall from Chapter 18 that compared with young people, older adults are often better equipped to handle these losses. They know that decline and death are expected in late adulthood, and they have had a lifetime of experience through which to develop effective coping strategies.

At a funeral service, a surviving father and children mourn the loss of family members and friends after a devastating earthquake struck their village in central Italy. Public tragedies can spark bereavement overload, leaving mourners at risk for prolonged, overwhelming grief.

Public tragedies—terrorist attacks, natural disasters, random murders in schools, or widely publicized kidnappings—can spark bereavement overload (Kristensen, Weisaeth, & Heir, 2012; Rynearson & Salloum, 2011). For example, many survivors who lost loved ones, co-workers, or friends in the September 11, 2001, terrorist attacks (including an estimated 3,000 children who lost a parent) experienced repeated images of horror and destruction, which impeded coming to terms with loss. Children and adolescents suffered profoundly—from intense shock, prolonged grief, frequent mental replays of the vicious attack and gruesome outcomes, and fear of the settings in which those events occurred (Nader, 2002; Webb, 2002). The greater the bereaved individual's exposure to the catastrophic death scene, the more severe these reactions.

Funerals and other bereavement rituals, illustrated in the Cultural Influences box on the following page, assist mourners of all ages in resolving grief with the help of family and friends. Those who remain preoccupied with loss and who have difficulty resuming interest in everyday activities benefit from special interventions designed to help them adjust.

Bereavement Interventions

Sympathy and understanding are sufficient to enable most people to undertake the tasks necessary to recover from grief (see Applying What We Know on page 670). Yet effective support is often difficult to provide, and relatives and friends can benefit from training in how to respond. Sometimes they give advice aimed at hastening recovery or ask questions aimed at managing their own anxiety ("Were you expecting him to die?" "Was she in a lot of pain?")—approaches that most bereaved people dislike (Kastenbaum, 2012). Listening patiently and assuring the bereaved of "being there" for them—"I'm here if you need to talk," "Let me know what I can do"—are among the best ways to help.

Bereavement interventions typically encourage people to draw on their existing social network, while providing additional social support through group or individual counseling. Bereaved adults who struggle with and surmount loss often experience stress-related personal growth, including greater awareness of their own strengths, enhanced appreciation of close relationships, and new spiritual insights (Calhoun et al., 2010).

Support groups that bring together grievers who have experienced the same type of loss seem highly effective in promoting recovery. In a program for recently widowed older adults based on the dual-process model of coping with loss, in which group members helped one another resolve grief and master tasks of daily living, participants readily bonded with one another and gained in sense of self-efficacy at managing their own lives (Caserta, Lund, & Rice, 1999). A widow expressed the many lasting benefits:

> We shared our anger at being left behind, … our fright of that aloneness. We shared our favorite pictures, so each of us could know the others' families and the fun we used to have. We shared our feelings of guilt if we had fun … and found out that

Cultural Influences

Cultural Variations in Mourning Behavior

The ceremonies that commemorated Sofie's and Nicholas's deaths—the first Jewish, the second Quaker—were strikingly different. Yet they served common goals: announcing that a death had occurred, ensuring social support, celebrating the life of the deceased, and conveying a philosophy of life after death.

At the funeral home, Sofie's body was washed and shrouded, a Jewish ritual signifying return to a state of purity. Then it was placed in a plain wooden (not metal) coffin, so as not to impede the natural process of decomposition. To underscore the finality of death, Jewish tradition does not permit viewing of the body; it remains in a closed coffin. Traditionally, the coffin is not left alone until burial; in honor of the deceased, the community maintains a day-and-night vigil.

To return the body quickly to the life-giving earth from which it sprang, Sofie's funeral was scheduled as soon as relatives could gather—just three days after death. Sofie's husband and children symbolized their grief by cutting a black ribbon and pinning it to their clothing. The rabbi recited psalms of comfort, followed by a eulogy. The service continued at the graveside. Once the coffin had been lowered into the ground, relatives and friends took turns shoveling earth onto it, each participating in the irrevocable act of burial. The service concluded with the *Kaddish* prayer, which affirms life while accepting death.

At home, the family lit a memorial candle, which burned throughout *shiva*, the seven-day mourning period. A meal of consolation prepared by others followed, creating a warm feeling of community. Jewish custom prescribes that after 30 days, life must gradually return to normal. When a parent dies, the mourning period is extended to 12 months.

In the Quaker tradition of simplicity, Nicholas was cremated promptly. During the next week, relatives and close friends gathered with Giselle and Sasha at their home. Together, they planned a memorial service to celebrate Nicholas's life.

When people arrived on the appointed day, a clerk of the Friends (Quaker) Meeting welcomed them and explained to newcomers the Quaker custom of worshipping silently, with those who feel moved to speak rising at any time to share thoughts and feelings. Many mourners offered personal statements about Nicholas or read poems and selections from Scripture. After concluding comments from Giselle and Sasha, everyone joined hands to conclude the service. A reception for the family followed.

Variations in mourning behavior are vast, both within and across societies. At African-American funerals, for example, grief is expressed freely: Sermons, eulogies, and music are designed to trigger release of deep emotion. Energetic congregant participation, including responsive "Amens," convey to family survivors that the entire community empathizes with them (Collins & Doolittle, 2006). In contrast, the Balinese of Indonesia believe they must remain calm in the face of death so that the gods can hear their prayers. While acknowledging their underlying grief, Balinese mourners work hard to maintain their composure (Rosenblatt, 2008).

Religions also render accounts of the aftermath of death that console both dying and bereaved individuals. Beliefs of tribal and village cultures typically include an elaborate array of ancestor spirits and customs designed to ease the journey of the deceased to the afterlife. The Kalash people of rural Pakistan, who practice the rites of an ancient religion, carry the body to the graveyard on the deceased's bed. Once the grave is filled, mourners invert the bed on it, leaving it for the dead person's use in the next world (Sheikh et al., 2014). Jewish tradition emphasizes personal survival through giving life and care to others. Unlike other Christian groups,

Kalash mourners in rural Pakistan surround the body of a community member, who is carried to his grave on his bed. Kalash funeral rites for men include drum beating and dancing, which are intended to ward off any troubles the dead may face on their final journey.

Quakers give little attention to hope of heaven or fear of hell, focusing mainly on "salvation by character"—working for peace, justice, and a loving community.

In recent years, "virtual cemeteries" have arisen on the Internet, which allow postings whenever bereaved individuals feel ready to convey their thoughts and feelings, creation of tributes at little or no cost, and continuous, easy access to the memorial. Most creators of Web tributes choose to tell personal stories, highlighting a laugh, a favorite joke, or a touching moment. Some speak directly to their lost loved one. Guestbooks offer a place for visitors to connect with other mourners (de Vries & Moldaw, 2012). Web cemeteries also provide a means for people excluded from traditional death rituals to engage in public mourning. The following "gravesite" message captures the unique qualities of this highly flexible medium for mourning:

> I wish I could maintain contact with you, to keep alive the vivid memories of your impact on my life.... Because I cannot visit your grave today, I use this means to tell you how much you are loved.

CHAPTER 19 Death, Dying, and Bereavement

Applying what we Know

Suggestions for Resolving Grief After a Loved One Dies

SUGGESTION	DESCRIPTION
Give yourself permission to feel the loss.	Permit yourself to confront all thoughts and emotions associated with the death. Make a conscious decision to overcome your grief, recognizing that this will take time.
Accept social support.	In the early part of grieving, let others reach out to you by making meals, running errands, and keeping you company. Be assertive; ask for what you need so people who would like to help will know what to do.
Be realistic about the course of grieving.	Expect to have some negative and intense reactions, such as feeling anguished, sad, and angry, that last from weeks to months and may occasionally resurface years after the death. There is no one way to grieve, so find the best way for you.
Remember the deceased.	Review your relationship to and experiences with the deceased, permitting yourself to see that you can no longer be with him or her as before. Form a new bond based on memories, keeping it alive through photographs, commemorative donations, prayers, and other symbols and actions.
When ready, invest in new activities and relationships, and master new tasks of daily living.	Identify the roles you must give up and the ones you must assume as a consequence of the death, and take deliberate steps to modify daily life accordingly. Set small goals at first, such as a night at the movies, a dinner date with a friend, a cooking or household repair class, or a week's vacation.

it was okay to keep on living! ... We cheered when one of us accomplished a new task. We also tried to lend a helping hand and heart when we would have one of our bad days! ... This group will always be there for me and I will always be there for them. I love you all! (Lund, 2005)

Follow-up research suggests that group sessions are best suited for fostering loss-oriented coping (confronting and resolving grief), whereas an individually tailored approach works best for restoration-oriented coping (reorganizing daily life) (Lund et al., 2010a). Bereaved adults differ widely in the new roles, relationships, and life skills they need most, and in the formats and schedules best suited to acquiring them.

LOOK and LISTEN

Arrange to sit in on a bereavement support group session sponsored by a local hospice program or hospital, noting both emotional and daily living challenges expressed by group members. Ask participants to explain how the group has helped them.

Interventions for children and adolescents following violent deaths must protect them from unnecessary reexposure and assist parents and teachers with their own distress so they can effectively offer comfort (Dowd, 2013). In the aftermath of horrific tragedies—such as the mass shootings at Sandy Hook Elementary School in Newtown, Connecticut, in 2012, and at the public health department in San Bernardino, California, in 2015—nurturing and caring relationships with adults are the most powerful way to help children recover from trauma.

A sudden, violent, and unexplainable death; the loss of a child; a death that the mourner feels he or she could have prevented; or an ambivalent or dependent relationship with the deceased makes it harder for bereaved people to overcome their loss. In cases of complicated grief, individual or family therapy with a specially trained professional can be helpful (Stroebe, Schut, & van den Bout, 2013). Assisting bereaved adults in finding some value in the grieving experience—for example, discovering their own capacity to cope with adversity, gaining insight into the meaning of relationships, or crystallizing a sense of purpose in life—is particularly effective (Neimeyer et al., 2010).

Most grieving individuals do not participate in bereavement interventions. In several studies, only 25 to 50 percent of family caregivers of dying patients made use of bereavement services—such as phone support, support groups, and referrals for counseling—even though these were readily available through hospice, hospitals, or other community organizations (Bergman, Haley, & Small, 2011; Ghesquiere, Thomas, & Bruce, 2016). Many who refused services were severely distressed yet did not realize that intervention could be helpful.

Death Education

19.7 Explain how death education can help people cope with death more effectively.

Preparatory steps can help people of all ages cope with death more effectively. The death awareness movement that sparked increased sensitivity to the needs of dying patients has also led to the rise of college and university courses in death, dying, and bereavement. Instruction has been integrated into the training of students or those currently working in the fields of counseling, education, funeral service, nursing, medicine, and ministry, as well as those volunteering in hospice programs. Some institutions offer a major or minor in thanatology, in which students complete a program of courses addressing a variety of death-related subjects (Corr, 2015a). Death education is also found in adult education programs in many communities.

Death education at all levels has the following goals:

- Increasing students' understanding of the physical and psychological changes that accompany dying
- Enhancing students' awareness of options in end-of-life care, funeral services, and memorial rituals
- Promoting understanding of important social and ethical issues, including advance medical directives, medical aid-in-dying, euthanasia, and organ donation
- Improving students' ability to communicate effectively with others about death-related concerns
- Helping to prepare students for their professional roles in caring for the dying and supporting the bereaved
- Fostering students' appreciation of how lifespan development interacts with death, dying, and bereavement issues (Corr & Corr, 2013; Kastenbaum, 2012)

Educational format varies widely. Some programs simply convey information. Others are experiential and include activities such as role-playing, discussions with the terminally ill, visits to mortuaries and cemeteries, and personal awareness exercises. Research reveals that although using a lecture style leads to gains in knowledge, it often leaves students more uncomfortable about death than when they entered (Hurtig & Stewin, 2006). In contrast, experiential programs that help students confront their own mortality and clarify basic values on living and dying are more likely to have a positive, lasting impact.

Whether acquired in the classroom or in our daily lives, our thoughts and feelings about death are forged through interactions with others. Becoming more aware of how we die and of our own mortality, we encounter our greatest loss, but we also gain. Dying people have at times confided in those close to them that awareness of the limits of their lifespan permitted them to dispense with superficial distractions and wasted energies and focus on what is truly important in their lives. As one terminally ill patient summed up, "[It's] kind of like life, just speeded up"—an accelerated process in which, over a period of weeks to months, one grapples with issues that normally would have taken years or decades to resolve (Selwyn, 1996, p. 36). Applying this lesson to ourselves, we learn that by being in touch with death and dying, we can live ever more fully.

Ask yourself

CONNECT Compare grieving individuals' reactions with terminally ill patients' thoughts and feelings as they move closer to death, described on page 653. Can a dying person's reactions be viewed as a form of grieving? Explain.

APPLY List features of self-help groups that contribute to their effectiveness in helping people cope with loss.

REFLECT Visit a Web cemetery, such as Virtual Memorials (www.virtualmemorials.com). Select examples of Web tributes, guestbook entries, and testimonials that illustrate the unique ways in which virtual cemeteries help people cope with death.

Summary / chapter 19

How We Die (p. 646)

19.1 *Describe the physical changes of dying, along with their implications for defining death and the meaning of death with dignity.*

- **Thanatology,** the study of death and dying, has expanded dramatically over the past three decades. As a result of life-saving technology, death is long and drawn-out for three-fourths of people—many more than in times past. Of those who die suddenly, 65 to 85 percent are victims of heart attacks.
- In general, dying takes place in three phases: the **agonal phase,** in which regular heartbeat disintegrates; **clinical death,** a short interval in which resuscitation is still possible; and **mortality,** or permanent death.
- In most industrialized nations, **brain death** is accepted as the definition of death. But for incurable patients who remain in a **persistent vegetative state,** the brain death standard does not solve the problem of when to halt treatment.

- We can best ensure death with dignity by supporting dying patients through their physical and psychological distress, being candid about death's certainty, and helping them learn enough about their condition to make reasoned choices about treatment.

Understanding of and Attitudes Toward Death (p. 648)

19.2 *Discuss age-related changes in conceptions of and attitudes toward death, and cite factors that influence death anxiety.*

- Compared with earlier generations, more young people reach adulthood having had little contact with death, contributing to a sense of unease about it.

- To understand death, children must have some basic notions of biology and must be able to distinguish between *dead, inanimate, unreal,* and *nonexistent.* Most children attain a sophisticated grasp of death by age 6, gradually mastering subconcepts of nonfunctionality, finality, universality, applicability, and causation during the preschool years. Cultural and religious teachings affect children's understanding, as do open, honest discussions.

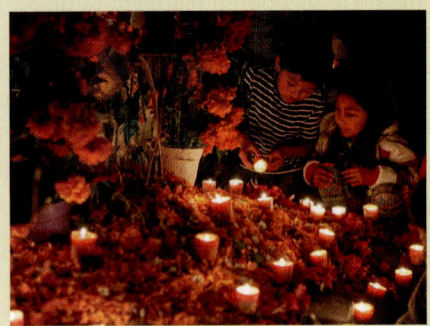

- Adolescents are aware that death happens to everyone and can occur at any time, but their high-risk activities suggest that they do not take death personally. Candid discussions can help teenagers build a bridge between death as a logical possibility and their everyday actions.
- In early adulthood, many people avoid thinking about death, but in midlife, they become more conscious that their own lives are finite. In late adulthood, as death nears, people are more apt to ponder the process of dying than the state of death.
- Wide individual and cultural variations exist in **death anxiety.** People with a sense of spirituality or a well-developed personal philosophy of death are less fearful, as are those with deep faith in a higher force or being. Older adults' greater ability to regulate negative emotion and their sense of symbolic immortality reduce death anxiety. Across cultures, women exhibit more death anxiety than men.

Thinking and Emotions of Dying People (p. 653)

19.3 *Describe and evaluate Kübler-Ross's theory of typical responses to dying, and cite factors that influence dying patients' responses.*

- Elisabeth Kübler-Ross proposed that dying people typically express five responses: denial, anger, bargaining, depression, and acceptance. These reactions do not occur in fixed sequence, and dying people often display other coping strategies. Still, Kübler-Ross convinced professionals and the general public that the dying are living people who usually have "unfinished needs" they want to address.
- The extent to which people attain an **appropriate death** depends on many contextual variables—nature of the disease, personality and coping style, family members' and health professionals' behavior, and spirituality, religion, and cultural background.

A Place to Die (p. 657)

19.4 *Evaluate the extent to which homes, hospitals, nursing homes, and the hospice approach meet the needs of dying people and their families.*

- Although most people say they want to die at home, only about one-fourth of Americans do. Even with professional help and hospital-supplied equipment, caring for a dying patient in the home is highly demanding.
- Sudden deaths typically occur in hospital emergency rooms, where sympathetic explanations from staff can reduce family members' anger, frustration, and confusion. Intensive care is especially depersonalizing for patients lingering between life and death while hooked to machines. Although hospital comprehensive treatment programs aimed at easing end-of-life suffering have increased over the past decade, about one-third of hospitals still do not have them.
- Though deaths in U.S. nursing homes are common, too often residents' end-of-life preferences are not followed.
- The **hospice** approach is a comprehensive program of support services that focuses on meeting the dying person's physical, emotional, social, and spiritual needs and providing **palliative,** or **comfort, care** rather than prolonging life. Hospice also contributes to improved family functioning and better psychological well-being among family survivors.

The Right to Die (p. 660)

19.5 *Discuss end-of-life medical practices, along with ethical controversies surrounding them.*

- Modern medical procedures can prolong inevitable death, diminishing quality of life and personal dignity. Ending life-sustaining treatment for terminally ill patients is widely accepted and practiced. People can best ensure that their wishes will be followed by preparing an **advance medical directive.** A **living will** contains instructions for treatment, whereas a **durable power of attorney for health care** names another person to make health-care decisions on one's behalf.

- **Medical aid-in-dying** is legal in five U.S. states, and public and physician support for it has recently increased. Opponents worry that health-care financial pressures or coercion from others might affect patient requests. Because the final act is solely the patient's, many supporters believe that legalizing medical aid-in-dying is preferable to legalizing voluntary euthanasia.
- Although public support for **voluntary euthanasia** is high in North America and Western Europe, the practice remains a criminal offense in most countries and has sparked heated controversy, fueled by fears that it will be applied involuntarily to vulnerable people.

Bereavement: Coping with the Death of a Loved One (p. 665)

19.6 *Describe the process of grieving, factors that contribute to individual variations, and bereavement interventions.*

- **Bereavement** refers to the experience of losing a loved one by death, **grief** to the intense physical and psychological distress that accompanies loss. **Mourning** is the culturally prescribed expression of the bereaved person's thoughts and feelings.

- Most bereaved individuals recover within a few months to a year. About 5 to 15 percent experience **complicated grief,** severe, prolonged distress, depression, and lack of acceptance of the death.

- The grief process is best conceived as a set of tasks to overcome rather than a series of orderly phases.

- According to the **dual-process model of coping with loss,** effective coping involves oscillating between dealing with the emotional consequences of loss and attending to life changes, which can have restorative effects. Bereaved individuals who experience positive as well as negative emotions cope more effectively.

- Grieving is affected by many personal and situational factors. Bereaved men express grief less directly than bereaved women. After a sudden, unanticipated death, avoidance may be especially pronounced and confrontation highly traumatic. In contrast, a prolonged, expected death allows time for **anticipatory grieving.**

- When a parent loses a child or a child loses a parent or sibling, grieving is often intense and prolonged. Because early loss of a life partner is a nonnormative event with a major impact on life plans, younger widowed individuals usually fare less well than their older counterparts. **Disenfranchised grief** can profoundly disrupt the grief process.

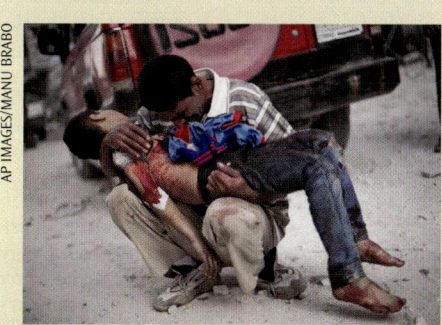

- People who experience several deaths at once or in close succession may suffer from bereavement overload. Those at risk include aging adults, individuals who have lost loved ones to public tragedies, and people who have witnessed unexpected, violent deaths.

- Sympathy and understanding are sufficient for most people to recover from grief. Support groups are highly effective in aiding recovery, whereas individually tailored approaches help mourners reorganize their daily lives. Interventions for children and adolescents following violent deaths must protect them from unnecessary reexposure and assist parents and teachers in offering comfort.

Death Education (p. 670)

19.7 *Explain how death education can help people cope with death more effectively.*

- Death education has been integrated into training for students and practitioners in diverse fields and for hospice volunteers. It can also be found in adult education programs. Goals include promoting understanding of end-of-life care options and important social and ethical issues (such as advance medical directives and euthanasia), and of how lifespan development interacts with death, dying, and bereavement.

Important Terms and Concepts

advance medical directive (p. 661)
agonal phase (p. 645)
anticipatory grieving (p. 666)
appropriate death (p. 654)
bereavement (p. 665)
brain death (p. 647)
clinical death (p. 645)
complicated grief (p. 665)

death anxiety (p. 651)
disenfranchised grief (p. 668)
dual-process model of coping with loss (p. 665)
durable power of attorney for health care (p. 662)
grief (p. 665)
hospice (p. 658)
living will (p. 661)
medical aid-in-dying (p. 662)

mortality (p. 645)
mourning (p. 665)
palliative, or comfort, care (p. 658)
persistent vegetative state (p. 647)
thanatology (p. 645)
voluntary euthanasia (p. 664)

Glossary

A

academic programs Preschool and kindergarten programs in which teachers structure children's learning, teaching academic skills through formal lessons that often involve repetition and drill. Distinguished from *child-centered programs*. (p. 246)

accommodation In Piaget's theory, the part of adaptation in which new schemes are created and old ones adjusted to produce a better fit with the environment. Distinguished from *assimilation*. (p. 150)

acculturative stress Psychological distress resulting from conflict between an individual's minority culture and the host culture. (p. 412)

activities of daily living (ADLs) Basic self-care tasks required to live on one's own, such as bathing, dressing, getting in and out of bed or a chair, and eating. (p. 573)

adaptation In Piaget's theory, the process of building schemes through direct interaction with the environment. Consists of two complementary activities: *assimilation* and *accommodation*. (p. 150)

adolescence The transition between childhood and adulthood that begins with puberty. It involves accepting one's full-grown body, acquiring adult ways of thinking, attaining greater independence from one's family, developing more mature ways of relating to peers of both sexes, and beginning to construct an identity. (p. 367)

advance medical directive A written statement of desired medical treatment should a person become incurably ill. (p. 661)

age-graded influences Influences on lifespan development that are strongly related to age and therefore fairly predictable in when they occur and how long they last. (p. 9)

age of viability The point at which the baby can first survive if born early, occurring sometime between 22 and 26 weeks. (p. 80)

aging in place In late adulthood, remaining in a familiar setting where one has control over one's everyday life. (p. 623)

agonal phase The phase of dying characterized by a rattled breathing sound, due to fluid buildup in the throat, and by gasps and muscle spasms during the first moments in which the regular heartbeat disintegrates. Distinguished from *clinical death* and *mortality*. (p. 645)

alcohol-related neurodevelopmental disorder (ARND) The least severe form of fetal alcohol spectrum disorder, involving brain injury but with typical physical growth and absence of facial abnormalities. Distinguished from *fetal alcohol syndrome (FAS)* and *partial fetal alcohol syndrome (p-FAS)*. (p. 84)

allele Each of two forms of a gene located at the same place on corresponding pairs of chromosomes. (p. 46)

Alzheimer's disease The most common form of dementia, in which structural and chemical brain deterioration is associated with gradual loss of many aspects of thought and behavior, including memory, skilled and purposeful movements, and comprehension and production of speech. (p. 588)

amnion The inner membrane that encloses the developing organism in *amniotic fluid*, which helps keep the temperature of the prenatal world constant and provides a cushion against jolts caused by the woman's movements. (p. 77)

amygdala An inner-brain structure that plays a central role in processing of novelty and emotional information. (p. 218)

amyloid plaques A structural change in the cerebral cortex associated with Alzheimer's disease, in which dense deposits of a deteriorated protein called *amyloid* develop, surrounded by clumps of dead nerve and glial cells. (p. 588)

androgyny The gender identity held by individuals who score high on both traditionally masculine and traditionally feminine personality characteristics. (p. 279)

anorexia nervosa An eating disorder in which young people, mainly females, starve themselves because of a compulsive fear of getting fat and an extremely distorted body image. (p. 378)

anoxia Inadequate oxygen supply. (p. 96)

anticipatory grieving During prolonged dying, the bereaved person's acknowledgment that the loss is inevitable, and emotional preparation for it. (p. 666)

Apgar Scale A rating system used to assess a newborn baby's physical condition immediately after birth on the basis of five characteristics: heart rate, respiratory effort, reflex irritability, muscle tone, and color. (p. 94)

applied behavior analysis Careful observations of individual behavior and related environmental events, followed by systematic changes in those events based on procedures of conditioning and modeling. The goal is to eliminate undesirable behaviors and increase desirable responses. (p. 17)

appropriate death A death that makes sense in terms of the individual's pattern of living and values, preserves or restores significant relationships, and is as free of suffering as possible. (p. 654)

assimilation In Piaget's theory, the part of adaptation in which current schemes are used to interpret the external world. Distinguished from *accommodation*. (p. 150)

assisted living Homelike housing arrangements for older adults who require more help than can be provided at home but less than is usually provided in nursing homes. (p. 593)

assistive technology An array of devices that permit people with disabilities, including older adults, to improve their functioning. (p. 579)

associative memory deficit Age-related difficulty creating and retrieving links between pieces of information—for example, two items or an item and its context. (p. 596)

associative play A form of social interaction in which children engage in separate activities but exchange toys and comment on one another's behavior. Distinguished from *nonsocial activity*, *parallel play*, and *cooperative play*. (p. 263)

attachment The strong affectionate tie we have with special people in our lives, which leads us to feel pleasure when interacting with them and to be comforted by their nearness in times of stress. (p. 196)

Attachment Q-Sort A method for assessing the quality of attachment in children between 1 and 5 years of age through home observations of a variety of attachment-related behaviors. (p. 198)

attention-deficit hyperactivity disorder (ADHD) A childhood disorder involving inattention, impulsivity, and excessive motor activity, resulting in academic and social problems. (p. 309)

authoritarian child-rearing style A child-rearing style that is low in acceptance and involvement, high in coercive and psychological control, and low in autonomy granting. Distinguished from *authoritative, permissive,* and *uninvolved child-rearing styles*. (p. 283)

authoritative child-rearing style A child-rearing style that is high in acceptance and involvement, adaptive control techniques, and appropriate autonomy granting. Distinguished from *authoritarian, permissive,* and *uninvolved child-rearing styles*. (p. 282)

autobiographical memory Long-lasting recollections of personally meaningful one-time events from both the recent and the distant past. (p. 164)

autoimmune response A malfunction of the immune system in which it turns against normal body tissues. (p. 577)

automatic processes Cognitive activities that are so well-learned that they require no space in working memory and, therefore, permit an individual to focus on other information while performing them. (p. 161)

autonomy At adolescence, a sense of oneself as a separate, self-governing individual. Involves relying more on oneself and less on parents for support and guidance and engaging in careful, well-reasoned decision making. (p. 420)

autonomy versus shame and doubt In Erikson's theory, the psychological conflict of toddlerhood, which is resolved favorably when parents provide young children with suitable guidance and reasonable choices. (p. 184)

autosomes The 22 matching pairs of chromosomes in each human cell. (p. 45)

average healthy life expectancy The number of years that an individual born in a particular year can expect to live in full health, without disease or injury. Distinguished from *maximum lifespan* and *average life expectancy*. (p. 571)

average life expectancy The number of years that an individual born in a particular year can expect to live, starting at any age. Distinguished from *maximum lifespan* and *average healthy life expectancy*. (p. 570)

G-1

B

babbling Infants' repetition of consonant–vowel combinations, beginning around 6 months of age. (p. 175)

basal metabolic rate (BMR) The amount of energy the body uses at complete rest. (p. 446)

basic emotions Emotions such as happiness, interest, surprise, fear, anger, sadness, and disgust that are universal in humans and other primates and have a long evolutionary history of promoting survival. (p. 185)

basic trust versus mistrust In Erikson's theory, the psychological conflict of infancy, which is resolved positively when the balance of care is sympathetic and loving. (p. 184)

behavioral genetics A field devoted to uncovering the contributions of nature and nurture to the diversity of human traits and abilities. (p. 66)

behaviorism An approach that regards directly observable events—stimuli and responses—as the appropriate focus of study and views the development of behavior as taking place through classical and operant conditioning. (p. 16)

bereavement The experience of losing a loved one by death. (p. 665)

bicultural identity The identity constructed by exploring and adopting values from both the individual's subculture and the dominant culture. (p. 412)

"big five" personality traits Five basic factors into which hundreds of personality traits have been organized: neuroticism, extroversion, openness to experience, agreeableness, and conscientiousness. (p. 548)

biological aging, or senescence Genetically influenced, age-related declines in the functioning of organs and systems that are universal in all members of our species. Sometimes called *primary aging.* (p. 438)

binge-eating disorder An eating disorder in which young people binge at least once a week for three months or longer, without compensatory purging, exercise, or fasting. (p. 379)

blended, or reconstituted, family A family structure resulting from remarriage or cohabitation that includes parent, child, and steprelatives. (p. 356)

body image Conception of and attitude toward one's physical appearance. (p. 377)

brain death Irreversible cessation of all activity in the brain and the brain stem. The definition of death accepted in most industrialized nations. (p. 647)

brain plasticity The capacity of various parts of the cerebral cortex to take over functions of damaged regions. Declines as hemispheres of the cerebral cortex lateralize. (p. 121)

breech position A position of the baby in the uterus that would cause the buttocks or feet to be delivered first. (p. 96)

bulimia nervosa An eating disorder in which individuals, mainly females, engage in binge eating, followed by compensatory efforts to avoid weight gain, such as deliberate vomiting, purging with laxatives, excessive exercise, or fasting. (p. 379)

burnout A condition in which long-term job stress leads to mental exhaustion, a sense of loss of personal control, and feelings of reduced accomplishment. (p. 560)

C

cardinality The mathematical principle specifying that the last number in a counting sequence indicates the quantity of items in the set. (p. 244)

carriers Heterozygous individuals who can pass a recessive trait to their offspring. (p. 46)

cataracts Cloudy areas in the lens of the eye that increase from middle to late adulthood, resulting in foggy vision and (without surgery) eventual blindness. (p. 574)

categorical self Classification of the self on the basis of prominent ways in which people differ, such as age, sex, physical characteristics, goodness versus badness, and competencies. Develops between 18 and 30 months. (p. 208)

central executive In information processing, the conscious, reflective part of our mental system that directs the flow of information, coordinating incoming information with information already in the system and selecting, applying, and monitoring strategies that facilitate memory storage, comprehension, reasoning, and problem solving. (p. 161)

centration In Piaget's theory, the tendency of preoperational children to focus on one aspect of a situation while neglecting other important features. (p. 230)

cephalocaudal trend An organized pattern of physical growth that proceeds from the upper to the lower part of the body ("head to tail"). Distinguished from *proximodistal trend.* (p. 117)

cerebellum A structure at the rear and base of the brain that aids in balance and control of body movement. (p. 218)

cerebral cortex The largest, most complex structure of the human brain, which contains the greatest number of neurons and synapses and accounts for the highly developed intelligence of the human species. (p. 120)

cesarean delivery A surgical birth, in which the doctor makes an incision in the mother's abdomen and lifts the baby out of the uterus. (p. 97)

child-centered programs Preschool and kindergarten programs in which teachers provide a variety of activities from which children select, and much learning takes place through play. Distinguished from *academic programs.* (p. 246)

child-rearing styles Combinations of parenting behaviors that occur over a wide range of situations, creating an enduring child-rearing climate. (p. 282)

chorion The outer membrane that surrounds the amnion, forming a protective covering around the developing organism. It sends out tiny fingerlike *villi,* from which the placenta begins to develop. (p. 78)

chromosomes Rodlike structures in the cell nucleus that store and transmit genetic information. (p. 44)

chronosystem In ecological systems theory, the temporal dimension of the environment, in which life changes can either be imposed externally or, alternatively, can arise from within the person. Distinguished from *microsystem, mesosystem, exosystem,* and *macrosystem.* (p. 26)

circular reaction In Piaget's theory, a means of building schemes in which infants try to repeat a chance event caused by their own motor activity. (p. 151)

classical conditioning A form of learning that involves associating a neutral stimulus with a stimulus that leads to a reflexive response. Once the nervous system makes the connection between the two stimuli, the neutral stimulus alone produces the behavior. (p. 130)

climacteric The midlife transition in which fertility declines, bringing an end to reproductive capacity in women and diminished fertility in men. (p. 510)

clinical death The phase of dying in which heartbeat, circulation, breathing, and brain functioning stop, but resuscitation is still possible. Distinguished from *agonal phase* and *mortality.* (p. 645)

clinical interview An interview method in which the researcher uses a flexible, conversational style to probe for the participant's point of view. Distinguished from *structured interview.* (p. 29)

clinical, or case study, method A research method in which the aim is to obtain as complete a picture as possible of one individual's psychological functioning and the experiences that led up to it by bringing together interview data, observations, and test scores. (p. 30)

clique A group of about five to seven members who are friends and, therefore, usually resemble one another in family background, attitudes, values, and interests. (p. 425)

cognitive-affective complexity In Labouvie-Vief's theory, a form of thinking that increases from adolescence through middle adulthood, involving awareness of conflicting positive and negative feelings and coordination of them into a complex, organized structure that recognizes the uniqueness of individual experiences. (p. 458)

cognitive-developmental theory Piaget's view that children actively construct knowledge as they manipulate and explore their world and that cognitive development takes place in stages. (p. 17)

cognitive maps Mental representations of familiar spaces, such as a classroom, school, or neighborhood. (p. 304)

cognitive reserve Reorganization of brain areas devoted to cognitive processes and richer synaptic connections, resulting from the complex cognitive activities of better-educated people, which give the aging brain greater tolerance for injury before it crosses the threshold into mental disability. (p. 590)

cognitive self-regulation The process of continuously monitoring progress toward a goal, checking outcomes, and redirecting unsuccessful efforts. (p. 312)

cohabitation The lifestyle of unmarried couples who have a sexually intimate relationship and who share a residence. (p. 494)

cohort effects The effects of cultural–historical change on the accuracy of longitudinal and cross-sectional research findings. Results based on one cohort—individuals developing in the same time period, who are influenced by particular historical and cultural conditions—may not apply to other cohorts. (p. 35)

commitment within relativistic thinking In Perry's theory, the mature individual's formulation of a perspective that synthesizes contradictions between opposing views, rather than choosing between them. (p. 457)

companionate love Love based on warm, trusting affection and valuing of the other. Distinguished from *passionate love* and *compassionate love*. (p. 479)

compassionate love Love based on concern for the other's well-being, expressed through caring efforts to alleviate the other's distress and promote the other's growth and flourishing. (p. 479)

compliance Voluntary obedience to requests and commands. (p. 209)

complicated grief A bereaved person's severe, prolonged distress, depression, and lack of acceptance of the death that persists for years, impairing physical and mental health. (p. 665)

compression of morbidity The public health goal of reducing the average period of diminished vigor before death as life expectancy extends. Medical advances and improved socioeconomic conditions promote this goal. (p. 582)

concrete operational stage Piaget's third stage of cognitive development, extending from about 7 to 11 years, during which thought becomes logical, flexible, and organized in its application to concrete information, but the capacity for abstract thinking is not yet present. (p. 304)

conditioned response (CR) In classical conditioning, a new response elicited by a conditioned stimulus (CS) that is similar to the unconditioned, or reflexive, response (UCR). (p. 131)

conditioned stimulus (CS) In classical conditioning, a neutral stimulus that, through pairing with an unconditioned stimulus (UCS), leads to a new, conditioned response. (CR). (p. 131)

conservation The understanding that certain physical characteristics of objects remain the same, even when their outward appearance changes. (p. 229)

constructivist classroom A classroom grounded in Piaget's view of children as active agents who construct their own knowledge. Features include richly equipped learning centers, small groups and individuals solving self-chosen problems, a teacher who guides and supports in response to children's needs, and evaluation based on individual students' progress in relation to their own prior development. Distinguished from *traditional* and *social-constructivist classrooms*. (p. 324)

contexts Unique combinations of personal and environmental circumstances that can result in different paths of development. (p. 6)

continuity theory A social theory of aging that states that most aging adults, in their choice of everyday activities and social relationships, strive to maintain a personal system—an identity and a set of personality dispositions, interests, roles, and skills—that promotes life satisfaction by ensuring consistency between their past and anticipated future. (p. 620)

continuous development The view that development is a process of gradually augmenting the same types of skills that were there to begin with. Distinguished from *discontinuous development*. (p. 6)

contrast sensitivity A general principle accounting for early pattern preferences, which states that if babies can detect the contrast in two or more patterns, they prefer the pattern with more contrast. (p. 141)

controversial children Children who receive many votes, both positive and negative, on self-report measures of peer acceptance, indicating that they are both liked and disliked. Distinguished from *popular, neglected,* and *rejected children*. (p. 347)

conventional level Kohlberg's second level of moral development, in which moral understanding is based on conformity to social rules to ensure positive human relationships and maintain societal order. (p. 414)

convergent thinking The type of cognition emphasized on intelligence tests, which involves arriving at a single correct answer to a problem. Distinguished from *divergent thinking*. (p. 328)

cooing Pleasant vowel-like noises made by infants beginning around 2 months of age. (p. 175)

cooperative learning Collaboration on a task by a small group of classmates who work toward common goals by considering one another's ideas, appropriately challenging one another, providing sufficient explanations to correct misunderstandings, and resolving differences of opinion on the basis of reasons and evidence. (p. 325)

cooperative play A form of social interaction in which children orient toward a common goal, such as acting out a make-believe theme. Distinguished from *nonsocial activity, parallel play,* and *associative play.* (p. 263)

coparenting Parents' mutual support of each other's parenting behaviors. (p. 57)

coregulation A form of supervision in which parents exercise general oversight while letting children take charge of moment-by-moment decision making. (p. 352)

core knowledge perspective A perspective that states that infants are born with a set of innate knowledge systems, or core domains of thought, each of which permits a ready grasp of new, related information and therefore supports early, rapid development of certain aspects of cognition. (p. 158)

corpus callosum The large bundle of fibers connecting the two hemispheres of the cerebral cortex. Supports smooth coordination of movements on both sides of the body and integration of many aspects of thinking. (p. 219)

correlational design A research design in which investigators gather information on individuals without altering their experiences and then examine relationships between participants' characteristics and their behavior or development. Does not permit inferences about cause and effect. (p. 31)

correlation coefficient A number, ranging from +1.00 to –1.00, that describes the strength and direction of the relationship between two variables. (p. 33)

creativity The ability to produce work that is *original* yet *appropriate*—something others have not thought of that is useful in some way. (p. 328)

cross-linkage theory of aging A theory of biological aging asserting that the formation of bonds, or links, between normally separate protein fibers causes the body's connective tissue to become less elastic over time, leading to many negative physical outcomes. (p. 440)

cross-sectional design A research design in which groups of participants differing in age are studied at the same point in time. Distinguished from *longitudinal design*. (p. 36)

crowd A large, loosely organized social group consisting of several cliques with similar values. Membership is based on reputation and stereotype. (p. 425)

crystallized intelligence Intellectual skills that depend on accumulated knowledge and experience, good judgment, and mastery of social conventions—abilities acquired because they are valued by the individual's culture. Distinguished from *fluid intelligence.* (p. 525)

D

death anxiety Fear and apprehension of death. (p. 651)

deferred imitation The ability to remember and copy the behavior of models who are not present. (p. 153)

delay of gratification The ability to wait for an appropriate time and place to engage in a tempting act. (p. 209)

dementia A set of disorders occurring almost entirely in old age in which many aspects of thought and behavior are so impaired that everyday activities are disrupted. (p. 587)

deoxyribonucleic acid (DNA) Long, double-stranded molecules that make up chromosomes. (p. 44)

dependency–support script A predictable pattern of interaction in which caregivers attend to older adults' dependent behaviors immediately, thereby reinforcing those behaviors, while ignoring independent behaviors. Distinguished from *independence–ignore script*. (p. 616)

dependent variable The variable the researcher expects to be influenced by the independent variable in an experiment. Distinguished from *independent variable.* (p. 33)

developmental cognitive neuroscience An area of investigation that brings together researchers from psychology, biology, neuroscience, and medicine to study the relationship between changes in the brain and the developing person's cognitive processing and behavior patterns. (p. 20)

developmentally appropriate practice A set of standards devised by the U.S. National Association for the Education of Young Children, specifying program characteristics that serve young children's developmental and individual needs, based on current research and consensus among experts. (p. 171)

developmental quotient (DQ) A score on an infant intelligence test, computed in the same manner as an IQ but labeled more conservatively because it does not tap the same dimensions of intelligence assessed in older children. (p. 169)

developmental science An interdisciplinary field devoted to understanding constancy and change throughout the lifespan. (p. 5)

developmental social neuroscience A new field devoted to studying the relationship between changes in the brain and emotional and social development. (p. 20)

differentiation theory The view that perceptual development involves the detection of increasingly fine-grained, invariant features in the environment. (p. 144)

difficult child A child whose temperament is characterized by irregularity in daily routines, slowness in accepting new experiences, and a tendency to react negatively and intensely. Distinguished from *easy child* and *slow-to-warm-up child*. (p. 190)

discontinuous development The view that development is a process in which new ways of understanding and responding to the world emerge at specific times. Distinguished from *continuous development*. (p. 6)

disenfranchised grief A sense of loss without the opportunity to mourn publicly and benefit from others' support. (p. 668)

disorganized/disoriented attachment The attachment pattern reflecting the greatest insecurity, characterizing infants who show confused, contradictory responses when reunited with the parent after a separation. Distinguished from *secure, avoidant,* and *resistant attachment*. (p. 198)

displaced reference The realization that words can be used to cue mental images of things that are not physically present. (p. 156)

divergent thinking The type of thinking associated with creativity, which involves generating multiple and unusual possibilities when faced with a task or problem. Distinguished from *convergent thinking*. (p. 328)

dominance hierarchy A stable ordering of group members that predicts who will win when conflict arises. (p. 302)

dominant cerebral hemisphere The hemisphere of the cerebral cortex responsible for skilled motor action and other important abilities. In right-handed individuals, the left hemisphere is dominant; in left-handed individuals, motor and language skills are often shared between the hemispheres. (p. 218)

dominant–recessive inheritance A pattern of inheritance in which, under heterozygous conditions, only one allele, called *dominant*, affects the child's characteristics. The second allele, which has no effect, is called *recessive*. (p. 46)

dualistic thinking In Perry's theory, the cognitive approach typical of younger college students, who divide information, values, and authority into right and wrong, good and bad, we and they. Distinguished from *relativistic thinking*. (p. 456)

dual-process model of coping with loss A perspective that assumes that effective coping requires bereaved people to oscillate between dealing with the emotional consequences of loss and attending to life changes, which—when handled successfully—have restorative, or healing, effects. (p. 665)

dual representation The ability to view a symbolic object as both an object in its own right and a symbol. (p. 229)

durable power of attorney for health care A written statement authorizing appointment of another person (usually, though not always, a family member) to make health-care decisions on one's behalf. (p. 662)

dynamic assessment An approach to testing consistent with Vygotsky's zone of proximal development, in which purposeful teaching is introduced into the testing situation to find out what the child can attain with social support. (p. 320)

dynamic systems theory of motor development A theory that views mastery of motor skills as a process of acquiring increasingly complex *systems of action*, in which separate abilities blend together, each cooperating with others to produce more effective ways of exploring and controlling the environment. Each new skill is a joint product of central nervous system development, the body's movement capacities, the child's goals, and environmental supports for the skill. (p. 135)

E

easy child A child whose temperament is characterized by quick establishment of regular routines in infancy, general cheerfulness, and easy adaptation to new experiences. Distinguished from *difficult child* and *slow-to-warm-up child*. (p. 190)

ecological systems theory Bronfenbrenner's approach, which views the person as developing within a complex system of relationships affected by multiple levels of the surrounding environment, from immediate settings of family and school to broad cultural values and programs. (p. 23)

educational self-fulfilling prophecies Teachers' positive or negative views of individual children, who tend to adopt and start to live up to those views. (p. 326)

effortful control The self-regulatory dimension of temperament, involving the capacity to voluntarily suppress a dominant response in order to plan and execute a more adaptive response. (p. 191)

egalitarian marriage A form of marriage in which partners relate as equals, sharing power and authority. Both try to balance the time and energy they devote to their occupations, their children, and their relationship. Distinguished from *traditional marriage*. (p. 486)

egocentrism Failure to distinguish others' symbolic viewpoints from one's own. (p. 229)

ego integrity versus despair In Erikson's theory, the psychological conflict of late adulthood, which is resolved positively when older adults come to terms with their lives and feel whole, complete, and satisfied with their achievements. (p. 610)

elaboration A memory strategy that involves creating a relationship, or shared meaning, between two or more pieces of information that do not belong to the same category. (p. 310)

embryo The prenatal organism from 2 to 8 weeks after conception—the period when the groundwork is laid for all body structures and internal organs. (p. 78)

emergent literacy Children's active efforts to construct literacy knowledge through informal experiences. (p. 242)

emerging adulthood A new transitional period of development, extending from the late teens to the mid- to late twenties, during which young people have left adolescence but have not yet assumed adult responsibilities. Rather, they explore alternatives in education, work, and personal values and behavior more intensely than they did in adolescence. (p. 470)

emotional self-regulation Strategies for adjusting our emotional state to a comfortable level of intensity so we can accomplish our goals. (p. 189)

emotion-centered coping A strategy for managing emotion that is internal, private, and aimed at controlling distress when little can be done about an outcome. Distinguished from *problem-centered coping*. (p. 342)

empathy The ability to understand another's emotional state and *feel with* that person, or respond emotionally in a similar way. (p. 208)

epigenesis Development resulting from ongoing, bidirectional exchanges between heredity and all levels of the environment. (p. 70)

episodic memory Memory for everyday experiences. Distinguished from *semantic memory*. (p. 240)

epistemic cognition Reflections on how one arrived at facts, beliefs, and ideas. (p. 456)

ethnic identity A sense of ethnic group membership and the attitudes, beliefs, and feelings associated with that membership, as an enduring aspect of the self. (p. 412)

ethnography A research method in which the researcher attempts to understand a culture or a distinct social group through *participant observation*—living with its members and gathering field notes over an extended period of time. (p. 30)

ethological theory of attachment Bowlby's theory, the most widely accepted view of attachment, which recognizes the infant's emotional tie to the caregiver as an evolved response that promotes survival. (p. 196)

ethology An approach concerned with the adaptive, or survival, value of behavior and its evolutionary history. (p. 21)

evolutionary developmental psychology An area of research that seeks to understand the adaptive value of species-wide cognitive, emotional, and social competencies as those competencies change with age. (p. 22)

executive function In information processing, the diverse cognitive operations and strategies that enable us to achieve our goals in cognitively challenging situations. These include controlling attention by inhibiting impulses and irrelevant actions and by flexibly directing thought and behavior to suit the demands of a task; coordinating information in working memory; and planning. (p. 161)

exosystem In ecological systems theory, the level of the environment consisting of social settings that do not contain the developing person but nevertheless affect experiences in immediate settings. Distinguished from *microsystem, mesosystem, macrosystem,* and *chronosystem.* (p. 24)

expansions Adult responses that elaborate on children's speech, increasing its complexity. (p. 252)

experience-dependent brain growth Growth and refinement of established brain structures as a result of specific learning experiences that vary widely across individuals and cultures. Distinguished from *experience-expectant brain growth.* (p. 124)

experience-expectant brain growth The young brain's rapidly developing organization, which depends on ordinary experiences—opportunities to explore the environment, interact with people, and hear language and other sounds. Distinguished from *experience-dependent brain growth.* (p. 124)

experimental design A research design in which investigators randomly assign participants to two or more treatment conditions and then study the effect that manipulating an independent variable has on a dependent variable. Permits inferences about cause and effect. (p. 33)

expertise Acquisition of extensive knowledge in a field or endeavor. (p. 458)

explicit memory Memory that requires controlled, strategic processing. Distinguished from *implicit memory.* (p. 596)

expressive style of language learning A style of early language learning in which toddlers use language mainly to talk about their own and others' feelings and needs, with an initial vocabulary emphasizing social formulas and pronouns. Distinguished from *referential style of language learning.* (p. 178)

extended-family households Households in which parent and child live with one or more adult relatives. (p. 62)

F

family life cycle A series of phases characterizing the development of most families around the world. In early adulthood, people typically live on their own, marry, and bear and rear children. In middle age, parenting responsibilities diminish. Late adulthood brings retirement, growing old, and (more often for women) death of one's spouse. (p. 484)

fantasy period Period of vocational development in which children gain insight into career options by fantasizing about them. Distinguished from *tentative period* and *realistic period.* (p. 462)

fast-mapping Children's ability to connect new words with their underlying concepts after only a brief encounter. (p. 250)

feminization of poverty A trend in which women who support themselves or their families have become the majority of the adult population living in poverty, regardless of age and ethnic group. (p. 550)

fetal alcohol spectrum disorder (FASD) A range of physical, mental, and behavioral outcomes caused by prenatal alcohol exposure, including *fetal alcohol syndrome (FAS), partial fetal alcohol syndrome (p-FAS),* and *alcohol-related neurodevelopmental disorder (ARND).* (p. 84)

fetal alcohol syndrome (FAS) The most severe form of fetal alcohol spectrum disorder, distinguished by slow physical growth, facial abnormalities, and brain injury. Usually affects children whose mothers drank heavily throughout pregnancy. Distinguished from *partial fetal alcohol syndrome (p-FAS)* and *alcohol-related neurodevelopmental disorder (ARND).* (p. 84)

fetal monitors Electronic instruments that track the baby's heart rate during labor. (p. 96)

fetus The developing organism from the ninth week to the end of pregnancy—the period during which body structures are completed and dramatic growth in size occurs. (p. 79)

fluid intelligence Intellectual skills that largely depend on basic information-processing skills—ability to detect relationships among visual stimuli, speed of analyzing information, and capacity of working memory. Influenced less by culture than by conditions in the brain and by learning unique to the individual. Distinguished from *crystallized intelligence.* (p. 525)

Flynn effect The steady increase in IQ from one generation to the next. (p. 319)

formal operational stage Piaget's highest stage of cognitive development, beginning around age 11, in which young people develop the capacity for abstract, systematic, scientific thinking. (p. 388)

frailty Weakened functioning of diverse organs and body systems, which profoundly interferes with everyday competence and leaves older adults highly vulnerable in the face of infection, extremely hot or cold weather, or injury. (p. 585)

fraternal, or dizygotic, twins Twins resulting from the release and fertilization of two ova. They are genetically no more alike than ordinary siblings. Distinguished from *identical, or monozygotic, twins.* (p. 45)

free radicals Naturally occurring, highly reactive chemicals that form in the presence of oxygen within cells and, at toxic levels, cause DNA and cellular damage, increasing vulnerability to wide-ranging disorders of aging. (p. 440)

functional age Actual competence and performance of an older adult, as distinguished from chronological age. (p. 570)

G

gametes The sex cells, or sperm and ovum, which contain half as many chromosomes as regular body cells. (p. 44)

gender constancy A full understanding of the biologically based permanence of one's gender, including the realization that sex remains the same even if clothing, hairstyle, and play activities change. (p. 279)

gender identity An image of oneself as relatively masculine or feminine in characteristics. (p. 279)

gender schema theory An information-processing approach to gender typing that combines social learning and cognitive-developmental features to explain how environmental pressures and children's cognitions work together to shape gender-role development. (p. 279)

gender typing Any association of objects, roles, or traits with one sex or the other in ways that conform to cultural stereotypes. (p. 276)

gene A segment of DNA along the length of the chromosome containing instructions for making proteins that contribute to body growth and functioning. (p. 44)

gene–environment correlation The idea that individuals' genes influence the environments to which they are exposed. (p. 68)

gene–environment interaction The view that because of their genetic makeup, individuals differ in their responsiveness to qualities of the environment. (p. 68)

generativity versus stagnation In Erikson's theory, the psychological conflict of midlife, which is resolved positively if the adult can integrate personal goals with the welfare of the larger social world. The resulting strength is the capacity to give to and guide the next generation. (p. 538)

genetic counseling A communication process designed to help couples assess their chances of giving birth to a baby with a hereditary disorder and choose the best course of action in view of risks and family goals. (p. 51)

genomic imprinting A pattern of inheritance in which alleles are imprinted, or chemically marked, in such a way that one pair member is activated, regardless of its makeup. (p. 49)

genotype An individual's genetic makeup. Distinguished from *phenotype.* (p. 43)

gerotranscendence According to Joan Erikson, a psychosocial stage representing development beyond ego integrity, characterized by a cosmic and transcendent perspective directed beyond the self to affinity with past and future generations and oneness with the universe. (p. 611)

gifted Displaying exceptional intellectual strengths, such as high IQ, high potential for creativity, or specialized talent. (p. 328)

glass ceiling Invisible barrier to advancement up the corporate ladder, faced by women and ethnic minorities. (p. 561)

glaucoma A disease in which poor fluid drainage leads to a buildup of pressure within the eye, damaging the optic nerve. A leading cause of blindness among older adults. (p. 509)

glial cells Cells that are responsible for myelination of neural fibers, which improves the efficiency of message transfer. (p. 118)

goodness-of-fit model A model proposed by Thomas and Chess to explain how favorable adjustment depends on an effective match, or good fit, between a child's temperament and the child-rearing environment. (p. 195)

grief Intense physical and psychological distress following the death of a loved one. (p. 665)

growth hormone (GH) A pituitary hormone that affects the development of almost all body tissues. (p. 219)

growth spurt Rapid gain in height and weight that is the first outward sign of puberty. (p. 369)

guided participation Shared endeavors between more expert and less expert participants, without specifying the precise features of communication, thereby allowing for variations across situations and cultures. A broader concept than *scaffolding*. (p. 236)

H

habituation A gradual reduction in the strength of a response due to repetitive stimulation. (p. 131)

hardiness A set of three personal qualities—control, commitment, and challenge—that, together, help people cope adaptively with stress brought on by inevitable life changes. (p. 522)

heritability estimate A statistic that measures the extent to which individual differences in complex traits, such as intelligence or personality, in a specific population are due to genetic factors. (p. 67)

heterozygous Having two different alleles at the same place on a pair of chromosomes. Distinguished from *homozygous*. (p. 46)

hierarchical classification The organization of objects into classes and subclasses on the basis of similarities and differences. (p. 230)

hippocampus An inner-brain structure that plays a vital role in memory and in images of space that help us find our way. (p. 218)

history-graded influences Influences on lifespan development that are unique to a particular historical era and explain why people born around the same time (called a *cohort*) tend to be alike in ways that set them apart from people born at other times. (p. 9)

Home Observation for Measurement of the Environment (HOME) A checklist for gathering information about the quality of children's home lives through observation and parental interview. (p. 170)

homozygous Having two identical alleles at the same place on a pair of chromosomes. Distinguished from *heterozygous*. (p. 46)

hormone therapy Low daily doses of estrogen, either alone or in combination with progesterone, aimed at reducing the physical discomforts of menopause. (p. 512)

hospice A comprehensive program of support services for terminally ill people and their families, which regards the patient and family as a unit of care and emphasizes meeting the patient's physical, emotional, social, and spiritual needs while also providing follow-up bereavement services to the family. (p. 658)

hypothetico-deductive reasoning A formal operational problem-solving strategy in which adolescents begin with a *hypothesis,* or prediction about variables that might affect an outcome, from which they *deduce* logical, testable inferences. Then they systematically isolate and combine variables to see which of those inferences are confirmed in the real world. (p. 388)

I

identical, or monozygotic, twins Twins that result when a zygote that has started to duplicate separates into two clusters of cells with the same genetic makeup, which develop into two individuals. Distinguished from *fraternal, or dizygotic, twins*. (p. 46)

identity A well-organized conception of the self that defines who one is, what one values, and what directions one chooses to pursue in life. (p. 408)

identity achievement The identity status of individuals who, after a period of exploration, have committed themselves to a clearly formulated set of self-chosen values and goals. Distinguished from *identity moratorium, identity foreclosure,* and *identity diffusion*. (p. 408)

identity diffusion The identity status of individuals who do not engage in exploration and are not committed to values and goals. Distinguished from *identity achievement, identity moratorium,* and *identity foreclosure*. (p. 408)

identity foreclosure The identity status of individuals who do not engage in exploration but, instead, are committed to ready-made values and goals chosen for them by authority figures. Distinguished from *identity achievement, identity moratorium,* and *identity diffusion*. (p. 408)

identity moratorium The identity status of individuals who are exploring but not yet committed to self-chosen values and goals. Distinguished from *identity achievement, identity foreclosure,* and *identity diffusion*. (p. 408)

identity versus role confusion In Erikson's theory, the psychological conflict of adolescence, which is resolved positively when adolescents achieve an identity through a process of exploration and inner soul-searching. (p. 408)

imaginary audience Adolescents' belief that they are the focus of everyone else's attention and concern. (p. 392)

imitation Learning by copying the behavior of another person. (p. 132)

implantation Attachment of the blastocyst to the uterine lining, which occurs 7 to 9 days after fertilization. (p. 77)

implicit memory Memory without conscious awareness. Distinguished from *explicit memory*. (p. 596)

inclusive classrooms Classrooms in which students with learning difficulties learn alongside typical students in the regular educational setting for all or part of the school day—a practice designed to prepare them for participation in society and to combat prejudices against individuals with disabilities. (p. 326)

incomplete dominance A pattern of inheritance in which both alleles are expressed in the phenotype, resulting in a combined trait, or one that is intermediate between the two. (p. 48)

independence–ignore script A predictable pattern of interaction in which older adults' independent behaviors are mostly ignored and, as a result, occur less often. Distinguished from *dependency–support script*. (p. 616)

independent living communities Assisted living arrangements for older adults that provide a variety of hotel-like support services, including meals in a common dining room, housekeeping, laundry services, transportation assistance, and recreational activities. (p. 623)

independent variable In an experiment, the variable the investigator expects to cause changes in another variable and that the researcher manipulates by randomly assigning participants to different treatment conditions. Distinguished from *dependent variable*. (p. 33)

induction A type of discipline in which an adult helps make the child aware of feelings by pointing out the effects of the child's misbehavior on others. (p. 267)

industry versus inferiority In Erikson's theory, the psychological conflict of middle childhood, which is resolved positively when experiences lead children to develop a sense of competence at useful skills and tasks. (p. 336)

infant-directed speech (IDS) A form of communication used by adults to speak to infants and toddlers, consisting of short sentences with high-pitched, exaggerated expression, clear pronunciation, distinct pauses between speech segments, and repetition of new words in a variety of contexts. (p. 179)

infantile amnesia The inability of most older children and adults to retrieve events that happened before age 2 to 3. (p. 164)

infant mortality The number of deaths in the first year of life per 1,000 live births. (p. 102)

information processing A perspective that views the human mind as a symbol-manipulating system through which information flows and that regards cognitive development as a continuous process. (p. 19)

inhibited, or shy, children Children whose temperament is such that they react negatively to and withdraw from novel stimuli. Distinguished from *uninhibited, or sociable, children*. (p. 191)

initiative versus guilt In Erikson's theory, the psychological conflict of early childhood, which is resolved positively through play experiences that foster a healthy sense of initiative and through development of a superego, or conscience, that is not overly strict and guilt-ridden. (p. 258)

insecure–avoidant attachment The attachment pattern characterizing infants who seem unresponsive to the parent when she is present, are usually not distressed by parental separation, react to the stranger in much the same way as to the parent, and avoid or are slow to greet the parent when she returns. Distinguished from *secure, insecure–resistant,* and *disorganized/disoriented attachment*. (p. 198)

insecure–resistant attachment The attachment pattern characterizing infants who seek closeness to the parent and fail to explore before separation, are usually distressed when the parent leaves, and combine clinginess with angry, resistive behavior when the parent returns. Distinguished from *secure, insecure–avoidant,* and *disorganized/disoriented attachment*. (p. 198)

instrumental activities of daily living (IADLs) Tasks necessary to conduct the business of daily life and also requiring some cognitive competence, such as telephoning, shopping, food preparation, housekeeping, and paying bills. (p. 573)

intelligence quotient (IQ) A score that permits an individual's performance on an intelligence test to be compared to the performances of other individuals of the same age. (p. 169)

intentional, or goal-directed, behavior A sequence of actions in which schemes are deliberately coordinated to solve a problem. (p. 152)

interactional synchrony A form of communication in which the caregiver responds to infant signals in a well-timed, rhythmic, appropriate fashion and both partners match emotional states, especially the positive ones. (p. 200)

intermodal perception The process of making sense of simultaneous input from more than one modality, or sensory system, perceiving these separate streams of information as an integrated whole. (p. 143)

internal working model A set of expectations about the availability of attachment figures and their likelihood of providing support in times of stress. It becomes a vital part of personality, serving as a guide for all future close relationships. (p. 197)

intimacy versus isolation In Erikson's theory, the psychological conflict of early adulthood, evident in the young person's thoughts and feelings about making a long-term commitment to an intimate partner and in close, mutually gratifying friendships. (p. 476)

irreversibility The inability to mentally go through a series of steps in a problem and then reverse direction, returning to the starting point. Distinguished from *reversibility*. (p. 230)

J

joint attention A state in which the child attends to the same object or event as the caregiver, who often labels it. Contributes to early language development. (p. 176)

K

kinkeeper Role assumed by members of the middle generation, especially mothers, who take responsibility for gathering the family for celebrations and making sure everyone stays in touch. (p. 552)

kinship studies Studies that compare the characteristics of family members to determine the importance of heredity in complex human characteristics. (p. 67)

kwashiorkor A disease caused by an unbalanced diet very low in protein that usually appears after weaning, between 1 and 3 years of age. Symptoms include an enlarged belly, swollen feet, hair loss, skin rash, and irritable, listless behavior. (p. 129)

L

language acquisition device (LAD) In Chomsky's theory, an innate system containing a universal grammar, or set of rules common to all languages, that enables children, no matter which language they hear, to understand and speak in a rule-oriented fashion as soon as they pick up enough words. (p. 174)

lanugo White, downy hair that covers the entire body of the fetus, helping the vernix stick to the skin. (p. 79)

lateralization Specialization of functions in the two hemispheres of the cerebral cortex. (p. 121)

learned helplessness Attribution of success to external factors, such as luck, and failure to low ability, which is fixed and cannot be improved by trying hard. Distinguished from *mastery-oriented attributions*. (p. 339)

learning disabilities Great difficulty with one or more aspects of learning, usually reading, resulting in achievement that is considerably behind what would be expected on the basis of a child's IQ. (p. 327)

life-care communities Assisted living arrangements for older adults that offer a continuum of housing alternatives: independent living, residences providing personal and health-related services to accommodate older adults with physical and mental disabilities, and full nursing home care. Guarantees that individuals' changing needs will be met within the same facility as they age. (p. 623)

lifespan perspective A developmental systems approach that assumes development is lifelong, multidimensional and multidirectional, highly plastic, and affected by multiple interacting forces. (p. 7)

living will A written statement specifying the treatments a person does or does not want in case of a terminal illness, coma, or other near-death situation. (p. 661)

longitudinal design A research design in which participants are studied repeatedly, and changes are noted as they get older. Distinguished from *cross-sectional design*. (p. 35)

long-term memory In information processing, the largest storage area in memory, containing our permanent knowledge base. (p. 161)

M

macrosystem In ecological systems theory, the outermost level of the environment, consisting of cultural values, laws, customs, and resources that influence individuals' experiences and interactions at inner levels. Distinguished from *microsystem, mesosystem, exosystem,* and *chronosystem*. (p. 24)

macular degeneration Blurring and eventual loss of central vision due to a breakdown of light-sensitive cells in the macula, or central region of the retina. (p. 575)

make-believe play A type of play in which children act out everyday and imaginary activities. (p. 153)

marasmus A wasted condition of the body caused by a diet low in all essential nutrients, which usually appears in the first year of life when the mother is too malnourished to produce enough breast milk and bottle-feeding is also inadequate. (p. 129)

mastery-oriented attributions Attributions that credit success to ability, which can be improved through effort, and failure to factors that can be changed or controlled, such as insufficient effort or a difficult task. Distinguished from *learned helplessness*. (p. 339)

matters of personal choice Concerns such as choice of friends, hairstyle, and leisure activities, which do not violate rights and are up to the individual. Distinguished from *moral imperatives* and *social conventions*. (p. 272)

maximum lifespan The species-specific biological limit to length of life (in years), corresponding to the age at which the oldest known individual died. Distinguished from *average life expectancy* and *average healthy life expectancy*. (p. 572)

medical aid-in-dying At an incurably ill patient's request, a doctor's provision of a prescription for a lethal dose of drugs, which the patient self-administers to end his or her life. (p. 662)

meiosis The process of cell division through which gametes are formed, in which the number of chromosomes normally present in each cell is halved. (p. 45)

memory strategies Deliberate mental activities that improve the likelihood of remembering. (p. 240)

menarche First menstruation. (p. 371)

menopause The end of menstruation and, therefore, of a woman's reproductive capacity. (p. 510)

mental representations Internal depictions of information that the mind can manipulate, including images and concepts. (p. 152)

mesosystem In ecological systems theory, the second level of the environment, encompassing connections between an individual's microsystems, or immediate settings. Distinguished from *microsystem, exosystem, macrosystem,* and *chronosystem*. (p. 24)

metacognition Thinking about thought; a theory of mind, or coherent set of ideas about mental activities. (p. 241)

methylation A biochemical process triggered by certain experiences, in which a set of chemical compounds (called a methyl group) lands on top of a gene and changes its impact, reducing or silencing its expression. (p. 70)

microsystem In ecological systems theory, the innermost level of the environment, consisting of activities and interaction patterns in the person's immediate surroundings. Distinguished from *mesosystem, exosystem, macrosystem,* and *chronosystem*. (p. 23)

midlife crisis Self-doubt and stress that prompt major restructuring of the personality during the transition to middle adulthood. Characterizes the experience of only a minority of adults. (p. 542)

mirror neurons Specialized cells in motor areas of the cerebral cortex in primates that may underlie early imitative capacities by firing identically when a primate hears or sees an action and when it carries out the action on its own. (p. 132)

moral identity The degree to which morality is central to an individual's self-concept. (p. 418)

moral imperatives Rules and expectations that protect people's rights and welfare. Distinguished from *social conventions* and *matters of personal choice*. (p. 272)

mortality The phase of dying in which the individual passes into permanent death. Distinguished from *agonal phase* and *clinical death*. (p. 645)

mourning The culturally specified expression of the bereaved person's thoughts and feelings through funerals and other rituals. (p. 665)

mutation A sudden but permanent change in a segment of DNA. (p. 49)

myelination The coating of neural fibers with an insulating fatty sheath, called *myelin,* that improves the efficiency of message transfer. (p. 118)

N

naturalistic observation A research method in which the investigator goes into the field, or natural environment, and records the behavior of interest. Distinguished from *structured observation*. (p. 28)

natural, or prepared, childbirth A group of techniques aimed at reducing pain and medical intervention and making childbirth a rewarding experience. (p. 95)

nature–nurture controversy Disagreement among theorists about whether genetic or environmental factors are more important influences on development. (p. 7)

neglected children Children who are seldom mentioned, either positively or negatively, on self-report measures of peer acceptance. Distinguished from *popular, rejected,* and *controversial children*. (p. 347)

Neonatal Behavioral Assessment Scale (NBAS) A test used to evaluate a newborn's reflexes, muscle tone, state changes, responsiveness to physical and social stimuli, and other reactions. (p. 110)

neural tube During the period of the embryo, the primitive spinal cord that develops from the ectoderm, the top of which swells to form the brain. (p. 78)

neurofibrillary tangles A structural change in the cerebral cortex associated with Alzheimer's disease, in which bundles of twisted threads appear that are the product of collapsed neural structures and that contain abnormal forms of a protein called tau. (p. 588)

neurons Nerve cells that store and transmit information. (p. 117)

neurotransmitters Chemicals released by neurons that cross the synapse to send messages to other neurons. (p. 117)

niche-picking A type of gene–environment correlation in which individuals actively choose environments that complement their heredity. (p. 69)

nonnormative influences Influences on lifespan development that are irregular, in that they happen to just one person or a few people and do not follow a predictable timetable. (p. 10)

non-rapid-eye-movement (NREM) sleep A "regular" sleep state during which the body is almost motionless and heart rate, breathing, and brain-wave activity are slow and even. Distinguished from *rapid-eye-movement (REM) sleep*. (p. 104)

nonsocial activity Unoccupied, onlooker behavior and solitary play. Distinguished from *parallel, associative,* and *cooperative play*. (p. 263)

normal distribution The bell-shaped distribution that results when researchers measure individual differences in large samples. Most scores cluster around the mean, or average, with progressively fewer falling toward the extremes. (p. 169)

normative approach An approach in which measures of behavior are taken on large numbers of individuals, and age-related averages are computed to represent typical development. (p. 14)

O

obesity A greater-than-20-percent increase over healthy weight, based on body mass index (BMI), a ratio of weight to height associated with body fat. (p. 295)

object permanence The understanding that objects continue to exist when out of sight. (p. 152)

operant conditioning A form of learning in which a spontaneous behavior is followed by a stimulus that changes the probability that the behavior will occur again. (p. 131)

ordinality The mathematical principle specifying order relationships (more than and less than) between quantities. (p. 244)

organization In Piaget's theory, the internal rearrangement and linking of schemes to create a strongly interconnected cognitive system. In information processing, a memory strategy that involves grouping related items together to improve recall. (p. 150, p. 310)

osteoarthritis A form of arthritis that involves deteriorating cartilage on the ends of bones of frequently used joints, leading to swelling, stiffness, and loss of flexibility. Also known as "wear-and-tear" arthritis or "degenerative joint disease." Distinguished from *rheumatoid arthritis*. (p. 585)

osteoporosis Severe age-related bone loss, which greatly magnifies the risk of bone fractures. (p. 519)

overextension An early vocabulary error in which young children apply a word too broadly, to a wider collection of objects and events than is appropriate. Distinguished from *underextension*. (p. 177)

overregularization Overextension of regular grammatical rules to words that are exceptions. (p. 251)

P

palliative, or comfort, care Care for terminally ill, suffering patients that relieves pain and other symptoms (nausea, breathing difficulties, insomnia, and depression), with the goal of protecting the patient's quality of remaining life rather than prolonging life. (p. 658)

parallel play A form of limited social participation in which a child plays near other children with similar materials but does not try to influence their behavior. Distinguished from *nonsocial activity, associative play,* and *cooperative play*. (p. 263)

partial fetal alcohol syndrome (p-FAS) A form of fetal alcohol spectrum disorder characterized by facial abnormalities and brain injury, but less severe than fetal alcohol syndrome. Usually affects children whose mothers drank alcohol in smaller quantities during pregnancy. Distinguished from *fetal alcohol syndrome (FAS)* and *alcohol-related neurodevelopmental disorder (ARND)*. (p. 84)

passionate love Love based on intense sexual attraction. Distinguished from *companionate love* and *compassionate love*. (p. 479)

peer acceptance Likability, or the extent to which a child is viewed by a group of agemates as a worthy social partner. (p. 347)

peer groups Collectives of peers who generate unique values and standards for behavior and a social structure of leaders and followers. (p. 346)

peer victimization A destructive form of peer interaction in which certain children become frequent targets of verbal and physical attacks or other forms of abuse. (p. 349)

perceptual narrowing effect Perceptual sensitivity that becomes increasingly attuned with age to information most often encountered. (p. 139)

permissive child-rearing style A child-rearing style that is warm and accepting but uninvolved, low in control (either overindulgent or inattentive), and lenient rather than appropriate in autonomy granting. Distinguished from *authoritative, authoritarian,* and *uninvolved child-rearing styles*. (p. 283)

persistent vegetative state A state in which the cerebral cortex no longer registers electrical activity but the brain stem remains active. The person is unconscious and displays no voluntary movements. (p. 647)

personal fable Adolescents' inflated opinion of their own importance—a feeling that they are special and unique. (p. 386)

person–environment fit A good match between older adults' abilities and the demands of their living environments, which promotes adaptive behavior and psychological well-being. (p. 616)

person praise Praise that emphasizes a child's traits, such as "You're so smart!" Distinguished from *process praise*. (p. 339)

phenotype An individual's directly observable physical and behavioral characteristics, which are determined by both genetic and environmental factors. Distinguished from *genotype*. (p. 43)

phobia An intense, unmanageable fear that leads to persistent avoidance of the feared situation. (p. 358)

phonics approach An approach to beginning reading instruction that emphasizes coaching children on *phonics*—the basic rules for translating written symbols into sounds—before exposing them to complex reading material. Distinguished from *whole-language approach*. (p. 313)

phonological awareness The ability to reflect on and manipulate the sound structure of spoken language, as indicated by sensitivity to changes in sounds within words, to rhyming, and to incorrect pronunciation. A strong predictor of emergent literacy knowledge. (p. 244)

physical aggression A form of aggression that harms others through physical injury to themselves or their property. Distinguished from *verbal aggression* and *relational aggression*. (p. 272)

pituitary gland A gland located at the base of the brain that releases hormones that induce physical growth. (p. 219)

placenta The organ that permits food and oxygen to reach the developing organism and waste products to be carried away, while also preventing the mother's and embryo's blood from mixing directly. (p. 78)

plasticity Openness of development to change in response to influential experiences. (p. 7)

polygenic inheritance A pattern of inheritance in which many genes influence a characteristic. (p. 50)

popular-antisocial children A subgroup of popular children who are admired for their socially adept yet belligerent behavior. Includes "tough" boys—athletically skilled but poor students who cause trouble and defy authority—and relationally aggressive boys and girls who enhance their own status by ignoring, excluding, and spreading rumors about other children. Distinguished from *popular-prosocial children*. (p. 348)

popular children Children who receive many positive votes on self-report measures of peer acceptance, indicating they are well-liked. Distinguished from *rejected, controversial,* and *neglected children*. (p. 347)

popular-prosocial children A subgroup of popular children who combine academic and social competence and are both well-liked and admired. Distinguished from *popular-antisocial children*. (p. 348)

positivity effect An emotional strength of older adults who, compared with younger people, selectively attend to and better recall emotionally positive over negative information. (p. 611)

possible selves The temporal dimension of self-concept—future-oriented representations of what one is striving for and what one is attempting to avoid. (p. 544)

postconventional level Kohlberg's highest level of moral development, in which individuals define morality in terms of abstract principles and values that apply to all situations and societies. (p. 415)

postformal thought Cognitive development beyond Piaget's formal operational stage. (p. 456)

practical problem solving Problem solving that requires people to size up real-world situations and analyze how best to achieve goals that have a high degree of uncertainty. (p. 530)

pragmatics The practical, social side of language, concerned with how to engage in effective and appropriate communication. (p. 252)

pragmatic thought In Labouvie-Vief's theory, a structural advance in thinking in adulthood, in which logic becomes a tool for solving real-world problems and contradictions are accepted as part of existence. (p. 458)

preconventional level Kohlberg's first level of moral development, in which children accept the rules of authority figures and judge actions by their consequences, viewing behaviors that result in punishment as bad and those that lead to rewards as good. (p. 414)

prefrontal cortex The region of the cerebral cortex, lying in front of areas controlling body movement, that is responsible for thought—in particular, consciousness, inhibition of impulses, integration of information, and memory, reasoning, planning, and problem-solving strategies. (p. 120)

prenatal diagnostic methods Medical procedures that permit detection of developmental problems before birth. (p. 53)

preoperational stage Piaget's second stage of cognitive development, extending from about 2 to 7 years of age, in which children undergo an extraordinary increase in representational, or symbolic, activity, although thought is not yet logical. (p. 227)

presbycusis Age-related hearing impairment, beginning around age 50 with a noticeable decline in sensitivity to high-frequency sounds, which gradually extends to all frequencies. (p. 509)

presbyopia A condition of aging in which, around age 60, the lens of the eye loses its capacity to adjust to objects at varying distances. (p. 508)

preterm infants Infants born several weeks or more before their due date. (p. 98)

primary aging Genetically influenced age-related declines in the functioning of organs and systems that affect all members of our species and occur even in the context of overall good health. Also called *biological aging*. Distinguished from *secondary aging*. (p. 585)

primary sexual characteristics Physical features that involve the reproductive organs (ovaries, uterus, and vagina in females; penis, scrotum, and testes in males). Distinguished from *secondary sexual characteristics*. (p. 371)

private speech Self-directed speech that children use to plan and guide their own behavior. (p. 234)

proactive aggression A type of aggression in which children act to fulfill a need or desire—to obtain an object, privilege, space, or social reward, such as adult or peer attention—and unemotionally attack a person to achieve their goal. Also called *instrumental aggression*. Distinguished from *reactive aggression*. (p. 272)

problem-centered coping A strategy for managing emotion that involves appraising the situation as changeable, identifying the difficulty, and deciding what to do about it. Distinguished from *emotion-centered coping*. (p. 342)

process praise Praise that emphasizes behavior and effort, such as "You figured it out!" Distinguished from *person praise*. (p. 339)

programmed cell death An aspect of brain growth in which, as synapses form, many surrounding neurons die, making space for these connective structures. (p. 118)

Project Head Start The most extensive U.S. federally funded preschool program, which provides low-SES children with a year or two of preschool education, along with nutritional and health services, and encourages parent involvement in children's learning and development. (p. 246)

propositional thought A type of formal operational reasoning involving the ability to evaluate the logic of propositions, or verbal statements, without referring to real-world circumstances. (p. 389)

prosocial, or altruistic, behavior Actions that benefit another person without any expected reward for the self. (p. 262)

prospective memory Recall that involves remembering to engage in planned actions in the future. (p. 598)

protein-coding genes Genes that directly affect our body's characteristics by sending instructions for making a rich assortment of proteins to the cytoplasm surrounding the cell nucleus. (p. 44)

proximodistal trend An organized pattern of physical growth that proceeds from the center of the body outward ("near to far"). Distinguished from *cephalocaudal trend*. (p. 117)

psychoanalytic perspective An approach to personality development introduced by Freud that assumes people move through a series of stages in which they confront conflicts between biological drives and social expectations. How these conflicts are resolved determines the person's ability to learn, to get along with others, and to cope with anxiety. (p. 14)

psychological control Parental behaviors that intrude on and manipulate children's verbal expressions, individuality, and attachments to parents. (p. 283)

psychosexual theory Freud's theory, which emphasizes that how parents manage children's sexual and aggressive drives in the first few years is crucial for healthy personality development. (p. 14)

psychosocial theory Erikson's theory, which emphasizes that in each Freudian stage, individuals not only develop a unique personality but also acquire attitudes and skills that make them active, contributing members of their society. Recognizes the lifespan nature of development. (p. 15)

puberty Biological changes at adolescence that lead to an adult-sized body and sexual maturity. (p. 367)

public policies Laws and government programs designed to improve current conditions. (p. 64)

punishment In operant conditioning, removal of a desirable stimulus or presentation of an unpleasant one to decrease the occurrence of a response. (p. 131)

R

random assignment An unbiased procedure for assigning participants to treatment conditions in an experiment, such as drawing numbers out of a hat or flipping a coin. Increases the chances that participants' characteristics will be equally distributed across treatment groups. (p. 33)

rapid-eye-movement (REM) sleep An irregular sleep state in which brain-wave activity is similar to that of the waking state. Distinguished from *non-rapid-eye-movement (NREM) sleep*. (p. 104)

reactive aggression An angry, defensive response to provocation or a blocked goal, which is meant to hurt another person. Also called *hostile aggression*. Distinguished from *proactive aggression*. (p. 272)

realistic period Period of vocational development in which older adolescents and young adults narrow their vocational options, engaging in further exploration before focusing on a general vocational category and, slightly later, settling on a single occupation. Distinguished from *fantasy period* and *tentative period*. (p. 462)

recall A type of memory that involves remembering something that is not present. Distinguished from *recognition*. (p. 163)

recasts Adult responses that restructure children's grammatically inaccurate speech into correct form. (p. 252)

recognition A type of memory that involves noticing when a stimulus is identical or similar to one previously experienced. Distinguished from *recall*. (p. 163)

recovery Following habituation, an increase in responsiveness to a new stimulus. (p. 131)

recursive thought A form of perspective taking that involves the ability to view a situation from at least two perspectives—that is, to reason simultaneously about what two or more people are thinking. (p. 312)

referential style of language learning A style of early language learning in which toddlers use language mainly to name things, producing many words that refer to objects. Distinguished from *expressive style of language learning*. (p. 178)

reflex An inborn, automatic response to a particular form of stimulation. (p. 101)

regulator genes Genes that modify the instructions given by protein-coding genes, greatly complicating their genetic impact. (p. 44)

rehearsal A memory strategy that involves repeating information to oneself. (p. 310)

reinforcer In operant conditioning, a stimulus that increases the occurrence of a response. (p. 131)

rejected-aggressive children A subgroup of rejected children who show high rates of conflict, physical and relational aggression, and hyperactive, inattentive, and impulsive behavior. Distinguished from *rejected-withdrawn children*. (p. 348)

rejected children Children who receive many negative votes on self-report measures of peer acceptance, indicating they are actively disliked. Distinguished from *popular, controversial,* and *neglected children*. (p. 347)

rejected-withdrawn children A subgroup of rejected children who are passive and socially awkward. Distinguished from *rejected-aggressive children*. (p. 348)

relational aggression A form of aggression that damages another's peer relationships through social exclusion, malicious gossip, or friendship manipulation. Distinguished from *physical aggression* and *verbal aggression*. (p. 272)

relativistic thinking In Perry's theory, the cognitive approach typical of older college students, who view all knowledge as embedded in a framework of thought and, therefore, give up the possibility of absolute truth in favor of multiple truths, each relative to its context. Distinguished from *dualistic thinking*. (p. 457)

reminiscence The process of telling stories about people and events from the past and reporting associated thoughts and feelings. (p. 612)

reminiscence bump Older adults' heightened autobiographical memory for events that occurred between ages 10 and 30. (p. 597)

remote memory Very long-term episodic recall. (p. 597)

resilience The ability to adapt effectively in the face of threats to development. (p. 10)

reticular formation A structure in the brain stem that maintains alertness and consciousness. (p. 218)

reversibility The capacity to think through a series of steps in a problem and then mentally reverse direction, returning to the starting point. Distinguished from *irreversibility*. (p. 304)

rheumatoid arthritis A form of arthritis in which an autoimmune response leads to inflammation of connective tissue, particularly the membranes that line the joints, resulting in overall aching, inflammation, and stiffness. Leads to deformed joints and often serious loss of mobility. Distinguished from *osteoarthritis*. (p. 585)

Rh factor incompatibility A condition that arises when the Rh protein is present in the fetus's blood but not in the mother's, causing the mother to build up antibodies. If these enter the fetus's system, they destroy red blood cells, reducing the oxygen supply to organs and tissues. Intellectual disability, miscarriage, heart damage, and infant death can occur. (p. 89)

rough-and-tumble play A form of peer interaction involving friendly chasing and play-fighting that emerges in the preschool years and peaks in middle childhood. In our evolutionary past, it may have been important for developing fighting skill. (p. 302)

S

sandwich generation A term used to describe middle-aged adults who must care for multiple generations above and below them at the same time. (p. 555)

scaffolding Adjusting the support offered during a teaching session to fit the learner's current level of performance. As competence increases, effective scaffolders gradually and sensitively withdraw support, turning over responsibility to the learner. (p. 235)

scale errors Toddlers' attempts to do things that their body size makes impossible, such as trying to put on dolls' clothes, sit in a doll-sized chair, or walk through a door too narrow to pass through. (p. 207)

schemes In Piaget's theory, specific psychological structures, or organized ways of making sense of experience, that change with age. (p. 150)

scripts General descriptions of what occurs and when it occurs in a particular situation, used to organize and interpret routine experiences. (p. 240)

secondary aging Age-related declines due to hereditary defects and environmental influences, such as poor diet, lack of exercise, disease, substance abuse, environmental pollution, and psychological stress. Distinguished from *primary aging*. (p. 585)

secondary friends People who are not intimates but with whom an individual spends time occasionally, such as a group that meets for lunch, bridge, or museum tours. (p. 631)

secondary sexual characteristics Physical features visible on the outside of the body that serve as signs of sexual maturity but do not involve the reproductive organs (for example, breast development in females, appearance of underarm and pubic hair in both sexes). Distinguished from *primary sexual characteristics*. (p. 371)

secular trend A change from one generation to the next in an aspect of development, such as body size or pubertal timing. (p. 373)

secure attachment The attachment pattern characterizing infants who use the parent as a secure base from which to explore, may be distressed by separation from the parent, but convey clear pleasure and are easily comforted when the parent returns. Distinguished from *insecure–avoidant, insecure–resistant,* and *disorganized/disoriented attachment*. (p. 198)

secure base The familiar caregiver as a point from which the baby explores, venturing into the environment and then returning for emotional support. (p. 186)

selective optimization with compensation A set of strategies used by older adults who sustain high levels of functioning. Narrowing their goals, they *select* personally valued activities to *optimize* (or maximize) returns from their diminishing energy and also find new ways to *compensate* for losses. (p. 595)

self-care children Children who are without adult supervision for some period of time after school. (p. 351)

self-concept The set of attributes, abilities, attitudes, and values that an individual believes defines who he or she is. (p. 258)

self-conscious emotions Emotions involving injury to or enhancement of the sense of self, including guilt, shame, embarrassment, envy, and pride. (p. 188)

self-esteem An aspect of self-concept that involves judgments about one's own worth and the feelings associated with those judgments. (p. 260)

self-recognition Identification of the self as a physically unique being. (p. 207)

semantic memory Memory for information removed from the context in which it was first learned that has become part of an individual's general knowledge base. Distinguished from *episodic memory*. (p. 240)

sensitive caregiving Caregiving that involves responding promptly, consistently, and appropriately to infants and holding them tenderly and carefully. (p. 200)

sensitive period A time that is biologically optimal for certain capacities to emerge because the individual is especially responsive to environmental influences. Development can occur later, but it is harder to induce. (p. 21)

sensorimotor stage Piaget's first stage, spanning the first two years of life, during which infants and toddlers "think" with their eyes, ears, hands, and other sensorimotor equipment. (p. 152)

sensory register The part of the information-processing system in which sights and sounds are represented directly and stored briefly. (p. 160)

separation anxiety An infant's distressed reaction to the departure of the familiar caregiver. (p. 197)

seriation The ability to order items along a quantitative dimension, such as length or weight. (p. 304)

sequential designs Developmental designs in which investigators conduct several similar cross-sectional or longitudinal studies (called *sequences*) at varying times, sometimes combining longitudinal and cross-sectional strategies. (p. 36)

sex chromosomes The twenty-third pair of chromosomes, which determines the sex of the individual. In females, it is called *XX*; in males, *XY*. (p. 45)

short-term memory store The part of the mind in which attended-to information is retained briefly so we can actively "work on" it to reach our goals. (p. 160)

skipped-generation family A family structure in which children live with grandparents but apart from parents. (p. 554)

sleep apnea A condition in which breathing ceases for 10 seconds or longer during sleep, resulting in many brief awakenings. (p. 577)

slow-to-warm-up child A child whose temperament is characterized by inactivity; mild, low-key reactions to environmental stimuli; negative mood; and slow adjustment to new experiences. Distinguished from *easy child* and *difficult child*. (p. 190)

small-for-date infants Infants whose birth weight is below their expected weight considering length of the pregnancy. Some are full-term; others are preterm infants who are especially underweight. (p. 98)

social clock Age-graded expectations for major life events, such as beginning a first job, getting married, birth of the first child, buying a home, and retiring. (p. 478)

social comparisons Judgments of one's own appearance, abilities, and behavior in relation to those of others. (p. 336)

social-constructivist classroom A classroom grounded in Vygotsky's sociocultural theory, in which children participate in a wide range of challenging activities with teachers and peers, with whom they jointly construct understandings. Distinguished from *traditional* and *constructivist classrooms*. (p. 325)

social conventions Customs determined solely by consensus within a society, such as table manners and politeness rituals. Distinguished from *moral imperatives* and *matters of personal choice*. (p. 272)

social convoy A model of age-related changes in social networks, which views the individual as moving through life within a cluster of relationships, with close ties in the inner circle and less close ties on the outside. With age, people change places in the convoy, new ties are added, and some drift off. (p. 625)

social learning theory An approach that emphasizes the role of *modeling*, also known as *imitation* or *observational learning*, as a powerful source of development. (p. 17)

social referencing Actively seeking emotional information from a trusted person in an uncertain situation. (p. 188)

social smile The infant's broad grin, evoked by the parent's communication, that first appears between 6 and 10 weeks of age. (p. 185)

sociocultural theory Vygotsky's theory, in which children acquire the ways of thinking and behaving that make up their community's culture through *social interaction*—in particular, cooperative dialogues with more knowledgeable members of society. (p. 22)

sociodramatic play The make-believe with others that is under way by the end of the second year and increases rapidly in complexity during early childhood. (p. 228)

socioeconomic status (SES) A measure of an individual's or a family's social position and economic well-being that combines three related, but not completely overlapping, variables: years of education, the prestige of one's job and the skill it requires, and income. (p. 58)

socioemotional selectivity theory A social theory of aging that states that social interaction in late adulthood extends lifelong selection processes. Aging leads to an increased emphasis on the emotion-regulating function of social interaction, causing older adults to prefer familiar social partners with whom they have developed pleasurable relationships. (p. 620)

spermarche First ejaculation of seminal fluid. (p. 372)

stages Qualitative changes in thinking, feeling, and behaving that characterize specific periods of development. (p. 6)

standardization The practice of giving a newly constructed test to a large, representative sample and using the results as the standard for interpreting individual scores. (p. 169)

states of arousal Different degrees of sleep and wakefulness. (p. 108)

statistical learning capacity Infants' capacity to analyze the speech stream for patterns—repeatedly occurring sequences of sounds—through which they acquire a stock of speech structures for which they will later learn meanings. (p. 138)

stereotype threat The fear of being judged on the basis of a negative stereotype, which can trigger anxiety that interferes with performance. (p. 320)

stranger anxiety The infant's expression of fear in response to unfamiliar adults, which appears in many babies in the second half of the first year. (p. 186)

Strange Situation A laboratory procedure used to assess the quality of attachment between 1 and 2 years of age by observing the baby's response to eight short episodes involving brief separations from and reunions with the caregiver in an unfamiliar playroom. (p. 197)

structured interview An interview method in which the researcher asks each participant the same set of questions in the same way. Distinguished from *clinical interview*. (p. 30)

structured observation A research method in which the investigator sets up a laboratory situation that evokes the behavior of interest so that every participant has equal opportunity to display the response. Distinguished from *naturalistic observation*. (p. 28)

subcultures Groups of people with beliefs and customs that differ from those of the larger culture. (p. 62)

successful aging Aging in which gains are maximized and losses minimized, enabling realization of individual potential. (p. 637)

sudden infant death syndrome (SIDS) The unexpected death, usually during the night, of an infant younger than 1 year of age that remains unexplained after thorough investigation. (p. 106)

sympathy Feelings of concern or sorrow for another's plight. (p. 263)

synapses The gaps between neurons, across which chemical messages are sent. (p. 117)

synaptic pruning A process in which neurons that are seldom stimulated lose their synapses and are returned to an uncommitted state so they can support future development. (p. 118)

T

talent Outstanding performance in a specific field. (p. 328)

telegraphic speech Toddlers' two-word utterances that, like a telegram, focus on high-content words while omitting smaller, less important words. (p. 177)

telomeres A special type of DNA located at the ends of chromosomes—serving as a "cap" to protect the ends from destruction—that shortens with each cell duplication. Eventually, so little remains that the cells no longer duplicate at all. (p. 438)

temperament Early-appearing, stable individual differences in reactivity (quickness and intensity of emotional arousal, attention, and motor activity) and self-regulation (strategies that modify that reactivity). (p. 190)

tentative period Period of vocational development in which adolescents begin to evaluate vocational options in terms of their interests, abilities, and values. Distinguished from *fantasy period* and *realistic period*. (p. 462)

teratogen Any environmental agent that causes damage during the prenatal period. (p. 81)

terminal decline Acceleration in deterioration of cognitive functioning prior to death. (p. 601)

thanatology An interdisciplinary field devoted to the study of death and dying. (p. 645)

theory An orderly, integrated set of statements that describes, explains, and predicts behavior. (p. 5)

theory of multiple intelligences Gardner's theory, which identifies at least eight independent intelligences—linguistic, logico-mathematical, musical, spatial, bodily-kinesthetic, naturalist, interpersonal, and intrapersonal—defined in terms of distinct sets of processing operations that permit individuals to engage in a wide range of culturally valued activities. (p. 316)

Third Age A new phase of late adulthood extending from ages 65 to 79 or longer, resulting from added years of longevity and health plus financial stability, in which older adults pursue personally enriching interests and goals. (p. 613)

thyroid-stimulating hormone (TSH) A pituitary hormone that prompts the thyroid gland to release *thyroxine,* which is necessary for brain development and for growth hormone to have its full impact on body size. (p. 219)

time out A form of mild punishment that involves removing children from the immediate setting until they are ready to act appropriately. (p. 269)

traditional classroom A classroom in which the teacher is the sole authority for knowledge, rules, and decision making and students are relatively passive learners whose progress is evaluated by how well they keep pace with a uniform set of standards for their grade. Distinguished from *constructivist* and *social-constructivist classrooms.* (p. 324)

traditional marriage A form of marriage involving clear division of roles—husband as head of household responsible for family economic well-being, wife as caregiver and homemaker. Distinguished from *egalitarian marriage.* (p. 486)

transitive inference The ability to seriate, or order items along a quantitative dimension, mentally. (p. 304)

triangular theory of love Sternberg's view of love as including three components—*passion, intimacy,* and *commitment*—that shift in emphasis as romantic relationships develop. (p. 479)

triarchic theory of successful intelligence Sternberg's theory, in which intelligent behavior involves balancing three broad, interacting intelligences—analytical, creative, and practical—to achieve success in life according to one's personal goals and the requirements of one's cultural community. (p. 316)

trimesters Three equal time periods, each lasting three months, into which prenatal development is sometimes divided. (p. 79)

Type A behavior pattern A behavior pattern characterized by extreme competitiveness, ambition, impatience, hostility, angry outbursts, and a sense of eagerness, hurriedness, and time pressure. (p. 519)

U

umbilical cord The long cord connecting the developing organism to the placenta that delivers nutrients and removes waste products. (p. 78)

unconditioned response (UCR) In classical conditioning, a reflexive response that is consistently produced by an unconditioned stimulus (UCS). Distinguished from *conditioned response.* (p. 130)

unconditioned stimulus (UCS) In classical conditioning, a stimulus that consistently produces a reflexive response. Distinguished from *conditioned stimulus.* (p. 130)

underextension An early vocabulary error in which young children apply a word too narrowly, to a smaller number of objects and events than is appropriate. Distinguished from *overextension.* (p. 177)

uninhibited, or **sociable, children** Children whose temperament is such that they display positive emotion to and approach novel stimuli. Distinguished from *inhibited,* or *shy, children.* (p. 191)

uninvolved child-rearing style A child-rearing style that combines low acceptance and involvement with little control and general indifference to issues of autonomy. Distinguished from *authoritative, authoritarian,* and *permissive child-rearing styles.* (p. 283)

V

vascular dementia A form of dementia that develops when a series of strokes leaves areas of dead brain cells, producing step-by-step degeneration of mental ability, with each step occurring abruptly after a stroke. (p. 590)

verbal aggression A type of aggression that harms others through threats of physical aggression, name-calling, or hostile teasing. Distinguished from *physical aggression* and *relational aggression.* (p. 272)

vernix A white, cheeselike substance that covers the fetus, preventing the skin from chapping due to constant exposure to amniotic fluid. (p. 79)

video deficit effect In toddlers, poorer performance on tasks after watching a video than after seeing a live demonstration. (p. 157)

violation-of-expectation method A method in which researchers show babies an expected event (one that is consistent with reality) and an unexpected event (a variation of the first event that violates reality). Heightened attention to the unexpected event suggests that the infant is "surprised" by a deviation from physical reality and, therefore, is aware of that aspect of the physical world. (p. 153)

visual acuity Fineness of visual discrimination. (p. 109)

voluntary euthanasia At a patient's request, the practice of actively taking the patient's life in a painless way for the purpose of relieving suffering. (p. 664)

W

whole-language approach An approach to beginning reading instruction in which children are exposed to text in its complete form, using reading materials that are whole and meaningful, to promote appreciation of the communicative function of written language. Distinguished from *phonics approach.* (p. 313)

wisdom A capacity made up of multiple cognitive and personality traits, combining breadth and depth of practical knowledge; ability to reflect on and apply that knowledge in ways that make life more bearable and worthwhile; emotional maturity, including the ability to listen patiently and empathetically and give sound advice; and an altruistic form of creativity that involves contributing to humanity and enriching others' lives. (p. 600)

working memory The number of items that can be briefly held in mind while also engaging in some effort to monitor or manipulate those items—a "mental workspace" that we use to accomplish many activities in daily life. A contemporary view of the short-term memory store. (p. 161)

X

X-linked inheritance A pattern of inheritance in which a harmful allele is carried on the X chromosome, so that males are more likely than females to be affected. (p. 48)

Z

zone of proximal development In Vygotsky's theory, a range of tasks too difficult for a child to handle alone but possible with the help of more skilled partners. (p. 166)

zygote The newly fertilized cell formed by the union of sperm and ovum at conception. (p. 45)

References

A

Aalsma, M., Lapsley, D. K., & Flannery, D. J. (2006). Personal fables, narcissism, and adolescent adjustment. *Psychology in the Schools, 43,* 481–491.

Aarhus, L., Tambs, K., Kvestad, E., & Engdahl, B. (2015). Childhood otitis media: A cohort study with 30-year follow-up of hearing (the Hunt Study). *Ear and Hearing, 36,* 302–308.

AARP. (2015). *Caregiving in the U.S.* Washington, DC: AARP Public Policy Institute. Retrieved from www.aarp.org/content/dam/aarp/ppi/2015/caregiving-in-the-united-states-2015-report-revised.pdf

Abakoumkin, G., Stroebe, W., & Stroebe, M. (2010). Does relationship quality moderate the impact of marital bereavement on depressive symptoms? *Journal of Social and Clinical Psychology, 29,* 510–526.

Abbey, A., & Jacques-Tiura, A. J. (2011). Sexual assault perpetrators' tactics: Associations with their personal characteristics and aspects of the incident. *Journal of Interpersonal Violence, 26,* 2866–2889.

Abele, A. E. (2014). How gender influences objective career success and subjective career satisfaction: The impact of self-concept and of parenthood. In I. Schoon & J. S. Eccles (Eds.), *Gender differences in aspirations and attainment: A life course perspective* (pp. 412–426). New York: Cambridge University Press.

Abele, A. E., & Spurk, D. (2011). The dual impact of gender and the influence of timing of parenthood on men's and women's career development: Longitudinal findings. *International Journal of Behavioral Development, 35,* 225–232.

Aber, L., Brown, J. L., Jones, S. M., Berg, J., & Torrente, C. (2011). School-based strategies to prevent violence, trauma, and psychopathology: The challenges of going to scale. *Development and Psychopathology, 23,* 411–421.

Abner, K. S., Gordon, R. A., Kaestner, R., & Korenman, S. (2013). Does child-care quality mediate associations between type of care and development? *Journal of Marriage and Family, 75,* 1203–1217.

Aboud, F. E. (2008). A social-cognitive developmental theory of prejudice. In S. M. Quintana & C. McKown (Eds.), *Handbook of race, racism, and the developing child* (pp. 55–71). Hoboken, NJ: Wiley.

Aboud, F. E., & Brown, C. S. (2013). Positive and negative intergroup contact among children and its effect on attitudes. In G. Hodson & M. Hewstone (Eds.), *Advances in intergroup contact* (pp. 176–199). New York: Psychology Press.

Aboud, F. E., & Doyle, A. (1996). Parental and peer influences on children's racial attitudes. *International Journal of Intercultural Relations, 20,* 371–383.

Abo-Zena, M. M., & Barry, C. M. (2013). Religion and immigrant-origin youth: A resource and a challenge. *Research in Human Development, 10,* 353–371.

Acevedo, E. O. (2012). Exercise psychology: Understanding the mental health benefits of physical activity and the public health challenges of inactivity. In E. O. Acevedo (Ed.), *Oxford handbook of exercise psychology* (pp. 3–8). New York: Oxford University Press.

Achenbach, T. M., Howell, C. T., & Aoki, M. F. (1993). Nine-year outcome of the Vermont Intervention Program for low birth weight infants, *Pediatrics, 91,* 45–55.

Acker, M. M., & O'Leary, S. G. (1996). Inconsistency of mothers' feedback and toddlers' misbehavior and negative affect. *Journal of Abnormal Child Psychology, 24,* 703–714.

Ackerman, J. P., Riggins, T., & Black, M. M. (2010). A review of the effects of prenatal cocaine exposure among school-aged children. *Pediatrics, 125,* 554–565.

Adams, G. A., & Rau, B. L. (2011). Putting off tomorrow to do what you want today: Planning for retirement. *American Psychologist, 66,* 180–192.

Adams, K. B., Sanders, S., & Auth, E. A. (2004). Loneliness and depression in independent living retirement communities: Risk and resilience factors. *Aging and Mental Health, 8,* 475–485.

Adams, R. G., & Laursen, B. (2001). The organization and dynamics of adolescent conflict with parents and friends. *Journal of Marriage and the Family, 63,* 97–110.

Addati, L., Cassirer, N., & Gilchrist, K. (2014). *Maternity and paternity at work: Law and practice across the world.* Geneva, Switzerland: International Labour Organization.

Adelson, S. L. (2012). Practice parameter on gay, lesbian, or bisexual sexual orientation, gender nonconformity, and gender discordance in children and adolescents. *Journal of the American Academy of Child and Adolescent Psychiatry, 51,* 957–974.

Adelstein, S. J. (2014). Radiation risk. In S. T. Treves (Ed.), *Pediatric nuclear medicine and molecular imaging* (pp. 675–682). New York: Springer Science + Business.

Ades, P. A. (2015). A lifestyle program of exercise and weight loss is effective in preventing and treating type 2 diabetes mellitus: Why are programs not more available? *Preventive Medicine, 80,* 50–52.

Adhikari, B., Kahende, J., Malarcher, A., Pechacek, T., & Tong, V. (2009). Smoking-attributable mortality, years of potential life lost, and productivity losses. *Oncology Times, 31,* 40–43.

Adolph, K. E. (2008). Learning to move. *Current Directions in Psychological Science, 17,* 213–218.

Adolph, K. E., Cole, W. G., Komati, M., Garciaguirre, J. S., Badaly, D., Lingeman, J. M., et al. (2012). How do you learn to walk? Thousands of steps and hundreds of falls per day. *Psychological Science, 23,* 1387–1394.

Adolph, K. E., Karasik, L. B., & Tamis-LeMonda, C. S. (2010). Motor skill. In M. H. Bornstein (Ed.), *Handbook of cultural developmental science* (pp. 61–88). New York: Psychology Press.

Adolph, K. E., & Kretch, K. S. (2012). Infants on the edge: Beyond the visual cliff. In A. Slater & P. Quinn (Eds.), *Developmental psychology: Revisiting the classic studies* (pp. 36–55). London: Sage.

Adolph, K. E., Kretch, K. S., & LoBue, V. (2014). Fear of heights in infants? *Current Directions in Psychological Science, 23,* 60–66.

Adolph, K. E., & Robinson, S. R. (2013). The road to walking: What learning to walk tells us about development. In P. Zelazo (Ed.), *Oxford handbook of developmental psychology* (pp. 403–443). New York: Oxford University Press.

Adolph, K. E., & Robinson, S. R. (2015). Perceptual development. In L. S. Liben & U. Müller (Eds.), *Handbook of child psychology and developmental science: Vol. 2. Cognitive processes* (7th ed., pp. 113–157). Hoboken, NJ: Wiley.

Adolph, K. E., Tamis-LeMonda, C. S., Ishak, S., Karasik, L. B., & Lobo, S. A. (2008). Locomotor experience and use of social information is posture specific. *Developmental Psychology, 44,* 1705–1714.

Adolphs, R. (2010). What does the amygdala contribute to social cognition? *Annals of the New York Academy of Sciences, 119,* 42–61.

Afifi, T. O., Mota, M., MacMillan, H. L., & Sareen, J. (2013). Harsh physical punishment in childhood and adult physical health. *Pediatrics, 132,* e333–e340.

Agarwal, S., Driscoll, J. C., Gabaix, X., & Laibson, D. (2007). *The age of reason: Financial decisions over the lifecycle* (NBER Working Paper No. 13191). Cambridge, MA: National Bureau of Economic Research. Retrieved from www.nber.org/papers/w13191

Agigoroaei, S. (2016). Physical health and social class. In S. K. Whitbourne (Ed.), *Encyclopedia of adulthood and aging* (Vol. 3, pp. 1085–1088). Malden, MA: Wiley Blackwell.

Agree, E. M. (2014). The potential for technology to enhance independence for those aging with a disability. *Disability and Health Journal, 7,* S33–S39.

Agronick, G., Stueve, A., Vargo, S., & O'Donnell, L. (2007). New York City young adults' psychological reactions to 9/11: Findings from the Reach for Health longitudinal study. *American Journal of Community Psychology, 39,* 79–90.

Aguiar, A., & Baillargeon, R. (2002). Developments in young infants' reasoning about occluded objects. *Cognitive Psychology, 45,* 267–336.

Ahmadlou, M., Gharib, M., Hemmti, S., Vameghi, R., & Sajedi, F. (2013). Disrupted small-world brain network in children with Down syndrome. *Clinical Neurophysiology, 124,* 1755–1764.

Ahola, K., & Hakanen, J. (2014). Burnout and health. In M. P. Leiter, A. B. Bakker, & C. Maslach (Eds.), *Burnout at work: A psychological perspective* (pp. 10–31). New York: Psychology Press.

Ahrens, C. J. C., & Ryff, C. D. (2006). Multiple roles and well-being: Sociodemographic and psychological moderators. *Sex Roles, 55,* 801–815.

Ai, A. L., Wink, P., & Ardelt, M. (2010). Spirituality and aging: A journey for meaning through deep interconnection in humanity. In J. C. Cavanaugh & C. K. Cavanaugh (Eds.), *Aging in America: Vol. 3. Societal issues* (pp. 222–246). Santa Barbara, CA: Praeger.

Aikens, J. W., Bierman, K. L., & Parker, J. G. (2005). Navigating the transition to junior high school: The influence of pre-transition friendship and self-system characteristics. *Social Development, 14,* 42–60.

Ainsworth, M. D. S., Blehar, M. C., Waters, E., & Wall, S. (1978). *Patterns of attachment.* Hillsdale, NJ: Erlbaum.

Ajrouch, K. J. (2007). Health disparities and Arab-American elders: Does intergenerational support buffer the inequality–health link? *Journal of Social Issues, 63,* 745–758.

Akers, A. Y., Gold, M. A., Bost, J. E., Adimore, A. A., Orr, D. P., & Fortenberry, J. D. (2011). Variation in sexual behaviors in a cohort of adolescent females: The role of personal, perceived peer, and perceived family attitudes. *Journal of Adolescent Health, 48,* 87–93.

Akolekar, R., Beta, J., Picciarelli, G., Ogilvie, C., & D'Antonio, F. (2015). Procedure-related risk of miscarriage following amniocentesis and chorionic villus sampling: A systematic review and meta-analysis. *Ultrasound in Obstetrics and Gynecology, 45,* 16–26.

Akutagawa-Martins, G. C., Salatino-Oliveira, A., Kieling, C. C., Rohde, L. A., & Hutz, M. H. (2013). Genetics of attention-deficit/hyperactivity disorder: Current findings and future directions. *Expert Review of Neurotherapeutics, 13,* 435–445.

Alati, R., Smith, G. D., Lewis, S. J., Sayal, K., Draper, E. S., Golding, J., et al. (2013). Effect of prenatal alcohol exposure on childhood academic outcomes: Contrasting maternal and paternal associations in the ALSPAC Study. *PLOS ONE, 8*(10), e74844.

Albareda-Castellot, B., Pons, F., & Sebastián-Gallés, N. (2010). The acquisition of phonetic categories in bilingual infants: New data from an anticipatory eye movement paradigm. *Developmental Science, 14,* 395–401.

Albers, C. A., & Grieve, A. J. (2007). Test review: Bayley, N. (2006). Bayley Scales of Infant and Toddler Development–Third Edition. San Antonio, TX: Harcourt Assessment. *Journal of Psychoeducational Assessment, 25,* 180–190.

Albert, D., Chein, J., & Steinberg, L. (2013). The teenage brain: Peer influences on adolescent decision making. *Current Directions in Psychological Science, 22,* 114–120.

Alberts, A., Elkind, D., & Ginsberg, S. (2007). The personal fable and risk-taking in early adolescence. *Journal of Youth and Adolescence, 36,* 71–76.

Aldridge, M. A., Stillman, R. D., & Bower, T. G. R. (2001). Newborn categorization of vowel-like sounds. *Developmental Science, 4,* 220–232.

Aldwin, C. M., & Yancura, L. (2011). Stress, coping, and adult development. In R. J. Contrada & A. Baum (Eds.), *Handbook of stress science: Biology, psychology, and health* (pp. 263–274). New York: Springer.

Aldwin, C. M., Yancura, L. A., & Boeninger, D. K. (2010). Coping across the life span. In M. E. Lamb, A. M. Freund, & R. M. Lerner (Eds.), *Handbook of life-span development: Vol. 2. Social and emotional development* (pp. 298–340). Hoboken, NJ: Wiley.

Alessandri, S. M., Sullivan, M. W., & Lewis, M. (1990). Violation of expectancy and frustration in early infancy. *Developmental Psychology, 26,* 738–744.

Alexander, J. M., Fabricius, W. V., Fleming, V. M., Zwahr, M., & Brown, S. A. (2003). The development of metacognitive causal explanations. *Learning and Individual Differences, 13,* 227–238.

Alfirevic, Z., Devane, D., & Gyte, G. M. L. (2013). Continuous cardiotocography (CTG) as a form of electronic fetal monitoring (EFM) for fetal assessment during labour. *Cochrane Database of Systematic Reviews,* Issue 5, Art. No.: CD006066.

Ali, L., & Scelfo, J. (2002, December 9). Choosing virginity. *Newsweek,* pp. 60–65.

Alink, L. R. A., Mesman, J., van Zeijl, J., Stolk, M. N., Juffer, F., & Koot, H. M. (2006). The early childhood aggression curve: Development of physical aggression in 10- to 50-month-old children. *Child Development, 77,* 954–966.

Alishaire, J. A., Beltrán-Sánchez, H., & Crimmins, E. M. (2015). Becoming centenarians: Disease and functioning trajectories of older U.S. adults as they survive to 100. *Journals of Gerontology, 70A,* 193–201.

Alkema, G. E., Wilber, K. H., & Enguidanos, S. M. (2007). Community- and facility-based care. In J. A. Blackburn & C. N. Dulmus (Eds.), *Handbook of gerontology: Evidence-based approaches to theory, practice, and policy* (pp. 455–497). Hoboken, NJ: Wiley.

Allely, C. S., Gillberg, C., & Wilson, P. (2014). Neurobiological abnormalities in the first few years of life in individuals later diagnosed with autism spectrum disorder: A review of recent data. *Behavioural Neurology.* Retrieved from www.hindawi.com/journals/bn/2014/210780

Allemand, M., Zimprich, D., & Martin, M. (2008). Long-term correlated change in personality traits in old age. *Psychology and Aging, 23,* 545–557.

Allen, J. P., Chango, J., Szwedo, D. E., Schad, M. M., & Marston, E. G. (2012). Predictors of susceptibility to peer influence regarding substance use in adolescence. *Child Development, 83,* 337–350.

Allen, J. P., & Loeb, E. L. (2015). The autonomy–connection challenge in adolescent–peer relationships. *Child Development Perspectives, 9,* 101–105.

Allen, J. P., & Philliber, S. (2001). Who benefits most from a broadly targeted prevention program? Differential efficacy across populations in the Teen Outreach Program. *Journal of Community Psychology, 29,* 637–655.

Allen, J. P., Philliber, S., Herrling, S., & Kuperminc, G. P. (1997). Preventing teen pregnancy and academic failure: Experimental evaluation of a developmentally based approach. *Child Development, 64,* 729–742.

Allen, S. E. M., & Crago, M. B. (1996). Early passive acquisition in Inukitut. *Journal of Child Language, 23,* 129–156.

Allison, B. N., & Schultz, J. B. (2004). Parent–adolescent conflict in early adolescence. *Adolescence, 39,* 101–119.

Alloway, T. P., Bibile, V., & Lau, G. (2013). Computerized working memory training: Can it lead to gains in cognitive skills in students? *Computers in Human Behavior, 29,* 632–638.

Alloway, T. P., Gathercole, S. E., Kirkwood, H., & Elliott, J. (2009). The cognitive and behavioral characteristics of children with low working memory. *Child Development, 80,* 606–621.

Almeida, D. M., & Horn, M. C. (2004). Is daily life more stressful during middle adulthood? In O. G. Brim, C. D. Ryff, & R. C. Kessler (Eds.), *How healthy are we? A national study of well-being at midlife* (pp. 425–451). Chicago: University of Chicago Press.

Alonso-Fernández, P., & De la Fuente, M. (2011). Role of the immune system in aging and longevity. *Current Aging Science, 4,* 78–100.

Alsaker, F. D. (1995). Timing of puberty and reactions to pubertal changes. In M. Rutter (Ed.), *Psychosocial disturbances in young people* (pp. 37–82). New York: Cambridge University Press.

Alterovitz, S. S. R., & Mendelsohn, G. A. (2013). Relationship goals of middle-aged, young–old, and old–old Internet daters: An analysis of online personal ads. *Journal of Aging Studies, 27,* 159–165.

Alzheimer's Association. (2016a). *2016 Alzheimer's disease facts and figures.* Retrieved from www.alz.org/documents_custom/2016-facts-and-figures.pdf

Alzheimer's Association. (2016b). *Communication and Alzheimer's.* Retrieved from www.alz.org/care/dementia-communication-tips.asp

Amato, P. R. (2010). Research on divorce: Continuing trends and new developments. *Journal of Marriage and Family, 72,* 650–666.

Amato, P. R. (2014). Tradition, commitment, and individualism in American marriages. *Psychological Inquiry, 25,* 42–46.

Amato, P. R., & Booth, A. (1995). Change in gender role attitudes and perceived marital quality. *American Sociological Review, 60,* 58–66.

Amato, P. R., & Dorius, C. (2010). Father, children, and divorce. In M. E. Lamb (Ed.), *The role of the father in child development* (5th ed., pp. 177–200). Hoboken, NJ: Wiley.

Amato, P. R., & Fowler, F. (2002). Parenting practices, child adjustment, and family diversity. *Journal of Marriage and the Family, 64,* 703–716.

Amato, P. R., & Rogers, S. J. (1997). A longitudinal study of marital problems and subsequent divorce. *Journal of Marriage and the Family, 59,* 612–624.

Amato, P. R., & Sobolewski, J. M. (2004). The effects of divorce on fathers and children: Nonresidential fathers and stepfathers. In M. E. Lamb (Ed.), *The role of the father in child development* (4th ed., pp. 341–367). Hoboken, NJ: Wiley.

Ambler, G. (2013). Normal physical development and growth at puberty. In K. Steinbeck & M. Kohn (Eds.), *A clinical handbook in adolescent medicine* (pp. 1–13). Hackensack, NJ: World Scientific Publishing.

American Academy of Hospice and Palliative Medicine. (2016). *Statement on physician-assisted dying.* Retrieved from aahpm.org/positions/pad

American Academy of Pediatrics. (2001). Committee on Public Education: Children, adolescents, and television. *Pediatrics, 104,* 341–343.

American Academy of Pediatrics. (2012a). Breastfeeding and the use of human milk. *Pediatrics, 129,* e827–e841.

American Academy of Pediatrics. (2012b). SIDS and other sleep-related infant deaths: Expansion of recommendations for a safe sleep environment. *Pediatrics, 128,* e1341.

American Cancer Society. (2015a). *The American Cancer Society encourages people to make health lifestyle choices that can help reduce their risk of cancer.* Retrieved from www.cancer.org/healthy/index

American Cancer Society. (2015b). *Breast cancer risk factors you cannot change.* Retrieved from www.cancer.org/cancer/breastcancer/moreinformation/breastcancerearlydetection/breast-cancer-early-detection-risk-factors-you-cannot-change

American Cancer Society. (2015c). *Cancer facts and figures.* Retrieved from www.oralcancerfoundation.org/facts/pdf/Us_Cancer_Facts.pdf

American College of Obstetricians and Gynecologists. (2014). Female age-related fertility decline. *Obstetrics and Gynecology, 589,* 719–721.

American Express Open. (2014). *The 2014 state of women-owned businesses report.* Retrieved from www.womenable.com/content/userfiles/2014_State_of_Women-owned_Businesses_public.pdf

American Foundation for Suicide Prevention. (2016). *Suicide statistics.* Retrieved from www.afsp.org/about-suicide/suicide-statistics

American Hospice Foundation. (2013). *Talking about hospice: Tips for physicians.* Washington, DC: Author.

American Medical Association. (2016). *AMA code of medical ethics: Chapter 5. Opinions on caring for patients at the end of life.* Retrieved from www.ama-assn.org/ama/pub/physician-resources/medical-ethics/code-medical-ethics.page

American Psychiatric Association. (2013). *Diagnostic and statistical manual of mental disorders* (5th ed.). Arlington, VA: Author.

American Psychological Association. (2010). *Ethical principles of psychologists and code of conduct.* Retrieved from www.apa.org/ethics/code/index.aspx

Amsel, E., & Brock, S. (1996). The development of evidence evaluation skills. *Cognitive Development, 11,* 523–550.

An, J. S., & Cooney, T. M. (2006). Psychological well-being in mid to late life: The role of generativity development and parent–child relationships across the lifespan. *International Journal of Behavioral Development, 30,* 410–421.

Anand, V., Downs, S. M., Bauer, N. S., & Carroll, A. E. (2014). Prevalence of infant television viewing and maternal depression symptoms. *Journal of Developmental and Behavioral Pediatrics, 35,* 216–224.

Ananth, C. V., Chauhan, S. P., Chen, H.-Y., & D'Alton, M. E. (2013). Electronic fetal monitoring in the United States: Temporal trends and adverse perinatal outcomes. *Obstetrics and Gynecology, 121,* 927–933.

Ananth, C. V., Friedman, A. M., & Gyamfi-Bannerman, C. (2013). Epidemiology of moderate preterm, late preterm and early term delivery. *Clinics in Perinatology, 40,* 601–610.

Anderson, C. A., Shibuya, A., Ihori, N., Swing, E. L., Bushman, B. J., Sakamoto, A., et al. (2010). Violent video game effects on aggression, empathy, and prosocial behavior in Eastern and Western countries: A meta-analytic review. *Psychological Bulletin, 136,* 151–173.

Anderson, C. B., Hughes, S. O., & Fuemmeler, B. F. (2009). Parent–child attitude congruence on type and intensity of physical activity: Testing multiple mediators of sedentary behavior in older children. *Health Psychology, 28,* 428–438.

Anderson, C. M. (2012). The diversity, strengths, and challenges of single-parent households. In F. Walsh (Ed.), *Normal family processes: Growing diversity and complexity* (4th ed., pp. 128–148). New York: Guilford.

Anderson, D. M., Huston, A. C., Schmitt, K. L., Linebarger, D. L., & Wright, J. C. (2001). Early childhood television viewing and adolescent behavior. *Monographs of the Society for Research in Child Development, 66*(1, Serial No. 264).

Anderson, E. (2000). Exploring register knowledge: The value of "controlled improvisation." In L. Menn & N. B. Ratner (Eds.), *Methods for studying language production* (pp. 225–248). Mahwah, NJ: Erlbaum.

Anderson, J. R., Van Ryzin, M. J., & Doherty, W. J. (2010). Developmental trajectories of marital happiness in continuously married individuals: A group-based modeling approach. *Journal of Family Psychology, 24,* 587–596.

Anderson, R. C., Wilson, P. T., & Fielding, L. G. (1988). Growth in reading and how children spend their time outside of school. *Reading Research Quarterly, 23,* 285–303.

Anderson, V., & Beauchamp, M. H. (2013). A theoretical model of developmental social neuroscience. In V. Anderson & M. H. Beauchamp (Eds.), *Developmental social neuroscience and childhood brain insult: Theory and practice* (pp. 3–20). New York: Guilford.

Anderson, V., Spencer-Smith, M., & Wood, A. (2011). Do children really recover better? Neurobehavioural plasticity after early brain insult. *Brain, 134,* 2197–2221.

Andreoletti, C., & Lachman, M. E. (2004). Susceptibility and resilience to memory aging stereotypes: Education matters more than age. *Experimental Aging Research, 30,* 129–148.

Andrews, G., & Halford, G. S. (1998). Children's ability to make transitive inferences: The importance of premise integration and structural complexity. *Cognitive Development, 13,* 479–513.

Andrews, G., & Halford, G. S. (2002). A cognitive complexity metric applied to cognitive development. *Cognitive Psychology, 45,* 475–506.

Andrews, G., & Halford, G. S. (2011). Recent advances in relational complexity theory and its application to cognitive development. In P. Barrouillet & V. Gaillard (Eds.), *Cognitive development and working memory: A dialogue between neo-Piagetian and cognitive approaches* (pp. 47–68). Hove, UK: Psychology Press.

Ang, S., Rodgers, J. L., & Wänström, L. (2010). The Flynn effect within subgroups in the U.S.: Gender, race, income, education, and urbanization differences in the NLSY-Children data. *Intelligence, 38,* 367–384.

Angel, R. J., Angel, J. L., & Hill, T. D. (2009). Subjective control and health among Mexican-origin elders in Mexico and the United States: Structural considerations in comparative research. *Journals of Gerontology, 64B,* 390–401.

Angold, A., Costello, E. J., Erkanli, A., & Worthman, C. M. (1999). Pubertal changes in hormone levels and depression in girls. *Psychological Medicine, 29,* 1043–1053.

Anisfeld, M. (2005). No compelling evidence to dispute Piaget's timetable of the development of representational imitation in infancy. In S. Hurley & N. Chater (Eds.), *Perspectives on imitation: From neuroscience to social science: Vol. 2. Imitation, human development, and culture* (pp. 107–131). Cambridge, MA: MIT Press.

Anthonysamy, A., & Zimmer-Gembeck, M. J. (2007). Peer status and behaviors of maltreated children and their classmates in the early years of school. *Child Abuse & Neglect, 31,* 971–991.

Antonini, F. M., Magnolfi, S. U., Petruzzi, E., Pinzani, P., Malentacchi, F., Petruzzi, I., & Masotti, G. (2008). Physical performance and creative activities of centenarians. *Archives of Gerontology and Geriatrics, 46,* 253–261.

Antonucci, T. C., Ajrouch, K. J., & Birditt, K. S. (2008). Social relations in the Third Age: Assessing strengths and challenges using the convoy model. In J. B. James & P. Wink (Eds.), *Annual review of gerontology and geriatrics* (Vol. 26, pp. 193–209). New York: Springer.

Antonucci, T. C., & Akiyama, H. (1995). Convoys of social relations: Family and friendships within a life span context. In R. Blieszner & V. H. Bedford (Eds.), *Handbook of aging and the family* (pp. 355–371). Westport, CT: Greenwood Press.

Antonucci, T. C., Akiyama, H., & Merline, A. (2002). Dynamics of social relationships in midlife. In M. E. Lachman (Ed.), *Handbook of midlife development* (pp. 571–598). New York: Wiley.

Antonucci, T. C., Akiyama, H., & Takahashi, K. (2004). Attachment and close relationships across the lifespan. *Attachment and Human Development, 6,* 353–370.

Antonucci, T. C., Birditt, K. S., & Ajrouch, K. J. (2011). Convoys of social relations: Past, present, and future. In K. L. Fingerman, C. A. Berg, J. Smith, & T. C. Antonucci (Eds.), *Handbook of life-span development* (pp. 161–182). New York: Springer.

Antonucci, T. C., Birditt, K. S., & Akiyama, H. (2009). Convoys of social relations: An interdisciplinary approach. In V. Bengston, M. Silverstein, N. Putney, & D. Gans (Eds.), *Handbook of theories of aging* (pp. 247–260). New York: Springer.

Antonucci, T. C., Blieszner, R., & Denmark, F. L. (2010). Psychological perspectives on older women. In H. Landrine & N. F. Russo (Eds.), *Handbook of diversity in feminist psychology* (pp. 233–257). New York: Springer.

Antshel, K. M., Hier, B. O., & Barkley, R. A. (2015). Executive functioning theory and ADHD. In S. Goldstein & J. A. Naglieri (Eds.), *Handbook of executive functioning* (pp. 107–120). New York: Springer Science + Business Media.

Anzures, G., Quinn, P. C., Pascalis, O., Slater, A. M., Tanaka, J. W., & Lee, K. (2013). Developmental origins of the other-race effect. *Current Directions in Psychological Science, 22,* 173–178.

Apfelbaum, E. P., Pauker, K., Ambady, N., Sommers, S. R., & Norton, M. I. (2008). Learning (not) to talk about race: When older children underperform in social categorization. *Developmental Psychology, 44,* 1513–1518.

Apgar, V. (1953). A proposal for a new method of evaluation in the newborn infant. *Current Research in Anesthesia and Analgesia, 32,* 260–267.

Aquilino, W. S. (2006). Family relationships and support systems in emerging adulthood. In J. J. Arnett & J. L. Tanner (Eds.), *Emerging adults in America: Coming of age in the 21st century* (pp. 193–218). Washington, DC: American Psychological Association.

Archer, T., Fredriksson, A., Schütz, E., & Kostrzewa, R. M. (2011). Influence of physical exercise on neuroimmunological functioning and health: Aging and stress. *Neurotoxicity Research, 20,* 69–83.

Archibald, A. B., Graber, J. A., & Brooks-Gunn, J. (2006). Pubertal processes and physiological growth in adolescence. In G. R. Adams & M. D. Berzonsky (Eds.), *Blackwell handbook of adolescence* (pp. 24–48). Malden, MA: Blackwell.

Arcus, D., & Chambers, P. (2008). Childhood risks associated with adoption. In T. P. Gullotta & G. M. Blau (Eds.), *Family influences on childhood behavior and development* (pp. 117–142). New York: Routledge.

Ardelt, M. (2003). Effects of religion and purpose in life on elders' subjective well-being and attitudes toward death. *Journal of Religious Gerontology, 14,* 55–77.

Ardelt, M., & Ferrari, M. (2015). Wisdom and emotions. In M. A. Skinner, C. A. Berg, & B. N. Uchino (Eds.), *Oxford handbook of emotion, social cognition, and problem solving in adulthood* (pp. 256–272). New York: Oxford University Press.

Ardila-Rey, A., & Killen, M. (2001). Middle-class Colombian children's evaluations of personal, moral, and social-conventional interactions in the classroom. *International Journal of Behavioral Development, 25,* 246–255.

Arem, H., Moore, S. C., Patel, A., Hartge, P., de Gonzales, A. B., Visvanathan, K., et al. (2015). Leisure time physical activity and mortality: A detailed pooled analysis of the dose–response relationship. *JAMA Internal Medicine, 175,* 959–967.

Arias, E. (2015). United States life tables, 2011. *National Vital Statistics Reports, 61*(11). Retrieved from www.cdc.gov/nchs/data/nvsr/nvsr64/nvsr64_11.pdf

Arija, V., Esparó, G., Fernández-Ballart, J., Murphy, M. M., Biarnés, E., & Canals, J. (2006). Nutritional status and performance in test of verbal and non-verbal intelligence in 6 year old children. *Intelligence, 34,* 141–149.

Arim, R. G., Tamonte, L., Shapka, J. D., Dahinten, V. S., & Willms, J. D. (2011). The family antecedents and the subsequent outcomes of early puberty. *Journal of Youth and Adolescence, 40,* 1423–1435.

Arking, R. (2006). *Biology of aging: Observations and principles* (3rd ed.). New York: Oxford University Press.

Armstrong, K. L., Quinn, R. A., & Dadds, M. R. (1994). The sleep patterns of normal children. *Medical Journal of Australia, 161,* 202–206.

Armstrong, T. D., & Crowther, M. R. (2002). Spirituality among older African Americans. *Journal of Adult Development, 9,* 3–12.

Arnett, J. J. (2007a). Emerging adulthood, a 21st century theory: A rejoinder to Hendry and Kloep. *Child Development Perspectives, 1,* 80–82.

Arnett, J. J. (2007b). Emerging adulthood: What is it and what is it good for? *Child Development Perspectives, 1,* 68–73.

Arnett, J. J. (2011). Emerging adulthood(s): The cultural psychology of a new life stage. In L. A. Jensen (Ed.), *Bridging cultural and developmental psychology: New syntheses in theory, research, and policy* (pp. 255–275). New York: Oxford University Press.

Arnett, J. J. (2013). The evidence for Generation We and against Generation Me. *Emerging Adulthood, 1,* 5–10.

Arnett, J. J. (2015). *Emerging adulthood: The winding road from the late teens through the twenties* (2nd ed.). New York: Oxford University Press.

Arnett, J. J., & Schwab, J. (2013). *Clark University poll of emerging adults, 2012: Thriving, struggling, and hopeful.* Worcester, MA: Clark University.

Arnett, J. J., & Tanner, J. L. (2011). Themes and variations in emerging adulthood across social classes. In J. J. Arnett, M. Kloep, L. B. Hendry, & J. L. Tanner (Eds.), *Debating emerging adulthood: Stage or process?* (pp. 31–51). New York: Oxford University Press.

Arnett, J. J., Trzesniewski, K. H., & Donnellan, M. B. (2013). The dangers of generational myth-making: Rejoinder to Twenge. *Emerging Adulthood, 1,* 17–20.

Arnold, A. P. (2009). The organizational–activational hypothesis as the foundation for a unified theory of sexual differentiation of all mammalian tissues. *Hormones and Behavior, 55,* 570–578.

Arnold, D. H., McWilliams, L., & Harvey-Arnold, E. (1998). Teacher discipline and child misbehavior in daycare: Untangling causality with correlational data. *Developmental Psychology, 34,* 276–287.

Arnon, S., Shapsa, A., Forman, L., Regev, R., Bauer, S., & Litmanovitz, I. (2006). Live music is beneficial to preterm infants in the neonatal intensive care unit. *Birth, 33,* 131–136.

Arseth, A. K., Kroger, J., Martinussen, M., & Marcia, J. E. (2009). Meta-analytic studies of identity status and the relational issues of attachment and intimacy. *Identity, 9,* 1–32.

Artal, R. (2015). The role of exercise in reducing the risks of gestational diabetes mellitus in obese women. *Best Practice & Research, 29,* 123–132.

Artman, L., & Cahan, S. (1993). Schooling and the development of transitive inference. *Developmental Psychology, 29,* 753–759.

Artman, L., Cahan, S., & Avni-Babad, D. (2006). Age, schooling, and conditional reasoning. *Cognitive Development, 21,* 131–145.

Arum, R., & Roksa, J. (2014). *Aspiring adults adrift: Tentative transitions of college graduates.* Chicago: University of Chicago Press.

Asendorpf, J. B., Denissen, J. J. A., & van Aken, M. A. G. (2008). Inhibited and aggressive preschool children at 23 years of age: Personality and social transition into adulthood. *Developmental Psychology, 44,* 997–1011.

Asher, S. R., & Rose, A. J. (1997). Promoting children's social-emotional adjustment with peers. In P. Salovey & D. J. Sluyter (Eds.), *Emotional development and emotional intelligence* (pp. 193–195). New York: Basic Books.

Aslin, R. N., Jusczyk, P. W., & Pisoni, D. B. (1998). Speech and auditory processing during infancy: Constraints on and precursors to language. In D. Kuhn & R. S. Siegler (Eds.), *Handbook of child psychology: Vol. 2. Cognition, perception, and language* (5th ed., pp. 147–198). New York: Wiley.

Aslin, R. N., & Newport, E. L. (2012). Statistical learning: From acquiring specific items to forming general rules. *Psychological Science, 21,* 170–176.

Astington, J. W., & Hughes, C. (2013). Theory of mind: Self-reflection and social understanding. In S. M. Carlson, P. D. Zelazo, & S. Faja (Eds.), *Oxford handbook of developmental psychology: Vol. 2. Self and other* (pp. 398–424). New York: Oxford University Press.

Astington, J. W., & Pelletier, J. (2005). Theory of mind, language, and learning in the early years: Developmental origins of school readiness. In B. D. Homer & C. S. Tamis-LeMonda (Eds.), *The development of social cognition and communication* (pp. 205–230). Mahwah, NJ: Erlbaum.

Astington, J. W., Pelletier, J., & Homer, B. (2002). Theory of mind and epistemological development: The relation between children's second-order false belief understanding and their ability to reason about evidence. *New Ideas in Psychology, 20,* 131–144.

Atance, C. M., & Meltzoff, A. N. (2005). My future self: Young children's ability to anticipate and explain future states. *Cognitive Development, 20,* 341–361.

Atchley, R. C. (1989). A continuity theory of normal aging. *Gerontologist, 29,* 183–190.

Atchley, R. C. (1999). *Continuity and adaptation in aging: Creating positive experiences.* Baltimore, MD: Johns Hopkins University Press.

Attems, J., Walker, L., & Jellinger, K. A. (2015). Olfaction and aging: A mini-review. *Gerontology, 61,* 485–490.

Au, T. K., Sidle, A. L., & Rollins, K. B. (1993). Developing an intuitive understanding of conservation and contamination: Invisible particles as a plausible mechanism. *Developmental Psychology, 29,* 286–299.

Audretsch, D. B., & Lehmann, E. E. (2016). *The seven secrets of Germany: Economic resilience in an era of global turbulence.* New York: Oxford University Press.

Aunola, K., Stattin, H., & Nurmi, J.-E. (2000). Parenting styles and adolescents' achievement strategies. *Journal of Adolescence, 23,* 205–222.

Avendano, M., & Kawachi, I. (2014). Why do Americans have shorter life expectancy and worse health than people in other high-income countries? *Annual Review of Public Health, 35,* 307–325.

Averhart, C. J., & Bigler, R. S. (1997). Shades of meaning: Skin tone, racial attitudes, and constructive memory in African-American children. *Journal of Experimental Child Psychology, 67,* 368–388.

Avis, N. E., Assmann, S. F., Kravitz, H. M., Ganz, P. A., & Ory, M. (2004). Quality of life in diverse groups of midlife women: Assessing the influence of menopause, health status and psychosocial and demographic factors. *Quality of Life Research, 13,* 933–946.

Avis, N. E., & Crawford, S. (2006). Menopause: Recent research findings. In S. K. Whitbourne & S. L. Willis (Eds.), *The baby boomers grow up: Contemporary perspectives on midlife* (pp. 75–109). Mahwah, NJ: Erlbaum.

Avolio, B. J., & Sosik, J. J. (1999). A lifespan framework for assessing the impact of work on white-collar workers. In S. L. Willis & J. D. Reid (Eds.), *Life in the middle* (pp. 249–274). San Diego, CA: Academic Press.

B

Bacallao, M. L., & Smokowski, P. R. (2007). The costs of getting ahead: Mexican family system changes after immigration. *Family Relations, 56,* 52–66.

Bachman, J. G., Johnston, L. D., & O'Malley, P. M. (2014). *Monitoring the Future: Questionnaire responses from the nation's high school seniors: 2012.* Ann Arbor, MI: Institute for Social Research, University of Michigan.

Bachman, J. G., O'Malley, P. M., Freedman-Doan, P., Trzesniewski, K. H., & Donnellan, M. B. (2011). Adolescent self-esteem: Differences by race/ethnicity, gender, and age. *Self and Identity, 10,* 445–473.

Bachstetter, A. D., Watterson, D. M., & Van Eldik, L. J. (2014). Target engagement analysis and link to pharmacodynamic endpoint for a novel class of CNS-penetrant and efficacious p38 MAPK inhibitors. *Journal of Neuroimmune Pharmacology, 9,* 454–460.

Badanes, L. S., Dmitrieva, J., & Watamura, S. E. (2012). Understanding cortisol reactivity across the day at child care: The potential buffering role of secure attachments to caregivers. *Early Childhood Research Quarterly, 27,* 156–165.

Baddeley, J., & Singer, J. A. (2015). Charting the life story's path: Narrative identity across the life span. In J. D. Clandinin (Ed.), *Handbook of narrative inquiry: Mapping a methodology* (pp. 177–202). Thousand Oaks, CA: Sage.

Badiee, Z., Asghari, M., & Mohammadizadeh, M. (2013). The calming effect of maternal breast milk odor on premature infants. *Pediatrics and Neonatology, 54,* 322–325.

Baenninger, M., & Newcombe, N. (1995). Environmental input to the development of sex-related differences in spatial and mathematical ability. *Learning and Individual Differences, 7,* 363–379.

Baglietto-Vargas, D., Shi, J., Yaeger, D. M., Ager, R., & LaFerla, F. M. (2016). Diabetes and Alzheimer's disease crosstalk. *Neuroscience and Biobehavioral Reviews, 64,* 272–287.

Bagwell, C. L., & Schmidt, M. E. (2011). *Friendships in childhood and adolescence.* New York: Guilford.

Bahrick, L. E. (2010). Intermodal perception and selective attention to intersensory redundancy: Implications for typical social development and autism. In G. Bremner & T. D. Wachs (Eds.), *Wiley-Blackwell handbook of infant development: Vol. 1. Basic research* (2nd ed., pp. 120–166). Oxford, UK: Wiley-Blackwell.

Bahrick, L. E., Hernandez-Reif, M., & Flom, R. (2005). The development of infant learning about specific face–voice relations. *Developmental Psychology, 41,* 541–552.

Bahrick, L. E., Hernandez-Reif, M., & Pickens, J. N. (1997). The effect of retrieval cues on visual preferences and memory in infancy: Evidence for a four-phase attention function. *Journal of Experimental Child Psychology, 67,* 1–20.

Bahrick, L. E., & Lickliter, R. (2012). The role of intersensory redundancy in early perceptual, cognitive, and social development. In A. J. Bremner, D. J. Lewkowicz, & C. Spence (Eds.), *Multisensory development* (pp. 183–206). Oxford, UK: Oxford University Press.

Bailar-Heath, M., & Valley-Gray, S. (2010). Accident prevention. In P. C. McCabe & S. R. Shaw (Eds.), *Pediatric disorders* (pp. 123–132). Thousand Oaks, CA; Corwin Press.

Bailey, J. M., Bobrow, D., Wolfe, M., & Mikach, S. (1995). Sexual orientation of adult sons of gay fathers. *Developmental Psychology, 31,* 124–129.

Baillargeon, R., & DeVos, J. (1991). Object permanence in young infants: Further evidence. *Child Development, 62,* 1227–1246.

Baillargeon, R., Li, J., Gertner, Y., & Wu, D. (2011). How do infants reason about physical events? In U. Goswami (Ed.), *Wiley-Blackwell handbook of childhood cognitive development* (2nd ed., pp. 11–48). Chichester, UK: Wiley-Blackwell.

Baillargeon, R., Li, J., Ng, W., & Yuan, S. (2009). An account of infants' physical reasoning. In A. Woodward & A. Needham (Eds.), *Learning and the infant mind* (pp. 66–116). New York: Oxford University Press.

Baillargeon, R. H., Zoccolillo, M., Keenan, K., Côté, S., Pérusse, D., Wu, H.-X., & Boivin, M. (2007). Gender differences in physical aggression: A prospective population-based survey of children before and after 2 years of age. *Developmental Psychology, 43,* 13–26.

Bair, D. (2007). *Calling it quits: Late-life divorce and starting over.* New York: Random House.

Baker, F. C., Willoughby, A. R., Sassoon, S. A., Colrain, I. M., & de Zambotti, M. (2015). Insomnia in women approaching menopause: Beyond perception. *Psychoneuroendocrinology, 60,* 96–104.

Baker, M. (2005). Facilitating forgiveness and peaceful closure: The therapeutic value of psychosocial intervention in end-of-life care. *Journal of Social Work and End of Life Palliative Care, 1,* 83–96.

Baker, T., & Mingo, C. A. (2016). Arthritis. In S. K. Whitbourne (Ed.), *Encyclopedia of adulthood and aging* (Vol. 1, pp. 85–90). Malden, MA: Wiley Blackwell.

Bakermans-Kranenburg, M. J., Steele, H., Zeanah, C. H., Muhamedrahimov, R. J., Vorria, P., & Dobrova-Krol, N. A. (2011). Attachment and emotional development in institutional care: Characteristics and catch up. In R. B. McCall, M. H. van IJzendoorn, F. Juffer, C. J. Groark, & V. K. Groza (Eds.), Children without permanent parents: Research, practice, and policy. *Monographs of the Society for Research in Child Development, 76*(4, Serial No. 301), 62–91.

Bakermans-Kranenburg, M. J., & van IJzendoorn, M. H. (2015). The hidden efficacy of interventions: Gene × environment experiments from a differential susceptibility perspective. *Annual Review of Psychology, 66,* 381–409.

Bakermans-Kranenburg, M. J., van IJzendoorn, M. H., Mesman, J., Alink, L. R. A., & Juffer, F. (2008a). Effects of an attachment-based intervention on daily cortisol moderated by dopamine receptor D4: A randomized control trial on 1- to 3-year-olds screened for externalizing behavior. *Development and Psychopathology, 20,* 805–820.

Bakermans-Kranenburg, M. J., van IJzendoorn, M. H., Pijlman, F. T. A., Mesman, J., & Juffer, F. (2008b). Experimental evidence for differential susceptibility: Dopamine D4 receptor polymorphism (DRD4 VNTR) moderates intervention effects on toddlers' externalizing behavior in a randomized control trial. *Developmental Psychology, 44,* 293–300.

Baker-Sennett, J., Matusov, E., & Rogoff, B. (2008). Children's planning of classroom plays with adult or child direction. *Social Development, 17,* 998–1018.

Balasch, J. (2010). Ageing and infertility: An overview. *Gynecological Endocrinology, 26,* 855–860.

Balfanz, R., Herzog, L., & MacIver, D. J. (2007). Preventing student disengagement and keeping students on the graduation path in urban middle-grades schools: Early identification and effective interventions. *Educational Psychologist, 42,* 223–235.

Ball, H. (2006). Parent–infant bed-sharing behavior: Effects of feeding type and presence of father. *Human Nature, 17,* 301–318.

Ball, H. L., & Volpe, L. E. (2013). Sudden infant death syndrome (SIDS) risk reduction and infant sleep location—moving the discussion forward. *Social Science and Medicine, 79,* 84–91.

Ball, M. M., Perkins, M. M., Hollingsworth, C., Whittington, F. J., & King, S. V. (2009). Pathways to assisted living: The influence of race and class. *Journal of Applied Gerontology, 28,* 81–108.

Baltes, M. M. (1995, February). Dependency in old age: Gains and losses. *Psychological Science, 4*(1), 14–19.

Baltes, M. M. (1996). *The many faces of dependency in old age.* New York: Cambridge University Press.

Baltes, M. M., Wahl, H.-W., & Reichert, M. (1992). Successful aging in long-term care institutions. In K. W. Schaie & M. P. Lawton (Eds.), *Annual review* of gerontology and geriatrics (pp. 311–337). New York: Springer.

Baltes, P. B., Lindenberger, U., & Staudinger, U. M. (2006). Life span theory in developmental psychology. In R. M. Lerner (Ed.), *Handbook of child psychology: Vol. 1. Theoretical models of human development* (6th ed., pp. 569–664). Hoboken, NJ: Wiley.

Baltes, P. B., & Smith, J. (2003). New frontiers in the future of aging: From successful aging of the young old to the dilemmas of the fourth age. *Gerontology, 49,* 123–135.

Baltes, P. B., & Smith, J. (2008). The fascination of wisdom. *Perspectives on Psychological Science, 3,* 56–64.

Baltes, P. B., & Staudinger, U. M. (2000). Wisdom: A metaheuristic (pragmatic) to orchestrate mind and virtue toward excellence. *American Psychologist, 55,* 122–136.

Bamford, C., & Lagattuta, K. H. (2012). Looking on the bright side: Children's knowledge about the benefits of positive versus negative thinking. *Child Development, 83,* 667–682.

Bamidis, P. D., Vivas, A. B., Styliadis, C., Frantzidis, C., Klados, M., Schlee, W., et al. (2014). A review of physical and cognitive interventions in aging. *Neuroscience and Biobehavioral Reviews, 44,* 206–220.

Bandstra, E. S., Morrow, C. E., Accornero, V. H., Mansoor, E., Xue, L., & Anthony, J. C. (2011). Estimated effects of in utero cocaine exposure on language development through early adolescence. *Neurotoxicology and Teratology, 33,* 25–35.

Bandstra, E. S., Morrow, C. E., Mansoor, E., & Accornero, V. H. (2010). Prenatal drug exposure: Infant and toddler outcomes. *Journal of Addictive Diseases, 29,* 245–258.

Bandura, A. (1977). *Social learning theory.* Englewood Cliffs, NJ: Prentice-Hall.

Bandura, A. (1992). Perceived self-efficacy in cognitive development and functioning. *Educational Psychologist, 28,* 117–148.

Bandura, A. (2001). Social cognitive theory: An agentic perspective. *Annual Review of Psychology, 52,* 1–26.

Bandura, A. (2011). Social cognitive theory. In P. A. M. Van Lange, A. W. Kruglanski, & E. T. Higgins (Eds.), *Handbook of theories of social psychology* (Vol. 1, pp. 349–373). Thousand Oaks, CA: Sage.

Banerjee, D., & Perrucci, C. C. (2012). Employee benefits and policies: Do they make a difference for work/family conflict? *Journal of Sociology & Social Welfare, 39,* 133–147.

Bangerter, L. R., & Waldron, V. R. (2014). Turning points in long distance grandparent–grandchild relationships. *Journal of Aging Studies, 29,* 88–97.

Banish, M. T., & Heller, W. (1998). Evolving perspectives on lateralization of function. *Current Directions in Psychological Science, 7,* 1–2.

Banks, M. S. (1980). The development of visual accommodation during early infancy. *Child Development, 51,* 646–666.

Banks, M. S., & Ginsburg, A. P. (1985). Early visual preferences: A review and new theoretical treatment. In H. W. Reese (Ed.), *Advances in child development and behavior* (Vol. 19, pp. 207–246). New York: Academic Press.

Bannard, C., Lieven, E., & Tomasello, M. (2009). Modeling children's early grammatical knowledge. *Proceedings of the National Academy of Sciences, 106,* 17284–17289.

Banse, R., Gawronski, B., Rebetez, C., Gutt, H., & Morton, J. B. (2010). The development of spontaneous gender stereotyping in childhood: Relations to stereotype knowledge and stereotype flexibility. *Developmental Science, 13,* 298–306.

Barber, B. K., & Olsen, J. A. (1997). Socialization in context: Connection, regulation, and autonomy in the family, school, and neighborhood, and with peers. *Journal of Adolescent Research, 12,* 287–315.

Barber, B. K., & Olsen, J. A. (2004). Assessing the transitions to middle and high school. *Journal of Adolescent Research, 19,* 3–30.

Barber, B. K., Stolz, H. E., & Olsen, J. A. (2005). Parental support, psychological control, and behavioral control: Assessing relevance across time, culture, and method. *Monographs of the Society for Research in Child Development, 70*(4, Serial No. 282).

Barber, B. K., & Xia, M. (2013). The centrality of control to parenting and its effects. In R. E. Larzelere, A. S. Morris, & A. W. Harrist (Eds.), *Authoritative parenting: Synthesizing nurturance and discipline for optimal child development* (pp. 61–88). Washington, DC: American Psychological Association.

Barber, B. L., Stone, M. R., Hunt, J. E., & Eccles, J. S. (2005). Benefits of activity participation: The roles of identity affirmation and peer group norm sharing. In J. L. Mahoney, R. W. Larson, & J. S. Eccles (Eds.), *Organized activities as contexts of development: Extracurricular activities, after-school and community programs* (pp. 185–210). Mahwah, NJ: Erlbaum.

Bard, K. A., Todd, B. K., Bernier, C., Love, J., & Leavens, D. A. (2006). Self-awareness in human and chimpanzee infants: What is measured and what is meant by the mark and mirror test? *Infancy, 9,* 191–219.

Barelds, D. P. H., & Dijkstra, P. (2011). Positive illusions about a partner's personality and relationship quality. *Journal of Research in Personality, 45,* 37–43.

Barnes, J., Katz, I., Korbin, J. E., & O'Brien, M. (2007). *Children and families in communities: Theory, research, policy and practice.* Hoboken, NJ: Wiley.

Barnes, R., Josefowitz, N., & Cole, E. (2006). Residential schools: Impact on Aboriginal students' academic and cognitive development. *Canadian Journal of School Psychology, 21,* 18–32.

Barnes-Farrell, J., & Matthews, R. A. (2007). Age and work attitudes. In K. S. Shultz & G. A. Adams (Eds.), *Aging and work in the 21st century* (pp. 139–162). Mahwah, NJ: Erlbaum.

Barnett, W. S. (2011). Effectiveness of early educational intervention. *Science, 333,* 975–978.

Baron-Cohen, S. (2011). What is theory of mind, and is it impaired in ASC? In S. Bolte & J. Hallmayer (Eds.), *Autism spectrum conditions: FAQs on autism, Asperger syndrome, and atypical autism answered by international experts* (pp. 136–138). Cambridge, MA: Hogrefe Publishing.

Baron-Cohen, S., & Belmonte, M. K. (2005). Autism: A window onto the development of the social and the analytic brain. *Annual Review of Neuroscience, 28,* 109–126.

Barr, H. M., Streissguth, A. P., Darby, B. L., & Sampson, P. D. (1990). Prenatal exposure to alcohol, caffeine, tobacco, and aspirin: Effects on fine and gross motor performance in 4-year-old children. *Developmental Psychology, 26,* 339–348.

Barr, R., & Hayne, H. (2003). It's not what you know, it's who you know: Older siblings facilitate imitation during infancy. *International Journal of Early Years Education, 11,* 7–21.

Barr, R., Marrott, H., & Rovee-Collier, C. (2003). The role of sensory preconditioning in memory retrieval by preverbal infants. *Learning and Behavior, 31,* 111–123.

Barr, R., Muentener, P., & Garcia, A. (2007). Age-related changes in deferred imitation from television by 6- to 18-month-olds. *Developmental Science, 10,* 10–921.

Barr, R. G. (2001). "Colic" is something infants do, rather than a condition they "have": A developmental approach to crying phenomena patterns, pacification and (patho)genesis. In R. G. Barr, I. St. James-Roberts, & M. R. Keefe (Eds.), *New evidence on unexplained infant crying* (pp. 87–104). St. Louis: Johnson & Johnson Pediatric Institute.

Barr, R. G., Fairbrother, N., Pauwels, J., Green, J., Chen, M., & Brant, R. (2014). Maternal frustration, emotional and behavioural responses to prolonged infant crying. *Infant Behavior and Development, 37,* 652–664.

Barrera, M., Alam, R., D'Agostino, N. M., Nicholas, D. B., & Schneiderman, G. (2013). Parental perceptions of siblings' grieving after a childhood cancer death: A longitudinal study. *Death Studies, 37,* 25–46.

Barreto, M., Ryan, M. K., & Schmitt, M. T. (2009). *The glass ceiling in the 21st century: Understanding barriers to gender equality.* Washington, DC: American Psychological Association.

Barrett, K. C. (2005). The origins of social emotions and self-regulation in toddlerhood: New evidence. *Cognition and Emotion, 19,* 953–979.

Barrouillet, P., & Gaillard, V. (2011a). Advances and issues: Some thoughts about controversial questions. In P. Barrouillet & V. Gaillard (Eds.), *Cognitive development and working memory: A dialogue between neo-Piagetian and cognitive approaches* (pp. 263–271). Hove, UK: Psychology Press.

Barrouillet, P., & Gaillard, V. (Eds.). (2011b). *Cognitive development and working memory: A dialogue between neo-Piagetian and cognitive approaches.* Hove, UK: Psychology Press.

Barry, C. M., & Abo-Zena, M. M. (2014). Emerging adults' religious and spiritual development. In C. M. Barry & M. Abo-Zena (Eds.), *Emerging adults' religiousness and spirituality: Meaning-making in an age of transition* (pp. 21–38). New York: Oxford University Press.

Barry, C. M., & Abo-Zena, M. M. (2016). The experience of meaning-making: The role of religiousness and spirituality in emerging adults' lives. In J. J. Arnett (Ed.), *Oxford handbook of emerging adulthood* (pp. 464–480). New York: Oxford University Press.

Barry, C. M., & Christofferson, J. L. (2014). The role of peer relationships in emerging adults' religiousness and spirituality. In C. M. Barry & M. Abo-Zena (Eds.), *Emerging adults' religiousness and spirituality: Meaning-making in an age of transition* (pp. 76–92). New York: Oxford University Press.

Barry, C. M., Madsen, S., & DeGrace, A. (2016). Growing up with a little help from their friends in emerging adulthood. In J. J. Arnett (Ed.), *Oxford handbook of emerging adulthood* (pp. 215–229). New York: Oxford University Press.

Barry, C. M., & Wentzel, K. R. (2006). Friend influence on prosocial behavior: The role of motivational factors and friendship characteristics. *Developmental Psychology, 42,* 153–163.

Barsman, S. G., Dowling, D. A., Damato, E. G., & Czeck, P. (2015). Neonatal nurses' beliefs, knowledge, and practices in relation to sudden infant death syndrome risk-reduction recommendations. *Advances in Neonatal Care, 15,* 209–219.

Barthell, J. E., & Mrozek, J. D. (2013). Neonatal drug withdrawal. *Minnesota Medicine, 96,* 48–50.

Bartholomew, K., Cobb, R. J., & Dutton, D. G. (2015). Established and emerging perspectives on violence in intimate relationships. In M. Mikulincer & P. R. Shaver (Eds.), *Handbook of personality and social psychology: Vol. 3. Interpersonal relations* (pp. 605–630). Washington, DC: American Psychological Association.

Bartick, M., & Smith, L. J. (2014). Speaking out on safe sleep: Evidence-based infant sleep recommendations. *Breastfeeding Medicine, 9,* 417–422.

Bartocci, M., Berggvist, L. L., Lagercrantz, H., & Anand, K. J. (2006). Pain activates cortical areas in the preterm newborn brain. *Pain, 122,* 109–117.

Bartrip, J., Morton, J., & de Schonen, S. (2001). Responses to mother's face in 3-week- to 5-month-old infants. *British Journal of Developmental Psychology, 19,* 219–232.

Bartsch, K., & Wellman, H. (1995). *Children talk about the mind.* New York: Oxford University Press.

Barzilai, S., & Zohar, A. (2015). Epistemic (meta) cognition: Ways of thinking about knowledge and knowing. In J. A. Greene, W. A. Sandoval &

I. Bråten (Eds.), *Handbook of epistemic cognition* (pp. 409–424). New York, NY: Routledge

Basak, C., & Verhaeghen, P. (2011). Aging and switching the focus of attention in working memory: Age differences in item availability but not in item accessibility. *Journals of Gerontology, 66B,* 519–526.

Basilio, C. D., Knight, G. P., O'Donnell, M., Roosa, M. W., Gonzales, N. A., Umaña-Taylor, A. J., & Torres, M. (2014). The Mexican American Biculturalism Scale: Bicultural comfort, facility, and advantages for adolescents and adults. *Psychological Assessment, 26,* 539–554.

Basinger, B. (2013). Low-income and minority children with asthma. In L. Rubin & J. Merrick (Eds.), *Environmental health disparities with children: Asthma, obesity and food* (pp. 61–72). Hauppauge, NY: Nova Science.

Bass, S. (2011). From retirement to "productive aging" and back to work again. In D. C. Carr & K. Komp (Eds.), *Gerontology in the era of the Third Age: Implications and next steps* (pp. 169–188). New York: Springer.

Bass-Ringdahl, S. M. (2010). The relationship of audibility and the development of canonical babbling in young children with hearing impairment. *Journal of Deaf Studies and Deaf Education, 15,* 287–310.

Bastawrous, M., Gignac, M. A., Kapral, M. K., & Camerson, J. I. (2015). Factors that contribute to adult children caregivers' well-being: A coping review. *Health and Social Care in the Community, 23,* 449–466.

Basten, S., & Jiang, Q. (2015). Fertility in China: An uncertain future. *Population Studies, 69,* S97–S105.

Bastin, C., Diana, R. A., Simon, J., Collette, F., Yonelinas, A. P., & Salmon, E. (2013). Associative memory in aging: The effect of unitization on source memory. *Psychology and Aging, 28,* 275–283.

Basu, R., Hochhalter, A. K., & Stevens, A. B. (2015). The impact of the REACH II intervention on caregivers' perceived health. *Journal of Applied Gerontology, 34,* 590–608.

Bates, E., Marchman, V., Thal, D., Fenson, L., Dale, P., Reznick, J. S., Reilly, J., & Hartung, J. (1994). Developmental and stylistic variation in the composition of early vocabulary. *Journal of Child Language, 21,* 85–123.

Bates, J. E., Wachs, T. D., & Emde, R. N. (1994). Toward practical uses for biological concepts. In J. E. Bates & T. D. Wachs (Eds.), *Temperament: Individual differences at the interface of biology and behavior* (pp. 275–306). Washington, DC: American Psychological Association.

Bathelt, J., O'Reilly, H., Clayden, J. D., Cross, J. H., & de Haan, M. (2013). Functional brain network organization of children between 2 and 5 years derived from reconstructed activity of cortical sources of high-density EEG recordings. *NeuroImage, 82,* 595–604.

Bauer, P. J. (2006). Event memory. In D. Kuhn & R. Siegler (Eds.), *Handbook of child psychology: Vol. 2. Cognition, perception, and language* (6th ed., pp. 373–425). Hoboken, NJ: Wiley.

Bauer, P. J. (2013). Memory. In S. M. Carlson, P. D. Zelazo, & S. Faja (Eds.), *Oxford handbook of developmental psychology: Vol. 1. Body and mind* (pp. 505–541). New York: Oxford University Press.

Bauer, P. J., Larkina, M., & Deocampo, J. (2011). Early memory development. In U. Goswami (Ed.), *Wiley-Blackwell handbook of childhood cognitive development* (2nd ed., pp. 153–179). Chichester, UK: Wiley-Blackwell.

Baum, N., Rahav, G., & Sharon, D. (2005). Changes in the self-concepts of divorced women. *Journal of Divorce and Remarriage, 43,* 47–61.

Baumbusch, J. L. (2004). Unclaimed treasures: Older women's reflections on lifelong singlehood. *Journal of Women and Aging, 16,* 105–121.

Baumeister, R. F., Campbell, J. D., Krueger, J. I., & Vohs, K. D. (2003). Does high self-esteem cause better performance, interpersonal success, happiness, or healthier lifestyles? *Psychological Science in the Public Interest, 4*(1), 1–44.

Baumgart, M., Snyder, H. M., Carrillo, M. C., Fazio, S., Kim, H., & Johns, H. (2015). Summary of the evidence on modifiable risk factors for cognitive decline and dementia: A population-based perspective. *Alzheimer's & Dementia, 11,* 18–26.

Baumgartner, H. A., & Oakes, L. M. (2011). Infants' developing sensitivity to object function: Attention to features and feature correlations. *Journal of Cognition and Development, 12,* 275–298.

Baumgartner, M. S., & Schneider, D. E. (2010). Perceptions of women in management: A thematic analysis of razing the glass ceiling. *Journal of Career Development, 37,* 559–576.

Baumgartner, S. E., Weeda, W. D., van der Heijden, L. L., & Huizinga, M. (2014). The relationship between media multitasking and executive function in early adolescence. *Journal of Early Adolescence, 34,* 1120–1144.

Baumrind, D. (1971). Current patterns of parental authority. *Developmental Psychology Monograph, 4*(No. 1, Pt. 2).

Baumrind, D. (2013). Authoritative parenting revisited: History and current status. In R. E. Larzelere, A. S. Morris, & A. W. Harrist (Eds.), *Authoritative parenting: Synthesizing nurturance and discipline for optimal child development* (pp. 11–34). Washington, DC: American Psychological Association.

Baumrind, D., Lazelere, R. E., & Owens, E. B. (2010). Effects of preschool parents' power assertive patterns and practices on adolescent development. *Parenting, 10,* 157–201.

Baumwell, L., Tamis-LeMonda, C. S., & Bornstein, M. H. (1997). Maternal verbal sensitivity and child language comprehension. *Infant Behavior and Development, 20,* 247–258.

Bauserman, R. (2002). Child adjustment in joint-custody versus sole-custody arrangements: A meta-analytic review. *Journal of Family Psychology, 16,* 91–102.

Bauserman, R. (2012). A meta-analysis of parental satisfaction, adjustment, and conflict in joint custody and sole custody following divorce. *Journal of Divorce & Remarriage, 53,* 464–488.

Bayer, A., & Tadd, W. (2000). Unjustified exclusion of elderly people from studies submitted to research ethics committee for approval: Descriptive study. *British Medical Journal, 321,* 992–993.

Bayley, N. (1969). *Bayley Scales of Infant Development.* New York: Psychological Corporation.

Bayley, N. (1993). *Bayley Scales of Infant Development* (2nd ed.). San Antonio, TX: Psychological Corporation.

Bayley, N. (2005). *Bayley Scales of Infant and Toddler Development* (3rd ed.). San Antonio, TX: Harcourt Assessment.

Be, D., Whisman, M. A., & Uebelacker, L. A. (2013). Prospective associations between marital adjustment and life satisfaction. *Personal Relationships, 20,* 728–739.

Bean, R. A., Barber, B. K., & Crane, D. R. (2007). Parental support, behavioral control, and psychological control among African American youth: The relationships to academic grades, delinquency, and depression. *Journal of Family Issues, 27,* 1335–1355.

Beauchamp, G. K., & Mennella, J. A. (2011). Flavor perception in human infants: Development and functional significance. *Digestion, 83*(Suppl. 1), 1–6.

Beaulieu, M., Leclerc, N., & Dube, M. (2003). Fear of crime among the elderly: An analysis of mental health issues. *Journal of Gerontological Social Work, 40,* 121–138.

Beckett, C., Maughan, B., Rutter, M., Castle, J., Colvert, E., & Groothues, C. (2006). Do the effects of early severe deprivation on cognition persist into early adolescence? Findings from the English and Romanian adoptees study. *Child Development, 77,* 696–711.

Bedard, K., & Dhuey, E. (2006). The persistence of early childhood maturity: International evidence of long-run age effects. *Quarterly Journal of Economics, 121,* 1437–1472.

Bedford, V. H., & Avioli, P. S. (2006). "Shooting the bull": Cohort comparisons of fraternal intimacy in midlife and old age. In V. H. Bedford & B. F. Turner (Eds.), *Men in relationships* (pp. 81–101). New York: Springer.

Bedford, V. H., & Avioli, P. S. (2016). Sibling ties. In S. K. Whitbourne (Ed.), *Encyclopedia of adulthood and aging* (Vol. 3, pp. 1305–1309). Malden, MA: Wiley Blackwell.

Beelmann, A., & Heinemann, K. S. (2014). Preventing prejudice and improving intergroup attitudes: A meta-analysis of child and adolescent training programs. *Journal of Applied Developmental Psychology, 35,* 10–24.

Behm, I., Kabir, Z., Connolly, G. N., & Alpert, H. R. (2012). Increasing prevalence of smoke-free homes and decreasing rates of sudden infant death syndrome in the United States: An ecological association study. *Tobacco Control, 21,* 6–11.

Behnke, M., & Smith, V. C. (2013). Prenatal substance abuse: Short- and long-term effects on the exposed fetus. *Pediatrics, 131,* e1009–1024.

Behrens, K. Y., Hesse, E., & Main, M. (2007). Mothers' attachment status as determined by the Adult Attachment Interview predicts their 6-year-olds' reunion responses: A study conducted in Japan. *Developmental Psychology, 43*(6), 1553–1567.

Beier, M. E., & Ackerman, P. L. (2005). Age, ability, and the role of prior knowledge on the acquisition of new domain knowledge: Promising results in a real-world learning environment. *Psychology and Aging, 20,* 341–355.

Bekhet, A. K. (2016). Relocation adjustment in older adults. In S. K. Whitbourne (Ed.), *Encyclopedia of adulthood and aging* (Vol. 3, pp. 1189–1193). Malden, MA: Wiley Blackwell.

Bekkouche, N. S., Holmes, S., Whittaker, K. S., & Krantz, D. S. (2011). Stress and the heart: Psychosocial stress and coronary heart disease. In R. J. Contrada & A. Baum (Eds.), *Handbook of stress science: Biology, psychology, and health* (pp. 385–398). New York: Springer.

Bélanger, M. J., Atance, C. M., Varghese, A. L., Nguyen, V., & Vendetti, C. (2014). What will I like best when I'm all grown up? Preschoolers' understanding of future preferences. *Child Development, 85,* 2419–2431.

Belcher, D., Lee, A., Solmon, M., & Harrison, L. (2003). The influence of gender-related beliefs and conceptions of ability on women learning the hockey wrist shot. *Research Quarterly for Exercise and Sport, 74,* 183–192.

Belfort, M. B., Rifas-Shiman, S. L., Kleinman, K. P., Guthrie, L. B., Bellinger, D. C., Taveras, E. M., et al. (2013). Infant feeding and childhood cognition at ages 3 and 7 years: Effects of breastfeeding duration and exclusivity. *JAMA Pediatrics, 167,* 836–844.

Bell, J. H., & Bromnick, R. D. (2003). The social reality of the imaginary audience: A grounded theory approach. *Adolescence, 38,* 205–219.

Bell, M. A. (1998). Frontal lobe function during infancy: Implications for the development of cognition and attention. In J. E. Richards (Ed.), *Cognitive neuroscience of attention: A developmental perspective* (pp. 327–362). Mahwah, NJ: Erlbaum.

Bell, M. A., & Fox, N. A. (1996). Crawling experience is related to changes in cortical organization during infancy: Evidence from EEG coherence. *Developmental Psychobiology, 29,* 551–561.

Bellagamba, F., Camaioni, L., & Colonnesi, C. (2006). Change in children's understanding of others' intentional actions. *Developmental Science, 9,* 182–188.

Bellagamba, F., Laghi, F., Lonigro, A., & Pace, C. S. (2012). Re-enactment of intended acts from a video presentation by 18- and 24-month-old children. *Cognitive Processes, 13,* 381–386.

Belle, S. H., Burgio, L., Burns, R., Coon, D., Czaja, S. J., Gallagher-Thompson, D., & Gitlin, L. N. (2006). Enhancing quality of life of dementia caregivers from different ethnic or racial groups: A randomized, controlled trial. *Annals of Internal Medicine, 145,* 727–738.

Belloc, S., Hazout, A., Zini, A., Merviel, P., Cabry, R., Chahine, H., et al. (2014). How to overcome male infertility after 40: Influence of paternal age on fertility. *Maturitas, 78,* 22–29.

Belsky, J. (2005). Attachment theory and research in ecological perspective: Insights from the Pennsylvania Infant and Family Development Project and the NICHD Study of Early Child Care. In K. E. Grossmann, K. Grossmann, & E. Waters (Eds.), *Attachment from infancy to adulthood: The major longitudinal studies* (pp. 71–97). New York: Guilford.

Belsky, J., & de Haan, M. (2011). Parenting and children's brain development: The end of the beginning. *Journal of Child Psychology and Psychiatry, 52,* 409–428.

Belsky, J., & Fearon, R. M. P. (2002). Early attachment security, subsequent maternal sensitivity, and later child development: Does continuity in development depend on caregiving? *Attachment and Human Development, 4,* 361–387.

Belsky, J., & Fearon, R. M. P. (2008). Precursors of attachment security. In J. Cassidy & P. R. Shaver (Eds.), *Handbook of attachment: Theory, research, and clinical applications* (2nd ed., pp. 295–316). New York: Guilford.

Belsky, J., Schlomer, G. L., & Ellis, B. J. (2012). Beyond cumulative risk: Distinguishing harshness and unpredictability as determinants of parenting and early life history strategy. *Developmental Psychology, 48,* 662–673.

Belsky, J., Steinberg, L. D., Houts, R. M., Friedman, S. L., DeHart, G., Cauffman, E., Roisman, G. I., & Halpern-Felsher, B. (2007a). Family rearing antecedents of pubertal timing. *Child Development, 78,* 1302–1321.

Belsky, J., Steinberg, L., Houts, R. M., & Halpern-Felsher, B. L. (2010). The development of reproductive strategy in females: Early maternal harshness → earlier menarche → increased sexual risk taking. *Developmental Psychology, 46,* 120–128.

Belsky, J., Vandell, D. L., Burchinal, M., Clarke-Stewart, K. A., McCartney, K., & Owen, M. T. (2007b). Are there long-term effects of early child care? *Child Development, 78,* 681–701.

Bender, H. L., Allen, J. P., McElhaney, K. B., Antonishak, J., Moore, C. M., Kelly, H. L., & Davis, S. M. (2007). Use of harsh physical discipline and developmental outcomes in adolescence. *Development and Psychopathology, 19,* 227–242.

Benenson, J. F., & Christakos, A. (2003). The greater fragility of females' versus males' closest same-sex friendships. *Child Development, 74,* 1123–1129.

Benigno, J. P., Byrd, D. L., McNamara, P. H., Berg, W. K., & Farrar, M. J. (2011). Talking through transitions: Microgenetic changes in preschoolers' private speech. *Child Language Teaching and Therapy, 27,* 269–285.

Benner, A. D. (2011). The transition to high school: Current knowledge, future directions. *Educational Psychology Review, 23,* 299–328.

Benner, A. D., & Graham, S. (2009). The transition to high school as a developmental process among multiethnic urban youth. *Child Development, 80,* 356–376.

Benner, A. D., & Wang, Y. (2014). Shifting attendance trajectories from middle to high school: Influences of school transitions and changing school contexts. *Developmental Psychology, 50,* 1288–1301.

Bennett, C., Barlow, J., Huband, N., Smailagic, N., & Roloff, V. (2013). Group-based parenting programs for improving parenting and psychological functioning: A systematic review. *Journal of the Society for Social Work and Research, 4,* 300–332.

Bennett, D. A., Schneider, J. A., Tang, Y., Arnold, S. E., & Wilson, R. S. (2006). The effect of social networks on the relation between Alzheimer's disease pathology and level of cognitive function in old people: A longitudinal cohort study. *Lancet Neurology, 5,* 406–412.

Bennett, K. M. (2007). "No sissy stuff": Toward a theory of masculinity and emotional expression in older widowed men. *Journal of Aging Studies, 21,* 347–356.

Bennett, K. M., & Soulsby, L. K. (2012). Well-being in bereavement and widowhood. *Illness, Crisis & Loss, 20,* 321–337.

Benoit, A., Lacourse, E., & Claes, M. (2013). Pubertal timing and depressive symptoms in late adolescence: The moderating role of individual, peer, and parental factors. *Development and Psychopathology, 25,* 455–471.

Benson, J. E., Sabbagh, M. A., Carlson, S. M., & Zelazo, P. D. (2013). Individual differences in executive functioning predict preschoolers' improvement from theory-of-mind training. *Developmental Psychology, 49,* 1615–1627.

Bera, A., Ghosh, J., Singh, A. K., Hazra, A., Mukherjee, S., & Mukherjee, R. (2014). Effect of kangaroo mother care on growth and development of low birthweight babies up to 12 months of age: A controlled clinical trial. *Acta Paediatrica, 103,* 643–650.

Beratis, I. N., Rabavilas, A. D., Kyprianou, M., Papadimitriou, G. N., & Papageorgiou, C. (2013). Investigation of the link between higher order cognitive functions and handedness. *Journal of Clinical and Experimental Neuropsychology, 35,* 393–403.

Berenbaum, S. A., & Beltz, A. M. (2011). Sexual differentiation in human behavior: Effects of prenatal and pubertal organizational hormones. *Frontiers in Neuroendocrinology, 32,* 183–200.

Berg, C. A., & Strough, J. (2011). Problem solving across the life span. In K. L. Fingerman, C. A. Berg, J. Smith, & T. C. Antonucci (Eds.), *Handbook of life-span development* (pp. 239–267). New York: Springer.

Bergen, D. (2013). Does pretend play matter? Searching for evidence: Comment on Lillard et al. (2013). *Psychological Bulletin, 139,* 45–48.

Berger, L. M., Paxson, C., & Waldfogel, J. (2009). Income and child development. *Children and Youth Services Review, 31,* 978–989.

Berger, S. E. (2010). Locomotor expertise predicts infants' perseverative errors. *Developmental Psychology, 46,* 326–336.

Berger, S. E., Theuring, C., & Adolph, K. E. (2007). How and when infants learn to climb stairs. *Infant Behavior and Development, 30,* 36–49.

Bergman, E. J., Haley, W. E., & Small, B. J. (2010). The role of grief, anxiety, and depressive symptoms in the utilization of bereavement services. *Death Studies, 34,* 441–458.

Bergman, I., Blomberg, M., & Almkvist, O. (2007). The importance of impaired physical health and age in normal cognitive aging. *Scandinavian Journal of Psychology, 48,* 115–125.

Bergman, M. J., Rose, K. J., & Shuck, M. B. (2015). Adult degree programs: Factors impacting student persistence. In J. K. Holtz, S. B. Springer, & C. J. Boden-McGill (Eds.), *Building sustainable futures for adult learners* (pp. 27–50). Charlotte, NC: Information Age Publishing.

Bergman, R. (2004). Identity as motivation. In D. K. Lapsley & D. Narvaez (Eds.), *Moral development, self, and identity* (pp. 21–46). Mahwah, NJ: Erlbaum.

Bering, J. M., & Bjorklund, D. F. (2004). The natural emergence of reasoning about the afterlife as a developmental regularity. *Developmental Psychology, 40,* 217–233.

Berk, L. E. (2001). *Awakening children's minds: How parents and teachers can make a difference.* New York: Oxford University Press.

Berk, L. E. (2006). Looking at kindergarten children. In D. Gullo (Ed.), *K today: Teaching and learning in the kindergarten year* (pp. 11–25). Washington, DC: National Association for the Education of Young Children.

Berk, L. E. (2015). Make-believe play and children's self-regulation. *Speaking about … Psychology On-Demand Webinars.* Hoboken, NJ: Pearson Education. Retrieved from www.pearsoned.com/events-and-webinars/higher-education-events-and-webinars/speaking-about-webinars/on-demand-webinars/psychology

Berk, L. E., & Meyers, A. B. (2013). The role of make-believe play in the development of executive function: Status of research and future directions. *American Journal of Play, 6,* 98–110.

Berk, L. E., & Spuhl, S. (1995). Maternal interaction, private speech, and task performance in preschool children. *Early Childhood Research Quarterly, 10,* 145–169.

Berkeley, S., Mastropieri, M. A., & Scruggs, T. E. (2011). Reading comprehension strategy instruction and attribution retraining for secondary students with learning and other mild disabilities. *Journal of Learning Disabilities, 44,* 18–31.

Berkowitz, M. W., & Gibbs, J. C. (1983). Measuring the developmental features of moral discussion. *Merrill-Palmer Quarterly, 29,* 399–410.

Berkowitz, R. L., Roberts, J., & Minkoff, H. (2006). Challenging the strategy of maternal age-based prenatal genetic counseling. *JAMA, 295,* 1446–1448.

Berlin, L. J., Ipsa, J. M., Fine, M. A., Malone, P. S., Brooks-Gunn, J., Brady-Smith, C., et al. (2009). Correlates and consequences of spanking and verbal punishment for low-income white, African-American, and Mexican-American toddlers. *Child Development, 80,* 1403–1420.

Berman, R. A. (2007). Developing linguistic knowledge and language use across adolescence. In K. Hirsh-Pasek & R. M. Golinkoff (Eds.), *Action meets word: How children learn verbs* (pp. 347–367). New York: Oxford University Press.

Berndt, T. J. (2004). Children's friendships: Shifts over a half-century in perspectives on their development and effects. *Merrill-Palmer Quarterly, 50,* 206–223.

Bernier, A., Larose, S., & Whipple, N. (2005). Leaving home for college: A potential stressful event for adolescents with preoccupied attachment patterns. *Attachment and Human Development, 7,* 171–185.

Bern-Klug, M., & Manthai, T. (2016). Nursing homes. In S. K. Whitbourne (Ed.), *Encyclopedia of adulthood and aging* (Vol. 2, pp. 985–988). Malden, MA: Wiley Blackwell.

Bernstein, N. (2014). *Burning down the house: The end of juvenile prison.* New York: New Press.

Berry, P., & Griffie, J. (2016). Planning for the actual death. In N. Coyle & B. R. Ferrell (Eds.), *Social aspects of care* (pp. 73–98). New York: Oxford University Press.

Berscheid, E. (2010). Love in the fourth dimension. *Annual Review of Psychology, 61,* 1–25.

Bertenthal, B. I. (1993). Infants' perception of biomechanical motions: Intrinsic image and knowledge-based constraints. In C. Granrud (Ed.), *Visual perception and cognition in infancy* (pp. 175–214). Hillsdale, NJ: Erlbaum.

Bertenthal, B. I., Gredebäck, G., & Boyer, T. W. (2013). Differential contributions of development and learning to infants' knowledge of object continuity and discontinuity. *Child Development, 84,* 413–421.

Bertenthal, B. I., Longo, M. R., & Kenny, S. (2007). Phenomenal permanence and the development of predictive tracking in infancy. *Child Development, 78,* 350–363.

Bertrand, J., & Dang, E. P. (2012). Fetal alcohol spectrum disorders: Review of teratogenicity, diagnosis and treatment issues. In D. Hollar (Ed.), *Handbook of children with special health care needs* (pp. 231–258). New York: Springer Science + Business Media.

Bertrand, M., & Mullainathan, S. (2004). *Are Emily and Brendan more employable than Lakisha and Jamal? A field experiment on labor market discrimination.* Unpublished manuscript, University of Chicago.

Berzin, S. C., & De Marco, A. C. (2010). Understanding the impact of poverty on critical events in emerging adulthood. *Youth and Society, 42,* 278–300.

Berzlanovich, A. M., Keil, W. W., Sim, T., Fasching, P., & Fazeny-Dorner, B. (2005). Do centenarians die healthy? An autopsy study. *Journals of Gerontology, 60A,* 862–865.

Berzonsky, M. D. (2011). A social-cognitive perspective on identity construction. In S. J. Schwartz, K. Luyckz, & V. L. Vignoles (Eds.), *Handbook of identity theory and research* (pp. 55–76). New York: Springer.

Berzonsky, M. D., Cieciuch, J., Duriez, B., & Soenens, B. (2011). The how and what of identity formation: Associations between identity styles and value orientations. *Personality and Individual Differences, 50,* 295–299.

Best, C., & Fortenberry, J. D. (2013). Adolescent sexuality and sexual behavior. In W. T. O'Donohue, L. T. Benuto, & L. Woodward Tolle (Eds.), *Handbook of adolescent health psychology* (pp. 271–291). New York: Springer.

Best, D. (2009). From the American Academy of Pediatrics: Technical report—secondhand and prenatal tobacco smoke exposure. *Pediatrics, 124,* e1017–e1044.

Best, D. L. (2001). Gender concepts: Convergence in cross-cultural research and methodologies. *Cross-cultural Research: The Journal of Comparative Social Science, 35,* 23–43.

Beydoun, M. E., Beydoun, H. A., Gamaldo, A. A., Teel, A., & Zonderman, A. B. (2014). Epidemiologic studies of modifiable factors associated with cognition and dementia: Systematic review and meta-analysis. *BMC Public Health, 14,* 643.

Beyene, Y. (1992). Menopause: A biocultural event. In A. J. Dan & L. L. Lewis (Eds.), *Menstrual health in women's lives* (pp. 169–177). Urbana, IL: University of Illinois Press.

Beyene, Y., & Martin, M. C. (2001). Menopausal experiences and bone density of Mayan women in Yucatan, Mexico. *American Journal of Human Biology, 13,* 47–71.

Beyers, J. M., Bates, J. E., Pettit, G. S., & Dodge, K. A. (2003). Neighborhood structure, parenting processes, and the development of youths' externalizing behaviors: A multilevel analysis. *American Journal of Community Psychology, 31,* 35–53.

Beyers, W., & Luyckx, K. (2016). Ruminative exploration and reconsideration of commitment as risk factors for suboptimal identity development in adolescence and emerging adulthood. *Journal of Adolescence, 47,* 169–178.

Beyers, W., & Seiffge-Krenke, I. (2010). Does identity precede intimacy? Testing Erikson's theory of romantic development in emerging adults of the 21st century. *Journal of Adolescent Research, 25,* 387–415.

Bhargava, S., & Witherspoon, D. P. (2015). Parental involvement across middle and high school: Exploring contributions of individual and neighborhood characteristics. *Journal of Youth and Adolescence, 44,* 1702–1719.

Bhat, A., Heathcock, J., & Galloway, J. C. (2005). Toy-oriented changes in hand and joint kinematics during the emergence of purposeful reaching. *Infant Behavior and Development, 28,* 445–465.

Bhatt, R. S., Rovee-Collier, C., & Weiner, S. (1994). Developmental changes in the interface between perception and memory retrieval. *Developmental Psychology, 30,* 151–162.

Bhatt, R. S., Wilk, A., Hill, D., & Rovee-Collier, C. (2004). Correlated attributes and categorization in the first half-year of life. *Developmental Psychobiology, 44,* 103–115.

Bherer, L. (2012). Physical activity and exercise in older adults. In E. O. Acevedo (Ed.), *Oxford handbook of exercise psychology* (pp. 359–384). New York: Oxford University Press.

Bherer, L., Kramer, A. F., Peterson, M. S., Colcombe, S., Erickson, K., & Becic, E. (2006). Training effects on dual-task performance: Are there age-related differences in plasticity of attentional control? *Psychology and Aging, 20,* 695–709.

Bialystok, E. (2011). Reshaping the mind: The benefits of bilingualism. *Canadian Journal of Experimental Psychology, 65,* 229–235.

Bialystok, E. (2013). The impact of bilingualism on language and literacy development. In T. K. Bhatia & W. C. Ritchie (Eds.), *Handbook of bilingualism and multilingualism* (pp. 624–648). Chichester, UK: Wiley-Blackwell.

Bialystok, E., Craik, F. I. M., & Luk, G. (2012). Bilingualism: Consequences for mind and brain. *Trends in Cognitive Sciences, 16,* 240–250.

Bialystok, E., & Martin, M. M. (2003). Notation to symbol: Development in children's understanding of print. *Journal of Experimental Child Psychology, 86,* 223–243.

Bianchi, S. M. (2011). Family change and time allocation in American families. *Annals of the American Academy of Political and Social Science, 638,* 21–44.

Bick, J., Dozier, M., Bernard, K., Grasso, D., & Simons, R. (2013). Foster mother–infant bonding: Associations between foster mothers' oxytocin production, electrophysiological brain activity, feelings of commitment, and caregiving quality. *Child Development, 84,* 826–840.

Biederman, J., Fried, R., Petty, C., Mahoney, L., & Faraone, S. V. (2012). An examination of the impact of attention-deficit hyperactivity disorder on IQ: A large controlled family-based analysis. *Canadian Journal of Psychiatry, 57,* 608–616.

Bielak, A. A. M., Hultsch, D. F., Strauss, E., MacDonald, S. W. S., & Hunter, M. A. (2010). Intraindividual variability in reaction time predicts cognitive outcomes 5 years later. *Neuropsychology, 24,* 731–741.

Bierman, K. L., Domitrovich, C. E., Nix, R. L., Gest, S. D., Welsh, J. A., Greenberg, M. T., et al. (2008). Promoting academic and social-emotional school readiness: The Head Start REDI program. *Child Development, 79,* 1802–1817.

Bierman, K. L., Nix, R. L., Heinrichs, B. S., Domitrovich, C. E., Gest, S. D., Welsh, J. A., et al. (2014). Effects of Head Start REDI on children's outcomes 1 year later in different kindergarten contexts. *Child Development, 85,* 140–159.

Bierman, K. L., & Powers, L. M. (2009). Social skills training to improve peer relations. In K. H. Rubin, W. M. Bukowski, & B. Laursen (Eds.), *Handbook of peer interactions, relationships, and groups* (pp. 603–621). New York: Guilford Press.

Bifulco, R., Cobb, C. D., & Bell, C. (2009). Can interdistrict choice boost student achievement? The case of Connecticut's interdistrict magnet school program. *Educational Evaluation and Policy Analysis, 31,* 323–345.

Bigelow, A. E., MacLean, K., Proctor, J., Myatt, T., Gillis, R., & Power, M. (2010). Maternal sensitivity throughout infancy: Continuity and relation to attachment security. *Infant Behavior and Development, 33,* 50–60.

Bigelow, A. E., & Power, M. (2014). Effects of maternal responsiveness on infant responsiveness and behavior in the still-face task. *Infancy, 19,* 558–584.

Bigler, R. S. (2007, June). Personal communication.

Bigler, R. S. (2013). Understanding and reducing social stereotyping and prejudice among children. In M. Banaji & S. A. Gelman (Eds.), *Navigating the social world: What infants, children, and other species can teach us* (pp. 327–33). New York: Oxford University Press.

Bilgel, M., An, Y., Lang, A., Prince, J., Ferrucci, L., Jedynak, B., & Risnick, S. M. (2014). Trajectories of Alzheimer disease-related cognitive measures in a longitudinal sample. *Alzheimer's & Dementia, 10,* 735–742.

Birbeck, D., & Drummond, M. (2015). Research methods and ethics working with young children. In O. N. Saracho (Ed.), *Handbook of research methods in early childhood education: Vol. 2. Review of research methodologies* (pp. 607–632). Charlotte, NC: IAP Information Age Publishing.

Birch, L. L., & Fisher, J. A. (1995). Appetite and eating behavior in children. *Pediatric Clinics of North America, 42,* 931–953.

Birch, L. L., Fisher, J. O., & Davison, K. K. (2003). Learning to overeat: Maternal use of restrictive feeding practices promotes girls' eating in the absence of hunger. *American Journal of Clinical Nutrition, 78,* 215–220.

Birch, L. L., Zimmerman, S., & Hind, H. (1980). The influence of social-affective context on preschool children's food preferences. *Child Development, 51,* 856–861.

Bird, A., & Reese, E. (2006). Emotional reminiscing and the development of an autobiographical self. *Developmental Psychology, 42,* 613–626.

Birditt, K. S., & Antonucci, T. C. (2007). Relationship quality profiles and well-being among married adults. *Journal of Family Psychology, 21,* 595–604.

Birditt, K. S., & Fingerman, K. L. (2005). Do we get better at picking our battles? Age group differences in descriptions of behavioral reactions to interpersonal tensions. *Journals of Gerontology, 60B,* P121–P128.

Birditt, K. S., Jackey, L. M. H., & Antonucci, T. C. (2009). Longitudinal patterns of negative relationship quality across adulthood. *Journals of Gerontology, 64B,* 55–64.

Biringen, Z., Altenhofen, S., Aberle, J., Baker, M., Brosal, A., Bennett, S., et al. (2012). Emotional availability, attachment, and intervention in center-based child care for infants and toddlers. *Development and Psychopathology, 24,* 23–34.

Biringen, Z., Emde, R. N., Campos, J. J., & Appelbaum, M. I. (1995). Affective reorganization in the infant, the mother, and the dyad: The role of upright locomotion and its timing. *Child Development, 66,* 499–514.

Birkeland, M. S., Breivik, K., & Wold, B. (2014). Peer acceptance protects global self-esteem from negative effects of low closeness to parents during adolescence and early adulthood. *Journal of Youth and Adolescence, 43,* 70–80.

Birkeland, M. S., Melkevik, O., Holsen, I., & Wold, B. (2012). Trajectories of global self-esteem development during adolescence. *Journal of Adolescence, 35,* 43–54.

Birney, D. P., & Sternberg, R. J. (2011). The development of cognitive abilities. In M. H. Bornstein & M. E. Lamb (Eds.), *Developmental science: An advanced textbook* (6th ed., pp. 353–388). New York: Psychology Press.

Biro, F. M., & Wien, M. (2010). Childhood obesity and adult morbidities. *American Journal of Clinical Nutrition, 91,* 1499S–1505S.

Birren, J. E. (2009). Gifts and talents of elderly people: The persimmon's promise. In F. D. Horowitz, R. F. Subotnik, & D. J. Matthews (Eds.), *The development of giftedness and talent across the life span* (pp. 171–185). Washington, DC: American Psychological Association.

Bjelakovic, G., Nikolova, D., & Gluud, C. (2013). Antioxidant supplements to prevent mortality. *JAMA, 310,* 1178–1179.

Bjorklund, D. F. (2012). *Children's thinking* (5th ed.). Belmont, CA: Wadsworth Cengage Learning.

Bjorklund, D. F., Causey, K., & Periss, V. (2009). The evolution and development of human social cognition. In P. Kappeler & J. Silk (Eds.), *Mind the gap: Racing the origins of human universals* (pp. 351–371). Berlin: Springer Verlag.

Bjorklund, D. F., Schneider, W., Cassel, W. S., & Ashley, E. (1994). Training and extension of a memory strategy: Evidence for utilization deficiencies in high- and low-IQ children. *Child Development, 65*, 951–965.

Black, M. C. (2011). Intimate partner violence and adverse health consequences: Implications for clinicians. *American Journal of Lifestyle Medicine, 5*, 428–439.

Black, M. C., Basile, K. C., Breiding, M. J., Smith, S. G., Walters, M. L., Merrick, M. T., et al. (2011). *The National Intimate Partner and Sexual Violence Survey: 2010 summary report.* Atlanta, GA: Centers for Disease Control and Prevention. Retrieved from www.cdc.gov/violenceprevention/pdf/nisvs_executive_summary-a.pdf

Black, R. E., Victora, C. G., Walker, S. P., Bhutta, Z. A., Christian, P., de Onis, M., et al. (2013). Maternal and child undernutrition and overweight in low-income and middle-income countries. *Lancet, 382*, 427–451.

Black, R. E., Williams, S. M., Jones, I. E., & Goulding, A. (2002). Children who avoid drinking cow milk have low dietary calcium intakes and poor bone health. *American Journal of Clinical Nutrition, 76*, 675–680.

Blackwell, R., Moscovis, S., Hall, S., Burns, C., & Scott, R. J. (2015). Exploring the risk factors for sudden infant deaths and their role in inflammatory responses to infection. *Frontiers in Immunology, 6*(44), 1–8.

Blair, B. L., Perry, N. B., O'Brien, M., Calkins, S. D., Keane, S. P., & Shanahan, L. (2014). The indirect effects of maternal emotion socialization on friendship quality in middle childhood. *Developmental Psychology, 50*, 566–576.

Blair, C., Grander, D. A., Willoughby, M., Mills-Koonce, R., Cox, M., Greenberg, M. T., et al. (2011). Salivary cortisol mediates effects of poverty and parenting on executive functions in early childhood. *Child Development, 82*, 1970–1984.

Blair, C., & Raver, C. C. (2012). Child development in the context of adversity: Experiential canalization of brain and behavior. *American Psychologist, 67*, 309–318.

Blair, C., & Razza, R. P. (2007). Relating effortful control, executive function, and false belief understanding to emerging math and literacy ability in kindergarten. *Developmental Psychology, 78*, 647–663.

Blake, A. B., & Castel, A. D. (2016). Metamemory. In S. K. Whitbourne (Ed.), *Encyclopedia of adulthood and aging* (Vol. 2, pp. 903–907). Hoboken, NJ: Wiley Blackwell.

Blakemore, J. E. O. (2003). Children's beliefs about violating gender norms: Boys shouldn't look like girls, and girls shouldn't act like boys. *Sex Roles, 48*, 411–419.

Blakemore, J. E. O., Berenbaum, S. A., & Liben, L. S. (2009). *Gender development.* New York: Psychology Press.

Blakemore, J. E. O., & Hill, C. A. (2008). The Child Gender Socialization Scale: A measure to compare traditional and feminist parents. *Sex Roles, 58*, 192–207.

Blakemore, S.-J. (2012). Imaging brain development: The adolescent brain. *NeuroImage, 61*, 397–406.

Blanchard-Fields, F. (2007). Everyday problem solving and emotion: An adult developmental perspective. *Current Directions in Psychological Science, 16*, 26–31.

Blanchard-Fields, F., & Coats, A. H. (2008). The experience of anger and sadness in everyday problems impacts age differences in emotion regulation. *Developmental Psychology, 44*, 1547–1556.

Blasi, A. (1994). Moral identity: Its role in moral functioning. In B. Puka (Ed.), *Fundamental research in moral development: A compendium* (Vol. 2, pp. 123–167). New York: Garland.

Blasi, C. H., & Bjorklund, D. F. (2003). Evolutionary developmental psychology: A new tool for better understanding human ontogeny. *Human Development, 46*, 259–281.

Blass, E. M., Ganchrow, J. R., & Steiner, J. E. (1984). Classical conditioning in newborn humans 2–48 hours of age. *Infant Behavior and Development, 7*, 223–235.

Blatteis, C. M. (2012). Age-dependent changes in temperature regulation—a mini review. *Gerontology, 58*, 289–295.

Blau, D., & Goldstein, R. (2007). *What explains trends in labor force participation of older men in the United States?* Discussion Paper No. 2991. Bonn, Germany: Institute for the Study of Labor.

Bleske, A. L., & Buss, D. M. (2000). Can men and women be just friends? *Personal Relationships, 7*, 131–151.

Blieszner, R., & Roberto, K. A. (2012). Partners and friends in adulthood. In S. K. Whitbourne & M. J. Sliwinski (Eds.), *The Wiley-Blackwell handbook of adulthood and aging* (pp. 381–398). Malden, MA: Wiley-Blackwell.

Block, C. C. (2012). Proven and promising reading instruction. In J. S. Carlson & J. R. Levin (Eds.), *Instructional strategies for improving students' learning* (pp. 3–41). Charlotte, NC: Information Age Publishing.

Block, J. (2011). The five-factor framing of personality and beyond: Some ruminations. *Psychological Inquiry, 21*, 2–25.

Blondell, S. J., Hammersley-Mather, R., & Veerman, J. L. (2014). Does physical activity prevent cognitive decline and dementia? A systematic review and meta-analysis of longitudinal studies. *BMC Public Health, 14*, 510.

Blood-Siegfried, J. (2009). The role of infection and inflammation in sudden infant death syndrome. *Immunopharmacology and Immunotoxicology, 31*, 516–523.

Bloom, L. (2000). The intentionality model of language development: How to learn a word, any word. In R. Golinkoff, K. Hirsh-Pasek, N. Akhtar, L. Bloom, G. Hollich, L. Smith, M. Tomasello, & A. Woodward (Eds.), *Becoming a word learner: A debate on lexical acquisition.* New York: Oxford University Press.

Bloom, T., Glass, N., Curry, M. A., Hernandez, R., & Houck, G. (2013). Maternal stress exposures, reactions, and priorities for stress reduction among low-income, urban women. *Journal of Midwifery and Women's Health, 58*, 167–174.

Bluck, S., Dirk, J., Mackay, M. M., & Hux, A. (2008). Life experience with death: Relation to death attitudes and to the use of death-related memories. *Death Studies, 32*, 524–549.

Bluebond-Langner, M. (1977). Meanings of death to children. In H. Feifel (Ed.), *New meanings of death* (pp. 47–66). New York: McGraw-Hill.

Blumenfeld, P. C., Marx, R. W., & Harris, C. J. (2006). Learning environments. In K. A. Renninger & I. E. Sigel (Eds.), *Handbook of child psychology: Vol. 4. Child psychology in practice* (6th ed., pp. 297–342). Hoboken, NJ: Wiley.

Blumenthal, H., Leen-Feldner, E. W., Babson, K. A., Gahr, J. L., Trainor, C. D., & Frala, J. L. (2011). Elevated social anxiety among early maturing girls. *Developmental Psychology, 47*, 1133–1140.

Bodell, L. P., Joiner, T. F., & Keel, P. K. (2013). Comorbidity-independent risk for suicidality increases with bulimia nervosa but not anorexia nervosa. *Journal of Psychiatric Research, 47*, 617–621.

Bodner, E., Shrira, A., Bergman, Y. S., & Cohen-Fridel, S. (2015). Anxieties about aging and death and psychological distress. The protective role of emotional complexity. *Personality and Individual Differences, 83*, 91–96.

Bodrova, E., & Leong, D. J. (2007). *Tools of the mind: The Vygotskian approach to early childhood education* (2nd ed.). Upper Saddle River, NJ: Merrill/Prentice Hall.

Boerner, K., Jopp, D. S., Carr, D., Sosinsky, L., & Kim, S.-K. (2014). "His" and "her" marriage? The role of positive and negative marital characteristics in global marital satisfaction among older adults. *Journals of Gerontology, 69*, 579–589.

Bogaert, A. F., & Skorska, M. (2011). Sexual orientation, fraternal birth order, and the maternal immune hypothesis: A review. *Frontiers in Neuroendocrinology, 32*, 247–254.

Bogin, B. (2001). *The growth of humanity.* New York: Wiley-Liss.

Bohannon, J. N., III, & Bonvillian, J. D. (2013). Theoretical approaches to language acquisition. In J. B. Gleason & N. B. Ratner (Eds.), *The development of language* (8th ed., pp. 190–240). Upper Saddle River, NJ: Pearson.

Bohannon, J. N., III, & Stanowicz, L. (1988). The issue of negative evidence: Adult responses to children's language errors. *Developmental Psychology, 24*, 684–689.

Bolisetty, S., Bajuk, B., Me, A.-L., Vincent, T., Sutton, L., & Lui, K. (2006). Preterm outcome table (POT): A simple tool to aid counselling parents of very preterm infants. *Australian and New Zealand Journal of Obstetrics and Gynaecology, 46*, 189–192.

Bolkan, C., & Hooker, K. (2012). Self-regulation and social cognition in adulthood: The gyroscope of personality. In S. K. Whitbourne & M. J. Sliwinski (Eds.), *Wiley-Blackwell handbook of adulthood and aging* (pp. 357–380). Malden, MA: Wiley-Blackwell.

Bonanno, G. A. (2004). Loss, trauma, and human resilience. *American Psychologist, 59*, 20–28.

Bonanno, G. A., Westphal, M., & Mancini, A. D. (2011). Resilience to loss and potential trauma. *Annual Review of Clinical Psychology, 7*, 511–535.

Bonanno, G. A., Wortman, C. B., Lehman, D. R., Tweed, R. G., Haring, M., Sonnega, J., et al. (2002). Resilience to loss and chronic grief: A prospective study from preloss to 18-months postloss. *Journal of Personality and Social Psychology, 83*, 260–271.

Bookman, A., & Kimbrel, D. (2011). Families and elder care in the twenty-first century. *Future of Children, 21*, 117–140.

Boom, J., Wouters, H., & Keller, M. (2007). A cross-cultural validation of stage development: A Rasch re-analysis of longitudinal socio-moral reasoning data. *Cognitive Development, 22*, 213–229.

Booren, L. M., Downer, J. T., & Vitiello, V. E. (2012). Observations of children's interactions with teachers, peers, and tasks across preschool classroom activity settings. *Early Education and Development, 23*, 517–538.

Booth, A., Scott, M. E., & King, V. (2010). Father residence and adolescent problem behavior: Are youth always better off in two-parent families? *Journal of Family Issues, 31*, 585–605.

Booth, R. D. L., & Happé, F. G. E. (2016). Evidence of reduced global processing in autism spectrum disorder. *Journal of Autism and Developmental Disorders, 46*, ISSN 1573-3472.

Booth-LaForce, C., Groh, A. M., Burchinal, M. R., Roisman, G. I., Owen, M. T., & Cox, M. J. (2014). Caregiving and contextual sources of continuity and change in attachment security from infancy to late adolescence. In C. Booth-LaForce & G. I. Roisman (Eds.), *The Adult Attachment Interview: Psychometrics, stability and change from infancy, and developmental origins. Monographs of the Society for Research in Child Development, 79*(3, Serial No. 314), 67–84.

Borchert, S., Lamm, B., Graf, F., & Knopf, M. (2013). Deferred imitation in 18-month-olds from two cultural contexts: The case of Cameroonian Nso farmer and German-middle class infants. *Infant Behavior and Development, 36,* 717–727.

Borghese, M. M., Tremblay, M. S., Katzmarzyk, P. T., Tudor-Locke, C., Schuna, J. M., Jr., Leduc, G., et al. (2015). Mediating role of television time, diet patterns, physical activity and sleep duration in the association between television in the bedroom and adiposity in 10-year-old children. *International Journal of Behavioral Nutrition and Physical Activity, 12,* Article ID 60.

Bornstein, M. H. (2015). Children's parents. In M. H. Bornstein & T. Leventhal (Eds.), *Handbook of child psychology and developmental science: Vol. 4. Ecological settings and processes* (7th ed., pp. 55–132). Hoboken, NJ: Wiley.

Bornstein, M. H., & Arterberry, M. E. (1999). Perceptual development. In M. H. Bornstein & M. E. Lamb (Eds.), *Developmental psychology: An advanced textbook* (pp. 231–274). Mahwah, NJ: Erlbaum.

Bornstein, M. H., & Arterberry, M. E. (2003). Recognition, discrimination, and categorization of smiling by 5-month-old infants. *Developmental Science, 6,* 585–599.

Bornstein, M. H., Arterberry, M. E., & Mash, C. (2010). Infant object categorization transcends object–context relations. *Infant Behavior and Development, 33,* 7–15.

Bornstein, M. H., Vibbert, M., Tal, J., & O'Donnell, K. (1992). Toddler language and play in the second year: Stability, covariation, and influences of parenting. *First Language, 12,* 323–338.

Borst, C. G. (1995). *Catching babies: The professionalization of childbirth, 1870–1920.* Cambridge, MA: Harvard University Press.

Borst, G., Poirel, N., Pineau, A., Cassotti, M., & Houdé, O. (2013). Inhibitory control efficiency in a Piaget-like class-inclusion task in school-age children and adults: A developmental negative priming study. *Developmental Psychology, 49,* 1366–1374.

Bos, H. (2013). Lesbian-mother families formed through donor insemination. In A. E. Goldberg & K. R. Allen (Eds.), *LGBT-parent families: Innovations in research and implications for practice* (pp. 21–37). New York: Springer.

Bos, H. M. W., & Sandfort, T. G. M. (2010). Children's gender identity in lesbian and heterosexual two-parent families. *Sex Roles, 62,* 114–126.

Bos, H. M. W., van Balen, F., & van den Boom, D. C. (2004). Experience of parenthood, couple relationship, social support, and child-rearing goals in planned lesbian mother families. *Journal of Child Psychology and Psychiatry, 25,* 755–764.

Bost, K. K., Shin, N., McBride, B. A., Brown, G. L., Vaughn, B. E., & Coppola, G. (2006). Maternal secure base scripts, children's attachment security, and mother–child narrative styles. *Attachment and Human Development, 8,* 241–260.

Boswell, G. H., Kahana, E., & Dilworth-Anderson, P. (2006). Spirituality and healthy lifestyle behaviors: Stress counter-balancing effects on the well-being of older adults. *Journal of Religion and Health, 45,* 587–602.

Boswell, H. (2014). Normal pubertal physiology in females. In J. E. Dietrich (Ed.), *Female puberty: A comprehensive guide for clinicians* (pp. 7–30). New York: Springer.

Bouazzaoui, B., Follenfant, A., Ric, F., Fay, S., Croizet, J.-C., Atzeni, T., & Taconnat, L. (2015). Ageing-related stereotypes in memory: When the beliefs come true. *Memory, 24,* 659–668.

Bouchard, T. J. (2004). Genetic influence on human psychological traits: A survey. *Current Directions in Psychological Science, 13,* 148–151.

Boucher, O., Bastien, C. H., Saint-Amour, D., Dewailly, E., Ayotte, P., Jacobson, J. L., Jacobson, et al. (2010). Prenatal exposure to methylmercury and PCBs affects distinct stages of information processing: An event-related potential study with Inuit children. *Neurotoxicology, 31,* 373–384.

Boucher, O., Jacobson, S. W., Plusquellec, P., Dewailly, E., Ayotte, P., Forget-Dubois, N., et al. (2012). Prenatal methylmercury, postnatal lead exposure, and evidence of attention deficit/hyperactivity disorder among Inuit children in Arctic Québec. *Environmental Health Perspectives, 120,* 1456–1461.

Boucher, O., Muckle, G., & Bastien, C. H. (2009). Prenatal exposure to polychlorinated biphenyls: A neuropsychologic analysis. *Environmental Health Perspectives, 117,* 7–16.

Bouldin, P. (2006). An investigation of the fantasy predisposition and fantasy style of children with imaginary companions. *Journal of Genetic Psychology, 167,* 17–29.

Bourassa, K. J., Sbarra, D. A., & Whisman, M. A. (2015). Women in very low quality marriages gain life satisfaction following divorce. *Journal of Family Psychology, 29,* 490–499.

Boutwell, B. B., Franklin, C. A., Barnes, J. C., & Beaver, K. M. (2011). Physical punishment and childhood aggression: The role of gender and gene–environment interplay. *Aggressive Behavior, 37,* 559–568.

Bowen, C. E., Noack, M. G., & Staudinger, U. M. (2011). Aging in the work context. In K. W. Schaie & S. L. Willis (Eds.), *Handbook of the psychology of aging* (7th ed., pp. 263–277). San Diego, CA: Academic Press.

Bowlby, J. (1969). *Attachment and loss: Vol. 1. Attachment.* New York: Basic Books.

Bowlby, J. (1980). *Attachment and loss: Vol. 3. Loss: Sadness and depression.* New York: Basic Books.

Bowman, N. A. (2011a). College diversity experiences and cognitive development: A meta-analysis. *Review of Educational Research, 80,* 4–33.

Bowman, N. A. (2011b). Promoting participation in a diverse democracy: A meta-analysis of college diversity experiences and civic engagement. *Review of Educational Research, 81,* 29–68.

Boyatzis, C. J. (2000). The artistic evolution of mommy: A longitudinal case study of symbolic and social processes. In C. J. Boyatzis & M. W. Watson (Eds.), *Symbolic and social constraints on the development of children's artistic style* (pp. 5–29). San Francisco: Jossey-Bass.

Boyd-Franklin, N. (2006). *Black families in therapy* (2nd ed.). New York: Guilford.

Boyle, C. A., Boulet, S., Schieve, L. A., Cohen, R. A., Blumberg, S. J., Yeargin-Allsopp, M., et al. (2011). Trends in the prevalence of developmental disabilities in U.S. children, 1997–2008. *Pediatrics, 127,* 1034–1042.

Boynton-Jarrett, R., Wright, R. J., Putnam, F. W., Lividoti Hibert, E., Michels, K. B., Forman, M. R., & Rich-Edwards, J. (2013). Child abuse and age at menarche. *Journal of Adolescent Health, 52,* 241–247.

Boysson-Bardies, B. de, & Vihman, M. M. (1991). Adaptation to language: Evidence from babbling and first words in four languages. *Language, 67,* 297–319.

Bozionelos, N., Bozionelos, G., Kostopoulos, K., & Polychroniou, P. (2011). How providing mentoring relates to career success and organizational commitment: A study in the general managerial population. *Career Development International, 16,* 446–468.

Bracken, B. A., & Nagle, R. J. (2006). *Psychoeducational assessment of preschool children.* New York: Routledge.

Brackett, M. A., Rivers, S. E., & Salovey, P. (2011). Emotional intelligence: Implications for personal, social, academic, and workplace success. *Social and Personality Compass, 5,* 88–103.

Bradley, R. H. (1994). The HOME Inventory: Review and reflections. In H. W. Reese (Ed.), *Advances in child development and behavior* (Vol. 25, pp. 241–288). San Diego, CA: Academic Press.

Bradley, R. H., & Caldwell, B. M. (1982). The consistency of the home environment and its relation to child development. *International Journal of Behavioral Development, 5,* 445–465.

Bradley, R. H., Corwyn, R. F., McAdoo, H. P., & Garcia-Coll, C. (2001). The home environments of children in the United States. Part I: Variations by age, ethnicity, and poverty status. *Child Development, 72,* 1844–1867.

Bradley, R. H., Whiteside, L., Mundfrom, D. J., Casey, P. H., Kelleher, K. J., & Pope, S. K. (1994). Early indications of resilience and their relation to experiences in the home environments of low birthweight, premature children living in poverty. *Child Development, 65,* 346–360.

Brady, K. T., & Lawson, K. M. (2012). Substance use disorders in women throughout the lifespan. In N. Rowe (Ed.), *Clinical updates in women's health care.* Washington, DC: American College of Obstetricians and Gynecologists.

Brady, S. A. (2011). Efficacy of phonics teaching for reading outcomes: Indications from post-NRP research. In S. A. Brady, D. Braze, & C. A. Fowler (Eds.), *Explaining individual differences in reading: Theory and evidence* (pp. 69–96). New York: Psychology Press.

Braine, L. G., Schauble, L., Kugelmass, S., & Winter, A. (1993). Representation of depth by children: Spatial strategies and lateral biases. *Developmental Psychology, 29,* 466–479.

Brainerd, C. J. (2003). Jean Piaget, learning, research, and American education. In B. J. Zimmerman (Ed.), *Educational psychology: A century of contributions* (pp. 251–287). Mahwah, NJ: Erlbaum.

Brand, S., Gerber, M., Beck, J., Hatzinger, M., Puhse, U., & Holsboer-Trachsler, E. (2010). High exercise levels are related to favorable sleep and psychological functioning in adolescence: A comparison of athletes and controls. *Journal of Adolescent Health, 46,* 133–141.

Brand, S. R., Schechter, J. C., Hammen, C. L., Brocque, R. L., & Brennan, P. A. (2011). Do adolescent offspring of women with PTSD experience higher levels of chronic and episodic stress? *Journal of Trauma and Stress, 24,* 399–404.

Braswell, G. S. (2006). Sociocultural contexts for the early development of semiotic production. *Psychological Bulletin, 132,* 877–894.

Braswell, G. S., & Callanan, M. A. (2003). Learning to draw recognizable graphic representations during mother–child interactions. *Merrill-Palmer Quarterly, 49,* 471–494.

Braungart-Rieker, J. M., Hill-Soderlund, A. L., & Karrass, J. (2010). Fear and anger reactivity trajectories from 4 to 16 months: The roles of temperament, regulation, and maternal sensitivity. *Developmental Psychology, 46,* 791–804.

Braver, S. L., & Lamb, M. E. (2013). Marital dissolution. In G. W. Peterson & K. R. Bush (Eds.), *Handbook of marriage and the family* (3rd ed., pp. 487–516). New York: Springer Science+Business Media.

Brazelton, T. B., Koslowski, B., & Tronick, E. (1976). Neonatal behavior among urban Zambians and Americans. *Journal of the American Academy of Child Psychiatry, 15,* 97–107.

Brazelton, T. B., & Nugent, J. K. (2011). *Neonatal Behavioral Assessment Scale* (4th ed.). London: Mac Keith Press.

Brazelton, T. B., Nugent, J. K., & Lester, B. M. (1987). Neonatal Behavioral Assessment Scale. In J. D. Osofsky (Ed.), *Handbook of infant development* (2nd ed., pp. 780–817). New York: Wiley.

Bregman, H. R., Malik, N. M., Page, M. J. L., Makynen, E., & Lindahl, K. M. (2013). Identity profiles in lesbian, gay, and bisexual youth: The role of family influences. *Journal of Youth and Adolescence, 42,* 417–430.

Brehmer, Y., Westerberg, H., & Bäckman, L. (2012). Working-memory training in younger and older adults: Training gains, transfer, and maintenance. *Frontiers in Human Neuroscience, 6,* 63.

Bremner, J. G. (2010). Cognitive development: Knowledge of the physical world. In J. G. Bremner

& T. D. Wachs (Eds.), *Wiley-Blackwell handbook of infant development: Vol. 1. Basic research* (2nd ed., pp. 204–242). Oxford, UK: Wiley-Blackwell.

Bremner, J. G., Slater, A. M., & Johnson, S. P. (2015). Perception of object persistence: The origins of object permanence in infancy. *Child Development Perspectives, 9,* 7–13.

Brendgen, M., Boivin, M., Dionne, G., Barker, E. D., Vitaro, F., Girard, A., et al. (2011). Gene–environment processes linking aggression, peer victimization, and the teacher–child relationship. *Child Development, 82,* 2021–2036.

Brendgen, M., Markiewicz, D., Doyle, A. B., & Bukowski, W. M. (2001). The relations between friendship quality, ranked-friendship preference, and adolescents' behavior with their friends. *Merrill-Palmer Quarterly, 47,* 395–415.

Brennan, L. M., Shelleby, E. C., Shaw, D. S., Gardner, F., Dishion, T. J., & Wilson, M. (2013). Indirect effects of the family check-up on school-age academic achievement through improvements in parenting in early childhood. *Journal of Educational Psychology, 105,* 762–773.

Brennan, W. M., Ames, E. W., & Moore, R. W. (1966). Age differences in infants' attention to patterns of different complexities. *Science, 151,* 354–356.

Brenner, E., & Salovey, P. (1997). Emotional regulation during childhood: Developmental, interpersonal, and individual considerations. In P. Salovey & D. Sluyter (Eds.), *Emotional literacy and emotional development* (pp. 168–192). New York: Basic Books.

Brent, S. B., Speece, M. W., Lin, C., Dong, Q., & Yang, C. (1996). The development of the concept of death among Chinese and U.S. children 3–17 years of age: From binary to "fuzzy" concepts? *Omega, 33,* 67–83.

Breslau, N., Kessler, R. C., Chilcoat, H. D., Schultz, L. R., Davis, G. C., & Andreski, P. (1998). Trauma and posttraumatic stress disorder in the community: The 1996 Detroit Area Survey of Trauma. *Archives of General Psychiatry, 55,* 626–632.

Bretherton, I., & Munholland, K. A. (2008). Internal working models in attachment relationships. In J. Cassidy & P. R. Shaver (Eds.), *Handbook of attachment: Theory, research, and clinical applications* (2nd ed., pp. 102–127). New York: Guilford.

Brewster, K. L., Tillman, K. H., & Jokinen-Gordon, H. (2014). Demographic characteristics of lesbian parents in the United States. *Population Research and Policy Review, 33,* 485–502.

Bridgett, D. J., Gartstein, M. A., Putnam, S. P., McKay, T., Iddins, R., Robertson, C., et al. (2009). Maternal and contextual influences and the effect of temperament development during infancy on parenting in toddlerhood. *Infant Behavior and Development, 32,* 103–116.

Bright, G. M., Mendoza, J. R., & Rosenfeld, R. G. (2009). Recombinant human insulin-like growth factor-1 treatment: Ready for primetime. *Endocrinology and Metabolism Clinics of North America, 38,* 625–638.

Brint, S., & Cantwell, A. M. (2010). Undergraduate time use and academic outcomes: Results from the University of California Undergraduate Experience Survey 2006. *Teachers College Record, 112,* 2441–2470.

Brisch, K. H., Bechinger, D., Betzler, S., Heineman, H., Kachele, H., Pohlandt, F., Schmucker, G., & Buchheim, A. (2005). Attachment quality in very low-birth-weight premature infants in relation to maternal attachment representations and neurological development. *Parenting: Science and Practice, 5,* 11–32.

Broadhead, G. K., Grigg, J. R., Chang, A. A., & McCluskey, P. (2015). Dietary modification and supplementation for the treatment of age-related macular degeneration. *Nutrition Reviews, 73,* 448–462.

Brodaty, H., Seeher, K., & Gibson, L. (2012). Dementia time to death: A systematic literature review on survival time and years of life lost in people with dementia. *International Psychogeriatrics, 24,* 1034–1045.

Brody, G. H., Beach, S. R. H., Philibert, R. A., Chen, Y., & Murry, V. M. (2009). Prevention effects moderate the association of 5-HTTLPR and youth risk behavior initiation: Gene x environment hypotheses tested via a randomized preventive design. *Child Development, 80,* 645–661.

Brody, G. H., Chen, Y., Beach, S. R. H., Kogan, S. M., Yu, T., DiClemente, R. J., et al. (2014). Differential sensitivity to prevention programming: A dopaminergic polymorphism-enhanced prevention effect on protective parenting and adolescent substance use. *Health Psychology, 33,* 182–191.

Brody, G. H., & Murry, V. M. (2001). Sibling socialization of competence in rural, single-parent African American families. *Journal of Marriage and Family, 63,* 996–1008.

Brody, G. H., Stoneman, Z., & McCoy, J. K. (1994). Forecasting sibling relationships in early adolescence from child temperaments and family processes in middle childhood. *Child Development, 65,* 771–784.

Brody, L. (1999). *Gender, emotion, and the family.* Cambridge, MA: Harvard University Press.

Brodzinsky, D. M. (2011). Children's understanding of adoption: Developmental and clinical implications. *Professional Psychology: Research and Practice, 42,* 200–207.

Broidy, L. M., Nagin, D. S., Tremblay, R. E., Bates, J. E., Brame, B., Dodge, K. A., et al. (2003). Developmental trajectories of childhood disruptive behaviors and adolescent delinquency: A six-site, cross-national study. *Developmental Psychology, 39,* 222–245.

Bromberger, J. T., Kravitz, H. M., Chang, Y. F., Cyranowski, J. M., Brown, C., & Matthews, K. A. (2011). Major depression during and after the menopausal transition: Study of Women's Health Across the Nation (SWAN). *Psychological Medicine, 41,* 1897–1898.

Bronfenbrenner, U., & Morris, P. A. (2006). The bioecological model of human development. In R. M. Lerner (Ed.), *Handbook of child psychology: Vol. 1. Theoretical models of human development* (6th ed., pp. 297–342). Hoboken, NJ: Wiley.

Bronson, G. W. (1994). Infants' transitions toward adult-like scanning. *Child Development, 65,* 1243–1261.

Brook, J. S., Lee, J. Y., & Brook, D. W. (2015). Trajectories of marijuana use beginning in adolescence predict tobacco dependence in adulthood. *Substance Abuse, 36,* 470–477.

Brooker, R. J., Buss, K. A., Lemery-Chalfant, K., Aksan, N., Davidson, R. J., & Goldsmith, H. H. (2013). The development of stranger fear in infancy and toddlerhood: Normative development, individual differences, antecedents, and outcomes. *Developmental Science, 16,* 864–878.

Brooks, R., & Meltzoff, A. N. (2005). The development of gaze following and its relation to language. *Developmental Science, 8,* 535–543.

Brooks-Gunn, J. (1988). Antecedents and consequences of variations in girls' maturational timing. *Journal of Adolescent Health Care, 9,* 365–373.

Brooks-Gunn, J., Han, W.-J., & Waldfogel, J. (2010). First-year maternal employment and child development in the first 7 years. *Monographs of the Society for Research in Child Development, 75*(No. 2, Serial No. 296), 59–69.

Brooks-Gunn, J., Klebanov, P. K., Smith, J., Duncan, G. J., & Lee, K. (2003). The black–white test score gap in young children. Contributions of test and family characteristics. *Applied Developmental Science, 7,* 239–252.

Brown, A., & Harries, V. (2015). Infant sleep and night feeding patterns during later infancy: Association with breastfeeding frequency, daytime complementary food intake, and infant weight. *Breastfeeding Medicine, 10,* 246–252.

Brown, A. M., & Miracle, J. A. (2003). Early binocular vision in human infants: Limitations on the generality of the superposition hypothesis. *Vision Research, 43,* 1563–1574.

Brown, B. B., & Dietz, E. L. (2009). Informal peer groups in middle childhood and adolescence. In K. H. Rubin, W. M. Bukowski, & B. Laursen (Eds.), *Handbook of peer interactions, relationships, and groups* (pp. 361–376). New York: Guilford Press.

Brown, B. B., Herman, M., Hamm, J. V., & Heck, D. (2008). Ethnicity and image: Correlates of minority adolescents' affiliation with individual-based versus ethnically defined peer crowds. *Child Development, 79,* 529–546.

Brown, B. B., & Larson, J. (2009). Peer relationships in adolescence. In R. M. Lerner & L. Steinberg (Eds.), *Handbook of adolescent psychology* (3rd ed., pp. 74–103). New York: Wiley.

Brown, C., & Lowis, M. J. (2003). Psychosocial development in the elderly: An investigation into Erikson's ninth stage. *Journal of Aging Studies, 17,* 415–426.

Brown, C. A. (2016a). Successful aging. In S. K. Whitbourne (Ed.), *Encyclopedia of adulthood and aging* (Vol. 3, pp. 1377–1381). Malden, MA: Wiley Blackwell.

Brown, C. S., & Bigler, R. S. (2004). Children's perceptions of gender discrimination. *Developmental Psychology, 40,* 714–726.

Brown, E. R. (2016b). Possible selves. In S. K. Whitbourne (Ed.), *Encyclopedia of adulthood and aging* (Vol. 3, pp. 1114–1118). Malden, MA: Wiley Blackwell.

Brown, G. L., Mangelsdorf, S. C., & Neff, C. (2012). Father involvement, paternal sensitivity, and father–child attachment security in the first 3 years. *Journal of Family Psychology, 26,* 421–430.

Brown, G. L., Schoppe-Sullivan, S. J., Mangelsdorf, S. C., & Neff, C. (2010). Observed and reported supportive coparenting as predictors of infant–mother and infant–father attachment security. *Early Child Development and Care, 180,* 121–137.

Brown, J. A., Rowles, G. D., & McIlwain, A. S. (2016). Environmental design and assistive technologies. In G. D. Rowles & P. B. Teaster (Eds.), *Long-term care in an aging society: Theory and practice* (pp. 205–229). New York: Springer.

Brown, J. D., Harris, S. K., Woods, E. R., Buman, M. P., & Cox, J. E. (2012). Longitudinal study of depressive symptoms and social support in adolescent mothers. *Maternal and Child Health Journal, 16,* 894–901.

Brown, J. D., & L'Engle, K. L. (2009). X-rated: Attitudes and behaviors associated with U.S. early adolescents' exposure to sexually explicit media. *Communication Research, 36,* 129–151.

Brown, L. H., & Rodin, P. A. (2004). Grandparent–grandchild relationships and the life course perspective. In J. Demick & C. Andreoletti (Eds.), *Handbook of adult development* (pp. 459–474). New York: Springer.

Brown, R. M., & Brown, S. L. (2014). Informal caregiving: A reappraisal of effects on caregivers. *Social Issues and Policy Review, 8,* 74–102.

Brown, R. W. (1973). *A first language: The early stages.* Cambridge, MA: Harvard University Press.

Brown, S. A., & Ramo, D. E. (2005). Clinical course of youth following treatment for alcohol and drug problems. In H. A. Liddle & C. L. Rowe (Eds.), *Adolescent substance abuse: Research and clinical advances* (pp. 79–103). Cambridge, UK: Cambridge University Press.

Brown, S. L., Bulanda, J. R., & Lee, G. R. (2012). Transitions into and out of cohabitation in later life. *Journal of Marriage and Family, 74,* 774–793.

Brown, S. L., & Kawamura, S. (2010). Relationships quality among cohabitors and marrieds in older adulthood. *Social Science Research, 39,* 777–786.

Brown, S. L., & Lin, I.-F. (2012). *Divorce in middle and later life: New estimates from the 2009 American*

Community Survey. Bowling Green, OH: Center for Family and Demographic Research, Bowling Green University.

Brown, S. L., & Lin, I.-F. (2013). *The gray divorce revolution: Rising divorce among middle-aged and older adults, 1990–2010.* Bowling Green, OH: National Center for Family & Marriage Research, Bowling Green University.

Brown, S. L., Nesse, R. M., Vinokur, A. D., & Smith, D. M. (2003). Providing social support may be more beneficial than receiving it: Results from a prospective study of mortality. *Psychological Science, 14,* 320–327.

Brown, S. L., & Shinohara, S. K. (2013). Dating relationships in older adulthood: A national portrait. *Journal of Marriage and Family, 75,* 1194–1202.

Brown, T. M., & Rodriguez, L. F. (2009). School and the co-construction of dropout. *International Journal of Qualitative Studies in Education, 22,* 221–242.

Browne, J. V., & Talmi, A. (2005). Family-based intervention to enhance infant–parent relationships in the neonatal intensive care unit. *Journal of Pediatric Psychology, 30,* 667–677.

Brownell, C. A., Zerwas, S., & Ramani, G. B. (2007). "So big": The development of body self-awareness in toddlers. *Child Development, 78,* 1426–1440.

Brownell, M. D., Nickel, N. C., Chateau, D., Martens, P. J., Taylor, C., Crockett, L., et al. (2015). Long-term benefits of full-day kindergarten: A longitudinal study. *Early Child Development and Care, 185,* 291–316.

Brucker, E., & Leppel, K. (2013). Retirement plans: Planners and nonplanners. *Educational Gerontology, 39,* 1–11.

Bruine de Bruin, W. (2012). Judgment and decision making in adolescents. In M. Dhami, A. Schlottmann, & M. R. Waldmann (Eds.), *Judgment and decision-making as a skill: Learning, development, and evolution* (pp. 85–111). New York: Cambridge University Press.

Brumariu, L. E., Kerns, K. A., & Seibert, A. (2012). Mother–child attachment, emotion regulation, and anxiety symptoms in middle childhood. *Personal Relationships, 19,* 569–585.

Brummelman, E., Thomaes, S., Overbeek, G., Orobio de Castro, B., van den Hout, M. A., & Bushman, B. J. (2014). On feeding those hungry for praise: Person praise backfires in children with low self-esteem. *Journal of Experimental Psychology: General, 143,* 9–14.

Bruschweiler-Stern, N. (2004). A multifocal neonatal intervention. In A. J. Sameroff, S. C. McDonough, & K. L. Rosenblum (Eds.), *Treating parent–infant relationship problems* (pp. 188–212). New York: Guilford.

Brussoni, M. J., & Boon, S. D. (1998). Grandparental impact in young adults' relationships with their closest grandparents: The role of relationship strength and emotional closeness. *International Journal of Aging and Human Development, 45,* 267–286.

Bruzzese, J.-M., & Fisher, C. B. (2003). Assessing and enhancing the research consent capacity of children and youth. *Applied Developmental Science, 7,* 13–26.

Bryan, A. E., & Dix, T. (2009). Mothers' emotions and behavioral support during interactions with toddlers: The role of child temperament. *Social Development, 18,* 647–670.

Bryant, B. K., Zvonkovic, A. M., & Reynolds, P. (2006). Parenting in relation to child and adolescent vocational development. *Journal of Vocational Behavior, 69,* 149–175.

Bryant, D. M., Hoeft, F., Lai, S., Lackey, J., Roeltgen, D., Ross, J., et al. (2012). Sex chromosomes and the brain: A study of neuroanatomy in XYY syndrome. *Developmental Medicine and Child Neurology, 54,* 1149–1156.

Bryant, N. B., & Gómez, R. L. (2015). The teen sleep loss epidemic: What can be done? *Translational Issues in Psychological Science, 1,* 115–125.

Bryant, P., & Nunes, T. (2002). Children's understanding of mathematics. In U. Goswami (Ed.), *Blackwell handbook of childhood cognitive development* (pp. 412–439). Malden, MA: Blackwell.

Brydges, C. R., Reid, C. L., Fox, A. M., & Anderson, M. (2012). A unitary executive function predicts intelligence in children. *Intelligence, 40,* 458–469.

Bryk, R. L., & Fisher, P. A. (2012). Training the brain: Practical applications of neural plasticity from the intersection of cognitive neuroscience, developmental psychology, and prevention science. *American Psychologist, 67,* 87–100.

Buchanan, C. M., Maccoby, E. E., & Dornbusch, S. M. (1996). *Adolescents after divorce.* Cambridge, MA: Harvard University Press.

Buchanan-Barrow, E., & Barrett, M. (1998). Children's rule discrimination within the context of the school. *British Journal of Developmental Psychology, 16,* 539–551.

Buchsbaum, D., Dridgers, S., Weisberg, D. S., & Gopnik, A. (2012). The power of possibility: Causal learning, counterfactual reasoning, and pretend play. *Philosophical Transactions of the Royal Society B, 367,* 2202–2212.

Buckingham-Howes, S., Berger, S. S., Scaletti, L. A., & Black, M. M. (2013). Systematic review of prenatal cocaine exposure and adolescent development. *Pediatrics, 131,* e1917–1936.

Buehler, C., & O'Brien, M. (2011). Mothers' part-time employment: Associations with mother and family well-being. *Journal of Family Psychology, 25,* 895–906.

Bugental, D. B., Corpuz, R., & Schwartz, A. (2012). Preventing children's aggression: Outcomes of an early intervention. *Developmental Psychology, 48,* 1443–1449.

Bugental, D. B., & Happaney, K. (2004). Predicting infant maltreatment in low-income families: The interactive effects of maternal attributions and child status at birth. *Developmental Psychology, 40,* 234–243.

Buhl, H. M., & Lanz, M. (2007). Emerging adulthood in Europe: Common traits and variability across five European countries. *Journal of Adolescent Research, 22,* 439–443.

Buhrmester, D., & Furman, W. (1990). Perceptions of sibling relationships during middle childhood and adolescence. *Child Development, 61,* 1387–1398.

Buhs, E. S., Ladd, G. W., & Herald-Brown, S. L. (2010). Victimization and exclusion: Links to peer rejection, classroom engagement, and achievement. In S. R. Jimerson, S. M. Swearer, & D. L. Espelage (Eds.), *Handbook of bullying in schools: An international perspective* (pp. 163–172). New York: Routledge.

Bukacha, C. M., Gauthier, S., & Tarr, M. J. (2006). Beyond faces and modularity: The power of an expertise framework. *Trends in Cognitive Sciences, 10,* 159–166.

Bunting, H., Drew, H., Lasseigne, A., & Anderson-Butcher, D. (2013). Enhancing parental involvement and family resources. In C. Franklin, M. B. Harris, & P. Allen-Meares (Eds.), *School services sourcebook: A guide for school-based professionals* (2nd ed., pp. 633–643). New York: Oxford University Press.

Burchinal, M., Kainz, K., & Cai, Y. (2011). How well do our measures of quality predict child outcomes? A meta-analysis and coordinated analysis of data from large-scale studies of early childhood settings. In M. Zeslow (Ed.), *Reasons to take stock and strengthen our measures of quality* (pp. 11–31). Baltimore, MD: Paul H. Brookes.

Burchinal, M., Magnuson, K., Powell, D., & Hong, S. S. (2015). Early childcare and education. In M. H. Bornstein & T. Leventhal (Eds.), *Handbook of child psychology and developmental science: Vol. 4. Ecological settings and processes* (7th ed., pp. 223–267). Hoboken, NJ: Wiley.

Burden, M. J., Jacobson, S. W., & Jacobson, J. L. (2005). Relation of prenatal alcohol exposure to cognitive processing speed and efficiency in childhood. *Alcoholism: Clinical and Experimental Research, 29,* 1473–1483.

Burgess-Champoux, T. L., Larson, N., Neumark-Sztainer, D., Hannan, P. J., & Story, M. (2009). Are family meal patterns associated with overall diet quality during the transition from early to middle adolescence? *Journal of Nutrition Education and Behavior, 41,* 79–86.

Burke, D. M., & Shafto, M. A. (2004). Aging and language production. *Current Directions in Psychological Science, 13,* 21–24.

Burleson, B. R., & Kunkel, A. W. (2006). Revisiting the different cultures thesis: An assessment of sex differences and similarities in communication. In K. Dindia & D. J. Canary (Eds.), *Sex differences and similarities in communication* (2nd ed., pp. 137–159). Mahwah, NJ: Erlbaum.

Burman, D. D., Bitan, T., & Booth, J. R. (2008). Sex differences in neural processing of language among children. *Neuropsychologia, 46,* 1349–1362.

Burts, D.C., Hart, C. H., Charlesworth, R., Fleege, P. O., Mosely, J., & Thomasson, R. H. (1992). Observed activities and stress behaviors of children in developmentally appropriate and inappropriate kindergarten classrooms. *Early Childhood Research Quarterly, 7,* 297–318.

Bush, K. R., & Peterson, G. W. (2008). Family influences on child development. In T. P. Gullotta & G. M. Blau (Eds.), *Handbook of child behavioral issues: Evidence-based approaches to prevention and treatment* (pp. 43–67). New York: Routledge.

Bushman, B. J., & Huesmann, L. R. (2012). Effects of violent media on aggression. In D. G. Singer & J. L. Singer (Eds.), *Handbook of children and the media* (2nd ed., pp. 231–248). Thousand Oaks, CA: Sage.

Bushnell, E. W., & Boudreau, J. P. (1993). Motor development and the mind: The potential role of motor abilities as a determinant of aspects of perceptual development. *Child Development, 64,* 1005–1021.

Buss, D. (2012). *Evolutionary psychology: The new science of the mind* (4th ed.). Upper Saddle River, NJ: Pearson.

Buss, D. M., Shackelford, T. K., Kirkpatrick, L. A., & Larsen, R. J. (2001). A half century of mate preferences: The cultural evolution of values. *Journal of Marriage and Family, 63,* 491–503.

Bussey, K. (1992). Lying and truthfulness: Children's definitions, standards, and evaluative reactions. *Child Development, 63,* 129–137.

Buswell, S. D., & Spatz, D. L. (2007). Parent–infant co-sleeping and its relationship to breastfeeding. *Journal of Pediatric Health Care, 21,* 22–28.

Butler, R. N. (1968). The life review: An interpretation of reminiscence in the aged. In B. Neugarten (Ed.), *Middle age and aging* (pp. 486–496). Chicago: University of Chicago Press.

Buttelmann, D., & Böhm, R. (2014). The ontogeny of the motivation that underlies in-group bias. *Psychological Science, 25,* 921–927.

Buttelmann, D., Over, H., Carpenter, M., & Tomasello, M. (2014). Eighteen-month-olds understand false beliefs in an unexpected-contents task. *Journal of Experimental Child Psychology, 119,* 120–126.

Butterworth, P., & Rodgers, B. (2006). Concordance in the mental health of spouses: Analysis of a large national household panel survey. *Psychological Medicine, 36,* 685–697.

Butts, M. M., Casper, W. J., & Yang, T. S. (2013). How important are work–family support policies? A meta-analytic investigation of their effects on employee outcomes. *Journal of Applied Psychology, 98,* 1–25.

Bybee, J. A., & Wells, Y. V. (2003). The development of possible selves during adulthood. In J. Demick & C. Andreoletti (Eds.), *Handbook of adult development* (pp. 257–270). New York: Springer.

Byne, W., Bradley, S. J., Coleman, E., Eyler, A. E., Green, R., Menvielle, E. J., et al. (2012). Report of the American Psychiatric Association Task Force on

Treatment of Gender Identity Disorder. *Archives of Sexual Behavior, 41,* 759–796.

Byrnes, J. P., & Wasik, B. A. (2009). *Language and literacy development: What educators need to know.* New York: Guilford.

C

Cabell, S. Q., Justice, L. M., Logan, J. A. R., & Konold, T. R. (2013). Emergent literacy profiles among prekindergarten children from low-SES backgrounds: Longitudinal considerations. *Early Childhood Research Quarterly, 28,* 608–620.

Cabrera, N. J., Aldoney, D., & Tamis-LeMonda, C. S. (2014). Latino fathers. In N. J. Cabrera & C. S. Tamis-LeMonda (Eds.), *Handbook of father involvement: Multidisciplinary perspectives* (2nd ed., pp. 244–250). New York: Routledge.

Cabrera, N. J., & Bradley, R. H. (2012). Latino fathers and their children. *Child Development Perspectives, 6,* 232–238.

Cabrera, N. J., Shannon, J. D., & Tamis-LeMonda, C. (2007). Fathers' influence on their children's cognitive and emotional development: From toddlers to pre-K. *Applied Developmental Science, 11,* 208–213.

Cain, K., & Oakhill, J. (2011). Matthew effects in young readers: Reading comprehension and reading experience aid vocabulary development. *Journal of Learning Disabilities, 44,* 431–443.

Cain, M. A., Bornick, P., & Whiteman, V. (2013). The maternal, fetal, and neonatal effects of cocaine exposure in pregnancy. *Clinical Obstetrics and Gynecology, 56,* 124–132.

Cairns, R. B., & Cairns, B. D. (2006). The making of developmental psychology. In R. M. Lerner (Ed.), *Handbook of child psychology: Vol. 1. Theoretical models of human development* (6th ed., pp. 89–165). Hoboken, NJ: Wiley.

Calabrese, S. K., Rosenberger, J. G., Schick, V. R., & Novak, D. S. (2015). Pleasure, affection, and love among black men who have sex with men (MSM) versus MSM of other races: Countering dehumanizing stereotypes via cross-race comparisons of reported sexual experience at last sexual event. *Archives of Sexual Behavior, 44,* 2001–2014.

Caldwell, B. M., & Bradley, R. H. (1994). Environmental issues in developmental follow-up research. In S. L. Friedman & H. C. Haywood (Eds.), *Developmental follow-up* (pp. 235–256). San Diego: Academic Press.

Calhoun, L. G., Tedeschi, R. G., Cann, A., & Hanks, E. A. (2010). Positive outcomes following bereavement: Paths to posttraumatic growth. *Psychologica Belgica, 50,* 125–143.

Callanan, M. A., & Sabbagh, M. A. (2004). Multiple labels for objects in conversations with young children: Parents' language and children's developing expectations about word meanings. *Developmental Psychology, 40,* 746–763.

Calvert, S. L. (2015). Children and digital media. In M. H. Bornstein & T. Leventhal (Eds.), *Handbook of cultural developmental science: Vol. 4. Ecological settings and processes* (pp. 299–322). New York: Psychology Press.

Cameron, C. A., Lau, C., Fu, G., & Lee, K. (2012). Development of children's moral evaluations of modesty and self-promotion in diverse cultural settings. *Journal of Moral Education, 41,* 61–78.

Cameron, C. A., & Lee, K. (1997). The development of children's telephone communication. *Journal of Applied Developmental Psychology, 18,* 55–70.

Cameron, P. A., & Gallup, G. G. (1988). Shadow recognition in human infants. *Infant Behavior and Development, 11,* 465–471.

Camp, C. J., Cohen-Mansfield, J., & Capezuti, E. A. (2002). Use of nonpharmacologic interventions among nursing home residents with dementia. *Psychiatric Services, 53,* 1397–1401.

Campbell, A., Shirley, L., & Candy, J. (2004). A longitudinal study of gender-related cognition and behaviour. *Developmental Science, 7,* 1–9.

Campbell, A. L., & Binstock, R. H. (2011). Politics and aging in the United States. In R. H. Binstock & L. K. George (Eds.), *Handbook of aging and the social sciences* (pp. 265–280). San Diego, CA: Academic Press.

Campbell, D. A., Lake, M. F., Falk, M., & Backstrand, J. R. (2006). A randomized control trial of continuous support in labor by a lay doula. *Journal of Obstetrics and Gynecology and Neonatal Nursing, 35,* 456–464.

Campbell, D. A., Scott, K. D., Klaus, M. H., & Falk, M. (2007). Female relatives or friends trained as labor doulas: Outcomes at 6 to 8 weeks postpartum. *Birth, 34,* 220–227.

Campbell, F. A., Pungello, E. P., Kainz, K., Burchinal, M., Pan, Y., Wasik, B. H., et al. (2012). Adult outcomes as a function of an early childhood educational program: An Abecedarian Project follow-up. *Developmental Psychology, 48,* 1033–1043.

Campbell, F. A., Pungello, E. P., Miller-Johnson, S., Burchinal, M., & Ramey, C. T. (2001). The development of cognitive and academic abilities: Growth curves from an early childhood educational experiment. *Developmental Psychology, 37,* 231–242.

Campbell, F. A., Ramey, C. T., Pungello, E. P., Sparling, J., & Miller-Johnson, S. (2002). Early childhood education: Young adult outcomes from the Abecedarian Project. *Applied Developmental Science, 6,* 42–57.

Campbell, S. B., Brownell, C. A., Hungerford, A., Spieker, S. J., Mohan, R., & Blessing, J. S. (2004). The course of maternal depressive symptoms and maternal sensitivity as predictors of attachment security at 36 months. *Development and Psychopathology, 16,* 231–252.

Campos, J. J., Anderson, D. I., Barbu-Roth, M. A., Hubbard, E. M., Hertenstein, J. J., & Witherington, D. (2000). Travel broadens the mind. *Infancy, 1,* 149–219.

Campos, J. J., Frankel, C. B., & Camras, L. (2004). On the nature of emotion regulation. *Child Development, 75,* 377–394.

Campos, J. J., Witherington, D., Anderson, D. I., Frankel, C. I., Uchiyama, I., & Barbu-Roth, M. (2008). Rediscovering development in infancy. *Child Development, 79,* 1625–1632.

Camras, L. (2011). Differentiation, dynamical integration and functional emotional development. *Emotion Review, 3,* 138–146.

Camras, L. A., Oster, H., Campos, J. J., & Bakeman, R. (2003). Emotional facial expressions in European-American, Japanese, and Chinese infants. *Annals of the New York Academy of Sciences, 1000,* 1–17.

Camras, L. A., Oster, H., Campos, J. J., Miyake, K., & Bradshaw, D. (1992). Japanese and American infants' responses to arm restraint. *Developmental Psychology, 28,* 578–583.

Camras, L. A., & Shuster, M. M. (2013). Current emotion research in developmental psychology. *Emotion Review, 5,* 321–329.

Camras, L. A., & Shutter, J. M. (2010). Emotional facial expressions in infancy. *Emotion Review, 2,* 120–129.

Cancian, M., & Haskins, R (2013). Changes in family composition: Implications for income, poverty, and public policy. *Annals of the American Academy of Political and Social Science, 654,* 31–47.

Candelaria, M., Teti, D. M., & Black, M. M. (2011). Multi-risk infants: Predicting attachment security from sociodemographic, psychosocial, and health risk among African-American preterm infants. *Journal of Child Psychology and Psychiatry, 52,* 870–877.

Candy, B., Holman, A., Leurent, S., & Jones, D. L. (2011). Hospice care delivered at home, in nursing homes and in dedicated hospice facilities: A systematic review of quantitative and qualitative evidence. *International Journal of Nursing Studies, 48,* 121–133.

Cao, S., Moineddin, R., Urquia, M. L., Razak, F., & Ray, J. G. (2014). J-shapedness: An often missed, often miscalculated relation: The example of weight and mortality. *Journal of Epidemiology and Community Health, 68,* 683–690.

Capirci, O., Contaldo, A., Caselli, M. C., & Volterra, V. (2005). From action to language through gesture. *Gesture, 5,* 155–177.

Caplan, M., Vespo, J., Pedersen, J., & Jay, D. F. (1991). Conflict and its resolution in small groups of one- and two-year-olds. *Child Development, 62,* 1513–1524.

Cappeliez, P., Rivard, V., & Guindon, S. (2007). Functions of reminiscence in later life: Proposition of a model and applications. European *Review of Applied Psychology, 57,* 151–156.

Cappelli, P., & Novelli, B. (2010). *Managing the older worker: How to prepare for the new organizational order.* Boston: Harvard Business School Publishing.

Carballo, J. J., Muñoz-Lorenzo, L., Blasco-Fontecilla, H., Lopez-Castroman, J., García-Nieto, R., Dervic, K., et al. (2011). Continuity of depressive disorders from childhood and adolescence to adulthood: A naturalistic study in community mental health centers. *Primary Care Companion for CNS Disorders, 13,* PCC.11m01150.

Card, N. A., Stucky, B. D., Sawalani, G. M., & Little, T. D. (2008). Direct and indirect aggression during childhood and adolescence: A meta-analytic review of gender differences, intercorrelations, and relations to maladjustment. *Child Development, 79,* 1185–1229.

Cardona Cano, S., Tiemeier, H., Van Hoeken, D., Tharner, A., Jaddoe, V. W., Hofman, A., et al. (2015). Trajectories of picky eating during childhood: A general population study. *International Journal of Eating Disorders, 48,* 570–579.

Carey, S. (2009). *The origins of concepts.* Oxford, UK: Oxford University Press.

Carey, S., & Markman, E. M. (1999). Cognitive development. In B. M. Bly & D. E. Rumelhart (Eds.), *Cognitive science* (pp. 201–254). San Diego: Academic Press.

Carli, L. L. (2015). Women and leadership. In A. M. Broadbridge & S. L. Fielden (Eds.), *Handbook of gendered careers in management* (pp. 290–304). Cheltenham, UK: Edward Elgar Publishing.

Carlo, G. (2014). The development and correlates of prosocial moral behaviors. In M. Killen & J. G. Smetana (Eds.), *Handbook of moral development* (2nd ed., pp. 208–234). New York: Psychology Press.

Carlo, G., Mestre, M. V., Samper, P., Tur, A., & Armenta, B. E. (2011). The longitudinal relations among dimensions of parenting styles, sympathy, prosocial moral reasoning, and prosocial behaviors. *International Journal of Behavioral Development, 35,* 116–124.

Carlson, M. C., Erikson, K. I., Kramer, A. F., Voss, M. W., Bolea, N., Mielke, M., et al. (2009). Evidence for neurocognitive plasticity in at-risk older adults: The Experience Corps program. *Journals of Gerontology, 64A,* 1275–1282.

Carlson, M. C., Kuo, J. H., Yi-Fang, C., Varma, V. R., Harris, G., Albert, M. S., et al. (2015). Impact of the Baltimore Experience Corps trial on cortical and hippocampal volumes. *Alzheimer's & Dementia, 11,* 1340–1348.

Carlson, S. M., & Meltzoff, A. N. (2008). Bilingual experience and executive functioning in young children. *Developmental Science, 11,* 282–298.

Carlson, S. M., Moses, L. J., & Claxton, S. J. (2004). Individual differences in executive functioning and theory of mind: An investigation of inhibitory control and planning ability. *Journal of Experimental Child Psychology, 87,* 299–319.

Carlson, S. M., & White, R. E. (2013). Executive function, pretend play, and imagination. In R. E. White & S. M. Carlson (Eds.), *Oxford handbook of the development of imagination* (pp. 161–174). New York: Oxford University Press.

Carlson, S. M., White, R. E., & Davis-Unger, A. (2014). Evidence for a relation between executive function and pretense representation in preschool children. *Cognitive Development, 29,* 1–16.

Carlson, S. M., Zelazo, P. D., & Faja, S. (2013). Executive function. In P. D. Zelazo (Ed.), *Oxford handbook of developmental psychology: Vol. 1. Body and mind* (pp. 706–743). New York: Oxford University Press.

Carlson, V. J., & Harwood, R. L. (2003). Attachment, culture, and the caregiving system: The cultural patterning of everyday experiences among Anglo and Puerto Rican mother–infant pairs. *Infant Mental Health Journal, 24,* 53–73.

Carnelley, K. B., Wortman, C. B., Bolger, N., & Burke, C. T. (2006). The time course of grief reactions to spousal loss: Evidence from a national probability sample. *Journal of Personality and Social Psychology, 91,* 476–492.

Carpenter, M., Nagell, K., & Tomasello, M. (1998). Social cognition, joint attention, and communicative competence. *Monographs of the Society for Research in Child Development, 63*(4, Serial No. 255).

Carpenter, R., McGarvey, C., Mitchell, E. A., Tappin, D. M., Vennemann, M. M., Smuk, M., & Carpenter, J. R. (2013). Bed sharing when parents do not smoke: Is there a risk of SIDS? An individual level analysis of five major case-control studies. *British Medical Journal, 3,* e002299.

Carpenter, T. P., Fennema, E., Fuson, K., Hiebert, J., Human, P., & Murray, H. (1999). Learning basic number concepts and skills as problem solving. In E. Fennema & T. A. Romberg (Eds.), *Mathematics classrooms that promote understanding: Studies in mathematical thinking and learning series* (pp. 45–61). Mahwah, NJ: Erlbaum.

Carr, D. (2003). A "good death" for whom? Quality of spouse's death and psychological distress among older widowed persons. *Journal of Health and Social Behavior, 44,* 215–232.

Carr, D. (2004). Psychological well-being across three cohorts: A response to shifting work–family opportunities and expectations? In O. G. Brim, C. D. Ryff, & R. C. Kessler (Eds.), *How healthy are we? A national study of well-being at midlife* (pp. 452–484). Chicago: University of Chicago Press.

Carr, D., House, J. S., Kessler, R. C., Nesse, R. M., Sonnega, J., & Wortman, C. (2000). Marital quality and psychological adjustment to widowhood among older adults: A longitudinal analysis. *Journals of Gerontology, 55B,* S197–S207.

Carr, J. (2002). Down syndrome. In P. Howlin & O. Udwin (Eds.), *Outcomes in neurodevelopmental and genetic disorders* (pp. 169–197). New York: Cambridge University Press.

Carroll, D., Phillips, A. C., Hunt, K., & Der, G. (2007). Symptoms of depression and cardiovascular reactions to acute psychological stress: Evidence from a population study. *Biological Psychology, 75,* 68–74.

Carroll, J. B. (2005). The three-stratum theory of cognitive abilities. In D. P. Flanagan & P. L. Harrison (Eds.), *Contemporary intellectual assessment: Theories, tests, and issues* (2nd ed., pp. 69–76). New York: Guilford.

Carskadon, M. A. (2011). Sleep in adolescents: The perfect storm. *Pediatric Clinics of North America, 58,* 637–647.

Carson, S., Peterson, J. B., & Higgins, D. M. (2003). Decreased latent inhibition is associated with increased creative achievement in high-functioning individuals. *Journal of Personality and Social Psychology, 85,* 499–506.

Carstensen, L. L. (2006). The influence of sense of time on human development. *Science, 312,* 1913–1915.

Carstensen, L. L., Turan, B., Scheibe, S., Ram, N., Ersner-Hershfield, H., Samanez-Larkin, G. R., et al. (2011). Emotional experience improves with age: Evidence based on over 10 years of experience sampling. *Psychology and Aging, 26,* 21–33.

Carter, B. D., Abnet, C. C., Feskanich, D., Freedman, N. D., Hartge, P., Lewis, C. E., et al. (2015). Smoking and mortality—beyond established causes. *New England Journal of Medicine, 372,* 631–640.

Carter, C. S., Hofer, T., Seo, A. Y., & Leeuwenburgh, C. (2007). Molecular mechanisms of life- and healthspan extension: Role of calorie restriction and exercise intervention. *Applied Physiology, Nutrition, and Metabolism, 32,* 954–966.

Carver, K., Joyner, K., & Udry, J. R. (2003). National estimates of adolescent romantic relationships. In P. Florsheim (Ed.), *Adolescent romantic relations and sexual behavior: Theory, research, and practical implications* (pp. 23–56). Mahwah, NJ: Erlbaum.

Casalin, S., Luyten, P., Vliegen, N., & Meurs, P. (2012). The structure and stability of temperament from infancy to toddlerhood: A one-year prospective study. *Infant Behavior and Development, 35,* 94–108.

Casasola, M., & Park, Y. (2013). Developmental changes in infant spatial categorization: When more is best and when less is enough. *Child Development, 84,* 1004–1019.

Case, A. D., Todd, N. R., & Kral, M. J. (2014). Ethnography in community psychology: Promises and tensions. *American Journal of Community Psychology, 54,* 60–71.

Case, R. (1996). Introduction: Reconceptualizing the nature of children's conceptual structures and their development in middle childhood. In R. Case & Y. Okamoto (Eds.), The role of central conceptual structures in the development of children's thought. *Monographs of the Society for Research in Child Development, 246*(61, Serial No. 246), pp. 1–26.

Case, R. (1998). The development of central conceptual structures. In D. Kuhn & R. Siegler (Eds.), *Handbook of child psychology: Vol. 2. Cognition, perception, and language* (5th ed., pp. 745–800). New York: Wiley.

Case, R., & Okamoto, Y. (Eds.). (1996). The role of central conceptual structures in the development of children's thought. *Monographs of the Society for Research in Child Development, 61*(1–2, Serial No. 246).

Caserta, D., Graziano, A., Lo Monte, G., Bordi, G., & Moscarini, M. (2013). Heavy metals and placental fetal–maternal barrier: A mini-review on the major concerns. *European Review for Medical and Pharmacological Sciences, 17,* 2198–2206.

Caserta, M., Lund, D., Utz, R., & de Vries, B. (2009). Stress-related growth among the recently bereaved. *Aging and Mental Health, 13,* 463–476.

Caserta, M. S., & Lund, D. A. (2002). Video Respite® in an Alzheimer's care center: Group versus solitary viewing. *Activities, Adaptation & Aging, 27,* 13–28.

Caserta, M. S., Lund, D. A., & Obray, S. J. (2004). Promoting self-care and daily living skills among older widows and widowers: Evidence from the Pathfinders Demonstration Project. *Omega, 49,* 217–236.

Caserta, M. S., Lund, D. A., & Rice, S. J. (1999). Pathfinders: A self-care and health education program for older widows and widowers. *Gerontologist, 39,* 615–620.

Casey, B. J., Jones, R. M., & Somerville, L. H. (2011). Braking and accelerating of the adolescent brain. *Journal of Research on Adolescence, 21,* 21–33.

Casper, L. M., & Smith, K. E. (2002). Dispelling the myths: Self-care, class, and race. *Journal of Family Issues, 23,* 716–727.

Caspi, A., Elder, G. H., Jr., & Bem, D. J. (1987). Moving against the world: Life-course patterns of explosive children. *Developmental Psychology, 23,* 308–313.

Caspi, A., Elder, G. H., Jr., & Bem, D. J. (1988). Moving away from the world: Life-course patterns of shy children. *Developmental Psychology, 24,* 824–831.

Caspi, A., Harrington, H., Milne, B., Amell, J. W., Theodore, R. F., & Moffitt, T. E. (2003). Children's behavioral styles at age 3 are linked to their adult personality traits at age 26. *Journal of Personality, 71,* 495–513.

Caspi, A., Moffitt, T. E., Morgan, J., Rutter, M., Taylor, A., Kim-Cohen, J., & Polo-Tomas, M. (2004). Maternal expressed emotion predicts children's antisocial behavior problems: Using monozygotic-twin differences to identify environmental effects on behavioral development. *Developmental Psychology, 40,* 149–161.

Caspi, A., & Roberts, B. W. (2001). Personality development across the life course: The argument for change and continuity. *Psychological Inquiry, 12,* 49–66.

Caspi, A., & Shiner, R. L. (2006). Personality development. In N. Eisenberg (Ed.), *Handbook of child psychology: Vol. 3. Social, emotional, and personality development* (6th ed., pp. 300–365). Hoboken, NJ: Wiley.

Cassia, V. M., Turati, C., & Simion, F. (2004). Can a nonspecific bias toward top-heavy patterns explain newborns' face preference? *Psychological Science, 15,* 379–383.

Cassidy, J. (2001). Adult romantic attachments: A developmental perspective on individual differences. *Review of General Psychology, 4,* 111–131.

Cassidy, J., & Berlin, L. J. (1994). The insecure/ambivalent pattern of attachment: Theory and research. *Child Development, 65,* 971–991.

Catalano, R., Ahern, J., Bruckner, T., Anderson, E., & Saxton, K. (2009). Gender-specific selection in utero among contemporary human birth cohorts. *Paediatric and Perinatal Epidemiology, 23,* 273–278.

Catalano, R., Zilko, C. E., Saxton, K. B., & Bruckner, T. (2010). Selection in utero: A biological response to mass layoffs. *American Journal of Human Biology, 22,* 396–400.

Cauley, J. A. (2013). Public health impact of osteoporosis. *Journals of Gerontology, 68B,* 1243–1251.

Ceci, S. J., Bruck, M., & Battin, D. B. (2000). The suggestibility of children's testimony. In D. F. Bjorklund (Ed.), *False-memory creation in children and adults* (pp. 169–201). Mahwah, NJ: Erlbaum.

Ceci, S. J., Kulkofsky, S., Klemfuss, J. Z., Sweeney, C. D., & Bruck, M. (2007). Unwarranted assumptions about children's testimonial accuracy. *Annual Review of Clinical Psychology, 3,* 311–328.

Ceci, S. J., Rosenblum, T. B., & Kumpf, M. (1998). The shrinking gap between high- and low-scoring groups: Current trends and possible causes. In U. Neisser (Ed.), *The rising curve* (pp. 287–302). Washington, DC: American Psychological Association.

Ceci, S. J., & Williams, W. M. (2010). *The mathematics of sex: How biology and society conspire to limit talented women and girls.* New York: Oxford University Press.

Cecil, J. E., Watt, P., Murrie, I. S. L., Wrieden, W., Wallis, D. J., Hetherington, M. M., Bolton-Smith, C., & Palmer, C. N. A. (2005). Childhood obesity and socioeconomic status: A novel role for height growth limitation. *International Journal of Obesity, 29,* 1199–1203.

Ceda, G. P., Dall'Aglio, E., Morganti, S., Denti, L., Maggio M., Lauretani, F., et al. (2010). Update on new therapeutic options for the somatopause. *Atenei Parmensis, 81*(Suppl. 1), 67–72.

Cederholm, T., Salem, N., Jr., & Palmblad, J. (2013). ω-3 fatty acids in the prevention of cognitive decline in humans. *Advances in Nutrition, 4,* 672–676.

Center for Communication and Social Policy (Ed.). (1998). *National Television Violence Study* (Vol. 2). Newbury Park, CA: Sage.

Center for Hearing and Communication. (2016). *Facts about hearing loss.* Retrieved from chchearing.org/facts-about-hearing-loss

Centers for Disease Control and Prevention. (2014a). *Breastfeeding report card: United States/2014.* Retrieved from www.cdc.gov/breastfeeding/pdf/2014breastfeedingreportcard.pdf

Centers for Disease Control and Prevention. (2014b). *Bridging the Gap Research Program: Supporting recess in elementary schools.* Atlanta, GA: U.S. Department of Health and Human Services.

Centers for Disease Control and Prevention. (2014c). *National diabetes statistics report, 2014.* Retrieved from www.cdc.gov/diabetes/pubs/statsreport14/national-diabetes-report-web.pdf

Centers for Disease Control and Prevention. (2014d, September 5). Prevalence and characteristics of sexual violence, stalking and intimate partner violence victimization—National Intimate Partner Sexual Violence Survey, United States, 2011. *Morbidity and Mortality Weekly Report, 63*(SS08), 1–18.

Centers for Disease Control and Prevention. (2014e). QuickStats: Rate of nonfatal fall injuries receiving medical attention by age group—National Health Interview Survey, United States, 2012. *Morbidity and Mortality Weekly Report, 63*(29), 641.

Centers for Disease Control and Prevention. (2014f). *State indicator report on physical activity: 2014.* Retrieved from www.cdc.gov/physicalactivity/downloads/pa_state_indicator_report_2014.pdf

Centers for Disease Control and Prevention. (2015a). *Asthma surveillance data.* Retrieved from www.cdc.gov/asthma/asthmadata.htm

Centers for Disease Control and Prevention. (2015b). *CDC fact sheet: Reported STDs in the United States.* Retrieved from www.cdc.gov/std/stats14/std-trends-508.pdf

Centers for Disease Control and Prevention. (2015c). *Child maltreatment: Risk and protective factors.* Retrieved from www.cdc.gov/violenceprevention/childmaltreatment/riskprotectivefactors.html

Centers for Disease Control and Prevention. (2015d). *Current cigarette smoking among adults in the United States.* Retrieved from www.cdc.gov/tobacco/data_statistics/fact_sheets/adult_data/cig_smoking

Centers for Disease Control and Prevention. (2015e). *Dental caries and sealant prevalence in children and adolescents in the United States,* 2011–2012. Retrieved from www.cdc.gov/nchs/data/databriefs/db191.htm

Centers for Disease Control and Prevention. (2015f). *Hip fractures among older adults.* Retrieved from www.cdc.gov/homeandrecreationalsafety/falls/adulthipfx.html

Centers for Disease Control and Prevention. (2015g). *HIV in the United States: At a glance.* Retrieved from www.cdc.gov/hiv/statistics/overview/ataglance.html

Centers for Disease Control and Prevention. (2015h). *HIV/AIDS: Statistics center.* Retrieved from www.cdc.gov/hiv/statistics/surveillance/incidence.html

Centers for Disease Control and Prevention. (2015i). Infant mortality statistics from the 2013 period linked birth/infant death data set. *National Vital Statistics Reports, 64*(9), 1–29. Retrieved from www.cdc.gov/nchs/data/nvsr/nvsr64/nvsr64_09.pdf

Centers for Disease Control and Prevention. (2015j). National, state, and selected local area vaccination coverage among children aged 19–35 months—United States 2014. *Morbidity and Mortality Weekly Report, 64,* 889–896.

Centers for Disease Control and Prevention. (2015k). *National suicide statistics.* Retrieved from www.cdc.gov/violenceprevention/suicide/statistics/index.html

Centers for Disease Control and Prevention. (2015l). *Sexually transmitted disease surveillance 2014.* Retrieved from www.cdc.gov/std/stats14/surv-2014-print.pdf

Centers for Disease Control and Prevention. (2015m). *Sickle cell disease: Data and statistics.* Retrieved from www.cdc.gov/ncbddd/sicklecell/data.html

Centers for Disease Control and Prevention. (2015n). *Tobacco use and pregnancy.* Retrieved from www.cdc.gov/reproductivehealth/maternalinfanthealth/tobaccousepregnancy/index.htm

Centers for Disease Control and Prevention. (2015o, October 16). Trends in quit attempts among adult cigarette smokers—United States, 2001–2013. *Morbidity and Mortality Weekly Report, 64,* 1129–1135.

Centers for Disease Control and Prevention. (2015p). *WISQARS fatal injury reports, national and regional, 1999–2014.* Retrieved from webappa.cdc.gov/sasweb/ncipc/mortrate10_us.html

Centers for Disease Control and Prevention. (2016a). *CDC fact sheet: Trends in U.S. HIV diagnoses, 2005–2014.* Retrieved from www.cdc.gov/nchhstp/newsroom/docs/factsheets/hiv-data-trends-fact-sheet-508.pdf

Centers for Disease Control and Prevention. (2016b). *Changes in life expectancy by race and Hispanic origin in the United States.* Retrieved from www.cdc.gov/nchs/products/databriefs/db244.htm

Centers for Disease Control and Prevention. (2016c). *Important facts about falls.* Retrieved from www.cdc.gov/HomeandRecreationalSafety/Falls/adultfalls.html

Centers for Disease Control and Prevention. (2016d). *Increase in suicide in the United States, 1999–2014: Key findings.* Retrieved from www.cdc.gov/nchs/products/databriefs/db241.htm

Centers for Disease Control and Prevention. (2016e). *Multiple cause of death, 1999–2014.* Retrieved from wonder.cdc.gov/wonder/help/mcd.html

Centers for Disease Control and Prevention. (2016f). *Pedestrian safety.* Retrieved from www.cdc.gov/motorvehiclesafety/pedestrian_safety

Centers for Medicare and Medicaid Services. (2013). *Nursing home data compendium, 2013 edition.* Retrieved from www.cms.gov/Medicare/Provider-Enrollment-and-Certification/CertificationandComplianc/downloads/nursinghomedatacompendium_508.pdf

Centers for Medicare and Medicaid Services. (2016). *NHE [National health expenditure] fact sheet.* Retrieved from www.cms.gov/research-statistics-data-and-systems/statistics-trends-and-reports/nationalhealthexpenddata/nhe-fact-sheet.html

Cernoch, J. M., & Porter, R. H. (1985). Recognition of maternal axillary odors by infants. *Child Development 56,* 1593–1598.

Cespedes, E. M., Gillman, M. W., Kleinman, D., Rifas-Shiman, S. L., Redline, S., & Taveras, E. M. (2014). Television viewing, bedroom television, and sleep duration from infancy to mid-childhood. *Pediatrics, 133,* e1163–1171.

Cetinkaya, M. B., Siano, L. J., & Benadiva, C. (2013). Reproductive outcome of women 43 years and beyond undergoing ART treatment with their own oocytes in two Connecticut university programs. *Journal of Assisted Reproductive Genetics, 30,* 673–678.

Cevenini, E., Invidia, L., Lescai, F., Salvioli, S., Tieri, P., Castellani, G., & Franceschi, G. (2008). Human models of aging and longevity. *Expert Opinion on Biological Therapy, 8,* 1393–1405.

Chaddock, L., Erickson, K. I., Prakash, R. S., Kim, J. S., Voss, M. W., Van Patter, M., et al. (2010a). A neuroimaging investigation of the association between aerobic fitness and hippocampal volume and memory performance in preadolescent children. *Brain Research, 1358,* 172–183.

Chaddock, L., Erickson, K. I., Prakash, R. S., VanPatter, M., Voss, M. V., Pontifex, M. B., et al. (2010b). Basal ganglia volume is associated with aerobic fitness in preadolescent children. *Developmental Neuroscience, 32,* 249–256.

Chaddock, L., Erickson, K. I., Prakash, R. S., Voss, M. V., VanPatter, M., Pontifex, M. B., et al. (2012). A functional MRI investigation of the association between childhood aerobic fitness and neurocognitive control. *Biological Psychology, 89,* 260–268.

Chaddock, L., Pontifex, M. B., Hillman, C. H., & Kramer, A. F. (2011). A review of the relation of aerobic fitness and physical activity to brain structure and function in children. *Journal of the International Neuropsychological Society, 17,* 1–11.

Chaddock-Heyman, L., Erickson, K. I., Holtrop, J. L., Voss, M W., Pontifex, M. B., Raine, L. B., et al. (2014). Aerobic fitness is associated with greater white matter integrity in children. *Frontiers in Human Neuroscience, 8,* 584.

Chaddock-Heyman, L., Erickson, K. I., Voss, M. W., Knecht, A. M., Pontifex, M. B., Castelli, D. M., et al. (2013). The effects of physical activity on functional MRI activation associated with cognitive control in children: A randomized controlled intervention. *Frontiers in Human Neuroscience, 7,* 72.

Chae, D. H., Nuru-Jeter, A. M., Adler, N. E., Brody, G. H., Lin, J., Blackburn, E. H., & Epel, E. S. (2014). Discrimination, racial bias, and telomere length in African-American men. *American Journal of Preventive Medicine, 46,* 103–111.

Chakravarty, E. F., Hubert, H. B., Krishnan, E., Bruce, B. B., Lingala, V. B., & Fries, J. F. (2012). Lifestyle risk factors predict disability and death in healthy aging adults. *American Journal of Medicine, 125,* 190–197.

Chakravorty, S., & Williams, T. N. (2015). Sickle cell disease: A neglected chronic disease of increasing global health importance. *Archives of Disease in Childhood, 100,* 48–53.

Chalabaev, A., Sarrazin, P., & Fontayne, P. (2009). Stereotype endorsement and perceived ability as mediators of the girls' gender orientation–soccer performance relationship. *Psychology of Sport and Exercise, 10,* 297–299.

Chambaere, K., Vander Stichele, R., Mortier, F., Cohen, J., & Deliens, L. (2015). Recent trends in euthanasia and other end-of-life practices in Belgium. *New England Journal of Medicine, 372,* 1179–1181.

Chamberlain, P. (2003). Antisocial behavior and delinquency in girls. In P. Chamberlain (Ed.), *Treating chronic juvenile offenders* (pp. 109–127). Washington, DC: American Psychological Association.

Chan, A., Meints, K., Lieven, E., & Tomasello, M. (2010). Young children's comprehension of English SVO word order revisited: Testing the same children in act-out and intermodal preferential looking tasks. *Cognitive Development, 25,* 30–45.

Chan, C. C. Y., Brandone, A. C., & Tardif, T. (2009). Culture, context, or behavioral control? English- and Mandarin-speaking mothers' use of nouns and verbs in joint book reading. *Journal of Cross-Cultural Psychology, 40,* 584–602.

Chan, C. C. Y., Tardif, T., Chen, J., Pulverman, R. B., Zhu, L., & Meng, X. (2011). English- and Chinese-learning infants map novel labels to objects and actions differently. *Developmental Psychology, 47,* 1459–1471.

Chan, S. M. (2010). Aggressive behaviour in early elementary school children: Relations to authoritarian parenting, children's negative emotionality and coping strategies. *Early Child Development and Care, 180,* 1253–1269.

Chan, T. W., & Koo, A. (2011). Parenting style and youth outcomes in the UK. *European Sociological Review, 27,* 385–399.

Chandra, A., Copen, C. E., & Stephen, E. H. (2013, August 14). Infertility and impaired fecundity in the United States, 1982–2010: Date from the National Survey of Family Growth. *National Health Statistics Reports,* No. 67. Retrieved from www.cdc.gov/nchs/data/nhsr/nhsr067.pdf

Chang, E., Wilber, K. H., & Silverstein, M. (2010). The effects of childlessness on the care and psychological well-being of older adults with disabilities. *Aging and Mental Health, 14,* 712–719.

Chang, P. F., Choi, Y. H., Bazarova, N. N., & Löckenhoff, C. E. (2015). Age differences in online social networking: Extending socioemotional selectivity theory to social network sites. *Journal of Broadcasting & Electronic Media, 59,* 221–239.

Chang, Y. T., Hayter, M., & Wu, S. C. (2010). A systematic review and meta-ethnography of the qualitative literature: Experiences of the menarche. *Journal of Clinical Nursing, 19,* 447–460.

Chao, R. K., & Good, G. E. (2004). Nontraditional students' perspectives on college education: A qualitative study. *Journal of College Counseling, 7,* 5–12.

Chapman, R. S. (2006). Children's language learning: An interactionist perspective. In R. Paul (Ed.), *Language disorders from a developmental perspective* (pp. 1–53). Mahwah, NJ: Erlbaum.

Charity, A. H., Scarborough, H. S., & Griffin, D. M. (2004). Familiarity with school English in African American children and its relation to early reading achievement. *Child Development, 75,* 1340–1356.

Charles, D., Whitaker, D. J., Le, B., Swahn, M., & DiClemente, R. J. (2011). Differences between perpetrators of bidirectional and unidirectional physical intimate partner violence. *Partner Abuse, 2,* 344–364.

Charles, S. T. (2010). Strength and vulnerability integration: A model of emotional well-being across adulthood. *Psychological Bulletin, 136,* 1068–1091.

Charles, S. T. (2011). Emotional experience and regulation in later life. In K. W. Schaie & S. L. Willis (Eds.), *Handbook of the psychology of aging* (7th ed., pp. 295–310). San Diego, CA: Academic Press.

Charles, S. T., & Carstensen, L. L. (2009). Socioemotional selectivity theory. In H. Reis & S. Sprecher (Eds.), *Encyclopedia of human relationships* (pp. 1578–1581). Thousand Oaks, CA: Sage.

Charles, S. T., & Carstensen, L. L. (2010). Social and emotional aging. *Annual Review of Psychology, 61,* 383–409.

Charles, S. T., & Carstensen, L. L. (2014). Emotion regulation and aging. In J. J. Gross (Ed.), *Handbook of emotion regulation* (pp. 203–218). New York: Guilford Press.

Charles, S. T., & Luong, G. (2013). Emotional experience across adulthood: The theoretical model of strength and vulnerability integration. *Current Directions in Psychological Science, 22,* 443–448.

Charles, S. T., Piazza, J. R., Luong, G., & Almeida, D. M. (2009). Now you see it, now you don't: Age differences in affective reactivity to social tensions. *Psychology and Aging, 24,* 645–653.

Charlier, R., Mertens, E., Lefevre, J., & Thomis, M. (2015). Muscle mass and muscle function over the adult life span: A cross-sectional study in Flemish adults. *Archives of Gerontology and Geriatrics, 61,* 161–167.

Charman, T., Baron-Cohen, S., Swettenham, J., Baird, G., Cox, A., & Drew, A. (2001). Testing joint attention, imitation, and play as infancy precursors to language and theory of mind. *Cognitive Development, 15,* 481–49.

Charman, W. N. (2008). The eye in focus: Accommodation and presbyopia. *Optometry, 91,* 207–225.

Charness, N., & Boot, W. R. (2016). Technology, gaming, and social networking. In K. W. Schaie & S. L. Willis (Eds.), *Handbook of the psychology of aging* (8th ed., pp. 390–407). London, UK: Academic Press.

Chase-Lansdale, P. L., Gordon, R., Brooks-Gunn, J., & Klebanov, P. K. (1997). Neighborhood and family influences on the intellectual and behavioral competence of preschool and early school-age children. In J. Brooks-Gunn, G. Duncan, & J. L. Aber (Eds.), *Neighborhood poverty: Context and consequences for development* (pp. 79–118). New York: Russell Sage Foundation.

Chatterji, P., & Markowitz, S. (2012). Family leave after childbirth and the mental health of new mothers. *Journal of Mental Health Policy and Economics, 15,* 61–76.

Chatters, L. M., Taylor, R. J., Woodward, A. T., & Nicklett, E. J. (2015). Social support from church and family members and depressive symptoms among older African Americans. *American Journal of Geriatric Psychiatry, 23,* 559–567.

Chauhan, G. S., Shastri, J., & Mohite, P. (2005). Development of gender constancy in preschoolers. *Psychological Studies, 50,* 62–71.

Chavajay, P., & Rogoff, B. (1999). Cultural variation in management of attention by children and their caregivers. *Developmental Psychology, 35,* 1079–1090.

Chavajay, P., & Rogoff, B. (2002). Schooling and traditional collaborative social organization of problem solving by Mayan mothers and children. *Developmental Psychology, 38,* 55–66.

Chavarria, M. C., Sánchez, F. J., Chou, Y. Y., Thompson, P. M., & Luders, E. (2014). Puberty in the corpus callosum. *Neuroscience, 265,* 1–8.

Chawarska, K., Macari, S., & Shic, F. (2013). Decreased spontaneous attention to social scenes in 6-month-old infants later diagnosed with autism spectrum disorders. *Biological Psychiatry, 74,* 195–203.

Cheah, C. S. L., Leung, C. Y. Y., Tahseen, M., & Schultz, D. (2009). Authoritative parenting among immigrant Chinese mothers of preschoolers. *Journal of Family Psychology, 23,* 311–320.

Cheah, C. S. L., & Li, J. (2010). Parenting of young immigrant Chinese children: Challenges facing their social-emotional and intellectual development. In E. L. Grigorenko & R. Takanishi (Eds.), *Immigration, diversity, and education* (pp. 225–241). New York: Routledge.

Checkley, W., Epstein, L. D., Gilman, R. H., Cabrera, L., & Black, R. E. (2003). Effects of acute diarrhea on linear growth in Peruvian children. *American Journal of Epidemiology, 157,* 166–175.

Chen, B., Vansteenkiste, M., Beyers, W., Soenens, B., & Van Petegem, S. (2013). Autonomy in family decision making for Chinese adolescents: Disentangling the dual meaning of autonomy. *Journal of Cross-Cultural Psychology, 44,* 1184–1209.

Chen, E. S. L., & Rao, N. (2011). Gender socialization in Chinese kindergartens: Teachers' contributions. *Sex Roles, 64,* 103–116.

Chen, J. J., Howard, K. S., & Brooks-Gunn, J. (2011). How do neighborhoods matter across the life span? In K. L. Fingerman, C. A. Berg, J. Smith, & T. C. Antonucci (Eds.), *Handbook of life-span development* (pp. 805–836). New York: Springer.

Chen, L.-C., Metcalfe, J. S., Jeka, J. J., & Clark, J. E. (2007). Two steps forward and one back: Learning to walk affects infants' sitting posture. *Infant Behavior and Development, 30,* 16–25.

Chen, R. (2012). Institutional characteristics and college student dropout risks: A multilevel event history analysis. *Research in Higher Education, 53,* 487–505.

Chen, X. (2012). Culture, peer interaction, and socioemotional development. *Child Development Perspectives, 6,* 27–34.

Chen, X., Cen, G., Li, D., & He, Y. (2005). Social functioning and adjustment in Chinese children: The imprint of historical time. *Child Development, 76,* 182–195.

Chen, X., DeSouza, A. T., Chen, H., & Wang, L. (2006). Reticent behavior and experiences in peer interactions in Chinese and Canadian children. *Developmental Psychology, 42,* 656–665.

Chen, X., Rubin, K. H., Liu, M., Chen, H., Wang, L., Li, D., et al. (2003). Compliance in Chinese and Canadian toddlers: A cross-cultural study. *International Journal of Behavioral Development, 27,* 428–436.

Chen, X., & Schmidt, L. A. (2015). Temperament and personality. In M. E. Lamb (Ed.), *Handbook of child psychology and developmental science: Vol. 3. Socioemotional processes* (7th ed., pp. 152–200). Hoboken, NJ: Wiley.

Chen, X., Wang, L., & Cao, R. (2011). Shyness-sensitivity and unsociability in rural Chinese children: Relations with social, school, and psychological adjustment. *Child Development, 82,* 1531–1543.

Chen, X., Wang, L., & DeSouza, A. (2006). Temperament, socioemotional functioning, and peer relationships in Chinese and North American children. In X. Chen, D. C. French, & B. H. Schneider (Eds.), *Peer relationships in cultural context* (pp. 123–147). New York: Cambridge University Press.

Chen, Y., Li, H., & Meng, L. (2013). Prenatal sex selection and missing girls in China: Evidence from the diffusion of diagnostic ultrasound. *Journal of Human Resources, 48,* 36–70.

Chen, Y.-C., Yu, M.-L., Rogan, W., Gladen, B., & Hsu, C.-C. (1994). A 6-year follow-up of behavior and activity disorders in the Taiwan Yu-cheng children. *American Journal of Public Health, 84,* 415–421.

Chen, Y.-J., & Hsu, C.-C. (1994). Effects of prenatal exposure to PCBs on the neurological function of children: A neuropsychological and neurophysiological study. *Developmental Medicine and Child Neurology, 36,* 312–320.

Chen, Z., Sanchez, R. P., & Campbell, T. (1997). From beyond to within their grasp: The rudiments of analogical problem solving in 10- to 13-month-olds. *Developmental Psychology, 33,* 790–801.

Cheng, G., Huang, C., Deng, H., & Wang, H. (2012). Diabetes as a risk factor for dementia and mild cognitive impairment: A meta-analysis of longitudinal studies. *Internal Medicine Journal, 42,* 484–491.

Cherlin, A. J. (2010). Demographic trends in the United States: A review of research in the 2000s. *Journal of Marriage and Family, 72*(3), 403–419.

Chess, S., & Thomas, A. (1984). *Origins and evolution of behavior disorders.* New York: Brunner/Mazel.

Chessell, Z. J., Rathbone, C. J., Souchay, C., Charlesworth, L., & Moulin, C. J. A. (2014). Autobiographical memory, past and future events, and self-images in younger and older adults. *Self and Identity, 13,* 380–397.

Chetty, R., Stepner, M., Abraham, S., Lin, S., Scuderi, B., Turner, N., et al. (2016). The association between income and life expectancy in the United States, 2001–2014. *JAMA, 315,* 1750–1766.

Cheung, F. M., & Halpern, D. F. (2010). Women at the top: Powerful leaders define success as work + family in a culture of gender. *American Psychologist, 65,* 182–193.

Chevalier, N. (2015). The development of executive function: Toward more optimal coordination of control with age. *Child Development Perspectives, 9,* 239–244.

Cheyney, M., Bovbjerg, M., Everson, C., Gordon, W., Hannibal, D., & Vedam, S. (2014). Outcomes of care for 16,924 planned home births in the United States: The Midwives Alliance of North America Statistics Project, 2004 to 2009. *Journal of Midwifery and Women's Health, 59,* 17–27.

Chhin, C. S., Bleeker, M. M., & Jacobs, J. E. (2008). Gender-typed occupational choices: The long-term impact of parents' beliefs and expectations. In H. M. G. Watt & J. S. Eccles (Eds.), *Gender and occupational outcomes: Longitudinal assessments of individual, social, and cultural influences* (pp. 215–234). Washington, DC: American Psychological Association.

Chi, M. T. H. (2006). Laboratory methods for assessing experts' and novices' knowledge. In K. A. Ericsson, N. Charness, P. J. Feltovich, & R. R. Hoffman (Eds.), *The Cambridge handbook of expertise and expert performance* (pp. 167–184). New York: Cambridge University Press.

Chiang, T., Schultz, R. M., & Lampson, M. A. (2012). Meiotic origins of maternal age-related aneuploidy. *Biology of Reproduction, 86,* 1–7.

Child Care Aware. (2015). *Parents and the high cost of child care: 2014 report.* Retrieved from usa.childcareaware.org

Child Trends. (2013). *Family meals.* Retrieved from www.childtrends.org/wp-content/uploads/2012/09/96_Family_Meals.pdf

Child Trends. (2014a). *Births to unmarried women.* Retrieved from www.childtrends.org/?indicators=births-to-unmarried-women

Child Trends. (2014b). *Early childhood program enrollment.* Retrieved from www.childtrends.org/?indicators=early-childhood-program-enrollment

Child Trends. (2014c). *Unintentional injuries: Indicators on children and youth.* Retrieved from www.childtrends.org/wp-content/uploads/2014/08/122_Unintentional_Injuries.pdf

Child Trends. (2015a). *Births to unmarried women*. Retrieved from www.childtrends.org/wp-content/uploads/2015/03/75_Births_to_Unmarried_Women.pdf

Child Trends. (2015b). *Full-day kindergarten*. Retrieved from www.childtrends.org/?indicators=full-day-kindergarten

Child Trends. (2015c). *Late or no prenatal care*. Retrieved from www.childtrends.org/wp-content/uploads/2014/07/25_Prenatal_Care.pdf

Chin, H. B., Sipe, T. A., Elder, R., Mercer, S. L., Chattopadhyay, S. K., Jacob, V., et al. (2012). The effectiveness of group-based comprehensive risk-reduction and abstinence education interventions to prevent or reduce the risk of adolescent pregnancy, human immunodeficiency virus, and sexually transmitted infections: Two systematic reviews for the guide to community preventive services. *American Journal of Preventive Medicine, 42*, 272–294.

Chinn, C. A., & Malhotra, B. A. (2002). Children's responses to anomalous scientific data: How is conceptual change impeded? *Journal of Educational Psychology, 94*, 327–343.

Chiu, D., Beru, Y., Wately, E., Wubu, S., Simson, E., Kessinger, R., et al. (2008). Seventh-grade students' self-beliefs and social comparisons. *Journal of Educational Research, 102*, 125–136.

Choe, D. E., Olson, S. L., & Sameroff, A. J. (2013). The interplay between externalizing problems and physical discipline and inductive discipline during childhood. *Developmental Psychology, 49*, 2029–2039.

Choi, N., & Kim, J. (2011). The effect of time volunteering and charitable donations in later life on psychological well-being. *Ageing and Society, 31*, 590–611.

Choi, N. G., & Landeros, C. (2011). Wisdom from life's challenges: Qualitative interviews with low- and moderate-income older adults who were nominated as being wise. *Journal of Gerontological Social Work, 54*, 592–64.

Choi, S., & Gopnik, A. (1995). Early acquisition of verbs in Korean: A cross-linguistic study. *Journal of Child Language, 22*, 497–529.

Choi, S., McDonough, L., Bowerman, M., & Mandler, J. M. (1999). Early sensitivity to language-specific spatial categories in English and Korean. *Cognitive Development, 14*, 241–268.

Chomsky, C. (1969). *The acquisition of syntax in children from five to ten*. Cambridge, MA: MIT Press.

Chomsky, N. (1957). *Syntactic structures*. The Hague: Mouton.

Chouinard, M. M. (2007). Children's questions: A mechanism for cognitive development. *Monographs of the Society for Research in Child Development, 72*(1, Serial No. 286).

Chouinard, M. M., & Clark, E. V. (2003). Adult reformulations of child errors as negative evidence. *Journal of Child Language, 30*, 637–669.

Chrisler, J. C., Barney, A., & Palatino, B. (2016). Ageism can be hazardous to women's health: Ageism, sexism, and stereotypes of older women in the healthcare system. *Journal of Social Issues, 72*, 86–104.

Christ, G. H., Siegel, K., & Christ, A. E. (2002). "It never really hit me ... until it actually happened." *JAMA, 288*, 1269–1278.

Christakis, D. A., Garrison, M. M., Herrenkohl, T., Haggerty, K., Rivara, F. P., Zhou, C., & Liekweg, K. (2013). Modifying media content for preschool children: A randomized controlled trial. *Pediatrics, 131*, 431–438.

Christakis, D. A., Zimmerman, F. J., DiGiuseppe, D. L., & McCarty, C. A. (2004). Early television exposure and subsequent attentional problems in children. *Pediatrics, 113*, 708–713.

Christakou, A., Gershman, S. J., Niv, Y., Simmons, A., Brammer, M., & Rubia, K. (2013). Neural and psychological maturation of decision-making in adolescence and young adulthood. *Journal of Cognitive Neuroscience, 25*, 1807–1823.

Christie, C. A., Jolivette, K., & Nelson, M. (2007). School characteristics related to high school dropout rates. *Remedial and Special Education, 28*, 325–339.

Christoffersen, M. N. (2012). A study of adopted children, their environment, and development: A systematic review. *Adoption Quarterly, 15*, 220–237.

Chu, C. Y. C., Xie, Y., & Yu, R. R. (2011). Coresidence with elderly parents: A comparative study of southeast China and Taiwan. *Journal of Marriage and Family, 73*, 120–135.

Chung, H. L., Mulvey, E. P., & Steinberg, L. (2011). Understanding the school outcomes of juvenile offenders: An exploration of neighborhood influences and motivational resources. *Journal of Youth and Adolescence, 40*, 1025–1038.

Chung, K. W., Kim, D. H., Park, M. H., Choi, Y. J., Kim, N. D., Lee, J., et al. (2013). Recent advances in calorie restriction research on aging. *Experimental Gerontology, 48*, 1049–1053.

Church, E. (2004). *Understanding stepmothers: Women share their struggles, successes, and insights*. Toronto: HarperCollins.

Churchman, R., York, G. S., Woodard, B., Wainright, C., & Rau-Foster, M. (2014). Revisiting perceptions of quality of hospice care: Managing for the ultimate referral. *American Journal of Hospice & Palliative Medicine, 31*, 521–526.

Ciarrochi, J., Parker, P., Sahdra, B., Marshall, S., Jackson, C., Gloster, A. T., & Heaven, P. (2016). The development of compulsive Internet use and mental health: A four-year study of adolescence. *Developmental Psychology, 52*, 272–283.

Cicchetti, D., & Toth, S. L. (2015). Child maltreatment. In M. E. Lamb (Ed.), *Handbook of child psychology and developmental science: Vol. 3. Socioemotional processes* (7th ed., pp. 513–563). Hoboken, NJ: Wiley.

Cicirelli, V. G. (1995). *Sibling relationships across the life span*. New York: Plenum.

Cicirelli, V. G. (2001). Personal meanings of death in older adults and young adults in relation to their fears of death. *Death Studies, 25*, 663–683.

Cicirelli, V. G. (2002). *Older adults' views on death*. New York: Springer.

Cillessen, A. H. N. (2009). Sociometric methods. In K. H. Rubin & W. M. Bukowski (Eds.), *Handbook of peer interactions, relationships, and groups* (pp. 82–99). New York: Guilford.

Cillessen, A. H. N., & Bellmore, A. D. (2004). Social skills and interpersonal perception in early and middle childhood. In P. K. Smith & C. H. Hart (Eds.), *Blackwell handbook of childhood social development* (pp. 355–374). Malden, MA: Blackwell.

Cipriano, E. A., & Stifter, C. A. (2010). Predicting preschool effortful control from toddler temperament and parenting behavior. *Journal of Applied Developmental Psychology, 31*, 221–230.

Circle (Center for Information & Research on Civic Learning & Engagement). (2013). *Youth voting*. Retrieved from www.civicyouth.org/quick-facts/youth-voting

Claes, R., & Heymans, M. (2008). HR professionals' views on work motivation and retention of older workers: A focus group study. *Career Development International, 13*, 95–111.

Clark, S. M., Ghulmiyyah, L. M., & Hankins, G. D. (2008). Antenatal antecedents and the impact of obstetric care in the etiology of cerebral palsy. *Clinical Obstetrics and Gynecology, 51*, 775–786.

Clarke, B. L., & Khosla, S. (2010). Physiology of bone loss. *Radiologic Clinics of North America, 48*, 483–495.

Clarke, M. J., Marks, A. D. J., & Lykins, A. D. (2015). Effects of gender group norms on the endorsement of same-sex attraction, behavior, and identity. *Journal of Bisexuality, 15*, 319–345.

Clarke, P., & Smith, J. (2011). Aging in a cultural context: Cross-national differences in disability and the moderating role of personal control among older adults in the United States and England. *Journals of Gerontology, 66B*, 457–467.

Clarke-Stewart, K. A., & Hayward, C. (1996). Advantages of father custody and contact for the psychological well-being of school-age children. *Journal of Applied Developmental Psychology, 17*, 239–270.

Claxton, A., O'Rourke, N., Smith, J. Z., & DeLongis, A. (2011). Personality traits and marital satisfaction within enduring relationships: An intra-couple discrepancy approach. *Journal of Social and Personal Relationships, 29*, 375–396.

Claxton, L. J., Keen, R., & McCarty, M. E. (2003). Evidence of motor planning in infant reaching behavior. *Psychological Science, 14*, 354–356.

Clay, R. A. (2009). Mini-multitaskers. *Monitor on Psychology, 40*(2), 38–40.

Clearfield, M. W. (2011). Learning to walk changes infants' social interactions. *Infant Behavior and Development, 34*, 15–25.

Clearfield, M. W., & Nelson, N. M. (2006). Sex differences in mothers' speech and play behavior with 6-, 9-, and 14-month-old infants. *Sex Roles, 54*, 127–137.

Clearfield, M. W., & Westfahl, S. M.-C. (2006). Familiarization in infants' perception of addition problems. *Journal of Cognition and Development, 7*, 27–43.

Clements, D. H., & Sarama, J. (2012). Learning and teaching early and elementary mathematics. In J. S. Carlson & J. R. Levin (Eds.), *Instructional strategies for improving students' learning* (pp. 205–212). Charlotte, NC: Information Age Publishing.

Clements, D. H., Sarama, J., Spitler, M. E., Lange, A. A., & Wolfe, C. B. (2011). Mathematics learned by young children in an intervention based on learning trajectories: A large-scale cluster randomized trial. *Journal for Research in Mathematics Education, 42*, 127–166.

Clifton, R. K., Rochat, P., Robin, D. J., & Berthier, N. E. (1994). Multimodal perception in the control of infant reaching. *Journal of Experimental Psychology: Human Perception and Performance, 20*, 876–886.

Clinchy, B. M. (2002). Revisiting women's ways of knowing. In B. K. Hofer & P. R. Pintrich (Eds.), *Personal epistemology: The psychological beliefs about knowledge and knowing* (pp. 63–87). Mahwah, NJ: Erlbaum.

Clincy, A. R., & Mills-Koonce, W. R. (2013). Trajectories of intrusive parenting during infancy and toddlerhood as predictors of rural, low-income African American boys' school-related outcomes. *American Journal of Orthopsychiatry, 83*, 194–206.

Coall, D. A., Callan, A. C., Dickins, T. E., & Chisholm, J. S. (2015). Evolution and prenatal development: An evolutionary perspective. In M. E. Lamb (Ed.), *Handbook of child psychology and developmental science: Vol. 3. Socioemotional processes* (7th ed., pp. 57–105). Hoboken, NJ: Wiley.

Cohen, D. A. (2014). *A big crisis: The hidden forces behind the obesity epidemic—and how we can end it*. New York: Nation Books.

Cohen, G. L., Garcia, J., & Master, A. (2006). Reducing the racial achievement gap: A social-psychological intervention. *Science, 313*, 1307–1310.

Cohen, J., Van Landeghem, P., Carpentier, N., & Delins, L. (2014). Different trends in euthanasia acceptance across Europe: A study of 13 western and 10 central and eastern European countries. *European Journal of Public Health, 23*, 378–380.

Cohen, L. B. (2003). Commentary on Part I: Unresolved issues in infant categorization. In D. H. Rakison & L. M. Oakes (Eds.), *Early category and concept development: Making sense of the blooming, buzzing confusion* (pp. 193–209). New York: Oxford University Press.

Cohen, L. B. (2010). A bottom-up approach to infant perception and cognition: A summary of evidence and discussion of issues. In S. P. Johnson (Ed.), *Neoconstructivism: The new science of cognitive development* (pp. 335–346). New York: Oxford University Press.

Cohen, L. B., & Brunt, J. (2009). Early word learning and categorization: Methodological issues and recent empirical evidence. In J. Colombo, P. McCardle, & L. Freund (Eds.), *Infant pathways to language: Methods, models, and research disorders* (pp. 245–266). New York: Psychology Press.

Cohen-Bendahan, C. C. C., van Doornen, L. J. P., & de Weerth, C. (2014). Young adults' reactions to infant crying. *Infant Behavior and Development, 37,* 33–43.

Cohn, N. (2014). Framing "I can't draw": The influence of cultural frames on the development of drawing. *Culture and Psychology, 20,* 102–117.

Colbert, J. A., Schulte, J., & Adler, J. N. (2013). Clinical decisions: Physician-assisted suicide—polling results. *New England Journal of Medicine, 369:* e15.

Colbert, L. G. (2014, May). Taking care of mom: A son's journey. *Aging Today.* San Francisco: American Society on Aging. Retrieved from www.asaging.org/blog/taking-care-mom-sons-journey

Colby, A., Kohlberg, L., Gibbs, J., & Lieberman, M. (1983). A longitudinal study of moral judgment. *Monographs of the Society for Research in Child Development, 48*(1–2, Serial No. 200).

Colby, S. L., & Ortman, J. M. (2014, May). The baby boom cohort in the United States: 2012 to 2060: Population estimates and projections. *Current Population Reports* (P25-1141). Washington, DC: U.S. Census Bureau.

Cole, D. A., Maxwell, S. E., Martin, J. M., Peeke, L. G., Seroczynski, A. D., & Tram, J. M. (2001). The development of multiple domains of child and adolescent self-concept: A cohort sequential longitudinal design. *Child Development, 72,* 1723–1746.

Cole, E. R., & Stewart, A. J. (1996). Meanings of political participation among black and white women: Political identity and social responsibility. *Journal of Personality and Social Psychology, 71,* 130–140.

Cole, M. (1990). Cognitive development and formal schooling: The evidence from cross-cultural research. In L. C. Moll (Ed.), *Vygotsky and education* (pp. 89–110). New York: Cambridge University Press.

Cole, M. (2006). Culture and cognitive development in phylogenetic, historical, and ontogenetic perspective. In R. M. Lerner (Ed.), *Handbook of child psychology: Vol. 1. Theoretical models of human development* (6th ed., pp. 636–685). Hoboken, NJ: Wiley.

Cole, P. M., Armstrong, L. M., & Pemberton, C. K. (2010). The role of language in the development of emotion regulation. In S. D. Calkins & M. A. Bell (Eds.), *Child development at the intersection of emotion and cognition* (pp. 59–77). Washington, DC: American Psychological Association.

Cole, P. M., LeDonne, E. N., & Tan, P. Z. (2013). A longitudinal examination of maternal emotions in relation to young children's developing self-regulation. *Parenting: Science and Practice, 13,* 113–132.

Coleman, M., Ganong, L., & Leon, K. (2006). Divorce and postdivorce relationships. In A. L. Vangelisti & D. Perlman (Eds.), *The Cambridge handbook of personal relationships* (pp. 157–173). New York: Cambridge University Press.

Coleman, M., Ganong, L., & Russell, L. T. (2013). Resilience in stepfamilies. In D. S. Becvar (Ed.), *Handbook of family resilience* (pp. 85–103). New York: Springer.

Coleman, P. G., Ivani-Chalian, C., & Robinson, M. (2004). Religious attitudes among British older people: Stability and change in a 20-year longitudinal study. *Ageing and Society, 24,* 167–188.

Coley, R. L., Morris, J. E., & Hernandez, D. (2004). Out-of-school care and problem behavior trajectories among low-income adolescents: Individual, family, and neighborhood characteristics as added risks. *Child Development, 75,* 948–965.

Collings, P. (2001). "If you got everything, it's good enough": Perspectives on successful aging in a Canadian Inuit community. *Journal of Cross-Cultural Gerontology, 16,* 127–155.

Collins, N. L., & Feeney, B. C. (2010). An attachment theoretical perspective on social support dynamics in couples: Normative processes and individual differences. In K. Sullivan & J. Davila (Eds.), *Support processes in intimate relationships* (pp. 89–120). New York: Oxford University Press.

Collins, W., & Doolittle, A. (2006). Personal reflections of funeral rituals and spirituality in a Kentucky African American family. *Death Studies, 30,* 957–969.

Collins, W. A., & Laursen, B. (2004). Parent–adolescent relationships and influences. In R. M. Lerner & L. Steinberg (Eds.), *Handbook of adolescent psychology* (2nd ed., pp. 331–361). New York: Wiley.

Collins, W. A., & Madsen, S. D. (2006). Personal relationships in adolescence and early adulthood. In A. L. Vangelisti & D. Perlman (Eds.), *The Cambridge handbook of personal relationships* (pp. 191–209). New York: Cambridge University Press.

Collins, W. A., Madsen, S. D., & Susman-Stillman, A. (2002). Parenting during middle childhood. In M. H. Bornstein (Ed.), *Handbook of parenting: Vol. 1* (2nd ed., pp. 73–101). Mahwah, NJ: Erlbaum.

Collins, W. A., & van Dulmen, M. (2006a). "The course of true love(s) ...": Origins and pathways in the development of romantic relationships. In A. Booth & A. Crouter (Eds.), *Romance and sex in adolescence and emerging adulthood: Risks and opportunities* (pp. 63–86). Mahwah, NJ: Erlbaum.

Collins, W. A., & van Dulmen, M. (2006b). Friendships and romantic relationships in emerging adulthood: Continuities and discontinuities. In J. J. Arnett & J. Tanner (Eds.), *Emerging adults in America: Coming of age in the 21st century* (pp. 219–234). Washington, DC: American Psychological Association.

Collins, W. A., Welsh, D. P., & Furman, W. (2009). Adolescent romantic relationships. *Annual Review of Psychology, 60,* 631–652.

Collins, W. K., & Steinberg, L. (2006). Adolescent development in interpersonal context. In N. Eisenberg (Ed.), *Handbook of child psychology: Vol. 3. Social, emotional, and personality development* (6th ed., pp. 1003–1067). Hoboken, NJ: Wiley.

Collin-Vézina, D., Daigneault, I., & Hébert, M. (2013). Lessons learned from child sexual abuse research: Prevalence, outcomes, and preventive strategies. *Child and Adolescent Psychiatry and Mental Health, 7,* 1–9.

Colman, R. J., Anderson, R. M., Johnson, S. C., Kastman, E. K., Kosmatka, K. J., Beasley, T. M., et al. (2009). Caloric restriction delays disease onset and mortality in rhesus monkeys. *Science, 325,* 201–204.

Colombo, J. (2002). Infant attention grows up: The emergence of a developmental cognitive neuroscience perspective. *Current Directions in Psychological Science, 11,* 196–199.

Colombo, J., Brez, C. C., & Curtindale, L. M. (2013). Infant perception and cognition. In R. M. Lerner, M. A. Easterbrooks, & J. Mistry (Eds.), *Handbook of psychology: Vol. 6. Developmental psychology* (pp. 61–89). Hoboken, NJ: Wiley.

Colombo, J., Kapa, L., & Curtindale, L. (2011). Varieties of attention in infancy. In L. M. Oakes, C. H. Cashon, M. Casasola, & D. Rakison (Eds.), *Infant perception and cognition* (pp. 3–25). New York: Oxford University Press.

Colombo, J., Shaddy, D. J., Richman, W. A., Maikranz, J. M., & Blaga, O. M. (2004). The developmental course of habituation in infancy and preschool outcome. *Infancy, 5,* 1–38.

Colson, E. R., Willinger, M., Rybin, D., Heeren, T., Smith, L. A., Lister, G., et al. (2013). Trends and factors associated with infant bed sharing, 1993–2010. The National Infant Sleep Position Study. *JAMA Pediatrics, 167,* 1032–1037.

Comeau, L., Genesee, F., & Mendelson, M. (2010). A comparison of bilingual and monolingual children's conversational repairs. *First Language, 30,* 354–374.

Commendador, K. A. (2010). Parental influences on adolescent decision-making and condom use. *Pediatric Nursing, 36,* 147–170.

Common Sense Media. (2013). *Zero to eight: Children's media use in America 2013.* San Francisco: Author. Retrieved from www.commonsensemedia.org/research/zero-to-eight-childrens-media-use-in-america-2013

Compas, B. E., Jaser, S. S., Dunn, M. J., & Rodriguez, E. M. (2012). Coping with chronic illness in childhood and adolescence. *Annual Review of Clinical Psychology, 8,* 455–480.

Compton, J. I., Cox, E., & Laanan, F. S. (2006). Adult learners in transition. In F. S. Laanan (Eds.), *New directions for student services* (Vol. 114, pp. 73–80). San Francisco: Jossey-Bass.

Comstock, G. (2008). A sociological perspective on television violence and aggression. *American Behavioral Scientist, 51,* 1137–1154.

Comunian, A. L., & Gielen, U. P. (2000). Sociomoral reflection and prosocial and antisocial behavior: Two Italian studies. *Psychological Reports, 87,* 161–175.

Comunian, A. L., & Gielen, U. P. (2006). Promotion of moral judgment maturity through stimulation of social role-taking and social reflection: An Italian intervention study. *Journal of Moral Education, 35,* 51–69.

Conchas, G. Q. (2006). *The color of success: Race and high-achieving urban youth.* New York: Teachers College Press.

Conde-Agudelo, A., Belizan, J. M., and Diaz-Rossello, J. (2011). Kangaroo mother care to reduce morbidity and mortality in low birthweight infants. *Cochrane Database of Systematic Reviews,* Issue 3, Art. No.: CD002771.

Condron, D. J. (2013). Affluence, inequality, and educational achievement: A structural analysis of 97 jurisdictions, across the globe. *Sociological Spectrum, 33,* 73–97.

Conduct Problems Prevention Research Group. (2014). Trajectories of risk for early sexual activity and early substance use in the Fast Track Prevention Program. *Prevention Sciences, 15*(Suppl. 1), S33–S46.

Conger, K. J., Stocker, C., & McGuire, S. (2009). Sibling socialization: The effects of stressful life events and experiences. In L. Kramer & K. J. Conger (Eds.), *Siblings as agents of socialization: New directions for child and adolescent development* (No. 126, pp. 44–60). San Francisco: Jossey-Bass.

Conger, R. D., & Donnellan, M. B. (2007). An interactionist perspective on the socioeconomic context of human development. *Annual Review of Psychology, 58,* 175–199.

Conner, D. B., & Cross, D. R. (2003). Longitudinal analysis of the presence, efficacy, and stability of maternal scaffolding during informal problem-solving interactions. *British Journal of Developmental Psychology, 21,* 315–334.

Connidis, I. A. (2010). *Family ties and aging* (2nd ed.). Thousand Oaks, CA: Pine Forge Press.

Connolly, J., & Goldberg, A. (1999). Romantic relationships in adolescence: The role of friends and peers in their emergence and development. In W. Furman, B. B. Brown, & C. Feiring (Eds.), *The development of romantic relationships in adolescence* (pp. 266–290). New York: Cambridge University Press.

Connolly, J., & McIsaac, C. (2011). Romantic relationships in adolescence. In M. K. Underwood & L. H. Rosen (Eds.), *Social development: Relationships in infancy, childhood, and adolescence* (pp. 180–203). New York: Guilford.

Connor, D. F. (2015). Stimulant and nonstimulant medications for childhood ADHD. In R. A. Barkley (Ed.), *Attention-deficit hyperactivity disorder: A* handbook for diagnosis and treatment (4th ed., pp. 666–685). New York: Guilford.

Connor, S. R., Pyenson, B., Fitch, K., Spence, C., & Iwasaki, K. (2007). Comparing hospice and nonhospice patient survival among patients who die within a three-year window. *Journal of Pain and Symptom Management, 33,* 238–246.

Conroy-Beam, D., Buss, D. M., Pham, M. N., & Shackelford, T. K. (2015). How sexually dimorphic are human mate preferences? *Personality and Social Psychology Bulletin, 41,* 1082–1093.

Conway, C. C., Rancourt, D., Adelman, C. B., Burk, W. J., & Prinstein, M. J. (2011). Depression socialization within friendship groups at the transition to adolescence: The roles of gender and group centrality as moderators of peer influence. *Journal of Abnormal Psychology, 120,* 857–867.

Conway, L. (2007, April 5). Drop the Barbie: Ken Zucker's reparatist treatment of gender-variant children. *Trans News Updates.* Retrieved from ai.eecs.umich.edu/people/conway/TS/News/Drop%20the%20Barbie.htm

Conway, M. A., Wang, Q., Hanyu, K., & Haque, S. (2005). A cross-cultural investigation of autobiographical memory. On the universality and cultural variation of the reminiscence bump. *Journal of Cross-Cultural Psychology, 36,* 739–749.

Conwell, Y., Duberstein, P. R., Hirsch, J., & Conner, K. R. (2010). Health status and suicide in the second half of life. *Geriatric Psychiatry, 25,* 371–379.

Conwell, Y., & O'Reilly, A. (2013). The challenge of suicide prevention in later life. In H. Lavretsky, M. Sajatovic, & C. F. Reynolds, III (Eds.), *Late-life mood disorders* (pp. 206–219). New York: Oxford University Press.

Conwell, Y., Van Orden, K., & Caine, E. D. (2011). Suicide in older adults. *Psychiatric Clinics of North America, 34,* 451–468.

Cook, C. R., Williams, K. R., Guerra, N. G., & Kim, T. E. (2010). Variability in the prevalence of bullying and victimization: A cross-national and methodological analysis. In S. R. Jimerson, S. M. Swearer, & D. L. Espelage (Eds.), *Handbook of bullying in schools: An international perspective* (pp. 347–362). New York: Routledge.

Cooke, L. P. (2010). The politics of housework. In J. Treas & S. Drobnic (Eds.), *Dividing the domestic: Men, women, and household work in cross-national perspective* (pp. 59–78). Stanford, CA: Stanford University Press.

Cooper, C., Sayer, A. A., & Dennison, E. M. (2006). The developmental environment: Clinical perspectives on effects on the musculoskeletal system. In P. Gluckman & M. Hanson (Eds.), *Developmental origins of health and disease* (pp. 392–405). Cambridge, UK: Cambridge University Press.

Cooper, H., Batts, A., Patall, E. A., & Dent, A. L. (2010). Effects of full-day kindergarten on academic achievement and social development. *Review of Educational Research, 80,* 54–70.

Copeland, W., Shanahan, L., Miller, S., Costello, E. J., Angold, A., & Maughan, B. (2010). Do the negative effects of early pubertal timing on adolescent girls continue into young adulthood? *American Journal of Psychiatry, 167,* 1218–1225.

Copen, C. E., Chandra, A., & Febo-Vazquez, I. (2016). Sexual behavior, sexual attraction, and sexual orientation among adults aged 18–44 in the United States: Data from the 2011–2013 National Survey of Family Growth. *National Health Statistics Reports,* No. 88. Retrieved from www.cdc.gov/nchs/data/nhsr/nhsr088.pdf

Copen, C. E., Daniels, K., & Mosher, W. D. (2013). *First premarital cohabitation in the United States: 2006–2010 National Survey of Family Growth. National Health Statistics Reports,* No. 64. Hyattsville, MD: National Center for Health Statistics.

Coplan, R. J., & Arbeau, K. A. (2008). The stresses of a "brave new world": Shyness and school adjustment in kindergarten. *Journal of Research in Childhood Education, 22,* 377–389.

Coplan, R. J., & Armer, M. (2007). A "multitude" of solitude: A closer look at social withdrawal and nonsocial play in early childhood. *Child Development Perspectives, 1,* 26–32.

Coplan, R. J., Gavinsky-Molina, M. H., Lagace Seguin, D., & Wichmann, C. (2001). When girls versus boys play alone: Gender differences in the associates of nonsocial play in kindergarten. *Developmental Psychology, 37,* 464–474.

Coplan, R. J., & Ooi, L. (2014). The causes and consequences of "playing alone" in childhood. In R. J. Coplan & J. C. Bowker (Eds.), *The handbook of solitude: Psychological perspectives on social isolation, social withdrawal, and being alone* (pp. 111–128). Chichester, UK: Wiley-Blackwell.

Coplan, R. J., Prakash, K., O'Neil, K., & Armer, M. (2004). Do you "want" to play? Distinguishing between conflicted shyness and social disinterest in early childhood. *Developmental Psychology, 40,* 244–258.

Copple, C., & Bredekamp, S. (2009). *Developmentally appropriate practice in early childhood programs* (3rd ed.). Washington, DC: National Association for the Education of Young Children.

Corbett, B., & Alda, M. (2015). On telomeres long and short. *Journal of Psychiatry Neuroscience, 40,* 3–4.

Corby, B. C., Hodges, E. V., & Perry, D. G. (2007). Gender identity and adjustment in black, Hispanic, and white preadolescents. *Developmental Psychology, 26,* 261–266.

Corenblum, B. (2003). What children remember about ingroup and outgroup peers: Effects of stereotypes on children's processing of information about group members. *Journal of Experimental Child Psychology, 86,* 32–66.

Cornell, K. H. (2013). Adolescent pregnancy and parenthood. In J. Sandoval (Ed.), *Crisis counseling, intervention, and prevention in the schools* (3rd ed., pp. 291–313). New York: Routledge.

Cornoldi, C., Giofré, D., Orsini, A., & Pezzuti, L. (2014). Differences in the intellectual profile of children with intellectual vs. learning disability. *Research in Developmental Disabilities, 35,* 2224–2230.

Cornwell, A. C., & Feigenbaum, P. (2006). Sleep biological rhythms in normal infants and those at high risk for SIDS. *Chronobiology International, 23,* 935–961.

Cornwell, B., & Laumann, E. O. (2015). The health benefits of network growth: New evidence from a national survey of older adults. *Social Science and Medicine, 125,* 94–106.

Corr, C. A. (2015a). Death education at the college and university level. In J. M. Stillion & T. Attig (Eds.), *Death, dying, and bereavement: Contemporary perspectives, institutions, and practices* (pp. 207–219). New York: Springer.

Corr, C. A. (2015b). Let's stop "staging" persons who are coping with loss. *Illness, Crisis, & Loss, 23,* 226–241.

Corr, C. A., & Corr, D. M. (2007). Historical and contemporary perspectives on loss, grief, and mourning. In C. A. Corr & D. M. Corr (Eds.), *Handbook of thanatology* (pp. 131–142). New York: Routledge.

Corr, C. A., & Corr, D. M. (2013). *Death and dying, life and living* (7th ed.). Belmont, CA: Wadsworth/Cengage Learning.

Correa-Chávez, M., Roberts, A. L. D., & Perez, M. M. (2011). Cultural patterns in children's learning through keen observation and participation in their communities. In J. B. Benson (Ed.), *Advances in child development and behavior* (Vol. 40, pp. 209–241). San Diego, CA: Elsevier Academic Press.

Correia, C., Lopez, K. J., Wroblewski, K. E., Huisingh-Scheetz, M., Kern, D. W., Chen, R. C., et al. (2016). Global sensory impairment in older adults in the United States. *Journal of the American Geriatrics Society, 64,* 306–313.

Cosentino, S., Schupf, N., Christensen, K., Andersen, S. L., Newman, A., & Mayeux, R. (2013). Reduced prevalence of cognitive impairment in families with exceptional longevity. *JAMA Neurology, 70,* 867–874.

Costa, A., & Sebastián-Gallés, N. (2014). How does the bilingual experience sculpt the brain? *Nature Reviews Neuroscience, 15,* 336–345.

Costacurta, M., Sicuro, L., Di Renzo, L., & Condo, R. (2012). Childhood obesity and skeletal-dental maturity. *European Journal of Paediatric Dentistry, 13,* 128–132.

Côté, J. E. (2006). Emerging adulthood as an institutionalized moratorium: Risks and benefits to identity formation. In J. J. Arnett (Ed.), *Emerging adults in America: Coming of age in the 21st century* (pp. 85–116). Washington, DC: American Psychological Association.

Côté, J. E. (2014). The dangerous myth of emerging adulthood: An evidence-based critique of a flawed developmental theory. *Applied Developmental Science, 18,* 177–188.

Côté, J. E., & Bynner, J. M. (2008). Changes in the transition to adulthood in the UK and Canada: The role of structure and agency in emerging adulthood. *Journal of Youth Studies, 11,* 251–268.

Cote, L. R., & Bornstein, M. H. (2009). Child and mother play in three U.S. cultural groups: Comparisons and associations. *Journal of Family Psychology, 23,* 355–363.

Côté, S. M., Vaillancourt, T., Barker, E. D., Nagin, D., & Tremblay, R. E. (2007). The joint development of physical and indirect aggression: Predictors of continuity and change during childhood. *Development and Psychopathology, 19,* 37–55.

Coubart, A., Izard, V., Spelke, E. S., Marie, J., & Streri, A. (2014). Dissociation between small and large numerosities in newborn infants. *Developmental Science, 17,* 11–22.

Couch, S. C., Glanz, K., Zhou, C., Sallis, J. F., & Saelens, B. E. (2014). Home food environment in relation to children's diet quality and weight status. *Journal of the Academy of Nutrition and Dietetics, 114,* 1569–1579.

Coudin, G., & Alexopoulos, T. (2010). "Help me! I'm old": How negative aging stereotypes create dependency among older adults. *Aging and Mental Health, 14,* 516–523.

Courage, M. L., & Howe, M. L. (2010). To watch or not to watch: Infants and toddlers in a brave new electronic world. *Developmental Review, 30,* 101–115.

Courchesne, E., Mouton, P. R., Calhoun, M. E., Semendeferi, K., Ahrens-Barbeau, C., Hallet, M. J., et al. (2011). Neuron number and size in prefrontal cortex of children with autism. *JAMA, 306,* 2001–2010.

Coursolle, K. M., Sweeney, M. M., Raymo, J. M., & Ho, J.-H. (2010). The association between retirement and emotional well-being: Does prior work–family conflict matter? *Journals of Gerontology, 65B,* 609–620.

Cowan, C. P., & Cowan, P. A. (1997). Working with couples during stressful transitions. In S. Dreman (Ed.), *The family on the threshold of the 21st century* (pp. 17–47). Mahwah, NJ: Erlbaum.

Cowan, N., & Alloway, T. P. (2009). Development of working memory in childhood. In M. L. Courage & N. Cowan (Eds.), *Development of memory in infancy and childhood* (pp. 303–342). Hove, UK: Psychology Press.

Cowan, P. A., & Cowan, C. P. (2002). Interventions as tests of family systems theories: Marital and family relationships in children's development and psychopathology. *Development and Psychopathology, 14,* 731–759.

Cox, B. D. (2013). The past and future of epigenesis in psychology. *New Ideas in Psychology, 31,* 351–354.

Coyle, J. T. (2013). Brain structural alterations induced by fetal exposure to cocaine persist into adolescence and affect behavior. *JAMA Psychiatry, 70,* 1113–1114.

Coyle, T. R. (2013). Effects of processing speed on intelligence may be underestimated: Comment on Demetriou et al. (2013). *Intelligence, 41,* 732–734.

Coyne, S. M., Robinson, S. L., & Nelson, D. A. (2010). Does reality backbite? Verbal and relational aggression in reality television programs. *Journal of Broadcasting and Electronic Media, 54,* 282–298.

Crago, M. B., Annahatak, B., & Ningiuruvik, L. (1993). Changing patterns of language socialization in Inuit homes. *Anthropology and Education Quarterly, 24,* 205–223.

Craig, C. M., & Lee, D. N. (1999). Neonatal control of sucking pressure: Evidence for an intrinsic tau guide. *Experimental Brain Research, 124,* 371–382.

Craig, H. K., & Washington, J. A. (2006). *Malik goes to school: Examining the language skills of African American students from preschool–5th grade.* Mahwah, NJ: Erlbaum.

Craig, W. M., Pepler, D., & Atlas, R. (2000). Observations of bullying in the playground and in the classroom. *School Psychology International, 21,* 22–36.

Crain, W. (2010). *Theories of development: Concepts and applications* (6th ed.). Upper Saddle River, NJ: Pearson.

Crair, M. C., Gillespie, D. C., & Stryker, M. P. (1998). The role of visual experience in the development of columns in cat visual cortex. *Science, 279,* 566–570.

Cratty, B. J. (1986). *Perceptual and motor development in infants and children* (3rd ed.), Englewood Cliffs, NJ: Prentice-Hall.

Crick, N. R., Ostrov, J. M., Burr, J. E., Cullerton-Sen, C., Jansen-Yeh, E., & Ralston, P. (2006). A longitudinal study of relational and physical aggression in preschool. *Journal of Applied Developmental Psychology, 27,* 254–268.

Crick, N. R., Ostrov, J. M., & Werner, N. E. (2006). A longitudinal study of relational aggression, physical aggression, and social-psychological adjustment. *Journal of Abnormal Child Psychology, 34,* 131–142.

Criss, M. M., & Shaw, D. S. (2005). Sibling relationships as contexts for delinquency training in low income families. *Journal of Family Psychology, 19,* 592–600.

Crocetti, E., Cieciuch, J., Gao, C.-H., Klimstra, T., Lin, C.-L., Matos, P. M., et al. (2015). National and gender measurement invariance of the Utrecht-Management of Identity Commitments Scale (U-MICS): A 10-nation study with university students. *Assessment, 22,* 753–768.

Crocetti, E., Jahromi, P., & Meeus, W. (2012). Identity and civic engagement in adolescence. *Journal of Adolescence, 35,* 521–532.

Crocetti, E., & Meeus, W. (2015). The identity statuses: Strengths of a person-centered approach. In K. C. McLean & M. Syed (Eds.), *Oxford handbook of identity development* (pp. 97–114). New York: Oxford University Press.

Crocetti, E., Meeus, W. H. J., Ritchie, R. A., Meca, A., & Schwartz, S. J. (2014). Adolescent identity: Is this the key to unraveling associations between family relationships and problem behaviors? In L. M. Scheier & W. B. Hansen (Eds.), *Parenting and teen drug use: The most recent findings from research, prevention, and treatment* (pp. 92–109). New York: Oxford University Press.

Crocetti, E., Rabaglietti, E., & Sica, L. S. (2012). Personal identity in Italy. In S. J. Schwartz (Ed.), *New directions for child and adolescent development* (pp. 87–102). New York: Wiley.

Crocetti, E., Sica, L. S., Schwartz, S. J., Serafini, T., & Meeus, W. (2013). Identity styles, dimensions, statuses, and functions: Making connections among identity conceptualizations. *European Review of Applied Psychology, 63,* 1–13.

Crockenberg, S., & Leerkes, E. (2003). Infant negative emotionality, caregiving, and family relationships. In A. C. Crouter & A. Booth (Eds.), *Children's influence on family dynamics* (pp. 57–78). Mahwah, NJ: Erlbaum.

Crockenberg, S., & Leerkes, E. (2004). Infant and maternal behaviors regulate infant reactivity to novelty at 6 months. *Developmental Psychology, 40,* 1123–1132.

Croft, D. P., Brent, L. J. N., Franks, D. W., & Cant, M. A. (2015). The evolution of prolonged life after reproduction. *Trends in Ecology and Evolution, 30,* 407–416.

Croker, R. (2007). *The boomer century: 1946–2046: How America's most influential generation changed everything.* New York: Springboard Press.

Crosnoe, R., & Benner, A. D. (2015). Children at school. In M. H. Bornstein & T. Leventhal (Eds.), *Handbook of child psychology and developmental science: Vol. 4. Ecological settings and processes* (7th ed., pp. 268–304). Hoboken, NJ: Wiley.

Crosnoe, R., Johnson, M. K., & Elder, G. H., Jr. (2004). School size and the interpersonal side of education: An examination of race/ethnicity and organizational context. *Social Science Quarterly, 85,* 1259–1274.

Cross, S., & Markus, H. (1991). Possible selves across the life span. *Human Development, 34,* 230–255.

Crouch, J. L., Skowronski, J. J., Milner, J. S., & Harris, B. (2008). Parental responses to infant crying: The influence of child physical abuse risk and hostile priming. *Child Abuse and Neglect, 32,* 702–710.

Croucher, K., Hicks, L., & Jackson, K. (2006) *Housing with care for later life: A literature review.* London, UK: Joseph Rowntree Foundation.

Crouter, A. C., & Head, M. R. (2002). Parental monitoring and knowledge of children. In M. H. Bornstein (Ed.), *Handbook of parenting: Vol. 3. Being and becoming a parent* (2nd ed., pp. 461–483). Mahwah, NJ: Erlbaum.

Crouter, A. C., Whiteman, S. D., McHale, S. M., & Osgood, D. W. (2007). Development of gender attitude traditionality across middle childhood and adolescence. *Child Development, 78,* 911–926.

Crowley, K. (2011). Sleep and sleep disorders in older adults. *Neuropsychological Review, 21,* 41–53.

Cruces, J., Venero, C., Pereda-Pérez, I., & De la Fuente, M. (2014). The effect of psychological stress and social isolation on neuroimmunoendocrine communication. *Current Pharmaceutical Design, 20,* 4608–4628.

Crystal, D. S., Killen, M., & Ruck, M. D. (2010). Fair treatment by authorities is related to children's and adolescents' evaluations of interracial exclusion. *Applied Developmental Science, 14,* 125–136.

Csibra, G., & Gergely, G. (2011). Natural pedagogy as evolutionary adaptation. *Philosophical Transactions of the Royal Society B, 366,* 1149–1157.

Csikszentmihalyi, M., & Nakamura, J. (2005). The role of emotions in the development of wisdom. In R. J. Sternberg & J. Jordan (Eds.), *A handbook of wisdom: Psychological perspectives* (pp. 220–242). New York: Cambridge University Press.

Cubanski, J., Casillas, G., & Damico, A. (2015). *Poverty among seniors: An updated analysis of national and state level poverty rates under the official and supplemental poverty measures.* Menlo Park, CA: Kaiser Family Foundation. Retrieved from kff.org/report-section/poverty-among-seniors-issue-brief

Cui, M., & Donnellan, M. B. (2009). Trajectories of conflict over raising adolescent children and marital satisfaction. *Journal of Marriage and Family, 71,* 478–494.

Cumming, E., & Henry, W. E. (1961). *Growing old: The process of disengagement.* New York: Basic Books.

Cummings, E. M., & Davies, P. T. (2010). *Marital conflict and children: An emotional security perspective.* New York: Guilford.

Cummings, E. M., Goeke-Morey, M. C., & Papp, L. M. (2004). Everyday marital conflict and child aggression. *Journal of Abnormal Child Psychology, 32,* 91–202.

Cummings, E. M., & Miller-Graff, L. E. (2015). Emotional security theory: An emerging theoretical model for youths' psychological and physiological responses across multiple developmental contexts. *Current Directions in Psychological Science, 24,* 208–213.

Curby, T. W., LoCasale-Crouch, J., Konold, T. R., Pianta, R. C., Howes, C., Burchinal, M., et al. (2009). The relations of observed pre-K classroom quality profiles to children's achievement and social competence. *Early Education and Development, 20,* 346–372.

Curl, A. L., Stowe, J. D., Cooney, T. M., & Proulx, C. M. (2014). Giving up the keys: How driving cessation affects engagement in later life. *Gerontologist, 54,* 423–433.

Curlin, F. A., Nwodim, C., Vance, J. L., Chin, M. H., & Lantos, J. D. (2008). To die, to sleep: U.S. physicians' religious and other objections to physician-assisted suicide, terminal sedation, and withdrawal of life support. *American Journal of Hospice and Palliative Medicine, 25,* 112–120.

Curtin, S., & Werker, J. F. (2007). The perceptual foundations of phonological development. In G. Gaskell (Ed.), *Oxford handbook of psycholinguistics* (pp. 579–599). Oxford, UK: Oxford University Press.

Curtin, S. C., Ventura, S. J., & Martinez, G. M. (2014, August). *Recent declines in nonmarital childbearing in the United States* (NCHS Data Brief No. 162). Hyattsville, MD: National Center for Health Statistics. Retrieved from www.cdc.gov/nchs/data/databriefs/db162.pdf

Curtiss, K., Hayslip, B., Jr., & Dolan, D. C. (2007). Motivational style, length of residence, voluntariness, and gender as influences on adjustment to long term care: A pilot study. *Journal of Human Behavior in the Social Environment, 15,* 13–34.

Curtiss, S., & Schaeffer, J. (2005). Syntactic development in children with hemispherectomy: The I-, D-, and C-systems. *Brain and Language, 94,* 147–166.

Cutchin, M. P. (2013). The complex process of becoming at-home in assisted living. In G. D. Rowles & M. Bernard (Eds.), *Environmental gerontology: Making meaningful places in old age* (pp. 105–124). New York: Springer.

Cutler, D. M., & Lleras-Muney, A. (2010). Understanding differences in health behaviors by education. *Journal of Health Economics, 29,* 1–28.

Cutler, S. J., Hendricks, J., & O'Neill, G. (2011). Civic engagement and aging. In R. H. Binstock & L. K. George (Eds.), *Handbook of aging and the social sciences* (7th ed., pp. 221–233). San Diego, CA: Academic Press.

Cutuli, J. J., Herbers, J. E., Rinaldi, M., Masten, A. S., & Oberg, C. N. (2010). Asthma and behavior in homeless 4- to 7-year-olds. *Pediatrics, 125,* e145–e151.

Cvencek, D., Meltzoff, A. N., & Greenwald, A. G. (2011). Math-gender stereotypes in elementary school children. *Child Development, 82,* 766–779.

Cyr, C., Euser, E. M., Bakermans-Kranenburg, M. J., & van IJzendoorn, M. H. (2010). Attachment security and disorganization in maltreating and high-risk families: Implications for developmental theory. *Development and Psychopathology, 14,* 843–860.

Czaja, S. J. (2016). Long-term care services and support systems for older adults: The role of technology. *American Psychologist, 71,* 294–301.

D

Daatland, S. O. (2007). Marital history and intergenerational solidarity: The impact of divorce and unmarried cohabitation. *Journal of Social Issues, 63,* 809–825.

Dabrowska, E. (2000). From formula to schema: The acquisition of English questions. *Cognitive Linguistics, 11,* 1–20.

Daher, M. (2012). Cultural beliefs and values in cancer patients. *Annals of Oncology, 23*(Suppl. 3), 66–69.

Dahl, A., Hassing, L. B., Fransson, E., Berg, S., Gatz, M., Reynolds, C. A., et al. (2010). Being overweight in midlife is associated with lower cognitive ability and steeper cognitive decline in late life. *Journals of Gerontology, 65A,* 57–62.

Dakil, S. R., Cox, M., Lin, H., & Flores, G. (2012). Physical abuse in U.S. children: Risk factors and deficiencies in referrals to support services. *Journal of Aggression, Maltreatment, and Trauma, 21,* 555–569.

Daley, T. C., Whaley, S. E., Sigman, M. D., Espinosa, M. P., & Neumann, C. (2003). IQ on the rise: The Flynn effect in rural Kenyan children. *Psychological Science, 14,* 215–219.

Dallman, M. F., Pecoraro, N., Akana, S. F., la Fleur, S. E., Gomez, F., Houshyar, H., et al. (2003). Chronic stress and obesity: A new view of "comfort food." *Proceedings of the National Academy of Sciences, 100,* 11696–11701.

Damon, W. (1988a). *The moral child.* New York: Free Press.

Damon, W. (1988b). *Self-understanding in childhood and adolescence.* New York: Cambridge University Press.

Damon, W. (1990). Self-concept, adolescent. In R. M. Lerner, A. C. Petersen, & J. Brooks-Gunn (Eds.), *The encyclopedia of adolescence* (Vol. 2, pp. 87–91). New York: Garland.

Dane, E., Baer, M., Pratt, M. G., & Oldham, G. R. (2011). Rational versus intuitive problem solving: How thinking "off the beaten path" can stimulate creativity. *Psychology of Aesthetics, Creativity, and the Arts, 5,* 3–12.

Danesh, D., Paskett, E. D., & Ferketich, A. K. (2014). Disparities in receipt of advice to quit smoking from health care providers: 2010 National Health Interview Survey. *Preventing Chronic Disease, 11,* 140053.

Daniels, E., & Leaper, C. (2006). A longitudinal investigation of sport participation, peer acceptance, and self-esteem among adolescent girls and boys. *Sex Roles, 55,* 875–880.

Daniels, H. (2011). Vygotsky and psychology. In U. Goswami (Ed.), *The Wiley-Blackwell handbook of childhood cognitive development* (2nd ed., pp. 673–696). Malden, MA: Wiley-Blackwell.

Dannemiller, J. L., & Stephens, B. R. (1988). A critical test of infant pattern preference models. *Child Development, 59,* 210–216.

Danzer, E., & Johnson, M. P. (2014). Fetal surgery for neural tube defects. *Seminars in Fetal and Neonatal Medicine, 19,* 2–8.

Darcy, A. (2012). Gender issues in child and adolescent eating disorders. In J. Lock (Ed.), *Oxford handbook of child and adolescent eating disorders: Developmental perspectives* (pp. 88–105). New York: Oxford University Press.

Darling, N., & Steinberg, L. (1997). Community influences on adolescent achievement and deviance. In J. Brooks-Gunn, G. Duncan, & L. Aber (Eds.), *Neighborhood poverty: Context and consequences for children: Conceptual, ethological, and policy approaches to studying neighborhoods* (Vol. 2, pp. 120–131). New York: Russell Sage Foundation.

Darling-Hammond, L. (2010). *The flat world and education: How America's commitment to equity will determine our future.* New York: Teachers College Press.

Darwin, C. (1936). *On the origin of species by means of natural selection.* New York: Modern Library. (Original work published 1859)

Das, A., Waite, L. J., & Laumann, E. O. (2012). Sexual expression over the life course: Results from three landmark surveys. In L. M. Carpenter & J. DeLamater (Eds.), *Sex for life* (pp. 236–259). New York: New York University Press.

Daskalakis, N., & Yehuda, R. (2014). Site-specific methylation changes in the glucocorticoid receptor exon 1F promoter in relation to life adversity: Systematic review of contributing factors. *Frontiers in Neuroscience, 8.* Retrieved from journal.frontiersin.org/article/10.3389/fnins.2014.00369/full

Datar, A., & Sturm, R. (2006). Childhood overweight and elementary school outcomes. *International Journal of Obesity, 30,* 1449–1460.

D'Augelli, A. R. (2006). Developmental and contextual factors and mental health among lesbian, gay, and bisexual youths. In A. M. Omoto & H. S. Howard (Eds.), *Sexual orientation and mental health: Examining identity and development in lesbian, gay, and bisexual people* (pp. 37–53). Washington, DC: American Psychological Association.

Daugherty, J., & Copen, C. (2016). Trends in attitudes about marriage, childbearing, and sexual behavior: United States, 2002, 2006–2010, and 2011–2013. *National Health Statistics Reports,* No. 92. Retrieved from www.cdc.gov/nchs/data/nhsr/nhsr092.pdf

Davey, A., & Takagi, E. (2013). Adulthood and aging in families. In G. W. Peterson & K. R. Bush (Eds.), *Handbook of marriage and family* (pp. 377–399). New York: Springer.

David, K. M., & Murphy, B. C. (2007). Interparental conflict and preschoolers' peer relations: The moderating roles of temperament and gender. *Social Development, 16,* 1–23.

Davies, J. (2008). Differential teacher positive and negative interactions with male and female pupils in the primary school setting. *Educational and Child Psychology, 25,* 17–26.

Davies, P. T., & Cicchetti, D. (2014). How and why does the 5-HTTLPR gender moderate associations between maternal unresponsiveness and children's disruptive problems? *Child Development, 85,* 484–500.

Davis, A., Kimball, W., & Gould, E. (2015, May 27). *The class of 2015: Despite an improving economy, young grads still face an uphill climb.* Washington, DC: Economic Policy Institute. Retrieved from www.epi.org/publication/the-class-of-2015

Davis, E. L., & Buss, K. A. (2012). Moderators of the relation between shyness and behavior with peers: Cortisol dysregulation and maternal emotion socialization. *Social Development, 21,* 801–820.

Davis, E. L., Levine, L. J., Lench, H. C., & Quas, J. A. (2010). Metacognitive emotion regulation: Children's awareness that changing thoughts and goals can alleviate negative emotions. *Emotion, 10,* 498–510.

Davis, K., Schoen, C., & Bandeali, F. (2015). *Medicare: 50 years of ensuring coverage and care.* New York: The Commonwealth Fund.

Davis, K. F., Parker, K. P., & Montgomery, G. L. (2004). Sleep in infants and young children. Part 1: Normal sleep. *Journal of Pediatric Health Care, 18,* 65–71.

Davis, P. E., Meins, E., & Fernyhough, C. (2014). Children with imaginary companions focus on mental characteristics when describing their real-life friends. *Infant and Child Development, 23,* 622–633.

Dawson, T. L. (2002). New tools, new insights: Kohlberg's moral judgment stages revisited. *International Journal of Behavioral Development, 26,* 154–166.

Dayton, C. J., Walsh, T. B., Oh, W., & Volling, B. (2015). Hush now baby: Mothers' and fathers' strategies for soothing their infants and associated parenting outcomes. *Journal of Pediatric Health Care, 29,* 145–155.

DeAngeleo, L., Hurtado, S., & Pryor, J. H. (2010). *Your first college year: National norms for the 2008 YFCY Survey.* Los Angeles: Higher Education Research Institute, UCLA.

Dearing, E., McCartney, K., & Taylor, B. A. (2009). Does higher quality early child care promote low-income children's math and reading achievement in middle childhood? *Child Development, 80,* 1329–1349.

Dearing, E., Wimer, C., Simpkins, S. D., Lund, T., Bouffard, S. M., Caronongan, P., & Kreider, H. (2009). Do neighborhood and home contexts help explain why low-income children miss opportunities to participate in activities outside of school? *Developmental Psychology, 45,* 1545–1562.

Deary, I. J., Strand, S., Smith, P., & Fernandes, C. (2007). Intelligence and educational achievement. *Intelligence, 35,* 13–21.

Deary, I. J., Yang, J., Davies, G., Harris, S. E., Tenesa, A., Liewald, D., et al. (2012). Genetic contributions to stability and change in intelligence from childhood to old age. *Nature, 481,* 212–215.

Deas, S., Power, K., Collin, P., Yellowlees, A., & Grierson, D. (2011). The relationship between disordered eating, perceived parenting, and perfectionistic schemas. *Cognitive Therapy Research, 35,* 414–424.

Deater-Deckard, K., Lansford, J. E., Dodge, K. A., Pettit, G. S., & Bates, J. E. (2003). The development of attitudes about physical punishment: An 8-year longitudinal study. *Journal of Family Psychology, 17,* 351–360.

Deaton, A. S. (2009). *Aging religion, and health* (Working Paper 15271). Retrieved from www.nber.org/papers/w15271.pdf

DeBoer, T., Scott, L. S., & Nelson, C. A. (2007). Methods for acquiring and analyzing infant event-related potentials. In M. de Haan (Ed.), *Infant EEG and event-related potentials* (pp. 5–37). New York: Psychology Press.

Debrabant, J., Gheysen, F., Vingerhoets, G., & Van Waelvelde, H. (2012). Age-related differences in predictive response timing in children: Evidence from regularly relative to irregularly paced reaction time performance. *Human Movement Science, 31,* 801–810.

de Bruyn, E. H. (2005). Role strain, engagement and academic achievement in early adolescence. *Educational Studies, 31,* 15–27.

de Bruyn, E. H., & Cillessen, A. H. N. (2006). Popularity in early adolescence: Prosocial and antisocial subtypes. *Journal of Adolescent Research, 21,* 607–627.

de Bruyn, E. H., Deković, M., & Meijnen, G. W. (2003). Parenting, goal orientations, classroom behavior, and school success in early adolescence. *Journal of Applied Developmental Psychology, 24,* 393–412.

de Calignon, A., Polydoro, M., Suárez-Calvet, M., William, C., Adamowicz, D. H., Kopeikina, K. J., et al. (2012). Propagation of tau pathology in a model of early Alzheimer's disease. *Neuron, 73,* 685–697.

DeCasper, A. J., & Spence, M. J. (1986). Prenatal maternal speech influences newborns' perception of speech sounds. *Infant Behavior and Development, 9,* 133–150.

Dechanet, C., Anahory, T., Mathieu, T., Mathieu, D. J. C., Quantin, X., Ryftmann, L., et al. (2011). Effects of cigarette smoking on reproduction. *Human Reproduction Update, 17,* 76–95.

Declercq, E. R., Sakala, C., Corry, M. P., Applebaum, S., & Herrlich, A. (2014). Major survey findings of Listening to Mothers (SM) III: Pregnancy and Birth. *Journal of Perinatal Education, 23,* 9–16.

de Cock, E. S. A., Henrichs, J., Rijk, C. H. A. M., & van Bakel, H. J. A. (2015). Baby please stop crying: An experimental approach to infant crying, affect, and expected parent self-efficacy. *Journal of Reproductive and Infant Psychology, 33,* 414–425.

De Corte, E., & Verschaffel, L. (2006). Mathematical thinking and learning. In K. A. Renninger & I. E. Sigel (Eds.), *Handbook of child psychology: Vol. 4. Child psychology in practice* (6th ed., pp. 103–152). Hoboken, NJ: Wiley.

Deeg, D. J. H. (2016). Gender and physical health in later life. In S. K. Whitbourne (Ed.), *Encyclopedia of adulthood and aging* (Vol. 2, pp. 537–542). Malden, MA: Wiley Blackwell.

DeFlorio, L., & Beliakoff, A. (2015). Socioeconomic status and preschoolers' mathematical knowledge: The contribution of home activities and parent beliefs. *Early Education and Development, 25,* 319–341.

Defoe, I. N., Dubas, J. S., Figner, B., & van Aken, M. A. G. (2015). A meta-analysis on age differences in risky decision making: Adolescents versus children and adults. *Psychological Bulletin, 141,* 48–84.

de Frias, C. M. (2014). Memory compensation in older adults: The role of health, emotion regulation, and trait mindfulness. *Journals of Gerontology, 69B,* 678–685.

De Goede, I. H. A., Branje, S. J. T., & Meeus, W. H. J. (2009). Developmental changes and gender differences in adolescents' perceptions of friendships. *Journal of Adolescence, 32,* 1105–1123.

de Haan, M. (2015). Neuroscientific methods with children. In P. D. Zelazo (Ed.), *Oxford handbook of developmental psychology: Vol. 1. Body and mind* (pp. 683–712). New York: Oxford University Press.

de Haan, M., & Gunnar, M. R. (2009). The brain in a social environment: Why study development? In M. de Haan & M. R. Gunnar (Eds.), *Handbook of developmental social neuroscience* (pp. 3–12). New York: Guilford.

De Jager, P. L., Srivastava, G., Lunnon, K., Burgess, J., Schalkwyk, L. C., Yu, L., et al. (2014). Alzheimer's disease: Early alterations in brain DNA methylation at ANK1, BIN1, RHBDF2 and other loci. *Nature Neuroscience, 17,* 1156–1163.

deJong, A., & Franklin, B. A. (2004). Prescribing exercise for the elderly: Current research and recommendations. *Current Sports Medicine Reports, 3,* 337–343.

DeKosky, S. T., Williamson, J. D., Fitzpatrick, A. L., Kronmal, R. A., Ives, D. G., & Saxton, J. A. (2008). Ginkgo biloba for prevention of dementia: A randomized controlled trial. *JAMA, 300,* 2253–2262.

Deković, M., Noom, M. J., & Meeus, W. (1997). Expectations regarding development during adolescence: Parent and adolescent perceptions. *Journal of Youth and Adolescence, 26,* 253–271.

De Laet, S. Doumen, S., Vervoort, E., Colpin, H., Van Leeuwen, K., Goossens, L., & Verschueren, K. (2014). Transactional links between teacher–child relationship quality and perceived versus sociometric popularity: A three-wave longitudinal study. *Child Development, 85,* 1647–1662.

Delahunty, K. M., McKay, D. W., Noseworthy, D. E., & Storey, A. E. (2007). Prolactin responses to infant cues in men and women: Effects of parental experience and recent infant contact. *Hormones and Behavior, 51,* 213–220.

DeLamater, J. (2012). Sexual expression in later life: A review and synthesis. *Journal of Sex Research, 49,* 125–141.

DeLamater, J., & Koepsel, E. (2014). Relationships and sexual expression in later life: A biopsychosocial perspective. *Sexual and Relationship Therapy, 30,* 37–59.

de la Monte, S. M., & Kril, J. J. (2014). Human alcohol-related neuropathology. *Acta Neuropathologica, 127,* 71–90.

Delaney, R. K. (2014). National Survey of Midlife Development in the United States. *International Journal of Aging, 79,* 329–331.

de Lima, C., Alves, L. E., Iagher, F., Machado, A. F., Bonatto, S. J., & Kuczera, D. (2008). Anaerobic exercise reduces tumor growth, cancer cachexia and increases macrophage and lymphocyte response in Walker 256 tumor-bearing rats. *European Journal of Applied Physiology, 104,* 957–964.

DeLoache, J. S. (1987). Rapid change in symbolic functioning of very young children. *Science, 238,* 1556–1557.

DeLoache, J. S. (2002). The symbol-mindedness of young children. In W. Hartup & R. A. Weinberg (Eds.), *Minnesota symposia on child psychology* (Vol. 32, pp. 73–101). Mahwah, NJ: Erlbaum.

DeLoache, J. S., Chiong, C., Sherman, K., Islam, N., Vanderborght, M., Troseth, G. L., et al. (2010). Do babies learn from baby media? *Psychological Science, 21,* 1570–1574.

DeLoache, J. S., & Ganea, P. A. (2009). Symbol-based learning in infancy. In A. Woodward & A. Needham (Eds.), *Learning and the infant mind* (pp. 263–285). New York: Oxford University Press.

DeLoache, J. S., LoBue, V., Vanderborght, M., & Chiong, C. (2013). On the validity and robustness of the scale error phenomenon in early childhood. *Infant Behavior and Development, 36,* 63–70.

DeMarie, D., & Lopez, L. M. (2014). Memory in schools. In P. J. Bauer & R. Fivush (Eds.), *Wiley handbook on the development of children's memory* (Vol. 2, pp. 836–864). Malden, MA: Wiley-Blackwell.

DeMarie, D., Miller, P. H., Ferron, J., & Cunningham, W. R. (2004). Path analysis tests of theoretical models of children's memory performance. *Journal of Cognition and Development, 5,* 461–492.

Demetriou, A., Christou, C., Spanoudis, G., & Platsidou, M. (2002). The development of mental processing: Efficiency, working memory, and thinking. *Monographs of the Society for Research in Child Development, 67*(1, Serial No. 268).

Demetriou, A., Efklides, A., Papadaki, M., Papantoniou, G., & Economou, A. (1993). Structure and development of causal thought: From early adolescence to youth. *Developmental Psychology, 29,* 480–497.

Demetriou, A., Pachaury, A., Metallidou, Y., & Kazi, S. (1996). Universals and specificities in the structure and development of quantitative-relational thought: A cross-cultural study in Greece and India. *International Journal of Behavioral Development, 19,* 255–290.

Demiray, B., & Bluck, S. (2014). Time since birth and time left to live: Opposing forces in constructing psychological well-being. *Ageing and Society, 34,* 1193–1218.

Demiray, B., Gülgöz, S., & Bluck, S. (2009). Examining the life story account of the reminiscence bump: Why we remember more from young adulthood. *Memory, 17,* 708–723.

Denham, B. E. (2012). Anabolic-androgenic steroids and adolescents: Recent developments. *Journal of Addictions Nursing, 23,* 167–171.

Denham, S., Warren, H., von Salisch, M., Benga, O., Chin, J., & Geangu, E. (2011). Emotions and social development in childhood. In P. K. Smith & C. H. Hart (Eds.), *Wiley-Blackwell handbook of childhood social development* (2nd ed., pp. 413–433). Chichester, UK: Wiley-Blackwell.

Denissen, J. J. A., Zarrett, N. R., & Eccles, J. S. (2007). I like to do it, I'm able, and I know I am: Longitudinal couplings between domain-specific achievement, self-concept, and interest. *Child Development, 78,* 430–447.

Denkinger, M. D., Leins, H., Schirmbeck, R., Florian, M. C., & Geiger, H. (2015). HSC aging and senescent immune remodeling. *Trends in Immunology, 36,* 815–824.

Denmark, F. L., & Klara, M. D. (2007). Empowerment: A prime time for women over 50. In V. Mulhbauer & J. C. Chrisler (Eds.), *Women over 50* (pp. 182–203). New York: Springer.

Dennerstein, L., & Lehert, P. (2004). Modeling midaged women's sexual functioning: A prospective, population-based study. *Journal of Sex and Marriage Therapy, 30,* 173–183.

Dennis, T. A., & Kelemen, D. A. (2009). Preschool children's views on emotion regulation: Functional associations and implications for social–emotional adjustment. *International Journal of Behavioral Development, 33,* 243–252.

Dennis, W. (1960). Causes of retardation among institutionalized children: Iran. *Journal of Genetic Psychology, 96,* 47–59.

Dennison, R. P., Koerner, S. S., & Segrin, C. (2014). A dyadic examination of family-of-origin influence on newlyweds' marital satisfaction. *Journal of Family Psychology, 28,* 429–435.

DePaulo, B. M., & Morris, W. L. (2005). Singles in society and in science. *Psychological Inquiry, 16,* 142–149.

Deprest, J. A., Devlieger, R., Srisupundit, K., Beck, V., Sandaite, I., Rusconi, S., et al. (2010). Fetal surgery is a clinical reality. *Seminars in Fetal and Neonatal Medicine, 15,* 58–67.

DeRoche, K., & Welsh, M. (2008). Twenty-five years of research on neurocognitive outcomes in early-treated phenylketonuria: Intelligence and executive function. *Developmental Neuropsychology, 33,* 474–504.

DeRose, L. M., & Brooks-Gunn, J. (2006). Transition into adolescence: The role of pubertal processes. In L. Balter & C. S. Tamis-LeMonda (Eds.), *Child psychology: A handbook of contemporary issues* (2nd ed., pp. 385–414). New York: Psychology Press.

DeRosier, M. E. (2007). Peer-rejected and bullied children: A safe schools initiative for elementary school students. In J. E. Zins, M. J. Elias, & C. A. Maher (Eds.), *Bullying, victimization, and peer harassment* (pp. 257–276). New York: Haworth.

de Rosnay, M., Copper, P. J., Tsigaras, N., & Murray, L. (2006). Transmission of social anxiety from mother to infant: An experimental study using a social referencing paradigm. *Behavior Research and Therapy, 44,* 1165–1175.

de Rosnay, M., & Hughes, C. (2006). Conversation and theory of mind: Do children talk their way to socio-cognitive understanding? *British Journal of Developmental Psychology, 24,* 7–37.

De Souza, E., Alberman, E., & Morris, J. K. (2009). Down syndrome and paternal age, a new analysis of case-control data collected in the 1960s. *American Journal of Medical Genetics, 149A,* 1205–1208.

Dessens, A. B., Slijper, F. M. E., & Drop, S. L. S. (2005). Gender dysphoria and gender change in chromosomal females with congenital adrenal hyperplasia. *Archives of Sexual Behavior, 34,* 389–397.

Deutsch, A. R., Crockett, L. J., Wolff, J. M., & Russell, S. T. (2012). Parent and peer pathways to adolescent delinquency: Variations by ethnicity and neighborhood context. *Journal of Youth and Adolescence, 41,* 1078–1094.

Deutsch, N. L., & Schmertz, B. (2011). "Starting from Ground Zero: Constraints and experiences of adult women returning to college. *Review of Higher Education, 34,* 477–504.

Deveson, A. (1994). *Coming of age: Twenty-one interviews about growing older.* Newham, Australia: Scribe.

de Vries, B., & Moldaw, S. (2012). Virtual memorials and cyber funerals: Contemporary expressions of ageless experiences. In C. J. Sofka, I. N. Cupit, & K. R. Gilbert (Eds.), *Dying death, and grief in an online universe: For counselors and educators* (pp. 135–148). New York: Springer.

de Vries, B., Utz, R., Caserta, M., & Lund, D. (2014). Friend and family contact and support in early widowhood. *Journals of Gerontology, 69B,* 75–84.

DeVries, R. (2001). Constructivist education in preschool and elementary school: The sociomoral atmosphere as the first educational goal. In S. L. Golbeck (Ed.), *Psychological perspectives on early childhood education* (pp. 153–180). Mahwah, NJ: Erlbaum.

de Waal, F. B. M. (2001). *Tree of origin.* Cambridge, MA: Harvard University Press.

De Wit, D. J., Karioja, K., Rye, B. J., & Shain, M. (2011). Perceptions of declining classmate and teacher support following the transition to high school: Potential correlates of increasing student mental health difficulties. *Psychology in the Schools, 48,* 556–572.

Diamond, A. (2004). Normal development of prefrontal cortex from birth to young adulthood: Cognitive functions, anatomy, and biochemistry. In D. T. Stuff & R. T. Knight (Eds.), *Principles of frontal lobe function* (pp. 466–503). New York: Oxford University Press.

Diamond, A., Cruttenden, L., & Neiderman, D. (1994). AB with multiple wells: 1. Why are multiple wells sometimes easier than two wells? 2. Memory or memory + inhibition. *Developmental Psychology, 30,* 192–205.

Diamond, L. M. (2006). The intimate same-sex relationships of sexual minorities. In A. L. Vangelisti & D. Perlman (Eds.), *The Cambridge handbook of personal relationships* (pp. 293–312). New York: Cambridge University Press.

Diamond, L. M. (2008). Female bisexuality from adolescence to adulthood: Results from a 10-year longitudinal study. *Developmental Psychology, 44,* 5–14.

Diamond, L. M., Bonner, S. B., & Dickenson, J. (2015). The development of sexuality. In M. E. Lamb (Ed.), *Handbook of child psychology and developmental science: Vol. 3. Socioemotional processes* (7th ed., pp. 888–931). Hoboken, NJ: Wiley.

Diamond, L. M., Fagundes, C. P., & Butterworth, M. R. (2010). Intimate relationships across the lifespan. In M. E. Lamb, A. M. Freund, & R. M. Lerner, (Eds.), *The handbook of life-span development: Vol. 2, Social and emotional development* (pp. 379–433). Hoboken, NJ: Wiley.

Dias, M. G., & Harris, P. L. (1988). The effect of make-believe play on deductive reasoning. *British Journal of Developmental Psychology, 6,* 207–221.

Dias, M. G., & Harris, P. L. (1990). The influence of the imagination on reasoning by young children. *British Journal of Developmental Psychology, 8,* 305–318.

DiBiase, A.-M., Gibbs, J. C., Potter, G. B., & Blount, M. R. (2011). Teaching adolescents to think and act responsibly: *The EQUIP approach.* Champaign, IL: Research Press.

Di Ceglie, D. (2014). Care for gender-dysphoric children. In B. P. C. Kreukels, T. D. Steensma, & A. L. C. deVries (Eds.), *Gender dysphoria and disorders of sex development: Progress in care and knowledge* (pp. 151–169). New York: Springer Science + Business Media.

Dickinson, D. K., Golinkoff, R. M., & Hirsh-Pasek, K. (2010). Speaking out for language: Why language is central to reading development. *Educational Researcher, 39,* 305–310.

Dickinson, D. K., & McCabe, A. (2001). Bringing it all together: The multiple origins, skills, and environmental supports of early literacy. *Learning Disabilities Research and Practice, 16,* 186–202.

Dickinson, D. K., McCabe, A., Anastasopoulos, L., Peisner-Feinberg, E. S., & Poe, M. D. (2003). The comprehensive language approach to early literacy: The interrelationships among vocabulary, phonological sensitivity, and print knowledge among preschool-age children. *Journal of Educational Psychology, 95,* 465–481.

Dick-Read, G. (1959). *Childbirth without fear.* New York: Harper & Row.

Dickson, R. A., Pillemer, D. B., & Bruehl, E. C. (2011). The reminiscence bump for salient personal memories: Is a cultural life script required? *Memory and Cognition, 39,* 977–991.

DiDonato, M. D., & Berenbaum, S. A. (2011). The benefits and drawbacks of gender typing: How different dimensions are related to psychological adjustment. *Archives of Sexual Behavior, 40,* 457–463.

Diehl, M., & Berg, K. M. (2007). Personality and involvement in leisure activities during the Third Age: Findings from the Ohio Longitudinal Study. In J. B. James & P. Wink (Eds.), *Annual review of gerontology and geriatrics* (Vol. 26, pp. 211–226). New York: Springer.

Diehl, M., Coyle, N., & Labouvie-Vief, G. (1996). Age and sex differences in strategies of coping and defense across the life span. *Psychology and Aging, 11,* 127–139.

Diehl, M., Youngblade, L. M., Hay, E. L., & Chui, H. (2011). The development of self-representations across the life span. In K. L. Fingergman, C. A. Berg, J. Smith, & H. Chui (Eds.), *Handbook of lifespan development* (pp. 611–646). New York: Springer.

Diekmann, A., & Schmidheiny, K. (2013). The intergenerational transmission of divorce: A fifteen-country study with the fertility and family survey. *Comparative Sociology, 12,* 211–235.

Diener, E., Gohm, C. L., Suh, E., & Oishi, S. (2000). Similarity of the relations between marital status and subjective well-being across cultures. *Journal of Cross-Cultural Psychology, 31,* 419–436.

Diggs, J. (2008). The cross-linkage theory of aging. In S. J. D. Loue & M. Sajatovic (Eds.), *Encyclopedia of aging and public health* (pp. 250–252). New York: Springer.

Di Giuseppe, D., Discacciati, A., Orsini, N., & Wolk, A. (2014). Cigarette smoking and risk of rheumatoid arthritis: A dose–response meta-analysis. *Arthritis Research & Therapy, 16,* R61.

DiLalla, L. F., Bersted, K., & John, S. G. (2015). Evidence of reactive gene–environment correlation in preschoolers' prosocial play with unfamiliar peers. *Developmental Psychology, 51,* 1464–1475.

DiLisi, R., & Gallagher, A. M. (1991). Understanding of gender stability and constancy in Argentinian children. *Merrill-Palmer Quarterly, 37,* 483–502.

Dilworth-Anderson, P., Goodwin, P. Y., & Williams, S. W. (2004). Can culture help explain the physical health effects of caregiving over time among African American caregivers? *Journals of Gerontology, 59B,* S138–S145.

Dimitry, L. (2012) A systematic review on the mental health of children and adolescents in areas of armed conflict in the Middle East. *Child: Care, Health, and Development, 38,* 153–161.

DiPietro, J. A., Bornstein, M. H., Costigan, K. A., Pressman, E. K., Hahn, C.-S., & Painter, K. (2002). What does fetal movement predict about behavior during the first two years of life? *Developmental Psychobiology, 40,* 358–371.

DiPietro, J. A., Caulfield, L. E., Irizarry, R. A., Chen, P., Merialdi, M., & Zavaleta, N. (2006). Prenatal development of intrafetal and maternal–fetal synchrony. *Behavioral Neuroscience, 120,* 687–701.

DiPietro, J. A., Costigan, K. A., & Voegtline, K. M. (2015). Studies in fetal behavior: Revisited, renewed, and reimagined. *Monographs of the Society for Research in Child Development, 80*(3, Serial No. 318).

DiPietro, J. A., Hodgson, D. M., Costigan, K. A., & Hilton, S. C. (1996). Fetal neurobehavioral development. *Child Development, 67,* 2553–2567.

Dishion, T. J., Shaw, D., Connell, A., Gardner, F., Weaver, C., & Wilson, M. (2008). The Family Check-Up with high-risk indigent families: Preventing problem behavior by increasing parents' positive behavior support in early childhood. *Child Development, 79,* 1395–1414.

Dittmar, M., Abbot-Smith, K., Lieven, E., & Tomasello, M. (2014). Familiar verbs are not always easier than novel verbs: How German preschool children comprehend active and passive sentences. *Cognitive Science, 38,* 128–151.

Dix, T., Stewart, A. D., Gershoff, E. T., & Day, W. H. (2007). Autonomy and children's reactions to being controlled: Evidence that both compliance and defiance may be positive markers in early development. *Child Development, 78,* 1204–1221.

Dixon, P. (2009). Marriage among African Americans: What does the research reveal? *Journal of African American Studies, 13,* 29–46.

Dixon, R. A., de Frias, C. M., & Bäckman, L. (2001). Characteristics of self-reported memory compensation in older adults. *Journal of Clinical and Experimental Neuropsychology, 23,* 650–661.

Dodd, V. L. (2005). Implications of kangaroo care for growth and development in preterm infants. *Journal of Obstetric, Gynecologic and Neonatal Nursing, 34,* 218–232.

Dodge, K. A., Coie, J. D., & Lynam, D. (2006). Aggression and antisocial behavior in youth. In N. Eisenberg (Ed.), *Handbook of child psychology: Vol. 3. Social, emotional, and personality development* (6th ed., pp. 719–788). New York: Wiley.

Dodge, K. A., & Haskins, R. (2015). Children and government. In M. H. Bornstein & T. Leventhal (Eds.), *Handbook of child psychology and developmental science: Vol. 4. Ecological settings and processes* (7th ed., pp. 654–703). Hoboken, NJ: Wiley.

Dodge, K. A., Malone, P. S., Greenberg, M. T., & Conduct Problems Prevention Research Group. (2008). Testing an idealized dynamic cascade model of the development of serious violence in adolescence. *Child Development, 97,* 1907–1027.

Dodge, K. A., McLoyd, V. C., & Lansford, J. E. (2006). The cultural context of physically disciplining children. In V. C. McLoyd, N. E. Hill, & K. A. Dodge (Eds.), *African-American family life: Ecological and cultural diversity* (pp. 245–263). New York: Guilford.

Dodson, T. A., & Borders, L. D. (2006). Men in traditional and nontraditional careers: Gender role attitudes, gender role conflict, and job satisfaction. *Career Development Quarterly, 54,* 283–296.

Dohnt, H., & Tiggemann, M. (2006). The contribution of peer and media influences to the development of body satisfaction and self-esteem in young girls: A prospective study. *Developmental Psychology, 42,* 929–936.

Doka, K. J. (2008). Disenfranchised grief in historical and cultural perspective. In M. S. Stroebe, R. O. Hansson, H. Schut, & W. Stroebe (Eds.), *Handbook of bereavement research and practice* (pp. 223–240). Washington, DC: American Psychological Association.

Doka, K. J., & Martin, T. L. (2010). *Grieving beyond gender: Understanding the ways men and women mourn* (rev. ed.). New York: Routledge.

Dolbin-MacNab, M. L. (2006). Just like raising your own? Grandmothers' perceptions of parenting a second time around. *Family Relations, 55,* 564–575.

Dombrovski, A. Y., Butters, M. A., Reynolds, C. F., III, Houck, P. R., Clark, L., Mazumdar, S., & Szanto, K. (2008). Cognitive performance in suicidal depressed elderly: Preliminary report. *American Journal of Geriatric Psychiatry, 16,* 109–115.

Domellöf, E., Johansson, A., & Rönnqvist, L. (2011). Handedness in preterm born children: A systematic review and meta-analysis. *Neuropsychologia, 49,* 2299–2310.

Domingo, J. P., Matamoros, N. E., Danés, C. F., Abelló, H. V., Carranza, J. M., Ripoll, A. I. R., et al. (2015). Effectiveness of music therapy in advanced cancer patients admitted to a palliative care unit: A non-randomized controlled, clinical trial. *Music & Medicine, 7,* 23–31.

Domitrovich, C. E., Gest, S. D., Gill, S., Bierman, K. L., Welsh, J. A., & Jones, D. (2009). Fostering high-quality teaching with an enriched curriculum and professional development support: The Head Start REDI program. *American Educational Research Journal, 46,* 567–597.

Donaldson, M., & Jones, J. (2013). Optimizing outcome in congenital hypothyroidism: Current opinions on best practice in initial assessment and subsequent management. *Journal of Clinical Research in Pediatric Endocrinology, 5*(Suppl. 12), 13–22.

Donatelle, R. J. (2012). *Health: The basics* (10th ed.). San Francisco: Benjamin Cummings.

Donatelle, R. J. (2015). *Health: The basics* (11th ed.). Hoboken, NJ: Pearson.

Dondi, M., Simion, F., & Caltran, G. (1999). Can newborns discriminate between their own cry and the cry of another newborn infant? *Developmental Psychology, 35,* 418–426.

Dong, X., Simon, M., Rajan, K., & Evans, D. A. (2011). Association of cognitive function and risk for elder abuse in a community-dwelling population. *Dementia and Geriatric Cognitive Disorders, 32,* 209–215.

Donnellan, M. B., Larsen-Rife, D., & Conger, R. D. (2005). Personality, family history, and competence in early adult romantic relationships. *Journal of Personality and Social Psychology, 88,* 562–576.

Donnellan, M. B., & Lucas, R. E. (2008). Age differences in the big five across the life span: Evidence from two national samples. *Psychology and Aging, 23,* 558–566.

Donnellan, M. B., Trzesniewski, K. H., Robins, R. W., Moffitt, T. E., & Caspi, A. (2005). Low self-esteem is related to aggression, antisocial behavior, and delinquency. *Psychological Science, 16,* 328–335.

Doornwaard, S. M., Branje, S., Meeus, W. H. J., & ter Bogt, T. F. M. (2012). Development of adolescents' peer crowd identification in relation to changes in problem behaviors. *Developmental Psychology, 48,* 1366–1380.

Dorfman, L. T. (2016). Retirement, leisure activities in. In S. K. Whitbourne (Ed.), *Encyclopedia of adulthood and aging* (Vol. 3, pp. 1251–1255). Malden, MA: Wiley Blackwell.

Dorris, M. (1989). *The broken cord.* New York: Harper & Row.

Dorwie, F. M., & Pacquiao, D. F. (2014). Practices of traditional birth attendants in Sierra Leone and perceptions by mothers and health professionals familiar with their care. *Journal of Transcultural Nursing, 25,* 33–41.

Doss, B. D., Rhoades, G. K., Stanley, S. M., & Markman, H. J. (2009). The effect of the transition to parenthood on relationship quality: An 8-year prospective study. *Journal of Personality and Social Psychology, 96,* 601–619.

Double, E. B., Mabuchi, K., Cullings, H. M., Preston, D. L., Kodama, K., Shimizu, Y., et al. (2011). Long-term radiation-related health effects in a unique human population: Lessons learned from the atomic bomb survivors of Hiroshima and Nagasaki. *Disaster Medicine and Public Health Preparedness, 5*(Suppl. 1), S122–S133.

Douglas, E. M. (2006). *Mending broken families: Social policies for divorced families.* Lanham, MD: Rowman & Littlefield.

Douglass, S., & Umaña-Taylor, A. J. (2015). Development of ethnic–racial identity among Latino adolescents and the role of the family. *Journal of Applied Developmental Psychology, 41,* 90–98.

Dowd, M. D. (2013). Prevention and treatment of traumatic stress in children: Few answers, many questions. *Pediatrics, 31,* 591–592.

Dowling, E. M., Gestsdottir, S., Anderson, P. M., von Eye, A., Almerigi, J., & Lerner, R. M. (2004). Structural relations among spirituality, religiosity, and thriving in adolescence. *Applied Developmental Psychology, 8,* 7–16.

Downing, J. E. (2010). *Academic instruction for students with moderate and severe intellectual disabilities.* Thousand Oaks, CA: Corwin.

Downs, A. C., & Fuller, M. J. (1991). Recollections of spermarche: An exploratory investigation. *Current Psychology: Research and Reviews, 10,* 93–102.

Dragowski, E. A., Halkitis, P. N., Grossman, A. H., & D'Augelli, A. R. (2011). Sexual orientation victimization and posttraumatic stress symptoms among lesbian, gay, and bisexual youth. *Journal of Gay and Lesbian Social Services, 23,* 226–249.

Drake, K., Belsky, J., & Fearon, R. M. P. (2014). From early attachment to engagement with learning in school: The role of self-regulation and persistence. *Developmental Psychology, 50,* 1350–1361.

Drake, M. T., Clark, B. L., & Lewiecki, E. M. (2015). The pathophysiology and treatment of osteoporosis. *Clinical Therapeutics, 37,* 1837–1850.

Draper, B. M. (2014). Suicidal behavior and suicide prevention in later life. *Maturitas, 79,* 179–183.

Drayton, S., Turley-Ames, K. J., & Guajardo, N. R. (2011). Counterfactual thinking and false belief: The role of executive function. *Journal of Experimental Child Psychology, 108,* 532–548.

Driver, J., Tabares, A., Shapiro, A. F., & Gottman, J. M. (2012). Couple interaction in happy and unhappy marriages: Gottman Laboratory studies. In F. Walsh (Ed.), *Normal family processes: Growing diversity and complexity* (pp. 57–77). New York: Guilford.

Druet, C., Stettler, N., Sharp, S., Simmons, R. K., Cooper, C., Smith, G. D., et al. (2012). Prediction of childhood obesity by infancy weight gain: An individual-level meta-analysis. *Paediatric and Perinatal Epidemiology, 26,* 19–26.

Drury, S. S., Mabile, E., Brett, Z. H., Esteves, K., Jones, E., Shirtcliff, E. A., & Theall, K. P. (2014). The association of telomere length with family violence and disruption. *Pediatrics, 134,* e128–e137.

DuBois, D. L., Felner, R. D., Brand, S., & George, G. R. (1999). Profiles of self-esteem in early adolescence: Identification and investigation of adaptive correlates. *American Journal of Community Psychology, 27,* 899–932.

Dubois, L., Kyvik, K. O., Girard, M., Tatone-Tokuda, F., Pérusse, D., Hjelmborg, J., et al. (2012). Genetic and environmental contributions to weight, height, and BMI from birth to 19 years of age: An international study of over 12,000 twin pairs. *PLOS ONE, 7*(2), e30153.

Dubois, M.-F., Bravo, C., Graham, J., Wildeman, S., Cohen, C., Painter, K., et al. (2011). Comfort with proxy consent to research involving decisionally impaired older adults: Do type of proxy and risk–benefit profile matter? *International Psychogeriatrics, 23,* 1479–1488.

du Bois-Reymond, M. (2016). Emerging adulthood theory and social class. In J. J. Arnett (Ed.), *Oxford handbook of emerging adulthood* (pp. 47–61). New York: Oxford University Press.

Duckworth, A. L., Quinn, P. D., & Tsukayama, E. (2012). What No Child Left Behind leaves behind: The roles of IQ and self-control in predicting standardized achievement test scores and report card grades. *Journal of Educational Psychology, 104,* 439–451.

Dudani, A., Macpherson, A., & Tamim, H. (2010). Childhood behavior problems and unintentional injury: A longitudinal, population-based study. *Journal of Developmental and Behavioral Pediatrics, 31,* 276–285.

Dugan, A. (2015). *In U.S., support up for doctor-assisted suicide.* Retrieved from www.gallup.com/poll/183425/support-doctor-assisted-suicide.aspx

Dumanovsky, T., Augustin, R., Rogers, M., Lettang, K., Meier, D. E., & Morrison, R. S. (2016). The growth of palliative care in U.S. hospitals: A status report. *Journal of Palliative Medicine, 19,* 8–15.

Duncan, G. J., Dowsett, C. J., Claessens, A., Magnuson, K., Huston, A. C., Klebanov, P., et al. (2007). School readiness and later achievement. *Developmental Psychology, 43,* 1428–1446.

Duncan, G. J., & Magnuson, K. A. (2003). Off with Hollingshead: Socioeconomic resources, parenting, and child development. In M. H. Bornstein & R. H. Bradley (Eds.), *Socioeconomic status, parenting, and child development* (pp. 83–106). Mahwah, NJ: Erlbaum.

Duncan, G. J., Magnuson, K., & Votruba-Drzal, E. (2015). Children and socioeconomic status. In M. H. Bornstein & T. Leventhal (Eds.), *Handbook of child psychology and developmental science: Vol. 4. Ecological settings and processes* (7th ed., pp. 534–573). Hoboken, NJ: Wiley.

Duncan, L. E., Pollastri, A. R., & Smoller, J. W. (2014). Mind the gap: Why many geneticists and psychological scientists have discrepant views about gene–environment interaction (GXE) research. *American Psychologist, 69,* 249–268.

Duncan, M., Vandelanotte, C., Kolt, G. S., Rosenkranz, R. R., Caperchione, C. M., George, E. S., et al. (2014). Effectiveness of a web- and mobile phone-based intervention to promote physical activity and healthy eating in middle-aged males: Randomized controlled trial of the ManUp study. *Journal of Medical Internet Research, 16,* e136.

Dundek, L. H. (2006). Establishment of a Somali doula program at a large metropolitan hospital. *Journal of Perinatal and Neonatal Nursing, 20,* 128–137.

Dunham, Y., Baron, A. S., & Banaji, M. R. (2006). From American city to Japanese village: A cross-cultural investigation of implicit race attitudes. *Child Development, 77,* 1268–1281.

Dunham, Y., Baron, A. S., & Carey, S. (2011). Consequences of "minimal" group affiliations in children. *Child Development, 82,* 793–811.

Dunham, Y., Chen, E. E., & Banaji, M. R. (2013). Two signatures of implicit intergroup attitudes: Developmental invariance and early enculturation. *Psychological Science, 24,* 860–868.

Dunkel-Shetter, C., & Lobel, M. (2012). Pregnancy and birth: A multilevel analysis of stress and birth weight. In T. A. Revenson, A. Baum, & J. Singer (Eds.), *Handbook of health psychology* (2nd ed., pp. 431–463). London: Psychology Press.

Dunn, J. (1989). Siblings and the development of social understanding in early childhood. In P. G. Zukow (Ed.), *Sibling interaction across cultures* (pp. 106–116). New York: Springer-Verlag.

Dunn, J. (1994). Temperament, siblings, and the development of relationships. In W. B. Carey & S. C. McDevitt (Eds.), *Prevention and early intervention* (pp. 50–58). New York: Brunner/Mazel.

Dunn, J. (2002). The adjustment of children in stepfamilies: Lessons from community studies. *Child and Adolescent Mental Health, 7,* 154–161.

Dunn, J. (2004a). *Children's friendships: The beginnings of intimacy.* Oxford, UK: Blackwell.

Dunn, J. (2004b). Sibling relationships. In P. K. Smith & C. H. Hart (Eds.), *Handbook of childhood social development* (pp. 223–237). Malden, MA: Blackwell.

Dunn, J. (2005). Moral development in early childhood and social interaction in the family. In M. Killen & J. G. Smetana (Eds.), *Handbook of moral development* (pp. 331–350). Mahwah, NJ: Erlbaum.

Dunn, J. (2014). Moral development in early childhood and social interaction in the family. In M. Killen & J. G. Smetana (Eds.), *Handbook of moral development* (2nd ed., pp. 135–159). New York: Psychology Press.

Dunn, J., Cheng, H., O'Connor, T. G., & Bridges, L. (2004). Children's perspectives on their relationships with their nonresident fathers: Influences, outcomes and implications. *Journal of Child Psychology and Psychiatry, 45,* 553–566.

Dunn, J., Cutting, A. L., & Demetriou, H. (2000). Moral sensibility, understanding others, and children's friendship interactions in the preschool period. *British Journal of Developmental Psychology, 18,* 159–177.

Dunn, J. R., Schaefer-McDaniel, N. J., & Ramsay, J. T. (2010). Neighborhood chaos and children's development: Questions and contradictions. In G. W. Evans & T. D. Wachs (Eds.), *Chaos and its influence on children's development: An ecological perspective* (pp. 173–189). Washington, DC: American Psychological Association.

Dunne, E. J., & Dunne-Maxim, K. (2004). Working with families in the aftermath of suicide. In F. Walsh & M. McGoldrick (Eds.), *Living beyond loss: Death in the family* (2nd ed., pp. 272–284). New York: Norton.

duRivage, N., Keyes, K., Leray, E., Pez, O., Bilfoi, A., Koç, C., et al. (2015). Parental use of corporal punishment in Europe: Intersection between public health and policy. *PLOS ONE, 10*(2), e0118059.

Durlak, J. A., Weissberg, R. P., Dymnicki, A. B., Taylor, R. D., & Schellinger, K. B. (2011). The impact of enhancing students' social and emotional learning: A meta-analysis of school-based universal interventions. *Child Development, 82,* 405–432.

Durlak, J. A., Weissberg, R. P., & Pachan, M. (2010). A meta-analysis of after-school programs that seek to promote personal and social skills of children and adolescents. *American Journal of Community Psychology, 45,* 294–309.

Durrant, J. E., Plateau, D. P., Ateah, C., Stewart-Tufescu, A., Jones, A., Ly, G., et al. (2014). Preventing punitive violence: Preliminary data on the Positive Discipline in Everyday Parenting (PDEP) Program. *Canadian Journal of Community Mental Health, 33,* 109–125.

Duszak, R. S. (2009). Congenital rubella syndrome—major review. *Optometry, 80,* 36–43.

Dutta, A., Henley, W., Lang, I., Llewellyn, D., Guralnik, J., Wallace, R. B., et al. (2011). Predictors of extraordinary survival in the Iowa Established Populations for Epidemiological Study of the Elderly: Cohort follow-up to "extinction." *Journal of the American Geriatrics Society, 59,* 963–971.

Dutton, D., Tetreault, C., Karakanta, C., & White, K. (2015). Psychological factors in intimate partner violence. In C. A. Pietz & C. A. Mattson (Eds.), *Violent offenders: Understanding and assessment* (pp. 186–215). New York: Oxford University Press.

Dutton, D. G. (2012). The case against the role of gender in intimate partner violence. *Aggression and Violent Behavior, 17,* 99–104.

Duxbury, F. (2014). Domestic violence and abuse. In S. Bewley & J. Welch (Ed.), *ABC of domestic and sexual violence* (pp. 9–16). Chichester, UK: Wiley-Blackwell.

Dweck, C. S., & Molden, D. C. (2013). Self-theories: Their impact on competence motivation and acquisition. In A. J. Elliott & C. J. Dweck (Eds.), *Handbook of confidence and motivation* (pp. 122–140). New York: Guilford.

Dykiert, D., Der, G., Starr, J. M., & Deary, I. J. (2012). Sex differences in reaction time mean and intraindividual variability across the life span. *Developmental Psychology, 48,* 1262–1276.

Dykstra, P. A. (2006). Off the beaten track: Childlessness and social integration in late life. *Research on Aging, 28,* 749–767.

Dykstra, P. A., & Hagestad, G. O. (2007). Roads less taken: Developing a nuanced view of older adults without children. *Journal of Family Issues, 28,* 1275–1310.

Dyregrov, K., Grad, O., De Leo, D., & Cimitan, A. (2014). Surviving suicide. In D. De Leo, A. Cimitan, K. Dyregrov, O. Grad, & K. Andriessen (Eds.), *Bereavement after traumatic death: Helping the survivors* (pp. 37–48). Boston: Hogrefe Publishing.

Dzurova, D., & Pikhart, H. (2005). Down syndrome, paternal age and education: Comparison of California and the Czech Republic. *BMC Public Health, 5,* 69.

E

Eagan, K., Lozano, J. B., Hurtado, S., & Case, M. H. (2013). *The American freshman: National norms, Fall 2013.* Los Angeles: Higher Education Research Institute, UCLA.

Eagly, A. H., Eastwick, P. W., & Johannesen-Schmidt, M. (2009). Possible selves in marital roles: The impact of the anticipated division of labor on mate preferences of women and men. *Personality and Social Psychology Bulletin, 35,* 403–414.

Eagly, A. H., & Wood, W. (2012). Social role theory. In P. A. M. Van Lange, A. W. Kruglanski, & E. T. Higgins (Eds.), *Handbook of theories of social psychology* (Vol. 2, pp. 458–476). Thousand Oaks, CA: Sage.

Eagly, A. H., & Wood, W. (2013). Feminism and evolutionary psychology: Moving forward. *Sex Roles, 69,* 549–556.

Eaker, E. D., Sullivan, L. M., Kelly-Hayes, M., D'Agostino, R. B., & Benjamin, E. J. (2004). Anger and hostility predict the development of atrial fibrillation in men in the Framingham Offspring Study. *Circulation, 109,* 1267–1271.

Eaker, E. D., Sullivan, L. M., Kelly-Hayes, M., D'Agostino, R. B., & Benjamin, E. J. (2007). Marital status, marital strain, and risk of coronary heart disease or total mortality: The Framingham Offspring Study. *Psychosomatic Medicine, 69,* 509–513.

Easterbrooks, M. A., Kotake, C., Raskin, M., & Bumgarner, E. (2016). Patterns of depression among adolescent mothers: Resilience related to father support and home visiting program. *American Journal of Orthopsychiatry, 86,* 61–68.

Eaves, L., Silberg, J., Foley, D., Bulik, C., Maes, H., & Erkanli, A. (2004). Genetic and environmental influences on the relative timing of pubertal change. *Twin Research, 7,* 471–481.

Ebeling, K. S., & Gelman, S. A. (1994). Children's use of context in interpreting "big" and "little." *Child Development, 65,* 1178–1192.

Ebner, N. C., Freund, A. M., & Baltes, P. B. (2006). Developmental changes in personal goal orientation from young to late adulthood: From striving for gains to maintenance and prevention of losses. *Psychology and Aging, 21,* 664–678.

Eccles, J. S. (2004). Schools, academic motivation, and stage–environment fit. In R. M. Lerner & L. Steinberg (Eds.), *Handbook of adolescent psychology* (2nd ed., pp. 125–154). Hoboken, NJ: Wiley.

Eccles, J. S., Jacobs, J. E., & Harold, R. D. (1990). Gender-role stereotypes, expectancy effects, and parents' role in the socialization of gender differences in self-perceptions and skill acquisition. *Journal of Social Issues, 46,* 183–201.

Eccles, J. S., & Roeser, R. W. (2009). Schools, academic motivation, and stage–environment fit. In R. M. Lerner & L. Steinberg (Eds.), *Handbook of adolescent psychology* (Vol. 1, pp. 404–434). Hoboken, NJ: Wiley.

Eccles, J. S., Templeton, J., Barber, B., & Stone, M. (2003). Adolescence and emerging adulthood: The critical passageways to adulthood. In M. H. Bornstein, L. Davidson, C. L. M., Keyes, K. A. Moore, & the Center for Child Well-Being (Eds.), *Well-being: Positive development across the life course* (pp. 383–406). Mahwah, NJ: Erlbaum.

Eccles, J. S., Vida, M. N., & Barber, B. (2004). The relation of early adolescents' college plans and both academic ability and task-value beliefs to subsequent college enrollment. *Journal of Early Adolescence, 24,* 63–77.

Eder, R. A., & Mangelsdorf, S. C. (1997). The emotional basis of early personality development: Implications for the emergent self-concept. In R. Hogan, J. Johnson, & S. Briggs (Eds.), *Handbook of personality psychology* (pp. 209–240). San Diego, CA: Academic Press.

Edwards, O. W., & Oakland, T. D. (2006). Factorial invariance of Woodcock-Johnson III scores for African Americans and Caucasian Americans. *Journal of Psychoeducational Assessment, 24,* 358–366.

Efstathiou, N., & Clifford, C. (2011). The critical care nurse's role in end-of-life care: Issues and challenges. *Nursing in Critical Care, 16,* 116–123.

Eggebeen, D. J., Dew, J., & Knoester, C. (2010). Fatherhood and men's lives at middle age. *Journal of Family Issues, 31,* 113–130.

Eggenberger, E., Heimerl, K., & Bennett, M. I. (2013). Communication skills training in dementia care: A systematic review of effectiveness, training content, and didactic methods in different settings. *International Psychogeriatrics, 25,* 345–358.

Ehrensaft, M. K. (2009). Family and relationship predictors of psychological and physical aggression. In D. K. O'Leary & E. M. Woodin (Eds.), *Psychological and physical aggression in couples: Causes and interventions* (pp. 99–118). Washington, DC: American Psychological Association.

Ehri, L. C., & Roberts, T. (2006). The roots of learning to read and write: Acquisition of letters and phonemic awareness. In D. K. Dikinson & S. B. Neuman (Eds.), *Handbook of early literacy research* (Vol. 2, pp. 113–131). New York: Guildford.

Eibich, P., Krekel, C., Demuth, I., & Wagner, G. G. (2016). Associations between neighborhood characteristics, well-being and health vary over the life course. *Gerontology, 62,* 362–370.

Eichstedt, J. A., Serbin, L. A., Poulin-Dubois, D., & Sen, M. G. (2002). Of bears and men: Infants' knowledge of conventional and metaphorical gender stereotypes. *Infant Behavior and Development, 25,* 296–310.

Einstein, G. O., McDaniel, M. A., & Scullin, M. K. (2012). Prospective memory and aging: Understanding the variability. In M. Naveh-Benjamin & N. Ohta (Eds.), *Memory and aging: Current issues and future directions* (pp. 153–179). New York: Psychology Press.

Eisbach, A. O. (2004). Children's developing awareness of diversity in people's trains of thought. *Child Development, 75,* 1694–1707.

Eisenberg, N. (2003). Prosocial behavior, empathy, and sympathy. In M. H. Bornstein & L. Davidson (Eds.), *Well-being: Positive development across the life course* (pp. 253–265). Mahwah, NJ: Erlbaum.

Eisenberg, N. (2006). Emotion-related regulation. In H. E. Fitzgerald, B. M. Lester, & B. Zuckerman (Eds.), *The crisis in youth mental health: Critical issues and effective programs: Vol. 1. Childhood disorders* (pp. 133–155). Westport, CT: Praeger.

Eisenberg, N. (2010). Empathy-related responding: Links with self-regulation, moral judgment, and moral behavior. In M. Mikulincer & P. R. Shaver (Eds.), *Prosocial motives, emotions, and behavior: The better angels of our nature* (pp. 129–148). Washington, DC: American Psychological Association.

Eisenberg, N., Eggum, N. D., & Edwards, A. (2010). Empathy-related responding and moral development. In W. F. Arsenio & E. A. Lemerise (Eds.), *Emotions, aggression, and morality in children* (pp. 115–135). Washington, DC: American Psychological Association.

Eisenberg, N., & Silver, R. C. (2011). Growing up in the shadow of terrorism. *American Psychologist, 66,* 468–481.

Eisenberg, N., Spinrad, T. L., & Knafo-Noam, A. (2015). Prosocial development. In M. E. Lamb (Ed.), *Handbook of child psychology and developmental science: Vol. 3. Socioemotional processes* (7th ed., pp. 610–656). Hoboken, NJ: Wiley.

Eisenberg, N., Zhou, Q., Spinrad, T. L., Valiente, C., Fabes, R. A., & Liew, J. (2005). Relations among positive parenting, children's effortful control, and externalizing problems: A three-wave longitudinal study. *Child Development, 76,* 1055–1071.

Eisma, M. C., Stroebe, M. S., Schut, H. A. W., Stroebe, W., Boelen, P. A., & van den Bout, J. (2013). Avoidance processes mediate the relationship between rumination and symptoms of complicated grief and depression following loss. *Journal of Abnormal Psychology, 122,* 961–970.

Eisner, M. P., & Malti, T. (2015). Aggressive and violent behavior. In M. E. Lamb (Ed.), *Handbook of child psychology and developmental science: Vol. 3. Socioemotional processes* (7th ed., pp. 794–841). Hoboken, NJ: Wiley.

Eivers, A. R., Brendgen, M., Vitaro, F., & Borge, A. I. H. (2012). Concurrent and longitudinal links between children's and their friends' antisocial and prosocial behavior in preschool. *Early Childhood Research Quarterly, 27,* 137–146.

Ekas, N. V., Lickenbrock, D. M., & Braungart-Rieker, J. M. (2013). Developmental trajectories of emotion regulation across infancy: Do age and the social partner influence temporal patterns? *Infancy, 18,* 729–754.

Ekman, P., & Friesen, W. (1972). Constants across culture in the face of emotion. *Journal of Personality and Social Psychology, 17,* 124–129.

Ekman, P., & Matsumoto, D. (2011). Reading faces: The universality of emotional expression. In M. A. Gernsbacher, R. W. Pew, L. M. Hough, & J. R. Pomerantz (Eds.), *Psychology and the real world: Essays illustrating fundamental contributions to society* (pp. 140–146). New York: Worth.

Elavsky, S., & McAuley, E. (2007). Physical activity and mental health outcomes during menopause: A randomized controlled trial. *Annals of Behavioral Medicine, 33,* 132–142.

Elder, G. H., Jr., Nguyen, T. V., & Caspi, A. (1985). Linking family hardship to children's lives. *Child Development, 56,* 361–375.

Elder, G. H., Jr., & Shanahan, M. J. (2006). The life course and human development. In R. M. Lerner (Ed.), *Handbook of child psychology: Vol. 1.*

Theoretical models of human development (6th ed., pp. 665–715). Hoboken, NJ: Wiley.

Elder, G. H., Jr., Shanahan, M. J., & Jennings, J. A. (2015). Human development in time and place. In M. H. Bornstein & T. Leventhal (Eds.), *Handbook of child psychology: Vol. 4. Ecological settings and processes* (7th ed., pp. 6–54). Hoboken, NJ: Wiley.

Elfenbein, D. S., & Felice, M. E. (2003). Adolescent pregnancy. *Pediatric Clinics of North America, 50*, 781–800.

Elias, C. L., & Berk, L. E. (2002). Self-regulation in young children: Is there a role for sociodramatic play? *Early Childhood Research Quarterly, 17*, 1–17.

Elias, V. L., Fullerton, A. S., & Simpson, J. M. (2013). Long-term changes in attitudes toward premarital sex in the United States: Reexamining the role of cohort replacement. *Journal of Sex Research, 52*, 129–139. Retrieved from www.tandfonline.com/doi/pdf/10.1080/00224499.2013.798610#.VG49Z1fF9rE

Elicker, J., Englund, M., & Sroufe, L. A. (1992). Predicting peer competence and peer relationships in childhood from early parent–child relationships. In R. D. Parke & G. W. Ladd (Eds.), *Family–peer relationships: Modes of linkage* (pp. 77–106). Hillsdale, NJ: Erlbaum.

Elkind, D. (1994). *A sympathetic understanding of the child: Birth to sixteen* (3rd ed.). Boston: Allyn and Bacon.

Elkind, D., & Bowen, R. (1979). Imaginary audience behavior in children and adolescents. *Developmental Psychology, 15*, 33–44.

Ellin, A. (2015, March 20). Finding success, well past the age of wonderkind. *New York Times*, p. B5.

Elliott, A. F., Burgio, L. D., & DeCoster, J. (2010). Enhancing caregiver health: Findings from the Resources for Enhancing Alzheimer's Care Health II intervention. *Journal of the American Geriatric Society, 58*, 30–37.

Elliott, J. G. (1999). School refusal: Issues of conceptualization, assessment, and treatment. *Journal of Child Psychology and Psychiatry and Allied Disciplines, 40*, 1001–1012.

Ellis, A. E., & Oakes, L. M. (2006). Infants flexibly use different dimensions to categorize objects. *Developmental Psychology, 42*, 1000–1011.

Ellis, B. J., & Essex, M. J. (2007). Family environments, adrenarche, and sexual maturation: A longitudinal test of a life history model. *Child Development, 78*, 1799–1817.

Ellis, B. J., Shirtcliff, E. A., Boyce, W. T., Deardorff, J., & Essex, M. J. (2011). Quality of early family relationships and the timing and tempo of puberty: Effects depend on biological sensitivity to context. *Development and Psychopathology, 23*, 85–99.

Ellis, L., & Bonin, S. L. (2003). Genetics and occupation-related preferences: Evidence from adoptive and non-adoptive families. *Personality and Individual Differences, 35*, 929–937.

Ellis, R. R., & Simmons, T. (2014). *Coresident grandparents and their grandchildren: 2012*. Washington, DC: U.S. Census Bureau. Retrieved from www.census.gov/content/dam/Census/library/publications/2014/demo/p20-576.pdf

Ellis, W. E., & Zarbatany, L. (2007). Explaining friendship formation and friendship stability: The role of children's and friends' aggression and victimization. *Merrill-Palmer Quarterly, 53*, 79–104.

Else-Quest, N. M. (2012). Gender differences in temperament. In M. Zentner & R. L. Shiner (Eds.), *Handbook of temperament* (pp. 479–496). New York: Guilford.

Else-Quest, N. M., Hyde, J. S., Goldsmith, H. H., & Van Hulle, C. A. (2006). Gender differences in temperament: A meta-analysis. *Psychological Bulletin, 132*, 33–72.

Else-Quest, N. M., Hyde, J. S., & Linn, M. C. (2010). Cross-national patterns of gender differences in mathematics: A meta-analysis. *Psychological Bulletin, 136*, 103–127.

Else-Quest, N. M., & Morse, E. (2015). Variations in parental ethnic socialization and adolescent ethnic identity: A longitudinal study. *Cultural Diversity and Ethnic Minority Psychology, 21*, 54–64.

El-Sheikh, M., Cummings, E. M., & Reiter, S. (1996). Preschoolers' responses to ongoing interadult conflict: The role of prior exposure to resolved versus unresolved arguments. *Journal of Abnormal Child Psychology, 24*, 665–679.

Eltzschig, H. K., Lieberman, E. S., & Camann, W. R. (2003). Regional anesthesia and analgesia for labor and delivery. *New England Journal of Medicine, 384*, 319–332.

Elwert, F., & Christakis, N. A. (2006). Widowhood and race. *American Sociological Review, 71*, 16–41.

Emanuel, E. J., Onwuteaka-Pilipsen, B. D., Urwin, J. W., & Cohen, J. (2016). Attitudes and practices of euthanasia and physician-assisted suicide in the United States, Canada & Europe. *JAMA, 316*, 79–89.

Emery, R. E., Sbarra, D., & Grover, T. (2005). Divorce mediation: Research and reflections. *Family Court Review, 43*, 22–37.

English, T., & Carstensen, L. L. (2014). Selective narrowing of social networks across adulthood is associated with improved emotional experience in daily life. *International Journal of Behavioral Development, 38*, 195–202.

Ennemoser, M., & Schneider, W. (2007). Relations of television viewing and reading: Findings from a 4-year longitudinal study. *Journal of Educational Psychology, 99*, 349–368.

Entringer, S., Epel, E. S., Kumsta, R., Lin, J., Hellhammer, D. H., Blackburn, E. H., et al. (2011). Stress exposure in intrauterine life is associated with shorter telomere length in young adulthood. *Proceedings of the National Academy of Sciences, 108*, e513–e518.

Entringer, S., Epel, E. S., Lin, J., Buss, C., Shahbaba, B., Blackburn, E. H., et al. (2012). Maternal psychosocial stress during pregnancy is associated with newborn leukocyte telomere length. *American Journal of Obstetrics and Gynecology, 208*, 134.e1–134.e7.

Entwisle, D. R., Alexander, K. L., & Olson, L. S. (2005). First grade and educational attainment by age 22: A new story. *American Journal of Sociology, 110*, 1458–1502.

Epel, E. S., Linn, J., Wilhelm, F., Mendes, W., Adler, N., & Dolbier, C. (2006). Cell aging in relation to stress arousal and cardiovascular disease risk factors. *Psychoneuroendocrinology, 31*, 277–287.

Epel, E. S., Merkin, S. S., Cawthon, R., Blackburn, E. H., Adler, N., Pletcher, M. J., & Seeman, T. S. (2009). The rate of leukocyte telomere shortening predicts mortality from cardiovascular disease in elderly men: A novel demonstration. *Aging, 1*, 81–88.

Epstein, L. H., Roemmich, J. N., & Raynor, H. A. (2001). Behavioral therapy in the treatment of pediatric obesity. *Pediatric Clinics of North America, 48*, 981–983.

Epstein, R., Pandit, M., & Thakar, M. (2013). How love emerges in arranged marriages: Two cross-cultural studies. *Journal of Comparative Family Studies, 44*, 341–360.

Erdogan, B., Bauer, T. N., Truxillo, D. M., & Mansfield, L. R. (2012). Whistle while you work: A review of the life satisfaction literature. *Journal of Management, 38*, 1038–1083.

Erickson, K. I., Colcombe, S. J., Wadhwa, R., Bherer, L., Peterson, M. S., & Scalf, P. E. (2007). Training-induced plasticity in older adults: Effects of training on hemispheric asymmetry. *Neurobiology of Aging, 28*, 272–283.

Erickson, K. I., Leckie, R. L., & Weinstein, A. M. (2014). Physical activity, fitness, and gray matter volume. *Neurobiology of Aging, 35*, 530–528.

Erickson, K. I., Raji, C. A., Lopez, O. L., Becker, J. T., Rosano, C., Newman, A. B., et al. (2010). Physical activity predicts gray matter volume in late adulthood: The Cardiovascular Health Study. *Neurology, 75*, 1415–1422.

Erikson, E. H. (1950). *Childhood and society*. New York: Norton.

Erikson, E. H. (1968). *Identity, youth, and crisis*. New York: Norton.

Erikson, E. H. (1998). *The life cycle completed. Extended version with new chapters on the ninth stage by Joan M. Erikson*. New York: Norton.

Erol, R. Y., & Orth, U. (2011). Self-esteem development from age 14 to 30 years: A longitudinal study. *Journal of Personality and Social Psychology, 101*, 607–619.

Esposito-Smythers, C., Weismoore, J., Zimmermann, R. P., & Spirito, A. (2014). Suicidal behaviors among children and adolescents. In M. Nock (Ed.), *Oxford handbook of suicide and self-injury* (pp. 61–81). New York: Oxford University Press.

Espy, K. A., Fang, H., Johnson, C., Stopp, C., & Wiebe, S. A. (2011). Prenatal tobacco exposure: Developmental outcomes in the neonatal period. *Developmental Psychology, 47*, 153–156.

Espy, K. A., Molfese, V. J., & DiLalla, L. F. (2001). Effects of environmental measures on intelligence in young children: Growth curve modeling of longitudinal data. *Merrill-Palmer Quarterly, 47*, 42–73.

Esquivel-Santoveña, E. E., Lambert, T. L., & Hamel, J. (2013). Partner abuse worldwide. *Partner Abuse, 4*, 6–75.

Etaugh, C. (2013). Midlife career transitions for women. In W. Patton (Ed.), *Conceptualising women's working lives* (pp. 105–117). Rotterdam, Netherlands: Sense Publishers.

Etnier, J. L., & Labban, J. D. (2012). Physical activity and cognitive function: Theoretical bases, mechanisms, and moderators. In E. O. Acebedo (Ed.), *Oxford Handbook of exercise psychology* (pp. 76–96). New York: Oxford University Press.

Evanoo, G. (2007). Infant crying: A clinical conundrum. *Journal of Pediatric Health Care, 21*, 333–338.

Evans, G. W. (2003). A multimethodological analysis of cumulative risk and allostatic load among rural children. *Developmental Psychology, 39*, 924–933.

Evans, G. W. (2006). Child development and the physical environment. *Annual Review of Psychology, 57*, 424–451.

Evans, G. W., Fuller-Rowell, T. E., & Doan, S. N. (2012). Childhood cumulative risk and obesity: The mediating role of self-regulatory ability. *Pediatrics, 129*, e68–e73.

Evans, G. W., Gonnella, C., Marcynyszn, L. A., Gentile, L., & Slapekar, N. (2005). The role of chaos in poverty and children's socioemotional adjustment. *Psychological Science, 16*, 560–565.

Evans, G. W., & Schamberg, M A. (2009). Childhood poverty, chronic stress, and adult working memory. *Proceedings of the National Academy of Sciences, 106*, 6545–6549.

Evans, N., & Levinson, S. C. (2009). The myth of language universals: Language diversity and its importance for cognitive science. *Behavioral and Brain Sciences, 32*, 429–492.

Even-Zohar, A. (2011). Intergenerational solidarity between adult grandchildren and their grandparents with different levels of functional ability. *Journal of Intergenerational Relationships, 9*, 128–145.

Evert, J., Lawler, E., Bogan, H., & Perls, T. (2003). Morbidity profiles of centenarians: Survivors, delayers, and escapers. *Journals of Gerontology, 58A*, 232–237.

Ewald, P. W., & Ewald, H. A. S. (2012). Infection, mutation, and cancer evolution. *Journal of Molecular Medicine, 90*, 535–541.

Ewing, S. W. F., & Bryan, A. D. (2015). A question of love and trust? The role of relationship factors in adolescent sexual decision making. *Journal of Developmental and Behavioral Pediatrics, 36*, 628–634.

Exner-Cortens, D., Eckenrode, J., & Rothman, E. (2012). Longitudinal associations between teen dating violence victimization and adverse health outcomes. *Pediatrics, 131,* 71–78.

Eyler, A. A., Haire-Joshu, D., Brownson, R. C., & Nanney, M. S. (2004). Correlates of fat intake among urban, low-income African Americans. *American Journal of Health Behavior, 28,* 410–417.

Eyler, L. T., Pierce, K., & Courchesne, E. (2012). A failure of left temporal cortex to specialize for language is an early emerging and fundamental property of autism. *Brain, 135,* 949–960.

F

Fabes, R. A., Eisenberg, N., Hanish, L. D., & Spinrad, T. L. (2001). Preschoolers' spontaneous emotion vocabulary: Relations to likeability. *Early Education and Development, 12,* 11–27.

Fabes, R. A., Eisenberg, N., McCormick, S. E., & Wilson, M. S. (1988). Preschoolers' attributions of the situational determinants of others' naturally occurring emotions. *Developmental Psychology, 24,* 376–385.

Fabiani, M. (2012). It was the best of times, it was the worst of times: A psychophysiologist's view of cognitive aging. *Psychophysiology, 49,* 283–304.

Fagan, J. F., & Holland, C. R. (2007). Racial equality in intelligence: Predictions from a theory of intelligence as processing. *Intelligence, 35,* 319–334.

Fagan, J. F., Holland, C. R., & Wheeler, K. (2007). The prediction, from infancy, of adult IQ and achievement. *Intelligence, 35,* 225–231.

Fagard, J., & Pezé, A. (1997). Age changes in interlimb coupling and the development of bimanual coordination. *Journal of Motor Behavior, 29,* 199–208.

Fagard, J., Spelke, E., & von Hofsten, C. (2009). Reaching and grasping a moving object in 6-, 8-, and 10-month-old infants: Laterality and performance. *Infant Behavior and Development, 32,* 137–146.

Fagot, B. I. (1985). Changes in thinking about early sex role development. *Developmental Review, 5,* 83–98.

Fagot, B. I., & Hagan, R. I. (1991). Observations of parent reactions to sex-stereotyped behaviors: Age and sex effects. *Child Development, 62,* 617–628.

Fahrmeier, E. D. (1978). The development of concrete operations among the Hausa. *Journal of Cross-Cultural Psychology, 9,* 23–44.

Faircloth, B. S., & Hamm, J. V. (2005). Sense of belonging among high school students representing four ethnic groups. *Journal of Youth and Adolescence, 34,* 293–309.

Falagas, M. E., & Zarkadoulia, E. (2008). Factors associated with suboptimal compliance to vaccinations in children in developed countries: A systematic review. *Current Medical Research and Opinion, 24,* 1719–1741.

Falbo, T. (2012). Only children: An updated review. *Journal of Individual Psychology, 68,* 38–49.

Falbo, T., Poston, D. L., Jr., Triscari, R. S., & Zhang, X. (1997). Self-enhancing illusions among Chinese schoolchildren. *Journal of Cross-Cultural Psychology, 28,* 172–191.

Falk, D. (2005). Brain lateralization in primates and its evolution in hominids. *American Journal of Physical Anthropology, 30,* 107–125.

Fanslow, C. A. (1981). Death: A natural facet of the life continuum. In D. Krieger (Ed.), *Foundations for holistic health nursing practices: The renaissance nurse* (pp. 249–272). Philadelphia: Lippincott.

Fantz, R. L. (1961, May). The origin of form perception. *Scientific American, 204*(5), 66–72.

Faraone, S. V., Biederman, J., & Mick, E. (2006). The age-dependent decline of attention deficit hyperactivity disorder: A meta-analysis of follow-up studies. *Psychological Medicine, 36,* 159–165.

Farmer, T. W., Irvin, M. J., Leung, M.-C., Hall, C. M., Hutchins, B. C., & McDonough, E. (2010). Social preference, social prominence, and group membership in late elementary school: Homophilic concentration and peer affiliation configurations. *Social Psychology of Education, 13,* 271–293.

Farr, R. J., Forssell, S. L., & Patterson, C. J. (2010). Parenting and child development in adoptive families: Does parental sexual orientation matter? *Applied Developmental Science, 14,* 164–178.

Farrell, C. (2014). *Unretirement: How baby boomers are changing the way we think about work, community, and the good life.* New York: Bloomsbury Press.

Farrington, D. P. (2009). Conduct disorder, aggression and delinquency. In R. M. Lerner & L. Steinberg (Eds.), *Handbook of adolescent psychology: Vol. 1. Individual bases of adolescent development* (3rd ed., pp. 683–722). Hoboken, NJ: Wiley.

Farrington, D. P., Ttofi, M. M., & Coid, J. W. (2009). Development of adolescence-limited, late-onset, and persistent offenders from age 8 to age 48. *Aggressive Behavior, 35,* 150–163.

Farroni, T., Csibra, G., Simion, F., & Johnson, M. H. (2002). Eye contact detection in humans from birth. *Proceedings of the National Academy of Sciences, 99,* 9602–9605.

Farroni, T., Massaccesi, S., Menon, E., & Johnson, M. H. (2007). Direct gaze modulates face recognition in young infants. *Cognition, 102,* 396–404.

Farver, J. M., & Branstetter, W. H. (1994). Preschoolers' prosocial responses to their peers' distress. *Developmental Psychology, 30,* 334–341.

Fassino, S., Amianto, F., Rocca, G., & Daga, G. A. (2010). Parental bonding and eating psychopathology in bulimia nervosa: Personality traits as possible mediators. *Epidemiology and Psychiatric Sciences, 19,* 214–222.

Faulkner, J. A., Larkin, L. M., Claflin, D. R., & Brooks, S. V. (2007). Age-related changes in the structure and function of skeletal muscles. *Clinical and Experimental Pharmacology and Physiology, 34,* 1091–1096.

Fearon, R. P., Bakermans-Kranenburg, M. J., Lapsley, A., & Roisman, G. I. (2010). The significance of insecure attachment and disorganization in the development of children's externalizing behavior: A meta-analytic study. *Child Development, 81,* 435–456.

Federal Interagency Forum on Aging Related Statistics. (2012). *Older Americans: Key indicators of well-being.* Washington, DC: U.S. Government Printing Office.

Fedewa, S. A., Sauer, A. G., Siegel, R. L., & Jemal, A. (2015). Prevalence of major risk factors and use of screening tests for cancer in the United States. *Cancer Epidemiology Biomarkers & Prevention, 24,* 637–652.

Fedina, L., Holmes, J. L., & Backes, B. L. (2016). Campus sexual assault: A systematic review of prevalence research from 2000 to 2015. *Trauma, Violence, & Abuse, 17,* (epub ahead of print).

Fehr, B., Harasymchuk, C., & Sprecher, S. (2014). Compassionate love in romantic relationships: A review and some new findings. *Journal of Social and Personal Relationships, 31,* 575–600.

Fehr, B., & Sprecher, S. (2013). Compassionate love: What we know so far. In M. Hojjat & D. Cramer (Eds.), *Positive psychology of love* (pp. 106–120). New York: Oxford University Press.

Feigelman, W., & Gorman, B. S. (2008). Assessing the effects of peer suicide on youth suicide. *Suicide and Life-Threatening Behavior, 38,* 181–194.

Feinberg, M. E., McHale, S. M., Crouter, A. C., & Cumsille, P. (2003). Sibling differentiation: Sibling and parent relationship trajectories in adolescence. *Child Development, 74,* 1261–1274.

Feldman, A. F., & Matjasko, J. L. (2007). Profiles and portfolios of adolescent school-based extracurricular activity participation. *Journal of Adolescence, 30,* 313–332.

Feldman, D. C., & Beehr, T. A. (2011). A three-phase model of retirement decision making. *American Psychologist, 66,* 193–203.

Feldman, D. C., & Vogel, R. M. (2009). The aging process and person–environment fit. In S. G. Baugh & S. E. Sullivan (Eds.), *Research in careers* (pp. 1–25). Charlotte, NC: Information Age Press.

Feldman, R. (2003). Infant–mother and infant–father synchrony: The coregulation of positive arousal. *Infant Mental Health Journal, 24,* 1–23.

Feldman, R. (2006). From biological rhythms to social rhythms: Physiological precursors of mother–infant synchrony. *Developmental Psychology, 42,* 175–188.

Feldman, R. (2007). Maternal versus child risk and the development of parent–child and family relationships in five high-risk populations. *Development and Psychopathology, 19,* 293–312.

Feldman, R., Eidelman, A. I., & Rotenberg, N. (2004). Parenting stress, infant emotion regulation, maternal sensitivity, and the cognitive development of triplets: A model for parent and child influences in a unique ecology. *Child Development, 75,* 1774–1791.

Feldman, R., Gordon, I., Schneiderman, I., Weisman, O., & Zagoory-Sharon, O. (2010). Natural variations in maternal and paternal care are associated with systematic changes in oxytocin following parent–infant contact. *Psychoneuroendocrinology, 35,* 1133–1141.

Feldman, R., & Klein, P. S. (2003). Toddlers' self-regulated compliance to mothers, caregivers, and fathers: Implications for theories of socialization. *Developmental Psychology, 39,* 680–692.

Feldman, R., Rosenthal, Z., & Eidelman, A. (2014). Maternal–preterm skin-to-skin contact enhances child physiologic organization and cognitive control across the first 10 years of life. *Biological Psychiatry, 75,* 56–64.

Feldman, R., Sussman, A. L., & Zigler, E. (2004). Parental leave and work adaptation at the transition to parenthood: Individual, marital, and social correlates. *Applied Developmental Psychology, 25,* 459–479.

Felner, R. D., Favazza, A., Shim, M., Brand, S., Gu, K., & Noonan, N. (2002). Whole school improvement and restructuring as prevention and promotion: Lessons from STEP and the Project on High Performance Learning Communities. *Journal of School Psychology, 39,* 177–202.

Feng, P., Huang, L., & Wang, H. (2013). Taste bud homeostasis in health, disease, and aging. *Chemical Senses, 39,* 3–16.

Fenn, A. M., Corona, A. W., & Godbout, J. P. (2014). Aging and the immune system. In A. W. Kusnecov & H. Anisman (Eds.), *Wiley-Blackwell handbook of psychoneuroimmunology* (pp. 313–329). Malden, MA: Wiley Blackwell.

Ferguson, L. R. (2010). Meat and cancer. *Meat Science, 84,* 308–313.

Ferguson, T. J., Stegge, H., & Damhuis, I. (1991). Children's understanding of guilt and shame. *Child Development, 62,* 827–839.

Fernald, A., & Marchman, V. A. (2012). Individual differences in lexical processing at 18 months predict vocabulary growth in typically developing and late-talking toddlers. *Child Development, 82,* 203–222.

Fernald, A., Marchman, V. A., & Weisleder, A. (2013). SES differences in language processing skill and vocabulary are evident at 18 months. *Developmental Science, 16,* 234–248.

Fernald, A., & Morikawa, H. (1993). Common themes and cultural variations in Japanese and American mothers' speech to infants. *Child Development, 64,* 637–656.

Fernald, A., Taeschner, T., Dunn, J., Papousek, M., Boyssen-Bardies, B., & Fukui, I. (1989). A cross-language study of prosodic modifications in mothers' and fathers' speech to preverbal infants. *Journal of Child Language, 16,* 477–502.

Fernald, L. C., & Grantham-McGregor, S. M. (1998). Stress response in school-age children who have been growth-retarded since early childhood. *American Journal of Clinical Nutrition, 68,* 691–698.

Fernandes, M., Stein, A., Srinivasan, K., Menezes, G., & Ramchandani, P. J. (2015). Foetal exposure to maternal depression predicts cortisol responses in infants: Findings from rural South India. *Child: Care, Health and Development, 41,* 677–686.

Fernandes-Taylor, S., & Bloom, J. R. (2015). A psychosocial perspective on socioeconomic disparities in cancer. In J. C. Holland, W. S. Breitbart, P. N. Butow, P. B. Jacobsen, M. J. Loscalzo, & R. McCorkle (Eds.), *Psycho-oncology* (3rd ed., pp. 28–34). New York: Oxford University Press.

Ferrando, M., Prieto, M. D., Almeida, L. S., Ferrándiz, C., Bermejo, R., López-Pina, J. A., et al. (2011). Trait emotional intelligence and academic performance: Controlling for the effects of IQ, personality, and self-concept. *Journal of Psychoeducational Assessment, 29,* 150–159.

Ferrari, P. F., & Coudé, G. (2011). Mirror neurons and imitation from a developmental and evolutionary perspective. In A. Vilain, C. Abry, J.-L. Schwartz, & J. Vauclair (Eds.), *Primate communication and human language* (pp. 121–138). Amsterdam, Netherlands: John Benjamins.

Ferrari, P. F., Tramacere, A., Simpson, E. A., & Iriki, A. (2013). Mirror neurons through the lens of epigenetics. *Trends in Cognitive Sciences, 17,* 450–457.

Ferrari, P. F., Visalberghi E., Paukner A., Fogassi L., Ruggiero A., Suomi, S. (2006). Neonatal imitation in rhesus macaques. *PLoS Biology, 4,* e302.

Ferry, A. L., Hespos, S. J., & Waxman, S. R. (2010). Categorization in 3- and 4-month-old infants: An advantage of words over tones. *Child Development, 81,* 472–479.

Ficca, G., Fagioli, I., Giganti, F., & Salzarulo, P. (1999). Spontaneous awakenings from sleep in the first year of life. *Early Human Development, 55,* 219–228.

Field, D. (1997). "Looking back, what portion of your life brought you the most satisfaction?" *International Journal of Aging and Human Development, 45,* 169–194.

Field, D. (1999). Stability of older women's friendships: A commentary on Roberto. *International Journal of Aging and Human Development, 48,* 81–83.

Field, T. (2001). Massage therapy facilitates weight gain in preterm infants. *Current Directions in Psychological Science, 10,* 51–54.

Field, T. (2011). Prenatal depression effects on early development: A review. *Infant Behavior and Development, 34,* 1–14.

Field, T., Hernandez-Reif, M., & Freedman, J. (2004). Stimulation programs for preterm infants. *Social Policy Report of the Society for Research in Child Development, 18*(1).

Fiese, B. H., Foley, K. P., & Spagnola, M. (2006). Routine and ritual elements in family mealtimes: Contexts for child well-being and family identity. *New Directions for Child and Adolescent Development, 111,* 67–90.

Fiese, B. H., & Schwartz, M. (2008). Reclaiming the family table: Mealtimes and child health and well-being. *Social Policy Report of the Society for Research in Child Development, 22*(4), 3–18.

Fiese, B. H., & Winter, M. A. (2010). The dynamics of family chaos and its relation to children's socioemotional well-being. In G. W. Evans & T. D. Wachs (Eds.), *Chaos and its influence on children's development: An ecological perspective* (pp. 49–66). Washington, DC: American Psychological Association.

Fifer, W. P., Byrd, D. L., Kaku, M., Eigsti, I. M., Isler, J. R., Grose-Fifer, J., et al. (2010). Newborn infants learn during sleep. *Proceedings of the National Academy of Sciences, 107,* 10320–10323.

Figner, B., Mackinlay, R. J., Wilkening, F., & Weber, E. U. (2009). Affective and deliberative processes in risky choice: Age differences in risk taking in the Columbia Card Task. *Journal of Experimental Psychology: Learning, Memory, and Cognition, 35,* 709–770.

Fincham, F. D., & Bradbury, T. N. (2004). Marital satisfaction, depression, and attributions: A longitudinal analysis. In R. M. Kowalski & M. R. Leary (Eds.), *The interface of social and clinical psychology: Key readings* (pp. 129–146). New York: Psychology Press.

Finchum, T., & Weber, J. A. (2000). Applying continuity theory to elder adult friendships. *Journal of Aging and Identity, 5,* 159–168.

Fingerman, K. L. (2004). The role of offspring and in-laws in grandparents' ties to their grandchildren. *Journal of Family Issues, 25,* 1026–1049.

Fingerman, K. L., & Birditt, K. S. (2003). Do we get better at picking our battles? Age group differences in descriptions of behavioral reactions to interpersonal tensions. *Journals of Gerontology, 60B,* P121–P128.

Fingerman, K. L., & Birditt, K. S. (2011). Relationships between adults and their aging parents. In K. W. Schaie & S. L. Willis (Eds.), *Handbook of the psychology of aging* (pp. 219–232). San Diego, CA: Academic Press.

Fingerman, K. L., Chen, P.-C., Hay, E., Cichy, K. E., & Lefkowitz, E. S. (2006). Ambivalent reactions in the parent and offspring relationship. *Journals of Gerontology, 61B,* P152–P160.

Fingerman, K. L., Cheng, Y.-P., Birditt, K., & Zarit, S. (2012a). Only as happy as the least happy child: Multiple grown children's problems and successes and middle-aged parents' well-being. *Journals of Gerontology, 67B,* 184–193.

Fingerman, K. L., Cheng, Y-P., Tighe, L., Birditt, K. S., & Zarit, S. (2012b). Relationships between young adults and their parents. In A. Booth, S. L. Brown, N. S. Landale, W. D. Manning, & S. M. McHale (Eds.), *Early adulthood in a family context* (pp. 59–85). New York: Springer.

Fingerman, K. L., Cheng, Y-P., Wesselmann, D., Zarit, S., Furstenberg, F., & Birditt, K. S. (2012c). Helicopter parents and landing pad kids: Intense parental support of grown children. *Journal of Marriage and Family, 74,* 880–896.

Fingerman, K. L., Gilligan, M., VanderDrift, L., & Pitzer, L. (2012d). In-law relationships before and after marriage: Husbands, wives, and their mothers-in-law. *Research in Human Development, 9,* 106–125.

Fingerman, K. L., Hay, E. L., Dush, C. M. K., Cichy, K. E., & Hosterman, S. J. (2007). Parents' and offspring's perceptions of change and continuity when parents experience the transition to old age. *Advances in Life Course Research, 12,* 275–305.

Fingerman, K. L., Kim, K., Birditt, K. S., & Zarit, S. H. (2016). The ties that bind: Midlife parents' daily experiences with grown children. *Journal of Marriage and Family, 78,* 431–450.

Fingerman, K. L., Kim, K., Davis, E. M., Furstenberg, F. F., Jr., Birditt, K. S., & Zarit, S. H. (2015). "I'll give you the world": Socioeconomic differences in parental support of adult children. *Journal of Marriage and Family, 77,* 844–865.

Fingerman, K. L., Miller, L., Birditt, K., & Zarit, S. (2009). Giving to the good and the needy: Parental support of grown children. *Journal of Marriage and Family, 71,* 1220–1233.

Fingerman, K. L., Pitzer, L. M., Chan, W., Birditt, K., Franks, M. M., & Zarit, S. (2011a). Who gets what and why? Help middle-aged adults provide to parents and grown children. *Journals of Gerontology, 66B,* 87–98.

Fingerman, K. L., Pitzer, L., Lefkowitz, E. S., Birditt, K. S., & Mroczek, D. (2008). Ambivalent relationship qualities between adults and their parents: Implications for both parties' well-being. *Journals of Gerontology, 63B,* P362–P371.

Fingerman, K. L., VanderDrift, L. E., Dotterer, A. M., Birditt, K. S., & Zarit, S. H. (2011b). Support to aging parents and grown children in black and white families. *Gerontologist, 51,* 441–452.

Finkel, D., Gerritsen, L., Reynolds, C. A., Dahl, A. K., & Pedersen, N. L. (2014). Etiology of individual differences in human health and longevity. In R. L. Sprott (Ed.), *Annual Review of Gerontology and Geriatrics* (Vol. 34, pp. 189–227). New York: Springer.

Finkel, D., Reynolds, C. A., McArdle, J. J., Hamagami, F., & Pedersen, N. L. (2009). Genetic variance in processing speed drives variation in aging of spatial and memory abilities. *Developmental Psychology, 45,* 820–834.

Finkel, E. J., Eastwick, P. W., Karney, B. R., Reis, H. T., & Sprecher, S. (2012). Online dating: A critical analysis from the perspective of psychological science. *Psychological Science in the Public Interest, 13,* 3–66.

Finkelhor, D. (2009). The prevention of childhood sexual abuse. *Future of Children, 19,* 169–194.

Finucane, M. L., Mertz, C. K., Slovic, P., & Schmidt, E. S. (2005). Task complexity and older adults' decision-making competence. *Psychology and Aging, 20,* 71–84.

Fiocco, A. J., Peck, K., & Mallya, S. (2016). Central nervous system. In S. K. Whitbourne (Ed.), *Encyclopedia of adulthood and aging* (Vol. 1, pp. 184–188). Malden, MA: Wiley Blackwell.

Fiori, K. L., Antonucci, T., & Cortina, K. S. (2006). Social network typologies and mental health among older adults. *Journals of Gerontology, 61B,* 25–32.

Fiori, K. L., & Denckla, C. A. (2015). Friendship and happiness among middle-aged adults. In M. Demir (Ed.), *Friendship and happiness: Across the life-span and cultures* (pp. 137–154). New York: Springer Science+Business Media.

Fiori, K. L., Smith, J., & Antonucci, T. C. (2007). Social network types among older adults: A multidimensional approach. *Journals of Gerontology, 62B,* P322–P330.

Fischer, K. (2013, March 12). A college degree sorts applicants, but employers wish it meant more. *Chronicle of Higher Education.* Retrieved from chronicle.com/article/The-Employment-Mismatch/137625/#id=overview

Fischer, K. W., & Bidell, T. (1991). Constraining nativist inferences about cognitive capacities. In S. Carey & R. Gelman (Eds.), *The epigenesis of mind: Essays on biology and cognition* (pp. 199–235). Hillsdale, NJ: Erlbaum.

Fischman, M. G., Moore, J. B., & Steele, K. H. (1992). Children's one-hand catching as a function of age, gender, and ball location. *Research Quarterly for Exercise and Sport, 63,* 349–355.

Fish, M. (2004). Attachment in infancy and preschool in low socioeconomic status rural Appalachian children: Stability and change and relations to preschool and kindergarten competence. *Development and Psychopathology, 16,* 293–312.

Fisher, C. B., Hoagwood, K., Boyce, C., Duster, T., Frank, D. A., & Grisso, T. (2002). Research ethics for mental health science involving ethnic minority children and youths. *American Psychologist, 57,* 1024–1040.

Fisher, G. G., Stachowski, A., Infurna, F. J., Faul, J. D., Grosch, J., & Tetrick, L. E. (2014). Mental work demands, retirement, and longitudinal trajectories of cognitive functioning. *Journal of Occupational Health Psychology, 19,* 231–242.

Fisher, S. K., Easterly, S., & Lazear, K. J. (2008). Lesbian, gay, bisexual and transgender families and their children. In T. P. Gullotta & G. M. Blau (Eds.), *Family influences on child behavior and development: Evidence-based prevention and treatment approaches* (pp. 187–208). New York: Routledge.

Fivush, R., & Haden, C. A. (2005). Parent–child reminiscing and the construction of a subjective self. In B. D. Homer & C. S. Tamis-LeMonda (Eds.), *The development of social cognition and communication* (pp. 315–336). Mahwah, NJ: Erlbaum.

Fivush, R., & Wang, Q. (2005). Emotion talk in mother–child conversations of the shared past: The effects of culture, gender, and event valence. *Journal of Cognition and Development, 6,* 489–506.

Fivush, R., & Zaman, W. (2014). Gender, subjective perspective, and autobiographical consciousness. In

P. J. Bauer & R. Fivush (Eds.), *Wiley handbook on the development of children's memory* (pp. 586–604). Hoboken, NJ: Wiley-Blackwell.

Flak, A. L., Su, S., Bertrand, J., Denny, C. H., Kesmodel, U. S., & Cogswell, M. E. (2014). The association of mild, moderate, and binge prenatal alcohol exposure and child neuropsychological outcomes: A meta-analysis. *Alcoholism: Clinical and Experimental Research, 38,* 214–226.

Flanagan, C., & Levine, P. (2010). Civic engagement and the transition to adulthood. *Future of Children, 20,* 159–179.

Flanagan, C. A., Stout, M., & Gallay, L. S. (2008). It's my body and none of your business: Developmental changes in adolescents' perceptions of rights concerning health. *Journal of Social Issues, 64,* 815–834.

Flanagan, C. A., & Tucker, C. J. (1999). Adolescents' explanations for political issues: Concordance with their views of self and society. *Developmental Psychology, 35,* 1198–1209.

Flannery, D. J., Hussey, D. L., Biebelhausen, L., & Wester, K. L. (2003). Crime, delinquency, and youth gangs. In G. R. Adams & M. D. Berzonsky (Eds.), *Blackwell handbook of adolescence* (pp. 502–522). Malden, MA: Blackwell.

Flavell, J. H., Flavell, E. R., & Green, F. L. (2001). Development of children's understanding of connections between thinking and feeling. *Psychological Science, 12,* 430–432.

Flavell, J. H., Green, F. L., & Flavell, E. R. (1995). Young children's knowledge about thinking. *Monographs of the Society for Research in Child Development, 60*(1, Serial No. 243).

Flavell, J. H., Green, F. L., & Flavell, E. R. (2000). Development of children's awareness of their own thoughts. *Journal of Cognition and Development, 1,* 97–112.

Fleeson, W. (2004). The quality of American life at the end of the century. In O. G. Birm, C. D. Ryff, & R. C. Kessler (Eds.), *How healthy are we? A national study of well-being at midlife* (pp. 252–272). Chicago: University of Chicago Press.

Fletcher, E. N., Whitaker, R. C., Marino, A. J., & Anderson, S. E. (2014). Screen time at home and school among low-income children attending Head Start. *Child Indicators Research, 7,* 421–436.

Floccia, C., Christophe, A., & Bertoncini, J. (1997). High-amplitude sucking and newborns: The quest for underlying mechanisms. *Journal of Experimental Child Psychology, 64,* 175–198.

Flom, R. (2013). Intersensory perception of faces and voices in infants. In P. Belin, S. Campanella, & T. Ethofer (Eds.), *Integrating face and voice in person perception* (pp. 71–93). New York: Springer.

Flom, R., & Bahrick, L. E. (2007). The development of infant discrimination of affect in multimodal and unimodal stimulation: The role of intersensory redundancy. *Developmental Psychology, 43,* 238–252.

Flom, R., & Bahrick, L. E. (2010). The effects of intersensory redundancy on attention and memory: Infants' long-term memory for orientation in audiovisual events. *Developmental Psychology, 46,* 428–436.

Flom, R., & Pick, A. D. (2003). Verbal encouragement and joint attention in 18-month-old infants. *Infant Behavior and Development, 26,* 121–134.

Flood, D. G., & Coleman, P. D. (1988). Cell type heterogeneity of changes in dendritic extent in the hippocampal region of the human brain in normal aging and in Alzheimer's disease. In T. L. Petit & G. O. Ivy (Ed.), *Neural plasticity: A lifespan approach* (pp. 265–281). New York: Alan R. Liss.

Florian, V., & Kravetz, S. (1985). Children's concepts of death: A cross-cultural comparison among Muslims, Druze, Christians, and Jews in Israel. *Journal of Cross-Cultural Psychology, 16,* 174–179.

Florian, V., & Mikulincer, M. (1998). Symbolic immortality and the management of the terror of death: The moderating role of attachment style. *Journal of Personality and Social Psychology, 74,* 725–734.

Flynn, J. R. (1999). Searching for justice: The discovery of IQ gains over time. *American Psychologist, 54,* 5–20.

Flynn, J. R. (2007). *What is intelligence? Beyond the Flynn effect.* New York: Cambridge University Press.

Flynn, J. R., & Rossi-Casé, L. (2011). Modern women match men on Raven's Progressive Matrices. *Personality and Individual Differences, 50,* 799–803.

Foehr, U. G. (2006). *Media multitasking among American youth: Prevalence, predictors, and pairings.* Menlo Park. CA: Kaiser Family Foundation.

Foerde, K., Knowlton, B. J., & Poldrack, R. A. (2006). Modulation of competing memory systems by distraction. *Proceedings of the National Academy of Sciences, 103,* 11778–11783.

Fomon, S. J., & Nelson, S. E. (2002). Body composition of the male and female reference infants. *Annual Review of Nutrition, 22,* 1–17.

Fonnesbeck, C. J., McPheeters, M. L., Krishnaswami, S., Lindegren, M. L., & Reimschisel, T. (2013). Estimating the probability of IQ impairment from blood phenylalanine for phenylketonuria patients: A hierarchical meta-analysis. *Journal of Inherited Metabolic Disease, 36,* 757–766.

Fontana, L. (2008). Calorie restriction and cardiometabolic health. *European Journal of Cardiovascular Prevention and Rehabilitation, 15,* 3–9.

Fontana, L., & Hu, F. B. (2014). Optimal body weight for health and longevity: Bridging basic, clinical, and population research. *Aging Cell, 13,* 391–400.

Fontana, L., Klein, S., & Holloszy, J. O. (2010). Effects of long-term calorie restriction and endurance exercise on glucose tolerance, insulin action, and adipokine production. *Age, 32,* 97–108.

Forcada-Guex, M., Pierrehumbert, B., Borghini, A., Moessinger, A., & Muller-Nix, C. (2006). Early dyadic patterns of mother–infant interactions and outcomes of prematurity at 18 months. *Pediatrics, 118e,* 107–114.

Ford, D. Y. (2012). Gifted and talented education: History, issues, and recommendations. In K. R. Harris, S. Graham, T. Urdan, S. Graham, J. M. Royer, & M. Zeidner (Eds.), *APA educational psychology handbook: Vol. 2. Individual differences and cultural contextual factors* (pp. 83–110). Washington, DC: American Psychological Association.

Ford, L., Kozey, M. L., & Negreiros, J. (2012). Cognitive assessment in early childhood: Theoretical and practical perspectives. In D. P. Flanagan & P. L. Harrison (Eds.), *Contemporary intellectual assessment: Theories, tests, and issues* (pp. 585–622). New York: Guilford.

Forman, D. R., Aksan, N., & Kochanska, G. (2004). Toddlers' responsive imitation predicts preschool-age conscience. *Psychological Science, 15,* 699–704.

Formosa, M. (2014). Four decades of Universities of the Third Age: Past, present, and future. *Aging & Society, 34,* 42–66.

Fowler, C. (2009). Motives for sibling communication across the lifespan. *Communication Quarterly, 57,* 51–66.

Fowler, J. W., & Dell, M. L. (2006). Stages of faith from infancy through adolescence: Reflections on three decades of faith development theory. In E. C. Roehlkepartain, P. E. King, L. Wagener, & P. L. Benson (Eds.), *Handbook of spiritual development in childhood and adolescence* (pp. 34–45). Thousand Oaks, CA: Sage.

Fox, C. L., & Boulton, M. J. (2006). Friendship as a moderator of the relationship between social skills problems and peer victimization. *Aggressive Behavior, 32,* 110–121.

Fox, N. A., & Davidson, R. J. (1986). Taste-elicited changes in facial signs of emotion and the asymmetry of brain electrical activity in newborn infants. *Neuropsychologia, 24,* 417–422.

Fox, N. A., Henderson, H. A., Pérez-Edgar, K., & White, L. K. (2008). The biology of temperament: An integrative approach. In C. A. Nelson & M. Luciana (Eds.), *Handbook of developmental cognitive neuroscience* (2nd ed., pp. 839–853). Cambridge, MA: MIT Press.

Fox, N. A., Nelson, C. A., III, & Zeanah, C. H. (2013). The effects of early severe psychosocial deprivation on children's cognitive and social development: Lessons from the Bucharest Early Intervention Project. In N. S. Landale, S. M. McHale, & A. Booth (Eds.), *Families and child health* (pp. 33–41). New York: Springer Science + Business Media.

Franceschi, C., & Campisi, J. (2014). Chronic inflammation (inflammaging) and its potential contribution to age-associated diseases. *Journals of Gerontology, 69A*(Suppl. 1), S4–S9.

Franchak, J. M., & Adolph, K. E. (2012). What infants know and what they do: Perceiving possibilities for walking through openings. *Developmental Psychology, 48,* 1254–1261.

Frank, M. C., Amso, D., & Johnson, S. P. (2014). Visual search and attention to faces during early infancy. *Journal of Experimental Child Psychology, 118,* 13–26.

Frankel, L. A., Umemura, T., Jacobvitz, D., & Hazen, N. (2015). Marital conflict and parental responses to infant negative emotions: Relations with toddler emotional regulation. *Infant Behavior and Development, 40,* 73–83.

Franklin, V. P. (2012). "The teachers' unions strike back?" No need to wait for "Superman": Magnet schools have brought success to urban public school students for over 30 years. In D. T. Slaughter-Defoe, H. C. Stevenson, E. G. Arrington, & D. J. Johnson (Eds.), *Black educational choice: Assessing the private and public alternatives to traditional K–12 public schools* (pp. 217–220). Santa Barbara, CA: Praeger.

Frazier, L., Barreto, M., & Newman, F. (2012). Self-regulation and eudaimonic well-being across adulthood. *Experimental Aging Research, 38,* 394–410.

Frazier, L. D. (2002). Perceptions of control over health: Implications for sense of self in healthy and ill older adults. In S. P. Shohov (Ed.), *Advances in psychology research* (Vol. 10, pp. 145–163). Huntington, NY: Nova Science Publishers.

Frazier, L. D., & Hooker, K. (2006). Possible selves in adult development: Linking theory and research. In C. Dunkel & J. Kerpelman (Eds.), *Possible selves: Theory, research and applications* (pp. 41–59). Hauppauge, NY: Nova Science.

Frederickson, B. L., & Carstensen, L. L. (1990). Relationship classification using grade of membership analysis: A typology of sibling relationships in later life. *Journals of Gerontology, 45,* S43–S51.

Fredricks, J. A. (2012). Extracurricular participation and academic outcomes: Testing the over-scheduling hypothesis. *Journal of Youth and Adolescence, 41,* 295–306.

Fredricks, J. A., & Eccles, J. S. (2002). Children's competence and value beliefs from childhood through adolescence: Growth trajectories in two male-sex-typed domains. *Developmental Psychology, 38,* 519–533.

Fredricks, J. A., & Eccles, J. S. (2006). Is extracurricular participation associated with beneficial outcomes? Concurrent and longitudinal relations. *Developmental Psychology, 42,* 698–713.

Freedman, V. A., & Spillman, B. C. (2014). The residential continuum from home to nursing home: Size, characteristics and unmet needs of older adults. *Journals of Gerontology, 69B,* S42–S50.

Freeman, D. (1983). *Margaret Mead and Samoa: The making and unmaking of an anthropological myth.* Cambridge, MA: Harvard University Press.

Freeman, E. W., Sammel, M. D., Boorman, D. W., & Zhang, R. (2014). Longitudinal pattern of depressive symptoms around natural menopause. *JAMA Psychiatry, 71,* 36–43.

Freeman, E. W., Sammel, M. D., Lin, H., & Nelson, D. B. (2006). Associations of hormones and menopausal status with depressed mood in women with no history of depression. *Archives of General Psychiatry, 63,* 375–382.

Freeman, H., & Newland, L. A. (2010). New directions in father attachment. *Early Child Development and Care, 180,* 1–8.

Freitag, C. M., Rohde, L. A., Lempp, T., & Romanos, M. (2010). Phenotypic and measurement influences on heritability estimates in childhood ADHD. *European Child and Adolescent Psychiatry, 19,* 311–323.

Freitas, A. A., & Magalhães, J. P. de. (2011). A review and appraisal of the DNA damage theory of ageing. *Mutation Research, 728,* 1–2, 12–22.

Frejka, T., Sobotka, T., Hoem, J. M., & Toulemon, L. (2008). Childbearing trends and policies in Europe. *Demographic Research, 19,* 5–14.

French, B. H., Tilghman, J. D., & Malebranche, D. A. (2015). Sexual coercion context and psychosocial correlates among diverse males. *Psychology of Men & Masculinity, 16,* 42–53.

French, D. C., Chen, X., Chung, J., Li, M., Chen, H., & Li, D. (2011). Four children and one toy: Chinese and Canadian children faced with potential conflict over a limited resource. *Child Development, 82,* 830–841.

French, D. J., Sargent-Cox, K., & Luszcz, M. A. (2012). Correlates of subjective health across the aging lifespan: Understanding self-rated health in the oldest old. *Journal of Aging and Health, 24,* 1449–1469.

French, S. A., & Story, M. (2013). Commentary on nutrition standards in the national school lunch and breakfast programs. *JAMA Pediatrics, 167,* 8–9.

Freud, S. (1973). *An outline of psychoanalysis.* London: Hogarth. (Original work published 1938)

Freund, A. M., & Baltes, P. B. (1998). Selection, optimization, and compensation as strategies of life management: Correlations with subjective indicators of successful aging. *Psychology and Aging, 13,* 531–543.

Freund, A. M., & Ritter, J. O. (2009). Midlife crisis: A debate. *Gerontology, 55,* 582–591.

Freund, A. M., & Smith, J. (1999). Content and function of the self-definition in old and very old age. *Journals of Gerontology, 54B,* P55–P67.

Frey, A., Ruchkin, V., Martin, A., & Schwab-Stone, M. (2009). Adolescents in transition: School and family characteristics in the development of violent behaviors entering high school. *Child Psychiatry and Human Development, 40,* 1–13.

Fried, L. P., Carlson, M. C., Freedman, M., Frick, K. D., Glass, T. A., Hill, J., et al. (2004). A social model for health promotion for an aging population: Initial evidence on the Experience Corps model. *Journal of Urban Health, 81,* 64–78.

Fried, L. P., Xue, Q-L., Cappola, A. R., Ferrucci, L., Chaves, P., Varadhan, R., et al. (2009). Nonlinear multisystem physiological dysregulation associated with frailty in older women: Implications for etiology and treatment. *Journals of Gerontology, 64A,* 1049–1052.

Friedlmeier, W., Corapci, F., & Cole, P. M. (2011). Socialization of emotions in cross-cultural perspective. *Social and Personality Psychology Compass, 5,* 410–427.

Friedman, C., McGwin, G., Jr., Ball, K. K., & Owsley, C. (2013). Association between higher-order visual processing abilities and a history of motor vehicle collision involvement by drivers age 70 and over. *Investigative Ophthalmology and Visual Science, 54,* 778–782.

Fries, J. F., Bruce, B., & Chakravarty, E. (2011). Compression of morbidity 1980–2011: A focused review of paradigms and progress. *Journal of Aging Research,* Article ID 261702. Retrieved from www.hindawi.com/journals/jar/2011/261702

Frisell, T., Saevarsdottir, S., & Askling, J. (2016). Family history of rheumatoid arthritis: An old concept with new developments. *Nature Reviews Rheumatology, 12,* 335–343.

Frontline. (2012). *Poor kids.* Retrieved from www.pbs.org/wgbh/pages/frontline/poor-kids

Fruhauf, C. A., Jarrott, S. E., & Allen, K. R. (2006). Grandchildren's perception of caring for grandparents. *Journal of Family Issues, 27,* 887–911.

Fry, C. L. (1985). Culture, behavior, and aging in the comparative perspective. In J. E. Birren & K. W. Schaie (Eds.), *Handbook of the psychology of aging* (2nd ed., pp. 216–244). New York: Van Nostrand Reinhold.

Fry, D. P. (2014). Environment of evolutionary adaptedness, rough-and-tumble play, and the selection of restraint in human aggression. In D. Narvaez, K. Valentino, A. Fuentes, J. J. McKenna, & P. Gray (Eds.), *Ancestral landscapes in human evolution: Culture, childrearing and social wellbeing* (pp. 169–188). New York: Oxford University Press.

Fry, P. S. (2003). Perceived self-efficacy domains as predictors of fear of the unknown and fear of dying among older adults. *Psychology and Aging, 18,* 474–486.

Fry, P. S., & Debats, D. L. (2006). Sources of life strengths as predictors of late-life mortality and survivorship. *International Journal of Aging and Human Development, 62,* 303–334.

Fry, P. S., & Debats, D. L. (2010). Sources of human strengths, resilience, and health. In P. S. Fry & C. L. Keyes (Eds.), *New frontiers in resilient aging: Life strengths and well-being in late life* (pp. 15–59). New York: Cambridge University Press.

Fu, G., Xiao, W. S., Killen, M., & Lee, K. (2014). Moral judgment and its relation to second-order theory of mind. *Developmental Psychology, 50,* 2085–2092.

Fu, G., Xu, F., Cameron, C. A., Heyman, G., & Lee, K. (2007). Cross-cultural differences in children's choices, categorizations, and evaluations of truths and lies. *Developmental Psychology, 43,* 278–293.

Fuh, M.-H., Wang, S.-J., Wang, P.-H., & Fuh, J.-L. (2005). Attitudes toward menopause among middle-aged women: A community survey in an island of Taiwan. *Maturitas, 52,* 348–355.

Fulcher, M., Sutfin, E. L., & Patterson, C. J. (2008). Individual differences in gender development: Associations with parental sexual orientation, attitudes, and division of labor. *Sex Roles, 58,* 330–341.

Fuligni, A. J. (2004). The adaptation and acculturation of children from immigrant families. In U. P. Gielen & J. Roopnarine (Eds.), *Childhood and adolescence: Cross-cultural perspectives* (pp. 297–318). Westport, CT: Praeger.

Fuligni, A. J., & Tsai, K. M. (2014). Developmental flexibility in the age of globalization: Autonomy and identity development among immigrant adolescents. *Annual Review of Psychology, 66,* 411–431.

Fuligni, A. S., Han, W.-J., & Brooks-Gunn, J. (2004). The Infant-Toddler HOME in the 2nd and 3rd years of life. *Parenting: Science and Practice, 4,* 139–159.

Fuller-Iglesias, H. (2010, November). Coping across borders: Transnational families in Mexico. In M. Mulso, *Families Coping across Borders.* Paper presented at the National Council on Family Relations Annual Conference, Minneapolis, MN.

Fuller-Iglesias, H. R., Webster, N. J., & Antonucci, T. C. (2015). The complex nature of family support across the life span: Implications for psychological well-being. *Developmental Psychology, 51,* 277–288.

Fuller-Thomson, E., & Minkler, M. (2005). Native American grandparents raising grandchildren: Findings from the Census 2000 Supplementary Survey and implications for social work practice. *Social Work, 50,* 131–139.

Fuller-Thomson, E., & Minkler, M. (2007). Mexican American grandparents raising grandchildren: Findings from the Census 2000 American Community Survey. *Families in Society, 88,* 567–574.

Fuqua, J. S., & Rogol, A. D. (2013). Puberty: Its role in adolescent maturation. In W. T. O'Donohue, L. T. Benuto, & L. Woodword Tolle (Eds.), *Handbook of adolescent health psychology* (pp. 245–270). New York: Springer.

Furman, W., & Collins, W. A. (2009). Adolescent romantic relationships and experiences. In K. Rubin, W. M. Bukowski, & B. Laursen (Eds.), *Handbook of peer interactions, relationships, and groups* (pp. 341–360). New York: Guilford Press.

Furman, W., & Rose, A. J. (2015). Friendships, romantic relationships, and peer relationships. In M. E. Lamb (Ed.), *Handbook of child psychology and developmental science: Vol. 3. Socioemotional processes* (7th ed., pp. 932–974). Hoboken, NJ: Wiley.

Furnham, A. (2009). Sex differences in mate selection preferences. *Personality and Individual Differences, 47,* 262–267.

Furstenberg, F. F. (2010). On a new schedule: Transitions to adulthood and family change. *Future of Children, 20,* 67–87.

Fushiki, S. (2013). Radiation hazards in children—lessons from Chernobyl, Three Mile Island and Fukushima. *Brain & Development, 35,* 220–227.

Fuson, K. C. (2009). Avoiding misinterpretations of Piaget and Vygotsky: Mathematical teaching without learning, learning without teaching, or helpful learning-path teaching? *Cognitive Development, 24,* 343–361.

Futris, T. G., Nielsen, R. B., & Olmstead, S. B. (2010). No degree no job: Adolescent mothers' perceptions of the impact that adolescent fathers' human capital has on paternal financial and social capital. *Child & Adolescent Social Work Journal, 27,* 1–20.

G

Gabbay, S. G., & Wahler, J. J. (2002). Lesbian aging: Review of a growing literature. *Journal of Gay and Lesbian Social Services, 14,* 1–21.

Gabriel, Z., & Bowling, A. (2004). Quality of life from the perspectives of older people. *Ageing and Society, 24,* 675–691.

Gailliot, M. T., Schmeichel, B. J., & Baumeister, R. F. (2006). Self-regulatory processes defend against the threat of death: Effects of self-control depletion and trait self-control on thoughts and fears of dying. *Journal of Personality and Social Psychology, 91,* 49–62.

Galambos, N. L., Fang, S., Krahn, H., Johnson, M. D., & Lachman, M. E. (2015). Up, not down: The age curve in happiness from early adulthood to midlife in two longitudinal studies. *Developmental Psychology, 11,* 1664–1671.

Galanki, E. P., & Christopoulos, A. (2011). The imaginary audience and the personal fable in relation to the separation-individuation process during adolescence. *Psychology, the Journal of the Hellenic Psychological Society, 18,* 85–103.

Galbally, M., Lewis, J., van IJzendoorn, M., & Permezel, M. (2011). The role of oxytocin in mother–infant relations: A systematic review of human studies. *Harvard Review of Psychiatry, 19,* 1–14.

Galetta, F., Franzoni, F., Abraham, N., Guidotti, E., Russo, M. A., Camici, M., et al. (2012). Age related cardiovascular dysfunction and effects of physical activity. *Frontiers in Bioscience, 4,* 2617–2637.

Galinsky, E., Aumann, K., & Bond, J. T. (2009). *Times are changing: Gender and generation at work and at home.* New York: Families and Work Institute.

Galland, B. C., Taylor, B. J., Elder, D. E., & Herbison, P. (2012). Normal sleep patterns in infants and children: A systematic review. *Sleep Medicine Reviews, 16,* 213–222.

Galler, J. R., Bryce, C. P., Waber, D. P., Hock, R. S., Harrison, R., Eaglesfield, G. D., et al. (2012). Infant malnutrition predicts conduct problems in adolescents. *Nutritional Neuroscience, 15,* 186–192.

Galler, J. R., Ramsey, C. F., Morley, D. S., Archer, E., & Salt, P. (1990). The long-term effects of early kwashiorkor compared with marasmus. IV. Performance on the National High School Entrance Examination. *Pediatric Research, 28,* 235–239.

Gallo, W. T., Bradley, E. H., Dubin, J. A., Jones, R. N., Falba, T. A., Teng, H.-M., & Kasl, S. V. (2006). The persistence of depressive symptoms in older workers who experience involuntary job loss: Results from the Health and Retirement Survey. *Journals of Gerontology, 61B,* S221–S228.

Galloway, J., & Thelen, E. (2004). Feet first: Object exploration in young infants. *Infant Behavior and Development, 27,* 107–112.

Gallup. (2013). *Desire for children still norm in U.S.* Retrieved from www.gallup.com/poll/164618/desire-children-norm.aspx

Gallup. (2014). *Many baby boomers reluctant to retire.* Retrieved from www.gallup.com/poll/166952/baby-boomers-reluctant-retire.aspx

Gallup. (2015a). *Americans greatly overestimate percent gay and lesbian in the United States.* Retrieved from www.gallup.com/poll/183383/americans-greatly-overestimate-percent-gay-lesbian.aspx

Gallup. (2015b). *Fewer young people say I do—to any relationship.* Retrieved from www.gallup.com/poll/183515/fewer-young-people-say-relationship.aspx

Gallup. (2015c). *Same-sex marriages up after Supreme Court ruling.* Retrieved from www.gallup.com/poll/186518/sex-marriages-supreme-court-ruling.aspx?utm_source=alert&utm_medium=email&utm_content=morelink&utm_campaign=syndication

Galvao, T. F., Silva, M. T., Zimmermann, I. R., Souza, K. M., Martins, S. S., & Pereira, M. G. (2014). Pubertal timing in girls and depression: A systematic review. *Journal of Affective Disorders, 155,* 13–19.

Galvao, T. F., Thees, M. F., Pontes, R. F., Silva, M. T., & Pereira, M. G. (2013). Zinc supplementation for treating diarrhea in children: A systematic review and meta-analysis. *Pan American Journal of Public Health, 33,* 370–377.

Ganea, P. A., Allen, M. L., Butler, L., Carey, S., & DeLoache, J. S. (2009). Toddlers' referential understanding of pictures. *Journal of Experimental Child Psychology, 104,* 283–295.

Ganea, P. A., Ma, L., & DeLoache, J. S. (2011). Young children's learning and transfer of biological information from picture books to real animals. *Child Development, 82,* 1421–1433.

Ganea, P. A., Shutts, K., Spelke, E., & DeLoache, J. S. (2007). Thinking of things unseen: Infants' use of language to update object representations. *Psychological Science, 8,* 734–739.

Ganger, J., & Brent, M. R. (2004). Reexamining the vocabulary spurt. *Developmental Psychology, 40,* 621–632.

Gannon, L., & Ekstrom, B. (1993). Attitudes toward menopause: The influence of sociocultural paradigms. *Psychology of Women Quarterly, 17,* 275–288.

Ganong, L., Coleman, M., Fine, M., & Martin, P. (1999). Step-parents' affinity-seeking and affinity-maintaining strategies with stepchildren. *Journal of Family Issues, 20,* 299–327.

Ganong, L. H., & Coleman, M. (2004). *Stepfamily relationships: Development, dynamics, and interventions.* New York: Kluwer/Plenum.

Ganong, L. H., Coleman, M., & Jamison, Y. (2011). Patterns of stepchild–stepparent relationship development. *Journal of Marriage and Family, 73,* 396–413.

Garcia, A. J., Koschnitzky, J. E., & Ramirez, J. M. (2013). The physiological determinants of sudden infant death syndrome. *Respiratory Physiology and Neurobiology, 189,* 288–300.

García Coll, C., & Marks, A. K. (2009). *Immigrant stories: Ethnicity and academics in middle childhood.* New York: Oxford University Press.

Garcia-Pinillos, F., Cozar-Barba, M., Munoz-Jimenez, M., Soto-Hermoso, V., & Latorre-Roman, P. (2016). Gait speed in older people: An easy test for detecting cognitive impairment, functional independence, and health state. *Psychogeriatrics, 16,* 165–171.

Gardner, H. (1983). *Frames of mind: The theory of multiple intelligences.* New York: Basic Books.

Gardner, H. (1993). *Multiple intelligences: The theory in practice.* New York: Basic Books.

Gardner, H. (2011). The theory of multiple intelligences. In M. A. Gernsbacher, R. W. Pew, L. M. Hough, & J. R. Pomerantz (Eds.), *Psychology and the real world: Essays illustrating fundamental contributions to society* (pp. 122–130). New York: Worth.

Gardner, H. E. (2000). *Intelligence reframed: Multiple intelligences for the twenty-first century.* New York: Basic Books.

Gardner, R. S., Mainetti, M., & Ascoli, G. A. (2015). Older adults report moderately more detailed autobiographical memories. *Frontiers in Psychology, 6:* Article 631.

Garner, P. W. (1996). The relations of emotional role taking, affective/moral attributions, and emotional display rule knowledge to low-income school-age children's social competence. *Journal of Applied Developmental Psychology, 17,* 19–36.

Garner, P. W. (2003). Child and family correlates of toddlers' emotional and behavioral responses to a mishap. *Infant Mental Health Journal, 24,* 580–596.

Garner, P. W., & Estep, K. (2001). Emotional competence, emotion socialization, and young children's peer-related social competence. *Early Education and Development, 12,* 29–48.

Gartrell, N. K., Bos, H. M. W., & Goldberg, N. G. (2011). Adolescents of the U.S. National Longitudinal Lesbian Family Study: Sexual orientation, sexual behavior, and sexual risk exposure. *Archives of Sexual Behavior, 40,* 1199–1209.

Gartstein, M. A., Gonzalez, C., Carranza, J. A., Ahadi, S. A., Ye, R., Rothbart, M. K., & Yang, S. W. (2006). Studying cross-cultural differences in the development of infant temperament: People's Republic of China, the United States of America, and Spain. *Child Psychiatry and Human Development, 37,* 145–161.

Gartstein, M. A., Slobodskaya, H. R., Zylicz, P. O., Gosztyla, D., & Nakagawa, A. (2010). A cross-cultural evaluation of temperament: Japan, USA, Poland and Russia. *International Journal of Psychology and Psychological Therapy, 10,* 55–75.

Gaskill, R. L., & Perry, B. D. (2012). Child sexual abuse, traumatic experiences, and their impact on the developing brain. In P. Goodyear-Brown (Ed.), *Handbook of child sexual abuse: Identification, assessment, and treatment* (pp. 29–47). Hoboken, NJ: Wiley.

Gaskins, S. (1999). Children's daily lives in a Mayan village: A case study of culturally constructed roles and activities. In R. Göncü (Ed.), *Children's engagement in the world: Sociocultural perspectives* (pp. 25–61). Cambridge, UK: Cambridge University Press.

Gaskins, S. (2013). Pretend play as culturally constructed activity. In M. Taylor (Ed.), *Oxford handbook on the development of the imagination* (pp. 224–251). Oxford, UK: Oxford University Press.

Gaskins, S. (2014). Children's play as cultural activity. In L. Brooker, M. Blaise, & S. Edwards (Eds.), *Sage handbook of play and learning in early childhood* (pp. 31–42). London: Sage.

Gaskins, S., Haight, W., & Lancy, D. F. (2007). The cultural construction of play. In A. Göncü & S. Gaskins (Eds.), *Play and development: Evolutionary, sociocultural, and functional perspectives* (pp. 179–202). Mahwah, NJ: Erlbaum.

Gates, G. J. (2013). *LGBT parenting in the United States.* Los Angeles: Williams Institute, UCLA School of Law. Retrieved from http://williamsinstitute.law.ucla.edu/wp-content/uploads/LGBT-Parenting.pdf

Gathercole, S. E., & Alloway, T. P. (2008). Working memory and classroom learning. In S. K. Thurman & C. A. Fiorello (Eds.), *Applied cognitive research in K–3 classrooms* (pp. 17–40). New York: Routledge/Taylor & Francis Group.

Gathercole, S. E., Lamont, E., & Alloway, T. P. (2006). Working memory in the classroom. In S. Pickering (Ed.), *Working memory and education* (pp. 219–240). San Diego: Elsevier.

Gathercole, V., Sebastián, E., & Soto, P. (1999). The early acquisition of Spanish verb morphology: Across-the-board or piecemeal knowledge? *International Journal of Bilingualism, 3,* 133–182.

Gati, I., & Perez, M. (2014). Gender differences in career preferences from 1990 to 2010: Gaps reduced but not eliminated. *Journal of Counseling Psychology, 61,* 63–80.

Gattis, M. N., Morrow-Howell, N., McCrary, S., Lee, M., Johnson-Reid, M., Tamar, K., et al. (2010). Examining the effects of New York Experience Corps® on young readers. *Literacy Research and Instruction, 49,* 299–314.

Gauvain, M., de la Ossa, J. L., & Hurtado-Ortiz, M. T. (2001). Parental guidance as children learn to use cultural tools: The case of pictorial plans. *Cognitive Development, 16,* 551–575.

Gauvain, M., & Munroe, R. L. (2009). Contributions of societal modernity to cognitive development: A comparison of four cultures. *Child Development, 80,* 1628–1642.

Gauvain, M., Perez, S. M., & Beebe, H. (2013). Authoritative parenting and parental support for children's cognitive development. In R. E. Larzelere, A. S. Morris, & A. W. Harrist (Eds.), *Authoritative parenting: Synthesizing nurturance and discipline for optimal child development* (pp. 211–233). Washington, DC: American Psychological Association.

Gavey, N., & Senn, C. Y. (2014). Sexuality and sexual violence. In D. L. Tolman, L. M. Diamond, J. A. Bauermeister, W. H. George, J. G. Pfaus, & L. M. Ward (Eds.), *APA handbook of sexuality and psychology: Vol. 1. Person-based approaches* (pp. 269–315). Washington, DC: American Psychological Association.

Gavrilova, N. S., & Gavrilov, L. A. (2012). Comments on dietary restriction, Okinawa diet and longevity. *Gerontology, 58,* 221–223.

Gazzaley, A., Cooney, J. W., Rissman, J., & D'Esposito, M. (2005). Top-down suppression deficit underlies working memory impairment in normal aging. *Nature Neuroscience, 8,* 1298–1300.

Ge, X., Brody, G. H., Conger, R. D., Simons, R. L., & Murry, V. (2002). Contextual amplification of the effects of pubertal transition on African American children's deviant peer affiliation and externalized behavioral problems. *Developmental Psychology, 38,* 42–54.

Ge, X., Conger, R. D., & Elder, G. H., Jr. (1996). Coming of age too early: Pubertal influences on girls' vulnerability to psychological distress. *Child Development, 67,* 3386–3400.

Geangu, E., Benga, O., Stahl, D., & Striano, T. (2010). Contagious crying beyond the first days of life. *Infant Behavior and Development, 33,* 279–288.

Gee, C. B., & Rhodes, J. E. (2003). Adolescent mothers' relationship with their children's biological fathers: Social support, social strain, and relationship continuity. *Journal of Family Psychology, 17,* 370–383.

Geerts, C. C., Bots, M. L., van der Ent, C. K., Grobbee, D. E., & Uiterwaal, C. S. (2012). Parental smoking and vascular damage in their 5-year-old children. *Pediatrics, 129,* 45–54.

Gelman, R. (1972). Logical capacity of very young children: Number invariance rules. *Child Development, 43,* 75–90.

Gelman, R., & Shatz, M. (1978). Appropriate speech adjustments: The operation of conversational constraints on talk to two-year-olds. In M. Lewis & L. A. Rosenblum (Eds.), *Interaction, conversation, and the development of language* (pp. 27–61). New York: Wiley.

Gelman, S. A. (2003). *The essential child.* New York: Oxford University Press.

Gelman, S. A., & Kalish, C. W. (2006). Conceptual development. In D. Kuhn & R. Siegler (Eds.), *Handbook of child psychology: Vol. 2. Cognition, perception, and language* (6th ed., pp. 687–733). Hoboken, NJ: Wiley.

Gelman, S. A., Taylor, M. G., & Nguyen, S. P. (2004). Mother–child conversations about gender. *Monographs of the Society for Research in Child Development, 69*(1, Serial No. 275), pp. 1–127.

Gendler, M. N., Witherington, D. C., & Edwards, A. (2008). The development of affect specificity in infants' use of emotion cues. *Infancy, 13,* 456–468.

Genesee, F., & Jared, D. (2008). Literacy development in early French immersion programs. *Canadian Psychology, 49,* 140–147.

Gentile, B., Twenge, J. M., & Campbell, W. K. (2010). Birth cohort differences in self-esteem, 1988–2008: A cross-temporal meta-analysis. *Review of General Psychology, 14,* 261–268.

Genzler, A. L., & Kerns, K. A. (2004). Associations between insecure attachment and sexual experiences. *Personal Relationships, 11,* 249–265.

Geraci, A., & Surian, L. (2011). The developmental roots of fairness: Infants' reactions to equal and unequal distributions of resources. *Developmental Science, 14,* 1012–1020.

Gere, J., Schimmack, U., Pinkus, R. T., & Lockwood, P. (2011). The effects of romantic partners' goal congruence on affective well-being. *Journal of Research in Personality, 45,* 549–559.

Gergely, G., & Watson, J. (1999). Early socioemotional development: Contingency perception and the social-biofeedback model. In P. Rochat (Ed.), *Early social cognition: Understanding others in the first months of life* (pp. 101–136). Mahwah, NJ: Erlbaum.

Gershoff, E. T., Grogan-Kaylor, A., Lansford, J. E., Chang, L., Zelli, A., Deater-Deckard, K., et al. (2010). Parent discipline practices in an international sample: Associations with child behaviors and moderation by perceived normativeness. *Child Development, 81,* 487–502.

Gershoff, E. T., Lansford, J. E., Sexton, H. R., Davis-Kean, P., & Sameroff, A. J. (2012). Longitudinal links between spanking and children's externalizing behaviors in a national sample of white, black, Hispanic, and Asian American families. *Child Development, 83,* 838–843.

Gershon, E. S., & Alliey-Rodriguez, N. (2013). New ethical issues for genetic counseling in common mental disorders. *American Journal of Psychiatry, 170,* 968–976.

Gerstorf, D., Heckhausen, J., Ram, N., Infurna, F. J., Schupp, J., & Wagner, G. G. (2014). Perceived personal control buffers terminal decline in well-being. *Psychology and Aging, 29,* 612–625.

Gerstorf, D., & Ram, N. (2013). Inquiry into terminal decline: Five objectives for future study. *Gerontologist, 53,* 727–737.

Gesell, A. (1933). Maturation and patterning of behavior. In C. Murchison (Ed.), *A handbook of child psychology.* Worcester, MA: Clark University Press.

Geuze, R. H., Schaafsma, S. M., Lust, J. M., Bouma, A., Schiefenhovel, W., Groothuis, T. G. G., et al. (2012). Plasticity of lateralization: Schooling predicts hand preference but not hand skill asymmetry in a non-industrial society. *Neuropsychologia, 50,* 612–620.

Gewirtz, A., Forgatch, M. S., & Wieling, E. (2008). Parenting practices as potential mechanisms for child adjustment following mass trauma. *Journal of Marital and Family Therapy, 34,* 177–192.

Ghavami, N., Fingerhut, A., Peplau, L. A., Grant, S. K., & Wittig, M. A. (2011). Testing a model of minority identity achievement, identity affirmation, and psychological well-being among ethnic minority and sexual minority individuals. *Cultural Diversity and Ethnic Minority Psychology, 17,* 79–88.

Ghesquiere, A., Thomas, J., & Bruce, M. L. (2016). Utilization of hospice bereavement support by at-risk family members. *American Journal of Hospice & Palliative Medicine, 33,* 124–129.

Ghim, H. R. (1990). Evidence for perceptual organization in infants: Perception of subjective contours by young infants. *Infant Behavior and Development, 13,* 221–248.

Gibbs, J. C. (2010). Beyond the conventionally moral. *Journal of Applied Developmental Psychology, 31,* 106–108.

Gibbs, J. C. (2014). *Moral development and reality: Beyond the theories of Kohlberg, Hoffman, and Haidt* (3rd ed.). New York: Oxford University Press.

Gibbs, J. C., Basinger, K. S., Grime, R. L., & Snarey, J. R. (2007). Moral judgment development across cultures: Revisiting Kohlberg's universality claims. *Developmental Review, 24,* 443–500.

Gibbs, J. C., Moshman, D., Berkowitz, M. W., Basinger, K. S., & Grime, R. L. (2009). Taking development seriously: Critique of the 2008 *JME* special issue on moral functioning. *Journal of Moral Education, 38,* 271–282.

Gibson, C. J., Joffe, H., Bromberger, J. T., Thurston, R. C., Lewis, T. T., Khalil, N., & Matthews, K. A. (2012). Mood symptoms after natural menopause and hysterectomy with and without bilateral oophorectomy among women in midlife. *Obstetrics and Gynecology, 119,* 935–941.

Gibson, E. J. (1970). The development of perception as an adaptive process. *American Scientist, 58,* 98–107.

Gibson, E. J. (2003). The world is so full of a number of things: On specification and perceptual learning. *Ecological Psychology, 15,* 283–287.

Gibson, E. J., & Walk, R. D. (1960). The "visual cliff." *Scientific American, 202,* 64–71.

Gibson, J. J. (1979). *The ecological approach to visual perception.* Boston: Houghton Mifflin.

Gibson, P. A. (2005). Intergenerational parenting from the perspective of American grandmothers. *Family Relations, 54,* 280–297.

Gibson-Davis, C., & Rackin, H. (2014). Marriage or carriage? Trends in union context and birth type by education. *Journal of Marriage and Family, 76,* 506–519.

Giedd, J. N., Lalonde, F. M., Celano, M. J., White, S. L., Wallace, G. L., Lee, N. R., et al. (2009). Anatomical brain magnetic resonance imaging of typically developing children and adolescents. *Journal of the American Academy of Child and Adolescent Psychiatry, 48,* 465–470.

Giles, A., & Rovee-Collier, C. (2011). Infant long-term memory for associations formed during mere exposure. *Infant Behavior and Development, 34,* 327–338.

Giles, J. W., & Heyman, G. D. (2005). Young children's beliefs about the relationship between gender and aggressive behavior. *Child Development, 76,* 107–121.

Giles-Sims, J., Straus, M. A., & Sugarman, D. B. (1995). Child, maternal, and family characteristics associated with spanking. *Family Relations, 44,* 170–176.

Gilleard, C., & Higgs, P. (2011). The Third Age as a cultural field. In D. C. Carr & K. Komp (Eds.), *Gerontology in the era of the Third Age* (pp. 33–49). New York: Springer.

Gillies, R. M. (2003). The behaviors, interactions, and perceptions of junior high school students during small-group learning. *Journal of Educational Psychology, 95,* 137–147.

Gillies, R. M., & Ashman, A. F. (1996). Teaching collaborative skills to primary school children in classroom-based workgroups. *Learning and Instruction, 6,* 187–200.

Gilligan, C. F. (1982). *In a different voice.* Cambridge, MA: Harvard University Press.

Gilligan, M., Suitor, J. J., Kim, S., & Pillemer, K. (2013). Differential effects of perceptions of mothers' and fathers' favoritism on sibling tension in adulthood. *Journals of Gerontology, 68B,* 593–598.

Gilligan, M., Suitor, J. J., & Nam, S. (2015). Maternal differential treatment in later life families and within-family variations in adult sibling closeness. *Journals of Gerontology, 70B,* 167–177.

Gilliom, M., Shaw, D. S., Beck, J. E., Schonberg, M. A., & Lukon, J. L. (2002). Anger regulation in disadvantaged preschool boys: Strategies, antecedents, and the development of self-control. *Developmental Psychology, 38,* 222–235.

Gilmore, J. H., Shi, F., Woolson, S. L., Knickmeyer, R. C., Short, S. J., Lin, W., et al. (2012). Longitudinal development of cortical and subcortical gray matter from birth to 2 years. *Cerebral Cortex, 22,* 2478–2485.

Ginsburg, H. P., Lee, J. S., & Boyd, J. S. (2008). Mathematics education for young children: What it is and how to promote it. *Social Policy Report of the Society for Research in Child Development, 12*(1).

Gitlin, L. N., Belle, S. H., Burgio, L. D., Szaja, S. J., Mahoney, D., & Gallagher-Thompson, D. (2003). Effect of multicomponent interventions on caregiver burden and depression: The REACH multisite initiative at 6-month follow-up. *Psychology and Aging, 18,* 361–374.

Gleason, T. R. (2013). Imaginary relationships. In M. Taylor (Ed.), *Oxford handbook of the development of imagination* (pp. 251–271). New York: Oxford University Press.

Gleitman, L. R., Cassidy, K., Nappa, R., Papfragou, A., & Trueswell, J. C. (2005). Hard words. *Language Learning and Development, 1,* 23–64.

Glenright, M., & Pexman, P. M. (2010). Development of children's ability to distinguish sarcasm and verbal irony. *Journal of Child Language, 37,* 429–451.

Glover, J. A., Galliher, R. V., & Lamere, T. G. (2009). Identity development and exploration among sexual minority adolescents: Examination of a multidimensional model. *Journal of Homosexuality, 56,* 77–101.

Gluckman, P. D., Sizonenko, S. V., & Bassett, N. S. (1999). The transition from fetus to neonate—an endocrine perspective. *Acta Paediatrica Supplement, 88*(428), 7–11.

Gnepp, J. (1983). Children's social sensitivity: Inferring emotions from conflicting cues. *Developmental Psychology, 19,* 805–814.

Gnoth, C., Maxrath, B., Skonieczny, T., Friol, K., Godehardt, E., & Tigges, J. (2011). Final ART success rates: A 10 years survey. *Human Reproduction, 26,* 2239–2246.

Goble, P., Martin, C. L., Hanish, L. D., & Fabes, R. A. (2012). Children's gender-typed activity choices across preschool social contexts. *Sex Roles, 67,* 435–451.

Goddings, A.-L., & Giedd, J. N. (2014). Structural brain development during childhood and adolescence. In A.-L. Goddings & J. N. Giedd (Eds.), *The cognitive neurosciences* (5th ed., pp. 15–22). Cambridge, MA: Cambridge University Press.

Goedert, M. (2015). Alzheimer's and Parkinson's diseases: The prion concept in relation to assembled Aβ, tau, and α-synuclein. *Science, 349,* 601.

Goeke-Morey, M. C., Papp, L. M., & Cummings, E. M. (2013). Changes in marital conflict and youths' responses across childhood and adolescence: A test of sensitization. *Development and Psychopathology, 25,* 241–251.

Goering, J. (Ed.). (2003). *Choosing a better life? How public housing tenants selected a HUD experiment to improve their lives and those of their children: The Moving to Opportunity Demonstration Program.* Washington, DC: Urban Institute Press.

Gogate, L. J., & Bahrick, L. E. (2001). Intersensory redundancy and 7-month-old infants' memory for arbitrary syllable–object relations. *Infancy, 2,* 219–231.

Goh, Y. I., & Koren, G. (2008). Folic acid in pregnancy and fetal outcomes. *Journal of Obstetrics and Gynaecology, 28,* 3–13.

Goin, M. (2015). The Buddhist way of death. In C. M. Parkes, P. Laungani, & B. Young (Eds.), *Death and bereavement across cultures* (2nd ed., pp. 61–75). New York: Routledge.

Gold, D. T. (2016). Bone. In S. K. Whitbourne (Ed.), *Encyclopedia of adulthood and aging* (Vol. 1, pp. 130–135). Malden, MA: Wiley Blackwell.

Gold, J. M. (2012). The experiences of childfree and childless couples in a pronatalistic society: Implications for family counselors. *Counseling and Therapy for Couples and Families, 21,* 223–229.

Goldberg, A. E. (2010). *Lesbian and gay parents and their children: Research on the family life cycle.* Washington, DC: American Psychological Association.

Goldberg, A. E., Kashy, D. A., & Smith, J. Z. (2012). Gender-typed play behavior in early childhood: Adopted children with lesbian, gay, and heterosexual parents. *Sex Roles, 67,* 503–513.

Goldberg, A. E., & Perry-Jenkins, M. (2003). Division of labor and working-class women's well-being across the transition to parenthood. *Journal of Family Psychology, 18,* 225–236.

Goldfield, B. A. (1987). The contributions of child and caregiver to referential and expressive language. *Applied Psycholinguistics, 8,* 267–280.

Goldschmidt, L., Richardson, G. A., Cornelius, M. D., & Day, N. L. (2004). Prenatal marijuana and alcohol exposure and academic achievement at age 10. *Neurotoxicology and Teratology, 26,* 521–532.

Goldsteen, M., Houtepen, R., Proot, I. M., Abu-Saad, H. H., Spreeuwenberg, C., & Widdershoven, G. (2006). What is a good death? Terminally ill patients dealing with normative expectations around death and dying. *Patient Education and Counseling, 64,* 378–386.

Goldstein, M. H., & Schwade, J. A. (2008). Social feedback to infants' babbling facilitates rapid phonological learning. *Psychological Science, 19,* 515–523.

Goldstein, S. (2011). Attention-deficit/hyperactivity disorder. In S. Goldstein & C. R. Reynolds (Eds.), *Handbook of neurodevelopmental and genetic disorders in children* (2nd ed., pp. 131–150). New York: Guilford.

Goldston, D. B., Molock, S. D., Whitbeck, L. B., Murakami, J. L., Zayas, L. H., & Hall, G. C. N. (2008). Cultural considerations in adolescent suicide prevention and psychosocial treatment. *American Psychologist, 63,* 14–31.

Golinkoff, R. M., & Hirsh-Pasek, K. (2006). Baby wordsmith: From associationist to social sophisticate. *Current Directions in Psychological Science, 15,* 30–33.

Golomb, C. (2004). *The child's creation of a pictorial world* (2nd ed.). Mahwah, NJ: Erlbaum.

Golombok, S., Blake, L., Casey, P., Roman, G., & Jadva, V. (2013). Children born through reproductive donation: A longitudinal study of psychological adjustment. *Journal of Child Psychology and Psychiatry, 54,* 653–660.

Golombok, S., Readings, J., Blake, L., Casey, P., Mellish, L., Marks, A., & Jadva, V. (2011). Children conceived by gamete donation: Psychological adjustment and mother–child relationships at age 7. *Journal of Family Psychology, 25,* 230–239.

Golombok, S., Rust, J., Zervoulis, K., Croudace, T., Golding, J., & Hines, M. (2008). Developmental trajectories of sex-typed behavior in boys and girls: A longitudinal general population study of children aged 2.5–8 years. *Child Development, 79,* 1583–1593.

Golombok, S., & Tasker, F. (2015). Socioemotional development in changing families. In M. E. Lamb (Ed.), *Handbook of child psychology and developmental science: Vol. 3. Socioemotional processes* (7th ed., pp. 419–463). Hoboken, NJ: Wiley.

Gomez, H. L., Iyer, P., Batto, L. L., & Jensen-Campbell, L. A. (2011). Friendships and adjustment. In R. J. R. Levesque (Ed.), *Encyclopedia of adolescence: Vol. 2. Adolescents' social and personal relationships.* New York: Springer Science + Business Media.

Gomez-Perez, E., & Ostrosky-Solis, F. (2006). Attention and memory evaluation across the life span: Heterogeneous effects of age and education. *Journal of Clinical and Experimental Neuropsychology, 28,* 477–494.

Gonzalez, A.-L., & Wolters, C. A. (2006). The relation between perceived parenting practices and achievement motivation in mathematics. *Journal of Research in Childhood Education, 21,* 203–217.

Gonzalez-Feliciano, A. G., Maisonet, M., & Marcus, M. (2013). The relationship of BMI to menarche. In L. E. Rubin (Ed.), *Break the cycle of environmental health disparities: Maternal and child health aspects* (pp. 13–21). Hauppauge, NY: Nova Science Publishers.

Good, M., & Willoughby, T. (2014). Institutional and personal spirituality/religiosity and psychosocial adjustment in adolescence: Concurrent and longitudinal associations. *Journal of Youth and Adolescence, 43,* 757–774.

Goodman, A., Schorge, J., & Greene, M. F. (2011). The long-term effects of in utero exposures—the DES story. *New England Journal of Medicine, 364,* 2083–2084.

Goodman, C., & Silverstein, M. (2006). Grandmothers raising grandchildren: Ethnic and racial differences in well-being among custodial and coparenting families. *Journal of Family Issues, 27,* 1605–1626.

Goodman, C. C. (2012). Caregiving grandmothers and their grandchildren: Well-being nine years later. *Children and Youth Services Review, 34,* 648–654.

Goodman, G. S., Ogle, C. M., McWilliams, K., Narr, R. K., & Paz-Alonso, P. M. (2014). Memory development in the forensic context. In P. J. Bauer & R. Fivush (Eds.), *Wiley handbook on the development of children's memory* (pp. 921–941). Hoboken, NJ: Wiley.

Goodman, J., Dale, P., & Li, P. (2008). Does frequency count? Parental input and the acquisition of vocabulary. *Journal of Child Language, 35,* 515–531.

Goodman, J. H., Prager, J., Goldstein, R., & Freeman, M. (2015). Perinatal dyadic psychotherapy for postpartum depression: A randomized controlled pilot trial. *Archives of Women's Mental Health, 18,* 493–506.

Goodman, S. H., Rouse, M. H., Long, Q., Shuang, J., & Brand, S. R. (2011). Deconstructing antenatal depression: What is it that matters for neonatal behavioral functioning? *Infant Mental Health Journal, 32,* 339–361.

Goodvin, R., & Romdall, L. (2013). Associations of mother–child reminiscing about negative past events, coping, and self-concept in early childhood. *Infant and Child Development, 22,* 383–400.

Goodwin, M. H. (1998). Games of stance: Conflict and footing in hopscotch. In S. Hoyle & C. T. Adger (Eds.), *Language practices of older children* (pp. 23–46). New York: Oxford University Press.

Gooren, E. M. J. C., Pol, A. C., Stegge, H., Terwogt, M. M., & Koot, H. M. (2011). The development of conduct problems and depressive symptoms in early elementary school children: The role of peer rejection. *Journal of Clinical Child and Adolescent Psychology, 40,* 245–253.

Gopnik, A., & Choi, S. (1990). Do linguistic differences lead to cognitive differences? A cross-linguistic study of semantic and cognitive development. *First Language, 11,* 199–215.

Gopnik, A., & Nazzi, T. (2003). Words, kinds, and causal powers: A theory theory perspective on early naming and categorization. In D. H. Rakison & L. M. Oakes (Eds.), *Early category and concept development* (p. 303–329). New York: Oxford University Press.

Gopnik, A., & Tenenbaum, J. B. (2007). Bayesian networks, Bayesian learning and cognitive development. *Developmental Science, 10,* 281–287.

Gorchoff, S. M. (2016). Close/romantic relationships. In S. K. Whitbourne (Ed.), *Encyclopedia of adulthood and aging* (Vol. 1, pp. 201–206). Malden, MA: Wiley Blackwell.

Gordon, I., Zagoory-Sharon, O., Leckman, J. F., & Feldman, R. (2010). Oxytocin and the development of parenting in humans. *Biological Psychiatry, 68,* 377–382.

Gordon, R. A., Chase-Lansdale, P. L., & Brooks-Gunn, J. (2004). Extended households and the life course of young mothers: Understanding the associations using a sample of mothers with premature, low-birth-weight babies. *Child Development, 75,* 1013–1038.

Gormally, S., Barr, R. G., Wertheim, L., Alkawaf, R., Calinoiu, N., & Young, S. N. (2001). Contact and nutrient caregiving effects on newborn infant pain responses. *Developmental Medicine and Child Neurology, 43,* 28–38.

Gorman, B. K., Fiestas, C. E., Peña, E. D., & Clark, M. R. (2011). Creative and stylistic devices employed by children during a storybook narrative task: A cross-cultural study. *Language, Speech, and Hearing Services in Schools, 42,* 167–181.

Gormley, W. T., Jr., & Phillips, D. (2009). *The effects of pre-K on child development: Lessons from Oklahoma.* Washington, DC: National Summit on Early Childhood Education, Georgetown University.

Goronzy, J. J., Shao, L., & Weyand, C. M. (2010). Immune aging and rheumatoid arthritis. *Rheumatoid Disease Clinics of North America, 36,* 297–310.

Gosselin, P. A., & Gagne, J.-P. (2011). Older adults expend more listening effort than young adults recognizing audiovisual speech in noise. *International Journal of Audiology, 50,* 786–792.

Goswami, U. (1996). Analogical reasoning and cognitive development. In H. Reese (Ed.), *Advances in child development and behavior* (Vol. 26, pp. 91–138). New York: Academic Press.

Gothe, N., Mullen, S. P., Wójcicki, T. R., Mailey, E. L., White, S. M., & Olson, E. A. (2011). Trajectories of change in self-esteem in older adults: Exercise intervention effects. *Journal of Behavioral Medicine, 34,* 298–306.

Gott, M., & Hinchliff, S. (2003). How important is sex in later life? The views of older people. *Social Science and Medicine, 56,* 1617–1628.

Gottfredson, L. S. (2005). Applying Gottfredson's theory of circumscription and compromise in career guidance and counseling. In S. D. Brown & R. W. Lent (Eds.), *Career development and counseling* (pp. 71–100). Hoboken, NJ: Wiley.

Gottlieb, G. (1998). Normally occurring environmental and behavioral influences on gene activity: From central dogma to probabilistic epigenesis. *Psychological Review, 105,* 792–802.

Gottlieb, G. (2007). Probabilistic epigenesis. *Developmental Science, 10,* 1–11.

Gottlieb, G., Wahlsten, D., & Lickliter, R. (2006). The significance of biology for human development: A developmental psychobiological systems view. In R. M. Lerner (Ed.), *Handbook of child psychology: Vol. 1. Theoretical models of human development* (6th ed., pp. 210–257). Hoboken, NJ: Wiley.

Gottman, J. M. (2011). *The science of trust: Emotional attunement for couples.* New York: Norton.

Gottman, J. M., Driver, J., & Tabares, A. (2015). Repair during marital conflict in newlyweds: How couples move from attack–defend to collaboration. *Journal of Family Psychotherapy, 26,* 85–108.

Gottman, J. M., & Gottman, J. S. (2015). Gottman couple therapy. In A. S. Gurman, J. L. Lebow, & D. K. Snyder (Eds.), *Clinical handbook of couple therapy* (5th ed., pp. 129–157). New York: Guilford.

Gottman, J. M., Gottman, J. S., & Shapiro, A. (2010). A new couples approach to interventions for the transition to parenthood. In M. S. Schulz, M. K. Pruett, P. K. Kerig, & R. D. Parke (Eds.), *Strengthening couple relationships for optimal child development* (pp. 165–179). Washington, DC: American Psychological Association.

Gould, J. L., & Keeton, W. T. (1996). *Biological science* (6th ed.). New York: Norton.

Government Accountability Office. (2015). *Advance directives: Information on federal oversight, provider implementation, and prevalence.* Washington, DC: Author. Retrieved from www.gao.gov/assets/670/669906.pdf

Graber, J. A. (2004). Internalizing problems during adolescence. In R. M. Lerner & L. Steinberg (Eds.), *Handbook of adolescent psychology* (2nd ed., pp. 587–626). Hoboken, NJ: Wiley.

Graber, J. A., Brooks-Gunn, J., & Warren, M. P. (2006). Pubertal effects on adjustment in girls: Moving from demonstrating effects to identifying pathways. *Journal of Youth and Adolescence, 35,* 413–423.

Graber, J. A., Nichols, T., Lynne, S. D., Brooks-Gunn, J., & Botwin, G. J. (2006). A longitudinal examination of family, friend, and media influences on competent versus problem behaviors among urban minority youth. *Applied Developmental Science, 10,* 75–85.

Graber, J. A., Seeley, J. R., Brooks-Gunn, J., & Lewinsohn, P. M. (2004). Is pubertal timing associated with psychopathology in young adulthood? *Journal of the American Academy of Child and Adolescent Psychiatry, 43,* 718–726.

Graham-Bermann, S. A., & Howell, K. H. (2011). Child maltreatment in the context of intimate partner violence. In J. E. B. Myers (Ed.), *Child maltreatment* (3rd ed., pp. 167–180). Thousand Oaks, CA: Sage.

Gralinski, J. H., & Kopp, C. B. (1993). Everyday rules for behavior: Mothers' requests to young children. *Developmental Psychology, 29,* 573–584.

Grande, G., Cucumo, V., Cova, I., Ghiretti, R., Maggiore, L., Lacorte, E., et al. (2016). Reversible mild cognitive impairment: The role of comorbidities at baseline. *Journal of Alzheimer's Disease, 51,* 57–67.

Granier-Deferre, C., Bassereau, S., Ribeiro, A., Jacquet, A.-Y., & Lecanuet, J.-P. (2003). *Cardiac "orienting" response in fetuses and babies following in utero melody-learning.* Paper presented at the 11th European Conference on Developmental Psychology, Milan, Italy.

Grant, K. B., & Ray, J. A. (2010). *Home, school, and community collaboration: Culturally responsive family involvement.* Thousand Oaks, CA: Sage Publications.

Grantham-McGregor, S., Walker, S. P., & Chang, S. (2000). Nutritional deficiencies and later behavioral development. *Proceedings of the Nutrition Society, 59,* 47–54.

Gratier, M., & Devouche, E. (2011). Imitation and repetition of prosodic contour in vocal interaction at 3 months. *Developmental Psychology, 47,* 67–76.

Graves, L. M., Ohlott, P. J., & Ruderman, M. N. (2007). Commitment to family roles: Effects on managers' attitudes and performance. *Journal of Applied Psychology, 92,* 44–56.

Gray, K. A., Day, N. L., Leech, S., & Richardson, G. A. (2005). Prenatal marijuana exposure: Effect on child depressive symptoms at ten years of age. *Neurotoxicology and Teratology, 27,* 439–448.

Gray, M. R., & Steinberg, L. (1999). Unpacking authoritative parenting: Reassessing a multidimensional construct. *Journal of Marriage and the Family, 61,* 574–587.

Gray-Little, B., & Carels, R. (1997). The effects of racial and socioeconomic consonance on self-esteem and achievement in elementary, junior high, and high school students. *Journal of Research on Adolescence, 7,* 109–131.

Gray-Little, B., & Hafdahl, A. R. (2000). Factors influencing racial comparisons of self-esteem: A quantitative review. *Psychological Bulletin, 126,* 26–54.

Green, B. L., Tarte, J. M., Harrison, P. M., Nygren, M., & Sanders, M. B. (2014). Results from a randomized trial of the Healthy Families Oregon accredited statewide program: Early program impacts on parenting. *Children and Youth Services Review, 44,* 288–298.

Green, G. E., Irwin, J. R., & Gustafson, G. E. (2000). Acoustic cry analysis, neonatal status and long-term developmental outcomes. In R. G. Barr, B. Hopkins, & J. A. Green (Eds.), *Crying as a sign, a symptom, and a signal* (pp. 137–156). Cambridge, UK: Cambridge University Press.

Greenberg, J. P. (2013). Determinants of after-school programming for school-age immigrant children. *Children and Schools, 35,* 101–111.

Greendorfer, S. L., Lewko, J. H., & Rosengren, K. S. (1996). Family and gender-based socialization of children and adolescents. In F. L. Smoll & R. E. Smith (Eds.), *Children and youth in sport: A biopsychosocial perspective* (pp. 89–111). Dubuque, IA: Brown & Benchmark.

Greene, J. A., Torney-Purta, J., & Azevedo, R. (2010). Empirical evidence regarding relations among a model of epistemic and ontological cognition, academic performance, and educational level. *Journal of Educational Psychology, 102,* 234–255.

Greene, K., Krcmar, M., Walters, L. H., Rubin, D. L., Hale, J., & Hale, L. (2000). Targeting adolescent risk-taking behaviors: The contributions of egocentrism and sensation-seeking. *Journal of Adolescence, 23,* 439–461.

Greene, S. M., Anderson, E. R., Forgatch, M. S., DeGarmo, D. S., & Hetherington, E. M. (2012). Risk and resilience after divorce. In F. Walsh (Ed.), *Normal family processes: Growing diversity and complexity* (4th ed., pp. 102–127). New York: Guilford.

Greenfield, P. (1992, June). *Notes and references for developmental psychology.* Conference on Making Basic Texts in Psychology More Culture-Inclusive and Culture-Sensitive, Western Washington University, Bellingham, WA.

Greenfield, P. M. (2004). *Weaving generations together: Evolving creativity in the Maya of Chiapas.* Santa Fe, NM: School of American Research.

Greenfield, P. M., Suzuki, L. K., & Rothstein-Fish, C. (2006). Cultural pathways through human development. In K. A. Renninger & I. E. Sigel (Eds.), *Handbook of child psychology: Vol. 4. Child psychology in practice* (6th ed., pp. 655–699). Hoboken, NJ: Wiley.

Greenough, W. T., & Black, J. E. (1992). Induction of brain structure by experience: Substrates for cognitive development. In M. R. Gunnar & C. A. Nelson (Eds.), *Minnesota Symposia on Child Psychology* (pp. 155–200). Hillsdale, NJ: Erlbaum.

Gregory, A., & Huang, F. (2013). It takes a village: The effects of 10th grade college-going expectations of students, parents, and teachers four years later. *American Journal of Community Psychology, 52,* 41–55.

Gregory, A., & Weinstein, R. S. (2004). Connection and regulation at home and in school: Predicting growth in achievement for adolescents. *Journal of Adolescent Research, 19,* 405–427.

Greydanus, D. E., Omar, H., & Pratt, H. D. (2010). The adolescent female athlete: Current concepts and conundrums. *Pediatric Clinics of North America, 57,* 697–718.

Greydanus, D. E., Seyler, J., Omar, H. A., & Dodich, C. B. (2012). Sexually transmitted diseases in adolescence. *International Journal of Child and Adolescent Health, 5,* 379–401.

Griffin, B., Loh, V., & Hesketh, B. (2013). Age, gender, and the retirement process. In M. Wang (Ed.), *Oxford handbook of retirement* (pp. 202–214). New York: Oxford University Press.

Griffin, Z. M., & Spieler, D. H. (2006). Observing the what and when of language production for different age groups by monitoring speakers' eye movements. *Brain and Language, 99,* 272–288.

Grigoriadis, S., VonderPorten, E. H., Mamisashvili, L., Eady, A., Tomlinson, G., Dennis, C. L., et al. (2013). The effect of prenatal antidepressant exposure on neonatal adaptation: A systematic review and meta-analysis. *Journal of Clinical Psychiatry, 74,* e309–320.

Groh, A. M., Roisman, G. I., Booth-LaForce, C., Fraley, R. C., Owen, M. T., Cox, M. J., et al. (2014). Stability of attachment security from infancy to late adolescence. In C. Booth-LaForce & G. I. Roisman (Eds.), The Adult Attachment Interview: Psychometrics, stability and change from infancy, and developmental origins. *Monographs of the Society for Research in Child Development, 79*(3, Serial No. 314), 51–68.

Grönholm-Nyman, P. (2015). Can executive functions be trained in healthy older adults and in older adults with mild cognitive impairment? In A. K. Leist, J. Kulmala, & F. Nyqvist (Eds.), *Health and cognition in old age: From biomedical and life course factors to policy and practice* (pp. 223–243). Cham, Switzerland: Springer.

Grossbaum, M. F., & Bates, G. W. (2002). Correlates of psychological well-being at midlife: The role of generativity, agency and communion, and narrative themes. *International Journal of Behavioral Development, 26,* 120–127.

Grossmann, K., Grossmann, K. E., Kindler, H., & Zimmermann, P. (2008). A wider view of attachment and exploration: The influence of mothers and fathers on the development of psychological security from infancy to young adulthood. In J. Cassidy & P. R. Shaver (Eds.), *Handbook of attachment: Theory, research, and clinical applications* (2nd ed., pp. 880–905). New York: Guilford.

Grossmann, K., Grossmann, K. E., Spangler, G., Suess, G., & Unzner, L. (1985). Maternal sensitivity and newborns' orientation responses as related to quality of attachment in Northern Germany. In I. Bretherton & E. Waters (Eds.), Growing points of attachment theory and research. *Monographs of the Society for Research in Child Development, 50*(1–2, Serial No. 209).

Grossniklaus, H. E., Nickerson, J. M., Edelhauser, H. F., Bergman, L. A. M. K., & Berglin, L. (2013). Anatomic alterations in aging and age-related diseases of the eye. *Investigative Ophthalmology and Visual Science, 54,* 23–27.

Grossniklaus, U., Kelly, B., Ferguson-Smith, A. C., Pembrey, M., & Lindquist, S. (2013) Transgenerational epigenetic inheritance: How important is it? *Nature Reviews, 14,* 228–235.

Gruendel, J., & Aber, J. L. (2007). Bridging the gap between research and child policy change: The role of strategic communications in policy advocacy. In J. L. Aber, S. J. Bishop-Josef, S. M. Jones, K. T. McLearn, & D. Phillips (Eds.), *Child development and social policy: Knowledge for action* (pp. 43–58). Washington, DC: American Psychological Association.

Grundy, E. (2005). Reciprocity in relationships: Socio-economic and health influences on intergenerational exchanges between Third Age parents and their adult children in Great Britain. *British Journal of Sociology, 56,* 233–255.

Grünebaum, A., McCullough, L. B., Brent, R. L., Arabin, B., Levene, M. I., & Chervenak, F. A. (2015). Perinatal risks of planned home births in the United States. *American Journal of Obstetrics and Gynecology, 212*(350), e1–e6.

Grusec, J. E. (2006). The development of moral behavior and conscience from a socialization perspective. In M. Killen & J. Smetana (Eds.), *Handbook of moral development* (pp. 243–265). Philadelphia: Erlbaum.

Guasch-Ferré, M., Babio, N., Martínez-Gonzáles, M. A., Corella, D., Ros, E., Martín-Peláez, S., et al. (2015). Dietary fat intake and risk of cardiovascular disease and all-cause mortality in a population at high risk of cardiovascular disease. *American Journal of Clinical Nutrition, 102,* 1563–1573.

Guedes, G., Tsai, J. C., & Loewen, N. A. (2011). Glaucoma and aging. *Current Aging Science, 4,* 110–117.

Guedes, M., Pereira, M., Pires, R., Carvalho, P., & Canavarro, M. C. (2013). Childbearing motivations scale: Construction of a new measure and its preliminary psychometric properties. *Journal of Family Studies.* Retrieved from link.springer.com/article/10.1007%2Fs10826-013-9824-0

Guerra, N. G., Graham, S., & Tolan, P. H. (2011). Raising healthy children: Translating child development research into practice. *Child Development, 82,* 7–16.

Guerra, N. G., Williams, K. R., & Sadek, S. (2011). Understanding bullying and victimization during childhood and adolescence: A mixed methods study. *Child Development, 82,* 295–310.

Guerrero, N., Mendes de Leon, C. F., & Evans, D. A. (2015). Determinants of trust in health care in an older population. *Journal of the American Geriatric Society, 63,* 553–557.

Guest, A. M. (2013). Cultures of play during middle childhood: Interpretive perspectives from two distinct marginalized communities. *Sport, Education and Society, 18,* 167–183.

Guez, J., & Lev, D. (2016). A picture is worth a thousand words? Not when it comes to associative memory of older adults. *Psychology and Aging, 31,* 37–41.

Guggenheim, J. A., St Pourcain, B., McMahon, G., Timpson, N. J., Evans, D. M., & Williams, C. (2015). Assumption-free estimation of the genetic contribution to refractive error across childhood. *Molecular Vision, 21,* 621–632.

Guglielmi, R. S. (2008). Native language proficiency, English literacy, academic achievement, and occupational attainment in limited-English-proficient students: A latent growth modeling perspective. *Journal of Educational Psychology, 100,* 322–342.

Guignard, J.-H., & Lubart, T. (2006). Is it reasonable to be creative? In J. C. Kaufman & J. Baer (Eds.), *Creativity and reason in cognitive development* (pp. 269–281). New York: Cambridge University Press.

Guildner, S. H., Loeb, S., Morris, D., Penrod, J., Bramlett, M., Johnston, L., & Schlotzhauer, P. (2001). A comparison of life satisfaction and mood in nursing home residents and community-dwelling elders. *Archives of Psychiatric Nursing, 15,* 232–240.

Guilford, J. P. (1985). The structure-of-intellect model. In B. B. Wolman (Ed.), *Handbook of intelligence* (pp. 225–266). New York: Wiley.

Guiso, L., Mont, F., Sapienza, P., & Zingales, L. (2008). Culture, gender, and math. *Science, 320,* 1164–1165.

Gullone, E. (2000). The development of normal fear: A century of research. *Clinical Psychology Review, 20,* 429–451.

Gunderson, E. A., Ramirez, G., Levine, S. C., & Beilock, S. L. (2012). The role of parents and teachers in the development of gender-related math attitudes. *Sex Roles, 66,* 153–166.

Gunes, S., Hekim, G. N., Arslan, M. A., & Asci, R. (2016). Effects of aging on the male reproductive system. *Journal of Assisted Reproduction and Genetics, 33,* 441–454.

Gunnar, M. R., & Cheatham, C. L. (2003). Brain and behavior interfaces: Stress and the developing brain. *Infant Mental Health Journal, 24,* 195–211.

Gunnar, M. R., & de Haan, M. (2009). Methods in social neuroscience: Issues in studying development. In M. de Haan & M. R. Gunnar (Eds.), *Handbook of developmental social neuroscience* (pp. 13–37). New York: Guilford.

Gunnar, M. R., Doom, J. R., & Esposito, E. A. (2015). Psychoneuroendocrinology of stress: Normative development and individual differences. In M. E. Lamb (Eds.), *Handbook of child psychology and developmental science: Vol. 3. Socioemotional processes* (pp. 106–151). Hoboken, NJ: Wiley.

Gunnar, M. R., Morison, S. J., Chisholm, K., & Schuder, M. (2001). Salivary cortisol levels in children adopted from Romanian orphanages. *Development and Psychopathology, 13,* 611–628.

Gunnarsdottir, I., Schack-Nielsen, L., Michaelson, K. F., Sørensen, T. I., & Thorsdottir, I. (2010). Infant weight gain, duration of exclusive breast-feeding, and childhood BMI—two similar follow-up cohorts. *Public Health Nutrition, 13,* 201–207.

Guo, M., Chi, I., & Silverstein, M. (2013). Sources of older parents' ambivalent feelings toward their adult children: The case of rural China. *Journals of Gerontology, 68B,* 420–430.

Guralnick, M. J. (2012). Preventive interventions for preterm children: Effectiveness and developmental mechanisms. *Journal of Developmental and Behavioral Pediatrics, 33,* 352–364.

Gure, A., Ucanok, Z., & Sayil, M. (2006). The associations among perceived pubertal timing, parental relations and self-perception in Turkish adolescents. *Journal of Youth and Adolescence, 35,* 541–550.

Gustafson, G. E., Green, J. A., & Cleland, J. W. (1994). Robustness of individual identity in the cries of human infants. *Developmental Psychobiology, 27,* 1–9.

Gustavson, K., Nilsen, W., Ørstavik, R., & Røysamb, E. (2014). Relationship quality, divorce, and well-being: Findings from a three-year longitudinal study. *Journal of Positive Psychology, 9,* 163–174.

Guterman, N. B., Lee, S. J., Taylor, C. A., & Rathouz, P. J. (2009). Parental perceptions of neighborhood processes, stress, personal control, and risk for physical child abuse and neglect. *Child Abuse and Neglect, 33,* 897–906.

Gutgsell, K. J., Schluchter, M., Margevicius, S., DeGolia, P. A., McLaughlin, B., Harris, M., et al. (2013). Music therapy reduces pain in palliative care patients: A randomized control trial. *Journal of Pain and Symptom Management, 45,* 822–831.

Gutiérrez, I. T., Rosengren, K. S., & Miller, P. J. (2014). Mexican American immigrants in the Centerville region: Teachers, children, and parents. In K. Rosengren, P. J. Miller, I. T. Guiérrez, P. I. Chow, S. S. Schein, & K. N. Anderson (Eds.), *Children's understanding of death: Toward a contextualized, integrated account. Monographs of the Society for Research in Child Development, 79*(1, Serial No. 312), pp. 97–112.

Gutierrez-Galve, L., Stein, A., Hanington, L., Heron, J., & Ramchandani, P. (2015). Paternal depression in the postnatal period and child development: Mediators and moderators. *Pediatrics, 135,* e339–e347.

Gutman, L. M. (2006). How student and parent goal orientations and classroom goal structures influence the math achievement of African Americans during the high school transition. *Contemporary Educational Psychology, 31,* 44–63.

Gutmann, D. (1977). The cross-cultural perspective: Notes toward a comparative psychology of aging. In J. E. Birren & K. W. Schaie (Eds.), *Handbook of the psychology of aging* (pp. 302–326). New York: Van Nostrand Reinhold.

Guttmacher Institute. (2013). *Unintended pregnancy in the United States.* Retrieved from www.guttmacher.org/pubs/FB-Unintended-Pregnancy-US.html

Guttmacher Institute. (2015). *Teen pregnancy rates declined in many countries between the mid-1990s and 2011: United States lags behind many other developed nations.* Retrieved from www.guttmacher.org/media/nr/2015/01/23

Guzzo, K. B. (2014). Trends in cohabitation outcomes: Compositional changes and engagement among never-married young adults. *Journal of Marriage and Family, 76,* 826–842.

Gwiazda, J., & Birch, E. E. (2001). Perceptual development: Vision. In E. B. Goldstein (Ed.), *Blackwell handbook of perception* (pp. 636–668). Oxford, UK: Blackwell.

H

Haas, A. P., Rodgers, P. L., & Herman, J. L. (2014). *Suicide attempts among transgender and gender non-conforming adults.* Los Angeles: The Williams Institute, UCLA School of Law.

Haas, S. M., & Whitton, S. W. (2015). The significance of living together and importance of marriage in same-sex couples. *Journal of Homosexuality, 62,* 1241–1263.

Hagberg, B., & Samuelsson, G. (2008). Survival after 100 years of age: A multivariate model of exceptional survival in Swedish centenarians. *Journals of Gerontology, 63A,* 1219–1226.

Hagerman, R. J., Berry-Kravis, E., Kaufmann, W. E., Ono, M. Y., Tartaglia, N., & Lachiewicz, A. (2009). Advances in the treatment of fragile X syndrome. *Pediatrics, 123,* 378–390.

Haidt, J. (2013). Moral psychology for the twenty-first century. *Journal of Moral Education, 42,* 281–297.

Haines, C. J., Xing, S. M., Park, K. H., Holinka, C. F., & Ausmanas, M. K. (2005). Prevalence of menopausal symptoms in different ethnic groups of Asian women and responsiveness to therapy with three doses of conjugated estrogens/medroxyprogesterone acetate: The pan-Asian menopause (PAM) study. *Maturitas, 52,* 264–276.

Hainline, L. (1998). The development of basic visual abilities. In A. Slater (Ed.), *Perceptual development: Visual, auditory, and speech perception in infancy* (pp. 37–44). Hove, UK: Psychology Press.

Hakim, F., Kheirandish-Gozal, L., & Gozal, D. (2015). Obesity and altered sleep: A pathway to metabolic derangements in children? *Seminars in Pediatric Neurology, 22,* 77–85.

Hakuta, K., Bialystok, E., & Wiley, E. (2003). Critical evidence: A test of the critical-period hypothesis for second-language acquisitions. *Psychological Science, 14,* 31–38.

Hale, C. M., & Tager-Flusberg, H. (2003). The influence of language on theory of mind: A training study. *Developmental Science, 6,* 346–359.

Hale, S., Rose, N. S., Myerson, J., Strube, M. J., Sommers, M., Tye-Murray, N., et al. (2011). The structure of working memory abilities across the adult life span. *Psychology and Aging, 26,* 92–110.

Haley, B. (2016, April 8). *Hereditary breast cancer: The basics of BRCA and beyond* (Internal Medicine Grand Rounds). Retrieved from repositories.tdl.org/utswmed-ir/handle/2152.5/3095

Haley, W. E. (2013). Family caregiving at end-of-life: Current status and future directions. In R. C. Talley & R. J. V. Montgomery (Eds.), *Caregiving across the lifespan: Research, practice, and policy* (pp. 157–175). New York: Springer.

Halfon, N., & McLearn, K. T. (2002). Families with children under 3: What we know and implications for results and policy. In N. Halfon & K. T. McLearn (Eds.), *Child rearing in America: Challenges facing parents with young children* (pp. 367–412). New York: Cambridge University Press.

Halford, G. S., & Andrews, G. (2010). Information-processing models of cognitive development. In J. G. Bremner & T. D. Wachs (Eds.), *Wiley-Blackwell handbook of infant development: Vol. 1. Basic research* (2nd ed., pp. 698–722). Oxford, UK: Wiley-Blackwell.

Halford, G. S., & Andrews, G. (2011). Information-processing models of cognitive development. In U. Goswami (Ed.), *Wiley-Blackwell handbook of childhood cognitive development* (2nd ed., pp. 697–722). Hoboken, NJ: Wiley-Blackwell.

Halim, M. L., & Ruble, D. (2010). Gender identity and stereotyping in early and middle childhood. In J. C. Chrisler & D. R. McCreary (Eds.), *Handbook of gender research in psychology* (pp. 495–525). New York: Springer.

Halim, M. L., Ruble, D., Tamis-LeMonda, C., & Shrout, P. E. (2013). Rigidity in gender-typed behaviors in early childhood: A longitudinal study of ethnic minority children. *Child Development, 84,* 1269–1284.

Hall, C. B., Lipton, R. B., Sliwinski, M., Katz, M. J., Derby, C. A., & Verghese, J. (2009). Cognitive activities delay onset of memory decline in persons who develop dementia. *Neurology, 73,* 356–361.

Hall, D. T., & Las Heras, M. (2011). Personal growth through career work: A positive approach to careers. In K. S. Cameron & G. M. Spreitzer (Eds.), *Oxford handbook of positive organizational scholarship* (pp. 507–518). New York: Oxford University Press.

Hall, G. S. (1904). *Adolescence.* New York: Appleton.

Hall, J. A. (2011). Sex differences in friendship expectations: A meta-analysis. *Journal of Personal and Social Relationships 28,* 723–747.

Hall, K., Murrell, J., Ogunniyi, A., Deeg, M., Baiyewu, O., & Gao, S. (2006). Cholesterol, APOE genotype, and Alzheimer disease: An epidemiologic study of Nigerian Yoruba. *Neurology, 66,* 223–227.

Haller, J. (2005). Vitamins and brain function. In H. R. Lieberman, R. B. Kanarek, & C. Prasad (2005). *Nutritional neuroscience* (pp. 207–233). Philadelphia: Taylor & Francis.

Halpern, C. T., & Kaestle, C. E. (2014). Sexuality in emerging adulthood. In D. L. Tolman & L. M. Diamond (Eds.), *APA handbook of sexuality and psychology* (pp. 487–522). Washington, DC: American Psychological Association.

Halpern, C. T., & Kaestle, C. E. (2015). Sexuality and sexual violence. In D. L. Tolman, L. M. Diamond, J. A. Bauermeister, W. H. George, J. G. Pfaus, & L. M. Ward (Eds.), *APA handbook of sexuality and psychology: Vol. 1. Person-based approaches* (pp. 487–522). Washington, DC: American Psychological Association.

Halpern, D. F. (2005). How time-flexible work policies can reduce stress, improve health, and save money. *Stress and Health, 21,* 157–168.

Halpern, D. F. (2012). *Sex differences in cognitive abilities* (4th ed.). New York: Psychology Press.

Halpern, D. F., Benbow, C. P., Geary, D. C., Gur, R. C., Hyde, J. S., & Gernsbacher, M. A. (2007). The science of sex differences in science and mathematics. *Psychological Science in the Public Interest, 8,* 1–51.

Halpern-Felsher, B. L., Biehl, M., Kropp, R. Y., & Rubinstein, M. L. (2004). Perceived risks and benefits of smoking: Differences among adolescents with different smoking experiences and intentions. *Preventive Medicine, 39,* 559–567.

Hamberger, L. K., Lohr, J. M., Parker, L. M., & Witte, T. (2009). Treatment approaches for men who batter their partners. In C. Mitchell & D. Anglin (Eds.), *Intimate partner violence: A health-based perspective* (pp. 459–471). New York: Oxford University Press.

Hamel, J. (2014). *Gender-inclusive treatment of intimate partner abuse: Evidence-based approaches* (2nd ed.). New York: Springer.

Hamer, D. H., Hu, S., Magnuson, V. L., Hu, N., & Pattatucci, A. M. L. (1993). A linkage between DNA markers on the X chromosome and male sexual orientation. *Science, 261,* 321–327.

Hamilton, B. E., Martin, J. A., Osterman, J. K., Curtin, S. C., & Mathews, T. J. (2015). Births: Final data for 2014. *National Vital Statistics Report, 64*(12), 1–64. Retrieved from www.cdc.gov/nchs/data/nvsr/nvsr64/nvsr64_12.pdf

Hamilton, S. F., & Hamilton, M. A. (2000). Research, intervention, and social change: Improving adolescents' career opportunities. In L. J. Crockett & R. K. Silbereisen (Eds.), *Negotiating adolescence in times of social change* (pp. 267–283). New York: Cambridge University Press.

Hamlin, J. K., Hallinan, E. V., & Woodward, A. L. (2008). Do as I do: 7-month-old infants selectively reproduce others' goals. *Developmental Science, 11,* 487–494.

Hammond, S. I., Müller, U., Carpendale, J. I. M., Bibok, M. B., & Lieberman-Finestone, D. (2012). The effects of parental scaffolding on preschoolers' executive function. *Developmental Psychology, 48,* 271–281.

Hammons, A. J., & Fiese, B. H. (2011). Is frequency of shared family meals related to the nutritional health of children and adolescents? *Pediatrics, 127,* e1565–e1574.

Hampton, T. (2014). Studies probe links between childhood asthma and obesity. *JAMA, 311,* 1718–1719.

Hanioka, T., Ojima, M., Tanaka, K., & Yamamoto, M. (2011). Does secondhand smoke affect the development of dental caries in children? A systematic review. *International Journal of Environmental Research and Public Health, 8,* 1503–1509.

Hank, K., & Wagner, M. (2013). Parenthood, marital status, and well-being in later life: Evidence from SHARE. *Social Indicators Research, 114,* 639–653.

Hankin, B. L., Stone, L., & Wright, P. A. (2010). Co-rumination, interpersonal stress generation, and internalizing symptoms: Accumulating effects and transactional influences in a multiwave study of adolescents. *Development and Psychopathology, 22,* 217–235.

Hannon, E. E., & Johnson, S. P. (2004). Infants use meter to categorize rhythms and melodies: Implications for musical structure learning. *Cognitive Psychology, 50,* 354–377.

Hannon, E. E., & Trehub, S. E. (2005a). Metrical categories in infancy and adulthood. *Psychological Science, 16,* 48–55.

Hannon, E. E., & Trehub, S. E. (2005b). Tuning in to musical rhythms: Infants learn more readily than adults. *Proceedings of the National Academy of Sciences, 102,* 12639–12643.

Hans, S. L., & Jeremy, R. J. (2001). Postneonatal mental and motor development of infants exposed in utero to opiate drugs. *Infant Mental Health Journal, 22,* 300–315.

Hansen, M. B., & Markman, E. M. (2009). Children's use of mutual exclusivity to learn labels for parts of objects. *Developmental Psychology, 45,* 592–596.

Hansen, T., Moum, T., & Shapiro, A. (2007). Relational and individual well-being among cohabitors and married individuals in midlife: Recent trends from Norway. *Journal of Family Issues, 28,* 910–933.

Hansson, R. O., & Stroebe, M. S. (2007). The dual process model of coping with bereavement and development of an integrative risk factor framework. In R. O. Hansson & M. S. Stroebe (Eds.), *Bereavement in late life: Coping, adaptation, and developmental influences* (pp. 41–60). Washington, DC: American Psychological Association.

Hao, L., & Woo, H. S. (2012). Distinct trajectories in the transition to adulthood: Are children of immigrants advantaged? *Child Development, 83,* 1623–1639.

Harachi, T. W., Fleming, C. B., White, H. R., Ensminger, M. E., Abbott, R. D., Catalano, R. F., & Haggerty, K. P. (2006). Aggressive behavior among girls and boys during middle childhood: Predictors and sequelae of trajectory group membership. *Aggressive Behavior, 32,* 279–293.

Harden, K. P. (2014). A sex-positive framework for research on adolescent sexuality. *Perspectives on Psychological Science, 9,* 455–469.

Harden, K. P., & Tucker-Drob, E. M. (2011). Individual differences in the development of sensation seeking and impulsivity during adolescence: Further evidence for a dual systems model. *Developmental Psychology, 47,* 739–746.

Hardie, J. H. (2015). Women's work? Predictors of young men's aspirations for entering traditionally female-dominated occupations. *Sex Roles, 72,* 349–362.

Hardy, S. A., & Carlo, G. (2005). Religiosity and prosocial behaviours in adolescence: The mediating role of prosocial values. *Journal of Moral Education, 34,* 231–249.

Hardy, S. A., & Carlo, G. (2011). Moral identity: What is it, how does it develop, and is it linked to moral action? *Child Development Perspectives, 5,* 212–218.

Hardy, S. A., Pratt, M. W., Pancer, S. M., Olsen, J. A., & Lawford, H. L. (2011). Community and religious involvement as contexts of identity change across late adolescence and emerging adulthood. *International Journal of Behavioral Development, 35,* 125–135.

Hardy, S. A., Walker, L. J., Gray, A., Ruchty, J. A., & Olsen, J. A. (2012, March). A possible selves approach to adolescent moral identity. In S. A. Hardy (Chair), *Moral identity in adolescence and emerging adulthood: Conceptualization, measurement, and validation.* Symposium presented at the meeting of the Society for Research on Adolescence, Vancouver.

Harlow, H. F., & Zimmerman, R. (1959). Affectional responses in the infant monkey. *Science, 130,* 421–432.

Harris, P. L. (2011). Death in Spain, Madagascar, and beyond. In V. Talwar, P. L. Harris, & M. Schleifer (Eds.), *Children's understanding of death* (pp. 19–40). New York: Cambridge University Press.

Harris, P. L., & Giménez, M. (2005). Children's acceptance of conflicting testimony: The case of death. *Journal of Cognition and Culture, 5,* 143–164.

Harris-Kojetin, L., Sengupta, M., Park-Lee, E., Valverde, R., Caffrey, C., Rome, V., & Lendon, J. (2016). Long-term care providers and services users in the United States: Data from the National Study of Long-Term Care Providers, 2013–2014. *Vital Health Statistics, 3*(38).

Harris-McKoy, D., & Cui, M. (2013). Parental control, adolescent delinquency, and young adult criminal behavior. *Journal of Child and Family Studies, 22,* 836–843.

Harris Poll. (2013, December). *Americans' belief in God, miracles and heaven declines.* Retrieved from www.theharrispoll.com/health-and-life/Americans__Belief_in_God__Miracles_and_Heaven_Declines.html

Hart, B., & Risley, T. R. (1995). *Meaningful differences in the everyday experience of young American children.* Baltimore, MD: Paul H. Brookes.

Hart, C. H., Burts, D. C., Durland, M. A., Charlesworth, R., DeWolf, M., & Fleege, P. O. (1998). Stress behaviors and activity type participation of preschoolers in more and less developmentally appropriate classrooms: SES and sex differences. *Journal of Research in Childhood Education, 13,* 176–196.

Hart, C. H., Newell, L. D., & Olsen, S. F. (2003). Parenting skills and social–communicative competence in childhood. In J. O. Greene & B. R. Burleson (Eds.), *Handbook of communication and social interaction skills* (pp. 753–797). Mahwah, NJ: Erlbaum.

Hart, C. H., Yang, C., Charlesworth, R., & Burts, D. C. (2003, April). *Kindergarten teaching practices: Associations with later child academic and social/emotional adjustment to school.* Paper presented at the biennial meeting of the Society for Research in Child Development, Tampa, FL.

Hart, D., Atkins, R., & Donnelly, T. M. (2006). Community service and moral development. In M. Killen & J. G. Smetana (Eds.), *Handbook of moral development* (pp. 633–656). Philadelphia: Erlbaum.

Hart, D., Atkins, R., & Matsuba, M. K. (2008). The association of neighborhood poverty with personality change in childhood. *Journal of Personality and Social Psychology, 44,* 1048–1061.

Hart, D., Donnelly, T. M., Youniss, J., & Atkins, R. (2007). High school community service as a predictor of adult voting and volunteering. *American Educational Research Journal, 44,* 197–219.

Hart, D., & Fegley, S. (1995). Prosocial behavior and caring in adolescence: Relations to self-understanding and social judgment. *Child Development, 66,* 1346–1359.

Hart, H. M., McAdams, D. P., Hirsch, B. J., & Bauer, J. J. (2001). Generativity and social involvement among African Americans and white adults. *Journal of Research in Personality, 35,* 208–230.

Hart, S. L., & Charles, S. T. (2013). Age-related patterns in negative affect and appraisals about colorectal cancer over time. *Health Psychology, 32,* 302–310.

Harter, S. (1999). *The construction of self: A developmental perspective.* New York: Guilford.

Harter, S. (2012). *The construction of the self: Developmental and sociocultural foundations* (2nd ed.). New York: Guilford.

Hartl, A. C., Laursen, B., & Cillessen, A. H. N. (2015). A survival analysis of adolescent friendships: The downside of dissimilarity. *Psychological Science, 26,* 1304–1315.

Hartley, A. (2006). Changing role of the speed of processing construct. In J. E. Birren & K. W. Schaie (Eds.), *Handbook of the psychology of aging* (6th ed., pp. 183–207). Burlington, MA: Academic Press.

Hartley, D., Blumenthal, T., Carrillo, M., DiPaolo, G., Esralew, L., Gardiner, K., et al. (2015). Down syndrome and Alzheimer's disease: Common pathways, common goals. *Alzheimer's and Dementia, 11,* 700–709.

Hartman, J., & Warren, L. H. (2005). Explaining age differences in temporal working memory. *Psychology and Aging, 20,* 645–656.

Hartshorn, K., Rovee-Collier, C., Gerhardstein, P., Bhatt, R. S., Wondoloski, T. L., Klein, P., et al. (1998). The ontogeny of long-term memory over the first year-and-a-half of life. *Developmental Psychobiology, 32,* 69–89.

Hartshorne, J. K., & Germine, L. T. (2015). When does cognitive functioning peak? The asynchronous rise and fall of different cognitive abilities across the life span. *Psychological Science, 26,* 433–443.

Hartup, W. W. (2006). Relationships in early and middle childhood. In A. L. Vangelisti & D. Perlman (Eds.), *Cambridge handbook of personal relationships* (pp. 177–190). New York: Cambridge University Press.

Hartup, W. W., & Abecassis, M. (2004). Friends and enemies. In P. K. Smith & C. H. Hart (Eds.), *Blackwell handbook of childhood social development* (pp. 285–306). Malden, MA: Blackwell.

Harwood, J. (2001). Comparing grandchildren's and grandparents' stake in their relationship. *International Journal of Aging and Human Development, 53,* 195–210.

Hasebe, Y., Nucci, L., & Nucci, M. S. (2004). Parental control of the personal domain and adolescent symptoms of psychopathology: A cross-national study in the United States and Japan. *Child Development, 75,* 815–828.

Hasher, L., Lustig, C., & Zacks, R. T. (2007). Inhibitory mechanisms and the control of attention. In A. R. A. Conway, C. Jarrold, M. Kane, A. Miyake, & J. N. Towse (Eds.), *Variation in working memory* (pp. 227–249). New York: Oxford University Press.

Hastings, E. C., & West, R. L. (2009). The relative success of a self-help and a group-based memory training program for older adults. *Psychology and Aging, 24,* 586–594.

Hastrup, B. (2007). Healthy aging in Denmark? In M. Robinson, W. Novelli, C. Pearson, & L. Norris (Eds.), *Global health and global aging* (pp. 71–84). San Francisco: Jossey-Bass.

Hatch, L. R., & Bulcroft, K. (2004). Does long-term marriage bring less frequent disagreements? *Journal of Family Issues, 25,* 465–495.

Hatfield, E., Mo, Y.-M., & Rapson, R. L. (2015). Love, sex, and marriage across cultures. In L. A. Jensen (Ed.), *Oxford handbook of human development and culture* (pp. 570–585). New York: Oxford University Press.

Hatfield, E., Rapson, R. L., & Martel, L. D. (2007). Passionate love and sexual desire. In S. Kitayama & D. Cohen (Eds.), *Handbook of cultural psychology* (pp. 760–779). New York: Guilford.

Hau, K.-T., & Ho, I. T. (2010). Chinese students' motivation and achievement. In M. H. Bond (Ed.), *Oxford handbook of Chinese psychology* (pp. 187–204). New York: Oxford University Press.

Hauf, P., Aschersleben, G., & Prinz, W. (2007). Baby do–baby see! How action production influences action perception in infants. *Cognitive Development, 22,* 16–32.

Haukkala, A., Konttinen, H., Laatikainen, T., Kawachi, I., & Uutela, A. (2010). Hostility, anger control, and anger expression as predictors of cardiovascular disease. *Psychosomatic Medicine, 72,* 556–562.

Hauser-Cram, P., Warfield, M. E., Stadler, J., & Sirin, S. R. (2006). School environments and the diverging pathways of students living in poverty. In A. C. Huston & M. N. Ripke (Eds.), *Developmental contexts in middle childhood* (pp. 198–216). New York: Cambridge University Press.

Hauspie, R., & Roelants, M. (2012). Adolescent growth. In N. Cameron & R. Bogin (Eds.), *Human growth and development* (2nd ed., pp. 57–79). London: Elsevier.

Havstad, S. L., Johnson, D. D., Zoratti, E. M., Ezell, J. M., Woodcroft, K., Ownby, D. R., et al. (2012). Tobacco smoke exposure and allergic sensitization in children: A propensity score analysis. *Respirology, 17,* 1068–1072.

Haw, C., Harwood, D., & Hawton, K. (2009). Dementia and suicidal behavior: A review of the literature. *International Psychogeriatrics, 21,* 440–453.

Hawkins, R. L., Jaccard, J., & Needle, E. (2013). Nonacademic factors associated with dropping out of high school: Adolescent problem behaviors. *Journal of the Society for Social Work and Research, 4,* 58–75.

Hawsawi, A. M., Bryant, L. O., & Goodfellow, L. T. (2015). Association between exposure to secondhand smoke during pregnancy and low birthweight: A narrative review. *Respiratory Care, 60,* 135–140.

Hawton, A., Green, C., Dickens, A. P., Richards, S. H., Taylor, R. S., & Edwards, R. (2011). The impact of social isolation on the health status and health-related quality of life of older people. *Quality of Life Research, 20,* 57–67.

Hay, D. F., Pawlby, S., Waters, C. S., Perra, O., & Sharp, D. (2010). Mothers' antenatal depression and their children's antisocial outcomes. *Child Development, 81,* 149–165.

Hay, E. L., & Diehl, M. (2010). Reactivity to daily stressors in adulthood: The importance of stressor type in characterizing risk factors. *Psychology and Aging, 25,* 118–131.

Hay, P., & Bacaltchuk, J. (2004). Bulimia nervosa. *Clinical Evidence, 12,* 1326–1347.

Hayflick, L. (1994). *How and why we age.* New York: Ballantine.

Hayflick, L. (1998). How and why we age. *Experimental Gerontology, 33,* 639–653.

Hayne, H., & Gross, J. (2015). 24-month-olds use conceptual similarity to solve new problems after a delay. *International Journal of Behavioral Development, 39,* 339–345.

Hayne, H., Herbert, J., & Simcock, G. (2003). Imitation from television by 24- and 30-month-olds. *Developmental Science, 6,* 254–261.

Hayne, H., Rovee-Collier, C., & Perris, E. E. (1987). Categorization and memory retrieval by three-month-olds. *Child Development, 58,* 750–767.

Hayslip, B., Blumenthal, H., & Garner, A. (2014). Health and grandparent–grandchild well-being: One-year longitudinal findings for custodial grandfamilies. *Journal of Aging and Health, 26,* 559–582.

Hayslip, B., Blumenthal, H., & Garner, A. (2015). Social support and grandparent caregiver health: One-year longitudinal findings for grandparents raising their grandchildren. *Journals of Gerontology, 70B,* 804–812.

Hayslip, B., Jr., & Kaminski, P. L. (2005). Grandparents raising their grandchildren. *Marriage and Family Review, 37,* 147–169.

Hayward, R. D., & Krause, N. (2013a). Changes in church-based social support relationships during older adulthood. *Journals of Gerontology, 68B,* 85–96.

Hayward, R. D., & Krause, N. (2013b). Trajectories of late life change in God-mediated control: Evidence of compensation for declining personal control. *Journals of Gerontology, 68B,* 49–58.

Haywood, H. C., & Lidz, C. S. (2007). *Dynamic assessment in practice.* New York: Cambridge University Press.

Haywood, K., & Getchell, N. (2014). *Life span motor development* (6th ed.). Champaign, IL: Human Kinetics.

Hazel, N. A., Oppenheimer, C. W., Young, J. R., & Technow, J. R. (2014). Parent relationship quality buffers against the effect of peer stressors on depressive symptoms from middle childhood to adolescence. *Developmental Psychology, 50,* 2115–2123.

Hazen, N. L., McFarland, L., Jacobvitz, D., & Boyd-Soisson, E. (2010). Fathers' frightening behaviours and sensitivity with infants: Relations with fathers' attachment representations, father–infant attachment, and children's later outcomes. *Early Child Development and Care, 180,* 51–69.

Healthy Families America. (2011). *Healthy Families America FAQ.* Retrieved from www.healthyfamiliesamerica.org/about_us/faq.shtml

Hebblethwaite, S., & Norris, J. (2011). Expressions of generativity through family leisure: Experiences of grandparents and adult grandchildren. *Family Relations, 60,* 121–133.

Hebert, K., Moore, H., & Rooney, J. (2011). The nurse advocate in end-of-life care. *Ochsner Journal, 11,* 325–329.

Heckhausen, J., Wrosch, C., & Schultz, R. (2010). A motivational theory of life-span development. *Psychological Review, 117,* 32–60.

Heilbrun, K., Lee, R., & Cottle, C. C. (2005). Risk factors and intervention outcomes: Meta-analyses of juvenile offending. In K. Heilbrun, N. E. S. Goldstein, & R. E. Redding (Eds.), *Juvenile delinquency: Prevention, assessment, and intervention* (pp. 111–133). New York: Oxford University Press.

Hein, S., Reich, J., & Grigorenko, E. (2015). Cultural manifestation of intelligence in formal and informal learning environments during childhood. In L. A. Jensen (Ed.), *Oxford handbook of human development and culture* (pp. 214–229). New York: Oxford University Press.

Heino, R., Ellison, N., & Gibbs, J. (2010). Relationshopping: Investigating the market metaphor in online dating. *Journal of Social and Personal Relationships, 27,* 427–447.

Heinrich-Weltzien, R., Zorn, C., Monse, B., & Kromeyer-Hauschild, K. (2013). Relationship between malnutrition and the number of permanent teeth in Filipino 10- to 13-year-olds. *BioMed Research International, 2013,* Article ID 205950.

Hellemans, K. G., Sliwowska, J. H., Verma, P., & Weinberg, J. (2010). Prenatal alcohol exposure: Fetal programming and later life vulnerability to stress, expression and anxiety disorders. *Neuroscience and Biobehavioral Reviews, 34,* 791–807.

Heller, D., Watson, D., & Ilies, R. (2004). The role of person vs. situation in life satisfaction: A critical examination. *Psychological Bulletin, 130,* 574–600.

Helm, H. M., Hays, J. C., Flint, E. P., Koenig, H. G., & Blazer, D. G. (2000). Does private religious activity prolong survival? A six-year follow-up study of 3,851 older adults. *Journals of Gerontology, 55A,* M400–M405.

Helson, R., Jones, C. J., & Kwan, V. S. Y. (2002). Personality change over 40 years of adulthood: Hierarchical linear modeling analyses of two longitudinal samples. *Journal of Personality and Social Psychology, 83,* 752–766.

Helwig, C. C. (2006). Rights, civil liberties, and democracy across cultures. In M. Killen & J. G. Smetana (Eds.), *Handbook of moral development* (pp. 185–210). Philadelphia: Erlbaum.

Helwig, C. C., & Jasiobedzka, U. (2001). The relation between law and morality: Children's reasoning about socially beneficial and unjust laws. *Child Development, 72,* 1382–1393.

Helwig, C. C., Ruck, M. D., & Peterson-Badali, M. (2014). Rights, civil liberties, and democracy. In M. Killen & J. G. Smetana (Eds.), *Handbook of moral development* (2nd ed., pp. 46–69). New York: Psychology Press.

Helwig, C. C., & Turiel, E. (2004). Children's social and moral reasoning. In P. K. Smith & C. H. Hart (Eds.), *Blackwell handbook of childhood social development* (pp. 476–490). Malden, MA: Blackwell.

Helwig, C. C., & Turiel, E. (2011). Children's social and moral reasoning. In P. K. Smith & C. H. Hart (Eds.), *The Wiley-Blackwell handbook of childhood social development* (2nd ed., pp. 567–583). Chichester, UK: John Wiley & Sons.

Helwig, C. C., Zelazo, P. D., & Wilson, M. (2001). Children's judgments of psychological harm in normal and canonical situations. *Child Development, 72,* 66–81.

Henderson, T. L., & Bailey, S. J. (2015). Grandparents rearing grandchildren: A culturally variant perspective. In S. Browning & K. Pasley (Eds.), *Contemporary families: Translating research into practice* (pp. 230–247). New York: Routledge.

Hendrick, S. S., & Hendrick, C. (2002). Love. In C. R. Snyder & S. J. Lopez (Eds.), *Handbook of positive psychology* (pp. 472–484). New York: Oxford University Press.

Hendricks, J., & Cutler, S. J. (2004). Volunteerism and socioemotional selectivity in later life. *Journals of Gerontology, 59B,* S251–S257.

Hendrie, H. C., Murrell, J., Baiyewu, O., Lane, K., Purnell, C., Oqunniyi, A., et al. (2014). APOE ε4 and the risk for Alzheimer disease and cognitive decline in African Americans and Yoruba. *International Psychogeriatrics, 26,* 977–985.

Hendry, M., Paserfield, D., Lewis, R., Carter, B., Hodgson, D., & Wilinson, C. (2012). Why do we want the right to die? A systematic review of the international literature on the views of patients, carers and the public on assisted dying. *Palliative Medicine, 27,* 13–26.

Henggeler, S. W., Schoenwald, S. K., Bourduin, C. M., Rowland, M. D., & Cunningham, P. B. (2009). *Multisystemic therapy for antisocial behavior in children and adolescents* (2nd ed.). New York: Guilford.

Henig, R. M., & Henig, S. (2012). *Twenty something: Why do young adults seem stuck?* New York: Hudson Street Press.

Henk, T., Schönbeck, Y., van Dommelen, P., Bakker, B., van Buuren, S., & HiraSing, R. A. (2013). Trends in menarcheal age between 1955 and 2009 in the Netherlands. *PLOS ONE, 8*(4), e60056.

Henning, A., Spinath, F. M., & Aschersleben, G. (2011). The link between preschoolers' executive function and theory of mind and the role of epistemic states. *Journal of Experimental Psychology, 108,* 513–531.

Henning, K., Jones, A. R., & Holdford, R. (2005). Attributions of blame among male and female domestic violence offenders. *Journal of Family Violence, 20,* 131–139.

Henning-Smith, C. (2016). Quality of life and psychological distress among older adults: The role of living arrangements. *Journal of Applied Gerontology, 35,* 39–61.

Henrich, C. C., Kuperminc, G. P., Sack, A., Blatt, S. J., & Leadbeater, B. J. (2000). Characteristics and homogeneity of early adolescent friendship groups: A comparison of male and female clique and nonclique members. *Applied Developmental Science, 4,* 15–26.

Henricsson, L., & Rydell, A.-M. (2004). Elementary school children with behavior problems: Teacher–child relations and self-perception. A prospective study. *Merrill-Palmer Quarterly, 50,* 111–138.

Henry, M., Cortes, A., Shivji, A., & Buck, K. (2014). *The 2014 Annual Homeless Assessment Report (AHAR) to Congress: Part 1. Point-in-time estimates of homelessness in the U.S.* Washington, DC: U.S. Department of Housing and Urban Development. Retrieved from www.hudexchange.info/resource/4074/2014-ahar-part-1-pit-estimates-of-homelessness

Hensley, E., & Briars, L. (2010). Closer look at autism and the measles-mumps-rubella vaccine. *Journal of the American Pharmacists Association, 50,* 736–741.

Hepper, P. (2015). Behavior during the prenatal period: Adaptive for development and survival. *Child Development Perspectives, 9,* 38–43.

Hepper, P. G., Dornan, J., & Lynch, C. (2012). Sex differences in fetal habituation. *Developmental Science, 15,* 373–383.

Heppner, M. J. (2013). Women, men and work: The long road to gender equality. In S. D. Brown & R. W. Lent (Eds.), *Career development and counseling: Putting theory and research to work* (2nd ed., pp. 215–244). New York: Wiley.

Heppner, M. J., & Jung, A.-K. (2013). Gender and social class: Powerful predictors of a life journey. In W. B. Walsh, M. L. Savickas, & P. J. Hartung (Eds.), *Handbook of vocational psychology: Theory, research, and practice* (4th ed., pp. 81–102). New York: Routledge.

Heraghty, J., Hilliard, T. N., Henderson, A. J., & Fleming, P. J. (2008). The physiology of sleep in infants. *Archives of Disease in Childhood, 93,* 982–985.

Herbenick, D., Reece, M., Schick, V., Sanders, S. A., Dodge, B., & Fortenberry, J. D. (2010). Sexual behavior in the United States: Results from a national probability sample of men and women ages 14–94. *Journal of Sexual Medicine, 7*(Suppl. 5), 255–265.

Herghelegiu, A. M., & Prada, G. I. (2014). Impact of metabolic control on cognitive function and health-related quality of life in older diabetics. In A. K. Leist, J. Kulmala, & F. Nyqvist (Eds.), *Health and cognition in old age: From biomedical and life course factors to policy and practice* (pp. 25–40). Cham, Switzerland: Springer.

Herman, M. (2004). Forced to choose: Some determinants of racial identification in multiracial adolescents. *Child Development, 75,* 730–748.

Herman-Giddens, M. E. (2006). Recent data on pubertal milestones in United States children: The secular trend toward earlier development. *International Journal of Andrology, 29,* 241–246.

Herman-Giddens, M. E., Steffes, J., Harris, D., Slora, E., Hussey, M., Dowshen, S. A., et al. (2012). Secondary sexual characteristics in boys: Data from the Pediatric Research in Office Settings Network. *Pediatrics, 130,* e1058–e1068.

Hernandez, D. J., Denton, N. A., & Blanchard, V. L. (2011). Children in the United States of America: A statistical portrait by race-ethnicity, immigrant origins, and language. *Annals of the American Academy of Political and Social Science, 633,* 102–127.

Hernandez, D. J., Denton, N. A., Macartney, S., & Blanchard, V. L. (2012). Children in immigrant families: Demography, policy, and evidence for the immigrant paradox. In C. García Coll & A. K. Marks (Eds.), *The immigrant paradox in children and adolescents: Is becoming American a developmental risk?* (pp. 17–36). Washington, DC: American Psychological Association.

Hernandez-Tejada, M., Amstadter, A., Muzzy, W., & Acierno, R. (2013). The national elder mistreatment study: Race and ethnicity findings. *Journal of Elder Abuse and Neglect, 25,* 281–293.

Hernando-Herraez, I., Prado-Martinez, J., Garg, P., Fernandez-Callejo, M., Heyn, H., Hvilsom, C., et al. (2013). Dynamics of DNA methylation in recent human and great ape evolution. *PLOS Genetics, 9*(9), e1003763.

Herndler-Brandstetter, D. (2014). How the aging process affects our immune system: Mechanisms, consequences, and perspectives for intervention. In A. K. Leist, J. Kulmala, & F. Nyqvist (Eds.), *Health and cognition in old age: From biomedical and life course factors to policy and practice* (pp. 55–69). Cham, Switzerland: Springer.

Herne, M. A., Bartholomew, M. L., & Weahkee, R. L. (2014). Suicide mortality among American Indians and Alaska Natives, 1999–2009. *American Journal of Public Health, 104,* S336–S342.

Heron, M. (2015, August 31). Deaths: Leading causes for 2012. *National Vital Statistics Report, 64*(10). Retrieved from www.cdc.gov/nchs/data/nvsr/nvsr64/nvsr64_10.pdf

Heron, T. E., Hewar, W. L., & Cooper, J. O. (2013). *Applied behavior analysis.* Upper Saddle River, NJ: Pearson.

Heron-Delaney, M., Anzures, G., Herbert, J. S., Quinn, P. C., Slater, A. M., Tanaka, J. W., et al. (2011). Perceptual training prevents the emergence of the other race effect during infancy. *PLOS ONE, 6,* 231–255.

Herrnstein, R. J., & Murray, C. (1994). *The bell curve.* New York: Free Press.

Hershey, D. A., Jacobs-Lawson, J. M., McArdle, J. J., & Hamagami, F. (2007). Psychological foundations of financial planning for retirement. *Journal of Adult Development, 14,* 26–36.

Hertzog, C., McGuire, C. L., Horhota, M., & Jopp, D. (2010). Does believing in "use it or lose it" relate to self-rated memory control, strategy use, and recall? *International Journal of Aging and Human Development, 70,* 61–87.

Hespos, S. J., Ferry, A. L., Cannistraci, C. J., Gore, J., & Park, S. (2010). Using optical imaging to investigate functional cortical activity in human infants. In A. W. Roe (Ed.), *Imaging the brain with optical methods* (pp. 159–176). New York: Springer Science + Business Media.

Hesse, E., & Main, M. (2000). Disorganized infant, child, and adult attachment: Collapse in behavioral and attentional strategies. *Journal of the American Psychoanalytic Association, 48,* 1097–1127.

Hesse, E., & Main, M. (2006). Frightening, threatening, and dissociative parental behavior in low-risk samples: Description, discussion, and interpretations. *Development and Psychopathology, 18,* 309–343.

Hetherington, E. M. (2003). Social support and the adjustment of children in divorced and remarried families. *Childhood, 10,* 237–254

Hetherington, E. M., & Clingempeel, W. G. (1992). Coping with marital transitions: A family systems perspective. *Monographs of the Society for Research in Child Development, 57*(2–3, Serial No. 227).

Hetherington, E. M., & Kelly, J. (2002). *For better or for worse: Divorce reconsidered.* New York: Norton.

Hetherington, E. M., & Stanley-Hagan, M. (2000). Diversity among stepfamilies. In D. H. Demo, K. R. Allen, & M. A. Fine (Eds.), *Handbook of family diversity* (pp. 173–196). New York: Oxford University Press.

Hewlett, B. S. (1992). Husband–wife reciprocity and the father–infant relationship among Aka pygmies. In B. S. Hewlett (Ed.), *Father–child relations: Cultural and biosocial contexts* (pp. 153–176). New York: Aldine de Gruyter.

Heyder, A., & Kessels, U. (2015). Do teachers equate male and masculine with lower academic engagement? How students' gender enactment triggers gender stereotypes at school. *Social Psychology of Education, 18,* 467–485.

Heyes, C. (2005). Imitation by association. In S. Hurley & N. Chater (Eds.), *From neuroscience to social science: Vol. 1. Mechanisms of imitation and imitation in animals* (pp. 157–177). Cambridge, MA: MIT Press.

Heyes, C. M. (2010). Where do mirror neurons come from? *Neuroscience and Biobehavioral Reviews, 34,* 575–583.

Heyman, G. D., & Legare, C. H. (2004). Children's beliefs about gender differences in the academic and social domains. *Sex Roles, 50,* 227–239.

Hicken, B. L., Smith, D., Luptak, M., & Hill, R. D. (2014). Health and aging in rural America. In J. Warren & K. B. Smalley (Eds.), *Rural public health: Best practices and preventive models* (pp. 241–254). New York: Springer.

Hickling, A. K., & Wellman, H. M. (2001). The emergence of children's causal explanations and theories: Evidence from everyday conversation. *Developmental Psychology, 37,* 668–683.

Higginbottom, G. M. A. (2006). "Pressure of life": Ethnicity as a mediating factor in mid-life and older peoples' experience of high blood pressure. *Sociology of Health and Illness, 28,* 583–610.

Higgins, C. A., Duxbury, L. E., & Lyons, S. T. (2010). Coping with overload and stress: Men and women in dual-earner families. *Journal of Marriage and Family 72,* 847–859.

Higginson, I. J., Sarmento, V. P., Calanzani, N., Benalia, H., & Gomes, B. (2013). Dying at home—is it better: A narrative appraisal of the state of the science. *Palliative Medicine, 27,* 918–924.

Hilbert, D. D., & Eis, S. D. (2014). Early intervention for emergent literacy development in a collaborative community pre-kindergarten. *Early Childhood Education Journal, 42,* 105–113.

Hildreth, K., & Rovee-Collier, C. (2002). Forgetting functions of reactivated memories over the first year of life. *Developmental Psychobiology, 41,* 277–288.

Hilimire, M. R., Mienaltowski, A., Blanchard-Fields, F., & Corballis, P. M. (2014). Age-related differences in event-related potential for early visual processing of emotional faces. *Social Cognitive and Affective Neuroscience, 9,* 969–976.

Hill, D. B., Menvielle, E., Sica, K. M., & Johnson, A. (2010). An affirmative intervention for families with gender variant children: Parental ratings of child mental health and gender. *Journal of Sex and Marital Therapy, 36,* 6–23.

Hill, E. J., Mead, N. T., Dean, L. R., Hafen, D. M., Gadd, R., & Palmer, A. A. (2006). Researching the 60-hour dual-earner workweek. *American Behavioral Scientist, 49,* 1184–1203.

Hill, J. L., Brooks-Gunn, J., & Waldfogel, J. (2003). Sustained effects of high participation in an early intervention for low-birth-weight premature infants. *Developmental Psychology, 39,* 730–744.

Hill, N. E., & Taylor, L. C. (2004). Parental school involvement and children's academic achievement: Pragmatics and issues. *Current Directions in Psychological Science, 13,* 161–164.

Hilliard, L. J., & Liben, L. S. (2010). Differing levels of gender salience in preschool classrooms: Effects on children's gender attitudes and intergroup bias. *Child Development, 81,* 1787–1798.

Hillis, S. D., Anda, R. F., Dube, S. R., Felitti, V. J., Marchbanks, P. A., & Marks, J. S. (2004). The association between adverse childhood experiences and adolescent pregnancy, long-term psychosocial consequences, and fetal death. *Pediatrics, 113,* 320–327.

Hillman, K. M. (2011). End-of-life care in acute hospitals. *Australian Health Review, 35,* 176–177.

Hines, M. (2011a). Gender development and the human brain. *Annual Review of Neuroscience, 34,* 67–86.

Hines, M. (2011b). Prenatal endocrine influences on sexual orientation and on sexually differentiated childhood behavior. *Neuroendocrinology, 32,* 170–182.

Hines, M. (2015). Gendered development. In M. E. Lamb (Ed.), *Handbook of child psychology and developmental science: Vol. 3. Socioemotional processes* (7th ed., pp. 842–887). Hoboken, NJ: Wiley.

Hinrichsen, G. A. (2016). Depression. In S. K. Whitbourne (Ed.), *Encyclopedia of adulthood and aging* (Vol. 1, pp. 327–331). Malden, MA: Wiley Blackwell.

Hinsta, T., Jokela, M., Pulkki-Råback, L., & Keltikangas-Järvinen, L. (2014). Age- and cohort-related variance of Type-A behavior over 24 years: The Young Finns Study. *International Journal of Behavioral Medicine, 21,* 927–935.

Hipfner-Boucher, K., Milburn, T., Weitzman, E., Greenberg, J., Pelletier, J., & Girolametto, L. (2014). Relationships between preschoolers' oral language and phonological awareness. *First Language, 34,* 178–197.

Hirasawa, R., & Feil, R. (2010). Genomic imprinting and human disease. *Essays in Biochemistry, 48,* 187–200.

Hirsh-Pasek, K., & Burchinal, M. (2006). Mother and caregiver sensitivity over time: Predicting language and academic outcomes with variable- and person-centered approaches. *Merrill-Palmer Quarterly, 52,* 449–485.

Hoang, D. H., Pagnier, A., Guichardet, K., Dubois-Teklali, F., Schiff, I., Lyard, G., et al. (2014). Cognitive disorders in pediatric medulloblastoma: What neuroimaging has to offer. *Journal of Neurosurgery, 14,* 136–144.

Hobbs, S. D., & Goodman, G. S. (2014). Child witnesses in the legal system: Improving child interviews and understanding juror decisions. *Behavioral Sciences & the Law, 32,* 681–685.

Hochwarter, W. A., Ferris, G. R., Perrewe, P. L., Witt, L. A., & Kiewitz, C. (2001). A note on the nonlinearity of the age–job satisfaction relationship. *Journal of Applied Social Psychology, 31,* 1223–1237.

Hodel, A. S., Hunt, R. H., Cowell, R. A., Van Den Heuvel, S. E., Gunnar, M. R., & Thomas, K. M. (2014). Duration of early adversity and structural brain development in post-institutionalized adolescents. *NeuroImage, 105,* 112–119.

Hodges, J., & Tizard, B. (1989). Social and family relationships of ex-institutional adolescents. *Journal of Child Psychology and Psychiatry, 30,* 77–97.

Hodnett, E. D., Gates, S., Hofmeyr, G. J., & Sakala, C. (2012). Continuous support for women during childbirth. *Cochrane Database of Systematic Reviews,* Issue 7, Art. No.: CD003766.

Hoeft, T. J., Hinton, L., Liu, J., & Unützer, J. (2016). Directions for effectiveness research to improve health services for late-life depression in the United States. *American Journal of Geriatric Psychiatry, 24,* 18–30.

Hoeppner, B. B., Paskausky, A. L., Jackson, K. M., & Barnett, N. P. (2013). Sex differences in college student adherence to NIAAA drinking guidelines. *Alcohol Clinical and Experimental Research, 37,* 1779–1786.

Hoerr, T. (2004). How MI informs teaching at New City School. *Teachers College Record, 106,* 40–48.

Hoff, E. (2003). The specificity of environmental influence: Socioeconomic status affects early vocabulary development via maternal speech. *Child Development, 74,* 1368–1378.

Hoff, E. (2013). Interpreting the early language trajectories of children from low-SES and language minority homes: Implications for closing achievement gaps. *Developmental Psychology, 49,* 4–14.

Hoff, E., Core, C., Place, S., Rumiche, R., Senor, M., & Parra, M. (2012). Dual language exposure and early bilingual development. *Journal of Child Language, 39,* 1–27.

Hoff, E., Laursen, B., & Tardif, T. (2002). Socioeconomic status and parenting. In M. H. Bornstein (Ed.), *Handbook of parenting* (pp. 231–252). Mahwah, NJ: Erlbaum.

Hofferth, S. L. (2003). Race/ethnic differences in father involvement in two-parent families: Culture, context, or economy? *Journal of Family Issues, 24,* 185–216.

Hofferth, S. L. (2010). Home media and children's achievement and behavior. *Child Development, 81,* 1598–1619.

Hofferth, S. L., & Anderson, K. G. (2003). Are all dads equal? Biology versus marriage as a basis for paternal investment. *Journal of Marriage and Family, 65,* 213–232.

Hofferth, S. L., Forry, N. D., & Peters, H. E. (2010). Child support, father–child contact, and preteens' involvement with nonresidential fathers: Racial/ethnic differences. *Journal of Family Economic Issues, 31,* 14–32.

Hoffman, L. W. (2000). Maternal employment: Effects of social context. In R. D. Taylor & M. C. Wang (Eds.), *Resilience across contexts: Family, work, culture, and community* (pp. 147–176). Mahwah, NJ: Erlbaum.

Hoffman, M. L. (2000). *Empathy and moral development.* New York: Cambridge University Press.

Hoffner, C., & Badzinski, D. M. (1989). Children's integration of facial and situational cues to emotion. *Child Development, 60,* 411–422.

Hogan, B. E., & Linden, W. (2004). Anger response styles and blood pressure: At least don't ruminate about it! *Annals of Behavioral Medicine, 27,* 38–49.

Hokoda, A., & Fincham, F. D. (1995). Origins of children's helpless and mastery achievement patterns in the family. *Journal of Educational Psychology, 87,* 375–385.

Holden, G. W., Williamson, P. A., & Holland, G. W. O. (2014). Eavesdropping on the family: A pilot investigation of corporal punishment in the home. *Journal of Family Psychology, 28,* 401–406.

Holditch-Davis, D., Belyea, M., & Edwards, L. J. (2005). Prediction of 3-year developmental outcomes from sleep development over the preterm period. *Infant Behavior and Development, 7,* 49–58.

Holdren, J. P., & Lander, E. (2012). *Engage to excel: Producing one million additional college graduates with degrees in science, technology, engineering, and mathematics.* Washington, DC: President's Council of Advisors on Science and Technology.

Holland, J. L. (1985). *Making vocational choices: A theory of vocational personalities and work environments.* Englewood Cliffs, NJ: Prentice-Hall.

Holland, J. L. (1997). *Making vocational choices: A theory of vocational personalities and work environments* (3rd ed.). Odessa, FL: Psychological Assessment Resources.

Hollenstein, T., & Lougheed, J. P. (2013). Beyond storm and stress: Typicality, transactions, timing, and temperament to account for adolescent change. *American Psychologist, 68,* 444–454.

Hollich, G. J., Hirsh-Pasek, K., & Golinkoff, R. M. (2000). Breaking the language barrier: An emergentist coalition model for the origins of word learning. *Monographs of the Society for Research in Child Development, 65*(3, Serial No. 262).

Höllwarth, M. E. (2013). Prevention of unintentional injuries: A global role for pediatricians. *Pediatrics, 132,* 4–7.

Holmes, J., Gathercole, S. E., & Dunning, D. L. (2010). Poor working memory: Impact and interventions. In P. Bauer (Ed.), *Advances in child development and behavior* (Vol. 39, pp. 1–43). London: Academic Press.

Holt-Lunstad, J., Smith, T. B., & Layton, J. B. (2010). Social relationships and mortality risk: A meta-analytic review. *PLOS ONE, 7,* e1000316

Hong, D. S., Hoeft, F., Marzelli, M. J., Lepage, J.-F., Roeltgen, D., Ross, J., et al. (2014). Influence of the X-chromosome on neuroanatomy: Evidence from Turner and Klinefelter syndromes. *Journal of Neuroscience, 34,* 3509–3516.

Hong, S. I., & Morrill-Howell, N. (2010). Health outcomes of Experience Corps: A high-commitment volunteer program. *Social Science and Medicine, 71,* 414–420.

Hong, T., Mitchell, P., Burlutsky, G., Liew, G., & Wang, J. J. (2016). Visual impairment, hearing loss and cognitive function in an older population: Longitudinal findings from the Blue Mountains Eye Study. *PLOS ONE, 11*(1), e017646.

Hoobler, J. M., Lemmon, G., & Wayne, S. J. (2011). Women's underrepresentation in upper management:

New insights on a persistent problem. *Organizational Dynamics, 40,* 151–156.

Hood, M., Conlon, E., & Andrews, G. (2008). Preschool home literacy practices and children's literacy development: A longitudinal analysis. *Journal of Educational Psychology, 100,* 252–271.

Hootman, J. M., Helmick, C. G., Barbour, K. E., Theis, K. A., & Boring, M. A. (2016). Updated projected prevalence of self-reported doctor-diagnosed arthritis and arthritis-attributable activity limitation among U.S. adults, 2015–2040. *Arthritis & Rheumatology, 68,* 1582–1587.

Hooyman, N., Kawamoto, K. S., & Kiyak, H. A. S. (2015). *Aging matters: An introduction to social gerontology.* Hoboken, NJ: Pearson.

Hopf, L., Quraan, M. A., Cheung, M. J., Taylor, M. J., Ryan, J. D., & Moses, S. N. (2013). Hippocampal lateralization and memory in children and adults. *Journal of the International Neuropsychological Society, 19,* 1042–1052.

Hopkins, B., & Westra, T. (1988). Maternal handling and motor development: An intracultural study. *Genetic, Social and General Psychology Monographs, 14,* 377–420.

Hoppmann, C. A., Gerstorf, D., Smith, J., & Klumb, P. L. (2007). Linking possible selves and behavior: Do domain-specific hopes and fears translate into daily activities in very old age? *Journals of Gerontology, 62B,* P104–P111.

Horhota, M., Lineweaver, T., Ositelu, M., Summers, K., & Hertzog, C. (2012). Young and older adults' beliefs about effective ways to mitigate age-related memory decline. *Psychology and Aging, 27,* 293–304.

Horn, J. L., & Noll, J. (1997). Human cognitive capabilities: Gf-Gc theory. In D. P. Flanagan, J. L., Genshaft, & P. L. Harrison (Eds.), *Beyond traditional intellectual assessment* (pp. 53–91). New York: Guilford.

Horn, K., Branstetter, S., Zhang, J., Jarett, T., Tompkins, N. O., Anesetti-Rothermel, A., et al. (2013). Understanding physical activity outcomes as a function of teen smoking cessation. *Journal of Adolescent Health, 53,* 125–131.

Horn, S. S., & Heinze, J. (2011). She can't help it, she was born that way: Adolescents' beliefs about the origins of homosexuality and sexual prejudice. *Anales de Psichología, 27,* 688–697.

Horn, S. S., & Sinno, S. M. (2014). Gender, sexual orientation, and discrimination based on gender. In M. Killen & J. G. Smetana (Eds.), *Handbook of moral development* (2nd ed., pp. 317–349). New York: Psychology Press.

Horn, S. S., & Szalacha, L. A. (2009). School differences in heterosexual students' attitudes about homosexuality and prejudice based on sexual orientation. *International Journal of Developmental Science, 3,* 64–79.

Horner, T. M. (1980). Two methods of studying stranger reactivity in infants: A review. *Journal of Child Psychology and Psychiatry, 21,* 203–219.

Horne-Thompson, A., & Grocke, D. (2008). The effect of music therapy on anxiety in patients who are terminally ill. *Journal of Palliative Medicine, 11,* 582–590.

Horowitz, R., Gramling, R., & Quill, T. (2014). Palliative care education in U.S. medical schools. *Medical Education, 48,* 59–66.

Hospice Foundation of America. (2011). *A caregiver's guide to the dying process.* Retrieved from hospicefoundation.org/hfa/media/Files/Hospice_TheDyingProcess_Docutech-READERSPREADS.pdf

Hospice Foundation of America. (2016). *Paying for care.* Retrieved from hospicefoundation.org/End-of-Life-Support-and-Resources/Coping-with-Terminal-Illness/Paying-for-Care

Hoste, R. R., & Le Grange, D. (2013). Eating disorders in adolescence. In W. T. Donohue, L. T. Benuto, & L. Woodword Tolle (Eds.), *Handbook of adolescent health psychology* (pp. 495–506). New York: Springer.

Hostetler, A. J., & Sweet, S., & Moen, P. (2007). Gendered career paths: A life course perspective on returning to school. *Sex Roles, 56,* 85–103.

Houlihan, J., Kropp, T., Wiles, R., Gray, S., & Campbell, C. (2005). *Body burden: The pollution in newborns.* Washington, DC: Environmental Working Group.

Houts, R. M., Barnett-Walker, K. C., Paley, B., & Cox, M. J. (2008). Patterns of couple interaction during the transition to parenthood. *Personal Relationships, 15,* 103–122.

Hovdenak, N., & Haram, K. (2012). Influence of mineral and vitamin supplements on pregnancy outcome. *European Journal of Obstetrics & Gynecology and Reproductive Biology, 164,* 127–132.

Howard, K., & Walsh, M. E. (2010). Conceptions of career choice and attainment: Developmental levels in how children think about careers. *Journal of Vocational Behavior, 76,* 143–152.

Howe, M. L. (2014). The co-emergence of self and autobiographical memory: An adaptive view of early memory. In P. J. Bauer & R. Fivush (Eds.), *Wiley handbook on the development of children's memory* (pp. 545–567). Hoboken, NJ: Wiley-Blackwell.

Howe, M. L. (2015). Memory development. In L. S. Liben & U. Müller (Eds.), *Handbook of child psychology and developmental science: Vol. 2. Cognitive processes* (7th ed., pp. 203–249). Hoboken, NJ: Wiley.

Howe, N., Aquan-Assee, J., & Bukowski, W. M. (2001). Predicting sibling relations over time: Synchrony between maternal management styles and sibling relationship quality. *Merrill-Palmer Quarterly, 47,* 121–141.

Howell, K. K., Coles, C. D., & Kable, J. A. (2008). The medical and developmental consequences of prenatal drug exposure. In J. Brick (Ed.), *Handbook of the medical consequences of alcohol and drug abuse* (2nd ed., pp. 219–249). New York: Haworth Press.

Howell, S. R., & Becker, S. (2014). Grammar from the lexicon: Evidence from neural network simulations of language acquisition. In D. Bittner & N. Ruhlig (Eds.), *Lexical bootstrapping: The role of lexis and semantics in child language* (pp. 245–264). Berlin: Walter de Gruyter.

Howell, T. M., & Yuille, J. C. (2004). Healing and treatment of Aboriginal offenders: A Canadian example. *American Journal of Forensic Psychology, 22,* 53–76.

Høybe, C., Cohen, P., Hoffman, A. R., Ross, R., Biller, B. M., & Christiansen, J. S. (2015). Status of long-acting-growth hormone preparations—2015. *Growth Hormone & IGF Research, 25,* 201–206.

Hoyer, W. J., & Verhaeghen, P. (2006). Memory aging. In J. E. Birren & K. W. Schaie (Eds.), *Handbook of the psychology of aging* (6th ed., pp. 209–232). Burlington, MA: Elsevier Academic Press.

HSBC & Oxford Institute of Ageing. (2007). *The future of retirement.* London: HSBC Insurance.

Hsu, A. S., Chater, N., & Vitányi, P. (2013). Language learning from positive evidence, reconsidered: A simplicity-based approach. *Topics in Cognitive Science, 5,* 35–55.

Huang, C.-C. (2006). Child support enforcement and father involvement for children in never-married mother families. *Fathering, 4,* 97–111.

Huang, C. Y., & Stormshak, E. A. (2011). A longitudinal examination of early adolescence ethnic identity trajectories. *Cultural Diversity and Ethnic Minority Psychology, 17,* 261–270.

Huang, H., Coleman, S., Bridge, J. A., Yonkers, K., & Katon, W. (2014). A meta-analysis of the relationship between antidepressant use in pregnancy and the risk of preterm birth and low birth weight. *General Hospital Psychiatry, 36,* 13–18.

Huang, K.-E. (2010). Menopause perspective and treatment of Asian women. *Seminars in Reproductive Medicine, 28,* 396–403.

Huang, Q., & Sverke, M. (2007). Women's occupational career patterns over 27 years: Relations to family of origin, life careers, and wellness. *Journal of Vocational Behavior, 70,* 369–397.

Hubbard, P., Gorman-Murray, A., & Nash, C. J. (2015). Cities and sexualities. In J. DeLatamer & R. F. Plante (Eds.), *Handbook of the sociology of sexualities* (pp. 287–303). New York: Springer.

Hubbs-Tait, L., Nation, J. R., Krebs, N. F., & Bellinger, D. C. (2005). Neurotoxicants, micronutrients, and social environments: Individual and combined effects on children's development. *Psychological Science in the Public Interest, 6,* 57–121.

Huddleston, J., & Ge, X. (2003). Boys at puberty: Psychosocial implications. In C. Hayward (Ed.), *Gender differences at puberty* (pp. 113–134). New York: Cambridge University Press.

Hudson, J. A., Fivush, R., & Kuebli, J. (1992). Scripts and episodes: The development of event memory. *Applied Cognitive Psychology, 6,* 483–505.

Hudson, J. A., & Mayhew, E. M. Y. (2009). The development of memory for recurring events. In M. L. Courage & N. Cowan (Eds.), *The development of memory in infancy and childhood* (pp. 69–91). Hove, UK: Psychology Press.

Hudson, N. W., & Fraley, R. C. (2016). Changing for the better? Longitudinal associations between volitional personality change and psychological well-being. *Personality and Social Psychology Bulletin, 42,* 603–615.

Huebner, C. E., & Payne, K. (2010). Home support for emergent literacy: Follow-up of a community-based implementation of dialogic reading. *Journal of Applied Developmental Psychology, 31,* 195–201.

Huesmann, L. R., Moise-Titus, J., Podolski, C. & Eron, L. D. (2003). Longitudinal relations between children's exposure to TV violence and their aggressive and violent behavior in young adulthood: 1977–1992. *Developmental Psychology, 39,* 201–221.

Huffman, M. L. (2012). Introduction: Gender, race, and management. *Annals of the American Academy of Political and Social Science, 639,* 6–12.

Hughes, C. (2010). Conduct disorder and antisocial behavior in the under-5s. In C. L. Cooper, J. Field, U. Goswami, R. Jenkins, & B. J. Sahakian (Eds.), *Mental capital and well-being* (pp. 821–827). Malden, MA: Wiley-Blackwell.

Hughes, C., & Ensor, R. (2010). Do early social cognition and executive function predict individual differences in preschoolers' prosocial and antisocial behavior? In B. W. Sokol, U. Müller, J. I. M. Carpendale, A. R. Young, & G. Iarocci (Eds.), *Social interaction and the development of social understanding and executive functions* (pp. 418–441). New York: Oxford University Press.

Hughes, C., Ensor, R., & Marks, A. (2010). Individual differences in false belief understanding are stable from 3 to 6 years of age and predict children's mental state talk with school friends. *Journal of Experimental Child Psychology, 108,* 96–112.

Hughes, C., Marks, A., Ensor, R., & Lecce, S. (2010). A longitudinal study of conflict and inner state talk in children's conversations with mothers and younger siblings. *Social Development, 19,* 822–837.

Hughes, J. N. (2011). Longitudinal effects of teacher and student perceptions of teacher–student relationship qualities on academic adjustment. *Elementary School Journal, 112,* 38–60.

Hughes, J. N., Cavell, T. A., & Grossman, P. B. (1997). A positive view of self: Risk or protection for aggressive children? *Development and Psychopathology, 9,* 75–94.

Hughes, J. N., & Kwok, O. (2006). Classroom engagement mediates the effect of teacher–student support on elementary students' peer acceptance. *Journal of School Psychology, 43,* 465–480.

Hughes, J. N., Wu, J.-Y., Kwok, O., Villarreal, V., & Johnson, A. Y. (2012). Indirect effects of child reports of teacher–student relationship on achievement. *Journal of Educational Psychology, 104,* 350–365.

Hughes, J. N., Zhang, D., & Hill, C. R. (2006). Peer assessments of normative and individual teacher–student support predict social acceptance and engagement among low-achieving children. *Journal of School Psychology, 43,* 447–463.

Huizenga, H., Crone, E. A., & Jansen, B. (2007). Decision making in healthy children, adolescents and adults explained by the use of increasingly complex proportional reasoning rules. *Developmental Science, 10,* 814–825.

Hultsch, D. F., Hertzog, C., Dixon, R. A., & Small, B. J. (1998). *Memory change in the aged.* New York: Cambridge University Press.

Hunnius, S., & Geuze, R. H. (2004a). Developmental changes in visual scanning of dynamic faces and abstract stimuli in infants: A longitudinal study. *Infancy, 6,* 231–255.

Hunnius, S., & Geuze, R. H. (2004b). Gaze shifting in infancy: A longitudinal study using dynamic faces and abstract stimuli. *Infant Behavior and Development, 27,* 397–416.

Hunt, C. E., & Hauck, F. R. (2006). Sudden infant death syndrome. *Canadian Medical Association Journal, 174,* 1861–1869.

Hunt, E. (2011). *Human intelligence.* New York: Cambridge University Press.

Hunt, J. S. (2015). Race in the justice system. In B. L. Cutler & P. A. Zapf (Eds.), *APA handbook of forensic psychology: Vol. 2. Criminal investigation, adjudication, and sentencing outcomes* (pp. 125–161). Washington, DC: American Psychological Association.

Hunter, L. A. (2014). Vaginal breech birth: Can we move beyond the term breech trial? *Journal of Midwifery and Women's Health, 59,* 320–327.

Huntsinger, C., Jose, P. E., Krieg, D. B., & Luo, Z. (2011). Cultural differences in Chinese American and European American children's drawing skills over time. *Early Childhood Research Quarterly, 26,* 134–145.

Hurtig, W. A., & Stewin, L. (2006). The effect of death education and experience on nursing students' attitude toward death. *Journal of Advanced Nursing, 15,* 29–34.

Huston, A. C., Wright, J. C., Marquis, J., & Green, S. B. (1999). How young children spend their time: Television and other activities. *Developmental Psychology, 35,* 912–925.

Huston, T. L., Caughlin, J. P., Houts, R. M., Smith, S. E., & George, L. J. (2001). The connubial crucible: Newlywed years as predictors of marital delight, distress, and divorce. *Journal of Personality and Social Psychology, 80,* 237–252.

Hutchinson, E. A., De Luca, C. R., Doyle, L. W., Roberts, G., & Anderson, P. J. (2013). School-age outcomes of extremely preterm or extremely low birth weight children. *Pediatrics, 131,* e1053–1061.

Huttenlocher, J., Waterfall, H., Veasilyeva, M., Vevea, J., & Hedges, L. (2010). Sources of variability in children's language growth. *Cognitive Psychology, 61,* 343–365.

Huttenlocher, P. R. (2002). *Neural plasticity: The effects of environment on the development of the cerebral cortex.* Cambridge, MA: Harvard University Press.

Huxhold, O., Miche, M., & Schüz, B. (2014). Benefits of having friends in older ages: Differential effects of informal social activities on well-being in middle-aged and older adults. *Journals of Gerontology, 69B,* 366–375.

Huyck, M. H. (1996). Continuities and discontinuities in gender identity in midlife. In V. L. Bengtson (Ed.), *Adulthood and aging* (pp. 98–121). New York: Springer-Verlag.

Huyck, M. H. (1998). Gender roles and gender identity in midlife. In S. L. Willis & J. D. Reid (Eds.), *Life in the middle* (pp. 209–232). San Diego: Academic Press.

Hyde, J. S. (2014). Gender similarities and differences. *Annual Review of Psychology, 65,* 373–398.

Hyde, J. S., Mezulis, A. H., & Abramson, L. Y. (2008). The ABCs of depression: Integrating affective, biological, and cognitive models to explain the emergence of the gender difference in depression. *Psychological Review, 115,* 291–313.

Hyman, B. T., Phelps, C. H., Beach, T. G., Bigio, E. H., Cairns, N. J., Carrillo, M. C., et al. (2012). National Institute on Aging–Alzheimer's Association guidelines for the neuropathologic assessment of Alzheimer's disease. *Alzheimer's and Dementia, 8,* 1–13.

Hymel, S., Schonert-Reichl, K. A., Bonanno, R. A., Vaillancourt, T., & Henderson, N. R. (2010). Bullying and morality: Understanding how good kids can behave badly. In S. Jimerson, S. M. Swearer, & D. L. Espelage (Eds.), *Handbook of bullying in schools: An international perspective* (pp. 101–118). New York: Routledge.

I

Ibanez, G., Bernard, J. Y., Rondet, C., Peyre, H., Forhan, A., Kaminski, M., & Saurel-Cubizolles, M.-J. (2015). Effects of antenatal maternal depression and anxiety on children's early cognitive development: A prospective cohort study. *PLOS ONE, 10,* e0135849.

Ickes, M. J. (2011). Stigmatization of overweight and obese individuals: Implications for mental health promotion. *International Journal of Mental Health Promotion, 13,* 37–45.

Ikejima, C., Ikeda, M., Hashimoto, M., Ogawa, Y., Tanimukai, S., Kashibayashi, T., et al. (2014). Multicenter population-based study on the prevalence of early onset dementia in Japan: Vascular dementia as its prominent cause. *Psychiatry and Clinical Neuroscience, 68,* 216–224.

Imai, M., & Haryu, E. (2004). The nature of word-learning biases and their roles for lexical development: From a cross-linguistic perspective. In D. G. Hall & S. R. Waxman (Eds.), *Weaving a lexicon* (pp. 411–444). Cambridge, MA: MIT Press.

Impett, E. A., & Peplau, L. A. (2006). "His" and "her" relationships? A review of the empirical evidence. In A. L. Vangelisti & D. Perlman (Eds.), *The Cambridge handbook of personal relationships* (pp. 273–292). New York: Cambridge University Press.

Impett, E. A., Sorsoli, L., Schooler, D., Henson, J. M., & Tolman, D. L. (2008). Girls' relationship authenticity and self-esteem across adolescence. *Developmental Psychology, 44,* 722–733.

Ingoldsby, E. M., Shelleby, E., Lane, T., & Shaw, D. S. (2012). Extrafamilial contexts and children's conduct problems. In V. Maholmes & R. B. King (Eds.), *Oxford handbook of poverty and child development* (pp. 404–422). New York: Oxford University Press.

Ingram, D. K., & Roth, G. S. (2015). Calorie restriction mimetics: Can you have your cake and eat it, too? *Ageing Research Reviews, 20,* 46–62.

Inhelder, B., & Piaget, J. (1958). *The growth of logical thinking from childhood to adolescence: An essay on the construction of formal operational structures.* New York: Basic Books. (Original work published 1955)

Insana, S. P., & Montgomery-Downs, H. E. (2012). Sleep and sleepiness among first-time postpartum parents: A field- and laboratory-based multimethod assessment. *Developmental Psychobiology, 55,* 361–372.

Institute of Medicine. (2015). *Cognitive aging: Progress in understanding and opportunity for action.* Washington, DC: National Academies Press.

Ip, S., Chung, M., Raman, G., Trikalinos, T. A., & Lau, J. (2009). A summary of the Agency for Healthcare Research and Quality's evidence report on breastfeeding in developed countries. *Breastfeeding Medicine, 4*(Suppl. 1), S17–S30.

Irvine, A. B., Ary, D. V., & Bourgeois, M. S. (2003). An interactive multimedia program to train professional caregivers. *Journal of Applied Gerontology, 22,* 269–288.

Isabella, R., & Belsky, J. (1991). Interactional synchrony and the origins of infant–mother attachment: A replication study. *Child Development, 62,* 373–384.

Ishida, M., & Moore, G. E. (2013). The role of imprinted genes in humans. *Molecular Aspects of Medicine, 34,* 826–840.

Ishihara, K., Warita, K., Tanida, T., Sugawara, T., Kitagawa, H., & Hoshi, N. (2007). Does paternal exposure to 2, 3, 7, 8-tetrachlorodibenzo-p-dioxin (TCDD) affect the sex ratio of offspring? *Journal of Veterinary Medical Science, 69,* 347–352.

Iyer-Eimerbrink, P., & Nurnberger, J. I., Jr. (2014). Genetics of alcoholism. *Current Psychiatry Reports, 16,* 518.

Izard, C. E., King, P. A., Trentacosta, C. J., Laurenceau, J. P., Morgan, J. K., Krauthamer-Ewing, E. S., & Finlon, K. J. (2008). Accelerating the development of emotion competence in Head Start children. *Development and Psychopathology, 20,* 369–397.

Izard, V., Sann, C., Spelke, E. S., & Streri, A. (2009). Newborn infants perceive abstract numbers. *Proceedings of the National Academy of Sciences, 106,* 10382–10385.

J

Jabès, A., & Nelson, C. A. (2014). Neuroscience and child well-being. In A. Ben-Arieh, F. Casas, I. Frønes, & J. E. Korbin (Eds.), *Handbook of child well-being: Vol. 1* (pp. 219–247) Dordrecht, Germany: Springer Reference.

Jack, F., Simcock, G., & Hayne, G. (2012). Magic memories: Young children's verbal recall after a 6-year delay. *Child Development, 83,* 159–172.

Jackson, J. B., Miller, R. B., Oka, M., & Henry, R. G. (2014). Gender differences in marital satisfaction: A meta-analysis. *Journal of Marriage and Family, 76,* 105–129.

Jackson, J. J., Hill, P. L., Payne, B. R., Roberts, B. W., & Steine-Morrow, E. A. L. (2012). Can an old dog learn (and want to experience) new tricks? Cognitive training increases openness to experience in older adults. *Psychology and Aging, 27,* 286–292.

Jackson, K. J., Muldoon, P. P., De Biasi, M., & Damaj, M. I. (2015). New mechanisms and perspectives in nicotine withdrawal. *Neuropharmacology, 96*(Pt. B), 223–234.

Jackson, S. L., & Hafemeister, T. L. (2012). Pure financial exploitation vs. hybrid financial exploitation co-occurring with physical abuse and/or neglect of elderly persons. *Psychology of Violence, 2,* 285–296.

Jackson, V. A., Sullivan, A. M., Gadmer, N. M., Seltzer, D., Mitchell, A. M., & Lakoma, M. D. (2005). "It was haunting … ": Physicians' descriptions of emotionally powerful patient deaths. *Academic Medicine, 80,* 648–656.

Jacobs, J. E., & Klaczynski, P. A. (2002). The development of judgment and decision making during childhood and adolescence. *Current Directions in Psychological Science, 11,* 145–149.

Jacobs, J. E., Lanza, S., Osgood, D. W., Eccles, J. S., & Wigfield, A. (2002). Changes in children's self-competence and values: Gender and domain differences across grades one through twelve. *Child Development, 73,* 509–527.

Jadallah, M., Anderson, R. C., Nguyen-Jahiel, K., Miller, B. W., Kim, I.-H., Kuo, L.-J., et al. (2011). Influence of a teacher's scaffolding moves during child-led small-group discussions. *American Educational Research Journal, 48,* 194–230.

Jadva, V., Casey, P., & Golombok, S. (2012). Surrogacy families 10 years on: Relationship with the surrogate, decisions over disclosure and children's understanding of their surrogacy origins. *Human Reproduction, 27,* 3008–3014.

Jaffe, M., Gullone, E., & Hughes, E. K. (2010). The roles of temperamental dispositions and perceived parenting behaviours in the use of two emotion regulation strategies in late childhood. *Journal of Applied Developmental Psychology, 31,* 47–59.

Jaffee, S. R., Bowes, L., Ouellet-Morin, I., Fisher, H. L., Moffitt, T. E., Merrick, M. T., & Arseneault, L. (2013). Safe, stable, nurturing relationships break the intergenerational cycle of abuse: A prospective nationally representative cohort of children in the United Kingdom. *Journal of Adolescent Health, 53,* S4–S10.

Jaffee, S. R., & Christian, C. W. (2014). The biological embedding of child abuse and neglect: Implications for policy and practice. *Society for Research in Child Development Social Policy Report, 28*(1).

Jahanfar, S., Lye, M.-S., & Krishnarajah, I. S. (2013). Genetic and environmental effects on age at menarche, and its relationship with reproductive health in twins. *Indian Journal of Human Genetics, 19,* 245–250.

Jambon, M., & Smetana, J. G. (2014). Moral complexity in middle childhood: Children's evaluations of necessary harm. *Developmental Psychology, 50,* 22–33.

James, J., Ellis, B. J., Schlomer, G. L., & Garber, J. (2012). Sex-specific pathways to early puberty, sexual debut, and sexual risk taking: Tests of an integrated evolutionary–developmental model. *Developmental Psychology, 48,* 687–702.

James, J. B., Lewkowicz, C., Libhaber, J., & Lachman, M. (1995). Rethinking the gender identity crossover hypothesis: A test of a new model. *Sex Roles, 32,* 185–207.

James, J. B., & Zarrett, N. (2007). Ego integrity in the lives of older women. *Journal of Adult Development, 13,* 61–75.

Jansen, J., de Weerth, C., & Riksen-Walraven, J. M. (2008). Breastfeeding and the mother–infant relationship. *Developmental Review, 28,* 503–521.

Jansen, P. W., Roza, S. J., Jaddoe, V. W. V., Mackenbach, J. D., Raat, H., Hofman, A., et al. (2012). Children's eating behavior, feeding practices of parents and weight problems in early childhood: Results from the population-based Generation R Study. *International Journal of Behavioral Nutrition and Physical Activity, 9,* 130–138.

Janssen, S. M., Rubin, D. C., & St. Jacques, P. L. (2011). The temporal distribution of autobiographical memory: Changes in reliving and vividness over the life span do not explain the reminiscence bump. *Memory and Cognition, 39,* 1–11.

Janssens, J. M. A. M., & Deković, M. (1997). Child rearing, prosocial moral reasoning, and prosocial behaviour. *International Journal of Behavioral Development, 20,* 509–527.

Jarvis, J. F., & van Heerden, H. G. (1967). The acuity of hearing in the Kalahari Bushman: A pilot study. *Journal of Laryngology and Otology, 81,* 63–68.

Jaudes, P. K., & Mackey-Bilaver, L. (2008). Do chronic conditions increase young children's risk of being maltreated? *Child Abuse and Neglect, 32,* 671–681.

Jedrychowski, W., Perera, F. P., Jankowski, J., Mrozek-Budzyn, D., Mroz, E., Flak, E., et al. (2009). Very low prenatal exposure to lead and mental development of children in infancy and early childhood. *Neuroepidemiology, 32,* 270–278.

Jenkins, C., Lapelle, N., Zapka, J. G., & Kurent, J. E. (2005). End-of-life care and African Americans: Voices from the community. *Journal of Palliative Medicine, 8,* 585–592.

Jenkins, C. L., Edmundson, A., Averett, P., & Yoon, I. (2014). Older lesbians and bereavement. *Journal of Gerontological Social Work, 57,* 273–287.

Jenkins, J. M., Rasbash, J., & O'Connor, T. G. (2003). The role of the shared family context in differential parenting. *Developmental Psychology, 39,* 99–113.

Jenkins, K. R., Pienta, A. M., & Horgas, A. L. (2002). Activity and health-related quality of life in continuing care retirement communities. *Research on Aging, 24,* 124–149.

Jensen, A. R. (1969). How much can we boost IQ and scholastic achievement? *Harvard Educational Review, 39,* 1–123.

Jensen, A. R. (2001). Spearman's hypothesis. In J. M. Collis & S. Messick (Eds.), *Intelligence and personality: Bridging the gap in theory and measurement* (pp. 3–24). Mahwah, NJ: Erlbaum.

Jensen, A. R. (2002). Galton's legacy to research on intelligence. *Journal of Biosocial Science, 34,* 145–172.

Jerome, E. M., Hamre, B. K., & Pianta, R. C. (2009). Teacher–child relationships from kindergarten to sixth grade: Early childhood predictors of teacher-perceived conflict and closeness. *Social Development, 18,* 915–945.

Jipson, J. L., & Gelman, S. A. (2007). Robots and rodents: Children's inferences about living and nonliving kinds. *Child Development, 78,* 1675–1688.

Joe, G. W., Kalling Knight, D., Becan, J. E., & Flynn, P. M. (2014). Recovery among adolescents: Models for post-treatment gains in drug abuse treatments. *Journal of Substance Abuse Treatment, 46,* 362–373.

Jogerst, G. J., Daly, J. M., Galloway, L. J., Zheng, S., & Xu, Y. (2012). Substance abuse associated with elder abuse in the United States. *American Journal of Drug and Alcohol Abuse, 38,* 63–69.

Joh, A. S., & Adolph, K. E. (2006). Learning from falling. *Child Development, 77,* 89–102.

Johansson, A. K., & Grimby, A. (2013). Anticipatory grief among close relatives of patients in hospice and palliative wards. *American Journal of Hospice and Palliative Medicine, 29,* 134–138.

Johnson, A. D., Ryan, R. M., & Brooks-Gunn, J. (2012). Child-care subsidies: Do they impact the quality of care children experience? *Child Development, 83,* 1444–1461.

Johnson, C. L., & Troll, L. E. (1994). Constraints and facilitators to friendships in late life. *Gerontologist, 34,* 79–87.

Johnson, E. K., & Seidl, A. (2008). Clause segmentation by 6-month-old infants: A crosslinguistic perspective. *Infancy, 13,* 440–455.

Johnson, E. K., & Tyler, M. D. (2010). Testing the limits of statistical learning for word segmentation. *Developmental Science, 13,* 339–345.

Johnson, J. G., Cohen, P., Smailes, E. M., Kasen, S., & Brook, J. S. (2002). Television viewing and aggressive behavior during adolescence and adulthood. *Science, 295,* 2468–2471.

Johnson, M. H. (1999). Ontogenetic constraints on neural and behavioral plasticity: Evidence from imprinting and face processing. *Canadian Journal of Experimental Psychology, 55,* 77–90.

Johnson, M. H. (2001). The development and neural basis of face recognition: Comment and speculation. *Infant and Child Development, 10,* 31–33.

Johnson, M. H. (2011). Developmental neuroscience, psychophysiology, and genetics. In M H Bornstein & M. E. Lamb (Eds.), *Developmental science: An advanced textbook* (6th ed., pp. 187–222). Mahwah, NJ: Erlbaum.

Johnson, M. H., & de Haan, M. (2015). *Developmental cognitive neuroscience: An introduction* (4th ed.). Chichester, UK: Wiley-Blackwell.

Johnson, R. C., & Schoeni, R. F. (2011). Early-life origins of adult disease: National longitudinal population-based study of the United States. *American Journal of Public Health, 101,* 2317–2324.

Johnson, S. C., Dweck, C. S., & Chen, F. S. (2007). Evidence for infants' internal working models of attachment. *Psychological Science, 18,* 501–502.

Johnson, S. C., Dweck, C., Chen, F. S., Stern, H. L., Ok, S.-J., & Barth, M. (2010). At the intersection of social and cognitive development: Internal working models of attachment in infancy. *Cognitive Science, 34,* 807–825.

Johnson, S. L. (2000). Improving preschoolers' self-regulation of energy intake. *Pediatrics, 106,* 1429–1435.

Johnson, S. P., & Hannon, E. E. (2015). Perceptual development. In L. S. Liben & U. Müller (Eds.), *Handbook of child psychology and developmental science: Vol. 2. Cognitive processes* (7th ed., pp. 63–112). Hoboken, NJ: Wiley.

Johnson, S. P., Slemmer, J. A., & Amso, D. (2004). Where infants look determines how they see: Eye movements and object perception performance in 3-month-olds. *Infancy, 6,* 185–201.

Johnston, L. D., O'Malley, P. M., Miech, R. A., Bachman, J. G., & Schulenberg, J. E. (2014). *National survey results on drug use: 1975–2013. Key findings on adolescent drug use.* Retrieved from www.monitoringthefuture.org/pubs/monographs/mtf-overview2013.pdf

Johnston, L. D., O'Malley, P. M., Miech, R. A., Bachman, J. G., & Schulenberg, J. E. (2015). *Monitoring the Future national survey results on drug use, 1975–2015: Overview: Key findings on adolescent drug use.* Ann Arbor: Institute for Social Research, University of Michigan.

Johnston, M., Pollard, B., Morrison, V., & MacWalter, R. (2004). Functional limitations and survival following stroke: Psychological and clinical predictors of 3-year outcome. *International Journal of Behavioral Medicine, 11,* 187–196.

Johnston, M. V., Nishimura, A., Harum, K., Pekar, J., & Blue, M. E. (2001). Sculpting the developing brain. *Advances in Pediatrics, 48,* 1–38.

Jokhi, R. P., & Whitby, E. H. (2011). Magnetic resonance imaging of the fetus. *Developmental Medicine and Child Neurology, 53,* 18–28.

Jome, L. M., Surething, N. A., & Taylor, K. K. (2005). Relationally oriented masculinity, gender nontraditional interests, and occupational traditionality of employed men. *Journal of Career Development, 32,* 183–197.

Jones, A., Charles, P., & Benson, K. (2013). A model for supporting at-risk couples during the transition to parenthood. *Families in Society, 94,* 166–173.

Jones, A. R., Parkinson, K. N., Drewett, R. F., Hyland, R. M., Pearce, M. S., & Adamson, A. J. (2011). Parental perceptions of weight status in children: The Gateshead Millennium Study. *International Journal of Obesity, 35,* 953–962.

Jones, B. K., & McAdams, D. P. (2013). Becoming generative: Socializing influences recalled in life stories in late midlife. *Journal of Adult Development, 20,* 158–172.

Jones, C. J., Peskin, H., & Livson, N. (2011). Men's and women's change and individual differences in change in femininity from age 33 to 85: Results from the Intergenerational Studies. *Journal of Adult Development, 18,* 155–163.

Jones, D. J., & Lindahl, K. M. (2011). Coparenting in extended kinship systems: African American, Hispanic, Asian heritage, and Native American families. In J. P. McHale & K. M. Lindahl (Eds.), *Coparenting* (pp. 61–79). Washington, DC: American Psychological Association.

Jones, M. C., & Mussen, P. H. (1958). Self-conceptions, motivations, and interpersonal attitudes of early and late-maturing girls. *Child Development, 29,* 491–501.

Jones, S. (2009). The development of imitation in infancy. *Philosophical Transactions of the Royal Society B, 364,* 2325–2335.

Jopp, D., & Rott, C. (2006). Adaptation in very old age: Exploring the role of resources, beliefs, and attitudes for centenarians' happiness. *Psychology and Aging, 21,* 266–280.

Josselyn, S. A., & Frankland, P. W. (2012). Infantile amnesia: A neurogenic hypothesis. *Learning and Memory, 19,* 423–433.

Joyner, K., Manning, W., & Prince, B. (2015). *The qualities of same-sex and different-sex couples in young adulthood* (CFDR Working Paper 2015-22). Bowling Green, OH: Center for Family and Demographic Research, Bowling Green State University.

Juby, H., Billette, J.-M., Laplante, B., & Le Bourdais, C. (2007). Nonresident fathers and children: Parents' new unions and frequency of contact. *Journal of Family Issues, 28,* 1220–1245.

Judson, S. S., Johnson, D. M., & Perez, A. L. C. (2013). Perceptions of adult sexual coercion as a function of victim gender. *Psychology of Men & Masculinity, 14,* 335–344.

Juffer, F., & van IJzendoorn, M. H. (2012). Review of meta-analytical studies on the physical, emotional, and cognitive outcomes of intercountry adoptees. In J. L. Gibbons & K. S. Rotabi (Eds.), *Intercountry adoption: Policies, practices, and outcomes* (pp. 175–186). Burlington, VT: Ashgate Publishing.

Jukic, A. M., Evenson, K. R., Daniels, J. L., Herring, A. H., Wilcox, A. J., Harmann, K. E., et al. (2012). A prospective study of the association between vigorous physical activity during pregnancy and length of gestation and birthweight. *Maternal and Child Health Journal, 16,* 1031–1044.

Junge, C., Kooijman, V., Hagoort, P., & Cutler, A. (2012). Rapid recognition at 10 months as a predictor of language development. *Developmental Science, 15,* 463–473.

Juntunen, C. L., Wegner, K. E., & Matthews, L. G. (2002). Promoting positive career change in midlife. In C. L. Juntunen & D. R. Atkinson (Eds.), *Counseling across the lifespan* (pp. 329–347). Thousand Oaks, CA: Sage.

Jürgensen, M., Hiort, O., Holterhus, P.-M., & Thyen, U. (2007). Gender role behavior in children with XY karyotype and disorders of sex development. *Hormones and Behavior, 51,* 443–453.

Jusczyk, P. W. (2002). Some critical developments in acquiring native language sound organization. *Annals of Otology, Rhinology and Laryngology, 189,* 11–15.

Jusczyk, P. W., & Hohne, E. A. (1997). Infants' memory for spoken words. *Science, 277,* 1984–1986.

Jusczyk, P. W., & Luce, P. A. (2002). Speech perception. In H. Pashler & S. Yantis (Eds.), *Stevens' handbook of experimental psychology: Vol. 1. Sensation and perception* (3rd ed., pp. 493–536). New York: Wiley.

Jutras-Aswad, D., DiNieri, J. A., Harkany, T., & Hurd, Y. L. (2009). Neurobiological consequences of maternal cannabis on human fetal development and its neuropsychiatric outcome. *European Archives of Psychiatry and Clinical Neuroscience, 259,* 395–412.

K

Kaczmarczyk, M. M., Miller, M. J., & Freund, G. G. (2012). The health benefits of dietary fiber: Beyond the usual suspects of type 2 diabetes mellitus, cardiovascular disease and colon cancer. *Metabolism: Clinical and Experimental, 61,* 1058–1066.

Kaffashi, F., Scher, M. S., Ludington-Hoe, S. M., & Loparo, K. A. (2013). An analysis of the kangaroo care intervention using neonatal EEG complexity: A preliminary study. *Clinical Neurophysiology, 124,* 238–246.

Kagan, J. (2003). Behavioral inhibition as a temperamental category. In R. J. Davidson, K. R. Scherer, & H. H. Goldsmith (Eds.), *Handbook of affective science* (pp. 320–331). New York: Oxford University Press.

Kagan, J. (2010). Emotions and temperament. In M. H. Bornstein (Ed.), *Handbook of cultural developmental science* (pp. 175-194). New York: Psychology Press.

Kagan, J. (2013a). Contextualizing experience. *Developmental Review, 33,* 273–278.

Kagan, J. (2013b). Equal time for psychological and biological contributions to human variation. *Review of General Psychology, 17,* 351–357.

Kagan, J. (2013c). *The human spark: The science of human development.* New York: Basic Books.

Kagan, J. (2013d). Temperamental contributions to inhibited and uninhibited profiles. In P. D. Zelazo (Ed.), *The Oxford handbook of developmental psychology* (142–164). New York: Oxford University Press.

Kagan, J., Snidman, N., Kahn, V., & Towsley, S. (2007). The preservation of two infant temperaments into adolescence. *Monographs of the Society for Research in Child Development, 72*(2, Serial No. 287).

Kahana, E., King, C., Kahana, B., Menne, H., Webster, N. J., & Dan, A. (2005). Successful aging in the face of chronic disease. In M. L. Wykle, P. J. Whitehouse, & D. L. Morris (Eds.), *Successful aging through the life span* (pp. 101–126). New York: Springer.

Kahn, U. R., Sengoelge, M., Zia, N., Razzak, J. A., Hasselberg, M., & Laflamme, L. (2015). Country level economic disparities in child injury mortality. *Archives of Disease in Childhood, 100,* s29–s33.

Kahne, J. E., & Sporte, S. E. (2008). Developing citizens: The impact of civic learning opportunities on students' commitments to civic participation. *American Educational Research Journal, 45,* 738–766.

Kail, R. V. (2003). Information processing and memory. In M. H. Bornstein, L. Davidson, C. L. M. Keyes, K. A. Moore, and the Center for Child Well-Being (Eds.), *Well-being: Positive development across the life course* (pp. 269–280). Mahwah, NJ: Erlbaum.

Kail, R. V., & Ferrer, E. F. (2007). Processing speed in childhood and adolescence: Longitudinal models for examining developmental change. *Child Development, 78,* 1760–1770.

Kail, R. V., McBride-Chang, C., Ferrer, E., Cho, J.-R., & Shu, H. (2013). Cultural differences in the development of processing speed. *Developmental Science, 16,* 476–483.

Kaiser Family Foundation. (2015). *How will the uninsured fare under the Affordable Care Act?* Retrieved from www.kff.org/health-reform/fact-sheet/how-will-the-uninsured-fare-under-the-affordable-care-act

Kakihara, F., Tilton-Weaver, L., Kerr, M., & Stattin, H. (2010). The relationship of parental control to youth adjustment: Do youths' feelings about their parents play a role? *Journal of Youth and Adolescence, 39,* 1442–1456.

Kalil, A., Levine, J. A., & Ziol-Guest, K. M. (2005). Following in their parents' footsteps: How characteristics of parental work predict adolescents' interest in parents' working jobs. In B. Schneider & L. J. Waite (Eds.), *Being together, working apart: Dual-career families and the work–life balance* (pp. 422–442). New York: Cambridge University Press.

Kalisch, T., Kattenstroth, J.-C., Kowalewski, R., Tegenthoff, M., & Dinse, H. R. (2012). *PLoS ONE, 7*(1), e30420.

Kalogrides, D., & Loeb, S. (2013). Different teachers, different peers: The magnitude of student sorting within schools. *Educational Researcher, 42,* 306–316.

Kalpouzos, G., & Nyberg, L. (2012). *Multimodal neuroimaging in normal aging: Structure–function interactions* (pp. 273–304). New York: Psychology Press.

Kalra, L., & Ratan, R. (2007). Recent advances in stroke rehabilitation. *Stroke, 38,* 235–237.

Kaminski, J. W., Puddy, R. W., Hall, D. M., Cashman, S. Y., Crosby, A. E., & Ortega, L. G. (2010). The relative influence of different domains of social connectedness on self-directed violence in adolescence. *Journal of Youth and Adolescence, 39,* 460–473.

Kaminsky, Z., Petronis, A., Wang, S.-C., Levine, B., Ghaffar, O., Floden, D., et al. (2007). Epigenetics of personality traits: An illustrative study of identical twins discordant for risk-taking behavior. *Twin Research and Human Genetics, 11,* 1–11.

Kanazawa, S. (2015). Breastfeeding is positively associated with child intelligence even net of parental IQ. *Developmental Psychology, 51,* 1683–1689.

Kandler, C., Kornadt, A. E., Hagemeyer, B., & Neyer, F. J. (2015). Patterns and sources of personality development in old age. *Journal of Personality and Social Psychology, 109,* 175–191.

Kane, L. (2014) *Medscape ethics report 2014, Part 1: Life, death, and pain.* Retrieved from www.medscape.com/features/slideshow/public

Kane, P., & Garber, J. (2004). The relations among depression in fathers, children's psychopathology, and father–child conflict: A meta-analysis. *Clinical Psychology Review, 24,* 339–360.

Kane, R. A., Lum, T. Y., Cutler, L. J., Degenholtz, H. B., & Yu, T.-C. (2007). Resident outcomes in small-house nursing homes: A longitudinal evaluation of the initial Green House program. *Journal of the American Geriatrics Society, 55,* 836–839.

Kanfer, R., Beier, M. E., & Ackerman, P. L. (2013). Goals and motivation related to work in later adulthood: An organizing framework. *Journal of Work and Organizational Psychology, 22,* 835–847.

Kang, N. H., & Hong, M. (2008). Achieving excellence in teacher workforce and equity in learning opportunities in South Korea. *Educational Researcher, 37,* 200–207.

Kann, L., Kinchen, S., Shanklin, S. L., Flint, K. H., Hawkins, J., Harris, W. A., et al. (2014). Youth risk behavior surveillance—United States, 2013. *Morbidity and Mortality Weekly Report, 63*(4). Retrieved from www.cdc.gov/mmwr/pdf/ss/ss6304.pdf

Kann, L., McManus, T., Harris, W. A., Shanklin, S. L., Flint, K. H., Hawkins, J., et al. (2016). Youth risk behavior surveillance—United States, 2015. *Morbidity and Mortality Weekly Report, 65*(6). Retrieved from www.cdc.gov/healthyyouth/data/yrbs/pdf/2015/ss6506_updated.pdf

Kann, L., Olsen, E. O., McManus, T., Kinchen, S., Chyen, D., Harris, W. A., et al. (2011). Sexual identity, sex of sexual contacts, and health-risk behaviors among students in grades 9–12. Youth Risk Behavior Surveillance, Selected Sites, United States, 2001–2009. *Morbidity and Mortality Weekly Report, 60,* 1–127.

Kantaoka, S., & Vandell, D. L. (2013). Quality of afterschool activities and relative change in adolescent functioning over two years. *Applied Developmental Science, 17,* 123–134.

Kanters, M. A., Bocarro, J. N., Edwards, M., Casper, J., & Floyd, M. F. (2013). School sport participation under two school sport policies: Comparisons by race/ethnicity, gender, and socioeconomic status. *Annals of Behavioral Medicine, 45*(Suppl. 1), S113–S121.

Kaplan, D. B., & Pillemer, K. (2015). Fulfilling the promise of the Elder Justice Act: Priority goals for the White House Conference on Aging. *Public Policy & Aging Report, 25,* 63–66.

Kaplan, D. L., Jones, E. J., Olson, E. C., & Yunzal-Butler, C. B. (2013). Early age of first sex and health risk in an urban adolescent population. *Journal of School Health, 83,* 350–356.

Kaplowitz, P. B. (2008). Link between body fat and timing of puberty. *Pediatrics, 121,* S208–S217.

Karafantis, D. M., & Levy, S. R. (2004). The role of children's lay theories about the malleability of human attributes in beliefs about and volunteering for disadvantaged groups. *Child Development, 75,* 236–250.

Karasawa, M., Curhan, K. B., Markus, H. R., Kitayama, S. S., Love, G. D., Radler, B. T., et al. (2011). Cultural perspectives on aging and well-being: A comparison of Japan and the U.S. *International Journal of Aging and Human Development, 73,* 73–98.

Karasik, L. B., Adolph, K. E., Tamis-LeMonda, C. S., & Zuckerman, A. L. (2012). Carry on: Spontaneous object carrying in 13-month-old crawling and walking infants. *Developmental Psychology, 48,* 389–397.

Karasik, L. B., Tamis-LeMonda, C. S., & Adolph, K. E. (2011). Transition from crawling to walking affects infants' social actions with objects. *Child Development, 82,* 1199–1209.

Karasik, L. B., Tamis-LeMonda, C. S., Adolph, K. E., & Dimitroupoulou, K. A. (2008). How mothers encourage and discourage infants' motor actions. *Infancy, 13,* 366–392.

Karbach, J., & Küper, K. (2016). Cognitive reserve. In S. K. Whitbourne (Ed.), *Encyclopedia of adulthood and aging* (Vol. 1, pp. 47–51). Malden, MA: Wiley Blackwell.

Karel, M. J., Gatz, M., & Smyer, M. A. (2012). Aging and mental health in the decade ahead: What psychologists need to know. *American Psychologist, 67,* 184–198.

Karemaker, A., Pitchford, N., & O'Malley, C. (2010). Enhanced recognition of written words and enjoyment of reading in struggling beginner readers through whole-word multimedia software. *Computers and Education, 54,* 199–208.

Karevold, E., Ystrom, E., Coplan, R. J., Sanson, A. V., & Mathiesen, K. S. (2012). A prospective longitudinal study of shyness from infancy to adolescence: Stability, age-related changes, and prediction of socio-emotional functioning. *Journal of Abnormal Child Psychology, 40,* 1167–1177.

Karg, K., Burmeister, M., Shedden, K., & Sen, S. (2011). The serotonin transporter promoter variant (5-HTTLPR), stress, and depression meta-analysis revisited: Evidence of genetic moderation. *Archives of General Psychiatry, 68,* 444–454.

Karger, H. J., & Stoesz, D. (2011). *American social welfare policy* (7th ed.). Upper Saddle River, NJ: Pearson Education.

Karila, L., Megarbane, B., Cottencin, O., & Lejoyeux, M. (2015). Synthetic cathinones: A new public health problem. *Current Neuropharmacology, 13,* 12–20.

Karkhaneh, M., Rowe, B. H., Saunders, L. D., Voaklander, D. C., & Hagel, B. E. (2013). Trends in head injuries associated with mandatory bicycle helmet legislation targeting children and adolescents. *Accident Analysis and Prevention, 59,* 206–212.

Karlsson, C., & Berggren, I. (2011). Dignified end-of-life care in the patients' own homes. *Nursing Ethics, 18,* 374–385.

Kärnä, A., Voeten, M., Little, T. D., Poskiparta, E., Kaljonen, A., & Salmivalli, C. (2011). A large-scale evaluation of the KiVa antibullying program: Grades 4–6. *Child Development, 82,* 311–330.

Karraker, A., & DeLamater, J. (2013). Past-year sexual inactivity among older married persons and their partners. *Journal of Marriage and Family, 75,* 142–163.

Kärtner, J., Holodynski, M., & Wörmann, V. (2013). Parental ethnotheories, social practice and the culture-specific development of social smiling in infants. *Mind, Culture, and Activity, 20,* 79–95.

Kärtner, J., Keller, H., Chaudhary, N., & Yovsi, R. D. (2012). The development of mirror self-recognition in different sociocultural contexts. *Monographs of the Society for Research in Child Development, 77*(4, Serial No. 305).

Kashdan, T. B., & Nezlek, J. B. (2012). Whether, when, and how is spirituality related to well-being? Moving beyond single occasion questionnaires to understanding daily process. *Personality and Social Psychology Bulletin, 38,* 1523–1535.

Kassel, J. D., Weinstein, S., Skitch, S. A., Veilleux, J., & Mermelstein, R. (2005). The development of substance abuse in adolescence: Correlates, causes, and consequences. In J. D. Kassel, S. Weinstein, S. A. Skitch, J. Veilleux, & R. Mermelstein (Eds.), *Development of psychopathology: A vulnerability-stress perspective* (pp. 355–384). Thousand Oaks, CA: Sage.

Kastenbaum, R. J. (2012). *Death, society, and human experience* (11th ed.). Upper Saddle River, NJ: Pearson.

Kataoka, S., & Vandell, D. L. (2013). Quality of afterschool activities and relative change in adolescent functioning over two years. *Applied Developmental Science, 17,* 123–134.

Katz, J., Lee, A. C. C., Lawn, J. E., Cousens, S., Blencowe, H., Ezzati, M., et al. (2013). Mortality risk in preterm and small-for-gestational-age infants in low-income and middle-income countries: A pooled country analysis. *Lancet, 382,* 417–425.

Katz-Wise, S. L., Priess, H. A., & Hyde, J. S. (2010). Gender-role attitudes and behavior across the transition to parenthood. *Developmental Psychology, 46,* 18–28.

Kaufman, A. S. (2001). WAIS-III IQs, Horn's theory, and generational changes from young adulthood to old age. *Intelligence, 29,* 131–167.

Kaufman, J. C., & Sternberg, R. J. (2007, July/August). Resource review: Creativity. *Change, 39,* 55–58.

Kaufmann, K. B., Büning, H., Galy, A., Schambach, A., & Grez, M. (2013). Gene therapy on the move. *EMBO Molecular Medicine, 5,* 1642–1661.

Kavanaugh, R. D. (2006). Pretend play. In B. Spodek & O. N. Saracho (Eds.), *Handbook of research on the education of young children* (2nd ed., pp. 269–278). Mahwah, NJ: Erlbaum.

Kavšek, M. (2004). Predicting later IQ from infant visual habituation and dishabituation: A meta-analysis. *Journal of Applied Developmental Psychology, 25,* 369–393.

Kavšek, M., & Bornstein, M. H. (2010). Visual habituation and dishabituation in preterm infants: A review and meta-analysis. *Research in Developmental Disabilities, 31,* 951–975.

Kavšek, M., Yonas, A., & Granrud, C. E. (2012). Infants' sensitivity to pictorial depth cues: A review and meta-analysis. *Infant Behavior and Development, 35,* 109–128.

Kaye, W. (2008). Neurobiology of anorexia and bulimia nervosa. *Physiology and Behavior, 94,* 121–135.

Kayed, N. S., & Van der Meer, A. L. H. (2009). A longitudinal study of prospective control in catching by full-term and preterm infants. *Experimental Brain Research, 194,* 245–258.

Kearney, C. A., Spear, M., & Mihalas, S. (2014). School refusal behavior. In L. Grossman & S. Walfish (Eds.), *Translating psychological research into practice* (pp. 83–88). New York: Springer.

Keating, D. P. (2004). Cognitive and brain development. In R. M. Lerner & L. Steinberg (Eds.), *Handbook of adolescent psychology* (2nd ed., pp. 45–84). Hoboken, NJ: Wiley.

Keating, D. P. (2012). Cognitive and brain development in adolescence. *Enfance, 64,* 267–279.

Keegan, L., & Drick, C. A. (2011). *End of life: Nursing solutions for death with dignity.* New York: Springer.

Keen, R. (2011). The development of problem solving in young children: A critical cognitive skill. *Annual Review of Psychology, 62,* 1–24.

Keil, F. C. (1986). Conceptual domains and the acquisition of metaphor. *Cognitive Development, 1,* 73–96.

Keller, H., Borke, Y. J., Kärtner, J., Jensen, H., & Papaligoura, Z. (2004). Developmental consequences of early parenting experiences: Self-recognition and self-regulation in three cultural communities. *Child Development, 75,* 1745–1760.

Keller, P. A., & Lusardi, A. (2012). Employee retirement savings: What we know and are discovering for helping people prepare for life after work. In G. D. Mick, S. Pettigrew, C. Pechmann, & J. L. Ozanne (Eds.), *Transformative consumer research for personal and collective well-being* (pp. 445–464). New York: Routledge.

Kelley, S. A., Brownell, C. A., & Campbell, S. B. (2000). Mastery motivation and self-evaluative affect in toddlers: Longitudinal relations with maternal behavior. *Child Development, 71,* 1061–1071.

Kelly, D. J., Liu, S., Ge, L., Quinn, P. C., Slater, A. M., Lee, K., Liu, Q., & Pascalis, O. (2007). Cross-race preferences for same-race faces extend beyond the African versus Caucasian contrast in 3-month-old infants. *Infancy, 11,* 87–95.

Kelly, D. J., Quinn, P. C., Slater, A. M., Lee, K., Ge, L., & Pascalis, O. (2009). Development of the other-race effect during infancy: Evidence toward universality? *Journal of Experimental Child Psychology, 104,* 105–114.

Kelly, E. L., Moen, P., Oakes, J. M., Fan, W., Okechukwu, C., Davis, K. D., et al. (2014). Changing work and work–family conflict: Evidence from the work, family, and health network. *American Sociological Review, 79,* 485–516.

Kelly, R., & Hammond, S. (2011). The relationship between symbolic play and executive function in young children. *Australasian Journal of Early Childhood, 36*(2), 21–27.

Kelly, S., & Price, H. (2011). The correlates of tracking policy: Opportunity hoarding, status competition, or a technical-functional explanation? *American Educational Research Journal, 48,* 560–585.

Kelly, S. J., & Ismail, M. (2015). Stress and type 2 diabetes: A review of how stress contributes to the development of type 2 diabetes. *Annual Review of Public Health, 36,* 441–462.

Kempe, C. H., Silverman, B. F., Steele, P. W., Droegemueller, P. W., & Silver, H. K. (1962). The battered-child syndrome. *JAMA, 181,* 17–24.

Kemper, S. (2015). Language production in late life. In A. Gerstenberg & A. Voeste (Eds.), *Language development: The lifespan perspective* (pp. 59–75). Amsterdam, Netherlands: John Benjamins Publishing.

Kemper, S. (2016). Language production. In S. K. Whitbourne (Ed.), *Encyclopedia of adulthood and aging* (Vol. 2, pp. 726–731). Malden, MA: Wiley Blackwell.

Kemper, S., Rash, S. R., Kynette, D., & Norman, S. (1990). Telling stories: The structure of adults' narratives. *European Journal of Cognitive Psychology, 2,* 205–228.

Kendig, H., Dykstra, P. A., van Gaalen, R. I., & Melkas, T. (2007). Health of aging parents and childless individuals. *Journal of Family Issues, 28,* 1457–1486.

Kendler, K. S., Thornton, L. M., Gilman, S. E., & Kessler, R. C. (2000). Sexual orientation in a U.S. national sample of twin and non-twin sibling pairs. *American Journal of Psychiatry, 157,* 1843–1846.

Kendrick, D., Barlow, J., Hampshire, A., Stewart-Brown, S., & Polnay, L. (2008). Parenting interventions and the prevention of unintentional injuries in childhood: Systematic review and meta-analysis. *Child: Care, Health and Development, 34,* 682–695.

Kennell, J., Klaus, M., McGrath, S., Robertson, S., & Hinkley, C. (1991). Continuous emotional support during labor in a U.S. hospital. *JAMA, 265,* 2197–2201.

Kenney-Benson, G. A., Pomerantz, E. M. Ryan, A. M., & Patrick, H. (2006). Sex differences in math performance: The role of children's approach to schoolwork. *Developmental Psychology, 42,* 11–26.

Kenyon, B. L. (2001). Current research in children's conceptions of death: A critical review. *Omega, 43,* 63–91.

Keren, M., Feldman, R., Namdari-Weinbaum, I., Spitzer, S., & Tyano, S. (2005). Relations between parents' interactive style in dyadic and triadic play and toddlers' symbolic capacity. *American Journal of Orthopsychiatry, 75,* 599–607.

Kerestes, M., Youniss, J., & Metz, E. (2004). Longitudinal patterns of religious perspective and civic integration. *Applied Developmental Science, 8,* 39–46.

Kernis, M. H. (2002). Self-esteem as a multifaceted construct. In T. M. Brinthaupt & R. P. Lipka (Eds.), *Understanding early adolescent self and identity* (pp. 57–88). Albany: State University of New York Press.

Kerns, K. A., Brumariu, L. E., & Seibert, A. (2011). Multi-method assessment of mother–child attachment: Links to parenting and child depressive symptoms in middle childhood. *Attachment and Human Development, 13,* 315–333.

Kerpelman, J. L., Shoffner, M. F., & Ross-Griffin, S. (2002). African American mothers' and daughters' beliefs about possible selves and their strategies for reaching the adolescent's future academic and career goals. *Journal of Youth and Adolescence, 31,* 289–302.

Kettl, P. (1998). Alaska Native suicide: Lessons for elder suicide. *International Psychogeriatrics, 10,* 205–211.

Kew, K., Ivory, G., Muniz, M. M., & Quiz, F. Z. (2012). No Child Left Behind as school reform: Intended and unintended consequences. In M. A. Acker-Hocevar, J. Ballenger, W. A. Place, & G. Ivory (Eds.), *Snapshots of school leadership in the 21st century: Perils and promises of leading for social justice, school improvement, and democratic community* (pp. 13–30). Charlotte, NC: IAP Information Age Publishing.

Key, J. D., Gebregziabher, M. G., Marsh, L. D., & O'Rourke, K. M. (2008). Effectiveness of an intensive, school-based intervention for teen mothers. *Journal of Adolescent Health, 42,* 394–400.

Keyes, C. L. M., & Ryff, C. D. (1998a). Generativity and adult lives: Social structural contours and quality of life consequences. In D. P. McAdams & E. de St. Aubin (Eds.), *Generativity and adult development: How and why we care for the next generation* (pp. 227–263). Washington, DC: American Psychological Association.

Keyes, C. L. M., & Ryff, C. D. (1998b). Psychological well-being in midlife. In S. L. Willis & J. D. Reid (Eds.), *Life in the middle* (pp. 161–180). San Diego: Academic Press.

Keyes, C. L. M., Shmotkin, D., & Ryff, C. D. (2002). Optimizing well-being: The empirical encounter of two traditions. *Journal of Personality and Social Psychology, 82,* 1007–1022.

Keyes, C. L. M., & Westerhof, G. J. (2012). Chronological and subjective age differences in flourishing mental health and major depressive episode. *Aging and Mental Health, 16,* 67–74.

Khaleefa, O., Sulman, A., & Lynn, R. (2009). An increase of intelligence in Sudan, 1987–2007. *Journal of Biosocial Science, 41,* 279–283.

Khaleque, A., & Rohner, R. P. (2002). Perceived parental acceptance–rejection and psychological adjustment: A meta-analysis of cross cultural and intracultural studies. *Journal of Marriage and Family, 64,* 54–64.

Khaleque, A., & Rohner, R. P. (2012). Pancultural associations between perceived parental acceptance and psychological adjustment of children and adults: A meta-analytic review of worldwide research. *Journal of Cross-Cultural Psychology, 43,* 784–800.

Khashan, A. S., Baker, P. N., & Kenny, L. C. (2010). Preterm birth and reduced birthweight in first and second teenage pregnancies: A register-based cohort study. *BMC Pregnancy and Childbirth, 10,* 36.

Khavkin, J., & Ellis, D. A. (2011). Aging skin: Histology, physiology, and pathology. *Facial Plastic Surgery Clinics of North America, 19,* 229–234.

Khurana, A., Romer, D., Betancourt, L. M., Brodsky, N. L., Giannetta, J. M., & Hurt, H. (2015). Experimentation versus progression in adolescent drug use: A test of an emerging neurobehavioral imbalance model. *Development and Psychopathology, 27,* 901–913.

Kidwai, R., Mancham, B. E., Brown, Q. L., & Eaton, W. W. (2014). The effect of spirituality and religious attendance on the relationship between psychological distress and negative life events. *Social Psychiatry and Psychiatric Epidemiology, 49,* 487–497.

Kiernan, K. (2002). Cohabitation in Western Europe: Trends, issues, and implications. In A. Booth & A. C. Crouter (Eds.), *Just living together* (pp. 3–32). Mahwah, NJ: Erlbaum.

Killen, M., Crystal, D., & Watanabe, H. (2002). The individual and the group: Japanese and American children's evaluations of peer exclusion, tolerance of difference, and prescriptions for conformity. *Child Development, 73,* 1788–1802.

Killen, M., Henning, A., Kelly, M. C., Crystal, D., & Ruck, M. (2007). Evaluations of interracial peer encounters by majority and minority U.S. children and adolescents. *International Journal of Behavioral Development, 31,* 491–500.

Killen, M., Lee-Kim, J., McGlothlin, H., & Stangor, C. (2002). How children and adolescents evaluate gender and racial exclusion. *Monographs of the Society for Research in Child Development, 67*(4, Serial No. 271).

Killen, M., Margie, N. G., & Sinno, S. (2006). Morality in the context of intergroup relationships. In M. Killen & J. G. Smetana (Eds.), *Handbook of moral development* (pp. 155–183). Mahwah, NJ: Erlbaum.

Killen, M., Mulvey, K. L., Richardson, C., Jampol, N., & Woodward, A. (2011). The accidental transgressor: Morally relevant theory of mind. *Cognition, 119,* 197–215.

Killen, M., Rutland, A., & Ruck, M. (2011). Promoting equity, tolerance, and justice in childhood. *Society for Research in Child Development Social Policy Report, 25*(4).

Killen, M., & Smetana, J. G. (2015). Origins and development of morality. In M. E. Lamb (Ed.), *Handbook of child psychology and developmental science: Vol. 3. Socioemotional processes* (pp. 701–749). Hoboken, NJ: Wiley.

Killoren, S. E., Thayer, S. M., & Updegraff, K. A. (2008). Conflict resolution between Mexican origin adolescent siblings. *Journal of Marriage and Family, 70,* 1200–1212.

Kilmer, R. P., Cook, J. R., Crusto, C., Strater, K. P., & Haber, M. G. (2012). Understanding the ecology and development of children and families experiencing homelessness: Implications for practice, supportive services, and policy. *American Journal of Orthopsychiatry, 82,* 389–401.

Kilpatrick, S. D., Bissonnette, V. L., & Rusbult, C. E. (2002). Empathic accuracy and accommodative behavior among newly married couples. *Personal Relationships, 9,* 369–393.

Kim, G., Walden, T. A., & Knieps, L. J. (2010). Impact and characteristics of positive and fearful emotional messages during infant social referencing. *Infant Behavior and Development, 33,* 189–195.

Kim, H. Y., Schwartz, K., Cappella, E., & Seidman, E. (2014). Navigating middle grades: Role of social contexts in middle grade school climate. *American Journal of Community Psychology, 54,* 28–45.

Kim, J., & Cicchetti, D. (2006). Longitudinal trajectories of self-system processes and depressive symptoms among maltreated and nonmaltreated children. *Child Development, 77,* 624–639.

Kim, J. E., & Moen, P. (2002). Is retirement good or bad for subjective well-being? *Current Directions in Psychological Science, 10,* 83–86.

Kim, J. M. (1998). Korean children's concepts of adult and peer authority and moral reasoning. *Developmental Psychology, 34,* 947–955.

Kim, J. W., & Choi, Y. J. (2013). Feminisation of poverty in 12 welfare states: Consolidating cross-regime variations? *International Journal of Social Welfare, 22,* 347–359.

Kim, J.-Y., McHale, S. M., Crouter, A. C., & Osgood, D. W. (2007). Longitudinal linkages between sibling relationships and adjustment from middle childhood through adolescence. *Developmental Psychology, 43,* 960–973.

Kim, J.-Y., McHale, S. M., Osgood, D. W., & Crouter, A. C. (2006). Longitudinal course and family correlates of sibling relationships from childhood through adolescence. *Child Development, 77,* 1746–1761.

Kim, K., Zarit, S. H., Fingerman, K. L., & Han, G. (2015). Intergenerational exchanges of middle-aged adults with their parents and parents-in-law in Korea. *Journal of Marriage and Family, 77,* 791–805.

Kim, S., & Kochanska, G. (2012). Child temperament moderates effects of parent–child mutuality on self-regulation: A relationship-based path for emotionally negative infants. *Child Development, 83,* 1275–1289.

Kim, Y. S., Park, Y. S., Allegrante, J. P., Marks, R., Ok, H., Cho, K. O., & Garber, C. E. (2012). Relationship between physical activity and general mental health. *Preventive Medicine, 55,* 458–463.

Kimhi, Y., Shoam-Kugelmas, D., Agam Ben-Artzi, G., Ben-Moshe, I., & Bauminger-Zviely, N. (2014). Theory of mind and executive function in preschoolers with typical development versus intellectually able preschoolers with autism spectrum disorder. *Journal of Autism and Developmental Disorders, 44,* 2341–2354.

King, A. C., & Bjorklund, D. F. (2010). Evolutionary developmental psychology. *Psicothema, 22,* 22–27.

King, L. A., & Hicks, J. A. (2007). Whatever happened to "What might have been"? *American Psychologist, 62,* 625–636.

King, P. E., & Furrow, J. L. (2004). Religion as a resource for positive youth development: Religion, social capital, and moral outcomes. *Developmental Psychology, 40,* 703–713.

King, P. M., & Kitchener, K. S. (2002). The reflective judgment model: Twenty years of research on epistemic cognition. In B. K. Hofer & P. R. Pintrich (Eds.), *Personal epistemology: The psychological beliefs about knowledge and knowing* (pp. 37–61). Mahwah, NJ: Erlbaum.

King, V. (2007). When children have two mothers: Relationships with nonresident mothers, stepmothers, and fathers. *Journal of Marriage and Family, 69,* 1178–1193.

King, V. (2009). Stepfamily formation: Implications for adolescent ties to mothers, nonresident fathers, and stepfathers. *Journal of Marriage and Family, 71,* 954–968.

Kinney, H. C. (2009). Brainstem mechanisms underlying the sudden infant death syndrome: Evidence from human pathologic studies. *Developmental Psychobiology, 51,* 223–233.

Kinnunen, M.-L., Pietiläinen, K., & Rissanen, A. (2006). Body size and overweight from birth to adulthood. In L. Pulkkinen & J. Kaprio (Eds.), *Socioemotional development and health from adolescence to adulthood* (pp. 95–107). New York: Cambridge University Press.

Kins, E., Beyers, W., Soenens, B., & Vansteenkiste, M. (2009). Patterns of home leaving and subjective well-being in emerging adulthood: The role of motivational processes and parental autonomy support. *Developmental Psychology, 45,* 1416–1429.

Kinsella, M. T., & Monk, C. (2009). Impact of maternal stress, depression and anxiety on fetal neurobehavioral development. *Clinical Obstetrics and Gynecology, 52,* 425–440.

Kinser, K., & Deitchman, J. (2007). Tenacious persisters: Returning adult students in higher education. *Journal of College Student Retention, 9,* 75–94.

Kirby, D. (2002). Effective approaches to reducing adolescent unprotected sex, pregnancy, and childbearing. *Journal of Sex Research, 39,* 51–57.

Kirby, D. B. (2008). The impact of abstinence and comprehensive sex and STD/HIV education programs on adolescent sexual behavior. *Sexuality Research and Social Policy, 5,* 18–27.

Kiriakidis, S. P., & Kavoura, A. (2010). Cyberbullying: A review of the literature on harassment through the Internet and other electronic means. *Family and Community Health, 33,* 82–93.

Kirkham, N. Z., Cruess, L., & Diamond, A. (2003). Helping children apply their knowledge to their behavior on a dimension-switching task. *Developmental Science, 6,* 449–476.

Kirshenbaum, A. P., Olsen, D. M., & Bickel, W. K. (2009). A quantitative review of the ubiquitous relapse curve. *Journal of Substance Abuse Treatment, 36,* 8–17.

Kirshner, B. (2009). "Power in numbers": Youth organizing as a context for exploring civic identity. *Journal of Research on Adolescence, 19,* 414–440.

Kisilevsky, B. S., & Hains, S. M. J. (2011). Onset and maturation of fetal heart rate response to the mother's voice over late gestation. *Developmental Science, 14,* 214–223.

Kisilevsky, B. S., Hains, S. M. J., Brown, C. A., Lee, C. T., Cowperthwaite, B., & Stutzman, S. S. (2009). Fetal sensitivity to properties of maternal speech and language. *Infant Behavior and Development, 32,* 59–71.

Kit, B. K., Ogden, C. L., & Flegal, K. M. (2014). Epidemiology of obesity. In W. Ahrens & I. Pigeot (Eds.), *Handbook of epidemiology* (2nd ed., pp. 2229–2262). New York: Springer Science + Business Media.

Kite, M. E., Stockdale, G. D., Whitley, B. E., Jr., & Johnson, B. T. (2005). Attitudes toward younger and older adults: An updated meta-analytic review. *Journal of Social Issues, 61,* 241–266.

Kitsantas, P., Gaffney, K. F., & Cheema, J. (2012). Life stressors and barriers to timely prenatal care for women with high-risk pregnancies residing in rural and nonrural areas. *Women's Health Issues, 22,* e455–e460.

Kitzman, H. J., Olds, D. L., Cole, R. E., Hanks, C. A., Anson, E. A., Arcoleo, K. J., et al. (2010). Enduring effects of prenatal and infancy home visiting by nurses on children: Follow-up of a randomized trial among children at age 12 years. *Archives of Pediatric and Adolescent Medicine, 164,* 412–418.

Kitzmann, K. M., Cohen, R., & Lockwood, R. L. (2002). Are only children missing out? Comparison of the peer-related social competence of only children and siblings. *Journal of Social and Personal Relationships, 19,* 299–316.

Kiuru, N., Aunola, K., Vuori, J., & Nurmi, J.-E. (2009). The role of peer groups in adolescents' educational expectation and adjustment. *Journal of Youth and Adolescence, 36,* 995–1009.

Kjønniksen, L., Anderssen, N., & Wold, B. (2009). Organized youth sport as a predictor of physical activity in adulthood. *Scandinavian Journal of Medicine and Science in Sports, 19,* 646–654.

Kjønniksen, L., Torsheim, T., & Wold, B. (2008). Tracking of leisure-time physical activity during adolescence and young adulthood: A 10-year longitudinal study. *International Journal of Behavioral Nutrition and Physical Activity, 5,* 69.

Klaczynski, P. A. (2001). Framing effects on adolescent task representations, analytic and heuristic processing, and decision making: Implications for the normative/descriptive gap. *Applied Developmental Psychology, 22,* 289–309.

Klaczynski, P. A., Schuneman, M. J., & Daniel, D. B. (2004). Theories of conditional reasoning: A developmental examination of competing hypotheses. *Developmental Psychology, 40,* 559–571.

Klahr, D., Matlen, B., & Jirout, J. (2013). Children as scientific thinkers. In G. J. Feist & M. E. Gorman (Eds.), *Handbook of the psychology of science* (pp. 223–247). New York: Springer.

Klass, D. (2004). The inner representation of the dead child in the psychic and social narratives of bereaved parents. In R. A. Neimeyer (Ed.), *Meaning reconstruction and the experience of loss* (pp. 77–94). Washington, DC: American Psychological Association.

Klaw, E. L., Rhodes, J. E., & Fitzgerald, L. F. (2003). Natural mentors in the lives of African-American adolescent mothers: Tracking relationships over time. *Journal of Youth and Adolescence, 32,* 223–232.

Klebanov, P. K., Brooks-Gunn, J., McCarton, C., & McCormick, M. C. (1998). The contribution of neighborhood and family income to developmental test scores over the first three years of life. *Child Development, 69,* 1420–1436.

Kleespies, P. M. (2004). Concluding thoughts on suffering, dying and choice. In P. M. Kleespies (Ed.), *Life and death decisions: Psychological and ethical considerations in end-of-life care* (pp. 163–167). Washington, DC: American Psychological Association.

Kleffer, M. J. (2013). Development of reading and math skills in early adolescents: Do K–8 public schools make a difference? *Journal of Research on Educational Effectiveness, 6,* 361–379.

Kleiber, M. L., Diehl, E. J., Laufer, B. I., Mantha, K., Chokroborty-Hoque, A., Alberry, B., et al. (2014). Long-term genomic and epigenomic dysregulation as a consequence of prenatal alcohol exposure: A model for fetal alcohol spectrum disorders. *Frontiers in Genetics, 5* (161), 1–12.

Kleinsorge, C., & Covitz, L. M. (2012). Impact of divorce on children: Developmental considerations. *Pediatrics in Review, 33,* 147–155.

Kleinspehn-Ammerlahn, A., Kotter-Grühn, D., & Smith, J. (2008). Self-perceptions of aging: Do subjective age and satisfaction with aging change during old age? *Journals of Gerontology Series B: Psychological Sciences and Social Sciences, 63,* 377–385.

Klemfuss, J. Z., & Ceci, S. J. (2012). Legal and psychological perspectives on children's competence to testify in court. *Developmental Review, 32,* 81–204.

Kliegel, M., Jäger, T., & Phillips, L. H. (2008). Adult age differences in event-based prospective memory: A meta-analysis on the role of focal versus nonfocal cues. *Psychology and Aging, 23,* 203–208.

Kliegman, R. M., Stanton, B. F., St. Geme, J. W., & Schor, N. (Eds.). (2015). *Nelson textbook of pediatrics* (20th ed.). Philadelphia: Saunders.

Kliewer, W., Fearnow, M. D., & Miller, P. A. (1996). Coping socialization in middle childhood: Tests of maternal and paternal influences. *Child Development, 67,* 2339–2357.

Klimstra, T. A., Hale, W. W., III, Raaijmakers, Q. A. W., Branje, S. J. T., & Meeus, W. H. J. (2010). Identity formation in adolescence: Change or stability? *Journal of Youth and Adolescence, 39,* 150–162.

Kloep, M., & Hendry, L. B. (2007). Retirement: A new beginning? *The Psychologist, 20,* 742–745.

Kloep, M., & Hendry, L. B. (2011). A systemic approach to the transitions to adulthood. In J. J. Arnett, M. Kloep, L. B. Hendry & J. L. Tanner (Eds.), *Debating emerging adulthood: Stage or process?* (pp. 53–75). New York: Oxford University Press.

Kloess, J. A., Beech, A. R., & Harkins, L. (2014). Online child sexual exploitation: Prevalence, process, and offender characteristics. *Trauma, Violence, & Abuse, 15,* 126–139.

Kluwer, E. S., & Johnson, M. D. (2007). Conflict frequency and relationship quality across the transition to parenthood. *Journal of Marriage and Family, 69,* 1089–1106.

Kmec, J. A., O'Connor, L. T., & Schieman, S. (2014). Not ideal: The association between working anything but full time and perceived unfair treatment. *Work and Occupations, 41,* 63–85.

Knafo, A., & Plomin, R. (2006). Parental discipline and affection and children's prosocial behavior: Genetic and environmental links. *Journal of Personality and Social Psychology, 90,* 147–164.

Knafo, A., Zahn-Waxler, C., Davidov, M., Hulle, C. V., Robinson, J. L., & Rhee, S. H. (2009). Empathy in early childhood: Genetic, environmental, and affective contributions. In O. Vilarroya, S. Altran, A. Navarro, K. Ochsner, & A. Tobena (Eds.), *Values, empathy, and fairness across social barriers* (pp. 103–114). New York: New York Academy of Sciences.

Knight, B. J., & Sayegh, P. (2010). Cultural values and caregiving: The updated sociocultural stress and coping model. *Journals of Gerontology, 65B,* 5–13.

Knobloch, H., & Pasamanick, B. (Eds.). (1974). *Gesell and Amatruda's developmental diagnosis.* Hagerstown, MD: Harper & Row.

Knopf, M., Kraus, U., & Kressley-Mba, R. A. (2006). Relational information processing of novel unrelated actions by infants. *Infant Behavior and Development, 29,* 44–53.

Knowles, M. S., Swanson, R. A., & Holton, E. F. (2011). *The adult learner: The definitive classic in adult education and human resource development.* Burlington, MA: Butterworth-Heinemann.

Knudsen, E. I. (2004). Sensitive periods in the development of the brain and behavior. *Journal of Cognitive Neuroscience, 16,* 1412–1425.

Ko, E., Nelson-Becker, H., Shin, M., & Park, Y. (2014). Preferences and expectations for delivering bad news among Korean older adults. *Journal of Social Service Research, 40,* 402–414.

Ko, H.-J., Mejía, S., & Hooker, K. (2014). Social possible selves, self-regulation, and social goal progress in older adulthood. *International Journal of Behavioral Development, 38,* 219–227.

Kobayashi, T., Hiraki, K., & Hasegawa, T. (2005). Auditory-visual intermodal matching of small numerosities in 6-month-old infants. *Developmental Science, 8,* 409–419.

Kochanska, G. (1991). Socialization and temperament in the development of guilt and conscience. *Child Development, 62,* 1379–1392.

Kochanska, G., & Aksan, N. (2006). Children's conscience and self-regulation. *Journal of Personality, 74,* 1587–1617.

Kochanska, G., Aksan, N., & Carlson, J. J. (2005). Temperament, relationships, and young children's receptive cooperation with their parents. *Developmental Psychology, 41*(4), 648–660.

Kochanska, G., Aksan, N., & Nichols, K. E. (2003). Maternal power assertion in discipline and moral discourse contexts: Commonalities, differences, and implications for children's moral conduct and cognition. *Developmental Psychology, 39,* 949–963.

Kochanska, G., Aksan, N., Prisco, T. R., & Adams, E. E. (2008). Mother–child and father–child mutually responsive orientation in the first 2 years and children's outcomes at preschool age: Mechanisms of influence. *Child Development, 79,* 30–44.

Kochanska, G., Forman, D. R., Aksan, N., & Dunbar, S. B. (2005). Pathways to conscience: Early mother–child mutually responsive orientation and children's moral emotion, conduct, and cognition. *Journal of Child Psychology and Psychiatry, 46,* 19–34.

Kochanska, G., Gross, J. N., Lin, M.-H., & Nichols, K. E. (2002). Guilt in young children: Development, determinants, and relations with broader system standards. *Child Development, 73,* 461–482.

Kochanska, G., & Kim, S. (2014). A complex interplay among the parent–child relationship, effortful control, and internalized rule-compatible conduct in young children: Evidence from two studies. *Developmental Psychology, 50,* 8–21.

Kochanska, G., Kim, S., Barry, R. A., & Philibert, R. A. (2011). Children's genotypes interact with maternal responsive care in predicting children's competence: Diathesis-stress or differential susceptibility? *Development and Psychopathology, 23,* 605–616.

Kochanska, G., & Knaack, A. (2003). Effortful control as a personality characteristic of young children: Antecedents, correlates, and consequences. *Journal of Personality, 71,* 1087–1112.

Kochanska, G., Murray, K. T., & Harlan, E. T. (2000). Effortful control in early childhood: Continuity and change, antecedents, and implications for social development. *Developmental Psychology, 36,* 220–232.

Kochel, K. P., Ladd, G. W., & Rudolph, K. D. (2012). Longitudinal associations among youth depressive symptoms, peer victimization, and low peer acceptance: An interpersonal process perspective. *Child Development, 83,* 637–650.

Koen, J., & Yonelinas, A. (2013). Recollection and familiarity declines in healthy aging, aMCI, and AD. *Journal of Cognitive Neuroscience, 25*(Suppl.), 197.

Kohen, D. E., Leventhal, T., Dahinten, V. S., & McIntosh, C. N. (2008). Neighborhood disadvantage: Pathways of effects for young children. *Child Development, 79,* 156–169.

Kohlberg, L., Levine, C., & Hewer, A. (1983). *Moral stages: A current formulation and a response to critics.* Basel, Switzerland: Karger.

Kohn, M. L. (2006). *Change and stability: A crossnational analysis of social structure and personality.* Greenbrae, CA: Paradigm Press.

Kohn, M. L., Naoi, A., Schoenbach, C., Schooler, C., & Slomczynski, K. M. (1990). Position in the class structure and psychological functioning in the United States, Japan, and Poland. *American Journal of Sociology, 95,* 964–1008.

Kojima, G. (2016). Frailty as a predictor of nursing home placement among community-dwelling older adults: A systematic review and meta-analysis. *Journal of Geriatric Physical Therapy, 23,* (epub ahead of print).

Kojola, E., & Moen, P. (2016). No more lock-step retirement: Boomers' shifting meanings of work and retirement. *Journal of Aging Studies, 36,* 59–70.

Kolak, A. M., & Volling, B. L. (2011). Sibling jealousy in early childhood: Longitudinal links to sibling relationship quality. *Infant and Child Development, 20,* 213–226.

Koletzko, B., Beyer, J., Brands, B., Demmelmair, H., Grote, V., Haile, G., et al. (2013). Early influences of nutrition on postnatal growth. *Nestlé Nutrition Institute Workshop Series, 71,* 11–27.

Kollmann, M., Haeusler, M., Haas, J., Csapo, B., Lang, U., & Klaritsch, P. (2013). Procedure-related complications after genetic amniocentesis and chorionic villus sampling. *Ultraschall in der Medizen, 34,* 345–348.

Komp, D. M. (1996). The changing face of death in children. In H. M. Spiro, M. G. M. Curnen, & L. P. Wandel (Eds.), *Facing death: Where culture, religion, and medicine meet* (pp. 66–76). New Haven: Yale University Press.

Kon, A. A. (2011). Palliative sedation: It's not a panacea. *American Journal of Bioethics, 11,* 41–42

Konner, M. (2010). *The evolution of childhood: Relationships, emotion, mind.* Cambridge, MA: Harvard University Press.

Kooijman, V., Hagoort, P., & Cutler, A. (2009). Prosodic structure in early word segmentation: ERP evidence from Dutch ten-month-olds. *Infancy, 14,* 591–612.

Kopeikina, K. J., Carlson, G. A., Pitstick, R., Ludvigson, A. E., Peters, A., et al. (2011). Tau accumulation causes mitochondrial distribution deficits in neurons in a mouse model of tauopathy and in human Alzheimer's disease brain. *American Journal of Pathology 179,* 2071–2082.

Kopp, C. B., & Neufeld, S. J. (2003). Emotional development during infancy. In R. Davidson, K. R. Scherer, & H. H. Goldsmith (Eds.), *Handbook of affective sciences* (pp. 347–374). Oxford, UK: Oxford University Press.

Koppel, J., & Berntsen, D. (2014). The peaks of life: The differential temporal locations of the reminiscence bump across disparate cueing methods. *Journal of Applied Research in Memory and Cognition, 4,* 66–80.

Koppel, J., & Rubin, D. C. (2016). Recent advances in understanding the reminiscence bump: The importance of cues in guiding recall from autobiographical memory. *Current Directions in Psychological Science, 25,* 135–140.

Koren, C. (2014). Together and apart: A typology of re-partnering in old age. *International Psychogeriatrics, 26,* 1327–1350.

Koss, K. J., Hostinar, C. E., Donzella, B., & Gunnar, M. R. (2014). Social deprivation and the HPA axis in early deprivation. *Psychoneuroendocrinology, 50,* 1–13.

Kotkin, J. (2012, July 16). Are Millennials the screwed generation? *Newsweek.* Retrieved from www.thedailybeast.com/newsweek/2012/07/15/are-millennials-the-screwed-generation.html

Kotre, J. (1999). *Make it count: How to generate a legacy that gives meaning to your life.* New York: Free Press.

Kotter-Grühn, D. (2015). Changing negative views of aging: Implications for intervention and translational research. *Annual Review of Gerontology and Geriatrics, 35,* 167–186.

Kowalski, R. M., & Limber, S. P. (2013). Psychological, physical, and academic correlates of cyberbullying and traditional bullying. *Journal of Adolescent Health, 53,* S13–S20.

Kowalski, R. M., Limber, S. P., & Agatston, P. W. (2008). *Cyber bullying: Bullying in the digital age.* Malden, MA: Blackwell.

Kozbelt, A. (2016). Creativity. In S. K. Whitbourne (Ed.), *Encyclopedia of adulthood and aging* (Vol. 1, pp. 265–269). Malden, MA: Wiley Blackwell.

Kozer, E., Costei, A. M., Boskovic, R., Nulman, I., Nikfar, S., & Koren, G. (2003). Effects of aspirin consumption during pregnancy on pregnancy outcomes: Meta-analysis. *Birth Defects Research, Part B, Developmental and Reproductive Toxicology, 68,* 70–84.

Kozulin, A. (Ed.). (2003). *Vygotsky's educational theory in cultural context.* Cambridge, UK: Cambridge University Press.

Krafft, K., & Berk, L. E. (1998). Private speech in two preschools: Significance of open-ended activities and make-believe play for verbal self-regulation. *Early Childhood Research Quarterly, 13,* 637–658.

Kragstrup, T. W., Kjaer, M., & Mackey, A. L. (2011). Structural, biochemical, cellular, and functional changes in skeletal muscle extracellular matrix with aging. *Scandinavian Journal of Medicine and Science in Sports, 21,* 749–757.

Krähenbühl, S., Blades, M., & Eiser, C. (2009). The effect of repeated questioning on children's accuracy and consistency in eyewitness testimony. *Legal and Criminological Psychology, 14,* 263–278.

Krakauer, J. (2015). *Rape and the justice system in a college town.* New York: Doubleday.

Kramer, A. F., Fabiani, M., & Colcombe, S. J. (2006). Contributions of cognitive neuroscience to the understanding of behavior and aging. In J. E. Birren & K. W. Schaie (Eds.), *Handbook of the psychology of aging* (6th ed., pp. 57–83). Burlington, MA: Elsevier Academic Press.

Kramer, A. F., Hahn, S., & Gopher, D. (1998). Task coordination and aging: Explorations of executive control processes in the task switching paradigm. *Acta Psychologica, 101,* 339–378.

Kramer, A. F., & Madden, D. J. (2008). Attention. In F. I. M. Craik & T. A. Salthouse (Eds.), *Handbook of aging and cognition* (pp. 189–249). New York: Psychology Press.

Kramer, D. A. (2003). The ontogeny of wisdom in its variations. In J. Demick & C. Andreoletti (Eds.), *Handbook of adult development* (pp. 131–151). New York: Springer.

Kramer, S. E., Kapteyn, T. S., Kuik, D. J., & Deeg, D. J. (2002). The association of hearing impairment and chronic diseases with psychosocial health status in older age. *Journal of Aging and Health, 14,* 122–137.

Krampe, R. T., & Charness, N. (2007). Aging and expertise. In K. A. Ericsson, N. Charness, P. J. Feltovich, & R. R. Hoffman (Eds.), *Cambridge handbook of expertise and expert performance* (pp. 723–742). New York: Cambridge University Press.

Krause, N. (2004). Neighborhoods, health, and well-being in later life. In H.-W. Wahl, R. J. Scheidt, & P. G. Windley (Eds.), *Aging in context: Socio-physical environments* (pp. 223–249). New York: Springer.

Krause, N. (2012). Religious involvement, humility, and change in self-rated health over time. *Journal of Psychology and Theology, 40,* 199–210.

Krause, N., & Hayward, R. D. (2016). Religion, health, and aging. In L. K. George & K. F. Ferraro (Eds.), *Handbook of aging and the social sciences* (8th ed., pp. 251–270). New York: Academic Press.

Krause, N., Hayward, R. D., Bruce, D., & Woolever, C. (2013). Church involvement, spiritual growth, meaning in life, and health. *Archive for the Psychology of Religion, 35,* 169–191.

Krcmar, M., Grela, B., & Linn, K. (2007). Can toddlers learn vocabulary from television? An experimental approach. *Media Psychology, 10,* 41–63.

Krebs, D. L. (2011). *The origins of morality: An evolutionary account.* New York: Oxford University Press.

Kreider, R. M., & Ellis, R. (2011). Living arrangements of children: 2009. *Current Population Reports* (P70–126). Washington, DC: U.S. Census Bureau. Retrieved from www.census.gov/prod/2011pubs/p70-126.pdf

Kreppner, J. M., Kumsta, R., Rutter, M., Beckett, C., Castle, J., Stevens, S., et al. (2010). Developmental course of deprivation specific psychological patterns: Early manifestations, persistence to age 15, and clinical features. *Monographs of the Society for Research in Child Development, 75*(1, Serial No. 295), 79–101.

Kreppner, J. M., Rutter, M., Beckett, C., Castle, J., Colvert, E., Groothues, C., Hawkins, A., & O'Connor, T. G. (2007). Normality and impairment following profound early institutional deprivation: A longitudinal follow-up into early adolescence. *Developmental Psychology, 43,* 931–946.

Kretch, K. S., & Adolph, K. E. (2013). Cliff or step? Posture-specific learning at the edge of a drop-off. *Child Development, 84,* 226–240.

Kretch, K. S., Franchak, J. M., & Adolph, K. E. (2014). Crawling and walking infants see the world differently. *Child Development, 85,* 1503–1518.

Krettenauer, T., Colasante, T., Buchmann, M., & Malti, T. (2014). The development of moral emotions and decision-making from adolescence to early adulthood: A 6-year longitudinal study. *Journal of Youth and Adolescence, 43,* 583–596.

Kristensen, P., Weisaeth, L., & Heir, T. (2012). Bereavement and mental health after sudden and violent losses: A review. *Psychiatry, 75,* 76–97.

Kroger, J. (2012). The status of identity: Developments in identity status research. In P. K. Kerig, M. S. Schulz, & S. T. Hauser (Eds.), *Adolescence and beyond: Family processes and development* (pp. 64–83). New York: Oxford University Press.

Kroger, J., Martinussen, M., & Marcia, J. E. (2010). Identity status change during adolescence and young adulthood: A meta-analysis. *Journal of Adolescence, 33,* 683–698.

Kropf, N. P., & Pugh, K. L. (1995). Beyond life expectancy: Social work with centenarians. *Journal of Gerontological Social Work, 23,* 121–137.

Krueger, R. F., & Johnson, W. (2008). Behavior genetics and personality. In L. Q. Pervin, O. P. John, & R. W. Robins (Eds.), *Handbook of personality: Theory and research* (3rd ed., pp. 287–310). New York: Guilford.

Krumhansl, C. L., & Jusczyk, P. W. (1990). Infants' perception of phrase structure in music. *Psychological Science, 1,* 70–73.

Kubicek, B., Korunka, C., Raymo, J. M., & Hoonakker, P. (2011). Psychological well-being in retirement: The effects of personal and gendered contextual resources. *Journal of Occupational Health Psychology, 16,* 230–246.

Kübler-Ross, E. (1969). *On death and dying.* New York: Macmillan.

Kubotera, T. (2004). Japanese religion in changing society: The spirits of the dead. In J. D. Morgan & P. Laungani (Eds.), *Death and bereavement around the world: Vol. 4. Asia, Australia, and New Zealand* (pp. 95–99). Amityville, NY: Baywood Publishing Company.

Kubzansky, L. D., & Boehm, J. K. (2016). Positive psychological functioning: An enduring asset for healthy aging. In A. D. Ong & C. E. Löckenhoff (Eds.), *Emotion, aging, and health* (pp. 163–183). Washington, DC: American Psychological Association.

Kuczynski, L. (1984). Socialization goals and mother–child interaction: Strategies for long-term and short-term compliance. *Developmental Psychology, 20*, 1061–1073.

Kuczynski, L., & Lollis, S. (2002). Four foundations for a dynamic model of parenting. In J. R. M. Gerris (Ed.), *Dynamics of parenting*. Hillsdale, NJ: Erlbaum.

Kuh, G. D., Cruce, T. M., & Shoup, R. (2008). Unmasking the effects of student engagement on first-year college grades and persistence. *Journal of Higher Education, 79*, 540–553.

Kuhl, P. K., Ramirez, R. R., Bosseler, A., Lin, J. L., & Imada, T. (2014). Infants' brain responses to speech suggest analysis by synthesis. *Proceedings of the National Academy of Sciences, 111*, 11238–11245.

Kuhl, P. K., Tsao, F.-M., & Liu, H.-M. (2003). Foreign language experience in infancy: Effects of short-term exposure and social interaction on phonetic learning. *Proceedings of the National Academy of Sciences, 100*, 9096–9101.

Kuhn, D. (2000). Theory of mind, metacognition, and reasoning: A life-span perspective. In P. Mitchell & K. J. Riggs (Eds.), *Children's reasoning and the mind* (pp. 301–326). Hove, UK: Psychology Press.

Kuhn, D. (2002). What is scientific thinking, and how does it develop? In U. Goswami (Ed.), *Blackwell handbook of childhood cognitive development* (pp. 371–393). Malden, MA: Blackwell.

Kuhn, D. (2009). Adolescent thinking. In R. M. Lerner & L. Steinberg (Eds.), *Handbook of adolescent psychology: Vol. 1. Individual bases of adolescent development* (3rd ed., pp. 152–186). Hoboken, NJ: Wiley.

Kuhn, D. (2011). What is scientific reasoning and how does it develop? In U. Goswami (Ed.), *Wiley-Blackwell handbook of childhood cognitive development* (2nd ed., pp. 497–523). Hoboken, NJ: Wiley-Blackwell.

Kuhn, D. (2013). Reasoning. In P. D. Zelazo (Ed.), *Oxford handbook of developmental psychology: Vol. 1. Body and mind* (pp. 744–764). New York: Oxford University Press.

Kuhn, D., Amsel, E., & O'Loughlin, M. (1988). *The development of scientific thinking skills*. Orlando, FL: Academic Press.

Kuhn, D., & Dean, D. (2004). Connecting scientific reasoning and causal inference. *Journal of Cognition and Development, 5*, 261–288.

Kuhn, D., & Franklin, S. (2006). The second decade: What develops (and how)? In D. Kuhn & R. S. Siegler (Eds.), *Handbook of child psychology: Vol. 2. Cognition, perception, and language* (6th ed.). Hoboken, NJ: Wiley.

Kuhn, D., Iordanou, K., Pease, M., & Wirkala, C. (2008). Beyond control of variables: What needs to develop to achieve skilled scientific thinking? *Cognitive Development, 23*, 435–451.

Kulkarni, A. D., Jamieson, D. J., Jones, H. W., Jr., Kissin, D. M., Gallo, M. F., Macaluso, M., et al. (2013). Fertility treatments and multiple births in the United States. *New England Journal of Medicine, 369*, 2218–2225.

Kumaido, K., Sugiyama, S., & Tsutsumi, H. (2015). Brain death and organ donation. In H. Uchino, K. Ushijima, & Y. Ikeda (Eds.), *Neuroanesthesia and cerebrospinal protection* (pp. 701–707). Tokyo: Springer Japan.

Kumar, M., Chandra, S., Ijaz, Z., & Senthilselvan, A. (2014). Epidural analgesia in labour and neonatal respiratory distress: A case-control study. *Archives of Disease in Childhood—Fetal and Neonatal Edition, 99*, F116–F119.

Kunnen, E. S., Sappa, V., van Gert, P. L. C., & Bonica, L. (2008). The shapes of commitment development in emerging adulthood. *Journal of Adult Development, 15*, 113–131.

Kunzmann, U. (2016). Wisdom, Berlin model. In S. K. Whitbourne (Ed.), *Encyclopedia of adulthood and aging* (Vol. 2, pp. 1437–1441). Malden, MA: Wiley Blackwell.

Kuperberg, A. (2014). Age at coresidence, premarital cohabitation, and marriage dissolution: 1985–2009. *Journal of Marriage and Family, 76*, 352–369.

Kuppens, S., Laurent, L., Heyvaert, M., & Onghena, P. (2013). Associations between parental control and relational aggression in children and adolescents: A multilevel and sequential meta-analysis. *Developmental Psychology, 49*, 1697–1712.

Kurdek, L. A. (2004). Gay men and lesbians: The family context. In M. Coleman & L. H. Ganong (Eds.), *Handbook of contemporary families: Considering the past, contemplating the future* (pp. 96–115). Thousand Oaks, CA: Sage.

Kurganskaya, M. E. (2011). Manual asymmetry in children is related to parameters of early development and familial sinistrality. *Human Physiology, 37*, 654–657.

Kurtz-Costes, B., Copping, K. E., Rowley, S. J., & Kinlaw, C. R. (2014). Gender and age differences in awareness and endorsement of gender stereotypes. *European Journal of Psychology and Education, 29*, 603–618.

Kurtz-Costes, B., Rowley, S. J., Harris-Britt, A., & Woods, T. A. (2008). Gender stereotypes about mathematics and science and self-perceptions of ability in late childhood and early adolescence. *Merrill-Palmer Quarterly, 54*, 386–409.

Kushner, R. F. (2012). Clinical assessment and management of adult obesity. *Circulation, 126*, 2870–2877.

Kyratzis, A., & Guo, J. (2001). Preschool girls' and boys' verbal conflict strategies in the United States and China. *Research on Language and Social Interaction, 34*, 45–74.

L

Labouvie-Vief, G. (1980). Beyond formal operations: Uses and limits of pure logic in life-span development. *Human Development, 23*, 141–160.

Labouvie-Vief, G. (1985). Logic and self-regulation from youth to maturity: A model. In M. Commons, F. Richards, & C. Armon (Eds.), *Beyond formal operations: Late adolescent and adult cognitive development* (pp. 158–180). New York: Praeger.

Labouvie-Vief, G. (2003). Dynamic integration: Affect, cognition, and the self in adulthood. *Current Directions in Psychological Science, 12*, 201–206.

Labouvie-Vief, G. (2005). Self-with-other representations and the organization of the self. *Journal of Research in Personality, 39*, 185–205.

Labouvie-Vief, G. (2006). Emerging structures of adult thought. In J. J. Arnett & J. L. Tanner (Eds.), *Emerging adults in America: Coming of age in the 21st century* (pp. 59–84). Washington, DC: American Psychological Association.

Labouvie-Vief, G. (2008). When differentiation and negative affect lead to integration and growth. *American Psychologist, 63*, 564–565.

Labouvie-Vief, G. (2015). *Integrating emotions and cognition throughout the lifespan*. Cham, Switzerland: Springer.

Labouvie-Vief, G., Diehl, M., Jain, E., & Zhang, F. (2007). Six-year change in affect optimization and affect complexity across the adult life span: A further examination. *Psychology and Aging, 22*, 738–751.

Labouvie-Vief, G., Grühn, S., & Studer, J. (2010). Dynamic integration of emotion and cognition: Equilibrium regulation in development and aging. In W. Overton & R. M. Lerner (Eds.), *Handbook of life-span development: Vol. 2. Social and emotional development* (pp. 79–115). Hoboken, NJ: Wiley.

Lachance, J. A., & Mazzocco, M. M. M. (2006). A longitudinal analysis of sex differences in math and spatial skills in primary school age children. *Learning and Individual Differences, 16*, 195–216.

Lachman, M. E. (2004). Development in midlife. *Annual Review of Psychology, 55*, 305–331.

Lachman, M. E., & Bertrand, R. M. (2002). Personality and self in midlife. In M. E. Lachman (Ed.), *Handbook of midlife development* (pp. 279–309). New York: Wiley.

Lachman, M. E., Neupert, S. D., & Agrigoroaei, S. (2011). The relevance of control beliefs for health and aging. In K. W. Schaie & S. L. Willis (Eds.), *Handbook of the psychology of aging* (7th ed., pp. 175–190). San Diego, CA: Elsevier.

Lachs, M., Bachman, R., Williams, C. S., Kossack, A., Bove, C., & O'Leary, J. (2006). Violent crime victimization increases the risk of nursing home placement in older adults. *Gerontologist, 46*, 583–589.

Ladd, G. W. (2005). *Children's peer relationships and social competence: A century of progress*. New Haven, CT: Yale University Press.

Ladd, G. W., Birch, S. H., & Buhs, E. S. (1999). Children's social and scholastic lives in kindergarten: Related spheres of influence? *Child Development, 70*, 1373–1400.

Ladd, G. W., Buhs, E. S., & Seid, M. (2000). Children's initial sentiments about kindergarten: Is school liking an antecedent of early classroom participation and achievement? *Merrill-Palmer Quarterly, 46*, 255–279.

Ladd, G. W., & Burgess, K. B. (1999). Charting the relationship trajectories of aggressive, withdrawn, and aggressive/withdrawn children during early grade school. *Child Development, 70*, 910–929.

Ladd, G. W., Kochenderfer-Ladd, B., Eggum, N. D., Kochel, K. P., & McConnell, E. M. (2011). Characterizing and comparing the friendships of anxious-solitary and unsociable preadolescents. *Child Development, 82*, 1434–1453.

Ladd, G. W., LeSieur, K., & Profilet, S. M. (1993). Direct parental influences on young children's peer relations. In S. Duck (Ed.), *Learning about relationships* (Vol. 2, pp. 152–183). London: Sage.

LaFreniere, L., & Cain, A. (2015). Parentally bereaved children and adolescents: The question of peer support. *OMEGA, 71*, 245–271.

Lagattuta, K. H., Sayfan, L., & Blattman, A. J. (2010). Forgetting common ground: Six- to seven-year-olds have an overinterpretive theory of mind. *Developmental Psychology, 46*, 1417–1432.

Lagattuta, K. H., & Thompson, R. A. (2007). The development of self-conscious emotions: Cognitive processes and social influences. In J. L. Tracy, R. W. Robins, & J. P. Tangney (Eds.), *The self-conscious emotions: Theory and research* (pp. 91–113). New York: Guilford.

Laible, D. (2007). Attachment with parents and peers in late adolescence: Links with emotional competence and social behavior. *Personality and Individual Differences, 43*, 1185–1197.

Laible, D. (2011). Does it matter if preschool children and mothers discuss positive vs. negative events during reminiscing? Links with mother-reported attachment, family emotional climate, and socioemotional development. *Social Development, 20*, 394–411.

Laible, D., & Song, J. (2006). Constructing emotional and relational understanding: The role of affect and mother–child discourse. *Merrill-Palmer Quarterly, 52*, 44–69.

Laible, D., & Thompson, R. A. (2002). Mother–child conflict in the toddler years: Lessons in emotion, morality, and relationships. *Child Development, 73*, 1187–1203.

Laird, R. D., Pettit, G. S., Dodge, K. A., & Bates, J. E. (2005). Peer relationship antecedents of delinquent behavior in late adolescence: Is there evidence of demographic group differences in developmental processes? *Development and Psychopathology, 17*, 127–144.

Lakshman, R., Elks, C. E., & Ong, K. K. (2012). Childhood obesity. *Circulation, 126*, 1770–1779.

Lalonde, C. E., & Chandler, M. J. (2002). Children's understanding of interpretation. *New Ideas in Psychology, 20*, 163–198.

Lalonde, C. E., & Chandler, M. J. (2005). Culture, selves, and time: Theories of personal persistence in native and non-native youth. In C. Lightfoot, C. Lalonde,

& M. Chandler (Eds.), *Changing conceptions of psychological life* (pp. 207–229). Mahwah, NJ: Erlbaum.

Lam, C. B., McHale, S. M., & Crouter, A. C. (2012). Parent–child shared time from middle childhood to late adolescence: Developmental course and adjustment correlates. *Child Development, 83,* 2089–2103.

Lam, C. B., Solmeyer, A. R., & McHale, S. M. (2012). Sibling relationships and empathy across the transition to adolescence. *Journal of Youth and Adolescence, 41,* 1657–1670.

Lam, H. S., Kwok, K. M., Chan, P. H., So, H. K., Li, A. M., Ng, P. C., et al. (2013). Long term neurocognitive impact of low dose prenatal methylmercury exposure in Hong Kong. *Environment International, 54,* 59–64.

Lam, J. (2015). Picky eating in children. *Frontiers in Pediatrics, 3:* 41.

Lamaze, F. (1958). *Painless childbirth.* London: Burke.

Lamb, M. E. (2012). Mothers, fathers, families, and circumstances: Factors affecting children's adjustment. *Applied Developmental Science, 16,* 98–111.

Lamb, M. E., & Lewis, C. (2013). Father–child relationships. In N. J. Cabrera & C. S. Tamis-LeMonda (Eds.), *Handbook of father involvement* (2nd ed., pp. 119–134). New York: Routledge.

Lamb, M. E., Thompson, R. A., Gardner, W., Charnov, E. L., & Connell, J. P. (1985). Infant–mother attachment: The origins and developmental significance of individual differences in the Strange Situation: Its study and biological interpretation. *Behavioral and Brain Sciences, 7,* 127–147.

Lambda, N., & Anderson-Nelson, S. (2014). Medication induced retinal side effects. *Disease-a-Month, 60,* 263–267.

Lamberg, L. (2007). Menopause not always to blame for sleep problems in midlife women. *JAMA, 297,* 1865–1866.

Lamers, S. M. A., Bohlmeijer, E. T., Korte, J., & Westerhof, G. J. (2015). The efficacy of life-review as online-guided self-help for adults: A randomized trial. *Journals of Gerontology, 70B,* 24–34.

Lamkaddem, M., van der Straten, A., Essink-Bot, M. L., van Eijsden, M., & Vrijkotte, T. (2014). Etnische verschillen in het gebruik van kraamzorg [Ethnic differences in uptake of professional maternity care assistance]. *Nederlands Tijdschrift voor Geneeskunde, 158*(A7718).

Lamminmaki, A., Hines, M., Kuiri-Hanninen, T., Kilpelainen, L., Dunkel, L., & Sankilampi, U. (2012). Testosterone measured in infancy predicts subsequent sex-typed behavior in boys and girls. *Hormones and Behavior, 61,* 611–616.

Lampl, M. (1993). Evidence of saltatory growth in infancy. *American Journal of Human Biology, 5,* 641–652.

Lampl, M., & Johnson, M. L. (2011). Infant growth in length follows prolonged sleep and increased naps. *Sleep, 34,* 641–650.

Lancy, D. F. (2008). *The anthropology of childhood.* Cambridge, UK: Cambridge University Press.

Lane, J. D., Wellman, H. N., Olson, S. L., Labounty, J., & Kerr, D. C. R. (2010). Theory of mind and emotion understanding predict moral development in early childhood. *British Journal of Developmental Psychology, 28,* 871–889.

Lang, A., Gottlieb, L. N., & Amsel, R. (1996). Predictors of husbands' and wives' grief reactions following infant death: The role of marital intimacy. *Death Studies, 20,* 33–57.

Lang, F. (2016). Control beliefs across adulthood. In K. S. Whitbourne Ed.), *Encyclopedia of adulthood and aging* (Vol. 1, pp. 252–256). Malden, MA: Blackwell.

Lang, F. R., & Baltes, M. M. (1997). Being with people and being alone in later life: Costs and benefits for everyday functioning. *International Journal of Behavioral Development, 21,* 729–749.

Lang, F. R., Rohr, M. K., & Williger, B. (2011). Modeling success in life-span psychology: The principles of selection, optimization, and compensation. In L. Fingerman, C. A. Berg, J. Smith, & T. C. Antonucci (Eds.), *Handbook of life-span development* (pp. 57–85). New York: Springer.

Lang, I. A., Llewellyn, D. J., Langa, K. M., Wallace, R. B., Huppert, F. A., & Melzer, D. (2008). Neighborhood deprivation, individual socioeconomic status, and cognitive function in older people: Analyses from the English Longitudinal Study of Ageing. *Journal of the American Geriatric Society, 56,* 191–198.

Lang, M. (2010). Can mentoring assist in the school-to-work transition? *Education + Training, 52,* 359–367.

Langer, G. (2004). *ABC New Prime Time Live Poll: The American Sex Survey.* Retrieved from abcnews.go.com/Primetime/News/story?id=174461&page=1

Langer, J., Gillette, P., & Arriaga, R. I. (2003). Toddlers' cognition of adding and subtracting objects in action and in perception. *Cognitive Development, 18,* 233–246.

Långström, N., Rahman, Q., Carlström, E., & Lichtenstein, P. (2010). Genetic and environmental effects on same-sex sexual behavior: A population study of twins in Sweden. *Archives of Sexual Behavior, 39,* 75–80.

Lansford, J. E. (2009). Parental divorce and children's adjustment. *Perspectives on Psychological Science, 4,* 140–152.

Lansford, J. E., Criss, M. M., Dodge, K. A., Shaw, D. S., Pettit, G. S., & Bates, J. E. (2009). Trajectories of physical discipline: Early childhood antecedents and developmental outcomes. *Child Development, 80,* 1385–1402.

Lansford, J. E., Criss, M. M., Laird, R. D., Shaw, D. S., Pettit, G. S., Bates, J. E., & Dodge, K. A. (2011). Reciprocal relations between parents' physical discipline and children's externalizing behavior during middle childhood and adolescence. *Development and Psychopathology, 23,* 225–238.

Lansford, J. E., Criss, M. M., Pettit, G. S., Dodge, K. A., & Bates, J. E. (2003). Friendship quality, peer group affiliation, and peer antisocial behavior as moderators of the link between negative parenting and adolescent externalizing behavior. *Journal of Research on Adolescence, 13,* 161–184.

Lansford, J. E., Laird, R. D., Pettit, G. S., Bates, J. E., & Dodge, K. A. (2014). Mothers' and fathers' autonomy-relevant parenting: Longitudinal links with adolescents' externalizing and internalizing behavior. *Journal of Youth and Adolescence, 43,* 1877–1889.

Lansford, J. E., Malone, P. S., Castellino, D. R., Dodge, K. A., Pettit, G., & Bates, J. E. (2006). Trajectories of internalizing, externalizing, and grades for children who have and have not experienced their parents' divorce or separation. *Journal of Family Psychology, 20,* 292–301.

Lansford, J. E., Wagner, L. B., Bates, J. E., Dodge, K. A., & Pettit, G. S. (2012). Parental reasoning, denying privileges, yelling, and spanking: Ethnic differences and associations with child externalizing behavior. *Parenting: Science and Practice, 12,* 42–56.

Laranjo, J., Bernier, A., Meins, E., & Carlson, S. M. (2010). Early manifestations of children's theory of mind: The roles of maternal mind-mindedness and infant security of attachment. *Infancy, 15,* 300–323.

Larsen, J. A., & Nippold, M. A. (2007). Morphological analysis in school-age children: Dynamic assessment of a word learning strategy. *Language, Speech, and Hearing Services in Schools, 38,* 201–212.

Larsen, P. (2009, January). A review of cardiovascular changes in the older adult. *Gerontology Update, December 2008/January 2009, 3,* 9.

Larson, R. W. (2001). How U.S. children and adolescents spend time: What it does (and doesn't) tell us about their development. *Current Directions in Psychological Science, 10,* 160–164.

Larson, R. W., & Ham, M. (1993). Stress and "storm and stress" in early adolescence: The relationship of negative events with dysphoric affect. *Developmental Psychology, 29,* 130–140.

Larson, R. W., & Lampman-Petraitis, C. (1989). Daily emotional states as reported by children and adolescents. *Child Development, 60,* 1250–1260.

Larson, R. W., Moneta, G., Richards, M. H., & Wilson, S. (2002). Continuity, stability, and change in daily emotional experience across adolescence. *Child Development, 73,* 1151–1165.

Larson, R. W., & Richards, M. (1998). Waiting for the weekend: Friday and Saturday night as the emotional climax of the week. In A. C. Crouter & R. Larson (Eds.), *Temporal rhythms in adolescence: Clocks, calendars, and the coordination of daily life* (pp. 37–51). San Francisco: Jossey-Bass.

Larson, R. W., Richards, M. H., Sims, B., & Dworkin, J. (2001). How urban African-American young adolescents spend their time: Time budgets for locations, activities, and companionship. *American Journal of Community Psychology, 29,* 565–597.

Larsson, M., Öberg, C., & Bäckman, L. (2005). Odor identification in old age: Demographic, sensory and cognitive correlates. *Aging, Neuropsychology, and Cognition, 12,* 231–244.

Larzelere, R. E., Cox, R. B., Jr., & Mandara, J. (2013). Responding to misbehavior in young children: How authoritative parents enhance reasoning with firm control. In R. E. Larzelere, A. S. Morris, & A. W. Harrist (Eds.), *Authoritative parenting: Synthesizing nurturance and discipline for optimal child development* (pp. 89–111). Washington, DC: American Psychological Association.

Larzelere, R. E., Schneider, W. N., Larson, D. B., & Pike, P. L. (1996). The effects of discipline responses in delaying toddler misbehavior recurrences. *Child and Family Behavior Therapy, 18,* 35–57.

Lashley, F. R. (2007). *Essentials of clinical genetics in nursing practice.* New York: Springer.

Latorre, J. M., Serrano, J. P., Ricarte, J., Bonete, B., Ros, L., & Sitges, E. (2015). Life review based on remembering specific positive events in active aging. *Journal of Aging and Health, 27,* 140–157.

Lau, Y. L., Cameron, C. A., Chieh, K. M., O'Leary, J., Fu, G., & Lee, K. (2012). Cultural differences in moral justifications enhance understanding of Chinese and Canadian children's moral decisions. *Journal of Cross-Cultural Psychology, 44,* 461–477.

Lauer, P. A., Akiba, M., Wilkerson, S. B., Apthorp, H. S., Snow, D., & Martin-Glenn, M. (2006). Out-of-school time programs: A meta-analysis of effects for at-risk students. *Review of Educational Research, 76,* 275–313.

Laughlin, L. (2013). *Who's minding the kids? Child care arrangements: Spring 2011. Current Population Reports* (P70–135). Washington, DC: U.S. Census Bureau.

Laumann, E. O., Gagnon, J. H., Michael, R. T., & Michaels, S. (1994). *The social organization of sexuality.* Chicago: University of Chicago Press.

Laurent, H., Kim, H., & Capaldi, D. (2008). Prospective effects of interparental conflict on child attachment security and the moderating role of parents' romantic attachment. *Journal of Family Psychology, 22,* 377–388.

Laureys, S., & Boly, M. (2007). What is it like to be vegetative or minimally conscious? *Current Opinion in Neurology, 20,* 609–613.

Lauricella, A. R., Gola, A. A. H., & Calvert, S. L. (2011). Toddlers' learning from socially meaningful video characters. *Media Psychology, 14,* 216–232.

Lautenschlager, N. T., Cox, K. L., Flicker, L., Foster, J. K., van Bockxmeer, F. M., Xiao, J., Greenop, K. R., & Almeida, O. P. (2008). Effect of physical activity on cognitive function in older adults at risk for Alzheimer disease: A randomized trial. *JAMA, 300,* 1027–1037.

Lavelli, M., & Fogel, A. (2005). Developmental changes in the relationship between the infant's attention and emotion during early face-to-face communication: The 2-month transition. *Developmental Psychology, 41,* 265–280.

Lavner, J. A., & Bradbury, T. N. (2012). Why do even satisfied newlyweds eventually go on to divorce? *Journal of Family Psychology, 26,* 1–10.

Lavner, J. A., Karney, B. R., & Bradbury, T. N. (2013). Relationship problems over the early years of marriage: Stability or change? *Journal of Family Psychology, 28,* 979–985.

Law, E. C., Sideridis, G. D., Prock, L. A., & Sheridan, M. A. (2014). Attention-deficit/hyperactivity disorder in young children: Predictors of diagnostic stability. *Pediatrics, 133,* 659–667.

Law, K. L., Stroud, L. R., Niaura, R., LaGasse, L. L., Giu, J., & Lester, B. M. (2003). Smoking during pregnancy and newborn neurobehavior. *Pediatrics, 111,* 1318–1323.

Lawn, J. E., Blencowe, H., Oza, S., You, D., Lee, A. C., Waiswa, P., et al. (2014). Every newborn: Progress, priorities, and potential beyond survival. *Lancet, 12,* 189–205.

Lawrence, A. R., & Schigelone, A. R. S. (2002). Reciprocity beyond dyadic relationships: Aging-related communal coping. *Research on Aging, 24,* 684–704.

Lawrence, E., Rothman, A. D., Cobb, R. J., & Rothman, M. T. (2008). Marital satisfaction across the transition to parenthood. *Journal of Family Psychology, 22,* 41–50.

Lawson, J. F., James, C., Jannson, A.-U. C., Koyama, N. F., & Hill, R. A. (2014). A comparison of heterosexual and homosexual mating preferences in personal advertisements. *Evolution and Human Behavior, 35,* 408–414.

Lazar, A., & Torney-Purta, J. (1991). The development of the subconcepts of death in young children: A short-term longitudinal study. *Child Development, 62,* 1321–1333.

Lazar, I., & Darlington, R. (1982). Lasting effects of early education: A report from the Consortium for Longitudinal Studies. *Monographs of the Society for Research in Child Development, 47*(2–3, Serial No. 195).

Lazarus, R. S., & Lazarus, B. N. (1994). *Passion and reason.* New York: Oxford University Press.

Lazinski, M. J., Shea, A. K., & Steiner, M. (2008). Effects of maternal prenatal stress on offspring development: A commentary. *Archives of Women's Mental Health, 11,* 363–375.

Leaper, C. (1994). Exploring the correlates and consequences of gender segregation: Social relationships in childhood, adolescence, and adulthood. In C. Leaper (Ed.), *New directions for child development* (No. 65, pp. 67–86). San Francisco: Jossey-Bass.

Leaper, C. (2000). Gender, affiliation, assertion, and the interactive context of parent–child play. *Developmental Psychology, 36,* 381–393.

Leaper, C. (2013). Gender development during childhood. In P. D. Zelazo (Ed.), *Oxford handbook of developmental psychology: Vol. 2. Self and other* (pp. 326–377). New York: Oxford University Press.

Leaper, C., Anderson, K. J., & Sanders, P. (1998). Moderators of gender effects on parents' talk to their children: A meta-analysis. *Developmental Psychology, 34,* 3–27.

Leaper, C., & Friedman, C. K. (2007). The socialization of gender. In J. E. Grusec & P. D. Hastings (Eds.), *Handbook of socialization: Theory and research* (pp. 561–587). New York: Guilford.

Leaper, C., Tenenbaum, H. R., & Shaffer, T. G. (1999). Communication patterns of African-American girls and boys from low-income, urban backgrounds. *Child Development, 70,* 1489–1503.

Leavell, A. S., Tamis-LeMonda, C. S., Ruble, D. N., Zosuls, K. M, & Cabrera, N. J. (2011). African American, White, and Latino fathers' activities with their sons and daughters in early childhood. *Sex Roles, 66,* 53–65.

Lebel, C., & Beaulieu, C. (2011). Longitudinal development of human brain wiring continues from childhood into adulthood. *Journal of Neuroscience, 31,* 10937–10947.

Lecanuet, J.-P., Granier-Deferre, C., Jacquet, A.-Y., Capponi, I., & Ledru, L. (1993). Prenatal discrimination of a male and female voice uttering the same sentence. *Early Development and Parenting, 2,* 217–228.

LeCroy, C. W., & Krysik, J. (2011). Randomized trial of the Healthy Families Arizona home visiting program. *Children and Youth Services Review, 33,* 1761–1766.

LeCuyer, E., & Houck, G. M. (2006). Maternal limit-setting in toddlerhood: Socialization strategies for the development of self-regulation. *Infant Mental Health Journal, 27,* 344–370.

LeCuyer, E. A., Christensen, J. J., Kearney, M. H., & Kitzman, H. J. (2011). African American mothers' self-described discipline strategies with young children. *Issues in Comprehensive Pediatric Nursing, 34,* 144–162.

Lee, C.-Y. S., & Doherty, W. J. (2007). Marital satisfaction and father involvement during the transition to parenthood. *Fathering, 5,* 75–96.

Lee, E. E., & Farran, C. J. (2004). Depression among Korean, Korean American, and Caucasian American family caregivers. *Journal of Transcultural Nursing, 15,* 18–25.

Lee, E. H., Zhou, Q., Eisenberg, N., & Wang, Y. (2012). Bidirectional relations between temperament and parenting styles in Chinese children. *International Journal of Behavioral Development, 37,* 57–67.

Lee, G. Y., & Kisilevsky, B. S. (2013). Fetuses respond to father's voice but prefer mother's voice after birth. *Developmental Psychobiology, 56,* 1–11.

Lee, H. Y., & Hans, S. L. (2015). Prenatal depression and young low-income mothers' perception of their children from pregnancy through early childhood. *Infant Behavior and Development, 40,* 183–192.

Lee, K., Xu, F., Fu, G., Cameron, C. A., & Chen, S. (2001). Taiwan and Mainland Chinese and Canadian children's categorization and evaluation of lie and truth-telling: A modesty effect. *British Journal of Developmental Psychology, 19,* 525–542.

Lee, S. J., Ralston, H. J., Partridge, J. C., & Rosen, M. A. (2005). Fetal pain: A systematic multidisciplinary review of the evidence. *JAMA, 294,* 947–954.

Lee, S. J., Taylor, C. A., Altschul, I., & Rice, J. C. (2013). Parental spanking and subsequent risk for child aggression in father-involved families of young children. *Children and Youth Services Review, 35,* 1476–1485.

Lee, S. L., Morrow-Howell, N., Jonson-Reid, M., & McCrary, S. (2012). The effect of the Experience Corps® program on student reading outcomes. *Education and Urban Society, 44,* 97–118.

Lee, V. E., & Burkam, D. T. (2002). *Inequality at the starting gate.* Washington, DC: Economic Policy Institute.

Lee, Y. (2013). Adolescent motherhood and capital: Interaction effects of race/ethnicity on harsh parenting. *Journal of Community Psychology, 41,* 102–116.

Leerkes, E. M. (2010). Predictors of maternal sensitivity to infant distress. *Parenting: Science and Practice, 10,* 219–239.

Lefkovics, E., Baji, I., & Rigó, J. (2014). Impact of maternal depression on pregnancies and on early attachment. *Infant Mental Health Journal, 35,* 354–365.

Lefkowitz, E. S., & Gillen, M. M. (2006). "Sex is just a normal part of life": Sexuality in emerging adulthood. In J. J. Arnett & J. L. Tanner (Eds.), *Emerging adults in America* (pp. 235–256). Washington, DC: American Psychological Association.

Lefkowitz, E. S., Vukman, S. N., & Loken, E. (2012). Young adults in a wireless world. In A. Booth, S. L. Brown, N. S. Landale, W. D. Manning, & S. M. McHale (Eds.), *Early adulthood in a family context* (pp. 45–57). New York: Springer.

Legge, G. E., Madison, C., Vaughn, B. N., Cheong, A. M. Y., and Miller, J. C. (2008). Retention of high tactile acuity throughout the life span in blindness. *Perception and Psychophysics, 70,* 1471–1488.

Lehman, D. R., & Nisbett, R. E. (1990). A longitudinal study of the effects of undergraduate training on reasoning. *Developmental Psychology, 26,* 952–960.

Lehman, M., & Hasselhorn, M. (2012). Rehearsal dynamics in elementary school children. *Journal of Experimental Child Psychology, 111,* 552–560.

Lehnung, M., Leplow, B., Ekroll, V., Herzog, A., Mehdorn, M., & Ferstl, R. (2003). The role of locomotion in the acquisition and transfer of spatial knowledge in children. *Scandinavian Journal of Psychology, 44,* 79–86.

Lehr, V. T., Zeskind, P. S., Ofenstein, J. P., Cepeda, E., Warrier, I., & Aranda, J. V. (2007). Neonatal facial coding system scores and spectral characteristics of infant crying during newborn circumcision. *Clinical Journal of Pain, 23,* 417–424.

Lehrer, E. L., & Chen, Y. (2011). *Women's age at first marriage and marital instability: Evidence from the 2006–2008 National Survey of Family Growth.* Discussion Paper No. 5954. Chicago: University of Illinois at Chicago.

Lehrer, J. A., Pantell, R., Tebb, K., & Shafer, M. A. (2007). Forgone health care among U.S. adolescents: Associations between risk characteristics and confidentiality. *Journal of Adolescent Health, 40,* 218–226.

Lehrer, R., & Schauble, L. (2015). The development of scientific thinking. In L. S. Liben & U. Müller (Eds.), *Handbook of child psychology: Vol. 2. Cognitive processes* (7th ed., pp. 671–714). Hoboken, NJ: Wiley.

Leibowitz, S., & de Vries, A. L. C. (2016). Gender dysphoria in adolescence. *International Review of Psychiatry, 28,* 21–35.

Lejeune, F., Marcus, L., Berne-Audeoud, F., Streri, A., Debillon, T., & Gentaz, E. (2012). Intermanual transfer of shapes in preterm human infants from 33 to 34 + 6 weeks postconceptional age. *Child Development, 83,* 794–800.

Lemaitre, H., Goldman, A. L., Sambataro, F., Verchinski, B. A., Meyer-Lindenberg, A., & Mattay, V. S. (2012). Normal age-related brain morphometric changes: Nonuniformity across cortical thickness, surface area and gray matter volume? *Neurobiology of Aging, 33,* 617.

Leman, P. J. (2005). Authority and moral reasons: Parenting style and children's perceptions of adult rule justifications. *International Journal of Behavioral Development, 29,* 265–270.

Lemaster, P., Delaney, R., & Strough, J. (2015). Crossover, degendering, or … ? A multidimensional approach to life-span gender development. *Sex Roles,* 1–13. Retrieved from link.springer.com/article/10.1007%2Fs11199-015-0563-0

Lemay, M. (2015, February 26). *A letter to my son Jacob on his 5th birthday.* Retrieved from www.boston.com/life/moms/2015/02/26/letter-son-jacob-his-birthday/a2Jynr9Jhc3W8VQ9lVFx8N/story.html

Lemche, E., Lennertz, I., Orthmann, C., Ari, A., Grote, K., Hafker, J., & Klann-Delius, G. (2003). Emotion-regulatory process in evoked play narratives: Their relation with mental representations and family interactions. *Praxis der Kinderpsychologie und Kinderpsychiatrie, 52,* 156–171.

Lemish, D., & Muhlbauer, V. (2012). "Can't have it all": Representations of older women in popular culture. *Women & Therapy, 35,* 165–180.

Lemola, S. (2015). Long-term outcomes of very preterm birth: Mechanisms and interventions. *European Psychologist, 20,* 128–137.

Lenhart, A., Ling, R., Campbell, S., & Purcell, K. (2010). *Teens and mobile phones*. Washington, DC: Pew Internet & American Life Project.

Lenhart, A., & Page, D. (2015). *Teens, social media & technology overview 2015*. Washington, DC: Pew Research Center. Retrieved from www.pewinternet.org/files/2015/04/PI_TeensandTech_Update2015_0409151.pdf

Lenhart, A., Smith, A., Anderson, M., Duggan, M., & Perrin, A. (2015). *Teens, technology & friendships*. Washington, DC: Pew Research Center. Retrieved from www.pewinternet.org/files/2015/08/Teens-and-Friendships-FINAL2.pdf

Lenroot, R. K., & Giedd, J. N. (2006). Brain development in children and adolescents: Insights from anatomical magnetic resonance imaging. *Neuroscience and Biobehavioral Reviews, 30*, 718–729.

Lenzi, M., Vieno, A., Perkins, D. D., Santinello, M., Elgar, F. J., Morgan, A., et al. (2012). Family affluence, school and neighborhood contexts and adolescents' civic engagement: A cross-national study. *American Journal of Community Psychology, 50*, 197–210.

Leonesio, M. V., Bridges, B., Gesumaria, R., & Del Bene, L. (2012). The increasing labor force participation of older workers and its effect on the income of the aged. *Social Security Bulletin, 72*(1). Retrieved from www.ssa.gov/policy/docs/ssb/v72n1/v72n1p59.html

Leopold, T., & Skopek, J. (2015). The demography of grandparenthood: An international profile. *Social Forces, 94*, 801–832.

Lepers, R., Knechtle, B., & Stapley, P. J. (2013). Trends in triathlon performance: Effects of sex and age. *Sports Medicine, 43*, 851–863.

Lerman, R. I. (2010). Capabilities and contributions of unwed fathers. *Future of Children, 20*, 63–85.

Lerner, R. M. (2015). Preface. In W. F. Overton & P. C. Molenaar (Eds.), *Handbook of child psychology and developmental science: Vol. 1. Theory and method* (pp. xv–xxi). Hoboken, NJ: Wiley.

Lerner, R. M., Agans, J. P., DeSouza, L. M., & Hershberg, R. M. (2014). Developmental science in 2025: A predictive review. *Research in Human Development, 11*, 255–272.

Lernout, T., Theeten, H., Hens, N., Braeckman, T., Roelants, M., Hoppenbrouwers, K., & Van Damme, P. (2013). Timeliness of infant vaccination and factors related with delay in Flanders, Belgium. *Vaccine, 32*, 284–289.

Leslie, A. M. (2004). Who's for learning? *Developmental Science, 7*, 417–419.

Letherby, G. (2002). Childless and bereft? Stereotypes and realities in relation to "voluntary" and "involuntary" childlessness and womanhood. *Sociological Inquiry, 72*, 7–20.

Leuner, B., Glasper, E. R., & Gould, E. (2010). Parenting and plasticity. *Trends in Neuroscience, 33*, 465–473.

LeVay, S. (1993). *The sexual brain*. Cambridge, MA: MIT Press.

Levendosky, A. A., Bogat, G. A., Huth-Bocks, A. C., Rosenblum, K., & von Eye, A. (2011). The effects of domestic violence on the stability of attachment from infancy to preschool. *Journal of Clinical Child and Adolescent Psychology, 40*, 398–410.

Leventhal, T., & Brooks-Gunn, J. (2003). Children and youth in neighborhood contexts. *Current Directions in Psychological Science, 12*, 27–31.

Leventhal, T., & Dupéré, V. (2011). Moving to opportunity: Does long-term exposure to "low-poverty" neighborhoods make a difference for adolescents? *Social Science and Medicine, 73*, 737–743.

Leventhal, T., Dupéré, V., & Brooks-Gunn, J. (2009). Neighborhood influences on adolescent development. In R. M. Lerner & L. Steinberg (Eds.), *Handbook of adolescent psychology: Vol. 2* (3rd ed., pp. 411–443). Hoboken, NJ: Wiley.

Leventhal, T., Dupéré, V., & Shuey, E. A. (2015). Children in neighborhoods. In M. H. Bornstein & T. Leventhal (Eds.), *Handbook of child psychology: Vol. 4. Ecological settings and processes* (7th ed., pp. 493–533). Hoboken, NJ: Wiley.

Levin, B. (2012). *More high school graduates: How schools can save students from dropping out*. Thousand Oaks, CA: Sage.

Levine, K. A., & Sutherland, D. (2013). History repeats itself: Parental involvement in children's career exploration. *Canadian Journal of Counselling and Psychotherapy, 47*, 239–255.

LeVine, R. A., Dixon, S., LeVine, S., Richman, A., Leiderman, P. H., Keefer, C. H., & Brazelton, T. B. (1994). *Child care and culture: Lessons from Africa*. New York: Cambridge University Press.

Levine, S. C., Huttenlocher, J., Taylor, A., & Langrock, A. (1999). Early sex differences in spatial skill. *Developmental Psychology, 35*, 940–949.

Levine, S. C., Ratliff, K. R., Huttenlocher, J., & Cannon, J. (2012). Early puzzle play: A predictor of preschoolers' spatial transformation skill. *Developmental Psychology, 48*, 530–542.

Levinson, D. J. (1978). *The seasons of a man's life*. New York: Knopf.

Levinson, D. J. (1996). *The seasons of a woman's life*. New York: Knopf.

Levitt, M. J., & Cici-Gokaltun, A. (2011). Close relationships across the lifespan. In K. Fingerman, C. A. Berg, J. Smith, & T. C. Antonucci (Eds.), *Handbook of life-span development* (pp. 457–486). New York: Springer.

Levy, B. R., & Leifheit-Limson, E. (2009). The stereotype-matching effect: Greater influence on functioning when age stereotypes correspond to outcomes. *Psychology and Aging, 24*, 230–233.

Levy, B. R., Slade, M. D., Kunkel, S. R., & Kasl, S. V. (2002). Longevity increased by positive self-perceptions of aging. *Journal of Personality and Social Psychology, 83*, 261–270.

Levy, B. R., Zonderman, A. B., Slade, M. D., & Ferrucci, L. (2012). Memory shaped by age stereotypes over time. *Journals of Gerontology, 67B*, 432–436.

Levy, S. R., & Dweck, C. S. (1999). The impact of children's static vs. dynamic conceptions of people on stereotype formation. *Child Development, 70*, 1163–1180.

Lewiecki, E. M., & Miller, S. A. (2013). Suicide, guns, and public policy. *American Journal of Public Health, 103*, 27–31.

Lewis, J. M., & Kreider, R. M. (2015). *Remarriage in the United States* (American Community Service Reports No. ACS–30). Washington, DC: U.S. Census Bureau. Retrieved from www.census.gov/content/dam/Census/library/publications/2015/acs/acs-30.pdf

Lewis, M. (1995). Embarrassment: The emotion of self-exposure and evaluation. In J. P. Tangney & K. W. Fischer (Eds.), *Self-conscious emotions* (pp. 198–218). New York: Guilford.

Lewis, M. (1998). Emotional competence and development. In D. Pushkar, W. M. Bukowski, A. E. Schwartzman, E. M. Stack, & D. R. White (Eds.), *Improving competence across the lifespan* (pp. 27–36). New York: Plenum.

Lewis, M. (2014). *The rise of consciousness and the development of emotional life*. New York: Guilford.

Lewis, M., & Brooks-Gunn, J. (1979). *Social cognition and the acquisition of self*. New York: Plenum.

Lewis, M., & Ramsay, D. (2004). Development of self-recognition, personal pronoun use, and pretend play during the 2nd year. *Child Development, 75*, 1821–1831.

Lewis, M., Ramsay, D. S., & Kawakami, K. (1993). Differences between Japanese infants and Caucasian American infants in behavioral and cortisol response to inoculation. *Child Development, 64*, 1722–1731.

Lewis, M. A., Granato, H., Blayney, J. A., Lostutter, T. W., & Kilmer, J. R. (2012). Predictors of hooking up sexual behaviors and emotional reactions among U.S. college students. *Archives of Sexual Behavior, 41*, 1219–1229.

Lewis, M. D. (2008). Emotional habits in brain and behavior: A window on personality development. In A. Fogel, B. J. King, & S. G. Shanker (Eds.), *Human development in the twenty-first century* (pp. 72–80). New York: Cambridge University Press.

Lewis, T. L., & Maurer, D. (2005). Multiple sensitive periods in human visual development: Evidence from visually deprived children. *Developmental Psychobiology, 46*, 163–183.

Lew-Williams, C., Pelucchi, B., & Saffran, J. R. (2011). Isolated words enhance statistical language learning in infancy. *Developmental Science, 14*, 1323–1329.

Leyk, D., Rüther, T., Wunderlich, M., Sievert, A., Ebfeld, D., Witzki, A., et al. (2010). Physical performance in middle age and old age. *Deutsches Ärzteblatt International, 107*, 809–816.

Li, D.-K., Willinger, M., Petitti, D. B., Odouli, R., Liu, L., & Hoffman, H. J. (2006). Use of a dummy (pacifier) during sleep and risk of sudden infant death syndrome (SIDS): Population based case-control study. *British Medical Journal, 332*, 18–21.

Li, J., Johnson, S. E., Han, W., Andrews, S., Kendall, G., Strazdins, L., & Dockery, A. (2014). Parents' nonstandard work schedules and child well-being: A critical review of the literature. *Journal of Primary Prevention, 35*, 53–73.

Li, J. J., Berk, M. S., & Lee, S. S. (2013). Differential susceptibility in longitudinal models of gene–environment interaction for adolescent depression. *Developmental Psychopathology, 25*, 991–1003.

Li, K., Zhu, D., Guo, L., Li, Z., Lynch, M. E., Coles, C., et al. (2013). Connectomics signatures of prenatal cocaine exposure affected adolescent brains. *Human Brain Mapping, 34*, 2494–2510.

Li, K. Z. H., & Bruce, H. (2016). Sensorimotor–cognitive interactions. In S. K. Whitbourne (Ed.), *Encyclopedia of adulthood and aging* (Vol. 3, pp. 1292–1296). Malden, MA: Wiley Blackwell.

Li, S.-C., Lindenberger, U., Hommel, B., Aschersleben, G., Prinz, W., & Baltes, P. B. (2004). Transformation in the couplings among intellectual abilities and constituent cognitive processes across the life span. *Psychological Science, 15*, 155–163.

Li, W., Farkas, G., Duncan, G. J., Burchinal, M. R., & Vandell, D. L. (2013). Timing of high-quality child care and cognitive, language, and preacademic development. *Developmental Psychology, 49*, 1440–1451.

Li, X., Atkins, M. S., & Stanton, B. (2006). Effects of home and school computer use on school readiness and cognitive development among Head Start children: A randomized control trial. *Merrill-Palmer Quarterly, 52*, 239–263.

Liang, J., Matheson, B. E., Kaye, W. H., & Boutelle, K. N. (2014). Neurocognitive correlates of obesity and obesity-related behaviors in children and adolescents. *International Journal of Obesity, 38*, 494–506.

Liben, L. S. (2006). Education for spatial thinking. In K. A. Renninger & I. E. Sigel (Eds.), *Handbook of child psychology: Vol. 4. Child psychology in practice* (6th ed., pp. 197–247). Hoboken, NJ: Wiley.

Liben, L. S. (2009). The road to understanding maps. *Current Directions in Psychological Science, 18*, 310–315.

Liben, L. S., & Bigler, R. S. (2002). The developmental course of gender differentiation: Conceptualizing, measuring, and evaluating constructs and pathways. *Monographs of the Society for Research in Child Development, 6*(4, Serial No. 271).

Liben, L. S., Bigler, R. S., & Krogh, H. R. (2001). Pink and blue collar jobs: Children's judgments of job status and job aspirations in relation to sex of worker. *Journal of Experimental Child Psychology, 79*, 346–363.

Liben, L. S., & Downs, R. M. (1993). Understanding person–space–map relations: Cartographic and developmental perspectives. *Developmental Psychology, 29*, 739–752.

Liben, L. S., Myers, L. J., Christensen, A. E., & Bower, C. A. (2013). Environmental-scale map use in middle childhood: Links to spatial skills, strategies, and gender. *Child Development, 84,* 2047–2063.

Lichtenberg, P. A. (2016). Financial exploitation, financial capacity, and Alzheimer's disease. *American Psychologist, 71,* 312–320.

Lickliter, R., & Honeycutt, H. (2013). A developmental evolutionary framework for psychology. *Review of General Psychology, 17,* 184–189.

Lickliter, R., & Honeycutt, H. (2015). Biology, development, and human systems. In W. F. Overton & P. C. M. Molenaar (Eds.), *Handbook of child psychology and developmental science: Vol. 1. Theory and method* (7th ed., pp. 162–207). Hoboken, NJ: Wiley.

Lidstone, J. S. M., Meins, E., & Fernyhough, C. (2010). The roles of private speech and inner speech in planning during middle childhood: Evidence from a dual task paradigm. *Journal of Experimental Child Psychology, 107,* 438–451.

Lidz, J. (2007). The abstract nature of syntactic representations. In E. Hoff & M. Shatz (Eds.), *Blackwell handbook of language development* (pp. 277–303). Malden, MA: Blackwell.

Lidz, J., Gleitman, H., & Gleitman, L. (2004). Kidz in the 'hood: Syntactic bootstrapping and the mental lexicon. In D. G. Hall & S. R. Waxman (Eds.), *Weaving a lexicon* (pp. 603–636). Cambridge, MA: MIT Press.

Liew, J., Eisenberg, N., Spinrad, T. L., Eggum, N. D., Haugen, R. G., Kupfer, A., et al. (2010). Physiological regulation and fearfulness as predictors of young children's empathy-related reactions. *Social Development, 20,* 111–134.

Li-Grining, C. P. (2007). Effortful control among low-income preschoolers in three cities: Stability, change, and individual differences. *Developmental Psychology, 43,* 208–221.

Li-Korotky, H.-S. (2012). Age-related hearing loss: Quality of care for quality of life. *Gerontologist, 52,* 265–271.

Lilgendahl, J. P., & McAdams, D. P. (2011). Constructing stories of self-growth: How individual differences in patterns of autobiographical reasoning relate to well-being in midlife. *Journal of Personality, 79,* 391–428.

Lillard, A. (2007). *Montessori: The science behind the genius.* New York: Oxford University Press.

Lillard, A. S., Lerner, M. D., Hopkins, E. J., Dore, R. A., Smith, E. D., & Palmquist, C. M. (2013). The impact of pretend play on children's development: A review of the evidence. *Psychological Bulletin, 139,* 1–34.

Lillard, A. S., & Peterson, J. (2011). The immediate impact of different types of television on young children's executive function. *Pediatrics, 128,* 644–649.

Lin, I.-F., & Wu, H.-S. (2014). Activity limitations, use of assistive devices or personal help, and well-being: Variation by education. *Journals of Gerontology, 69B,* S16–S25.

Lin, J., Epel, E., & Blackburn, E. (2012). Telomeres and lifestyle factors: Roles in cellular aging. *Mutation Research/Fundamental and Molecular Mechanisms of Mutagenesis, 730,* 85–89.

Lin, K.-H., & Lundquist, J. (2013). Mate selection in cyberspace: The intersection of race, gender, and education. *American Journal of Sociology, 119,* 183–215.

Lind, J. N., Li, R., Perrine, C. G., & Shieve, L. A. (2014). Breastfeeding and later psychosocial development of children at 6 years of age. *Pediatrics, 134,* S36–S41.

Lindau, S. T., Schumm, L. P., Laumann, E. O., Levinson, W., O'Muircheartaigh, C. A., & Waite, L. J. (2007). A study of sexuality and health among older adults in the United States. *New England Journal of Medicine, 357,* 762–774.

Lindauer, M. S., Orwoll, L., & Kelley, M. C. (1997). Aging artists on the creativity of their old age. *Creativity Research Journal, 10,* 133–152.

Lindberg, S. M., Hyde, J. S., Linn, M. C., & Petersen, J. L. (2010). New trends in gender and mathematics performance: A meta-analysis. *Psychological Bulletin, 136,* 1123–1135.

Linder, J. R., & Collins, W. A. (2005). Parent and peer predictors of physical aggression and conflict management in romantic relationships in early adulthood. *Journal of Family Psychology, 19,* 252–262.

Lindsey, E. W., & Colwell, M. J. (2013). Pretend and physical play: Links to preschoolers' affective social competence. *Merrill-Palmer Quarterly, 59,* 330–360.

Lindsey, E. W., Colwell, M. J., Frabutt, J. M., Chambers, J. C., & MacKinnon-Lewis, C. (2008). Mother–child dyadic synchrony in European-American families during early adolescence: Relations with self-esteem and prosocial behavior. *Merrill-Palmer Quarterly, 54,* 289–315.

Lindsey, E. W., & Mize, J. (2000). Parent–child physical and pretense play: Links to children's social competence. *Merrill-Palmer Quarterly, 46,* 565–591.

Linebarger, D. L., & Piotrowski, J. T. (2010). Structure and strategies in children's educational television: The roles of program type and learning strategies in children's learning. *Child Development, 81,* 1582–1597.

Linebarger, J. S., Sahler, O. J., & Egan, K. A. Coping with death. *Pediatrics in Review, 30,* 350–355.

Linver, M. R., Martin, A., & Brooks-Gunn, J. (2004). Measuring infants' home environment: The ITHOME for infants between birth and 12 months in four national data sets. *Parenting: Science and Practice, 4,* 115–137.

Lionetti, F., Pastore, M., & Barone, L. (2015). Attachment in institutionalized children: A review and meta-analysis. *Child Abuse and Neglect, 42,* 135–145.

Lippold, M. A., Greenberg, M. T., Graham, J. W., & Feinberg, M. E. (2014). Unpacking the effect of parental monitoring on early adolescent problem behavior: Mediation by parental knowledge and moderation by parent–youth warmth. *Journal of Family Issues, 35,* 1800–1823.

Lips, H. M. (2013). The gender pay gap: Challenging the rationalizations. Perceived equity, discrimination, and the limits of human capital models. *Sex Roles, 68,* 169–185.

Lipton, J. S., & Spelke, E. S. (2003). Origins of number sense: Large-number discrimination in human infants. *Psychological Science, 14,* 396–401.

Liszkowski, U., Carpenter, M., & Tomasello, M. (2007). Pointing out new news, old news, and absent referents at 12 months of age. *Developmental Science, 10,* F1–F7.

Lithopoulos, A., Rathwell, S., & Young, B. W. (2015). Examining the effects of gain-framed messages on the activation and elaboration of possible sport selves in middle-aged adults. *Journal of Applied Sport Psychology, 27,* 140–155.

Liu, C.-C., Kanekiyo, T., Xu, H., & Bu, G. (2013). Apolipoprotein E and Alzheimer disease: Risk, mechanisms and therapy. *Nature Reviews Neurology, 9,* 106–118.

Liu, J., Raine, A., Venables, P. H., Dalais, C., & Mednick, S. A. (2003). Malnutrition at age 3 years and lower cognitive ability at age 11 years. *Archives of Paediatric and Adolescent Medicine, 157,* 593–600.

Liu, J., Raine, A., Venables, P. H., & Mednick, S. A. (2004). Malnutrition at age 3 years and externalizing behavior problems at age 8, 11, and 17 years. *American Journal of Psychiatry, 161,* 2006–2013.

Liu, K., Daviglus, M. L., Loria, C. M., Colangelo, L. A., Spring, B., Moller, A. C., et al. (2012). Healthy lifestyle through young adulthood and the presence of low cardiovascular disease risk profile in middle age: The Coronary Artery Risk Development in (Young) Adults (CARDIA) study. *Circulation, 125,* 996–1004.

Liu, L., Drouet, V., Wu, J. W., Witter, M. P., Small, S. A., Clelland C., et al. (2012). Trans-synaptic spread of tau pathology in vivo. *PLoS One, 7,* e31302.

Liu, R. T., & Mustanski, B. (2012). Suicidal ideation and self-harm in lesbian, gay, bisexual, and transgender youth. *American Journal of Preventive Medicine, 42,* 221–228.

Liu, Y., Long, J., & Liu, J. (2014). Mitochondrial free radical theory of aging: Who moved my premise? *Geriatrics and Gerontology International, 14,* 740–749.

Lleras, C., & Rangel, C. (2009). Ability grouping practices in elementary school and African American/Hispanic achievement. *American Journal of Education, 115,* 279–304.

Lloyd, G. M., Sailor, J. L., & Carney, W. (2014). A phenomenological study of postdivorce adjustment in midlife. *Journal of Divorce and Remarriage, 55,* 441–450.

Lloyd, M. E., Doydum, A. O., & Newcombe, N. S. (2009). Memory binding in early childhood: Evidence for a retrieval deficit. *Child Development, 80,* 1321–1328.

Lochman, J. E., & Dodge K. A. (1998). Distorted perceptions in dyadic interactions of aggressive and nonaggressive boys: Effects of prior expectations, context, and boys' age. *Development and Psychopathology, 10,* 495–512.

Lockhart, S. N., & DeCarli, C. (2014). Structural imaging measures of brain aging. *Neuropsychological Review, 24,* 271–289.

Lodi-Smith, J., & Roberts, B. W. (2007). Social investment and personality: A meta-analysis of the relationship of personality traits to investment in work, family, religion, and volunteerism. *Personality and Social Psychology Review, 11,* 68–86.

Loehlin, J. C., Horn, J. M., & Willerman, L. (1997). Heredity, environment, and IQ in the Texas Adoption Project. In R. J. Sternberg & E. L. Grigorenko (Eds.), *Intelligence, heredity, and environment* (pp. 105–125). New York: Cambridge University Press.

Loehlin, J. C., Jonsson, E. G., Gustavsson, J. P., Stallings, M. C., Gillespie, N. A., Wright, M. J., & Martin, N. G. (2005). Psychological masculinity–femininity via the gender diagnosticity approach: Heritability and consistency across ages and populations. *Journal of Personality, 73,* 1295–1319.

Loehlin, J. C., & Martin, N. G. (2001). Age changes in personality traits and their heritabilities during the adult years: Evidence from Australian twin registry samples. *Personality and Individual Differences, 30,* 1147–1160.

Loganovskaja, T. K., & Loganovsky, K. N. (1999). EEG, cognitive and psychopathological abnormalities in children irradiated in utero. *International Journal of Psychophysiology, 34,* 211–224.

Loganovsky, K. N., Loganovskaja, T. K., Nechayev, S. Y., Antipchuk, Y. Y., & Bomko, M. A. (2008). Disrupted development of the dominant hemisphere following prenatal irradiation. *Journal of Neuropsychiatry and Clinical Neurosciences, 20,* 274–291.

Loman, M. M., & Gunnar, M. R. (2010). Early experience and the development of stress reactivity and regulation in children. *Neuroscience and Biobehavioral Reviews, 34,* 867–876.

Lombardi, C. M., & Coley, R. L. (2013). Low-income mothers' employment experiences: Prospective links with young children's development. *Family Relations, 62,* 514–528.

Long, D. D. (1985). A cross-cultural examination of fears of death among Saudi Arabians. *Omega, 16,* 43–50.

Lonigan, C. J. (2015). Literacy development. In L. S. Liben & U. Müller (Eds.), *Handbook of child psychology and developmental science: Vol. 2. Cognitive processes* (7th ed., pp. 763–805). Hoboken, NJ: Wiley.

Lonigan, C. J., Purpura, D. J., Wilson, S. B., Walker, J., & Clancy-Menchetti, J. (2013). Evaluating the components of an emergent literacy intervention for preschool children at risk for reading difficulties. *Journal of Experimental Child Psychology, 114,* 111–130.

Looker, D., & Thiessen, V. (2003). *The digital divide in Canadian schools: Factors affecting student access to and use of information technology.* Ottawa: Canadian Education Statistics Council.

Lopez, C. M., Driscoll, K. A., & Kistner, J. A. (2009). Sex differences and response styles: Subtypes of rumination and associations with depressive symptoms. *Journal of Clinical Child and Adolescent Psychology, 38,* 27–35.

Lopresti, A. L., & Drummond, P. D. (2013). Obesity and psychiatric disorders: Commonalities in dysregulated biological pathways and their implications for treatment. *Progress in Neuro-Psychopharmacology & Biological Psychiatry, 45,* 92–99.

Lora, K. R., Sisson, S. B., DeGrace, B. W., & Morris, A. S. (2014). Frequency of family meals and 6–11-year-old children's social behaviors. *Journal of Family Psychology, 28,* 577–582.

Lorber, M. F., & Egeland, B. (2011). Parenting and infant difficulty: Testing a mutual exacerbation hypothesis to predict early onset conduct problems. *Child Development, 82,* 2006–2020.

Lorch, R. F., Jr., Lorch, E. P., Calderhead, W. J., Dunlap, E. E., Hodell, E. C., & Freer, B. D. (2010). Learning the control of variables strategy in higher- and lower-achieving classrooms: Contributions of explicit instruction and experimentation. *Journal of Educational Psychology, 102,* 90–101.

Lorentzen, C. (2014). College enrollment decision for nontraditional female students. *College of Professional Studies Professional Projects* (Paper 68). Retrieved from epublications.marquette.edu/cgi/viewcontent.cgi?article=1069&context=cps_professional

Lorenz, K. (1952). *King Solomon's ring.* New York: Crowell.

Lorntz, B., Soares, A. M., Moore, S. R., Pinkerton, R., Gansneder, B., Bovbjerg, V. E., et al. (2006). Early childhood diarrhea predicts impaired school performance. *Pediatric Infectious Disease Journal, 25,* 513–520.

Lou, E., Lalonde, R. N., & Giguère, B. (2012). Making the decision to move out: Bicultural young adults and the negotiation of cultural demands and family relationships. *Journal of Cross-Cultural Psychology, 43,* 663–670.

Lou, K., Yao, Y., Hoye, A. T., James, M. J., Cornec, A. S., Hyde, E., et al. (2014). Brain-penetrant, orally bioavailable microtubule-stabilizing small molecules are potential candidate therapeutics for Alzheimer's disease and related tauopathies. *Journal of Medicinal Chemistry, 57,* 6116–6127.

Louie, V. (2001). Parents' aspirations and investment: The role of social class in the educational experiences of 1.5- and second generation Chinese Americans. *Harvard Educational Review, 71,* 438–474.

Louis, J., Cannard, C., Bastuji, H., & Challemel, M. J. (1997). Sleep ontogenesis revisited: A longitudinal 24-hour home polygraphic study on 15 normal infants during the first two years of life. *Sleep, 20,* 323–333.

Lourenço, O. (2003). Making sense of Turiel's dispute with Kohlberg: The case of the child's moral competence. *New Ideas in Psychology, 21,* 43–68.

Lourenço, O. (2012). Piaget and Vygotsky: Many resemblances, and a crucial difference. *New Ideas in Psychology, 30,* 281–295.

Lourida, I., Soni, M., Thompson-Coon, J., Purandare, N., Lang, I. A., Ukoumunne, O. C., & Llewellyn, D. J. (2013). Mediterranean diet, cognitive function, and dementia: A systematic review. *Epidemiology, 24,* 479–489.

Lövdén, M., Bergman, L., Adolfsson, R., Lindenberger, U., & Nilsson, L.-G. (2005). Studying individual aging in an interindividual context: Typical paths of age-related, dementia-related, and mortality-related cognitive development in old age. *Psychology and Aging, 20,* 303–316.

Lövdén, M., Schmiedek, F., Kennedy, K. M., Rodrigue, K. M., Lindenberger, U., & Raz, N. (2012). Does variability in cognitive performance correlated with frontal brain volume? *NeuroImage, 64,* 209–215.

Love, J. M., Chazan-Cohen, R., & Raikes, H. (2007). Forty years of research knowledge and use: From Head Start to Early Head Start and beyond. In J. L. Aber, S. J. Bishop-Josef, S. M. Jones, K. T. McLearn, & D. Phillips (Eds.), *Child development and social policy: Knowledge for action* (pp. 79–95). Washington, DC: American Psychological Association.

Love, J. M., Harrison, L., Sagi-Schwartz, A., van IJzendoorn, M. H., Ross, C., & Ungerer, J. A. (2003). Child care quality matters: How conclusions may vary with context. *Child Development, 74,* 1021–1033.

Love, J. M., Kisker, E. E., Ross, C., Raikes, H., Constantine, J., Boller, K., & Brooks-Gunn, J. (2005). The effectiveness of Early Head Start for 3-year-old children and their parents: Lessons for policy and programs. *Developmental Psychology, 41,* 885–901.

Lovejoy, M., & Stone, P. (2012). Opting back in: The influence of time at home on professional women's career redirection after opting out. *Gender, Work and Organization, 19,* 632–653.

Low, M., Farrell, A., Biggs, B., & Pasricha, S. (2013). Effects of daily iron supplementation in primary-school-aged children: Systematic review and meta-analysis of randomized controlled trials. *Canadian Medical Association Journal, 185,* E791–E802.

Low, S. H., & Goh, E. C. L. (2015). Granny as nanny: Positive outcomes for grandparents providing childcare for dual-income families: Fact or myth? *Journal of Intergenerational Relationships, 13,* 302–319.

Low, S. M., & Stocker, C. (2012). Family functioning and children's adjustment: Associations among parents' depressed mood, marital hostility, parent–child hostility, and children's adjustment. *Journal of Family Psychology, 19,* 394–403.

Lowenstein, A., Katz, R., & Gur-Yaish, N. (2007). Reciprocity in parent–child exchange and life satisfaction among the elderly: A cross-national perspective. *Journal of Social Issues, 63,* 865–883.

Lowery, E. M., Brubaker, A. L., Kuhlmann, E., & Kovacs, E. J. (2013). The aging lung. *Clinical Interventions in Aging, 8,* 1489–1496.

Loy, C. T., Schofield, P. R., Turner, A. M., & Kwok, J. B. J. (2014). Genetics of dementia. *Lancet, 383,* 828–840.

Lu, P. H., Lee, G. J., Tishler, T. A., Meghpara, M., Thompson, P. M., & Bartzokis, G. (2013). Myelin breakdown mediates age-related slowing in cognitive processing speed in healthy elderly men. *Brain and Cognition, 81,* 131–138.

Lubart, T. I., Georgsdottir, A., & Besançon, M. (2009). The nature of creative giftedness and talent. In T. Balchin, B. Hymer, & D. J. Matthews (Eds.), *The Routledge international companion to gifted education* (pp. 42–49). New York: Routledge.

Lubart, T. I., & Sternberg, R. J. (1998). Life span creativity: An investment theory approach. In C. E. Adams-Price (Ed.), *Creativity and successful aging.* New York: Springer.

Luby, J., Belden, A., Sullivan, J., Hayen, R., McCadney, A., & Spitznagel, E. (2009). Shame and guilt in preschool depression: Evidence for elevations in self-conscious emotions in depression as early as age 3. *Journal of Child Psychology and Psychiatry, 50,* 1156–1166.

Lucassen, N., Tharner, A., Van IJzendoorn, M. H., Bakermans-Kranenburg, M. J., Volling, B. L., Verhulst, F. C., et al. (2011). The association between paternal sensitivity and infant–father attachment security: A meta-analysis of three decades of research. *Journal of Family Psychology, 25,* 986–992.

Lucas-Thompson, R., & Clarke-Stewart, K. A. (2007). Forecasting friendship: How marital quality, maternal mood, and attachment security are linked to children's peer relationships. *Journal of Applied Developmental Psychology, 28,* 499–514.

Lucas-Thompson, R. G., Goldberg, W. A., & Prause, J. (2010). Maternal work early in the lives of children and its distal associations with achievement and behavior problems: A meta-analysis. *Psychological Bulletin, 136,* 915–942.

Luciana, M., Collins, P. F., Muetzel, R. L., & Lim, K. O. (2013). Effects of alcohol use initiation on brain structure in typically developing adolescents. *American Journal of Drug and Alcohol Abuse, 39,* 345–355.

Ludlow, A. T., Ludlow, L. W., & Roth, S. M. (2013). Do telomeres adapt to physiological stress? Exploring the effect of exercise on telomere length and telomere-related proteins. *BioMed Research International,* Article ID 601368.

Luecken, L. J. (2008). Long-term consequences of parental death in childhood: Psychological and physiological manifestations. In M. S. Stroebe, R. O. Hansson, H. Schut, & W. Stroebe (Eds.), *Handbook of bereavement research and practice* (pp. 397–416). Washington, DC: American Psychological Association.

Luecken, L. J., Lin, B., Coburn, S. S., MacKinnon, D. P., Gonzales, N. A., & Crnic, K. A. (2013). Prenatal stress, partner support, and infant cortisol reactivity in low-income Mexican American families. *Psychoneuroendocrinology, 38,* 3092–3101.

Lugton, J. (2002). *Communicating with dying people.* Oxon, UK: Radcliffe Medical Press.

Luhmann, M., Hofmann, W., Eid, M., & Lucas, R. E. (2012). Subjective well-being and adaptation to life events: A meta-analysis. *Journal of Personality and Social Psychology, 102,* 592–615.

Luk, B. H., & Loke, A. Y. (2015). The impact of infertility on the psychological well-being, marital relationships, sexual relationships, and quality of life of couples: A systematic review. *Journal of Sex & Marital Therapy, 41,* 610–625.

Lukas, C., & Seiden, H. M. (2007). *Silent grief: Living in the wake of suicide* (rev. ed.). London, UK: Jessica Kingsley.

Luke, A., Cooper, R. S., Prewitt, T. E., Adeyemo, A. A., & Forrester, T. E. (2001). Nutritional consequences of the African diaspora. *Annual Review of Nutrition, 21,* 47–71.

Lukowski, A. F., Koss, M., Burden, M. J., Jonides, J., Nelson, C. A., Kaciroti, N., et al. (2010). Iron deficiency in infancy and neurocognitive functioning at 19 years: Evidence of long-term deficits in executive function and recognition memory. *Nutritional Neuroscience, 13,* 54–70.

Luna, B., Padmanabhan, A., & Geier, C. (2014). The adolescent sensation-seeking period: Development of reward processing and its effects on cognitive control. In V. F. Reyna & V. Zayas (Eds.), *The neuroscience of risky decision making* (pp. 93–121). Washington, DC: American Psychological Association.

Luna, B., Thulborn, K. R., Monoz, D. P., Merriam, E. P., Garver, K. E., Minshew, N. J., et al. (2001). Maturation of widely distributed brain function subserves cognitive development. *Neuroimage, 13,* 786–793.

Lund, D., Caserta, M., Utz, R., & de Vries, B. (2010a). Experiences and early coping of bereaved spouses/partners in an intervention based on the dual process model (DPM). *Omega, 61,* 291–313.

Lund, D. A. (2005). *My journey* [Sue's letter]. Unpublished document. Salt Lake City, UT: University of Utah.

Lund, D. A., & Caserta, M. S. (2004). Facing life alone: Loss of a significant other in later life. In D. Doda (Ed.), *Living with grief: Loss in later life* (pp. 207–223). Washington, DC: Hospice Foundation of America.

Lund, D. A., Caserta, M. S., & Dimond, M. F. (1993). The course of spousal bereavement in later life. In M. S. Stroebe, W. Stroebe, & R. O. Hansson (Eds.), *Handbook of bereavement* (pp. 240–245). New York: Cambridge University Press.

Lund, D. A., Utz, R., Caserta, M., & de Vries, B. (2008–2009). Humor, laughter, and happiness in the daily lives of recently bereaved spouses. *Omega, 58,* 87–105.

Lund, D. A., Utz, R., Caserta, M. S., & Wright, S. D. (2009). Examining what caregivers do during respite time to make respite more effective. *Journal of Applied Gerontology, 28,* 109–131.

Lund, D. A., Wright, S. D., Caserta, M. S., Utz, R. L., Lindfelt, C., Bright, O., et al. (2010b). *Respite services: Enhancing the quality of daily life for caregivers and care receivers.* San Bernardino, CA: California State University at San Bernardino.

Lundberg, S., & Pollak, R. A. (2015). The evolving role of marriage: 1950–2010. *Future of Children, 25*(2), 29–50.

Luo, L. Z., Li, H., & Lee, K. (2011). Are children's faces really more appealing than those of adults? Testing the baby schema hypothesis beyond infancy. *Journal of Experimental Child Psychology, 110,* 115–124.

Luong, G., Charles, S. T., & Fingerman, K. L. (2011). Better with age: Social relationships across adulthood. *Journal of Social and Personal Relationships, 28,* 9–23.

Luster, T., & Haddow, J. L. (2005). Adolescent mothers and their children: An ecological perspective. In T. Luster & J. L. Haddow (Eds.), *Parenting: An ecological perspective* (2nd ed., pp. 73–101). Mahwah, NJ: Erlbaum.

Lustig, C., & Lin, Z. (2016). Memory: Behavior and neural basis. In K. W. Schaie & S. L. Willis (Eds.), *Handbook of the psychology of aging* (8th ed., pp. 147–163). Waltham, MA: Elsevier.

Luthar, S. S., & Barkin, S. H. (2012). Are affluent youths truly "at risk"? Vulnerability and resilience across three diverse samples. *Development and Psychopathology, 24,* 429–449.

Luthar, S. S., Barkin, S., & Crossman, E. J. (2013). "I can, therefore I must": Fragility in the upper-middle classes. *Development and Psychopathology, 25,* 1529–1549.

Luthar, S. S., Crossman, E. J., & Small, P. J. (2015). Resilience and adversity. In M. E. Lamb (Ed.), *Handbook of child psychology and developmental science: Vol. 3. Socioemotional processes* (7th ed., pp. 247–286). Hoboken, NJ: Wiley.

Luthar, S. S., & Latendresse, S. J. (2005b). Comparable "risks" at the socioeconomic status extremes: Preadolescents' perceptions of parenting. *Development and Psychopathology, 17,* 207–230.

Luxembourg Income Study. (2015). *LIS database.* Retrieved from www.lisdatacenter.org/our-data/lis-database

Luyckx, K., Goossens, L., & Soenens, B. (2006). A developmental contextual perspective on identity construction in emerging adulthood: Change dynamics in commitment formation and commitment evaluation. *Developmental Psychology, 42,* 366–380.

Luyckx, K., Goossens, L., Soenens, B., & Beyers, W. (2006). Unpacking commitment and exploration: Preliminary validation of an integrative model of late adolescent identity formation. *Journal of Adolescence, 29,* 361–378.

Luyckx, K., & Robitschek, C. (2014). Personal growth initiative and identity formation in adolescence through young adulthood: Mediating processes on the pathway to well-being. *Journal of Adolescence, 37,* 973–981.

Luyckx, K., Schwartz, S. J., Goossens, L., Byers, W., & Missotten, L. (2011). Processes of personal identity formation and evaluation. In S. J. Schwartz, K. Luyckx, & V. L. Vignoles (Eds.), *Handbook of identity theory and research* (pp. 77–98). New York: Springer.

Luyckx, K., Soenens, B., Vansteenkiste, M., Goossens, L., & Berzonsky, M. D. (2007). Parental psychological control and dimensions of identity formation in emerging adulthood. *Journal of Family Psychology, 21,* 546–550.

Lyness, K. S., & Heilman, M. E. (2006). When fit is fundamental: Performance evaluations and promotions of upper-level female and male managers. *Journal of Applied Psychology, 90,* 777–785.

Lyngstad, T. H. (2013). Bereavement and divorce: Does the death of a child affect parents' marital stability? *Family Science, 4,* 79–86.

Lyon, T. D., & Flavell, J. H. (1994). Young children's understanding of "remember" and "forget." *Child Development, 65,* 1357–1371.

Lyster, R., & Genesee, F. (2012). Immersion education. In Carol A. Chapelle (Ed.), *Encyclopedia of applied linguistics* (pp. 2608–2614). Hoboken, NJ: Wiley.

Lytton, H., & Gallagher, L. (2002). Parenting twins and the genetics of parenting. In M. H. Bornstein (Ed.), *Handbook of parenting* (Vol. 1, pp. 227–253). Mahwah, NJ: Erlbaum.

M

Ma, F., Xu, F., Heyman, G. D., & Lee, K. (2011). Chinese children's evaluations of white lies: Weighing the consequences for recipients. *Journal of Experimental Child Psychology, 108,* 308–321.

Ma, L., & Lillard, A. S. (2006). Where is the real cheese? Young children's ability to discriminate between real and pretend acts. *Child Development, 77,* 1762–1777.

Ma, W., Golinkoff, R. M., Hirsh-Pasek, K., McDonough, C., & Tardif, T. (2009). Imagine that! Imageability predicts the age of acquisition of verbs in Chinese children. *Journal of Child Language, 36,* 405–423.

Maas, F. K. (2008). Children's understanding of promising, lying, and false belief. *Journal of General Psychology, 13,* 301–321.

Maccoby, E. E. (1998). *The two sexes: Growing up apart, coming together.* Cambridge, MA: Belknap.

Maccoby, E. E. (2002). Gender and group process: A developmental perspective. *Current Directions in Psychological Science, 11,* 54–58.

MacDonald, J. L., & Levy, S. R. (2016). Ageism in the workplace: The role of psychosocial factors in predicting job satisfaction, commitment, and engagement. *Journal of Social Issues, 72,* 169–190.

MacDonald, S. W. S., Hultsch, D. F., & Dixon, R. A. (2011). Aging and the shape of cognitive change before death: Terminal decline or terminal drop? *Journals of Gerontology, 66,* 292–301.

MacDonald, S. W. S., Li, S-C., & Bäckman, L. (2009). Neural underpinnings of within-person variability in cognitive functioning. *Psychology and Aging, 24,* 792–808.

MacDonald, S. W. S., & Stawski, R. S. (2016). Methodological considerations for the study of adult development and aging. In K. W. Schaie & S. L. Willis (Eds.), *Handbook of the psychology of aging* (8th ed., pp. 15–40). San Diego: Academic Press.

MacDorman, M. F., & Gregory, E. C. W. (2015). Fetal and perinatal mortality: United States, 2013. *National Vital Statistics Reports, 64*(8). Retrieved from www.cdc.gov/nchs/data/nvsr/nvsr64/nvsr64_08.pdf

MacKenzie, M. J., Nicklas, E., Waldfogel, J., & Brooks-Gunn, J. (2013). Spanking and child development across the first decade of life. *Pediatrics, 132,* e1118–e1125. Retrieved from http://pediatrics.aappublications.org/content/132/5/e1118

Mackey, K., Arnold, M. L., & Pratt, M. W. (2001). Adolescents' stories of decision making in more and less authoritative families: Representing the voices of parents in narrative. *Journal of Adolescent Research, 16,* 243–268.

Mackey, R. A., Diemer, M. A., & O'Brien, B. A. (2000). Psychological intimacy in the lasting relationships of heterosexual and same-gender couples. *Sex Roles, 43,* 201–227.

Mackie, S., Show, P., Lenroot, R., Pierson, R., Greenstein, D. K., & Nugent, T. F., III. (2007). Cerebellar development and clinical outcome in attention deficit hyperactivity disorder. *American Journal of Psychiatry, 164,* 647–655.

Mackinnon, S. P., De Pasquale, D., & Pratt, M. W. (2015). Predicting generative concern in young adulthood from narrative intimacy: A 5-year follow-up. *Journal of Adult Development, 23,* 27–35.

MacLean, P. S., Bergouignan, A., Cornier, M.-A., & Jackman, M. R. (2011). Biology's response to dieting: The impetus for weight gain. *American Journal of Physiology—Regular, Integrated, and Comparative Physiology, 301,* R581–R600.

MacWhinney, B. (2005). Language development. In M. H. Bornstein & M. E. Lamb (Eds.), *Developmental science: An advanced textbook* (5th ed., pp. 359–387). Mahwah, NJ: Erlbaum.

MacWhinney, B. (2015). Language development. In L. S. Liben & U. Müller (Eds.), *Handbook of child psychology and developmental science: Vol. 2. Cognitive processes* (7th ed., pp. 296–338). Hoboken, NJ: Wiley.

Macy, M. L., Butchart, A. T., Singer, D C., Gebremariam, A., Clark, S. J., & Davis, M. M. (2015). Looking back on rear-facing car seats: Surveying U.S. parents in 2011 and 2013. *Academic Pediatrics, 15,* 526–533.

Madathil, J., & Benshoff, J. M. (2008). Importance of marital characteristics and marital satisfaction: A comparison of Asian Indians in arranged marriages and Americans in marriages of choice. *Family Journal, 16,* 222–230.

Madden, M., Lenhart, A., Cortesi, S., Gasser, U., Duggan, M., Smith, A., et al. (2013). *Teens, social media, and privacy: Part 1. Teens and social media use.* Washington, DC: Pew Research Center's Internet and American Life Project. Retrieved from www.pewinternet.org/2013/05/21/part-1-teens-and-social-media-use

Maddi, S. R. (2006). Hardiness: The courage to be resilient. In J. C. Thomas, D. L. Segal, & M. Hersen (Eds.), *Comprehensive handbook of personality and psychopathology: Vol. 1. Personality and everyday functioning* (pp. 306–321). Hoboken, NJ: Wiley.

Maddi, S. R. (2007). The story of hardiness: Twenty years of theorizing, research, and practice. In A. Monat, R. S. Lazarus, & G. Reevy (Eds.), *Praeger handbook on stress and coping* (Vol. 2, pp. 327–340). Westport, CT: Praeger.

Maddi, S. R. (2011). Personality hardiness as a pathway to resilience under educational stresses. In G. M. Reevy & E. Frydenberg (Eds.), *Personality, stress, and coping: Implications for education* (pp. 293–313). Charlotte, NC: Information Age Publishing.

Maddi, S. R. (2016). Hardiness. In S. K. Whitbourne (Ed.), *Encyclopedia of adulthood and aging* (Vol. 2, pp. 594–598). Malden, MA: Wiley Blackwell.

Maddox, G. L. (1963). Activity and morale: A longitudinal study of selected elderly subjects. *Social Forces, 42,* 195–204.

Madigan, S., Bakermans-Kranenburg, M. J., van IJzendoorn, M. H., Moran, G., Pederson, D. R., & Benoit, D. (2006). Unresolved states of mind, anomalous parental behavior, and disorganized attachment: A review and meta-analysis of a transmission gap. *Attachment and Human Development, 8,* 89–111.

Madnawat, A. V. S., & Kachhawa, P. S. (2007). Age, gender, and living circumstances: Discriminating older adults on death anxiety. *Death Studies, 31,* 763–769.

Madole, K. L., Oakes, L. M., & Rakison, D. H. (2011). Information-processing approaches to infants' developing representation of dynamic features. In L. M. Oakes, C. H. Cashon, M. Casasola, & D. Rakison (Eds.), *Infant perception and cognition* (153–178). New York: Oxford University Press.

Maeda, Y., & Yoon, S. Y. (2013). A meta-analysis on gender differences in mental rotation ability measured by the Purdue Spatial Visualization Tests: Visualization of Rotations (PSV:R). *Educational Psychology Review, 25*, 69–94.

Magolda, M. B., Abes, E., & Torres, V. (2009). Epistemological, intrapersonal, and interpersonal development in the college years and young adulthood. In M. C. Smith & N. DeFrates-Densch (Eds.), *Handbook of research on adult learning and development* (pp. 183–219). New York: Routledge.

Magolda, M. B. B., King, P. M., Taylor, K. B., & Wakefield, K. M. (2012). Decreasing authority dependence during the first year of college. *Journal of College Student Development, 53*, 418–435.

Magyar-Russell, G., Deal, P. J., & Brown, A. I. (2014). Potential benefits and detriments of religiousness and spirituality to emerging adults. In C. M. Barry & M. M. Abo-Zena (Eds.), *Emerging adults' religiousness and spirituality* (pp 21–38). New York: Oxford University Press.

Mahady, G. B., Locklear, T. D., Doyle, B. J., Huang, Y., Perez, A. L., & Caceres, A. (2008). Menopause, a universal female experience: Lessons from Mexico and Central America. *Current Women's Health Reviews, 4*, 3–8.

Mahay, J., & Lewin, A. C. (2007). Age and the desire to marry. *Journal of Family Issues, 28*, 706–723.

Mahne, K., & Huxhold, O. (2015). Grandparenthood and subjective well-being: Effects of educational level. *Journals of Gerontology, 70B*, 782–792.

Mahon, M. M., Goldberg, E. Z., & Washington, S. K. (1999). Concept of death in a sample of Israeli kibbutz children. *Death Studies, 23*, 43–59.

Main, M., & Goldwyn, R. (1998). *Adult attachment classification system*. London: University College.

Main, M., & Solomon, J. (1990). Procedures for identifying infants as disorganized/disoriented during the Ainsworth Strange Situation. In M. Greenberg, D. Cicchetti, & M. Cummings (Eds.), *Attachment in the preschool years: Theory, research, and intervention* (pp. 121–160). Chicago: University of Chicago Press.

Mainiero, L. A., & Sullivan, S. E. (2005). Kaleidoscope careers: An alternate explanation for the "opt-out" revolution. *Academy of Management Executive, 19*, 106–123.

Maitland, S. B., Intrieri, R. C., Schaie, K. W., & Willis, S. L. (2000). Gender differences and changes in cognitive abilities across the adult life span. *Aging, Neuropsychology, and Cognition, 7*, 32–53.

Majdandžić, M., & van den Boom, D. C. (2007). Multimethod longitudinal assessment of temperament in early childhood. *Journal of Personality, 75*, 12.

Malatesta, C. Z., Grigoryev, P., Lamb, C., Albin, M., & Culver, C. (1986). Emotion socialization and expressive development in preterm and full-term infants. *Child Development, 57*, 316–330.

Malone, M. M. (1982). Consciousness of dying and projective fantasy of young children with malignant disease. *Developmental and Behavioral Pediatrics, 3*, 55–60.

Malta, S., & Farquharson, K. (2014). The initiation and progression of late-life romantic relationships. *Journal of Sociology, 50*, 237–251.

Malti, T., & Krettenauer, T. (2013). The relation of moral emotion attributions to prosocial and antisocial behavior: A meta-analysis. *Child Development, 84*, 397–412.

Mandara, J., Varner, F., Greene, N., & Richman, S. (2009). Intergenerational family predictors of the black–white achievement gap. *Journal of Educational Psychology, 101*, 867–878.

Mandel, D. R., Jusczyk, P. W., & Pisoni, D. B. (1995). Infants' recognition of the sound patterns of their own names. *Psychological Science, 6*, 314–317.

Mandler, J. M. (2004). Thought before language. *Trends in Cognitive Sciences, 8*, 508–513.

Mandler, J. M., & McDonough, L. (1998). On developing a knowledge base in infancy. *Developmental Psychology, 34*, 1274–1288.

Mangelsdorf, S. C., Schoppe, S. J., & Buur, H. (2000). The meaning of parental reports: A contextual approach to the study of temperament and behavior problems. In V. J. Molfese & D. L. Molfese (Eds.), *Temperament and personality across the life span* (pp. 121–140). Mahwah, NJ: Erlbaum.

Mani, T. M., Bedwell, J. S., & Miller, L. S. (2005). Age-related decrements in performance on a brief continuous performance task. *Archives of Clinical Neuropsychology, 20*, 575–586.

Manning, W. D., Longmore, M. A., Copp, J., & Giordano, P. C. (2014). The complexities of adolescent dating and sexual relationships: Fluidity, meaning(s), and implications for young adults' well-being. In E. S. Lefkowicz & S. A. Vasilenko (Eds.), *New directions for child and adolescent development* (Vol. 144, pp. 53–69). San Francisco: Jossey-Bass.

Manole, M. D., & Hickey, R. W. (2006). Preterminal gasping and effects on the cardiac function. *Critical Care Medicine, 34*(Suppl.), S438–S441.

Maquestiaux, F. (2016). Qualitative attentional changes with age in doing two tasks at once. *Psychonomic Bulletin and Review, 23*, 54–61.

Maratsos, M. (2000). More overregularizations after all: New data and discussion on Marcus, Pinker, Ullman, Hollander, Rosen, & Xu. *Journal of Child Language, 27*, 183–212.

Marceau, K., Ram, N., & Susman, E. J. (2015). Development and lability in the parent–child relationship during adolescence: Associations with pubertal timing and tempo. *Journal of Research on Adolescence, 25*, 474–489.

Marcia, J. E. (1980). Identity in adolescence. In J. Adelson (Ed.), *Handbook of adolescent psychology* (pp. 159–187). New York: Wiley.

Marcus, G. F. (1995). Children's overregularization of English plurals: A quantitative analysis. *Journal of Child Language, 22*, 447–459.

Marcus-Newhall, A., Thompson, S., & Thomas, C. (2001). Examining a gender stereotype: Menopausal women. *Journal of Applied Social Psychology, 31*, 698–719.

Mares, M.-L., & Pan, Z. (2013). Effects of *Sesame Street*: A meta-analysis of children's learning in 15 countries. *Journal of Applied Developmental Psychology, 34*, 140–151.

Margolis, J., Matthews, R. A., & Lapierre, L. M. (2014). Examining the antecedents of family-supportive supervisory behaviors. *Academy of Management Proceedings* (Meeting Abstract Supplement). Retrieved from proceedings.aom.org/content/2014/1/12906.short

Margolis, R. (2016). The changing demography of grandparenthood. *Journal of Marriage and Family, 78*, 611–622.

Margrett, J. A., Daugherty, K., Martin, P., MacDonald, M., Davey, A., Woodard, J. L., et al. (2011). Affect and loneliness among centenarians and the oldest old: The role of individual and social resources. *Aging and Mental Health, 15*, 385–396.

Marin, M. M., Rapisardi, G., & Tani, F. (2015). Two-day-old newborn infants recognize their mother by her axillary odour. *Acta Paediatrica, 104*, 237–240.

Marin, T. J., Chen, E., Munch, T., & Miller, G. (2009). Double exposure to acute stress and chronic family stress is associated with immune changes in children with asthma. *Psychosomatic Medicine, 71*, 378–384.

Marjoribanks, J., Farquhar, C., Roberts, H., & Lethaby, A. (2012). Long term hormone therapy for perimenopausal and postmenopausal women. *Cochrane Database of Systematic Reviews*, Issue 7, Art. No.: CD004143.

Markant, J. C., & Thomas, K. M. (2013). Postnatal brain development. In P. D. Zelazo (Ed.), *Oxford handbook of developmental psychology: Vol. 1. Body and mind* (pp. 129–163). New York: Oxford University Press.

Markman, E. M. (1992). Constraints on word learning: Speculations about their nature, origins, and domain specificity. In M. R. Gunnar & M. P. Maratsos (Eds.), *Minnesota Symposia on Child Psychology* (Vol. 25, pp. 59–101). Hillsdale, NJ: Erlbaum.

Markova, G., & Legerstee, M. (2006). Contingency, imitation, and affect sharing: Foundations of infants' social awareness. *Developmental Psychology, 42*, 132–141.

Markovits, H., & Vachon, R. (1990). Conditional reasoning, representation, and level of abstraction. *Developmental Psychology, 26*, 942–951.

Marks, N. F. (1996). Caregiving across the lifespan: National prevalence and predictors. *Family Relations, 45*, 27–36.

Marks, N. F., Bumpass, L. L., & Jun, H. (2004). Family roles and well-being during the middle life course. In O. G. Brim, C. D. Ryff, & R.C. Kessler (Eds.), *How healthy are we? A national study of well-being at midlife* (pp. 514–549). Chicago: University of Chicago Press.

Marks, N. F., & Greenfield, E. A. (2009). The influence of family relationships on adult psychological well-being and generativity. In M. C. Smith & N. DeFrates-Densch (Eds.), *Handbook of research on adult learning and development* (pp. 306–349). New York: Routledge.

Marks, N. F., & Lambert, J. D. (1998). Marital status continuity and change among young and midlife adults. *Journal of Family Issues, 19*, 652–686.

Markstrom, C. A., & Kalmanir, H. M. (2001). Linkages between the psychosocial stages of identity and intimacy and the ego strengths of fidelity and love. *Identity, 1*, 179–196.

Markstrom, C. A., Sabino, V., Turner, B., & Berman, R. (1997). The Psychosocial Inventory of Ego Strengths: Development and validation of a new Eriksonian measure. *Journal of Youth and Adolescence, 26*, 705–732.

Markunas, C. A., Xu, Z., Harlid, S., Wade, P. A., Lie, R. T., Taylor, J. A., & Wilcox, A. J. (2014). Identification of DNA methylation changes in newborns related to maternal smoking during pregnancy. *Environmental Health Perspectives, 10*, 1147–1153.

Markus, H. R., & Herzog, A. R. (1991). The role of self-concept in aging. In K. W. Schaie & M. P. Lawton (Eds.), *Annual review of gerontology and geriatrics* (pp. 110–143). New York: Springer.

Marlier, L., & Schaal, B. (2005). Human newborns prefer human milk: Conspecific milk odor is attractive without postnatal exposure. *Child Development, 76*, 155–168.

Marra, R., & Palmer, B. (2004). Encouraging intellectual growth: Senior college student profiles. *Journal of Adult Development, 11*, 111–122.

Marsee, M. A., & Frick, P. J. (2010). Callous-unemotional traits and aggression in youth. In W. F. Arsenio & E. A. Lemerise (Eds.), *Emotions, aggression, and morality in children: Bridging development and psychopathology* (pp. 137–156). Washington, DC: American Psychological Association.

Marsh, H. W. (1990). The structure of academic self-concept: The Marsh/Shavelson model. *Journal of Educational Psychology, 82*, 623–636.

Marsh, H. W., & Ayotte, V. (2003). Do multiple dimensions of self-concept become more differentiated with age? The differential distinctiveness hypothesis. *Journal of Educational Psychology, 95*, 687–706.

Marsh, H. W., Craven, R., & Debus, R. (1998). Structure, stability, and development of young children's self-concepts: A multicohort–multioccasion study. *Child Development, 69*, 1030–1053.

Marsh, H. W., Ellis, L. A., & Craven, R. G. (2002). How do preschool children feel about themselves? Unraveling measurement and multidimensional self-concept structure. *Developmental Psychology, 38*, 376–393.

Marsh, H. W., & Kleitman, S. (2005). Consequences of employment during high school: Character building, subversion of academic goals, or a threshold? *American Educational Research Journal, 42,* 331–369.

Marsh, H. W., Parada, R. H., & Ayotte, V. (2004). A multidimensional perspective of relations between self-concept (Self Description Questionnaire II) and adolescent mental health (Youth Self Report). *Psychological Assessment, 16,* 27–41.

Marsh, H. W., Trautwein, U., Lüdtke, O., Koller, O., & Baumert, J. (2005). Academic self-concept, interest, grades, and standardized test scores: Reciprocal effects models of causal ordering. *Child Development, 76,* 397–416.

Marshall, B. J., & Davies, B. (2011). Bereavement in children and adults following the death of a sibling. In R. Neimeyer, D. Harris, H. Winokuer, & G. Thornton (Eds.), *Grief and bereavement in contemporary society: Bridging research and practice* (pp. 107–116). New York: Routledge.

Marshall, E. A., & Butler, K. (2016). School-to-work transitions in emerging adulthood. In J. J. Arnett (Ed.), *Oxford handbook of emerging adulthood* (pp. 316–333). New York: Oxford University Press.

Marshall, P. J., & Meltzoff, A. N. (2011). Neural mirroring systems: Exploring the EEG mu rhythm in human infancy. *Developmental Cognitive Neuroscience, 1,* 110–123.

Marshall-Baker, A., Lickliter, R., & Cooper, R. P. (1998). Prolonged exposure to a visual pattern may promote behavioral organization in preterm infants. *Journal of Perinatal and Neonatal Nursing, 12,* 50–62.

Martin, A., Brazil, A., & Brooks-Gunn, J. (2012). The socioemotional outcomes of young children of teenage mothers by paternal coresidence. *Journal of Family Issues, 34,* 1217–1237.

Martin, A., Razza, R. A., & Brooks-Gunn, J. (2012). Specifying the links between household chaos and preschool children's development. *Early Child Development and Care, 182,* 1247–1263.

Martin, C. L., & Fabes, R. A. (2001). The stability and consequences of young children's same-sex peer interactions. *Developmental Psychology, 37,* 431–446.

Martin, C. L., Fabes, R. A., Hanish, L., Leonard, S., & Dinella, L. M. (2011). Experienced and expected similarity to same-gender peers: Moving toward a comprehensive model of gender segregation. *Sex Roles, 65,* 421–434.

Martin, C. L., & Halverson, C. F. (1987). The role of cognition in sex role acquisition. In D. B. Carter (Ed.), *Current conceptions of sex roles and sex typing: Theory and research* (pp. 123–137). New York: Praeger.

Martin, C. L., Kornienko, O., Schaefer, D. R., Hanish, L. D., Fabes, R. A., & Goble, P. (2013). The role of sex of peers and gender-typed activities in young children's peer affiliative networks: A longitudinal analysis of selection and influence. *Child Development, 84,* 921–937.

Martin, C. L., & Ruble, D. (2004). Children's search for gender cues: Cognitive perspectives on gender development. *Current Directions in Psychological Science, 13,* 67–70.

Martin, C. L., Ruble, D. N., & Szkrybalo, J. (2002). Cognitive theories of early gender development. *Psychological Bulletin, 128,* 903–933.

Martin, J. A., Hamilton, B. E., Osterman, M. J. K., Curtin, S. C., & Mathews, T. J. (2015). Births: Final data for 2013. *National Vital Statistics Reports, 64*(1). Hyattsville, MD: National Center for Health Statistics. Retrieved from www.cdc.gov/nchs/data/nvsr/nvsr64/nvsr64_01.pdf

Martin, J. L., Groth, G., Longo, L., & Rocha, T. L. (2015). Disordered eating and alcohol use among college women: Associations with race and big five traits. *Eating Behaviors, 17,* 149–152.

Martin, K. A. (1996). *Puberty, sexuality and the self: Girls and boys at adolescence.* New York: Routledge.

Martin, P., Long, M. V., & Poon, L. W. (2002). Age changes and differences in personality traits and states of the old and very old. *Journals of Gerontology, 57B,* P144–P152.

Martinez, G. M., & Abma, J. C. (2015). *Sexual activity, contraceptive use, and childbearing of teenagers aged 15–19 in the United States* (NCHS Data Brief No. 209). Hyattsville, MD: National Center for Health Statistics. Retrieved from www.cdc.gov/nchs/data/databriefs/db209.pdf

Martinez-Frias, M. L., Bermejo, E., Rodríguez Pinilla, E., & Frías, J. L. (2004). Risk for congenital anomalies associated with different sporadic and daily doses of alcohol consumption during pregnancy: A case-control study. *Birth Defects Research, Part A, Clinical and Molecular Teratology, 70,* 194–200.

Martinot, D., Bagès, C., & Désert, M. (2012). French children's awareness of gender stereotypes about mathematics and reading: When girls improve their reputation in math. *Sex Roles, 66,* 210–219.

Martinson, I. M., Davies, E., & McClowry, S. G. (1987). The long-term effect of sibling death on self-concept. *Journal of Pediatric Nursing, 2,* 227–235.

Martlew, M., & Connolly, K. J. (1996). Human figure drawings by schooled and unschooled children in Papua New Guinea. *Child Development, 67,* 2743–2762.

Maruna, S., LeBel, T. P., & Lanier, C. S. (2004). Generativity behind bars: Some "redemptive truths" about prison society. In E. de St. Aubin, D. P. McAdams, & T.-C. Kim (Eds.), *The generative society* (pp. 131–151). Washington, DC: American Psychological Association.

Maruta, T., Colligan, R. C., Malinchoc, M., & Offord, K. P. (2002). Optimism–pessimism assessed in the 1960s and self-reported health status 30 years later. *Mayo Clinic Proceedings, 77,* 748–753.

Marván, M. L., & Alcalá-Herrera, V. (2014). Age at menarche, reactions to menarche and attitudes towards menstruation among Mexican adolescent girls. *Journal of Pediatric and Adolescent Gynecology, 27,* 61–66.

Marván, M. L., Castillo-López, R., & Arroyo, L. (2013). Mexican beliefs and attitudes toward menopause and menopausal-related symptoms. *Journal of Psychosomatic Obstetrics & Gynecology, 34,* 39–45.

Marzolf, D. P., & DeLoache, J. S. (1994). Transfer in young children's understanding of spatial representations. *Child Development, 65,* 1–15.

Masataka, N. (1996). Perception of motherese in a signed language by 6-month-old deaf infants. *Developmental Psychology, 32,* 874–879.

Mascolo, M. F., & Fischer, K. W. (2007). The codevelopment of self and sociomoral emotions during the toddler years. In C. A. Brownell & C. B. Kopp (Eds.), *Socioemotional development in the toddler years: Transitions and transformations* (pp. 66–99). New York: Guilford.

Mascolo, M. F., & Fischer, K. W. (2015). Dynamic development of thinking, feeling, and acting. In W. F. Overton & P. C. Molenaar (Eds.), *Handbook of child psychology and developmental science: Vol. 1. Theory and method* (pp. 113–121). Hoboken, NJ: Wiley.

Mashburn, A. J., Pianta, R. C., Mamre, B. K., Downer, J. T., Barbarin, O. A., Bryant, D., et al. (2008). Measures of classroom quality in prekindergarten and children's development of academic, language, and social skills. *Child Development, 79,* 732–749.

Mason, C. A., Walker-Barnes, C. J., Tu, S., Simons, J., & Martisez-Arrue, R. (2004). Ethnic differences in the affective meaning of parental control behaviors. *Journal of Primary Prevention, 25,* 601–631.

Mason, M. G., & Gibbs, J. C. (1993a). Role-taking opportunities and the transition to advanced moral judgment. *Moral Education Forum, 18,* 1–12.

Mason, M. G., & Gibbs, J. C. (1993b). Social perspective taking and moral judgment among college students. *Journal of Adolescent Research, 8,* 109–123.

Masten, A. (2013). Risk and resilience in development. In P. D. Zelazo (Ed.), *Oxford handbook of developmental psychology: Vol. 2. Self and other* (pp. 579–607). New York: Oxford University Press.

Masten, A. S. (2014). Global perspectives on resilience in children and youth. *Child Development, 85,* 6–20.

Masten, A. S., & Cicchetti, D. (2010). Developmental cascades. *Development and Psychopathology, 22,* 491–495.

Masten, A. S., Narayan, A. J., Silverman, W. K., & Osofsky, J. D. (2015). Children in war and disaster. In M. H. Bornstein & T. Leventhal (Eds.), *Handbook of child psychology and developmental science: Vol. 4. Ecological settings and processes* (7th ed., pp. 704–745). Hoboken, NJ: Wiley.

Masters, R. K. (2012). Uncrossing the U.S. black–white mortality crossover: The role of cohort forces in life course mortality risk. *Demography, 49,* 773–796.

Mastropieri, D., & Turkewitz, G. (1999). Prenatal experience and neonatal responsiveness to vocal expression of emotion. *Developmental Psychobiology, 35,* 204–214.

Mastropieri, M. A., Scruggs, T. E., Guckert, M., Thompson, C. C., & Weiss, M. P. (2013). Inclusion and learning disabilities: Will the past be prologue? In J. P. Bakken, F. E. Oblakor, & A. Rotatori (Eds.), *Advances in special education* (Vol. 25, pp. 1–17). Bingley, UK: Emerald Group Publishing.

Masur, E. F., & Rodemaker, J. E. (1999). Mothers' and infants' spontaneous vocal, verbal, and action imitation during the second year. *Merrill-Palmer Quarterly, 45,* 392–412.

Mather, M. (2010, May). *U.S. children in single-mother families* (PRB Data Brief). Washington, DC: Population Reference Bureau.

Mather, M., & Carstensen, L. L. (2005). Aging and motivated cognition: The positivity effect in attention and memory. *Trends in Cognitive Sciences, 9,* 496–502.

Mather, M., Jacobsen, L. A., & Pollard, K. M. (2015). Aging in the United States. *Population Bulletin, 70*(2). Retrieve from http://www.prb.org/pdf16/aging-us-population-bulletin.pdf

Matlen, B. J., & Klahr, D. (2013). Sequential effects of high and low instructional guidance on children's acquisition of experimentation skills: Is it all in the timing? *Instructional Science, 41,* 621–634.

Matsuba, M. K., Murzyn, T., & Hart, D. (2014). Moral identity development and community. In M. Killen & J. G. Smetana (Eds.), *Handbook of moral development* (2nd ed., pp. 520–537). New York: Psychology Press.

Matthews, H. (2014, January 14). *A billion dollar boost for child care and early learning.* CLASP: Policy solutions that work for low-income people. Retrieved from www.clasp.org/issues/child-care-and-early-education/in-focus/a-billion-dollar-boost-for-child-care-and-early-learning

Matthews, K. A., & Gallo, L. C. (2011). Psychological perspectives on pathways linking socioeconomic status and physical healthy. *Annual Review of Psychology, 62,* 501–530.

Matthews, K. A., Gump, B. B., Harris, K. F., Haney, T. L., & Barefoot, J. C. (2004). Hostile behaviors predict cardiovascular mortality among men enrolled in the Multiple Risk Factor Intervention Trial. *Circulation, 109,* 66–70.

Mattison, J. A., Roth, G. S., Beasley, T. M., Tilmont, E. M., Handy, A. M., Herbert, R. L., et al. (2012). Impact of caloric restriction on health and survival in rhesus monkeys from the NIA study. *Nature, 489,* 318–321.

Mattson, S. N., Calarco, K. E., & Lang, A. R. (2006). Focused and shifting attention in children with heavy prenatal alcohol exposure. *Neuropsychology, 20,* 361–369.

Mattson, S. N., Crocker, N., & Nguyen, T. T. (2012). Fetal alcohol spectrum disorders: Neuropsychological and behavioral features. *Neuropsychological Review, 21,* 81–101.

Mattsson, N., Insel, P. S., Donohue, M., Landau, S., Jagust, W. J., Shaw, L. M., et al. (2015). Independent information from cerebrospinal fluid amyloid-β and florbetapir imaging in Alzheimer's disease. *Brain, 138,* 772–783.

Mauratore, A. M., & Earl, J. K. (2015). Improving retirement outcomes: The role of resources, pre-retirement planning and transition characteristics. *Aging & Society, 35,* 2100–2140.

Maurer, D., & Lewis, T. (2013). Human visual plasticity: Lessons from children treated for congenital cataracts. In J. K. E. Steeves & L. R. Harris (Eds.), *Plasticity in sensory systems* (pp. 75–93). New York: Cambridge University Press.

Maurer, D., Mondloch, C. J., & Lewis, T. L. (2007). Sleeper effects. *Developmental Science, 10,* 40–47.

Maurer, T. J., Wrenn, K. A., & Weiss, E. M. (2003). Toward understanding and managing stereotypical beliefs about older workers' ability and desire for learning and development. In J. J. Martocchio & G. R. Ferris (Eds.), *Research in personnel and human resources management* (Vol. 22, pp. 253–285). Stamford, CT: JAI Press.

Maxwell, R., & Lynn, S. J. (2015). Exercise: A path to physical and psychological well-being. In S. J. Lynn, W. T. O'Donohue, & S. O. Lilienfeld (Eds.), *Health, happiness, and well-being: Better living through psychological science* (pp. 223–248). Thousand Oaks, CA: Sage.

Mayberry, R. I. (2010). Early language acquisition and adult language ability: What sign language reveals about the critical period for language. In M. Marshark & P. E. Spencer (Eds.), *Oxford handbook of deaf studies, language, and education* (Vol. 2, pp. 281–291). New York: Oxford University Press.

Mayer, R. E. (2013). Problem solving. In D. Reisberg (Ed.), *Oxford handbook of cognitive psychology* (pp. 769–778). New York: Oxford University Press.

Mayeux, L., & Cillessen, A. H. N. (2003). Development of social problem solving in early childhood: Stability, change, and associations with social competence. *Journal of Genetic Psychology, 164,* 153–173.

Mayeux, L., Houser, J. J., & Dyches, K. D. (2011). Social acceptance and popularity: Two distinct forms of peer status. In A. H. N. Cillessen, D. Schwartz, & L. Mayeux (Eds.), *Popularity in the peer system* (pp. 79–102). New York: Guilford.

Maynard, A. E. (2002). Cultural teaching: The development of teaching skills in Maya sibling interactions. *Child Development, 73,* 969–982.

Maynard, A. E., & Greenfield, P. M. (2003). Implicit cognitive development in cultural tools and children: Lessons from Maya Mexico. *Cognitive Development, 18,* 489–510.

Maynard, B. (2014, November 2). My right to death with dignity at 29. *CNN Opinion.* Retrieved from www.cnn.com/2014/10/07/opinion/maynard-assisted-suicide-cancer-dignity

Mazerolle, M., Régner, I., Rigalleau, F., & Huguet, P. (2015). Stereotype that alters the subjective experience of memory. *Experimental Psychology, 62,* 395–402.

McAdams, D. P. (2011). Life narratives. In K. L. Fingerman, C. A. Berg, J. Smith, & T. C. Antonucci (Eds.), *Handbook of life-span development* (pp. 589–610). New York: Springer.

McAdams, D. P. (2013a). The positive psychology of adult generativity: Caring for the next generation and constructing a redemptive life. In J. D. Sinnott (Ed.), *Positive psychology: Advances in understanding adult motivation* (pp. 191–205). New York: Springer.

McAdams, D. P. (2013b). *The redemptive self: Stories Americans live by* (rev. ed.). New York: Oxford University Press.

McAdams, D. P. (2014). The life narrative at midlife. In B. Schiff (Ed.), *Rereading personal narrative and the life course* (pp. 57–69). Hoboken, NJ: Wiley Periodicals.

McAdams, D. P., & de St. Aubin, E. (1992). A theory of generativity and its assessment through self-report, behavioral acts, and narrative themes in autobiography. *Journal of Personality and Social Psychology, 62,* 1003–1015.

McAdams, D. P., Diamond, A., de St. Aubin, E., & Mansfield, E. (1997). Stories of commitment: The psychosocial construction of generative lives. *Journal of Personality and Social Psychology, 72,* 678–694.

McAdams, D. P., & Guo, J. (2015). Narrating the generative life. *Psychological Science, 26,* 475–483.

McAdams, D. P., Hart, H. M., & Maruna, S. (1998). The anatomy of generativity. In D. P. McAdams & E. de St. Aubin (Eds.), *Generativity and adult development* (pp. 7–43). Washington, DC: American Psychological Association.

McAdams, D. P., & Logan, R. L. (2004). What is generativity? In E. de St. Aubin & D. P. McAdams (Eds.), *The generative society: Caring for future generations* (pp. 15–31). Washington, DC: American Psychological Association.

McAdoo, H. P., & Younge, S. N. (2009). Black families. In H. A. Neville, B. M. Tynes, & S. O. Utsey (Eds.), *Handbook of African American psychology* (pp. 103–115). Thousand Oaks, CA: Sage.

McAlister, A., & Peterson, C. C. (2006). Mental playmates: Siblings, executive functioning and theory of mind. *British Journal of Developmental Psychology, 24,* 733–751.

McAlister, A., & Peterson, C. C. (2007). A longitudinal study of child siblings and theory of mind development. *Cognitive Development, 22,* 258–270.

McArdle, J. J., Ferrer-Caja, E., Hamagami, F., & Woodcock, R. W. (2002). Comparative longitudinal structural analyses of the growth and decline of multiple intellectual abilities over the life span. *Developmental Psychology, 38,* 115–142.

McAuley, E., & Elavsky, S. (2008). Self-efficacy, physical activity, and cognitive function. In W. W. Spirduso, L. W. Poon, & W. Chodzko-Zajko (Eds.), *Exercise and its mediating effects on cognition* (pp. 69–84). Champaign, IL: Human Kinetics.

McCabe, A. (1997). Developmental and cross-cultural aspects of children's narration. In M. Bamberg (Ed.), *Narrative development: Six approaches* (pp. 137–174). Mahwah, NJ: Erlbaum.

McCabe, A., Tamis-LeMonda, C. S., Bornstein, M. H., Cates, C. B., Golinkoff, R., Guerra, A. W., et al. (2013). Multilingual children: Beyond myths and toward best practices. *Society for Research in Child Development Social Policy Report, 27*(4).

McCarthy, J. (2014). *Seven in 10 Americans back euthanasia.* Retrieved from www.gallup.com/poll/171704/seven-americans-back-euthanasia.aspx

McCartney, K., Dearing, E., Taylor, B., & Bub, K. (2007). Quality child care supports the achievement of low-income children: Direct and indirect pathways through caregiving and the home environment. *Journal of Applied Developmental Psychology, 28,* 411–426.

McCartney, K., Owen, M., Booth, C., Clarke-Stewart, A., & Vandell, D. (2004). Testing a maternal attachment model of behavior problems in early childhood. *Journal of Child Psychology and Psychiatry, 45,* 765–778.

McCarton, C. (1998). Behavioral outcomes in low birth weight infants. *Pediatrics, 102,* 1293–1297.

McCarty, M. E., & Ashmead, D. H. (1999). Visual control of reaching and grasping in infants. *Developmental Psychology, 35,* 620–631.

McCarty, M. E., & Keen, R. (2005). Facilitating problem-solving performance among 9- and 12-month-old infants. *Journal of Cognition and Development, 6,* 209–228.

McClain, C. S., Rosenfeld, B., & Breitbart, W. (2003). Effect of spiritual well-being on end-of-life despair in terminally ill cancer patients. *Lancet, 361,* 1603–1607.

McClain-Jacobson, C., Rosenfeld, B., Kosinski, A., Pessin, H., Cimino, J. E., & Breitbart, W. (2004). Belief in an afterlife, spiritual well-being and end-of-life despair in patients with advanced cancer. *General Hospital Psychiatry, 26,* 484–486.

McColgan, K. L., & McCormack, T. (2008). Searching and planning: Young children's reasoning about past and future event sequences. *Child Development, 79,* 1477–1479.

McCormack, M., Anderson, E., & Adams, A. (2014). Cohort effect on the coming out experiences of bisexual men. *Sociology, 48,* 1207–1223.

McCormack, T., & Atance, C. M. (2011). Planning in young children: A review and synthesis. *Developmental Review, 31,* 1–31.

McCrae, C., Roth, A. J., Zamora, R., Dautovich, N. D., & Lichstein, K. L. (2015). Late life sleep and sleep disorders. In P. A. Lichtenberg, B. T. Mast, B. D. Carpenter, & J. Loebach Wetherell (Eds.), *APA handbook of clinical geropsychology: Vol. 2. Assessment, treatment, and issues in later life* (pp. 369–394). Washington, DC: American Psychological Association.

McCrae, R., & Costa, P. T., Jr. (2006). Cross-cultural perspectives on adult personality trait development. In D. K. Mroczek & T. D. Little (Eds.), *Handbook of personality development* (pp. 129–146). Mahwah, NJ: Erlbaum.

McCune, L. (1993). The development of play as the development of consciousness. In M. H. Bornstein & A. O'Reilly (Eds.), *New directions for child development* (No. 59, pp. 67–79). San Francisco: Jossey-Bass.

McDaniel, M. A., Maier, S. F., & Einstein, G. O. (2002). "Brain-specific" nutrients: A memory cure? *Psychological Science in the Public Interest, 3,* 12–38.

McDill, T., Hall, S. K., & Turell, S. C. (2006). Aging and creating families: Never-married heterosexual women over forty. *Journal of Women and Aging, 18,* 37–50.

McDonald, K., Malti, T., Killen, M., & Rubin, K. (2104). Best friends' discussion of social dilemmas. *Journal of Youth and Adolescence, 43,* 233–244.

McDonough, C., Song, L., Hirsh-Pasek, K., & Golinkoff, R. M. (2011). An image is worth a thousand words: Why nouns tend to dominate verbs in early word learning. *Developmental Science, 14,* 181–189.

McDonough, L. (1999). Early declarative memory for location. *British Journal of Developmental Psychology, 17,* 381–402.

McDowell, D. J., & Parke, R. D. (2000). Differential knowledge of display rules for positive and negative emotions: Influences from parents, influences on peers. *Social Development, 9,* 415–432.

McEachern, A. D., & Snyder, J. (2012). Gender differences in predicting antisocial behaviors: Developmental consequences of physical and relational aggression. *Journal of Abnormal Child Psychology, 40,* 501–512.

McElhaney, K. B., & Allen, J. P. (2001). Autonomy and adolescent social functioning: The moderating effect of risk. *Child Development, 72,* 220–235.

McElhaney, K. B., Allen, J. P., Stephenson, J. C., & Hare, A. L. (2009). Attachment and autonomy during adolescence. In R. M. Lerner & L. Steiberg (Eds.), *Handbook of adolescent psychology: Vol. 1. Individual bases of adolescent development* (3rd ed., pp. 358–403). Hoboken, NJ: Wiley.

McElwain, N. L., & Booth-LaForce, C. (2006). Maternal sensitivity to infant distress and nondistress as predictors of infant–mother attachment security. *Journal of Family Psychology, 20,* 247–255.

McFarland-Piazza, L., Hazen, N., Jacobvitz, D., & Boyd-Soisson, E. (2012). The development of father–child attachment: Associations between adult attachment representations, recollections of childhood experiences and caregiving. *Early Child Development and Care, 182,* 701–721.

McGarrity, L. A. (2014). Socioeconomic status as context for minority stress and health disparities among lesbian, gay, and bisexual individuals. *Psychology of Sexual Orientation and Gender Diversity, 1,* 383–397.

McGee, L. M., & Richgels, D. J. (2012). *Literacy's beginnings: Supporting young readers and writers* (6th ed.). Boston: Allyn and Bacon.

McGoldrick, M., & Shibusawa, T. (2012). The family life cycle. In F. Walsh (Ed.), *Normal family processes: Growing diversity and complexity* (pp. 375–398). New York: Guilford.

McGonigle-Chalmers, M., Slater, H., & Smith, A. (2014). Rethinking private speech in preschoolers: The effects of social presence. *Developmental Psychology, 50,* 829–836.

McGregor, R. A., Cameron-Smith, D., & Poppitt, S. D. (2014). It is not just muscle mass: A review of muscle quality, composition and metabolism during ageing as determinants of muscle function and mobility in later life. *Longevity and Healthspan, 3,* 9.

McGue, M., Elkins, I., Walden, B., & Iacono, W. G. (2005). Perceptions of the parent–adolescent relationship: A longitudinal investigation. *Developmental Psychology, 41,* 971–984.

McHale, J. P., Kazali, C., Rotman, T., Talbot, J., Carleton, M., & Lieberson, R. (2004). The transition to coparenthood: Parents' prebirth expectations and early coparental adjustment at 3 months postpartum. *Development and Psychopathology, 16,* 711–733.

McHale, J. P., Kuersten-Hogan, R., & Rao, N. (2004). Growing points for coparenting theory and research. *Journal of Adult Development, 11,* 221–234.

McHale, J. P., & Rotman, T. (2007). Is seeing believing? Expectant parents' outlooks on coparenting and later coparenting solidarity. *Infant Behavior and Development, 30,* 63–81.

McHale, S. M., Updegraff, K. A., & Whiteman, S. D. (2012). Sibling relationships and influences in childhood and adolescence. *Journal of Marriage and Family, 74,* 913–930.

McIntosh, H., Metz, E., & Youniss, J. (2005). Community service and identity formation in adolescents. In J. S. Mahoney, R. W. Larson, & J. S. Eccles (Eds.), *Organized activities as contexts of development: Extracurricular activities, after-school and community programs* (pp. 331–351). Mahwah, NJ: Erlbaum.

McIntosh, W. D., Locker, L., Briley, K., Ryan, R., & Scott, A. J. (2011). What do older adults seek in their potential romantic partners? Evidence from online personal ads. *International Journal of Aging and Human Development, 72,* 67–82.

McIntyre, S., Blair, E., Badawi, N., Keogh, J., & Nelson, K. B. (2013). Antecedents of cerebral palsy and perinatal death in term and late preterm singletons. *Obstetrics and Gynecology, 122,* 869–877.

Mckee, A. C., & Daneshvar, D. H. (2015). The neuropathology of traumatic brain injury. *Handbook of Clinical Neurology, 127,* 45–66.

McKee-Ryan, F. M., Virick, M., Prussia, G. E., Harvey, J., & Lilly, J. D. (2009). Life after the layoff: Getting a job worth keeping. *Journal of Organizational Behavior, 30,* 561–580.

McKenna, J. J. (2002, September/October). Breast-feeding and bedsharing still useful (and important) after all these years. *Mothering, 114.* Retrieved from www.mothering.com/articles/new_baby/sleep/mckenna.html

McKenna, J. J., & McDade, T. (2005). Why babies should never sleep alone: A review of the co-sleeping controversy in relation to SIDS, bedsharing, and breastfeeding. *Paediatric Respiratory Reviews, 6,* 134–152.

McKenna, J. J., & Volpe, L. E. (2007). Sleeping with baby: An Internet-based sampling of parental experiences, choices, perceptions, and interpretations in a Western industrialized context. *Infant and Child Development, 16,* 359–385.

McKeown, M. G., & Beck, I. L. (2009). The role of metacognition in understanding and supporting reading comprehension. In D. J. Hacker, J. Dunlosky, & A. C. Graesser (Eds.), *Handbook of metacognition in education* (pp. 7–25). New York: Routledge.

McKim, W. A., & Hancock, S. (2013). *Drugs and behavior* (7th ed.). Upper Saddle River, NJ: Pearson.

McKinney, C., Donnelly, R., & Renk, K. (2008). Perceived parenting, positive and negative perceptions of parents, and late adolescent emotional adjustment. *Child and Adolescent Mental health, 13,* 66–73.

McKown, C. (2013). Social equity theory and racial-ethnic achievement gaps. *Child Development, 84,* 1120–1136.

McKown, C., Gregory, A., & Weinstein, R. S. (2010). Expectations, stereotypes, and self-fulfilling prophecies in classroom and school life. In J. L. Meece & J. S. Eccles (Eds.), *Handbook of research on schools, schooling and human development* (pp. 256–274). New York: Routledge.

McKown, C., & Strambler, M. J. (2009). Developmental antecedents and social and academic consequences of stereotype-consciousness in middle childhood. *Child Development, 80,* 1643–1659.

McKown, C., & Weinstein, R. S. (2003). The development and consequences of stereotype consciousness in middle childhood. *Child Development, 74,* 498–515.

McKown, C., & Weinstein, R. S. (2008). Teacher expectations, classroom context, and the achievement gap. *Journal of School Psychology, 46,* 235–261.

McLanahan, S. (1999). Father absence and the welfare of children. In E. M. Hetherington (Ed.), *Coping with divorce, single parenting, and remarriage: A risk and resiliency perspective* (pp. 117–145). Mahwah, NJ: Erlbaum.

McLaughlin, K. A., Fox, N. A., Zeanah, C. H., & Nelson, C. A. (2011). Adverse rearing environments and neural development in children: The development of frontal electroencephalogram asymmetry. *Biological Psychiatry, 70,* 1008–1015.

McLaughlin, K. A., Sheridan, M. A., Tibu, F., Fox, N. A., Zeanah, C. H., & Nelson, C. H., III. (2015). Causal effects of the early caregiving environment on development of stress response systems in children. *Proceedings of the National Academy of Sciences, 112,* 5637–5642.

McLaughlin, K. A., Sheridan, M. A., Winter, W., Fox, N. A., Zeanah, C. H., Nelson, C. H., III, et al. (2014). Widespread reductions in cortical thickness following severe early-life deprivation: A neurodevelopmental pathway to attention-deficit hyperactivity disorder. *Biological Psychiatry, 76,* 629–638.

McLean, K. C. (2008). Stories of the young and the old: Personal continuity and narrative identity. *Developmental Psychology, 44,* 254–264.

McLeskey, J., & Waldron, N. L. (2011). Educational programs for elementary students with learning disabilities: Can they be both effective and inclusive? *Learning Disabilities: Research and Practice, 26,* 48–57.

McLoyd, V. C., Kaplan, R., Hardaway, C. R., & Wood, D. (2007). Does endorsement of physical discipline matter? Assessing moderating influences on the maternal and child psychological correlates of physical discipline in African-American families. *Journal of Family Psychology, 21,* 165–175.

McLoyd, V. C., & Smith, J. (2002). Physical discipline and behavior problems in African-American, European-American, and Hispanic children: Emotional support as a moderator. *Journal of Marriage and Family, 64,* 40–53.

McNeil, D. G., Jr. (2014, March 5). Early treatment is found to clear H.I.V. in a 2nd baby. *New York Times,* p. A1.

Mead, E. L., Doorenbos, A. Z., Javid, S. H., Haozous, E. A., Alvord, L. A., Flum, D. R., & Morris, A. M. (2013). Shared decision-making for cancer care among racial and ethnic minorities: A systematic review. *American Journal of Public Health, 103,* e15–e29.

Mead, G. H. (1934). *Mind, self, and society.* Chicago: University of Chicago Press.

Mead, M. (1928). *Coming of age in Samoa.* Ann Arbor, MI: Morrow.

Meade, C. S., Kershaw, T. S., & Ickovics, J. R. (2008). The intergenerational cycle of teenage motherhood: An ecological approach. *Health Psychology, 27,* 419–429.

Meadus, R. J., & Twomey, J. C. (2011). Men student nurses: The nursing education experience. *Nursing Forum, 46,* 269–279.

Meeus, W., Oosterwegel, A., & Vollebergh, W. (2002). Parental and peer attachment and identity development in adolescence. *Journal of Adolescence, 25,* 93–106.

Meeus, W., van de Schoot, R., Keijsers, L., & Branje, S. (2012). Identity statuses as developmental trajectories: A five-wave longitudinal study in early-to-middle and middle-to-late adolescents. *Journal of Youth and Adolescence, 41,* 1008–1021.

Meeus, W., van de Schoot, R., Keijsers, L., Schwartz, S. J., & Branje, S. (2010). On the progression and stability of adolescent identity formation: A five-wave longitudinal study in early-to-middle and middle-to-late adolescence. *Child Development, 81,* 1565–1581.

Mehanna, E., Hamik, A., & Josephson, R. A. (2016). Cardiorespiratory fitness and atherosclerosis: Recent data and future directions. *Current Atherosclerosis Reports, 18*(5), 26.

Mehlson, M., Platz, M., & Fromholt, P. (2003). Life satisfaction across the life course: Evaluations of the most and least satisfying decades of life. *International Journal of Aging and Human Development, 57,* 217–236.

Mehta, C. M., & Strough, J. (2009). Sex segregation in friendships and normative contexts across the life span. *Developmental Review, 29,* 21–220.

Mehta, L. S., Beckie, T. M., DeVon, H. A., Grines, C. L., Krumholz, H. M., Johnson, M. N., et al. (2016). Acute myocardial infarction in women: A scientific statement from the American Heart Association. *Circulation, 133,* 916–947.

Mehta, N. K., Sudharsanan, N., & Elo, I. T. (2014). Race/ethnicity and disability among older Americans. In K. E. Whitfield & Tamara A. Baker (Eds.), *Handbook of minority aging* (pp. 111–129). New York: Springer.

Mei, J. (1994). The Northern Chinese custom of rearing babies in sandbags: Implications for motor and intellectual development. In J. H. A. van Rossum & J. I. Laszlo (Eds.), *Motor development: Aspects of normal and delayed development* (pp. 41–48). Amsterdam, Netherlands: VU Uitgeverij.

Meier, A., & Allen, G. (2009). Romantic relationships from adolescence to young adulthood: Evidence from the National Longitudinal Study of Adolescent Health. *Sociological Quarterly, 50,* 308–335.

Meins, E. (2013). Sensitive attunement to infants' internal states: Operationalizing the construct of mind-mindedness. *Attachment & Human Development, 15,* 524–544.

Meins, E., Fernyhough, C., de Rosnay, M., Arnott, B., Leekam, S. R., & Turner, M. (2012). Mind-mindedness as a multidimensional construct: Appropriate and nonattuned mind-related comments independently predict infant–mother attachment in a socially diverse sample. *Infancy, 17,* 393–415.

Meins, E., Fernyhough, C., Wainwright, R., Clark-Carter, D., Gupta, M. D., Fradley, E., & Tucker, M. (2003). Pathways to understanding mind: Construct validity and predictive validity of maternal mind-mindedness. *Child Development, 74,* 1194–1211.

Melby, M. K., Lock, M., & Kaufert, P. (2005). Culture and symptom reporting at menopause. *Human Reproduction Update, 11,* 495–512.

Melby-Lervag, M., & Hulme, C. (2010). Serial and free recall in children can be improved by training: Evidence for the importance of phonological and semantic representations in immediate memory tasks. *Psychological Science, 21,* 1694–1700.

Meldrum, R. C., Barnes, J. C., & Hay, C. (2015). Sleep deprivation, low self-control, and delinquency: A test of the strength model of self-control. *Journal of Youth and Adolescence, 44,* 465–477.

Meltzoff, A. (2013). Origins of social cognition: Bidirectional self-other mapping and the "like-me" hypothesis. In M. Banaji & S. A. Gelman (Eds.), *Navigating the social world: What infants, children, and other species can teach us* (pp. 139–144). New York: Oxford University Press.

Meltzoff, A. N., & Kuhl, P. K. (1994). Faces and speech: Intermodal processing of biologically relevant signals in infants and adults. In D. J. Lewkowicz & R. Lickliter (Eds.), *The development of intersensory perception* (pp. 335–369). Hillsdale, NJ: Erlbaum.

Meltzoff, A. N., & Moore, M. K. (1977). Imitation of facial and manual gestures by human neonates. *Science, 198,* 75–78.

Meltzoff, A. N., & Moore, M. K. (1994). Imitation, memory, and the representation of persons. *Infant Behavior and Development, 17,* 83–99.

Meltzoff, A. N., & Williamson, R. A. (2010). The importance of imitation for theories of social-cognitive development. In J. G. Bremner & T. D. Wachs (Eds.), *Wiley-Blackwell handbook of infant development* (2nd ed., pp. 345–364). Oxford, UK: Wiley-Blackwell.

Meltzoff, A. N., & Williamson, R. A. (2013). Imitation: Social, cognitive, and theoretical perspectives. In P. D. Zelazo (Ed.), *Oxford handbook of developmental psychology: Vol. 1. Body and mind* (pp. 651–682). New York: Oxford University Press.

Melzi, G., & Schick, A. R. (2013). Language and literacy in the school years. In J. B. Gleason & N. B. Ratner (Eds.), *Development of language* (8th ed., pp. 329–365). Upper Saddle River, NJ: Pearson.

Memo, L., Gnoato, E., Caminiti, S., Pichini, S., & Tarani, L. (2013). Fetal alcohol spectrum disorders and fetal alcohol syndrome: The state of the art and new diagnostic tools. *Early Human Development, 89S1,* S40–S43.

Mendle, J., Turkheimer, E., & Emery, R. E. (2007). Detrimental psychological outcomes associated with early pubertal timing in adolescent girls. *Developmental Review, 27,* 151–171.

Menesini, E., Calussi, P., & Nocentini, A. (2012). Cyberbullying and traditional bullying: Unique, additive, and synergistic effects on psychological health symptoms. In L. Qing, D. Cross, & P. K. Smith (Eds.), *Cyberbullying in the global playground: Research from international perspectives* (pp. 245–262). Malden, MA: Wiley-Blackwell.

Menesini, E., & Spiel, C. (2012). Introduction: Cyberbullying: Development, consequences, risk and protective factors. *European Journal of Developmental Psychology, 9,* 163–167.

Mennella, J. A., & Beauchamp, G. K. (1998). Early flavor experiences: Research update. *Nutrition Reviews, 56,* 205–211.

Menon, U. (2001). Middle adulthood in cultural perspective: The imagined and the experienced in three cultures. In M. E. Lachman (Ed.), *Handbook of midlife development* (pp. 40–74). New York: Wiley.

Ment, L. R., Vohr, B., Allan, W., Katz, K. H., Schneider, K. C., Westerveld, M., Cuncan, C. C., & Makuch, R. W. (2003). Change in cognitive function over time in very low-birth-weight infants. *JAMA, 289,* 705–711.

Merikangas, K. R., He, J-P. Burstein, M., Swanson, S. A. Avenevoli, S., Cui, L., Benjet, C., et al. (2010). Lifetime prevalence of mental disorders in U.S. adolescents: Results from the National Comorbidity Survey Replication—Adolescent Supplement (NCS-A). *Journal of the American Academy of Child and Adolescent Psychiatry, 49,* 980–989.

Messinger, D. S., & Fogel, A. (2007). The interactive development of social smiling. In R. Kail (Ed.), *Advances in child development and behavior* (Vol. 35, pp. 327–366). Oxford, UK: Elsevier.

Metheny, J., McWhirter, E. H., & O'Neil, M. E. (2008). Measuring perceived teacher support and its influence on adolescent career development. *Journal of Career Assessment, 16,* 218–237.

Methven, L., Allen, V. J., Withers, C. A., & Gosney, M. A. (2012). Aging and taste. *Proceedings of the Nutrition Society, 71,* 556–565.

MetLife. (2011a). *MetLife study of caregiving costs to working caregivers: Double jeopardy for baby boomers caring for their parents.* Westport, CT: National Alliance for Caregiving and MetLife Mature Market Institute.

MetLife. (2011b). *MetLife study of elder financial abuse: Crimes of occasion, desperation and predation against America's elders.* Retrieved from www.metlife.com/assets/cao/mmi/publications/studies/2011/mmi-elder-financial-abuse.pdf

Meyer, B. J. F., Russo, C., & Talbot, A. (1995). Discourse comprehension and problem solving: Decisions about the treatment of breast cancer by women across the lifespan. *Psychology and Aging, 10,* 84–103.

Meyer, B. J. F., Talbot, A. P., & Ranalli, C. (2007). Why older adults make more immediate treatment decisions about cancer than younger adults. *Psychology and Aging, 22,* 505–524.

Meyer, R. (2009). Infant feeding in the first year. 1: Feeding practices in the first six months of life. *Journal of Family Health Care, 19,* 13–16.

Meyer, S., Raikes, H. A., Virmani, E. A., Waters, S., & Thompson, R. A. (2014). Parent emotion representations and the socialization of emotion regulation in the family. *International Journal of Behavioral Development, 38,* 164–173.

Meyers, A. B., & Berk, L. E. (2014). Make-believe play and self-regulation. In L. Brooker, M. Blaise, & S. Edwards (Eds.), *Sage handbook of play and learning in early childhood* (pp. 43–55). London: Sage.

Michalik, N. M., Eisenberg, N., Spinrad, T. L., Ladd, B., Thompson, M., & Valiente, C. (2007). Longitudinal relations among parental emotional expressivity and sympathy and prosocial behavior in adolescence. *Social Development, 16,* 286–309.

Michiels, D., Grietens, H., Onghena, P., & Kuppens, S. (2010). Perceptions of maternal and paternal attachment security in middle childhood: Links with positive parental affection and psychological adjustment. *Early Child Development and Care, 180,* 211–225.

Mienaltowski, A. (2011). Everyday problem solving across the adult life span. *Annals of the New York Academy of Sciences, 1235,* 75–85.

Miga, E. M., Gdula, J. A., & Allen, J. P. (2012). Fighting fair: Adaptive marital conflict strategies as predictors of future adolescent peer and romantic relationship quality. *Social Development, 21,* 443–460.

Mikami, A. Y., Lerner, M. D., & Lun, J. (2010). Social context influences on children's rejection by their peers. *Child Development Perspectives, 4,* 123–130.

Mikami, A. Y., Szwedo, D. E., Allen, J. P., Evans, M. A., & Hare, A. L. (2010). Adolescent peer relationships and behavior problems predict young adults' communication on social networking websites. *Developmental Psychology, 46,* 46–56.

Mikkola, T. M., Portegijs, E., Rantakokko, M., Gagné, J.-P., Rantanen, T., & Viljanen, A. (2015). Association of self-reported hearing difficulty to objective and perceived participation outside the home in older community-dwelling adults. *Journal of Aging and Health, 27,* 103–122.

Mikulincer, M., Florian, V., & Hirschberger, G. (2003). The existential function of close relationships: Introducing death into the science of love. *Personality and Social Psychology Review, 7,* 20–40.

Mikulincer, M., & Shaver, P. R. (2008). An attachment perspective on bereavement. In M. S. Stroebe, R. O. Hansson, H. Schut, & W. Stroebe (Eds.), *Handbook of bereavement research and practice* (pp. 87–112). Washington, DC: American Psychological Association.

Milevsky, A., Schlechter, M., Netter, S., & Keehn, D. (2007). Maternal and paternal parenting styles in adolescents: Associations with self-esteem, depression, and life satisfaction. *Journal of Child and Family Studies, 16,* 39–47.

Milkie, M. A., Bierman, A., & Schieman, S. (2008). How adult children influence older parents' mental health: Integrating stress-process and life-course perspectives. *Social Psychology Quarterly, 71,* 86–105.

Milkie, M. A., Nomaguchi, K. M., & Denny, K. E. (2015). Does the amount of time mothers spend with children or adolescents matter? *Journal of Marriage and Family, 77,* 355–372.

Miller, D. I., & Halpern, D. F. (2014). The new science of cognitive sex differences. *Trends in Cognitive Sciences, 18,* 37–44.

Miller, D. I., Taler, V., Davidson, P. S. R., & Messier, C. (2012). Measuring the impact of exercise on cognitive aging: Methodological issues. *Neurobiology of Aging, 33,* 622.e29–622.e43.

Miller, D. N. (2011). *Child and adolescent suicidal behavior: School-based prevention, assessment, and intervention.* New York: Guilford.

Miller, G. E., Chen, E., Fok, A. K., Walker, H., Lim, A., Hiholls, E. F., et al. (2009). Low early-life social class leaves a biological residue manifested by decreased glucocorticoid and increased proinflammatory signaling. *Proceedings of the National Academy of Sciences, 106,* 14716–14721.

Miller, J., Slomczynski, K. M., & Kohn, M. L. (1985). Continuity of learning-generalization: The effect of job on men's intellective process in the United States and Poland. *American Journal of Sociology, 91,* 593–615.

Miller, J. G., & Bersoff, D. M. (1995). Development in the context of everyday family relationships: Culture, interpersonal morality, and adaptation. In M. Killen & D. Hart (Eds.), *Morality in everyday life: Developmental perspectives* (pp. 259–282). Cambridge, UK: Cambridge University Press.

Miller, J. G., & Bland, C. G. (2014). A cultural psychology perspective on moral development. In M. Killen & J. G. Smetana (Eds.), *Handbook of moral development* (2nd ed., pp. 208–234). New York: Psychology Press.

Miller, L. E., Grabell, A., Thomas, A., Bermann, E., & Graham-Bermann, S. A. (2012a). The associations between community violence, television violence, parent–child aggression, and aggression in sibling relationships of a sample of preschoolers. *Psychology of Violence, 2,* 165–178.

Miller, L. J., Myers, A., Prinzi, L., & Mittenberg, W. (2009). Changes in intellectual functioning associated with normal aging. *Archives of Clinical Neuropsychology, 24,* 681–688.

Miller, P. H. (2009). *Theories of developmental psychology* (5th ed.). New York: Worth.

Miller, P. J. (2014). Entries into meaning: Socialization via narrative in the early years. In M. J. Gelfand, C.-Y. Chiu, & Y.-Y. Hong (Eds.), *Advances in culture and psychology* (Vol. 4, pp. 124–176). New York: Oxford University Press.

Miller, P. J., Fung, H., Lin, S., Chen, E. C., & Boldt, B. R. (2012b). How socialization happens on the ground: Narrative practices as alternate socializing pathways in Taiwanese and European-American families. *Monographs of the Society for Research in Child Development, 77*(1, Serial No. 302).

Miller, P. J., Fung, H., & Mintz, J. (1996). Self-construction through narrative practices: A Chinese and American comparison of early socialization. *Ethos, 24,* 1–44.

Miller, P. J., Gutiérrez, I. T., Chow, P. I., & Schein, S. S. (2014). European Americans in Centerville: Community and family contexts. In K. Rosengren,

P. J. Miller, I. T. Guiérrez, P. I. Chow, S. S. Schein, & K. N. Anderson (Eds.), Children's understanding of death: Toward a contextualized, integrated account. *Monographs of the Society for Research in Child Development, 79*(1, Serial No. 312), pp. 19–42.

Miller, P. J., Wang, S., Sandel, T., & Cho, G. E. (2002). Self-esteem as folk theory: A comparison of European American and Taiwanese mothers' beliefs. *Parenting: Science and Practice, 2,* 209–239.

Miller, P. J., Wiley, A. R., Fung, H., & Liang, C. H. (1997). Personal storytelling as a medium of socialization in Chinese and American families. *Child Development, 68,* 557–568.

Miller, S., Lansford, J. E., Costanzo, P., Malone, P. S., Golonka, M., & Killeya-Jones, L. A. (2009). Early adolescent romantic partner status, peer standing, and problem behaviors. *Journal of Early Adolescence, 29,* 839–861.

Miller, S. A., Hardin, C. A., & Montgomery, D. E. (2003). Young children's understanding of the conditions for knowledge acquisition. *Journal of Cognition and Development, 4,* 325–356.

Miller, S. C., Lima, J. C., & Thompson, S. A. (2015). End-of-life care in nursing homes with greater versus less palliative care knowledge and practice. *Journal of Palliative Medicine, 18,* 527–534.

Miller, T. R. (2015). Projected outcomes of Nurse–Family Partnership home visitation during 1996–2013, USA. *Prevention Science, 16,* 765–777.

Milligan, C., Turner, M., Blake, S., Brearley, S., Seamark, D., Thomas, C., et al. (2016). Unpacking the impact of older adults' home death on family caregivers' experiences of home. *Health & Place, 38,* 103–111.

Milligan, K., Astington, J. W., & Dack, L. A. (2007). Language and theory of mind: Meta-analysis of the relation between language ability and falsebelief understanding. *Child Development, 78,* 622–646.

Mills, C. M. (2013). Knowing when to doubt: Developing a critical stance when learning from others. *Developmental Psychology, 49,* 404–418.

Mills, D., Plunkett, K., Prat, C., & Schafer, G. (2005). Watching the infant brain learn words: Effects of language and experience. *Cognitive Development, 20,* 19–31.

Min, J., Chiu, D. T., & Wang, T. (2013). Variation in the heritability of body mass index based on diverse twin studies: A systematic review. *Obesity Review, 14,* 871–882.

Mindell, J. A., Li, A. M., Sadeh, A., Kwon, R., & Goh, D. Y. T. (2015). Bedtime routines for young children: A dose-dependent association with sleep outcomes. *Sleep, 38,* 717–722.

Mineka, S., & Zinbarg, R. (2006). A contemporary learning theory perspective on the etiology of anxiety disorders: It's not what you thought it was. *American Psychologist, 61,* 10–26.

Miner-Rubino, K., Winter, D. G., & Stewart, A. J. (2004). Gender, social class, and the subjective experience of aging: Self-perceived personality change from early adulthood to late midlife. *Personality and Social Psychology Bulletin, 30,* 1599–1610.

Minnotte, K. L., Minnotte, M. C., & Bonstrom, J. (2015). Work–family conflicts and marital satisfaction among U.S. workers: Does stress amplification matter? *Journal of Family Economic Issues, 36,* 21–33.

Mintziori, G., Lambrinoudaki, I., Goulis, D. G., Ceausu, I., Depypere, H., Erel, C. T., et al. (2015). EMAS position statement: Non-hormonal management of menopausal vasomotor symptoms. *Maturitas, 81,* 410–4123.

Mireault, G. C., Crockenberg, S. C., Sparrow, J. E., Cousineau, K., Pettinato, C., & Woodard, K. (2015). Laughing matters: Infant humor in the context of parental affect. *Journal of Experimental Child Psychology, 136,* 30–41.

Mirkin, S., Archer, D. F., Pickar, J. H., & Komm, B. S. (2014). Recent advances help understand and improve the safety of menopausal therapies. *Menopause, 22,* 351–360.

Misailidi, P. (2006). Young children's display rule knowledge: Understanding the distinction between apparent and real emotions and the motives underlying the use of display rules. *Social Behavior and Personality, 34,* 1285–1296.

Mischel, W., & Liebert, R. M. (1966). Effects of discrepancies between observed and imposed reward criteria on their acquisition and transmission. *Journal of Personality and Social Psychology, 3,* 45–53.

Mishra, G., & Kuh, D. (2006). Perceived change in quality of life during the menopause. *Social Science and Medicine, 62,* 93–102.

Mistry, J., & Dutta, R. (2015). Human development and culture. In W. F. Overton & P. C. Molenaar (Eds.), *Handbook of child psychology and developmental science: Vol. 1. Theory and method* (pp. 369–406). Hoboken, NJ: Wiley.

Mistry, R. S., Biesanz, J. C., Chien, N., Howes, C., & Benner, A. D. (2008). Socioeconomic status, parental investments, and the cognitive and behavioral outcomes of low-income children from immigrant and native households. *Early Childhood Research Quarterly, 23,* 193–212.

Mitchell, B. A. (2016). Intergenerational and family ties of baby boomers. In K. S. Whitbourne Ed.), *Encyclopedia of adulthood and aging* (Vol. 2, pp. 669–678). Malden, MA: Blackwell.

Mitchell, B. A., & Lovegreen, L. D. (2009). The empty nest syndrome in midlife families: A multimethod exploration of parental gender differences and cultural dynamics. *Journal of Family Issues, 30,* 1651–1670.

Mitchell, B. D., Hsueh, W. C., King, T. M., Pollin, T. I., Sorkin, J., Agarwala, R., Schäffer, A. A., & Shuldiner, A. R. (2001). Heritability of life span in the Old Order Amish. *American Journal of Medical Genetics, 102,* 346–352.

Mitchell, M. E., Eby, L. T., & Lorys, A. (2015). Feeling work at home: A transactional model of women and men's negative affective spillover from work to family. In M. J. Mills (Ed.), *Gender and the work–family experience* (pp. 121–140). New York: Springer.

Miu, D. K. Y., & Chan, C. K. M. (2011). Prognostic value of depressive symptoms on mortality, morbidity and nursing home admission in older people. *Geriatrics and Gerontology International, 11,* 174–179.

Miura, I. T., & Okamoto, Y. (2003). Language supports for mathematics understanding and performance. In A. J. Baroody & A. Dowker (Eds.), *The development of arithmetic concepts and skills* (pp. 229–242). Mahwah, NJ: Erlbaum.

Mize, J., & Pettit, G. S. (2010). The mother–child playgroup as socialisation context: A short-term longitudinal study of mother–child–peer relationship dynamics. *Early Child Development and Care, 180,* 1271–1284.

Mo, H. N., Shin, D. W., Woo, J. H., Choi, J. Y., Kang, J., Baik, Y. J., et al. (2011). Is patient autonomy a critical determinant of quality of life in Korea? End-of-life decision making from the perspective of the patient. *Palliative Medicine, 26,* 222–231.

Modrek, S., & Cullen, M. R. (2012). *Job demand and early retirement.* Chestnut Hill, MA: Center for Retirement Research at Boston College. Retrieved from ssrn.com/abstract=2127722

Moen, P., Kelly, E. L., Tranby, E., & Huang, Q. (2011). Changing work, changing health: Can real work-time flexibility promote health behaviors and well-being? *Journal of Health and Social Behavior, 52,* 404–429.

Moffitt, T. E. (2007). Life-course-persistent vs. adolescence-limited antisocial behavior. In D. Cicchetti & D. J. Cohen (Eds.), *Developmental psychopathology* (2nd ed., pp. 570–598). Hoboken, NJ: Wiley.

Mohr, J. J., & Daly, C. A. (2008). Sexual minority stress and changes in relationship quality in same-sex couples. *Journal of Social and Personal Relationships, 25,* 989–1007.

Mohr, J. J., & Fassinger, R. E. (2006). Sexual orientation identity and romantic relationship quality in same-sex couples. *Personality and Social Psychology Bulletin, 32,* 1085–1099.

Mok, M. M. C., Kennedy, K. J., & Moore, P. J. (2011). Academic attribution of secondary students: Gender, year level and achievement level. *Educational Psychology, 31,* 87–104.

Mola, J. R. (2015). Erectile dysfunction in the older adult male. *Urological Nursing, 35,* 87–93.

Moll, H., & Meltzoff, A. N. (2011). How does it look? Level 2 perspective-taking at 36 months of age. *Child Development, 82,* 661–673.

Moll, K., Ramus, F., Bartling, J., Bruder, J., Kunze, S., Neuhoff, N., et al. (2014). Cognitive mechanisms underlying reading and spelling development in five European orthographies. *Learning and Instruction, 29,* 65–77.

Mollenkopf, H., Hieber, A., & Wahl, H.-W. (2011). Continuity and change in older adults' perceptions of out-of-home mobility over ten years: A qualitative–quantitative approach. *Ageing and Society, 31,* 782–802.

Moller, K., Hwang, C. P., & Wickberg, B. (2008). Couple relationship and transition to parenthood: Does workload at home matter? *Journal of Reproductive and Infant Psychology, 26,* 57–68.

Molloy, C. S., Wilson-Ching, M., Anderson, V. A., Roberts, G., Anderson, P. J., Doyle, L. W., et al. (2013). Visual processing in adolescents born extremely low birth weight and/or extremely preterm. *Pediatrics, 132,* e704–e712.

Molnar, D. S., Levitt, A., Eiden, R. D., & Schuetze, P. (2014). Prenatal cocaine exposure and trajectories of externalizing behavior problems in early childhood: Examining the role of maternal negative affect. *Development and Psychopathology, 26,* 515–528.

Monahan, K. C., Lee, J. M., & Steinberg, L. (2011). Revisiting the impact of part-time work on adolescent adjustment: Distinguishing between selection and socialization using propensity score matching. *Child Development, 82,* 96–112.

Mondloch, C. J., Lewis, T., Budreau, D. R., Maurer, D., Dannemiller, J. L., Stephens, B. R., & Kleiner-Gathercoal, K. A. (1999). Face perception during early infancy. *Psychological Science, 10,* 419–422.

Monin, J. K., & Schulz, R. (2009). Interpersonal effects of suffering in older adult caregiving relationships. *Psychology and Aging, 24,* 681–695.

Monk, C., Georgieff, M. K., & Osterholm, E. A. (2013). Research review: Maternal prenatal distress and poor nutrition—mutually influencing risk factors affecting infant neurocognitive development. *Journal of Child Psychology and Psychiatry, 54,* 115–130.

Monk, C., Sloan, R., Myers, M. M., Ellman, L., Werner, E., Jeon, J., et al. (2010). Neural circuitry of emotional face processing in autism spectrum disorders. *Journal of Psychiatry and Neuroscience, 35,* 105–114.

Monsour, M. (2002). *Women and men as friends.* Mahwah, NJ: Erlbaum.

Montague, D. P. F., & Walker-Andrews, A. S. (2001). Peekaboo: A new look at infants' perception of emotion expressions. *Developmental Psychology, 37,* 826–838.

Montepare, J. M. (2006). Body consciousness across the adult years: Variations with actual and subjective age. *Journal of Adult Development, 13,* 102–107.

Montgomery, D. E., & Koeltzow, T. E. (2010). A review of the day–night task: The Stroop paradigm and interference control in young children. *Developmental Review, 30,* 308–330.

Montgomery, M. J. (2005). Psychosocial intimacy and identity: From early adolescence to emerging adulthood. *Journal of Adolescent Research, 20,* 346–374.

Montgomery, M. J., & Côté, J. E. (2003). College as a transition to adulthood. In G. R. Adams &

M. D. Berzonsky (Eds.), *Blackwell handbook of adolescence* (pp. 149–172). Malden, MA: Blackwell.

Moon, C., Cooper, R. P., & Fifer, W. P. (1993). Two-day-old infants prefer their native language. *Infant Behavior and Development, 16,* 495–500.

Moore, A., & Stratton, D. C. (2002). *Resilient widowers.* New York: Springer.

Moore, D. S. (2013). Behavioral genetics, genetics, and epigenetics. In P. D. Zelazo (Ed.), *Oxford handbook of developmental psychology: Vol. 1. Body and mind* (pp. 91–128). New York: Oxford University Press.

Moore, D. S., & Johnson, S. P. (2011). Mental rotation of dynamic, three-dimensional stimuli by 3-month-old infants. *Infancy, 16,* 435–445.

Moore, E. G. J. (1986). Family socialization and the IQ test performance of traditionally and transracially adopted black children. *Developmental Psychology, 22,* 317–326.

Moore, J. A., Cooper, B. R., Domitrovich, C. E., Morgan, N. R., Cleveland, M. J., Shah, H., et al. (2015). Effects of exposure to an enhanced preschool program on the social-emotional functioning of at-risk children. *Early Childhood Research Quarterly, 32,* 127–138.

Moore, K. L., Persaud, T. V. N., & Torchia, M. G. (2016a). *Before we are born: Essentials of embryology and birth defects* (9th ed.). Philadelphia: Elsevier.

Moore, K. L., Persaud, T. V. N., & Torchia, M. G. (2016b). *The developing human: Clinically oriented embryology.* Philadelphia: Elsevier.

Moore, M. K., & Meltzoff, A. N. (2004). Object permanence after a 24-hr delay and leaving the locale of disappearance: The role of memory, space, and identity. *Developmental Psychology, 40,* 606–620.

Moore, M. K., & Meltzoff, A. N. (2008). Factors affecting infants' manual search for occluded objects and the genesis of object permanence. *Infant Behavior and Development, 31,* 168–180.

Moore, M. R., & Stambolis-Ruhstorfer, M. (2013). LGBT sexuality and families at the start of the twenty-first century. *Annual Review of Sociology, 39,* 491–507.

Moorehouse, P., & Mallery, L. (2016). Care planning in frailty. In S. K. Whitbourne (Ed.), *Encyclopedia of adulthood and aging* (Vol. 1, pp. 171–180). Malden, MA: Wiley Blackwell.

Moran, S., & Gardner, H. (2006). Extraordinary achievements: A developmental and systems analysis. In D. Kuhn & R. Siegler (Eds.), *Handbook of child psychology: Vol. 2. Cognition, perception, and language* (6th ed., pp. 905–949). Hoboken, NJ: Wiley.

Morawska, A., & Sanders, M. (2011). Parental use of time out revisited: A useful or harmful parenting strategy? *Journal of Child and Family Studies, 20,* 1–8.

Morelli, G. (2015). The evolution of attachment theory and cultures of human attachment in infancy and early childhood. In L. A. Jensen (Ed.), *Oxford handbook of human development and culture: An interdisciplinary perspective* (pp. 149–164). New York: Oxford University Press.

Morelli, G., Rogoff, B., Oppenheim, D., & Goldsmith, D. (1992). Cultural variation in infants' sleeping arrangements: Questions of independence. *Developmental Psychology, 28,* 604–613.

Morelli, G. A., Rogoff, B., & Angelillo, C. (2003). Cultural variation in young children's access to work or involvement in specialized child-focused activities. *International Journal of Behavioral Development, 27,* 264–274.

Moreno, A. J., Klute, M. M., & Robinson, J. L. (2008). Relational and individual resources as predictors of empathy in early childhood. *Social Development, 17,* 613–637.

Morgan, I. G., Ohno-Matsui, K., & Saw, S.-M. (2012). Myopia. *Lancet, 379,* 1739–1748.

Morgan, J. D., Laungani, P., & Palmer, S. (2009). General introduction to series. In J. D. Morgan, P. Laungani, & S. Palmer (Eds.), *Death and bereavement around the world: Vol. 5. Reflective essays* (pp. 1–4). Amityville, NY: Baywood.

Morgan, P. J., Collins, C. E., Plotnickoff, R. C., Cook, A. T., Berthon, B., Mitchell, S., & Callister, R. (2011). Efficacy of a workplace-based weight loss program for overweight male shift workers: The Workplace POWER (Preventing Obesity without Eating Like a Rabbit) randomized control trial. *Preventive Medicine, 52,* 317–325.

Morgan, P. L., Farkas, G., Hillemeier, M. M., & Maczuga, S. (2009). Risk factors for learning-related behavior problems at 24 months of age: Population-based estimates. *Journal of Abnormal Child Psychology, 37,* 401–413.

Moriarty, H. J., Carroll, R., & Controneo, M. (1996). Differences in bereavement reactions within couples following death of a child. *Research in Nursing & Health, 19,* 461–469.

Morinis, J., Carson, C., & Quigley, M. A. (2013). Effect of teenage motherhood on cognitive outcomes in children: A population-based cohort study. *Archives of Disease in Childhood, 98,* 959–964.

Moro-García, M. A., Alonso-Arias, R., López Vázquez, A., Suárez-García, F. M., Solano-Jaurrieta, J. J., Baltar, J., et al. (2012). Relationship between functional ability in older people, immune system status, and intensity of response to CMV. *Age, 34,* 479–495.

Morrill, M. I., Hines, D. A., Mahmood, S., & Córdova, J. V. (2010). Pathways between marriage and parenting for wives and husbands: The role of coparenting. *Family Process, 49,* 59–73.

Morris, A. S., Silk, J. S., Morris, M. D. S., & Steinberg, L. (2011). The influence of mother–child emotion regulation strategies on children's expression of anger and sadness. *Developmental Psychology, 47,* 213–225.

Morris, A. S., Silk, J. S., Steinberg, L., Myers, S. S., & Robinson, L. R. (2007). The role of the family context in the development of emotion regulation. *Social Development, 16,* 362–388.

Morris, J. (2011). Communication skills training in end-of-life care. *Nursing Times, 107,* 16–17.

Morris, M. C., Brockman, J., Schneider, J. A., Wang, Y., Bennett, D. A., Tangney, C. C., & van de Rest, O. (2016). Association of seafood consumption, brain mercury level, and APOE ε4 status with brain neuropathology in older adults. *JAMA, 315,* 489–497.

Morris, M. C., Tangney, C. C., Wang, Y., Sacks, F. M., Bennett, D. A., & Aggarwal, N. T. (2015). MIND diet associated with reduced incidence of Alzheimer's disease. *Alzheimer's & Dementia, 11,* 1007–1014.

Morris, W. L., DePaulo, B. M., Hertel, J., & Taylor, L. C. (2008). Singlism—another problem that has no name: Prejudice, stereotypes and discrimination against singles. In M. A. Morrison & T. G. Morrison (Eds.), *The psychology of modern prejudice* (pp. 165–194). Hauppauge, NY: Nova Science Publishers.

Morrison, M., & Roese, N. J. (2011). Regrets of the typical American: Findings from a nationally representative sample. *Social Psychological & Personality Science, 2,* 576–583.

Morrison, V. (2008). Ageing and physical health. In B. Woods & L. Clare (Eds.), *Handbook of the clinical psychology of ageing* (2nd ed., pp. 57–74). Chichester, UK: Wiley.

Morrissey, T., Dunifon, R. E., & Kalil, A. (2011). Maternal employment, work schedules, and children's body mass index. *Child Development, 82,* 66–81.

Morrongiello, B. A., Fenwick, K. D., & Chance, G. (1998). Crossmodal learning in newborn infants: Inferences about properties of auditory-visual events. *Infant Behavior and Development, 21,* 543–554.

Morrongiello, B. A., Midgett, C., & Shields, R. (2001). Don't run with scissors: Young children's knowledge of home safety rules. *Journal of Pediatric Psychology, 26,* 105–115.

Morrongiello, B. A., Ondejko, L., & Littlejohn, A. (2004). Understanding toddlers' in-home injuries: I. Context, correlates, and determinants. *Journal of Pediatric Psychology, 29,* 415–431.

Morrongiello, B. A., Widdifield, R., Munroe, K., & Zdzieborski, D. (2014). Parents teaching young children home safety rules: Implications for childhood injury risk. *Journal of Applied Developmental Psychology, 35,* 254–261.

Morse, S. B., Zheng, H., Tang, Y., & Roth, J. (2009). Early school-age outcomes of late preterm infants. *Pediatrics, 123,* e622–e629.

Morton, R. H. (2014). A decline in anaerobic distance capacity of champion athletes over the years? *International Journal of Sports Science & Coaching, 9,* 1057–1065.

Mosby, L., Rawls, A. W., Meehan, A. J., Mays, E., & Pettinari, C. J. (1999). Troubles in interracial talk about discipline: An examination of African American child rearing narratives. *Journal of Comparative Family Studies, 30,* 489–521.

Mosely-Howard, G. S., & Evans, C. B. (2000). Relationships and contemporary experiences of the African-American family: An ethnographic case study. *Journal of Black Studies, 30,* 428–451.

Moshman, D. (1998). Identity as a theory of oneself. *Genetic Epistemologist, 26*(3), 1–9.

Moshman, D. (2005). *Adolescent psychological development: Rationality, morality, and identity* (2nd ed.). Mahwah, NJ: Erlbaum.

Moshman, D. (2011). *Adolescent rationality and development: Cognition, morality, and identity* (3rd ed.). New York: Psychology Press.

Moshman, D. (2013). Epistemic cognition and development. In P. Barrouillet & C. Gauffroy (Eds.), *The development of thinking and reasoning* (pp. 13–33). New York: Psychology Press.

Moshman, D., & Franks, B. A. (1986). Development of the concept of inferential validity. *Child Development, 57,* 153–165.

Moshman, D., & Geil, M. (1998). Collaborative reasoning: Evidence for collective rationality. *Thinking and Reasoning, 4,* 231–248.

Moss, E., Cyr, C., Bureau, J.-F., Tarabulsy, G. M., & Dubois-Comtois, K. (2005). Stability of attachment during the preschool period. *Developmental Psychology, 41,* 773–783.

Moss, E., Smolla, N., Guerra, I., Mazzarello, T., Chayer, D., & Berthiaume, C. (2006). Attachment and self-reported internalizing and externalizing behavior problems in a school period. *Canadian Journal of Behavioural Science, 38,* 142–157.

Mossey, P. A., Little, J., Munger, R. G., Dixon, M. J., & Shaw, W. C. (2009). Cleft lip and palate. *Lancet, 374,* 1773–1785.

Moss-Racusin, C. A., Dovidio, J. F., Brescoll, V. L., Graham, M. J., & Handelsman, J. (2012). Science faculty's subtle gender biases favor male students. *Proceedings of the National Academy of Sciences, 109,* 16474–16479.

Motl, R. W., Dishman, R. K., Saunders, R. P., Dowda, M., Felton, G., Ward, D. S., & Pate, R. R. (2002). Examining social–cognitive determinants of intention and physical activity among black and white adolescent girls using structural equation modeling. *Health Psychology, 21,* 459–467.

Mottus, R., Indus, K., & Allik, J. (2008). Accuracy of only children stereotype. *Journal of Research in Personality, 42,* 1047–1052.

Mottweiler, C. M., & Taylor, M. (2014). Elaborated role play and creativity in preschool age children. *Psychology of Aesthetics, Creativity, and the Arts, 8,* 277–286.

Mõttus, R., Johnson, W., & Deary, I. J. (2012). Personality traits in old age: Measurement and rank-order stability and some mean-level change. *Psychology and Aging, 27,* 243–249.

Mounts, N. S., & Steinberg, L. (1995). An ecological analysis of peer influence on adolescent grade point average and drug use. *Developmental Psychology, 31,* 915–922.

Mounts, N. S., Valentiner, D. P., Anderson, K. L., & Boswell, M. K. (2006). Shyness, sociability, and parental support for the college transition: Relation to adolescents' adjustment. *Journal of Youth and Adolescence, 35,* 71–80.

Mozaffarian, D., Arnett, D. K., Cushman, M., Després, J.-P., Howard, V. J., Isasi, C. R., et al. (2016). Heart disease and stroke statistics—2016 update: A report from the American Heart Association. *Circulation, 133,* 38–60.

Mozaffarian, D., Benjamin, E. J., Go, A. S., Arnett, D. K., Blaha, M. J., Cushman, M., et al. (2015). Heart disease and stroke statistics—2015 update: A report from the American Heart Association. *Circulation, 129,* e229–e322.

Mroczek, D. K., & Spiro, A., III. (2005). Change in life satisfaction during adulthood: Findings from the Veterans Affairs Normative Aging Study. *Journal of Personality and Social Psychology, 88,* 189–202.

Mroczek, D. K., Spiro, A., & Turiano, N. A. (2009). Do health behaviors explain the effect of neuroticism on mortality? *Journal of Research in Personality, 43,* 653–659.

Mrug, S., Elliott, M. N., Daies, S., Tortolero, S. R., Cuccaro, P., & Schuster, M. A. (2014). Early puberty, negative peer influence, and problem behaviors in adolescent girls. *Pediatrics, 133,* 7–14.

Mrug, S., Hoza, B., & Gerdes, A. C. (2001). Children with attention-deficit/hyperactivity disorder: Peer relationships and peer-oriented interventions. In D. W. Nangle & C. A. Erdley (Eds.), *The role of friendship in psychological adjustment* (pp. 51–77). San Francisco: Jossey-Bass.

Mu, Q., & Fehring, R. J. (2014). Efficacy of achieving pregnancy with fertility-focused intercourse. *American Journal of Maternal Child Nursing, 39,* 35–40.

Mueller, B. R., & Bale, T. L. (2008). Sex-specific programming of offspring emotionality after stress early in pregnancy. *Journal of Neuroscience, 28,* 9055–9065.

Muenssinger, J., Matuz, T., Schleger, F., Kiefer-Schmidt, I., Goelz, R., Wacker-Gussmann, A., et al. (2013). Auditory habituation in the fetus and neonate: An fMEG study. *Developmental Science, 16,* 287–295.

Muise, A., Schimmack, U., & Impett, E. A. (2015). Sexual frequency predicts greater well-being, but more is not always better. *Social Psychological and Personality Science.* Retrieved from spp.sagepub .com/content/early/2015/11/16/1948550615616462 .full.pdf+html

Müller, O., & Krawinkel, M. (2005). Malnutrition and health in developing countries. *Canadian Medical Association Journal, 173,* 279–286.

Müller, U., & Kerns, K. (2015). The development of executive function. In L. S. Liben & U. Müller (Eds.), *Handbook of child psychology and developmental science: Vol. 2. Cognitive processes* (7th ed., pp. 571–623). Hoboken, NJ: Wiley.

Müller, U., Liebermann-Finestone, D. P., Carpendale, J. I. M., Hammond, S. I., & Bibok, M. B. (2012). Knowing minds, controlling actions: The developmental relations between theory of mind and executive function from 2 to 4 years of age. *Journal of Experimental Child Psychology, 111,* 331–348.

Müller, U., Overton, W. F., & Reese, K. (2001). Development of conditional reasoning: A longitudinal study. *Journal of Cognition and Development, 2,* 27–49.

Mullett-Hume, E., Anshel, D., Guevara, V., & Cloitre, M. (2008). Cumulative trauma and posttraumatic stress disorder among children exposed to the 9/11 World Trade Center attack. *American Journal of Orthopsychiatry, 78,* 103–108.

Mulvaney, M. K., McCartney, K., Bub, K. L., & Marshall, N. L. (2006). Determinants of dyadic scaffolding and cognitive outcomes in first graders. *Parenting: Science and Practice, 6,* 297–310.

Mulvaney, M. K., & Mebert, C. J. (2007). Parental corporal punishment predicts behavior problems in early childhood. *Journal of Family Psychology, 21,* 389–397.

Mumme, D. L., Bushnell, E. W., DiCorcia, J. A., & Lariviere, L. A. (2007). Infants' use of gaze cues to interpret others' actions and emotional reactions. In R. Flom, K. Lee, & D. Muir (Eds.), *Gaze-following: Its development and significance* (pp. 143–170). Mahwah, NJ: Erlbaum.

Munakata, Y. (2006). Information processing approaches to development. In D. Kuhn & R. S. Siegler (Eds.), *Handbook of child psychology: Vol. 3. Cognition, perception, and language* (6th ed., pp. 426–463). Hoboken, NJ: Wiley.

Munnell, A. H., Webb, A., Delorme, L., & Golub-Sass, F. (2012). *National retirement risk index: How much longer do we need to work?* Chestnut Hill, MA: Center for Retirement Research at Boston College. Retrieved from crr.bc.edu/briefs/national-retirement -risk-index-how-much-longer-do-we-need-to-work

Munroe, R. L., & Romney, A. K. (2006). Gender and age differences in same-sex aggregation and social behavior. *Journal of Cross-Cultural Psychology, 37,* 3–19.

Muret-Wagstaff, S., & Moore, S. G. (1989). The Hmong in America: Infant behavior and rearing practices. In J. K. Nugent, B. M. Lester, & T. B. Brazelton (Eds.), *Biology, culture, and development* (Vol. 1, pp. 319–339). Norwood, NJ: Ablex.

Muris, P., & Field, A. P. (2011). The "normal" development of fear. In W. K. Silverman & A. P. Field (Eds.), *Anxiety disorders in children and adolescents* (2nd ed., pp. 76–89). Cambridge, UK: Cambridge University Press.

Muris, P., & Meesters, C. (2014). Small or big in the eyes of the other: On the developmental psychopathology of self-conscious emotions as shame, guilt, and pride. *Clinical Child and Family Psychology Review, 17,* 19–40.

Murphy, J. B. (2013). Access to in vitro fertilization deserves increased regulation in the United States. *Journal of Sex and Marital Therapy, 39,* 85–92.

Murphy, S. A. (2008). The loss of a child: Sudden death and extended illness perspectives. In M. S. Stroebe, R. O. Hansson, H. Schut, & W. Stroebe (Eds.), *Handbook of bereavement research and practice* (pp. 375–396). Washington, DC: American Psychological Association.

Murphy, T. H., & Corbett, D. (2009). Plasticity during recovery: From synapse to behaviour. *Nature Reviews Neuroscience, 10,* 861–872.

Murphy, T. P., & Laible, D. J. (2013). The influence of attachment security on preschool children's empathic concern. *International Journal of Behavioral Development, 37,* 436–440.

Murray, L. K., Nguyen, A., & Cohen, J. A. (2014). Child sexual abuse. *Pediatric Clinics of North America, 23,* 321–337.

Murray, M. W. E., & Isaacowitz, D. M. (2016). Emotions and aging. In S. K. Whitbourne (Ed.), *Encyclopedia of adulthood and aging* (Vol. 1, pp. 423–428). Malden, MA: Wiley Blackwell.

Murray, S. A., & McLoughlin, P. (2012). Illness trajectories and palliative care: Implications for holistic service provision for all in the last year of life. In L. Sallnow, S. Kumar, & A. Kellehear (Eds.), *International perspectives on public health and palliative care* (pp. 30–51). New York: Routledge.

Murray, S. L. (2008). Risk regulation in relationships: Self-esteem and the if–then contingencies of interdependent life. In J. V. Wood, A. Tesser, & J. G. Holmes (Eds.), *The self and social relationships* (pp. 3–25). New York: Psychology Press.

Mussen, P., & Eisenberg-Berg, N. (1977). *Roots of caring, sharing, and helping.* San Francisco: Freeman.

Mutchler, J. E., Baker, L. A., & Lee, S. (2007). Grandparents responsible for grandchildren in Native-American families. *Social Science Quarterly, 88,* 990–1009.

Mutchler, J. E., Burr, J. A., & Caro, F. G. (2003). From paid worker to volunteer: Leaving the paid workforce and volunteering in later life. *Social Forces, 81,* 1267–1293.

Mutran, E. J., Danis, M., Bratton, K. A., Sudha, S., & Hanson, L. (1997). Attitudes of the critically ill toward prolonging life: The role of social support. *Gerontologist, 37,* 192–199.

Myers, L. J., & Liben, L. S. (2008). The role of intentionality and iconicity in children's developing comprehension and production of cartographic symbols. *Child Development, 79,* 668–684.

Myerson, J., Hale, S., Wagstaff, D., Poon, L. W., & Smith, G. A. (1990). The information-loss model: A mathematical theory of age-related cognitive slowing. *Psychological Review, 97,* 475–487.

Myowa-Yamakoshi, M., Tomonaga, M., Tanaka, M., & Matsuzawa, T. (2004). Imitation in neonatal chimpanzees *(Pan troglodytes). Developmental Science, 7,* 437–442.

N

Nadel, J., Prepin, K., & Okanda, M. (2005). Experiencing contingency and agency: First step toward self-understanding in making a mind? *Interaction Studies, 6,* 447–462.

Nader, K. (2002). Treating children after violence in schools and communities. In N. B. Webb (Ed.), *Helping bereaved children: A handbook for practitioners* (pp. 214–244). New York: Guilford.

Nader, P. R., O'Brien, M., Houts, R., Bradley, R., Belsky, J., Crosnoe, R., et al. (2006). Identifying risk for obesity in early childhood. *Pediatrics, 118,* e594–e601.

Naerde, A., Ogden, T., Janson, H., & Zachrisson, H. D. (2014). Normative development of physical aggression from 8 to 26 months. *Developmental Psychology, 6,* 1710–1720.

Nagy, E., Compagne, H., Orvos, H., Pal, A., Molnar, P., & Janszky, I. (2005). Index finger movement imitation by human neonates: Motivation, learning, and left-hand preference. *Pediatric Research, 58,* 749–753.

Nagy, W. E., & Scott, J. A. (2000). Vocabulary processes. In M. L. Kamil & P. B. Mosenthal (Eds.), *Handbook of reading research* (Vol. 3, pp. 269–284). Mahwah, NJ: Erlbaum.

Naigles, L. G., & Gelman, S. A. (1995). Overextensions in comprehension and production revisited: Preferential-looking in a study of dog, cat, and cow. *Journal of Child Language, 22,* 19–46.

Naigles, L. R., & Swenson, L. D. (2007). Syntactic supports for word learning. In E. Hoff & M. Shatz (Eds.), *Blackwell handbook of language development* (pp. 212–231). Malden, MA: Blackwell.

Naito, M., & Seki, Y. (2009). The relationship between second-order false belief and display rules reasoning: Integration of cognitive and affective social understanding. *Developmental Science, 12,* 150–164.

Nakamura, J., & Csikszentmihalyi, M. (2009). Flow theory and research. In C. R. Snyder & S. J. Lopez (Eds.), *Oxford handbook of positive psychology* (2nd ed., pp. 195–206). New York: Oxford University Press.

Nan, C., Piek, J., Warner, C., Mellers, D., Krone, R. E., Barrett, T., & Zeegers, M. P. (2013). Trajectories and predictors of developmental skills in healthy twins up to 24 months of age. *Infant Behavior and Development, 36,* 670–678.

Nánez, J., Sr., & Yonas, A. (1994). Effects of luminance and texture motion on infant defensive reactions to optical collision. *Infant Behavior and Development, 17,* 165–174.

Napolitano, C. M., & Freund, A. M. (2016). Model of selection, optimization, and compensation. In S. K. Whitbourne (Ed.), *Encyclopedia of adulthood and aging* (Vol. 2, pp. 929–933). Malden, MA: Wiley Blackwell.

Narayan, A. J., Englund, M. M., Carlson, E. A., & Egeland, B. (2014). Adolescent conflict as a developmental process in the prospective pathway from exposure to interparental violence to dating violence. *Journal of Abnormal Child Psychology, 42,* 239–250.

Narayan, A. J., Englund, M. M., & Egeland, B. (2013). Developmental timing and continuity of exposure to interparental violence and externalizing behavior as prospective predictors of dating violence. *Development and Psychopathology, 25,* 973–990.

Narr, K. L., Woods, R. P., Lin J., Kim, J., Phillips, O. R., Del'Homme, M., et al. (2009). Widespread cortical thinning is a robust anatomical marker for attention-deficit/hyperactivity disorder. *Journal of the American Academy of Child and Adolescent Psychiatry, 48,* 1014–1022.

National Center for Assisted Living. (2013, March). *Assisted living state regulatory review 2013.* Retrieved from www.ahcancal.org/ncal/resources/Documents/2013_reg_review.pdf

National Center for Biotechnology Information. (2015). *Online Mendelian inheritance in man.* Retrieved from www.omim.org

National Center on Elder Abuse. (2016). *Frequently asked questions.* Retrieved from ncea.acl.gov/faq

National Coalition for the Homeless. (2012). *Education of homeless children and youth.* Retrieved from www.nationalhomeless.org/factsheets/education.html

National Federation of State High School Associations. (2016). *2014–2015 High School Athletics Participation Survey.* Retrieved from www.nfhs.org/ParticipationStatistics/PDF/2014-15_Participation_Survey_Results.pdf

National Institute on Aging. (2016). *2014–2015 Alzheimer's disease progress report: Advancing research toward a cure.* Retrieved from www.nia.nih.gov/alzheimers/publication/2014-2015-alzheimers-disease-progress-report

National Institute on Alcohol Abuse and Alcoholism. (2015). *Alcohol facts and statistics.* Retrieved from www.niaaa.nih.gov/alcohol-health/overview-alcohol-consumption/alcohol-facts-and-statistics

National Institute on Drug Abuse. (2016a). *Drug facts: MDMA (Ecstasy/Molly).* Retrieved from www.drugabuse.gov/publications/drugfacts/mdma-ecstasymolly

National Institute on Drug Abuse. (2016b). *Is marijuana addictive?* Retrieved from www.drugabuse.gov/publications/research-reports/marijuana/marijuana-addictive

National Institute on Retirement Security. (2016). *Women 80% more likely to be impoverished in retirement.* Retrieved from www.nirsonline.org/index.php?option=content&task=view&id=913

National Institutes of Health. (2015). *Genes and disease.* Retrieved from www.ncbi.nlm.nih.gov/books/NBK22183

National Research Council. (2007). *Race conscious policies for assigning students to schools: Social science research and the Supreme Court cases.* Washington, DC: National Academy Press.

Natsuaki, M. N., Biehl, M. C., & Ge, X. (2009). Trajectories of depressed mood from early adolescence to young adulthood: The effects of pubertal timing and adolescent dating. *Journal of Research on Adolescence, 19,* 47–74.

Natsuaki, M. N., Samuels, D., & Leve, L. D. (2014). Puberty, identity, and context: A biopsychosocial perspective on internalizing psychopathology in early adolescent girls. In K. C. McLean & M. Syed (Eds.), *Oxford handbook of identity development* (pp. 389–405). New York: Oxford University Press.

Natsuaki, M. N., Shaw, D. S., Neiderhiser, J. M., Ganiban, J. M., Harold, G. T., Reiss, D., et al. (2014). Raised by depressed parents: Is it an environmental risk?

Clinical Child and Family Psychology Review, 17, 357–367.

Nauta, J., van Mechelen, W., Otten, R. H. J., & Verhagen, E. A. L. M. (2014). A systematic review on the effectiveness of school and community-based injury prevention programmes on risk behaviour and injury risk in 8–12 year old children. *Journal of Science and Medicine in Sport, 17,* 165–172.

Naveh-Benjamin, M. (2012). Age-related differences in explicit associative memory: Contributions of effortful-strategic and automatic processes. In M. Naveh-Benjamin & N. Ohta (Eds.), *Memory and aging: Current issues and future directions* (pp. 71–95). New York: Psychology Press.

Naveh-Benjamin, M., Brav, T. K., & Levy, D. (2007). The associative memory deficit of older adults: The role of strategy utilization. *Psychology and Aging, 22,* 202–208.

Naveh-Benjamin, M., Craik, F. I. M., Guez, J., & Kreuger, S. (2005). Divided attention in younger and older adults: Effects of strategy and relatedness on memory performance and secondary task costs. *Journal of Experimental Psychology: Learning, Memory, and Cognition, 31,* 520–537.

Naveh-Benjamin, M., & Kilb, A. (2014). Age-related differences in associative memory: The role of sensory decline. *Psychology and Aging, 29,* 672–683.

Neal, M. B., & Hammer, L. B. (2007). *Working couples caring for children and aging parents.* Mahwah, NJ: Erlbaum.

Needham, B. L., & Austin, E. L. (2010). Sexual orientation, parental support, and health during the transition to young adulthood. *Journal of Youth and Adolescence, 39,* 1189–1198.

Neff, L. A., & Karney, B. R. (2008). Compassionate love in early marriage. In B. Fehr, S. Sprecher, & L. G. Underwood, (Eds.), *The science of compassionate love: Theory, research, and applications* (pp. 201–221). Malden, MA: Wiley-Blackwell.

Negriff, S., Susman, E. J., & Trickett, P. K. (2011). The developmental pathway from pubertal timing to delinquency and sexual activity from early to late adolescence. *Journal of Youth and Adolescence, 40,* 1343–1356.

Neimeyer, R., Currier, J. M., Coleman, R., Tomer, A., & Samuel, E. (2011). Confronting suffering and death at the end of life: The impact of religiosity, psychosocial factors, and life regret among hospice patients. *Death Studies, 35,* 777–800.

Neimeyer, R. A. (Ed.). (1994). *Death anxiety handbook.* Washington, DC: Taylor & Francis.

Neimeyer, R. A. (2001). The language of loss: Grief therapy as a process of meaning reconstruction. In R. A. Neimeyer (Ed.), *Meaning reconstruction and the experience of loss* (pp. 261–292). Washington, DC: American Psychological Association.

Neimeyer, R. A., Burke, L. A., Mackay, M. M., & van Dyke Stringer, J. G. (2010). Grief therapy and the reconstruction of meaning: From principles to practice. *Journal of Contemporary Psychotherapy, 40,* 73–83.

Neimeyer, R. A., & Van Brunt, D. (1995). Death anxiety. In H. Waas & R. A. Neimeyer (Eds.), *Dying: Facing the facts* (3rd ed., pp. 49–88). Washington, DC: Taylor & Francis.

Neitzel, C., & Stright, A. D. (2003). Mothers' scaffolding of children's problem solving: Establishing a foundation of academic self-regulatory competence. *Journal of Family Psychology, 17,* 147–159.

Nelson, C. A. (2007). A neurobiological perspective on early human deprivation. *Child Development Perspectives, 1,* 13–18.

Nelson, C. A., & Bosquet, M. (2000). Neurobiology of fetal and infant development: Implications for infant mental health. In C. H. Zeanah, Jr. (Ed.), *Handbook of infant mental health* (2nd ed., pp. 37–59). New York: Guilford.

Nelson, C. A., Fox, N. A., & Zeanah, C. H. (2014). *Romania's abandoned children: Deprivation,*

brain development, and the struggle for recovery. Cambridge, MA: Harvard University Press.

Nelson, C. A., Thomas, K. M., & de Haan, M. (2006). Neural bases of cognitive development. In D. Kuhn & R. Siegler (Eds.), *Handbook of child psychology: Vol. 2. Cognition, perception, and language* (6th ed., pp. 3–57). Hoboken, NJ: Wiley.

Nelson, D. A., Nelson, L. J., Hart, C. H., Yang, C., & Jin, S. (2006). Parenting and peer-group behavior in cultural context. In X. Chen, D. French, & B. Schneider (Eds.), *Peer relations in cultural context* (pp. 213–246). New York: Cambridge University Press.

Nelson, D. A., Robinson, C. C., & Hart, C. H. (2005). Relational and physical aggression of preschool-age children: Peer status linkages across informants. *Early Education and Development, 16,* 115–139.

Nelson, D. A., Yang, C., Coyne, S. M., Olsen, J. A., & Hart, C. H. (2013). Parental psychological control dimensions: Connections with Russian preschoolers' physical and relational aggression. *Journal of Applied Developmental Psychology, 34,* 1–8.

Nelson, E. L., Campbell, J. M., & Michel, G. F. (2013). Unimanual to bimanual: Tracking the development of handedness from 6 to 24 months. *Infant Behavior and Development, 36,* 181–188.

Nelson, K. (2003). Narrative and the emergence of a consciousness of self. In G. D. Fireman & T. E. McVay, Jr. (Eds.), *Narrative and consciousness: Literature, psychology, and the brain* (pp. 17–36). London: Oxford University Press.

Nelson, L. J. (2009). An examination of emerging adulthood in Romanian college students. *International Journal of Behavioral Development, 33,* 402–411.

Nelson, L. J. (2014). The role of parents in the religious and spiritual development of emerging adults. In C. M. Barry & M. M. Abo-Zena (Eds.), *Emerging adults' religiousness and spirituality* (pp 59–75). New York: Oxford University Press.

Nelson, L. J., & Luster, S. S. (2016). "Adulthood" by whose definition?: The complexity of emerging adults' conceptions of adulthood. In J. J. Arnett (Ed.), *Oxford handbook of emerging adulthood* (pp. 421–437). New York: Oxford University Press.

Nelson, L. J., & Padilla-Walker, L. M. (2013). Flourishing and floundering in emerging adult college students. *Emerging Adulthood, 1,* 67–78.

Nelson, L. J., Padilla-Walker, L. M., Christensen, K. J., Evans, C. A., & Carroll, J. S. (2011). Parenting in emerging adulthood: An examination of parenting clusters and correlates. *Journal of Youth and Adolescence, 40,* 730–743.

Nelson, S. K., Kushlev, K., English, T., Dunn, E. W., & Lyubomirsky, S. (2013). In defense of parenthood: Children are associated with more joy than misery. *Psychological Science, 24,* 3–10.

Nepomnyaschy, L., & Waldfogel, J. (2007). Paternity leave and fathers' involvement with their young children. *Community, Work and Family, 10,* 427–453.

Nesdale, D., Durkin, K., Maas, A., & Griffiths, J. (2004). Group status, outgroup ethnicity, and children's ethnic attitudes. *Applied Developmental Psychology, 25,* 237–251.

Netz, Y., Wu, M.-J., Becker, B. J., & Tenenbaum, G. (2005). Physical activity and psychological well-being in advanced age: A meta-analysis of intervention studies. *Psychology and Aging, 20,* 272–284.

Neugarten, B. L. (1979). Time, age, and the life cycle. *American Journal of Psychiatry, 136,* 887–894.

Neugarten, B. L. (1996). The middle years. In D. A. Neugarten (Ed.), *The meanings of age: Selected papers of Bernice L. Neugarten.* Chicago: University of Chicago Press.

Neugebauer, R., Fisher, P. W., Turner, J. B., Yamabe, S., Sarsfield, J. A., & Stehling-Ariza, T. (2009). Post-traumatic stress reactions among Rwandan children and adolescents in the early aftermath of genocide. *International Journal of Epidemiology, 38,* 1033–1045.

Neuhouser, M. L., Wasserthel-Smoller, S., Thomson, C., Aragaki, A., Anderson, G. L., & Manson, J. E. (2009). Multivitamin use and risk of cancer and cardiovascular disease in the Women's Health Initiative cohorts. *Archives of Internal Medicine, 169,* 294–304.

Neuman, S. B. (2003). From rhetoric to reality: The case for high-quality compensatory prekindergarten programs. *Phi Delta Kappan, 85*(4), pp. 286–291.

Neville, H. J., & Bavelier, D. (2002). Human brain plasticity: Evidence from sensory deprivation and altered language experience. In M. A. Hofman, G. J. Boer, A. J. G. D. Holtmaat, E. J. W. van Someren, J. Berhaagen, & D. F. Swaab (Eds.), *Plasticity in the adult brain: From genes to neurotherapy* (pp. 177–188). Amsterdam: Elsevier Science.

Newcombe, N. S., Sluzenski, J., & Huttenlocher, J. (2005). Preexisting knowledge versus on-line learning: What do young infants really know about spatial location? *Psychological Science, 16,* 222–227.

Newheiser, A., Dunham, Y., Merrill, A., Hoosain, L., & Olson, K. R. (2014). Preference for high status predicts implicit outgroup bias among children from low-status groups. *Developmental Psychology, 50,* 1081–1090.

Newland, L. A., Coyl, D. D., & Freeman, H. (2008). Predicting preschoolers' attachment security from fathers' involvement, internal working models, and use of social support. *Early Child Development and Care, 178,* 785–801.

Newnham, C. A., Milgrom, J., & Skouteris, H. (2009). Effectiveness of a modified mother–infant transaction program on outcomes for preterm infants from 3 to 24 months of age. *Infant Behavior and Development, 32,* 17–26.

Newport, E. L. (1991). Contrasting conceptions of the critical period for language. In S. Cary & R. Gelman (Eds.), *The epigenesis of mind: Essays on biology and cognition* (pp. 111–130). Hillsdale, NJ: Erlbaum.

Newsom, J. T., & Schulz, R. (1998). Caregiving from the recipient's perspective: Negative reactions to being helped. *Health Psychology, 17,* 172–181.

Newson, R. S., Boelen, P. A., Hek, K., Hofman, A., & Tiemeier, H. (2011). The prevalence and characteristics of complicated grief in older adults. *Journal of Affective Disorders, 132,* 231–238.

New Strategist Editors. (2015). *The baby boom: Americans born 1946 to 1964.* Amityville, NY: New Strategists Press.

Newton, E. K., Laible, D., Carlo, G., Steele, J. S., & McGinley, M. (2014). Do sensitive parents foster kind children, or vice versa? Bidirectional influences between children's prosocial behavior and parental sensitivity. *Developmental Psychology, 50,* 1808–1816.

Newton, N. J., & Jones, B. K. (2016). Passing on: Personal attributes associated with midlife expressions of intended legacies. *Developmental Psychology, 52,* 341–353.

Newton, N. J., & Stewart, A. J. (2010). The middle ages: Change in women's personalities and social roles. *Psychology of Women Quarterly, 34,* 75–84.

Ng, A. S., & Kaye, K. (2012). *Why it matters: Teen childbearing, single parenthood, and father involvement.* Washington, DC: The National Campaign to Prevent Unplanned and Teenage Pregnancy.

Ng, F. F., Pomerantz, E. M., & Deng, C. (2014). Why are Chinese mothers more controlling than American mothers?: "My child is my report card." *Child Development, 85,* 355–369.

Ng, F. F., Pomerantz, E. M., & Lam, S. (2007). European American and Chinese parents' responses to children's success and failure: Implications for children's responses. *Developmental Psychology, 43,* 1239–1255.

Ng, T. W. H., & Feldman, D. C. (2008). The relationship of age to ten dimensions of job performance. *Journal of Applied Psychology, 93,* 392–423.

Ngata, P. (2004). Death, dying, and grief: A Maori perspective. In J. D. Morgan & P. Laungani (Eds.), *Death and bereavement around the world: Vol. 4. Asia, Australia, and New Zealand* (pp. 95–99). Amityville, NY: Baywood.

Nguyen, S., & Rosengren, K. S. (2004). Parental reports of children's biological knowledge and misconceptions. *International Journal of Behavioral Development, 28,* 411–420.

NHPCO (National Hospice and Palliative Care Organization). (2013). *NHPCO's facts and figures: Hospice care in America—2013 edition.* Retrieved from www.nhpco.org/sites/default/files/public/Statistics_Research/2013_Facts_Figures.pdf

NICHD (National Institute of Child Health and Human Development) Early Child Care Research Network. (1997). The effects of infant child care on infant–mother attachment security: Results of the NICHD Study of Early Child Care. *Child Development, 68,* 860–879.

NICHD (National Institute of Child Health and Human Development) Early Child Care Research Network. (1998). Relations between family predictors and child outcomes: Are they weaker for children in child care? *Developmental Psychology, 34,* 1119–1128.

NICHD (National Institute of Child Health and Human Development) Early Child Care Research Network. (1999). Child care and mother–child interaction in the first 3 years of life. *Developmental Psychology, 35,* 1399–1413.

NICHD (National Institute of Child Health and Human Development) Early Child Care Research Network. (2000a). Characteristics and quality of child care for toddlers and preschoolers. *Applied Developmental Science, 4,* 116–135.

NICHD (National Institute of Child Health and Human Development) Early Child Care Research Network. (2000b). The relation of child care to cognitive and language development. *Child Development, 71,* 960–980.

NICHD (National Institute of Child Health and Human Development) Early Child Care Research Network. (2001). Before Head Start: Income and ethnicity, family characteristics, child care experiences, and child development. *Early Education and Development, 12,* 545–575.

NICHD (National Institute of Child Health and Human Development) Early Child Care Research Network. (2002a). Child-care structure ▯ process ▯ outcome: Direct and indirect effects of childcare quality on young children's development. *Psychological Science, 13,* 199–206.

NICHD (National Institute of Child Health and Human Development) Early Child Care Research Network. (2002b). The interaction of child care and family risk in relation to child development at 24 and 36 months. *Applied Developmental Science, 6,* 144–156.

NICHD (National Institute of Child Health and Human Development) Early Child Care Research Network. (2003a). Does amount of time spent in child care predict socioemotional adjustment during the transition to kindergarten? *Child Development, 74,* 976–1005.

NICHD (National Institute of Child Health and Human Development) Early Child Care Research Network. (2003b). Does quality of child care affect child outcomes at age 4½? *Developmental Psychology, 39,* 451–469.

NICHD (National Institute of Child Health and Human Development) Early Child Care Research Network. (2004). Trajectories of physical aggression from toddlerhood to middle childhood. *Monographs of the Society for Research in Child Development, 69*(4, Serial No. 278).

NICHD (National Institute of Child Health and Development) Early Child Care Research Network. (2005). *Child care and development: Results from the NICHD Study of Early Child Care and Youth Development.* New York: Guilford.

NICHD (National Institute of Child Health and Human Development) Early Child Care Research Network. (2006). Child-care effect sizes for the NICHD Study of Early Child Care and Youth Development. *American Psychologist, 61,* 99–116.

Nichols, K. E., Fox, N., & Mundy, P. (2005). Joint attention, self-recognition, and neurocognitive function in toddlers. *Infancy, 7,* 35–51.

Nickels, A., & Kowalski-Braun, M. (2012). Examining NIARA: How a student-designated program for women of color is impacting mentors. *Advances in Developing Human Resources, 14,* 188–204.

Nickman, S. L., Rosenfeld, A. A., Fine, P., MacIntyre, J. C., Pilowsky, D. J., & Howe, R. A. (2005). Children in adoptive families: Overview and update. *Journal of the American Academy of Child and Adolescent Psychiatry, 44,* 987–995.

Nicolopoulou, A., & Ilgaz, H. (2013). What do we know about pretend play and narrative development? A response to Lillard, Lerner, Hopkins, Dore, Smith, and Palmquist on "The impact of pretend play on children's development: A review of the evidence." *American Journal of Play, 6,* 55–81.

Nielsen, M. (2012). Imitation, pretend play, and childhood: Essential elements in the evolution of human culture? *Journal of Comparative Psychology, 126,* 170–181.

Nielsen, N. M., Hansen, A. V., Simonsen, J., & Hviid, A. (2011). Prenatal stress and risk of infectious diseases in offspring. *American Journal of Epidemiology, 173,* 990–997.

Nielson, D. (2012). Discussing death with pediatric patients: Implications for nurses. *Journal of Pediatric Nursing, 27,* e59–e64.

Nikulina, V., & Widom, C. S. (2013). Child maltreatment and executive functioning in middle adulthood: A prospective examination. *Neuropsychology, 27,* 417–427.

Nikulina, V., Widom, C. S., & Czaja, S. (2011). The role of childhood neglect and childhood poverty in predicting academic achievement and crime in adulthood. *American Journal of Community Psychology, 48,* 309–321.

Nippold, M. A., Taylor, C. L., & Baker, J. M. (1996). Idiom understanding in Australian youth: A cross-cultural comparison. *Journal of Speech and Hearing Research, 39,* 442–447.

Nisbett, R. E. (2009). *Intelligence and how to get it.* New York: Norton.

Nisbett, R. E., Aronson, J., Blair, C., Dickens, W., Flynn, J., Halpern, D. F., et al. (2012). Intelligence: New findings and theoretical developments. *American Psychologist, 67,* 130–159.

Nishitani, S., Miyamura, T., Tagawa, M., Sumi, M., Takase, R., Doi, H., et al. (2009). The calming effect of a maternal breast milk odor on the human newborn infant. *Neuroscience Research, 63,* 66–71.

Nissan, J., Liewald, D., & Deary, I. J. (2013). Reaction time and intelligence: Comparing associations based on the two response modes. *Intelligence, 41,* 622–630.

Nissen, N. K., & Holm, L. (2015). Literature review: Perceptions and management of body size among normal weight and moderately overweight people. *Obesity Reviews, 16,* 150–160.

Noble, K. G., Fifer, W. P., Rauh, V. A., Nomura, Y., & Andrews, H. F. (2012). Academic achievement varies with gestational age among children born at term. *Pediatrics, 130,* e257–e264.

Noel-Miller, C. (2015, October). *Medicare beneficiaries' out-of-pocket spending for health care.* Washington, DC: AARP Public Policy Institute. Retrieved from www.aarp.org/content/dam/aarp/ppi/2015/medicare-beneficiaries-out-of-pocket-spending-for-health-care.pdf

Noice, H., & Noice, T. (2006). What studies of actors and acting can tell us about memory and cognitive functioning. *Current Directions in Psychological Science, 15,* 14–18.

Noice, H., & Noice, T. (2013). Extending the reach of an evidence-based theatrical intervention. *Experimental Aging Research, 39,* 398–418.

Noice, H., Noice, T., & Staines, G. (2004). A short-term intervention to enhance cognitive and affective functioning in older adults. *Journal of Aging and Health, 16,* 562–585.

Noice, T., Noice, H., & Kramer, A. F. (2014). Participatory arts for older adults: A review of benefits and challenges. *Gerontologist, 54,* 741–753.

Nolen-Hoeksema, S., & Aldao, A. (2011). Gender and age differences in emotion regulation and their relationship to depressive symptoms. *Personality and Individual Differences, 51,* 704–708.

Noll, J. G., & Shenk, C. E. (2013). Teen birth rates in sexually abused and neglected females. *Pediatrics, 131,* e1181–e1187.

Nomaguchi, K. M., & Brown, S. L. (2011). Parental strains and rewards among mothers: The role of education. *Journal of Marriage and Family, 73,* 621–636.

Nomaguchi, K. M., & Milkie, M. A. (2003). Costs and rewards of children: The effects of becoming a parent on adults' lives. *Journal of Marriage and Family, 65,* 356–374.

Noppe, I. C., & Noppe, L. D. (1997). Evolving meanings of death during early, middle, and later adolescence. *Death Studies, 21,* 253–275.

Noroozian, M., Shadloo, B., Shakiba, A., & Panahi, P. (2012). Educational achievement and other controversial issues in left-handedness: A neuropsychological and psychiatric view. In T. Dutta & M. K. Mandal (Eds.), *Bias in human behavior* (pp. 41–82). Hauppauge, NY: Nova Science.

Northstone, K., Joinson, C., Emmett, P., Ness, A., & Paus, T. (2012). Are dietary patterns in childhood associated with IQ at 8 years of age? A population-based cohort study. *Journal of Epidemiological Community Health, 66,* 624–628.

Nosek, B. A., Smyth, F. L., Siriram, N., Lindner, N. M., Devos, T., Ayala, A., et al. (2009). National differences in gender–science stereotypes predict national sex differences in science and math achievement. *Proceedings of the National Academy of Sciences, 106,* 10593–10597.

Noterdaeme, M., Mildenberger, K., Minow, F., & Amorosa, H. (2002). Evaluation of neuromotor deficits in children with autism and children with a specific speech and language disorder. *European Child and Adolescent Psychiatry, 11,* 219–225.

Nowicki, E. A., Brown, J., & Stepien, M. (2014). Children's thoughts on the social exclusion of peers with intellectual or learning disabilities. *Journal of Intellectual Disability Research, 58,* 346–357.

Nucci, L. (2008). *Nice is not enough: Facilitating moral development.* Upper Saddle River, NJ: Prentice Hall.

Nucci, L. P. (2001). *Education in the moral domain.* New York: Cambridge University Press.

Nucci, L. P. (2005). Culture, context, and the psychological sources of human rights concepts. In W. Edelstein & G. Nunner-Winkler (Eds.), *Morality in context* (pp. 365–394). Amsterdam, Netherlands: Elsevier.

Nucci, L. P., & Gingo, M. (2011). The development of moral reasoning. In U. Goswami (Ed.), *The Wiley-Blackwell handbook of childhood cognitive development* (2nd ed., pp. 420–444). Hoboken, NJ: Wiley.

Nuland, S. B. (1993). *How we die.* New York: Random House.

Núñez, J., & Flanagan, C. (2016). Political beliefs and civic engagement in emerging adulthood. In J. J. Arnett (Ed.), *Oxford handbook of emerging adulthood* (pp. 481–496). New York: Oxford University Press.

Nuttall, R. L., Casey, M. B., & Pezaris, E. (2005). Spatial ability as a mediator of gender differences on mathematics tests: A biological–environmental framework. In A. M. Gallagher & J. C. Kaufman (Eds.), *Gender differences in mathematics: An integrated psychological approach* (pp. 121–142). New York: Cambridge University Press.

O

Oakes, L. M., Ross-Sheehy, S., & Luck, S. J. (2007). The development of visual short-term memory in infancy. In L. M. Oakes & P. J. Bauer (Eds.), *Short- and long-term memory in infancy and early childhood* (pp. 75–102). New York: Oxford University Press.

Obeidallah, D., Brennan, R. T., Brooks-Gunn, J., & Earls, F. (2004). Links between pubertal timing and neighborhood contexts: Implications for girls' violent behavior. *Journal of the American Academy of Child and Adolescent Psychiatry, 43,* 1460–1468.

Oberecker, R., & Friederici, A. D. (2006). Syntactic event-related potential components in 24-month-olds' sentence comprehension. *NeuroReport, 17,* 1017–1021.

Obermeyer, C. M. (2000). Menopause across cultures: A review of the evidence. *Menopause, 7,* 184–192.

Obradović, J., Long, J. D., Cutuli, J. J., Chan, C. K., Hinz, E., Heistad, D., & Masten, A. S. (2009). Academic achievement of homeless and highly mobile children in an urban school district: Longitudinal evidence on risk, growth, and resilience. *Development and Psychopathology, 21,* 493–518.

Obradović, J., & Masten, A. S. (2007). Developmental antecedents of young adult civic engagement. *Applied Developmental Science, 11,* 2–19.

O'Brien, K. M., Franco, M. G., & Dunn, M. G. (2014). Women of color in the workplace: Supports, barriers, and interventions. In M. L. Miville & A. D. Ferguson (Eds.), *Handbook of race–ethnicity and gender in psychology* (pp. 247–270). New York: Springer Science+Business Media.

O'Brien, M., Weaver, J. M., Burchinal, M., Clarke-Stewart, K. A., & Vandell, D. L. (2014). Women's work and child care: Perspectives and prospects. In E. T. Gershoff, R. S. Mistry, & D. A. Crosby (Eds.), *Societal contexts of child development: Pathways of influence and implications for practice and policy* (pp. 37–53). New York: Oxford University Press.

O'Brien, M., Weaver, J. M., Nelson, J. A., Calkins, S. D., Leerkes, E. M., & Marcovitch, S. (2011). Longitudinal associations between children's understanding of emotions and theory of mind. *Cognition and Emotion, 25,* 1074–1086.

O'Brien, M. A., Hsing, C., & Konrath, S. (2010, May). *Empathy is declining in American college students.* Poster presented at the annual meeting of the Association for Psychological Science, Boston.

O'Connor, E., & McCartney, K. (2007). Examining teacher–child relationships and achievement as part of an ecological model of development. *American Educational Research Journal, 44,* 340–369.

O'Connor, M. K., & Kraft, M. L. (2013). Lifestyle factors and successful cognitive aging in older adults. In J. J. Randolph (Ed.), *Positive neuropsychology: Evidence-based perspectives on promoting cognitive health* (pp. 121–141). New York: Springer Science + Business Media.

O'Connor, P. G. (2012). Alcohol abuse and dependence. In L. Goldman & D. A. Ausiello (Eds.), *Cecil Medicine* (23rd ed.), Philadelphia: Elsevier.

O'Connor, T. G., Marvin, R. S., Rutter, M., Olrich, J. T., Britner, P. A., & the English and Romanian Adoptees Study Team. (2003). Child–parent attachment following early institutional deprivation. *Development and Psychopathology, 15,* 19–38.

O'Connor, T. G., Rutter, M., Beckett, C., Keaveney, L., Dreppner, J. M., & the English and Romanian Adoptees Study Team. (2000). The effects of global severe privation on cognitive competence: Extension and longitudinal follow-up. *Child Development, 71,* 376–390.

O'Dea, J. A. (2012). Body image and self-esteem. In T. F. Cash (Ed.), *Encyclopedia of body image and human appearance* (pp. 141–147). London: Elsevier.

O'Doherty, D., Troseth, G. L., Shimpi, P. M., Goldenberg, E., Saylor, M. M., & Akhtr, N. (2011). Third-party social interaction and word learning from video. *Child Development, 82,* 902–915.

OECD (Organisation for Economic Cooperation and Development). (2012). *Education at a glance 2012: OECD indicators.* Paris: Author.

OECD (Organisation for Economic Cooperation and Development). (2013a). *Education at a glance 2013: OECD indicators.* Retrieved from www.oecd.org/edu/eag2013%20(eng)--FINAL%2020%20June%202013.pdf

OECD (Organisation for Economic Cooperation and Development). (2013b). *Health at a glance 2013: OECD indicators.* Retrieved from www.oecd.org/els/health-systems/Health-at-a-Glance-2013.pdf

OECD (Organisation for Economic Cooperation and Development). (2013c). *PISA 2012 results: Excellence through equity: Vol. 2. Giving every student the chance to succeed.* Retrieved from www.oecd.org/pisa/keyfindings/pisa-2012-results-volume-II.pdf

OECD (Organisation for Economic Cooperation and Development). (2014). *Education at a glance 2014: OECD indicators.* Retrieved from www.oecd.org/edu/Education-at-a-Glance-2014.pdf2

OECD (Organisation for Economic Cooperation and Development). (2015a). *Country note: How does health spending in the United States compare?* Retrieved from www.oecd.org/unitedstates/Country-Note-UNITED%20STATES-OECD-Health-Statistics-2015.pdf

OECD (Organisation for Economic Cooperation and Development). (2015b). *Gender equality.* Retrieved from www.oecd.org/gender/data/genderwagegap.htm

OECD (Organisation for Economic Cooperation and Development). (2015c). *Health at a glance 2015: OECD indicators.* Paris, France: OECD Publishing.

OECD (Organisation for Economic Cooperation and Development). (2015d). *OECD Health statistics 2015: Online database.* Retrieved from www.oecd.org/els/health-systems/health-data.htm

OECD (Organisation for Economic Cooperation and Development). (2016). *Long-term care resources and utilisation: Long-term care recipients.* Retrieved from stats.oecd.org/Index.aspx?DataSetCode=HEALTH_LTCR

Oetzel, J. G., Simpson, M., Berryman, K., & Reddy, R. (2015). Differences in ideal communication behaviours during end-of-life care for Maori carers/patients and palliative care workers. *Palliative Medicine, 29,* 764–766.

Offer, S. (2013). Family time activities and adolescents' emotional well-being. *Journal of Marriage and Family, 75,* 26–41.

Offer, S., & Schneider, B. (2011). Revisiting the gender gap in time-use patterns: Multitasking and well-being among mothers and fathers in dual-earner families. *American Sociological Review, 76,* 809–833.

Office of Head Start. (2014). *Head Start program facts: Fiscal year 2013.* Retrieved from eclkc.ohs.acf.hhs.gov/hslc/data/factsheets/2013-hs-program-factsheet.html

Ogbu, J. U. (2003). *Black American students in an affluent suburb: A study of academic disengagement.* Mahwah, NJ: Erlbaum.

Ogden, C. L., Carroll, M. D., Kit, B. K., & Flegal, K. M. (2014). Prevalence of childhood and adult obesity. *JAMA, 311,* 806–814.

Ogolsky, B., Dennison, R. P., & Monk, J. K. (2014). The role of couple discrepancies in cognitive and behavioral egalitarianism in marital quality. *Sex Roles, 70,* 329–342.

Oh, J.-H., & Kim, S. (2009). Aging, neighborhood attachment, and fear of crime: Testing reciprocal effects. *Journal of Community Psychology, 37,* 21–40.

O'Halloran, C. M., & Altmaier, E. M. (1996). Awareness of death among children: Does a life-threatening illness alter the process of discovery? *Journal of Counseling and Development, 74,* 259–262.

Ohannessian, C. M., & Hesselbrock, V. M. (2008). Paternal alcoholism and youth substance abuse: The indirect effects of negative affect, conduct problems, and risk taking. *Journal of Adolescent Health, 42,* 198–200.

Ohgi, S., Arisawa, K., Takahashi, T., Kusumoto, T., Goto, Y., Akiyama, T., & Saito, H. (2003a). Neonatal behavioral assessment scale as a predictor of later developmental disabilities of low-birth-weight and/ or premature infants. *Brain and Development, 25,* 313–321.

Ohgi, S., Takahashi, T., Nugent, J. K., Arisawa, K., & Akiyama, T. (2003b). Neonatal behavioral characteristics and later behavioral problems. *Clinical Pediatrics, 42,* 679–686.

Okagaki, L., & Sternberg, R. J. (1993). Parental beliefs and children's school performance. *Child Development, 64,* 36–56.

Okami, P., Weisner, T., & Olmstead, R. (2002). Outcome correlates of parent–child bedsharing: An eighteen-year longitudinal study. *Developmental and Behavioral Pediatrics, 23,* 244–253.

Okeke-Adeyanju, N., Taylor, L., Craig, A. B., Smith, R. E., Thomas, A., Boyle, A. E., et al. (2014). Celebrating the strengths of black youth: Increasing self-esteem and implications for prevention. *Journal of Primary Prevention, 35,* 357–369.

Okuro, M., & Moritmoto, S. (2014). Sleep apnea in the elderly. *Current Opinion in Psychiatry, 27,* 472–477.

Olafson, E. (2011). Child sexual abuse: Demography, impact, and interventions. *Journal of Child and Adolescent Trauma, 4,* 8–21.

Old, S. R., & Naveh-Benjamin, M. (2008). Age-related changes in memory: Experimental approaches. In S. M. Hofer & D. F. Alwin (Eds.), *Handbook of cognitive aging: Interdisciplinary perspectives* (pp. 151–167). Thousand Oaks, CA: Sage.

Olds, D. L., Eckenrode, J., Henderson, C., Kitzman, H., Cole, R., Luckey, D., et al. (2009). Preventing child abuse and neglect with home visiting by nurses. In K. A. Dodge & D. L. Coleman (Eds.), *Preventing child maltreatment* (pp. 29–54). New York: Guilford.

Olds, D. L., Kitzman, H., Cole, R., Robinson, J., Sidora, R., Luckey, D. W., et al. (2004). Effects of nurse home-visiting on maternal life course and child development: Age 6 follow-up results of a randomized trial. *Pediatrics, 114,* 1550–1559.

Olds, D. L., Kitzman, H., Hanks, C., Cole, R., Anson, E., Sidora-Arcoleo, K., et al. (2007). Effects of nurse home visiting on maternal and child functioning: Age-9 follow-up of a randomized trial. *Pediatrics, 120,* e832–e845.

Olds, D. L., Robinson, J., O'Brien, R., Luckey, D. W., Pettitt, L. M., Henderson, C. R., Jr., et al. (2002). Home visiting by paraprofessionals and by nurses: A randomized, controlled trial. *Pediatrics, 110,* 486–496.

Olfman, S., & Robbins, B. D. (Eds.). (2012). *Drugging our children.* New York: Praeger.

Olineck, K. M., & Poulin-Dubois, D. (2009). Infants' understanding of intention from 10 to 14 months: Interrelations among violation of expectancy and imitation tasks. *Infant Behavior and Development, 32,* 404–415.

Olino, T. M., Durbin, C. E., Klein, D. N., Hayden, E. P., & Dyson, M. W. (2013). Gender differences in young children's temperamental traits: Comparisons across observational and parent-report methods. *Journal of Personality, 81,* 119–129.

Oliveira, F. L., Patin, R. V., & Escrivao, M. A. (2010). Atherosclerosis prevention and treatment in children and adolescents. *Expert Review of Cardiovascular Therapy, 8,* 513–528.

Ollendick, T. H., King, N. J., & Muris, P. (2002). Fears and phobias in children: Phenomenology, epidemiology, and aetiology. *Child and Adolescent Mental Health, 7,* 98–106.

Oller, D. K. (2000). *The emergence of the speech capacity.* Mahwah, NJ: Erlbaum.

Olshansky, S. J. (2011). Trends in longevity and prospects for the future. In R. H. Binstock & L. K. George (Eds.), *Handbook of aging and the social sciences* (7th ed., pp. 47–56). San Diego, CA: Academic Press.

Olshansky, S. J., Hayflick, L., & Perls, T. T. (2004). Antiaging medicine: The hype and the reality—Part II. *Journals of Gerontology, 59A,* 649–651.

Olson, K. R., Key, A. C., & Eaton, N. R. (2015). Gender cognition in transgender children. *Psychological Science, 26,* 467–474.

Olson, S. L., Lopez-Duran, N., Lunkenheimer, E. S., Chang, H., & Sameroff, A. J. (2011). Individual differences in the development of early peer aggression: Integrating contributions of self-regulation, theory of mind, and parenting. *Development and Psychopathology, 23,* 253–266.

Olsson, B., Lautner, R., Andreasson, U., Öhrfelt, A., Portelius, E., Bjerke, M., et al. (2016). CSF and blood biomarkers for the diagnosis of Alzheimer's disease: A systematic review and meta-analysis. *Lancet, 15,* 673–684.

Omar, H., McElderry, D., & Zakharia, R. (2003). Educating adolescents about puberty: What are we missing? *International Journal of Adolescent Medicine and Health, 15,* 79–83.

O'Neill, M., Bard, K. A., Kinnell, M., & Fluck, M. (2005). Maternal gestures with 20-month-old infants in two contexts. *Developmental Science, 8,* 352–359.

O'Neill, R., Welsh, M., Parke, R. D., Wang, S., & Strand, C. (1997). A longitudinal assessment of the academic correlates of early peer acceptance and rejection. *Journal of Clinical Child Psychology, 26,* 290–303.

Ong, A. D., Bergeman, C. S., & Bisconti, T. L. (2004). The role of daily positive emotions during conjugal bereavement. *Journals of Gerontology, 59B,* 168–176.

Ong, A. D., Mroczek, D. K., & Riffin, C. (2011). The health significance of positive emotions in adulthood and later life. *Social and Personality Psychology Compass, 5/8,* 538–551.

Ontai, L. L., & Thompson, R. A. (2008). Attachment, parent–child discourse and theory-of-mind development. *Social Development, 17,* 47–60.

Onwuteaka-Philipsen, B. D., Brinkman-Stoppelenburg, A., Penning, C., de Jong-Krul, G. J., van Delden, J. J., & van der Heide, A. (2012). Trends in end-of-life practices before and after the enactment of the euthanasia law in the Netherlands from 1990 to 2010: A repeated cross-sectional survey. *Lancet, 380,* 908–915.

Oosterwegel, A., & Oppenheimer, L. (1993). *The self-system: Developmental changes between and within self-concepts.* Hillsdale, NJ: Erlbaum.

Opinion Research Corporation. (2009). *American teens say they want quality time with parents.* Retrieved from www.napsnet.com/pdf_archive/47/68753.pdf

Orbio de Castro, B., Veerman, J. W., Koops, W., Bosch, J. D., & Monshouwer, H. J. (2002). Hostile attribution of intent and aggressive behavior: A meta-analysis. *Child Development, 73,* 916–934.

Ordonana, J. R., Caspi, A., & Moffitt, T. E. (2008). Unintentional injuries in a twin study of preschool children: Environmental, not genetic risk factors. *Journal of Pediatric Psychology, 33,* 185–194.

Oregon Public Health Division. (2016). *Oregon's Death with Dignity Act—2014.* Retrieved from public.health.oregon.gov/ProviderPartnerResources/EvaluationResearch/DeathwithDignityAct/Documents/year17.pdf

Ormel, J., Petukhova, M., Chatterji, S., Aguilar Gaxiola, S., Alonso, J., & Angermeyer, M. C. (2008). Disability and treatment of specific mental and physical disorders across the world. *British Journal of Psychiatry, 192,* 368–375.

O'Rourke, N., Cappeliez, P., & Claxton, A. (2011). Functions of reminiscence and the psychological well-being of young–old and older adults over time. *Aging and Mental Health, 15,* 272–281.

Orth, U., Robins, R. W., & Widaman, K. F. (2012). Life-span development of self-esteem and its effects on important life outcomes. *Personality Processes and Individual Differences, 102,* 1271–1288.

Orth, U., Trzesniewski, K. H., & Robins, R. W. (2010). Self-esteem development from young adulthood to old age: A cohort-sequential longitudinal study. *Journal of Personality and Social Psychology, 98,* 645–658.

Osherson, D. N., & Markman, E. M. (1975). Language and the ability to evaluate contradictions and tautologies. *Cognition, 2,* 213–226.

Osterholm, E. A., Hostinar, C. E., & Gunnar, M. R. (2012). Alterations in stress responses of the hypothalamic-pituitary-adrenal axis in small for gestational age infants. *Psychoneuroendocrinology, 37,* 1719–1725.

Ostir, G. V., Carlson, J. E., Black, S. A., Rudkin, L., Goodwin, J. S., & Markides, K. S. (1999). Disability in older adults 1: Prevalence, causes, and consequences. *Behavioral Medicine, 24,* 147–156.

Ostrov, J. M., Crick, N. R., & Stauffacher, K. (2006). Relational aggression in sibling and peer relationships during early childhood. *Applied Developmental Psychology, 27,* 241–253.

Ostrov, J. M., Murray-Close, D., Godleski, S. A., & Hart, E. J. (2013). Prospective associations between forms and functions of aggression and social and affective processes during early childhood. *Journal of Experimental Child Psychology, 116,* 19–36.

Oswald, F., & Wahl, H.-W. (2013). Creating and sustaining homelike places in residential living. In G. D. Rowles & M. Bernard (Eds.), *Environmental gerontology: Making meaningful places in old age* (pp. 53–78). New York: Springer.

Otis, N., Grouzet, F. M. E., & Pelletier, L. G. (2005). Latent motivational change in an academic setting: A three-year longitudinal study. *Journal of Educational Psychology, 97,* 170–183.

Otter, M., Schrander-Stempel, C. T. R. M., Didden, R., & Curfs, L. M. G. (2013). The psychiatric phenotype in triple X syndrome: New hypotheses illustrated in two cases. *Developmental Neurorehabilitation, 15,* 233–238.

Otto, H., & Keller, H. (Eds.). (2014). *Different faces of attachment: Cultural variation of a universal human need.* Cambridge, UK: Cambridge University Press.

Ouko, L. A., Shantikumar, K., Knezovich, J., Haycock, P., Schnugh, D. J., & Ramsay, M. (2009). Effect of alcohol consumption on CpG methylation in the differentially methylated regions of H19 and IG-DMR in male gametes: Implications for fetal alcohol spectrum disorders. *Alcoholism, Clinical and Experimental Research, 33,* 1615–1627.

Overton, W. F., & Molenaar, P. C. M. (2015). Concepts, theory, and method in developmental science: A view of the issues. In W. F. Overton & P. C. Molenaar (Eds.), *Handbook of child psychology and developmental science: Vol. 1. Theory and method* (pp. 1–8). Hoboken, NJ: Wiley.

Owen, C. G., Whincup, P. H., Kaye, S. J., Martin, R. M., Smith, G. D., Cook, D. G., et al. (2008). Does initial breastfeeding lead to lower blood cholesterol in adult life? A quantitative review of the evidence. *American Journal of Clinical Nutrition, 88,* 305–314.

Owsley, C. (2011). Aging and vision. *Vision Research, 51,* 1610–1622.

Oyserman, D., Bybee, D., Mowbray, C., & Hart-Johnson, T. (2005). When mothers have serious mental health problems: Parenting as a proximal mediator. *Journal of Adolescence, 28,* 443–463.

Özçaliskan, S. (2005). On learning to draw the distinction between physical and metaphorical motion: Is metaphor an early emerging cognitive and linguistic capacity? *Journal of Child Language, 32,* 291–318.

Ozer, E. M., & Irwin, C. E., Jr. (2009). Adolescent and young adult health: From basic health status to clinical interventions. In R. M. Lerner & L. Steinberg (Eds.), *Handbook of adolescent psychology: Vol. 1. Individual bases of adolescent development* (pp. 618–641). Hoboken, NJ: Wiley.

Ozmerai, E. J., Eddins, A. C., Frisina, R., Sr., & Eddins, D. A. (2016). Large cross-sectional study of presbycusis reveals rapid progressive decline in auditory temporal acuity. *Neurobiology of Aging, 43,* 72–78.

P

Pacanowski, C. R., Senso, M. M., Oriogun, K., Crain, A. L., & Sherwood, N. E. (2014). Binge eating behavior and weight loss maintenance over a 2-year period. *Journal of Obesity,* Article ID 249315.

Padilla-Walker, L. M., Harper, J. M., & Jensen, A. C. (2010). Self-regulation as mediators between parenting and adolescents' prosocial behaviors. *Journal of Research on Adolescence, 22,* 400–408.

Padilla-Walker, L. M., & Nelson, L. J. (2012). Black Hawk down?: Establishing helicopter parenting as a distinct construct from other forms of parental control during emerging adulthood. *Journal of Adolescence, 35,* 1177–1190.

Páez, M., & Hunter, C. (2015). Bilingualism and language learning for immigrant-origin children and youth. In C. Suárez-Orozco, M. Abo-Zena, & A. K. Marks (Eds.), *Transitions: The development of children of immigrants* (pp. 165–183). New York: New York University Press.

Pagani, L. S., Japel, C., Vitaro, F., Tremblay, R. E., Larose, S., & McDuff, P. (2008). When predictions fail: The case of unexpected pathways toward high school dropout. *Journal of Social Issues, 64,* 175–193.

Pager, D., & Pedulla, D. S. (2015). Race, self-selection, and the job search process. *American Journal of Sociology, 120,* 1005–1054.

Pager, D., & Shepherd, H. (2008). The sociology of discrimination: Racial discrimination in employment, housing, credit, and consumer markets. *Annual Review of Sociology, 34,* 181–209.

Pager, D., Western, B., & Bonikowski, B. (2009). Discrimination in a low-wage labor market: A field experiment. *American Sociological Review, 74,* 777–799.

Pahlke, E., Bigler, R. S., & Suizzo, M.-A. (2012). Relations between colorblind socialization and children's racial bias: Evidence from European American mothers and their preschool children. *Child Development, 83,* 1164–1179.

Paik, A. (2010). "Hookups," dating, and relationship quality: Does the type of sexual involvement matter? *Social Science Research, 39,* 739–753.

Painter, J. A., Allison, L., Dhingra, P., Daughtery, J., Cogdill, K., & Trujillo, L. G. (2012). Fear of falling and its relationship with anxiety, depression, and activity engagement among community-dwelling older adults. *American Journal of Occupational Therapy, 66,* 169–176.

Palacios, J., & Brodzinsky, D. M. (2010). Adoption research: Trends, topics, outcomes. *International Journal of Behavioral Development, 34,* 270–284.

Palkovitz, R., Fagan, J., & Hull, J. (2013). Coparenting and children's well-being. In N. Cabrera and C. S. LeMonda (Eds.), *Handbook of father involvement: Multidisciplinary perspectives* (2nd ed., pp. 202–219). New York: Routledge.

Pan, H. W. (1994). Children's play in Taiwan. In J. L. Roopnarine, J. E. Johnson, & F. H. Hooper (Eds.), *Children's play in diverse cultures* (pp. 31–50). Albany, NY: SUNY Press.

Panagiotaki, G., Nobes, G., Ashraf, A., & Aubby, H. (2015). British and Pakistani children's understanding of death: Cultural and developmental influences. *British Journal of Developmental Psychology, 33,* 31–44.

Panish, J. B., & Stricker, G. (2002). Perceptions of childhood and adult sibling relationships. *NYS Psychologist, 14,* 33–36.

Papp, K. V., Kaplan, R. F., Springate, B., Moscufo, N., Wakefield, D. B., Guttmann, R. G., & Wolfson, L. (2014). Processing speed in normal aging: Effects of white matter hyperintensities and hippocampal volume loss. *Aging, Neuropsychology, and Cognition, 21,* 197–213.

Paradis, J., Genesee, F., & Crago, M. B. (2011). *Dual language development and disorders: A handbook on bilingualism and learning* (2nd ed.). Baltimore, MD: Brookes.

Paradise, R., & Rogoff, B. (2009). Side by side: Learning by observing and pitching in. *Ethos, 27,* 102–138.

Paramei, G. V. (2012). Color discrimination across four life decades assessed by the Cambridge Color Test. *Journal of the Optical Society of America, 29,* A290–A297.

Parameswaran, G. (2003). Experimenter instructions as a mediator in the effects of culture on mapping one's neighborhood. *Journal of Environmental Psychology, 23,* 409–417.

Parent, A., Teilmann, G., Juul, A., Skakkebaek, N. E., Toppari, J., & Bourguignon, J. (2003). The timing of normal puberty and the age limits of sexual precocity: Variations around the world, secular trends, and changes after migration. *Endocrine Reviews, 24,* 668–693.

Paris, S. G., & Paris, A. H. (2006). Assessments of early reading. In K. A. Renninger & I. E. Sigel (Eds.), *Handbook of child psychology: Vol. 4. Child psychology in practice* (6th ed., pp. 48–74). Hoboken, NJ: Wiley.

Parish-Morris, J., Golinkoff, R. M., & Hirsh-Pasek, K. (2013). From coo to code: A brief story of language development. In P. D. Zelazo (Ed.), *Oxford handbook of developmental psychology: Vol. 1. Body and mind* (pp. 867–908). New York: Oxford University Press.

Parish-Morris, J., Pruden, S., Ma, W., Hirsh-Pasek, K., & Golinkoff, R. M. (2010). A world of relations: Relational words. In B. Malt & P. Wolf (Eds.), *Words and the mind: How words capture human experience* (pp. 219–242). New York: Oxford University Press.

Park, D. C. (2002). Judging meaning improves function in the aging brain. *Trends in Cognitive Sciences, 6,* 227–229.

Park, D. C., Lautenschlager, G., Hedden, T., Davidson, N. S., Smith, A. D., & Smith, P. K. (2002). Models of visuospatial and verbal memory across the adult life span. *Psychology and Aging, 17,* 299–320.

Park, W. (2009). Acculturative stress and mental health among Korean adolescents in the United States. *Journal of Human Behavior in the Social Environment, 19,* 626–634.

Parke, R. D. (2002). Fathers and families. In M. H. Bornstein (Ed.), *Handbook of parenting: Vol. 3* (2nd ed., pp. 27–73). Mahwah, NJ: Erlbaum.

Parke, R. D., Simpkins, S. D., McDowell, D. J., Kim, M., Killian, C., Dennis, J., Flyr, M. L., Wild, M., & Rah, Y. (2004). Relative contributions of families and peers to children's social development. In P. K. Smith & C. H. Hart (Eds.), *Blackwell handbook of childhood social development* (pp. 156–177). Malden, MA: Blackwell.

Parker, E. T., & Pascarella, E. T. (2013). Effects of diversity experiences on socially responsible leadership over four years of college. *Journal of Diversity in Higher Education, 6,* 219–230.

Parker, J. G., Low, C. M., Walker, A. R., & Gamm, B. K. (2005). Friendship jealousy in young adolescents: Individual differences and links to sex, self-esteem, aggression, and social adjustment. *Developmental Psychology, 41,* 235–250.

Parker, P. D., Schoon, I., Tsai, Y-M., Nagy, G., Trautwein, U., & Eccles, J. (2012). Achievement, agency, gender, and socioeconomic background as predictors of postschool choices: A multicontext study. *Developmental Psychology, 48,* 1629–1642.

Parschau, L., Fleig, L., Warner, L. M., Pomp, S., Barz, M., Knoll, N., et al. (2014). Positive exercise experience facilitates behavior change via self-efficacy. *Health Education & Behavior, 41,* 414–442.

Parten, M. (1932). Social participation among preschool children. *Journal of Abnormal and Social Psychology, 27,* 243–269.

Pascalis, O., de Haan, M., & Nelson, C. A. (2002). Is face processing species-specific during the first year of life? *Science, 296,* 1321–1323.

Pascarella, E. T., & Terenzini, P. T. (1991). *How college affects students.* San Francisco: Jossey-Bass.

Pascarella, E. T., & Terenzini, P. T. (2005). *How college affects students: Vol. 2. A third decade of research.* San Francisco: Jossey-Bass.

Pasley, K., & Garneau, C. (2012). Remarriage and stepfamily life. In F. Walsh (Ed.), *Normal family processes: Growing diversity and complexity* (4th ed., pp. 149–171). New York: Guilford.

Patel, S., Gaylord, S., & Fagen, J. (2013). Generalization of deferred imitation in 6-, 9-, and 12-month-old infants using visual and auditory memory contexts. *Infant Behavior and Development, 36,* 25–31.

Pathman, T., Larkina, M., Burch, M. M., & Bauer, P. J. (2013). Young children's memory for the times of personal past events. *Journal of Cognition and Development, 14,* 120–140.

Patock-Peckam, J. A., & Morgan-Lopez, A. A. (2009). Mediational links among parenting styles, perceptions of parental confidence, self-esteem, and depression on alcohol-related problems in emerging adulthood. *Journal of Studies on Alcohol and Drugs, 70,* 215–226.

Patrick, M. E., & Schulenberg, J. E. (2014). Prevalence and predictors of adolescent alcohol use and binge drinking in the United States. *Alcohol Research: Current Reviews, 35,* 193–200.

Patrick, R. B., & Gibbs, J. C. (2011). Inductive discipline, parental expression of disappointed expectations, and moral identity in adolescence. *Journal of Youth and Adolescence, 41,* 973–983.

Patterson, C. J. (2013). Family lives of lesbian and gay adults. In G. W. Peterson & K. R. Bush (Eds.), *Handbook of marriage and family* (pp. 659–681). New York: Springer.

Patterson, G. R., & Fisher, P. A. (2002). Recent developments in our understanding of parenting: Bidirectional effects, causal models, and the search for parsimony. In M. H. Bornstein (Ed.), *Handbook of parenting* (Vol. 5, pp. 59–88). Mahwah, NJ: Erlbaum.

Patton, G. C., Coffey, C., Cappa, C., Currie, D., Riley, L., Gore, F., et al. (2012). Health of the world's adolescents: A synthesis of internationally comparable data. *Lancet, 379,* 1665–1675.

Patton, G. C., Coffey, C., Carlin, J. B., Sawyer, S. M., Williams, J., Olsson, C. A., et al. (2011). Overweight and obesity between adolescence and young adulthood: A 10-year prospective cohort study. *Journal of Adolescent Health, 48,* 275–280.

Paukner, A., Ferrari, P. F., & Suomi, S. J. (2011). Delayed imitation of lipsmacking gestures by infant rhesus macaques (*Macaca mulatta*). *PLoS ONE 6*(12), e28848.

Paul, J. J., & Cillessen, A. H. N. (2003). Dynamics of peer victimization in early adolescence: Results from a four-year longitudinal study. *Journal of Applied School Psychology, 19,* 25–43.

Paulsen, J. A., Syed, M., Trzesniewski, K. H., & Donnellan, M. B. (2016). Generational perspectives on emerging adulthood: A focus on narcissism. In J. J. Arnett (Ed.), *Oxford handbook of emerging adulthood* (pp. 26–44). New York: Oxford University Press.

Paulussen-Hoogeboom, M. C., Stams, G. J. J. M., Hermanns, J. M. A., & Peetsma, T. T. D. (2007). Child negative emotionality and parenting from infancy to preschool: A meta-analytic review. *Developmental Psychology, 43,* 438–453.

Payne, B. R., Gao, X., Noh, S. R., Anderson, C. J., & Stine-Morrow, E. A. L. (2012). The effects of print exposure on sentence processing and memory in older adults: Evidence for efficiency and reserve. *Aging, Neuropsychology, and Cognition, 19,* 122–149.

Pea, R., Nass, C., Meheula, L., Rance, M., Kumar, A., Bamford, H., et al. (2012). Media use, face-to-face communication, media multitasking, and social well-being among 8- to 12-year-old girls. *Developmental Psychology, 48,* 327–336.

Pearson, C. M., Wonderlich, S. A., & Smith, G. T. (2015). A risk and maintenance model for bulimia nervosa: From impulsive action to compulsive behavior. *Psychological Review, 122,* 516–535.

Peck, R. C. (1968). Psychological developments in the second half of life. In B. L. Neugarten (Ed.), *Middle age and aging* (pp. 88–92). Chicago: University of Chicago Press.

Pedersen, S., Vitaro, F., Barker, E. D., & Anne, I. H. (2007). The timing of middle-childhood peer rejection and friendship: Linking early behavior to early adolescent adjustment. *Child Development, 78,* 1037–1051.

Pederson, D. R., & Moran, G. (1996). Expressions of the attachment relationship outside of the Strange Situation. *Child Development, 67,* 915–927.

Peguero, A. A. (2011). Violence, schools, and dropping out: Racial and ethnic disparities in the educational consequence of student victimization. *Journal of Interpersonal Violence, 26,* 3753–3772.

Peirano, P., Algarin, C., & Uauy, R. (2003). Sleep–wake states and their regulatory mechanisms throughout early human development. *Journal of Pediatrics, 43,* S70–S79.

Peiró, J., Tordera, N., & Potocnik, K. (2012). Retirement practices in different countries. In M. Wang (Ed.), *Oxford handbook of retirement* (pp. 509–540). New York: Oxford University Press.

Pellegrini, A. D. (2003). Perceptions and functions of play and real fighting in early adolescence. *Child Development, 74,* 1522–1533.

Pellegrini, A. D. (2006). The development and function of rough-and-tumble play in childhood and adolescence: A sexual selection theory. In A. Göncü & S. Gaskins (Eds.), *Play and development: Evolutionary, sociocultural, and functional perspectives* (pp. 77–98). Mahwah, NJ: Erlbaum.

Peltonen, K., & Punamäki, R.-L. (2010). Preventive interventions among children exposed to trauma of armed conflict: A literature review. *Aggressive Behavior, 36,* 95–116.

Pennington, B. F. (2015). Atypical cognitive development. In L. S. Liben & U. Müller (Eds.), *Handbook of child psychology and developmental science: Vol. 2. Cognitive processes* (7th ed., pp. 995–1042). Hoboken, NJ: Wiley.

Pennisi, E. (2012). ENCODE Project writes eulogy for junk DNA. *Science, 337,* 1160–1161.

Penny, H., & Haddock, G. (2007). Anti-fat prejudice among children: The 'mere proximity' effect in 5–10 year olds. *Journal of Experimental Social Psychology, 43,* 678–683.

Peralta de Mendoza, O. A., & Salsa, A. M. (2003). Instruction in early comprehension and use of a symbol–referent relation. *Cognitive Development, 18,* 269–284.

Perdue, C. W. (2016). Ageism. In S. K. Whitbourne (Ed.), *Encyclopedia of adulthood and aging* (Vol. 1, pp. 47–51). Malden, MA: Wiley Blackwell.

Perelli-Harris, B., & Gassen, N. S. (2012). How similar are cohabitation and marriage? Legal approaches to cohabitation across Western Europe. *Population and Development Review, 38,* 435–467.

Perlman, D., Stevens, N. L., & Carcedo, R. J. (2015). Friendship. In M. Mikulincer, P. R. Shaver, J. A. Simpson, & J. F. Dovidio (Eds.), *APA handbook of personality and social psychology: Vol. 3. Interpersonal relations* (pp. 463–493). Washington, DC: American Psychological Association.

Perlmutter, M. (1984). Continuities and discontinuities in early human memory: Paradigms, processes, and performances. In R. V. Kail, Jr., & N. R. Spear (Eds.), *Comparative perspectives on the development of memory* (pp. 253–287). Hillsdale, NJ: Erlbaum.

Perlmutter, M., Kaplan, M., & Nyquist, L. (1990). Development of adaptive competence in adulthood. *Human Development, 33,* 185–197.

Perls, T., Levenson, R., Regan, M., & Puca, A. (2002). What does it take to live to 100? *Mechanisms of Ageing and Development, 123,* 231–242.

Perls, T., & Terry, D. (2003). Understanding the determinants of exceptional longevity. *Annals of Internal Medicine, 139,* 445–449.

Perls, T., Terry, D. F., Silver, M., Shea, M., Bowen, J., & Joyce, E. (2000). Centenarians and the genetics of longevity. *Results and Problems in Cell Differentiation, 29,* 1–20.

Perone, S., Madole, K. L., Ross-Sheehy, S., Carey, M., & Oakes, L. M. (2008). The relation between infants' activity with objects and attention to object appearance. *Developmental Psychology, 44,* 1242–1248.

Perrin, A. (2015, October 8). *Social media usage: 2005–2015* (Internet & American Life Project). Washington, DC: Pew Research Center.

Perroud, N., Rutembesa, E., Paoloni-Giacobino, A., Mutabaruka, J., Mutesa, L., Stenz, L., et al. (2014). The Tutsi genocide and transgenerational transmission of maternal stress: Epigenetics and biology of the HPA axis. *World Journal of Biological Psychiatry, 15,* 334–345.

Perry, W. G., Jr. (1981). Cognitive and ethical growth. In A. Chickering (Ed.), *The modern American college* (pp. 76–116). San Francisco: Jossey-Bass.

Perry, W. G., Jr. (1998). *Forms of intellectual and ethical development in the college years: A scheme.* San Francisco: Jossey-Bass. (Originally published 1970)

Peshkin, A. (1997). *Places of memory: Whiteman's schools and Native American communities.* Mahwah, NJ: Erlbaum.

Pesonen, A.-K., Räikkönen, K., Heinonen, K., & Komsi, N. (2008). A transactional model of temperamental development: Evidence of a relationship between child temperament and maternal stress over five years. *Social Development, 17,* 326–340.

Peters, L., Cant, R., Payne, S., O'Connor, M., McDermott, F., Hood, K., et al. (2013). How death anxiety impacts nurses' caring for patients at the end of life: A review of literature. *Open Nursing Journal, 7,* 14–21.

Peters, R. D. (2005). A community-based approach to promoting resilience in young children, their families, and their neighborhoods. In R. D. Paters, B. Leadbeater, & R. J. McMahon (Eds.), *Resilience in children, families, and communities: Linking context to practice and policy* (pp. 157–176). New York: Kluwer Academic.

Peters, R. D., Bradshaw, A. J., Petrunka, K., Nelson, G., Herry, Y., Craig, W. M., et al. (2010). The Better Beginnings, Better Futures Project: Findings from grade 3 to grade 9. *Monographs of the Society for Research in Child Development, 75*(3, Serial No. 297).

Peters, R. D., Petrunka, K., & Arnold, R. (2003). The Better Beginnings, Better Futures Project: A universal, comprehensive, community-based prevention approach for primary school children and their families. *Journal of Clinical Child and Adolescent Psychology, 32,* 215–227.

Peterson, B. E. (2002). Longitudinal analysis of midlife generativity, intergenerational roles, and caregiving. *Psychology and Aging, 17,* 161–168.

Peterson, B. E. (2006). Generativity and successful parenting: An analysis of young adult outcomes. *Journal of Personality, 74,* 847–869.

Peterson, B. E., & Duncan, L. E. (2007). Midlife women's generativity and authoritarianism: Marriage, motherhood, and 10 years of aging. *Psychology and Aging, 22,* 411–419.

Peterson, C., & Rideout, R. (1998). Memory for medical emergencies experienced by 1- and 2-year-olds. *Developmental Psychology, 34,* 1059–1072.

Peterson, C., & Roberts, C. (2003). Like mother, like daughter: Similarities in narrative style. *Developmental Psychology, 39,* 551–562.

Peterson, C., Warren, K. L., & Short, M. M. (2011). Infantile amnesia across the years: A 2-year follow-up of children's earliest memories. *Child Development, 82,* 1092–1105.

Peter-Wight, M., & Martin, M. (2011). Older spouses' individual and dyadic problem solving. *European Psychologist, 16,* 288–294.

Petitto, L. A., Holowka, S., Sergio, L. E., & Ostry, D. (2001, September 6). Language rhythms in babies' hand movements. *Nature, 413,* 35–36.

Petitto, L. A., & Marentette, P. F. (1991). Babbling in the manual mode: Evidence for the ontogeny of language. *Science, 251,* 1493–1496.

Petrill, S. A., & Deater-Deckard, K. (2004). The heritability of general cognitive ability: A within-family adoption design. *Intelligence, 32,* 403–409.

Petrofsky, J., Berk, L., & Al-Nakhli, H. (2012). The influence of autonomic dysfunction associated with aging and type 2 diabetes on daily life activities. *Experimental Diabetes Research,* Article ID 657103.

Pettigrew, T. F., & Tropp, L. R. (2006). A meta-analytic test of intergroup contact theory. *Journal of Personality and Social Psychology, 90,* 751–783.

Pettit, G. S., Brown, E. G., Mize, J., & Lindsey, E. (1998). Mothers' and fathers' socializing behaviors in three contexts: Links with children's peer competence. *Merrill-Palmer Quarterly, 44,* 173–193.

Petty, F., Hayslip, B., Jr., Caballero, D. M., & Jenkins, S. R. (2015). Development of a scale to measure death perspectives: Overcoming and participating. *OMEGA, 7,* 146–168.

Pew Research Center. (2006). *Strong public support for right to die.* Retrieved from http://people-press.org/reports

Pew Research Center. (2010a). *College and marital stability.* Retrieved from www.pewsocialtrends.org/2010/10/07/iv-college-and-marital-stability

Pew Research Center. (2010b). *Gay marriage gains more acceptance.* Washington, DC: Author. Retrieved from www.pewresearch.org/2010/10/06/gay-marriage-gains-more-acceptance

Pew Research Center. (2010c). *Religion among the millennials.* Washington, DC: Pew Form on Religion and Public Life.

Pew Research Center. (2012). *"Nones" on the rise: One-in-five adults have no religious affiliation.* Washington, DC: Author.

Pew Research Center. (2013a). *Love and marriage.* Retrieved from www.pewsocialtrends.org/2013/02/13/love-and-marriage

Pew Research Center. (2013b). *Online dating & relationships.* Washington, DC: Author. Retrieved from pewinternet.org/Reports/2013/Online-Dating.aspx

Pew Research Center. (2013c). *The sandwich generation: Rising financial burdens for middle-aged Americans.* Retrieved from www.pewsocialtrends.org/2013/01/30/the-sandwich-generation

Pew Research Center. (2013d). *A survey of LGBT Americans: Attitudes, experiences, and values in changing times.* Retrieved from www.pewsocialtrends.org/files/2013/06/SDT_LGBT-Americans_06-2013.pdf

Pew Research Center. (2014a). *Millennials in adulthood: Detached from institutions, networked with friends.* Washington, DC: Author.

Pew Research Center. (2014b). *Record share of Americans have never married.* Retrieved from www.pewsocialtrends.org/2014/09/24/record-share-of-americans-have-never-married

Pew Research Center. (2015a). *America's changing religious landscape*. Washington, DC: Pew Research Center. Retrieved from www.pewforum.org/files/2015/05/RLS-08-26-full-report.pdf

Pew Research Center. (2015b). *Childlessness*. Retrieved from www.pewsocialtrends.org/2015/05/07/childlessness

Pew Research Center. (2015c). *5 Facts about today's fathers*. Retrieved from www.pewresearch.org/fact-tank/2015/06/18/5-facts-about-todays-fathers

Pew Research Center. (2015d). *Interracial marriage: Who is marrying out?* Retrieved from http://www.pewresearch.org/fact-tank/2015/06/12/interracial-marriage-who-is-marrying-out

Pew Research Center. (2015e). *Modern parenthood: Roles of moms and dads converge as they balance work and family*. Retrieved from www.pewsocialtrends.org/2013/03/14/modern-parenthood-roles-of-moms-and-dads-converge-as-they-balance-work-and-family

Pew Research Center. (2015f). *Same-sex marriage detailed tables*. Washington, DC: Author. Retrieved from www.people-press.org/2015/06/08/same-sex-marriage-detailed-tables

Pew Research Center. (2015g). *Teens, social media & technology overview 2015: Smartphones facilitate shift in communication landscape for teens*. Retrieved from www.pewinternet.org/files/2015/04/PI_TeensandTech_Update2015_0409151.pdf

Pew Research Center. (2016a). *For first time in modern era, living with parents edges out other living arrangements for 18- to 34-year olds*. Retrieved from file:///Users/lauraberk/Downloads/2016-05-24_living-arrangemnet-final.pdf

Pew Research Center. (2016b). *Millennials match Baby Boomers as largest generation in U.S. electorate, but will they vote?* Retrieved from www.pewresearch.org/fact-tank/2016/05/16/millennials-match-baby-boomers-as-largest-generation-in-u-s-electorate-but-will-they-vote

Pew Research Center. (2016c). *Religious landscape study*. Retrieved from www.pewforum.org/religious-landscape-study

Pew Research Center. (2016d). *Social media usage: 2005–2015*. Retrieved from www.pewinternet.org/2015/10/08/social-networking-usage-2005-2015

Pfeifer, J. H., Ruble, D. N., Bachman, M. A., Alvarez, J. M., Cameron, J. A., & Fuligni, A. J. (2007). Social identities and intergroup bias in immigrant and nonimmigrant children. *Developmental Psychology, 43,* 496–507.

Pfeiffer, S. I., & Yermish, A. (2014). Gifted children. In L. Grossman & S. Walfish (Eds.), *Translating psychological research into practice* (pp. 57–64). New York: Springer.

Phelan, A. (2013). Elder abuse: An introduction. In A. Phelan (Ed.), *International perspectives on elder abuse* (pp. 1–31). London, UK: Routledge.

Phillipou, A., Rossell, S. L., & Castle, D. J. (2014). The neurobiology of anorexia nervosa: A systematic review. *Australian and New Zealand Journal of Psychiatry, 48,* 128–152.

Phillips, D. A., & Lowenstein, A. E. (2011). Early care, education, and child development. *Annual Review of Psychology, 62,* 483–500.

Phinney, J. S. (2007). Ethnic identity exploration in emerging adulthood. In J. J. Arnett & J. L. Tanner (Eds.), *Emerging adults in America: Coming of age in the 21st century* (pp. 117–134). Washington, DC: American Psychological Association.

Phinney, J. S., Ong, A., & Madden, T. (2000). Cultural values and intergenerational value discrepancies in immigrant and non-immigrant families. *Child Development, 71,* 528–539.

Phuong, D. D., Frank, R., & Finch, B. R. (2012). Does SES explain more of the black/white health gap than we thought? Revisiting our approach toward understanding racial disparities in health. *Social Science and Medicine, 74,* 1385–1393.

Piaget, J. (1926). *The language and thought of the child*. New York: Harcourt, Brace & World. (Original work published 1923)

Piaget, J. (1930). *The child's conception of the world*. New York: Harcourt, Brace, & World. (Original work published 1926)

Piaget, J. (1951). *Play, dreams, and imitation in childhood*. New York: Norton. (Original work published 1945)

Piaget, J. (1952). *The origins of intelligence in children*. New York: International Universities Press. (Original work published 1936)

Piaget, J. (1967). *Six psychological studies*. New York: Vintage.

Piaget, J. (1971). *Biology and knowledge*. Chicago: University of Chicago Press.

Picho, K., Rodriguez, A., & Finnie, L. (2013). Exploring the moderating role of context on the mathematics performance of females under stereotype threat: A meta-analysis. *Journal of Social Psychology, 153,* 299–333.

Pickel, G. (2013). *Religion monitor: Understanding common ground. An international comparison of religious belief*. Gütersloh, Germany: Bertelsmann Foundation.

Pickens, J., Field, T., & Nawrocki, T. (2001). Frontal EEG asymmetry in response to emotional vignettes in preschool age children. *International Journal of Behavioral Development, 25,* 105–112.

Piernas, C., & Popkin, B. M. (2011). Increased portion sizes from energy-dense foods affect total energy intake at eating occasions in U.S. children and adolescents: Patterns and trends by age group and sociodemographic characteristics, 1977–2006. *American Journal of Clinical Nutrition, 94,* 1324–1332.

Pierroutsakos, S. L., & Troseth, G. L. (2003). Video verité: Infants' manual investigation of objects on video. *Infant Behavior and Development, 26,* 183–199.

Pietromonaco, P. R., & Beck, L. A. (2015). Attachment processes in adult relationships. In M. Mikulincer & P. R. Shaver (Eds.), *APA handbook of personality and social psychology: Vol. 3. Interpersonal relations* (pp. 33–64). Washington, DC: American Psychological Association.

Piirto, J. (2007). *Talented children and adults* (3rd ed.). Waco, TX: Prufrock Press.

Pike, K. M., Hoek, H. W., & Dunne, P. E. (2014). Cultural trends in eating disorders. *Current Opinion in Psychiatry, 27,* 436–442.

Pillemer, K., & Suitor, J. J. (2013). Who provides care? A prospective study of caregiving among adult siblings. *Gerontologist, 54,* 589–598.

Pillow, B. (2002). Children's and adults' evaluation of the certainty of deductive inferences, inductive inferences, and guesses. *Child Development, 73,* 779–792.

Ping, R. M., & Goldin-Meadow, S. (2008). Hands in the air: Using ungrounded iconic gestures to teach children conservation of quantity. *Developmental Psychology, 44,* 1277–1287.

Pinheiro, A. P., Root, T., & Bulik, C. M. (2011). The genetics of anorexia nervosa: Current findings and future perspectives. In J. Merrick (Ed.), *Child and adolescent health yearbook, 2009* (pp. 173–186). New York: Nova Biomedical Books.

Pinker, S. (1999). *Words and rules: The ingredients of language*. New York: Basic Books.

Pinquart, M. (2003). Loneliness in married, widowed, divorced, and never-married older adults. *Journal of Social and Personal Relationships, 20,* 31–53.

Pinquart, M. (2016). Associations of parenting styles and dimensions with academic achievement in children and adolescents: A meta-analysis. *Educational Psychology Review, 28,* 475–493.

Pinquart, M., & Forstmeier, S. (2012). Effects of reminiscence interventions on psychosocial outcomes: A meta-analysis. *Aging & Mental Health, 16,* 541–558.

Pinquart, M., & Schindler, I. (2009). Change of leisure satisfaction in the transition to retirement: A latent-class analysis. *Leisure Sciences, 31,* 311–329.

Pinquart, M., & Sörensen, S. (2006). Gender differences in caregiver stressor, social resources, and health: An updated meta-analysis. *Journals of Gerontology, 61B,* P33–P45.

Pirie, K., Peto, R., Reeves, G. K., Green, J., Beral, V., & the Million Women Study Collaborators. (2013). The 21st century hazards of smoking and benefits of stopping: A prospective study of one million women in the UK. *Lancet, 381,* 133–141.

Pitkin, J. (2010). Cultural issues and the menopause. *Menopause International, 16,* 156–161.

Plante, I., Théoret, M., & Favreau, O. E. (2009). Student gender stereotypes: Contrasting the perceived maleness and femaleness of mathematics and language. *Educational Psychology, 29,* 385–405.

Platt, M. P. W. (2014). Neonatology and obstetric anaesthesia. *Archives of Disease in Childhood—Fetal and Neonatal Edition, 99,* F98.

Pleck, J. H. (2012). Integrating father involvement in parenting research. *Parenting: Science and Practice, 12,* 243–253.

Ploeg, J., Campbell, L., Denton, M., Joshi, A., & Davies, S. (2004). Helping to build and rebuild secure lives and futures: Financial transfers from parents to adult children and grandchildren. *Canadian Journal on Aging, 23,* S131–S143.

Plomin, R. (2013). Commentary: Missing heritability, polygenic scores, and gene–environment interactions. *Journal of Child Psychology and Psychiatry and Allied Disciplines, 54,* 1147–1149.

Plomin, R., & Deary, I. J. (2015). Genetics and intelligence differences: Five special findings. *Molecular Psychiatry, 20,* 98–108.

Plomin, R., DeFries, J. C., & Knopik, V. S. (2013). *Behavioral genetics* (6th ed.). New York: Worth.

Plomin, R., & Spinath, F. M. (2004). Intelligence: Genetics, genes, and genomics. *Journal of Personality and Social Psychology, 86,* 112–129.

Plucker, J. A., & Makel, M. C. (2010). Assessment of creativity. In J. C. Kaufman & R. J. Sternberg (Eds.), *Cambridge handbook of creativity* (pp. 48–73). New York: Cambridge University Press.

Pluess, M., & Belsky, J. (2011). Prenatal programming of postnatal plasticity? *Development and Psychopathology, 23,* 29–38.

Poehlmann, J., Schwichtenberg, A. J. M., Shlafer, R. J., Hahn, E., Bianchi, J.-P., & Warner, R. (2011). Emerging self-regulation in toddlers born preterm or low birth weight: Differential susceptibility to parenting. *Developmental and Psychopathology, 23,* 177–193.

Poelman, M. P., de Vet, E., Velema, E., Seidell, J. C., & Steenhuis, I. H. M. (2014). Behavioural strategies to control the amount of food selected and consumed. *Appetite, 72,* 156–165.

Polakowski, L. L., Akinbami, L. J., & Mendola, P. (2009). Prenatal smoking cessation and the risk of delivering preterm and small-for-gestational-age newborns. *Obstetrics and Gynecology, 114,* 318–325.

Polanska, K., Jurewicz, J., & Hanke, W. (2013). Review of current evidence on the impact of pesticides, polychlorinated biphenyls and selected metals on attention deficit/hyperactivity disorder in children. *International Journal of Occupational Medicine and Environmental Health, 26,* 16–38.

Polderman, T. J. C., de Geus, J. C., Hoekstra, R. A., Bartels, M., van Leeuwen, M., Verhulst, F. C., et al. (2009). Attention problems, inhibitory control, and intelligence index overlapping genetic factors: A study in 9-, 12-, and 18-year-old twins. *Neuropsychology, 23,* 381–391.

Pomerantz, E. M., & Dong, W. (2006). Effects of mothers' perceptions of children's competence: The moderating role of mothers' theories of competence. *Developmental Psychology, 42,* 950–961.

Pomerantz, E. M., Grolnick, W. S., & Price, C. E. (2013). The role of parents in how children approach achievement: A dynamic process perspective. In A. J. Elliott & C. J. Dweck (Eds.), *Handbook of confidence and motivation* (pp. 259–278). New York: Guilford.

Pomerantz, E. M., & Kempner, S. G. (2013). Mothers' daily person and process praise: Implications for children's theory of intelligence and motivation. *Developmental Psychology, 13,* 2040–2046.

Pomerantz, E. M., & Saxon, J. L. (2001). Conceptions of ability as stable and self-evaluative processes: A longitudinal examination. *Child Development, 72,* 152–173.

Pong, S., Johnston, J., & Chen, V. (2010). Authoritarian parenting and Asian adolescent school performance. *International Journal of Behavioral Development, 34,* 62–72.

Pong, S., & Landale, N. S. (2012). Academic achievement of legal immigrants' children: The roles of parents' pre- and postmigration characteristics in origin-group differences. *Child Development, 83,* 1543–1559.

Ponnappan, S., & Ponnappan, U. (2011). Aging and immune function: Molecular mechanisms to interventions. *Antioxidants & Redox Signaling, 14,* 1551–1585.

Pons, F., Lawson, J., Harris, P. L., & de Rosnay, M. (2003). Individual differences in children's emotion understanding: Effects of age and language. *Scandinavian Journal of Psychology, 44,* 347–353.

Poobalan, A. S., Aucott, L. S., Precious, E., Crombie, I. K., & Smith, W. C. S. (2010). Weight loss interventions in young people (18 to 25 year olds): A systematic review. *Obesity Reviews, 11,* 580–592.

Poole, D. A., & Bruck, M. (2012). Divining testimony? The impact of interviewing props on children's reports of touching. *Developmental Review, 32,* 165–180.

Portes, A., & Rumbaut, R. G. (2005). Introduction: The second generation and the Children of Immigrants Longitudinal Study. *Ethnic and Racial Studies, 28,* 983–999.

Posner, M. I., & Rothbart, M. K. (2007). Temperament and learning. In M. I. Posner & M. K. Rothbart (Eds.), *Educating the human brain* (pp. 121–146). Washington, DC: American Psychological Association.

Posthuma, R. A., & Campion, M. A. (2009). Age stereotypes in the workplace: Common stereotypes, moderators, and future research directions. *Journal of Management, 35,* 158–188.

Poti, J. M., Slining, M. M., & Popkin, B. M. (2014). Where are kids getting their empty calories? Stores, schools, and fast-food restaurants each played an important role in empty calorie intake among US children during 2009–2010. *Journal of the Academy of Nutrition and Dietetics, 114,* 908–917.

Potter, D. (2012). Same-sex parent families and children's academic achievement. *Journal of Marriage and Family, 74,* 556–571.

Potter, G. G., Helms, M. J., & Plassman, B. L. (2008). Associations of job demands and intelligence with cognitive performance among men in late life. *Neurology, 70,* 1803–1808.

Poulin-Dubois, D., Serbin, L. A., Eichstedt, J. A., Sen, M. G., & Beissel, C. F. (2002). Men don't put on make-up: Toddlers' knowledge of the gender stereotyping of household activities. *Social Development, 11,* 166–181.

Prager, K. J., & Bailey, J. M. (1985). Androgyny, ego development, and psychological crisis resolution. *Sex Roles, 13,* 525–535.

Pratt, M. W., Norris, J. E., Hebblethwaite, S., & Arnold, M. L. (2008). Intergenerational transmission of values: Family generativity and adolescents' narratives of parent and grandparent value teaching. *Journal of Personality, 76,* 171–198.

Pratt, M. W., Skoe, E. E., & Arnold, M. L. (2004). Care reasoning development and family socialization patterns in later adolescence: A longitudinal analysis. *International Journal of Behavioral Development, 28,* 139–147.

Prechtl, H. F. R., & Beintema, D. (1965). *The neurological examination of the full-term newborn infant.* London: Heinemann Medical Books.

Preece, J., & Findsen, B. (2007). Keeping people active: Continuing education programs that work. In M. Robinson, W. Novelli, C. Pearson, & L. Norris (Eds.), *Global health and global aging* (pp. 313–322). San Francisco: Jossey-Bass.

Pressley, M., & Hilden, D. (2006). Cognitive strategies. In D. Kuhn & R. Siegler (Eds.), *Handbook of child psychology: Vol. 2. Cognition, perception, and language* (6th ed., pp. 511–556). Hoboken, NJ: Wiley.

Preuss, T. M. (2012). Human brain evolution: From gene discovery to phenotype discovery. *Proceedings of the National Academy of Sciences, 109*(Suppl. 1), 10709–10716.

Prevatt, F. (2003). Dropping out of school: A review of intervention programs. *Journal of School Psychology, 41,* 377–399.

Price, J., Jordan, J., Prior, L., & Parkes, J. (2011). Living through the death of a child: A qualitative study of bereaved parents' experiences. *International Journal of Nursing Studies, 48,* 1384–1392.

Price, J. E., & Jones, A. M. (2015). Living through the life-altering loss of a child: A narrative review. *Issues in Comprehensive Pediatric Nursing, 38,* 222–240.

Price, L. H., Kao, H.-T., Burgers, D. E., Carpenter, L. L., & Tyrka, A. R. (2013). Telomeres and early-life stress: An overview. *Biological Psychiatry, 73,* 15–23.

Priess, H. A., Lindberg, S. M., & Hyde, J. S. (2009). Adolescent gender-role identity and mental health: Gender intensification revisited. *Child Development, 80,* 1531–1544.

Prince, M., Bryce, R., Albanese, E., Wimo, A., Ribeiro, W., & Ferri, C. P. (2013). The global prevalence of dementia: A systematic review and meta-analysis. *Alzheimer's and Dementia, 9,* 63–75.

Prince-Paul, M. J., Zyzanski, S., & Exline, J. J. (2013). The RelCom-S: A Screening instrument to assess personal relationships and communication in advanced cancer. *Journal of Hospice and Palliative Nursing, 15,* 298–306.

Principe, G. F. (2011). *Your brain on childhood: The unexpected side effects of classrooms, ballparks, family rooms, and the minivan.* Amherst, NY: Prometheus Books.

Prinstein, M. J., & La Greca, A. M. (2002). Peer crowd affiliation and internalizing distress in childhood and adolescence: A longitudinal follow-back study. *Journal of Research on Adolescence, 12,* 325–351.

Proctor, M. H., Moore, L. L., Gao, D., Cupples, L. A., Bradlee, M. L., Hood, M. Y., & Ellison, R. C. (2003). Television viewing and change in body fat from preschool to early adolescence: The Framingham Children's Study. *International Journal of Obesity, 27,* 827–833.

Programme for International Student Assessment. (2012). *PISA 2012 results.* Retrieved from nces.ed.gov/surveys/pisa/pisa2012/index.asp

Proietti, E., Röösli, M., Frey, U., & Latzin, P. (2013). Air pollution during pregnancy and neonatal outcome: A review. *Journal of Aerosol Medicine and Pulmonary Drug Delivery, 26,* 9–23.

Proulx, C. M. (2016). Marital trajectories. In In S. K. Whitbourne (Ed.), *Encyclopedia of adulthood and aging* (Vol. 2, pp. 842–846). Malden, MA: Wiley Blackwell.

Proulx, J., & Aldwin, C. M. (2016). Effects of coping on psychological and physical health. In S. K. Whitbourne (Ed.), *Encyclopedia of adulthood and aging* (Vol. 1, pp. 397–402). Hoboken, NJ: Wiley Blackwell.

Proulx, K., & Jacelon, C. (2004). Dying with dignity: The good patient versus the good death. *American Journal of Hospice and Palliative Care, 21,* 116–120.

Proulx, M., & Poulin, F. (2013). Stability and change in kindergartners' friendships: Examination of links with social functioning. *Social Development, 22,* 111–125.

Pruden, S. M., Hirsh-Pasek, K., Golinkoff, R. M., & Hennon, E. A. (2006). The birth of words: Ten-month-olds learn words through perceptual salience. *Child Development, 77,* 266–280.

Pruett, M. K., & Donsky, T. (2011). Coparenting after divorce: Paving pathways for parental cooperation, conflict resolution, and redefined family roles. In J. P. McHale & K. M. Lindahl (Eds.), *Coparenting: A conceptual and clinical examination of family systems* (pp. 231–250). Washington, DC: American Psychological Association.

Pryor, J. (2014). *Stepfamilies: A global perspective on research, policy, and practice.* New York: Routledge.

Public Health Agency of Canada. (2015). *Executive summary: Report on sexually transmitted infections in Canada: 2012.* Retrieved from www.phac-aspc.gc.ca/sti-its-surv-epi/rep-rap-2012/sum-som-eng.php

Pudrovska, T. (2009). Parenthood, stress, and mental health in late midlife and early old age. *International Journal of Aging and Human Development, 68,* 127–147.

Pugliese, C. E., Anthony, L. G., Strang, J. F., Dudley, K., Wallace, G. L., Naiman, D. Q., et al. (2016). Longitudinal examination of adaptive behavior in autism spectrum disorders: Influence of executive function. *Journal of Autism and Developmental Disorders, 13,* 467–477.

Puhl, R. M., Heuer, C. A., & Brownell, D. K. (2010). Stigma and social consequences of obesity. In P. G. Kopelman, I. D. Caterson, & W. H. Dietz (Eds.), *Clinical obesity in adults and children* (3rd ed., pp. 25–40). Hoboken, NJ: Wiley.

Puhl, R. M., & Latner, J. D. (2007). Stigma, obesity, and the health of the nation's children. *Psychological Bulletin, 133,* 557–580.

Pujol, J., Soriano-Mas, C., Ortiz, H., Sebastián-Gallés, N., Losilla, J. M., & Deus, J. (2006). Myelination of language-related areas in the developing brain. *Neurology, 66,* 339–343.

Puma, M., Bell, S., Cook, R., Heid, C., Broene, P., Jenkins, F., et al. (2012). *Third grade follow-up to the Head Start Impact Study final report* (OPRE Report #2012-45b). Washington, DC: U.S. Department of Health and Human Services.

Punamaki, R. L. (2006). Ante- and perinatal factors and child characteristics predicting parenting experience among formerly infertile couples during the child's first year: A controlled study. *Journal of Family Psychology, 20,* 670–679.

Putallaz, M., Grimes, C. L., Foster, K. J., Kupersmidt, J. B., Coie, J. D., & Dearing, K. (2007). Overt and relational aggression and victimization: Multiple perspectives within the school setting. *Journal of School Psychology, 45,* 523–547.

Putnam, S. P., Sanson, A. V., & Rothbart, M. K. (2000). Child temperament and parenting. In V. J. Molfese & D. L. Molfese (Eds.), *Temperament and personality across the life span* (pp. 255–277). Mahwah, NJ: Erlbaum.

Pyka, G., Lindenberger, E., Charette, S., & Marcus, R. (1994). Muscle strength and fiber adaptations to a year-long resistance training program in elderly men and women. *Journals of Gerontology, 49,* M22–27.

Pyszczynski, T., Greenberg, J., Solomon, S., Arndt, J., & Schimel, J. (2004). Why do people need self-esteem? A theoretical and empirical view. *Psychological Bulletin, 130,* 435–468.

Q

Qian, Z., & Lichter, D. T. (2011). Changing patterns of interracial marriage in a multiracial society. *Journal of Marriage and Family, 73,* 1065–1084.

Qin, L., & Pomerantz, E. M. (2013). Reciprocal pathways between American and Chinese early adolescents' sense of responsibility and disclosure to parents. *Child Development, 84,* 1887–1895.

Qouta, S. R., Palosaari, E., Diab, M., & Punamäki, R.-L. (2012). Intervention effectiveness among war-affected children: A cluster randomized controlled trial on improving mental health. *Journal of Traumatic Stress, 25,* 288–298.

Qu, Y., & Pomerantz, E. M. (2015). Divergent school trajectories in early adolescence in the United States and China: An examination of underlying mechanisms. *Journal of Youth and Adolescence, 44,* 2095–2109.

Quas, J. A., Malloy, L. C., Melinder, A., Goodman, G. S., & D'Mello, M. (2007). Developmental differences in the effects of repeated interviews and interviewer bias on young children's event memory and false reports. *Developmental Psychology, 43,* 823–837.

Qui, C. (2014). Lifestyle factors in the prevention of dementia: A life course perspective. In A. K. Leist, J. Kulmala, & F. Nyqvist (Eds.), *Health and cognition in old age: From biomedical and life course factors to policy and practice* (pp. 161–175). Cham, Switzerland: Springer.

Quinn, P. C. (2008). In defense of core competencies, quantitative change, and continuity. *Child Development, 79,* 1633–1638.

Quinn, P. C., Kelly, D. J., Lee, K., Pascalis, O., & Slater, A. (2008). Preference for attractive faces extends beyond conspecifics. *Developmental Science, 11,* 76–83.

Quinn, P. C., & Liben, L. S. (2014). A sex difference in mental rotation in infants: Convergent evidence. *Infancy, 19,* 103–116.

R

Raabe, T., & Beelmann, A. (2011). Development of ethnic, racial, and national prejudice in childhood and adolescence: A multinational meta-analysis of age differences. *Child Development, 82,* 1715–1737.

Raaijmakers, Q. A. W., Engels, R. C. M. E., & van Hoof, A. (2005). Delinquency and moral reasoning in adolescence and young adulthood. *International Journal of Behavioral Development, 29,* 247–258.

Rabbitt, P., Lunn, M., & Wong, D. (2008). Death, dropout, and longitudinal measurements of cognitive change in old age. *Journals of Gerontology, 63B,* P271–P278.

Rabig, J., Thomas, W., Kane, R., Cutler, L. J., & McAlilly, S. (2006). Radical redesign of nursing homes: Applying the Green House concept in Tupelo, Mississippi. *Gerontologist, 46,* 533–539.

Raby, K. L., Steele, R. D., Carlson, E. A., & Sroufe, L. (2015). Continuities and changes in infant attachment patterns across two generations. *Attachment & Human Development, 17,* 414–428.

Racz, S. J., McMahon, R. J., & Luthar, S. S. (2011). Risky behavior in affluent youth: Examining the co-occurrence and consequences of multiple problem behaviors. *Journal of Child and Family Studies, 20,* 120–128.

Radesky, J. S., Kistin, C. J., Zuckerman, B., Nitzberg, K., Gross, J., Kaplan-Sanoff, M., et al. (2014). Patterns of mobile device use by caregivers and children during meals in fast food restaurants. *Pediatrics, 133,* e843–e849.

Radey, M., & Randolph, K. A. (2009). Parenting sources: How do parents differ in their effort to learn about parenting? *Family Relations, 58,* 536–548.

Raevuori, A., Hoek, H. W., Susser, E., Kaprio, J., Rissanen, A., & Keski-Rahkonen, A. (2009). Epidemiology of anorexia nervosa in men: A nationwide study of Finnish twins. *PLoS ONE, 4,* e4402.

Ragow-O'Brien, D., Hayslip, B., Jr., & Guarnaccia, C. A. (2000). The impact of hospice on attitudes toward funerals and subsequent bereavement adjustment. *Omega, 41,* 291–305.

Rahi, J. S., Cumberland, P. M., & Peckham, C. S. (2011). Myopia over the life course: Prevalence and early life influences in the 1958 British birth cohort. *Ophthalmology, 118,* 797–804.

Rahman, Q., & Wilson, G. D. (2003). Born gay? The psychobiology of human sexual orientation. *Personality and Individual Differences, 34,* 1337–1382.

Raikes, H. A., Robinson, J. L., Bradley, R. H., Raikes, H. H., & Ayoub, C. C. (2007). Developmental trends in self-regulation among low-income toddlers. *Social Development, 16,* 128–149.

Raikes, H. H., Chazan-Cohen, R., Love, J. M., & Brooks-Gunn, J. (2010). Early Head Start impacts at age 3 and a description of the age 5 follow-up study. In A. J. Reynolds, A. J. Rolnick, M. M. Englund, & J. Temple (Eds.), *Childhood programs and practices in the first decade of life: A human capital integration* (pp. 99–118). New York: Cambridge University Press.

Räikkönen, K., Matthews, K. A., Flory, J. D., Owens, J. F., & Gump, B. B. (1999). Effects of optimism, pessimism, and trait anxiety on ambulatory blood pressure and mood during everyday life. *Journal of Personality and Social Psychology, 76,* 104–113.

Räikkönen, K., Matthews, K. A., Sutton-Tyrrell, K., & Kuller, L. H. (2004). Trait anger and the metabolic syndrome predict progression of carotid atherosclerosis in healthy middle-aged women. *Psychosomatic Medicine, 66,* 903–908.

Rakison, D. H. (2005). Developing knowledge of objects' motion properties in infancy. *Cognition, 96,* 183–214.

Rakison, D. H. (2010). Perceptual categorization and concepts. In J. G. Bremner & T. D. Wachs (Eds.), *Wiley-Blackwell handbook of infant development* (2nd ed., pp. 243–270). Oxford, UK: Wiley-Blackwell.

Rakison, D. H., & Lawson, C. A. (2013). Categorization. In P. D. Zelazo (Ed.), *Oxford handbook of developmental psychology: Vol. 1. Body and mind* (pp. 591–627). New York: Oxford University Press.

Rakoczy, H., Tomasello, M., & Striano, T. (2004). Young children know that trying is not pretending: A test of the "behaving-as-if" construal of children's early concept of pretense. *Developmental Psychology, 40,* 388–399.

Rakoczy, H., Tomasello, M., & Striano, T. (2005). How children turn objects into symbols: A cultural learning account. In L. Namy (Ed.), *Symbol use and symbol representation* (pp. 67–97). New York: Erlbaum.

Raley, R. K., Sweeney, M. M., & Wondra, D. (2015). The growing racial and ethnic divide in U.S. marriage patterns. *Future of Children, 25,* 89–105.

Ralston, S. H., & Uitterlinden, A. G. (2010). Genetics of osteoporosis. *Endocrine Reviews, 31,* 629–662.

Ramachandrappa, A., & Jain, L. (2008). Elective cesarean section: Its impact on neonatal respiratory outcome. *Clinics in Perinatology, 35,* 373–393.

Ramaswami, A., Dreher, G. F., Bretz, R., & Wiethoff, C. (2010). Gender, mentoring, and career success: The importance of organizational context. *Personnel Psychology, 63,* 385–405.

Ramchandani, P. G., Stein, A., O'Connor, T. G., Heron, J., Murray, L., & Evans, J. (2008). Depression in men in the postnatal period and later child psychopathology: A population cohort study. *Journal of the American Academy of Child and Adolescent Psychiatry, 47,* 390–398.

Ramey, C. T., Ramey, S. L., & Lanzi, R. G. (2006). Children's health and education. In K. A. Renninger & I. E. Sigel (Eds.), *Handbook of child psychology: Vol. 4. Child psychology in practice* (6th ed., pp. 864–892). Hoboken, NJ: Wiley.

Ramnitz, M. S., & Lodish, M. B. (2013). Racial disparities in pubertal development. *Seminars in Reproductive Medicine, 31,* 333–339.

Ramos, M. C., Guerin, D. W., Gottfried, A. W., Bathurst, K., & Oliver, P. H. (2005). Family conflict and children's behavior problems: The moderating role of child temperament. *Structural Equation Modeling, 12,* 278–298.

Ramsey-Rennels, J. L., & Langlois, J. H. (2006). Differential processing of female and male faces. *Current Directions in Psychological Science, 15,* 59–62.

Ramus, F. (2002). Language discrimination by newborns: Teasing apart phonotactic, rhythmic, and intonational cues. *Annual Review of Language Acquisition, 2,* 85–115.

Rando, T. A. (1995). Grief and mourning: Accommodating to loss. In H. Wass & R. A. Neimeyer (Eds.), *Dying: Facing the facts* (3rd ed., pp. 211–241). Washington, DC: Taylor & Francis.

Raqib, R., Alam, D. S., Sarker, P., Ahmad, S. M., Ara, G., & Yunus, M. (2007). Low birth weight is associated with altered immune function in rural Bangladeshi children: A birth cohort study. *American Journal of Clinical Nutrition, 85,* 845–852.

Rasmus, S., Allen, J., & Ford, T. (2014). "Where I have to learn the ways how to live:" Youth resilience in a Yup'ik village in Alaska. *Transcultural Psychiatry, 51,* 735–756.

Rasmussen, C., Ho, E., & Bisanz, J. (2003). Use of the mathematical principle of inversion in young children. *Journal of Experimental Child Psychology, 85,* 89–102.

Ratcliff, R., & McKoon, G. (2015). Aging effects in item and associative recognition memory for pictures and words. *Psychology and Aging, 30,* 669–674.

Rathunde, K., & Csikszentmihalyi, M. (2005). The social context of middle school: Teachers, friends, and activities in Montessori and traditional school environments. *Elementary School Journal, 106,* 59–79.

Rauer, A. J., & Albers, L. K. (2016). Marital happiness. In S. Whitbourne (Ed.), *Encyclopedia of adulthood and aging* (Vol. 2, pp. 833–842). Malden, MA: Wiley Blackwell.

Rauers, A., Riediger, M., Schmiedek, F., & Lindenberger, U. (2011). With a little help from my spouse: Does spousal collaboration compensate for the effects of cognitive aging? *Gerontology, 57,* 161–166.

Rawlins, W. K. (2004). Friendships in later life. In J. F. Nussbaum & J. Coupland (Eds.), *Handbook of communication and aging research* (2nd ed., pp. 273–299). Mahwah, NJ: Erlbaum.

Ray, E., & Heyes, C. (2011). Imitation in infancy: The wealth of the stimulus. *Developmental Science, 14,* 92–105.

Rayner, K., Pollatsek, A., & Starr, M. S. (2003). Reading. In A. F. Healy & R. W. Proctor (Eds.), *Handbook of psychology: Experimental psychology* (Vol. 4, pp. 549–574). New York: Wiley.

Read, S., Braam, A. W., Lyyra, T.-M., & Dee, D. J. H. (2014). Do negative life events promote gerotranscendence in the second half of life? *Aging & Mental Health, 18,* 117–124.

Reagan, P. B., Salsberry, P. J., Fang, M. Z., Gardner, W. P., & Pajer, K. (2012). African-American/white differences in the age of menarche: Accounting for the difference. *Social Science and Medicine, 75,* 1263–1270.

Ream, G. L., & Rodriguez, E. M. (2014). Sexual minorities. In C. M. Barry & M. M. Abo-Zena (Eds.), *Emerging adults' religiousness and spirituality* (pp. 204–219). New York: Oxford University Press.

Reay, A. C., & Browne, K. D. (2008). Elder abuse and neglect. In B. Woods & L. Clare (Eds.), *Handbook of the clinical psychology of ageing* (pp. 311–322). Chichester, UK: Wiley.

Rebok, G. W., Ball, K., Guey, L. T., Jones, R. N., Kim, H.-Y., King, J. W., et al. (2014). Ten-year effects of the Advanced Cognitive Training from Independent and Vital Elderly Cognitive Training Trial on cognition and everyday functioning in older adults. *Journal of the American Geriatrics Society, 62,* 16–24.

Rebok, G. W., Carlson, M. C., Frick, K. D., Giuriceo, K. D., Gruenewald, T. L., McGill, S., et al. (2014). The Experience Corps: Intergenerational interventions to enhance well-being among retired people. In F. A. Huppert & C. L. Cooper (Eds.), *Interventions and policies to enhance wellbeing: A complete reference guide* (Vol. 6, pp. 307–330). Malden, MA: Wiley Blackwell.

Redman, L. M., & Ravussin, E. (2011). Caloric restriction in humans: Impact on physiological, psychological, and behavioral outcomes. *Antioxidants & Redox Signaling, 14,* 275–287.

Reed, C. E., & Fenton, S. E. (2013). Exposure to diethylstilbestrol during sensitive life stages: A legacy of heritable health effects. *Birth Defects Research. Part C, Embryo Today: Reviews, 99,* 134–146.

Reef, J., Diamantopoulou, S., van Meurs, I., Verhulst, F. C., & van der Ende, J. (2011). Developmental trajectories of child to adolescent externalizing behavior and adult DSM–IV disorder: Results of a 24-year longitudinal study. *Social Psychiatry and Psychiatric Epidemiology, 46,* 1233–1241.

Reese E. (2002). A model of the origins of autobiographical memory. In J. W. Fagen & H. Hayne (Eds.), *Progress in Infancy Research* (Vol. 2, pp. 215–60). Mahwah, NJ: Erlbaum.

Reich, S. M., Subrahmanyam, K., & Espinoza, G. (2012). Friending, IMing, and hanging out face-to-face: Overlap in adolescents' online and offline social networks. *Developmental Psychology, 48,* 356–368.

Reid, K. F., & Fielding, R. A. (2012). Skeletal muscle power: A critical determinant of physical functioning in older adults. *Exercise and Sports Sciences Reviews, 40,* 4–12.

Reilly, D. (2012). Gender, culture, and sex-typed cognitive abilities. *PLOS ONE, 7,* e39904.

Reilly, D., Neumann, D. L., & Andrews, G. (2016). Sex and sex-role differences in specific cognitive abilities. *Intelligence, 54,* 147–158.

Reinke, L. F., Uman, J., Udris, E. M., Moss, B. R., & Au, D. H. (2013). Preferences for death and dying among veterans with chronic obstructive pulmonary disease. *American Journal of Hospice & Palliative Medicine, 30,* 768–772.

Reis, S. M. (2004). We can't change what we don't recognize: Understanding the special needs of gifted females. In S. Baum (Ed.), *Twice-exceptional and special populations of gifted students* (pp. 67–80). Thousand Oaks, CA: Corwin Press.

Reiss, D. (2003). Child effects on family systems: Behavioral genetic strategies. In A. C. Crouter & A. Booth (Eds.), *Children's influence on family dynamics: The neglected side of family relationships* (pp. 3–36). Mahwah, NJ: Erlbaum.

Reiss, N. S., & Tishler, C. L. (2008). Suicidality in nursing home residents: Part II. Prevalence, risk factors, methods, assessment, and management. *Professional Psychology: Research and Practice, 39,* 271–275.

Reitzes, D. C., & Mutran, E. J. (2002). Self-concept as the organization of roles: Importance, centrality, and balance. *Sociological Quarterly, 43,* 647–667.

Reitzes, D. C., & Mutran, E. J. (2004). Grandparenthood: Factors influencing frequency of grandparent-grandchildren contact and grandparent role satisfaction. *Journals of Gerontology, 59,* S9–S16.

Rentner, T. L., Dixon, L. D., & Lengel, L. (2012). Critiquing fetal alcohol syndrome health communication campaigns targeted to American Indians. *Journal of Health Communication, 17,* 6–21.

Repacholi, B. M., & Gopnik, A. (1997). Early reasoning about desires: Evidence from 14- and 18-month-olds. *Developmental Psychology, 33,* 12–21.

Repetti, R. L., & Wang, S.-W. (2014). Employment and parenting. *Parenting: Science and Practice, 14,* 121–132.

Reppucci, N. D., Meyer, J. R., & Kostelnik, J. O. (2011). Tales of terror from juvenile justice and education. In M. S. Aber, K. I. Maton, & E. Seidman (Eds.), *Empowering settings and voices for social change* (pp. 155–172). New York: Oxford University Press.

Resnick, G. (2010). Project Head Start: Quality and links to child outcomes. In A. J. Reynolds, A. J. Rolnick, M. M. Englund, & J. Temple (Eds.), *Childhood programs and practices in the first decade of life: A human capital integration* (pp. 121–156). New York: Cambridge University Press.

Resnick, M., & Silverman, B. (2005). Some reflections on designing construction kits for kids. Proceedings of the Conference on Interaction Design and Children, Boulder, CO.

Rest, J. R. (1979). *Development in judging moral issues.* Minneapolis: University of Minnesota Press.

Reuter-Lorenz, P. A., & Cappell, K. A. (2008). Neurocognitive aging and the compensation hypothesis. *Current Directions in Psychological Science, 17,* 177–182.

Reuter-Lorenz, P. A., Festini, S. B., & Jantz, T. K. (2016). Executive functions and neurocognitive aging. In K. W. Schaie & S. L. Willis (Eds.), *Handbook of the psychology of aging* (8th ed., pp. 245–262). London, UK: Elsevier.

Reyna, V. F., & Farley, F. (2006). Risk and rationality in adolescent decision making: Implications for theory, practice, and public policy. *Psychological Science in the Public Interest, 7,* 1–44.

Reynolds, R. M. (2013). Programming effects of glucocorticoids. *Clinical Obstetrics and Gynecology, 56,* 602–609.

Rhoades, B. L., Greenberg, M. T., & Domitrovich, C. E. (2009). The contribution of inhibitory control to preschoolers' social-emotional competence. *Journal of Applied Developmental Psychology, 30,* 310–320.

Ribarič, S. (2016). The rationale for insulin therapy in Alzheimer's disease. *Molecules, 21,* 689.

Rich, G. J. (2013). Finding flow: The history and future of a positive psychology concept. In J. D. Sinnott (Ed.), *Positive psychology: Advances in understanding adult motivation* (pp. 43–60). New York: Springer Science+Business Media.

Rich, P. (2015). *Physician perspective on end-of-life issues fully aired.* Retrieved from www.cma.ca/En/Pages/Physician-perspective-on-end-of-life-issues-fully-aired.aspx

Richard, C. A., & Brown, A. H. (2006). Configurations of informal social support among older lesbians. *Journal of Women and Aging, 18,* 49–65.

Richard-Davis, G., & Wellons, M. (2013). Racial and ethnic differences in the physiology and clinical symptoms of menopause. *Seminars in Reproductive Medicine, 31,* 380–386.

Richardson, H. L., Walker, A. M., & Horne, R. S. C. (2008). Sleep position alters arousal processes maximally at the high-risk age for sudden infant death syndrome. *Journal of Sleep Research, 17,* 450–457.

Richardson, K., & Norgate, S. H. (2006). A critical analysis of IQ studies of adopted children. *Human Development, 49,* 339–350.

Richardson, V. E. (2007). A dual process model of grief counseling: Findings from the changing lives of older couples (CLOC) study. *Journal of Gerontological Social Work, 48,* 311–329.

Richie, B. S., Fassinger, R. E., Linn, S. G., Johnson, J., Prosser, J., & Robinson, S. (1997). Persistence, connection, and passion: A qualitative study of the career development of highly achieving African American–black and white women. *Journal of Counseling Psychology, 44,* 133–148.

Richler, J., Luyster, R., Risi, S., Hsu, W.-L., Dawson, G., & Bernier, R. (2006). Is there a "regressive phenotype" of autism spectrum disorder associated with the measles-mumps-rubella vaccine? A CPEA study. *Journal of Autism and Developmental Disorders, 36,* 299–316.

Richmond, J., Colombo, M., & Hayne, H. (2007). Interpreting visual preferences in the visual paired-comparison task. *Journal of Experimental Psychology: Learning, Memory, and Cognition, 33,* 823–831.

Rideout, V., & Hamel, E. (2006). *The media family: Electronic media in the lives of infants, toddlers, preschoolers and their parents.* Menlo Park, CA: Henry J. Kaiser Family Foundation.

Rideout, V. J., Foehr, U. G., & Roberts, D. F. (2010). *Generation M2: Media in the lives of 8- to 18-year-olds.* Menlo Park. CA: Henry J. Kaiser Family Foundation.

Riediger, M., Li, S.-C., & Lindenberger, U. (2006). Selection, optimization, and compensation as developmental mechanisms of adaptive resource allocation: Review and preview. In J. E. Birren & K. W. Schaire (Eds.), *Handbook of the psychology of aging* (6th ed., pp. 289–313). Burlington, MA: Academic Press.

Rieffe, C., Terwogt, M. M., & Cowan, R. (2005). Children's understanding of mental states as causes of emotions. *Infant and Child Development, 14,* 259–272.

Rifkin, R. (2014, May 30). *New record highs in moral acceptability: Premarital sex, embryonic stem cell research, euthanasia growing in acceptance.* Retrieved from www.gallup.com/poll/170789/new-record-highs-moral-acceptability.aspx

Riggins, T., Miller, N. C., Bauer, P., Georgieff, M. K., & Nelson, C. A. (2009). Consequences of low neonatal iron status due to maternal diabetes mellitus on explicit memory performance in childhood. *Developmental Neuropsychology, 34,* 762–779.

Rijlaarsdam, J., Stevens, G. W. J. M., van der Ende, J., Arends, L. R., Hofman, A., Jaddoe, V. W. V., et al. (2012). A brief observational instrument for the assessment of infant home environment: Development and psychometric testing. *International Journal of Methods in Psychiatric Research, 21,* 195–204.

Rinaldo, L. A., & Ferraro, K. F. (2012). Inequality, health. In G. Ritzer (Ed.), *Wiley-Blackwell encyclopedia of globalization.* Hoboken, NJ: Wiley-Blackwell.

Rindermann, H., & Ceci, S. J. (2008). *Education policy and country outcomes in international cognitive competence studies.* Graz, Austria: Institute of Psychology, Karl-Franzens-University Graz.

Ripley, A. (2013). *The smartest kids in the world: And how they got that way.* New York: Simon and Schuster.

Ripple, C. H., & Zigler, E. (2003). Research, policy, and the federal role in prevention initiatives for children. *American Psychologist, 58,* 482–490.

Ristic, J., & Enns, J. T. (2015). Attentional development. In L. S. Liben & U. Müller (Eds.), *Handbook of child psychology and developmental science: Vol. 2. Cognitive processes* (pp. 158–202). Hoboken, NJ: Wiley.

Ristori, J., & Steensma, T. D. (2016). Gender dysphoria in childhood. *International Review of Psychiatry, 28,* 13–20.

Ritchie, L. D., Spector, P., Stevens, M. J., Schmidt, M. M., Schreiber, G. B., Striegel-Moore, R. H., et al. (2007). Dietary patterns in adolescence are related to adiposity in young adulthood in black and white females. *Journal of Nutrition, 137,* 399–406.

Ritchie, S. J., Dickie, D. A., Cox, S. R., Valdes Hernandez, M. del C., Corley, J., Royle, N. A., et al. (2015). Brain volumetric changes and cognitive ageing during the eighth decade of life. *Human Brain Mapping, 36,* 4910–4925.

Rith, K. A., & Diamond, L. M. (2013). Same-sex relationships. In M. A. Fine & F. D. Fincham (Eds.), *Handbook of family theories: A content-based approach* (pp. 123–144). New York: Routledge.

Ritz, B., Oiu, J., Lee, P. C., Lurmann, F., Penfold, B., Erin Weiss, R., et al. (2014). Prenatal air pollution exposure and ultrasound measures of fetal growth in Los Angeles, California. *Environmental Research, 130,* 7–13.

Rivas-Drake, D., Seaton, E. K., Markstrom, C., Quintana, S., Syed, M., Lee, R. M., et al. (2014). Ethnic and racial identity in adolescence: Implications for psychosocial, academic, and health outcomes. *Child Development, 85,* 40–57.

Rivkees, S. A. (2003). Developing circadian rhythmicity in infants. *Pediatrics, 112,* 373–381.

Rizza, W., Veronese, N., & Fontana, L. (2014). What are the roles of calorie restriction and diet quality in promoting healthy longevity? *Ageing Research Reviews, 13,* 38–45.

Rizzoli, R., Abraham, C., & Brandi, M. L. (2014). Nutrition and bone health: Turning knowledge and beliefs into healthy behavior. *Current Medical Research and Opinion, 30,* 131–141.

Roben, C. K. P., Bass, A. J., Moore, G. A., Murray-Kolb, L., Tan, P. Z., Gilmore, R. O., et al. (2012). Let me go: The influences of crawling experience and temperament on the development of anger expression. *Infancy, 17,* 558–577.

Robert, L., Labat-Robert, J., & Robert, A.-M. (2009). Physiology of skin aging. *Pathologie Biologie, 57,* 336–341.

Roberto, K. A. (2016a). Abusive relationships in late life. In L. K. George & K. F. Ferraro (Eds.), *Handbook of aging and the social sciences* (8th ed., pp. 337–355). New York: Academic Press.

Roberto, K. A. (2016b). The complexities of elder abuse. *American Psychologist, 71,* 302–311.

Roberto, K. A., & Jarrott, S. E. (2008). Family caregivers of older adults: A life span perspective. *Family Relations, 57,* 100–111.

Roberto, K. A., Teaster, P. B., McPherson, M., Mancini, J. A., & Savla, J. (2015). A community capacity framework for enhancing a criminal justice response to elder abuse. *Journal of Criminal Justice, 38,* 9–26.

Roberts, B. W., & DelVecchio, W. E. (2000). The rank-order consistency of personality traits from childhood to old age: A quantitative review of longitudinal studies. *Psychological Bulletin, 126,* 3–25.

Roberts, B. W., Kuncel, N., Shiner, R., Caspi, A., & Goldberg, L. R. (2007). The power of personality: A comparative analysis of the predictive validity of personality traits, SES, and IQ. *Perspectives on Psychological Science, 2,* 313–345.

Roberts, B. W., & Mroczek, D. (2008). Personality and trait change in adulthood. *Current Directions in Psychological Science, 17,* 31–35.

Roberts, B. W., Walton, K. E., & Viechtbauer, W. (2006). Patterns of mean-level change in personality traits across the life course: A meta-analysis of longitudinal studies. *Psychological Bulletin, 132,* 3–25.

Roberts, D. F., Foehr, U. G., & Rideout, V. (2005). *Generation M: Media in the lives of 8–18 year olds.* Menlo Park, CA: Henry J. Kaiser Family Foundation.

Roberts, D. F., Henriksen, L., & Foehr, U. G. (2009). Adolescence, adolescents, and media. In R. M. Lerner & L. Steinberg (Eds.), *Handbook of adolescent psychology: Vol. 2. Contextual influences on adolescent development* (3rd ed., pp. 314–344). Hoboken, NJ: Wiley.

Roberts, H., & Hickey, M. (2016). Managing the menopause: An update. *Maturitas, 86,* 53–58.

Roberts, J. E., Burchinal, M. R., & Durham, M. (1999). Parents' report of vocabulary and grammatical development of American preschoolers: Child and environment associations. *Child Development, 70,* 92–106.

Robertson, J. (2008). Stepfathers in families. In J. Pryor (Ed.), *International handbook of stepfamilies: Policy and practice in legal, research, and clinical environments* (pp. 125–150). Hoboken, NJ: Wiley.

Robine, J.-M., & Allard, M. (1999). Jeanne Louise Calment: Validation of the duration of her life. In B. Jeune & J. W. Vaupel (Ed.), *Validation of exceptional longevity.* Odense, Denmark: Odense University Press.

Robins, R. W., Tracy, J. L., Trzesniewski, K., Potter, J., & Gosling, S. D. (2001). Personality correlates of self-esteem. *Journal of Research in Personality, 35,* 463–482.

Robins, R. W., & Trzesniewski, K. H. (2005). Self-esteem development across the lifespan. *Current Directions in Psychological Science, 14,* 158–162.

Robinson, C. C., Anderson, G. T., Porter, C. L., Hart, C. H., & Wouden-Miller, M. (2003). Sequential transition patterns of preschoolers' social interactions during child-initiated play: Is parallel-aware play a bi-directional bridge to other play states? *Early Childhood Research Quarterly, 18,* 3–21.

Robinson, G. E. (2015). Controversies about the use of antidepressants in pregnancy. *Journal of Nervous and Mental Disease, 203,* 159–163.

Robinson, K. M. (2010). Policy issues in mental health among the elderly. *Nursing Clinics of North America, 45,* 627–634.

Robinson, S., Goddard, L., Dritschel, B., Wisley, M., & Howlin, P. (2009). Executive functions in children with autism spectrum disorders. *Brain and Cognition, 71,* 362–368.

Robinson-Cimpian, J. P., Lubienski, S. T., Ganley, C. M., & Copur-Gencturk, Y. (2014). Teachers' perceptions of students' mathematics proficiency may exacerbate early gender gaps in achievement. *Developmental Psychology, 50,* 1262–1281.

Robinson-Zañartu, C., & Carlson, J. (2013). Dynamic assessment. In K. F. Geisinger (Ed.), *APA handbook of testing and assessment in psychology: Vol. 3. Testing and assessment in school psychology and education* (pp. 149–168). Washington, DC: American Psychological Association.

Rocha, N. A. C. F., de Campos, A. C., Silva, F. P. dos Santos, & Tudella, E. (2013). Adaptive actions of young infants in the task of reaching for objects. *Developmental Psychobiology, 55,* 275–282.

Rochat, P. (1989). Object manipulation and exploration in 2- to 5-month-old infants. *Developmental Psychology, 25,* 871–884.

Rochat, P. (1998). Self-perception and action in infancy. *Experimental Brain Research, 123,* 102–109.

Rochat, P. (2013). Self-conceptualizing in development. In P. Zelazo (Ed.), *Oxford handbook of developmental psychology* (Vol. 2, pp. 378–397). New York: Oxford University Press.

Rochat, P., & Goubet, N. (1995). Development of sitting and reaching in 5- to 6-month-old infants. *Infant Behavior and Development, 18,* 53–68.

Rochat, P., & Hespos, S. J. (1997). Differential rooting responses by neonates: Evidence for an early sense of self. *Early Development and Parenting, 6,* 105–112.

Rochat, P., & Striano, T. (2002). Who's in the mirror? Self–other discrimination in specular images by four- and nine-month-old infants. *Infant and Child Development, 11,* 289–303.

Roche, K. M., Ensminger, M. E., & Cherlin, A. J. (2007). Variations in parenting and adolescent outcomes among African American and Latino families living in low-income, urban areas. *Journal of Family Issues, 28,* 882–909.

Roche, L., MacCann, C., & Croot, K. (2016). Predictive factors for the uptake of coping strategies by spousal dementia caregivers: A systematic review. *Alzheimer Disease & Associated Disorders, 30,* 80–91.

Rochelle, T. L., Yeung, D. K. Y., Bond, M. H., & Li, L. M. (2015). Predictors of the gender gap in life expectancy across 54 nations. *Psychology, Health & Medicine, 20,* 129–138.

Rodgers, J. L., & Wänström, L. (2007). Identification of a Flynn effect in the NLSY: Moving from the center to the boundaries. *Intelligence, 35,* 187–196.

Rodkin, P. C., Farmer, T. W., Pearl, R., & Van Acker, R. (2006). They're cool: Social status and peer group supports for aggressive boys and girls. *Social Development, 15,* 175–204.

Rodrigue, K. M., & Kennedy, K. M. (2011). The cognitive consequences of structural changes to the aging brain. In K. W. Schaie & S. L. Willis (Eds.), *Handbook of the psychology of aging* (7th ed., pp. 73–91). San Diego, CA: Academic Press.

Rodríguez, B., & López, M. J. R. (2011). El "nido repleto": La resolución de conflictos familiares cuando los hijos mayores se quedan en el hogar. [The "full nest": The resolution of family conflicts when older children remain in the home.] *Cultura y Educación, 23,* 89–104.

Rodriguez, E. M., Dunn, M. J., & Compas, B. E. (2012). Cancer-related sources of stress for children with cancer and their parents. *Journal of Pediatric Psychology, 37,* 185–197.

Roelfsema, N. M., Hop, W. C., Boito, S. M., & Wladimiroff, J. W. (2004). Three-dimensional sonographic measurement of normal fetal brain volume during the second half of pregnancy. *American Journal of Obstetrics and Gynecology, 190,* 275–280.

Roeser, R. W., Eccles, J. S., & Freedman-Doan, C. (1999). Academic functioning and mental health in adolescence: Patterns, progressions, and routes from childhood. *Journal of Adolescent Research, 14,* 135–174.

Rogoff, B. (2003). *The cultural nature of human development.* New York: Oxford University Press.

Rogoff, B., Correa-Chavez, M., & Silva, K. G. (2011). Cultural variation in children's attention and learning. In M. A. Gernsbacher, R. W. Pew, L. M. Hough, & J. R. Pomerantz (Eds.), *Psychology and the real world: Essays illustrating fundamental contributions to society* (pp. 154–163). New York: Worth.

Rogol, A. D., Roemmich, J. N., & Clark, P. A. (2002). Growth at puberty. *Journal of Adolescent Health, 31,* 192–200.

Rohde, P., Stice, E., & Marti, C. N. (2014). Development and predictive effects of eating disorder risk factors during adolescence: Implications for prevention efforts. *International Journal of Eating Disorders, 47,* 187–198.

Rohner, R. P., & Veneziano, R. A. (2001). The importance of father love: History and contemporary evidence. *Review of General Psychology, 5,* 382–405.

Roid, G. (2003). *The Stanford-Binet Intelligence Scales, Fifth Edition, interpretive manual.* Itasca, IL: Riverside Publishing.

Roid, G. H., & Pomplun, M. (2012). The Stanford-Binet Intelligence Scales, Fifth Edition. In D. P. Flanagan & P. L. Harrison (Eds.), *Contemporary intellectual assessment: Theories, tests and issues* (pp. 249–268). New York: Guilford.

Roisman, G. I., & Fraley, R. C. (2008). Behavior-genetic study of parenting quality, infant-attachment security, and their covariation in a nationally representative sample. *Developmental Psychology, 44,* 831–839.

Roisman, G. I., Madsen, S. D., Hennighausen, K. H., Sroufe, L. A., & Collins, W. A. (2001). The coherence of dyadic behavior across parent–child and romantic relationships as mediated by the internalized representation of experience. *Attachment and Human Development, 3,* 156–172.

Roisman, R., & Fraley, C. (2006). The limits of genetic influence: A behavior-genetic analysis of infant–caregiver relationship quality and temperament. *Child Development, 77,* 1656–1667.

Rokach, R., Cohen, O., & Dreman, S. (2004). Who pulls the trigger? Who initiates divorce among over 45-year-olds. *Journal of Divorce and Remarriage, 42,* 61–83.

Romano, E., Babchishin, L., Pagani, L. S., & Kohen, D. (2010). School readiness and later achievement: Replication and extension using a nationwide Canadian survey. *Developmental Psychology, 46,* 995–1007.

Roman-Rodriguez, C. F., Toussaint, T., Sherlock, D. J., Fogel, J., & Hsu, C.-D. (2014). Preemptive penile ring block with sucrose analgesia reduces pain response to neonatal circumcision. *Urology, 83,* 893–898.

Romero, A. J., & Roberts, R. E. (2003). The impact of multiple dimensions of ethnic identity on discrimination and adolescents' self-esteem. *Journal of Applied Social Psychology, 33,* 2288–2305.

Ronald, A., & Hoekstra, R. (2014). Progress in understanding the causes of autism spectrum disorders and autistic traits: Twin studies from 1977 to the present day. In S. H. Rhee & A. Ronald (Eds.), *Advances in Behavior Genetics* (Vol. 2, pp. 33–65). New York: Springer.

Rönnqvist, L., & Domellöf, E. (2006). Quantitative assessment of right and left reaching movements in infants: A longitudinal study from 6 to 36 months. *Developmental Psychobiology, 48,* 444–459.

Roopnarine, J. L., & Evans, M. E. (2007). Family structural organization, mother–child and father–child relationships and psychological outcomes in English-speaking African Caribbean and Indo Caribbean families. In M. Sutherland (Ed.), *Psychological of development in the Caribbean*. Kingston, Jamaica: Ian Randle.

Roopnarine, J. L., Hossain, Z., Gill, P., & Brophy, H. (1994). Play in the East Indian context. In J. L. Roopnarine, J. E. Johnson, & F. H. Hooper (Eds.), *Children's play in diverse cultures* (pp. 9–30). Albany: State University of New York Press.

Røsand, G.-M. B., Slinning, K., Røysamb, E., & Tambs, K. (2014). Relationship dissatisfaction and other risk factors for future relationship dissolution: A population-based study of 18,523 couples. *Social Psychiatry and Psychiatric Epidemiology, 49*, 109–119.

Rosario, M., & Schrimshaw, E. W. (2013). The sexual identity development and health of lesbian, gay, and bisexual adolescents: An ecological perspective. In C. J. Patterson & A. R. D'Augelli (Eds.), *Handbook of psychology and sexual orientation*. New York: Oxford University Press.

Rose, A. J., Schwartz-Mette, R. A., Glick, G. C., & Smith, R. (2014). An observational study of co-rumination in adolescent friendships. *Developmental Psychology, 50*, 2199–2209.

Rose, A. J., Swenson, L. P., & Waller, E. M. (2004). Overt and relational aggression and perceived popularity: Developmental differences in concurrent and prospective relations. *Developmental Psychology, 40*, 378–387.

Rose, S. A., Jankowski, J. J., & Senior, G. J. (1997). Infants' recognition of contour-deleted figures. *Journal of Experimental Psychology: Human Perception and Performance, 23*, 1206–1216.

Roseberry, S., Hirsh-Pasek, K., & Golinkoff, R. M. (2014). Skype me! Socially contingent interactions help toddlers learn language. *Child Development, 85*, 956–970.

Rosen, A. B., & Rozin, P. (1993). Now you see it, now you don't: The preschool child's conception of invisible particles in the context of dissolving. *Developmental Psychology, 29*, 300–311.

Rosen, C. S., & Cohen, M. (2010). Subgroups of New York City children at high risk of PTSD after the September 11 attacks: A signal detection analysis. *Psychiatric Services, 61*, 64–69.

Rosen, D. (2003). Eating disorders in children and young adolescents: Etiology, classification, clinical features, and treatment. *Adolescent Medicine: State of the Art Reviews, 14*, 49–59.

Rosen, L. D., Carrier, L. M., & Cheever, N. A. (2013). Facebook and texting made me do it: Media-induced task-switching while studying. *Computers in Human Behavior, 29*, 948–958.

Rosen, S., Bergman, M., & Plester, D. (1962). Presbycusis study of a relatively noise-free population in the Sudan. *Transactions of the American Otological Society, 50*, 135–152.

Rosenbaum, J. E. (2009). Patient teenagers? A comparison of the sexual behavior of virginity pledgers and matched nonpledgers. *Pediatrics, 123*, e110–e120.

Rosenblatt, P. C. (2008). Grief across cultures: A review and research agenda. In M. S. Stroebe, R. O. Hansson, H. Schut, & W. Stroebe (Eds.), *Handbook of bereavement research and practice* (pp. 207–222). Washington, DC: American Psychological Association.

Rosengren, K., Gutiérrez, I. T., & Schein, S. S. (2014). Cognitive dimensions of death in context. In K. Rosengren, P. J. Miller, I. T. Guíerrez, P. I. Chow, S. S. Schein, & K. N. Anderson (Eds.), Children's understanding of death: Toward a contextualized, integrated account. *Monographs of the Society for Research in Child Development, 79*(1, Serial No. 312), pp. 62–82.

Rosenman, R. H., Brand, R. J., Jenkins, C. D., Friedman, M., Strauss, R., & Wurm, M. (1975). Coronary heart disease in the Western Collaborative Group Study: Final follow-up experience of 8½ years. *JAMA, 223*, 872–877.

Rosenstein, D. L. (2011). Depression and end-of-life care for patients with cancer. *Dialogues in Clinical Neuroscience, 13*, 101–108.

Roseth, C. J., Pellegrini, A. D., Bohn, C. M., van Ryzin, M., & Vance, N. (2007). Preschoolers' aggression, affiliation, and social dominance relationships: An observational, longitudinal study. *Journal of School Psychology, 45*, 479–497.

Roskos, K. A., & Christie, J. F. (2013). Gaining ground in understanding the play–literacy relationship. *American Journal of Play, 6*, 82–97.

Ross, C. E., & Mirowsky, J. (2012). The sense of personal control: Social structural causes and emotional consequences. In C. S. Aneschensel, J. C. Phelan, & A. Bierman (Eds.), *Handbook of the sociology of mental health* (2nd ed., pp. 379–402). New York: Springer.

Ross, J. L., Roeltgen, D. P., Kushner, H., Zinn, A. R., Reiss, A., Bardsley, M. Z., et al. (2012). Behavioral and social phenotypes in boys with 47, XYY syndrome or 47, XXY Klinefelter syndrome. *Pediatrics, 129*, 769–778.

Ross, N., Medin, D. L., Coley, J. D., & Atran, S. (2003). Cultural and experiential differences in the development of folkbiological induction. *Cognitive Development, 18*, 25–47.

Rossen, E. K., Knafl, K. A., & Flood, M. (2008). Older women's perceptions of successful aging. *Activities, Adaptation and Aging, 32*, 73–88.

Rossi, A. S. (Ed.). (2001). *Caring and doing for others: Social responsibility in the domains of family, work, and community*. Chicago: University of Chicago Press.

Rossi, A. S. (2004a). The menopausal transition and aging processes. In O. G. Brim, C. D. Ryff, & R. C. Kessler (Eds.), *How healthy are we? A national study of well-being at midlife* (pp. 153–201). Chicago: University of Chicago Press.

Rossi, A. S. (2004b). Social responsibility to family and community. In O. G. Brim, C. D. Ryff, & R. C. Kessler (Eds.), *How healthy are we? A national study of well-being at midlife* (pp. 550–585). Chicago: University of Chicago Press.

Rossi, B. V. (2014). Donor insemination. In J. M. Goldfarb (Ed.), *Third-party reproduction* (pp. 133–142). New York: Springer.

Rostan, S. M. (1994). Problem finding, problem solving, and cognitive controls: An empirical investigation of critically acclaimed productivity. *Creativity Research Journal, 7*, 97–110.

Rostgaard, T. (2012). Quality reforms in Danish home care—balancing between standardisation and individualisation. *Health & Social Care in the Community, 20*, 247–254.

Roszel, E. L. (2015). Central nervous system deficits in fetal alcohol spectrum disorder. *Nurse Practitioner, 40*(4), 24–33.

Rotblatt, L. J., Sumida, C. A., Van Etten, E. J., Turk, E. P., Tolentino, J. C., & Gilbert, P. E. (2015). Differences in temporal order memory among young, middle-aged, and older adults may depend on the level of interference. *Frontiers in Aging Neuroscience, 7*: Article 28.

Rote, W. M., & Smetana, J. G. (2015). Parenting, adolescent–parent relationships, and social domain theory: Implications for identity development. In K. C. McLean & M. Syed (Eds.), *Oxford handbook of identity development* (pp. 437–453). New York: Oxford University Press.

Roth, D. L., Dilworth-Anderson, P., Huang, J., Gross, A. L., & Gitlin, L. N. (2015). Positive aspects of family caregiving for dementia: Differential item functioning by race. *Journals of Gerontology, 70B*, 813–819.

Roth, D. L., Skarupski, K. A., Crews, D. C., Howard, V. J., & Locher, J. L. (2016). Distinct age and self-rated health crossover mortality effects for African Americans: Evidence from a national cohort study. *Social Science & Medicine, 156*, 12–20.

Rothbart, M. K. (2003). Temperament and the pursuit of an integrated developmental psychology. *Merrill-Palmer Quarterly, 50*, 492–505.

Rothbart, M. K. (2011). *Becoming who we are: Temperament and personality in development*. New York: Guilford.

Rothbart, M. K., Ahadi, S. A., & Evans, D. E. (2000). Temperament and personality: Origins and outcome. *Journal of Personality and Social Psychology, 78*, 122–135.

Rothbart, M. K., & Bates, J. E. (2006). Temperament. In N. Eisenberg (Ed.), *Handbook of child psychology: Vol. 3. Social, emotional, and personality development* (6th ed., pp. 99–166). Hoboken, NJ: Wiley.

Rothbart, M. K., Posner, M. I., & Kieras, J. (2006). Temperament, attention, and the development of self-regulation. In K. McCartney & D. Phillips (Eds.), *Blackwell handbook of early childhood development* (pp. 338–357). Malden, MA: Blackwell.

Rothbaum, F., Morelli, G., & Rusk, N. (2011). Attachment, learning, and coping: The interplay of cultural similarities and differences. In M. J. Gelfand, C.-Y. Chiu, & Y.-Y. Horng (Eds.), *Advances in culture and psychology* (pp. 153–215). Oxford, UK: Oxford University Press.

Rothman, S. M., & Mattson, M. P. (2012). Sleep disturbances in Alzheimer's and Parkinson's diseases. *Neuromolecular Medicine, 14*, 194–204.

Rouselle, L., Palmers, E., & Noël, M.-P. (2004). Magnitude comparison in preschoolers: What counts? Influence of perceptual variables. *Journal of Experimental Child Psychology, 87*, 57–84.

Routledge, C., & Juhl, J. (2010). When death thoughts lead to death fears: Mortality salience increases death anxiety for individuals who lack meaning in life. *Cognition and Emotion, 24*, 848–854.

Rovee-Collier, C. K. (1999). The development of infant memory. *Current Directions in Psychological Science, 8*, 80–85.

Rovee-Collier, C. K., & Barr, R. (2001). Infant learning and memory. In G. Bremner & A. Fogel (Eds.), *Blackwell handbook of infant development* (pp. 139–168). Oxford, UK: Blackwell.

Rovee-Collier, C. K., & Bhatt, R. S. (1993). Evidence of long-term memory in infancy. *Annals of Child Development, 9*, 1–45.

Rovee-Collier, C., & Cuevas, K. (2009a). The development of infant memory. In M. Courage & N. Cowan (Eds.), *The development of memory in infancy and childhood* (pp. 11–41). Hove, UK: Psychology Press.

Rowe, M. L. (2008). Child-directed speech: Relation to socioeconomic status, knowledge of child development and child vocabulary skill. *Journal of Child Language, 35*, 185–205.

Rowe, M. L., & Goldin-Meadow, S. (2009). Early gesture selectively predicts later language learning. *Developmental Science, 12*, 182–187.

Rowe, M. L., Raudenbush, S. W., & Goldin-Meadow, S. (2012). The pace of vocabulary growth helps predict later vocabulary skill. *Child Development, 83*, 508–525.

Rowland, C. F. (2007). Explaining errors in children's questions. *Cognition, 104*, 106–134.

Rowland, C. F., & Pine, J. M. (2000). Subject-auxiliary inversion errors and wh-question acquisition: "What children do know?" *Journal of Child Language, 27*, 157–181.

Rowley, S. J., Kurtz-Costes, B., Mistry, R., & Feagans, L. (2007). Social status as a predictor of race and gender stereotypes in late childhood and early adolescence. *Social Development, 16*, 150–168.

Roy, K. M., & Lucas, K. (2006). Generativity as second chance: Low-income fathers and transformation of the difficult past. *Research in Human Development, 3,* 139–159.

Rozen, G. S. (2012). Healthy eating among adolescents. In Y. Latzer & O. Tzischinsky (Eds.), *The dance of sleeping and eating among adolescents: Normal and pathological perspectives* (pp. 3–15). New York: Nova Science Publishers.

Rubens, D., & Sarnat, H. B. (2013). Sudden infant death syndrome: An update and new perspectives of etiology. *Handbook of Clinical Neurology, 112,* 867–874.

Rubenstein, L. Z., Stevens, J. A., & Scott, V. (2008). Interventions to prevent falls among older adults. In L. S. Doll, S. E. Bonzo, D. A. Sleet, J. A. Mercy, & E. N. Haas (Eds.), *Handbook of injury and violence prevention* (pp. 37–53). New York: Springer.

Rubin, C., Maisonet, M., Kieszak, S., Monteilh, C., Holmes A., Flanders, D., et al. (2009). Timing of maturation and predictors of menarche in girls enrolled in a contemporary British cohort. *Paediatric and Perinatal Epidemiology, 23,* 492–504.

Rubin, D., Downes, K., O'Reilly, A., Mekonnen, R., Luan, X., & Localio, R. (2008). Impact of kinship care on behavioral well-being for children in out of home care. *Archives of Pediatrics and Adolescent Medicine, 162,* 550–556.

Rubin, D. M., O'Reilly, A. L., Luan, X., Dai, D., Localio, A. R., et al. (2011). Variation in pregnancy outcomes following statewide implementation of a prenatal home visitation program. *Archives of Pediatrics and Adolescent Medicine, 165,* 198–204.

Rubin, K. H., Bowker, J. C., McDonald, K. L., & Menzer, M. (2013). Peer relationships in childhood. In P. D. Zelazo (Ed.), *Oxford handbook of developmental psychology: Vol. 2. Self and other* (pp. 242–275). New York: Oxford University Press.

Rubin, K. H., Bukowski, W. M., & Parker, J. G. (2006). Peer interactions, relationships, and groups. In N. Eisenberg (Ed.), *Handbook of child psychology: Vol. 3. Social, emotional, and personality development* (6th ed., pp. 571–645). Hoboken, NJ: Wiley.

Rubin, K. H., & Burgess, K. B. (2002). Parents of aggressive and withdrawn children. In M. Bornstein (Ed.), *Handbook of parenting* (2nd ed., pp. 383–418). Hillsdale, NJ: Erlbaum.

Rubin, K. H., Coplan, R. J., & Bowker, J. C. (2009). Social withdrawal in childhood. *Annual Review of Psychology, 60,* 141–171.

Rubin, K. H., Fein, G. G., & Vandenberg, B. (1983). Play. In E. M. Hetherington (Ed.), *Handbook of child psychology: Vol. 4. Socialization, personality, and social development* (4th ed., pp. 693–744). New York: Wiley.

Rubin, K. H., Watson, K. S., & Jambor, T. W. (1978). Free-play behaviors in preschool and kindergarten children. *Child Development, 49,* 539–536.

Rubin, S. E., & Wooten, H. R. (2007). Highly educated stay-at-home mothers: A study of commitment and conflict. *Counseling and Therapy for Couples and Families, 15,* 336–345.

Ruble, D. N., Alvarez, J., Bachman, M., Cameron, J., Fuligni, A., García Coll, C., & Rhee, E. (2004). The development of a sense of "we": The emergence and implications of children's collective identity. In M. Bennett & F. Sani (Eds.), *The development of the social self* (pp. 29–76). Hove, UK: Psychology Press.

Ruble, D. N., Taylor, L. J., Cyphers, L., Greulich, F. K., Lurye, L. E., & Shrout, P. E. (2007). The role of gender constancy in early gender development. *Child Development, 78,* 1121–1136.

Ruck, M. D., Park, H., Killen, M., & Crystal, D. S. (2011). Intergroup contact and evaluations of race-based exclusion in urban minority children and adolescents. *Journal of Youth and Adolescence, 40,* 633–643.

Rudolph, C. W., & Toomey, E. (2016). Bridge employment. In S. K. Whitbourne (Ed.), *Encyclopedia of adulthood and aging* (Vol. 1, pp. 135–138). Malden, MA: Wiley Blackwell.

Rudolph, K. D., Caldwell, M. S., & Conley, C. S. (2005). Need for approval and children's well-being. *Child Development, 76,* 309–323.

Rueda, H. A., Lindsay, M., & Williams, L. R. (2015). "She posted it on Facebook": Mexican American adolescents' experiences with technology and romantic relationship conflict. *Journal of Adolescent Research, 30,* 419–445.

Ruedinger, E., & Cox, J. E. (2012). Adolescent childbearing: Consequences and interventions. *Current Opinions in Pediatrics, 24,* 446–452.

Ruff, H. A., & Capozzoli, M. C. (2003). Development of attention and distractibility in the first 4 years of life. *Developmental Psychology, 39,* 877–890.

Ruffman, T., & Langman, L. (2002). Infants' reaching in a multi-well A not B task. *Infant Behavior and Development, 25,* 237–246.

Ruffman, T., Perner, J., Olson, D. R., & Doherty, M. (1993). Reflecting on scientific thinking: Children's understanding of the hypothesis–evidence relation. *Child Development, 64,* 1617–1636.

Ruffman, T., Slade, L., Devitt, K., & Crowe, E. (2006). What mothers say and what they do: The relation between parenting, theory of mind, language, and conflict/cooperation. *British Journal of Developmental Psychology, 24,* 105–124.

Runco, M. A. (1992). Children's divergent thinking and creative ideation. *Developmental Review, 12,* 233–264.

Runco, M. A., Cramond, B., & Pagnani, A. R. (2010). Gender and creativity. In J. C. Chrisler & D. R. McCreary (Eds.), *Handbook of gender research in psychology* (Vol. 1, pp. 343–357). New York: Springer.

Rushton, J. P. (2012). No narrowing in mean black–white IQ differences—predicted by heritable g. *American Psychologist, 67,* 500–501.

Rushton, J. P., & Bons, T. A. (2005). Mate choice and friendship in twins. *Psychological Science, 16,* 555–559.

Rushton, J. P., & Jensen, A. R. (2006). The totality of available evidence shows the race IQ gap still remains. *Psychological Science, 17,* 921–924.

Rushton, J. P., & Jensen, A. R. (2010). The rise and fall of the Flynn effect as a reason to expect a narrowing of the black–white IQ gap. *Intelligence, 38,* 213–219.

Russac, R. J., Gatliff, C., Reece, M., & Spottswood, D. (2007). Death anxiety across the adult years: An examination of age and gender effects. *Death Studies, 31,* 549–561.

Russell, A. (2014). Parent–child relationships and influences. In P. K. Smith & C. H. Hart (Eds.), *Wiley-Blackwell handbook of childhood social development* (2nd ed., pp. 337–355). Malden, MA: Wiley-Blackwell.

Russell, A., Mize, J., & Bissaker, K. (2004). Parent–child relationships. In P. K. Smith & C. H. Hart (Eds.), *Blackwell handbook of childhood social development* (pp. 204–222). Malden, MA: Blackwell.

Russell, S. T., & Muraco, J. A. (2013). Representative data sets to study LGBT-parent families. In A. E. Goldberg & K. R. Allen (Eds.), *LGBT-parent families: Innovations in research and implications for practice* (pp. 343–356). New York: Springer.

Russo, A., Semeraro, F., Romano, M. R., Mastropasqua, R., Dell'Omo, R., & Costagliola, C. (2014). Myopia onset and progression: Can it be prevented? *International Ophthalmology, 34,* 693–705.

Ruthsatz, J., & Urbach, J. B. (2012). Child prodigy: A novel cognitive profile places elevated general intelligence, exceptional working memory and attention to detail at the root of prodigiousness. *Intelligence, 40,* 419–426.

Rutland, A., Killen, M., & Abrams, D. (2010). A new social-cognitive developmental perspective on prejudice: The interplay between morality and group identity. *Perspectives on Psychological Science, 5,* 279–291.

Rutter, M. (2011). Biological and experiential influences on psychological development. In D. P. Keating (Ed.), *Nature and nurture in early child development* (pp. 7–44). New York: Cambridge University Press.

Rutter, M., Colvert, E., Kreppner, J., Beckett, C., Castle, J., & Groothues, C. (2007). Early adolescent outcomes for institutionally deprived and nondeprived adoptees. I: Disinhibited attachment. *Journal of Child Psychology and Psychiatry, 48,* 17–30.

Rutter, M., & the English and Romanian Adoptees Study Team. (1998). Developmental catch-up, and deficit, following adoption after severe global early privation. *Journal of Child Psychology and Psychiatry, 39,* 465–476.

Rutter, M., O'Connor, T. G., & English and Romanian Adoptees (ERA) Study Team. (2004). Are there biological programming effects for psychological development? Findings from a study of Romanian adoptees. *Developmental Psychology, 40,* 81–94.

Rutter, M., Sonuga-Barke, E. J, Beckett, C., Castle, J., Kreppner, J., Kumsta, R., et al. (2010). Deprivation-specific psychological patterns: Effects of institutional deprivation. *Monographs of the Society for Research in Child Development, 75*(1, Serial No. 295), 48–78.

Ryan, A. M., Shim, S. S., & Makara, K. A. (2013). Changes in academic adjustment and relational self-worth across the transition to middle school. *Journal of Youth and Adolescence, 42,* 1372–1384.

Ryan, M. K., David, B., & Reynolds, K. J. (2004). Who cares? The effect of gender and context on the self and moral reasoning. *Psychology of Women Quarterly, 28,* 246–255.

Rybash, J. M., & Hrubi-Bopp, K. L. (2000). Isolating the neural mechanisms of age-related changes in human working memory. *Nature Neuroscience, 3,* 509–515.

Ryding, M., Konradsson, K., Kalm, O., & Prellner, K. (2002). Auditory consequences of recurrent acute purulent otitis media. *Annals of Otology, Rhinology, and Laryngology, 111*(3, Pt. 1), 261–266.

Ryff, C. D., Friedman, E., Fuller-Rowell, T., Love, G., Miyamoto, Y., Morozink, J., et al. (2012). Varieties of resilience in MIDUS. *Social and Personality Psychology Compass, 6,* 792–806.

Ryff, C. D., & Keyes, C. L. M. (1995). The structure of psychological well-being revisited. *Journal of Personality and Social Psychology, 69,* 719–727.

Ryff, C. D., Singer, B. H., & Seltzer, M. M. (2002). Pathways through challenge: Implications for well-being and health. In L. Pulkkinen & A. Caspi (Eds.), *Paths to successful development* (pp. 302–328). Cambridge, UK: Cambridge University Press.

Rynearson, E. K., & Salloum, A. (2011). Restorative retelling: Revising the narrative of violent death. In R. A. Neimeyer, D. L. Harris, H. R. Winokuer, & G. F. Thornton (Eds.), *Grief and bereavement in contemporary society: Bridging research and practice* (pp. 177–188). New York: Routledge.

S

Saarni, C., Campos, J. J., Camras, L. A., & Witherington, D. (2006). Emotional development: Action, communication, and understanding. In N. Eisenberg (Ed.), *Handbook of child psychology: Vol. 3. Social, emotional, and personality development* (6th ed., pp. 226–299). Hoboken, NJ: Wiley.

Sabo, D., and Veliz, P. (2011). *Progress without equity: The provision of high school athletic opportunity in the United States, by gender 1993–94 through 2005–06.* East Meadow, NY: Women's Sports Foundation.

Sacks, D. W., Stevenson, B., & Wolfers, J. (2012). The new stylized facts about income and subjective well-being. *Emotion, 12,* 1181–1187.

Sadeh, A. (1997). Sleep and melatonin in infants: A preliminary study. *Sleep, 20,* 185–191.

Sadler, P., Ethier, N., & Woody, E. (2011). Interpersonal complementarity. In L. M. Horowitz & S. Strack

(Eds.), *Handbook of interpersonal psychology* (pp. 123–156). Hoboken, NJ: Wiley.

Sadler, P. M., Sonnert, G., Hazari, Z., & Tai, R. (2012). Stability and volatility of STEM career interest in high school: A gender study. *Science Education, 96,* 411–427.

Sadler, T. W. (2014). *Langman's medical embryology* (13th ed.). Baltimore, MD: Lippincott Williams & Wilkins.

Safe Kids Worldwide. (2011). *A look inside American family vehicles: National study of 79,000 car seats, 2009–2010.* Retrieved from www.safekids.org/assets/docs/safety-basics/safety-tips-by-risk-area/sk-car-seat-report-2011.pdf

Safe Kids Worldwide. (2015). *Overview of childhood injury morbidity and mortality in the U.S.: Fact sheet 2015.* Retrieved from www.safekids.org/sites/default/files/documents/skw_overview_fact_sheet_november_2014.pdf

Saffran, J. R. (2009). Acquiring grammatical patterns: Constraints on learning. In J. Colombo, P. McCardle, & L. Freund (Eds.), *Infant pathways to language: Methods, models, and research disorders* (pp. 31–47). New York: Psychology Press.

Saffran, J. R., Aslin, R. N., & Newport, E. L. (1996). Statistical learning by 8-month-old infants. *Science, 27,* 1926–1928.

Saffran, J. R., & Thiessen, E. D. (2003). Pattern induction by infant language learners. *Developmental Psychology, 39,* 484–494.

Saffran, J. R., Werker, J. F., & Werner, L. A. (2006). The infant's auditory world: Hearing, speech, and the beginnings of language. In D. Kuhn & R. Siegler (Eds.), *Handbook of child psychology: Vol. 2. Cognition, perception, and language* (6th ed., pp. 58–108). Hoboken, NJ: Wiley.

Safren, S. A., & Pantalone, D. W. (2006). Social anxiety and barriers to resilience among lesbian, gay, and bisexual adolescents. In A. M. Omoto & H. S. Kurtzman (Eds.), *Sexual orientation and mental health: Examining identity and development in lesbian, gay, and bisexual young people* (pp. 55–71). Washington, DC: American Psychological Association.

Sagare, A. P., Bell, R. D., Zhao, Z., Ma, Q., Winkler, E. A., Ramanathan, A., & Zlokovic, B. V. (2013). Pericyte loss influences Alzheimer-like neurodegeneration in mice. *Nature Communications, 4,* 2932.

Saginak, K. A., & Saginak, M. A. (2005). Balancing work and family: Equity, gender, and marital satisfaction. *Counseling and Therapy for Couples and Families, 13,* 162–166.

Sahathevan, R., Brodtmann, A., & Donnan, G. (2011). Dementia, stroke, and vascular risk factors: A review. *International Journal of Stroke, 7,* 61–73.

Saito, Y., Auestad, R. A., & Waerness, K. (2010). *Meeting the challenges of elder care: Japan and Norway.* Kyoto, Japan: Kyoto University Press.

Saitta, N. M., & Hodge, S. D., Jr. (2013). What are the consequences of disregarding a "do not resuscitate directive" in the United States? *Medicine and Law, 32,* 441–458.

Sakraida, T. J. (2005). Divorce transition differences of midlife women. *Issues in Mental Health Nursing, 26,* 225–249.

Sala, P., Prefumo, F., Pastorino, D., Buffi, D., Gaggero, R., Foppiano, M., & De Biasio, P. (2014). Fetal surgery: An overview. *Obstetrical and Gynecological Survey, 69,* 218–228.

Salami, A., Eriksson, J., Nilsson, L.-G., & Nyberg, L. (2012). Age-related white matter microstructural differences partly mediate age-related decline in processing speed but not cognition. *Biochemica and Biophysica Acta, 1822,* 408–415.

Salami, S. O. (2010). Retirement context and psychological factors as predictors of well-being among retired teachers. *Europe's Journal of Psychology, 6,* 47–64.

Salari, S. (2011). Elder mistreatment. In R. A. Settersten, Jr., & J. L. Angel (Eds.), *Handbook of sociology of aging* (pp. 415–430). New York: Springer.

Salas-Wright, C. P., Vaughn, M. G., & Maynard, B. R. (2014). Religiosity and violence among adolescents in the United States: Findings from the National Survey on Drug Use and Health, 2006–2010. *Journal of Interpersonal Violence, 29,* 1178–1200.

Salas-Wright, C. P., Vaughn, M. G., & Maynard, B. R. (2015). Profiles of religiosity and their association with risk behavior among emerging adults in the United States. *Emerging Adulthood, 3,* 67–84.

Sale, A., Berardi, N., & Maffei, L. (2009). Enrich the environment to empower the brain. *Trends in Neurosciences, 32,* 233–239.

Salihu, H. M., Shumpert, M. N., Slay, M., Kirby, R. S., & Alexander, G. R. (2003). Childbearing beyond maternal age 50 and fetal outcomes in the United States. *Obstetrics and Gynecology, 102,* 1006–1014.

Salmivalli, C. (2010). Bullying and the peer group: A review. *Aggression and Violent Behavior, 15,* 112–120.

Salmivalli, C., & Voeten, M. (2004). Connections between attitudes, group norms, and behaviour in bullying situations. *International Journal of Behavioral Development, 28,* 246–258.

Salomo, D., & Liszkowski, U. (2013). Sociocultural settings influence the emergence of prelinguistic deictic gestures. *Child Development, 84,* 1296–1307.

Salomon, J. A., Wang, H., Freeman, M. K., Vos, T., Flaxman, A. D., Lopez, A. D., & Murray, C. J. (2012). Healthy life expectancy for 187 countries, 1990–2010: A systematic analysis for the Global Burden Disease Study 2010. *Lancet, 380,* 2144–2162.

Salomonis, N. (2014). Systems-level perspective of sudden infant death syndrome. *Pediatric Research, 76,* 220–229.

Salthouse, T. A. (1984). Effects of age and skill in typing. *Journal of Experimental Psychology: General, 113,* 345–371.

Salthouse, T. A. (2006). Aging of thought. In E. Bialystok & F. I. M. Craik (Eds.), *Lifespan cognition: Mechanisms of change* (pp. 274–284). New York: Oxford University Press.

Salthouse, T. A. (2011). Neuroanatomical substrates of age-related cognitive decline. *Psychological Bulletin, 137,* 753–784.

Salthouse, T. A., & Madden, D. J. (2008). Information processing speed and aging. In J. DeLuca & J. H. Kalmar (Eds.), *Information processing speed in clinical populations* (pp. 221–242). New York: Taylor & Francis.

Salvioli, S., Capri, M., Santoro, A., Raule, N., Sevini, F., & Lukas, S. (2008). The impact of mitochondrial DNA on human lifespan: A view from studies on centenarians. *Biotechnology Journal, 3,* 740–749.

Samarel, N. (1991). *Caring for life and death.* Washington, DC: Hemisphere.

Sampaio, R. C., & Truwit, C. L. (2001). Myelination in the developing human brain. In C. A. Nelson & M. Luciana (Eds.), *Handbook of developmental cognitive neuroscience* (pp. 35–44). Cambridge, MA: MIT Press.

Sampselle, C. M., Harris, V., Harlow, S. D., & Sowers, M. (2002). Midlife development and menopause in African-American and Caucasian women. *Health Care for Women International, 23,* 351–363.

Samuolis, J., Griffin, K. W., Williams, C., Cesario, B., & Botvin, G. J. (2013). Work intensity and substance use among adolescents employed part-time in entry-level jobs. In J. Merrick (Eds.), *Child and adolescent health yearbook, 2011* (pp. 81–88). Hauppauge, NY: Nova Biomedical Books.

Sanchis-Gomar, F., Perez-Quilis, C., Leischik, R., & Lucia, A. (2016). Epidemiology of coronary heart disease and acute coronary syndrome. *Annals of Translational Medicine, 4,* 256.

Sandberg-Thoma, S. E., Snyder, A., & Jang, B. J. (2015). Exiting and returning to the parental home for boomerang kids. *Journal of Marriage and Family, 77,* 806–818.

Sanders, O. (2006). *Evaluating the Keeping Ourselves Safe Programme.* Wellington, NZ: Youth Education Service, New Zealand Police. Retrieved from www.nzfvc.org.nz/accan/papers-presentations/abstract11v.shtml

Sandri, M., Protasi, F., Carraro, U., & Kern, H. (2014). Lifelong physical exercise delays age-associated skeletal muscle decline. *Journals of Gerontology, 70A,* 163–173.

Sandström, A., Rhodin, N., Lundberg, M., Olsson, T., & Nyberg, L. (2005). Impaired cognitive performance in patients with chronic burnout syndrome. *Biological Psychology, 69,* 271–279.

San Juan, V., & Astington, J. W. (2012). Bridging the gap between implicit and explicit understanding: How language development promotes the processing and representation of false belief. *British Journal of Developmental Psychology, 30,* 105–122.

Sann, C., & Streri, A. (2007). Perception of object shape and texture in human newborns: Evidence from cross-modal transfer tasks. *Developmental Science, 10,* 399–410.

Sansavini, A., Bertoncini, J., & Giovanelli, G. (1997). Newborns discriminate the rhythm of multisyllabic stressed words. *Developmental Psychology, 33,* 3–11.

Sarason, S. B. (1977). *Work, aging, and social change.* New York: Free Press.

Sarnecka, B. W., & Gelman, S. A. (2004). Six does not just mean a lot: Preschoolers see number words as specific. *Cognition, 92,* 329–352.

Sarnecka, B. W., & Wright, C. E. (2013). The idea of an exact number: Children's understanding of cardinality and equinumerosity. *Cognitive Science, 37,* 1493–1506.

Sasser-Coen, J. A. (1993). Qualitative changes in creativity in the second half of life: A life-span developmental perspective. *Journal of Creative Behavior, 27,* 18–27.

Satin, J. R., Linden, W., Phillips, M. J. (2009). Depression as a predictor of disease progression and mortality in cancer patients. *Cancer, 115,* 5349–5361.

Sattler, C., Toro, P., Schönknecht, P., & Schröder, J. (2012). Cognitive activity, education and socioeconomic status as preventive factors for mild cognitive impairment and Alzheimer's disease. *Psychiatry Research, 196,* 90–95.

Sattler, F. R. (2013). Growth hormone in the aging male. *Best Practice & Research Clinical Endocrinology & Metabolism, 27,* 541–555.

Saucier, J. F., Sylvestre, R., Doucet, H., Lambert, J., Frappier, J. Y., Charbonneau, L., & Malus, M. (2002). Cultural identity and adaptation to adolescence in Montreal. In F. J. C. Azima & N. Grizenko (Eds.), *Immigrant and refugee children and their families: Clinical, research, and training issues* (pp. 133–154). Madison, WI: International Universities Press.

Saudino, K. J. (2003). Parent ratings of infant temperament: Lessons from twin studies. *Infant Behavior and Development, 26,* 100–107.

Saudino, K. J., & Plomin, R. (1997). Cognitive and temperamental mediators of genetic contributions to the home environment during infancy. *Merrill-Palmer Quarterly, 43,* 1–23.

Saunders, B. E. (2012). Determining best practice for treating sexually victimized children. In P. Goodyear-Brown (Ed.), *Handbook of child sexual abuse: Identification, assessment, and treatment* (pp. 173–198). Hoboken, NJ: Wiley.

Sautter, J. M., Thomas, P. A., Dupre, M., & George, L. K. (2012). Socioeconomic status and the black–white mortality crossover. *American Journal of Public Health, 102,* 1566–1571.

Sawyer, A. M., & Borduin, C. M. (2011). Effects of multisystemic therapy through midlife: A 21.9-year follow-up to a randomized clinical trial with serious and violent juvenile offenders. *Journal of Consulting and Clinical Psychology, 79,* 643–652.

Saxe, G. B. (1988, August–September). Candy selling and math learning. *Educational Researcher, 17*(6), 14–21.

Saxton, M., Backley, P., & Gallaway, C. (2005). Negative input for grammatical errors: Effects after a lag of 12 weeks. *Journal of Child Language, 32,* 643–672.

Sayer, L. C. (2010). Trends in housework. In J. Treas & S. Drobnic (Eds.), *Dividing the domestic: Men, women, and household work in cross-national perspective* (pp. 19–38). Stanford, CA: Stanford University Press.

Saygin, A. P., Leech, R., & Dick, F. (2010). Nonverbal auditory agnosia with lesion to Wernicke's area. *Neuropsychologia, 48,* 107–113.

Saylor, M. M. (2004). Twelve- and 16-month-old infants recognize properties of mentioned absent things. *Developmental Science, 7,* 599–611.

Saylor, M. M., & Troseth, G. L. (2006). Preschoolers use information about speakers' desires to learn new words. *Cognitive Development, 21,* 214–231.

Scarlett, W. G., & Warren, A. E. A. (2010). Religious and spiritual development across the life span: A behavioral and social science perspective. In M. Lamb & A. Freund (Eds.), *Handbook of life-span development: Vol. 2. Social and emotional development* (pp. 631–682). Hoboken, NJ: Wiley.

Scarr, S., & McCartney, K. (1983). How people make their own environments: A theory of genotype environment effects. *Child Development, 54,* 424–435.

Scarr, S., & Weinberg, R. A. (1983). The Minnesota Adoption Studies: Genetic differences and malleability. *Child Development, 54,* 260–267.

Schaal, B., Marlier, L., & Soussignan, R. (2000). Human fetuses learn odours from their pregnant mother's diet. *Chemical Senses, 25,* 729–737.

Schaal, S., Dusingizemungu, J.-P., Jacob, N., & Elbert, T. (2011). Rates of trauma spectrum disorders and risks of posttraumatic stress disorder in a sample of orphaned and widowed genocide survivors. *European Journal of Psychotraumatology, 2.* Retrieved from www.ncbi.nlm.nih.gov/pmc/articles/PMC3402134

Schaie, K. W. (1994). The course of adult intellectual development. *American Psychologist, 49,* 304–313.

Schaie, K. W. (1998). The Seattle Longitudinal Studies of Adult Intelligence. In M. P. Lawton & T. A. Salthouse (Eds.), *Essential papers on the psychology of aging* (pp. 263–271). New York: New York University Press.

Schaie, K. W. (2005). *Developmental influences on adult intelligence: The Seattle Longitudinal Study.* New York: Oxford University Press.

Schaie, K. W. (2011). Historical influences on aging and behavior. In K. W. Schaie & S. L. Willis (Eds.), *Handbook of the psychology of aging* (7th ed., pp. 41–55). San Diego, CA: Academic Press.

Schaie, K. W. (2013). *Developmental influences on adult intelligence: The Seattle Longitudinal Study* (2nd ed.). New York: Oxford University Press.

Schaie, K. W. (2016). Seattle Longitudinal Study findings. In S. K. Whitbourne (Ed.), *Encyclopedia of adulthood and aging* (Vol. 3, pp. 1274–1278). Malden, MA: Wiley Blackwell.

Schalet, A. (2007). Adolescent sexuality viewed through two different cultural lenses. In M. S. Tepper & A. F. Owens (Eds.), *Sexual health: Vol. 3. Moral and cultural foundations* (pp. 365–387). Westport, CT: Praeger.

Scher, A., Epstein, R., & Tirosh, E. (2004). Stability and changes in sleep regulation: A longitudinal study from 3 months to 3 years. *International Journal of Behavioral Development, 28,* 268–274.

Scher, A., Tirosh, E., Jaffe, M., Rubin, L., Sadeh, A., & Lavie, P. (1995). Sleep patterns of infants and young children in Israel. *International Journal of Behavioral Development, 18,* 701–711.

Schewe, P. A. (2007). Interventions to prevent sexual violence. In L. S. Doll, S. E. Bonzo, D. A. Sleet, & J. A. Mercy (Eds.), *Handbook of injury and violence prevention* (pp. 223–240). New York: Springer Science + Business Media.

Schiamberg, L. B., Barboza, G. G., Oehmke, J., Zhang, Z., Griffore, R. J., Weatherhill, R. P., et al. (2011). Elder abuse in nursing homes: An ecological perspective. *Journal of Elder Abuse and Neglect, 23,* 190–211.

Schiebe, S., & Carstensen, L. L. (2010). Emotional aging: Recent findings and future trends. *Journals of Gerontology, 65B,* 135–144.

Schiebe, S., & Epstude, K. (2016). Life regret and Sehnsucht. In S. Whitbourne (Ed.), *Encyclopedia of adulthood and aging* (Vol. 2, pp. 771–775). Malden, MA: Wiley Blackwell.

Schieman, S., Bierman, A., & Ellison, C. G. (2010). Religious involvement, beliefs about God, and the sense of mattering among older adults. *Journal for the Scientific Study of Religion, 49,* 517–535.

Schieman, S., Bierman, A., & Ellison, C. G. (2013). Religion and mental health. In C. S., Aneshensel, J. C. Phelan, & A. Bierman (Eds.), *Handbook of the sociology of mental health* (2nd ed., pp. 457–478). New York: Springer Science + Business Media.

Schieman, S., & Plickert, G. (2007). Functional limitations and changes in levels of depression among older adults: A multiple-hierarchy stratification perspective. *Journals of Gerontology, 62B,* S36–S42.

Schilling, O. K., Wahl, H.-W., & Wiegering, S. (2013). Affective development in advanced old age: Analyses of terminal change in positive and negative affect. *Developmental Psychology, 49,* 1011–1020.

Schlagmüller, M., & Schneider, W. (2002). The development of organizational strategies in children: Evidence from a microgenetic longitudinal study. *Journal of Experimental Child Psychology, 81,* 298–319.

Schlegel, A., & Barry, H., III. (1991). *Adolescence: An anthropological inquiry.* New York: Free Press.

Schmidt, K.-H., Neubach, B., & Heuer, H. (2007). Self-control demands, cognitive control deficits, and burnout. *Work and Stress, 21,* 142–154.

Schmidt, L. A., Fox, N. A., Schulkin, J., & Gold, P. W. (1999). Behavioral and psychophysiological correlates of self-presentation in temperamentally shy children. *Developmental Psychobiology, 30,* 127–140.

Schmidt, L. A., Santesso, D. L., Schulkin, J., & Segalowitz, S. J. (2007). Shyness is a necessary but not sufficient condition for high salivary cortisol in typically developing 10-year-old children. *Personality and Individual Differences, 43,* 1541–1551.

Schmidt, M. E., Crawley-Davis, A. M., & Anderson, D. R. (2007). Two-year-olds' object retrieval based on television: Testing a perceptual account. *Media Psychology, 9,* 389–409.

Schmitt, D. P., Allik, J., McCrae, R. R., & Benet-Martínez, V. (2007). The geographic distribution of the Big Five personality traits: Patterns and profiles of human self-description across 56 countries. *Journal of Cross-Cultural Psychology, 38,* 173–212.

Schmitz, S., Fulker, D. W., Plomin, R., Zahn-Waxler, C., Emde, R. N., & DeFries, J. C. (1999). Temperament and problem behaviour during early childhood. *International Journal of Behavioural Development, 23,* 333–355.

Schneider, B. H., Atkinson, L., & Tardif, C. (2001). Child–parent attachment and children's peer relations: A quantitative review. *Developmental Psychology, 37,* 87–100.

Schneider, D. (2006). Smart as we can get? *American Scientist, 94,* 311–312.

Schneider, W. (2002). Memory development in childhood. In U. Goswami (Ed.), *Blackwell handbook of childhood cognitive development* (pp. 236–256). Malden, MA: Blackwell.

Schneider, W., & Bjorklund, D. F. (1992). Expertise, aptitude, and strategic remembering. *Child Development, 63,* 461–473.

Schneider, W., & Bjorklund, D. F. (1998). Memory. In D. Kuhn & R. S. Siegler (Eds.), *Handbook of child psychology: Vol. 2. Cognition, perception, and language* (5th ed., pp. 467–521). New York: Wiley.

Schneider, W., & Pressley, M. (1997). *Memory development between two and twenty* (2nd ed.). Mahwah, NJ: Erlbaum.

Schneller, D. P., & Arditti, J.A. (2004). After the breakup: Interpreting divorce and rethinking intimacy. *Journal of Divorce and Remarriage, 42,* 1–37.

Schnitzspahn, K. M., Ihle, A., Henry, J. D., Rendell, P. G., & Kliegel, M. (2011). The age-prospective memory-paradox: A comprehensive exploration of possible mechanisms. *International Psychogeriatrics, 23,* 583–592.

Schnitzspahn, K. M., Scholz, U., Ballhausen, N., Hering, A., Ihle, A., Lagner, P., & Kliegel, M. (2016). Age differences in prospective memory of everyday life intentions: A diary approach. *Memory, 24,* 444–454.

Schnohr, P., Nyboe, J., Lange, P., & Jensen, G. (1998). Longevity and gray hair, baldness, facial wrinkles, and arcus senilis in 13,000 men and women: The Copenhagen City Heart Study. *Journals of Gerontology, 53,* M347–350.

Schnohr, P., Scharling, H., & Jensen, J. S. (2003). Changes in leisure-time physical activity and risk of death: An observational study of 7,000 men and women. *American Journal of Epidemiology, 158,* 639–644.

Schonberg, R. L. (2012). Birth defects and prenatal diagnosis. In M. L. Batshaw, N. J. Roizen, & G. R. Lotrecchiano (Eds.), *Children with disabilities* (7th ed., pp. 47–60). Baltimore, MD: Paul H. Brookes.

Schonert-Reichl, K. A. (1999). Relations of peer acceptance, friendship adjustment, and social behavior to moral reasoning during early adolescence. *Journal of Early Adolescence, 19,* 249–279.

Schonert-Reichl, K. A., & Lawlor, M. S. (2010). The effects of a mindfulness-based education program on pre- and early adolescents' well-being and social and emotional competence. *Mindfulness, 1,* 137–151.

Schonert-Reichl, K. A., Oberle, E., Lawlor, M. S., Abbott, D., Thomson, K., Oberlander, T. F., et al. (2015). Enhancing cognitive and social-emotional development through a simple-to-administer mindfulness-based school program for elementary school children: A randomized controlled trial. *Developmental Psychology, 51,* 52–66.

Schooler, C., Mulatu, M. S., & Oates, G. (1999). The continuing effects of substantively complex work on the intellectual functioning of older workers. *Psychology and Aging, 14,* 483–506.

Schoon, I., Jones, E., Cheng, H., & Maughan, B. (2012). Family hardship, family instability, and cognitive development. *Journal of Epidemiology and Community Health, 66,* 716–722.

Schoon, L., & Parsons, S. (2002). Teenage aspirations for future careers and occupational outcomes. *Journal of Vocational Behavior, 60,* 262–288.

Schoppe-Sullivan, S. J., Brown, G. L., Cannon, E. A., Mangelsdorf, S. C., & Sokolowski, M. S. (2008). Maternal gatekeeping, coparenting quality, and fathering behavior in families with infants. *Journal of Family Psychology, 22,* 389–398.

Schott, J. M., & Rossor, M. N. (2003). The grasp and other primitive reflexes. *Journal of Neurological and Neurosurgical Psychiatry, 74,* 558–560.

Schroeder, R. D., Bulanda, R. E., Giordano, P. C., & Cernkovich, S. A. (2010). Parenting and adult criminality: An examination of direct and indirect effects by race. *Journal of Adolescent Research, 25,* 64–98.

Schull, W. J. (2003). The children of atomic bomb survivors: A synopsis. *Journal of Radiological Protection, 23,* 369–394.

Schultz, R., Burgio, L., Burns, R., Eisdorfer, C., Gallagher-Thompson, D., Gitlin, L. N., & Mahoney, D. F. (2003). Resources for enhancing Alzheimer's caregiver health (REACH): Overview, site-specific outcomes, and future directions. *Gerontologist, 43,* 514–520.

Schulz, M. S., Cowan, C. P., & Cowan, P. A. (2006). Promoting healthy beginnings: A randomized controlled trial. *Journal of Consulting and Clinical Psychology, 74,* 20–31.

Schulz, R., & Curnow, C. (1988). Peak performance and age among superathletes: Track and field, swimming, baseball, tennis, and golf. *Journals of Gerontology, 43,* P113–P120.

Schulze, C., Grassmann, S., & Tomasello, M. (2013). 3-year-old children make relevant inferences in indirect verbal communication. *Child Development, 84,* 2079–2093.

Schunk, D. H., & Zimmerman, B. J. (2013). Self-regulation and learning. In W. M. Reynolds, G. E. Miller, & I. B. Weiner (Eds.), *Handbook of psychology: Vol. 7. Educational psychology* (pp. 45–68). Hoboken, NJ: Wiley.

Schwanenflugel, P. J., Henderson, R. L., & Fabricius, W. V. (1998). Developing organization of mental verbs and theory of mind in middle childhood: Evidence from extensions. *Developmental Psychology, 34,* 512–524.

Schwartz, B. L., & Frazier, L. D. (2005). Tip-of-the-tongue states and aging: Contrasting psycholinguistic and metacognitive perspectives. *Journal of General Psychology, 132,* 377–391.

Schwartz, C. E., Kunwar, P. S., Greve, D. N., Kagan, J., Snidman, N. C., & Bloch, R. B. (2012). A phenotype of early infancy predicts reactivity of the amygdala in male adults. *Molecular Psychiatry, 17,* 1042–1050.

Schwartz, C. R., & Han, H. (2014). The reversal of the gender gap in education and trends in marital dissolution. *American Sociological Review, 79,* 605–629.

Schwartz, S. A. (2007). The relationship between love and marital satisfaction in arranged and romantic Jewish couples. *Dissertation Abstracts International: Section B: The Sciences and Engineering, 68*(4–B), 2716.

Schwartz, S. G., Hampton, B. M., Kovach, J. L., & Brantley, M. A., Jr. (2016). Genetics and age-related macular degeneration: A practical review for the clinician. *Clinical Ophthalmology, 10,* 1229–1235.

Schwartz, S. J., Beyers, W., Luyckx, K., Soenens, B. Zamboanga, B. L., Forthun, L. F., et al. (2011). Examining the light and dark sides of emerging adults' identity: A study of identity status differences in positive and negative psychosocial functioning. *Journal of Youth and Adolescence, 40,* 839–859.

Schwartz, S. J., Donnellan, M. B., Ravert, R. D., Luyckx, K., & Zamboanga, B. L. (2013). Identity development, personality, and well-being in adolescence and emerging adulthood: Theory, research, and recent advances. In R. M. Lerner, M. A. Easterbrooks, & J. Mistry (Eds.), *Handbook of psychology: Vol. 6. Developmental psychology* (pp. 339–364). Hoboken, NJ: Wiley.

Schwartz, S. J., Zamboanga, B. L., Luyckx, K., Meca, A., & Ritchie, R. A. (2013). Identity in emerging adulthood: Reviewing the field and looking forward. *Emerging Adulthood, 1,* 96–113.

Schwarz, N. (2008). Self-reports: How the questions shape the answers. In R. H. Fazio & R. E. Petty (Eds.), *Attitudes: Their structure, function, and consequences* (pp. 49–67). New York: Psychology Press.

Schwarzer, G., Freitag, C., & Schum, N. (2013). How crawling and manual object exploration are related to the mental rotation abilities of 9-month-old infants. *Frontiers in Psychology, 4,* D97.

Schwebel, D. C., & Brezausek, C. M. (2007). Father transitions in the household and young children's injury risk. *Psychology of Men and Masculinity, 8,* 173–184.

Schwebel, D. C., & Gaines, J. (2007). Pediatric unintentional injury: Behavioral risk factors and implications for prevention. *Journal of Developmental and Behavioral Pediatrics, 28,* 245–254.

Schwebel, D. C., Roth, D. L., Elliott, M. N., Chien, A. T., Mrug, S., Shipp, E., et al. (2012). Marital conflict and fifth-graders' risk for injury. *Accident Analysis and Prevention, 47,* 30–35.

Schwebel, D. C., Roth, D. L., Elliott, M. N., Windle, M., Grunbaum, J. A., Low, B., et al. (2011). The association of activity level, parent mental distress, and parental involvement and monitoring with unintentional injury risk in fifth graders. *Accident Analysis and Prevention, 43,* 848–852.

Schweinhart, L. J. (2010). The challenge of the High/Scope Perry Preschool study. In A. J. Reynolds, A. J. Rolnick, M. M. Englund, & J. Temple (Eds.), *Childhood programs and practices in the first decade of life: A human capital integration* (pp. 199–213). New York: Cambridge University Press.

Schweinhart, L. J., Montie, J., Xiang, Z., Barnett, W. S., Belfield, C. R., & Nores, M. (2005). *Lifetime effects: The High/Scope Perry Preschool Study through age 40.* Ypsilanti, MI: High/Scope Press.

Schweizer, K., Moosbrugger, H., & Goldhammer, F. (2006). The structure of the relationship between attention and intelligence. *Intelligence, 33,* 589–611.

Schwenck, C., Bjorklund, D. F., & Schneider, W. (2007). Factors influencing the incidence of utilization deficiencies and other patterns of recall/strategy-use relations in a strategic memory task. *Child Development, 22,* 197–212.

Schwerdt, G., & West, M. R. (2013). The impact of alternative grade configurations on student outcomes through middle and high school. *Journal of Public Economics, 97,* 308–326.

Schwier, C., van Maanen, C., Carpenter, M., & Tomasello, M. (2006). Rational imitation in 12-month-old infants. *Infancy, 10,* 303–311.

Sciarra, D. T., & Ambrosino, K. E. (2011). Post-secondary expectations and educational attainment. *Professional School Counseling, 14,* 231–241.

Scocco, P., Rapattoni, M., & Fantoni, G. (2006). Nursing home institutionalization: A source of eustress or distress for the elderly? *International Journal of Geriatric Psychiatry, 21,* 281–287.

Scott, L. D. (2003). The relation of racial identity and racial socialization to coping with discrimination among African Americans. *Journal of Black Studies, 20,* 520–538.

Scott, L. S., & Monesson, A. (2009). The origin of biases in face perception. *Psychological Science, 20,* 676–680.

Scott, R. M., & Fisher, C. (2012). 2.5-year-olds use cross-situational consistency to learn verbs under referential uncertainty. *Cognition, 122,* 163–180.

Scrutton, D. (2005). Influence of supine sleep positioning on early motor milestone acquisition. *Developmental Medicine and Child Neurology, 47,* 364.

Scullin, M. K., Bugg, J. M., McDaniel, M. A., & Einstein, G. O. (2011). Prospective memory and aging: Preserved spontaneous retrieval, but impaired deactivation, in older adults. *Memory and Cognition, 39,* 1232–1240.

Seburg, E., Olson-Bullis, B., Bredeson, D., Hayes, M., & Sherwood, N. (2015). A review of primary care-based childhood prevention and treatment interventions. *Current Obesity Reports, 4,* 157–173.

Sedgh, G., Finer, L. B., Bankole, A., Eilers, M. A., & Singh, S. (2015). Adolescent pregnancy, birth, and abortion rates across countries: Levels and recent trends. *Journal of Adolescent Health, 56,* 223–230.

Seery, M. D., Holman, E. A., & Silver, R. C. (2010). Whatever does not kill us: Cumulative lifetime adversity, vulnerability, and resilience. *Journal of Personality and Social Psychology, 99,* 1025–1041.

Seethaler, P. M., Fuchs, L. S., Fuchs, D., & Compton, D. L. (2012). Predicting first graders' development of calculation versus word-problem performance: The role of dynamic assessment. *Journal of Educational Psychology, 104,* 224–234.

Sehlstedt, I., Ignell, H., Wasling, B., Ackerley, R., Olausson, H., & Croy, I. (2016). Gentle touch perception across the lifespan. *Psychology and Aging, 31,* 176–184.

Seibert, A. C., & Kerns, K. A. (2009). Attachment figures in middle childhood. *International Journal of Behavioral Development, 33,* 347–355.

Seidl, A., Hollich, G., & Jusczyk, P. (2003). Early understanding of subject and object wh-questions. *Infancy, 4,* 423–436.

Seidman, E., Aber, J. L., & French, S. E. (2004). Assessing the transitions to middle and high school. *Journal of Adolescent Research, 19,* 3–30.

Seidman, E., Lambert, L. E., Allen, L., & Aber, J. L. (2003). Urban adolescents' transition to junior high school and protective family transactions. *Journal of Early Adolescence, 23,* 166–193.

Seiffge-Krenke, I. (2006). Leaving home or still in the nest? Parent–child relationships and psychological health as predictors of different leaving home patterns. *Developmental Psychology, 42,* 864–876.

Seiffge-Krenke, I. (2013). "She's leaving home …" Antecedents, consequences, and cultural patterns in the leaving home process. *Emerging Adulthood, 1,* 114–124.

Seki, Y., Yamazaki, Y., Mizota, Y., & Inoue, Y. (2009). How families in Japan view the disclosure of terminal illness: A study of iatrogenic HIV infection. *AIDS Care, 21,* 422–430.

Sekita, A., Ninomiya, T., Tanizaki, Y., Doi, Y., Hata, J., Yonemoto, K., et al. (2010). Trends in prevalence of Alzheimer's disease and vascular dementia in a Japanese community: the Hisayama Study. *Acta Psychiatrica Scandivavica, 122,* 319–325.

Selman, L., Speck, P., Gysels, M., Agupio, G., Dinat, N., Downing, J., et al. (2013). "Peace" and "life worthwhile" as measures of spiritual well-being in African palliative care: A mixed-methods study. *Health and Quality of Life Outcomes, 11,* 94.

Selwood, A., & Cooper, C. (2009). Abuse of people with dementia. *Reviews in Clinical Gerontology, 19,* 35–43.

Selwood, A., Johnston, K., Katona, C., Lyketsos, C., & Livingston, G. (2007). Systematic review of the effect of psychological interventions on family caregivers of people with dementia. *Journal of Affective Disorders, 101,* 75–89.

Selwyn, P. A. (1996). Before their time: A clinician's reflections on death and AIDS. In H. M. Spiro, M. G. M. Curnen, & L. P. Wandel (Eds.), *Facing death: Where culture, religion, and medicine meet* (pp. 33–37). New Haven, CT: Yale University Press.

Semanik, P. A., Chang, R. W., & Dunlop, D. D. (2012). Aerobic activity in prevention and symptom control of osteoarthritis. *PM&R, 4,* S37–S44.

Senechal, M., & LeFevre, J. (2002). Parental involvement in the development of children's reading skill: A five-year longitudinal study. *Child Development, 73,* 445–460.

Sengpiel, V., Elind, E., Bacelis, J., Nilsson, S., Grove, J., Myhre, R., et al. (2013). Maternal caffeine intake during pregnancy is associated with birth weight but not with gestational length: Results from a large prospective observational cohort study. *BMC Medicine, 11,* 42.

Senju, A., Csibra, G., & Johnson, M. H. (2008). Understanding the referential nature of looking: Infants' preference for object-directed gaze. *Cognition, 108,* 303–319.

Senn, T. E., Espy, K. A., & Kaufmann, P. M. (2004). Using path analysis to understand executive function organization in preschool children. *Developmental Neuropsychology, 26,* 445–464.

Serbin, L. A., Powlishta, K. K., & Gulko, J. (1993). The development of sex typing in middle childhood. *Monographs of the Society for Research in Child Development, 58*(2, Serial No. 232).

Sermon, K., Van Steirteghem, A., & Liebaers, I. (2004). Preimplantation genetic diagnosis. *Lancet, 363,* 1633–1641.

Serra, L., Perri, R., Cercignani, M., Spano, B., Fadda, L., Marra, C. et al. (2010). Are behavioral symptoms of Alzheimer's disease directly associated with neurodegeneration? *Journal of Alzheimer's Disease, 21,* 627–639.

Sesame Workshop. (2015). *Where we work: All locations.* Retrieved from www.sesameworkshop.org/where-we-work/all-locations

Settersten, R. A. (2003). Age structuring and the rhythm of the life course. In J. T. Mortimer & M. J. Shanahan (Eds.), *Handbook of the life course* (pp. 81–98). New York: Kluwer Academic.

Settersten, R. A. (2007). The new landscape of adult life: Road maps, signposts, and speed lines. *Research in Human Development, 4,* 239–252.

Sevigny, P. R., & Loutzenhiser, L. (2010). Predictors of parenting self-efficacy in mothers and fathers of toddlers. Child Care, *Health and Development, 36,* 179–189.

SFIA (Sports & Fitness Industry Association). (2015). *2015 U.S. trends in team sports report.* Silver Spring, MD: Author.

Shafer, R. J., Raby, K. L., Lawler, J. M., Hesemeyer, P. S., & Roisman, G. I. (2015). Longitudinal associations between adult attachment states of mind and parenting quality. *Attachment & Human Development, 17,* 83–95.

Shalev, I., Entringer, S., Wadhwa, P. D., Wokowitz, O. M., Puterman, E., Lin, J., & Epel, E. S. (2013). Stress and telomere biology: A lifespan perspective. *Psychoneuroendocrinology, 38,* 1835–1842.

Shamloul, R., & Ghanem, H. (2013). Erectile dysfunction. *Lancet, 381,* 153–165.

Shapka, J. D., & Keating, D. P. (2005). Structure and change in self-concept during adolescence. *Canadian Journal of Behavioural Science, 37,* 83–96.

Sharf, R. S. (2013). Advances in theories of career development. In W. B. Walsh, M. L. Savickas, & P. J. Hartung (Eds.), *Handbook of vocational psychology: Theory, research, and practice* (4th ed., pp. 3–32). New York: Routledge.

Sharma, A. (2015). Divorce/separation in later-life: A fixed effects analysis of economic well-being by gender. *Journal of Family Economic Issues, 36,* 299–306.

Sharp, C., Beckstein, A., Limb, G., & Bullock, Z. (2015). Completing the circle of life: Death and grief among Native Americans. In J. Cacciatore & J. DeFrain (Eds.), *The world of bereavement: Cultural perspectives on death in families* (pp. 221–239). Cham, Switzerland: Springer International Publishing.

Sharp, E. A., & Ganong, L. (2011). "I'm a loser, I'm not married, let's just all look at me": Ever-single women's perceptions of their social environment. *Journal of Family Issues, 32,* 956–980.

Sharp, E. H., Coatsworth, J. D., Darling, N., Cumsille, P., & Ranieri, S. (2007). Gender differences in the self-defining activities and identity experiences of adolescents and emerging adults. *Journal of Adolescence, 30,* 251–269.

Sharp, K. L., Williams, A. J., Rhyner, K. T., & Hardi, S. S. (2013). The clinical interview. In K. F. Geisinger, B. A. Bracken, J. F. Carlson, J. C. Hansen, N. R. Kuncel, S. P. Reise, et al. (Eds.), *APA handbook of testing and assessment in psychology* (Vol. 2, pp. 103–117). Washington, DC: American Psychological Association.

Shaul, S., & Schwartz, M. (2014). The role of executive functions in school readiness among preschool-age children. *Reading and Writing, 27,* 749–768.

Shaw, B. A. (2005). Anticipated support from neighbors and physical functioning during later life. *Research on Aging, 27,* 503–525.

Shaw, D. S., Hyde, L. W., & Brennan, L. M. (2012). Early predictors of boys' antisocial trajectories. *Development and Psychopathology, 24,* 871–888.

Shaw, P., Eckstrand, K., Sharp, W., Blumenthal, J., Lerch, J. P., & Greenstein, D. (2007). Attention-deficit/hyperactivity disorder is characterized by a delay in cortical maturation. *Proceedings of the National Academy of Sciences Online.* Retrieved from www.pnas.org/cgi/content/abstract/0707741104v1

Sheehan, G., Darlington, Y., Noller, P., & Feeney, J. (2004). Children's perceptions of their sibling relationships during parental separation and divorce. *Journal of Divorce and Remarriage, 41,* 69–94.

Sheehan, N. W., & Petrovic, K. (2008). Grandparents and their adult grandchildren: Recurring themes from the literature. *Marriage and Family Review, 44,* 99–124.

Sheikh, I., Naz, A., Hazirullah, Khan, Q., Kahn, W., & Khan, N. (2014). An ethnographic analysis of death and burial customs in Kalash community of Chitral District of Khyber Pakhtunkhwa Pakistan. *Middle-East Journal of Scientific Research, 21,* 1937–1946.

Shellman, J., Ennis, E., & Bailey-Addison, K. (2011). A contextual examination of reminiscence functions in older African Americans. *Journal of Aging Studies, 25,* 348–354.

Shepperd, S., Goncalves-Bradley, D. C., Straus, S. E., & Wee, B. (2016). Hospital at home: Home-based end of life care. *Cochrane Database of Systematic Reviews,* Issue 7, Art. No.: CD009231.

Sherman, A. M., de Vries, B., & Lansford, J. E. (2000). Friendship in childhood and adulthood: Lessons across the life span. *International Journal of Aging and Human Development, 51,* 31–51.

Sherman, A. M., Lansford, J. E., & Volling, B. L. (2006). Sibling relationships and best friendships in young adulthood: Warmth, conflict, and well-being. *Personal Relationships, 13,* 151–165.

Sherrod, L. R., & Spiewak, G. S. (2008). Possible interrelationships between civic engagement, positive youth development, and spirituality/religiosity. In R. M. Lerner, R. W. Roeser, & E. Phelps (Eds.), *Positive youth development and spirituality: From theory to research* (pp. 322–338). West Conshohocken, PA: Templeton Foundation Press.

Shimada, S., & Hiraki, K. (2006). Infant's brain responses to live and televised action. *NeuroImage, 32,* 930–939.

Shimizu, H. (2001). Japanese adolescent boys' senses of empathy (omoiyari) and Carol Gilligan's perspectives on the morality of care: A phenomenological approach. *Culture and Psychology, 7,* 453–475.

Shin, N., Kim, M., Goetz, S., & Vaughn, B. E. (2014). Dyadic analyses of preschool-aged children's friendships: Convergence and differences between friendship classifications from peer sociometric data and teacher reports. *Social Development, 23,* 178–195.

Shokolenko, I. N., Wilson, G. L., & Alexeyev, M. F. (2014). Aging: A mitochondrial DNA perspective, critical analysis and an update. *World Journal of Experimental Medicine, 20,* 46–57.

Shonkoff, J. P., & Bales, S. N. (2011). Science does not speak for itself: Translating child development research for the public and its policymakers. *Child Development, 82,* 17–32.

Shonkoff, J. P., & Garner, A. S. (2012). The lifelong effects of early childhood adversity and toxic stress. *Pediatrics, 129,* e232–e246.

Shor, E., Roelfs, D. J., Curreli, M., Clemow, L., Burg, M. M., & Schwartz, J. E. (2012). Widowhood and mortality: A meta-analysis and meta-regression. *Demography, 49,* 575–606.

Shriver, L. H., Harrist, A. W., Page, M., Hubbs-Tait, L., Moulton, M., & Topham, G. (2013). Differences in body esteem by weight status, gender, and physical activity among young elementary school-aged children. *Body Image, 10,* 78–84.

Shuey, K., & Hardy, M. A. (2003). Assistance to aging parents and parents-in-law: Does lineage affect family allocation decisions? *Journal of Marriage and Family, 65,* 418–431.

Shultz, K. S., & Wang, M. (2007). The influence of specific physical health conditions on retirement decisions. *International Journal of Aging and Human Development, 65,* 149–161.

Shwalb, D. W., Nakawaza, J., Yamamoto, T., & Hyun, J.-H. (2004). Fathering in Japanese, Chinese, and Korean cultures: A review of the research literature. In M. E. Lamb (Ed.), *The role of the father in child development* (4th ed., pp. 146–181). Hoboken, NJ: Wiley.

Siberry, G. K. (2015). Preventing and managing HIV infection in infants, children, and adolescents in the United States. *Pediatrics in Review, 35,* 268–286.

Sidebotham, P., Heron, J., & the ALSPAC Study Team. (2003). Child maltreatment in the "children of the nineties": The role of the child. *Child Abuse and Neglect, 27,* 337–352.

Siegal, M., Iozzi, L., & Surian, L. (2009). Bilingualism and conversational understanding in young children. *Cognition, 110,* 115–122.

Siega-Riz, A. M., Deming, D. M., Reidy, K. C., Fox, M. K., Condon, E., & Briefel, R. R. (2010). Food consumption patterns of infants and toddlers: Where are we now? *Journal of the American Dietetic Association, 110,* S38–S51.

Siegel, J. S. (2012). *The demography and epidemiology of human health and aging.* New York: Springer.

Siegel, R. L., Miller, K. D., & Jemal, A. (2016). Cancer statistics, 2016. *CA: A Cancer Journal for Clinicians, 66,* 7–30.

Siegler, R. S. (2009). Improving preschoolers' number sense using information-processing theory. In O. A. Barbarin & B. H. Wasik (Eds.), *Handbook of child development and early education* (pp. 429–454). New York: Guilford.

Siegler, R. S., & Mu, Y. (2008). Chinese children excel on novel mathematics problems even before elementary school. *Psychological Science, 19,* 759–763.

Siegler, R. S., & Svetina, M. (2006). What leads children to adopt new strategies? A microgenetic/cross-sectional study of class inclusion. *Child Development, 77,* 997–1015.

Sieri, S., Chiodini, P., Agnoli, C., Pala, V., Berrino, F., Trichopoulou, A., et al. (2014). Dietary fat intake and development of specific breast cancer subtypes. *Journal of the National Cancer Institute, 106*(5), dju068.

Sievert, L. L., & Espinosa-Hernandez, G. (2003). Attitudes toward menopause in relation to symptom experience in Puebla, Mexico. *Women & Health, 38,* 93–106.

Sikora, J., & Pokropek, A. (2012). Gender segregation of adolescent science career plans in 50 countries. *Science Education, 96,* 234–264.

Silvén, M. (2001). Attention in very young infants predicts learning of first words. *Infant Behavior and Development, 24,* 229–237.

Silver, M. H., & Perls, T. T. (2000). Is dementia the price of a long life? An optimistic report from centenarians. *Journal of Geriatric Psychiatry, 33,* 71–79.

Silverman, I., Choi, J., & Peters, M. (2007). The hunter-gatherer theory of sex differences in spatial abilities. *Archives of Sexual behavior, 36,* 261–268.

Silverman, P. R. (2004). Dying and bereavement in historical perspective. In J. Berzoff & P. R. Silverman (Eds.), *Living with dying: A handbook for end-of-life healthcare practitioners* (pp. 128–149). New York: Columbia University Press.

Silverman, P. R., & Nickman, S. L. (1996). Children's construction of their dead parents. In D. Klass, P. R. Silverman, & S. L. Nickman (Eds.), *Continuing bonds: New understandings of grief* (pp. 73–86). Washington, DC: Taylor & Francis.

Silverstein, M., & Giarrusso, R. (2010). Aging and family life: A decade review. *Journal of Marriage and Family, 72,* 1039–1058.

Silverstein, M., & Marenco, A. (2001). How Americans enact the grandparent role across the family life course. *Journal of Family Issues, 22,* 493–522.

Simcock, G., & DeLoache, J. (2006). Get the picture? The effects of iconicity on toddlers' reenactment from picture books. *Developmental Psychology, 42,* 1352–1357.

Simcock, G., Garrity, K., & Barr, R. (2011). The effect of narrative cues on infants' imitation from television and picture books. *Child Development, 82,* 1607–1619.

Simcock, G., & Hayne, H. (2003). Age-related changes in verbal and nonverbal memory during early childhood. *Developmental Psychology, 39,* 805–814.

Simoneau, M., & Markovits, H. (2003). Reasoning with premises that are not empirically true: Evidence for the role of inhibition and retrieval. *Developmental Psychology, 39,* 964–975.

Simonton, D. K. (2012). Creative productivity and aging. In S. K. Whitbourne & M. J. Sliwinski (Eds.), *Wiley-Blackwell handbook of adulthood and aging* (pp. 477–496). Malden, MA: Blackwell Publishing.

Simonton, D. K., & Damian, R. I. (2013). Creativity. In D. Reisberg (Ed.), *Oxford handbook of cognitive psychology* (pp. 795–807). New York: Oxford University Press.

Simpson, E. A., Varga, K., Frick, J. E., & Fragaszy, D. (2011). Infants experience perceptual narrowing for nonprimate faces. *Infancy, 16,* 318–328.

Simpson, J. A., & Overall, N. C. (2014). Partner buffering of attachment insecurity. *Current Directions in Psychological Science, 23,* 54–59.

Simpson, R. (2004). Masculinity at work: The experiences of men in female dominated occupations. *Work, Employment and Society, 18,* 349–368.

Simpson, R. (2005). Men in non-traditional occupations: Career entry, career orientation and experience of role strain. *Gender, Work and Organization, 12,* 363–380.

Sims, M., & Rofail, M. (2013). The experiences of grandparents who have limited or no contact with their grandchildren. *Journal of Aging Studies, 27,* 377–386.

Singer, L. T., Minnes, S., Min, M. O., Lewis, B. A., & Short, E. J. (2015). Prenatal cocaine exposure and child outcomes: A conference report based on a prospective study from Cleveland. *Human Psychopharmacology, 30,* 285–289.

Singh, G. K., & Linn, S. C. (2013). Dramatic increases in obesity and overweight prevalence among Asian subgroups in the United States, 1992–2011. *ISRN Preventive Medicine,* Article ID 898691.

Singleton, J. L., & Newport, E. L. (2004). When learners surpass their models: The acquisition of American Sign Language from inconsistent input. *Cognitive Psychology, 49,* 370–407.

Sinkkonen, J., Anttila, R., & Siimes, M. A. (1998). Pubertal maturation and changes in self-image in early adolescent Finnish boys. *Journal of Youth and Adolescence, 27,* 209–211.

Sinnott, J. D. (2003). Postformal thought and adult development: Living in balance. In J. Demick & C. Andreoletti (Eds.), *Handbook of adult development* (pp. 221–238). New York: Kluwer Academic.

Sirsch, U., Erher, E., Mayr, E., & Willinger, U. (2009). What does it take to be an adult in Austria? *Journal of Adolescent Research, 24,* 275–292.

Skinner, E. A., Zimmer-Gembeck, M. J., & Connell, J. P. (1998). Individual differences and the development of perceived control. *Monographs of the Society for Research in Child Development, 63*(2–3, Serial No. 254).

Skinner, M., Berg, C. A., & Uchino, B. N. (2014). Contextual variation in adults' emotion regulation during everyday problem solving. In M. A. Skinner, C. A. Berg, & B. N. Uchino (Eds.), *Oxford handbook of emotion, social cognition, and problem solving in adulthood* (pp. 175–189). New York: Oxford University Press.

Slagsvold, B., & Sørensen, A. (2013). Changes in sense of control in the second half of life: Results from a 5-year panel study. *International Journal of Aging and Human Development, 77,* 289–308.

Slater, A., Quinn, P. C., Kelly, D. J., Lee, K., Longmore, C. A., McDonald, P. R., & Pascalis, O. (2011). The shaping of the face space in early infancy: Becoming a native face processor. *Child Development Perspectives, 4,* 205–211.

Slater, A., Riddell, P., Quinn, P. C., Pascalis, O., Lee, K., & Kelly, D. J. (2010). Visual perception. In J. G. Bremner & T. D. Wachs (Eds.), *Wiley-Blackwell handbook of infant development: Vol. 1. Basic research* (2nd ed., pp. 40–80). Oxford, UK: Wiley-Blackwell.

Slaughter, V., & Griffiths, M. (2007). Death understanding and fear of death in young children. *Clinical Child Psychology and Psychiatry, 12,* 525–535.

Slaughter, V., Jaakkola, R., & Carey, S. (1999). Constructing a coherent theory: Children's biological understanding of life and death. In M. Siegel & C. C. Petersen (Eds.), *Children's understanding of biology and health* (pp. 71–96). Cambridge, UK: Cambridge University Press.

Slaughter, V., & Lyons, M. (2003). Learning about life and death in early childhood. *Cognitive Psychology, 46,* 1–30.

Slevin, K. F., & Mowery, C. E. (2012). Exploring embodied aging and ageism among old lesbians and gay men. In L. Carpenter & J. DeLamater (Eds.), *Sex for life: From virginity to Viagra, how sexuality changes throughout our lives* (pp. 260–277). New York: NYU Press.

Slining, M. M., Mathias, K. C., & Popkin, B. M. (2013). Trends in food and beverage sources among U.S. children and adolescents: 1989–2010. *Journal of the Academy of Nutrition and Dietetics, 113,* 1683–1694.

Slonims, V., & McConachie, H. (2006). Analysis of mother–infant interaction in infants with Down syndrome and typically developing infants. *American Journal of Mental Retardation, 111,* 273–289.

Sloutsky, V. (2015). Conceptual development. In L. S. Liben & U. Müller (Eds.), *Handbook of child psychology and developmental science: Vol. 2. Cognitive processes* (7th ed., pp. 469–518). Hoboken, NJ: Wiley.

Slusher, M. P., Mayer, C. J., & Dunkle, R. E. (1996). Gays and lesbians older and wiser (GLOW): A support group for older gay people. *Gerontologist, 36,* 118–123.

Slutske, W. S., Hunt-Carter, E. E., Nabors-Oberg, R. E., Sher, K. J., Bucholz, K. K., & Madden, P. A. F. (2004). Do college students drink more than their non-college-attending peers? Evidence from a population-based longitudinal female twin study. *Journal of Abnormal Psychology, 113,* 530–540.

Smahel, D., Brown, B. B., & Blinka, L. (2012). Associations between online friendship and Internet addiction among adolescents and emerging adults. *Developmental Psychology, 48,* 381–388.

Small, B. J., Rawson, K. S., Eisel, S., & McEvoy, C. L. (2012). Memory and aging. In S. K. Whitbourne & M. J. Sliwinski (Eds.), *Wiley-Blackwell handbook of adulthood and aging* (pp. 174–189). Malden, MA: Wiley-Blackwell.

Small, M. (1998). *Our babies, ourselves.* New York: Anchor.

Smetana, J. G. (2002). Culture, autonomy, and personal jurisdiction in adolescent–parent relationships. In R. V. Kail & H. W. Reese (Eds.), *Advances in child development and behavior* (Vol. 29, pp. 51–87). San Diego, CA: Academic Press.

Smetana, J. G. (2006). Social-cognitive domain theory: Consistencies and variations in children's moral and social judgments. In M. Killen & J. G. Smetana (Eds.), *Handbook of moral development* (pp. 119–154). Mahwah, NJ: Erlbaum.

Smetana, J. G., Metzger, A., & Campione-Barr, N. (2004). African-American late adolescents' relationships with parents: Developmental transitions and longitudinal patterns. *Child Development, 75,* 932–947.

Smink, R. F. E., van Hoeken, D., Oldehinkel, A. J., & Hoek, H. W. (2014). Prevalence and severity of DSM-5 eating disorders in a community cohort of adolescents. *International Journal of Eating Disorders, 47,* 610–619.

Smit, D. J. A., Boersma, M., Schnack, H. G., Micheloyannis, S., Doomsma, D. I., Pol, H. E. H., et al. (2012). The brain matures with stronger functional connectivity and decreased randomness of its network. *PLOS ONE, 7*(5), e36896.

Smith, A. (2014). *Older adults and technology use.* Washington, DC: Pew Research Center. Retrieved from www.pewinternet.org/2014/04/03/older-adults-and-technology-use

Smith, B. H., & Shapiro, C. J. (2015). Combined treatments for ADHD. In R. A. Barkley (Ed.), *Attention-deficit hyperactivity disorder: A handbook for diagnosis and treatment* (4th ed., pp. 686–704). New York: Guilford.

Smith, C., Christoffersen, K., Davidson, H., & Herzog, P. S. (2011). *Lost in transition: The dark side of emerging adulthood.* New York: Oxford University Press.

Smith, C., Perou, R., & Lesesne, C. (2002). Parent education. M. H. Bornstein (Ed.), *Handbook of parenting* (Vol. 4, pp. 389–410). Mahwah, NJ: Erlbaum.

Smith, C., & Snell, P. (2009). *Souls in transition: The religious & spiritual lives of emerging adults.* New York: Oxford University Press.

Smith, D. G., Xiao, L., & Bechara, A. (2012). Decision making in children and adolescents: Impaired Iowa gambling task performance in early adolescence. *Developmental Psychology, 48,* 1180–1187.

Smith, E., Hay, P., Campbell, L., & Trollor, J. N. (2011). A review of the association between obesity and cognitive function across the lifespan: Implications for novel approaches to prevention and treatment. *Obesity Reviews, 12,* 740–755.

Smith, G. C. (2016). Grandparents raising grandchildren. In S. Whitbourne (Ed.), *Encyclopedia of adulthood and aging* (Vol. 2, pp. 581–586). Malden, MA: Wiley Blackwell.

Smith, G. C., Rodriguez, J. M., & Palmieri, P. A. (2010). Patterns and predictors of support group use by custodial grandmothers and grandchildren. *Families in Society, 91,* 385–393.

Smith, J., & Baltes, P. B. (1999). Life-span perspectives on development. In M. H. Bornstein & M. E. Lamb (Eds.), *Developmental psychology: An advanced textbook* (4th ed., pp. 275–311). Mahwah, NJ: Erlbaum.

Smith, J., & Freund, A. M. (2002). The dynamics of possible selves in old age. *Journals of Gerontology, 57B,* P492–P500.

Smith, J., & Infurna, F. J. (2011). Early precursors of later health. In K. L. Fingerman, C. A. Berg, J. Smith, & T. C. Antonucci (Eds.), *Handbook of life-span development* (pp. 213–238). New York: Springer.

Smith, J. C., Nielson, K. A., Woodard, J. L., Seidenberg, M., & Rao, S. M. (2013). Physical activity and brain function in older adults at increased risk for Alzheimer's disease. *Brain Science, 3,* 54–83.

Smith, J. P., & Forrester, R. (2013). Who pays for the health benefits of exclusive breastfeeding? An analysis of maternal time costs. *Journal of Human Lactation, 29,* 547–555.

Smith, L. B., Jones, S. S., Gershkoff-Stowe, L., & Samuelson, L. (2002). Object name learning provides on-the-job training for attention. *Psychological Science, 13,* 13–19.

Smith, N., Young, A., & Lee, C. (2004). Optimism, health-related hardiness and well-being among older Australian women. *Journal of Health Psychology, 9,* 741–752.

Smith, P. K., Mahdavi, J., Carvalho, M., Fisher, S., Russell, S., & Tippett, N. (2008). Cyberbullying: Its nature and impact in secondary school pupils. *Journal of Child Psychology and Psychiatry, 49,* 376–385.

Smith, T. W. (2006). Personality as risk and resilience in physical health. *Current Directions in Psychological Science, 15,* 227–231.

Smith, T. W., & Cundiff, J. M. (2011). An interpersonal perspective on risk for coronary heart disease. In L. Horowitz & S. Strack (Eds.), *Handbook of interpersonal psychology: Theory, research, assessment, and therapeutic interventions* (pp. 471–489). Hoboken, NJ: Wiley.

Smith, T. W., Glazer, K., Ruiz, J. M., & Gallo, L. C. (2004). Hostility, anger, aggressiveness, and coronary heart disease: An interpersonal perspective on personality, emotion, and health. *Journal of Personality, 72,* 1217–1270.

Smith, T. W., & Mackenzie, J. (2006). Personality and risk of physical illness. *Annual Review of Clinical Psychology, 2,* 435–467.

Smith, T. W., Marsden, P., Hout, M., & Kim, J. (1972–2014). *General Social Surveys, 1972–2014.* Sponsored by the National Science Foundation. Chicago: NORC at the University of Chicago. Data accessed from the GSS Data Explorer website at gssdataexplorer.norc.org

Smith, T. W., Uchino, B. N., Berg, C. A., & Florsheim, P. (2012). Marital discord and coronary artery disease: A comparison of behaviorally defined discrete groups. *Journal of Consulting and Clinical Psychology, 80,* 87–92.

Smits, J., & Monden, C. (2011). Twinning across the developing world. *PLOS ONE, 6*(9), e25239.

Smyke, A. T., Zeanah, C. H., Fox, N. A., Nelson, C. A., & Guthrie, D. (2010). Placement in foster care enhances quality of attachment among young institutionalized children. *Child Development, 81,* 212–223.

Smyth, A. C., & Naveh-Benjamin, M. (2016). Can DRYAD explain age-related associative memory deficits? *Psychology and Aging, 31,* 1–13.

Sneed, J. R., Whitbourne, S. K., & Culang, M. E. (2006). Trust, identity, and ego integrity: Modeling Erikson's core stages over 34 years. *Journal of Adult Development, 13,* 148–157.

Sneed, J. R., Whitbourne, S. K., Schwartz, S. J., & Huang, S. (2012). The relationship between identity, intimacy, and midlife well-being: Findings from the Rochester Adult Longitudinal Study. *Psychology and Aging, 27,* 318–323.

Snidman, N., Kagan, J., Riordan, L., & Shannon, D. C. (1995). Cardiac function and behavioral reactivity. *Psychophysiology, 32,* 199–207.

Snow, C. E., & Beals, D. E. (2006). Mealtime talk that supports literacy development. In R. W. Larson, A. R. Wiley, & K. R. Branscomb (Eds.), *Family mealtime as a context of development and socialization* (pp. 51–66). San Francisco: Jossey-Bass.

Snow, C. E., Pan, B. A., Imbens-Bailey, A., & Herman, J. (1996). Learning how to say what one means: A longitudinal study of children's speech act use. *Social Development, 5,* 56–84.

Snyder, J., Brooker, M., Patrick, M. R., Snyder, A., Schrepferman, L., & Stoolmiller, M. (2003). Observed peer victimization during early elementary school: Continuity, growth, and relation to risk for child antisocial and depressive behavior. *Child Development, 74,* 1881–1898.

Snyder, J. S., & Cameron, H. A. (2012). Could adult hippocampal neurogenesis be relevant for human behavior? *Behavioural Brain Research, 227,* 384–390.

Sobel, D. M. (2006). How fantasy benefits young children's understanding of pretense. *Developmental Science, 9,* 63–75.

Sobiraj, S., Rigotti, T., Weseler, D., & Mohr, G. (2015). Masculinity ideology and psychological strain: Considering men's social stressors in female-dominated occupations. *Psychology of Men and Masculinity, 16,* 54–66.

Society for Research in Child Development. (2007). *SRCD ethical standards for research with children.* Retrieved from www.srcd.org/index.php?option=com_content&task=view&id=68&Itemid=110

Soderstrom, M., Dolbier, C., Leiferman, J., & Steinhardt, M. (2000). The relationship of hardiness, coping strategies, and perceived stress to symptoms of illness. *Journal of Behavioral Medicine, 23,* 311–328.

Soderstrom, M., Seidl, A., Nelson, D. G. K., & Jusczyk, P. W. (2003). The prosodic bootstrapping of phrases: Evidence from prelinguistic infants. *Journal of Memory and Language, 49,* 249–267.

Soli, A. R., McHale, S. M., & Feinberg, M. E. (2009). Risk and protective effects of sibling relationships among African American adolescents. *Family Relations, 58,* 578–592.

Solmeyer, A. R., McHale, S. M., & Crouter, A. C. (2014). Longitudinal association between sibling relationship qualities and risky behavior across adolescence. *Developmental Psychology, 50,* 600–610.

Solomon, J., & George, C. (2011). The disorganized attachment-caregiving system. In J. Solomon & C. George (Eds.), *Disorganized attachment and caregiving* (pp. 3–24). New York: Guilford.

Solomon, J. C., & Marx, J. (1995). "To grandmother's house we go": Health and school adjustment of children raised solely by grandparents. *Gerontologist, 35,* 386–394.

Somers, M., Ophoff, R. A., Aukes, M. F., Cantor, R. M., Boks, M. P., Dauwan, M., et al. (2015). Linkage analysis in a Dutch population isolate shows no major gene for left-handedness or atypical language lateralization. *Journal of Neuroscience, 35,* 8730–8736.

Somerville, L. H. (2013). The teenage brain: Sensitivity to social evaluation. *Current Directions in Psychological Science, 22,* 121–127.

Son, J., & Wilson, J. (2011). Generativity and volunteering. *Sociological Forum, 26,* 644–667.

Song, C., Benin, M., & Glick, J. (2012). Dropping out of high school: The effects of family structure and family transitions. *Journal of Divorce and Remarriage, 53,* 18–33.

Song, J., Lindquist, L. A., Chang, R. W., Semanik, P. A., Ehrlich-Jones, L. S., Lee, J., et al. (2015). Sedentary behavior as a risk factor for physical frailty independent of moderate activity: Results from the osteoarthritis initiative. *American Journal of Public Health, 10,* 1439–1445.

Soos, I., Biddle, S. J. H., Ling, J., Hamar, P., Sandor, I., Boros-Balint, I., et al. (2014). Physical activity, sedentary behaviour, use of electronic media, and snacking among youth: An international study. *Kinesiology, 46,* 155–163.

Sørensen, K., Mouritsen, A., Aksgaede, L., Hagen, C. P., Mogensen, S. S., & Juul, A. (2012). Recent secular trends in pubertal timing: Implications for evaluation and diagnosis of precocious puberty. *Hormone Research in Paediatrics, 77,* 137–145.

Sörensen, S., White, K., & Ramchandran, R. S. (2016). Vision in mid and late life. In S. K. Whitbourne (Ed.), *Encyclopedia of adulthood and aging* (Vol. 3, pp. 1427–1431). Malden, MA: Wiley Blackwell.

Sorkhabi, N., & Mandara, J. (2013). Are the effects of Baumrind's parenting styles culturally specific or culturally equivalent? In R. E. Larzelere, A. S. Morris, & A. W. Harrist (Eds.), *Authoritative parenting: Synthesizing nurturance and discipline for optimal child development* (pp. 113–135). Washington, DC: American Psychological Association.

Sosa, R., Kennell, J., Klaus, M., Robertson, S., & Urrutia, J. (1980). The effect of a supportive companion on perinatal problems, length of labor, and mother–infant interaction. *New England Journal of Medicine, 303,* 597–600.

Soska, K. C., Adolph, K. E., & Johnson, S. P. (2010). Systems in development: Motor skill acquisition facilitates three-dimensional object completion. *Developmental Psychology, 46,* 129–138.

Soto, C. J., John, O. P., Gosling, S. D., & Potter, J. (2011). Age differences in personality traits from 10 to 65: Big five domains and facets in a large cross-sectional sample. *Journal of Personality and Social Psychology, 100,* 330–348.

Soto, C. J., Kronauer, A., & Liang, J. K. (2016). Five-factor model of personality. In K. S. Whitbourne Ed.), *Encyclopedia of adulthood and aging* (Vol. 2, pp. 506–511). Malden, MA: Blackwell.

South Africa Department of Health. (2013). *The 2012 National Antenatal Sentinel HIV and Herpes Simplex Type-2 Prevalence Survey in South Africa.* Pretoria: Author. Retrieved from www.health-e.org.za/wp-content/uploads/2014/05/ASHIVHerp_Report2014_22May2014.pdf

Sowers, M. F., Zheng, H., Tomey, K., Karvonen-Gutierrez, M. J., Li, X., Matheos, Y., & Symons, J. (2007). Changes in body composition in women over six years at midlife: Ovarian and chronological aging. *Journal of Clinical Endocrinology and Metabolism, 92,* 895–901.

Sowislo, J. F., & Orth, U. (2013). Does low self-esteem predict depression and anxiety? A meta-analysis of longitudinal studies. *Psychological Bulletin, 139,* 213–240.

Spangler, G., Fremmer-Bomik, E., & Grossmann, K. (1996). Social and individual determinants of attachment security and disorganization during the first year. *Infant Mental Health Journal, 17,* 127–139.

Spangler, G., Johann, M., Ronai, Z., & Zimmermann, P. (2009). Genetic and environmental influence on attachment disorganization. *Journal of Child Psychology and Psychiatry, 50,* 952–961.

Speece, D. L., Ritchey, K. D., Cooper, D. H., Roth, F. P., & Schatschneider, C. (2004). Growth in early reading skills from kindergarten to third grade. *Contemporary Educational Psychology, 29,* 312–332.

Spelke, E. S., & Kinzler, K. D. (2007). Core knowledge. *Developmental Science, 10,* 89–96.

Spelke, E. S., & Kinzler, K. D. (2013). Core knowledge. In S. M. Downes & E. Machery (Eds.), *Arguing about human nature: Contemporary debates* (pp. 107–116). New York: Routledge.

Spelke, E. S., Phillips, A. T., & Woodward, A. L. (1995). Infants' knowledge of object motion and human action. In A. Premack (Ed.), *Causal understanding in cognition and culture* (pp. 4–78). Oxford, UK: Clarendon Press.

Spence, I., & Feng, J. (2010). Video games and spatial cognition. *Review of General Psychology, 14,* 92–104.

Spence, M. J., & DeCasper, A. J. (1987). Prenatal experience with low-frequency maternal voice sounds influences neonatal perception of maternal voice samples. *Infant Behavior and Development, 10,* 133–142.

Spencer, J. P., Perone, S., & Buss, A. T. (2011). Twenty years and going strong: A dynamic systems revolution in motor and cognitive development. *Child Development Perspectives, 5,* 260–266.

Spere, K. A., Schmidt, L. A., Theall-Honey, L. A., & Martin-Chang, S. (2004). Expressive and receptive language skills of temperamentally shy preschoolers. *Infant and Child Development, 13,* 123–133.

Spieker, S. J., Campbell, S. B., Vandergrift, N., Pierce, K. M., Cauffman, E., Susman, E. J., & Roisman, G. I. (2012). Relational aggression in middle childhood: Predictors and adolescent outcomes. *Social Development, 21,* 354–375.

Spilt, J., Hughes, J. N., Wu, J.-Y., & Kwok, O.-M. (2012). Dynamics of teacher–student relationships: Stability and change across elementary school and the influence on children's academic success. *Child Development, 83,* 1180–1195.

Spirito, A., Esposito-Smythers, C., Weismoore, J., & Miller, A. (2012). Adolescent suicide behavior. In P. C. Kendall (Ed.), *Child and adolescent therapy: Cognitive behavioral procedures* (4th ed., pp. 234–256). New York: Guilford.

Spitze, G., & Gallant, M. P. (2004). "The bitter with the sweet": Older adults' strategies for handling ambivalence in relations with their adult children. *Research on Aging, 26,* 387–412.

Spock, B., & Needlman, R. (2012). *Dr. Spock's baby and child care* (9th ed.). New York: Gallery Books.

Spoelstra, M. N., Mari, A., Mendel, M., Senga, E., van Rheenen, P., van Dijk, T. H., et al. (2012). Kwashiorkor and marasmus are both associated with impaired glucose clearance related to pancreatic β-cell dysfunction. *Metabolism: Clinical and Experimental, 61,* 1224–1230.

Spokane, A. R., & Cruza-Guet, M. C. (2005). Holland's theory of vocational personalities in work environments. In S. D. Brown & R. W. Lent (Eds.), *Career development and counseling* (pp. 24–41). Hoboken, NJ: Wiley.

Sprecher, S. (1999). "I love you more today than yesterday": Romantic partners' perceptions of changes in love and related affect over time. *Journal of Personality and Social Psychology, 76,* 46–53.

Sprecher, S. (2011). The influence of social networks on romantic relationships: Through the lens of the social network. *Personal Relationships, 18,* 630–644.

Sprecher, S. (2013). Attachment style and sexual permissiveness: The moderating role of gender. *Personality and Individual Differences, 55,* 428–432.

Sprecher, S., & Fehr, B. (2005). Compassionate love for close others and humanity. *Journal of Social and Personal Relationships, 22,* 629–652.

Sprecher, S., & Fehr, B. (2011). Dispositional attachment and relationship-specific attachment as predictors of compassionate love for partner. *Journal of Social and Personal Relationships, 28,* 558–574.

Sprecher, S., Felmlee, D., Metts, S., & Cupach, W. (2015). Relationship initiation and development. In M. Mikulincer, P. R. Shaver, J. A. Simpson, & J. F. Dovidio (Eds.), *APA handbook of personality and social psychology: Vol. 3. Interpersonal relations* (pp. 211–245). Washington, DC: American Psychological Association.

Sprecher, S., Harris, G., & Meyers, A. (2008). Perceptions of sources of sex education and targets of sex communication: Socio-demographic and cohort effects. *Journal of Sex Research, 45,* 17–26.

Sprecher, S., & Regan, P. C. (1998). Passionate and companionate love in courting and young married couples. *Sociological Inquiry, 68,* 163–185.

Srivastava, S., John, O. P., Gosling, S. D., & Potter, J. (2003). Development of personality in early and middle adulthood: Set like plaster or persistent change? *Journal of Personality and Social Psychology, 84,* 1041–1053.

Sroufe, L. A. (2002). From infant attachment to promotion of adolescent autonomy: Prospective, longitudinal data on the role of parents in development. In J. G. Borkowski & S. L. Ramey (Eds.), *Parenting and the child's world* (pp. 187–202). Mahwah, NJ: Erlbaum.

Sroufe, L. A., Coffino, B., & Carlson, E. A. (2010). Conceptualizing the role of early experience: Lessons from the Minnesota Longitudinal Study. *Developmental Review, 30,* 36–51.

Sroufe, L. A., Egeland, B., Carlson, E., & Collins, W. (2005). *Minnesota Study of Risk and Adaptation from birth to maturity: The development of the person.* New York: Guilford.

Stackert, R. A., & Bursik, K. (2003). Why am I unsatisfied? Adult attachment style, gendered irrational relationship beliefs, and young adult romantic relationship satisfaction. *Personality and Individual Differences, 34,* 1419–1429.

Staff, J., Mont'Alvao, A., & Mortimer, J. T. (2015). Children at work. In M. H. Bornstein, T. Leventhal, & R. M. Lerner (Eds.), *Handbook of child psychology and developmental science: Vol. 4. Ecological settings and processes* (7th ed., pp. 345–374). Hoboken, NJ: Wiley.

Staff, J., & Mortimer, J. T. (2007). Educational and work strategies from adolescence to early adulthood: Consequences for educational attainment. *Social Forces, 85,* 1169–1194.

Staff, J., & Uggen, C. (2003). The fruits of good work: Early work experiences and adolescent deviance. *Journal of Research in Crime and Delinquency, 40,* 263–290.

Stams, G. J. M., Brugman, D., Deković, M., van Rosmalen, L., van der Laan, P., & Gibbs, J. C. (2006). The moral judgment of juvenile delinquents: A meta-analysis. *Journal of Abnormal Child Psychology, 34,* 697–713.

Stams, G. J. M., Juffer, F., & van IJzendoorn, M. H. (2002). Maternal sensitivity, infant attachment, and temperament in early childhood predict adjustment in middle childhood: The case of adopted children and their biologically unrelated parents. *Developmental Psychology, 38,* 806–821.

Stanovich, K. E. (2013). *How to think straight about psychology* (10th ed.). Upper Saddle River, NJ: Pearson.

Stark, P., & Noel, A. M. (2015). *Trends in high school dropout and completion rates in the United States: 1972–2012* (NCES 2015–015). Washington, DC: U.S. Department of Education.

Starks, T. J., Newcomb, M. E., & Mustanski, B. (2015). A longitudinal study of interpersonal relationships among lesbian, gay, and bisexual adolescents and young adults. *Archives of Sexual Behavior, 44,* 1821–1831.

Staub, F. C., & Stern, E. (2002). The nature of teachers' pedagogical content beliefs matters for students' achievement gains: Quasi-experimental evidence from elementary mathematics. *Journal of Educational Psychology, 94,* 344–355.

Staudinger, U. M. (1996). Wisdom and the social-interactive foundation of the mind. In P. B. Baltes & U. M. Staudinger (Eds.), *Interactive minds: Life-span perspectives on the social foundation of cognition* (pp. 276–315). New York: Cambridge University Press.

Staudinger, U. M. (2008). A psychology of wisdom: History and recent developments. *Research in Human Development, 5,* 107–120.

Staudinger, U. M., & Bowen, C. E. (2010). Life-span perspectives on positive personality development in adulthood and old age. In M. E. Lamb, A. M. Freund, & R. M. Lerner (Eds.), *Handbook of life-span development: Vol. 2. Social and emotional development* (pp. 254–297). Hoboken, NJ: Wiley.

Staudinger, U. M., Dörner, J., & Mickler, C. (2005). Wisdom and personality. In R. J. Sternberg & J. Jordan (Eds.), *A handbook of wisdom: Psychological perspectives* (pp 191–219). New York: Cambridge University Press.

Staudinger, U. M., & Glück, J. (2011). Psychological wisdom research: Commonalities and differences in a growing field. *Annual Review of Psychology, 62,* 215–241.

Staudinger, U. M., & Lindenberger, U. (2003). Understanding human development takes a metatheory and multiple disciplines. In U. M. Staudinger & U. Lindenberger (Eds.), *Understanding human development: Dialogues with life span psychology* (pp. 1–13). Norwell, MA: Kluwer.

Steele, H., & Steele, M. (2014). Attachment disorders: Theory, research, and treatment considerations. In M. Lewis & K. D. Rudolph (Eds.), *Handbook of developmental psychopathology* (3rd ed., pp. 357–370). New York: Springer Science + Business Media.

Steele, L. C. (2012). The forensic interview: A challenging intervention. In P. Goodyear-Brown (Ed.), *Handbook of child sexual abuse: Identification, assessment, and treatment* (pp. 99–119). Hoboken, NJ: Wiley.

Steele, S., Joseph, R. M., & Tager-Flusberg, H. (2003). Developmental change in theory of mind abilities in children with autism. *Journal of Autism and Developmental Disorders, 33,* 461–467.

Steensma, T. D., Biemond, R., de Boer, F., & Cohen-Kettenis, P T. (2011). Desisting and persisting gender dysphoria after childhood: A qualitative follow-up study. *Clinical Child Psychology and Psychiatry, 16,* 499–516.

Steensma, T. D., & Cohen-Kettenis, P. T. (2015). More than two developmental pathways in children with gender dysphoria? *Journal of the American Academy of Child and Adolescent Psychiatry, 54,* 147.

Steinberg, L. (2008). A social neuroscience perspective on adolescent risk-taking. *Developmental Review, 28,* 78–106.

Steinberg, L., Blatt-Eisengart, I., & Cauffman, E. (2006). Patterns of competence and adjustment among adolescents from authoritative, authoritarian, indulgent, and neglectful homes: A replication in a sample of serious juvenile offenders. *Journal of Research on Adolescence, 16,* 47–58.

Steinberg, L., Graham, S., O'Brien, L., Woolard, J., Cauffman, E., & Banich, M. (2009). Age differences in future orientation and delay discounting. *Child Development, 80,* 28–44.

Steinberg, L., & Monahan, K. C. (2011). Adolescents' exposure to sexy media does not hasten the initiation of sexual intercourse. *Developmental Psychology, 47,* 562–576.

Steinberg, L. D. (2001). We know some things: Parent-adolescent relationships in retrospect and prospect. *Journal of Research on Adolescence, 11,* 1–19.

Steiner, J. E. (1979). Human facial expression in response to taste and smell stimulation. In H. W. Reese & L. P. Lipsitt (Eds.), *Advances in child development and behavior* (Vol. 13, pp. 257–295). New York: Academic Press.

Steiner, J. E., Glaser, D., Hawilo, M. E., & Berridge, D. C. (2001). Comparative expression of hedonic impact: Affective reactions to taste by human infants and other primates. *Neuroscience and Biobehavioral Review, 25,* 53–74.

Stenberg, C. (2003). Effects of maternal inattentiveness on infant social referencing. *Infant and Child Development, 12,* 399–419.

Stenberg, C., & Campos, J. J. (1990). The development of anger expressions in infancy. In N. Stein, B. Leventhal, & T. Trabasso (Eds.), *Psychological and biological approaches to emotion* (pp. 247–282). Hillsdale, NJ: Erlbaum.

Stephens, B. E., & Vohr, B. R. (2009). Neurodevelopmental outcome of the premature infant. *Pediatric Clinics of North America, 56,* 631–646.

Stephens, M. A. P., Franks, M. M., Martire, L. M., Norton, T. R., & Atienza, A. A. (2009). Women at midlife: Stress and rewards of balancing parent care with employment and family roles. In K. Shifren (Ed.), *How caregiving affects development* (pp. 147–167). Washington, DC: American Psychological Association.

Stephens, P. C., Sloboda, Z., Stephens, R. C., Teasdale, B., Grey, S. F., Hawthorne, R. D., & Williams, J. (2009). Universal school-based substance abuse prevention programs: Modeling targeted mediators and outcomes for adolescent cigarette, alcohol, and marijuana use. *Drug and Alcohol Dependence, 102,* 19–29.

Stepler, R. (2015). *5 facts about family caregivers.* Washington, DC: Pew Research Center. Retrieved from www.pewresearch.org/fact-tank/2015/11/18/5-facts-about-family-caregivers

Stepler, R. (2016). *World's centenarian population projected to grow eightfold by 2050.* Retrieved from www.pewresearch.org/fact-tank/2016/04/21/worlds-centenarian-population-projected-to-grow-eightfold-by-2050

Sternberg, R. J. (2005). The triarchic theory of successful intelligence. In D. P. Flanagan & P. L. Harrison (Eds.), *Contemporary intellectual assessment: Theories, tests, and issues* (pp. 103–119). New York: Guilford.

Sternberg, R. J. (2006). A duplex theory of love. In R. J. Sternberg & K. Weis (Eds.), *The new psychology of* love (pp. 184–199). New Haven, CT: Yale University Press.

Sternberg, R. J. (2008). The triarchic theory of successful intelligence. In N. Salkind (Ed.), *Encyclopedia of educational psychology* (Vol. 2, pp. 988–994). Thousand Oaks, CA: Sage.

Sternberg, R. J. (2011). The theory of successful intelligence. In R. J. Sternberg & S. B. Kaufman (Eds.), *Cambridge handbook of intelligence* (pp. 504–527). New York: Cambridge University Press.

Sternberg, R. J. (2013). Contemporary theories of intelligence. In W. M. Reynolds & G. E. Miller (Eds.), *Handbook of psychology: Vol. 7. Educational psychology* (2nd ed., pp. 23–44). Hoboken, NJ: Wiley.

Sternberg, R. J., & Lubart, T. I. (2001). Wisdom and creativity. In J. E. Birren & K. W. Schaie (Eds.), *Handbook of the psychology of aging* (pp. 500–522). San Diego: Academic Press.

Sterns, H. L., & McQuown, C. K. (2015). Retirement redefined. In P. A. Lichtenberg, B. T. Mast, B. D. Carpenter, & J. L. Wetherell (Eds.), *APA handbook of clinical geropsychology: Vol. 2. Assessment, treatment, and issues of later life* (pp. 601–616). Washington, DC: American Psychological Association.

Stevens, J., Katz, E. G., & Huxley, R. R. (2010). Associations between gender, age and waist circumference. *European Journal of Clinical Nutrition, 64,* 6–15.

Stevens, J. C., & Cruz, L. A. (1996). Spatial acuity of touch: Ubiquitous decline with aging revealed by repeated threshold testing. *Somatosensory and Motor Research, 13,* 1–10.

Stevenson, R., & Pollitt, C. (1987). The acquisition of temporal terms. *Journal of Child Language, 14,* 533–545.

Stewart, A. J., & Malley, J. E. (2004). Women of the greatest generation. In C. Daiute & C. Lightfoot (Eds.), *Narrative analysis: Studying the development of individuals in society* (pp. 223–244). Thousand Oaks, CA: Sage.

Stewart, A. L., Verboncoeur, C. J., McLellan, B. Y., Gillis, D. E., Rush, S., & Mills, K. M. (2001). Physical activity outcomes of CHAMPS II: A physical activity promotion program for older adults. *Journals of Gerontology, 56A,* M465–M470.

Stewart, P. W., Lonky, E., Reihman, J., Pagano, J., Gump, B. B., & Darvill, T. (2008). The relationship between prenatal PCB exposure and intelligence (IQ). *Environmental Health Perspectives, 116,* 1416–1422.

Stewart, R. B., Jr. (1990). *The second child: Family transition and adjustment.* Newbury Park, CA: Sage.

Stewart, S., Lim, D. H., & Kim, J. (2015). Factors influencing college persistence for first-time students. *Journal of Developmental Education, 38*(3), 12–20.

Stice, E. (2003). Puberty and body image. In C. Hayward (Ed.), *Gender differences at puberty* (pp. 61–76). New York: Cambridge University Press.

Stice, E., Marti, C. N., & Rohde, P. (2013). Prevalence, incidence, impairment, and course of the proposed DSM-5 eating disorder diagnoses in an 8-year prospective community study of young women. *Journal of Abnormal Psychology, 122,* 455–457.

Stiles, J. (2012). The effects of injury to dynamic neural networks in the mature and developing brain. *Developmental Psychobiology, 54,* 343–349.

Stiles, J., Brown, T. T., Haist, F., & Jernigan, T. L. (2015). Brain and cognitive development. In L. S. Liben & U. Müller (Eds.), *Handbook of child psychology and developmental science: Vol. 2. Cognitive processes* (7th ed., pp. 9–62). Hoboken, NJ: Wiley.

Stiles, J., Moses, P., Roe, K., Akshoomoff, N. A., Trauner, D., & Hesselink, J. (2003). Alternative brain organization after prenatal cerebral injury: Convergent fMRI and cognitive data. *Journal of the International Neuropsychological Society, 9,* 604–622.

Stiles, J., Nass, R. D., Levine, S. C., Moses, P., & Reilly, J. S. (2009). Perinatal stroke: Effects and outcomes. In K. O. Yeates, M. D. Ris, H. G. Taylor, & B. Pennington (Eds.), *Pediatric neuropsychology: Research, theory and practice* (2nd ed., pp. 181–210). New York: Guilford.

Stiles, J., Reilly, J. S., & Levine, S. C. (2012). *Neural plasticity and cognitive development.* New York: Oxford University Press.

Stiles, J., Reilly, J., Paul, B., & Moses, P. (2005). Cognitive development following early brain injury: Evidence for neural adaptation. *Trends in Cognitive Sciences, 9,* 136–143.

Stiles, J., Stern, C., Appelbaum, M., & Nass, R. (2008). Effects of early focal brain injury on memory for visuospatial patterns: Selective deficits of global–local processing. *Neuropsychology, 22,* 61–73.

Stiles-Shields, C., & Carroll, R. A. (2015). Same-sex domestic violence: Prevalence, unique aspects, and clinical implications. *Journal of Sex and Marital Therapy, 41,* 636–648.

Stine-Morrow, E. A. L., & Payne, B. R. (2016). Age differences in language segmentation. *Experimental Aging Research. 42,* 107–125.

Stine-Morrow, E. A. L., Payne, B. R., Roberts, B. W., Kramer, A. F., Morrow, D. G., Payne, L., et al. (2014). Training versus engagement as paths to cognitive enrichment with aging. *Psychology and Aging, 29,* 891–906.

Stipek, D. (2011). Classroom practices and children's motivation to learn. In E. Zigler, W. S. Gilliam, & W. S. Barnett (Eds.), *The pre-K debates: Current controversies and issues* (pp. 98–103). Baltimore, MD: Paul H. Brookes.

Stipek, D. J., Feiler, R., Daniels, D., & Milburn, S. (1995). Effects of different instructional approaches on young children's achievement and motivation. *Child Development, 66,* 209–223.

Stipek, D. J., Gralinski, J. H., & Kopp, C. B. (1990). Self-concept development in the toddler years. *Developmental Psychology, 26,* 972–977.

St James-Roberts, I. (2007). Helping parents to manage infant crying and sleeping: A review of the evidence and its implications for services. *Child Abuse Review, 16,* 47–69.

St James-Roberts, I. (2012). *The origins, prevention and treatment of infant crying and sleep problems.* London: Routledge.

Stochholm, K., Bojesen, A., Jensen, A. S., Juul, S., & Grayholt, C. H. (2012). Criminality in men with Klinefelter's syndrome and XYY syndrome: A cohort study. *British Medical Journal, 2,* e000650.

Stoet, G., & Geary, D. C. (2013). Sex differences in mathematics and reading achievement are inversely related: Within- and across-nation assessment of 10 years of PISA data. *PLOS ONE, 8,* e57988.

Stohs, S. J. (2011). The role of free radicals in toxicity and disease. *Journal of Basic and Clinical Physiology and Pharmacology, 6,* 205–228.

Stone, A. A., Schwartz, J. E., Broderick, J. E., & Deaton, A. (2010). A snapshot of the age distribution of psychological well-being in the United States. *Proceedings of the National Academy of Sciences, 107,* 9985–9990.

Stone, M. R., & Brown, B. B. (1999). Identity claims and projections: Descriptions of self and crowds in secondary school. In J. A. McLellan & M. J. V. Pugh (Eds.), *The role of peer groups in adolescent social identity: Exploring the importance of stability and change* (pp. 7–20). San Francisco: Jossey-Bass.

Stoner, R., Chow, M. L., Boyle, M. P., Sunkin, S. M., Mouton, P. R., Roy, S., et al. (2014). Patches of disorganization in the neocortex of children with autism. *New England Journal of Medicine, 370,* 1209–1219.

Storch, S. A., & Whitehurst, G. J. (2001). The role of family and home in the literacy development of children from low-income backgrounds. In P. R. Britto & J. Brooks-Gunn (Eds.), *New directions for child and adolescent development* (No. 92, pp. 53–71). San Francisco: Jossey-Bass.

Strapp, C. M., & Federico, A. (2000). Imitations and repetitions: What do children say following recasts? *First Language, 20,* 273–290.

Strasburger, V. C. (2012). Children, adolescents, drugs, and the media. In D. G. Singer & J. L. Singer (Eds.), *Handbook of children and the media* (2nd ed., pp. 419–454). Thousand Oaks, CA: Sage.

Straus, M. A., & Stewart, J. H. (1999). Corporal punishment by American parents: National data on prevalence, chronicity, severity, and duration, in relation to child and family characteristics. *Clinical Child and Family Psychology Review, 2,* 55–70.

Strazdins, L., Clements, M. S., Korda, R. J., Broom, D. H., & D'Souza, R. M. (2006). Unsociable work? Nonstandard work schedules, family relationships, and children's well-being. *Journal of Marriage and the Family, 68,* 394–410.

Strazdins, L., O'Brien, L. V., Lucas, N., & Rodgers, B. (2013). Combining work and family: Rewards or risks for children's mental health? *Social Science and Medicine, 87,* 99–107.

Street, A. E., Bell, M., & Ready, C. B. (2011). Sexual assault. In D. Benedek & G. Wynn (Eds.), *Clinical manual for the management of PTSD* (pp. 325–348). Arlington, VA: American Psychiatric Press.

Striano, T., & Rochat, P. (2000). Emergence of selective social referencing in infancy. *Infancy, 1,* 253–264.

Striano, T., Tomasello, M., & Rochat, P. (2001). Social and object support for early symbolic play. *Developmental Science, 4,* 442–455.

Stright, A. D., Herr, M. Y., & Neitzel, C. (2009). Maternal scaffolding of children's problem solving and children's adjustment in kindergarten: Hmong families in the United States. *Journal of Educational Psychology, 101,* 207–218.

Stright, A. D., Neitzel, C., Sears, K. G., & Hoke-Sinex, L. (2002). Instruction begins in the home: Relations between parental instruction and children's self-regulation in the classroom. *Journal of Educational Psychology, 93,* 456–466.

Stringer, K., Kerpelman, J., & Skorikov, V. (2011). Career preparation: A longitudinal, process-oriented examination. *Journal of Vocational Behavior, 79,* 158–169.

Stringer, K. J., & Kerpelman, J. L. (2010). Career identity development in college students: Decision making, parental support, and work experience. *Identity, 10,* 181–200.

Stroebe, M., & Schut, H. (2010). The dual process model of coping with bereavement: A decade on. *Omega, 61,* 273–289.

Stroebe, M., Schut, H., & van den Bout, J. (2013). Complicated grief: Assessment of scientific knowledge and implications for research and practice. In M. Stroebe, H. Schut, & J. van den Bout (Eds.), *Complicated grief* (pp. 295–311). New York: Routledge.

Stroebe, M. S., & Schut, H. (1999). The dual process model of coping with bereavement: Rationale and description. *Death Studies, 23,* 197–224.

Strohmaier, J., van Dongen, J., Willemsen, G., Nyholt, D. R., Zhu, G., Codd, V., et al. (2015). Low birth weight in MZ twins discordant for birth weight is associated with shorter telomere length and lower IQ, but not anxiety/depression in later life. *Twin Research and Human Genetics, 18,* 198–209.

Strohschein, L. (2005). Parental divorce and child mental health trajectories. *Journal of Marriage and Family, 67,* 1286–1300.

Stronach, E. P., Toth, S. L., Rogosch, F., Oshri, A., Manle, J. T., & Cicchetti, D. (2011). Child maltreatment, attachment security and internal representations of mother and mother–child relationships. *Child Maltreatment, 16,* 137–154.

Stroub, K. J., & Richards, M. P. (2013). From resegregation to reintegration: Trends in the racial/

ethnic segregation of metropolitan public schools, 1993–2009. *American Educational Research Journal, 50,* 497–531.

Strough, J., Hicks, P. J., Swenson, L. M., Cheng, S., & Barnes, K. A. (2003). Collaborative everyday problem solving: Interpersonal relationships and problem dimensions. *International Journal of Aging and Human Development, 56,* 43–66.

Strough, J., Leszczynski, J. P., Neely, T. L., Flinn, J. A., & Margrett, J. (2007). From adolescence to later adulthood: Femininity, masculinity, and androgyny in six age groups. *Sex Roles, 57,* 385–396.

Strough, J., McFall, J. P., Flinn, J. A., & Schuller, K. L. (2008). Collaborative everyday problem solving among same-gender friends in early and later adulthood. *Psychology and Aging, 23,* 517–530.

Strouse, D. L. (1999). Adolescent crowd orientations: A social and temporal analysis. In J. A. McLellan & M. J. V. Pugh (Eds.), *The role of peer groups in adolescent social identity: Exploring the importance of stability and change* (pp. 37–54). San Francisco: Jossey-Bass.

Sturge-Apple, M. L., Davies, P. T., Winter, M. A., Cummings, E. M., & Schermerhorn, A. (2008). Interparental conflict and children's school adjustment: The explanatory role of children's internal representations of interparental and parent–child relationships. *Developmental Psychology, 44,* 1678–1690.

Su, T. F., & Costigan, C. L. (2008). The development of children's ethnic identity in immigrant Chinese families in Canada: The role of parenting practices and children's perceptions of parental family obligation expectations. *Journal of Early Adolescence, 29,* 638–663.

Suarez-Morales, L., & Lopez, B. (2009). The impact of acculturative stress and daily hassles on preadolescent psychological adjustment: Examining anxiety symptoms. *Journal of Primary Prevention, 30,* 335–349.

Suárez-Orozco, C., Pimental, A., & Martin, M. (2009). The significance of relationships: Academic engagement and achievement among newcomer immigrant youth. *Teachers College Record, 111,* 712–749.

Subrahmanyam, K., Gelman, R., & Lafosse, A. (2002). Animate and other separably moveable things. In G. Humphreys (Ed.), *Category-specificity in brain and mind* (pp. 341–371). London: Psychology Press.

Substance Abuse and Mental Health Services Administration. (2014). *Results from the 2013 National Survey on Drug Use and Health: Summary of national findings.* NSDUH Series H-48, HHS Publication No. (SMA) 14-4863. Rockville, MD: Author.

Suddendorf, T., Simcock, G., & Nielsen, M. (2007). Visual self-recognition in mirrors and live videos: Evidence for a developmental asynchrony. *Cognitive Development, 22,* 185–196.

Suitor, J. J., Con, G., Johnson, K., Peng, S., & Gilligan, M. (2016). Parent–child relations. In S. Whitbourne (Ed.), *Encyclopedia of adulthood and aging* (Vol. 3, pp. 1011–1015). Malden, MA: Wiley Blackwell.

Suitor, J. J., Gilligan, M., Johnson, K., & Pillemer, K. (2013). Caregiving, perceptions of maternal favoritism, and tension among siblings. *Gerontologist, 54,* 580–588.

Suitor, J. J., Gilligan, M., & Pillemer, K. (2015). Stability, change, and complexity in later life families. In L. K. George & K. F. Ferraro (Eds.), *Handbook of aging and the social sciences* (8th ed., pp. 205–226). New York: Elsevier.

Suitor, J. J., Sechrist, J., Plikuhn, M., Pardo, S. T., Gilligan, M., & Pillemer, K. (2009). The role of perceived maternal favoritism in sibling relations in midlife. *Journal of Marriage and Family, 71,* 1026–1038.

Sullivan, A. R. (2010). Mortality differentials and religion in the United States: Religious affiliation and attendance. *Journal for the Scientific Study of Religion, 49,* 740–753.

Sullivan, A. R., & Fenelon, A. (2014). Patterns of widowhood mortality. *Journals of Gerontology, 69B,* 53–62.

Sullivan, J., Beech, A. R., Craig, L. A., & Gannon, T. A. (2011). Comparing intra-familial and extra-familial child sexual abusers with professionals who have sexually abused children with whom they work. *International Journal of Offender Therapy and Comparative Criminology, 55,* 56–74.

Sullivan, K. J., & Elias, M. F. (2016). Vascular dementia. In S. K. Whitbourne (Ed.), *Encyclopedia of adulthood and aging* (Vol. 3, pp. 1417–1421). Malden, MA: Wiley Blackwell.

Sullivan, K. T., Pasch, L. A., Johnson, M. D., & Bradbury, T. N. (2010). Social support, problem solving, and the longitudinal course of newlywed marriage. *Journal of Personality and Social Psychology, 98,* 631–644.

Sullivan, M. C., McGrath, M. M. Hawes, K., & Lester, B. M. (2008). Growth trajectories of preterm infants: Birth to 12 years. *Journal of Pediatric Health Care, 22,* 83–93.

Sulliveram, M. W., & Lewis, M. (2003). Contextual determinants of anger and other negative expressions in young infants. *Developmental Psychology, 39,* 693–705.

Sullivan, P. F., Daly, M. J., & O'Donovan, M. (2012). Genetic architectures of psychiatric disorders: The emerging picture and its implications. *Nature Reviews Genetics, 13,* 537–551.

Sun, H., Ma, Y., Han, D., Pan, C. W., & Xu, Y. (2014). Prevalence and trends in obesity among China's children and adolescents, 1985–2010. *PLOS ONE, 9*(8), e105469.

Sunderam, S., Kissin, D. M., Crawford, S. B., Folger, S. G., Jamieson, D. J., Warner, L., et al. (2015). Assisted reproductive technology surveillance—United States, 2012. *Morbidity and Mortality Weekly Report, 64*(SS06), 1–29. Retrieved from www.cdc.gov/mmwr/preview/mmwrhtml/ss6406a1.htm

Sundet, J. M., Barlaug, D. G., & Torjussen, T. M. (2004). The end of the Flynn effect? A study of secular trends in mean intelligence test scores of Norwegian conscripts during half a century. *Intelligence, 32,* 349–362.

Super, C. M. (1981). Behavioral development in infancy. In R. H. Monroe, R. L. Monroe, & B. B. Whiting (Eds.), *Handbook of cross-cultural human development* (pp. 181–270). New York: Garland.

Super, C. M., & Harkness, S. (2009). The developmental niche of the newborn in rural Kenya. In J. K. Nugent, B. J. Petrauskas, & T. B. Brazelton (Eds.), *The newborn as a person: Enabling healthy development worldwide* (pp. 85–97). Hoboken, NJ: Wiley.

Super, C. M., & Harkness, S. (2010). Culture and infancy. In J. G. Bremner & T. D. Wachs (Eds.), *Wiley-Blackwell handbook of infant development: Vol. 1. Basic research* (2nd ed., pp. 623–649). Oxford, UK: Wiley-Blackwell.

Super, C. M., Harkness, S., van Tijen, N., van der Vlugt, E., Fintelman, M., & Dijkstra, J. (1996). The three R's of Dutch childrearing and the socialization of infant arousal. In S. Harkness & C. M. Super (Eds.), *Parents' cultural belief systems* (pp. 447–466). New York: Guilford.

Super, D. E. (1994). A life span, life space perspective on convergence. In M. L. Savikas & R. W. Lent (Eds.), *Convergence in career development theories* (pp. 62–71). Palo Alto, CA: Consulting Psychologists Press.

Supple, A. J., Ghazarian, S. R., Peterson, G. W., & Bush, K. R. (2009). Assessing the cross-cultural validity of a parental autonomy granting measure: Comparing adolescents in the United States, China, Mexico, and India. *Journal of Cross-Cultural Psychology, 40,* 816–833.

Supple, A. J., & Small, S. A. (2006). The influence of parental support, knowledge, and authoritative parenting on Hmong and European American adolescent development. *Journal of Family Issues, 27,* 1214–1232.

Susman, E. J., & Dorn, L. D. (2009). Puberty: Its role in development. In R. M. Lerner & L. Steinberg (Eds.), *Handbook of adolescent psychology: Vol. 1. Individual bases of adolescent development* (3rd ed., pp. 116–151). Hoboken, NJ: Wiley.

Sussman, S., Pokhrel, P., Ashmore, R. D., & Brown, B. B. (2007). Adolescent peer group identification and characteristics: A review of the literature. *Addictive Behaviors, 32,* 1602–1627.

Sussman, S., Skara, S., & Ames, S. L. (2008). Substance abuse among adolescents. *Substance Use and Misuse, 43,* 1802–1828.

Sutin, A. R., & Terracciano, A. (2013). Perceived weight discrimination and obesity. *PLOS ONE, 8*(7), e70048.

Suzuki, K., & Ando, J. (2014). Genetic and environmental structure of individual differences in hand, foot, and ear preferences: A twin study. *Laterality, 19,* 113–128.

Sveen, C.-A., & Walby, F. A. (2008). Suicide survivors' mental health and grief reactions: A systematic review of controlled studies. *Suicide and Life-Threatening Behavior, 38,* 13–29.

Swain, M. E. (2014). Surrogacy and gestational carrier arrangements: Legal aspects. In J. M. Goldfarb (Ed.), *Third-party reproduction* (pp. 133–142). New York: Springer.

Swank, E., Frost, D. M., & Fahs, B. (2012). Rural location and exposure to minority stress among sexual minorities in the United States. *Psychology & Sexuality, 3,* 226–243.

Swedish Institute. (2016). *Elderly care: A challenge for the future.* Retrieved from sweden.se/wp-content/uploads/2013/11/Elderly-care-low-resolution.pdf

Sweet, M. A., & Appelbaum, M. L. (2004). Is home visiting an effective strategy? A meta-analytic review of home visiting programs for families with young children. *Child Development, 75,* 1435–1456.

Sweet, S., & Moen, P. (2007). Integrating educational careers in work and family. *Community, Work and Family, 10,* 231–250.

Swinson, J., & Harrop, A. (2009). Teacher talk directed to boys and girls and its relationship to their behaviour. *Educational Studies, 35,* 515–524.

Syed, M., & Juan, M. J. D. (2012). Birds of an ethnic feather? Ethnic identity homophily among college-age friends. *Journal of Adolescence, 35,* 1505–1514.

Syvertsen, A. K., Wray-Lake, L., Flanagan, C. A., Osgood, D. W., & Briddell, L. (2011). Thirty-year trends in U.S. adolescents' civic engagement: A story of changing participation and educational differences. *Journal of Research on Adolescence, 21,* 586–594.

Szaflarski, J. P., Rajogopal, A., Altaye, M., Byars, A. W., Jacola, L., Schmithorst, V. J., et al. (2012). Left-handedness and language lateralization in children. *Brain Research, 1433,* 85–97.

T

Taber-Thomas, B., & Perez-Edgar, K. (2016). Emerging adulthood brain development. In J. J. Arnett (Ed.), *Oxford handbook of emerging adulthood* (pp. 126–141). New York: Oxford University Press.

Tabibi, Z., & Pfeffer, K. (2007). Finding a safe place to cross the road: The effect of distractors and the role of attention in children's identification of safe and dangerous road-crossing sites. *Infant and Child Development, 16,* 193–206.

Taga, G., Asakawa, K., Maki, A., Konishi, Y., & Koizumi, H. (2003). Brain imaging in awake infants by near-infrared optical topography. *Proceedings of the National Academy of Sciences, 100,* 10722–10727.

Tager-Flusberg, H. (2014). Autism spectrum disorder: Developmental approaches from infancy through early childhood. In M. Lewis & K. D. Rudolph

(Eds.), *Handbook of Developmental Psychopathology* (pp. 651–664). New York: Springer.

Tahir, L., & Gruber, H. E. (2003). Developmental trajectories and creative work in late life. In J. Demick & C. Andreoletti (Eds.), *Handbook of adult development* (pp. 239–255). New York: Springer.

Takagi, E., & Silverstein, M. (2011). Purchasing piety? Coresidence of married children with their older parents in Japan. *Demography, 48,* 1559–1579.

Takahashi, K. (1990). Are the key assumptions of the "Strange Situation" procedure universal? A view from Japanese research. *Human Development, 33,* 23–30.

Takahashi, T. A., & Johnson, K. M. (2015). Menopause. *Medical Clinics of North America, 99,* 521–534.

Talaulikar, V. S., & Arulkumaran, S. (2011). Folic acid in obstetric review. *Obstetrics and Gynecological Survey, 66,* 240–247.

Talwar, V. (2011). Talking to children about death in educational settings. In V. Talwar, P. L. Harris, & M. Schleifer (Eds.), *Children's understanding of death: From biological to religious conceptions* (pp. 98–115). Cambridge, UK: Cambridge University Press.

Tamis-LeMonda, C. S., & Bornstein, M. H. (1989). Habituation and maternal encouragement of attention in infancy as predictors of toddler language, play, and representational competence. *Child Development, 60,* 738–751.

Tamis-LeMonda, C. S., & McFadden, K. E. (2010). The United States of America. In M. H. Bornstein & T. Leventhal (Eds.), *Handbook of cultural developmental science: Vol. 4. Ecological settings and processes* (pp. 299–322). New York: Psychology Press.

Tamm, L., Nakonezny, P. A., & Hughes, C. W. (2014). An open trial of metacognitive executive function training for young children with ADHD. *Journal of Attention Disorders, 18,* 551–559.

Tammelin, T., Näyhä, S., Hills, A. P., & Järvelin, M. (2003). Adolescent participation in sports and adult physical activity. *American Journal of Preventive Medicine, 24,* 22–28.

Tanaka, H., & Seals, D. R. (2003). Dynamic exercise performance in master athletes: Insight into the effects of primary human aging on physiological functional capacity. *Journal of Applied Physiology, 95,* 2152–2162.

Tanaka, H., & Seals, D. R. (2008). Endurance exercise performance in Masters athletes: Age associated changes and underlying physiological mechanisms. *Journal of Physiology, 586,* 55–63.

Tandon, S. D., Colon, L., Vega, P., Murphy, J., & Alonso, A. (2012). Birth outcomes associated with receipt of group prenatal care among low-income Hispanic women. *Journal of Midwifery & Women's Health, 57,* 476–481.

Tang, M. (2009). Examining the application of Holland's theory to vocational interests and choices of Chinese college students. *Journal of Career Assessment, 17,* 86–98.

Tangney, J. P., Stuewig, J., & Mashek, D. J. (2007). Moral emotions and moral behavior. *Annual Review of Psychology, 58,* 345–372.

Tanner, J. L. (2016). Mental health in emerging adulthood. In J. J. Arnett (Ed.), *Oxford handbook of emerging adulthood* (pp. 499–520). New York: Oxford University Press.

Tanner, J. L., & Arnett, J. J. (2011). Presenting "emerging adulthood": What makes it developmentally distinctive? In J. J. Arnett, M. Kloep, L. B. Hendry, & J. L. Tanner (Eds.), *Debating emerging adulthood: Stage or process?* (pp. 13–30). New York: Oxford University Press.

Tanner, J. L., Arnett, J. J., & Leis, J. A. (2009). Emerging adulthood: Learning and development during the first stage of adulthood. In M. C. Smith & N. DeFrates-Densch (Eds.), *Handbook of research on adult learning and development* (pp. 34–67). New York: Routledge.

Tanner, J. M., Healy, M., & Cameron, N. (2001). *Assessment of skeletal maturity and prediction of adult height (TW3 method)* (3rd ed.). Philadelphia: Saunders.

Taras, V., Sarala, R., Muchinsky, P., Kemmelmeier, M., Singelis, T. M., Avsec, A., et al. (2014). Opposite ends of the same stick? Multi-method test of the dimensionality of individualism and collectivism. *Journal of Cross-Cultural Psychology, 45,* 213–245.

Tardif, T., Fletcher, P., Liang, W., Zhang, Z., Kaciroti, N., & Marchman, V. A. (2008). Baby's first 10 words. *Developmental Psychology, 44,* 929–938.

Tarry-Adkins, J. L., Martin-Gronert, M. S., Chen, J. H., Cripps, R. L., & Ozanne, S. E. (2008). Maternal diet influences DNA damage, aortic telomere length, oxidative stress, and antioxidant defense capacity in rats. *FASEB Journal, 22,* 2037–2044.

Tarullo, A. R., Balsam, P. D., & Fifer, W. P. (2011). Sleep and infant learning. *Infant and Child Development, 20,* 35–46.

Taylor, C. A., Manganello, J. A., Lee, S. J., & Rice, J. C. (2010). Mother's spanking of 3-year-old children and subsequent risk of children's aggressive behavior. *Pediatrics, 125,* e1057–e1065.

Taylor, J. L. (2009). Midlife impacts of adolescent parenthood. *Journal of Family Issues, 30,* 484–510.

Taylor, M., Carlson, S. M., Maring, B. L., Gerow, L., & Charley, C. M. (2004). The characteristics and correlates of fantasy in school-age children: Imaginary companions, impersonation, and social understanding. *Developmental Psychology, 40,* 1173–1187.

Taylor, M. C., & Hall, J. A. (1982). Psychological androgyny: Theories, methods, and conclusions. *Psychological Bulletin, 92,* 347–366.

Taylor, M. G., & Lynch, S. M. (2011). Cohort differences and chronic disease profiles of differential disability trajectories. *Journals of Gerontology, 66B,* 729–738.

Taylor, M. G., Rhodes, M., & Gelman, S. A. (2009). Boys will be boys; cows will be cows: Children's essentialist reasoning about gender categories and animal species. *Child Development, 80,* 461–481.

Taylor, R. D. (2010). Risk and resilience in low-income African American families: Moderating effects of kinship social support. *Cultural Diversity and Ethnic Minority Psychology, 16,* 344–351.

Taylor, R. L. (2000). Diversity within African-American families. In D. H. Demo & K. R. Allen (Eds.), *Handbook of family diversity* (pp. 232–251). New York: Oxford University Press.

Taylor, W. C., Sallis, J. F., Lees, E., Hepworth, J. T., Feliz, K., Volding, D. C., et al. (2007). Changing social and built environments to promote physical activity: Recommendations from low-income, urban women. *Journal of Physical Activity and Health, 4,* 54–65.

Taylor, Z. E., Eisenberg, N., Spinrad, T. L., Eggum, N. D., & Sulik, M. J. (2013). The relations of ego-resiliency and emotion socialization to the development of empathy and prosocial behavior across early childhood. *Emotion, 15,* 822–831.

Tchkonia, T., Zhu, Y., van Deursen, J., Campisi, J., & Kirkland, J. L. (2013). Cellular senescence and the senescent secretory phenotype: Therapeutic opportunities. *Journal of Clinical Investigation, 123,* 966–972.

Team Up for Youth. (2014). *The perils of poverty: The health crisis facing our low-income girls ... and the power of sports to help.* Retrieved from www.afterschoolnetwork.org/sites/main/files/file-attachments/perils_poverty.pdf

Tecwyn, E. C., Thorpe, S. K. S., & Chappell, J. (2014). Development of planning in 4- to 10-year-old children: Reducing inhibitory demands does not improve performance. *Journal of Experimental Child Psychology, 125,* 85–101.

Telama, R., Yang, X., Viikari, J., Valimaki, I., Wanne, O., & Raitakari, O. (2005). Physical activity from childhood to adulthood: A 21-year tracking study. *American Journal of Preventive Medicine, 28,* 267–273.

Temple, C. M., & Shephard, E. E. (2012). Exceptional lexical skills but executive language deficits in school starters and young adults with Turner syndrome: Implications for X chromosome effects on brain function. *Brain and Language, 120,* 345–359.

Temple, J. L., Giacomelli, A. M., Roemmich, J. N., & Epstein, L. H. (2007). Overweight children habituate slower than nonoverweight children to food. *Physiology and Behavior, 9,* 250–254.

Templeton, L. (2011). Dilemmas facing grandparents with grandchildren affected by parental substance misuse. *Drugs: Education, Prevention, and Policy, 19,* 11–18.

ten Brummelhuis, L. L., ter Hoeven, C. L., De Jong, M. D. T., & Peper, B. (2013). Exploring the linkage between the home domain and absence from work: Health, motivation, or both? *Journal of Organizational Behavior, 34,* 273–290.

Tenenbaum, H. R., Hill, D., Joseph, N., & Roche, E. (2010). "It's a boy because he's painting a picture": Age differences in children's conventional and unconventional gender schemas. *British Journal of Psychology, 101,* 137–154.

Tenenbaum, H. R., & Leaper, C. (2002). Are parents' gender schemas related to their children's gender-related cognitions? A meta-analysis. *Developmental Psychology, 38,* 615–630.

Tenenbaum, H. R., & Leaper, C. (2003). Parent–child conversations about science: The socialization of gender inequities? *Developmental Psychology, 39,* 34–47.

Tenenbaum, H. R., Snow, C. E., Roach, K. A., & Kurland, B. (2005). Talking and reading science: Longitudinal data on sex differences in mother–child conversations in low-income families. *Journal of Applied Developmental Psychology, 26,* 1–19.

Tennstedt, S. L., & Unverzagt, F. W. (2013). The ACTIVE Study: Study overview and major findings. *Journal of Aging and Health, 25,* 3S–20S.

Teno, J. M., Gozalo, P. L., Bynum, J. P. W., Leland, N. E., Miller, S. C. Morden, N. E., et al. (2013). Change in end-of-life care for Medicare beneficiaries: Site of death, place of care, and health care transitions in 2000, 2005, and 2009. *JAMA, 209,* 470–477.

ten Tusscher, G. W., & Koppe, J. G. (2004). Perinatal dioxin exposure and later effects—a review. *Chemosphere, 54,* 1329–1336.

Teske, S. C. (2011). A study of zero tolerance policies in schools: A multi-integrated systems approach to improve outcomes for adolescents. *Journal of Child and Adolescent Psychiatric Nursing, 24,* 88–97.

Teti, D. M., Saken, J. W., Kucera, E., & Corns, K. M. (1996). And baby makes four: Predictors of attachment security among preschool-age firstborns during the transition to siblinghood. *Child Development, 67,* 579–596.

Thakur, G. A., Sengupta, S. M., Grizenko, N., Schmitz, N., Pagé, V., & Joober, R. (2013). Maternal smoking during pregnancy and ADHD: A comprehensive clinical and neurocognitive characterization. *Nicotine & Tobacco Research, 15,* 149–157.

Tharenou, P. (2013). The work of feminists is not yet done: The gender pay gap—a stubborn anachronism. *Sex Roles, 68,* 198–206.

Tharpar, A., Collishaw, S., Pine, D. S., & Tharpar, A. K. (2012). Depression in adolescence. *Lancet, 379,* 1056–1066.

Thatcher, R. W., Walker, R. A., & Giudice, S. (1987). Human cerebral hemispheres develop at different rates and ages. *Science, 236,* 1110–1113.

Thelen, E., Fisher, D. M., & Ridley-Johnson, R. (1984). The relationship between physical growth and a newborn reflex. *Infant Behavior and Development, 7,* 479–493.

Thelen, E., Schöner, G., Scheier, C., & Smith, L. B. (2001). The dynamics of embodiment: A field theory of infant perseverative reaching. *Behavioral and Brain Sciences, 24,* 1–34.

Thelen, E., & Smith, L. B. (1998). Dynamic systems theories. In R. M. Lerner (Ed.), *Handbook of child psychology: Vol. 1. Theoretical models of human development* (5th ed., pp. 563–634). New York: Wiley.

Thelen, E., & Smith, L. B. (2006). Dynamic systems theories. In R. M. Lerner (Ed.), *Handbook of child psychology: Vol. 1. Theoretical models of human development* (6th ed., pp. 258–312). Hoboken, NJ: Wiley.

Thiessen, E. D., & Saffran, J. R. (2007). Learning to learn: Infants' acquisition of stress-based strategies for work segmentation. *Language Learning and Development, 3,* 73–100.

Thoermer, C., Woodward, A., Sodian, B., & Perst, H. (2013). To get the grasp: Seven-month-olds encode and selectively reproduce goal-directed grasping. *Journal of Experimental Child Psychology, 116,* 499–509.

Thomaes, S., Brummelman, E., Reijntjes, A., & Bushman, B. J. (2013). When Narcissus was a boy: Origins, nature, and consequences of childhood narcissism. *Child Developmental Perspectives, 7,* 22–26.

Thomaes, S., Stegge, H., Bushman, B. J., & Olthof, T. (2008). Trumping shame by blasts of noise: Narcissism, self-esteem, shame, and aggression in young adolescents. *Child Development, 79,* 1792–1801.

Thomas, A., & Chess, S. (1977). *Temperament and development.* New York: Brunner/Mazel.

Thomas, H. N., Hess, R., & Thurston, R. C. (2015). Correlates of sexual activity and satisfaction in midlife and older women. *Annals of Family Medicine, 13,* 336–342.

Thomas, K. A., & Tessler, R. C. (2007). Bicultural socialization among adoptive families: Where there is a will, there is a way. *Journal of Family Issues, 28,* 1189–1219.

Thomas, S. R., O'Brien, K. A., Clarke, T. L., Liu, Y., & Chronis-Tuscano, A. (2015). Maternal depression history moderates parenting responses to compliant and noncompliant behaviors of children with ADHD. *Journal of Abnormal Child Psychology, 43,* 1257–1269.

Thombs, B. D., Roseman, M., & Arthurs, E. (2010). Prenatal and postpartum depression in fathers and mothers. *JAMA, 304,* 961.

Thomeer, M. B., Mudrazija, S., & Angel, J. L. (2014). How do race and Hispanic ethnicity affect nursing home admission? Evidence from the Health and Retirement Study. *Journals of Gerontology, 70B,* 628–638.

Thompson, A., Hollis, C., & Richards, D. (2003). Authoritarian parenting attitudes as a risk for conduct problems: Results of a British national cohort study. *European Child and Adolescent Psychiatry, 12,* 84–91.

Thompson, J., & Lakhani, N. (2015). Cataracts. *Primary Care, 42,* 409–423.

Thompson, J. M., Waldie, K. E., Wall, C. R., Murphy, R., & Mitchell, E. A. (2014). Associations between acetaminophen use during pregnancy and ADHD symptoms measured at ages 7 and 11 years. *PLOS ONE, 9,* e108210.

Thompson, P. M., Giedd, J. N., Woods, R. P., MacDonald, D., Evans, A. C., & Toga, A. W. (2000). Growth patterns in the developing brain detected by using continuum mechanical tensor maps. *Nature, 404,* 190–192.

Thompson, R. A. (2006). The development of the person: Social understanding, relationships, conscience, self. In N. Eisenberg (Ed.), *Handbook of child psychology: Vol. 3. Social, emotional, and personality development* (6th ed., pp. 24–98). Hoboken, NJ: Wiley.

Thompson, R. A. (2013). Attachment theory and research: Précis and prospect. In P. D. Zelazo (Ed.), *Oxford handbook of developmental psychology: Vol. 2. Self and other* (pp. 191–216). New York: Oxford University Press.

Thompson, R. A. (2014). Conscience development in early childhood. In M. Killen & J. G. Smetana (Eds.), *Handbook of moral development* (2nd ed., pp. 73–92). New York: Psychology Press.

Thompson, R. A. (2015). Relationships, regulation, and early development. In M. E. Lamb (Ed.), *Handbook of child psychology and developmental science: Vol. 3. Socioemotional processes* (7th ed., pp. 201–246). Hoboken, NJ: Wiley.

Thompson, R. A., & Goodman, M. (2010). Development of emotion regulation: More than meets the eye. In A. M. Kring & D. M. Sloan (Eds.), *Emotion regulation and psychopathology: A transdiagnostic approach to etiology and treatment* (pp. 38–58). New York: Guilford.

Thompson, R. A., & Goodvin, R. (2007). Taming the tempest in the teapot. In C. A. Brownell & C. B. Kopp (Eds.), *Socioemotional development in the toddler years: Transitions and transformations* (pp. 320–341). New York: Guilford.

Thompson, R. A., & Meyer, S. (2007). Socialization of emotion regulation in the family. In J. J. Gross (Ed.), *Handbook of emotion regulation* (pp. 249–268). New York: Guilford.

Thompson, R. A., Meyer, S., & McGinley, M. (2006). Understanding values in relationships: The development of conscience. In M. Killen & J. G. Smetana (Eds.), *Handbook of moral development* (pp. 267–298). Mahwah, NJ: Erlbaum.

Thompson, R. A., & Nelson, C. A. (2001). Developmental science and the media. *American Psychologist, 56,* 5–15.

Thompson, R. A., Winer, A. C., & Goodvin, R. (2011). The individual child: Temperament, emotion, self, and personality. In M. H. Bornstein & M. E. Lamb (Eds.), *Developmental science: An advanced textbook* (6th ed., pp. 427–468). Hoboken, NJ: Taylor & Francis.

Thompson, W. W., Price, C., Goodson, B., Shay, D. K., Benson, P., Hinrichsen, V. L., et al. (2007). Early thimerosal exposure and neuropsychological outcomes at 7 to 10 years. *New England Journal of Medicine, 357,* 1281–1292.

Thorne, B. (1993). *Gender play: Girls and boys in school.* New Brunswick, NJ: Rutgers University Press.

Thornton, K., Chervenak, J., & Neal-Perry, G. (2015). Menopause and sexuality. *Endocrinology and Metabolism Clinics of North America, 44,* 649–661.

Thornton, L. M., Mazzeo, S. E., & Bulik, C. M. (2011). The heritability of eating disorders: Methods and current findings. In R. A. H. Adan & W. H. Kaye (Eds.), *Behavioral neurobiology of eating disorders* (pp. 141–156). New York: Springer.

Thornton, M. J. (2013). Estrogens and aging skin. *Dermato-Endocrinology, 5,* 264–270.

Thornton, S. (1999). Creating conditions for cognitive change: The interaction between task structures and specific strategies. *Child Development, 70,* 588–603.

Thornton, W. L., Paterson, T. S. E., & Yeung, S. E. (2013). Age differences in everyday problem solving: The role of problem context. *International Journal of Behavioral Development, 37,* 13–20.

Thorson, J. A., & Powell, F. C. (1994). A revised death anxiety scale. In R. A. Neimeyer (Ed.), *Death anxiety handbook* (pp. 31–43). Washington, DC: Taylor & Francis.

Tien, A. (2013). Bootstrapping and the acquisition of Mandarin Chinese: A natural semantic metalanguage perspective. In D. Bittner & N. Ruhlig (Eds.), *Lexical bootstrapping: The role of lexis and semantics in child language* (pp. 39–72). Berlin: Walter de Gruyter.

Tienari, P., Wahlberg, K. E., & Wynne, L. C. (2006). Finnish adoption study of schizophrenia: Implications for family interventions. *Families, Systems, and Health, 24,* 442–451.

Tienari, P., Wynne, L. C., Lasky, K., Moring, J., Nieminen, P., & Sorri, A. (2003). Genetic boundaries of the schizophrenia spectrum: Evidence from the Finnish adoptive family study of schizophrenia. *American Journal of Psychiatry, 160,* 1587–1594.

Tiggemann, M., & Anesbury, T. (2000). Negative stereotyping of obesity in children: The role of controllability beliefs. *Journal of Applied Social Psychology, 30,* 1977–1993.

Tincoff, R., & Jusczyk, P. W. (1999). Some beginnings of word comprehension in 6-month-olds. *Psychological Science, 10,* 172–175.

Tishkoff, S. A., & Kidd, K. K. (2004). Implications of biogeography of human populations for "race" and medicine. *Nature Genetics, 36*(Suppl. 11), S21–S27.

Tizard, B., & Rees, J. (1975). The effect of early institutional rearing on the behaviour problems and affectional relationships of four-year-old children. *Journal of Child Psychology and Psychiatry, 16,* 61–73.

Tomasello, M. (2003). *Constructing a language: A usage-based theory of language acquisition.* Cambridge, MA: Harvard University Press.

Tomasello, M. (2006). Acquiring linguistic constructions. In D. Kuhn & R. Siegler (Eds.), *Handbook of child psychology: Vol. 2. Cognition, perception, and language* (6th ed., pp. 255–298). Hoboken, NJ: Wiley.

Tomasello, M. (2011). Language development. In U. Goswami (Ed.), *Wiley-Blackwell handbook of childhood cognitive development* (2nd ed., pp. 239–257). Malden, MA: Wiley-Blackwell.

Tomasello, M., & Akhtar, N. (1995). Two-year-olds use pragmatic cues to differentiate reference to objects and actions. *Cognitive Development, 10,* 201–224.

Tomasello, M., Call, J., & Hare, B. (2003). Chimpanzees understand psychological states—the question is which ones and to what extent. *Trends in Cognitive Sciences, 7,* 153–156.

Tomasello, M., Carpenter, M., & Liszkowski, U. (2007). A new look at infant pointing. *Child Development, 78,* 705–722.

Tomasetto, C., Alparone, F. R., & Cadinu, M. (2011). Girls' math performance under stereotype threat: The moderating role of mothers' gender stereotypes. *Developmental Psychology, 47,* 943–949.

Tomer, A., Eliason, G., & Smith, J. (2000). Beliefs about the self, life, and death: Testing aspects of a comprehensive model of death anxiety and death attitudes. In A. Tomer (Ed.), *Death attitudes and the older adult: Theories, concepts, and applications* (pp. 109–122). Philadelphia: Taylor & Francis.

Tomyr, L., Ouimet, C., & Ugnat, A. (2012). A review of findings from the Canadian Incidence Study of reported child abuse and neglect. *Canadian Journal of Public Health, 103,* 103–112.

Tong, S., Baghurst, P., Vimpani, G., & McMichael, A. (2007). Socioeconomic position, maternal IQ, home environment, and cognitive development. *Journal of Pediatrics, 151,* 284–288.

Torges, C. M., Stewart, A. J., & Miner-Rubino, K. (2005). Personality after the prime of life: Men and women coming to terms with regrets. *Journal of Research in Personality, 39,* 148–165.

Torney-Purta, J., Barber, C. H., & Wilkenfeld, B. (2007). Latino adolescents' civic development in the United States: Research results from the IEA Civic Education Study. *Journal of Youth and Adolescence, 36,* 111–125.

Tornstam, L. (2000). Transcendence in later life. *Generations, 23*(10), 10–14.

Tornstam, L. (2011). Maturing into gerotranscendence. *Journal of TransPersonal Psychology, 43,* 166–180.

Toro-Morn, M., & Sprecher, S. (2003). A cross-cultural comparison of mate preferences among university students: The United States vs. the People's Republic of China (PRC). *Journal of Comparative Family Studies, 34,* 151–170.

Torquati, J. C., Raikes, H. H., Huddleston-Casas, C. A., Bovaird, J. A., & Harris, B. A. (2011). Family income, parent education, and perceived constraints as predictors of observed program quality and parent rated program quality. *Early Childhood Research Quality, 26,* 453–464.

Torrance, E. P. (1988). The nature of creativity as manifest in its testing. In R. J. Sternberg (Ed.), *The nature of creativity: Contemporary psychological perspectives* (pp. 43–75). New York: Cambridge University Press.

Tottenham, N., Hare, T. A., & Casey, B. J. (2009). A developmental perspective on human amygdala function. In P. J. Whalen & E. A. Phelps (Eds.), *The human amygdala* (pp. 107–117). New York: Guilford.

Tottenham, N., Hare, T. A., Millner, A., Gilhooly, T., Zevin, J. D., & Casey, B. J. (2011). Elevated amygdala response to faces following early deprivation. *Developmental Science, 14,* 190–204.

Tracy, J. L., Robins, R. W., & Lagattuta, K. H. (2005). Can children recognize pride? *Emotion, 5,* 251–257.

Tran, P., & Subrahmanyam, K. (2013). Evidence-based guidelines for informal use of computers by children to promote the development of academic, cognitive and social skills. *Ergonomics, 56,* 1349–1362.

Trappe, S. (2007). Marathon runners: How do they age? *Sports Medicine, 37,* 302–305.

Träuble, B., & Pauen, S. (2011). Cause or effect: What matters? How 12-month-old infants learn to categorize artifacts. *British Journal of Developmental Psychology, 29,* 357–374.

Trautner, H. M., Ruble, D. N., Cyphers, L., Kirsten, B., Behrendt, R., & Hartmann, P. (2005). Rigidity and flexibility of gender stereotypes in childhood: Developmental or differential? *Infant and Child Development, 14,* 365–381.

Treas, J., & Tai, T. (2016). Gender inequality in housework across 20 European nations: Lessons from gender stratification theories. *Sex Roles, 74,* 495–511.

Trehub, S. E. (2001). Musical predispositions in infancy. *Annals of the New York Academy of Sciences, 930,* 1–16.

Tremblay, R. E. (2000). The development of aggressive behaviour during childhood: What have we learned in the past century? *International Journal of Behavioral Development, 24,* 129–141.

Trenholm, C., Devaney B., Fortson, K., Clark, M., Quay, L., & Wheeler, J. (2008). Impacts of abstinence education on teen sexual activity, risk of pregnancy, and risk of sexually transmitted diseases. *Journal of Policy Analysis and Management, 27,* 255–276.

Trentacosta, C. J., & Shaw, D. S. (2009). Emotional self-regulation, peer rejection, and antisocial behavior: Developmental associations from early childhood to early adolescence. *Journal of Applied Developmental Psychology, 30,* 356–365.

Triandis, H. C., & Gelfand, M. J. (2012). A theory of individualism and collectivism. In P. A. M. Van Lange, A. W. Kruglanski, & E. T. Higgins (Eds.), *Handbook of theories of social psychology* (Vol. 2, pp. 498–520). Thousand Oaks, CA: Sage.

Trickett, P. K., Noll, J. G., & Putnam, F. W. (2011). The impact of sexual abuse on female development: Lessons from a multigenerational, longitudinal research study. *Development and Psychopathology, 23,* 453–476.

Trocmé, N., & Wolfe, D. (2002). *Child maltreatment in Canada: The Canadian Incidence Study of Reported Child Abuse and Neglect.* Retrieved from www.hc-sc.gc.ca/pphb-dgspsp/cm-vee

Troilo, J., & Coleman, M. (2012). Full-time, part-time full-time, and part-time fathers: Father identities following divorce. *Family Relations, 61,* 601–614.

Tronick, E., & Lester, B. M. (2013). Grandchild of the NBAS: The NICU Network Neurobehavioral Scale (NNNS): A review of the research using the NNNS. *Journal of Child and Adolescent Psychiatric Nursing, 26,* 193–203.

Tronick, E., Morelli, G., & Ivey, P. (1992). The Efe forager infant and toddler's pattern of social relationships: Multiple and simultaneous. *Developmental Psychology, 28,* 568–577.

Tronick, E. Z., Thomas, R. B., & Daltabuit, M. (1994). The Quechua manta pouch: A caretaking practice for buffering the Peruvian infant against the multiple stressors of high altitude. *Child Development, 65,* 1005–1013.

Tropp, L. R., & Page-Gould, E. (2015). Contact between groups. In M. Mikulincer & P. R. Shaver (Eds.), *APA handbook of personality and social psychology: Vol. 2. Group processes* (pp. 535–560). Washington, DC: American Psychological Association.

Troop-Gordon, W., & Asher, S. R. (2005). Modifications in children's goals when encountering obstacles to conflict resolution. *Child Development, 76,* 568–582.

Troseth, G. L. (2003). Getting a clear picture: Young children's understanding of a televised image. *Developmental Science, 6,* 247–253.

Troseth, G. L., & DeLoache, J. S. (1998). The medium can obscure the message: Young children's understanding of video. *Child Development, 69,* 950–965.

Troseth, G. L., Saylor, M. M., & Archer, A. H. (2006). Young children's use of video as a source of socially relevant information. *Child Development, 77,* 786–799.

Troutman, D. R., & Fletcher, A. C. (2010). Context and companionship in children's short-term versus long-term friendships. *Journal of Social and Personal Relationships, 27,* 1060–1074.

Troyer, A. K., Häfliger, A., Cadieux, M. J., & Craik, F. I. M. (2006). Name and face learning in older adults: Effects of level of processing, self-generation, and intention to learn. *Journals of Gerontology, 61B,* P67–P74.

True, M. M., Pisani, L., & Oumar, F. (2001). Infant–mother attachment among the Dogon of Mali. *Child Development, 72,* 1451–1466.

Trzesniewski, K. H., & Donnellan, M. B. (2010). Rethinking "generation me": A study of cohort effects from 1976–2006. *Perspectives on Psychological Science, 5,* 58–75.

Trzesniewski, K. H., Donnellan, M. B., & Robins, R. W. (2003). Stability of self-esteem across the life span. *Journal of Personality and Social Psychology, 84,* 205–220.

Tsang, C. D., & Conrad, N. J. (2010). Does the message matter? The effect of song type on infants' pitch preferences for lullabies and playsongs. *Infant Behavior and Development, 33,* 96–100.

Tsang, P. S., & Shaner, T. L. (1998). Age, attention, expertise, and time-sharing performance. *Psychology and Aging, 13,* 323–347.

Turati, C., Cassia, V. M., Simion, F., & Leo, I. (2006). Newborns' face recognition: Role of inner and outer facial features. *Child Development, 77,* 297–311.

Turiel, E., & Killen, M. (2010). Taking emotions seriously: The role of emotions in moral development. In W. F. Arsenio & E. A. Lemerise (Eds.), *Emotions, aggression, and morality in children: Bridging development and psychopathology* (pp. 33–52). Washington, DC: American Psychological Association.

Turner, P. J., & Gervai, J. (1995). A multidimensional study of gender typing in preschool children and their parents: Personality, attitudes, preferences, behavior, and cultural differences. *British Journal of Developmental Psychology, 11,* 323–342.

Turner, R. N., Hewstone, M., & Voci, A. (2007). Reducing explicit and implicit outgroup prejudice via direct and extended contact: The mediating role of self-disclosure and intergroup anxiety. *Journal of Personality and Social Psychology, 93,* 369–388.

Tustin, K., & Hayne, H. (2010). Defining the boundary: Age-related changes in childhood amnesia. *Developmental Psychology, 46,* 1046–1061.

Tveito, M., Correll, C. U., Bramness, J. G., Engedal, K., Lorentzen, B., Refsum, H., et al. (2016). Correlates of major medication side effects interfering with daily performance: Results from a cross-sectional cohort study of older psychiatric patients. *International Psychogeriatrics, 28,* 331–340.

Twenge, J. M. (2001). Changes in women's assertiveness in response to status and roles: A crosstemporal meta-analysis, 1931–1993. *Journal of Personality and Social Psychology, 81,* 133–145.

Twenge, J. M. (2013). The evidence for Generation Me and against Generation We. *Emerging Adulthood, 1,* 11–16.

Twenge, J. M., & Crocker, J. (2002). Race and self-esteem: Meta-analyses comparing whites, blacks, Hispanics, Asians, and America Indians and comment on Gray-Little and Hafdahl (2000). *Psychological Bulletin, 128,* 371–408.

Twenge, J. M., Sherman, R. A., & Wells, B. E. (2015). Changes in American adults' sexual behavior and attitudes. *Archives of Sexual Behavior, 44,* 2273–2285.

Twyman, R. (2014). *Principles of proteomics* (2nd ed.). New York: Garland Science.

Tyler, C. P., Paneth, N., Allred, E. N., Hirtz, D., Kuban, K., McElrath, T., et al. (2012). Brain damage in preterm newborns and maternal medication: The ELGAN Study. *American Journal of Obstetrics and Gynecology, 207*(192), e1–9. Retrieved from www.ajog.org/article/S0002-9378(12)00713-2/pdfSummary

Tzuriel, D., & Egozi, G. (2010). Gender differences in spatial ability of young children: The effects of training and processing strategies. *Child Development, 81,* 1417–1430.

U

Uccelli, P., & Pan, B. A. (2013). Semantic development. In J. B. Gleason & N. B. Ratner (Eds.), *Development of language* (8th ed., pp. 89–119). Upper Saddle River, NJ: Pearson.

Uchino, B. N. (2009). Understanding the links between social support and physical health. *Perspectives on Psychological Science, 4,* 236–255.

Uhlenberg, P., & Hammill, B. G. (1998). Frequency of grandparent contact with grandchild sets: Six factors that make a difference. *Gerontologist, 38,* 276–285.

Ukrainetz, T. A., Justice, L. M., Kaderavek, J. N., Eisenberg, S. L., Gillam, R., & Harm, H. M. (2005). The development of expressive elaboration in fictional narratives. *Journal of Speech, Language, and Hearing Research, 48,* 1363–1377.

Underwood, M. K. (2003). *Social aggression among girls.* New York: Guilford.

Unger, C. C., Salam, S. S., Sarker, M. S. A., Black, R., Cravioto, A., & Arifeen, S. E. (2014). Treating diarrheal disease in children under five: The global picture. *Archives of Diseases of Childhood, 99,* 273–278.

UNICEF (United Nations Children's Fund). (2011). *Children in conflict and emergencies.* Retrieved from www.unicef.org/protection/armedconflict.html

UNICEF (United Nations Children's Fund). (2013). *UNICEF data: Monitoring the situation of children and women.* Retrieved from www.childinfo.org/statistical_tables.html

UNICEF (United Nations Children's Fund). (2015). *UNICEF data: Monitoring the situation of children and women—infant and young child feeding.* Retrieved from data.unicef.org/nutrition/iycf.html

United Nations. (2015). *World population prospects: Key findings & advance tables.* Retrieved from esa.un.org/unpd/wpp/Publications/Files/Key_Findings_WPP_2015.pdf

U.S. Bureau of Labor Statistics. (2016). *Volunteering in the United States, 2015.* Retrieved from www.bls.gov/news.release/volun.nr0.htm

U.S. Census Bureau. (2011). *Marital events of Americans: 2009.* Retrieved from www.census.gov/prod/2011pubs/acs-13.pdf

U.S. Census Bureau. (2014). *American Community Survey (ACS) 2014 release*. Retrieved from www.census.gov/programs-surveys/acs/news/data-releases.2014.html

U.S. Census Bureau. (2015a). *Families and living arrangements: Living arrangements of adults*. Retrieved from www.census.gov/hhes/families/data/adults.html

U.S. Census Bureau. (2015b). *Fertility of women in the United States: 2014*. Retrieved from http://www.census.gov/hhes/fertility/data/cps/2014.html

U.S. Census Bureau. (2015c). *International data base*. Retrieved from www.census.gov/population/international/data/idb/informationGateway.php

U.S. Census Bureau. (2015d). *Statistical Abstracts series*. Retrieved from www.census.gov/library/publications/time-series/statistical_abstracts.html

U.S. Census Bureau. (2016a). *America's families and living arrangements: 2015*. Retrieved from www.census.gov/hhes/families/data/cps2015.html

U.S. Census Bureau. (2016b). *Median age at first marriage: 1890 to present*. Retrieved from www.census.gov/hhes/families/files/graphics/MS-2.pdf

U.S. Census Bureau. (2016c). *Population estimates*. Retrieved from www.census.gov/popest/data/state/asrh/2015/index.html

U.S. Department of Agriculture. (2014). *Expenditures on children by families, 2013*. Retrieved from www.cnpp.usda.gov/sites/default/files/expenditures_on_children_by_families/crc2013.pdf

U.S. Department of Agriculture. (2015a). *Food security in the U.S.: Key statistics and graphics*. Retrieved from www.ers.usda.gov/topics/food-nutrition-assistance/food-security-in-the-us/key-statistics-graphics.aspx

U.S. Department of Agriculture. (2015b). *Women, Infants and Children (WIC): About WIC–WIC at a glance*. Retrieved from www.fns.usda.gov/wic/about-wic-wic-glance

U.S. Department of Agriculture. (2016). *Dietary guidelines for Americans 2015–2020* (8th ed.). Retrieved from www.cnpp.usda.gov/2015-2020-dietary-guidelines-americans

U.S. Department of Education. (2012a). *The nation's report card: Science 2011* (NCES 2012–465). Washington, DC: Institute of Education Sciences.

U.S. Department of Education. (2012b). *The nation's report card: Writing 2011* (NCES 2012–470). Washington, DC: Institute of Education Sciences.

U.S. Department of Education. (2015). *Digest of education statistics: 2013*. Washington, DC: U.S. Government Printing Office.

U.S. Department of Education. (2016). *The nation's report card: 2015 Mathematics and reading assessments, national results overview*. Retrieved from www.nationsreportcard.gov/reading_math_2015/#reading?grade=4

U.S. Department of Health and Human Services. (2006). *Research to practice: Preliminary findings from the Early Head Start Prekindergarten Follow-Up, Early Head Start Research and Evaluation Project*. Washington, DC: Author.

U.S. Department of Health and Human Services. (2010). *Head Start Impact Study: Final report*. Washington, DC: U.S. Government Printing Office.

U.S. Department of Health and Human Services. (2011). *Your guide to breastfeeding*. Retrieved from womenshealth.gov/publications/our-publications/breastfeeding-guide/BreastfeedingGuide-General-English.pdf

U.S. Department of Health and Human Services. (2014, April 3). *The TEDS Report: Gender differences in primary substance of abuse across age groups*. Retrieved from www.samhsa.gov/data/sites/default/files/sr077-gender-differences-2014.pdf

U.S. Department of Health and Human Services. (2015a). *Behavioral health trends in the United States: Results from the 2014 National Survey on Drug Use and Health* (HHS Publication No. SMA 15-4927, NSDUH Series H-50). Retrieved from www.samhsa.gov/data/sites/default/files/NSDUH-FRR1-2014/NSDUH-FRR1-2014.pdf

U.S. Department of Health and Human Services. (2015b). *Child health USA 2014*. Rockville, MD: Author. Retrieved from mchb.hrsa.gov/chusa14/dl/chusa14.pdf

U.S. Department of Health and Human Services. (2015c). *Child maltreatment: 2013*. Rockville, MD: Author. Retrieved from www.acf.hhs.gov/sites/default/files/cb/cm2013.pdf

U.S. Department of Health and Human Services. (2015d). *Health, United States, 2014*. Retrieved from www.cdc.gov/nchs/data/hus/hus14.pdf

U.S. Department of Health and Human Services. (2015e). *A profile of older Americans: 2014*. Retrieved from www.aoa.acl.gov/Aging_Statistics/Profile/2014/docs/2014-Profile.pdf

U.S. Department of Health and Human Services. (2015f). *What causes Down syndrome?* www.nichd.nih.gov/health/topics/down/conditioninfo/Pages/causes.aspx

U.S. Department of Health and Human Services. (2016a). *About teen pregnancy*. Retrieved from www.cdc.gov/teenpregnancy/about/index.htm

U.S. Department of Health and Human Services. (2016b). *Growing older in America: The health and retirement study*. Retrieved from www.nia.nih.gov/health/publication/growing-older-america-health-and-retirement-study/preface

U.S. Department of Health and Human Services. (2016c). *Long-term care providers and services users in the United States: Data from the National Study of Long-Term Care Providers, 2013–2014*. Vital and Health Statistics, Series 3, No. 38. Retrieved from www.cdc.gov/nchs/data/series/sr_03/sr03_038.pdf

U.S. Department of Justice. (2015). *Crime in the United States: 2014*. Retrieved from www.fbi.gov/about-us/cjis/ucr/crime-in-the-u.s/2014/crime-in-the-u.s.-2014

U.S. Department of Labor. (2015a). *College enrollment and work activity of 2014 high school graduates*. Retrieved from www.bls.gov/news.release/pdf/hsgec.toc.htm

U.S. Department of Labor. (2015b). Women in the labor force: A databook. *BLS Reports,* No. 1059. Retrieved from www.bls.gov/opub/reports/womens-databook/archive/women-in-the-labor-force-a-databook-2015.pdf

U.S. Department of Labor. (2016a). *Labor force statistics from the Current Population Survey: 11. Employed persons by detailed occupation, sex, race, and Hispanic or Latino ethnicity*. Retrieved from www.bls.gov/cps/cpsaat11.htm

U.S. Department of Labor. (2016b). *Occupational noise exposure*. Retrieved from www.osha.gov/SLTC/noisehearingconservation

U.S. Department of Transportation. (2014). *Traffic safety facts: Alcohol-impaired driving*. Retrieved from www-nrd.nhtsa.dot.gov/Pubs/812102.pdf

Usta, I. M., & Nassar, A. H. (2008). Advanced maternal age. Part I: Obstetric complications. *American Journal of Perinatology, 25,* 521–534.

Uttal, D. H., Meadow, N. G., Tipton, E., Hand, L. L., Alden, A. R., Warren, C., & Newcombe, N. S. (2013). The malleability of spatial skills: A meta-analysis of training studies. *Psychological Bulletin, 139,* 352–402.

Utz, R. L., & Tabler, J. (2016). Compression of morbidity. In S. K. Whitbourne (Ed.), *Encyclopedia of adulthood and aging* (Vol. 1, pp. 235–239). Malden, MA: Wiley Blackwell.

Uziel, Y., Chapnick, G., Oren-Ziv, A., Jaber, L., Nemet, D., & Hashkes, P. J. (2012). Bone strength in children with growing pains: Long-term follow-up. *Clinical and Experimental Rheumatology, 30,* 137–140.

V

Vacha-Haase, T., Hill, R. D., & Bermingham, D. W. (2012). Aging theory and research. In N. A. Fouad, J. A. Carter, & L. M. Subich (Eds.), *APA handbook of counseling psychology: Vol. 1. Theories, research, and methods* (pp. 491–505). Washington, DC: American Psychological Association.

Vaever, M. S., Krogh, M. T., Smith-Nielsen, J., Christensen, T. T., & Tharner, A. (2015). Infants of depressed mothers show reduced gaze activity during mother–infant interaction at 4 months. *Infancy, 20,* 445–454.

Vaillancourt, T., & Hymel, S. (2006). Aggression and social status: The moderating roles of sex and peer-valued characteristics. *Aggressive Behavior, 32,* 396–408.

Vaillancourt, T., Hymel, S., & McDougall, P. (2013). The biological underpinnings of peer victimization: Understanding why and how the effects of bullying can last a lifetime. *Theory into Practice, 52,* 241–248.

Vaillant, G. E. (1977). *Adaptation to life*. Boston: Little, Brown.

Vaillant, G. E. (2002). *Aging well*. Boston: Little, Brown.

Vaillant, G. E. (2012). *Triumphs of experience: The men of the Harvard Grant Study*. Cambridge, MA: Belknap Press.

Vaillant, G. E., & Mukamal, K. (2001). Successful aging. *American Journal of Psychiatry, 158,* 839–847.

Vaish, A., Missana, M., & Tomasello, M. (2011). Three-year-old children intervene in third-party moral transgressions. *British Journal of Developmental Psychology, 29,* 124–130.

Vaish, A., & Striano, T. (2004). Is visual reference necessary? Contributions of facial versus vocal cues in 12-month-olds' social referencing behavior. *Developmental Science, 7,* 261–269.

Vakil, E., Blachstein, H., Sheinman, M., & Greenstein, Y. (2009). Developmental changes in attention tests norms: Implications for the structure of attention. *Child Neuropsychology, 15,* 21–39.

Valentine, J. C., DuBois, D. L., & Cooper, H. (2004). The relation between self-beliefs and academic achievement: A meta-analytic review. *Educational Psychologist, 39,* 111–133.

Valian, V. (1999). Input and language acquisition. In W. C. Ritchie & T. K. Bhatia (Eds.), *Handbook of child language acquisition* (pp. 497–530). San Diego: Academic Press.

Valiente, C., Eisenberg, N., Fabes, R. A., Shepard, S. A., Cumberland, A., & Losoya, S. H. (2004). Prediction of children's empathy-related responding from their effortful control and parents' expressivity. *Developmental Psychology, 40,* 911–926.

Valiente, C., Lemery-Chalfant, K., & Swanson, J. (2010). Prediction of kindergartners' academic achievement from their effortful control and emotionality: Evidence for direct and moderated relations. *Journal of Educational Psychology, 102,* 550–560.

Valkenburg, P. M., & Peter, J. (2009). Social consequences of the Internet for adolescents: A decade of research. *Current Directions in Psychological Science, 18,* 1–5.

Valle, C. G., Tate, D. F., Mayer, D. K., Allicock, M., Cai, J., & Campbell, M. K. (2015). Physical activity in young adults: A signal detection analysis of Health Information National Trends Survey (HINTS) 2007 data. *Journal of Health Communication, 20,* 134–146.

Valli, L., Croninger, R. G., & Buese, D. (2012). Studying high-quality teaching in a highly charged policy environment. *Teachers College Record, 114*(4), 1–33.

van Aken, C., Junger, M., Verhoeven, M., van Aken, M. A. G., & Deković, M. (2007). The interactive effects of temperament and maternal parenting on toddlers' externalizing behaviours. *Infant and Child Development, 16,* 553–572.

van Baarsen, B. (2002). Theories on coping with loss: The impact of social support and self-esteem on adjustment to emotional and social loneliness following a partner's death in later life. *Journals of Gerontology, 57B,* S33–S42.

Van Beijsterveldt, C. E., Hudziak, J. J., & Boomsma, D. I. (2006). Genetic and environmental influences on cross-gender behavior and relation to behavior problems: A study of Dutch twins at ages 7 and 10 years. *Archives of Sexual Behavior, 35,* 647–658.

Vandell, D. L., Belsky, J., Burchinal, M., Steinberg, L., Vandergrift, N., & NICHD Early Child Care Research Network. (2010). Do effects of early child care extend to age 15 years? Results from the NICHD Study of Early Child Care and Youth Development. *Child Development, 81,* 737–756.

Vandell, D. L., & Posner, J. K. (1999). Conceptualization and measurement of children's after-school environments. In S. L. Friedman & T. D. Wachs (Eds.), *Measuring environment across the life span* (pp. 167–196). Washington, DC: American Psychological Association.

Vandell, D. L., Reisner, E. R., & Pierce, K. M. (2007). *Outcomes linked to high-quality after-school programs: Longitudinal findings from the Study of Promising After-School Programs.* Retrieved from www.gse.uci.edu/childcare/pdf/afterschool/PP%20Longitudinal%20Findings%20Final%20Report.pdf

Vandell, D. L., Reisner, E. R., Pierce, K. M., Brown, B. B., Lee, R., Bolt, D., & Pechman, E. M. (2006). *The study of promising after-school programs: Examination of longer term outcomes after two years of program experiences.* Madison, WI: University of Wisconsin. Retrieved from www.wcer.wisc.edu/childcare/statements.html

Vandell, D. L., & Shumow, L. (1999). After-school child care programs. *Future of Children, 9*(2), 64–80.

van den Akker, A. L. Deković, M., Prinzie, P., & Asscher, J. J. (2010). Toddlers' temperament profiles: Stability and relations to negative and positive parenting. *Journal of Abnormal Child Psychology, 38,* 485–495.

Van den Bergh, B. R. H., & De Rycke, L. (2003). Measuring the multidimensional self-concept and global self-worth of 6- to 8-year-olds. *Journal of Genetic Psychology, 164,* 201–225.

Vandenbosch, L., & Eggermont, S. (2013). Sexually explicit websites and sexual initiation: Reciprocal relationships and the moderating role of pubertal status. *Journal of Research on Adolescence, 23,* 621–634.

van den Dries, L., Juffer, F., van IJzendoorn, M. H., & Bakermans-Kranenburg, M. J. (2009). Fostering security? A meta-analysis of attachment in adopted children. *Children and Youth Services Review, 31,* 410–421.

van den Eijnden, R., Vermulst, A., van Rooij, A. J., Scholte, R., & van de Mheen, D. (2014). The bidirectional relationships between online victimization and psychosocial problems in adolescents: A comparison with real-life victimization. *Journal of Youth and Adolescence, 43,* 790–802.

Van der Heide, A. L. J., & Onwuteaka-Philipsen, B. (2012). *Second evaluation of the euthanasia law.* The Hague, Netherlands: ZonMw.

VanderLaan, D. P., Blanchard, R., Wood, H., & Zucker, K. J. (2014). Birth order and sibling sex ratio of children and adolescents referred to a gender identity service. *PLOS ONE, 9,* 1–9.

Van der Lippe, T. (2010). Women's employment and housework. In J. Treas & S. Drobnic (Eds.), *Dividing the Domestic: Men, women, and household work in cross-national perspective* (pp. 41–58). Stanford, CA: Stanford University Press.

van der Pers, M., Mulder, C. H., & Steverink, N. (2015). Geographic proximity of adult children and the well-being of older persons. *Research on Aging, 37,* 524–551.

van de Vijver, F. J. R. (2011). Bias and real difference in cross-cultural differences: Neither friends nor foes. In F. J. R. van de Vijver, A. Chasiotis, & H. F. Byrnes (Eds.), *Fundamental questions in cross-cultural psychology* (pp. 235–258). Cambridge, UK: Cambridge University Press.

Van Doorn, M. D., Branje, S. J. T., & Meeus, W. H. J. (2011). Developmental changes in conflict resolution styles in parent–adolescent relationships: A four-wave longitudinal study. *Journal of Youth and Adolescence, 40,* 97–107.

van Eeden-Moorefield, B., & Pasley, B. K. (2013). Remarriage and stepfamily life. In G. W. Peterson & K. R. Bush (Eds.), *Handbook of marriage and the family* (3rd ed., pp. 517–546). New York: Springer Science+Business Media.

Van Eyken, E., Van Camp, G., & Van Laer, L. (2007). The complexity of age-related hearing impairment: Contributing environmental and genetic factors. *Audiology and Neurotology, 12,* 345–358.

van Geel, M., & Vedder, P. (2011). The role of family obligations and school adjustment in explaining the immigrant paradox. *Journal of Youth and Adolescence, 40,* 187–196.

van Gelderen, L., Bos, H. M. W., Gartrell, N., Hermanns, J., & Perrin, E. C. (2012). Quality of life of adolescents raised from birth by lesbian mothers: The U.S. National Longitudinal Family Study. *Journal of Developmental and Behavioral Pediatrics, 33,* 17–23.

van Goethem, A. A. J., van Hoof, A., van Aken, M. A. G., de Castro, B. O., & Raaijmakers, Q. A. W. (2014). Socialising adolescent volunteering: How important are parents and friends? Age-dependent effects of parents and friends on adolescents' volunteering behaviours. *Journal of Applied Developmental Psychology, 35,* 94–101.

van Grieken, A., Renders, C. M., Wijtzes, A. I., Hirasing, R. A., & Raat, H. (2013). Overweight, obesity and underweight is associated with adverse psychosocial and physical health outcomes among 7-year-old children: The "Be Active, Eat Right" Study. *PLOS ONE, 8,* e67383.

Van Hiel, A., & Vansteenkiste, M. (2009). Ambitions fulfilled? The effects of intrinsic and extrinsic goal attainment on older adults' ego integrity and death attitudes. *International Journal of Aging and Human Development, 68,* 27–51.

Van Hulle, C. A., Goldsmith, H. H., & Lemery, K. S. (2004). Genetic, environmental, and gender effects on individual differences in toddler expressive language. *Journal of Speech, Language, and Hearing Research, 47,* 904–912.

van IJzendoorn, M. H., & Bakermans-Kranenburg, M. J. (2006). DRD4 7-repeat polymorphism moderates the association between maternal unresolved loss or trauma and infant disorganization. *Attachment and Human Development, 8,* 291–307.

van IJzendoorn, M. H., & Bakermans-Kranenburg, M. J. (2015). Genetic differential susceptibility on trial: Meta-analytic support from randomized controlled experiments. *Development and Psychopathology, 27,* 151–162.

van IJzendoorn, M. H., Bakermans-Kranenburg, M. J., & Ebstein, R. P. (2011). Methylation matters in child development: Toward developmental behavioral epigenetics. *Child Development Perspectives, 5,* 305–310.

van IJzendoorn, M. H., Belsky, J., & Bakermans-Kranenburg, M. J. (2012). Serotonin transporter genotype 5-HTTLPR as a marker of differential susceptibility: A meta-analysis of child and adolescent gene-by-environment studies. *Translational Psychiatry, 2,* e147.

van IJzendoorn, M. H., Juffer, F., & Poelhuis, C. W. K. (2005). Adoption and cognitive development: A meta-analytic comparison of adopted and nonadopted children's IQ and school performance. *Psychological Bulletin, 131,* 301–316.

van IJzendoorn, M. H., & Kroonenberg, P. M. (1988). Cross-cultural patterns of attachment: A meta-analysis of the Strange Situation. *Child Development, 59,* 147–156.

van IJzendoorn, M. H., & Sagi-Schwartz, A. (2008). Cross-cultural patterns of attachment: Universal and contextual dimensions. In J. Cassidy & P. R. Shaver (Eds.), *Handbook of attachment* (2nd ed., pp. 880–905). New York: Guilford.

van IJzendoorn, M. H., Vereijken, C. M. J. L., Bakermans-Kranenburg, M. J., & Riksen-Walraven, J. M. (2004). Assessing attachment security with the Attachment Q Sort: Meta-analytic evidence for the validity of the Observer AQS. *Child Development, 75,* 1188–1213.

Van Laningham, J., Johnson, D. R., & Amato, P. R. (2001). Marital happiness, marital duration, and the U-shaped curve: Evidence from a five-wave panel study. *Social Forces, 79,* 1313–1341.

van Solinge, H. (2013). Adjustment to retirement. In M. Wang (Ed.), *Oxford handbook of retirement* (pp. 311–324). New York: Oxford University Press.

van Solinge, H., & Henkens, K. (2008). Adjustment to and satisfaction with retirement: Two of a kind? *Psychology and Aging, 23,* 422–434.

Van Volkom, M. (2006). Sibling relationships in middle and older adulthood: A review of the literature. *Marriage and Family Review, 40,* 151–170.

Varnhagen, C. (2007). Children and the Web. In J. Gackenbach (Ed.), *Psychology and the Internet* (2nd ed., pp, 37–54). Amsterdam: Elsevier.

Värnik, P., Sisask, M., Värnik, A., Arensman, E., Van Audenhove, C., van deer Feltz-Cornelis, C. M., et al. (2012). Validity of suicide statistics in Europe in relation to undetermined deaths: Developing the 2–20 benchmark. *Injury Prevention, 18,* 321–325.

Vartanian, L. R., & Powlishta, K. K. (1996). A longitudinal examination of the social-cognitive foundations of adolescent egocentrism. *Journal of Early Adolescence, 16,* 157–178.

Vasilenko, S. A., Kugler, K. C., Butera, N. M., & Lanza, S. T. (2014). Patterns of adolescent sexual behavior predicting young adult sexually transmitted infections: A latent class analysis approach. *Archives of Sexual Behavior, 43,* ISSN 1573-2800.

Vaughn, B. E., Bost, K. K., & van IJzendoorn, M. H. (2008). Attachment and temperament. In J. Cassidy & P. R. Shaver (Eds.), *Handbook of attachment: Theory, research, and clinical applications* (2nd ed., pp. 192–216). New York: Guilford.

Vaughn, B. E., Kopp, C. B., & Krakow, J. B. (1984). The emergence and consolidation of self-control from eighteen to thirty months of age: Normative trends and individual differences. *Child Development, 55,* 990–1004.

Vazsonyi, A. T., Hibbert, J. R., & Snider, J. B. (2003). Exotic enterprise no more? Adolescent reports of family and parenting processes from youth in four countries. *Journal of Research on Adolescence, 13,* 129–160.

Vedova, A. M. (2014). Maternal psychological state and infant's temperament at three months. *Journal of Reproductive and Infant Psychology, 32,* 520–534.

Veenstra, R., Lindenberg, S., Munniksma, A., & Dijkstra, J. K. (2010). The complex relation between bullying, victimization, acceptance, and rejection: Giving special attention to status, affection, and sex differences. *Child Development, 81,* 480–486.

Velez, C. E., Wolchik, S. A., Tien, J., & Sandler, I. (2011). Protecting children from the consequences of divorce: A longitudinal study of the effects of parenting on children's coping processes. *Child Development, 82,* 244–257.

Venet, M., & Markovits, H. (2001). Understanding uncertainty with abstract conditional premises. *Merrill-Palmer Quarterly, 47,* 74–99.

Veneziano, R. A. (2003). The importance of paternal warmth. *Cross-Cultural Research, 37,* 265–281.

Verhaak, P. F. M., Dekkeer, J. H., de Waal, M. W. M., van Marwijk, H. W. J., & Comijs, H. C. (2014). Depression, disability and somatic diseases among elderly. *Journal of Affective Disorders, 167,* 187–191.

Verhaeghen, P. (2012). Working memory still working: Age-related differences in working-memory functioning and cognitive control. In M. Naveh-Benjamin & N. Ohta (Eds.), *Memory and aging: Current issues and future directions* (pp. 3–30). New York: Psychology Press.

Verhaeghen, P. (2014). *The elements of cognitive aging: Meta-analyses of age-related differences in processing speed and their consequences.* New York: Oxford University Press.

Verhaeghen, P. (2016). Working memory. In S. K. Whitbourne (Ed.), *Encyclopedia of adulthood and aging* (Vol. 3, pp. 1458–1463). Malden, MA: Wiley Blackwell.

Verhaeghen, P., & Cerella, J. (2002). Aging, executive control, and attention: A review of meta-analysis. *Neuroscience and Biobehavioral Reviews, 26,* 849–857.

Verhaeghen, P., & Cerella, J. (2008). Everything we know about aging and response times: A meta-analytic integration. In S. M. Hofer & D. F. Alwin (Eds.), *Handbook of cognitive aging: Interdisciplinary perspectives* (pp. 134–150). Thousand Oaks, CA: Sage.

Verhulst, F. C. (2008). International adoption and mental health: Long-term behavioral outcome. In M. E. Garralda & J.-P. Raynaud (Eds.), *Culture and conflict and adolescent mental health* (pp. 83–105). Lanham, MD: Jason Aronson.

Veríssimo, M., & Salvaterra, F. (2006). Maternal secure-base scripts and children's attachment security in an adopted sample. *Attachment and Human Development, 8,* 261–273.

Vernon-Feagans, L., & Cox, M. (2013). The Family Life Project: An epidemiological and developmental study of young children living in poor rural communities. *Monographs of the Society for Research in Child Development, 78*(5, Serial No. 310).

Versey, H. S., & Newton, N. J. (2013). Generativity and productive pursuits: Pathways to successful aging in late midlife African American and white women. *Journal of Adult Development, 20,* 185–196.

Vespa, J. (2012). Union formation in later life: Economic determinants of cohabitation and remarriage among older adults. *Demography, 49,* 1103–1125.

Vespa, J. (2014). Historical trends in the marital intentions of one-time and serial cohabitors. *Journal of Marriage and Family, 76,* 207–217.

Vest, A. R., & Cho, L. S. (2012). Hypertension in pregnancy. *Cardiology Clinics, 30,* 407–423.

Viddal, K. R., Berg-Nielsen, T. S., Wan, M. W., Green, J., Hygen, B. W., Wichstrøm, L., et al. (2015). Secure attachment promotes the development of effortful control in boys. *Attachment & Human Development, 17,* 319–335.

Vinden, P. G. (1996). Junín Quechua children's understanding of mind. *Child Development, 67,* 1707–1716.

Vinik, J., Almas, A., & Grusec, J. (2011). Mothers' knowledge of what distresses and what comforts their children predicts children's coping, empathy, and prosocial behavior. *Parenting: Science and Practice, 11,* 56–71.

Virant-Klun, I. (2015). Postnatal oogenesis in humans: A review of recent findings. *Stem Cells and Cloning: Advances and Applications, 8,* 49–60.

Visher, E. B., Visher, J. S., & Pasley, K. (2003). Remarriage, families and stepparenting. In F. Walsh (Ed.), *Normal family processes* (pp. 153–175). New York: Guilford.

Vistad, I., Cvancarova, M., Hustad, B. L., & Henriksen, T. (2013). Vaginal breech delivery: Results of a prospective registration study. *BMC Pregnancy and Children, 13,* 153.

Vitali, P., Migliaccio, R., Agosta, F., Rosen, H. J., & Geschwind, M. D. (2008). Neuroimaging in dementia. *Seminars in Neurology, 28,* 467–483.

Vitaro, F., Boivin, M., Brendgen, M., Girard, A., & Dionner, G. (2012). Social experiences in kindergarten and academic achievement in grade 1: A monozygotic twin difference study. *Journal of Educational Development, 2,* 366–380.

Vitaro, F., & Brendgen, M. (2012). Subtypes of aggressive behaviors: Etiologies, development, and consequences. In T. Bliesner, A. Beelmann, & M. Stemmler (Eds.), *Antisocial behavior and crime: Contributions of developmental and evaluation research to prevention and intervention* (pp. 17–38). Cambridge, MA: Hogrefe.

Vitrup, B., & Holden, G. W. (2010). Children's assessments of corporal punishment and other disciplinary practices: The role of age, race, SES, and exposure to spanking. *Journal of Applied Developmental Psychology, 31,* 211–220.

Vivian-Taylor, J., & Hickey, M. (2014). Menopause and depression: Is there a link? *Maturitas, 79,* 142–146.

Voegtline, K. M., Costigan, K. A., Pater, H. A., & DiPietro, J. A. (2013). Near-term fetal response to maternal spoken voice. *Infant Behavior and Development, 36,* 526–533.

Vogel, C. A., Xue, Y., Maiduddin, E. M., Carlson, B. L., & Kisker, E. E. (2010). *Early Head Start children in grade 5: Long-term follow-up of the Early Head Start Research and Evaluation Study sample* (OPRE Report No. 2011-8). Washington, DC: U.S. Department of Health and Human Services.

Volling, B. L. (2001). Early attachment relationships as predictors of preschool children's emotion regulation with a distressed sibling. *Early Education and Development, 12,* 185–207.

Volling, B. L. (2012). Family transitions following the birth of a sibling: An empirical review of changes in the firstborn's adjustment. *Psychological Bulletin, 138,* 497–528.

Volling, B. L., & Belsky, J. (1992). Contribution of mother–child and father–child relationships to the quality of sibling interaction: A longitudinal study. *Child Development, 63,* 1209–1222.

Volling, B. L., Mahoney, A., & Rauer, A. J. (2009). Sanctification of parenting, moral socialization, and young children's conscience development. *Psychology of Religion and Spirituality, 1,* 53–68.

Volling, B. L., McElwain, N. L., & Miller, A. L. (2002). Emotion regulation in context: The jealousy complex between young siblings and its relations with child and family characteristics. *Child Development, 73,* 581–600.

von Hofsten, C. (2004). An action perspective on motor development. *Trends in Cognitive Sciences, 8,* 266–272.

von Hofsten, C., & Rosander, K. (1998). The establishment of gaze control in early infancy. In S. Simion & S. G. Butterworth (Eds.), *The development of sensory, motor and cognitive capacities in early infancy* (pp. 49–66). Hove, UK: Psychology Press.

Vouloumanos, A. (2010). Three-month-olds prefer speech to other naturally occurring signals. *Language Learning and Development, 6,* 241–257.

Vranekovic, J., Bozovic, I. B., Grubic, Z., Wagner, J., Pavlinic, D., Dahoun, S., et al. (2012). Down syndrome: Parental origin, recombination, and maternal age. *Genetic Testing and Molecular Biomarkers, 16,* 70–73.

Vukasović, T., & Bratko, D. (2015). Heritability of personality: A meta-analysis of behavior genetic studies. *Psychological Bulletin, 141,* 769–785.

Vygotsky, L. S. (1978). *Mind in society: The development of higher mental processes.* Cambridge, MA: Harvard University Press. (Original works published 1930, 1933, and 1935)

Vygotsky, L. S. (1987). Thinking and speech. In R. W. Rieber & A. S. Carton (Eds.), & N. Minick (Trans.), *The collected works of L. S. Vygotsky: Vol. 1. Problems of general psychology* (pp. 37–285). New York: Plenum. (Original work published 1934)

W

Waber, D. P. (2010). *Rethinking learning disabilities.* New York: Guilford.

Waber, D. P., Bryce, C. P., Girard, J. M., Zichlin, M., Fitzmaurice, G. M., & Galler, J. R. (2014). Impaired IQ and academic skills in adults who experienced moderate to severe infantile malnutrition: A 40-year study. *Nutritional Neuroscience, 17,* 58–64.

Wadden, T. A., Webb, V. L., Moran, C. H., & Bailer, B. A. (2012). Lifestyle modification for obesity. *Circulation, 125,* 1157–1170.

Wadell, P. M., Hagerman, R. J., & Hessl, D. R. (2013). Fragile X syndrome: Psychiatric manifestations, assessment and emerging therapies. *Current Psychiatry Reviews, 9,* 53–58.

Wagenaar, K., van Wessenbruch, M. M., van Leeuwen, F. E., Cohen-Kettenis, P. T., Delemarre-van de Waal, H. A., Schats, R., et al. (2011). Self-reported behavioral and socioemotional functioning of 11- to 18-year-old adolescents conceived by in vitro fertilization. *Fertility and Sterility, 95,* 611–616.

Wahlheim, C. N., & Huff, M. J. (2015). Age differences in the focus of retrieval: Evidence from dual-list free recall. *Psychology and Aging, 30,* 768–780.

Wahlstrom, K., Dretzke, B., Gordon, M., Peterson, K., Edwards, K., & Gdula, J. (2014). *Examining the impact of later school start times on the health and academic performance of high school students: A multi-site study.* St Paul, MN: Center for Applied Research and Educational Improvement, University of Minnesota.

Wai, J. (2014). Experts are born, then made: Combining prospective and retrospective longitudinal data shows that cognitive ability matters. *Intelligence, 45,* 74–80.

Wai, J., Cacchio, M., Putallaz, M., & Makel, M. C. (2010). Sex differences in the right tail of cognitive abilities: A 30-year examination. *Intelligence, 38,* 412–423.

Wai, J., Lubinski, D., & Benbow, C. P. (2009). Spatial ability for STEM domains: Aligning over 50 years of cumulative psychological knowledge solidifies its importance. *Journal of Educational Psychology, 101,* 817–835.

Waite, L., & Das, A. (2013). Families, social life, and well-being at older ages. *Demography, 47,* S87–S109.

Waite, L. J., Laumann, E. O., Das, A., & Schumm, L. P. (2009). Sexuality: Measures of partnerships, practices, attitudes, and problems in the National Social Life, Health, and Aging Study. *Journals of Gerontology, 64B,* i56–i66.

Walberg, H. J. (1986). Synthesis of research on teaching. In M. C. Wittrock (Ed.), *Handbook of research on teaching* (3rd ed., pp. 214–229). New York: Macmillan.

Walden, T., Kim, G., McCoy, C., & Karrass, J. (2007). Do you believe in magic? Infants' social looking during violations of expectations. *Developmental Science, 10,* 654–663.

Waldfogel, J., Craigie, T. A., & Brooks-Gunn, J. (2010). Fragile families and child well-being. *Future of Children, 20,* 87–112.

Waldfogel, J., & Zhai, F. (2008). Effects of public preschool expenditures on the test scores of fourth graders: Evidence from TIMMS. *Educational Research and Evaluation, 14,* 9–28.

Waldorf, K. M. A., & McAdams, R. M. (2013). Influence of infection during pregnancy on fetal development. *Reproduction, 146,* R151–R162.

Walfisch, A., Sermer, C., Cressman, A., & Koren, G. (2013). Breast milk and cognitive *development—the role of confounders: A systematic review. British Medical Journal, 3,* e003259.

Walker, C. (2014). *Early Head Start participants, programs, families and staff in 2013.* Retrieved from www.clasp.org/resources-and-publications/publication-1/HSpreschool-PIR-2013-Fact-Sheet.pdf

Walker, C. M., Walker, L. B., & Ganea, P. A. (2012). The role of symbol-based experience in early learning and transfer from pictures: Evidence from Tanzania. *Developmental Psychology, 49,* 1315–1324.

Walker, J., Hansen, C. H., Martin, P., Symeonides, S., Ramessur, R., Murray, G., & Sharpe, M. (2014). Prevalence, associations, and adequacy of treatment of major depression in patients with cancer: A cross-sectional analysis of routinely collected clinical data. *Lancet Psychiatry, 1,* 343–350.

Walker, L. J. (1995). Sexism in Kohlberg's moral psychology? In W. M. Kurtines & J. L. Gewirtz (Eds.), *Moral development: An introduction* (pp. 83–107). Boston: Allyn and Bacon.

Walker, L. J. (2004). Progress and prospects in the psychology of moral development. *Merrill-Palmer Quarterly, 50,* 546–557.

Walker, L. J. (2006). Gender and morality. In M. Killen & J. G. Smetana (Eds.), *Handbook of moral development* (pp. 93–118). Philadelphia: Erlbaum.

Walker, L. J., & Taylor, J. H. (1991b). Stage transitions in moral reasoning: A longitudinal study of developmental processes. *Developmental Psychology, 27,* 330–337.

Walker, O. L., & Henderson, H. A. (2012). Temperament and social problem solving competence in preschool: Influences on academic skills in early elementary school. *Social Development, 21,* 761–779.

Walker, S. M. (2013). Biological and neurodevelopmental implications of neonatal pain. *Clinics in Perinatology, 40,* 471–491.

Wall, M., & Côté, J. (2007). Developmental activities that lead to dropout and investment in sport. *Physical Education and Sport Pedagogy, 12,* 77–87.

Wall, M. I., Carlson, S. A., Stein, A. D., Lee, S. M., & Fulton, J. E. (2011). Trends by age in youth physical activity: Youth Media Campaign Longitudinal Survey. *Medicine and Science in Sports and Exercise, 40,* 2140–2147.

Wallon, M., Peron, F., Cornu, C., Vinault, S., Abrahamowicz, M., Kopp C. B., et al. (2013). Congenital toxoplasma infections: Monthly prenatal screening decreases transmission rate and improves clinical outcome at age 3 years. *Clinics in Infectious Disease, 56,* 1223–1231.

Walsh, C. A., Ploeg, J., Lohfeld, L., Horne, J., MacMillan, H., & Lai, D. (2007). Violence across the lifespan: Interconnections among forms of abuse as described by marginalized Canadian elders and their caregivers. *British Journal of Social Work, 37,* 491–514.

Walsh, F., & McGoldrick, M. (2004). Loss and the family: A systemic perspective. In F. Walsh & M. McGoldrick (Eds.), *Living beyond loss: Death in the family* (2nd ed., pp. 3–26). New York: Norton.

Wanberg, C. R., Kanfer, R., Hamann, D. J., & Zhang, Z. (2016). Age and reemployment success after job loss: An integrative model and meta-analysis. *Psychological Bulletin, 142,* 400–426.

Wang, H.-X., Jin, Y., Hendrie, H. C., Liang, C., Yang, L., Cheng, Y., et al. (2013). Late life leisure activities and risk of cognitive decline. *Journals of Gerontology, 68A,* 205–213.

Wang, K.-Y., Kercher, K., Huang, J.-Y., & Kosloski, K. (2014). Aging and religious participation in late life. *Journal of Religious Health, 53,* 1514–1528.

Wang, M. (2007). Profiling retirees in the retirement transition and adjustment process: Examining the longitudinal change patterns of retirees' psychological well-being. *Journal of Applied Psychology, 92,* 455–474.

Wang, M., Olson, D. A., & Shultz, K. S. (2013). *Mid and late career issues: An integrative perspective.* New York: Routledge.

Wang, M., & Shi, J. (2016). Work, retirement and aging. In K. W. Schaie & S. L. Willis (Eds.), *Handbook of the psychology of aging* (8th ed., pp. 339–359). San Diego, CA: Academic Press.

Wang, M., & Shultz, K. (2010). Employee retirement: A review and recommendations for future investigation. *Journal of Management, 36,* 172–206.

Wang, M.-T., & Kenny, S. (2014). Parental physical punishment and adolescent adjustment: Bidirectionality and the moderation effects of child ethnicity and parental warmth. *Journal of Abnormal Child Psychology, 42,* 717–730.

Wang, M.-T., & Sheikh-Khalil, S. (2014). Does parental involvement matter for student achievement and mental health in high school? *Child Development, 85,* 610–625.

Wang, Q. (2006). Relations of maternal style and child self-concept to autobiographical memories in Chinese, Chinese immigrant, and European American 3-year-olds. *Child Development, 77,* 1794–1809.

Wang, Q. (2008). Emotion knowledge and autobiographical memory across the preschool years: A cross-cultural longitudinal investigation. *Cognition, 108,* 117–135.

Wang, Q., Pomerantz, E. M., & Chen, H. (2007). The role of parents' control in early adolescents' psychological functioning: A longitudinal investigation in the United States and China. *Child Development, 78,* 1592–1610.

Wang, Q., Shao, Y., & Li, Y. J. (2010). "My way or mom's way?" The bilingual and bicultural self in Hong Kong Chinese children and adolescents. *Child Development, 81,* 555–567.

Wang, S., Baillargeon, R., & Paterson, S. (2005). Detecting continuity violations in infancy: A new account and new evidence from covering and tube events. *Cognition, 95,* 129–173.

Wang, Z., & Deater-Deckard, K. (2013). Resilience in gene–environment transactions. In S. Goldstein & R. Brooks (Eds.), *Handbook of resilience in children* (2nd ed., pp. 57–72). New York: Springer Science + Business Media.

Ward, E. V., Berry, C. J., & Shanks, D. R. (2013). Age effects on explicit and implicit memory. *Frontiers in Psychology, 4:* Article 639.

Ward, M. M. (2013). Sense of control and self-reported health in a population-based sample of older Americans: Assessment of potential confounding by affect, personality, and social support. *International Journal of Behavioral Medicine, 20,* 140–147.

Ward, R. A., Spitze, G., & Deane, G. (2009). The more the merrier? Multiple parent–adult child relations. *Journal of Marriage and Family, 71,* 161–173.

Ward, T. C. S. (2015). Reasons for mother–infant bedsharing: A systematic narrative synthesis of the literature and implications for future research. *Maternal and Child Health Journal, 19,* 675–690.

Warneken, F., & Tomasello, M. (2009). Varieties of altruism in children and chimpanzees. *Trends in Cognitive Sciences, 13,* 397.

Warneken, F., & Tomasello, M. (2013). Parental presence and encouragement do not influence helping in young children. *Infancy, 18,* 345–368.

Warner, L. A., Valdez, A., Vega, W. A., de la Rosa, M., Turner, R. J., & Canino, G. (2006). Hispanic drug abuse in an evolving cultural context: An agenda for research. *Drug and Alcohol Dependence, 84*(Suppl. 1), S8–S16.

Warner, L. M., Ziegelmann, J. P., Schüz, B., Wurm, S., Tesch-Römer, C., & Schwarzer, R. (2011). Maintaining autonomy despite multimorbidity: Self-efficacy and the two faces of social support. *European Journal of Ageing, 8,* 3–12.

Warnock, F., & Sandrin, D. (2004). Comprehensive description of newborn distress behavior in response to acute pain (newborn male circumcision). *Pain, 107,* 242–255.

Warr, P. (2001). Age and work behavior: Physical attributes, cognitive abilities, knowledge, personality traits, and motives. *International Review of Industrial and Organizational Psychology, 16,* 1–36.

Warr, P. (2007). *Work, happiness, and unhappiness.* Mahwah, NJ: Erlbaum.

Warren, S. L., & Simmens, S. J. (2005). Predicting toddler anxiety/depressive symptoms: Effects of caregiver sensitivity on temperamentally vulnerable children. *Infant Mental Health Journal, 26,* 40–55.

Warreyn, P., Roeyers, H., & De Groote, I. (2005). Early social communicative behaviours of preschoolers with autism spectrum disorder during interaction with their mothers. *Autism, 9,* 342–361.

Warshaw, C., Brashler, P., & Gil, J. (2009). Mental health consequences of intimate partner violence. In C. Mitchell & D. Anglin (Eds.), *Intimate partner violence: A health-based perspective* (pp. 147–171). New York: Oxford University Press.

Washington, J. A., & Thomas-Tate, S. (2009). How research informs cultural-linguistic differences in the classroom: The bi-dialectal African American child. In S. Rosenfield & V. Berninger (Eds.), *Implementing evidence-based academic interventions in school settings* (pp. 147–164). New York: Oxford University Press.

Washington, T., Gleeson, J. P., & Rulison, K. L. (2013). Competence and African American children in informal kinship care: The role of family. *Children and Youth Services Review, 35,* 1305–1312.

Wasserman, E. A., & Rovee-Collier, C. (2001). Pick the flowers and mind your As and 2s! Categorization by pigeons and infants. In M. E. Carroll & J. B. Overmier (Eds.), *Animal research and human health: Advancing human welfare through behavioral science* (pp. 263–279). Washington, DC: American Psychological Association.

Wasylyshyn, C., Verhaeghen, P., & Sliwinski, M. J. (2011). Aging and task switching: A meta-analysis. *Psychology and Aging, 26,* 15–20.

Watamura, S. E., Donzella, B., Alwin, J., & Gunnar, M. R. (2003). Morning-to-afternoon increases in cortisol concentrations for infants and toddlers at child care: Age differences and behavioral correlates. *Child Development, 74,* 1006–1020.

Watamura, S. E., Phillips, D., Morrissey, T. W., McCartney, K., & Bub, K. (2011). Double jeopardy: Poorer social-emotional outcomes for children in the NICHD SECCYD experiencing home and childcare environments that confer risk. *Child Development, 82,* 48–65.

Waterman, A. S., & Whitbourne, S. K. (1982). Androgyny and psychosocial development among college students and adults. *Journal of Personality, 50,* 121–133.

Waters, E., de Silva-Sanigorski, A., Brown, T., Campbell, K. J., Goa, Y., Armstrong, R., et al. (2011). Interventions for preventing obesity in children. *Cochrane Database of Systematic Reviews,* Issue 12, Art. No.: CD011871.

Waters, E., Merrick, S., Treboux, D., Crowell, J., & Albersheim, L. (2000). Attachment security in infancy and early adulthood: A twenty-year longitudinal study. *Child Development, 71,* 684–689.

Waters, E., Vaughn, B. E., Posada, G., & Kondo-Ikemura, K. (Eds.). (1995). Caregiving, cultural, and cognitive perspectives on secure-base behavior and working models: New growing points of attachment theory and research. *Monographs of the Society for Research in Child Development, 60*(2–3, Serial No. 244).

Waters, E., Lester, L., & Cross, D. (2014). How does support from peers compare with support from adults as students transition to secondary school? *Journal of Adolescent Health, 54,* 543–549.

Waters, S. F., & Thompson, R. A. (2014). Children's perceptions of the effectiveness of strategies for regulating anger and sadness. *International Journal of Behavioral Development, 38,* 174–181.

Watrin, J. P., & Darwich, R. (2012). On behaviorism in the cognitive revolution: Myth and reactions. *Review of General Psychology, 16,* 269–282.

Watson, D., Klohnen, E. C., Casillas, A., Simms, E. N., Haig, J., & Berry, D. S. (2004). Match makers and deal breakers: Analyses of assortative mating in newlywed couples. *Journal of Personality, 72,* 1029–1068.

Watson, J. B., & Raynor, R. (1920). Conditioned emotional reactions. *Journal of Experimental Psychology, 3,* 1–14.

Waxman, S. R., & Senghas, A. (1992). Relations among word meanings in early lexical development. *Developmental Psychology, 28,* 862–873.

Way, N. (2013). Boys' friendships during adolescence: Intimacy, desire, and loss. *Journal of Research on Adolescence, 23,* 201–213.

Way, N., Cressen, J., Bodian, S., Preston, J., Nelson, J., & Hughes, D. (2014). "It might be nice to be a girl … then you wouldn't have to be emotionless": Boys' resistance to norms of masculinity during adolescence. *Psychology of Men and Masculinity, 15,* 241–252.

Weaver, J. M., & Schofield, T. J. (2015). Mediation and moderation of divorce effects on children's behavior problems. *Journal of Family Psychology, 29,* 39–48.

Webb, A. R., Heller, H. T., Benson, C. B., & Lahav, A. (2015). Mother's voice and heartbeat sounds elicit auditory plasticity in the human brain before full gestation. *Proceedings of the National Academy of Sciences, 112,* 3152–3157.

Webb, N. B. (2002). September 11, 2001. In N. B. Webb (Ed.), *Helping bereaved children: A handbook for practitioners* (pp. 365–384). New York: Guilford.

Webb, N. M., Franke, M. L., Ing, M., Chan, A., De, T., Freund, D., & Battey, D. (2008). The role of teacher instructional practices in student collaboration. *Contemporary Educational Psychology, 33,* 360–381.

Webb, S. J., Monk, C. S., & Nelson, C. A. (2001). Mechanisms of postnatal neurobiological development: Implications for human development. *Developmental Neuropsychology, 19,* 147–171.

Weber, C., Hahne, A., Friedrich, M., & Friederici, A. (2004). Discrimination of word stress in early infant perception: Electrophysiological evidence. *Cognitive Brain Research, 18,* 149–161.

Webster, G. D., Graber, J. A., Gesselman, A. N., Crosier, B. J., & Schember, T. O. (2014). A life history theory of father absence and menarche: A meta-analysis. *Evolutionary Psychology, 12,* 273–294.

Webster, J. D. (2002). Reminiscence function in adulthood: Age, ethnic, and family dynamics correlates. In J. D. Webster & B. K. Haight (Eds.), *Critical advances in reminiscence work* (pp. 140–142). New York: Springer.

Webster-Stratton, C., & Reid, M. J. (2010b). The Incredible Years program for children from infancy to pre-adolescence: Prevention and treatment of behavior problems. In R. C. Murrihy, A. D. Kidman, & T. H. Ollendick (Eds.), *Clinical handbook of assessing and treating conduct problems in youth* (pp. 117–138). New York: Springer Science + Business Media.

Webster-Stratton, C., Rinaldi, J., & Reid, J. M. (2011). Long-term outcomes of Incredible Years parenting program: Predictors of adolescent adjustment. *Child and Adolescent Mental Health, 16,* 38–46.

Wechsler, D. (2012). *Wechsler Preschool and Primary Scale of Intelligence—Fourth Edition (WPPSI–IV).* Upper Saddle River, NJ: Pearson.

Weech-Maldonado, R., Pradhan, R., & Powell, M. P. (2014). Medicare and health care utilization. In K. Whitfield & T. A. Baker (Eds.), *Handbook of minority aging* (pp. 539–556). New York: Springer.

Weems, C. F., & Costa, N. M. (2005). Developmental differences in the expression of childhood anxiety symptoms and fears. *Journal of the American Academy of Child and Adolescent Psychiatry, 44,* 656–663.

Wei, W., Lu, H., Zhao, H., Chen, C., Dong, Q., & Zhou, X. (2012). Gender differences in children's arithmetic performance are accounted for by gender differences in language abilities. *Psychological Science, 23,* 320–330.

Weiland, C., & Yoshikawa, H. (2013). Impacts of a prekindergarten program on children's mathematics, language, literacy, executive function, and emotional skills. *Child Development, 84,* 2112–2130.

Weinberg, M. K., & Tronick, E. Z. (1994). Beyond the face: An empirical study of infant affective configurations of facial, vocal, gestural, and regulatory behaviors. *Child Development, 65,* 1503–1515.

Weinberger, M. I., & Whitbourne, S. K. (2010). Depressive symptoms, self-reported physical functioning, and identity in community-dwelling older adults. *Aging International, 35,* 276–285.

Weinfield, N. S., Sroufe, L. A., & Egeland, B. (2000). Attachment from infancy to early adulthood in a high-risk sample: Continuity, discontinuity, and their correlates. *Child Development, 71,* 695–702.

Weinfield, N. S., Whaley, G. J. L., & Egeland, B. (2004). Continuity, discontinuity, and coherence in attachment from infancy to late adolescence: Sequelae of organization and disorganization. *Attachment and Human Development, 6,* 73–97.

Weinstein, A. A., Lydick, S. E., & Biswabharati, S. (2014). Exercise and its relationship to psychological health and well-being. In A. R. Gomes, R. Resende, & A. Albuquerque (Eds.), *Positive human functioning from a multidisciplinary perspective: Vol. 2. Promoting healthy lifestyles* (pp. 147–166). Hauppauge, NY: Nova Science.

Weinstein, R. S. (2002). *Reaching higher: The power of expectations in schooling.* Cambridge, MA: Harvard University Press.

Weinstock, M. (2008). The long-term behavioural consequences of prenatal stress. *Neuroscience and Biobehavioral Reviews, 32,* 1073–1086.

Weisgram, E. S., Bigler, R. S., & Liben, L. S. (2010). Gender, values, and occupational interests among children, adolescents, and adults. *Child Development, 81,* 778–796.

Weisman, O., Magori-Cohen, R., Louzoun, Y., Eidelman, A. I., & Feldman, R. (2011). Sleep–wake transitions in premature neonates predict early development. *Pediatrics, 128,* 706–714.

Weiss, A., Costa, P. T., Jr., Karuza, J., Duberstein, P. R., Friedman, B., & McCrae, R. M. (2005). Crosssectional age differences in personality among Medicare patients aged 65 to 100. *Psychology and Aging, 20,* 182–185.

Weiss, K. M. (2005). Cryptic causation of human disease: Reading between the germ lines. *Trends in Genetics, 21,* 82–88.

Weiss, L., Saklofske, D., Holdnack, J., & Prifitera, A. (2015). *WISC-V assessment and interpretation.* San Diego, CA: Academic Press.

Weissberg, R. W. (2006). Modes of expertise in creative thinking: Evidence from case studies. In K. A. Ericsson, N. Charness, P. J. Feltovich, & R. R. Hoffman (Eds.), *The Cambridge handbook of expertise and expert performance* (pp. 761–787). New York: Cambridge University Press.

Weiss-Numeroff, G. (2013). *Extraordinary centenarians in America: Their secrets to living a long and vibrant life.* Victoria, Canada: Agio Publishing.

Wekerle, C., & Wolfe, D. A. (2003). Child maltreatment. In E. J. Mash & R. A. Barkley (Eds.), *Child psychopathology* (2nd ed., pp. 632–684). New York: Guilford.

Wellman, H. M. (2011). Developing a theory of mind. In U. Goswami (Ed.), *Wiley-Blackwell handbook of childhood cognitive development* (2nd ed., pp. 258–284). Malden, MA: Wiley-Blackwell.

Wellman, H. M. (2012). Theory of mind: Better methods, clearer findings, more development. *European Journal of Developmental Psychology, 9,* 313–330.

Wellman, H. M., & Hickling, A. K. (1994). The mind's "I": Children's conception of the mind as an active agent. *Child Development, 65,* 1564–1580.

Wenger, G. C. (2009). Childlessness at the end of life: Evidence from rural Wales. *Ageing and Society, 29,* 1243–1259.

Wennberg, A. M., Canham, S. L., Smith, M. T., & Spira, A. P. (2013). Optimizing sleep in older adults: Treating insomnia. *Maturitas, 76,* 247–252.

Wentworth, N., Benson, J. B., & Haith, M. M. (2000). The development of infants' reaches for stationary and moving targets. *Child Development, 71,* 576–601.

Wentzel, K. R., Barry, C. M., & Caldwell, K. A. (2004). Friendships in middle school: Influences on motivation and school adjustment. *Journal of Educational Psychology, 96,* 195–203.

Wentzel, K. R., & Brophy, J. E. (2014). *Motivating students to learn.* Hoboken, NJ: Taylor & Francis.

Werner, E. E. (1991). Grandparent–grandchild relationships amongst U.S. ethnic groups. In P. K. Smith (Ed.), *The psychology of grandparenthood: An international perspective* (pp. 68–82). London: Routledge.

Werner, E. E. (2013). What can we learn about resilience from large-scale longitudinal studies? In S. Goldstein & R. Brooks (Eds.), *Handbook of resilience in children* (2nd ed., pp. 87–102). New York: Springer Science + Business Media.

Werner, N. E., & Crick, N. R. (2004). Maladaptive peer relationships and the development of relational and physical aggression during middle childhood. *Social Development, 13,* 495–514.

West, R. L., Bagwell, D. K., & Dark-Freudeman, A. (2008). Memory and goal-setting: The response of older and younger adults to positive and objective feedback. *Psychology and Aging, 20,* 195–201.

Westerhof, G. J. (2008). Age identity. In D. Carr (Ed.), *Encyclopedia of the life course and human development* (pp. 10–14). Farmington Hills, MI: Macmillan.

Westerhof, G. J., & Barrett, A. E. (2005). Age identity and subjective well-being: A comparison of the United States and Germany. *Journals of Gerontology, 60S,* 129–136.

Westerhof, G. J., & Bohlmeijer, E. T. (2014). Celebrating fifty years of research and applications in reminiscence and life review: State of the art and new directions. *Journal of Aging Studies, 29,* 107–114.

Westerhof, G. J., Bohlmeijer, E., & Webster, J. D. (2010). Reminiscence and mental health: A review of recent progress in theory, research and interventions. *Ageing and Society, 30,* 697–721.

Westerhof, G. J., Miche, M., Brothers, A. F., Barrett, A. E., Diehl, M., Montepare, J. M., et al. (2014). The influence of subjective aging on health and longevity: A meta-analysis of longitudinal data. *Psychology and Aging, 29,* 793–802.

Westerhof, G. J., Whitbourne, S. K., & Freeman, G. P. (2012). The aging self in a cultural context: The relation of conceptions of aging to identity processes and self-esteem in the United States and the Netherlands. *Journals of Gerontology, 67B,* 52–60.

Westermann, G., Sirois, S., Shultz, T. R., & Mareschal, D. (2006). Modeling developmental cognitive neuroscience. *Trends in Cognitive Sciences, 10,* 227–232.

Westermeyer, J. F. (2004). Predictors and characteristics of Erikson's life cycle model among men: A 32-year longitudinal study. *International Journal of Aging and Human Development, 58,* 29–48.

Wetmore, C. M., & Mokdad, A. H. (2012). In denial: Misperceptions of weight change among adults in the United States. *Preventive Medicine, 55,* 93–100.

Wettstein, M., & Wahl, H.-W. (2016). Hearing. In S. K. Whitbourne (Ed.), *Encyclopedia of adulthood and aging* (Vol. 2, pp. 608–613). Malden, MA: Wiley Blackwell.

Wexler, J., & Pyle, N. (2013). Effective approaches to increase student engagement. In C. Franklin, M. B. Harris, & P. Allen-Meares (Eds.), *School services sourcebook: A guide for school-based professionals* (2nd ed., pp. 381–394). New York: Oxford University Press.

Wheeler, I. (2001). Parental bereavement: The crisis of meaning. *Death Studies, 25,* 51–66.

Whipple, E. E. (2006). Child abuse and neglect: Consequences of physical, sexual, and emotional abuse of children. In H. E. Fitzgerald, B. M. Lester, & B. Zuckerman (Eds.), *The crisis in youth mental health: Critical issues and effective programs: Vol. 1. Childhood disorders* (pp. 205–229). Westport, CT: Praeger.

Whipple, N., Bernier, A., & Mageau, G. A. (2011). Broadening the study of infant security of attachment:

Maternal autonomy-support in the context of infant exploration. *Social Development, 20,* 17–32.

Whitbourne, S. K. (2002). *The aging individual: Physical and psychological perspectives.* New York: Springer.

Whitbourne, S. K., & Meeks, S. (2011). Psychopathology, bereavement, and aging. In K. W. Schaie & S. L. Willis (Eds.), *Handbook of the psychology of aging* (7th ed., pp. 311–323). San Diego, CA: Elsevier.

Whitbourne, S. K., Zuschlag, M. K., Elliot, L. B., & Waterman, A. S. (1992). Psychosocial development in adulthood: A 22-year sequential study. *Journal of Personality and Social Psychology, 63,* 260–271.

White, L. (2001). Sibling relationships over the life course: A panel analysis. *Journal of Marriage and Family, 63,* 555–568.

Whiteman, S. D., McHale, S. M., & Crouter, A. C. (2010). Family relationships from adolescence to early adulthood: Changes in the family system following firstborns' leaving home. *Journal of Research on Adolescence, 21,* 461–474.

Whiteman, S. D., Solmeyer, A. R., & McHale, S. M. (2015). Sibling relationships and adolescent adjustment: Longitudinal associations in two-parent African American families. *Journal of Youth and Adolescence, 44,* 2042–2053.

Whitesell, N. R., Mitchell, C. M., Spicer, P., and the Voices of Indian Teens Project Team. (2009). A longitudinal study of self-esteem, cultural identity, and academic success among American Indian adolescents. *Cultural Diversity and Ethnic Minority Psychology, 15,* 38–50.

Whitfield, K. E., Thorpe, R., & Szanton, S. (2011). Health disparities, social class, and aging. In K. Warner Schaie & S. L. Willis (Eds.), *Handbook of the psychology of aging* (7th ed., pp. 207–218). San Diego, CA: Academic Press.

Whiting, B., & Edwards, C. P. (1988). A cross-cultural analysis of sex differences in the behavior of children aged 3 through 11. In G. Handel (Ed.), *Childhood socialization* (pp. 281–297). New York: Aldine de Gruyter.

Whitney, C. G., Zhou, F., Singleton, J., & Schuchat, A. (2014). Benefits from immunization during the Vaccines for Children Program Era—United States, 1994–2013. *Morbidity and Mortality Weekly Report, 63,* 352–355.

Whitton, S. W., Waldinger, R. J., Schulz, M. S., Allen, J. P., Crowell, J. A., & Hauser, S. T. (2008). Prospective associations from family-of-origin interactions to adult marital interactions and relationship adjustment. *Journal of Family Psychology, 22,* 274–286.

Wicher, C. P., & Meeker, M. A. (2012). What influences African American end-of-life preferences? *Journal of Health Care for the Poor and Underserved, 23,* 28–58.

Wichmann, C., Coplan, R. J., & Daniels, T. (2004). The social cognitions of socially withdrawn children. *Social Development, 13,* 377–392.

Wickrama, K. A. S., Lee, T. K., O'Neal, C. W., & Kwon, J. A. (2015). Stress and resource pathways connecting early socioeconomic adversity to young adults' physical health risk. *Journal of Youth and Adolescence, 44,* 1109–1124.

Widen, S. C., & Russell, J. A. (2011). In building a script for an emotion do preschoolers add its cause before its behavior consequence? *Social Development, 20,* 471–485.

Widman, L., Choukas-Bradley, S., Helms, S. W., Golin, C. E., & Prinstein, M. J. (2014). Sexual communication between early adolescents and their dating partners, parents, and best friends. *Journal of Sex Research, 51,* 731–741.

Wiemers, E. E., & Bianchi, S. M. (2015). Competing demands from aging parents and adult children in two cohorts of American women. *Population Development and Review, 41,* 127–146.

Wigfield, A., Eccles, J. S., Schiefele, U., Roeser, R. W., & Davis-Kean, P. (2006). Development of achievement motivation. In N. Eisenberg (Ed.), *Handbook of child psychology: Vol. 3. Social, emotional, and personality development* (6th ed., pp. 933–1002). Hoboken, NJ: Wiley.

Wigfield, A., Eccles, J. S., Yoon, K. S., Harold, R. D., Arbreton, A. J., Freedman-Doan, C., & Blumenfeld, P. C. (1997). Changes in children's competence beliefs and subjective task values across the elementary school years: A three-year study. *Journal of Educational Psychology, 89,* 451–469.

Wight, R. G., LeBlanc, A. J., & Lee Badget, M. V. (2013). Same-sex legal marriage and psychological well-being: Findings from the California Health Interview Survey. *American Journal of Public Health, 103,* 339–346.

Wight, V. R., Bianchi, S. M., & Hunt, B. R. (2012). Explaining racial/ethnic variation in partnered women's and men's housework: Does one size fit all? *Journal of Family Issues, 34,* 394–427.

Wikby, A., Maxson, P., Olsson, J., Johansson, B., & Ferguson, F. G. (1998). Changes in CD8 and CD4 lymphocyte subsets, T cell proliferation responses and non-survival in the very old: The Swedish longitudinal OCTO-immune study. *Mechanisms of Ageing and Development, 102,* 187–198.

Wilbur, J., Chandler, P. J., Dancy, B., & Lee, H. (2003). Correlates of physical activity in urban Midwestern African-American women. *American Journal of Preventive Medicine, 25,* 45–52.

Wildsmith, E., Manlove, J., Jekielek, S., Moore, K. A., & Mincieli, L. (2012). Teenage childbearing among youth born to teenage mothers. *Youth and Society, 44,* 258–283.

Wilkie, S. S., Guenette, J. A., Dominelli, P. B., & Sheel, A. W. (2012). Effects of an aging pulmonary system on expiratory flow limitation and dyspnoea during exercise in healthy women. *European Journal of Applied Physiology, 112,* 2195–2204.

Wilkinson, K., Ross, E., & Diamond, A. (2003). Fast mapping of multiple words: Insights into when "the information provided" does and does not equal "the information perceived." *Applied Developmental Psychology, 24,* 739–762.

Wilkinson, R. B. (2004). The role of parental and peer attachment in the psychological health and self-esteem of adolescents. *Journal of Youth and Adolescence, 33,* 479–493.

Willatts, P. (1999). Development of means–end behavior in young infants: Pulling a support to retrieve a distant object. *Developmental Psychology, 35,* 651–667.

Williams, C. L. (2013). The glass escalator, revisited: Gender inequality in neoliberal times *Gender & Society, 27,* 609–629.

Williams, J. M., & Currie, C. (2000). Self-esteem and physical development in early adolescence: Pubertal timing and body image. *Journal of Early Adolescence, 20,* 129–149.

Williams, K., & Dunne-Bryant, A. (2006). Divorce and adult psychological well-being: Clarifying the role of gender and age. *Journal of Marriage and Family, 68,* 1178–1196.

Williams, K. N., Herman, R., Gajewski, B., & Wilson, K. (2008). Elderspeak communication: Impact on dementia care. *American Journal of Alzheimer's Disease and Other Dementias, 24,* 11–20.

Williams, M. E., & Fredriksen-Goldsen, K. I. (2014). Same-sex partnerships and the health of older adults. *Journal of Community Psychology, 42,* 558–570.

Williams, N., & Torrez, D. J. (1998). Grandparenthood among Hispanics. In M. E. Szinovacz (Ed.), *Handbook on grandparenthood* (pp. 87–96). Westport, CT: Greenwood Press.

Williams, S., & Dale, J. (2006). The effectiveness of treatment for depression/depressive symptoms in adults with cancer: A systematic review. *British Journal of Cancer, 94,* 372–390.

Willis, S. L., & Belleville, S. (2016). Cognitive training in later adulthood. In K. W. Schaie & S. L. Willis (Eds.), *Handbook of the psychology of aging* (8th ed., pp. 219–243). Waltham, MA: Elsevier.

Willoughby, B. J., & Carroll, J. S. (2016). On the horizon: Marriage timing, beliefs, and consequences in emerging adulthood. In J. J. Arnett (Ed.), *Oxford handbook of emerging adulthood* (pp. 280–295). New York: Oxford University Press.

Willoughby, J., Kupersmidt, J. B., & Bryant, D. (2001). Overt and covert dimensions of antisocial behavior. *Journal of Abnormal Child Psychology, 29,* 177–187.

Wilmot, K. A., O'Flaherty, M., Capewell, S., Ford, E. S., & Vaccarino, V. (2016). Coronary heart disease mortality declines in the United States through 2011: Evidence for stagnation in young adults, especially women. *Circulation, 134,* 997–1002.

Wilson, D. J., Mitchell, J. M., Kemp, B. J., Adkins, R. H., & Mann, W. (2009). Effects of assistive technology on functional decline in people aging with a disability. *Assistive Technology, 21,* 208–217.

Wilson, E. K., Dalberth, B. T., Koo, H. P., & Gard, J. C. (2010). Parents' perspectives on talking to preteenage children about sex. *Perspectives on Sexual and Reproductive Health, 42,* 56–63.

Wilson, S. J., & Tanner-Smith, E. E. (2013). Dropout prevention and intervention programs for improving school completion among school-aged children and youth: A systematic review. *Journal of the Society for Social Work and Research, 4,* 357–372.

Wilson-Ching, M., Molloy, C. S., Anderson, V. A., Burnett, A., Roberts, G., Cheong, J. L., et al. (2013). Attention difficulties in a contemporary geographic cohort of adolescents born extremely preterm/extremely low birth weight. *Journal of the International Neuropsychological Society, 19,* 1097–1108.

Wimmer, M. B. (2013). *Evidence-based practices for school refusal and truancy.* Bethesda, MD: National Association of School Psychologists.

Wincze, J. P., & Weisberg, R. B. (2015). *Sexual dysfunction* (3rd ed.). New York: Guilford.

Windsor, T. D., Anstey, K. J., & Rodgers, B. (2008). Volunteering and psychological well-being among young–old adults: How much is too much? *Gerontology, 48,* 59–70.

Wink, P. (2006). Who is afraid of death? Religiousness, spirituality, and death anxiety in late adulthood. *Journal of Religion, Spirituality and Aging, 18,* 93–111.

Wink, P. (2007). Everyday life in the Third Age. In J. B. James & P. Wink (Eds.), *Annual review of gerontology and geriatrics* (Vol. 26, pp. 243–261). New York: Springer.

Wink, P., & Dillon, M. (2008). Religiousness, spirituality, and psychosocial functioning in late adulthood: Findings from a longitudinal study. *Psychology of Religion and Spirituality 5,* 102–115.

Wink, P., & Helson, R. (1993). Personality change in women and their partners. *Journal of Personality and Social Psychology, 65,* 597–605.

Wink, P., & Scott, J. (2005). Does religiousness buffer against the fear of death and dying in late adulthood? Findings from a longitudinal study. *Journals of Gerontology, 60B,* P207–P214.

Wink, P., & Staudinger, U. M. (2016). Wisdom and psychosocial functioning in later life. *Journal of Personality, 84,* 306–318.

Winkler, I., Háden, G. P., Ladinig, O., Sziller, I., & Honing, H. (2009). Newborn infants detect the beat in music. *Proceedings of the National Academy of Sciences, 106,* 2468–2471.

Winner, E. (1986). Where pelicans kiss seals. *Psychology Today, 20*(8), 25–35.

Winner, E. (2003). Creativity and talent. In M. H. Bornstein, L. Davidson, C. L. M. Keyes, K. A. Moore, & the Center for Child Well-Being (Eds.), *Well-being: Positive development across the life course* (pp. 371–380). Mahwah, NJ: Erlbaum.

Winsler, A. (2009). Still talking to ourselves after all these years: A review of current research on private speech. In A. Winsler, C. Fernyhough, & I. Montero (Eds.), *Private speech executive functioning, and the development of self-regulation.* New York: Cambridge University Press.

Winsler, A., Fernyhough, C., & Montero, I. (Eds.). (2009). *Private speech, executive functioning, and the development of verbal self-regulation.* New York: Cambridge University Press.

Winter, D. G., Torges, C. M., Stewart, A. J., Henderson-King, D., & Henderson-King, E. (2007). Pathways toward the Third Age: Studying a cohort from the "golden age." In J. B. James & P. Wink (Eds.), *The crown of life: Dynamics of the early postretirement period* (pp. 103–130). New York: Springer.

Wiringa, A. E., Gondwe, T., & Haggerty, C. L. (2015). Reproductive health. In S. K. Whitbourne (Ed.), *Encyclopedia of adulthood and aging* (Vol. 3, pp. 1085–1088). Malden, MA: Wiley Blackwell.

Witherington, D. C. (2005). The development of prospective grasping control between 5 and 7 months: A longitudinal study. *Infancy, 7,* 143–161.

Witherington, D. C., Campos, J. J., Harriger, J. A., Bryan, C., & Margett, T. E. (2010). Emotion and its development in infancy. In G. Bremner & T. D. Wachs (Eds.), *Wiley-Blackwell handbook of infant development: Vol. 1. Basic research* (2nd ed., pp. 568–591). Oxford, UK: Wiley-Blackwell.

Wöhrman, A. M., Deller, J., & Wang, M. (2013). Outcome expectations and work design characteristics in post-retirement work planning. *Journal of Vocational Behavior, 83,* 219–228.

Wolak, J., Mitchell, K., & Finkelhor, D. (2007). Unwanted and wanted exposure to online pornography in a national sample of youth Internet users. *Pediatrics, 119,* 247–257.

Wolfe, D. A. (2005). *Child abuse* (2nd ed.). Thousand Oaks, CA: Sage.

Wolff, P. H. (1966). The causes, controls and organization of behavior in the neonate. *Psychological Issues, 5*(1, Serial No. 17).

Wolff, P. H., & Fesseha, G. (1999). The orphans of Eritrea: A five-year follow-up study. *Journal of Child Psychology and Psychiatry and Allied Disciplines, 40,* 1231–1237.

Wolinsky, F. D., Unverzagt, F. W., Smith, D. M., Jones R., Stoddard, A., & Tennstedt, S. L. (2006). The ACTIVE cognitive training trail and health-related quality of life: Protection that lasts for 5 years. *Journals of Gerontology, 61A,* 1324–1329.

Wong, C. A., Eccles, J. S., & Sameroff, A. (2003). The influence of ethnic discrimination and ethnic identification on African American adolescents' school and socioemotional adjustment. *Journal of Personality, 71,* 1197–1232.

Wood, E., Desmarais, S., & Gugula, S. (2002). The impact of parenting experience on gender stereotyped toy play of children. *Sex Roles, 47,* 39–49.

Wood, J. J., Emmerson, N. A., & Cowan, P. A. (2004). Is early attachment security carried forward into relationships with preschool peers? *British Journal of Developmental Psychology, 22,* 245–253.

Wood, J. T. (2009). Communication, gender differences in. In H. T. Reis & S. K. Sprecher (Eds.), *Encyclopedia of human relationships* (Vol. 1, pp. 252–256). Thousand Oaks, CA: Sage.

Wood, R. M. (2009). Changes in cry acoustics and distress ratings while the infant is crying. *Infant and Child Development, 18,* 163–177.

Woolley, J. D., Browne, C. A., & Boerger, E. A. (2006). Constraints on children's judgments of magical causality. *Journal of Cognition and Development, 7,* 253–277.

Woolley, J. D., & Cornelius, C. A. (2013). Beliefs in magical beings and cultural myths. In M. Taylor (Ed.), *Oxford handbook of the development of imagination* (pp. 61–74). New York: Oxford University Press.

Woolley, J. D., & Cox, V. (2007). Development of beliefs about storybook reality. *Developmental Science, 10,* 681–693.

Worden, J. W. (2000). Toward an appropriate death. In T. A. Rando (Ed.), *Clinical dimensions of anticipatory mourning* (pp. 267–277). Champaign, IL: Research Press.

Worden, J. W. (2009). *Grief counseling and grief therapy* (4th ed.). New York: Springer.

World Bank. (2016). *Fertility rate, total (births per woman).* Retrieved from data.worldbank.org/indicator/SP.DYN.TFRT.IN?page=6

World Health Organization. (2015a). *HIV/AIDS: Data and statistics.* Retrieved from http://www.who.int/hiv/data/en

World Health Organization. (2015b). *Immunization, vaccines, and biologicals: Data, statistics and graphics.* Retrieved from www.who.int/immunization/monitoring_surveillance/data/en

World Health Organization. (2015c). *Levels and trends in child malnutrition: Key findings of the 2015 edition.* Retrieved from www.who.int/nutgrowthdb/jme_brochure2015.pdf?ua=1

World Health Organization. (2015d). *Levels and trends in child mortality: Report 2015.* Geneva, Switzerland: Author.

World Health Organization. (2015e). *Rubella: Fact sheet No. 367.* Retrieved from www.who.int/mediacentre/factsheets/fs367/en

World Health Organization. (2015f). *The World Health Organization's infant feeding recommendation.* Retrieved from www.who.int/nutrition/topics/infantfeeding_recommendation/en

World Health Organization. (2015g). *World health statistics 2015.* Retrieved from www.who.int/gho/publications/world_health_statistics/2015/en

World Health Organization. (2015h). *The world's women: Trends and statistics.* Retrieved from http://unstats.un.org/unsd/gender/downloads/WorldsWomen2015_report.pdf

Worthy, J., Hungerford-Kresser, H., & Hampton, A. (2009). Tracking and ability grouping. In L. Christenbury, R. Bomer, & P. Smargorinsky (Eds.), *Handbook of adolescent literacy research* (pp. 220–235). New York: Guilford.

Wortman, J., Lucas, R. E., & Donellan, M. B. (2012). Stability and change in the Big Five personality domains: Evidence from a longitudinal study of Australians. *Psychology and Aging, 27,* 867–874.

Worton, S. K., Caplan, R., Nelson, G., Pancer, S. M., Loomis, C., Peters, R. D., & Hayward, K. (2014). Better Beginnings, Better Futures: Theory, research, and knowledge transfer of a community-based initiative for children and families. *Psychosocial Intervention, 23,* 135–143.

WPCA (Worldwide Palliative Care Alliance). (2014). *Global atlas of palliative care at the end of life.* London, UK: Author. Retrieved from www.thewhpca.org/resources/global-atlas-on-end-of-life-care

Wray, S. (2007). Health, exercise, and well-being: The experiences of midlife women from diverse ethnic backgrounds. *Social Theory and Health, 5,* 126–144.

Wright, A. A., Zang, B., Ray, A., Mack, J. W., Trice, E., Balboni, T., et al. (2008). Associations between end-of-life discussions, patient mental health, medical care near death, and caregiver bereavement adjustment. *JAMA, 300,* 1665–1673.

Wright, B. C. (2006). On the emergence of the discriminative mode for transitive inference. *European Journal of Cognitive Psychology, 18,* 776–800.

Wright, B. C., Robertson, S., & Hadfield, L. (2011). Transitivity for height versus speed: To what extent do the under-7s really have a transitive capacity? *Thinking and Reasoning, 17,* 57–81.

Wright, J. C., Huston, A. C., Murphy, K. C., St. Peters, M., Pinon, M., Scantlin, R., & Kotler, J. (2001). The relations of early television viewing to school readiness and vocabulary of children from low-income families: The Early Window Project. *Child Development, 72,* 1347–1366.

Wright, K. (2003). Relationships with death: The terminally ill talk about dying. *Journal of Marital and Family Therapy, 29,* 439–454.

Wright, N. C., Looker, A. C., Saag, K. G., Curtis, J. R., Delzell, E. S., Randall, S., & Dawson-Hughes, B. (2014). The recent prevalence of osteoporosis and low bone mass in the United States based on bone mineral density at the femoral neck or lumbar spine. *Journal of Bone and Mineral Research, 29,* 2520–2526.

Wright, P. J., Malamuth, N. M., & Donnerstein, E. (2012). Research on sex in the media: What do we know about effects on children and adolescents? In D. G. Singer & J. L. Singer (Eds.), *Handbook of children and the media* (2nd ed., pp. 273–302). Thousand Oaks, CA: Sage.

Wright, W. E. (2013). Bilingual education. In T. K. Bhatia & W. C. Ritchie (Eds.), *Handbook of bilingualism and multilingualism* (pp. 598–623). Chichester, UK: Wiley-Blackwell.

Wrotniak, B. H., Epstein, L. H., Raluch, R. A., & Roemmich, J. N. (2004). Parent weight change as a predictor of child weight change in family-based behavioral obesity treatment. *Archives of Pediatric and Adolescent Medicine, 158,* 342–347.

Wrzus, C., Hänel, M., Wagner, J., & Neyer, F. J. (2013). Social network changes and life events across the life span: A meta-analysis. *Psychological Bulletin, 139,* 53–80.

Wu, A. M. S., Tang, C. S. K., & Kwok, T. C. Y. (2002). Death anxiety among Chinese elderly people in Hong Kong. *Journal of Aging and Health, 14,* 42–56.

Wu, J. H., Lemaitre, R. N., King, I. B., Song, X., Psaty, B. M., Siscovick, D. S., & Mozaffarian, D. (2014). Circulating omega-6 polyunsaturated fatty acids and total and cause-specific mortality: The Cardiovascular Health Study. *Circulation, 130,* 1245–1253.

Wu, L. L., Bumpass, L. L., & Musick, K. (2001). Historical and life course trajectories of nonmarital childbearing. In L. L. Wu & B. Wolfe (Eds.), *Out of wedlock: Causes and consequences of nonmarital fertility* (pp. 3–48). New York: Russell Sage Foundation.

Wu, Z., & Schimmele, C. M. (2007). Uncoupling in late life. *Generations, 31,* 41–46.

Wulczyn, F. (2009). Epidemiological perspectives on maltreatment prevention. *Future of Children, 19,* 39–66.

Wuyts, D., Vansteenkiste, M., Soenens, B., & Assor, A. (2015). An examination of the dynamics involved in parental child-invested contingent self-esteem. *Parenting: Science and Practice, 15,* 55–74.

Wyman, E., Rakoczy, H., & Tomasello, M. (2009). Normativity and context in young children's pretend play. *Cognitive Development, 24,* 146–155.

Wynn, K. (1992). Addition and subtraction by human infants. *Nature, 358,* 749–750.

Wynn, K., Bloom, P., & Chiang, W.-C. (2002). Enumeration of collective entities by 5-month-old infants. *Cognition, 83,* B55–B62.

Wynne-Edwards, K. E. (2001). Hormonal changes in mammalian fathers. *Hormones and Behavior, 40,* 139–145.

Wysong, A., Lee, P. P., & Sloan, F. A. (2009). Longitudinal incidence of adverse outcomes of age-related macular degeneration. *Archives of Ophthalmology, 127,* 320–327.

X

Xu, F., Han, Y., Sabbagh, M. A., Wang, T., Ren, X., & Li, C. (2013). Developmental differences in the structure of executive function in middle childhood and adolescence. *PLOS ONE, 8,* e77770.

Xu, F., Spelke, E. S., & Goddard, S. (2005). Number sense in human infants. *Developmental Science, 8,* 88–101.

Xu, X., & Lai, S.-C. (2004). Gender ideologies, marital roles, and marital quality in Taiwan. *Journal of Family Issues, 25,* 318–355.

Y

Yamaguchi, S., Gelfand, M., Ohashi, M. M., & Zemba, Y. (2005). The cultural psychology of control: Illusions of personal versus collective control in the United States and Japan. *Journal of Cross-Cultural Psychology, 36,* 750–761.

Yan, L. L., Liu, K., Matthews, K. A., Daviglus, M. L., Ferguson, T. F., & Kiefe, C. I. (2003). Psychosocial factors and risk of hypertension: The Coronary Artery Risk Development in Young Adults (CARDIA) study. *JAMA, 290,* 2138–2148.

Yang, B., Ollendick, T. H., Dong, Q., Xia, Y., & Lin, L. (1995). Only children and children with siblings in the People's Republic of China: Levels of fear, anxiety, and depression. *Child Development, 66,* 1301–1311.

Yang, C.-K., & Hahn, H.-M. (2002). Cosleeping in young Korean children. *Developmental and Behavioral Pediatrics, 23,* 151–157.

Yang, F.-Y., & Tsai, C.-C. (2010). Reasoning about science-related uncertain issues and epistemological perspectives among children. *Instructional Science, 38,* 325–354.

Yang, Q., & Miller, G. (2015). East–West differences in perception of brain death: Review of history, current understandings, and directions for research. *Journal of Bioethical Inquiry, 2,* 211–215.

Yang, S. C., & Chen, S.-F. (2002). A phenomenographic approach to the meaning of death: A Chinese perspective. *Death Studies, 26,* 143–175.

Yanovski, J. A. (2015). Pediatric obesity. An introduction. *Appetite, 93,* 3–12.

Yap, M. B. H., Allen, N. B., & Ladouceur, C. D. (2008). Maternal socialization of positive affect: The impact of invalidation on adolescent emotion regulation and depressive symptomatology. *Child Development, 79,* 1415–1431.

Yarrow, M. R., Scott, P. M., & Waxler, C. Z. (1973). Learning concern for others. *Developmental Psychology, 8,* 240–260.

Yarwood, A., Han, B., Raychaudhuri, S., Bowes, J., Lunt, M., Pappas, D. A., et al. (2015). A weighted genetic risk score using all known susceptibility variants to estimate rheumatoid arthritis risk. *Annals of Rheumatic Diseases, 74,* 170–176.

Yates, L. B., Djousée, L., Kurth, T., Buring, J. E., & Gaziano, J. M. (2008). Exceptional longevity in men: Modifiable factors associated with survival and function to age 90 years. *Archives of Internal Medicine, 168,* 284–290.

Yau, J. P., Tasopoulos-Chan, M., & Smetana, J. G. (2009). Disclosure to parents about everyday activities among American adolescents from Mexican, Chinese, and European backgrounds. *Child Development, 80,* 1481–1498.

Yavorsky, J. E., Dush, C. M. K., & Schoppe-Sullivan, S. J. (2015). The production of inequality: The gender division of labor across the transition to parenthood. *Journal of Marriage and Family, 77,* 662–679.

Yehuda, R., & Bierer, L. M. (2009). The relevance of epigenetics to PTSD: Implications for DSM-V. *Journal of Trauma and Stress, 22,* 427–434.

Yeung, D. Y., Fung, H. H., & Lang, F. R. (2008). Self-construal moderates age differences in social network characteristics. *Psychology and Aging, 23,* 222–226.

Yeung, J. W. K., Cheung, C.-K., Kwok, S. Y. C. L., & Leung, J. T. Y. (2016). Socialization effects of authoritative parenting and its discrepancy on children. *Journal of Child and Family Studies, 25,* 1980–1990.

Yip, S. Y., Cheung, Y. T., Chau, P. H., & Law, Y. W. (2010). The impact of epidemic outbreak: The case of severe acute respiratory syndrome (SARS) and suicidal behavior among older adults in Hong Kong. *International Psychogeriatrics, 21,* 86–92.

Yip, T., Douglass, S., & Shelton, J. N. (2013). Daily intragroup contact in diverse settings: Implications for Asian adolescents' ethnic identity. *Child Development, 84,* 1425–1441.

Yirmiya, N., Erel, O., Shaked, M., & Solomonica-Levi, D. (1998). Meta-analyses comparing theory of mind abilities of individuals with autism, individuals with mental retardation, and normally developing individuals. *Psychological Bulletin, 124,* 283–307.

Yong, M. H., & Ruffman, T. (2014). Emotional contagion: Dogs and humans show a similar physiological response to human infant crying. *Behavioural Processes, 108,* 155–165.

Yook, J.-H., Han, J.-Y., Choi, J.-S., Ahn, H.-K., Lee, S.-W., Kim, M.-Y., et al. (2012). Pregnancy outcomes and factors associated with voluntary pregnancy termination in women who had been treated for acne with isotretinoin. *Clinical Toxicology, 50,* 896–901.

Yorgason, J. B., & Stott, K. L. (2016). Physical health and marital status. In S. K. Whitbourne (Ed.), *Encyclopedia of adulthood and aging* (Vol. 3, pp. 1180–1184). Malden, MA: Wiley Blackwell.

Yoshida, H., & Smith, L. B. (2003). Known and novel noun extensions: Attention at two levels of abstraction. *Child Development, 74,* 564–577.

Yoshikawa, H., Aber, J. L., & Beardslee, W. R. (2012). The effects of poverty on the mental, emotional, and behavioral health of children and youth: Implications for prevention. *American Psychologist, 67,* 272–284.

Yoshikawa, H., Weiland, C., Brooks-Gunn, J., Burchinal, M. R., Espinosa, L. M., Gormley, W. T., et al. (2013). *Investing in our future: The evidence base on preschool education.* Ann Arbor, MI: Society for Research in Child Development. Retrieved from fcd-us.org/sites/default/files/Evidence%20Base%20on%20Preschool%20Education%20FINAL.pdf

You, D., Maeda, Y., & Bebeau, M. J. (2011). Gender differences in moral sensitivity: A meta-analysis. *Ethics and Behavior, 21,* 263–282.

Youn, G., Knight, B. G., Jeon, H., & Benton, D. (1999). Differences in familism values and caregiving outcomes among Korean, Korean American, and White American dementia caregivers. *Psychology and Aging, 14,* 355–364.

Youn, M. J., Leon, J., & Lee, K. J. (2012). The influence of maternal employment on children's learning growth and the role of parental involvement. *Early Child Development and Care, 182,* 1227–1246.

Young, J. B., & Rodgers, R. F. (1997). A model of radical career change in the context of psychosocial development. *Journal of Career Assessment, 5,* 167–172.

Young, S. E., Friedman, N. P., Miyake, A., Willcutt, E. G., Corley, R. P., Haberstick, B. C., et al. (2009). Behavioral disinhibition: Liability for externalizing spectrum disorders and its genetic and environmental relation to response inhibition across adolescence. *Journal of Abnormal Psychology, 118,* 117–130.

Yousafzai, A. K., Yakoob, M. Y., & Bhutta, Z. A. (2013). Nutrition-based approaches to early childhood development. In P. R. Britto, P. L. Engle, & C. M. Super (Eds.), *Handbook of early childhood development research and its impact on global policy* (pp. 202–226). New York: Oxford University Press.

Yu, R. (2002). On the reform of elementary school education in China. *Educational Exploration, 129,* 56–57.

Yuan, A. S. V., & Hamilton, H. A. (2006). Stepfather involvement and adolescent well-being: Do mothers and nonresidential fathers matter? *Journal of Family Issues, 27,* 1191–1213.

Yumoto, C., Jacobson, S. W., & Jacobson, J. L. (2008). Fetal substance exposure and cumulative environmental risk in an African American cohort. *Child Development, 79,* 1761–1776.

Yunger, J. L., Carver, P. R., & Perry, D. G. (2004). Does gender identity influence children's psychological well-being? *Developmental Psychology, 40,* 572–582.

Yur'yev, A., Leppik, L., Tooding, L.-M., Sisask, M., Värnik, P., Wu, J., & Värnik, A. (2010). Social inclusion affects elderly suicide mortality. *International Psychogeriatrics, 22,* 1337–1343.

Z

Zaccagni, L., Onisto, N., & Gualdi-Russo, E. (2009). Biological characteristics and ageing in former elite volleyball players. *Journal of Science and Medicine in Sport, 12,* 667–672.

Zacher, H., Rosing, K., Henning, T., & Frese, M. (2011). Establishing the next generation at work: Leader generativity as a moderator of the relationship between leader age, leader–member exchange, and leadership success. *Psychology and Aging, 26,* 241–252.

Zachrisson, H. D., Dearing, E., Lekhal, R., & Toppelberg, C. O. (2013). Little evidence that time in child care causes externalizing problems during early childhood in Norway. *Child Development, 84,* 1152–1170.

Zacks, R. T., & Hasher, L. (2006). Aging and long-term memory: Deficits are not inevitable. In E. Bialystok & F. I. M. Craik (Eds.), *Lifespan cognition: Mechanisms of change* (pp. 162–177). New York: Oxford University Press.

Zadjel, R. T., Bloom, J. M., Fireman, G., & Larsen, J. T. (2013). Children's understanding and experience of mixed emotions: The roles of age, gender, and empathy. *Journal of Genetic Psychology, 174,* 582–603.

Zaff, J. F., Hart, D., Flanagan, C. A., Youniss, J., & Levine, P. (2010). Developing civic engagement within a civic context. In M. Lamb & A. Freund (Eds.), *Handbook of life-span development: Vol. 2. Social and emotional development* (pp. 590–630). Hoboken, NJ: Wiley.

Zahn-Waxler, C., Kochanska, G., Krupnick, J., & McKnew, D. (1990). Patterns of guilt in children of depressed and well mothers. *Developmental Psychology, 26,* 51–59.

Zajac, R., O'Neill, S., & Hayne, H. (2012). Disorder in the courtroom? Child witnesses under cross-examination. *Developmental Review, 32,* 181–204.

Zajacova, A., & Woo, H. (2016). Examination of age variations in the predictive validity of self-rated health. *Journals of Gerontology, 71B,* 551–557.

Zakowski, S. G., Hall, M. H., Klein, L. C., & Baum, A. (2001). Appraised control, coping, and stress in a community sample: A test of the goodness-of-fit hypothesis. *Annals of Behavioral Medicine, 23,* 158–165.

Zalewski, M., Lengua, L. J., Wilson, A. C., Trancik, A., & Bazinet, A. (2011). Emotion regulation profiles, temperament, and adjustment problems in preadolescents. *Child Development, 82,* 951–966.

Zaretsky, M. D. (2003). Communication between identical twins: Health behavior and social factors are associated with longevity that is greater among identical than fraternal U.S. World War II veteran twins. *Journals of Gerontology, 58,* 566–572.

Zarit, S. H., & Eggebeen, D. J. (2002). Parent–child relationships in adulthood and later years. In M. H. Bornstein (Ed.), *Handbook of parenting, Vol. 1* (2nd ed., pp. 135–161). Mahwah, NJ: Erlbaum.

Zaslow, M. J., Weinfield, N. S., Gallagher, M., Hair, E. C., Ogawa, J. R., Egeland, B., Tabors, P. O., & De Temple, J. M. (2006). Longitudinal prediction of child outcomes from differing measures of parenting in a low-income sample. *Developmental Psychology, 42,* 27–37.

Zayas, V., Mischel, W., Shoda, Y., & Aber, J. L. (2011). Roots of adult attachment: Maternal caregiving at 18 months predicts adult peer and partner attachment. *Social Psychological and Personality Science, 2,* 289–297.

Zdaniuk, B., & Smith, C. (2016). Same-sex relationships in middle and late adulthood. In J. Bookwala

(Ed.), *Couple relationships in the middle and later years* (pp. 95–114). Washington, DC: American Psychological Association.

Zelazo, N. A., Zelazo, P. R., Cohen, K. M., & Zelazo, P. D. (1993). Specificity of practice effects on elementary neuromotor patterns. *Developmental Psychology, 29,* 686–691.

Zelazo, P., & Paus, T. (2010). Developmental social neuroscience: An introduction. In M. K. Underwood & L. H. Rosen (Eds.), *Social development: Relationships in infancy, childhood, and adolescence* (pp. 29–43). New York: Guilford.

Zelazo, P. D. (2006). The Dimensional Change Card Sort (DCCS): A method of assessing executive function in children. *Nature Protocols, 1,* 297–301.

Zelazo, P. D., Anderson, J. A. Richler, J., Wallner-Allen, K., Beaumont, J. L., & Weintraub, S. (2013). NIH Toolbox Cognition Battery (CB): Measuring executive function and attention. In P. D. Zelazo & P. J. Bauer (Eds.), National Institutes of Health Toolbox Cognition Battery (NIH Toolbox CB): Validation for children between 3 and 15 years. *Monographs of the Society for Research in Child Development, 78*(4, Serial No. 309), 16–33.

Zelazo, P. D., & Lyons, K. E. (2012). The potential benefits of mindfulness training in early childhood: A developmental social cognitive neuroscience perspective. *Child Development Perspectives, 6,* 154–160.

Zeller, M. H., & Modi, A. C. (2006). Predictors of health-related quality of life in obese youth. *Obesity Research, 14,* 122–130.

Zellner, D. A., Loaiza, S., Gonzales, Z., Pita, J., Morales, J., Pecora, D., & Wolf, A. (2006). Food selection changes under stress. *Physiology & Behavior, 87,* 789–793.

Zeskind, P. S., & Barr, R. G. (1997). Acoustic characteristics of naturally occurring cries of infants with "colic." *Child Development, 68,* 394–403.

Zhang, L., & Sternberg, R. J. (2011). Revisiting the investment theory of creativity. *Creativity Research Journal, 23,* 229–238.

Zhang, X., Geng, J., Zheng, J., Peng, B., Che, J., & Liang, C. (2012). Photoselective vaporization versus transurethral resection of the prostate for benign prostatic hyperplasia: A meta-analysis. *Journal of Endourology, 26,* 1109–1117.

Zhang, Z., Gu, D., & Luo, Y. (2014). Coresidence with elderly parents in contemporary China: The role of filial piety, reciprocity, socioeconomic resources, and parental needs. *Cross Cultural Gerontology, 29,* 259–276.

Zhao, J., Settles, B. H., & Sheng, X. (2011). Family-to-work conflict: Gender, equity and workplace policies. *Journal of Comparative Family Studies, 42,* 723–738.

Zheng, N. T., Mukamel, D. B., Caprio, T. V., & Temkin-Greener, H. (2012). Hospice utilization in nursing homes: Association with facility end-of-life care practices. *Gerontologist, 52.* Retrieved from gerontologist.oxfordjournals.org.libproxy.lib.ilstu.edu/search?fulltext=Zheng&submit=yes&x=13&y=9

Zheng, N. T., Mukamel, D. B., Friedman, B., Caprio, T. V., & Temkin-Greener, H. (2015). The effect of hospice on hospitalizations of nursing home residents. *Journal of the American Medical Directors Association, 16,* 155–159.

Zhou, X., Huang, J., Wang, Z., Wang, B., Zhao, Z., Yang, L., & Zheng-zheng, Y. (2006). Parent–child interaction and children's number learning. *Early Child Development and Care, 176,* 763–775.

Zhu, H., Sun, H.-P., Pan, C.-W., & Xu, Y. (2016). Secular trends of age at menarche from 1985 to 2010 among Chinese urban and rural girls. *Universal Journal of Public Health, 4,* 1–7.

Zickuhr, K., & Madden, M. (2012). *Pew Internet: Older adults and Internet use.* Washington, DC: Pew Research Center.

Ziemer, C. J., Plumert, J. M., & Pick, A. D. (2012). To grasp or not to grasp: Infants' actions toward objects and pictures. *Infancy, 17,* 479–497.

Zimmer-Gembeck, M., & Helfand, M. J. (2008). Ten years of longitudinal research on U.S. adolescent sexual behavior: Developmental correlates of sexual intercourse, and the importance of age, gender and ethnic background. *Developmental Review, 28,* 153–224.

Zimmerman, B. J., & Labuhn, A. S. (2012). Self-regulation of learning: Process approaches to personal development. In K. R. Harris, S. Graham, T. Urdan, C. B. McCormick, G. M. Sinatra, & J. Sweller (Eds.), *APA educational psychology handbook: Vol. 1. Theories, constructs, and critical issues* (pp. 399–425). Washington, DC: American Psychological Association.

Zimmerman, B. J., & Moylan, A. R. (2009). Self-regulation: Where metacognition and motivation intersect. In D. J. Hacker, J. Dunlosky, & A. C. Graesser (Eds.), *Handbook of metacognition in education* (pp. 299–315). New York: Routledge.

Zimmerman, C. (2012). Acceptance of dying: A discourse analysis of palliative care literature. *Social Science and Medicine, 78,* 217–224.

Zimmerman, C., & Croker, S. (2013). In G. J. Feist & M. E. Gorman (Eds.), *Handbook of the psychology of science* (pp. 49–70). New York: Springer.

Zimmerman, F. J., & Christakis, D. A. (2005). Children's television viewing and cognitive outcomes. *Archives of Pediatrics and Adolescent Medicine, 159,* 619–625.

Zimmerman, F. J., Christakis, D. A., & Meltzoff, A. N. (2007). Television and DVD/video viewing in children younger than 2 years. *Archives of Pediatrics and Adolescent Medicine, 161,* 473–479.

Zimmermann, L. K., & Stansbury, K. (2004). The influence of emotion regulation, level of shyness, and habituation on the neuroendocrine response of three-year-old children. *Psychoneuroendocrinology, 29,* 973–982.

Zitzmann, M. (2013). Effects of age on male fertility. *Best Practice & Research Clinical Endocrinology and Metabolism, 27,* 617–628.

Ziv, Y. (2013). Social information processing patterns, social skills, and school readiness in preschool children. *Journal of Experimental Child Psychology, 114,* 306–320.

Zolotor, A. J., & Puzia, M. E. (2010). Bans against corporal punishment: A systematic review of the laws, changes in attitudes and behaviours. *Child Abuse Review, 19,* 229–247.

Zolotor, A. J., Theodore, A. D., Runyan, D. K., Chang, J. J., & Laskey, A. L. (2011). Corporal punishment and physical abuse: Population-based trends for three-to-11-year-old children in the United States. *Child Abuse Review, 20,* 57–66.

Zosuls, K. M., Ruble, D. N., Bornstein, M. H., & Greulich, F. K. (2009). The acquisition of gender labels in infancy: Implications for gender-typed play. *Developmental Psychology, 45,* 688–701.

Zukow-Goldring, P. (2002). Sibling caregiving. In M. H. Bornstein (Ed.), *Handbook of parenting: Vol. 3* (2nd ed., pp. 253–286). Hillsdale, NJ: Erlbaum.

Zukowski, A. (2013). Putting words together. In J. B. Gleason & N. B. Ratner (Eds.), *The development of language* (8th ed., pp. 120–162). Upper Saddle River, NJ: Pearson.

Name Index

Italic n *following page number indicates page with an illustration or table.*

A

Aalsma, M., 393
Aarhus, L., 298
AARP, 556, 557, 592
Abakoumkin, G., 666
Abbey, A., 454
Abecassis, M., 346
Abele, A. E., 490
Aber, J. L., 59, 62, 398
Aber, L., 360
Abes, E., 456
Abma, J. C., 380, 381*n*
Abner, K. S., 248
Aboud, F. E., 344, 345
Abo-Zena, M. M., 418, 472
Abraham, C., 510
Abrams, D., 345, 416
Abramson, L. Y., 427, 428
Acevedo, E. O., 448
Achenbach, T. M., 100
Acker, M. M., 269
Ackerman, J. P., 83
Ackerman, P. L., 529, 562
Adams, A., 383
Adams, G. A., 564
Adams, K. B., 624
Adams, R. G., 376
Addati, L., 103
Adelson, S. L., 281
Adelstein, S. J., 49
Ades, P. A., 586
Adhikari, B., 449
Adolph, K. E., 134, 135, 136, 141, 145, 207
Adolphs, R., 218
Afifi, T. O., 269
Agarwal, S., 530
Agatston, P. W., 349
Agigoroaei, S., 444, 515
Agree, E. M., 580
Agrigoroaei, S., 546, 579, 583, 616
Agronick, G., 359
Aguiar, E., 154
Ahadi, S. A., 191
Ahmadlou, M., 50
Ahola, K., 560
Ahrens, C. J. C., 547
Ai, A. L., 615
Aikens, J. W., 398
Ainsworth, M. D. S., 198, 198*n*, 200
Ajrouch, K. J., 617, 625, 631
Akers, A. Y., 380
Akhtar, N., 250
Akinbami, L. J., 84
Akiyama, H., 549, 557, 559, 620, 625
Akolekar, R., 54*n*
Aksan, N., 191, 209, 268, 269
Akutagava-Martins, G. C., 309
Alati, R., 84
Albareda-Castellot, B., 138
Alberman, E., 50
Albers, C. A., 169
Albers, L. K., 547
Albert, D., 373
Alberts, A., 393

Alcalá-Herrera, V., 374
Alda, M., 439
Aldao, A., 455
Aldoney, D., 204
Aldridge, M. A., 109
Aldwin, C. M., 521, 545
Alessandri, S. M., 186
Alexander, J. M., 311
Alexander, K. L., 402
Alexeyev, M. F., 440
Alexopoulos, T., 580, 616
Alfirevic, Z., 97
Algarin, C., 104
Ali, L., 380
Alink, L. R. A., 273
Alkema, G. E., 594
Allard, M., 572
Allely, C. S., 243
Allemand, M., 614
Allen, G., 426
Allen, J., 31
Allen, J. P., 385, 421, 422, 425, 426
Allen, K. R., 632
Allen, N. B., 428
Alliey-Rodriguez, N., 52
Allik, J., 352
Allison, B. N., 376
Alloway, T. P., 161, 308, 310
Almas, A., 342
Almeida, D. M., 545, 545*n*
Almkvist, O., 579
Al-Nakhli, H., 586
Alonso-Fernández, P., 440
Alparone, F. R., 340
Alsaker, F. D., 377
Alterovitz, S. S. R., 627, 627*n*
Altmaier, E. M., 652
Alzheimer's Association, 587, 588, 590, 592, 593
Amato, P. R., 282, 354, 355, 356, 488, 495, 496, 550, 625
Ambler, G., 369
Ambrosina, K. E., 463
American Academy of Hospice and Palliative Medicine, 664
American Academy of Pediatrics, 126, 128*n*, 157
American Cancer Society, 516, 517, 517*n*
American College of Obstetricians and Gynecologists, 444
American Express Open, 561
American Foundation for Suicide Prevention, 618
American Hospice Foundation, 648
American Psychiatric Association, 243, 309, 327, 378, 379, 427
American Psychological Association, 37, 38*n*
American Society for Suicide Prevention, 546

Ames, E. W., 141
Ames, S. L., 387
Amsel, E., 391, 391*n*
Amsel, R., 667
Amso, D., 140, 161
An, J. S., 539
Anand, S. S., 157
Ananth, C. V., 96, 98
Anderson, C. A., 274
Anderson, C. B., 301
Anderson, D. M., 248
Anderson, D. R., 157
Anderson, E., 252, 383, 497
Anderson, J. R., 626, 626*n*
Anderson, K. G., 356
Anderson, K. J., 177
Anderson, R. C., 322
Anderson, V., 20, 122
Anderson-Nelson, S., 513
Anderssen, N., 302
Ando, J., 218
Andreoletti, C., 580
Andrews, G., 19, 20, 161, 233, 244, 307, 395
Anesbury, T., 297
Ang, S., 319
Angel, J. L., 579, 593
Angel, R. J., 579
Angelillo, C., 237
Angold, A., 427
Anisfeld, M., 132
Annahatak, B., 319
Anstey, K. J., 637
Anthonysamy, A., 263
Antonini, F. M., 573
Antonucci, T. C., 483, 484, 523, 547, 549, 557, 559, 617, 620, 625, 626, 630, 631
Antshel, K. M., 309
Anttila, R., 377
Anzures, G., 143
Aoki, M. F., 100
Apfelbaum, E. P., 344
Apgar, V., 94*n*, 95
Appelbaum, M. L., 172
Aquan-Assee, J., 205
Aquilino, W. S., 475
Arbeau, K. A., 192, 264
Archer, A. H., 157
Archer, T., 577
Archibald, A. B., 372
Arcus, D., 56
Ardelt, M., 601, 615, 651
Ardila-Rey, A., 344
Arditti, J. A., 550, 551
Arem, H., 521
Arias, E., 571, 572
Arija, V., 295
Arim, R. G., 376
Arking, R., 438, 441*n*, 442
Armer, M., 264
Armstrong, K. L., 125
Armstrong, L. M., 190
Armstrong, T. D., 615
Arnett, J. J., 470, 470*n*, 471, 472, 473, 474, 476, 480
Arnold, A. P., 277
Arnold, D. H., 273

Arnold, M. L., 282, 416
Arnold, R., 61
Arnon, S., 99
Arriaga, R. I., 158
Arroyo, L., 513
Arseth, A. K., 410, 411
Artal, R., 88
Arterberry, M. E., 143, 163, 225
Arthurs, E., 187
Artman, L., 306, 390
Arulkumaran, S., 89
Arum, R., 461, 474
Ary, D. V., 593
Asakawa, K., 120*n*
Aschersleben, G., 137, 238
Ascoli, G. A., 598
Asendorpf, J. B., 36
Asghari, M., 108
Asher, S. R., 348
Ashman, A. F., 401
Ashmead, D. H., 137
Askling, J., 586
Aslin, R. N., 139, 140, 175, 179
Astington, J. W., 241, 242, 311, 312*n*
Atance, C. M., 238, 260
Atchley, R. C., 620
Atkins, M. S., 249
Atkins, R., 59, 419
Atkinson, L., 205
Atlas, R., 29
Attems, J., 576
Au, T. K., 231
Audretsch, D. B., 465
Auestad, R. A., 557
Aumann, K., 202, 357
Aunola, K., 282, 283
Austin, E. L., 383
Auth, E. A., 624
Avendano, M., 445
Averhart, C. J., 344
Avioli, P. S., 558, 630
Avis, N. E., 513
Avni-Babad, D., 390
Avolio, B. J., 531, 560
Ayotte, V., 337, 409
Azevedo, R., 458

B

Bacallao, M. L., 32
Bacaltchuk, J., 379
Bachman, J. G., 401, 409
Bachstetter, A. D., 590
Backes, B. L., 454
Backley, P., 252
Bäckman, L., 576, 598, 601, 602
Badanes, L. S., 203
Baddeley, J., 337
Badiee, Z., 108
Badzinski, D. M., 261
Baenninger, M., 397
Bagès, C., 350
Baglietto-Vargas, D., 586
Bagwell, C. L., 423, 425
Bagwell, D. K., 602
Bahrick, L. E., 132, 144, 158, 162

Bailar-Heath, M., 299
Bailey, J. M., 382, 548
Bailey, S. J., 554
Bailey-Addison, K., 612
Baillargeon, R., 153*n*, 154, 158
Baillargeon, R. H., 273
Bair, D., 627
Baji, I., 187
Baker, F. C., 512
Baker, J. M., 322
Baker, L. A., 62
Baker, M., 655
Baker, P. N., 384
Baker, T., 585
Bakermans-Kranenburg, M. J., 68, 72, 195, 199, 201
Baker-Sennett, J., 310
Balasch, J., 444
Bale, T. L., 71
Bales, S. N., 66
Balfanz, R., 402
Ball, H., 126
Ball, M. M., 624
Balsam, P. D., 104
Baltes, M. M., 616, 624
Baltes, P. B., 7, 8, 68, 595, 595*n*, 600, 637
Bamford, C., 261
Bamidis, P. D., 9
Banaji, M. R., 344
Bandeali, F., 65
Bandstra, E. S., 83
Bandura, A., 17, 268
Banerjee, D., 501
Bangerter, L. R., 553
Banish, M. T., 121
Banks, M. S., 110, 141, 142*n*
Bannard, C., 177
Banse, R., 276
Barber, B. K., 283, 397, 421, 461
Barber, B. L., 411
Barber, C. H., 419
Bard, K. A., 207
Barelds, D. P. H., 488
Barkin, S. H., 60
Barkley, R. A., 309
Barlaug, D. G., 319
Barnes, J., 61
Barnes, J. C., 374
Barnes, R., 429
Barnes-Farrell, J., 560, 561
Barnett, W. S., 173, 247
Barney, A., 523
Baron, A. S., 344
Baron-Cohen, S., 243
Barone, L., 199
Barr, H. M., 83
Barr, R., 131, 154, 156, 157, 162*n*, 168
Barr, R. G., 105, 108
Barrera, M., 667
Barreto, M., 508, 561
Barrett, A. E., 541
Barrett, K. C., 188
Barrett, M., 343
Barrouillet, P., 307

NI-1

Barry, C. M., 418, 425, 472, 473, 476, 482, 484
Barry, H., III, 376
Barsman, S. G., 106
Barthell, J. E., 83
Bartholomew, K., 488
Bartholomew, M. L., 618
Bartick, M., 126
Bartocci, M., 108
Bartrip, J., 143
Bartsch, K., 241
Barzilai, S., 457
Basak, C., 529
Basilio, C. D., 412
Basinger, B., 298
Bass, S., 613
Bassett, N. S., 94
Bass-Ringdahl, S. M., 176
Bastawrous, M., 557
Basten, S., 48
Bastien, C. H., 86
Bastin, C., 597
Basu, R., 593
Bates, E., 178
Bates, G. W., 539
Bates, J. E., 190, 191
Bathelt, J., 217
Battin, D. B., 361
Bauer, P. J., 155, 163, 240
Baum, N., 551
Baumbusch, J. L., 493
Baumeister, R. F., 345, 652
Baumgart, M., 589
Baumgartner, H. A., 163
Baumgartner, M. S., 561
Baumgartner, S. E., 400
Baumrind, D., 282, 283
Baumwell, L., 179
Bauserman, R., 355
Bavelier, D., 121
Bayer, A., 38
Bayley, N., 134n, 137n, 167
Be, D., 547
Beals, D. E., 323
Bean, R. A., 421
Beardslee, W. R., 59
Beauchamp, G. K., 108, 109
Beauchamp, M. H., 20
Beaulieu, C., 217
Beaulieu, M., 623
Bebeau, M. J., 415
Bechara, A., 373
Beck, I. L., 313
Beck, L. A., 480
Becker, S., 252
Beckett, C., 123, 123n
Bedard, K., 320
Bedford, V. H., 558, 630
Bedwell, J. S., 528
Beebe, H., 398
Beech, A. R., 358
Beehr, T. A., 635
Beelmann, A., 344, 345
Behm, I., 106
Behnke, M., 83, 84
Behrens, K. Y., 202
Beier, M. E., 529, 562
Beintema, D., 101n
Bekhet, A. K., 623
Bekkouche, N. S., 455
Bélanger, M. J., 260
Belcher, D., 301
Belfort, M. B., 128

Beliakoff, A., 245
Belizan, J. M., 99
Bell, C., 327
Bell, J. H., 393
Bell, M., 455
Bell, M. A., 141, 154
Bellagamba, F., 155, 157
Belle, S. H., 593
Belleville, S., 9
Bellmore, A. D., 348
Belloc, S., 444
Belmonte, M. K., 243
Belsky, J., 58, 124, 171, 195, 200, 202, 205, 206, 247, 373
Beltrán-Sánchez, H., 572
Beltz, A. M., 277
Belyea, M., 105
Bem, D. J., 35
Benadiva, C., 52
Benbow, C. P., 395
Bender, H. L., 269
Benenson, J. F., 423
Benigno, J. P., 235
Benin, M., 402
Benner, A. D., 62, 396, 397, 401
Bennett, C., 492
Bennett, D. A., 590
Bennett, K. M., 628, 629
Bennett, M. I., 593
Benoit, A., 377
Benshoff, J. M., 482
Benson, J. B., 137
Benson, J. E., 242
Benson, K., 491
Bera, A., 100
Berardi, N., 121
Beratis, I. N., 218
Berenbaum, S. A., 276, 277, 279
Berg, C. A., 599
Berg, K. M., 636
Bergeman, C. S., 666
Bergen, D., 228
Berger, L. M., 246
Berger, S. E., 135, 154
Berggren, I., 657
Bergman, E. J., 670
Bergman, I., 579
Bergman, M., 509
Bergman, M. J., 532, 533
Bergman, R., 414
Bering, J. M., 649
Berk, L., 586
Berk, L. E., 168, 225, 228, 235, 236, 264, 271n, 328n
Berk, M. S., 428
Berkeley, S., 340
Berkowitz, M. W., 417
Berkowitz, R. L., 51
Berlin, L. J., 201, 269
Berman, R. A., 322
Bermingham, D. W., 620
Berndt, T. J., 347
Bernier, A., 201, 485
Bern-Klug, M., 624
Bernstein, N., 431
Berntsen, D., 597, 597n
Berry, C. J., 596
Berry, P., 659
Berscheid, E., 479

Bersoff, D. M., 417
Bersted, K., 69
Bertenthal, B. I., 142, 154
Bertoncini, J., 109, 131
Bertrand, J., 85
Bertrand, M., 500
Bertrand, R. M., 544
Berzin, S. C., 485
Berzlanovich, A. M., 573
Berzonsky, M. D., 410, 411
Besançon, M., 328
Best, C., 369, 380, 381
Best, D., 84
Best, D. L., 350
Beydoun, M. E., 590
Beyene, Y., 514
Beyers, J. M., 431
Beyers, W., 410, 476
Bhargava, S., 399
Bhat, A., 136
Bhatt, R. S., 162, 163, 163n
Bhutta, Z. A., 220
Bialystok, E., 244, 323
Bianchi, S. M., 25, 487, 554
Bibile, V., 310
Bick, J., 111
Bickel, W. K., 450
Biderman, J., 309
Biehl, M. C., 375, 376, 377
Bielak, A. A. M., 601
Bierer, L. M., 71
Bierman, A., 615, 631
Bierman, K. L., 247, 275, 398
Bifulco, R., 327
Bigelow, A. E., 185, 188, 200
Bigler, R. S., 279, 280, 344, 345, 347, 351
Bilgel, M., 588
Binstock, R. H., 637
Birbeck, D., 38
Birch, E. E., 142
Birch, L. L., 219, 220
Birch, S. H., 265
Bird, A., 240
Birditt, K. S., 483, 484, 551, 555, 611, 617, 621, 625, 626
Biringen, Z., 133, 203
Birkelund, M. S., 409
Birney, D. P., 19, 160
Biro, F. M., 297
Birren, J. E., 600
Bisanz, J., 245
Bisconti, T. L., 666
Bissaker, K., 282, 351
Bissonnette, V. L., 481
Biswabharati, S., 546
Bitan, T., 394
Bjelakovic, G., 440
Bjorklund, D. F., 22, 159, 310, 311, 649
Black, J. E., 124
Black, M. C., 454, 489
Black, M. M., 83, 201
Black, R. E., 129, 220
Blackburn, E., 439
Blackwell, C., 106
Blades, M., 361
Blair, B. L., 347
Blair, C., 189, 237, 239
Blake, A. B., 529, 602

Blakemore, J. E. O., 276, 277, 278, 350
Blakemore, S.-J., 373
Blanchard, V. L., 32
Blanchard-Fields, F., 611, 621
Bland, C. G., 417
Blasi, A., 414
Blasi, C. H., 22
Blass, E. M., 131
Blatteis, C. M., 574
Blatt-Eisengart, I., 283
Blattman, A. J., 312
Blau, D., 562
Bleeker, M. M., 464
Bleske, A. L., 483
Bliesener, R., 483, 523, 631
Blinka, L., 424
Block, C. C., 313
Block, J., 549
Blomberg, M., 579
Blondell, S. J., 590
Blood-Siegfried, J., 106
Bloom, J. R., 517
Bloom, L., 177
Bloom, P., 158
Bloom, T., 89
Bluck, S., 508, 597, 655
Bluebond-Langner, M., 655
Blumenthal, H., 376, 554
Bodell, L. P., 379
Bodner, E., 652
Bodrova, E., 166, 325
Boehm, J. K., 581
Boeninger, D. K., 521
Boerger, E. A., 231
Boerner, K., 626
Bogaert, A. F., 382
Bogin, B., 117, 219
Bohannon, J. N., III, 175, 252
Bohlmeijer, E. T., 612
Böhm, R., 344
Bolisetty, S., 98, 98n
Bolkan, C., 544, 580
Boly, M., 647
Bonanno, G. A., 665, 666
Bond, J. T., 202, 357
Bonikowski, B., 500, 500n
Bonin, S. L., 463
Bonner, S. B., 381
Bons, T. A., 69
Bonstrom, J., 488
Bonvillian, J. D., 175
Bookman, A., 557
Boom, J., 415
Boomsma, D. I., 281
Boon, S. D., 553
Booren, L. M., 266
Boot, W. R., 605
Booth, A., 488, 497
Booth, J. R., 394
Booth, R. D. L., 243
Booth-LaForce, C., 199, 200
Borchert, S., 167
Borders, L. D., 464
Borduin, C. M., 432, 432n
Borghese, M. M., 297
Bornick, P., 83
Bornstein, M. H., 131, 143, 163, 167, 168, 170, 179, 203, 205, 225, 357
Borst, C. G., 95
Borst, G., 304
Bos, H., 497, 498

Bosquet, M., 121
Bost, K. K., 201, 240
Boswell, G. H., 615
Boswell, H., 372n
Bouazzaoui, B., 580
Bouchard, T. J., 69
Boucher, O., 86
Boudreau, J. P., 141
Bouldin, P., 228
Boulton, M., 349
Bourassa, K. J., 496, 550
Bourgeois, M. S., 593
Boutwell, B. B., 269
Bowen, C. E., 531, 546, 561
Bowen, R., 392
Bower, T. G. R., 109
Bowker, J. C., 171
Bowlby, J., 7, 22, 196, 197, 203, 665
Bowling, A., 622
Bowman, N. A., 460
Boyatzis, C. J., 225
Boyd, J. S., 245
Boyd-Franklin, N., 63
Boyer, T. W., 154
Boyle, C. A., 48
Boynton-Jarrett, R., 373
Boysson-Bardies, B. de, 176
Bozionelos, N., 499
Bracken, B. A., 245
Brackett, M. A., 317
Bradbury, T. N., 481, 488
Bradley, R. H., 100, 170, 246, 284
Brady, K. T., 449
Brady, S. A., 313
Braine, L. G., 300
Brainerd, C. J., 234
Brand, S., 371
Brand, S. R., 71
Brandi, M. L., 510
Brandone, A. C., 178
Branje, S. J. T., 376, 423
Branstetter, W. H., 28
Brashler, P., 489
Braswell, G. S., 224, 225
Bratko, D., 67
Braungart-Rieker, J. M., 185, 186, 189
Brav, T. K., 529, 597
Braver, S. L., 496
Brazelton, T. B., 110
Brazil, A., 386
Bredekamp, S., 172n, 226, 248n, 325n
Bregman, H. R., 383
Brehmer, Y., 602
Breitbart, W., 656
Breivik, K., 409
Bremner, J. G., 153, 158
Brendgen, M., 266, 272, 273, 423
Brennan, L. M., 34
Brennan, W. M., 141
Brenner, E., 342
Brent, M. R., 177
Brent, S. B., 650
Breslau, N., 666
Bretherton, I., 197, 202
Brewster, K. L., 497
Brez, C. C., 132
Brezausek, C. M., 222
Briars, L., 221

Bridgett, D. J., 193
Bright, G. M., 219
Brint, S., 461
Brisch, K. H., 201
Broadhead, G. K., 575
Brock, S., 391
Brodaty, H., 588
Brodtmann, A., 591
Brody, G. H., 204, 352, 387
Brody, L., 277
Brodzinsky, D. M., 55, 56
Broidy, L. M., 431
Bromberger, J. T., 512
Bromnick, R. D., 393
Bronfenbrenner, U., 23, 57, 68
Bronson, G. W., 142
Brook, D. W., 449
Brook, J. S., 449
Brooker, R. J., 186
Brooks, R., 176
Brooks-Gunn, J., 25, 60, 61, 63, 100, 170, 171, 203, 207, 318, 360, 372, 374, 375, 376, 386, 430, 497
Brophy, J. E., 339, 340, 341*n*
Brown, A., 125
Brown, A. H., 627
Brown, A. I., 473
Brown, A. M., 141
Brown, B. B., 259, 423, 424, 425
Brown, C., 611
Brown, C. A., 637
Brown, C. S., 280, 345
Brown, E. R., 614
Brown, G. L., 203, 204, 205
Brown, J., 328
Brown, J. A., 580
Brown, J. D., 380, 385
Brown, L. H., 553
Brown, R. M., 557
Brown, R. W., 251
Brown, S. A., 387
Brown, S. L., 491, 550, 557, 617, 627, 628
Brown, T. M., 402
Browne, C. A., 231
Browne, J. V., 110
Browne, K. D., 634
Brownell, C. A., 207, 260, 262
Brownell, D. K., 446
Brownell, M. D., 246
Bruce, B., 582
Bruce, H., 576
Bruce, M. L., 670
Bruck, M., 361
Brucker, E., 563
Bruehl, E. C., 597
Bruine de Bruin, W., 394
Brumariu, L. E., 338, 352
Brummelman, E., 339
Brunt, J., 165
Bruschweiler-Stern, N., 110
Brussoni, M. J., 553
Bruzzese, J.-M., 38
Bryan, A. D., 381
Bryan, A. E., 195
Bryant, B. K., 463
Bryant, D., 431
Bryant, D. M., 51
Bryant, L. O., 84
Bryant, N. B., 374
Bryant, P., 244

Brydges, C. R., 316
Bryk, R. L., 118
Buchanan, C. M., 356
Buchanan-Barrow, E., 343
Buchsbaum, D., 228
Buckingham-Howes, S., 83
Buehler, C., 357
Buese, D., 326
Bugental, D. B., 276, 286
Buhl, H. M., 470
Buhrmester, D., 36
Buhs, E. S., 265, 266, 346, 348
Bukacha, C. M., 143
Bukowski, W. M., 205, 263, 423
Bulanda, J. R., 627, 628
Bulcroft, K., 626
Bulik, C. M., 379
Bumpass, L. L., 497, 539
Bunting, H., 399
Burchinal, M. R., 29, 64, 171, 246, 247
Burden, M. J., 85
Burgess, K. B., 192, 283, 348
Burgess-Champoux, T. L., 295, 378
Burgio, L. D., 593
Burkam, D. T., 244*n*
Burke, D. M., 599
Burleson, B. R., 481
Burman, D. D., 394
Burr, J. A., 637
Bursik, K., 480
Burts, D. C., 246
Bush, K. R., 58
Bushman, B. J., 274
Bushnell, E. W., 141
Buss, A. T., 135, 166
Buss, D. M., 479, 483
Buss, K. A., 192
Bussey, K., 271
Buswell, S. D., 126
Butler, K., 473
Butler, R., 612
Buttelmann, D., 241, 344
Butterworth, M. R., 487*n*
Butterworth, P., 479
Butts, M. M., 357
Buur, H., 191
Bybee, J. A., 508, 544
Byne, W., 281
Bynner, J. M., 474
Byrnes, J. P., 250

C
Cabell, S. Q., 244
Cabrera, N. J., 179, 204, 284
Cadinu, M., 340
Cahan, S., 306, 390
Cai, Y., 171
Cain, A., 667
Cain, K., 322
Cain, M. A., 83
Caine, E. D., 618
Cairns, B. D., 14
Cairns, R. B., 14
Calabrese, S. K., 453
Calarco, K. E., 85
Caldwell, B. M., 170, 246
Caldwell, K. A., 425
Caldwell, M. S., 409
Calhoun, L. G., 668

Call, J., 174
Callanan, M. A., 224, 250
Caltran, G., 105
Calussi, P., 349
Calvert, S. L., 157, 274, 279, 297
Camaioni, L., 155
Camann, W. R., 97
Cameron, C. A., 252, 343
Cameron, H. A., 574
Cameron, N., 117
Cameron, P. A., 207
Cameron-Smith, D., 578
Camp, C. J., 590
Campbell, A., 278
Campbell, A. L., 637
Campbell, D. A., 96
Campbell, F. A., 173
Campbell, J. M., 218
Campbell, S. B., 201, 260, 262
Campbell, T., 155
Campbell, W. K., 339, 471
Campion, M. A., 559
Campione-Barr, N., 485
Campisi, J., 440
Campos, J. J., 141, 153, 185, 186
Camras, L. A., 185, 186
Cancian, M., 62
Candelaria, M., 201
Candy, B., 659
Candy, J., 278
Cantwell, A. M., 461
Cao, R., 195
Cao, S., 447
Capaldi, D., 204
Capezuti, E. A., 590
Capirci, O., 176
Caplan, M., 208
Capozzoli, M. C., 162
Cappeliez, P., 612
Cappell, K. A., 574
Cappelli, P., 561
Carballo, J. J., 427
Carcedo, R. J., 483
Card, N. A., 273
Cardona Cano, S., 219
Carels, R., 338, 409
Carey, S., 151, 158, 344, 648
Carli, L. L., 561
Carlo, G., 416, 418
Carlson, E. A., 7
Carlson, J. J., 209, 321
Carlson, M. C., 638
Carlson, S. M., 20, 161, 228, 236, 238, 242, 308, 323
Carlson, V. J., 201
Carnelley, K. B., 668
Carney, W., 551
Caro, F. G., 637
Carpenter, M., 176, 177
Carpenter, R., 126
Carpenter, T. P., 314
Carr, D., 545, 629, 666
Carr, J., 50
Carrier, L. M., 400
Carroll, D., 455
Carroll, J. B., 315
Carroll, J. S., 476
Carroll, R., 667
Carroll, R. A., 488
Carskadon, M. A., 374

Carson, C., 385
Carson, S., 459
Carstensen, L. L., 611, 612, 620, 621, 621*n*
Carter, B. D., 449
Carter, C. S., 511
Carver, K., 426, 426*n*
Carver, P. R., 351
Casalin, S., 191
Casasola, M., 163
Case, A. D., 31
Case, R., 19, 233, 300, 307
Caserta, D., 86
Caserta, M. S., 593, 615, 628, 629, 668
Casey, B. J., 218, 373
Casey, M. B., 396
Casey, P., 53
Casillas, G., 581, 613
Casper, L. M., 357
Casper, W. J., 357
Caspi, A., 12, 35, 70, 191, 193, 221
Cassia, V. M., 142, 143*n*
Cassidy, J., 201, 480
Cassirer, N., 103
Castel, A. D., 529, 602
Castillo-López, R., 513
Castle, D. J., 379
Catalano, R., 48, 49
Cauffman, E., 283
Cauley, J. A., 519
Causey, K., 22
Cavell, T. A., 339
Ceci, S. J., 246, 318, 361, 395
Cecil, J. E., 220
Ceda, G. P., 440
Cederholm, T., 583
Center for Communication and Social Policy, 274
Center for Hearing and Communication, 509
Centers for Disease Control and Prevention, 48, 84, 106, 127, 217, 221, 285*n*, 298, 299*n*, 303, 383, 428, 449, 453, 454, 515, 546, 570, 586, 587, 618, 657
Centers for Medicare and Medicaid Services, 591, 593
Cerella, J., 528, 529
Cernoch, J. M., 109
Cespedes, E. M., 157
Cetinkaya, M. B., 52
Cevenini, E., 571
Chaddock, L., 300
Chaddock-Heyman, L., 300
Chae, D. H., 439
Chakravarty, E., 582
Chakravarty, E. F., 582, 582*n*
Chakravorty, S., 48
Chalabaev, A., 301
Chambaere, K., 664
Chamberlain, P., 431
Chambers, P., 56
Chan, A., 251
Chan, C. C. Y., 178, 250
Chan, C. K. M., 617
Chan, S. M., 284
Chan, T. W., 398
Chance, G., 144
Chandler, M. J., 312, 411

Chandra, A., 443, 450, 451
Chang, E., 630
Chang, J. J., 269*n*
Chang, P. F., 631
Chang, R. W., 586
Chang, S., 295
Chang, Y. T., 374
Chao, R. K., 533
Chapman, R. S., 175
Chappell, J. J., 310
Charity, A. H., 319
Charles, D., 488
Charles, P., 491
Charles, S. T., 611, 612, 617, 620, 621, 622
Charlier, R., 510
Charman, T., 167
Charman, W. N., 508
Charness, N., 528, 530, 605
Chase-Lansdale, P. L., 63, 170
Chater, N., 175
Chatterji, P., 103
Chatters, L. M., 618
Chauhan, G. S., 279
Chavajay, P., 167, 319
Chavarria, M. C., 373
Chawarska, K., 243
Chazan-Cohen, R., 173
Cheah, C. S. L., 284
Cheatham, C. L., 123
Checkley, W., 221
Cheema, J., 91
Cheever, N. A., 400
Chein, J., 373
Chen, B., 421
Chen, E. E., 344
Chen, E. S. L., 278
Chen, F. S., 197
Chen, H., 421
Chen, J. J., 60, 360
Chen, L.-C., 135
Chen, R., 265, 461
Chen, S.-F., 650
Chen, W., 284
Chen, X., 191, 193, 195, 265
Chen, Y., 48, 486
Chen, Y.-C., 86
Chen, Y.-J., 86
Chen, Z., 155
Cheng, G., 586
Cherlin, A. J., 284, 497
Chervenak, J., 512
Chess, S., 190, 195
Chessell, Z. J., 544
Chetty, R., 570
Cheung, F. M., 561
Chevalier, N., 20, 161
Cheyney, M., 96
Chhin, C. S., 464
Chi, I., 632
Chi, M. T. H., 459
Chiang, T., 50
Chiang, W.-C., 158
Child Care Aware, 171
Child Trends, 25, 91, 221, 222, 246, 247, 384, 497
Chin, H. B., 385
Chinn, C. A., 391
Chiu, D., 401
Chiu, D. T., 295
Cho, L. S., 91
Choe, D. E., 267
Choi, J., 397

Choi, N. G., 547, 601
Choi, S., 165, 178
Choi, Y. J., 550
Chomsky, C., 322
Chomsky, N., 174
Chouinard, M. M., 232, 252
Chrisler, J. C., 523
Christ, A. E., 667
Christ, G. H., 667
Christakis, D. A., 157, 275
Christakis, N. A., 629
Christakos, A., 423
Christakou, A., 393
Christensen, A.-D., 542
Christian, C. W., 287
Christie, C. A., 402
Christie, J. F., 228
Christofferson, M. N., 56
Christofferson, J. L., 472, 473
Christophe, A., 131
Christopoulos, A., 393
Chu, C. Y. C., 556
Chung, H. L., 430
Chung, K. W., 511
Church, E., 497
Churchman, R., 659
Ciarrochi, J., 424
Cicchetti, D., 195, 195n, 286, 287, 337, 360
Cici-Gokaltun, A., 559
Cicirelli, V. G., 558, 651, 652
Cillessen, A. H. N., 346, 347, 348, 349, 423
Cipriano, E. A., 195, 283
Circle (Center for Information & Research on Civic Learning & Engagement), 472
Claes, M., 377
Claes, R., 561
Clark, B. L., 519
Clark, E. V., 252
Clark, P. A., 369, 372, 372n
Clark, S. M., 96
Clarke, B. L., 510
Clarke, M. J., 452
Clarke, P., 579
Clarke-Stewart, K. A., 266, 355
Claxton, A., 489, 612
Claxton, L. J., 137
Claxton, S. J., 242
Clay, R. A., 400
Clearfield, M. W., 133, 158, 277
Cleland, J. W., 105
Clements, D. H., 245, 313
Clifford, C., 655
Clifton, R. K., 136
Clinchy, B. M., 457
Clincy, A. R., 171
Clingempeel, W. G., 497
Coall, D. A., 89
Coats, A. H., 621
Cobb, C. D., 327
Cobb, R. J., 488
Coffino, B., 7
Cohen, D. A., 446
Cohen, G. L., 321n
Cohen, J., 664
Cohen, J. A., 358
Cohen, L. B., 158, 159, 164, 165

Cohen, M., 36, 359
Cohen, O., 549
Cohen, R., 353
Cohen-Bendahan, C. C. C., 107
Cohen-Kettenis, P. T., 281
Cohen-Mansfield, J., 590
Cohn, N., 226
Coid, J. W., 431
Coie, J. D., 348
Colbert, L. G., 557
Colby, A., 414
Colby, S. L., 12
Colcombe, S. J., 574
Cole, D. A., 409
Cole, E., 429
Cole, E. R., 13
Cole, M., 201, 390
Cole, P. M., 189, 190, 209, 262
Coleman, M., 354, 496, 497
Coleman, P. D., 574
Coleman, P. G., 615
Coles, C. D., 84
Coley, R. L., 356, 357
Collings, P., 581
Collins, N. L., 480
Collins, W., 669
Collins, W. A., 352, 420, 422, 423, 426, 427
Collins, W. K., 398, 421
Collin-Vézina, D., 358, 360
Colman, R. J., 511
Colombo, J., 132, 161, 169
Colombo, M., 132
Colonnesi, C., 155
Colson, E. R., 126
Colwell, M. J., 228, 265
Comeau, L., 252
Commendador, K. A., 380
Common Sense Media, 249
Compas, B. E., 298
Compton, J. I., 532
Comstock, G., 274
Comunian, A. L., 417, 418
Conchas, G. Q., 400
Conde-Agudelo, A., 99
Condron, D. J., 327, 330
Conduct Problems Prevention Research Group, 381
Conger, K. J., 352
Conger, R. D., 58, 59, 376, 480
Conley, C. S., 409
Conlon, E., 244
Connell, J. P., 339
Conner, D. B., 235
Connidis, I. A., 628, 630
Connolly, J., 425, 426, 426n, 427
Connolly, K. J., 225
Connor, D. F., 309
Connor, S. R., 659
Conrad, N. J., 138
Conroy-Beam, D., 479
Conway, C. C., 428
Conway, L., 351
Conway, M. A., 597
Conwell, Y., 618, 619
Cook, C. R., 349
Cooke, L. P., 487
Cooney, T. M., 539
Cooper, C., 369, 633
Cooper, H., 246, 337

Cooper, J. O., 17
Cooper, R. P., 99, 109
Copeland, W., 377
Copen, C. E., 443, 450, 451, 494
Coplan, R. J., 171, 192, 264, 348
Copple, C., 172n, 226, 248n, 325n
Corapci, F., 189, 262
Corbett, D., 121, 122
Corbett, N., 439
Corby, B. C., 351
Corenblum, B., 344
Cornelius, C. A., 231
Cornell, K. H., 385
Cornoldi, C., 327
Cornwell, A. C., 106
Cornwell, B., 625
Corona, A. W., 443
Corpuz, R., 276
Corr, C. A., 650, 653, 666, 671
Corr, D. M., 650, 653, 666, 671
Correa-Chavez, M., 167, 236
Correia, C., 576
Cortina, K. S., 547
Cosentino, S., 573
Costa, A., 323
Costa, N. M., 358
Costa, P. T., Jr., 548, 548n
Costacurta, M., 217
Costigan, C. L., 32
Côté, J., 302
Côté, J. E., 410, 460, 470, 474
Cote, L. R., 168
Côté, S. M., 273, 346
Cotroneo, M., 667
Cottle, C. C., 432
Coubart, A., 159
Couch, S. C., 296
Coudé, G., 132
Coudin, G., 580, 616
Courage, M. L., 249
Courchesne, E., 243
Coursolle, K. M., 636
Covitz, L. M., 354
Cowan, C. P., 422, 491
Cowan, N., 161
Cowan, P. A., 266, 422, 491
Cowan, R., 260
Cox, B. D., 70
Cox, E., 532
Cox, J. E., 384, 385
Cox, M., 59
Cox, R. B., Jr., 283
Cox, V., 231
Coyl, D. D., 204
Coyle, J. T., 83, 315
Coyle, N., 545
Coyne, S. M., 274
Crago, M. B., 319, 324
Craig, C. M., 101
Craig, H. K., 319
Craig, W. M., 29
Craigie, T. A., 497
Craik, F. I. M., 323
Crain, W., 16
Crair, M. C., 121
Cramond, B., 548
Crane, D. R., 421
Cratty, B. J., 223n

Craven, R. G., 260, 337
Crawford, S., 513
Crawley-Davis, A. M., 157
Crick, N. R., 273, 347, 352, 431
Crimmins, E. M., 572
Criss, M. M., 422
Crocetti, E., 410, 411, 419, 470, 471, 551
Crockenberg, S., 23, 189
Crocker, J., 337
Crocker, N., 84
Croft, D. P., 22
Croker, R., 12, 613
Croker, S., 391
Crone, E. A., 393
Croninger, R. G., 326
Croot, K., 592
Crosnoe, R., 62, 401, 403
Cross, D., 398
Cross, D. R., 235
Cross, S., 544
Crossman, E. J., 11, 60, 284, 360, 422
Crouch, J. L., 286
Croucher, K., 624
Crouter, A. C., 350, 352, 421, 422, 485
Crowley, K., 577
Crowther, M. R., 615
Cruce, T. M., 461
Cruces, J., 443
Cruess, L., 238
Cruttenden, L., 154
Cruz, L. A., 576
Cruza-Guet, M. C., 463
Crystal, D. S., 346, 417
Csibra, G., 166, 176
Csikszentmihalyi, M., 325, 546, 600
Cubanski, J., 581, 613
Cuevas, K., 155, 162, 163
Cui, M., 430, 492
Culang, M. E., 36, 543
Cullen, M. R., 562
Cumberland, P. M., 298
Cumming, E., 620
Cummings, E. M., 23, 33, 57
Cundiff, J. M., 520
Curby, T. W., 266
Curl, A. L., 587
Curlin, F. A., 661
Curnow, C., 442
Currie, C., 377
Curtin, S., 138
Curtin, S. C., 497
Curtindale, L. M., 132, 161
Curtiss, K., 616
Curtiss, S., 175
Cutchin, M. P., 624
Cutler, A., 140
Cutler, D. M., 62
Cutler, S. J., 636, 637
Cutting, A. L., 272
Cutuli, J. J., 59
Cvencek, D., 350
Cyr, C., 201
Czaja, S., 286
Czaja, S. J., 579, 592

D

Daatland, S. O., 628
Dabrowska, E., 251

Dack, L. A., 242
Dadds, M. R., 125
Daher, M., 518
Dahl, A., 601
Daigneault, I., 358, 360
Dakil, S. R., 286
Dale, J., 654
Dale, P., 177
Daley, T. C., 319
Dallman, M. F., 296
Daltabuit, M., 107
Daly, C. A., 481
Daly, M. J., 67
Damhuis, I., 341
Damian, R. I., 459
Damico, A., 581, 613
Damon, W., 265, 346, 408
Dane, E., 459
Danesh, D., 449
Daneshvar, D. H., 589
Dang, E. P., 85
Daniel, D. B., 389
Daniels, E., 302
Daniels, H., 23, 236
Daniels, K., 494
Daniels, T., 348
Dannemiller, J. L., 143
Danzer, E., 54
Darcy, A., 378
Dark-Freudeman, A., 602
Darling, N., 62
Darling-Hammond, L., 330
Darlington, R., 246
Darwich, R., 17
Darwin, C., 13
Das, A., 515, 631
Daskalakis, N., 71
Datar, A., 297
D'Augelli, A. R., 382
Daugherty, J., 494
Davey, A., 555
David, B., 416
David, K. M., 191
Davidson, R. J., 121
Davies, B., 667
Davies, E., 667
Davies, J., 278
Davies, P. T., 23, 195, 195n
Davis, A., 474
Davis, E. L., 192, 261
Davis, K., 65
Davis, K. F., 104
Davis, P. E., 228
Davison, K. K., 220
Davis-Unger, A., 228
Dawson, T. L., 415
Dayton, C. J., 107n
Deal, P. J., 473
Dean, D., 391
Deane, G., 555
DeAngelo, L., 471
Dearing, E., 61, 171, 247
Deary, I. J., 67, 314, 527, 601, 614
Deas, S., 379
Deater-Deckard, K., 11, 67, 269
Deaton, A. S., 614
Debats, D. L., 616, 617
DeBoer, T., 119
Debrabant, J., 300
de Bruyn, E. H., 348, 397, 398
Debus, R., 337

de Calignon, A., 589
DeCarli, C., 574
DeCasper, A. J., 81, 109
Dechanet, C., 449
Declercq, E. R., 97
de Cock, E. S. A., 105
De Corte, E., 314
DeCoster, J., 593
Deeg, D. J. H., 570, 582
DeFlorio, L., 245
Defoe, I. N., 393
de Frias, C. M., 8, 598
DeFries, J. C., 67
De Goede, I. H. A., 423
DeGrace, A., 476, 482, 484
De Groote, I., 243
de Haan, M., 20, 21, 119, 120, 121, 124, 139, 139n, 217, 219
Deitchman, J., 532
De Jager, P. L., 590
deJong, A., 583
DeKosky, S. T., 583
Deković, M., 272, 376, 398
De Laet, S., 348
De la Fuente, M., 440
Delahunty, K. M., 111
DeLamater, J., 515, 584, 584n
de la Monte, S. M., 85
Delaney, R. K., 538, 547
de la Ossa, J. L., 239
de Lima, C., 448
Dell, M. L., 615
Deller, J., 564
DeLoache, J. S., 156, 157, 179, 207, 229
DelVecchio, W. E., 193
De Marco, A. C., 485
DeMarie, D., 308, 312
Demetriou, A., 390, 392
Demetriou, H., 272
Demiray, B., 508, 597
Denckla, C. A., 558
Deng, C., 284
Denham, B. E., 370
Denham, S., 260
Denissen, J. J. A., 36, 337
Denkinger, M. D., 443
Denmark, F. L., 523
Dennerstein, L., 515
Dennis, T. A., 261
Dennis, W., 136
Dennison, E. M., 369
Dennison, R. P., 481, 488
Denny, K. E., 25, 422
Denton, N. A., 32
Deocampo, J., 163
De Pasquale, D., 476
DePaulo, B. M., 493
Deprest, J. A., 54
DeRoche, K., 46
DeRose, L. M., 374, 375
DeRosier, M. E., 348
de Rosnay, M., 188, 242
De Rycke, L., 337
de St. Aubin, E., 539
de Schonen, S., 143
Désert, M., 350
Desmarais, S., 278
DeSouza, A., 193, 195
De Souza, E., 50
Dessens, A. B., 281
Deutsch, A. R., 430

Deutsch, N. L., 532
Devane, D., 97
Deveson, A., 630
DeVos, J., 153n, 154
Devouche, E., 176
de Vries, A. L. C., 281
de Vries, B., 483, 628, 669
DeVries, R., 325
Dew, J., 492
de Waal, F. B. M., 277
de Weerth, C., 107, 128
De Wit, D. J., 397
Dhuey, E., 320
Diamond, A., 154, 218, 237, 238, 238n, 250
Diamond, L. M., 381, 383, 483, 486, 487n
Dias, M. G., 389
Diaz-Rossello, J., 100
DiBiase, A.-M., 432
Di Ceglie, D., 281
Dick, F., 175
Dickenson, J., 381
Dickinson, D. K., 244
Dick-Read, G., 95
Dickson, R. A., 597
DiDonato, M. D., 279
Diehl, M., 545, 612, 636
Diekmann, A., 495
Diemer, M. A., 550
Diener, E., 547
Dietz, E. L., 425
Diggs, J., 440
Di Giuseppe, D., 586
Dijkstra, P., 488
DiLalla, L. F., 69, 246
DiLisi, R., 279
Dillon, M., 541
Dilworth-Anderson, P., 557, 615
Dimitry, L., 359
Dimond, M. F., 615
DiPietro, J. A., 79, 80
Dishion, T. J., 34
Dittmar, M., 251
Dix, T., 195, 209
Dixon, L. D., 85
Dixon, P., 497
Dixon, R. A., 598, 601
Dmitrieva, J., 203
Dodd, V. L., 100
Dodge, K. A., 62, 270, 274, 348, 431
Dodson, T. A., 464
Doherty, W. J., 491, 626, 626n
Dohnt, H., 338
Doka, K. J., 666, 668
Dolan, D. C., 616
Dolbin-MacNab, M. L., 554
Dombrovski, A. Y., 619
Domellöf, E., 218
Domingo, J. P., 659
Domitrovich, C. E., 237, 247
Donaldson, M., 219
Donatelle, R. J., 445, 448, 450, 455
Dondi, M., 105
Donellan, M. B., 614
Dong, W., 339
Dong, X., 633
Donnan, G., 591
Donnellan, M. B., 58, 59, 337, 339, 471, 480, 492, 614

Donnelly, R., 409
Donnelly, T. M., 419
Donnerstein, E., 380
Donsky, T., 57
Doolittle, A., 669
Doom, J. R., 20
Doornwaard, S. M., 425, 426
Dorfman, L. T., 636
Dorius, C., 354
Dorn, L. D., 376
Dornan, J., 81
Dornbusch, S. M., 356
Dörner, J., 601
Dorris, M., 84
Dorwie, F. M., 95
Doss, B. D., 490
Double, E. B., 85
Douglas, E. M., 355
Douglass, S., 412
Dowd, M. D., 670
Dowling, E. M., 418
Downer, J. T., 266
Downing, J. E., 327
Downs, A. C., 375
Downs, R. M., 305
Doydum, A. O., 240
Doyle, A., 344
Dragowski, E. A., 383
Drake, K., 206
Drake, M. T., 519
Draper, B. M., 619
Drayton, S., 242
Dreman, S., 549
Drick, C. A., 647
Driscoll, K. A., 428
Driver, J., 481, 489, 490
Drop, S. L. S., 281
Druet, C., 128, 128n
Drummond, M., 38
Drummond, P. D., 297
Drury, S. S., 439
Dube, M., 623
DuBois, D. L., 337, 409
Dubois, L., 127
Dubois, M.-F., 38
du Bois-Reymond, M., 474
Duckworth, A. L., 320
Dudani, A., 222
Dugan, A., 663
Dumanovsky, T., 658
Duncan, G. J., 58, 59, 237, 245
Duncan, L. E., 72, 539
Duncan, M., 522
Dundek, L. H., 96
Dunham, Y., 344
Dunifon, R. E., 296
Dunkel-Shetter, C., 89
Dunkle, R. E., 627
Dunlop, D. D., 586
Dunn, J., 204, 208, 265, 267, 272, 352, 354, 356
Dunn, J. R., 60
Dunn, M. G., 500
Dunn, M. J., 298
Dunne, E. J., 666
Dunne, P. E., 378
Dunne-Bryant, A., 354
Dunne-Maxim, K., 666
Dunning, D. L., 308
Dupéré, V., 11, 59, 61, 430
Durham, M., 246
duRivage, N., 286

Durlak, J. A., 61, 357, 360
Durrant, J. E., 271
Dush, C. M. K., 490
Duszak, R. S., 87
Dutta, A., 438
Dutta, R., 6, 22
Dutton, D. G., 488
Duxbury, F., 489
Duxbury, L. E., 501
Dweck, C. S., 197, 339, 345
Dyches, K. D., 347, 348
Dykiert, D., 527
Dykstra, P. A., 495, 630
Dyregrov, K., 666
Dzurova, D., 50

E

Eagan, K., 471
Eagly, A. H., 479
Eaker, E. D., 520
Earl, J. K., 563
Easterbrooks, M. A., 386
Easterly, S., 498
Eastwick, P. W., 479
Eaton, N. R., 281
Eaves, L., 372
Ebeling, K. S., 231
Ebner, N. C., 595, 595n
Ebstein, R. P., 72
Eby, L. T., 500
Eccles, J. S., 301, 337, 350, 397, 399, 401, 403, 410, 461
Eckenrode, J., 426
Eder, R. A., 258
Edwards, A., 188, 268, 274
Edwards, C. P., 277
Edwards, L. J., 105
Edwards, O. W., 318
Efstathiou, N., 655
Egan, K. A., 649
Egeland, B., 57, 199, 202, 426
Eggebeen, D. J., 492, 551
Eggenberger, E., 593
Eggermont, S., 380
Eggum, N. D., 268, 274
Egozi, G., 397
Ehrensaft, M. K., 488
Ehri, L. C., 225, 244
Eibich, P., 622
Eichstedt, J. A., 276
Eidelman, A. I., 46, 100
Einstein, G. O., 583, 598
Eis, S. D., 244
Eisbach, A. O., 242
Eisenberg, N., 189, 191, 262, 263, 268, 274, 359, 421
Eisenberg-Berg, N., 268
Eiser, C., 361
Eisma, M. C., 665
Eisner, M. P., 272, 273, 429, 431
Ekas, N. V., 189
Ekman, P., 185
Ekstrom, B., 514
Elavsky, S., 513, 522
Elder, G. H., Jr., 5, 6, 12, 35, 376, 403
Elfenbein, D. S., 384
Elias, C. L., 236
Elias, M. F., 591
Elias, V. L., 380

Eliason, G., 651, 652, 652n
Elicker, J., 205
Elkind, D., 392, 393
Elks, C. E., 297
Ellin, A., 613
Elliott, A. F., 593
Elliott, J. G., 358
Ellis, A. E., 164
Ellis, B. J., 58, 373
Ellis, D. A., 510
Ellis, L., 463
Ellis, L. A., 260
Ellis, R., 353
Ellis, R. R., 554
Ellis, W. E., 347
Ellison, C. G., 615
Ellison, N., 451
Elo, I. T., 581
Else-Quest, N. M., 189, 195, 209, 276, 395, 412
El-Sheikh, M., 33
Eltzschig, H. K., 97
Elwert, F., 629
Emanuel, E. J., 663, 664
Emde, R. N., 190
Emery, R. E., 355, 377
Emmerson, N. A., 266
Engels, R. C. M. E., 418
English, T., 621, 621n
Englund, M. M., 205, 426
Enguidanos, S. M., 594
Ennemoser, M., 248, 249
Ennis, E., 612
Enns, J. T., 19
Ensminger, M. E., 284
Ensor, R., 241, 261
Entringer, S., 439
Entwisle, D. R., 402
Epel, E. S., 439
Epstein, L. H., 297
Epstein, R., 125, 482
Epstude, K., 543
Erdogan, B., 501
Erickson, K. I., 529, 583
Erikson, E. H., 258, 336, 408, 538, 610, 611
Erol, R. Y., 409
Escrivao, M. A., 442
Espinosa-Hernandez, G., 513
Espinoza, G., 424
Esposito, E. A., 21
Esposito-Smythers, C., 428
Espy, K. A., 84, 238, 246
Esquivel-Santoveña, E. E., 488, 489
Essex, M. J., 373
Estep, K., 261
Etaugh, C., 541
Ethier, K., 479
Etnier, J. L., 448
Evanoo, G., 107n
Evans, C. B., 63
Evans, D. A., 582
Evans, D. E., 191
Evans, G. W., 62, 296, 308
Evans, M. E., 284
Evans, N., 174
Even-Zohar, A., 632
Evert, J., 573
Ewald, H. A. S., 516
Ewald, P. W., 516
Ewing, S. W. F., 381
Exline, J. J., 655

Exner-Cortens, D., 426
Eyler, A. A., 447
Eyler, L. T., 243

F
Fabes, R. A., 261, 277
Fabiani, M., 574
Fabricius, W. V., 312
Fagan, J., 57
Fagan, J. F., 169, 320
Fagard, J., 137
Fagen, J., 154
Fagot, B. I., 277, 279
Fagundes, C. P., 487n
Fahrmeier, E. D., 306
Fahs, B., 453
Faircloth, B. S., 399
Faja, S., 20, 161, 236, 238, 308
Falagas, M. E., 221
Falbo, T., 337, 353
Falk, D., 121
Fanslow, C. A., 656
Fantoni, G., 617
Fantz, R. L., 141
Faraone, S. V., 309
Farley, F., 394
Farmer, T. W., 346
Farquharson, K., 628
Farr, R. J., 498
Farran, C. J., 557
Farrell, C., 13
Farrington, D. P., 430, 431
Farroni, T., 142, 143
Farver, J. M., 28
Fassinger, R. E., 481
Fassino, S., 379
Faulkner, K. A., 443
Favreau, O. E., 350
Fearnow, M. D., 342
Fearon, R. M. P., 200, 205, 206
Febo-Vazquez, I., 450, 451
Federal Interagency Forum on Aging Related Statistics, 623
Federico, A., 252
Fedewa, S. A., 448
Fedina, L., 454
Feency, B. C., 480
Fehr, B., 479, 480, 481
Fehring, R. J., 76
Feigelman, W., 429
Feigenbaum, P., 106
Feil, R., 49
Fein, G. G., 263, 264n
Feinberg, M. E., 352
Feldman, A. F., 403
Feldman, D. C., 559, 635
Feldman, R., 33, 46, 99, 100, 103, 105, 111, 203, 491
Felice, M. E., 384
Felner, R. D., 398
Fenelon, A., 629
Feng, J., 397
Feng, P., 441n
Fenn, A. M., 443
Fenton, S. E., 83
Fenwick, K. D., 144
Ferguson, L. R., 447
Ferguson, T. J., 341
Ferketich, A. K., 449

Fernald, A., 177, 178, 179
Fernald, L. C., 129
Fernandes, M., 187
Fernandes-Taylor, S., 517
Fernyhough, C., 22, 228, 235
Ferrando, M., 317
Ferrari, M., 601
Ferrari, P. F., 132, 133
Ferraro, K. F., 582
Ferrer, E. F., 308
Ferry, A. L., 165
Fesseha, G., 359
Festini, S. B., 528
Ficca, G., 125
Field, A. P., 358
Field, D., 612, 630
Field, T., 89, 99, 187, 263
Fielding, L. G., 322
Fielding, R. A., 578
Fiese, B. H., 25, 295, 378
Fifer, W. P., 104, 109
Figner, B., 393
Finch, B. R., 445
Fincham, F. D., 339, 488
Finchum, T., 620
Findsen, B., 605
Fingerman, K. L., 485, 551, 552, 553, 555, 556, 611, 621, 622, 632
Finkel, D., 438, 526
Finkel, E. J., 451
Finkelhor, D., 360, 380
Finnie, L., 395
Finucane, M. L., 599
Fiocco, A. J., 574
Fiori, K. L., 547, 558, 625, 630, 631
Fischer, K., 461
Fischer, K. W., 19, 186, 189, 262, 306, 307
Fischman, M. G., 225
Fish, M., 199
Fisher, C., 250
Fisher, C. B., 38
Fisher, D. M., 101n, 103
Fisher, G. G., 531
Fisher, J. A., 219
Fisher, J. O., 220
Fisher, P. A., 118, 177
Fisher, S. K., 498
Fitzgerald, L. F., 385
Fivush, R., 240, 241, 261
Flak, A. L., 85
Flanagan, C. A., 416, 419, 471, 472
Flannery, D. J., 393, 429
Flavell, E. R., 241, 242, 341
Flavell, J. H., 241, 242, 341
Fleeson, W., 550
Flegal, K. M., 296
Fletcher, A. C., 347
Fletcher, E. N., 249
Floccia, C., 131
Flom, R., 132, 144, 176
Flood, D. G., 574
Flood, M., 614
Florian, V., 649, 652
Flynn, J. R., 319
Foehr, U. G., 248, 249, 275, 380, 395, 400
Foerde, K., 400
Fogel, A., 185
Foley, K. P., 25

Fomon, S. J., 117
Fonnesbeck, C. J., 46
Fontana, L., 511
Fontayne, P., 301
Forcada-Guex, M., 99
Ford, D. Y., 329
Ford, L., 245
Ford, T., 31
Forgatch, M. S., 359
Forman, D. R., 268
Formosa, M., 604
Forrester, R., 127
Forry, N. D., 355
Forssell, S. L., 498
Forstmeier, S., 612
Fortenberry, J. D., 369, 380, 381
Fowler, C., 558
Fowler, F., 282
Fowler, J. W., 615
Fox, C. L., 349
Fox, N. A., 121, 124, 141, 192, 207
Fraley, C., 193
Fraley, R. C., 201, 549
Franceschi, C., 440
Franchak, J. M., 136, 207
Franco, M. G., 500
Frank, M. C., 161
Frank, R., 445
Frankel, C. B., 185
Frankel, L. A., 189
Frankland, P. W., 164
Franklin, B. A., 583
Franklin, S., 390
Franklin, V. P., 327
Franks, B. A., 389
Frazier, L. D., 508, 544, 581, 599, 614
Frederickson, B. L., 621
Fredricks, J. A., 301, 403
Fredriksen-Goldsen, K. I., 626
Freedman, J., 99
Freedman, V. A., 623, 624
Freedman-Doan, C., 397
Freeman, D., 368
Freeman, E. W., 512, 512n
Freeman, G. P., 541
Freeman, H., 203, 204
Freitag, C., 141
Freitag, J. R., 309
Freitas, A. A., 440
Frejka, T., 490
Fremmer-Bomik, E., 201
French, B. H., 454
French, D. C., 265
French, D. J., 581
French, S. A., 378
French, S. E., 398
Freud, S., 15
Freund, A. M., 543, 595, 595n, 614, 637
Freund, G. G., 447
Frey, A., 430
Frick, P. J., 274
Fried, L. P., 585, 638
Friederici, A. D., 175
Friedlmeier, W., 189, 262
Friedman, A. M., 98
Friedman, C., 586
Friedman, C. K., 277
Fries, J. F., 582
Friesen, W., 185

Frisell, T., 586
Fromholt, P., 612
Frontline, 58
Frost, D. M., 453
Fruhauf, C. A., 632
Fry, C. L., 547
Fry, D. P., 302
Fry, P. S., 616, 617, 652
Fu, G., 343
Fuemmeler, B. F., 301
Fuh, M.-H., 514
Fulcher, M., 278
Fuligni, A. J., 32, 421
Fuligni, A. S., 170
Fuller, M. J., 375
Fuller-Iglesias, H. R., 484, 547
Fuller-Thomson, E., 554
Fullerton, A. S., 380
Fung, H., 259
Fung, H. H., 622
Fuqua, J. S., 371
Furman, W., 11, 36, 265, 347, 425, 426, 427
Furnham, A., 479
Furrow, J. L., 418
Furstenberg, F. F., 484
Fushiki, S., 85
Fuson, K. C., 313
Futris, T. G., 384

G
Gabbay, S. G., 626
Gabriel, Z., 622
Gaffney, K. F., 91
Gagne, J.-P., 575
Gaillard, V., 307
Gailliot, M. T., 652
Gaines, J., 221
Galambos, N. L., 545
Galanki, E. P., 393
Galbally, M., 111
Galetta, F., 577
Gagne, J.-P., 575
Galinsky, E., 202, 357
Gallagher, A. M., 279
Gallagher, L., 46
Galland, B. C., 125
Gallant, M. P., 631
Gallaway, C., 252
Gallay, L. S., 416
Galler, J. R., 129
Galliher, R. V., 426
Gallo, L. C., 445
Gallo, W. T., 562
Galloway, J. C., 135, 136
Gallup, 453, 485, 490, 494, 563
Gallup, G. G., 207
Galvao, T. F., 221, 376
Ganchrow, J. R., 131
Ganea, P. A., 156
Ganger, J., 177
Gannon, L., 514
Ganong, L., 494, 496, 497
Garber, J., 187
Garcia, A., 157
Garcia, A. J., 106
Garcia, J., 321n
García Coll, C., 32
Garcia-Pinillos, F., 579
Gardner, H., 30, 224n, 316, 317, 317n, 328, 329
Gardner, R. S., 598

Garneau, C., 356
Garner, A., 554
Garner, A. S., 11
Garner, P. W., 29, 188, 261, 342
Garrity, K., 156
Garstein, M. A., 193
Gartrell, N. K., 498
Gartstein, M. A., 189
Gaskill, R. L., 359
Gaskins, S., 168, 237, 258, 265
Gassen, N. S., 494
Gates, G. J., 497
Gathercole, S. E., 308
Gathercole, V., 251
Gati, I., 463
Gattis, M. N., 638
Gatz, M., 617
Gauthier, S., 143
Gauvain, M., 239, 311, 398
Gavey, N., 454
Gavrilov, L. A., 511
Gavrilova, N. S., 511
Gaylord, S., 154
Gazzaley, A., 528
Gdula, J. A., 426
Ge, X., 375, 376, 377
Geangu, E., 105
Geary, D. C., 394
Gee, C. B., 386
Geerts, C. C., 84
Geier, C., 373
Geil, M., 457
Gelfand, M. J., 63
Gelman, R., 231
Gelman, S. A., 177, 231, 232, 244, 278, 350
Gendler, M. N., 188
Genesee, F., 252, 323, 324
Gentile, B., 339, 471
Genzler, A. L., 480
George, C., 201
Georgieff, M. K., 88, 89
Georgsdottir, A., 328
Geraci, A., 267
Gerdes, A. C., 348
Gere, J., 487n
Gergely, G., 166, 185
Germine, L. T., 525
Gershoff, E. T., 269, 270, 273
Gershon, E. S., 52
Gerstorf, D., 579, 602, 616
Gervai, J., 277
Gesell, A., 14
Getchell, N., 223n, 225, 300, 301, 370
Geuze, R. H., 142, 218
Gewirtz, A., 359
Ghanem, H., 513
Ghavami, N., 412
Ghesquiere, A., 670
Ghim, H. R., 142, 142n
Ghulmiyyah, L. M., 96
Giarrusso, R., 558
Gibbs, J. C., 271, 415, 417, 418, 419, 420, 451
Gibson, C. J., 512
Gibson, E. J., 140, 144, 145
Gibson, J. J., 144
Gibson, L., 588
Gibson, P. A., 554
Gibson-Davis, C., 497

Giedd, J. N., 307, 373, 456
Gielen, U. P., 417, 418
Giguère, B., 485
Gil, J., 489
Gilchrist, K., 103
Giles, A., 154
Giles, J. W., 276
Giles-Sims, J., 269
Gillberg, C., 243
Gilleard, C., 613
Gillen, M. M., 451
Gillespie, D. C., 121
Gillette, P., 158
Gillies, R. M., 401
Gilligan, C. F., 415
Gilligan, M., 555, 557
Gilliom, M., 261
Gilmore, J. H., 117, 120
Giménez, M., 649
Gingo, M., 272
Ginsberg, S., 393
Ginsburg, A. P., 141
Ginsburg, H. P., 245
Giovanelli, G., 109
Gitlin, L. N., 593
Giudice, S., 217
Glasper, E. R., 111
Gleason, T. R., 228
Gleeson, J. P., 63
Gleitman, H., 250
Gleitman, L. R., 250
Glenright, M., 322
Glick, J., 402
Glover, J. A., 426
Glück, J., 601
Gluckman, P. D., 94
Gluud, C., 440
Gnepp, J., 261
Gnoth, C., 52
Goble, P., 280
Godbout, J. P., 443
Goddard, S., 158
Goddings, A.-L., 373
Goedert, M., 587
Goeke-Morey, M. C., 57
Goering, J., 61
Gogate, L. J., 144
Goh, D. Y. T., 125n
Goh, E. C. L., 553
Goh, Y. I., 89
Goin, M., 656
Gola, A. A. H., 157
Gold, D. T., 510
Gold, J. M., 495
Goldberg, A., 425
Goldberg, A. E., 278, 490, 498
Goldberg, E. Z., 649
Goldberg, N. G., 498
Goldberg, W. A., 356
Goldfield, B. A., 178
Goldhammer, F., 316
Goldin-Meadow, S., 176, 178, 233
Goldschmidt, L., 84
Goldsmith, H. H., 177
Goldsteen, M., 654
Goldstein, M. H., 176
Goldstein, R., 562
Goldstein, S., 309
Goldston, D. B., 429
Goldwyn, R., 202
Golinkoff, R. M., 174, 177, 179, 244, 250, 251

Golomb, C., 224, 226
Golombok, S., 52, 53, 350, 354
Gomez, H. L., 422
Gómez, R. L., 374
Gomez-Perez, E., 308
Gondwe, T., 453
Gonzalez, A.-L., 282
Gonzalez-Feliciano, A. G., 373
Good, G. E., 533
Good, M., 418
Goodfellow, L. T., 84
Goodman, A., 83
Goodman, C. C., 63, 554
Goodman, G. S., 361
Goodman, J., 177
Goodman, J. H., 187
Goodman, M., 261, 342
Goodman, S. H., 187
Goodwin, R., 189, 259, 260
Goodwin, M. H., 278
Goodwin, P. Y., 557
Gooren, E. M. J. C., 348
Goossens, L., 411
Gopher, D., 529
Gopnik, A., 19, 165, 178, 188, 232
Gorchoff, S. M., 479
Gordon, I., 111
Gordon, R. A., 63
Gormally, S., 108
Gorman, B. K., 323
Gorman, B. S., 429
Gorman-Murray, A., 453
Gormley, W. T., Jr., 246
Goronzy, J. J., 585
Gosselin, P. A., 575
Goswami, U., 232
Gothe, N., 522
Gott, M., 515
Gottfredson, L. S., 462, 463
Gottlieb, G., 68, 70, 70n
Gottlieb, L. N., 667
Gottman, J. M., 481, 489, 491, 495, 549
Gottman, J. S., 491, 495, 549
Goubet, N., 137
Gould, E., 111, 474
Gould, J. L., 45
Government Accountability Office, 662
Gozal, D., 296
Graber, J. A., 274, 372, 375, 376, 377, 428
Graham, S., 27, 397
Graham-Bermann, S. A., 286
Gralinski, J. H., 208, 209
Gramling, R., 658
Grande, G., 591
Granier-Deferre, C., 81
Granrud, C. E., 141
Grant, K. B., 62
Grantham-McGregor, S. M., 129, 295
Grassmann, S., 252
Gratier, M., 176
Graves, L. M., 501
Gray, K. A., 84
Gray, M. R., 282
Gray-Little, B., 338, 409
Gredebäck, G., 154
Green, B. L., 287

Green, F. L., 241, 242, 341
Green, G. E., 108
Green, J. A., 105
Green, M. A., 632
Greenberg, J. P., 357
Greenberg, M. T., 237
Greendorfer, S. L., 225
Greene, J. A., 458
Greene, K., 393
Greene, M. F., 83
Greene, S. M., 353
Greenfield, E. A., 547, 551
Greenfield, P. M., 23, 136, 306, 320
Greenough, W. T., 124
Greenwald, A. G., 350
Gregory, A., 326, 398, 463
Gregory, E. C. W., 48
Grela, B., 157
Greydanus, D. E., 369, 370, 383
Grieve, A. J., 169
Griffie, J., 659
Griffin, B., 635
Griffin, D. M., 319
Griffin, Z. M., 599
Griffiths, M., 648
Grigorenko, E., 316
Grigoriadis, S., 83
Grimby, A., 666
Grocke, D., 659
Groh, A. M., 199, 206
Grolnick, W. S., 339
Grönholm-Nyman, P., 602
Gross, J., 165
Grossbaum, M. F., 539
Grossman, P. B., 339
Grossmann, K., 199, 201, 204
Grossniklaus, H. E., 509
Grossniklaus, U., 70
Grouzet, F. M. E., 397
Grover, T., 355
Gruber, H. E., 531
Gruendel, J., 62
Grühn, S., 458
Grundy, E., 631
Grünebaum, A., 96
Grusec, J. E., 268, 271n, 342
Gu, D., 555
Guajardo, N. R., 242
Gualdi-Russo, E., 443
Guarnaccia, C. A., 659
Guasch-Ferré, M., 447
Guedes, G., 509
Guedes, M., 490
Guerra, N. G., 27, 349
Guerrero, N., 582
Guest, A. M., 301
Guez, J., 596, 597n
Guggenheim, J. A., 298
Guglielmi, R. S., 324
Gugula, S., 278
Guignard, J.-H., 329
Guildner, S. H., 624
Guilford, J. P., 328
Guindon, S., 612
Guiso, L., 395, 395n
Gülgöz, S., 597
Gulko, J., 351
Gullone, E., 282, 358
Gunderson, E. A., 340
Gunes, S., 513
Gunnar, M. R., 20, 98, 119, 120, 123

Gunnarsdottir, I., 128
Guo, J., 278, 540
Guo, M., 632
Guralnick, M. J., 100
Gure, A., 376
Gur-Yaish, N., 631
Gustafson, G. E., 105, 108
Gustavson, K., 496
Guterman, N. B., 286
Gutgsell, K. J., 659
Gutiérrez, I. T., 649
Gutierrez-Galve, L., 187
Gutman, L. M., 398
Gutmann, D., 547
Guttmacher Institute, 384, 490
Guzzo, K. B., 494
Gwiazda, J., 142
Gyamfi-Bannerman, C., 98
Gyte, G. M. L., 97

H

Haas, A. P., 281
Haas, S. M., 486, 494
Haddock, G., 297
Haddow, J. L., 384
Haden, C. A., 261
Hadfield, L., 304
Hafdahl, A. R., 338, 409
Hafemeister, T. L., 633
Hagan, R. I., 277
Hagberg, B., 573
Hagerman, R. J., 49
Hagestad, G. O., 495
Haggerty, C. L., 453
Hagoort, P., 140
Hahn, H.-M., 126
Hahn, S., 529
Haidt, J., 420
Haight, W., 237
Haines, C. J., 514
Hainline, L., 110
Hains, S. M. J., 81
Haith, M. M., 137
Hakanen, J., 560
Hakim, F., 296
Hakuta, K., 323
Hale, C. M., 242
Hale, S., 528
Haley, B., 517
Haley, W. E., 661, 670
Halfon, N., 62
Halford, G. S., 19, 20, 161, 233, 307
Halim, M. L., 276, 350
Hall, C. B., 590
Hall, D. T., 499
Hall, G. S., 14, 368
Hall, J. A., 279, 423
Hall, M., 590
Hall, S. K., 630
Haller, J., 129
Hallinan, E. V., 155
Halpern, C. T., 451, 452
Halpern, D. F., 394, 395, 396, 501, 561
Halpern-Felsher, B. L., 394
Halverson, C. F., 279
Ham, M., 375
Hamberger, L. K., 489
Hamel, E., 249, 275
Hamel, J., 488, 489
Hamer, D. H., 382
Hamik, A., 448

Hamilton, B. E., 444n, 497
Hamilton, H. A., 356
Hamilton, M. A., 401
Hamilton, S. F., 401
Hamlin, J. K., 155
Hamm, J. V., 399
Hammer, L. B., 556
Hammersley-Mather, R., 590
Hammill, B. G., 553
Hammond, S., 236
Hammond, S. I., 238
Hammons, A. J., 295
Hampton, A., 326, 401
Hampton, T., 298
Hamre, B. K., 326
Han, H., 495
Han, W.-J., 170, 203
Hancock, S., 450
Hanioka, T., 217
Hank, K., 630
Hanke, W., 86
Hankin, B. L., 423
Hankins, G. D., 96
Hannon, E. E., 109, 110, 138, 139, 140, 145
Hans, S. L., 83, 187
Hansen, M. B., 250
Hansen, T., 547
Hansson, R. O., 665
Hao, L., 32
Happaney, K., 286
Happé, F. G. E., 243
Harachi, T. W., 431
Haram, K., 89
Harasymchuk, C., 481
Harden, K. P., 373, 373n, 381
Hardie, J. H., 464
Hardin, C. A., 242, 312
Hardy, M. A., 556
Hardy, S. A., 411, 418
Hare, B., 174
Hare, T. A., 218
Harkins, L., 358
Harkness, S., 110, 125
Harlan, E. T., 193, 209
Harlow, H. F., 196
Harold, R. D., 350
Harper, J. M., 352
Harries, V., 125
Harris, G., 380
Harris, P. L., 389, 649
Harris-Kojetin, L., 592
Harris-McKoy, D., 430
Harris Poll, 649
Harrop, A., 278
Hart, B., 170, 252
Hart, C. H., 246, 273, 282, 283, 353
Hart, D., 59, 418, 419
Hart, H. M., 539, 541
Hart, S., 611
Harter, S., 258, 260, 279, 336, 337, 341, 342, 377, 408, 409
Hartl, A. C., 423
Hartley, A., 527
Hartley, D., 50
Hartman, J., 596
Hartshorn, K., 162
Hartshorne, J. K., 525
Hartup, W. W., 265, 346
Harvey-Arnold, E., 273
Harwood, D., 619

Harwood, J., 632
Harwood, R. L., 201
Haryu, E., 250
Hasebe, Y., 344
Hasegawa, T., 158
Hasher, L., 528, 529, 596
Haskins, R., 62
Hasselhorn, M., 310
Hastings, E. C., 602
Hastrup, B., 594
Hatch, L. R., 626
Hatfield, E., 481, 482
Hau, K.-T., 330
Hauck, F. R., 106
Hauf, P., 137
Haukkala, A., 520
Hauser-Cram, P., 62
Hauspie, R., 294
Havstad, S. L., 84
Haw, C., 619
Hawkins, R. L., 402
Hawsawi, A. M., 84
Hawton, A., 591
Hawton, K., 619
Hay, C., 374
Hay, D. F., 187
Hay, E. L., 545
Hay, P., 379
Hayflick, L., 438, 571, 579
Hayne, G., 164
Hayne, H., 132, 157, 163n, 164, 165, 165n, 168, 361
Hayslip, B., 554
Hayslip, B., Jr., 554, 616, 659
Hayter, M., 374
Hayward, C., 355
Hayward, R. D., 615, 618
Haywood, H. C., 321
Haywood, K. M., 223n, 225, 300, 301, 370
Hazel, N. A., 352
Hazen, N. L., 204
Head, M. R., 421
Healthy Families America, 287
Healy, M., 117
Heathcock, J., 136
Hebblethwaite, S., 552
Hebert, K., 655
Hébert, M., 358, 360
Heckhausen, J., 19, 616
Heilbrun, K., 432
Heilman, M. E., 561
Heimerl, K., 593
Hein, S., 316
Heinemann, K. S., 345
Heino, R., 451
Heinrich-Weltzien, R., 217
Heinze, J., 416
Heir, T., 668
Helfand, M. J., 381
Hellemans, K. G., 85
Heller, D., 550
Heller, W., 121
Helm, H. M., 615
Helms, M. J., 531
Helson, R., 544, 548
Helwig, C. C., 271, 272, 343, 416
Henderson, H. A., 266
Henderson, R. L., 312
Henderson, T. L., 554
Hendrick, C., 481

Hendrick, S. S., 481
Hendricks, J., 636, 637
Hendrie, H. C., 589
Hendry, L. B., 474, 636
Hendry, M., 663
Henggeler, S. W., 432
Henig, R. M., 483
Henig, S., 483
Henk, T., 373
Henkens, K., 636
Henning, A., 238
Henning, K., 488
Henning-Smith, C., 617
Henrich, C. C., 425
Henricsson, L., 326
Henriksen, L., 380
Henry, J. D., 59
Henry, W. E., 620
Hensley, E., 221
Hepper, P. G., 79, 81
Heppner, M. J., 477, 498
Heraghty, J. L., 104
Herald-Brown, S. L., 346, 348
Herbenick, D., 452
Herbert, J., 157
Herghelegiu, A. M., 579
Herman, J. L., 281
Herman, M., 412
Herman-Giddens, M. E., 372n, 373
Hernandez, D., 357
Hernandez, D. J., 32
Hernandez-Reif, M., 99, 144, 162
Hernandez-Tejada, M., 633
Hernando-Herraez, I., 44
Herndler-Brandstetter, D., 577
Herne, M. A., 618
Heron, M., 444n, 516, 516n, 518, 584n, 585, 586
Heron, T. E., 17
Heron-Delaney, M., 143
Herr, M. Y., 235
Herrnstein, R. J., 318
Hershey, D. A., 563
Hertzog, C., 529
Herzog, A. R., 614
Herzog, L., 402
Hesketh, B., 635
Hespos, S. J., 101, 119, 121, 165, 207
Hess, R., 515, 515n
Hesse, E., 199, 201, 202
Hesselbrock, V. M., 386
Hessl, D. R., 49
Hetherington, E. M., 354, 355, 356, 497
Heuer, C. A., 446
Heuer, H., 560
Hewar, W. L., 17
Hewer, A., 414
Hewlett, B. S., 205
Hewstone, M., 345
Heyder, A., 350
Heyes, C., 132, 133
Heyman, G. D., 276, 350
Heymans, M., 561
Hibbert, J. R., 421
Hicken, B. L., 59
Hickey, M., 512, 513
Hickey, R. W., 646
Hickling, A. K., 231, 322
Hicks, J. A., 543

Hicks, L., 624
Hieber, A., 622
Hier, B. O., 309
Higginbottom, G. M. A., 31
Higgins, C. A., 501
Higgins, D. M., 459
Higginson, I. J., 657
Higgs, P., 613
Hilbert, D., 244
Hilden, D., 161
Hildreth, K., 162
Hilimire, M. R., 611
Hill, C. A., 277, 278
Hill, C. R., 326
Hill, D. B., 351
Hill, E. J., 261
Hill, J. L., 100
Hill, N. E., 398
Hill, R. D., 620
Hill, T. D., 579
Hilliard, L. J., 278
Hillis, S. D., 384
Hillman, K. M., 658
Hill-Soderlund, A. L., 185, 186, 189
Hinchliff, S., 515
Hind, H., 219
Hines, M., 195, 208, 277, 280, 382, 397
Hinrichsen, G. A., 591
Hinsta, T., 520
Hipfner-Boucher, K., 244
Hiraki, K., 132, 158
Hirasawa, R., 49
Hirschberger, G., 652
Hirsh-Pasek, K., 29, 174, 177, 179, 244, 250, 251
Ho, E., 245
Ho, I. T., 330
Hoang, D. H., 218
Hobbs, S. D., 361
Hochhalter, A. K., 593
Hochwarter, W. A., 560n
Hodel, A. S., 123
Hodge, S. D., Jr., 661
Hodges, E. V., 351
Hodges, J., 199
Hodnett, E. D., 96
Hoeft, T. J., 617
Hoek, H. W., 378
Hoekstra, R., 67
Hoeppner, B. B., 449
Hoerr, T., 329
Hoff, E., 33, 58, 170, 244, 323
Hofferth, S. L., 204, 274, 355, 356
Hoffman, L. W., 208, 267, 342, 356
Hoffner, C., 261
Hogan, B. E., 520
Hohne, E. A., 138
Hokoda, A., 339
Holden, G. W., 268, 269
Holdford, R., 488
Holditch-Davis, D., 105
Holdren, J. P., 465
Holland, C. R., 169, 320
Holland, G. W. O., 268
Holland, J. L., 462
Hollenstein, T., 368, 374
Hollich, G. J., 251
Hollis, C., 283
Holloszy, J. O., 511

Höllwarth, M. E., 222
Holm, L., 447
Holman, E. A., 523, 523n
Holmes, J., 308
Holmes, J. L., 454
Holodynski, M., 189
Holt-Lunstad, J., 626
Holton, E. F., 533
Homer, B., 312n
Honeycutt, H., 22, 66
Hong, D. S., 51
Hong, M., 330
Hong, S. I., 638
Hong, T., 576
Hoobler, J. M., 561
Hood, M., 244
Hooker, K., 544, 580
Hootman, J. M., 586
Hooyman, N., 13, 61, 622, 632
Hopf, L., 219
Hopkins, B., 136
Hoppmann, C. A., 614
Horgas, A. L., 624
Horhota, M., 529
Horn, J. L., 525
Horn, J. M., 318
Horn, K., 387
Horn, M. C., 545, 545n
Horn, S. S., 416, 417
Horne, R. S. C., 106
Horne-Thompson, A., 659
Horner, T. M., 186
Horowitz, R., 658
Hospice Foundation of America, 646, 659
Hoste, R. R., 379
Hostetler, A. J., 532
Hostinar, C. E., 98
Houck, G. M., 189
Houlihan, J., 86
Houser, J. J., 347, 348
Houts, R. M., 490
Hovdenak, N., 89
Howard, A. S., 123
Howard, K., 462
Howard, K. S., 60, 360
Howe, M. L., 163, 165, 249
Howe, N., 205
Howell, C. T., 100
Howell, K. H., 286
Howell, K. K., 84
Howell, S. R., 252
Howell, T. M., 429
Høybe, C., 219
Hoyer, W. J., 596
Hoza, B., 348
Hrubi-Bopp, K. L., 596
HSBC, 637
Hsu, A. S., 175
Hsu, C.-C., 86
Hu, F. B., 511
Huang, C. Y., 412
Huang, C.-C., 497
Huang, F., 463
Huang, H., 83
Huang, K.-E., 514
Huang, L., 441n
Huang, Q., 498
Hubbard, P., 453
Hubbs-Tait, L., 86
Huddleston, J., 376
Hudson, J. A., 240
Hudson, N. W., 549
Hudziak, J. J., 281

Huebner, C. E., 244
Huesmann, L. R., 274
Huff, M. J., 596
Huffman, M. L., 561
Hughes, C., 241, 242, 261, 311, 431
Hughes, C. W., 309
Hughes, E. K., 282
Hughes, J. N., 326, 339
Hughes, S. O., 301
Huizenga, H., 393
Hull, J., 57
Hulme, C., 240
Hultsch, D. F., 529, 601
Hungerford-Kresser, H., 326, 401
Hunnius, S., 142
Hunt, B. R., 487
Hunt, C. E., 106
Hunt, E., 318
Hunt, J. S., 430
Hunter, C., 323
Hunter, L. A., 97
Huntsinger, C., 226
Hurtado, S., 471
Hurtado-Ortiz, M. T., 239
Hurtig, W. A., 671
Huston, A. C., 249
Huston, T. L., 481
Hutchinson, E. A., 98
Huttenlocher, J., 154, 176, 177, 252
Huttenlocher, P. R., 122, 124
Huxhold, O., 630, 632
Huxley, R. R., 510
Huyck, M. H., 279, 547
Hwang, C. P., 490
Hyde, J. S., 394, 395, 427, 428, 490
Hyman, B. T., 588
Hymel, S., 348, 349

I
Ibanez, G., 187
Ickes, M. J., 446
Ickovics, J. R., 384
Ikejima, C., 591
Ilgaz, H., 228
Ilies, R., 550
Imai, M., 250
Impett, E. A., 409, 452, 479
Indus, K., 352
Infurna, F. J., 445
Ingoldsby, E. M., 60
Ingram, D. K., 511
Inhelder, B., 388, 392
Insana, S. P., 111
Institute of Medicine, 589
Iozzi, L., 323
Ip, S., 128n
Irvine, A. B., 593
Irwin, C. E., Jr., 378
Irwin, J. R., 108
Isaacowitz, D. M., 611
Isabella, R., 200
Ishida, M., 49
Ishihara, K., 86
Ismail, M., 455
Ivani-Chalian, C., 615
Ivey, P., 186
Iyer-Eimerbrink, P., 450
Izard, C. E., 275
Izard, V., 159

J

Jaakkola, R., 648
Jabès, A., 79, 118, 121, 163
Jaccard, J., 402
Jacelon, C., 654
Jack, F., 164
Jackey, L. M. H., 626
Jackson, J. B., 488
Jackson, J. J., 614
Jackson, K., 624
Jackson, K. J., 449
Jackson, S. L., 633
Jackson, V. A., 655
Jacobs, J. E., 337, 338, 350, 393, 464
Jacobsen, L. A., 627, 628, 629, 634
Jacobson, J. L., 82, 85
Jacobson, S. W., 82, 85
Jacques-Tiura, A. J., 454
Jadallah, M., 326
Jadva, V., 53
Jaffe, M., 282
Jaffee, S. R., 285, 287
Jäger, T., 598
Jahanfar, S., 372
Jahromi, P., 419
Jain, L., 97
Jambon, M., 343
Jambor, T. W., 264
James, J., 373
James, J. B., 547, 610
Jamison, Y., 497
Jang, B. J., 484
Jankowski, J. J., 142, 142n
Jansen, B., 393
Jansen, J., 128
Jansen, P. W., 220, 220n, 296
Janssen, S. M., 597
Janssens, J. M. A. M., 272
Jantz, T. K., 528
Jared, D., 323
Jarrott, S. E., 557, 632
Jarvis, J. F., 509
Jasiobedzka, U., 343
Jaudes, P. K., 285
Jedrychowski, W., 86
Jellinger, K. A., 576
Jemal, A., 516n, 517
Jenkins, C., 656
Jenkins, C. L., 668
Jenkins, J. M., 352
Jenkins, K. R., 624
Jennings, J. A., 6
Jensen, A. C., 352
Jensen, A. R., 67, 318
Jensen, J. S., 448
Jeremy, R. J., 83
Jerome, E. M., 326
Jiang, Q., 48
Jipson, J. L., 231
Jirout, J., 19
Joe, G. W., 387
Jogerst, G. J., 633
Joh, A. S., 141
Johannesen-Schmidt, M., 479
Johansson, A., 218
Johansson, A. K., 666
John, S. G., 69
Johnson, A. D., 171
Johnson, C. L., 631
Johnson, D. M., 454
Johnson, D. R., 625
Johnson, E. K., 138, 139
Johnson, J. G., 274, 274n
Johnson, K. M., 512
Johnson, M. D., 490
Johnson, M. H., 21, 118, 142, 143n, 176
Johnson, M. L., 403
Johnson, M. L., 117
Johnson, M. P., 54
Johnson, R. C., 88, 88n
Johnson, S. C., 197
Johnson, S. L., 296
Johnson, S. P., 109, 110, 138, 140, 141, 145, 153, 158, 161, 397
Johnson, W., 193, 614
Johnston, J., 284
Johnston, L. D., 370, 386, 401, 449
Johnston, M., 581
Johnston, M. V., 119
Joiner, T. F., 379
Jokhi, R. P., 54n
Jokinen-Gordon, H., 497
Jolivette, K., 402
Jome, L. M., 464
Jones, A., 491
Jones, A. M., 666
Jones, A. R. (2005), 488
Jones, A. R. (2011), 297
Jones, B. K., 539, 539f, 541
Jones, C. J., 544, 547
Jones, D. J., 62
Jones, J., 219
Jones, K. M., 541
Jones, M. C., 376
Jones, R. M., 373
Jones, S., 132
Jopp, D., 573
Josefowitz, N., 429
Joseph, R. M., 243
Josephson, R. A., 448
Josselyn, S. A., 164
Joyner, K., 426, 426n, 453
Juan, M. J. D., 412
Juby, H., 356
Judson, S. S., 454
Juffer, F., 55, 56, 205
Juhl, J., 651
Jukic, A. M., 88
Jun, H., 539
Jung, A.-K., 498
Junge, C., 140
Juntunen, C. L., 562
Jurewicz, J., 86
Jürgensen, M., 277
Jusczyk, P. W., 109, 138, 176, 177, 179, 251
Jutras-Aswad, D., 84

K

Kable, J. A., 84
Kachhawa, P. S., 652
Kaczmarczyk, M. M., 447
Kaestle, C. E., 451, 452
Kaffashi, F., 100
Kagan, J., 6, 21, 60, 120, 158, 192, 193
Kahana, E., 615, 637
Kahn, U. R., 222
Kahne, J. E., 419
Kail, R. V., 300, 308
Kainz, K., 171
Kaiser Family Foundation, 64
Kakihara, F., 283
Kalil, A., 296, 463
Kalisch, T., 576
Kalish, C. W., 232
Kalmanir, H. M., 476
Kalogrides, D., 401
Kalpouzos, G., 528
Kalra, L., 122
Kaminski, J. W., 429
Kaminski, P. L., 554
Kaminsky, Z., 70
Kanazawa, S., 128
Kandler, C., 616
Kane, L., 664
Kane, P., 187
Kane, R. A., 625
Kanfer, R., 562
Kang, N. H., 330
Kann, L., 371, 381, 381n, 382, 383
Kantaoka, S., 357
Kanters, M. A., 301
Kapa, L., 161
Kaplan, D. B., 633
Kaplan, D. L., 381
Kaplan, M., 530
Kaplowitz, P. B., 372
Karafantis, D. M., 345
Karasawa, M., 544, 545
Karasik, L. B., 133, 134, 136
Karbach, J., 590
Karel, M. J., 617
Karemaker, A., 249
Karevold, E., 36, 192
Karg, K., 428
Karger, H. J., 65
Karila, L., 448
Karkhaneh, M., 299
Karlsson, C., 657
Kärnä, A., 349
Karney, B. R., 481
Karraker, A., 515, 584, 584n
Karrass, J., 185, 186, 189
Kärtner, J., 189, 207, 208n
Kashdan, T. B., 615
Kashy, D. A., 278
Kassel, J. D., 387
Kastenbaum, R. J., 650, 653, 655, 668, 671
Kataoka, S., 61
Katz, E. G., 510
Katz, J., 98
Katz, R., 631
Katz-Wise, S. L., 490
Kaufert, P., 513
Kaufman, A. S., 525
Kaufman, J. C., 328
Kaufmann, K. B., 55
Kaufmann, P. M., 238
Kavanaugh, R. D., 228
Kavoura, A., 349
Kavšek, M., 131, 141, 169
Kawachi, I., 445
Kawakami, K., 193
Kawamoto, K. S., 13, 61, 622, 632
Kawamura, S., 628
Kaye, K., 386
Kaye, W., 379
Kayed, N. S., 137
Kearney, C. A., 358
Keating, D. P., 337, 388, 390, 409
Keegan, L., 647
Keel, P. K., 379
Keen, R., 137, 155
Keeton, W. T., 45
Keil, F. C., 250
Kelemen, D. A., 261
Keller, H., 200, 208
Keller, M., 415
Keller, P. A., 563
Kelley, M. C., 531
Kelley, S. A., 260, 262
Kelly, D. J., 143
Kelly, E. L., 560
Kelly, J., 354
Kelly, R., 236
Kelly, S., 401
Kelly, S. J., 455
Kempe, C. H., 285
Kemper, S., 598, 599
Kempner, S. G., 339
Kendig, H., 630
Kendler, K. S., 382
Kendrick, D., 222
Kennedy, K. J., 340
Kennedy, K. M., 574
Kennell, J. H., 96
Kenney-Benson, G. A., 395
Kenny, L. C., 384
Kenny, S., 154, 270
Kenyon, B. L., 649
Keren, M., 168
Kerestes, M., 418
Kernis, M. H., 339, 409
Kerns, K., 20, 161, 217, 238, 310
Kerns, K. A., 204, 338, 352, 480
Kerpelman, J. L., 462, 463
Kershaw, T. S., 384
Kessels, U., 350
Kessler, R. C., 542
Kettl, P., 618
Kew, K., 325, 330
Key, A. C., 281
Key, J. D., 385
Keyes, C. L. M., 539, 541, 544, 545, 579
Khaleefa, O., 319
Khaleque, A., 57, 283
Khashan, A. S., 384
Khavkin, J., 510
Kheirandish-Gozal, L., 296
Khosla, S., 510
Khurana, A., 386, 387n
Kidd, K. K., 44
Kidwai, R., 615
Kieras, J., 189
Kiernan, K., 494
Kilb, A., 597
Killen, M., 272, 320, 343, 344, 345, 346, 416, 417
Killoren, S. E., 422
Kilmer, R. P., 59
Kilpatrick, S. D., 481
Kim, G., 188
Kim, H., 204
Kim, H. Y., 398
Kim, Jinseok, 547
Kim, Joyun, 461
Kim, Jungmeen, 337
Kim, J. E., 636
Kim, J. M., 344
Kim, J. W., 550
Kim, J.-Y., 36, 352, 422
Kim, K., 555
Kim, S., 193, 209, 268, 623
Kim, Y. S., 448
Kimball, W., 474
Kimbrel, D., 557
Kimhi, Y., 243
King, A. C., 22
King, L. A., 543
King, N. J., 358
King, P. E., 418
King, P. M., 456, 458
King, V., 356, 497
Kinney, H. C., 106
Kinnunen, M.-L., 127
Kins, E., 475
Kinsella, M. T., 89
Kinser, K., 532
Kinzler, K. D., 158
Kirby, D. B., 385
Kiriakidis, S. P., 349
Kirkham, N. Z., 238
Kirshenbaum, A. P., 450
Kirshner, B., 419
Kisilevsky, B. S., 81
Kistner, J. A., 428
Kit, B. K., 296
Kitchener, K. S., 456, 458
Kite, M. E., 523, 580
Kitsantas, P., 91
Kitzman, H. J., 90
Kitzmann, K. M., 353
Kiuru, N., 399
Kiyak, H. A. S., 13, 61, 622, 632
Kjaer, M., 440
Kjønniksen, L., 302, 303
Klaczynski, P. A., 389, 393
Klahr, D., 19, 389
Klara, M. D., 523
Klass, D., 667
Klaw, E. L., 385
Klebanov, P. K., 170
Kleespies, P. M., 654
Kleffer, M. J., 398
Kleiber, M. L., 85
Klein, P. S., 33
Klein, S., 511
Kleinsorge, C., 354
Kleinspehn-Ammerlahn, A., 579
Kleitman, S., 401
Klemfuss, J. Z., 361
Kliegel, M., 598
Kliegman, R. M., 47n, 87n
Kliewer, W., 342
Klimstra, T. A., 410
Kloep, M., 474, 636
Kloess, J. A., 358
Klute, M. M., 208
Kluwer, E. S., 490
Kmec, J. A., 560
Knaack, A., 191, 193
Knafl, K. A., 614
Knafo, A., 263, 268
Knafo-Noam, A., 262, 263, 268
Knechtle, B., 443
Knieps, L. J., 188
Knight, B. J., 557
Knobloch, H., 101n

Knoester, C., 492
Knopf, M., 155
Knopik, V. S., 67
Knowles, M. S., 533
Knowlton, B. J., 400
Knudsen, E. I., 21
Ko, E., 655
Ko, H.-J., 544
Kobayashi, T., 158
Kochanska, G., 191, 193, 195, 209, 267, 268, 269, 271
Kochel, K. P., 349
Koeltzow, T. E., 237
Koen, J., 596
Koepsel, E., 584
Koerner, S. S., 481
Kohen, D. E., 59
Kohlberg, L., 414
Kohn, M. L., 531
Koisumi, H., 120n
Kojima, G., 592
Kojola, E., 563
Kolak, A. M., 352
Koletzko, B., 128
Kollmann, M., 54n
Komp, D. M., 653
Kon, A. A., 664
Konishi, Y., 120n
Konner, M., 277
Koo, A., 398
Kooijman, V., 140
Kopeikina, K. J., 589
Kopp, C. B., 189, 208, 209
Koppe, J. G., 86
Koppel, J., 597, 597n
Koren, C., 628
Koren, G., 89
Koschnitzky, J. E., 106
Koslowski, B., 110
Koss, K. J., 123
Kostelnik, J. O., 430
Kotkin, J., 474
Kotre, J., 539
Kotter-Grühn, D., 579, 580
Kowalski, R. M., 349
Kowalski-Braun, M., 500
Kozbelt, A., 531
Kozer, E., 83
Kozey, M. L., 245
Kozulin, A., 23
Krafft, K., 236
Kraft, M. L., 601
Kragstrup, T. W., 440
Krähenbühl, S., 361
Krakauer, J., 454
Krakow, J. B., 209
Kral, M. J., 31
Kramer, A. F., 529, 574, 602, 603
Kramer, D. A., 601
Kramer, S. E., 575
Krampe, R. T., 528, 530
Kraus, U., 155
Krause, N., 615, 618, 622
Kravetz, S., 649
Krawinkel, M., 129
Krcmar, M., 157
Krebs, D. L., 420
Kreider, R. M., 353, 495
Kreppner, J. M., 123, 200
Kressley-Mba, R. A., 155
Kretch, K. S., 136, 141, 145
Krettenauer, T., 418, 431

Kril, J. J., 85
Krishnarajah, I. S., 372
Kristensen, P., 668
Kroger, J., 408, 410
Krogh, H. R., 351
Kronauer, A., 548n
Kroonenberg, P. M., 199n
Kropf, N. P., 573
Krueger, R. F., 193
Krumhansl, C. L., 138
Krysik, J., 287
Kubicek, B., 636
Kübler-Ross, E., 653
Kubotera, T., 656
Kubzansky, L. D., 581
Kuczynski, L., 268, 282
Kuebli, J., 240
Kuersten-Hogan, R., 492
Kuh, D., 513
Kuh, G. D., 461
Kuhl, P. K., 132, 138, 139
Kuhn, D., 388, 390, 391, 391n
Kulkarni, A. D., 45n, 46, 52
Kumaido, K., 647
Kumar, M., 97
Kumpf, M., 318
Kunkel, A. W., 481
Kunnen, E. S., 471
Kunzmann, U., 600
Küper, K., 590
Kuperberg, A., 494
Kupersmidt, J. B., 431
Kuppens, S., 273, 283
Kurdek, L. A., 481
Kurganskaya, M. E., 218
Kurtz-Costes, B., 338, 350
Kushner, R. F., 446, 447
Kwan, V. S. Y., 544
Kwok, O., 326
Kwok, T. C. Y., 652
Kwon, R., 125n
Kyratzis, A., 278

L
Laanan, F. S., 532
Labat-Robert, J., 578
Labban, J. D., 448
Labouvie-Vief, G., 458, 458n, 470, 544, 545, 621
Labuhn, A. S., 312
Lachance, J. A., 395
Lachman, M. E., 543, 544, 546, 579, 580, 583, 616
Lachs, M., 623
Lacourse, E., 377
Ladd, G. W., 265, 266, 346, 347, 348, 349
Ladouceur, C. D., 428
Lafosse, A., 231
LaFreniere, L., 667
Lagattuta, K. H., 261, 262, 312, 342
La Greca, A. M., 425
Lai, S.-C., 488
Laible, D. J., 261, 263, 266
Laird, R. D., 430
Lakhani, N., 575
Lakshman, R., 297
Lalonde, C. E., 312, 411
Lalonde, R. N., 485
Lam, C. B., 352, 422
Lam, H. S., 86
Lam, J., 219

Lam, S., 340, 340n
Lamaze, F., 95
Lamb, M. E., 205, 206, 353, 354, 355, 357, 496, 497
Lambda, N., 513
Lamberg, L., 512
Lambert, J. D., 547, 550
Lambert, T. L., 488, 489
Lamere, T. G., 426
Lamers, S. M. A., 612
Lamkaddem, M., 102
Lamminmaki, A., 277
Lamont, E., 308
Lampl, M., 117
Lampman-Petraitis, C., 375
Lampson, M. A., 50
Lancy, D. F., 237, 368, 376
Landale, N. S., 32
Lander, E., 465
Landeros, C., 601
Lane, J. D., 272
Lang, A., 667
Lang, A. R., 85
Lang, F. R., 546, 616, 622, 637
Lang, I. A., 60
Lang, M., 465
Langer, G., 452
Langer, J., 158
Langlois, J. H., 143
Langman, L., 154
Långström, N., 382
Lanier, C. S., 540
Lansford, J. E., 268, 269, 270, 354, 421, 425, 483, 484
Lanz, M., 470
Lanzi, R. G., 172, 247
Lapierre, L. M., 560
Lapsley, D. K., 393
Laranjo, J., 242
Larkina, M., 163
Larose, S., 485
Larsen, J. A., 321
Larsen, J. E., 542
Larsen, P., 576
Larsen-Rife, D., 480
Larson, J., 423
Larson, R. W., 375, 422
Larsson, M., 576
Larzelere, R. E., 271, 283
Las Heras, M., 576
Lashley, F. R., 45n, 46, 47n
Laskey, A. L., 269n
Latendresse, S. J., 60, 60n
Latner, J. D., 297
Latorre, J. M., 612
Lau, G., 310
Lau, Y. L., 343
Lauer, P. A., 357
Laughlin, L., 357
Laumann, E. O., 453, 515, 625
Laungani, P., 648
Laurent, H., 204
Laureys, S., 647
Lauricella, A. R., 157
Laursen, B., 58, 376, 420, 422, 423
Lautenschlager, N. T., 590
Lavelli, M., 185
Lavner, J. A., 481
Law, E. C., 309
Law, K. L., 84

Lawlor, M. S., 310
Lawn, J. E., 98
Lawrence, A. R., 624
Lawrence, E., 490
Lawson, C. A., 232
Lawson, J. F., 479
Lawson, K. M., 449
Layton, J. B., 626
Lazar, A., 649
Lazar, I., 246
Lazarus, B. N., 342
Lazarus, R. S., 342
Lazear, K. J., 498
Lazinski, M. J., 89
Leaper, C., 177, 277, 278, 279, 302, 350
Leavell, A. S., 277
Lebel, C., 217
LeBel, T. P., 540
LeBlanc, A. J., 626
Lecanuet, J.-P., 81
Leckie, R. L., 583
Leclerc, N., 623
LeCroy, C. W., 287
LeCuyer, E. A., 189, 270
LeDonne, E. N., 209
Lee, C., 522
Lee, C.-Y. S., 491
Lee, D. N., 101
Lee, E. E., 557
Lee, E. H., 195, 284
Lee, G. R., 627, 628
Lee, G. Y., 81
Lee, H. Y., 187
Lee, J. M., 401
Lee, J. S., 245
Lee, J. Y., 449
Lee, K., 94, 252, 343
Lee, K. J., 357
Lee, P. P., 575
Lee, R., 432
Lee, S., 62
Lee, Susan J., 81
Lee, Shawna J., 269
Lee, S. L., 638
Lee, S. S., 428
Lee, V. E., 244n
Lee, Y., 384
Lee Badget, M. V., 626
Leech, R., 175
Leerkes, E. M., 23, 107, 189
LeFevre, J., 244
Lefkovics, E., 187
Lefkowitz, E. S., 451, 483
Legare, C. H., 350
Legerstee, M., 188
Legge, G. E., 576
Le Grange, D., 379
Lehert, P., 515
Lehman, D. R., 390
Lehman, M., 310
Lehmann, E. E., 465
Lehnung, M., 305
Lehr, V. T., 108
Lehrer, E. L., 486
Lehrer, J. A., 382
Lehrer, R., 391
Leibowitz, S., 281
Leifheit-Limson, E., 580
Leis, J. A., 473
Lejeune, F., 108
Lemaitre, H., 441n
Leman, P. J., 416

Lemaster, P., 547
Lemay, M., 281
Lemche, E., 236
Lemery, K. S., 177
Lemery-Chalfant, K., 191
Lemish, D., 523
Lemmon, G., 561
Lemola, S., 98
Lengel, L., 85
L'Engle, K. L., 380
Lenhart, A., 395, 423, 424, 424n
Lenroot, R. K., 456
Lenzi, M., 419
Leon, J., 357
Leon, K., 496
Leonesio, M. V., 559
Leong, D. J., 166, 325
Leopold, T., 552
Lepers, R., 443
Leppel, K., 563
Lerman, R. I., 497
Lerner, M. D., 348
Lerner, R. M., 5, 7
Lernout, T., 221
Lesesne, C., 492
LeSieur, K., 266
Leslie, A. M., 158
Lester, B. M., 110
Lester, L., 398
Letherby, G., 495
Leuner, B., 111
Lev, D., 596, 597n
LeVay, S., 382
Leve, L. D., 428
Levendosky, A. A., 199
Leventhal, T., 11, 59, 61, 430
Levin, P., 402
Levine, C., 414
Levine, J. A., 463
Levine, K. A., 463
Levine, P., 471, 472
LeVine, R. A., 200
Levine, S. C., 122, 397
Levinson, D. J., 477, 542
Levinson, S. C., 174
Levitt, M. J., 559
Levy, B. R., 580
Levy, D., 529, 597
Levy, S. R., 345, 561
Lewiecki, E. M., 429, 519
Lewin, A. C., 628
Lewis, C., 205, 357
Lewis, J. M., 495
Lewis, M., 186, 188, 189, 193, 207, 262
Lewis, M. A., 451
Lewis, M. D., 632
Lewis, T. L., 121
Lewko, J. H., 225
Lew-Williams, C., 140
Leyk, D., 443
Li, A. M., 125n
Li, D.-K., 106
Li, H., 48, 94
Li, Jianghong, 357
Li, Jin, 284
Li, J. J., 428
Li, K., 83, 171
Li, K. Z. H., 576
Li, P., 177
Li, S.-C., 315, 527, 527n, 595, 601

Name Index

Li, W., 171, 171n
Li, X., 249
Li, Y. J., 337
Liang, J., 296
Liang, J. K., 548n
Liben, L. S., 276, 278, 279, 305, 351, 397
Lichtenberg, P. A., 633
Lichter, D. T., 486
Lickenbrock, D. M., 189
Lickliter, R., 22, 66, 68, 99, 144
Lidstone, J. S. M., 235
Lidz, C. S., 321
Lidz, J., 175, 250
Liebaers, I., 54n
Lieberman, E. S., 97
Liebert, R. M., 268
Lieven, E., 177
Liew, J., 263
Liewald, D., 527
Li-Grining, C. P., 193
Li-Korotky, H.-S., 509
Lilgendahl, J. P., 540
Lillard, A. S., 168, 228, 248
Lim, D. H., 461
Lima, J. C., 658
Limber, S. P., 349
Lin, I.-F., 550, 580, 627
Lin, J., 439
Lin, K.-H., 479
Lin, Z., 21
Lind, J. N., 128
Lindahl, K. M., 62
Lindau, S. T., 515
Lindauer, M. S., 531
Lindberg, S. M., 395, 428
Linden, W., 520, 654
Lindenberger, U., 7, 8, 68, 595
Linder, J. R., 426
Lindsay, M., 424
Lindsey, E. W., 228, 265, 266, 409
Linebarger, D. L., 248
Linebarger, J. S., 649
Linn, K., 157
Linn, M. C., 395
Linn, S. C., 445
Linver, M. R., 170
Lionetti, F., 199
Lippold, M. A., 421
Lips, H. M., 499
Lipton, J. S., 158
Liszkowski, U., 176, 177
Lithopoulos, A., 522
Littlejohn, A., 222
Liu, C.-C., 589
Liu, H.-M., 139
Liu, J., 220, 295, 440
Liu, K., 442
Liu, L., 589
Liu, R. T., 428
Liu, Y., 440
Livson, N., 547
Lleras, C., 326
Lleras-Muney, A., 62
Lloyd, G. M., 551
Lloyd, M. E., 240
Lobel, M., 89
LoBue, V., 145
Lochman, J. E., 274
Lock, M., 513
Lockhart, S. N., 574

Lockwood, R. L., 353
Lodish, M. B., 373
Lodi-Smith, J., 549
Loeb, E. L., 425
Loeb, S., 401
Loehlin, J. C., 67, 195, 318
Loewen, N. A., 509
Logan, R. L., 539, 540
Loganovskaja, T. K., 85
Loganovsky, K. N., 85
Loh, V., 635
Loke, A. Y., 495
Loken, E., 483
Lollis, S., 282
Loman, M. M., 123
Lombardi, C. M., 356
Long, D. D., 651
Long, J., 440
Long, M. V., 573
Longo, M. R., 154
Lonigan, C. J., 244, 313
Looker, D., 395
Lopez, B., 421
Lopez, C. M., 428
Lopez, L. M., 308
López, M. J. R., 485
Lopresti, A. L., 297
Lora, K. R., 25
Lorber, M. F., 57
Lorch, R. F., Jr., 389
Lorentzen, C., 532
Lorenz, K., 21
Lorntz, B., 221
Lorys, A., 500
Lou, E., 485
Lou, K., 590
Loughead, J. P., 368, 374
Louie, V., 32
Louis, J., 104
Lourenço, O., 22, 272, 325
Lourida, I., 590
Loutzenhiser, L., 205
Lövdén, M., 601
Love, J. M., 173, 203
Lovegreen, L. D., 551
Lovejoy, M., 499
Low, M., 295
Low, S. H., 553
Low, S. M., 23
Lowenstein, A., 631
Lowenstein, A. E., 64, 68
Lowery, E. M., 442
Lewis, M. J., 611
Loy, C. T., 589
Lu, P. H., 527
Lubart, T. I., 328, 329, 531
Lubinski, D., 395
Luby, J., 262
Lucas, K., 539
Lucas, R. E., 614
Lucassen, N., 203
Lucas-Thompson, R. G., 266, 356
Luce, P. A., 109
Luciana, M., 387
Luck, S. J., 162
Ludlow, A. T., 439
Ludlow, L. W., 439
Luecken, L. J., 89, 667
Lugton, J., 656n
Luhmann, M., 490
Luk, B. H., 495
Luk, G., 323

Lukas, C., 666
Luke, A., 447, 447n
Lukowski, A. F., 220
Lun, J., 348
Luna, B., 121, 373
Lund, D. A., 593, 615, 628, 629, 666, 668, 670
Lundberg, S., 353, 353n
Lundquist, J., 479
Lunn, M., 601
Luo, L. Z., 94
Luo, Y., 555
Luong, G., 611, 612, 621
Lusardi, A., 563
Luster, S. S., 474
Luster, T., 384
Lustig, C., 21, 528, 529
Luszcz, M. A., 581
Luthar, S. S., 11, 60, 60n, 284, 360, 422
Luxembourg Income Study, 65n
Luyckx, K., 410, 411, 470, 471, 475
Lydick, S. E., 546
Lye, M.-S., 372
Lykins, A. D., 452
Lynam, D., 348
Lynch, C., 81
Lynch, S. M., 582
Lyness, K. S., 561
Lyngstad, T. H., 667
Lynn, R., 319
Lynn, S. J., 546
Lyon, T. D., 242
Lyons, K. E., 310
Lyons, M., 648, 650
Lyons, S. T., 501
Lyster, R., 323
Lytton, H., 46

M

Ma, F., 179, 343
Ma, L., 156, 168
Ma, W., 250
Maas, F. K., 271
Macari, S., 243
MacCann, C., 592
Maccoby, E. E., 277, 278, 356
MacDonald, J. L., 561
MacDonald, S. W. S., 36, 601
MacDorman, M. F., 48
MacIver, D. J., 402
Mackenzie, J., 520
MacKenzie, M. J., 269, 270
Mackey, A. L., 440
Mackey, K., 282
Mackey, R. A., 550
Mackey-Bilaver, L., 285
Mackie, S., 309
Mackinnon, S. P., 476
MacLean, P. S., 446, 447
Macpherson, A., 222
MacWhinney, B., 138, 158, 173, 174, 177, 250, 252, 323
Macy, M. L., 222
Madathil, J., 482
Madden, D. J., 527, 529
Madden, M., 424, 632
Madden, T., 412
Maddi, S. R., 522
Maddox, G. L., 620

Madigan, S., 201
Madnawat, A. V. S., 652
Madole, K. L., 165
Madsen, S. D., 352, 423, 476, 482, 484
Maeda, Y., 396, 415
Maffei, L., 121
Magalhães, J. P. de, 440
Mageau, G. A., 201
Magnuson, K., 58, 59
Magolda, M. B. B., 456
Magyar-Russell, G., 473
Mahady, G. B., 514
Mahay, J., 628
Mahne, K., 632
Mahon, M., 649
Mahoney, A., 267
Maier, S. F., 583
Main, M., 198, 199, 201, 202
Mainetti, M., 598
Mainiero, L. A., 562
Maisonet, M., 373
Maitland, S. B., 526
Majdandžić, M., 191
Makara, K. A., 396
Makel, M. C., 328
Maki, A., 120n
Malamuth, N. M., 380
Malatesta, C. Z., 189
Malebranche, D. A., 454
Malhotra, B. A., 391
Mallery, L., 585
Malley, J. E., 12
Mallya, S., 574
Malone, M. M., 652
Malta, S., 628
Malti, T., 272, 273, 429, 431
Mancini, A. D., 665
Mandara, J., 58, 283, 284
Mandel, D. R., 176
Mandler, J. M., 164, 165
Mangelsdorf, S. C., 191, 203, 258
Mani, T. M., 528
Manning, W. D., 426, 453
Manole, M. D., 646
Manthai, T., 624
Maquestiaux, F., 529
Maratsos, M., 251
Marceau, K., 376
Marchman, V. A., 177, 178
Marcia, J. E., 409, 410
Marcus, G. F., 251
Marcus, M., 373
Marcus-Newhall, A., 523
Marenco, A., 553
Marentette, P. F., 176
Mares, M.-L., 248
Margie, N. G., 272
Margolis, J., 560
Margolis, R., 552
Margrett, J. A., 573
Marin, M. M., 109
Marin, T. J., 298
Marjoribanks, J., 512
Markant, J. C., 217
Markman, E. M., 151, 250, 389
Markova, G., 188
Markovits, H., 389, 390
Markowitz, S., 103
Marks, A., 241
Marks, A. D. J., 452

Marks, A. K., 32
Marks, N. F., 539, 547, 550, 551, 556
Markstrom, C. A., 476
Markunas, C. A., 70
Markus, H. R., 544, 614
Marlier, L., 108, 109, 109n
Marra, R., 457
Marrott, H., 154
Marsee, M. A., 274
Marsh, H. W., 260, 337, 339, 401, 409
Marshall, B. J., 667
Marshall, E. A., 473
Marshall, P. J., 133
Marshall-Baker, A., 99
Martel, L. D., 481, 482
Marti, C. N., 378, 379
Martin, A., 25, 170, 386
Martin, C. L., 277, 278, 279
Martin, J. A., 45, 49, 96, 97, 98
Martin, J. L., 378
Martin, K. A., 375
Martin, Mike, 600, 614
Martin, Margary, 32
Martin, M. C., 514
Martin, M. M., 244
Martin, N. G., 195
Martin, P., 573
Martin, T. L., 666
Martinez, G. M., 380, 381n, 497
Martinez-Frias, M. L., 85
Martinot, D., 350
Martinson, I. M., 667
Martinussen, M., 410
Martlew, M., 225
Maruna, S., 539, 540
Maruta, T., 522
Marván, M. L., 374, 513
Marx, J., 554
Marzolf, D. P., 229
Masataka, N., 179
Mascolo, M. F., 19, 186, 189, 262, 307
Mash, C., 163
Mashburn, A. J., 266
Mashek, D. J., 262
Mason, C. A., 284
Mason, M. G., 417
Masten, A. S., 10, 11, 359, 360, 419, 553
Master, A., 321n
Masters, R. K., 571
Mastropieri, D., 109
Mastropieri, M. A., 328, 340
Masur, E. F., 178
Mather, M., 497, 611, 627, 628, 629, 634
Mathias, K. C., 378
Matjasko, J. L., 403
Matlen, B. J., 19, 389
Matsuba, M. K., 59, 418
Matsumoto, D., 185
Matthews, H., 172
Matthews, K. A., 445, 520
Matthews, L. G., 562
Matthews, R. A., 560, 561
Mattison, J. A., 511
Mattson, M. P., 589
Mattson, S. N., 84, 85
Mattsson, N., 588
Matusov, E., 310

Mauratore, A. M., 563
Maurer, D., 121
Maurer, T. J., 561
Maxwell, R., 546
Mayberry, R. I., 174
Mayer, C. J., 627
Mayer, R. E., 459
Mayeux, L., 346, 347, 348
Mayhew, E. M. Y., 240
Maynard, A. E., 168, 306
Maynard, B. R., 418, 473
Mazerolle, M., 580
Mazzeo, S. E., 379
Mazzocco, M. M. M., 395
McAdams, D. P., 538, 539, 539f, 540, 541, 543
McAdams, R. M., 87, 87n
McAdoo, H. P., 63
McAlister, A., 242
McArdle, J. J., 526
McAuley, E., 513, 522
McCabe, A., 244, 323
McCarthy, J., 664
McCartney, K., 68, 69, 171, 205, 247, 326
McCarton, C., 100
McCarty, M. E., 137, 155
McClain, C. S., 656
McClain-Jacobson, C., 656
McClowry, S. G., 667
McColgan, K. L., 238, 239n
McConachie, H., 50
McCormack, M., 383
McCormack, T., 238, 239n
McCoy, J. K., 204
McCrae, C., 577
McCrae, R., 548, 548n
McCune, L., 228
McDade, T., 126
McDaniel, M. A., 583, 598
McDill, T., 630
McDonald, K., 344
McDonough, C., 250
McDonough, L., 154, 164
McDougall, P., 349
McDowell, D. J., 342
McEachern, A. D., 431
McElderry, D., 374, 375
McElhaney, K. B., 420, 422
McElwain, N. L., 200, 205
McFadden, K. E., 284
McFarland-Piazza, L., 202
McGarrity, L. A., 453
McGee, L. M., 244
McGinley, M., 262
McGoldrick, M., 484, 657
McGonigle-Chalmers, M., 235
McGrath, S. K., 96
McGregor, R. A., 578
McGue, M., 376
McGuire, S., 352
McHale, J. P., 490, 492
McHale, S. M., 36, 352, 422, 485
McIlwain, A. S., 580
McIntosh, H., 411
McIntosh, W. D., 627
McIntyre, S., 96
McIsaac, C., 426n, 427
Mckee, A. C., 589
McKee-Ryan, F. M., 562
McKenna, J. J., 126

McKeown, M. G., 313
McKim, W. A., 630
McKinney, C., 409
McKoon, G., 596
McKown, C., 318, 320, 326
McLanahan, S., 355
McLaughlin, K. A., 123, 124
McLean, K. C., 613
McLearn, K. T., 62
McLeskey, J., 328
McLoughlin, P., 646
McLoyd, V. C., 270
McMahon, R. J., 60
McNeil, D. G., Jr., 88
McQuown, C. K., 635
McWhirter, E. H., 463
McWilliams, L., 273
Mead, E. L., 655
Mead, G. H., 337
Mead, M., 368
Meade, C. S., 384
Meadus, R. J., 464
Meaney, M. J., 70
Mebert, C. J., 269
Meeker, M. A., 661
Meeks, S., 617
Meesters, C., 262
Meeus, W. H. J., 376, 410, 411, 419, 423, 470
Mehanna, E., 448
Mehlson, M., 612
Mehta, C. M., 277
Mehta, L. S., 519
Mehta, N. K., 581
Mei, J., 136
Meier, A., 426
Meijnen, G. W., 398
Mejía, S., 544
Melby, M. K., 513
Melby-Lervag, M., 240
Meldrum, R. C., 374
Meltzoff, A. N., 132, 133, 133n, 154, 157, 176, 188, 231, 260, 323, 350
Melzi, G., 322
Memo, L., 85
Mendelsohn, G. A., 627, 627n
Mendelson, M., 252
Mendes de Leon, C. F., 582
Mendle, J., 377
Mendola, P., 84
Mendoza, J. R., 219
Menesini, E., 349
Meng, L., 48
Mennella, J. A., 108, 109
Menkler, M., 554
Minkoff, H., 51
Minnotte, K. L., 488
Minnotte, M. C., 488
Mintz, J., 259
Mintziori, G., 512
Miracle, J. A., 141
Mireault, G. C., 185
Mirkin, S., 512
Mirowsky, J., 469
Misailidi, P., 342
Mischel, W., 268
Mishra, G., 513
Missana, M., 271
Mistry, J., 6, 22
Mistry, R. S., 58, 246
Mitchell, B. A., 538, 551
Mitchell, B. D., 571
Mitchell, K. J., 380
Mitchell, M. E., 500
Miu, D. K. Y., 617
Miura, I. T., 314
Mize, J., 266, 282, 351
Mo, H. N., 655
Mo, Y.-M., 482

Michalik, N. M., 263
Miche, M., 630
Michel, G. F., 218
Michiels, D., 205
Mick, E., 309
Mickler, C., 601
Midgett, C., 222
Mienaltowski, A., 530
Miga, E. M., 426
Mihalas, S., 358
Mikami, A. Y., 348, 424
Mikkola, T. M., 575
Mikulincer, M., 652, 666
Milevsky, A., 282
Milgrom, J., 100
Milkie, M. A., 25, 422, 492, 631
Miller, A. L., 205
Miller, D. I., 396, 583
Miller, D. N., 19, 429
Miller, G., 647
Miller, G. E., 70
Miller, J., 531
Miller, J. G., 417
Miller, K. D., 516n, 517
Miller, L. E., 273
Miller, L. J., 525
Miller, L. S., 528
Miller, M. J., 447
Miller, P. A., 342
Miller, P. H., 236, 312
Miller, P. J., 259, 649
Miller, S., 426
Miller, Sara A., 429
Miller, Scott A., 242, 312
Miller, S. C., 658
Miller, T. R., 90
Miller-Graff, L. E., 57
Milligan, C., 657
Milligan, K., 242
Mills, C. M., 343
Mills, D., 121
Mills-Koonce, W. R., 171
Min, J., 295
Mindell, J. A., 125, 125n
Mineka, S., 523
Miner-Rubino, K., 541, 543
Mingo, C. A., 585

Modi, A. C., 297
Modrek, S., 562
Moen, P., 532, 560, 563, 636
Moffitt, T. E., 221, 431
Mohammadizadeh, M., 108
Mohite, P., 279
Mohr, J. J., 481
Mok, M. M. C., 340
Mokdad, A. H., 446
Mola, J. R., 513
Moldaw, S., 669
Molden, D. C., 339
Molenaar, P. C. M., 5, 7
Molfese, V. J., 246
Moll, H., 231
Moll, K., 313
Mollenkopf, H., 622
Moller, K., 490
Molloy, C. S., 298
Molnar, D. S., 84
Monahan, K. C., 380, 401
Monden, C., 45n
Mondloch, C. J., 121, 142, 143n
Monesson, A., 139
Monin, J. K., 592
Monk, C., 88, 89
Monk, C. S., 118, 243
Monk, J. K., 488
Monsour, M., 483, 631
Montague, D. P. F., 188
Mont'Alvao, A., 401
Montepare, J. M., 579
Montero, I., 22
Montgomery, D. E., 237, 242, 312
Montgomery, G. L., 104
Montgomery, M. J., 410, 460, 476
Montgomery-Downs, H. E., 111
Moon, C., 109
Moore, A., 628
Moore, D. S., 66, 397
Moore, E. C. G., 318
Moore, G. E., 49
Moore, H., 655
Moore, J. A., 275
Moore, J. B., 225
Moore, K. L., 45, 54n, 76n, 77, 77n, 78, 79, 80, 82, 82n, 117
Moore, M. K., 132, 133n, 154
Moore, M. R., 498
Moore, P. J., 340
Moore, R. W., 141
Moore, S. G., 110
Moorehouse, P., 585
Moosebrugger, H., 316
Moran, G., 200
Moran, S., 30, 328, 329
Morawska, A., 269
Morelli, G. A., 126, 186, 199, 200, 237
Moreno, A. J., 208
Morgan, I. G., 298
Morgan, J. D., 648
Morgan, P. J., 522
Morgan, P. L., 59
Morgan-Lopez, A. A., 475
Moriarty, H. J., 667
Morikawa, H., 178
Morimoto, S., 577

Morinis, J., 385
Moro-García, M. A., 577
Morrill, M. I., 57
Morrill-Howell, N., 638
Morris, A. S., 261, 342
Morris, J., 655
Morris, J. E., 357
Morris, J. K., 50
Morris, M. C., 583, 590
Morris, P. A., 23, 57, 68
Morris, W. L., 493
Morrison, M., 542, 543, 543n
Morrison, V., 617
Morrissey, T., 296
Morrongiello, B. A., 144, 222
Morse, E., 412
Morse, S. B., 98
Mortimer, J. T., 401
Morton, J., 143
Morton, R. H., 442
Mosby, L., 270
Mosely-Howard, G. S., 63
Moses, L., 242
Mosher, W. D., 494
Moshman, D., 19, 389, 390, 391, 408, 457
Moss, E., 201, 206
Mossey, P. A., 84
Moss-Racusin, C. A., 499
Motl, R. W., 371
Mottus, R., 352
Mottweiler, C. M., 228
Mõtus, R., 614
Moum, T., 547
Mounts, N. S., 36, 426
Mowery, C. E., 584
Moylan, A. R., 313
Mozaffarian, D., 441, 442, 518, 518n, 646
Mroczek, D. K., 545, 614, 618
Mrozek, J. D., 83
Mrug, S., 348, 376
Mu, Q., 76
Mu, Y., 314
Muckle, G., 86
Mudrazija, S., 593
Mueller, B. R., 71
Muenssinger, J., 81
Muentener, P., 157
Muhlbauer, V., 523
Muise, A., 452
Mukamal, K., 638
Mulatu, M. S., 531
Mulder, C. H., 631
Mullainathan, S., 500
Müller, O., 129
Müller, U., 20, 161, 217, 238, 242, 310, 390
Mullett-Hume, E., 36
Mulvaney, M. K., 235, 269
Mulvey, E. P., 430
Mumme, D. L., 188
Munakata, Y., 19, 20, 174
Mundy, P., 207
Munholland, K. A., 197, 202
Munnell, A. H., 563
Munroe, R. L., 277, 311
Muraco, J. A., 498
Muret-Wagstaff, S., 110
Muris, P., 262, 358
Murphy, B. C., 191
Murphy, J. B., 52, 53
Murphy, S. A., 667

Name Index

Murphy, T. H., 121, 122
Murphy, T. P., 263
Murray, C., 318
Murray, K. T., 193, 209
Murray, L. K., 358
Murray, M. W. E., 611
Murray, S. A., 646
Murray, S. L., 489
Murry, V. M., 352
Murzyn, T., 418
Musick, K., 497
Mussen, P. H., 268, 376
Mustanski, B., 426, 428
Mutchler, J. E., 62, 637
Mutran, E. J., 552, 553, 655
Myers, L. J., 305
Myerson, J., 527
Myowa-Yamakoshi, M., 132, 133n

N

Nadel, J., 207
Nader, K., 668
Nader, P. R., 295
Naerde, A., 272
Nagell, K., 176
Nagle, R. J., 245
Nagy, E., 132
Nagy, W. E., 321
Naigles, L. G., 177
Naigles, L. R., 250
Naito, M., 312
Nakamura, J., 546, 600
Nakonezny, P. A., 309
Nam, S., 557
Nan, C., 46
Nánez, J., Sr., 140
Napolitano, C. M., 595
Narayan, A. J., 426
Narr, K. L., 309
Nash, C. J., 453
Nassar, A. H., 91
National Center for Assisted Living, 624
National Center for Biotechnology Information, 47n, 49
National Center on Elder Abuse, 634
National Coalition for the Homeless, 59
National Federation of State High School Associations, 370
National Institute on Aging, 588, 589, 590
National Institute on Alcohol Abuse and Alcoholism, 449
National Institute on Drug Abuse, 448, 449
National Institute on Retirement Security, 623
National Institutes of Health, 55
National Research Council, 398
Natsuaki, M. N., 187, 375, 376, 377, 428
Nauta, J., 299
Naveh-Benjamin, M., 529, 595, 596, 597
Nawrocki, T., 263

Nazzi, T., 232
Neal, M. B., 556
Neal-Perry, G., 512
Needham, B. L., 383
Needle, E., 402
Needlman, R., 126
Neff, C., 203
Neff, L. A., 481
Negreiros, J., 245
Negriff, S., 376
Neiderman, D., 154
Neimeyer, R. A., 651, 652, 665, 670
Neitzel, C., 235
Nelson, C. A., 79, 118, 118n, 119, 121, 123, 124, 139, 139n, 163, 217, 219
Nelson, D. A., 273, 274, 283
Nelson, E. L., 218
Nelson, K., 259
Nelson, L. J., 470, 473, 474, 475
Nelson, M., 402
Nelson, N. M., 277
Nelson, S. E., 117
Nelson, S. K., 492
Nepomnyaschy, L., 103
Nesdale, D., 344
Netz, Y., 546
Neubach, B., 560
Neufeld, S. J., 189
Neugarten, B. L., 478, 508
Neugebauer, R., 71
Neuhouser, M. L., 583
Neuman, S. B., 178
Neumann, D. L., 395
Neupert, S. D., 546, 579, 583, 616
Neville, H. J., 121
Newcomb, M. E., 426
Newcombe, N. S., 154, 240, 397
Newell, L. D., 282, 283, 353
Newheiser, A., 344
Newland, L. A., 203, 204
Newman, F., 508
Newnham, C. A., 100
Newport, E. L., 139, 140, 174, 175
Newsom, J. T., 616
Newson, R. S., 665
New Strategist Editors, 13
Newton, E. K., 263
Newton, N. J., 539, 541
Nezlek, J. B., 615
Ng, A. S., 386
Ng, F. F., 284, 340, 340n
Ng, T. W. H., 559
Ngata, P., 656
Nguyen, A., 358
Nguyen, S., 649
Nguyen, S. P., 278
Nguyen, T. T., 84
Nguyen, T. V., 12
NHPCO (National Hospice and Palliative Care Organization), 657, 658, 659, 660
NICHD Early Child Care Research Network, 171, 202, 203, 247
Nichols, K. E., 207, 269
Nickels, A., 500

Nickman, S. L., 56, 667
Nicolopoulou, A., 228
Nielsen, M., 168, 207
Nielsen, R. B., 384
Nielson, D., 649
Nikolova, D., 440
Nikulina, V., 286
Ningiuruvik, L., 319
Nippold, M. A., 321, 322
Nisbett, R. E., 318, 319, 390
Nishitani, S., 108
Nissan, J., 527
Nissen, N. K., 447
Noack, M. G., 531, 561
Noble, K. G., 98
Nocentini, A., 349
Noel, A. M., 402n
Noël, M.-P., 233
Noel-Miller, C., 582
Noice, H., 602, 603
Noice, T., 602, 603
Nolen-Hoeksema, S., 455
Noll, J., 525
Noll, J. G., 360, 384
Nomaguchi, K. M., 25, 422, 491, 492
Noom, M. J., 376
Noppe, I. C., 650
Noppe, L. D., 650
Norgate, S. H., 67
Noroozian, M., 218
Norris, J., 552
Northstone, K., 295
Nosek, B. A., 395
Noterdaeme, M., 218
Novelli, B., 561
Nowicki, E. A., 328
Nucci, L. P., 272, 343, 344, 416
Nucci, M. S., 344
Nugent, J. K., 110
Nuland, S. B., 646
Nunes, T., 244
Núñez, J., 472
Nurmi, J.-E., 282, 283
Nurnberger, J. I., Jr., 450
Nuttall, R. L., 396
Nyberg, L., 528
Nyquist, L., 530

O

Oakes, L. M., 162, 163, 164, 165
Oakhill, J., 322
Oakland, T. D., 318
Oates, G., 531
Obeidallah, D., 377
Oberecker, R., 175
Öberg, C., 576
Obermeyer, C. M., 512
Obradović, J., 11, 419
Obray, S. J., 629
O'Brian, M., 357
O'Brien, B. A., 550
O'Brien, K. M., 500
O'Brien, M., 202, 261
O'Connor, E., 326
O'Connor, L. T., 560
O'Connor, M. K., 601
O'Connor, P. G., 450
O'Connor, T. G., 123, 199, 352
O'Dea, J. A., 337
O'Doherty, D., 179

O'Donovan, M., 67
OECD (Organisation for Economic Cooperation and Development), 64n, 97, 395, 395n, 401, 444, 445, 453, 460, 499, 516, 592
Oetzel, J. G., 656
Offer, S., 25, 422
Office of Head Start, 246
Ogbu, J. U., 401
Ogden, C. L., 295, 296, 445
Ogolsky, B., 488
Oh, J.-H., 623
O'Halloran, C. M., 652
Ohannessian, C. M., 386
Ohgi, S., 110
Ohlott, P. J., 501
Ohno-Matsui, K., 298
Okagaki, L., 316
Okami, P., 126
Okamoto, Y., 233, 300, 314
Okanda, M., 207
Okeke-Adeyanju, N., 338
Okuro, M., 577
Olafson, E., 358
Old, S. R., 596
Olds, D. L., 90, 287
O'Leary, S. G., 269
Olfman, S., 386
Olineck, K. M., 155
Olino, T. M., 195
Oliveira, F. L., 442
Ollendick, T. H., 358
Oller, D. K., 176
Olmstead, R., 126
Olmstead, S. B., 384
O'Loughlin, M., 391n
Olsen, D. M., 450
Olsen, J. A., 283, 397, 421
Olsen, S. F., 282, 283, 353
Olshansky, S. J., 572, 579
Olson, D. A., 635
Olson, K. R., 281
Olson, L. S., 402
Olson, S. L., 267, 273
Olsson, B., 588
O'Malley, C., 249
O'Malley, P. M., 401
Omar, H., 369, 370, 374, 375
Ondejko, L., 222
O'Neil, M. E., 463
O'Neill, G., 636
O'Neill, M., 179
O'Neill, R., 348
O'Neill, S., 361
Ong, A. D., 412, 614, 666
Ong, K. K., 297
Onisto, N., 443
Ontai, L. L., 242
Onwuteaka-Philipsen, B. D., 664
Ooi, L., 264
Oosterwegel, A., 337, 411
Opinion Research Corporation, 25
Oppenheimer, L., 337
Orbio de Castro, B., 274
Ordonana, J. R., 221
Oregon Public Health Division, 663, 663n
O'Reilly, A., 618
Ormel, J., 617

O'Rourke, N., 612
Orth, U., 337, 409, 470, 471
Ortman, J. M., 12
Orwoll, L., 531
Osherson, D. N., 389
Osterholm, E. A., 88, 89, 98
Ostir, G. V., 581
Ostrosky-Solis, F., 308
Ostrov, J. M., 273, 352
Oswald, F., 624
Otis, N., 397
Otter, M., 51
Otto, H., 200
Ouimet, C., 24, 286
Ouko, L. A., 84
Oumar, F., 199
Overall, N. C., 480
Overton, W. F., 5, 7, 390
Owen, C. G., 128n
Owens, E. B., 283
Owsley, C., 508, 509, 575
Oxford Institute of Ageing, 637
Oyserman, D., 283
Özçaliskan, S., 250
Ozer, E. M., 378
Ozmerai, E. J., 509

P

Pacanowski, C. R., 446
Pachan, M., 61, 357
Pacquiao, D. F., 95
Padilla-Walker, L. M., 352, 473, 475
Padmanabhan, A., 373
Páez, M., 323
Pagani, L. S., 402
Page, D., 423, 424n
Page-Gould, E., 345
Pager, D., 500, 500n
Pagnani, A. R., 548
Pahlke, E., 344, 347
Paik, A., 452
Painter, J. A., 587
Palacios, J., 55
Palatino, B., 523
Palkovitz, R., 57
Palmblad, J., 583
Palmer, B., 457
Palmer, S., 648
Palmers, E., 233
Palmieri, P. A., 554
Pan, B. A., 322
Pan, H. W., 264
Pan, Z., 248
Panagiotaki, G., 649
Pandit, M., 482
Panish, J. B., 484
Pantalone, D. W., 382
Papadakis, A. A., 428
Papp, K. V., 527
Papp, L. M., 57
Parada, R. H., 409
Paradis, J., 324
Paradise, R., 319
Paramei, G. V., 509
Parameswaran, G., 305, 305n
Parent, A., 372
Paris, A. H., 244
Paris, S. G., 244
Parish-Morris, J., 174, 250, 251
Park, D. C., 525, 603
Park, W., 421

Park, Y., 163
Parke, R. D., 203, 266, 342
Parker, E. T., 460
Parker, J. G., 200, 263, 398, 423
Parker, K. P., 104
Parker, P. D., 395
Parschau, L., 522
Parsons, S., 463
Parten, M., 263
Pasamanick, B., 101*n*
Pascalis, O., 139, 139*n*
Pascarella, E. T., 460
Paskett, E. D., 449
Pasley, B. K., 497
Pasley, K., 356
Pastore, M., 199
Patel, S., 154
Paterson, S., 154
Paterson, T. S. E., 530
Pathman, T., 240
Patin, R. V., 442
Patock-Peckam, J. A., 475
Patrick, M. E., 386
Patrick, R. B., 418
Patterson, C. J., 278, 487, 498
Patterson, G. R., 177
Patton, G. C., 295, 428
Pauen, S., 165
Paukner, A., 132
Paul, J. J., 349
Paulsen, J. A., 471
Paulussen-Hoogeboom, M. C., 195
Paus, T., 20
Paxson, C., 246
Payne, B. R., 598
Payne, K., 244
Pea, R., 424
Pearson, C. M., 379
Peck, K., 574
Peck, R. C., 610
Peckham, C. S., 298
Pedersen, S., 348
Pederson, D. R., 200
Pedulla, D. S., 500
Peguero, A. A., 402
Peirano, P., 104
Peiró, J., 636
Pellegrini, A. D., 302, 303
Pelletier, J., 241, 312*n*
Pelletier, L. G., 397
Peltonen, K., 359
Pelucchi, B., 140
Pemberton, C. K., 190
Pennington, B. F., 122
Pennisi, E., 44
Penny, H., 297
Peplau, L. A., 479
Pepler, D., 29
Peralta de Mendoza, O. A., 229
Perdue, C. W., 580
Perelli-Harris, B., 494
Perez, A. L. C., 454
Perez, M., 463
Perez, M. M., 167
Perez, S. M., 398
Perez-Edgar, K., 456
Periss, V., 22
Perlman, D., 483
Perlmutter, M., 239, 530
Perls, T. T., 573, 579
Perone, S., 135, 145, 166

Perou, R., 492
Perrin, A., 559, 559*n*, 605
Perris, E. E., 163*n*
Perroud, N., 71, 71*n*
Perrucci, C. C., 501
Perry, B. D., 359
Perry, D. G., 351
Perry, W. G., Jr., 19, 456, 457
Perry-Jenkins, M., 490
Persaud, T. V. N., 45, 54*n*, 76*n*, 77, 77*n*, 78, 79, 80, 82, 82*n*, 117
Peshkin, A., 31
Peskin, H., 547
Pesonen, A.-K., 195
Peter, J., 424
Peters, H. E., 355
Peters, L., 655
Peters, M., 397
Peters, R. D., 61
Peterson, B. E., 539
Peterson, C., 164, 361, 394
Peterson, C. C., 242
Peterson, G. W., 58
Peterson, J., 248
Peterson, J. B., 459
Peterson-Badali, M., 416
Peter-Wight, M., 600
Petitto, L. A., 176
Petrill, S. A., 67
Petrofsky, J., 586
Petrovic, K., 632
Petrunka, K., 61
Pettigrew, T. F., 345
Pettit, G. S., 266
Petty, E., 651
Pew Research Center, 25, 62, 204, 204*n*, 352, 382, 400, 418, 451, 452, 452*n*, 472, 472*n*, 483, 485, 486, 493, 495, 555, 614, 615, 627, 661
Pexman, P. M., 322
Pezaris, E., 396
Pezé, A., 137
Pfeffer, K., 308
Pfeifer, J. H., 345
Pfeiffer, S. I., 328, 329
Phelan, A., 633
Philliber, S., 385
Phillipou, A., 379
Phillips, A. T., 163
Phillips, D. A., 64, 68, 246
Phillips, L. H., 598
Phillips, M. J., 654
Phinney, J. S., 412
Phuong, D. D., 445
Piaget, J., 17, 29, 151, 152, 227, 229, 231, 234, 388, 392, 456
Pianta, R. C., 326
Picho, K., 395
Pick, A. D., 156, 176
Pickel, B., 418
Pickens, J. N., 162, 263
Pienta, A. M., 624
Pierce, K., 243
Pierce, K. M., 61
Piernas, C., 378
Pierroutsakos, S. L., 157
Pietilainen, K., 127
Pietromonaco, P. R., 480
Piirto, J., 317

Pike, K. M., 378
Pikhart, H., 50
Pillemer, D. B., 597
Pillemer, K., 555, 556, 633
Pillow, B., 389
Pimental, A., 32
Pine, J. M., 251
Ping, R. M., 233
Pinheiro, A. P., 379
Pinker, S., 252
Pinquart, M., 398, 493, 556, 557, 592, 612, 636
Piotrowski, J. T., 248
Pirie, K., 449
Pisani, L., 199
Pisoni, D. B., 176, 179
Pitchford, N., 249
Pitkin, J., 513
Pixley, J. E., 542
Plante, I., 350
Plassman, B. L., 531
Platt, M. P. W., 97
Platz, M., 612
Pleck, J. H., 203
Plester, D., 509
Plickert, G., 617
Ploeg, J., 551
Plomin, R., 66, 67, 170, 263
Plucker, J. A., 328
Pluess, M., 195
Plumert, J. M., 156
Poehlmann, J., 99
Poelhuis, C. W. K., 55
Poelman, M. P., 447
Pokropek, A., 465
Polakowski, L. L., 84
Polanska, K., 86
Polderman, T. J. C., 307
Poldrack, R. A., 400
Pollak, R. A., 353, 353*n*
Pollard, K. M., 627, 628, 629, 634
Pollastri, A. R., 72
Pollatsek, A., 313
Pollitt, C., 250
Pomerantz, E. M., 30, 284, 339, 340, 340*n*, 421
Pomplun, M., 315
Pong, S., 32, 284
Ponnappan, S., 577
Ponnappan, U., 577
Pons, F., 138, 342
Poobalan, A. S., 446, 447
Poole, D. A., 361
Poon, L. W., 573
Popkin, B. M., 378
Poppitt, S. D., 578
Porter, R. H., 109
Portes, A., 32
Posner, J. K., 357
Posner, M. I., 161, 189, 191
Posthuma, R. A., 559
Poti, J. M., 378
Potocnik, K., 636
Potter, D., 498
Potter, G. G., 531
Poulin, F., 265
Poulin-Dubois, D., 155, 276
Powell, F. C., 651
Powell, M. P., 581
Power, M., 185, 188
Powers, L. M., 275
Powlishta, K. K., 351, 392

Prada, G. I., 579
Pradhan, R., 581
Prager, K. J., 548
Pratt, H. D., 369, 370
Pratt, M. W., 282, 416, 476, 539
Prause, J., 356
Prechtl, H. F. R., 101*n*
Preece, J., 605
Prepin, K., 207
Pressley, M., 161, 311
Preuss, T. M., 44
Prevatt, F., 402
Price, C. E., 339
Price, H., 401
Price, J. E., 666, 667
Price, L. H., 439
Priess, H. A., 428, 490
Prince, B., 453
Prince, M. J., 587
Prince-Paul, M. J., 655
Principe, G. F., 124
Prinstein, M. J., 425
Prinz, W., 137
Proctor, M. H., 297
Profilet, S. M., 266
Programme for International Student Assessment, 329, 329*n*
Proietti, E., 86
Proulx, C. M., 625
Proulx, J., 521, 545
Proulx, K., 654
Proulx, M., 265
Pruden, S. M., 251
Pruett, M. K., 57
Pryor, J., 356, 496, 497
Pryor, J. H., 471
Public Health Agency of Canada, 383
Pudrovska, T., 555
Pugh, K. L., 573
Pugliese, C. E., 243
Puhl, R. M., 297, 446
Pujol, J., 120
Puma, M., 247
Punamäki, R.-L., 52, 359
Putallaz, M., 348
Putnam, F. W., 360
Putnam, S. P., 193
Puzia, M. E., 286
Pyka, G., 583
Pyle, N., 402
Pyszczynski, T., 652

Q
Qian, Z., 486
Qin, L., 30
Qouta, S. R., 359
Qu, Y., 340
Quas, J. A., 361
Qui, C., 579
Quigley, M. A., 385
Quill, T., 658
Quinn, P. C., 142, 164, 397
Quinn, P. D., 320
Quinn, R. A., 125

R
Raabe, T., 344
Raaijmakers, Q. A. W., 418
Rabaglietti, E., 471, 551
Rabbitt, P., 601

Rabig, J., 624
Raby, K. L., 199
Rackin, H., 497
Racz, S. J., 60
Radesky, J. S., 275
Radey, M., 492
Raevuori, A., 378
Ragow-O'Brien, D., 659
Rahav, G., 551
Rahi, J. S., 298
Rahman, Q., 382
Raikes, H. A., 195
Raikes, H. H., 173
Räikkönen, K., 520, 522
Rakison, D. H., 158, 163, 164, 165, 232
Rakoczy, H., 228
Raley, R. K., 353
Ralston, S. H., 519
Ram, N., 376, 602
Ramachandrappa, A., 97
Ramani, G. B., 207
Ramaswami, A., 499
Ramchandani, P. G., 187
Ramchandran, R. S., 508, 575
Ramey, C. T., 172, 247
Ramey, S. L., 172, 247
Ramirez, J. M., 106
Ramnitz, M. S., 373
Ramo, D. E., 387
Ramos, M. C., 190
Ramsay, D. S., 193, 207
Ramsay, J. T., 60
Ramsey-Rennels, J. L., 143
Ramus, F., 109
Ranalli, C., 600
Rando, T. A., 665
Randolph, K. A., 492
Rangel, C., 326
Rao, N., 278, 492
Rapattoni, M., 617
Rapisardi, G., 109
Rapson, R. L., 481, 482
Raqib, R., 439
Rasbash, J., 352
Rasmus, S., 31
Rasmussen, C., 245
Ratan, R., 122
Ratcliff, R., 596
Rathunde, K., 325
Rathwell, S., 522
Rau, B. L., 564
Raudenbush, S. W., 178
Rauer, A. J., 267, 547
Rauers, A., 600
Raver, C. C., 189
Ravussin, E., 511
Rawlins, W. K., 630
Ray, E., 133
Ray, J. A., 62
Rayner, K., 313
Raynor, H. A., 297
Raynor, R., 16
Razza, R. A., 25
Razza, R. P., 237
Read, S., 611
Ready, C. B., 455
Reagan, P. B., 373
Ream, G. L., 473
Reay, A. C., 634
Rebok, G. W., 602, 638
Redman, L. M., 511
Reed, C. E., 83

Reef, J., 431
Rees, J., 199
Reese, E., 240
Reese, K., 390
Regan, P. C., 479
Reich, J., 316
Reich, S. M., 424
Reichert, M., 624
Reid, J. M., 275
Reid, K. F., 578
Reid, M. J., 275
Reilly, D., 394, 395
Reilly, J. S., 122
Reinke, L. F., 654
Reis, S. M., 329
Reisner, E. R., 61
Reiss, D., 69, 69n
Reiss, N. S., 618
Reiter, S., 33
Reitzes, D. C., 552, 553
Renk, K., 409
Rentner, T. L., 85
Repacholi, B. M., 188
Repetti, R., 501
Reppucci, N. D., 430
Resnick, G., 247
Resnick, M., 249
Rest, J. R., 415
Reuter-Lorenz, P. A., 528, 574
Reyna, V. F., 394
Reynolds, K. J., 416
Reynolds, P., 463
Reynolds, R. M., 89
Rhoades, B. L., 237
Rhodes, J. E., 385, 386
Rhodes, M., 350
Ribarič, S., 590
Rice, S. J., 668
Rich, G. J., 547
Richard, C. A., 627
Richard-Davis, G., 512
Richards, D., 283
Richards, M., 375
Richards, M. P., 327
Richardson, H. L., 106
Richardson, K., 67
Richardson, V. E., 666
Richgels, D. J., 244
Richie, B. S., 500
Richler, J., 221
Richmond, J., 132
Rideout, R., 361
Rideout, V. J., 248, 249, 275, 395, 400
Ridley-Johnson, R., 101n, 103
Riediger, M., 595
Rieffe, C., 260
Riffin, C., 614
Rifkin, R., 380
Riggins, T., 83, 91
Rigó, J., 187
Rijlaarsdam, J., 170
Riksen-Walraven, J. M., 128
Rinaldi, J., 275
Rinaldo, L. A., 582
Rindermann, H., 246
Ripley, A., 330
Ripple, C. H., 64
Risley, T. R., 170, 252
Rissanen, A., 127
Ristic, J., 19
Ristori, J., 281
Ritchie, L. D., 378

Ritchie, S. J., 574
Rith, K. A., 486
Ritter, J. O., 543
Ritz, B., 86
Rivard, V., 612
Rivas-Drake, D., 412
Rivers, S. E., 317
Rivkees, S. A., 80
Rizza, W., 511
Rizzoli, R., 510
Robbins, B. D., 386
Roben, C. K. P., 186
Robert, A.-M., 578
Robert, L., 578
Roberto, K. A., 483, 557, 631, 633, 634
Roberts, A. L. D., 167
Roberts, B. W., 35, 193, 545, 548, 549
Roberts, C., 394
Roberts, D. F., 248, 249, 275, 380, 395, 400
Roberts, H., 513
Roberts, J., 51
Roberts, J. E., 246
Roberts, R. E., 412
Roberts, T., 225, 244
Robertson, J., 356
Robertson, S., 304
Robine, J.-M., 572
Robins, R. W., 337, 342, 470, 471, 544
Robinson, C. C., 263, 273
Robinson, G. E., 83
Robinson, J. L., 208
Robinson, K. M., 591
Robinson, M., 615
Robinson, S., 243
Robinson, S. L., 274
Robinson, S. R., 134, 135
Robinson-Cimpian, J. P., 350
Robinson-Zañartu, C., 321
Robitschek, C., 471
Rochat, N. A. C. F., 137
Rochat, P., 101, 137, 137n, 188, 207, 228
Roche, K. M., 284
Roche, L., 592
Rochelle, T. L., 570
Rodemaker, J. E., 178
Rodgers, B., 479, 637
Rodgers, J. L., 319
Rodgers, P. L., 281
Rodgers, R. F., 562
Rodin, P. A., 553
Rodkin, P. C., 348
Rodrigue, K. M., 574
Rodriguez, A., 395
Rodríguez, B., 485
Rodriguez, E. M., 298, 473
Rodriguez, J. M., 554
Rodriguez, L. F., 402
Roelants, M., 294
Roelfsema, N. M., 79
Roemmich, J. N., 297, 369, 372, 372n
Roese, N. J., 542, 543, 543n
Roeser, R. W., 397
Roeyers, H., 243
Rofail, M., 553
Rogers, S. J., 495
Rogoff, B., 23, 166, 167, 236, 237, 306, 310, 311, 319

Rogol, A. D., 369, 371, 372, 372n
Rohde, P., 378, 379
Rohner, R. P., 57, 205, 283
Rohr, M. K., 637
Roid, G., 245, 315
Roisman, G. I., 201, 480
Roisman, R., 193
Rokach, R., 549
Roksa, J., 461, 474
Rollins, K. B., 231
Romano, E., 245
Roman-Rodriguez, C. F., 108
Romdall, L., 259
Romero, A. J., 412
Romney, A. K., 277
Ronald, A., 67
Rönnqvist, L., 218
Rooney, J., 655
Roopnarine, J. L., 265, 284
Root, T., 379
Røsand, G.-M. B., 486
Rosander, K., 110, 140
Rosario, M., 383
Rose, A. J., 11, 265, 347, 348, 423, 425
Rose, K. J., 532, 533
Rose, S. A., 142, 142n
Roseberry, S., 179
Roseman, M., 187
Rosen, A. B., 231
Rosen, C. S., 36, 359
Rosen, D., 377
Rosen, L. D., 400
Rosen, S., 509
Rosenbaum, J. E., 385
Rosenblatt, P. C., 669
Rosenblum, T. B., 318
Rosenfeld, B., 656
Rosenfeld, R. G., 219
Rosengren, K. S., 225, 649
Rosenman, R. H., 519
Rosenstein, D. L., 654
Rosenthal, Z., 100
Roseth, C. J., 302
Roskos, K. A., 228
Ross, C. E., 469
Ross, E., 250
Ross, J. L., 51
Ross, N., 232
Rossell, S. L., 379
Rossen, E. K., 614
Ross-Griffin, S., 463
Rossi, A. S., 510, 513, 539, 541
Rossi, B. V., 52
Rossi-Casé, L., 319
Rossor, M. N., 104
Ross-Sheehy, S., 162
Rostan, S. M., 459
Rostgaard, T., 594
Roszel, E. L., 85
Rotblatt, L. J., 596
Rote, W. M., 416
Rotenberg, N., 46
Roth, D. L., 556, 557, 571
Roth, G. S., 511
Roth, S. M., 439
Rothbart, M. K., 161, 189, 190, 191, 193
Rothbaum, F., 199
Rothman, E., 426
Rothman, S. M., 589

Rothstein-Fish, C., 320
Rotman, T., 490
Rott, C., 573
Rouselle, L., 233
Routledge, C., 651
Rovee-Collier, C. K., 131, 154, 155, 162, 162n, 163, 163n
Rowe, M. L., 176, 178, 179
Rowland, C. F., 251
Rowles, G. D., 580
Rowley, S. J., 350
Roy, K. M., 539
Rozen, G. S., 378
Rozin, P., 231
Rubens, D., 106
Rubenstein, L. Z., 587
Rubin, C., 372, 372n
Rubin, D., 554
Rubin, D. C., 597
Rubin, D. M., 90
Rubin, K. H., 171, 192, 263, 264, 264n, 283, 346, 347, 348, 397, 399, 423
Rubin, S. E., 499
Ruble, D. N., 276, 279, 344, 350
Ruck, M. D., 320, 416, 417
Ruderman, M. N., 501
Rudolph, C. W., 634
Rudolph, K. D., 349, 409
Rueda, H. A., 424
Ruedinger, E., 384, 385
Ruff, H. A., 162
Ruffman, T., 105, 154, 242, 389
Rulison, K. L., 63
Rumbaut, R. G., 32
Runco, M. A., 328, 548
Runyan, D. K., 269n
Rusbult, C. E., 481
Rushton, J. P., 67, 69, 318
Rusk, N., 199
Russac, R. J., 651, 652
Russell, A., 57, 282, 351
Russell, J. A., 260
Russell, L. T., 496
Russell, S. T., 498
Russo, A., 298
Russo, C., 600
Ruthsatz, J., 30
Rutland, A., 320, 345, 416
Rutter, M., 68, 70, 123, 200
Ryan, A. M., 396
Ryan, M. K., 416, 561
Ryan, R. M., 171
Rybash, J. M., 596
Rydell, A.-M., 326
Ryding, M., 298
Ryff, C. D., 539, 544, 545, 547, 552
Rynearson, E. K., 668

S
Saarni, C., 184, 186
Sabbagh, M. A., 250
Sabo, D., 301
Sacks, D. W., 547
Sadeh, A., 125, 125n
Sadek, S., 349
Sadler, F., 479
Sadler, P. M., 464
Sadler, T. W., 78, 79

Saevarsdottir, S., 586
Safe Kids Worldwide, 221, 222
Saffran, J. R., 81, 109, 139, 140, 174
Safren, S. A., 382
Sagare, A. P., 588
Saginak, K. A., 501
Saginak, M. A., 501
Sagi-Schwartz, A., 199, 199n
Sahathevan, R., 591
Sahler, O. J., 649
Sailor, J. L., 551
St. Jacques, P. L., 597
St James-Roberts, I., 107n, 108
Saito, Y., 557
Saitta, N. M., 661
Sakraida, T. J., 550
Sala, P., 53
Salami, A., 527
Salami, S. O., 636
Salapatek, P., 142n
Salari, S., 633
Salas-Wright, C. P., 418, 473
Sale, A., 121
Salem, N., Jr., 583
Salihu, H. M., 91, 91n
Salloum, A., 668
Salmivalli, C., 347, 349
Salomo, D., 176
Salomon, J. A., 571, 571n
Salomonis, N., 106
Salovey, P., 317, 342
Salsa, A. M., 229
Salthouse, T. A., 526, 527, 528
Salvaterra, F., 56
Salvioli, S., 49
Samarel, N., 656
Sameroff, A. J., 267, 399
Sampaio, R. C., 218
Sampselle, C. M., 513
Samuels, D., 428
Samuelson, G., 573
Samuolis, J., 401
Sanchez, R. P., 155
Sanchis-Gomar, F., 646
Sandberg-Thoma, S. E., 484
Sanders, M., 269
Sanders, O., 360
Sanders, P., 177
Sanders, S., 624
Sandfort, T. G. M., 498
Sandri, M., 578
Sandrin, D., 108
Sandström, A., 560
San Juan, V., 242
Sann, C., 108, 144
Sansavini, A., 109
Sanson, A. V., 193
Sarama, J., 313
Sarason, S. B., 562
Sargent-Cox, K., 581
Sarnat, H. B., 106
Sarnecka, B. W., 244
Sarrazin, P., 301
Sasser-Coen, J. A., 531
Satin, J. R., 654
Sattler, C., 590
Sattler, F. R., 440
Saucier, J. F., 32
Saudino, K. J., 170, 195
Saunders, B. E., 360

Sautter, J. M., 571
Saw, S.-M., 298
Sawyer, A. M., 432, 432n
Saxe, G. B., 23
Saxon, J. L., 339
Saxton, M., 252
Sayegh, P., 557
Sayer, A. A., 369
Sayer, L. C., 486
Sayfan, L., 312
Saygin, A. P., 175
Sayil, M., 376
Saylor, M. M., 156, 157, 250
Sbarra, D. A., 355, 496, 550
Scarborough, H. S., 319
Scarlett, W. G., 418
Scarr, S., 68, 69, 318
Scelfo, J., 380
Schaal, B., 108, 109, 109n
Schaal, S., 71
Schaefer-McDaniel, N. J., 60
Schaeffer, J., 175
Schaie, K. W., 524, 525, 525n, 526, 526n, 595, 601, 602
Schalet, A., 385
Schamberg, M. A., 308
Scharling, H., 448
Schauble, L., 391
Schein, S. S., 649
Scher, A., 125
Schewe, P. A., 454
Schiamberg, L. B., 633, 634
Schick, A. R., 322
Schiebe, S., 543, 611
Schieman, S., 560, 615, 617, 631
Schigelone, A. R. S., 624
Schilling, O. K., 602
Schimmack, U., 452
Schimmele, C. M., 628
Schindler, I., 636
Schlagmüller, M., 312
Schlegel, A., 376
Schlomer, G. L., 58
Schmeichel, B. J., 652
Schmertz, B., 532
Schmidheiny, K., 495
Schmidt, K.-H., 560
Schmidt, L. A., 191, 192, 548
Schmidt, M. E., 157, 423, 425
Schmitt, M. T., 561
Schmitz, S., 190
Schneider, B., 25
Schneider, B. H., 205
Schneider, D., 319
Schneider, D. E., 561
Schneider, W., 248, 249, 310, 311, 312
Schneller, D. P., 550, 551
Schnitzspahn, K. M., 598
Schnohr, P., 448, 579
Schoen, C., 65
Schoeni, R. F., 88, 88n
Schofield, T. J., 354
Schonberg, R. L., 51n
Schonert-Reichl, K. A., 310, 417
Schooler, C., 531
Schoon, I., 172
Schoon, L., 463
Schoppe, S. J., 191
Schoppe-Sullivan, S. J., 490, 491

Schorge, J., 83
Schott, J. M., 104
Schrimshaw, E. W., 383
Schroeder, R. D., 283
Schulenberg, J. E., 386
Schull, W. J., 85
Schultz, J. B., 376
Schultz, R., 593, 616
Schultz, R. M., 50
Schulz, M. S., 491
Schulz, R., 19, 442, 592, 616
Schulze, C., 252
Schum, N., 141
Schuneman, M. J., 389
Schunk, D. H., 313
Schut, H., 665, 670
Schüz, B., 630
Schwab, J., 470n, 471, 476, 480
Schwade, J. A., 176
Schwanenflugel, P. J., 312
Schwartz, A., 276
Schwartz, B. L., 599
Schwartz, C. E., 192
Schwartz, C. R., 495
Schwartz, M., 25, 236, 378
Schwartz, T. L., 529
Schwartz, S. A., 482
Schwartz, S. G., 575
Schwartz, S. J., 411, 470, 471
Schwarz, N., 30
Schwarzer, G., 141
Schwebel, D. C., 221, 222, 299
Schweinhart, L. J., 247
Schweizer, K., 316
Schwenck, C., 310
Schwerdt, G., 396, 398
Schwier, C., 155
Sciarra, D. T., 463
Scocco, P., 617
Scott, J., 651
Scott, J. A., 321
Scott, L. D., 412
Scott, L. S., 119, 139
Scott, M. E., 497
Scott, P. M., 268
Scott, R. M., 250
Scott, V., 587
Scruggs, T. E., 340
Scrutton, D., 136
Scullin, M. K., 598
Seals, D. R., 442, 442n
Sebastián, E., 251
Sebastián-Gallés, N., 138, 323
Seburg, E., 297
Sedgh, G., 64n, 384, 384n
Seeher, K., 588
Seery, M. D., 523, 523n
Seethaler, P. M., 321
Segrin, C., 481
Sehlstedt, I., 576
Seibert, A. C., 204, 338, 352
Seid, M., 266
Seiden, H. M., 666
Seidl, A., 138, 251
Seidman, E., 397, 398
Seiffge-Krenke, I., 410, 476, 484, 485
Seki, Y., 312, 655
Sekita, A., 591
Selman, L., 656
Seltzer, M. M., 552
Selwood, A., 592, 633

Selwyn, P. A., 671
Semanik, P. A., 586
Senechal, M., 244
Senghas, A., 250
Sengpiel, V., 83
Senior, G. J., 142, 142n
Senju, A., 176
Senn, C. Y., 454
Senn, T. E., 238
Serbin, L. A., 351
Sermon, K., 54n
Serra, L., 588
Sesame Workshop, 248
Settersten, R. A., 478, 551
Settles, B. H., 500
Sevigny, P. R., 205
SFIA (Sports & Fitness Industry Association), 301
Shafer, R. J., 202
Shaffer, T. G., 278
Shafto, M. A., 599
Shalev, I., 439
Shamloul, R., 513
Shanahan, M. J., 5, 6
Shaner, T. L., 529
Shanks, D. R., 596
Shannon, J. D., 179
Shao, L., 585
Shao, Y., 337
Shapiro, A., 491, 547
Shapiro, C. J., 309
Shapka, J. D., 337, 409
Sharf, R. S., 462
Sharma, A., 627
Sharon, D., 551
Sharp, C., 656
Sharp, E. A., 494
Sharp, E. H., 411
Sharp, K. L., 29
Shastri, J., 279
Shatz, M., 231
Shaul, S., 236
Shaver, P. R., 666
Shaw, B. A., 622
Shaw, D. S., 57, 347, 422
Shaw, P., 309
Shea, A. K., 89
Sheehan, N. W., 632
Sheikh, I., 669
Sheikh-Khalil, S., 24, 399
Shellman, J., 612
Shelton, J. N., 412
Shenck, C. E., 384
Sheng, X., 500
Shephard, E. E., 51
Shepherd, H., 500
Shepperd, S., 657
Sherman, A. M., 483, 484
Sherman, R. A., 451
Sherrod, L. R., 418
Shi, J., 557
Shibusawa, T., 484
Shic, F., 243
Shields, R., 222
Shim, S. S., 396
Shimada, S., 132
Shimizu, H., 417
Shin, N., 265
Shiner, R. L., 193
Shinohara, S. K., 627
Shirley, L., 278
Shmotkin, D., 545

Shoffner, M. F., 463
Shokolenko, I. N., 440
Shonkoff, J. P., 11, 66
Shor, E., 629
Short, M. M., 164
Shoup, R., 461
Shriver, L. H., 338
Shuck, M. B., 532, 533
Shuey, E. A., 11, 59
Shuey, K., 556
Shultz, K. S., 635, 636
Shumow, L., 346
Shuster, M. M., 185
Shutter, J. M., 185
Shwalb, D. W., 204, 284
Siano, L. J., 52
Siberry, G. K., 88
Sica, L. S., 471, 551
Sidebotham, P., 285
Sidle, A. L., 231
Siegal, M., 323
Siega-Riz, A. M., 128
Siegel, J. S., 510
Siegel, K., 667
Siegel, R. L., 516n, 517
Siegler, R. S., 19, 314
Sieri, S., 447
Sievert, L. L., 513
Siimes, M. A., 377
Sikora, J., 465
Silva, K. G., 236
Silvén, M., 176
Silver, M. H., 573
Silver, R. C., 359, 523, 523n
Silverman, B., 249
Silverman, I., 397
Silverman, P. R., 653, 667
Silverstein, M., 63, 553, 558, 623, 630, 632
Simcock, G., 156, 157, 164, 165n, 207, 229
Simion, F., 105, 142, 143n
Simmens, S. J., 193
Simmons, T., 554
Simoneau, M., 389
Simonton, D. K., 459
Simpson, E. A., 139
Simpson, J. A., 480
Simpson, J. M., 380
Simpson, R., 464
Sims, M., 553
Singer, B. H., 552
Singer, J. A., 337
Singer, L. T., 83
Singh, G. K., 445
Singleton, J. L., 174
Sinkkonen, J., 377
Sinno, S. M., 272, 417
Sinnott, J. D., 457
Sirsch, U., 470
Sizonenko, S. V., 94
Skara, S., 387
Skinner, E. A., 339
Skinner, M., 599
Skoe, E. E., 416
Skopek, J., 552
Skorikov, V., 462
Skorska, M., 382
Skouteris, H., 100
Skultety, K. M., 541
Slagsvold, B., 579
Slater, A. M., 110, 140, 142, 153, 158

Slater, H., 235
Slaughter, V., 648, 650
Slemmer, J. A., 140
Slevin, K. F., 584
Slijper, F. M. E., 281
Slining, M. M., 378
Sliwinski, M. J., 529
Sloan, F. A., 575
Slomczynski, K. M., 531
Slonims, V., 50
Sloutsky, V., 163
Slusher, M. P., 627
Slutske, W. S., 450
Sluzenski, J., 154
Smahel, D., 424
Small, B. J., 596, 670
Small, M., 110
Small, P. J., 11, 284, 360, 422
Small, S. A., 32
Smetana, J. G., 272, 343, 416, 421, 485
Smink, R. F. E., 379
Smit, D. J. A., 307
Smith, A., 235, 605
Smith, B. H., 309
Smith, Camille, 550
Smith, Christian, 472, 473, 474, 492
Smith, Christine, 627
Smith, C. L., 33
Smith, D. G., 373
Smith, G. C., 554
Smith, G. T., 379
Smith, Jacqui, 8, 445, 579, 595, 600, 614, 625, 630, 631
Smith, Jason, 651, 652, 652n
Smith, Julia, 270
Smith, J. C., 590, 601
Smith, J. P., 127
Smith, J. Z., 278
Smith, K. E., 357
Smith, L. B., 135, 166, 250
Smith, L. J., 126
Smith, N., 522
Smith, P. K., 349
Smith, T. B., 626
Smith, T. W., 450, 451n, 520
Smith, V. C., 83, 84
Smits, J., 45n
Smokowski, P. R., 32
Smoller, J. W., 72
Smyer, M. A., 617
Smyke, A. T., 199
Smyth, A. C., 596
Sneed, J. R., 36, 542, 543
Snell, P., 472
Snider, J. B., 421
Snidman, N., 192
Snow, C. E., 252, 323
Snyder, A., 484
Snyder, J., 349, 431
Snyder, J. S., 574
Sobel, D. M., 228
Sobiraj, S., 464
Sobolewski, J. M., 355
Society for Research in Child Development, 37, 38, 38n
Soderstrom, M., 138, 522
Soenens, B., 411
Soli, A. R., 352
Solmeyer, A. R., 352, 422

Solomon, J., 198, 201
Solomon, J. C., 554
Somers, M., 218
Somerville, L. H., 373
Son, J., 541
Song, C., 402
Song, J., 261, 585
Soos, I., 297
Sørensen, A., 579
Sørensen, K., 373
Sörensen, S., 508, 556, 557, 575, 592
Sorkhabi, N., 284
Sosa, R., 96
Sosik, J. J., 531, 560
Soska, K. C., 141
Soto, C. J., 548, 548n
Soto, P., 251
Soulsby, L. K., 628
Soussignan, R., 108, 109n
South Africa Department of Health, 87
Sowers, M. F., 510
Sowislo, J. F., 337
Spagnola, M., 25
Spangler, G., 201
Spatz, D. L., 126
Spear, M., 358
Speece, D. L., 244
Spelke, E. S., 137, 158, 163
Spence, I., 397
Spence, M. J., 81, 109
Spencer, J. P., 135, 166
Spencer-Smith, M., 122
Spere, K. A., 177
Spieker, S. J., 431
Spiel, C., 349
Spieler, D. H., 599
Spiewak, G. S., 418
Spillman, B. C., 623, 624
Spilt, J., 326
Spinath, F. M., 67, 238
Spinrad, T. L., 262, 263, 268
Spirito, A., 429
Spiro, A., III, 614, 618
Spitz, G., 555
Spitze, G., 631
Spock, B., 126
Spoelstra, M. N., 129
Spokane, A. R., 463
Sporte, S. E., 419
Sprecher, S., 380, 451, 479, 480, 481
Spuhl, S., 235
Spurk, D., 490
Srivastava, S., 543, 548
Sroufe, L. A., 7, 199, 202, 205
Stackert, R. A., 480
Staff, J., 401
Staines, G., 603
Stambolis-Ruhstorfer, M., 498
Stams, G. J. M., 205, 418
Stanley-Hagan, M., 356
Stanovich, K. E., 30
Stanowicz, L., 252
Stansbury, K., 192
Stanton, B., 249
Stapley, P. J., 443
Stark, P., 402n
Starks, T. J., 426
Starr, M. S., 313
Stattin, H., 282, 283
Staub, F. C., 314

Staudinger, U. M., 7, 8, 68, 531, 546, 561, 595, 600, 601
Stauffacher, K., 352
Stawski, R. S., 36
Steele, H., 206
Steele, K. H., 225
Steele, L. C., 361
Steele, M., 206
Steele, S., 243
Steensma, T. D., 281
Stegge, H., 341
Steinberg, L., 62, 282, 283, 373, 377, 380, 398, 401, 421, 426, 430
Steiner, J. E., 108, 131
Steiner, M., 89
Stenberg, C., 186, 188
Stephen, E. H., 443
Stephens, B. E., 98
Stephens, B. R., 143
Stephens, M. A. P., 555
Stephens, P. C., 387
Stepien, M., 328
Stepler, R., 555
Stern, E., 314
Sternberg, R. J., 19, 160, 315, 316, 318, 328, 459, 479, 531
Sterns, H. L., 635
Stevens, A. B., 593
Stevens, J., 510
Stevens, J. A., 587
Stevens, J. C., 576
Stevens, N. L., 483
Stevenson, B., 547
Stevenson, R., 250
Steverink, N., 631
Stewart, A. J., 12, 13, 539, 541, 543
Stewart, A. L., 557
Stewart, J. H., 269
Stewart, P. W., 86
Stewart, R. B., Jr., 491
Stewart, S., 461
Stewin, L., 671
Stice, E., 377, 378, 379
Stifter, C. A., 195, 283
Stiles, J., 122, 143
Stiles-Shields, C., 488
Stillman, R. D., 109
Stine-Morrow, E. A. L., 8, 598
Stipek, D. J., 208, 246
Stochholm, K., 51, 51n
Stocker, C., 23, 352
Stoesz, D., 65
Stoet, G., 394
Stohs, S. J., 440
Stolz, H. E., 283, 421
Stone, A. A., 545
Stone, L., 423
Stone, M. R., 425
Stone, P., 499
Stoneman, Z., 204
Stoner, R., 21
Storch, S. A., 244
Stormshak, E. A., 412
Story, M., 378
Stott, K. L., 626
Stout, M., 416
Strambler, M. J., 320
Strapp, C. M., 252
Strasburger, V. C., 386

Stratton, D. C., 628
Straus, M. A., 269
Strazdins, L., 24, 357
Street, A. E., 455
Streri, A., 108, 144
Striano, T., 188, 207, 228
Stricker, G., 484
Stright, A. D., 235, 313
Stringer, K. J., 462, 463
Stroebe, M., 665, 666, 670
Stroebe, W., 666
Strohmaier, J., 439
Strohschein, L., 355
Stronach, E. P., 286
Stroub, K. J., 327
Strough, J., 277, 547, 599, 600
Stryker, M. P., 121
Studer, J., 458
Stuewig, J., 262
Sturge-Apple, M. L., 187
Sturm, R., 297
Su, T. F., 32
Suarez-Morales, L., 421
Suárez-Orozco, C., 32
Subrahmanyam, K., 231, 249, 424
Substance Abuse and Mental Health Services Administration, 83
Suddendorf, T., 207
Sudharsanan, N., 581
Sugarman, D. B., 269
Sugiyama, S., 647
Suitor, J. J., 555, 556, 557, 558
Suizzo, M.-A., 344, 347
Sullivan, A. R., 615, 629
Sullivan, J., 358
Sullivan, K. J., 591
Sullivan, K. T., 481
Sullivan, M. C., 98
Sullivan, M. W., 186
Sullivan, P. F., 67
Sullivan, S. E., 562
Sulman, A., 319
Sun, H., 295
Sunderam, S., 52
Sundet, J. M., 319
Suomi, S. J., 132
Super, C. M., 110, 125, 136
Super, D. E., 462
Supple, A. J., 32, 421
Surething, N. A., 464
Surian, L., 267, 323
Susman, E. J., 376
Susman-Stillman, A., 352
Sussman, A. L., 103, 491
Sussman, S., 387, 425
Sutfin, E. L., 278
Sutherland, D., 463
Sutin, A. R., 446
Suzuki, K., 218
Suzuki, L. K., 320
Sveen, C.-A., 666
Sverke, M., 498
Svetina, M., 19
Swain, M. E., 53
Swank, E., 453
Swanson, J., 191
Swanson, R. A., 533
Swedish Institute, 580
Sweeny, M. M., 353
Sweet, M. A., 172
Sweet, S., 532

Swenson, L. D., 250
Swenson, L. P., 348
Swinson, J., 278
Syed, M., 412
Syvertsen, A. K., 419
Szaflarski, J. P., 218
Szalacha, L. A., 417
Szanton, S., 570
Szkrybalo, J., 279

T

Tabares, A., 481
Taber-Thomas, B., 456
Tabibi, Z., 308
Tabler, J., 582
Tadd, W., 38
Taga, G., 120n
Tager-Flusberg, H., 242, 243
Tahir, L., 531
Tai, T., 486, 487, 487n
Takagi, E., 555, 623
Takahashi, K., 199, 549, 620
Takahashi, T. A., 512
Talaulikar, V. S., 89
Talbot, A. P., 600
Talmi, A., 110
Talwar, V., 650
Tamim, H., 222
Tamis-LeMonda, C. S., 136, 167, 179, 204, 284
Tamm, L., 309
Tammelin, T., 371
Tan, P. Z., 209
Tanaka, A., 442, 442n
Tandon, S. D., 92
Tang, C. S. K., 652
Tang, M., 463
Tangney, J. P., 262
Tani, F., 109
Tanner, J. L., 473, 474, 476
Tanner, J. M., 117
Tanner-Smith, E. E., 402
Taras, V., 63
Tardif, C., 205
Tardif, T., 58, 177, 178
Tarr, M. J., 143
Tarry-Adkins, J. L., 439
Tarullo, A. R., 104
Tasker, F., 354
Tasopoulos-Chan, M., 421
Taylor, B. A., 171, 247
Taylor, C. A., 269
Taylor, C. L., 322
Taylor, J. H., 415
Taylor, J. L., 384
Taylor, K. K., 464
Taylor, L. C., 398
Taylor, M., 228
Taylor, M. C., 279
Taylor, Marianne G., 278, 350
Taylor, Miles G., 582
Taylor, R. D., 11, 63
Taylor, R. L., 63
Taylor, W. C., 522
Taylor, Z. E., 263
Tchkonia, T., 439
Team Up for Youth, 302
Tecwyn, E. C., 310
Telama, R., 371
Temple, C. M., 51
Temple, J. L., 296
Templeton, L., 554
ten Brummelhuis, L. L., 501

Tenenbaum, H. R., 278, 280, 350
Tenenbaum, J. B., 19
Tennstedt, S. L., 602
Teno, J. M., 657
ten Tusscher, G. W., 86
Terenzini, P. T., 460
Terracciano, A., 446
Terry, D., 573
Terwogt, M. M., 260
Teske, S. C., 430
Tessler, R. C., 56
Teti, D. M., 201, 204
Thakar, M., 482
Thakur, G. A., 84
Tharenou, P., 499
Tharpar, A., 427
Thatcher, R. W., 217
Thayer, S. M., 422
Thelen, E., 101n, 103, 135, 154, 166
Theodore, A. D., 269n
Théoret, M., 350
Theuring, C., 135
Thiessen, E. D., 139, 140
Thiessen, V., 395
Thoermer, C., 155
Thomaes, S., 339
Thomas, A., 190, 195
Thomas, C., 523
Thomas, H. N., 515, 515n
Thomas, J., 670
Thomas, K. A., 56
Thomas, K. M., 121, 217, 219
Thomas, R. B., 107
Thomas, S. R., 187
Thomas-Tate, S., 319
Thombs, B. D., 187
Thomeer, M. B., 593
Thompson, A., 283
Thompson, J., 575
Thompson, J. M., 83
Thompson, P. M., 219
Thompson, R. A., 22, 118n, 188, 189, 198, 201, 206, 242, 260, 261, 262, 271, 342
Thompson, S., 523
Thompson, S. A., 658
Thompson, W. W., 221
Thorne, B., 278
Thornton, K., 512
Thornton, L. M., 379
Thornton, M. J., 510
Thornton, S., 19, 20n
Thornton, W. L., 530
Thorpe, R., 570
Thorpe, S. K. S., 310
Thorson, J. A., 651
Thurston, R. C., 515, 515n
Tien, A., 252
Tienari, P., 70
Tiggemann, M., 297, 338
Tilghman, J. D., 454
Tillman, K. H., 497
Tincoff, R., 177
Tirosh, E., 125
Tishkoff, S. A., 44
Tishler, C. L., 618
Tizard, B., 199
Todd, N. R., 31
Tolan, P. H., 27

Tomasello, M., 174, 175, 176, 177, 228, 250, 251, 252, 268, 271, 322
Tomasetto, C., 340
Tomer, A., 651, 652, 652n
Tomyr, L., 24, 286
Tong, S., 170
Toomey, E., 634
Torchia, M. G., 45, 54n, 76n, 77, 77n, 78, 79, 80, 82, 82n, 117
Tordera, N., 636
Torges, C. M., 543
Torjussen, T. M., 319
Torney-Purta, J., 419, 458, 649
Tornstam, L., 611
Toro-Morn, M., 479
Torquati, J. C., 171, 172
Torrance, E. P., 328
Torres, V., 456
Torrez, D. J., 553
Torsheim, T., 303
Toth, S. L., 286, 287
Tottenham, N., 200, 218
Tracy, J. L., 342
Tran, P., 249
Trappe, S., 442
Träuble, B., 165
Trautner, H. M., 276, 350
Treas, J., 486, 487, 487n
Trehub, S. E., 109, 138, 139
Tremblay, R. E., 273
Trenholm, C., 385
Trentacosta, C. J., 347
Triandis, H. C., 63
Trickett, P. K., 360, 376
Trocmé, N., 285
Troilo, J., 354
Troll, L. E., 631
Tronick, E. Z., 107, 110, 185, 186
Troop-Gordon, W., 348
Tropp, L. R., 345
Troseth, G. L., 157, 250
Troutman, D. R., 347
Troyer, A. K., 529
True, M. M., 199
Truwit, C. L., 218
Trzesniewski, K. H., 337, 471, 544
Tsai, C.-C., 391
Tsai, J. C., 509
Tsai, K. M., 421
Tsang, C. D., 138
Tsang, P. S., 529
Tsao, F.-M., 139
Tsukayama, E., 320
Tsutsumi, H., 647
Ttofi, M. M., 431
Tucker, C. J., 419
Tucker-Drob, E. M., 373, 373n
Turati, C., 142, 143n
Turell, S. C., 630
Turiano, N. A., 614
Turiel, E., 271, 272
Turkewitz, G., 109
Turkheimer, E., 377
Turley-Ames, K. J., 242
Turner, P. J., 277
Turner, R. N., 345
Tustin, K., 165
Tveito, M., 591

Twenge, J. M., 13, 337, 339, 451, 471
Twomey, J. C., 464
Twyman, R., 55
Tyler, C. P., 83
Tyler, M. D., 139
Tzuriel, D., 397

U
Uauy, R., 104
Ucanok, Z., 376
Uccelli, P., 322
Uchino, B. N., 599, 618
Udry, J. R., 426, 426n
Uebelacker, L. A., 547
Uggen, C., 401
Ugnat, A., 24, 286
Uhlenberg, P., 553
Uitterlinden, A. G., 519
Ukrainetz, T. A., 322
Umaña-Taylor, A. J., 412
Underwood, M. K., 273
Unger, C. C., 221
UNICEF, 59, 62, 64n, 127, 359
United Nations, 48
Unverzagt, F. W., 602
Updegraff, K. A., 36, 352, 422
Urbach, J. B., 30
U.S. Bureau of Labor Statistics, 637
U.S. Census Bureau, 7, 53, 59, 61, 64n, 65, 102, 102n, 171, 204, 246, 248, 323, 353, 354, 356, 484, 485, 490, 495, 549, 571, 574n, 575
U.S. Department of Agriculture, 89, 129, 447, 490
U.S. Department of Education, 64, 330, 394, 395, 401, 402, 403, 460, 470, 532
U.S. Department of Health and Human Services, 50, 65, 106, 127, 173, 247, 285, 287, 358, 384, 448, 449, 450, 522, 555, 571, 573, 581, 583, 591, 622, 623
U.S. Department of Justice, 429, 430, 623
U.S. Department of Labor, 463n, 464, 465, 499, 509, 561
U.S. Department of Transportation, 450
Usta, I. M., 91
Uttal, D. H., 320, 397
Utz, R. L., 582
Uziel, Y., 294

V
Vacha-Haase, T., 620
Vachon, R., 390
Vaever, M. S., 187
Vaillancourt, T., 348, 349
Vaillant, G. E., 477, 478, 542, 610, 611, 638
Vaish, A., 188, 271
Vakil, E., 308
Valentine, J. C., 337
Valian, V., 252

Valiente, C., 191, 263
Valkenburg, P. M., 424
Valle, C. D., 448
Valley-Gray, S., 299
Valli, L., 326
van Aken, M. A. G., 36
van Baarsen, B., 628
van Balen, F., 498
Van Beijsterveldt, C. E., 281
Van Brunt, D., 652
Van Camp, G., 509
Vandell, D. L., 61, 171, 247, 346, 357
van den Akker, A. L., 193
Vandenberg, B., 263, 264n
Van den Bergh, B. R. H., 337
van den Boom, D. C., 191, 193, 498
Vandenbosch, L., 380
van den Bout, J., 670
van den Dries, L., 55, 199
van den Eijnden, R., 349
Van der Heide, A. L. J., 664
VanderLaan, D. P., 382
Van der Lippe, T., 487
Van der Meer, A. L. H., 137
van der Pers, M., 631
van de Vijver, J. F. R., 30
Van Doorn, M. D., 376
van Doornen, L. J. P., 107
van Dulmen, M., 426
van Eeden-Moorefield, B., 497
Van Eldik, L. J., 590
Van Eyken, E., 509
van Geel, M., 32
van Gelderen, L., 498
van Goethem, A. A. J., 419
van Grieken, A., 297
van Heerden, H. G., 509
Van Hiel, A., 610
van Hoof, A., 418
Van Hulle, C. A., 177
van IJzendoorn, M. H., 55, 56, 68, 72, 195, 198, 199, 199n, 200, 201, 205
Van Laer, L., 509
VanLaningham, J., 625
Van Orden, K., 618
Van Ryzin, M. J., 626, 626n
van Solinge, H., 636
Vansteenkiste, M., 610
Van Steirteghem, A., 54n
Van Volkom, M., 630
Varnhagen, C., 275
Värnik, P., 428
Vartanian, L. R., 392
Vasilenko, S. A., 384
Vaughn, B. E., 201, 209
Vaughn, M. G., 418, 473
Vazsonyi, A. T., 421
Vedder, P., 32
Vedova, A. M., 187
Veenstra, R., 349
Veerman, J. L., 590
Velez, C. E., 354
Veliz, P., 301
Venet, M., 390
Veneziano, R. A., 205
Ventura, S. J., 497
Verhaak, P. F. M., 617
Verhaeghen, P., 528, 529, 595, 596

Verhulst, F. C., 56
Veríssimo, M., 56
Vernon-Feagans, L., 59
Veronese, N., 511
Verschaffel, L., 314
Versey, H. S., 539
Vespa, J., 494, 628
Vest, A. R., 91
Vida, M. N., 461
Viddal, K. R., 206
Viechtbauer, W., 548
Vihman, M. M., 176
Vinden, P. G., 242
Vinik, J., 342
Virant-Klun, I., 45
Visher, E. B., 356
Visher, J. S., 356
Vistad, I., 97
Vitali, P., 588
Vitányi, P., 175
Vitaro, F., 266, 272, 273
Vitiello, V. E., 266
Vitrup, B., 269
Vivian-Taylor, J., 512
Voci, A., 345
Voegtline, K. M., 81
Voeten, M., 349
Vogel, C. A., 173
Vogel, R. M., 635
Vohr, B. R., 98
Vollebergh, W., 411
Volling, B. L., 204, 205, 267, 352, 484
Volpe, L. E., 126
von Hofsten, C., 110, 136, 137, 140
Votruba-Drzal, E., 58, 59
Vouloumanos, A., 109
Vraneković, J., 50
Vukasović, T., 67
Vukman, S. N., 483
Vygotsky, L. S., 22, 234, 236

W
Waber, D. P., 129, 327
Wachs, T. D., 190
Wadden, T. A., 446
Wadell, P. M., 49
Waerness, K., 557
Wagenaar, K., 52
Wagner, M., 630
Wahl, H.-W., 509, 575, 602, 622, 624
Wahlberg, K. E., 70
Wahler, J. J., 626
Wahlheim, C. N., 596
Wahlsten, D., 68
Wahlstrom, K., 374
Wai, J., 394, 395, 530
Waite, L. J., 515, 631
Walberg, H. J., 325
Walby, F. A., 666
Walden, T. A., 158, 188
Waldfogel, J., 100, 103, 203, 246, 497
Waldorf, K. M. A., 87, 87n
Waldron, N. L., 328
Waldron, V. R., 553
Walfisch, A., 128
Walk, R. D., 140
Walker, A. M., 106
Walker, C., 173
Walker, C. M., 156

Walker, J., 654
Walker, L., 576
Walker, L. B., 156
Walker, L. J., 415
Walker, O. L., 266
Walker, R. A., 217
Walker, S. M., 108
Walker, S. P., 295
Walker-Andrews, A. S., 188
Wall, M., 302
Wall, M. I., 371, 371n
Waller, E. M., 348
Wallon, M., 88
Walsh, C. A., 634
Walsh, F., 657
Walsh, M. E., 462
Walton, K. E., 548
Wanberg, C. R., 562
Wang, H., 441n
Wang, H.-X., 601
Wang, K.-Y., 615
Wang, L., 193, 195
Wang, M., 557, 564, 635, 636
Wang, M.-T., 24, 270, 399
Wang, Q., 241, 337, 421
Wang, S., 154, 501
Wang, T., 295
Wang, Y., 396
Wang, Z., 11
Wänstrom, L., 319
Ward, E. V., 596
Ward, M. M., 579
Ward, R. A., 555
Ward, T. C. S., 126
Warneken, F., 268
Warner, L. A., 421
Warner, L. M., 617
Warnock, F., 108
Warr, P., 560
Warren, A. E. A., 418
Warren, K. L., 164
Warren, L. H., 596
Warren, M. P., 375, 376
Warren, S. L., 193
Warreyn, P., 243
Warshaw, C., 489
Washington, J. A., 319
Washington, S. K., 649
Washington, T., 63
Wasik, B. A., 250
Wasserman, E. A., 163
Wasylyshyn, C., 529
Watamura, S. E., 202, 203
Watanabe, H., 346
Waterman, A. S., 548
Waters, E., 198, 202, 298
Waters, S., 398
Waters, S. F., 342
Watrin, J. P., 17
Watson, D., 479, 550
Watson, J., 185
Watson, J. B., 16
Watson, K. S., 264
Watterson, D. M., 590
Waxler, C. Z., 268
Waxman, S. R., 165, 250
Way, N., 423
Wayne, S. J., 561
Weahkee, R. L., 618
Weaver, J. M., 354
Webb, A. R., 99, 99n
Webb, N. B., 668
Webb, N. M., 326

Webb, S. J., 118
Weber, C., 138
Weber, J. A., 620
Webster, G. D., 373
Webster, J. D., 612
Webster, N. J., 547
Webster-Stratton, C., 275
Wechsler, D., 245
Weech-Maldonado, R., 581
Weems, C. F., 358
Wegner, K. E., 562
Wei, W., 395
Weiland, C., 246
Weinberg, M. K., 185
Weinberg, R. A., 318
Weinberger, M. I., 617
Weiner, S., 163n
Weinfield, N. S., 199, 202
Weinstein, A. A., 546
Weinstein, A. M., 583
Weinstein, R. S., 320, 326, 398
Weinstock, M., 89
Weisaeth, L., 668
Weisberg, R. B., 452
Weisgram, E. S., 351
Weisleder, A., 178
Weisman, O., 105
Weisner, T., 126
Weiss, A., 614
Weiss, E. M., 561
Weiss, K. M., 49
Weiss, L., 315
Weissberg, R. P., 61, 357
Weissberg, R. W., 459
Weiss-Numeroff, G., 573
Wekerle, C., 285n
Wellman, H. M., 231, 241, 322
Wellons, M., 512
Wells, B. E., 451
Wells, Y. V., 508, 544
Welsh, D. P., 426, 427
Welsh, M., 46
Wenger, G. C., 630
Wennberg, A. M., 577
Wentworth, N., 137
Wentzel, K. R., 339, 340, 341n, 425
Werker, J. F., 81, 109, 138
Werner, E. E., 10, 553
Werner, L. A., 81, 109
Werner, N. E., 273, 347, 431
West, M. R., 396, 398
West, R. L., 602
Westerberg, H., 602
Westerhof, G. J., 541, 579, 612
Westermann, G., 19
Westermeyer, J. F., 539
Western, B., 500, 500n
Westfahl, S. M.-C., 158
Westphal, M., 665
Westra, T., 136
Wethington, E., 542
Wetmore, C. M., 446
Wettstein, M., 509, 575
Wexler, J., 402
Weyand, C. M., 585
Whaley, G. J. L., 199

Wheeler, I., 667
Wheeler, K., 169
Whipple, E. E., 285n
Whipple, N., 201, 485
Whisman, M. A., 496, 547, 550
Whitbourne, S. K., 36, 541, 543, 548, 574, 578, 617
Whitby, E. H., 54n
White, K., 508, 575
White, L., 557
White, R. E., 228
Whitehurst, G. J., 244
Whiteman, S. D., 36, 352, 422, 485
Whiteman, V., 83
Whitesell, N. R., 337
Whitfield, K. E., 570
Whiting, B., 277
Whitney, C. G., 221
Whitton, S. W., 426, 486, 494
Wicher, C. P., 661
Wichmann, C., 348
Wickberg, B., 490
Wickrama, K. A. S., 445
Widaman, K. F., 470, 471
Widen, S. C., 260
Widman, L., 380, 381
Widom, C. S., 286
Wiegering, S., 602
Wieling, E., 359
Wiemers, E. E., 554
Wien, M., 297
Wigfield, A., 337, 341n
Wight, R. G., 626
Wight, V. R., 487
Wikby, A., 577
Wilber, K. H., 594, 630
Wilbur, J., 522
Wildsmith, E., 381, 384
Wiley, E., 323
Wilkenfeld, B., 419
Wilkie, S. S., 442
Wilkinson, K., 250
Wilkinson, R. B., 409
Willatts, P., 155
Willerman, L., 318
Williams, C. L., 464
Williams, J. M., 377
Williams, K., 354
Williams, K. N., 599
Williams, K. R., 349
Williams, L. R., 424
Williams, M. E., 626
Williams, N., 553
Williams, S., 654
Williams, S. W., 557
Williams, T. N., 48
Williams, W. M., 395
Williamson, P. A., 268
Williamson, R. A., 132, 133, 154
Williger, B., 637
Willis, S. L., 9
Willoughby, B. J., 476
Willoughby, J., 431
Willoughby, T., 418
Wilmot, K. A., 570
Wilson, D. J., 580
Wilson, E. K., 380

Wilson, G. D., 382
Wilson, G. L., 440
Wilson, J., 541
Wilson, M., 271
Wilson, P., 243
Wilson, P. T., 322
Wilson, S. J., 402
Wilson-Ching, M., 98
Wimmer, M. B., 358
Wincze, J. P., 452
Windsor, T. D., 637
Winer, A. C., 260
Wink, P., 541, 548, 601, 612, 615, 651
Winkler, I., 109
Winner, E., 224, 329
Winsler, A., 22, 235
Winter, D. G., 541, 613
Winter, M. A., 25
Wiringa, A. E., 453
Witherington, D. C., 137, 143, 188
Witherspoon, D. P., 399
Wöhrman, A. M., 564
Wolak, J., 380
Wold, B., 302, 303, 409
Wolfe, D. A., 285, 285n, 286
Wolfers, J., 547
Wolff, P. H., 105n, 359
Wolinsky, F. D., 602
Wolters, C. A., 282
Wonderlich, S. A., 379
Wondra, D., 353
Wong, C. A., 399
Wong, D., 601
Woo, H., 514
Woo, H. S., 32
Wood, A., 122
Wood, E., 278
Wood, J. J., 266
Wood, J. T., 481
Wood, R. M., 105
Wood, W., 479
Woodward, A. L., 155, 163
Woody, E., 479
Woolley, J. D., 231
Wooten, H. R., 499
Worden, J. W., 612, 654, 665
World Bank, 490
World Health Organization, 87, 88, 127, 129, 220, 221, 295, 474
Wörmann, V., 189
Worthy, J., 326, 401
Wortman, J., 614
Worton, S. K., 61
Wouters, H., 415
WPCA (Worldwide Palliative Care Alliance), 660
Wray, S., 547
Wrenn, K. A., 561
Wright, A. A., 659
Wright, B. C., 304
Wright, C. E., 244
Wright, J. C., 249
Wright, K., 653, 654
Wright, N. C., 519
Wright, P. A., 423
Wright, P. J., 380
Wright, W. E., 324

Wrosch, C., 19, 616
Wrotniak, B. H., 297
Wrzus, C., 621
Wu, A. M. S., 652
Wu, H.-S., 580
Wu, J. H., 447
Wu, L. L., 497
Wu, S. C., 374
Wu, Z., 628
Wulczyn, F., 286
Wuyts, D., 339
Wyman, E., 228
Wynn, K., 158, 159n
Wynne, L. C., 70
Wynne-Edwards, K. E., 111
Wysong, A., 575

X

Xia, M., 283
Xiao, L., 373
Xie, Y., 556
Xu, F., 158, 307
Xu, X., 488

Y

Yakoob, M. Y., 220
Yamaguchi, S., 579
Yan, L. L., 520
Yancura, L. A., 521
Yang, B., 353
Yang, C.-K., 126
Yang, F.-Y., 391
Yang, Q., 647
Yang, S. C., 650
Yang, T. S., 357
Yanovski, J. A., 297
Yap, M. B. H., 428
Yarrow, M. R., 268
Yarwood, A., 586
Yates, L. B., 572
Yau, J. P., 421
Yavorsky, J. E., 490
Yehuda, R., 71
Yermish, A., 328, 329
Yeung, D. Y., 622
Yeung, J. W. K., 339
Yeung, S. E., 530
Yip, P. S., 619
Yip, T., 412
Yirmiya, N., 243
Yonas, A., 140, 141
Yonelinas, A., 596
Yong, M. H., 105
Yook, J.-H., 83
Yoon, S. Y., 396
Yorgason, J. B., 626
Yoshida, H., 250
Yoshikawa, H., 59, 246, 247
You, D., 415
Youn, G., 557
Youn, M. J., 357
Young, A., 522
Young, B. W., 522
Young, J. B., 562
Young, S. E., 307
Younge, S. N., 63
Youniss, J., 411, 418
Yousafzai, A. K., 220
Yu, R., 195
Yu, R. R., 556

Yuan, A. S. V., 356
Yuille, J. C., 429
Yumoto, C., 82
Yunger, J. L., 351
Yur'yev, A., 619

Z

Zaccagni, L., 443
Zacher, H., 539
Zachrisson, H. D., 203
Zacks, R. T., 528, 529, 596
Zadjel, R. T., 342
Zaff, J. F., 419
Zahn-Waxler, C., 267
Zajac, R., 361
Zajacova, A., 514
Zakharia, R., 374, 375
Zakowski, S. G., 520
Zalewski, M., 342
Zaman, W., 241
Zarbatany, L., 347
Zaretsky, M. D., 572
Zarit, S. H., 551
Zarkadoulia, E., 221
Zarrett, N., 610
Zarrett, N. R., 337
Zaslow, M. J., 246
Zayas, V., 480
Zdaniuk, B., 550, 627
Zeanah, C. H., 124
Zelazo, N. A., 103
Zelazo, P. D., 20, 161, 236, 238, 271, 308, 310
Zeller, M. H., 297
Zellner, D. A., 296
Zerwas, S., 207
Zeskind, P. S., 108
Zhai, F., 246
Zhang, D., 326
Zhang, L., 459
Zhang, T.-Y., 70
Zhang, X., 577
Zhang, Z., 555
Zhao, J., 500
Zheng, N. T., 658
Zhou, X., 314
Zhu, H., 372
Zickuhr, K., 632
Ziemer, C. J., 156
Zigler, E., 64, 103, 491
Zimmer-Gembeck, M. J., 263, 339, 381
Zimmerman, B. J., 312, 313
Zimmerman, C., 391, 655
Zimmerman, F. J., 157
Zimmerman, R., 196
Zimmerman, S., 219
Zimmermann, L. K., 192
Zimprich, D., 614
Zinbarg, R., 523
Ziol-Guest, K. M., 463
Zitzmann, M., 51
Ziv, Y., 266
Zohar, A., 457
Zolotor, A. J., 269, 269n, 286
Zosuls, K. M., 208
Zukow-Goldring, P., 168
Zukowski, A., 251
Zvonkovic, A. M., 463
Zyzanski, S., 655

Subject Index

Figures and tables are indicated by f and t following page numbers.

A

A-not-B search error in sensorimotor stage, 152, 154
AARP, 66, 638
Abortion
 in adolescent pregnancy, 384, 385
 sex-selective, 48
 spontaneous. See Miscarriage
Abstinence from sexual activity, 380, 385
Abstract thinking
 in adolescence, 18, 388–390, 392, 395, 408, 415
 in early adulthood, 459
 in middle adulthood, 530, 531
Abuse
 of child. See Child maltreatment
 in dating relationships, 426
 of older adults, 633
 of partner, 488–489
 of substances. See Substance abuse
Academic achievement, 62
 in adolescence, 394–396, 398–401
 of affluent youths, 60
 in bilingualism, 323–324
 child-rearing style affecting, 283, 284, 398
 and clique membership, 425
 cognitive self-regulation in, 312–313
 in cooperative learning, 326
 cultural influences on, 330, 337, 399
 divorce of parents affecting, 354
 and dropout rates, 402
 early intervention programs affecting, 246–247
 ethnic stereotypes on, 412
 in Experience Corps intervention, 638
 family beliefs on, 23
 gender stereotypes on, 278, 350, 464–465
 of immigrant youths, 32
 in inclusive classrooms, 327
 intelligence quotient as predictor of, 169, 318, 327
 international comparison of, 329f, 329–330
 in magnet schools, 327
 mathematical abilities affecting, 245
 Nurse–Family Partnership affecting, 90
 of only children, 353
 and peer acceptance, 348
 in poverty, 61, 62
 reading skills affecting, 244
 of rejected children, 348
 school transitions affecting, 397
 self-affirmation intervention affecting, 321, 321f
 and self-esteem, 313, 337, 338, 402, 409
 self-fulfilling prophecies in, 326
 and social skills, 266
 stereotype threat affecting, 326
 teacher–student interactions in, 326, 399, 400
Academic engagement in college, 461
Academic learning, 313–314. *See also* Education

Academic programs in preschool and kindergarten, 246
Acceptance
 of change in late adulthood, 611, 614
 in child rearing, 282, 282t, 283, 284
 of death, 610, 653, 654
 of gender nonconformity, 281, 351
 in peer relations, 347–348. See also Peer acceptance
 of self. See Self-acceptance
Accidental injuries. See Injuries, unintentional
Accommodation, Piaget on, 150, 229
Accommodation of eyes, 508
Acculturative stress, 412, 421
Acetylcholine, 589, 590, 591
Achievement
 ability and effort in, 339, 340
 academic. See Academic achievement
 and anorexia nervosa, 379
 attributions related to, 339–340, 398
 and identity, 409, 410, 410t, 411, 412, 476
 and learned helplessness, 339, 340
 person praise and process praise in, 339
 pride in, 189
 and self-esteem, 339–340
 of siblings, 352
Acquired immune deficiency syndrome. See AIDS
Active gene–environment correlation, 69
ACTIVE study, 602
Activities of daily living in late adulthood. See Daily living activities in late adulthood
Activity level and temperament, 191, 191t, 193
Activity theory of aging, 620
Actors, memory strategies of, 603
Adaptation
 of baby to labor and delivery, 94
 coping strategies in. See Coping strategies
 Darwin on, 13
 to dying, contextual influences on, 654–656
 in early adulthood, 477–478
 ethology of, 21
 evolutionary developmental psychology on, 22
 to family changes, 57–58
 and habituation, 81
 of immigrant youths, 32
 in late adulthood, 578–581, 599–600, 614, 628, 629
 in middle adulthood, 520–524, 542, 543
 Piaget on, 17, 150
 and practical intelligence, 316
 and resilience, 10–11
 Vaillant on, 477–478, 542
 in widowhood, 628, 629

Adaptation to Life (Vaillant), 477
Addiction, 386, 449
 to alcohol, 450
 of infants, 83
 in tobacco use, 449
Adjustment
 in adolescence, 368, 376, 383, 396, 409, 424–425
 affluence affecting, 60, 60f
 attachment security affecting, 206
 child-care facilities affecting, 202–203
 child maltreatment affecting, 286
 child-rearing styles affecting, 283, 339
 of child sexual abuse victims, 359
 to death of loved one, 666
 depression of parent affecting, 187
 divorce of parents affecting, 354, 356
 early intervention programs affecting, 247
 family mealtimes affecting, 60, 60f
 family stress affecting, 25
 and friendships, 265, 424–425
 and gender identity, 279
 of gifted and talented children, 329
 of immigrant youths, 32
 and infant sleeping arrangements, 126
 in lesbian and gay families, 498
 to parenthood, 111
 and peer acceptance, 347, 348
 religious and spiritual beliefs affecting, 473
 to retirement, 636
 in school transitions, 396, 397
 of self-care children, 357
 in single-parent families, 497
 and temperament, 190, 193
Adolescence (11 to 18 years old), 8t, 366–467
 academic achievement in, 394–396, 398–401
 in adoption, 56
 in affluence, 60
 aggression in, 303, 430, 431
 arousal states in, 374
 athletic activities in, 369, 370–371, 371f, 372
 authoritarian parents in, 283
 authoritative parents in, 282
 autonomy in, 379, 398, 420–421, 422, 423, 425, 492
 bereavement in, 668, 670
 biological perspective of, 366
 in blended families, 356
 body composition in, 369, 372
 body image in, 377, 378, 379
 body proportions in, 370f
 body size in, 369, 370f
 brain development in, 373–374, 386–387, 393–394, 650
 causes of death in, 650
 civic engagement in, 418, 419
 cognitive–affective complexity in, 458, 458f

cognitive development in, 18t, 373, 381, 386, 387f, 388–403
contraceptive use in, 381f, 381–382, 385
cultural influences on, 368, 374–375, 377, 380, 411, 412, 421
dating in, 380–381, 382, 426f, 426–427
death concept in, 649, 650, 652
death of parent or sibling during, 667
decision making in, 393–394
delinquency in, 429–432, 488
depression in, 376, 377, 379, 393, 427–428
divorce of parents during, 354, 495
dropping out of school during, 402–403
early phase of, 368, 393, 415
eating disorders in, 378–379
emotional and social development in, 406–433
employment in, 401
family in, 373, 377, 393, 420–422, 492
fetal drug and alcohol exposure affecting, 84, 85
formal operational stage in, 18t, 388–390
free time in, 422
friendships in, 398, 411, 417, 422–426, 428
gender dysphoria in, 281
gender identity in, 428
grandparent relationships during, 553
health issues in, 372, 373, 378–387
hormone changes in, 369, 377, 380, 426, 427
hypothetico-deductive reasoning in, 388, 389, 389f
idealism and criticism in, 393
identity development in, 408, 409–413
identity versus role confusion in, 15t, 408
of immigrant youths, 32
impulsivity and sensation seeking in, 373f, 373–374, 379, 386, 387f, 393, 650
information processing in, 390–392
initiation ceremonies in, 375
injuries in, 221, 650
language development in, 389
late phase of, 368
learning in school during, 396–403
maltreatment in, 285
mathematical abilities in, 395f, 395–396
media multitasking in, 400
memory of events in late adulthood, 597
middle phase of, 368, 415
milestones of development, 434–435
moodiness in, 375
moral development in, 344, 413–420
motor development in, 370–371
nutrition in, 372, 378–379

SI-1

Adolescence (continued)
　　overweight and obesity in, 295, 297, 372, 445
　　parent relationships in, 376, 420–422. *See also* Parent–adolescent relationships
　　part-time work during, 401
　　peer relations in, 373, 377, 386, 398, 399–400, 411, 422–427
　　physical attractiveness in, 377
　　physical development in, 368–387
　　play in, 303
　　post-traumatic stress in, 359
　　pregnancy in, 384–386. *See also* Adolescent pregnancy and parenthood
　　propositional thought in, 389, 390
　　psychosexual and psychosocial development in, 15t, 368
　　puberty in, 367, 368–377. *See also* Puberty
　　religious involvement in, 418
　　school transitions in, 396–398, 409
　　scientific reasoning in, 391f, 391–392
　　self-consciousness and self-focusing in, 392–393
　　self-esteem in, 338, 370, 377, 393, 408–409, 412
　　self-understanding in, 408–411
　　sex differences in, 368–372, 372t, 376, 377, 378, 394–396, 415–416
　　sexual abuse in, 358, 359, 360, 426
　　sexuality in, 379–386
　　sexually transmitted infections in, 383–384
　　sexual maturation in, 369, 371–372, 372t
　　sexual orientation in, 382–383, 411, 426
　　shyness in, 192
　　sibling relationships in, 422
　　single parent during, 497
　　sleep schedule in, 374
　　social perspective of, 366
　　spatial abilities in, 396f, 396–397
　　storm-and-stress perspective of, 368, 427
　　substance use and abuse in, 370, 386–387, 428, 429, 449
　　suicide in, 378, 382, 393, 428–429, 618, 650
　　television viewing in, 274, 274f
　　time spent with family in, 422
　　uninvolved parents in, 283
　　verbal abilities in, 394
　　violent delinquency in, 488
　　vocational choice in, 462, 465
Adolescent pregnancy and parenthood, 371, 384f, 384–386
　　and contraceptive use, 381, 385
　　international differences in, 64t, 384, 385
　　Nurse–Family Partnership in, 90
　　prenatal development in, 91, 384
　　safety of children in, 222
Adoption, 55–56
　　alcoholism research in, 449
　　attachment security in, 199–200
　　deprivation prior to, 121, 123, 123f
　　and environmental influences on gene expression, 70
　　heritability research in, 67, 68

　　hormone response of new parents in, 111
　　intelligence and IQ research in, 68, 123, 123f, 318
　　by lesbian and gay couples, 497
　　schizophrenia research in, 67
　　in surrogate motherhood, 53
　　weight of children and parents in, 127, 295
Adrenal androgens, 369
Adult Development and Enrichment Project (ADEPT), 602
Adulthood
　　brain plasticity in, 122
　　death concept in, 650–651
　　diversity of lifestyles in, 492–498
　　early, 8t, 436–505. *See also* Early adulthood
　　late, 8t, 568–641. *See also* Late adulthood
　　middle, 8t, 506–565. *See also* Middle adulthood
Adult-organized youth sports, 301–302
Advanced Cognitive Training for Independent and Vital Elderly (ACTIVE) study, 602
Advance medical directives, 661–662
Adversity
　　in life stories of generative adults, 540
　　outcomes in exposure to, 523, 523f, 601
Affluence, 60, 60f
Affordable Care Act, 64, 91, 103, 221
Afghanistan, 359, 571
Africa. *See also specific countries*.
　　age-related hearing loss in, 509
　　Alzheimer's disease in, 589–590
　　breastfeeding and bottle-feeding in, 127
　　dietary fat and heart disease in, 447, 447f
　　eating disorders in, 378
　　emerging adulthood in, 473
　　menopause in, 512
　　neonatal behavioral assessment in, 110
　　play of children in, 301
　　pubertal development in, 372
African Americans
　　academic achievement of, 321, 321f, 326, 399, 400, 401
　　adolescent, 372–373, 374–375, 381, 385, 387, 401, 422
　　as adolescent parents, 385
　　aging parents of, 555, 556, 557
　　Alzheimer's disease of, 589–590
　　anorexia nervosa of, 378
　　asthma of, 298
　　body growth of, 117
　　body image of, 377
　　cancer of, 517
　　cardiovascular disease of, 440–441, 442, 447, 447f, 455, 519
　　caregivers for older adults, 617–618, 623
　　child-rearing practices of, 270, 284, 422
　　communication style of, 319, 322–323
　　cosleeping of parents and infants, 126
　　death beliefs of, 656, 661, 669

　　dementia of, 587
　　departure from parental home, 485
　　diabetes of, 586
　　discipline and punishment of children, 270, 284
　　discrimination and prejudice against, 344, 500, 500f
　　divorce of, 353
　　extended families of, 62–63, 497, 553, 623
　　food insecurity of, 129
　　friendships of, 423
　　gay relationships of, 453
　　gender roles and housework hours of, 487
　　gender stereotypes of, 278
　　generativity of, 539f, 541
　　glaucoma of, 509
　　grandparents as caregivers of, 553, 554
　　health problems in late adulthood, 581
　　high school dropout rates for, 402f
　　HIV infection in, 453
　　infant mortality rate of, 102
　　intelligence and IQ of, 67–68, 246, 318, 320, 321
　　late adulthood of, 581, 593, 617–618, 623
　　life expectancy of, 570, 571
　　long-term care of older adults, 593
　　menarche of, 372–373, 374–375
　　menopause of, 513
　　moral identity of, 418
　　narrative style of, 322–323
　　never-married, 493, 497
　　osteoporosis of, 519
　　overweight and obesity of, 295, 445
　　parent–adolescent relationships of, 422
　　partner abuse of, 489
　　poverty of, 59, 63
　　puberty of, 372–373, 374–375, 377
　　religiosity of, 472, 615, 618
　　reminiscence in late adulthood, 612
　　school transitions of, 397
　　self-affirmation intervention for, 321, 321f
　　self-esteem of, 338, 409
　　sexual activity in adolescence, 381
　　sickle cell anemia of, 48
　　singlehood lifestyle of, 493
　　in single-parent families, 497
　　skeletal age of, 117
　　stereotype threat affecting, 320, 321
　　stress of, 455
　　substance abuse prevention and treatment for, 387
　　suicide rate of, 428
　　teacher–student interaction of, 319, 326, 401
　　vocational choice of, 463
　　widowhood of, 629
Afterlife beliefs, 649, 651, 669
After-school programs, 357
Age
　　in adolescence, 8t. *See also* Adolescence
　　in adoption, 55, 56, 123f
　　and death anxiety, 651–652, 652f
　　in departure from parental home, 484
　　during divorce of parents, 354, 356

　　of earliest memory, 165
　　in early adulthood, 8t. *See also* Early adulthood
　　in early childhood, 8t. *See also* Early childhood
　　in emerging adulthood, 470, 470f. *See also* Emerging adulthood
　　in eyewitness testimony of children, 361
　　of fetal viability, 80
　　First Age, 613
　　of first marriage, 485, 486
　　Fourth Age, 613
　　functional, 570
　　in grandparenthood, 552
　　and impulsive behavior, 373f, 373–374
　　in infancy and toddlerhood, 8t. *See also* Infancy and toddlerhood
　　and job discrimination, 562
　　and job satisfaction, 560, 560f
　　in late adulthood, 8t. *See also* Late adulthood
　　in lifespan perspective of development, 9
　　in major periods of development, 8t
　　maternal. *See* Maternal age
　　and maximum lifespan, 572
　　in middle adulthood, 8t. *See also* Middle adulthood
　　in middle childhood, 8t. *See also* Middle childhood
　　and number of social partners, 620–621, 621f
　　paternal, 45, 50, 51, 444
　　in pubertal development, 372t
　　of retirement, 563, 634, 635
　　Second Age, 604n, 613
　　skeletal, 117, 217
　　and social clock, 478
　　subjective, 541, 579
　　and teratogen impact, 81, 82f
　　Third Age, 604, 604n, 613
Age-graded influences, 9, 10, 474
Age spots on skin, 510, 578
Aggression
　　in adolescence, 303, 430, 431
　　bullying in, 349
　　in early childhood, 272–276
　　in middle childhood, 269, 270, 346, 347, 348, 349
　　partner abuse in, 488
　　twin studies of, 70
　　and violence in media, 274f, 274–275
Agility in motor development, 300
Aging
　　of baby boom generation, 13
　　basal metabolic rate in, 446
　　continuity theory of, 620, 623, 636
　　double standard of, 523–524, 541
　　in early adulthood, 438–444
　　functional age in, 570
　　in late adulthood, 611, 620–625, 632, 637–639
　　multidimensional and multidirectional influences in, 438, 538
　　of parents, 554–557
　　plasticity of development in, 9, 524
　　primary or biological, 438–444, 585
　　secondary, 585
　　stereotypes of. *See* Stereotypes of aging

subjective age in, 541, 579
successful, 637–639
suicide in, 618–619
Aging in place, 623, 624, 625
Aging Well (Vaillant), 477
Agonal phase in dying, 646
Agreeableness
in late adulthood, 614
and longevity, 572
in middle adulthood, 548, 548t, 549
Aid-in-dying, medical, 662–664
AIDS
in adolescence, 383
in early adulthood, 453
in middle childhood, 298
in pregnancy, 87t, 87–88
Air pollution, 86, 298
Aka of Central Africa, 205
Alaskan Natives, 618
Alcoholics Anonymous, 450
Alcoholism, 449
Alcohol-related neurodevelopmental disorder (ARND), 84
Alcohol use and abuse
in adolescence, 386, 425
in early adulthood, 448, 449–450, 489
in late adulthood, 584, 591
in middle adulthood, 519
paternal, at time of conception, 84
in pregnancy, 84–85
telomere length in, 439
Alertness of infants, 104, 105t
Alleles, 46–48, 47t, 49
Altruistic behavior, 262, 418, 419. *See also* Prosocial behavior
Alzheimer's disease, 587–590
caregivers in, 590, 592–593
as cause of death, 584f, 585
in Down syndrome, 50, 589
glucose blood levels in, 586, 590
in late adulthood, 584f, 585
long-term care in, 592
nutrition in, 583
recognition of living will in, 661
risk factors for, 512, 589–590
American Medical Association, 661
American Samoa, 311
American Sign Language, 174
Amnesia, infantile, 163, 164–165
Amniocentesis, 53, 54t
Amnion, 77, 77t
Amniotic fluid, 77, 79, 81, 108
Amodal sensory properties, 143, 144
Amphetamine use in adolescence, 386
Amygdala
in adopted children, 200
in autism, 243
in early childhood, 218, 218f, 243
in shyness and sociability, 192
Amyloid plaque, 588–589, 590
Anabolic steroid use in adolescence, 370
Analgesic drugs, 97, 586
Analogical problem solving, 155, 165, 232
Anal stage of psychosexual development, 15t
Analytical intelligence, 316, 316f
Andorra, 102f, 571f
Androgens
adrenal, 369
and aggression, 273

and gender roles, 277
in new fathers, 111
prenatal exposure to, 277, 281, 302, 382
in puberty, 369, 380
Androgyny
in early childhood, 279
in middle adulthood, 541, 547–548
in middle childhood, 350–351
Androstenedione, 370
Anemia, 47t, 298, 378
Anencephaly, 89
Anesthesia
during childbirth, 97
for newborns, 108
Anger
of dying people, 653, 655
in infancy and toddlerhood, 185–186, 189, 193, 194, 194f
in late adulthood, 610
in middle adulthood, 519–520, 521
Angina pectoris, 518
Angioplasty, 518
Angola, 301
Animals, nonhuman
aging at DNA level in, 440
anti-aging effects of calorie restriction in, 510, 511
attachment of, 196
environmental influences on gene expression in, 70
free radicals in, 440
imitation by, 132, 133f
imprinting in, 21, 196
language acquisition of, 174
life expectancy variations in, 440
play activities of, 302
puberty of, 376
sensory deprivation studies of, 121
sex differences in behavior of, 277
Animistic thinking in preoperational stage, 229, 231
Anorexia nervosa, 378–379
Anoxia of infant during childbirth, 96
Anti-aging effects of calorie restriction, 510, 511
Antibodies, 81, 89, 382, 443
Anticipatory grieving, 666
Antidepressant drugs
in adolescent depression, 429
in Alzheimer's disease, 590
in bulimia, 379
in menopause, 513
in parental depression, 187
in pregnancy, 83
in suicidal behavior, 619
Antigens, 443
Antioxidants, 440, 590
Antiretroviral drug therapy, 88
Antisocial behavior, 67, 70
in adolescence, 429, 430, 431
in depression of parent, 187
in middle childhood, 348
Anxiety
death anxiety, 648, 649, 650, 651–652, 652f
in early adulthood, 448
in infancy and toddlerhood, 186, 197, 198
in middle childhood, 358
in pregnancy, 89

Apgar Scale, 94t, 94–95, 96, 97
Apnea, sleep, 577
APOE ε4 gene in Alzheimer's disease, 589, 590
Appearance and attractiveness
in adolescence, 377, 392, 393, 409
in late adulthood, 578, 579
in mate selection, 479
in middle adulthood, 523, 541
in middle childhood, 337, 338
of newborn, 94
social bias on, 142
Appetite
in adolescence, 378–379
depression affecting, 427
in early childhood, 219
malnutrition affecting, 129
of sexual abuse victims, 359
stress affecting, 296
Applicability, and death concept, 648, 649
Applied behavior analysis, 17
Apprenticeship programs in vocational preparation, 465
Appropriate or good death, 648, 654
Area Agencies on Aging, 65
Argentina, 319, 398, 486
Arousal states
in adolescence, 374
in infancy and toddlerhood, 104–108, 105t, 125, 125f
Arrhythmias, 518, 646
Art education, 226
Arthritis, 440, 511
in late adulthood, 582, 585–586
in middle childhood, 298
Artistic expression
creativity in. *See* Creativity
drawing in. *See* Drawing
in early childhood, 224f, 224–225, 226
in middle childhood, 300, 300f, 301
Artistic personality, vocational choice in, 462
Asia. *See also specific countries.*
academic achievement in, 330
achievement-related attributions in, 340
aging parents in, 555, 556
autobiographical memory in, 241
bedtime routines and sleep of infants in, 125, 125f
dating in, 426
death concept and attitudes in, 656
departure from family home in, 485
drawing skills of children in, 225, 226
eating disorders in, 378
emerging adulthood in, 473
growth norms in, 117
immigrant youths from, 32
language development in, 177, 178
mathematics instruction in, 314
menopause in, 512, 514
myopia in, 298
neonatal behavioral assessment in, 110
pubertal development in, 372
romantic relationships in, 481–482
self-concept in, 259, 337
self-conscious emotions in, 189, 262
self-esteem in, 409
sense of control in, 579

sensitivity toward infants in, 200
temperament of children in, 193
terminally ill patients in, 655
Asian Americans
academic achievement of, 399
aging parents of, 555, 556, 623
anorexia nervosa of, 378
ethnic identity of, 412
extended-family households of, 62, 623
friendships of, 423
gender roles and housework hours of, 487
intelligence quotient of, 318
long-term care of older adults, 593
suicide rate of, 428
Asian Pacific Islanders, 284, 558
Aspirin in pregnancy, 83
Assimilation, Piaget on, 150
Assisted discovery learning, 235
Assisted-living facilities, 572, 593–594, 623, 624
Assisted suicide, 663. *See also* Medical aid-in-dying
Assistive technology and devices, 579–580
Associative memory in late adulthood, 596–597, 597f, 599
Associative play, 263
Asthma, 49, 298
Atherosclerosis, 442, 447, 452, 518–519, 576
hearing changes in, 509
hostility as risk for, 520
vision changes in, 575
Athletic activities
in adolescence, 369, 370–371, 371f, 372, 382, 409, 425
in early adulthood, 442f, 442–443
in late adulthood, 578
of lesbian, gay, and bisexual youths, 382
in middle adulthood, 510, 522
in middle childhood, 301–302, 337
in pregnancy, 88
Attachment, 5, 196–206
Bowlby on, 22, 196–197, 480
cultural differences in, 196, 198, 199, 199f, 200–201, 480
and dating, 426
disorganized/disoriented, 198, 201, 206
and empathy, 263
ethological theory of, 22, 196–197, 205, 426
and false-belief tasks, 242
insecure–avoidant, 198, 199, 201, 480, 485
insecure–resistant, 198, 199, 201, 480
internal working models of, 197, 202, 480
psychoanalytic perspective on, 196, 205
quality of caregiving affecting, 200–201, 202–203
and romantic relationships of adults, 480
secure, 198, 200–201, 480
security of, 197–198. *See also* Security of attachment
Attachment-in-the-making phase, 197
Attachment Q-Sort, 198

Attendance in school. *See* School attendance
Attention
  in adolescence, 390, 392, 400
  in autism, 243
  in early childhood, 237–238, 238*f*, 242, 261
  in infancy and toddlerhood, 141–142, 160, 161–162, 167, 176, 189, 190, 191, 207
  in late adulthood, 587, 594, 602
  in middle adulthood, 528–529
  in middle childhood, 307, 308, 309, 310
Attention-deficit hyperactivity disorder (ADHD), 309, 431
Attractiveness. *See* Appearance and attractiveness
Attributions, 339–340, 341
  achievement-related, 339–340, 398
Australia
  academic achievement in, 398
  adolescent suicide in, 428
  caregiving roles of parents in, 203
  cesarean delivery rate in, 97
  child care in, 171, 203
  childhood attachment patterns and adult romantic relationships in, 480
  housework hours and gender roles in, 487*f*
  immunization rate in, 221
  infant mortality rate in, 102*f*
  life expectancy in, 571*f*
  lifelong learning in, 604
  long-term care for older adults in, 592, 593
  math achievement scores in, 329*f*
  midlife mortality in, 546
  Nurse–Family Partnership in, 90
  parent–infant interactions in, 203
  poverty rate in, 65*f*
  prenatal health care in, 91
  reproductive technologies in, 53
  sleep patterns of infants in, 125
Austria, 102*f*, 329*f*, 465, 571*f*
Authoritarian child-rearing style, 282*t*, 283, 284
  academic achievement in, 398
  and peer relations in adolescence, 425–426
Authoritative child-rearing style, 282, 282*t*, 283–284, 351
  academic achievement in, 398
  during divorce, 354
  and peer relations in adolescence, 425–426
  and religious beliefs in emerging adulthood, 473
  self-care of children in, 357
  self-esteem in, 338, 409
Authority understanding in moral development, 414
Autism
  developmental social neuroscience research on, 21
  false beliefs in, 242
  in fragile X syndrome, 49
  genetic counseling on, 51
  heritability research on, 67
  in relatives of prodigies, 30
  and vaccinations, 221
Autism spectrum disorder, 243

Autobiographical memory, 164
  in early childhood, 240–241
  and infantile amnesia, 164–165
  in late adulthood, 597*f*, 597–598, 613–614
Autoimmune disorders, 577, 585
Automatic processes in information processing, 161
Autonomic nervous system, 192, 574, 584
Autonomous child-rearing goals, 208
Autonomy issues
  in adolescence, 379, 398, 420–421, 422, 423, 425, 492
  in child-rearing styles, 282, 283, 284
  in infancy and toddlerhood, 15*t*, 184
  in late adulthood, 616, 617, 618, 624
  in medical aid-in-dying, 663, 663*f*, 664
  in middle adulthood, 539, 541, 544
Autosomes, 45, 47*t*, 50
Average life expectancy, 7, 53, 438, 570, 571, 571*f*, 572
Aversion therapy in alcoholism, 450
Avoidance in grief process, 665
Avoidant attachment, 198, 199, 201, 480, 485

B

Babbling, 175–176, 178
Babinski reflex, 101*t*
Baby and Child Care (Spock), 14, 126
Baby boom generation, 12–13, 452*f*, 538
  aging of, 541
  Alzheimer's disease of, 588
  caring for aging parents, 556, 556*f*
  children of, 472
  cohabitation of, 628
  cohort effects in, 10, 12–13
  divorce of, 627
  environmental mastery of, 545
  history-graded influences on, 10
  late adulthood cognitive changes of, 601
  life expectancy of, 571
  middle adulthood cognitive changes of, 526
  retirement of, 563, 613, 634
  self-acceptance of, 545
  sibling relationships in, 558
  Third Age of, 613
  trailing edge of, 13
  vocational life of, 559
Baby fat, 116*f*, 117, 216
Baby teeth, 217
Bacterial diseases in pregnancy, 87*t*, 88
Baka of West Africa, 258
Balance in motor development, 136, 145, 300
Balinese of Indonesia, 669
Ball skills in motor development, 223, 225, 299, 300
Bandura, Albert, 17
Bangladesh, 597
Bargaining in coping with dying, 653
Bar mitzvah, 375
Basal metabolic rate, 446, 510, 511
Bases in DNA, 44, 45*f*
Bat mitzvah, 375
Bayley Scales of Infant and Toddler Development, 167, 169

B cells, 443
Bedsharing of parents and infants, 126
Bedtime routines and sleep of infants, 125, 125*f*
Behavioral control in child rearing styles, 282, 282*t*, 283
Behavioral genetics, 66
Behaviorism, 16, 17, 27*t*, 196
Belarus, 102*f*
Belgium
  adolescent birth rate in, 384*f*
  euthanasia in, 664
  infant mortality rate in, 102*f*
  life expectancy in, 571*f*
  long-term care for older adults in, 592
  marriage of same-sex couples in, 486
  math achievement scores in, 329*f*
  medical aid-in-dying in, 663
Beliefs
  and desires in theory of mind, 241
  false. *See* False beliefs
  gender stereotypes in, 276–280
  religious. *See* Religion
Belize, 311, 614
Bell-shaped distribution of intelligence test scores, 169, 169*f*
Bereavement, 612, 650, 665–670
Better Beginnings, Better Futures Project, 61
Bhatto Bhatto game in India, 265
Bias
  cultural, in intelligence tests, 245, 315, 318–321
  egocentric, 229
  in eyewitness testimony of children, 361
  in-group and out-group, 344–345
  mutual exclusivity, in vocabulary development, 250
  racial and ethnic, 344–345
  in research, 30, 31, 33, 35
  self-serving, 391
  shape, in vocabulary development, 250
  stereotypes in. *See* Stereotypes
  of teachers, 326
Bicultural identity, 412
Bicycle riding, childhood injuries in, 299
Bidirectional influences
  in ecological systems theory, 23, 57
  in epigenesis, 70, 70*f*
  in family, 23, 57
  in prenatal development, 82
  in reciprocal relationships. *See* Reciprocal relationships
"Big five" personality traits, 548*t*, 548–549
Bilingualism, 323–324
Binet, Alfred, 14, 167, 315
Binge eating, 379, 446
Binocular depth cues, 140–141
Biocultural event, menopause as, 514
Bioecological model, 23
Biological aging, 438–444, 585. *See also* Aging
Biological influences
  on adolescence, 368
  on gender typing, 277, 280, 281
  genetic. *See* Genetic factors
  on sexual orientation, 382, 383

Bipolar disorder, 51, 67
Biracial adolescents, 412
Birth
  complications of. *See* Birth complications
  defects at time of. *See* Birth defects
  labor and delivery in. *See* Childbirth
  low weight at time of. *See* Low birth weight
  preterm. *See* Preterm infants
Birth centers, freestanding, 95
Birth complications
  in adolescent pregnancy, 384
  crying of infants in, 108
  in fetal medicine interventions, 54
  in home delivery, 96
  maternal age in, 91, 91*f*
  prenatal health care reducing, 91
  in preterm and low-birth-weight infants, 97–100
Birth control, 381*f*, 381–382, 385, 490
Birth defects
  in chromosomal abnormalities, 48, 50
  folic acid in prevention of, 89
  in malnutrition, 88
  neonatal mortality rates in, 102
  in reproductive technologies, 52
  sex differences in, 48
  in teratogen exposure, 81–88
Birth order, and sexual orientation, 382
Birthrate
  among adolescents, 384, 384*f*
  by maternal age, 444*f*
Birth sex ratio, 48
Birth weight
  low, 97–100. *See also* Low birth weight
  of small-for-date infants, 98
  and survival rate, 98
Bisexuals. *See* Lesbian, gay, and bisexual people
Blastocyst, 76*f*, 77, 77*t*
Blended families, 355–356, 496–497
Blindness
  in cataracts, 574
  in diabetes, 297
  in glaucoma, 509
  in macular degeneration, 575, 585
  touch sensitivity in, 576
Blood pressure
  calorie restriction affecting, 511
  dietary fat affecting, 447, 447*f*
  in hypertension. *See* Hypertension
  in preeclampsia, 91
  in shyness and sociability, 192
Blood tests
  in phenylketonuria, 46
  in pregnancy, 53, 54*t*
Bodily-kinesthetic intelligence, 317*t*, 329
Body composition changes
  in early adulthood, 440
  in early childhood, 216, 216*f*
  in infancy and toddlerhood, 117
  in late adulthood, 578
  in middle adulthood, 510
  in middle childhood, 294
  in puberty, 369, 372
Body image
  in adolescence, 377, 378, 379
  in middle childhood, 338

Body mass index in obesity, 295, 296, 445
Body proportions
 in adolescence, 369, 370f
 in early childhood, 216, 216f
 in infancy and toddlerhood, 116f, 117
 in middle childhood, 294
Body size
 in early childhood, 216f, 216–217
 height in. See Height
 in infancy and toddlerhood, 116f, 116–117
 in middle childhood, 294, 294f
 nutrition affecting, 127–129
 in puberty, 369, 370f
 weight in. See Weight
Body transcendence in late adulthood, 611
Bonding. See Attachment
Bones. See Skeletal system
Bosnia, 102f, 359
Botswana, !Kung society of, 126
Bottle-feeding, 109, 127–128
Bowlby, John, 22, 196–197, 480
Braille reading, 576
Brain
 in adolescence, 373–374, 386–387, 393–394, 650
 alcohol use affecting, 450
 in Alzheimer's disease, 587–590
 in arousal states, 104, 125
 in attention-deficit hyperactivity disorder, 309
 in autism, 243
 cerebellum of. See Cerebellum
 cerebral cortex of. See Cerebral cortex
 cerebral hemispheres of. See Cerebral hemispheres
 childhood maltreatment affecting, 286–287
 cognitive-control network in, 373–374, 386, 387f, 393, 394, 456, 650
 developmental neuroscience research on, 20–21
 in Down syndrome, 50
 in early adulthood, 456
 in early childhood, 217–219, 218f
 electroencephalography of. See Electroencephalography
 emotional/social network in, 373, 374, 386, 387f, 393
 exercise affecting, 300, 448, 583, 590
 experience-dependent growth of, 124, 456
 experience-expectant growth of, 124
 in fetal alcohol spectrum disorder, 85
 functional MRI of. See Functional magnetic resonance imaging of brain
 in handedness, 217–218
 hormones affecting development of, 219
 imaging of, 119t, 119–120, 120f
 in infancy and toddlerhood, 98, 106, 117–125, 138, 189
 information-processing speed of, 161, 315–316, 526, 527

 language areas of, 120, 121, 122, 174, 218, 323, 394
 in late adulthood, 574, 576, 577, 583, 601, 638
 lateralization of, 121, 122, 217–218
 measures of functioning, 119t, 119–120, 120f
 in middle adulthood, 527
 in middle childhood, 306, 307
 milestones of development, 117–118, 118f
 neurobiological research on, 119, 123
 neurons in, 117–119, 164
 in Parkinson's disease, 587, 587n
 in persistent vegetative state, 647
 plasticity of, 121, 122, 595, 638
 prenatal development of, 78, 79–80, 81, 84, 85, 86, 88, 117, 118
 programmed cell death in, 118
 sensitive periods in development of, 121–124
 sex chromosome abnormalities affecting, 51
 in shy and sociable children, 192
 size changes of, 118, 217
 in small-for-date infants, 98
 in speech perception of infants, 138
 stimulation affecting development of, 118, 123–124
 stress affecting, 308, 455
 sudden infant death syndrome in impaired function of, 106
 in vascular dementia, 590–591
Brain death, 647
Brazil, 23, 221, 486
Breast cancer, 447, 516, 517
Breast development, 369, 371, 372, 372t
Breastfeeding, 101, 101t, 130f, 130–131
 compared to bottle-feeding, 127–128
 in cosleeping parents and infants, 126
 and smell sense of newborn, 109
 by Yurok Indians, 16
Breast milk odor, infant response to, 108, 109
Breathing techniques in natural childbirth, 95
Breech position, 96, 97
Bridge jobs prior to retirement, 634, 635
The Broken Cord (Dorris), 84
Bronfenbrenner, Urie, 23–26, 56, 57
Bucharest Early Intervention Project, 123–124
Buddhism, 615, 647, 656
Building Blocks math curriculum, 245
Bulgaria, 103, 487f
Bulimia nervosa, 379
Bullying, 29, 348, 349, 498
Burial practices, 669
Burnout from job stress, 560

C

Caffeine, and prenatal development, 83
Calcium, 378, 519, 582
Caloric intake
 anti-aging effects of restriction, 510, 511

 in early adulthood, 446
 in infancy and toddlerhood, 127, 128, 129
 in middle adulthood, 510, 511
 in middle childhood, 295, 296, 297
Cambodian immigrants, 32, 316, 632
Cameroon, 167, 189, 207–208, 208f
Canada
 academic achievement in, 329, 329f
 adolescent birth rate in, 384f
 adolescent contraceptive use in, 385
 adolescent suicide in, 428
 bilingualism in, 323, 324
 caregiving roles of parents in, 203
 cesarean delivery rate in, 97
 child maltreatment in, 287
 college education in, 460
 cosleeping of parents and infants, 126
 dual-earner families in, 501
 family size in, 490
 gender stereotypes in, 350
 hospice programs in, 660
 immunization rate in, 221
 infant mortality rate in, 102f
 life expectancy in, 7, 571f
 long-term care for older adults in, 593
 male birth rate in, 48
 marriage of same-sex couples in, 486
 math achievement scores in, 329f
 medical aid-in-dying in, 663
 midlife mortality in, 546
 moral development in, 343
 natives of, 126, 319, 411
 Nurse–Family Partnership in, 90
 obesity in, 295
 out-group prejudice in, 344
 parent–infant interaction in, 203
 personality traits in, 548
 poverty in, 61, 65f
 prenatal health care in, 91
 religious involvement in, 418
 reproductive technologies in, 53
 retirement programs in, 636
 sexually transmitted infections in, 383
 thalidomide use in, 82
 voluntary euthanasia opinions in, 664
Canadian Virtual Hospice, 660
Cancer, 49, 55, 84, 85
 annual death rate from, 444f, 584f, 646
 calorie-restricted diet affecting risk for, 511
 in children, 297, 298
 in diethylstilbestrol exposure, 83
 in dioxin exposure, 86
 in early adulthood, 440, 444f, 446, 447, 448, 449, 450, 455
 end-of-life care in, 654, 655, 658, 659, 663
 in late adulthood, 584f, 585
 in middle adulthood, 512, 515, 516f, 516–518
 telomere shortening in, 439
Car accidents. See Motor vehicle accidents
Cardinality, 244
Cardiovascular system
 annual death rate from diseases of, 444f, 516f, 584f, 646

 atherosclerosis of. See Atherosclerosis
 calorie-restricted diet affecting, 511
 in early adulthood, 440–442, 444f, 447, 447f, 448, 449, 455
 in late adulthood, 570, 576–577, 584, 585, 590–591
 low birth weight affecting risk for disease of, 88, 88f
 in middle adulthood, 515, 516f, 518–519, 520
 in physical changes of aging, 441t
 physical changes of dying in disease of, 646
 prenatal development of, 80, 81
 telomere shortening in disease of, 439
Career. See Employment
Caregivers
 abandonment of older adults with severe disabilities, 633
 of aging parents, 554–557, 558, 617, 623, 631
 of dementia victims, 590, 592–593
 dependency and control issues in late adulthood, 616
 of dying person, 653, 655, 657
 elder maltreatment by, 633–634
 siblings as, 630
 and social support in late adulthood, 617–618
 of terminally ill patients, 655
Care orientation in moral development, 415–416
Caribbean countries
 adaptation of immigrant youths from, 32
 child-rearing styles in, 284
 dietary fat and heart disease in, 447, 447f
 generational IQ gains in, 319
Carolina Abecedarian Project, 172–173
Carotenoids, 575
Carriers of inherited traits, 46, 48, 48f, 49f, 51
Car safety seats, 221, 222
Case studies, 16, 28t, 30
Cataracts
 free radicals in, 440
 in infancy, 50, 121
 in late adulthood, 574–575
Catch-up growth, 117, 127, 219
Categorical self, 208
Categorization abilities
 in early childhood, 230, 230f, 232
 in infancy and toddlerhood, 163f, 163–165, 166, 169, 208
 in middle childhood, 304, 310
Catholicism, 615, 661
The Cat in the Hat (Seuss), 81
Causation, and death concept, 648, 649
Cell phone use, 349, 400, 423–424, 424f
Cells, 44
 aging at level of, 438–440
 duplication of, 76f, 76–77
 glial, 79, 118
 in immune system, 439, 443
 meiosis of, 45
 nerve. See Neurons
 programmed death of, 118
 sex cells, 44–45

Cemeteries, 669
Centenarians, 572–573
Central nervous system
　brain in. See Brain
　childhood maltreatment affecting, 286–287
　in dynamic systems theory of motor development, 135
　genetic disorders affecting, 46, 47t, 48, 55
　in late adulthood, 574
　of newborn, 104, 105, 108
　prenatal development of, 78, 79–80, 82, 83, 84, 88, 106
　sexual abuse affecting, 359
Centration in preoperational stage, 230
Cephalocaudal trend in growth, 117, 369
Cerebellum
　childhood maltreatment affecting, 287
　in early childhood, 218, 218f, 287
　in late adulthood, 574
Cerebral cortex
　in adolescence, 373, 394
　in Alzheimer's disease, 588–589
　in early adulthood, 448, 456
　in early childhood, 217, 218, 219, 287
　electrical activity in, 119, 119t
　in infancy and toddlerhood, 120f, 120–121, 122, 123, 132, 163, 174
　in late adulthood, 574, 583, 587
　in middle childhood, 323
　in persistent vegetative state, 647
　prenatal development of, 80, 81
Cerebral hemispheres
　in autism, 243
　in early childhood, 217, 218
　in infancy and toddlerhood, 121, 174, 175
　in middle childhood, 323
Cerebral palsy, 96
Cerebrovascular disorders, stroke in. See Stroke
Certified nurse–midwives, 96
Cervix of uterus, 76, 76f, 93, 93f
Cesarean delivery, 97
Cessation of smoking, 449
Chaos in family, 25
Chernobyl nuclear power plant accident, 85
Chickenpox in pregnancy, 87t
Child abuse. See Child maltreatment
Childbearing
　decisions about, 489–490, 495
　maternal age in. See Maternal age
　pregnancy in. See Pregnancy
　transition to parenthood in, 111, 490–491
Childbirth, 92–97
　age of viability in, 80
　complications during. See Birth complications
　parental leave from employment after, 103, 203
　of preterm and low-birth-weight infant, 97–100
　stages of, 93f, 93–94
　and transition to parenthood, 111, 490–491
Child-care programs, 246, 247–248
　and attachment, 202–203

developmentally appropriate practice standards in, 171, 172, 248
　naturalistic observation of behavior in, 28
　public policies on, 64
　quality of care in, 171f, 171–172, 202–203, 247–248
　weekly hours in, 202, 203
Child-centered programs in preschool and kindergarten, 246
Childlessness
　in early adulthood, 489–490, 493–494, 495
　in late adulthood, 629–630
　in middle adulthood, 539
Child maltreatment, 283, 285t, 285–287
　by adolescent parents, 384
　alcohol abuse by victims of, 450
　attachment insecurity in, 201
　corporal punishment in, 269, 270, 286
　emotional self-regulation of child in, 263
　eyewitness testimony of children on, 361
　of preterm infants, 99, 108, 285
　sexual abuse in, 285, 358–360
Child-rearing costs, 490
Child-rearing practices
　and adjustment to emerging adulthood, 475
　and attachment security of child, 199–205, 206
　in blended families, 356, 496
　cultural influences on, 16, 62, 136, 186, 200–201, 203–204, 208, 237, 270, 284
　and delinquency, 430, 431
　differential susceptibility to, 194–195
　discipline in. See Discipline
　education on, 491, 492
　effective coparenting in, 57, 491
　and emotional self-regulation of child, 263
　in extended families, 63
　of fathers, 203–204
　gender typing in, 277–278
　goodness-of-fit model on, 195, 209
　of grandparents, 553, 554
　helicopter parenting in, 475
　in maternal employment, 202, 203
　in middle childhood, 351–352
　and mirror self-recognition by toddlers, 208
　and moral development, 416, 418
　and motor development, 136, 225
　and newborn behavior, 110
　normative approach to, 14
　and overweight and obesity, 296, 297
　positive parenting in, 271, 275
　and self-conscious emotions, 267
　and self-control, 209
　and self-esteem, 338–339
　and sibling relationships, 204–205
　sleeping arrangements and bedtime routines in, 125, 125f, 126
　socioeconomic status affecting, 58
　and stranger anxiety, 186

　and temperament of child, 190, 192, 193, 194f, 194–195, 209
　and vocational choice, 463
　warmth in, 11, 271, 339
Child-rearing styles, 282t, 282–285
　and academic achievement, 283, 284, 398
　in attention-deficit hyperactivity disorder, 309
　authoritarian, 282t, 283, 284, 398, 425–426
　authoritative. See Authoritative child-rearing style
　cultural variations in, 284
　and peer relations in adolescence, 425–426
　permissive, 282t, 283, 398
　uninvolved, 282t, 283, 398
Children and War Foundation, 359
Children's Defense Fund, 66
Children's Health Insurance Program (CHIP), 64
Child support payments, 353, 355, 386, 497
Chimpanzees, 132, 133f, 174
China
　academic achievement in, 329, 329f, 337, 398
　academic and vocational tracks in, 401
　achievement attributions in, 340, 340f
　aging parents in, 555, 632
　autobiographical memory in, 597
　child-rearing practices in, 136, 284
　child-rearing styles in, 398
　death concept and attitudes in, 647, 652, 656
　drawing skills of children in, 226
　emotional self-regulation in, 189, 193
　first words of infants in, 177
　gender typing in, 278
　immigrant youths from, 32
　language development in, 177, 178, 250
　mate selection in, 479
　math achievement in, 314, 329f
　moral development in, 343, 344
　motor development of infants in, 136
　obesity in, 295
　older parent–adult child relationships in, 632
　one-child families in, 48, 353
　peer relations in, 265
　play activities in, 265
　reminiscence of immigrants from, 612
　romantic relationships in, 479, 481–482
　self-concept in, 337
　self-conscious emotions in, 189
　self-esteem in, 337
　storytelling practices in, 259
　temperament of children in, 193, 195
　terminally ill patients in, 655
Chlamydia in pregnancy, 87t
Cholesterol, 442, 447, 448, 511, 512, 590
Chomsky, Noam, 174, 175, 252
Chorion, 77t, 78

Chorionic villi, 78
　sampling of, 53, 54t, 78n
Christian beliefs, death concept in, 649, 651, 669
Chromosomes, 44
　abnormalities of, 50–51, 51f, 589
　autosomes, 45, 47t, 50
　biological aging of, 438–439, 439f
　karyotype of, 44f
　in meiosis, 45
　and patterns of inheritance, 46–50
　sex, 45, 47t, 48–49, 49f, 50–51
　telomeres of, 438–439, 439f
Chronosystem, 24f, 26, 57
Cigarette smoking. See Smoking
Circular reactions in sensorimotor development, 151, 151t, 152
Circumcision, 108
Civic engagement
　in adolescence, 418, 419
　in college experience, 460
　in emerging adulthood, 471–472
　in late adulthood, 573, 613, 637
　in middle adulthood, 539, 539f
Classical conditioning, 16, 130f, 130–131
Classification
　categorization abilities in. See Categorization abilities
　in concrete operational stage, 304
Class inclusion problems, 230, 230f, 304
Classrooms. See Schools
Cleft lip and palate, 84, 89
Climacteric, 510. See also Menopause
Clinical death, 646
Clinical interviews, 18, 28t, 29, 413
Clinical research method, 16, 28t, 30
Cliques and crowds in adolescence, 425–426
Cocaine, 83–84, 386
Coercion, sexual, 453–455
Cognitive-affective complexity, 458, 458f, 611
Cognitive-control network, prefrontal
　in adolescence, 373–374, 386, 387f, 393, 394, 650
　in early adulthood, 456
Cognitive development, 8, 9f
　and academic learning, 313–314, 324–330, 396–403
　in adolescence, 18t, 373, 381, 386, 387f, 388–403
　animistic thinking in, 229, 231
　assimilation in, 150
　attention in, 161–162, 237–238. See also Attention
　in autism, 243
　brain injury affecting, 122
　categorization in. See Categorization abilities
　child-care quality affecting, 171–173, 247–248
　cognitive-affective complexity in, 458, 458f, 611
　in college experience, 460–461
　concrete operational stage in, 18, 18t, 304–307, 388
　as continuous or discontinuous process, 6, 159, 307
　core knowledge perspective of, 158–159
　creativity in, 459, 530–531

crystallized and fluid intelligence in, 525–526, 527, 527f
cultural influences on, 167, 235, 236, 237, 305–306, 311, 318–321, 390, 531
decision making in, 393–394
definition of, 9f
dualistic thinking in, 456–457
dynamic systems view of, 166
in early adulthood, 456–465
in early childhood, 17–18, 217, 218, 219, 224, 227–253, 264
early deprivation affecting, 123, 123f
early interventions in, 172–173, 246–247
emotional intelligence in, 317, 458
environmental influences on, 123, 169–173, 245–249
epistemic cognition in, 456–458
executive function in. See Executive function
expertise in. See Expertise
in fetal alcohol spectrum disorder, 85
formal operational stage in, 18, 18t, 388–390, 456
imitation in, 152, 153, 154–155, 155f
individual differences in, 167–173, 234, 245–249, 314–321, 526–527
in infancy and toddlerhood, 17, 18t, 19, 148–181, 158t, 186
infectious diseases affecting, 221
information-processing approach to. See Information processing
intelligence tests of, 167–169, 314–321
and language development. See Language development
in late adulthood, 574, 576, 586, 587–591, 594–605, 614, 638
lateralization of brain functions in, 121
lead exposure affecting, 86
lifelong learning in, 602–605
literacy in, 242–244
in low birth weight, 98
maintenance and loss prevention in late adulthood, 601–602
mathematical abilities in. See Mathematical abilities
memory in. See Memory
mental representations in, 151t, 152–153, 154–156, 227
metacognition in, 241–242
in middle adulthood, 524–533
in middle childhood, 18t, 295, 303–330
milestones in, 158t, 233t
and moral development, 271–272, 343
and motor development, 300
neo-Piagetian theory of, 233
neuroscience approach to, 20–21
nutrition affecting, 129, 220, 221, 295
of only children, 353
organization in, 150–151
peer interaction affecting, 457
and perceptual development, 142, 145
in phenylketonuria, 46

Piaget on, 17–19, 18t, 150–159, 227–234, 304–307
planning in, 238–239, 310
play in, 168, 227–228, 236, 264, 264t
postformal thought in, 456
pragmatic thought in, 458
prenatal drug exposure affecting, 82, 83, 84, 85
preoperational stage in. See Preoperational stage
of preterm infants, 98, 100
problem solving in, 155, 229, 229f, 530, 599–600
propositional thought in, 389
and questions asked by preschoolers, 232
reaching by infants in, 136–137, 154
relativistic thinking in, 457
scientific reasoning in, 391f, 391–392
self-concept in, 336–337, 392–393
and self-regulation, 312–313, 390
sensorimotor stage in. See Sensorimotor stage
sex chromosome abnormalities affecting, 51
sex differences in, 394–396
social context of, 166–167, 234–236
social learning theory on, 17
as socially mediated process, 22
sociocultural theory on, 22–23, 166–167, 234–236
spatial abilities in, 304–306
and suicidal behavior, 429
symbolic understanding in, 155–156, 228–229
television viewing time affecting, 157, 248–249
theory of mind in, 241–242, 311–312
verbal abilities in, 394, 525, 525f
and vocational choice, 462–465
and vocational life, 531–532
Vygotsky on, 22–23, 166–167, 234–236
wisdom in, 600–601
Cognitive-developmental theory, 17–19, 18t, 27t, 150–159
concrete operational stage in, 18, 18t, 304–307
contributions and limitations of, 18–19
evaluation of, 156–159
formal operational stage in, 18, 18t, 388–390
on gender identity, 279
on gender typing, 276
on moral behavior, 271–272, 343, 413, 414, 417, 420
and postformal thought, 456
preoperational stage in, 18, 18t, 227–234
sensorimotor stage in, 18, 18t, 150, 151–153
Cognitive maps in concrete operational stage, 304
Cognitive neuroscience, developmental, 20, 21
Cognitive reserve, 590
Cognitive self-regulation, 312–313
Cohabitation, 356
in early adulthood, 450, 451, 452, 494, 497

in late adulthood, 628
in middle adulthood, 515, 547, 549
and psychological well-being, 547
Cohort effects, 524–525, 525f
in androgynous gender identity, 547
in baby boom generation, 10, 12–13
in cross-sectional research, 524–525, 525f
history-graded influences in, 10
in longitudinal research, 35–36, 524–525, 525f, 625
in sequential research, 36–37, 37f, 524–525, 525f
Colic, 108
Collectivist societies, 63
interdependence in, 63. See also Interdependence, as cultural value
College enrollment, 394, 460, 532–533
College experience, 460–461
of adults as returning students, 532–533
alcohol use during, 449, 450
civic engagement in, 471
dualistic thinking in, 456–457
educational preparation for, 401, 402
and emerging adulthood, 474
epistemic cognition in, 456–457, 460
friendships in, 483
identity development in, 410, 470–471
moral development in, 417, 460
peer interactions in, 457, 460
relativistic thinking in, 457
sex differences in, 464–465
sexual encounters during, 451–452
smoking during, 449
vocational choice in, 462, 464
Colon cancer, 447, 448, 517, 611
Color vision, 110, 140, 509, 574
Colombia, 344, 486, 663
Communication
of caregivers and older adults with dementia, 593
with cell phones, 423–424, 424f
with children and adolescents about death, 649–650, 651, 652
collaborative style of, 319
in coregulation, 352
cultural influences on, 319–320
with dying person, 647–648, 652, 655–656
elderspeak in, 599
expressive style of, 178
hierarchical style of, 319–320
infant-directed speech in, 179
interactional synchrony in, 200
and language development. See Language development
in late adulthood, 598–599
in marital relationships, 481, 488–489, 495
in online interactions, 423–424, 424f
in parent–adult-child relationships, 551
preverbal gestures in, 176
referential style of, 178
and social interactionist view of language development, 175
sociocultural theory on, 22, 166–167, 235
topic-associating style of, 323
topic-focused style of, 322

Community influences, 24, 60–61
on child maltreatment, 285t, 286
on civic engagement, 419
on delinquency, 430
on early sexual activity, 381
on immigrant youths, 32
on late adulthood, 622–623
on resilient children, 11, 360
Community service. See Volunteer work
Companionate love, 479, 481
Compassionate love, 479, 481
Compensatory techniques of older adults, 8, 528, 529, 602
in language processing, 598, 599
in memory difficulties, 598
in selective optimization with compensation, 595, 616, 639
Competence, emotional, 260
Compliance in toddlerhood, 33, 209
Comprehension
compared to production of language, 177
of reading, 323
Compression of morbidity in late adulthood, 582
Computer use
in assistive technology and devices, 579
Internet in. See Internet use
in late adulthood, 605, 632
learning in, 249
and media multitasking, 400
and myopia, 298
parental supervision of, 275
sex differences in, 395
violent video games in, 274
Conception, 45, 76
maternal age at time of. See Maternal age
paternal alcohol use at time of, 84
radiation exposure prior to, 49
Conceptual categorization in infancy and toddlerhood, 165
Concrete operational stage, 18, 18t, 304–307, 305f, 388
Conditioned response, 130f, 131
Conditioned stimulus, 130f, 131
Conditioning
classical, 16, 130f, 130–131
operant, 16, 131, 153, 162, 162f, 163, 163f
Conduct problems, 430, 431
Cones and rods, 509
Confidentiality in research, 38, 38t
Conflict
in adolescence, 368, 376
in divorce of parents, 354, 355
in late adulthood, 600, 611, 621, 626
in marital relationships, 426, 481, 626
Confrontation in grief process, 665, 670
Confucian beliefs, 647
Congo, Republic of, 186, 237
Connective tissue changes in aging, 440
Conscience
and moral development, 267. See also Moral development
and superego, 15, 258, 267
Conscientiousness, as personality trait, 548, 548t, 549

Consent to research, 37, 38, 38t
Conservation
  in concrete operational stage, 304, 306, 307
  and gender constancy, 279
  in preoperational stage, 229–230, 230f
Constancy, gender, 279
Constructive play, 264t
Constructivist classrooms, 324, 325
Continuity theory of aging, 620, 623, 636
Continuous course of development, 7, 8, 27t, 159
  compared to discontinuous development, 6, 6f, 307
Continuous performance tasks, 528
Contraception, 381f, 381–382, 385, 490
Contractions of uterus in childbirth, 93f, 93–94
Contrast sensitivity, 141–142, 142f
Control
  in child rearing, 282–283, 284
  effortful. *See* Effortful control
  and hardiness as personal quality, 522
  in late adulthood, 579, 583, 587, 616, 636, 639
  in middle adulthood, 546
  in self-regulation. *See* Self-regulation
Controversial children, 347, 348
Conventional level of moral development, 414–415
Conventional personality, vocational choice in, 462
Convergent thinking, 328
Cooing, 175
Cooley's anemia, 47t
Cooperative learning, 325–326
Coparenting, effective, 57, 355, 356, 491
Coping strategies
  in adolescence, 387
  in bereavement interventions, 668, 670
  of caregivers, 557, 592
  in death of loved one, 657, 665–670
  dual-process model of, 665–666, 668
  of dying people, 653, 654–655
  in early adulthood, 455
  in early childhood, 261
  in late adulthood, 575, 579, 611, 614, 615, 617, 639
  of lesbian and gay couples, 626
  in middle adulthood, 520–521, 522, 545–546, 548, 560
  in middle childhood, 342
Coregulation in middle childhood, 352
Core knowledge perspective, 158–159, 159f, 242
Cornea, 574
Corporal punishment, 268–269, 269f, 270, 284, 286
Corpus callosum
  in early childhood, 218f, 219, 287
  in late adulthood, 574
  in middle childhood, 307
Corpus luteum, 76
Correlational research design, 31–33, 33f, 34t

Correlation coefficient, 33, 33f
Cortex, cerebral. *See* Cerebral cortex
Cortisol
  in bullying victims, 349
  in childbirth, 94
  child-care effects on, 203
  in child maltreatment victims, 287
  in early deprivation, 123, 124
  in family stress and overeating, 296
  in flight or fight response, 89
  in infants of depressed mothers, 187
  in poverty, 239, 308
  in pregnancy, 89
  in preterm infants, 100
  in response to crying infant, 105
  in shyness and sociability, 192
Corumination, 423, 428
Cosleeping arrangements, 126
Costa Rica, 571f
Counseling
  academic, 401, 411
  in adolescent delinquency, 432
  in alcoholism, 450
  in bereavement interventions, 670
  on birth control, 382
  of blended families, 356, 496
  on childbearing decisions, 490
  in chronic childhood illness, 298
  in dropout prevention programs, 402, 461
  in early pubertal timing, 377
  in elder maltreatment prevention, 634
  of foster parents, 124
  genetic, 51–52, 56
  on infant care, 102, 491
  on marital relationships, 489
  in partner abuse, 489
  in retirement planning, 563
  in school transitions, 398
  in smoking cessation, 449
  in suicide prevention, 429
  in unemployment, 562
  vocational, 465, 561
  in weight loss programs, 447
Counting skills in early childhood, 244–245
Court proceedings, eyewitness testimony of children in, 361
Crawling, 133, 134, 135
  cultural variations in, 136
  and depth perception, 140, 141
  and differentiation theory of perceptual development, 145
  and emotional self-regulation by infants, 186, 189
  and temperament, 193
Creativity
  in early adulthood, 459
  in early childhood, 226
  in middle adulthood, 530–531
  in middle childhood, 316, 316f, 328f, 328–329
Critical periods of development, 21
Croatia, 102f, 487, 487f
Cross-cultural research. *See* Cultural influences
Cross-linkage theory of aging, 440
Cross-sectional research design, 34t, 36
  cohort effects in, 36, 524–525, 525f
  sequential designs, 36, 37f, 524–525, 525f

Crowds and cliques in adolescence, 425–426
Crying of infants, 104, 105t, 105–108
  in drug addiction, 83
  and maternal smoking during pregnancy, 84
Crystallized intelligence, 525–526, 526f, 527, 527f, 594–595
Cuba, 102f
Cults, religious, 418
Cultural bias in intelligence tests, 245, 315, 318–321
Cultural influences, 6, 62–66
  on academic achievement, 330, 337, 399
  on achievement attributions, 340
  on adolescence, 368, 374–375, 377, 380, 411, 412, 421
  on aging stereotypes, 580–581
  on alcohol use, 450
  on attachment patterns, 196, 198, 199, 199f, 200–201, 480
  on bereavement, 669
  on body image, 377
  on breastfeeding practices, 16
  on caring for aging parent, 555, 556, 557, 623
  on categorization skills, 165, 232
  on childbirth practices, 95–96
  on child maltreatment, 285t, 286
  on child-rearing practices and styles, 16, 62, 136, 186, 200–201, 203–204, 208, 237, 270, 284
  on cognitive development, 167, 235, 236, 237, 305–306, 311, 318–321, 390, 531
  on cohabitation, 494
  on communication styles, 319–320
  on concrete operational stage, 305f, 305–306
  on coresidence of aging parents and children, 555
  on dating, 426
  on death understanding and attitudes, 647, 648, 649, 650, 651, 652, 656, 659–660, 666, 669
  on departure from parental home, 484, 485, 551
  on divorce, 496
  on drawings in early childhood, 225, 226
  ecological systems theory on, 24
  on education and schools, 236
  on emerging adulthood, 471, 473, 474
  on emotional self-regulation, 189
  ethnographic research on, 28t, 30–31
  on extended families, 62–63
  on false beliefs, 242
  on fathers as caregivers, 203–204, 205
  on fears of children, 358
  on food preferences, 219–220
  on formal operational stage, 390
  on friendships, 423
  on gender identity, 547
  on gender stereotypes, 278, 280
  on generativity, 539
  on grandparents as caregivers, 553
  on hand preference, 218
  on hospice care, 659–660
  on identity development, 411, 412, 471

  on imitation of adult behaviors, 167
  on immigrant youths, 32
  on intelligence assessment, 315, 318–321
  on language development, 177–178, 250, 318–319, 320, 322–323
  on late adulthood, 579, 580–581, 584, 600
  on learning, 23, 139, 167, 237
  in macrosystem, 24
  on make-believe play, 168, 237, 265
  on map making, 305f, 305–306
  on mate selection, 479, 482
  on memory and memory strategies, 241
  on menopause, 512, 513, 514
  on midlife crisis, 542
  on moral development, 267, 344, 416, 417, 418
  on motor development, 136
  on neonatal behavior, 110
  on observational learning, 237
  on older parent–adult child relationships, 631, 632
  on one-child families, 353
  on parenthood decisions, 490
  on partner abuse, 489
  on peer relations, 265
  on personality traits, 548
  on play, 168, 237, 258, 264, 265
  on prenatal health care, 91
  on psychological well-being, 545
  on punishment, 269, 270, 284, 286
  on religiosity, 472
  on reminiscence in late adulthood, 612
  research methods on, 30–31
  on respect for older adults, 580–581, 630
  on romantic relationships, 480, 481–482
  on scaffolding, 235
  on self-concept, 259, 262, 337, 339
  on self-conscious emotions, 189, 262
  on self-esteem, 259, 337, 339, 340, 409
  on self-recognition, 207–208, 208f
  self-report measures on, 30, 31
  on sense of control over health, 579
  on sensitivity toward infants, 201–202
  on sexual coercion, 454
  on sexuality, 368, 380, 584
  on sibling relationships, 422, 558
  on sleep, 125, 126
  on social relationships of older adults, 622
  sociocultural theory on, 22–23, 167
  on soothing of crying infants, 107–108
  on storytelling practices, 259
  on stranger anxiety, 186
  in subcultures, 62
  on suicidal behavior, 428, 429
  on temperament, 193, 195
  in tribal cultures. *See* Tribal cultures
  in village cultures. *See* Village cultures
  on vocational choice, 463
Custody of children, 355, 356, 497, 554
Cyberbullying, 349

Cyprus, 571*f*
Cystic fibrosis, 47*t*, 298
Cytomegalovirus infection in pregnancy, 87*t*, 88
Cytoplasm, 44
Czech Republic
  housework hours and gender roles in, 487*f*
  infant mortality rate in, 102*f*
  life expectancy in, 571*f*
  math achievement scores in, 329*f*
  poverty rate in, 65*f*

D

Daily living activities in late adulthood, 573, 575, 576
  Alzheimer's disease affecting, 588
  cognitive interventions affecting, 602
  control versus dependency in, 616
  exercise affecting, 583
  mental health problems affecting, 617
  problem solving in, 599–600
  widowhood affecting, 629
Dark adaptation in late adulthood, 575
Darwin, Charles, 12–14, 368
Dating
  in adolescence, 380–381, 382, 426*f*, 426–427
  in early adulthood, 450–451
  in late adulthood, 627, 627*f*
Day care programs. *See* Child-care programs
Day of the Dead celebration, 649
Death and dying, 644–673
  in adolescence, 221, 378, 646
  adolescent concept of, 650, 651, 652
  adult concept of, 650–651, 652
  advance medical directives on, 661–662
  and afterlife beliefs, 649, 651, 669
  agonal phase in, 646
  anticipatory grieving in, 666
  anxiety about, 648, 649, 650, 651–652, 652*f*
  appropriate or good death in, 648, 654
  bereavement in, 665–670
  brain death in, 647
  caregivers in, 653, 655, 657
  of child, 221, 287, 298, 299*f*, 666–667
  childhood concept of, 648–650, 651
  clinical death in, 646
  communication with children and adolescents about, 649–650, 651, 652
  communication with dying person in, 647–648, 652, 655–656
  contextual influences on adaptations to, 654–656
  coping of dying person in, 653, 654–655
  coping with death of loved one, 665–670
  definition of, 646–647
  with dignity, 646, 647–648
  and disengagement theory of aging, 620
  in early adulthood, 440–442, 444, 444*f*, 449
  education on, 648, 649–650, 651, 670–671

end-of-life care decisions in, 647, 660–664
in family, 655–656, 657, 659
funerals in, 668, 669
hospice approach to, 657, 658–660
in infancy, 102, 103. *See also* Infant mortality
of intimate partner, 667–668
in involuntary euthanasia, 660*t*, 664
in late adulthood, 570, 584*f*, 584–585, 586, 587, 610
leading causes of death, 221, 516*f*, 584*f*, 644*f*
medical aid in, 660*t*, 662–664
in middle adulthood, 515, 516–517
music therapy in, 659
nature of disease in, 654
pain management in, 646, 654, 657, 658, 659, 661
palliative care in, 658, 659
of parent, 667
participatory perspective of, 651
and persistent vegetative state, 647, 660
physical changes in, 646
place of, 657–660, 662
religious and spiritual beliefs on, 647, 649, 650, 651, 656, 661, 669
and right to die, 660–664
of sibling, 667
of spouse, 623, 627, 628–629, 666, 667–668
stages of, 653
sudden death in, 657, 666, 670
in suicide, 428, 666. *See also* Suicide
terminal decline prior to, 601–602
and thoughts and emotions of dying people, 653–656
understanding of and attitudes toward, 648–653
in voluntary euthanasia, 660*t*, 664
Debriefing in research, 39
Decentration in concrete operational stage, 304
Deception in research, 39
Decision making
  in adolescence, 393–394
  on end-of-life care, 647, 648, 660–664
  on health care, 600, 627
  on moral issues, 413–420
  on parenthood, 489–490, 495
  on retirement, 635, 635*f*
Deferred imitation in sensorimotor stage, 153, 154–155, 155*f*
Delay of gratification, 209
Delinquency, 376, 377, 429–432, 432*f*, 488
Delivery of baby, 93*f*, 93–94. *See also* Childbirth
Dementia, 587–591, 592–593
  in Alzheimer's disease, 585. *See also* Alzheimer's disease
  euthanasia in, 664
  suicide in, 619
Denial, in coping with dying, 653, 655
Denmark
  adolescent pregnancy in, 384*f*
  caring for aging parents in, 557
  housework hours and gender roles in, 487*f*
  immunization rate in, 221

infant mortality rate in, 102*f*
life expectancy in, 571*f*
long-term care of older adults in, 594
marriage of same-sex couples in, 486
math achievement scores in, 329*f*
physical activity in, 448
poverty rate in, 65*f*
reproductive technologies in, 53
retirement programs in, 636
vocational education in, 465
Deoxyribonucleic acid. *See* DNA
Dependency in late adulthood, 616, 617, 631, 633, 639
Dependency–support script, 616, 617
Dependent variable in experimental research design, 33
Depression, 67, 71
  in adolescence, 376, 377, 379, 393, 427–428, 429
  in Alzheimer's disease, 588
  in cancer, 654
  in caring for aging parent, 557
  in children with depressed parent, 187
  in death of loved one, 665, 666, 667
  in dying, 653
  in early adulthood, 446, 448, 455
  in late adulthood, 591, 616, 617, 618–619, 624, 630, 636, 638
  in menopause, 512, 512*f*
  in middle childhood, 297
  in parent, 187
  in pregnancy, 83
  in sexual coercion victims, 454
  suicide in, 428–429. *See also* Suicide
  in widowhood, 628, 629
Depth perception
  in infancy, 140*f*, 140–141
  in late adulthood, 575, 579
Dermis, 509, 510
Design of research, 27, 31–37, 34*t*
Despair in late adulthood, 15*t*, 610
Destruction–creation developmental tasks, 541
Developmental cognitive neuroscience, 20, 21
Developmentally appropriate practice standards, 171, 172, 248
Developmental quotients (DQs), 169
Developmental science, 5–6
  historical studies in, 12–19
  recent theories in, 19–26
Developmental social neuroscience, 20–21
Diabetes, 49, 88, 88*f*
  calorie-restricted diet affecting risk for, 511
  in early adulthood, 446, 448, 452
  in late adulthood, 584, 585, 586
  in middle childhood, 297, 298
  in pregnancy, 91
  telomere length in, 439
Diabetes insipidus, 47*t*
Diarrhea, 221
Diet. *See* Nutrition
Diethylstilbestrol (DES), 82–83
Differentiation theory of perceptual development, 144–145
Difficult child, as temperament type, 190, 195, 201, 354

Diffuse-avoidant cognitive style, 411
Diffusion of identity, 409, 410, 410*t*, 411
Dignity, death with, 646, 647–648
Dilation and effacement of cervix in childbirth, 93, 93*f*
Dinner and mealtimes in family. *See* Mealtimes in family
Dioxins, prenatal exposure to, 86
Disabilities
  assistive technology and devices in, 579–580
  intellectual. *See* Intellectual disabilities
  in late adulthood, 579–580, 581, 582, 582*f*, 584–591, 617, 633
  learning, 48
  in middle adulthood, 515–519, 562
  of preterm infants, 98, 98*f*
Discipline
  in blended families, 496
  in child-rearing styles, 282, 283
  cultural influences on, 269, 270, 284
  in delinquency, 430
  inductive, 267–268
  and moral development, 267–268
  in positive parenting, 271
  punishment in. *See* Punishment
  and socioeconomic status, 58
  and temperament, 269
Discontinuous career path, 498
Discontinuous course of development, 6, 7, 8, 27*t*
  compared to continuous development, 6, 6*f*, 307
Discovery learning, 19, 233
  assisted, 235
Discrimination
  adolescent moral understanding of, 416, 417
  age-related, 562, 580
  in career opportunities, 499–500, 500*f*, 559, 561, 562
  ethnic and racial, 344, 412, 500, 500*f*
  gender-related, 499–500, 559, 561
  in homosexuality, 498, 627
  in obesity, 297, 446
  religious, 418
Diseases, infectious. *See* Infectious diseases
Disenfranchised grief, 668
Disengagement theory of aging, 620
Disequilibrium in cognitive development, 150
Disorganized/disoriented attachment, 198, 199, 201, 206
Displaced reference, and symbolic understanding of infants, 156
Distractibility, temperament in, 190
Divergent thinking, 328, 328*f*
Diversity and inequality, childhood understanding of, 344–345
Divorce, 353–355
  after death of child, 667
  age at time of marriage in, 486, 495
  age differences in response to parental divorce, 354, 356
  cohabitation after, 495
  and cohabitation prior to marriage, 494, 495
  consequences of, 496
  departure from parental home in, 484

Subject Index

Divorce (*continued*)
  in early adulthood, 491, 495–496
  feminization of poverty in, 550
  grandparent–grandchild contact after, 553
  in late adulthood, 627–628
  in middle adulthood, 550–551
  remarriage in, 356, 495–496, 550, 627–628
  in second marriage, 353, 356, 496, 497, 550, 628
  sex differences in response to, 354–355, 356, 496
  singlehood lifestyle after, 493
  in transition to parenthood, 491
Dizygotic twins, 45. *See also* Twins
DNA (deoxyribonucleic acid), 44, 45*f*, 70, 438–440
  mutations in, 49–50, 439–440, 516
Dogmatic inflexible cognitive style in identity development, 410–411
Dogon people of Mali, 199
Domestic violence, 488–489
Dominance hierarchy in peer relations, 302
Dominant cerebral hemisphere, 218
Dominant–recessive inheritance, 46–48, 47*t*, 48*f*
Donor insemination, 52
Dopamine in attention-deficit hyperactivity disorder, 309
Dorris, Michael, 84
Double standard of aging, 523–524, 541
Doula support during childbirth, 96
Down syndrome, 50, 51*f*, 589
Drawing
  in early childhood, 224*f*, 224–225, 226
  in middle childhood, 300, 300*f*, 301, 328, 328*f*
DRD4 7-repeat gene, 201, 387
Dreaming in REM sleep, 104
Dream of adult life in early adulthood, 477
Dressing skills in early childhood, 224
Dropping out
  from college, 460–461
  from high school, 402*f*, 402–403, 430, 431
Drowsiness of infants, 105*t*
Drug abuse. *See* Substance abuse
Drug therapy
  in AIDS, 88
  in Alzheimer's disease, 590
  analgesic, 97, 586
  antidepressant. *See* Antidepressant drugs
  in attention-deficit hyperactivity disorder, 309
  in bulimia, 379
  during childbirth, 97
  dementia-like symptoms from, 591
  in depression, 429
  in erectile dysfunction, 513, 584
  in infertility, fraternal twinning related to, 45, 45*t*
  in medical aid-in-dying, 663
  in menopause, 513
  in pregnancy, 82–83, 88
  in rheumatoid arthritis, 586
  in sleep disturbances, 577
  and taste perception, 576

Druze culture, 547, 649
Dual-cycle model of identity development, 471
Dual-earner households, 356–357, 486
  attachment security of infants in, 202
  combining work and family in, 500–501
  transition to parenthood in, 490–491
Dualistic thinking, 456–457
Dual-process model of coping with loss, 665–666
Dual representation in preoperational stage, 229
Duchenne muscular dystrophy, 47*t*
Durable power of attorney for health care, 661, 662
Dutch children
  clique and crowd membership of, 425
  feeding practices and weight of, 220, 220*f*
  gender dysphoria of, 281
  sleep schedule for infants, 125
Dying. *See* Death and dying
Dynamic assessment of intelligence, 320–321
Dynamic systems perspective
  cognitive development in, 166
  early adulthood in, 478
  ecological systems theory in, 26
  emerging adulthood in, 478
  emotional development in, 185, 189
  family in, 57–58
  motor development in, 135–136, 223

E

Ear, and hearing. *See* Hearing
Early adolescence (11 to 14 years old), 368, 393, 415
Early adulthood (18 to 40 years old), 8*t*, 436–505
  adaptation to life in, 477–478
  biological aging in, 438–444
  brain development in, 456
  cardiovascular and respiratory changes in, 440–442
  career development in, 470, 498–501
  childlessness in, 489–490, 493–494, 495
  civic and political commitments in, 471–472
  cognitive-affective complexity in, 458, 458*f*
  cognitive development in, 456–465
  cohabitation in, 494
  college experience in, 460–461
  combining work and family in, 500–501
  cultural influences in, 473, 474, 481–482
  death concept in, 650, 652*f*
  death of intimate partner in, 667–668
  diversity of lifestyles in, 492–498
  divorce and remarriage in, 495–496
  emotional and social development in, 468–503
  endocrine system in, 440

epistemic cognition in, 456–458
exercise in, 440, 442*f*, 442–443, 446, 447–448
expertise and creativity in, 458–459
exploration in, 470–473, 474
family life cycle in, 484–492
friendships in, 476, 482–484, 493
health and fitness in, 444–456
identity development in, 470–471
immune system in, 439, 440, 441*t*, 443
intimacy versus isolation in, 15*t*, 476
leading causes of death in, 444, 444*f*
leaving parental home in, 471, 484–485
loneliness in, 476
marriage in, 450, 452, 474, 476, 485–489, 495–496
mate selection in, 479
memory of events in, in late adulthood, 597
milestones of development in, 504–505
motor performance in, 442–443
nutrition in, 445–447
obesity in, 445–447, 448
parenthood in, 473, 474, 489–492, 496–498
parent relationships, 475, 485
partner abuse in, 488–489
physical development in, 438–456
postformal thought in, 456
pragmatic thought and cognitive-affective complexity in, 458
pregnancy in, 443–444, 444*f*
psychosocial development in, 15*t*, 476–478
religion and spirituality in, 472*f*, 472–473
reproductive capacity in, 443–444
risk and resilience in, 473–476
romantic relationships in, 476, 478–482
and seasons of life theory, 477
sexuality in, 450–455
singlehood in, 493–494
social clock in, 478, 493
stress in, 455–456
substance abuse in, 448–450
vocational choice in, 462–465
Early Childhood Longitudinal Study, 171
Early childhood (2 to 6 years old), 8*t*, 214–291
aggression in, 272–276
attention in, 237–238
body composition in, 216, 216*f*
body proportions in, 216, 216*f*
body size in, 216*f*, 216–217
brain development in, 217–219
child-rearing styles of parents during, 282–287
cognitive-developmental perspective on, 271–272
cognitive development in, 17–18, 217, 218, 219, 224, 227–253, 264
death concept in, 648–650
discipline in, 267–268
drawing in, 224*f*, 224–225, 226
educational media in, 248–249

emotional and social development in, 256–289
emotional self-regulation in, 261
empathy in, 260, 262–263
executive function in, 217, 228, 236–239, 242, 248, 261, 273, 286
false beliefs in, 241*f*, 241–242, 272
fear in, 262
friendships in, 265
gender dysphoria in, 281
gender identity in, 279–280, 281
gender typing in, 276–280
hand preference in, 217–218
home environment in, 245–246
infectious diseases in, 220–221
information processing in, 236–245
inhibition in, 237, 238*f*, 242
initiative versus guilt in, 15*t*, 258
injuries in, 221–222
language development in, 217, 225, 227, 234–235, 240, 242–244, 249–253, 261
mathematical reasoning in, 233, 244–245
memory in, 164–165, 165*f*, 238, 239–241
milestones of development in, 233*t*, 290–291
moral development in, 267–272
motor development in, 218, 219, 222–226, 223*t*
nutrition in, 217, 219–220
parent relationships in. *See* Parent–child relationships
peer relations in, 263–266
physical development in, 216–226
planning in, 238–239, 239*f*
play in, 225, 227–228, 237, 242, 258, 263–265
preoperational stage in, 18*t*, 227–234. *See also* Preoperational stage
punishment in, 268–271
questions asked in, 232, 251
school readiness in, 266
self-concept in, 258–260
self-conscious emotions in, 260, 262
self-control in, 237, 238*f*
self-esteem in, 260
self-help skills in, 224
sociocultural theory on, 234–236
symbol–real world relations in, 228–229
theory of mind in, 241–242, 272
of transgender children, 281
vocational choice in, 462
Early Head Start program, 173, 246–247
Early intervention programs, 172–173, 244, 246–247
  in telomere shortening, 439
Easy child, as temperament type, 190
Eating habits. *See also* Nutrition
  in adolescence, 378–379
  in early adulthood, 445–447
  in early childhood, 219–220
  in middle childhood, 295–296, 297
  and telomere length, 439
Ecological systems theory, 23–26, 24*f*, 27*t*, 56, 57, 60
  on childhood injuries, 221
  on child maltreatment, 285–286
  on family chaos, 25

Economic status. *See* Socioeconomic status
Ecstasy (MDMA), 386, 448
Ectoderm, 78
Education
 academic achievement in. *See* Academic achievement
 in adolescence, 391, 396–403
 and adolescent pregnancy, 384, 385
 in aggression interventions, 275
 on Alzheimer's disease, 590
 and Alzheimer's disease risk, 590
 for caregivers of older adults with dementia, 592, 593
 in childbirth classes, 95
 and civic engagement, 419
 and cognitive changes of late adulthood, 601
 on death, 648, 649–650, 651, 670–671
 and divorce rate, 353, 353*f*
 in early adulthood, 460–461, 464–465, 470–471, 473
 in early childhood, 233–234, 235–236, 246–247
 in elder maltreatment prevention, 634
 on immunizations, 221
 in infancy and toddlerhood, 172–173
 international comparisons of, 64*t,* 329*f,* 329–330
 in late adulthood, 602–605
 in middle adulthood, 532–533
 in middle childhood, 323–329, 330
 and moral development, 417
 in obesity interventions, 446–447
 on parenthood, 100, 491, 492
 on prenatal health care, 91
 on preterm infant caregiving skills, 100
 public expenditure on, 64*t*
 religious, 418
 in schools. *See* Schools
 in sexual abuse interventions, 360
 on sexuality, 584. *See also* Sex education
 and socioeconomic status, 58, 62
 in substance abuse prevention, 387
 on sudden infant death syndrome, 106
 television programs in, 157, 248–249
 vocational, 62, 400, 401, 402, 411, 465, 560–561
 in widowhood, in informational classes, 629
EEG. *See* Electroencephalography
Efe of Republic of Congo, 186, 237
Effortful control
 and delay of gratification, 209
 and emotional self-regulation, 189
 and self-awareness, 208–209
 sex differences in, 194
 and temperament, 189, 191, 191*t,* 193
Egalitarian marriages, 486, 487
Ego, 14–15
Egocentrism
 in adolescence, 392
 in early childhood, 229, 231, 234
 generational changes in, 471
Ego differentiation in late adulthood, 610

Ego integrity in late adulthood, 15*t,* 610–611, 613, 614, 652
 and continuity theory of aging, 620
 and life-review reminiscence, 612
Ego transcendence in late adulthood, 611
Ejaculation, first (spermarche), 372, 372*t,* 375
Elaboration as memory strategy, 240, 310–311, 529, 597, 603
Elder maltreatment, 632–634
Elderspeak, 599
Electra conflict, 15*t,* 258
Electroencephalography (EEG), 119, 119*t,* 141, 217
 in childhood maltreatment, 286
 in exercise and cerebral neural activity, 448
 in late adulthood, 574
 in shyness and sociability, 192
Embarrassment in infancy and toddlerhood, 188
Embryonic development, 77*t,* 78–79, 81, 82*f*
Embryonic disk, 77, 78
Emerging adulthood, 469, 470–476
 civic and political commitments in, 471–472
 cultural influences on, 473, 474
 as distinct period of development, 473, 474
 exploration in, 470–473, 474
 features of, 470
 identity development in, 470–471
 parent relationships in, 475
 religion and spirituality in, 472*f,* 472–473
 risk and resilience in, 473–476
 survey responses on, 470, 470*f*
 worldview in, 471–473
Emotional abuse, 285, 633
Emotional and social development, 8, 9*f*
 acceptance of change in, 614
 adaptation to life in, 477–478, 542
 in adolescence, 406–432
 of adopted children, 55–56
 aggression in, 272–276
 agreeableness in, 548, 548*t,* 549, 614
 attachment in, 196–206. *See also* Attachment
 autonomy in, 15*t,* 184, 544. *See also* Autonomy issues
 basic emotions in, 185–186, 260–261
 and career changes, 562
 and career development, 498–501, 560–561
 categorical self in, 208
 child-care quality affecting, 202–203
 child-rearing styles affecting, 282*t,* 282–285
 civic engagement in, 419, 471–472
 cognitive-affective complexity in, 458, 458*f*
 common problems in, 358–360, 427–432
 competence in, 260
 continuity theory of, 620
 control versus dependency in, 616

 coping strategies in, 545–546. *See also* Coping strategies
 cultural influences on, 471, 473, 481–482
 dating in, 426–427
 and delinquency, 429–432
 depression in, 427–428
 depression of parent affecting, 187
 disengagement theory of, 620
 and diversity of adult lifestyles, 492–498
 divorce of parents affecting, 353–355
 dynamic systems perspective of, 185, 189
 in early adulthood, 468–503
 in early childhood, 256–289
 early deprivation affecting, 123
 ego integrity in, 610–611
 in emerging adulthood, 470–476
 emotional competence in, 260
 emotional intelligence in, 317
 empathy and sympathy in, 208, 262–263
 environmental mastery in, 544
 ethology on, 22
 evolutionary developmental psychology on, 22
 exploration in, 470–473
 and eyewitness testimony of children, 361
 family influences on, 351–357, 420–422
 in family life cycle, 484–492
 fear in, 262, 358
 friendships in. *See* Friendships
 gender identity in, 279–280, 350–351, 546–548
 gender typing in, 276–280, 350–351
 generativity versus stagnation in, 15*t,* 538–541
 gerotranscendence in, 610–611
 in grandparenthood, 552–553, 554
 identity development in, 409–413, 470–471
 identity versus role confusion in, 15*t,* 408
 indirect influences on, 57, 266
 industry versus inferiority in, 15*t,* 336
 in infancy and toddlerhood, 182–211
 initiative versus guilt in, 15*t,* 258
 integrity versus despair in, 15*t,* 610
 intimacy versus isolation in, 15*t,* 476
 job satisfaction in, 560
 in late adulthood, 608–641
 leaving parental home in, 471, 484–485
 of lesbian and gay couples, 626–627
 maltreatment affecting, 285–287
 marriage in, 485–489, 549–551, 625–626. *See also* Marital relationships
 in middle adulthood, 536–565
 in middle childhood, 334–363
 midlife crisis in, 542–543
 and moral development, 267–276, 342–345, 413–420
 negative life changes affecting, 617
 neuroscience research on, 20–21

 of never-married, childless older adults, 629–630
 nonsocial activities in, 263, 264
 of only children, 352–353
 openness to experience in, 614
 parental warmth affecting, 205, 209
 parent–child relationships affecting, 205, 209, 351–352
 parenthood in, 489–492
 parent–infant relationships affecting, 187, 189
 peer relations in, 263–266, 345–349, 422–427. *See also* Peer relations
 personal agency in, 471, 474
 personality in, 184, 548–549
 physical health affecting, 617
 political commitments in, 471–472
 positivity effect in, 611–612
 possible selves in, 544, 614
 psychological well-being in. *See* Psychological well-being
 and relationships in early adulthood, 478–484
 and relationships in late adulthood, 625–634
 and relationships in middle adulthood, 549–559
 reminiscence in, 612
 resilience in, 360, 473–476
 in retirement, 634–637
 and retirement planning, 562–564
 romantic relationships in, 479–482
 and school readiness, 266
 in seasons of life theory, 477, 541–542
 self-acceptance in, 544
 self-awareness in, 206–208
 self-concept in. *See* Self-concept
 self-conscious emotions in, 188–189, 262, 341, 342
 self-control in, 208–209
 self-esteem in, 260, 337–341, 408–409
 self-regulation of emotions in, 189–190, 261, 342
 self-understanding in, 258–260, 336–341, 408–411
 sequential research on, 36
 sexual abuse affecting, 358–360
 shyness and sociability in, 192
 sibling relationships in, 557–558, 630
 social clock in, 477–478
 and social contexts of aging, 622–625
 social referencing in, 188
 social support affecting, 617–618
 and social theories of aging, 620–622
 socioemotional selectivity theory of, 620–622
 spirituality and religiosity in, 418, 472*f,* 472–473, 614–615
 stage or life events approach to, 543
 and suicide, 428–429, 618–619
 temperament in, 190–195
 trust versus mistrust in, 15*t,* 184
 understanding and responding to emotions of others in, 188, 260–261, 342
 and unemployment, 562
 and vocational life, 559–564
 and widowhood, 628–629
 worldview in, 471–473

Emotional expression, facial, 143, 185, 200, 342
Emotional intelligence, 317, 458
Emotional self-regulation, 193, 199
and death anxiety, 652
in early childhood, 261
in infancy and toddlerhood, 189–190
in late adulthood, 611, 639
in middle childhood, 342, 352
Emotional well-being. *See* Psychological well-being
Emotion-centered coping
in late adulthood, 579, 611
in middle adulthood, 520–521, 522, 545
in middle childhood, 342
Emotions. *See also specific emotions.*
in adolescence, 375
anger, 185–186
facial expressions of, 143, 185, 200, 342
fear, 186, 262
happiness, 185
in infancy and toddlerhood, 184–190
of others, understanding and responding to, 188, 260–261, 342
sadness, 186
self-conscious, 188–189, 260, 341, 342
self-regulation of, 189–190
Empathy
in early childhood, 260, 262–263, 268
in infancy and toddlerhood, 105, 208
in middle childhood, 342, 344
Emphysema, 585
Employment
in adolescence, 401
age climate in, 561
apprenticeship programs in, 465
in baby boom generation, 13
bridge jobs prior to retirement in, 634, 635
burnout from job stress in, 560
and caring for aging parents, 556, 556f, 557
and child care, 171f, 171–172, 202–203, 246, 491–492
cognitive flexibility in, 531–532
college experience in transition to, 461
combining family with, 356–357, 477, 490–492, 499, 500–501
discontinuous career path in, 498
in dual-earner families, 356–357. *See also* Dual-earner households
in early adulthood, 462–465, 470, 473, 477, 490–501
and eating habits, 446
educational preparation for, 62, 400, 401, 402, 411, 461, 465, 560–561
equal pay and opportunities in, 357
establishment of career in, 498–499
ethnic and racial differences in, 500, 500f
exosystem in, 24
in families with young children, 491–492
flexible time policies in, 357, 501
gender pay gap in, 499, 550

gender stereotypes in, 280, 351, 463t, 463–465, 499–500, 561
glass ceiling in, 561
hearing loss related to, 509
of high school dropouts, 402
and identity, 410
job satisfaction in, 560, 560f
and marital roles, 356–357, 486–487
mentoring relationships in, 499
in middle adulthood, 531–532, 541, 542, 556, 556f, 559–564
of mothers, 103, 171, 202, 203, 204, 246, 356–357, 490–492, 499
nontraditional jobs of men in, 464
observation and participation of children in, 237
parental leave from, 103, 203, 491
and parenthood decisions, 490
professions of women in, 463, 463t
retirement from. *See* Retirement
and self-care children, 357
sex differences in, 463t, 463–465, 477, 499–501, 542, 561
and socioeconomic status, 58
and time spent per day with children, 357
and unemployment, 562
vocational choice in, 462–465
Empty nest phase, 549
Endocrine system. *See* Hormones
Endoderm, 78
End-of-life care, 644–671
advance medical directives on, 661f, 661–662
communication with dying person in, 647–648, 652, 655–656
decision making on, 647, 648, 660–664
dignity in, 646, 647–648
and right to die, 660–664
Endorphins, 108
Engagement
academic, in college experience, 461
civic. *See* Civic engagement
and separateness in seasons of life theory, 541
England, 96, 278, 319, 579
Enterprising personality, vocational choice in, 462
Environmental influences, 56–66
on Alzheimer's disease, 589, 590
on antisocial behavior, 70
on asthma, 298
on attachment security, 201, 202–203
on attention-deficit hyperactivity disorder, 309
on cancer, 516
on childhood injuries, 221, 222
on child maltreatment, 286
on cognitive development, 123, 169–173, 245–249
cultural, 62–66. *See also* Cultural influences
on delinquency, 430
ecological systems theory on, 23–26, 56, 60
in epigenesis, 70–72
evolutionary developmental psychology on, 22
evolutionary theory of Darwin on, 13
on executive function, 308

family as, 57–60
on gender typing, 277–279
and gene correlation, 68–69, 69f, 70
on gene expression, 70–72
and gene interactions, 68, 68f, 70
on genetic mutations, 49
on health in early adulthood, 445
on hearing loss, 509
in home, 245–246. *See also* Home environment
and intelligence and IQ, 67–68, 70, 123, 169–173, 318–321
on life expectancy, 571, 572
on motor development, 301
on multiple births, 45, 45t, 46
neighborhoods as, 60–61
and person–environment fit, 580, 616, 618, 623, 624, 625, 639
on prenatal development, 70, 71, 71f, 81–88
on pubertal development, 372–373, 377
and relative influence of nature and nurture, 7, 27t, 66–72, 318–321
and resilience, 10–11
schools as, 61–62
in sensitive periods, 21, 121–124
on sexual activity of adolescents, 381
on sexual orientation, 382
socioeconomic, 58–60. *See also* Socioeconomic status
on substance abuse, 386
on sudden infant death syndrome, 106
on temperament, 68, 192, 193–195
teratogens in, 81–88
on vascular dementia, 591
Environmental mastery in middle adulthood, 544, 545, 547
Envy in infancy and toddlerhood, 188
Epidermis, 509
Epidural analgesia during childbirth, 97
Epigenesis, 70f, 70–72, 85, 89
of Alzheimer's disease, 590
Epinephrine in stress response, 89
Epiphyses, 217, 369
Episodic memory, 240, 596, 597, 602
Epistemic cognition, 456–458, 460
Equilibrium in cognitive development, 18, 150
Erectile dysfunction, 513, 584
Erikson, Erik, 15t, 15–16, 36
on autonomy versus shame and doubt, 15t, 184
on generativity versus stagnation, 15t, 538–541
on identity versus role confusion, 15t, 408
on industry versus inferiority, 15t, 336
on initiative versus guilt, 15t, 258
on integrity versus despair, 15t, 610
on intimacy versus isolation, 15t, 476
on trust versus mistrust, 15t, 184
Erikson, Joan, 611
Eritrea, 359
Eskimo people, 316
Estonia, 65f, 102f, 329f
Estrogens
in early adulthood, 440

in middle adulthood, 510, 512, 519
in new fathers, 111
prenatal exposure to, 382
in puberty, 369
Ethical issues
in reproductive technologies, 52, 53
in research, 16, 37–39, 38t, 121
in right to die, 660–664
and universal principles in moral development, 415
Ethiopia, 129
Ethnic and racial differences
in academic achievement, 399–400, 401
in body size, 117
in career opportunities, 499–500, 500f, 561
in caregiving for older adults, 617–618
in caring for aging parents, 555, 556
in cliques and crowds, 425
in college dropout rates, 460
in community and neighborhood, 622
in corporal punishment, 270
in cosleeping of parents and infants, 126
in death concept of children, 649
in delinquency, 430
in dementia, 587
in departure from parental home, 485
in early adulthood health, 445
in family structure, 62
in fraternal twinning, 45t
in friendships, 423
in gay relationships, 453
in grandparent–grandchild relationships, 553, 554
heritability research on, 67–68
in high school dropout rates, 402, 402f
in identity, 412
in infant mortality rate, 102
in intelligence test results, 318–321
in late adulthood health, 581, 582, 587
in marriage partners, 486
in menopause, 513
and middle childhood understanding of diversity, 344–345
in nutrition and obesity, 295–296, 445
in parent–adult-child relationships, 551, 631
in partner abuse, 489
in prenatal health care, 91
in pubertal development, 372–373
in religiosity, 472, 615, 618
in retirement decisions, 635
in right-to-die issues, 661
in school transitions, 397, 398
in self-esteem, 338, 409
in singlehood, 493
in single-parent families, 497
in socioeconomic status, 59
stereotypes on, 320, 344, 350, 412, 532
in suicide, 428, 618
in teacher–student interactions, 326, 340, 401
in temperament, 193
in widowhood, 628, 629

Ethnographic research, 28t, 30–31, 32
Ethology, 21–22, 27t
  attachment theory in, 22, 196–197, 205, 426, 480
Europe. *See also specific countries.*
  academic and vocational tracks in, 401
  adoption in, 55
  anorexia nervosa in, 378
  caring for aging parents in, 623
  child care in, 171
  childhood injury rates in, 222
  cliques and crowds of adolescents in, 425
  cohabitation in, 494, 547
  collectivism in, 63
  contraceptive use of adolescents in, 385
  corporal punishment in, 286
  departure from parental home in, 551
  early deprivation of institutionalized orphans in, 199
  elder suicide in, 619
  health care for parents and newborn in, 102
  housework hours and gender roles in, 486–487, 487f
  intelligence quotient gains in, 319
  lifelong learning in, 604
  long-term care for older adults in, 593
  male birth rate in, 48
  marital roles in, 486
  menopause in, 512
  midlife mortality in, 546
  moral development in, 417
  natural childbirth movement in, 95
  nursing home care in, 624
  physical development of adolescents in, 369, 371, 373
  poverty rate in, 59
  prenatal health care in, 91, 102
  preschool programs in, 246
  psychological well-being in, 547
  reproductive technologies in, 53
  retirement in, 563
  sexual activity of adolescents in, 385
  sexually transmitted infections in, 383, 453
  temperament of children in, 193
  terminally ill patients in, 655
  thalidomide use in, 82
  Third Age in, 604, 613
  vocational education in, 401, 465
  voluntary euthanasia in, 664
European Americans
  academic achievement of, 399
  adolescent, 372, 374, 399
  aging parents of, 556, 557
  anorexia nervosa of, 378
  body image of, 377
  cancer of, 517
  as caregivers of older adults with dementia, 593
  categorization abilities of children, 232
  communication style of, 322
  community and neighborhood of, 622
  death concept of, 649
  divorce of, 353
  drawing skills of children, 226
  gay relationships of, 453
  gender roles and housework hours of, 487
  gender typing by, 278
  generativity of, 539f, 541
  glaucoma of, 509
  grandparents as caregivers of, 554
  in-group and out-group biases of, 344
  intelligence quotient of, 318, 320
  life expectancy of, 570, 571
  long-term care of older adults, 593
  menarche of, 374
  menopause of, 513
  moral development of, 413
  narrative style of, 322
  neonatal behavioral assessment, 110
  parent–infant interactions of, 193
  physical development in infancy and toddlerhood, 117
  puberty of, 372, 374, 377
  punishment of children by parents, 270
  and racial stereotypes, 320
  religiosity of, 615
  reminiscence in late adulthood, 612
  scaffolding interactions of, 235
  self-esteem of, 338, 409
  shyness and sociability of, 192
  singlehood lifestyle of, 493
  stereotype threat affecting, 320
  suicide rate of, 428
  temperament of, 192, 193
Eustachian tube, 298
Euthanasia, 660t, 664
  and medical aid-in-dying, 662–664
Event-based prospective memory tasks, 598
Event-related potentials (ERPs), 119, 119t, 121
  in emotional responses, 200, 611
  in speech perception of infants, 138, 175
Every Child Succeeds Act, 324–325
Evocative gene–environment correlation, 68–69
Evolution, theories of, 12–14, 368
  attachment in, 22, 196
  in ethology, 22, 196
  gender roles in, 277
  generativity in, 539
  mate selection in, 479
  play activities in, 302–303
  wisdom of older adults in, 600
Evolutionary developmental psychology, 22, 27t
Executive function, 20
  and academic and social skills, 236, 308
  in adolescence, 373, 374, 386, 387f, 390, 400, 431
  and aggressive behavior, 273
  in attention-deficit hyperactivity disorder, 309
  in autism, 243
  in bilingualism, 323
  and brain development, 217, 307, 373, 574
  components of, 161, 217, 236, 316
  in continuous performance tasks, 528
  and delinquency, 431
  in early childhood, 217, 228, 236–239, 242, 248, 261, 273, 286
  educational media affecting, 248
  and effortful control, 191
  and emotional self-regulation, 261
  exercise affecting, 300, 310, 546, 583
  of Experience Corps volunteers, 638
  and flexible shifting of attention, 237–238, 242, 261, 307, 308, 390, 528–529, 594
  genetic factors affecting, 308–309
  in infancy and toddlerhood, 160f, 161, 191
  and inhibition, 237, 242, 261, 307, 308, 390, 528, 594
  and intelligence, 316
  and language skills, 217, 323
  in late adulthood, 574, 576, 583, 586, 594, 602, 619, 638
  make-believe play affecting, 228
  of maltreated children, 286
  measures of, 161, 237–238
  media multitasking affecting, 400
  in middle adulthood, 527, 528–529, 546
  in middle childhood, 300, 307–310, 316, 323
  and motor vehicle accidents, 586
  parenting affecting, 238–239, 286
  and planning, 238, 242, 307, 310, 390
  poverty affecting, 239, 308
  prefrontal cortex in, 574
  prenatal influences on, 308
  and sensory (hearing and vision) declines, 576
  and sleep, 374
  and speed of information processing, 527, 528, 576
  and substance abuse, 386, 387f
  and theory of mind, 242
  training of, 308–310, 529, 602
  and working memory, 238, 261, 307, 308, 310, 390, 528, 594, 602
Exercise
  in adolescence, 370–371, 371f, 372
  and Alzheimer's disease risk, 590
  athletic activities in. *See* Athletic activities
  in early adulthood, 440, 442f, 442–443, 446, 447–448
  in late adulthood, 572, 573, 575, 577, 578, 582f, 583, 586, 590
  in middle adulthood, 510, 519, 521–522, 546, 547
  in middle childhood, 297, 300, 303, 310
  in pregnancy, 88
  and telomere length, 439
Exosystem, 24, 24f, 25, 60
Expansion of morbidity in late adulthood, 582
Expansion strategy in grammar development, 252
Experience Corps, 638
Experience-dependent brain growth, 124, 456
Experience-expectant brain growth, 124
Experimental research design, 31, 33–34, 34t
  combined with developmental research, 37
Expertise
  in early adulthood, 458–459
  in late adulthood, 600, 621
  in middle adulthood, 530, 531
  in middle childhood, 329
Explicit memory, 239, 400, 596
Explicit self-awareness, 207–208
Exploration in early adulthood, 470–473, 474
  and vocational choice, 462, 470
Exploration in infancy and toddlerhood
  attachment security affecting, 197
  attention in, 161
  and categorization, 165
  circular reactions in, 152
  eye movements in, 110
  intentional behavior in, 152
  and motor development, 133–137, 141
  and perceptual development, 140–141, 145
  of pictures and images, 156, 157
  secure base for, 186, 197, 198
  and temperament, 193
  visual cliff studies of, 140, 140f
Explosive children, longitudinal study of, 35
Expressive style of communication, 178
Extended families, 62–63
  of African Americans, 62–63, 497, 553, 623
  caregiving for older adults in, 623
  and departure from parental home, 485, 551
  in divorce, 355
  in exosystem, 24, 24f
  of families with young children, 492
  and generativity in middle adulthood, 541
  grandparents in, 62–63, 553
  of lesbian and gay couples, 498
  long-term care of older adults in, 593
  marital roles in, 486
  of single mothers, 63, 497
  and social context of aging, 623
  of stepfamilies, 497
  suicide prevention in, 428
  in widowhood, 628, 629
Externalizing difficulties, 57, 60, 123, 202, 206, 270, 341
Extinction in classical conditioning, 131
Extracurricular activities, 11, 403, 419
Extramarital sex, attitudes toward, 451f, 452
Extroversion, 548, 548t, 612, 614, 618
Eye blink reflex, 101t
Eye movements
  in infancy and toddlerhood, 110, 154, 161, 176
  in sleep, 104, 105, 105t, 125, 577
Eyes
  in late adulthood, 574–575
  in middle adulthood, 508–509
  of newborn, 109–110
  and vision. *See* Vision
Eyewitness testimony by children, 361

F

Fables, personal, 392, 393, 429
Face, aging of, 509–510, 578

Facebook use
  in adolescence, 423, 424
  in early adulthood, 483
  in late adulthood, 605, 631, 632
  in middle adulthood, 559, 559f
Face perception, 139, 139f, 142–143, 143f
  early vision loss affecting, 121
  intermodal, 144
Facial expressions
  brain activity in response to, 200
  in disorganized/disoriented attachment, 198
  emotions associated with, 143, 185, 200, 342
  infant perception of, 143, 185, 188
  newborn imitation of, 132–133, 133f
  in odor response of infants, 108, 109f
  systematic observation of, 29
  in taste response of infants, 108
Facial hair development, 369, 372, 372t
Factor analysis of intelligence tests, 315
Faith, spiritual and religious
  death concept in, 651
  in late adulthood, 615, 639
Fallopian tubes, 76, 76f
Falls
  in infancy and toddlerhood, 135, 136, 141, 145
  in late adulthood, 575, 577, 587
  in middle adulthood, 515
False beliefs
  in autism, 242
  in early childhood, 241f, 241–242, 272
  in middle childhood, 312, 312f, 343
Familiarity preference of infants, 131–132, 132f
Familism, cultural ideal of, 63, 422
Family, 57–60
  adaptation to changes in, 57–58
  adjustment to parenthood in, 111, 490–491
  of adolescents, 373, 377, 393, 420–422, 432, 492
  adoptive. See Adoption
  and aggression, 273–274, 275–276
  aging parents in, 554–557
  Alzheimer's disease in, 589, 592–593
  in anorexia nervosa therapy, 379
  attachment quality in, 201–202
  attention-deficit hyperactivity disorder in, 309
  bereavement interventions in, 670
  bidirectional influences in, 23, 57
  blended, 355–356, 496–497
  chaos in, 25
  child maltreatment in, 285t, 285–287, 358–360
  child-rearing practices in. See Child-rearing practices
  chronic illness in, 298
  and civic engagement, 419
  combining work with, 356–357, 477, 490–492, 499, 500–501
  death and dying in, 655–656, 657, 659, 666–668, 670
  of dementia victims, 590, 592–593
  direct influences of, 57

divorce in, 353–355. See also Divorce
  dual-earner, 356–357, 486. See also Dual-earner households
  in early adulthood, 484–492
  elder maltreatment in, 633–634
  ethnic identity of, 412
  extended, 62. See also Extended families
  and generativity in middle adulthood, 538–539, 540
  genetic mutations in, 49
  grandparents in, 552–554. See also Grandparents
  home environment of. See Home environment
  of immigrant youths, 32
  indirect influences of, 57
  in-laws in, 552, 553, 555
  kinkeeper role in, 552, 553, 628, 629
  in late adulthood, 619, 622, 625–628, 630, 631–632, 633–634
  of lesbian and gay couples, 497–498, 626–627
  life cycle of, 484–492, 549
  longevity in, 571, 572, 573
  marital roles in, 486–487
  mealtimes in. See Mealtimes in family
  in middle adulthood, 545, 547, 549–558
  in middle childhood, 351–357
  in multisystemic therapy for adolescent delinquency, 432
  of never-married childless older adults, 629
  with one child, 352–353
  parents in. See Parent(s)
  partner abuse in, 286
  pedigree of, 51
  and pubertal growth, 373, 377
  of resilient children, 11
  sexual abuse in, 358–360
  siblings in, 352, 484, 490. See also Siblings
  single-parent. See Single-parent families
  size of, 12, 58, 204, 484, 490
  skipped-generation, 554
  socioeconomic status of, 58–60. See also Socioeconomic status
  stepparents in, 356, 496–497
  stressful circumstances in, 275–276, 296, 422
  and substance abuse, 386
  and suicide, 429
  as system, 57–58, 421
  twins in, 45t, 46. See also Twins
  violence in, 488–489, 633–634
  and vocational choice, 463
  with young children, 491–492
Family Check-Up intervention, 34
Family pedigree in genetic counseling, 51
Family therapy, 432, 593
Fantasy period in vocational choice, 462
Fast-mapping process in vocabulary development, 250
Fast-twitch muscle fibers, 443, 510, 578
Fat, body
  in anorexia nervosa, 378

baby fat, 116f, 117, 216
  in early adulthood, 440, 448
  in late adulthood, 578
  in middle adulthood, 510
  in middle childhood, 294, 297
  in puberty, 369, 372
Fat, dietary
  and Alzheimer's disease, 590
  in early adulthood, 442, 446, 447, 447f
  in late adulthood, 591
Fathers
  adjustment to role as, 111, 385, 490–491
  adolescent, 384, 386
  age of, 45, 50, 51, 444
  alcohol use of, at time of conception, 84
  androgynous gender identity of, 547
  and attachment security of infant, 202, 203–204
  bereavement in loss of child, 667
  in blended families, 356, 497
  cultural influences on role of, 203–204, 205
  depression of, 187
  dioxin in bloodstream of, 86
  divorce of, 353, 354, 355, 356, 496
  in dual-earner marriages, 357, 490–491
  education on child rearing, 492
  employment leave time for, 103
  gender typing of children by, 277, 278, 350, 351
  generativity in middle adulthood, 539
  as grandparents, 553
  leave time from employment, 103
  marital roles of, 486, 490–491
  in maternal employment, 357
  play activities of, 203–204, 266, 277, 302
  radiation exposure of, 49
  relationships with adult children, 632
  self-acceptance of, 545
  and sibling relationships, 352, 557
  in single-parent families, 353
  as stepparents, 356, 497
  time spent in child-care activities, 204, 204f, 205, 357, 497
  time spent with sons, 352
  unwed, 497
  warmth of, 205
Father–stepmother families, 356
Favoritism
  sibling preference in, 352, 557–558
  toward in-groups, 278, 344, 345
  toward out-groups, 344
Fear
  of death, 651
  in early childhood, 262
  in infancy and toddlerhood, 16, 131, 186, 190, 191, 191t, 193
  in late adulthood, 587, 622–623
  in middle childhood, 358
Feeding practices
  and attachment, 196
  bottle-feeding in, 127–128
  breastfeeding in. See Breastfeeding
  and obesity, 220, 220f, 296
  overfeeding in, 128
Feet-first reaching, 135, 135f

Feminine traits
  in adolescence, 394, 428
  in early adulthood, 483
  in early childhood, 277, 279
  in middle adulthood, 541, 546–548, 556
  in middle childhood, 350–351
Feminization of poverty, 550, 623
Fertility
  and childlessness in infertility, 495
  in early adulthood, 443–444
  in middle adulthood, 510
  prenatal DES exposure affecting, 83
  in puberty, 371, 372
  and reproductive technologies, 45, 45t, 52–53
Fertilization, 76, 76f
  in reproductive technologies, 45, 45t, 52, 53
Fetal alcohol spectrum disorder (FASD), 84–85
Fetal alcohol syndrome (FAS), 84, 85
Fetal development, 77t, 79–81
  alcohol exposure affecting, 84–85
  diagnosis and treatment of problems in, 53–55, 54t
  habituation in, 81, 131
  maternal age affecting, 91f
  nicotine exposure affecting, 84
  stress hormones affecting, 89
  teratogens affecting, 81, 82f
Fetal medicine, 53–55, 54t
Fetal monitoring, 96–97
Fetoscopy, 54t, 80
Fibrillation, 646
Fibrosis, cystic, 47t, 298
Field experiments, 34
Fight or flight response, 89
Fiji, 267
Filipinos, 32, 316
Finality, and death concept, 648
Financial abuse of older adults, 633, 634
Financial planning for retirement, 562–564
Fine-motor development
  in early childhood, 223t, 224f, 224–225, 226
  in infancy and toddlerhood, 134, 134t, 136–137
  in middle childhood, 300, 300f, 301
Finland
  academic achievement in, 329, 329f, 330
  adolescent suicide in, 428
  adoption study of mental illness in, 70
  cesarean delivery rate in, 97
  housework hours and gender roles in, 486, 487f
  infant mortality rate in, 102f
  poverty rate in, 65f
  retirement programs in, 636
First Age, 613
Firstborn
  arrival of new sibling affecting, 204
  transition to parenthood in, 111, 490–491
First marriage, age at time of, 485, 486
First pregnancy, 111, 443, 444f, 490–491
First words, 176–177

Flexibility changes in motor development, 299
Flexible shifting of attention, 237–238, 242, 261, 307, 308, 390, 528–529, 594
Flight or fight response, 89
Flowcharts on information processing, 19, 20*f*
Flow state in middle adulthood, 546–547
Fluid intelligence, 525–526, 527, 527*f*, 594–595
Fluoride treatments and fluoridated water, 217
Flynn effect, 319
Folic acid in prenatal nutrition, 88–89
Food. *See also* Eating habits; Nutrition
  insecurity concerning, 129
  mercury exposure from, 86
  PCB exposure from, 86
  supplement programs, 89
  taste and odor of, 108–109, 109*f*, 576
  toxoplasmosis from, 88
Foreclosure status in identity development, 409, 410*t*, 410–411
Formal operational stage, 18, 18*t*, 388–390, 389*f*
  and postformal thought, 456
Formula feeding of infants, 127–128
Foster care, 124
4Rs (Reading, Writing, Respect, and Resolution) Program, 360
Fourth Age, 613
Fowler, James, on faith development, 615
Fractures
  in late adulthood, 587
  in middle adulthood, 510, 519
Fragile X syndrome, 49
Frailty in late adulthood, 585, 623, 633
France
  adolescent birth rate in, 384*f*
  gender stereotypes in, 350
  housework hours and gender roles in, 487*f*
  infant mortality rate in, 102*f*
  life expectancy in, 571*f*
  lifetime exposure to adversity in, 523, 523*f*
  marriage of same-sex couples in, 486
  math achievement scores in, 329*f*, 395*f*
  poverty rate in, 65*f*
  reproductive technologies in, 53
  retirement programs in, 636
  smell sense of newborn in, 108
Fraternal twins, 45. *See also* Twins
Free radicals, 440, 511
Freestanding birth centers, 95
Freud, Sigmund, 14–15, 184
  on attachment, 196
  on moral development, 267–268
  on psychosexual stages of development, 14–15, 15*t*, 258, 368
Friendships
  in adolescence, 398, 411, 417, 422–426, 428
  in early adulthood, 476, 482–484, 493, 496
  in early childhood, 265, 276

in late adulthood, 620–621, 621*f*, 630–631
in middle adulthood, 558–559
in middle childhood, 344, 346–347, 349
online. *See* Online friendships
Frontal lobes, 120, 120*f*, 175, 574
Full inclusion of students with learning difficulties, 327
Functional age, 570
Functional magnetic resonance imaging of brain, 119, 119*t*, 120*f*
  in adolescence, 373
  in autism, 243
  in childhood maltreatment, 286
  in early adulthood, 456
  in early childhood, 217
  in exercise, 448
  in Experience Corps volunteers, 638
  in infancy, 120*f*
  language-specific areas in, 394
  in late adulthood, 574, 603
  lateralization in, 121
  in middle adulthood, 527
  in multitasking, 400
Functional play, 264*t*
Funerals, 668, 669, 671

G

Gabapentin in menopause, 513
Games, 249, 301. *See also* Play
Gametes, 44–45, 52, 53
Gardner, Howard, 316–317, 317*t*, 329
Gay people. *See* Lesbian, gay, and bisexual people
Gender constancy, 279
Gender contentedness, 351
Gender differences. *See* Sex differences
Gender dysphoria, 281, 351
Gender identity
  in adolescence, 428
  in early childhood, 279–280, 281
  feminine traits in. *See* Feminine traits
  masculine traits in. *See* Masculine traits
  in middle adulthood, 541, 546–548
  in middle childhood, 350–351
  of transgender children, 280, 281
Gender roles
  in adolescence, 423, 428
  in caring for aging parents, 555, 556
  in early adulthood, 452, 463, 479, 486–487, 490–491, 495–496
  in early childhood, 264, 273, 276, 277, 278, 279, 280
  in employment opportunities, 463, 464, 499–500, 561
  in lesbian and gay partnerships, 278, 452, 487
  in marital relationships, 356–357, 486–487, 488, 490–491, 495–496, 500–501, 629
  in maternal employment, 356, 357, 463, 490
  in middle adulthood, 532, 543, 545, 555, 556, 558, 561
  in middle childhood, 350, 351
  in partner abuse, 489
  stereotypes on. *See* Gender stereotypes
  in toddler play, 208

of transgender children, 281
in widowhood, 629
Gender-salience filter, 279, 280*f*
Gender schema theory, 276, 279–280, 280*f*
Gender stereotypes
  in adolescence, 395
  in early adulthood, 463*t*, 463–465, 499–500
  in early childhood, 273, 276–280, 280*f*
  in infancy and toddlerhood, 208
  in middle adulthood, 513, 523–524, 532, 541, 561
  in middle childhood, 301, 338, 340, 350, 351
Gender typicality, 351
Gender typing
  in early childhood, 276–280, 281
  in infancy and toddlerhood, 208
  in middle childhood, 350–351
  stereotypes in. *See* Gender stereotypes
Gene–environment correlation, 68–69, 69*f*, 70, 193
Gene–environment interaction, 68, 68*f*, 70, 194, 201
Gene–gene interactions, 46–50
"Generation me," 471
Generation X, 452*f*
Generativity
  in early adulthood, 476, 538
  in late adulthood, 610
  in middle adulthood, 15*t*, 538–541, 542, 543
Generic utterances, 277–278
Genes, 44–51
  dominant and recessive, 46–48, 47*t*, 48*f*
  expression of, 44, 70–72
  Human Genome Project on, 54
  methylation of, 70, 71, 71*f*, 85, 89, 590
  mutations of, 49–50. *See also* Mutations
  programmed effects of, 438
Gene therapy, 55
Genetic code, 44
Genetic engineering, 54
Genetic factors, 44–51
  in aggression, 431
  in aging, 438–440, 585
  in alcoholism, 449
  in Alzheimer's disease, 589, 590
  in anorexia nervosa, 378
  in antisocial behavior, 67
  in attachment security, 201
  in attention-deficit hyperactivity disorder, 309
  in behavioral genetics, 66
  in cancer, 49, 55, 516, 517, 518
  in cognitive changes of late adulthood, 601
  counseling on, 51–52, 56
  in depression, 67, 427, 428
  in diabetes, 586
  dominant and recessive genes in, 46–48, 47*t*, 48*f*
  in empathy, 268
  and environment correlation, 68–69, 69*f*, 70, 193
  and environment interactions, 68, 68*f*, 70, 194, 201

in epigenesis, 70–72
in executive function, 307–308
in glaucoma, 509
in hand preference, 218
heritability estimates on, 67–68
in intelligence and IQ, 67–68, 68*f*, 318
in life expectancy, 438, 440, 570, 571, 572, 573
in multiple offspring, 45–46
in myopia, 298
in obesity, 295, 446
in osteoporosis, 519
in patterns of inheritance, 46–50
in personality traits, 67, 68, 193, 548, 549
in physical growth, 127, 217, 219
in pubertal changes, 368, 373
and relative influence of nature and nurture, 7, 27*t*, 66–72, 318–321
and resilience, 10, 11
in rheumatoid arthritis, 586
in sexual orientation, 382
in spatial abilities, 397
in substance abuse, 386, 387
in temperament, 68, 192, 193–195, 194*f*, 201
and teratogen impact, 81
in vascular dementia, 591
in X-linked inheritance, 48–49, 49*f*
Genetic markers, 51–52
Genitals
  herpes simplex virus infection of, 87*t*, 88
  in menopause, 512
  prenatal development of, 82, 82*f*, 83, 84
  in puberty, 371, 372, 372*t*
Genital stage of psychosexual development, 15*t*, 368
Genocide, epigenetic transmission of maternal stress in, 71, 71*f*
Genomewide testing methods, 52
Genomic imprinting, 49
Genotype, 43, 194, 194*f*
German measles (rubella), 86–87, 87*t*, 221
Germany
  adolescent birth rate in, 384*f*
  attachment patterns in, 199, 199*f*
  caregiving roles of parents in, 203, 204
  child imitation of adult behaviors in, 167
  control sense and life satisfaction in, 616
  family size in, 490
  housework hours and gender roles in, 487*f*
  infant mortality rate in, 102*f*
  life expectancy in, 571*f*
  math achievement scores in, 329*f*
  obesity in, 295
  parental leave time from employment in, 103
  parent–infant interactions in, 189, 203
  personality traits in, 548
  religious involvement in, 418, 614
  retirement programs in, 636
  self-recognition by toddlers in, 207–208, 208*f*
  vocational education in, 465

Germinal period in prenatal development, 76f, 76–78, 77t
teratogen exposure in, 81, 82f
Germline mutations, 49, 516
Gerotranscendence, 611
Gesell, Arnold, 14
Gestures
and emotional expression, 185
preverbal, 176
in sign language, 174, 176
Gifted children and prodigies, 30, 328–329
Gilligan, Carol, 415
Glass ceiling in employment opportunities, 561
Glaucoma, 509
Glial cells, 79, 118
Global identity, 473
Globalization, 473
Glucose blood levels
in Alzheimer's disease, 586, 590
calorie restriction affecting, 511
in diabetes, 586
Goal-directed behavior of infants, 152, 162–163
Golden Rule, 414
Good boy–good girl orientation in moral development, 414
Goodness-of-fit model on child rearing, 195, 209
Government policy. See Public policy
Graduation rates for high schools, 402
Grammatical development
in early childhood, 251–252
in infancy and toddlerhood, 174, 175, 177
in middle childhood, 322
Grandparents, 552–554, 632
in extended family, 62–63, 553
as indirect influence, 57
of resilient children, 11, 553
Grasping of infants and newborn, 136–137, 137f, 154
as reflex, 101, 101t, 102
Gratification, delayed, 209
Great Britain
hospice care in, 658
housework hours and gender roles in, 487f
religious involvement in, 418, 615
smoking cessation in, 449
Greece
adolescent suicide in, 428
departure from parental home in, 551
infant mortality rate in, 102f
life expectancy in, 571f
math achievement scores in, 329f
menopause in, 514
obesity in, 295
poverty rate in, 65f
Green House model of nursing-home care, 624–625
GR gene methylation, 71, 71f
Grief, 665–666
complicated, 665, 670
in suicide, 429, 666
Gross-motor development
in early childhood, 223, 223t, 225
in infancy and toddlerhood, 134, 134t
in middle childhood, 299–300, 301

Groups
in-groups and out-groups, 344–345
intelligence tests administered in, 315
peer. See Peer groups
prenatal health care in, 91
rape therapy sessions in, 454–455
in schools, 326, 327, 401
Growing pains in middle childhood, 294
Growth, physical. See Physical development
Growth hormone, 219, 369, 440
Growth norms, 117
Growth spurts
in infancy and toddlerhood, 116–117
in puberty, 369, 370f, 371, 372, 372t, 378
in vocabulary, 177
Guatemala
attention style in, 167
childbirth practices in, 96
communication style in, 319
cosleeping of parents and infants in, 126
gender identity in, 547
observational learning in, 237
Guidance Study, 35
Guided participation, 236
Guilt
in bulimia nervosa, 379
in early childhood, 15t, 258, 262, 267, 268
in infancy and toddlerhood, 188, 189
in middle childhood, 341
in suicidal loss, 666
Gun control legislation, 429, 444
Gusii of Kenya, 136, 200

H

Habituation, 131–132, 132f
and attention, 161
and categorization, 163
and discrimination of human and monkey faces, 139, 139f
and intelligence, 169
and operant conditioning of infants, 162
in prenatal development, 81, 131
and violation-of-expectation method, 153, 153f
Hair
inheritance of characteristics, 46, 48f
in physical changes of aging, 441t, 578, 579
in puberty, 369, 370, 371, 372, 372t
Haiti, 571
Hall, G. Stanley, 14
Hand preference, 121, 217–218
Happiness
in infancy and toddlerhood, 185
in marital relationships, 487t, 487–489, 495, 550
in middle adulthood, 546, 547, 550
in middle childhood, 342
in retirement, 563
in singlehood lifestyle, 493
Hardiness, as personal quality, 522–523
Hausa of Nigeria, 306

Head injuries, 299, 589
Head Start programs, 173, 246–247
Health
in adolescence, 372, 373, 378–387
in early adulthood, 443, 444–456
in early childhood, 219–222
in infancy and toddlerhood, 127–130
international comparisons of indicators on, 64, 64t
in late adulthood, 572, 573, 581–594, 601, 617, 618–619, 626, 635, 636, 638
in middle adulthood, 514–520, 546
in middle childhood, 295–299
in prenatal period, 91–92
and telomere length, 439
Health care
in Alzheimer's disease, 590
drug therapy in. See Drug therapy
in early childhood, 220, 221
at end of life, 658, 659, 660–664
fetal medicine in, 53–55, 54t
immunizations in, 87, 220, 221
in late adulthood, 579–580, 581–582, 586, 591–594, 600, 627, 639
in middle adulthood, 512–513, 519
for parents and newborn, 102–103
prenatal, 91–92. See also Prenatal health care
reproductive technologies in. See Reproductive technologies
universal access to, 91, 103
Health-care proxy, 662
Health insurance
for adolescents, 91, 385
for children, 64, 221, 295
hospice benefits in, 659
lack of, 64, 295, 444, 445, 516
for older adults, 65
public policies on, 64, 65
in retirement planning, 563
Healthy Families America, 287
Hearing
in early adulthood, 441t
in infancy and toddlerhood, 109, 121, 138–140, 143–144, 174, 176
in late adulthood, 574f, 575–576, 597
in middle adulthood, 509
in middle childhood, 298
in physical changes of aging, 441t
in prenatal development, 81, 99, 99f, 109
Hearing aids, 509
Heart, 440–442, 518–519, 576. See also Cardiovascular system
Heart attack, 442, 518–519
Heart rate
age-related changes in, 442
in arrhythmias, 518, 646
fetal, 80, 81, 96–97
in shyness and sociability, 192
Height
in early adulthood, 441t
in early childhood, 216f, 216–217, 219
in infancy and toddlerhood, 116–117
in late adulthood, 578
in middle adulthood, 510
in middle childhood, 294, 294f

in physical changes of aging, 441t
in puberty, 369, 371, 372t
Heinz dilemma, 413–414, 415
Helicopter parenting, 475
Helmet use, 299
Helpfulness. See Prosocial behavior
Helplessness, learned. See Learned helplessness
Hemispheres, cerebral. See Cerebral hemispheres
Hemophilia, 47t, 48, 55
Heredity. See also Genetic factors
and heritability estimates. See Heritability estimates
and relative influence of nature and nurture, 7, 27t, 66–72
stability of characteristics in, 7
Heritability estimates, 67–68
of intelligence, 67–68, 318
of longevity, 438
of myopia, 298
of personality traits, 67, 193
of temperament, 192, 193
Heroin, 83, 386
Herpes simplex virus, 87t, 88
Heterozygous genes, 46
Hidden objects, searching for, in sensorimotor stage, 151, 152, 153, 154
Hierarchical classification in preoperational stage, 230, 230f
Hierarchical communication style, 319–320
High-density lipoproteins, 448
High/Scope Perry Preschool Project, 247
High-stakes testing movement, 394
Hip fractures, 519
Hippocampus, 164
in adolescence, 373, 400
in early childhood, 218f, 218–219, 287
in late adulthood, 574, 583
in middle childhood, 308
Hispanics
academic achievement of, 326, 399, 401
adolescent initiation ceremonies of, 375
aging parents of, 555, 556, 623
anorexia nervosa of, 378
bilingual, 323
body image of, 377
as caregivers of older adults with dementia, 593
child-rearing styles of, 284
communication style of, 319
departure from parental home, 485
discipline and punishment of children, 270
discrimination in career opportunities, 500, 500f
divorce of, 353
extended-family households of, 62, 63, 623
familism ideal of, 63, 422
father–child relationships of, 204, 284
food insecurity of, 129
friendships of, 423
gay relationships of, 453
gender roles and housework hours of, 487

gender typing of, 278
glaucoma of, 509
grandparents as caregivers of, 554
health problems in late adulthood, 581
high school dropout rates for, 402, 402f
HIV infection of, 453
intelligence quotient of, 318, 320
late adulthood of, 581
long-term care of older adults, 593
Mexican American. *See* Mexican Americans
moral reasoning of, 418
overweight and obese, 295, 445
part-time employment in adolescence, 401
poverty of, 59
puberty of, 375, 377
religiosity of, 472, 615
school transitions of, 397
stereotype threat affecting, 320
suicide rate of, 428
teacher–student interaction of, 326
Historical development of child development theories, 12–19
History-graded influences, 9–10
HIV infection and AIDS. *See* AIDS
Hmong immigrants, 32, 235
Home births, 95, 96
Home environment
  for aging in place, 623
  assisted-living facilities as, 593–594
  assistive technology and devices in, 579–580
  attachment assessment in, 198
  caring for aging parent in, 557
  chaos in, 25
  childbirth in, 95, 96
  and cognitive development, 244, 245–246
  communication style in, 319–320
  death and dying in, 657, 658
  hospice care in, 658
  and intelligence, 68, 170–171
  in late adulthood, 623–625
  leaving parental home, 471, 484–485, 547, 549, 551
  marital roles in, 486–487, 487f
  and mathematics skills, 245
  person–environment fit in, 616, 618, 623, 624, 625
  and reading readiness, 244, 244f
  in residential communities for older adults, 623–624
  of resilient children, 11
  and return to parental home, 484
Homelessness, 59
Home Observation for Measurement of the Environment (HOME), 170–171, 202, 245–246
Home visitation program
  in Healthy Families America, 287
  in Infant Health and Development Program, 100
  in Nurse–Family Partnership, 90, 287, 385
  for parental care, 557
Homicide rates, 444, 444f
Homophobia, 383
Homosexuals. *See* Lesbian, gay, and bisexual people
Homozygous genes, 46

Hong Kong, 329f, 622
Hope in dying people, 656
Hopi Indians, 258
Hormones
  in early adulthood, 440, 443
  in early childhood, 219
  in middle adulthood, 510, 512–513, 519
  in new parents, 111
  prenatal exposure to, 277, 281, 302, 382
  in puberty, 369, 377, 380, 426, 427
  in stress, 89. *See also* Stress hormones
Hospice programs, 657, 658–660
Hospitals
  abandonment of older adults at, 633
  childbirth in, 95, 96, 97
  death and dying in, 657–658, 662
  hospice care in, 658
Hot flashes in menopause, 512, 513, 514
Housework and household chores, 357, 486–487, 487f, 488, 500–501
5-HTTLPR gene, 194f, 194–195, 201, 428
Human Genome Project, 54
Human immunodeficiency virus (HIV) infections. *See* AIDS
Humor, and language development, 322
Hungary, 102f, 329f
Hunger, infant crying in, 105
Huntington's disease, 47t, 48
Hyperactivity, in attention-deficit hyperactivity disorder, 309
Hypertension, 441
  and dietary fat, 447, 447f
  hostility as risk for, 519, 520
  low birth weight as risk for, 88, 88f
  in pregnancy, 91
Hypodermis, 509
Hypotheses, 26, 388, 389
Hypothetico-deductive reasoning in formal operational stage, 388, 389, 389f

I

Iceland
  housework hours and gender roles in, 487, 487f
  infant mortality rate in, 102f
  marriage of same-sex couples in, 486
  math achievement scores in, 329f, 395, 395f
Id, 14–15
Idealism in adolescence, 393
Ideal reciprocity, 414, 415, 420
Ideal self, 337, 418
Identical twins, 46. *See also* Twins
Identity
  in adolescence, 15t, 382–383, 408, 409–413, 416, 418, 419, 425
  in early adulthood, 470–471, 473, 474, 476
  in emerging adulthood, 470–471, 474
  gender-related. *See* Gender identity
  in middle adulthood, 541–542, 559
  sequential design of research on, 36

Imaginary audience in adolescence, 392
Imaginary companions, 228
Imitation
  cultural variations in, 167
  deferred, 153, 154–155, 155f
  emotional self-regulation in, 189
  give-and-take interactions and language development in, 176
  infant memory of, 154–155, 155f, 163
  inferred, 155
  and intentional behavior of infants, 152
  mirror neurons in, 132
  by newborn, 132–133, 133f
  social learning theory on, 17
  understanding and responding to emotions of others in, 188
Immigrants
  academic achievement of, 32
  acculturative stress of, 412, 421
  adaptation of, 32
  bilingual development of, 323
  child-rearing styles of, 421
  feeding practices and nutrition of, 296
  identity development of, 412
  intelligence definition of, 316
  overweight and obese, 445
  parenting practices of, 421
  prejudice against, 32, 418
Immortality, symbolic, 539, 552, 652
Immune system, 88
  in early adulthood, 439, 440, 441t, 443, 448, 455
  in early childhood, 220
  in late adulthood, 573, 574, 577
  in middle adulthood, 511
  in middle childhood, 298
  in physical changes of aging, 441t
Immunization, 87, 220, 221
Implantation of blastocyst, 76f, 77–78
Implicit memory, 239, 400, 596
Impotence, 449, 513
Imprinting, 21, 196
  genomic, 49
Impulsivity
  in adolescence, 373f, 373–374, 379, 386, 387f, 650
  in early childhood, 266, 268, 273, 274, 276, 283
  in middle childhood, 299, 308, 309, 310, 348
  in prenatal teratogen exposure, 84, 308
Incest, 359
Inclusive classrooms, 326–328
Income
  and retirement decisions, 635
  and socioeconomic status, 58
Incomplete dominance in genetic inheritance, 48
Incredible Years program, 275
Independence, as cultural value, 62, 126
  art education in, 226
  attachment patterns of infants in, 199
  individualism in, 63
  infant caregiving in, 200
  late adulthood in, 616
  moral development in, 417

scaffolding in, 235
self-concept in, 337
Independence–ignore script, 616
Independent living
  in late adulthood, 616, 623
  in leaving parental home, 471, 484–485
Independent variable in experimental research design, 33
India
  caregiving roles of parents in, 203
  death concept and attitudes in, 656
  immigrant youths from, 32
  maps drawn by children in, 305f, 305–306
  moral development in, 417
  parent–infant interactions in, 203
  play and peer sociability in, 265
  religious involvement in, 614
  romantic relationships in, 482
  self-recognition by toddlers in, 207–208, 208f
Individualism, as cultural value, 63
  childbearing decisions in, 490
  control sense in, 579
  departure from parental home in, 485
  divorce in, 496
  generativity in, 541
  infant sleeping arrangements in, 126
  moral development in, 417
  peer sociability in, 265
  romantic relationships in, 481
  youthful self-image in, 541
Indonesia, 168, 669
Inductive discipline, 267–268
Inductive reasoning, 526, 526f, 602
Industry versus inferiority in middle childhood, 15t, 336
Inequality, understanding of, in middle childhood, 344–345
Infancy and toddlerhood (birth to 2 years old), 8t, 114–211
  adjustment of parents in, 111, 490–491
  amnesia about events in, 163, 164–165
  arousal states in, 104–108, 105t, 125, 125f
  attachment in, 5, 22, 196–206. *See also* Attachment
  attention in, 141–142, 161–162, 176, 189, 207
  autonomy versus shame and doubt in, 15t, 184
  behavioral assessment in, 110
  body composition in, 117
  body proportions in, 116f, 117
  body size in, 116f, 116–117
  brain development in, 117–125
  breastfeeding and bottle-feeding in, 127–128
  categorical self in, 208
  categorization in, 163f, 163–165, 166, 169
  child-care settings in, 171f, 171–173, 202–203
  classical conditioning in, 16, 130f, 130–131
  cognitive development in, 17, 18t, 19, 148–181, 158t, 186
  core knowledge in, 158–159
  cosleeping arrangements in, 126

Infancy and toddlerhood (*continued*)
  crying in, 104, 105*t*, 105–108
  depression of parent in, 187
  deprivation and enrichment in, 121–123
  Down syndrome in, 50
  early intervention programs in, 123–124, 172–173
  emotional development in, 184–190
  empathy in, 105
  exploration in. *See* Exploration in infancy and toddlerhood
  fear in, 16, 131, 186
  growth spurts in, 116–117
  habituation and recovery in, 131–132, 132*f*, 153, 153*f*, 161, 162
  hand preference in, 217–218
  heredity affecting growth in, 127
  home environment in, 170–171
  imitation in, 132–133, 133*f*, 152, 153, 154–155, 155*f*, 167, 188
  individual and group differences in, 117, 167–173, 177–178
  information processing in, 160–166
  intelligence tests in, 167–169
  language development in, 109, 120, 121, 138–140, 144, 155–156, 158, 165, 170, 173–179, 208
  learning capacities in, 130–133, 138–139, 157
  linguistic knowledge in, 158
  maltreatment in, 285
  mathematics in, 158–159, 159*f*
  memory in, 131–132, 154–155, 162*f*, 162–163, 166
  mental representations in, 151*t*, 152–153, 154–156, 158
  milestones of development in, 134*t*, 158*t*, 175*t*, 212–213
  mortality in. *See* Infant mortality
  motor development in, 110, 133–137, 141
  newborn infants. *See* Newborns
  novelty preference in, 131, 132*f*, 139
  numerical knowledge in, 158–159, 159*f*
  nutrition in, 127–129
  object permanence in, 152, 153*f*, 153–154, 169
  observational research on behavior in, 29
  operant conditioning in, 131, 162, 162*f*, 163, 163*f*
  pain sensitivity in, 108
  parent relationships in. *See* Parent–infant relationships
  perceptual development in, 137–146
  personality in, 184
  physical development in, 114–147
  physical knowledge in, 158
  plasticity of brain in, 121, 122
  play in, 168, 176
  preterm infants, 97–100. *See also* Preterm infants
  problem solving in, 137, 152–153, 155
  psychological knowledge in, 158
  reflexes in, 101*t*, 101–104, 151, 151*t*
  self-awareness in, 188–189, 206–208
  self-control in, 208–209
  as sensitive period of development, 121–124
  sensorimotor stage in, 18*t*, 150, 151–153. *See also* Sensorimotor stage
  sensory system in, 108–110
  sleep in, 83, 104–105, 105*t*, 106, 125, 125*f*, 126
  social referencing in, 188
  sociocultural theory on, 166–167
  statistical learning capacity in, 138–140
  sudden infant death syndrome in, 105, 106, 126, 136, 666
  symbolic understanding in, 155–156
  television viewing in, 157
  temperament in, 186, 190–195
  trust versus mistrust in, 15*t*, 184
  visual impairment in, 50, 121
Infant Health and Development Program, 100
Infantile amnesia, 163, 164–165
Infant mortality, 102, 103
  in cosleeping of parents and infants, 126
  in home delivery, 96
  international differences in, 64*t*, 102, 102*f*
  in malnutrition, 129
  in Rh factor incompatibility, 89
  sex differences in, 117
  of small-for-date infants, 98
  in sudden infant death syndrome, 105, 106, 126, 136
Infant–parent relationships. *See* Parent–infant relationships
Infectious diseases
  AIDS. *See* AIDS
  breastfeeding in protection against, 127
  in early adulthood, immune response to, 443
  in early childhood, 220–221
  immunization against, 87, 220, 221
  in middle childhood, 298
  in pregnancy, 86–88, 87*t*
  sexually transmitted, 383–384, 453
Inferences
  in early childhood, 242
  in middle childhood, 304, 306, 312
Inferiority versus industry in middle childhood, 15*t*, 336
Inferred imitation, 155
Infertility
  adoption in, 55
  childlessness in, 495
  in prenatal DES exposure, 83
  reproductive technologies in, 45, 45*t*, 52–53
Infinitive phrases in language development, 322
Inflammation, calorie restriction affecting, 511
Information-gathering cognitive style in identity development, 410
Information-loss view of information processing speed, 527
Information processing, 19–20, 27*t*
  in academic learning, 313–314
  in adolescence, 390–392
  and analytical intelligence, 316
  attention in, 160, 161–162, 237–238, 390, 528–529
  in autism, 243
  automatic, 161
  capacity of working memory in, 161, 238, 308, 310, 529
  categorization in, 163–165
  and cognitive self-regulation, 312–323, 390
  compensatory strategies in, 528, 529
  and concrete operational thought, 306–307
  in continuous performance tasks, 528
  creativity in, 530–531
  in early adulthood, 456
  in early childhood, 236–245
  executive function in, 160*f*, 161, 236–239, 307–310, 528–529
  expertise in, 530
  flowcharts on, 19, 20*f*
  and fluid intelligence, 525, 526, 527
  and gender schema theory, 279
  general model of, 160*f*, 160–161
  in infancy and toddlerhood, 160–166
  and language development, 174–175, 252
  and literacy development, 242–244
  mathematical reasoning in, 244–245, 313–314
  memory in, 160–161, 162–163, 239–241, 308, 310–311, 390, 529–530
  mental strategies in, 160, 390
  in middle adulthood, 526, 526*f*, 527–531
  in middle childhood, 300, 307–314
  in motor performance, 300
  problem solving in, 530
  scientific reasoning in, 391*f*, 391–392
  sensory register in, 160, 160*f*, 161
  speed of. *See* Speed of information processing
  and theory of mind, 241–242, 311–312
Informed consent of research participants, 38, 38*t*
In-groups, 344
  favoritism toward, 278, 344, 345
Inhalant drug use in adolescence, 386
Inheritance, 46–50. *See also* Genetic factors
  of chromosomal abnormalities, 50–51
  dominant–recessive, 46–48, 47*t*, 48*f*
  polygenic, 50, 66
  X-linked, 48–49, 49*f*
Inhibition
  in adolescence, 390
  in attention-deficit hyperactivity disorder, 309
  in early childhood, 237, 238*f*, 242, 261
  in infancy and toddlerhood, 191, 192, 208–209
  in late adulthood, 594
  in middle adulthood, 528–529
  in middle childhood, 307, 308, 309
Initiation ceremonies in adolescence, 375
Initiative in early childhood, 15*t*, 258, 260
Injuries, unintentional, 646
  in adolescence, 221, 650
  in early adulthood, 444*f*
  in early childhood, 221–222
  in late adulthood, 585, 586–587
  in middle adulthood, 515, 516*f*
  in middle childhood, 298–299, 299*f*
Innate knowledge, 158–159
Inner speech, 234
Insecure–avoidant attachment, 198
Insecure–resistant attachment, 198
Insomnia in late adulthood, 577
Institutionalization
  attachment security in, 199–200
  early deprivation in, 121, 123, 123*f*
  motor development in, 136
  stress in, 123
  temperament development in, 193
Institutional review boards, 38
Instrumental activities of daily living, 573
Instrumental aggression, 272
Instrumental purpose orientation in moral development, 414, 420
Insulin, 296, 439, 511, 590
Insurance, health. *See* Health insurance
Integration of schools, 327
Integrity versus despair in late adulthood, 15*t*, 610
Intellectual development. *See* Cognitive development
Intellectual disabilities
  of aging parents, 557
  classroom inclusion in, 327
  in dementia, 587–591
  in Down syndrome, 50
  in fragile X syndrome, 49
  handedness in, 218
  infectious diseases during pregnancy associated with, 87*t*
  in phenylketonuria, 46
  in Prader-Willi syndrome, 49
  in sex chromosome abnormalities, 51
  sex differences in, 48
Intelligence
  analytical, 316, 316*f*
  creative, 316, 316*f*, 328
  crystallized, 525–526, 526*f*, 527, 527*f*, 594–595
  definitions of, 314–317
  dynamic assessment of, 320–321
  emotional, 317, 458
  environmental influences on, 67–68, 70, 123, 169–173, 318–321
  fluid, 525–526, 527, 527*f*, 594–595
  gene–environment interactions in, 68, 68*f*, 318
  general (g), 314–315, 316
  genetic factors in, 67–68, 68*f*, 318
  heritability estimates on, 67–68, 318
  home environment affecting, 68, 170–171
  measurement of, 167–169, 314–321
  multiple intelligences theory of Gardner, 316–317, 317*t*, 329
  practical, 316, 316*f*, 530
  triarchic theory of, 316, 316*f*, 530
Intelligence quotient (IQ), 169, 314–321
  and academic achievement, 169, 318, 327
  in attention-deficit hyperactivity disorder, 309

Subject Index SI-19

bell-shaped distribution of, 169, 169*f*
and early intervention programs, 172–173, 246, 247
environmental influences on, 169–173, 318–321
ethnic and racial differences in, 318–321
Flynn effect in, 319
genetic influences on, 318
of gifted children, 328
heritability estimates of, 318
home environment affecting, 170–171
in learning disabilities, 327
in middle childhood, 314–315
normal distribution of, 169, 169*f*
nutrition affecting, 295
predictive value of, 169, 318
secular trends in, 319
and socioeconomic status, 170, 172–173, 245, 318, 320
in twins, 318
Intelligence tests, 314–321
in attention-deficit hyperactivity disorder, 309
of crystallized intelligence, 525
cultural bias in, 245, 315, 318–321
dynamic assessment in, 320–321
early deprivation affecting scores on, 123, 123*f*
factor analysis of, 315
of fluid intelligence, 525
group administered, 315
historical development of, 14
individually administered, 315
for infants, 167–169
intelligence quotient derived from. *See* Intelligence quotient
in middle childhood, 314–321
normal distribution of scores, 169, 169*f*
predictive value of, 169, 318
socioeconomic status affecting performance on, 245, 295, 318, 320
standardization of, 169
stereotype threat affecting performance on, 320, 321
verbal and nonverbal components of, 245, 315, 315*f*, 320
Intensive care units, dying in, 657, 658
Intentional behavior of infants, 152
and sustained attention, 161–162
Interactional synchrony, and attachment security, 200
Interactionist theories of language development, 174–175, 178
Intercourse. *See also* Sexual attitudes and behavior
contraceptive use in, 381*f*, 381–382
first, age at time of, 380, 381, 381*f*
frequency of, 452, 453, 515, 515*f*, 583–584, 584*f*
sexual dysfunction in, 449, 513
Interdependence, as cultural value, 337, 622
academic achievement in, 330
autobiographical memory in, 241
autonomy of adolescents in, 421
collectivism in, 63, 622
coresidence of aging parents and children in, 555

cosleeping of parent and infant in, 126
identity development in, 412
infant-rearing practices in, 186
infant sleeping arrangements in, 126
late adulthood in, 622
moral development in, 417
older parent–adult child relationships in, 632
peer sociability in, 265
psychological well-being in, 545
romantic relationships in, 481–482
same-sex peer relations in, 278
scaffolding in, 235
self-concept in, 337
self-conscious emotions in, 189, 262
social relationships of older adults in, 622
time spent with family in, 422
Intergenerational patterns
in adolescent parenthood, 384–385
in attachment, 199, 202
in corporal punishment, 269
in divorce, 495
in family violence, 633–634
in intelligence quotient, 318
in partner abuse, 488–489
in sexual abuse, 360
social clock in, 478
Intermodal perception, 143–144, 207, 576
Internalizing difficulties, 57, 60, 123, 192, 206, 341
Internal working models of attachment, 197, 202, 480
Internet use
in bereavement, 669
communication with friends in, 423–424, 424*f*
cyberbullying in, 349
dating services in, 451, 627, 627*f*
hospice services in, 660
in late adulthood, 605, 627, 627*f*, 632
media multitasking in, 400
online friendships in. *See* Online friendships
parent regulation of, 275
personal ads placed in, 627, 627*f*
safety in, 424
sex education in, 380
sexual abuse of children in, 358
social networking sites in. *See* Social networking sites
Interpersonal intelligence, 317, 317*t*
Interviews
clinical, 18, 28*t*, 29, 413
structured, 28*t*, 30
suggestibility of children in, 361
Intimacy, 36
in adolescence, 410, 422, 424, 425, 426
in early adulthood, 15*t*, 451, 476–484, 489, 493, 494
in late adulthood, 583, 584, 611, 626, 628, 630, 631
in middle adulthood, 550
Intrapersonal intelligence, 317, 317*t*
Inuit, 126, 319, 580–581
Invariant features in differentiation theory, 144, 145
Investigative personality, vocational choice in, 462

Invisible displacement in sensorimotor stage, 153
In vitro fertilization, 45, 45*t*, 52, 53, 54*t*
Involuntary euthanasia, 660*t*, 664
Involvement in child rearing, 282, 282*t*, 283
in uninvolved style, 282*t*, 283, 398
Iranian orphans, 136
Iraq, 359
Ireland
adolescent suicide in, 428
housework hours and gender roles in, 487*f*
infant mortality rate in, 102*f*
life expectancy in, 571*f*
math achievement scores in, 329*f*
obesity in, 295
poverty rate in, 65*f*
Irish-American storytelling practices, 259
Iron deficiency, 378
Irreversibility of thought in preoperational stage, 230
Irritability
child-rearing practices in, 193, 195, 201
and effortful control, 193
genetic factors in, 193, 201
risk for childhood injuries in, 221
temperament in, 190, 191, 191*t*, 193, 195
Isolation
in early adulthood, versus intimacy, 15*t*, 476
of gifted children, 329
of lesbian and gay youths, 382
in middle childhood, 346
Isotretinoin, 83
Israel
adolescent birth rate in, 384*f*
adolescent propositional thought in, 390
attachment patterns and romantic relationships in, 480
caregiving roles of parents in, 203
death concept in, 649, 652
infant mortality rate in, 102*f*
life expectancy in, 571*f*
math achievement scores in, 329*f*
obesity in, 295
parent–infant interactions in, 203
sleep patterns of infants in, 125
stranger anxiety of infants in, 186
Italy
adolescent suicide in, 428
caregiving roles of parents in, 203
departure from parental home in, 471, 551
family size in, 490
infant mortality rate in, 102*f*
life expectancy in, 571*f*
math achievement scores in, 329*f*, 395*f*
parent–infant interactions in, 203
personality traits in, 548
poverty rate in, 65*f*
reproductive technologies in, 53

J

Jamaican West Indian infants, 136
Japan
academic achievement in, 329, 329*f*, 330, 337

academic and vocational tracks in, 401
adolescent suicide in, 428
aging parents in, 555, 557
attachment patterns in, 199, 199*f*
autobiographical memory of older adults from, 597
calorie-restricted diet in, 511
caregiving roles of parents in, 203, 204
college education in, 460
cosleeping of parents and infants in, 126
death definition in, 647
drawing skills of children in, 226
emotional self-regulation in, 189, 193
family size in, 490
immigrant youths from, 32
infant mortality rate in, 102*f*
language development in, 178, 250
late adulthood in, 623
life expectancy in, 571, 571*f*
mate selection in, 479
menopause in, 514
midlife emotional and social development in, 538, 545
moral development in, 417
parent–infant interactions in, 203
personality traits in, 548
prenatal health care in, 91
psychological well-being in, 545
respect for older adults in, 581
romantic relationships in, 481–482
self-conscious emotions in, 189
self-esteem in, 337
temperament of children in, 193
terminally ill patients in, 655
vascular dementia in, 591
vocational life and cognitive development in, 531
Jarara of South America, 95
Jealousy
in avoidant attachment, 480
in friendships, 347, 424
in marital relationships, 488, 495, 496
in resistant attachment, 480
in sibling relationships, 111, 205
Jewish beliefs, 375, 669
Jimi Valley (Papua New Guinea), 225
Job. *See* Employment
Joint attention of infant and caregiver, 176, 207
Joint custody of children, 355
Judaism, 375, 669
Justice, and moral reasoning, 271, 272, 343, 415, 417
Juvenile delinquency, 429–432

K

Kaddish prayer, 669
Kalash people of Pakistan, 669
Kangaroo care for preterm infants, 99–100
Kanreki ritual, 580–581
Karakia ceremony, 656
Karyotype, 44*f*
Keeping Ourselves Safe, 360

Subject Index

Kenya
- intelligence in, 316, 319
- modernization in, 311, 319
- mother–infant relationship and attachment security in, 200
- motor development of infants in, 110, 136

Kibbutzim, 186, 649
Kindergarten, 246–248
Kinesthetic intelligence, 317*t*, 329
Kinkeeper role, 552, 553, 628, 629
Kinship studies, 67, 318, 438
- twins in, 67. *See also* Twins

Kipsigis of Kenya, 110, 136
Klinefelter syndrome, 51
Knowledge
- in adolescence, 390
- in early adulthood, 458–459
- in infancy and toddlerhood, 158–159, 159*f*
- in late adulthood, 600–601, 612
- metacognitive. *See* Metacognition
- in middle adulthood, 529, 530
- in middle childhood, 311, 313, 320

Kohlberg, Lawrence, 413–415, 417, 420
Korea
- academic achievement in, 329, 329*f*, 330
- aging parents in, 553, 555, 557
- categorization skills in, 165
- college education in, 460
- cosleeping of parents and infants in, 126
- drawing skills of children in, 226
- immigrant youths from, 32
- infant mortality rate in, 102*f*
- language development in, 178, 250
- life expectancy in, 571*f*
- math achievement scores in, 329*f*, 395*f*
- moral development in, 344
- personality traits in, 548
- psychological well-being in, 545
- terminally ill patients in, 655

Korean Americans, 557, 655
Kübler-Ross, Elisabeth, 653
!Kung of Botswana, 126
Kwashiorkor, 129

L

Labor and delivery, 92–97. *See also* Childbirth
Laboratory experiments, 16, 33
Labouvie-Vief, Gisella, 458
Lamaze childbirth method, 95
Language acquisition device (LAD), 174
Language areas in cerebral cortex, 120, 121, 122, 174, 218, 323, 394
Language development
- in adolescence, 389, 394
- in autism, 243
- babbling in, 175–176
- in bilingualism, 323–324
- brain areas in, 120, 121, 122, 174, 218, 323, 394
- and categorization skills, 165, 208, 232
- child-care quality affecting, 171*f*
- comprehension and production of words in, 177
- conversational skills in, 176, 252
- core knowledge perspective of, 158
- cultural influences on, 177–178, 250, 318–319, 320, 322–323
- delay in, 178
- in early childhood, 217, 225, 227, 234–235, 240, 242–244, 249–253, 261
- early intervention programs affecting, 247
- early printing in, 225
- emergent literacy in, 242–244, 244*f*
- and emotional self-regulation, 189–190
- emotion words in, 261
- and false beliefs, 242
- first speech sounds in, 175–177
- first words in, 176–177
- and gender typing, 277–278
- generic references to gender in, 277–278
- give-and-take interactions in, 176
- grammar in. *See* Grammatical development
- in hearing loss, 121, 174, 176
- home environment affecting, 170, 319–320
- individual differences in, 177–178
- in infancy and toddlerhood, 109, 120, 121, 138–140, 144, 155–156, 165, 170, 173–179, 208
- infant-directed speech in, 179
- information-processing theories of, 174–175, 252
- interactionist theories of, 174–175, 178
- intermodal perception in, 144
- joint attention in, 176
- in late adulthood, 598–599
- and memory, 164, 165*f*, 240
- in middle childhood, 321–324
- milestones of, 175*t*
- nativist theory of, 174, 175, 252
- phonological, 244, 313
- pragmatic, 252, 322–323
- preverbal gestures in, 176
- private speech in, 234–235, 236
- reading in, 313. *See also* Reading
- sensitive period in, 174, 323
- sex differences in, 177, 394
- in social interaction, 175, 176, 179, 252
- sociocultural theory on, 23
- speech perception and analysis in, 138–140
- and symbolic understanding, 155–156
- theories of, 174–175
- two-word utterances in, 177
- underextension and overextension errors in, 177
- vocabulary in, 250–251, 321–322. *See also* Vocabulary

Language immersion programs in bilingualism, 323, 324
Lanugo, 79, 81
Laos, 32
Late adolescence (16 to 18 years old), 368
Late adulthood (65 years old to death), 8*t*, 568–643
- acceptance of change in, 611, 614
- activity theory of, 620
- adaptation in, 578–581, 599–600, 614, 628, 629
- adult children as caregivers in, 555–557, 623
- age range in, 8*t*
- aging in place in, 623, 624, 625
- agreeableness in, 614
- Alzheimer's disease in, 587–590
- appearance in, 578
- arthritis in, 585–586
- assistive technology in, 579–580
- bereavement overload in, 668
- body composition changes in, 578
- brain development in, 574
- cardiovascular system in, 576–577
- causes of death in, 584*f*, 584–585
- of centenarians, 572–573
- cognitive development in, 574, 576, 587–591, 594–605, 614, 638
- cognitive interventions in, 602, 603
- cognitive maintenance and loss prevention in, 595, 595*f*, 601–602, 603
- cohabitation in, 628
- community and neighborhood in, 61, 622
- compression of morbidity in, 582
- contact with adult children in, 555–556
- continuity theory of, 620, 623, 636
- control versus dependency in, 616
- coping strategies in, 575, 579, 611, 614, 615, 617, 639
- cultural influences on, 579, 580–581, 600
- daily living activities in. *See* Daily living activities in late adulthood
- death concept in, 610, 650, 652, 652*f*
- dementia in, 587–591, 592–593
- dependency in, 616
- depression in, 591, 616, 617, 618–619, 624, 630, 636, 638
- diabetes in, 586
- disabilities in, 579–580, 581, 582, 582*f*, 584–591, 617, 633
- disengagement theory of, 620
- divorce in, 627–628
- emotional and social development in, 608–641
- emotional expertise in, 621
- ethical issues in research on, 38
- exercise in, 578, 583, 586
- falls in, 575, 577, 587
- family relationships in, 619, 622, 625–628, 630, 631–632, 633–634
- frailty in, 585, 623, 633
- friendships in, 620–621, 621*f*, 630–631
- functional age in, 570
- gerotranscendence in, 610–611
- grandchildren and great-grandchildren in, 632
- health and fitness in, 572, 573, 581–594, 617, 618–619, 626, 635, 636, 638
- health care in, 579, 580, 581–582, 591–594, 600, 627, 639
- hearing changes in, 574*f*, 575–576, 597
- housing arrangements in, 623–625
- immune system in, 573, 574, 577
- injuries in, unintentional, 586–587
- integrity versus despair in, 15*t*, 610
- language processing in, 598–599
- leisure and volunteer activities in, 575, 578, 635, 636–637, 639
- of lesbian and gay couples, 584, 626–627
- life expectancy in, 570–573
- lifelong learning in, 602–605
- long-term care in, 591, 592–594
- maltreatment in, 632–634
- marriage in, 573, 625–626, 626*f*, 627–628, 636
- maximum lifespan in, 572
- memory in, 573–574, 576, 577, 580, 583, 588, 594, 595–599, 602, 612, 613
- mental disabilities in, 587–591
- milestones of development in, 642–643
- mobility in. *See* Mobility in late adulthood
- motor vehicle accidents in, 586–587
- negative life changes in, 612, 615, 617
- nervous system development in, 573–574, 583
- of never-married childless adults, 629–630
- number of social partners in, 620–621, 621*f*
- nursing home care in, 592–594, 624–625, 658
- nutrition in, 573, 576, 582–583, 586
- openness to experience in, 612, 614
- personality traits in, 612, 614
- person–environment fit in, 580, 616, 618, 623, 624, 625, 639
- physical development in, 570–594
- physical disabilities in, 584–587
- plasticity of development in, 602
- positivity effect in, 611–612, 621
- possible selves in, 581, 614
- poverty in, 65, 65*f*, 582, 623
- problem solving in, 599–600, 601, 614
- psychological well-being in, 615–619
- psychosocial theories of, 610–612
- public policies on, 64–65, 66, 579, 580, 591–594, 613, 623, 624, 635–636, 639
- quality of life in, 571, 575
- quality of relationships in, 620, 622, 639
- relationships with adult children in, 631–632, 633
- remarriage in, 627–628
- reminiscence in, 597, 597*f*, 612
- respiratory system in, 576–577
- retirement in, 613, 618, 634–637, 638
- self-concept in, 580, 612–614, 639
- sensory system changes in, 574–576
- sexuality in, 583–584
- siblings in, 630
- in singlehood, 629–630
- sleep in, 574, 577
- smell sense in, 576
- social context of aging in, 622–625
- social support in, 573, 615, 617–618, 619, 620, 628, 629–630, 636
- social theories of aging in, 620–622

socioemotional selectivity theory of, 620–622, 632
spirituality and religiosity in, 614–615, 617
stereotypes of aging in, 580–581. *See also* Stereotypes of aging
stroke in, 590–591
subjective age in, 579
successful aging in, 637–639
suicide in, 617, 618–619
taste sense in, 576
terminal decline in, 601–602
as Third Age, 613
touch sense in, 576
vascular dementia in, 590–591
victimization and fear of crime in, 622–623
vision changes in, 574–575, 576, 579, 585, 586, 597
widowhood in, 623, 628–629, 667
wisdom in, 600–601
Latency stage of psychosexual development, 15*t*
Lateralization of brain, 121, 122, 217–218
Latin America, 32, 127
Latvia, 102*f*, 487, 487*f*
Laughter in infancy and toddlerhood, 185
Layoff from job, 499, 532, 542, 562
Lead exposure, prenatal, 86
Learned helplessness
achievement-related attributions in, 339
attribution retraining in, 340
and cognitive self-regulation, 313
and depression, 428
of rejected-withdrawn children, 348
Learning
achievement-related attributions in, 339
in adolescence, 396–403
in classical conditioning, 16, 130*f*, 130–131
cognitive-developmental theory on, 17–19, 150–159
and cognitive self-regulation, 312–313
in college experience, 461
with computers, 249
cooperative, 325–326
cultural influences on, 23, 139, 167, 237
definition of, 130
by discovery, 19, 233, 235
in dualistic thinking, 457
early interventions for, 172–173, 244
and epistemic cognition, 456–457
in guided participation, 236
in habituation, 131–132, 132*f*
in imitation, 132–133, 133*f*
individual differences in, 234
in infancy and toddlerhood, 130–133, 157, 179
information processing in, 19–20, 160–166, 313–314
in job training during middle adulthood, 561
of language, 173–179, 250, 321–324
in late adulthood, 602–605
lifelong, 602–605, 639
malnutrition affecting, 129

mastery-oriented approach to, 339, 340, 341
of mathematics, 23, 313–314
media multitasking affecting, 400
and memory, 162–163, 308, 310, 311
in middle adulthood, 529, 532–533, 561
observational, 17, 237
in operant conditioning, 16, 131, 162
in Piagetian classrooms, 233–234
readiness for, 234
reading in, 313
by returning students in middle adulthood, 532–533
in scaffolding, 166, 235
in school, 313–314, 324–330, 396–403
of second language, 323–324
in service-learning programs, 419
social-cognitive, 17
social learning theory on, 17. *See also* Social learning theory
sociocultural theory on, 22–23, 166–167, 235–236
statistical learning capacity in infants, 138–140
symbolic understanding in, 155–156, 228–229
from television and videos, 157, 179
vocabulary development in, 177, 250, 321
working memory in, 308, 310
Learning difficulties, 326–328
Learning disabilities, 48, 327
Left-handedness, 121, 218
Leisure activities in late adulthood, 578
in retirement, 635, 636–637
in successful aging, 639
vision loss affecting, 575
Lens of eye, 109, 508
in cataracts, 574–575
Leptin, 372
Lesbian, gay, and bisexual people
adolescence of, 382–383, 411, 426
affection and love in relationships of, 453
anorexia nervosa of, 378
bulimia nervosa of, 379
cohabitation of, 494
dating of, 426
death of intimate partner, 668
early adulthood of, 452–453, 497–498
friendships of, 483
gender-equitable expectations and behavior of, 278
health-care decisions for partners of, 627
identity development of, 411
late adulthood of, 584, 626–627
marriage of. *See* Same-sex marriage
mate selection of, 453, 479
middle adulthood of, 550
moral reasoning of adolescents about, 416, 417
as parents, 278, 497–498
partner abuse of, 488
romantic relationships of, 453, 481, 483

sexually transmitted infections of, 383, 453
suicide of, 382, 428
Levinson, Daniel, 477, 541–542
Life-care communities, 623–624
Life cycle of family, 484–492, 549
Life expectancy, 570–573
and adaptive value of longevity, 22
and aging parents of middle-aged children, 554
in Alzheimer's disease, 588
and anti-aging effects of calorie restriction, 511
average, 7, 53, 438, 570, 571, 571*f*, 572
in Down syndrome, 50
exercise affecting, 521–522
genetic factors in, 438, 440, 570, 571, 572, 573
and maximum lifespan, 572
and retirement trends, 634
in sickle cell anemia, 48
smoking affecting, 449
variations in, 570–571, 571*f*
worldwide trends in, 7
Lifelong learning, 602–605, 639
Life review
in cancer and depression, 654
in late adulthood, 612
in middle adulthood, 539, 540, 542–543, 543*f*, 545
Lifespan perspective, 7–12, 11*f*, 27*t*
age-graded influences in, 9
biological aging in, 438
early adulthood cognitive development in, 456
emerging adulthood in, 474
history-graded influences in, 9–10
as lifelong process, 7, 8
major periods of development in, 8, 8*t*
midlife psychological well-being in, 546
multidimensional and multidirectional influences in, 8, 10, 438, 474, 524, 538
nonnormative influences in, 10–11
plasticity in, 9
and public policies, 64–66
Life stories of generative adults, 540
Life structure, Levinson on, 477
Lifestyle
of adults, diversity of, 492–498
and Alzheimer's disease risk, 590
and cancer incidence, 517
of centenarians, 573
in childlessness, 495
in cohabitation, 494
and compression of morbidity in late adulthood, 582
daily living activities in, 573
in diabetes, 586
and health in middle adulthood, 510, 515
in obesity, 445–446
and osteoporosis, 519
in singlehood, 493–494
Life-sustaining treatment, withholding or withdrawal of, 660*t*, 660–662
Linguistic intelligence, 317, 317*t*, 329
Linguistic knowledge in core-knowledge perspective, 158
Lipoproteins, 448

Literacy
in adolescence, 394
emergent, 242–244, 244*f*
reading skills in. *See* Reading
writing skills in. *See* Writing
Lithuania, 102*f*, 487, 487*f*
Living apart together, in late adulthood, 628
Living will, 661*f*, 661–662
Logical necessity in propositional thought, 389
Logical thought
in formal operational stage, 388, 389, 390
in preoperational stage, 231–232, 233
Logico-mathematical intelligence, 317, 317*t*
Loneliness
in adolescence, 375, 431
in divorce, 496
of dying person, 652
in early adulthood, 476, 493, 496
in early childhood, 273
in late adulthood, 575, 618, 619, 628, 630
in middle childhood, 348, 349
in shyness, 192
Longevity. *See* Life expectancy
Longitudinal research design, 35–36
on adaptation to life, 542
on agreeableness in late adulthood, 614
on Alzheimer's disease, 586, 590
on amount of daily exercise, 371*f*
on athletic performance in aging, 442*f*
on attachment, 202, 205, 242, 480
on authoritative child rearing, 283
on calorie restriction diets, 511
on cardiovascular disease, 442
on centenarians, 572
on child-care quality, 171
on child-rearing style, 283
on clique and crowd membership in adolescence, 425
on cognitive maintenance and change in late adulthood, 601, 602
cohort effects in, 35–36, 524–525, 525*f*, 625
compared to other research designs, 34*t*, 36
on control sense and life satisfaction, 616
on corporal punishment, 269, 270
on crystallized and fluid intelligence, 525–526
on depression in menopause, 512
on diabetes, 586
on divorce, 495, 550
on exercise benefits, 448, 521–522, 590
on gender identity and behavior, 351
on gender typing, 350
on gerotranscendence, 611
on health and disability in late adulthood, 581
on impulsivity and sensation-seeking behavior, 373*f*, 373–374
on Internet use, 424
limitations of, 35–36

Longitudinal research design (*continued*)
  on marital relationships, 426, 481, 547, 625
  on math achievement, 395
  on mental abilities, 524–526, 525f, 526f
  on midlife emotional and social development, 538, 545
  on moral development, 413, 415
  on neighborhood poverty, 61
  in New York Longitudinal Study, 190
  on nutrition in middle childhood, 295
  on parent–child conflict resolution, 376
  on peer sociability, 263
  on personality traits, 35, 548
  on physical changes of aging, 440, 442, 442f, 574, 581
  on possible selves, 614
  practice effects in, 35
  on pubertal timing, 373
  on resilience, 473–475
  in Seattle Longitudinal Study, 524, 526, 526f, 602
  on self-esteem, 351, 409
  sequential design, 36, 37f, 524–525, 525f
  on sexual activity, 515
  on sibling relationships, 36
  on smoking, 601
  on social interaction in late adulthood, 620
  on spirituality and religiosity, 614–615
  on stereotypes of aging, 580
  on substance abuse, 386
  on teacher–student interactions, 462
  on television viewing, 274
  on temperament, 190, 192, 283
  on theory of mind, 242
  on verbal ability, 525, 525f
Long-term care
  in late adulthood, 591, 592–594
  in nursing homes. *See* Nursing home care
Long-term memory, 160, 160f, 161, 529, 598
Lorenz, Konrad, 21, 196
Love, 479–482
  in same-sex relationships, 453
Low birth weight, 97–100
  behavioral assessment in, 110
  and disease risk in adulthood, 88, 88f
  drugs associated with, 83
  and exercise during pregnancy, 88
  infectious diseases associated with, 87t
  maternal age in, 91f
  mortality rate in, 102
  myopia in, 298
  in reproductive technologies, 52
  of small-for-date infants, 98
  smoking associated with, 84
  sudden infant death syndrome in, 106
  telomere length in, 439
Low-density lipoproteins, 448
Loyalty in friendships, 423, 482
LSD, 448

Lungs
  age-related changes in, 441t, 442, 576–577
  cancer of, 516, 516f, 517
  emphysema of, 585
Luxembourg
  infant mortality rate in, 102f
  life expectancy in, 571f
  marriage of same-sex couples in, 486
  math achievement scores in, 329f
  medical aid-in-dying in, 663
  poverty rate in, 65f
  voluntary euthanasia in, 664
Lying, and moral development in middle childhood, 343

M

Macrosystem, 24, 24f, 26, 56, 62
  in family chaos, 25
Macular degeneration, 575, 585
Magical thinking in preoperational stage, 231
Magnesium deficiency in adolescence, 378
Magnetic resonance imaging
  in Alzheimer's disease, 588
  functional. *See* Functional magnetic resonance imaging of brain
  ultrafast, in pregnancy, 54t
Magnet schools, 326, 327
Make-believe play
  in autism, 243
  in early childhood, 227–228, 236, 237, 242, 264, 264t, 265
  in infancy and toddlerhood, 153, 168
Malaria, 48, 49, 87t
Mali, 199
Malnutrition
  in anorexia nervosa, 378–379
  in early childhood, 217, 220–221
  in infancy and toddlerhood, 117, 129, 193
  in late adulthood, 583
  in middle childhood, 295
  prenatal, 88–89, 129
  in puberty, 372
Malta, 102f, 571f
Maltreatment
  of children, 285t, 285–287. *See also* Child maltreatment
  of elderly, 632–634
Management positions, glass ceiling in, 561
Maori of New Zealand, 656
Mapping of human genome, 54
Map skills, 304–306, 305f
Marasmus, 129
Marfan syndrome, 47t
Marijuana use, 84, 386, 448, 449
Marital relationships
  abuse in, 286, 488–489
  and adolescent delinquency, 430
  and adolescent pregnancy, 384
  of adult learners, 532
  in arranged marriages, 482
  in blended families, 356
  childlessness in, 489–490
  cohabitation as alternative to, 494, 628
  cohabitation prior to, 494

communication in, 481, 488–489, 495
conflicts in, 426, 481, 626
cultural influences on, 481–482
death of child affecting, 667
death of spouse in, 623, 627, 628–629, 666, 667–668
and divorce, 353–355, 495–496. *See also* Divorce
in dual-earner families, 356–357, 486
in early adulthood, 450, 452, 474, 476, 481, 485–489, 495–496
egalitarian, 486, 487, 496
first, age at time of, 485, 486
frequency of sex in, 515
gender roles in, 356–357, 486–487, 488, 490–491, 495–496, 500–501, 629
as indirect influence on development, 57
of interracial couples, 486
in late adulthood, 573, 625–626, 626f, 627–628, 636
leaving parental home for, 484, 485
living apart together in, 628
and mate selection, 479, 489
in middle adulthood, 515, 532, 547, 549–551
and never-married adults, 493, 497, 629–630
and parenthood, 489–492
and parent–infant relationships, 205
and psychological well-being, 547, 550
and remarriage. *See* Remarriage
in retirement, 636
of returning students, 532
romantic love in, 481
of same-sex couples. *See* Same-sex marriage
satisfaction with, in early adulthood, 452, 481, 487t, 487–489, 490, 495–496
satisfaction with, in late adulthood, 625–626, 626f, 628, 636
satisfaction with, in middle adulthood, 515, 547, 550
sexual frequency in, 452, 515
sexual satisfaction in, 452
and sibling relationships, 205
in traditional marriage, 486
in transition to parenthood, 111, 490–491
Masculine traits
  in adolescence, 395, 423, 428
  in early adulthood, 464, 483, 499, 500
  in early childhood, 277, 279
  in middle adulthood, 541, 546–548, 556
  in middle childhood, 350–351
Mastery-oriented attributions, 339, 340, 341, 398
Maternal age, 443–444, 444f
  in adolescent pregnancy, 384–386. *See also* Adolescent pregnancy and parenthood
  in Down syndrome, 50, 51, 51f
  in first pregnancy, 443, 444f
  in fraternal twinning, 45, 45t
  late childbearing associated with longevity, 573

and prenatal development, 89–91, 91f
in reproductive technologies, 52, 53
and transition to parenthood, 490–491
Maternal factors. *See* Mothers
Mate selection, 479, 482, 489
Mathematical abilities, 23
  in adolescence, 329f, 395f, 395–396
  in early adulthood, 464
  in early childhood, 233, 244–245
  in infancy and toddlerhood, 158–159, 159f
  in middle childhood, 313–314, 350
Matters of personal choice, 272, 416, 421
Maximum lifespan, 572
Mayans
  attention style of, 167
  communication style of, 319
  cosleeping of parents and infants, 126
  gender identity of, 547
  menopause of, 514
  observational learning of, 237
  play of, 265
MDMA (Ecstasy), 386, 448
Mead, Margaret, 368
Mealtimes in family, 25, 60, 60f
  in adolescence, 378, 422
  in middle childhood, 295, 323
Mealtimes in school, 297, 378
Means–end action sequences in sensorimotor stage, 152
Measles, 220
  German measles (rubella), 86–87, 87t, 221
Media
  and cell phone use, 349, 400, 423–424, 424f
  and computer use. *See* Computer use
  educational, 248–249
  gender stereotypes in, 279
  and Internet use. *See* Internet use
  and multitasking, 400, 528–529
  sexual content in, 380
  strategies regulating use of, 275
  television. *See* Television
  violence on, 274f, 274–275
Mediation services in divorce, 355
Medicaid, 592–593, 659
Medical aid-in-dying, 660t, 662–664, 663f
Medical care. *See* Health care
Medical insurance. *See* Health insurance
Medicare, 65, 581, 591–592, 639, 659
Medications. *See* Drug therapy
Mediterranean countries, 484, 590
Meiosis, 45
Melatonin, 125
Memory
  of actors, 603
  in adolescence, 400
  in Alzheimer's disease, 588, 590
  in attention-deficit hyperactivity disorder, 309
  autobiographical. *See* Autobiographical memory
  of childhood attachment patterns, 480

in early childhood, 164–165, 165f, 238, 239–241
and eyewitness testimony by children, 361
in fetal development, 81
in infancy, 131–132, 154–155, 162f, 162–163, 166, 169
and infantile amnesia, 163, 164–165
in information processing, 160–161, 162–163, 239–241, 308, 310–311, 390, 527, 529–530
language development affecting, 164, 165f, 240
in late adulthood, 573–574, 576, 577, 580, 583, 588, 594, 595–599, 602, 612, 613
long-term, 160, 160f, 161, 529, 598
in middle adulthood, 528, 529–530
in middle childhood, 300, 307, 308, 310–311, 312, 322
nonverbal, 164, 165f
recall. See Recall memory
reconstructed, 202
retrieval of information from, 161, 311, 529, 596, 598, 599
semantic, 240, 311, 529, 596
short-term, 160f, 160–161, 162, 163
strategies for, 240, 310–311, 312, 390, 529–530, 597, 603
working. See Working memory
Menarche, 371
age at time of, 371, 372, 372t
individual and group differences in, 372, 373
reactions to, 374–375
Mende of Sierra Leone, 95
Menopause, 510–513, 514, 519
death anxiety in, 652
depression in, 512, 512f
reproductive technologies in, 53
stress in, 512, 513, 514, 521
Menstrual cycle
in early adulthood, 444
eating disorders affecting, 378
estrogen in, 369
first, 371, 372t, 374. See also Menarche
in middle adulthood, 510, 512
Mental development. See Cognitive development
Mental representations
in early childhood, 227, 228, 229
in infancy and toddlerhood, 151t, 152–153, 154–156, 158, 163, 227
Mental rotation tasks, sex differences in, 396f, 396–397
Mental strategies in information processing, 160
Mental testing movement, 14. See also Intelligence tests
Mentor relationships, 477, 499, 638
Mercury exposure, 86, 221
Mesoderm, 78
Mesosystem, 24, 24f, 25, 60
Metabolic rate, basal, 446, 510, 511
Metacognition
in adolescence, 390, 391, 392, 394
in early adulthood, 457
in early childhood, 241–242
in late adulthood, 602
in middle adulthood, 529
in middle childhood, 311, 312, 313

Metaphors in vocabulary development, 250, 322
Methadone in pregnancy, 83
Methylation of genes, 70, 71, 71f, 85, 89
in Alzheimer's disease, 590
Mexican Americans
death and dying concept of, 649, 655
diabetes of, 586
ethnic identity of, 412
grandparents as caregivers, 553
intelligence definition of, 316
sibling relationships of, 422
Mexico
concrete operational stage in, 306
Day of the Dead celebration in, 649
food preferences in, 219
immigrant youths from, 32
make-believe play in, 168
menopause in, 514
motor development of infants in, 136
observational learning in, 237
sense of control in, 579
Zinacanteco Indians in, 23, 136, 168, 306
Microsystem, 23, 24f, 25, 56, 57
Middle adolescence (14 to 16 years old), 368, 415
Middle adulthood (40 to 65 years old), 8t, 506–567
adaptation in, 520–524, 542, 543
attention in, 528–529
autonomy in, 539, 541, 544
body composition changes in, 510
career in, 531–532, 541, 542, 559–564
cognitive development in, 524–533
cohort effects in, 524–525
creativity in, 530–531
crystallized and fluid intelligence in, 525–526, 527, 527f
death concept in, 650
death of intimate partner in, 667–668
divorce in, 550–551
emotional and social development in, 536–565
environmental mastery in, 544, 545, 547
executive function in, 527, 528–529, 546
exercise in, 510, 519, 521–522, 546, 547
expertise in, 530
family in, 545, 547, 549–558
flow state in, 546–547
friendships in, 558–559
gender identity in, 541, 546–548
gender stereotypes on aging in, 523–524
generativity versus stagnation in, 15t, 538–541
grandparenthood in, 552–553, 554
hardiness in, 522–523
health and fitness in, 514–520, 546
hearing changes in, 509
hostility and anger in, 519–520
illness and disability in, 515–519

individual and group differences in, 526–527
information processing in, 526, 526f, 527–531
job satisfaction in, 560
job training in, 560–561
learning as returning student in, 532–533
life satisfaction in, 539, 540, 542, 543, 547
life stories in, 540
marital relationships in, 515, 532, 547, 549–551, 549–552
memory in, 528, 529–530
menopause in, 510–513, 514
mental abilities in, 524–527
midlife crisis in, 542–543, 562
milestones of development in, 566–567
multiple roles in, 545, 547, 555
nutrition in, 510, 511
optimism in, 522–523
parent–child relationships in, with adult children, 551–552
parent–child relationships in, with aging parents, 554–557
personality traits in, 519–520, 543, 544, 548t, 548–549
personal life investment in, 546–547
physical development in, 508–524
possible selves in, 544
practical problem solving in, 530, 550
as prime of life, 545
psychological well-being in, 539, 545, 546–547, 550
regrets in, 542–543, 543f
reproductive system in, 510–514
retirement planning in, 562–564
role overload in, 545
in sandwich generation, 555–556
seasons of life in, 541–542
self-acceptance in, 539, 544, 545
self-concept in, 541, 543–545, 546–548
sense of control in, 546
sexuality in, 515, 515f
siblings in, 557–558
skeletal changes in, 510, 519
skin changes in, 509–510
social relationships in, 549–559
speed of information processing in, 527–528
stage or life events approach to, 543
stress in, 516, 517, 520–521, 522–523, 545–546, 550
suicide in, 546, 618
turning points in, 542–543
unemployment in, 562
vision changes in, 508–509, 515
vocational life in, 531–532, 542, 559–564
Middle childhood (6 to 11 years old), 8t, 292–365
attention in, 308, 310
body composition in, 294
body growth in, 294
body proportions in, 294
cognitive development in, 18t, 295, 303–330
cognitive self-regulation in, 312–313

concrete operational stage in, 18t, 304–307
death concept in, 649
death of sibling during, 667
divorce of parents during, 353–355
emotional and social development in, 334–363
executive function in, 300, 307–310, 316, 323
eyewitness testimony during, 361
family influences in, 351–357
fears and anxieties in, 358
gender typing in, 350–351
grammar in, 322
health problems in, 295–299
hearing in, 298
height in, 294
individual differences in, 314–321
industry versus inferiority in, 15t, 336
information processing in, 300, 307–314
injuries in, unintentional, 298–299
intelligence in, 295, 314–321
language development in, 321–324
learning in, 313–314, 323–330
memory in, 300, 307, 308, 310–311, 312, 322
milestones of development in, 364–365
moral development in, 342–345
motor development in, 299–303
nutrition in, 295–298
of only children, 352–353
parent relationships in, 337, 338–340, 351–352. See also Parent–child relationships
peer relations in, 345–349
physical development in, 294–303
physical education in, 303
play in, 299–303
resilience in, 360
school attendance in, 311, 324–330
self-care in, 357
self-conscious emotions in, 341
self-regulation in, emotional, 342
self-understanding in, 336–341
sex differences in, 294, 294f, 301
sexual abuse during, 358–360
theory of mind in, 311–312
vision in, 298
vocabulary in, 321–322
vocational choice in, 462
weight in, 294, 295–298
Middle East, 127, 378, 512, 547
Midlife crisis, 542–543, 562
Midlife Development in the United States (MIDUS) survey, 538, 539, 542, 545, 547
Midwives, 96
Milestones of development
in adolescence, 434–435
in brain development, 117–118, 118f
in cognitive development, 158t, 233t
in early adulthood, 504–505
in early childhood, 290–291
in infancy and toddlerhood, 134t, 158t, 175t, 212–213
in language development, 175t
in late adulthood, 642–643
in middle adulthood, 566–567
in middle childhood, 364–365
prenatal, 77t

Millennial generation, 452, 452f, 471, 472
Mind, theory of. *See* Theory of mind
Mindfulness training, 310
Minerals, dietary, 88, 220
Mirror neurons, 132
Mirror self-recognition of infants, 207–208, 208f
Miscarriage
  drugs associated with, 83
  drugs in prevention of, 82, 382
  in fetal medicine and diagnostic procedures, 54, 54t
  genetic factors in, 48, 50, 51
  in infectious diseases, 87t
  maternal age in, 89, 443, 444
  paternal age in, 444
  in radiation exposure, 49, 85
  in reproductive technologies, 52
  in Rh factor incompatibility, 89
  in smoking, 84
  in stress, 48–49, 89
Mistrust, 15t, 184
Mobility in late adulthood, 578
  Alzheimer's disease affecting, 588
  arthritis affecting, 585
  falls affecting, 587
  vision affecting, 575
Modeling
  of empathy and sympathy, 263
  gender typing in, 279
  of mobile device use, 275
  of moral behavior, 268
  social learning theory on, 17, 268
Modernization, societal, performance on cognitive tasks in, 311, 319
Monkeys
  anti-aging effects of calorie restriction in, 511
  attachment of, 196
  discrimination of human and monkey faces, 139, 139f
Monozygotic twins, 46. *See also* Twins
Moods, 375, 512, 513
Moral development, 37
  in adolescence, 344, 413–420
  and aggression, 272–276
  and behavior, 417–418
  care orientation in, 415–416
  child-rearing practices affecting, 416, 418, 419
  and civic engagement, 418, 419
  cognitive-developmental theory of, 271–272, 343, 413, 414, 417, 420
  in college experience, 417, 460
  cultural influences on, 267, 344, 416, 417, 418
  diversity and inequality understanding in, 344–345
  in early childhood, 267–272
  and middle adulthood generativity, 540, 541
  identity in, 416, 418, 419
  individual rights in, 343–344
  Kohlberg on, 413–415, 417, 420
  in middle childhood, 342–345
  peer interaction affecting, 417
  pragmatic approach to, 420
  psychoanalytic theory of, 267–268
  religion in, 418
  schooling affecting, 417, 419
  sex differences in, 415–416
  social learning theory of, 267, 268–271
Moral imperatives, 272, 343, 416
Moratorium in identity development, 409, 410, 410t, 411, 476
Morbidity
  compression in late adulthood, 582
  expansion of, 582
Moro reflex, 101, 101t
Mortality, 646. *See also* Death and dying
Mothers
  adjustment to role as, 111, 490–491
  adolescent, 384–386
  age of. *See* Maternal age
  and attachment security of infant, 200–201
  bereavement in loss of child, 667
  in blended families, 356, 496–497
  depression of, 187
  divorce of, 353, 354, 355, 356, 496
  in dual-earner marriages, 356–357, 490–491
  education on child rearing, 492
  emotional sensitivity of, 29
  employment leave time for, 103, 203, 491
  employment of, 103, 171, 202, 203, 204, 246, 356–357, 490–492, 499
  gender typing of children by, 350, 351
  as grandparents, 553
  infant perception of face of, 143
  intelligence quotient of, 318
  kinkeeper role of, 552, 553
  marital roles of, 486, 491
  and maternal mind-mindedness, 200, 242
  never-married, 497
  play activities of, 168, 203, 266
  pregnancy of. *See* Pregnancy
  radiation exposure of, 49
  relationships with adult children, 632
  and sibling relationships, 204–205, 352, 557–558
  in single-parent families, 353, 497
  as stepparents, 356, 496–497
  time spent in child-care activities, 204, 204f
  time spent with daughters, 352
  transition to parenthood, 111, 490–491
  and vocational choice of daughters, 463
  warmth of, 187, 204
Mother–stepfather families, 356
Motion, infant perception of, 140
Motivation
  of adult learners, 532
  attachment affecting, 206
  awareness of, in emotional intelligence, 458
  in bilingual development, 323
  in career, 464, 465, 561
  childbearing, 490
  classroom experiences affecting, 401
  in drug abuse treatment, 387
  ethnic identity affecting, 412
  in generativity, 539, 540
  grouping practices affecting, 326
  and identity development, 470
  for imitation, 17
  in make-believe play, 228
  maltreatment in childhood affecting, 286
  moral, 418, 420
  and motor performance, 442
  of only children, 352
  in parenthood decisions, 490
  peer influences on, 399
  and personality traits, 549
  and physical activity in middle adulthood, 522
  possible selves as, 544
  and practical intelligence, 316
  preschool and kindergarten programs affecting, 246
  and resilience in middle childhood, 360
  of returning students, 532
  of school dropouts, 460, 461
  school transitions affecting, 397, 398
  and self-esteem, 339, 397
  stereotypes affecting, 320, 326, 399
  teacher–student interactions affecting, 325, 326
  in test-taking, 319
  tracking programs affecting, 401
  unconscious, 14
Motor development
  in adulthood, 442f, 442–443
  in early childhood, 218, 219, 222–226, 223t
  fine-motor skills in. *See* Fine-motor development
  gross-motor skills in. *See* Gross-motor development
  in infancy and toddlerhood, 110, 133–137, 134t, 140, 141, 145
  in middle childhood, 299–303
  in puberty, 370–371
Motor vehicle accidents
  in adolescence, 374
  childhood injuries in, 221, 298, 299f
  in early adulthood, 444f, 450
  in late adulthood, 586–587, 602
  sudden unanticipated death in, 666
Mourning behavior, 665. *See also* Bereavement
Multicultural research, 30. *See also* Cultural influences
Multidirectional and multidimensional aspects of lifespan development, 8, 10
  in early adulthood, 438, 474
  in middle adulthood, 524, 538
Multiple attachments, 203–205
Multiple births, 45t, 45–46
  low birth weight in, 98
  preterm, 46, 98
  in reproductive technologies, 45, 45t, 52
  twin. *See* Twins
Multiple intelligences theory of Gardner, 316–317, 317t, 329
Multisystemic therapy in delinquency, 432, 432f
Multitasking, 25, 400, 528–529
Mumps in pregnancy, 87t
Muscles
  in early adulthood, 440, 441t, 442, 443, 448
  in early childhood, 216
  in infancy and toddlerhood, 117
  in late adulthood, 578, 583
  in middle adulthood, 510
  in middle childhood, 294
  in physical changes of aging, 441t
  in puberty, 369, 372t
Muscular dystrophy, Duchenne, 47t
Music
  in Alzheimer's disease, 590, 593
  in multiple intelligences theory, 317t
  as palliative care for dying person, 659
  perception in infancy, 99, 109, 138, 139
Muslims, 418, 649, 651
Mutations, 49–50, 439–440, 516, 518
Mutual exclusivity bias in vocabulary development, 250
Myelination of nerves, 118f
  in adolescence, 373
  in early adulthood, 456
  in early childhood, 217, 218, 219
  in infancy and toddlerhood, 118, 120
  in middle adulthood, 527
  in middle childhood, 300, 307, 308
Myopia, 298, 508

N

Narcissism, 12, 471
Narratives
  in adolescence, 411
  in early childhood, 240–241, 259
  in late adulthood, 599
  in middle childhood, 322–323
Narrowing effect in perceptual development, 139
National Association for the Education of Young Children, 171
National Center for Children in Poverty, 66
National Institute of Child Health and Development, 202
National Resource Center for Safe Aging, 587
National Social Life, Health, and Aging Project, 583–584, 584f
Native Americans
  academic achievement of, 401
  aging parents of, 623
  attention style of, 167
  categorization abilities of children, 232
  communication style of, 319
  death beliefs of, 656
  departure from parental home, 485
  diabetes of, 586
  divorce of, 353
  extended-family households of, 62, 623
  fetal alcohol syndrome of, 85
  gender identity of, 547
  grandparents as caregivers of, 553, 554
  health problems in late adulthood, 581
  high school dropout rates of, 402, 402f
  long-term care of older adults, 593
  neonatal behavioral assessment of, 110
  overweight and obese, 295, 445
  partner abuse of, 489

poverty of, 59
religiosity of, 615
suicide of, 428, 429
Native Canadians, 126, 319, 411
Nativist theory of language development, 174, 175, 252
Natural childbirth, 95–96
Natural experiments, 34
Naturalistic observation research method, 28, 28t
Naturalist intelligence, 317t
Natural selection, 13
Nature, and relative influence of nurture, 7, 27t, 66–72
heritability estimates on, 67–68, 318
in intelligence, 318–321
Near-infrared spectroscopy (NIRS), 119, 119t, 120f, 121, 217
Nearsightedness, 298, 508
Neglect
in child maltreatment, 283, 285, 286
in elder maltreatment, 633, 634
by peers, 347, 348
in uninvolved child rearing, 283
Neighborhood influences, 60–61, 622–623. *See also* Community influences
Neighborhood Watch programs, 623
Neonatal Behavioral Assessment Scale (NBAS), 110, 201
Neonatal Intensive Care Unit Network Neurobehavioral Scale (NNNS), 110
Neonates. *See* Newborns
Neo-Piagetian theory, 233, 307
Nepal, 311
Nervous system
autonomic, 574, 584
brain in. *See* Brain
in early adulthood, 443
in infancy, reflex testing of, 103–104
in late adulthood, 573–574
in middle adulthood, 509, 513, 526
neurons in. *See* Neurons
optic nerve in, 109, 509, 575
in physical changes of aging, 441t
Netherlands
academic achievement in, 329, 329f, 398
adolescent birth rate in, 384f
child-rearing styles in, 398
cohabitation in, 494
euthanasia in, 664
health care for parents and newborn in, 102–103
home births in, 96
immunization rate in, 221
infant mortality rate in, 102f
life expectancy in, 571f
long-term care for older adults in, 592, 594
marriage of same-sex couples in, 486
medical aid-in-dying in, 663
Nurse–Family Partnership in, 90
poverty rate in, 65f
Neural network view of information processing, 307
Neural tube, 78, 79, 117, 118
in fetal alcohol spectrum disorder, 85
folic acid affecting, 89

Neurobiological research, 20, 119
on early deprivation, 123
Experience Corps volunteers in, 638
on stress, 308
on temperament, 191, 192
Neurofibrillary tangles in Alzheimer's disease, 588, 589
Neuroimaging techniques, 119t, 119–120, 120f
Neurons
in Alzheimer's disease, 588–589
and brain plasticity, 122
development of, 79, 117–119
in fetal alcohol spectrum disorder, 85
hippocampal, 164
in late adulthood, 574, 576
mirror, 132
stimulation of, 118
synapses of, 79, 117, 118, 118f
Neuroscience, developmental, 20–21
Neuroticism, 548, 548t, 549, 614
Neurotransmitters, 117
in adolescence, 373, 378, 379
in Alzheimer's disease, 589, 590
in anorexia nervosa, 378, 379
Neutral stimulus in classical conditioning, 130f, 131
Never-married adults, 497, 629–630
Newborns
adaptation to labor and delivery, 94
Apgar Scale on, 94t, 94–95, 96, 97
appearance of, 94
arousal states of, 104–108, 105t
attachment development in, 196–197, 201
behavioral assessment of, 110
brain lateralization in, 121
breastfeeding of. *See* Breastfeeding
core knowledge perspective of, 158
crying of, 104, 105t, 105–108
distress response of, 185
empathy of, 105
employment leave time for parents of, 103, 491
eye movements and gaze of, 176
face perception of, 142–143, 143f
family adjustment to, 111, 490–491
and first-time parents, 111
habituation and recovery of, 131, 161
hand movements and prereaching of, 136, 137f
imitation by, 132–133, 133f
intermodal perception of, 143–144, 207
low birth weight of, 97–100. *See also* Low birth weight
mortality rate for, 102
pain sensitivity of, 108
pattern perception of, 141
perceptual development of, 108–110, 137–146
preterm, 97–100. *See also* Preterm infants
reflexes of, 94t, 101t, 101–104, 151, 151t
self-awareness of, 207
sensory capacities of, 108–110
sleep patterns of, 104–105, 105t, 106, 125
small for date, 98
smiling of, 185
New Guinea, 218, 225

New York Longitudinal Study, 190
New Zealand
adolescent birth rate in, 384f
adolescent suicide in, 428
cesarean delivery rate in, 97
child care in, 171
death beliefs in, 656
infant mortality rate in, 102f
life expectancy in, 571f
long-term care for older adults in, 592, 593
make-believe play in, 168
marriage of same-sex couples in, 486
math achievement scores in, 329f
obesity in, 295
reproductive technologies in, 53
sexual abuse prevention programs in, 360
Niche-picking, 69
Nicotine, 84, 449. *See also* Smoking
Nigeria, 306, 589–590
Night sweats, 512, 514
Night vision, 508, 575, 586
No Child Left Behind Act, 324
Noise exposure, hearing loss in, 509
Nonfunctionality, and death concept, 648
Nonnormative influences, 10–11, 474
Non-rapid-eye-movement (NREM) sleep, 104, 105, 105t, 577
Nonverbal memory, 164, 165f
Norms, 10
age-graded influences on, 9, 10, 474
in Hall and Gesell approach, 14
history-graded influences on, 9–10
in intelligence test scores, 169, 169f
and nonnormative influences, 10–11, 474
in physical growth, 117
Norway
adolescent birth rate in, 384f
adolescent suicide in, 428
child care in, 203
cohabitation in, 494
housework hours and gender roles in, 486, 487f
immunization rate in, 221
infant mortality rate in, 102f
intelligence quotient in, 319
marriage of same-sex couples in, 486
math achievement scores in, 329f, 395f
poverty rate in, 65f
Nouns in language development, 177, 178, 250
Novelty
preference for, 131, 132f, 139, 161
temperament affecting reaction to, 192
Nso people of Cameroon, 167, 189, 207–208, 208f
Nuclear power plant accidents, radiation exposure in, 85
Nucleus of cells, 44
Numerical knowledge, 158–159, 159f, 313. *See also* Mathematical abilities
Nurse–Family Partnership, 90, 287, 385
Nurse–midwives, certified, 96

Nursing home care, 557, 592–594, 624–625
death and dying in, 657, 658
maltreatment in, 633, 634
quality of life in, 617
sexuality in, 584
suicide in, 619
Nurture, 7
and relative influence of nature, 7, 27t, 66–72, 318–321
Nutrition
in adolescence, 372, 378–379
and Alzheimer's disease risk, 589–590
in early adulthood, 440, 442, 445–447
in early childhood, 217, 219–220, 220f
in infancy and toddlerhood, 109, 109f, 117, 127–129, 193
in late adulthood, 572, 573, 575, 576, 577, 582–583, 586, 591
and malnutrition. *See* Malnutrition
in middle adulthood, 510, 511, 512, 519
in middle childhood, 295–298
in phenylketonuria, 46, 47t
in pregnancy, 45t, 86, 88–89, 98, 108, 109f, 129, 439
and telomere length, 439
vitamins in. *See* Vitamins

O

Obedience, in moral development, 413, 414
Obesity
in adolescence, 372, 373, 379, 445
in early adulthood, 445–447, 448
in early childhood, 220, 220f
in late adulthood, 575, 577, 582, 582f, 585, 586, 589
in middle childhood, 295–298
in Prader-Willi syndrome, 49
telomere length in, 439
and weight in infancy, 128
Object permanence in infancy and toddlerhood, 152, 153f, 153–154, 169
Observational learning, 17, 237
Observational research, 28t, 28–29, 30
on attachment-related behaviors, 198
on cultural influences, 30, 31
participant observations in, 31
on temperament, 191
Occipital lobe, 574
Occupation. *See* Employment
Odor perception
in infancy and toddlerhood, 108–109, 109f
in late adulthood, 576
in physical changes of aging, 441t
Oedipus conflict, 15t, 258
Older adults. *See* Late adulthood
Omega-3 fatty acids, 575, 583
Oncogenes, 516
One-child families, 48, 352–353
Online dating services, 451, 627, 627f
Online friendships, 559f
in adolescence, 423–424, 424f
in early adulthood, 483
in late adulthood, 631
in middle adulthood, 559

Openness to experience as personality trait, 548, 548t, 612, 614
Operant conditioning, 16, 131, 153
 and categorization by infants, 163, 163f
 and memory of infants, 162, 162f
Operations, 229
 and concrete operational stage, 304, 306
 and formal operational stage, 388–390
 and preoperational stage, 227–234
Optic nerve, 109, 509, 575
Optimal aging, 638
Optimism
 in late adulthood, 581, 582, 611, 614, 639
 in middle adulthood, 522–523
Oral rehydration therapy (ORT), 221
Oral stage of psychosexual development, 15t
Ordinality, 244
Organ donation, death definition for, 647
Organization
 in cognitive development, 150–151
 as memory strategy, 240, 310, 311, 529
Orgasm, 515
Orphans
 attachment insecurity of, 199–200
 early deprivation of, 121, 123, 136, 193
 genetic and environmental influences on, 193
 motor development of, 136
 stress of, 123, 359
Osher Lifelong Learning Institutes, 604
Osteoarthritis, 585, 586
Osteoporosis, 510, 519, 582, 585
Other-focused reminiscence in late adulthood, 612
Other-sex friendships, 483–484
Out-groups, 344–345
Ovaries, 76, 76f, 369, 371, 444
Overcoming perspective of death, 651
Overextensions in language development, 177
Overregularization in grammatical development, 251
Overweight
 in adolescence, 373, 379, 445
 in early adulthood, 445–447, 448
 in early childhood, 220, 220f
 in infancy, 128
 in middle childhood, 295–298
Ovulation, 76
Ovum, 44, 45, 76, 77, 444
 in multiple offspring, 45, 46
 in reproductive technologies, 52, 53
OxyContin, 448
Oxygen deprivation, 83
 in cocaine use during pregnancy, 83
 in fetal alcohol syndrome, 85
 of infant during childbirth, 94, 96
 in sickle cell anemia, 48
 sudden infant death syndrome in, 106
Oxytocin, 111

Islanders, 95, 284, 368, 558
 101, 106

Pain
 in cancer, 654
 in childbirth, 97
 of dying person, 646, 654, 657, 658, 659, 661, 663, 664
 fetal sensitivity to, 81
 medical aid-in-dying in, 663, 664
 newborn sensitivity to, 108
Pakistan, 398, 669
Palate, cleft, 84, 89
Palliative care, 658, 659, 661
Palmar grasp reflex, 101, 101t, 102
Papua New Guinea, 225
Parallel play, 263–264
Parasitic diseases in pregnancy, 87t, 88
Parent(s), 489–492. See also Fathers; Mothers
 abusive relationships of, 488–489
 adjustment to role as, 111, 490–491
 and adolescent relationships. See Parent–adolescent relationships
 adolescents as, 384–386. See also Adolescent pregnancy and parenthood
 adoption by. See Adoption
 aging, 554–557, 623
 attachment experiences of, 199, 202
 in blended families, 356, 496–497
 child-rearing practices of. See Child-rearing practices
 and child relationships. See Parent–child relationships
 children leaving home of, 471, 484–485, 547, 549, 551
 civic engagement of, 419
 combining work and family, 356–357, 477, 490–492, 499, 500–501
 consent to research on children, 38
 and decision to have children, 489–490
 depression of, 187
 direct influence of, 57, 266
 divorce of, 353–355
 in dual-earner families. See Dual-earner households
 early adults as, 473, 474, 489–492, 496–498
 in early interventions for at-risk preschoolers, 246
 education on child rearing, 491, 492
 effective coparenting of, 57, 355, 356, 491
 emotional self-regulation of, 261
 gender identity of, 547
 generativity of, 538–539
 as grandparents, 552–554
 grief in death of child, 666–667
 grief of children in death of, 667
 indirect influence of, 57, 266
 and infant relationships. See Parent–infant relationships
 intelligence quotient of, 318
 involvement in school activities, 62, 398–399
 involvement in youth sports programs, 302
 leave time from employment, 103, 203, 491
 lesbian and gay, 278, 497–498
 marital interactions of, 426
 moral behavior of, 267, 268, 416
 multitasking of, 25

never-married, 497
 in observational research, 29
 overweight and obese, 297
 of preterm infants, 98–100
 reports on temperament of child, 191
 reproductive choices of, 51–56
 and return to parental home, 484
 sibling favored by, 352, 557–558
 in single-parent families. See Single-parent families
 as stepparents, 356, 496–497
 vocational choice of, 463
 warmth of, 11, 271, 339
Parent–adolescent relationships, 376, 420–422, 492
 and academic achievement, 398–399
 in anorexia nervosa, 379
 autonomy issues in, 379, 420–421, 425
 and civic engagement, 419
 and clique membership, 425–426
 conflict resolution in, 376
 and contraceptive use of adolescent, 381–382
 cultural influences on, 421
 and dating relationships, 426
 in delinquency, 430, 431, 432
 and dropout rates, 402, 403
 in effective parenting, 420–421
 idealism and criticism in, 393
 and identity development, 411, 412
 of lesbian, gay, and bisexual youths, 383
 and moral development, 416, 418, 419
 and pubertal timing, 373
 and reactions to pubertal changes, 374–375, 377
 in school transitions, 398
 and self-esteem, 409
 sex differences in, 376
 sex education in, 380
 and sexual activity of adolescents, 384
 shared activities in, 422
Parent–adult-child relationships
 in middle adulthood of parents, 551–552
 of middle-aged children and aging parents, 554–557
Parent–child relationships
 and achievement attributions, 339, 340, 340f
 in adolescence. See Parent–adolescent relationships
 in adoption, 56
 and aggression, 273–274
 attachment in. See Attachment
 in attention-deficit hyperactivity disorder, 309
 and autobiographical memory of child, 240–241
 in baby boom generation, 12
 bidirectional influences in, 23, 57
 in blended families, 356, 496–497
 and childhood injuries, 221–222
 child-rearing practices in. See Child-rearing practices
 child-rearing styles in, 282t, 282–285
 in chronic illness of child, 298
 communication style in, 319–320

 conflict resolution in, 376
 coregulation in, 352
 depression of parent affecting, 187
 direct influences of, 57, 266
 divorce affecting, 354–355
 in early adulthood of child, 475, 485
 and eating habits, 219–220, 220f, 296
 and emotional development, 260, 261, 262
 and emotional self-regulation of child, 261, 342
 and empathy development, 263
 and executive function skills of children, 238–239
 family chaos affecting, 25
 gender typing in, 277–278, 350, 351
 of gifted and talented children, 329
 and grandparent–grandchild relationships, 552–554, 632
 indirect influences of, 266
 in infancy. See Parent–infant relationships
 and language development, 177–178
 in late adulthood, with adult children, 617, 631–632, 633
 in lesbian and gay parents, 498
 maltreatment in, 285t, 285–287
 in maternal employment, 357
 of middle-aged children and aging parents, 554–557
 of middle-aged parents and adult children, 551–552
 in middle childhood, 337, 338–340, 351–352
 mobile device use affecting, 275
 and moral development, 267–272
 observation of, 29
 in one-child families, 352–353
 and peer relations, 266
 in planning tasks, 238–239
 play in, 29, 168, 203–204, 266, 302
 in positive parenting, 271
 in psychosexual theory of development, 15, 258
 punishment in, 268–271
 questions asked by children in, 232
 of rejected children, 348
 reproductive technologies affecting, 52
 of resilient children, 11
 and romantic relationships as adults, 480
 in sandwich generation, 555–556
 scaffolding in, 235, 238
 and self-concept, 259, 262, 337, 338–340
 and self-conscious emotions, 262
 and self-esteem, 337, 338–340
 and sibling relationships, 352
 socioeconomic status affecting, 58, 60
 storytelling practices in, 259
 and theory of mind, 242
 warmth and attention in, 11, 271, 339
 in war-related violence, 359
Parent–emerging adult relationships, 475
Parent–infant relationships
 angry reactions in, 186
 attachment in, 22, 196–206
 in breastfeeding and bottle-feeding, 128

classical conditioning in, 130f, 130–131
and cognitive development of infants, 170–171
in cosleeping arrangements, 126
cultural variations in, 110, 203, 205
depression of parent affecting, 187
in Down syndrome, 50
and emotional self-regulation by infant, 189
facial expressions in, 185
in first child, 111, 490–491
infant characteristics affecting, 201
infant-directed speech in, 179
interactional synchrony in, 200
and language development, 176, 177–178
and motor development of infants, 110
operant conditioning in, 131
play activities in, 168, 203–204
in preterm infants, 98–100
quality of caregiving in, 184, 200–201
reflexes affecting, 101
in sensitive caregiving, 184, 185, 200–201
and sleeping arrangements, 126
smiling and laughter in, 185
social referencing in, 188
and soothing of crying infant, 105, 107–108
and temperament of child, 192, 194–195
transition to parenthood affecting, 111, 490–491
trust in, 184
Parenting practices. *See* Child-rearing practices
Parenting styles. *See* Child-rearing styles
Parents Anonymous, 287
Parent–school partnerships, 398–399
Parietal lobe, 574
Parkinson's disease, 587, 587n
Partial fetal alcohol syndrome, 84
Participant observation in ethnography, 31
Participatory perspective of death, 651
Partner abuse, 286, 488–489
Passion, in triangular theory of love, 479
Passionate love, 479, 481
Passive correlation of genetic and environmental factors, 68
Passive smoking, 84
Passive voice in language development, 174, 322
Paternal factors. *See* Fathers
Pattern perception, 141–142, 142f, 144
and face perception, 142–143, 143f
Pavlov, Ivan, 16
PCBs (polychlorinated biphenyls), 86
Peck, Robert, 610–611
Pedigree in genetic counseling, 51
Peer acceptance, 347–348
learning disability affecting, 327–328
in nontraditional careers of men, 464
obesity affecting, 297
of only children, 353
pubertal timing affecting, 377

in school transitions, 398
and self-esteem, 409
Peer collaboration in education, 235, 325
Peer culture, 346
Peer groups, 425–426
exclusion from, 417
and in-group favoritism, 278
in middle childhood, 346
suicide in, 429
Peer relations
and academic achievement, 399–400
acceptance in, 347–348. *See also* Peer acceptance
in adolescence, 373, 377, 386, 397, 398, 399–400, 409, 411, 412, 422–427
aggression in, 272, 273, 274, 346
bullying in, 348, 349
in college experience, 457, 460
cooperative learning in, 325–326
dating in, 426f, 426–427
in delinquency, 429, 430, 431
in early adulthood, 457–458, 460, 464
in early childhood, 263–266, 272, 273, 274, 276, 277, 278
friendships in, 265, 346–347, 422–425
of lesbian, gay, and bisexual youths, 383
gender typing in, 276, 277, 278
of gifted children, 329
and identity development, 411, 412
in middle childhood, 297, 302, 317, 325–326, 327–328, 329, 344
learning disability affecting, 327–328, 345–349, 351
and moral development, 417
in obesity, 297
of resilient children, 11
of same-ethnicity peers, 412
of same-sex peers, 277, 278, 351
and school readiness, 266
in school transitions, 397, 398
sex differences in, 278, 346, 349
and sibling relationships, 352, 353
and suicidal behavior, 428, 429
Peer sociability, 263–265
Peer victimization, 349
Pendulum problem, 388, 389f
Penis
in late adulthood, 584
in middle adulthood, 513
in puberty, 371, 372, 372t
Perception, 137–146
amodal, 143, 144
deprivation affecting, 121
differentiation theory of, 144–145
hearing in. *See* Hearing
intermodal, 143–144, 207, 576
narrowing effect in, 139, 143
smell sense in. *See* Smell sense
taste sense in. *See* Taste sense
touch in. *See* Touch
vision in. *See* Vision
Performance-enhancing drug use in adolescence, 370
Permanence of objects in sensorimotor stage, 152, 153f, 153–154
Permissive child-rearing style, 282t, 283, 398
Perry, William, 456, 458

Persistence, and temperament, 190, 191, 191t
Persistent vegetative state, 647, 660, 661
Personal agency, 471, 474
Personal choice, matters of, 272, 343–344, 416, 421
Personal fable, 392, 393, 429, 650
Personality traits, 35, 67, 68
in adolescence, 408, 411
in Alzheimer's disease, 588
in baby boom generation, 12
of dying people, and coping styles, 654–655
in early adulthood, 459, 462–463
in early childhood, 276, 277, 279
in infancy and toddlerhood, 184, 193
in late adulthood, 572, 573, 612, 614
in middle adulthood, 519–520, 543, 544, 548t, 548–549
in middle childhood, 345, 350, 352
prenatal development of, 80
of resilient children, 10–11
of romantic partners, 479
of siblings, 195
Person–environment fit in late adulthood, 580, 616, 618, 624, 625, 639
Person–environment system, 22
Person praise, 339
Perspective taking
in adolescence, 380, 392, 414, 417
in infancy and toddlerhood, 208
in middle childhood, 301, 312, 322, 337, 342, 343, 346, 348
Peru, 107, 221, 242
Phallic stage of psychosexual development, 15t
Phencyclidine (PCP), 386
Phenotype, 43, 46, 48, 70
Phenylalanine, 46, 47t
Phenylketonuria (PKU), 46, 47t, 48f
Philippines, 226
Phobias in middle childhood, 358
Phonics approach to reading, 313
Phonological awareness, 244, 313, 323
Physical abuse
of children, 285. *See also* Child maltreatment
of elderly, 633
Physical activities. *See* Exercise
Physical aggression, 272, 273
Physical development, 8, 9f
adaptation to changes in, 520–524, 578–581
in adolescence, 368–387
and biological aging, 438–444
body composition changes in. *See* Body composition changes
body proportion changes in. *See* Body proportion
body size changes in. *See* Body size
brain changes in, 217–219, 373–374
cardiovascular and respiratory changes in, 440–442, 576–577
cephalocaudal trend in, 117
in early adulthood, 438–456
in early childhood, 216–226
exercise affecting, 370–371, 447–448, 521–522, 583
gender stereotypes on, 523–524
genetic influences on, 127, 217, 219
hand preference in, 217–218

hardiness in, 522–523
health and fitness in, 378–387, 444–456, 514–520, 581–605
hearing changes in, 441t, 509, 575–576
hormonal influences on, 219, 369
illness and disability in, 515–519
immune system in, 441t, 443, 577
in infancy and toddlerhood, 114–147
infectious diseases affecting, 87t, 220–221, 383–384
in late adulthood, 570–594
and life expectancy, 570–573
in lifespan perspective, 8, 11f
in middle adulthood, 508–524
in middle childhood, 294–303
motor skills in. *See* Motor development
nervous system changes in, 441t, 573–574
of newborn, assessment of, 94t, 94–95
nutrition affecting, 127–129, 217, 219–220, 378–379, 445–447, 511, 582–583
prenatal. *See* Prenatal development
proximodistal trend in, 117
in puberty, 366–377
reproductive system in, 371–372, 441t, 443–444, 510–514
sex differences in, 117, 216, 216f, 217, 294, 294f, 368–372
sexuality in, 379–386, 450–455, 515, 583–584
skeletal changes in, 217, 441t, 510
skin changes in, 441t, 509–510, 578
sleep affecting, 577
smell sense in, 441t, 576
stress affecting, 455–456, 520–521
substance abuse affecting, 386–387, 448–450
taste sense in, 441t, 576
vision changes in, 441t, 508–509, 574–575
Physical education classes, 303, 371
Physical knowledge in infancy, 158
Piaget, Jean, 17, 324
clinical interviews of, 18, 29
cognitive-developmental theory of. *See* Cognitive-developmental theory
legacy of, 159
on moral development, 413, 414
Pictorial depth cues, 141
Pictures, and symbolic understanding of infants, 156
Pincer grasp, 137, 137f
Pituitary hormones, 219
Placenta, 77t, 78, 93f, 94
Planning
in adolescence, 390
in early childhood, 238–239, 239f
in middle adulthood, for retirement, 562–564
in middle childhood, 310
Plaque
amyloid, in Alzheimer's disease, 588–589, 590
in atherosclerosis, 442, 447
Plasticity
of brain, 121, 122, 595, 638
of development, 7, 9, 194–195, 524, 532, 602

Play
  in adolescence, 303, 397
  in autism, 243
  cross-gender activities in, 278
  in early childhood, 225, 227–228, 236, 237, 242, 258, 263–265, 264t, 266
  emotional understanding in, 261
  gender roles in, 208, 264, 276, 277
  gender segregation in, 277, 278
  gender-typed activities in, 276, 277, 278, 279, 280f, 350, 397
  in infancy and toddlerhood, 124, 153, 164, 168, 176, 200, 203–204, 208
  make-believe. See Make-believe play
  in middle childhood, 299–303, 350, 351
  of parent and child, 29, 168, 203–204, 266, 302
  with same-sex playmates, 277, 278, 351
Playground safety, 222
Pluralistic orientation in emerging adulthood, 471–472
Poland
  housework hours and gender roles in, 487, 487f
  infant mortality rate in, 102f
  math achievement scores in, 329f, 395f
  poverty rate in, 65f
  vocational life and cognitive development in, 531
Political involvement
  in emerging adulthood, 471–472
  in late adulthood, 637
  in middle adulthood, 539f
Pollution, prenatal exposure to, 86
Polychlorinated biphenyls (PCBs), 86
Polygenic inheritance, 50, 66
Popular children, 347, 348, 376
Pornography, 380, 454
Portion size in eating habits, 446, 447
Portugal
  infant mortality rate in, 102f
  life expectancy in, 571f
  marriage of same-sex couples in, 486
  math achievement scores in, 329f, 395f
Positive parenting, 271, 275
Positivity effect in late adulthood, 611–612, 621
Positron emission tomography (PET), 119, 119t, 588
Possible selves, 544, 581, 614
Postconventional level of moral development, 415
Postformal thought, 456, 459
Postpartum depression, 187
Post-traumatic stress disorder, 71, 286, 359
Poverty, 58–60
  academic achievement in, 61, 62
  and adolescent pregnancy, 90, 384
  asthma in, 298
  athletic activities of children in, 302
  breastfeeding of infants in, 127
  child-care quality in, 171
  childhood injuries in, 222

  cognitive development in, 172–173, 239, 246–247
  community influences in, 60–61
  and delinquency, 430
  dental caries in, 217
  early intervention and intellectual development in, 172–173, 246–247
  early sexual activity in, 381
  executive function development in, 239, 308
  extended family support in, 63
  feminization of, 550, 623
  fetal alcohol syndrome in, 85
  genetic and environmental influences in, 194
  of grandparents rearing grandchildren, 554
  and health problems, 217, 220, 221, 295, 296, 298, 445, 586
  homelessness in, 59
  immunizations in, 221
  infant mortality rate in, 102
  international differences in, 64t
  in late adulthood, 65, 65f, 582, 623
  leaving parental home in, 485
  life expectancy in, 571
  malnutrition in, 89, 295
  partner abuse in, 489
  physical development in, 217, 372
  preterm infants born into, 98, 99, 100
  pubertal growth in, 372
  of single-parent families, 59, 353, 355, 497
  sudden infant death syndrome in, 106
  suicide rate in, 546
  supplemental food program in, 89
  susceptibility to poor parenting in, 194–195
  working-memory capacity in, 308
Power of attorney for health care, 661, 662
Practical intelligence, 316, 316f, 530
Practical problem solving in middle adulthood, 530, 550
Practice effects in longitudinal research, 35
Prader-Willi syndrome, 49
Pragmatic approach to morality, 420
Pragmatic language development, 252, 322–323
Pragmatic thought, 458
Preattachment phase, 196–197
Preconventional level of moral development, 414
Preeclampsia, 91, 91f
Prefrontal cortex, 120, 120f
  in adolescence, 373–374, 386, 393, 394, 650
  in attention-deficit hyperactivity disorder, 309
  in autism, 243
  cognitive-control network in, 373–374, 386, 387f, 393, 394, 456, 650
  in early adulthood, 456
  in early childhood, 217, 218, 219
  in infancy and toddlerhood, 120, 123, 163, 189, 193
  in late adulthood, 574, 583, 601
  in middle childhood, 307, 308, 323

  recovery after injury of, 122
  in shy children, 192
Pregnancy, 76–97
  in adolescence, 371, 384–386. See also Adolescent pregnancy and parenthood
  age at time of, 89–91, 91f, 443. See also Maternal age
  alcohol use in, 84–85
  childbirth in, 92–97. See also Childbirth
  counseling on parenthood during, 102, 491
  diabetes in, 91
  diagnosis and treatment of fetal problems in, 53–55, 54t
  drug use in, 82–85, 106
  in early adulthood, 443–444, 444f
  embryo period in, 77t, 78–79
  environmental influences in, 70, 71, 71f, 81–88
  fetal period in, 77t, 79–81
  first, 111, 443, 444f, 490–491
  germinal period in, 76f, 76–78, 77t
  infectious diseases in, 86–88, 87t
  leave time from employment in, 103
  miscarriage in. See Miscarriage
  Nurse–Family Partnership in, 90
  nutrition in, 86, 88–89, 98, 108, 109f, 129, 439
  prenatal development in, 76–92. See also Prenatal development
  prenatal health care in. See Prenatal health care
  radiation exposure in, 49, 85–86
  in reproductive technologies, 52–53
  Rh factor incompatibility in, 89
  smoking in, 84
  social support in, 89, 90
  stress in, 48–49, 70, 71, 71f, 89, 90, 439
  in surrogate motherhood, 53
  teratogen exposure in, 81–88
  toxemia of, 91
  and transition to parenthood, 111, 490–491
  trimesters in, 77t, 79–81
Preimplantation genetic diagnosis, 54t
Prejudice, 344–345
  against lesbian, gay, and bisexual people, 382, 383, 453, 627
  against older adults, 580
  against religious communities, 418
Prekindergarten, universal, 246
Premarital sex, attitudes toward, 451, 451f
Premature infants. See Preterm infants
Prenatal development, 8t, 76–92
  in adolescent pregnancy, 384
  age of viability in, 80
  antibodies in, 81, 89, 382
  and conception, 76, 76f
  Darwin on, 13
  definition of, 8t
  diagnosis and treatment of problems in, 53–55, 54t
  drug exposure affecting, 82–85, 106
  embryonic, 77t, 78–79
  environmental influences on, 70, 71, 71f, 81–88
  fetal, 77t, 79–81
  germinal period in, 76f, 76–78, 77t
  habituation in, 81

  and hand preference, 218
  hearing in, 81, 99, 99f, 109
  hormone exposure affecting, 277, 281, 302, 382
  infectious diseases affecting, 86–88, 87t
  maternal age affecting, 89–91, 91f
  milestones of, 77t
  nutrition affecting, 86, 88–89, 98, 129, 439
  Rh factor incompatibility affecting, 89
  sensitive periods in, 81, 82f
  of small-for-date infants, 98
  stress affecting, 70, 71, 71f, 89, 90, 439
  teratogens affecting, 81–88, 308, 309
  trimesters in, 77t, 79–81
Prenatal health care, 91–92, 98, 102
  in adolescent pregnancy, 91, 384
  diagnostic tests in, 53–55, 54t
  exercise in, 88
  and infant mortality rates, 102
  long-term consequences of, 439
  nutrition in, 86, 88–89, 98, 129, 439
  and small-for-date infants, 98
  stress reduction in, 89, 90
Preoperational stage, 18, 18t, 227–234
  accommodation in, 229
  animistic thinking in, 229, 231
  categorization in, 230, 230f, 232
  centration in, 230
  conservation in, 229–230, 230f
  dual representation in, 229
  education in, 233–234
  egocentrism in, 229, 231, 234
  evaluation of, 232–233
  hierarchal classification in, 230, 230f
  irreversibility of thought in, 230
  learning in, 233–234
  limitations of thought in, 229–230
  logical thought in, 231–232, 233
  magical thinking in, 231
  make-believe play in, 227–228
  mental representations in, 227, 228
  problem solving in, 229, 229f, 230, 230f, 233
  questions asked by children in, 232
  research on, 231–232
  symbol–real-world relations in, 228–229
Prepared childbirth, 95–96
Prereaching movements of newborn, 137f
Presbycusis, 509
Presbyopia, 508
Preschool programs, 172, 246–247, 266
Preschool years. See Early childhood
Preterm infants, 97–100
  attachment insecurity of, 201
  behavioral assessment of, 110
  caregiving for, 46, 98–100, 108
  crying of, 108
  disabilities of, 98, 98f
  and drug use during pregnancy, 83
  habituation of, 131, 161
  and infectious diseases during pregnancy, 87t
  interventions for, 99f, 99–100
  kangaroo care of, 99–100

maltreatment and abuse of, 99, 108, 285
pain sensitivity of, 108
sleep of, 104
sudden infant death syndrome of, 106
twins, 46, 98
Preverbal gestures, 176
Pride
  in early childhood, 262
  in infancy and toddlerhood, 188, 189
  in middle childhood, 341, 342
Primary aging, 438–444, 585. *See also* Aging
Primary circular reaction in sensorimotor stage, 151, 151*t*
Primary sexual characteristics, 371
Primary teeth, 217
Principled level of moral development, 415
Private speech, 234–235, 236
Proactive aggression, 272, 273
Problem-centered coping
  in late adulthood, 579
  in middle adulthood, 520–521, 522, 545
  in middle childhood, 342
Problem solving
  in adolescence, 388, 389, 391–392, 393–394, 395, 413–414, 415, 416
  in early adulthood, 447, 457, 459
  in early childhood, 19, 20*f,* 229, 230, 232, 233, 238, 244–245
  in infancy and toddlerhood, 137, 152–153, 155, 165
  in late adulthood, 599–600, 601, 614
  in middle adulthood, 530, 550
  in middle childhood, 304, 306, 313, 314, 321, 328, 342
Procedural knowledge in middle adulthood, 529
Procedural memory, 529
Processing capacity, 161, 238, 308, 310
Processing speed. *See* Speed of information processing
Process praise, 339
Prodigies and gifted children, 30, 328–329
Production of language, compared to comprehension, 177
Progesterone in menopause therapy, 512
Programmed cell death in brain development, 118
Project Head Start, 173, 246–247
Prolactin, 111
Prolonged death, compared to sudden unexpected death, 666
Propositional thought, 389, 390
Prosocial behavior
  in adolescence, 417–418, 420
  in early adulthood, 471–472
  in early childhood, 262, 263, 268
  in middle childhood, 343, 346, 347, 348
Prospective memory in late adulthood, 598
Prostate gland, 372, 516, 517, 577
Protein
  in Alzheimer's disease, 588, 589
  in breastfeeding, 128

cross-linkage theory of aging on, 440
free radicals affecting, 440
and gene activity, 44, 54, 55
in kwashiorkor, 129
leptin, 372
in phenylketonuria, 46, 47*t*
Rh factor, 89
in weight loss diets, 446
Proteomics, 55
Proximal care of infants, 108
Proximodistal trend in growth, 117
Pruning, synaptic, 118, 118*f,* 119, 217, 456
Psychoanalytic perspective, 14–16, 27*t*
  attachment in, 196, 205
  clinical or case study research in, 16
  contributions and limitations of, 16
  moral development in, 267–268
  stages of development in, 15*t*
Psychological control in authoritarian child-rearing style, 283
Psychological knowledge in infancy, 158
Psychological well-being
  acceptance of change in, 614
  balance between work and family in, 501, 545
  of caregivers in Alzheimer's disease, 593
  in caregiving for older parents, 557
  child rearing in, 492
  community influences on, 60, 622
  contextual influences on, 615–619
  coping with stress in, 545, 617
  cultural influences on, 545
  in departure of children from parental home, 549, 551
  in divorce, 496, 550, 627
  of dying patients, 655, 659
  ego integrity in, 610
  executive processes in, 20
  exercise affecting, 448, 546
  factors promoting, 546–547
  family affecting, 25, 57, 60, 559
  fear of falls affecting, 587
  and flow state, 546–547
  friendships in, 424–425, 482, 483, 559, 630–631
  gender identity affecting, 351, 548
  generativity affecting, 539
  in gerotranscendence, 611
  of grandparents, 632
  and health, 546, 581, 617
  and identity status in adolescence, 410–411
  of lesbian, gay, and bisexual people, 383, 626
  life regrets affecting, 543
  marital relationships in, 489, 547, 550
  mastery of multiple roles in, 547, 555
  of never-married childless older adults, 630
  in nursing homes, 594
  parents affecting, 206, 475
  in personal life investment, 546–547
  person–environment fit in, 580, 616
  positivity effect in, 611
  possible selves affecting, 544
  prenatal stress affecting, 89

psychosocial theories of, 539, 610, 611, 612
in puberty, 374–377
relationships with grown children affecting, 551, 631
religious involvement in, 473, 615, 618
reminiscence and life review in, 612
in retirement, 563, 635, 636
romantic love in, 479
self-acceptance in, 545
self-concept in, 614
sense of control in, 546, 616
sex differences in, 545, 550, 617
sibling relationships in, 484, 630
in social perspective of adolescence, 368
social relationships in, 547, 620, 631
social support affecting, 557, 617–618, 631
subjective age in, 541, 579
in successful aging, 638–639
in terminal decline, 601
volunteer work in, 547
in widowhood, 629
Psychosexual stages of development, 14–15, 15*t*, 258, 368
  compared to psychosocial stages, 15*t,* 15–16
Psychosocial development, 15*t*, 15–16
  adaptation to life in, 477–478, 542
  autonomy versus shame and doubt in, 15*t*, 184
  compared to psychosexual development, 15*t*, 15–16
  death anxiety in, 651–652
  generativity versus stagnation in, 15*t,* 538–541
  gerotranscendence in, 611
  identity versus role confusion in, 15*t,* 408
  industry versus inferiority in, 15*t,* 336
  initiative versus guilt in, 15*t,* 258
  integrity versus despair in, 15*t,* 610
  intimacy versus isolation in, 15*t,* 476
  positivity effect in, 611–612
  reminiscence in, 612
  in seasons of life, 477, 541–542
  sequential research on, 36
  trust versus mistrust in, 15*t,* 184
Puberty, 367, 368–377
  antisocial behavior in, 431
  arousal states in, 374
  body composition in, 369, 372
  body image in, 377
  body proportions in, 369
  body size in, 369, 370*f*
  brain development in, 373–374
  depression in, 376, 377, 427–428
  early versus late timing of, 376–377, 379
  hormone changes in, 369, 377, 380, 426, 427
  individual and group differences in, 372–373
  moodiness in, 375
  motor development in, 370–371
  peer relations in, 377
  psychological impact of, 374–377
  reactions to changes in, 374–375

relationships with parents during, 376, 420
secular trends in, 373
sex differences in, 368–372, 372*t,* 373, 376, 377, 378
sexual maturation in, 369, 371–372, 372*t*
sexual orientation in, 382–383
timing of, 373, 376–377
Pubic hair development, 369, 371, 372, 372*t*
Public education programs
  on elder maltreatment, 634
  on immunizations, 221
  on nutrition, 447
  on prenatal health care, 91
  on sudden infant death syndrome, 106
Public policy, 64–66
  on adolescent suicide, 429
  on assisted-living facilities, 624
  on bilingual education, 323–324
  on caring for aging parents, 557
  for children, youths, and families, 64
  on early intervention programs, 173, 246–247
  and feminization of poverty, 550
  future trends in, 65–66
  on health care for parents and newborn, 102–103
  on health care in late adulthood, 579, 580, 591–592
  on hospice care, 659
  on immunizations, 221
  and infant mortality rates, 102, 103
  on long-term care in late adulthood, 592–594
  on Nurse–Family Partnership, 90
  for older adults, 64–65, 579, 580, 591–594, 613, 623, 624, 635–636, 639
  on parental leave time from employment, 103
  on reproductive technologies, 53
  on retirement benefits, 562–563, 635–636
  on surrogate motherhood, 53
  on universal health care, 91, 103
  on universal prekindergarten, 246
Puerto Rico, 103, 200–201
Pukapukans of Pacific Islands, 95
Punishment
  and aggression, 269, 270, 273
  consistency in, 269
  corporal, 268–269, 269*f,* 270
  cultural influences on, 269, 270, 284, 286
  in delinquency, 430
  explanations to child for, 271
  and moral development, 268–271, 414
  in operant conditioning, 16, 131
  in social learning theory, 17, 268–271
  time out technique in, 269, 270
  undesirable effects of, 269
  withdrawal of privileges in, 269, 270

Q

Q-Sort method in attachment assessment, 198
Quaker beliefs, 669
Quasi-experimental research, 34
Quechua of Peru, 107, 242

Questionnaires in research, 28t, 30, 36
Quinceañera, 375
Quinlan, Karen Ann, 660, 662

R

Racial differences. *See* Ethnic and racial differences
Radiation exposure, 49, 85–86
Random assignment in experimental research, 33–34
Random events theory of aging, 438, 439–440
Rape, 453–455
Rapid-eye-movement (REM) sleep, 104, 105, 105t, 125
Reaching in infancy and toddlerhood, 135, 135f, 136–137, 137f, 154
REACH (Resources for Enhancing Alzheimer's Caregiver Health) initiative, 593
Reactive aggression, 272, 273
Reactivity, and temperament, 190, 191t, 193, 194f
Readiness
 for learning, 234
 for reading, 244, 244f
 for school, 266
Reading
 in adolescence, 394, 464
 in early childhood, 225, 242–244, 244f
 in middle childhood, 313, 322, 323
Reading, Writing, Respect, and Resolution (4 Rs) Program, 360
Realistic period in vocational choice, 462
Realistic personality, vocational choice in, 462
Reasoning
 abstract. *See* Abstract thinking
 in early childhood, 232
 hypothetico-deductive, 388, 389, 389f
 inductive, 526, 526f
 in late adulthood, 614
 mathematical, 244–245. *See also* Mathematical abilities
 in middle childhood, 304–305
 moral, 272, 413–420
 propositional thought in, 389, 390
 scientific, 391f, 391–392
 spatial. *See* Spatial reasoning and skills
Recall memory
 in early childhood, 239–240
 in infancy and toddlerhood, 163
 in late adulthood, 596, 597
 in middle childhood, 529
Recast strategy in grammar correction, 252
Recent memory of infants, in habituation, 131
Recessive and dominant inheritance, 46–48, 47t, 48f
Recess time at school, 303
Reciprocal relationships
 ecological systems theory on, 23, 57
 ethological theory of attachment on, 197
 ideal reciprocity in, 414, 415, 416, 420
 morality of cooperation in, 414

Reciprocity, ideal, 414, 415, 416, 420
Recognition memory, 163, 239, 596, 597
Reconstituted families, 355–356
Recovery and habituation, 131, 132, 169
Recursive thought, 312, 322, 337, 342, 343, 346
Redemption events in life stories, 540
REDI (Research-Based Developmentally Information) curriculum, 247
Referential communication, 178
Reflexes
 classical conditioning of, 16, 130–131
 of infants and newborn, 94t, 101t, 101–104, 151, 151t
Regrets, in middle adulthood, 542–543, 543f
Regulator genes, 44
Rehearsal as memory strategy, 161, 240, 310, 529
Reinforcement
 in operant conditioning, 16, 131
 in social learning theory, 17, 268
Rejected children, 347, 348, 349, 351
Relational aggression, 272, 273, 346, 348, 431
Relational child-rearing goals, 208
Relativistic thinking, 457, 458
Religion
 adolescent rites of passage in, 375
 death concept in, 647, 649, 650, 651, 656, 661, 669
 in emerging adulthood, 472f, 472–473
 freedom in choice of, 343, 416
 and generativity, 539f, 541
 in late adulthood, 614–615, 617, 618
 of marriage partners, 487t, 496
 in middle adulthood, 539f, 541
 and moral development, 343, 418
 of romantic partners, 451, 479
Remarriage, 356
 in early adulthood, 495–497
 in late adulthood, 627–628, 629
 in middle adulthood, 550
Reminiscence in late adulthood, 597, 597f, 612
Remote memory, 132, 597f, 597–598
Repetition as memory strategy, 240
Representations, mental. *See* Mental representations
Reproductive capacity, age-related changes in, 443–444, 444f
Reproductive choices, 51–56
Reproductive system
 conception and prenatal development in, 76f, 76–81
 in early adulthood, 441t, 443–444, 444f
 in middle adulthood, 510–514
 in physical changes of aging, 441t
 in puberty, 369, 371–372, 372t
Reproductive technologies, 52–53, 443
 in early adulthood, 443, 444, 494
 for lesbian and gay families, 497
 multiple births in, 45, 45t, 52
 preimplantation genetic diagnosis in, 54t
 sex sorter methods in, 52
 in singlehood, 494

Research designs, 27, 31–37
 strengths and limitations of, 34, 34t
Research methods, 27, 28t, 28–31
Residential communities, older adults in, 623–624, 636
Resilience, 10–11
 in adolescence, 398, 412, 422
 in African-American families, 62
 in authoritative child-rearing style, 284
 in bereavement, 666
 in emerging adulthood, 473–476
 grandparents as source of, 553
 in late adulthood, 611, 614, 628
 in middle adulthood, 522–523
 in middle childhood, 352, 360
Resistant attachment, 198, 201, 480, 485
Resources for Enhancing Alzheimer's Caregiver Health (REACH) initiative, 593
Respiratory system
 in early adulthood, 441t, 442, 443
 in infancy and toddlerhood, 94t, 106
 in late adulthood, 576–577, 584f, 585
 in physical changes of aging, 441t
 in sleep apnea, 577
Respite services, 593, 634
Restoration task in grief process, 665–666, 670
Reticular formation in early childhood, 218, 218f
Retina, 121n
 in early adulthood, 449
 in late adulthood, 575
 in middle adulthood, 508, 509, 513
 in newborn, 109
Retirement, 613, 634–637
 average age of, 563, 634, 635
 of baby boom generation, 13
 cognitive changes in, 532
 and continuity theory of aging, 620
 decision making on, 635, 635f
 Experience Corps program in, 638
 leisure and volunteer activities in, 613, 635, 636–637, 638
 planning for, 562–564
 residential communities in, 623, 636
 suicide in, 618
 Third Age in, 613
Retrieval of information from memory, 161, 311, 529
 in late adulthood, 596, 598, 599
Reversibility
 in concrete operational stage, 304
 in preoperational stage, 230
Rheumatoid arthritis, 585, 586
Rh factor incompatibility, 89
Riboflavin deficiency in adolescence, 378
Right-handedness, 121, 218
Rights
 adolescent understanding of, 414, 415, 416
 childhood understanding of, 343–344
 in death and dying issues, 660t, 660–664
 of research participants, 37–39, 38t
Risks and benefits of research, 38–39
Risk-taking behavior
 in adolescence, 373f, 373–374, 393, 394, 650
 in middle childhood, 299

Rituals and ceremonies
 in mourning, 668, 669, 671
 in puberty onset, 375
 respect for older adults in, 581
Road Scholar program, 603–604
Robotic devices, 579
Rods and cones, 509
Role confusion and identity in adolescence, 15t, 408
Romania, 123, 123f, 329f, 384f
Romantic relationships
 in adolescence, 410, 426f, 426–427
 in early adulthood, 476, 478–482, 483, 484, 485
 in late adulthood, 627, 628
Rooting reflex, 101, 101t, 207
Rothbart model of temperament, 190–191, 191t
Rough-and-tumble play, 265, 302–303
Rubella (German measles), 86–87, 87t, 221
Rule-use tasks, flexible shifting in, 237–238, 308
Running, age-related changes in, 442f, 442–443
Rural areas, community influences in, 59, 622
Russia
 adolescent suicide in, 428
 math achievement scores in, 329f
 personality traits in, 548
 poverty rate in, 65f
 religious involvement in, 614
Rwanda, 71, 71f, 359

S

Sadness in infancy, 186
Safe to Sleep campaign, 106
Safety seats in cars, 221, 222
Same-sex caregivers for aging parents, 556
Same-sex couples, 453, 481, 483
 cohabitation of, 494
 gender-equitable expectations and behavior of, 278, 487
 grief in death of partner, 668
 health-care decisions of, 627
 marriage of. *See* Same-sex marriage
 mate selection of, 453, 479
 middle adulthood of, 550
 as parents, 278, 497–498
 partner abuse in, 488
Same-sex friendships, 423, 425, 483, 493
Same-sex marriage, 486, 494
 cohabitation prior to, 494
 happiness in, 486
 legalization of, 486, 494
 public support of, 451, 452f
Samoans, 311, 368
Sandwich generation, 555–556
Sarcasm, in pragmatic language development, 322
Saudi Arabia, 651
Scaffolding, 260
 and autobiographical memory of children, 240
 and executive function skills, 238, 308, 310
 in make-believe play, 168
 in sociocultural theory, 166, 235
Scale errors, 207

Schemes in cognitive development, 150
Schiavo, Terri, 660, 661, 662
Schizophrenia, 51, 67, 70
School attendance, 402–403
  and dropping out, 402f, 402–403, 430, 431
  and intelligence test scores, 320
  school transitions affecting, 397
School refusal, 358
Schools, 61–62
  academic achievement in, 62, 398–401. See also Academic achievement
  achievement attributions in, 339–340
  adult learners in, 532–533
  athletic activities in, 370
  bilingual programs in, 323–324
  bullying in, 29, 349
  career-related curriculum in, 400
  child-centered programs in, 246
  children with special needs in, 326–329
  and civic engagement, 419
  cliques and crowds in, 425–426
  cognitive self-regulation in, 312–313
  college. See College experience
  community service opportunities in, 419
  concrete operational thought in, 306
  constructivist classrooms in, 324, 325
  cooperative learning in, 325–326
  corporal punishment in, 286
  delinquency prevention and treatment strategies in, 430, 432
  diversity understanding in, 345
  dropping out from, 402–403, 430, 431, 460–461
  early literacy activities in, 244
  educational philosophies in, 324–326
  ethnic and racial diversity in, 345, 417
  Experience Corps intervention in, 638
  formal operational thought in, 390
  friendships in, 346–347, 398, 425
  gender typing in, 278, 350
  gifted children in, 328–329
  graduation rate from, 402
  grouping practices in, 326, 327, 401
  heterogeneous groups in, 326, 327
  high-quality, signs of, 325
  homogeneous groups in, 326
  identity development in, 411
  inclusive classrooms in, 326–328
  information processing in, 313–314
  integration of, 327
  international comparisons of, 329–330
  learning in, 313–314, 324–330
  magnet, 326, 327
  mathematics instruction in, 313–314, 395–396
  meals served in, 297, 378
  memory strategies in, 313
  moral development in, 417, 419
  Native-American culture in, 429
  obesity prevention strategies in, 297–298

  parent involvement with, 62, 398–399
  peer acceptance in, 347–348
  peer groups in, 266
  physical education classes in, 303, 371
  Piagetian classrooms in, 233–234
  preschool and kindergarten programs in, 246–247
  readiness for, 234, 266
  reading instruction in, 313
  recess time in, 303
  resilience interventions in, 360
  resource rooms in, 328
  service-learning programs in, 419
  sexual abuse prevention programs in, 360
  social-constructivist classrooms in, 325
  suicide prevention strategies in, 429
  teacher–student interactions in, 326. See also Teacher–student interactions
  tracking in, 401, 402
  traditional classrooms in, 324, 325
  transitions in, 396–398, 409
  trauma curriculum in, 359
  vocational programs in, 400, 401, 402, 411
  Vygotskian classrooms in, 235–236
  work–study programs in, 401
  zero tolerance policies in, 430
Science achievement, sex differences in, 395, 464–465
Scientific reasoning, 391f, 391–392
Scripts, memory of, 240
Scrotum, 76, 371
The Seasons of a Man's Life (Levinson), 477
The Seasons of a Woman's Life (Levinson), 477
Seasons of life theory, 477, 541–542
Seattle Longitudinal Study, 524, 526, 526f, 602
Second Age of midlife, 604n, 613
Secondary aging, 585
Secondary circular reaction in sensorimotor stage, 151t, 152
Secondary friends, 631
Secondary sexual characteristics, 371
Second language learning, 323–324
Second-order false beliefs, 312, 312f, 343
Secure base for infant exploration, 186, 197, 198
Security of attachment, 197–203
  cultural variations in, 199, 199f, 200–201
  and dating, 426
  and empathy, 263
  and false-belief tasks, 242
  and identity development in adolescence, 411
  and later development, 200, 202–203, 205–206
  measurement of, 197–198, 198t, 199, 199f
  and peer relations, 266
  and romantic relationships of adults, 480
  and self-concept, 259

Selective optimization with compensation, 595, 616, 639
Self-acceptance
  in late adulthood, 614, 639
  of lesbian, gay, and bisexual youths, 382–383
  in middle adulthood, 539, 544
Self-affirmation intervention, 321, 321f
Self-awareness
  in early childhood, 258–260
  in infancy and toddlerhood, 164–165, 188–189, 206–208
  in middle childhood, 336–337
Self-care children, 357
Self-concept, 17
  in adolescence, 392–393, 408, 418, 425
  in early adulthood, 477
  in early childhood, 258–260, 262
  in emerging adulthood, 470
  gender identity in. See Gender identity
  in late adulthood, 580, 612–614, 639
  in middle adulthood, 541, 543–545, 546–548
  in middle childhood, 336–341
  self-esteem in. See Self-esteem
Self-conscious emotions
  in early childhood, 260, 262
  in infancy and toddlerhood, 188–189
  in middle childhood, 341, 342
Self-consciousness in adolescence, 392–393
Self-control. See also Self-regulation
  in early childhood, 237, 238f, 265, 267, 268
  in infancy and toddlerhood, 208–209
Self-disclosure in friendships, 423, 424, 483
Self-efficacy, 17
  in adolescence, 371
  in late adulthood, 581, 582, 602
  in middle adulthood, 522, 546, 561
  in middle childhood, 313, 342
Self-esteem
  in adolescence, 370, 377, 393, 397, 401, 402, 403, 408–409, 412
  in bullying, 349
  in early childhood, 259, 260, 279, 282, 283, 284, 286
  in emerging adulthood, 470, 471, 473, 475
  in middle adulthood, 522, 540, 541, 542, 544, 548, 559
  in middle childhood, 302, 313, 326, 337–341, 338f, 345
  in obesity, 446, 447
  in retirement, 635, 636
Self-focusing
  in adolescence, 392–393
  in emerging adulthood, 470
  in late adulthood, 612
Self-fulfilling prophecy, educational, 326
Self-help skills in early childhood, 224, 237
Self-recognition, 207–208, 208f
Self-regulation
  in adolescence, 373, 390

  in early childhood, 237, 238f, 261, 267, 268
  emotional. See Emotional self-regulation
  in infancy and toddlerhood, 189, 190, 191t, 208–209
  in middle childhood, 296, 312–313, 340, 342, 352
Self-report research methods, 28t, 29–30, 31
Self-understanding
  in adolescence, 408–411
  in early childhood, 258–260
  in middle childhood, 336–341
Semantic memory, 240, 311, 529, 596
Semen, 444
Senescence, 438. See also Aging
Senior Corps, 613
Sensation-seeking behavior in adolescence, 373f, 373–374, 379, 386, 387f, 393, 650
Sensitive caregiving
  attachment in, 200–201, 203, 206
  autonomy of toddler in, 184
  emotional expressions of infant in, 185
  executive function skills of children in, 238
  goodness-of-fit model on, 195
  language development in, 252
  for preterm infants, 99
  in soothing of crying infant, 107
  trust of infant in, 184
Sensitive periods of development, 21
  in brain development, 121–124
  in culture-specific learning, 139
  deprivation in, 121, 123
  in language development, 174, 323
  in perceptual development, 138, 139
  telomere changes in, 439
  teratogen exposure in, 81, 82f
Sensorimotor stage, 18, 18t, 150, 151–153
  circular reactions in, 151, 151t, 152
  evaluation of, 156–159
  imitation in, 152, 153, 154–155, 155f
  intentional behavior in, 152
  mental representation in, 151t, 152–153, 154–156, 158, 227
  object permanence in, 152, 153f, 153–154
  problem solving in, 152–153, 155
  repeating chance behaviors in, 151–152
  searching for hidden objects in, 151, 152, 153, 154
  substages in, 151, 151t
  symbolic understanding in, 155–156
Sensory register in information processing, 160, 160f, 161
Separation, marital. See Divorce
Separation anxiety, 197, 198
September 11, 2001
  terrorist attacks, 36, 359, 668
Sequential research designs, 36–37
  cohort effects in, 36–37, 37f, 524–525, 525f
  compared to other research designs, 34t
Seriation in concrete operational stage, 304

Serotonin
  in Alzheimer's disease, 589, 590
  in attention-deficit hyperactivity disorder, 309
  in sudden infant death syndrome, 106
  and temperament, 194
Service-learning programs, 419
Sesame Street, 248
Sex cells, 44–45
Sex chromosomes, 45, 48–49, 49*f*
  abnormalities of, 50–51
  diseases linked to, 47*t*
Sex differences
  in achievement attributions, 340, 350
  in adult learners, 532
  in age trends in mental abilities, 526
  in aggression, 273, 274, 276
  in aging stereotypes, 523–524, 541
  in alcohol use, 449
  in asthma, 298
  in athletic activities, 301, 369, 370–371, 371*f*
  in attention-deficit hyperactivity disorder, 309
  in autobiographical memory, 241
  in bereavement, 666, 667
  in birth rate, 48
  in blended families, 356
  in body composition of muscle and fat, 294, 369, 510
  in body proportion changes, 369, 370*f*
  in body size, 117, 216, 216*f*, 294, 369, 370*f*
  in bullying, 349
  in cancer, 516, 516*f*, 517
  in cardiovascular disease, 442, 518–519
  in careers, 477, 499–501, 542, 561
  in caring for aging parents, 556, 556*f*
  in childhood injuries, 221
  in cliques, 425
  in college enrollment, 394
  in computer use, 249
  in conflict resolution, 481
  in death anxiety, 652, 652*f*
  in delinquency, 430, 431
  in dementia rate, 587
  in depression, 427, 428, 618
  in divorce, 496, 550–551, 627, 628
  in dream of adult life in early adulthood, 477
  in emotional expression, 189
  in exercise, 448
  in fears during middle childhood, 358
  in friendships, 346, 347, 423, 424, 483–484, 493, 558, 559, 631
  and gender typing, 276–280
  in generativity in middle adulthood, 539
  in genomic imprinting, 49
  in glaucoma, 509
  in grandparent–grandchild relationships, 553, 554
  in hearing loss, age-related, 509, 574*f*
  in high school dropout rates, 402
  in HIV infection and AIDS, 453
  in housework hours, 486–487, 487*f*
  in identity development, 350–351, 410
  in infant mortality rate, 117
  and infant preference for female faces, 143
  in intimacy, 479
  in job satisfaction, 560
  in language development, 177, 394
  in late adulthood health, 582, 586, 587
  in life expectancy, 570, 571, 571*f*, 572
  in marital roles, 356–357, 486–487, 487*f*, 490–491, 629
  in marital satisfaction, 488, 550, 626
  in mate selection, 479
  in mathematical abilities, 395*f*, 395–396
  in mental abilities, 394–396
  middle adulthood health problems, 516
  in moral development, 415–416
  in motor development, 225, 301, 370
  in never-married childless older adults, 630
  in number of sexual partners, 451
  in obesity rate, 445
  in older parent–adult child relationships, 632
  in osteoporosis, 519
  in parenting education, 492
  in partner abuse, 488, 489
  pay gap in, 499, 550
  in personality traits, 276, 277
  in physical development, 117, 216, 216*f*, 217, 294, 294*f*, 368–372
  in play activities, 203–204, 225, 264, 265, 266, 277, 302, 350
  in puberty, 368–372, 372*t*, 373, 376, 377, 378
  in relationships with aging parents, 555
  in religiosity, 472, 615
  in remarriage, 496, 628
  in reproductive system changes, 371–372, 372*t*, 443–444, 510–513
  in response to divorce of parents, 354–355, 356
  in retirement decisions, 635, 636
  in retirement planning, 564
  in seasons of life theory, 477
  in self-acceptance, 545
  in self-control, 209
  in self-esteem, 338, 409
  in sensory system changes in aging, 574*f*
  in sexual abuse, 426
  in sexual attitudes and behaviors, 381*f*, 451, 452, 583–584, 584*f*
  in sexual coercion, 454
  in sexual dysfunction, 452
  in sexually transmitted infections, 453
  in sexual maturation, 371–372, 372*t*
  in shyness, 35
  in sibling relationships, 558, 630
  in singlehood, 493
  in skeletal changes, age-related, 510
  in skin changes, age-related, 510
  in sleep disturbances, 577
  in smoking, 449
  in social media use, 424
  in spatial reasoning and skills, 395, 396*f*, 396–397
  stereotyped beliefs on, 277–278. *See also* Gender stereotypes
  in stress, 428, 545, 545*f*, 615, 617
  in suicidal behavior, 428, 618
  in temperament, 193–194
  in unintentional injuries, 298, 299, 299*f*
  in vascular dementia, 591
  in verbal abilities, 394
  in violent media viewing, 275
  in visual impairments, age-related, 574*f*
  in vocation, 463*t*, 463–465, 561
  in widowhood, 628, 629
  in X-linked inheritance, 48, 49
Sex education
  on contraception, 381–382, 385
  cultural influences on, 380
  in prevention of adolescent pregnancy, 385
  and reactions to pubertal changes, 374–375
  on sexually transmitted infections, 383–384, 453
Sex hormones
  and aggression, 273
  estrogen. *See* Estrogen
  in puberty, 369
  and sexual orientation, 382
  testosterone, 369, 510, 513, 519
Sex roles. *See* Gender roles
Sex stereotypes. *See* Gender stereotypes
Sex typing. *See* Gender typing
Sexual abuse
  in adolescent dating relationships, 426
  and alcohol abuse, 450, 454
  in early adulthood, 453–455
  in early childhood, 285
  eyewitness memory of children on, 361
  in late adulthood, 633
  in middle childhood, 358–360
  prevention and treatment of, 360
  sexual dysfunction of victim after, 452
Sexual attitudes and behavior, 379–386
  and adolescent pregnancy, 384–386
  coercion in, 453–455
  and contraceptive use, 381*f*, 381–382
  cultural influences on, 368, 380, 584
  divorce of parents affecting, 354
  in early adulthood, 450–455
  in late adulthood, 583–584
  lifetime number of sexual partners in, 451
  in middle adulthood, 512, 513, 515, 515*f*, 547
  in passionate love, 479
  psychosexual theory of Freud on, 15
  sexual abuse affecting, 359–360, 452, 454
  and sexually transmitted infections, 383–384, 453
  and sexual orientation, 452–453
  timing of puberty affecting, 377
  trends in, 451, 451*f*
Sexual characteristics, primary and secondary, 371
Sexual coercion, 453–455
Sexual dysfunction, 449, 452, 513
Sexual identity of homosexual youths, 382–383
Sexually transmitted infections
  in adolescence, 383–384
  AIDS, 383. *See also* AIDS
  in early adulthood, 453
Sexual maturation, 371–372, 372*t*
  hormone changes in, 369
  initiation ceremonies in, 375
  reactions to, 374–375
  timing of, 376–377
Sexual orientation
  in adolescence, 382–383, 411, 426
  of children of homosexual parents, 498
  in early adulthood, 452–453
  lesbian, gay, and bisexual. *See* Lesbian, gay, and bisexual people
  religious beliefs on, 473
Shame
  in early childhood, 260, 262
  in infancy and toddlerhood, 15*t*, 184, 188, 189
  in middle childhood, 341
  in suicidal loss, 666
Shape bias in vocabulary development, 250
Shinto beliefs about death, 647
Shiva mourning period, 669
Shoe tying in early childhood, 224
Short-term memory, 160*f*, 160–161, 162, 163
Shyness, 191, 192
  cultural influences on, 195, 265
  longitudinal study of, 35–36
Siblings
  in adolescence, 422
  affectionate ties between, 206
  aggression of, 273
  arrival of new sibling, 204
  attachment patterns of, 201, 204–205
  in blended families, 355–356
  of centenarians, 573
  cross-sectional studies of, 36
  death of, 667
  in early adulthood, 484
  and false beliefs, 242
  as friends, 484
  gene–environment correlation in studies of, 69, 69*f*
  genetic variability between, 45
  glaucoma in, 509
  in late adulthood, 630
  longitudinal studies of, 36
  in middle adulthood, 557
  in middle childhood, 352
  number of, 12, 204, 484, 490
  and one-child families, 48, 352–353
  play of, 168
  rivalry between, 352, 484, 557–558
  sexual orientation of, 382
  temperament and personality of, 195, 204
  twin. *See* Twins
Sickle cell anemia, 47*t*, 48, 298
Sickle cell trait, 48, 49
SIDS (sudden infant death syndrome), 105, 106, 126, 136, 666
Sierra Leone, 571
Sign language, 121, 174, 176
Simon, Theodore, 14
Singapore, 329*f*, 571*f*
Singlehood
  in early adulthood, 493–494
  frequency of sexual activity in, 515
  in middle adulthood, 515
  and widowhood, 668
Single-parent families
  in adolescent pregnancy, 384

Subject Index   SI-33

chaos in, 25
in divorce, 353, 355
extended family relationships of, 63
food insecurity in, 129
grandparents in, 553
interventions for, 491
leave time from employment, 103
in never-married parents, 497
and parents as adult learners, 532
poverty of, 59, 353, 355, 497
Size of family, 12, 58, 204, 484, 490
Skeletal age, 117, 217
Skeletal system
in early adulthood, 440, 441*t*
in early childhood, 217
in late adulthood, 578, 585, 587
in middle adulthood, 510, 512, 519
in physical changes of aging, 441*t*
in puberty, 369
Skin
in early adulthood, 440, 441*t*
in late adulthood, 578
in middle adulthood, 509–510, 512
in physical changes of aging, 441*t*
Skinner, B. F., 16
Skin surface temperature, in shyness and sociability, 192
Skipped-generation families, 554
Sleep
in adolescence, 374
of fetus, 80
insufficient, weight gain in, 296
in late adulthood, 574, 577
in menopause, 512
of newborn and infants, 83, 104–105, 105*t*, 106, 125, 125*f*, 126
non-rapid-eye-movement, 104, 105, 105*t*, 577
rapid-eye-movement, 104, 105, 105*t*, 125
sudden infant death in, 106, 136
Slovakia, 102*f*, 487*f*
Slovenia
housework hours and gender roles in, 487, 487*f*
infant mortality rate in, 102*f*
life expectancy in, 571*f*
math achievement scores in, 329*f*
poverty rate in, 65*f*
Slow-to-warm-up temperament, 190
Slow-twitch muscle fibers, 443, 578
Small-for-date infants, 98
Smart home technologies, 579–580
Smartphones, 579
Smell sense
in infancy and toddlerhood, 108–109, 109*f*
in late adulthood, 576
in physical changes of aging, 441*t*
Smiling in infancy, 131, 185
Smoking, 49
in adolescence, 376, 386, 387, 416
in early adulthood, 442, 448, 449, 454
exposure of children to smoke from, 217
in late adulthood, 575, 576, 577, 582*f*, 584, 586, 591, 601
in middle adulthood, 509, 516, 519
in pregnancy, 70, 84, 91
and sudden infant death syndrome, 106
telomere length in, 439

Sociability, 191, 192
cultural influences on, 195, 265
in peer relations, 263–265
Social clock, 478, 493, 539, 551, 562
Social-cognitive learning theory, 17
Social comparisons
gender identity in, 351
in-group and out-group biases in, 344–345
in middle childhood, 336, 337, 351
and self-esteem, 337, 544
Social-constructivist classrooms, 325
Social contract orientation in moral development, 415
Social conventions and moral development, 272, 343, 416
Social convoy model, 625
Social development. *See* Emotional and social development
Social interaction
language development in, 175, 176
sociocultural theory on, 22–23
Social learning theory, 17, 27*t*
on gender identity, 279
on gender typing, 276
on moral development, 267, 268–271
Social networking sites
in adolescence, 423–424, 424*f*
in early adulthood, 451, 483
Facebook. *See* Facebook use
in late adulthood, 605, 631, 632
in middle adulthood, 559, 559*f*
online friendships in. *See* Online friendships
Social neuroscience, developmental, 20–21
Social order-maintaining orientation in moral development, 414–415, 420
Social personality, vocational choice in, 462
Social preference measure of peer acceptance, 347
Social referencing in infancy and toddlerhood, 188
Social Security benefits, 64–65, 563, 635
Social smile, 185
Social support
of adolescent parents, 385, 386
and attachment security of children, 201
in bereavement interventions, 668
for caregivers, 557, 593
in childhood injury prevention, 222
in child maltreatment prevention, 286
in early adulthood, 447, 456, 473, 483, 484
in ecological systems, 24
in elder maltreatment prevention, 634
extended family relationships in, 63
in late adulthood, 573, 615, 617–618, 619, 620, 628, 629–630, 636
in middle adulthood, 532–533
neighborhood resources in, 61
in partner abuse interventions, 489
during pregnancy and childbirth, 89, 90, 96
of resilient children, 11
Social theories of aging, 620–622
Sociocultural theory, 22–23, 27*t*, 166–167, 234–236
on education, 235–236, 325

evaluation of, 236
on play, 168, 236
on private speech, 234–235
on scaffolding, 166, 235
on zone of proximal development, 166, 235, 325
Sociodramatic play in early childhood, 228, 236, 264–265
Socioeconomic status, 58–60
and academic achievement, 325, 326, 330, 401
and academic tracking, 401
and access to high-quality education, 327
in adolescent pregnancy, 90, 384
and adolescent sexual activity, 381
of adult learners as returning students, 532, 533
in affluence, 60
and after-school programs, 357
and age trends in mental abilities, 526
and athletic activities of children, 301–302
and attachment security, 198–199
and bilingual education, 323
and cancer incidence, 516–517
and child-care quality, 171
and child-rearing practices, 284
and civic engagement, 419
and cognitive development, 170, 239
and college experience, 460, 461
and computer use, 249
and delinquency, 430
and departure from parental home, 485, 551
divorce affecting, 353, 355, 550
and dropout rates, 402
and early intervention programs for at-risk preschoolers, 172–173, 245–247
and emerging adulthood, 474
and exercise, 448
factors considered in, 58
and family functioning, 58–60
and flexible abstract thinking, 531
and friendships, 346
and generativity in middle adulthood, 539
and grandparent–grandchild relationships, 553
and grouping practices in schools, 326, 340
and health in early adulthood, 444–445
and health in late adulthood, 575, 581
and health in middle adulthood, 515–516
and health in middle childhood, 298
and IQ, 170, 172–173, 245, 318, 319, 320
and knowledge development, 320
in late adulthood, 581, 623
and life expectancy, 570, 571
and mathematics skills, 245
and myopia, 298
and neighborhood influences, 60–61
and nutrition problems, 220, 295–296, 378
and parent–adult-child relationships, 551–552

and part-time work of adolescents, 401
and play activities, 301
in poverty, 58–60. *See also* Poverty
and pubertal growth variations, 372, 373
and reading skills, 244, 244*f*
and religious activities, 615
in retirement, 563
and self-care children, 357
and self-esteem, 338, 340
and service-learning programs, 419
of single-parent families, 59, 353, 355, 497
and storytelling practices, 259
and stress, 455
and suicide rate, 546
in surrogate motherhood, 53
and teacher–student interactions, 326
and television viewing time, 249
and vocabulary development, 178
and vocational choice, 463
Socioemotional selectivity theory of aging, 620–622, 632
Somatic mutation, 49, 516
Son-in-law, 552, 553
Soothing of child, 105, 107–108, 189
South Africa, 87, 486
South America, 473
South Korea, 102*f*, 460, 548, 571*f*
Spain
adolescent birth rate in, 384*f*
adolescent suicide in, 428
departure from parental home in, 551
infant mortality rate in, 102*f*
life expectancy in, 571*f*
marriage of same-sex couples in, 486
math achievement scores in, 329*f*
poverty rate in, 65*f*
Spanking, 270
Spatial reasoning and skills, 121, 122
in adolescence, 395, 396*f*, 396–397
in early childhood, 217
intelligence tests of, 315, 315*f*, 319, 320
in late adulthood, 602
in middle adulthood, 528
in middle childhood, 304–305, 315, 317, 319, 320, 329
in multiple intelligences theory, 317, 317*t*, 329
Special needs, teaching children with, 326–329
Special Supplemental Food Program for Women, Infants, and Children, U.S. (WIC), 89
Spectroscopy, near-infrared (NIRS), 119, 119*t*, 120*f*, 121
Speech
age-related decline in perception of, 575
comprehension and production of, 177
egocentric, 234
first sounds of, 175–177
infant attention to, 109, 121
infant-directed, 179
infant perception of, 138–140
inner, 234
in late adulthood, 598, 599
private, 234–235, 236
telegraphic, 177
two-word utterances in, 177

Speed of information processing, 161
 in late adulthood, 602
 in middle adulthood, 526, 526f, 527–528, 531
 in middle childhood, 315f, 315–316
Sperm, 44, 45, 76, 77, 372, 372t
 age-related changes in, 444, 513
 and conception, 45, 76
 in reproductive technologies, 52, 53
Spermarche, 372, 372t, 375
Spina bifida, 89
Spinal column changes in middle adulthood, 510
Spirituality
 death concept in, 649, 650, 656
 in emerging adulthood, 472f, 472–473
 in late adulthood, 614–615, 639
Spock, Benjamin, 14, 126
Sports activities, 301–302, 370–371. *See also* Athletic activities
Spouses. *See* Marital relationships
Stability genes in cancer, 516
Stability of characteristics, 7
 in attachment, 198–199
 compared to plasticity, 7
 in temperament, 191–193
Stages of development
 cognitive, 17–19, 18t
 concrete operational. *See* Concrete operational stage
 in discontinuous perspective, 6
 formal operational. *See* Formal operational stage
 in middle adulthood, 543
 moral, 414–415
 preoperational. *See* Preoperational stage
 psychosexual, 14–15, 15t
 psychosocial, 15t, 15–16
 sensorimotor. *See* Sensorimotor stage
 in sociocultural theory, 23
Stages of dying, 653
Stagnation versus generativity in middle adulthood, 15t, 538–541
Standardization of intelligence tests, 169
Stanford-Binet Intelligence Scale, 14, 315
States of arousal
 in adolescence, 374
 in infancy and toddlerhood, 104–108, 105t, 125, 125f
Statistical learning capacity in infants, 138–140
STEM careers, 395, 464–465
Stepfamilies, 356, 496–497
Stepping reflex, 101t, 102
Stereotypes
 of aging. *See* Stereotypes of aging
 on childlessness, 495
 ethnic and racial, 320, 344, 350, 412, 532
 gender-related. *See* Gender stereotypes
 on homosexuality and bisexuality, 382–383
 in obesity, 297
 on religious communities, 418
 and stereotype threat, 320, 321, 326, 395, 580

Stereotypes of aging, 523–524, 580–581
 and anxiety of returning students, 532
 continuing education affecting, 605
 cultural influences on, 580–581
 dependency in, 616
 elder maltreatment in, 634
 elderspeak in, 599
 friendships affecting, 630
 and socioemotional selectivity theory, 621
 in vocational setting, 531, 561
Sternberg triarchic theory of successful intelligence, 316, 316f, 530
Steroids, anabolic, adolescents using, 370
Stimulant drug use, 309, 386, 448
Storytelling, 259, 599, 612
Stranger anxiety, 186
Strange Situation procedure, 197–198, 198t, 199, 199f
Stress
 in adolescence, 373, 376, 377, 387, 412, 421, 428, 429
 of bullying victims, 349
 calorie-restriction diet affecting response to, 511
 of caregivers of aging parents, 557, 558
 of caregivers of older adults with dementia, 590, 592–593
 of caregivers of preterm infants, 99, 108
 of caregivers of terminally ill patients, 655
 in childbirth, 94
 of child maltreatment victims, 287
 in chronic illness of child, 298
 coping strategies in, 520–521. *See also* Coping strategies
 cortisol levels in. *See* Cortisol
 in early adulthood, 443, 445, 448, 452, 455–456, 493
 in early childhood, 263
 in family circumstances, 275–276, 296, 422
 of grandparents rearing grandchildren, 554
 in infancy and toddlerhood, 108, 123, 129, 193, 203
 in late adulthood, 577, 612, 614, 615, 617
 in life stories, 540
 and lifetime exposure to adversity, 523, 523f
 in menopause, 512, 513, 514, 521
 in middle adulthood, 516, 517, 520–521, 522–523, 532, 545–546, 550, 560
 in middle childhood, 308, 353, 359, 360
 obesity in, 296
 of parents, 25, 187, 222, 286, 287
 in poverty, 59, 222, 239, 308
 in pregnancy, 48–49, 70, 71, 71f, 89, 90, 439
 resilience in, 10–11, 360
 in retirement, 636
 of shy children, 192
 telomere length in, 439
 in unemployment, 562
 in war-related violence, 359

Stress hormones. *See also* Cortisol
 in early deprivation, 123
 in labor and delivery, 94
 in late adulthood, 574
 in overeating, 296
 in post-traumatic stress disorder, 71
 in pregnancy, 89
Stroke, 584f, 585
 brain plasticity in, 122
 dementia in, 590–591
 signs and symptoms of, 591
Strong African American Families (SAAF) program, 387
Structured interviews research method, 28t, 30
Structured observation research method, 28t, 28–29
Subcultures, 62
Subjective age, 541, 579
Substance abuse, 386–387
 in adolescence, 370, 386–387, 428, 429, 449
 in affluence, 60
 AIDS in, 453
 of alcohol. *See* Alcohol use and abuse
 of anabolic steroids, 370
 and clique membership, 425
 and dating, 426
 in early adulthood, 448–450
 in early pubertal maturation, 376
 of lesbian, gay, and bisexual youths, 382
 in peer group, 386, 425
 during pregnancy, 82–85, 106
 prevention and treatment of, 387
 and smoking. *See* Smoking
 and suicide, 428, 429
 telomere length in, 439
Suburban communities, older adults in, 622
Successful aging, 637–639
Sucking reflex, 101, 101t, 130f, 130–131
Sudan, 319, 359
Sudden death
 bereavement interventions in, 670
 compared to prolonged death, 666
 in hospital, 657
 of infant, 105, 106, 126, 136, 666
Sudden infant death syndrome (SIDS), 105, 106, 126, 136, 666
Suggestibility affecting eyewitness memory of children, 361
Suicide
 in adolescence, 378, 382, 393, 428–429, 618, 650
 in anorexia nervosa, 378
 in bulimia nervosa, 379
 in early adulthood, 444f
 grief of survivors in, 429, 666
 in late adulthood, 617, 618–619
 of lesbian, gay, and bisexual youths, 382, 428
 of maltreatment victims, 286
 in middle adulthood, 546, 618
 in obesity, 297
 physician-assisted, 663
 prevention and treatment strategies, 429, 619
 of transgender adults, 281
 warning signs in, 429, 429t, 619
Sun exposure, skin aging in, 510

Superego, 14–15, 258, 267
Surrogate motherhood, 53
Survival of the fittest, 13
Swaddling of infants, 107
Sweden
 adolescent birth rate in, 384f
 assistive technology in, 580
 caring for aging parents in, 557
 cohabitation in, 494
 family size in, 490
 health care in, 580
 home births in, 96
 immunization rate in, 221
 infant mortality rate in, 102f
 intelligence quotient in, 319
 life expectancy in, 571, 571f
 long-term care for older adults in, 592
 marital roles in, 486, 487f
 marriage of same-sex couples in, 486
 math achievement scores in, 329f, 395, 395f
 parental leave in, 103
 poverty rate in, 65f
 religious involvement in, 418
 retirement programs in, 636
Switzerland
 academic achievement in, 329, 329f
 adolescent birth rate in, 384f
 housework hours and gender roles in, 487f
 infant mortality rate in, 102f
 life expectancy in, 571f
 long-term care for older adults in, 592
 medical aid-in-dying in, 663
 vocational education in, 465
Symbolic understanding, 155–156, 228–229
Sympathetic nervous system in shy infants, 192
Sympathy in early childhood, 263
Synapses, 79, 117, 118, 118f, 119
 in Alzheimer's disease, 589
 in late adulthood, 574
 pruning process, 118, 118f, 119, 217, 456
 stimulation of, 118
Syphilis in pregnancy, 87t
Syria, 359
Systems approach, 7
 in dynamic systems perspective. *See* Dynamic systems perspective
 in ecological systems theory, 23–26. *See also* Ecological systems theory
 family as system, 57–58, 421
 in lifespan perspective, 7–8

T

Taiwan
 academic achievement in, 330
 drawing skills of children in, 226
 life expectancy in, 571f
 math achievement scores in, 329f
 play activities in, 264
 prenatal exposure to PCBs in, 86
 storytelling practices in, 259
Talent and creativity, 328–329
Tanzania, 156
Taste sense
 in infancy and toddlerhood, 108–109
 in late adulthood, 576
 in physical changes of aging, 441t

Tau in neurofibrillary tangles, 588, 589, 590
Taxonomic categories as memory strategy, 310
Tay-Sachs disease, 47t, 56
T cells, 443, 577
Teacher–student interactions, 326
    and academic achievement, 326, 399, 400
    achievement attributions in, 339, 340
    in bullying, 349
    and civic engagement, 419
    in college experience, 461
    in constructivist classrooms, 324
    and dropout rates, 402
    gender typing in, 278, 280, 350
    international differences in, 330
    and moral reasoning, 417, 419
    in preschool and kindergarten programs, 246, 266
    of rejected children, 348
    in resource room, 328
    in school transitions, 397, 398
    self-fulfilling prophecies in, 326
    in social-constructivist classrooms, 325
    suicide prevention strategies in, 429
    in traditional classrooms, 324, 325
    and vocational choice, 463
Team approach in hospice care, 658
Teenage pregnancy and parenthood, 371, 384–386. *See also* Adolescent pregnancy and parenthood
Teen Outreach, 385
Teeth
    in early childhood, 217, 219
    in late adulthood, 573, 578
    in middle childhood, 294
Telegraphic speech, 177
Television
    daily viewing time, 128, 157, 248–249, 274, 274f, 297
    death depictions in programs on, 649
    educational programs on, 157, 248–249
    infant and toddler learning from, 157, 179
    and media multitasking, impact on learning, 400
    and myopia, 298
    and obesity, 128, 297
    roles of older adults on, 580
    sexual content of programs on, 380
    substance use in programs on, 386
    and video deficit effect, 157
    violence on, 274f, 274–275
Telomerase, 439
Telomeres, 438–439, 439f
Temperament, 68
    and aggression, 273
    and attachment security, 201
    of bullying victims, 349
    and childhood injuries, 221
    and child-rearing practices, 190, 192, 193, 195, 209
    cultural variations in, 193, 195
    in adolescent delinquency, 430
    of bullying victims, 349
    and empathy, 263
    gene–environment correlations in, 193
    gene–environment interactions in, 68, 194
    genetic influences on, 68, 192, 193–195, 194f, 201
    goodness-of-fit model on, 195, 209
    in early childhood, 221, 263, 268, 269, 273, 283
    in infancy and toddlerhood, 177, 186, 189, 190–195, 201, 209
    and language development, 177
    of maltreatment victims, 285
    models of, 190–191, 191t, 195, 209
    and moral development, 268
    prenatal development of, 80
    of resilient children, 10–11
    and response to divorce of parents, 354
    of siblings, 195, 204
    stability of, 191–193
Temperature adaptation in late adulthood, 574, 578
Temper tantrums, 189
Temporal lobes, 175, 243, 574
Tentative period in vocational choice, 462
Teratogens, 81–88, 308, 309
Terminal decline in late adulthood, 601–602
Terminal illness
    behavior of health professionals in, 655
    caregiver stress in, 655
    in children, 649, 652, 655, 659
    coping with dying in, 653, 654–655
    death anxiety in, 652
    in family member, 655–656
    home death in, 657
    hospice care in, 658–660
    informing patient about, 652, 655
    personality and coping style in, 654–655
    religious and spiritual beliefs in, 656
    right to die in, 660–664
    stages of dying in, 653
Terrorism
    bereavement overload in, 668
    death concept of children experiencing, 649
    impact on children, 36, 359
    sudden unanticipated death in, 666
Tertiary circular reaction in sensorimotor stage, 151t
Testes, 76
    in puberty, 369, 371, 372, 372t
Testimony, eyewitness, by children, 361
Testing methods, 27, 28t, 29, 30
    Flynn effect in, 319
    on intelligence. *See* Intelligence tests
    practice effects in, 35
Testosterone
    in middle adulthood, 510, 513, 519
    in puberty, 369
Text messaging, 423–424, 424f
Thailand, immigrant youths from, 32
Thalidomide, 82
Thanatology, 645, 671
    music, 659
Theories of development, 5–27. *See also specific theories.*
    on attachment, 6

behaviorism, 16
cognitive-developmental, 17–19
comparison of, 26, 27t
as continuous or discontinuous process, 6, 6f, 27t
on course of development, 6, 27t
definition of, 5
developmental neuroscience, 20–21
ecological systems, 23–26
ethology, 21–22
evolutionary developmental psychology, 22
historical foundations of, 12–19
information processing, 19–20
psychoanalytic, 14–16
recent perspectives, 19–26
on relative influence of nature and nurture, 7, 27t
scientific verification of, 6
social learning, 17
sociocultural, 22–23
Theory of mind
    in autism, 242, 243
    in early childhood, 241–242, 272
    in middle childhood, 311–312, 312f
Third Age, 604, 604n, 613
Third parties in microsystem, 23, 57
Three-mountains problem, 229, 229f
Thymus, 443
Thyroid-stimulating hormone (TSH), 219
Thyroxine, 219, 369
Time-based prospective memory tasks, 598
Time out as punishment technique, 269, 270
Tinbergen, Niko, 21
Tip-of-the-tongue state in late adulthood, 598, 599
Tobacco use, 84, 448, 449. *See also* Smoking
Toddlerhood. *See* Infancy and toddlerhood
Togo, 614
Toilet training, 184
Tonic neck reflex, 101t, 102
Tooth conditions. *See* Teeth
Topic-associating narrative style, 323
Topic-focused narrative style, 322
Touch
    in infancy, 99, 108, 143–144
    in late adulthood, 576
    in physical changes of aging, 441t
Toxemia of pregnancy, 91
Toxoplasmosis in pregnancy, 87t, 88
Tracking, academic, 401, 402
Traditional classrooms, 324, 325
Traditional marriages, 486
Training. *See* Education
Transgender children, 280, 281
Transitive inferences in concrete operational stage, 304, 306
Triangular theory of love, 479
Triarchic theory of successful intelligence, 316, 316f
Tribal cultures
    adolescence in, 368, 375, 376
    childbirth practices in, 95
    crying of infants in, 107–108
    death beliefs in, 656
    formal operational stage in, 390
    hand preference in, 218
    initiation ceremonies in, 375
    mourning behavior in, 669
    observation and participation in adult work by children in, 237
    wisdom of older adults in, 600
Trimesters in prenatal development, 77t, 79–81
Triplets, 46, 52, 98
Triple X syndrome, 51
Trisomy 21 (Down syndrome), 50, 51f, 589
Triumphs of Experience (Vaillant), 477
Trophoblast, 77, 78
Trust
    in early adulthood, 482
    in infancy and toddlerhood, 15t, 184, 197
    in middle childhood, 346
Truth telling, and moral development in middle childhood, 343
Tuberculosis in pregnancy, 87t
Tumor suppressor genes, in cancer, 516, 517
Turkey, 329f, 597
Turner syndrome, 51
Tutsi genocide, 71, 71f
Twins, 45t, 45–46
    alcoholism of, 449
    anorexia nervosa of, 378
    attention-deficit hyperactivity disorder of, 309
    bulimia nervosa of, 379
    corporal punishment of, 269
    depression of, 427
    empathy of, 268
    environmental influences on gene expression in, 70
    gene–environment correlation in studies of, 69, 69f
    heritability estimate studies of, 67–68, 318
    intelligence and IQ of, 67–68, 70, 318
    kinship studies of, 67
    life expectancy of, 438, 571
    lifespan of, 438
    low birth weight of, 98
    maternal factors linked to, 45, 45t
    myopia of, 298
    niche-picking of, 69
    obesity of, 295
    osteoporosis of, 519
    personality traits of, 67
    physical growth of, 127
    preterm birth of, 46, 98
    puberty of, 372
    rheumatoid arthritis of, 586
    schizophrenia of, 67
    sexual orientation of, 382
    temperament and personality of, 193, 195
Twitter use, 424
Type A behavior pattern, 519–520
Type B behavior pattern, 519

U

Ulnar grasp, 137, 137f
Ultrasound in pregnancy, 54t
Umbilical cord, 77t, 78
Unconditioned response, 130, 130f
Unconditioned stimulus, 130, 130f
Underarm hair growth in puberty, 369, 371, 372

Underextensions in language development, 177
Underweight, in early childhood, 220, 220f
Unemployment, 49, 474, 562
Uninhibited child, temperament of, 191
Unintentional injuries. See Injuries, unintentional
Uninvolved child-rearing style, 282t, 283, 398
United Kingdom
  adolescent birth rate in, 384f
  child-rearing styles and academic achievement in, 398
  family size in, 490
  immunization rate in, 221
  infant mortality rate in, 102f
  life expectancy in, 571f
  marriage of same-sex couples in, 486
  math achievement scores in, 329f
  Nurse–Family Partnership in, 90
  obesity in, 295
  poverty rate in, 65f
Universal ethical principle orientation in moral development, 415
Universal grammar, 174
Universality, and death concept, 648–649
University education. See College experience
University of the Third Age, 604
Urban areas, community influences in, 59, 622–623
Uruguay, 486
Uterus, 76, 76f, 77, 369, 371
  age-related changes in, 443
  contractions in childbirth, 93f, 93–94
Utku Indians, 267

V
Vaccinations, 87, 220, 221
Vagina, 369, 371, 512
Vaillant, George, 611
  on adaptation to life, 477–478, 542
  on successful aging, 638–639
Values, cultural. See Cultural influences
Variables in research, 33
Vascular dementia, 590–591
Vegetative state, persistent, 647, 660
  recognition of living will in, 661
Verbal abilities
  cohort effects in, 525, 525f
  sex differences in, 394
  working memory in, 528
Verbal aggression, 272, 273
Verbs in language development, 241, 250, 251
Vernix, 79
Video deficit effect, 157
Video games, 274, 320, 397
Video Respite, 593
Video viewing
  in Alzheimer's disease, 593
  infant and toddler learning from, 157, 179
Vietnam, 32, 126, 226, 316
Village cultures
  adolescence in, 368, 375, 376
  childbirth practices in, 95

concrete operational stage in, 306
conservation in, 306
course of development in, 6
crying of infants in, 107–108
emotional expression of infants in, 189, 200
formal operational stage in, 390
gender identity in, 547
hand preference in, 218
initiation ceremonies in, 375
learning by observation and imitation in, 167
memory strategies in, 311
moral development in, 417
mourning behavior in, 669
observation and participation in adult work by children in, 237
parent–infant interactions in, 167, 189, 200
pictorial understanding in, 156
play in, 237, 265, 301
practical intelligence in, 316
sibling relationships in, 558
wisdom of older adults in, 600
Violation-of-expectation research method, 153f, 153–154, 158–159, 159f
Violence
  in adolescent dating relationships, 426
  in adolescent delinquency, 430, 431, 432f, 488
  bereavement interventions in, 670
  bereavement overload in, 668
  ethnic and political, impact on children, 359, 652
  in family, risk for elder maltreatment in, 633–634
  fear of, in late adulthood, 622–623
  in partner abuse, 488–489
  in sexual coercion, 454
  sudden unanticipated death in, 666
  on television, 274f, 274–275
  in video games, 274
Viral diseases
  AIDS. See AIDS
  in pregnancy, 86–88, 87t
Virtual cemeteries, 669
Vision
  in infancy and toddlerhood, 109–110, 121, 137, 139, 140–144
  in late adulthood, 574–575, 576, 579, 585, 586, 597
  in middle adulthood, 508–509, 515
  in middle childhood, 298
  in physical changes of aging, 441t
Visual acuity
  in infancy, 109–110, 140
  in late adulthood, 575
Visual cliff, 140, 140f
Vital capacity of lungs, 442, 443, 576
Vitamins
  in adolescence, 378
  in early adulthood, 440
  in early childhood, 220
  in late adulthood, 575, 582–583
  in middle adulthood, 519
  in pregnancy, 84, 88–89
Vitreous changes in middle adulthood, 508–509
Vocabulary
  in early childhood, 232, 250–251, 261

in infancy and toddlerhood, 155–156, 165, 173, 176–177, 178, 189
in late adulthood, 598, 599
in middle childhood, 313, 320, 321–322
Vocation. See Employment
Voice
  effortful control of, 193
  and emotional expression, 185, 188
  fetal response to, 81
  hearing loss affecting perception of, 509
  infant response to, 81, 108, 109, 144, 188
  in preterm infant stimulation, 99, 99f, 100
  in puberty, 372, 372t
Voluntary euthanasia, 660t, 664
Volunteers in Medicine, 613
Volunteer work
  in adolescence, 385, 418, 419
  in emerging adulthood, 471
  in late adulthood, 613, 635, 636–637, 638, 639
  in middle adulthood, 539, 539f, 547
  in middle childhood, 345
  and resilience, 11
Voting participation, 419, 472, 539f, 637
Vygotsky, Lev, 22
  sociocultural theory of. See Sociocultural theory

W
Walking
  in early childhood, 223t
  in infancy, 133–134, 135, 136, 141, 145
  in late adulthood, 578
  and stepping reflex, 101t, 102
War, and impact of violence on children, 359, 652
Water, fluoridated, 217
Watson, John, 16
Wechsler Intelligence Scale for Children, 315
Weight
  in anorexia nervosa, 378
  at birth, low, 97–100. See also Low birth weight
  in bulimia nervosa, 379
  in early adulthood, 441t, 445–447
  in early childhood, 216f, 216–217
  of fetus, 81
  genetic factors affecting, 127
  in infancy and toddlerhood, 116, 117, 127, 128–129
  in late adulthood, 578
  in middle adulthood, 510
  in middle childhood, 294, 295–299
  in obesity. See Obesity
  in physical changes of aging, 441t
  in puberty, 369, 372, 372t, 373
  sleep affecting, 296
Welfare benefits, 64, 90, 384
Well-being
  and health. See Health
  international comparisons of indicators on, 64, 64t
  psychological. See Psychological well-being
West Indians of Jamaica, 136

White blood cells, 439, 443
Whole-language approach to reading, 313
Whooping cough, 221
WIC program, 89
Widowhood, 623, 628–629
  bereavement in, 666, 667–668
  remarriage in, 627, 628, 629
Wisdom, 8
  in late adulthood, 600–601
Withdrawal of privileges as punishment technique, 269, 270
Withdrawal symptoms
  from marijuana, 449
  from nicotine, 449
Withholding or withdrawal of life-sustaining treatment, 660t, 660–662
Women's Health Initiative, 515
Work. See Employment
Working memory
  in adolescence, 390, 391
  in attention-deficit hyperactivity disorder, 309
  in early childhood, 238, 261
  in infancy and toddlerhood, 161
  intelligence tests of, 315, 315f
  in late adulthood, 596, 597, 598, 602
  in middle adulthood, 528, 529
  in middle childhood, 307, 308, 310, 311, 313, 315
World Health Organization, 127
World Trade Center terrorist attacks, 36, 359, 668
Worldview in emerging adulthood, 471–473
Writing
  in adolescence, 394, 464
  in early childhood, 225, 242–244
  in middle childhood, 300, 301

X
X chromosome, 45
  abnormalities of, 50–51
  diseases linked to, 47t, 48, 49f
  in fragile X syndrome, 49
XX chromosomes, 45
XXX syndrome, 51
XY chromosomes, 45
XYY syndrome, 51

Y
Y chromosome, 45, 48, 50–51
Yolk sac, 77, 77t
Yoruba of Nigeria, 589–590
Young–old developmental tasks in seasons of life theory, 541
Yucatán Mayans, 237, 514
Yup'ik Eskimos, 316
Yurok Indians, 16

Z
Zambia, 110
Zero tolerance policies, 430
Zinacanteco Indians, 23, 136, 168, 306
Zinc, 221
Zone of proximal development, 166, 179, 235, 325
Zygote, 45, 76f, 76–77, 77t
  in fraternal or dizygotic twins, 45
  in identical or monozygotic twins, 46
  teratogen exposure affecting, 82f

Brief Contents

PART I: THEORY AND RESEARCH IN HUMAN DEVELOPMENT
1. History, Theory, and Research Strategies   2

PART II: FOUNDATIONS OF DEVELOPMENT
2. Genetic and Environmental Foundations   42
3. Prenatal Development, Birth, and the Newborn Baby   74

PART III: INFANCY AND TODDLERHOOD: THE FIRST TWO YEARS
4. Physical Development in Infancy and Toddlerhood   114
5. Cognitive Development in Infancy and Toddlerhood   148
6. Emotional and Social Development in Infancy and Toddlerhood   182

PART IV: EARLY CHILDHOOD: TWO TO SIX YEARS
7. Physical and Cognitive Development in Early Childhood   214
8. Emotional and Social Development in Early Childhood   256

PART V: MIDDLE CHILDHOOD: SIX TO ELEVEN YEARS
9. Physical and Cognitive Development in Middle Childhood   292
10. Emotional and Social Development in Middle Childhood   334

PART VI: ADOLESCENCE: THE TRANSITION TO ADULTHOOD
11. Physical and Cognitive Development in Adolescence   366
12. Emotional and Social Development in Adolescence   406

PART VII: EARLY ADULTHOOD
13. Physical and Cognitive Development in Early Adulthood   436
14. Emotional and Social Development in Early Adulthood   468

PART VIII: MIDDLE ADULTHOOD
15. Physical and Cognitive Development in Middle Adulthood   506
16. Emotional and Social Development in Middle Adulthood   536

PART IX: LATE ADULTHOOD
17. Physical and Cognitive Development in Late Adulthood   568
18. Emotional and Social Development in Late Adulthood   608

PART X: THE END OF LIFE
19. Death, Dying, and Bereavement   644